Collins [NEW]

WORLD**ATLAS**

COLLINS NEW WORLD ATLAS

This edition published in 2002 for DMG,
Unit 5, Bestwood Business Park, Nottingham NG6 8AN

An imprint of HarperCollins*Publishers*
77-85 Fulham Palace Road
London
W6 8JB

First Published 2001

Copyright © HarperCollins*Publishers* 2001
Maps © Bartholomew Ltd 2001

Collins® is a registered trademark of HarperCollins*Publishers* Ltd

The contents of this edition of the Collins New World Atlas are believed
correct at the time of printing. Nevertheless the publisher can accept
no responsibility for errors or omissions, changes in the detail given,
or for any expense or loss thereby caused.

Printed in Spain

British Library Cataloguing in Publication Data.
A catalogue record for this book is available from the British Library.

ISBN 0 00 766907 0

The maps in this product are also available for purchase in digital format
from Bartholomew Mapping Solutions. For details and information visit
http://www.bartholomewmaps.com

or contact
Bartholomew Mapping Solutions
Tel: +44 (0) 141 306 3162
Fax: +44 (0) 141 306 3104
e-mail: bartholomew@harpercollins.co.uk

www.**fire**and**water**.com
Visit the book lover's website

[NEW]
WORLD**ATLAS**

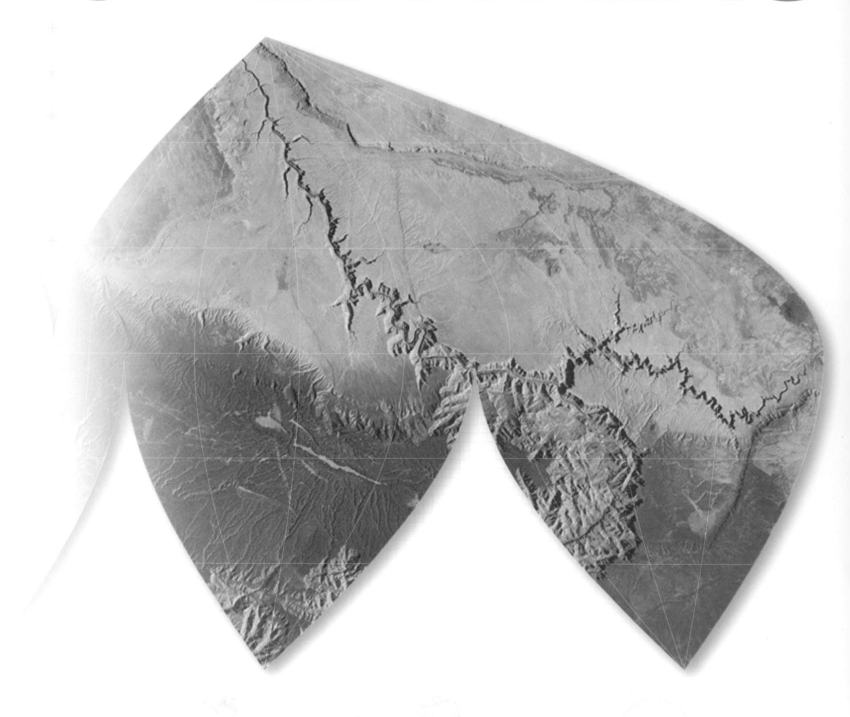

CONTENTS

The atlas is arranged into a world thematic section and continental sections as defined in the contents list below. Full details of the contents of each section can be found on the introductory spread within the section. As indicated on the contents list, each section is distinctively colour-coded to allow easy identification.

The continental sections contain detailed, comprehensive reference maps of the continent, which are preceded by introductory pages consisting of a mixture of statistical and thematic maps, geographical statistics, and photographs and images illustrating specific themes. Each map and thematic spread contains a 'connections' box, which indicates links to other pages in the atlas containing related information.

title	pages		title	pages
world	6–7		oceania	134–135
[physical features]	8–9		[landscapes]	136–137
[countries]	10–11		[countries]	138–139
[land images]	12–13		[threats]	140–141
[earthquakes and volcanoes]	14–15		[features]	142–143
[climate and weather]	16–17		[reference maps]	144–153
[land cover]	18–19			
[changes]	20–21		northamerica	154–155
[population]	22–23		[landscapes]	156–157
[cities]	24–25		[countries]	158–159
[communications]	26–27		[threats]	160–161
			[environments]	162–163
europe	28–29		[reference maps]	164–187
[landscapes]	30–31			
[countries]	32–33		southamerica	188–189
[countries/issues]	34–35		[landscapes]	190–191
[environments]	36–37		[countries]	192–193
[reference maps]	38–59		[contrasts]	194–195
			[impacts]	196–197
asia	60–61		[reference maps]	198-207
[landscapes]	62–63			
[countries]	64–65		oceans and poles	208–209
[countries/issues]	66–67		oceans [features]	210–211
[changes]	68–69		antarctica [features]	212–213
[threats]	70–71		the arctic [features]	214–215
[reference maps]	72–109		oceans and poles [reference maps]	216–224
			index	225–335
africa	110–111			
[landscapes]	112–113		acknowledgements	336
[countries]	114–115			
[countries/issues]	116–117			
[locations]	118–119			
[reference maps]	120–133			

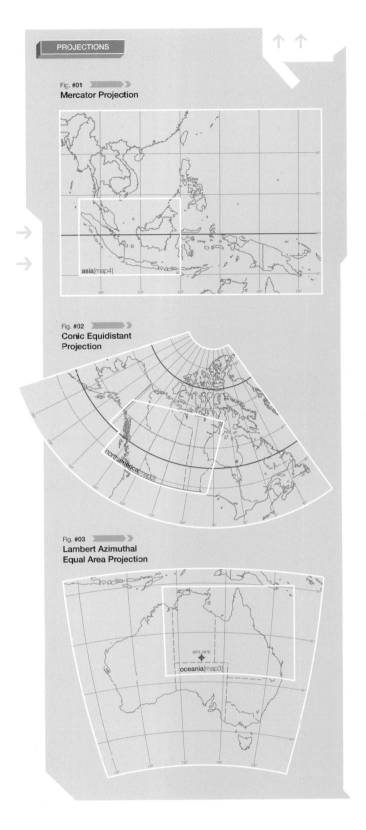

PROJECTIONS

Fig. #01
Mercator Projection

asia[map4]

Fig. #02
Conic Equidistant Projection

northamerica[map1]

Fig. #03
Lambert Azimuthal Equal Area Projection

oceania[map3]

REFERENCE MAPS

Symbols and generalization

Maps show information by using signs, or symbols, which are designed to reflect the features on the Earth which they represent. Symbols can be in the form of points, lines, or areas and variations in the size, shape and colour of the symbols allow a great range of information to be shown. The symbols used on the reference maps are explained opposite.

Not all features on the ground can be shown, nor can all characteristics of a feature be depicted. Much detail has to be generalized to be clearly shown on the maps, the degree of generalization being determined largely by the scale of the map. As map scale decreases, fewer features can be shown, and their depiction becomes less detailed. The most common generalization techniques are selection and simplification. Selection is the inclusion of some features and the omission of others of less importance. Smaller scale maps can show fewer features than larger scales, and therefore only the more important features are selected. Simplification is the process of smoothing lines, combining areas, or slightly displacing symbols to add clarity. Smaller scale maps require more simplification. These techniques are carried out in such a way that the overall character of the area mapped is retained.

Scale

The amount of detail shown on a map is determined by its scale – the relationship between the size of an area shown on the map and the actual size of the area on the ground. Larger scales show more detail, smaller scales require more generalization and show less. The scale can be used to measure the distance between two points and to calculate comparative areas.

Scales used for the reference maps range from 1:3M (large scale) to 1:48M (small scale). Insets are used to show areas of the world of particular interest or which cannot be included in the page layouts in their true position. The scale used is indicated in the margin of each map.

Map projections

The 'projection' of the three-dimensional globe onto a two-dimensional map is always a problem for cartographers. All map projections introduce distortions to either shape, area or distances. Projections for the maps in this atlas have been specifically selected to minimize these distortions. The diagrams above illustrate three types of projection used. The red lines represent the 'centres' of the projections where there is no distortion and scale is correct.

Each reference map is cut to the shape of the graticule (the lines of latitude and longitude), which is determined by the projection used. This gives each map a unique shape, suggesting its position on the globe, as illustrated by the examples on the diagrams.

Geographical names

There is no single standard way of spelling names or of converting them from one alphabet, or symbol set, to another. Instead, conventional ways of spelling have evolved, and the results often differ significantly from the original name in the local language. Familiar examples in English include Munich (München in German), Florence (Firenze in Italian) and Moscow (Moskva from Russian). A further complication is that in many countries different languages are in use in different regions.

These factors, and any changes in official languages, have to be taken into account when creating maps. The policy in this atlas is generally to use local name forms which are officially recognized by the governments of the countries concerned. This is a basic principle laid down by the Permanent Committee on Geographical Names (PCGN) – the body responsible for determining official UK government policy on place names around the world. PCGN rules are also applied to the conversion of non-roman alphabet names, for example in the Russian Federation, into the roman alphabet used in English.

However, English conventional name forms are used for the most well-known places for which such a form is in common use. In these cases, the local form is included in brackets on the map and appears as a cross-reference in the index. Other alternative names, such as well-known historical names or those in other languages, may also be included in brackets. All country names and those for international physical features appear in their English forms.

Boundaries

The status of nations and their boundaries, and the names associated with them, are shown in this atlas as they are in reality at the time of going to press, as far as can be ascertained. All recent changes of the status of nations and their boundaries have been taken into account. Where international boundaries are the subject of dispute, the aim is to take a strictly neutral viewpoint and every reasonable attempt is made to show where an active territorial dispute exists. Generally, prominence is given to the situation as it exists on the ground (the *de facto* situation). The depiction on the maps of boundaries and their current status varies accordingly.

International boundaries are shown on all the reference maps, and those of a large enough scale also include internal administrative boundaries of selected countries. The delineation of international boundaries in the sea is often a very contentious issue, and in many cases an official alignment is not defined. Boundaries in the sea are generally only shown where they are required to clarify the ownership of specific islands or island groups.

Indexing

All names appearing on the reference maps are included in the index and can be easily found from the information included in the index entry. Details of all alternative name forms are included in the index entries and as cross-references. Gazetteer entries, with important geographical information, are included for selected places and features. Full details of index policies and content can be found in the Introduction to the Index on page 225.

SETTLEMENTS

Population	National Capital	Administrative Capital	Other City or Town
over 5 million	BEIJING ✵	Tianjin ◉	New York ◉
1 million to 5 million	KĀBUL ✵	Sydney ◉	Kaohsiung ◉
500 000 to 1 million	BANGUI ✵	Trujillo ◎	Jeddah ◉
100 000 to 500 000	WELLINGTON ✵	Mansa ○	Apucarana ○
50 000 to 100 000	PORT OF SPAIN ✵	Potenza ○	Arecibo ○
10 000 to 50 000	MALABO ✿	Chinhoyi ○	Ceres ○
1 000 to 10 000	VALLETTA ✿	Asi ○	Venta ○
under 1000		Chhukha ○	Shapki ○

◌ Built-up area

BOUNDARIES

▪▪▪▪ International boundary

▪▫▪▫ Disputed international boundary or alignment unconfirmed

▬▬▬ Administrative boundary

••••• Ceasefire line

MISCELLANEOUS

---------- National park

·········· Reserve or Regional park

✿ Site of specific interest

▭▭▭▭ Wall

LAND AND SEA FEATURES

Desert

Oasis

Lava field

1234 Volcano
height in metres

Marsh

Ice cap / Glacier

Escarpment

Coral reef

1234 Pass
height in metres

LAKES AND RIVERS

Lake

Impermanent lake

Salt lake or lagoon

Impermanent salt lake

Dry salt lake or salt pan

123 Lake height
surface height above sea level, in metres

—— River

------ Impermanent river or watercourse

‖ Waterfall

— Dam

| Barrage

RELIEF

Contour intervals and layer colours

Continents

>6000m
5000-6000m
4000-5000m
3000-4000m
2000-3000m
1500-2000m
1000-1500m
500-1000m
200-500m
100-200m
0-100m
<0m
0-50m
50-100m
100-200m
200-500m
500-1000m
1000-2000m
2000-3000m
3000-4000m
4000-5000m
5000-6000m
>6000m

Oceans and Poles

>6000m
5000-6000m
4000-5000m
3000-4000m
2000-3000m
1000-2000m
500-1000m
200-500m
0-200m
<0m
0-200m
200-2000m
2000-3000m
3000-4000m
4000-5000m
5000-6000m
6000-7000m
>7000m

1234 △ Summit
height in metres

-123 Spot height
height in metres

123 Ocean deep
height in metres

TRANSPORT

▬▬▬ ===== Motorway (tunnel; under construction)

▬▬▬ ----- Main road (tunnel; under construction)

▬▬▬ ----- Secondary road (tunnel; under construction)

·········· Track

▬▬▬ ----- Main railway (tunnel; under construction)

▬▬▬ ----- Secondary railway (tunnel; under construction)

▬▬▬ ----- Other railway (tunnel; under construction)

——— Canal

✈ Main airport

✈ Regional airport

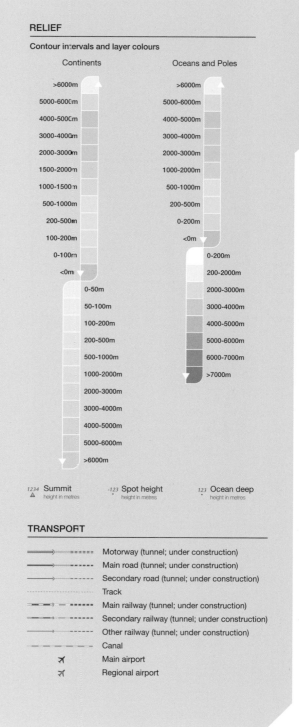

SATELLITE IMAGERY

MAIN SATELLITES/SENSORS

satellite/sensor name	launch dates	owner	aims and applications	wavelengths	resolution of imagery	web address
Landsat 4, 5, 7	July 1972-April 1999	National Aeronautics and Space Administration (NASA), USA	The first satellite to be designed specifically for observing the Earth's surface. Originally set up to produce images of use for agriculture and geology. Today is of use for numerous environmental and scientific applications.	Visible, near-infrared, short-wave and thermal infrared wavelength bands.	15m in the panchromatic band (only on Landsat 7), 30m in the six visible, near and short-wave infrared bands and 60m in the thermal infrared band.	geo.arc.nasa.gov ls7pm3.gsfc.nasa.gov
SPOT 1, 2, 3, 4 (Satellite Pour l'Observation de la Terre)	February 1986-March 1998	Centre National d'Etudes Spatiales (CNES) and Spot Image, France	Particularly useful for monitoring land use, water resources research, coastal studies and cartography.	Visible and near infrared.	Panchromatic 10m. Multispectral 20m.	www.cnes.fr www.spotimage.fr
Space Shuttle	Regular launches from 1981	NASA, USA	Each shuttle mission has separate aims. Astronauts take photographs with high specification hand held cameras. The Shuttle Radar Topography Mission (SRTM) in 2000 obtained the most complete near-global high-resolution database of the earth's topography.	Visible with hand held cameras. Radar on SRTM Mission.	SRTM: 30m for US and 90m for rest of the world.	science.ksc.nasa.gov/shuttle/countdown www.jpl.nasa.gov/srtm
IKONOS	September 1999	Space Imaging	First commercial high-resolution satellite. Useful for a variety of applications mainly Cartography, Defence, Urban Planning, Agriculture, Forestry and Insurance	Visible and near infrared.	Panchromatic 1m. Multispectral 4m.	www.spaceimaging.com

ADDITIONAL IMAGERY

satellite/sensor name	web address
ASTER	asterweb.jpl.nasa.gov www.nasda.go.jp
SeaWIFS	seawifs.gsfc.nasa.gov
Radarsat	www.rsi.ca
MODIS	modis.gsfc.nasa.gov
TOPEX/Poseidon	topex-www.jpl.nasa.gov
ERS-1 (European Space Agency) Earth Resources Satellite	earthnet.esrin.esa.it

PHOTOGRAPHS AND IMAGES

The thematic pages of the atlas contain a wide variety of photographs and images. These are a mixture of 3-D perspective views, terrestrial and aerial photographs and satellite imagery. All are used to illustrate specific themes and to give an indication of the variety of imagery, and different means of visualizing the Earth, available today. The main types of imagery used in the atlas are described in the table above.

Satellite imagery, and the related science of satellite remote sensing – the acquisition, processing and interpretation of images captured by satellites – is a particularly valuable tool in observing and monitoring the Earth. Satellite sensors can capture electromagnetic radiation in a variety of wavelengths, including those visible to the eye (colours), infrared wavelengths and microwave and radio radiation as detected by radar sensors. The data received by the sensors can be processed in different ways to allow detailed interpretation of the landscape and environmental conditions. Panchromatic images represent a single wavelength in values of grey (black and white) while multispectral sensors can combine several wavelengths in a single image. Imagery also varies in the amount of detail it can show. The ability to distinguish visual detail, and the size of the smallest feature which can be detected, is known as the image's resolution, and is usually expressed in metres.

SPOT

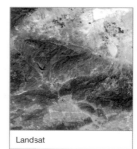
Landsat

Space Shuttle

IKONOS

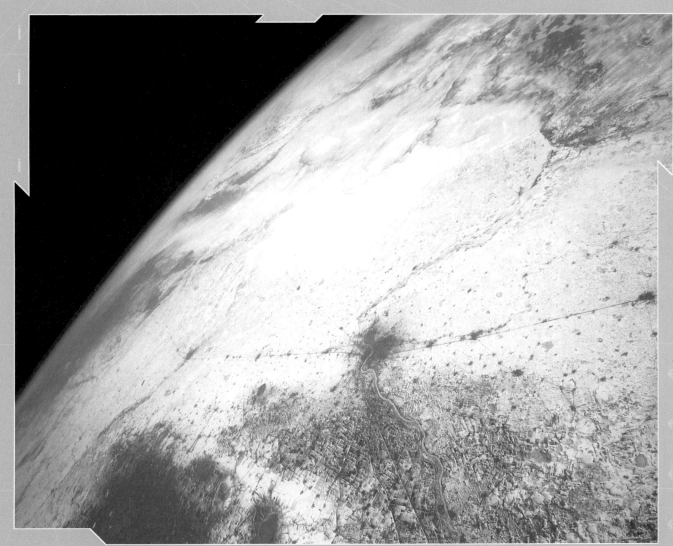

Omsk, *Russian Federation*

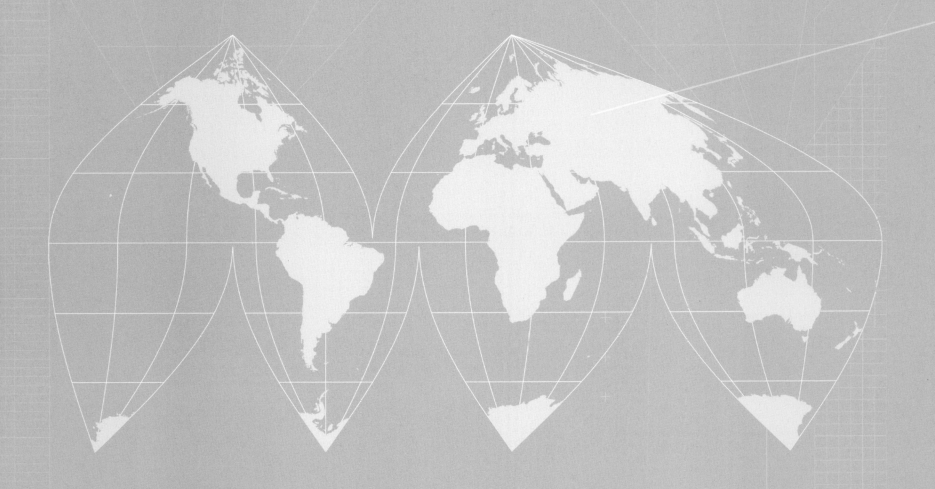

world

[contents]

1   Nile Delta and Sinai Peninsula, *Africa/Asia*

Several distinct physical features can be seen in this oblique Shuttle photograph which looks southeast from above the Mediterranean Sea over northeast Africa and southwest Asia. The dark, triangular area at the bottom of the photograph is the Nile delta. The Sinai peninsula in the centre of the image is flanked by the two elongated water bodies of the Gulf of Aqaba on the left, and the Gulf of Suez on the right. These gulfs merge to form the Red Sea. The Dead Sea is also visible on the left edge of the image.

Satellite/Sensor : Space Shuttle

2   Himalayas, *Asia*

The Himalayan mountain chain forms a major physical barrier across Jammu and Kashmir, northern India, Nepal and Bhutan and contains the world's highest mountains. This Space Shuttle photograph looks west along the mountains. The low plains on the left contain three major rivers, the Ganges, Indus and Brahmaputra. To the right of the permanently snow-capped mountains is the Plateau of Tibet, a vast barren area over 4 000 m above sea level.

Satellite/Sensor : Space Shuttle

NORTH AMERICA

Coast Ranges — Rocky Mountains — Great Plains — Lake Michigan — Lake Huron — Lake Erie — Chesapeake Bay — Appalachian Mountains — Long Island — Cape Cod — Nova Scotia

SOUTH AMERICA

Andes — Selvas — Mato Grosso — Bahia de São Marcos — Ponta do Calcanhar

AFRICA

CapVert — Sahara — Hoggar — Tibesti — Marra Plateau — Ethiopian Highlands — Red Sea — Arabian Peninsula — Socotra

Fig. #01
World physical features

>6000m
5000-6000m
4000-5000m
3000-4000m
2000-3000m
1000-2000m
500-1000m
200-500m
0-200m
<0m

0-200m
200-2000m
2000-3000m
3000-4000m
4000-5000m
5000-6000m
6000-7000m
>7000m

HIGHEST MOUNTAINS

	m	ft	location	map
Mt Everest	8 848	29 028	China/Nepal	97 E4
K2	8 611	28 251	China/Jammu and Kashmir	96 C2
Kangchenjunga	8 586	28 169	India/Nepal	97 F4
Lhotse	8 516	27 939	China/Nepal	97 E3
Makalu	8 463	27 765	China/Nepal	97 E4
Cho Oyu	8 201	26 906	China/Nepal	97 E3
Dhaulagiri	8 167	26 794	Nepal	97 D3
Manaslu	8 163	26 781	Nepal	97 E3
Nanga Parbat	8 126	26 660	Jammu and Kashmir	96 B2
Annapurna I	8 091	26 545	Nepal	97 D3

LONGEST RIVERS

	km	miles	continent	map
Nile	6 695	4 160	Africa	121 F2
Amazon	6 516	4 049	South America	202 B1
Yangtze	6 380	3 964	Asia	87 G2
Mississipi-Missouri	5 969	3 709	North America	179 E7
Ob'-Irtysh	5 568	3 459	Asia	38 G3-39 I5
Yenisey-Angara-Selenga	5 550	3 448	Asia	39 I2-K4
Yellow	5 464	3 395	Asia	85 H4
Congo	4 667	2 900	Africa	127 B6
Rio de la Plata - Parana	4 500	2 796	South America	204 F4
Irtysh	4 440	2 759	Asia	38 G3

LARGEST ISLANDS

	sq km	sq miles	location	map
Greenland	2 175 600	840 004	North America	165 O3
New Guinea	808 510	312 167	Oceania	73 J8
Borneo	745 561	287 863	Asia	77 F2
Madagascar	587 040	226 657	Africa	131 J3
Baffin Island	507 451	195 927	North America	165 L2
Sumatra	473 606	182 860	Asia	76 C3
Honshu	227 414	87 805	Asia	91 F6
Great Britain	218 476	84 354	Europe	47 J9
Victoria Island	217 291	83 897	North America	165 H2
Ellesmere Island	196 236	75 767	North America	165 K2

LARGEST LAKES

	sq km	sq miles	continent	map
Caspian Sea	371 000	143 243	Asia / Europe	102 B4
Lake Superior	82 100	31 698	North America	172 D3
Lake Victoria	68 800	26 563	Africa	128 B5
Lake Huron	59 600	23 011	North America	173 I6
Lake Michigan	57 800	22 316	North America	172 E7
Aral Sea	33 640	12 988	Asia	102 D3
Lake Tanganyika	32 900	12 702	Africa	129 A6
Great Bear Lake	31 328	12 095	North America	166 F1
Lake Baikal	30 500	11 776	Asia	39 K4
Lake Nyasa	30 044	11 600	Africa	129 B7

EARTH'S DIMENSIONS

Equatorial diameter	12 756.274 km (7 926.381 miles)
Polar diameter	12 713.505 km (7 899.806 miles)
Mass	5.974 X 10²¹ tonnes
Total area	509 450 000 sq km/196 672 000 sq miles
Land area	149 450 000 sq km/57 688 000 sq miles
Water area	360 000 000 sq km/138 984 000 sq miles
Volume	1 083 207 X 10⁶ cubic km/259 875 X 10⁶ cubic miles

EUROPE — Cordillera Cantabrica, Land's End, Bay of Biscay, Pyrenees, Massif Central, Alps, Adriatic Sea, Carpathian Mountains, Black Sea, Crimea, Sea of Azov, Caucasus

ASIA — Mediterranean Sea, Cyprus, Caucasus, Caspian Sea, Turan Lowlands, Tien Shan, Tarim Basin, Plateau of Tibet, Gobi, Yellow Sea, Sea of Japan, Honshu

OCEANIA — Joseph Bonaparte Gulf, Melville Island, Arnhem Land, Gulf of Carpentaria, Cape York Peninsula, Great Dividing Range, Tasman Sea, North Cape, North Island, Cook Strait

CONNECTIONS

► subject	page#
► Europe landscapes	30–31
► Asia landscapes	62–63
► Africa landscapes	112–113
► Oceania landscapes	136–137
► North America landscapes	156–157
► South America landscapes	190–191

world[countries]

ARCTIC OCEA

Svalbard
(Norway)

Greenland
(Denmark)

Bjørnøya
(Norway)

Beaufort Sea

Ellesmere Island

Baffin
Bay

Jan Mayen
(Norway)

Point Hope

Victoria
Island

Baffin Island

ICELAND

REYKJAVIK

NORWAY SWEDEN FINLAND
Shetland OSLO STOCKHOLM HELSINKI
Islands EST. TALLIN
Faroe Islands RIGA LAT.
NUUK

Inuvik

Great Bear
Lake

Iqaluit

Anchorage

U.S.A.

Yukon

Whitehorse

Great Slave
Lake

Hudson
Bay

Edinburgh
DUBLIN

UNITED
KINGDOM

DENMARK
COPENHAGEN

LITH.
VILNIUS
MINSK
R.F.

C A N A D A

Vancouver

Calgary

Edmonton

Winnipeg

Lake
Superior

Newfoundland

St Pierre and
Miquelon
(France)

Belfast

REPUBLIC
OF IRELAND

LONDON

AMSTERDAM
THE HAGUE
BRUSSELS

HAMBURG
BERLIN

GERMANY

BEL.

PRAGUE
CZ.R.

WARSAW
POLAND

Lviv

BELARUS

U

Portland

Seattle

Boise

Missouri

Lake
Michigan

OTTAWA

Lake
Huron

Montreal

Toronto

St John's

PARIS

BERN
SW.

LIECH.
VIENNA
LJUBLJANA
ZAGREB

BRATISLAVA
BUDAPEST

HUN. ROM.

UKRAINE

KIEV

CHISINAU

MOL.

BUCHAREST

San Francisco

UNITED STATES
OF AMERICA

Denver

Chicago

Detroit

Cleveland

Lake Ontario

Lake Erie

New York

FRANCE

Marseille

B.H.

SARAJEVO

YU.
BELGRADE

SOFIA

BULG.

Los Angeles

Phoenix

St Louis

Indianapolis

Philadelphia

WASHINGTON D.C.

PORTUGAL

LISBON

MADRID

SPAIN

Barcelona

Valencia

ROME
ITALY

TIRANA

SKOPJE

GREECE

ATHEN

San Diego

El Paso

Dallas

Memphis

Atlanta

Azores
(Portugal)

Sevilla

Palermo

Mediterranean Sea

Baja California

San Antonio

Houston

New
Orleans

Jacksonville

Bermuda
(U.K.)

Madeira
(Portugal)

RABAT
Casablanca

ALGIERS

TUNIS

TUNISIA

TRIPOLI

Oran

Guadalupe
(Mexico)

Gulf of
Mexico

Miami

NASSAU

THE BAHAMAS

Canary Islands
(Spain)

LAÂYOUNE

MOROCCO

ALGERIA

LIBYA

Tropic of Cancer

Hawaiian Islands
(U.S.A.)

Guadalajara

MEXICO

HAVANA

CUBA

DOMINICAN
REP.

Puerto Rico
(U.S.A.)

WESTERN
SAHARA

Islas
Revillagigedo

MEXICO
CITY

GUATEMALA

HAITI

KINGSTON

JAMAICA

SANTO
DOMINGO

ANTIGUA

Guadeloupe (France)

DOMINICA

Martinique (France)

MAURITANIA

NOUAKCHOTT

MALI

NIGER

CHAD

PACIFIC

BELIZE

BELMOPAN

HONDURAS

CAPE VERDE

PRAIA

SENEGAL

DAKAR

NIAMEY

Kano

GUA EMALA CITY

SAN SALVADOR

TEGUCIGALPA

EL SALVADOR

NICARAGUA

MANAGUA

Caribbean
Sea

BARBADOS

ST VINCE'T

GRENADA

ST LUCIA

THE GAMBIA

BISSAU

BANJUL

BAMAKO

BURKINA

OUAGADOUGOU

NIGERIA

ABUJA

NDJAMENA

Ile Clipperton

SAN JOSÉ

PANAMA CITY

TRINIDAD
AND TOBAGO

CARACAS

GUINEA-BISSAU

CONAKRY

GUINEA

FREETOWN

CÔTE

D'IVOIRE

YAMOUSSOUKRO

GHANA

TOGO

BENIN

LOME

CAMEROON

CENTRAL
AFRICAN
REPUBLIC

OCEAN

COSTA RICA

PANAMA

Maracaibo

VENEZUELA

Barranquilla

GEORGETOWN

PARAMARIBO

SUR.

CAYENNE

SIERRA LEONE

MONROVIA

LIBERIA

Abidjan

ACCRA

MALABO

PORTO-NOVO

EQUATORIAL
GUINEA

YAOUNDE

BANGUI

LIBREVILLE

DEM. R

OF

CON

Equator

KIRIBATI

Line Islands

INTERNATIONAL DATE LINE

Galapagos
Islands
(Ecuador)

QUITO

ECUADOR

Guayaquil

Medellin

BOGOTÁ

Cali

COLOMBIA

French Guiana

Manaus

Amazon

Belém

Amazonas

SÃO TOMÉ
AND PRÍNCIPE

GABON

CONGO

BRAZZAVILLE

KINSHASA

BUJU

Fortaleza

Teresina

Fernando de Noronha
(Brazil)

Natal

Ascension
(U.K.)

LUANDA

American
Samoa

Niue
(N.Z.)

Cook
Islands
(N.Z.)

Marquesas
Islands

Tahiti

Society
Islands

Tuamotu Islands

French
Polynesia

Trujillo

PERU

LIMA

Arequipa

LA PAZ

BOLIVIA

SUCRE

Santa Cruz

B R A Z I L

BRASÍLIA

Goiânia

Recife

Salvador

Belo Horizonte

Ilhas Martin Vas
(Brazil)

St Helena
(U.K.)

ATLANTIC

ANGOLA

ZA

LUS

NAMIBIA

Bula

BOTSW

WINDHOEK

GABORONE

Johannesb

SW

OCEAN

Rarotonga
(N.Z.)

Tropic of Capricorn

Tubuai Islands

Pitcairn Is
(U.K.)

Isla de Pascua
(Easter Island)
(Chile)

Isla Sala y Gómez
(Chile)

Archipélago
Juan Fernández
(Chile)

PARAGUAY

ASUNCIÓN

São Paulo

Curitiba

Rio de Janeiro

Trindade
(Brazil)

Porto Alegre

Tristan da Cunha
(U.K.)

Gough Island
(U.K.)

REPUBLIC

SOUTH AF

CAPE
TOWN

MASE

Cape Agul

SANTIAGO

Córdoba

URUGUAY

MONTEVIDEO

BUENOS
AIRES

Mar del Plata

ARGENTINA

CHILE

San Miguel
de Tucumán

Rosario

OCEAN

South Georgia
and
South Sandwich
Islands
(U.K.)

Bouvetøya
(Norway)

S O U T

Punta
Arenas

STANLEY

Falkland
Islands
(U.K.)

Cape
Horn

South Shetland
Islands
(U.K.)

South Orkney
Islands
(U.K.)

Weddell
Sea

Antarctic
Peninsula

A N T A R C T

CONNECTIONS

► subject	page#
► World population	22–23
► World cities	24–25
► Europe countries	32–35
► Asia countries	64–67
► Africa countries	114–117
► Oceania countries	138–139
► North America countries	158–159
► South America countries	192–193

1 Beijing, *China*

This infrared SPOT satellite image of Beijing shows the extent of the capital city of China spreading out from the Forbidden City and Tiananmen Square, just to the right of the lake in the centre. The central city has a very marked grid-iron street pattern, with very densely packed low-rise buildings. On the outskirts, areas of intensive cultivation are represented in shades of red.

Satellite/Sensor : SPOT

2 Washington, D.C., *United States of America*

The capital of the United States, Washington, D.C., is shown in this infrared aerial photograph. The city is situated on the confluence of the Potomac and Anacostia rivers, seen here to the left and bottom of the photograph respectively. It has become a leading political, educational and research centre. The Pentagon, home of the US Department of Defense is at the far left of the photograph and The Mall, the Capitol, the White House and Union Station can all be seen in the centre.

3 La Paz, *Bolivia*

This infrared satellite image shows the highest capital in the world, La Paz, which lies at a height of over 3 500 metres above sea level. It is located at the edge of the Altiplano between two mountain belts within the Andes mountains. The mountains seen at the top of the image have year-round snow cover. The grey-blue area to the right of centre is the urban area of La Paz, with the city's airport clearly visible to the west.

Satellite/Sensor : SPOT

4 Mauritania/Senegal, *Africa*

The Senegal river creates a natural border between the northeast African countries of Mauritania and Senegal. The top of this infrared satellite image shows the southern edge of the Sahara desert in Mauritania. The semi-desert southern fringe of the Sahara, the Sahel, stretches east from Mauritania to Chad. The orange-red colour in the bottom half of the image represents mixed scrub and bush savanna vegetation of Senegal.

Satellite/Sensor : SPOT

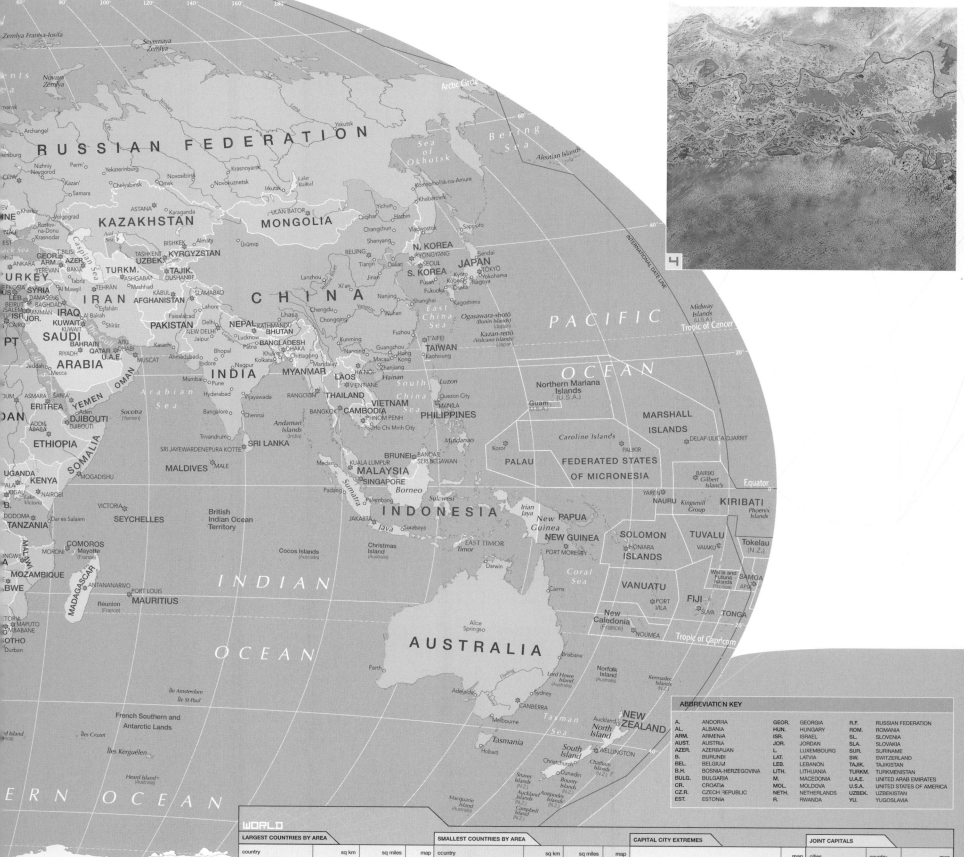

ABBREVIATION KEY

A.	ANDORRA	GEOR.	GEORGIA	R.F.	RUSSIAN FEDERATION
AL.	ALBANIA	HUN.	HUNGARY	ROM.	ROMANIA
ARM.	ARMENIA	ISR.	ISRAEL	SL.	SLOVENIA
AUST.	AUSTRIA	JOR.	JORDAN	SLA.	SLOVAKIA
AZER.	AZERBAIJAN	L.	LUXEMBOURG	SUR.	SURINAME
B.	BURUNDI	LAT.	LATVIA	SW.	SWITZERLAND
BEL.	BELGIUM	LEB.	LEBANON	TAJIK.	TAJIKISTAN
B.H.	BOSNIA-HERZEGOVINA	LITH.	LITHUANIA	TURKM.	TURKMENISTAN
BULG.	BULGARIA	M.	MACEDONIA	U.A.E.	UNITED ARAB EMIRATES
CR.	CROATIA	MOL.	MOLDOVA	U.S.A.	UNITED STATES OF AMERICA
CZ.R.	CZECH REPUBLIC	NETH.	NETHERLANDS	UZBEK.	UZBEKISTAN
EST.	ESTONIA	R.	RWANDA	YU.	YUGOSLAVIA

WORLD

LARGEST COUNTRIES BY AREA

country	sq km	sq miles	map
1. Russian Federation	17 075 400	6 592 849	38–39
2. Canada	9 970 610	3 849 674	164–165
3. United States of America	9 809 378	3 787 422	170–171
4. China	9 584 492	3 700 593	80–81
5. Brazil	8 547 379	3 300 161	202–203
6. Australia	7 682 395	2 966 189	144–145
7. India	3 065 027	1 183 414	92–93
8. Argentina	2 766 889	1 068 302	204–205
9. Kazakhstan	2 717 300	1 049 155	102–103
10. Sudan	2 505 813	967 500	120–121

SMALLEST COUNTRIES BY AREA

country	sq km	sq miles	map
1. Vatican City	0.5	0.2	56
2. Monaco	2	1	51
3. Nauru	21	8	145
4. Tuvalu	25	10	145
5. San Marino	61	24	56
6. Liechtenstein	160	62	51
7. St Kitts and Nevis	261	101	187
8. Maldives	298	115	93
9. Grenada	378	146	187
10. St Vincent and the Grenadines	389	150	187

CAPITAL CITY EXTREMES

			map
Most populous	Tōkyō, Japan	26 444 000	91 F7
Least populous	Yaren, Nauru	600	145 F2
Highest	La Paz, Bolivia	3 636m / 11 910ft	200 C4
Lowest	Manama, Bahrain and Male, Maldives	0.9m / 3ft	100 B5 / 93 D10
Furthest north	Nuuk, Greenland	64° 11'N	165 N3
Furthest south	Wellington, New Zealand	41° 18'S	152 I9
Furthest east	Funafuti, Tuvalu	179° 13'E	145 G2
Furthest west	Nuku'alofa, Tonga	175° 12'W	145 H4

JOINT CAPITALS

cities	country	map
Amsterdam/The Hague	Netherlands	48 C3 / 48 B3
La Paz/Sucre	Bolivia	200 C4 / 200 D4
Pretoria/Cape Town	South Africa	133 M2 / 132 C10

1 Orinoco River, *South America*

The Orinoco river flows from right to left in this Shuttle photograph which looks towards the southeast. The upper section of the image shows the dense forests of the western edge of the Guiana Highlands. The main tributary joining the Orinoco is the Meta river with the town of Puerto Páez at the confluence. The Orinoco and the Meta form part of the boundary between Colombia and Venezuela.

Satellite/Sensor : Space Shuttle

2 Zaskar Mountains, *Asia*

The brackish waters of Tso Morari lake, surrounded by the Zaskar Mountains, can be seen at the left hand edge of this Shuttle photograph. North is to the right of the image. The mountains form one of the ranges at the western end of the Himalayas in the disputed area of Jammu and Kashmir. The lake is more than 4 000 m above sea level, the surrounding mountains rise to over 6 000 m.

Satellite/Sensor : Space Shuttle

3 Altiplano, *South America*

The Altiplano is a high plateau which stretches from western Bolivia to southern Peru. It has an average height of over 3 600 m and is bordered to the west and east by two main ridges of the Andes mountains. This Shuttle photograph shows part of Lake Coipasa. Unusually, the water level is high. The lake is normally a dry lakebed for the majority of the year. The photograph shows individual volcanoes which are common in this region.

Satellite/Sensor : Space Shuttle

1

2

CONNECTIONS

► subject		page#
► Types of imagery		4-5
► World physical features		8-9
► Volcanoes		14-15
► Land cover types		18-19
► Coral reefs		140-141

4

3

5

4 French Polynesia, *Oceania*

This view of Bora-Bora, an island group within the Society Islands of French Polynesia in the southern Pacific Ocean, is typical of this area which consists of many scattered groups of islands. The main island, just visible at the top of the photograph, lies in a large lagoon surrounded by numerous coral reefs and small islands.

5 Greenland, *North America*

Icebergs are usually formed either by sections breaking off glaciers which flow into the sea, or from the breaking up of ice-sheets as temperatures start to rise in spring. This one, off the northwest coast of Greenland in the Arctic Ocean, is surrounded by flat sections of broken up sea ice.

6 Namib Desert, *Africa*

This satellite image of the west coast of Africa clearly shows the natural barrier formed by the Kuiseb river at the northern edge of the Namib Desert in Namibia. To the north of the river are the Khomas Highlands which are rich in minerals, including uranium, to the south are the extensive dunes within the desert. The town of Walvis Bay is at the mouth of the river with the area's capital of Swakopmund just to the north.

Satellite/Sensor : Landsat

7 Canyonlands, *North America*

In this infrared satellite image of the Canyonlands region of the USA, vegetation shows as red, and forests as brown. The pale colours to the lower left of the image mark the area known as the Painted Desert. North is at the bottom. The image shows the upper reaches of the Grand Canyon, formed as a result of erosion by the Colorado River. The canyon ranges from six to twenty nine kilometres across.

Satellite/Sensor : SPOT

8 Taklimakan Desert, *Asia*

This image looks east over the Kunlun Shan mountains towards the Taklimakan Desert in the Tarim Pendi basin in China. The mountains mark the northern edge of the Plateau of Tibet. The southern edge of the plateau is the Himalayas. The dark areas in the desert at the top and on the left edge of the image are fertile areas, fed by intermittent rivers, around the towns of Hotan and Shache.

Satellite/Sensor : Space Shuttle

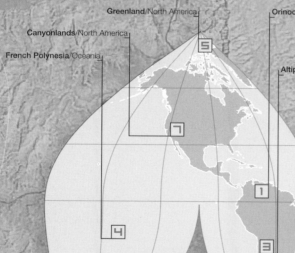

Greenland/North America

Canyonlands/North America

French Polynesia/Oceania

Orinoco River/South America

Altiplano/South America

Taklimakan Desert/Asia

Zaskar Mountains/Asia

Namib Desert/Africa

Sinusoidal Projection

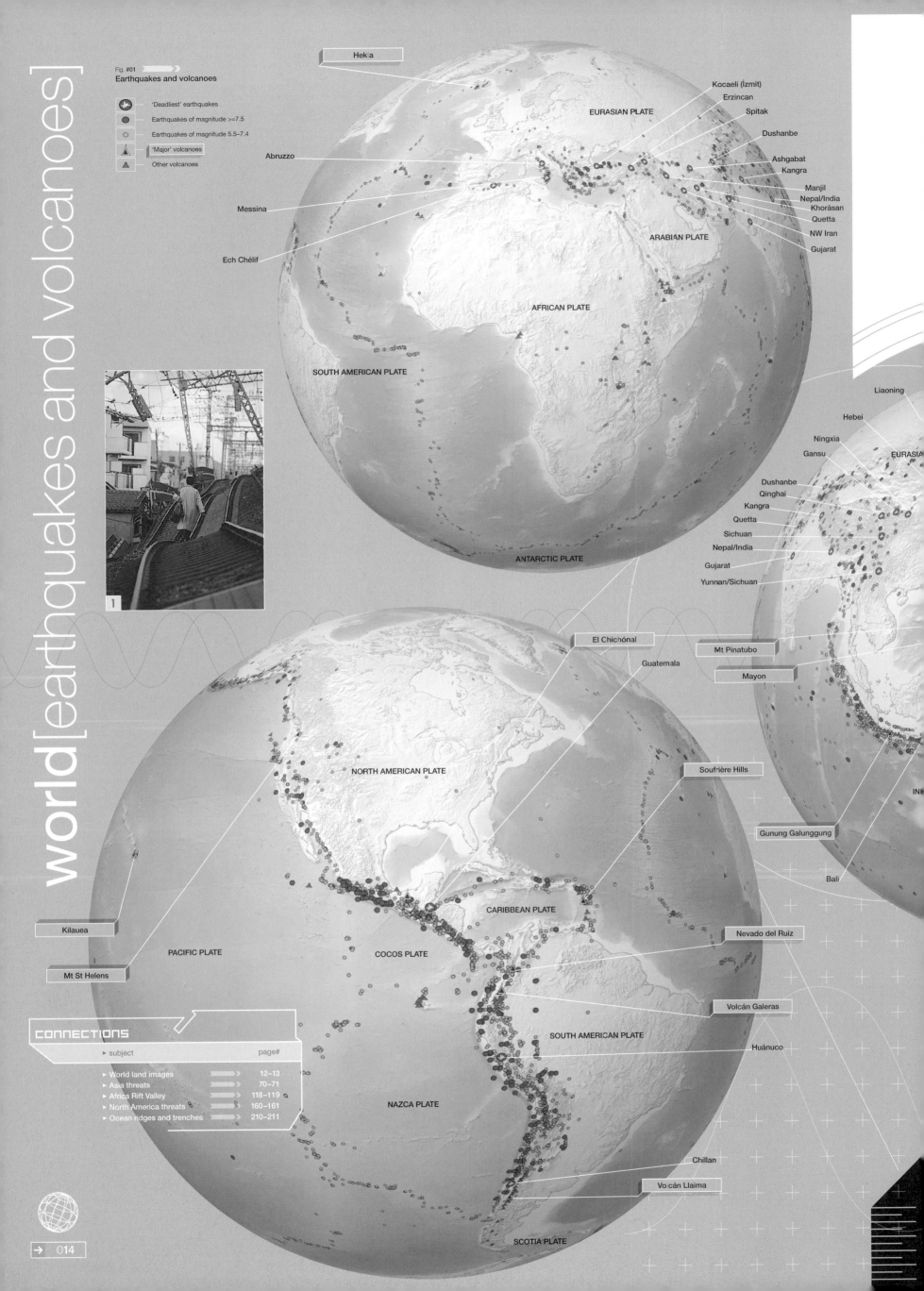

Fig. #01
Earthquakes and volcanoes

- 'Deadliest' earthquakes
- Earthquakes of magnitude >=7.5
- Earthquakes of magnitude 5.5–7.4
- 'Major' volcanoes
- Other volcanoes

Hekla

Kocaeli (Izmit)
Erzincan
Spitak
Dushanbe
Ashgabat
Kangra
Manjil
Nepal/India
Khorāsan
Quetta
NW Iran
Gujarat

EURASIAN PLATE

Abruzzo

Messina

ARABIAN PLATE

Ech Chélif

AFRICAN PLATE

SOUTH AMERICAN PLATE

Liaoning
Hebei
Ningxia
Gansu
EURASIA

Dushanbe
Qinghai
Kangra
Quetta
Sichuan
Nepal/India
Gujarat
Yunnan/Sichuan

ANTARCTIC PLATE

El Chichónal
Guatemala

Mt Pinatubo
Mayon

NORTH AMERICAN PLATE

Soufrière Hills

Gunung Galunggung

Bali

IN

Kilauea

PACIFIC PLATE

CARIBBEAN PLATE

Nevado del Ruiz

Mt St Helens

COCOS PLATE

SOUTH AMERICAN PLATE

Volcán Galeras

Huánuco

NAZCA PLATE

Chillan

Volcán Llaima

SCOTIA PLATE

CONNECTIONS

▸ subject	page#
▸ World land images	12–13
▸ Asia threats	70–71
▸ Africa Rift Valley	118–119
▸ North America threats	160–161
▸ Ocean ridges and trenches	210–211

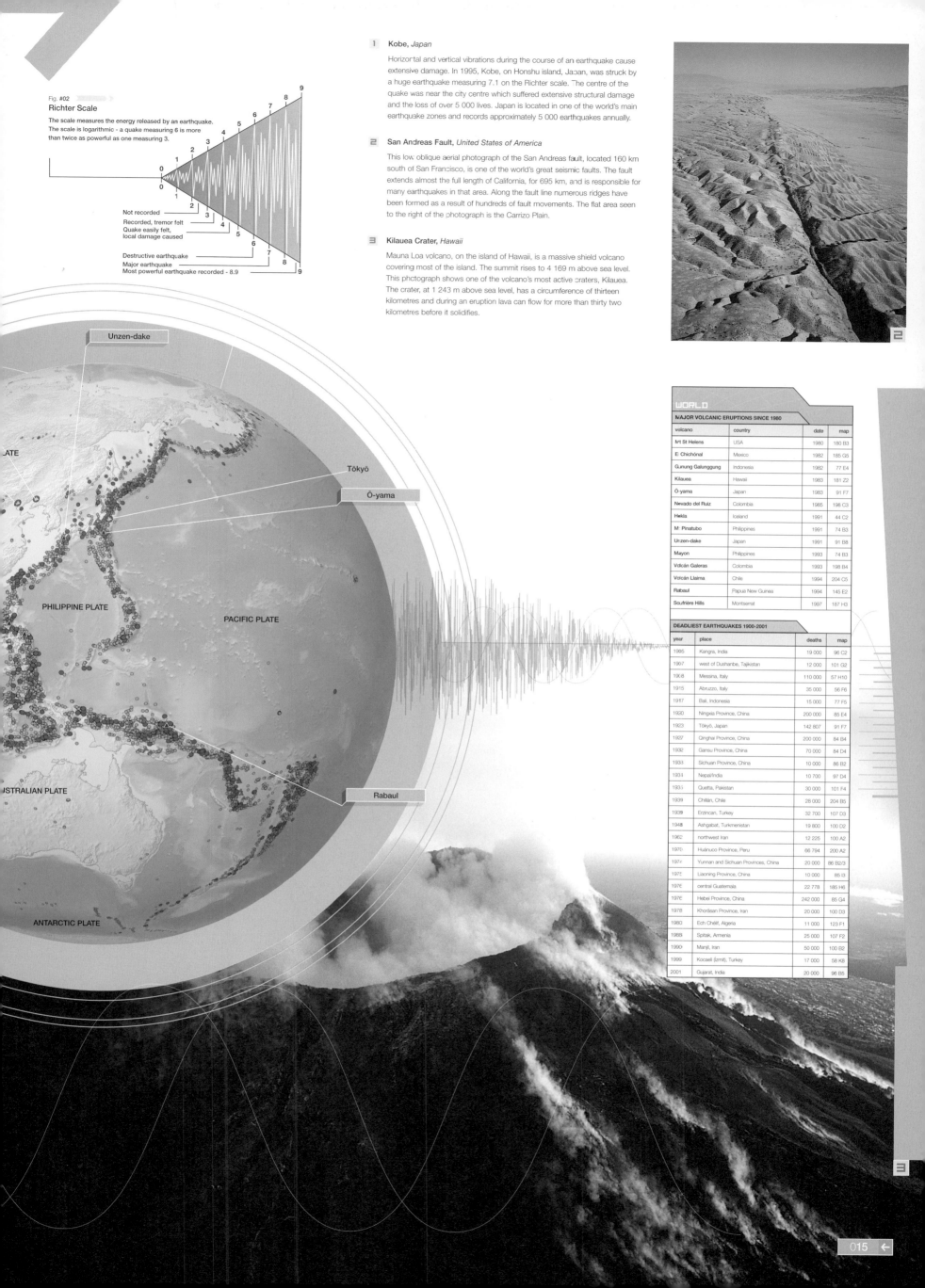

Fig. #02
Richter Scale

The scale measures the energy released by an earthquake.
The scale is logarithmic - a quake measuring 6 is more
than twice as powerful as one measuring 3.

Not recorded
Recorded, tremor felt
Quake easily felt,
local damage caused
Destructive earthquake
Major earthquake
Most powerful earthquake recorded - 8.9

1 Kobe, Japan

Horizontal and vertical vibrations during the course of an earthquake cause
extensive damage. In 1995, Kobe, on Honshu island, Japan, was struck by
a huge earthquake measuring 7.1 on the Richter scale. The centre of the
quake was near the city centre which suffered extensive structural damage
and the loss of over 5 000 lives. Japan is located in one of the world's main
earthquake zones and records approximately 5 000 earthquakes annually.

2 San Andreas Fault, United States of America

This low oblique aerial photograph of the San Andreas fault, located 160 km
south of San Francisco, is one of the world's great seismic faults. The fault
extends almost the full length of California, for 695 km, and is responsible for
many earthquakes in that area. Along the fault line numerous ridges have
been formed as a result of hundreds of fault movements. The flat area seen
to the right of the photograph is the Carrizo Plain.

3 Kilauea Crater, Hawaii

Mauna Loa volcano, on the island of Hawaii, is a massive shield volcano
covering most of the island. The summit rises to 4 169 m above sea level.
This photograph shows one of the volcano's most active craters, Kilauea.
The crater, at 1 243 m above sea level, has a circumference of thirteen
kilometres and during an eruption lava can flow for more than thirty two
kilometres before it solidifies.

Unzen-dake
Tōkyō
Ō-yama
Rabaul

PHILIPPINE PLATE
PACIFIC PLATE
AUSTRALIAN PLATE
ANTARCTIC PLATE

WORLD

MAJOR VOLCANIC ERUPTIONS SINCE 1980

volcano	country	date	map
Mt St Helens	USA	1980	180 B3
El Chichónal	Mexico	1982	185 G5
Gunung Galunggung	Indonesia	1982	77 E4
Kilauea	Hawaii	1983	181 Z2
Ō-yama	Japan	1983	91 F7
Nevado del Ruiz	Colombia	1985	198 C3
Hekla	Iceland	1991	44 C2
Mt Pinatubo	Philippines	1991	74 B3
Unzen-dake	Japan	1991	91 B8
Mayon	Philippines	1993	74 B3
Volcán Galeras	Colombia	1993	198 B4
Volcán Llaima	Chile	1994	204 C5
Rabaul	Papua New Guinea	1994	145 E2
Soufrière Hills	Montserrat	1997	187 H3

DEADLIEST EARTHQUAKES 1900-2001

year	place	deaths	map
1905	Kangra, India	19 000	96 C2
1907	west of Dushanbe, Tajikistan	12 000	101 G2
1908	Messina, Italy	110 000	57 H10
1915	Abruzzo, Italy	35 000	56 F6
1917	Bali, Indonesia	15 000	77 F5
1920	Ningxia Province, China	200 000	85 E4
1923	Tōkyō, Japan	142 807	91 F7
1927	Qinghai Province, China	200 000	84 B4
1932	Gansu Province, China	70 000	84 D4
1933	Sichuan Province, China	10 000	86 B2
1934	Nepal/India	10 700	97 D4
1935	Quetta, Pakistan	30 000	101 F4
1939	Chillán, Chile	28 000	204 B5
1939	Erzincan, Turkey	32 700	107 D3
1948	Ashgabat, Turkmenistan	19 800	100 D2
1962	northwest Iran	12 225	100 A2
1970	Huánuco Province, Peru	66 794	200 A2
1974	Yunnan and Sichuan Provinces, China	20 000	86 B2/3
1975	Liaoning Province, China	10 000	85 I3
1976	central Guatemala	22 778	185 H6
1976	Hebei Province, China	242 000	85 G4
1978	Khorāsan Province, Iran	20 000	100 D3
1980	Ech Chélif, Algeria	11 000	123 F1
1988	Spitak, Armenia	25 000	107 F2
1990	Manjil, Iran	50 000	100 B2
1999	Kocaeli (İzmit), Turkey	17 000	58 K8
2001	Gujarat, India	20 000	96 B5

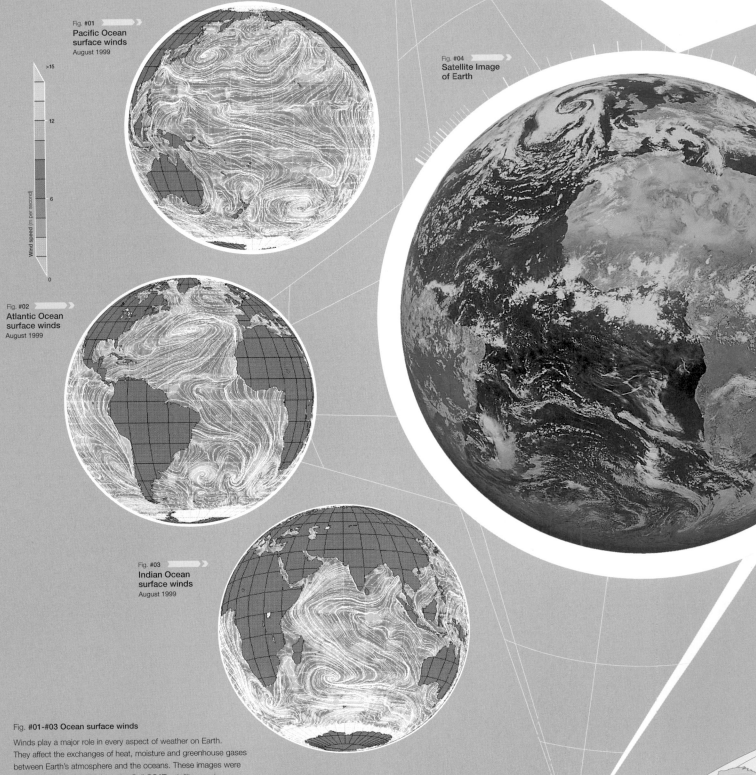

Fig. #01
Pacific Ocean
surface winds
August 1999

Wind speed (m per second)

>15

12

6

0

Fig. #02
Atlantic Ocean
surface winds
August 1999

Fig. #03
Indian Ocean
surface winds
August 1999

Fig. #04
Satellite Image
of Earth

Fig. #01-#03 Ocean surface winds

Winds play a major role in every aspect of weather on Earth.
They affect the exchanges of heat, moisture and greenhouse gases
between Earth's atmosphere and the oceans. These images were
taken on 1 August 1999 from the QuikSCAT satellite carrying a
radar instrument called a scatterometer which can record surface
wind speeds in the oceans. In the image of the Pacific Ocean
yellow spirals representing typhoon Olga can be seen moving
around South Korea and the East China Sea. Intense winter
storms can also be seen around Antarctica in all three images.

Satellite/Sensor : QuikSCAT/SeaWinds

Fig. #04 Satellite image of Earth

Images such as this from the Meteosat satellite provide valuable
meteorological information on a global scale. Dense clouds appear
white, thinner cloud cover as pink . A swirling frontal weather system
is clearly seen in the Atlantic Ocean to the west of Europe.

Satellite/Sensor : Meteosat

Fig. #10-#11 Climate change in the future

Future climate change will depend to a large extent on the effect
human activities have on the chemical composition of the
atmosphere. As greenhouse gases and aerosol emissions increase
the atmospheric temperatures rise. The map of predicted
temperature in the 2050s shows that average annual temperatures
may rise by as much as 5°C in some areas if current emission rates
continue. The map of precipitation change shows some areas are
likely to experience a significant increase in precipitation of over 3
mm per day, while others will experience a decrease. Such changes
are likely to have significant impacts on sea level which could rise
by as much as 50 cm in the next century. The changes would also
have implications for water resources, food production and health.

Fig. #05
Major climatic regions and sub-types

Köppen classification system

A   Rainy climate with no winter:
    coolest month above 18°C (64.4°F).
B   Dry climates; limits are defined by formulae
    based on rainfall effectiveness:
    BS Steppe or semi-arid climate.
    BW Desert or arid climate.
*C Rainy climates with mild winters:
    coolest month above 0°C (32°F), but
    below 18°C (64.4°F); warmest month
    above 10°C (50°F).
*D Rainy climates with severe winters:
    coldest month below 0°C (32°F);
    warmest month above 10°C (50°F).
E   Polar climates with no warm season:
    warmest month below 10°C (50°F).
    ET Tundra climate: warmest month
    below 10°C (50°F) but above
    0°C (32°F).
    EF Perpetual frost: all months below
    0°C (32°F).
a   Warmest month above 22°C (71.6°F).
b   Warmest month below 22°C (71.6°F).
c   Less than four months over 10°C (50°F).
d   As 'c', but with severe cold: coldest
    month below -38°C (-36.4°F).
f   Constantly moist rainfall throughout the year.
*h Warmer dry: all months above 0°C (32°F).
*k Cooler dry: at least one month below
    0°C (32°F).
m   Monsoon rain: short dry season, but is
    compensated by heavy rains during rest
    of the year.
n   Frequent fog.
s   Dry season in summer.
w   Dry season in winter.

* Modification of Köppen definition

Polar

EF Ice cap

ET Tundra

Cooler humid

Dc Dd Subarctic

Db Continental cool summer

Da Continental warm summer

Warmer humid

Cb Cc Temperate

Ca Humid subtropical

Cs Mediterranean

Dry

BS Steppe

BW Desert

Tropical humid

Aw As Savanna

Af Am Rain forest

CONNECTIONS

► subject   page#

► Asia threats   70–71
► Africa issues   116–117
► North America threats   160–161
► South America impacts   196–197
► Antarctica features   212–213
► Arctic features   214–215

Fig. #06

Tracks of tropical storms
Wind speeds often over
160km per hour

⇨ Cyclone track ⇨ Willy-willies ▢ Source area of tropical storms
⇨ Typhoon track ⇨ Hurricane track ● Major tropical storm (1994-2000)

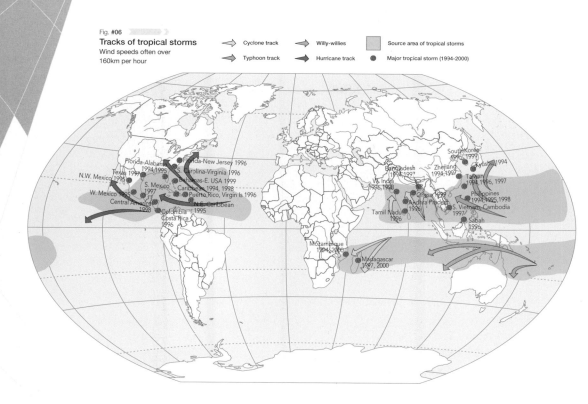

Fig. #07
Actual surface temperature
January

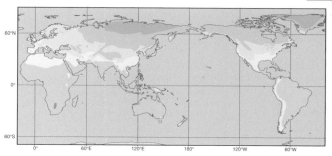

Fig. #08

Actual surface temperature
July

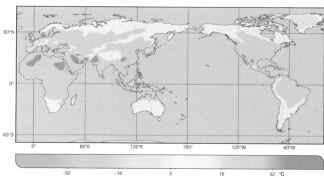

-32   -16   0   16   32 °C

Fig. #09

Average annual precipitation

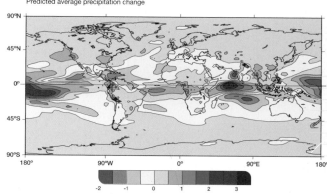

0   2.5   5   7.5   10
Precipitation (mm per day)

WORLD

WEATHER EXTREMES

Highest shade temperature	57.8°C/136°F Al 'Azīzīyah, Libya (13th September 1922)
Hottest place — Annual mean	34.4°C/93.9°F Dalol, Ethiopia
Driest place — Annual mean	0.1 mm/0.004 inches Atacama Desert, Chile
Most sunshine — Annual mean	90% Yuma, Arizona, USA (over 4 000 hours)
Least sunshine	Nil for 182 days each year, South Pole
Lowest screen temperature	-89.2°C/-128.6°F Vostok Station, Antarctica (21st July 1983)
Coldest place — Annual mean	-56.6°C/-69.9°F Plateau Station, Antarctica
Wettest place — Annual mean	11 873 mm/467.4 inches Meghalaya, India
Most rainy days	Up to 350 per year Mount Waialeale, Hawaii, USA
Windiest place	322 km per hour/200 miles per hour in gales, Commonwealth Bay, Antarctica
Highest surface wind speed	
High altitude	372 km per hour/231 miles per hour Mount Washington, New Hampshire, USA (12th April 1934)
Low altitude	333 km per hour/207 miles per hour Qaanaaq (Thule), Greenland (8th March 1972)
Tornado	512 km per hour/318 miles per hour Oklahoma City, Oklahoma, USA (3rd May 1999)
Greatest snowfall	31 102 mm/1 224.5 inches Mount Rainier, Washington, USA (19th February 1971—18th February 1972)
Heaviest hailstones	1 kg/2.21 lb Gopalganj, Bangladesh (14th April 1986)
Thunder-days Average	251 days per year Tororo, Uganda
Highest barometric pressure	1 083.8 mb Agata, Siberia, Russian Federation (31st December 1968)
Lowest barometric pressure	870 mb 483 km/300 miles west of Guam, Pacific Ocean (12th October 1979)

Fig. #10 -#11

Climate changes in the future

#10 Precipitation in 2050s
Predicted average precipitation change

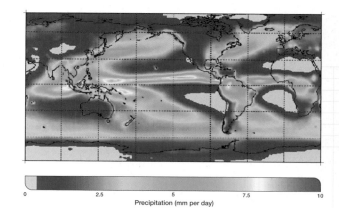

-2 -1 0 1 2 3
Average precipitation change (mm per day)

#11 Temperature in 2050s
Predicted annual mean temperature change

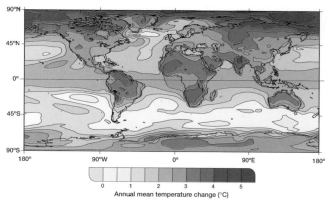

0 1 2 3 4 5
Annual mean temperature change (°C)

1 Wetland

Wetland areas make up less than 1 per cent of world land cover. This aerial photograph of the Okavango Delta in Botswana shows an unusual environment. Set in the centre of southern Africa, the Okavango river drains into this low lying area, not into the sea. The extent of the wetland varies with the amount of rainfall in the catchment area. The high water table allows for a wide diversity of vegetation to grow in an area surrounded by grassland.

2 Crops/Mosaic

Fertile land which is cultivated by man often produces geometric patterns. The infrared satellite image shows part of the Everglades swamp in Florida, USA, east of Lake Okeechobee. Bare fields appear as dark pink and planted fields as green. The pattern continues into the urban areas depicted in blue. Regular field systems such as these enable mechanized agriculture and crop diversification. The dark mottled area to the top right of the image is an undeveloped part of the Everglades.

Satellite/Sensor : Landsat

3 Urban

Representing approximately 0.2 per cent of total world land cover, the urban environment is probably the farthest removed from the Earth's original, natural land cover. This aerial view of Manhattan in New York, USA, shows the 'grid iron' street pattern typical of many modern cities. Major natural features, such as the Hudson River in this image, interrupt this regular plan. Parkland areas, such as that appearing at the top left of the image, are manufactured rather than natural.

4 Grass/Savanna

This view of Ngorongoro, Tanzania is typical of tropical savanna grasslands. Over 25 per cent of Africa's land cover falls within this category. Large areas of tropical grasslands also occur in South America and northern Australia, with temperate grasslands in North America (prairie) and Asia (steppe). Seasonal rainfall provides a regular cycle of lush, tall grass interspersed by scattered trees and shrubs. The savanna areas of east Africa support large numbers of wild animals.

5 Forest/Woodland

The type of woodland coverage in this photograph is tropical rainforest or jungle. This accounts for over 40 per cent of land cover in South America. Dense coverage includes tall hardwood trees which provide a high canopy over smaller trees and shrubs capable of surviving with little direct sunlight. Natural forest or woodland areas such as the Amazon are under continuous threat from the external pressures of agriculture, mineral exploration or urbanization.

6 Barren

The Hoggar region of Algeria is part of the 30 per cent of barren land in Africa, the most extensive land cover type on the continent. This area is a plateau of bare rock lying at a height of over 2 000 m above sea level. It is surrounded by the sandy desert of the Sahara. Rainfall is negligible and the extreme temperatures result in little, or no vegetation and wildlife.

7 Shrubland

Shrubland areas, shown here around Ayers Rock in central Australia, develop on the fringes of desert regions. Sporadic rainfall and less severe temperatures than in the deserts, are enough for hardy plants and shrubs to grow in the thin soil. Moving away from the desert areas, as conditions become less harsh, the vegetation changes and the range of plants increases.

8 Snow/Ice

The continent of Antarctica is almost completely covered by snow and ice. In the northern hemisphere, Spitsbergen, shown here, is one of a large group of islands within the Arctic Circle which is also permanently covered. There is no vegetation on land and any wildlife must survive on food caught in the sea. Although inhospitable areas at the polar extremes see little human interaction, they are affected by global increases in temperature. Resultant melting of glaciers and icecaps threatens a rise in sea level.

CONNECTIONS

► subject	page#
► Changes to land cover	20–21
► World cities	24–25
► North America environments	162–163
► South America contrasts	194–195
► Arctic regions	210–211

Fig. #01
Continental land cover composition

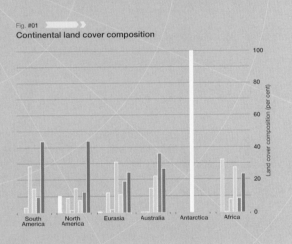

Land cover composition (per cent)

South America · North America · Eurasia · Australia · Antarctica · Africa

Urban
Wetland
Snow/Ice
Barren
Grass/Savanna
Shrubland
Crops/Mosaic
Forest/Woodland

Fig. #02
Global land cover composition

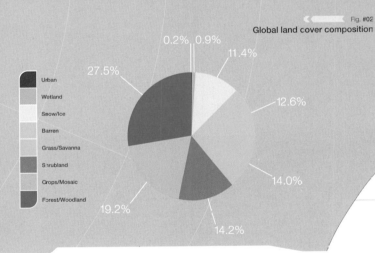

0.2% 0.9% 11.4% 12.6% 27.5% 14.0% 19.2% 14.2%

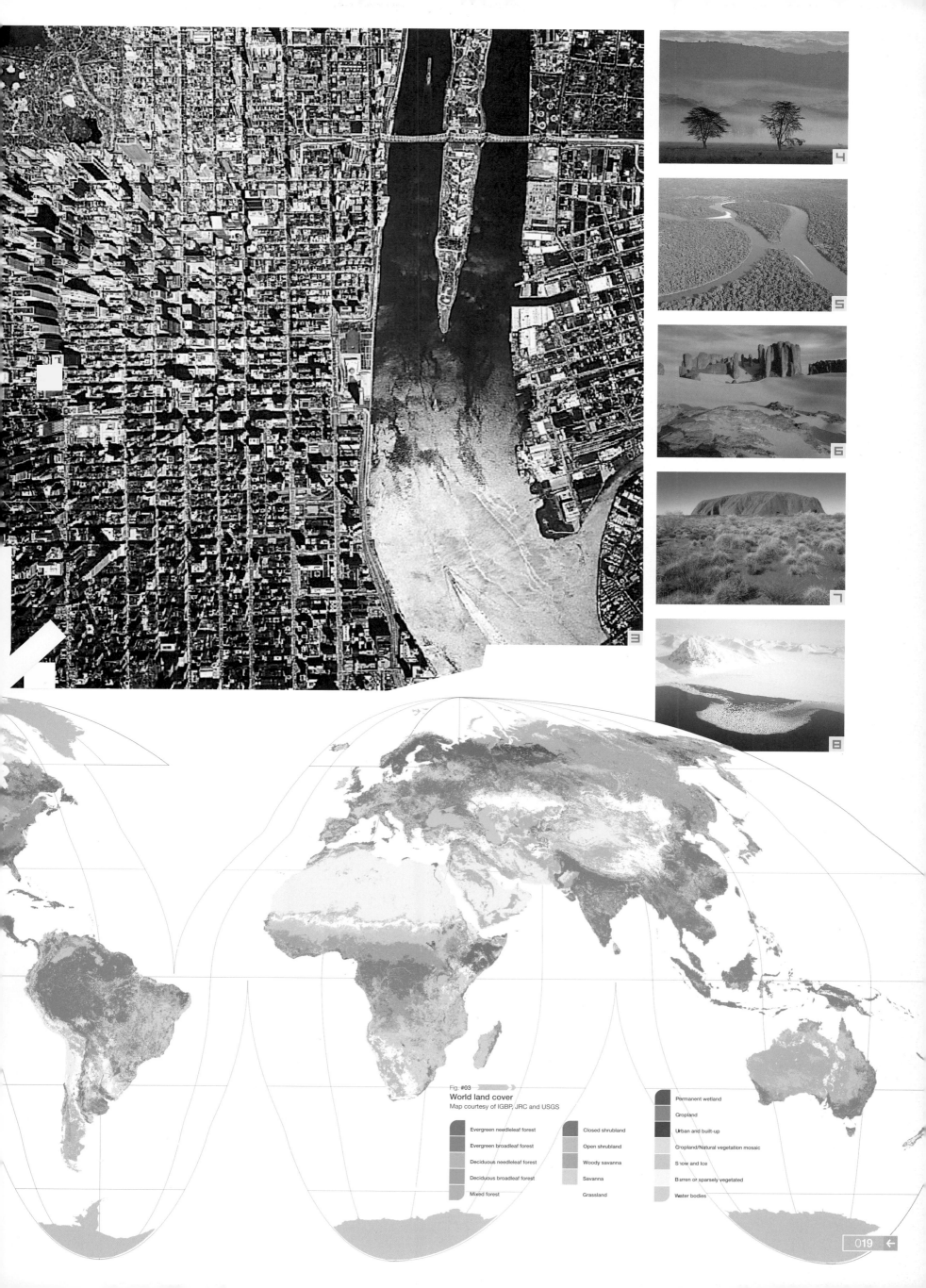

Fig. #03

World land cover
Map courtesy of IGBP, JRC and USGS

Evergreen needleleaf forest	Closed shrubland	Permanent wetland
Evergreen broadleaf forest	Open shrubland	Cropland
Deciduous needleleaf forest	Woody savanna	Urban and built-up
Deciduous broadleaf forest	Savanna	Cropland/Natural vegetation mosaic
Mixed forest	Grassland	Snow and Ice
		Barren or sparsely vegetated
		Water bodies

world[changes]

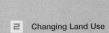

Changing Land Use

The changes in land use between Alberta, Canada (top) and Montana, USA (bottom) can be seen on this infrared satellite image. The straight international boundary runs diagonally from centre left to upper right. Intense cultivation on the US side has created regular field patterns, whereas on the Canadian side plantations of forest and thick mountain vegetation cover extensive areas.

Satellite/Sensor : Landsat

Deforestation

This aerial photograph shows the dramatic effect the clearcut logging method of deforestation can have on a landscape. The change in appearance and the effects on the immediate environment can be dramatic. It shows part of the northwest US state of Washington, which has large areas of thick forest, particularly on the western slopes of the Cascade mountain range. More than half of the state is forested and lumber and lumber-related products form the basis of much of the state's economic activity.

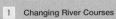

Changing River Courses

This aerial infrared photograph shows a small section of the Mississippi river near Lake Providence in Louisiana state. The pattern of old loops and bends identifies old courses of the river, showing changes which have occurred over many years. Some loops have become isolated 'oxbow' lakes as shown on the west bank of the river in the left of the image. At the bottom right one former loop of the river can be identified within the cultivated area.

Urban Growth

These Landsat images illustrate how such imagery can be used to monitor environmental change. They show the rapid urban growth which has taken place in and around Shenzhen, China, between 1988 (left) and 1996 (right). This city has benefited greatly from its location adjacent to Hong Kong. One of the most obvious changes is the development along the coastline, where huge off-shore structures and large areas of reclaimed land can be seen in the 1996 image. Much of the vegetation (red) in the left image has been cleared and replaced by urban development, leaving only scattered patches of the original vegetation.

Satellite/Sensor : Landsat

5 Environmental Effects of War

These two images of Kuwait were taken in 1984 (left) and 1998 (right) and show the impact of oil fires during the 1991 Gulf War. In the course of this war hundreds of oil wells were set on fire, and oil lakes, visible at the bottom of the 1998 mage, were formed. The soot from the fires combined with sand and oil to leave a black layer of 'tarcrete' on almost five per cent of the country's area. Traces of this can be seen on the 1998 image to the southeast of the oilfield. Time-sequence satellite imagery such as this can reveal such drastic effects of war, and assist in monitoring changes.

Satellite/Sensor : Landsat

Washington State   Alberta/Montana   Kuwait

Mississippi   Shenzhen

CONNECTIONS

▶ subject		page#
▶ World cities		24–25
▶ Asia changes		68–69
▶ North America countries		158–159
▶ North America environments		162–163
▶ South America impacts		196–197

— 2050
— 1998

80+
75-79
70-74
65-69
60-64
55-59
50-54
45-49
40-44
35-39
30-34
25-29
20-24
15-19
10-14
5-9
0-4

300 250 200 150 100 50 0   0 50 100 150 200 250 300

millions   millions

Fig. #01
Age pyramid
Less developed countries

1 Village Settlement, *Botswana*

The Kalahari Desert stretches across the southwest and central part of Botswana and into Namibia and South Africa. This photograph shows a small village settlement in this very isolated and sparsely populated region. Such villages are usually temporary with the area's people living nomadic lives, moving on to new locations when food sources run low. Although surface water is practically non-existent in the desert, underlying groundwater supports deep-rooted shrubs and trees.

2 Tokyo, *Japan*

A small section of Tokyo, the world's largest city and the capital of Japan, is shown in this aerial photograph mosaic. The contrasting pattern of high-rise development and densely packed low-rise buildings is typical of many major Asian cities. While displaying all the characteristics of a modern city, it has retained much of its cultural and historical identity. It is renowned for its excellent transport systems and is the centre of government, industry, commerce and education in Japan.

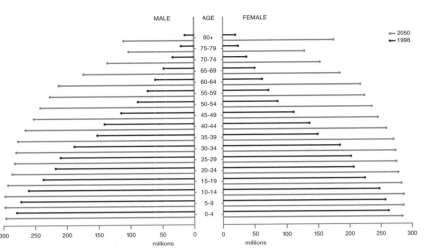

CONNECTIONS

▸ subject   page#

▸ World countries   10–11
▸ World cities   24–25
▸ Chinese migration   66–67
▸ Ethnic groups in the Balkans   34–35
▸ Arctic peoples   214–215

Fig. #03
World population growth by continent
1750-2050

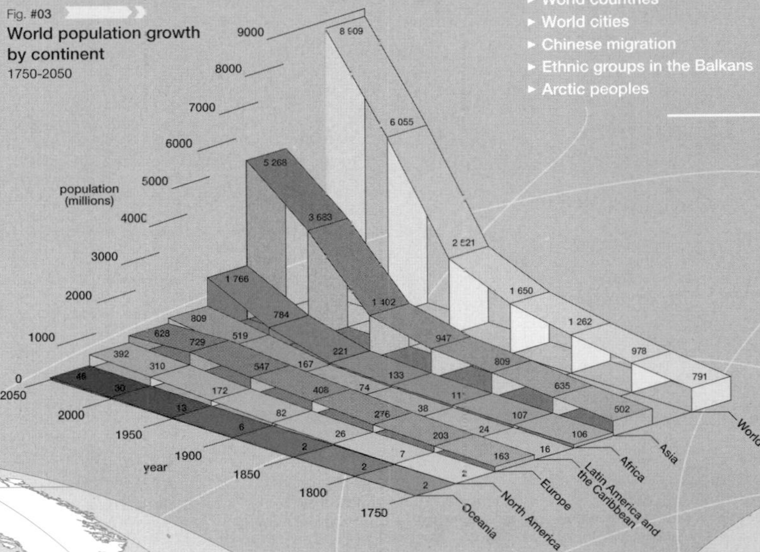

9000
8000
7000
6000
population (millions) 5000
4000
3000
2000
1000
0

Fig. #04
World population distribution

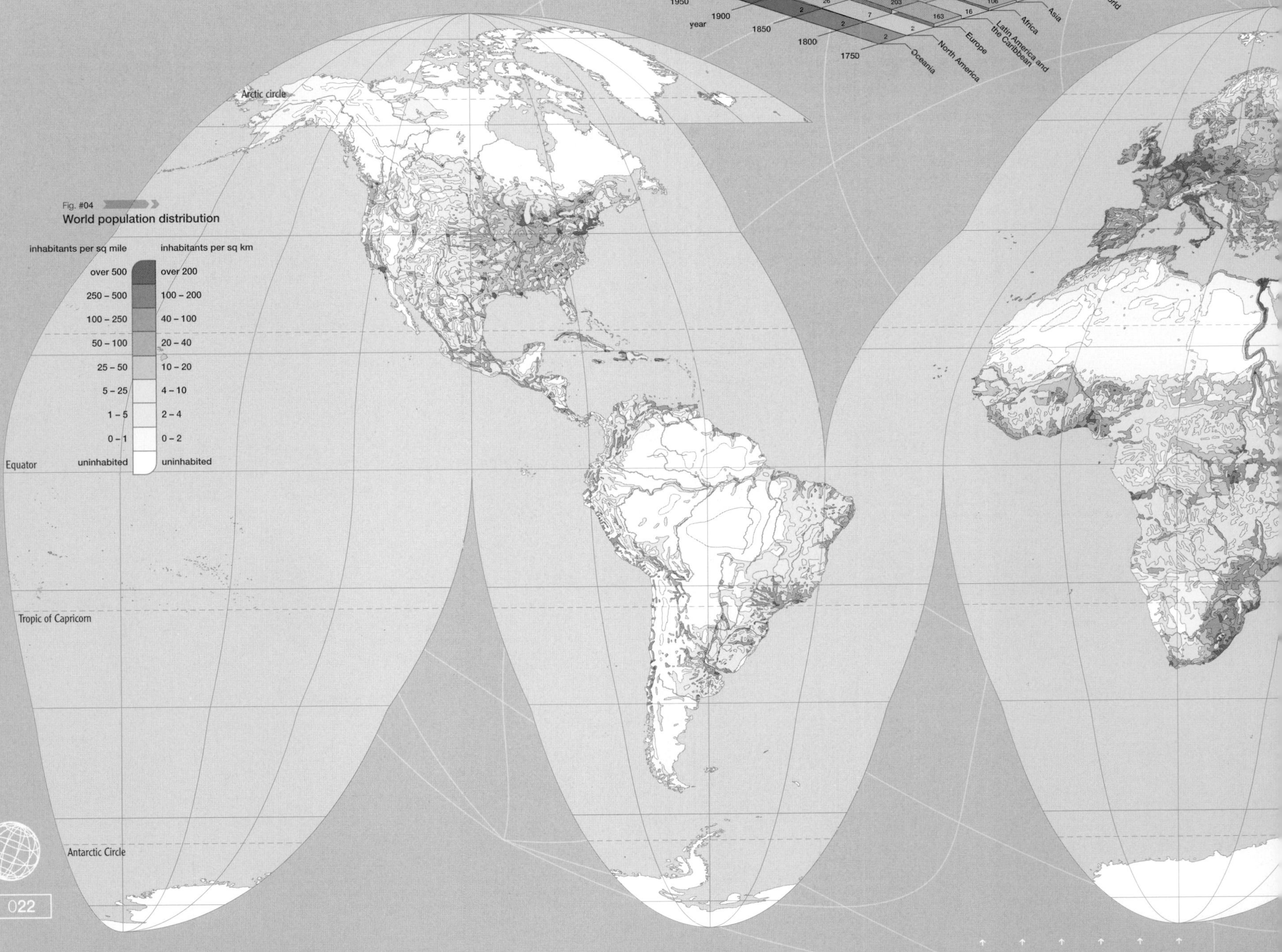

inhabitants per sq mile	inhabitants per sq km
over 500	over 200
250 – 500	100 – 200
100 – 250	40 – 100
50 – 100	20 – 40
25 – 50	10 – 20
5 – 25	4 – 10
1 – 5	2 – 4
0 – 1	0 – 2
uninhabited	uninhabited

Arctic circle

Equator

Tropic of Capricorn

Antarctic Circle

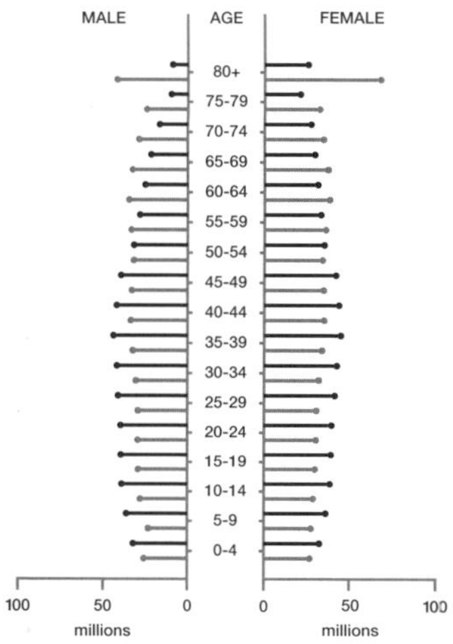

2

MALE | AGE | FEMALE

80+
75-79
70-74
65-69
60-64
55-59
50-54
45-49
40-44
35-39
30-34
25-29
20-24
15-19
10-14
5-9
0-4

100 50 0   0 50 100
millions   millions

Fig. #02

Age pyramid
More developed countries

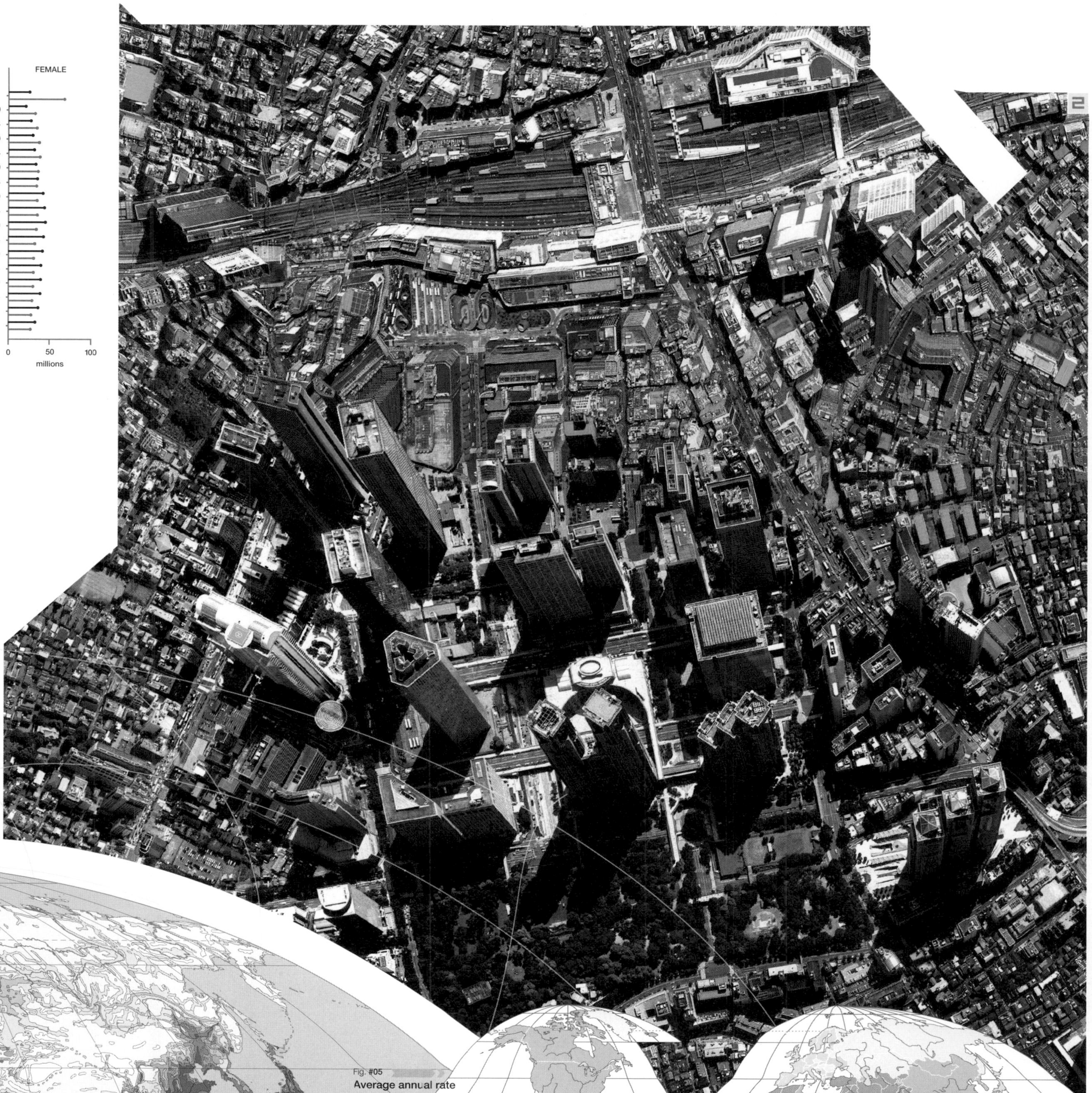

Fig. #05

Average annual rate
of population change
1995-2000

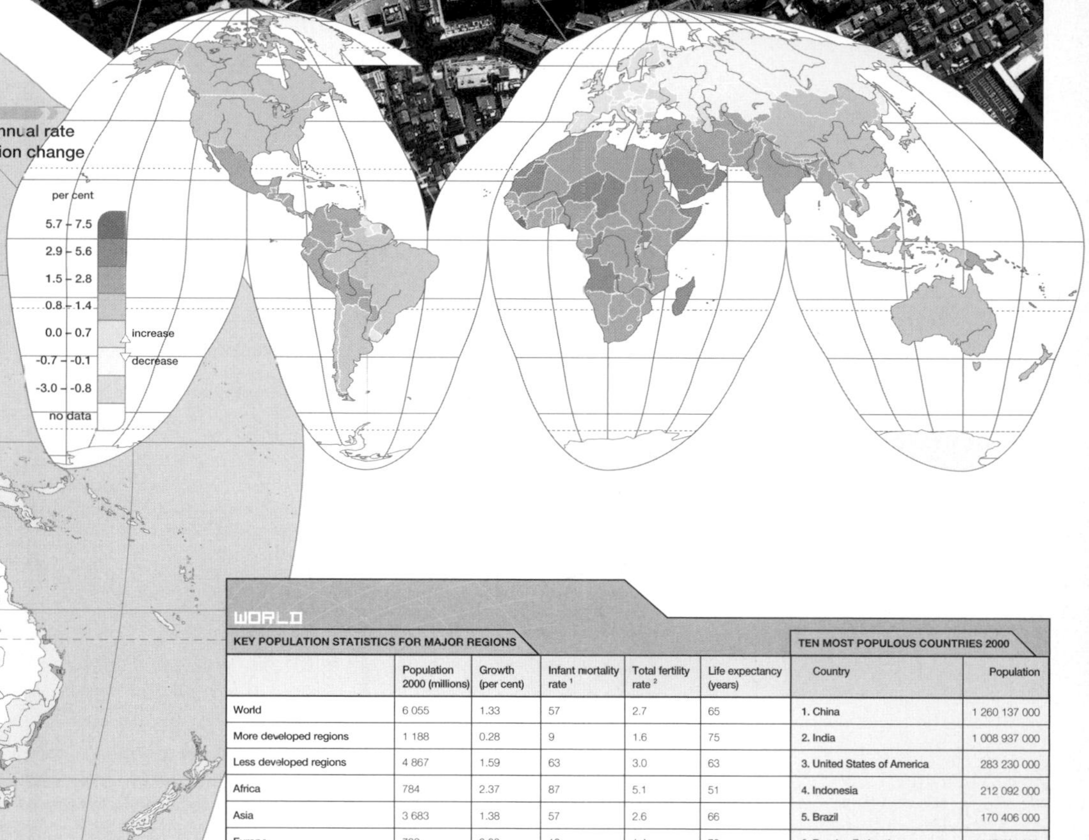

per cent
5.7 – 7.5
2.9 – 5.6
1.5 – 2.8
0.8 – 1.4
0.0 – 0.7   increase
-0.7 – -0.1   decrease
-3.0 – -0.8
no data

WORLD

KEY POPULATION STATISTICS FOR MAJOR REGIONS

TEN MOST POPULOUS COUNTRIES 2000

	Population 2000 (millions)	Growth (per cent)	Infant mortality rate [1]	Total fertility rate [2]	Life expectancy (years)	Country	Population
World	6 055	1.33	57	2.7	65	1. China	1 260 137 000
More developed regions	1 188	0.28	9	1.6	75	2. India	1 008 937 000
Less developed regions	4 867	1.59	63	3.0	63	3. United States of America	283 230 000
Africa	784	2.37	87	5.1	51	4. Indonesia	212 092 000
Asia	3 683	1.38	57	2.6	66	5. Brazil	170 406 000
Europe	729	0.03	12	1.4	73	6. Russian Federation	145 491 000
Latin America and the Caribbean	519	1.57	36	2.7	69	7. Pakistan	141 256 000
North America	310	0.85	7	1.9	77	8. Bangladesh	137 439 000
Oceania	30	1.3	24	2.4	74	9. Japan	127 096 000
						10. Nigeria	113 862 000

[1] Deaths of infants less than one year old per 1 000 live births
[2] Estimate of number of children a woman will bear through her child-bearing years

1 San Francisco, *United States of America*

The city of San Francisco is situated on the peninsula which lies to the western side of San Francisco Bay. The Golden Gate, upper left, bridges the entrance to the bay and three other bridges are visible in the image. San Francisco has frequently suffered extensive damage from earthquakes and the two lakes south of the city mark the line of the San Andreas fault. The southern end of the bay is surrounded by a green patchwork of salt beds.

Satellite/Sensor : Landsat

2 Hong Kong, *China*

A British colony until 1997, Hong Kong is now a Special Administrative Region of China. This high resolution satellite image is centred on Hong Kong Harbour, with the Kowloon Peninsula to the north (top) and Hong Kong Island to the south. Much of the coastline shown is reclaimed land, including the old Kai Tak airport, seen in the top right of the image. This airport has been closed since the completion of the new Hong Kong International airport 25 kilometres west of the harbour.

Satellite/Sensor : IKONOS

3 Cairo, *Egypt*

This oblique aerial photograph looks north across the suburbs of southwest Cairo. There has been a major expansion of the city and its suburbs over the last fifty years and the city now has a population of over 10 million. The urban expansion brings the city up against the important historical site of the Giza Pyramids. The Pyramid of Khufu and the Great Sphinx can be seen at the left of the photograph.

4 Tokyo, *Japan*

This false-colour infrared image of Tokyo shows the northwest edge of Tokyo Bay. It shows just a small part of the vast expanse of Tokyo, the world's largest city with over 26 million inhabitants. The amount of land reclamation in the bay is obvious, and the reclaimed land includes Tokyo International (Haneda) Airport, at the bottom of the image. Vegetation shows as red, making the grounds of the Imperial Palace clearly visible in the top left.

Satellite/Sensor : Terra/ASTER

CONNECTIONS

▶ subject	page#
▶ World countries	10–11
▶ World land cover	18–19
▶ Urban growth	20–21
▶ World population	22–23
▶ Oceania capitals	138–139

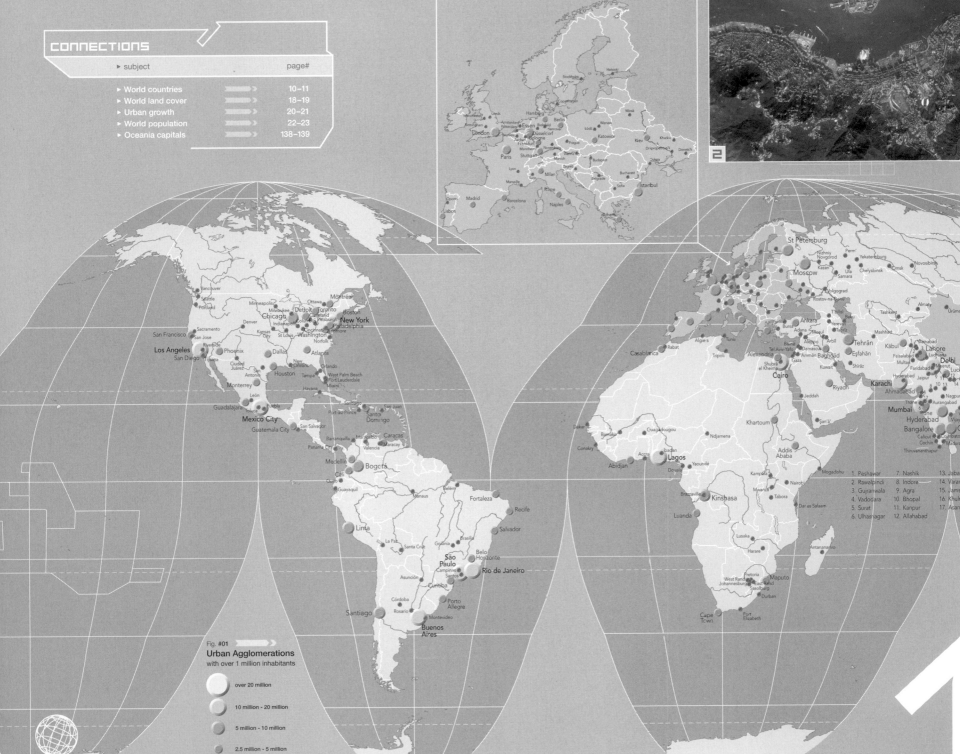

EUROPE

Fig. #01

Urban Agglomerations
with over 1 million inhabitants

- over 20 million
- 10 million – 20 million
- 5 million – 10 million
- 2.5 million – 5 million
- 1 million – 2.5 million

1. Peshawar
2. Rawalpindi
3. Gujranwala
4. Vadodara
5. Surat
6. Ulhasnagar
7. Nashik
8. Indore
9. Agra
10. Bhopal
11. Kanpur
12. Allahabad
13. Jabalpur
14. Varanasi
15. Jamshedpur
16. Khulna
17. Asansol

Fig. #02

10 Million Cities
Dates at which cities attained 10 million population
1950-2015

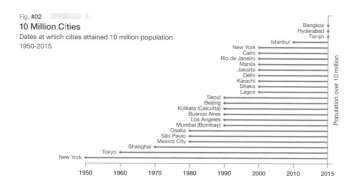

Bangkok
Hyderabad
Tianjin
Istanbul
New York
Cairo
Rio de Janeiro
Manila
Jakarta
Delhi
Karachi
Dhaka
Lagos
Seoul
Beijing
Kolkata (Calcutta)
Buenos Aires
Los Angeles
Mumbai (Bombay)
Osaka
Mexico City
Shanghai
Tokyo
New York

Population over 10 million

1950 1960 1970 1980 1990 2000 2010 2015

Fig. #03

World Top 10 Cities
1900-2015

World Rank

1 2 3 4 5 6 7 8 9 10

1900 1930 1950 1960 1970 1980 1990 2000 2010 2015

- London
- New York
- Berlin
- Chigago
- Wuhan
- Tokyo
- Philadelphia
- St Petersburg
- Paris
- Moscow
- Shanghai
- Osaka
- Buenos Aires
- Essen
- Kolkata (Calcutta)
- Beijing
- Los Angeles
- Mexico City
- São Paulo
- Mumbai (Bombay)
- Lagos
- Dhaka
- Karachi
- Jakarta

WORLD

THE WORLD'S LARGEST CITIES 2000

city	country	population
Tōkyō	Japan	26 444 000
Mexico City	Mexico	18 131 000
Mumbai (Bombay)	India	18 066 000
São Paulo	Brazil	17 755 000
New York	United States of America	16 640 000
Lagos	Nigeria	13 427 000
Los Angeles	United States of America	13 140 000
Kolkata (Calcutta)	India	12 918 000
Shanghai	China	12 887 000
Buenos Aires	Argentina	12 560 000
Dhaka	Bangladesh	12 317 000
Karachi	Pakistan	11 794 000
Delhi	India	11 695 000
Jakarta	Indonesia	11 018 000
Ōsaka	Japan	11 013 000
Manla	Philippines	10 870 000
Beijing	China	10 839 000
Rio de Janeiro	Brazil	10 582 000
Cairo	Egypt	10 552 000
Seoul	South Korea	9 888 000

CHINA AND JAPAN

Fig. #01
Communications
satellites

Fig. #01 Communications Satellites

This graphic shows the current distribution of major communications satellites in orbit around the Earth. These satellites relay radio, telephone and television signals between ground stations or to other satellites. They are generally in 'geostationary' orbits above the equator, remaining above a fixed point on the Earth and completing an orbit every 24 hours. Their specific locations are determined by the demands for signal coverage. Two coincident equatorial orbits are indicated as examples – Intelsat 605 positioned above 27°30'W and Astra 1F at 19°12'E.

INTELSAT 605

Fig. #02
World telecommunications equipment
1970-2000

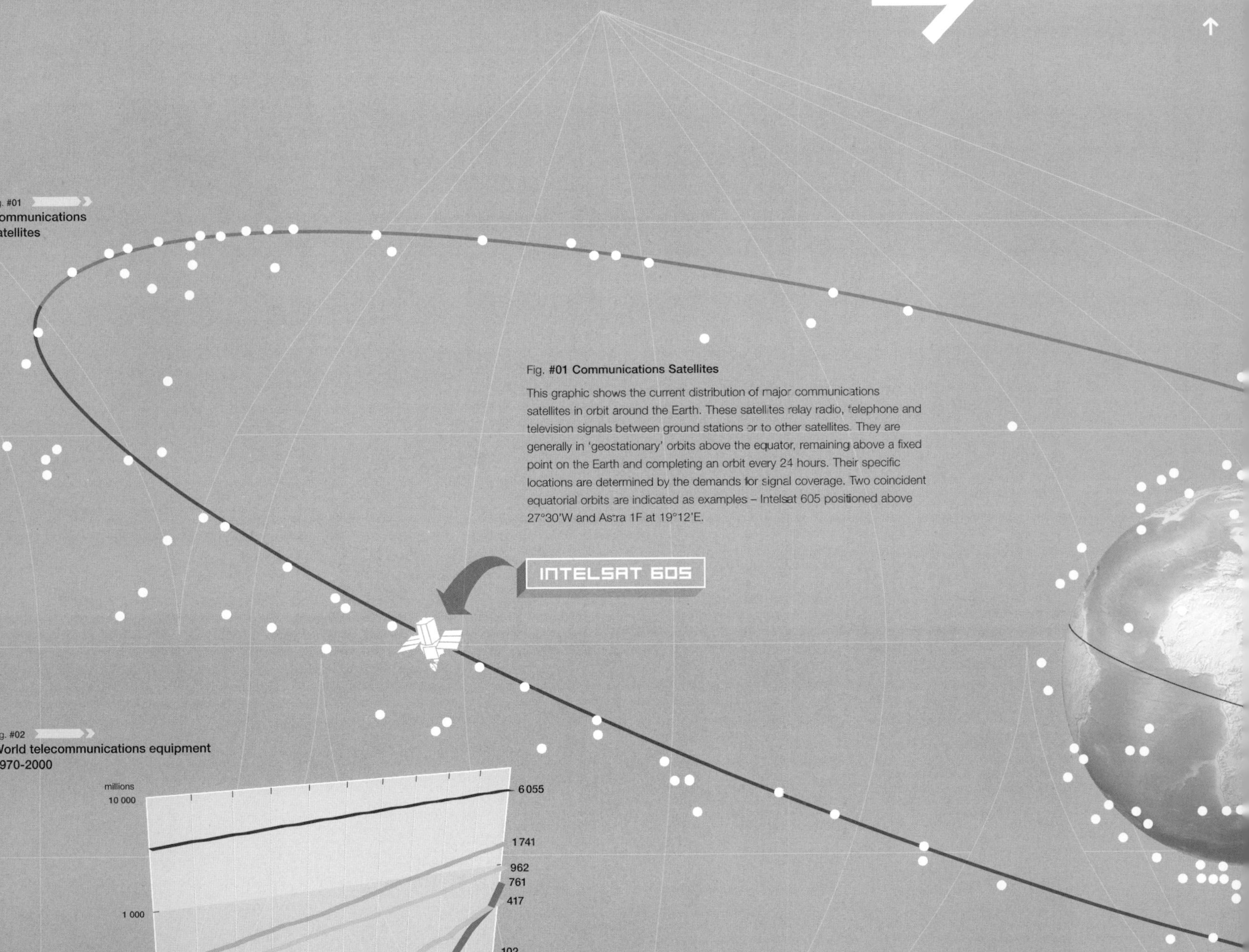

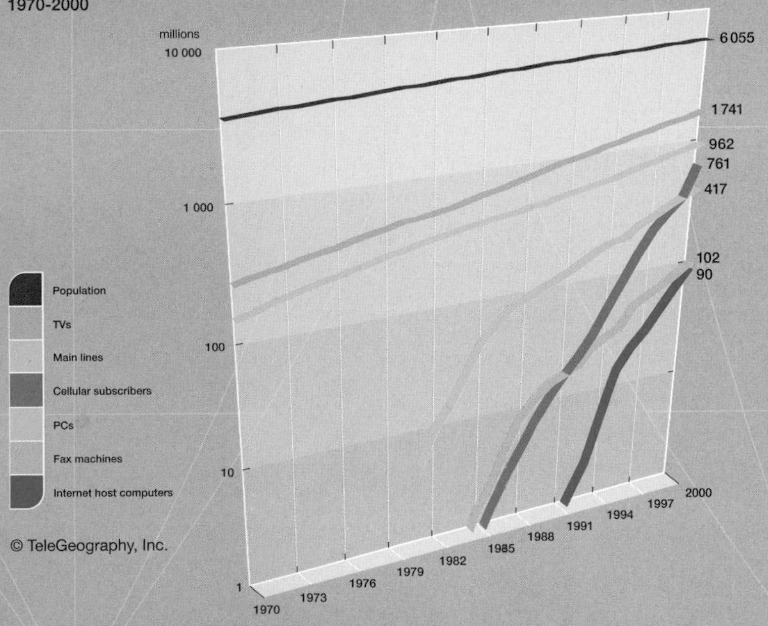

millions
10 000

6 055
1 741
962
761
417
102
90

1 000

100

10

1

| Population |
| TVs |
| Main lines |
| Cellular subscribers |
| PCs |
| Fax machines |
| Internet host computers |

© TeleGeography, Inc.

1970 1973 1976 1979 1982 1985 1988 1991 1994 1997 2000

CONNECTIONS

► subject   page#

► World countries   10–11
► World population   22–23
► World cities   24–25

Fig. #03
International telecommunications traffic 1999
Each band is proportional to the total annual traffic on the
public telephone network in both directions

Million minutes of telecommunications traffic (mMiTTs)

2 500   1 000   500   100

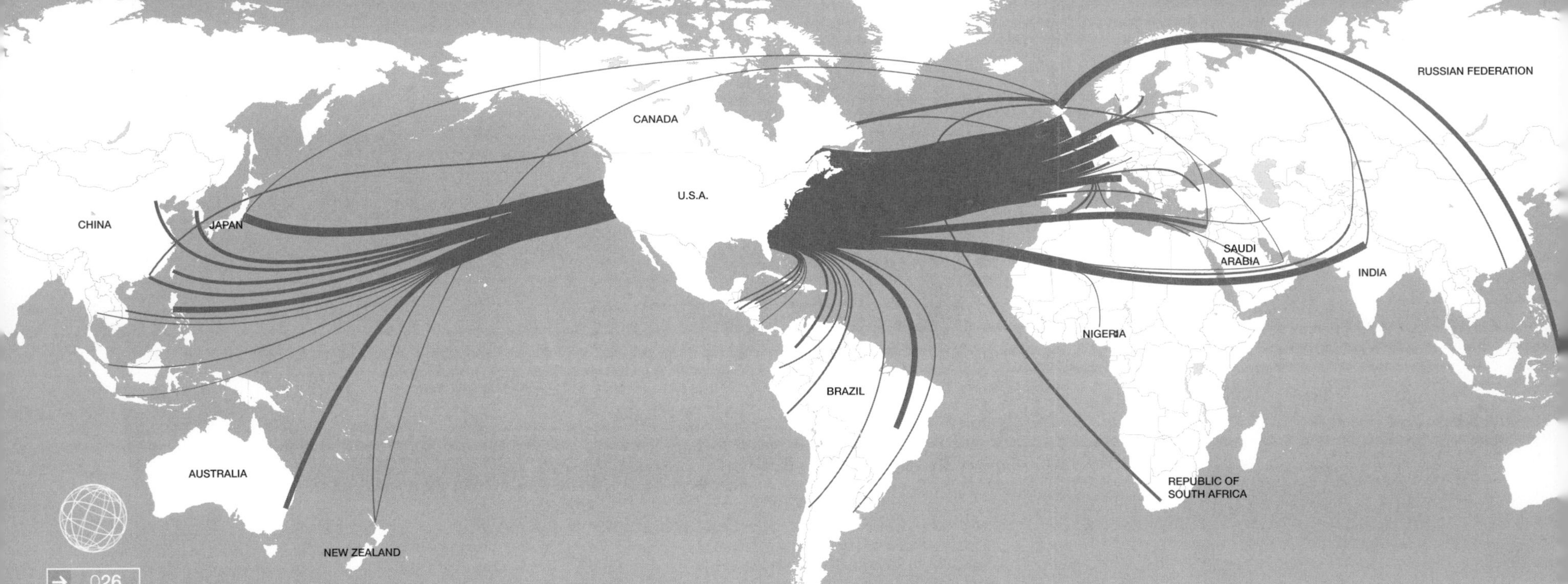

RUSSIAN FEDERATION

CANADA

CHINA

JAPAN

U.S.A.

SAUDI
ARABIA

INDIA

NIGERIA

BRAZIL

AUSTRALIA

REPUBLIC OF
SOUTH AFRICA

NEW ZEALAND

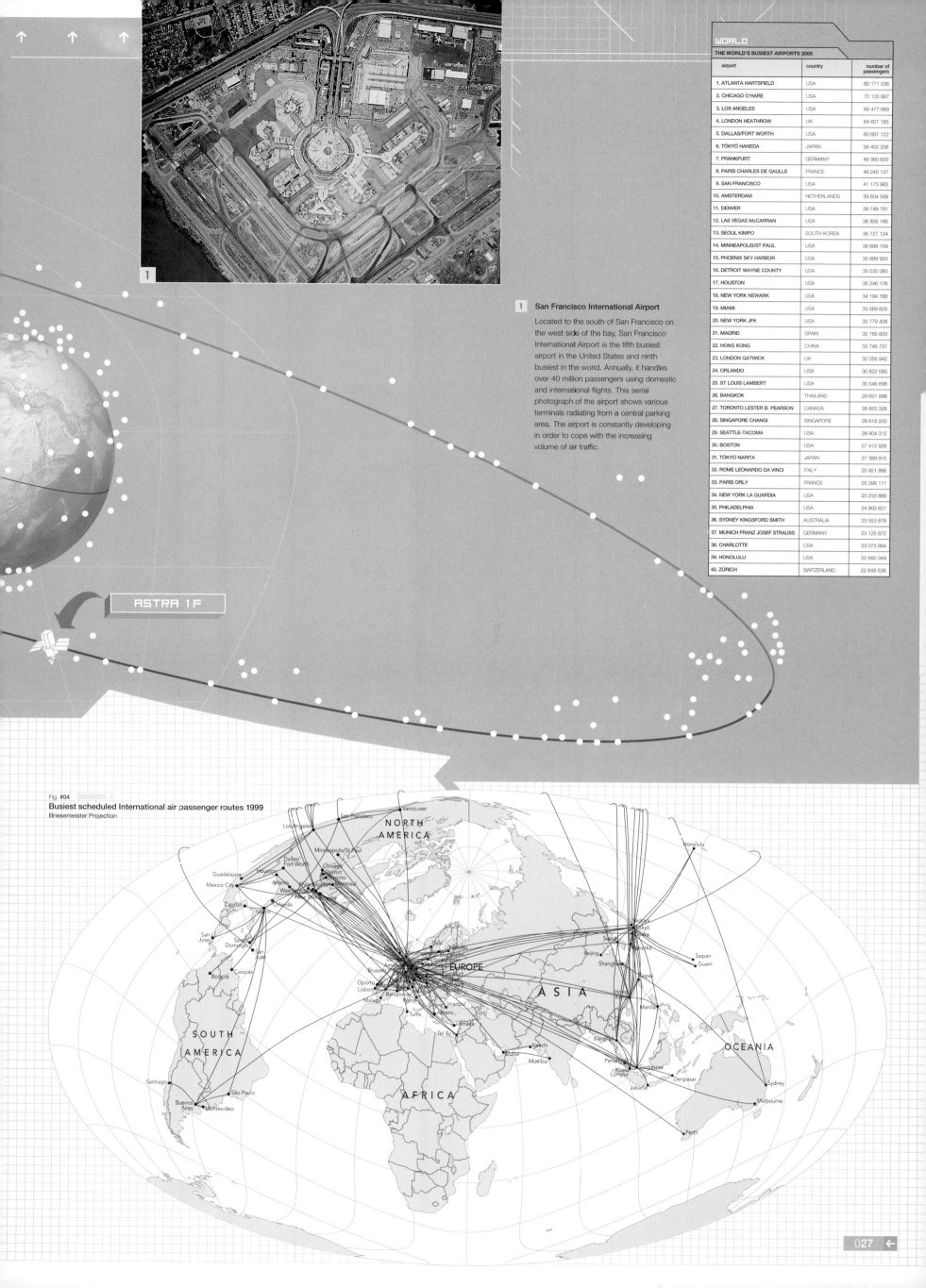

THE WORLD'S BUSIEST AIRPORTS 2000

airport	country	number of passengers
1. ATLANTA HARTSFIELD	USA	80 171 036
2. CHICAGO O'HARE	USA	72 135 887
3. LOS ANGELES	USA	68 477 689
4. LONDON HEATHROW	UK	64 607 185
5. DALLAS/FORT WORTH	USA	60 687 122
6. TŌKYŌ HANEDA	JAPAN	56 402 206
7. FRANKFURT	GERMANY	49 360 620
8. PARIS CHARLES DE GAULLE	FRANCE	48 240 137
9. SAN FRANCISCO	USA	41 173 983
10. AMSTERDAM	NETHERLANDS	39 604 589
11. DENVER	USA	38 748 781
12. LAS VEGAS McCARRAN	USA	36 856 186
13. SEOUL KIMPO	SOUTH KOREA	36 727 124
14. MINNEAPOLIS/ST PAUL	USA	36 688 159
15. PHOENIX SKY HARBOR	USA	35 889 933
16. DETROIT WAYNE COUNTY	USA	35 535 080
17. HOUSTON	USA	35 246 176
18. NEW YORK NEWARK	USA	34 194 788
19. MIAMI	USA	33 569 625
20. NEW YORK JFK	USA	32 779 428
21. MADRID	SPAIN	32 765 820
22. HONG KONG	CHINA	32 746 737
23. LONDON GATWICK	UK	32 056 942
24. ORLANDO	USA	30 822 580
25. ST LOUIS LAMBERT	USA	30 546 698
26. BANGKOK	THAILAND	29 621 898
27. TORONTO LESTER B. PEARSON	CANADA	28 820 326
28. SINGAPORE CHANGI	SINGAPORE	28 618 200
29. SEATTLE-TACOMA	USA	28 404 312
30. BOSTON	USA	27 412 926
31. TŌKYŌ NARITA	JAPAN	27 389 915
32. ROME LEONARDO DA VINCI	ITALY	25 921 886
33. PARIS ORLY	FRANCE	25 399 111
34. NEW YORK LA GUARDIA	USA	25 233 889
35. PHILADELPHIA	USA	24 900 621
36. SYDNEY KINGSFORD SMITH	AUSTRALIA	23 553 878
37. MUNICH FRANZ JOSEF STRAUSS	GERMANY	23 125 872
38. CHARLOTTE	USA	23 073 894
39. HONOLULU	USA	22 660 349
40. ZÜRICH	SWITZERLAND	22 649 539

1 **San Francisco International Airport**

Located to the south of San Francisco on the west side of the bay, San Francisco International Airport is the fifth busiest airport in the United States and ninth busiest in the world. Annually, it handles over 40 million passengers using domestic and international flights. This aerial photograph of the airport shows various terminals radiating from a central parking area. The airport is constantly developing in order to cope with the increasing volume of air traffic.

ASTRA 1F

Fig. #04
Busiest scheduled International air passenger routes 1999
Briesemeister Projection

Alps, *France*

europe

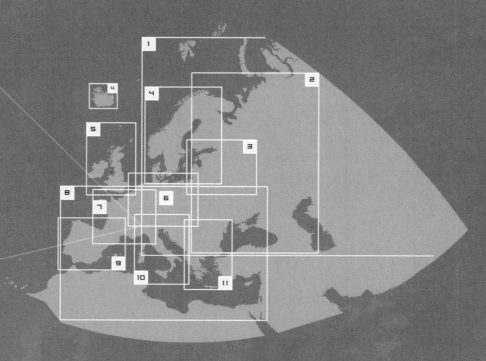

[contents]

		page#
europe [landscapes]		30–31
europe [countries]		32–33
europe [countries/issues]		34–35
europe [environments]		36–37

	map coverage	scale	page#
europe [map 1]	RUSSIAN FEDERATION	1:18 000 000	38–39
europe [map 2]	RUSSIAN FEDERATION West	1:7 500 000	40–41
europe [map 3]	ESTONIA, LATVIA, LITHUANIA and the MOSCOW REGION	1:3 000 000	42–43
europe [map 4]	ICELAND, NORWAY, SWEDEN, FINLAND and DENMARK	1:4 500 000	44–45
europe [map 5]	UNITED KINGDOM and REPUBLIC OF IRELAND	1:3 000 000	46–47
europe [map 6]	EUROPE North Central	1:3 000 000	48–49
europe [map 7]	FRANCE and SWITZERLAND	1:3 000 000	50–51
europe [map 8]	EUROPE South and the MEDITERRANEAN	1:9 000 000	52–53
europe [map 9]	SPAIN and PORTUGAL	1:3 000 000	54–55
europe [map 10]	ITALY, SLOVENIA, CROATIA and BOSNIA-HERZEGOVINA	1:3 000 000	56–57
europe [map 11]	EUROPE Southeast	1:3 000 000	58–59

europe[landscapes]

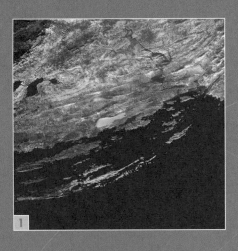

1 **Dalmatia,** *Croatia*

The Dalmatian coast of Croatia joins the Adriatic Sea in a series of mountainous limestone ridges running parallel to the coast. The mountains continue into the sea leaving strings of long, thin fragmented islands. The Krka river, to the right of this image, is one of a very few rivers which cross this remote region. The soil is thin and patchy but such a coastline provides many sheltered harbours. The large lake which appears green has a high salt content which has seeped through from the sea.

Satellite/Sensor : Space Shuttle

Europe, the world's second smallest continent, is located on the western tip of the vast Eurasian land-mass. The curve of mountain ranges, which includes the Alps, the Pyrenees and the Carpathians divides the north of the continent from the south. The highest peak in Europe, Mt Elbrus (5 642 m) lies in the Caucasus, the mountain range between the Black Sea and the Caspian Sea. North of these mountains, the rolling plains of Ukraine and European Russia extend to the Ural Mountains which, together with the Caucasus and the Bosporus in Turkey, form the physical boundary between Europe and Asia.

The Mediterranean Sea, in the south, is a large inland sea which is enclosed by mainland Europe to the north and west, Africa to the south, and Asia to the east. The Strait of Gibraltar connects the Mediterranean to the Atlantic Ocean on the west and in the southeast the Suez canal is the seaway to the Red Sea.

Largest island
Great Britain
218 476 sq km / 84 354 sq miles
Map reference 47 J7

CONNECTIONS

► subject	page#
► Types of imagery	4–5
► World physical features	8–9
► Arctic land cover	18–19
► European states and territories	32–33
► Reference maps of Europe	38–59

Spitsbergen

Norwegian Sea

Scandinavia

Gu
Bot

Faroe Islands

North Sea

Elbe River

Rhine River

Great Britain

Ireland

Seine River

English Channel

Loire River

Massif Central

Bay of Biscay

Pyrenees

Bale

Atlantic Ocean

Iberian Peninsula

Tagus River

Strait of Gibraltar

Alps, *Europe*

The snow-capped crescent-shaped Alps, seen here in early spring, separate Italy from the rest of central Europe. The valley in the lower centre of the image is that of the Po river and also visible are Lake Garda, right of centre, and Lake Geneva left of the snow covered area. The Alps are the source of several major European rivers including the Danube, Rhine and Rhone. The highest peak in the mountain range, Mont Blanc 4 804 m, is located on the France/Italy border, centre left on the image.

Satellite/Sensor : MODIS

Volga Delta, *Russian Federation*

The Volga river flows south into the Caspian Sea, over 3 000 km from its source, making it Europe's longest river. In this high oblique shuttle photograph the river delta, viewed from the north, fans out into the landlocked Caspian Sea. The city of Astrakhan is situated at the head of the delta on the west bank of the river. The silt from the delta provides a rich environment for flora and fauna.

Satellite/Sensor : Space Shuttle

Barents Sea

Novaya Zemlya

Lappland

Ural Mountains

Lake Ladoga

Baltic Sea

North European Plain

Vistula River

Volga River

Caspian Sea

Don River

Elbrus

Dnieper River

Carpathian Mountains

Crimea

Caucasus

Danube River

Black Sea

Alps

Bosporus

Po River

Dalmatia

Adriatic Sea

Apennines

Corsica

Sardinia

Sicily

Crete

Mediterranean Sea

...slands

Highest point

Elbrus
Russian Federation
5 642 m / 18 510 feet
Map reference 107 E2

Longest river

Volga
3 688 km / 2 291 miles
Drainage basin
1 380 000 sq km / 533 000 sq miles
Map reference 41 I7

Largest lake

Caspian Sea
371 000sq km / 143 243 sq miles
Map reference 102 B4

EUROPE

HIGHEST MOUNTAINS				
	m	ft	location	map
Elbrus	5 642	18 510	Russian Federation	107 E2
Gora Dykh-Tau	5 204	17 073	Russian Federation	41 G8
Shkhara	5 201	17 063	Georgia/Russian Federation	41 G8
Kazbek	5 047	16 558	Georgia/Russian Federation	107 F2
Mont Blanc	4 808	15 774	France/Italy	51 M7
Durfourspitze	4 634	15 203	Italy/Switzerland	51 N7

LARGEST ISLANDS			
	sq km	sq miles	map
Great Britain	218 476	84 354	47 J9
Iceland	102 820	39 699	44 inset
Novaya Zemlya	90 650	35 000	38 T2
Irelanc	83 045	32 064	47 D11
Spitzbergen	37 814	14 600	38 B2
Sicily	25 426	9 817	57 F1

LONGEST RIVERS			
	km	miles	map
Volga	3 688	2 291	41 I7
Danube	2 850	1 770	58 K3
Dnieper	2 285	1 419	41 E7
Kama	2 028	1 260	40 J4
Don	1 931	1 199	41 F7
Pechora	1 802	1 119	38 F3

LAKES			
	sq km	sq miles	map
Caspian Sea	371 000	143 243	102 B4
Lake Ladoga	18 390	7 100	40 D3
Lake Onega	9 600	3 706	40 E3
Vanern	5 585	2 156	45 C4
Rybinskoye Vodokhranilishche	5 180	2 000	43 T3

LAND AREA		
		map
Most northerly point	Ostrov Rudol'fa, Russian Federation	38 F1
Most southerly point	Gavdos, Crete, Greece	59 F14
Most westerly point	Bjargtangar, Iceland	44 A2
Most easterly point	Mys Flissingskiy, Russian Federation	39 G2
Total land area: 9 908 599 sq km / 3 825 731 sq miles		

EUROPE
COUNTRIES

		area sq km	area sq miles	population	capital	languages	religions	currency	map
ALBANIA		28 748	11 100	3 134 000	Tirana (Tiranë)	Albanian, Greek	Sunni Muslim, Albanian Orthodox, Roman Catholic	Lek	58–59
ANDORRA		465	180	86 000	Andorra la Vella	Spanish, Catalan, French	Roman Catholic	French franc, Spanish peseta	55
AUSTRIA		83 855	32 377	8 080 000	Vienna (Wien)	German, Croatian, Turkish	Roman Catholic, Protestant	Schilling, Euro	48–49
BELARUS		207 600	80 155	10 187 000	Minsk	Belorussian, Russian	Belorussian Orthodox, Roman Catholic	Rouble	42–43
BELGIUM		30 520	11 784	10 249 000	Brussels (Bruxelles)	Dutch (Flemish), French (Walloon), German	Roman Catholic, Protestant	Franc, Euro	51
BOSNIA-HERZEGOVINA		51 130	19 741	3 977 000	Sarajevo	Bosnian, Serbian, Croatian	Sunni Muslim, Serbian Orthodox, Roman Catholic, Protestant	Marka	56
BULGARIA		110 994	42 855	7 949 000	Sofia (Sofiya)	Bulgarian, Turkish, Romany, Macedonian	Bulgarian Orthodox, Sunni Muslim	Lev	58
CROATIA		56 538	21 829	4 654 000	Zagreb	Croatian, Serbian	Roman Catholic, Serbian Orthodox, Sunni Muslim	Kuna	56
CZECH REPUBLIC		78 864	30 450	10 272 000	Prague (Praha)	Czech, Moravian, Slovak	Roman Catholic, Protestant	Koruna	49
DENMARK		43 075	16 631	5 320 000	Copenhagen (København)	Danish	Protestant	Krone	45
ESTONIA		45 200	17 452	1 393 000	Tallinn	Estonian, Russian	Protestant, Estonian and Russian Orthodox	Kroon	42
FINLAND		338 145	130 559	5 172 000	Helsinki (Helsingfors)	Finnish, Swedish	Protestant, Greek Orthodox	Markka, Euro	44–45
FRANCE		543 965	210 026	59 238 000	Paris	French, Arabic	Roman Catholic, Protestant, Sunni Muslim	Franc, Euro	50–51
GERMANY		357 028	137 849	82 017 000	Berlin	German, Turkish	Protestant, Roman Catholic	Mark, Euro	48–49
GREECE		131 957	50 949	10 610 000	Athens (Athína)	Greek	Greek Orthodox, Sunni Muslim	Drachma	58–59
HUNGARY		93 030	35 919	9 968 000	Budapest	Hungarian	Roman Catholic, Protestant	Forint	49
ICELAND		102 820	39 699	279 000	Reykjavik	Icelandic	Protestant	Króna	44
IRELAND, REPUBLIC OF		70 282	27 136	3 803 000	Dublin (Baile Átha Cliath)	English, Irish	Roman Catholic, Protestant	Punt, Euro	46–47
ITALY		301 245	116 311	57 530 000	Rome (Roma)	Italian	Roman Catholic	Lira, Euro	56–57
LATVIA		63 700	24 595	2 421 000	Riga	Latvian, Russian	Protestant, Roman Catholic, Russian Orthodox	Lat	42
LIECHTENSTEIN		160	62	33 000	Vaduz	German	Roman Catholic, Protestant	Swiss franc	51
LITHUANIA		65 200	25 174	3 696 000	Vilnius	Lithuanian, Russian, Polish	Roman Catholic, Protestant, Russian Orthodox	Litas	42
LUXEMBOURG		2 586	998	437 000	Luxembourg	Letzeburgish, German, French	Roman Catholic	Franc, Euro	51
MACEDONIA (F.Y.R.O.M.)		25 713	9 928	2 034 000	Skopje	Macedonian, Albanian, Turkish	Macedonian Orthodox, Sunni Muslim	Denar	58
MALTA		316	122	390 000	Valletta	Maltese, English	Roman Catholic	Lira	57
MOLDOVA		33 700	13 012	4 295 000	Chişinău (Kishinev)	Romanian, Ukrainian, Gagauz, Russian	Romanian Orthodox, Russian Orthodox	Leu	41
MONACO		2	1	33 000	Monaco-Ville	French, Monegasque, Italian	Roman Catholic	French franc	51
NETHERLANDS		41 526	16 033	15 864 000	Amsterdam/The Hague	Dutch, Frisian	Roman Catholic, Protestant, Sunni Muslim	Guilder, Euro	48
NORWAY		323 878	125 050	4 469 000	Oslo	Norwegian	Protestant, Roman Catholic	Krone	44–45

CONNECTIONS

▶ subject		page#
▶ World countries		10–11
▶ Europe landscapes		30–31
▶ Europe issues		34–35
▶ Reference maps of Europe		38–59
▶ Atlantic Ocean		216–217

1 Rock of Gibraltar, *Gibraltar, Europe*

The narrow passage of water, appearing as a horizontal band of blue across the centre of this photograph is the 13 km wide Strait of Gibraltar which connects the Atlantic Ocean to the Mediterranean Sea. The strait forms a physical boundary between the continents of Europe and Africa. The photograph shows the 426 m high Rock of Gibraltar, viewed from Ceuta, a small Spanish enclave in Morocco, on the northern coast of Africa.

2 Bosporus, *Turkey, Europe/Asia*

The continents of Europe and Asia are physically separated by a narrow strait of water, the Bosporus, in Turkey. The strait, which at its narrowest point is less than 1 km wide, is 31 km long and connects the Sea of Marmara in the north to the Black Sea in the south. It is straddled by the city of Istanbul. The strait and the city are clearly shown in this SPOT satellite image. Istanbul airport is located near the coast toward the lower left of the image.

Satellite/Sensor : SPOT

EUROPE

TOP 10 COUNTRIES BY AREA

	sq km	sq miles	map	world rank
1. RUSSIAN FEDERATION	17 075 400	6 592 849	38–39	1
2. UKRAINE	603 700	233 090	41	44
3. FRANCE	543 965	210 026	50–51	48
4. SPAIN	504 782	194 897	54–55	51
5. SWEDEN	449 964	173 732	44–45	55
6. GERMANY	357 028	137 849	48–49	62
7. FINLAND	338 145	130 559	44–45	64
8. NORWAY	323 878	125 050	44–45	67
9. POLAND	312 683	120 728	49	69
10. ITALY	301 245	116 311	56–57	71

TOP 10 COUNTRIES BY POPULATION

	population	map	world rank
1. RUSSIAN FEDERATION	145 491 000	38–39	6
2. GERMANY	82 017 000	48–49	12
3. UNITED KINGDOM	59 634 000	46–47	20
4. FRANCE	59 238 000	50–51	21
5. ITALY	57 530 000	56–57	22
6. UKRAINE	49 568 000	41	24
7. SPAIN	39 910 000	54–55	29
8. POLAND	38 605 000	49	30
9. ROMANIA	22 438 000	58	44
10. NETHERLANDS	15 864 000	48	58

Berlin, *Germany*

Berlin, Germany's capital city until 1945, is now the national capital of the reunified Germany. In this near true-colour SPOT satellite image the path of the wall which formerly divided the city for over 25 years, can be seen on the northern outskirts of the city. In the top right, northeast of the river Spree which can be seen running across the centre of the image, is a large development of tower blocks built in the former Eastern sector.

Satellite/Sensor : SPOT

COUNTRIES

		area sq km	area sq miles	population	capital	languages	religions	currency	map
POLAND		312 683	120 728	38 605 000	Warsaw (Warszawa)	Polish, German	Roman Catholic, Polish Orthodox	Złoty	49
PORTUGAL		88 940	34 340	10 016 000	Lisbon (Lisboa)	Portuguese	Roman Catholic, Protestant	Escudo, Euro	54
ROMANIA		237 500	91 699	22 438 000	Bucharest (București)	Romanian, Hungarian	Romanian Orthodox, Protestant, Roman Catholic	Leu	58
RUSSIAN FEDERATION		17 075 400	6 592 849	145 491 000	Moscow (Moskva)	Russian, Tatar, Ukrainian, local languages	Russian Orthodox, Sunni Muslim, Protestant	Rouble	38–39
SAN MARINO		61	24	27 000	San Marino	Italian	Roman Catholic	Italian lira	56
SLOVAKIA		49 035	18 933	5 399 000	Bratislava	Slovak, Hungarian, Czech	Roman Catholic, Protestant, Orthodox	Koruna	49
SLOVENIA		20 251	7 819	1 988 000	Ljubljana	Slovene, Croatian, Serbian	Roman Catholic, Protestant	Tólar	56
SPAIN		504 782	194 897	39 910 000	Madrid	Castilian, Catalan, Galician, Basque	Roman Catholic	Peseta, Euro	54–55
SWEDEN		449 964	173 732	8 842 000	Stockholm	Swedish	Protestant, Roman Catholic	Krona	44–45
SWITZERLAND		41 293	15 943	7 170 000	Bern (Berne)	German, French, Italian, Romansch	Roman Catholic, Protestant	Franc	51
UKRAINE		603 700	233 090	49 568 000	Kiev (Kyiv)	Ukrainian, Russian	Ukrainian Orthodox, Ukrainian Catholic, Roman Catholic	Hryvnia	41
UNITED KINGDOM		244 082	94 241	59 634 000	London	English, Welsh, Gaelic	Protestant, Roman Catholic, Muslim	Pound	46–47
VATICAN CITY		0.5	0.2	480	Vatican City	Italian	Roman Catholic	Italian lira	56
YUGOSLAVIA		102 173	39 449	10 552 000	Belgrade (Beograd)	Serbian, Albanian, Hungarian	Serbian Orthodox, Montenegrin Orthodox, Sunni Muslim	Dinar	58

DEPENDENT TERRITORIES

		territorial status	area sq km	area sq miles	population	capital	languages	religions	currency	map
Azores (Arquipélago dos Açores)		Autonomous Region of Portugal	2 300	888	243 600	Ponta Delgada	Portuguese	Roman Catholic, Protestant	Port. Escudo	216
Faroe Islands		Self-governing Danish Territory	1 399	540	46 000	Tóshavn (Thorshavn)	Faroese, Danish	Protestant	Danish krone	46
Gibraltar		United Kingdom Overseas Territory	7	3	27 000	Gibraltar	English, Spanish	Roman Catholic, Protestant, Sunni Muslim	Pound	54
Guernsey		United Kingdom Crown Dependency	78	30	64 555	St Peter Port	English, French	Protestant, Roman Catholic	Pound	50
Isle of Man		United Kingdom Crown Dependency	572	221	77 000	Douglas	English	Protestant, Roman Catholic	Pound	47
Jersey		United Kingdom Crown Dependency	116	45	89 136	St Helier	English, French	Protestant, Roman Catholic	Pound	50

i The European Union

The European Union (EU) is a union of fifteen independent European states. It was founded as the European Economic Commission by the Treaty of Rome in 1957. Its purpose is to enhance political, economic and social cooperation. As shown on the map, the EU has grown from six to fifteen members and thirteen new applicants are currently negotiating for membership. The headquarters of the EU, in the Belgian capital Brussels, is the curved glass roofed building, known as the Hémicycle Européen, shown in the photograph.

Fig. #01
The European Union

- Founder members (1957)
- Joined in 1973
- Joined in 1981
- Joined in 1986
- Joined in 1995
- Current applicant
- Non-member

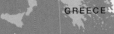

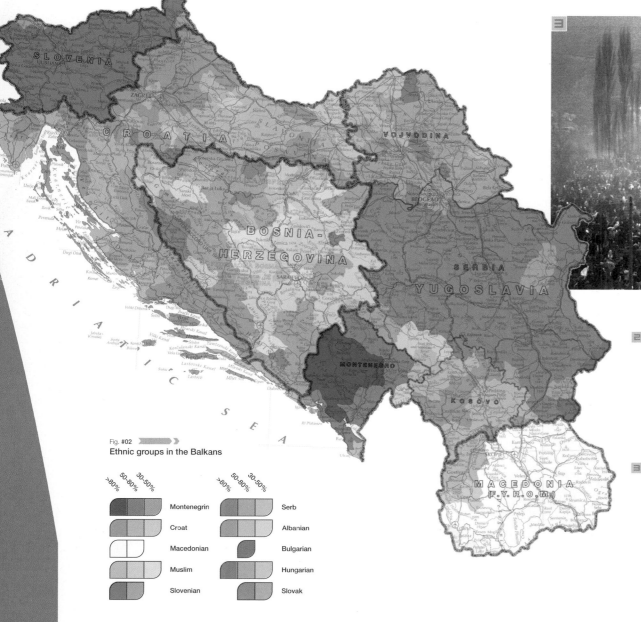

Fig. #02
Ethnic groups in the Balkans

	>80%	50-80%	30-50%			>80%	50-80%	30-50%
Montenegrin					Serb			
Croat					Albanian			
Macedonian					Bulgarian			
Muslim					Hungarian			
Slovenian					Slovak			

```
CONNECTIONS
```
► subject	page#
► World physical features	8–9
► World countries	10–11
► Europe landscapes	30–31
► Europe countries	32–33
► Reference maps of Europe	38–59

Caucasus, *Europe/Asia*

The Caucasus mountains extend from the eastern shores of the Black Sea to the southwest coast of the Caspian Sea and form an almost impenetrable barrier between Europe in the north, and Asia in the south. Europe's highest mountain, Elbrus, reaches 5 642 m in the western end of the range. The plains lying north of the Caucasus, seen in the lower half of this Shuttle photograph, are part of the Russian Federation and include the region of Chechnia. On the southern slopes of the mountains are the countries of Georgia and Azerbaijan.

Satellite/Sensor : Space Shuttle

The Balkans, *Europe*

The region of the Balkans has a long history of instability and ethnic conflict. The map shows the underlying complexity of the ethnic composition of the former country of Yugoslavia. The 1990 Yugoslav elections uncovered these divisions and over the next three years, four of the six Yugoslav republics – Croatia, Slovenia, Bosnia-Herzegovina and Macedonia – each declared their independence. The civil war continued until 1995 when the Dayton Peace Accord was established. In Kosovo, a sub-division of the Yugoslav republic of Serbia, the majority population of Muslim Albanians were forced to accept direct Serbian rule, and as a result support grew for the independence-seeking rebel Kosovo Liberation Army. In 1998 and 1999 the Serbs reacted through 'ethnic cleansing' of Kosovo, when many Kosovans were killed and, as shown in the photograph, thousands were forced to flee their homes. After NATO action, an agreement for Serb withdrawal was reached in June 1999.

europe[environments]

1 Lakelands, *Finland*

This aerial photograph, taken to the east of Kuopio, shows an environment typical of the lakeland areas of central Finland. The country is mostly lowland, with many lakes, marshes, and low hills. The vast forested interior plateau includes approximately 60 000 lakes, many of which are linked by short rivers, or canals to form commercial waterways.

2 Volcanic Environment, *Iceland*

The steam rising from the mountain side in this photograph is a result of volcanic activity. Iceland is a country with nearly 200 volcanoes, many of them still active. These create, and have created, great lava fields and rough mountainous terrain. Perhaps the most notable volcano is Hekla which rises to 1 491 m and had a major eruption in 1991. Hot springs and geysers are also common, and their geothermal energy is commonly used for domestic heating.

3 Mediterranean Island, *Europe*

This satellite image of the French island of Corsica in the Mediterranean Sea shows a mountainous island with some flat areas in the form of lagoons and marshes on the eastern coast. The highest point of the island is Monte Cinto, 2 706 m, which is towards the north of the pale, mountainous area.

Satellite/sensor : SPOT

4 Agricultural Region, *Italy*

The numerous rectangles in this satellite image are a patchwork of fields found in the Fucino plain, to the east of Avezzano, Italy. This area was formerly a lake which was drained in the mid-nineteenth century and now provides over 160 square kilometres of fertile farmland. Today the area is intensely cultivated with a variety of crops being grown, including cereals, potatoes, sugar beet, grapes and fruit.

Satellite/Sensor : Landsat

5 Planned Village, *The Netherlands*

This aerial photograph shows the village of Bourtange located in the extreme south-east of Groningen province in the Netherlands, less than 2 km from the German border. The star-shaped fortress dates back to the late sixteenth century. The old core of the village was restored in 1967 and has since been protected as a national monument.

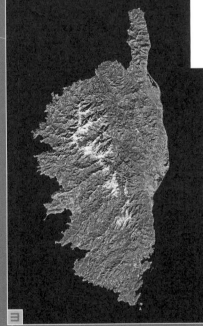

6 Mountainous Coastline, *United Kingdom*

This satellite image of the west coast of Scotland clearly shows the effect of the last ice age on this landscape. Retreating glaciers left long, deep valleys, high mountains and a very rugged, indented coastline. The barren mountains are clearly identified as the white areas of bare rock. Water appears as darker areas with Loch Maree being the largest loch in the centre of the image.

Satellite/Sensor : Landsat

7 Urban Environment, *United Kingdom*

This aerial photograph shows part of the centre of London, the capital city of the United Kingdom. Westminster, the seat of the British government, is located on the left bank of the River Thames at the bottom of the photograph. Other notable features are Buckingham Palace (bottom left), St James's Park, Waterloo Station (bottom right) and the London Eye observation wheel in its flat construction position over the river, prior to its final erection and completion.

CONNECTIONS

► subject	page#
► World land cover types	18–19
► World cities	24–25
► Europe landscapes	30–31
► Reference maps of Europe	38–59
► North America environments	162–163

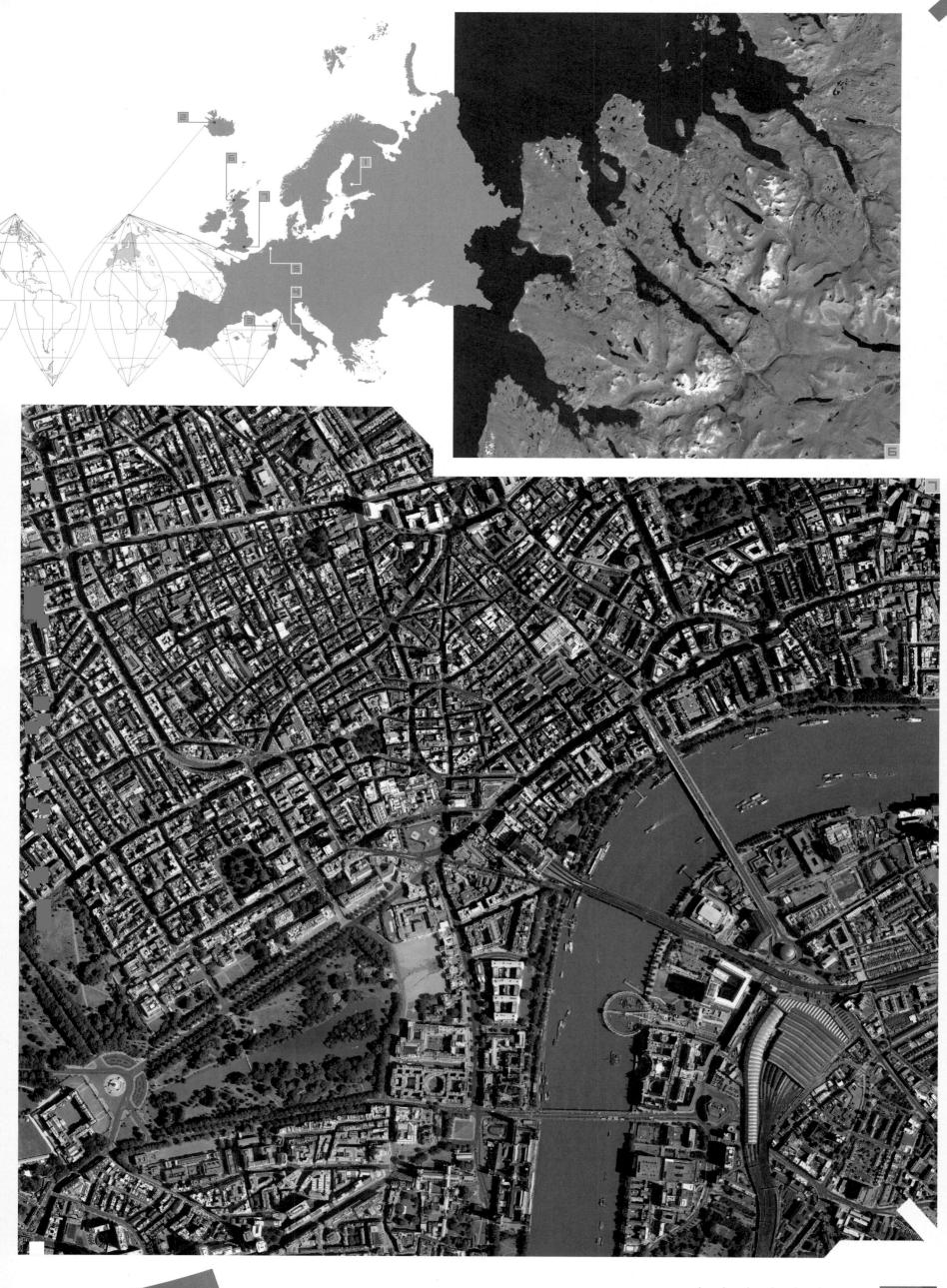

Ural Mountains
(Ural'skiy Khrebet)

RUSSIAN

Barents Sea

Pechorskoye More

Novaya Zemlya

Kola Peninsula
(Kol'skiy Poluostrov)

White Sea
(Beloye More)

ARKHANGEL'SKAYA OBLAST

RESPUBLIKA KARELIYA

Lake Ladoga
(Ladozhskoye)

Lake Onega
(Onezhskoye Ozero)

VOLOGODSKAYA OBLAST

LENINGRADSKAYA OBLAST

St Petersburg
(Sankt-Peterburg)

MOSCOW

TVERSKAYA OBLAST

NOVGORODSKAYA OBLAST

PSKOVSKAYA OBLAST

NORWAY

SWEDEN

FINLAND

Gulf of Bothnia

HELSINKI
(Helsingfors)

Gulf of Finland

TALLINN

ESTONIA

Baltic Sea

Gulf of Riga

RIGA

LATVIA

LITHUANIA

VILNIUS

NENETSKIY AVTONOMNYY OKRUG

MURMANSKAYA OBLAST'

Murmansk

Arctic Circle

CONNECTIONS

▶ subject   page#

▲▲ World cities   24–25
▲▲▲ Europe landscapes   30–31
▲▲▲ Europe countries   32–35
▲▲▲ Europe environments   36–37

048-049

europe[map2]

41°-71°N / 20°-54°E

100-101 ▶
106-107 ▶

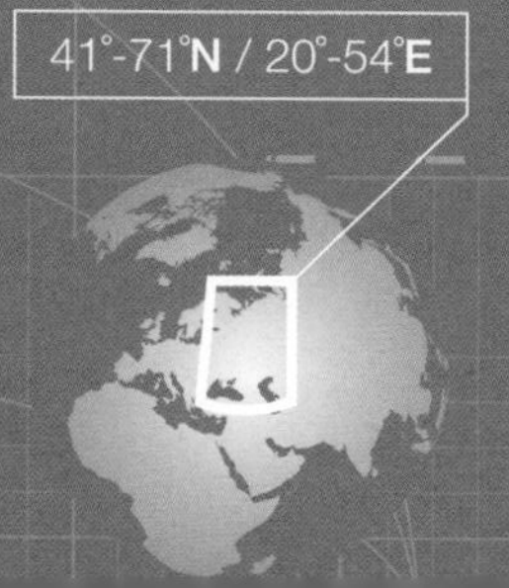

1:7 500 000

Conic Equidistant Projection

miles
0 100 200 300
km
0 100 200 300 400 500

Administrative divisions in Russian Federation numbered on the map:

1. RESPUBLIKA ADYGEYA (G7)
2. CHECHENSKAYA RESPUBLIKA (CHECHNIA) (H8)
3. RESPUBLIKA INGUSHETIYA (INGUSHETIA) (H8)
4. KABARDINO-BALKARSKAYA RESPUBLIKA (G8)
5. KARACHAYEVO-CHERKESSAYA RESPUBLIKA (G8)
6. RESPUBLIKA SEVERNAYA OSETIYA-ALANIYA (NORTH OSSETIA) (H8)

Elevation legend:
>6000m
5000-6000m
4000-5000m
3000-4000m
2000-3000m
1000-2000m
500-1000m
200-500m
0-200m
<0m
0-200m
200-500m
500-1000m
1000-2000m
2000-3000m
3000-4000m
4000-5000m
5000-6000m
>6000m

POLAND
BELARUS
RUSSIAN FEDERATION
UKRAINE
MOLDOVA
ROMANIA
BULGARIA
GREECE
TURKEY
GEORGIA
AZERBAIJAN
TURKMENISTAN
KAZAKHSTAN

Black Sea
Caspian Sea
Sea of Azov
Caucasus
Carpathian Mountains

europe[map3]

52°–61°N / 20°–40°E

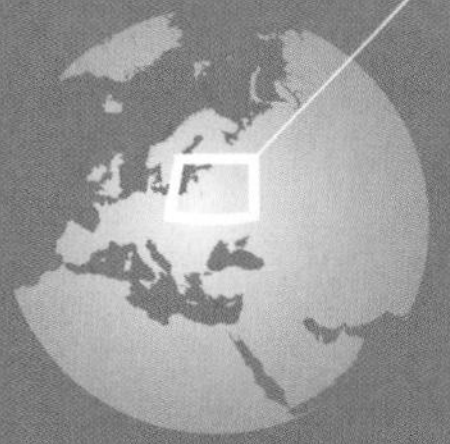

>6000m
5000-6000m
4000-5000m
3000-4000m
2000-3000m
1500-2000m
1000-1500m
500-1000m
200-500m
100-200m
0-100m
<0m
0-50m
50-100m
100-200m
200-500m
500-1000m
1000-2000m
2000-3000m
3000-4000m
4000-5000m
5000-6000m
>6000m

048-049

miles
0 25 50 75 100 125
1:3 000 000
0 25 50 75 100 125 150 175 200
km

Conic Equidistant Projection

Gulf of Bothnia
Åland Islands
FINLAND
LÄNSI-SUOMI
ITÄ-SUOMI
HELSINKI (Helsingfors)
Gulf of Finland
TALLINN
ESTONIA
Lake Peipus
Hiiumaa
Saaremaa
Gulf of Riga
Baltic Sea
Irbe Strait
Ventspils
LATVIA
RĪGA
Jūrmala
Liepāja
Vidzemes Centrālā Augstiene
LITHUANIA
Klaipėda
Palanga
Šiauliai
Panevėžys
Daugavpils
KAUNAS
VILNIUS
RUSSIAN FEDERATION
KALININGRADSKAYA OBLAST
Kaliningrad
Gulf of Gdańsk
POLAND
MAZURSKIE
POJEZIERZE
WARSAW
Mazowiecka Nizina
MINSK
BELARUS
HRODZYENSKAYA VOBLASTS
BRESTSKAYA VOBLASTS
MINSKAYA VOBLASTS

ARCTIC OCEAN

Barents Sea

RUSSIAN FEDERATION

FINLAND

NORRBOTTEN

VÄSTERBOTTEN

Norwegian Sea

CONNECTIONS

▶ subject   page#

▲ World countries   10-11
▲ World earthquakes and volcanoes   14-15
▲ Europe landscapes   30-31
▲ Europe countries   32-35
▲ Europe environments   36-37

ICELAND

Breiðafjörður

Faxaflói

REYKJAVÍK

Arctic Circle

1:4 500 000

miles 0   30
km   0   50

>6000m
5000-6000m
4000-5000m
3000-4000m
2000-3000m
1500-2000m
1000-1500m
500-1000m
200-500m
100-200m
0-100m

0-50m
50-100m
100-200m
200-500m
500-1000m
1000-2000m
2000-3000m
3000-4000m
4000-5000m
5000-6000m
>6000m

europe[map4]

048-049 ▶

54°-72°N / 4°-28°E

RUSSIAN FEDERATION

St Petersburg
Sankt-Peterburg

F i n l a n d

Gulf of Finland

HELSINKI
(Helsingfors)

TALLINN

E S T O N I A

Gulf
of Riga
(Estonia)

Saaremaa

Gulf

Åland Islands

L A T V I A

R I G A

B a l t i c   S e a

Gotland
(Sweden)

L I T H U A N I A

STOCKHOLM

Öland

B E L A R U S

RUSSIAN FEDERATION

Gulf
of
Gdańsk

Gdańsk
Gdynia

POLAND

Bornholm
(Denmark)

Hanöbukten

COPENHAGEN
København

Zealand

D E N M A R K

Kattegat
(Denmark)

Gothenburg
(Göteborg)

S W E D E N

D A L A R N A

O P P L A N D
H E D M A R K

Skagerrak

Jutland

North Frisian
Islands

1:4 500 000

Conic Equidistant Projection

miles
km

I   J   K   L   M   N

UNITED KINGDOM

G r e a t   B r i t a i n

E N G L A N D

WALES

Cambrian Mountains

NORTHERN IRELAND

REPUBLIC OF IRELAND

CONNAUGHT

ULSTER

LEINSTER

MUNSTER

I r e l a n d

FRANCE

PICARDIE

HAUTE NORMANDIE

BELGIUM

North Sea

Irish Sea

Celtic Sea

English Channel (La Manche)

St George's Channel

Bristol Channel

Cardigan Bay

Lyme Bay

Baie de Seine

Solway Firth

Isle of Man (U.K.)

DOUGLAS

LONDON

DUBLIN (Baile Átha Cliath)

Dún Laoghaire

Cardiff

Swansea

Bristol

Bath

Plymouth

Liverpool

Birkenhead

Blackpool

Southport

Newcastle upon Tyne

South Shields

Sunderland

Hartlepool

Redcar

Scarborough

Bridlington

Hull

Kingston upon Hull

Grimsby

Skegness

Great Yarmouth

Lowestoft

Norwich

Ipswich

Felixstowe

Harwich

Clacton-on-Sea

Southend-on-Sea

Margate

Ramsgate

Deal

Dover

Strait of Dover (Pas de Calais)

Folkestone

Hastings

Eastbourne

Brighton

Worthing

Portsmouth

Isle of Wight

Bournemouth

Weymouth

Isle of Portland

Torquay

Newquay

St Ives

Land's End

Lizard Point

Belfast

Carlisle

Whitehaven

Workington

Barrow-in-Furness

Fleetwood

Aberystwyth

Holyhead

Caernarfon

Galway

Limerick

Cork

Waterford

Wexford

Tralee

Dunkirk (Dunkerque)

Calais

Boulogne-sur-Mer

Le Touquet-Paris-Plage

Dieppe

Fécamp

Cap de la Hague

Cherbourg

1:3 000 000

Conic Equidistant Projection

miles 0 25 50 75 100 125

km 0 25 50 75 100 125 150 175 200

46°–55°N / 4°–22°E

North
Sea

>6000m
5000-6000m
4000-5000m
3000-4000m
2000-3000m
1500-2000m
1000-1500m
500-1000m
200-500m
100-200m
0-100m
<0m

0-50m
50-100m
100-200m
200-500m
500-1000m
1000-2000m
2000-3000m
3000-4000m
4000-5000m
5000-6000m
>6000m

DENMARK
NETHERLANDS
BELGIUM
LUXEMBOURG
GERMANY
FRANCE
SWITZERLAND
LIECHTENSTEIN
ALPS
ITALIA

1 : 3 000 000

miles
0   25   50   75   100   125
0   25   50   75   100 125 150 175 200
km

Conic Equidistant Projection

050–051

056-057

europe[map7]

43°-51°N / 6°W-11°E

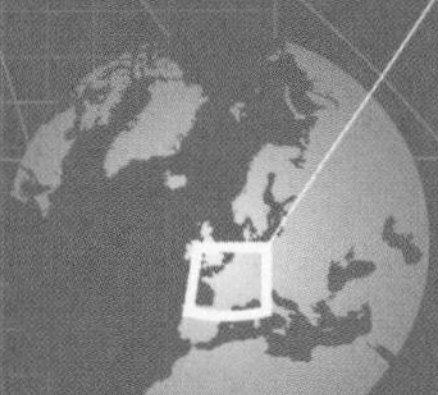

CONNECTIONS

English Channel
(La Manche)

UNITED KINGDOM

LONDON

Channel Islands
(Îles Normandes)

Guernsey (U.K.)
ST PETER PORT
Jersey (U.K.)
ST HELIER

Baie
de
Seine

BASSE-NORMANDIE

BRETAGNE

PAYS DE LÉON

CORNOUAILLE

PAYS DE LA LOIRE

FRANCE

ANJOU

TOURAINE

POITOU

CHARENTES

Bay of Biscay

Gulf of Gascony
(Golfe de Gascogne)

Mar Cantábrico

AQUITAINE

MIDI-PYRÉNÉES

ASTURIAS

CANTABRIA

PAÍS VASCO

NAVARRA

CASTILLA LEÓN

LA RIOJA

ARAGÓN

SPAIN

PYRÉNÉES

ANDORRA
ANDORRA LA VELLA

Santander

Donostia-
San Sebastián

Bordeaux

Pamplona

Burgos

Elevation scale

>6000m
5000-6000m
4000-5000m
3000-4000m
2000-3000m
1500-2000m
1000-1500m
500-1000m
200-500m
100-200m
0-100m
<0m

0-50m
50-100m
100-200m
200-500m
500-1000m
1000-2000m
2000-3000m
3000-4000m
4000-5000m
5000-6000m
>6000m

1:3 000 000

miles
0 25 50 75 100

km
0 25 50 75 100 125 150

Conic Equidistant Projection

054-055

GERMANY · POLAND · BELARUS · RUSSIAN FEDERATION

CZECH REPUBLIC · SLOVAKIA · UKRAINE

BERLIN · WARSAW · Łódź · KIEV (Kyiv)

PRAGUE · VIENNA · BRATISLAVA · BUDAPEST · CHISINAU · Odesa

AUSTRIA · HUNGARY · SLOVENIA · CROATIA · ROMANIA · MOLDOVA

Sea of Azov

ZAGREB · BELGRADE (Beograd) · BUCHAREST (Bucureşti) · Constanţa

SLOVENIA · BOSNIA · HERZEGOVINA · YUGOSLAVIA · SARAJEVO

Black Sea

SAN MARINO · VATICAN CITY · ROME (Roma)

Balkan Mountains · BULGARIA · SOFIA (Sofiya)

Adriatic Sea · SKOPJE · ALBANIA · MACEDONIA · TIRANA (Tiranë)

ISTANBUL · ANKARA · TURKEY

Tyrrhenian Sea · Naples (Napoli) · ITALY

Aegean Sea · Lesbos · İzmir (Smyrna) · Chios

Ionian Sea · GREECE · ATHENS (Athina) · Taurus Mountains

Cephalonia (Kefallonia) · Andros

Cyclades (Kykládes) · Dodecanese (Dodekánisos) · Rhodes (Rodos)

Sicily (Sicilia) · Palermo · Catania · Syracuse (Siracusa)

Krytiko Pelagos · Karpathos · CYPRUS · NICOSIA · SYRIA · Aleppo (Halab)

MALTA · VALLETTA

Crete (Kríti) · Iraklion (Irakleio)

LEBANON · BEIRUT

Gavdos

DAMASCUS

Mediterranean Sea

ISRAEL · Tel Aviv-Yafo · JERUSALEM · AMMAN · JORDAN · GAZA

TRIPOLI (Ṭarābulus) · Al Khums · Mişrātah · Benghazi

Gulf of Sirte (Khalīj Surt) · CYRENAICA

Alexandria (El Iskandarîya)

CAIRO (El Qâhira) · Shubrâ el Khema

TRIPOLITANIA · Libyan Plateau

SINAI · Gebel et Tîh · Gulf of Suez

LIBYA · Great Sand Sea · EGYPT

Qattâra Depression

Western Desert (Ṣahara el Gharbîya)

Eastern Desert (Ṣahara el Sharqîya) · Red Sea

AS SARIR

Libyan Desert

E · 15° · F · 20° · G · H · 30° · I

miles
1 : 9 000 000
0   100   200   300   400
0   100   200   300   400   500   600
km

Conic Equidistant Projection

35°-44°N / 11°W-5°E

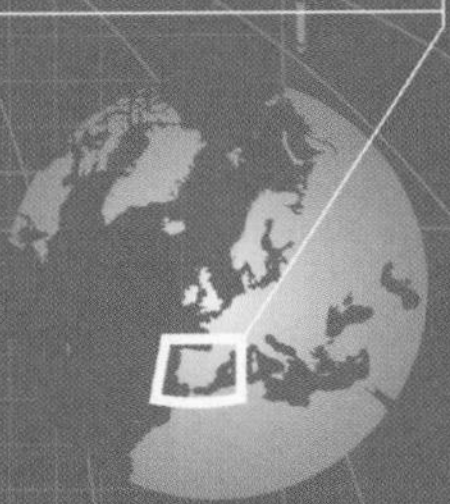

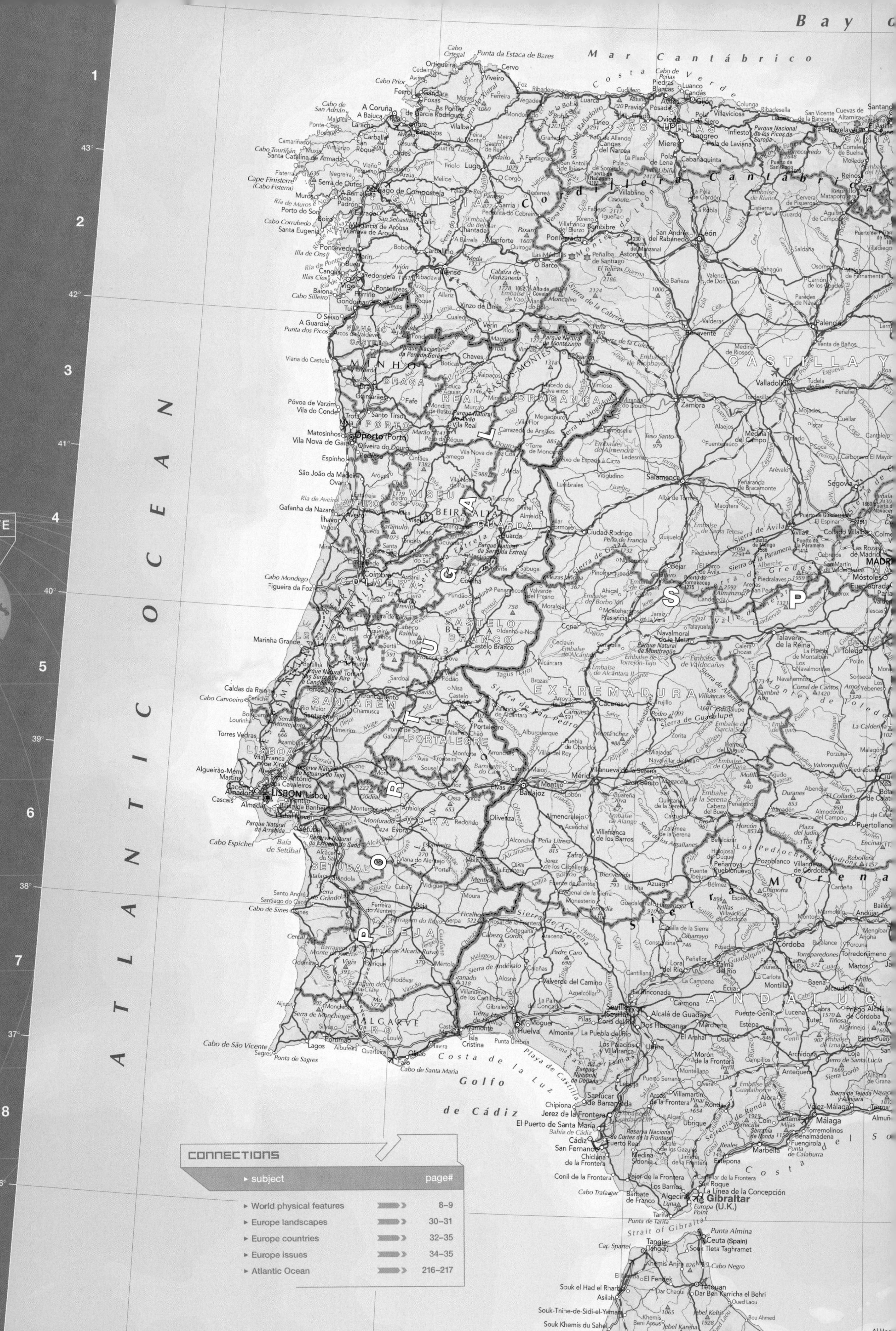

ATLANTIC OCEAN

Elevation legend

>6000m	
5000-6000m	
4000-5000m	
3000-4000m	
2000-3000m	
1500-2000m	
1000-1500m	
500-1000m	
200-500m	
100-200m	
0-100m	
<0m	

0-50m	
50-100m	
100-200m	
200-500m	
500-1000m	
1000-2000m	
2000-3000m	
3000-4000m	
4000-5000m	
5000-6000m	
>6000m	

CONNECTIONS

miles
0 25 50 75 100 125

1:3 000 000

km
0 25 50 75 100 125 150 175 200

Conic Equidistant Projection

CONNECTIONS

subject	page#
▶ World physical features	8–9
▶ World cities	24–25
▶ Europe landscapes	30–31
▶ Europe countries	32–35
▶ Europe issues	34–35
▶ Europe environments	36–37

35°48N / 8°19E

1:3 000 000   Conic Equidistant Projection

miles
km

Seas and water bodies

f Otranto
Tyrrhenian Sea
Ionian Sea
Mediterranean Sea
Sicilian Channel
Golfo di Taranto
Golfo di Napoli
Golfo di Cagliari
Golfe de Tunis
Golfe de Hammamet
Canal de la Galite

Islands / regions

SARDINIA (SARDEGNA) (Italy)
SICILY (SICILIA)
CALABRIA
BASILICATA
Appennino Lucano
Isole Lipari
Isola Stromboli
Isola Vulcano
Isole Egadi
Isola di Pantelleria (Italy)
Isole Pelagie (Italy)
Isola di Lampedusa
Isola di Linosa
Isola di Ustica
Isola Alicudi
Isola Filicudi
Isola Salina
Isola Lipari
Gozo (Ghawdex)
MALTA
VALLETTA
Kemmuna (Comino)
Hal Saflieni Hypogeum

Mainland cities / places (Italy)

Brindisi
Taranto
Lecce
Gallipoli
Matera
Crotone
Catanzaro
Cosenza
Reggio di Calabria
Messina
Catania
Siracusa (Syracuse)
Palermo
Trapani
Marsala
Agrigento
Gela
Ragusa
Modica
Cagliari
Oristano
Sassari
Alghero
Salerno

Tunisia / North Africa

TUNISIA
ALGERIA
TUNIS
Bizerte
Hammamet
Sousse
Kairouan
Cap Bon
Monastir
Mahdia

122–123

057

europe[map]11

35°47'N / 19°-29°E

1:3 000 000
Conic Equidistant Projection

miles
km

CONNECTIONS

▶ subject	page#
▲ Europe landscapes	30–31
▲ Europe countries	32–33
▲ Europe issues	34–35
▲ Mediterranean Sea	52–53

TURKEY

BALIKESIR · BURSA · KÜTAHYA · UŞAK · MANISA · AYDIN · IZMIR · SMYRNA · MUĞLA · ÇANAKKALE · DENIZLI

GREECE

MAKEDONIA · IPEIROS · THESSALIA · STEREA ELLAS · DYTIKI ELLAS · ATTIKI · PELOPONNISOS · VOREIO AIGAIO · NOTIO AIGAIO

Pindus Mountains · ATHENS (Atína) · Piraeus · Chalkída · Évvoia · Lárisa · Vólos · Pátrai · Sparti · Kalámai · Trípoli · Argos · Náfplio · Korinthos · Gulf of Corinth

Aegean Sea

Límnos · Lésvos (Lésvos) · Chíos · Sámos · Ikaría · Skyros · Andros · Tínos · Mykonos · Naxos · Paros · Sífnos · Mílos · Sérifos · Kéa · Kythnos

Cyclades (Kykládes)

Dodecanese (Dodekánisos)

Pátmos · Léros · Kálymnos · Kos · Astypálaia · Tílos · Símy · Rhodes (Ródos) · Kárpathos · Kastellóri

Krytikó Pelagos

Crete (Kríti)

Chaniá · Réthymno · Iráklion · Ierápetra · Gávdos

Ionian Sea

Corfu (Kérkyra) · Lefkáda · Cephalonia (Kefalloniá) · Zákynthos (Zante) · Ithaki · Páxoi · Antípaxoi

Ionian Islands

Voreíoi Sporádes · Skópelos · Skíathos · Alónnisos

Mirtóö Pelagos

Kýthira · Antikýthira

Mediterranean Sea

Megísti (Greece)

Osaka, *Japan*

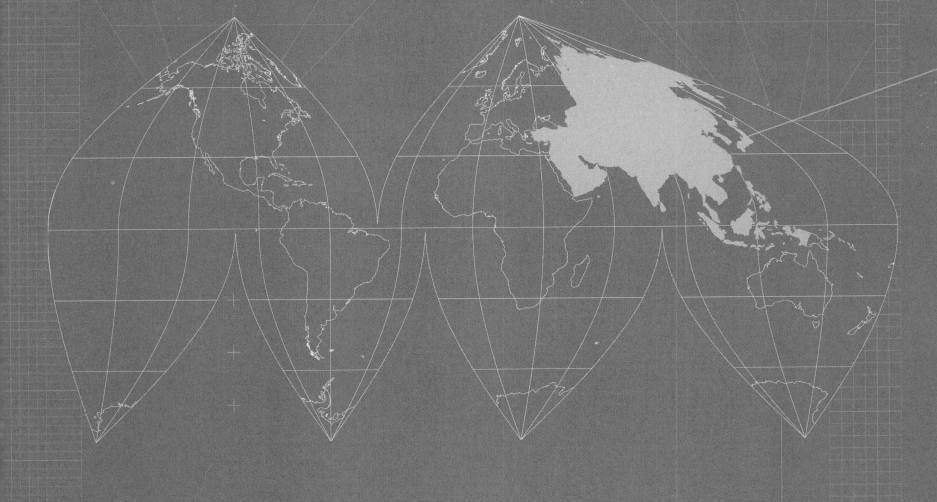

asia

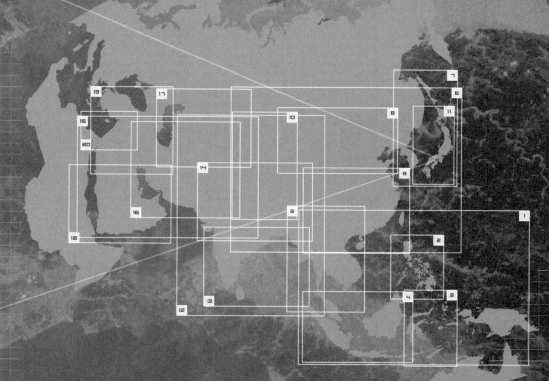

[contents]

		page#
asia [landscapes]		62–63
asia [countries]		64–65
asia [countries/issues]		66–67
asia [changes]		68–69
asia [threats]		70–71

	map coverage	scale	page#
asia [map 1]	ASIA Southeast	1:13 000 000	72–73
asia [map 2]	PHILIPPINES	1:6 000 000	74
asia [map 3]	INDONESIA Central	1:6 000 000	75
asia [map 4]	INDONESIA West, MALAYSIA and SINGAPORE	1:6 000 000	76–77
asia [map 5]	MYANMAR, THAILAND, LAOS and VIETNAM	1:6 000 000	78–79
asia [map 6]	ASIA East	1:13 000 000	80–81
asia [map 7]	ASIA Northeast	1:6 000 000	82–83
asia [map 8]	CHINA North and MONGOLIA	1:6 000 000	84–85
asia [map 9]	CHINA South	1:6 000 000	86–87
asia [map 10]	CHINA West	1:6 000 000	88–89
asia [map 11]	JAPAN	1:4 000 000	90–91
asia [map 12]	ASIA Central and South	1:12 000 000	92–93
asia [map 13]	INDIA South and SRI LANKA	1:6 000 000	94–95
asia [map 14]	INDIA North, BANGLADESH and NEPAL	1:6 000 000	96–97
asia [map 15]	ASIA Southwest	1:11 000 000	98–99
asia [map 16]	IRAN, AFGHANISTAN and PAKISTAN	1:6 000 000	100–101
asia [map 17]	KAZAKHSTAN, UZBEKISTAN and KYRGYZSTAN	1:6 000 000	102–103
asia [map 18]	SAUDI ARABIA and THE GULF STATES	1:6 000 000	104–105
asia [map 19]	TURKEY, IRAQ, and TRANS-CAUCASIAN REPUBLICS	1:6 000 000	106–107
asia [map 20]	MIDDLE EAST	1:3 000 000	108–109

Mediterranean Sea

Black Sea

Caucasus

Kirghiz Steppe

Ural Mountains

Ob' River

Yenisey River

Sibería

Euphrates River

Elburz Mountains

Caspian Sea

Aral Sea

Irtysh River

West Siberian Plain

Tigris River

Zagros Mountains

Central Siberian Plateau

Lake Balkhash

Arabian Peninsula

The Gulf

Hindu Kush

Tien Shan

Altai Mountains

Lake Baikal

Tarim Pendi

Kunlun Shan

Plateau of Tibet

Gobi

Indus River

Himalaya

Yellow River

Mount Everest

Ganges River

Arabian Sea

Yangtze River

Sri Lanka

Bay of Bengal

Eas

Irrawaddy River

Indian Ocean

Ryuky

Gulf of Thailand

Malay Peninsula

South China Sea

Mekong River

Sumatra

Philippines

Borneo

Java

Java Sea

Celebes

Palau

Timor

New Guinea

Largest drainage basin

Ob'-Irtysh
2 990 000 sq km / 1 154 000 sq miles
Map reference 38 G3-39 I5

Largest lake

Caspian Sea
371 000 sq km / 143 243 sq miles
Map reference 102 B4

Highest point

Mt Everest
China/Nepal
8 848 m / 29 028 ft
Map reference 97 E4

Longest river

Yangtze
6 380 km / 3 964 miles
Map reference 87 G2

Largest island

Borneo
745 561 sq km / 287 863 sq miles
Map reference 77 F2

CONNECTIONS

► subject		pages
► World physical features		10–11
► Asian states and territories		64–65
► Water issues		66–67
► Tropical storms in Asia		70–71
► Reference maps of Asia		72–109

Arctic Ocean

Lena River

Argun River

Heilong Jiang River

Sea of Okhotsk

Kamchatka Peninsula

Sea of Japan

China

a

Honshu

lands

Pacific Ocean

Northern Mariana Islands

Asia is the world's largest continent and its huge range of physical features is evident in this perspective view from the southeast. These include in southwest Asia the Arabian Peninsula, in southern Asia the Indian subcontinent, in southeast Asia the vast Indonesian archipelago, in central Asia the Plateau of Tibet and the Gobi desert and in east Asia the volcanic islands of Japan and the Kamchatka Peninsula.

North to south, the continent extends over 76 degrees of latitude from the Arctic Ocean in the north to the southern tip of Indonesia in the south. The Ural Mountains and the Caucasus in the west form the boundary with Europe. Asia's most impressive mountain range is the Himalaya, which contains the world's highest peaks. The continent is drained by some of the world's longest rivers and the Caspian Sea is the world's largest lake or inland sea.

1 **Himalayas**, *China/Nepal*

This view of the Himalayas shows Mount Everest, at 8 848 m the world's highest mountain. The photograph looks south from the Plateau of Tibet, with its typical barren landscape in the foreground. The plateau lies at a height of over 4 000 m. The Himalayas mark the southern limit of the plateau and stretch for over 2 000 km, forming the northern limit of the Indian sub-continent.

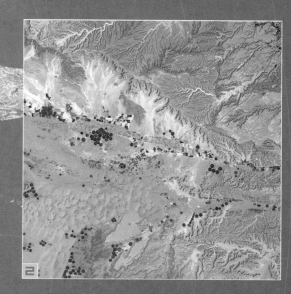

2 **Arabian Desert**, *Saudi Arabia*

The arid desert areas to the southwest of Riyadh, Saudi Arabia are shown in this infrared satellite image. Sand shows as yellow and bare rock as grey. Extensive drainage patterns belie the fact that this area only receives 100 mm of rain each year. These are dry river beds for most of the year. The red dots are circular fields with centre-pivot irrigation systems. Water is fed through large revolving sprinklers.

Satellite/Sensor : SPOT

3 **Ganges Delta**, *India*

This infrared satellite image shows the Hugli river in the western part of the Ganges delta, flowing into the Bay of Bengal. Vegetation shows as red in the image and the pale blue areas depict water full of sediment. The strong red indicates areas of mangrove swamp. The delta is a huge area, over 300 km across. The fertile soil is intensively farmed but the area is often flooded, particularly as a result of tropical cyclones.

Satellite/Sensor : SPOT

ASIA

HIGHEST MOUNTAINS

	m	ft	location	map
Mt Everest	8 848	29 028	China/Nepal	97 E4
K2	8 611	28 251	China/Jammu and Kashmir	96 C2
Kangchenjunga	8 586	28 169	India/Nepal	97 F4
Lhotse	8 516	27 939	China/Nepal	97 E3
Makalu	8 463	27 765	China/Nepal	97 E4
Cho Oyu	8 201	26 906	China/Nepal	97 E3
Dhaulagiri	8 167	26 794	Nepal	97 D3
Manaslu	8 163	26 781	Nepal	97 E3
Nanga Parbat	8 126	26 660	Jammu and Kashmir	96 B2
Annapurna 1	8 091	26 545	Nepal	97 D3

LARGEST ISLANDS

	sq km	sq miles	map
Borneo	745 561	287 863	77 F2
Sumatra	473 606	182 860	76 C3
Honshu	227 414	87 805	91 F6
Celebes	189 216	73 057	75 B3
Java	132 188	51 038	77 E4
Luzon	104 690	40 421	76 B2
Mindanao	94 630	36 537	74 C5
Hokkaido	78 073	30 144	90 H3
Sakhalin	76 400	29 498	82 F2
Sri Lanka	65 610	25 332	94 D5
Kyushu	36 554	14 114	91 B8
Taiwan	35 873	13 851	87 G4

LONGEST RIVERS

	km	miles	map
Yangtze	6 380	3 964	87 G2
Ob'-Irtysh	5 568	3 459	38 G3 –39 I5
Yenisey-Angara-Selenga	5 550	3 448	39 I2–K4
Yellow	5 464	3 395	85 H4
Irtysh	4 440	2 759	38 G3
Mekong	4 425	2 749	79 D6
Heilong Jiang -Argun'	4 416	2 744	81 M3
Lena-Kirenga	4 400	2 734	39 M2 –K4
Yenisey	4 090	2 541	39 I2
Ob'	3 701	2 300	38 H3

LAKES

	sq km	sq miles	map
Caspian Sea	371 000	143 243	102 B4
Aral Sea	33 640	12 988	102 D3
Lake Baikal	30 500	11 776	39 K4
Lake Balkhash	17 400	6 718	103 H3
Ysyk-Köl	6 200	2 393	103 I4

LAND AREA

		map
Most northerly point	Mys Arkticheskiy, Russian Federation	39 J1
Most southerly point	Pamana, Indonesia	75 B5
Most westerly point	Bozcaada, Turkey	59 H9
Most easterly point	Mys Dezhneva, Russian Federation	39 T3

Total land area: 45 036 492 sq km / 17 388 686 sq miles

asia[countries]

COUNTRIES		area sq km	area sq miles	population	capital	languages	religions	currency	map
AFGHANISTAN		652 225	251 825	21 765 000	Kābul	Dari, Pushtu, Uzbek, Turkmen	Sunni Muslim, Shi'a Muslim	Afghani	101
ARMENIA		29 800	11 506	3 787 000	Yerevan (Erevan)	Armenian, Azeri	Armenian Orthodox	Dram	107
AZERBAIJAN		86 600	33 436	8 041 000	Baku	Azeri, Armenian, Russian, Lezgian	Shi'a Muslim, Sunni Muslim, Russian and Armenian Orthodox	Manat	107
BAHRAIN		691	267	640 000	Manama (Al Manāmah)	Arabic, English	Shi'a Muslim, Sunni Muslim, Christian	Dinar	105
BANGLADESH		143 998	55 598	137 439 000	Dhaka (Dacca)	Bengali, English	Sunni Muslim, Hindu	Taka	97
BHUTAN		46 620	18 000	2 085 000	Thimphu	Dzongkha, Nepali, Assamese	Buddhist, Hindu	Ngultrum	97
BRUNEI		5 765	2 226	328 000	Bandar Seri Begawan	Malay, English, Chinese	Sunni Muslim, Buddhist, Christian	Dollar	77
CAMBODIA		181 000	69 884	13 104 000	Phnom Penh	Khmer, Vietnamese	Buddhist, Roman Catholic, Sunni Muslim	Riel	79
CHINA		9 584 492	3 700 593	1 260 137 000	Beijing (Peking)	Mandarin, Wu, Cantonese, Hsiang, regional languages	Confucian, Taoist, Buddhist, Christian, Sunni Muslim	Yuan	80–81
CYPRUS		9 251	3 572	784 000	Nicosia (Lefkosia)	Greek, Turkish, English	Greek Orthodox, Sunni Muslim	Pound	108
GEORGIA		69 700	26 911	5 262 000	T'bilisi	Georgian, Russian, Armenian, Azeri, Ossetian, Abkhaz	Georgian Orthodox, Russian Orthodox, Sunni Muslim	Lari	107
INDIA		3 065 027	1 183 414	1 008 937 000	New Delhi	Hindi, English, many regional languages	Hindu, Sunni Muslim, Shi'a Muslim, Sikh, Christian	Rupee	92–93
INDONESIA		1 919 445	741 102	212 092 000	Jakarta	Indonesian, local languages	Sunni Muslim, Protestant, Roman Catholic, Hindu, Buddhist	Rupiah	72–73
IRAN		1 648 000	636 296	70 330 000	Tehrān	Farsi, Azeri, Kurdish, regional languages	Shi'a Muslim, Sunni Muslim	Rial	100–101
IRAQ		438 317	169 235	22 946 000	Baghdād	Arabic, Kurdish, Turkmen	Shi'a Muslim, Sunni Muslim, Christian	Dinar	107
ISRAEL		20 770	8 019	6 040 000	Jerusalem (Yerushalayim) (El Quds)	Hebrew, Arabic	Jewish, Sunni Muslim, Christian, Druze	Shekel	108
JAPAN		377 727	145 841	127 096 000	Tōkyō	Japanese	Shintoist, Buddhist, Christian	Yen	90–91
JORDAN		89 206	34 443	4 913 000	'Ammān	Arabic	Sunni Muslim, Christian	Dinar	108–109
KAZAKHSTAN		2 717 300	1 049 155	16 172 000	Astana (Akmola)	Kazakh, Russian, Ukrainian, German, Uzbek, Tatar	Sunni Muslim, Russian Orthodox, Protestant	Tenge	102–103
KUWAIT		17 818	6 880	1 914 000	Kuwait (Al Kuwayt)	Arabic	Sunni Muslim, Shi'a Muslim, Christian, Hindu	Dinar	107
KYRGYZSTAN		198 500	76 641	4 921 000	Bishkek (Frunze)	Kyrgyz, Russian, Uzbek	Sunni Muslim, Russian Orthodox	Som	103
LAOS		236 800	91 429	5 279 000	Vientiane (Viangchan)	Lao, local languages	Buddhist, traditional beliefs	Kip	78–79
LEBANON		10 452	4 036	3 496 000	Beirut (Beyrouth)	Arabic, Armenian, French	Shi'a Muslim, Sunni Muslim, Christian	Pound	108–109
MALAYSIA		332 965	128 559	22 218 000	Kuala Lumpur	Malay, English, Chinese, Tamil, local languages	Sunni Muslim, Buddhist, Hindu, Christian, traditional beliefs	Ringgit	76–77
MALDIVES		298	115	291 000	Male	Divehi (Maldivian)	Sunni Muslim	Rufiyaa	93
MONGOLIA		1 565 000	604 250	2 533 000	Ulan Bator (Ulaanbaatar)	Khalka (Mongolian), Kazakh, local languages	Buddhist, Sunni Muslim	Tugrik	84–85
MYANMAR		676 577	261 228	47 749 000	Rangoon (Yangôn)	Burmese, Shan, Karen, local languages	Buddhist, Christian, Sunni Muslim	Kyat	78–79
NEPAL		147 181	56 827	23 043 000	Kathmandu	Nepali, Maithili, Bhojpuri, English, local languages	Hindu, Buddhist, Sunni Muslim	Rupee	96–97
NORTH KOREA		120 538	46 540	22 268 000	P'yŏngyang	Korean	Traditional beliefs, Chondoist, Buddhist	Won	82–83
OMAN		309 500	119 499	2 538 000	Muscat (Masqaṭ)	Arabic, Baluchi, Indian languages	Ibadhi Muslim, Sunni Muslim	Rial	105

1 Middle East Boundaries

International boundaries are often visible from space because of differences in land use. In this Shuttle photograph the borders between Egypt, Gaza and Israel can be clearly identified. Grazing is the predominant agricultural activity in this part of Egypt, to the bottom of the image, and in Gaza in the centre, and has removed much of the vegetation. In contrast, Israel, to the east of the boundary, appears darker and more cultivated because of irrigation from the Jordan river.

Satellite/Sensor : Space Shuttle

2 Egypt/Gaza Border, *Middle East*

Borders between countries frequently follow the alignment of natural physical features, such as rivers, mountains or lake shores. Some borders, however, are demarcated only by man-made features, such as this fence at Rafah on the boundary between Egypt and Gaza. Gaza is a small semi-autonomous region on the southeast shore of the Mediterranean Sea. It is home to about 1 million Palestinian Arabs and was formerly under complete Israeli control.

3 The Great Wall, *China*

The Great Wall of China was built in various stages and forms over a period of 1 000 years from the third century BC. It is one of China's most distinctive and spectacular features. The wall is visible in this aerial photograph as a light coloured line running across the hills from lower right to upper left. Stretching a total length of over 2 400 km from the coast east of Beijing, to the Gobi desert in Gansu province, the wall was first built to protect China from the Mongols and nomadic peoples to the north of the country.

CONNECTIONS

▶ subject	page#
▶ World physical features	8–9
▶ World countries	10–11
▶ Asia landscapes	62–63
▶ Asia issues	66–67
▶ Reference maps of Asia	72–109

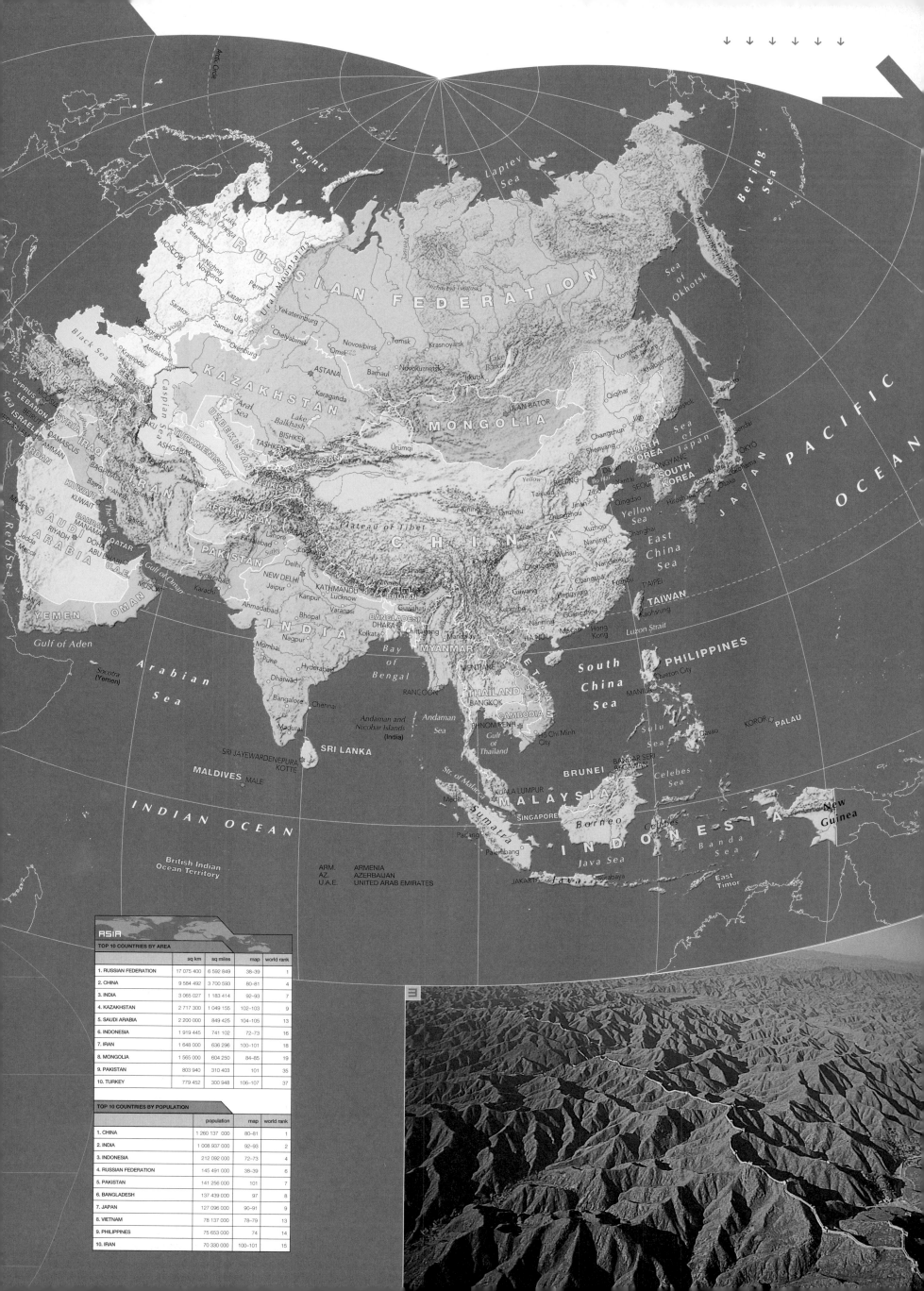

ASIA

TOP 10 COUNTRIES BY AREA

	sq km	sq miles	map	world rank
1. RUSSIAN FEDERATION	17 075 400	6 592 849	38–39	1
2. CHINA	9 584 492	3 700 593	80–81	4
3. INDIA	3 065 027	1 183 414	92–93	7
4. KAZAKHSTAN	2 717 300	1 049 155	102–103	9
5. SAUDI ARABIA	2 200 000	849 425	104–105	13
6. INDONESIA	1 919 445	741 102	72–73	16
7. IRAN	1 648 000	636 296	100–101	18
8. MONGOLIA	1 565 000	604 250	84–85	19
9. PAKISTAN	803 940	310 403	101	35
10. TURKEY	779 452	300 948	106–107	37

TOP 10 COUNTRIES BY POPULATION

	population	map	world rank
1. CHINA	1 260 137 000	80–81	1
2. INDIA	1 008 937 000	92–93	2
3. INDONESIA	212 092 000	72–73	4
4. RUSSIAN FEDERATION	145 491 000	38–39	6
5. PAKISTAN	141 256 000	101	7
6. BANGLADESH	137 439 000	97	8
7. JAPAN	127 096 000	90–91	9
8. VIETNAM	78 137 000	78–79	13
9. PHILIPPINES	75 653 000	74	14
10. IRAN	70 330 000	100–101	15

ARM. ARMENIA
AZ. AZERBAIJAN
U.A.E. UNITED ARAB EMIRATES

ASIA
COUNTRIES

		area sq km	area sq miles	population	capital	languages	religions	currency	map
PAKISTAN		803 940	310 403	141 256 000	Islamabad	Urdu, Punjabi, Sindhi, Pushtu, English	Sunni Muslim, Shi'a Muslim, Christian, Hindu	Rupee	101
PALAU		497	192	19 000	Koror	Palauan, English	Roman Catholic, Protestant, traditional beliefs	US dollar	73
PHILIPPINES		300 000	115 831	75 653 000	Manila	English, Pilipino, Cebuano, local languages	Roman Catholic, Protestant, Sunni Muslim, Aglipayan	Peso	74
QATAR		11 437	4 416	565 000	Doha (Ad Dawḩah)	Arabic	Sunni Muslim	Riyal	105
RUSSIAN FEDERATION		17 075 400	6 592 849	145 491 000	Moscow (Moskva)	Russian, Tatar, Ukrainian, local languages	Russian Orthodox, Sunni Muslim, Protestant	Rouble	38–39
SAUDI ARABIA		2 200 000	849 425	20 346 000	Riyadh (Ar Riyāḑ)	Arabic	Sunni Muslim, Shi'a Muslim	Riyal	104–105
SINGAPORE		639	247	4 018 000	Singapore	Chinese, English, Malay, Tamil	Buddhist, Taoist, Sunni Muslim, Christian, Hindu	Dollar	76
SOUTH KOREA		99 274	38 330	46 740 000	Seoul (Sŏul)	Korean	Buddhist, Protestant, Roman Catholic	Won	83
SRI LANKA		65 610	25 332	18 924 000	Sri Jayewardenepura Kotte	Sinhalese, Tamil, English	Buddhist, Hindu, Sunni Muslim, Roman Catholic	Rupee	94
SYRIA		185 180	71 498	16 189 000	Damascus (Dimashq)	Arabic, Kurdish, Armenian	Sunni Muslim, Shi'a Muslim, Christian	Pound	108–109
TAIWAN		36 179	13 969	22 300 000	T'aipei	Mandarin, Min, Hakka, local languages	Buddhist, Taoist, Confucian, Christian	Dollar	87
TAJIKISTAN		143 100	55 251	6 087 000	Dushanbe	Tajik, Uzbek, Russian	Sunni Muslim	Rouble	101
THAILAND		513 115	198 115	62 806 000	Bangkok (Krung Thep)	Thai, Lao, Chinese, Malay, Mon-Khmer languages	Buddhist, Sunni Muslim	Baht	78–79
TURKEY		779 452	300 948	66 668 000	Ankara	Turkish, Kurdish	Sunni Muslim, Shi'a Muslim	Lira	106–107
TURKMENISTAN		488 100	188 456	4 737 000	Ashgabat (Ashkhabad)	Turkmen, Uzbek, Russian	Sunni Muslim, Russian Orthodox	Manat	102–103
UNITED ARAB EMIRATES		83 600	32 278	2 606 000	Abu Dhabi (Abū Ẓabī)	Arabic, English	Sunni Muslim, Shi'a Muslim	Dirham	105
UZBEKISTAN		447 400	172 742	24 881 000	Tashkent	Uzbek, Russian, Tajik, Kazakh	Sunni Muslim, Russian Orthodox	Sum	102–103
VIETNAM		329 565	127 246	78 137 000	Ha Nôi	Vietnamese, Thai, Khmer, Chinese, local languages	Buddhist, Taoist, Roman Catholic, Cao Dai, Hoa Hao	Dong	78–79
YEMEN		527 968	203 850	18 349 000	Şan'ā'	Arabic	Sunni Muslim, Shi'a Muslim	Rial	104–105

DEPENDENT AND DISPUTED TERRITORIES

		territorial status	area sq km	area sq miles	population	capital	languages	religions	currency	map
British Indian Ocean Territory		United Kingdom Overseas Territory	60	23	uninhabited					219
Christmas Island		Australian External Territory	135	52	2 195	The Settlement	English	Buddhist, Sunni Muslim, Protestant, Roman Catholic	Australian dollar	72
Cocos Islands (Keeling Islands)		Australian External Territory	14	5	637	West Island	English	Sunni Muslim, Christian	Australian dollar	218
East Timor		under UN Transitional Administration	14 874	5 743	737 000	Dili	Portuguese, Tetun, English	Roman Catholic		75
French Southern and Antarctic Lands		French Overseas Territory	439 580	169 723	uninhabited					219
Gaza		semi-autonomous region	363	140	3 191 000*	Gaza	Arabic	Sunni Muslim, Shi'a Muslim	Israeli shekel	108
Heard and McDonald Islands		Australian External Territory	412	159	uninhabited					219
Jammu and Kashmir		Disputed territory (India/Pakistan)	222 236	85 806	13 000 000					96–97
West Bank		Disputed territory	5 860	2 263			Arabic, Hebrew	Sunni Muslim, Jewish, Shi'a Muslim, Christian		108

*includes occupied West Bank

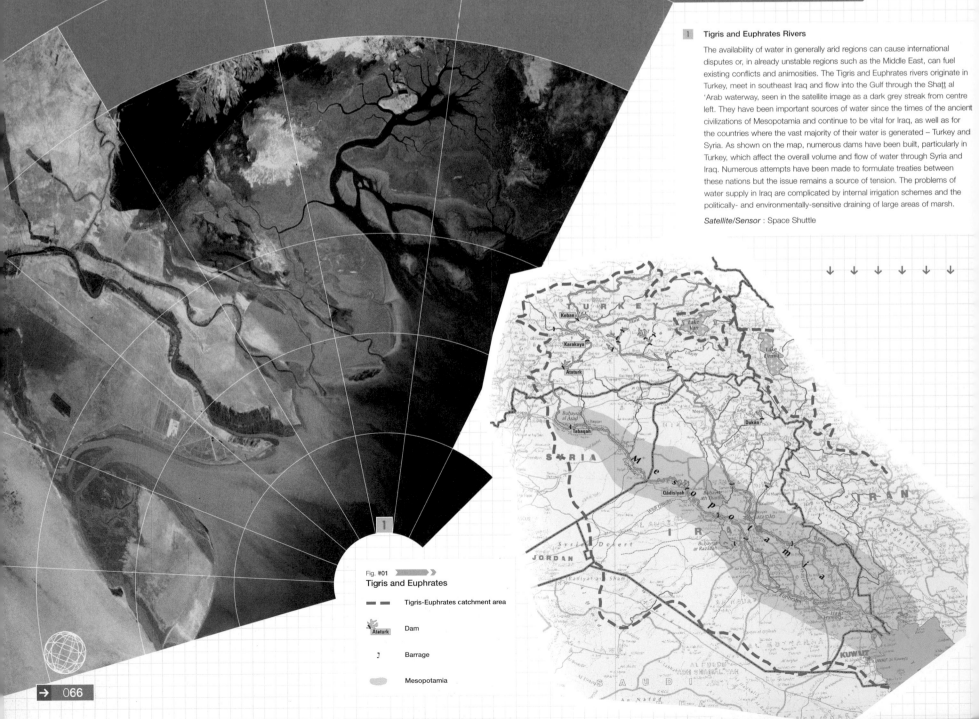

1 Tigris and Euphrates Rivers

The availability of water in generally arid regions can cause international disputes or, in already unstable regions such as the Middle East, can fuel existing conflicts and animosities. The Tigris and Euphrates rivers originate in Turkey, meet in southeast Iraq and flow into the Gulf through the Shaṭṭ al 'Arab waterway, seen in the satellite image as a dark grey streak from centre left. They have been important sources of water since the times of the ancient civilizations of Mesopotamia and continue to be vital for Iraq, as well as for the countries where the vast majority of their water is generated – Turkey and Syria. As shown on the map, numerous dams have been built, particularly in Turkey, which affect the overall volume and flow of water through Syria and Iraq. Numerous attempts have been made to formulate treaties between these nations but the issue remains a source of tension. The problems of water supply in Iraq are complicated by internal irrigation schemes and the politically- and environmentally-sensitive draining of large areas of marsh.

Satellite/Sensor : Space Shuttle

Fig. #01
Tigris and Euphrates

- – – Tigris-Euphrates catchment area
- Dam
- Barrage
- Mesopotamia

Fig. #02
Jerusalem

General place of interest

Place of worship

Transport location

Academic/municipal building

Jerusalem

The city of Jerusalem is a holy city for Jews, Muslims and Christians alike, and remains a focus of the ongoing conflicts between Israelis and Palestinians. This aerial photograph shows the Old City outlined by the city walls, the full outline of which is shown on the map. The Old City is divided into the Jewish, Muslim, Christian and Armenian quarters. The Muslim quarter, seen on the right of this photograph, is the busiest and most densely populated area. Just left of centre is the distinctive golden-roofed Dome of the Rock and to the left of this the El-Aqsa Mosque.

Fig. #03

Chinese migration

Main regions of Chinese emigration

Main destination countries

Principal overseas communities

CONNECTIONS

▸ subject	page#
▸ World countries	10–11
▸ Asia landscapes	62–63
▸ Asia countries	64–65
▸ Reference maps of Asia	72–109

Chinese migration

There has been a pattern of population migration from China since the early nineteenth century. This has resulted in a large overseas Chinese population, or *diaspora*, today estimated at over 30 million. Historically, the most common reasons for this population movement have been economic hardship, famine and political instability. As can be seen from the map, the majority of migrants settle in southeast Asia, mainly in Indonesia, Thailand, Malaysia and Singapore. In some countries this can create tensions between ethnic groups. Over eighty per cent of the Chinese overseas population lives in Asia, with most of them living in Chinese communities within the major cities. Europe and North America have also been important destinations, where the immigrants have again created distinctive communities in large cities, such as Chinatown in San Francisco, part of which is shown in the photograph.

asia[changes]

CONNECTIONS

► subject   page#

► Types of imagery   4–5
► World changes   20–21
► Asia landscapes   62–63
► Asia issues   66–67
► Reference maps of Asia   72–109

1 **Three Gorges Dam Project,** *China*

The Three Gorges Dam Project on the Yangtze river is the world's largest hydroelectric project. The term refers to a 190 km stretch of the Yangtze river where it flows through the precipitous Quitang, Wu and Xiling gorges, as shown on the satellite image and map. The photograph at the top shows part of the project area before construction began in 1997. The centre photograph shows part of the construction work and gives some idea of the effect it will have on the landscape. When complete, the dam will be over two kilometres wide and will create a 620 km long reservoir which will engulf over 400 sq km of farmland, thirteen cities, hundreds of villages, and archaeological sites. While the project, due for completion in 2009, will improve flood management, generate electricity and transfer water to dry areas further north, it raises many social and environmental issues, including the resettlement of between 1–2 million people, the potential accumulation of pollutants and the destruction of precious natural habitats.

Satellite/Sensor : Landsat (bottom)

Fig. #01
Three Gorges Dam project

SHAANXI

HUBEI

0   miles   50
0   kilometres   100

Area to be inundated

Area affected by Three Gorges Dam project

Three Gorges Dam

Gorge

Inundated town

Provincial boundary

Wuxi

Xingshan

Xiang He

Daning He

Wushan

Zigui

Kaixian

Fengjie

Badong

Xiling Gorge

Gezhouba Dam

Quitang Gorge

Wu Gorge

Sandouping

Yichang

Yunyang

SICHUAN

Wanxian

Yangtze

Dong He

Zhongxian

Shizhu

Fengdu

Jialing Jiang

Changshou

Fuling

Jiangbei

CHONGQING

Chongqing

Mudong

Wu Jiang

Ba Xian

Wulong

GUIZHOU

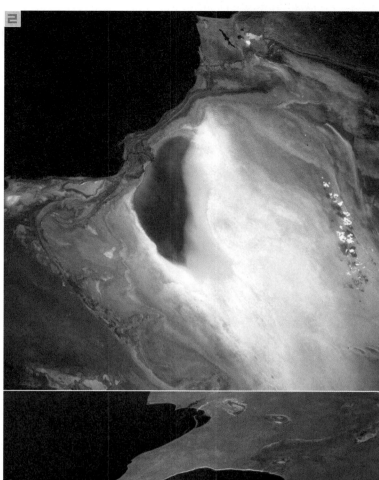

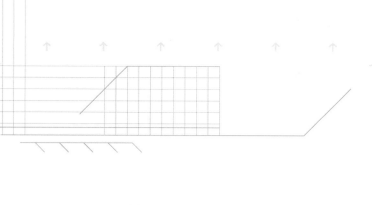

2 Lake Level Variations

A natural evaporation basin, the Kara-Bogaz-Gol is located in a semi-arid region of Turkmenistan on the eastern shore of the Caspian Sea. In these northwest-looking oblique Shuttle photographs the difference in water level, due to both evaporation and variation in the flow of water from the Caspian Sea into the basin, is striking. The 1985 image (top) shows water in only a small section near the western end. In contrast to this, the 1995 image (bottom) shows the water level to be high in the whole basin. The level of the Caspian Sea is normally approximately three metres above that of the basin, and water flows from one to the other through a dyke built in the late 1970s. However, low rainfall in the region can result in exceptionally low water levels in the Caspian Sea, which dramatically affect the amount of water flowing into the basin.

Satellite/Sensor : Space Shuttle

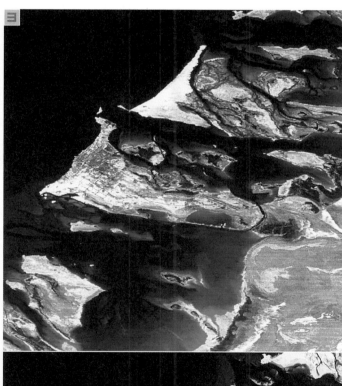

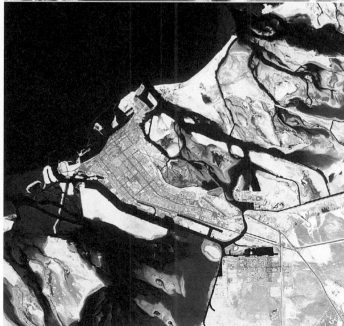

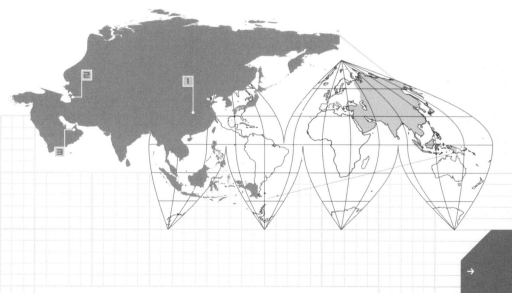

3 Urban Development and Land Reclamation

These satellite images show the development of the capital of the United Arab Emirates, Abu Dhabi. In the 1950s the town was little more than a small fishing village, but this changed after the discovery of offshore oil in the early 1960s. The changes, particularly to the extent of the city and to the coastline, in the period between the image at the top (1972) and the one below (1989), are dramatic. A national development program was implemented to help improve the city's harbour and to construct buildings, roads, and an international airport.

Satellite/Sensor : Landsat

1

CONNECTIONS

► subject   page#

► World earthquakes and volcanoes   14–15
► World tropical storms   16–17
► Mozambique floods   116–117
► North America threats   160–161

2

1 Tropical Storms

Tropical storms are among the most powerful and destructive weather systems on Earth. Worldwide between eighty and one hundred develop over tropical oceans each year. The northwest Pacific area experiences an average of thirty one typhoons annually and most of these occur between July and October. If they reach land they can cause extensive damage to property or loss of life as a result of high winds and heavy rain. This image gives an idea of the overall size of a typhoon as it moves westwards across the Pacific Ocean towards the island of Guam. Wind speeds in this typhoon reached over 370 km per hour.

Satellite/Sensor : GOES

2 Tropical Cyclone Hudah, *Southwest Indian Ocean*

Tropical cyclone Hudah was one of the most powerful storms ever seen in the Indian Ocean and was typical of the storms which frequently occur in the Pacific and Indian Oceans and which threaten the coasts of Asia and Africa. At the end of March 2000 the storm began a fairly straight westerly track across the entire south Indian Ocean, as shown on the map, struck Madagascar as an intense tropical cyclone, weakened, then regained intensity in the Mozambique Channel before making a final landfall in Mozambique on 9 April. This image was taken just before the cyclone hit the coast of Madagascar where wind gusts reached over 296 km per hour causing the destruction of 90% of the city of Antalaha.

Satellite/Sensor : MODIS

3 Bangladesh Cyclone Damage

Bangladesh, lying at the northern edge of the Bay of Bengal often experiences extreme climatic conditions which can wreak havoc. Cyclones regularly occur in the Bay of Bengal often having devastating effects on the flat coastal regions as shown in this photograph. In 1991 the country was hit by a massive cyclone which killed more than 140 000 people.

4 Klyuchevskaya Volcano, *Russian Federation*

Klyuchevskaya is the highest mountain in eastern Russian Federation and one of the most active volcanoes on the Kamchatka Peninsula. This view shows the major eruption of 1994 when the eruption cloud reached 18 300 m above sea level and the winds carried ash as far as 1 030 km to the southeast. The Kamchatka Peninsula is a sparsely populated area and the volcano's threat to human life is not serious. However, it lies on a major airline route and volcanic eruptions frequently cause aircraft to divert around the region.

Satellite/Sensor : Space Shuttle

Fig. #01
Tracks of tropical cyclones in the southwest Indian Ocean 2000

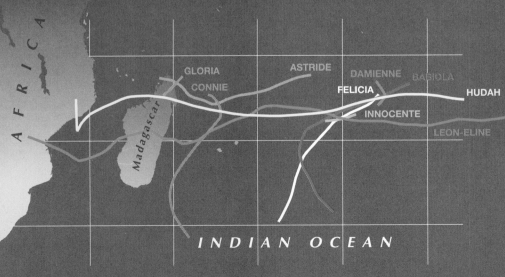

AFRICA

GLORIA
CONNIE
ASTRIDE
DAMIENNE
BASIOLA
FELICIA
INNOCENTE
HUDAH
LEON-ELINE

Madagascar

INDIAN OCEAN

3

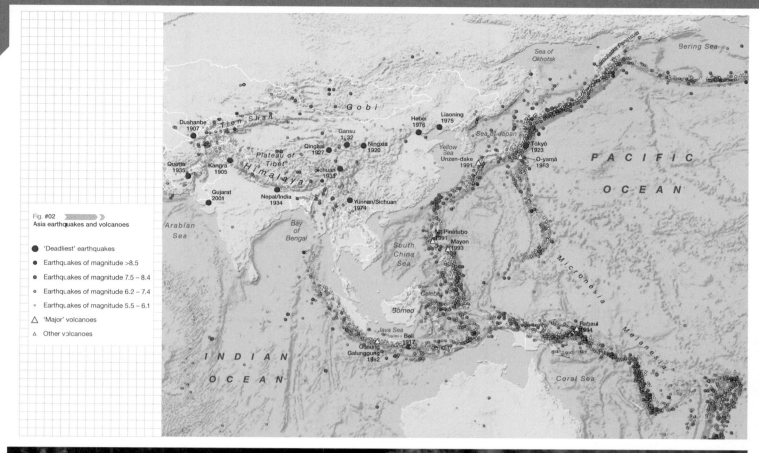

Fig. #02
Asia earthquakes and volcanoes

● 'Deadliest' earthquakes
● Earthquakes of magnitude >8.5
● Earthquakes of magnitude 7.5 – 8.4
● Earthquakes of magnitude 6.2 – 7.4
• Earthquakes of magnitude 5.5 – 6.1
△ 'Major' volcanoes
△ Other volcanoes

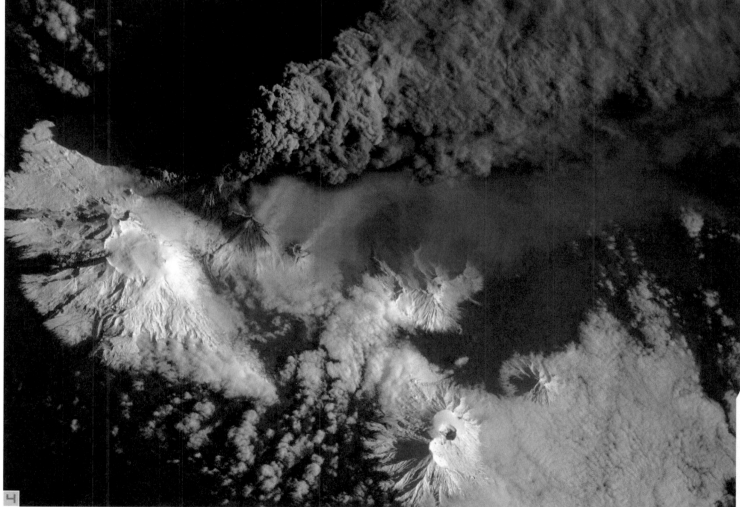

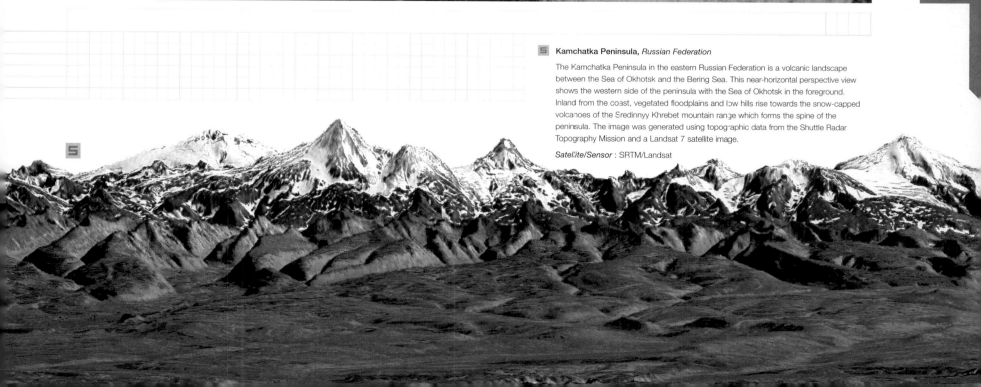

5 Kamchatka Peninsula, *Russian Federation*

The Kamchatka Peninsula in the eastern Russian Federation is a volcanic landscape
between the Sea of Okhotsk and the Bering Sea. This near-horizontal perspective view
shows the western side of the peninsula with the Sea of Okhotsk in the foreground.
Inland from the coast, vegetated floodplains and low hills rise towards the snow-capped
volcanoes of the Sredinnyy Khrebet mountain range which forms the spine of the
peninsula. The image was generated using topographic data from the Shuttle Radar
Topography Mission and a Landsat 7 satellite image.

Satellite/Sensor : SRTM/Landsat

11°S-26°N / 95°-147°E

080-081

092-093

Elevation scale (left legend)

>6000m
5000-6000m
4000-5000m
3000-4000m
2000-3000m
1000-2000m
500-1000m
200-500m
0-200m
<0m

0-200m
200-500m
500-1000m
1000-2000m
2000-3000m
3000-4000m
4000-5000m
5000-6000m
>6000m

5°–21°N / 117°–128°E

CONNECTIONS

▸ subject   page#

▸ World tropical storms   ➤   16–17
▸ World cities   ➤   24–25
▸ Asia countries   ➤   64–67
▸ Asia threats   ➤   70–71

PHILIPPINES

Luzon

Mindoro

Palawan

Panay

Negros

Samar

Mindanao

MANILA

Quezon City

MALAYSIA

INDONESIA

Philippine Sea

South China Sea

Sulu Sea

Celebes Sea

Luzon Strait

Batan Islands

Babuyan Islands

Balintang Channel

Babuyan Channel

Visayan Sea

Bohol Sea

Moro Gulf

Sibuyan Sea

Davao Gulf

Leyte Gulf

Sulu Archipelago

Mercator Projection

1 : 6 000 000

miles
0   50   100   150   200   250

km
0   50   100   150   200   250   300   350   400

>6000m
5000-6000m
4000-5000m
3000-4000m
2000-3000m
1000-2000m
500-1000m
200-500m
0-200m
<0m

0-200m
200-500m
500-1000m
1000-2000m
2000-3000m
3000-4000m
4000-5000m
5000-6000m
>6000m

076-077

075

asia[map4]

8°N–10°S / 95°–120°E

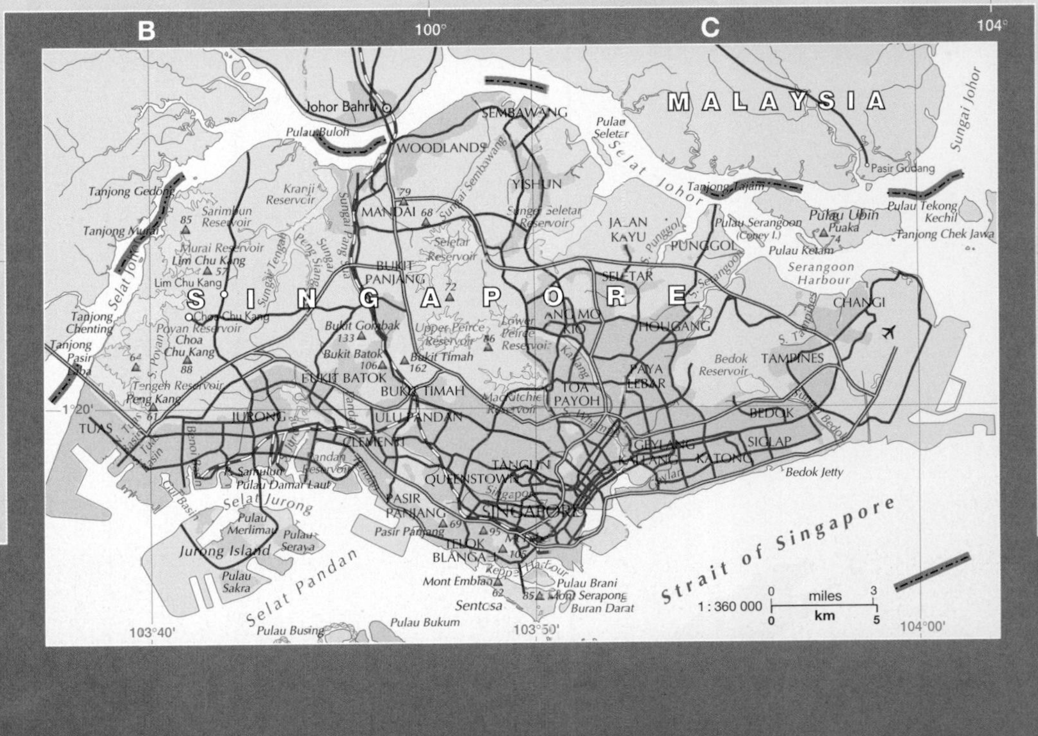

INDIAN

OCEAN

THAILAND

MALAYSIA

Peninsular
Malaysia

KUALA LUMPUR

SINGAPORE

SUMATERA
UTARA

SUMATERA
BARAT

Medan

Padang

Palembang

Legend (elevation):
>6000m
5000-6000m
4000-5000m
3000-4000m
2000-3000m
1000-2000m
500-1000m
200-500m
0-200m
<0m

0-200m
200-500m
500-1000m
1000-2000m
2000-3000m
3000-4000m
4000-5000m
5000-6000m
>6000m

Equator

Singapore inset:

MALAYSIA

SINGAPORE

Johor Bahru
WOODLANDS
SEMBAWANG
YISHUN
MANDAI
BUKIT PANJANG
JURONG
BUKIT BATOK
BEDOK
TAMPINES
CHANGI
TOA PAYOH
QUEENSTOWN
KATONG

Strait of Singapore

Selat Pandan

1 : 360 000
miles
km

1:6 000 000

Mercator Projection

asia[map5]

CONNECTIONS

▶ subject	page#
▲ Asia landscapes	62–63
▲ Asia countries	64–67
▲ Chinese migration	66–67
▲ Asia threats	70–71
▲ Indian Ocean	218–219

5°-29'N / 92°-110'E

076–077

1:6 000 000

Mercator Projection

miles
km

>6000m
5000–6000m
4000–5000m
3000–4000m
2000–3000m
1000–2000m
500–1000m
200–500m
0–200m
<0m
0–200m
200–500m
500–1000m
1000–2000m
2000–3000m
3000–4000m
4000–5000m
5000–6000m
>6000m

079

Selected geographic labels:

VIETNAM

CHINA

CAMBODIA

PHNOM PENH

BANGKOK (Krung Thep)

THAILAND

Gulf of Thailand

Bight of Bangkok

South China Sea

MALAYSIA

INDONESIA

Sumatra (Sumatera)

ACEH

Andaman Sea

ANDAMAN AND NICOBAR ISLANDS
(India)

Andaman Islands

Nicobar Islands

Mergui Archipelago

Strait of Malacca

INDIAN OCEAN

Ho Chi Minh City (Saigon)

Mouths of the Mekong

Kuala Terengganu

asia[map6]

18°-55°N / 73°-140°E

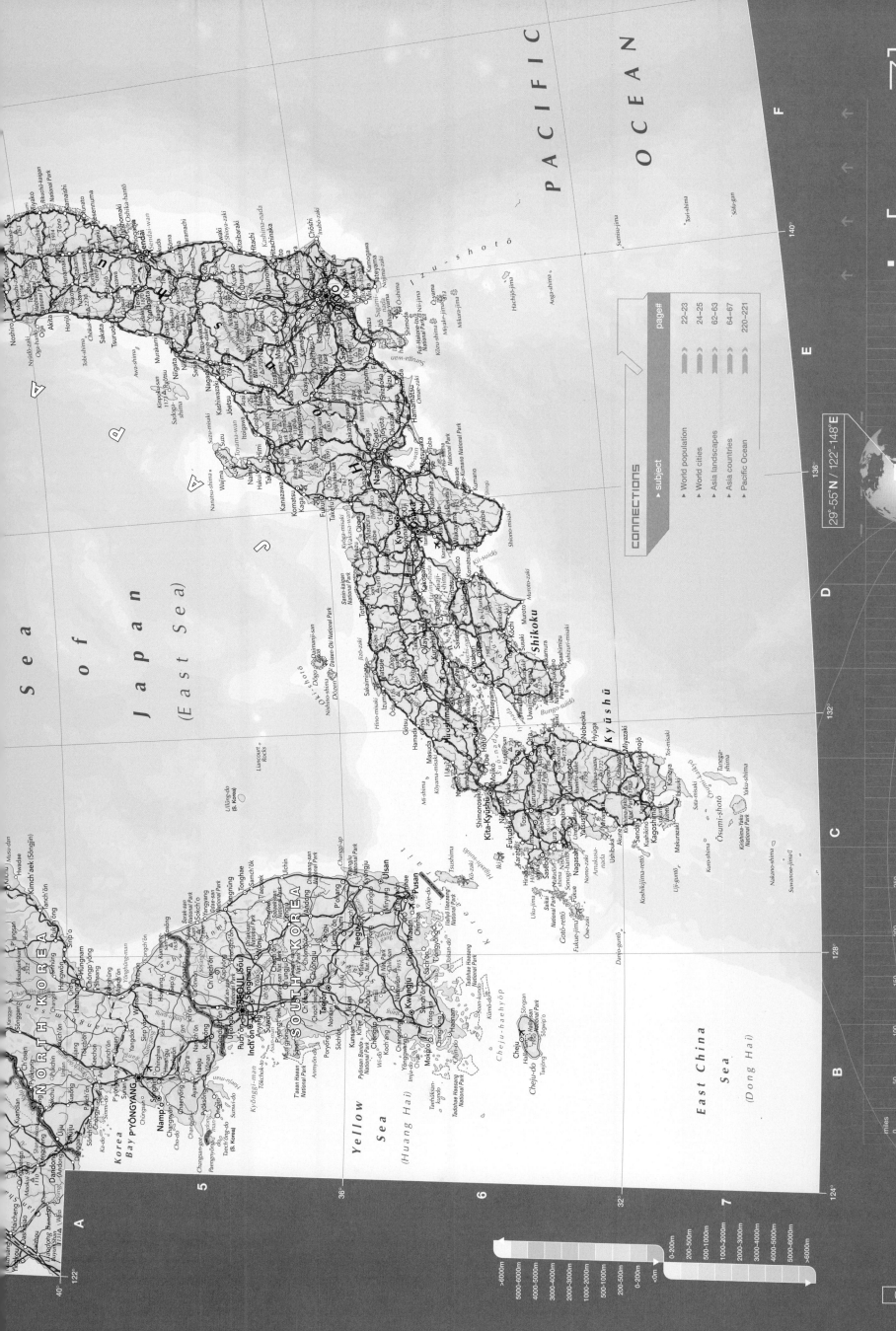

asia[map8]

34°-52°N / 92°-122°E

>6000m
5000-6000m
4000-5000m
3000-4000m
2000-3000m
1000-2000m
500-1000m
200-500m
0-200m
<0m

0-200m
200-500m
500-1000m
1000-2000m
2000-3000m
3000-4000m
4000-5000m
5000-6000m
>6000m

asia[map9]

18°-36°N / 96°-122°E

>6000m
5000-6000m
4000-5000m
3000-4000m
2000-3000m
1000-2000m
500-1000m
200-500m
0-200m
<0m

0-200m
200-500m
500-1000m
1000-2000m
2000-3000m
3000-4000m
4000-5000m
5000-6000m
>6000m

1:6 000 000

miles
0   50   100   150   200   250
0 50 100 150 200 250 300 350 400
km

Conic Equidistant Projection

084-085

088-089

078-079

078-079

QINGHAI

GANSU

XIZANG ZIZHIQU (TIBET)

SICHUAN

INDIA

KACHIN

The Triangle

MYANMAR

SHAN

YUNNAN

GUIZHOU

KAYAH

THAILAND

LAOS

VIETNAM

TONKIN

Lanzhou (Lanchow)

Chengdu

Chongq

Kunming

Guiyang

Mandalay

Chiang Mai

HA NÔI

Hai Phong

Vinh

Lhasa

Tianshui

1

2

3

4

5

32°

28°

24°

20°

18°

96°

100°

104°

A

B

C

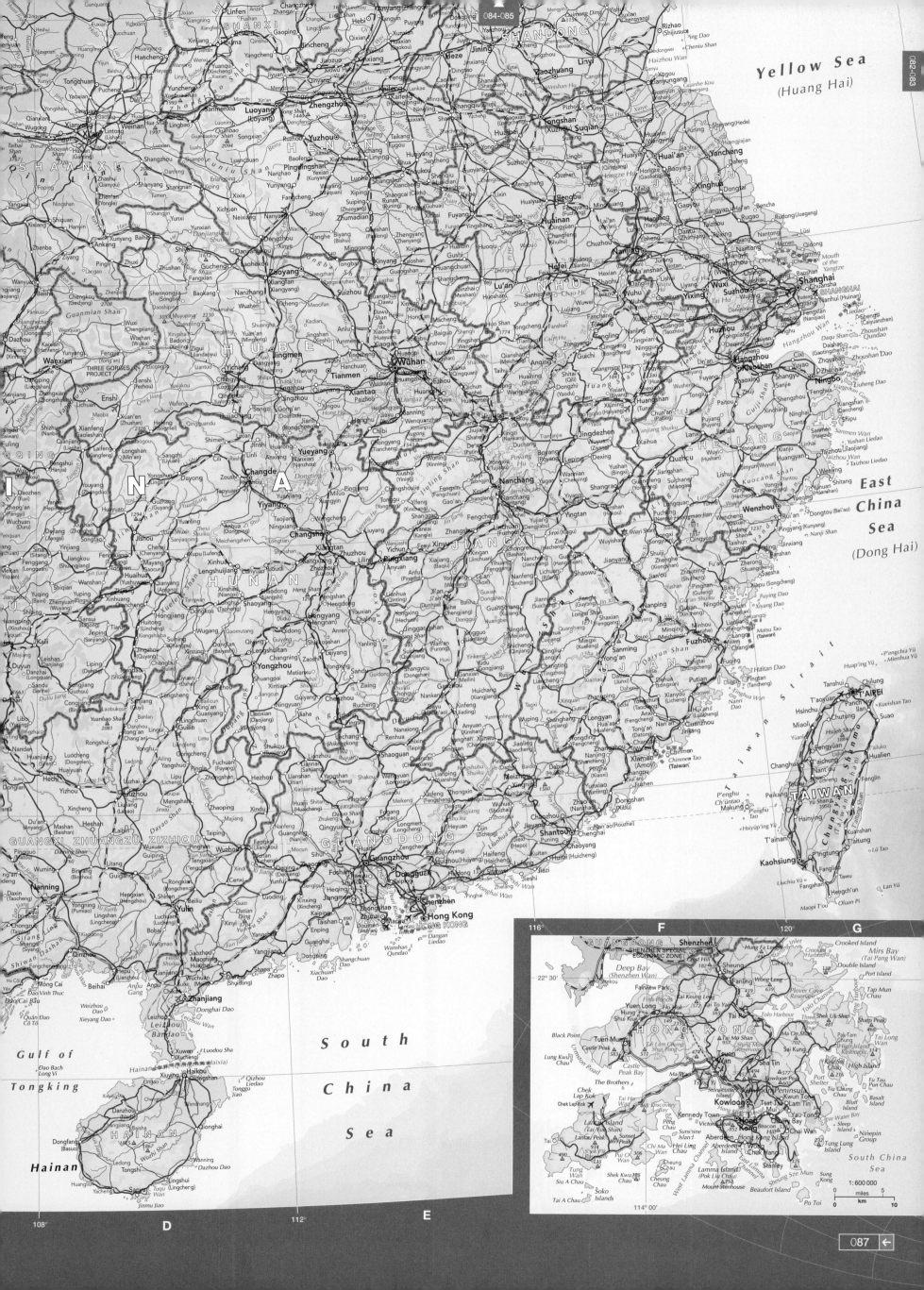

asia[map10]

26°-51'N / 74°-96'E

CONNECTIONS

	page#
▶ subject	
▲ World physical features	8–9
▲ World land images	12–13
▲ Asia landscapes	62–63
▲ Asia countries	64–67

1:6 000 000

Conic Equidistant Projection

miles
0   50   100   150   200   250

km
0   100   150   200   250   300   350   400

QINGHAI

Shan

Kunlun Shan

Plateau of Tibet

Qing Zang Gaoyuan

XIZANG (TIBET)

Gangdise Shan

Nyainqêntanglha Shan

BHUTAN

THIMPHU

SIKKIM

NEPAL

KATHMANDU

AKSAI CHIN
CLAIMED BY INDIA
UNDER CHINESE
ADMINISTRATION

JAMMU AND KASHMIR

NORTHERN AREAS

BALTISTAN

LADAKH Range

ZASKAR Range

Pir Panjal Range

LINE OF CONTROL

Srinagar

HIMACHAL PRADESH

UTTARANCHAL

PUNJAB

Mahabharat Range

Siwalik Range

Lahore

Delhi

Ludhiana

Meerut

Lucknow

Jaipur

INDIA

UTTAR PRADESH

Gwalior

100-101

096-097

A   B   C   D   E   F

5   6   7

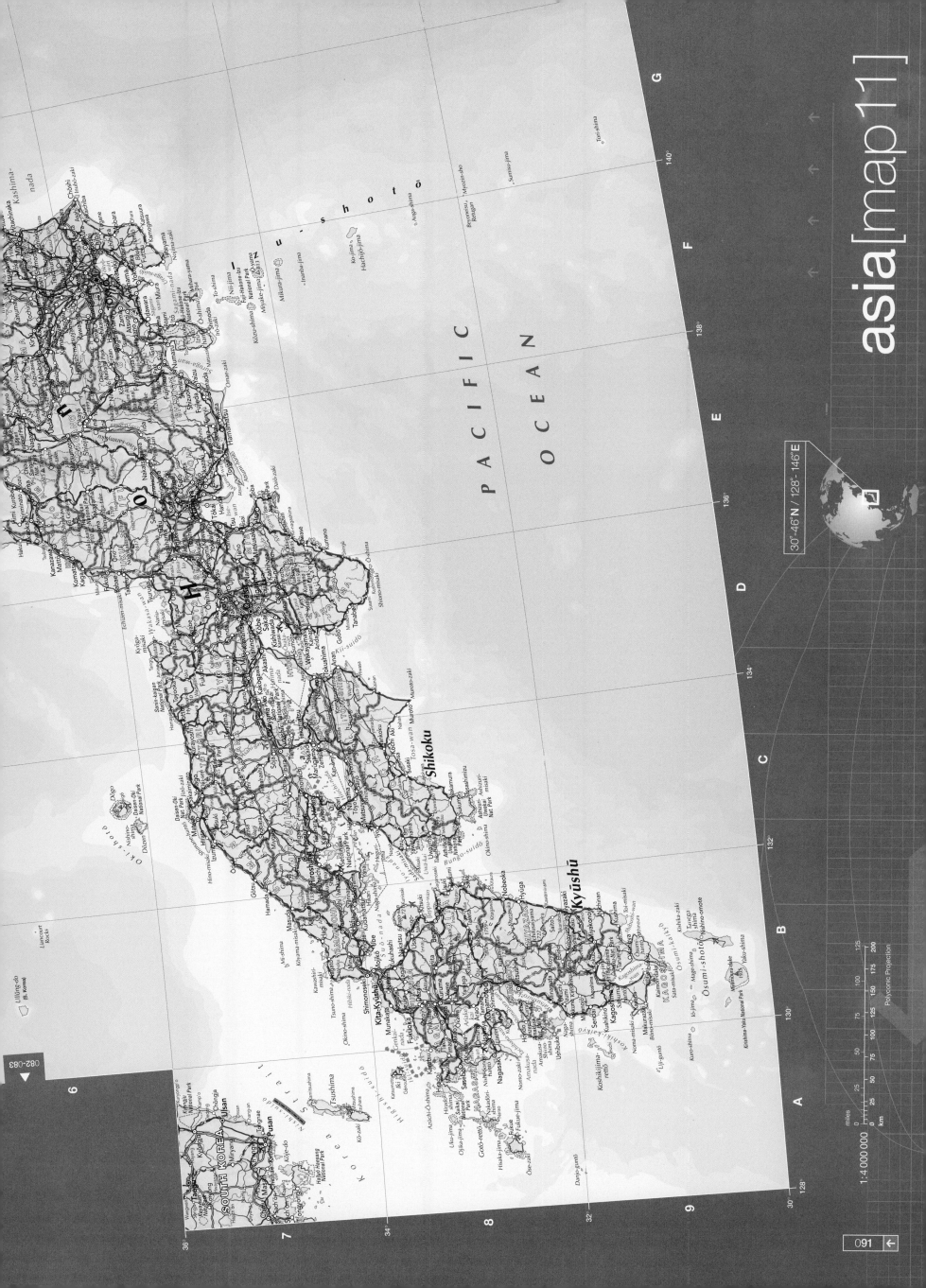

PACIFIC

OCEAN

Shikoku

Kyūshū

SOUTH KOREA

Ullŭng-do
(S. Korea)

Liancourt
Rocks

Korea Strait

Tsushima

Nihon-suido Strait

Pusan

Ulsan

I-z-u-s-h-o-t-ō

Oki-shotō

Dōgo

Daisen-Oki
National Park

Sanin-kaigan
National Park

Shimonoseki

Kita-Kyūshū
Fukuoka

Nagasaki
Sasebo

KAGOSHIMA

Kumamoto

Ōsumi-shotō

Yaku-shima

Kirishima-Yaku National Park

Kinko-wan

Kagoshima

Sendai

Miyazaki

Nobeoka

Hyūga

Kōchi

Tosa-wan

Ashizuri-Uwakai
Nat. Park

Bungo-suidō

30° 46'N / 128°–146°E

1:4 000 000

Polyconic Projection

082–083

091

asia[map12]

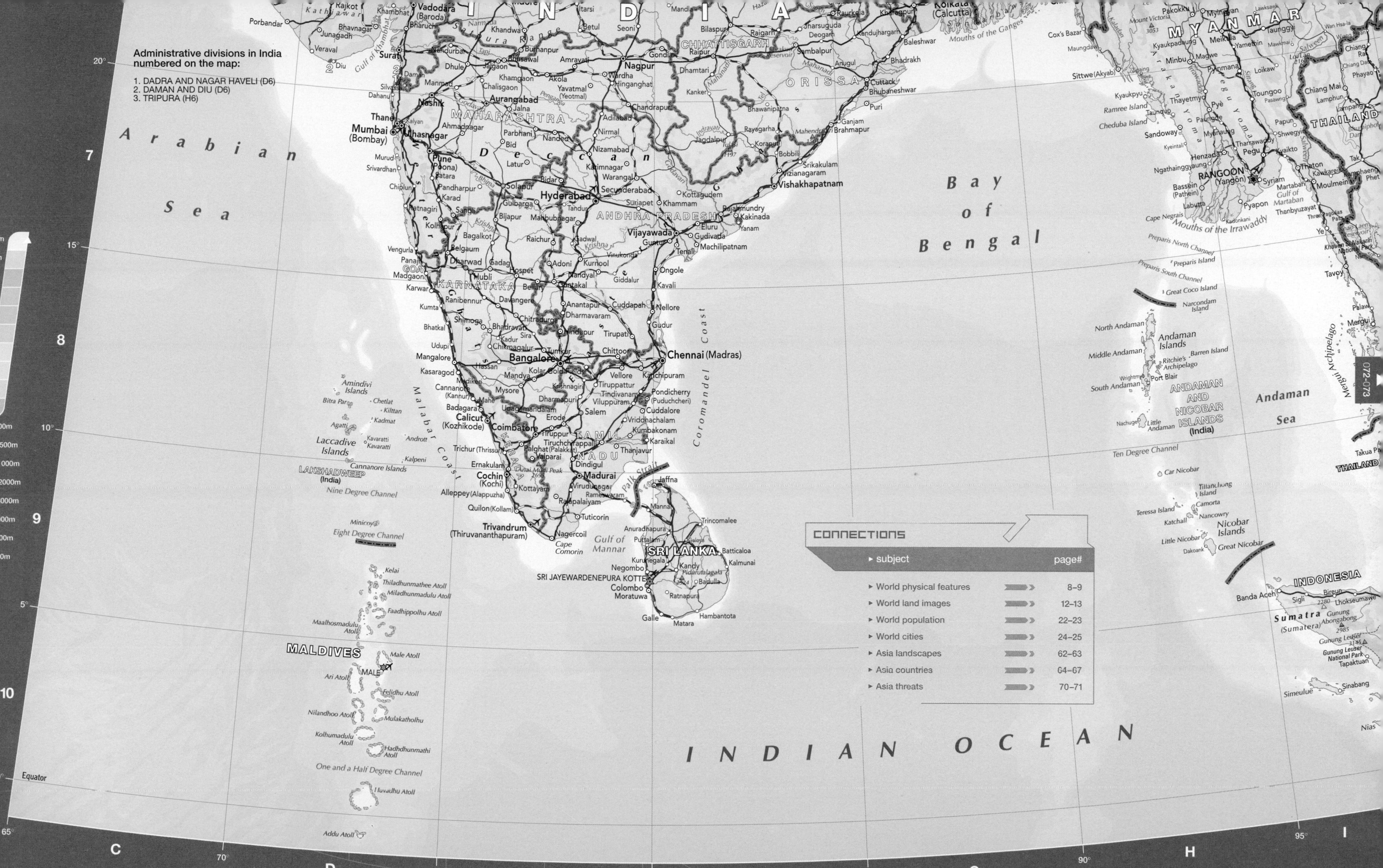

1:12 000 000

1°S–50°N 60°–97°E

Albers Equal Area Conic Projection

miles
0 100 200 300 400 500
km
0 100 200 300 400 500 600 700 800

CONNECTIONS

► subject	page#
▲ World physical features	8–9
▲ World land images	12–13
▲ World population	22–23
▲ World cities	24–25
▲ Asia landscapes	62–63
▲ Asia countries	64–67
▲ Asia threats	70–71

Administrative divisions in India numbered on the map:
1. DADRA AND NAGAR HAVELI (D6)
2. DAMAN AND DIU (D6)
3. TRIPURA (H6)

Elevation scale (metres):
>6000m
5000–6000m
4000–5000m
3000–4000m
2000–3000m
1000–2000m
500–1000m
200–500m
0–200m
<0m
0–200m
200–500m
500–1000m
1000–2000m
2000–3000m
3000–4000m
4000–5000m
5000–6000m
>6000m

Countries and regions

THAILAND
MYANMAR
RANGOON (Yangon)
INDIA
ORISSA
CHHATTISGARH
ANDHRA PRADESH
MAHARASHTRA
KARNATAKA
GOA
KERALA
TAMIL NADU
LAKSHADWEEP (India)
MALDIVES
MALE
SRI LANKA
SRI JAYEWARDENEPURA KOTTE
INDONESIA
Sumatra (Sumatera)

Seas and oceans

Arabian Sea
Bay of Bengal
Andaman Sea
INDIAN OCEAN
Gulf of Kutch
Gulf of Khambhat
Gulf of Mannar
Palk Strait
Laccadive Islands
Amindivi Islands
Cannanore Islands
Nine Degree Channel
Eight Degree Channel
One and a Half Degree Channel
Mouths of the Ganges
Mouths of the Irrawaddy
Gulf of Martaban
Mergui Archipelago
Ten Degree Channel
Great Channel

Andaman and Nicobar Islands (India)

ANDAMAN AND NICOBAR ISLANDS (India)
Andaman Islands
North Andaman
Middle Andaman
South Andaman
Port Blair
Ritchie's Archipelago
Barren Island
Little Andaman
Nicobar Islands
Car Nicobar
Teressa Island
Nancowry
Katchall
Little Nicobar
Great Nicobar
Preparis Island
Preparis North Channel
Preparis South Channel
Coco Islands
Great Coco Island
Cape Negrais

Cities (selected)

Mumbai (Bombay)
Pune (Poona)
Nashik
Thane
Surat
Vadodara (Baroda)
Nagpur
Hyderabad
Secunderabad
Vijayawada
Visakhapatnam
Chennai (Madras)
Bangalore
Mysore
Calicut (Kozhikode)
Cochin (Kochi)
Trivandrum (Thiruvananthapuram)
Madurai
Coimbatore
Pondicherry (Puducherry)
Cuddalore
Tiruchchirappalli
Thanjavur
Salem
Vellore
Kolkata (Calcutta)
Bhubaneshwar
Cuttack
Kolhapur
Belgaum
Mangalore
Cape Comorin
Colombo
Moratuwa
Negombo
Jaffna
Trincomalee
Batticaloa
Galle
Matara
Hambantota
Kandy
Ratnapura
Anuradhapura

Deccan

Malabar Coast
Coromandel Coast

Equator

asia[map13]

5°-22°N / 70°-96°E

Elevation legend (left, meters):
>6000m
5000-6000m
4000-5000m
3000-4000m
2000-3000m
1000-2000m
500-1000m
200-500m
0-200m
<0m

Bathymetry legend:
0-200m
200-500m
500-1000m
1000-2000m
2000-3000m
3000-4000m
4000-5000m
5000-6000m
>6000m

Arabian Sea

MAHARASHTRA

INDIA

DECCAN

KARNATAKA

ANDHRA PRADESH

GOA

KERALA

TAMIL NADU

Coromandel Coast

LAKSHADWEEP (India)

Laccadive Islands

MALDIVES

SRI LANKA

Major cities and towns:
Vadodara (Baroda), Surat, Navsari, Nashik, Aurangabad, Thane, Mumbai (Bombay), Pune, Kolhapur, Panaji, Madgaon, Karwar, Mangalore, Hubli, Belgaum, Dharwad, Bellary, Hyderabad, Secunderabad, Kurnool, Bijapur, Gulbarga, Raichur, Anantapur, Bangalore, Mysore, Chikmagalur, Udupi, Chennai (Madras), Tiruvottiyur, Kanchipuram, Chengalpattu, Pondicherry (Puducherry), Cuddalore, Chidambaram, Coimbatore, Calicut (Kozhikode), Cochin (Kochi), Alleppey (Alappuzha), Kollam (Quilon), Trivandrum (Thiruvananthapuram), Nagercoil, Cape Comorin, Madurai, Tuticorin, Rameswaram, Tiruchchirappalli, Thanjavur, Nagore, Nagapattinam, Jaffna, Trincomalee, Anuradhapura, Polonnaruwa, Kurunegala, Kandy, Colombo, Sri Jayewardenepura Kotte, Moratuwa, Galle, Hambantota, Matara

Water features:
Gulf of Khambhat, Gulf of Mannar, Palk Strait, Nine Degree Channel, Eight Degree Channel, Coromandel Coast, Malabar Coast

Islands / banks:
Diu, Sesostris Bank, Bassas de Pedro Padua Bank, Cherbaniani Reef, Byramgore Reef, Chetlat, Bitra Par, Kiltan, Amindivi Islands, Kadmat, Amini, Andrott, Kavaratti, Kalpeni, Cheriyam, Cannanore Islands, Minicoy, Thiladhunmathee Atoll, Maalhosmadulu Atoll, Faadhippolhu Atoll

asia[map14]

20°-38°N / 68°-96°E

>6000m
5000-6000m
4000-5000m
3000-4000m
2000-3000m
1000-2000m
500-1000m
200-500m
0-200m
<0m

0-200m
200-500m
500-1000m
1000-2000m
2000-3000m
3000-4000m
4000-5000m
5000-6000m
>6000m

Administrative divisions in India
numbered on the map:

1. DADRA AND NAGAR HAVELI (B5)
2. DAMAN AND DIU (A5, B5)

13°-42°N / 30°-80°E

052-053

040-041

120-121

128-129

>6000m
5000-6000m
4000-5000m
3000-4000m
2000-3000m
1000-2000m
500-1000m
200-500m
0-200m
<0m

0-200m
200-500m
500-1000m
1000-2000m
2000-3000m
3000-4000m
4000-5000m
5000-6000m
>6000m

Administrative divisions in India
numbered on the map:

1. DADRA AND NAGAR HAVELI (I5)
2. DAMAN AND DIU (I5)

CONNECTIONS

► subject	page#
► World changes	20–21
► Asia landscapes	62–63
► Asia countries	64–67
► Asia issues	66–67
► Asia changes	68–69

1:11 000 000

miles
0   100   200   300   400

0   100   200   300   400   500   600   700
km

Albers Conic Equal Area Projection

asia[map16]

102-103

Administrative divisions numbered on the map

AFGHANISTAN
1. KÁBUL (G3)
2. KÁPISÁ (G3)
3. LAGHMÁN (G3)
4. LOWGAR (G3)
5. PARVÁN (G3)

IRAN
6. CHAHÁR MAHÁLL VÄ BAKHTIÁRÍ (B3)
7. KOHKÍLÚYEH VA BÚYER AHMADÍ (B4)

UZBEKISTAN
8. ANDIZHANSKAYA OBLAST' (H1)
9. FERGANSKAYA OBLAST' (G1)
10. RESPUBLIKA KARAKALPAKISTAN (E1)
11. KHOREZMSKAYA OBLAST' (E1)
12. NAMANGANSKAYA OBLAST' (G1)
13. SYRDAR'INSKAYA OBLAST' (G1)
14. TASHKENTSKAYA OBLAST' (G1)

23°-40°N / 44°-76°E

>6000m
5000-6000m
4000-5000m
3000-4000m
2000-3000m
1000-2000m
500-1000m
200-500m
0-200m
<0m

0-200m
200-500m
500-1000m
1000-2000m
2000-3000m
3000-4000m
4000-5000m
5000-6000m
>6000m

→ 100

104-105

106-107

CONNECTIONS

▶ subject	page#
▶ World earthquakes	14–15
▶ World changes	20–21
▶ Asia countries	64–67

1:6 000 000

miles
0   50   100   150   200   250

km
0   50   100   150   200   250   300   350   400

Conic Equidistant Projection

asia[map17]

36°-54°N / 46°-79°E

CONNECTIONS

subject	page#
▶ World physical features	8–9
▶ Volga Delta	30–31
▶ Asia landscapes	62–63
▶ Asia countries	64–67
▶ Asia changes	68–69

>6000m
5000-6000m
4000-5000m
3000-4000m
2000-3000m
1000-2000m
500-1000m
200-500m
0-200m
<0m
0-200m
200-500m
500-1000m
1000-2000m
2000-3000m
3000-4000m
4000-5000m
5000-6000m
>6000m

Administrative regions in Uzbekistan
numbered on the map:

1. ANDIZHANSKAYA OBLAST' (H4)
2. DZHIZAKSKAYA OBLAST' (F5)
3. FERGANSKAYA OBLAST' (G4)
4. KASHKADAR'INSKAYA OBLAST' (F5)
5. NAMANGANSKAYA OBLAST' (G4)
6. SAMARKANDSKAYA OBLAST' (F5)
7. SYRDAR'INSKAYA OBLAST' (G4)
8. TASHKENTSKAYA OBLAST' (G4)

asia[map18]

12°-29°N / 33°-60°E

108-109
120-121
128-129
JORDAN
EGYPT
SUDAN
ERITREA
ETHIOPIA
DJIBOUTI
Red Sea
HALAIB TRIANGLE UNDER SUDANESE ADMINISTRATION
Nubian Desert
Gulf of Suez
Gulf of Aqaba
An Nafūd
AL JAWF
HĀ'IL
TABŪK
AL MADĪNAH
MAKKAH
AL BĀḤAH
'ASĪR
JĪZĀN
NAJRĀN
AL QAṢĪM
AL ḤUDŪD ASH SHAMĀLĪYAH
Medina (Al Madīnah)
Jeddah (Jiddah)
Mecca (Makkah)
Aţ Ţā'if
Ḥā'il
Tabūk
Yanbu' al Baḥr
Abhā
Jīzān
Buraydah
Port Sudan (Būr Sudan)
Suakin
Kassala
Atbara
Berber
Gedaref
Wad Medani
Sennar
ASMARA
Massawa
Keren
Mek'ele
Gonder
Hurghada
Dahlak Archipelago
Suakin Archipelago
Farasān
Hodeidah (Al Ḥudaydah)
SAN'A'
Ta'izz
Tropic of Cancer
KHARTOUM
RED SEA
NILE
KASSALA
GEDAREF
SENNAR
EL GEZIRA
BLUE NILE
ASWĀN
QENA
EL BAHR EL AHMAR
JANŪB SĪNĀ'
TIGRAY
AMHARA
AFAR
DANKALIA
HAJJAH
ṢA'DAH
Dinder National Park
28°
24°
20°
16°
12°
33°
36°
40°
44°
A
B
C
1
2
3
4
5

>6000m
5000-6000m
4000-5000m
3000-4000m
2000-3000m
1000-2000m
500-1000m
200-500m
0-200m
<0m
0-200m
200-500m
500-1000m
1000-2000m
2000-3000m
3000-4000m
4000-5000m
5000-6000m
>6000m

asia[map19]

27°-44°N / 24°-52°E

Administrative divisions numbered on the map

EGYPT
10. EL ISKANDARÎYA (C5)
11. BEHEIRA (C5)
12. EL QÂHIRA (C5)
13. DAQAHLÎYA (C5)
14. DUMYÂT (C5)
15. GHARBÎYA (C5)
16. ISMÂ'ÎLÎYA (D5)
17. KAFR EL SHEIKH (C5)
18. MINÛFÎYA (C5)
19. BÛR SA'ÎD (D5)
20. QALYÛBÎYA (C5)
21. SHARQÎYA (C5)
22. EL SUWEIS (D5)

IRAN
23. CHAHÂR MAHÀLL VA BAKHTÎARÎ (G4)
24. KOHKÎLÛYEH VA BÛYER AHMADÎ (G5)

>6000m
5000-6000m
4000-5000m
3000-4000m
2000-3000m
1000-2000m
500-1000m
200-500m
0-200m
<0m

0-200m
200-500m
500-1000m
1000-2000m
2000-3000m
3000-4000m
4000-5000m
5000-6000m
>6000m

CONNECTIONS

Administrative divisions in Egypt
numbered on the map

1. BÛR SA'ÏD (D6)
2. DUMYÄT (C6)
3. KAFR EL SHEIKH (B6)
4. GHARBÏYA (C7)
5. MINÜFÏYA (C7)
6. QALYÜBÏYA (C7)

Mediterranean Sea

>6000m
5000-6000m
4000-5000m
3000-4000m
2000-3000m
1500-2000m
1000-1500m
500-1000m
200-500m
100-200m
0-100m
0-0m
<0m

0-200m
200-500m
500-1000m
1000-2000m
2000-3000m
3000-4000m
4000-5000m
5000-6000m
>6000m

058-059

120-121

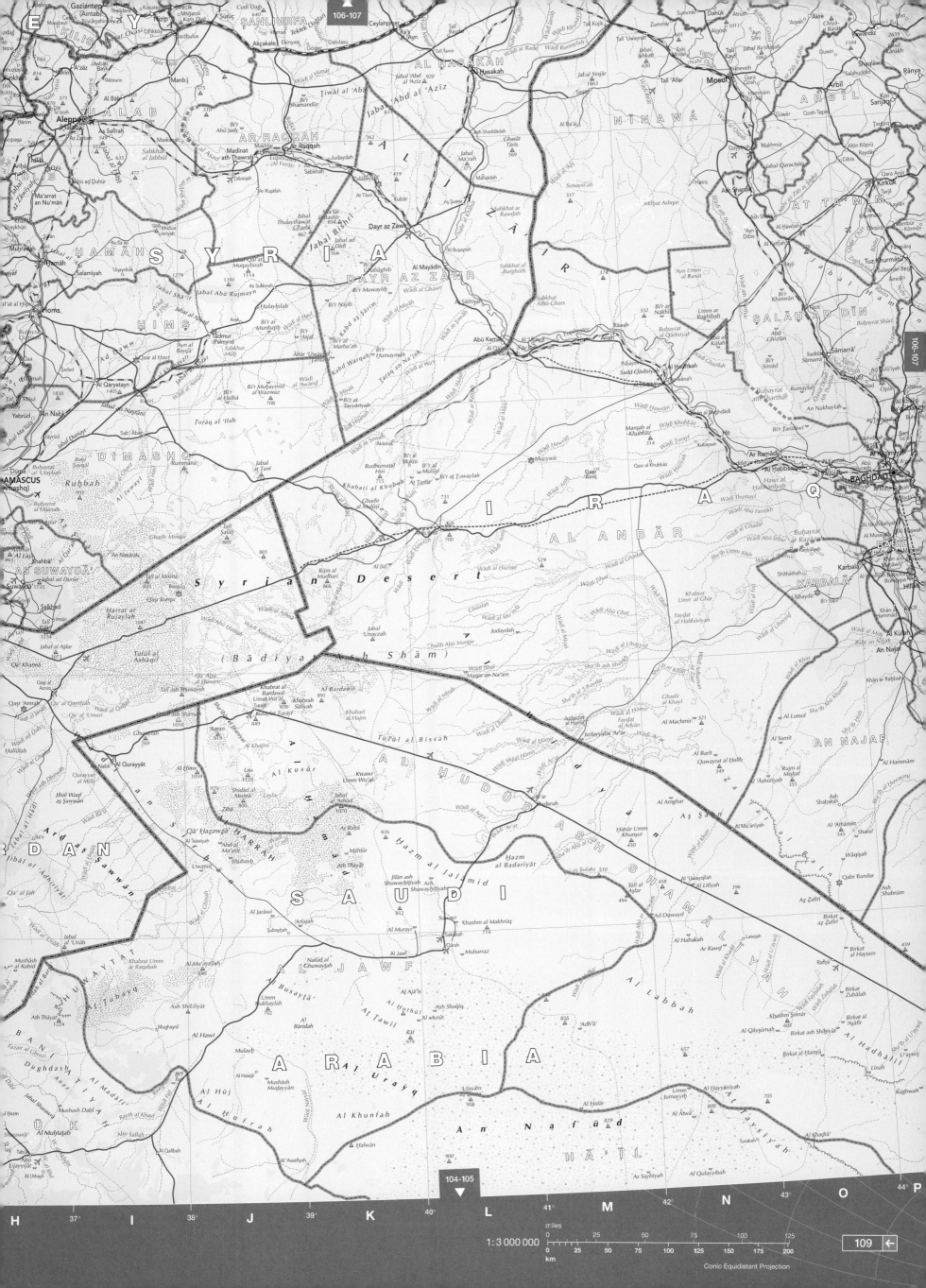

Rift Valley, *Eritrea*

africa

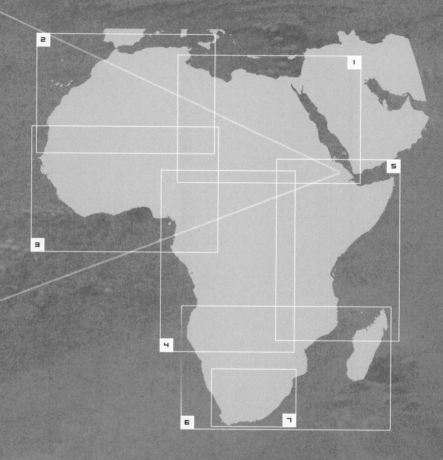

[contents]

	page#
africa [landscapes]	112–113
africa [countries]	114–115
africa [countries/issues]	116–117
africa [locations]	118–119

	map coverage	scale	page#
africa [map 1]	AFRICA Northeast	1:8 000 000	120–121
africa [map 2]	AFRICA Northwest	1:8 000 000	122–123
africa [map 3]	AFRICA West	1:8 000 000	124–125
africa [map 4]	AFRICA West Central	1:8 000 000	126–127
africa [map 5]	AFRICA East Central	1:8 000 000	128–129
africa [map 6]	AFRICA South	1:8 000 000	130–131
africa [map 7]	REPUBLIC OF SOUTH AFRICA	1:3 500 000	132–133

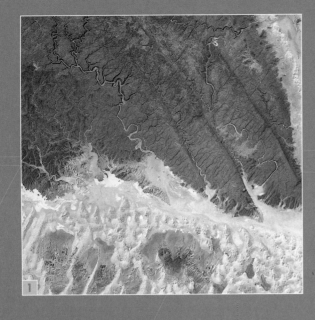

Africa, viewed here from above the southern Indian Ocean, is dominated by several striking physical features. The Sahara desert extends over most of the north and in the east the geological feature, known as the Great Rift Valley, extends from the valley of the river Jordan in Southwest Asia to Mozambique. The valley contains a string of major lakes including Lake Turkana, Lake Tanganyika and Lake Nyasa.

The river basin of the Congo, in central Africa draining into the Atlantic Ocean, is the second largest river basin in the world. The land south of the equator is higher than in the north and forms a massive plateau dissected by several large rivers which flow east to the Indian Ocean or west to the Atlantic. The most distinctive feature in the south is the Drakensberg, a range of mountains which run southwest to northeast through Lesotho and South Africa. The large island separated from Africa by the Mozambique Channel is Madagascar, the fourth largest island in the world.

1 Sahara Desert, *Algeria*

The Sahara desert crosses the continent of Africa from the Atlantic Ocean to the Red Sea. Within this vast area there is a great variety in topography with heights from 30 m below sea level to mountains over 3 300 m. This satellite image of east central Algeria shows the sand dunes stopping at the higher ground of the dark base rock. Although rain is scarce, dry river beds can be seen cutting through the rock.

Satellite/Sensor : SPOT

2 Congo River, *Democratic Republic of Congo*

This satellite image shows broken clouds above a heavily braided Congo river in Congo. The river is over 4 600 km long and has many long tributaries which result in a drainage basin of approximately 3 700 000 sq km. In this tropical area the river acts as a highway between communities where roads do not exist. The river flows into the Atlantic Ocean, forming the boundary between Angola and the Democratic Republic of Congo.

Satellite/Sensor : Space Shuttle

3 Atlas Mountains, *Morocco*

The Atlas Mountains of Morocco in northwest Africa form a major boundary between the Sahara desert and the fertile coastal plain. They are a composite of several ranges created from extensive fault movements and earthquakes, resulting in distinct rock layers and folds, as seen in this image. The dark areas are sandy beds of a seasonal river system.

Satellite/Sensor : SIR-C/X-SAR

Canary Islands

Atlas Mountains

Cape Verde Islands

Volta

Benue River

Largest desert in the world

Sahara
9 065 000 sq km / 3 500 000 sq miles
Map reference 123 F4

Niger River

Gulf of Guinea

Bioco

São Tome

Atlantic Ocean

Congo River

Largest drainage basin

Congo Basin
3 700 000 sq km / 1 429 000 sq miles
Map reference 126 C5

Bié Plateau

Victoria Falls

Namib Desert

Okavango Delta

Orange River

Kalahari Desert

Great Karoo

Drakensberg

Limpo

Cape of Good Hope

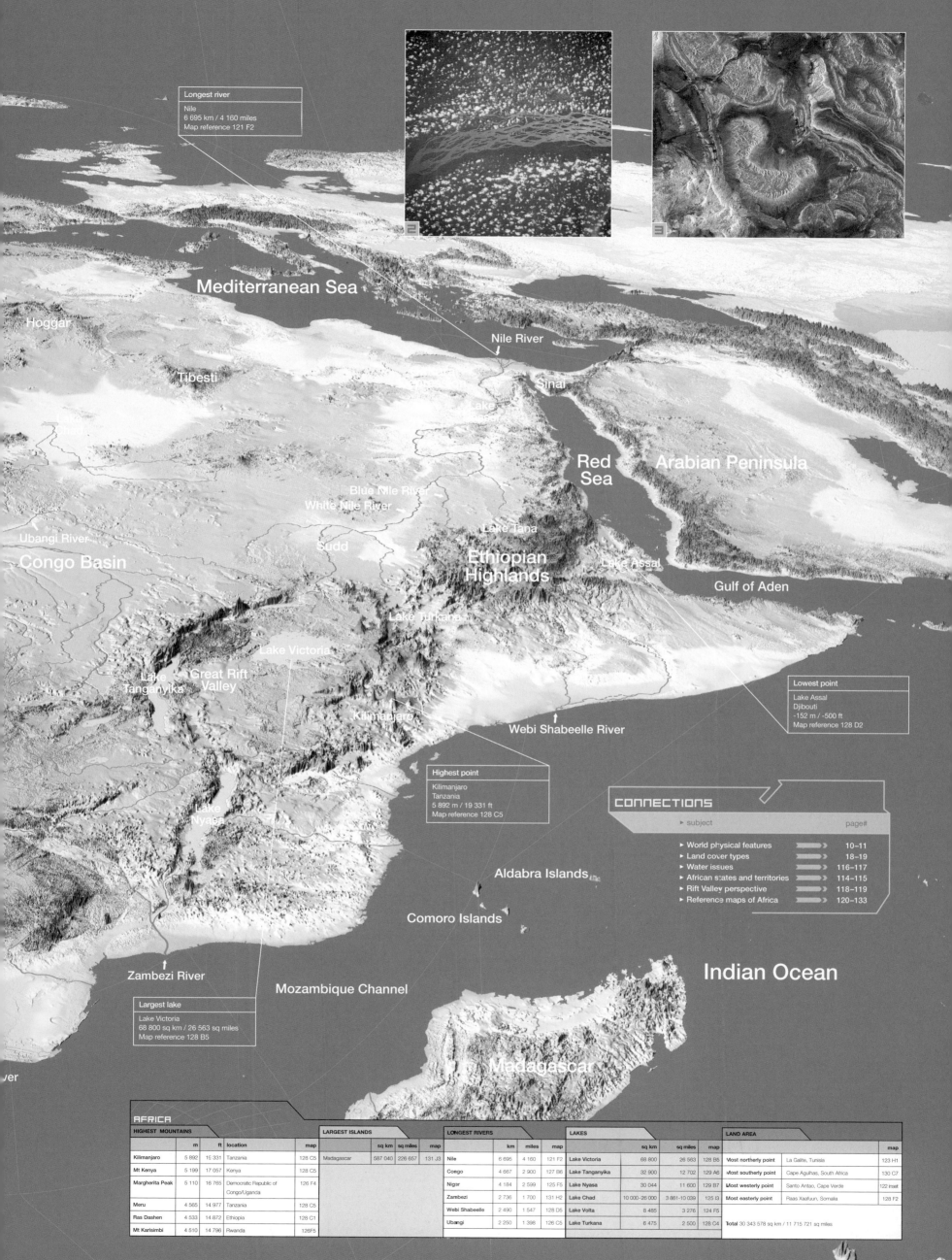

Mediterranean Sea

Hoggar

Tibesti

Lake
Chad

Nile River

Sinai

Lake

Red
Sea

Arabian Peninsula

Blue Nile River

White Nile River

Lake Tana

Ubangi River

Congo Basin

Sudd

Ethiopian
Highlands

Lake Assal

Gulf of Aden

Lake Turkana

Lake Victoria

Great Rift
Valley

Lake
Tanganyika

Kilimanjaro

Webi Shabeelle River

Lake
Nyasa

Aldabra Islands

Comoro Islands

Zambezi River

Mozambique Channel

Indian Ocean

Madagascar

Longest river
Nile
6 695 km / 4 160 miles
Map reference 121 F2

Lowest point
Lake Assal
Djibouti
-152 m / -500 ft
Map reference 128 D2

Highest point
Kilimanjaro
Tanzania
5 892 m / 19 331 ft
Map reference 128 C5

Largest lake
Lake Victoria
68 800 sq km / 26 563 sq miles
Map reference 128 B5

CONNECTIONS

▶ subject	page#
▶ World physical features	10–11
▶ Land cover types	18–19
▶ Water issues	116–117
▶ African states and territories	114–115
▶ Rift Valley perspective	118–119
▶ Reference maps of Africa	120–133

AFRICA

HIGHEST MOUNTAINS

	m	ft	location	map
Kilimanjaro	5 892	19 331	Tanzania	128 C5
Mt Kenya	5 199	17 057	Kenya	128 C5
Margherita Peak	5 110	16 765	Democratic Republic of Congo/Uganda	126 F4
Meru	4 565	14 977	Tanzania	128 C5
Ras Dashen	4 533	14 872	Ethiopia	128 C1
Mt Karisimbi	4 510	14 796	Rwanda	126 F5

LARGEST ISLANDS

	sq km	sq miles	map
Madagascar	587 040	226 657	131 J3

LONGEST RIVERS

	km	miles	map
Nile	6 695	4 160	121 F2
Congo	4 667	2 900	127 B6
Niger	4 184	2 599	125 F5
Zambezi	2 736	1 700	131 H2
Webi Shabeelle	2 490	1 547	128 D5
Ubangi	2 250	1 398	126 C5

LAKES

	sq km	sq miles	map
Lake Victoria	68 800	26 563	128 B5
Lake Tanganyika	32 900	12 702	129 A6
Lake Nyasa	30 044	11 600	129 B7
Lake Chad	10 000–26 000	3 861–10 039	125 G3
Lake Volta	8 485	3 276	124 F5
Lake Turkana	6 475	2 500	128 C4

LAND AREA

		map
Most northerly point	La Galite, Tunisia	123 H1
Most southerly point	Cape Agulhas, South Africa	130 C7
Most westerly point	Santo Antao, Cape Verde	122 inset
Most easterly point	Raas Xaafuun, Somalia	128 F2
Total 30 343 578 sq km / 11 715 721 sq miles		

1 **Border Post,** *Algeria/Niger*

The border between Algeria and Niger lies in the centre of the Sahel region of Africa. Both countries have largely geometric borders in the relatively featureless landscape which offers no obvious physical boundaries. As a result simple indicators of the presence of a border, such as the marker shown in this photograph taken south of the actual boundary line, are the only features which advise of the passage from one country to the other.

2 **Refugee Camp,** *Tanzania*

Much internal migration in Africa has been instigated by war, ethnic conflict, economic disparities and famine. In 1994 over 2 million Rwandans fled to the neighbouring countries of Tanzania and the Democratic Republic of Congo to escape tribal war between Hutus and Tutsis. This photograph shows a refugee camp in Tanzania just across the border from Rwanda and gives an indication of the difficult conditions in such centres. Tanzania is currently one of East Africa's most important host countries with a refugee population of nearly half a million.

AFRICA
COUNTRIES

		area sq km	area sq miles	population	capital	languages	religions	currency	map
ALGERIA		2 381 741	919 595	30 291 000	Algiers (Alger)	Arabic, French, Berber	Sunni Muslim	Dinar	122–123
ANGOLA		1 246 700	481 354	13 134 000	Luanda	Portuguese, Bantu, local languages	Roman Catholic, Protestant, traditional beliefs	Kwanza	127
BENIN		112 620	43 483	6 272 000	Porto-Novo	French, Fon, Yoruba, Adja, local languages	Traditional beliefs, Roman Catholic, Sunni Muslim	CFA franc	125
BOTSWANA		581 370	224 468	1 541 000	Gaborone	English, Setswana, Shona, local languages	Traditional beliefs, Protestant, Roman Catholic	Pula	130–131
BURKINA		274 200	105 869	11 535 000	Ouagadougou	French, Moore (Mossi), Fulani, local languages	Sunni Muslim, traditional beliefs, Roman Catholic	CFA franc	124–125
BURUNDI		27 835	10 747	6 356 000	Bujumbura	Kirundi (Hutu, Tutsi), French	Roman Catholic, traditional beliefs, Protestant	Franc	126
CAMEROON		475 442	183 569	14 876 000	Yaoundé	French, English, Fang, Bamileke, local languages	Roman Catholic, traditional beliefs, Sunni Muslim, Protestant	CFA franc	126
CAPE VERDE		4 033	1 557	427 000	Praia	Portuguese, creole	Roman Catholic, Protestant	Escudo	124
CENTRAL AFRICAN REPUBLIC		622 436	240 324	3 717 000	Bangui	French, Sango, Banda, Baya, local languages	Protestant, Roman Catholic, traditional beliefs, Sunni Muslim	CFA franc	126
CHAD		1 284 000	495 755	7 885 000	Ndjamena	Arabic, French, Sara, local languages	Sunni Muslim, Roman Catholic, Protestant, traditional beliefs	CFA franc	120
COMOROS		1 862	719	706 000	Moroni	Comorian, French, Arabic	Sunni Muslim, Roman Catholic	Franc	129
CONGO		342 000	132 047	3 018 000	Brazzaville	French, Kongo, Monokutuba, local languages	Roman Catholic, Protestant, traditional beliefs, Sunni Muslim	CFA franc	126–127
CONGO, DEMOCRATIC REPUBLIC OF		2 345 410	905 568	50 948 000	Kinshasa	French, Lingala, Swahili, Kongo, local languages	Christian, Sunni Muslim	Franc	126–127
CÔTE D'IVOIRE		322 463	124 504	16 013 000	Yamoussoukro	French, creole, Akan, local languages	Sunni Muslim, Roman Catholic, traditional beliefs, Protestant	CFA franc	124
DJIBOUTI		23 200	8 958	632 000	Djibouti	Somali, Afar, French, Arabic	Sunni Muslim, Christian	Franc	128
EGYPT		1 000 250	386 199	67 884 000	Cairo (El Qâhira)	Arabic	Sunni Muslim, Coptic Christian	Pound	120–121
EQUATORIAL GUINEA		28 051	10 831	457 000	Malabo	Spanish, French, Fang	Roman Catholic, traditional beliefs	CFA franc	125
ERITREA		117 400	45 328	3 659 000	Asmara	Tigrinya, Tigre	Sunni Muslim, Coptic Christian	Nakfa	121
ETHIOPIA		1 133 880	437 794	62 908 000	Addis Ababa (Ādīs Ābeba)	Oromo, Amharic, Tigrinya, local languages	Ethiopian Orthodox, Sunni Muslim, traditional beliefs	Birr	128
GABON		267 667	103 347	1 230 000	Libreville	French, Fang, local languages	Roman Catholic, Protestant, traditional beliefs	CFA franc	126
THE GAMBIA		11 295	4 361	1 303 000	Banjul	English, Malinke, Fulani, Wolof	Sunni Muslim, Protestant	Dalasi	124
GHANA		238 537	92 100	19 306 000	Accra	English, Hausa, Akan, local languages	Christian, Sunni Muslim, traditional beliefs	Cedi	124–125
GUINEA		245 857	94 926	8 154 000	Conakry	French, Fulani, Malinke, local languages	Sunni Muslim, traditional beliefs, Christian	Franc	124
GUINEA–BISSAU		36 125	13 948	1 199 000	Bissau	Portuguese, crioulo, local languages	Traditional beliefs, Sunni Muslim, Christian	CFA franc	124
KENYA		582 646	224 961	30 669 000	Nairobi	Swahili, English, local languages	Christian, traditional beliefs	Shilling	128–129
LESOTHO		30 355	11 720	2 035 000	Maseru	Sesotho, English, Zulu	Christian, traditional beliefs	Loti	133
LIBERIA		111 369	43 000	2 913 000	Monrovia	English, creole, local languages	Traditional beliefs, Christian, Sunni Muslim	Dollar	124
LIBYA		1 759 540	679 362	5 290 000	Tripoli (Ṭarābulus)	Arabic, Berber	Sunni Muslim	Dinar	120
MADAGASCAR		587 041	226 658	15 970 000	Antananarivo	Malagasy, French	Traditional beliefs, Christian, Sunni Muslim	Franc	131
MALAWI		118 484	45 747	11 308 000	Lilongwe	Chichewa, English, local languages	Christian, traditional beliefs, Sunni Muslim	Kwacha	129
MALI		1 240 140	478 821	11 351 000	Bamako	French, Bambara, local languages	Sunni Muslim, traditional beliefs, Christian	CFA franc	124–125
MAURITANIA		1 030 700	397 955	2 665 000	Nouakchott	Arabic, French, local languages	Sunni Muslim	Ouguiya	122
MAURITIUS		2 040	788	1 161 000	Port Louis	English, creole, Hindi, Bhojpuri, French	Hindu, Roman Catholic, Sunni Muslim	Rupee	218
MOROCCO		446 550	172 414	29 878 000	Rabat	Arabic, Berber, French	Sunni Muslim	Dirham	122–123
MOZAMBIQUE		799 380	308 642	18 292 000	Maputo	Portuguese, Makua, Tsonga, local languages	Traditional beliefs, Roman Catholic, Sunni Muslim	Metical	131
NAMIBIA		824 292	318 261	1 757 000	Windhoek	English, Afrikaans, German, Ovambo, local languages	Protestant, Roman Catholic	Dollar	130
NIGER		1 267 000	489 191	10 832 000	Niamey	French, Hausa, Fulani, local languages	Sunni Muslim, traditional beliefs	CFA franc	125
NIGERIA		923 768	356 669	113 862 000	Abuja	English, Hausa, Yoruba, Ibo, Fulani, local languages	Sunni Muslim, Christian, traditional beliefs	Naira	125
RWANDA		26 338	10 169	7 609 000	Kigali	Kinyarwanda, French, English	Roman Catholic, traditional beliefs, Protestant	Franc	126
SÃO TOMÉ AND PRÍNCIPE		964	372	138 000	São Tomé	Portuguese, creole	Roman Catholic, Protestant	Dobra	125
SENEGAL		196 720	75 954	9 421 000	Dakar	French, Wolof, Fulani, local languages	Sunni Muslim, Roman Catholic, traditional beliefs	CFA franc	124
SEYCHELLES		455	176	80 000	Victoria	English, French, creole	Roman Catholic, Protestant	Rupee	218
SIERRA LEONE		71 740	27 699	4 405 000	Freetown	English, creole, Mende, Temne, local languages	Sunni Muslim, traditional beliefs	Leone	124
SOMALIA		637 657	246 201	8 778 000	Mogadishu (Muqdisho)	Somali, Arabic	Sunni Muslim	Shilling	128
SOUTH AFRICA, REPUBLIC OF		1 219 090	470 693	43 309 000	Pretoria/Cape Town	Afrikaans, English, nine official local languages	Protestant, Roman Catholic, Sunni Muslim, Hindu	Rand	130–131
SUDAN		2 505 813	967 500	31 095 000	Khartoum	Arabic, Dinka, Nubian, Beja, Nuer, local languages	Sunni Muslim, traditional beliefs, Christian	Dinar	120–121
SWAZILAND		17 364	6 704	925 000	Mbabane	Swazi, English	Christian, traditional beliefs	Lilangeni	133
TANZANIA		945 087	364 900	35 119 000	Dodoma	Swahili, English, Nyamwezi, local languages	Shi'a Muslim, Sunni Muslim, traditional beliefs, Christian	Shilling	128–129
TOGO		56 785	21 925	4 527 000	Lomé	French, Ewe, Kabre, local languages	Traditional beliefs, Christian, Sunni Muslim	CFA franc	125
TUNISIA		164 150	63 379	9 459 000	Tunis	Arabic, French	Sunni Muslim	Dinar	123
UGANDA		241 038	93 065	23 300 000	Kampala	English, Swahili, Luganda, local languages	Roman Catholic, Protestant, Sunni Muslim, traditional beliefs	Shilling	128
ZAMBIA		752 614	290 586	10 421 000	Lusaka	English, Bemba, Nyanja, Tonga, local languages	Christian, traditional beliefs	Kwacha	127
ZIMBABWE		390 759	150 873	12 627 000	Harare	English, Shona, Ndebele	Christian, traditional beliefs	Dollar	131

Equator

Trop

CONNECTIONS

subject	page#
▶ World physical features	8–9
▶ World countries	10–11
▶ Africa issues	116–117
▶ Reference maps of Africa	120–133

AFRICA

TOP 10 COUNTRIES BY AREA

	sq km	sq miles	map	world rank
1. SUDAN	2 505 813	967 500	120–121	10
2. ALGERIA	2 381 741	919 595	122–123	11
3. CONGO, DEMOCRATIC REPUBLIC OF	2 345 410	905 563	126–127	12
4. LIBYA	1 759 540	679 362	120	17
5. CHAD	1 284 000	495 755	120	21
6. NIGER	1 267 000	489 19·	125	22
7. ANGOLA	1 246 700	481 35·	127	23
8. MALI	1 240 140	478 821	124–125	24
9. SOUTH AFRICA, REPUBLIC OF	1 219 090	470 693	130–131	25
10. ETHIOPIA	1 133 880	437 794	128	27

TOP 10 COUNTRIES BY POPULATION

	population	map	world rank
1. NIGERIA	113 862 000	125	10
2. EGYPT	67 884 000	120–121	16
3. ETHIOPIA	62 908 000	128	18
4. CONGO, DEMOCRATIC REPUBLIC OF	50 948 000	126–127	23
5. SOUTH AFRICA, REPUBLIC OF	43 309 000	130–131	27
6. TANZANIA	35 119 000	128–129	32
7. SUDAN	31 095 000	120–121	33
8. KENYA	30 669 000	128–129	35
9. ALGERIA	30 291 000	122–123	36
10. MOROCCO	29 878 000	122–123	37

DEPENDENT AND DISPUTED TERRITORIES		territorial status	area sq km	area sq miles	population	capital	languages	religions	currency	map
Canary Islands (Islas Canarias)		Autonomous Community of Spain	7 447	2 875	1 606 522	Santa Cruz de Tenerife, Las Palmas	Spanish	Roman Catholic	Peseta	122
Ceuta		Spanish Territory	19	7	68 796	Ceuta	Spanish, Arabic	Roman Catholic, Muslim	Peseta	122
Madeira		Autonomous Region of Portugal	779	301	259 000	Funchal	Portuguese	Roman Catholic, Protestant	Port. escudo	122
Mayotte		French Territorial Collectivity	373	144	144 944	Dzaoudzi	French, Mahorian	Sunni Muslim, Christian	French franc	129
Melilla		Spanish Territory	13	5	59 576	Melilla	Spanish, Arabic	Roman Catholic, Muslim	Peseta	123
Réunion		French Overseas Department	2 551	985	721 000	St-Denis	French, creole	Roman Catholic	French franc	218
St Helena and Dependencies		United Kingdom Overseas Territory	121	47	6 000	Jamestown	English	Protestant, Roman Catholic	Pound sterling	216
Western Sahara		Disputed territory (Morocco)	266 000	102 703	252 000	Laâyoune	Arabic	Sunni Muslim	Moroccan dirham	122

1

Okavango Delta, Botswana

This Shuttle photograph shows the world's largest inland delta, the Okavango Delta in Botswana. The Okavango river originates in southeast Angola and ends in this spectacular and unique alluvial plain covering 10 000 square kilometres. The river is fed by rains from October to March which produce rich seasonal vegetation and support great numbers of wildlife. Scientists have identified this to be one of the most ecologically sensitive areas on Earth.

Satellite/Sensor : Space Shuttle

CONNECTIONS

► subject		page#
► World physical features		8–9
► World countries		10–11
► World land cover types		18–19
► Africa countries		114–115
► Reference maps of Africa		120–133
► South America impacts		196–197

Nile Valley, *Egypt*

The Nile river winds through Egypt in this satellite image, ending in the distinctive triangular delta on the Mediterranean coast. The dark blue water and green vegetation of the irrigated valley and delta provide a striking contrast to the surrounding desert. Thick layers of silt carried downstream for thousands of years provide the delta with the most fertile soil in Africa. The Suez Canal is also visible on the image, providing a link between the Mediterranean Sea at the top of the image and the Gulf of Suez and the Red Sea to the right.

Satellite/Sensor : MODIS

Flooded Village, *Kenya*

This village near Garsen was flooded when the Tana river burst its banks. An increase in extreme weather patterns occurred throughout the world in 1998. Some cases were blamed on the periodic warming of Pacific Ocean waters known as El Niño. In east Africa the regular problems of drought were replaced by excessive rainfall which led to the destruction of crops and the threat of famine. This village felt the affect of Kenya's annual rainfall increasing by over 1000mm in 1998.

Fig. #01

Safe water
Percentage of total population using
improved drinking water sources 1999

per cent

91–100	
66 – 90	
52 – 65	
31 – 51	
0 – 30	
no data	

4 Water Well, *Burkina*

This scene in the Silmiougou Valley in Burkina is common across
much of Africa. Such basic wells and hand water pumps provide
an essential source of fresh water in large parts of the continent.
Finding sufficient water of good quality is a major challenge facing
much of Africa's population, particularly in sub-Saharan Africa.
The map indicates the extent of this problem, with Africa having
some of the worst figures in the world for availability of improved
water. Impure water is a major contributory factor to disease, and
drought, with resultant food shortages, is a regular threat to the
lives of many people in the region.

5 Mozambique Floods

This pair of SPOT satellite images illustrates the large scale
flooding which hit Mozambique in early 2000. The course of
the Incomati river can clearly be seen in the 1998 image (left),
however the valley is flooded extensively in the 2000 image
(right) and is visible as a wide green feature down the centre of
the image. The flooding hit large areas of southern Africa and
left thousands homeless. Mozambique was the country worst
affected, particularly in the northern Maputo region shown in
the images.

Satellite/Sensor : SPOT

africa[locations]

1 Cape Town, *Republic of South Africa*

Cape Town is the legislative capital of South Africa, the capital city of Western Cape Province and is located 40 km from the Cape of Good Hope. This view from Table Mountain shows the full extent of the city spreading out to the waterfront area on the shores of Table Bay.

2 Cairo, *Egypt*

The largest city in Africa and capital of Egypt, Cairo is situated on the right bank of the river Nile. The main built-up area appears grey in this image. The famous pyramids and the suburb of Giza are visible to the lower left where the city meets the desert. Cairo airport can be seen at the upper right. Agricultural areas, achieved by extensive irrigation, show as deep red around the city.

Satellite/Sensor : SPOT

3 The Great Rift Valley, *Africa*

The Great Rift Valley is a huge, linear depression which marks a series of geological faults resulting from tectonic activity. The section of the valley shown in this 3-D perspective view extends from Lake Nyasa in the south to the Red Sea coast in the north. The valley splits into two branches north of Lake Nyasa and then combines again through the Ethiopian Highlands. The western branch is very prominent in the image and contains several lakes, including Lake Tanganyika. The eastern branch passes to the west of Kilimanjaro, the highest mountain to the right of the image, and contains Lake Turkana on the northern border of Kenya.

4 Victoria Falls, *Zambia/Zimbabwe*

The Victoria Falls are located in the Zambezi river on the Zambia/Zimbabwe border near the town of Livingstone. The river is over 1.7 km wide at the point where the falls drop 108 m over a precipice into a narrow chasm. The volume of water in the falls varies with the seasons. Land on the Zimbabwe side of the falls is preserved as a national park.

5 Sahara Desert, *Africa*

This photograph was taken in the eastern Sahara in Libya and illustrates sharp contrasts in the landscape. At the top are huge sand dunes which have been shaped by the wind. The area in the middle view has been planted with trees, to prevent the movement of sand and soil, and the irrigated area in the near view is typical of a fertile oasis, where the land has been worked to produce crops and to support livestock.

6 The Pyramids, *Egypt*

The suburbs of Giza, shown on the left of this satellite image, spread out from the city of Cairo to an arid plateau on which stand the famous Great Pyramids. The largest, shown at the bottom centre of the image, is the Great Pyramic of Cheops. To the left of this are three small pyramids collectively known as the Pyramids of Queens. Above them is the Great Sphinx. The pyramid at the centre right of the image is Chephren and the small one at the top right is Mycerinus.

Satellite/Sensor : IKONOS

CONNECTIONS

► subject		page#
► Types of imagery	⟹	4–5
► World physical features	⟹	8–9
► World cities	⟹	24–25
► Africa landscapes	⟹	112–113
► Africa countries	⟹	114–117

122-123

Mediterranean Sea

TUNISIA

TRIPOLI
(Tarābulus)

Al Khums
Leptis Magna
Zlītan
Misrātah

Gulf of Sirte
(Khalīj Surt)

Benghazi

Cyrene
Al Bayḍā'
Shaḥḥāt
Darnah
Ra's at Tīn

Al Marj
Ajal al Akhḍar
Al Mukhaylī
Tubruq
Al 'Adam

Crete
(Kriti)
(Greece)

Akra Líthino
Gavdos

CYRENAICA

Marmarica

TRIPOLITANIA

Jabal Nafūsa

Wādī Zamzam

Mizdah

Al Qaddāḥīyah

Sirte (Surt)

As Sidrah

Ajdābiyā

Marsa
al Burayqah

Bīr Tānjidar
Abyār al Hakīm

Az Zuwaytīnah

Sulṭān

Zāwīyat Masūs

Bīr adh Dhakar

Al 'Uqaylah

Sabkhat
Ghuzayyil

Al Jaghbūb

Great Sand Sea

Sarīr Water
Wells Field

AS SARĪR

L I B Y A

Lib

Des

Calansio Sand Sea

Al Jaghbūb

Sabkhat
al Qunayyin

Rebiana
Sand Sea
(Ramlat Rabyānah)

Al Khufrah
Oasis

Al Jawf
Al Ghazāl

S a h a r a

Jabal Bin Ghanīmah

Waw al Kabīr

Waw an Nāmūs

Ramlat al Wīgh

Sarīr
Tibesti

Hosenofu

Jabal al Uwaynāt

Jebel Uweinat

ALGERIA

Tropic of Cancer

Djanet

Jabal Atī

Mountains
of Tummo

Toummo

Plateau du Manguéni

Plateau
du Djado

Plateau
du Tchigai

Enneri Tārsū

Bardaï
Zouar

T i b e s t i

Emi Koussi

BORKOU-ENNEDI-TIBESTI

Dépression du Mourdi

Ennedi

Erg du Djourab

Plateau de Basso

Massif
Ennedi

Kapka

N I G E R

Réserve Naturelle
Intégrale dite
Sanctuaire
des Addax

Ténéré
du
Tafassàsset

A G A D E Z

Réserve Naturelle
Nationale
de l'Aïr et du Ténéré

Erg de Bilma

Erg du Ténéré

D I F F A

Massif
de Termit

Z I N D E R

Zinder

Lake Chad

C H A D

K A N E M

BATHA

Abéché

BILTINE

Massif
du Kapka
Guéréda

OUADDAÏ

**WESTERN
DARFUR**

Marra
Plateau

Jebel Marra

Geneina

NIGERIA

BORNO

YOBE

Maiduguri

CAMEROON

NDJAMENA

**CHARI-
BAGUIRMI**

GUÉRA

SALAMAT

National
de Waza

JIGAWA

BAUCHI

L A C

B O D É L É

126-127

Elevation scale:
>6000m
5000-6000m
4000-5000m
3000-4000m
2000-3000m
1000-2000m
500-1000m
200-500m
0-200m
<0m

0-200m
200-500m
500-1000m
1000-2000m
2000-3000m
3000-4000m
4000-5000m
5000-6000m
>6000m

africa[map2]

16°-40°N / 20°W-16°E

CONNECTIONS

► subject	page#
► Land cover types	18–19
► Mediterranean map	52–53
► Africa landscapes	112–113
► Africa countries	114–117
► Algeria/Niger border	114–115

ATLANTIC OCEAN

PORTUGAL
LISBON (Lisboa)
SPAIN
MOROCCO
RABAT
Casablanca
Arquipélago da Madeira
Madeira (Portugal)
FUNCHAL
Canary Islands (Spain)
Islas Canarias
Tenerife
Gran Canaria
Lanzarote
Fuerteventura
La Palma
El Hierro
La Gomera
LAÂYOUNE
WESTERN SAHARA
Tropic of Cancer
Nouâdhibou
MAURITANIA
NOUAKCHOTT
SENEGAL
St-Louis

>6000m
5000-6000m
4000-5000m
3000-4000m
2000-3000m
1000-2000m
500-1000m
200-500m
0-200m
<0m

→ 122

WESTERN SAHARA

Nouâdhibou
Cansado
Râs
Nouâdhibou
DÂKHLAT
NOUÂDHIBOU
Parc
National
du Banc
d'Arguin
Châmi
Azzeffâl
TIIIRÎT
Akchâr
INCHIRI

Ntanu
Dhar Amîîn
Amîla

Chreirîk
El Beyyed
Oued el Rêchât
Ouadâne 465

El Ghallâoulya
OUARÂNE

El Gçaib
Erg Atouila
'Oglât el Khnâchîch
Bir Ounâne

Iouîk
Râs Timirist
Nouâmghâr
Akjoujt
Oujeft
Terjît
Chinguetti
Adrar 455
far'aoun

li âfêne
El Fçâl
Aïoûn el 'Atroûs

S
a

Gôur Oulad
Ahmed

Oued el Hajâr

MAURITANIA

El Moinane
El Khnâchîch
S
a

NOUAKCHOTT
Oued Nâga
Boû Nâga
Tintâne
El Melhes
El Gheddîya
Magta'Lahjar
Boutilimit
Aleg
Mederdra
Bôû Naga
Tîdjikja
El Houeïât
TAGANT
Tichît

Aghouavil
HODH
ECH CHARGUI

Araouane
Sidi el Mokhtâr
TOMBOUCTO

Tagânet Keyna
Azâ
'Oglât

TRARZA
BRAKNA
ASSABA

El Beyyed
El Abîod
Guérou
'Ayoûn el 'Atroûs
Kiffa
Koubenni
Diêgräga
El Mraïig

HÔD
HODH
EL GHARBI

Kobenni
Nampala

M

SENEGAL

ATLANTIC OCEAN

africa[map4]

14°N-20°S / 8°-32°E

1:8 000 000

Lambert Azimuthal Equal Area Projection

130-131

CONNECTIONS

▶ subject	page#
▶ World physical features	8-9
▶ Africa landscapes	112-113
▶ Africa countries	114-117
▶ Africa locations	118-119

miles

km

>6000m
5000-6000m
4000-5000m
3000-4000m
2000-3000m
1000-2000m
500-1000m
200-500m
0-200m
<0m

0-200m
200-500m
500-1000m
1000-2000m
2000-3000m
3000-4000m
4000-5000m
5000-6000m
>6000m

120-121

126-127

africa[map7]

25°-35°S / 17°-33°E

>6000m
5000-6000m
4000-5000m
3000-4000m
2000-3000m
1500-2000m
1000-1500m
500-1000m
200-500m
100-200m
0-100m
<0m

0-200m
200-500m
500-1000m
1000-2000m
2000-3000m
3000-4000m
4000-5000m
5000-6000m
>6000m

NAMIBIA

GREAT NAMAQUALAND

HARDAP

KALAHARI DESERT

Kalahari Gemsbok
National Park

Gemsbok National Park

KGALAGADI

BOTSWANA

KARAS

NAMAQUALAND

Richtersveld
National Park

Augrabies Falls
National Park

REPUBLIC OF

NORTHERN

CAPE

GRIQUALAND W

Keetmanshoop

Ai-Ais Hot Springs
and Fish River
Canyon Park

Great Karoo

Roggeveld

WESTERN CAPE

Little Karoo

ATLANTIC

OCEAN

Cape Columbine

Saldanha Bay

West Coast
National Park

Robben Island
Table Bay

CAPE TOWN
Table Mountain

False Bay

Cape of Good Hope
Nature Reserve

Cape
of Good Hope

Danger Point

Quoin Point

Struis Bay

Cape Agulhas

Cape Infanta

Mossel Bay

Wilderness
National Park

Goukamma
Nature Reserve

Cape Seal

Tsitsikamma
Forest and Coast
National Park

A B C D E F G H

1 2 3 4 5 6 7 8 9 10 11

1:3 500 000

miles
0 25 50 75 100 125

km
0 25 50 75 100 125 150 175 200

Lambert Azimuthal Equal Area Projection

Great Barrier Reef, *Australia*

oceania

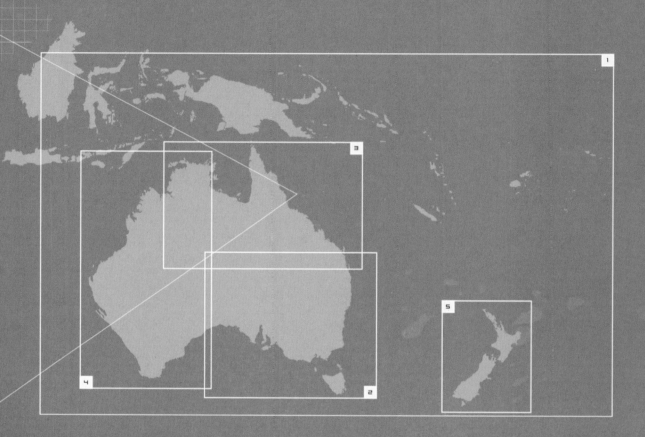

[contents]

	page#
oceania [landscapes]	136–137
oceania [countries]	138–139
oceania [threats]	140–141
oceania [features]	142–143

	map coverage	scale	page#
oceania [map 1]	AUSTRALIA and PACIFIC Southwest	1:18 000 000	144–145
oceania [map 2]	AUSTRALIA Southeast	1:6 000 000	146–147
oceania [map 3]	AUSTRALIA Northeast	1:6 000 000	148–149
oceania [map 4]	AUSTRALIA West	1:6 000 000	150–151
oceania [map 5]	NEW ZEALAND	1:3 250 000	152–153

Highest point
Puncak Jaya
Indonesia
5030 m / 16 502 ft
Map reference 73 I7

Largest island
New Guinea
808 510 sq km / 312 167 sq miles
Map reference 73 J8

Solomon Islands

New Guinea

Puncak Jaya

Cape York Peninsula

Great Barrier Reef

Arafura Sea

Gulf of
Carpentaria

Great Div

Arnhem Land

Timor Sea

Kimberley Plateau

Macdonnell
Ranges

Lake Eyre

Fitzroy River

Musgrave
Ranges

Indian Ocean

Great Victoria
Desert

Nullarbor
Plain

Fortescue River

Great Australian
Bight

Largest lake and lowest point
Lake Eyre
0 - 8 900 sq km / 0 - 3 436 sq miles
16 m / 53 ft below sea level
Map reference 146 C2

Fiji

New Caledonia

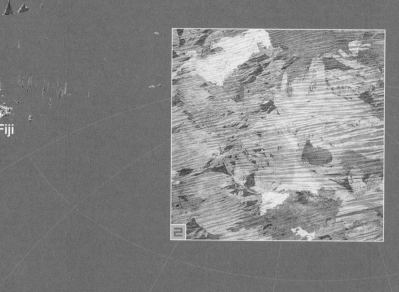

Coral Sea

Pacific Ocean

North Island

Mount Cook

South Island

Tasman Sea

Mount Kosciuszko

Murray River

Tasmania

Darling River

Longest river

Murray-Darling
3 750 km / 2 330 miles
Map reference 146 C3

CONNECTIONS

► subject		page#
► World physical features	➤	8–9
► Pacific island landscape	➤	12–13
► Oceania states and territories	➤	138–139
► Coral reefs	➤	140–141
► Reference maps of Oceania	➤	144–153

The continent of Oceania comprises Australia, the islands of New Zealand, New Guinea and numerous small islands and island groups in the Pacific Ocean, including Micronesia, Melanesia and Polynesia. The main landmass of Australia is largely desert, with many salt lakes and a low artesian basin in the east central area. The mountains of the Great Dividing Range run parallel to the east coast and are the source of the main river system, the Murray-Darling. The Great Barrier Reef, which stretches off the coast of Queensland, Australia, is the world's largest deposit of coral.

New Guinea is a mountainous island, most of which is covered with tropical forest. New Zealand has a great variety of landscape types, from tropical environments in the north of North Island to sub-Antarctic conditions in the south of South Island. North Island has extensive volcanic areas and South Island is mountainous, being dominated by the Southern Alps range.

1 Great Barrier Reef, *Australia*

This photograph shows the Great Barrier Reef which stretches for over 2 000 km off the coast of Queensland, Australia. This is the largest area of coral reefs in the world, and consists of a mixture of small islands, reefs and atolls. Whitsunday Island, shown here, is typical of the landscape. Beyond the reef is the Coral Sea.

2 Gibson Desert, *Australia*

The Gibson Desert in Western Australia has distinctive long, thin dune-like ridges which are covered with resilient desert grasses. The different coloured patches are due to a combination of seasonal new growth and fire damage. The dark areas on this image indicate the most recent summer fire outbreaks. The darkness fades as new growth appears.

Satellite/Sensor : SPOT

3 Mount Cook, *New Zealand*

Mount Cook on South Island, New Zealand is the highest peak in the country at 3 754 m. This photograph looks southeast towards Lake Pukaki, close to the horizon on the left. The peak is part of the Southern Alps mountain range and the National Park surrounding Mount Cook is designated a World Heritage area. The bare rock face below the summit resulted from a major avalanche in 1991 which reduced the height of the mountain by 20 m.

OCEANIA

HIGHEST MOUNTAINS

	m	ft	location	map
Puncak Jaya	5 030	16 502	Indonesia	73 I7
Puncak Trikora	4 730	15 518	Indonesia	73 I7
Puncak Mandala	4 700	15 420	Indonesia	73 J7
Puncak Yamin	4 595	15 075	Indonesia	73 I7
Mt Wilhelm	4 509	14 793	Papua New Guinea	73 J8
Mt Kubor	4 359	14 301	Papua New Guinea	73 J8

LARGEST ISLANDS

	sq km	sq miles	map
New Guinea	808 510	312 167	73 J8
South Island, New Zealand	151 215	58 384	153 F11
North Island, New Zealand	115 777	44 702	152 J6
Tasmania	67 800	26 178	147 E5

LONGEST RIVERS

	km	miles	map
Murray-Darling	3 750	2 330	146 C3
Darling	2 739	1 702	146 D3
Murray	2 589	1 608	146 C3
Murrumbidgee	1 690	1 050	147 E3
Lachlan	1 480	919	147 D3
Macquarie	950	590	147 E2

LAKES

	sq km	sq miles	map
Lake Eyre	0-8 900	0-3 436	146 C2
Lake Torrens	0-5 780	0-2 232	146 C2

LAND AREA

		map
Most northerly point	Eastern Island, North Pacific Ocean	220 H4
Most southerly point	Macquarie Island, South Pacific Ocean	220 F9
Most westerly point	Cape Inscription, Australia	151 A5
Most easterly point	Ile Clipperton, North Pacific Ocean	221 L5

Total land area: 8 844 516 sq km / 3 414 887 sq miles
(includes New Guinea and Pacific Island nations)

OCEANIA

COUNTRIES

		area sq km	area sq miles	population	capital	languages	religions	currency	map
AUSTRALIA		7 682 395	2 966 189	19 138 000	Canberra	English, Italian, Greek	Protestant, Roman Catholic, Orthodox	Dollar	144–145
FIJI		18 330	7 077	814 000	Suva	English, Fijian, Hindi	Christian, Hindu, Sunni Muslim	Dollar	145
KIRIBATI		717	277	83 000	Bairiki	Gilbertese, English	Roman Catholic, Protestant	Australian dollar	145
MARSHALL ISLANDS		181	70	51 000	Delap-Uliga-Djarrit	English, Marshallese	Protestant, Roman Catholic	US dollar	220
MICRONESIA, FEDERATED STATES OF		701	271	123 000	Palikir	English, Chuukese, Pohnpeian, local languages	Roman Catholic, Protestant	US dollar	220
NAURU		21	8	12 000	Yaren	Nauruan, English	Protestant, Roman Catholic	Australian dollar	145
NEW ZEALAND		270 534	104 454	3 778 000	Wellington	English, Maori	Protestant, Roman Catholic	Dollar	152–153
PAPUA NEW GUINEA		462 840	178 704	4 809 000	Port Moresby	English, Tok Pisin (creole), local languages	Protestant, Roman Catholic, traditional beliefs	Kina	144–145
SAMOA		2 831	1 093	159 000	Apia	Samoan, English	Protestant, Roman Catholic	Tala	145
SOLOMON ISLANDS		28 370	10 954	447 000	Honiara	English, creole, local languages	Protestant, Roman Catholic	Dollar	145
TONGA		748	289	99 000	Nuku'alofa	Tongan, English	Protestant, Roman Catholic	Pa'anga	145
TUVALU		25	10	11 000	Vaiaku	Tuvaluan, English	Protestant	Dollar	145
VANUATU		12 190	4 707	197 000	Port Vila	English, Bislama (creole), French	Protestant, Roman Catholic, traditional beliefs	Vatu	145

DEPENDENT TERRITORIES

		territorial status	area sq km	area sq miles	population	capital	languages	religions	currency	map
American Samoa		United States Unincorporated Territory	197	76	68 000	Fagatoga	Samoan, English	Protestant, Roman Catholic	US dollar	145
Ashmore and Cartier Islands		Australian External Territory	5	2	uninhabited					150
Baker Island		United States Unincorporated Territory	1	0.4	uninhabited					145
Cook Islands		Self-governing New Zealand Territory	293	113	20 000	Avarua	English, Maori	Protestant, Roman Catholic	Dollar	221
Coral Sea Islands Territory		Australian External Territory	22	8	uninhabited					145
French Polynesia		French Overseas Territory	3 265	1 261	233 000	Papeete	French, Tahitian, Polynesian languages	Protestant, Roman Catholic	Pacific franc	221
Guam		United States Unincorporated Territory	541	209	155 000	Agana	Chamorro, English, Tagalog	Roman Catholic	US dollar	73
Howland Island		United States Unincorporated Territory	2	1	uninhabited					145
Jarvis Island		United States Unincorporated Territory	5	2	uninhabited					221
Johnston Atoll		United States Unincorporated Territory	3	1	uninhabited					221
Kingman Reef		United States Unincorporated Territory	1	0.4	uninhabited					221
Midway Islands		United States Unincorporated Territory	6	2	uninhabited					220
New Caledonia		French Overseas Territory	19 058	7 358	215 000	Nouméa	French, local	Roman Catholic, Protestant, Sunni Muslim	Pacific franc	145
Niue		Self-governing New Zealand Overseas Territory	258	100	2 000	Alofi	English, Polynesian	Christian	NZ dollar	145
Norfolk Island		Australian External Territory	35	14	2 000	Kingston	English	Protestant, Roman Catholic	Australian Dollar	145
Northern Mariana Islands		United States Commonwealth	477	184	73 000	Capitol Hill	English, Chamorro, local languages	Roman Catholic	US dollar	73
Palmyra Atoll		United States Unincorporated Territory	12	5	uninhabited					221
Pitcairn Islands		United Kingdom Overseas Territory	45	17	68	Adamstown	English	Protestant	NZ dollar	221
Tokelau		New Zealand Overseas Territory	10	4	1 000		English, Tokelauan	Christian	NZ dollar	145
Wake Island		United States Unincorporated Territory	7	3	uninhabited					220
Wallis and Futuna Islands		French Overseas Territory	274	106	14 000	Matā'utu	French, Wallisian, Futunian	Roman Catholic	Pacific franc	145

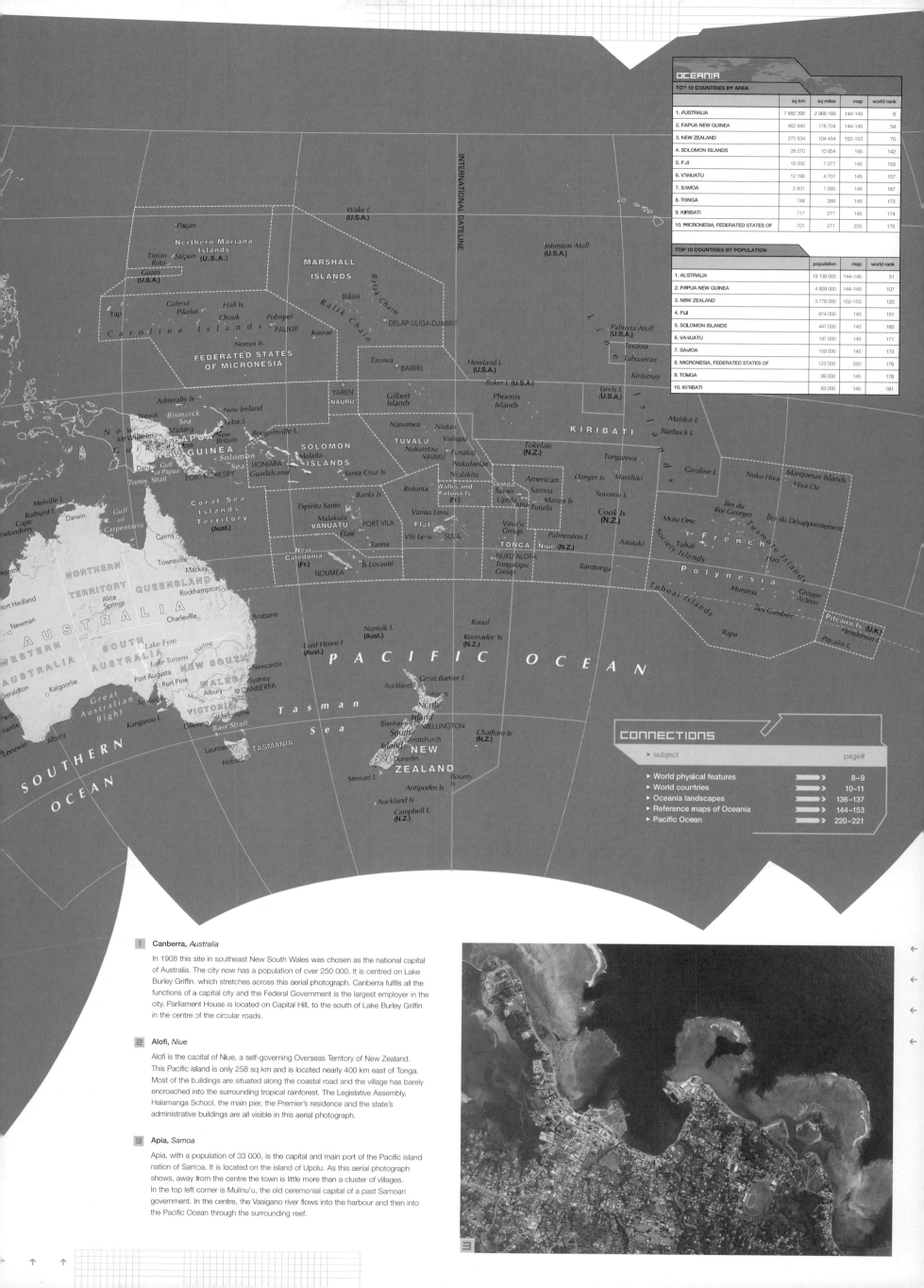

OCEANIA

TOP 10 COUNTRIES BY AREA

	sq km	sq miles	map	world rank
1. AUSTRALIA	7 682 395	2 966 189	144–145	6
2. PAPUA NEW GUINEA	462 840	178 704	144–145	54
3. NEW ZEALAND	270 534	104 454	152–153	75
4. SOLOMON ISLANDS	28 370	10 954	145	142
5. FIJI	18 330	7 077	145	153
6. VANUATU	12 190	4 707	145	157
7. SAMOA	2 831	1 093	145	167
8. TONGA	748	289	145	173
9. KIRIBATI	717	277	145	174
10. MICRONESIA, FEDERATED STATES OF	701	271	220	175

TOP 10 COUNTRIES BY POPULATION

	population	map	world rank
1. AUSTRALIA	19 138 000	144–145	51
2. PAPUA NEW GUINEA	4 809 000	144–145	107
3. NEW ZEALAND	3 778 000	152–153	120
4. FIJI	814 000	145	151
5. SOLOMON ISLANDS	447 000	145	160
6. VANUATU	197 000	145	171
7. SAMOA	159 000	145	173
8. MICRONESIA, FEDERATED STATES OF	123 000	220	176
9. TONGA	99 000	145	178
10. KIRIBATI	83 000	145	181

CONNECTIONS

► subject	page#
► World physical features	8–9
► World countries	10–11
► Oceania landscapes	136–137
► Reference maps of Oceania	144–153
► Pacific Ocean	220–221

1 Canberra, Australia

In 1908 this site in southeast New South Wales was chosen as the national capital of Australia. The city now has a population of over 250 000. It is centred on Lake Burley Griffin, which stretches across this aerial photograph. Canberra fulfils all the functions of a capital city and the Federal Government is the largest employer in the city. Parliament House is located on Capital Hill, to the south of Lake Burley Griffin in the centre of the circular roads.

2 Alofi, Niue

Alofi is the capital of Niue, a self-governing Overseas Territory of New Zealand. This Pacific island is only 258 sq km and is located nearly 400 km east of Tonga. Most of the buildings are situated along the coastal road and the village has barely encroached into the surrounding tropical rainforest. The Legislative Assembly, Halamanga School, the main pier, the Premier's residence and the state's administrative buildings are all visible in this aerial photograph.

3 Apia, Samoa

Apia, with a population of 33 000, is the capital and main port of the Pacific island nation of Samoa. It is located on the island of Upolu. As this aerial photograph shows, away from the centre the town is little more than a cluster of villages. In the top left corner is Mulinu'u, the old ceremonial capital of a past Samoan government. In the centre, the Vasigano river flows into the harbour and then into the Pacific Ocean through the surrounding reef.

1 Australian Bushfires

Bushfires are an annual threat in the arid and savanna regions of Australia. Although fire can be of great benefit environmentally and ecologically, if it is not managed and controlled effectively it can have dramatic effects and can directly threaten settlements. In 1994 the suburbs of Sydney were affected by bushfires which destroyed 4 000 sq km of bush and grassland and in northern Australia over 300 000 sq km are affected each year. Satellite imagery, such as this image of a fire in northern Queensland, is an important tool in monitoring and managing bushfires. Imagery can be used to detect and map areas at risk, to map fire occurrences and to monitor post-fire recovery of the environment.

Satellite/Sensor : Apollo 7

CONNECTIONS

► subject	page#
► World land cover types	18–19
► World climate and weather	16–17
► Oceania landscapes	136–137
► Oceania features	142–143
► Pacific Ocean	220–221

Fig. #01
Australia salinity hazard

Cropland or pasture
Cropland

Irrigated areas
- ○ >100 000ha
- ○ 50 000 - 100 000ha
- ○ 20 000 - 50 000ha
- · 10 000 - 20 000ha

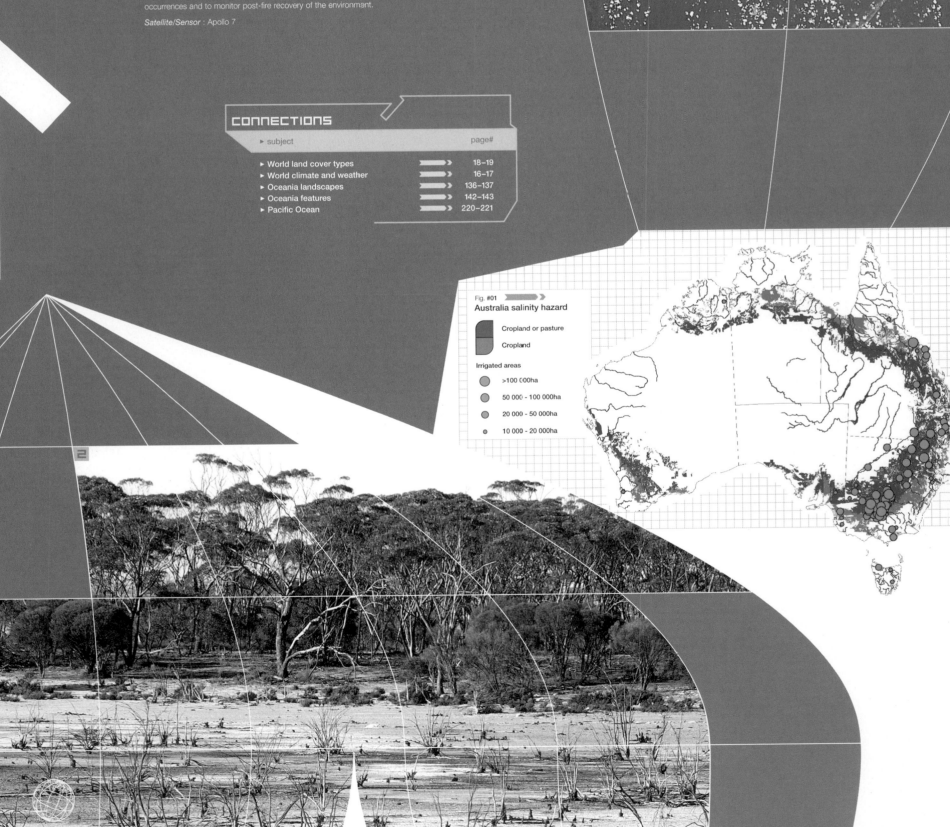

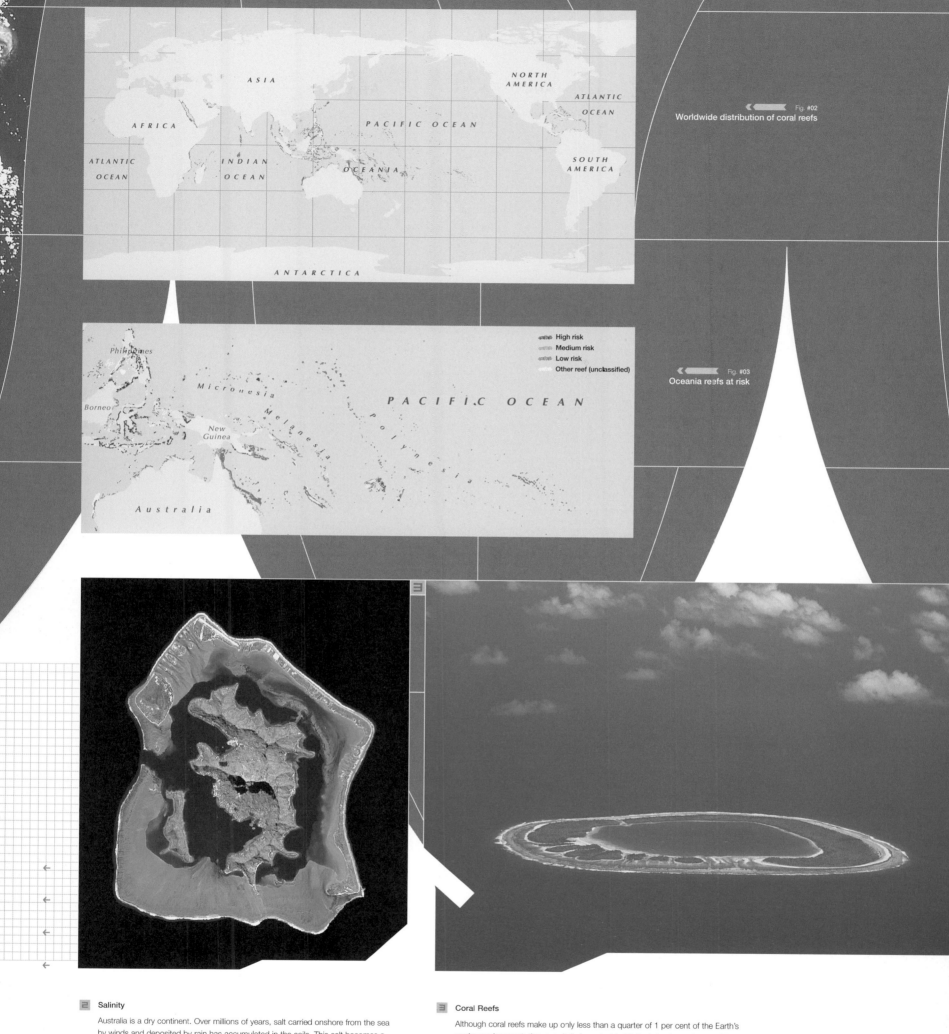

High risk
Medium risk
Low risk
Other reef (unclassified)

ASIA
NORTH AMERICA
ATLANTIC OCEAN
AFRICA
PACIFIC OCEAN
ATLANTIC OCEAN
INDIAN OCEAN
OCEANIA
SOUTH AMERICA
ANTARCTICA

Philippines
Micronesia
Borneo
New Guinea
Melanesia
Polynesia
PACIFIC OCEAN
Australia

Salinity

Australia is a dry continent. Over millions of years, salt carried onshore from the sea by winds and deposited by rain has accumulated in the soils. This salt becomes a problem when native vegetation is cleared, allowing excess water to percolate through the soil. This raises groundwater levels, bringing the salt to the surface and leaching salt into streams and rivers. Irrigation schemes add more water, making the problem worse. Salt kills crops and pastureland, damages roads and buildings, impairs water quality for both irrigation and human consumption and reduces biodiversity. The photograph shows an area badly affected by salinity near Kellerberrin, Western Australia. Approximately 5.7 million hectares of Australia's farmland is currently affected by salinity and it is predicted that, unless effective solutions are implemented, 17 million hectares of land and 20 000 km of streams could be salinized by 2050. The map shows areas where salt stored in the landscape is being mobilised by surplus water, creating the risk of salinity.

Coral Reefs

Although coral reefs make up only less than a quarter of 1 per cent of the Earth's marine environment, they are vitally important habitats, being home to over 25 per cent of all known marine fish species. They are also important sources of food and tourist income, and they provide physical protection for vulnerable coastlines. Reefs are widely distributed around the world (Fig. #02) with major concentrations in the Caribbean Sea, the Indian Ocean, southeast Asia and the Pacific Ocean.

Reefs are fragile environments, and many are under threat from coastal development, pollution and overexploitation of marine resources. The degree of risk varies, with the reefs of southeast Asia under the greatest threat. Over 25 per cent of the world's reefs are judged to be at high risk. In the Pacific Ocean over 40 per cent of reefs are at risk (Fig. #03). The beauty and fragility of these environments are suggested in the images above. The aerial photograph (right) shows the coral island of Mataiva and the SPOT satellite image (left) shows the island and reefs of Bora-Bora. Both are in the Pacific territory of French Polynesia.

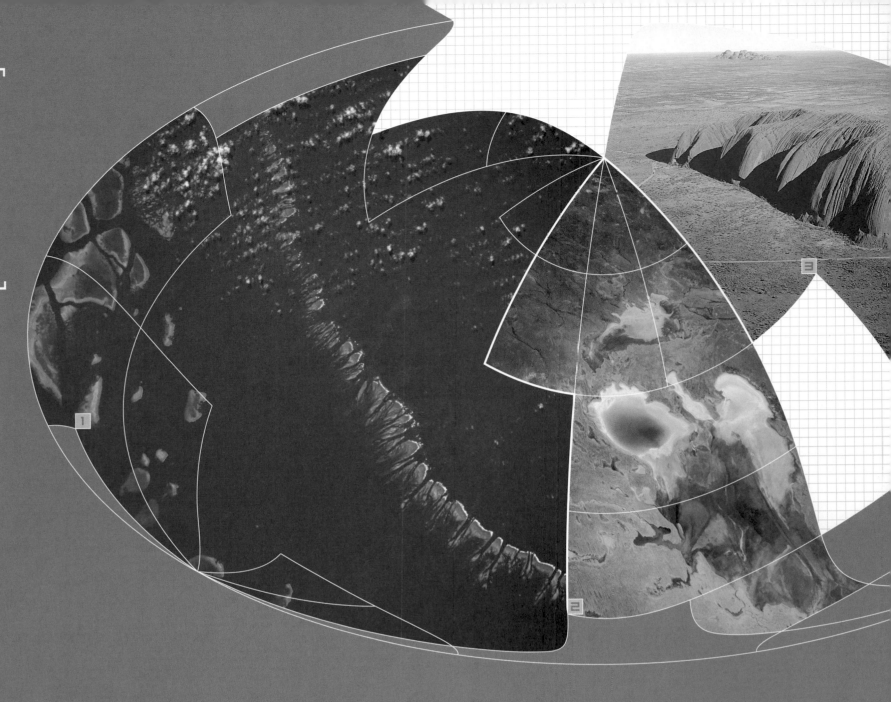

1   **Great Barrier Reef,** *Queensland, Australia*

This Shuttle photograph of the northern end of the Great Barrier Reef shows two separate reef zones. The line of unbroken coral reefs, at the bottom right of the image contrasts to the randomly spaced reefs in the shallow waters off the coast of the Cape York Peninsula, at the left hand edge. The image captures only a tiny fraction of the whole reef which extends over 2 000 km along the northeast coast of Queensland.

Satellite/Sensor : Space Shuttle

2   **Lake Eyre,** *South Australia, Australia*

Lake Eyre, situated in one of the driest regions in South Australia, is the largest salt lake in Australia. The lake actually comprises two lakes, Lake Eyre North and the much smaller Lake Eyre South. Salt has been washed into the lake from underlying marine sediments and when dry, which is its usual state, the lake bed is a glistening sheet of white salt. In this photograph, the lake, viewed from the north, is in the process of drying out after being at a higher level.

Satellite/Sensor : Space Shuttle

3   **Uluru (Ayers Rock),** *Northern Territory, Australia*

Uluru (Ayers Rock), is a large single rock outcrop which rises 350 m above the vast plain of central Australia. This aerial photograph, looking west, shows how the steep, almost vertical walls of the rock rise from the flat surrounding land. The rock is composed of a collection of vertically bedded strata. In the far distance of the photograph, a similar rock formation, the Olgas, can be seen.

4   **Banks Peninsula,** *New Zealand*

The only recognizable volcanic feature on South Island, New Zealand is Banks Peninsula. It has been extensively eroded over the years yet it still possess the circular shape and radial drainage pattern typical of many volcanoes. The peninsula has been formed by two overlapping volcanic centres which are separated by a large harbour, Akaroa Harbour. In this aerial photograph, the peninsula is viewed from the east and at the top the Canterbury Plains are just visible.

5 **Palm Valley,** *Northern Territory, Australia*

The dark brown and blue area of this radar image, is a broad valley located in the arid landscape of central Australia, approximately 50 km south west of Alice Springs. Palm Valley, the oval shaped feature at the top left of the image, contains many rare species of palms. The mountains of the Macdonnell Ranges are seen as curving bands of folded sedimentary outcrops. In the top right of the image, the river Finke cuts across the mountain ridge and continues in a deep canyon to the lower centre of the image.

Satellite/Sensor : Space Shuttle/SIR-C/X-SAR

6 **Sydney,** *Australia*

Sydney, the largest city in Australia and capital of New South Wales state, has one of the world's finest natural harbours. It is Australia's chief port, and its main cultural and industrial centre. This satellite image of the city, in which north is at the bottom, was captured by the IKONOS satellite in late 1999. The image highlights the renowned Sydney Opera house, located on Bennelong Point. Also clearly visible are the Royal Botanical Gardens and west of these the main urban area of the city centre.

Satellite/Sensor : IKONOS

7 **New Caledonia and Vanuatu,** *Pacific Ocean*

The long narrow island of New Caledonia lies in the southern Pacific Ocean approximately 1 500 km east of Queensland, Australia. The territory comprises one large island and several smaller ones. This SeaWiFS satellite image clearly shows the extensive reef formations which extend far out into the ocean. The island has a landscape of rugged mountains with little flat land. Almost obscured by clouds, at the top right of this image, is a group of islands which collectively make up the small republic of Vanuatu.

Satellite/Sensor : OrbView2/SeaWiFS

CONNECTIONS

► subject		page#
► Uluru (Ayers Rock)		18–19
► Oceania landscapes		136–137
► Oceania countries		138–139
► Coral reefs		140–141
► Southwest Pacific Ocean		144–145
► Pacific Ocean		220–221

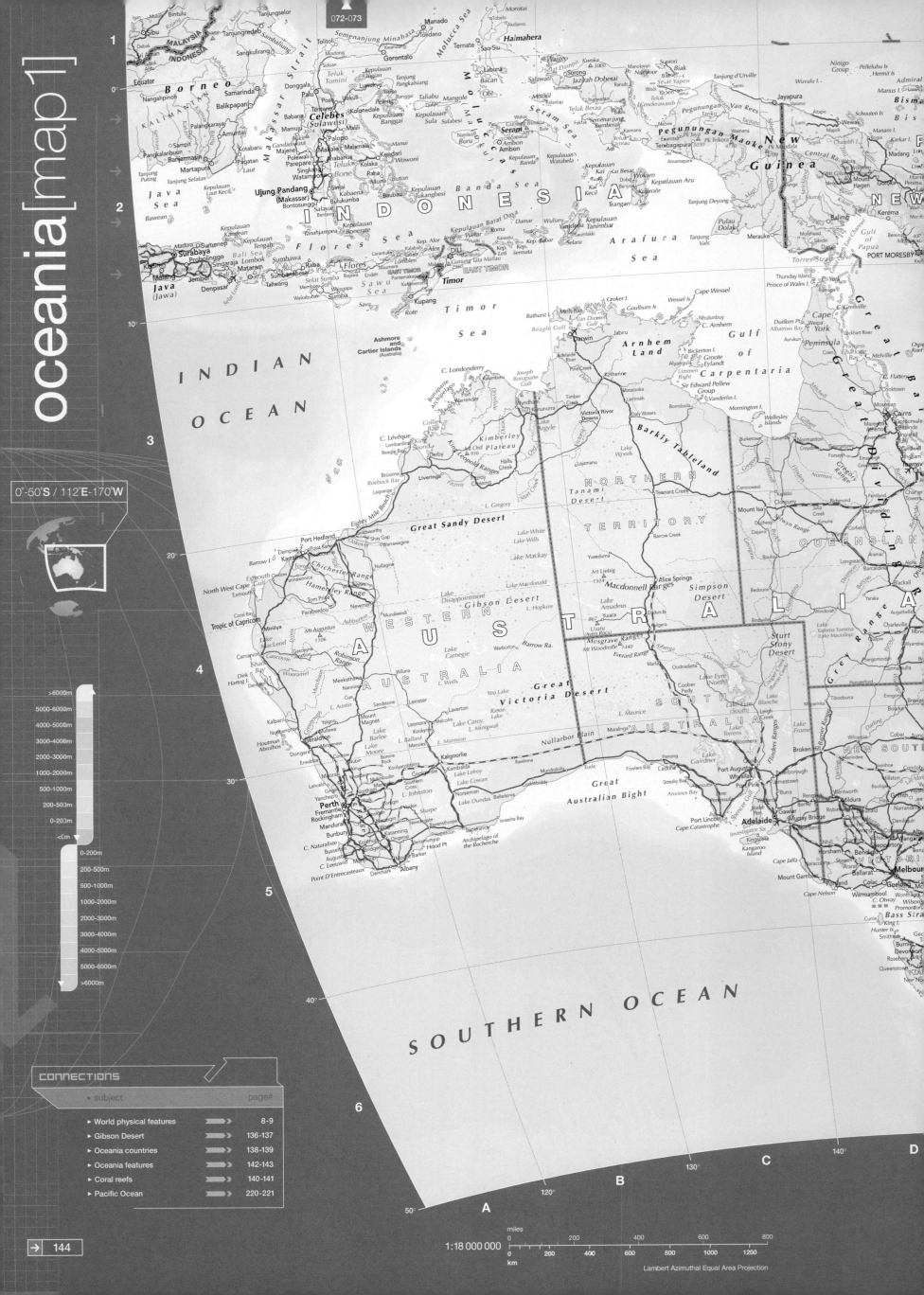

oceania [map 1]

CONNECTIONS

→ 144

1:18 000 000

Lambert Azimuthal Equal Area Projection

Kapingamarangi
(Micronesia)

Abaiang Marakei
Marakei
BAIRIKI Tarawa
Maiana

Howland I.
(U.S.A.)

Baker I.
(U.S.A.)

Mussau I.
St Matthias
Group
nbuyo I.

Lyra Reef

Nauru
YAREN

Banaba
(Ocean I.)

Kuria Abemama
Aranuka

Nonouti

NAURU

K I R I B A T I

Phoenix
Islands

Kanton
Enderbury

Archipelago
ck
rk

New
Hanover

Tabar Is
New Lihir Group
Ireland
Tanga Is
Nematanai

Feni Is

Tabiteuea Beru Nikunau
Onotoa Kingsmill Group
Tamana

Arorae

McKean Birnie
Rawaki

PAPUA

Rabaul C. St George
New 532
Britain Buka I.
Gloucester Sohano
Hoskins

Nukumanu Is

Nanumea

Nikumaroro

Orona Manra

New Ireland
Green I.
Tauu Is

Ontong Java
Atoll

Nanumanga
Niutao

GUINEA

chhafen
Kandrian

Bougainville
Island
Arawa

Choiseul

Roncador
Reef

Nui
Vaitupu

TUVALU

Lusancay
Islands
and Reefs

Vella Lavella
Ranongga
New
Georgia

Santa
Isabel
Malu'u
Malaita

Nukufetau
Funafuti
VAIAKU

Swains I.

Trobriand Is
Woodlark I.

Kolombangara

SOLOMON

Stewart
Islands

Nukulaelae

Tokelau
(New Zealand)

Atafu
Nukunonu

Fakaofo

Goodenough I.
Fergusson I.
Normanby I.
D'Entrecasteaux Is

New Georgia
Islands

ISLANDS

Niulakita

r Stanley Ra

HONIARA
Guadalcanal

Apio

Kirakira

San Cristobal
(Makira)

Rennell

Duff Islands
Swallow Islands
Nupani
Lata Ndeni
Santa Cruz Islands
Utupua
Vanikoro Is

Rotuma
(Fiji)

Wallis and
Futuna Islands
(France)

MATĀ'UTU
Île Futuna
Îles Wallis

SAMOA

Savai'i Mt Silisili
Faleolo
Apia

American
Samoa
(U.S.A.)

Manua
Maia
Tau

Conflict Group

Louisiade Archipelago

Tagula I.

Cherry I.
Mitre I.

Niulakita

Coral
Sea

Indispensable
Reefs

Torres Is
Vanua Lava
Mota Lava
797 Banks Islands
Santa María I.

Île de Hoorn Île Alofi
Île Futuna Sigave

210

Niuatoputapu
Tafahi

Tutuila FAGATOGO
Poutasi
Upolu

Coral Sea
Islands
Territory
(Australia)

Flinders
Reefs

Espíritu Santo

Aoba
Maéwo

Cikobia
Vetauua
Yasawa

Great Sea Reef
Vanua Levu

Somosomo

Niuafo'ou
Hihifo

Niuatoputapu

Marion Reef

Îles Chesterfield

VANUATU

Mt Marum
Luganville
Malakula

Pentecost I.

Ambrym

Yasawa
Group
Bligh
Water

Lautoka

Qelelevu

Rabi
Koro

Tavenui

Northern
Lau Group

Vanua Balavu

Vava'u Group
Vava'u

Neiafu
110

Tokú

Ambae

Milgo
Ufai

TONGA

Fonualei

SAMOA

Bowen
Airdale
Townsville
Datlome
Mackay
Sarina

Swain
Reefs

Saumarez
Reef

PORT VILA

Récifs
d'Entrecasteaux

Récifs
de
Français

Efaté

Erromango

Shepherd Is

Viti Levu

Sigatoka
Vatulele

Koro
Sea

Nadi SUVA
Levuka

Ba

Kadavu Passage

Moala

Matuku
Kadavu

Totoya

Southern
Lau Group

150
Late I.

Fonuafo'ou
(Falcon I.)

Kao 500
Tofua

Vava'u

Ha'ano
Ha'apai Group

ALOFI

Tuvana-i-Ra

Grand Passage
Grand
Récif
Îles de Cook

Nouvelle Calédonie

Koumac

Olive
Fayaoué

Récifs
de
l'Astrolabe

Îles Loyauté

Lifou
Maré

Aratom
(Aneityum)

Futuna

Ceva-i-Ra

Ono-i-Lau

Tuvana-i-Colo
Vatoa

Dovi
100
Fonuafo'ou

Tofua
Nomuka
Kotu

Tongatapu
Group

Niue
(New Zealand)

NUKU'ALOFA
Tongatapu
Eua

Ata

Rockhampton
Gladstone

Marble

Rma

Taroom

Yeppoon

Bundaberg
Fraser Island

FIJI

NOUMÉA
Dumbéa
Mont-Dore
Grand Récif
du Sud
Île des Pins

Humboldt 1618
Bouloupari

Hunter I.
100

Minerva
Reefs

Minoche
Morto
Childe
Maryborough
Gympie
Tewantin
Murgon
Nambour
Kingaroy
Maroochydore
Caboolture

P A C I F I C

O C E A N

Surat
Dalby
Toowoomba
Oakey
Brisbane
Goondiwindi
Beaudesert
Beenleigh
Gold Coast

Darling

Warialda
Glen
Inverell
Innes

Casino
Lismore
Murwillumbah
Ballina

Middleton Reef

Norfolk Island
(Australia)

Narrabri
Coonabarabran
Gunnedah

Grafton
Coffs Harbour

Elizabeth Reef

ghtning

Armidale

WALES

Walgett
Wee Waa

Tamworth

Kempsey
Macksville

Raoul I.
Macauley I.
Curtis I.

Kermadec Islands
(New Zealand)

Wellington
Orange
Bathurst

Mount
Singleton
Maitland
Newcastle

Nowra
CANBERRA

Gosford
The Entrance

Port Macquarie
Taree
Forster

Havre Rock
L'Espérance Rock

Dubbo

2230

Goulburn
Ulladulla
Batemans Bay
Moruya

Sydney
Wollongong

JERVIS BAY TERRITORY

Kosciuszko

Cooma
Bega
Eden

Naroona

Cape Howe

T a s m a n   S e a

Three Kings
Islands

Cape Maria van Diemen

North Cape

Furneaux
Group
Flinders I.

dale
eston

Port Arthur

East

Lord Howe I.
(Australia)

Awanui

Dargaville
Kawakawa
Whangarei

Great Barrier I.

Takapuna
Auckland
Manukau

East Cape

Cape Farewell

Hamilton
Te Awamutu

Te Kuiti

Thames
1075
Whakaari

Tauranga
Whakatane

North Island

Rotorua

Gisborne

Tokoroa

Taupo

New Plymouth

Mt Taranaki
(Mt Egmont)

Taumarunui

Ruapehu
2518

Hawke Bay

Cape Providence

Takaka
Riwaka

Wanganui

Feilding

Napier
Hastings

Tasman
Bay

Levin

Palmerston
North

Masterton

NEW
ZEALAND

Nelson
Motueka
Richmond
Blenheim

Greymouth
Hokitika

Lower Hutt
WELLINGTON
C. Palliser

Chatham Islands
(New Zealand)

Chatham I.

South Island

Mt Cook
(Aoraki)
3754

Rangiora
Christchurch

Waitangi

Pitt I.

Mt Aspiring
3030

Ashburton

Banks Peninsula

Queenstown

Timaru
Waimate

Cape Providence

Alexandra
Gore

Oamaru
Milton
Port Chalmers
Dunedin
Balclutha

Invercargill
Bluff

Stewart I.

South West
Cape

Chaslands
Mistake

Snares
Islands

Bounty Islands
(New Zealand)

150°
E

160°
F

170°
G

180°
H

170°

160°

Antipodes Islands
(New Zealand)

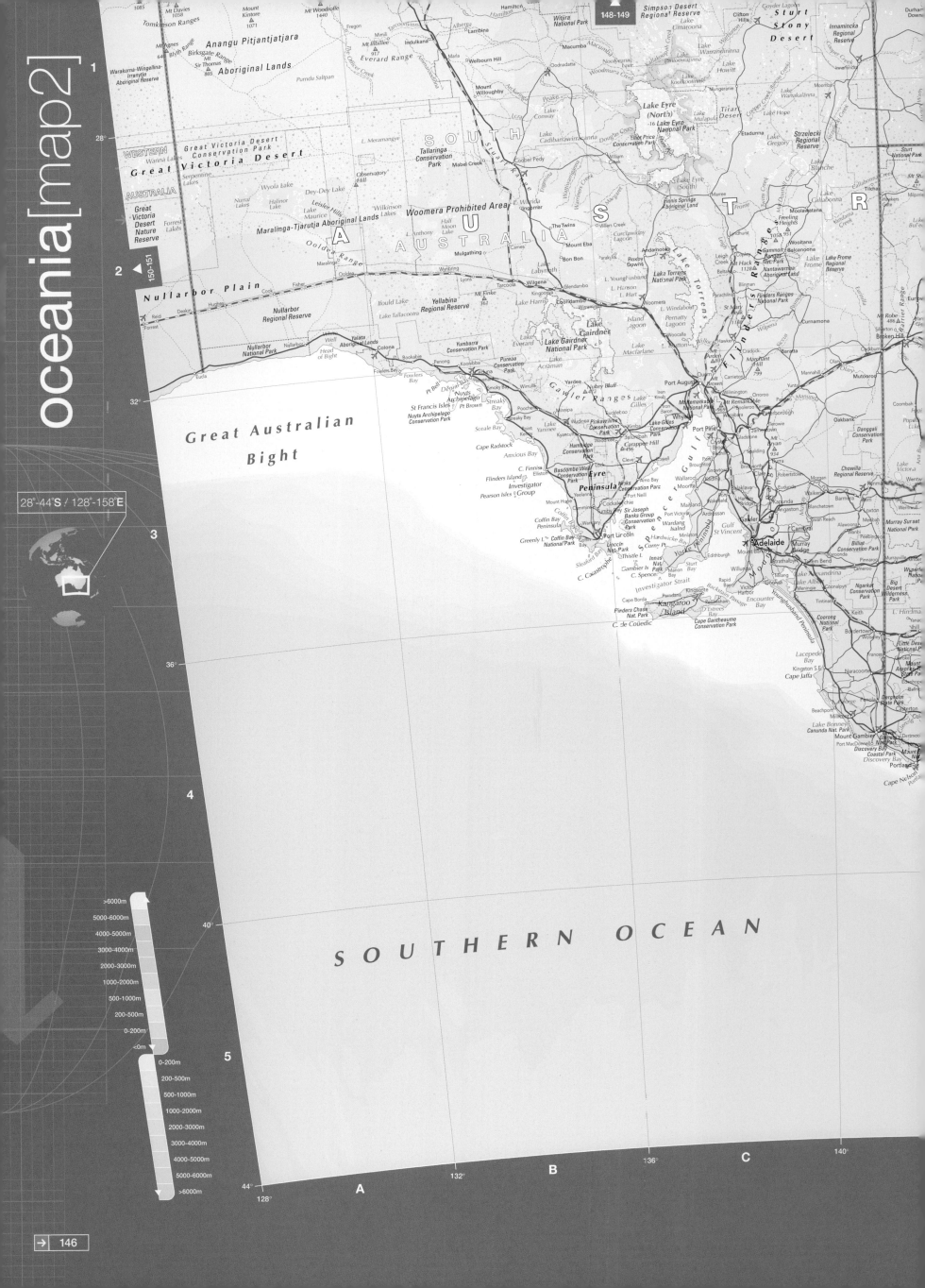

11°–28°S / 128°–154°E

1

C. Van Diemen
St Asaph Bay
Radford Pt
Pt Jahleel
Port Essington
Trepang Bay
C. Croker
C. Croker I
Cobourg Pen.
Gurig National Park
Greenhill I.
Goulburn Islands
Braithwaite Pt
Junction Bay
Boucaut Bay
C. Stewart
Drysdale I.
Wessel Islands
Cape Wessel
The English Company's Is
Wilberforce
Melville Bay
Nhulunbuy
Gove Pen. Yirrkala
Cape Arnhem
Mt Alexander
Port Bradshaw
Caledon Bay
C. Grey
C. Shield

Bathurst Island
Gordon Bay
Mitchell Pt
Ngului
Tiwi Aboriginal Land
Melville Island
C. Keith
Van Diemen Gulf
Wellington Ra.
Maningrida
Goyder R.
Cooper

Beagle Gulf
Clarence Strait
Vernon Is
Pt Hotham
Chambers Bay
Finke Bay
Field I.
West Alligator
Spencer Range
East Alligator
Cumberton Bay
Gapuwiyak
Mt Catt
Mt Marumba

Timor Sea

Charles Pt
Port Darwin
Darwin
Howard Springs
Palmerston
Humpty Doo
Jabiluka Aboriginal Land
Jabiru
Kakadu National Park
Oenpelli
Mann
Blue Mud Bay

12°

Arnhem Land
Arnhem Land
Aboriginal Land

Gulf
of
Carpenta

Fog Bay
Pt Blaze
Batchelor
Adelaide River
Mary R.
Goodparla
Mt Saunders
305
Katherine
Bulman Gorge
Bulman
Bickerton I.
Alyangula
Umbakumba
213
Groote Eylandt

2

Joseph Bonaparte Gulf

Hyland Bay
Peron Is
Anson Bay
Malak Malak Aboriginal Land
C. Scott
Daly River
Pine Creek
Edith Falls
Barnjarn Aboriginal Land
Nitmiluk Nat. Park
Beswick
Beswick Aboriginal Land
Mainoru
Numbulwar
Edward I.
Limmen Bight
Port Roper
Maria I.
Sir Edward Pellew Group
Vanderlin I.
C. Beatrice

16°

Daly River/ Port Keats Aboriginal Land
Pearce Pt
Keyling Inlet
Fitzmaurice
Queens Channel
Wadeye
Wingate Mountains
Macadam Range
Dorisvale
Fitzroy
Flora
Katherine
King
Mataranka
Roper Bar
Roper Bar Aboriginal Land
Marra Aboriginal Land
Wada Wadalla Aboriginal Land
Bing Bong
Wurralibi
Narwinbi Aboriginal Land
McArthur
Aboriginal Land

C. Dussejour
Cambridge Gulf
C. Donnett
Ord River Nature Res.
Adolphus I.
Parry Lagoons Nature Res.
Wyndham
Ivanhoe
Kununurra
Keep River Nat. Park
Timber Creek
Victoria
Fitzroy
Gregory Nat. Park
Waninim Aboriginal Land
Stokes Range
Daly Waters
Dunmarra
Broadmere
Hodgson Downs Aboriginal Land
Hodgson Downs
Alawa Aboriginal Land
Larrimah
Nutwood Downs
Minamia
Borroloola
Manangoora
Wellesley Islands Aboriginal Reserve
Mornington I.
Forsyth Is
Wellesley Island
Bentinck I.
Bayley Pt Aboriginal Reserve
South Wellesley Is
Tarrant
Doomadgee
Doomadgee Aboriginal Reserve
Nicholson

3

Knob Peak
Doon Doon Aboriginal Reserve
Glen Hill Aboriginal Reserve
Lake Argyle
Bow River Aboriginal Res.
Purnululu National Park
Stirling Ra.
Turner River Park
Nicholson
Antrim Plateau
Gordon Downs
Birrindudu
Western Desert Aboriginal Land
Gardiner Range
Sturt Creek
NORTHERN
Gregory National Park
Victoria River Downs
Yarralin Aboriginal Land
Montejinnie
Murranji Aboriginal Land
Mount Samford
Wave Hill
Kalkaringi
Daguragu Aboriginal Land
Inverway
Hooker Creek Aboriginal Land
Lajamanu
Sturt Plain
Newcastle Creek
Elliot
Lake Woods
Renner Springs
Muckaty Aboriginal Land
Banka Banka
Barkly Tableland
Anthony Lagoon
Cresswell Downs
Brunette Downs
Tarrabool L.
Corella Lake
Lake Sylvester
Connells Lagoon Conservation Reserve
Alroy Downs
Herbert
Lawn Hill National Park
Lawn Hill
Gregory Downs
Riversleigh
Thorntonia

16°

Limbunya

NORTHERN TERRITORY

WESTERN AUSTRALIA

4

Central Australia Aboriginal Reserve
Lake Mackay
Lake Mackay Aboriginal Land
Lake Hazlett
Lake Wills
Lake White
Lake Dennis
Balgo Aboriginal Reserve
Tanami Downs Aboriginal Land
Yiningarra Aboriginal Land
Lewis Range
Tanami Desert
Central Desert Aboriginal Land
Rabbit Flat
Mount Davidson
464
436
Tanami
Wirliyajarrayi Aboriginal Land Trust
Willowra
584
Mala Aboriginal Land
Pawu Aboriginal Land
844
Mt Singleton
844
Truer Range
Vaughan Springs 817
Yuendumu Aboriginal Land
Yalpirakinu Aboriginal Land
Napperby
958
Yunkanjini Aboriginal Land
Mt Stanley
887
Stuart Bluff Range
Central Mount Wedge
1067
Mount Wedge
615
Anmatjere Aboriginal Land
Tea Tree
Woolla
Stirling
Barrow Creek
Alyawarra Aboriginal Land
Crawford Range
Mt Strzelecki 636
Warrari Aboriginal Land
Hatches Creek
Elkidra
Murray Downs
Anurrere Aboriginal Land
Davenport Range
Wauchope
South Aboriginal Land
Karlantijpa
Kantijji Aboriginal Land
Kanturga
Mungkarta Aboriginal Land
Tennant Creek
Warumungu Aboriginal Land
Kurundi
Wakaya Aboriginal Land
Arruwurra Aboriginal Land
Austral Downs
Soudan
Wonarah
Buckley
Ranken
Lake Nash
Alpurrurulam
Austral Downs
Argadargada
339
Lucy Creek
Anatye Aboriginal Land
Tobermorey
Marqua
Jervois Range
Irramarne Aboriginal Land
Angarapa Aboriginal Land
Urapuntja
Delmore Downs
Waite River
Aileron
Mt Laughlen
Harts Range
Mt Brasser 1728
Ross River
Santa Teresa
Atnetye Aboriginal Land
Sandringham
Urandangi
Headingly
Mount Isa
Camooweal
Camooweal Caves National Park
Mingera Cr.
Yaringa

20°

Central Desert Aboriginal Land
Tanami Desert

TERRITORY

SOUTH AUSTRALIA

Tropic of Capricorn

Lake Macdonald
Lake Amadeus
Mt Liebig
881
1524
West MacDonnell Nat. Park
Mt Zeil 1510
Haasts Bluff Aboriginal Land
Papunya
Hamilton Downs
1249
Mt Everard
Alice Springs
Undoolya
Illogwa
Harts Range
Mt Eaglebeak
1166
Macdonnell Ranges
Ehrenberg Ra.
Gardiner's Range
Hermannsburg
Iwupataka Aboriginal Land
James Ranges
Wallace Rockhole
Waterhouse Range
Finke Gorge Nat. Park
Hale
Llyentye Apurte Aboriginal Land
Pmere Nyente Aboriginal Land
Simpson Desert

24°

Lake Orantjugurr
Lake Anec
Lake Neale
Watarrka Nat. Park
Winnalls Ridge
Kings Canyon
Seymour Range
George Gills Ra.
McMinns Cr.
Palmer
Henbury
Tempe Downs
Basedow Range
Idracowra
Finke
Maryvale
Horseshoe Bend
Finke Aboriginal Land
Finke
Simpson Desert National Park
Poeppel Corner

Lake Hopkins
Mount Harris
Bloods Range
Petermann Aboriginal Land
Giles Meteorological Station
Mount Deering 1219
Kaltukatjara
Kernot Range
Angas Downs
Erldunda
Black Hill Range
Umbeara
Mulga Park
Victory Downs
Kulgera
Lake Thomas
Simpson Desert Regional Reserve
Poolowanna
Peera Peera Poolanna Lake

Petermann Ranges
Olia Chain
Mt Olga 1069
Yulara
Uluru 867
Uluru National Park
Mt Conner 863

5

Mt Aloysius 1005
Mt Mann
Mt Davies 1174
Tomkinson Ranges
Mt Whinham 1231
Mt Woodroffe 1440
Mt Everard 1174
Amata
Musgrave Ranges
Tieyon
Marryat
Witjira National Park
Dalhousie
Lake Eyabarinie

Warakurna-Wingellina-Irrunytju Aboriginal Reserve
Warburton
Mt Agnes 392
Mt Lindsay
Birksgate Range
Mt Sir Thomas 805
Blyth Range
Anangu Pitjantjatjara
Aboriginal Lands
Mt Kintore 1071
Fregon
Mimili
Mt Illbillee
Everard Range
Indulkana
Marla
Welbourn Hill
Oodnadatta
Macumba
Lake Woodnadutta

Pundu Saltpan
Mount Willoughby

SOUTH AUSTRALIA

28°

128° **A** **132°** **B** **136°** **C**

150–151
146–147

Elevation scale:
>6000m
5000–6000m
4000–5000m
3000–4000m
2000–3000m
1000–2000m
500–1000m
200–500m
0–200m
<0m

0–200m
200–500m
500–1000m
1000–2000m
2000–3000m
3000–4000m
4000–5000m
5000–6000m
>6000m

1 : 6 000 000

miles
0   50   100   150   200   250
km
0 50 100 150 200 250 300 350 400

Lambert Azimuthal Equal Area Projection

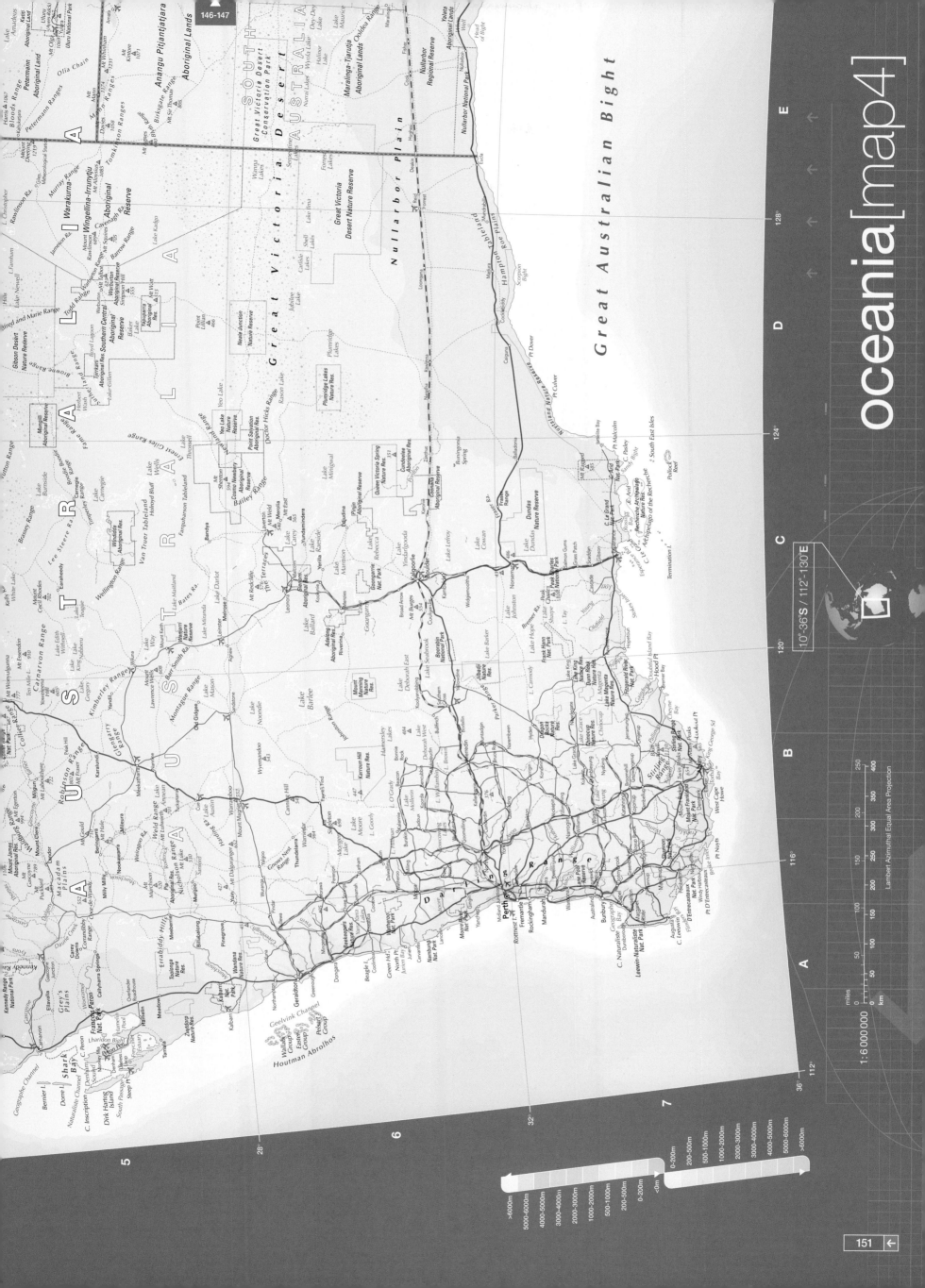

Monument Valley, *Arizona, USA*

north**america**

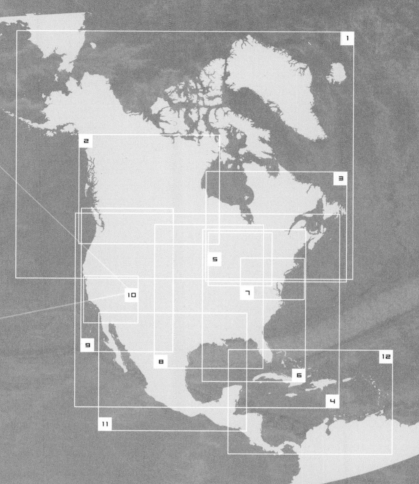

[contents]

		page#
north**america** [landscapes]		156–157
north**america** [countries]		158–159
north**america** [threats]		160–161
north**america** [environments]		162–163

	map coverage	scale	page#
north**america** [map 1]	CANADA	1:15 000 000	164–165
north**america** [map 2]	CANADA West	1:6 500 000	166–167
north**america** [map 3]	CANADA Central and East	1:6 500 000	168–169
north**america** [map 4]	UNITED STATES OF AMERICA	1:12 000 000	170–171
north**america** [map 5]	THE GREAT LAKES	1:3 000 000	172–173
north**america** [map 6]	UNITED STATES OF AMERICA East	1:6 500 000	174–175
north**america** [map 7]	UNITED STATES OF AMERICA Northeast	1:3 000 000	176–177
north**america** [map 8]	UNITED STATES OF AMERICA Central	1:6 500 000	178–179
north**america** [map 9]	UNITED STATES OF AMERICA West	1:6 500 000	180–181
north**america** [map 10]	UNITED STATES OF AMERICA Southwest	1:3 000 000	182–183
north**america** [map 11]	MEXICO	1:7 000 000	184–185
north**america** [map 12]	CENTRAL AMERICA and the CARIBBEAN	1:7 000 000	186–187

Arctic Ocean

Mount McKinley

Mackenzie River

Gulf of Alaska

Coast Mountains

Peace River

Pacific Ocean

Rocky Mountains

Snake River

Great Basin

Great Plains

Grand Canyon

Death Valley

Platte River

Colorado River

Baja California

Gulf of California

Sierra Madre Occidental

Highest point
Mt McKinley
United States of America
6 194 m / 20 321 ft
Map reference 164 D3

Lowest point
Death Valley
86 m / 282 ft below sea level
Map reference 181 C5

North America is the largest continent in the western hemisphere. This view illustrates how the west coast is dominated by the Rocky Mountains which stretch from Alaska in the north through Canada, USA, Mexico and Central America. The Great Plains stretch gradually east of the Rockies, and extend from the Arctic Ocean to the Gulf of Mexico. The Appalachian Mountains dominate the east of the USA, with lowlands skirting the east coast of the continent and the Gulf of Mexico.

Major water bodies are the Great Lakes, and Great Slave Lake and Great Bear Lake in the Arctic regions of Canada. In the northeast, Hudson Bay is a huge inland sea connected to the Atlantic Ocean by the Hudson Strait. The large purple feature at the centre top of the image is the high, snow-covered plateau in Greenland. The Caribbean Sea contains numerous islands, stretching from the Bahamas to the north coast of South America. In the south the Isthmus of Panama forms the link between Central and South America.

Grand Canyon, Arizona, USA

The Grand Canyon in northern Arizona, USA, is the largest canyon in the world and one of the most famous World Heritage Sites. It has been established as a National Park since 1919. This aerial view shows how the canyon has been carved out by the Colorado river, exposing many layers of sedimentary rock. The canyon reaches depths of over 1.5 km and there are many peaks and smaller canyons within the main gorge.

Mackenzie River Delta, Canada

This photograph looks west across the delta of the Mackenzie river towards the Richardson Mountains in the Northwest Territories of Canada. The isolated village of Alavik is located inside the tight bend in the river. The severe climate means that the river is only navigable here between June and October. The Mackenzie, including the Peace and Finlay rivers to the east of the Great Slave Lake, is the second longest river system in North America.

Appalachian Mountains, USA

This photograph from the Space Shuttle shows the heavily wooded ridges of the Appalachian Mountains in southwest Virginia. This narrow range, which is only approximately 160 km wide, forms the principal mountains in the eastern United States and runs parallel to the Atlantic coast. In the area shown in this image, some peaks exceed 1 200 m in height. The valleys between the mountain ridges have rich agricultural soils

Satellite/Sensor: Space Shuttle

CONNECTIONS

▶ subject	page#
▶ World physical features	8–9
▶ World land images	12–13
▶ North American countries	158–159
▶ USA protected areas	162–163
▶ Reference maps of North America	164–187

Greenland

Iceland

Baffin Bay

Baffin Island

Davis Strait

Hudson
Bay

Newfoundland

Canadian Shield

St Lawrence River

Great Lakes

Appalachian Mountains

Atlantic Ocean

Red River

Mississippi River

Brazos River

Florida

The Bahamas

Rio Grande River

Gulf of
Mexico

Cuba

Sierra Madre
Oriental

Hispaniola

Yucatan

Bahía de Campeche

Caribbean Sea

Isthmus
of Panama

NORTH AMERICA

HIGHEST MOUNTAINS	m	ft	location	map
Mt McKinley	6 194	20 321	USA	164 D3
Mt Logan	5 959	19 550	Canada	166 A2
Pico de Orizaba	5 747	18 855	Mexico	185 F5
Mt St Elias	5 489	18 008	USA	166 A2
Volcan Popocatepetl	5 452	17 887	Mexico	185 F5
Mt Foraker	5 303	17 398	USA	164 D3

LARGEST ISLANDS	sq km	sq miles	map
Greenland	2 175 600	840 004	165 O3
Baffin Island	507 451	195 927	165 L2
Victoria Island	217 291	83 897	165 H2
Elesmere Island	196 236	75 767	165 K2
Cuba	110 860	42 803	186 D2
Newfoundland	108 860	42 031	169 J3
Hispaniola	76 192	29 418	187 F3

LONGEST RIVERS	km	miles	map
Mississippi-Missouri	5 969	3 709	179 E7
Mackenzie-Peace-Finlay	4 241	2 635	164 F3
Missouri	4 086	2 539	178 E5
Mississippi	3 765	2 339	179 F7
Yukon	3 185	1 979	164 C3
Rio Grande	3 057	1 899	171 E8

LARGEST LAKES	sq km	sq miles	map
Lake Superior	82 100	31 698	172 D3
Lake Huron	59 600	23 011	173 I6
Lake Michigan	57 800	22 315	172 E7
Great Bear Lake	31 328	12 095	166 F1
Great Slave Lake	28 568	11 030	167 H2
Lake Erie	25 700	9 922	173 K9
Lake Winnipeg	24 387	9 415	167 L4
Lake Ontario	18 960	7 320	173 N7

LAND AREA		map
Most northerly point	Kap Morris Jessup, Greenland	165 P1
Most southerly point	Punta Mariato, Panama	186 C8
Most westerly point	Attu Island, Aleutian Islands	220 G2
Most easterly point	Nordostrundingen, Greenland	224 X1
Total land area: 24 680 331 sq km / 9 529 129 sq miles		

NORTH AMERICA

COUNTRIES

		area sq km	area sq miles	population	capital	languages	religions	currency	map
ANTIGUA AND BARBUDA		442	171	65 000	St John's	English, creole	Protestant, Roman Catholic	E. Carib. dollar	187
THE BAHAMAS		13 939	5 382	304 000	Nassau	English, creole	Protestant, Roman Catholic	Dollar	186–187
BARBADOS		430	166	267 000	Bridgetown	English, creole	Protestant, Roman Catholic	Dollar	187
BELIZE		22 965	8 867	226 000	Belmopan	English, Spanish, Mayan, creole	Roman Catholic, Protestant	Dollar	185
CANADA		9 970 610	3 849 674	30 757 000	Ottawa	English, French	Roman Catholic, Protestant, Eastern Orthodox, Jewish	Dollar	164–165
COSTA RICA		51 100	19 730	4 024 000	San José	Spanish	Roman Catholic, Protestant	Colón	186
CUBA		110 860	42 803	11 199 000	Havana (La Habana)	Spanish	Roman Catholic, Protestant	Peso	186–187
DOMINICA		750	290	71 000	Roseau	English, creole	Roman Catholic, Protestant	E. Carib. dollar	187
DOMINICAN REPUBLIC		48 442	18 704	8 373 000	Santo Domingo	Spanish, creole	Roman Catholic, Protestant	Peso	187
EL SALVADOR		21 041	8 124	6 278 000	San Salvador	Spanish	Roman Catholic, Protestant	Colón	185
GRENADA		378	146	94 000	St George's	English, creole	Roman Catholic, Protestant	E. Carib. dollar	187
GUATEMALA		108 890	42 043	11 385 000	Guatemala City	Spanish, Mayan languages	Roman Catholic, Protestant	Quetzal	185
HAITI		27 750	10 714	8 142 000	Port-au-Prince	French, creole	Roman Catholic, Protestant, Voodoo	Gourde	186
HONDURAS		112 088	43 277	6 417 000	Tegucigalpa	Spanish, Amerindian languages	Roman Catholic, Protestant	Lempira	186
JAMAICA		10 991	4 244	2 576 000	Kingston	English, creole	Protestant, Roman Catholic	Dollar	186
MEXICO		1 972 545	761 604	98 872 000	Mexico City	Spanish, Amerindian languages	Roman Catholic, Protestant	Peso	184–185
NICARAGUA		130 000	50 193	5 071 000	Managua	Spanish, Amerindian languages	Roman Catholic, Protestant	Córdoba	186
PANAMA		77 082	29 762	2 856 000	Panama City	Spanish, English, Amerindian languages	Roman Catholic, Protestant, Sunni Muslim	Balboa	186
ST KITTS AND NEVIS		261	101	38 000	Basseterre	English, creole	Protestant, Roman Catholic	E. Carib. dollar	187
ST LUCIA		616	238	148 000	Castries	English, creole	Roman Catholic, Protestant	E. Carib. dollar	187
ST VINCENT AND THE GRENADINES		389	150	112 000	Kingstown	English, creole	Protestant, Roman Catholic	E. Carib. dollar	187
TRINIDAD AND TOBAGO		5 130	1 981	1 294 000	Port of Spain	English, creole, Hindi	Roman Catholic, Hindu, Protestant, Sunni Muslim	Dollar	187
UNITED STATES OF AMERICA		9 809 378	3 787 422	283 230 000	Washington	English, Spanish	Protestant, Roman Catholic, Sunni Muslim, Jewish	Dollar	170–171

DEPENDENT TERRITORIES

		territorial status	area sq km	area sq miles	population	capital	languages	religions	currency	map
Anguilla		United Kingdom Overseas Territory	155	60	11 000	The Valley	English	Protestant, Roman Catholic	E. Carib. Dollar	187
Aruba		Self-governing Netherlands Territory	193	75	101 000	Oranjestad	Papiamento, Dutch, English	Roman Catholic, Protestant	Florin	187
Bermuda		United Kingdom Overseas Territory	54	21	63 000	Hamilton	English	Protestant, Roman Catholic	Dollar	171
Cayman Islands		United Kingdom Overseas Territory	259	100	38 000	George Town	English	Protestant, Roman Catholic	Dollar	186
Clipperton, Île		French Overseas Territory	7	3	uninhabited					221
Greenland		Self-governing Danish Territory	2 175 600	840 004	56 000	Nuuk (Godthåb)	Greenlandic, Danish	Protestant	Danish krone	165
Guadeloupe		French Overseas Department	1 780	687	428 000	Basse-Terre	French, creole	Roman Catholic	French franc	187
Martinique		French Overseas Department	1 079	417	383 000	Fort-de-France	French, creole	Roman Catholic, traditional beliefs	French franc	187
Montserrat		United Kingdom Overseas Territory	100	39	4 000	Plymouth	English	Protestant, Roman Catholic	E. Carib. Dollar	187
Navassa Island		United States Unincorporated Territory	5	2	uninhabited					186
Netherlands Antilles		Self-governing Netherlands Territory	800	309	215 000	Willemstad	Dutch, Papiamento, English	Roman Catholic, Protestant	NA guilder	187
Puerto Rico		United States Commonwealth	9 104	3 515	3 915 000	San Juan	Spanish, English	Roman Catholic, Protestant	US dollar	187
St Pierre and Miquelon		French Territorial Collectivity	242	93	7 000	St-Pierre	French	Roman Catholic	French franc	169
Turks and Caicos Islands		United Kingdom Overseas Territory	430	166	17 000	Grand Turk	English	Protestant	US dollar	187
Virgin Islands (U.K.)		United Kingdom Overseas Territory	153	59	24 000	Road Town	English	Protestant, Roman Catholic	US dollar	187
Virgin Islands (U.S.A.)		United States Unincorporated Territory	352	136	121 000	Charlotte Amalie	English, Spanish	Protestant, Roman Catholic	US dollar	187

1

Tropic of Cancer

Hawaiian Islands (U.S.A.)
Honolulu

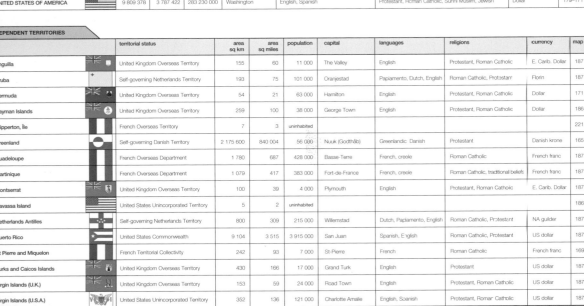
2

3

CONNECTIONS

► subject	page#
► World physical features	8–9
► World countries	10–11
► North America landscapes	156–157
► North America environments	162–163
► Reference maps of North America	164–187

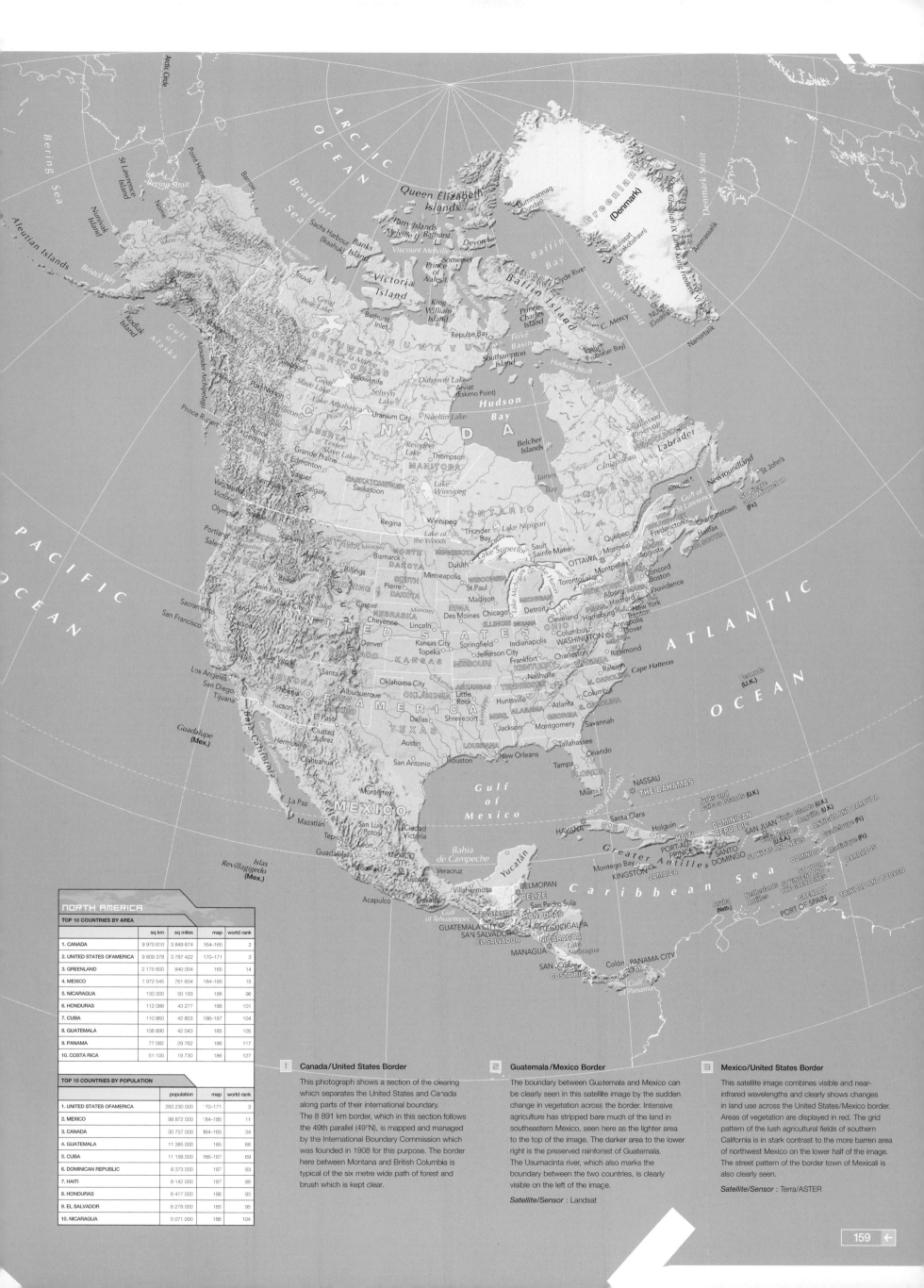

NORTH AMERICA

TOP 10 COUNTRIES BY AREA

	sq km	sq miles	map	world rank
1. CANADA	9 970 610	3 849 674	164–165	2
2. UNITED STATES OF AMERICA	9 809 378	3 787 422	170–171	3
3. GREENLAND	2 175 600	840 004	165	14
4. MEXICO	1 972 545	761 604	184–185	15
5. NICARAGUA	130 000	50 193	186	96
6. HONDURAS	112 088	43 277	186	101
7. CUBA	110 860	42 803	186–187	104
8. GUATEMALA	108 890	42 043	185	105
9. PANAMA	77 082	29 762	186	117
10. COSTA RICA	51 100	19 730	186	127

TOP 10 COUNTRIES BY POPULATION

	population	map	world rank
1. UNITED STATES OF AMERICA	283 230 000	70–171	3
2. MEXICO	98 872 000	184–185	11
3. CANADA	30 757 000	164–165	34
4. GUATEMALA	11 385 000	185	66
5. CUBA	11 199 000	186–187	69
6. DOMINICAN REPUBLIC	8 373 000	187	83
7. HAITI	8 142 000	187	86
8. HONDURAS	6 417 000	186	93
9. EL SALVADOR	6 278 000	185	95
10. NICARAGUA	5 071 000	186	104

1 Canada/United States Border

This photograph shows a section of the clearing which separates the United States and Canada along parts of their international boundary.
The 8 891 km border, which in this section follows the 49th parallel (49°N), is mapped and managed by the International Boundary Commission which was founded in 1908 for this purpose. The border here between Montana and British Columbia is typical of the six metre wide path of forest and brush which is kept clear.

2 Guatemala/Mexico Border

The boundary between Guatemala and Mexico can be clearly seen in this satellite image by the sudden change in vegetation across the border. Intensive agriculture has stripped bare much of the land in southeastern Mexico, seen here as the lighter area to the top of the image. The darker area to the lower right is the preserved rainforest of Guatemala.
The Usumacinta river, which also marks the boundary between the two countries, is clearly visible on the left of the image.

Satellite/Sensor : Landsat

3 Mexico/United States Border

This satellite image combines visible and near-infrared wavelengths and clearly shows changes in land use across the United States/Mexico border. Areas of vegetation are displayed in red. The grid pattern of the lush agricultural fields of southern California is in stark contrast to the more barren area of northwest Mexico on the lower half of the image. The street pattern of the border town of Mexicali is also clearly seen.

Satellite/Sensor : Terra/ASTER

1 San Andreas Fault, *California, USA*

The San Andreas fault is a large break in the Earth's crust between the North American and Pacific plates. It runs for over 950 km from northwest California to the Gulf of California. Movement between the two plates causes earthquakes which present a serious threat to this part of the United States. The fault runs diagonally across this satellite image from left to right, with the supplementary Garlock fault stretching to the top of the image. The proximity of the faults to Los Angeles, the large grey area at the bottom of the image, is obvious.

Satellite/Sensor : Landsat

2 Mount St Helens, *Washington, USA*

After lying dormant since 1857, Mount St Helens in the Cascade mountain range in Washington state, USA erupted violently in May 1980. The eruption was one of the largest volcanic events in North American history and caused the loss of sixty lives. The explosion reduced the height of the mountain by 390 m and flattened trees and killed wildlife over an area of twenty five kilometres radius. The result was the new horseshoe-shaped crater seen in this aerial photograph.

3 Popocatépetl, *Mexico*

This false-colour satellite image shows the Mexican volcano Popocatépetl four days after its eruption in December 2000. The eruption sent molten rock high into the air and over 50 000 people were evacuated from the surrounding area. The bright green spot in the crater indicates that its temperature is still very high. The volcano lies only seventy kilometres southeast of Mexico City, and its name, which is the Aztec word for 'smoking mountain' is suggestive of the threat it presents.

Satellite/Sensor : SPOT

4 Atlantic Hurricanes

Tropical storms have different names in different parts of the world – typhoons in the northwest Pacific Ocean, cyclones in the Indian Ocean region and hurricanes in the Atlantic Ocean and east Pacific. The effects of their strong winds and heavy rain can be devastating.

The Atlantic hurricane season lasts from June to November, with the majority of storms occurring between August and October. The storms present a threat to the islands of the Caribbean and Bermuda and to the east coast of the United States of America. In both 1999 and 2000 there were eight tropical storms which reached hurricane force, as shown on the map Fig. #01. The most severe of these was Hurricane Floyd which developed during early September 1999. It achieved maximum sustained wind speeds of 249 km per hour and made landfall near Cape Fear, North Carolina, USA. Although wind speeds had dropped to around 166 km per hour, it had a devastating effect and fifty seven deaths were directly attributed to the hurricane, making it the deadliest US hurricane since 1972. The computer-generated images show Floyd just off the Florida coast and the inset image indicates wind directions and rainfall levels (yellow-orange over 10mm per hour) at the centre of the hurricane.

CONNECTIONS

► subject	page#
► World earthquakes and volcanoes	14–15
► World climate and weather	16–17
► Asia threats	70–71
► North America landscapes	156–157
► North America environments	162–163

Fig. #01
Atlantic hurricane tracks
1999-2000

Hurricane Strength
1999
2000

29.0 N
65.0 W

20

17.0 N
77.0 W

NORTH AMERICA

ATLANTIC OCEAN

FLORENCE
MICHAEL

DENNIS

CINDY
GERT

BRET
GORDON
IRENE
KEITH
LENNY

FLOYD
DEBBY

ISAAC
JOYCE ALBERTO

JOSE

SOUTH AMERICA

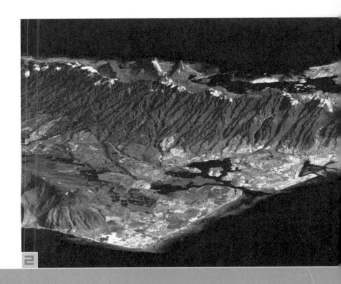

northamerica[environments]

1 Suburbia, California, *USA*

A new housing development west of Stockton, California is shown in this vertical aerial photograph. Water-front properties are in great demand in this area and each house on the finger-like promontories has its own berth, with access via canals to the California Delta waterways of the Sacramento and San Joaquin rivers. Development is continuing on the empty plots at the lower right of the photograph.

2 Island Environment, Hawaii, *USA*

This image shows a perspective view of Honolulu and surrounding area on the Hawaiian island of Oahu. The three-dimensional effect is a result of using height data collected during the Shuttle Radar Topography Mission (SRTM) of the Space Shuttle Endeavour. This height data has been combined with a Landsat 7 satellite image which has been draped over the surface of the elevation model. Honolulu, Pearl Harbour, the Koolau mountain range and offshore reef patterns are all visible on the image.

Satellite/Sensor : Space Shuttle and Landsat

3 Great Plains, Montana, *USA*

A wheat farm on the Great Plains of Montana is shown in this aerial photograph. The high grasses of the Great Plains once sustained large herds of buffalo and the cattle and sheep of large ranches. Today the environment is dominated by large farms using modern extensive farming techniques.

4 Arctic Coastline, *Greenland*

This Space Shuttle photograph gives a northeast view of the south-southeast tip of Greenland. This is a typical scene of the glaciated coastline which surrounds the world's largest island. The dark elongated fingers are inlets, or fjords, which stretch from the North Atlantic Ocean towards the interior. Large white areas to the top of the image mark the start of the permanent ice cap which stretches north across the island to the Arctic Ocean.

Satellite/Sensor : Space Shuttle

5 Protected Environment, Yellowstone National Park, *USA*

The Lower Falls in the Grand Canyon of the Yellowstone River are one of many spectacular features in Yellowstone National Park, Wyoming. The park mainly lies within a volcanically active basin in the Rocky Mountains. It became the world's first national park in 1872 with the purpose of preserving this area of great natural beauty. As well as many geysers, hot springs, lakes and waterfalls the park has a rich variety of flora and fauna.

6 Irrigation, Wyoming, *USA*

This aerial photograph shows fields watered by centre-pivot irrigation next to the Bighorn river in northern Wyoming. This method of irrigation has created circular patterns in the landscape. Each circle is fed from a rotating structure of up to 300 m in length. The flow is carefully controlled so that the whole area is supplied with an equal amount of water. The system makes it possible to grow crops in otherwise infertile parts of the state.

CONNECTIONS

► subject	page#
► Land cover types	18–19
► World land use patterns	20–21
► Europe environments	36–37
► North America landscapes	156–157
► Reference maps of North America	164–187
► Arctic features	214–215

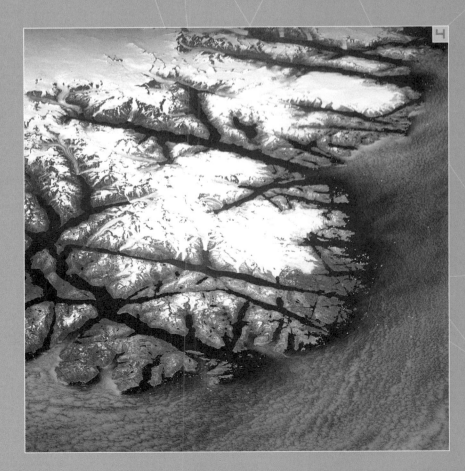

Fig. #01
Land protected by the
US Federal Government

ALASKA

Kobuk Valley
N.P.
Gates of the
Arctic N.P.

Denali
N.P.

Wrangell-
St Elias N.P.

Kenai Fjords N.P.

Katmai
N.P.

Glacier
Bay N.P.

Kauai

Oahu

Maui

Haleakala
N.P.

Hawaiian
Islands

Hawaii

Hawaii
Volcanoes
N.P.

North
Cascades
N.P.

Olympic N.P.

Coville

Glacier
N.P.

Mount
Rainier N.P.

Yakima
I.R.

Blackfeet
I.R.

Flathead
I.R.

Fort Peck
I.R.

Voyageurs
N.P.

Isle Royale
N.P.

Crater
Lake N.P.

Yellowstone
N.P.

Grand Teton
N.P.

Wind
River
I.R.

Northern
Cheyenne I.R.

Crow I.R.

Standing Rock
I.R.

Cheyenne River
I.R.

Lake Traverse
I.R.

Badlands
N.P.

Pine Rosebud
Ridge I.R.
I.R.

Rocky Mountain
N.P.

Yosemite
N.F.

Kings Canyon
N.P.

Sequoia
N.P.

Death
Valley
N.P.

Capitol
Reef N.P.

Bryce
Canyon N.P.

Uintah &
Ouray I.R.

Canyonlands N.P.

Sherandoah
N.P.

Mojave
N.P.

Grand
Canyon N.P.

Navajo I.R.

Hopi I.R.

Osage
I.R.

Great Smoky
Mts N.P.

Joshua Tree
N.P.

Channel Is
N.P.

Organ Pipe
Cactus N.P.

Fort Apache I.R.

San Carlos I.R.

White Sands
Nat. Mon.

Big Bend
N.P.

Everglades
N.P.

National forest

National grassland

National wildlife refuge

National park

Indian reservation

Bureau of Land Management land

Military reservation

National wild and scenic river

40°-85°N / 10°-180°W

RUSSIAN FEDERATION

ARCTIC OCEAN

Beaufort Sea

Chukchi Sea

Bering Strait

Aleutian Islands

Fox Islands

ALASKA

Brooks Range

Philip Smith Mountains

Alaska Range

Aleutian Range

Kuskokwim Mountains

Ahklun Mts

Bristol Bay

Gulf of Alaska

YUKON TERRITORY

NORTHWEST TERRITORIES

Great Bear Lake

Great Slave Lake

Mackenzie Mountains

Cassiar Mountains

BRITISH COLUMBIA

ALBERTA

SASKATCHEWAN

ROCKY MOUNTAINS

Queen Charlotte Islands

Prince of Wales Island

Alexander Archipelago

Vancouver Island

PACIFIC OCEAN

WASHINGTON

OREGON

IDAHO

MONTANA

NEVADA

CALIFORNIA

UTAH

WYOMING

COLORADO

UNITED STATES OF

Seattle

Portland

Vancouver

CONNECTIONS

170–171

>6000m
5000-6000m
4000-5000m
3000-4000m
2000-3000m
1000-2000m
500-1000m
200-500m
0-200m
<0m

0-200m
200-500m
500-1000m
1000-2000m
2000-3000m
3000-4000m
4000-5000m
5000-6000m
>6000m

miles
0   200   400   600

1:15 000 000

km
0   200   400   600   800   1000

Lambert Conformal Conic Projection

48°-65°N / 92°-142°W

CONNECTIONS

▶ subject	page#
▸ World physical features	8–9
▸ World changes	20–21
▸ North America landscapes	156–157
▸ North America countries	158–159

40°-57°N / 52°-95°W

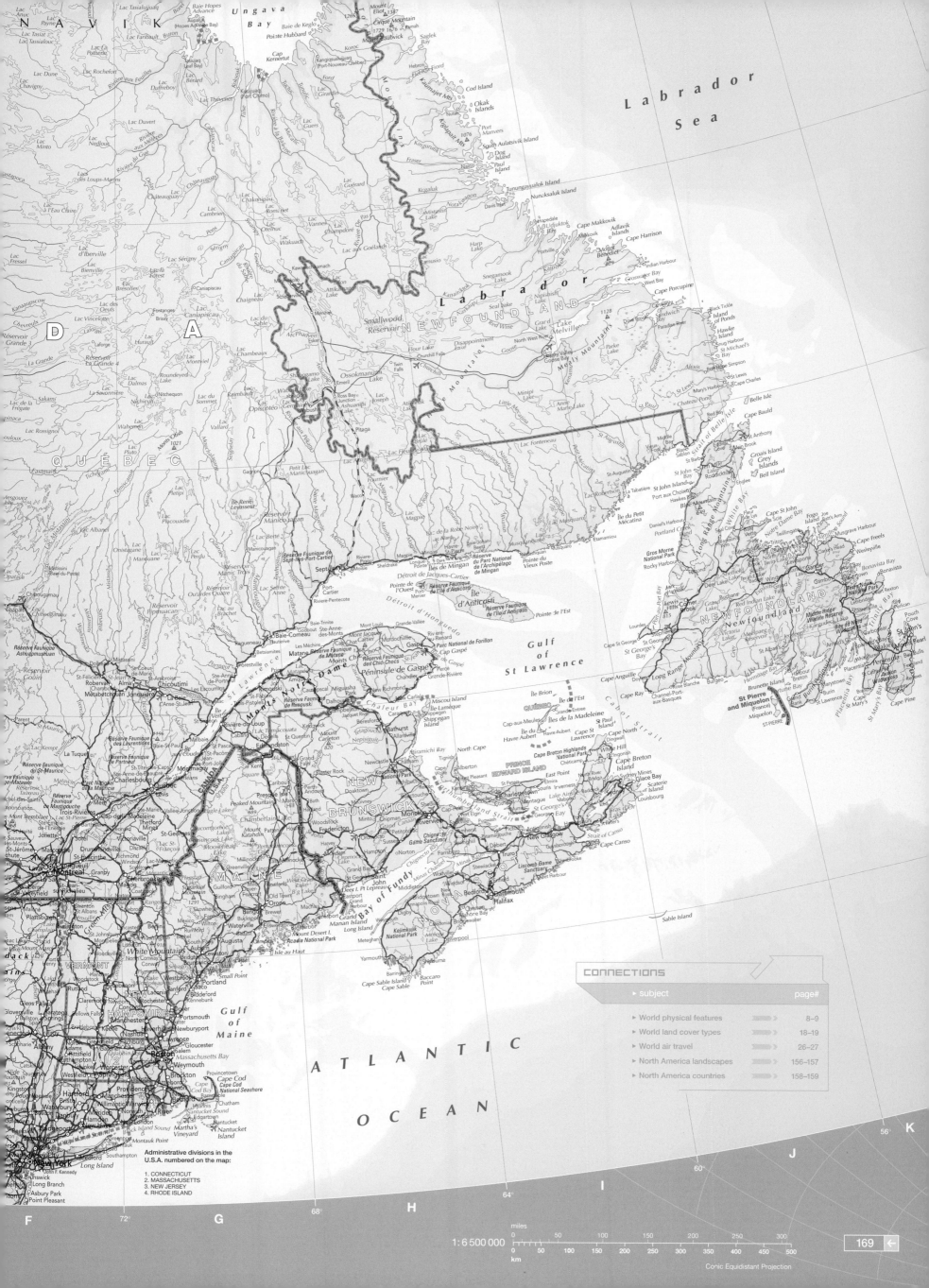

northamerica[map4]

17°-50°N / 67°-125°W

→ 170

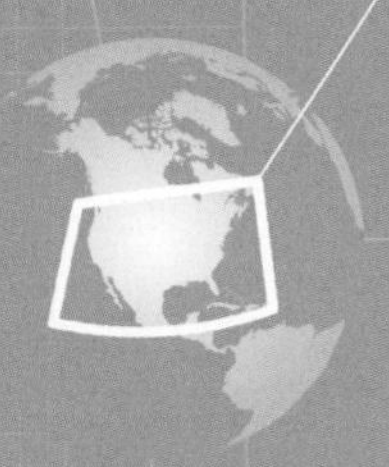

>6000m
5000-6000m
4000-5000m
3000-4000m
2000-3000m
1000-2000m
500-1000m
200-500m
0-200m
<0m
0-200m
200-500m
500-1000m
1000-2000m
2000-3000m
3000-4000m
4000-5000m
5000-6000m
>6000m

PACIFIC
OCEAN

MEXICO

Tropic of Cancer

miles
100 200 300 400 500
1:12 000 000
100 200 300 400 500 600 700 800
km

Lambert Conformal Conic Projection

>6000m
5000–6000m
4000–5000m
3000–4000m
2000–3000m
1500–2000m
1000–1500m
500–1000m
200–500m
100–200m
0–100m
<0m

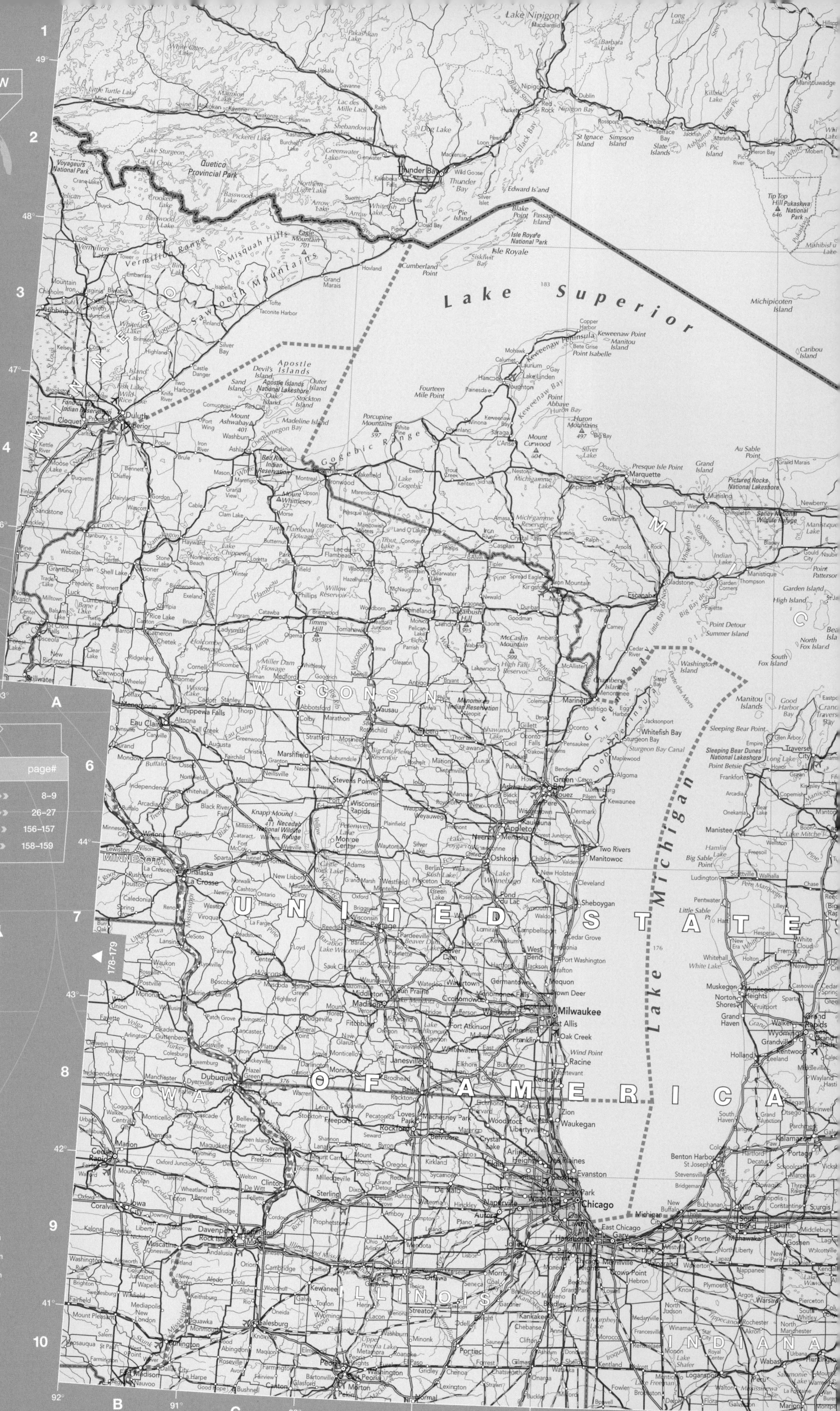

0–50m
50–100m
100–200m
200–500m
500–1000m
1000–2000m
2000–3000m
3000–4000m
4000–5000m
5000–6000m
>6000m

178–179

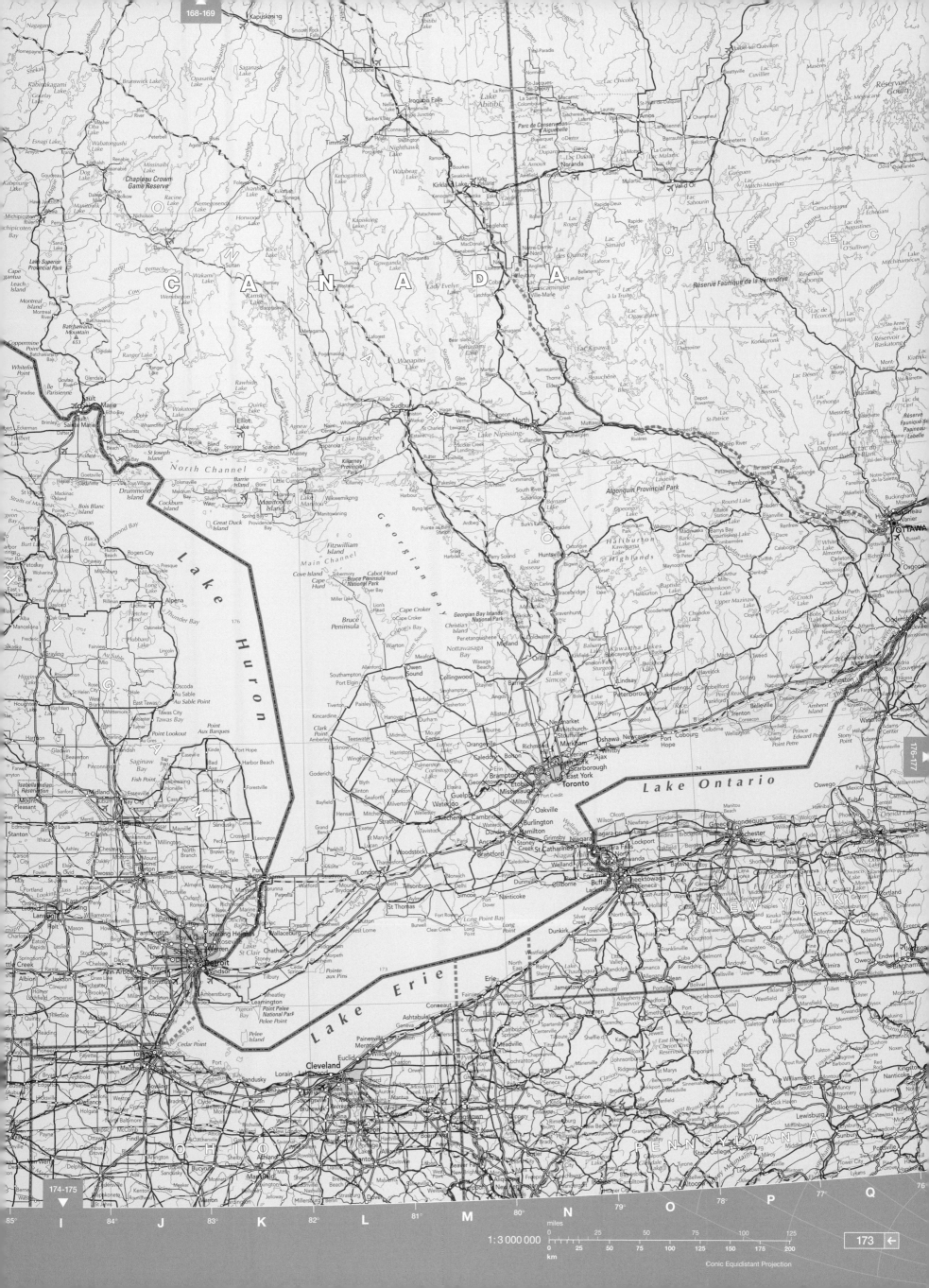

Administrative divisions in the U.S.A.
numbered on map:

1. CONNECTICUT
2. MASSACHUSETTS
3. RHODE ISLAND
4. DELAWARE

CONNECTIONS

	subject	page#
▲	World land cover types	18–19
▲	World cities	24–25
▲	North America landscapes	156–157
▲	North America countries	158–159
▲	North America threats	160–161
▲	Atlantic Ocean	216–217

22°48'N / 92°–70'W

186–187

ATLANTIC OCEAN

THE BAHAMAS

Gulf of Mexico

CUBA

HAVANA (La Habana)

NASSAU

FLORIDA

GEORGIA

ALABAMA

SOUTH CAROLINA

LOUISIANA

MISSISSIPPI

Straits of Florida

Great Bahama Bank

Little Bahama Bank

Tongue of the Ocean

Tropic of Cancer

Miami

Fort Lauderdale

West Palm Beach

Orlando

Tampa

St Petersburg

Jacksonville

Tallahassee

New Orleans

Mobile

Pensacola

Charleston

elevation legend:
>6000m
5000–6000m
4000–5000m
3000–4000m
2000–3000m
1000–2000m
500–1000m
200–500m
0–200m
<0m

depth legend:
0–200m
200–500m
500–1000m
1000–2000m
2000–3000m
3000–4000m
4000–5000m
5000–6000m
>6000m

miles: 0 50 100 150 200 250 300
km: 0 50 100 150 200 250 300 350 400 450 500

1:6 500 000

Lambert Conformal Conic Projection

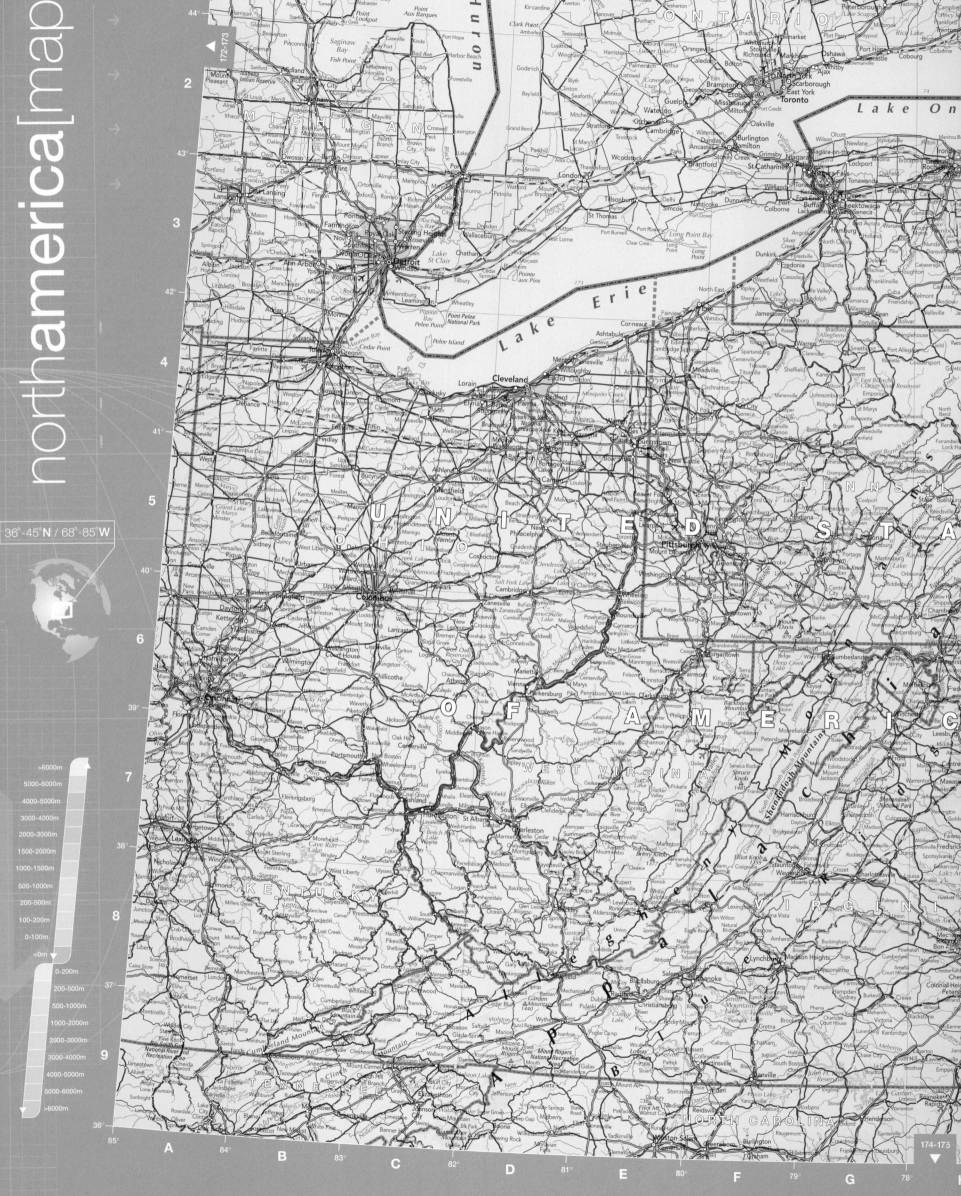

>6000m
5000-6000m
4000-5000m
3000-4000m
2000-3000m
1500-2000m
1000-1500m
500-1000m
200-500m
100-200m
0-100m
<0m

0-200m
200-500m
500-1000m
1000-2000m
2000-3000m
3000-4000m
4000-5000m
5000-6000m
>6000m

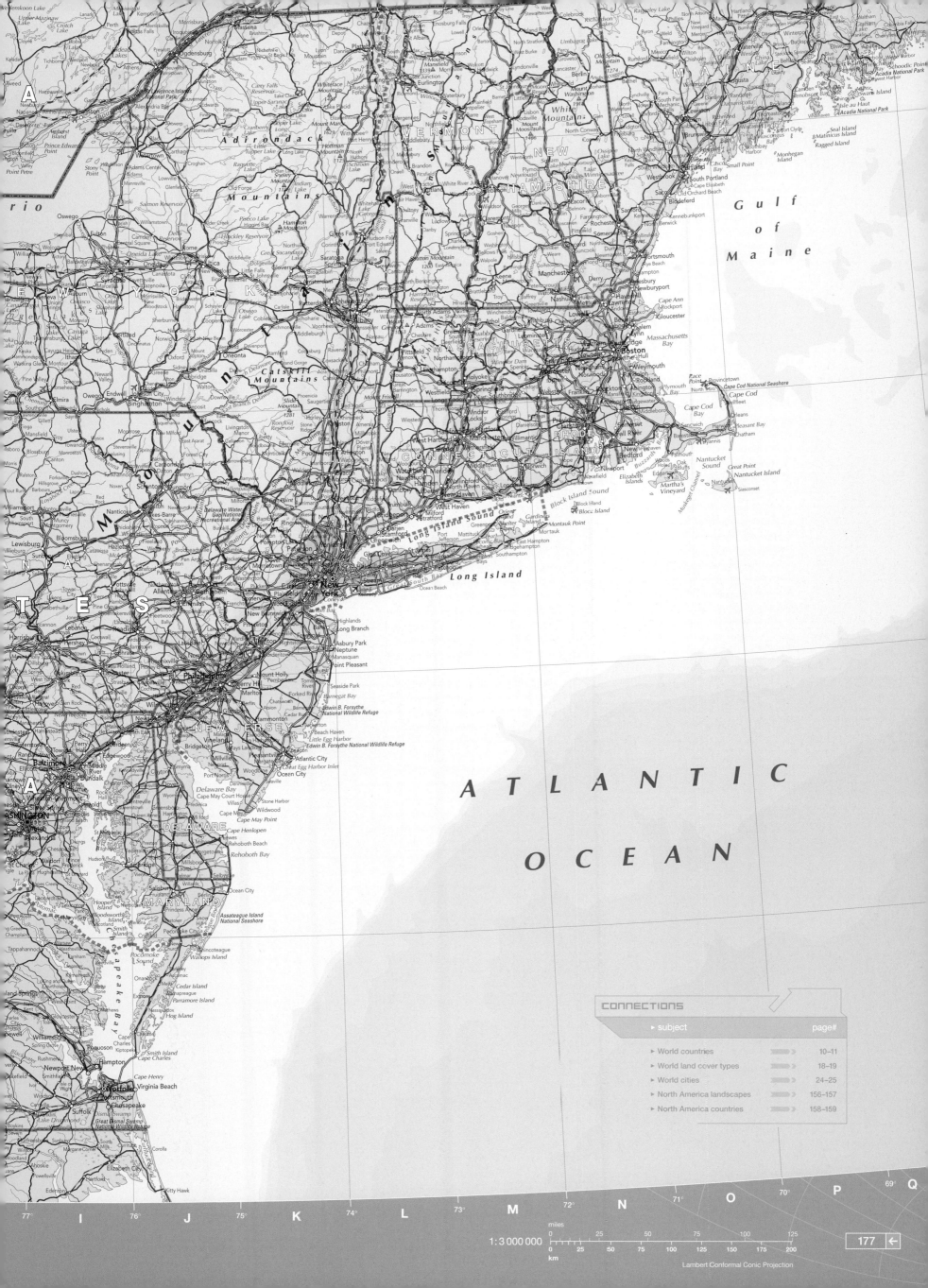

ATLANTIC

OCEAN

*Gulf
of
Maine*

*Massachusetts
Bay*

*Cape Cod
Bay*

*Nantucket
Sound*

Nantucket Island

*Martha's
Vineyard*

Long Island Sound

Long Island

Great South Bay

Delaware Bay

Chesapeake Bay

CONNECTIONS

▸ subject	page#
▸ World countries	10–11
▸ World land cover types	18–19
▸ World cities	24–25
▸ North America landscapes	156–157
▸ North America countries	158–159

miles
1:3 000 000

km

Lambert Conformal Conic Projection

166-167
180-181

northamerica[map8]

1:6 500 000

25°52'N / 82°-104°W

Lambert Conformal Conic Projection

CONNECTIONS

subject	page#
► World physical features	8–9
► World changes	20–21
► North America countries	158–159
► North America environments	162–163

Gulf of Mexico

TENNESSEE

GEORGIA

ALABAMA

FLORIDA

MISSISSIPPI

LOUISIANA

ARKANSAS

OKLAHOMA

TEXAS

NORTH AMERICA

MEXICO

COAHUILA

NUEVO LEÓN

Sierra Madre Oriental

Edwards Plateau

Stockton Plateau

Ouachita Mountains

New Orleans

Houston

San Antonio

Dallas

Fort Worth

Corpus Christi

Galveston

Monterrey

Matamoros

Reynosa

Nuevo Laredo

Brownsville

Gulf of Mexico

Mississippi Delta

Chandeleur Islands

Delta National Wildlife Refuge

Rockefeller National Wildlife Refuge

Padre Island National Seashore

Laguna Madre

>6000m
5000-6000m
4000-5000m
3000-4000m
2000-3000m
1000-2000m
500-1000m
200-500m
0-200m

0-200m
200-500m
500-1000m
1000-2000m
2000-3000m
3000-4000m
4000-5000m
5000-6000m
>6000m

<0m

miles
0 50 100 150 200 250 300

km
0 50 100 150 200 250 300 350 400 450 500

166-167

27° 53'N / 103°-126°W

▼ 184–185

CONNECTIONS

▶ subject	page#
World land images	12–13
World earthquakes	14–15
North America countries	158–159
North America threats	160–161
North America environments	162–163

Lambert Conformal Conic Projection

U N I T E D   S T A T E S   O F   A M E R I C A

MEXICO

NORTE DE MEXICO

CALIFORNIA

ARIZONA

NEW MEXICO

TEXAS

SONORA

CHIHUAHUA

COAHUILA

BAJA CALIFORNIA

BAJA CALIFORNIA NORTE

Gulf of California

PACIFIC OCEAN

Gulf of Mexico

HAWAII (U.S.A.)

PACIFIC OCEAN

1:6 500 000

miles
km

Elevation legend (metres)

>6000m
5000–6000m
4000–5000m
3000–4000m
2000–3000m
1000–2000m
500–1000m
200–500m
0–200m
<0m

Grid references: A B C D E F G / 1 2 3 4 5 6 7 8 / Y Z

32°-40°N / 109°-124°W

PACIFIC

OCEAN

Elevation legend:
>6000m
5000–6000m
4000–5000m
3000–4000m
2000–3000m
1500–2000m
1000–1500m
500–1000m
200–500m
100–200m
0–100m
<0m

0–200m
200–500m
500–1000m
1000–2000m
2000–3000m
3000–4000m
4000–5000m
5000–6000m
>6000m

CONNECTIONS

UNITED

NEW MEXICO

ARIZONA

SONORA

CHIHUAHUA

BAJA CALIFORNIA NORTE

BAJA CALIFORNIA SUR

SINALOA

DURANGO

NAYARIT

COLIMA

Tropic of Cancer

PACIFIC OCEAN

Islas Revillagigedo

Isla San Benedicto
Isla Socorro
Volcán Everman
1050
Isla Roca Partida
I. Clarión
390

Chula Vista
Tijuana
Rosarito
Tecate
Ensenada
Rodolfo Sanchez Toboada
Uruapan
San Antonio del Mar
Punta Baja
Cabo San Quintín
Isla Cedros
Isla Natividad
Punta Eugenia
Bahía Tortugas

Mexicali
San Luis Río Colorado
Yuma
Puerto Peñasco
San Felipe
Puerto Libertad

Tucson
Nogales
Douglas
Ciudad Juárez
El Paso
Las Cruces
Carlsbad Caverns National Park

Hermosillo
Guaymas
Ciudad Obregón
Navojoa
Los Mochis
Guasave
Culiacán
Mazatlán
Tepic

Chihuahua
Ciudad Delicias
Hidalgo del Parral
Durango
Gómez Palacio
Ciudad Lerdo

La Paz
Cabo San Lucas
San José del Cabo
Todos Santos
Santiago

Rocas Alijos

Isla María Madre
Islas Marías
Isla María Magdalena
Isla María Cleofas

Puerto Vallarta
Bahía de Banderas
Cabo Corrientes
Manzanillo

Elevation legend:
>6000m
5000-6000m
4000-5000m
3000-4000m
2000-3000m
1000-2000m
500-1000m
200-500m
0-200m
<0m

0-200m
200-500m
500-1000m
1000-2000m
2000-3000m
3000-4000m
4000-5000m
5000-6000m
>6000m

6°-26°N / 60°-89°W

184-185

Gulf of Mexico

U.S.A.
FLORIDA
North Port
Englewood
Fort Myers
Cape Coral
Bonita Springs
Naples
Ten Thousand Islands
Everglades National Park
Florida Bay
Cape Sable
Marathon
Dry Tortugas
Marquesas Keys
Key West
Boca Chica Key

Port
Hobe Sound
Jupiter
West Palm Beach
Delray Beach
Boca Raton
Fort Lauderdale
Hollywood
Miami
Miami Beach
Kendall
Cutter Ridge
Homestead
Key Largo National Marine Sanctuary

THE BAHAMAS
Walker Cay
Little Abaco
Cooper's Town
Great Abaco
Marsh Harbour
Cherokee
Grand Bahama
Freeport City
Great Harbour
NASSAU
New Providence
Andros
Eleuthera
Great Exuma
Exuma Cays

Gulf of Mexico

HAVANA (La Habana)
Marianao
Guanabacoa
Varadero
Cárdenas
Pinar del Río
CUBA
Cienfuegos
Sancti Spíritus
Ciego de Ávila
Camagüey
Holguín
Bayamo
Manzanillo
Santiago de Cuba
Sierra Maestra

Cayman Islands (U.K.)
Grand Cayman
GEORGE TOWN

JAMAICA
Montego Bay
KINGSTON
Spanish Town

Yucatan Channel

MEXICO
YUCATÁN
Cancún
Cozumel
Isla de Cozumel
Chichén Itzá
Tulum
QUINTANA ROO
Chetumal

BELIZE
BELMOPAN
Belize
Dangriga

Gulf of Honduras
Islas de la Bahía
Roatán

HONDURAS
San Pedro Sula
La Ceiba
Trujillo
TEGUCIGALPA
MOSQUITIA
Puerto Cabezas

GUATEMALA

EL SALVADOR
SAN SALVADOR
San Miguel

NICARAGUA
MANAGUA
León
Masaya
Granada
Lake Nicaragua
Isla de Ometepe
Bluefields
El Bluff

Costa del Mosquito

COSTA RICA
SAN JOSÉ
Liberia
Puntarenas
Limón
Península de Nicoya

PANAMA
PANAMA CITY
Colón
David
CHOCÓ

Gulf of Panama

Caribbean Sea

1:7 000 000
Lambert Conformal Conic Projection

miles 0 50 100 150 200 250 300
km 0 50 100 150 200 250 300 350 400 450 500

Elevation:
>6000m
5000-6000m
4000-5000m
3000-4000m
2000-3000m
1000-2000m
500-1000m
200-500m
0-200m
<0m

ATLANTIC OCEAN

CONNECTIONS

▶ subject	page#
▶ World land images	12–13
▶ World volcanoes	14–15
▶ North America countries	158–159
▶ North America threats	160–161
▶ Atlantic Ocean	216–217

West Indies

Leeward Islands

Greater Antilles

Caribbean Sea

Lesser Antilles

Windward Islands

San Salvador
Long Island
Crooked Island
Acklins Island
Plana Cays
Mayaguana
Great Inagua
Little Inagua
Matthew Town
Samana Cay

Turks and Caicos Islands (U.K.)
North Caicos
Grand Caicos
East Caicos
West Caicos
GRAND TURK (Cockburn Town)
Ambergris Cays

Silver Bank
Mouchoir Bank

Moa
Guantánamo
Maisi
Baracoa

HAITI
PORT-AU-PRINCE
Cap-Haïtien
Gonaïves
St Marc
Jérémie
Les Cayes
Jacmel
Île de la Gonâve
Île de la Tortue
Dame Marie

DOMINICAN REPUBLIC
SANTO DOMINGO
Santiago
San Francisco de Macorís
Barahona
San Cristóbal
San Pedro de Macorís
La Romana
Puerto Plata
Monte Cristi
Salcedo
Parque Nacional del Este
Isla Saona
Isla Beata
Cabo Beata

Hispaniola

Puerto Rico (U.S.A.)
SAN JUAN
Bayamón
Arecibo
Aguadilla
Mayagüez
San Germán
Ponce
Guánica
Guayama
Humacao
Caguas
Vieques
Isla Mona
Cabo Rojo

Virgin Is (U.K.)
ROAD TOWN
Tortola
Virgin Gorda
Anegada

Virgin Is (U.S.A.)
CHARLOTTE AMALIE
St Thomas
St John
St Croix
Christiansted
Frederiksted

Sombrero
Anguilla (U.K.)
THE VALLEY
Saint Martin (Fr.)
St Maarten (Neth.)
St-Barthélemy (Fr.)
Barbuda
Saba (Neth.)
St Eustatius (Neth.)

ST KITTS AND NEVIS
BASSETERRE
St Kitts
Nevis
Redonda

ANTIGUA AND BARBUDA
ST JOHN'S
Antigua
Falmouth

Montserrat (U.K.)
PLYMOUTH
Soufrière Hills

Guadeloupe (France)
BASSE-TERRE
Grande-Terre
Basse-Terre
La Désirade
Marie-Galante
Îles des Saintes
Grand Bourg
Pointe Noire
Ste-Rose
Moule
Port Louis

DOMINICA
ROSEAU
Portsmouth
Marigot
Scotts Head

Martinique (France)
FORT-DE-FRANCE
Ste-Marie
St-Robert
Montagne
Rivière-Pilote

ST LUCIA
CASTRIES
Soufrière
Vieux Fort
Micoud
Gros Islet

ST VINCENT AND THE GRENADINES
KINGSTOWN
St Vincent
Bequia
Mustique
Canouan
The Grenadines
Carriacou

GRENADA
ST GEORGE'S
Hillsborough
Grenville
Ronde

BARBADOS
BRIDGETOWN
Speightstown
Six Cross Roads

Anegada Passage
Guadeloupe Passage
Dominica Passage
Martinique Passage
St Lucia Channel
St Vincent Passage
Windward Passage
Mona Passage

Aves (Venezuela)

Aruba (Neth.)
ORANJESTAD
St Nicolaas

Netherlands Antilles
WILLEMSTAD
Curaçao
Bonaire
Parque Nacional
Santa Catarina

Isla La Tortuga
Isla Blanquilla
Islas Los Roques
Islas Las Aves
Isla Orchila
Los Testigos
Los Hermanos

Isla de Margarita
NUEVA ESPARTA
La Asunción
Porlamar
Coche
Isla Cubagua
Isla Coche

TRINIDAD AND TOBAGO
PORT OF SPAIN
Trinidad
Tobago
Scarborough
Charlotteville
Galera Pt
Diego Martin
San Fernando

Tortuguero
Charlottesville
Gulf of Paria
Serpent's Mouth
Boca Grande

VENEZUELA
CARACAS
DISTRITO FEDERAL
Maracaibo
Valencia
Maracay
Barquisimeto
Maiquetía
Puerto Cabello
Barcelona
Cumaná
Barinas
Mérida
Cúcuta
San Cristóbal
Ciudad Bolívar
Ciudad Guayana
El Tigre
Anaco
Maturín
Carúpano
San Fernando de Apure
San Carlos
Guanare
San Felipe
Puerto La Cruz

States: ZULIA, FALCÓN, LARA, YARACUY, CARABOBO, ARAGUA, MIRANDA, ANZOÁTEGUI, MONAGAS, SUCRE, GUÁRICO, COJEDES, PORTUGUESA, BARINAS, APURE, TÁCHIRA, MÉRIDA, TRUJILLO, BOLÍVAR, DELTA AMACURO

Lake Maracaibo
Golfo de Venezuela
Península de Paria
Orinoco
Delta Amacuro
Embalse de Guri

Parque Nacional Sierra Nevada
Parque Nacional Médanos de Coro
Parque Nacional Macuira
Parque Nacional Mochima
Parque Nacional Canaima
Parque Nacional Cinaruco-Capanaparo
Sierra de Perijá
Cordillera Oriental

COLOMBIA
Santa Marta
Riohacha
Valledupar
Barranquilla
Maicao
Magangué
El Banco

Depts: MAGDALENA, CESAR, GUAJIRA, NORTE DE SANTANDER, BOLÍVAR, SANTANDER, ARAUCA

Cabo de la Vela
Punta Gallinas
Bahía Honda

GUYANA
Kaieteur Falls
Serranía de Imataca
Waini Point

Llanos

Cabo San Román
Cabo Codera
Boca Grande

Canaima National Park, *Venezuela*

southamerica

[contents]

		page#
southamerica [landscapes]		190–191
southamerica [countries]		192–193
southamerica [contrasts]		194–195
southamerica [impacts]		196–197

	map coverage	scale	page#
southamerica [map 1]	SOUTH AMERICA North	1:8 000 000	198–199
southamerica [map 2]	SOUTH AMERICA Central	1:8 000 000	200–201
southamerica [map 3]	SOUTH AMERICA East	1:8 000 000	202–203
southamerica [map 4]	SOUTH AMERICA South	1:8 000 000	204–205
southamerica [map 5]	BRAZIL Southeast	1:3 300 000	206–207

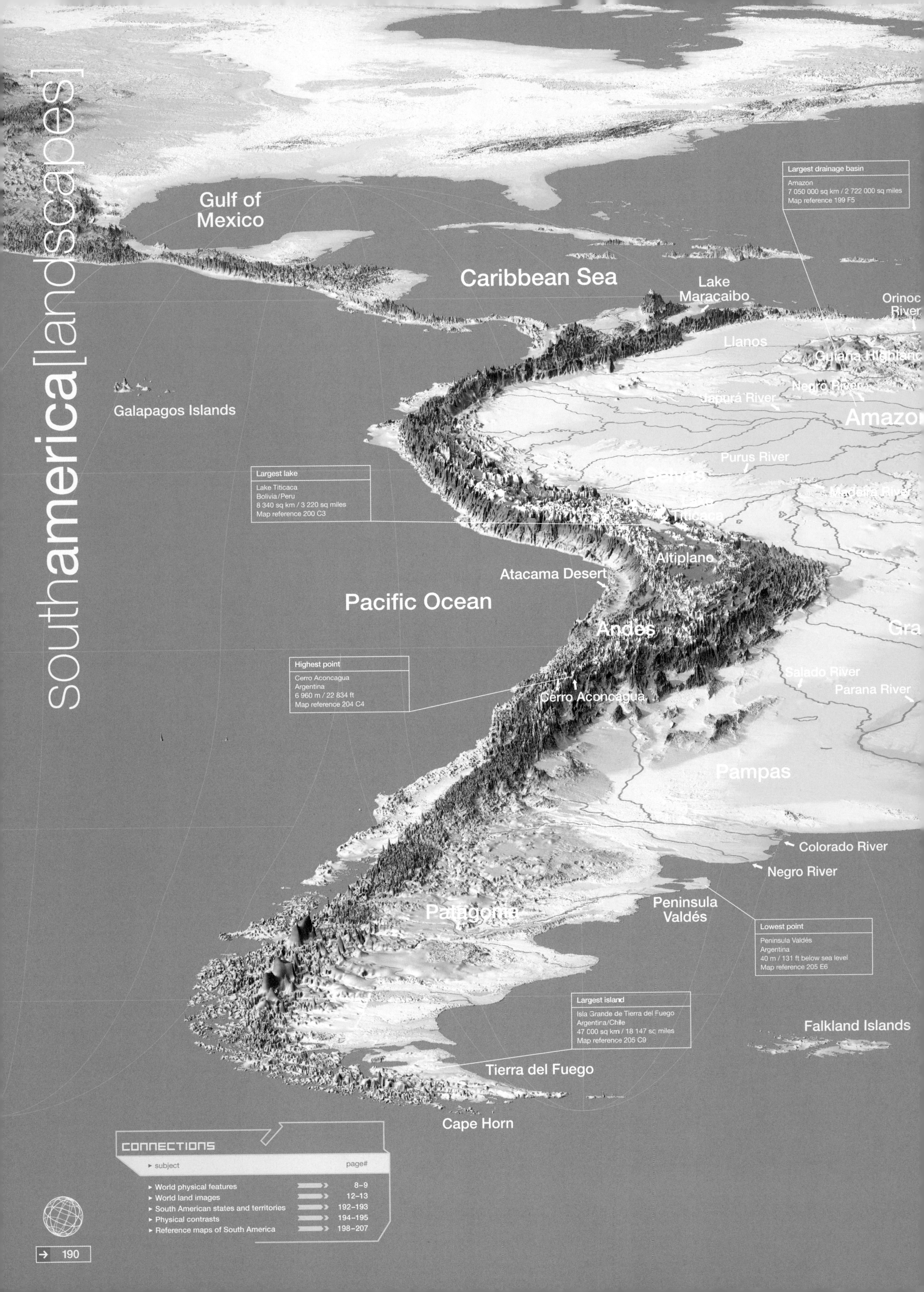

Gulf of Mexico

Caribbean Sea

Lake Maracaibo

Orinoco River

Largest drainage basin

Amazon
7 050 000 sq km / 2 722 000 sq miles
Map reference 199 F5

Llanos

Guiana Highlands

Negro River

Japurá River

Amazon

Galapagos Islands

Purus River

Madeira River

Largest lake

Lake Titicaca
Bolivia/Peru
8 340 sq km / 3 220 sq miles
Map reference 200 C3

Titicaca

Altiplano

Atacama Desert

Pacific Ocean

Andes

Gra

Highest point

Cerro Aconcagua
Argentina
6 960 m / 22 834 ft
Map reference 204 C4

Cerro Aconcagua

Salado River

Parana River

Pampas

Colorado River

Negro River

Patagonia

Peninsula Valdés

Lowest point

Peninsula Valdés
Argentina
40 m / 131 ft below sea level
Map reference 205 E6

Largest island

Isla Grande de Tierra del Fuego
Argentina/Chile
47 000 sq km / 18 147 sq miles
Map reference 205 C9

Falkland Islands

Tierra del Fuego

Cape Horn

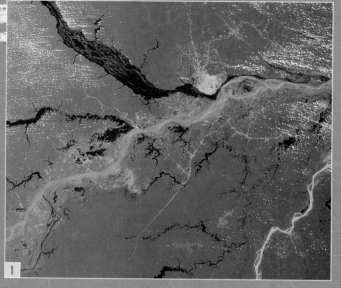

← Orinoco River Delta

Angel Falls

← Mouths of the Amazon

Basin

Amazon River

Longest river
Amazon
6 516 km / 4 049 miles
Map reference 202 B1

Mato Grosso

Tocantins River

Sao Francisco River

Chaco

Brazilian Highlands

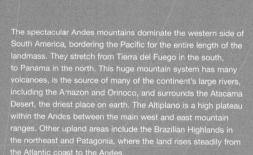

Uruguay River

Atlantic Ocean

← Rio de la Plata

The spectacular Andes mountains dominate the western side of South America, bordering the Pacific for the entire length of the landmass. They stretch from Tierra del Fuego in the south, to Panama in the north. This huge mountain system has many volcanoes, is the source of many of the continent's large rivers, including the Amazon and Orinoco, and surrounds the Atacama Desert, the driest place on earth. The Altiplano is a high plateau within the Andes between the main west and east mountain ranges. Other upland areas include the Brazilian Highlands in the northeast and Patagonia, where the land rises steadily from the Atlantic coast to the Andes.

The Amazon Basin is a large lowland area, lying just south of the equator, through which the Amazon river and its many tributaries flow towards the huge delta on the Atlantic coast. The region contains vast areas of tropical rain forest. Huge, sparsely populated plains known as Llanos in the north and Pampas in the south provide further contrasts in the landscapes of the continent.

1 Amazon River, *Brazil*

The grey area on this satellite image is the isolated city of Manaus in northern Brazil. It sits at the confluence of the Amazon and Negro rivers. The Amazon, flowing from west to east, originates in the Andes mountains in Peru and carries a thick solution of silt and sand giving it a brown colour. The Negro river flows over hard base rock giving little sediment so the water is clearer, appearing dark in this image. The waters do not combine immediately but flow side by side for some distance before merging.

Satellite/Sensor : Terra, MISR

2 Pampas, *Argentina*

The Pampas grassland plains of Argentina stretch from the foothills of the Andes mountains to the east coast. This photograph shows the Pampas in Neuquen Province. Eastern areas tend to be better irrigated but the whole area supports a major livestock industry.

3 Lake Viedma, *Argentina*

Lake Viedma in the centre of this image, Lake Argentino to the left, and Lake San Martin to the right are situated in southern Argentina. This image looks southwest and shows the lakes being fed by meltwater from the glaciers of the Andes Mountains. Lake Viedma is over 300 m above sea level. Waters from it flow into Lake Argentino then into the Santa Cruz river, across the Patagonia plateau to the Atlantic Ocean. The snow-capped ridge behind the lakes forms the boundary between Argentina and Chile.

Satellite/Sensor : Space Shuttle

SOUTH AMERICA

HIGHEST MOUNTAINS

	m	ft	location	map
Cerro Aconcagua	6 960	22 834	Argentina	204 C4
Nevado Ojos del Salado	6 908	22 664	Argentina/Chile	2C4 C2
Cerro Bonete	6 872	22 546	Argentina	204 C2
Cerro Pissis	6 858	22 500	Argentina	204 C2
Cerro Tupungato	6 800	22 309	Argentina/Chile	204 C4
Cerro Meredario	6 770	22 211	Argentina	204 B3

LARGEST ISLANDS

	sq km	sq miles	map
Isla Grande de Tierra del Fuego	47 000	18 147	205 C9
Isla de Chiloe	8 394	3 240	205 B6
East Falkland	6 760	2 610	205 F8
West Falkland	5 413	2 090	205 E8

LONGEST RIVERS

	km	miles	map
Amazon	6 516	4 049	202 B1
Rio de la Plata-Parana	4 500	2 796	204 F4
Purus	3 218	1 999	199 F5
Madeira	3 200	1 988	199 G5
Sao Francisco	2 900	1 802	202 E4
Tocantins	2 750	1 708	202 B2

LAKES

	sq km	sq miles	map
Lake Titicaca	8 340	3 220	200 C3

LAND AREA

		map
Most northerly point	Punta Gallinas, Colombia	198 D1
Most southerly point	Cape Horn, Chile	205 D9
Most westerly point	Galapgos Islands, Ecuador	216 H6
Most easterly point	Ilhas Martin Vaz, Atlantic Ocean	216 M7

Total land area: 17 815 420 sq km / 6 878 572 sq miles

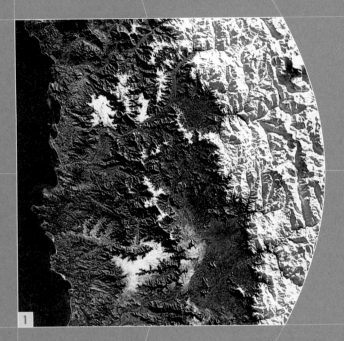

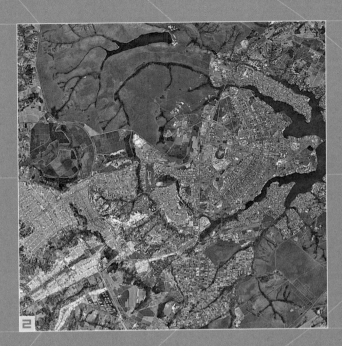

CONNECTIONS

► subject	page#
► World physical features	8–9
► World countries	10–11
► South America landscapes	190–191
► South America contrasts	194–195
► Reference maps of South America	198–207

SOUTH AMERICA

COUNTRIES

		area sq km	area sq miles	population	capital	languages	religions	currency	map
ARGENTINA		2 766 889	1 068 302	37 032 000	Buenos Aires	Spanish, Italian, Amerindian languages	Roman Catholic, Protestant	Peso	204–205
BOLIVIA		1 098 581	424 164	8 329 000	La Paz/Sucre	Spanish, Quechua, Aymara	Roman Catholic, Protestant, Baha'i	Boliviano	200–201
BRAZIL		8 547 379	3 300 161	170 406 000	Brasília	Portuguese	Roman Catholic, Protestant	Real	202–203
CHILE		756 945	292 258	15 211 000	Santiago	Spanish, Amerindian languages	Roman Catholic, Protestant	Peso	204–205
COLOMBIA		1 141 748	440 831	42 105 000	Bogotá	Spanish, Amerindian languages	Roman Catholic, Protestant	Peso	198
ECUADOR		272 045	105 037	12 646 000	Quito	Spanish, Quechua, other Amerindian languages	Roman Catholic	Sucre	198
GUYANA		214 969	83 000	761 000	Georgetown	English, creole, Amerindian languages	Protestant, Hindu, Roman Catholic, Sunni Muslim	Dollar	199
PARAGUAY		406 752	157 048	5 496 000	Asunción	Spanish, Guarani	Roman Catholic, Protestant	Guaraní	201
PERU		1 285 216	496 225	25 662 000	Lima	Spanish, Quechua, Aymara	Roman Catholic, Protestant	Sol	200
SURINAME		163 820	63 251	417 000	Paramaribo	Dutch, Surinamese, English, Hindi	Hindu, Roman Catholic, Protestant, Sunni Muslim	Guilder	199
URUGUAY		176 215	68 037	3 337 000	Montevideo	Spanish	Roman Catholic, Protestant, Jewish	Peso	204
VENEZUELA		912 050	352 144	24 170 000	Caracas	Spanish, Amerindian languages	Roman Catholic, Protestant	Bolívar	198–199

DEPENDENT TERRITORIES

		territorial status	sq km	sq miles	population	capital	languages	religions	currency	map
Falkland Islands		United Kingdom Overseas Territory	12 170	4 699	2 000	Stanley	English	Protestant, Roman Catholic	Pound	205
French Guiana		French Overseas Department	90 000	34 749	165 000	Cayenne	French, creole	Roman Catholic	French franc	199
South Georgia and South Sandwich Islands		United Kingdom Overseas Territory	4 066	1 570	uninhabited					217

1 Santiago, *Chile*

In this Landsat satellite image, Santiago, capital city and main industrial centre of Chile, can be seen to the left of the snow-capped Andes mountains which form a natural boundary between Chile and its easterly neighbour, Argentina. The city, which has suffered many earthquakes and floods, was established as Chile's capital when the country became independent in 1818.

Satellite/Sensor : Landsat

2 Brasília, *Brazil*

Construction of Brasília as the administrative and political centre of Brazil began in 1956 and four years later it replaced Rio de Janeiro as the capital city of Brazil, South America's largest country. It is located on the Paraná, a headstream of the Tocantins river. In this infrared satellite image the city is in the centre, where buildings appear as light blue-grey. Lakes to the north and east of the city are blue-black, and vegetation along the small tributaries shows as red.

Satellite/Sensor : SPOT

3 Lake Titicaca, *Bolivia/Peru*

Lake Titicaca, located in a depression within the high plains (Altiplano) of South America, is the largest freshwater lake on the continent. The international boundary between Bolivia and Peru passes through the lake. In this oblique Shuttle photograph, the Andes mountains can be seen in the top right and bottom left. Persistent drought in the area has caused water levels to drop and expose the bottom of the lake, shown as white patches on the lake shore.

Satellite/Sensor : Space Shuttle

SOUTH AMERICA

TOP 10 COUNTRIES BY AREA

	sq km	sq miles	map	world rank
1. BRAZIL	8 547 379	3 300 161	202–203	5
2. ARGENTINA	2 766 889	1 068 302	204–205	8
3. PERU	1 285 216	496 225	200	20
4. COLOMBIA	1 141 748	440 831	198	26
5. BOLIVIA	1 098 581	424 164	200–201	28
6. VENEZUELA	912 050	352 144	198–199	33
7. CHILE	756 945	292 258	204–205	38
8. PARAGUAY	406 752	157 048	201	59
9. ECUADOR	272 045	105 037	198	74
10. GUYANA	214 969	83 000	199	83

TOP 10 COUNTRIES BY POPULATION

	population	map	world rank
1. BRAZIL	170 406 000	202–203	5
2. COLOMBIA	42 105 000	198	28
3. ARGENTINA	37 032 000	204–205	31
4. PERU	25 662 000	200	38
5. VENEZUELA	24 170 000	198–199	40
6. CHILE	15 211 000	204–205	59
7. ECUADOR	12 646 000	198	63
8. BOLIVIA	8 329 000	200–201	84
9. PARAGUAY	5 496 000	201	97
10. URUGUAY	3 337 000	204	125

1 La Paz, *Bolivia*

The Bolivian city of La Paz is the highest capital city in the world. It lies just southeast of Lake Titicaca, in a valley between the Cordillera Oriental and the Andes, sheltered from the severe winds and weather of the Altiplano. It has a population of over 1 million. The city was established by the Spanish conquistadors in the mid 1500's.

2 Farmland, *Ecuador*

On the western slopes of the Andes, erosion of the high volcanic peaks has created rich soils for farming, as seen here in Ecuador. The scattered farms are worked by indigenous Indian people who gather to sell, buy and barter at local weekly markets. Over 30 per cent of Ecuador's population is employed in agriculture and agricultural products account for almost half of the country's exports.

3 Glacier, *Patagonia*

Glaciers such as this, in the region of Patagonia, which straddles the Chile/Argentina border, are a great influence on the landscape. The surface of the glacier is deeply scarred by crevasses and patterns of debris within the ice indicate its current flow. Braided streams carry fine sediment away from the glacier.

Satellite/Sensor : Terra/ASTER

4 Galapagos Islands, *Ecuador*

This satellite image shows part of the Galapagos Islands, a group of islands created by volcanic activity. The craters of volcanoes on the main island of Isla Isabela and on Isla Fernandina to the west, can be clearly seen. Vegetation, which appears red, is limited as the landscape is dominated by lava flows. The Galapagos Islands are a group of isolated islands lying over 1 000 km west of the coast of Ecuador. They are renowned for their rich and unique wildlife.

Satellite/Sensor : SPOT

5 Andes Mountains

The Andes mountain range forms a formidable barrier down the whole length of the western side of the South American continent. This is clearly seen in this dramatic visualization created from digital terrain data. The western edge of the Andes descends steeply towards the Pacific Ocean with very little coastal lowland. Likewise to the east, the transition from high ground to low, flatter areas is also sudden, emphasizing the barrier of the mountains. To the south, the lowland areas form the grassy plains of the Pampas and to the north, the Amazon basin.

CONNECTIONS

► subject		page#
► La Paz	⟫	10–11
► World weather extremes	⟫	16–17
► Land cover types	⟫	18–19
► World's largest cities	⟫	24–25
► South America landscapes	⟫	190–191
► South America countries	⟫	192–193
► South America impacts	⟫	196–197

6 Atacama Desert, *Chile*

The Atacama Desert in north central Chile is the driest place on Earth and is a very barren area. The volcanic ground has produced an area rich in minerals and the region is a major source of the world's nitrates. This satellite image shows many dry river courses, carved out by seasonal rains which carry minerals to the salt pans which appear white. The dark area at centre top is a more recent lava flow from the Napa volcano.

Satellite/Sensor : SPOT

7 Amazon River Basin, *Brazil*

The Amazon river, from its source in the Andes of southern Peru extends across a vast area of the equatorial region of Brazil. The river and its tributaries form the largest river basin in the world of over 7 million square kilometres. High temperatures and plentiful rainfall result in dense, lush vegetation. This aerial photograph shows the great variety of trees which form a thick canopy in the rainforest.

8 Ranches, *Brazil*

This Space Shuttle photograph shows recent forest clearing to create ranch land in the Brazilian state of Mato Grosso. The photograph shows part of the Serra do Tombador plateau where there is good drainage and rich soils. Land cleared close to the river Sargue at the bottom of the picture is under water for almost three months of the year. The area suffers from soil erosion and can only be worked on in the dry season.

Satellite/Sensor : Space Shuttle

9 Escondida Mine, *Chile*

The Esconcida copper, gold and silver mine is located in the arid, northern Atacama Desert of Chile, 160 km south of the port of Antofagasta. It is situated 3 050 m above sea level. The mine is a conventional open-pit operation, employs over 2 000 people and produces 127 000 tons of ore per day. The initial processing of ore is carried out on site, then concentrates are sent through a 170 km pipe to the Pacific coast for further processing.

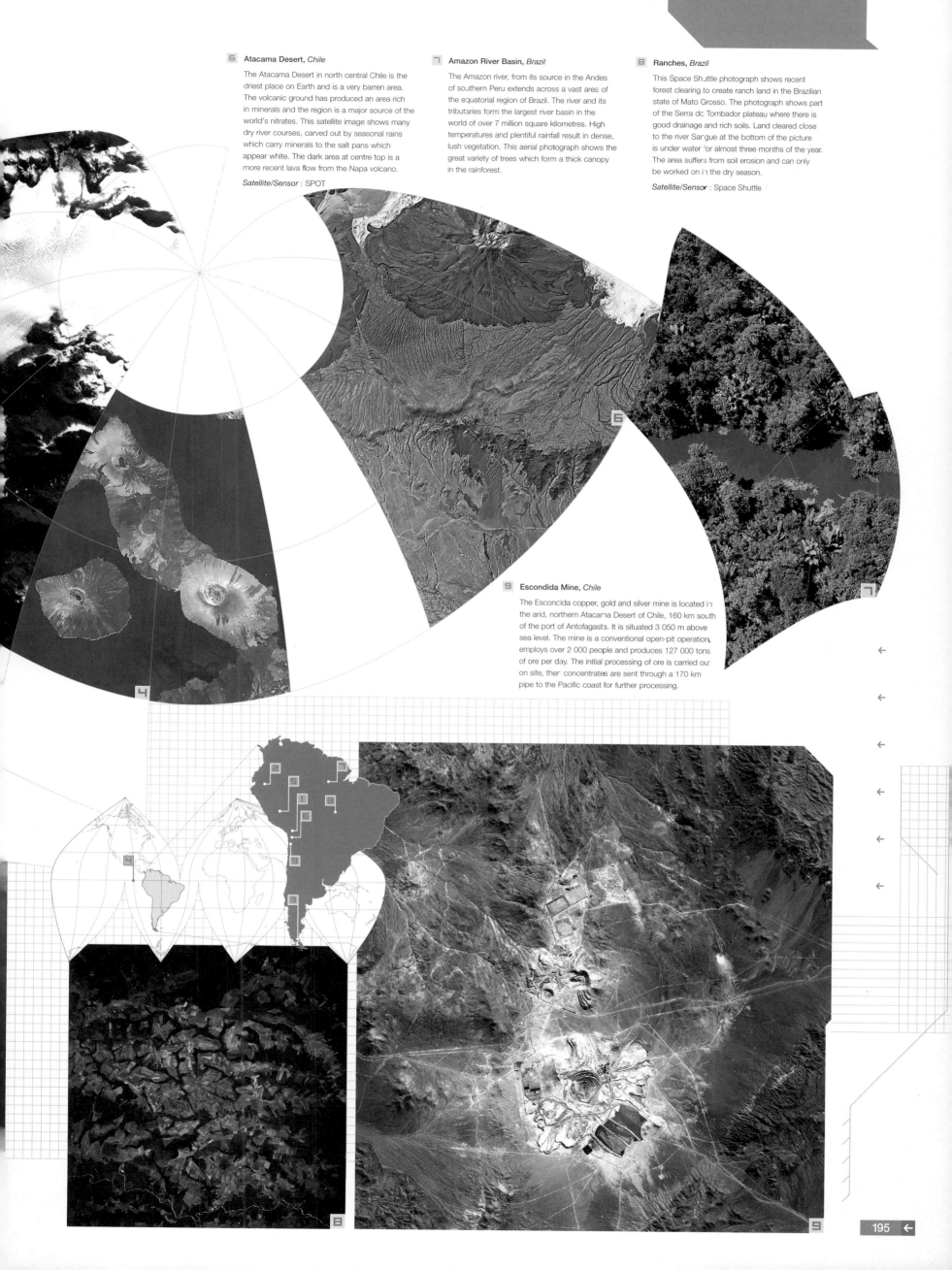

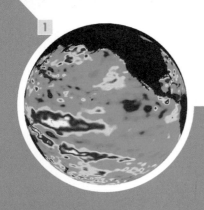
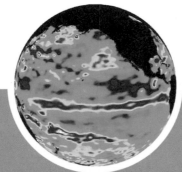
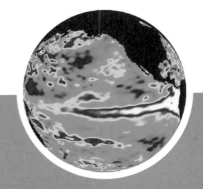
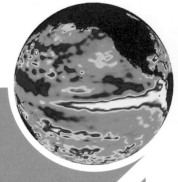

1

1 El Niño, *South America*

Periodically, atmospheric pressure becomes abnormally low in the middle of the Pacific Ocean and abnormally high over northern Australia. This results in the prevailing easterly winds weakening and changing direction. As a result, water off the west coast of South America becomes warmer by 4°–5°C. This phenomenon, known as El Niño, can have a dramatic effect on the world's climate, including higher rainfall in east Africa, and much lower rainfall and higher temperatures than normal in Australia.

The satellite images of the Earth show the development of El Niño during 1997. The red/white areas represent El Niño moving eastwards across the Pacific Ocean. The impacts of this on South America were drier conditions along the north coast, higher temperatures on the east and more rain in the northwest and southeast. The area most severely affected was the northwest coast. High river levels and flash floods were frequent and mudslides destroyed villages. Over 30 000 homes were lost in Peru during the course of the 1997–1998 El Niño event.

Satellite/Sensor : TOPEX/Poseidon

2 Mining, *South America*

The mineral distribution map of South America (Fig. #01) shows the great concentration of copper mining along the Andes mountain range. Large quantities of bauxite, the main ore for the production of aluminium, are mined in those areas with a tropical humid climate in the north of the continent. Symbol sizes on the map are proportional to mineral production as a percentage of world production, the largest representing over five per cent. While mining contributes enormously to the overall economy of South America, it also depletes natural resources and damages the environment. The photograph of the Bon Futuro tin mine in the Rondônia region of Brazil (number 7 on the map) shows how landscapes can be scarred by mining activities. Additional impacts can be the displacement of communities and the pollution of rivers and lakes.

Fig. #01
South America minerals

Metallic minerals

- Iron **Fe**
- Copper **Cu**
- Gold **Au**
- Aluminium **Al**
- Manganese **Mn**
- Lead **Pb**, Zinc **Zn**, Silver **Ag**
- Tin **Sn**, Antimony **Sb**
- Nickel **Ni**, Molybdenum **Mo**, Niobium **Nb**, Chromium **Cr**, Tungsten **W**

Industrial (non metallic) minerals

- Phosphate **P**, Borates **B**,
- Fluorspar **F**
- Diamonds **Diam.**

Symbol sizes reflect level of production from less than 1% to over 5% of world production.

Argentina
1 Aguilar, **Pb, Zn, Ag**
2 Bajo de la Alumbrera **Cu, Mo, Au**
3 El Pachon, **Cu, Mo, Au**
4 Northern Provinces, **B**

Bolivia
5 Potosí, Oruro, **Sn, Sb, Pb, Zn, Ag, W**

Brazil
6 Trombetas, **Al**
7 Rondônia, **Sn**
8 Carajás, **Fe**
9 Igarapé Azul, Carajás, **Mn**
10 Caraíba, **Cu**
11 Campo Formoso, **Cr**
12 Cana Brava, **Cr**
13 Niquelândia, **Ni**
14 Morro do Niquel, **Ni**
15 Tocantins, **Ni**
16 Urucum, **Mn, Fe**
17 Vazante, **Pb, Zn**
18 Boquira, **Pb, Zn**
19 Jequitinhonha, **Diam.**
20 Araxá, **Nb, P**
21 Morro Velho, **Au**
22 Iron Quadrilateral, **Fe**
23 Morro da Fumaça, **F**
24 Roraima, **Diam.**

Chile
25 Chuquicamata, **Abra, Cu, Mo**
26 Escondida, El Salvador, **Cu, Mo, Au**
27 Disputada, Ancina, Pelambres, **Cu, Mo**
28 El Teniente, **Cu, Mc**
29 Cerro Colorado, Quebrada Blanca, **Cu, Mo**
30 La Candelaria, **Cu, Mo, Au**
31 Atacama, **Fe**

Colombia
32 Titiribi, **Au**
33 Cerro Matoso, **Ni**

Ecuador
34 Portovelo, **Au**

Guyana
35 Guyana, **Al**
36 Omai, **Au**

Peru
37 Northern Peru, **Pb, Zn, Ag, Cu, Mo**
38 Cerro de Pasco, central Peru, **Pb, Zn, Ag, Cu, Mo**
39 Cuajone, Toquepala, **Cu, Mo**
40 Tintaya, **Cu, Mo**
41 Cerro Verde, **Cu, Mo**
42 Marcona, **Fe**
43 Yanacocha, **Au**

Suriname
44 Suriname, **Al**

Venezuela
45 Cedeno, **Al**
46 Cerro Bolivar, San Isidro, **Fe**
47 Cristinas, **Au, Cu**

2

Deforestation, *Bolivia*

The two Landsat satellite images below were produced fifteen years apart. The upper image shows an area of tropical rainforest near the Bolivian city of Santa Cruz in 1984. The Piray river is the dark blue line in the bottom left of the image. Forest and natural vegetation appears as green, bare ground as red. The lower image, dated 1998, demonstrates the impact of deforestation in the region. Huge areas of the forest east of the river have been completely cleared for agriculture, in a similar way to that shown in the aerial photograph. Destruction of the rainforest is a major environmental issue and interrupting the forest canopy in this way causes humidity to drop rapidly and huge areas of forest become vulnerable to fire.

Satellite/Sensor : Landsat

CONNECTIONS

► subject	page#
► World climate and weather	16–17
► World land cover types	18–19
► World changes	20–21
► South America landscapes	190–191
► South America countries	192–193
► South America contrasts	194–195

8°S-14°N / 51°-82°W

Administrative regions
numbered on the map:
COLOMBIA
1. QUINDÍO (C3)
2. RISARALDA (C3)
3. SANTAFÉ DE BOGOTÁ (C3)
ECUADOR
4. BOLÍVAR (B5)
5. CHIMBORAZO (B5)
6. TUNGURAHUA (B5)
7. ZAMORA-CHINCHIPE (B5)

>6000m
5000-6000m
4000-5000m
3000-4000m
2000-3000m
1000-2000m
500-1000m
200-500m
0-200m
<0m

0-200m
200-500m
500-1000m
1000-2000m
2000-3000m
3000-4000m
4000-5000m
5000-6000m
>6000m

PACIFIC

OCEAN

Caribbean

Lesser

PANAMA

COLOMBIA

ECUADOR

PERU

Gulf of
Panama

Golfo de
Guayaquil

6°-28°S / 48°-80°W

1

2

3

4

5

6

>6000m
5000-6000m
4000-5000m
3000-4000m
2000-3000m
1000-2000m
500-1000m
200-500m
0-200m
<0m

0-200m
200-500m
500-1000m
1000-2000m
2000-3000m
3000-4000m
4000-5000m
5000-6000m
>6000m

→ 200

PACIFIC

OCEAN

Tropic of Capricorn

CONNECTIONS

▶ subject   page#

▶ World cities   24–25
▶ South America landscapes   190–191
▶ South America countries   192–193
▶ South America contrasts   194–195
▶ South America impacts   196–197

PERU

CHILE

BOLIVIA

AMAZONAS

LORETO

SAN MARTIN

UCAYALI

ACRE

PANDO

MADRE DE DIOS

CUSCO

PUNO

LA PAZ

BENI

COCHABAMBA

ANCASH

HUANUCO

PASCO

JUNIN

LIMA

HUANCAVELICA

AYACUCHO

APURIMAC

AREQUIPA

MOQUEGUA

TACNA

ORURO

POTOSI

SUCRE

TARAPACA

ANTOFAGASTA

ATACAMA

CATAMARCA

CAJAMARCA

LA LIBERTAD

LIMA

LA PAZ

Lake Titicaca

Salar de Uyuni

Cruzeiro do Sul

Pucallpa

Rio Branco

Arequipa

Tacna

Arica

Iquique

Tocopilla

Antofagasta

Chimbote

Huaraz

Trujillo

Callao

Chincha Alta

Pisco

Ica

Nazca

Cusco

Puno

Juliaca

Oruro

Calama

Copiapó

Chañaral

southamerica[map3]

CONNECTIONS

subject	page#
► World countries	10–11
▲ World population distribution	22–23
▲ World cities	24–25
▲ South America countries	192–193
▲ Atlantic Ocean	216–217

ATLANTIC

OCEAN

Rio de Janeiro

MINAS GERAIS

Planalto do Brasil

SÃO PAULO

PARANÁ

MATO GROSSO DO SUL

RIO GRANDE DO SUL

PARAGUAY

ARGENTINA

MISIONES

200–201

204–205

>6000m
5000–6000m
4000–5000m
3000–4000m
2000–3000m
1000–2000m
500–1000m
200–500m
0–200m
<0m

0–200m
200–500m
500–1000m
1000–2000m
2000–3000m
3000–4000m
4000–5000m
5000–6000m
>6000m

miles
km

southamerica[map4]

South Georgia (U.K.)

1:8 000 000

24°–56°S / 48°–80°W

Lambert Azimuthal Equal Area Projection

15°-24°S / 38°-53°W

202-203

Elevation legend (above sea level):
- >6000m
- 5000-6000m
- 4000-5000m
- 3000-4000m
- 2000-3000m
- 1500-2000m
- 1000-1500m
- 500-1000m
- 200-500m
- 100-200m
- 0-100m
- <0m

Elevation legend (below sea level):
- 0-200m
- 200-500m
- 500-1000m
- 1000-2000m
- 2000-3000m
- 3000-4000m
- 4000-5000m
- 5000-6000m
- >6000m

202-203

Tropic of Capricorn

ATLANTIC

OCEAN

miles
1:3 300 000

km

Conic Equidistant Projection

Paradise Bay, *Antarctica*

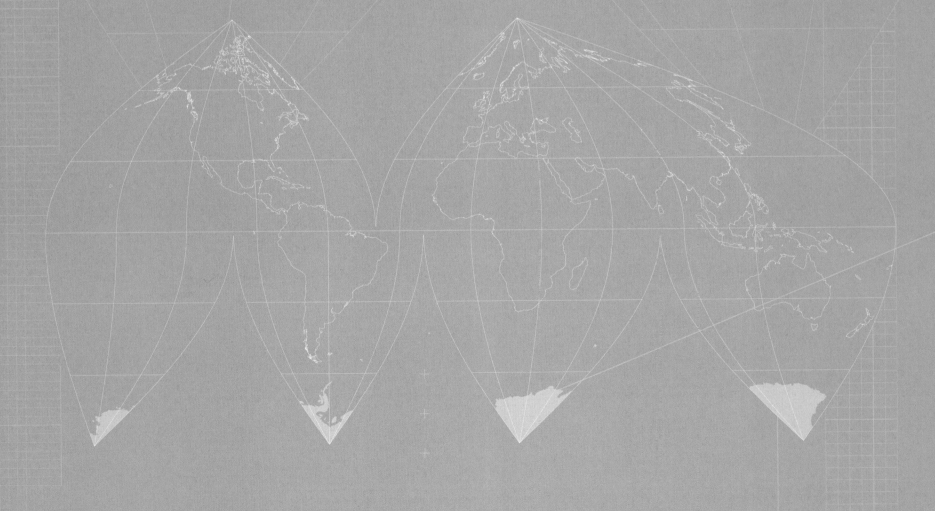

oceansandpoles

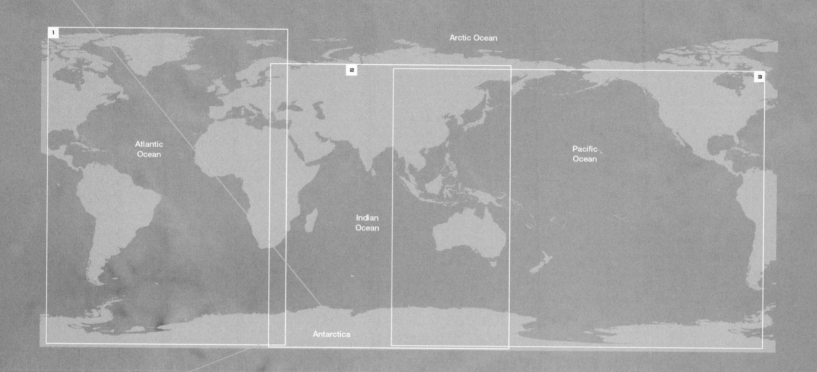

Arctic Ocean

Atlantic
Ocean

Indian
Ocean

Pacific
Ocean

Antarctica

[contents]

		page#
oceans [features]		210–211
antarctica [features]		212–213
thearctic [features]		214–215

	map coverage	scale	page#
oceans [map1]	ATLANTIC OCEAN	1:40 000 000	216–217
oceans [map 2]	INDIAN OCEAN	1:40 000 000	218–219
oceans [map 3]	PACIFIC OCEAN	1:45 000 000	220–221
antarctica [map 1]	ANTARCTICA	1:18 000 000	222–223
thearctic [map 1]	ARCTIC OCEAN	1:24 000 000	224

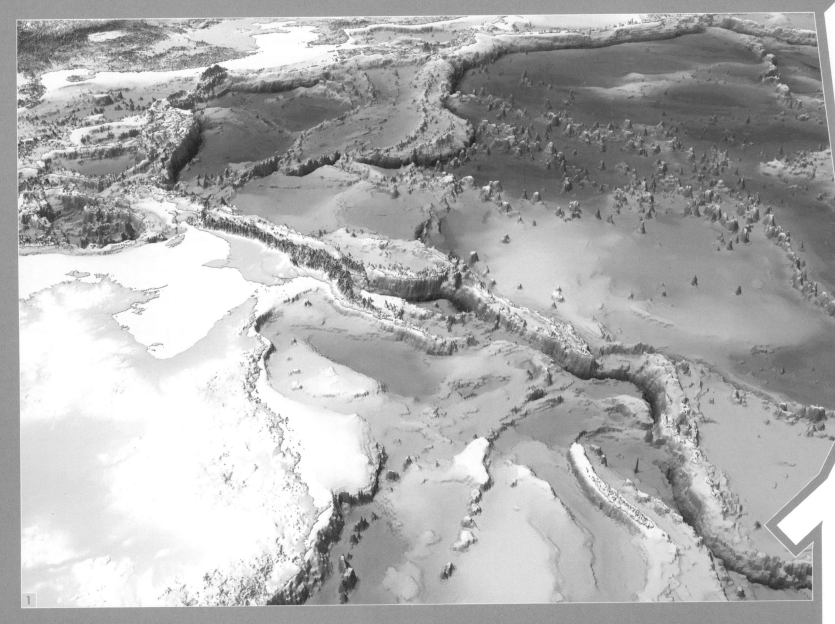

1

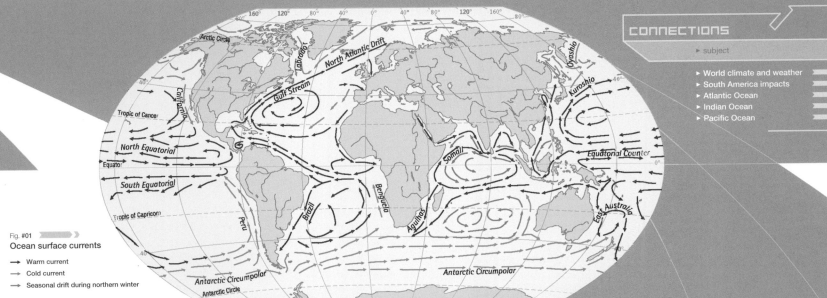

CONNECTIONS

► subject | page#

► World climate and weather | 16–17
► South America impacts | 196–197
► Atlantic Ocean | 216–217
► Indian Ocean | 218–219
► Pacific Ocean | 220–221

Fig. #01
Ocean surface currents

→ Warm current
→ Cold current
→ Seasonal drift during northern winter

Arctic Circle
North Atlantic Drift
Labrador
Gulf Stream
California
Kuroshio
Oyashio
Tropic of Cancer
North Equatorial
Equatorial Counter
Equator
South Equatorial
Somali
Tropic of Capricorn
Peru
Brazil
Benguela
Agulhas
East Australia
Antarctic Circumpolar
Antarctic Circumpolar
Antarctic Circle

Fig. #02
Sea surface height

Fig. #01–#02 Sea surface currents and height

Most of the Earth's incoming solar radiation is absorbed by the surface waters of the oceans. The resultant warming is greatest around the equator and ocean surface currents, as shown on the map above (Fig. #01), redistribute the heat around the globe. They are influenced by winds, by density gradients caused by variations in temperature and salinity, and by the Earth's rotation which tends to deflect currents to the right in the northern hemisphere and to the left in the southern hemisphere. The circulation of ocean currents is a major influence on the world's climate. Sea surface circulation is reflected in variations in sea surface height (Fig. #02) which can vary greatly across currents. Currents flow along the slopes and are strongest where the slopes are steepest.

Satellite/Sensor : TOPEX/POSEIDON

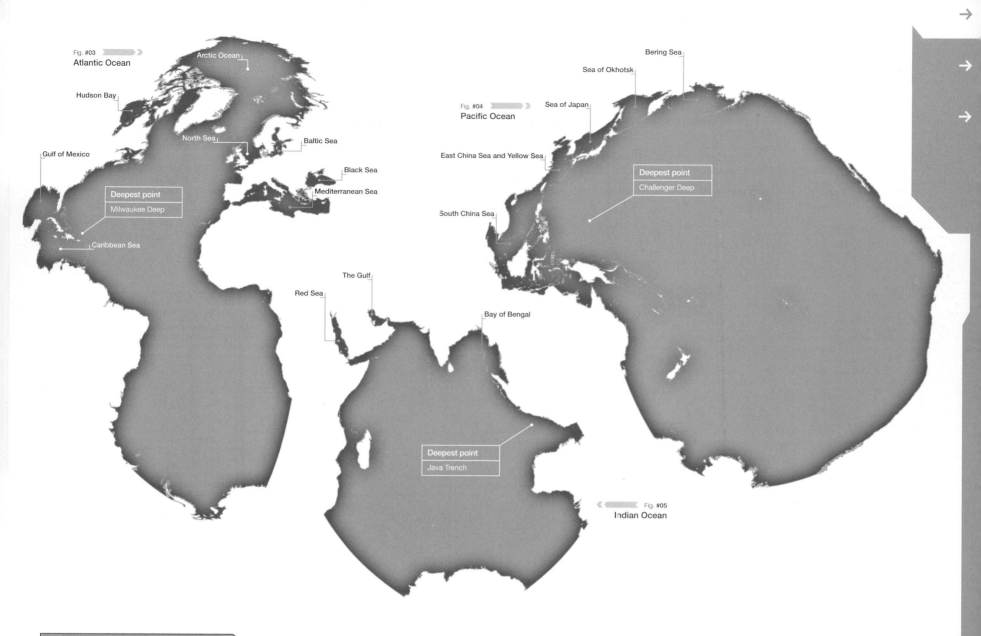

Fig. #03 → Atlantic Ocean

Arctic Ocean
Hudson Bay
North Sea
Baltic Sea
Gulf of Mexico
Black Sea
Mediterranean Sea
Deepest point — Milwaukee Deep
Caribbean Sea

Bering Sea
Sea of Okhotsk
Sea of Japan
Fig. #04 → Pacific Ocean
East China Sea and Yellow Sea
Deepest point — Challenger Deep
South China Sea

The Gulf
Red Sea
Bay of Bengal
Deepest point — Java Trench
← Fig. #05 Indian Ocean

OCEANS

ATLANTIC OCEAN	area sq km	area sq miles	maximum depth metres	maximum depth feet
Atlantic Ocean	86 557 000	33 420 000	8 605	28 231
Arctic Ocean	9 485 000	3 662 000	5 450	17 880
Caribbean Sea	2 512 000	970 000	7 680	25 196
Mediterranean Sea	2 510 000	969 000	5 121	16 800
Gulf of Mexico	1 544 000	596 000	3 504	11 495
Hudson Bay	1 233 000	476 000	259	849
North Sea	575 000	222 000	661	2 168
Black Sea	508 000	196 000	2 245	7 365
Baltic Sea	382 000	147 000	460	1 509

INDIAN OCEAN	area sq km	area sq miles	maximum depth metres	maximum depth feet
Indian Ocean	73 427 000	28 350 000	7 125	23 376
Bay of Bengal	2 172 000	839 000	4 500	14 763
Red Sea	453 000	175 000	3 040	9 973
The Gulf	238 000	92 000	73	239

PACIFIC OCEAN	area sq km	area sq miles	maximum depth metres	maximum depth feet
Pacific Ocean	166 241 000	64 186 000	10 920	35 826
South China Sea	2 590 000	1 000 000	5 514	18 090
Bering Sea	2 261 000	873 000	4 150	13 615
Sea of Okhotsk (Okhotskoye More)	1 392 000	537 000	3 363	11 033
East China Sea (Dong Hai) and Yellow Sea (Huang Hai)	1 202 000	464 000	2 717	8 913
Sea of Japan (East Sea)	1 013 000	391 000	3 743	12 280

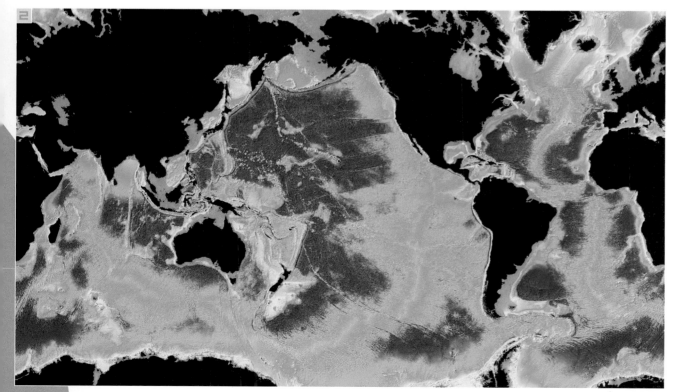

1 Perspective View, Pacific Ocean

This 3-D perspective view shows the sea trenches, ridges and basins of the western side of the Pacific Ocean. The image has been generated using sea depth values and extends from Australia and Melanesia at the bottom to Japan and the Kamchatka Peninsula at the top. Severe variations in depth of the sea bed are clearly seen. Deep trenches are shown by the darker areas. The New Hebrides, South Solomon and New Britain Trenches are visible at the bottom of the image and the Mariana Trench, the world's deepest, in the upper centre.

2 Global Seafloor Topography

This image has been produced from a combination of shipboard depth soundings and gravity data derived from satellite altimetry from the ERS-1 and Geosat satellites. The range of colours represents different depths of the ocean – from orange and yellow on the shallow continental shelves to dark blues in the deepest ocean trenches. The heavily fractured mid-ocean ridges (ranging from green to yellow) are particularly prominent.

antarctica[features]

ANTARCTICA		
HIGHEST MOUNTAINS		
	m	ft
Vinson Massif	4 897	16 066
Mt Tyree	4 852	15 918
Mt Kirkpatrick	4 528	14 855
Mt Markham	4 351	14 275
Mt Jackson	4 190	13 747
Mt Sidley	4 181	13 717
AREA		
	sq km	sq miles
Total land area (excluding ice shelves)	12 093 000	4 669 292
Ice shelves	1 559 000	601 954
Exposed rock	49 000	18 920
HEIGHTS		
	m	ft
Lowest bedrock elevation (Bentley Subglacial Trench)	-2 496	-8 189
Maximum ice thickness (Astrolabe Subglacial Basin)	4 776	15 669
Mean ice thickness (including ice shelves)	1 859	6 099
VOLUME		
	cubic km	cubic miles
Ice sheet (including ice shelves)	25 400 000	10 160 000
CLIMATE		
	°C	°F
Lowest screen temperature (Vostok Station, 21st July 1983)	-89.2	-128.6
Coldest place – Annual mean (Plateau Station)	-56.6	-69.9

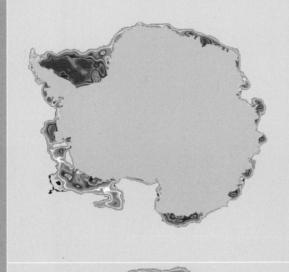

1 Ozone Depletion

Since the 1970s, measurements have shown a thinning of the protective ozone layer in the Earth's atmosphere and the appearance of an ozone 'hole' over Antarctica. A major cause of this appears to be emissions of CFCs chlorofluorocarbons (CFCs) and halon gasses. This image from the Total Ozone Mapping Spectrometer (TOMS) sensor shows the ozone hole (blue) at its maximum extent of 11 million square miles in 2000. The unit of measurement for Ozone is the Dobson Unit (DU) with 300 being an average figure. In the image, yellow and orange represent high levels of 300–340DU, and dark blue low levels of 100–200 DU.

Satellite/Sensor : TOMS

2 Sea Ice Concentration

These images have been derived from data collected by the Special Sensor Microwave Imager (SSM/I) carried on US Department of Defense meteorological satellites. The colours represent ice concentration, ranging from the purple and red areas with a concentration of over 80 per cent, through to the green and yellow areas with concentrations between 20 and 40 per cent. The top image shows the ice at its lowest 2000 level in February, towards the end of the Antarctic summer. Ice builds up through the winter and by September (bottom), the ice is at its most extensive. In places the sea is frozen to a distance of over 1 000 km from the land.

Satellite/Sensor : SSM/I

3 Larsen Ice Shelf

This satellite image shows the edge of the Larsen Ice Shelf on the eastern side of the Antarctic Peninsula, and icebergs which have split, or 'calved' from the shelf. Ice shelves, which account for about 2 per cent of all Antarctic ice, typically undergo cycles of advance and retreat over many decades. Warmer surface temperatures over just a few months can cause an ice shelf to splinter and may prime it for a major collapse. This process can be expected to become more widespread if global, and particularly Antarctic summer, temperatures increase.

Satellite/Sensor : Landsat

4 Ice Sheet Thickness

Antarctica is covered by a permanent ice sheet that is in places more that 4 500 m thick. This map shows the thickness of ice, with the orange/red areas representing ice over 3 000 m thick. The thinnest ice is around the coast and on the high mountains, represented by the blue areas. The cross-section shows the ice cap (pale blue) in relation to the bedrock of Antarctica. This clearly shows that the thickest ice occurs above the deep glacial trenches, where the bedrock lies well below sea level.

5 Radar Image of Antarctica

This image of the whole of Antarctica is derived from data gathered by the Canadian RADARSAT satellite. In the image, light and dark areas represent relative measurements of radar reflectivity. Areas of finely powdered snow and smooth ice with few imperfections tend not to scatter radar waves projected against it, hence they appear dark. Irregular surfaces such as old, pitted ice, rock slides, and crevasses scatter the radar beam, giving a strong radar signal and thus appearing bright. Images such as this are valuable tools in the study of ice flow and stability on the continent.

Satellite/Sensor : RADARSAT

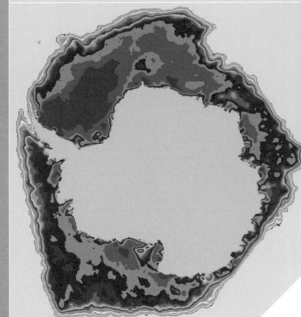
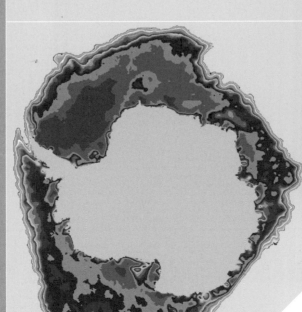

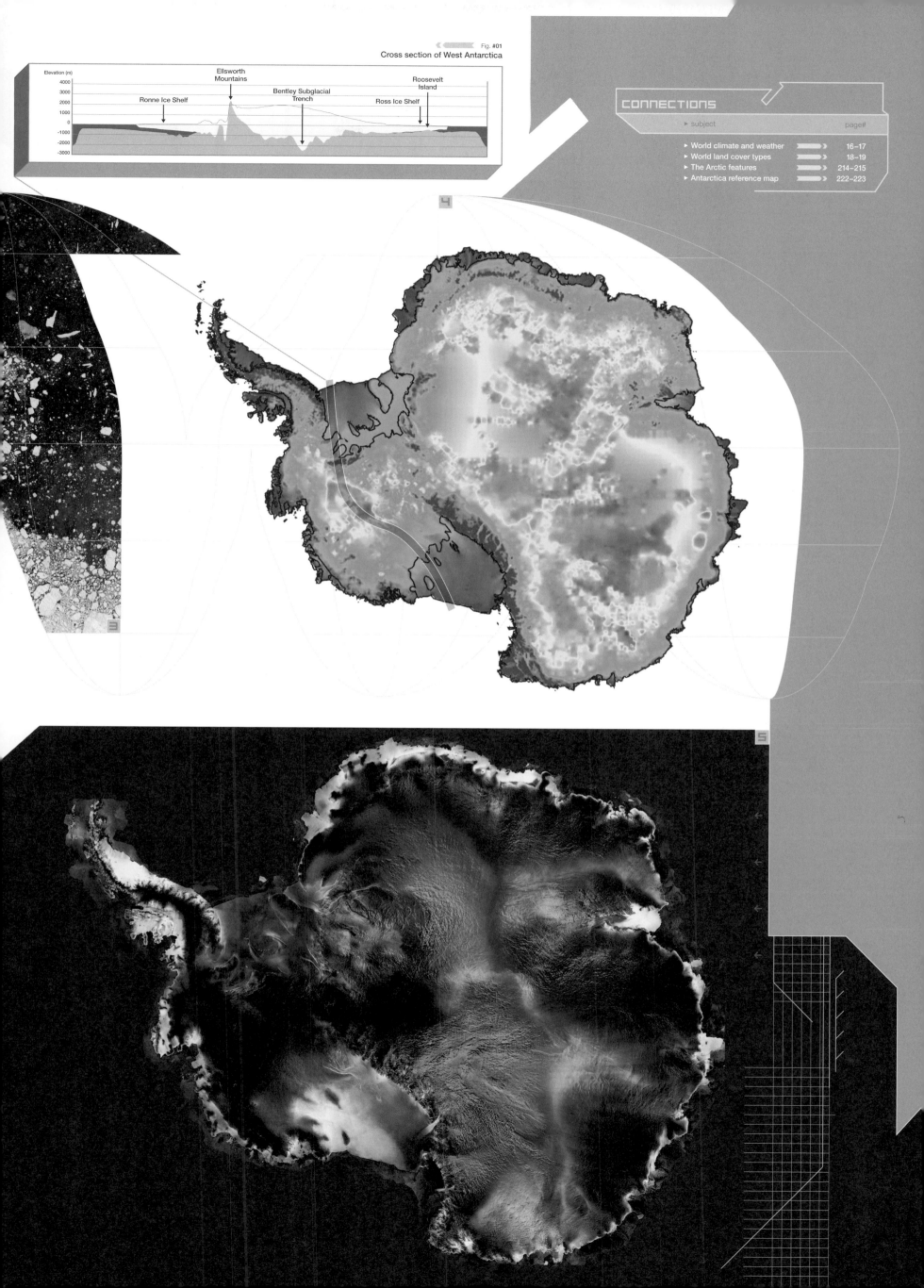

Fig. #01
Cross section of West Antarctica

Elevation (m)
4000
3000
2000
1000
0
-1000
-2000
-3000

Ellsworth
Mountains

Bentley Subglacial
Trench

Roosevelt
Island

Ronne Ice Shelf

Ross Ice Shelf

4

3

5

thearctic[features]

1

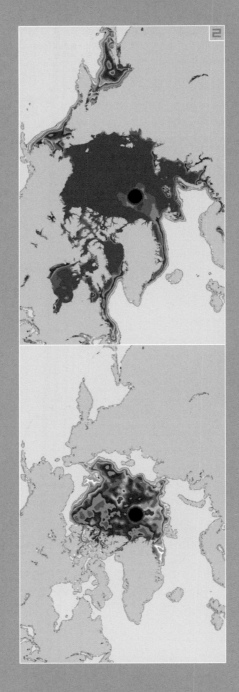

2

1 Tundra Landscape

Lakes and meandering rivers in a tundra landscape are shown in this photograph, taken in the short Arctic summer. Tundra is a cold-climate landscape type characterized by very low winter temperatures and short, cool summers. It is found in the region between 60°N and the Arctic ice cap and also at high altitudes beyond the climatic limits of tree growth. Tundra vegetation consists of dwarf shrubs, low herbaceous plants, lichens and mosses, on a permanently frozen subsoil.

2 Sea Ice Concentration

Although much of the Arctic Ocean is constantly frozen, there are wide variations in the amount of sea ice throughout the year, as shown by these images from the Special Sensor Microwave Imager (SSM/I). The purple areas show almost completely frozen sea (over ninety six per cent concentration) which extends as far south as Hudson Bay, Canada in February (top). By the end of the summer most of this ice has melted, as seen in the September image (bottom). The remaining sea ice at this time is thinner and more fragmented, even near the North Pole. Pink and brown areas represent concentrations of between sixty and eighty per cent.

Satellite/Sensor : SSM/I

Fig. #01
Peoples of the Arctic

The Arctic regions of Alaska, northern Canada, Greenland, and northern Scandinavia and Russian Federation contain the homelands of a diverse range of indigenous peoples. The main groups are shown on this map. These native peoples have subsisted for thousands of years on the resources of land and sea, as hunters, fishermen and reindeer herders. More recently, conflicts have arisen with governments eager to exploit the rich natural resources of the Arctic. There have also been moves towards greater autonomy for such groups. Most notably, in 1992 the Tungavik Federation of Nunavut and the government of Canada signed an agreement which addressed Inuit land claims and harvesting rights and established the new territory of Nunavut.

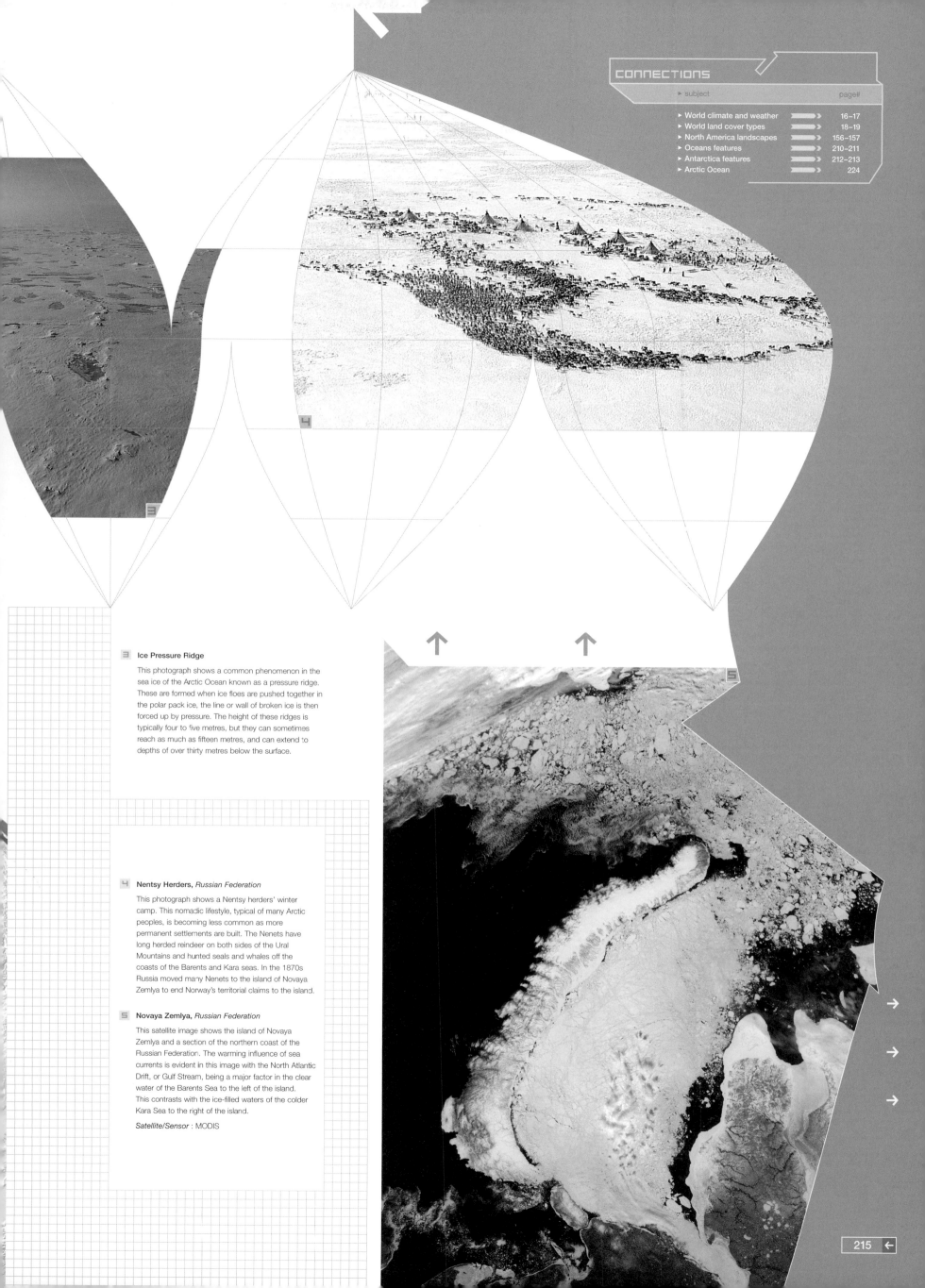

CONNECTIONS

▶ subject   page#

▶ World climate and weather   ▬▬▶   16–17
▶ World land cover types   ▬▬▶   18–19
▶ North America landscapes   ▬▬▶   156–157
▶ Oceans features   ▬▬▶   210–211
▶ Antarctica features   ▬▬▶   212–213
▶ Arctic Ocean   ▬▬▶   224

∃ Ice Pressure Ridge

This photograph shows a common phenomenon in the sea ice of the Arctic Ocean known as a pressure ridge. These are formed when ice floes are pushed together in the polar pack ice, the line or wall of broken ice is then forced up by pressure. The height of these ridges is typically four to five metres, but they can sometimes reach as much as fifteen metres, and can extend to depths of over thirty metres below the surface.

४ Nentsy Herders, *Russian Federation*

This photograph shows a Nentsy herders' winter camp. This nomadic lifestyle, typical of many Arctic peoples, is becoming less common as more permanent settlements are built. The Nenets have long herded reindeer on both sides of the Ural Mountains and hunted seals and whales off the coasts of the Barents and Kara seas. In the 1870s Russia moved many Nenets to the island of Novaya Zemlya to end Norway's territorial claims to the island.

५ Novaya Zemlya, *Russian Federation*

This satellite image shows the island of Novaya Zemlya and a section of the northern coast of the Russian Federation. The warming influence of sea currents is evident in this image with the North Atlantic Drift, or Gulf Stream, being a major factor in the clear water of the Barents Sea to the left of the island. This contrasts with the ice-filled waters of the colder Kara Sea to the right of the island.

Satellite/Sensor : MODIS

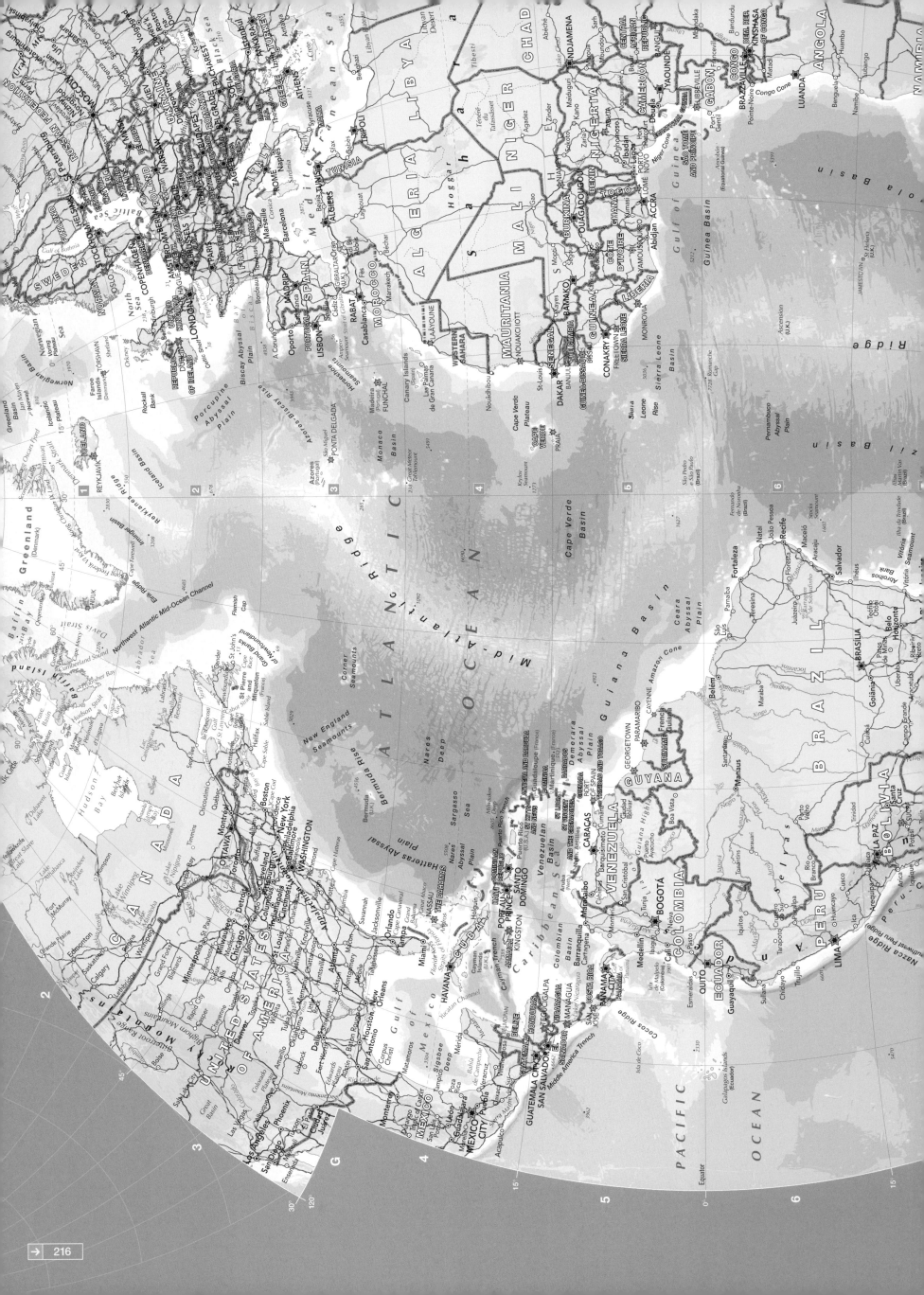

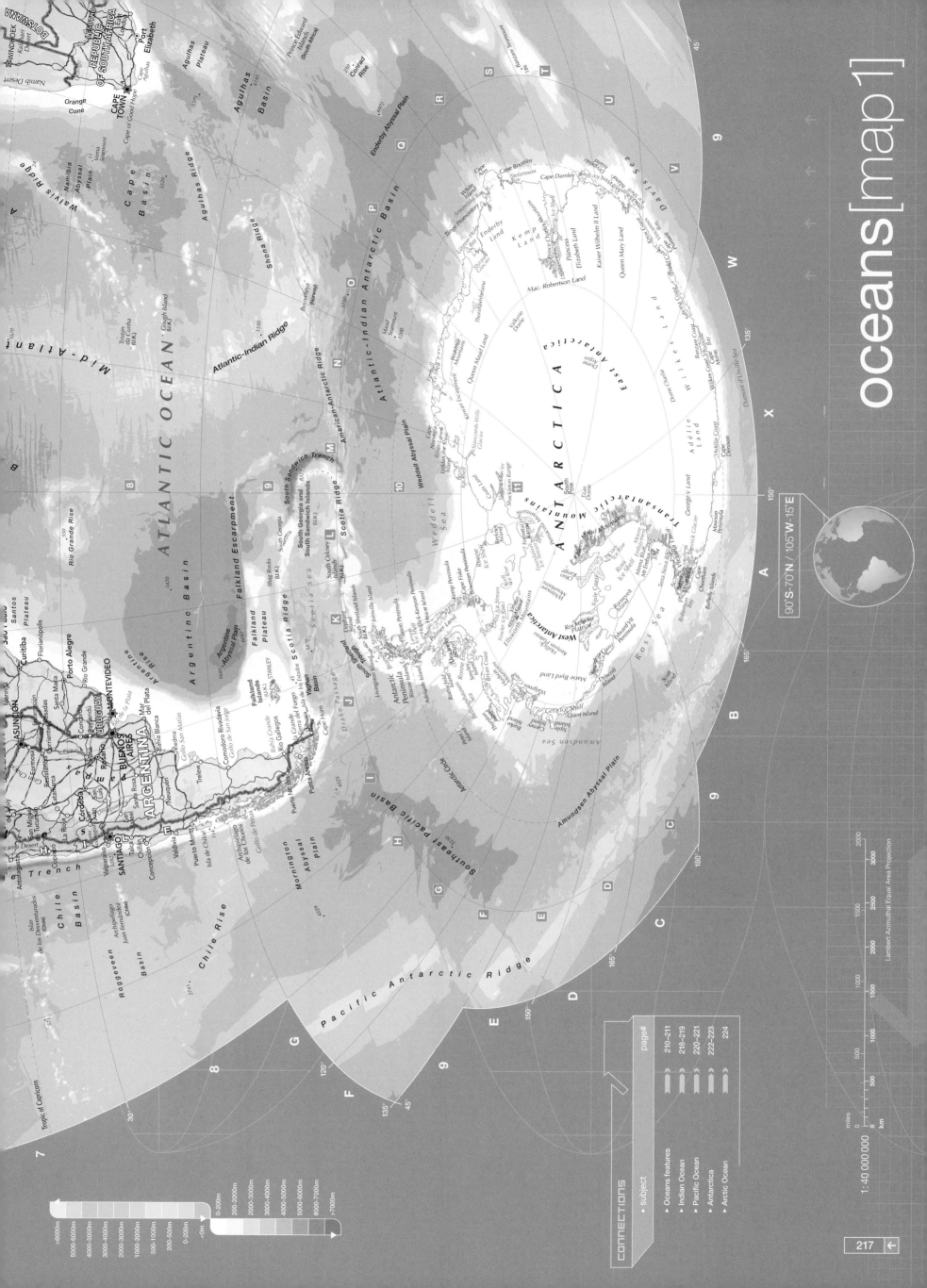

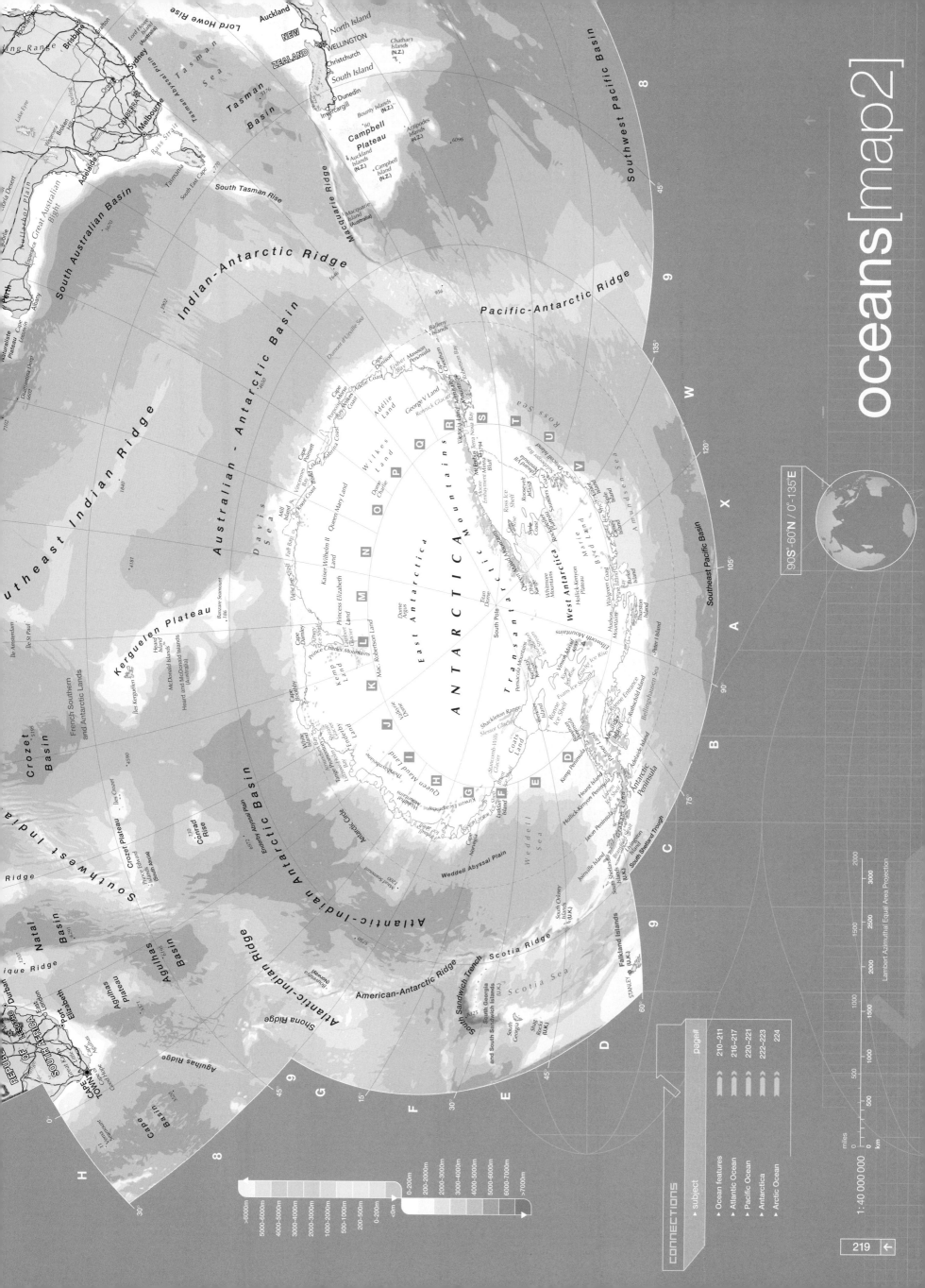

antarctica[map1]

50°-90°**S** / 0°-180°-0°

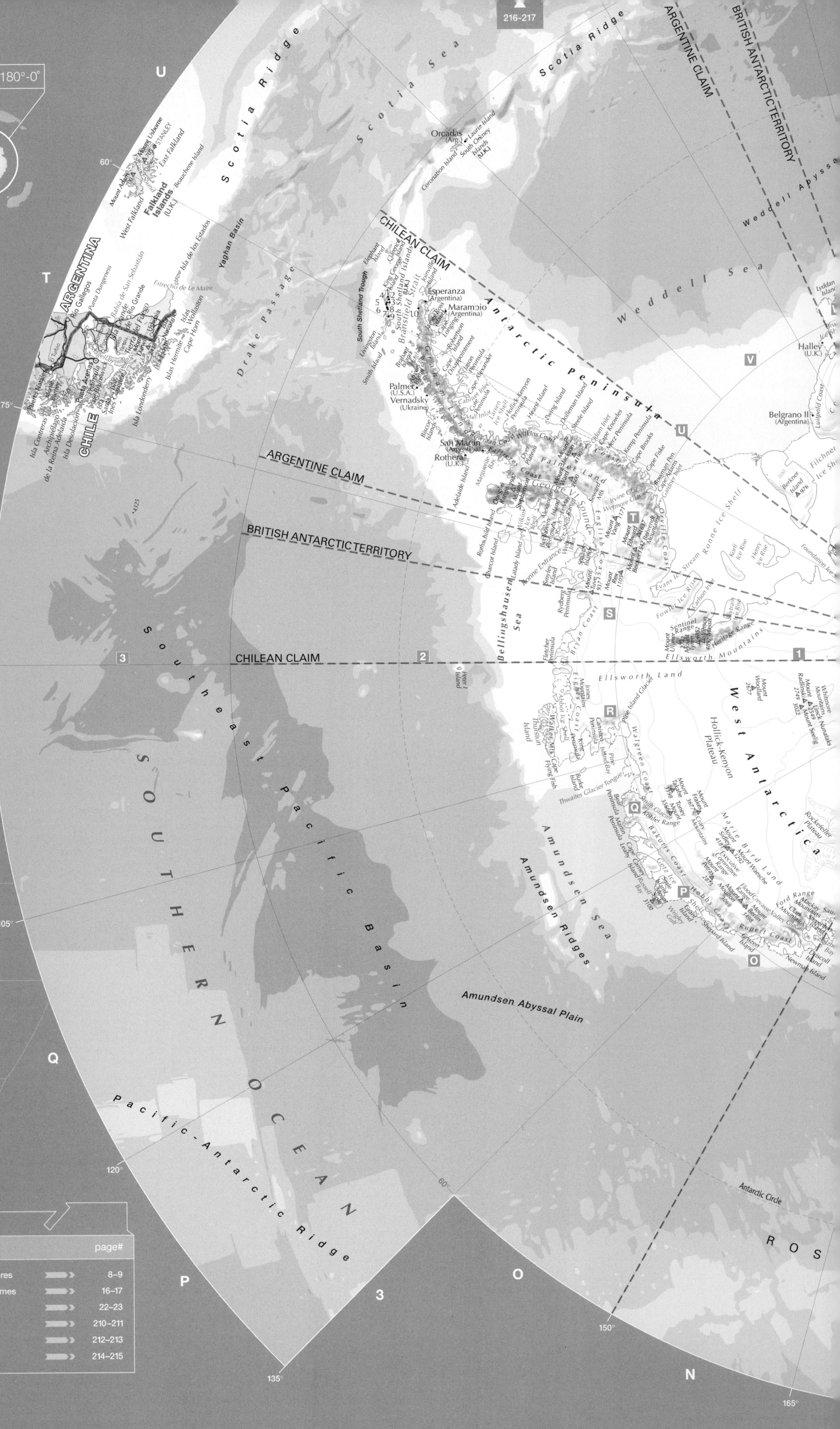

ARGENTINE CLAIM

BRITISH ANTARCTIC TERRITORY

Scotia Ridge

Scotia Sea

Scotia Ridge

Weddell Abyssal

Weddell Sea

Orcadas (Arg.)
Laurie Island
South Orkney
Coronation Island
Islands (U.K.)

Mount Usborne
West Falkland
Mount Adam
East Falkland
Beauchene Island
Falkland Islands (U.K.)

60°

CHILEAN CLAIM

Elephant Island
Clarence Island
King George Island
Esperanza (Argentina)
Marambio (Argentina)
South Shetland Islands (U.K.)
Livingston Island
Brabant Island
Anvers Island
Palmer (U.S.A.)
Vernadsky (Ukraine)
Bransfield Strait

Antarctic Peninsula

Lyddan Island

Halley (U.K.)

Belgrano II (Argentina)

Luitpold Coast

Berkner Island

Filchner Ice Shelf

Yaghan Basin

ARGENTINA
Río Gallegos
Isla de San Sebastián
Punta Dungeness
Bahía de San Sebastián
Río Grande
Tierra del Fuego
Ushuaia
CHILE
Punta Arenas
Isla Contreras
Archipiélago de la Reina Adelaida
Isla Desolación
Islas Hermite
Cape Horn
Islas Wollaston
Islas Londonderry

60°
75°

Estrecho de Le Maire
Isla de los Estados

Drake Passage

South Shetland Trough

San Martín (Argentina)
Rothera (U.K.)
Adelaide Island
Alexander Island
George VI Sound
Palmer Land
Wilkins Coast
Wilkins Ice Shelf
Ronne Ice Shelf
Foundation Ice Stream
Henry Ice Rise
Korff Ice Rise
Fowler Ice Rise
Evans Ice Stream

ARGENTINE CLAIM

75°

BRITISH ANTARCTIC TERRITORY

Bellingshausen Sea
Charcot Island
Ellsworth Land
Ellsworth Mountains
Sentinel Range
Heritage Range

CHILEAN CLAIM

90°

Peter I Øy

West Antarctica
Hollick-Kenyon Plateau
Mount Woollard

Southeast Pacific Basin

Thurston Island
Walgreen Coast
Marie Byrd Land
Amundsen Sea
Amundsen Ridges
Kohler Range
Bakutis Coast
Ford Ranges
Rockefeller Plateau
Ruppert Coast
Saunders Coast

S O U T H E R N   O C E A N

105°

Amundsen Abyssal Plain

R O S S

120°

Pacific-Antarctic Ridge

60°

Antarctic Circle

135°

150°

165°

>6000m
5000-6000m
4000-5000m
3000-4000m
2000-3000m
1000-2000m
500-1000m
200-500m
0-200m
<0m

0-200m
200-2000m
2000-3000m
3000-4000m
4000-5000m
5000-6000m
6000-7000m
>7000m

U
T
S
R
Q
P

V
U
T
S
1
R
Q
P
O

2
3

N
O

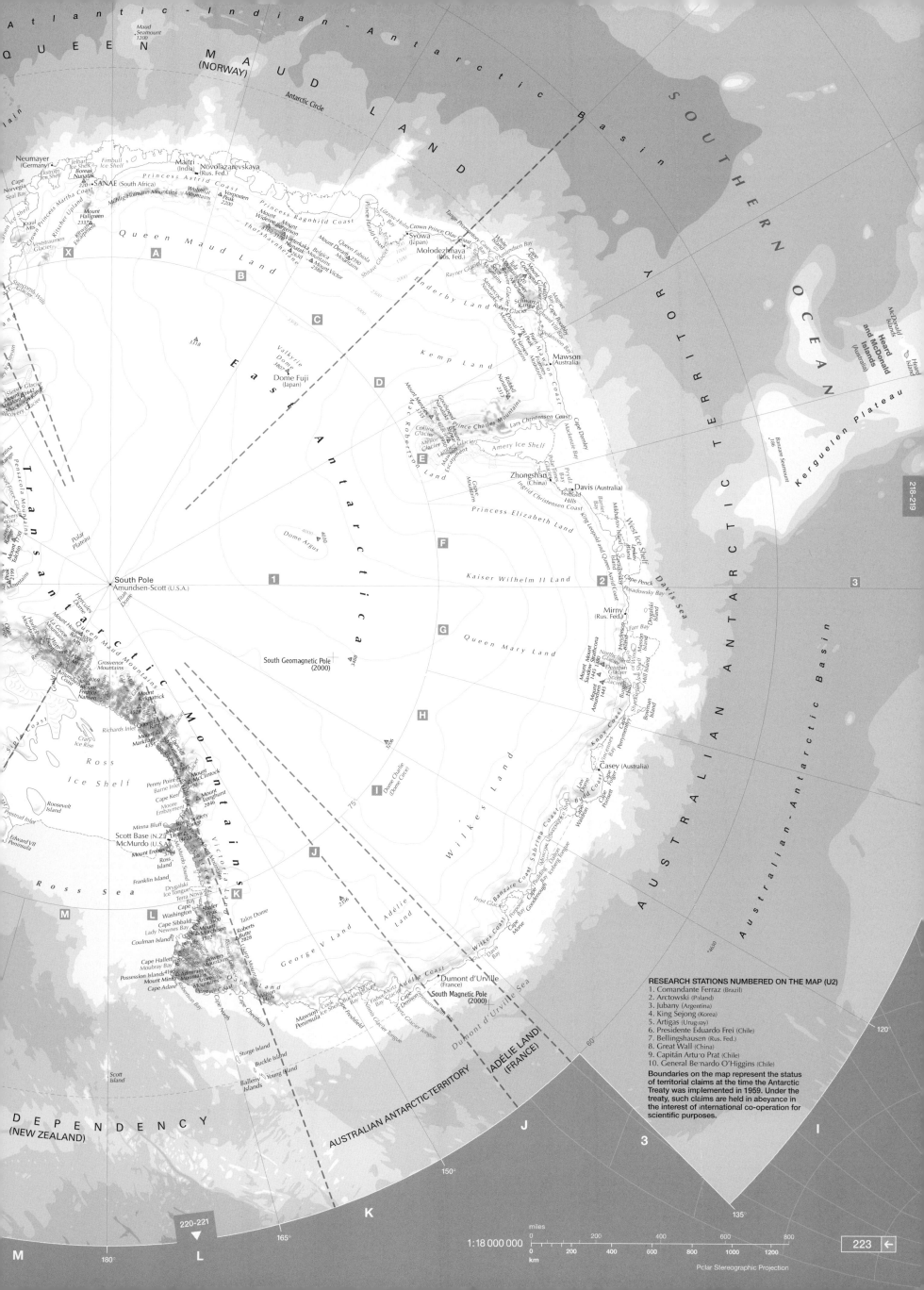

RESEARCH STATIONS NUMBERED ON THE MAP (U2)

1. Comandante Ferraz (Brazil)
2. Arctowski (Poland)
3. Jubany (Argentina)
4. King Sejong (Korea)
5. Artigas (Uruguay)
6. Presidente Eduardo Frei (Chile)
7. Bellingshausen (Rus. Fed.)
8. Great Wall (China)
9. Capitán Arturo Prat (Chile)
10. General Bernardo O'Higgins (Chile)

Boundaries on the map represent the status of territorial claims at the time the Antarctic Treaty was implemented in 1959. Under the treaty, such claims are held in abeyance in the interest of international co-operation for scientific purposes.

1:18 000 000

Polar Stereographic Projection

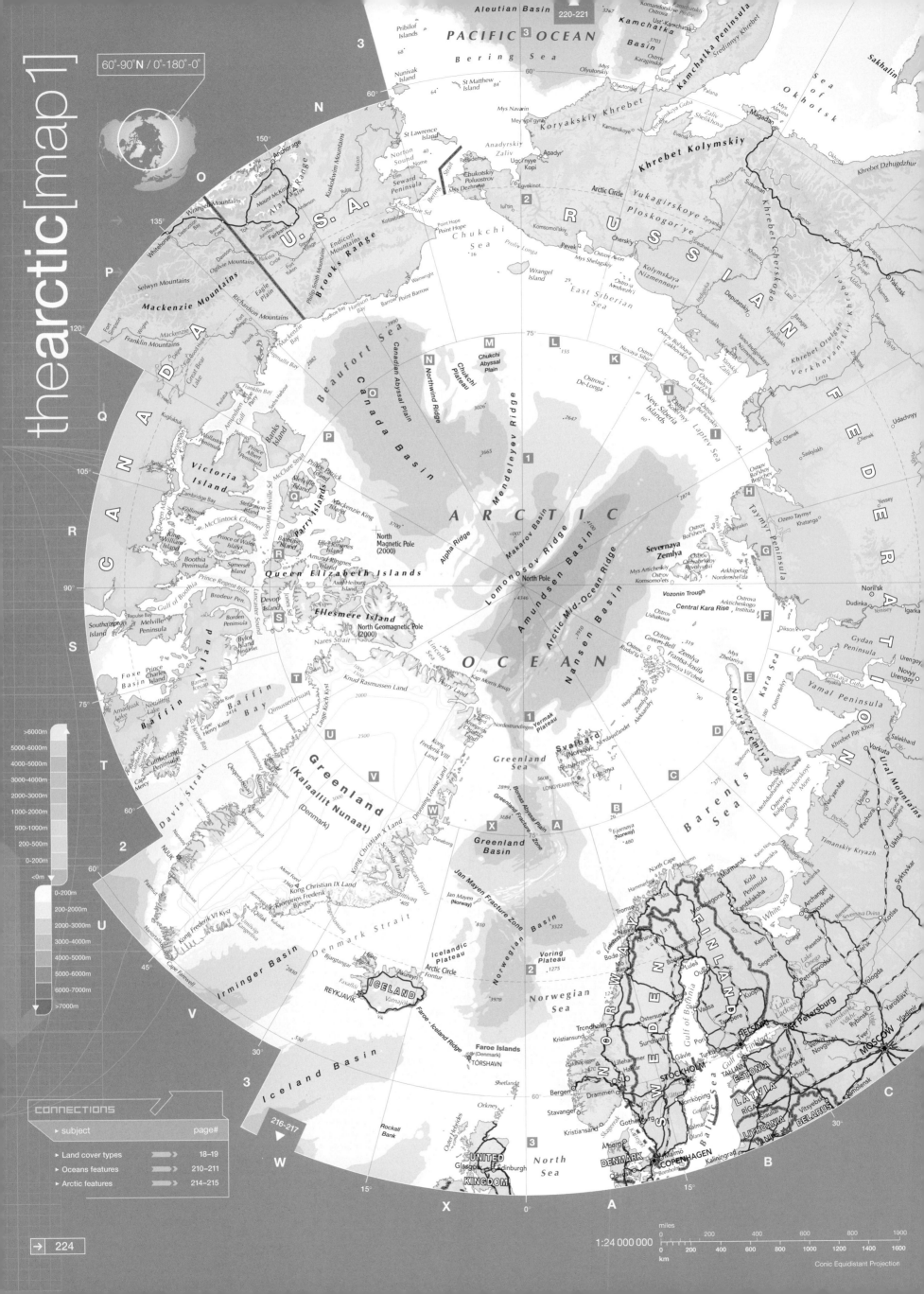

INTRODUCTION TO THE INDEX

The index includes all names shown on the reference maps in the atlas. Each entry includes the country or geographical area in which the feature is located, a page number and an alphanumeric reference. Additional entry details and aspects of the index are explained below.

Referencing

Names are referenced by page number and by grid reference. The grid reference relates to the alphanumeric values which appear in the margin of each map. These reflect the graticule on the map – the letter relates to longitude divisions, the number to latitude divisions.

Names are generally referenced to the largest scale map page on which they appear. For large geographical features, including countries, the reference is to the largest scale map on which the feature appears in its entirety, or on which the majority of it appears.

Rivers are referenced to their lowest downstream point – either their mouth or their confluence with another river. The river name will generally be positioned as close to this point as possible.

Alternative names

Alternative names appear as cross-references and refer the user to the index entry for the form of the name used on the map. Details of alternative names and their types also appear within the main entry. The different types of name form included are: alternative forms or spellings currently in common use; English conventional name forms normally used in English-language contexts; historical and former names; and long and short name forms.

For rivers with multiple names – for example those which flow through several countries – all alternative name forms are included within the main index entries, with details of the countries in which each form applies.

Administrative qualifiers

Administrative divisions are included in an entry to differentiate duplicate names – entries of exactly the same name and feature type within the one country – where these division names are shown on the maps. In such cases, duplicate names are alphabetized in the order of the administrative division names.

Additional qualifiers are included for names within selected geographical areas, to indicate more clearly their location.

Descriptors

Entries, other than those for towns and cities, include a descriptor indicating the type of geographical feature. Descriptors are not included where the type of feature is implicit in the name itself, unless there is a town or city of exactly the same name.

Insets

Where relevant, the index clearly indicates [inset] if a feature appears on an inset map.

Name forms and alphabetical order

Name forms are as they appear on the maps, with additional alternative forms included as cross-references. Names appear in full in the index, although they may appear in abbreviated form on the maps.

The Icelandic characters Þ and þ are transliterated and alphabetized as 'Th' and 'th'. The German character ß is alphabetized as 'ss'. Names beginning with Mac or Mc are alphabetized exactly as they appear. The terms Saint, Sainte, etc, are abbreviated to St, Ste, etc, but alphabetized as if in the full form.

Name form policies are explained in the Introduction to the Atlas (pp 4–5).

Numerical entries

Entries beginning with numerals appear at the beginning of the index, in numerical order. Elsewhere, numerals are alphabetized before 'a'.

Permuted terms

Names beginning with generic, geographical terms are permuted – the descriptive term is placed after, and the index alphabetized by, the main part of the name. For example, Mount Everest is indexed as Everest, Mount; Lake Superior as Superior, Lake. This policy is applied to all languages. Permuting has not been applied to names of towns, cities or administrative divisions beginning with such geographical terms. These remain in their full form, for example, Lake Isabella, USA.

Gazetteer entries and connections

Selected entries have been extended to include gazetteer-style information. Important geographical facts which relate specifically to the entry are included within the entry in coloured type.

Entries for features which also appear on, or which have a topical link to, the thematic pages of the atlas include a connection to those pages indicated by the symbol ▬▶.

Tables

Several tables, ranking geographical features by size, are included within the main index listing. Where possible these have been placed directly below the index entry for the feature ranked 1 in the table.

ABBREVIATIONS

admin. dist.	administrative district	imp. l.	impermanent lake	pref.	prefecture
admin. div.	administrative division	IN	Indiana	prov.	province
admin. reg.	administrative region	Indon.	Indonesia	pt	point
Afgh.	Afghanistan	Kazakh.	Kazakhstan	Qld	Queensland
AK	Alaska	KS	Kansas	Que.	Québec
AL	Alabama	KY	Kentucky	r.	river
Alg.	Algeria	Kyrg.	Kyrgyzstan	r. mouth	river mouth
AR	Arkansas	l.	lake	r. source	river source
Arg.	Argentina	LA	Louisiana	reg.	region
aut. comm.	autonomous community	lag.	lagoon	res.	reserve
aut. div.	autonomous division	Lith.	Lithuania	resr	reservoir
aut. reg.	autonomous region	Lux.	Luxembourg	RI	Rhode Island
aut. rep.	autonomous republic	MA	Massachusetts	Rus. Fed.	Russian Federation
AZ	Arizona	Madag.	Madagascar	S.	South
Azer.	Azerbaijan	Man.	Manitoba	S.A.	South Australia
b.	bay	MD	Maryland	salt l.	salt lake
B.C.	British Columbia	ME	Maine	Sask.	Saskatchewan
Bangl.	Bangladesh	Mex.	Mexico	SC	South Carolina
Bol.	Bolivia	MI	Michigan	SD	South Dakota
Bos.-Herz.	Bosnia-Herzegovina	MN	Minnesota	sea chan.	sea channel
Bulg.	Bulgaria	MO	Missouri	Sing.	Singapore
c.	cape	Moz.	Mozambique	Switz.	Switzerland
CA	California	MS	Mississippi	Tajik.	Tajikistan
Cent. Afr. Rep.	Central African Republic	MT	Montana	Tanz.	Tanzania
CO	Colorado	mt.	mountain	Tas.	Tasmania
Col.	Colombia	mts	mountains	terr.	territory
CT	Connecticut	N.	North	Thai.	Thailand
Czech Rep.	Czech Republic	N.B.	New Brunswick	TN	Tennessee
DC	District of Columbia	N.S.	Nova Scotia	Trin. and Tob.	Trinidad and Tobago
DE	Delaware	N.S.W.	New South Wales	Turkm.	Turkmenistan
Dem. Rep. Congo	Democratic Republic of Congo	N.T.	Northern Territory	TX	Texas
depr.	depression	N.W.T.	Northwest Territories	U.A.E.	United Arab Emirates
des.	desert	N.Z.	New Zealand	U.K.	United Kingdom
Dom. Rep.	Dominican Republic	nat. park	national park	U.S.A.	United States of America
E.	East, Eastern	nature res.	nature reserve	Ukr.	Ukraine
Equat. Guinea	Equatorial Guinea	NC	North Carolina	union terr.	union territory
esc.	escarpment	ND	North Dakota	UT	Utah
est.	estuary	NE	Nebraska	Uzbek.	Uzbekistan
Eth.	Ethiopia	Neth.	Netherlands	VA	Virginia
Fin.	Finland	NH	New Hampshire	Venez.	Venezuela
FL	Florida	NJ	New Jersey	Vic.	Victoria
for.	forest	NM	New Mexico	vol.	volcano
Fr. Guiana	French Guiana	NV	Nevada	vol. crater	volcanic crater
g.	gulf	NY	New York	VT	Vermont
GA	Georgia	OH	Ohio	W.	West, Western
Guat.	Guatemala	OK	Oklahoma	W.A.	Western Australia
H.K.	Hong Kong	OR	Oregon	WA	Washington
HI	Hawaii	P.E.I.	Prince Edward Island	WI	Wisconsin
Hond.	Honduras	P.N.G.	Papua New Guinea	WV	West Virginia
i.	island	PA	Pennsylvania	WY	Wyoming
IA	Iowa	pen.	peninsula	Y.T.	Yukon Territory
ID	Idaho	plat.	plateau	Yugo.	Yugoslavia
IL	Illinois	Port.	Portugal		

↓ 1

1st Cataract *rapids* Egypt **121** G3
2nd Cataract *rapids* Sudan **121** F4
3rd Cataract *rapids* Sudan **121** F5
4th Cataract *rapids* Sudan **121** G5
5th Cataract *rapids* Sudan **121** G5
9 de Julio Arg. **204** E4
long form Nueve de Julio
15th of May City Egypt *see*
Medinet 15 Mayo
25 de Mayo Buenos Aires Arg. **204** E4
long form Veinticinco de Mayo
25 de Mayo La Pampa Arg. **204** D5
long form Veinticinco de Mayo
25 de Mayo Mendoza Arg. **204** C4
long form Veinticinco de Mayo
26 Baki Komissari Azer. **107** G3
also known as imeni 26 Bakinskikh
Komissarov; *formerly known as* Neftechala;
long form İyirmi Altı Bakı Komissarı
42nd Hill S. Africa **133** N5
70 Mile House Canada **166** F5
100 Mile House Canada **166** F5
150 Mile House Canada **166** F4

↓ A

Aabenraa Denmark *see* Åbenrå
Aachen Germany **48** D5
formerly known as Aix-la-Chapelle;
historically known as Aquae Grani or
Aquisgranum
Aadan Yabaal Somalia **128** E4
Aalborg Denmark *see* Ålborg
Aalen Germany **48** H7
Aalesund Norway *see* Ålesund
Aaley Lebanon **51** K2
also spelt Alost
Aanaar Fin. *see* Inari
Äänekoski Fin. **44** N3
Aansluit S. Africa **132** G3
Aarau Switz. **51** O5
Aarberg Switz. **51** N5
Areavaara Sweden **44** M2
Aarhus Denmark *see* Århus
Aarlen Belgium *see* Arlon
Aarschot Belgium **51** K2
Aasiaat Greenland **165** N3
also known as Egedesminde
Aath Belgium *see* Ath
Aavasaksa Fin. **44** M2
Aba China **86** B1
also known as Ngawa
Aba Dem. Rep. Congo **126** F4
Aba Nigeria **125** G5
Abã ad Dūd Saudi Arabia **104** D2
Abã al Afan *oasis* Saudi Arabia **105** E4
Abã al Qūr, Sha'īb *watercourse*
Saudi Arabia **109** N6
Abã ar Ruwāth, Wādī *watercourse*
Saudi Arabia **109** N7
Abacaxis *r.* Brazil **199** G6
Ābādān Iran **100** B4
English form Abadan
Abadan Iran *see* Ābādān
Ābādān, Jazīreh *i.* Iran/Iraq **105** E1
Ābādeh Iran **100** C4
Ābādeh Tashk Iran **100** C4
Abadia dos Dourados Brazil **206** F5
Abadiânia Brazil **206** E3
Abadla Alg. **123** E3
Abádszalók Hungary **49** R8
Abaeté Brazil **207** H5
Abaeté *r.* Brazil **207** H5
Abaetetuba Brazil **202** B2
Abagnar Qi China *see* Xilinhot
Abag Qi China *see* Xin Hot
Abai Para. **201** G6
Abaiang *atoll* Kiribati **145** G1
also spelt Apaiang; *formerly known as* Apia
A Baiuca Spain **54** C1
Abaji Nigeria **125** G4
Abajo Peak U.S.A. **183** O4
Abakaliki Nigeria **125** H5
Abakan Rus. Fed. **80** F2
formerly known as Ust'-Abakanskoye
Abala Congo **126** B5
Abala Niger **125** F3
Abalak Niger **125** G3
Abalyanka *r.* Belarus **43** L7
Abana Turkey **106** C2
Abancay Peru **200** B3
Abanga *r.* Gabon **126** A5
Abapó Bol. **201** E4
Abaringa *i.* Kiribati *see* Kanton
Abarqū Iran **100** C4
A Barrela Spain **54** D2
Abarshahr Iran *see* Neyshābūr
Abār 'Uwayrid Tahtānī *well* Syria
109 K3
Abashiri Japan **90** I2
Abashiri-wan *b.* Japan **90** I2
Abasolo Mex. **185** F3
Abasula *waterhole* Kenya **128** C5
Abau P.N.G. **145** D3
Abava *r.* Latvia **42** C4
Abay Kazakh. **103** H2
also known as Churubay Nura; *formerly
known as* Abay Bazar
Abay Kazakh. *see* Karaul
Abaya, Lake Eth. **128** C3
also known as 'Abaya Hāyk'; *formerly known
as* Margherita, Lake
'Abaya Hāyk' *l.* Eth. *see* Abaya, Lake
Abay Bazar Kazakh. *see* Abay
Abay Wenz *r.* Eth./Sudan **128** C2 *see
Blue Nile*
Abaza Rus. Fed. **80** F2
Abba Cent. Afr. Rep. **126** B3
Abbadia San Salvatore Italy **56** D6
Abbāsābād Iran **100** D3
Abbasanta *Sardegna* Italy **57** A8
Abbatis Villa France *see* Abbeville
Abbaye, Point U.S.A. **172** E4
Abbe, Lake Djibouti/Eth. **128** D2
Abbeville France **51** H2
historically known as Abbatis Villa
Abbeville GA U.S.A. **175** D6
Abbeville LA U.S.A. **179** D6
Abbeville SC U.S.A. **175** D5
Abbey Canada **167** I5
Abbeyfeale Rep. of Ireland **47** C11
Abbiategrasso Italy **56** A3
Abborrträsk Sweden **44** L2
Abbot, Mount Australia **149** E4
Abbot Bay Australia **149** E3
Abbotsford Canada **166** F5
Abbotsford U.S.A. **172** D6
Abbott NM U.S.A. **181** F5
Abbott WV U.S.A. **176** E7
Abbottabad Pak. **101** H3
Abbott Ice Shelf Antarctica **222** R2
Abchuha Belarus **43** K7
Abd, Oued el *watercourse* Alg. **55** L9
'Abd al 'Azīz, Jabal *hill* Syria **109** K1
'Abd al 'Azīz, Jabal *plat.* Syria **109** K1
'Abd al Kūrī *i.* Yemen **105** F5
'Abd Allah, Khawr *sea chan.* Iraq/Kuwait
107 G5
Abd al Ma'asir *well* Saudi Arabia
109 J7
Ābdānān Iran **100** A3
Abdollāhābād Iran **100** D2
Abdulino Rus. Fed. **41** J5

Abéché Chad **120** D6
also known as Abesher
Abejukolo Nigeria **125** G5
Abelbod *well* Mali **125** E2
Abellinum Italy *see* Avellino
Abel Tasman National Park N.Z. **152** H8
Abemama *atoll* Kiribati **145** G1
also spelt Apamama
Abenab Namibia **130** C3
Abengourou Côte d'Ivoire **124** E5
Abenójar Spain **54** G4
Abenrå Denmark **45** J5
also spelt Aabenraa
Abensberg Germany **48** I7
Abeokuta Nigeria **125** F5
Abera Eth. **128** B3
Aberaeron U.K. **47** H11
Aberchirder U.K. **46** J6
Abercorn Zambia *see* Mbala
Abercrombie *r.* Australia **147** F3
Aberdare U.K. **47** I12
Aberdare National Park Kenya **128** C5
Aberdaron U.K. **47** H11
Aberdaugleddau U.K. *see* Milford Haven
Aberdeen Australia **147** F3
Aberdeen Hong Kong China **87** [inset]
also known as Heung Kong Tsai
Aberdeen S. Africa **132** H9
Aberdeen U.K. **46** J7
historically known as Devana
Aberdeen MD U.S.A. **177** I6
Aberdeen MS U.S.A. **175** B5
Aberdeen OH U.S.A. **176** B7
Aberdeen SD U.S.A. **178** C2
Aberdeen WA U.S.A. **180** B3
Aberdeen Island Hong Kong China **87** [inset]
Aberdeen Lake Canada **167** L1
Aberdeen Road S. Africa **133** I9
Aberfeldy U.K. **46** I7
Aberfoyle U.K. **46** H7
Abergavenny U.K. **47** I12
also known as Y Fenni; *historically known as*
Gobannium
Abergelê Eth. **104** B5
Abergwaun U.K. *see* Fishguard
Aberhonddu U.K. *see* Brecon
Abermaw U.K. *see* Barmouth
Abernathy U.S.A. **179** B5
Abertawe U.K. *see* Swansea
Aberteifi U.K. *see* Cardigan
Abeshr Chad *see* Abéché
Abez' Rus. Fed. **40** J2
Abhã Saudi Arabia **104** C4
Abhã, Jabal *hill* Saudi Arabia **104** C2
Abhanpur India **97** D5
Abhar Iran **100** B2
Abhar Rūd *r.* Iran **100** B3
Abia *state* Nigeria **125** G5
Abiad, Bahr el *r.* Sudan/Uganda **128** B2 *see*
White Nile
Ābīata Hāyk' *l.* Eth. **128** C3
Abi-i Bazuft *r.* Iran **100** B4
Abibe, Serranía de *mts* Col. **198** B2
Abidjan Côte d'Ivoire **124** D5
Former capital of Côte d'Ivoire.
Abiekwasputs *salt pan* S. Africa **132** E4
Ab-i-Istada *l.* Afgh. **101** G4
Abijatta-Shalla National Park Eth. **128** C3
also known as Rift Valley Lakes National
Park
Ab-i-Kavir *salt flat* Iran **100** D3
Abiko Japan **91** G7
Abilene KS U.S.A. **178** C4
Abilene TX U.S.A. **179** C5
Abingdon U.K. **47** K12
Abingdon IL U.S.A. **172** C10
Abingdon VA U.S.A. **176** C9
Abington U.S.A. **177** O3
Abington Reef Australia **149** F3
Abinsk Rus. Fed. **41** F7
Ab-i-Panja *r.* Afgh./Tajik. *see* Pyandzh
Ab-i-Safed *r.* Afgh. **101** F3
Abiseo, Parque Nacional *nat. park* Peru
200 A1
Abisko nationalpark *nat. park* Sweden **44** L1
Abitibi *r.* Canada **168** D3
Abitibi, Lake Canada **168** D3
Åb Naft *r.* Iraq **107** F4
also known as Naft
Abnūb Egypt **121** F3
Åbo Fin. *see* Turku
Abohar India **96** B3
Aboisso Côte d'Ivoire **124** E5
Aboke Sudan **128** B3
Abomey Benin **125** F5
Abongabong, Gunung *mt.* Indon. **76** B1
Abong Mbang Cameroon **125** I6
Aboot Oman **105** F4
Aborlan Phil. **74** A4
Abou Déia Chad **126** C2
Abou Goulem Chad **120** D6
Aboumi Gabon **126** B5
Abqaiq Saudi Arabia **105** E2
also known as Buqayq
Abra, Lago del *l.* Arg. **204** E6
Abrād, Wādī *watercourse* Yemen **105** D5
Abraka Nigeria **125** G5
Abrams U.S.A. **172** E6
Abra Pampa Arg. **200** D5
Abre Campo Brazil **207** K7
Abreojos, Punta of Mex. **184** B3
'Abrī Sudan **121** F4
Abrolhos, Arquipélago dos *is* Brazil **207** O5
Abrosovo Rus. Fed. **43** Q3
Abrud Romania **58** F2
Abruka *i.* Estonia **42** D3
Abruzzi *admin. reg.* Italy *see* Abruzzo
Abruzzo *admin. reg.* Italy **56** F6
also spelt Abruzzi
Abruzzo, Parco Nazionale d' *nat. park* Italy
56 F7
'Abs Yemen **104** C4
Absalom, Mount Antarctica **223** W1
Absaroka Range *mts* U.S.A. **180** E3
Absecon U.S.A. **177** K6
Abşeron Yarımadası *pen.* Azer. **107** G2
also known as Apsheronskiy Poluostrov
Absterna, Vozyera *l.* Belarus **42** I6
Abtar, Jabal al *hills* Syria **109** I3
Abū ad Duhūr Syria **109** I2
Abū al Husayn, Qā' *imp. l.* Jordan **109** J5
Abū'Alī *i.* Saudi Arabia **105** E2
Abu al Jirab *i.* U.A.E. **105** F2
Abū al Kūfah *watercourse* Iraq **109** N3
Abū 'Āmūd, Wādī *watercourse* Jordan
108 H7
Abū 'Arīsh Saudi Arabia **104** C4
Abū 'Aweigila *well* Egypt **108** F7
Abu Ballūs *hill* Egypt **121** E3
Abū Dā'ir *des.* Yemen **105** D4
Abu Deleiq Sudan **121** G6
Abu Dhabi U.A.E. **105** F2
*Capital of the United Arab Emirates. Also
spelt* Abū Zaby.
asia [changes] ▶ 68–69
Abū Dībā' *watercourse* Saudi Arabia **104** B3
Abu Durba Egypt **108** E9
Abu el Matāmir Egypt **108** B7
Abufari Brazil **199** F6
Abū Farrūkh, Wādī *watercourse* Iraq
109 O4
Abu Gabra Sudan **126** E2
Abu Gamel Sudan **121** G6
Abū Ghar, Wādī *watercourse* Iraq **109** M5
Abū Ghizlān *waterhole* Iraq **109** O3

Abū Ghurayb Iraq **109** P4
Abu Gubeiha Sudan **128** A2
Abū Hād, Wādī *watercourse* Egypt **108** E9
Abū Hafnah, Wādī *watercourse* Jordan
109 H6
Abu Haggag Egypt **121** E2
Abū Hallūfah, Jabal *hill* Jordan **109** H6
Abu Hamed Sudan **121** G5
Abū Hammād Egypt **108** C7
Abu Haraz Sudan **121** G6
Abu Hashim Sudan **121** G6
Abu Higar Sudan **121** G6
Abu Hummus Egypt **108** B6
Abu Huswa, Gebel *hill* Egypt **108** E9
Abuja Nigeria **125** G4
Capital of Nigeria.
Abū Jahaf, Wādī *watercourse* Iraq **109** O5
Abū Kamāl Syria **109** L3
Abū Kammāsh Libya **120** A1
Abu Khamsāt, Sha'īb *watercourse* Iraq
109 O6
Abu La'ot *watercourse* Sudan **121** F6
Abū Latt Island Saudi Arabia **104** C4
Abū Madd, Ra's *hd* Saudi Arabia **104** C4
Abu Matariq Sudan **126** E2
Abu Mena *tourist site* Egypt **121** F2
Abū Mīnā *tourist site* Egypt **108** A7
Abumombazi Dem. Rep. Congo **126** D4
Abu Musa *i.* The Gulf **105** F2
also known as Abū Mūsá, Jazīreh-ye
Abū Mūsá, Jazīreh-ye *i.* The Gulf *see*
Abu Musa
Abunã *r.* Bol. **200** D2
Abunã Brazil **200** D2
Abunai Brazil **199** E5
Abū Na'im *well* Libya **120** C2
Ābune Yosēf *mt.* Eth. **128** C1
Abū Nujaym Libya **120** B2
Abū Qīr, Khalīg *b.* Egypt **108** B6
Abū Qurīn Libya **120** B2
Abū Rāqah *well* Saudi Arabia **104** B2
Aburo *mt.* Dem. Rep. Congo **126** F4
Abu Road India **96** B4
also known as Kharari
Abū Rubayq Saudi Arabia **104** B3
Abū Rujmayn, Jabal *mts* Syria **109** J3
Abū Rūtha, Gebel *mt.* Egypt **108** F8
Abū Sallah *watercourse* Saudi Arabia **109** I9
Abū Sawādah *well* Saudi Arabia **105** E2
Abu Shagara, Ras *pt* Sudan **121** H4
Abu Simbel Egypt **121** F4
Abu Simbel Temple *tourist site* Egypt **121** F4
Abū Sukhayr Iraq **107** F5
Abū Sultān Egypt **108** D7
Abu Tabaq *well* Sudan **121** G4
Abu Tarfa, Wādī *watercourse* Egypt **108** E8
Abut Head N.Z. **153** E11
Abū Tīyūr, Gebel *mt.* Egypt **121** G3
Abū Ujayyijāt *well* Saudi Arabia **109** H9
Abuye Meda *mt.* Eth. **128** C2
Abu Zabad Sudan **121** F6
Abū Zabī U.A.E. *see* Abu Dhabi
Abū Zenīma Egypt **121** G2
Abwong Sudan **128** B2
Aby Sweden **45** L4
Abyad Sudan **121** F6
Abyaḍ, Jabal al *hill* Saudi Arabia **108** G9
Abyaḍ, Jabal al *mts* Syria **109** I3
Abyār al Hakīm *well* Libya **120** D1
Abyār an Nakhīlan *well* Libya **120** D2
Abyār Banī Murr *well* Saudi Arabia **108** G9
Abydos Australia **150** B4
Abyei Sudan **126** F3
Abym Sweden **44** M2
Abyssinia *country* Africa *see* Ethiopia
Abzakovo Rus. Fed. **102** D1
Abzanovo Rus. Fed. **102** D2
Acacias Col. **198** C3
Academician Vernadskiy *research station*
Antarctica *see* Vernadsky
Academy Bay Rus. Fed. *see* Akademii, Zal v
Acadia *prov.* Canada *see* Nova Scotia
Acadia National Park U.S.A. **177** Q1
Açailāndia Brazil **202** C2
Acajutla El Salvador **185** H6
Acala Mex. **185** G5
Acamarachi *mt.* Chile *see* Pili, Cerro
Acámbaro Mex. **185** E4
Acampamento de Caça do Mucusso
Angola **127** D9
Acancéh Mex. **185** H4
Acandí Col. **198** B2
Acaponeta Mex. **184** D4
Acapulco Mex. **185** F5
long form Acapulco de Juárez
Acapulco de Juárez Mex. *see* Acapulco
Acará Brazil **202** B2
Acará *r.* Brazil **202** B2
Acará Miri *r.* Brazil **202** B2
Acaraú Brazil **202** D2
Acaraú *r.* Brazil **202** D2
Acaray, Represa de *resr* Para. **201** G6
Acari *r.* Brazil **207** H2
Acari Peru **200** B3
Acari, Peru **200** B3
Acari, Serra *hills* Brazil/Guyana **199** G4
Acarigua Venez. **198** D2
Acatlan Mex. **185** F5
Acatzingo Mex. **185** F5
Acay, Nevado de *mt.* Arg. **200** D6
Acayucan Mex. **185** G5
Accho Israel *see* 'Akko
Accomac U.S.A. **177** J8
also spelt Accomack
Accomack U.S.A. *see* Accomac
Accra Ghana **125** E5
Capital of Ghana.
Aceguá Brazil **204** G3
Aceh *admin. dist.* Indon. **76** B1
formerly spelt Acheh or Atjeh; *historically
known as* Achin
Aceuchal Spain **54** E6
Achacachi Bol. **200** D4
Achaguas Venez. **199** D3
Achalpur India **96** C5
formerly known as Dadra or Elichpur
Achampet India **94** C2
Achan Rus. Fed. **82** E2
formerly known as Bolon'
Achanta India **94** D2
Achayvayam Rus. Fed. **39** R3
Acheh *admin. dist.* Indon. *see* Aceh
Achemelmel *well* Mali **123** F5
Achemmim *well* Mauritania **124** D2
Acheng China **82** B3
Achern Germany **48** E7
Achhota India **94** D1
Achigh-Kol *salt l.* China **84** C4
Achill Island Rep. of Ireland **47** B10
Achim Germany **48** G2
Achin *admin. dist.* Indon. *see* Aceh
Achinsk Rus. Fed. **80** F2
Achisay Kazakh. **103** G4
also spelt Ashchysay
Achit Rus. Fed. **40** K4
Achit Nuur *l.* Mongolia **84** A1
Achkhoy-Martan Rus. Fed. **107** F2
formerly known as Novoselskoye
Achlades, Akra *pt* Greece **59** G12

Achnasheen U.K. **46** G6
Achosa-Rudnya Belarus **43** M9
Aci Castello *Sicilia* Italy **57** H11
Aci Catena *Sicilia* Italy **57** H11
Acıgöl *l.* Turkey **105** B3
Acıpayam Turkey **106** B3
Acireale *Sicilia* Italy **57** H11
Ackerman U.S.A. **175** B5
Ackley U.S.A. **174** A3
Acklins Island Bahamas **187** E2
Acobamba *Huancavelica* Peru **200** B3
Acobamba *Junín* Peru **200** B2
Acomayo *Cusco* Peru **200** C3
Acomayo *Huánuco* Peru **200** A2
Aconcagua, Cerro *mt.* Arg. **204** C4
Highest mountain in South America.
southamerica [landscapes] ▶▶ 190–191
Acopiara Brazil **202** E3
Acora Peru **200** C4
A Coruña Spain **54** C1
English form Corunna; *also spelt* La Coruña
Acostambo Peru **200** B3
Acoyapa Nicaragua **186** B5
Acqui Terme Italy **56** A4
historically known as Aquae Statiellae
Acra U.S.A. **177** K3
Acragas *Sicilia* Italy *see* Agrigento
Acre *r.* Brazil **200** D2
formerly known as Aquiry
Acre *state* Brazil **200** C2
Acre, Israel *see* 'Akko
Acreúna Brazil **206** C4
Acri Italy **57** I9
Ács Hungary **49** P8
Actaeon Group *is* Fr. Polynesia *see*
Actéon, Groupe
Acton Canada **173** M7
Acton U.S.A. **182** F7
Actopán Mex. **185** F4
Açu *r.* Brazil **201** D1
Açucena Brazil **207** K6
Acuman Acusio France *see* Montélimar
Acurenam Equat. Guinea **125** H6
Açuriqua Brazil **201** F3
Ada *Vojvodina, Srbija* Yugo. **58** B3
Ada MN U.S.A. **178** C2
Ada OH U.S.A. **176** B5
Ada OK U.S.A. **179** C5
Adaba Eth. **128** C3
Adabazar Turkey *see* Sakarya
Adabiya Egypt **108** D8
Adaf, Djebel *mts* Alg. **123** H5
Adeja *r.* Spain **54** G3
Adak Sweden **44** L2
Adalia Turkey *see* Antalya
Adam Oman **105** F3
Adam, Mount *hill* Falkland Is **205** F8
Adamantina Brazil **206** B8
Adamaoua *prov.* Cameroon **125** I5
Adamas Greece **59** F12
also known as Adámas
Adamawa *state* Nigeria **125** H4
Adamclisi Romania **58** I4
Adamello *mt.* Italy **56** C2
Adamello-Brenta, Parco Naturale
nature res. Italy **56** C2
Adaminaby Australia **147** F4
Adamówka Rus. Fed. **102** D2
Adams KY U.S.A. **176** C8
Adams MA U.S.A. **177** L3
Adams NY U.S.A. **177** I2
Adams WI U.S.A. **172** D7
Adams, Cape Antarctica **222** T2
Adams, Mount N.Z. **153** E11
Adam's Bridge *sea feature* India/Sri Lanka
94 C4
Adams Center U.S.A. **177** I2
Adams Lake Canada **166** G5
Adams McGill Reservoir U.S.A. **183** I3
also known as Samanala or Sri Pada
Adam's Peak Sri Lanka **94** D5
Adams Peak U.S.A. **182** D2
Adamstown Pitcairn Is **221** J7
Capital of the Pitcairn Islands.
Adamstown U.S.A. **177** I5
'Adan Yemen *see* Aden
Adana Turkey **106** C3
also known as Seyhan; *historically known as*
Ataniya
Adana *prov.* Turkey **106** G1
Adana Yemen *see* Aden
'Adan as Sughra Yemen **104** D5
English form Little Aden
Adang, Teluk *b.* Indon. **77** G3
Adani Nigeria **125** G5
Adapazarı Turkey *see* Sakarya
Adaran, Jabal *mt.* Yemen **105** D5
Adare, Cape Antarctica **223** L2
Adarmo, Khawr *watercourse* Sudan **104** A3
Adatara-san *vol.* Japan **90** G6
Adavale Australia **149** E5
Ādāzī Latvia **42** F4
Adbān Afgh. **101** G2
Adda *r.* Italy **56** B3
Ad Dabbah Sudan *see* Ed Debba
Ad Dafīnah Saudi Arabia **104** C3
Ad Daghghārah Iraq **107** F4
Ad Dahnā' *des.* Saudi Arabia **105** D3
also spelt Dahana
Ad Dākhilīyah *admin. reg.* Oman **105** G3
Ad Dakhla W. Sahara **122** B5
also spelt Dakhla; *formerly known as* Villa
Cisneros
Ad Dāli' Yemen **104** D5
Ad Damir Sudan *see* Ed Damer
Ad Dammām Saudi Arabia *see* Dammam
Addanki India **94** C3
Ad Dār al Hamrā' Saudi Arabia **104** B2
Ad Darb Saudi Arabia **104** C4
Adda Sud, Parco dell' *park* Italy **56** B3
Addatigaia India **94** C4
Ad Dawādimī Saudi Arabia **104** D2
Ad Dawhah Qatar *see* Doha
Ad Daww *plain* Syria **109** J3
**Addax, Réserve Naturelle Intégrale dite
Sanctuaire des** *nature res.* Niger **125** H2
Ad Dibdibah *plain* Saudi Arabia **107** G5
Ad Dibin Yemen **105** E4
Ad Dikākah *des.* Saudi Arabia **105** E4
Ad Dir'īyah Saudi Arabia **105** D2
Ad Dulū'īyah Iraq **109** P3
Ad Duwayd *well* Saudi Arabia **107** E5
Ad Duwayhirah Saudi Arabia **104** C2
Ad Duwaym Sudan *see* Ed Dueim

Ad Duwayris *well* Saudi Arabia **105** E3
Adel GA U.S.A. **175** D6
Adel IA U.S.A. **178** D3
Adelaide Australia **146** C3
State capital of South Australia.
Adelaide Bahamas **175** E7
Adelaide S. Africa **133** K9
Adelaide Island Antarctica **222** T2
Adelaide River Australia **148** A2
Adelebsen Germany **48** G4
Adele Island Australia **150** C2
Adelfoi *i.* Greece **59** I12
Adélie Coast Antarctica **223** J2
Adélie Coast *reg.* Antarctica *see*
Adélie Land
Adélie Land *reg.* Antarctica **223** J2
also known as Adélie Coast or Terre Adélie
Adelong Aboriginal Reserve Australia
151 C6
Adelsheim Germany **48** G6
Adelunga Uzbek. **103** G4
Aden Yemen **104** D5
also known as 'Adan; *historically known as* Adana
Aden, Gulf of Somalia/Yemen **128** E2
Adena U.S.A. **176** E5
Adenau Germany **48** D5
Adendorp S. Africa **133** I9
Aderbissinat Niger **125** G3
Aderno *Sicilia* Italy *see* Adrano
Adesar India **96** A5
'Adīd Umm Inderab *well* Sudan **121** F6
Adige *r.* Italy **56** E3
Adigey Autonomous Oblast *aut. rep.*
Rus. Fed. *see* Adygeya, Respublika
Ādigrat Eth. **128** C1
Adigüzel Barajı *resr* Turkey **106** B3
Adi Keyih Eritrea **121** H6
Adi Kwala Eritrea **121** H6
Adilabad India **94** C2
Adilang Uganda **128** B4
Adilcevaz Turkey **107** E3
Adin U.S.A. **180** B4
Adirī Libya **120** B3
Adirondack Mountains U.S.A. **177** K1
Ādīs Ābeba Eth. *see* Addis Ababa
Ādīs Zemen Eth. **128** C1
Adi Ugri Eritrea *see* Mendefera
Adıyaman Turkey **107** D3
Adjoantali *reg.* Alg. **123** G5
Adjud Romania **58** I2
Adjumani Uganda **128** A4
Adiawik Islands Canada **169** J2
Admiralty Gulf Australia **150** D2
Admiralty Gulf Aboriginal Reserve
Australia **150** D2
Admiralty Inlet Canada **165** K2
Admiralty Island Canada **165** I3
Admiralty Island U.S.A. **164** F4
**Admiralty Island National Monument -
Kootznoowoo Wilderness** *nat. park*
U.S.A. **164** F4
Admiralty Islands P.N.G. **73** K7
Admiralty Mountains Antarctica **223** L2
Ado Eth. **128** E3
Ado-Ekiti Nigeria **125** G5
Adok Sudan **128** A2
Adolfo Gonzáles Chaves Arg. **204** E5
Adolfsström Sweden **44** L2
Adolphus Island Australia **150** E2
Adonara *i.* Indon. **75** B5
also spelt Adunara
Adoni India **94** C3
Adour *r.* France **50** E9
Adra India **97** E5
Adra Spain **55** H8
Adra *r.* Spain **55** I8
Adramyttium Turkey *see* Edremit
Adramyttium, Gulf of Turkey *see*
Edremit Körfezi
Adrano *Sicilia* Italy **57** G11
also spelt Aderno; *historically known as*
Hadranum
Adrar Alg. **123** E4
Adrar *mts* Alg. **123** G4
Adrar *hills* Mali *see* Îfôghas, Adrar des
Adrar *admin. reg.* Mauritania **122** C5
Adraskand *r.* Afgh. **101** E3
Adrasmon Tajik. **101** G1
Adré Chad **120** D6
Adrian MI U.S.A. **173** I9
Adrian TX U.S.A. **179** B5
Adrianople Turkey *see* Edirne
Adrianopolis Turkey *see* Edirne
Adriatic Sea Europe **56** F4
Adua Eth. *see* Ādwa
Adunara *i.* Indon. *see* Adonara
Adur India **94** C4
Adusa Dem. Rep. Congo **126** F4
Adutiškis Lith. **42** H6
Aduwa Eth. *see* Ādwa
Adverse Well Australia **150** C4
Ādwa Eth. **128** C1
also known as Adua; *also spelt* Adua
Adwufia Ghana **124** E5
Adycha *r.* Rus. Fed. **39** N3
Adygeya *aut. rep.* Rus. Fed. *see*
Adygeya, Respublika
Adygeya, Respublika *aut. rep.* Rus. Fed.
41 F7
formerly known as Adigey Autonomous
Oblast or Adygeyskaya Avtonomnaya
Oblast'; *short form* Adygeya
Adygeysk Rus. Fed. **41** F7
formerly known as Teuchezhsk
Adygeyskaya Avtonomnaya Oblast'
aut. rep. Rus. Fed. *see* Adygeya, Respublika
Adyk Rus. Fed. **41** I7
formerly known as Yuzhnyy
Adzhiyan Turkm. **102** C5
Adzopé Côte d'Ivoire **124** E5
Adz'va *r.* Rus. Fed. **40** L2
Adz'vavom Rus. Fed. **40** K2
Aegean Sea Greece/Turkey **59** F10
Aegina *i.* Greece *see* Aigina
Aegna *i.* Estonia **42** F2
Aegviidu Estonia **42** G2
Aegyptus *country* Africa *see* Egypt
Aela Jordan *see* Al 'Aqabah
Aelana Jordan *see* Al 'Aqabah
Aelia Capitolina Israel/West Bank *see*
Jerusalem
Aelōninglap *atoll* Marshall Is *see*
Ailinglaplap
Aenus Turkey *see* Enez
Ærø *i.* Denmark **48** H1
Aerzen Germany **48** G3
Aesernia Italy *see* Isernia
A Estrada Spain **54** C2
Åetsä Fin. **45** M3
Afabet Eritrea **121** H5
Afal *watercourse* Saudi Arabia *see*
'Ifāl, Wādī
Afanas'yevo Rus. Fed. **40** J4
Afandou Greece *see* Afantou
Afantou Greece **59** J12
also spelt Afándou

Afar admin. reg. Eth. 128 D1
Afar Oman 105 G3
Afar Depression Eritrea/Eth. 121 I6
Āfdem Eth. 128 D2
Afféri Côte d'Ivoire 124 E5
Affreville Alg. see Khemis Miliana
Afghānestān country Asia see Afghanistan
▶Afghanistan country Asia 101 E3
spelt Afghānestān in Dari and Pushtu
asia [countries] ▶▶ 64–67
Afgooye Somalia 128 E4
'Afīf Saudi Arabia 104 C3
Afikpo Nigeria 125 G5
Afim'ino Rus. Fed. 43 P4
Afiun Karahissar Turkey see Afyon
Åfjord Norway 44 J3
Aflou Alg. 123 F2
Afmadow Somalia 128 D4
Afognak Island U.S.A. 164 D4
Afojjar well Mauritania 124 B2
A Fonsagrada Spain 54 D1
also known as Fonsagrada
Afonso Cláudio Brazil 207 L7
Afragola Italy 56 G8
Afrânio Brazil 202 D4
Āfrēra Terara vol. Eth. 128 D1
Āfrēra YeChe'ew Hāyk' l. Eth. 128 D1
Africa Nova country Africa see Tunisia
'Afrīn Syria 109 H1
'Afrīn, Nahr r. Syria/Turkey 109 H1
Afşar Barajı resr Turkey 59 J10
Afşin Turkey 107 D3
also known as Efsus
Afsluitdijk barrage Neth. 48 C3
Aftol well Eth. 128 E3
Afton NY U.S.A. 177 J3
Afton WY U.S.A. 180 E4
Aftoût Faï depr. Mauritania 124 B2
Afuá Brazil 202 B2
'Afula Israel 108 G5
Afyon Turkey 106 B3
also known as Afyonkarahisar; historically known as Afiun Karahissar
Afyonkarahisar Turkey see Afyon
Aga Egypt 108 C7
Aga r. Rus. Fed. 85 G1
Aga-Buryat Autonomous Okrug admin. div. Rus. Fed. see
Aginskiy Buryatskiy Avtonomnyy Okrug
Agadem well Niger 125 I2
Agadès Niger see Agadez
Agadez Niger 125 G2
also spelt Agadès
Agadez dept Niger 125 H2
Agadir Morocco 122 C3
Agadyr' Kazakh. 103 H2
also spelt Aqadyr
Agaie Nigeria 125 G4
Agalega Islands Mauritius 218 K6
Agalta nat. park Hond. 186 B4
Agana Guam see Hagåtña
Agapovka Rus. Fed. 102 D1
Agar India 96 C5
Agârak well Niger 125 G2
Agâraktem well Mali 122 D5
Agaro Eth. 128 C3
Agartala India 97 F5
Agashi India 94 B2
Agassiz National Wildlife Refuge nature res. U.S.A. 178 D1
Agate Canada 168 D3
Agathe France see Agde
Agathonisi i. Greece 59 H11
Agatti i. India 94 B4
Agawa r. Canada 173 I3
Agbor Bojiboji Nigeria 125 G5
Agboville Côte d'Ivoire 124 D5
Ağcabädi Azer. 107 F2
also spelt Agdzhabedi
Ağdam Azer. 107 F3
Ağdaş Azer. 107 F2
also spelt Agdash
Agdash Azer. see Ağdaş
Agde France 51 J9
historically known as Agathe
Agdzhabedi Azer. see Ağcabädi
Agedabia Libya see Ajdābiyā
Agen France 50 G8
historically known as Aginum
Agenebode Nigeria 125 G5
Āgere Maryam Eth. 128 C3
Ageyevo Rus. Fed. 43 R7
Ageneys S. Africa 132 C6
Aggershus county Norway see Akershus
Aggteleki nat. park Hungary 49 R7
Agharri, Sha'īb al watercourse Iraq 109 L4
Aghezzaf well Mali 125 E2
also spelt Arezzaf
Aghil Pass China/Jammu and Kashmir 89 B4
Aghireşu Romania 58 E2
Aghouavil des. Mauritania 124 D2
Aghrîjît well Mauritania 124 C2
Aghzoumal, Sabkhat salt pan W. Sahara 122 B4
Agia Greece 59 D9
also spelt Ayiá
Agiabampo Mex. 184 C3
Agia Eirinis, Akra pt Greece 59 G9
Agia Marina Greece 59 H11
Agiasos Greece 59 H9
also spelt Ayiásos
Agia Vervara Greece 59 G13
Agigea Romania 58 J4
Agighiol Romania 58 J3
Agiguan i. N. Mariana Is see Aguijan
Ağın Turkey 107 D3
Aginskiy Buryatskiy Avtonomnyy Okrug admin. div. Rus. Fed. 85 G1
English form Aga-Buryat Autonomous Okrug
Aginskoye Rus. Fed. 85 G1
Aginum France see Agen
Agioi Apostoloi Greece 59 E10
Agios Dimitrios Greece 59 E11
also spelt Áyios Dhimítrios
Agios Dimitrios, Akra pt Greece 59 F11
also spelt Áyios Dhimítris, Ákra
Agios Efstratios Greece 59 F9
Agios Efstratios i. Greece 59 G9
also spelt Áyios Evstrátios
Agios Fokas, Akra pt Greece 59 H9
Agios Georgios i. Greece 59 E11
also spelt Áyios Yeóryios
Agios Ioannis, Akra pt Greece 59 G13
Agios Kirykos Greece 59 H11
Agios Konstantinos Greece 59 D10
Agios Nikolaos Greece 59 G13
also spelt Áyios Nikólaos
Agios Paraskevi Greece 59 H9
Agios Petros Greece 59 D11
Agiou Orous, Kolpos b. Greece 59 E8
Agirwat Hills Sudan 121 G5
Agisanang S. Africa 133 J3
Agly r. France 51 J10
Agnantero Greece 59 C9
Agnes, Mount hill Australia 146 A1
Agnew Australia 151 C6
Agnew Lake Canada 173 L4
Agnibilékrou Côte d'Ivoire 124 E5
Agnita Romania 58 F3
Agniye-Afanas'yevsk Rus. Fed. 82 E2
Agno r. Italy 56 D3
Agnone Italy 56 G7
Ago-Are Nigeria 125 F4
Agogo Ghana 125 E5
Agona Junction Ghana 125 E5
Agong China 84 D4
Agounni Jefal well Mali 124 E2
Agoura U.S.A. 182 F7
Agous-n-Ehsel well Mali 125 F2
also known as Ehcel
Agout r. France 51 H9
Agra India 96 C4
Agrakhanskiy Poluostrov pen. Rus. Fed. 102 A4
Agram Croatia see Zagreb
Agreda Spain 55 J3
Agri r. Italy 57 I8
Ağrı Turkey 107 E3
also known as Karaköse
Agria Gramvousa i. Greece 59 E13
Ağrı Dağı mt. Turkey see Ararat, Mount
Agrigan i. N. Mariana Is see Agrihan
Agrigento Sicilia Italy 57 F11
formerly known as Girgenti; historically known as Acragas or Agrigentum
Agrigentum Sicilia Italy see Agrigento
Agrihan i. N. Mariana Is 73 K3
also spelt Agrigan; formerly spelt Grigan
Agrii r. Romania 58 E1
Agrinio Greece 59 C10
Agropoli Italy 57 G8
Agryz Rus. Fed. 40 J4
Ågskaret Norway 44 K2
Ağstafa Azer. 107 F2
Ağsu Azer. 107 G2
also spelt Akhsu
Agtertang S. Africa 133 J7
Água Blanca Arg. 204 D5
Água Boa Brazil 207 K4
Agua Brava, Laguna lag. Mex. 184 D4
Agua Clara Bol. 200 D3
Água Clara Brazil 206 A7
Aguaclara Col. 198 C3
Aguada Mex. 185 H5
Aguadilla Puerto Rico 187 G3
Aguado Cecilio Arg. 204 D6
Agua Doce do Norte Brazil 207 L5
Aguados, Serra dos mts Brazil 206 D9
Agua Dulce Bol. 200 D3
Aguadulce Panama 186 C5
Agua Escondida Arg. 204 C5
Agua Fria r. U.S.A. 183 L8
Aguanaval r. Mex. 185 E3
Aguanga U.S.A. 183 H8
Aguanqueterique Hond. 186 B4
Aguanus r. Canada 169 I3
Aguapeí Brazil 201 F4
Aguapeí r. Brazil 206 B8
Aguapeí r. Mato Grosso do Sul Brazil 206 B8
also known as Feio
Aguapeí r. Brazil 201 F3
Aguapeí, Serra hills Brazil 201 F4
Agua Prieta Mex. 184 C2
Aguaray Arg. 201 E5
A Guarda Spain 54 C3
also spelt La Guardia
Aguaro-Guariquito, Parque Nacional nat. park Venez. 199 E2
Aguaruto Mex. 184 D3
Aguas r. Spain 55 J7
Águas Belas Brazil 202 E4
Aguascalientes Mex. 185 E4
Aguascalientes state Mex. 185 E4
Águas Formosas Brazil 203 D6
Águas Vermelhas Brazil 207 L2
Aguasvivas r. Spain 55 K3
Água Verde r. Brazil 201 F3
Água Vermelha, Represa resr Brazil 206 C6
Aguaytia Peru 200 B2
Agudo Spain 54 G6
Agudos Brazil 206 E9
Águeda Port. 54 C4
Águeda r. Port./Spain 54 E3
Aguelal Niger 125 H2
Aguelhok Mali 125 F2
Aguemour, Oued watercourse Alg. 123 F4
Aguessis well Niger 123 H6
Aguié Niger 125 G3
Aguijan i. N. Mariana Is 73 K4
also spelt Agiguan
Aguila mt. Spain 55 J4
Aguila U.S.A. 183 K8
Aguilar de Campóo Spain 54 G2
Águilas Spain 55 J7
Aguililla Mex. 185 E5
Aguisan Phil. 74 B4
Aguʻila Eth. 104 B5
Agulhas S. Africa 132 E11
▶Agulhas, Cape S. Africa 132 E11
Most southerly point of Africa.
Agulhas Negras mt. Brazil 203 C7
Aguntum Italy see San Candido
Agusan r. Phil. 74 C4
Agutaya i. Phil. 74 B4
Ağva Turkey 106 B2
Agvali Rus. Fed. 102 A4
Agwarra Nigeria 125 G4
Agwei r. Sudan 128 B3
Ahaggar plat. Alg. see Hoggar
Ahakeye Aboriginal Land res. Australia 148 B4
Ahar Iran 100 A2
Ahaura N.Z. 153 F10
Ahaura r. N.Z. 153 F10
Ahaus Germany 48 E3
Ahigal Spain 54 E4
Ahillo mt. Spain 54 G7
Ahimanawa Range mts N.Z. 152 K6
Ahioma P.N.G. 149 F1
Ahipara N.Z. 152 H3
Ahipara Bay N.Z. 152 H3
Ahiri India 94 D2
Ahititi N.Z. 152 I6
Ahja r. Estonia 42 I3
Ahklun Mountains U.S.A. 164 C4
Ahlat Turkey 107 E3
Ahlen Germany 48 E4
Ahmadabad India 96 B5
formerly spelt Ahmedabad
Aḩmadābād Iran 101 E3
Aḩmad al Bāqir, Jabal mt. Jordan 108 G8
Ahmadnagar India 94 B2
formerly spelt Ahmednagar
Ahmadpur India 94 C2
also known as Rajura
Ahmadpur East Pak. 101 G4
Ahmadpur Sial Pak. 101 G4
Ahmar Mountains Eth. 128 D2
Ahmedabad India see Ahmadabad
Ahmednagar India see Ahmadnagar
Ahmetli Turkey 59 I10
Ahoada Nigeria 125 G5
Ahome Mex. 184 C3
Ahore India 96 B4
Ahoskie U.S.A. 177 I9
Ahram Iran 100 B4
Ahrāmāt el Jîzah tourist site Egypt see Giza Pyramids
Ahraura India 97 D4
Ahrensburg Germany 48 H2
Ähtäri Fin. 40 C3
Ahtme Estonia 42 I2
Āhū Iran 100 B4
Ahuacatlán Mex. 184 D4
Ahuachapán El Salvador 185 H6
Ahualulco Jalisco Mex. 184 E4
Ahualulco San Luis Potosí Mex. 185 E4
Ahun France 51 I6
Ahunapalu Estonia 42 I3
Ahuriri r. N.Z. 153 E12
Ahvāz Iran 100 B4
also spelt Ahwāz
Ahvenanmaa is Fin. see Åland Islands
Ahwa India 94 B1
Aḩwar Yemen 105 D5
Ahwāz Iran see Ahvāz
Ai r. China 83 B4
Ai-Ais Namibia 130 C5
Ai-Ais Hot Springs and Fish River Canyon Park nature res. Namibia 130 C5
Aibag Gol r. China 85 F3
Aibetsu Japan 90 H3
Aichach Germany 48 I7
Aichi pref. Japan 91 E7
Aid U.S.A. 176 C7
Aida Japan 91 D7
Aidin Turkm. 102 C5
Aigiali Greece 59 G12
also spelt Aiyiáli
Aigialousa Cyprus 108 F2
also known as Yialousa
Aigina Greece 59 E11
Aigina i. Greece 59 E11
English form Aegina; also spelt Aíyina
Aiginio Greece 58 D8
also known as Aíyinion
Aigio Greece 59 D10
also known as Aíyion
Aigle Switz. 51 M6
Aigle de Chambeyron mt. France 51 M8
Aigoual, Mont mt. France 51 J8
Aiguá Uruguay 204 G4
Aiguebelle, Parc de Conservation d' nature res. Canada 173 O2
Aigües Tortes i Estany de St Maurici, Parque Nacional d' nat. park Spain 55 L2
Aiguille de Scolette mt. France/Italy 51 M7
Aiguilles d'Arves mts France 51 M7
Aiguille Verte mt. France 51 M7
Aigurande France 50 H6
Aihua China see Yunxian
Aihui China see Heihe
Aija Peru 200 A2
Aijal India see Aizawl
Aiken U.S.A. 175 D5
Ailao Shan mts China 86 B3
Aileron Australia 148 B4
Aileu East Timor 75 C5
Ailigandi Panama 186 D5
Ailing China 87 D3
Ailinglabelab atoll Marshall Is see Ailinglapalap
Ailinglapalap atoll Marshall Is 220 F6
also spelt Aelönlaplap or Ailinglebelab; formerly known as Lambert
Ailly-sur-Noye France 51 I3
Ailsa Craig Canada 173 L7
Ailsa Craig i. U.K. 47 G8
Aimogasta Arg. 204 D3
Aimorés, Serra dos hills Brazil 203 D6
Aïn Beïda Alg. 123 G2
Ain r. France 51 L7
'Aïn 'Amûr spring Egypt 121 F3
Ainaži Latvia 42 F4
Aïn Beïda Alg. 123 G2
formerly known as Daoud
Aïn Beni Mathar Morocco 123 E2
Aïn Ben Tili Mauritania 122 C4
Aïn Bessem Alg. 55 O8
Aïn Biré well Mauritania 124 C2
Aïn Boucif Alg. 55 O9
'Aïn Dalla spring Egypt 121 E3
Aïn Defla Alg. 123 F1
formerly known as Duperré
Aïn Deheb Alg. 123 F2
Aïn Draham Tunisia 57 A12
Aïn el Bâgha well Egypt 108 E8
'Aïn el Furtâga well Egypt 108 F8
Aïn el Hadjadj well Alg. 123 F3
'Aïn el Hadjadj well Alg. 123 G4
Aïn el Hadjel Alg. 123 F2
'Aïn el Maqfi spring Egypt 121 F3
Aïn Galakka spring Chad 120 C5
Aïn Mdila well Alg. 123 G2
Aïn-M'Lila Alg. 123 G1
Ainos nat. park Greece 59 B10
Aïn Oussera Alg. 123 F2
Aïn Salah Alg. see In Salah
Aïn Sefra Alg. 123 E2
Ainslie, Lake Canada 169 I4
Ainsworth IA U.S.A. 172 B9
Ainsworth NE U.S.A. 178 C3
Aintab Turkey see Gaziantep
Aïn Taya Alg. 55 O8
Aïn Tédélès Alg. 55 L9
Aïn Temouchent Alg. 123 E2
'Aïn Tibaghbagh spring Egypt 121 E2
'Aïn Timeira spring Egypt 121 E2
Aïn Ti-m Misaou well Alg. 123 F5
'Aïn Zeitûn Egypt 106 A5
Aipe Col. 198 C4
Aiquile Bol. 200 D4
Air i. Indon. 77 D2
also known as Raibu
Airão Brazil 199 F5
Airbangis Indon. 76 B2
Airdrie Canada 167 H5
Aire r. France 51 K3
Aire-sur-l'Adour France 50 F9
Air Force Island Canada 165 L3
Airgin Sum China 85 F3
Airhitam r. Indon. 77 E3
Airhitam, Teluk b. Indon. 77 E3
Airlie Beach Australia 149 F4
Airlie Island Australia 150 A4
Airolo Switz. 51 O6
Airpanas Indon. 75 C4
Air Ronge Canada 167 J4
Airvault France 50 F6
Aisatung Mountain Myanmar 78 A3
Aisch r. Germany 48 I6
Aisén admin. reg. Chile 205 B7
Aishalton Guyana 199 G4
Ai Shan hill China 85 I4
Aishihik Canada 166 B2
Aishihik Lake Canada 166 B2
Aisimi Greece see Aisymi
Aisne r. France 51 I3
Aïssa, Djebel mt. Alg. 123 E2
Aisymi Greece 58 G7
also spelt Aisími
Aitamännikkö Fin. 44 N2
Aitana mt. Spain 55 K6
Aitape P.N.G. 73 J7
also spelt Eitape
Aït Benhaddou tourist site Morocco 122 D3
Aitkin U.S.A. 174 A2
Aitoliko Greece 59 C10
Aitova Rus. Fed. 41 J5
Aiud Romania 58 E2
also known as Nagyenyed
Aivadzh Tajik. 101 G2
also spelt Ayvadzh
Aiviekste r. Latvia 42 G5
Aix France see Aix-en-Provence
Aix r. France 51 K7
Aix-en-Othe France 51 J4
Aix-en-Provence France 51 L9
historically known as Aquae Sextiae; short form Aix
Aixe-sur-Vienne France 50 H7
Aix-la-Chapelle Germany see Aachen
Aix-les-Bains France 51 L7
historically known as Aquae Gratianae
Āīy Ādī Eth. 128 C1
Aiyiáli Greece see Aigiali
Aíyina i. Greece see Aigina
Aíyinion Greece see Aiginio
Aíyion Greece see Aigio
Aizawl India 97 G5
formerly spelt Aijal
Aizenay France 50 E6
Aizkraukle Latvia 42 G5
formerly known as Stučka or Stuchka or imeni Petra Stuchki
Aizpute Latvia 42 C5
Aizu-wakamatsu Japan 90 F6
Ajā, Jibāl mts Saudi Arabia 104 C2
Ajaccio Corse France 52 D3
Ajaccio, Golfe d' b. Corse France 56 A7
Ajaigarh India 96 D4
Ajajú r. Col. 198 C4
Ajalpán Mex. 185 F5
Ajanta India 94 B1
Ajanta Range hills India see Sahyadriparvat Range
Ajasse Nigeria 125 G4
Ajax Canada 173 N7
Ajax, Mount N.Z. 153 G10
Ajayameru India see Ajmer
Ajban U.A.E. 105 F2
Aj Bogd Uul mts Mongolia 84 B2
Ajdābiyā Libya 120 D2
formerly spelt Agedabia
Ajdovščina Slovenia 56 F3
a-Jiddét des. Oman see Harāsīs, Jiddat al
Ajigasawa Japan 90 G4
'Ajīj, Wādī al watercourse Iraq 109 M2
Ajimganj India 97 F4
Ajka Hungary 49 O8
'Ajlūn Jordan 108 G5
Ajman U.A.E. 105 F2
Ajmer India 96 B4
formerly known as Ajayameru or Ajmer-Merwara
Ajmer-Merwara India see Ajmer
Ajo U.S.A. 183 L9
Ajo, Mount U.S.A. 183 L9
Ajra India 94 B2
Ajuy Phil. 74 B4
Akāashat Iraq 107 D4
Akabira Japan 90 H3
Akabli Alg. 123 F4
Akaboun well Mali 125 F2
Akademii, Zaliv b. Rus. Fed. 82 E1
English form Academy Bay
Akademii Nauk, Khrebet mt. Tajik. see Akademiyai Fanho, Qatorkŭhi
Akademiyai Fanho, Qatorkŭhi mt. Tajik. 101 G2
also known as Akademii Nauk, Khrebet
Akagera National Park Rwanda 126 F5
also known as Kagera, Parc National de la or L'Akagera, Parc National de
Akagi Japan 91 C7
Akaishi-dake mt. Japan 91 F7
Āk'ak'ī Beseka Eth. 128 C2
Akalkot India 94 C2
Akama, Akra c. Cyprus see Arnauti, Cape
Akamagaseki Japan see Shimonoseki
Akamkpa Nigeria 125 H5
Akan Japan 90 I3
Akan-ko l. Japan 90 H3
Akan National Park Japan 90 I3
Akarkar well Niger 125 G3
Akarnanika mts Greece 59 B10
Akaroa N.Z. 153 G11
Akaroa Harbour N.Z. 153 G11
Akas reg. India 97 G4
'Akāsh, Wādī watercourse Iraq 109 L3
Akasha Sudan 121 F4
'Akāshāt Iraq 109 K4
Akashi Japan 91 D7
Äkäsjokisuu Fin. 44 M2
Akbakay Kazakh. 103 H3
Akbalyk Kazakh. 103 I3
also spelt Aqbalyq
Akbarābād Iran 100 C4
Akbarpur Uttar Pradesh India 96 D4
Akbarpur Uttar Pradesh India 97 D4
Akbasty Kazakh. 102 E3
Akbaytal Tajik. 101 H2
also known as Rabatakbaytal or Rabotoqbaytal
Akbaytal Pass Tajik. 101 H2
Akbeit Kazakh. 103 G2
also spelt Aqbeyit
Akbou Alg. 55 P8
Akbulak Rus. Fed. 102 C2
Akçadağ Turkey 107 D3
Akçakale Turkey 107 D3
Akçakertikbeli Geçidi pass Turkey 59 J9
Akçakoca Turkey 106 B2
Akçalı Dağları mt. Turkey 106 C3
Akçalı Dağları mts Turkey 108 D1
Akçaova Turkey 59 I11
Akçay r. Turkey 59 J11
Akchakaya, Vpadina depr. Turkm. 102 D4
Akchâr reg. Mauritania 124 B2
Akchatau Kazakh. 103 H3
also known as Aqshatau
Akchi Kazakh. see Akshiy
Akdağ mt. Turkey 59 J9
Akdağlar mts Turkey 106 B3
Akdağmadeni Turkey 106 C3
Akdepe Turkm. 102 D4
formerly known as Leninsk
Akdere Turkey 108 E1
Ak Dovurak Rus. Fed. 84 A1
Akelamo Indon. 75 D2
Akele Guzai prov. Eritrea 104 B5
Akelo Sudan 128 B3
Åkersberga Sweden 45 L4
Akershus county Norway 45 J3
formerly spelt Aggershus
Åkerstrømmen Norway 45 J3
Akespe Kazakh. 103 E3
Aketi Dem. Rep. Congo 126 D4
Akgyr Erezi hills Turkm. see Akkyr, Gory
Akhalgori Georgia 107 F2
also known as Leningori
Akhalk'alak'i Georgia 107 E2
Akhal Oblast admin. div. Turkm. see Akhal'skaya Oblast'
Akhal'skaya Oblast' admin. div. Turkm. 102 D5
English form Akhal Oblast; formerly known as Ashkhabadskaya Oblast'
Akhalts'ikhe Georgia 107 E2
Akhḑar, Al Jabal al mts Libya 120 D2
Akhḑar, Jabal mts Oman 105 G3
Akhḑar, Wādī al watercourse Saudi Arabia 109 H9
Akheloy Bulg. 58 I6
Akhisar Turkey 106 A3
historically known as Thyatira
Akhmīm Egypt 121 F3
also spelt Ekhmīm; historically known as Chemmis or Panoplis
Akhnoor Jammu and Kashmir 96 B2
Akhsu Azer. see Ağsu
Akhta Armenia see Hrazdan
Akhtarīn Syria 109 I1
Akhtubinsk Rus. Fed. 102 A2
Akhty Rus. Fed. 102 A4
Akhtyrka Ukr. see Okhtyrka
Aki Japan 91 C8
Akiéni Gabon 126 B5
Akimiski Island Canada 168 D2
Akincilar Turkey see Selçuk
Akıncılar Turkey 107 D2
Åkirkeby Denmark 45 K5
Akishma r. Rus. Fed. 82 D1
Akita Japan 90 G5
Akita pref. Japan 90 G5
Akitio N.Z. 152 K8
Akjoujt Mauritania 124 B2
Akka Morocco 122 C3
Akkajaure l. Sweden 44 L2
Akkala Uzbek. 102 D4
also spelt Oqqal"a
Akkem Rus. Fed. 88 D1
Akkerman Ukr. see Bilhorod-Dnistrovs'kyy
Akkermanovka Rus. Fed. 102 D2
Akkeshi Japan 90 I3
Akkeshi-wan b. Japan 90 I3
'Akko Israel 108 G5
historically known as Accho or Acre or St-Jean-d'Acre or Ptolemais
Akkol' Akmolinskaya Oblast' Kazakh. 103 G1
also spelt Aqköl; formerly known as Alekseyevka
Akkol' Almatinskaya Oblast' Kazakh. 103 H3
Akkol' Atyrauskaya Oblast' Kazakh. 41 I7
also spelt Akkul' or Aqköl
Akkol' Zhambylskaya Oblast' Kazakh. 103 G4
Akköy Turkey 106 A3
Akköy Turkey 59 K11
Akku Kazakh. 103 I2
formerly known as Lebyazh'ye
Akkul' Kazakh. see Akkol'
Akkum Kazakh. 103 F3
Akkuş Turkey 107 D2
Akkyr, Gory hills Turkm. 102 C4
also known as Akgyr Erezi
Akkystau Kazakh. 102 B3
also known as Aqqystaū
Aklavik Canada 164 F3
Aklera India 96 C4
Aklub reg. Saudi Arabia 104 D4
Ak-Mechet Kazakh. see Kyzylorda
Akmena r. Lith. 42 D6
Akmenė Lith. 42 D5
Akmenrags pt Latvia 42 C5
Akmeqit China 89 B4
Akmola Kazakh. see Astana
Akmola Oblast admin. div. Kazakh. see Akmolinskaya Oblast'
Akmolinsk Kazakh. see Astana
Akmolinskaya Oblast' admin. div. Kazakh. 103 G2
English form Aqmola Oblast; also known as Aqmola Oblysy; formerly known as Akmola Oblast or Tselinogradskaya Oblast'
Aknīste Latvia 42 G5
Aknoul Morocco 122 E2
Akō Japan 91 D7
Akobo Sudan 128 B3
Akobo Wenz r. Eth./Sudan 128 B3
Akodia India 96 C5
Akola Maharashtra India 94 B2
Akola Maharashtra India 94 C1
Akom II Cameroon 125 H6
Akonolinga Cameroon 125 I6
Akop Sudan 126 F2
Akordat Eritrea 121 H6
Akören Turkey 106 C3
Akot India 96 C5
Akouménaye Fr. Guiana 199 H4
Akoupé Côte d'Ivoire 124 E5
Ak-Oyuk, Gora mt. Rus. Fed. 84 A1
Akpatok Island Canada 165 M3
Akqi China 88 B3
Akraifnio Greece 59 E10
Akranes Iceland 44 [inset] B2
Akrathos, Akra pt Greece 59 F8
Åkrē Iraq 109 O1
Akrérèb Niger 125 H2
Akritas, Akra pt Greece 59 C12
Akron CO U.S.A. 178 B3
Akron IN U.S.A. 172 G9
Akron OH U.S.A. 176 D4
Akrotiri Bay Cyprus 108 E3
also known as Akrotirion Bay or Akrotiriou, Kolpos
Akrotirion Bay Cyprus see Akrotiri Bay
Akrotiriou, Kolpos b. Cyprus see Akrotiri Bay
Akrotiri Sovereign Base Area military base Cyprus 108 D3
▶Aksai Chin terr. Asia 89 B5
Disputed territory (China/India). Also known as Aqsayqin Hit.
Aksakal Turkey 59 J8
Aksakovo Bulg. 58 I5
Aksakovo Rus. Fed. 40 J5
Aksaray Turkey 106 C3
Aksarka Rus. Fed. 38 G3
Aksay China 84 B4
also known as Hongliuwan
Aksay Kazakh. 102 C2
also spelt Aqsay; formerly known as Kazakhstan
Ak-Say r. Kyrg. 103 H4
Aksay Rus. Fed. 41 H7
Akşehir Turkey 106 B3
historically known as Philomelium
Akşehir Gölü l. Turkey 106 B3
Akseki Turkey 106 B3
Aksenovo Rus. Fed. 41 J5
Aks-e Rostam r. Iran 100 C4
Aksha Rus. Fed. 85 G1
Akshatau Kazakh. 102 C2
Akshiganak Kazakh. 103 E2
Akshiy Kazakh. 103 I4
also spelt Aqshi; formerly spelt Akchi
Akshukur Kazakh. 102 B4
Aksu Xinjiang China 88 C3
Aksu Xinjiang China 88 C3
Aksu Almatinskaya Oblast' Kazakh. 103 I3
Aksu Pavlodarskaya Oblast' Kazakh. 103 I1
also spelt Aqsū; formerly known as Ermak or Yermak
Aksu Severnyy Kazakhstan Kazakh. 103 G1
also spelt Aqsū
Aksu Zapadnyy Kazakhstan Kazakh. 102 C2
Aksu r. Kazakh. 103 I3
Aksu r. Tajik. see Oksu
Aksu Turkey 108 B1
Aksu r. Turkey 107 B3
Aksuat Kustanayskaya Oblast' Kazakh. 103 F2
Aksuat Vostochnyy Kazakhstan Kazakh. 88 C2
also spelt Aqsūat
Aksuat, Ozero salt l. Kazakh. see Bol'shoy Aksuat, Ozero
Aksu-Ayuly Kazakh. 103 H2
also spelt Aqsū-Ayuly
Aksuek Kazakh. 103 H3
Aksu He r. China 88 C3
Āksum Eth. 128 C1
historically known as Axum
Aksüme China 88 C2
Aksu-Zhabaglinskiy Zapovednik nature res. Kazakh. 103 G4
Aktag mt. China 89 D4
Ak-Tal Rus. Fed. 88 F1
Aktash Uzbek. 103 F5
also spelt Oqtosh
Aktau Karagandinskaya Oblast' Kazakh. 103 G3
Aktau Karagandinskaya Oblast' Kazakh. 103 H2
Aktau Mangistauskaya Oblast' Kazakh. 102 B4
also spelt Aqtaū; formerly known as Shevchenko
Aktepe Turkey 109 H1
Akto China 88 B4
Aktogay Karagandinskaya Oblast' Kazakh. 103 H2
also spelt Aqtoghay
Aktogay Pavlodarskaya Oblast' Kazakh. 103 H1
also spelt Aqtoghay; formerly known as Krasnokutsk or Krasnokutskoye
Aktogay Vostochnyy Kazakhstan Kazakh. 103 I3
Aktsyabrskaya Belarus 43 L6
also spelt Oktyabr'skaya
Aktsyabrski Belarus 43 J9
also spelt Oktyabr'skiy; formerly known as Karpilovka
Aktsyabrski Belarus 43 K7
also spelt Oktyabr'skiy
Aktumsyk Kazakh. 102 D3
Aktumsyk, Mys pt Uzbek. 102 D3
Ak-Tüz Kyrg. 103 H4
also spelt Aktyuz
Aktyubinsk Kazakh. 102 D2
also known as Aqtöbe
Aktyubinskaya Oblast' admin. div. Kazakh. 102 D2
English form Aktyubinsk Oblast; also known as Aqtöbe Oblysy
Aktyubinsk Oblast admin. div. Kazakh. see Aktyubinskaya Oblast'
Aktyuz Kyrg. see Ak-Tüz
Akujärvi Fin. 44 N1
Akula Dem. Rep. Congo 126 D4
Akulichi Rus. Fed. 43 O8
Akulivik Canada 165 L3
Akumadan Ghana 125 E5
Akune Japan 91 B8
Akur mt. Uganda 128 B4
Akure Nigeria 125 G5
Akureyri Iceland 44 [inset] C2
Akuroa N.Z. 152 I4
Akwa Ibom state Nigeria 125 G5
Akwanga Nigeria 125 H4
Akyab Myanmar see Sittwe
Ak"yar Rus. Fed. 102 D2
Akyatan Gölü salt l. Turkey 108 G1
Akzhal Karagandinskaya Oblast' Kazakh. 103 H3
Akzhal Vostochnyy Kazakhstan Kazakh. 103 J2
also spelt Aqzhal
Akzhar Kzyl-Ordinskaya Oblast' Kazakh. 103 F3
Akzhar Vostochnyy Kazakhstan Kazakh. 88 C2
also spelt Aqzhar
Akzhar Zhambylskaya Oblast' Kazakh. 103 G4
Akzhaykyn, Ozero salt l. Kazakh. 103 F3
also known as Aqzhayqyn Köli
Ål Norway 45 J3
Ala r. Belarus 43 K9
Ala Italy 56 D3
'Alā, Jabal al hills Syria 109 H2
Alabama r. U.S.A. 175 C6
Alabama state U.S.A. 175 C5
Alabaster AL U.S.A. 175 C5
Alabaster MI U.S.A. 173 J6
Al 'Abṭīyah well Iraq 107 F5
Ala-Buka Kyrg. 103 G4
Al Abyaḑ Libya 120 B3
Al Abyār Libya 120 D1
Alaca Turkey 106 C2
also known as Huseyinabat
Alacahan Turkey 107 D3
Alaçam Turkey 106 C2
Alaçam Dağları mts Turkey 59 J9
Alacant Spain see Alicante
Alaçatı Turkey 59 H10
Alacrán, Arrecife reef Mex. 185 H4
Aladag mt. Bulg. 58 G7
Aladağ Turkey 106 C3
also known as Bademli
Ala Dag mt. Turkey 107 E3
Ala Dağlar mts Turkey 107 E3
Ala Dağları mts Turkey 106 C3
Al 'Adam Libya 120 D2
Alaejos Spain 54 F3
Al Aflāj reg. Saudi Arabia 105 D3
Alagadiço Brazil 199 F4
Alagapuram India 94 C4
Alag Hayrhan Uul mt. Mongolia 84 B2
Alagir Rus. Fed. 41 H8
Alagoas state Brazil 202 E4
Alagoinhas Brazil 202 E5
Alagón Spain 55 J3
Alagón r. Spain 54 E5
Alah r. Phil. 74 C5
Alahanpanjang Indon. 76 C3
Alahärmä Fin. 44 M3
Al Aḩmadī Kuwait 107 G5
Alaid, Ostrov i. Rus. Fed. see Atlasova, Ostrov
Alaior Spain 55 P5
Alai Range mts Asia 99 I2
also known as Alay Kyrka Toosu or Alayskiy Khrebet or Oloy, Qatorkŭhi
Ālāivān Iran 100 C3
Al Ajā'iz oasis Oman 105 G4
Al 'Ajā'iz well Oman 105 G4
Al Ajām Saudi Arabia 105 E2
Alajärvi Fin. 44 M3
Alajaure naturreservat nature res. Sweden 44 M1
Al Ajfar Saudi Arabia 104 C2
Alajõgi r. Estonia 42 I2
Alajuela Costa Rica 186 B5
Alakanuk U.S.A. 164 C3
Alaknanda r. India 96 C3
Alakol', Ozero salt l. Kazakh. 88 C2
also known as Ala Kul
Ala Kul salt l. Kazakh. see Alakol', Ozero
Alakurtti Rus. Fed. 44 O2
Al 'Alamayn Egypt see El 'Alamein
Alalaú r. Brazil 199 F5
Al 'Alayyah Saudi Arabia 104 C4
Alama Somalia 128 D3
Al 'Amādīyah Iraq 107 E3
Alamagan i. N. Mariana Is 73 K3
also spelt Alamaguan
Alamaguan i. N. Mariana Is see Alamagan
Al 'Amār Saudi Arabia 104 D2
Al 'Amārah Iraq 107 F5
'Alāmarvdasht watercourse Iran 100 C4
Ālamat'ā Eth. 104 B5
'Alam el Rûm, Râs pt Egypt 121 E2
Al Amghar waterhole Iraq 107 F5
Al Amghar waterhole Saudi Arabia 109 N7
Alamicamba Nicaragua 186 B4
Alaminos Phil. 74 A2
Alamito Creek r. U.S.A. 181 F7
Al Amlah Saudi Arabia 104 C3
'Alam Nafaza hill Egypt 108 A7
Alamo U.S.A. 174 B5
Alamo Dam U.S.A. 183 K7
Alamogordo U.S.A. 181 F6
Alamo Heights U.S.A. 179 C6
Alamos Sonora Mex. 184 C2
Alamos Sonora Mex. 184 C3
Alamos r. Mex. 185 E3
Alamos, Sierra mts Mex. 184 C3
Alamosa U.S.A. 181 F5
Alamosa Creek r. U.S.A. 181 F6
Alamos de Peña Mex. 184 D2
Alampur India 94 C3
Al 'Anad Yemen 104 D5
Alanäs Sweden 44 K2
Al Anbār governorate Iraq 107 E4
Åland is Fin. see Åland Islands
Aland r. Germany 48 I2
Aland India 94 C2
Aland r. Iran 107 F3
Åland Islands Fin. 45 L3
also known as Ahvenanmaa; short form Åland
Ålands Hav sea chan. Fin./Sweden 45 L4
Alandur India 94 D3
Alangalang, Tanjung pt Indon. 77 G3
Alang Besar i. Indon. 76 C2
Alange, Embalse de resr Spain 54 E6
Alanggantang i. Indon. 76 D3
Alanson U.S.A. 173 I5
Alanya Turkey 106 C3
historically known as Coracesium
'Alā' od Dīn Iran 100 C4
Alapaha r. U.S.A. 175 D6
Alapakam India 94 C4
Alapli Turkey 41 D8
Alappuzha India see Alleppey
Alapur India 96 C4
Al 'Aqabah Jordan 108 G8
also spelt 'Aqaba; historically known as Aela or Aelana
Al 'Aqīq Saudi Arabia 104 C3
Al 'Āqūlah well Saudi Arabia 104 C4
Al 'Arabīyah i. Saudi Arabia 107 G6
Al 'Arabīyah as Sa'ūdīyah country Asia see Saudi Arabia
Alarcón, Embalse de resr Spain 55 I5
Al 'Arīḑah Saudi Arabia 104 C4
Al Arin Saudi Arabia 104 C4
Al Arṭāwīyah Saudi Arabia 105 D2
Alas Indon. 77 G5
Alas, Selat sea chan. Indon. 77 G5

index A

Alaşehir Turkey 106 B3
historically known as Philadelphia
Alash r. Rus. Fed. 88 E1
Alash, Plato plat. Rus. Fed. 88 E1
Alashiya country Asia see Cyprus
Al 'Āshūrīyah well Iraq 107 E5
Alaska state U.S.A. 164 E3
Alaska, Gulf of U.S.A. 164 E4
Alaska Highway Canada/U.S.A. 166 A2
Alaska Peninsula U.S.A. 164 C4
Alaska Range mts U.S.A. 164 E3
Al 'Assāfīyah Saudi Arabia 104 B1
Alassio Italy 56 A4
Älät Azer. 107 G3
Alat Uzbek. 103 E5
also spelt Olot
Alataw Shankou pass China/Kazakh. see Dzungarian Gate
Al 'Athāmīn hill Iraq 109 O7
Alatri Italy 56 F7
historically known as Aletrium
Al Atwā' well Saudi Arabia 104 C1
Alatyr' Rus. Fed. 40 H5
Alatyr' r. Rus. Fed. 40 H5
Alauksts l. Latvia 42 G4
Alausí Ecuador 198 B5
Alaverdi Armenia 107 F2
Alavieska Fin. 44 N2
Ala-Vuokki Fin. 44 O2
Alavus Fin. 44 M3
Alawa Aboriginal Land res. Australia 148 B2
Al Awābī Oman 105 G3
Al 'Awdah Saudi Arabia 105 D2
Alawoona Australia 146 D3
Al Awshazīyah Saudi Arabia 104 C2
Alaykel' Kyrg. see Alaykuu
Alaykuu Kyrg. 103 H4
also known as Kök-Art or Kögart or Kök-Art; formerly known as Alaykel'
Alay Kyrka Toosu mts Asia see Alai Range
Al 'Ayn Oman 105 G3
Al 'Ayn Saudi Arabia 104 B2
Al 'Ayn U.A.E. 105 F2
Alayskiy Khrebet mts Asia see Alai Range
Al A'zamīyah Iraq 109 P4
Alazani r. Azer./Georgia 107 F2
Alazeya r. Rus. Fed. 39 P2
Al 'Azīzīyah Iraq 107 F4

▶Al 'Azīzīyah Libya 120 B1
Highest recorded shade temperature in the world.
world [climate and weather] ➡ 16–17

Alba Italy 51 O8
Alba U.S.A. 173 I6
Alba Adriatica Italy 56 F6
Al Ba'ā'ith Saudi Arabia 104 C2
Al Ba'āj Iraq 109 M1
Al Bāb Syria 109 I1
Albacete Spain 55 J5
Al Badā'i' Saudi Arabia 104 B2
Alba de Tormes Spain 54 F4
Al Badī' Saudi Arabia 105 D3
Al Bādiyah al Janūbīyah hill Iraq 107 F5
Ålbæk Denmark 45 J4
Ålbæk Bugt b. Denmark 45 J4
Al'bagan, Gora mt. Rus. Fed. 88 D1
Al Bāhah prov. Saudi Arabia 104 C3
Al Bahrayn country Asia see Bahrain
Alba Iulia Romania 58 E2
also known as Gyulafehérvár; formerly known as Karlsburg; historically known as Apulum
Al Bajā' well U.A.E. 105 E2
Al Ba'jah Saudi Arabia 104 C2
Al Bakhrā well Saudi Arabia 105 D2
Al Bakkī Libya 120 B3
Albalate de Arzobispo Spain 55 K3
Albanel, Lac l. Canada 169 F3
▶Albania country Europe 58 A7
known as Republika e Shqipërisë in Albanian
europe [countries] ➡ 32–35
Albano Brazil 199 G5
Albany Australia 151 B7
Albany r. Canada 168 D2
Albany Jamaica 186 D3
Albany GA U.S.A. 175 C6
Albany MO U.S.A. 178 D3

▶Albany NY U.S.A. 177 L3
State capital of New York. Historically known as Fort Orange.

Albany OH U.S.A. 176 C6
Albany OR U.S.A. 180 B3
Albany TX U.S.A. 179 C5
Albany Downs Australia 147 F1
Albardão do João Maria coastal area Brazil 204 G4
Al Bardawīl depr. Saudi Arabia 109 K6
Al Bardī Libya 120 E2
Al Bāridah hills Saudi Arabia 109 K8
Al Barīt waterhole Iraq 109 N6
Al Barrah Saudi Arabia 105 D2
Al Başrah Iraq see Basra
Al Başrah governorate Iraq 107 F5
Al Bat'ha' marsh Iraq 107 F5
Al Bāţinah admin. reg. Oman 105 G3
Al Bāţinah reg. Oman 105 G2
Al Bāţinah i. Saudi Arabia 105 E2
Albatross Bay Australia 149 D2
Albatross Island Australia 147 E5
Albatross Point N.Z. 152 I6
Al Bayḑā' Libya 120 D1
also spelt Beida
Al Bayḑā' Yemen 105 D5
Al Bayḑā' governorate Yemen 105 D5
Albay Gulf Phil. 74 B3
Albemarle U.S.A. 174 D5
Albemarle Sound sea chan. U.S.A. 174 E5
Albenga Italy 56 A4
Alberche r. Spain 54 G5
Alberdi Para. 201 F6
Alberga watercourse Australia 146 B1
Albergaria-a-Velha Port. 54 C4
Albergian, Monte mt. Italy 51 M7
Albert Australia 147 E3
Albert r. Australia 148 C3
Albert France 51 I3
Albert, Lake Australia 146 C3
Albert, Lake Dem. Rep. Congo/Uganda 128 A4
formerly known as Mobutu, Lake or Mobutu Sese Seko, Lake
Albert, Parc National nat. park Dem. Rep. Congo see Virunga, Parc National des
Alberta prov. Canada 167 H4
Albert Falls Nature Reserve S. Africa 133 O6
Albertinia S. Africa 132 F11
Albertirsa Hungary 49 Q8
Albert Kanaal canal Belgium 51 L2
Albert Lea U.S.A. 174 A3
Albert Nile r. Sudan/Uganda 126 G4
Alberto de Agostini, Parque Nacional nat. park Chile 205 C9
Alberton Canada 169 H4
Alberto Oviedo Mota Mex. 183 I9
Albertshoek S. Africa 133 J4
Albert Town Bahamas 187 E2
Albertville Dem. Rep. Congo see Kalémié
Albertville France 51 M7
Albertville U.S.A. 174 C5
Albeşti Romania 58 I2
Albi France 51 I9
Albia U.S.A. 174 A3
Al Bi'ār Saudi Arabia 104 B3
Al Bidah des. Saudi Arabia 105 E2
Albignasego Italy 56 D3
Albina Suriname 199 H3
Albino Italy 56 B3
Albion CA U.S.A. 182 A2
Albion IN U.S.A. 174 C3
Albion MI U.S.A. 173 I8
Albion NE U.S.A. 178 C3
Albion NY U.S.A. 176 G2
Albion PA U.S.A. 176 E4
Al Bi'r Saudi Arabia 104 B1
also known as Bi'r Ibn Hirmās
Al Birk Saudi Arabia 104 C4
Al Birkah Saudi Arabia 104 C3
Al Biyāḑh reg. Saudi Arabia 105 D3
Alborán, Isla de i. Spain 55 H9
Ålborg Denmark 45 J4
also spelt Aalborg
Ålborg Bugt b. Denmark 45 J4
Alborz, Reshteh-ye mts Iran see Elburz Mountains
Albota Romania 58 F4
Albox Spain 55 I7
Albro Australia 149 E4
Albstadt Germany 48 G7
Al Budayyi Bahrain 105 E2
Albufeira Port. 54 C7
Ālbū Ghars, Sabkhat salt l. Iraq 109 M3
Al Bukayrīyah Saudi Arabia 104 C2
Albula Alpen mts Switz. 51 P6
Albuñol Spain 55 H8
Albuquerque U.S.A. 181 F6
Albuquerque, Cayos de is Caribbean Sea 186 C4
Al Buraymī Oman 105 F2
Alburg U.S.A. 177 L1
Alburno, Monte mt. Italy 57 H8
Alburquerque Spain 54 E5
Albury Australia 147 E4
Al'bu Kyrg. 153 E12
Al Buşayrah Syria 109 L2
also spelt Buseire
Al Busayṭā' plain Saudi Arabia 107 D5
Al Buşayyah Iraq 107 F5
Al Bushūk well Saudi Arabia 104 D1
Al Buţayn plain Saudi Arabia 105 D2
Al Buwi well Oman 105 G4
Alca Peru 200 B3
Alcácer do Sal Port. 54 C6
Alcáçovas r. Port. 54 C6
Alcalá de Chivert Spain 55 L4
Alcalá de Guadaira Spain 54 F7
Alcalá de Henares Spain 55 H4
Alcalá de los Gazules Spain 54 F8
Alcalá la Real Spain 54 H7
Alcalde, Punta pt Chile 204 C3
Alcamo Sicilia Italy 57 E11
Alcanadre r. Spain 55 L3
Alcanar Spain 55 L4
Alcañiz Spain 55 K3
Alcântara Brazil 202 C2
Alcántara Spain 54 E5
Alcántara, Embalse de resr Spain 54 E5
Alcántara II, Embalse de resr Spain 54 E5
Alcantara Lake Canada 167 I2
Alcantarilla Spain 55 J7
Alcaraz Spain 55 I6
Alcaraz, Sierra de mts Spain 55 I6
Alcaria Ruiva hill Port. 54 D7
Alcarrache r. Port./Spain 54 D6
Alcatrazes, Ilha de i. Brazil 207 H11
Alcaudete Spain 54 G7
Alcázar de San Juan Spain 55 H5
Alcazarquivir Morocco see Ksar el Kebir
Alchevs'k Ukr. 41 F6
formerly known as Kommunarsk or Voroshilovsk
Alcira Arg. 204 D4
Alcira Spain see Alzira
Alcobaça Brazil 203 E6
Alconchel Spain 54 D6
Alcora Spain 55 K4
Alcorneo r. Port./Spain 54 E5
Alcorta Arg. 204 E4
Alcoy Spain 55 K6
Alcubierre, Sierra de mts Spain 55 K3
Alcúdia Spain 55 O5
Aldabra Atoll Seychelles 129 E7
Aldabra Islands Seychelles 129 E7
Aldama Chihuahua Mex. 184 D2
Aldama Tamaulipas Mex. 185 F4
Aldan Rus. Fed. 39 M4
Aldan r. Rus. Fed. 39 M3
Aldeburgh U.K. 47 N11
Aldeia Velha Brazil 202 B4
Aldeia Viçosa Angola 127 B7
Alder Creek U.S.A. 177 J2
Alderney i. Channel Is 50 D3
also known as Aurigny
Alder Peak U.S.A. 182 C6
Aldershot U.K. 47 L12
Alderson U.S.A. 176 E8
Al Dhafrah reg. U.A.E. 105 F3
Aldie Eth. 128 D3
Aledo U.S.A. 174 B3
Aleg Mauritania 124 B2
Alegre Brazil 203 D7
Alegre Brazil 203 A9
Alegres Mountain U.S.A. 181 E6
Alejandro Korn Arg. 204 F4
Alekhovshchina Rus. Fed. 43 O1
Aleksandra, Mys hd Rus. Fed. 82 E1
Aleksandra Bekovicha-Cherkasskogo, Zaliv b. Kazakh. 102 B4
Aleksandriya Ukr. see Oleksandriya
Aleksandropol Armenia see Gyumri
Aleksandrov Rus. Fed. 43 T5
Aleksandrovac Srbija Yugo. 58 C5
Aleksandrov Gay Rus. Fed. 102 B2
Aleksandrovka Rus. Fed. 41 J5
Aleksandrovo Bulg. 58 G5
Aleksandrovo Bulg. 58 F5
Aleksandrovsk Rus. Fed. 40 K4
formerly known as Aleksandrovskiy
Aleksandrovsk Ukr. see Zaporizhzhya
Aleksandrovskaya Rus. Fed. 43 R2
Aleksandrovskiy Rus. Fed. see Aleksandrovsk
Aleksandrovskoye Stavropol'skiy Kray Rus. Fed. 41 G7
Aleksandrovskoye Stavropol'skiy Kray Rus. Fed. 41 H7
Aleksandrovskoye Tomskaya Oblast' Rus. Fed. 38 H3
Aleksandrovsk-Sakhalinskiy Rus. Fed. 82 F2
Aleksandrów Kujawski Poland 49 P3
Aleksandrów Łódzki Poland 49 Q4
Aleksandry, Zemlya i. Rus. Fed. 38 E1
English form Alexandra Land
Alekseyevka Kazakh. see Akkol'
Alekseyevka Kazakh. 103 H2
Alekseyevka Kazakh. see Terekty
Alekseyevka Belgorodskaya Oblast' Rus. Fed. 41 F6
Alekseyevka Belgorodskaya Oblast' Rus. Fed. 41 F6
Alekseyevka Bryanskaya Oblast' Rus. Fed. 43 N8
Alekseyevskaya Rus. Fed. 41 G6
Aleksin Rus. Fed. 43 S7
Aleksinac Srbija Yugo. 58 C5
Aleksino-Shatur Rus. Fed. 43 U6
Alèmbé Gabon 126 A5
'Alem Ketema Eth. 128 C2
'Alem Maya Eth. 128 D2
Além Paraíba Brazil 203 D7
Ålen Norway 44 J3
Alençon France 50 G4
Alenquer Brazil 199 H5
Alentejo reg. Port. 54 C6
Alenuihaha Channel U.S.A. 181 [inset] Z1
Alep Syria see Aleppo
Alépé Côte d'Ivoire 124 E5
Aleppo Syria 109 I1
also known as Ḩalab or Yamkhad; also spelt Alep; historically known as Beroea
Aler r. India 94 C2
Alert Canada 165 M1
Alerta Peru 200 C2
Alert Bay Canada 166 E5
Alès France 51 K8
Aleşd Romania 58 D1
Aleshki Ukr. see Tsyurupyns'k
Aleshnya Rus. Fed. 43 O8
Aleşkirt Turkey see Eleşkirt
Alessandria Italy 56 A4
Alessio Albania see Lezhë
Ålesund Norway 44 I3
also spelt Aalesund
Aletrium Italy see Alatri
Aletschhorn mt. Switz. 51 N6
Aleutian Islands U.S.A. 220 G2
Aleutian Range mts U.S.A. 164 D4
Alevina, Mys c. Rus. Fed. 39 P4
Alevişik Turkey see Samandağı
Alexander, Cape Antarctica 222 T2
Alexander, Mount hill Australia 148 C2
Alexander Archipelago is U.S.A. 164 F4
Alexander Bay S. Africa 130 C6
Alexander City U.S.A. 175 C5
Alexander Island Antarctica 222 T2
Alexandra Australia 147 E4
Alexandra r. Australia 149 C3
Alexandra N.Z. 153 D13
Alexandra, Cape S. Georgia 205 [inset]
Alexandra Channel India 95 G3
Alexandra Falls Canada 167 G2
Alexandra Land i. Rus. Fed. see Aleksandry, Zemlya
Alexandreia Greece 58 D8
Alexandretta Turkey see İskenderun
Alexandria Afgh. see Ghaznī
Alexandria B.C. Canada 166 F4
Alexandria Ont. Canada 169 F4

▶Alexandria Egypt 121 F2
4th most populous city in Africa. Also known as Al Iskandarīyah; also spelt El Iskandarîya.
world [cities] ➡ 24–25

Alexandria Romania 58 G5
Alexandria S. Africa 133 K10
Alexandria Turkm. see Mary
Alexandria U.K. 46 H8
Alexandria KY U.S.A. 176 A7
Alexandria LA U.S.A. 179 D6
Alexandria MN U.S.A. 178 D2
Alexandria SD U.S.A. 178 C3
Alexandria VA U.S.A. 177 H7
Alexandria Arachoton Afgh. see Kandahār
Alexandria Areion Afgh. see Herāt
Alexandria Bay U.S.A. 177 J1
Alexandria Prophthasia Afgh. see Farāh
Alexandrina, Lake Australia 146 C3
Alexandroupoli Greece 58 G8
Alexânia Brazil 206 E3
Alexis r. Canada 169 J2
'Āley Lebanon 108 G4
also spelt Aaley
Aley r. Rus. Fed. 103 J1
Aleyak Iran 100 D2
Aleysk Rus. Fed. 103 J1
Al Fallūjah Iraq 109 O4
Alfambra r. Spain 55 J4
Al Fardah Yemen 105 E5
Alfaro Spain 55 J2
Alfarràs Spain 55 L3
Alfatar Bulg. 58 I5
Al Fathah Iraq 107 E4
Al Fatk Yemen 105 F4
Al Fāw Iraq 107 G5
Al Fayyūm Egypt see El Faiyûm
Al Fāzih Yemen 104 C5
Alfeios r. Greece 59 C11
also spelt Alfios
Alfeld (Leine) Germany 48 G4
Alfenas Brazil 203 C7
Alfios r. Greece see Alfeios
Alföld plain Hungary 49 R9
Alford U.K. 46 J6
Alfred U.S.A. 177 O2
Alfred and Marie Range hills Australia 151 D5
Alfred M. Terrazas Mex. 185 F4
Alfredo Chaves Brazil 207 M7
Alfredton N.Z. 152 J8
Alfta Sweden 45 L3
Al Fujayrah U.A.E. see Fujairah
Al Fuqahā' Libya 120 C3
Al Furāt r. Iraq/Syria see Euphrates
Alga Kazakh. 102 D2
also spelt Algha
Algabas Kazakh. 102 C2
Algar Spain 54 F8
Ålgård Norway 45 I4
Algarinejo Spain 54 G7
Algarrobal Chile 204 C3
Algarrobo del Aguilla Arg. 204 D5
Algarve reg. Port. 54 C7
Algasovo Rus. Fed. 41 G5
Algeciras Spain 54 F8
Algemesí Spain 55 K5
Algena Eritrea 121 H5
Alger Alg. see Algiers
Alger U.S.A. 173 I6

▶Algeria country Africa 123 E4
2nd largest country in Africa.
africa [countries] ➡ 114–117

Algha Kazakh. see Alga
Al Ghāfāt Oman 105 G3
Al Ghardaqah Egypt see Hurghada
Al Gharith Saudi Arabia 104 C3
Al Ghāţ Saudi Arabia 105 D2
Al Ghawr plain Jordan/West Bank 108 G7
also spelt El Ghor
Al Ghaydah Yemen 105 F4
Al Ghayl Saudi Arabia 105 D3
Alghero Sardegna Italy 57 A8
Al Ghubr reg. Oman 105 G4
Al Ghuwayr well Qatar 105 E2
Al Ghwaybiyah Saudi Arabia 105 E2

▶Algiers Alg. 123 F1
Capital of Algeria. Also known as Al Jaza'ir or Argel or El Djezair; also spelt Alger; historically known as Icosium.

Alginet Spain 55 K5
Algoa Bay S. Africa 133 J10
Algodón r. Peru 198 D5
Algodor r. Spain 54 H5
Algoma U.S.A. 172 F6
Algona U.S.A. 178 D3
Algonac U.S.A. 173 K8
Algonquin Park Canada 168 E4
Algonquin Provincial Park Canada 173 O5
Algorta (Guecho) Spain 55 I1
Algosh Iraq 109 O1
Al 'grūd Egypt 108 D7
Älgsjö Sweden 44 L2
Algueirao Moz. see Hacufera
Algueirão-Mem Martins Port. 54 B6
Al Habakah well Saudi Arabia 107 E5
Al Habbānīyah Iraq 107 E4
Al Hadaqah well Saudi Arabia 104 D1
Al Hadbah reg. Saudi Arabia 104 C3
Al Hadd Bahrain 105 E2
Al Haddār Saudi Arabia 105 D3
Al Hadhālil plat. Saudi Arabia 107 E5
Al Ḩadīthah Iraq 107 E4
Al Ḩaḑr Iraq see Hatra
Al Ḩafar well Saudi Arabia 104 C1
Al Haffah Syria 108 H2
Al Haggounia W. Sahara 122 B4
Al Ḩā'ir Saudi Arabia 105 D2
Al Hajar Oman 105 G3
Al Ḩajar al Gharbī mts Oman 105 G2
Al Ḩajar ash Sharqī mts Oman 105 G3
Al Ḩajr Yemen 105 D4
Al Ḩallānīyah i. Oman 105 G4
Alhama r. Spain 55 J2
Al Ḩamād plain Asia 98 B3
Al Ḩamādah al Ḩamrā' plat. Libya 120 A2
Alhama de Granada Spain 54 H7
Alhama de Murcia Spain 55 J7
Al Ḩamar Saudi Arabia 105 D3
Al Ḩāmī Yemen 105 E5
Alhamilla, Sierra hills Spain 55 I8
Al Ḩammām well Iraq 107 E5
Al Ḩamrā' Saudi Arabia 104 B3
Al Ḩanākīyah Saudi Arabia 104 C2
Al Ḩanish al Kabīr i. Yemen 104 C5
Al Ḩanīyah esc. Iraq 107 F5
Al Ḩaqlānīyah Iraq 109 N3
Al Ḩaqū Saudi Arabia 104 C4
Al Ḩariq Saudi Arabia 105 D3
Al Ḩarrah reg. Saudi Arabia 109 J7
Al Ḩarūj al Aswad hills Libya 120 C3
Al Ḩasa reg. Saudi Arabia 105 E2
Al Ḩasakah Syria 109 L1
Al Ḩasakah governorate Syria 109 L1
Al Ḩasānī i. Saudi Arabia 104 B2
Al Ḩāshimīyah Iraq 107 F4
Al Ḩasī well Saudi Arabia 105 D3
Al Ḩāsikīyah i. Oman 105 F4
Al Ḩaşwah Iraq 109 P5
Al Ḩatīfah plain Saudi Arabia 105 D2
Al Ḩawāyā des. Saudi Arabia 105 E3
Al Ḩawi salt pan Saudi Arabia 109 J8
Al Ḩawījah Iraq 109 O2
Al Ḩawīyah Saudi Arabia 104 C3
Al Ḩawjā' Saudi Arabia 109 J9
Al Ḩawrā Yemen 105 D5
Al Ḩawtah reg. Saudi Arabia 105 D3
Al Ḩayy Iraq 107 F4
Al Ḩayyānīyah waterhole Saudi Arabia 109 N9
Al Ḩazm Saudi Arabia 104 B1
Al Ḩazm al-Jawf Yemen 104 D4
Alheit S. Africa 132 E5
Al Ḩibāk des. Saudi Arabia 105 F4
Al Ḩillah Iraq see Hillah
Al Ḩillah governorate Iraq see Bābil
Al Ḩillah Saudi Arabia 105 D3
Al Ḩilwah Saudi Arabia 105 D3
Al Ḩimārah well Saudi Arabia 105 E2
Al Hindīyah Iraq 107 F4
Al Ḩinnāh Saudi Arabia 105 E2
Al Ḩinw mt. Saudi Arabia 107 D5
Al Ḩirrah well Saudi Arabia 105 E3
Al Ḩishwah hills Yemen 104 D4
Al Ḩismā plain Saudi Arabia 104 A1
Al Ḩişn Jordan 108 G5
also spelt Husn
Al Ḩişn Yemen 105 D5
Al Hoceima Morocco 122 E2
formerly known as Villa Sanjurjo
Alhuampa Arg. 204 E2
Al Ḩudaydah Yemen see Hodeidah
Al Ḩudaydah governorate Yemen 104 C5
Al Ḩudūd ash Shamālīyah prov. Saudi Arabia 104 C1
Al Ḩufayrah well Saudi Arabia 105 E2
Al Ḩufrah reg. Saudi Arabia 104 B1
Al Ḩufūf Saudi Arabia 105 E2
also spelt Hofūf
Al Ḩūj hills Saudi Arabia 104 B1
Al Ḩulayq al Kabīr hills Libya 120 C3
Al Ḩumayshah Yemen 105 D5
Al Ḩumrah reg. U.A.E. 105 F3
Al Ḩunayy Saudi Arabia 105 E2
Al Husayfin Oman 105 G2
Al Ḩuthūl hill Saudi Arabia 109 K8
Al Ḩuwatsah Oman 105 G3
Al Ḩuwaylah Qatar 105 E2
Al Ḩuwaymī Yemen 105 D5
Al Ḩuwayyit Saudi Arabia 104 C2
Al Ḩuwayz Syria 109 H2
Al Ḩuwwah Saudi Arabia 105 D3
Ali China 89 B5
also known as Shiquanhe
'Alīābād Afgh. 101 G2
'Alīābād Golestān Iran 100 C2
'Alīābād Hormozgan Iran 100 C4
'Alīābād Khorāsan Iran 100 D3
'Alīābād Khorāsan Iran 101 E4
'Alīābād Kordestān Iran 100 A3
'Alīābād Qom Iran 100 B3
'Alīābād, Kūh-e mt. Iran 100 B3
Aliağa Turkey 106 A3
Aliakmonas r. Greece 59 D8
Aliakmonas, Limni l. Greece 59 C8
Alialbamba East Timor 75 C5
Aliartos Greece 59 E10
Alibag India 94 B2
Āli Bayramlı Azer. 107 G3
Alibey Adası i. Turkey 59 H9
Alibunar Vojvodina, Srbija Yugo. 58 B3
Alicante Spain 55 K6
also spelt Alacant
Alice Australia 149 E4
Alice r. Australia 149 D2
Alice watercourse Australia 149 E5
Alice S. Africa 133 K9
Alice U.S.A. 179 C7
Alice, Punta pt Italy 57 J9
Alice Arm Canada 166 D4
Alicedale S. Africa 133 K10
Alice Springs Australia 148 B4
Alice Town Bahamas 186 D1
Aliceville U.S.A. 175 B5
Alichur Tajik. 101 H2
Alichur r. Tajik. 101 H2
Alichuri Janubi, Qatorkŭhi mts Tajik. 101 H2
also known as Yuzhno-Alichurskiy, Khrebet
Alicia Phil. 74 B5
Alick Creek r. Australia 149 D4
Alicoto Fr. Guiana 199 H4
Alicudi, Isola i. Isole Lipari Italy 57 G10
Al 'Idd U.A.E. 105 F3
Al 'Idwah well Saudi Arabia 104 C2
Aliero Nigeria 125 G3
Alife Italy 56 G7
Aligarh India 96 C4
Alīgūdarz Iran 100 B3
Alihe China 85 I1
also known as Oroqen Zizhiqi
Alījūq, Kūh-e mt. Iran 100 B4
'Alī Kheyl Afgh. 101 G3
Al Ikhwān is Yemen 105 F5
English form The Brothers
Alima r. Congo 126 C5
Al Imām Iraq 109 P5
Al Imārāt al 'Arabīyah at Muttaḩidah country Asia see United Arab Emirates
Alimia i. Greece 59 I12
Alindao Cent. Afr. Rep. 126 D3
Alinghar r. Afgh. 101 G3
Alingsås Sweden 45 K4
Alintale well Eth. 128 D3
Aliova r. Turkey 106 B3
Alipur India 94 C1
Alipur Pak. 101 G4
Alipur Duar India 97 F4
Aliquippa U.S.A. 176 E5
Alirajpur India 96 B5
Ali Sabieh Djibouti 128 D2
Al 'Īsāwīyah Saudi Arabia 107 D5
Al Iskandarīyah Egypt see Alexandria
Al Iskandarīyah Iraq 107 F4
Aliskerovo Rus. Fed. 39 Q3
Al Ismā'īlīyah Egypt see Ismâ'ilîya
Aliste r. Spain 54 E3
Alitaive mt. Sweden 44 L2
Al Ittihab Yemen see Madīnat ash Sha'b
Aliveri Greece 59 F10
Aliwal North S. Africa 133 K7
Alix Canada 167 H4
Aliyaha r. Ukr. 53 K3
Al Jafr Jordan 109 H7
Al Jāfūrah des. Saudi Arabia 105 E2
Al Jaghbūb Libya 120 E2
Al Jahrah Kuwait 107 F5
Al Jamalīyah Qatar 105 E2
Al Jarāwī well Saudi Arabia 109 J7
Al Jarf mts Saudi Arabia 104 B2
Al Jawārah well Oman 105 G4
Al Jawb reg. Saudi Arabia 105 E3
Al Jawf Libya 120 D3
Al Jawf Al Jawf Saudi Arabia 107 D5
also spelt Al Jauf
Al Jawf prov. Saudi Arabia 104 B1
Al Jawf governorate Yemen 105 D4
Al Jawsh Libya 120 A1
Al Jaza'ir Alg. see Algiers
Al Jazā'ir reg. Iraq/Syria 109 K1
Alj Beyk Iran 100 C2
Aljezur Port. 54 C7
Al Jībān reg. Saudi Arabia 105 E2
Al Jid well Iraq 109 K5
Al Jilh esc. Saudi Arabia 104 D2
Al Jisr Iraq 109 P4
Al Jithāmīyah Saudi Arabia 104 C2
Al Jīzah Egypt see Giza
Aljucén r. Spain 54 E6
Al Jufra Oasis Libya 120 B2
Al Julaydah well Saudi Arabia 105 D1
Al Jumūm Saudi Arabia 104 B3
Al Junaynah Saudi Arabia 104 C3
Al Jurayd i. Saudi Arabia 105 E2
Al Jurayfah Saudi Arabia 105 D2
Al Jurayr well Saudi Arabia 104 C3
Al Jurdhāwīyah Saudi Arabia 104 C2
Al Juwayf depr. Syria 109 I4
Al Juwayfah well Saudi Arabia 105 E3
Al Kahfah Saudi Arabia 104 C2
Al Kalban Oman 105 G3
Alkali Flat salt flat NV U.S.A. 182 G1
Alkali Flat salt flat NV U.S.A. 183 G3
Alkaliya r. Ukr. 58 L3
Alkamari Niger 125 H3
Al Kāmil Oman 105 G3
Al Karābilah Iraq 109 M3
Al Karak Jordan 108 G6
also spelt Karak
Al Karāmah Jordan 108 G6
Al Karmah Iraq 109 O4
Al Kāzimīyah Iraq 107 F4
also known as Kādhimain
Al Khābūrah Oman 105 G3
Al Khadrā' well Saudi Arabia 104 C1
Al Khafaq well Saudi Arabia 105 D2
Al Khafqān salt pan Saudi Arabia 104 C3
Al Khalf Saudi Arabia 104 C2
Al Khalīf Oman 105 G3
Al Khalīl West Bank see Hebron
Al Khāliş Iraq 107 F4
Al Khamāsīn Saudi Arabia 104 D3
Al Kharfah Saudi Arabia 105 D3
Al Khārijah Egypt see El Khârga
Al Kharj reg. Saudi Arabia 105 D3
Al Kharkhayr oasis Saudi Arabia 105 E4
Al Kharrārah Qatar 105 E2
Al Khaşab Oman 105 G2
Al Khasfah well Oman 105 F4
Al Khāşirah Saudi Arabia 104 C3
Al-Khatam reg. U.A.E. 105 F2
Al Khaţīnī vol. Saudi Arabia 109 J6
Al Khawkhah Yemen 104 C5
Al Khawr Qatar 105 E2
Al Khawţamah i. Yemen 104 C5
Al Khişah well Saudi Arabia 105 E2
Al Khiẕāmī well Saudi Arabia 105 E2
Al Khobar Saudi Arabia 105 E2
Al Khubrah Saudi Arabia 105 E2
Al Khuff reg. Saudi Arabia 104 D2
Al Khufrah Libya 120 D3
Al Khufrah Oasis Libya 120 D3
Al Khums Libya 120 B1
also spelt Homs
Al Khunfah sand area Saudi Arabia 104 B1
Al Khunn Saudi Arabia 105 E3
Al Khuwayr Qatar 105 E2
Al Kidan well Saudi Arabia 105 F3
Al Kifl Iraq 107 F4
Al Kir'ānah Qatar 105 E2
Alkmaar Neth. 48 B3
Al Kūfah Iraq 107 F4
Al Kufla well Saudi Arabia 105 E3
Al Kumayt Iraq 107 F4
Al Kūrā lava field Saudi Arabia 104 B2
Al Kūsūr hills Saudi Arabia 109 J6
Al Kūt Iraq 107 F4
also known as Kut-al-Imara
Al Kuwayt country Asia see Kuwait
Al Kuwayt Kuwait see Kuwait
Al Labbah plain Saudi Arabia 107 E5
Allada Benin 125 F5
Al Lādhiqīyah Syria see Latakia
Al Lādhiqīyah governorate Syria 108 G2
Allagadda India 94 C3
Allahabad India 97 D4
Al Lajā lava field Syria 109 H5
Allakh-Yun' Rus. Fed. 39 N3
Allanmyo Myanmar 78 A4
Allanridge S. Africa 133 K4
Allapalli India 94 D2
'Allāqī, Wādī el watercourse Egypt 121 G4
Allardt U.S.A. 176 A9
Allardville Canada 169 H4
Allariz Spain 54 D2
Al Latakhīyah well Yemen 105 E4
Alldays S. Africa 131 F4
Allegan U.S.A. 172 H8
Allegany U.S.A. 176 G3
Allegheny r. U.S.A. 176 F5
Allegheny Mountains U.S.A. 176 C9
Allegheny Reservoir U.S.A. 176 G4
Allemanskraaldam resr S. Africa 133 L5
Allen Phil. 74 C3
Allen, Lough l. Rep. of Ireland 47 D9
Allen, Mount hill N.Z. 153 B15
Allen, Mount U.S.A. 166 A2
Allendale U.S.A. 175 D5
Allende Coahuila Mex. 185 E2
Allende Nuevo León Mex. 185 E3
Allendorf (Lumda) Germany 51 O2
Allenford Canada 173 L6
Allenstein Poland see Olsztyn
Allensville OH U.S.A. 176 C6
Allensville PA U.S.A. 176 H5
Allentown U.S.A. 177 J5
Alleppey India 94 C4
also known as Alappuzha
Aller r. Germany 48 G3
Allianc Suriname 199 H3
Alliance NE U.S.A. 178 B3
Alliance OH U.S.A. 176 D5
Al Lībīyah country Africa see Libya
Allier r. France 51 J6
Al Lifīyah well Iraq 107 E5
Alligator Point Australia 149 D3
Al Lihābah well Saudi Arabia 105 D2
Allikher India 94 C2
Allinge-Sandvig Denmark 45 K5
Al Lişāfah well Saudi Arabia 105 D2
Al Lisān pen. Jordan 108 G6
Allison U.S.A. 174 A3
Alliston Canada 173 N6
Al Līth Saudi Arabia 104 C3
Al Liwā' oasis U.A.E. 105 F3
Alloa U.K. 46 I7
Allones Pays de la Loire France 50 G5
Allones Pays de la Loire France 50 G5
Allora Australia 147 G2
Allouez U.S.A. 172 E6
Allschwil Switz. 51 N5
Allu Indon. 75 A4
Al Luḩayyah Yemen 104 C5
Allumettes, Île aux i. Canada 173 P5
Allur India 94 D3
Alluru Kottapatnam India 94 D3
Al Lussuf well Iraq 107 E5
Alma Canada 169 G3
formerly known as St-Joseph-d'Alma
Alma KS U.S.A. 178 C4
Alma MI U.S.A. 173 I7
Alma NE U.S.A. 178 C3
Al Ma'ānīyah Iraq 107 E5
Alma-Ata Kazakh. see Almaty
Alma-Ata Oblast admin. div. Kazakh. see Almatinskaya Oblast'
Almacelles Spain 55 L3
Al Machmin waterhole Iraq 109 N6
Almada Port. 54 B6
Al Madāfi' plat. Saudi Arabia 104 B1
Al Madā'in Iraq 109 P4
Al Ma'danīyāt well Iraq 107 F5
Al Maḑāyā Saudi Arabia 104 C4
Almaden Australia 149 E3
Almadén Spain 54 G6
Almadina Brazil 207 N1
Al Madīnah Iraq 100 A4
Al Madīnah Saudi Arabia see Medina
Al Madīnah prov. Saudi Arabia 104 B2
Al Mafraq Jordan 108 H5
also spelt Mafraq
Al Maghrib reg. U.A.E. 105 F3
Almagro i. Phil. 74 C4
Al Mahākik reg. Saudi Arabia 105 E3
Al Maḩāwīl Iraq 109 P5
Al Mahbas W. Sahara 122 C4
Al Mahdam Saudi Arabia 104 C3
Al Maḩiā depr. Saudi Arabia 104 B2
Al Maḩmūdīyah Iraq 107 F4
Al Mahrah governorate Yemen 105 E4
Al Mahrah reg. Yemen 105 E5
Al Maḩwīt Yemen 104 C5
Al Maḩwīt governorate Yemen 104 C5
Al Majma'ah Saudi Arabia 105 D2
Almăjului, Munţii mts Romania 58 D4
Al Malsūnīyah reg. Saudi Arabia 105 E2
Almalyk Uzbek. 103 G4
also spelt Olmaliq
Al Manadir reg. Oman 105 F3
Al Manāmah Bahrain see Manama
Al Manjūr well Saudi Arabia 105 D3
Almanor, Lake U.S.A. 182 C1
Almansa Spain 55 J6
Al Manşūrah Egypt see El Manşûra
Almanzor mt. Spain 54 F4
Almanzora r. Spain 55 J7
Al Ma'qil Iraq 107 F5
Almar Afgh. 101 F3
Almar r. Spain 54 F4
Al Mariyyah U.A.E. 105 F3
Al Marj Libya 120 D1
also known as Barce
Almas r. Romania 58 E1
Almas, Rio das r. Brazil 206 D1
Al Masana'a Oman 105 G3
Almatinskaya Oblast' admin. div. Kazakh. 103 I3
English form Almaty Oblast; also known as Almaty Oblysy; formerly known as Alma-Ata Oblast
Al Matmarfag W. Sahara 122 B4

▶Almaty Kazakh. 103 I4
Former capital of Kazakhstan. English form Alma-Ata; formerly known as Vernyy.

Almaty Oblast admin. div. Kazakh. see Almatinskaya Oblast'
Almaty Oblysy admin. div. Kazakh. see Almatinskaya Oblast'
Al Mawşil Iraq see Mosul
Al Mayādīn Syria 109 L2
Almazán Spain 55 I3
Almeida Port. 54 E4
Almeirim Brazil 199 H5
Almeirim Port. 54 C5
Almelo Neth. 48 D3
Almenara Brazil 202 D6
Almenara Spain 55 K5
Almenara, Sierra de hills Spain 55 J7
Almendra, Embalse de resr Spain 54 E3
Almendralejo Spain 54 E6
Almere Neth. 48 C3
Almería Spain 55 I8
Almería, Golfo de b. Spain 55 I8
Almetievsk Rus. Fed. see Al'met'yevsk
Al'met'yevsk Rus. Fed. 40 J5
also spelt Almetievsk
Älmhult Sweden 45 K4
Al Midhnab Saudi Arabia 104 D2
Al Miḩrāḑ reg. Saudi Arabia 105 E3
Almina, Punta pt Spain 54 F9
Al Mindak Saudi Arabia 104 C3
Al Mintirib Oman 105 G3
Almirantazgo, Seno del sea chan. Chile 205 C9
Almirante Panama 186 C5
Al-Mirfa U.A.E. 105 F2
Almirós Greece see Almyros
Al Mish'āb Saudi Arabia 105 E1
Al Mismīyah Syria 109 H4
Almodôvar Port. 54 C7
Almodóvar del Campo Spain 54 G6
Almoloya Mex. 185 E4
Almont U.S.A. 173 J8
Almonte Canada 173 Q5
Almonte Spain 54 E7
Almonte r. Spain 54 E5

Almora India 96 C3
Almoradi Spain 55 K6
Almorox Spain 54 G4
Al Mota *well* Niger 125 G3
Almoustarat Mali 125 F2
Al Mu'ayzilah *hill* Saudi Arabia 109 J8
Al Mubarrez Saudi Arabia 105 E2
Al Muḍairib Oman 105 G3
Al Mudawwarah Jordan 108 H8
Al Muhtalab *depr.* Saudi Arabia 109 H9
Al Mukallā Yemen *see* Mukalla
Al Mukhā Yemen *see* Mocha
Al Munbaṭiḥ *des.* Saudi Arabia 105 D4
Al Mundafan *pass* Saudi Arabia 105 D4
Almuñécar Spain 54 H8
historically known as Sexi
Al Muqdādīyah Iraq 107 F4
Al Murayr *well* Saudi Arabia 109 K7
Al Mūrītānīyah *country* Africa *see*
Mauritania
Al Murūt *well* Saudi Arabia 107 D5
Almus Turkey 107 D2
also known as Tozanlı
Al Musannāh *ridge* Saudi Arabia 105 D1
Al Musayjid Saudi Arabia 104 B2
Al Musayyib Iraq 109 P5
Al Muthanná *governorate* Iraq 107 F5
Al Muwayh Saudi Arabia 104 C2
Al Muwaylih Saudi Arabia 104 B2
Almyropotamos Greece 59 F10
Almyros Greece 59 F10
also spelt Almirós
Almyrou, Ormos *b.* Greece 59 F13
Alness U.K. 46 H6
Alnwick U.K. 46 H6

▶ Alofi Niue 145 I3
Capital of Niue.
oceania [countries] ⮕ 138–139

Aloi Uganda 128 B4
Aloja Latvia 42 F4
Alol' Rus. Fed. 43 K5
Alolya r. Rus. Fed. 43 J5
Along India 97 G3
Alonnisos i. Greece 59 E9
Alonso r. Brazil 206 B11
Alor i. Indon. 75 C5
Alor, Selat sea chan. Indon. 75 B5
Alora Spain 54 G8
Alor Setar Malaysia 76 C1
also spelt Alur Setar; *formerly spelt* Alor Star
Alor Star Malaysia *see* Alor Setar
Alosno Spain 54 D7
Alost Belgium *see* Aalst
Alot India 96 B5
Alota Bol. 200 D5
Alotau P.N.G. 149 F1
Aloysius, Mount Australia 151 E5
Alpachiri Arg. 204 E5
Alpagut Turkey 59 J9
Alpaugh U.S.A. 182 E5
Alpena U.S.A. 173 J5
Alpercatas, Serra das hills Brazil 202 C3
Alpha Australia 149 E4
Alpha S. Africa 133 O4
Alpha U.S.A. 172 C9
Alpi Apuane, Parco Naturale delle
nature res. Italy 56 C4
Alpine AZ U.S.A. 183 O8
Alpine CA U.S.A. 183 H9
Alpine NY U.S.A. 177 I3
Alpine TX U.S.A. 179 B6
Alpine WY U.S.A. 180 E4
Alpine National Park Australia 147 E4
Alpinópolis Brazil 206 G7

▶ Alps mts Europe 51 M7
europe [landscapes] ⮕ 30–31

Al Qā' Saudi Arabia 104 C3
Al Qaddāhīyah Libya 120 B2
Al Qādisīyah governorate Iraq 107 F5
formerly known as Ad Dīwānīyah
Al Qadmūs Syria 108 H2
Al Qaffay i. U.A.E. 105 E3
Al Qafrah Yemen 105 D5
Al Qāhirah Egypt *see* Cairo
Al Qaḩmah Saudi Arabia 104 C4
Al Qā'im Iraq 109 L3
Al Qā'īyah Saudi Arabia 104 C3
Al Qā'īyah well Saudi Arabia 105 D2
Al Qalībah Saudi Arabia 104 B1
Al Qāmishlī Syria 107 I3
Al Qar'ah well Saudi Arabia 105 D2
Al Qar'ah lava field Syria 109 H5
Al Qarn Yemen 105 D5
Al Qaryatayn Syria 109 I3
Al Qaṣim prov. Saudi Arabia 104 C2
Al Qaṣr Saudi Arabia 104 C2
Al Qaṭif Saudi Arabia 105 E2
Al Qaṭn Yemen 105 E5
Al Qaṭrānah Jordan 108 H6
Al Qawnas reg. Saudi Arabia 105 D1
Al Qayṣūmah Saudi Arabia 105 D1
Al Qayṣūmah well Saudi Arabia 107 E5
Al Qiblīyah i. Oman 105 G4
Al Qulayyibah waterhole Saudi Arabia
109 N9
Al Qumur country Africa *see* Comoros
Al Qunayṭirah Syria 108 G4
Al Qunayṭirah governorate Syria 108 G4
Al Qunfidhah Saudi Arabia 104 C4
Al Qurayn Saudi Arabia 104 C3
Al Qurayni oasis Saudi Arabia 105 F3
Al Qurayyah Saudi Arabia 104 C3
Al Qurnah Iraq 107 F5
Al Qurrah i. U.A.E. 105 G2
Al Qurayyāt Saudi Arabia 107 D5
Al Quwārah Saudi Arabia 104 C2
Al Quwayi' Saudi Arabia 105 D3
Al Quwayrah Jordan 108 G8
Al Quzah Yemen 105 E5
Al Rabbād i. U.A.E. 105 F3
Alrar Est Alg. 123 H3
Alroy Downs Australia 148 C3
Alsace admin. reg. France 51 N4
Alsace, Plaine d' valley France 51 N5
Al Samha U.A.E. 105 E3
Al Samit well Iraq 107 E5
Alsask Canada 167 I5
Al'skiy Khrebet mt. Rus. Fed. 82 E1
Alston U.K. 47 J9
Alstonville Australia 147 G2
Alsuku Nigeria 125 H5
Alsunga Latvia 42 C5
Alsvīķi Latvia 42 H4
Alta Norway 44 M1
Alta, Mount N.Z. 153 C12
Altadena U.S.A. 182 F7
Altaelva r. Norway 44 M1
Altafjorden sea chan. Norway 44 M1
Alta Floresta Brazil 201 G6
Alta Gracia Arg. 204 D3
Alta Gracia Nicaragua 186 B5
Altai mts Asia 88 D3
also known as Altayskiy Khrebet
Altai Mountains Asia *see* Altai
Altamaha r. U.S.A. 175 D6
Altamira Amazonas Brazil 199 G4
Altamira Pará Brazil 199 H5
Altamira Chile 204 C2
Altamira Col. 198 C4
Altamira Costa Rica 186 B5

Altamira Mex. 185 F4
Altamira, Cuevas de tourist site Spain 54 G1
Altamira, Sierra de mts Spain 54 F5
Altamonte Springs City U.S.A. 175 D6
Altamura Italy 57 H8
Altan Rus. Fed. 85 F1
Altanbulag Mongolia 85 E2
Altan Emel China 85 H1
also known as Xin Barag Youqi
Altan Ovoo mt. China/Mongolia 84 A2
Altan Shiret China 85 E3
also known as Ejin Horo Qi; also spelt Altan
Xiret
Altan Xiret China *see* Altan Shiret
Alta Paraiso de Goiás Brazil 202 C5
Altapirire Venez. 199 E2
Altar Mex. 184 C2
Altar r. Mex. 181 E7
Altar, Desierto de des. Mex. 184 B1
Altata Mex. 184 C3
Altavista U.S.A. 176 F8
Altay China 84 A2
Altay Mongolia 84 C2
Altay, Respublika aut. rep. Rus. Fed. 84 A1
English form Altay Republic; formerly known as
Gorno-Altayskaya Avtonomnaya Oblast'
or Gornyy Altay
Altay Kray admin. div. Rus. Fed. *see*
Altayskiy Kray
Altay Republic aut. rep. Rus. Fed. *see*
Altay, Respublika
Altayskiy Khrebet mts Asia *see*
Altai Mountains
Altayskiy Kray admin. div. Rus. Fed. 88 C2
English form Altay Kray
Altayskiy Zapovednik nature res. Rus. Fed.
84 A1
Altdorf Switz. 51 O6
Altea Spain 55 K6
Alteidet Norway 44 M1
Altenburg Germany 49 J5
Altenqoke China 84 B4
Altentreptow (Westerwald) Germany 48 E5
Alter do Chão Brazil 199 H5
Alter do Chão Port. 54 D5
Altevatnet l. Norway 44 L1
Altın Köprü Iraq 107 F4
Altınoluk Turkey 59 H9
Altinópolis Brazil 206 F8
Altınova Turkey 59 H9
Altınözü Turkey 108 H1
Altınyaka Turkey 106 B3
Altıntaş Turkey 106 B3
Altiplano plain Bol. 200 C4
Altmühltal park Germany 48 I7
Altnaharra U.K. 46 H5
Alto r. U.S.A. 172 H8
Alto Araguaia Brazil 203 A6
Alto Cedro Cuba 186 E2
Alto Chicapa Angola 127 C7
Alto Cruz mt. Spain 55 I3
Alto Cuchumatanes mts Guat. 185 H6
Alto de Cabezas mt. Spain 55 L4
Alto de Covelo pass Spain 54 D2
Alto del Moncayo mt. Spain 55 J3
Alto de Pencoso hills Arg. 204 D4
Alto do Trevim mt. Port. 54 C4
Alto Garças Brazil 202 A6
Alto Ligonha Moz. 131 H2
Alto Madidi, Parque Nacional nat. park
Bol. 200 C3
Alto Molócuè Moz. 131 H2
Alto r. U.K. 47 L12
Alton IL U.S.A. 174 B4
Alton KY U.S.A. 176 A7
Alton MO U.S.A. 174 B4
Alton NH U.S.A. 177 N2
Altona B.C. Canada 166 F3
Altona Man. Canada 167 L5
Altoona PA U.S.A. 176 G5
Altoona WI U.S.A. 172 B6
Alto Pacajá r. Brazil 199 G5
Alto Parnaíba Brazil 202 C4
Alto Purús r. Peru 200 C2
Alto Rio Doce Brazil 207 J8
Alto Rio Senguerr Arg. 205 C7
Altos Brazil 202 E3
Altos de Chacaya Chile 200 C4
Altos de Chinchilla mts Spain 55 J6
Alto Sucuriú Brazil 206 A6
Altotero mt. Spain 55 H2
Altotonga Mex. 185 F5
Altötting Germany 49 J7
Alto Uruguai Brazil 203 A8
Altukhovo Rus. Fed. 43 P9
Altun Ha tourist site Belize 185 H5
Altun Shan mt. China 84 B4
Altun Shan mts China 84 B4
also known as Astin Tag
Alturas U.S.A. 180 B4
Altus U.S.A. 179 C5
Altynkul' Uzbek. 102 D4
also spelt Oltinkül
Altyn-Topkan Tajik. *see* Oltintopkan
Alu Estonia 42 F2
Alua Moz. 131 H2
Al 'Ubaydī Iraq 109 M3
Alucra Turkey 107 D2
Al 'Uḍaylīyah Saudi Arabia 105 E2
Al Udayn Yemen 104 C5
Al 'Ulā Saudi Arabia 104 B2
Alūah Iran 100 B3
Alum Bridge U.S.A. 176 E6
Alum Creek Lake U.S.A. 176 C5
Alunda Sweden 45 L3
Aluniş Romania 58 F2
Alupka Ukr. 106 C1
Al 'Uqaylah Libya 120 C2
Al 'Uqaylah Saudi Arabia *see* An Nabk
Al 'Uqayr Saudi Arabia 105 E2
Al Uqşur Egypt *see* Luxor
Alur India 94 C3
Al Uruq al Mu'taridah des. Saudi Arabia 105 D5
Alur Setar Malaysia *see* Alor Setar
Al 'Urdun country Asia *see* Jordan
Alushta Ukr. 41 E7
Al Uthaylī Saudi Arabia 104 B1
Aluva India *see* Alwaye
Al 'Uwayja' well Saudi Arabia 105 E3
Al 'Uwaynah well Saudi Arabia 104 B2
Al 'Uwaynāt Libya 120 E4
Al 'Uwayniḑah i. Saudi Arabia 104 B2
Al 'Uwayqīlah Saudi Arabia 107 E5
Al 'Uyaynah Saudi Arabia 105 D2
Al 'Uẕam Saudi Arabia 104 C2
Al 'Uyūnah well Saudi Arabia 108 H9
Al 'Uzayr Iraq 107 F5
Alva r. U.S.A. 172 H8
Alva U.S.A. 178 C4
Alvand, Kūh-e mt. Iran 100 B3
Alvão, Parque Natural do nature res. Port.
54 D3
Alvarado Mex. 185 G5
Alvarado U.S.A. 179 C5
Alvares Machado Brazil 206 B9
Älvdalen Sweden 45 K3
Älvdalen valley Sweden 45 K3
Aledro airport Brazil 54 C1
Alverca Port. 54 B6
Alvesta Sweden 45 K4
Alvin TX U.S.A. 179 D6
Alvin WI U.S.A. 172 F5
Alvinópolis Brazil 207 J7
Älvkarleby Sweden 45 L3

Älvsbyn Sweden 44 M2
Al Wafrah Kuwait 107 F5
Al Wajh Saudi Arabia 104 B2
Al Wakrah Qatar 105 E2
Al Waqbá well Saudi Arabia 105 D1
Al Warī'ah Saudi Arabia 105 D2
Al Waţiyah Libya 120 A1
Alwar India 96 C4
Al Widyān plat. Iraq/Saudi Arabia 107 E4
Al Wigh Libya 120 B3
Al Wigh, Ramlat des. Libya 120 C3
Al Wusayl well Qatar 105 E2
Al Wusayt well Saudi Arabia 104 D1
Al Wusṭá admin. reg. Oman 105 G4
Alxa Youqi China *see* Ehen Hudag
Alxa Zuoqi China *see* Bayan Hot
Al Yamāmah Saudi Arabia 105 D2
Al Yāsat i. U.A.E. 105 E3
Al Yūsufīyah Iraq 109 P4
Alzada U.S.A. 178 A3
Alzey Germany 48 F6
Alzira Spain 55 K5
Amacayacu, Parque Nacional nat. park
Col. 198 D5
Āmādalen Sweden 45 K3
Amadeus, Lake salt flat Australia 148 A5
Amadi Sudan 128 A3
Amadjuak Lake Canada 165 L3
Amadora Port. 54 B6
Amadror plat. Alg. 123 G4
Amaga Col. 198 C3
Amagi Japan 91 B8
Amakusa-Kami-shima i. Japan 91 B8
Amakusa-nada b. Japan 91 A8
Amakusa-Shimo-shima i. Japan 91 B8
Amal Oman 105 F4
Åmål Sweden 45 K4
Amalaoulaou well Mali 125 F3
Amalapuram India 94 D2
Amalfi Col. 198 C3
Amaliada Greece 59 C11
Amalner India 96 B5
Amamapare Indon. 73 I7
Amambaí Brazil 201 G5
Amambai, Serra de hills Brazil/Para. 201 G5
Amami-Ō-shima i. Japan 81 L7
Amami-shotō is Japan 81 L7
Amamula Dem. Rep. Congo 126 E5
Āmān r. Sweden 45 K3
Amana, Lago l. Brazil 199 E5
Amanāb P.N.G. 73 J7
Amândji Aboriginal Land res. Australia
148 A3
Amanda U.S.A. 176 C6
Amandola Italy 56 F6
Amangel'dy Aktyubinskaya Oblast' Kazakh.
102 D2
also spelt Amankeldi
Amangel'dy Kustanayskaya Oblast' Kazakh.
103 F2
also spelt Amankeldi
Amankaragay Kazakh. 103 F1
also spelt Amanqaraghay
Amankeldi Kazakh. *see* Amangel'dy
Amankeldi Kazakh. *see* Amangel'dy
Amanotkel' Kazakh. 103 E3
Amanqaraghay Kazakh. *see* Amankaragay
Amantea Italy 57 I9
Amanzimtoti S. Africa 133 O7
Amapa Brazil 200 C3
Amapá Brazil 199 I4
Amapá state Brazil 199 I4
Amapala Hond. 186 B4
Amapari r. Brazil 199 I4
Amara Abu Sin Sudan 121 G6
Amaradia r. Romania 58 E4
Amaral Ferrador Brazil 203 A9
Amarante Brazil 202 C3
Amarante do Maranhão Brazil 202 C3
Amarapura Myanmar 78 B3
Amaravati r. India 94 C4
Amardalay Mongolia 85 E2
Amargosa Brazil 202 E5
Amargosa watercourse U.S.A. 181 C5
Amargosa Desert U.S.A. 183 H5
Amargosa Range mts U.S.A. 183 H5
Amargosa Valley U.S.A. 183 H5
Amarapura Island Tonga *see* Fonualei
Amarillo U.S.A. 179 B5
Amarkantak India 97 D5
Amaro, Monte mt. Italy 56 G6
Amarpur India 97 F5
Amarwara India 96 C5
Amasa U.S.A. 172 E4
Amasia Turkey *see* Amasya
Amasine W. Sahara 122 B4
Amasra Turkey 106 C2
Amassine well Mali 125 F2
Amasya Turkey 106 C2
historically known as Amasia
Amata Australia 151 E5
Amataurá Brazil 199 E5
Amatenango Mex. 185 G5
Amatikulu S. Africa 133 P6
Amatique, Bahía de b. Guat. 185 H6
Amatlán de Cañas Mex. 184 D4

▶ Amazon r. S. America 202 B1
Longest river in South America and 2nd in
the world. Also spelt Amazonas.
southamerica [landscapes] ⮕ 190–191
southamerica [contrasts] ⮕ 194–195

Amazon, Mouths of the Brazil 202 B1
Amazon, Source of the Peru 200 B3
Amazonas state Brazil 199 E6
Amazonas dept Col. 198 D5
Amazonas dept Peru 198 B6
Amazonas state Venez. 199 E4
Amazónia, Parque Nacional nat. park
Brazil 199 G6

Ambatosia Madag. 131 [inset] K2
Ambazac France 50 H7
Ambejogai India *see* Ambajogai
Ambelau i. Indon. 75 C4
Ambelón Greece *see* Ampelonas
Amberg Germany 48 I6
Ambergris Cay i. Belize 185 I5
Ambergris Cays is Turks and Caicos Is
187 F2
Amberieu-en-Bugey France 51 L7
Amberley Canada 173 L6
Amberley N.Z. 153 G11
Ambert France 51 J7
Ambgaon India 96 C5
Ambidédi Mali 124 B3
Ambikapur India 97 D5
Ambikol Sudan 121 F4
Ambikonar r. India *see* Ambikapur
Ambilobe Madag. 131 [inset] K2
Amble U.K. 47 K8
Ambleside U.K. 47 J9
Amblève r. Belgium 51 L2
Ambo Ethiopia *see* Hagere Hiywet
Ambo India 97 E5
Ambo Peru 200 A2
Amboasary Madag. 131 [inset] J5
Amboasary Gara Madag. 131 [inset] K3
Amboavory Madag. 131 [inset] K3
Ambodifotatra Madag. 131 [inset] K3
Ambodiharina Madag. 131 [inset] K3
Ambohidratrimo Madag. 131 [inset] J3
Ambohijanahary Madag. 131 [inset] J3
Ambohimahasoa Madag. 131 [inset] J4
Ambohipaky Madag. 131 [inset] J3
Ambohitra mt. Madag. 131 [inset] K2
Ambohitralanana Madag. 131 [inset] K3
Amboina Indon. *see* Ambon
Amboise France 50 G5
Ambon Indon. 75 C4
formerly known as Amboina
Ambon i. Indon. 75 C4
Amboró, Parque Nacional nat. park Bol.
201 D4
Amboseli National Park Kenya 128 C5
Ambositra Madag. 131 [inset] J4
Ambovombe Madag. 131 [inset] J5
Amboy CA U.S.A. 183 I7
Amboy IL U.S.A. 172 D9
Ambre, Cap d' c. Madag. see
Bobaomby, Tanjona
Ambriz Angola 127 B6
Ambriz, Coutada do nature res. Angola
127 B6
Ambrizete Angola *see* N'zeto
Ambrosio r. Sri Lanka 94 D5
Ambrym i. Vanuatu 145 F3
also spelt Ambrim
Ambunten Indon. 77 F4
Ambur India *see* Amaravati
Andals Verk Norway 45 J4
Am-Dam Chad 120 D6
Amderma Rus. Fed. 40 L1
Amdilis well Mali 125 F2
Am Djéména Chad 120 C6
Amdo China 89 E5
also known as Lhargarbo
Amealco Mex. 185 E4
Amecameca Mex. 185 F5
Amedamit mt. Ethiopia 128 C2
Ameghino Arg. 204 E4
Ameland i. Neth. 48 C2
Amelia Italy 56 E6
Amelia Court House U.S.A. 176 H8
Amellu India 96 D4
Amendolara Italy 57 I9
Amenia U.S.A. 177 L4
American, North Fork r. U.S.A. 182 C3
Americana Brazil 206 F9
American Falls U.S.A. 180 D4
American Falls Reservoir U.S.A. 180 D4
American Fork U.S.A. 183 M1

▶ American Samoa terr. S. Pacific Ocean
145 I3
United States Unincorporated Territory.
Formerly known as Eastern Samoa.
oceania [countries] ⮕ 138–139

Americus U.S.A. 175 C5
Ameringkogel mt. Austria 49 L8
Amersfoort Neth. 48 D3
Amersfoort S. Africa 133 N4
Amery Canada 167 M3
Amery Ice Shelf Antarctica 223 E2
Ames U.S.A. 174 A3
Amesbury U.S.A. 177 O3
Amet India 96 B4
Amethi India 97 D4
Amfilochia Greece 59 C10
Amfissa Greece 59 D10
Amga Rus. Fed. 39 N3
Amgalang China 85 H1
also known as Xin Barag Zuoqi
Amguema r. Rus. Fed. 39 S3
Amguid Alg. 123 G4
also known as Amadar'ya
Amgun' r. Rus. Fed. 82 E1
Amhara admin. reg. Ethiopia 128 C2
Amherst Canada 169 H4
Amherst MA U.S.A. 177 M3
Amherst OH U.S.A. 176 C4
Amherst VA U.S.A. 176 F8
Amherst, Mount hill Australia 150 D3
Amherstburg Canada 173 J8
Amherstdale U.S.A. 176 D8
Amherst Island Canada 173 Q6
also known as Hinchin Jiang
Amida Turkey *see* Diyarbakır
Amidon U.S.A. 178 B2
Amiens France 51 I3
historically known as Ambianum or
Samarobriva
'Āmij, Wādī watercourse Iraq 107 E4
Amik Ovası marsh Turkey 107 D3
Amīlḩayt, Wādī al r. Oman 105 F4
Amilly France 51 I5
Amīnābād Iran 100 C4
Amindaion Greece *see* Amyntaio
Amindivi is India *see* Amindivi
Amindivi Islands India 94 B4
Amini i. India 94 B4
Amino Japan 91 D7
Aminuis Namibia 130 C4
Amiou Lebanon 108 G3
Amipshahr India 96 C3
Amirābād Esfahān Iran 100 B3
Amirābād Īlām Iran 100 A3
Amirabad Iran see Fuladi Maialleh
Amirante Islands Seychelles 218 K6
Āmīrlī Iraq 107 F4
Amisk Lake Canada 167 K4
Amistad, Parque de resr Mex./U.S.A. see
Amistad Reservoir
Amistad Reservoir Mex./U.S.A. 185 E2
also known as Amistad, Represa de
Amite U.S.A. 175 B6
Amite r. U.S.A. 175 B6
Amla India 96 C5
also known as Sarni
Amlaḩ, Jabal al hill Saudi Arabia 104 C4
Amlamé Togo 125 F5
Amlash Iran 100 B2
Amlekhganj Nepal 97 E4
Āmli Norway 45 J4
Amlwch U.K. 47 H10
'Amm Adam Sudan 121 H5

Amman Jordan *see* 'Ammān

▶ 'Ammān Jordan 108 G6
Capital of Jordan. English form Amman;
historically known as Philadelphia or
Rabbath Ammon.

Ammanazar Turkm. 102 C5
Ammānsaari Fin. 44 O2
'Ammār, reg. Yemen 105 D5
'Ammār, Tall hill Syria 109 H5
Ammarnäs Sweden 44 J3
Ammassalik Greenland 165 P3
also known as Tasiilaq; also spelt
Angmagssalik
Ammer r. Germany 48 I8
Ammersee l. Germany 48 I8
Ammochostos Cyprus *see* Famagusta
Ammochostos Bay Cyprus 108 F2
also known as Famagusta Bay
Amne Machin Range mts China *see*
A'nyêmaqên Shan
Amnok-kang r. China/N. Korea *see*
Yalu Jiang
Amo India 96 B5
Amo r. China 86 B4
Amol Iran 100 C2
Amolar Brazil 201 F4
Amoliani i. Greece 59 E8
Amontada Brazil 202 E2
Amor mt. Spain 54 F4
Amorbieta Spain 55 I1
Amores r. Arg. 204 F3
Amorgos i. Greece 59 G12
Amorinópolis Brazil 206 B3
Amory U.S.A. 175 B5
Åmot Buskerud Norway 45 J4
Åmot Telemark Norway 45 I4
also known as Ytre Vinje
Amotape, Cerros de mts Peru 198 A6
Åmotfors Sweden 45 K4
Amouri Mauritania 124 C3
Amoy China see Xiamen
Ampah Indon. 77 F3
Ampani India 95 D2
Ampanefena Madag. 131 [inset] K2
Ampani India 95 D2
Ampanihy Madag. 131 [inset] J5
Ampapentoamaizina Madag. 131 [inset] K3
Amparafaravola Madag. 131 [inset] K3
Amparai Sri Lanka 94 D5
Amparo Brazil 206 B3
Ampasimanolotra Madag. 131 [inset] K3
formerly known as Vohibinany
Ampelonas Greece 59 D9
also known as Ambelón
Ampenan Indon. 77 G5
Amper r. Germany 48 I7
Amper Nigeria 125 H4
Amphitrite Group is Paracel Is 72 D3
Ampibaku Indon. 75 B3
Ampisikinana Madag. 131 [inset] K2
formerly spelt Ampitsikiana
Ampitsikinana Madag. see Ampisikinana
Ampoa Indon. 75 B3
Amposta Spain 55 L4
Amqui Canada 169 H3
Amrabad India 94 C2
Amrabadi India 94 C2
Amravati India 96 C1
formerly spelt Amraoti
Amreli India 96 A5
Am Rijā' Yemen 121 J6
Amritsar India 96 B3
Amroha India 96 C3
Amrum i. Germany 48 F1
Åmsele Sweden 44 L2
Amstelveen Neth. 48 B3
Amsterdam Neth. 48 B3

▶ Amsterdam Neth. 48 B3
Official capital of the Netherlands.
world [countries] ⮕ 10–11

Amsterdam S. Africa 133 O3
Amsterdam NY U.S.A. 177 K3
Amsterdam, Île i. Indian Ocean 219 M8
English form Amsterdam Island
Amsterdam Island Indian Ocean see
Amsterdam, Île
Amstetten Austria 49 L7
Am Timan Chad 126 D2
Āmū r. Col. 198 D4
Amu Co l. China 89 E5
'Āmūd, Jabal al mt. Saudi Arabia 109 K7
Amudar'ya r. Asia 99 D3
English form Amu Darya; also known as
Dar'yoi Amu; also spelt Amudaryo,
Amyderya; historically known as Oxus
Amu Darya r. Asia see Amudar'ya
Amudaryo r. Asia see Amudar'ya
Amund Ringnes Island Canada 165 J2
Amundsen, Mount Antarctica 223 G2
Amundsen Bay Antarctica 223 D2
Amundsen Coast Antarctica 223 J1
Amundsen Glacier Antarctica 223 N1
Amundsen Gulf Canada 164 G2
Amundsen-Scott research station
Antarctica 223 N1
Amundsen Sea Antarctica 222 Q2
Amuntai Indon. 77 F3
Amur r. Rus. Fed. 82 E1
also known as Heilong Jiang
'Amur, Wadi watercourse Sudan 121 G5
Amurang Indon. 75 C2
Amursk Rus. Fed. 82 E2
Amurskaya Oblast' admin. div. Rus. Fed.
82 C1
English form Amur Oblast
Amurskiy Rus. Fed. 102 D1
Amurskiy liman strait Rus. Fed. 82 F1
Amurzet Rus. Fed. 82 C3
Amvrakikos Kolpos b. Greece 59 D10
Amyderya r. Asia see Amudar'ya
Amyntaio Greece 59 C8
also known as Amíndhaion
Amyot Canada 173 L2
Amzacea Romania 58 J5
Amzéradd well Mali 125 F2
Am-Zoer Chad 120 D6
Ana r. Turkey 58 J7
Anaa atoll Fr. Polynesia 221 I7
Anabanua Indon. 75 B3
Anabar r. Rus. Fed. 39 L2
Anabta West Bank 108 G5
Anaca Venez. 199 E2
Anaco Venez. 199 E2
Anacortes U.S.A. 180 B2
Anacortes Turkey see Samsun
Anadarko U.S.A. 179 C5
Anadolu Dağları mts Turkey 107 D2
Anadyr' Rus. Fed. 39 R3
Anadyr, Gulf of Rus. Fed. 39 S3
Anadyrskiy Zaliv
Anadyrskiy Zaliv b. Rus. Fed. 39 S3
English form Anadyr, Gulf of
Anafi Greece *see* Antiparos
Anafi i. Greece 59 G12
Anáfi i. Greece 59 G12
Andia, Sierra de mts Spain 55 J2

Anagni Italy 56 F7
historically known as Anagnia
Anagnia Italy *see* Anagni
'Ānah Iraq 107 E4
Anaheim U.S.A. 182 G8
Anahim Lake Canada 166 E4
Anáhuac Nuevo León Mex. 185 E3
Anáhuac Veracruz Mex. 185 F4
Anahuac U.S.A. 179 D6
Anaimalai Hills India 94 C4
Anai Mudi Peak India 94 C4
Anaiteum i. Vanuatu see Anatom
Anajás Brazil 202 B2
Anajás, Ilha i. Brazil 202 B2
Anajatuba Brazil 202 C2
Anakao Madag. 131 [inset] I4
Anakapalle India 95 D2
Anakie Australia 149 E4
Analalava Madag. 131 [inset] I4
Analavelona mts Madag. 131 [inset] I4
Anamã Brazil 199 F5
Ana Maria, Golfo de b. Cuba 186 D2
Anambas, Kepulauan is Indon. 77 D2
Anambra state Nigeria 125 G5
Anamosa U.S.A. 174 B3
Anamur Turkey 106 C3
Anan Japan 91 D8
Anand India 96 B5
Anandapur India 97 E5
Anandpur r. India 97 E5
Ananes i. Greece 59 F12
Anan'ev Kyrg. see Anan'yevo
Anang Pitjantjatjara Aboriginal Lands
res. Australia 146 A1
Anantapur India 94 C3
Anantnag Jammu and Kashmir 96 B2
also known as Islamabad
Anant Peth India 96 C4
Ananyevo Kyrg. see Anan'yevo
Anan'yevo Ukr. 41 D7
also spelt Ananyev
Anapa Rus. Fed. 41 F7
Anápolis Brazil 206 D3
Anapú r. Brazil 199 I5
Anār Fin. see Inari
Anār Iran 100 C3
Anārak Iran 100 C3
Anarbar r. Iran 100 C3
Anardara Afgh. 101 E3
Anare Mountains Antarctica 223 K1
Anasco Puerto Rico 187 G3
Ânäset Sweden 44 M2
Anatahan i. N. Mariana Is 73 K3
formerly spelt Anatajan
Anatajan i. N. Mariana Is see Anatahan
Anatolia reg. Turkey 106 B3
Anatoliki Makedonia kai Thraki
admin. reg. Greece 58 G7
Anatom i. Vanuatu 145 F4
also known as Anetchom, Île or Aneytioum,
Île or Kéamu; also spelt Aneityum or
Anaiteum
Anatuya Arg. 204 E3
Anatye Aboriginal Land res. Australia 148 C4
Anauá r. Brazil 199 F4
Anaurilândia Brazil 206 B9
Anavilhanas, Arquipélago das is Brazil
199 F5
Anaypazarı Turkey see Gülnar
Anaz mts Saudi Arabia 109 H9
Anbei China 84 C3
Anbyon N. Korea 83 B5
Ancares, Serra dos mts Spain 54 D2
Ancash dept Peru 200 A2
Ancaster Canada 173 N7
Ancasti Arg. 204 D3
Ancasti, Sierra mts Arg. 204 D3
Ancenis France 50 E5
Anchang China see Anxian
Anchau Nigeria 125 H4
Ancheita Brazil 207 M7
Anchodaya Bol. 200 D4
Anchorage U.S.A. 164 E3
Anchorage Island atoll Cook Is see
Suwarrow
Anchorage Reefs P.N.G. 149 F1
Anchor Bay U.S.A. 173 K8
Anchuthengu India see Anjengo
Anci China see Langfang
Ančia r. Lith. 42 D6
Anclitas, Cayo i. Cuba 186 D2
An Cóbh Rep. of Ireland see Cóbh
Ancón Peru 200 A2
Ancona Italy 56 F5
Ancuabe Moz. 129 C8
Ancud Chile 205 B6
Ancud, Golfo de g. Chile 205 B6
Ancyra Turkey see Ankara
Anda China see Daqing
Anda i. Indon. 75 C1
Andacollo Chile 204 C3
Andahuaylas Peru 200 B3
Andal India 97 E5
also spelt Ondal
Andalgalá Arg. 204 D3
Andalsnes Norway 44 I3
Andalucía aut. comm. Spain 54 G7
English form Andalusia
Andalusia S. Africa see Jan Kempdorp
Andalusia aut. comm. Spain see Andalucía
Andalusia AL U.S.A. 175 C6
Andalusia IL U.S.A. 172 C9
Andām, Wādī r. Oman 105 G4
Andaman and Nicobar Islands union terr.
India 93 H9
Andaman and Nicobar Islands union terr.
India 93 H9
Andaman Islands India 95 G3
Andaman Sea Indian Ocean 79 A6
also known as Middle Strait
Andamooka Australia 146 C2
Andapa Madag. 131 [inset] K2
Andāráb Afgh. 101 F2
Andarab Tajik. 101 G2
also spelt Anderob
Andeba Ye Midir Zerf Chaf pt Eritrea
104 C5
Andeg Rus. Fed. 40 J2
Andegavum France see Angers
Andelle r. France 50 H3
Andenes Norway 44 L1
Andenne Belgium 51 L2
Andermatt Switz. 51 O6
Andernos-les-Bains France 50 E8
Anderob Tajik. see Andarob
Anderson r. Canada 164 G3
Anderson AK U.S.A. 164 E3
Anderson CA U.S.A. 182 B1
Anderson IN U.S.A. 174 C3
Anderson MO U.S.A. 178 D4
Anderson SC U.S.A. 174 D5
Anderson Bay Australia 147 E5
Anderson Reservoir U.S.A. 182 C4
Andes Col. 198 C3

▶ Andes mts S. America 200 C4
southamerica [contrasts] ⮕ 194–195

index A

Andijon Wiloyati *admin. div.* Uzbek. *see* **Andizhanskaya Oblast'**
Andikíra Greece *see* **Antikyra**
Andikithira *i.* Greece *see* **Antikythira**
Andilamena Madag. 131 [inset] K3
Andilanatoby Madag. 131 [inset] K3
Andīmeshk Iran 100 B3
Andímilos *i.* Greece *see* **Antimilos**
Andípaxoi *i.* Greece *see* **Antipaxoi**
Andípsara *i.* Greece *see* **Antipsara**
Andirá Brazil 206 C10
Andir He *r.* China 89 C4
Andırın Turkey 107 D3
Andirlangar China 89 C4
Andiyskoye Koysu *r.* Rus. Fed. 102 A4
Andiyur India 94 C4
Andizhan Uzbek. 103 H4
also spelt Andijon
Andizhan Oblast *admin. div.* Uzbek. *see* **Andizhanskaya Oblast'**
Andizhanskaya Oblast' *admin. div.* Uzbek. 103 H4
English form Andizhan Oblast; *also known as* Andijon Wiloyati
Andkhui *r.* Afgh. 101 F2
Andkhvoy Afgh. 101 F2
Andoany Madag. 131 [inset] K2
formerly known as Hell-Ville
Andoas Peru 198 B5
Andoas Nuevo Ecuador 198 B5
Andoga *r.* Rus. Fed. 43 S2
Andogskaya Gryada *hills* Rus. Fed. 43 S2
Andohahela, Réserve d' *nature res.* Madag. 131 [inset] J5
Andohajango Madag. 131 [inset] K2
Andol India 94 C2
Andola India 94 C2
Andong China *see* **Dandong**
Andong S. Korea 83 C5
Andongwei *Shandong* China 85 H5
Andoom Australia 149 D2
▶**Andorra** *country* Europe 55 M2
europe [countries] ➠ 32–35
Andorra Spain 55 K4

▶**Andorra la Vella** Andorra 55 M2
Capital of Andorra. Also spelt Andorra la Vieja.

Andorra la Vieja Andorra *see* **Andorra la Vella**
Andover U.K. 47 K12
Andover *MA* U.S.A. 177 N3
Andover *NH* U.S.A. 177 N2
Andover *NY* U.S.A. 176 H3
Andover *OH* U.S.A. 176 E4
Andøya *i.* Norway 44 K1
Andozero, Ozero *l.* Rus. Fed. 43 S2
Andradas Brazil 206 G9
Andrade U.S.A. 183 J9
Andradina Brazil 206 B7
Andramasina Madag. 131 [inset] J3
Andramy Madag. 131 [inset] J3
Andranomavo Madag. 131 [inset] J3
Andranomena Madag. 131 [inset] K3
Andranopasy Madag. 131 [inset] I4
Andranovondronina Madag. 131 [inset] K2
Andranovory Madag. 131 [inset] J4
Andreanof Islands U.S.A. 221 G2
Andreapol' Rus. Fed. 43 N5
André Félix, Parc National de *nat. park* Cent. Afr. Rep. 126 D2
André Fernandes Brazil 207 L2
Andrelândia Brazil 203 C7
Andrequicé Brazil 207 I5
Andrew Canada 167 H4
Andrew Bay Myanmar 78 A4
Andrews *SC* U.S.A. 175 E5
Andrews *TX* U.S.A. 179 B5
Andreyevka *Almatinskaya Oblast'* Kazakh. 103 J3
Andreyevka *Severnyy Kazakhstan* Kazakh. 103 F1
Andreyevka Rus. Fed. 102 B1
Andreyevskoye Rus. Fed. *see* **Dneprovskoye**
Andreykovichi Rus. Fed. 43 O9
Andreykovo Rus. Fed. 43 P6
Andria Italy 56 I7
Andriba Madag. 131 [inset] J3
Andrieskraal S. Africa 133 I10
Andriesvale S. Africa 132 E3
Andringitra *mts* Madag. 131 [inset] J4
Androka Madag. 131 [inset] J5
Androna *reg.* Madag. 131 [inset] K2
Androniki Rus. Fed. 43 U4
Andropov Rus. Fed. *see* **Rybinsk**
Andros *i.* Bahamas 186 D1
Andros Greece 59 F11
Andros *i.* Greece 59 F11
Androscoggin *r.* U.S.A. 177 P2
Androsovka Rus. Fed. 102 B1
Andros Town Bahamas 186 D1
Andrott *i.* India 94 B4
Andrushevka Ukr. *see* **Andrushivka**
Andrushivka Ukr. 41 D6
also spelt Andrushevka
Andrychów Poland 49 Q6
Andselv Norway 44 L1
Andsnes Norway 44 M1
Andújar Spain 54 G6
Andulo Angola 127 C7
Anec, Lake *salt flat* Australia 150 E4
Anecón Grande *mt.* Arg. 205 C6
Āneen-Kio *terr.* N. Pacific Ocean *see* **Wake Atoll**
Anéfis Mali 125 F2
Anéfis *well* Mali 125 E2
Anegada *i.* Virgin Is (U.K.) 187 G3
Anegada, Bahía *b.* Arg. 204 E6
Anegada Passage Virgin Is (U.K.) 187 H3
Anegam U.S.A. 183 L9
Aného Togo 125 F5
Aneityum *i.* Vanuatu *see* **Anatom**
'Aneiza, Jabal *hill* Iraq *see* **'Unayzah, Jabal**
Anekal India 94 C3
Añelo Arg. 204 C5
Anemourion *tourist site* Turkey 108 D1
Anesbaraka *well* Alg. 123 G6
Anet France 50 H4
Anetchom, Île *i.* Vanuatu *see* **Anatom**
Aneto *mt.* Spain 55 L2
Aney Niger 125 I2
Aneytioum, Île *i.* Vanuatu *see* **Anatom**
Anfile Bay Eritrea 121 I6
Anfu China 87 E3
also known as Pingdu
Angadippuram India 94 C4
Angadoka, Lohatanjona *hd* Madag. 131 [inset] J2
Angahook Lorne State Park *nature res.* Australia 147 D4
Angalarri *r.* Australia 148 A2
Angamma, Falaise d' *esc.* Chad 120 C5
Angamos, Isla *i.* Chile 205 B8
Angamos, Punta *pt* Chile 200 C5
Ang'angxi China 85 I2

▶**Angara** *r.* Rus. Fed. 84 E1
Part of the Yenisey-Angara-Selenga, 3rd longest river in Asia. English form Upper Tunguska; also known as Verkhnyaya Tunguska.
asia [landscapes] ➠ 62–63

Angaradébou Benin 125 F4
Angarapa Aboriginal Land *res.* Australia 148 B4
Angarsk Rus. Fed. 80 G2
Angas Downs Australia 148 B5
Angas Range *hills* Australia 150 E4
Angaston Australia 146 C3
Angat Phil. 74 B3
Angatuba Brazil 206 E10
Angaur *i.* Palau 73 H5
also spelt Ngeaur *or* Niaur
Ånge Sweden 44 K3
Ángel, Salto del *waterfall* Venez. *see* **Angel Falls**
Angel de la Guarda, Isla *i.* Mex. 184 B2
Angeles Phil. 74 B3

▶**Angel Falls** Venez. 199 F3
Highest waterfall in the world. Also known as Ángel, Salto del.

Ängelholm Sweden 45 K4
Angelina *r.* U.S.A. 179 D6
Angellala Creek *r.* Australia 149 E5
Angelo *r.* Australia 150 B4
Angels Camp U.S.A. 182 D3
Āngereb Eth. 104 B5
Āngereb Wenz *r.* Eth. 128 C1
Ångermanälven *r.* Sweden 44 L3
Angermünde Germany 49 L2
Angers France 50 F5
historically known as Andegavum *or* Juliomagus
Anggana Indon. 77 G3
Angical Brazil 202 C4
Angicos Brazil 202 E3
Angikuni Lake Canada 167 L2
Angiola U.S.A. 182 E6
Angkor *tourist site* Cambodia 79 C5
Anglem, Mount *hill* N.Z. 153 B14
also known as Hananui
Anglesey *i.* U.K. 47 H10
also known as Ynys Môn
Angleton U.S.A. 179 D6
Angliers Canada 173 N3
Anglin *r.* France 50 G6
Anglo-Egyptian Sudan *country* Africa *see* **Sudan**
Angmagssalik Greenland *see* **Ammassalik**
Ang Mo Kio Sing. 76 [inset]
Ango Dem. Rep. Congo 126 E3
Angoche Moz. 131 H3
formerly known as António Enes
Angohrān Iran 100 D5
Angol Chile 204 B5
▶**Angola** *country* Africa 127 C7
formerly known as Portuguese West Africa
africa [countries] ➠ 114–117
Angola *IN* U.S.A. 174 C3
Angola *NY* U.S.A. 176 F3
Angonia, Planalto de *plat.* Moz. 131 G2
Angoon U.S.A. 164 F4
Angora Turkey *see* **Ankara**
Angostura Mex. 184 C3
Angoulême France 50 G7
historically known as Iculisma
Angra dos Reis Brazil 207 I10
Angren Uzbek. 103 G4
Ängsö naturreservat *nature res.* Sweden 45 L4
Ang Thong Thai. 79 C5
Angu Dem. Rep. Congo 126 E4
Angualasto Arg. 204 C3
Anguang China 85 I2

▶**Anguilla** *terr.* West Indies 187 H3
United Kingdom Overseas Territory.
oceania [countries] ➠ 138–139

Anguilla Cays *is* Bahamas 186 D2
Anguille, Cape Canada 169 J4
Anguli Nur *l.* China 85 G3
Anguo China 85 G4
Angurugu Australia 148 C2
Angus Canada 173 N6
Angustura Brazil 201 E2
Angwin U.S.A. 182 B3
Anhanguera Brazil 206 E5
Anholt *i.* Denmark 45 J4
Anhua China 87 D2
also known as Dongping
Anhui *prov.* China 87 F1
English form Anhwei
Anhumas Brazil 202 A6
Anhwei *prov.* China *see* **Anhui**
Aniak U.S.A. 164 D3
Aniakchak National Monument and Preserve *nat. park* U.S.A. 164 D4
Anicuns Brazil 206 D3
Ánidhros *i.* Greece *see* **Anydro**
Anié Togo 125 F5
Anie, Pic d' *mt.* France 50 F10
Aniene *r.* Italy 56 E7
Anikhovka Rus. Fed. 103 E2
Anikovo Rus. Fed. 40 G4
Animas *r.* U.S.A. 181 E5
Anina Romania 58 C3
Anishino Rus. Fed. 43 S7
Añisoc Equat. Guinea 125 H6
Anitaguipan Point Phil. 74 C4
Anıtlı Turkey 108 D1
Aniva Rus. Fed. 82 F3
Aniva, Mys *c.* Rus. Fed. 82 F3
Aniva, Zaliv *b.* Rus. Fed. 82 F3
Anivorano Madag. 131 [inset] K3
Anivorano Avaratra Madag. 131 [inset] K2
Aniwa U.S.A. 172 D5
Anjad India 96 B5
Anjafy *mt.* Madag. 131 [inset] J3
Anjalankoski Fin. 45 N3
Anjangaon India 96 C5
Anjar India 96 A5
Anjengo India 94 C4
also known as Anchuthengu
Anji China 87 F2
also known as Dipu
Anji India 94 C1
Anjiang China *see* **Qianyang**
Anjihai China 88 D2
Anjir Avand Iran 100 C3
Anjō Japan 91 E7
Anjoman Iran 100 D3
Anjou *reg.* France 50 F5
Anjou, Val d' *valley* France 50 F5
Anjouan *i.* Comoros *see* **Nzwani**
Anjozorobe Madag. 131 [inset] J3
Anjŭ N. Korea 83 B5
Anjuman *reg.* Afgh. 101 G3
Anka Nigeria 125 G3
Ankaboa, Tanjona *pt* Madag. 131 [inset] I4
formerly known as St-Vincent, Cap
Ankang China 87 D1

▶**Ankara** Turkey 106 C3
Capital of Turkey. Historically known as Ancyra or Angora.

Ankaratra *mts* Madag. 131 [inset] J3
Ankarsrum Sweden 45 L4
Ankatafa Madag. 131 [inset] K2
Ankavandra Madag. 131 [inset] J3
Ankazoabo Madag. 131 [inset] J4
Ankazobe Madag. 131 [inset] J3
Ankeny U.S.A. 174 A3
Ankerika Madag. 131 [inset] J2
An Khê Vietnam 79 E5
formerly known as An Tuc
Ankiliabo Madag. 131 [inset] I4
Anklam Germany 49 K2
Ankleshwar India 96 B5
formerly spelt Anklesvar
Anklesvar India *see* **Ankleshwar**
Ankofa *mt.* Madag. 131 [inset] K3
Ankogel *mt.* Austria 49 K8
Ankola India 94 B3
Ankouzhen China 85 E5
An'kovo Rus. Fed. 43 U5
Ankpa Nigeria 125 G5
Anling China *see* **Yanling**
Anloga Ghana 125 F5
Anlong China 86 C3
Ânlong Vêng Cambodia 79 D5
Anlu China 87 E2
Anmoore U.S.A. 176 E6
An Muileann gCearr Rep. of Ireland *see* **Mullingar**
Anmyŏn-do *i.* S. Korea 83 B5
Ann, Cape Antarctica 223 D2
Ann, Cape U.S.A. 177 O3
Anna Rus. Fed. 41 G6
Anna U.S.A. 176 A5
Anna, Lake U.S.A. 176 H7
Annaba Alg. 123 G1
formerly known as Bône; *historically known as* Bona *or* Hippo Regius
Annaberg-Buchholtz Germany 49 K5
An Nabk Saudi Arabia 109 I6
also known as Al 'Uqaylah
An Nabk Syria 109 H3
An Nafūd *des.* Saudi Arabia 104 C1
Annai Guyana 199 G4
An Nā'ikah, Qarārat *depr.* Libya 120 C3
An Najaf Iraq 107 F5
An Najaf *governorate* Iraq 107 E5
An Najaf, Baḩr *l.* Iraq 109 P6
Annalee *r.* Rep. of Ireland 47 E9
Annam *reg.* Vietnam 78 D4
Annam Highlands *mts* Laos/Vietnam 78 D4
Annan U.K. 47 I9
Annan *r.* U.K. 47 I9
'Annān, Wādī al *watercourse* Syria 109 J3
Annandale U.S.A. 177 H7
Anna Plains Australia 150 C3

▶**Annapolis** U.S.A. 177 I7
State capital of Maryland. Historically known as Anne Arundel Town or Providence.

Annapolis Royal Canada 169 H4
Annapurna Conservation Area *nature res.* Nepal 97 E3

▶**Annapurna I** *mt.* Nepal 97 D3
10th highest mountain in the world and in Asia.
world [physical features] ➠ 8–9

Annapurna II *mt.* Nepal 97 E3
Ann Arbor U.S.A. 173 J8
Anna Regina Guyana 199 G3
An Nás Rep. of Ireland *see* **Naas**
An Nashū, Wādī *watercourse* Libya 120 B3
An Nāşirīyah Iraq 107 F5
Annaspan *imp. l.* S. Africa 133 J5
An Nawfalīyah Libya 120 C2
Annean, Lake *salt flat* Australia 151 B5
Anne Arundel Town U.S.A. *see* **Annapolis**
Annecy France 51 M7
Annecy, Lac d' *l.* France 51 M7
Annecy-le-Vieux France 51 M7
Anne Marie Lake Canada 169 I2
Annemasse France 51 M6
Annette Island U.S.A. 166 D4
Annie *r.* Australia 149 D2
Annikvere Estonia 42 H2
An Nimārah Syria 109 I5
An Nimāş Saudi Arabia 104 C4
Anning China 86 B3
formerly known as Lianran
Anning He *r.* China 86 B3
Annino Rus. Fed. 43 S2
Anniston U.S.A. 175 C5
Annobón *i.* Equat. Guinea 125 G7
formerly known as Pagalu
Annonay France 51 K7
Annotto Bay Jamaica 186 D3
An Nu'ayrīyah Saudi Arabia 105 E2
An Nukhaylah *waterhole* Iraq 109 P4
An Nu'mānīyah Iraq 107 F4
An Nuqay'ah Qatar 105 E2
An Nuşayrīyah, Jabal *mts* Syria 108 H2
Annville U.S.A. 176 B8
Anogeia Greece 59 F13
also spelt Anóyia
Anoka U.S.A. 174 A2
Anori Brazil 199 F5
Anorontany, Tanjona *hd* Madag. 131 [inset] I2
Anosibe An'Ala Madag. 131 [inset] K3
Anou I-n-Atei *well* Alg. 123 G5
Ânou Mellene *well* Mali 125 F2
Anou-n-Bidek *well* Alg. 123 G6
Ano Viannos Greece 59 G13
Anóyia Greece *see* **Anogeia**
Anpu China 87 D4
Anpu Gang *b.* China 87 D4
Anqing China 87 F2
Anqiu China 85 H4
Anren China 87 E3
Ansai China 85 F4
also known as Zhenwudong
Anse-à-Galets Haiti 187 E3
Anse-à-Pitre Haiti 187 F3
Anse-à-Veau Haiti 187 E3
Anseba Shet *watercourse* Eritrea 104 B4
Anse d'Hainault Haiti 187 E3
Anser Group *is* Australia 147 E4
Anserma Col. 198 C3
Anshan China 85 I3
Anshun China 86 C3
Anshunchang China 86 B2
Ansina Uruguay 204 G3
An Sirhān, Wādī *watercourse* Saudi Arabia 107 D5
Ansjö Sweden 44 L3
Anson U.S.A. 179 C5
Anson Bay Australia 148 A2
Ansongo Mali 125 F3
Ansongo-Ménaka, Réserve Partielle de Faune d' *nature res.* Mali 125 F3
Ansonia U.S.A. 176 A5
Ansonville Canada 173 M2
Ansted U.S.A. 176 D7
Anstruther U.K. 46 J7
Ansu China *see* **Xushui**
Anta India 96 C4
Anta Peru 200 B3
Antabamba Peru 200 B3
Antakya Turkey 106 D3
also known as Hatay; *historically known as* Antioch *or* Antiochia
Antalaha Madag. 131 [inset] K2
Antalya Turkey 106 B3
also spelt Adalia; *historically known as* Attalea *or* Attalia
Antalya *prov.* Turkey 108 B1
Antalya Körfezi *g.* Turkey 106 B3
Antanambao Manampotsy Madag. 131 [inset] K3
Antanambe Madag. 131 [inset] K3

▶**Antananarivo** Madag. 131 [inset] J3
Capital of Madagascar. Formerly spelt Tananarive; short form Tana.

Antananarivo *prov.* Madag. 131 [inset] J3
Antanifotsy Madag. 131 [inset] J3
Antanimora Atsimo Madag. 131 [inset] J5
Antantûr, Râs *pt* Egypt 108 F9
An tAonach Rep. of Ireland *see* **Nenagh**

▶**Antarctica** 222
Most southerly and coldest continent, and the continent with the highest average elevation.
world [land cover] ➠ 18–19
antarctica [features] ➠ 212–213

Antarctic Peninsula Antarctica 222 T2
Antaritarika Madag. 131 [inset] J5
Antelope Island U.S.A. 183 L1
Antelope Range *mts* U.S.A. 183 H2
Antequera Spain 54 G7
Anthony *KS* U.S.A. 178 C4
Anthony *NM* U.S.A. 181 F6
Anthony, Lake *salt flat* Australia 146 B2
Anthony Lagoon Australia 148 B3
Anti Atlas *mts* Morocco 122 C3
also known as Petit Atlas
Antibes France 51 N9
Anticosti, Île d' *i.* Canada 169 I3
English form Anticosti Island
Anticosti Island Canada *see* **Anticosti, Île d'**
Antifer, Cap d' *c.* France 50 G3
Antigo U.S.A. 172 D5
Antigonish Canada 169 I4
Antigua *i.* Antigua and Barbuda 187 H3
Antigua Guat. 185 H6
long form Antigua Guatemala
Antigua *country* West Indies *see* **Antigua and Barbuda**
▶**Antigua and Barbuda** *country* West Indies 187 H3
short form Antigua
northamerica [countries] ➠ 158–159
Antigua Guatemala Guat. *see* **Antigua**
Antiguo-Morelos Mex. 185 F4
Antikyra Greece 59 D10
also spelt Andikíra
Antikythira *i.* Greece 59 E13
also spelt Andikithira
Antikythiro, Steno *sea chan.* Greece 59 E13
Anti Lebanon *mts* Lebanon/Syria *see* **Sharqī, Jabal ash**
Antilla Arg. 204 D2
Antilla Cuba 186 E2
Antimilos *i.* Greece 59 F12
also spelt Andímilos
Antimony U.S.A. 183 M3
An tInbhear Mór Rep. of Ireland *see* **Arklow**
Antioch Turkey *see* **Antakya**
Antioch *CA* U.S.A. 182 C3
Antioch *IL* U.S.A. 172 E8
Antiocheia ad Cragum *tourist site* Turkey 108 D1
Antiochia Turkey *see* **Antakya**
Antioquia Col. 198 C3
Antioquia *dept* Col. 198 C3
Antiparos *i.* Greece 59 G11
also spelt Andhíparos
Antipaxoi *i.* Greece 59 B9
also spelt Andípaxoi
Antipino Rus. Fed. 43 O6
Antipodes Islands N.Z. 145 G6
Antipsara *i.* Greece 59 G10
also spelt Andípsara
Antitilos *i.* Greece 59 I12
Antium Italy *see* **Anzio**
Antlers U.S.A. 179 D5
An t-Ob U.K. *see* **Leverburgh**
Antofagasta Chile 200 C5
Antofagasta *admin. reg.* Chile 200 C5
Antofagasta de la Sierra Arg. 204 D2
Antonhibe Madag. 131 [inset] J2
Antônio Carlos Brazil 207 J8
Antonio de Biedma Arg. 205 D7
Antônio Dias Brazil 207 K6
António Enes Moz. *see* **Angoche**
Antônio Lemos Brazil 202 B2
Antón Recio Cuba 186 C2
Antopal' Belarus 42 F9
Antrim U.K. 47 F9
Antrim Hills U.K. 47 F8
Antrim Plateau Australia 150 E3
Antrodoco Italy 56 F6
Antropovo Rus. Fed. 40 G4
Antsahabe Madag. 131 [inset] K2
Antsalova Madag. 131 [inset] J3
Antsambalahy Madag. 131 [inset] K2
Antseranana Madag. *see* **Antsirañana**
Antsiferovo Rus. Fed. 43 O3
Antsirabe Madag. 131 [inset] J3
Antsirabe Avaratra Madag. 131 [inset] K2
Antsirañana Madag. 131 [inset] K2
formerly known as Diégo Suarez; *formerly spelt* Antseranana
Antsirañana *prov.* Madag. 131 [inset] K2
Antsla Estonia 42 H4
Antsohihy Madag. 131 [inset] J2
Antsohimbondrona Madag. 131 [inset] K2
formerly known as Port St-Louis
Antsondrodava Madag. 131 [inset] J3
Anttis Sweden 44 M2
Anttola Fin. 45 N3
Antu China *see* **Songjiang**
An Tuc Vietnam *see* **An Khê**
Antuco Chile 204 C5
Antuco, Volcán *vol.* Chile 204 C5
Antufash, Jazīrat *i.* Yemen 104 C5
English form Antufush Island
Antufush Island Yemen *see* **Antufash, Jazīrat**
Antwerp Belgium 51 K1
also known as Anvers; *also spelt* Antwerpen
Antwerp U.S.A. 177 J1
Antwerpen Belgium *see* **Antwerp**
An Uaimh Rep. of Ireland *see* **Navan**
Anuc, Lac *l.* Canada 169 F1
Anuchino Rus. Fed. 82 D4
Anueque, Sierra *mts* Arg. 205 C6
Anugul India 95 E1
Anupgarh India 96 B3
Anuradhapura Sri Lanka 94 D4
Anurrete Aboriginal Land *res.* Australia 148 B4
Anvers Belgium *see* **Antwerp**
Anvers Island Antarctica 222 T2
Anvil Range *mts* Canada 166 C2
Anxi *Fujian* China 87 F3
also known as Fengcheng
Anxi *Gansu* China 84 B3
also known as Yuanquan
Anxian China 86 C2
also known as Anchang
Anxiang China 87 E2
Anxin China 85 G4
also known as Xin'an
Anxious Bay Australia 146 B3
Anxur Italy *see* **Terracina**
Anyang China *see* **Du'an**
Anyang China 85 G4
also known as Zhangde
Anyang S. Korea 83 B5
Anyar Indon. 77 D4
Anydro *i.* Greece 59 G12
also known as Ánidhros
A'nyêmaqên Shan *mts* China 86 A1
English form Amne Machin Range
Anyi China 87 E2
also known as Longjin
Anykščiai Lith. 42 G6
Anyuan *Jiangxi* China 87 E3
also known as Xinshan
Anyuan *Jiangxi* China 87 E3
Anyue China 86 C2
also known as Yueyang
Anyuy *r.* Rus. Fed. 82 E2
Anyuysk Rus. Fed. 39 Q3
Anzac *Alta* Canada 167 I3
Anzac *B.C.* Canada 166 F4
Anze China 85 G4
Anzhero-Sudzhensk Rus. Fed. 80 D1
Anzi Dem. Rep. Congo 126 D5
Anzio Italy 56 E7
historically known as Antium
Anzoátegui *state* Venez. 199 E2
Aoba *i.* Vanuatu 145 F3
also known as Omba; *also spelt* Oba
Aob Luang National Park Thai. 78 B4
Aoga-shima *i.* Japan 91 F8
Aohan Qi China *see* **Xinhui**
Aomen China *see* **Macau**
Aomori Japan 90 G4
Aomori *pref.* Japan 90 G4
Aoos *r.* Greece 59 B8
Ao Phang Nga National Park Thai. 79 B6
Aoraki N.Z. *see* **Mount Cook**
Aoraki *mt.* N.Z. *see* **Cook, Mount**
Aôral, Phnum *mt.* Cambodia 79 D5
Aorangi *mt.* N.Z. *see* **Cook, Mount**
Aorere *r.* N.Z. 152 G8
Aosta Italy 51 N7
Aotearoa *country* Oceania *see* **New Zealand**
Aouderas Niger 125 H2
Aoufist W. Sahara 122 B4
Aouhinet bel Egra *well* Alg. 122 D4
Aouk, Bahr *r.* Cent. Afr. Rep./Chad 126 C2
Aoukalé *r.* Cent. Afr. Rep./Chad 126 D2
Aoukâr *reg.* Mali/Mauritania 122 D5
Aoukenek *well* Mali 125 F2
Aoulef Alg. 123 F4
Aoulime, Jbel *mt.* Morocco 122 C3
Aourou Mali 124 C3
Aoxi China *see* **Le'an**
Aoya Japan 91 D7
Aoyang China *see* **Shanggao**
Aozou Chad 120 C4
Apa *r.* Brazil 201 F5
Apac Uganda 128 B4
Apache U.S.A. 179 C5
Apache, Lake U.S.A. 183 M8
Apache Junction U.S.A. 183 M8
Apagado, Volcán *vol.* Bol. 200 D5
Apahida Romania 58 E2
Apaiaí *r.* Brazil 206 E10
Apaiang *atoll* Kiribati *see* **Abaiang**
Apalachee Bay U.S.A. 175 C6
Apalachicola U.S.A. 175 C6
Apalachicola *r.* U.S.A. 175 C6
Apalachicola Bay U.S.A. 175 C6
Apam Ghana 125 E5
Apamama *atoll* Kiribati *see* **Abemama**
Apamea Turkey *see* **Dinar**
Apan Mex. 185 F5
Apaporis *r.* Col. 198 D5
Apar, Teluk *b.* Indon. 77 G3
Aparecida do Rio Doce Brazil 206 B5
Aparecida do Tabuado Brazil 206 B7
Aparima N.Z. *see* **Riverton**
Aparima *r.* N.Z. 153 C14
Aparri Phil. 74 B2
Aparurén Venez. 199 F3
Apas, Sierra *hills* Arg. 205 D6
Apaščia *r.* Lith. 42 F5
Apatin *Vojvodina, Srbija* Yugo. 56 K3
Apatity Rus. Fed. 44 P2
Apatou Fr. Guiana 199 H3
Apatzingán Mex. 185 E5
Ape Latvia 42 H4
Apediá *r.* Brazil 201 E2
Apeldoorn Neth. 48 C3
Apennines *mts* Italy 53 D3
also known as Appennino
Apere *r.* Bol. 200 D3
Apex Mountain Canada 166 B2
Aphrodite's Birthplace *tourist site* Cyprus 108 D3
also known as Petra tou Romiou
Api Dem. Rep. Congo 126 E4
Api *mt.* Nepal 96 D3
Api, Tanjung *pt* Indon. 75 B3
Apia Col. 198 C3
Apia *atoll* Kiribati *see* **Abaiang**

▶**Apia** Samoa 145 H3
Capital of Samoa.
oceania [countries] ➠ 138–139

Apiacas, Serra dos *hills* Brazil 201 F2
Apiaí Brazil 203 B8
Apiaú, Serra do *mts* Brazil 199 F4
Apio Solomon Is 145 F2
Apipilulco Mex. 185 F5
Apishapa *r.* U.S.A. 178 B4
Apiti N.Z. 152 J7
Apizaco Mex. 185 F5
Apizolaya Mex. 179 B7
Aplao Peru 200 B4
Ap Lei Chau *i. Hong Kong* China *see* **Aberdeen Island**
Apo, Mount *vol.* Phil. 74 C5
Apodi Brazil 202 E3
Apodi, Chapada do *hills* Brazil 202 E3
Apo East Passage Phil. 74 B3
Apoera Suriname 199 G3
Apolda Germany 48 I4
Apollinopolis Magna Egypt *see* **Idfu**
Apollo Bay Australia 147 D4
Apollonia Bulg. *see* **Sozopol**
Apollonia Greece 59 F12
Apolo Bol. 200 C3
Apopka U.S.A. 175 D6
Aporé *r.* Brazil 206 C6
Apostle Islands U.S.A. 172 C4
Apostle Islands National Lakeshore *nature res.* U.S.A. 172 C3
Apostolens Tommelfinger *mt.* Greenland 165 O3
Apóstoles Arg. 204 G2
Apostolos Andreas, Cape Cyprus 108 F2
also known as Zafer Burnu
Apoteri Guyana 199 G3
Apo West Passage Phil. 74 B3
Appalachia U.S.A. 176 C9
▶**Appalachian Mountains** U.S.A. 176 B9
northamerica [landscapes] ➠ 156–157
Appalla *i.* Fiji *see* **Kabara**
Appennino *mts* Italy *see* **Apennines**
Appennino Abruzzese *mts* Italy 56 F6
Appennino Lucano *mts* Italy 57 H8
Appennino Napoletano *mts* Italy 56 H7
Appennino Tosco-Emiliano *mts* Italy 56 C5
Appiano sulla Strada del Vino Italy 56 D2
Applecross U.K. 46 G6
Appleton *MN* U.S.A. 178 C2
Appleton *WI* U.S.A. 172 E6
Apple Valley U.S.A. 183 G7
Appomattox U.S.A. 176 G8
Aprelevka Rus. Fed. 43 S6
Aprilia Italy 56 E7
Apsheronsk Rus. Fed. 41 F7
formerly known as Apsheronskaya
Apsheronskaya Rus. Fed. *see* **Apsheronsk**
Apsheronskiy Poluostrov *pen.* Azer. *see* **Abşeron Yarımadası**
Apsley Canada 173 O6
Apsley Strait Australia 148 A1
Apt France 51 L9
Apucarana Brazil 206 B10
Apucarana, Serra da *hills* Brazil 206 B10
Apulum Romania *see* **Alba Iulia**
Apurahuan Phil. 74 A4
Apure *r.* Venez. 198 E3
Apure *state* Venez. 198 D3
Apurímac *dept* Peru 200 B3
Apurimac *r.* Peru 200 B3
Apurito Venez. 198 D3
Aq"a Georgia *see* **Sokhumi**
'Aqaba Jordan *see* **Al 'Aqabah**
Aqaba, Gulf of Asia 104 A1
'Aqaba, Wâdi el *watercourse* Egypt 108 E7
Aqadyr Kazakh. *see* **Agadyr'**
Aqal China 88 B3
Aqbalyq Kazakh. *see* **Akbalyk**
Aqbeyit Kazakh. *see* **Akbeit**
Āqchah Afgh. 101 F2
Aq Chai *r.* Iran 107 F3
Āqdā Iran 100 C3
Aqdoghmish *r.* Iran 100 A2
Aqiq Sudan 121 H5
Aqiq, Khalîg *b.* Sudan 104 B4
Aqiq, Wādī al *watercourse* Saudi Arabia 104 C2
Aqitag *mt.* China 88 E3
Aqköl Kazakh. *see* **Akkol'**
Aqköl Kazakh. *see* **Akkol'**
Aqla *well* Saudi Arabia 104 B2
Aqmola Kazakh. *see* **Astana**
Aqmola Oblast *admin. div.* Kazakh. *see* **Akmolinskaya Oblast'**
Aqmola Oblysy *admin. div.* Kazakh. *see* **Akmolinskaya Oblast'**
Āq Qal'eh Iran 100 C2
formerly known as Pahlavī Dezh
Aqqan China 89 D4
formerly known as Atqan
Aqqikkol Hu *salt l.* China 89 E4
Aqqystaū Kazakh. *see* **Akkystau**
Aqra', Wādī al *watercourse* Saudi Arabia 109 L7
'Aqraba West Bank 108 G5
'Aqrah Iraq 107 E3
'Aqran *hill* Saudi Arabia 109 J6
Aqsay Kazakh. *see* **Aksay**
Aqsayqin Hit *terr.* Asia *see* **Aksai Chin**
Aqshataū Kazakh. *see* **Akchatau**
Aqshī Kazakh. *see* **Akshiy**
Aqshuqyr Kazakh. *see* **Akshukur**
Aqsū Kazakh. *see* **Aksu**
Aqsū Kazakh. *see* **Aksu**
Aqsū Kazakh. *see* **Aksu**
Aqsūat Kazakh. *see* **Aksuat**
Aqsū-Ayuly Kazakh. *see* **Aksu-Ayuly**
Aqtaū Kazakh. *see* **Aktau**
Aqtöbe Kazakh. *see* **Aktyubinsk**
Aqtöbe Oblysy *admin. div.* Kazakh. *see* **Aktyubinskaya Oblast'**
Aqtoghay Kazakh. *see* **Aktogay**
Aqtoghay Kazakh. *see* **Aktogay**
Aquae Grani Germany *see* **Aachen**
Aquae Gratianae France *see* **Aix-les-Bains**
Aquae Sextiae France *see* **Aix-en-Provence**
Aquae Statiellae Italy *see* **Acqui Terme**
Aquarius Mountains U.S.A. 183 K7
Aquarius Plateau U.S.A. 183 M4
Aquaviva delle Fonti Italy 56 I8
Aquidabánmi *r.* Para. 201 F5
Aquidauana Brazil 201 G5
Aquidauana *r.* Brazil 201 F4
Aquila Mex. 184 E5
Aquiles Mex. 184 D2
Aquin Haiti 187 E3
Aquincum Hungary *see* **Budapest**
Aquiry *r.* Brazil *see* **Acre**
Aquisgranum Germany *see* **Aachen**
Aquitaine *admin. reg.* France 50 F8
Aqzhal Kazakh. *see* **Akzhal**
Aqzhar Kazakh. *see* **Akzhar**
Aqzhayqyn Köli *salt l.* Kazakh. *see* **Akzhaykyn, Ozero**
Ara India 97 E4
formerly spelt Arrah
Ara *r.* Spain 55 L2
Āra Ārba Eth. 128 D3
Arab U.S.A. 174 C5
Arab, Bahr el *watercourse* Sudan 126 F2
'Arab, Khalîg el *b.* Egypt 121 F2
'Araba, Wâdi *watercourse* Egypt 108 D8
'Arabābād Iran 100 D3
Ara Bacalle *well* Eth. 128 D3
'Arabah, Wādī *r.* Yemen 105 E4
'Arabah, Wādī al *watercourse* Israel/Jordan 108 G8
also known as Ha 'Arava
Arabelo Venez. 199 E3
Arabian Gulf Asia *see* **The Gulf**
Arabian Oryx Sanctuary *tourist site* Saudi Arabia 105 G4
Arabian Sea Indian Ocean 99 H6
Ara Bonel Eth. 128 D3
Arabopó Venez. 199 F3
Araç Turkey 106 C2
Araça *r.* Brazil 199 F5
Aracaju Brazil 202 E4
Aracanguy, Montes de *hills* Para. 201 G6
Aracar, Volcán *vol.* Arg. 200 D6
Aracati Brazil 202 E3
Aracatu Brazil 202 D5
Araçatuba Brazil 206 C8
Aracena Spain 54 E7
Aracena, Isla *i.* Chile 205 C9
Aracena, Sierra de *hills* Spain 54 D7
Arachthos *r.* Greece 59 C9
also spelt Arakhthos
Aračinovo Macedonia 58 C6
Aracoiaba Brazil 202 E3
Aracruz Brazil 203 D6
Araçuaí Brazil 203 D6
Araçuaí *r.* Brazil 203 D6
'Arad Israel 108 G6
Arad Romania 58 C2
Arada Chad 120 D6
'Arādah U.A.E. 105 F3
Arādān Iran 100 C3
Aradeib, Wadi *watercourse* Sudan 120 D6
Arafura Sea Australia/Indon. 144 C2
Aragarças Brazil 206 A2
Aragón *aut. comm.* Spain 55 K3
Aragón *r.* Spain 55 J2
Aragoncillo *mt.* Spain 55 I4
Aragua *state* Venez. 199 E2
Araguacema Brazil 202 B4
Araguaçu Brazil 202 B5
Aragua de Barcelona Venez. 199 E2
Aragua de Maturín Venez. 199 F2
Araguaia *r.* Brazil 206 A3
Araguaia, Parque Nacional de *nat. park* Brazil 202 B4
Araguaiana Brazil 206 B2
Araguaína Brazil 202 B3
Araguana Brazil 202 B3
Araguao, Boca *r. mouth* Venez. 199 F2
Araguapiche, Punta *pt* Venez. 199 F2
Araguari Brazil 206 E5
Araguari *r. Amapá* Brazil 199 I4
Araguari *r. Minas Gerais* Brazil 206 E5
Araguatins Brazil 202 B3
Aragvi *r.* Georgia 107 F2
'Ārah, Ra's *pt* Yemen 104 C5

'Ārah, Wādī *r.* Oman **105** F4
Arai Japan **90** F6
Araif el Naga, Gebel *hill* Egypt **108** F7
Araiosos Brazil **202** D2
Arak Alg. **123** F4
Arāk Iran **100** B3
formerly known as Sultanabad
Arak Syria **109** J3
Arakai-yama *mt.* Japan **90** F6
Arakaka Guyana **199** F3
Arakan *state* Myanmar **78** A3
also known as Rakhaing or Rakhine or Yagaing
Arakan Yoma *mts* Myanmar **78** A3
Arakhthos *r.* Greece see **Arachthos**
Arakkonam India **94** C3
formerly spelt Arkonam
Aral China **88** C3
Aral Kazakh. see **Aral'sk**
Aral Tajik. see **Vose**

▶**Aral Sea** *salt l.* Kazakh./Uzbek. **102** D3
2nd largest lake in Asia and 6th in the world. Also known as Aral Tengizi or Orol Dengizi.
asia [landscapes] ➡ 62–63

Aral'sk Kazakh. **103** E3
also known as Aral
Aralsor, Ozero *l.* Kazakh. **102** B2
Aralsor, Ozero *salt l.* Kazakh. **102** C2
Aralsul'fat Kazakh. **103** E3
Aral Tengizi *salt l.* Kazakh./Uzbek. see **Aral Sea**
Aramac Australia **149** E4
Aramac Creek *watercourse* Australia **149** E4
Aramah *plat.* Saudi Arabia **105** D2
A Ramallosa Spain **54** C2
Aramberri Mex. **185** F3
Arame Brazil **202** C3
Aramia *r.* P.N.G. **73** J8
Aran *r.* India **94** C2
Arancibia Arg. **204** C3
Aranda de Duero Spain **55** H3
Aranđelovac *Srbija* Yugo. **58** B4
Arandis Namibia **130** B4
Arang India **97** D5
Arani India **94** C3
Aran Island Rep. of Ireland **47** D9
Aran Islands Rep. of Ireland **47** C10
Aranjuez Spain **55** H4
Aranos Namibia **130** C5
Aransas Pass U.S.A. **179** C7
Arantangi India **94** C4
Arantes *r.* Brazil **206** C6
Aranuka *atoll* Kiribati **145** G1
formerly known as Henderville
Aranyaprathet Thai. **79** C5
Arao Japan **91** B8
Araouane Mali **124** E2
Arapaho U.S.A. **179** C5
Arapahoe U.S.A. **178** C3
Arapari Brazil **199** H5
Arapawa Island N.Z. **152** I9
Arapicos Ecuador **198** B5
Arapiraca Brazil **202** E4
Arapis, Akra *pt* Greece **59** F8
Arapkir Turkey **107** D3
Arapongas Brazil **206** B10
Arapoti Brazil **206** D11
Arapsun Turkey see **Gülşehir**
Arapuá Brazil **206** A7
Arapuni N.Z. **152** J6
'Ar'ar Saudi Arabia **107** E5
'Ar'ar, Wādī *watercourse* Iraq/Saudi Arabia **107** E5
Arara *r.* Brazil **199** F5
Araracuara Col. **198** C5
Araracuara, Cerros de *hills* Col. **198** C5
Araranguá Brazil **203** B9
Araraquara Brazil **206** E8
Araras *Amazonas* Brazil **200** C2
Araras *Pará* Brazil **199** H6
Ararás Brazil **200** D2
Araras *São Paulo* Brazil **206** F9
Araras, Açude *resr* Brazil **202** D3
Araras, Serra das *hills* Brazil **203** A6
Araras, Serra das *mts* Brazil **203** A8
Ararat Armenia **107** F3
Ararat Australia **147** D4
Ararat, Mount Turkey **107** F3
also known as Ağrı Dağı
Arari Brazil **202** C2
Araria India **97** E4
Araripe Brazil **202** D3
Araripe, Chapada do *hills* Brazil **202** D3
Araripina Brazil **202** D3
Araruama Brazil **207** K9
Araruama, Lago de *lag.* Brazil **207** K9
Aras Turkey **107** E3
also known as Velibaba
Aras *r.* Turkey see **Araz**
Ar Asgat Mongolia **85** E1
Arațâne *well* Mauritania **124** C2
Arataú *r.* Brazil **202** B2
Aratürük China see **Yiwu**
Arauá *r.* Brazil **199** F6
Arauá *r.* Brazil **199** F6
Arauã *r.* Brazil **200** D2
Arauca Col. **198** D3
Arauca *dept* Col. **198** D3
Arauca *r.* Venez. **198** E3
Arauco Chile **204** B5
Arauco, Golfo de *b.* Chile **204** B5
Arauquita Col. **198** D3
Araure Venez. **198** D2
Aravaipa Creek *watercourse* U.S.A. **183** N9
Aravalli Range *mts* India **96** B4
Aravete Estonia **42** G2
Araviana *r.* Spain **55** I3
Aravissos Greece **58** D8
Arawa P.N.G. **145** E2
Arawale National Reserve *nature res.* Kenya **128** D5
Arawata *r.* N.Z. **153** C12
formerly spelt Arawhata
Arawhana *mt.* N.Z. **152** L6
Arawhata *r.* N.Z. see **Arawata**
Araxá Brazil **206** G6
Araxos, Akra *pt* Greece **59** C10
Araya, Península de *pen.* Venez. **199** E2
Arayıt Dağı *mt.* Turkey **106** B3
Araz *r.* Azer. **107** G2
also spelt Aras
Arba *r.* Spain **55** J3
Arbailu Iraq see **Arbīl**
Ārba Minch Eth. **128** C3
Arbela Iraq see **Arbīl**
Arbīl Iraq **107** F3
also known as Hawlêr; also spelt Irbil; historically known as Arbailu or Arbela
Arbīl *governorate* Iraq **107** E4
Arboga Sweden **45** K4
Arbois France **51** L6
Arboletes Col. **198** B2
Arbon Switz. **51** P5
Arborfield Canada **167** K4
Arborg Canada **167** L5
Arbrå Sweden **45** L3
Arbroath U.K. **46** J7
Arbuckle U.S.A. **182** B2
Arbu Lut, Dasht-e *des.* Afgh. **101** E4
Arc *r.* France **51** M7
Arcachon France **50** E8
Arcachon, Bassin d' *inlet* France **50** E8
Arcadia *FL* U.S.A. **175** D7
Arcadia *LA* U.S.A. **179** D5
Arcadia *MI* U.S.A. **172** G6
Arcadia *WI* U.S.A. **172** B6
Arcalod, Pointe d' *mt.* France **51** M7
Arcanum U.S.A. **176** A6
Arcas, Cayos *is* Mex. **185** H4
Arcata U.S.A. **180** A4
Arc Dome *mt.* U.S.A. **183** G3
Arcelia Mex. **185** E5
Archangel Rus. Fed. **40** G2
also known as Arkhangel'sk; historically known as Novyj Cholmogory or Novyj Holmogory or Novyy Kholmogory
Archangel Oblast *admin. div.* Rus. Fed. see **Arkhangel'skaya Oblast'**
Archangelos Greece **59** J12
Archar *r.* Bulg. **58** D5
Archbold U.S.A. **176** A4
Archena Spain **55** J6
Archer *r.* Australia **149** D2
Archer Bend National Park Australia **149** D2
Archer City U.S.A. **179** C5
Arches National Park U.S.A. **183** O3
Arch Henda *well* Mali **124** E2
Archidona Spain **54** G7
Archie Creek *r.* Australia **148** C3
Archman Turkm. **102** D5
Arci, Monte *hill Sardegna* Italy **57** A9
Arcipélago de la Maddalena, Parco Nazionale dell' *nat. park Sardegna* Italy **56** B7
Ärçivan Azer. **107** G3
Arckaringa *watercourse* Australia **146** B2
Arco Italy **56** C3
Arco U.S.A. **180** D4
Arcola U.S.A. **176** H7
Arconce *r.* France **51** J6
Arcos Brazil **207** H7
Arcos de Jalón Spain **55** I3
Arcos de la Frontera Spain **54** F8
Arcos de Valdevez Port. **54** C3
Arcot India **94** C3
Arcoverde Brazil **202** E4
Arctic Bay Canada **165** K2
Arctic Institute Islands Rus. Fed. see **Arkticheskogo Instituta, Ostrova**
▶**Arctic Ocean 224** O1
arctic [features] ➡ 214–215
Arctic Red *r.* Canada **166** C1
Arctic Red River Canada see **Tsiigehtchic**
Arctowski *research station* Antarctica **222** U2
long form Henryk Arctowski
Arda *r.* Bulg. **58** H7
also known as Ardas
Ardabīl Iran **100** B2
Ardabīl *prov.* Iran **100** A2
Ardahan Turkey **107** E2
Ardāk Iran **101** D2
Ardakān *Fārs* Iran **100** C4
Ardakān *Yazd* Iran **100** C3
Ardal Iran **100** B4
Årdal Norway **45** I3
Årdalstangen Norway **45** I3
Ardas *r.* Greece **58** H7
Ard aş Şawwān *plain* Jordan **109** I7
Ardatov *Nizhegorodskaya Oblast'* Rus. Fed. **40** G5
Ardatov *Respublika Mordoviya* Rus. Fed. **40** H5
Ardbeg Canada **173** M5
Ardèche *r.* France **51** K8
Ardee Rep. of Ireland **47** F10
Arden, Mount *hill* Australia **146** C3
Ardennes *plat.* Belgium **51** K3
also known as L'Ardenne, Plateau de
Ardentes France **50** H6
Arden Town U.S.A. **182** C3
Ardestān Iran **100** C3
Ardglass U.K. **47** G9
Ardila *r.* Port. **54** D6
Ardino Bulg. **58** G7
Ardkeen N.Z. **152** L6
Ardlethan Australia **147** E3
Ardmore U.S.A. **179** C5
Ardnamurchan, Point of U.K. **46** F7
Ardon Rus. Fed. **107** F2
Ardrossan Australia **146** C3
Ardrossan U.K. **46** H8
Ards Peninsula U.K. **47** G9
Ardvasar U.K. **46** G6
Are Sweden **44** K3
Areado Brazil **207** G8
Arebi Dem. Rep. Congo **126** F4
Arecibo Puerto Rico **187** G3
Arefino Rus. Fed. **43** U3
Arefu Romania **58** F3
Areguá Para. **201** F6
Areia Branca Brazil **202** E3
Arekhawsk Belarus **43** L7
also spelt Orekhovsk; formerly known as Orekhi-Vydritsa
Arel Belgium see **Arlon**
Arelas France see **Arles**
Arelate France see **Arles**
Arena *reef* Phil. **74** B4
Arena, Point U.S.A. **182** A3
Arena de la Ventana, Punta *pt* Mex. **184** C3
Arenal, Campo del *plain* Arg. **204** D2
Arenal, Puerto del *pass* Spain **55** I6
Arenal, Volcán *vol.* Costa Rica **186** B5
Arena Point Phil. **74** B3
Arenápolis Brazil **201** F3
Arenas, Punta de *pt* Arg. **205** C9
Arenas de San Pedro Spain **54** F4
Arendal Norway **45** J4
Arendsee (Altmark) Germany **48** I3
Arenys de Mar Spain **55** N3
Arenzano Italy **56** A4
Areopoli Greece **59** D12
Areponapuchi Mex. **181** F8
Arequipa Peru **200** C4
Arequipa *dept* Peru **200** B3
Arere Brazil **199** H5
Ārēro Eth. **128** C3
Aresa *r.* Belarus **42** J9
Arévalo Spain **54** G3
Areza Eritrea **104** B5
Arezzaf *well* Mali see **Aghezzaf**
Arezzo Italy **56** D5
historically known as Arretium
'Arfajah *well* Saudi Arabia **107** D5
Arfara Greece **59** D11
Arga *r.* Spain **55** J2
Argadargada Australia **148** C4
Argalant Mongolia **85** F2
Argalasti Greece **59** E9
Argan China **88** E3
Arganda Spain **55** H4
Arganil Port. **54** C4
Argao Phil. **74** B4
Argatay Mongolia **85** E2
Argel Alg. see **Algiers**
Argelès-Gazost France **50** F9
Argelès-sur-Mer France **51** J10
Argens *r.* France **51** M9
Argenta Italy **56** D4
Argentan France **50** F4
Argentario, Monte *hill* Italy **56** D6
Argentat France **51** H7
Argentera, Cima dell' *mt.* Italy **51** N8

▶**Argentina** *country* S. America **204** C4
2nd largest country in South America and 8th in the world. 3rd most populous country in South America. Long form Argentine Republic.
world [countries] ➡ 10–11
southamerica [countries] ➡ 192–193

Argentina Range *mts* Antarctica **223** V1
Argentine Republic *country* S. America see **Argentina**
Argentino, Lago *l.* Arg. **205** B8
Argenton *r.* France **50** F5
Argentoratum France see **Strasbourg**
Argentre France **50** F4
Argeş *r.* Romania **58** H4
Argeşel *r.* Romania **58** F4
Arghandab *r.* Afgh. **101** F4
Arghastan *r.* Afgh. **101** F4
Argolikos Kolpos *b.* Greece **59** D11
Argonne U.S.A. **172** E5
Argos Greece **59** D11
Argos U.S.A. **172** G9
Argos Orestiko Greece **59** C8
Argostoli Greece **59** B10
Arguedas Spain **55** J2
Argun' *r.* China/Rus. Fed. **85** H1
also known as Ergun He
Argun *r.* Georgia/Rus. Fed. **107** F2
Argun Rus. Fed. **107** F2
Argungu Nigeria **125** G3
Argunskiy Khrebet *mts* Rus. Fed. **85** H1
Argus Range *mts* U.S.A. **182** G6
Arguut Mongolia **84** D2
Argyle Canada **169** H5
Argyle *IA* U.S.A. **172** B10
Argyle *WI* U.S.A. **172** D8
Argyle, Lake Australia **150** E3
Argyrokastron Albania see **Gjirokastër**
Arhab *reg.* Yemen **104** D5
Arhangay *prov.* Mongolia **84** D2
Ar Horqin Qi China see **Tianshan**
Århus Denmark **45** J4
also spelt Aarhus
Aria N.Z. **152** I6
Ariaga *i.* Indon. **75** C1
Ariake-kai *b.* Japan **91** B8
Ariamsvlei Namibia **130** C6
Ariano Irpino Italy **56** H7
Arias Arg. **204** E4
Ari Atoll Maldives **93** D10
Ariaú Brazil **199** G5
Aribí *r.* Venez. **199** F2
Aribinda Burkina **125** E3
Arica Chile **200** C4
Arica Col. **198** D5
Aricagua Venez. **198** D2
Arid, Cape Australia **151** C7
Arida Japan **91** D7
Aridaia Greece **58** D8
Aridal, Sabkhat *salt pan* W. Sahara **122** B4
Arid Island N.Z. see **Rakitu Island**
Ariège *r.* France **50** H9
Aries *r.* Romania **58** E2
Arieşul Mic *r.* Romania **58** E2
Arigiyn Gol *r.* Mongolia **84** D1
Arīhā Syria **109** H2
Arīḥā West Bank see **Jericho**
Arikaree *r.* U.S.A. **178** B3
Arilje *Srbija* Yugo. **58** B5
Arima Trin. and Tob. **187** H5
Arimã Brazil **199** F6
Ariminum Italy see **Rimini**
Arimu Mine Guyana **199** G3
'Arīn, Wādī al *watercourse* Saudi Arabia **104** C4
Arinagour U.K. **46** F7
Arinos *Mato Grosso* Brazil **201** G3
Arinos *Minas Gerais* Brazil **202** C5
Arinos *r.* Brazil **201** F2
Ario de Rosáles Mex. **185** E5
Ariogala Lith. **42** E6
Aripao Venez. **199** E3
Aripo, Mount *hill* Trin. and Tob. **187** H5
Aripuanã Brazil **201** F2
Aripuanã *r.* Brazil **199** F6
Ariquemes Brazil **201** E2
Ariranhá *r.* Brazil **203** A6
Arisaig U.K. **46** G7
Arisaig, Sound of *sea chan.* U.K. **46** G7
Arisaru Falls Guyana **199** G3
'Arîsh, Wâdi el *watercourse* Egypt **108** E6
Arismendi Venez. **198** D2
Aristazabal Island Canada **166** D4
Aristizábal, Cabo *c.* Arg. **205** D7
Aristóbulo del Valle Arg. **201** G6
Aritwala Pak. **101** H4
Arivonimamo Madag. **131** [inset] J3
Arixang China see **Wenquan**
Ariya *waterhole* Kenya **128** C4
Ariyalur India **94** C4
Arizaro, Salar de *salt flat* Arg. **200** D6
Arizgoiti Spain **55** I1
Arizona Arg. **204** D4
Arizona *state* U.S.A. **183** M7
Arizpe Mex. **184** C2
'Arjah Saudi Arabia **104** D2
Årjäng Sweden **45** K4
Arjasa Indon. **77** F4
'Arjāwī, Wādī al *watercourse* Iraq **109** O5
Arjeplog Sweden **44** L2
Arjo Eth. **128** C2
Arjona Col. **198** C2
Arjona Spain **54** G7
Arjuni India **96** D5
Arkadak Rus. Fed. **41** G6
Arkadelphia U.S.A. **179** D5
Arkagala Rus. Fed. **39** O3
Arkalgud India **94** C3
Arkalochori Greece **59** G13
Arkalyk Kazakh. **103** F2
also spelt Arqalyq
Arkansas *r.* U.S.A. **179** E5
Arkansas *state* U.S.A. **174** A5
Arkansas City *AR* U.S.A. **175** B5
Arkansas City *KS* U.S.A. **178** C4
Arkata *r.* Bulg. **58** G7
Arkatag Shan *mts* China **89** E4
Arkell, Mount Canada **166** C2
Arkenu, Jabal *mt.* Libya **120** E4
Arkhangel'sk Rus. Fed. see **Archangel**
Arkhangel'skaya Oblast' *admin. div.* Rus. Fed. **40** G3
English form Archangel Oblast
Arkhangel'skoye *Respublika Bashkortostan* Rus. Fed. **40** K5
Arkhangel'skoye *Tul'skaya Oblast'* Rus. Fed. **43** S8
Arkhara Rus. Fed. **82** C2
Arkhara *r.* Rus. Fed. **82** C2
Arkhipovka Rus. Fed. **82** D3
Arkhipovka Rus. Fed. **43** M7
Árki *i.* Greece see **Arkoi**
Arklow Rep. of Ireland **47** F11
also known as An tInbhear Mór
Arkoi *i.* Greece **59** H11
also known as Árki
Arkona Canada **173** L7
Arkona, Kap *c.* Germany **49** K1
Arkonam India see **Arakkonam**
Arkösund Sweden **45** L4

▶**Arkticheskiy, Mys** *is* Rus. Fed. **39** J1
Most northerly point of Asia.

Arkticheskogo Instituta, Ostrova *is* Rus. Fed. **39** I2
English form Arctic Institute Islands
Arkul' Rus. Fed. **40** I4
Ärla Sweden **45** L4
Arlanc France **51** J7
Arlang, Gora *mt.* Turkm. **102** C5
Arlanza *r.* Spain **55** G2
Arlanzón *r.* Spain **54** G2
Arles France **51** K9
historically known as Arelas or Arelate
Arli Burkina **125** F4
Arlington *IA* U.S.A. **172** B8
Arlington *IL* U.S.A. **172** D9
Arlington *NY* U.S.A. **177** L4
Arlington *OH* U.S.A. **176** B5
Arlington *OR* U.S.A. **180** B3
Arlington *VA* U.S.A. **177** H7
Arlington *WI* U.S.A. **172** D7
Arlington Heights U.S.A. **174** B3
Arlit Niger **125** G2
Arlon Belgium **51** L3
also known as Arel; also spelt Aarlen
Arltunga Australia **148** B4
Arlyeya Belarus **43** K6
Arm *r.* Canada **167** J5
Armadale Australia **151** A7
Armadores *i.* Indon. **75** C1
Armageddon *tourist site* Israel see **Tel Megiddo**
Armagh U.K. **47** F9
Armah, Wādī *r.* Yemen **105** E4
Armançon *r.* France **51** J5
Armando Bermudez *nat. park* Dom. Rep. **187** F3
Armant Egypt **121** G3
historically known as Hermonthis
Armathia *i.* Greece **59** H13
Armavir Rus. Fed. **41** G7
▶**Armenia** *country* Asia **107** F2
known as Haikakan in Armenian; formerly known as Armyanskaya S.S.R.; historically known as Urartu
asia [countries] ➡ 64–67
Armenia Col. **198** C3
Armenistis, Akra *pt* Greece **59** I12
Armenki Rus. Fed. **43** V4
Armenopolis Romania see **Gherla**
Armeria Mex. **184** E5
Armi, Capo dell' *c.* Italy **57** H11
Armidale Australia **147** F2
Armit Lake Canada **167** N1
Armona U.S.A. **182** E5
Armori India **94** D1
Armorique, Parc Régional d' *park* France **50** C4
Armour U.S.A. **178** C3
Armstrong Arg. **204** E4
Armstrong *r.* Australia **148** A3
Armstrong *B.C.* Canada **166** G5
Armstrong *Ont.* Canada **168** B3
Armstrong, Mount Canada **166** C2
Armstrong Island Cook Is see **Rarotonga**
Armu *r.* Rus. Fed. **82** E3
Armur India **94** C2
Armutçuk Dağı *mts* Turkey **106** A3
Armutlu Turkey **58** J8
Armutova Turkey see **Gömeç**
Armyans'k Ukr. **41** E7
Armyanskaya S.S.R. *country* Asia see **Armenia**
Arnå *r.* Denmark **48** F1
Arna Greece **59** D12
Árnafjall *hill* Faroe Is **46** E1
Arnage France **50** G5
Arnaia Greece **58** E8
Arnaoutis, Cape Cyprus see **Arnauti, Cape**
Arnarfjörður *inlet* Iceland **44** [inset] A2
Arnaud *r.* Canada **169** G1
Arnauti, Cape Cyprus **108** D2
also known as Akama, Akra; also spelt Arnaoutis, Cape
Arnavutköy Turkey **58** J7
Arnay-le-Duc France **51** K5
Arnedo Spain **55** I2
Arneiroz Brazil **202** D3
Arnemark Sweden **44** M2
Årnes Norway **45** J3
Arnett U.S.A. **179** C4
Arnhem Neth. **48** C4
Arnhem, Cape Australia **148** C2
Arnhem Land *reg.* Australia **148** B2
Arnhem Land Aboriginal Land *res.* Australia **148** B2
Arnionys 1 Lith. **42** G6
Arnisdale U.K. **46** G6
Arnissa Greece **58** C8
Arno *r.* Italy **56** C5
Arno Bay Australia **146** C3
Arnoia *r.* Spain **54** C2
also spelt Arnoya
Arnold *MD* U.S.A. **177** I6
Arnold *MI* U.S.A. **172** F4
Arnold *MO* U.S.A. **174** B4
Arnold's Cove Canada **169** K4
Arnoldstein Austria **49** K9
Arnon *r.* France **51** I5
Arnon *r.* Jordan see **Mawjib, Wādī al**
Arnoux, Lac *l.* Canada **173** N2
Arnøya *i.* Norway **44** M1
Arnoya *r.* Spain see **Arnoia**
Arnprior Canada **168** E4
Arnsberg Germany **48** F4
Arnstadt Germany **48** H5
Arnstein Canada **173** N5
Arnstorf Germany **49** J7
Arntfield Canada **173** N2
Aro *r.* Venez. **199** E3
Aroab Namibia **130** C5
Aroania *mt.* Greece **59** D11
Aroeira Brazil **203** A7
Aroland Canada **168** C3
Arolsen Germany **48** G4
Aroma Sudan **104** B5
Aromas U.S.A. **182** C5
Aron *r.* France **51** J6
Aron India **96** C4
Arona Italy **56** A3
Arorae *i.* Kiribati **145** G2
also spelt Arore; formerly known as Hurd Island
Arore *i.* Kiribati see **Arorae**
Aroroy Phil. **74** B3
Aros *r.* Mex. **184** C2
Arosa, Ría de *est.* Spain see **Arousa, Ría de**
Arossi *i.* Solomon Is see **San Cristobal**
Arouca Port. **54** C4
Arouelli *well* Chad **120** D5
Arousa, Ría de *est.* Spain **54** B2
also spelt Arosa, Ría de
Arpa *r.* Armenia/Turkey **107** E2
Arpaçay Turkey **107** E2
Arpaçsakarlar Turkey **108** F1
Arpajon-sur-Cère France **51** I8
Arqalyq Kazakh. see **Arkalyk**
Arquata del Tronto Italy **56** F6
Arquipélago dos Açores *terr.* N. Atlantic Ocean see **Azores**
Arra *r.* Pak. **101** F5
Arrábida, Parque Natural da *nature res.* Port. **54** C6
Arrabury Australia **149** D5
Arrah Côte d'Ivoire **124** E5
Arrah India see **Ara**
Ar Rahá *hill* Saudi Arabia **109** K7
Ar Raḥḥālīyah Iraq **107** E4
Ar Rāhidah Yemen **104** D5
Arraias *r.* Brazil **202** A4
Arraias, Serra de *hills* Brazil **202** C5
Arraiolos Port. **54** D6
Ar Ramādī Iraq **107** E4
Ar Ramthā Jordan **108** H5
Arran *i.* U.K. **46** G8
Ar Raqqah Syria **109** K2
also spelt Raqqa; historically known as Nicephorium
Ar Raqqah *governorate* Syria **109** J1
Arras France **51** I2
historically known as Nemetocenna
Ar Ra's al Abyaḍ *pt* Saudi Arabia **104** B3
Arrasate Spain **55** I1
also known as Mondragón
Ar Rāshidīyah Iraq **109** P4
Ar-Rass Saudi Arabia **104** C2
Arrats *r.* France **50** G8
Ar Rawḍ *well* Saudi Arabia **107** E5
Ar Rawḍah Saudi Arabia **104** C3
Ar Rawḍah Yemen **105** D5
Ar Rāwuk Yemen **105** E4
Ar Rayḥānī Oman **105** F3
Ar Rayn Saudi Arabia **105** D3
Ar Rayyān Qatar **105** E2
Arrecifal Col. **198** D4
Arrecife Canary Is **122** B3
Arrecifes Arg. **204** E4
Arrée, Monts d' *hills* France **50** B4
Arretium Italy see **Arezzo**
Arriagá Mex. **185** G5
Arriaga Mex. **185** E4
Arribeños Arg. **204** E4
Ar Rifā'ī Iraq **107** F5
Ar Rihāb *salt flat* Iraq **107** F5
Ar Rimāl *des.* Saudi Arabia **105** F3
Arrington U.S.A. **176** G8
Ar Riyāḍ Saudi Arabia see **Riyadh**
Ar Riyāḍ *prov.* Saudi Arabia **104** D2
Arroio Grande Brazil **204** G4
Arronches Port. **54** D5
Arros *r.* France **50** F9
Arroux *r.* France **51** J6
Arrow *r.* Canada **172** D2
Arrow, Lough *l.* Rep. of Ireland **47** D9
Arrow Creek *r.* U.S.A. **180** E3
Arrow Lake Canada **172** C2
Arrowsmith, Mount N.Z. **153** E11
Arrowtown N.Z. **153** C12
Arroyo de la Luz Spain **54** E5
Arroyo Grande U.S.A. **182** D6
Arroyo Seco Mex. **185** F4
Ar Rubay'iyah Saudi Arabia **104** D2
Arruda Brazil **201** F3
Ar Rumādīyat Saudi Arabia **104** C2
Ar Rumaythā Bahrain **105** E2
Ar Rumaythah Iraq **107** F5
Ar Rummānah Iraq **109** M3
Ar Ruq'ī *well* Saudi Arabia **105** D1
Ar Ruşāfah Syria **109** J2
Ar Ruşayfah Jordan **108** H5
Ar Rustāq Oman **105** G3
Ar Ruṭbah Iraq **107** E4
Ar Ruwaybāt *well* Libya **120** C3
Ar Ruwaydah Saudi Arabia **104** D3
Arruwurra Aboriginal Land *res.* Australia **148** C4
Ārs Denmark **45** J4
Ars Iran **100** A2
Arsaköy Turkey **59** K12
Arsarybaba Erezi *hills* Turkm. see **Irsarybaba, Gory**
Arsenajān Iran **100** C4
Arseno Lake Canada **167** H1
Arsen'yev Rus. Fed. **82** D3
Arsen'yevo Rus. Fed. **43** R8
Arshanskaye Wzvyshsha *hills* Belarus **43** K7
Arsikere India **94** C3
Arsk Rus. Fed. **40** I4
Arslanköy Turkey **108** F1
Arta Greece **59** B9
Artashat Armenia **107** F3
formerly known as Kamarlu
Arteaga *Coahuila* Mex. **185** E3
Arteaga *Michoacán* Mex. **185** E5
Artem Rus. Fed. **82** D4
Artemisa Cuba **186** C2
Artemivs'k Ukr. **41** F6
also spelt Artemovsk; formerly known as Bakhmut
Artemovsk Ukr. see **Artemivs'k**
Artemovskiy Rus. Fed. **39** L4
Artemovskiy Rus. Fed. **82** D4
Artenay France **51** H4
Artesa de Segre Spain **55** M3
Artesia *AZ* U.S.A. **183** O9
Artesia *NM* U.S.A. **181** F6
Arthur Canada **173** M7
Arthur *NE* U.S.A. **178** B3
Arthur *TN* U.S.A. **176** B9
Arthur, Lake S. Africa **133** J9
Arthur, Lake U.S.A. **176** E5
Arthur Lake Australia **147** E5
Arthur Pieman Protected Area *nature res.* Australia **147** E5
Arthur's Pass N.Z. **153** F10
Arthur's Pass National Park N.Z. **153** F10
Arthur's Town Bahamas **186** E1
Artigas *research station* Antarctica **222** U2
Artigas Uruguay **204** F3
Art'ik Armenia **107** E2
Artillery Lake Canada **167** I2
Artisia Botswana **131** E5
Artjärvi Fin. **42** H1
Artos Dağı *mt.* Turkey **107** E3
Artova Turkey **107** D2
Artrutx, Cap d' *c.* Spain **55** O5
Artsakh *aut. reg.* Azer. see **Dağlıq Qarabağ**
Arts Bogd Uul *mts* Mongolia **84** D2
Artsiz Ukr. see **Artsyz**
Artsyz Ukr. **41** D7
also spelt Artsiz
Artur de Paiva Angola see **Kuvango**
Artux China **88** B4
Artvin Turkey **107** E2
also known as Çoruh
Artyk Turkm. **102** D5
Aru Dem. Rep. Congo **126** F4
Aru, Kepulauan *is* Indon. **73** H8
Arua Uganda **128** A4
Aruajá Brazil **199** E6
Aruanã Brazil **206** B1

▶**Aruba** *terr.* West Indies **198** D1
Self-governing Netherlands Territory.
oceania [countries] ➡ 138–139

Arudy France **50** F9
Arumã Brazil **199** F6
Arun *r.* China **85** J2
Arun *r.* Nepal **97** E4
Arunachal Pradesh *state* India **97** G4
formerly known as North-East Frontier Agency
Arun Qi China see **Naji**
Aruppukkottai India **94** C4
Arus, Tanjung *pt* Indon. **75** B2
Arusha Tanz. **128** C5
Arusha *admin. reg.* Tanz. **129** C5
Arusha National Park Tanz. **128** C5
Arut *r.* Indon. **77** E3
Arutí Brazil **199** E5
Aruwimi *r.* Dem. Rep. Congo **126** D4
Arvada U.S.A. **180** F5
Arvayheer Mongolia **84** D2
Arvi India **94** C1
Arviat Canada **167** M2
formerly known as Eskimo Point
Arvidsjaur Sweden **44** L2
Arvika Sweden **45** K4
Årviksand Norway **44** M1
Arvin U.S.A. **182** F6
Arvonia U.S.A. **176** G8
Arwā' Saudi Arabia **104** D3
Arwād *i.* Syria **108** G3
Arwala Indon. **75** C4
Arxan China **85** H2
Aryanah Tunisia see **L'Ariana**
Arykbalyk Kazakh. **103** G1
also spelt Aryqbayq
Aryqbayq Kazakh. see **Arykbalyk**
Arys' Kazakh. **103** G4
Arys' *r.* Kazakh. **103** G4
Arys, Ozero *salt l.* Kazakh. **103** F3
Aryskannyg-Aryg Rus. Fed. **88** E1
Arzamas Rus. Fed. **40** G5
Arzanah *i.* U.A.E. **105** F2
Arzew Alg. **123** E2
Arzew, Golfe d' *g.* Alg. **55** K9
Arzgir Rus. Fed. **41** H7
Arzila Morocco see **Asilah**
Arzúa Spain **54** C2
Arzubikha Rus. Fed. **43** V1
Aš Czech Rep. **49** J5
Asa *waterhole* Kenya **128** C5
Åsa Sweden **45** K4
Asab Namibia **132** B2
Asaba Nigeria **125** G5
Asad, Buḥayrat al *resr* Syria **109** J1
Asadābād Afgh. **101** G3
Asadābād *Hamadān* Iran **100** B3
Asadābād *Khorāsan* Iran **101** D3
Asagny, Parc National d' *nat. park* Côte d'Ivoire **124** D5
Asahan *r.* Indon. **76** B2
Asahi *Chiba* Japan **91** G7
Asahi *Toyama* Japan **91** E6
Asahi-dake *mt.* Japan **90** F5
Asahi-dake *vol.* Japan **90** H3
Asahi-gawa *r.* Japan **91** C7
Asahikawa Japan **90** H3
Asaka Uzbek. **103** H4
also spelt Assake; formerly known as Leninsk
Āsalē *l.* Eth. **128** D1
Asālem Iran **100** B2
Asama-yama *vol.* Japan **91** F6
Asankranguaa Ghana **124** E5
Asan-man *b.* S. Korea **83** B5
Asansol India **97** E5
Asanwenso Ghana **124** E5
Āsayita Eth. **128** D2
Asbestos Hill Canada see **Purtuniq**
Asbestos Mountains S. Africa **132** G6
Āsbe Teferī Eth. **128** D2
Asbury Park U.S.A. **177** K5
Ascalon Israel see **Ashqelon**
Ascea Italy **57** H8
Ascensión Bol. **201** E3
Ascensión *Chihuahua* Mex. **184** D2
Ascensión *Nuevo León* Mex. **185** F3
Ascension *atoll* Micronesia see **Pohnpei**

▶**Ascension** *i.* S. Atlantic Ocean **216** N6
Dependency of St Helena.

Aschaffenburg Germany **48** G6
Ascheberg Germany **48** E4
Aschersleben Germany **48** I4
Asciano Italy **56** D5
Ascoli Piceno Italy **56** F6
historically known as Asculum or Asculum Picenum
Ascoli Satriano Italy **56** H7
historically known as Ausculum or Ausculum Apulum
Ascotán Chile **200** C5
Ascotán, Salar de *salt flat* Chile **200** C5
Asculum Italy see **Ascoli Piceno**
Asculum Picenum Italy see **Ascoli Piceno**
Ascutney U.S.A. **177** M2
Åse Norway **44** K1
Āseb Eritrea see **Assab**
Asedjrad *plat.* Alg. **123** F4
Āsela Eth. **128** C3
Åsele Sweden **44** L2
Āsendabo Eth. **128** C3
Asenovgrad Bulg. **58** F6
Åseral Norway **45** I4
Aseri Estonia **42** H2
Aşfak Iran **100** D3
Aşfar, Jabal al *mt.* Jordan **109** H5
Aşfar, Tall al *hill* Saudi Arabia **109** M7
Aşfar, Tall al *hill* Syria **109** H4
Ásgarður Iceland **44** [inset] B2
Asha Rus. Fed. **40** K5
Ashanti *admin. reg.* Ghana **125** E5
Asharat Saudi Arabia **105** D2
Ashbourne U.K. **47** K10
Ashburn U.S.A. **175** D6
Ashburton *watercourse* Australia **150** A4
Ashburton N.Z. **153** F11
Ashburton *r.* N.Z. **153** F12
also known as Hakatere
Ashburton Bay Canada **172** G2
Ashburton Range *hills* Australia **148** B3
Ashchikol', Ozero *salt l.* Kazakh. **103** F3
Ashchikol', Ozero *salt l.* Kazakh. **103** G4
Ashchysay Kazakh. see **Achisay**
Ashcroft Canada **166** F5
Ashdod Israel **108** F6
historically known as Azotus
Ashdown U.S.A. **179** D5
Asheboro U.S.A. **174** E5
Ashern Canada **167** L5
Asheville U.S.A. **174** D5
Ashevo Rus. Fed. **43** K4
Asheweig *r.* Canada **168** C2
Ashford Australia **147** F2
Ashford U.K. **47** M12
Ash Fork U.S.A. **183** L6

▶**Ashgabat** Turkm. **102** D5
Capital of Turkmenistan. Formerly spelt Ashkhabad; historically known as Poltoratsk.

Ashhurst N.Z. **152** J8
Ashibetsu Japan **90** H3
Ashikaga Japan **91** F6
Ashington U.K. **47** K8
Ashiro Japan **90** G4
Ashizuri-misaki *pt* Japan **91** C8
Ashizuri-Uwakai National Park Japan **83** D6
Ashkazar Iran **100** C4
Ashkelon Israel see **Ashqelon**
Ashkhabad Turkm. see **Ashgabat**
Ashkhabadskaya Oblast' *admin. div.* Turkm. see **Akhal'skaya Oblast'**
Ashkidah Libya **120** B3
Ashkum U.S.A. **172** F10
Ashkun *reg.* Afgh. **101** G3
Ashland *AL* U.S.A. **175** C5
Ashland *KS* U.S.A. **178** C4
Ashland *KY* U.S.A. **176** C7
Ashland *ME* U.S.A. **174** H2
Ashland *NE* U.S.A. **178** C3
Ashland *NH* U.S.A. **177** N2
Ashland *OH* U.S.A. **176** C5
Ashland *OR* U.S.A. **180** B4
Ashland *VA* U.S.A. **176** H8
Ashland *WI* U.S.A. **172** C4
Ashland City U.S.A. **174** C4
Ashley *r.* N.Z. **153** G11
also known as Rakahuri
Ashley *IN* U.S.A. **173** H9
Ashley *MI* U.S.A. **173** I7
Ashley *ND* U.S.A. **178** C2
Ashley *OH* U.S.A. **176** C5

▶**Ashmore and Cartier Islands** *terr.* Australia **144** B3
Australian External Territory.
oceania [countries] ➡ 138–139

Ashmore Reef Australia **150** C2
Ashmūn Egypt **108** B7
Ashmyanskaye Wzvyshsha *hills* Belarus **42** G7
Ashmyany Belarus **42** G7
also spelt Oshmyany
Ashmyany Belarus **42** H7
Ashoknagar India **96** C4
Ashoro Japan **90** H3
Ashqelon Israel **108** F6
also spelt Ashkelon; historically known as Ascalon
Ash Sha'ār Saudi Arabia **104** C4
Ash Shabakah Iraq **107** E5
Ash Shabrūm *waterhole* Saudi Arabia **109** O7
Ash Shaddādah Syria **109** L1
Ash Shāfi' Saudi Arabia **104** C3
Ash Shakk Iraq **109** O2
Ash Sham Syria see **Damascus**
Ash Sha'm U.A.E. **105** G2
Ash Shanāfīyah Iraq **107** F5
also spelt Shināfiyah
Ash Shaqīq *well* Saudi Arabia **107** E5
Ash Sha'rā' Saudi Arabia **104** D2
Ash Sharawrah Saudi Arabia **105** D4
Ash Shāriqah U.A.E. see **Sharjah**
Ash Sharqāṭ Iraq **107** E4
also spelt Sharqāt; historically known as Ashur
Ash Sharqīyah *admin. reg.* Oman **105** G3
Ash Sharqīyah *reg.* Oman **105** G3

Ash Sharqiyah *prov.* Saudi Arabia 105 E3
Ash Shatrah Iraq 107 F5
Ash Shawbak Jordan 108 G7
also spelt Shaubak
Ash Shawr *hill* Libya 109 L4
Ash Shaykh 'Uthman Yemen 104 D5
English form Sheikh Othman
Ash Shihr Yemen 105 E5
Ash Shinas Oman 105 G2
Ash Shiqar *well* Oman 105 F4
Ash Shu'aybah Saudi Arabia 104 C2
Ash Shu'bah Saudi Arabia 104 D1
Ash Shubaykiyah Saudi Arabia 104 C2
Ash Shumlul Saudi Arabia 105 D2
Ash Shuqayq Saudi Arabia 104 C3
Ash Shurayf Saudi Arabia *see* Khaybar
Ash Shuwayrif Libya 120 L7
Ashta *Madhya Pradesh* India 96 C5
Ashta *Maharashtra* India 94 B2
Ashtabula U.S.A. 176 C4
Ashtarak Armenia 107 F2
Ashti *Maharashtra* India 94 B2
Ashti *Maharashtra* India 94 C2
Ashti *Maharashtra* India 96 C5
Ashton S. Africa 132 E10
Ashton U.S.A. 180 E3
Ashton IL U.S.A. 172 C9
Ashuanipi r. Canada 169 H2
Ashuanipi Lake Canada 169 H2
formerly known as Chamouchouane
Ashuapmushuan r. Canada 174 F1
formerly known as Chamouchouane
Ashuapmushuan, Réserve Faunique
nature res. Canada 169 F3
Ashur Iraq *see* Ash Sharqat
Ashusui *pass* Kyrg. 103 H4
also known as Chiyirchik, Pereval
Ashville U.S.A. 175 C5
Ashville ME U.S.A. 177 Q1
Ashville PA U.S.A. 176 G5
Ashwabay, Mount U.S.A. 172 C4
Ashwaubenon U.S.A. 172 E6
'Asi r. Lebanon/Syria *see* Orontes
'Asi, Nahr al r. Asia *see* Orontes
Asid Gulf Phil. 74 B3
Asientos Mex. 185 E4
Asifabad India 94 C2
Asika India 95 C5
Asikkala Fin. 45 N3
Asilah Morocco 54 E9
formerly spelt Arzila
Asillo Peru 200 C3
Asimi Greece 59 G13
Asinara, Golfo dell' *b.* Sardegna Italy 56 A8
Asinara, Isola *i.* Sardegna Italy 56 A7
Asind India 96 B4
Asino Rus. Fed. 39 I4
Asintorf Belarus 43 L7
Asipovichy Belarus 43 J8
also spelt Osipovichi
'Asir *prov.* Saudi Arabia 104 C3
'Asir *reg.* Saudi Arabia 104 C3
Asisium Italy *see* Assisi
Askainen Fin. 42 C1
Askale Turkey 107 E3
Askarovo Rus. Fed. 102 D1
Asker Norway 45 J4
Askersund Sweden 45 K4
Askim Norway 45 J4
Askino Rus. Fed. 40 K4
Askio *mt.* Greece 59 C8
Akira Nigeria 125 I4
Askival *hill* Scotland U.K. 46 F7
Askiz Rus. Fed. 80 E2
Askola Fin. 45 N3
Askol'd, Ostrov *i.* Rus. Fed. 90 C3
Askot India 96 C3
Askvoll Norway 45 I3
Aslam, Wadi *watercourse* Saudi Arabia 104 D3
Aslanduz Iran 100 A2
Aslankoy r. Turkey 108 F1
Aslik r. Belarus 43 K8
Aslókozpont Hungary *see* Mórahalom
Asmar Afgh. 101 G3
Asmar *reg.* Saudi Arabia 104 C4
► Asmara Eritrea 121 H6
Capital of Eritrea. Also spelt Asmera.

Äsmera Eritrea *see* Asmara
Åsnen *l.* Sweden 45 K4
As Neves Spain 54 C2
also spelt Niéves
Asoenangka Brazil 199 G4
Aso-Kuju National Park Japan 91 B8
Asola Italy 56 C3
Asopos r. Greece 59 D11
Asopos r. Greece 59 E10
Asosa Eth. 128 B2
Asoteriba, Jebel *mt.* Sudan 121 H4
Asotin U.S.A. 180 C3
Aspang-Markt Austria 49 N8
Aspara Kazakh. 103 H4
Asparukhovo Bulg. 58 I6
Aspås Sweden 44 K3
Aspe Spain 55 K6
Åspea Sweden 44 L3
Aspen U.S.A. 180 F5
Aspermont U.S.A. 179 B5

Aspiring, Mount N.Z. 153 C12
also known as Tititea
As Pontes de García Rodríguez Spain 54 D1
also spelt Puentes de García Rodríguez
Aspro, Cape Cyprus 108 D3
also known as Aspron, Cape
Asprokavos, Akra *pt* Greece 59 B9
Aspromonte, Parco Nazionale dell'
nat. park Italy 57 H10
Aspron, Cape Cyprus *see* Aspro, Cape
Asprovalta Greece 58 E8
Aspur India 96 B5
Asquith Canada 167 J4
Assa Morocco 122 C2
Assa r. Uganda 128 A4
Assab Eritrea 121 I6
also spelt Aseb
Assaba *admin. reg.* Mauritania 124 C2
Sab'an Saudi Arabia 104 C2
As Sabkhah Syria 109 K2
As Sabsab *well* Saudi Arabia 105 E2
Assabu Japan 90 G4
As Safa *lava field* Syria 109 H4
As Safaqis Tunisia *see* Sfax
As Safi Jordan 108 G6
As Safirah Syria 109 I1
As Sahaf Saudi Arabia 105 E2
As Sahif Yemen 104 C5
As Sahn *hills* Iraq/Saudi Arabia 109 N7
Assake Uzbek. *see* Asaka
Assake-Audan, Vpadina *depr.* Uzbek.
102 D4
'Assal, Lac *l.* Djibouti *see* Assal, Lake

► Assal, Lake Djibouti 128 D2
Lowest point in Africa. Also known as
'Assal, Lac.
africa [landscapes] ▶▶ 112–113

As Salamiyah Saudi Arabia 105 D2
As Salihiyah Syria 109 L3
also known as Dura Europos
As Salman Iraq 107 F5
As Salt Jordan 108 G5
also spelt Salt
Assam *state* India 97 F4
Assamakka Niger 125 G2
As Samawah Iraq 107 F5
As Sanam Saudi Arabia 105 E3
Assaq *watercourse* W. Sahara 122 B4
As Sarir *reg.* Libya 120 D3
Assateague Island National Seashore
nature res. U.S.A. 177 J8
As Sawadah Saudi Arabia 105 D3
As Sawda *i.* Oman 105 F4
As Sawrah Saudi Arabia 104 A2
As Saybiyah *waterhole* Saudi Arabia 109 M9
Assegaaibos S. Africa 133 I10
Assemini *Sardegna* Italy 57 B9
Assen Neth. 48 D2
Assens Denmark 45 J5
Assesse Belgium 51 L2
As Sidrah Libya 120 B2
As Sikak Saudi Arabia 105 E3
Assiniboia Canada 167 J5
Assiniboine r. Canada 167 L5
Assiniboine, Mount Canada 167 H5
Assinica, Lac *l.* Canada 168 F3
Assis Brazil 206 C9
Assisi Italy 56 E5
historically known as Asisium
Assomada Cape Verde 124 [inset]
Assouf Mellene *watercourse* Alg. 123 F4
As Subayhiyah Kuwait 107 F5
As Subaykhah Saudi Arabia 104 D1
As Sufal Yemen 105 E5
As Sufayri *well* Saudi Arabia 105 D1
As Sukhnah Syria 109 J3
As Sulaymaniyah Iraq 107 F4
As Sulaymaniyah *governorate* Iraq 107 F4
As Sulaymi Saudi Arabia 104 C2
As Sulayyil Saudi Arabia 105 D3
As Sulb *reg.* Saudi Arabia 105 E2
As Sultan Libya 120 C2
As Summan *plat.* Saudi Arabia 105 D2
As Summan *plat.* Saudi Arabia 105 E2
As Suq Saudi Arabia 104 C3
As Suriyah *country* Asia *see* Syria
As Suwar Syria 109 L2
As Suwayda' Syria 109 H5
As Suwayda' *governorate* Syria 109 H5
As Suwayh Oman 105 G3
As Suwayq Oman 105 G3
As Suwayrah Iraq 107 F4
As Suwayriqiyah Saudi Arabia 104 C3
As Suways Egypt *see* Suez
As Suwaydiyah Yemen 105 D5
Asta r. Norway 45 J3
Asta, Cima *d'* *mt.* Italy 56 D2
Astacus Turkey *see* Kocaeli
Astaffort France 50 G8
Astakida *i.* Greece 59 H13
Astakos Greece 59 C10
Astalu Island Pak. *see* Astola Island

► Astana Kazakh. 103 G2
Capital of Kazakhstan. Formerly known as
Akmola or Aqmola or Akmolinsk or
Tselinograd.

Astaneh Iran 100 B2
Astara Azer. 107 G3
Åsteby Sweden 45 K3
Asterabad Iran *see* Gorgan
Asti Italy 56 A4
Astica Arg. 204 D3
Astillero Peru 200 C3
Astin Tag *mts* China *see* Altun Shan
Astipalaia i. Greece *see* Astypalaia
Astola Island Pak. 101 E5
also spelt Astalu Island
Aston Bay S. Africa 133 I11
Astor Jammu and Kashmir 96 B2
Astor r. Pak. 101 H3
Astorga Brazil 206 B9
Astorga Spain 54 E2
historically known as Asturica Augusta
Astoria U.S.A. 180 B3
Astra Arg. 205 D7
Astrabad Iran *see* Gorgan
Astrakhan' Kazakh. *see* Astrakhanka
Astrakhan' Rus. Fed. 102 B3
Astrakhan' Bazar Azer. *see* Calilabad
Astrakhanka Kazakh. 103 G2
also known as Astrakhan'
Astrakhan Oblast *admin. div.* Rus. Fed.
see Astrakhanskaya Oblast'
Astrakhanskaya Oblast' *admin. div.*
Rus. Fed. 102 A3
English form Astrakhan Oblast
Astravyets Belarus 42 H7
Astrida Rwanda *see* Butare
Astrolabe, Récifs de l' *reef* New Caledonia
145 F3
Astros Greece 59 D11
Astryna Belarus 42 F8
Astsyer r. Belarus 43 M8
Asturias *aut. comm.* Spain 54 E1
Asturica Augusta Spain *see* Astorga
Astypalaia *i.* Greece 59 H12
also known as Astipálaia; *formerly known as*
Stampalia
Asubulak Kazakh. 88 C1
also spelt Asubulaq
Asubulaq Kazakh. *see* Asubulak
Asunción Bol. 200 D2
Asunción *r.* Mex. 181 D7
Asuncion *i.* N. Mariana Is 73 K3

Asunción Para. 201 F6
Capital of Paraguay.

Asunción Mita Guat. 185 H6
Asvyeya Belarus 42 J5
Asvyeyskaye, Vozyera *l.* Belarus 42 J5
Aswa r. Uganda 128 A4
Aswad Oman 105 G2
Aswad, Ar Ra's al *pt* Saudi Arabia 104 B3
Aswad, Wadi *watercourse* Oman 105 F3
Aswan Egypt 121 G3
Aswan *governorate* Egypt 104 A2
Aswan Dam Egypt 121 G3
Asyut Egypt 121 F3
historically known as Lycopolis
Asyut *governorate* Egypt 106 B6
Ata *i.* Tonga 145 H4
formerly known as Sola
Atabapo r. Col./Venez. 199 E3
Atabay Kazakh. 103 G4
Atacama *admin. reg.* Chile 200 C3
Atacama, Desierto de *des.* Chile *see*
Atacama Desert
Atacama, Salar de *salt flat* Chile 200 C5

► Atacama Desert Chile 204 C2
Driest place in the world. Also known as
Atacama, Desierto de.
world [climate and weather] ▶▶ 16–17
southamerica [contrasts] ▶▶ 194–195

Atacames Ecuador 198 B4
Ataco Col. 198 C4
Atafaitafa, Djebel *mt.* Alg. 123 G4
Atafu *atoll* Tokelau 145 H2
formerly known as Duke of York
Atairtir el Dahami, Gebel *mt.* Egypt 108 E9
Atakent Turkey 108 F1
Atakor *mts* Alg. 123 G5
Atakpamé Togo 125 F5
Atalaia Brazil 202 F4
Atalaia *hill* Port. 54 C6
Atalaia do Norte Brazil 198 D6
Atalaya Panama 186 C5
Atalaya *Madre de Dios* Peru 200 C3
Atalaya *Ucayali* Peru 200 B3
Ataléia Brazil 203 D6
Atamanovka Rus. Fed. 85 G1
Atami Japan 91 F7
Atamisqui Arg. 204 E3
Atammik Greenland 165 N3
Ataniya Turkey *see* Adana
Atapupu Indon. 75 C5
'Ataq Yemen 105 D5
'Ataqa, Gebel *hill* Egypt 108 D8
Atar Mauritania 122 B5
Ataran r. Myanmar 78 B4
Atascadero U.S.A. 182 D6
Atascosa *watercourse* U.S.A. 179 C6
Atasu Kazakh. 103 G2
Atatan He r. China 88 A4
Atatürk Milli Parkı *nat. park* Turkey 59 J12
Atauro *i.* East Timor 75 C5
formerly known as Kambing, Pulau
Atáviros *mt.* Greece *see* Attavyros
Atbara r. Sudan 121 G5
Atbara r. Sudan 121 G5
Atbasar Kazakh. 103 F1
At-Bashy Kyrg. 103 H4
Atchafalaya Bay U.S.A. 175 B6
Atchison U.S.A. 178 D4
Atebubu Ghana 125 E5
Ateca Spain 55 J3
Aten Bol. 200 C3
Atenguillo Mex. 184 D4
Aterno r. Italy 56 F6
Ateshan Iran 100 C3
Ateshkhaneh, Kuh-e *hill* Afgh. 101 E3
Atessa Italy 56 G6
Atfih Egypt 108 C8
Ath Belgium 51 J2
also spelt Aath
Athabasca Canada 167 H4
Athabasca r. Canada 167 I3
Athabasca, Lake Canada 167 I3
Athagarh India 95 E1
Athalia U.S.A. 176 C7
Athapapuskow Lake Canada 167 K4
Athboy Rep. of Ireland 47 F10
Athenae Greece *see* Athens
Athenry Rep. of Ireland 47 D10
Athens Canada 173 R6

► Athens Greece 59 E11
Capital of Greece. Also known as Athínai;
also spelt Athina; historically known as
Athenae.

Athens AL U.S.A. 174 C5
Athens GA U.S.A. 175 D5
Athens NY U.S.A. 177 L3
Athens OH U.S.A. 176 C6
Athens TN U.S.A. 174 C5
Athens TX U.S.A. 179 D5
Atherton Australia 149 E3
Athi r. Kenya 128 C5
Athina Greece *see* Athens
Athínai Greece *see* Athens
Athi River Kenya 128 C5
Athlone Rep. of Ireland 47 E10
also known as Baile Átha Luain
Athna', Wadi al *watercourse* Jordan 109 J5
Athni India 94 B2
Athol N.Z. 153 C13
Athol U.S.A. 177 L3
Athos *mt.* Greece 59 F8
Ath Tharthar, Wadi r. Iraq 107 E4
Ath Thayat *hills* Saudi Arabia 109 H8
Ath Thayat *mt.* Saudi Arabia 109 H8
Ath Thumami *well* Saudi Arabia 105 D2
Athy Rep. of Ireland 47 F11
Ati Chad 120 C6
Ati, Jabal *mts* Libya 120 B3
Atiak Uganda 128 B4
Atiamuri N.Z. 152 K6
Ati Ardébé Chad 120 C6
Atibaia Brazil 206 G10
Atico Peru 200 B4
Atico r. Peru 200 B4
Atienza Spain 55 H3
Atiko Sudan 126 E3
Atikameg Canada 167 H4
Atikameg r. Canada 168 D2
Atik Lake Canada 167 M4
Atikokan Canada 168 B3
Atikonak Lake Canada 169 H2
Atimonan Phil. 74 B3
Atina Italy 56 F7
Atirampattinam India 94 C4
Atitlán Guat. 185 H6
Atitlán, Parque Nacional *nat. park* Guat.
185 H6
Atjeh *admin. dist.* Indon. *see* Aceh
'Atk, Wadi al *watercourse* Saudi Arabia
105 D2
Atka Rus. Fed. 39 P4
Atkarsk Rus. Fed. 41 H6
Atkri Indon. 75 D3
Atlacomulco Mex. 185 F5
Atlanta S. Africa 133 L2

► Atlanta GA U.S.A. 175 C5
State capital of Georgia.

Atlanta TX U.S.A. 179 D5
Atlanta Turkey 106 C2
Atlantic IA U.S.A. 178 D3
Atlantic NC U.S.A. 177 O1
Atlantic City U.S.A. 177 K6
Atlántico *dept* Col. 198 C2

► Atlantic Ocean 216 K3
2nd largest ocean in the world.
oceans [features] ▶▶ 210–211

Atlantic Peak U.S.A. 180 E4
Atlantis S. Africa 132 C10
Atlas Bogd *mt.* Mongolia 84 C3
Atlas Méditerranéen *mts* Alg. *see*
Atlas Tellien

► Atlas Mountains Africa 122 D3
africa [landscapes] ▶▶ 112–113

Atlasova, Ostrov *i.* Rus. Fed. 39 P4
formerly known as Alaid, Ostrov
Atlas Saharien Alg. 123 F2
English form Saharan Atlas
Atlas Tellien Alg. 123 F2
also known as Atlas Méditerranéen or Tell
Atlas
Atlin Canada 166 C3
Atlin Lake Canada 166 C3
Atlin Provincial Park Canada 166 C3
'Atlit Israel 108 F5
Atlixco Mex. 185 F5
Atmakur *Andhra Pradesh* India 94 C3
Atmakur *Andhra Pradesh* India 94 C3
Atmore U.S.A. 175 C6
Atna Norway 45 J3
Atner India 96 C5
Ato Japan 91 B7
Atocha Bol. 200 D5
Atoka U.S.A. 179 C5
Atome Angola 127 B7
Atotonilco el Alto Mex. 185 E4
Atoua *mt.* Laos 78 D4
Atoyac de Álvarez Mex. 185 E5
Atpadi India 94 B2
Atqan China *see* Aqqan
Atqasuk U.S.A. 164 D2
Atrai r. India 97 F4
Atrak, Rud-e r. Iran/Turkm. *see* Atrek
Ätran r. Sweden 45 K4
Atranh India 96 C4
Atrato r. Col. 198 B3
Atrek r. Iran/Turkm. 100 C2
also known as Atrak, Rud-e or Etrek
Atri Italy 56 F6
Atropatene *country* Asia *see* Azerbaijan
Atrush Iraq 109 O1
Atsiki Greece 59 G9
Atsion U.S.A. 177 K6
Atsugi Japan 91 F7
Atsumi *Aichi* Japan 91 F7
Atsumi *Yamagata* Japan 90 F5
Atsumi-hanto *pen.* Japan 91 E7
Atsuta Japan 90 G3
At Taff *reg.* U.A.E. 105 F4
At Tafilah Jordan 108 G7
also spelt Tafila
At Ta'if Saudi Arabia 104 C3
At Taji Iraq 109 P4
Attalea Turkey *see* Antalya
Attalia Turkey *see* Antalya
Attalla U.S.A. 175 C5
At Tallab *oasis* Libya 120 D3
Ta'mim *salt flat* Saudi Arabia 104 C4
At Tamimi Libya 120 D1
Attapu Laos 79 D5
also spelt Attopeu
Attar, Oued et *watercourse* Alg. 123 G2
At Tarfat *waterhole* Iraq 109 L4
At Tarmiyah Iraq 109 P4
Attavyros *mt.* Greece 59 I12
also spelt Atáviros
Attawapiskat Canada 168 D2
Attawapiskat r. Canada 168 D2
Attawapiskat Lake Canada 168 C2
At Tawil *mts* Saudi Arabia 107 D5
At Taysiyah *plat.* Saudi Arabia 105 C1
At Tayyibah Jordan 108 G7
Attendorn Germany 48 E4
Atterbury S. Africa 133 M2
Attersee *l.* Austria 49 K8
At Tibni Syria 109 K2
Attica IN U.S.A. 174 C3
Attica NY U.S.A. 176 G3
Attica OH U.S.A. 176 C4
Attikamagen Lake Canada 169 H2
Attiki *admin. reg.* Greece 59 E11
At Tin, Ra's *pt* Libya 120 D1
Attingal India 94 C4
Attleboro U.S.A. 177 N4
Attock City Pak. 101 H3
Attopeu Laos *see* Attapu
Attu Greenland 165 N3
At Tubayq *reg.* Saudi Arabia 107 D5

► Attu Island U.S.A. 220 H1
Most westerly point of North America.

At Tulayhi *well* Saudi Arabia 104 D2
Attunga Australia 147 F2
At Tunisiyah *country* Africa *see* Tunisia
Attur *Tamil Nadu* India 94 C4
Attur *Tamil Nadu* India 94 C4
At Turbah Yemen 104 D5
At Turbah Yemen 104 D5
At Tuwayyah *well* Saudi Arabia 104 C4
Atud Yemen 105 E5
Atuel r. Arg. 204 D5
Atvidaberg Sweden 45 K4
Atwari Bangl. 97 F4
Atwater U.S.A. 182 D4
Atwood U.S.A. 178 B4
Atyrau Kazakh. 102 B3
formerly known as Atersank or Gur'yev
Atyrau Oblast *admin. div.* Kazakh. *see*
Atyrauskaya Oblast'
Atyrau Oblysy *admin. div.* Kazakh. *see*
Atyrauskaya Oblast'
Atyrauskaya Oblast' *admin. div.* Kazakh.
102 B3
English form Atyrau Oblast; *also known as*
Atyrau Ob ysy; *formerly known as*
Gur'yevskaya Oblast'
Auati-Paraná r. Brazil 199 E5
Aubagne France 51 L9
Aube r. France 51 K4
Aubenas France 51 K8
Aubigny-sur-Nère France 51 I5
Aubin France 51 I8
Aubinadong r. Canada 168 D4
Aubonne France 51 M6
Auboué France 51 L5
Aubrey Cliffs *mts* U.S.A. 183 L6
Aubry Lake Canada 164 G3
Auburn AL U.S.A. 175 C5
Auburn CA U.S.A. 182 C3
Auburn IL U.S.A. 174 B4
Auburn IN U.S.A. 174 C3
Auburn ME U.S.A. 177 O1
Auburn NE U.S.A. 178 D3
Auburn NY U.S.A. 177 I3
Auburn WA U.S.A. 180 B3
Auburn Range *hills* Australia 149 F5
Aubusson France 51 I7
Auca Mahuida, Sierra de *mt.* Arg. 204 C5
Auch France 50 G9
historically known as Augusta Auscorum or
Elimberrum
Auche Myanmar 78 B2
Auchi Nigeria 125 G5

► Auckland N.Z. 152 I4
5th most populous city in Oceania.
world [cities] ▶▶ 24–25

Auckland *admin. reg.* N.Z. 152 I4
Auckland Islands N.Z. 220 F9
Aude r. France 51 J9
Auden Canada 168 C3
Audenarde Belgium *see* Oudenaarde
Audierne, Baie d' *b.* France 50 B5
Audincourt France 51 M5
Audo Range *mts* Eth. 128 D3
Audru Estonia 42 F3
Audruicq France 51 I2
Audubon U.S.A. 178 D3
Aue r. Germany 48 G3
Aue Germany 51 S2
Auerbach in der Oberpfalz Germany 48
H6
Auersberg *mt.* Germany 51 S2
Augathella Australia 149 E5
Augrabies S. Africa 132 E5
Augrabies Falls S. Africa 132 E5
Augrabies Falls National Park S. Africa
132 E5
Au Gres U.S.A. 173 J6
Augsburg Germany 48 H7
historically known as Augusta Vindelicorum
Augsburg-Westliche Wälder *park* Germany
48 H7
Augšligatne Latvia 42 G4
Augšzemes Augstiene *hills* Latvia 42 H5
Augusta Australia 151 A7
Augusta Sicilia Italy 57 H11
Augusta AR U.S.A. 174 B5
Augusta GA U.S.A. 175 D5
Augusta KS U.S.A. 178 C4
Augusta KY U.S.A. 176 A7

► Augusta ME U.S.A. 177 P1
State capital of Maine.

Augusta WI U.S.A. 172 B6
Augusta WV U.S.A. 176 G6
Augusta, Golfo di *b.* Sicilia Italy 57 H11
Augusta Auscorum France *see* Auch
Augusta Cardosa Moz. *see* Metangula
Augusta Taurinorum Italy *see* Turin
Augusta Trevirorum Germany *see* Trier
Augusta Victoria Chile 200 C6
Augusta Vindelicorum Germany *see*
Augsburg
Augustin Cadazzi Col. 198 C2
Augustine Island U.S.A. 164 D4
Augusto Cardosa Moz. *see* Metangula
Augusto de Lima Brazil 207 I5
Augustodunum France *see* Autun
Augusto Severo Brazil 202 E3
Augustów Poland 49 T2
Augustowski, Kanał *canal* Poland 49 U2
Augustus, Mount Australia 151 B5
Augustus Island Australia 150 D2
Aukan Island Eritrea 104 C5
Aukstaitijos nacionalinis parkas *nat. park*
Lith. 42 H6
Aukstelke Lith. 42 E6
Aukstelke Lith. 42 E6
Auktsjaur Sweden 44 L2
Aulavik National Park Canada 165 H2
Auld, Lake *salt flat* Australia 150 C4
Auliye Ata Kazakh. *see* Taraz
Aulla Italy 56 B3
Aulneau Peninsula Canada 167 M5
Aulnoye-Aymeries France 51 J2
Aulon Albania *see* Vlorë
Ault France 50 H2
Aumale France 51 I3
Aumance r. France 51 I6
Aumund Germany 48 G2
Auna Nigeria 125 G3
Aungban Myanmar 78 B3
Auning Denmark 45 J4
Auob *watercourse* Namibia/S. Africa 132 E3
Aupaluk Canada 169 G1
formerly known as Hopes Advance Bay
Aur r. Malaysia 76 D2
Aura Fin. 45 M3
Aura r. Fin. 45 M3
Auraiya India 96 C4
Aurajoki r. Fin. 42 D1
Aurangabad *Bihar* India 97 E4
Aurangabad *Maharashtra* India 94 B2
Auray France 50 D5
Aure Norway 44 J3
Aure r. Norway 44 J3
Aurich Germany 48 E2
Auriflama Brazil 206 C7
Aurigny i. Channel Is *see* Alderney
Aurilândia Brazil 206 C3
Aurillac France 51 I8
Aurino r. Italy 56 D2
Auronzo di Cadore Italy 56 E2
Aurora S. Africa 132 C9
Aurora Phil. 74 B5
Aurora CO U.S.A. 180 F5
Aurora IL U.S.A. 174 B3
Aurora IN U.S.A. 176 A6
Aurora MN U.S.A. 174 A2
Aurora MO U.S.A. 178 D4
Aurora NE U.S.A. 178 C3
Aurora OH U.S.A. 176 D4
Aurora UT U.S.A. 183 M3
Aurora Island Vanuatu *see* Maéwo
Aurukun Australia 149 D2
Aurukun Aboriginal Reserve Australia
149 D2
Aus Namibia 130 C5
Ausa India 94 C2
Au Sable U.S.A. 173 J6
Au Sable r. U.S.A. 173 J6
Ausable r. U.S.A. 177 L1
Ausable Forks U.S.A. 177 L1
Au Sable Point MI U.S.A. 172 D3
Au Sable Point MI U.S.A. 173 J6
Auschwitz Poland *see* Oświęcim
Ausculum Italy *see* Ascoli Satriano
Ausculum Apulum Italy *see* Ascoli Satriano
Austafjord Norway 44 K1
Aust-Agder *county* Norway 45 J4
Austari-Jokulsa r. Iceland 44 [inset] C2
Austertana Norway 44 O1
Austin IN U.S.A. 174 A3
Austin NV U.S.A. 183 G2

► Austin TX U.S.A. 179 C6
State capital of Texas.

Austin, Lake *salt flat* Australia 151 B6
Austral Downs Australia 148 C4
Australes, Îles *is* Fr. Polynesia *see*
Tubuai Islands

► Australia *country* Oceania 144 A4
Largest country in Oceania and 6th in the
world. Most populous country in Oceania.
Historically known as New Holland.
world [countries] ▶▶ 10–11
oceania [countries] ▶▶ 138–139

Australian-Antarctic Basin *sea feature*
Indian Ocean 219 N9
Australian Antarctic Territory Antarctica
223 J2
Australian Capital Territory *admin. div.*
Australia 147 F3
Australind Australia 151 A7

► Austria *country* Europe 49 J8
known as Österreich in German
europe [countries] ▶▶ 32–35

Austrumkursas Augstiene *hills* Latvia 42 D5

Austurland *constituency* Iceland
44 [inset] D2
Austvagøy i. Norway 44 K1
Autazes Brazil 199 G5
Auterive France 50 H9
Autesiodorum France *see* Auxerre
Authie r. France 51 H2
Authier Canada 173 Q2
Autlán Mex. 184 D5
Autti Fin. 44 N2
Autun France 51 K6
historically known as Augustodunum
Auvergne *admin. reg.* France 51 J7
Auvergne, Monts d' *mts* France 51 I7
Auvézère r. France 50 G7
Auxerre France 51 J5
historically known as Autesiodorum
Auxonne France 51 L5
Auyan Tepui *plat.* Venez. 199 F3
Auyuittuq National Park Reserve Canada
165 M3
Auzoue r. France 50 G8
Auzzov Kazakh. 103 J2
Ava Myanmar 78 A3
Ava MO U.S.A. 178 D4
Ava NY U.S.A. 177 J2
Avaí Brazil 206 D9
Availles-Limouzine France 50 G6
Avallon France 51 J5
Avalon U.S.A. 182 F8
Avalon Peninsula Canada 169 K4
Avalon Wilderness *nature res.* Canada
169 K4
Avan Iran 100 A3
Avanashi India 94 C4
Avanganna *mt.* Guyana 199 G3
Avanigadda India 94 D2
Avanos Turkey 106 C3
Avarau *atoll* Cook Is *see* Palmerston
Avaré Brazil 206 E10
Avaricum France *see* Bourges
Avarskoye Koysu r. Rus. Fed. 102 A4

► Avarua Cook Is 221 H7
Capital of the Cook Islands, on Rarotonga
island.

Avatele Iran 100 A3
Avaträsk Sweden 44 L2
Avawatz Mountains U.S.A. 183 H6
Ave r. Port. 54 C3
Aveiro Brazil 199 H5
Aveiro Port. 54 C4
Aveiro *admin. dist.* Port. 54 C4
Aveiro, Ria de *est.* Port. 54 C4
Åvej Iran 100 B3
Avellaneda Arg. 204 F3
Avellino Italy 56 G8
historically known as Abellinum
Avenal U.S.A. 182 D5
Avenio France *see* Avignon
Averøya i. Norway 44 I3
Aversa Italy 56 G8
Aves *i.* West Indies 187 H4
Aves *i.* West Indies *see* Las Aves, Islas
Avesnes-sur-Helpe France 51 J2
Avesta Sweden 45 L3
Aveyron r. France 51 H8

► Avezzano Italy 56 F6
europe [environments] ▶▶ 36–37

Avgan Geçidi *pass* Turkey 108 E1
Avgo i. Kythira Greece 59 D13
Avgo i. Greece 59 G13
Aviá Terai Arg. 204 E2
Avidore U.K. 46 I6
Aviemore, Lake N.Z. 153 E12
Avigliano Italy 57 H8
Avignon France 51 K9
historically known as Avenio
Ávila Spain 54 G4
Ávila, Sierra de *mts* Spain 54 F4
Avilés Spain 54 F1
Aviño Spain 54 C1
Avinurme Estonia 42 H3
Avión *mt.* Spain 54 C2
Avis Port. 54 D5
Avisio r. Italy 56 D2
Avize France 51 K4
Avlama Daği *mt.* Turkey 108 E1
Avlemonas Greece 59 E12
Avlida Greece 59 E10
Avlona Albania *see* Vlorë
Avlum Denmark 45 J4
Avnyugskiy Rus. Fed. 40 H3
Avoca Australia 147 D4
Avoca r. Australia 147 D3
Avoca S. Africa 133 P2
Avoca IA U.S.A. 178 D3
Avoca NY U.S.A. 176 H3
Avola Sicilia Italy 57 H12
Avon r. Australia 151 B6
Avon r. England U.K. 47 J12
Avon r. England U.K. 47 J11
Avon r. England U.K. 47 K12
Avon IL U.S.A. 172 C10
Avon NY U.S.A. 176 H3
Avondale U.S.A. 183 L8
Avon Downs Australia 149 C4
Avonmore r. Rep. of Ireland 47 F11
Avon Park U.S.A. 175 D7
Avontuur S. Africa 132 H10
Avoti Latvia 42 F4
Avram Iancu Romania 58 C2
Avranches France 50 E4
Avre r. France 51 I3
Avrig Romania 58 F3
Avrillé France 50 F5
Avsuyu Turkey 109 H1
Avuavu Solomon Is 145 F2
Avveel Fin. *see* Ivalo
Avvil Fin. *see* Ivalo
A'waj r. Syria 108 G4
Awaji-shima i. Japan 91 D7
Awakeri N.Z. 152 K6
Awakino N.Z. 152 I5
Awali Bahrain 105 E2
Awang Indon. 77 G5
Awanui N.Z. 152 H3
Awarawar, Tanjung *pt* Indon. 77 F4
Awarë Eth. 128 D3
'Awarid, Wadi al *watercourse* Syria
109 J3
Awarua Point N.Z. 153 C12
Awasa Eth. 128 C3
Awash Eth. 128 D2
Awash r. Eth. 128 D2
Awa-shima i. Japan 90 F5
Awash National Park Eth. 128 C2
Awash West Wildlife Reserve *nature res.*
Eth. 128 C2
Awat China 88 C3
Awata Shet' r. Eth. 128 C3
Awatere r. N.Z. 153 I9
Awbari Libya 120 B3
Awd *reg.* Yemen 104 D5
'Awdah *well* Saudi Arabia 105 E3
'Awdah, Hawr al *imp. l.* Iraq 107 F5
Aw Dheegle Somalia 128 E4
Awdiinle Somalia 128 D4
Awe, Loch *l.* U.K. 46 G7
Aweil Sudan 126 E2
Awgu Nigeria 125 G5
Awka Nigeria 125 G5
Awlitis *watercourse* W. Sahara 122 B4
Awry Lake Canada 167 H2
Awserd W. Sahara 122 B5
Awu *vol.* Indon. 75 C2
Axe r. U.K. 47 I13
Axel Heiberg Glacier Antarctica 223 N1
Axel Heiberg Island Canada 165 J2
Axente Sever Romania 58 F2
Axim Ghana 125 E5
Axinim Brazil 199 G6

Axioma Brazil **199** E6
Axios *r.* Greece **58** D8
Axmars naturreservat *nature res.* Sweden **45** L3
Axum Eth. *see* **Āksum**
Ay Kazakh. **103** J3
Ayabe Japan **91** D7
Ayachi, Jbel *mt.* Morocco **122** D2
Ayacucho Arg. **204** F5
Ayacucho Peru **200** B3
Ayacucho dept Peru **200** B3
Ayadaw Myanmar **78** A3
Ayagoz Kazakh. **103** J3
also spelt Ayaköz; *formerly spelt* Ayaguz
Ayagoz *watercourse* Kazakh. **103** J3
Ayaguz Kazakh. *see* **Ayagoz**
Ayakagytma, Vpadina *depr.* Uzbek. **103** F4
Ayakkuduk Uzbek. **103** F4
also spelt Oyoqquduq
Ayakkum Hu *salt l.* China **89** E4
Ayaköz Kazakh. *see* **Ayagoz**
Ayamé Côte d'Ivoire **124** E5
Ayamiken Equat. Guinea **125** H6
Ayamonte Spain **54** D7
Ayan Rus. Fed. **39** N4
Ayancık Turkey **106** C2
Ayang N. Korea **83** B5
Ayangba Nigeria **125** G5
Ayanka Rus. Fed. **39** Q3
Ayapel, Serranía de *mts* Col. **198** C3
Ayaş Turkey **106** C2
Ayaviri Peru **200** C3
Ayayei Eth. **128** C1
Āybak Afgh. **101** G2
Aydabul Kazakh. **103** G1
Aydar *r.* Ukr. **41** F6
Aydarkul', Ozero *l.* Uzbek. **103** F4
Aydarly Kazakh. **103** F3
'Aydim, Wādī *r.* Oman **105** F4
Aydın Turkey **106** A3
Aydın *prov.* Turkey **59** J11
Aydıncık Turkey **108** E1
also known as Gilindire
Aydın Dağları *mts* Turkey **106** A3
Aydingkol Hu *marsh* China **88** E3
Ayeat, Gora *hill* Kazakh. **103** G3
Ayedo *mt.* Spain **55** I2
Āyelu Terara *vol.* Eth. **128** D2
Ayem Gabon **126** A5
Ayer U.S.A. **177** N3
Ayers Rock *hill* Australia *see* **Uluru**
Ayeyarwady *r.* Myanmar *see* **Irrawaddy**
Aygyrzhal Kazakh. **103** J2
Ayiá Greece *see* **Agia**
Ayiásos Greece *see* **Agiasos**
Ayila Ri'gyü *mts* China **89** B5
Áyios Dhimítrios Greece *see* **Agios Dimitrios**
Áyios Dhimítris, Ákra *pt* Greece *see* **Agios Dimitrios, Akra**
Áyios Evstrátios *i.* Greece *see* **Agios Efstratios**
Áyios Nikólaos Greece *see* **Agios Nikolaos**
Áyios Yeóryios *i.* Greece *see* **Agios Georgios**
Ayke, Ozero *l.* Kazakh. **103** E2
Āykel Eth. **128** C1
Aykhal Rus. Fed. **39** L3
Aykino Rus. Fed. **40** I3
Aykol China **88** C3
Aylesbury U.K. **47** L12
Aylett U.S.A. **177** H8
Ayllón, Sierra de *mts* Spain **55** H3
Aylmer Canada **173** M8
Aylmer Lake Canada **167** I1
Aymagambetov Kazakh. **103** E2
'Ayn, Ra's al *c.* Oman **105** G4
'Ayn, Wādī al *watercourse* Oman **105** F3
Ayna Peru **200** B3
Aynabulak Kazakh. **103** I3
'Ayn al 'Abd Libya **120** C2
'Ayn al 'Abd *well* Saudi Arabia **105** E1
'Ayn al Bayḍā' *well* Syria **109** I3
'Ayn al Ghazāl *spring* Libya **120** E4
'Ayn al Maẓr'ah *well* Saudi Arabia **104** B2
'Ayn Ba Ma'bad Yemen **105** D5
'Ayn Dībis Iraq **109** O2
'Ayn Hindī *oasis* Oman **105** G4
Ayni Tajik. **101** G2
'Aynīn *well* Saudi Arabia **104** C3
'Ayn Sifnī Iraq **109** O1
'Ayn Umm al Banāt *waterhole* Iraq **109** N3
'Ayn Zuwayyah *spring* Libya **120** E4
Ayon, Ostrov *i.* Rus. Fed. **39** Q3
Ayoquezco Mex. **185** F5
Ayora Spain **55** J5
Ayorou Niger **125** F3
Ayos Cameroon **125** I6
'Ayoûn 'Abd el Mâlek *well* Mauritania **122** D4
'Ayoûn el 'Atroûs Mauritania **124** C2
Ayr Australia **149** E3
Ayr U.K. **46** H8
Ayr *r.* U.K. **46** H8
Ayrag Nuur *salt l.* Mongolia **84** B1
Ayrancı Turkey **106** C3
Ayrancılar Turkey **59** I10
Ayre, Point of Isle of Man **47** H9
Aysarinskoye Kazakh. *see* **Zaozernyy**
Aysary Kazakh. *see* **Zaozernyy**
Āysha Eth. **128** D2
Ayteke Bi Kazakh. **103** E3
formerly known as Novokazalinsk *or* Zhangaqazaly
Aytos Bulg. **58** I6
Aytoska Reka *r.* Bulg. **58** I6
Aytré France **50** E6
Ayun Oman **105** F4
Ayuthia Thai. *see* **Ayutthaya**
Ayutla *Guerrero* Mex. **185** F5
Ayutla *Jalisco* Mex. **184** D4
Ayutthaya Thai. **79** C5
also known as Krungkao; *also spelt* Ayuthia; *long form* Phra Nakhon Si Ayutthaya
Ayvacık Turkey **106** A3
Ayvadzh Tajik. *see* **Aivadzh**
Ayvalı Turkey **107** D3
Ayvalık Turkey **106** A3
Aywat al Manāḥil, Wādī *r.* Yemen **105** E4
Aywat aş Şay'ar, Wādī *r.* Yemen **105** E4
Azacualpa Hond. **186** B4
Azak Rus. Fed. *see* **Azov**
Azambuja Port. **54** C5
Azamgarh India **97** D4
Azangaro Peru **200** C3
Azanja *Srbija* Yugo. **58** B4
Azaouâd *reg.* Mali **124** E2
Azaouagh, Vallée de *watercourse* Mali/Niger **125** F2
Azapa Chile **200** C4
Azar *watercourse* Niger **125** G2
Azaran Iran *see* **Hashtrud**
Azārbayjan *country* Asia *see* **Azerbaijan**
Āzarbāyjān-e Gharbī *prov.* Iran **100** A2
Āzarbāyjān-e Sharqī *prov.* Iran **100** A2
Azare Nigeria **125** H4
Azarychy Belarus **43** K9
Azatskoye, Ozero *l.* Rus. Fed. **43** S2
A'zāz Syria **109** I1
Azazga Alg. **55** P8
Azbine *mts* Niger *see* **L'Aïr, Massif de**
Azdavay Turkey **106** C2
Azélik *well* Niger **125** H2
Azemmour Morocco **122** C2
▶**Azerbaijan** *country* Asia **107** F2
spelt Azärbaycan *in Azeri; formerly known as* Azerbaydzhanskaya S.S.R.; *historically known as* Atropatene
asia [countries] ▶▶▶ 64–67
Azerbaydzhanskaya S.S.R. *country* Asia *see* **Azerbaijan**
Azergues *r.* France **51** K7
Āzezo Eth. **128** C1
Azhu-Tayga, Gora *mt.* Rus. Fed. **88** E1
Azilal Morocco **122** D2
Azilda Canada **173** L4
Azingo Gabon **126** A5
'Azīzābād Iran **100** D4
Azizbekov Armenia *see* **Vayk'**
Aziziye Turkey *see* **Pınarbaşı**
Azlam, Wādī *watercourse* Saudi Arabia **104** A2
Aznakayevo Rus. Fed. **40** J5
Aznalcóllar Spain **54** E7
Azogues Ecuador **198** B5
Azopol'ye Rus. Fed. **40** H2

▶**Azores** *terr.* N. Atlantic Ocean **216** M3
Autonomous Region of Portugal. Long form Arquipélago dos Açores.
europe [countries] ▶▶▶ 32–35

Azotus Israel *see* **Ashdod**
Azov Rus. Fed. **41** F7
historically known as Azak
Azov, Sea of Rus. Fed./Ukr. **41** F7
also known as Azovs'ke More *or* Azovskoye More
Azovo-Sivashskiy Zapovidnyk *nature res.* Ukr. **41** E7
Azovs'ke More *sea* Rus. Fed./Ukr. *see* **Azov, Sea of**
Azovskoye More *sea* Rus. Fed./Ukr. *see* **Azov, Sea of**
Azpeitia Spain **55** I1
Azraq, Bahr el *r.* Eth./Sudan **104** A5 *see* **Blue Nile**
Azrou Morocco **122** D2
Azrou, Oued *watercourse* Alg. **123** G5
Aztec U.S.A. **181** E5
Azua Dom. Rep. **187** F3
Azuaga Spain **54** F6
Azuay *prov.* Ecuador **198** B5
Azúcar *r.* Chile **204** C2
Azuchi-Ō-shima *i.* Japan **91** A8
Azuer *r.* Spain **55** H5
Azuero, Península de *pen.* Panama **186** C6
Azufre, Cerro del *mt.* Chile **204** C2
Azul Arg. **204** F5
Azul *r.* Mex. **185** H5
also known as Blue Creek
Azul, Cordillera *mts* Peru **200** B2
Azul, Serra *hills* Brazil **201** G3
Azuma-san *vol.* Japan **90** G6
Azurduy Bol. **201** D5
Azyory Belarus **42** F8
'Azza Gaza *see* **Gaza**
Az Zabadānī Syria **108** H4
Az Zabīrah *well* Saudi Arabia **104** C2
Az Zafīrī *reg.* Iraq **107** E5
Az Zāhirah *admin. reg.* Oman **105** G3
Az Zahrān Saudi Arabia *see* **Dhahran**
Az Zallāf, Wādī *watercourse* Libya **120** B3
Az Zallāq Bahrain **105** E2
Azzano Decimo Italy **56** E3
Az Zaqāzīq Egypt *see* **Zagazig**
Az Zarbah Syria **109** H1
Az Zarqā' Jordan **108** H5
also spelt Zarqā'
Az Zāwiyah Libya **120** B1
Az Zaydīyah Yemen **104** C5
Azzeffâl *hills* Mauritania/W. Sahara **122** B5
Azzel Matti, Sebkha *salt pan* Alg. **123** F4
Az Zilfī Saudi Arabia **104** D2
Az Zintān Libya **120** B2
Az Zubayr Iraq **107** F5
Az Zuhrah Yemen **104** C5
Az Zuqur *i.* Yemen **104** C5
English form Az Zuqur Island
Az Zuqurt *oasis* Saudi Arabia **105** E4
Az Zuwaytīnah Libya **120** D2

↓ B

Baa Indon. **75** B5
Baai *r.* Indon. **77** G2
Ba'albek Lebanon **108** H3
Ba'al Hazor *mt.* West Bank **108** G6
Baardheere Somalia **128** D4
formerly spelt Bardera
Bab India **96** C4
Baba *mt.* Bulg. **58** E6
Bābā, Kūh-e *mts* Afgh. **101** G3
Baba Burnu *pt* Turkey **59** H9
Babaçulândia Brazil **202** C3
Babadağ *mt.* Azer. **107** G2
Babadag Romania **58** J4
Babadağ Turkey **59** J11
Baba Dağ *mt.* Turkey **59** K12
Babadagului, Podișul *plat.* Romania **58** J4
Babadaykhan *Akhal'skaya Oblast'* Turkm. **102** E5
formerly known as Kirovsk
Babadaykhan *Akhal'skaya Oblast'* Turkm. **102** E5
formerly known as Kommuna
Babadurmaz Turkm. **102** D5
Babaeski Turkey **106** A2
Babahoyo Ecuador **198** B5
Babai *r.* Nepal **97** D3
Babai Gaxun China **84** E3
Babak Phil. **74** C5
Bābā Kalān Iran **100** B4
Babakourimigana *well* Niger **125** H3
Bāb al Mandab *strait* Africa/Asia **121** I6
Bab al Mandab, Cape Yemen *see* **Bāb al Mandab, Ra's**
Bāb al Mandab, Ra's *c.* Yemen **104** C5
English form Bab al Mandab, Cape
Babana Indon. **75** A3
Babanango S. Africa **133** P5
Babanki Cameroon **125** H5
Babanusa Sudan **126** E2
Babao China *see* **Qilian**
Babao China **86** C4
Babar *i.* Indon. **75** D4
Babar, Kepulauan *is* Indon. **75** D4
Babat Indon. **77** F4
Babati Tanz. **129** B6
Babau Indon. **75** B5
Babayevo Rus. Fed. **43** Q2
Babayurt Rus. Fed. **102** A4
Babeldaob *i.* Palau **73** H5
also spelt Babelthuap
Babelegi S. Africa **133** M2
Babelthuap *i.* Palau *see* **Babeldaob**
Băbeni Romania **58** F4
Baberu India **96** D4
Bab Ezzouar Alg. **55** O8
Babi, Pulau *i.* Indon. **76** B2
Babia Góra *mt.* Poland **49** Q6
Babian Jiang *r.* China **86** B4
Bābil Egypt **108** C7
Bābil *governorate* Iraq **107** F4
formerly known as Al Ḥillah
Babilē Eth. **128** D2
Babimost Poland **49** M3
Babinavichy Belarus **43** L7
Babinda Australia **149** E3
Babine *r.* Canada **166** E4
Babine Lake Canada **166** E4
Babine Range *mts* Canada **166** E4
Babinga Dem. Rep. Congo **126** C5
Babītes ezers *l.* Latvia **42** E5
Babo Indon. **73** H7
Bābol Iran **100** C2
Bābol Sar Iran **100** C2
Babonã *r.* Brazil **199** E6
Babongo Cameroon **125** I5
Baboon Point S. Africa **132** C9
Baboua Cent. Afr. Rep. **126** B3
Babruysk Belarus **43** K8
also spelt Bobruysk
Babstovo Rus. Fed. **82** D2
Babtai Lith. **42** E6
Bab Taza Morocco **54** F9
Babu China *see* **Hezhou**
Babuna Planina *mts* Macedonia **58** C7
Babusar Pass Pak. **101** H3
Babushkin Rus. Fed. **85** E1
formerly known as Mysovsk
Babušnica *Srbija* Yugo. **58** D5
Babuyan Phil. **74** A4
Babuyan *i.* Phil. **74** B2
Babuyan Channel Phil. **74** B2
Babuyan Islands Phil. **74** B2
Babylon *tourist site* Iraq **107** F4
Babynino Rus. Fed. **43** Q7
Bač *Vojvodina, Srbija* Yugo. **58** A3
Bacaadweyn Somalia **128** E3
Bacaba *r.* Brazil **198** D5
Bacabáchi Mex. **184** C3
Bacabal *Maranhão* Brazil **202** C3
Bacabal *Pará* Brazil **199** G6
Bacajá *r.* Brazil **199** I5
Bacakliyayla Tepesi *mt.* Turkey **106** B2
Bacalar Mex. **185** H5
Bacalar Chico, Boca *sea chan.* Mex. **185** I5
Bacan *i.* Indon. **75** C3
Bacanora Mex. **184** C2
Bacarra Phil. **74** B2
Bacău Romania **58** H2
Baccarat France **51** M4
Baccaro Point Canada **169** H5
Bacchiglione *r.* Italy **56** E3
Băc Giang Vietnam **78** D3
Bachaquero Venez. **198** D2
Bacheykava Belarus **43** K6
Bach Ice Shelf Antarctica **222** T2
Bachiniva Mex. **181** F7
Bach Long Vi, Đao *i.* Vietnam **78** D3
Bachu China **88** B4
formerly known as Maralbashi *or* Maralwexi
Bachuma Eth. **128** B3
Back *r.* Australia **149** D3
Back *r.* Canada **167** M1
Bačka *reg.* Hungary/Yugo. **58** A2
Bačka Palanka *Vojvodina, Srbija* Yugo. **58** A3
Bačka Topola *Vojvodina, Srbija* Yugo. **58** A3
Backbone Mountain U.S.A. **176** F6
Backbone Ranges *mts* Canada **166** D2
Backe Sweden **44** L3
Bäckefors Sweden **45** K4
Bäckhammar Sweden **45** K4
Bački Petrovac *Vojvodina, Srbija* Yugo. **58** A3
Backnang Germany **48** G7
Bačko Gradište *Vojvodina, Srbija* Yugo. **58** B3
Backstairs Passage Australia **146** C3
Bac Lac Vietnam **78** D3
Bac Liêu Vietnam **79** D6
Băc Ninh Vietnam **78** D3
Bacnotan Phil. **74** B2
Baco, Mount Phil. **74** B3
Bacoachi Mex. **184** C2
Bacoachi *watercourse* Mex. **181** E7
Bacobampo Mex. **184** C3
Bacolod Phil. **74** B4
Bắc Quang Vietnam **78** D3
Bacqueville-en-Caux France **50** G3
Bácsalmás Hungary **49** Q9
Bactra Afgh. *see* **Balkh**
Bacubirito Mex. **184** D3
Baculin Bay Phil. **74** C5
Baculin Point Phil. **74** C4
Bacuri Brazil **202** C2
Bad *r.* U.S.A. **178** B2
Bada China *see* **Xilin**
Bada *mt.* Eth. **128** C3
Bada *i.* Myanmar **79** B6
Badagara India **94** B4
Badain Jaran Shamo *des.* China **84** D3
Badajós *Amazonas* Brazil **199** F5
Badajós *Pará* Brazil **202** C2
Badajós, Lago *l.* Brazil **199** F5
Badajoz Spain **54** E6
Badakhshan *prov.* Afgh. **101** G2
Badakhshan *aut. rep.* Tajik. *see* **Kŭhistoni Badakhshon**
Badakhshoni Kŭhi *aut. rep.* Tajik. *see* **Kŭhistoni Badakhshon**
Badami India **94** B3
Badanah Saudi Arabia **107** E5
Badaojiang China *see* **Baishan**
Badarinath *mts* India *see* **Badrinath Peaks**
Badarīyāt, Ḥazm al *plat.* Saudi Arabia **109** L7
Badarpur India **97** G4
Badas, Kepulauan *is* Indon. **77** D2
Bad Aussee Austria **49** K8
Bad Axe U.S.A. **173** K7
Bad Bergzabern Germany **48** E6
Bad Berka Germany **48** I5
Bad Berleburg Germany **48** F4
Bad Bevensen Germany **48** H2
Baddeck Canada **169** I4
Badderen Norway **44** M1
Baddo *r.* Pak. **101** F4
Bad Doberan Germany **48** I1
Badéguichéri Niger **125** G3
Bademli Turkey *see* **Aladağ**
Bademli Geçidi *pass* Turkey **106** B3
Bad Ems Germany **48** E5
Baden Austria **49** N7
Baden Switz. **51** O5
Baden-Baden Germany **48** F7
Baden-Württemberg *land* Germany **48** F7
Badèr Niger **125** G3
Bad Freienwalde Germany **49** L3
Badgastein Austria **49** K8
Badger Canada **169** J3
Bādghīs *prov.* Afgh. **101** E3
Bad Harzburg Germany **48** H4
Bad Hersfeld Germany **48** G5
Bad Hofgastein Austria **49** K8
Bad Homburg vor der Höhe Germany **48** F5
Badi *r.* Guinea **124** B4
Badia Polesine Italy **56** D3
Badigeru Swamp Sudan **128** B3
Badin Pak. **101** G5
Badinko, Réserve du *nature res.* Mali **124** C3
Badiraguato Mex. **184** D3
Bad Ischl Austria **49** K8
Bādiyat ash Shām *des.* Asia *see* **Syrian Desert**
Badje-Sohppar Sweden *see* **Övre Soppero**
Badkhyzskiy Zapovednik *nature res.* Turkm. **101** E3
Bad Kissingen Germany **48** H5
Bad Königsdorff Poland *see* **Jastrzębie-Zdrój**
Bad Kreuznach Germany **48** E6
Bad Krozingen Germany **48** E8
Badlands *reg.* *ND* U.S.A. **178** B2
Badlands *reg.* *SD* U.S.A. **178** B3
Badlands National Park U.S.A. **178** B3
Bad Langensalza Germany **48** H4
Bad Lauterberg im Harz Germany **48** H4
Bad Liebenwerda Germany **49** K4
Bad Lippspringe Germany **48** F4
Bad Mergentheim Germany **48** G6
Bad Nauheim Germany **48** F5
Badnawar India **96** B5
Bad Neuenahr-Ahrweiler Germany **48** E5
Bad Neustadt an der Saale Germany **48** H5
Bad Oldesloe Germany **48** H2
Badong China **87** D2
also known as Xinling
Ba Đông Vietnam **79** D6
Badou Togo **125** F5
Badplaas S. Africa **133** O2
Bad Pyrmont Germany **48** G4
Bad Ragaz Switz. **51** P5
Badr City Egypt **108** C7
Bad Reichenhall Germany **49** J8
Badr Ḥunayn Saudi Arabia **104** B3
Badrinath Peaks India **96** C3
also known as Badarinath *or* Chaukhamba
Bad River Indian Reservation *res.* U.S.A. **172** C4
Bad Säckingen Germany **48** E8
Bad Salzuflen Germany **48** F3
Bad Salzungen Germany **48** H5
Bad Schwartau Germany **48** H2
Bad Segeberg Germany **48** H2
Badu China **87** F3
Badu Island Australia **73** J9
Badulla Sri Lanka **94** D5
Badvel India **94** C3
Bad Waldsee Germany **48** G8
Bad Windsheim Germany **48** H6
Badzhal'skiy Khrebet *mts* Rus. Fed. **82** D2
Bad Zwischenahn Germany **48** F2
Bae Colwyn U.K. *see* **Colwyn Bay**
Bæir Iceland **44** [inset] B2
Baena Spain **54** G7
Baeza Ecuador **198** B5
Baeza Spain **55** H7
Bafang Cameroon **125** H5
Bafatá Guinea-Bissau **124** B3
Bafa Pak. **101** H3
Baffin Bay *sea* Canada/Greenland **165** M2

▶**Baffin Island** Canada **165** L2
2nd largest island in North America and 5th in the world.
northamerica [landscapes] ▶▶▶ 156–157

Bafia Cameroon **125** H5
Bafilo Togo **125** F4
Bafing *r.* Guinea/Mali **124** C3
Bafing, Réserve du *nature res.* Mali **124** C3
Bafing Makana Mali **124** C3
Bafoulabé Mali **124** C3
Bafoussam Cameroon **125** H5
Bāfq Iran **100** C4
Bafra Turkey **106** C2
Bafra Burnu *pt* Turkey **106** C2
Bāft Iran **100** D4
Bafwasende Dem. Rep. Congo **126** E4
Baga Nigeria **125** I3
Baga Spain **55** M2
Baga Bogd Uul *mts* Mongolia **84** D2
Bagac Bay Phil. **74** B3
Bagaha India **97** E4
Bagahak *hill Sabah* Malaysia **77** G1
Bagalkot India **94** B2
Bagamoyo Tanz. **129** C6
Bagan China **86** A1
Bagan Datoh Malaysia *see* **Bagan Datuk**
Bagan Datuk Malaysia **76** C2
formerly known as Bagan Datoh
Baganga Phil. **74** C5
Bagani Namibia **130** D3
Baganian Peninsula Phil. **74** B5
Bagansiapiapi Indon. **76** C2
Bagar *watercourse* Kazakh. **88** C1
Bağarası Turkey **59** I11
Bagaré *well* Niger **125** G3
Bagaroua Niger **125** G3
Bagata Dem. Rep. Congo **126** C5
Bagazán Peru **198** C6
Bagbag Sudan **121** F6
Bagdad U.S.A. **183** K7
Bagé Brazil **204** G3
Bagepalli India **94** C3
Bagerhat Bangl. *see* **Bagherhat**
Bages et de Sigean, Étang de *lag.* France **51** I9
Bageshwar India **96** C3
Bagevadi India **94** C2
Baggå Sweden **45** K4
Baggs U.S.A. **180** F4
Bagh India **96** B5
Baghak Pak. **101** F4
Baghbaghū Iran **101** E2

▶**Baghdād** Iraq **107** F4
Capital of Iraq. English form Baghdad.

Baghdad Iraq *see* **Baghdād**
Bāgh-e Bābū'īyeh Iran **100** D4
Bagherhat Bangl. **97** F5
also spelt Bagerhat
Bagheria *Sicilia* Italy **57** F10
Bāghīn Iran **100** D4
Baghlān Afgh. **101** G2
Baghlān *prov.* Afgh. **101** G3
Bāghlī Da *hill* Iran **100** A2
Baginda, Tanjung *pt* Indon. **77** D3
Bağırsak Deresi *r.* Syria/Turkey *see* **Sājūr, Nahr**
Bagley U.S.A. **178** D2
Baglung Nepal **97** D3
Bagn Norway **45** J3
Bagnara Calabra Italy **57** H10
Bagnères-de-Bigorre France **50** G9
Bagnères-de-Luchon France **50** G10
Bagno di Romagna Italy **56** D5
Bagnolo Mella Italy **56** C3
Bagnols-sur-Cèze France **51** K8
Bagnuiti *r.* Nepal **97** E4
Bago Myanmar *see* **Pegu**
Bago *admin. div.* Myanmar *see* **Pegu**
Bago Phil. **74** B4
Bagoé *r.* Côte d'Ivoire/Mali **124** D3
Bagong China *see* **Sansui**
Bagrationovsk Rus. Fed. **42** B7
historically known as Eylau *or* Preussisch-Eylau
Bagrax China *see* **Bohu**
Bagrax Hu *l.* China *see* **Bosten Hu**
Bagre Brazil **202** B2
Bagua Peru **198** B6
Baguio Nigeria **125** G4
Baguio Phil. **74** B2
Baguio Point Phil. **74** B2
Bağyurdu Turkey **59** I10
Bagzane, Monts *mts* Niger **125** H2
Bahadurganj Nepal **89** C7
Bahadurgarh India **96** C3
Bahāmabād Iran *see* **Rafsanjān**
▶**Bahamas** *country* West Indies **186** D1
northamerica [countries] ▶▶▶ 158–159
Baharampur India **97** F4
formerly spelt Berhampur
Bahardipur Pak. **101** G5
Bahariya Oasis Egypt **121** F3
Bahau *r.* Indon. **77** G2
Bahau Malaysia **76** C2
Bahaur Indon. **77** F3
Bahawalnagar Pak. **101** H4
Bahawalpur Pak. **101** G4
Bahçe *Adana* Turkey **108** G1
Bahçe *Osmaniye* Turkey **107** D3
Ba He *r.* China **86** C2
Bāherden Turkm. *see* **Bakherden**
Baheri India **96** C3
Bahi Tanz. **129** B6
Bahia Brazil *see* **Salvador**
Bahia *state* Brazil **202** D5
Bahía Asunción Mex. **181** D8
Bahía Blanca Arg. **204** E5
Bahía Bustamante Arg. **205** D7
Bahía Kino Mex. **184** C2
Bahía Laura Arg. **205** D8
Bahía Negra Para. **201** F5
Bahía San Blas Arg. **204** E6
Bahía Tortugas Mex. **184** B3
Bahig Egypt **108** A7
Bahir Dar Eth. **128** C2
Bahlā Oman **105** G3
Bahluі *r.* Romania **58** I1
Bahmanshīr, Khowr-e *r.* Iran **100** B4
Bahomonte Indon. **75** B3
Bahr Saudi Arabia **104** C4
Bahraich India **97** D4
▶**Bahrain** *country* Asia **105** E2
spelt Al Baḥrayn *in Arabic*
asia [countries] ▶▶▶ 64–67
Bahrain, Gulf of Asia **105** E2
Bahrāmābād Iran **100** B2
Bahrāmjerd Iran **100** D4
Bahr el Jebel *state* Sudan **128** A3
Bahror India **96** C4
Bahuaja-Sonene, Parque Nacional *nat. park* Peru **200** C3
Bāhū Kālāt Iran **101** E5
Bahushewsk Belarus **43** L7
Baia Romania **58** H1
Baia Romania **58** J4
Baia de Aramă Romania **58** D4
Baia de Arieș Romania **58** E2
Baia dos Tigres Angola **127** A9
Baia Farta Angola **127** B8
Baia Mare Romania **53** G2
Baião Brazil **202** B2
Baiazeh Iran **100** C3
Baibeli *well* Chad **120** D5
Baibokoum Chad **126** B3
Baicheng China *see* **Xiping**
Baicheng *Jilin* China **85** I2
Baicheng *Xinjiang* China **88** C3
also known as Bay
Băicoi Romania **58** G3
Baidoa Somalia *see* **Baydhabo**
Baidoi Co *l.* China **89** D5
Baidu China **87** F3
Baidunzi China **84** B3
Baie-aux-Feuilles Canada *see* **Tasiujaq**
Baie-Comeau Canada **169** G3
Baie de Henne Haiti **187** E3
Baie-du-Poste Canada *see* **Mistissini**
Baie-Johan-Beetz Canada **169** I3
Baie-St-Paul Canada **169** G4
Baie-Trinité Canada **169** H3
Baie Verte Canada **169** J3
Baigou *r.* China **85** H4
Baiguan China *see* **Shangyu**
Baiguo China **87** E2
Baigura *mt.* Spain **55** J2
Baihanchang China **86** A3
Baihar India **96** D5
Baihe *Jilin* China **82** C4
formerly known as Erdaobaihe
Baihe *Shaanxi* China **87** D1
Bai He *r.* China **87** E1
Baiji Iraq *see* **Bayjī**
Baijiantan China **88** D2
Baijnath *Himachal Pradesh* India **96** C2
Baijnath *Uttaranchal* India **96** C3

▶**Baikal, Lake** Rus. Fed. **81** H2
Deepest lake in the world and in Asia. 3rd largest lake in Asia and 9th in the world. Also known as Baykal, Ozero.
world [physical features] ▶▶▶ 8–9

Baikanthpur India **97** D4
Baikouquan China **88** D2
Baikunthpur India **97** D5
Bailang China **85** I2
Bailanhe Shuiku *resr* China **87** E2
Baile Átha Cliath Rep. of Ireland *see* **Dublin**
Baile Átha Luain Rep. of Ireland *see* **Athlone**
Băile Govora Romania **58** F3
Băile Herculane Romania **58** D4
Bailén Spain **54** H6
Băile Olănești Romania **58** F3
Băilești Romania **58** E4
Băileștilor, Câmpia *plain* Romania **58** E4
Băile Tușnad Romania **58** G2
Bailey S. Africa **133** K8
Bailey Ice Stream Antarctica **223** W1
Bailey Range *hills* Australia **151** C6
Baileyton U.S.A. **176** C9
Bailicun China **87** D3
Bailingmiao China **85** F3
also known as Darhan Muminggan Lianheqi
Baillie *r.* Canada **167** J1
Bailong Jiang *r.* China **86** C1
Bailundo Angola **127** B8
formerly known as Teixeira da Silva
Baima China **86** B1
also known as Sêraitang
Baima China *see* **Baxoi**
Bainang China **89** E6
also known as Norkyung
Bainbridge *GA* U.S.A. **175** C6
Bainbridge *NY* U.S.A. **177** J3
Bainbridge *OH* U.S.A. **176** B6
Bain-de-Bretagne France **50** E5
Baindurur India **94** B3
Bainet Haiti **187** E3
Baingoin China **89** E6
also known as Porong
Baini China *see* **Yuqing**
Baiona Spain **54** C2
also spelt Bayona
Baiqên China **86** B1
Baiquan China **82** B3
Bā'ir Jordan **109** H7
Bā'ir, Wādī *watercourse* Jordan/Saudi Arabia **109** I6
Bairab Co *l.* China **89** C5
Bairagnia India **97** E4
Baird U.S.A. **179** C5
Baird, Mount Canada **166** C1
Baird Mountains U.S.A. **164** D3

▶**Bairiki** Kiribati **145** G1
Capital of Kiribati, on Tarawa atoll.

Bairin Qiao China **85** H3
formerly known as Balinqiao
Bairin Youqi China *see* **Daban**
Bairin Zuoqi China *see* **Lindong**
Bairkum Kazakh. **103** G4
also spelt Bayyrqum
Bairnsdale Australia **147** E4
Bais France **50** F4
Bais Phil. **74** B4
Baïse *r.* France **50** G8
Baisha *Chongqing* China **86** C2
Baisha *Hainan* China **87** D5
also known as Yacha
Baisha *Jiangxi* China **87** E3
Baisha *Sichuan* China **87** D2
Baishan China *see* **Mashan**
Baishan *Jilin* China **82** B4
formerly known as Badaojiang *or* Hunjiang
Baishan *Jilin* China **82** B4
Baishi China **85** F5
Baishui Jiang *r.* China **86** C1
Băișoara Romania **58** E2
Baisogala Lith. **42** E6
Baitadi Nepal **96** D3
Baitang China **86** A1
Bai Thuong Vietnam **78** D4
Baitle *r.* China **85** H5
Baixa da Banheira Port. **54** B6
Baixi China *see* **Yibin**
Baixiang China **85** G4
Baixingt China **85** I3
Baixo Guandu Brazil **207** M6
Baixo-Longa Angola **127** C8
Baiyang Dian *resr* China **85** H4
Baiyanghe China **88** E3
Baiyashi China *see* **Dong'an**
Baiyin China **84** E4
Baiyü China **86** A2
also known as Jianshe
Baiyuda Desert Sudan **121** G5
Baiyu Shan *mts* China **85** E4
Baja Hungary **49** P9
Baja, Punta *pt* Mex. **184** E2
Baja California *pen.* Mex. **184** B2
English form Lower California
Baja California Norte *state* Mex. **184** B2
Baja California Sur *state* Mex. **184** B3
Bajan Mex. **185** E3
Bajang Nepal **96** D3
Bajau *i.* Indon. **77** D2
Bajaur *reg.* Pak. **101** G3
Bajawa Indon. **75** B5
Baj Baj India **97** F5
Bājgīrān Iran **100** D2
Bājil Yemen **104** C5
Bajina Bašta *Srbija* Yugo. **58** A5
Bajitpur Bangl. **97** F4
Bajmok *Vojvodina, Srbija* Yugo. **58** A3
Bajna India **96** B5
Bajo Baudó Col. **198** B3
Bajo Boquete Panama **186** C5
Bajo Caracoles Arg. **205** C7
Bajoga Nigeria **125** H4
Bajo Grande Arg. **205** C7
Bajo Hondo Arg. **204** D3
Bajrakot India **97** E5
Bajram Curri Albania **58** B6
Baka, Bukit *mt.* Indon. **77** F3
Bakaba Chad **126** C2
Bakala Cent. Afr. Rep. **126** D3
Bakaly Rus. Fed. **40** J5
Bakanas Kazakh. **103** I3
Bakanas *watercourse* Kazakh. **103** I3
Bakau Gambia **124** A3
Bakayan, Gunung *mt.* Indon. **77** G2
Bakel Senegal **124** B3
Baker *CA* U.S.A. **183** H6
Baker *LA* U.S.A. **175** B6
Baker *MT* U.S.A. **180** F3
Baker *OR* U.S.A. **180** C3
Baker *WV* U.S.A. **176** G6
Baker, Mount *vol.* U.S.A. **180** B2
Baker Butte *mt.* U.S.A. **183** M7

▶**Baker Island** N. Pacific Ocean **145** H1
United States Unincorporated Territory.
oceania [countries] ▶▶▶ 138–139

Baker Island U.S.A. **166** C4
Baker Lake *salt flat* Australia **151** D5
Baker Lake Canada **167** M1
also known as Qamanittuaq
Baker Lake *l.* Canada **167** M1
Baker's Dozen Islands Canada **168** E1
Bakersfield U.S.A. **182** F6
Bakerville S. Africa **133** K2
Bakhā Oman **105** G2
Bakharden Turkm. *see* **Bakherden**
Bakhardok Turkm. **102** D5
also spelt Bokurdak
Bākharz *mts* Iran **101** E3
Bakhchisaray Ukr. *see* **Bakhchysaray**
Bakhchysaray Ukr. **41** E7
also spelt Bakhchisaray
Bakherden Turkm. **102** D5
also spelt Bäherden; *formerly spelt* Bakharden
Bakhirevo Rus. Fed. **82** C2
Bakhmach Ukr. **41** E6
Bakhmut Ukr. *see* **Artemivs'k**
Bakhmutovo Rus. Fed. **43** P5
Bakhta Rus. Fed. **39** I3
Bākhtarān Iran *see* **Kermānshāh**
Bākhtarān *prov.* Iran *see* **Kermānshāh**
Bakhtegan, Daryācheh-ye *l.* Iran **100** C4
Bakhtiari Country *reg.* Iran **100** B3
Bakhtiyarpur India **97** E4
Bakhty Kazakh. **88** C2
also spelt Baqty
Bakhuis Gebergte *mts* Suriname **199** G3
Baki Azer. *see* **Baku**
Baki *well* Chad **120** D5
Bakin Birji Niger **125** H3
Bakır *r.* Turkey **59** I10
Bakırköy Turkey **106** B2
Bakkaflói *b.* Iceland **44** [inset] D2
Baklan Turkey **59** K11
Baklanka Rus. Fed. **43** V3
Baklanovo Rus. Fed. **43** M6
Bakloh India **96** B2
Bako Côte d'Ivoire **124** D4
Bako Eth. **128** C2
Bako National Park *Sarawak* Malaysia **77** E2
Bakool *admin. reg.* Somalia **128** D4
Bakota Dem. Rep. Congo **126** D5
Bakouma Cent. Afr. Rep. **126** D3
Bakoumba Gabon **126** B5
Bakoy *r.* Mali **124** C3
Baksan Rus. Fed. **41** G8
Baktalórántháza Hungary **49** T8

▶**Baku** Azer. **107** G2
Capital of Azerbaijan. Also spelt Bakı or Baky.

Bakung *i.* Indon. **76** D2
Bakuny Belarus **42** F9
Bakuriani Georgia **107** E2
Bakutis Coast Antarctica **222** P2
Baky Azer. *see* **Baku**
Baky Uyandino *r.* Rus. Fed. **39** O3
Balā Turkey **106** C3
Bala U.K. **47** I11
also known as Y Bala
Bala, Cerros de *mts* Bol. **200** C3
Balabac *i.* Phil. **74** A5
Balabac Strait Malaysia/Phil. **77** G1
Bālābād, Gardaneh-ye *pass* Iran **100** C3
Balabalangan, Kepulauan *atolls* Indon. **77** G3
Balabanovo Rus. Fed. **43** R6
Bălăceanu Romania **58** I3
Bălăcița Romania **58** E4
Balad Iraq **107** F4
Bālā Deh Iran **100** B4
Baladeh *Māzandarān* Iran **100** B2
Baladeh *Māzandarān* Iran **100** B2
Balaghat India **96** D5
Balaghat Range *hills* India **94** B2
Balaguer Spain **55** L3
Bālā Howz Iran **100** D4
Balaiberkuak Indon. **77** E3
Balaikarangan Indon. **77** E2
Balaipungut Indon. **76** C2
Balairiam Indon. **77** E3
Balaïtous *mt.* France **50** F10
Balaka Malawi **129** B8
Balakän Azer. **107** F2
Balakhna Rus. Fed. **40** G4
Balakirevo Rus. Fed. **43** T5
Balaklava Australia **146** C3
Balaklava Ukr. **41** E7
Balakleya Ukr. *see* **Balakliya**
Balakliya Ukr. **41** F6
also spelt Balakleya
Balakovo Rus. Fed. **102** A1
Balama Moz. **131** H2
Balambangan *i. Sabah* Malaysia **77** G1
Bālā Morghāb Afgh. **101** E3
Balan India **96** A4
Bălan Romania **58** G2
Balancán Mex. **185** H5
Balanda Rus. Fed. *see* **Kalininsk**
Balan Dağı *hill* Turkey **59** J12
Balanga Phil. **74** B3
Balangala Dem. Rep. Congo **126** C4
Balangir India **95** D1
Balangoda Sri Lanka **94** D5
Balapur India **94** C1
Balarampur India **97** E5
Balase *r.* Indon. **75** B3
Bălășești Romania **58** I2
Balashi Rus. Fed. **102** B2
Balashikha Rus. Fed. **43** S6
Balashov Rus. Fed. **41** G6
Balasinor India **96** B5
Balassagyarmat Hungary **49** Q7
Balaton *l.* Hungary *see* **Balaton, Lake**

Balaton, Lake Hungary **49** O9
also known as Balaton
Balatonboglár Hungary **49** O9
Balatonfüred Hungary **49** O9
Balatonlelle Hungary **49** O9
Balauring Indon. **75** B5
Balazote Spain **55** I6
Balbina Brazil **199** G5
Balbina, Represa de *resr* Brazil **199** G5
Balbriggan Rep. of Ireland **47** F10
Balcad Somalia **128** E4
Balcanoona Australia **146** C4
Balcarce Arg. **204** F5
Balchik Bulg. **58** J5
Balclutha N.Z. **153** D14
Baldim Brazil **207** J6
Bald Knob *AR* U.S.A. **174** B5
Bald Knob *WV* U.S.A. **176** D8
Bald Mountain U.S.A. **183** I4
Baldock Lake Canada **167** L3
Baldwin U.S.A. **175** D6
Baldwinsville U.S.A. **177** I2
Baldwinville U.S.A. **177** M3
Baldy Mount Canada **166** G5
Baldy Mountain *hill* Canada **167** K5
Baldy Peak U.S.A. **183** O8
Bal'dzhikan Rus. Fed. **85** F1
Bale Indon. **76** C3
Bâle Switz. *see* Basel
Baléa Mali **124** C3
Baleares, Islas *is* Spain *see*
Balearic Islands
Baleares Insulae *is* Spain *see*
Balearic Islands
Balearic Islands *is* Spain **55** M5
also known as Baleares, Islas *or* Balears,
Illes; *historically known as* Baleares Insulae
Balears, Illes *is* Spain *see* Balearic Islands
Baleh *r.* Sarawak Malaysia **77** F2
Baleia, Ponta da *pt* Brazil **203** E6
Baleines, Pointe des *pt* France **50** E3
Bâlen Phil. **74** B4
Baler Phil. **74** B3
Baler Bay Phil. **74** B3
Balesa Kenya **128** C4
Baleshwar India **97** E5
Balestrand Norway **44** E1
Baley Rus. Fed. **85** H1
Baleyara Niger **125** F3
Balezino Rus. Fed. **40** J4
Balfate Hond. **186** B4
Balfe's Creek Australia **149** E4
Balfour Canada **167** G5
Balfour N.Z. **153** C13
Balfour *E. Cape* S. Africa **133** K9
Balfour *Mpumalanga* S. Africa **133** M3
Balfour Downs Australia **150** C4
Balgatay Mongolia **84** C2
formerly known as Shiluüstey
Balgazyn Rus. Fed. **88** F1
Balgo Australia **150** D4
Balgo Aboriginal Reserve Australia **150** E4
Balguda *well* Kenya **128** C5
Balguntay China **88** D3
Bâlhaf Yemen **105** G5
Balho Djibouti **128** D1
Bali India **96** B4
Bali *i.* Indon. **77** F5
Bali *prov.* Indon. **77** F5
Bali *reg.* Saudi Arabia **104** B2
Bali, Selat *sea chan.* Indon. **77** F5
Baliangao Phil. **74** B4
Baliapal India **97** E5
Balichak India **97** E5
Baliguda India **95** D1
Balihan China **85** H3
Balıkesir Turkey **106** A3
Balıkesir *prov.* Turkey **59** J9
Balık Gölü *l.* Turkey **107** F3
Balikh *r.* Syria/Turkey **109** K2
Balikkeşme Turkey **59** I8
Balikpapan Indon. **77** G3
Balikpapan, Teluk *b.* Indon. **77** G3
Bălileşti Romania **58** F3
Balimbing India **94** D2
Balimila Reservoir India **94** D2
Balimo P.N.G. **73** J8
Balin China **85** I1
Balingen Germany **48** F7
Balingian Sarawak Malaysia **77** F2
Balingian *r.* Sarawak Malaysia **77** F2
Balingiao China *see* Bairin Qiao
Balintang Channel Phil. **74** B2
Bali Sea Indon. **77** F4
Balitondo Cent. Afr. Rep. **126** D4
Baliungan *i.* Phil. **74** B5
Baljurshi Saudi Arabia **104** C4
Balkan Mountains Bulg./Yugo. **58** D5
also known as Stara Planina
europe [issues] ➤➤➤ 34–35
Balkan Oblast *admin. div.* Turkm. *see*
Balkanskaya Oblast'
Balkanskaya Oblast' *admin. div.* Turkm.
102 C4
English form Balkan Oblast; *formerly known*
as Krasnovodskaya Oblast'
Balkashino Kazakh. **103** G1
Balkh Afgh. **101** F2
historically known as Bactra *or* Zariaspa
Balkh *prov.* Afgh. **101** F2
Balkhab *r.* Afgh. **101** F2
Balkhash India **103** H3
also spelt Balqash

Balkhash, Ozero *l.* Kazakh. *see*
Balkhash, Lake
Balkonda India **94** C2
Balkuduk Kazakh. **102** A3
Balla Bangl. **97** F4
Balla Balla Zimbabwe *see* Mbalabala
Ballachulish U.K. **46** G7
Balladonia Australia **151** C7
Ballaghaderreen Rep. of Ireland **47** D10
Ballangen Norway **44** L1
Ballantrae U.K. **47** H8
Ballard, Lake *salt flat* Australia **151** C6
Ballarpur India **94** C2
Ballater U.K. **46** I6
Ballé Mali **124** C3
Ballena, Punta *pt* Chile **204** C2
Ballenero, Canal *sea chan.* Chile
205 C9
Balleny Islands Antarctica **223** K2
Ballia India **97** E4
Ballina Australia **147** G2
Ballina Rep. of Ireland **47** C9
also spelt Béal an Átha
Ballinasloe Rep. of Ireland **47** D10
also spelt Béal Átha na Sluaighe
Ballineen Rep. of Ireland **47** D12
Ballinger U.S.A. **179** C6
Ballinrobe Rep. of Ireland **47** C10
Ballons des Vosges, Parc Naturel
Régional des *nature res.* France **51** M5
Balsh Albania **58** A3
Ballston Spa U.S.A. **177** L2
Bally U.S.A. **177** J5
Ballybunnion Rep. of Ireland **47** C11
Ballycastle Rep. of Ireland **47** C9
Ballycastle U.K. **47** F8
Ballyhaunis Rep. of Ireland **47** D10
Ballymena U.K. **47** F9
Ballymoney U.K. **47** F8
Ballyshannon Rep. of Ireland **47** D9
Balmaceda *Aisén* Chile **205** C7
Balmaceda *Antofagasta* Chile **200** C6
Balmaseda Spain **55** H1
also spelt Valmaseda
Balmazújváros Hungary **49** S8
Balmer India *see* Barmer
Balmertown Canada **167** M5
Balmoral Australia **146** D4
Balmoral N.Z. **153** G10
Balnearia Arg. **204** E3
Baloa Indon. **75** B3
Balochistan *prov.* Pak. **101** F4
formerly spelt Baluchistan
Balod India **94** D1
Baloda India **97** D5
Baloda Bazar India **97** D5
Balok, Teluk *b.* Indon. **77** D3
Balombo Angola **127** B8
formerly known as Norton de Matos
Balonne *r.* Australia **147** F2
Balotra India **96** B4
Balpahari Reservoir India **97** E4
Balpyk Bi Kazakh. **103** I3
formerly known as Kirov *or* Kirovskiy
Balqash Kazakh. *see* Balkhash
Balqash *l.* Kazakh. *see* Balkhash, Lake
Balrampur India **97** D4
Balranald Australia **147** D3
Balş Romania **58** F4
Balsam Creek Canada **173** N4
Balsam Lake *l.* Canada **173** O6
Balsam Lake *l.* U.S.A. **172** A5
Balsapuerto Peru **198** B6
Balsareny Spain **55** M3
Balsas Brazil **202** C3
Balsas *r.* Mex. **185** E5
Balsas, Rio das *r.* Brazil **202** C3
Bal'shavik Belarus **43** L9
Bålsta Sweden **45** L4
Balta Ukr. **41** D7
Baltasi Rus. Fed. **40** I4
Baltasound U.K. **46** L3
Baltay Rus. Fed. **102** A1
Bălți Moldova **41** C7
formerly spelt Bel'ts' *or* Bel'tsy
Baltic Sea *g.* Europe **45** L5
Baltim Egypt **121** F2
Baltimore Rep. of Ireland **47** C12
Baltimore *MD* U.S.A. **177** I6
Baltimore *OH* U.S.A. **176** C6
Baltinava Latvia **42** I5
Baltinglass Rep. of Ireland **47** F11
Baltistan *reg.* Jammu and Kashmir **96** B2
Baltiysk Rus. Fed. **42** A7
historically known as Pillau
Baltoji Vokė Lith. **42** G7
Baltoro Glacier Jammu and Kashmir **96** C2
Baluarte Brazil **202** B4
Baluch Ab *well* Iran **100** D4
Balūchestān va Sīstān *prov.* Iran **101** E5
Baluchistan *reg.* Pak. *see* Balochistan
Balui *r.* Sarawak Malaysia **77** F2
Balumath India **97** E4
Balumbah Australia **146** C3
Balumundam Indon. **76** B2
Balupe *r.* Latvia **42** I5
Baluran, Gunung *mt.* Indon. **77** F3
Baluran National Park Indon. **77** F3
Balurghat India **97** F4
Balut *i.* Indon. **74** C5
Balvatnet *l.* Norway **44** K2
Balvi Latvia **42** I4
Balya Turkey **106** A3
Balyaga Rus. Fed. **85** F1
Balykchy Kyrg. **103** I4
formerly known as Issyk-Kul' *or* Ysyk-Köl *or*
Rybach'ye
Balykshi Kazakh. **102** B3
also spelt Balyasby
Balyktyg-Khem *r.* Rus. Fed. **84** C1
Balyqshy Kazakh. *see* Balykshi
Balzar Ecuador **198** B5
Bam Iran **100** D4
Bâm Iran **100** D2
Bama China **87** D4
Bama Nigeria **125** I4
Bamaga Australia **149** D1
Bamaji Lake Canada **168** B3
▶ **Bamako** Mali **124** C3
Capital of Mali.

Bamba *r.* Cent. Afr. Rep. **126** C3
Bamba Dem. Rep. Congo **127** C6
Bamba Mali **125** E2
Bambang Phil. **74** B2
Bambandand Angola **127** D9
Bambannan *i.* Phil. **74** B5
Bambari Cent. Afr. Rep. **126** D3
Bamberg Germany **48** H6
Bamberg U.S.A. **175** D5
Bambey Senegal **124** A3
Bambili Dem. Rep. Congo **126** E4
Bambio Cent. Afr. Rep. **126** B4
Bamboesberg *mts* S. Africa **133** K8
Bamboi Ghana **125** E4
Bamboo Creek Australia **150** C4
Bamboo *well* Mali **125** E2
Bambouk *reg.* Mali **124** C3
Bambouti Cent. Afr. Rep. **126** F3
Bambuí Brazil **203** C7
Bamda China **86** A2
Bamdezh Iran **100** B4
Bamenda Cameroon **125** H5
Bamendjing, Lac de *l.* Cameroon **125** H5
Bamfield Canada **166** E5

Bami Turkm. **102** D5
also spelt Bamy
Bāmiān Afgh. **101** F3
Bāmiān *prov.* Afgh. **101** F3
Bamiancheng China **85** J3
Bamiantong China *see* Muling
Bamingui Cent. Afr. Rep. **126** D3
Bamingui *r.* Cent. Afr. Rep. **126** C3
Bamingui-Bangoran *pref.* Cent. Afr. Rep.
126 D2
Bamingui-Bangoran, Parc National du
nat. park Cent. Afr. Rep. **126** C2
Bamiyan *r.* Afgh. **101** G3
Bammo *well* Niger **125** H3
Bamoa Mex. **184** C3
Bamor India **96** C4
Bam Posht *reg.* Iran **101** E5
Bam Posht, Küh-e *mts* Iran **101** E5
Bampūr Iran **101** E5
Bampūr *watercourse* Iran **101** D5
Bamy Turkm. *see* Bami
Bamyili Australia **148** B2
also known as Barunga
Ban Burkina **124** E3
Bana, Wādī *watercourse* Yemen **105** D5
Banaba *i.* Kiribati **145** F2
also known as Ocean Island; *also spelt*
Paanopa
Banahao, Mount *vol.* Phil. **74** B3
Banalia Dem. Rep. Congo **126** E4
Banamba Mali **124** D3
Banan China **86** C2
formerly known as Baxian
Banana Australia **149** F5
Bananal, Ilha do *i.* Brazil **202** B4
Banapa India **95** C3
Banapur India **95** E2
Banarlı Turkey **58** I7
Banas *r.* India **96** C4
Banās, Râs *pt* Egypt **121** G4
Banatski Karlovac *Vojvodina, Srbija* Yugo.
58 C3
Banawaya *i.* Indon. **75** A4
Banaz Turkey **106** B3
Banaz *r.* Turkey **59** K10
Banbar China **89** F6
also known as Domartang
Banbridge U.K. **47** F9
Ban Bua Yai Thai. **79** C5
Banbury U.K. **47** K11
Banca Romania **58** I2
Banc d'Arguin, Parc National du *nat. park*
Mauritania **122** A5
Ban Chiang *tourist site* Thai. **78** C4
Banchory U.K. **46** J6
Bancoran *i.* Phil. **74** A5
Bancroft Canada **168** E4
Bancroft Zambia *see* Chililabombwe
Band Iran **100** D3
Banda Dem. Rep. Congo **126** E3
Banda *Madhya Pradesh* India **96** C4
Banda *Uttar Pradesh* India **96** D4
Banda, Kepulauan *is* Indon. **75** D4
Banda Aceh Indon. **76** A1
formerly known as Kutaraja
Banda Banda, Mount Australia **147** G2
Bandahara, Gunung *mt.* Indon. **76** B2
Bandai-Asahi National Park Japan **90** F6
Bandama *r.* Côte d'Ivoire **124** D4
Bandama Blanc *r.* Côte d'Ivoire **124** D4
Bandān Iran **101** E4
Bandaneira Indon. **75** D4
Bandān Küh *mts* Iran **101** E4
Bandar India *see* Machilipatnam
Bandar Abbas Iran *see* Bandar-e 'Abbās
Bandaragung Indon. **76** D4
Bandar-e 'Abbās Iran **100** D5
English form Bandar Abbas; *historically*
known as Gombroon
Bandar-e Anzalī Iran **100** B2
formerly known as Bandar-e Pahlavī
Bandar-e Chārak Iran **100** D5
Bandar-e Deylam Iran **100** B4
Bandar-e Emām Khomeynī Iran **100** B4
formerly known as Bandar-e Shāhpūr
Bandar-e Lengeh Iran **100** C5
Bandar-e Maqām Iran **100** C5
Bandar-e Mashur Iran **100** B4
Bandar-e Moghūyeh Iran **100** C5
Bandar-e Pahlavī Iran *see* Bandar-e Anzalī
Bandar-e Rīg Iran **100** B4
Bandar-e Shāh Iran *see*
Bandar-e Torkeman
Bandar-e Shāhpūr Iran *see*
Bandar-e Emām Khomeynī
Bandar-e Torkeman Iran **100** C2
formerly known as Bandar-e Shāh
Bandar Lampung Indon. *see*
Tanjungkarang-Telukbetung
Bandar Murcaayo Somalia **128** F2
Bandarpunch *mt.* India **96** C3
▶ **Bandar Seri Begawan** Brunei **77** F1
Capital of Brunei. Formerly known as
Brunei.

Bandar Wanaag Somalia **128** E2
Banda Sea Indon. **75** D4
Bandeira Brazil **207** M2
Bandeirante Brazil **202** B3
Bandeirantes Brazil **206** C10
Bandeiras, Pico de *mt.* Brazil **203** D7
Bandera Arg. **204** D3
Bandera U.S.A. **179** C6
Banderas Mex. **184** D2
Banderas, Bahía de *b.* Mex. **184** D4
Bandhi Pak. **101** G5
Bandhogarh India **96** D5
Bandi *r.* India **96** B4
Bandiagara Mali **124** E3
Bandiagara, Falaise de *esc.* Mali **124** E3
Band-i-Amir *r.* Afgh. **101** F3
Band-i-Baba *mts* Afgh. **101** E3
Band-i-Husain Num *mts* Iran **100** C3
Bandikui India **96** C4
Bandikui Iran **101** D5
Bandipur Jammu and Kashmir **96** B2
Bandipur Nepal **97** D4
Bandipur National Park India **94** C4
Bandırma Turkey **106** A2
Band-i-Turkestan *mts* Afgh. **101** E3
Bandjarmasin Indon. *see* Banjarmasin
Bandjer *pass* Yugo. **58** A5
Bandon Rep. of Ireland **47** D12
Bandon *r.* Rep. of Ireland **47** D12
Ban Don Thai. *see* Surat Thani
Bandon U.S.A. **180** A4
Ban Don, Ao *b.* Thai. **79** B6
Band Qīr Iran **100** B4
Bandra India **94** B2
Bandua Moz. **131** G3
Bandula Moz. **131** G3
Bandundu Dem. Rep. Congo **126** C5
formerly known as Banningville
Bandundu *prov.* Dem. Rep. Congo **126** C5
Bandung Indon. **77** D4
Bandya Australia **151** C6
Băneasa Romania **58** H4
Banemo Indon. **75** D2
Banera India **96** B4

Banes Cuba **186** E2
Banff Canada **167** H5
Banff National Park Canada **167** G5
Banfora Burkina **124** D4
Bang Cent. Afr. Rep. **126** B3
Banga Angola **127** B7
Banga Dem. Rep. Congo **126** D5
Banga *r.* Phil. **74** C5
Bangai Point Phil. **74** C5
Bangalore India **94** C3
Banganapalle India **94** C3
Banganga *r.* India **96** C4
Bangangté Cameroon **125** H5
Bangaon India **97** F5
Bangar Brunei **77** F1
Bangar Phil. **74** B2
Bangara *r.* Angola **127** C9
Bangarapet India **94** C3
Bangassou Cent. Afr. Rep. **126** D3
Bangdag Co *salt l.* China **89** C5
Bangfai, Xé *r.* Laos **78** D4
Banggi Indon. **77** F4
Banggai *i.* Indon. **75** B3
Banggai, Kepulauan *is* Indon. **75** B3
Banggi *i.* Sabah Malaysia *see* Banghazi
Banghiang, Xé *r.* Laos **78** D4
Bangil Indon. **77** F4
Bangka *i.* Indon. **75** C2
Bangka *i.* Indon. **77** D3
Bangka, Selat *sea chan.* Indon. **77** D3
Bangkala, Teluk *b.* Indon. **75** A4
Bangkalan Indon. **77** F4
Bangkaru *i.* Indon. **76** B2
Bangkinang Indon. **76** C2
Bangkir Indon. **75** B2
Bangko Indon. **76** C3
Bangko Co *salt l.* China **89** E6
▶ **Bangkok** Thai. **79** C5
Capital of Thailand. Also known as Krung
Thep.

Bangkok, Bight of *b.* Thai. **79** C5
Bangkor China **89** D6
Bangkulu *i.* Indon. **75** B3
Bangla *state* India *see* West Bengal
▶ **Bangladesh** *country* Asia **97** F4
8th most populous country in the world.
Formerly known as East Bengal or East
Pakistan.
world [population] ➤➤➤ 22–23
asia [countries] ➤➤➤ 64–67

Bangma Shan China **86** A4
Bang Mun Nak Thai. **78** C4
Bàngnàs Sweden **44** K2
Bangolo Côte d'Ivoire **124** D5
Bangong Co *salt l.*
China/Jammu and Kashmir **89** B5
also spelt Pangong Tso
Bangor *Gwynedd, Wales* U.K. **47** H10
Bangor *Northern Ireland* U.K. **47** G9
Bangor *ME* U.S.A. **177** Q1
Bangor *MI* U.S.A. **172** G8
Bangor *PA* U.S.A. **177** J5
Bangriposi India **97** E5
Bangs, Embalse del *resr* Spain *see*
Vao, Embalse de
Bao'an China *see* Shenzhen
Bao'an China **84** D5
Baochang China *see* Taibus Qi
Baocheng China **85** G5
also known as Guozhen
Baoding China **85** G4
Baofeng China **87** E1
Baoji *Shaanxi* China **86** C1
Baoji *Shaanxi* China **87** D1
also known as Guozhen
Baokang *Hubei* China **87** D2
also known as Horqin Zuoyi Zhongqi
Baokang *Nei Mongol* China **85** I2
Baoqing China **82** D3
Baoro Cent. Afr. Rep. **126** B3
Baoshan *Shanghai* China **87** G2
Baoshan *Yunnan* China **86** A3
Baotou China **85** F3
Baoulé *r.* Mali **124** C3
Baoulé *r.* Mali **124** C3
Baoxing China **86** B2
Baoxiu China **86** B3
Baoying China **87** F1
Baoyou China *see* Ledong
Bap India **96** B4
Bapatla India **94** D3
Bapaume France **51** I2
Baptiste Lake Canada **173** O5
Bapu China *see* Meigu
Baqar, Bahr el *canal* Egypt **108** D6
Baqên *Xizang* China **89** F5
also known as Dartang
Baqên *Xizang* China **89** F5
also known as Yêtatang
Baqiu China *see* Le'an
Baqrān Saudi Arabia **104** C3
Baqty Kazakh. *see* Bakhty
Ba'qūbah Iraq **107** F4
Bar *Crna Gora* Yugo. **58** A4
Bara Nigeria **125** H4
Bara Sudan **121** F6
Bara *well* Sudan **128** C4
Baraawe Somalia **128** E4
Barabai Indon. **77** F3
Bara Banki India **96** D4
Barabanovo Rus. Fed. **43** T7
Barabash Rus. Fed. **90** B3
Barabhum India **97** E5
Barabinsk Rus. Fed. **80** B1
Baraboo U.S.A. **172** D7
Baraboo *r.* U.S.A. **172** C7
Baraboy *r.* Ukr. **58** L2
Baracoa Spain *see* Barakaldo
Baracoa Cuba **187** E2
Baradá, Nahr *r.* Syria **108** H4
Baradero Arg. **204** F4
Baradine *r.* Australia **147** F2
Baraga U.S.A. **172** E4
Baragoi Kenya **128** C4
Baragua, Sierra de *mts* Venez. **198** D2
Barahona Dom. Rep. **187** F3
Barail Range *mts* India **97** G4
Bara Issa *r.* Mali **124** E2
Barajevo *Srbija* Yugo. **58** B4
Barak Afgh. **101** G2
Barak *r.* India **97** G4
Baraka *watercourse* Eritrea/Sudan **121** H5
Barakaldo Spain **55** I1
also spelt Baracaldo
Baraki Baraki Afgh. **101** G3
Barakke S. Africa **133** I9
Barakot India **97** E5
Barakovo Rus. Fed. **43** U7
Barakpay Kazakh. **103** F1
also spelt Baraqbay
Baralaba Australia **149** F5
Bara Lacha Pass India **96** C2
Baram *r.* Sarawak Malaysia **77** F1
Baram, Tanjong *pt* Sarawak Malaysia **77** F1

Baramanni Guyana **199** G3
Baramati India **94** B2
Barambah *r.* Australia **149** F5
Barameiya Sudan **121** H5
Baramula Jammu and Kashmir **96** B2
Baran Belarus **43** L7
Baran India **96** C4
Baran *r.* Pak. **101** G5
Bārān, Küh-e *mts* Iran **101** E3
Baranavichy Belarus **42** H8
formerly known as Baranovichi; *formerly spelt*
Baranowicze
Barang, Dasht-i *des.* Afgh. **101** E3
Baranikha Rus. Fed. **39** Q3
Baranivka Ukr. **41** C6
Baranoa Col. **187** E5
Baranof Island U.S.A. **164** F4
Baranovichi Belarus *see* Baranavichy
Baranowicze Belarus *see* Baranavichy
Barão de Cocais Brazil **207** J6
Barão de Grajaú Brazil **202** D3
Barão de Melgaço Brazil **201** G4
Barão de Melgaço Brazil **201** E3
Baraolt Romania **58** G2
Baraqbay Kazakh. *see* Barakpay
Baraquville Serra *mts* Brazil **199** F4
Baraúna Brazil **202** E3
Barauna, Serra *mts* Brazil **199** F4
Baraut India **96** C3
Baraya Col. **198** C4
Barbacena *Minas Gerais* Brazil **203** D7
Barbacena *Pará* Brazil **199** H5
▶ **Barbados** *country* West Indies **187** I4
northamerica [countries] ➤➤➤ 158–159
Barbar, Gebel *el mt.* Egypt **108** E9
Barbara Lake Canada **168** C3
Barbaria, Cap de *c.* Spain **55** M6
Barbaros Turkey **58** I8
Barbastro Spain **55** L2
Barbate de Franco Spain **54** F8
Bärbele Latvia **42** F5
Barber's Bay Canada **173** M2
Barberspan Nature Reserve S. Africa
133 J3
Barberton S. Africa **133** O2
Barberton U.S.A. **176** D4
Barbezieux-St-Hilaire France **50** F7
Barbigha India **97** E4
Barbil India **97** E5
Barbosa Col. **198** D3
Barbour Bay Canada **167** M2
Barbours U.S.A. **177** I4
Barbourville U.S.A. **176** B9
Barboza Phil. **74** B4
Barbuda *i.* Antigua and Barbuda **187** H3
Bârca Romania **58** E5
Barcaldine Australia **149** E4
Barcău *r.* Romania **58** C1
Barce Libya *see* Al Marj
Barcelona Spain **55** N3
historically known as Barcino
Barcelona Venez. **199** E2
Barcelonnette France **51** M8
Barcelos Brazil **199** F5
Barcin Poland **49** O3
Barcino Spain *see* Barcelona
Barclay de Tolly *atoll* Fr. Polynesia *see*
Raroia
Barclayville Liberia **124** C5
Barcoo *watercourse* Australia **149** D5
Barcoo Creek *watercourse* Australia *see*
Cooper Creek
Barcoo National Park Australia *see*
Welford National Park
Barcs Hungary **56** J3
Barczewo Poland **49** R2
Bärdä Azer. **107** F2
Barda Rus. Fed. **40** J4
Bardaale Somalia **128** E3
Bárðarbunga *mt.* Iceland **44** [inset] C2
Bardas Blancas Arg. **204** C4
Bardaskan Iran **100** D3
Bardawil, Khabrat al *salt pan* Saudi Arabia
109 J6
Bardawil, Sabkhet el *lag.* Egypt **108** E6
Barddhaman India **97** E5
formerly spelt Burdwan
Bardejov Slovakia **49** S6
Bardera Somalia *see* Baardheere
Bardsey Island U.K. **47** H11
Bard Shah Iran **100** D3
Bardsir Iran **100** D4
Barðsneshorn *pt* Iceland **165** R3
Bardstown U.S.A. **174** C4
Barduli Italy *see* Barletta
Bardwell U.S.A. **174** C4
Barē Eth. **128** D3
Bareilly India **96** C3
Bareli India **96** C4
Barengapara India **97** F4
Barentin France **50** G3
Barenton France **50** F4
Barentsburg Svalbard **38** J2
Barents Island Svalbard *see* Barentsøya
Barentsøya *i.* Svalbard **38** C2
English form Barents Island
Barents Sea Arctic Ocean **38** G2
Barentu Eritrea **121** H6
Bareo Sarawak Malaysia **77** F1
Barfleur, Pointe de *pt* France **50** E3
Barga China **89** C6
Barga Italy **56** C3
Bargaal Somalia **128** F2
Bārgāh Iran **100** D5
Bargara Australia **149** G5
Bargē Eth. **128** C3
Barge Italy **51** N8
Bargi India **96** C4
Bargıri Turkey *see* Muradiye
Bargteheide Germany **48** H2
Barguna Bangl. **97** F5
Bargur India **94** C3
Barh India **97** E4
Barhaj India **97** D4
Barhalganj India **97** D4
Bar Harbor U.S.A. **177** Q1
Barharwa India **97** F4
Bari Dem. Rep. Congo **126** C4
Bari Italy **56** J7
historically known as Barium
Bari *admin. reg.* Somalia **128** E2
Ba Ria Vietnam **79** D6
Baridi, Ra's *hd* Saudi Arabia **104** B2
Bari Doab *lowland* Pak. **101** H4
Barik Oman **105** G3
Barika Alg. **123** G2
Barikot Afgh. **101** H3
Barikot Nepal **97** D3
Barim *i.* Yemen **104** C5
English form Perim Island
Barima *r.* Guyana **199** G2
Barima *r.* Venez. **187** H5
Barinas Venez. **198** D2
Barinas *state* Venez. **198** D2
Baringa Dem. Rep. Congo **126** D4
Baringo, Lake Kenya **128** C4
Baripada India **97** E5
Bariri Brazil **206** E9
Bari Sadri India **96** B4
Barisal Bangl. **97** F5
Barisal *admin. div.* Bangl. **97** F5
Barisan, Pegunungan *mts* Indon. **76** C3
Barito *r.* Indon. **77** F3
Barituú, Parque Nacional *nat. park* Arg.
201 D5
Barium Italy *see* Bari

Barjaude, Montagne de *mt.* France 51 M9
Barjols France 51 M9
Barjora India 97 E5
Barjúj, Wādī *watercourse* Libya 120 B3
Barka *r.* Eritrea 104 B4
Barkam China 84 B3
Barkan, Ra's-e *pt* Iran 100 B4
Barkava Latvia 42 G5
Barker, Lake *salt flat* Australia 151 C6
Barkerville Canada 166 F4
Barkéwol el Abiod Mauritania 124 B2
Barkham Pak. 101 G4
Barki Saraiya India 97 E4
Barkley, Lake U.S.A. 174 C4
Barkley Sound *inlet* Canada 166 E5
Barkly East S. Africa 133 L7
Barkly Pass S. Africa 133 L8
Barkly Tableland *reg.* Australia 148 B3
Barkly West S. Africa 133 I5
Barkol China 84 B3
Barkol Hu *salt l.* China 84 B3
Barkot India 96 C3
Bârlad Romania 58 I2
formerly spelt Bîrlad
Barlag Gol *watercourse* Mongolia 84 B2
Bar-le-Duc France 51 L4
Barlee, Lake *salt flat* Australia 151 B6
Barlee Range *hills* Australia 150 A4
Barlee Range Nature Reserve Australia 150 A4
Barletta Italy 56 I7
historically known as Barduli
Barlinek Poland 49 M3
Barlow Canada 166 B2
Barlow Lake Canada 167 K2
Barmedman Australia 147 E3
Barmen-Elberfeld Germany *see* Wuppertal
Barmer India 96 A4
also spelt Balmer
Barmera Australia 146 D3
Barm Fīrūz, Kūh-e *mt.* Iran 107 G3
Barmouth U.K. 47 H11
also known as Abermaw
Barmstedt Germany 48 G2
Barnagar India 96 B5
Barnala India 96 B3
Barnard, Mount Canada/U.S.A. 166 B3
Barnard Castle U.K. 47 K9
Barnato Australia 147 D3
Barnaul Rus. Fed. 80 C2
Barnegat U.S.A. 177 K6
Barnegat Bay U.S.A. 177 K6
Barnes Icecap Canada 165 L2
Barnesboro U.S.A. 176 F5
Barnesville *GA* U.S.A. 175 D5
Barnesville *MN* U.S.A. 178 C2
Barnet U.S.A. 177 M1
Barneveld Neth. 48 C3
Barney Top *mt.* U.S.A. 183 M4
Barnhart U.S.A. 179 B6
Barnjarm Aboriginal Land *res.* Australia 148 B2
Bârnova, Dealul *hill* Romania 58 I1
Barnsdall U.S.A. 178 C4
Barnsley U.K. 47 K10
Barnstable U.S.A. 177 O4
Barnstaple U.K. 47 H12
Barnstaple Bay U.K. *see* Bideford Bay
Barnwell U.S.A. 175 D5
Baro Nigeria 125 G4
Baroda India *see* Vadodara
Baroda India 96 C4
Baroda S. Africa 133 J8
Baroe S. Africa 133 I10
Baroghil Pass Afgh. 101 H2
Barong China 86 A2
Baron'ki Belarus 43 N8
Barons Range *hills* Australia 150 D5
Baroua Cent. Afr. Rep. 126 E3
Baro Wenz *r.* Eth. 128 B2
Barowka Belarus *r.* 42 H8
Barpeta India 97 F4
Bar Pla Soi Thai. *see* Chon Buri
Barqa, Gebel *hill* Egypt 108 F9
Barqā al Ashqar *reg.* Yemen 105 D4
Barqā 'Damaj *well* Saudi Arabia 109 H9
Barques, Point Aux U.S.A. 173 K6
Barquisimeto Venez. 198 D2
Barra *i.* Brazil 202 D4
Barra *i.* U.K. 46 E7
also spelt Barraigh
Barraba Australia 147 F2
Barra Bonita Brazil 206 E9
Barra Bonita, Represa *resr* Brazil 206 E9
Barração do Barreto Brazil 207 J4
Barrackville U.S.A. 176 E6
Barracouta, Cape S. Africa 132 F11
Barra da Estiva Brazil 202 D5
Barra de Navidad Mex. 184 D5
Barra de Santos *inlet* Brazil 206 G11
Barra de São João Brazil 207 L9
Barra do Bugres Brazil 201 F3
Barra do Corda Brazil 202 C3
Barra do Cuanza Angola 127 B7
Barra do Cuieté Brazil 207 L6
Barra do Garças Brazil 206 A2
Barrado Mendes Brazil 202 C4
Barra do Piraí Brazil 207 J9
Barra do Rocha Brazil 207 M1
Barra do São Manuel Brazil 201 F1
Barra do Una Brazil 206 F11
Barra Falsa, Ponta da *pt* Moz. 131 G4
Barraigh *i.* U.K. *see* Barra
Barra Kruta Hond. 186 C4
Barra Longa Brazil 207 J7
Barra Mansa Brazil 207 I9
Barrāmīya Egypt 121 G3
Barranca Peru 200 A2
Barranca Venez. 198 C2
Barrancabermeja Col. 198 C3
Barranca del Cobre, Parque Natural *nature res.* Mex. 184 D3
Barrancas *r.* Arg. 204 C5
Barrancas *Barinas* Venez. 198 D2
Barrancas *Monagas* Venez. 199 F2
Barranco de Loba Col. 198 C2
Barranqueras Arg. 204 F3
Barranquilla *Atlántico* Col. 198 C2
Barranquilla *Guaviare* Col. 198 C4
Barranquita Peru 198 B6
Barras Brazil 202 D3
Barraute Canada 173 P2
Barrax Spain 55 I5
Barre *MA* U.S.A. 177 M3
Barre *VT* U.S.A. 177 M1
Barre des Écrins *mt.* France 51 M8
Barreiras Brazil 202 C5
Barreirinha Brazil 199 G5
Barreiro *r.* Brazil 206 A2
Barreiro do Nascimento Brazil 202 B4
Barren Island India 95 G3
Barren Islands U.S.A. 164 D4
Barretos Brazil 206 E7
Barrett U.S.A. 183 H9
Barret, Mount *hill* Australia 147 H4
Barrhead Canada 167 H4
Barrhill N.Z. 153 F11
Barrie Canada 168 E4
Barrier Island Canada 173 K5
Barrier, Cape N.Z. 152 J4
Barrier Bay Antarctica 223 F2

Barrière Canada 166 F5
Barrier Range *hills* Australia 146 D2
Barrier Reef Belize 185 I5
Barrington S. Africa 132 G10
Barrington, Mount Australia 147 F3
Barrington Tops National Park Australia 147 F3
Barro Alto Brazil 206 E2
Barrocão Brazil 207 J3
Barrolândia Brazil 207 N3
Barron *r.* U.S.A. 172 C5
Barronett U.S.A. 172 B5
Barroso Brazil 207 I9
Barrow *r.* Rep. of Ireland 47 F11
Barrow U.S.A. 164 D2
Barrow, Point U.S.A. 164 D2
Barrow Creek Australia 148 B3
Barrow-in-Furness U.K. 47 I9
Barrow Island Australia 150 A4
Barrow Island Nature Reserve Australia 150 A4
Barrow Range *hills* Australia 151 D5
Barrow Strait Canada 165 J2
Barr Smith Range *hills* Australia 151 C5
Barry U.K. 47 I12
Barrydale S. Africa 132 E10
Barry Islands Canada 167 I1
Barry Mountains Australia 147 E4
Barrys Bay Canada 168 E4
Barryton U.S.A. 173 H7
Barryville N.Z. 152 J6
Barryville U.S.A. 177 K4
Barsakel'mes, Ostrov *i.* Kazakh. 102 D3
Barsakel'messkiy Zapovednik *nature res.* Kazakh. 102 E3
Barsalogo Burkina 125 E3
Barsalpur India 96 B3
Barshatas Kazakh. 103 I2
Barshi India *see* Barsi
Barstow U.S.A. 182 G7
Barstyčiai Lith. 42 C5
Barsuki Rus. Fed. 43 S7
Barsur India 94 D2
Bar-sur-Aube France 51 K4
Bar-sur-Seine France 51 K4
Bārta Latvia 42 C5
Bārta *r.* Latvia 42 C5
Bartang *r.* Tajik. 101 G2
Barth Germany 49 J1
Bartholomew, Bayou *r.* U.S.A. 175 A5
Bartica Guyana 199 G3
Bartın Turkey 106 C2
Bartle Frere, Mount Australia 149 E3
Bartles, Mount U.S.A. 176 C7
Bartles, Mount U.S.A. 183 N2
Bartlesville U.S.A. 178 C4
Bartlett *NH* U.S.A. 177 N1
Bartlett *NE* U.S.A. 178 C3
Bartlett Lake Canada 167 G2
Bartlett Reservoir U.S.A. 183 M8
Bartletts N.Z. 152 L6
Barton U.S.A. 177 M1
Bartonville U.S.A. 172 D10
Bartoszyce Poland 49 R1
Bartow U.S.A. 175 D7
Bartuva *r.* Lith. 42 C5
Baru, Isla de *i.* Col. 198 C2
Baruipur India 97 F5
Barūm Yemen 105 E5
Barumun *r.* Indon. 76 C2
Barung *i.* Indon. 76 E3
Barunga Australia *see* Bamyili
Barun-Torey, Ozero *l.* Rus. Fed. 85 G1
Barus Indon. 76 B2
Baruunharaa Mongolia 85 E2
Baruunsuu Mongolia 85 E3
Baruunturuun Mongolia 84 B1
Baruun Urt Mongolia 85 G2
Baruva India 95 E2
Barwa India 97 E5
Barwah India 96 C5
Barwala *Gujarat* India 96 A5
Barwala *Haryana* India 96 B3
Barwāni India 96 B5
Barwice Poland 49 N2
Barwon *r.* Australia 147 E2
Baryatino Rus. Fed. 43 P7
Barybino Rus. Fed. 43 S6
Barycz *r.* Poland 49 N4
Barygaza India *see* Bharuch
Barysaw Belarus 43 J7
also spelt Borisov
Barysh Rus. Fed. 41 H5
Basaga Turkm. 101 F2
formerly spelt Bossaga
Bāsa'īdū Iran 100 C5
Basail Arg. 204 F2
Basak, Tônlé *r.* Cambodia 79 D6
Basalt *i.* Australia 149 E3
Basalt Island *Hong Kong* China 87 [inset]
also known as Fo Shek Chau
Basanga Dem. Rep. Congo 126 E6
Basankusu Dem. Rep. Congo 126 C4
Basantpur India 97 E4
Basarabeasca Moldova 58 J2
formerly known as Romanovka; *formerly spelt* Bessarabka
Basarabi Romania 58 J4
Basargechar Armenia *see* Vardenis
Basavilbaso Arg. 204 F4
Basay Phil. 74 B4
Basco Phil. 74 B1
Bascombe Well Conservation Park *nature res.* Australia 146 B3
Bas-Congo *prov.* Dem. Rep. Congo 126 B7
formerly known as Bas-Zaïre
Bascuñán, Cabo *c.* Chile 204 C3
Bascuñana, Sierra de *mts* Spain 55 I4
Basedow Range *hills* Australia 150 D5
Basel Switz. 51 N5
English form Basle; *also spelt* Bâle
Basel-Mulhouse *airport* France 51 N5
Basentello *r.* Italy 56 I8
Basento *r.* Italy 57 I8
Basey Phil. 74 C4
Bashākerd, Kūhhā-ye *mts* Iran 100 D5
Bashan China *see* Chongren
Bashanta Rus. Fed. *see* Gorodovikovsk
Bashaw Canada 167 H4
Bashee *r.* S. Africa 133 M8
Bashee Bridge S. Africa 133 M8
Bashgul *r.* Afgh. 101 H3
Bāshī Iran 100 B4
Bashi Channel Taiwan 73 F2
Bashimuke Dem. Rep. Congo 127 D6
Ba'shiqah, Jabal *hill* Iraq 109 O1
Bashkaus *r.* Rus. Fed. 88 D1
Bashkiria *aut. rep.* Rus. Fed. *see* Bashkortostan, Respublika
Bashkirskaya A.S.S.R. *aut. rep.* Rus. Fed. *see* Bashkortostan, Respublika
Bashkirskiy Zapovednik *nature res.* Rus. Fed. 102 D1
Bashkortostan, Respublika *aut. rep.* Rus. Fed. 102 D1
formerly known as Bashkiria *or* Bashkirskaya A.S.S.R.
Bashmakovo Rus. Fed. 41 G5
Bāsht Iran 100 B4
Bashtanka Ukr. 41 E7
Bāshūri, Ra's *pt* Yemen 105 F5
Basi India 96 B3
Basia India 97 E5
Basilaki Island P.N.G. 149 F1

Basilan *i.* Phil. 74 B5
Basilan Strait Phil. 74 B5
Basildon U.K. 47 M12
Basile U.S.A. 179 D6
Basile, Pico *mt.* Equat. Guinea 125 H6
Basilicata *admin. reg.* Italy 57 H8
Basin U.S.A. 180 E3
Basingstoke U.K. 47 K12
Basin Lake Canada 167 J4
Bāsira *r.* Iraq 107 F5
Basirhat India 97 F5
Basīt, Ra's al *pt* Syria 108 G2
Baskahegan Lake U.S.A. 174 H2
Başkale Turkey 107 F3
Baskatong, Réservoir Canada 168 F4
Baskerville, Cape Australia 150 C3
Başkomutan Milli Parkı *nat. park* Turkey 106 B3
Baskunchak, Ozero *l.* Rus. Fed. 102 A2
Basle Switz. *see* Basel
Basmat India 94 C2
Baso *i.* Indon. 76 C3
Basoda India 96 C5
Basoko Dem. Rep. Congo 126 D4
Basongo Dem. Rep. Congo 126 D6
Basotu Tanz. 129 B6
Basque Country *aut. comm.* Spain *see* País Vasco
Basra Iraq 107 F5
also spelt Al Başrah
Bassano del Grappa Italy 56 D3
Bassano Canada 167 H5
Bassar Togo 125 F4
Bassas da India *reef* Indian Ocean 131 H4
Bassas de Pedro Padua Bank *sea feature* India 94 A3
Bassein Myanmar 78 A4
also spelt Pathein; *formerly spelt* Pathein
Bassein *r.* Myanmar 78 A4
Basse-Kotto Cent. Afr. Rep. 126 D3
Basse-Normandie *admin. reg.* France 50 F3
Basse Santa Su Gambia 124 B3
Basse-Terre Guadeloupe 187 H3
Capital of Guadeloupe.
Basse-Terre *i.* Guadeloupe 187 H3
Basseterre St Kitts and Nevis 187 H3
Capital of St Kitts and Nevis.
Bassett *NE* U.S.A. 178 C3
Bassett *VA* U.S.A. 176 F9
Bassett Peak U.S.A. 183 N9
Bassikounou Mauritania 124 C3
Bassila Benin 125 F4
Basso, Plateau de Chad 120 D5
Bass Strait Australia 147 E4
Basswood Lake Canada 168 B3
Basswood Lake U.S.A. 172 B2
Båstad Sweden 45 K4
Bastak Iran 100 C5
Bāstānābād Iran 100 A2
Basti India 97 D4
Bastia *Corse* France 51 P10
Bastia Italy 56 E5
Bastian U.S.A. 176 D8
Bastogne Belgium 51 L3
Bastos Brazil 206 C8
Bastrop *LA* U.S.A. 175 B5
Bastrop *TX* U.S.A. 179 C6
Basturträsk Sweden 44 M2
Basu, Tanjung *pt* Indon. 76 C3
Basul *r.* Pak. 101 F5
Basuo China *see* Dongfang
Basya *r.* Belarus 43 M8
Bas-Zaïre *prov.* Dem. Rep. Congo *see* Bas-Congo
Bat *r.* Croatia 56 I5
Bat, Al-Khutm and Al-Ayn *tourist site* Oman 105 G3
Bata Equat. Guinea 125 H6
Bataan Peninsula Phil. 74 B3
Batabanó, Golfo de *b.* Cuba 186 C2
Batac Phil. 74 B2
Batagay Rus. Fed. 39 N3
Batagay-Alyta Rus. Fed. 39 N3
Bataguaçu Brazil 206 A8
Batak Bulg. 58 F7
Batakan Indon. 77 F4
Batala India 96 B3
Batalha Brazil 202 E3
Batalha Port. 54 C5
formerly known as Belo Monte
Batam *i.* Indon. 76 C2
Batama Dem. Rep. Congo 126 E4
Batamay Rus. Fed. 39 M3
Batamshinskiy Kazakh. 102 D2
also known as Batamshy
Batamshy Kazakh. *see* Batamshinskiy
Batan *i.* Phil. 74 B1
Batan *i.* Phil. 74 B3
Batang China 86 A2
also known as Xiaqiong
Batangafo Cent. Afr. Rep. 126 C3
Batangas Phil. 74 B3
Batanghari *r.* Indon. 76 D3
Batangkehe *i.* Indon. 76 B2
Batangtoru Indon. 76 B2
Batan Islands Phil. 74 B1
Bataszék Hungary 49 P9
Batavia *r.* Brazil 206 E7
Batavia Indon. *see* Jakarta
Batavia *NY* U.S.A. 176 G3
Batavia *OH* U.S.A. 176 A6
Bataysk Rus. Fed. 41 F7
Batbatan *i.* Phil. 74 B4
Batchawana Canada 173 I3
Batchawana Bay Canada 173 I4
Batchawana Mountain *hill* Canada 168 C4
Batdâmbâng Cambodia 79 C5
also spelt Battambang
Bateemeucica, Gunung *mt.* Indon. 76 A1
Batéké, Plateaux Congo 126 B5
Batemans Bay Australia 147 F3
Batemburg U.S.A. 175 D5
Bates Range *hills* Australia 151 C5
Batesville *AR* U.S.A. 174 B5
Batesville *MS* U.S.A. 174 B5
Batetskiy Rus. Fed. 43 L3
Bath *N.B.* Canada 169 H4
Bath *Ont.* Canada 173 Q6
Bath U.K. 47 J12
Bath *NY* U.S.A. 177 H3
Bath *PA* U.S.A. 177 J5
Batha *pref.* Chad 120 C6
Batha *watercourse* Chad 120 C6
Bathinda India 96 B3
also spelt Bhatinda
Bathurst Australia 147 F3
Bathurst Canada 169 H4
Bathurst *Gambia see* Banjul
Bathurst S. Africa 133 K10
Bathurst, Cape Canada 164 F2
Bathurst Bay Australia 149 E2
Bathurst Inlet Canada 167 I1
Bathurst Inlet *inlet* Canada 167 I1
Bathurst Island Australia 148 A1
Bathurst Island Canada 165 J2
Batī Eth. 128 D6
Batia Benin 125 F4
Batié Burkina 124 E4

Batikala, Tanjung *pt* Indon. 75 B3
Bāti Menteşe Dağları *mts* Turkey 59 I11
Bāṭin, Wādī al *watercourse* Asia 105 D1
Batista, Serra da Brazil 202 D4
Bati Toroslar *mts* Turkey 106 B3
Bati *r.* Xar Bürd
Bayano, Lago *l.* Panama 186 D5
Bayan-Obo Kuanqçu China 85 F3
Bayan-Ölgiy *prov.* Mongolia 84 A1
Bayan Qagan China 85 F2
also known as Qahar Youyi Houqi
Bayansayr Mongolia 84 D1
Bayan Shan *mt.* China 84 C4
Bayanteeg Mongolia 84 D2
Bayan Tohoi China 85 H1
Bayan Ul Hot China 85 H2
Bayan Uul *mts* Mongolia 84 A1
Bayard *NE* U.S.A. 178 B3
Bayard *WV* U.S.A. 176 F6
Bayat Turkey 106 C3
Baybay Phil. 74 C4
Bay Bulls Canada 169 K4
Bayburt Turkey 107 E2
Baychunas Kazakh. 102 C3
also spelt Bayshonas
Bay City *MI* U.S.A. 173 J7
Bay City *TX* U.S.A. 179 D6
Baydā, Jabal al *mt.* Saudi Arabia 104 B2
Baydaratskaya Guba Rus. Fed. 40 M1
Baydhabo Somalia 128 D4
formerly known as Baidoa
Baydrag *r.* Mongolia 84 C2
Baydrag Gol *r.* Mongolia 84 C2
Bay du Nord Wilderness *nature res.* Canada 169 K3
Baydzhansay Kazakh. *see* Bayzhansay
Bayelsa *state* Nigeria 125 G5
Bayerische Rhön *park* Germany 48 G5
Bayerischer Wald *mts* Germany 49 K6
Bayerischer Wald *nat. park* Germany 49 J6
Bayern *land* Germany 51 J3
English form Bavaria
Bayern *reg.* Germany *see* Bavaria
Bayer Wald, Nationalpark *nat. park* Germany 49 K7
Bayeux France 50 F3
Bayeva Belarus 43 M7
Bayevo Rus. Fed. 103 J1
Bayfield Canada 173 L7
Bayganin Kazakh. 102 C2
formerly known as Karaulkel'dy
Baygora Kazakh. 103 I2
Bayhan al Qişāb Yemen 105 D5
Bayındır Turkey 106 A3
Bayingbike is *Hond. see* La Bahía, Islas de
Bayizhen China 89 F5
Bayji Iraq 107 E4
also known as Baiji
Baykadam Kazakh. *see* Saudakent
Baykal, Ozero *l.* Rus. Fed. *see* Baikal, Lake
Baykal-Amur Magistral Rus. Fed. 82 C1
Baykal Range *mts* Rus. Fed. *see* Baykal'skiy Khrebet
Baykal'skiy Zapovednik *nature res.* Rus. Fed. 85 E1
Baykan Turkey 107 E3
Bay-Khaak Rus. Fed. 84 B1
Bay-Khozha Kazakh. 103 E3
Baykibashevo Rus. Fed. 40 K5
Baykit Rus. Fed. 39 J3
Baykonur Karagandinskaya Oblast' Kazakh. 103 F3
Baykonur Kzyl-Ordinskaya Oblast' Kazakh. 103 E3
also spelt Baykonyr *or* Bayqongyr; *formerly known as* Leninsk *or* Toretam *or* Tyuratam
Baykonyr Kazakh. *see* Baykonur
Bayley Point Aboriginal Reserve Australia 148 C3
Baymak Rus. Fed. 102 D1
Bay Minette U.S.A. 175 C6
Baynūna'h *reg.* U.A.E. 105 E3
Bay of Islands Maritime and Historic Park *nature res.* N.Z. 152 I3
Bay of Plenty *admin. reg.* N.Z. 152 K5
Bayombong Phil. 74 B2
Bayona Spain *see* Baiona
Bayonne France 50 E9
historically known as Lapurdum
Bayonne U.S.A. 177 K5
Bayo Point Phil. 74 B4
Bayóvar Peru 198 A6
Bay Port U.S.A. 173 J7
Bayqadam Kazakh. *see* Saudakent
Bayqongyr Kazakh. *see* Baykonur
Bayramaly Turkm. 103 F5
Bayramic Turkey 106 A3
Bayreuth Germany 48 I5
Bayrūt Lebanon *see* Beirut
Bay St Louis U.S.A. 175 B6
Baysh *watercourse* Saudi Arabia 104 C4
Bayshonas Kazakh. *see* Baychunas
Bay Springs U.S.A. 175 B5
Baysun Uzbek. 103 F5
Baysuntau, Gory *mts* Uzbek. 103 F5
Baytik Egypt 121 F2
Baytik-Shan *mts* China 84 C2
Bayt Laḩm West Bank *see* Bethlehem
Baytown U.S.A. 179 D6
Bayu Indon. 75 B3
Bayunglincir Indon. 76 C3
Bayy al Kabir, Wādī *watercourse* Libya 120 B2
Bayyrqum Kazakh. *see* Bairkum
Bayzhansay Kazakh. 103 G4
also spelt Baydzhansay
Baza Spain 55 I7
Baza, Sierra de *mts* Spain 55 I7
Bazardyuzi Kazakh. 102 B2
formerly spelt Bazarshulan
Bazardchulan Kazakh. 102 B2
formerly spelt Bazarshulan
Bazardyuzi, Gora *mt.* Azer./Rus. Fed. 107 F2
Bāzār-e Māsāl Iran 100 B2
Bazarkhanym, Gora *mt.* Uzbek. 103 G5
Bazar-Korgon Kyrg. 103 H4
also known as Bazar Kurgan
Bazar Kurgan Kyrg. *see* Bazar-Korgon
Bazarnyy Karabulak Rus. Fed. 41 H5
Bazarnyy Syzgan Rus. Fed. 41 H5
Bazarshulan Kazakh. *see* Bazardchulan
Bazartobe Kazakh. 102 C2
Bazaruto, Ilha do *i.* Moz. 131 G4
Bazas France 50 F8
Bazhong China 86 B2
Bazhou China 85 H4
formerly known as Baxian
Bazin *r.* Canada 168 F3
Baziwehn Liberia 124 C4
Bazmān Iran 101 E5
Bazmān, Kūh-e *mt.* Iran 101 E4
Béal an Átha Rep. of Ireland *see* Ballina
Béal Átha na Sluaighe Rep. of Ireland *see* Ballinasloe
Beach U.S.A. 178 B2
Beach City U.S.A. 176 D5
Beachburg Canada 173 Q5

Beach Haven U.S.A. 177 K6
Beachport Australia 146 D4
Beachy Head U.K. 47 M13
Beacon Australia 151 B6
Beacon U.S.A. 177 L4
Beacon Bay S. Africa 133 L9
Beaconsfield Australia 147 E5
Beagle, Canal *sea chan.* Arg. 205 C9
Beagle Bank *reef* Australia 150 C2
Beagle Bay Australia 150 C3
Beagle Bay Aboriginal Reserve Australia 150 C3
Beagle Gulf Australia 148 A1
Beagle Island Australia 151 A6
Bealanana Madag. 131 [inset] J3
Béal an Átha Rep. of Ireland *see* Ballina
Béal Átha na Sluaighe Rep. of Ireland *see* Ballinasloe
Beallangaratra *mts* Madag. 131 [inset] J5
Beamdranzena Madag. 131 [inset] K2
Bear *r.* U.S.A. 180 D4
Bearalváhki Norway *see* Berlevåg
Bear Creek Canada 166 D4
Bear Creek *r.* U.S.A. 178 B4
Beardmore Glacier Antarctica 223 L1
Beardmore Reservoir Australia 147 F1
Beardstown U.S.A. 174 B3
Bear Island *i.* Arctic Ocean *see* Bjørnøya
Bear Island Canada 173 M4
Bear Island *i.* Canada 168 D2
Bear Island *i.* Rep. of Ireland 47 C12
Bear Lake *l.* Canada 167 L4
Bear Lake U.S.A. 172 G6
Bear Lake *l.* U.S.A. 180 E4
Bearma *r.* India 96 C4
Bear Mountain U.S.A. 178 B3
Bearnaraigh *i.* U.K. *see* Berneray
Bear Paw Mountain U.S.A. 180 E2
Bearpaw Mountains U.S.A. 180 E2
Bear Peninsula Antarctica 222 Q2
Beerskin Lake Canada 168 B2
Bears *r.* India 96 D3
Bear Lake *l.* Canada 167 L4
Beasain Spain 55 I1
Beata, Cabo *c.* Dom. Rep. 187 F3
Beata, Isla *i.* Dom. Rep. 187 F3
Beatrice Zimbabwe 131 F3
Beatrice, Cape Australia 148 C2
Beatton *r.* Canada 166 F3
Beatty U.S.A. 183 H5
Beattyville U.S.A. 168 E3
Beattyville U.S.A. 174 D5
Beauce *r.* France 51 K9
Beauceville Canada 173 O4
Beauchene Island Falkland Is 205 F9
Beaucourt France 51 N5
Beaudesert Australia 147 G1
Beaufort *Sabah* Malaysia 77 F1
Beaufort *NC* U.S.A. 174 E5
Beaufort *SC* U.S.A. 175 D5
Beaufort Castle *tourist site* Lebanon 108 G4
Beaufort Island *Hong Kong* China 87 [inset]
also known as Lo Chau
Beaufort Sea Canada/U.S.A. 164 C2
Beaufort West S. Africa 132 G9
Beaugency France 50 H5
Beaulieu *r.* Canada 167 H2
Beauly U.K. 46 H6
Beauly *r.* U.K. 46 H6
Beaumont Belgium 51 K2
Beaumont Belgium 51 K2
Beaumont N.Z. 153 D13
Beaumont *CA* U.S.A. 183 H8
Beaumont *MS* U.S.A. 175 B6
Beaumont *TX* U.S.A. 179 D6
Beaumont-de-Lomagne France 50 G9
Beaumont-le-Roger France 50 G3
Beaune France 51 K5
Beaune-La Rolande France 51 I4
Beauraing Belgium 51 K2
Beauséjour Canada 167 L5
Beauvais France 51 I3
Beauval Canada 167 J3
Beauvoir-sur-Mer France 50 D6
Beaver *r.* Alta/Sask. Canada 167 J4
Beaver *r.* Ont. Canada 168 C2
Beaver *r.* Y.T. Canada 166 D3
Beaver *r.* Y.T. Canada 166 C3
Beaver *OK* U.S.A. 178 B4
Beaver *UT* U.S.A. 183 L3
Beaver *r.* *OK* U.S.A. 178 B4
Beaver *r.* *UT* U.S.A. 183 L2
Beaver City U.S.A. 178 C3
Beaver Creek Canada 166 A2
Beaver Creek *r.* *MO* U.S.A. 178 D4
Beaver Creek *r.* *MT* U.S.A. 180 F2
Beaver Creek *r.* *ND* U.S.A. 178 B2
Beaver Creek *r.* *ND* U.S.A. 178 B2
Beaver Dam *WI* U.S.A. 172 E7
Beaver Dam *WI* U.S.A. 172 E7
Beaver Falls U.S.A. 176 E5
Beaver Glacier Antarctica 223 D2
Beaverhead *r.* U.S.A. 180 D3
Beaverhead Mountains U.S.A. 180 D3
Beaver Hill Lake Canada 167 N4
Beaver Island U.S.A. 172 H5
Beaverlodge Canada 166 G3
Beaver Run Reservoir U.S.A. 176 F5
Beaverton *MI* U.S.A. 173 I7
Beaverton *OR* U.S.A. 180 B3
Beawar India 96 B4
Beazley Arg. 204 D4
Bebedero, Salina del *salt pan* Arg. 204 D4
Bébédjia Chad 126 C2
Bebedouro Brazil 206 E7
Beberibe Brazil 202 E3
Bebra Germany 48 G5
Bêca China 86 A2
Beccles U.K. 47 N11
Bečej *Vojvodina, Srbija* Yugo. 58 B3
also known as Óbecse
Becerrá Spain 54 D2
Becerreá Spain 54 D2
Becerro, Cayos *is* Hond. 186 D4
Béchar Alg. 123 E3
formerly known as Colomb-Béchar
Becharof Lake U.S.A. 164 D4
Bechevinka Rus. Fed. 43 T2
Bechuanaland *country* Africa *see* Botswana
Beçin Turkey 59 I11
Becker, Mount Antarctica 222 T1
Beckley U.S.A. 176 D8
Becks N.Z. 153 D12
Becky Peak U.S.A. 183 J2
Beclean Romania 58 F1
Bečva *r.* Czech Rep. 49 O6
Beda Hāyk' *l.* Eth. 128 D2
Bédarieux France 51 J9
Bedau Alg. *see* Ras el Ma
Bedel', Pereval *pass* China/Kyrg. 88 B3
Bedel Pass China/Kyrg. 88 B3
also known as Bedel', Pereval
Bedford Canada 169 I4
Bedford S. Africa 133 K9
Bedford U.K. 47 L11
Bedford *IA* U.S.A. 178 D3
Bedford *IN* U.S.A. 174 C4
Bedford *KY* U.S.A. 174 C4
Bedford *NY* U.S.A. 177 L4
Bedford *PA* U.S.A. 176 G6
Bedford *VA* U.S.A. 176 F8
Bedford, Cape Australia 149 E2
Bedford Downs Australia 150 D3
Bedford Heights U.S.A. 176 D4
Bedi India 96 A5
Bedinggong Indon. 77 D3
Bednja *r.* Croatia 56 I2
Bednodem'yanovsk Rus. Fed. 41 G5

235 ←

Bedok Sing. **76** [inset]
Bedok, Sungai r. Sing. **76** [inset]
Bedok Jetty Sing. **76** [inset]
Bedok Reservoir Sing. **76** [inset]
Bedouaram well Niger **125** I3
Bedourie Australia **148** C5
Bedrock U.S.A. **183** P3
Bedum Neth. **48** D2
Beechal Creek watercourse Australia **147** E1
Beecher U.S.A. **172** F9
Beech Fork Lake U.S.A. **176** C7
Beechy Canada **167** J5
Beekeepers Nature Reserve Australia **151** A6
Beelitz Germany **49** J3
Beenleigh Australia **147** G1
Beer Somalia **128** E2
Beersheba Israel **108** F6
also spelt Be'ér Sheva'
Be'ér Sheva' Israel see **Beersheba**
Beer Sheva watercourse Israel **108** F6
Beervlei Dam S. Africa **132** H10
Beeskow Germany **49** L3
Beestekraal S. Africa **133** L2
Beetaloo Australia **148** B3
Beethoven Peninsula Antarctica **222** T2
Beeville U.S.A. **179** C6
Befale Dem. Rep. Congo **126** D4
Befandriana Atsimo Madag. **131** [inset] I4
Befandriana Avaratra Madag. **131** [inset] K2
Befori Dem. Rep. Congo **126** D4
Befotaka Madag. **131** [inset] J4
Bega Australia **147** F4
Bega r. Romania **58** C3
Begamganj Bangl. **97** F5
Bégard France **50** C4
Begari r. Pak. **101** G4
Begicheva, Ostrov i. Rus. Fed. see **Bol'shoy Begichev, Ostrov**
Begovat Uzbek. see **Bekabad**
Begun India **96** B4
Begusarai India **97** E4
Behābād Iran **101** D3
Béhague, Pointe pt Fr. Guiana **199** I3
Behbehān Iran **100** B4
Beheira governorate Egypt **108** B7
Behm Canal sea chan. U.S.A. **166** D4
Behrendt Mountains Antarctica **222** T2
Behshahr Iran **100** C2
Behsūd Afgh. **101** F3
Bei'an China **82** B2
Bei'ao China see **Dongtou**
Beiba China **86** C1
Beibei China **86** C2
Beichuan China **86** C2
also known as Qushan
Beida Libya see **Al Bayḍā'**
Beigang Taiwan see **Peikang**
Beihai China **87** D4
historically known as Pakhoi
Bei Hulsan Hu salt l. China **84** B4
Bei Jiang r. China **87** E4

▶**Beijing** China **85** H4
Capital of China. Formerly known as Peking; historically known as Khanbalik.
world [countries] ➡ 10–11
world [cities] ➡ 24–25

Beijing municipality China **85** H3
Beilen Neth. **48** D3
Beiliu China **87** D4
Béinamar Chad **126** B2
Beining China **85** I3
also known as Guangning; formerly known as Beizhen
Beinn Bhreac hill U.K. **46** G7
Beinn Mhòr hill U.K. **46** E6
Beinn na Faoghlia i. U.K. see **Benbecula**
Beipiao China **85** I3
Beira Moz. **131** G3
Beira prov. Moz. see **Sofala**
Beira Alta reg. Port. **54** D4
Beira Baixa reg. Port. **54** D5
Beira Litoral reg. Port. **54** C4
Beiru r. China **87** E1

▶**Beirut** Lebanon **108** G4
Capital of Lebanon. Also spelt Bayrūt or Beyrouth; historically known as Berytus.

Beiseker Canada **167** H5
Beishan China **84** C3
Bei Shan mt. China **84** B3
Bei Shan mts China **84** B3
Beitbridge Zimbabwe **131** F4
Beit Jālā West Bank **108** G6
Beitun China **88** D2
Beiuş Romania **58** D2
Beizhen China see **Beining**
Beja Brazil **202** B2
Beja Port. **54** D6
Beja admin. dist. Port. **54** C7
Béja Tunisia **123** H1
Bejaïa Alg. **123** G1
formerly known as Bougie; historically known as Saldae
Béjar Spain **54** F4
Bejestān Iran **100** D3
Beji r. Pak. **101** G4
Bejucos Mex. **185** E5
Béka Adamaoua Cameroon **125** I5
Béka Est Cameroon **125** I5
Béka Nord Cameroon **125** I4
Bekabad Uzbek. **92** C2
also spelt Bekobod; formerly spelt Begovat
Bekapaika Madag. **131** [inset] J3
Bekasi Indon. **77** D4
Bekdash Turkm. **102** C4
Beke Dem. Rep. Congo **127** E7
Békés Hungary **49** S9
Békéscsaba Hungary **49** S9
Beketovskaya Rus. Fed. **43** U1
Bekilli Turkey **59** K10
Bekily Madag. **131** [inset] J5
Bekitro Madag. **131** [inset] J5
Bekkai Japan **90** I3
Beklemishevo Rus. Fed. **85** G1
Bekobod Uzbek. see **Bekabad**
Bekopaka Madag. **131** [inset] J3
Bekoropoka-Antongo Madag. **131** [inset] I4
Bekovo Rus. Fed. **41** G5
Bekwai Ghana **125** E5
Bekyem Ghana **125** E5
Bela Bihar India **97** E4
Bela Uttar Pradesh India **97** D4
Bela Pak. **101** F5
Belab r. Pak. **101** G4
Bela-Bela S. Africa **133** M1
Bélabo Cameroon **125** I5
Bela Crkva Vojvodina, Srbija Yugo. **58** C4
Belaga Sarawak Malaysia **77** F2
Bel'agash Kazakh. **103** J2
Bel Air U.S.A. **177** I6
Belalcázar Spain **54** F6
Belang Indon. **75** C2
Belangiran Indon. **77** E3
Bela Palanka Srbija Yugo. **58** D5
Bělá pod Bezdězem Czech Rep. **49** L5
Belapur India **94** B2
▶**Belarus** country Europe **42** H8
formerly known as Belorussia or Belorusskaya S.S.R. or Byelorussia or White Russia
europe [countries] ➡ 32–35
Belasica mts Bulg./Macedonia **58** D7
also known as Kerkini Oros; also spelt Belasitsa
Belasitsa mts Bulg./Macedonia see **Belasica**
Belau country N. Pacific Ocean see **Palau**
Bela Vista Angola **127** B6
Bela Vista Amazonas Brazil **199** E4
Bela Vista Mato Grosso do Sul Brazil **201** F5
Bela Vista Moz. **131** G5
Bela Vista de Goiás Brazil **206** E3
Belawan Indon. **76** B2
Belaya r. Rus. Fed. **39** R3
Belaya Glina Rus. Fed. **41** G7
Belaya Kalitva Rus. Fed. **41** G6
Belaya Kholunitsa Rus. Fed. **40** I4
Belayan r. Indon. **77** G3
Belayan, Gunung mt. Indon. **77** F2
Belaya Rechka Rus. Fed. **43** U5
Belaya Tserkva Ukr. see **Bila Tserkva**
Belbédji Niger **125** G3
Belceşti Romania **58** I1
Bełchatów Poland **49** Q4
Belcher U.S.A. **176** C8
Belcher Islands Canada **168** E1
Belchiragh Afgh. **101** F3
Belcourt Canada **173** P2
Beldanga India **97** F5
Belden U.S.A. **182** C1
Beldibi Turkey **59** J12
Belding U.S.A. **173** H7
Beleapani reef India see **Cherbaniani Reef**
Belebey Rus. Fed. **40** J5
Beled Hungary **49** O8
Beledweyne Somalia **128** E3
Belek Turkm. **102** C5
Béléko Mali **124** D3
Bélèl Cameroon **125** I5
Belel Nigeria **125** I4
Belém Brazil **202** B2
Belén Arg. **204** D2
Belén Para. **201** F5
Belen Antalya Turkey **108** D1
Belen Hatay Turkey **106** D3
Belen U.S.A. **181** F6
Belén, Cuchilla de hills Uruguay **204** F3
Belene Bulg. **58** G5
Bélep, Îles is New Caledonia **145** F3
Belesar, Embalse de resr Spain **54** D2
Belev Rus. Fed. **43** R8
Belevi Turkey **59** I10
Belfast N.Z. **153** G11
Belfast S. Africa **133** O2

▶**Belfast** U.K. **47** G9
Capital of Northern Ireland.

Belfast U.S.A. **177** P1
Bēlfodiyo Eth. **128** B2
Belford U.K. **46** K8
Belfort France **51** M5
Belgaum India **94** B3
Belgian Congo country Africa see **Congo, Democratic Republic of**
Belgicafjella mts Antarctica see **Belgica Mountains**
Belgica Mountains Antarctica **223** C2
also known as Belgicafjella
België country Europe see **Belgium**
Belgique country Europe see **Belgium**
▶**Belgium** country Europe **51** K2
known as België in Dutch (Flemish) or Belgique in French; historically known as Spanish Netherlands
europe [countries] ➡ 32–35
Belgorod Rus. Fed. **41** F6
Belgorod-Dnestrovskyy Ukr. see **Bilhorod-Dnistrovs'kyy**
Belgorod Oblast admin. div. Rus. Fed. see **Belgorodskaya Oblast'**
Belgorodskaya Oblast' admin. div. Rus. Fed. **41** F6
English form Belgorod Oblast
Belgrade ME U.S.A. **177** P1
Belgrade MT U.S.A. **180** E3

▶**Belgrade** Srbija Yugo. **58** B4
Capital of Yugoslavia. Also spelt Beograd; historically known as Singidunum.

Belgrano II research station Antarctica **222** V1
long form General Belgrano II
Belhirane Alg. **123** G3
Béli Guinea-Bissau **124** B4
Beli Nigeria **125** H5
Belice r. Sicilia Italy **57** E11
Beli Drim r. Yugo. **58** B6
Beliliou i. Palau see **Peleliu**
Beli Lom r. Bulg. **58** H5
Beli Manastir Croatia **56** K3
Belin-Béliet France **50** F8
Belington U.S.A. **176** F6
Belingwe Zimbabwe see **Mberengwa**
Belinskiy Rus. Fed. **41** G5
Belinţ Romania **58** C3
Belinyu Indon. **77** D3
Beli Timok r. Yugo. **58** D4
Belitsa Bulg. **58** E7
Belitung i. Indon. **77** E3
also spelt Billiton
Belize Angola **126** B6

▶**Belize** Belize **185** H5
Former capital of Belize.

▶**Belize** country Central America **185** H5
formerly known as British Honduras
northamerica [countries] ➡ 158–159
Bélizon Fr. Guiana **199** H3
Beljak Austria see **Villach**
Beljanica mt. Yugo. **58** C4
Belkina, Mys pt Rus. Fed. **90** E2
Bel'kovskiy, Ostrov i. Rus. Fed. **39** N2
Bell Australia **149** F5
Bell r. Australia **147** F3
Bell r. Canada **168** E3
Bell S. Africa **133** L10
Bell, Point Australia **146** B3
Bella Bella Canada **166** D4
Bellac France **50** H6
Bella Coola Canada **166** E4
Bella Coola r. Canada **166** E4
Bellagio Italy **56** B3
Bellaire MI U.S.A. **173** H6
Bellaire TX U.S.A. **179** D6
Bellaria Italy **56** E4
Bellary India **94** C3
Bellata Australia **147** F2
Bella Unión Uruguay **204** F3
Bella Vista Corrientes Arg. **204** F3
Bella Vista Santa Cruz Arg. **205** C8
Bella Vista Bol. **201** E3
Bella Vista Para. **201** F5
Bellavista Peru **198** C5
Bella Vista U.S.A. **182** B1
Bella Vista, Salar de salt flat Chile **200** C5
Bell Block N.Z. **152** I7
Bell Cay reef Australia **149** F4
Belle U.S.A. **176** D7
Belle-Anse Haiti **187** E3
formerly known as Saltrou
Belledonne mts France **51** L7
Bellefontaine U.S.A. **176** B5
Belle Fourche U.S.A. **178** B2
Belle Fourche r. U.S.A. **178** B2
Bellegarde-sur-Valserine France **51** L6
Belle Glade U.S.A. **175** D7
Belle-Île i. France **50** C5
Belle Isle i. Canada **169** K3
Belle Isle, Strait of Canada **169** J3
Bellemont U.S.A. **183** M6
Belleterre Canada **168** E4
Belleville Canada **168** E4
Belleville France **51** K6
Belleville U.S.A. **178** C4
Bellevue IA U.S.A. **174** B3
Bellevue MI U.S.A. **173** H8
Bellevue NE U.S.A. **178** D3
Bellevue OH U.S.A. **176** C4
Bellevue WA U.S.A. **180** B3
Belley France **51** L7
Bellin Canada see **Kangirsuk**
Bellingen Australia **147** G2
Bellingham U.K. **47** J8
Bellingham U.S.A. **180** B2
Bellingshausen research station Antarctica **222** U2
Bellingshausen Sea Antarctica **222** S2
Bellinzona Switz. **51** P6
Bell Island Canada **169** K3
Bello Col. **198** C3
Bellows Falls U.S.A. **177** M2
Bellpat Pak. **101** G4
Belluno Italy **56** E2
Belluru India **94** C3
Bell Ville Arg. **204** E4
Bellville S. Africa **132** C10
Bellville OH U.S.A. **176** C5
Bellville TX U.S.A. **179** C6
Bellwood U.S.A. **176** G5
Belly r. Canada **167** H5
Bélmez Spain **54** F6
Belmont Australia **147** F3
Belmont S. Africa **133** I6
Belmont NH U.S.A. **177** N2
Belmont NY U.S.A. **176** G3
Belmonte Brazil **202** E5
Belmonte Port. **54** D4
Belmont-sur-Rance France **51** I9

▶**Belmopan** Belize **185** H5
Capital of Belize.

Belmore Creek r. Australia **149** D3
Belmullet Rep. of Ireland **47** C9
Belo Madag. **131** [inset] J4
Beloe More Rus. Fed. see **Beloye More**
Beloe More sea Rus. Fed. see **White Sea**
Beloevo Rus. Fed. see **Beloyevo**
Belogorsk Rus. Fed. **82** C2
formerly known as Kuybyshevka-Vostochnaya
Belogorsk Ukr. see **Bilohirs'k**
Belogor'ye Kazakh. **103** I2
Belogradchik Bulg. **58** D5
Beloha Madag. **131** [inset] J5
Belo Horizonte Amazonas Brazil **199** E5
Belo Horizonte Minas Gerais Brazil **203** D6
Beloit KS U.S.A. **178** C4
Beloit WI U.S.A. **172** D8
Belo Jardim Brazil **202** E4
Belo Monte Brazil **199** I5
Belo Monte Brazil see **Batalha**
Belomorsk Rus. Fed. **40** E2
Belonia India **97** F5
Beloomut Rus. Fed. **43** U7
Belo Oriente Brazil **207** K6
Beloozersk Belarus see **Byelaazyorsk**
Beloozerskiy Rus. Fed. **43** T6
Belopa Indon. **75** B3
Belorado Spain **55** H2
Belorechensk Rus. Fed. **41** F7
formerly known as Belorechenskaya
Belorechenskaya Rus. Fed. see **Belorechensk**
Belören Adıyaman Turkey **107** D3
Belören Konya Turkey **106** C3
also known as Sarıoğlan
Beloretsk Rus. Fed. **38** F4
Belorussia country Europe see **Belarus**
Belorusskaya S.S.R. country Europe see **Belarus**
Beloslav Bulg. **58** I5
Belostok Poland see **Białystok**
Belot, Lac l. Canada **166** E1
Belotintsi Bulg. **58** D5
Belo Tsiribihina Madag. **131** [inset] J3
Belousovka Kazakh. **88** C1
Belousovo Rus. Fed. **43** R6
Belo Vale Brazil **207** I7
Belovo Bulg. **58** F6
Belovo Rus. Fed. **80** D2
Beloyarovo Rus. Fed. **82** C2
Beloye Rus. Fed. **43** U3
Beloye, Ozero l. Rus. Fed. **43** S1
Beloye More Rus. Fed. **44** P2
also spelt Beloe More
Beloye More sea Rus. Fed. see **White Sea**
Beloyevo Rus. Fed. **40** J4
also spelt Beloevo
Belozerka Rus. Fed. **102** C1
Belozersk Rus. Fed. **43** S1
Belpre U.S.A. **176** D6
Beltana Australia **146** C2
Belted Range mts U.S.A. **183** H4
Belterra Brazil **199** H5
Beltes Gol r. Mongolia **84** C1
Belton MO U.S.A. **178** D4
Belton TX U.S.A. **179** C6
Bel'tsy Moldova see **Bălţi**
Bel'tsy Moldova see **Bălţi**
Belukha, Gora mt. Kazakh./Rus. Fed. **88** D1
Belur India **94** B3
Belush'ya Guba Rus. Fed. **40** J1
Belush'ye Rus. Fed. **40** H2
Beluzhiy Nos, Mys c. Rus. Fed. **40** M1
Belva U.S.A. **176** D7
Belvès France **50** H8
Belvidere IL U.S.A. **174** B3
Belvidere NJ U.S.A. **177** J5
Belyando r. Australia **149** E4
Belyando Crossing Australia **149** E4
Belyayevka Rus. Fed. **102** D2
Belyayevka Ukr. see **Bilyayivka**
Belyayevo Rus. Fed. **43** Q6
Belyayevo Rus. Fed. **43** M6
Belyuen Australia **148** A2
Bely Rus. Fed. **43** N6
Belyy, Ostrov i. Rus. Fed. **38** H2
Belyye Berega Rus. Fed. **43** P8
Belyye Stolby Rus. Fed. **43** S6
Belyy Gorodok Rus. Fed. **43** S5
Belyy Yar Rus. Fed. **39** I4
Belzig Germany **49** J3
Belzoni U.S.A. **175** B5
Bełżyce Poland **49** T4
Bemaraha, Plateau du Madag. **131** [inset] J3
Bembe Angola **127** B6
Bembèrèkè Benin **125** F4
Bembibre Spain **54** E2
Bemidji U.S.A. **178** D2
Béna Burkina **124** D3
Bena Dibele Dem. Rep. Congo **126** D6
Benagin Indon. **77** F3
Ben Alder mt. U.K. **46** H7
Benalla Australia **147** E4
Benalmádena Spain **54** G8
Ben 'Amira well Mauritania **122** B5
Benares India see **Varanasi**
Ben Arous Tunisia **123** H1
Bénat, Cap c. France **51** M9
Benavente Spain **54** F2
Benavides Bol. **200** D3
Benbecula i. U.K. **46** E6
also known as Beinn na Faoghlia
Ben Boyd National Park Australia **147** F4
Benbury hill Rep. of Ireland **47** C10
Bencha China **87** G1
Bencheng China see **Luannan**
Bencubbin Australia **151** B6
Bend U.S.A. **180** B3
Bendearg mt. S. Africa **133** L8
Bendela Dem. Rep. Congo **126** C5
Bender Moldova see **Tighina**
Bender-Bayla Somalia **128** F2
Benderville U.S.A. **172** F6
Bendery Moldova see **Tighina**
Bendigo Australia **147** E4
Bendoc Australia **147** F4
Bēne Latvia **42** E5
Bene Moz. **131** G2
Benedict, Mount hill Canada **169** J2
Benedítinos Brazil **202** D3
Benedito Leite Brazil **202** C3
Bénéna Mali **124** D3
Benenitra Madag. **131** [inset] J4
Benešov Czech Rep. **49** L6
Benevento Italy **56** G7
historically known as Beneventum
Beneventum Italy see **Benevento**
Benezette U.S.A. **176** G4
Benfeld France **51** N4
Beng r. China **85** H5
Beng, Nam r. Laos **78** C4
Benga Malawi **129** B8
Bengal, Bay of sea Indian Ocean **95** F2
Bengamisa Dem. Rep. Congo **126** E4
Bengbis Cameroon **125** I6
Bengbu China **87** F1
Benghazi Libya **120** D1
also spelt Banghāzī; historically known as Berenice
Benghisa Point Malta **57** G13
also known as Il-Ponta ta' Benghajsa
Bengkalis Indon. **76** C2
Bengkalis i. Indon. **76** C2
Bengkayang Indon. **77** E2
Bengkulu Indon. **76** C3
Bengkulu prov. Indon. **76** C3
Bengo Angola **127** C9
Bengo prov. Angola **127** B7
Bengtsfors Sweden **45** K4
Benguela Angola **127** B8
Benguela prov. Angola **127** B8
Ben Guerdane Tunisia **123** H2
Benguerir Morocco **122** D2
Benguérua, Ilha i. Moz. **131** G4
Benha Egypt **121** F2
also spelt Banhā
Ben Hiant hill U.K. **46** F7
Ben Hope hill U.K. **46** H5
Beni dept Bol. **200** D3
Beni r. Bol. **200** D2
Beni Dem. Rep. Congo **126** F4
Beni Nepal **97** D3
Beni-Abbès Alg. **123** E3
Beni Boufrah Morocco **54** G9
Benicarló Spain **55** L4
Benicasim Spain **55** L4
Benicia U.S.A. **182** B3
Benidorm Spain **55** K6
Beni Dourso well Niger **125** I1
Benifaió Spain **55** K5
also spelt Benifayo
Benifayo Spain see **Benifaió**
Benigánim Spain **55** K6
Beni Guil reg. Morocco **123** E2
Beni Hadifa Morocco **54** G9
Beni Mazâr Egypt **106** B5
Beni Mellal Morocco **122** D2
▶**Benin** country Africa **125** F4
formerly known as Dahomey
africa [countries] ➡ 114–117
Benin r. Nigeria **125** G5
Benin, Bight of g. Africa **125** F5
Benin City Nigeria **125** G5
Beni-Ounif Alg. **123** E3
Beni-Saf Alg. **123** E2
Benishangul admin. reg. Eth. **128** B2
Benisheikh Nigeria **125** I4
Benissa Spain **55** L6
Beni Suef Egypt **121** F2
also spelt Banī Suwayf
Beni Suef governorate Egypt **108** A9
Benithora r. India **94** C2
Benito r. Equat. Guinea see **Mbini**
Benito, Islas is Mex. **184** B2
Benito Juárez Arg. **204** F5
Benito Juárez Mex. **183** J9
Benito Soliven Phil. **74** B2
Benjamim Constant Brazil **198** D6
Benjamin U.S.A. **179** C5
Benjamín, Isla i. Chile **205** B7
Benjamin Hill Mex. **184** C2
Benjamín Zorrillo Arg. **204** D5
Benjina Indon. **73** H8
Benkei-misaki pt Japan **90** G3
Benkelman U.S.A. **178** B3
Benken Switz. **51** P5
Benkovac Croatia **56** H4
Benkovski Bulg. **58** I5
Ben Lawers mt. U.K. **46** H7
Ben Lomond mt. Australia **147** F2
Ben Lomond hill U.K. **46** H7
Ben Lomond U.S.A. **182** B4
Ben Lomond National Park Australia **147** E5
Ben Macdhui mt. Lesotho **133** L7
Ben Macdui mt. U.K. **46** I6
Ben Mahidi Alg. **57** A12
Benmara Australia **148** C3
Ben More mt. N.Z. **153** F11
Ben More hill U.K. **46** F7
Ben More mt. U.K. **46** H7
Benmore, Lake N.Z. **153** E12
Ben More Assynt hill U.K. **46** H5
Bennett Canada **166** C3
Bennett IA U.S.A. **172** C9
Bennett WI U.S.A. **172** B4
Bennett, Lake salt flat Australia **148** A4
Bennetta, Ostrov i. Rus. Fed. **39** O2
English form Bennett Island
Bennett Island Rus. Fed. see **Bennetta, Ostrov**
Bennett Lake Canada **166** C3
Bennettsville U.S.A. **174** E5
Ben Nevis mt. U.K. **46** G7
Benneydale N.Z. **152** J6
Bennington NH U.S.A. **177** N2
Bennington VT U.S.A. **177** L3
Ben Ohau Range mts N.Z. **153** D12
Benoi Basin dock Sing. **76** [inset]
Benoni S. Africa **133** M3
Bénoué r. Cameroon **125** I4
Bénoy Chad **126** C2
Ben Rinnes hill U.K. **46** I6
Bensheim Germany **48** F6
Ben Slimane Morocco **122** D2
formerly known as Boulhaut
Benson AZ U.S.A. **181** E7
Benson MN U.S.A. **178** D2
Bensonville Liberia **124** C5
Bens Run U.S.A. **176** D6
Bent Iran **101** D5
Benta Seberang Malaysia **76** C1
Benteng Indon. **75** B4
Bentiaba Angola **127** B8
formerly known as São Nicolau
Ben Tieb Morocco **55** H9
Bentinck Island Australia **148** C3
Bentinck Island Myanmar **79** B6
Bentiu Sudan **126** F2
Bent Jbail Lebanon **108** G4
Bentley Canada **167** H4
Bentleyville U.S.A. **176** E5
Bento Gomes r. Brazil **201** F4
Benton AR U.S.A. **179** D5
Benton CA U.S.A. **182** F4
Benton IL U.S.A. **174** B4
Benton KY U.S.A. **174** B4
Benton LA U.S.A. **179** D5
Benton MO U.S.A. **174** B4
Benton TN U.S.A. **174** C5
Bentong Malaysia see **Bentung**
Benton Harbor U.S.A. **172** G8
Bentonville U.S.A. **179** D4
Bên Tre Vietnam **79** D6
formerly known as Truc Giang
Bentsy Rus. Fed. **43** M5
Bentuang Karimun National Park Indon. **77** F2
Bentung Malaysia **76** C2
formerly spelt Bentong
Benua Indon. **75** B4
Benua i. Indon. **77** D2
Benuamartinus Indon. **77** F2
Benue r. Nigeria **125** G5
Benue state Nigeria **125** H5
Benum, Gunung mt. Malaysia **76** C2
Ben Vorlich hill U.K. **46** H7
Benwa Zambia **127** E7
Benwee Head Rep. of Ireland **47** C9
Benwood U.S.A. **176** E5
Ben Wyvis mt. U.K. **46** H6
Benxi China **82** A4
Ben Zireg Alg. **123** E3
Beograd Srbija Yugo. see **Belgrade**
Bechari India **97** D4
Bécumi Côte d'Ivoire **124** D5
Bepagut, Gunung mt. Indon. **76** C4
Bepian Jiang r. China **86** C3
Beppu Japan **91** B8
Beppu-wan b. Japan **91** B8
Bequia i. St Vincent **187** H4
Bequimão Brazil **202** C2
Bera Bangl. **97** F4
Berach r. India **96** B4
Beramanja Madag. **131** [inset] K2
Berane Crna Gora Yugo. **58** A6
formerly known as Ivangrad
Bérard, Lac l. Canada **169** G1
Berasia India **96** C5
Berastagi Indon. **76** B2
Berat Albania **58** A8
Beratus, Gunung mt. Indon. **77** G3
Berau r. Indon. **77** G2
Berau, Teluk b. Indon. **73** H7
Beravina Madag. **131** [inset] J3
also spelt Berevina
Berbak National Park Indon. **76** D3
Berber Sudan **121** G5
Berbera Somalia **128** E2
Berbérati Cent. Afr. Rep. **126** B3
Berbice S. Africa **133** P4
Bercel Hungary **49** Q8
Berceto Italy **56** B4
Berchi-Guélé well Chad **120** C5
Berchogur Kazakh. **102** D2
also spelt Birshoghyr
Berchtesgaden, Nationalpark nat. park Germany **49** J8
Berck France **50** H2
Berd Armenia **107** F2
Berdichev Ukr. see **Berdychiv**
Berdigestyakh Rus. Fed. **39** M3
Berdsk Rus. Fed. **80** C2
Berdyans'k Ukr. **41** F7
formerly known as Osipenko
Berdychiv Ukr. **41** D6
also spelt Berdichev
Béré Chad **126** C2
Berea KY U.S.A. **176** A8
Berea OH U.S.A. **176** D4
Berebere Indon. **75** D2
Bereg Rus. Fed. **43** S1
Beregdaróc Hungary **49** T7
Beregovo Ukr. see **Berehove**
Berehove Ukr. **49** T7
also spelt Beregovo
Bereina P.N.G. **73** K8
Bereketa Madag. **131** [inset] J4
Berekum Ghana **124** E5
Berel' Kazakh. **88** D1
Beremend Hungary **56** K3
Berendeyevo Rus. Fed. **43** U5
Berenguela Bol. **200** C4
Berenice Egypt **121** G4
Berenice Libya see **Benghazi**
Berens r. Canada **167** L4
Berens Island Canada **167** L4
Berens River Canada **167** L4
Berenty Madag. **131** [inset] J5
Beresford Canada **169** H4
Beresford U.S.A. **178** C3
Bereşti Romania **58** I2
Berettyó r. Hungary **49** S8
Berettyóújfalu Hungary **49** S8
Berevo Madag. **131** [inset] J3
Berevo-Ranobe Madag. **131** [inset] J3
Bereza Belarus see **Byaroza**
Berezayka Rus. Fed. **43** O4
Berezeni Romania **58** J2
Berezino Belarus see **Byerazino**
Berezino Belarus see **Byerazino**
Berezivka Ukr. **41** D7
also spelt Berezovka
Berezne Ukr. **41** C6
Bereznik Rus. Fed. **40** G3
also known as Semyonovskoye
Berezniki Rus. Fed. **40** K4
Berezov Rus. Fed. see **Berezovo**
Berezovaya r. Rus. Fed. **40** K3
Berezovka Belarus see **Byarozawka**
Berezovka Amurskaya Oblast' Rus. Fed. **82** B2
Berezovka Orenburgskaya Oblast' Rus. Fed. **102** D1
Berezovka Permskaya Oblast' Rus. Fed. **40** K4
Berezovka Ukr. see **Berezivka**
Berezovo Rus. Fed. **38** G3
formerly known as Berezov
Berezovyy Rus. Fed. **82** D2
Berezyne Ukr. **58** K2
Berga Spain **55** M2
Bergama Turkey **106** A3
Bergamo Italy **56** B3
historically known as Bergomum
Bergantes r. Spain **55** K4
Bergby Sweden **45** L3
Bergen Mecklenburg-Vorpommern Germany **49** K1
Bergen Niedersachsen Germany **48** G3
Bergen Norway **45** I3
Bergen S. Africa **133** N3
Bergen U.S.A. **176** H2
Bergen op Zoom Neth. **48** B4
Bergerac France **50** G8
Bergerson, Mount Antarctica **223** B2
Berghan Point N.Z. **152** H2
Bergheim (Erft) Germany **48** D5
Bergisch Gladbach Germany **48** E5
Bergland Namibia **130** C4
Bergnäs Sweden **44** L2
Bergnäsviken Sweden **44** L2
Bergomum Italy see **Bergamo**
Bergsjö Sweden **45** L3
Bergstraße-Odenwald park Germany **48** G6
Bergsviken Sweden **44** M2
Bergues France **51** I2
Bergville S. Africa **133** N5
Berh Mongolia **85** F2
Berhala, Selat sea chan. Indon. **76** C3
Berhampur India see **Baharampur**
Berheci r. Romania **58** I2
Berikat, Tanjung pt Indon. **77** D3
Berilo Brazil **207** K3
Beringa, Ostrov i. Rus. Fed. **220** F2
Beringarra Australia **151** B5
Beringen Belgium **51** L1
Bering Land Bridge National Preserve nature res. U.S.A. **164** C3
Beringovskiy Rus. Fed. **39** R3
Bering Sea N. Pacific Ocean **39** R4
Bering Strait Rus. Fed./U.S.A. **164** C3
Beris, Ra's pt Iran **101** E5
Berislav Ukr. see **Beryslav**
Berja Spain **55** I8
Berkåk Norway **44** J3
Berkane Morocco **123** E2
Berkel r. Neth. **48** D3
Berkeley r. Australia **150** D2
Berkeley U.S.A. **182** B4
Berkeley Springs U.S.A. **176** G6
Berkner Island Antarctica **222** U1
Berkovitsa Bulg. **58** E5
Berkshire Hills U.S.A. **177** L3
Berland r. Canada **166** G4
Berlevåg Norway **44** O1
also known as Bearalváhki

▶**Berlin** Germany **49** K3
Capital of Germany.
europe [countries] ➡ 32–33

Berlin MD U.S.A. **177** J7
Berlin NH U.S.A. **177** N1
Berlin NJ U.S.A. **177** K6
Berlin OH U.S.A. **176** D5
Berlin PA U.S.A. **176** G6
Berlin WI U.S.A. **172** E7
Berlin, Mount Antarctica **222** O1
Berlins N.Z. **153** F9
Berliște Romania **58** C4
Bermagui Australia **147** F4
Berme Turkm. **102** D5
Bermeja, Punta pt Arg. **204** E6
Bermejillo Mex. **184** E3
Bermejo r. Arg. **204** D4
Bermejo r. Arg./Bol. **201** F6
Bermejo Bol. **201** D5
Bermeo Spain **55** I1

▶**Bermuda** terr. N. Atlantic Ocean **216** J3
United Kingdom Overseas Territory.
oceania [countries] ➡ 138–139

▶**Bern** Switz. **51** N6
Capital of Switzerland. Also spelt Berne.

Bernalda Italy **57** I8
Bernalillo U.S.A. **181** F6
Bernardino de Campos Brazil **206** D10
Bernard Lake Canada **173** N5
Bernardo O'Higgins, Parque Nacional nat. park Chile **205** B8
Bernau Germany **49** K3
Bernau am Chiemsee Germany **49** J8
Bernay France **50** G3
Bernburg (Saale) Germany **48** I4
Berndorf Austria **49** N8
Berne Switz. see **Bern**
Berne U.S.A. **176** A5
Berner Alpen mts Switz. **51** N6
English form Bernese Alps
Berneray i. Western Isles, Scotland U.K. **46** E6
also known as Bhearnaraigh, Eilean
Berneray i. Western Isles, Scotland U.K. **46** E7
also spelt Bearnaraigh
Bernese Alps mts Switz. see **Berner Alpen**
Bernesga r. Spain **54** F2
Bernier Bay Canada **165** K2
Bernier Island Australia **151** A5
Bernina Pass Switz. **51** Q6
Berninches mt. Spain **55** I4
Bernkastel-Kues Germany **48** E6
Bernstadt U.S.A. **176** A8
Beroea Greece see **Veroia**
Beroea Syria see **Aleppo**
Beroroha Madag. **131** [inset] J4
Beroun Czech Rep. **49** L6
Berounka r. Czech Rep. **49** L6
Berovina Madag. see **Beravina**
Berovo Macedonia **58** D7
Berre, Étang de lag. France **51** L9
Berrechid Morocco **122** D2
Berri Australia **146** D3
Berriane Alg. **123** F2
Berridale Australia **147** F4
Berrigan Australia **147** E3
Berrouaghia Alg. **123** F1
Berry reg. France **50** H6
Berry Creek r. Canada **167** I5
Berryessa, Lake U.S.A. **182** B3
Berry Head U.K. **47** I13
Berry Islands Bahamas **186** D1
Berryville AR U.S.A. **179** D4
Berryville VA U.S.A. **176** H6
Berseba Namibia **132** B3
Bersenbrück Germany **48** E3
Bersuat Rus. Fed. **103** E1
Berté, Lac l. Canada **169** G3
Bertinho Brazil **202** B2
Bertolinía Brazil **202** D3
Bertópolis Brazil **207** M4
Bertoua Cameroon **125** I5
Bertraghboy Bay Rep. of Ireland **47** C10
Beru atoll Kiribati **145** G2
also spelt Peru; formerly known as Francis
Beruni Uzbek. **102** E4
formerly known as Shabbaz; formerly spelt Biruni
Beruri Brazil **199** F5
Beruwala Sri Lanka **94** C5
Berveni Romania **49** T8
Berwick-upon-Tweed U.K. **46** J8
Beryslav Ukr. **41** E7
also spelt Berislav
Berytus Lebanon see **Beirut**
Berzasca Romania **58** C4
Bērzaune Latvia **42** H5
Bērzpils Latvia **42** I5
Bès r. France **51** J8
Besah Indon. **77** G2
Besalampy Madag. **131** [inset] J3
Besalú Spain **55** N2
Besançon France **51** M5
historically known as Vesontio
Besar i. Indon. **75** B5
Besar, Gunung mt. Indon. **77** F3
Besar, Gunung mt. Malaysia **76** C1
Besbay Kazakh. **102** C3
Besbre r. France **51** J6
Besed' r. Rus. Fed. **43** M9
Beshariq Uzbek. see **Besharyk**
Besharyk Uzbek. **103** G4
also spelt Beshariq; formerly known as Kirovo

Beshir Turkm. 103 F5
Beshkent Uzbek. 103 F5
Beshneh Iran 100 C4
Besh-Ter, Gora *mt.* Kyrg./Uzbek. 103 G4
also known as Besh-Ter Toosu
or Beshtor Toghi
Besh-Ter Toosu *mt.* Kyrg./Uzbek. *see*
Besh-Ter, Gora
Beshtor Toghi *mt.* Kyrg./Uzbek. *see*
Besh-Ter, Gora
Besikama Indon. 75 C5
Beşiri Turkey 107 E3
Besitang Indon. 76 B1
Beskid Niski *hills* Poland 49 S6
Beskid Sądecki *mts* Poland 49 R6
Beskra Alg. *see* Biskra
Beslan Rus. Fed. 41 H8
Beslet *mt.* Bulg. 58 E7
Besna Kobila *mt.* Yugo. 58 D6
Besnard Lake Canada 167 J4
Besni Turkey 107 D3
Besor *watercourse* Israel 108 F6
Beşparmak Dağları *mts* Cyprus *see*
Pentadaktylos Range
Béssao Chad 126 B3
Bessarabka Moldova *see* Basarabeasca
Bessaye, Gora *mt.* Kazakh. 103 G4
Bessemer *AL* U.S.A. 175 C5
Bessemer *MI* U.S.A. 172 C4
Besshoky, Gora *hill* Kazakh. 102 C3
Bessines-sur-Gartempe France 50 H6
Bessonovka Rus. Fed. 41 H5
Bessou, Mont de *hill* France 51 I7
Bestamak *Aktyubinskaya Oblast'* Kazakh.
102 C2
Bestamak *Vostochnyy Kazakhstan* Kazakh.
103 I2
Bestobe Kazakh. 103 H1
Beswick Australia 148 B2
Beswick Aboriginal Land *res.* Australia
148 B2
Betafo Madag. 131 [inset] J3
Betanzos Bol. 200 D4
Betanzos Spain 54 C1
Bétaré Oya Cameroon 125 I5
Bete Grise U.S.A. 172 F3
Bete Hor Eth. 128 C2
Bétérou Benin 125 F4
Betet *i.* Indon. 76 B3
Beth, Oued *r.* Morocco 122 D2
Bethal S. Africa 133 N3
Bethanie Namibia 130 C5
Bethany *MO* U.S.A. 178 D3
Bethany *OK* U.S.A. 179 C5
Bethari Nepal 97 E4
Bethel *AK* U.S.A. 164 C3
Bethel *ME* U.S.A. 177 O1
Bethel *OH* U.S.A. 176 C3
Bethesda *MD* U.S.A. 177 H6
Bethesda *OH* U.S.A. 176 D5
Bethesdaweg S. Africa 132 H8
Bethlehem S. Africa 133 M5
Bethlehem U.S.A. 177 J5
Bethlehem West Bank 108 G6
also spelt Bayt Laḥm *or* Bet Leḥem
Bethlesdorp S. Africa 133 J10
Bethulie S. Africa 133 J7
Béthune France 51 I2
Betijoque Venez. 198 D2
Betim Brazil 207 I7
Betioky Madag. 131 [inset] J4
Betiri, Gunung *mt.* Indon. 77 F5
Bet Leḥem West Bank *see* Bethlehem
Betlitsa Rus. Fed. 43 O7
Betma India 96 B5
Betong Thai. 79 C7
Betoota Australia 149 D5
Bétou Congo 126 C4
Betpak-Dala *plain* Kazakh. 103 G3
Betrandraka Madag. 131 [inset] J3
Betroka Madag. 131 [inset] J4
Bet She'an Israel 108 G5
Betsiamites Canada 169 G3
Betsiamites *r.* Canada 169 G3
Betsiboka *r.* Madag. 131 [inset] J2
Betsie, Point U.S.A. 172 G6
Betsy Bay Bahamas 187 E2
Betsy Lake U.S.A. 173 H4
Bettendorf U.S.A. 172 C9
Bettiah India 97 E4
Betwa *r.* India 96 C4
Betws-y-coed U.K. 47 I10
Betygala Lith. 42 E6
Beulah U.S.A. 178 B2
Beurfou *well* Chad 120 B6
Beuthen Poland *see* Bytom
Beuvron *r.* France 50 H5
Beverley U.K. 47 L10
Beverly *MA* U.S.A. 177 N4
Beverly *OH* U.S.A. 176 D6
Beverly Hills U.S.A. 182 F7
Beverwijk Neth. 48 B3
Bex Switz. 51 N6
Bextograk China 88 D4
Beyağaç Turkey 59 J11
Beyazköy Turkey 58 I7
Beyce Turkey *see* Orhaneli
Beydağ Turkey 59 J10
Bey Dağları *mts* Turkey 106 B3
Beykonak Turkey 108 R1
Beykoz Turkey 106 B2
Beyla Guinea 124 C4
Beylagan Azer. *see* Beyläqan
Beyläqan Azer. 107 F3
also known as Beylagan; *formerly known as*
Zhdanovsk
Beylul Eritrea 121 I6
Beymeu Kazakh. 102 C3
Beyoneisu Retugan *i.* Japan 91 F9
Beypazarı Turkey 106 C2
Beypınarı Turkey 107 D3
Beypore India 94 B4
Beyra Somalia 128 E3
Beyram Iran 100 C4
Beyrouth Lebanon *see* Beirut
Beyşehir Turkey 106 B3
Beyşehir Gölü *l.* Turkey 106 B3
Beytüşşebap Turkey 107 F3
also known as Elki
Bezameh Iran 100 A3
Bezbozhnik Rus. Fed. 40 I4
Bezdan Vojvodina, Srbija Yugo. 56 K3
Bezenjān Iran 100 D4
Bezhanitskaya Vozvyshennost' *hills*
Rus. Fed. 43 K5
Bezhanitsy Rus. Fed. 43 K5
Bezhanovo Bulg. 58 F6
Bezhetsk Rus. Fed. 43 P4
Bezhetskiy Verkh *reg.* Rus. Fed. 43 P4
Béziers France 51 J9
Bezmein Turkm. *see* Byuzmeyin
Bezwada India *see* Vijayawada
Bhabhar India 96 A5
Bhabra India 96 B5
Bhabua India 97 D4
Bhachau India 96 A5
Bhadar *r.* India 96 A5
Bhadarwah Jammu and Kashmir 96 B2
Bhadaur India 101 H4
Bhadgaon Nepal *see* Bhaktapur
Bhadohi India 97 D4
Bhadra India 96 B3
Bhadrachalam India 94 D2
Bhadrachalam Road Station India *see*
Kottagudem
Bhadrakh India 97 E5
Bhadra Reservoir India 94 B3
Bhadravati India 94 B3
Bhag Pak. 101 F4

Bhagalpur India 97 E4
Ehagirathi *r.* India 97 F5
Ehainsdehi India 96 C5
Bhairab Bazar Bangl. 97 F4
Bhairawa Nepal 97 E4
also known as Siddharthanagar;
also spelt Bhairawaha
Bhairawaha Nepal *see* Bhairawa
Bhairi Hol *mt.* Pak. 101 F5
Bhakkar Pak. 101 G4
Bhaktapur Nepal 97 E4
also known as Bhadgaon
Bhalki India 94 C2
Bhalwal Pak. 101 H3
Bhamgarh India 96 C4
Bhamo Myanmar 78 B2
Bhandara India 96 C5
Bhander India 96 C4
Bhanjanagar India 95 E2
Bhanpura India 96 B4
Bhanrer Range *hills* India 96 C5
Bharat *country* Asia *see* India
Bharatpur India 96 C3
Bharatpur Nepal 97 E4
Bhareli *r.* Pak. 101 E5
Bharthana India 96 C4
Bharuch India 96 B5
formerly known as Broach; *historically known
as* Barygaza *or* Bhrigukaccha
Bhatapara India 97 D5
Bhatghar Lake India 94 B2
Bhatiapara Ghat Bangl. 97 F5
Bhatinda India *see* Bathinda
Bhatkal India 94 B3
Bhatnair India *see* Hanumangarh
Bhatpara India 97 F5
Bhaun Gharibwal Pak. 101 H3
Bhavani India 94 C4
Bhavani *r.* India 94 C4
Bhavani Sagar *l.* India 94 C4
Bhavnagar India 96 B5
Bhawana Pak. 101 H3
Bhawanipatna India 95 D2
Bhearnaraigh, Eilean *i.* U.K. *see* Berneray
Bheemavaram India *see* Bhimavaram
Bhekuzulu S. Africa 133 O4
Bhera India 101 H3
Bheri *r.* Nepal 97 D3
Bhilai India 96 D5
Bhildi India 96 B4
Bhilwara India 96 B4
Bhima *r.* India 94 C2
Bhimavaram India 94 D2
formerly spelt Bheemavaram
Bhimbar Pak. 101 H3
Bhinmal India 96 B4
Bhimphedi Nepal 97 E4
Bhind India 96 C4
Bhingar India 94 B2
Bhinmal India 96 B4
Bhiwandi India 94 B2
Bhiwani India 96 C3
Bhogat India 96 A5
Bhojpur Nepal 97 E4
Bhokardan India 94 B1
Bhola Bangl. 97 F5
Bhongaon India 96 C4
Bhongir India 94 C2
Bhongweni S. Africa 133 N7
Bhopal India 96 C5
Bhopalpatnam India 94 D2
Bhor India 94 B2
Bhrigukaccha India *see* Bharuch
Bhuban India 95 E1
Bhubaneswar India 95 E1
formerly spelt Bhubaneswar
Bhubaneswar India *see* Bhubaneswar
Bhuban Hills India 97 G4
Bhuj India 96 A5
Bhunya Swaziland 133 P3
Bhurgaon Bhutan 97 F4
Bhusawal India 96 B5
Bhutan *country* Asia 97 F4
known as Druk-Yul *in Dzongkha*
asia [countries] >> 64–67
Bhuttewala India 96 A4
Bhuvanagiri India 94 C4
Biá *r.* Brazil 199 E5
Bia, Monts *mts* Dem. Rep. Congo 127 E7
Bia, Phou *mt.* Laos 78 C3
Biabân *mts* Iran 100 D5
Biafra, Bight of *g.* Africa *see* Benin, Bight of
Biak *Irian Jaya* Indon. 73 I7
Biak *Sulawesi Tengah* Indon. 75 B3
Biak *i.* Indon. 73 I7
Biała *r.* Poland 49 Q6
Biała Piska Poland 49 T2
Biała Podlaska Poland 49 U3
Białobrzegi Poland 49 R4
Białogard Poland 49 M2
Białowieski Park Narodowy *nat. park*
Poland 49 U3
Biały Bór Poland 49 N2
Białystok Poland 58 G6
formerly spelt Belostok
Biancavilla *Sicilia* Italy 57 G11
Bianco Italy 57 I5
Bianco, Monte *mt.* France/Italy *see*
Blanc, Mont
Bianga Cent. Afr. Rep. 126 D3
Biankouma Côte d'Ivoire 124 D5
Bianouan Côte d'Ivoire 124 C5
Bianzhuang China *see* Cangshan
Biaora India 96 C5
Bi'ār Ghabāghib *well* Syria 109 K2
Biärjmand Iran 100 C2
Biaro *i.* Indon. 75 C2
Biarritz France 50 E5
Bi'ār Tabrāk *well* Saudi Arabia 105 D2
Biasca Switz. 51 O6
Biba Egypt 121 F2
Bibai Japan 90 G3
Bibala Angola 127 B8
formerly known as Vila Arriaga
Bibanagar India 96 C3
Bibas Gabon 126 A4
Bibbenluke Australia 147 F4
Bibbiena Italy 56 D5
Biberach an der Riß Germany 48 G7
Bibiani Ghana 124 E5
Bibirevo Rus. Fed. 43 N5
Bibiyana *r.* Bangl. 97 F4
Bicas Brazil 207 I5
Bicaz Romania 58 H2
Bicester U.K. 47 J8
Bichenc Australia 147 F5
Bichevaya Rus. Fed. 82 D3
Bichi Nigeria 125 H4
Bichi *r.* Rus. Fed. 82 E1
Bicholim India 94 B3
Bichura Rus. Fed. 85 E1
Bichvint'a Georgia 107 E2
also known as Pitsunda
Bickerton Island Australia 148 C2
Bicuari, Parque Nacional do *nat.*
Angola 127 B8
Bid India *see* Bhir
Bidache France 50 E5
Bidadari, Tanjong *pt* Sabah Malaysia 77 G1
Bidar Point Phil. 74 C4
Bilād Banī 'Alī Oman 105 G3
Bidar India 94 C2
Bidasar India 96 B4
Biddeford U.S.A. 177 O2
Bideford U.K. 47 H12
Bideford Bay U.K. 47 H12

Bilangbilangan *i.* Indon. 77 G2
also known as Barnstaple Bay
Bidente *r.* Italy 56 E4
Bidjovagge Norway 44 M1
Bidkhan, Kūh-e *mt.* Iran 100 D4
Bidokht Iran 100 D3
Bidon 5 *tourist site* Alg. 123 F5
Bidzhan Rus. Fed. 82 D3
Bidzhar *r.* Rus. Fed. 82 D3
Bié Angola *see* Kuito
Bié *prov.* Angola 127 C8
Biebrza *r.* Poland 49 T2
Biebrzański Park Narodowy *nat. park*
Poland 49 T2
Biedenkopf Germany 48 F5
Biel Switz. 51 N5
also known as Bienne
Bielawa Poland 49 N5
Bielefeld Germany 48 F3
Bielitz Poland *see* Bielsko-Biała
Biella Italy 56 A3
Bielsk Podlaski Poland 49 U3
Bielsko-Biała Poland 49 Q6
historically known as Bielitz
Bielsk Poland 49 U3
Bielstein *hill* Germany 51 P1
Bienenbüttel Germany 48 H2
Biên Hoa Vietnam 79 D6
Bienne *r.* France 51 L6
Bienne Switz. *see* Biel
Bienvenida Spain 54 E6
Bienvenue Fr. Guiana 199 H4
Bienville, Lac *l.* Canada 169 F2
Bierbank Australia 149 E5
Biesiesvlei S. Africa 133 J3
Bieszczady *mts* Poland 49 T6
Bieszczadzki Park Narodowy *nat. park*
Poland 49 T6
Bièvre Belgium 51 L3
Biferno *r.* Italy 56 H7
Bifoun Gabon 126 A5
Bifröst Iceland 44 [inset] B2
Bifuka Japan 90 H2
Big *r.* U.S.A. 182 A2
Biga Turkey 106 A2
Biga *r.* Turkey 59 I8
Bigadiç Turkey 106 B3
Biganos France 50 F8
Big Baldy Mountain U.S.A. 180 E3
Big Bay U.S.A. 172 F3
Big Bay de Noc U.S.A. 172 F5
Big Bear Lake U.S.A. 183 H7
Big Belt Mountains U.S.A. 180 E3
Big Bend Swaziland 133 P3
Big Bend National Park U.S.A. 179 B6
Big Black *r.* U.S.A. 175 B5
Big Blue *r.* U.S.A. 178 C3
Big Canyon *watercourse* U.S.A. 179 B6
Big Cypress National Preserve *nature res.*
U.S.A. 175 D7
Big Desert Wilderness Park *nature res.*
Australia 146 D3
Big Eau Pleine Reservoir U.S.A. 172 D6
Biger Nuur *salt l.* Mongolia 84 C2
Big Fork *r.* U.S.A. 174 A1
Biggar Canada 167 J4
Biggar U.K. 46 I8
Biggar, Lac *l.* Canada 168 F3
Biggarsberg S. Africa 133 N5
Bigge Island Australia 150 D2
Biggenden Australia 149 G5
Bigger, Mount Canada 166 B3
Biggleswade U.K. 47 L11
Biggs U.S.A. 182 C3
Big Hole *r.* U.S.A. 180 D3
Bighorn *r.* U.S.A. 180 F3
Bighorn Mountains U.S.A. 180 F3
Bigil'dino Rus. Fed. 43 U8
Big Island *i.* Nunavut Canada 165 L3
Big Island *i.* N.W.T. Canada 167 G2
Big Island U.S.A. 176 F8
Big Kalzas Lake Canada 166 C2
Big Lake *l.* Canada 179 B6
Big Lake *l.* U.S.A. 174 H2
Big Muddy Creek *r.* U.S.A. 180 F2
Bigonia Senegal 124 A3
Bigobe Dem. Rep. Congo 127 E6
Big Otter *r.* U.S.A. 176 F8
Big Pine U.S.A. 182 F4
Big Pine Peak U.S.A. 182 E7
Big Rapids U.S.A. 172 H7
Big Rib *r.* U.S.A. 172 D6
Big River Canada 167 J4
Big Sable Point U.S.A. 172 G6
Big Salmon Canada 166 C2
Big Salmon *r.* Canada 166 C2
Big Sand Lake Canada 167 L3
Big Sandy *r.* U.S.A. 180 E4
Big Sandy *watercourse* U.S.A. 183 K7
Big Sandy Creek *r.* U.S.A. 178 B4
Big Sandy Lake Canada 167 J4
Big Sioux *r.* U.S.A. 178 C3
Big Smokey Valley U.S.A. 183 G3
Big South Cape Island N.Z. 153 B15
Big South Fork National River and
Recreation Area *park* U.S.A. 176 A9
Big Spring U.S.A. 179 B5
Big Stone Canada 167 I5
Big Sur U.S.A. 182 C5
Big Thicket National Preserve *nature res.*
U.S.A. 179 D6
Big Timber U.S.A. 180 E3
Big Trout Lake Canada 168 B2
Big Trout Lake *l.* Canada 168 B2
Big Valley Canada 167 H4
Big Water U.S.A. 183 M4
Bigwin Canada 173 N5
Bihać Bos.-Herz. 56 H4
Bihar *state* India 97 E4
Biharganj India 97 E4
Bihar Sharif India 97 E4
Bihor, Vârful *mt.* Romania 58 D2
Bihoro Japan 90 I3
Bihpuriagaon India 97 G4
Bijagós, Arquipélago dos *is* Guinea-Bissau
124 A4
Bijainagar India 96 C4
Bijaipur India 96 C4
Bijapur India 94 B2
Bijar Iran 100 A3
Bijarpur India 94 D2
Bijawar India 96 C4
Bijbehara Jammu and Kashmir 96 B2
Bijeljina Bos.-Herz. 56 K4
Bijelolasica *mt.* Croatia 56 H3
Bijelo Polje Crna Gora Yugo. 58 A5
Bijie China 86 C3
Bijni India 97 F4
Bijnor India 96 C3
Bijolia India 96 B4
Bijrān *well* Saudi Arabia 105 E2
Bijrān, Khashm *hill* Saudi Arabia 105 E2
Bikampur India 96 B4
Bikaner India 96 B3
Bikbauli Kazakh. 103 E3
Bikfaiya Lebanon 108 G4
Bikin *r.* Rus. Fed. 82 D3
Bikin Rus. Fed. 82 D3
Bikini *atoll* Marshall Is 220 F4
Bikita Zimbabwe 131 F4
Bikori India 97 D5
Bikoro Dem. Rep. Congo 126 C5
Bikramganj India 97 E4
Bilaa Point Phil. 74 C4
Bilād Banī Bū Ḥasan Oman 105 G3
Bilād Oman 105 G3
Bilād Ghāmid *reg.* Saudi Arabia 104 C3
Bilād Zahran *reg.* Saudi Arabia 104 C3
Bilanga Burkina 125 E3

Bilara India 96 B3
Bilari India 96 C3
Bilaspur *Chhattisgarh* India 97 D5
Bilaspur *Himachal Pradesh* India 96 C3
Bilāsuvar Azer. 107 G3
formerly known as Pushkino
Bilatan *r.* Phil. 74 C5
Bila Tserkva Ukr. 41 D6
also spelt Belaya Tserkva
Bilauktaung Range *mts* Myanmar/Thai.
79 B5
Bilbao Spain 55 I1
also spelt Bilbo
Bilbeis Egypt 121 F2
Bilbor Romania 58 G2
Bilbor *r.* France 51 L6
Bilbo Spain *see* Bilbao
Bildudalur Iceland 44 [inset] B2
Bileća Bos.-Herz. 56 K6
Bilecik Turkey 106 B2
Biled Romania 58 B3
Bilesha Plain Kenya 128 D4
Bilgoraj Poland 49 T5
Bilharamulo Tanz. 128 A5
Bilhaur India 96 C4
Bilhorod-Dnistrovs'kyy Ukr. 41 D7
also spelt Belgorod-Dnestrovskyy; *formerly
known as* Akkerman, *historically known as*
Cetatea Albă *or* Tyras
Bili Chad 126 C2
Bili *r.* Dem. Rep. Congo 126 D3
Bilibino Rus. Fed. 39 Q3
Biliboa Moz. 129 D8
Bilikōl *l.* Kazakh. *see* Biylikol', Ozero
Bilin Myanmar 78 B4
Biliran *i.* Phil. 74 C4
Bilisht Albania 58 B8
Bilis Qooqaani Somalia 128 D4
Biliu *r.* China 85 I4
Bili *r.* as Sakhā *well* Saudi Arabia 104 C3
Billabalong Australia 151 A5
Billabong Creek *r.* Australia *see*
Moulamein Creek
Billdal Sweden 45 J4
Billère France 50 F9
Billiat Conservation Park *nature res.*
Australia 146 D3
Billiluna Australia 150 D3
Billiton *i.* Indon. *see* Belitung
Billings U.S.A. 180 E3
Bill of Portland *hd* U.K. 47 J13
also known as Portland Bill
Bilund *airport* Denmark 45 J5
Bill Williams *r.* U.S.A. 183 J7
Bill Williams Mountain U.S.A. 183 L6
Bilma Niger 125 I2
Bilo Eth. 128 C2
Biloela Australia 149 F5
Bilohirs'k Ukr. 41 F7
formerly known as Belogorsk; *formerly
known as* Karasubazar
Bilohir"ya Ukr. 41 C6
Biloku Guyana 199 G4
Biloli India 94 C2
Bilohuts'k Ukr. 41 F6
Bilovods'k Ukr. 41 F6
Biloxi U.S.A. 175 B6
Bilpa Morea Claypan *salt flat* Australia
148 C5
Bilqās Qism Auwal Egypt 108 C6
Bilshausen Germany 48 H4
Biltine Chad 120 D6
Biltine *pref.* Chad 120 D6
Bilugyun Island Myanmar 78 B4
Bilungala Indon. 75 B2
Bilwascarma Nicaragua 186 C4
Bilyayivka Ukr. 41 D7
also spelt Belyayevka
Bima Indon. 77 G5
Bima Dem. Rep. Congo 126 E4
Bima, Teluk *b.* Indon. 77 G5
Bimah, Wādī *watercourse* Oman 105 G3
Bimbe Angola 127 B7
Bimber Pak. 101 H3
Bimbila Ghana 125 F4
Bimini Islands Bahamas 186 D1
Bimlipatam India 95 D2
Bina-Etawa India 96 C4
Binaija, Gunung *mt.* Indon. 75 D3
Binalbagan Phil. 74 B4
Bīnālūd, Kūh-e *mts* Iran 100 D2
Binatang Sarawak Malaysia 77 E2
Binboğa Daği *mt.* Turkey 107 D3
Bincheng China 85 I4
also known as Binxian
Binchuan China 86 B3
Bindki India 96 C4
Bindu Dem. Rep. Congo 127 C6
Bindura Zimbabwe 131 F3
Binefar Spain 55 L3
Binga Zimbabwe 131 E3
Binga, Monte *mt.* Moz. 131 F3
Bingara Australia 147 F2
Bingara *i.* India 94 B4
Bing Bong Australia 148 C2
Bingcaowan China 84 D4
Bingen am Rhein Germany 48 E6
Bin Ghanīmah, Jabal *hills* Libya 120 B3
Bin Ghashir Libya 120 B1
Bingmei China *see* Congjiang
Bingöl Turkey 107 E3
Bingöl Daği *mt.* Turkey 107 E3
Bingxi China *see* Yushan
Bingxi China *see* Yushan
Binh Son Vietnam 79 E5
Binika Phil. 74 B4
Bini Erda *well* Chad 120 C4
Binika India 97 D5
Binjai Indon. 76 B2
Bin Jawwād Libya 120 C2
Binna, Raas *pt* Somalia 128 F2
Binnaway Australia 147 F3
Binongko *i.* Indon. 75 C4
Binpur India 97 E5
Bintan *i.* Indon. 76 C2
Bintang, Bukit *mts* Malaysia 76 C1
Bintuan Phil. 74 B3
Bintuhan Indon. 76 C4
Binubusan Phil. 74 B3
Binxian *Heilong.* China 82 B3
also known as Binzhou
Binxian *Shaanxi* China 87 D1
Binxian China *see* Bincheng
Binyang China 87 D4
also known as Binzhou
Birkat al Asfar *waterhole* Saudi Arabia
109 O8
Bin-Yauri Nigeria 125 G4
Binzhou China *see* Binyang
Binzhou China *see* Binxian
Binzhou China 85 H4
Bioco *i.* Equat. Guinea 125 H6
also spelt Bioko; *formerly known as*
Fernando Poó *or* Macías Nguema
Biograd na Moru Croatia 56 H5
Biogradska Gora *nat. park* Yugo. 58 A6
Bioko *i.* Equat. Guinea *see* Bioco
Biokovo *nature res.* Croatia 56 I5
Biópuhos Brazil 207 H5
Bir India *see* Bhir
Bir, Ras *pt* Djibouti 128 D2
Bira Rus. Fed. 82 D2
Bira *r.* Rus. Fed. 82 D2
Bi'r Abā al 'Ajjāj *well* Saudi Arabia 104 C2
Bīr Abraq *well* Egypt 121 G4

Bīr Abu Darag *well* Egypt 108 D8
Bīr Abu Garad *well* Sudan 121 F5
Bīr Abu Hashim *well* Egypt 121 G4
Bīr Abu Husein *well* Egypt 121 F4
Bīr Abū Minqār *well* Egypt 121 E3
Bi'r ad Damar *well* Libya 120 A3
Bi'r adh Dhakar *well* Saudi Arabia 104 C3
Bir Aïdiat *well* Mauritania 122 C4
Birak Libya 120 B3
Birakan Rus. Fed. 82 C2
Bi'r al Amir *well* Saudi Arabia 104 C3
Bi'r al 'Awadi *well* Saudi Arabia 104 B3
Bi'r al Ghanam Libya 120 B1
Bi'r al Halbā *well* Syria 109 J3
Bi'r al Ḥisw *well* Saudi Arabia 104 C3
Bi'r al Ikhwān *well* Libya 120 B3
Bi'r al Jadid *well* Libya 120 B3
Bi'r al Mashi *well* Saudi Arabia 104 C4
Bi'r al Marba'ah *well* Saudi Arabia 104 B2
Bi'r al Mastūtah *well* Libya 120 A2
Bi'r al Qurr *well* Saudi Arabia 104 C3
Bi'r al 'Alaqah *well* Libya 120 A2
Bi'r as Sakhā *well* Saudi Arabia 104 C3
Bi'r 'Arja *well* Saudi Arabia 104 C2
Bi'r Māfiyah *well* Saudi Arabia 104 C3
Birmingham U.K. 47 K1
Birmingham U.S.A. 175 C5
Bīr Misāha *well* Egypt 121 E4
Birmitrapur India 97 E5
Bi'r Mogreïn Mauritania 122 C2
formerly known as Fort Trinquet
Bi'r Muḥaymid al Wazwaz *well* Syria 109 K3
Bi'r Mujayfil *well* Saudi Arabia 108 G8
Bi'r Murra *well* Egypt 121 F4
Bi'r Muwaylih *well* Syria 109 K3
Bi'r Nabt *well* Saudi Arabia 104 B2
Bi'r Nagib *well* Egypt 121 F4
Bi'r Nāhid *oasis* Egypt 121 F2
Bi'r Nabk *well* Syria 109 K3
Birni Benin 125 F4
Birnie *i.* Kiribati 145 H2
Birnin-Gaouré Niger 125 F3
Birnin-Gwari Nigeria 125 G3
Birnin-Kebbi Nigeria 125 G3
Birnin Konni Niger 125 G3
Birnin Kudu Nigeria 125 H4
Birniwa Nigeria 125 H3
Bir Nukheila *well* Sudan 121 E5
Birobidzhan Rus. Fed. 82 D3
Birofel'd Rus. Fed. 82 D2
Bir Ounane *well* Mali 122 E5
Birpur India 97 E4
Bir Qasir el Sirr *well* Egypt 106 A5
Bir Quleib *well* Egypt 121 F3
Birr Rep. of Ireland 47 E10
Birrie *r.* Australia 147 F2
Birrindudu Australia 148 A3
Birriyel el Aşeifar Egypt 108 B6
Bir Röd Sālim *well* Egypt 108 E7
Bi'r Roumi *well* Alg. 123 G3
Bi'r Sābil Iraq 107 E4
Bi'r Sahara *well* Egypt 121 E4
Bi'r Salala *well* Sudan 121 G4
Birsay U.K. 46 I4
Bi'r Shalatein Egypt 121 G4
Bi'r Shamandūr *well* Syria 109 K1
Birshoghyr Kazakh. *see* Berchogur
Bi'r Shuwayrid *well* Iraq 109 P3
Birsk Rus. Fed. 40 J5
Bi'r Sohanit *well* Sudan 104 A3
Bi'r Tāba Egypt 108 F7
Bi'r Talhah *well* Saudi Arabia 105 D3
Bi'r Tanguer *well* Alg. 123 G3
Bi'r Tānjidar *well* Libya 120 D2
Bi'r Tarfāwi *well* Egypt 121 E4
Bi'r Tarūfāwi *waterhole* Iraq 109 O4
Bi'r Thāl *well* Egypt 123 E8
Birthday Mountain *hill* Australia 149 D2
Birtle Canada 167 K5
Biru China 89 F6
also known as Biruxiong
Bi'r Udeib *well* Egypt 100 D8
Biruintea Moldova *see* Ştefan Vodă
Bi'r Umm el Gharāniq Libya 120 D2
Bi'r Umm Fawākhir *well* Egypt 104 A2
Bi'r Umm Missā *well* Saudi Arabia 104 B2
Bi'r Ungāt *well* Egypt 121 G4
Biruni Uzbek. *see* Beruni
Birur India 94 B3
Bi'r Usayfian *well* Saudi Arabia 105 D3
Biruxiong China *see* Biru
Bi'r Wario *well* Sudan 121 G4
Bi'r Wedeb *well* Libya 120 B3
Bi'r Wurshah *well* Saudi Arabia 104 C4
Biryakovo Rus. Fed. 43 V2
Biržai Lith. 42 F5
Bi'r Zar *well* Tunisia 123 H3
Bisa *i.* Indon. 75 C3
Bisalpur India 96 C3
Bisbee U.S.A. 181 E7
Biscarrosse France 50 E8
Biscarrosse et de Parentis, Étang de *l.*
France 50 E8
Biscay, Bay of *sea* France/Spain 50 A7
Biscayne Bay U.S.A. 175 D7
Biscayne National Park U.S.A. 175 D7
Bischofshofen Austria 49 K8
Bischofswerda Germany 49 L4
Biscoe Islands Antarctica 222 T1
Biscotasing Canada 168 D4
Biser' r. Rus. Fed. 40 K4
Bisertsi Bulg. 58 H5
Biševo *i.* Croatia 56 H6
Bisezhai China 86 B4
Bisha Eritrea 121 H6
Bishah *reg.* Saudi Arabia 104 C4
Bishah, Wādī *watercourse* Saudi Arabia
104 D3
Bishan China 86 C2
also known as Bicheng
Bishbek Kyrg. *see* Bishkek
▶Bishkek Kyrg. 103 H4
Capital of Kyrgyzstan. *Also spelt* Bishbek *or*
Pishpek; *formerly known as* Frunze.

Bishnupur India 97 E5
Bisho S. Africa 133 L9
Bishop U.S.A. 182 F4
Bishop Auckland U.K. 47 K9
Bishop Lake Canada 167 G1
Bishop's Stortford U.K. 47 M12
Bishopville U.S.A. 175 D5
Bishri, Jabal *hills* Syria 109 K2
Bishui China 82 A1
Bishui China *see* Biyang
Bisi S. Africa 133 N7
Bisinaca Col. 198 D3
Biskra Alg. 123 G2
also spelt Beskra
Biskupiec Poland 49 R2
Bislig Phil. 74 C4
Bislig Bay Phil. 74 C4
▶Bismarck U.S.A. 178 B2
State capital of North Dakota.

Bismarck Archipelago *is* P.N.G. 73 K7
Bismarck Sea P.N.G. 73 K7
Bismil Turkey 107 E3
Bismo Norway 45 J3
Bison U.S.A. 178 B2
Bisotūn Iran 100 A3
Bispgården Sweden 44 L3
Bissa, Djebel *mt.* Alg. 55 M8
Bissamcuttak India 95 D2

▶Bissau Guinea-Bissau 124 A3
Capital of Guinea-Bissau.

Bissaula Nigeria 125 H5
Bissett Canada 167 M5
Bissikrima Guinea-Bissau 124 C3
Bissorã Guinea-Bissau 124 A3
Bistcho Lake Canada 167 G3
Bistra *mt.* Macedonia 58 B7
Bistra *r.* Romania 58 D3
Bistra *mt.* Yugo. 58 B6
Bistret Romania 58 E5
Bistret, Lacul *l.* Romania 58 E5

B

Bistrița Romania 58 F1
Bistrița r. Romania 58 H2
Bistrița Bârgăului Romania 58 F1
Bistriței, Munții mts Romania 58 G1
Bistrítsa r. Bulg. 58 E7
Biswan India 96 D4
Bisztynek Poland 49 R1
Bitam Gabon 126 A4
Bitata Eth. 128 C3
Bitburg Germany 48 D6
Bitche France 51 N3
Bitik Kazakh. 102 B2
Bitkine Chad 126 C2
Bitlis Turkey 107 E3
Bitola Macedonia 58 C7
  formerly known as Manastir or Monastir;
  formerly spelt Bitolj
Bitolj Macedonia see Bitola
Bitonto Italy 56 I7
Bitrān, Jabal hill Saudi Arabia 105 D3
Bitra Par reef India 94 B4
Bitter Creek r. WY U.S.A. 180 E4
Bitter Creek r. WY U.S.A. 183 O2
Bitterfontein S. Africa 132 C8
Bitterroot r. U.S.A. 180 D3
Bitterroot Range mts U.S.A. 180 D3
Bitterwater U.S.A. 182 D5
Bittou Burkina 125 F4
Bituca Brazil 202 F4
Bitung Indon. 75 C2
Bityl S. Africa 133 M8
Bityug r. Rus. Fed. 41 F6
Biu Nigeria 125 I4
Biula Angola 127 D7
Bivane r. S. Africa 133 P4
Biwabik U.S.A. 172 A3
Biwa-ko l. Japan 91 D7
Bixad Romania 58 G2
Biyala Egypt 108 C7
Biyang China see Yixian
Biyang China 87 E1
  also known as Bishui
Biye K'obē Eth. 128 D2
Biylikol', Ozero l. Kazakh. 103 G4
  also known as Bilikōl
Biyo Ado well Eth. 128 E3
Biysk Rus. Fed. 88 F2
Bizana S. Africa 133 N7
Bizen Japan 91 D7
Bizerta Tunisia see Bizerte
Bizerte Tunisia 123 H1
  English form Bizerta; also known as Banzart;
  historically known as Hippo Zarytus
Bizhanābād Iran 100 D3

▶Bjargtangar hd Iceland 44 [inset] A2
  Most westerly point of Europe.

Bjärkøy Norway 44 L1
Bjästa Sweden 44 L3
Bjelasica mts Yugo. 58 A6
Bjelašnica mts Bos.-Herz. 56 K5
Bjelovar Croatia 56 I3
Bjerkvik Norway 44 L1
Bjerringbro Denmark 45 J4
Bjøllånes Norway 44 K2
Bjoneroa Norway 45 J3
Bjørbo Sweden 45 K3
Bjørkelangen Norway 45 J4
Björkfjället mts Sweden 44 L2
Björkliden Sweden 44 L1
Björklinge Sweden 45 L3
Björksele Sweden 44 L2
Bjorli Norway 44 I3
Björna Sweden 44 L3
Bjornafjorden b. Norway 45 I3
Bjørneborg Fin. see Pori
Bjørnevatn Norway 44 O1
Bjørnfjell Norway 44 L1

▶Bjørnøya i. Arctic Ocean 38 B2
  Part of Norway. English form Bear Island.

Bjørnstad Norway 44 O1
Bjurholm Sweden 44 L3
Bjuröklubb pt Sweden 44 M2
Bjursås Sweden 45 K3
Blą Mali 124 D3
Blace Kosovo, Srbija Yugo. 58 B6
Blāce Srbija Yugo. 58 C5
Blachownia Poland 49 P5
Black r. Man. Canada 167 L4
Black r. Ont. Canada 168 D3
Black r. Ont. Canada 172 G2
Black r. AR U.S.A. 174 B5
Black r. AZ U.S.A. 183 N8
Black r. MI U.S.A. 173 K8
Black r. SC U.S.A. 175 E5
Black r. WI U.S.A. 172 B6
Blackall Australia 149 E5
Black Bay Ont. Canada 168 B3
Black Bay Sask. Canada 167 I3
Blackbear r. Canada 168 B2
Blackbull Australia 149 D3
Blackburn U.K. 47 I10
Black Butte mt. U.S.A. 182 B2
Black Butte Lake U.S.A. 182 B2
Black Canyon gorge U.S.A. 183 J6
Black Canyon of the Gunnison National Park U.S.A. 181 F5
Black Coast Antarctica 222 T2
Black Creek Canada 168 D5
Black Creek watercourse U.S.A. 183 O6
Black Dome mt. Canada 166 E4
Blackdown Tableland National Park Australia 149 F4
Blackfeet Indian Reservation res. U.S.A. 180 D2
Blackfoot U.S.A. 180 D4
Black Foot r. U.S.A. 180 D3
Blackfoot Reservoir U.S.A. 180 E4
Black Forest mts Germany 48 F8
  also known as Schwarzwald
Black Hill Range hills Australia 148 B5

Black Hills SD U.S.A. 180 F3
Black Island Canada 167 L5
Black Lake Canada 167 J3
Black Lake l. U.S.A. 173 I5
Black Mesa mt. U.S.A. 183 O8
Black Mesa ridge U.S.A. 183 N5
Black Mountain hill U.S.A. 47 I12
Black Mountain CA U.S.A. 182 G6
Black Mountain KY U.S.A. 176 C9
Black Mountain hills U.K. 47 H12
Black Mountains U.S.A. 183 J6
Black Nossob watercourse Namibia 130 C4
  also known as Swart Nossob
Black Pagoda India see Konarka
Black Point Hong Kong China 87 [inset]
  also known as Lan Kok Tsui
Blackpool U.K. 47 I10
Black Range State Park nature res. Australia 147 D4
Black River Jamaica 186 D3
Black River r. U.S.A. 177 J1
Black River r. Vietnam 78 D3
  also known as Da, Sông
Black River Falls U.S.A. 172 C6
Black Rock hill Jordan see 'Unāb, Jabal al
Black Rock Desert U.S.A. 182 E1
Blacksburg U.S.A. 176 E6
Black Sea Asia/Europe 41 F8
  also known as Chernoye More or Kara Deniz
Blacks Fork r. U.S.A. 180 E4
Blackshear U.S.A. 175 D6
Blacksod Bay Rep. of Ireland 47 B9
Black Springs U.S.A. 182 E2
Blackstone r. N.W.T. Canada 166 F2
Blackstone r. Y.T. Canada 166 B1
Blackstone U.S.A. 176 G8
Black Sturgeon r. Canada 172 E2
Black Sugarloaf mt. Australia 147 F2
Black Tickle Canada 169 K2
Black Umfolozi r. S. Africa 133 P5
Black Volta r. Africa 124 E4
  also known as Mouhoun; also known as Volta Noire
Blackwater Australia 149 F4
Blackwater watercourse Australia 149 E5
Blackwater r. Canada 166 E2
Blackwater r. Rep. of Ireland 47 E11
Blackwater r. U.S.A. 177 I9
Blackwater watercourse U.S.A. 179 B5
Blackwater Lake Canada 166 F2
Blackwood National Park Australia 149 E4
Bladensburg National Park Australia 149 D4
Blåfjellshatten mt. Norway 44 K2
Blagodarnyy Rus. Fed. 41 G7
Blagodatnoye Kazakh. 103 H2
Blagoevgrad Bulg. 58 E6
  formerly known as Gorna Dzhumaya
Blagoveshchenka Rus. Fed. 103 I1
Blagoveshchensk Rus. Fed. 82 B2
Blagoveshchensk Rus. Fed. 40 K5
Blagoveshchenskoye Kazakh. 103 H4
Blaikiston, Mount Canada 167 H5
Blain France 50 F5
Blain U.S.A. 176 H5
Blaine U.S.A. 176 B9
Blaine Lake Canada 167 J4
Blair NE U.S.A. 178 C3
Blair WI U.S.A. 172 B6
Blair Athol Australia 149 E4
Blair Atholl U.K. 46 I7
Blairbeth S. Africa 133 K2
Blairgowrie U.K. 46 I7
Blairsden U.S.A. 182 D2
Blairsville U.S.A. 174 D5
Blaj Romania 58 E2
Blak Rus. Fed. 103 E2
Blakang Mati, Pulau i. Sing. see Sentosa
Blakely U.S.A. 175 C6
Blake Point U.S.A. 172 E2
Blakeslee U.S.A. 177 J4
Blama Sierra Leone 124 C5
Blambangan, Semenanjung pen. Indon. 77 F5

▶Blanc, Mont mt. France/Italy 51 M7
  5th highest mountain in Europe. Also known as Bianco, Monte.
  europe [landscapes] ➤➤ 30–31

Blanca, Bahía b. Arg. 204 E5
Blanca, Cordillera mts Peru 200 A2
Blanca, Sierra mt. U.S.A. 181 F6
Blanca Peak U.S.A. 181 F5
Blanche, Lake salt flat S.A. Australia 146 C2
Blanche, Lake salt flat W.A. Australia 150 C4
Blanchester U.S.A. 176 B6
Blanchetown Australia 146 C3
Blanco r. Arg. 204 C3
Blanco r. Bol. 201 D3
Blanco r. Peru 198 C6
Blanco S. Africa 132 G10
Blanco r. Spain 54 F7
Blanco, Cabo c. Costa Rica 186 B5
Blanco, Cape U.S.A. 180 A4
Blanc-Sablon Canada 169 J3
Bland r. Australia 147 E3
  also known as Yeo Yeo
Bland U.S.A. 176 D8
Blanda r. Iceland 44 [inset] B2
Blandford Forum U.K. 47 J13
Blanding U.S.A. 183 O4
Blanes Spain 55 N3
Blaney Park U.S.A. 172 H4
Blangah, Telok b. Sing. 76 [inset]
Blangkejeren Indon. 76 B3
Blangpidie Indon. 76 B3
Blangy-sur-Bresle France 50 H3
Blanice r. Czech Rep. 49 L6
Blankenheim Germany 48 D5
Blanquefort France 50 F8
Blanquilla, Isla i. Venez. 199 E2
Blansko Czech Rep. 49 N6
Blantyre Malawi 129 B8
Blarney Rep. of Ireland 47 D12
Blåsjø l. Norway 45 I4
Blaskaven mt. Norway 45 I3
Blåstöten mt. Sweden 44 K3
Blaszki Poland 49 P4
Blatná Czech Rep. 49 K6
Blattniksele Sweden 44 L2
Blau r. Germany 48 G7
Blaubeuren Germany 48 G7
Blåvands Huk pt Denmark 45 J5
Blavet r. France 50 C5
Blawet r. Cape Verde 124 [inset]
Blaydon U.K. 47 K9
Blaye France 50 F7
Blayeul Sommet mt. France 51 M8
Blayney Australia 147 F3
Blaze, Point Australia 148 A2
Błażowa Poland 49 T6
Blega Indon. 77 F4
Bleik Norway 44 K1
Bleilochtalsperre resr Germany 51 F2
Blekinge county Sweden 45 K4
Blenheim Canada 168 D5
Blenheim N.Z. 152 H9
Blenheim Palace tourist site U.K. 47 K12
Bléré France 50 G5
Blesmanspos S. Africa 132 I4
Bletoppen mt. Norway 45 J4
Bleu, Lac l. Canada 173 O4
Bleus, Monts mts Dem. Rep. Congo 126 F4
Blida Alg. 123 F1
  also spelt El Boulaïda
Bligh Sound inlet N.Z. 153 B12
Bligh Water b. Fiji 145 G3
Blind River Canada 168 D4

Blinkwater S. Africa 133 K9
Blinman Australia 146 C2
  also spelt Bobrovitsa
Bliss U.S.A. 180 D4
Blissfield MI U.S.A. 173 J9
Blissfield OH U.S.A. 176 D5
Blitar Indon. 77 F5
Block Island U.S.A. 177 N4
Block Island l. U.S.A. 177 N4
Block Island Sound sea chan. U.S.A. 177 N4
Bloedrivier S. Africa 133 O4
Bloemfontein S. Africa 133 K6
Bloemhof S. Africa 133 J4
Bloemhof Dam S. Africa 133 J4
Bloemhof Dam Nature Reserve S. Africa 133 J4
Blois France 50 H5
Blomberg se Vloer salt pan S. Africa 132 E7
Blöndulón l. Iceland 44 [inset] C2
Blönduós Iceland 44 [inset] B2
Blongas Indon. 77 G5
Blonie Poland 49 R3
Bloods Range mts Australia 148 A5
Bloodsworth Island U.S.A. 177 I7
Bloodvein r. Canada 167 L5
Bloody Foreland pt Rep. of Ireland 47 D8
Bloomer U.S.A. 172 B5
Bloomfield Canada 173 P7
Bloomfield IA U.S.A. 174 A3
Bloomfield IN U.S.A. 174 C4
Bloomfield MO U.S.A. 174 B4
Bloomfield NM U.S.A. 181 F5
Blooming Prairie U.S.A. 174 A3
Bloomington IL U.S.A. 174 B3
Bloomington IN U.S.A. 174 C4
Bloomington MN U.S.A. 174 A2
Bloomsburg U.S.A. 177 I4
Bloomsbury Australia 149 F4
Blora Indon. 77 E4
Blossburg U.S.A. 177 H4
Blossom, Mys pt Rus. Fed. 39 R2
Blouberg Nature Reserve S. Africa 131 F4
Blountstown U.S.A. 175 C6
Blowing Rock U.S.A. 176 D9
Bludenz Austria 48 G8
Blue r. Canada 166 G3
Blue r. U.S.A. 179 D5
Blue Bell Knoll mt. U.S.A. 183 M3
Blueberry r. Canada 166 F3
Blue Cliff S. Africa 133 J10
Blue Creek r. Mex. see Azul
Blue Diamond U.S.A. 183 I5
Blue Earth U.S.A. 178 D3
Blue Earth r. U.S.A. 178 D2
Bluefield U.S.A. 176 D8
Bluefields Nicaragua 186 C4
Bluegums S. Africa 133 L7
Blue Hill U.S.A. 177 Q1
Blue Hills Turks and Caicos Is 187 E2
Blue Knob hill U.S.A. 176 G5
Blue Lagoon National Park Zambia 127 E8
Blue Mountain hill Canada 169 J3
Blue Mountain India 97 G5
Blue Mountain Pass Lesotho 133 L6
Blue Mountains Australia 147 F3
Blue Mountains N.Z. 153 D14
Blue Mountains U.S.A. 180 C3
Blue Mountains National Park Australia 147 F3
Blue Mud Bay Australia 148 C2
Blue Nile r. Eth./Sudan 104 A5
  also known as Ābay Wenz (Ethiopia), Azraq, Bahr el (Sudan)
Blue Nile state Sudan 128 B2
Bluenose Lake Canada 164 H3
Blue Rapids U.S.A. 178 C4
Blue Ridge GA U.S.A. 174 C5
Blue Ridge VA U.S.A. 176 F8
Blue Ridge mts U.S.A. 176 E9
Blue River Canada 166 G4
Blue Stack Mountains hills Rep. of Ireland 47 D9
Bluestone Lake U.S.A. 176 E8
Bluff Australia 149 F4
Bluff N.Z. 153 C14
Bluff City U.S.A. 176 C9
Bluffdale U.S.A. 183 M1
Bluff Face Range hills Australia 150 D3
Bluff Harbour N.Z. 153 C14
  also known as Sha Tong Hau Shan
Bluff Island Hong Kong China 87 [inset]
Bluff Knoll mt. Australia 151 B7
Bluffton IN U.S.A. 174 C3
Bluffton OH U.S.A. 176 B5
Blumberg Germany 48 F8
Blumenau Brazil 203 B8
Blustry Mountain Canada 166 F5
Blyde River Nature Reserve S. Africa 133 O1
Blyth r. Australia 148 B2
Blyth Canada 173 L7
Blythdale Beach S. Africa 133 P6
Blythe U.S.A. 183 J8
Blytheville U.S.A. 174 B5
Blyth Range hills Australia 151 E6
Bø Norway 45 J4
Bo Sierra Leone 124 C5
Boac Phil. 74 B3
Boaco Nicaragua 186 B4
Boa Esperança Minas Gerais Brazil 203 C7
Boa Esperança Roraima Brazil 199 F4
Boa Esperança, Açude resr Brazil 202 D3
Boa Esperança do Sul Brazil 206 E8
Boa Hora Brazil 202 D3
Boʻai Henan China 85 G5
  also known as Qinghua
Boʻai Yunnan China 86 A4
Boal Spain 54 E1
Boali Cent. Afr. Rep. 126 C3
Boalsburg U.S.A. 176 H5
Boane Moz. 133 Q3
Boano i. Indon. 75 C3
Boano, Selat sea chan. Indon. 75 C3
Boardman U.S.A. 176 E4
Boatlaname Botswana 131 E4
Boatman Australia 147 E1
Boa Viagem Brazil 202 E3
Boa Vista Amazonas Brazil 198 C6
Boa Vista Amazonas Brazil 199 E5
Boa Vista Pará Brazil 199 H5
Boa Vista Roraima Brazil 199 F4
Boa Vista i. Cape Verde 124 [inset]
Bobadah Australia 147 E3
Bobai China 87 D4

▶Bobaomby, Tanjona c. Madag. 131 [inset] K1
  formerly known as Ambre, Cap d'

Bobbili India 95 D2
Bobbio Italy 56 B4
Bobcaygeon Canada 173 O6
Bobia mt. Spain 54 E1
Bobigny France 51 I4
Bobkovo Rus. Fed. 43 U6
Bobo-Dioulasso Burkina 124 D4
Boboliche Poland 49 N2
Bobon Phil. 74 C3
Bobonong Botswana 131 F4
Boborás Spain 54 C2
Bobotov Kuk mt. Yugo. see Durmitor
Bobovdol Bulg. 58 D6
Boboyb, Gora mt. Uzbek. 103 G4
Bobr Belarus 43 K7
Bóbr r. Belarus 43 J7
Bóbr r. Poland 49 M3
Bobrik r. Rus. Fed. 41 G6
Bobrov Rus. Fed. 41 G6
Bobrovitsa Ukr. see Bobrovytsya

Bobrovytsya Ukr. 41 D6
  also spelt Bobrovitsa
Bobruysk Belarus see Babruysk
Bobryk r. Belarus 42 H9
Bobrynets' Ukr. 41 E6
  also spelt Bobrinets
Bobs Lake Canada 173 Q6
Bobso China 86 B1
Bobuk Sudan 128 B2
Bobures Venez. 198 D2
Boby mt. Madag. 131 [inset] J4
Boca Chica Key i. U.S.A. 175 D7
Boca de la Travesía Arg. 204 D6
Boca del Pao Venez. 199 E2
Boca del Río Mex. 185 F5
Boca de Macareo Venez. 199 F2
Boca de Uracoa Venez. 199 F2
Boca do Acre Brazil 200 D2
Boca do Capanã Brazil 199 F6
Boca do Curuquetê Brazil 200 D2
Boca do Jari Brazil 199 I5
Boca do Moaco Brazil 200 C1
Boca Grande r. mouth Trin. and Tob./Venez. 187 H5
Bocaina de Minas Brazil 207 I9
Bocaiúva Brazil 207 I5
Bocaiúva do Sul Brazil 203 B8
Boca Mavaca Venez. 199 E4
Bocanda Côte d'Ivoire 124 D5
Bocaranga Cent. Afr. Rep. 126 C3
Boca Raton U.S.A. 175 D7
Bocas del Toro Panama 186 C5
Bochnia Poland 49 R6
Bocholt Germany 48 D4
Bochum Germany 48 E4
Bochum S. Africa 131 F4
Bockenem Germany 48 H3
Bocoio Angola 127 B7
  formerly known as Sousa Lara
Boçsa Romania 58 C3
Böda Sweden 45 L4
Boda Cent. Afr. Rep. 126 C3
Bodallin Australia 151 B6
Bodalla Australia 147 F3
Bodaybo Rus. Fed. 39 L4
Bodden Town Cayman Is 186 C3
Bode r. Germany 48 H4
Bode-Sadu Nigeria 125 G4
Bodegi Romania 58 H1
Bodfish U.S.A. 182 F6
Bodhan India 94 C2
Bodh Gaya India 97 E4
Bodinayakkanur India 94 C4
Bodiom r. Spain 54 E6
Bodmin U.K. 47 H13
Bodø Norway 44 K2
Bodocó Brazil 202 E3
Bodoquena Mato Grosso do Sul Brazil 201 F5
Bodoquena, Serra da hills Brazil 201 F5
Bodoukpa Cent. Afr. Rep. 126 C3
Bodrog r. Hungary 49 S7
Bodrum Turkey 106 A3
  historically known as Halicarnassus
Bodsjö Sweden 44 K3
Bódva r. Hungary 49 R7
Bodva r. Slovakia 49 R7
Boë r. Guinea 124 B3
Boechout Belgium 51 K1
Boedo r. Spain 54 G2
Boende Dem. Rep. Congo 126 D5
Bo Epinang Indon. 75 B3
Boerne U.S.A. 179 C6
Boesmans r. S. Africa 133 K10
Boesmans hoekpass S. Africa 133 K8
Boeuf r. U.S.A. 175 B6
Bofete Brazil 206 E10
Boffa Guinea 124 B4
Boftsa Norway 44 O1
Bogale Myanmar 78 A4
Bogale r. Myanmar 78 A5
Bogalusa U.S.A. 175 B6
Bogan r. Australia 147 E3
Bogande Burkina 125 E3
Bogan Gate Australia 147 E3
Bogangolo Cent. Afr. Rep. 126 C3
Bogantungan Australia 149 E4
Bogatić Srbija Yugo. 58 A4
Bogazliyan Turkey 106 C3
Bogboua Dem. Rep. Congo 126 C4
Bogcang Zangbo r. China 89 D6
Bogda Feng mt. China 88 E3
Bogdan mt. Bulg. 58 F6
Bogdana Romania 58 G5
Bogdanovka Rus. Fed. 102 C1
Bogda Shan mts China 88 E3
Bogembay Kazakh. 103 H1
Bogen Norway 44 K1
Boggabri Australia 150 B4
Boggeragh Mountains hills Rep. of Ireland 47 C11
Boggola hill Australia 150 B4
Boghar Alg. 55 N9
Boghari Alg. see Ksar el Boukhari
Bogia P.N.G. 73 J7
Bogie r. Australia 149 E4
Bogny-sur-Meuse France 51 K3
Bogo Phil. 74 C4
Bogodukhov Ukr. see Bohodukhiv
Bogodukhovka Kazakh. 103 G1
Bogolyubovo Smolenskaya Oblast' Rus. Fed. 43 N6
Bogolyubovo Vladimirskaya Oblast' Rus. Fed. 43 V5
Bogong, Mount Australia 147 E4
Bogopol' Rus. Fed. 90 D2
Bogor Indon. 77 D4
Bogoroditsk Rus. Fed. 43 T8
Bogoroditskoye Rus. Fed. 43 Q8
Bogorodskoye Rus. Fed. 82 F1
Bogorodskoye Rus. Fed. 40 I4

▶Bogotá Col. 198 C3
  Capital of Colombia and 5th most populous city in South America. Long form Santa Fé de Bogotá.
  world [cities] ➤➤ 24–25

Bogotol Rus. Fed. 80 D1
Bogovarovo Rus. Fed. 40 H4
Bogoyavlenskoye Rus. Fed. see Pervomayskiy
Bogra Bangl. 97 F4
Boguchany Rus. Fed. 39 J4
Boguchar Rus. Fed. 41 G6
Bogué Mauritania 124 B2
Boh r. Indon. 77 F2
Bo Hai g. China 85 H4
  English form Chihli, Gulf of; formerly spelt Po Hai
Bohai Haixia sea chan. China 85 I4
  formerly known as Laotieshan Channel
Bohain-en-Vermandois France 51 J3
Bohai Wan b. China 85 H4
Bohemia reg. Czech Rep. 49 L5
Bohemia Downs Australia 150 D3
Bohemia Downs Aboriginal Reserve Australia 150 D3
Bohemian Forest mts Germany see Böhmer Wald

Bohicon Benin 125 F5
Bohinjska, Vozjera l. Belarus 42 H6
Bohlokong S. Africa 133 M5
Böhmen reg. Czech Rep. see Bohemia
Böhmer Wald mts Germany 49 J6
  English form Bohemian Forest
Bohodukhiv Ukr. 41 E6
  also spelt Bogodukhov
Bohol i. Phil. 74 C4
Bohol Sea Phil. 74 C4
Bohol Strait Phil. 74 B4
Böhöt Mongolia 85 F2
Bohu China 88 D3
  also known as Bagrax
Boi, Ponta do pt Brazil 207 H10
Boiaçu Brazil 199 F5
Boichoko S. Africa 132 H5
Boigu Island Australia 73 J8
Boikhutso S. Africa 133 K3
Boila Moz. 131 H3
Boileau, Cape Australia 150 C4
Boim Brazil 199 H5
Boinu r. Myanmar 78 A3
Boiro Spain 54 C2
Bois, Lac des l. Canada 166 E1
Bois Blanc Island U.S.A. 173 I5
Bois de Sioux r. U.S.A. 178 C2

▶Boise U.S.A. 130 C4
  State capital of Idaho.

Boise r. U.S.A. 180 D4
Boise City U.S.A. 178 B4
Boissevain Canada 167 K5
Boite r. Italy 56 E2
Boitumelong S. Africa 133 J4
Boizenburg Germany 48 H2
Bojador, Cape Western Sahara see Boujdour
Bojnk Srbija Yugo. 58 C5
Bojnūrd Iran 100 D2
Bojonegoro Indon. 77 E4
Bojuru Brazil 204 H3
Bokada Dem. Rep. Congo 126 C3
Bokadaban Feng mt. China 89 E4
Bokajan India 97 G4
Bokanda Congo 126 C5
Bokaro India 97 E5
Bokat Indon. 75 B2
Bokatola Dem. Rep. Congo 126 C5
Boké Guinea 124 B4
Bokhontein S. Africa 132 D9
Boknafjorden sea chan. Norway 45 I4
Boko Congo 127 C6
Boko Dem. Rep. Congo 127 C6
Bokoko Dem. Rep. Congo 126 C3
Bokolo Gabon 126 A5
Bokombayevskoye Kyrg. see Bökönbaev
Bökönbaev Kyrg. 103 I1
  also known as Bokombayevskoye or Bökönbayevo
Bökönbayevo Kyrg. see Bökönbaev
Bokong Lesotho 133 M6
Bokoro Chad 120 C6
Bokote Dem. Rep. Congo 126 D5
Bokovskaya Rus. Fed. 41 G6
Bokpyin Myanmar 79 B6
Boksburg S. Africa 133 M3
Bokspits S. Africa 132 E4
Boktor Rus. Fed. 82 E2
Bokungu Dem. Rep. Congo 126 D5
Bokurdak Turkm. see Bakhardok
Bokwankua Dem. Rep. Congo 126 D5
Bol Chad 120 B6
Bola, Bahr watercourse Chad 126 C1
Bolaiti Dem. Rep. Congo 126 E5
Bolama Guinea-Bissau 124 B4
Bolan r. Pak. 101 F4
Bolangir India see Balangir
Bolaños de Calatrava Spain 54 H6
Bolan Pass Pak. 101 F4
Bolbec France 50 G3
Boldu Romania 58 I3
Boldumsaz Turkm. 102 D4
  formerly known as Kalinin
Bole China 83 C2
Bole Ghana 124 E4
Boleko Dem. Rep. Congo 126 C5
Bolesławiec Poland 49 M4
Bolgar Rus. Fed. 40 I5
  also known as Kuybyshev; also spelt Bulgar
Bolgatanga Ghana 125 E4
Bolgatovo Rus. Fed. 43 J5
Bolgrad Ukr. see Bolhrad
Bolhrad Ukr. 41 D7
  also spelt Bolgrad
Boli China 82 D3
Boli Sudan 128 F3
Bolia Dem. Rep. Congo 126 C5
Boliden Sweden 44 M2
Bolinao Phil. 74 A2
Bolintin-Vale Romania 58 G4
Bolívar Antioquia Col. 198 B3
Bolívar Cauca Col. 198 B4
Bolívar dept Col. 198 C2
Bolívar Peru 200 A1
Bolivar MO U.S.A. 178 D4
Bolivar NY U.S.A. 176 G3
Bolivar TN U.S.A. 174 B5
Bolivar state Venez. 199 F3
Bolívia Cuba 175 E8

▶Bolivia country S. America 200 D4
  5th largest country in South America.
  world [land images] ➤➤ 12–13
  southamer [countries] ➤➤ 192–193
  southamer [impacts] ➤➤ 196–197

Boljevac Srbija Yugo. 58 C5
Bolkhov Rus. Fed. 43 R8
Bolków Poland 49 N5
Bollène France 51 K8
Bollnäs Sweden 45 L3
Bollon Australia 147 E1
Bollstabruk Sweden 44 L3
Bolmen l. Sweden 45 K4
Bolnisi Georgia 107 F2
Bolobo Dem. Rep. Congo 126 C5
Bolod Islands Phil. 74 B5
Bologna Italy 56 D4
  historically known as Bononia or Felsina
Bolognesi Loreto Peru 198 C6
Bolognesi Ucayali Peru 200 B2
Bologoye Rus. Fed. 43 N4
Bologovo Rus. Fed. 43 M5
Bolokanang S. Africa 133 J6
Bolokhovo Rus. Fed. 43 S7
Bolomba Dem. Rep. Congo 126 C4
Bolombo r. Dem. Rep. Congo 126 C5
Bolon' Rus. Fed. see Achan
Bolonchén de Rejón Mex. 185 H4
Bolondo Equat. Guinea 125 H6
Bolong Phil. 74 B5
Bolongongo Angola 127 B7
Bolotana Sardegna Italy 57 A8
Bolotnoye Rus. Fed. 80 D1
Bolotovo Rus. Fed. 43 N2
Bolovens, Phouphieng plat. Laos 79 D5
Bolozo Dem. Rep. Congo 126 C5
Bolpur India 97 E5

Bolsa, Cerro mt. Arg. 204 C3
Bolsena, Lago di l. Italy 56 D6
Bol'shaya Rus. Fed. 42 C7
Bol'shaya Bereyka Rus. Fed. 43 T9
Bol'shaya Chernigovka Rus. Fed. 102 B1
Bol'shaya Churakovka Kazakh. 103 F1
Bol'shaya Glushitsa Rus. Fed. 102 B1
Bol'shaya Imandra, Ozero l. Rus. Fed. 40 E2
Bol'shaya Kokshaga r. Rus. Fed. 40 H4
Bol'shaya Kosha Rus. Fed. 43 O5
Bol'shaya Rogovaya r. Rus. Fed. 40 L2
Bol'shaya Synya r. Rus. Fed. 40 K2
Bol'shaya Tsarevshchina Rus. Fed. see Volzhskiy
Bol'shaya Usa r. Rus. Fed. 40 J4
Bol'shaya Vishera Rus. Fed. 43 N3
Bol'shaya Vladimirovka Kazakh. 103 I2
  also known as Ülken Vladimirovka
Bol'shenarymskoye Kazakh. 88 D1
Bol'she-Ploskoye Rus. Fed. 43 Q4
Bol'sheretsk Rus. Fed. 39 P4
Bol'shevik, Ostrov i. Rus. Fed. 39 K2
Bol'shezemel'skaya Tundra lowland Rus. Fed. 40 J2
Bol'shie Barsuki, Peski des. Kazakh. 102 D3
Bol'shiye Chirki Rus. Fed. 40 H3
Bol'shiye Kozly Rus. Fed. 40 F2
Bol'shiye Medvedki Rus. Fed. 43 S8
Bol'shiye Peshnyye, Ostrova i. Kazakh. 102 B3
  formerly known as Peshnyye, Ostrova
Bol'shoy Aksu Kazakh. 103 I4
Bol'shoy Aksuat, Ozero salt l. Kazakh. 103 F2
  formerly known as Aksuat, Ozero
Bol'shoy Aluy r. Rus. Fed. 39 P3
Bol'shoy Anyuy r. Rus. Fed. 39 Q3
Bol'shoy Begichev, Ostrov i. Rus. Fed. 39 L2
Bol'shoy Berezovyy, Ostrov i. Rus. Fed. 43 J1
Bol'shoy Bukon' Kazakh. 88 C1
Bol'shoye Alekseyevskoye Rus. Fed. 43 T6
Bol'shoye Beresnevo Rus. Fed. 43 N6
Bol'shoye Korovino Rus. Fed. 43 U7
Bol'shoye Mikhaylovskoye Rus. Fed. 43 T5
Bol'shoye Murashkino Rus. Fed. 40 H5
Bol'shoye Ozerko Rus. Fed. 44 P1
Bol'shoye Polpino Rus. Fed. 43 P8
Bol'shoye Popovo Rus. Fed. 43 U9
Bol'shoye Topol'noye, Ozero salt l. Rus. Fed. 103 I1
Bol'shoye Zaborov'ye Rus. Fed. 43 O3
Bol'shoye Zhokovo Rus. Fed. 43 T7
Bol'shoy Ik r. Rus. Fed. 102 C2
Bol'shoy Irgiz r. Rus. Fed. 102 B1
Bol'shoy Kamen' Rus. Fed. 82 D4
Bol'shoy Kavkaz mts Asia/Europe see Caucasus
Bol'shoy Kokovichi Rus. Fed. 43 O1
Bol'shoy Luga Rus. Fed. 84 E1
Bol'shoy Lyakhovskiy, Ostrov i. Rus. Fed. 39 O2
Bol'shoy Porog Rus. Fed. 39 J3
Bol'shoy Shantar, Ostrov i. Rus. Fed. 82 E1
Bol'shoy Tokmak Kyrg. see Tokmak
Bol'shoy Tokmak Ukr. see Tokmak
Bol'shoy Tuder' r. Rus. Fed. 43 M4
Bol'shoy Uzen' r. Kazakh./Rus. Fed. 102 B2
  also known as Ülkenözen
Bol'shoy Yug r. Rus. Fed. 43 T2
Bol'shoy Zelenchuk r. Rus. Fed. 107 E1
Bolsward Neth. 48 C2
Bolton Canada 173 N7
Bolton Phil. 74 C5
Bolton U.K. 47 J10
Boltutino Rus. Fed. 43 N7
Bolu Turkey 106 B2
Bolungarvik Iceland 44 [inset] B2
Boluntay China 84 B4
Boluo China 87 E4
  also known as Luoyang
Bolus Head Rep. of Ireland 47 B12
Bolva r. Rus. Fed. 43 P8
Bolvadin Turkey 106 B3
Bolvanskiy Nos, Mys c. Rus. Fed. 40 K1
Bolyarovo Bulg. 58 H6
Bolzano Italy 56 D2
  also known as Bozen
Boma Dem. Rep. Congo 127 B6
Bomaderry Australia 147 F3
Bomai China 86 A2
Bombala Australia 147 F4
Bombarral Port. 54 B5
Bombay India see Mumbai
Bombay N.Z. 152 I5
Bombay Beach U.S.A. 183 I8
Bomberai, Semenanjung pen. Indon. 73 H7
  English form Bomberai Peninsula
Bomberai Peninsula Indon. see Bomberai, Semenanjung
Bombo r. Dem. Rep. Congo 126 B5
Bombo Uganda 128 B4
Bom Comércio Brazil 200 D2
Bom Despacho Brazil 207 H6
Bomdila India 97 G4
Bomi China 80 D2
  also known as Bowo or Zhamo
Bomili Dem. Rep. Congo 126 E4
Bom Jardim de Goiás Brazil 206 A3
Bom Jardim de Minas Brazil 207 I8
Bom Jesus Piauí Brazil 202 D3
Bom Jesus Rio Grande do Sul Brazil 203 B9
Bom Jesus da Gurgueia, Serra do hills Brazil 202 D3
Bom Jesus da Lapa Brazil 202 D5
Bom Jesus de Goiás Brazil 206 D5
Bom Jesus do Itabapoana Brazil 203 D7
Bomlo i. Norway 45 I4
Bomokandi r. Dem. Rep. Congo 126 E4
Bompas France 51 I10
Bom Retiro Brazil 203 B8
Bom Sucesso Minas Gerais Brazil 207 I8
Bom Sucesso Paraná Brazil 206 B10
Bon, Cap c. Tunisia 123 H1
Bona Alg. see Annaba
Bona, Mount U.S.A. 166 A2
Bonāb Iran 100 A2
Bona Bona Island P.N.G. 149 F1
Bon Air U.S.A. 176 H8
Bonaire i. Neth. Antilles 187 F4
Bonandolok Indon. 76 B2
Bonanza Nicaragua 186 B4
Bonaparte Archipelago is Australia 150 D2
Bonaparte Lake Canada 166 F5
Bonasse Trin. and Tob. 187 H5
Bonavista Canada 169 K3
Bonavista Bay Canada 169 K3
Bon Bon Australia 146 B2
Bondo Équateur Dem. Rep. Congo 126 D5
Bondo Orientale Dem. Rep. Congo 126 D3
Bondoc Peninsula Phil. 74 B3
Bondokodi Indon. 75 A5
Bondoukou Côte d'Ivoire 124 E4
Bondoukui Burkina 124 E4
Bondowoso Indon. 77 F4
Bonduel U.S.A. 172 E6
Bondyuzhskiy Rus. Fed. see Mendeleyevsk
Bône Alg. see Annaba
Bone Indon. 75 B4
Bone, Teluk b. Indon. 75 B4
Bonekrad S. Africa 132 E8
Bonelipu Indon. 75 B4
Bonerate i. Indon. 75 B4
Bonerate, Kepulauan is Indon. 75 B4

▶Bonete, Cerro mt. Arg. 204 C2
3rd highest mountain in South America.

Bonfim Brazil 207 I7
Bonfim r. Brazil 206 A4
Bonfinópolis de Minas Brazil 202 C6
Bonga Eth. 128 C3
Bongabong Phil. 74 B3
Bongaigaon India 97 F4
Bongandanga Dem. Rep. Congo 126 D4
Bongani S. Africa 132 H6
Bongao Phil. 74 A5
Bongba China 89 C5
Bong Co l. China 89 E6
Bongka r. Indon. 75 B3
Bongo i. Phil. 74 C5
Bongo, Massif des mts Cent. Afr. Rep. 126 D2
Bongo, Serra do mts Angola 127 B7
Bongolava mts Madag. 131 [inset] J3
Bongor Chad 126 B2
Bongouanou Côte d'Ivoire 124 D5
Bồng Sơn Vietnam 79 E5
Bonham U.S.A. 179 C5
Bönhamn Sweden 44 L3
Boni Mali 125 E3
Bonifacio Corse France 52 D3
Bonifacio, Bocche di strait France/Italy see Bonifacio, Strait of
Bonifacio, Bouches de strait France/Italy see Bonifacio, Strait of
Bonifacio, Strait of France/Italy 56 A7
also known as Bonifacio, Bocche di or Bonifacio, Bouches de
Boni National Reserve nature res. Kenya 128 D5

▶Bonin Islands N. Pacific Ocean 220 D4
Part of Japan. Also known as Ogasawara-shotō.

Bonita Springs U.S.A. 175 D7
Bonito Mato Grosso do Sul Brazil 201 F5
Bonito Minas Gerais Brazil 207 I2
Bonito r. Brazil 206 B3
Bonito r. Brazil 206 G2

▶Bonn Germany 48 E5
Former capital of Germany. Historically known as Bonna.

Bonna Germany see Bonn
Bonnat France 51 H6
Bonners Ferry U.S.A. 180 C2
Bonnet, Lac du resr Canada 167 M5
Bonnet Plume r. Canada 166 C1
Bonneval France 50 H4
Bonneville France 51 M6
Bonney, Lake Australia 146 D4
Bonnie Rock Australia 151 B6
Bonny Glen Aboriginal Holding res. Australia 149 E3
Bonny Ridge S. Africa 133 N7
Bonnyville Canada 167 I4
Bono Sardegna Italy 57 B8
Bōno-misaki pt Japan 91 B9
Bonom Mhai mt. Vietnam 79 D6
Bononia Italy see Bologna
Bonorva Sardegna Italy 57 A8
Bonoua Côte d'Ivoire 124 E5
Bonpland, Mount N.Z. 153 C12
Bonsall U.S.A. 183 G8
Bonshaw Australia 147 F2
Bontberg mt. S. Africa 132 F9
Bonteberg mts S. Africa 132 D10
Bontebok National Park S. Africa 132 E11
Bonthe Sierra Leone 124 B5
Bontoc Phil. 74 B2
Bontomatane Indon. 75 B4
Bontosunggu Indon. 75 A4
Bontrand S. Africa 133 N7
Bontrug S. Africa 133 J10
Bonvouloir Islands P.N.G. 149 F1
Bonyhád Hungary 49 P9
Boo Sweden 45 L4
Boo, Kepulauan is Indon. 75 D3
Boodie Boodie Range hills Australia 151 C5
Bookabie Australia 146 B2
Book Cliffs ridge U.S.A. 183 O2
Booker U.S.A. 178 B4
Boola Guinea 124 C4
Booleroo Centre Australia 146 C3
Booligal Australia 147 E3
Boologooro Australia 151 A5
Boomi Australia 147 F2
Boon U.S.A. 172 H6
Boonah Australia 147 G1
Boone IA U.S.A. 174 A3
Boone NC U.S.A. 176 D9
Boone Lake U.S.A. 176 C9
Boones Mill U.S.A. 176 F8
Booneville AR U.S.A. 179 D5
Booneville KY U.S.A. 176 B8
Booneville MS U.S.A. 174 B5
Boons S. Africa 133 L2
Boonsboro U.S.A. 176 H6
Böön Tsagaan Nuur salt l. Mongolia 84 C2
Boonville CA U.S.A. 182 A3
Boonville IN U.S.A. 174 C4
Boonville MO U.S.A. 178 D4
Boopi r. Bol. 200 D3
Boorabin National Park Australia 151 C6
Boorama Somalia 128 D2
Booroorban Australia 147 E3
Boorowa Australia 147 F3
Boosaaso Somalia 128 F2
Boothbay Harbor U.S.A. 177 P2
Boothby, Cape Antarctica 223 D2
Boothia, Gulf of Canada 165 K3
Boothia Peninsula Canada 165 J2
Booué Gabon 126 A5
Bopolu Liberia 124 C5
Boppard Germany 48 E5
Boqê China 89 E6
Boqueirão Brazil 204 G3
Boqueirão, Serra do hills Brazil 202 C5
Bor Rus. Fed. 40 H4
Bor Sudan 128 A3
Bor Turkey 106 C3
Bor Srbija Yugo. 58 D4
Boragi waterhole Kenya 128 C5
Borah Peak U.S.A. 180 D3
Borakalalo Nature Reserve S. Africa 133 L2
Boran Kazakh. see Buran
Boraraigh i. U.K. see Boreray
Borås Sweden 45 K4
Borasambar India 95 D1
Borāzjān Iran 100 B4
Borba Brazil 199 G6
Borba Port. 54 D6
Borbollón, Embalse del resr Spain 54 E4
Borbon Phil. 74 C4
Borborema Brazil 206 D8
Borborema, Planalto da plat. Brazil 202 E3
Borca Romania 58 G1
Borcea, Braţul watercourse Romania 58 I4
Borchalo Georgia see Marneuli
Borchgrevink Coast Antarctica 223 K2
Borçka Turkey 107 E2
also known as Yeniyol
Borda, Cape Australia 150 C3
Borda da Mata Brazil 207 G9
Bor Dağı mt. Turkey 59 K11
Bordeaux France 50 F8
historically known as Burdigala
Bordehi India 96 C5
Bordein Sudan 121 G6
Borden Canada 169 I4
Borden Island Canada 165 H2
Borden Peninsula Canada 165 K2
Bordentown U.S.A. 177 K5
Border Ranges National Park Australia 147 G2
Bordertown Australia 146 D4
Borðeyri Iceland 44 [inset] B2
Bordj Bou Arréridj Alg. 123 G1
Bordj Bounaama Alg. 55 M9
Bordj Flye Ste-Marie Alg. 123 E4
Bordj Messaouda Alg. 123 H3
Bordj Mokhtar Alg. 123 F5
Bordj Omar Driss Alg. see Bordj Omer Driss
Bordj Omer Driss Alg. 123 G3
formerly known as Fort Flatters or Zaouet el Kahla; formerly spelt Bordj Omar Driss
Bordj Zemoura Alg. 55 P8
Borðoy i. Faroe Is 46 F1
Bordu Kyrg. 103 H4
also known as Bordunskiy
Bordunskiy Kyrg. see Bordu
Bordușani Romania 58 I4
Boré Mali 124 E3
Boreas Nunatak Antarctica 223 X2
Borel r. Canada 169 G1
Borensberg Sweden 45 K4
Boreray i. U.K. 46 D6
also spelt Boraraigh
Borgå Fin. see Porvoo
Borgafjäll Sweden 44 K2
Borgarfjörður Iceland 44 [inset] D2
Borgarnes Iceland 44 [inset] B2
Børgefjell Nasjonalpark nat. park Norway 44 K2
Borger U.S.A. 179 B5
Borgholm Sweden 45 L4
Borgo Corse France 51 P10
Borgo a Mozzano Italy 56 C5
Borgomanero Italy 56 A3
Borgo San Dalmazzo Italy 51 N8
Borgo San Lorenzo Italy 56 D5
Borgosesia Italy 56 A3
Borgo Val di Taro Italy 56 B4
Borgo Valsugana Italy 56 D2
Borgsjåbrotet mt. Norway 45 J3
Bori India 94 C1
Bori r. India 96 B5
Börili Kazakh. see Burli
Borilovo Rus. Fed. 43 Q8
Borino Bulg. 58 F7
Borinskoye Rus. Fed. 43 U9
Borisoglebsk Rus. Fed. 41 G6
Borisoglebskiy Rus. Fed. 43 U4
Borisov Belarus see Barysaw
Borisovka Rus. Fed. 41 F6
Borisovo-Sudskoye Rus. Fed. 43 R2
Borispol' Ukr. see Boryspil'
Bo River Post Sudan 126 E3
Boriziny Madag. 131 [inset] J2
Borja mts Bos.-Herz. 56 J4
Borja Peru 198 B6
Borjas Blancas Spain see Les Borges Blanques
Borj Bourguiba Tunisia 123 H2
Borjomis Nakrdzali nature res. Georgia 107 E2
Borkavichy Belarus 43 J6
Borken Germany 48 D4
Borkenes Norway 44 L1
Borki Rus. Fed. 43 T9
Borkou-Ennedi-Tibesti pref. Chad 120 C5
Borkovskaya Rus. Fed. 40 I2
Borkum Germany 48 D2
Borkum i. Germany 48 D2
Borlänge Sweden 45 K3
Borlaug Norway 45 I3
Borlu Turkey 106 B3
Borna Germany 49 J4
Born-Berge hill Germany 48 H4
Borne Alg. 123 G4

▶Borneo i. Asia 77 F2
Largest island in Asia and 3rd in the world.
asia [landscapes] ⟶ 62–63

Bornes mts France 51 M7
Bornholm i. Denmark 45 K5
Bornholmsgattet strait Denmark/Sweden 45 K5
Borno state Nigeria 125 I4
Bornova Turkey 106 A3
Borobudur tourist site Indon. 77 E4
Borodino Krasnoyarskiy Kray Rus. Fed. 39 I3
Borodino Moskovskaya Oblast' Rus. Fed. 43 Q6
Borodino Ukr. 58 K2
Borodinskoye Rus. Fed. 43 K1
Borodyanka Ukr. 41 D6
Borogontsy Rus. Fed. 39 N3
Borohoro Shan mts China 88 C2
Borok Rus. Fed. 43 T3
Boroko Indon. 75 B2
Borok-Sulezhskiy Rus. Fed. 43 R4
Boromo Burkina 124 E4
Boron Mali 124 D3
Boron U.S.A. 182 G7
Borongan Phil. 74 C4
Bororen Australia 149 F5
Borovan Bulg. 58 E5
Borovenka Rus. Fed. 43 O3
Borovichi Rus. Fed. 43 O3
Borovo Selo Croatia 56 K3
Borovoy Kirovskaya Oblast' Rus. Fed. 40 I4
Borovoy Respublika Kareliya Rus. Fed. 40 E2
Borovoy Respublika Komi Rus. Fed. 40 J3
Borovoye Kazakh. 103 G1
Borovsk Rus. Fed. 43 R6
Borovskoy Kazakh. 103 F1
Borrachudo r. Brazil 207 H5
Borrazópolis Brazil 206 B10
Borrego Springs U.S.A. 183 H8
Borroloola Australia 148 C3
Børsa Norway 44 J3
Borşa Romania 58 E2
Borşa Romania 53 G2
Borsad India 96 B5
Borsec Romania 58 G2
Børselv Norway 44 N1
Borshchiv Ukr. 41 C6
Borshchovochnyy Khrebet mts Rus. Fed. 85 F1
Borsippa tourist site Iraq 107 F4
Borskoye Rus. Fed. 102 B1
Börßum Germany 48 H3
Bortala China see Bole
Bortala He r. China 88 C2
Bort-les-Orgues France 51 I7
Bor-Üdzüür Mongolia 84 B2
Borūjen Iran 100 B4
Borūjerd Iran 100 B3
Bor Ul Shan mts China 84 C3
Borun Iran 100 D3
Borushtitsa Bulg. 58 G6
Boryspil' Ukr. 40 D6
also spelt Borispol'
Borzna Ukr. 41 E6
Börzsönyi park Hungary 49 P8
Borzya Rus. Fed. 85 H1
Borzya r. Rus. Fed. 85 G1
Bosa Sardegna Italy 57 A8
Bosaga Kazakh. 103 H3
also spelt Bosagha; formerly known as Bosaginskiy
Bosagha Kazakh. see Bosaga
Bosaginskiy Kazakh. see Bosaga
Bosanska Dubica Bos.-Herz. 56 I3
also known as Kozarska Dubica
Bosanska Gradiška Bos.-Herz. 56 J3
also known as Gradiška
Bosanska Kostajnica Bos.-Herz. 56 I3
also known as Srpska Kostajnica
Bosanska Krupa Bos.-Herz. 56 I4
also known as Krupa or Krupa na Uni
Bosanski Brod Bos.-Herz. 56 K3
also known as Srpski Brod
Bosanski Novi Bos.-Herz. 56 I3
also known as Novi Grad
Bosanski Petrovac Bos.-Herz. 56 I4
also known as Petrovac
Bosanski Šamac Bos.-Herz. 56 K3
also known as Šamac
Bosberg mt. S. Africa 133 K5
Bosbokrand S. Africa 133 P1
Boscawen U.S.A. 177 N2
Boscawen Island Tonga see Niuatoputopu
Bosch Arg. 204 F5
Boscobel U.S.A. 172 C7
Bosduiflaagte salt pan S. Africa 132 E6
Bose China 86 C4
Bosencheve, Parque Nacional nat. park Mex. 185 E5
Boshchakul' Kazakh. see Bozshakol'
Boshnyakovo Rus. Fed. 82 F2
Boshoek S. Africa 133 L2
Boshof S. Africa 133 J5
Boshruyeh Iran 100 D3
Bosilegrad Srbija Yugo. 58 D6
formerly spelt Bosiljgrad
Bosiljgrad Srbija Yugo. see Bosilegrad
Boskol' Kazakh. 103 E1
also spelt Bozköl; formerly spelt Buskul'
Boskovice Czech Rep. 49 N6
Boslanti Suriname 199 H3
Bosna r. Bos.-Herz. 56 K3
Bosna hills Bulg. 58 I6
Bosna i Hercegovina country Europe see Bosnia-Herzegovina
Bosna Saray Bos.-Herz. see Sarajevo
▶Bosnia-Herzegovina country Europe 56 J4
known as Bosna i Hercegovina in Bosnian
europe [countries] ⟶ 32–35
Boso Dem. Rep. Congo 126 D4
Bosobogolo Pan salt pan Botswana 132 G2
Bosobolo Dem. Rep. Congo 126 C3
Bōsō-hantō pen. Japan 91 G7
Bososama Dem. Rep. Congo 126 D3
Bospoort S. Africa 133 K3
▶Bosporus strait Turkey 106 B2
also known as İstanbul Boğazı
europe [countries] ⟶ 32–33
Bosque Spain 54 C1
Bossaga Turkm. see Basaga
Bossangoa Cent. Afr. Rep. 126 C3
Bossembélé Cent. Afr. Rep. 126 C3
Bossemptélé Cent. Afr. Rep. see Bossentélé
Bossentélé Cent. Afr. Rep. 126 C3
formerly spelt Bossemptélé
Bossiekom S. Africa 132 E6
Bossier City U.S.A. 179 D5
Bossiesvlei Namibia 130 C5
Bosspruit S. Africa 133 L2
Bossut, Cape Australia 150 C3
Bostan China 89 D4
Bostān Iran 100 A4
Bosten Hu l. China 88 D3
also known as Bagrax Hu
Boston U.K. 47 L11

▶Boston U.S.A. 177 N3
State capital of Massachusetts.

Boston Creek Canada 173 N2
Boston Mountains U.S.A. 179 D5
Bosut r. Croatia 56 L3
Boswell IN U.S.A. 172 F10
Boswell PA U.S.A. 176 F5
Botad India 96 A5
Botata Liberia 124 C5
Boteå Sweden 44 L3
Boteler Point S. Africa 133 Q3
Boteni Romania 58 G3
Boteti r. Botswana 131 E4
Botev mt. Bulg. 58 F6
Botevgrad Bulg. 58 E6
Bothaville S. Africa 133 K4
Bothell U.S.A. 180 B3
Bothnia, Gulf of Fin./Sweden 44 L3
Bothwell Australia 147 E5
Bothwell Canada 173 L8
Boticas Port. 54 D3
Botin mt. Bos.-Herz. 56 K5
Botkins U.S.A. 176 A5
Botlikh Rus. Fed. 102 A4
Botna r. Moldova 58 K2
Botoșani Romania 53 H2
Botou China 85 H4
Bô Trach Vietnam 78 D4
Botro Côte d'Ivoire 124 D5
Botshabelo S. Africa 133 K6
Botsmark Sweden 44 M2
▶Botswana country Africa 130 D4
formerly known as Bechuanaland
world [population] ⟶ 22–23
africa [countries] ⟶ 114–117
Bottenviken g. Fin./Sweden 44 M2
Bottineau U.S.A. 178 B1
Bottle Creek Turks and Caicos Is 187 E2
Bottom Neth. Antilles 187 H3
Bottrop Germany 48 D4
Botucatu Brazil 206 E9
Botumirim Brazil 207 J3
Bouaflé Côte d'Ivoire 124 D5
Bou Ahmed Morocco 54 G9
Bouaké Côte d'Ivoire 124 D5
Boualem Alg. 123 F2
Bouandougou Côte d'Ivoire 124 D4
formerly spelt Buandougou
Bouanga Congo 126 C5
Bouar Cent. Afr. Rep. 126 B3
Bou Arada Tunisia 57 B12
Bouârfa Morocco 123 E2
Bou Aroua Alg. 123 G2
Bouba Ndjida, Parc National de nat. park Cameroon 125 I4
Boubin mt. Czech Rep. 49 K6
Boû Bleï'îne well Mauritania 124 C2
Boubout well Alg. 122 D4
Bouca Cent. Afr. Rep. 126 C3
Boucau France 50 E9
Boucaut Bay Australia 148 B2
Bouchette Canada 173 R4
Bouctouche Canada 169 H4
Boudinar Morocco 54 H9
Boû Djébéha well Mali 124 E2
Boudoua Cent. Afr. Rep. 126 C3
Boudry Switz. 51 M6
Bouenza admin. reg. Congo 126 B6
Bouenza r. Congo 126 B6
Boufore Cent. Afr. Rep. 126 C3
Bougainville, Cape Australia 150 D2
Bougainville Island P.N.G. 145 E2
Bougaroûn, Cap c. Alg. 123 G1
Boughessa Mali 125 F2
formerly spelt Bouressa
Bougie Alg. see Bejaïa
Bougoumen Chad 126 B2
Bougouni Mali 124 D4
Bougtob Alg. 123 F2
Boû Guendouz well Mali 124 D2
Bouguirat Alg. 55 L9
Bougzoul Alg. 55 N9
Bouillon Belgium 51 L3
Bouïra Alg. 123 F1
Bou Izakarn Morocco 122 C3
Boujdour W. Sahara 122 B4
Bou Kahil, Djebel mts Alg. 123 F2
Boukoumbé Benin 125 F4
Boukta Chad 126 C2
Boulder Australia 151 C6
Boulder CO U.S.A. 180 F4
Boulder MT U.S.A. 180 D3
Boulder UT U.S.A. 183 M4
Boulder Canyon gorge U.S.A. 183 J5
Boulder City U.S.A. 183 J6
Bou Legmaden, Oued watercourse Alg./Morocco 122 C3
Boulemane Morocco 122 D2
Boulemane Morocco 122 D2
Boulevard U.S.A. 183 H9
Boulhaut Morocco see Ben Slimane
Boulia Australia 148 C4
Boulogne France see Boulogne-sur-Mer
Boulogne r. France 50 E5
Boulogne-Billancourt France 51 I4
Boulogne-sur-Mer France 50 H2
historically known as Gesoriacum; short form Boulogne
Bouloui r. Cent. Afr. Rep. 126 E3
Boulouba Cent. Afr. Rep. 126 D3
Boulouparis New Caledonia 145 F4
Boulsa Burkina 125 E3
Boultoum Niger 125 H3
Boumango Gabon 126 B5
Boumba r. Cameroon 125 I6
Boumbé I r. Cent. Afr. Rep. 126 B3
Boumerdes Alg. 123 F1
Bouna Côte d'Ivoire 124 E4
Bou Naceur, Jbel mt. Morocco 122 E2
Boû Nâga Mauritania 124 B2
Boundary U.S.A. 166 A1
Boundary Peak U.S.A. 182 F4
Boundiali Côte d'Ivoire 124 D4
Boung r. Vietnam 79 E4
Boungou r. Cent. Afr. Rep. 126 D3
Bountiful U.S.A. 183 M1
Bounty Islands N.Z. 145 G6
Bourail New Caledonia 145 F4
Bourbince r. France 51 K6
Bourbon terr. Indian Ocean see Réunion
Bourbon-Lancy France 51 J6
Bourbonne-les-Bains France 51 L5
Bourbriac France 50 C4
Bourem Mali 125 E2
Bouressa Mali see Boughessa
Bourg France 50 F7
Bourganeuf France 50 H7
Bourg-en-Bresse France 51 L6
Bourges France 51 I5
historically known as Avaricum
Bourgmont Canada 173 R2
Bourgneuf, Baie de b. France 50 D5
Bourgogne admin. reg. France 51 K5
Bourgoin-Jallieu France 51 L7
Bourg-St-Andéol France 51 K8
Bourg-St-Maurice France 51 M7
Bourke Australia 147 E2
Bourkes Canada 173 M2
Bournemouth U.K. 47 K13
Bouroum-Bouroum Burkina 124 E4
Bourtoutou Chad 126 D2
Bourzanga Burkina 125 E3
Bou Saâda Alg. 123 G2
Bou Salem Tunisia 57 A12
Bouse U.S.A. 183 J8
Bouse Wash watercourse U.S.A. 183 J7
Boussé Burkina 125 E3
Bousso Chad 126 C2
Boû Tezâya well Mauritania 124 C2
Boutilimit Mauritania 124 B2
Boutougou Fara Senegal 124 B3
Bouvet Island terr. S. Atlantic Ocean see Bouvetøya

▶Bouvetøya terr. S. Atlantic Ocean 217 O9
Dependency of Norway. English form Bouvet Island.

Boven Kapuas Mountains Indon./Malaysia see Kapuas Hulu, Pegunungan
Bow r. Australia 150 E3
Bow r. Alta Canada 167 I5
Bowa China see Muli
Bowbells U.S.A. 178 B1
Bowden U.S.A. 176 F7
Bowditch atoll Tokelau see Fakaofo
Bowen Arg. 204 D4
Bowen Australia 149 F4
Bowen r. Australia 149 E4
Bowen, Mount Australia 147 F4
Bowen Downs Australia 149 E4
Bowen Strait Australia 148 B1
Bowers Mountains Antarctica 223 K2
Bowie AZ U.S.A. 183 O9
Bowie TX U.S.A. 179 C5
Bow Island Canada 167 I5
Bowkan Iran 100 A2
Bowling Green KY U.S.A. 174 C4
Bowling Green MO U.S.A. 174 B4
Bowling Green OH U.S.A. 176 B4
Bowling Green VA U.S.A. 177 H7
Bowling Green Bay Australia 149 E3
Bowling Green Bay National Park Australia 149 E3
Bowman U.S.A. 178 B2
Bowman, Mount Canada 166 F5
Bowman Coast Antarctica 222 T2
Bowman Island Antarctica 223 G2
Bowman Peninsula Antarctica 222 T2
Bowmanville Canada 173 O7
Bown Somalia 128 D2
Bowo China see Bomai
Bowo China see Bomi
Bow River Aboriginal Reserve Australia 150 D3
Bowron r. Canada 166 F4
Bowron Lake Provincial Park Canada 166 F4
Bowser Lake Canada 166 D3
Boxberg Germany 48 G6
Box Elder U.S.A. 178 B2
Box Elder r. U.S.A. 178 B2
Boxholm Sweden 45 K4
Boxing China 85 H4
Boxtel Neth. 48 C4
Boyabat Turkey 106 C2
Boyaca dept Col. 198 C3
Boyadzhik Bulg. 58 H6
Boyalıca Turkey 58 K8
Boyalık Turkey see Çiçekdağı
Boyana tourist site Bulg. 58 E6
Boyang China 87 F2
formerly known as Poyang
Boyanovichi Rus. Fed. 43 P8
Boyanovo Bulg. 58 H6
Boyd r. Australia 147 G2
Boyd Lagoon salt flat Australia 151 D5
Boyd Lake Canada 167 K2
Boydton U.S.A. 176 G9
Boyer r. U.S.A. 178 D3
Boyera Dem. Rep. Congo 126 C5
Boyertown U.S.A. 177 J5
Boykins U.S.A. 177 H9
Boyle Canada 167 H4
Boyle Rep. of Ireland 47 D10
Boyne r. Qld Australia 149 F4
Boyne r. Qld Australia 149 F5
Boyne r. Rep. of Ireland 47 F10
Boyne City U.S.A. 173 H5
Boyni Qara Afgh. 101 F2
Boyo Cent. Afr. Rep. 126 D3
Boyoma, Chutes waterfall Dem. Rep. Congo see Boyoma Falls
Boyoma Falls Dem. Rep. Congo 126 E4
also known as Boyoma, Chutes; formerly known as Stanley, Chutes
Boysun Uzbek. see Baysun
Boyuibe Bol. 201 E5
Böyük Hinaldağ mt. Azer. 100 A1
Boyup Brook Australia 151 B7
Bozashy Tübegi pen. Kazakh. see Buzachi, Poluostrov
Bozburun Turkey 106 B3

▶Bozcaada i. Turkey 106 A3
Most westerly point of Asia. Also known as Tenedos.

Bozdağ mt. Turkey 59 H10
Bozdağ mt. Turkey 109 H1
Boz Dağları mts Turkey 106 A3
Bozdoğan Turkey 106 B3
Bozeman U.S.A. 180 E3
Bozen Italy see Bolzano
Bozhou China 87 E1
Bozkır Turkey 106 C3
also known as Silistat
Bozköl Kazakh. see Boskol'
Bozkurt Turkey 59 K11
Bozouls France 51 I8
Bozoum Cent. Afr. Rep. 126 C3
Bozova Turkey 107 D3
also known as Hüvek
Bozovici Romania 58 D4
Bozqūsh, Kūh-e mts Iran 100 A2
Bozshakol' Kazakh. 103 H2
formerly spelt Boshchakul'
Boztumsyk Kazakh. 103 F2
Bozüyük Turkey 106 B3
Bozyazı Turkey 108 D1
Bra Italy 51 N8
Brabant Island Antarctica 222 T2
Brač i. Croatia 56 I5
Bracara Port. see Braga
Bracciano Italy 56 E6
Bracciano, Lago di l. Italy 56 E6
Bracebridge Canada 168 E4
Brachet, Lac au l. Canada 169 G3
Bräcke Sweden 44 K3
Brackettville U.S.A. 179 B6
Brački Kanal sea chan. Croatia 56 I5
Bracknell U.K. 47 L12
Braço Norte r. Brazil 201 G2
Brad Romania 58 D2
Bradano r. Italy 57 I8
Bradenton U.S.A. 175 D7
Bradford Canada 173 N6
Bradford U.K. 47 K10
Bradford PA U.S.A. 176 G4
Bradford VT U.S.A. 177 M2
Bradley U.S.A. 172 F9
Bradner U.S.A. 176 B4
Bradshaw U.S.A. 176 D8
Brady U.S.A. 179 C6
Brady Creek r. U.S.A. 179 C6
Brady Glacier U.S.A. 166 B3
Braemar U.K. 46 I6
Braga Port. 54 C3
historically known as Bracara
Braga admin. dist. Port. 54 C3
Bragado Arg. 204 E4
Bragança Brazil 202 C2
Bragança Port. 54 E3
Bragança admin. dist. Port. 54 E3
Bragança Paulista Brazil 206 G9
Brahin Belarus 41 D6
Brahmakund India 97 H4
Brahmanbaria Bangl. 97 F5
Brahmani r. India 95 E1
Brahmapur India 95 E2
Brahmaputra r. China/India 89 D6
also known as Dihang (India) or Yarlung Zangbo (China)
Braidwood Australia 147 F3
Braidwood U.S.A. 172 E9
Brăila Romania 58 I3
Brăilei, Insula Mare a i. Romania 58 I4
Braine France 51 J3
Brainerd U.S.A. 178 D2
Braintree U.K. 47 M12
Braithwaite Point Australia 148 B1
Braives Belgium 51 L2
Brak r. S. Africa 132 E10
Brak watercourse S. Africa 132 C5
Brake (Unterweser) Germany 48 F2
Brâkna admin. reg. Mauritania 124 B2
Brakpoort S. Africa 132 H8
Brakspruit S. Africa 133 K3
Brakwater Namibia 130 C4
Bralorne Canada 166 F5
Bramhapuri India 94 C1
Bramming Denmark 45 J5
Brampton Canada 168 E5
Brampton U.K. 47 J9
Bramsche Germany 48 F3
Bramsöfjärden l. Sweden 45 L3
Brancaleone Italy 57 I11
Branch Canada 169 K4
Branco r. Mato Grosso Brazil 201 E2
Branco r. Roraima Brazil 199 F5
Branco i. Cape Verde 124 [inset]
Brandberg mt. Namibia 130 B4
Brändbo Sweden 45 L3
Brandbu Norway 45 J3
Brande Denmark 45 J5
Brandenburg Germany 49 J3
Brandenburg land Germany 49 K3
Brandenburg U.S.A. 174 C4
Brandenburger Wald- und Seengebiet park Germany 49 J3
Brandfort S. Africa 133 K5
Brandkop S. Africa 132 D8
Brändö Fin. 45 M3
Brandon Canada 167 L5
Brandon MS U.S.A. 175 B5
Brandon SD U.S.A. 178 C3
Brandon VT U.S.A. 177 L2
Brandon Head Rep. of Ireland 47 B11
Brandon Mountain hill Rep. of Ireland 47 B11
Brandonville U.S.A. 176 F6
Brandvlei S. Africa 132 E7
Brandvlei Dam resr S. Africa 132 D10
Brandvoll Norway 44 L1
Brani, Pulau i. Sing. 76 [inset]
Braniewo Poland 49 Q1
Brännberg Sweden 44 M2
Brannenburg Germany 48 J8
Bransfield Strait Antarctica 222 T2
Brańsk Poland 49 T3
Brantas r. Indon. 77 F4
Brantford Canada 168 D5
Brantôme France 50 G7
Branxholm Australia 147 E5
Brás Brazil 199 G5
Brasaljce Kosovo, Srbija Yugo. 58 C6
Bras d'Or Lake Canada 169 I4
Brasil Brazil 198 D6
Brasil country S. America see Brazil
Brasil, Planalto do plat. Brazil 203 D6
Brasilândia Mato Grosso do Sul Brazil 206 A8
Brasilândia Minas Gerais Brazil 206 E2
Brasilândia Minas Gerais Brazil 207 G4
Brasileia Brazil 200 C2

▶Brasília Brazil 206 F2
Capital of Brazil.
southamerica [countries] ⟶ 192–193

Brasília de Minas Brazil 202 C6
Brasília Legal Brazil 199 H5
Brasla r. Latvia 42 F4
Braslav Belarus see Braslaw
Braslaw Belarus 42 I6
also spelt Braslav
Brașov Romania 58 G3
formerly known as Orașul Stalin; historically known as Kronstadt
Brasovo Rus. Fed. 43 P9
Brassey, Banjaran mts Sabah Malaysia 77 G1
Brassey, Mount Australia 148 B4
Brassey Range hills Australia 151 C5
Bratan mt. Bulg. 58 G6
Bratca Romania 58 D2

▶Bratislava Slovakia 49 O7
Capital of Slovakia. Also known as Pozsony; formerly known as Pressburg.

Bratsk Rus. Fed. 80 G1
Bratskoye Vodokhranilishche resr Rus. Fed. 80 G1
Brattleboro U.S.A. 177 M3
Brattmon Sweden 45 K3
Brattvåg Norway 44 I3
Bratunac Bos.-Herz. 56 L4
Braulio Carrillo, Parque Nacional nat. park Costa Rica 186 C5
Braúnas Brazil 207 K6
Braunau am Inn Austria 49 K7
Braunsbedra Germany 48 I4
Braunschweig Germany 48 H3
historically known as Brunswick
Brava i. Cape Verde 124 [inset]
Brave U.S.A. 176 E6
Bråviken inlet Sweden 45 L4
Bravo, Cerro mt. Bol. 201 D4
Bravo del Norte, Río r. Mex./U.S.A. 185 F3
also known as Rio Grande
Brawley U.S.A. 183 I9
Bray Rep. of Ireland 47 F10
also spelt Bré
Bray S. Africa 132 H2
Braye r. France 50 G5
Bray Island Canada 165 L3
Bray-sur-Seine France 51 J4
Brazeau r. Canada 167 H4
Brazeau, Mount Canada 167 G4

▶Brazil country S. America 202 B4
Largest country in South America and 5th in the world. Most populous country in South America and 5th in the world. Spelt Brasil in Portuguese.
world [countries] ⟶ 10–11
world [population] ⟶ 22–23
southamerica [countries] ⟶ 192–193

Brazil U.S.A. 174 C4
Brazos r. U.S.A. 179 D6

▶Brazzaville Congo 126 B6
Capital of Congo.

Brčko Bos.-Herz. 56 K4
Brda r. Poland 49 P2
Brdy hills Czech Rep. 49 K6
Bré Rep. of Ireland see Bray
Breakfast Vlei S. Africa 133 K10
Breaksea Sound inlet N.Z. 153 A13
Breaksea Spit Australia 149 G5
Bream Bay N.Z. 152 I3
Bream Head N.Z. 152 I3
Bream Tail c. N.Z. 152 I4
Breas Chile 204 C2
Breaza Romania 58 G3
Brebes Indon. 77 E4
Brechin U.K. 46 J7
Brecht Belgium 51 K1
Breckenridge CO U.S.A. 180 F5
Breckenridge MN U.S.A. 178 C2
Breckenridge TX U.S.A. 179 C5
Brecknock, Peninsula pen. Chile 205 B9
Břeclav Czech Rep. 49 N7
Brecon U.K. 47 I12
also known as Aberhonddu
Brecon Beacons reg. U.K. 47 I12
Brecon Beacons National Park U.K. 47 I12
Breda Neth. 48 B4
Bredasdorp S. Africa 132 E11
Bredbo Australia 147 F3
Bredviken Sweden 44 K2
Bredy Rus. Fed. 103 E1
Breede r. S. Africa 132 E11
Bregalnica r. Macedonia 58 C7
Bregenz Austria 48 G8
Bregovo Bulg. 58 D4
Bréhal France 50 E4
Breiðafjörður b. Iceland 44 [inset] A2
Breiðdalsvík Iceland 44 [inset] D2
Breil-sur-Roya France 51 N9
Breipaal S. Africa 133 K7
Breisach am Rhein Germany 48 E7
Breivikbotn Norway 44 M1
Breivikeidet Norway 44 L1
Brejinho de Nazaré Brazil 202 B4
Brejo Brazil 202 D2
Brejo r. Brazil 202 D4
Brejo da Porta Brazil 202 C4
Brekstad Norway 44 J3
Bremen Germany 48 F2
Bremen GA U.S.A. 175 C5
Bremen OH U.S.A. 176 C6
Bremer Bay Australia 151 B7
Bremerhaven Germany 48 F2
Bremer Range hills Australia 151 C7
Bremersdorp Swaziland see Manzini
Bremerton U.S.A. 180 B3
Bremervörde Germany 48 G2
Breń r. Poland 49 S5
Brenham U.S.A. 179 C6
Brenna Norway 44 K2
Brennero Italy 56 D2
Brennero, Passo di pass Austria/Italy see Brenner Pass
Brennerpaß pass Austria/Italy see Brenner Pass
Brenner Pass pass Austria/Italy 48 I9
also known as Brennero, Passo di or Brennerpaß
Breno Italy 56 C3
Brenta r. Italy 56 E3
Brenta, Gruppo di mts Italy 56 C2
Brentwood U.K. 47 M12
Brenzone Italy 56 C3
Brescia Italy 56 C3
historically known as Brixia
Breslau Poland see Wrocław
Bresle r. France 50 H2
Brésolles, Lac l. Canada 169 G2
Bressanone Italy 56 D2
Bressay i. U.K. 46 K3
Bressuire France 50 F6
Brest Belarus 42 E9
formerly known as Brest-Litovsk or Brześć nad Bugiem
Brest France 50 B4
Brest-Litovsk Belarus see Brest
Brest Oblast admin. div. Belarus see Brestskaya Voblasts'
Brestovac Srbija Yugo. 58 C5
Brestskaya Oblast' admin. div. Belarus see Brestskaya Voblasts'
Brestskaya Voblasts' admin. div. Belarus 42 G9
English form Brest Oblast; also known as Brestskaya Oblast'
Bretagne admin. reg. France 50 D4
English form Brittany
Bretagne reg. France see Brittany
Bretana Peru 198 C6
Bretcu Romania 58 H2
Breteuil Haute-Normandie France 50 G4
Breteuil Picardie France 51 I3
Brétigny-sur-Orge France 51 I4
Breton Canada 167 H4
Breton Sound b. U.S.A. 175 B6
Bretten Germany 48 F6
Breu r. Brazil/Peru 200 B2
Breueh, Pulau i. Indon. 76 A1
Brevard U.S.A. 174 D5
Breves Brazil 202 B2
Brewarrina Australia 147 E2
Brewer U.S.A. 177 Q1
Brewerville Liberia 124 C5
Brewster NE U.S.A. 178 C3
Brewster OH U.S.A. 176 D5
Brewster WA U.S.A. 180 C2
Brewster, Kap c. Greenland see Kangikajik
Brewster, Lake imp. l. Australia 147 E3

Brewton U.S.A. 175 C6
Breyten S. Africa 133 N3
Breytovo Rus. Fed. 43 S3
Brezhnev Rus. Fed. see Naberezhnyye Chelny
Brežice Slovenia 56 H3
Breznik Bulg. 58 D6
Breznita-Motru Romania 58 E4
Breznitsa Bulg. 58 E7
Brezno Slovakia 49 Q7
Brezovo Bulg. 58 G6
Brezovo Polje hill Croatia 56 J3
Bria Cent. Afr. Rep. 126 D3
Briakan Rus. Fed. 82 D1
Briançon France 51 M8
Brian Head mt. U.S.A. 183 L4
Briare France 51 I5
Bribie Island Australia 149 G5
Briceni Moldova 41 C6
formerly spelt Brichany
Brichany Moldova see Briceni
Bricquebec France 50 E3
Bridgehampton U.S.A. 177 M5
Bridgeman U.S.A. 172 G9
Bridgend U.K. 47 I12
also known as Pen-y-Bont ar Ogwr
Bridgeport AL U.S.A. 174 C5
Bridgeport CA U.S.A. 182 E3
Bridgeport CT U.S.A. 177 L4
Bridgeport MI U.S.A. 173 J7
Bridgeport NE U.S.A. 178 B3
Bridgeport TX U.S.A. 179 C5
Bridgeport Reservoir U.S.A. 182 E3
Bridger Peak U.S.A. 180 F4
Bridgeton U.S.A. 177 J6
Bridgetown Australia 151 B7

▶Bridgetown Barbados 187 I4
Capital of Barbados.

Bridgetown Canada 169 H4
Bridgeville U.S.A. 177 J7
Bridgewater Australia 147 E5
Bridgewater Canada 169 H4
Bridgewater MA U.S.A. 177 O4
Bridgewater NY U.S.A. 177 J3
Bridgewater VA U.S.A. 176 G7
Bridgton U.S.A. 177 O1
Bridgwater U.K. 47 I12
Bridgwater Bay U.K. 47 I12
Bridlington U.K. 47 L9
Bridport Australia 147 E5
Bridport U.K. 47 J13
Brie reg. France 51 I4
Briec France 50 C4
Brie-Comte-Robert France 51 I4
Brieg Poland see Brzeg
Brienne-le-Château France 51 K4
Brienzer See l. Switz. 51 N6
Briery Knob mt. U.S.A. 176 E7
Brig Switz. 51 N6
Briggsville U.S.A. 172 D7
Brigham City U.S.A. 180 D4
Brighton Canada 173 P6
Brighton N.Z. 153 E13
Brighton U.K. 47 L13
Brighton CO U.S.A. 180 F5
Brighton IA U.S.A. 172 B9
Brighton MI U.S.A. 173 J8
Brighton NY U.S.A. 176 H2
Brighton WV U.S.A. 176 C7
Brighton Downs Australia 149 D4
Brignoles France 51 M9
Brihuega Spain 55 I4
Brikama Gambia 124 A3
Brillion U.S.A. 172 E6
Brilon Germany 48 F4
Brimley U.S.A. 173 I4
Brimnes Iceland 44 [inset] D2
Brimson U.S.A. 172 B3
Brindisi Italy 57 J8
historically known as Brundisium
Brinje Croatia 56 H3
Brinkley U.S.A. 174 B5
Brinkworth Australia 146 C3
Brion, Île i. Canada 169 I4
Brionne France 50 G3
Brioude France 51 J7
Brisay Canada 169 G2

▶Brisbane Australia 147 G1
State capital of Queensland and 3rd most populous city in Oceania.
world [cities] ▶▶ 24–25

Brisighella Italy 56 D4
Bristol U.K. 47 J12
Bristol CT U.S.A. 177 M4
Bristol FL U.S.A. 175 C6
Bristol NH U.S.A. 177 N2
Bristol RI U.S.A. 177 N4
Bristol TN U.S.A. 176 C9
Bristol VT U.S.A. 177 L1
Bristol Bay U.S.A. 164 C4
Bristol Channel est. U.K. 47 H12
Bristol Lake U.S.A. 183 I7
Bristol Mountains U.S.A. 183 H7
Britânia Brazil 206 B2
Britannia Island New Caledonia see Maré
British Antarctic Territory Antarctica 222 S2
British Columbia prov. Canada 166 F5
British Empire Range mts Canada 165 K1
British Guiana country S. America see Guyana
British Honduras country Central America see Belize

▶British Indian Ocean Territory terr. Indian Ocean 218 L6
United Kingdom Overseas Territory.
asia [countries] ▶▶ 64–67

British Solomon Islands country S. Pacific Ocean see Solomon Islands
Brito Godins Angola see Kiwaba N'zogi
Brits S. Africa 133 L2
Britstown S. Africa 132 H7
Brittany admin. reg. France see Bretagne
Brittany reg. France 50 C4
also known as Bretagne
Britton U.S.A. 178 C2
Brive-la-Gaillarde France 50 H7
Briviesca Spain 55 H2
Brixham U.K. 47 I13
Brixia Italy see Brescia
Brlik Kazakh. see Birlik
Brlik Kazakh. 103 H4
also spelt Birlik
Brno Czech Rep. 49 N6
formerly spelt Brünn
Broach India see Bharuch
Broad r. U.S.A. 174 D5
Broadalbin U.S.A. 177 K2
Broad Arrow Australia 151 C6
Broadback r. Canada 168 E3
Broad Bay U.K. 46 F5
also known as Tuath, Loch a'
Broadford U.K. 46 G6
Broad Law hill U.K. 46 I8
Broadmere Australia 148 B3
Broad Sound sea chan. Australia 149 F4
Broad Sound Channel Australia 149 F4
Broadsound Range hills Australia 149 F4
Broadus U.S.A. 180 F3
Broadview Canada 167 K5
Broadwater U.S.A. 178 B3
Broadway U.S.A. 176 G7
Broadwood N.Z. 152 H3
Broby Sweden 45 K4
Broceni Latvia 42 D5
Brochet Canada 167 K3
Brocken mt. Germany 48 H4
Brockman, Mount Australia 150 B4
Brockport NY U.S.A. 176 H2
Brockport PA U.S.A. 176 G4
Brockton U.S.A. 177 N3
Brockville Canada 168 F4
Brockway U.S.A. 176 G4
Brod Macedonia 58 C7
Broderick Falls Kenya see Webuye
Brodeur Peninsula Canada 165 K2
Brodhead KY U.S.A. 176 A8
Brodhead WI U.S.A. 172 D8
Brodheadsville U.S.A. 177 J5
Brodick U.K. 46 G8
Brodnax U.S.A. 176 G9
Brodnica Poland 49 Q2
Brody Ukr. 41 C6
Broedersput S. Africa 133 J3
Brok r. Poland 49 S3
Broke Inlet Australia 151 B7
Broken Arrow U.S.A. 179 D4
Broken Bay Australia 147 F3
Broken Bow NE U.S.A. 178 C3
Broken Bow OK U.S.A. 179 D5
Broken Bow Reservoir U.S.A. 179 D5
Brokenburg U.S.A. 176 H7
Brokenhead r. Canada 167 L5
Broken Hill Australia 146 D2
Broken Hill Zambia see Kabwe
Brokopondo Suriname 199 H3
Brokopondo Stuwmeer resr Suriname see Professor van Blommestein Meer
Bromberg Poland see Bydgoszcz
Bromnes Norway 44 L1
Bromo Tengger Semeru National Park Indon. 77 F4
Bromsgrove U.K. 47 J11
Brønderslev Denmark 45 J4
Brong-Ahafo admin. reg. Ghana 125 E5
Bronkhorstspruit S. Africa 133 M2
Bronnitsy Rus. Fed. 43 T6
Brønnøysund Norway 44 K2
Bronson FL U.S.A. 175 D6
Bronson MI U.S.A. 173 H9
Bronte Sicilia Italy 57 G11
Brooke U.S.A. 176 H7
Brooke's Point Phil. 74 A4
Brookfield MO U.S.A. 178 D4
Brookfield WI U.S.A. 172 E7
Brookhaven U.S.A. 175 B6
Brookings OR U.S.A. 180 A4
Brookings SD U.S.A. 178 C2
Brookline U.S.A. 177 N3
Brooklyn U.S.A. 173 I8
Brooklyn Park U.S.A. 174 A2
Brookneal U.S.A. 176 G8
Brooks Canada 167 I5
Brooks ME U.S.A. 177 P1
Brooks WV U.S.A. 176 E8
Brooks, Cape Antarctica 222 T2
Brooks Brook Canada 166 C2
Brooks Range mts U.S.A. 164 E3
Brookston IN U.S.A. 172 G10
Brookston MN U.S.A. 172 A4
Brooksville FL U.S.A. 175 D6
Brooksville KY U.S.A. 176 A7
Brookton Australia 151 B7
Brookville U.S.A. 176 F4
Broom, Loch inlet U.K. 46 G6
Broome Australia 150 C3
Broomehill Australia 151 B7
Broons France 50 D4
Brora U.K. 46 I5
Brora r. U.K. 46 I5
Brøstadbotn Norway 44 L1
Broşteni Romania 58 G1
Brosville U.S.A. 176 F9
Brotas Brazil 206 E9
Brotas de Macaúbas Brazil 202 D5
Brothers U.S.A. 180 B4
Brou France 50 H4
Broughton Island Canada see Qikiqtarjuaq
Broulkou well Chad 120 C5
Brovary Ukr. 41 D6
Brown, Lake salt flat Australia 151 B6
Brown, Mount hill Australia 146 C3
Brown, Point Australia 146 B3
Brown City U.S.A. 173 K7
Brown Creek r. Australia 149 D3
Brown Deer U.S.A. 172 F7
Browne Range hills Australia 151 D5
Brownfield U.S.A. 179 B5
Brown Mountain U.S.A. 183 G6
Brown's Town Jamaica 186 D3
Brownstown U.S.A. 174 C4
Brownsville PA U.S.A. 176 F5
Brownsville TN U.S.A. 174 B5
Brownsville TX U.S.A. 179 C7
Brownsweg Suriname 199 H3
Brownwood U.S.A. 179 C6
Browse Island Australia 150 C2
Brozas Spain 54 E5
Brozha Belarus 43 K9
Bruay-la-Bussière France 51 I2
Bruce MS U.S.A. 174 B5
Bruce WI U.S.A. 172 B5
Bruce, Mount Australia 150 B4
Bruce Peninsula Canada 173 L6
Bruce Peninsula National Park Canada 173 L5
Bruce Rock Australia 151 B6
Bruchsal Germany 48 F6
Bruck an der Leitha Austria 49 N7
Bruck an der Mur Austria 49 M8
Bruges Belgium see Brugge
Brugge Belgium 51 J1
also spelt Bruges
Bruhagen Norway 44 I3
Bruin KY U.S.A. 176 B7
Bruin PA U.S.A. 176 F4
Bruin Point mt. U.S.A. 183 N2
Bruint India 97 H3
Brûk, Wâdi el watercourse Egypt 108 E7
Brukkaros Namibia 130 C5
Brukkaros, Mount Namibia 132 B2
Brûlé Canada 166 G4
Brule U.S.A. 172 B4
Brûlé, Lac l. Canada 169 I2
also known as Burnt Lake
Brumadinho Brazil 207 I7
Brumado Brazil 202 D5
Brumath France 51 N4
Brumer Islands P.N.G. 149 F1
Brumunddal Norway 45 J3
Brú Na Bóinne tourist site Rep. of Ireland 47 F10
Brundisium Italy see Brindisi
Bruneau r. U.S.A. 180 D4
Bruneau, West Fork r. U.S.A. 180 D4
▶Brunei country Asia 77 F1
asia [countries] ▶▶ 64–67
Brunei Brunei see Bandar Seri Begawan
Brunei Bay Malaysia 77 F1
Brunette Downs Australia 148 B3
Brunette Island Canada 169 K4
Brunflo Sweden 44 K3
Brunico Italy 56 D2
Brünn Czech Rep. see Brno
Brunna Sweden 45 L4
Brunner, Lake N.Z. 153 F10
Bruno Canada 167 J4
Bruno U.S.A. 172 A4
Brunsbüttel Germany 48 G2
Brunswick Germany see Braunschweig
Brunswick GA U.S.A. 175 D6
Brunswick MD U.S.A. 176 H6
Brunswick ME U.S.A. 177 P2
Brunswick MO U.S.A. 178 D4
Brunswick OH U.S.A. 176 D4
Brunswick, Peninsula de pen. Chile 205 C9
Brunswick Bay Australia 150 D2
Brunswick Head Australia 147 G2
Brunswick Junction Australia 151 A7
Brunswick Lake Canada 168 D3
Bruntál Czech Rep. 49 O6
Brunt Ice Shelf Antarctica 222 W2
Bruny Island Australia 147 E5
Brus Srbija Yugo. 58 C5
Brusa Turkey see Bursa
Brush U.S.A. 178 B3
Brushton U.S.A. 177 K1
Brusovo Rus. Fed. 43 Q4
Brusque Brazil 203 B8
Brussel Belgium see Brussels

▶Brussels Belgium 51 K2
Capital of Belgium. Also spelt Brussel or Bruxelles.
europe [issues] ▶▶ 34–35

Brusturi-Drăgăneşti Romania 58 H1
Brusy Poland 49 O2
Bruthen Australia 147 E4
Bruxelles Belgium see Brussels
Bruyères France 51 M4
Bruzual Venez. 198 D2
Bryan OH U.S.A. 176 A4
Bryan TX U.S.A. 179 C6
Bryan, Mount hill Australia 146 C3
Bryan Coast Antarctica 222 S2
Bryansk Rus. Fed. 43 P8
Bryanskaya Oblast' admin. div. Rus. Fed. 43 O8
English form Bryansk Oblast
Bryansk Oblast admin. div. Rus. Fed. see Bryanskaya Oblast'
Bryanskoye Rus. Fed. 102 A3
Bryant AR U.S.A. 179 D5
Bryant WI U.S.A. 172 D5
Bryant Creek r. U.S.A. 178 D4
Bryant Pond U.S.A. 177 O1
Bryce Canyon National Park U.S.A. 183 L4
Bryce Mountains U.S.A. 183 O8
Bryn' Rus. Fed. 43 Q8
Bryne Norway 45 I4
Bryson, Lac l. Canada 173 P4
Bryukhovetskaya Rus. Fed. 41 F7
Brzava r. Yugo. 58 B3
Brzeg Poland 49 O5
historically known as Brieg
Brzeg Dolny Poland 49 N4
Brześć nad Bugiem Belarus see Brest
Brzozów Poland 49 T6
Bū well Yemen 105 D4
Bua Angola 127 B6
Bua Sweden 45 K4
Bu'aale Somalia 128 D4
Buad i. Phil. 74 C4
Buala Solomon Is 145 E2
Buandougou Côte d'Ivoire see Bouandougou
Buang i. Indon. 75 C2
Buatan Indon. 76 C2
Bū Athlah well Libya 120 D2
Bu'ayj well Saudi Arabia 105 E2
Bu'ayrāt al Hasūn Libya 120 B2
Bubanza Burundi 126 F5
Bubi r. Zimbabwe 131 F4
Būbiyān Island Kuwait 107 G5
Bubuan i. Phil. 74 B5
Bubuan i. Phil. 74 B5
Buca Turkey 59 I10
Bucak Turkey 106 B3
Bucaramanga Col. 198 C3
Bucas Grande i. Phil. 74 C4
Buccaneer Archipelago is Australia 150 C3
Bucegi, Munţii mts Romania 58 G3
Buchan Australia 147 F4
Buchanan Liberia 124 C5
Buchanan MI U.S.A. 172 G9
Buchanan VA U.S.A. 176 F8
Buchanan, Lake salt flat Australia 149 E4
Buchanan, Lake U.S.A. 179 C6
Buchan Gulf Canada 165 L2
Buchans Canada 169 J3

▶Bucharest Romania 58 H4
Capital of Romania. Also spelt Bucureşti or Bukreş.

Buchen (Odenwald) Germany 48 G6
Bucholz in der Nordheide Germany 48 G2
Buchon, Point U.S.A. 182 D6
Buchy France 50 H3
Bucin, Pasul pass Romania 58 G2
Buckburn Draw watercourse U.S.A. 179 B6
Bückeburg Germany 48 G3
Buckeye U.S.A. 183 L8
Buckhannon U.S.A. 176 E7
Buckhannon r. U.S.A. 176 F6
Buckhaven U.K. 46 I7
Buckhorn Canada 173 O6
Buckhorn Lake Canada 173 O6
Buckie U.K. 46 J6
Buckingham Canada 173 R5
Buckingham U.K. 47 L11
Buckingham PA U.S.A. 177 J5
Buckingham VA U.S.A. 176 G8
Buckland U.S.A. 164 C3
Bucklands S. Africa 132 H6
Buckland Tableland reg. Australia 149 F5
Buckleboo Australia 146 C3
Buckle Island Antarctica 223 K2
Buckley watercourse Australia 148 C4
Buckley U.S.A. 172 E10
Buckley Bay Antarctica 223 J2
Buckskin Mountains U.S.A. 183 K7
Bucks Mountain U.S.A. 182 C2
Bucksport U.S.A. 177 Q1
Bučovice Czech Rep. 49 O6
Bucşani Romania 58 G4
Bucureşti Romania see Bucharest
Bucyrus U.S.A. 176 C5
Bud Norway 44 I3
Buda Rus. Fed. 43 P8
Buda, Illa de i. Spain 55 L4
Budai park Hungary 49 P8
Buda-Kashalyova Belarus 43 L9
Budalin Myanmar 78 A3

▶Budapest Hungary 49 Q8
Capital of Hungary. Historically known as Aquincum.

Budaun India 96 C3
Budayyi'ah well Saudi Arabia 104 C3
Bud Bud Somalia 128 E3
Budd Coast Antarctica 223 H2
Buddi Eth. 128 D3
Buddusò Sardegna Italy 57 B8
Bude U.K. 47 H13
Budennovsk Rus. Fed. 41 H7
Buderim Australia 149 G5
Budeşti Romania 58 H4
Budhīya, Gebel hills Egypt 108 E8
Budogoshch' Rus. Fed. 43 N2
Budongquan China 84 B5
Budoni Sardegna Italy 57 B8
Büdszentmihály Hungary see Tiszavasvári
Budū', Sabkhat al salt pan Saudi Arabia 105 E3
Budureasa Romania 58 D2
Budva Crna Gora Yugo. 56 K6
Budweis Czech Rep. see České Budějovice
Budzilava Belarus 43 K6
Buea Cameroon 125 H5
Buëch r. France 51 L8
Buellton U.S.A. 182 D7
Buena Esperanza Arg. 204 D4
Buenaventura Col. 198 B4
Buenaventura Mex. 184 D2
Buena Vista Bol. 201 E4
Buena Vista Mex. 185 E5
Buena Vista i. N. Mariana Is see Tinian
Buenavista Phil. 74 B3
Buena Vista CO U.S.A. 180 F5
Buena Vista GA U.S.A. 175 C5
Buena Vista VA U.S.A. 176 F8
Buena Vista, Bahía de b. Cuba 186 D2
Buendia, Embalse de resr Spain 55 I4
Buenga r. Angola 127 B6
Buengas Angola 127 B6
formerly known as Nova Esperança
Buenolândia Brazil 206 C2
Buenópolis Brazil 203 C6

▶Buenos Aires Arg. 204 F4
Capital of Argentina. 2nd most populous city in South America and 10th in the world.
world [cities] ▶▶ 24–25

Buenos Aires prov. Arg. 204 E5
Buenos Aires Brazil 200 B2
Buenos Aires Amazonas Col. 198 D5
Buenos Aires Guaviare Col. 198 C4
Buenos Aires Costa Rica 186 C5
Buenos Aires, Lago l. Arg./Chile 205 B7
Buenos Aires National Wildlife Refuge nature res. U.S.A. 181 E7
Buen Pasto Arg. 205 C7
Buen Tiempo, Cabo c. Arg. 205 C8
Buerarema Brazil 202 E5
Buesaco Col. 198 B4
Bueu Spain 54 C2
Buey, Cabeza de mt. Spain 55 H6
Búfalo Mex. 184 D3
Buffalo r. Canada 167 H2
Buffalo MO U.S.A. 178 D4
Buffalo NY U.S.A. 176 G3
Buffalo OH U.S.A. 176 D6
Buffalo OK U.S.A. 178 C4
Buffalo SD U.S.A. 180 G3
Buffalo TX U.S.A. 179 C6
Buffalo WI U.S.A. 172 B6
Buffalo WY U.S.A. 180 F3
Buffalo r. AR U.S.A. 179 D4
Buffalo r. TN U.S.A. 174 C5
Buffalo r. WI U.S.A. 172 B6
Buffalo Head Hills Canada 167 G3
Buffalo Head Prairie Canada 167 G3
Buffalo Hump mt. U.S.A. 180 D3
Buffalo Lake Alta Canada 167 H4
Buffalo Lake N.W.T. Canada 167 H2
Buffalo Narrows Canada 167 I4
Buffalo Range Zimbabwe 131 F4
Buffalo Valley U.S.A. 183 G1
Buffels r. Kwazulu-Natal S. Africa 133 O5
Buffels r. W. Cape S. Africa 132 E10
Buffels watercourse S. Africa 132 B6
Buffels Drift S. Africa 131 E4
Buford U.S.A. 175 C5
Buftea Romania 58 G4
Bug r. Poland 49 U4
Buga Col. 198 B4
Buga Mongolia 84 B2
Buga Nigeria 125 G4
Bugala Island Uganda 128 B5
Bugana Nigeria 125 G5
Bugant Mongolia 85 E1
Bugarach, Pic de mt. France 51 I10
Bugaz Ukr. see Zatoka
Bugdayli Turkm. 102 C5
Bugeat France 51 H7
Bugel, Tanjung pt Indon. 77 E4
Bugojno Bos.-Herz. 56 J4
Bugøyfjord Norway 44 O1
Bugrino Rus. Fed. 40 I1
Bugsuk i. Phil. 74 A4
Bugt China 85 I1
Buguey Phil. 74 B2
Bugui Point Phil. 74 B3
Bugul'ma Rus. Fed. 40 J5
Bugun' Kazakh. 103 E3
Būgür China see Luntai
Buguruslan Rus. Fed. 41 J5
Būhābād Iran 100 C4
Buharkent Turkey 59 J11
Buhera Zimbabwe 131 F3
Buh He r. China 84 C4
Buhi Phil. 74 B3
Bühl Germany 48 F7
Buhl ID U.S.A. 180 D4
Buhl MN U.S.A. 172 A3
Buhoro Flats plain Tanz. 129 B7
Buhriz Iraq 109 P4
Buhu r. Tanz. 129 B6
Buhuşi Romania 58 H2
Buia Italy 56 F2
Buick Canada 166 F3
Builth Wells U.K. 47 I11
Buin P.N.G. 145 E2
Bui National Park Ghana 124 E4
Buinsk Rus. Fed. 40 I5
Bu'īn Zahrā Iran 100 B3
Buir Nur l. Mongolia 85 H2
Buitepos Namibia 130 C4
Buivydžiai Lith. 42 G7
Bujalance Spain 54 G7
Bujanovac Srbija Yugo. 58 C6
Bujoru Romania 58 G5

▶Bujumbura Burundi 126 F5
Capital of Burundi. Formerly known as Usumbura.

Buk Poland 49 N3
Bukachacha Rus. Fed. 81 J2
Buka Island P.N.G. 145 E2
Bukama Dem. Rep. Congo 127 E7
Bukan' Rus. Fed. 43 P8
Būkand Iran 100 C4
Bukanskoye Rus. Fed. 103 J1
Bukantau, Gory hills Uzbek. 103 E4
Bukavu Dem. Rep. Congo 126 F5
formerly known as Costermansville
Buked Dem. Rep. Congo 127 C6
Bukene Tanz. 129 B6
Bukeya Dem. Rep. Congo 127 E7
Bukhara Uzbek. 103 F5
also spelt Bukhoro
Bukhara Oblast admin. div. Uzbek. see Bukharskaya Oblast'
Bukharskaya Oblast' admin. div. Uzbek. 103 E4
English form Bukhara Oblast; also known as Bukhoro Wiloyati
Bukhava Belarus 43 K6
Bukhoro Uzbek. see Bukhara
Bukhoro Wiloyati admin. div. Uzbek. see Bukharskaya Oblast'
Bukhtarminskoye Vodokhranilishche resr Kazakh. 88 D1
also known as Buqtyrma Bögeni
Bukide i. Indon. 75 C2
Bukima Tanz. 128 B5
Bukit Baka Bukit Raya National Park Indon. 77 F3
Bukit Timah Sing. 76 [inset]
Bukit Timah hill Sing. 76 [inset]
Bukittinggi Indon. 76 C3
also known as Fort de Kock
Bükk mts Hungary 49 R7
Bukkapatnam India 94 C3
Bükki nat. park Hungary 49 R7
Bükkszérc Hungary 49 R8
Bukoba Tanz. 128 A5
Bukonys Lith. 42 F6
Bukowa r. Poland 49 T5
Bukowo, Jezioro lag. Poland 49 N1
Bükreş Romania see Bucharest
Buku, Tanjung pt Indon. 76 D3
Bukum, Pulau i. Sing. 76 [inset]
Būl, Kūh-e mt. Iran 100 C4
Bula Guinea-Bissau 124 B3
Bula Indon. 73 H7
Bülach Switz. 51 O5
Bulag Mongolia 85 F1
Bulagtay Mongolia 85 E1
Bulahdelal Australia 147 G3
Bulalacao i. Phil. 74 B4
Bulan Phil. 74 B3
Bulan i. Phil. 74 B5
Bulancak Turkey 107 D2
Bulandshahr India 96 C3
Bulanık Turkey 107 E3
Bulanovo Rus. Fed. 102 C1
Bulava Rus. Fed. 82 F2
Bulawa, Gunung mt. Indon. 75 B2
Bulawayo Zimbabwe 131 F4
Bulbula waterhole Kenya 128 C5
Buldan Turkey 106 B3
Buldana India 94 C1
Buldibuyo Peru 200 A2
Buleda reg. Pak. 101 E5
Bulei well Eth. 128 E3
Bulembu Swaziland 133 P2
formerly known as Havelock
Bulgan Bulgan Mongolia 84 D1
Bulgan Mongolia see Bürenhayrhan
Bulgan Hovd Mongolia 84 B2
formerly known as Darvi
Bulgan Hövsgöl Mongolia 84 D1
Bulgan Ömnögovĭ Mongolia 84 D2
Bulgan prov. Mongolia 84 D1
Bulgan Gol r. Mongolia 84 A2
Bulgar Rus. Fed. see Bolgar
Bulgarevo Bulg. 58 J5
▶Bulgaria country Europe 58 F6
spelt Bulgariya in Bulgarian
europe [countries] ▶▶ 32–35
Bŭlgariya country Europe see Bulgaria
Bulghah Saudi Arabia 104 C2
Buli Indon. 75 D2
Buli, Teluk b. Indon. 75 D2
Buliluyan, Cape Phil. 74 A4
Bulkley Ranges mts Canada 166 D4
Bullaque r. Spain 54 G6
Bullas Spain 55 J6
Bullaxaar Somalia 128 E2
Bulle Switz. 51 N6
Bullea, Lake salt flat Australia 146 D2
Bullen r. Canada 167 K1
Buller r. N.Z. 153 F9
Bulleringa National Park Australia 149 D3
Bullfinch Australia 151 B6
Bullhead City U.S.A. 183 J6
Bullion Mountains U.S.A. 183 H7
Bullmark Sweden 44 M2
Bullo r. Australia 148 A2
Bulloo watercourse Australia 147 D2
Bulloo Downs Australia 147 D2
Bulloo Lake salt flat Australia 147 D2
Bulls N.Z. 152 J8
Bull Shoals Lake U.S.A. 179 D4
Büllspoort Namibia 130 C5
Bully Choop Mountain U.S.A. 182 B1
Bulman Australia 148 B2
Bulman Gorge Australia 148 B2
Bulmer Lake Canada 166 F2
Buloh, Pulau i. Sing. 76 [inset]
Buloke, Lake dry lake Australia 147 D4
Bulolo P.N.G. 73 K8
Bulqizë Albania 58 B7
Bultfontein S. Africa 133 K5
Bulu, Gunung mt. Indon. 77 G2
Buluan Phil. 74 C5
Bulubulu Indon. 75 B4
Buluk well Kenya 128 C3
Bulukumba Indon. 75 B4
Bulun Rus. Fed. 39 M2
Bulungu Bandundu Dem. Rep. Congo 126 C6
Bulungu Kasai Occidental Dem. Rep. Congo 127 D6
Bulungur Uzbek. 103 F5
formerly known as Krasnogvardeysk
Bulusan Phil. 74 C3
Bulwer S. Africa 133 N6
Bumba Bandundu Dem. Rep. Congo 127 C6
Bumba Équateur Dem. Rep. Congo 126 D4
Bumbah, Khalij b. Libya 120 D1
Bumbat Mongolia 84 E2
Bumbeşti-Jiu Romania 58 E3
Bumbuna Sierra Leone 124 C4
Bumhkang Myanmar 78 B2
Bumpha Bum mt. Myanmar 78 B2
Buna Dem. Rep. Congo 126 C5
Buna Kenya 128 C4
Bunayyān well Saudi Arabia 105 E3
Bunazi Tanz. 128 A5
Bunbury Australia 151 A7
Bunclody Rep. of Ireland 47 F11
formerly known as Newtownbarry
Buncrana Rep. of Ireland 47 E8
Bunda Tanz. 128 B5
Bundaberg Australia 149 G5
Bundaleer Australia 147 E2
Bundey watercourse Australia 148 B4
Bundi India 96 B4
Bundibugyo Uganda 128 A4
Bundjalung National Park Australia 147 G2
Bundoran Rep. of Ireland 47 D9
Bundu India 97 E5
Bunduqiya Sudan 128 A3
Bunë r. Albania/Yugo. 58 A7
Buner reg. Pak. 101 H3
Bunga r. Nigeria 125 H3
Bungalaut, Selat sea chan. Indon. 76 B3
Bung Boraphet l. Thai. 79 C5
Bungendore Australia 147 F3
Bunger Hills Antarctica 223 G2
Bungi Indon. 75 B4
Bungil Creek r. Australia 149 F5
Bungle Bungle National Park Australia see Purnululu National Park
Bungo Angola 127 B6
Bungoma Kenya 128 B4
Bungo-suidō sea chan. Japan 91 C8
Bungo-takada Japan 91 B8
Bunguran, Kepulauan is Indon. see Natuna, Kepulauan
Bunguran, Pulau i. Indon. see Natuna Besar
Bunia Dem. Rep. Congo 126 F4
Buningonia well Australia 151 C6
Bunji Jammu and Kashmir 96 B2
Bunker Group atolls Australia 149 G4
Bunkeya Dem. Rep. Congo 127 E7
Bunkie U.S.A. 179 D6
Bunkris Sweden 45 K3
Bunnell U.S.A. 175 D6
Bunnythorpe N.Z. 152 J8
Buñol Spain 55 K5
Bünsum China 89 C6
Bunsuru watercourse Nigeria 125 G3
Buntok Indon. 77 F3
Buntokecil Indon. 77 F3
Bununu Nigeria 125 H4
Bunya Mountains National Park Australia 149 F5
Bünyan Turkey 106 C3
Bunyu i. Indon. 77 G2
Bunza Nigeria 125 G3
Buoač Bos.-Herz. 56 J4
Buoddobohki Fin. see Patoniva
Buonconvento Italy 56 D5
Buôn Mê Thuôt Vietnam 79 E5
Buorkhaya, Guba b. Rus. Fed. 39 N2
Bup r. China 89 D6
Buqayq Saudi Arabia see Abqaiq
Buqbuq Egypt 121 E2
Buqtyrma Bögeni resr Kazakh. see Bukhtarminskoye Vodokhranilishche
Bura Kenya 128 C5
Buraan Somalia 128 F2
Burakin Australia 151 B6
Buram Sudan 126 E2
Buran Kazakh. 88 D1
also spelt Boran
Buran Darat reef Sing. 76 [inset]
Buranhaém r. Brazil 207 N3
Burannoye Rus. Fed. 102 C2
Burano r. Italy 56 E5
Burao Somalia 128 E2
Burauen Phil. 74 C4
Buraydah Saudi Arabia 104 C2
Burayevo Rus. Fed. 40 J5
Burbach Germany 48 F5
Burbank U.S.A. 182 F7
Burchell Lake Canada 172 C2
Burcher Australia 147 E3
Burdalyk Turkm. 103 F5
Burdekin r. Australia 149 E3
Burdekin Falls Australia 149 E4
Burdigala France see Bordeaux
Burdur Turkey 106 B3
Burdur Gölü l. Turkey 106 B3
Burdwan India see Barddhaman
Burē Eth. 128 C2
Bure r. U.K. 47 N11
Bureå Sweden 44 M2
Bureinskiy Khrebet mts Rus. Fed. 82 D2
English form Bureya Range
Bureiqa well Sudan 121 F5
Bürenhayrhan Mongolia 84 A2
formerly known as Bulgan
Bürentsogt Mongolia 85 F2
Bureya r. Rus. Fed. 82 C2
Bureya-Pristan' Rus. Fed. see Novobureyskiy
Bureya Range mts Rus. Fed. see Bureinskiy Khrebet
Bureyinski Zapovednik nature res. Rus. Fed. 82 D2
Burgaltay Mongolia 84 E1
Burgas Bulg. 58 I6
Burgaw U.S.A. 174 E5
Burg bei Magdeburg Germany 48 I3
Burgdorf Niedersachsen Germany 48 H3
Burgdorf Niedersachsen Germany 48 H3
Burgdorf Switz. 51 N5
Burg el 'Arab Egypt 108 A7
Burgeo Canada 169 J4
Burgersdorp S. Africa 133 K7
Burgersfort S. Africa 133 O1
Burgerville S. Africa 133 I7
Burges, Mount hill Australia 151 C6
Burgess U.S.A. 177 I8
Burget Tuyur waterhole Sudan 121 E4
Burghausen Germany 49 J7
Burghūth, Sabkhat al salt l. Syria 109 M3
Burgin U.S.A. 176 A8
Burglengenfeld Germany 48 J6
Burg Migheizil Egypt 108 B6
Burgos Mex. 185 F3
Burgos Spain 55 H2
Burgsvik Sweden 45 L4
Burhabalanga r. India 97 E5
Burhan Budai Shan mts China 84 B5
Burhaniye Turkey 106 A3
Burhanpur India 96 C5
Burhar-Dhanpuri India 97 D5
Burhave (Butjadingen) Germany 48 F2
Burhi Gandak r. India 97 E4
Buri Brazil 206 E10
Burias i. Phil. 74 B3
Buriat-Mongol Republic aut. rep. Rus. Fed. see Buryatiya, Respublika
Buribay Rus. Fed. 102 D2
Burica, Punta pt Costa Rica 186 C5
Burin Canada 169 K4
Burin Peninsula Canada 169 K4
Buriram Thai. 79 C5
Buritama Brazil 206 C8
Buriti Brazil 202 D2
Buriti r. Brazil 201 F3
Buriti Alegre Brazil 206 D5
Buriti Bravo Brazil 202 D3
Buritirama Brazil 202 D4
Buritis Brazil 206 G2
Buritizeiro Brazil 207 I4
Burjassot Spain 55 K5
Burkan-Suu r. Kyrg. 103 I4
also known as Buurakan
Burkburnett U.S.A. 179 C5
Burke watercourse Australia 149 C4
Burke U.S.A. 178 C3
Burke Channel Canada 166 E5
Burke Island Antarctica 222 Q2
Burke Pass N.Z. 153 E12
Burkesville U.S.A. 174 C4
Burketown Australia 148 C3
Burkeville U.S.A. 176 G8
Burkhala Rus. Fed. 39 O3
▶Burkina country Africa 125 E3
formerly known as Upper Volta or Haute-Volta; long form Burkina Faso
africa [countries] ▶▶ 114–117
Burkina Faso country Africa see Burkina
Burk's Falls Canada 168 E4
Burla Rus. Fed. 103 I1
Burley U.S.A. 180 D4
Burli Kazakh. 103 E1
also spelt Börili
Burlin Kazakh. 102 C2
Burlington Canada 168 E5
Burlington CO U.S.A. 178 B4
Burlington IA U.S.A. 174 B3
Burlington KS U.S.A. 178 D4
Burlington NC U.S.A. 176 F9
Burlington VT U.S.A. 177 L1

Burlington *WA* U.S.A. **180** B2
Burlington *WI* U.S.A. **172** E8
Burly Rus. Fed. **40** K5
Burma country Asia *see* Myanmar
Burmakino Rus. Fed. **43** V4
Burnaby Canada **166** F5
Burnet U.S.A. **179** C6
Burnett *r.* Australia **149** G5
Burney, Monte *vol.* Chile **205** B9
Burnham U.S.A. **177** P1
Burnie Australia **147** E5
Burning Springs U.S.A. **176** B8
Burnley U.K. **47** J10
Burnoye Kazakh. *see*
 Bauyrzhan Momysh-Uly
Burns U.S.A. **180** C4
Burnside *r.* Canada **167** I1
Burnside U.S.A. **176** A9
Burns, Lake *salt flat* Australia **151** C5
Burns Junction U.S.A. **180** C4
Burnsville U.S.A. **176** E7
Burnt *r.* U.S.A. **180** C4
Burnt Lake Canada *see* Brûlé, Lac
Burntwood *r.* Canada **167** L4
Burntwood Lake Canada **167** K4
Burog Co *l.* China **89** D5
Buron *r.* Canada **169** G1
Burovoy Uzbek. **103** E4
Burqin China **88** D2
Burqin *r.* China **88** D2
Burqu' Jordan **109** J5
Burra Australia **146** C3
Burra *i.* U.K. **46** K3
Burrel Albania **58** B7
Burrel U.S.A. **182** E5
Burrendong Reservoir Australia **147** F3
Burren Junction Australia **147** F2
Burriana Spain **55** K5
Burrinjuck Reservoir Australia **147** F3
Burro, Serranías del *mts* Mex. **185** C3
Burr Oak U.S.A. **172** B7
Burr Oak Reservoir U.S.A. **176** C6
Burro Creek *watercourse* U.S.A. **183** K7
Burrow Head U.K. **47** H9
Burruyacú Arg. **204** D2
Bursa Turkey **106** B2
 historically known as Brusa or Prusa
Bursa *prov.* Turkey **59** J8
Bür Safāga Egypt **121** G3
Bür Sa'īd Egypt *see* Port Said
Bür Sa'īd governorate Egypt **108** D6
Bursinskoye Vodokhranilishche *resr*
 Rus. Fed. **82** C2
Bür Sudan Sudan *see* Port Sudan
Burt Lake U.S.A. **173** I5
Burtnieku ezers *l.* Latvia **42** G4
Burton U.S.A. **173** J8
Burton, Lac *l.* Canada **168** E2
Burton upon Trent U.K. **47** K11
Burträsk Sweden **44** M2
Burtundy Australia **147** D3
Burt Well Australia **148** B4
Buru *i.* Indon. **75** C3
Burubaytal Kazakh. **88** A2
 also spelt Bürylbaytal
Burullus, Bahra el *lag.* Egypt *see*
 Burullus, Lake
Burullus, Lake *lag.* Egypt **108** B6
 also known as Bozhanis, Buheirat el
Burulokay China *see* Fuhai
Burün, Rās *pt* Egypt **108** E6
Burundi country Africa **126** F5
 formerly known as Urundi
 africa [countries] ⟶ 114–117
Burunniy Rus. Fed. *see* Tsagan Aman
Bururi Burundi **126** F5
Burwash Landing Canada **166** B2
Burwell U.S.A. **178** C3
Burwick U.K. **46** J5
Buryatia *aut. rep.* Rus. Fed. *see*
 Buryatiya, Respublika
Buryatiya, Respublika *aut. rep.* Rus. Fed.
 84 D1
 English form Buryatia; formerly known as
 Buriat-Mongol Republic or Buryatskaya
 Mongolskaya A.S.S.R.
Buryatskaya Mongolskaya A.S.S.R.
 aut. rep. Rus. Fed. see
 Buryatiya, Respublika
Bürylbaytal Kazakh. see Burubaytal
Buryn' Ukr. **41** E6
Burynshyk Kazakh. **102** B3
Bury St Edmunds U.K. **47** M11
Burzil Pass Jammu and Kashmir **96** B2
Busalla Italy **56** A4
Busan S. Korea see Pusan
Büs'an Yemen **104** C5
Busan Bay Phil. **74** B3
Busanga Dem. Rep. Congo **126** D5
Busca Italy **51** N8
Buseire Syria see Al Buṣayrah
Büshehr Iran **100** B4
 formerly spelt Bushire
Büshehr prov. Iran **100** B4
Bushenyi Uganda **128** A5
Bushire Iran see Büsheh r
Bushkill U.S.A. **177** J4
Bushnell *FL* U.S.A. **175** D6
Bushnell *IL* U.S.A. **172** C5
Bushuikha Rus. Fed. **43** V2
Busia Kenya **128** B4
Busing, Pulau *i.* Sing. **76** [inset]
Businga Dem. Rep. Congo **126** D4
Busira *r.* Dem. Rep. Congo **126** C5
Buskerud *admin. div.* Norway **45** J3
Busko-Zdrój Poland **49** R5
Buskul' Kazakh. see Boskol'
Busobuso Indon. **75** D2
Busselton Australia **151** A7
Bussol', Proliv *strait* Rus. Fed. **81** Q3
Bustamante Mex. **185** E3
Buşteni Romania **58** G3
Bustillos, Lago *l.* Mex. **184** D2
Busto Arsizio Italy **56** A3
Busu-Djanoa Dem. Rep. Congo **126** D4
Büsum Germany **48** F1
Busu Modanda Dem. Rep. Congo **126** C4
Buta Dem. Rep. Congo **126** E4
Butajira Eth. **128** C3
Butan Bulg. **58** E5
Butang Group *is* Thai. **79** B7
 formerly known as Astrida
Buta Ranquil Arg. **204** C5
Butare Rwanda **126** F5
 formerly known as Astrida
Butaritari atoll Kiribati **220** F6
 also known as Makin
Butauanan *pt* Phil. **74** B3
Bute *i.* U.K. **46** G8
Butea Romania **58** H1
Butedale Canada **166** D4
Bute Inlet Canada **166** E5
Butembo Dem. Rep. Congo **126** F4
Butha Buthe Lesotho **133** M5
Butha Qi China see Zalantun
Buthidaung Myanmar **78** A3
Butiá Brazil **203** B9
Butiaba Uganda **128** A4
Butler *AL* U.S.A. **175** C5
Butler *GA* U.S.A. **175** D5
Butler *IN* U.S.A. **173** H5
Butler *KY* U.S.A. **176** A7
Butler *MO* U.S.A. **178** D4
Butler *PA* U.S.A. **176** F5
Buton *i.* Indon. **75** C4
Buton, Selat *sea chan.* Indon. **75** B4
Butrimonys Lith. **42** G7
Butrint, Liqeni i *l.* Albania **59** B9

Buttahatchee *r.* U.S.A. **175** B5
Butte *MT* U.S.A. **180** D3
Butte *NE* U.S.A. **178** C3
Butternut U.S.A. **172** C4
Butterworth Malaysia **76** C1
Butterworth S. Africa **133** M9
Buttes, Sierra *mt.* U.S.A. **182** D2
Butt of Lewis *hd* U.K. **46** F5
 also known as Robhanais, Rubha
Button Bay Canada **167** M3
Button Islands Canada **165** M3
Buttonwillow U.S.A. **182** E6
Eutuan Phil. **74** C4
Butuan Bay Phil. **74** C4
Butuo China **86** B3
 also known as Tuomji
Buturlinovka Rus. Fed. **41** G6
Butwal Nepal **97** D4
Butzbach Germany **48** F5
Bützow Germany **48** I2
Buuhoodle Somalia **128** E2
Buulobarde Somalia **128** E4
Buurakan *r.* Kyrg. see Burkan-Suu
Buur Gaabo Somalia **128** D5
Buurhabaka Somalia **128** D3
Buvåg Norway **44** K1
Buvuma Island Uganda **128** B4
Buwārah, Jabal *mt.* Saudi Arabia **108** F9
Buwāṭah Saudi Arabia **104** B2
Buxar India **97** E4
Buxtehude Germany **48** G2
Buxton U.K. **47** K10
Buy Rus. Fed. **40** H4
Buy *r.* Rus. Fed. **40** J4
Buyant Bayanhongor Mongolia **84** C2
Buyant Bayan-Ölgiy Mongolia **84** A1
Buyant Hentiy Mongolia **85** F1
Buyant Gol *r.* Mongolia **84** C2
Buyant Gol *r.* Mongolia **84** G2
Buyant-Ovoo Mongolia **85** E2
Buyant-Uhaa Mongolia **85** F2
Buyck U.S.A. **172** A1
Buynaksk Rus. Fed. **102** A4
Buyo Côte d'Ivoire **124** D5
Buyo, Lac de *l.* Côte d'Ivoire **124** D5
Buyuan Jiang *r.* China **86** B4
Büyükada *i.* Turkey **58** K8
Büyük Egri Dağ *mt.* Turkey **108** E1
Büyükkarıştıran Turkey **58** I7
Büyükkonak Turkey **59** K11
Büyükmenderes *r.* Turkey **106** A3
Büyükorhan Turkey **59** J9
Büyükşahinbey Turkey **109** I1
Buyun Shan *mt.* China **85** I3
Buzachi, Poluostrov *pen.* Kazakh. **102** B3
 also known as Bozashy Tübegi
Buzançais France **50** H6
Buzău Romania **58** H3
Buzău *r.* Romania **58** H3
Buzaymah oasis Libya **120** D3
Buzdyak Rus. Fed. **102** A4
Búzi *r.* Moz. **131** G3
Búzi *r.* Moz. **131** G3
Buziaş Romania **58** C3
Búzios, Cabo dos *c.* Brazil **207** L9
Búz os, Ilha dos *i.* Brazil **207** H10
Büzmeyin Turkm. see Byuzmeyin
Buzuluk Rus. Fed. **102** C1
Buzuluk *r.* Rus. Fed. **41** G6
Buzzards Bay U.S.A. **177** O4
Bwagaoia P.N.G. **149** G1
Byadgi India **94** B3
Byahoml' Belarus **42** J7
Byakar Bhutan see Jakar
Byala Bulg. **58** G5
Byala Bulg. **58** I6
Byala Slatina Bulg. **58** E5
Byalynichy Belarus **43** M8
Byam Martin Island Canada **165** I2
Byarezina *r.* Belarus **42** G8
Byarezina *r.* Belarus **43** J7
Byaroza Belarus **42** F9
 also spelt Bereza
Byarezawka Belarus **42** G8
 also spelt Berezovka
Byblos tourist site Lebanon **108** G3
Bychawa Poland **49** T4
Byczyna Poland **49** P2
Bydgoszcz Poland **49** P2
 historically known as Bromberg
Byelaazyorsk Belarus **42** G9
Byelarus' country Europe see Belarus
Byelaruchy Belarus **43** K6
Byelaweyezhskaya Pushcha park Belarus
 42 E9
Byelitsk Belarus **43** N7
Byel'ki Belarus **42** I6
Byelorussia country Europe see Belarus
Byerastavitsa Belarus see Pahranichny
Byerazino Belarus **43** J8
 also spelt Berezino
Byerazino Belarus **43** J7
 also spelt Berezino
Byeraznyaki Belarus **42** I9
Byers U.S.A. **180** F5
Byershty Belarus **42** F8
Byeshankovichy Belarus **43** K6
Byesville U.S.A. **176** D6
Byesyedz' *r.* Belarus **43** M9
Byfield Australia **149** F4
Byfield National Park Australia **149** F4
Bygdeå Sweden **44** M2
Byglandsfjord Norway **45** I4
Bykhaw Belarus **43** L8
 also spelt Bykhov
Bykhov Belarus see Bykhaw
Bykle Norway **45** I4
Bykovo Rus. Fed. **41** H6
Bykovskiy Rus. Fed. **39** M2
Bylas U.S.A. **183** N8
Bylot Island Canada **165** L2
Byng Inlet Canada **173** M5
Bynoe *r.* Australia **149** D3
Bynoe Harbour Australia **150** E2
Byramgore Reef India **94** A4
Byrd Glacier Antarctica **223** K1
Byrka Rus. Fed. **85** H1
Byrkjelo Norway **45** I3
Byrock Australia **147** E2
Byron *IL* U.S.A. **172** D7
Byron *ME* U.S.A. **177** O1
Byron Bay Australia **147** G2
Byron Island Kiribati see Nikunau
Byrranga, Gory *mts* Rus. Fed. **39** J2
Byrne Ukr. **43** O9
Byske Sweden **44** M2
Byskeälven *r.* Sweden **44** M2
Byssa *r.* Rus. Fed. **85** M1
Bystrá *mt.* Slovakia **49** R6
Bystretsovo Rus. Fed. **43** J4
Bystřice nad Pernštejnem Czech Rep.
 49 N6
Bystrinski Golets, Gora *mt.* Rus. Fed.
 85 I1
Bystrovka Kyrg. see Kemin
Bystryy Tanyp *r.* Rus. Fed. **40** J5
Bystrzyca *r.* Poland **49** N4
Bystrzyca *r.* Poland **49** T4
Bytantay *r.* Rus. Fed. **39** N3
Bytča Slovakia **49** P6
Bytom Poland **49** P5
 historically known as Beuthen
Bytosh' Rus. Fed. **43** P8
Bytów Poland **49** O1
Byumba Rwanda **126** F5
Byurgyutli Turkm. **102** C5
Byuzmeyin Turkm. **102** D5
 also spelt Büzmeyin; formerly spelt Bezmein

Byxelkrok Sweden **45** L4
Byzantium Turkey see Istanbul
Bzura *r.* Poland **49** R3

↓ C

Ca, Sông *r.* Vietnam **78** D4
Caacupé Para. **201** F6
Caaguazú Para. **201** F6
Caaguazú, Cordillera de *hills* Para. **201** G6
Caála Angola **127** B8
 formerly known as Robert Williams
Caapiranga Brazil **199** F5
Caapucú Para. **201** F6
Caarapó Brazil **203** A7
Caatiba Brazil **207** M2
Caatinga Brazil **207** H4
Caazapá Para. **201** F6
Cabaçal *r.* Brazil **201** F3
Cabaiguán Cuba **186** D2
Caballas Rus. Fed. see
Caballo *mt.* Spain **55** H7
Cabana Áncash Peru **200** A2
Cabana Ayacucho Peru **200** C3
Cabanaconde Peru **200** C3
Cabañaquinta Spain **54** F1
Cabanatuan Phil. **74** B3
Cabanès *hill* France **50** H9
Cabano Canada **169** G4
Čabar Croatia **56** G3
Cabdul Qaadir Somalia **128** D2
Cabeceiras Brazil **206** G2
Cabeço Rainha *mt.* Port. **54** D5
Cabedelo Brazil **202** F3
Cabeza *r.* Spain Arg. **205** C6
Cabeza del Buey Spain **54** F6
Cabeza de Vaca, Punta *pt* Chile **204** C2
Cabeza Prieta National Wildlife Refuge
 nature res. U.S.A. **183** K9
Cabezas Bol. **201** E4
Cabezo Gordo *hill* Spain **54** D7
Cabimas Venez. **198** D2
Cabinda Angola **127** B6
Cabinda, Golfo di *b.* Sardegna Italy **57** B9
Cabinet Inlet Antarctica **222** T2
Cabinet Mountains U.S.A. **180** D2
Cabingan *i.* Phil. **74** B5
Cabistra Turkey see Ereğli
Cable U.S.A. **172** B4
Cabo Brazil **202** F4
Cabo Delgado *prov.* Moz. **131** H2
Cabo Frio Brazil **207** J7
Cabo Frio, Ilha do *i.* Brazil **207** L10
Cabonga, Réservoir Canada **168** E4
Cabool U.S.A. **178** D4
Cabo Orange, Parque Nacional de
 nat. park Brazil **199** I3
Cabo Pantoja Peru **198** C5
Cabora Bassa, Lake *resr* Moz. **131** F2
 also known as Cahora Bassa, Lago de
Cabo Raso Arg. **205** D7
Caborca Mex. **184** B2
Cabot Head Canada **173** L5
Cabot Strait Canada **169** I4
Cabo Verde country N. Atlantic Ocean see
 Cape Verde
Cabo Verde, Ilhas do *is* N. Atlantic Ocean see
 Cape Verde
Cabra *i.* Phil. **74** B3
Cabra Spain **54** G7
Cabra *r.* Spain **54** G7
Cabral Dom. Rep. **187** F3
Cabral, Serra do *mts* Brazil **203** C6
Cabras Sardegna Italy **57** A9
Cabrera *i.* Spain **55** N5
Cabrera *r.* Dom. Rep. **187** F3
Cabrera *r.* Spain **55** N5
Cabri Canada **167** I5
Cabriel *r.* Spain **55** J5
Cabrobó Brazil **202** E4
Cabruta Venez. **199** E3
Čabulja *mt.* Bos.-Herz. **56** J5
Cabullona Mex. **184** C2
Cacador Brazil **203** B8
Cacagoin China see Qagca
Cacahuatepec Mex. **185** F5
Čačak Srbija Yugo. **58** B5
Cacao Fr. Guiana **199** H3
Caçapava Brazil **207** H10
Caçapava do Sul Brazil **203** A9
Cacapon *r.* U.S.A. **176** G6
Cácares Col. **198** C3
Cacém Port. **54** B6
Cáceres Brazil **201** F4
Cáceres Spain **54** E5
Cachal Bol. **200** D3
Cache *r.* U.S.A. **174** B4
Cache *r.* Guinea-Bissau **124** A3
Cache Creek Canada **166** F5
Cache Creek *r.* U.S.A. **182** C3
Cache la Poudre *r.* U.S.A. **180** F4
Cacheu Guinea-Bissau **124** A3
Cachi Arg. **204** D2
Cachi, Nevados de *mts* Arg. **200** D6
Cachimbo Brazil **202** A4
Cachimbo, Serra do *hills* Brazil **202** A4
Cachimo Angola **127** D7
Cachina *r.* Chile **204** C2
Cachingues Angola **127** C8
Cáchira Col. **198** C3
Cachoeira *Bahia* Brazil **202** E5
Cachoeira *Mato Grosso do Sul* Brazil **206** B6
Cachoeira Alta Brazil **206** C5
Cachoeira de Goiás Brazil **206** C3
Cachoeira do Arari Brazil **202** C2
Cachoeira do Sul Brazil **203** A9
Cachoeiras de Macacu Brazil **207** K9
Cachoeiro de Itapemirim Brazil **203** D7
Cachos, Punta de *pt* Chile **204** C2
Cachuela Esperanza Bol. **200** D2
Cacine Guinea-Bissau **124** A3
Cacolo Angola **127** C7
Caconda Angola **127** B8
Cacongo Angola **127** B6
 formerly known as Guilherme Capelo or
 Landana
Cactus U.S.A. **179** B4
Cactus Range *mts* U.S.A. **183** G4
Caçu Brazil **206** B5
Cacuaco Angola **127** B7
Caculama Angola **127** C7
Caculé Brazil **202** D5
Cacumba *r.* Brazil **207** N4
Cacuso Angola **127** B7
Cadale Somalia **128** E4
Cadca Slovakia **49** P6
Caddabassa *l.* Eth. **128** C2
Caddo Lake U.S.A. **179** D5
Cadell *r.* Australia **148** B2
Cadell Creek *watercourse* Australia **149** D4
Cadenberge Germany **48** G2
Cadereyta Mex. **185** F3
Cadi, Serra de *mts* Spain **55** M2
Cadibarrawirracanna, Lake *salt flat*
 Australia **146** B2
Cadig Mountains Phil. **74** B3
Cadillac *Que.* Canada **173** O2
Cadillac *Sask.* Canada **167** J5
Cadillac France **50** F8
Cadillac U.S.A. **172** H6
Cadillal, Embalse el *resr* Arg. **204** D2

Cadiz Phil. **74** B4
Cádiz Spain **54** E8
 historically known as Gades
Cadiz *IL* U.S.A. **183** I7
Cadiz *KY* U.S.A. **174** B4
Cadiz *OH* U.S.A. **176** E5
Cádiz, Bahía de *b.* Spain **54** E8
Cádiz, Golfo de *g.* Spain **54** D8
Cadomin Canada **167** G4
Cadott U.S.A. **172** B6
Cadotte *r.* Canada **167** G3
Cadoux Australia **151** B6
Caen France **50** F3
Caerdydd U.K. see Cardiff
Caere Italy see Cerveteri
Caerfyrddin U.K. see Carmarthen
Caergybi U.K. see Holyhead
Caernarfon U.K. **47** H10
 formerly known as Caernarvon; historically
 known as Segontia or Segontium
Caernarfon Castle tourist site U.K.
 47 H10
Caernarvon U.K. see Caernarfon
Caesaraugusta Spain see Zaragoza
Caesarea Alg. see Cherchell
Caesarea tourist site Israel **108** F5
Caesarea Cappadociae Turkey see
 Kayseri
Caesarea Philippi Syria see Bāniyās
Caesarodunum France see Tours
Caesaromagus U.K. see Chelmsford
Caeté Brazil **207** J6
Caeté *r.* Brazil **200** C2
Caetité Brazil **202** D5
Cafau Germany **49** X4
Cafayate Arg. **204** D2
Cafelândia Brazil **206** D6
Caffa Ukr. see Feodosiya
Cafuini *r.* Brazil **199** G4
Cagayan *i.* Phil. **74** A3
Cagayan *r.* Phil. **74** B2
Cagayan de Oro Phil. **74** C4
Cagayan Islands Phil. **74** B4
Cagli Italy **56** E5
Cagliari Sardegna Italy **57** B9
 historically known as Carales or Caralis
Cagliari, Golfo di *b.* Sardegna Italy **57** B9
Cagnano Varano Italy **56** H7
Cagnes-sur-Mer France **51** N9
Caguán *r.* Col. **198** C5
Caguas Puerto Rico **187** G3
Cahaba *r.* U.S.A. **175** C5
Cahama Angola **127** B9
Caha Mountains *hills* Rep. of Ireland **47** C12
Cahersiveen Rep. of Ireland **47** B12
 also spelt Cahirciveen
Cahir Rep. of Ireland **47** E11
Cahirciveen Rep. of Ireland see
 Cahersiveen
Cahora Bassa, Lago de *resr* Moz. see
 Cabora Bassa, Lake
Cahore Point Rep. of Ireland **47** F11
Cahors France **50** H8
Cahuapanas Peru **198** B6
Cahul Moldova **58** J1
 formerly known as Vila Fontes
Caia Moz. **131** G3
Caia *r.* Port. **54** D5
 formerly known as Vila Fontes
Caia, Barragem do *resr* Port. **54** D5
Caiabis, Serra dos *hills* Brazil **201** F3
Caiapó *r.* Brazil **206** A4
Caiapônia Brazil **206** B3
Caiaza Angola **127** B8
Caibarién Cuba **186** D2
Cai Bâu, Đao *i.* Vietnam **78** D3
Cai Be Vietnam **79** D6
Caibiran Phil. **74** C4
Caicara Venez. **199** E2
Caicó Brazil **202** E3
Caicos Islands Turks and Caicos Is **187** F2
Caicos Passage
 Bahamas/Turks and Caicos Is **187** E2
Caidian China **87** E2
 formerly known as Hanyang
Caidu China see Shangcai
Caifuche Angola **127** D7
Caiguna Australia **151** D7
Caihua China **87** D2
Caiju China see Kozhikode
Cainnyigoin China **86** B1
Cains Store U.S.A. **176** A8
Caipe Arg. **200** C6
Caird Coast Antarctica **222** W1
Cairngorm Mountains U.K. **46** I6
Cairns Australia **149** E3
Cairnsmore of Carsphairn *hill* U.K. **47** H8

Cairo Egypt **121** F2
 Capital of Egypt and 2nd most populous
 city in Africa. Also known as El Qâhira or
 Al Qâhirah or Le Caire.
 world [cities] ⟶ 24–25
 africa [locations] ⟶ 118–119
Cairo *GA* U.S.A. **175** C6
Cairo *IL* U.S.A. **174** B4
Cairo, Monte *mt.* Italy **56** F7
Cairo Montenotte Italy **56** A4
Caisleán an Bharraigh Rep. of Ireland see
 Castlebar
Caistor U.K. **47** L10
Caitou Angola **127** B8
Caiundo Angola **127** C8
Caiwarro Australia **147** E2
Caixi China **87** F3
Caiyuanzhen China see Shengsi
Caiza Bol. **200** D5
Caizi Hu *l.* China **87** F2
Cajabamba Peru **200** A1
Cajamarca Peru **200** A1
 formerly known as Caxamarca
Cajamarca dept Peru **198** B6
Cajàpió Brazil **202** D2
Cajarc France **50** H8
Cajari Brazil **202** C2
Cajatambo Peru **200** A2
Cajàzeiras Brazil **202** E3
Čajetina Srbija Yugo. **58** A4
Cajidiocan Phil. **74** B3
Čajniče Bos.-Herz. **56** L5
Cajones, Cayos *is* Hond. **186** C3
Cajuata Bol. **200** D4
Caka China **84** C4
Caka'lho China see Yanjing
Caka Yanhu *l.* China **84** C4
Čakovec Croatia **56** I2
Čal Turkey **106** B3
Cala S. Africa **133** L8
Cala *r.* Spain **54** E7
Calabar Nigeria **125** H5
Calabogie Canada **173** Q5
Calabozo Venez. **199** E2
Calabria *admin. reg.* Italy **57** I10
Calabria, Parco Nazionale della *nat. park*
 Italy **57** I9
Calaburras, Punta de *pt* Spain **54** G8
Calacoto Bol. **200** C4
Calaf Spain **55** M3
Calafat Romania **58** D4
Calafate Arg. **205** B8
Cala Figuera, Cap de *c.* Spain **55** N5

Caltagirone Sicilia Italy **57** G11
Caltanissetta Sicilia Italy **57** G11
Calucinga Angola **127** C7
Caluire-et-Cuire France **51** K7
Calulo Angola **127** B7
Calumet U.S.A. **172** E3
Calunda Angola **127** D8
Calunga Angola **127** C9
Caluquembe Angola **127** B8
Calusa *i.* Phil. **74** B4
Caluula Somalia **128** F2
Caluula, Raas *pt* Somalia **128** F2
Calvert *r.* Australia **148** C3
Calvert Hills Australia **148** C3
Calvert Island Canada **166** D5
Calvert Range *hills* Australia **150** C4
Calvi Corse France **51** O10
Calvià Spain **55** N5
Calvinia S. Africa **132** D8
Calvi Risorta Italy **56** G7
Calvitero *mt.* Spain **54** F4
Calzada de Calatrava Spain **54** H6
Cam *r.* U.K. **47** M11
Camabatela Angola **127** C7
Camaçari Brazil **202** E5
Camaçari Brazil **202** E5
Camache Reservoir U.S.A. **182** D3
Camachigama *r.* Canada **168** E4
Camachigama, Lac *l.* Canada **173** Q3
Camacho Mex. **185** E3
Camacuio Angola **127** B8
Camacupa Angola **127** C8
 formerly known as General Machado
Camaguán Venez. **199** E2
Camagüey Cuba **186** D2
Camagüey, Archipiélago de *is* Cuba
 186 D2
Camah, Gunung *mt.* Malaysia **76** C1
Camaiú *r.* Brazil **199** G6
Camajuani Cuba **186** D2
Camalan Turkey see Gülek
Camana Peru **200** B4
Camaná *r.* Peru **200** B4
Camanongue Angola **127** D7
 formerly known as Vila Bugaço; formerly
 spelt Kamenongue
Camapuã Brazil **203** A6
Camaquã Brazil **203** B9
Camaquã *r.* Brazil **204** H3
Camãr Romania **58** D1
Camará Brazil **199** F5
Camararé *r.* Brazil **198** D6
Camarat, Cap *c.* France **51** M9
Camararé *r.* Brazil **201** F3
Camargo Bol. **200** D5
Camargo Mex. **185** F3
Camargo, Parque Natural *nature res.* Mex.
 185 F3
Camargue, Parc Naturel Régional de
 nature res. France **51** K9
Camarillo U.S.A. **182** F7
Camariñas Spain **54** B1
Camarón, Cabo *c.* Hond. **186** B4
Camarones Arg. **205** D7
Camarones, Bahía *b.* Arg. **205** D7
Camas U.S.A. **180** B3
Camas Creek *r.* U.S.A. **180** D4
Ca Mau Vietnam **79** D6
 formerly known as Quan Long
Camaxilo Angola **127** C7
Cambara Brazil **201** F4
Cambará Brazil **206** C10
Camberley U.K. **47** L12
Cambodia country Asia **79** C5
 formerly known as Kampuchea or Khmer
 Republic
 asia [countries] ⟶ 64–67
Camborne U.K. **47** G13
Cambrai Australia **146** C3
Cambrai France **51** J2
Cambre Spain **54** C1
Cambria S. Africa **133** I10
Cambria *admin. div.* U.K. see Wales
Cambria *i.* U.S.A. **182** D5
Cambrian Mountains *hills* U.K. **47** I11
Cambridge Canada **168** D5
Cambridge N.Z. **152** I5
Cambridge U.K. **47** M11
Cambridge *IL* U.S.A. **174** B3
Cambridge *MA* U.S.A. **177** N3
Cambridge *MD* U.S.A. **177** I7
Cambridge *MN* U.S.A. **174** A2
Cambridge *NY* U.S.A. **177** L2
Cambridge *OH* U.S.A. **176** D5
Cambridge *VT* U.S.A. **177** M1
Cambridge *WI* U.S.A. **172** D7
Cambridge Bay Canada **165** I3
Cambridge Gulf Australia **150** D2
Cambridge Springs U.S.A. **176** E4
Cambrien, Lac *l.* Canada **169** G1
Cambrils Spain **55** M3
Cambuí Brazil **207** I8
Cambulo Angola **127** D6
Cambundi-Catembo Angola **127** C7
 formerly known as Nova Gaia
Cambuquira Brazil **207** H8
Cambutal, Cerro *mt.* Panama **186** C5
Cam Co *r.* China **89** C5
Camden Australia **147** F3
Camden *AL* U.S.A. **175** C5
Camden *AR* U.S.A. **179** D5
Camden *ME* U.S.A. **177** P1
Camden *NC* U.S.A. **177** I8
Camden *NJ* U.S.A. **177** J5
Camden *NY* U.S.A. **177** J2
Camden *OH* U.S.A. **176** A6
Camden *SC* U.S.A. **175** D5
Camden *TN* U.S.A. **174** B4
Camden Bay U.S.A. **164** E2
Camden Sound *sea chan.* Australia **150** D2
Camdenton U.S.A. **178** D4
Cameia Angola **127** D7
Cameia, Parque Nacional da *nat. park*
 Angola **127** D7
 also spelt Kameia, Parque Nacional de
Çameli Turkey **59** K11
Cameron *AZ* U.S.A. **183** M6
Cameron *LA* U.S.A. **179** D6
Cameron *MO* U.S.A. **178** D4
Cameron *TX* U.S.A. **179** C6
Cameron *WI* U.S.A. **172** B5
Cameron *WV* U.S.A. **176** E6
Cameron Highlands Malaysia **76** C1
Cameron Highlands *mts* Malaysia **76** C1
Cameron Hills Canada **167** G3
Cameron Mountains N.Z. **153** A14
Cameron Park Canada **125** H5
Cameroon country Africa **125** H5
 spelt Cameroun in French
 africa [countries] ⟶ 114–117
Camérount country Africa see Cameroon
Cameroun, Mont *vol.* Cameroon **125** H5
Cametá *Amazonas* Brazil **199** G6
Cametá *Pará* Brazil **202** C2
Camfield *r.* Australia **148** A3
Camiçi Gölü *l.* Turkey **106** A3
Camiguin *i.* Phil. **74** B2
Camiguin *i.* Phil. **74** C4
Camiling Phil. **74** B3
Camilla U.S.A. **175** C6
Camiña Chile **200** C4
Camiranga Brazil **202** C2
Camiri Bol. **201** E5
Camisea Peru **200** B3
Camisea *r.* Peru **200** B2
Camissombo Angola **127** D7
 formerly known as Veríssimo Sarmento

241 ←

Cammarata, Monte *mt. Sicilia* Italy **57** F11
Cammin Poland *see* Kamień Pomorski
Camocim Brazil **202** D2
Camooweal Australia **148** C3
Camooweal Caves National Park Australia **148** C4
Campái Brazil **199** H4
Camorta *i.* India **95** G4
Camotes Sea *g.* Phil. **74** C4
Campagna Italy **57** H8
Campamento Hond. **186** B4
Campana, Isla *i.* Chile **205** B8
Campanário *Minas Gerais* Brazil **203** D6
Campanário *Mato Grosso do Sul* Brazil **201** G5
Campanella, Punta *pt* Italy **57** G8
Campania *admin. reg.* Italy **57** G8
Campania Island Canada **166** D4
Campanquiz, Cerro *hills* Peru **198** B6
Campaspe *r.* Australia **149** E4
Campbell S. Africa **132** H5
Campbell U.S.A. **176** C4
Campbell, Cape N.Z. **153** I9
Campbellford Canada **168** E4
Campbell Hill *hill* U.S.A. **176** B5
Campbell Range *hills* Australia **150** D2
Campbell Island N.Z. **220** B6
also known as Motu Ihupuku
Campbell Lake Canada **167** J2
Campbell Range *hills* Australia **150** D2
Campbell River Canada **166** E5
Campbellsport U.S.A. **172** F1
Campbellsville U.S.A. **176** A6
Campbellton Canada **169** H4
Campbell Town Australia **147** E5
Campbelltown Australia **147** F3
Campbeltown U.K. **46** G8
Camp Creek U.S.A. **178** D8
Campeche Mex. **185** H5
Campeche *state* Mex. **185** H5
Campeche, Bahía de *g.* Mex. **185** G5
Campechuela Cuba **186** D3
Câmpeni Romania **58** E2
formerly spelt Cîmpeni
Camperdown Australia **147** D4
Camperdown S. Africa **133** O6
Campestre Brazil **207** G8
Campia U.S.A. **172** B5
Câmpia Turzii Romania **58** E2
formerly spelt Cîmpia Turzii
Campiglia Marittima Italy **56** C5
Campillos Spain **54** G7
Campina Brazil **201** H1
Câmpina Romania **58** G3
formerly spelt Cîmpina
Campinaçu Brazil **202** B5
Campina Grande Brazil **202** F3
Campinas Brazil **206** F9
Campina Verde Brazil **206** D6
Camplong Indon. **75** B5
Campo Cameroon **125** H6
Campo *r.* Cameroon *see* Ntem
Campo, Réserve de *nature res.* Cameroon **125** H6
Campoalegre Col. **198** C4
Campo Alegre de Lourdes Brazil **202** D4
Campobasso Italy **56** G7
Campobello di Licata *Sicilia* Italy **57** F11
Campobello di Mazara *Sicilia* Italy **57** E11
Campo Belo Brazil **203** C7
Campo de Criptana Spain **55** H5
Campo de Diauarum Brazil **202** A4
Campodolcino Italy **56** B2
Campo Erê Brazil **203** A8
Campo Esperanza Para. **201** F5
Campo Florido Brazil **206** E6
Campo Formoso Brazil **202** D4
Campo Gallo Arg. **204** E2
Campo Grande *Amazonas* Brazil **201** F2
Campo Grande *Mato Grosso do Sul* Brazil **203** A7
Campolândia Brazil **206** B1
Campo Largo Brazil **203** B8
Campo Maior Brazil **202** D3
Campo Maior Port. **54** D5
Campomarino Italy **56** H7
Campo Mourão Brazil **206** A11
Campo Novo Brazil **203** A8
Campos Brazil **207** H8
Campos Altos Brazil **203** C6
Campos Belos Brazil **202** C5
Campos del Puerto Spain **55** O5
Campos do Jordão Brazil **207** H9
Campo Serio Peru **198** C5
Campos Gerais Brazil **207** H8
Campos Novos Paulista Brazil **206** D9
Campos Sales Brazil **202** D3
Campo Tencia *mt.* Switz. **51** O6
Campo Troco Col. **199** D3
Camprodon Spain **55** N2
Campton U.S.A. **176** B8
Câmpulung Romania **58** G3
formerly spelt Cîmpulung
Câmpulung Moldovenesc Romania **41** L7
formerly spelt Cîmpulung Moldovenesc
Campuya Peru **198** C5
Campuya *r.* Peru **198** C5
Cam Verde U.S.A. **183** M7
Cam Ranh Vietnam **79** E6
Camrose Canada **167** H4
Camsell Lake Canada **167** I2
Camsell Range *mts* Canada **166** F2
Camulodunum U.K. *see* Colchester
Çamuzkızılı Turkey **109** A1
Çan Turkey **106** A2
Canaan *r.* Canada **169** H4
Canaan Trin. and Tob. **187** H5
Canaan U.S.A. **177** L3
Canaan Peak U.S.A. **183** M4
Canabrava Brazil **207** I4
Caña Brava, Serra da *hills* Brazil **207** N3
Canabungan *i.* Phil. **74** A5
Canacona India **94** B3

▶Canada *country* N. America **164** G3
Largest country in North America and 2nd in the world. 3rd most populous country in North America.
world [countries] ➡ 10–11
world [changes] ➡ 20–21
northamerica [countries] ➡ 158–159

Cañada Honda Arg. **204** C3
Canadian U.S.A. **179** B5
Canadian *r.* U.S.A. **179** D5
Cañadón de las Vacas Arg. **205** C8
Cañadon Grande, Sierra *mts* Arg. **205** C8
Canaima, Parque Nacional *nat. park* Venez. **199** F3
Canajoharie U.S.A. **177** K3
Çanakkale Turkey **106** A2
formerly known as Chanak
Çanakkale *prov.* Turkey **59** H8
Çanakkale Boğazı *strait* Turkey *see* Dardanelles
Canal Flats Canada **167** H5
Canals Spain **55** K6
Canal Winchester U.S.A. **176** C6
Canamari Brazil **200** C2
Canandaigua U.S.A. **177** H3
Canandaigua Lake U.S.A. **177** H3
Cananea Mex. **184** C2
Canania Brazil **203** C8
Cananéia Brazil **207** H3
Canapiare, Cerro *hill* Col. **198** D4
Canápolis Brazil **206** D5
Cañar Ecuador **198** B5
Cañar *prov.* Ecuador **198** B5
Canarana Brazil **202** A5
Canarias, Islas *is* N. Atlantic Ocean **122** A3
also known as Canary Islands
Canarias, Islas *terr.* N. Atlantic Ocean *see* Canary Islands
Canary Islands *is* N. Atlantic Ocean *see* Canarias, Islas

▶Canary Islands *terr.* N. Atlantic Ocean **122** A3
Autonomous Community of Spain. Also known as Canarias, Islas.
africa [countries] ➡ 114–117

Canasayab Mex. **185** H5
Canaseraga U.S.A. **176** H3
Canastota U.S.A. **177** J2
Canastra, Serra da *mts* Brazil **206** G6
Canatlán Mex. **184** D3
Canaveral, Cape U.S.A. **175** D6
formerly known as Kennedy, Cape
Canaveral National Seashore *nature res.* U.S.A. **175** D6
Canavieiras Brazil **202** E5
Cañazas Panama **186** C5
Canbelego Australia **147** E2

▶Canberra Australia **147** F3
Capital of Australia.

Canby *CA* U.S.A. **180** B4
Canby *MN* U.S.A. **178** C2
Cancale France **50** E4
Canchas Chile **204** C2
Canchyuaya, Cerros de *hills* Peru **198** C6
Cancún Mex. **185** I4
Çandar Turkey *see* Kastamonu
Çandarave Peru **200** C4
Çandarlı Turkey **106** A3
Candás Spain **54** F1
Candé France **50** E5
Candeias Brazil **203** C7
Candeias *r.* Brazil **201** E2
Candela *r.* Mex. **179** B7
Candelaria Arg. **204** D2
Candelaria Mex. **185** H5
Candelaria Venez. **199** E3
Candelaro *r.* Italy **56** H7
Candeleda Spain **54** F4
Candelo Australia **147** E4
Candia Greece *see* Iraklion
Cândido Mendes Brazil **202** C2
Cândido Sales Brazil **207** L2
Çandır Turkey **106** C2
Candle Lake Canada **167** J4
Candle Lake *l.* Canada **167** J4
Candlewood, Lake U.S.A. **177** L4
Cando U.S.A. **178** C1
Candon Phil. **74** B2
Candover S. Africa **133** P4
Cândrelu, Vârful *mt.* Romania **58** E3
Cane *r.* Australia **150** A4
Canea Greece *see* Chania
Canela Baja Chile **204** C3
Canelli Italy **56** A4
Canelones Uruguay **204** F4
Canelos Ecuador **198** B5
Cañete Chile **204** B5
Caney U.S.A. **178** D4
Caney *r.* U.S.A. **178** D4
Cangallia Brazil **206** G3
Cangallo Peru **200** B3
Cangamba Angola **127** C8
formerly known as Vila de Aljustrel
Cangandala Angola **127** C7
Cangandala, Parque Nacional de *nat. park* Angola **127** C7
also spelt Kangandala, Parque Nacional de
Çangarāfa Mauritania **124** B2
Cangas Spain **54** C2
Cangas del Narcea Spain **54** E1
Cango Caves S. Africa **132** G10
Canguçu Brazil **204** G3
Canguçu, Serra do *hills* Brazil **204** G3
Cangzhou China **85** H4
Caniapiscau Canada **169** G2
Caniapiscau *r.* Canada **169** G1
Caniapiscau, Lac *l.* Canada **169** G2
Caniçado Moz. *see* Guija
Canicattì *Sicilia* Italy **57** F11
Canicattini Bagni *Sicilia* Italy **57** H11
Canigao Channel Phil. **74** C4
Canigou, Pic du *mt.* France **51** I10
Canilles Spain **55** I7
Canim Lake Canada **166** F5
Canindé *Ceará* Brazil **202** E2
Canindé *Pará* Brazil **202** B3
Canindé *r.* Brazil **202** D3
Canino Italy **56** D6
Canisteo U.S.A. **176** H3
Canisteo *r.* U.S.A. **176** H3
Canisteo Peninsula Antarctica **222** R2
Canister Falls Guyana **199** G3
Cañitas de Felipe Pescador Mex. **185** E4
Çankırı Turkey **106** C2
historically known as Gangra
Çankuzo Burundi **126** D5
Cankpon Phil. **74** B4
Canna *i.* U.K. **46** F6
Cannanore India **94** B4
also known as Kannur
Cannanore Islands India **94** B4
Cannes France **51** N9
Cannich U.K. **46** H6
Canning Hill *hill* Australia **151** B6
Cannobio Italy **56** A2
Cannonball *r.* U.S.A. **178** B2
Cannon Beach U.S.A. **180** B3
Cannon Rocks S. Africa **133** K10
Cannonsburg U.S.A. **176** C7
Cann River Australia **147** F4
Canoa Ecuador **198** A5
Canoas Brazil **203** B9

Caño Colorado Col. **198** D4
Caño Colorado Venez. **187** H5
Canoeiros Brazil **203** C6
Canoe Lake Canada **167** I4
Canoe Lake *l.* Canada **167** I4
Canoinhas Brazil **203** B8
Canon City U.S.A. **181** F5
Cañón del Río Blanco, Parque Nacional *nat. park* Mex. **185** F5
Cañón del Sumidero, Parque Nacional *nat. park* Mex. **185** G5
Cañón Largo *watercourse* U.S.A. **181** F5
Canoochia *r.* U.S.A. **175** D6
Canoona Australia **149** F4
Canora Canada **167** K5
Caño Riecito Venez. **198** D3
Canosa di Puglia Italy **56** I7
historically known as Canusium
Canouan *i.* St Vincent **187** H4
Canowindra Australia **147** F3
Cansado W. Sahara **122** A4
Canso Canada **169** I4
Canso, Cape Canada **169** I4
Canso, Strait of Canada **169** I4
Canta Peru **200** A2
Cantábria *aut. comm.* Spain **54** G1
Cantabrian Mountains Spain *see* Cantábrica, Cordillera
Cantabrian Sea Spain *see* Cantábrico, Mar
Cantábrica, Cordillera *mts* Spain **54** G1
English form Cantabrian Mountains
Cantábrico, Mar *sea* Spain **54** E1
English form Cantabrian Sea
Cantagalo Brazil **199** G6
Cantalejo Spain **54** H3
Cantanhede Port. **54** C4
Canteras *hill* Spain **55** I7
Canterbury *admin. reg.* N.Z. **153** G11
Canterbury U.K. **47** N12
historically known as Cantuaria or Durovernum
Canterbury Bight *b.* N.Z. **153** F12
Canterbury Plains N.Z. **153** F11
Cần Thơ Vietnam **79** D6
Cantil U.S.A. **182** G6
Cantilan Phil. **74** C4
Cantillana Spain **54** F7
Canto do Buriti Brazil **202** D4
Cañuelas Arg. **204** F4
Canumã *Amazonas* Brazil **199** F6
Canumã *Amazonas* Brazil **199** F6
Canunda National Park Australia **146** C4
Canusium Italy *see* Canosa di Puglia
Canutama Brazil **199** F5
Canvastown N.Z. **152** H9
Canwood Canada **167** J4
Cany-Barville France **50** F3
Cànyoles *r.* Spain **55** K5
Canyon Canada **166** B2
Canyon U.S.A. **179** B5
Canyon City U.S.A. **180** C3
Canyon Creek *r.* U.S.A. **182** C2
Canyondam U.S.A. **182** C1
Canyon de Chelly National Monument *nat. park* U.S.A. **183** O5
Canyon Ferry Lake U.S.A. **180** E3
Canyon Lake U.S.A. **183** M8
Canyonlands National Park U.S.A. **183** O3
Canyon Ranges *mts* Canada **166** E2
Canyonville U.S.A. **180** B4
Canzar Angola **127** D6
Cao *r.* China **83** B4
Cao Bằng Vietnam **78** D3
Caocheng China *see* Caoxian
Caohe China *see* Qichun
Caohu China **88** D3
Caojiahe China *see* Qichun
Caojian China **86** A3
Caombo Angola **127** C7
Cao Nguyên Đắc Lắc *plat.* Vietnam **79** E5
Caorle Italy **56** E3
Caoxian China **87** E1
also known as Caocheng
Caozhou China *see* Heze
Cap *i.* Phil. **74** B5
Capac U.S.A. **173** K7
Capaccio Italy **57** H8
Capaci *Sicilia* Italy **57** F10
Cap-à-Foux *c.* Haiti **187** I3
Capaia Angola **127** D7
Capalulu, Selat *sea chan.* Indon. **75** C3
Capanaparo *r.* Venez. **199** E3
Capanema Brazil **198** D3
Capanema *r.* Brazil **202** C2
Capanne, Monte *mt.* Italy **56** C4
Capão Bonito Brazil **206** D10
Caparaó, Serra do *mts* Brazil **207** L7
Caparo *r.* Venez. **198** D3
Capas Phil. **74** B3
Căpățânii, Munții *mts* Romania **58** E3
Capătărida Venez. **198** D2
Cap-aux-Meules Canada **169** I4
Capbreton France **50** E9
Cap-Chat Canada **169** H3
Cap-de-la-Madeleine Canada **169** F4
Capdenac-Gare France **51** I8
Capdepera Spain **55** O5
Cape *r.* Australia **149** E4
Cape Arid National Park Australia **151** C7
Cape Bald Canada *see* Cap-Pelé
Cape Barren Island Australia **147** F5
Cape Borda Australia **146** C3
Cape Bougainville Aboriginal Reserve Australia **150** D2
Cape Breton Highlands National Park Canada **169** I4
Cape Breton Island Canada **169** I4
historically known as Royale, Île
Cape Charles Canada **169** K2
Cape Charles U.S.A. **177** I7
Cape Coast Ghana **125** E5
also known as Cape Coast Castle
Cape Coast Castle Ghana *see* Cape Coast
Cape Cod Bay U.S.A. **177** O4
Cape Cod National Seashore *nature res.* U.S.A. **174** G3
Cape Coral U.S.A. **175** D7
Cape Crawford Australia **148** B3
Cape Croker Australia **173** L6
Cape Dorset Canada **165** L3
Cape Elizabeth U.S.A. **177** O2
Cape Fear *r.* U.S.A. **174** E5
Cape Girardeau U.S.A. **174** B4
Cape Juby Morocco *see* Tarfaya
Cape Krusenstern National Monument *nat. park* U.S.A. **164** C3
Capel Australia **151** A7
Cape Le Grand National Park Australia **151** C7
Capelinha Brazil **203** D6
Capella Australia **149** F4

Capelle aan de IJssel Neth. **48** B4
Capelongo Angola **127** B8
formerly known as Folgares
Capelongo Angola *see* Kuvango
Cape May U.S.A. **177** K7
Cape May Court House U.S.A. **177** K6
Cape May Point U.S.A. **177** K7
Cape Melville National Park Australia **149** E2
Capenda-Camulemba Angola **127** C7
Cape of Good Hope Nature Reserve S. Africa **132** C11
Cape Palmerston National Park Australia **149** F4
Cape Range *hills* Australia **150** A4
Cape Range National Park Australia **150** A4
Cape Romain National Wildlife Refuge *nature res.* U.S.A. **175** E5
Cape Sable Island Canada **169** H5
Cape St George Canada **169** J3
Capesterre Guadeloupe **187** H3

▶Cape Town S. Africa **132** C10
Legislative capital of South Africa. Also known as Kaapstad.
world [countries] ➡ 10–11
africa [locations] ➡ 118–119

Cape Tribulation National Park Australia **149** E2
Cape Upstart National Park Australia **149** E3
▶Cape Verde *country* N. Atlantic Ocean **124** [inset]
also known as Cabo Verde
africa [countries] ➡ 114–117
Cape Vincent U.S.A. **177** I1
Cape Wolfe Canada **169** H4
Cape York Peninsula Australia **149** D2
Cap-Haïtien Haiti **187** E3
Capibara Venez. **199** E4
Capim Brazil **202** C2
Capim *r.* Brazil **202** C2
Capinópolis Brazil **206** D5
Capinota Bol. **200** D4
Capitán Arturo Prat *research station* Antarctica **222** U2
Capitão Enéas Brazil **207** J3
Capitari Brazil **199** F6
▶Capitol Hill N. Mariana Is **73** K3
Capital of the Northern Mariana Islands, on Saipan.

Capitol Reef National Park U.S.A. **183** M3
Capivara, Represa *resr* Brazil **206** B9
Capivari *r. Bahia* Brazil **202** D4
Capivari *r. São Paulo* Brazil **206** F9
Čapljina Bos.-Herz. **56** J5
Capnoyan *i.* Phil. **74** C4
Capo d'Orlando *Sicilia* Italy **57** G10
Capoeira, Cachoeira das *waterfall* Brazil **199** G6
Capoterra *Sardegna* Italy **57** A9
Cap-Pelé Canada **169** H4
formerly known as Cape Bald
Capraia, Isola di *i.* Italy **56** B4
Caprara, Isola *i. Sardegna* Italy **56** B7
Capri Italy **57** G8
Capri, Isola di *i.* Italy **57** G8
Capricorn, Cape Australia **149** F4
Capricorn Channel Australia **149** F4
Capricorn Group *atolls* Australia **149** G4
Caprivi *admin. reg.* Namibia **130** D3
Caprivi Game Park *nature res.* Namibia **130** D3
Caprivi Strip *reg.* Namibia **130** D3
Capsa Tunisia *see* Gafsa
Captain Cook U.S.A. **181** [inset] Z2
Captieux France **50** F8
Capuava Brazil **206** F11
Capuna Angola **127** C8
Capunda Cavilongo Angola **127** B8
formerly known as Oliveança-a-Nova
Caqueta *dept* Col. **198** C4
Caquetá *r.* Col. **198** D5
Cáqueza Col. **198** C3
Carabao *i.* Phil. **74** B3
Carabaya, Cordillera de *mts* Peru **200** C3
Carabinani *r.* Brazil **199** F5
Carabobo *state* Venez. **199** E2
Caracal Romania **58** F4
Caracarai Brazil **199** F4

▶Caracas Venez. **199** E2
Capital of Venezuela.

Caracol *Mato Grosso do Sul* Brazil **201** F5
Caracol *Piauí* Brazil **202** D4
Caracol *Rondônia* Brazil **201** D2
Caracollí Col. **187** E5
Caracollo Bol. **200** D4
Caraga Phil. **74** C5
Caragabal Australia **147** E3
Caraguatatuba Brazil **207** H10
Carahue Chile **204** B5
Caraí Brazil **207** L4
Caraiva Brazil **207** N3
Carajari Brazil **199** H6
Carajás Brazil **202** B3
Carajás, Serra dos *hills* Brazil **199** I6
Carales *Sardegna* Italy *see* Cagliari
Caralis *Sardegna* Italy *see* Cagliari
Caramanta Colombia **198** B3
Caramoan Peninsula Phil. **74** B3
Caramulo *mt.* Port. **54** C4
Caranavi Bol. **200** D3
Carandaí Brazil **203** D7
Carandaíti Bol. **201** E5
Carandazal Brazil **201** F4
Carangola Brazil **203** D7
Caransebeş Romania **58** D3
Carapajó Brazil **202** B2
Cara Paraná *r.* Col. **198** C5
Carapeguá Para. **201** F6
Carapelle *r.* Italy **56** H7
Carappee Hill *hill* Australia **146** C3
Caraquet Canada **169** H4
Caráquez Ecuador **198** A5
Carare *r.* Col. **198** C3
Carasova Romania **58** C3
Carat, Tanjung *pt* Indon. **76** D3
Caratasca Hond. **186** C4
Caratasca, Laguna *lag.* Hond. **186** C4
Caratinga Brazil **207** K6
Caratuú *r.* Col. **198** D5
Carauari Brazil **199** E6
Caraúbas Brazil **202** E3
Caraúnã *mt.* Brazil *see* Grande, Serra
Caravaca de la Cruz Spain **55** J6
Caravelas Brazil **207** N2
Caraveli Peru **200** B3
Carballino Spain **54** C2
Carballo Spain **54** C1
Carberry Canada **167** L5
Carbó Mex. **184** C2
Carbon, Cap *c.* Alg. **55** K9
Carbonara, Capo *c. Sardegna* Italy **57** B9
Carbondale *CO* U.S.A. **180** F5
Carbondale *IL* U.S.A. **174** B4
Carbondale *PA* U.S.A. **177** J4
Carbonear Canada **169** J4
Carboneras Spain **55** J8
Carboneras Mex. **184** D2
Carbonia *Sardegna* Italy **57** A9
Carbonita Brazil **203** D6
Carbonne France **50** H9
Carcaixent Spain **55** K5
Carcajou Canada **167** G3
Carcajou *r.* Canada **166** D1
Carcaliu Romania **58** J3

Carcar Phil. **74** B4
Carcare Italy **56** A4
Carcassonne France **51** I9
Carcastillo Spain **55** J2
Carcross Canada **166** C2
▶Cardiff U.K. **47** I12
Capital of Wales. Also spelt Caerdydd.

Çardak Turkey **59** I11
Cardamomes, Chaîne des *mts* Cambodia *see* Cardamom Range
Cardamom Mountains Cambodia *see* Cardamom Range
Cardamom Range *mts* Cambodia **79** C5
also known as Cardamom Chain or Cardamomes, Chaîne des or Cardamom Mountains or Banthat or Krâvanh, Chuŏr Phnum
Cardamon Hills India **94** C4
Cardeña Spain **54** G6
Cárdenas Cuba **186** C2
Cárdenas *San Luis Potosí* Mex. **185** F4
Cárdenas *Tabasco* Mex. **185** G5
Cardenyabba *watercourse* Australia **147** D2
Çardı Turkey *see* Harmancık
Cardiel, Lago *l.* Arg. **205** C8

▶Cardiff U.K. **47** I12
Capital of Wales. Also spelt Caerdydd.

Cardiff U.S.A. **177** I6
Cardigan U.K. **47** H11
also known as Aberteifi
Cardigan Bay U.K. **47** H11
Cardinal Canada **173** J1
Cardinal Lake Canada **167** G3
Cardington U.S.A. **176** C5
Cardón, Cerro *hill* Mex. **184** B3
Cardona Spain **55** M3
Cardoso Brazil **206** D7
Cardoso, Ilha do *i.* Brazil **203** C8
Carcrona Brazil **203** D12
Carei Romania **49** T8
Careiro Brazil **199** G5
Careiro do Castanho Brazil **199** F5
Carén Chile **204** C3
Carentan France **50** E3
Carey U.S.A. **175** B5
Carey, Lake *salt flat* Australia **151** C6
Carey Downs Australia **151** A5
Carey Lake Canada **167** J3
Cargados Carajós Islands Mauritius **218** L7
Carhaix-Plouguer France **50** C4
Carhuamayo Peru **200** A2
Carhué Arg. **204** E5
Cariacica Brazil **203** D7
Cariaco Venez. **187** H5
Cariamanga Ecuador **198** B6
Cariango Angola **127** B7
Cariati Italy **57** I9
Carei Romania **49** T8
Cariba Brazil **199** G5
Caribbean Sea N. Atlantic Ocean **171** J8
Cariboo Mountains Canada **166** F4
Caribou *r. Man.* Canada **167** M3
Caribou *r. N.W.T.* Canada **166** G2
Caribou U.S.A. **174** G2
Caribou Island Canada **172** H3
Caribou Islands Canada **167** H2
Caribou Mountains Canada **167** H3
Carichic Mex. **184** D3
Carigara Phil. **74** C4
Carigara Bay Phil. **74** C4
Carignan France **51** L3
Carinda Australia **147** E2
Cariñena Spain **55** J3
Carinhanha Brazil **202** D5
Carinhanha *r.* Brazil **202** D5
Carini *Sicilia* Italy **57** F10
Cariño Spain **54** D1
Carinola Italy **56** F7
Carioca Brazil **202** C1
Cariparé Brazil **202** C4
Caripe Venez. **199** F2
Caripito Venez. **199** F2
Cariris Novos, Serra dos *hills* Brazil **202** D3
Caris *r.* Venez. **199** F2
Caritianas Brazil **201** E2
Carlabhagh U.K. *see* Carloway
Carleton U.S.A. **173** J8
Carleton, Mount *hill* Canada **169** H4
Carleton Place Canada **168** E4
Carletonville S. Africa **133** L3
Carlin U.S.A. **183** H1
Carlinville U.S.A. **174** B4
Carlisle U.K. **47** J9
Carlisle *KY* U.S.A. **176** A7
Carlisle *NY* U.S.A. **177** K3
Carlisle *PA* U.S.A. **177** H5
Carlisle Bridge S. Africa **133** K10
Carlisle Lakes *salt flat* Australia **151** D6
Carlit, Pic *mt.* France **50** H10
Carloforte *Sardegna* Italy **57** A9
Carlópolis Brazil **206** D10
Carlos Casares Arg. **204** E4
Carlos Chagas Brazil **203** D6
Carlos Tejedor Arg. **204** E4
Carlow Rep. of Ireland **47** F11
also spelt Ceatharlach
Carloway U.K. **46** F5
also spelt Carlabhagh
Carlsbad Czech Rep. *see* Karlovy Vary
Carlsbad *CA* U.S.A. **183** G8
Carlsbad *NM* U.S.A. **181** F6
Carlsbad *TX* U.S.A. **179** B6
Carlsbad Caverns National Park U.S.A. **181** F6
Carlson Inlet Antarctica **222** S1
Carlton U.S.A. **174** A2
Carlton Hills S. Africa **133** I8
Carlyle Canada **167** K5
Carlyle U.S.A. **174** B4
Carlyle Lake U.S.A. **174** B4
Carmacks Canada **166** B2
Carman Canada **167** L5
Carmana Iran *see* Kerman
Carmarthen U.K. **47** H12
also known as Caerfyrddin
Carmarthen Bay U.K. **47** H12
Carmaux France **51** I8
Carmel *IN* U.S.A. **174** C4
Carmel *ME* U.S.A. **177** P1
Carmel, Mount *hill* Israel **108** G5
also known as Har Karmel
Carmel-by-the-Sea U.S.A. **182** C5
Carmel Head U.K. **47** H10
Carmelita Guat. **185** H5
Carmelo Uruguay **204** F4
Carmel Valley U.S.A. **182** C5
Carmen Col. **198** B2
Carmen *r.* Mex. **184** D2
Carmen Phil. **74** C4
Carmen Uruguay **204** F4
Carmen, Isla *i.* Mex. **184** C3
Carmen, Isla del *i.* Mex. **185** H5
Carmen Alto Chile **200** C5
Carmen de Areco Arg. **204** F4
Carmen del Paraná Para. **201** F6
Carmen de Patagones Arg. **204** E6
Carmi Canada **166** G5
Carmi U.S.A. **174** C4
Carmichael U.S.A. **182** C3
Carmo Brazil **207** K8
Carmo da Cachoeira Brazil **207** H7
Carmo do Paranaíba Brazil **207** G5
Carmody, Lake *salt flat* Australia **151** B7
Carmona Angola *see* Uige
Carmona Costa Rica **186** B5

Carmona Spain **54** F7
Carmópolis do Minas Brazil **207** I7
Carnamah Australia **151** A6
Carnarvon Australia **151** A5
Carnarvon S. Africa **132** G7
Carnarvonleegte *salt pan* S. Africa **132** F7
Carnarvon National Park Australia **149** E5
Carnarvon Range *hills* Australia **151** C5
Carnarvon Range *mts* Australia **149** F5
Carnegie Australia **151** C5
Carnegie, Lake *salt flat* Australia **151** C5
Carn Eighe *mt.* U.K. **46** G6
Carnero, Bahía del *b.* Chile **204** B5
Carnes Australia **146** B2
Carnesville U.S.A. **174** D5
Carney U.S.A. **172** F5
Carney Island Antarctica **222** P2
Car Nicobar *i.* India **95** G4
Carnikava Latvia **42** F4
Carnot Cent. Afr. Rep. **126** B3
Carnot Bay Australia **150** C3
Carnoustie U.K. **46** I7
Carnsore Point Rep. of Ireland **47** F11
Caro U.S.A. **173** J7
Caroaebe *r.* Brazil **199** F4
Caroche *mt.* Spain *see* El Caroche
Carola Cay *reef* Australia **149** G3
Carol City U.S.A. **175** D7
Carolina Brazil **202** C3
Carolina S. Africa **133** O3
Carolina Beach U.S.A. **175** E5
Caroline Canada **167** H4
Caroline Island Kiribati **221** H6
also known as Millenium Island
Caroline Islands N. Pacific Ocean **73** J5
Caroline Peak N.Z. **153** B13
Carondelet Ecuador **198** B4
Caroní *r.* Venez. **199** F2
Carora Venez. **198** D2
C. A. Rosetti Romania **58** K3
Carpathian Mountains Europe **49** Q6
also known as Carpaţii or Karpaty
Carpaţii *mts* Europe *see* Carpathian Mountains
Carpaţii Meridionali *mts* Romania *see* Transylvanian Alps
Carpentaria, Gulf of Australia **148** C2
Carpentras Downs Australia **149** E3
Carpentras France **51** L8
Carpi Italy **56** C4
Carpina Brazil **202** F3
Cărpiniş Romania **58** B3
Carpinteria U.S.A. **182** F7
Carp Lake Provincial Park Canada **166** F4
Carquefou France **50** E5
Carquesa *hill* Spain **54** E5
Carraig na Siuire Rep. of Ireland *see* Carrick-on-Suir
Carraipia Col. **198** C2
Carrantuohill *mt.* Rep. of Ireland **47** C11
Carrara Italy **56** C4
Carrasco, Parque Nacional *nat. park* Bol. **200** D4
Carrazeda de Ansiães Port. **54** D3
Carr Boyd Range *hills* Australia **150** D3
Carrbridge U.K. **46** I6
Carregal do Sal Port. **54** D4
Carrhae Turkey *see* Harran
Carriacou *i.* Grenada **187** H4
Carrickmacross Rep. of Ireland **47** F10
Carrick-on-Shannon Rep. of Ireland **47** D10
Carrick-on-Suir Rep. of Ireland **47** E11
also known as Carraig na Siuire
Carrieton Australia **146** C3
Carrillo Mex. **184** D3
Carrington U.S.A. **178** C2
Carrión *r.* Spain **54** G2
Carrión de los Condes Spain **54** G2
Carrizal Col. **198** C2
Carrizal Bajo Chile **204** C2
Carrizo U.S.A. **183** N7
Carrizo Creek *r.* U.S.A. **179** B4
Carrizo Creek *watercourse* AZ U.S.A. **183** N8
Carrizo Creek *watercourse* U.S.A. **183** N8
Carrizos Mex. **185** F3
Carrizo Springs U.S.A. **179** C6
Carrizo Wash *watercourse* U.S.A. **183** O7
Carrizozo U.S.A. **181** F6
Carroll U.S.A. **178** D3
Carrollton *AL* U.S.A. **175** B5
Carrollton *GA* U.S.A. **175** C5
Carrollton *IL* U.S.A. **174** B4
Carrollton *KY* U.S.A. **174** C4
Carrollton *MO* U.S.A. **178** D4
Carrollton *MS* U.S.A. **175** B5
Carrolltown U.S.A. **176** F5
Carron *r.* Australia **149** D3
Carron *r.* U.K. **46** H6
Carrot *r.* Canada **167** K4
Carrot River Canada **167** K4
Carrsville U.S.A. **177** I9
Carruthersville U.S.A. **174** B4
Carry Falls Reservoir U.S.A. **177** K1
Carşamba Turkey **107** D2
Carson *r.* Australia **150** D2
Carson U.S.A. **178** B2
Carson *r.* U.S.A. **182** E2
Carson City *MI* U.S.A. **173** I7

▶Carson City *NV* U.S.A. **182** E2
State capital of Nevada.

Carson Escarpment Australia **150** D2
Carson Lake U.S.A. **182** F2
Carson River Aboriginal Reserve Australia **150** D2
Carson Sink U.S.A. **182** F2
Carsonville U.S.A. **173** K7
Carstensz-top *mt.* Indon. *see* Jaya, Puncak
Carswell Lake Canada **167** I3
Cartagena Chile **204** C4
Cartagena Col. **198** B2
Cartagena Spain **55** K7
historically known as Carthago Nova
Cartago Col. **198** B3
Cartago Costa Rica **186** C5
Cártama Spain **54** G8
Cartaxo Port. **54** C5
Cartaya, Cap *c.* France **51** M9
Carter, Mount *hill* Australia **149** D2
Carteret Group *is* P.N.G. *see* Kilinailau Islands
Carteret Island Solomon Is *see* Malaita
Carters Range *hills* Australia **149** D4
Cartersville U.S.A. **175** C5
Carterton N.Z. **152** I7
Carthage *tourist site* Tunisia **123** H1
historically known as Carthago
Carthage U.S.A. **174** B3
Carthage *MO* U.S.A. **178** D4
Carthage *MS* U.S.A. **175** B5
Carthage *NC* U.S.A. **174** E5
Carthage *TN* U.S.A. **174** C4
Carthage *TX* U.S.A. **179** D5
Carthago *tourist site* Tunisia *see* Carthage
Carthago Nova Spain *see* Cartagena
Cartier Canada **173** L4
Cartier Island Australia **150** C2
Cartwright *Man.* Canada **167** L5
Cartwright *Nfld.* Canada **169** J3
Caruachi Venez. **199** F2
Caruaru Brazil **202** F4
Caruçambaba Brazil **202** B2
Cǎrunta, Vârful *mt.* Romania **58** F3
Carúpano Venez. **199** F2
Carutapera Brazil **202** C2
Carvalho Brazil **199** I5
Carver U.S.A. **176** B4
Carvin France **51** I2
Carvoeiro Brazil **199** F5
Carvoeiro, Cabo *c.* Port. **54** B5

Carwell Australia 149 E5
Cary U.S.A. 174 E5
Caryapundy Swamp Australia 147 D2
Caryville TN U.S.A. 176 A9
Caryville WI U.S.A. 172 B6
Casabindo, Cerro de mt. Arg. 200 D5
Casablanca Chile 204 C4

▶Casablanca Morocco 122 D2
5th most populous city in Africa. Also known as Dar el Beida.
world [cities] ▶ 24–25

Casa Branca Brazil 206 F8
Casa de Janos Mex. 184 C2
Casa de Piedra, Embalse resr Arg. 204 D5
Casa Grande U.S.A. 183 M9
Casale Monferrato Italy 56 A3
Casalins Arg. 204 F5
Casalmaggiore Italy 56 C4
Casalpusterlengo Italy 56 B3
Casalvasco Brazil 201 E3
Casamance r. Senegal 124 A3
Casanare dept Col. 198 D3
Casanare r. Col. 198 D3
Casares Nicaragua 186 B5
Casas Grandes Mex. 184 D2
Casas Grandes r. Mex. 184 D2
Casas-Ibáñez Spain 55 J5
Casbas Arg. 204 E5
Casca Brazil 203 A9
Cascada de Bassaseachic, Parque Nacional nat. park Mex. 184 C2
Cascade Australia 151 C7
Cascade r. N.Z. 153 C12
Cascade IA U.S.A. 174 B3
Cascade ID U.S.A. 180 C3
Cascade Point N.Z. 153 C12
Cascade Range mts Canada/U.S.A. 164 G5
Cascade Reservoir U.S.A. 180 C3
Cascais Port. 54 B6
Cascal, Paso del pass Nicaragua 186 B5
Cascapédia r. Canada 169 H3
Cascavel Ceará Brazil 202 E3
Cascavel Paraná Brazil 203 A8
Căscioarele Romania 58 H4
Casco U.S.A. 172 F6
Casco Bay U.S.A. 177 P2
Caserta Italy 56 G7
Caseville U.S.A. 173 J7
Casey research station Antarctica 223 H2
Casey Bay Antarctica 223 D2
Caseyr, Raas c. Somalia 128 F2
English form Guardafui, Cape
Cashel Rep. of Ireland 47 E11
Cashmere Australia 147 F1
Cashton U.S.A. 172 C7
Casigua Falcón Venez. 198 D2
Casigua Zulia Venez. 198 C2
Casiguran Phil. 74 B2
Casiguran Sound sea chan. Phil. 74 B2
Casilda Arg. 204 E4
Casimcea Romania 58 J4
Casimcea r. Romania 58 J4
Casimiro de Abreu Brazil 207 K9
Casino Australia 147 G2
Casinos Spain 55 K5
Casita Mex. 181 E7
Čáslav Czech Rep. 49 M6
Casma Peru 200 A2
Casnewydd U.K. see Newport
Casnovia U.S.A. 172 H7
Casogoran Bay Phil. 74 C4
Casoli Italy 56 G6
Caspe Spain 55 K3
Casper U.S.A. 180 F4
Caspian U.S.A. 172 E4
Caspian Lowland Kazakh./Rus. Fed. 102 A3
also known as Kaspiy Mangy Oypaty or Prikaspiyskaya Nizmennost'

▶Caspian Sea Asia/Europe 102 B4
Largest lake in the world and in Asia/Europe. Lowest point in Europe. Also known as Kaspiyskoye More.
world [physical features] ▶ 8–9

largest lakes

	lake	area sq km	area sq miles	location	page#
1▶	Caspian Sea	371 000	143 243	Asia/Europe	▶ 102 B4
2▶	Lake Superior	82 100	31 698	North America	▶ 172 F3
3▶	Lake Victoria	68 800	26 563	Africa	▶ 128 B5
4▶	Lake Huron	59 600	23 011	North America	▶ 173 J5
5▶	Lake Michigan	57 800	22 316	North America	▶ 172 F7
6▶	Aral Sea	33 640	12 988	Asia	▶ 102 D3
7▶	Lake Tanganyika	32 900	12 702	Africa	▶ 127 F6
8▶	Great Bear Lake	31 328	12 095	North America	▶ 166 F1
9▶	Lake Baikal	30 500	11 776	Asia	▶ 81 H2
10▶	Lake Nyasa	30 044	11 600	Africa	▶ 129 B7

Cass r. U.S.A. 173 J7
Cassacatiza Moz. 131 G2
Cassadaga U.S.A. 176 F3
Cassai Angola 127 D7
Cassamba Angola 127 D8
Cassano allo Ionio Italy 57 I9
Cassara Brazil 201 E3
Cass City U.S.A. 173 J7
Casselman Canada 168 F4
Casselton U.S.A. 178 C2
Cássia Brazil 206 G7
Cassiar Mountains Canada 166 D3
Cassilândia Brazil 206 B6
Cassilis Australia 147 F3
Cassinga Angola 127 C8
also spelt Kassinga
Cassino Brazil 204 G4
Cassino Italy 56 F7
Cassis France 51 L9
Cassley r. U.K. 46 H6
Cassongue Angola 127 B7
Cassopolis U.S.A. 172 G9
Cassville MO U.S.A. 178 D4
Cassville WI U.S.A. 172 C8
Castalla Spain 55 K6
Castanhal Amazonas Brazil 199 F6
Castanhal Pará Brazil 202 B2
Castanheira de Pêra Port. 54 C4
Castanheiro Brazil 199 E5
Castanho Brazil 201 E1
Castaño Nuevo Arg. 204 C3
Castaños Mex. 185 E3
Castejón, Montes de mts Spain 55 J3
Castèl di Sangro Italy 56 G7
Castelfiorentino Italy 56 C5
Castelfranco Emilia Italy 56 D4
Castelfranco Veneto Italy 56 D3
Casteljaloux France 50 G8
Castellammare, Golfo di b. Sicilia Italy 57 E10
Castellammare di Stabia Italy 57 G8
Castellane France 51 M9
Castellaneta Italy 57 I8
Castellanos mt. Spain 55 I6
Castellar de la Frontera Spain 54 F8
Castelldefels Spain 55 M3
Castell de Ferro Spain 55 H8
Castelli Buenos Aires Arg. 204 F5
Castelli Chaco Arg. 204 E2
Castell-nedd U.K. see Neath
Castell Newydd Emlyn U.K. see Newcastle Emlyn
Castello de Ampurias Spain see Castelló d'Empúries
Castelló de la Plana Spain 55 K5
also spelt Castellón de la Plana
Castelló d'Empúries Spain 55 O2
also spelt Castello de Ampurias
Castellón de la Plana Spain see Castelló de la Plana
Castelnaudary France 51 H9
Castelnau-de-Médoc France 50 F7
Castelnovo ne'Monti Italy 56 C4
Castelo Brazil 207 L7
Castelo Branco Port. 54 D5
Castelo Branco admin. dist. Port. 54 D4
Castelo de Vide Port. 54 D5
Castelo do Piauí Brazil 202 D3
Castèl San Pietro Terme Italy 56 D4
Castelsardo Sardegna Italy 56 A8
Castelsarrasin France 50 H8
Casteltermini Sicilia Italy 57 F11
Castelvetrano Sicilia Italy 57 E11
Castèl Volturno Italy 56 F7
Casterton Australia 146 D4
Castets France 50 E9
Castiglione dei Pepoli Italy 56 D4
Castiglione del Lago Italy 56 E5
Castiglione della Pescaia Italy 56 C6
Castiglione delle Stiviere Italy 56 C3
Castiglion Fiorentino Italy 56 D5
Castile U.S.A. 176 G3
Castilho Brazil 206 B7
Castilla Chile 204 C2
Castilla Peru 198 A6
Castilla - La Mancha aut. comm. Spain 55 H5
Castilla y León aut. comm. Spain 55 G3
Castillejo Venez. 199 F3
Castilletes Col. 198 D2
Castillo, Canal del sea chan. Chile 205 B8
Castillo, Pampa del hills Arg. 205 C7
Castillos Uruguay 204 G4
Castillos, Lago de l. Uruguay 204 G4
Castlebar Rep. of Ireland 47 C10
also known as Caisleán an Bharraigh
Castleblayney Rep. of Ireland 47 F9
Castle Dale U.S.A. 183 M2
Castle Danger U.S.A. 172 B3
Castle Dome Mountains U.S.A. 183 J8
Castle Douglas U.K. 47 I9
Castlegar Canada 166 G5
Castle Island Bahamas 187 E2
Castleisland Rep. of Ireland 47 C11
Castlemaine Australia 147 E4
Castle Mountain Canada 166 H5
formerly known as Eisenhower, Mount
Castle Mountain U.S.A. 182 D6
Castle Peak hill Hong Kong China 87 [inset]
also known as Tsing Shan
Castle Peak Bay Hong Kong China 87 [inset]
also known as Tsing Shan Wan
Castlepoint N.Z. 152 K8
Castlepollard Rep. of Ireland 47 E10
Castlerea Rep. of Ireland 47 D10
Castlereagh r. Australia 147 E2
Castle Rock CO U.S.A. 180 F5
Castle Rock WA U.S.A. 180 B3
Castle Rock Lake U.S.A. 172 C7
Castor Canada 167 I4
Castor, Rivière du r. Canada 168 E2
Castor Creek r. U.S.A. 179 D6
Castra Regina Germany see Regensburg
Castres France 51 I9
Castricum Neth. 48 B3

▶Castries St Lucia 187 H4
Capital of St Lucia.

Castro Brazil 203 B8
Castro Chile 205 B6
Castro Alves Brazil 202 E5
Castrocaro Terme Italy 56 D4
Castro del Río Spain 54 G7
Castro de Rei Spain 54 D1
Castro Marim Port. 54 D7
Castro-Urdiales Spain 55 H1
Castro Verde Port. 54 C7
Castrovillari Italy 57 I9
Castroville U.S.A. 182 C5
Castrovirreyna Peru 200 B3
Castuera Spain 54 F6
Cast Uul mt. Mongolia 84 A1
Caswell Sound inlet N.Z. 153 B12
Çat Turkey 107 E3
Catabola Angola 127 C8
formerly known as Nova Sintra
Catacamas Hond. 186 B4
Catacaos Peru 198 A6
Catacocha Ecuador 198 B6
Cataguases Brazil 207 K8
Catahoula Lake U.S.A. 179 D6
Cataingan Phil. 74 B3
Çatak Turkey 107 E3
Catalão Brazil 206 F5
Çatalca Turkey 58 J7
Çatalca Yarımadası pen. Turkey 58 J7
Catalina U.S.A. 183 N9
Catalonia aut. comm. Spain see Cataluña
Cataluña aut. comm. Spain 55 M3
English form Catalonia; also spelt Catalunya
Catalunya aut. comm. Spain see Cataluña
Çatalzeytin Turkey 106 C2
Catamarca Arg. 204 D3
Catamarca prov. Arg. 204 D2
Catambia Moz. see Catandica
Catana Sicilia Italy see Catania
Catanauan Phil. 74 B3
Catandica Moz. 131 G3
formerly known as Catambia or Vila Gouveia
Catanduanes i. Phil. 74 C3
Catanduva Brazil 206 D8
Catanduvas Brazil 203 A8
Catania Sicilia Italy 57 H11
historically known as Catana
Catania, Golfo di g. Sicilia Italy 57 H11
Catán Lil Arg. 204 C5
Catanzaro Italy 57 I10
Cataqueamã Brazil 201 E2
Cataract U.S.A. 172 C6
Cataract Creek watercourse U.S.A. 183 L5
Catarina Brazil 202 E3
Catarina U.S.A. 179 C6
Catarino Rodriguez Mex. 185 E3
Catarman Phil. 74 C3
Catarroja Spain 55 K5
Catastrophe, Cape Australia 146 B3
Catata Nova Angola 127 B8
Catatumbo Bari nat. park Col. 198 C2
Catavi Bol. 200 D4
Catawba U.S.A. 172 C5
Catawba r. U.S.A. 174 D5
Catawissa U.S.A. 177 I5
Cat Ba, Đao i. Vietnam 78 D3
Catbalogan Phil. 74 C4
Cateel Phil. 74 C5
Cateel Bay Phil. 74 C5
Catemaco Mex. 185 G5
Catembe Moz. 133 Q3
Catengue Angola 127 B8
Catete Angola 127 B7
Catete r. Brazil 199 H6
Cathcart S. Africa 133 L9
Cathedral City U.S.A. 183 H8
Cathedral Peak Lesotho 133 N5
Cathedral Provincial Park Canada 166 F5
Catherine, Mount U.S.A. 183 L3
Catheys Valley U.S.A. 182 D4
Cathlamet U.S.A. 180 B3
Catió Guinea-Bissau 124 B4
Catisimiña Venez. 199 F3
Cat Island Bahamas 187 E1
Catlins Forest Park nature res. N.Z. 153 D14
Catoche, Cabo c. Mex. 185 I4
Catolé do Rocha Brazil 202 E3
Catolé Grande r. Brazil 207 M2
Catolo Angola 127 C7
Catorce Mex. 185 E4
Catota Angola 127 C8
Catoute mt. Spain 54 E2
Catria, Monte mt. Italy 56 E5
Catriló Arg. 204 E5
Catrimani Brazil 199 F4
Catrimani r. Brazil 199 F4
Catskill U.S.A. 177 L3
Catskill Mountains U.S.A. 177 K3
Cattenom France 51 M3
Cattle Creek N.Z. 153 E12
Cattolica Italy 56 E5
Catúa Arg. 200 D5
Catuane Moz. 131 G5
Catur Moz. 129 B8
Cauaxi r. Brazil 202 B2
Cauayan Phil. 74 B4
Caubvick, Mount Canada 169 I1
Cauca dept Col. 198 B4
Cauca r. Col. 198 C2
Caucaia Brazil 202 E2
Caucasia Col. 198 C3

▶Caucasus mts Asia/Europe 107 E2
also known as Bol'shoy Kavkaz
europe [countries] ▶ 32–33

Caucete Arg. 204 C3
Cauchari, Salar de salt flat Arg. 200 D5
Cauchon Lake Canada 167 L4
Caucomgomoc Lake U.S.A. 174 G2
Caudete Spain 55 K6
Caudry France 51 J2
Cauit Point Phil. 74 C4
Caulnes France 50 D4
Caulonia Italy 57 I10
Caunao r. Cuba 186 D2
Caungula Angola 127 C7
Cauno Angola 127 C8
Cauquenes Chile 204 B4
Caura r. Venez. 199 E3
Caurés r. Brazil 199 F5
Causapscal Canada 169 H3
Căuşeni Moldova 58 K2
formerly spelt Kaushany
Căuşeni prov. Moldova 53 H2
Caussade France 50 H8
Cautário r. Brazil 201 D3
Caution, Cape Canada 166 E5
Cauto r. Cuba 186 D2
Cava de'Tirreni Italy 57 G8
Cávado r. Port. 54 C3
Cavaglià Italy 56 A3
Cavaillon France 51 L9
Cavalcante Goiás Brazil 202 C5
Cavalcante Rondônia Brazil 201 E2
Cavalier U.S.A. 178 C1
Cavalleria, Cap de c. Spain 55 P4
Cavalli Islands N.Z. 152 H2
Cavally r. Côte d'Ivoire 124 D5
Cavan Rep. of Ireland 47 E10
Çavdarhisar Turkey 59 K9
Çavdır Turkey 106 B3
Cave N.Z. 153 E12
Cave City AR U.S.A. 174 B4
Cave City KY U.S.A. 174 C4
Cave Creek U.S.A. 183 M8
Caveira Brazil 207 J3
Cavenagh Range hills Australia 151 E5
Cavera, Serra do hills Brazil 203 A9
Cavernoso, Serra do mts Brazil 203 A8
Cave Run Lake U.S.A. 176 B7
Caviana, Ilha i. Brazil 202 B1
Cavili reef Phil. 74 B4
Cavite Phil. 74 B3
Cavo, Monte hill Italy 56 F7
Cavone r. Italy 57 I8
Cavongo Angola 127 C8
Çavuşçu Turkey 106 B3
Çavuşköy Turkey 108 B1
Cawndilla Lake imp. l. Australia 147 D3
Cawnpore India see Kanpur
Cawood U.S.A. 176 B9
Caxambu Brazil 207 I8
Caxias Amazonas Brazil 198 D6
Caxias Maranhão Brazil 202 D3
Caxias do Sul Brazil 203 B9
Caxito Angola 127 B7
Caxiuana, Baía de l. Brazil 199 I5
Çay Turkey 106 B3
Cayambe-Coca, Parque Nacional nat. park Ecuador 198 B5
Çaybaşı Turkey see Çayeli
Cayce U.S.A. 175 D5
Çaycuma Turkey 106 C2
Çayeli Turkey 107 E2
also known as Çaybaşı

▶Cayenne Fr. Guiana 199 H3
Capital of French Guiana.

Cayey Puerto Rico 187 G3
Çaygören Barajı resr Turkey 59 J9
Çayhan Turkey 106 C3
Çayhisar Turkey 59 J12
Çayırhan Turkey 106 B2
Caylus France 50 H8
Cayman Brac i. Cayman Is 186 D3

▶Cayman Islands terr. West Indies 186 C3
United Kingdom Overseas Territory.
oceania [countries] ▶ 138–139

Cay Sal i. Bahamas 186 C2
Cay Santa Domingo i. Bahamas 186 E2
Cayucos U.S.A. 182 D6
Cayuga Canada 173 N8
Cayuga Heights U.S.A. 177 I3
Cayuga Lake U.S.A. 177 I3
Cazage Angola 127 D7
also spelt Cazaje
Cazaje Angola see Cazage
Cazalla de la Sierra Spain 54 F7
Căzăneşti Romania 58 I4
Caza Pava Arg. 204 F3
Cazaux et de Sanguinet, Étang de l. France 50 E8
Cazê China 89 D6
Cazenovia U.S.A. 177 J3
Cazères France 50 H9
Čazma Croatia 56 I3
Cazombo Angola 127 D7
Cazorla Spain 55 I7
Cazula Moz. 131 G2
Cea r. Spain 54 F2
Ceadâr-Lunga Moldova see Ciadîr-Lunga
Ceananus Mór Rep. of Ireland see Kells
Ceará Brazil see Fortaleza
Ceará state Brazil 202 E3
Ceatalchioi Romania 58 J3
Ceatharlach Rep. of Ireland see Carlow
Ceballos Mex. 184 D3
Cebireis Dağı mt. Turkey 108 D1
Cebollar Arg. 204 D3
Ceboruco, Volcán vol. Mex. 184 D4
Cebreros Spain 54 G4
Cebu Phil. 74 B4
Cebu i. Phil. 74 B4
Ceccano Italy 56 F7
Cecil U.S.A. 172 E5
Cecil Plains Australia 147 F1
Cecil Rhodes, Mount hill Australia 151 C5
Cecilton U.S.A. 177 J6
Cecina Italy 56 C5
Cecina r. Italy 56 C5
Ceclavín Spain 54 E5
Cedar r. MI U.S.A. 173 I7
Cedar r. ND U.S.A. 178 B2
Cedar r. NE U.S.A. 178 C3
Cedarberg mts S. Africa 132 C9
Cedar Bluff U.S.A. 176 D8
Cedar City U.S.A. 183 K4
Cedar Creek Reservoir U.S.A. 179 C5
Cedaredge U.S.A. 180 F5
Cedar Falls U.S.A. 174 A3
Cedar Grove CA U.S.A. 182 F5
Cedar Grove IN U.S.A. 176 A6
Cedar Grove WI U.S.A. 172 F7
Cedar Grove WV U.S.A. 176 D7
Cedar Island U.S.A. 177 J8
Cedar Lake Man. Canada 167 K4
Cedar Lake Ont. Canada 173 O4
Cedar Point U.S.A. 176 B4
Cedar Rapids U.S.A. 174 B3
Cedar Ridge U.S.A. 183 M5
Cedar River U.S.A. 172 F5
Cedar Run U.S.A. 177 K6
Cedar Springs Canada 173 K8
Cedar Springs U.S.A. 172 H7
Cedarville S. Africa 133 N7
Cedarville IL U.S.A. 172 D8
Cedarville MI U.S.A. 173 I5
Cedarville OH U.S.A. 176 B6
Cedegolo Italy 56 C2
Cedeira Spain 54 C1
Cedeño Hond. 186 B4
Cedral Quintana Roo Mex. 185 I4
Cedral San Luis Potosí Mex. 185 E4
Cedro Brazil 202 E3
Cedros Hond. 186 B4
Cedros Mex. 185 E3
Cedros, Cerro mt. Mex. 181 D7
Cedros, Isla i. Mex. 184 B2
Ceduna Australia 146 B3
Cée Spain 54 B2
Ceelaayo Somalia 128 F2
Ceelbuur Somalia 128 E3
Ceel Dhaab Somalia 128 E2
Ceeldheere Somalia 128 E4
Ceel Gaal Bari Somalia 128 F2
Ceel Gaal Woqooyi Galbeed Somalia 128 D2
Ceel Huur Somalia 128 F3
Ceel Walaaq well Somalia 128 D4
Ceerigaabo Somalia 128 E2
Cefalù Sicilia Italy 57 G10
historically known as Cephaloedium
Cega r. Spain 54 G3
Cegléd Hungary 49 Q8
Čegrane Macedonia 58 B7
Ceheng China 86 C3
also known as Zhelou
Cehu Silvaniei Romania 58 E1
Ceira r. Port. 54 C4
Çekerek Turkey 106 C2
also known as Hacıköy
Celah, Gunung mt. Malaysia 76 C1
Celano Italy 56 F6
Celaque, Parque Nacional nat. park Hond. 186 A4
Celaya Mex. 185 E4
Celbridge Rep. of Ireland 47 F10
Céle r. France 50 H8

▶Celebes i. Indon. 75 B3
4th largest island in Asia. Also known as Sulawesi.
asia [landscapes] ▶ 62–63

Celebes Sea Indon./Phil. 75 B2
Celendín Peru 198 B6
Celina OH U.S.A. 176 A5
Celina TN U.S.A. 174 C4
Celje Slovenia 56 H2
Cella Spain 55 J4
Celldömölk Hungary 49 O8
Celle Germany 48 H3
Celles-sur-Belle France 50 F6
Cellina r. Italy 56 E2
Celone r. Italy 56 H7
Celovec Austria see Klagenfurt
Celtic Sea Rep. of Ireland/U.K. 47 F13
Cemaru, Gunung mt. Indon. 77 F2
Cemilbey Turkey 106 C2
Çemişgezek Turkey 107 D3
Čempi, Teluk b. Indon. 77 G5
Cenad Romania 58 B2
Cenajo, Embalse del resr Spain 55 J6
Cencenighe Agordino Italy 56 D2
Cenderawasih, Teluk b. Indon. 73 I7
also known as Irian, Teluk
Cenei Romania 58 B3
Cenis, Col du Mont pass France 51 M7
Ceno r. Italy 56 C4
Cenon France 50 F8
Čenta Vojvodina, Srbija Yugo. 58 B3
Centane S. Africa see Kentani
Centenário do Sul Brazil 206 B9
Centenary Zimbabwe 131 F3
Centennial Wash watercourse U.S.A. 183 L8
Center ND U.S.A. 178 B2
Center NE U.S.A. 178 C3
Center TX U.S.A. 179 D6
Centerburg U.S.A. 176 C5
Center City U.S.A. 178 D2
Centereach U.S.A. 177 L5
Center Hill Lake resr U.S.A. 174 C5
Center Point U.S.A. 175 C5
Centerville AL U.S.A. 175 C5
Centerville IA U.S.A. 174 A3
Centerville MO U.S.A. 174 B4
Centerville NC U.S.A. 176 G9
Centerville OH U.S.A. 176 C7
Centerville PA U.S.A. 176 F4
Centerville TN U.S.A. 174 C5
Centerville TX U.S.A. 179 D6
Centerville WV U.S.A. 176 E6
Cento Italy 56 D4
Centrafricaine, République country Africa see Central African Republic
Central admin. dist. Botswana 131 E4
Central Brazil 202 D4
Central Chile 200 C5
Central admin. reg. Ghana 125 E5
Central prov. Kenya 128 C5
Central admin. reg. Malawi 129 B8
Central U.S.A. 181 E6
Central prov. Zambia 127 F8
Central, Cordillera mts Bol. 200 D4
Central, Cordillera mts Col. 198 B4
Central, Cordillera mts Dom. Rep. 187 F3
Central, Cordillera mts Panama 186 C5
Central, Cordillera mts Peru 200 A2
Central, Cordillera mts Phil. 74 B2
Central African Empire country Africa see Central African Republic

▶Central African Republic country Africa 126 C3
known as Centrafricaine, République in French; formerly known as Central African Empire or Ubangi-Shari
africa [countries] ▶ 114–117

Central Australia Aboriginal Reserve Australia 150 E4
Central Brahui Range mts Pak. 101 F4
Central Butte Canada 167 J5
Central City IA U.S.A. 174 B3
Central City NE U.S.A. 178 C3
Central City PA U.S.A. 176 G5
Central de Minas Brazil 207 L5
Central Desert Aboriginal Land res. Australia 148 A4
Central Falls U.S.A. 177 N4
Centralia IL U.S.A. 174 B4
Centralia WA U.S.A. 180 B3
Central Islip U.S.A. 177 L5
Central Kalahari Game Reserve nature res. Botswana 131 D4
Central Makran Range mts Pak. 101 F5
Central Mount Wedge Australia 148 A4
Central'noolesnoy Zapovednik nature res. Rus. Fed. 43 N5
Central Plateau Conservation Area nature res. Australia 147 E5
Central Provinces state India see Madhya Pradesh
Central Range mts Lesotho 133 M6
Central Range mts P.N.G. 73 J7
Central Russian Upland hills Rus. Fed. 43 R7
also known as Sredne-Russkaya Vozvyshennost'
Central Siberian Plateau Rus. Fed. 39 L3
also known as Siberia or Sredne-Sibirskoye Ploskogor'ye
Central Square U.S.A. 177 I2
Central Valley U.S.A. 182 B1
Centre prov. Cameroon 125 H5
Centre admin. reg. France 50 H5
Centre U.S.A. 175 C5
Centreville MD U.S.A. 177 I6
Centreville VA U.S.A. 176 H7
Centurion S. Africa 133 M2
formerly known as Verwoerdburg
Cenxi China 87 D4
Ceos i. Greece see Kea
Céou r. France 50 H8
Cephaloedium Sicilia Italy see Cefalù
Cephalonia i. Greece 59 B10
also known as Kefallinía; also spelt Kefallonia
Čepin Croatia 56 K3
Čepkelių nature res. Lith. 42 F8
Ceprano Italy 56 F7
Cepu Indon. 77 E4
Cer hills Yugo. 58 A4
Ceram i. Indon. see Seram
Ceram Sea Indon. see Seram Sea
Cerbat Mountains U.S.A. 183 J6
Cerbol r. Spain see Servol
Cercal hill Port. 54 C7
Čerchov mt. Czech Rep. 49 J6
Cère r. France 51 H8
Cerea Italy 56 D3
Cereal Canada 167 I5
Cereales Arg. 204 E5
Ceres Arg. 204 E3
Ceres Brazil 206 D2
Ceres S. Africa 132 D10
Ceres U.S.A. 182 D4
Céret France 51 I10
Cereté Col. 198 C2
Cerf, Lac du l. Canada 173 R4
Cerignola Italy 56 H7
Cerigo i. Greece see Kythira
Çerikli Turkey 106 C3
Cêringgolêb China see Dongco
Çerkeş Turkey 106 C2
Çerkezköy Turkey 58 J7
Cerknica Slovenia 56 G3
Cermei Romania 58 C2
Çermik Turkey 107 D3
Cerna Romania 58 J3
Cerna r. Romania 58 D3
Cerna r. Romania 58 D4
Cerna r. Romania 58 F4
Cernat Romania 58 H3
Cernăuţi Ukr. see Chernivtsi
Cernavodă Romania 58 J4
Cernay France 51 N5
Cerqueira César Brazil 206 D10
Cerralvo Mex. 185 F3
Cerralvo, Isla i. Mex. 184 C3
Cërrik Albania 58 A7
Cerrillos Arg. 200 D6
Cerritos Mex. 185 E4
Cerro Azul Brazil 203 B8
Cerro Azul Mex. 185 F4
Cerro de Pasco Peru 200 A2
Cerro Hoya, Parque Nacional nat. park Panama 186 C6
Cerro Manantiales Chile 205 C9
Cerrón mt. Spain 55 H8
Cerrón, Cerro mt. Venez. 198 D2
Cerro Negro Chile 200 C5
Cerros Colorados, Embalse resr Arg. 204 C5
Cerros de Amotape, Parque Nacional nat. park Peru 198 A5
Certaldo Italy 56 D5
Certeju de Sus Romania 58 D3
Cervantes Australia 151 A6
Cervantes, Cerro mt. Arg. 205 B8
Cervaro r. Italy 56 H7
Cervati, Monte mt. Italy 57 H8
Cervenia Romania 58 G5
Cervera Spain 55 M3
Cervera de Pisuerga Spain 54 G2
Cerveteri Italy 56 E7
historically known as Caere
Cervia Italy 56 E4
Cervialto, Monte mt. Italy 57 H8
Cervignano del Friuli Italy 56 F3
Cervina, Punta mt. Italy 56 D2
Cervione Corse France 51 P10
Cervo Spain 54 D1
César dept Col. 198 C2
César r. Col. 198 C2
Cesarò Sicilia Italy 57 G11
Cesena Italy 56 E4
Cesenatico Italy 56 E4
Cēsis Latvia 42 G4
historically known as Wenden
Česká Lípa Czech Rep. 49 L5
Česká Republika country Europe see Czech Republic
České Budějovice Czech Rep. 49 L7
formerly known as Budweis
České Středohoří hills Czech Rep. 49 K5
Českomoravská Vysočina hills Czech Rep. 49 L6
Český Krumlov Czech Rep. 49 L7
Český Les mts Czech Rep./Germany 49 J6
Český Těšín Czech Rep. 49 P6
Česma r. Croatia 56 I3
Çeşme Turkey 106 A3
Cessnock Australia 147 F3
Cesson-Sévigné France 50 E4
Cestas France 50 F8
Cestos r. Liberia 124 C5
Cesuras Spain 54 C1
Cesvaine Latvia 42 H5
Cetar China 84 D4
formerly known as Qaidar
Cetate Romania 58 E4
Cetatea Albă Ukr. see Bilhorod-Dnistrovs'kyy
Cetina r. Croatia 56 I5
Cetinje Crna Gora Yugo. 56 K6
Cetraro Italy 57 H9

▶Ceuta N. Africa 54 F9
Spanish Territory.
africa [countries] ▶ 114–117

Ceva-i-Ra reef Fiji 145 G4
also spelt Theva-i-Ra
Cévennes mts France 51 J9
Cévennes, Parc National des nat. park France 51 J8
Čevetjävri Fin. see Sevettijärvi
Cevizli Turkey 109 I1
Cevizlik Turkey see Maçka
Ceyhan Turkey 106 C3
Ceyhan r. Turkey 107 C3
Ceyhan Boğazı r. mouth Turkey 108 G1
Ceylanpınar Turkey 107 E3
also known as Resulayn
Ceylon country Asia see Sri Lanka
Cèze r. France 51 K8
Chaacha Turkm. 102 E5
also spelt Chäche
Chābahār Iran 101 E5
Chablais mts France 51 M6
Chablé Mex. 185 H5
Chablis France 51 J5
Chabre ridge France 51 L8
Chabrol i. New Caledonia see Lifou
Chabyêr Caka salt l. China 89 D6
Chaca Chile 200 C4
Chacabuco Arg. 204 E4
Chacarilla Bol. 200 C4
Chachahuén, Sierra mt. Arg. 204 C5
Chachapoyas Peru 198 B6
Chachaura-Binaganj India 96 C4
Chäche Turkm. see Chaacha
Chachersk Belarus 43 L9
Chachevichy Belarus 43 K8
Chachoengsao Thai. 79 C5
Chaco prov. Arg. 204 E2
formerly known as Presidente Juan Perón
Chaco Boreal reg. Para. 201 F5
Chaco Culture National Historical Park nat. park U.S.A. 181 F5
Chacon, Cape U.S.A. 166 C4
Chacorão, Cachoeira da waterfall Brazil 199 G6
Chacra de Piros Peru 200 B2

▶Chad country Africa 120 C6
5th largest country in Africa. Also spelt Tchad or Tshad.
africa [countries] ▶ 114–117

▶Chad, Lake Africa 120 B6
4th largest lake in Africa.
africa [landscapes] ▶ 112–113

Chadaasan Mongolia 84 D2
Chadan Rus. Fed. 84 A1
Chadileo r. Arg. 204 D5
Chadron U.S.A. 178 B3
Chadyr-Lunga Moldova see Ciadîr-Lunga
Chae Hom Thai. 78 B4
Chaek Kyrg. 103 H4
also spelt Chayek
Chaeryŏng N. Korea 83 B5
Chae Son National Park Thai. 78 B4
Chaffee U.S.A. 174 B4
Chaffers, Isla i. Chile 205 B7
Chaffey U.S.A. 172 A4
Chafurray Col. 198 C4
Chagai Pak. 101 F4
Chagai Hills Afgh./Pak. 101 E4
Chagalamarri India 94 C3
Chagan Kzyl-Ordinskaya Oblast' Kazakh. 103 F3
Chagan Vostochnyy Kazakhstan Kazakh. 103 I2
also spelt Shaghan
Chaganuzun Rus. Fed. 84 A1
Chagdo Kangri reg. China 89 D5
Chaghā Khūr mt. Iran 100 B4
Chaghcharān Afgh. 101 F3
Chaglinka r. Kazakh. 103 G1
Chagny France 51 K6
Chagoda Rus. Fed. 43 Q2
Chagoda r. Rus. Fed. 43 Q2
Chagodoshcha r. Rus. Fed. 43 R3
Chagos Archipelago is Indian Ocean 218 L6
Chagoyan Rus. Fed. 82 C1
Chagra r. Rus. Fed. 102 B1
Chagrayskoye Plato plat. Kazakh. see Shagyray, Plato
Chagres, Parque Nacional nat. park Panama 186 D5
Chaguanas Trin. and Tob. 187 H5
Chaguaramas Venez. 199 E2
Chagyl Turkm. 102 C4
Chagyllyshor, Vpadina depr. Turkm. 102 C4
Chaha r. Ukr. 58 K3
Chahah Burjal Afgh. 101 E4
Chāh Ākhvor Iran 101 D3
Chaharbagh Afgh. 101 G3
Chahār Maḩāll vā Bakhtīārī prov. Iran 100 B3
Chah Baba well Iran 100 C3
Chāh Bahār, Khalīj-e b. Iran 101 E5
Chahbounia Alg. 55 N9
Chāh-e'Asalū well Iran 100 C4
Chāh-e Bābā well Iran 100 D3
Chāh-e Gonbad well Iran 100 C3
Chāh-e Kavīr well Iran 100 D3
Chāh-e Khorāsān well Iran 100 C3
Chāh-e Malek well Iran 100 C3
Chāh-e Malek Mīrzā well Iran 100 C4
Chāh-e Mīrzā well Iran 100 C3
Chāh-e Mūjān well Iran 100 C3
Chāh-e Nūklok Iran 100 C3
Chāh-e Nūklok well Iran 100 C3
Chāh-e Pansu well Iran 100 C3
Chāh-e Qeysar well Iran 100 C4
Chāh-e Qobād well Iran 100 C3
Chāh-e Raḩmān well Iran 101 D4
Chāh-e Shūr well Iran 100 C3
Chāh-e Ţāqestān well Iran 100 C4
Chāh-e Tūnī well Iran 100 D3
Chāh Haji Abdulla well Iran 100 C3
Chāh Ḩaqq Iran 100 C4
Chah-i-Ab Afgh. 101 G2
Chāh Pās well Iran 100 C3
Chāh Ru'i well Iran 101 D4
Chah Sandan Pak. 101 E4
Chahuites Mex. 185 G5
Chai r. China 82 A4
Chaibasa India 97 E5
Chaigneau, Lac l. Canada 169 H2
Chaigoubu China see Huai'an
Chaillu, Massif du mts Gabon 126 A5
Chainat Thai. 79 C5
Chainjoin Co l. China 89 D5
Chai Si r. Thai. 79 C5
Chaitén Chile 205 B6
Chai Wan Hong Kong China 87 [inset]
Chaiwopu China 88 D3
Chaiya Thai. 79 B6
Chaiyaphum Thai. 79 C5
Chajarí Arg. 204 F3
Chakai India 97 E4
Chakar r. Pak. 101 G4
Chakari Zimbabwe 131 F3
Chake Chake Tanz. 129 C6
Chakhānsūr Afgh. 101 E4
Chakia India 97 D4
Chak Jhumra Pak. 101 H4
Chakonipau, Lake Canada 169 G1
Chakradharpur India 97 E5
Chakulia India 97 E5
Chakwal Pak. 101 H3
Chala Peru 200 B3
Chala Tanz. 129 A6
Chalais France 50 G7
Chalap Dalan mts Afgh. 101 F3
Chalatenango El Salvador 185 H6
Chalaua Moz. 131 H3
Chalaxung China 86 A1
Chalbi Desert Kenya 128 C4
Chalcedon Turkey see Kadıköy
Chalengkou China 84 B4
Chaleur Bay inlet Canada 169 H3
also known as Chaleurs, Baie de

C

Chaleurs, Baie de inlet Canada see
Chaleur Bay
Chalia r. Arg. 205 C8
Chalib Abū Munţar watercourse Iraq
109 L5
Chaling China 87 E3
Chalinze Tanz. 129 C6
Chalisgaon India 94 B1
Chalisseri India 94 C4
Chalkar, Ozero salt l. Kazakh. see
Shalkar, Ozero
Chalki Greece 59 I12
Chalki l. Greece 59 I12
also spelt Khálki
Chalkída Greece 59 E10
also known as Khalkis
Chalkudysu Kazakh. 103 I4
Chalky Inlet N.Z. 153 A14
Challakere India 94 C3
Challans France 50 E6
Challapata Bol. 200 D4
▶ Challenger Deep sea feature
N. Pacific Ocean 220 D3
Deepest point in the world (Mariana Trench).
oceans (features) ▶ 210–211
Challis U.S.A. 180 D3
Chalmette U.S.A. 175 B6
Chal'mny-Varre Rus. Fed. 40 F2
Chalonnes-sur-Loire France 50 F5
Châlons-en-Champagne France 51 K4
formerly known as Châlons-sur-Marne
Châlons-sur-Marne France see
Châlons-en-Champagne
Chalon-sur-Saône France 51 K6
Chalt Jammu and Kashmir 96 B1
Chalumna S. Africa 133 L10
Chālūs France 50 G7
Chālūs Iran 100 B2
Cham Germany 49 J6
Chama U.S.A. 181 F5
Chama r. U.S.A. 181 F5
Chamamba Tanz. 129 B6
Chaman Pak. 101 F4
Chaman Bid Iran 100 D2
Chamao, Khao mt. Thai. 79 C5
Chamba India 96 C2
Chamba Tanz. 129 C7
Chambas Cuba 186 D2
Chambeaux, Lac l. Canada 169 G2
Chamberlain Canada 167 J5
Chamberlain r. Australia 150 D3
Chamberlain U.S.A. 178 C3
Chamberlain Lake U.S.A. 174 G2
Chambers U.S.A. 183 O6
Chambers Bay Australia 148 A2
Chambersburg U.S.A. 176 H6
Chambers Island U.S.A. 172 F6
Chambéry France 51 L7
Chambeshi Zambia 127 F7
Chamboshi r. Zambia 127 F8
Chambi, Jebel mt. Tunisia 123 H2
Chambira r. Peru 198 C6
Chambord Canada 169 F3
Chambri Lake P.N.G. 73 J7
Chamdo China see Qamdo
Chame Panama 186 D5
Chamechaude mt. France 51 L7
Chamela Mex. 184 D5
Chamical Arg. 204 D3
Chamili r. Greece 59 H13
Chamo Häyk' l. Eth. 128 C3
Chamoli India 96 C3
Chamonix-Mont-Blanc France 51 M7
Chamouchouane r. Canada see
Ashuapmushuan
Chamouse, Montagne de mt. France 51 L8
Champa India 97 D5
Champagne admin. reg. France
51 K4
Champagne Castle mt. S. Africa 133 N6
Champagnole France 51 L6
Champagny Islands Australia 150 D2
Champaign U.S.A. 174 B3
Champaqui, Cerro mt. Arg. 204 D3
Champara mt. Peru 200 A2
Champasak Laos 79 D5
Champdoré, Lac l. Canada 169 H2
Champhai India 97 G5
Champion Canada 167 H5
Champion U.S.A. 172 F4
Champlain U.S.A. 177 L1
Champlain VA U.S.A. 177 I7
Champlain, Lake Canada/U.S.A. 174 F2
Champlain Canal U.S.A. 177 L2
Champlitte France 51 L5
Champneuf Canada 173 P2
Champotón Mex. 185 H5
Chamrajnagar India 94 C4
Cham Siyāh Iran 100 B4
Chamusca Port. 54 C5
Chan, Ko i. Thai. 79 B6
Chana Thai. 79 C7
Chanak Turkey see Çanakkale
Chanal Mex. 185 G5
Chañar Arg. 204 C5
Chañaral Chile 204 C2
Chañaral, Isla i. Chile 204 C3
Chañarán Iran 101 D2
Chañaro, Cerro mt. Venez. 199 F3
Chança r. Port./Spain see Chanza
Chancay Peru 200 A2
Chanco Chile 204 B4
Chancos Peru 200 A2
Chanda India see Chandrapur
Chandalar r. U.S.A. 164 E3
Chandama Tanz. 129 C6
Chandausi India 96 C3
Chandbali India 95 E1
Chandeleur Islands U.S.A. 175 B6

Chanderi India 96 C4
Chandia India 96 D5
Chandigarh India 96 C3
Chandil India 97 E5
Chandler Canada 169 H3
Chandler AZ U.S.A. 183 M8
Chandler OK U.S.A. 179 C5
Chandless r. Brazil 200 C2
Chandmany Mongolia 84 C1
Chandos Lake Canada 173 P6
Chandpur Bangl. 97 F5
Chandpur India 96 C3
Chandragiri India 94 C3
Chandrapur India 94 C2
formerly known as Chanda
Chandur India 94 C1
Chandvad India 94 B1
Chandyr r. Turkm. 102 C5
also spelt Chendir
Chang, Ko i. Thai. 79 C5
Changalane Moz. 133 Q3
Chang'an China see Rong'an
Chang'an China 87 D1
also known as Weiqu
Chang-an S. Korea 91 A7
Changane r. Moz. 131 G5
Changara Moz. 131 G3
Changbai China 82 B4
Changbai Shan mts China/N. Korea 82 B4
formerly known as Ch'ang-pai Shan
Chang Cheng research station Antarctica
see Great Wall
Changchow China see Zhangzhou
Changchow China see Changzhou
Changchun China 82 B4
historically known as Hsinking
Changdao China 85 I4
also known as Nanchangshan; formerly
known as Shima
Changde China 87 D2
formerly spelt Changteh
Changfeng China 87 F1
also known as Shuihu
Changge China 87 E1
Changgi-ap pt S. Korea 83 C5
Changgo China 89 E6
Changhai China 85 I4
also known as Sikuaishi
Chang Hu l. China 85 I2
Changhua Taiwan 87 G3
also spelt Zhanghua
Changhua Jiang r. China 87 D5
Changhŭng S. Korea 83 B6
Changi Sing. 76 [inset]
Changii China 88 D3
Changjiang China 87 D5
Chang Jiang r. China see Yangtze
Changjiang Kou r. mouth China see
Yangtze, Mouth of the
Changjin N. Korea 83 B4
Changjin-gang r. N. Korea 83 B4
Changkiang China see Zhanjiang
Changle China 87 F3
Changleng China see Xinjiang
Changli China 85 H4
Changling China 85 I2
Changliushui China 85 E4
Changning Jammu and Kashmir 96 C3
Changning Hunan China 87 E3
Changning China see Xunwu
Changning Sichuan China 86 C2
Changnyŏn N. Korea 83 B5
Ch'ang-pai Shan mts China/N. Korea see
Changbai Shan
Changping China 85 H3
Changpu China see Suining
Changsan-got pt N. Korea 83 B5
Changsha China 87 E3
Changshan China 87 F2
Changshou China 86 C2
Changshoujie China 87 E2
Changshu China 87 G2
Changsŏng S. Korea 83 B6
Changtai China 87 F3
also known as Wu'an
Changteh China see Changde
Changting Fujian China 87 F3
also spelt Tingzhou
Changting Heilong. China 82 C3
Changtu China 82 B4
Changuinola Panama 186 C5
Ch'angwŏn S. Korea 83 C6
Changwu China 85 E5
also known as Zhaoren
Changxing China 87 G2
Changxing Dao i. China 85 I4
Changyang China 87 D2
also known as Longzhouping
Changyi China 85 H4
Changyŏn N. Korea 83 B5
Changyuan China see Rongchang
Changyuan China 85 G5
Changzhi Shanxi China 85 G4
Changzhi Shanxi China 85 G5
also known as Handian
Changzhou China 87 F2
also known as Wujin; formerly spelt
Changchow

Chapala Mex. 185 E4
Chapala, Laguna de l. Mex. 185 E4
Chapare r. Bol. 200 D3
Cháparra Peru 200 B3
Chaparral Col. 198 C4
Chapayevo Kazakh. 102 B2
Chapayevsk Rus. Fed. 102 B1
Chapayevskoye Kazakh. 103 H1
Chapecó Brazil 203 A8
Chapecó r. Brazil 203 A8
Chapel Hill U.S.A. 174 E5
Chapicuy Uruguay 204 F3
Chapimarca Peru 200 B3
Chapleau Canada 168 D4
Chapleau Crown Game Reserve
nature res. Canada 168 D3
Chaplin Canada 167 J5
Chaplin Lake dry lake Canada 167 J5
Chaplino Rus. Fed. 39 S3
Chaplygin Rus. Fed. 41 F5
Chapman, Mount Canada 166 G5
Chapmanville PA U.S.A. 176 F4
Chapmanville WV U.S.A. 176 C8
Chappell U.S.A. 178 B3
Chappell Islands Australia 147 E5
Chapra India see Chhapra
Chapri Pass Afgh. 101 F3
Charadai Arg. 204 F2
Charagua Bol. 201 E4
Charana Bol. 200 C4
Charapita Col. 198 C5
Charata Arg. 204 E2
Charbonnel, Pointe de mt. France 51 N7
Charcas Mex. 185 E4
Charcot Island Antarctica 222 S2
Chard Canada 167 I4
Chard U.K. 47 J13
Chardara Kazakh. see Shardara
Chardarinskoye Vodokhranilishche resr
Kazakh./Uzbek. 103 G4
also known as Shardara Bögeni
Chardon U.S.A. 176 D4
Chardzhev Turkm. 103 E5
also known as Turkmenabat; also spelt
Chärjew; formerly spelt Chardzhou
Chardzhou Turkm. see Chardzhev
Chardzhouskaya Oblast' admin. div. Turkm.
see Lebapskaya Oblast'
Char Chu r. Xizang China 89 F6
Charente r. France 50 E4
Charg Iran 100 C4
Chari r. Cameroon/Chad 125 I3
also spelt Shari
Chārīkār Afgh. 101 G3
Charikot Nepal 97 E4
Chariton U.S.A. 174 A3
Chariton r. U.S.A. 174 A4
Chärjew Turkm. see Chardzhev
Charkayuvom Rus. Fed. 40 J2
Charkhari India 96 C4
Charkhi Dadri India 96 C3
Charkhlik China see Ruoqiang
Charleroi Belgium 51 K2
Charles, Cape U.S.A. 177 J8
Charlesbourg Canada 169 G3
Charles City IA U.S.A. 174 A3
Charles City VA U.S.A. 177 H8
Charles de Gaulle airport France 51 I2
Charles Lake Canada 167 I3
Charles M. Russell National Wildlife
Refuge nature res. U.S.A. 180 F3
Charles Point Australia 148 A1
Charleston N.Z. 153 F9
Charleston IL U.S.A. 174 B4
Charleston MO U.S.A. 174 B4
Charleston MS U.S.A. 174 B5
Charleston SC U.S.A. 175 E5
▶ Charleston WV U.S.A. 176 D7
State capital of West Virginia.
Charleston Peak U.S.A. 183 I5
Charlestown St Kitts and Nevis 187 H3
Charlestown NH U.S.A. 177 M2
Charlestown RI U.S.A. 177 N4
Charles Town U.S.A. 176 H6
Charleville Australia 149 E5
Charleville Rep. of Ireland see Rathluirc
Charleville-Mézières France 51 K3
Charlevoix U.S.A. 172 H5
Charlie Lake Canada 166 F3
Charlotte MI U.S.A. 173 I8
Charlotte NC U.S.A. 174 D5
▶ Charlotte Amalie Virgin Is (U.S.A.) 187 G3
Capital of the U.S. Virgin Islands.
Charlotte Bank sea feature S. China Sea
77 D1
Charlotte Court House U.S.A. 176 G8
Charlotte Harbor b. U.S.A. 175 D7
Charlotte Lake Canada 166 E4
Charlottenberg Sweden 45 K4
Charlottesville U.S.A. 176 G7
▶ Charlottetown Canada 169 I4
Provincial capital of Prince Edward Island.
Charlotte Trin. and Tob. 187 H5
Charlton Australia 147 D4
Charlton Island Canada 168 E2
Charmes France 51 M4
Charnitsa r. Belarus 43 L7
Charnley r. Australia 150 D3
Charoenkhan Kazakh. see Shar
Charozero Rus. Fed. 43 T1
Charron Lake Canada 167 M4
Charsadda Pak. 101 G3
Charshanga Turkm. 103 F5
Charsk Kazakh. see Shar
Charters r. U.S.A. 176 F6
Charters Towers Australia 149 E4
Chartres France 51 I4
Charvaksoye Vodokhranilishche resr
Kazakh./Uzbek. 103 G4
also spelt Sharyn
Charyn Kazakh. 103 I4
Charysh r. Rus. Fed. 103 J1
Charyshskoye Rus. Fed. 88 C1
Chas India 97 E5
Chās Iran. Port. 54 C4
Chaschuil Arg. 204 C2
Chascomús Arg. 204 F4
Chase Canada 166 G5
Chase City U.S.A. 176 G9
Chashkent Turkm. 103 E5
Chashmeh-ye Abe-e Garm spring Iran
100 D3
Chashmeh-ye Garm Ab spring Iran
100 D3
Chashmeh-ye Magu well Iran 100 D3
Chashmeh-ye Safid spring Iran 100 D3
Chashmeh-ye Shotoran well Iran 100 C3
Chashniki Belarus 43 K7
Chasia reg. Greece 59 C9
Chasico Arg. 205 D6
Chaska U.S.A. 178 D2
Chaslands Mistake c. N.Z. 153 D14
Chasŏng N. Korea 83 B4
Chasovenskaya Rus. Fed. 43 O1
Chassezac r. France 51 K8
Chassiron, Pointe de pt France 50 E6
Chastab, Kūh-e mts Iran 100 B3
Chastye Rus. Fed. 40 J4
Chasuta Peru 198 B6
Chāt Iran 100 C2
Chatang China see Zhanang
Château-Arnoux France 51 L8

Châteaubriant France 50 E5
Château-Chinon France 51 J5
Château-du-Loir France 50 G5
Châteaudun France 50 H4
Châteaugiron France 50 E4
Château-Gontier France 50 F5
Châteauguay, Lac l. Canada 169 G1
Châteauguay r. Canada 169 G1
Châteaulin France 50 B4
Châteauneuf-en-Thymerais France 50 H4
Châteauneuf-sur-Loire France 51 I5
Château Pond l. Canada 169 J2
Châteauponsac France 50 H6
Châteaurenard France 51 K9
Château-Renault France 50 G5
Châteauroux France 50 H5
Château-Salins France 51 M4
Château-Thierry France 51 I3
Châtelaillon-Plage France 50 E6
Châtelet Belgium 51 K2
Châtellerault France 50 G6
Châtenois France 51 L4
Châtillon-sur-Indre France 50 H6
Châtillon-sur-Loire France 51 I5
Châtillon-sur-Seine France 51 K5
Chatkal r. Kyrg. 103 G4
Chatkal mts Kyrg. 103 G4
Chatom U.S.A. 175 B6
Chatra India 97 E4
Chatra Nepal 97 E4
Chatsu India 96 B4
Chatsworth Australia 149 D4
Chatsworth Canada 173 M6
Chatsworth GA U.S.A. 175 C5
Chatsworth IL U.S.A. 172 E10
Chatsworth NJ U.S.A. 177 K6
Chatsworth Zimbabwe 131 F3
Chattagam Bangl. see Chittagong
Chattahoochee U.S.A. 175 C6
Chattahoochee r. U.S.A. 179 F6
Chattanooga U.S.A. 174 C5
Chatto Creek N.Z. 153 D13
Chatturat Thai. 79 C5
Chatyrkël', Ozero l. Kyrg. see Chatyr-Köl
Chatyr-Köl l. Kyrg. 88 B1
also known as Chatyrkël', Ozero
Chatyr-Tash Kyrg. 103 I4
Châu Đốc Vietnam 79 D6
formerly known as Chau Phu
Chauffailles France 51 K6
Chauhtan India 96 A4
Chauk Myanmar 78 A3
Chauka r. India 96 D4
Chaukhamba mts India see
Badrinath Peaks
Chau Kung To i. Hong Kong China see
Sunshine Island
Chaumont France 51 L4
Chauncey U.S.A. 176 C7
Chaungwabyin Myanmar 79 B5
Chaunskaya Guba b. Rus. Fed. 39 Q3
Chauny France 51 J3
Chau Phu Vietnam see Châu Đốc
Chaurai India 96 C5
Chausey, Îles is France 50 E4
Chausy Belarus see Chavusy
Chautauqua, Lake U.S.A. 176 F3
Chauvay Kyrg. 103 H4
Chauvigny France 50 G6
Chauvin Canada 167 I4
Chavakachcheri Sri Lanka 94 D4
Chaval Brazil 202 D2
Chavan'ga Rus. Fed. 40 F2
Chavār Iran 100 A3
Chaves Brazil 202 C2
Chaves Port. 54 D3
Chaves Valdivia Peru 198 B6
Chavigny, Lac l. Canada 169 F1
Chaviva Col. 198 C3
Chavusy Belarus 43 L7
also spelt Chausy
Chawal r. Pak. 101 F4
Chāy r. Vietnam 78 D3
Chayan Kazakh. see Shayan
Chayanta r. Bol. 200 D4
Chayatyn, Khrebet ridge Rus. Fed. 82 E1
Chayek Kyrg. see Chaek
Chayevo Rus. Fed. 43 S5
Chaykovskiy Rus. Fed. 40 J4
Chazhegovo Rus. Fed. 40 J3
Chazón Arg. 204 E3
Chazy U.S.A. 177 L1
Cheat r. U.S.A. 176 F6
Cheb Czech Rep. 49 J5
Chebanse U.S.A. 172 F9
Chebbi l. Alg. 123 F4
Cheboksary Rus. Fed. 40 H4
Cheboygan U.S.A. 173 I5
Chebsara r. Rus. Fed. 43 T2
Chechen', Ostrov i. Rus. Fed. 102 A4
Chechnya aut. rep. Rus. Fed. see
Chechenskaya Respublika
Chechenskaya Respublika aut. rep.
Rus. Fed. 41 H8
short form Chechnya; English form Chechenia
or Chechnia; also known as Ichkeria
Cheche Pass Lesotho 133 M6
Chechnia aut. rep. Rus. Fed. see
Chechenskaya Respublika
Chech'ŏn S. Korea 83 C5
Chęciny Poland 49 R5
Checotah U.S.A. 179 D5
Cheder Rus. Fed. 84 E1
Cheduba Myanmar 78 A4
Cheduba Island Myanmar 78 A4
also known as Man-aung Kyun
Cheduba Strait Myanmar 78 A4
Chée r. France 51 L4
Cheektowaga U.S.A. 176 E3
Cheepash r. Canada 168 D3
Cheepie Australia 149 D5
Cheetham, Cape Antarctica 223 K2
Chef-Boutonne France 50 F6
Cheffadene well Niger 125 I2
Chefoo China see Yantai
Chefornak U.S.A. 164 C3
Chegdomyn Rus. Fed. 82 D2
Chegga Mauritania 122 D4
Cheggué watercourse Mauritania 124 C2
Cheggué T-n-Kerkâz des. Mauritania
124 D2
Chegutu Zimbabwe 131 F3
formerly known as Hartley
Chehalis U.S.A. 180 B3
Chehalis r. U.S.A. 180 B3
Chehardeh Iran 100 C2
Cheharīz tourist site Iraq 107 F4
Chehel Chashmeh, Kūh-e hill Iran 100 A3
Chehel Dokhtarān, Kūh-e mt. Iran 101 E4
Chehel'āyeh Iran 100 D4
Cheikria well Alg. 123 G3
Cheiron r. France 51 M8
Cheil Nerei-Beuşniţa nat. park Romania
58 C3
Cherkassy Ukr. see Cherkasy

Cheiron, Cime du mt. France 51 M9
Cheju S. Korea 83 B6
Cheju-do i. S. Korea 83 B6
English form Quelpart Island
Cheju-haehyŏp sea chan. S. Korea 83 B6
Chekalin Rus. Fed. 43 R7
Chek Chau i. Hong Kong China see
Port Island
Chekhov Rus. Fed. 43 S6
formerly known as Lopasnya
Chekhov Rus. Fed. 82 F3
Chekiang prov. China see Zhejiang
Chek Jawa, Tanjong pt Sing. 76 [inset]
Chek Lap Kok i. Hong Kong China 87 [inset]
Chek Mun Hoi Hap sea chan. Hong Kong
China see Tolo Channel
Chekshino Rus. Fed. 43 S4
Chela, Serra da mts Angola 127 B9
Chelan U.S.A. 180 B3
Chelan, Lake U.S.A. 180 B2
Cheleken Turkm. 102 C5
Chelkar Turkm. 102 D3
also known as Shalqar
Chelial Alg. 55 P9
Chélif, Oued r. Alg. 55 L8
Cheline Moz. 131 G4
Chelkar Kazakh. 102 C2
also known as Shalqar
Chełm Poland 53 G1
historically known as Kholm
Chelmer r. U.K. 47 M12
Chełmno Poland 49 P2
Chelmsford U.K. 47 M12
historically known as Caesaromagus
Chelmsford U.S.A. 177 N3
Chelmsford Dam S. Africa 133 N4
Chelmsford Public Resort Nature
Reserve S. Africa 133 N4
Chełmża Poland 49 P2
Chelsea U.S.A. 173 I8
Cheltenham N.Z. 152 J8
Cheltenham U.K. 47 J12
Chelva Spain 55 K5
Chelyabinsk Rus. Fed. 38 G4
Chelyabinskaya Oblast' admin. div.
Rus. Fed. 103 E1
English form Chelyabinsk Oblast
Chelyabinsk Oblast admin. div. Rus. Fed.
see Chelyabinskaya Oblast'
Chelyuskin Rus. Fed. 39 K2
Chelyuskin, Mys c. Rus. Fed. 39 K2
Chemaïa Morocco 122 C2
Chemax Mex. 185 I4
Chembe Zambia 127 F7
Chemchâm, Sebkhet salt flat Mauritania
122 B5
Chem Co l. China 89 B5
Chemenibit Turkm. 101 E3
Chemillé France 50 F5
Chemmis Egypt see Akhmim
Chemnitz Germany 49 J5
formerly known as Karl-Marx-Stadt
Chemulpo S. Korea see Inch'ŏn
Chemult U.S.A. 180 B4
Chemung r. U.S.A. 177 I4
Chenab r. India/Pak. 96 A3
Chenachane Alg. 122 D4
Chenachane, Oued watercourse Alg.
122 D4
Chenango r. U.S.A. 177 J3
Chenango Bridge U.S.A. 177 J3
Ch'ench'a Eth. 128 C3
Chendir r. Turkm. see Chandyr
Cheney U.S.A. 180 C3
Cheney Reservoir U.S.A. 178 C4
Chengalpattu India 94 D3
formerly known as Chingleput
Chengam India 94 C3
Cheng'an China 85 G4
Chengbihe Shuiku resr China 86 C3
Chengbu China 87 D3
Chengcheng China 85 F5
Chengchow China see Zhengzhou
Chengde China 85 H3
Chengdu China 86 C2
formerly spelt Chengtu
Chengel'dy Kazakh. see Shengel'dy
Chenggong China 86 B3
also known as Longcheng
Chenghai China 87 F4
Chengjiang China see Taihe
Chengjiang China 86 B3
also known as Gecheng
Chengkou China 87 D2
also known as Jinjiang
Chengmai China 87 D5
Chengqian China 85 H5
Chengqiao China see Chongming
Chengshou China see Yingshan
Chengtu China see Chengdu
Chengwu China 87 E1
Chengxian China 85 E4
Chengxiang China see Fuquan
Chengxiang China see Wuxi
Chengxiang China see Quannan
Chengxiang China see Tianquan
Chengyang China see Juxian
Chengzhong China see Ningming
Cheniu Shan i. China 85 H5
Chennai India 94 D3
formerly known as Madras
Chenoa U.S.A. 172 E9
Chenstokhov Poland see Częstochowa
Chentejn Nuruu mts Mongolia 85 E1
Chenting, Tanjong pt Sing. 76 [inset]
Chenxi China 87 D3
also known as Chenyang
Chenyang China see Chenxi
Chenying China see Wannian
Chenzhou China 87 E3
Cheom Ksan Cambodia see Chŏăm Khsant
Chepelare Bulg. 58 F7
Chepén Peru 200 A1
Chepes Arg. 204 D3
Chepo Panama 186 D5
Chepstow U.K. 47 J12
Cheptsa r. Rus. Fed. 40 I4
Chequamegon Bay U.S.A. 172 C4
Cher r. France 51 G5
Chera stare India see Kerala
Cherán Mex. 185 E5
Cherangany Hills Kenya 128 B4
Cheraw U.S.A. 174 E5
Cherbaniani Reef India 94 A3
also known as Beleapani
Cherbourg France 50 E3
Cherchell Alg. 123 F1
historically known as Caesarea
Cherchen China see Qiemo
Cherdakly Rus. Fed. 41 I5
Cherdyn' Rus. Fed. 40 K3
Chère r. France 50 E5
Cherepaani reef Indon. see Byramgore Reef
Cherekha r. Rus. Fed. 43 J4
Cheremisinovo Rus. Fed. 41 F6
Cheremshany Rus. Fed. 82 D4
formerly known as Sinancha
Cheremukhovka Rus. Fed. 40 I4
Cherepanovo Rus. Fed. 80 D2
Cherepovets Rus. Fed. 43 S2
Cherepvovo Rus. Fed. 40 G4
Chergui, Chott ech imp. l. Alg. 123 F2
Chéria Alg. 123 G2
Cherial India 94 C2
Cheriton U.S.A. 177 J8
Cheriyam i. India 94 B4
Cherkassy Ukr. see Cherkasy

Cherkasy Ukr. 41 E6
also spelt Cherkassy
Cherkessk Rus. Fed. 41 G7
Cherkutino Rus. Fed. 43 U5
Cherla India 94 D2
Chermenze Angola 127 D8
Chermoz Rus. Fed. 40 K4
Chern' Rus. Fed. 43 R8
Chern' r. Rus. Fed. 43 R8
Chernak Kazakh. 103 G4
also spelt Shornaq
Chernava Lipetskaya Oblast' Rus. Fed.
43 T9
Chernava Ryazanskaya Oblast' Rus. Fed.
43 U8
Chernaya Rus. Fed. 40 K1
Chernaya r. Rus. Fed. 40 K1
Chernaya r. Rus. Fed. 42 I3
Chernaya Kholunitsa Rus. Fed. 40 I4
Chernevo Moskovskaya Oblast' Rus. Fed.
43 T7
Chernevo Pskovskaya Oblast' Rus. Fed. 43 J3
Chernigov Ukr. see Chernihiv
Chernigovka Rus. Fed. 82 D3
Chernihiv Ukr. 41 D6
Chernihivka Rus. Fed. 58 G5
Chernivka Ukr. 41 F7
Cherni Vrŭkh mt. Bulg. 58 E6
Chernivtsi Ukr. 41 C6
also known as Czernowitz; also spelt
Chernovtsy; historically known as Cernăuţi
Chernobyl' Ukr. see Chornobyl'
Chernogorsk Rus. Fed. 80 E2
Chernoostrovskoye Kazakh. 103 I1
Chernorechenskiy Rus. Fed. 82 B3
Chernoretskoye Kazakh. 103 I1
Chernoshevo Rus. Fed. 43 I3
Chernovskoye Rus. Fed. 40 H4
Chernovtsy Ukr. see Chernivtsi
Chernoye sea Asia/Europe see
Black Sea
Chernushka Rus. Fed. 40 K4
Chernyakhiv Ukr. 41 D6
Chernyakhovsk Rus. Fed. 42 C7
historically known as Insterburg
Chernyanka Rus. Fed. 41 F6
Chernyayevo Rus. Fed. 82 D1
Chernysheva, Zaliv b. Kazakh. 102 D3
Chernyshevsk Rus. Fed. 81 J2
Chernyshevskiy Rus. Fed. 39 L3
Chernyshkovskiy Rus. Fed. 41 G6
Chernyy, Mys c. Rus. Fed. 40 J1
Chernyye Zemli reg. Rus. Fed. 41 H7
Chernyy Irtysh r. China/Kazakh. see
Ertix He
Chernyy Otrog Rus. Fed. 102 C2
Chernyy Porog Rus. Fed. 40 E3
Chernyy Rynok Rus. Fed. see Kochubey
Chernyy Yar Rus. Fed. 102 B3
Cherokee IA U.S.A. 178 D3
Cherokee OK U.S.A. 178 C4
Cherokee Lake U.S.A. 176 B9
Cherokees, Lake o' the U.S.A. 178 D4
Cherokee Sound Bahamas 186 D1
Cherpessa Rus. Fed. 43 L5
▶ Cherrapunji India 97 F4
Highest recorded annual rainfall in the world.
world (climate and weather) ▶ 16–17
Cherry Creek r. U.S.A. 178 B2
Cherry Creek Mountains U.S.A. 183 J1
Cherryfield U.S.A. 177 R1
Cherry Hill U.S.A. 177 K6
Cherry Island Solomon Is 145 F3
Cherry Lake U.S.A. 182 E3
Cherry Valley Canada 173 P7
Cherskaya Rus. Fed. 43 J4
Cherskiy Rus. Fed. 39 Q3
formerly known as Nizhniye Kresty
Cherskiy Range mts Rus. Fed. see
Cherskogo, Khrebet
Cherskogo, Khrebet mts Rus. Fed. 85 F1
English form Cherskiy Range
Cherskogo, Khrebet mts Rus. Fed. 81 J2
Chersonisos Methano pen. Greece 59 E11
Cherthala India see Shertally
Chertkov Ukr. see Chortkiv
Chertkovo Rus. Fed. 41 G6
Chertolino Rus. Fed. 43 O5
Chertsey N.Z. 153 F11
Cherusti Rus. Fed. 43 V6
Cherven Bryag Bulg. 58 F5
Chervonoarmeyskoye Ukr. see Vil'nyans'k
Chervonograd Ukr. see Chervonohrad
Chervonohrad Ukr. 41 C6
also spelt Chervonograd; formerly known as
Kristinopol' or Krystynopol
Chervonozavods'ke Ukr. 41 E6
Chervonoznam"yanka Ukr. 58 L1
Chervyen' Belarus 43 J8
Cherykaw Belarus 43 M8
Chesaning U.S.A. 173 I7
Chesapeake U.S.A. 177 I8
Chesapeake Bay U.S.A. 177 I7
Chesapeake Beach U.S.A. 177 I7
Cheshire U.S.A. 177 L3
Cheshme Vtoroy Turkm. 102 E5
Cheshskaya Guba b. Rus. Fed. 40 H2
Chesht-e Sharīf Afgh. 101 E3
Chesma Rus. Fed. 103 E1
Chesnokovka Rus. Fed. see Novoaltaysk
Chester Canada 169 H4
Chester U.K. 47 I10
historically known as Deva
Chester CA U.S.A. 182 C1
Chester IL U.S.A. 174 B4
Chester MT U.S.A. 180 E2
Chester NJ U.S.A. 177 K5
Chester OH U.S.A. 176 C7
Chester PA U.S.A. 177 J6
Chester SC U.S.A. 174 D5
Chester VA U.S.A. 176 H8
Chester r. U.S.A. 177 I7
Chesterfield U.K. 47 K10
Chesterfield MO U.S.A. 174 B4
Chesterfield SC U.S.A. 174 D5
Chesterfield VA U.S.A. 176 H8
Chesterfield, Îles is New Caledonia
145 E3
Chesterfield Inlet Canada 167 N2
also known as Igluligaarjuk
Chesterfield Inlet inlet Canada 167 M2
Chestertown U.S.A. 177 I6
Chestnut Ridge U.S.A. 176 F5
Chesuncook Lake U.S.A. 174 G2
Chetek U.S.A. 172 B5
Chéticamp Canada 169 I4
Chetlat i. India 94 B4
Chetopa U.S.A. 178 D4
Chetumal Mex. 185 H5
Chetwode Islands N.Z. 152 I8
Chetwynd Canada 166 F3
Cheung Chau Hong Kong China 87 [inset]
Chevelon Creek r. U.S.A. 183 N7
Cheviot N.Z. 153 H10
Cheviot U.S.A. 176 A6
Cheviot Hills U.K. 47 J8
Cheviot Range hills Australia 149 D5
Cheviot r. Canada 169 F2
Ch'ew Bahir salt l. Eth. 128 C3
Ch'ew Bahir Wildlife Reserve nature res.
Eth. 128 C3
Chewelah U.S.A. 180 C2
Cheyenne OK U.S.A. 179 C5
▶ Cheyenne WY U.S.A. 180 F4
State capital of Wyoming.
Cheyenne r. U.S.A. 178 B2

Cheyenne River Indian Reservation res. U.S.A. 178 B2
Cheyenne Wells U.S.A. 178 B4
Cheyne Bay Australia 151 B7
Cheyur India 94 D3
Cheyyar r. India 94 C3
Chezacut Canada 166 E4
Chhabra India 96 C4
Chhapar India 96 B4
Chhapra India 97 E4
formerly spelt Chapra
Chhata India 96 C4
Chhatarpur Jharkhand India 97 E4
Chhatarpur Madhya Pradesh India 96 C4
Chhatrapur India 95 E2
Chhattisgarh state India 97 D5
Chhay Arêng, Stœng r. Cambodia 79 C6
Chhibramau India 96 C4
Chhindwara India 96 C5
Chhipa Barod India 96 C4
Chhlong, Prêk r. Cambodia 79 D5
Chhota Chhindwara India 96 C5
Chhota Udepur India 96 B5
Chhuk Cambodia see Phumĭ Chhuk
Chhukha Bhutan 97 F4
Chiai Taiwan 87 G4
also spelt Jiayi
Ch'iak-san National Park S. Korea 83 C5
Chiang Dao Thai. 78 B4
Chiange Angola 127 B8
formerly known as Vila de Almoster
Chiang Kham Thai. 78 C4
Chiang Khan Thai. 78 C4
Chiang Mai Thai. 78 B4
also spelt Chiengmai
Chiang Rai Thai. 78 B4
Chiani r. Italy 56 E6
Chiapa Mex. 185 G5
Chiapas state Mex. 185 G5
Chiat'ura Georgia 107 E2
Chiautla Mex. 185 F5
Chiavari Italy 56 B3
Chiavenna Italy 56 B2
Chiba Japan 91 G7
Chiba pref. Japan 90 G7
Chibemba Angola 127 B8
Chibi China 87 E2
Chibia Angola 127 B8
formerly known as João de Almeida
Chibit Rus. Fed. 88 D1
Chibizovka Rus. Fed. see Zherdevka
Chiboma Moz. 131 G4
Chibougamau Canada 169 F3
Chibougamau, Lac l. Canada 169 F3
Chibu-Sangaku National Park Japan 91 E6
English form Japan Alps National Park
Chibuto Moz. 131 G5
Chibuzhang Hu l. China 89 E5
Chibwe Zambia 127 F8
Chicacole India see Srikakulam

Chicago U.S.A. 174 C3
4th most populous city in North America.
world [cities] ▶▶▶ 24–25

Chicago Heights U.S.A. 172 F9
Chicala Angola 127 C7
Chicamba Moz. 131 G3
Chicapa r. Angola 127 D6
Chic-Chocs, Monts mts Canada 169 H3
Chic-Chocs, Réserve Faunique des nature res. Canada 169 H3
Chicera Hamba hill Romania 58 F3
Chichagof Island U.S.A. 164 F4
Chichak r. Pak. 101 F5
Chichaoua Morocco 122 C3
Chicheng China see Pengxi
Chicheng China see Pengxi
Chichén Itzá tourist site Mex. 185 H4
Chichester U.K. 47 L13
Chichester Range mts Australia 150 B4
Chichgarh India 96 C5
Chichibu Japan 83 E6
Chichibu-Tama National Park Japan 91 F7
Chichirivichie Venez. 199 D2
Chicholi India 96 C5
Chickahominy r. U.S.A. 177 I8
Chickasawhay r. U.S.A. 175 B6
Chickasha U.S.A. 179 C5
Chiclana de la Frontera Spain 54 E8
Chiclayo Peru 198 B6
Chico r. Chubut Arg. 205 C6
Chico r. Chubut Arg. 205 D7
Chico r. Santa Cruz Arg. 205 C8
Chico U.S.A. 182 C2
Chicoa Moz. 131 G2
Chicobea i. Fiji see Cikobia
Chicobi, Lac l. Canada 173 O2
Chicomba Angola 127 B8
Chicomo Moz. 131 G5
Chicomucelo Mex. 185 G6
Chicononoe Moz. 129 B8
Chicopee U.S.A. 177 M3
Chico Sapocoy, Mount Phil. 74 B2
Chicoutimi Canada 169 G3
Chicoutimi r. Canada 169 G3
Chicualacuala Moz. 131 F4
formerly known as Malvérnia
Chicuma Angola 127 B8
Chicumbane India 94 C4
Chido S. Korea 83 B6
Chiede Angola 127 C9
Chiefland U.S.A. 175 D6
Chiemsee l. Germany 49 J8
Chiengi Zambia 127 F7
Chiengmai Thai. see Chiang Mai
Chienti r. Italy 56 F5
Chieo Lan Reservoir Thai. 79 B6
Chieri Italy 51 N7
Chiers r. France 51 L3
Chiese r. Italy 56 C3
Chieti Italy 56 G6
historically known as Teate
Chifeng China 85 H3
also known as Ulanhad
Chifre, Serra do mts Brazil 203 D6
Chifunde Moz. 131 G2
formerly known as Tembué
Chiganak Kazakh. 103 H3
formerly spelt Shyganaq
Chiginagak, Mount vol. U.S.A. 164 D4
Chignecto Bay Canada 169 H4
Chignecto Game Sanctuary nature res. Canada 169 H4
Chignik U.S.A. 164 D4
Chigorodó Col. 198 B3
Chigu China 89 E6
Chiguana Bol. 200 D5
Chigubo Moz. 131 G4
Chigu Co l. China 89 E6
Chihli, Gulf of China see Bo Hai
Chihuahua Mex. 184 D2
Chihuahua state Mex. 184 D2
Chiili Kazakh. 103 F3
also spelt Shieli
Chijinpu China 84 C3
Chikalda India 96 C5
Chikan China 87 D4
Chikaskia r. U.S.A. 178 C4
Chikhachevo Rus. Fed. 43 K4
Chikhli India 96 C5
Chikmagalur India 94 B3
Chikodi India 94 B3
Chikodi Road India 94 B3
Chikoy Rus. Fed. 85 F1

Chikoy r. Rus. Fed. 85 E1
Chikugo Japan 91 B8
Chikuma-gawa r. Japan 90 F6
Chikushino Japan 91 B8
Chikwa Zambia 129 B7
Chikwawa Malawi 129 B9
Chikyū-misaki pt Japan 90 G3
Chila Angola 127 B8
Chilanko r. Canada 166 E4
Chilanko Forks Canada 166 E4
Chilapa Mex. 185 F5
Chilas Jammu and Kashmir 96 B2
Chilaw Sri Lanka 94 C5
Chilca Peru 200 A3
Chilcaya Chile 200 C4
Chilcotin r. Canada 166 F5
Childers Australia 149 G5
Childress U.S.A. 179 B5
▶ Chile country S. America 205 B7
southamerica [countries] ▶▶▶ 192–193
Chile Chico Chile 205 C7
Chilecito Arg. 204 D3
Chilengue, Serra do mts Angola 127 B8
Chilete Peru 200 A1
Chilhowie U.S.A. 176 D9
Chilia-Nouă Ukr. see Kiliya
Chilia Veche Romania 58 K3
Chilik Kazakh. 103 I4
also spelt Shelek
Chilik r. Kazakh. 103 I4
Chilika Lake India 95 E2
Chililabombwe Zambia 127 E8
formerly known as Bancroft
Chiliomodi Greece 59 D11
also known as Khiliomódhion
Chilko r. Canada 166 E4
Chilko Lake Canada 166 E5
Chillagoe Australia 149 E3
Chillán Chile 204 B5
Chillar Arg. 204 E5
Chillicothe IL U.S.A. 172 D10
Chillicothe MO U.S.A. 178 D4
Chillicothe OH U.S.A. 176 C6
Chilliluico Peru 200 C4
Chillinji Jammu and Kashmir 96 B1
Chilliwack Canada 166 F5
Chil'mamedkum, Peski des. Turkm. 102 C4
Chilmari Bangl. 97 F4
Chiloé, Isla de i. Chile 205 B6
long form Chiloé, Isla Grande de i.
Chiloé, Isla Grande de i. Chile see Chiloé, Isla de
Chilombo Angola 127 D8
Chilonga Zambia 127 F8
Chiloquin U.S.A. 180 B4
Chilpancingo Mex. 185 F5
Chiltern Australia 147 E4
Chiltern Hills U.K. 47 L12
Chilton U.S.A. 172 E6
Chiluage Angola 127 D7
Chilubi Zambia 127 F7
Chilumba Malawi 129 B7
Chilung Taiwan 87 G3
English form Keelung; also spelt Jilong
Chilung Pass Jammu and Kashmir 96 C2
Chilwa, Lake Malawi 129 B9
Chimala Tanz. 129 B7
Chimaltenango Guat. 185 H6
Chimán Panama 186 D5
Chimanimani Zimbabwe 131 G3
formerly known as Mandidzuzure or Melsetter
Chi Ma Wan Hong Kong China 87 [inset]
Chimba Zambia 127 F7
Chimbas Arg. 204 C3
Chimbay Uzbek. 102 D4
also spelt Chimboy
Chimborazo mt. Ecuador 198 B5
Chimborazo prov. Ecuador 198 B5
Chimbote Peru 200 A2
Chimboy Uzbek. see Chimbay
Chimian Pak. 101 H4
Chimichaguá Col. 187 E5
Chimion Uzbek. 103 G4
Chimishliya Moldova see Cimişlia
Chimkent Kazakh. see Shymkent
Chimkentskaya Oblast' admin. div. Kazakh.
see Yuzhnyy Kazakhstan
Chimoio Moz. 131 G3
formerly known as Vila Pery
Chimorra hill Spain 54 E6
Chimpay Arg. 204 D5
Chimtargha, Qullai mt. Tajik. 101 G2
also known as Chimtorga, Gora
Chimtorga, Gora mt. Tajik. see Chimtargha, Qullai
Chin state Myanmar 78 A3

▶ China country Asia 80 D5
Most populous country in the world and in Asia. 2nd largest country in Asia and 4th largest in the world. Known in Chinese as Zhongguo; long form Zhongguo Renmin Gongheguo or Chung-hua Jen-min Kung-ho-kuo.
world [countries] ▶▶▶ 10–11
world [population] ▶▶▶ 22–23
asia [countries] ▶▶▶ 64–67

index C

Ciénagas del Catatumbo nat. park Venez. 198 D2
Cienfuegos Cuba 186 C2
Cies, Illas is Spain 54 C2
Cieszanów Poland 49 U5
Cieszyn Poland 49 P6
Cieza Spain 55 J6
Çiftlikköy Turkey 109 I1
Çiftlik Turkey see Kelkit
Çiftlikköy Turkey 58 J7
Cifuentes Spain 55 I4
Cigeulis Indon. 77 D4
Cigüela r. Spain 55 H5
Cihanbeyli Turkey 106 C3
also known as Inevi
Cihangazi Turkey 59 K9
Cihuatlán Mex. 184 D5
Cijara, Embalse de resr Spain 54 G5
Cikai China see Gongshan
Çikes, Maja e mt. Albania 59 A8
Cikobia i. Fiji 145 H3
also spelt Thikombia; formerly spelt Chicobea or Ticumbia or Tikumbia
Čikola r. Croatia 56 I5
Cilacap Indon. 77 E4
Cilangkahan Indon. 77 D4
Çıldır Turkey 107 E2
also known as Zurzuna
Çıldır Gölü l. Turkey 107 E2
Çıldıroba Turkey 109 I1
Ciledug Indon. 77 E4
Cilento e del Vallo di Diano, Parco Nazionale del nat. park Italy 57 H8
Cili China 87 D2
Cilician Gates pass Turkey see Gülek Boğazı
Cilieni Romania 58 F5
Cill Airne Rep. of Ireland see Killarney
Cill Chainnigh Rep. of Ireland see Kilkenny
Cill Mhantáin Rep. of Ireland see Wicklow
Cilo Dağı mt. Turkey 107 F3
Çiloy Adası i. Azer. 107 G2
Cima U.S.A. 183 I6
Cimahi Indon. 77 D4
Cimarron KS U.S.A. 178 B4
Cimarron NM U.S.A. 181 F5
Cimarron r. U.S.A. 179 C4
Cimarron Creek r. U.S.A. 181 F5
Cimino, Monte mt. Italy 56 E6
Cimişlia Moldova 58 J2
formerly spelt Chimishliya or Chymyshliya
Cimone, Monte mt. Italy 56 C4
Cimpeni Romania see Câmpeni
Cimpia Turzii Romania see Câmpia Turzii
Cimpina Romania see Câmpina
Cimpulung Romania see Câmpulung
Cimpulung Moldovenesc Romania see Câmpulung Moldovenesc
Cina, Tanjung c. Indon. 76 D4
Çınar Turkey 107 E3
also known as Hanakpınar
Çınarcık Turkey 58 K8
Cinaruco r. Venez. 198 E3
Cinaruco-Capanaparo, Parque Nacional nat. park Venez. 199 E3
Cinca r. Spain 55 L3
Cincar mt. Bos.-Herz. 56 J5
Cincinnati U.S.A. 176 A6
Cincinnatus U.S.A. 177 J3
Cinco-Balas, Cayos is Cuba 186 D2
Cinco de Outubro Angola see Xá-Muteba
Cincu Romania 58 F3
Çine Turkey 106 B3
Çine r. Turkey 59 I11
Ciney Belgium 51 L2
Cinfães Port. 54 C3
Cingoli Italy 56 F5
Cinque Island India 95 G4
Cintalapa Mex. 185 G5
Cinto, Monte mt. France 51 O10
Cintruénigo Spain 55 J2
Cinzas r. Brazil 206 C10
Ciolpani Romania 58 H4
Čiovo i. Croatia 56 I5
Cipatuja Indon. 77 E4
Ciping China see Jinggangshan
Cipó Brazil 202 E4
Cipo r. Brazil 207 I5
Cipolletti Arg. 204 D5
Cipotânea Brazil 207 J7
Circeo, Monte hill Italy 56 F7
Circeo, Parco Nazionale del nat. park Italy 56 E7
Circle AK U.S.A. 164 E3
Circle MT U.S.A. 180 F3
Circleville OH U.S.A. 176 C6
Circleville UT U.S.A. 183 L3
Cirebon Indon. 77 E4
formerly spelt Tjirebon
Cirencester U.K. 47 K12
historically known as Corinium
Cirene tourist site Libya see Cyrene
Ciriè Italy 51 N7
Cirišs l. Latvia 42 H5
Cirò Marina Italy 57 J9
Ciron r. France 50 F8
Cirque Mountain Canada 169 I1
Cirta Alg. see Constantine
Cisco U.S.A. 183 O3
Cisnădie Romania 58 F3
Cisterna di Latina Italy 56 E7
Cistierna Spain 54 F2
Citadelle Laferrière tourist site Haiti 187 E3
Citlaltépetl vol. Mex. see Orizaba, Pico de
Čitluk Bos.-Herz. 56 J5
Citronelle U.S.A. 175 B6
Citrusdal S. Africa 132 D9
Citrus Heights U.S.A. 182 C3
Cittadella Italy 56 D3
Città di Castello Italy 56 E5
Cittanova Italy 57 I10
City of Derry airport U.K. 47 E8
Ciucaş, Vârful mt. Romania 58 G3
Ciucea Romania 58 D2
Ciudad Acuña Mex. 185 E2
Ciudad Altamirano Mex. 185 E5
Ciudad Bolívar Venez. 199 F2
Ciudad Camargo Mex. 184 D3
Ciudad Constitución Mex. 184 C3
also known as Villa Constitución
Ciudad Cuauhtémoc Mex. 185 H6
Ciudad del Carmen Mex. 185 H5
Ciudad del Este Para. 201 G6
formerly known as Puerto Presidente Stroessner
Ciudad Delicias Mex. 184 D2
Ciudad del Maíz Mex. 185 F4
Ciudad de Valles Mex. 185 F4
Ciudad Guayana Venez. 199 F2
Ciudad Guzmán Mex. 184 E5
Ciudad Hidalgo Mex. 185 E5
Ciudad Ixtepec Mex. 185 G5
Ciudad Juárez Mex. 184 D2
Ciudad Lerdo Mex. 184 E3
Ciudad Madero Mex. 185 F4
Ciudad Mante Mex. 185 F4
Ciudad Mendoza Mex. 185 F5
Ciudad Mier Mex. 185 F3
Ciudad Obregón Mex. 184 C3
Ciudad Piar Venez. 199 F3
Ciudad Real Spain 54 H6
Ciudad Río Bravo Mex. 185 F3
Ciudad Rodrigo Spain 54 E4
Ciudad Trujillo Dom. Rep. see Santo Domingo
Ciudad Victoria Mex. 185 F4
Ciudanoviţa Romania 58 C3
Ciumani Romania 58 G2
Ciutadella de Menorca Spain 55 O4
Civa Burnu pt Turkey 107 D2
Civetta, Monte mt. Italy 56 E2
Cividale del Friuli Italy 56 F2
Civita Castellana Italy 56 E6
historically known as Falerii
Civitanova Marche Italy 56 F5
Civitavecchia Italy 56 D6
Civitella Roveto Italy 56 F7
Civray France 50 G6
Çivril Turkey 106 B3
Cixi China 87 G2
also known as Hushan
Cixian China 85 G4
also known as Cizhou
Ciyao China 85 H5
Cizhou China see Cixian
Cizre Turkey 107 E3
Clackamas r. U.S.A. 180 B3
Clacton-on-Sea U.K. 47 N12
Clain r. France 50 G6
Claire, Lake Canada 167 H3
Clair Engle Lake resr U.S.A. 180 B4
Clairmont Canada 166 G4
Claise r. France 50 G6
Clam Lake U.S.A. 172 C4
Clan Alpine Mountains U.S.A. 182 G2
Clanton U.S.A. 175 C5
Clanville S. Africa 133 L8
Clanwilliam S. Africa 132 C9
Clanwilliam Dam S. Africa 132 C9
Clara r. Australia 149 D3
Clara Rep. of Ireland 47 E10
Clara Island Myanmar 79 B6
Claraville Australia 149 D3
Clare N.S.W. Australia 147 D3
Clare S.A. Australia 146 C3
Clare r. Rep. of Ireland 47 C10
Clare U.S.A. 173 I7
Clare Island Rep. of Ireland 47 B10
Claremont U.S.A. 177 M2
Claremont Isles Australia 149 D2
Claremore U.S.A. 179 D4
Claremorris Rep. of Ireland 47 D10
Clarence r. Australia 147 G2
Clarence N.Z. 153 H10
Clarence r. N.Z. 153 H10
Clarence U.S.A. 172 B9
Clarence, Isla i. Chile 205 C9
Clarence Island Antarctica 222 U2
Clarence Strait Australia 148 A1
Clarence Strait U.S.A. 166 C3
Clarence Town Bahamas 187 E2
Clarendon N.Z. 153 E14
Clarendon AR U.S.A. 174 B5
Clarendon PA U.S.A. 176 F4
Clarendon TX U.S.A. 179 B5
Clarenville Canada 169 K3
Claresholm Canada 167 H5
Clarinda U.S.A. 178 D3
Clarington U.S.A. 176 E6
Clarion IA U.S.A. 174 A3
Clarion PA U.S.A. 176 F4
Clarion r. U.S.A. 176 F4
Clarión, Isla i. Mex. 184 B5
Claris N.Z. 152 J4
Clark U.S.A. 178 C2
Clark, Mount Canada 166 F1
Clarkdale U.S.A. 183 L7
Clarke r. Australia 149 E3
Clarkebury S. Africa 133 M8
Clarke Range mts Australia 149 E4
Clarke River Australia 149 E3
Clarkes Creek r. Australia 149 D3
Clarke's Head Canada 169 K3
Clark Fork r. ID U.S.A. 180 C2
Clark Fork r. MT U.S.A. 180 C2
Clark Hill Reservoir U.S.A. 175 D5
Clark Mountain U.S.A. 183 I6
Clark Mountains Antarctica 222 O1
Clark Point Canada 168 D4
Clarksburg U.S.A. 176 E6
Clarksdale U.S.A. 174 B5
Clark's Fork Yellowstone r. U.S.A. 180 E3
Clarks Junction N.Z. 153 E13
Clarkson S. Africa 133 I11
Clarkston U.S.A. 180 C3
Clarksville AR U.S.A. 179 D5
Clarksville TN U.S.A. 174 C4
Clarksville TX U.S.A. 179 D5
Claro r. Goiás Brazil 206 C6
Claro r. Mato Grosso Brazil 206 B2
Clatskanie U.S.A. 180 B3
Claude U.S.A. 179 B5
Cláudio Brazil 203 C7
Claveria Phil. 74 B2
Clavering Ø i. Greenland 165 Q2
Claxton U.S.A. 175 D5
Clay U.S.A. 176 D7
Clayburg U.S.A. 177 L1
Clay Center KS U.S.A. 178 C4
Clay Center NE U.S.A. 178 C3
Clay City U.S.A. 176 B8
Clayhole Wash watercourse U.S.A. 183 K4
Claymont U.S.A. 177 J6
Claypool U.S.A. 183 N8
Clay Springs U.S.A. 183 N7
Clayton DE U.S.A. 177 J6
Clayton GA U.S.A. 174 D5
Clayton NM U.S.A. 178 B4
Clayton NY U.S.A. 177 I1
Claytor Lake U.S.A. 176 E8
Clearco U.S.A. 176 E7
Clear Creek Canada 173 M8
Clear Creek U.S.A. 183 M2
Clear Creek r. AZ U.S.A. 183 N7
Clear Creek r. WY U.S.A. 180 F3
Clearfield PA U.S.A. 176 G4
Clearfield UT U.S.A. 180 D4
Clear Fork Brazos r. U.S.A. 179 C5
Clear Hills Canada 166 G3
Clear Island Rep. of Ireland 47 C12
Clear Lake IA U.S.A. 174 A3
Clear Lake SD U.S.A. 178 C2
Clear Lake WI U.S.A. 172 A5
Clear Lake l. CA U.S.A. 182 B2
Clear Lake l. UT U.S.A. 183 L2
Clearlake Oaks U.S.A. 182 B2
Clear Lake Reservoir U.S.A. 180 B4
Clearmont U.S.A. 180 F3
Clear Spring U.S.A. 176 H6
Clearwater Canada 166 G5
Clearwater r. Alta Canada 167 H4
Clearwater r. Alta/Sask. Canada 167 I3
Clearwater U.S.A. 175 D7
Clearwater r. ID U.S.A. 180 C3
Clearwater r. MN U.S.A. 178 C2
Clear Water Bay Hong Kong China 87 [inset]
also known as Tsing Shui Wan
Clearwater Lake l. Canada 167 K4
Clearwater Lake U.S.A. 172 D5
Clearwater Lake Provincial Park Canada 167 K4
Clearwater Mountains U.S.A. 180 D3
Clearwater River Provincial Park Canada 167 I3
Cleburne U.S.A. 179 C5
Cle Elum U.S.A. 180 B3
Cléguérec France 50 C4
Clejani Romania 58 G4
Clément Fr. Guiana 199 H4
Clementi Sing. 76 [inset]
Clementina Brazil 206 C8
Clemmons U.S.A. 176 E9
Clemson U.S.A. 174 D5
Clendenin U.S.A. 176 D7
Clendening Lake U.S.A. 176 D5
Cleopatra Needle mt. Phil. 74 A4
Clères France 50 H3
Clerf Lux. see Clervaux
Cléricy Canada 173 O2
Clerke Reef Australia 150 B3
Clermont Australia 149 E4
Clermont France 51 I3
Clermont U.S.A. 175 D6
Clermont-en-Argonne France 51 L3
Clermont-Ferrand France 51 J7
Clermont-l'Hérault France 51 J9
Clervaux Lux. 51 M2
also known as Clerf
Cles Italy 56 D2
Cleve Australia 146 C3
Cleveland r. Canada 167 O1
Cleveland GA U.S.A. 174 D5
Cleveland MS U.S.A. 175 B5
Cleveland OH U.S.A. 176 D4
Cleveland TN U.S.A. 174 C5
Cleveland TX U.S.A. 179 D6
Cleveland UT U.S.A. 183 N2
Cleveland VA U.S.A. 176 C9
Cleveland WI U.S.A. 172 F7
Cleveland, Cape Australia 149 E3
Cleveland, Mount U.S.A. 180 D2
Cleveland Bay Australia 149 E3
Cleveland Hills U.K. 47 K9
Clevelândia do Norte Brazil 199 I4
Cleveland Peninsula U.S.A. 166 C4
Cleves Germany see Kleve
Clew Bay Rep. of Ireland 47 C10
Clewiston U.S.A. 175 D7
Clifden Rep. of Ireland 47 B10
Cliffdale r. Australia 148 C3
Clifford S. Africa 133 L8
Clifftop U.S.A. 176 E7
Clifton Australia 147 F1
Clifton AZ U.S.A. 183 O8
Clifton IL U.S.A. 172 F10
Clifton Beach Australia 149 E3
Clifton Forge U.S.A. 176 F8
Clifton Hills Australia 146 C1
Clifton Park U.S.A. 177 L3
Climax Canada 167 I5
Climax U.S.A. 172 H8
Clinch r. U.S.A. 176 B9
Clinchco U.S.A. 176 C8
Clinch Mountain mts U.S.A. 176 C9
Clinchport U.S.A. 176 C9
Cline River Canada 167 G4
Clinton Canada 168 D5
Clinton N.Z. 153 D14
Clinton AR U.S.A. 179 D5
Clinton IA U.S.A. 174 B3
Clinton KY U.S.A. 174 B4
Clinton LA U.S.A. 175 B6
Clinton ME U.S.A. 177 P1
Clinton MI U.S.A. 173 J8
Clinton MO U.S.A. 178 D4
Clinton MS U.S.A. 175 B5
Clinton NC U.S.A. 174 E5
Clinton NY U.S.A. 177 J2
Clinton OK U.S.A. 179 C5
Clinton TN U.S.A. 176 A9
Clinton-Colden Lake Canada 167 J1
Clinton Creek Canada 166 A1
Clintonville WI U.S.A. 172 E6
Clintonville WV U.S.A. 176 E8
Clintwood U.S.A. 176 C8
Clio U.S.A. 173 J7

▶Clipperton, Île terr. N. Pacific Ocean 221 K5
French Overseas Territory. Most easterly point of Oceania. English form Clipperton Island.
oceania [countries] ▶▶ 138–139

Clipperton Island terr. N. Pacific Ocean see Clipperton, Île
Clishham hill U.K. 46 F6
Clisson France 50 E5
Clitheroe U.K. 47 J10
Clive N.Z. 152 K7
Clive Lake Canada 167 G2
Cliza Bol. 200 D4
Cloates, Point Australia 150 A4
Clocolan S. Africa 133 L5
Clonagh Australia 149 D4
Clonakilty Rep. of Ireland 47 D12
Cloncurry Australia 149 D4
Cloncurry r. Australia 149 D3
Clones Rep. of Ireland 47 E9
Clonmel Rep. of Ireland 47 E11
also spelt Cluain Meala
Cloppenburg Germany 48 F3
Cloquet U.S.A. 174 A2
Cloquet r. U.S.A. 174 A2
Clorinda Arg. 204 F2
Cloud Bay Canada 172 D2
Cloud Peak WY U.S.A. 180 F3
Cloudy Bay N.Z. 152 I9
Clova Canada 168 F3
Clover U.S.A. 183 L1
Cloverdale U.S.A. 182 A3
Clovis CA U.S.A. 182 E5
Clovis NM U.S.A. 179 B5
Cloyes-sur-le-Loir France 50 H5
Cloyne Canada 173 P6
Cluain Meala Rep. of Ireland see Clonmel
Cluanie, Loch l. U.K. 46 G6
Cluff Lake Mine Canada 167 I3
Cluj-Napoca Romania 58 E2
also known as Kolozsvár
Cluny Australia 148 C5
Cluny France 51 K6
Cluses France 51 M6
Clusone Italy 56 B3
Cluster Springs U.S.A. 176 G9
Clutha r. N.Z. 153 D14
Clut Lake Canada 167 G1
Clutterbuck Hills hill Australia 151 D5
Clwydian Range hills U.K. 47 I10
Clyde Canada 167 H4
Clyde r. U.K. 46 H8
Clyde NY U.S.A. 177 I2
Clyde OH U.S.A. 176 C4
Clyde, Firth of est. U.K. 46 H8
Clydebank U.K. 46 H8
Clyde River Canada 165 M2
Clydevale N.Z. 153 D14
Clyman U.S.A. 172 E7
Clymer U.S.A. 176 F5
Cnossus tourist site Greece see Knossos
Côa r. Port. 54 D3
Coachella Canal U.S.A. 183 I9
Coachella U.S.A. 183 H8
Coahuayutla de Guerrero Mex. 185 E5
Coahuila state Mex. 185 E3
Coal r. Canada 166 E3
Coal City U.S.A. 172 E9
Coaldale Canada 167 H5
Coalgate U.S.A. 179 C5
Coal Grove U.S.A. 176 C7
Coal Harbour Canada 166 E5
Coalinga U.S.A. 182 D5
Coalport U.S.A. 176 G5
Coal River Canada 166 E3
Coal Valley U.S.A. 183 I4
Coalville U.S.A. 183 M1
Coamo Puerto Rico 187 G3
Coaraci Brazil 207 N1
Coari Brazil 199 F6
Coari r. Brazil 199 F6
Coari, Lago l. Brazil 199 F6
Coarsegold U.S.A. 182 E4
Coast prov. Kenya 128 D5
Coast admin. reg. Tanz. see Pwani
Coastal Plain U.S.A. 175 A6
Coast Mountains Canada 166 E4
Coast Range hills Australia 149 F5
Coast Ranges mts U.S.A. 182 A1
Coatepec Mex. 185 F5
Coatepeque Guat. 185 H6
Coatesville U.S.A. 177 J6
Coaticook Canada 169 G4
Coats Island Canada 165 K3
Coats Land reg. Antarctica 222 V1
Coatzacoalcos Mex. 185 G5
formerly known as Puerto México
Coatzintla Mex. 185 F4
Cobadin Romania 58 J4
Cobalt Canada 173 N3
Cobán Guat. 185 H6
Cobar Australia 147 E2
Cobargo Australia 147 F4
Cobb, Lake salt flat Australia 150 D5
Cobden Canada 173 Q5
Cóbh Rep. of Ireland 47 D12
also spelt An Cóbh; formerly known as Queenstown
Cobham r. Canada 167 M4
Cobija Bol. 200 C2
Cobija Chile 200 C5
Coblenz Germany see Koblenz
Cobleskill U.S.A. 177 K3
Cobos Mex. 185 F4
Cobourg Canada 168 E5
Cobourg Peninsula Australia 148 B1
Cobquecura Chile 204 B5
Cobra Australia 150 B5
Cobram Australia 147 E3
Cobres Arg. 200 D5
Cóbuè Moz. 129 B8
Coburg Germany 48 H5
Coburg Island Canada 165 L2
Coca Spain 54 G3
Cocachacra Peru 200 C4
Cocal Brazil 202 D2
Cocalinho Brazil 202 B5
Cocanada India see Kakinada
Cocapata Bol. 200 D4
Cocentaina Spain 55 K6
Cochabamba Bol. 200 D4
Cochabamba dept Bol. 200 D4
Cochamó Chile 205 B6
Coche, Isla i. Venez. 199 F2
Cochem Germany 48 E5
Co Chiên, Sông r. mouth Vietnam 79 D6
Cochin India 94 C4
also known as Kochi
Cochin reg. Vietnam 79 D6
Cochinos, Bahía de b. Cuba see Pigs, Bay of
Cochise U.S.A. 183 O9
Cochise Head mt. U.S.A. 183 O9
Cochran U.S.A. 175 D5
Cochrane Alta Canada 167 H5
Cochrane Ont. Canada 168 D3
Cochrane r. Canada 167 K3
Cochrane Chile 205 B7
Cochrane, Lago l. Arg./Chile 205 B7
Cochranton U.S.A. 176 E4
Cochranville U.S.A. 177 J6
Cockaleechie Australia 146 B3
Cockburn Australia 146 D3
Cockburn Harbour Turks and Caicos Is 187 F2
Cockburn Island Canada 168 D4
Cockburn Town Bahamas 187 E1
Cockburn Town Turks and Caicos Is see Grand Turk
Cockermouth U.K. 47 I9
Cocklebiddy Australia 151 D7
Cockscomb mt. S. Africa 133 I10
Coclé del Norte Panama 186 C5
Coco r. Brazil 202 B4
Coco r. Hond./Nicaragua 186 C4
also known as Segovia
Coco, Cayo i. Cuba 186 D2
Coco, Isla de i. N. Pacific Ocean 221 M5
Cocobeach Gabon 126 A4
Coco Channel India 95 G3
Coconino Plateau U.S.A. 183 K6
Cocopara National Park Australia 147 E3
Cocorná Col. 198 C3
Cocos Brazil 202 C5

▶Cocos Islands terr. Indian Ocean 218 N6
Australian External Territory. Also known as Keeling Islands.
asia [countries] ▶▶ 64–67

Cocula Mex. 184 E4
Cod, Cape U.S.A. 177 O4
Codăeşti Romania 58 I2
Codajás Brazil 199 F5
Codera, Cabo c. Venez. 199 E2
Coderre Canada 167 J5
Codigoro Italy 56 E4
Cod Island Canada 169 I1
Codlea Romania 58 G3
Codó Brazil 202 D3
Codogno Italy 56 B3
Codrington Antigua and Barbuda 187 H3
Codrington, Mount Antarctica 223 D2
Codroipo Italy 56 E3
Codru Moldova 58 J2
Cody U.S.A. 180 E3
Coeburn U.S.A. 176 C9
Coega S. Africa 133 J10
Coelho Neto Brazil 202 D3
Coen Australia 149 D2
Coen r. Australia 149 D2
Coerney S. Africa 133 J10
Coeroeni r. Suriname 199 G4
Coesfeld Germany 48 E4
Coetzeesberg mts S. Africa 133 I9
Coetzersdam S. Africa 133 I3
Coeur d'Alene U.S.A. 180 C3
Coeur d'Alene r. U.S.A. 180 C3
Coeur d'Alene Indian Reservation res. U.S.A. 180 C3
Coeur d'Alene Lake U.S.A. 180 C3
Coffee Bay S. Africa 133 N8
Coffee Creek Canada 166 B2
Coffeyville U.S.A. 178 D4
Coffin Bay Australia 146 B3
Coffin Bay b. Australia 146 B3
Coffin Bay National Park Australia 146 B3
Coffin Bay Peninsula Australia 146 B3
Coffs Harbour Australia 147 G2
Cofimvaba S. Africa 133 L9
formerly known as St Mark's
Cofre de Perote, Parque Nacional nat. park Mex. 185 F5
Cogâlniceanu airport Romania see Kogălniceanu
Cogealac Romania 58 J4
Coggon U.S.A. 172 B8
Coghinas r. Sardegna Italy 57 A8
Coghlan S. Africa 133 M8
Coghlan, Mount hill Australia 150 D3
Cognac France 50 F7
Cogo Equat. Guinea 125 H6
Cogolin France 51 M9
Cogune Moz. 131 G5
Čohkkiras Sweden see Jukkasjärvi
Cohocton r. U.S.A. 177 H3
Cohoes U.S.A. 177 L3
Cohuna Australia 147 E3
Coiba, Isla i. Panama 186 C6
Coihaique Chile 205 B7
Coihaique Alto Chile 205 C7
Coimbatore India 94 C4
Coimbra Port. 54 C4
Coimbra admin. dist. Port. 54 C4
Coin Spain 54 G8
Coipasa, Salar de salt flat Bol. 200 C4
Coire Switz. see Chur
Cojasca Romania 58 G4
Cojata Peru 200 C3
Cojedes state Venez. 198 D2
Cojoro Venez. 187 F5
Cojudo Blanco, Cerro mt. Arg. 205 C7
Colac Australia 147 D4
Colac N.Z. 153 B14
Colair Lake India see Kolleru Lake
Colakli Turkey 108 C1
Colares Brazil 202 B2
Colatina Brazil 203 D6
Colborne Canada 173 P7
Colby KS U.S.A. 178 B4
Colby WI U.S.A. 172 C6
Colca r. Peru 200 B3
Colceag Romania 58 H4
Colchester S. Africa 133 J10
Colchester U.K. 47 M12
historically known as Camulodunum
Colchester U.S.A. 177 M4
Cold Bay U.S.A. 164 C4
also known as Fort Randall
Cold Lake Canada 167 I4
Cold Lake l. Canada 167 I4
Coldspring U.S.A. 179 D6
Cold Springs U.S.A. 182 G2
Coldstream Canada 166 G5
Coldstream N.Z. 153 F12
Coldstream U.K. 46 J8
Coldwater Canada 173 N6
Coldwater KS U.S.A. 178 C4
Coldwater MI U.S.A. 173 I9
Coldwater Creek r. U.S.A. 179 B4
Coldwell Canada 172 G2
Colebrook U.S.A. 177 N1
Coleford S. Africa 133 N6
Coleman r. Australia 149 D2
Coleman MI U.S.A. 173 I7
Coleman TX U.S.A. 179 C6
Coleman WI U.S.A. 172 E5
Çölemerik Turkey see Hakkâri
Colenso S. Africa 133 N5
Colentina r. Romania 58 G4
Cole Peninsula Antarctica 222 T2
Coleraine Australia 146 D4
Coleraine U.K. 47 F8
Coleroon r. India 94 C4
Coles, Punta de pt Peru 200 C4
Coles Bay Australia 147 F5
Colesberg S. Africa 133 J7
Colesburg U.S.A. 172 B8
Coleville U.S.A. 182 E3
Colfax CA U.S.A. 182 D2
Colfax LA U.S.A. 179 D6
Colfax WA U.S.A. 180 C3
Colfax WI U.S.A. 172 B6
Colhué Huapí, Lago l. Arg. 205 C7
Colibaşi Romania 58 F4
Colico Italy 56 B2
Coligny S. Africa 133 K3
Colima Mex. 184 E5
Colima state Mex. 184 E5
Colima, Nevado de vol. Mex. 184 E4
Colina Brazil 206 E7
Colinas Brazil 202 C3
Coliseu r. Brazil 202 A5
Coll i. U.K. 46 F7
Collado Bajo mt. Spain 55 J4
Collado Villalba Spain 54 H4
Collahuasi Chile 200 C5
Collalto mt. Austria/Italy 48 J9
also known as Hochgall
Collarenebri Australia 147 F2
Collecchio Italy 56 C4
Colle di Val d'Elsa Italy 56 D5
College Corner U.S.A. 176 A6
College Hill U.S.A. 176 A6
College Park U.S.A. 175 C5
College Station U.S.A. 179 C6
Collerina Australia 147 E2
Collesalvetti Italy 56 C5
Collie Australia 151 B7
Collier Bay Australia 150 D3
Collier Range hills Australia 151 B5
Collier Range National Park Australia 151 B5
Collierville U.S.A. 174 B5
Collingwood Canada 168 D4
Collingwood N.Z. 152 G8
Collins U.S.A. 175 B6
Collins Glacier Antarctica 223 E2
Collins Lake U.S.A. 182 C2
Collinson Peninsula Canada 165 I2
Collinsville Australia 149 E4
Collinsville OK U.S.A. 179 D4
Collinsville VA U.S.A. 176 F9
Collipulli Chile 204 B5
Collmberg hill Germany 49 K4
Collooney Rep. of Ireland 47 D9
Colmar France 51 N4
Colmena Arg. 204 E3
Colmenar de Oreja Spain 55 H4
Colmenar Viejo Spain 54 H4
Colne U.K. 47 J10
Colo r. Australia 147 F3
Cologne Germany 48 D5
also spelt Köln; historically known as Colonia Agrippina
Coloma MI U.S.A. 172 G8
Coloma WI U.S.A. 172 D6
Colomb-Béchar Alg. see Béchar
Colômbia Brazil 206 E7
Colombia Col. 198 C4
Colombia Mex. 185 F3

▶Colombia country S. America 198 C4
2nd most populous and 4th largest country in South America.
southamerica [countries] ▶▶ 192–193

▶Colombo Sri Lanka 94 C5
Former capital of Sri Lanka.

Colombourg Canada 173 N2
Colomiers France 50 H9
Colón Buenos Aires Arg. 204 E4
Colón Entre Ríos Arg. 204 F4
Colón Cuba 186 C2
Colón Panama 186 D5
Colon U.S.A. 172 H9
Colón, Archipiélago de is Pacific Ocean see Galapagos Islands
Colón, Isla de i. Panama 186 C5
Colona Australia 146 B2
Colonelganj India 97 D4
Colonel Hill Bahamas 187 E2
Colonet, Cabo c. Mex. 184 A2
Colonia Arg. 204 E2
Colônia r. Brazil 207 N1
Colonia Micronesia 73 I5
Colonia Agrippina Germany see Cologne
Colonia del Sacramento Uruguay 204 F4
Colonia Dora Arg. 204 E3
Colonia Emilio Mitre Arg. 204 D5
Colonia Julia Fenestris Italy see Fano
Colonia Las Heras Arg. 205 C7
Colonial Heights U.S.A. 176 H8
Colonia Suiza Uruguay 204 F4
Colonna, Capo c. Italy 57 J9
Colonsay i. U.K. 46 F7
Colorado r. La Rioja Arg. 204 D3
Colorado r. San Juan Arg. 204 C3
Colorado r. Arg. 204 E5
Colorado Brazil 206 B9
Colorado r. Mex./U.S.A. 184 B2
Colorado r. U.S.A. 179 C6
Colorado state U.S.A. 183 P2
Colorado City AZ U.S.A. 183 K5
Colorado City TX U.S.A. 179 B5
Colorado Desert U.S.A. 183 H8
Colorado National Monument nat. park U.S.A. 183 P2
Colorado Plateau U.S.A. 183 O4
Colorado River Aqueduct canal U.S.A. 183 J7
Colorado River Indian Reservation res. U.S.A. 183 J8
Colorados, Cerro mt. Arg. 204 C2
Colorado Springs U.S.A. 180 F5
Colorno Italy 56 C4
Colossae Turkey see Honaz
Colotlán Mex. 185 E4
Colquechaca Bol. 200 D4
Colquiri Bol. 200 D4
Colquitt U.S.A. 175 C6
Colson U.S.A. 176 C8
Colstrip U.S.A. 180 F3
Colton CA U.S.A. 183 G7
Colton NY U.S.A. 177 K1
Colton UT U.S.A. 183 M2
Columbia KY U.S.A. 174 C4
Columbia LA U.S.A. 179 D5
Columbia MD U.S.A. 177 I6
Columbia MO U.S.A. 178 D4
Columbia MS U.S.A. 175 B6
Columbia NC U.S.A. 174 E5
Columbia NJ U.S.A. 177 J5
Columbia PA U.S.A. 177 I5

▶Columbia SC U.S.A. 175 D5
State capital of South Carolina.

Columbia TN U.S.A. 174 C5
Columbia r. U.S.A. 180 B3
Columbia, Cape Canada 165 L1
Columbia, Mount Canada 167 G4
Columbia, Sierra mts Mex. 184 B2
Columbia City U.S.A. 174 C3
Columbia Falls ME U.S.A. 177 R1
Columbia Falls MT U.S.A. 180 D2
Columbia Mountains Canada 166 F4
Columbia Plateau U.S.A. 180 C3
Columbine, Cape S. Africa 132 B9
Columbretes, Islas is Spain 55 L5
Columbus GA U.S.A. 175 C5
Columbus IN U.S.A. 174 C4
Columbus KS U.S.A. 178 D4
Columbus MS U.S.A. 175 B5
Columbus MT U.S.A. 180 E3
Columbus NC U.S.A. 174 D5
Columbus NE U.S.A. 178 C3

▶Columbus OH U.S.A. 176 B6
State capital of Ohio.

Columbus PA U.S.A. 176 F4
Columbus TX U.S.A. 179 C6
Columbus WI U.S.A. 172 D7
Columbus Grove U.S.A. 176 A5
Columbus Junction U.S.A. 172 B9
Columbus Salt Marsh U.S.A. 182 F3
Coluna Brazil 207 K5
Colunga Spain 54 F1
Colusa U.S.A. 182 B2
Colville N.Z. 152 J4
Colville U.S.A. 180 C2
Colville r. U.S.A. 164 D2
Colville, Cape N.Z. 152 J4
Colville Channel N.Z. 152 J4
Colville Indian Reservation res. U.S.A. 180 C2
Colville Lake Canada 166 E1
Colwyn Bay U.K. 47 I10
also known as Bae Colwyn
Comacchio Italy 56 E4
Comacchio, Valli di lag. Italy 56 E4
Comai China 89 E6
also known as Damxoi
Comalcalco Mex. 185 G5
Comallo Arg. 204 C6
Comana Romania 58 H4
Comanche U.S.A. 179 C6
Comandante Ferraz research station Antarctica 222 U2
Comandante Fontana Arg. 204 F2
Comandante Luis Piedra Buena Arg. 205 C8
Comandante Salas Arg. 204 C4
Comăneşti Romania 58 H2
Comarnic Romania 58 G3
Comayagua Hond. 186 B4
Combahee r. U.S.A. 175 D5
Combarbalá Chile 204 C3
Comber U.K. 47 G9
Combermere Canada 173 P5
Combermere Bay Myanmar 78 A4
Combol i. Indon. 76 C2
Combourg France 50 E4
Comendador Gomes Brazil 206 D6
Comercinho Brazil 207 L3
Comet Australia 149 F4
Comet r. Australia 149 F4
Comfort TX U.S.A. 179 C6
Comfort WV U.S.A. 176 D7
Comilla Bangl. 97 F5
Comino i. Malta see Kemmuna
Comino, Capo c. Sardegna Italy 57 B8
Comiso Sicilia Italy 57 G12
Comitán de Domínguez Mex. 185 G5
Commanda Canada 173 N5
Commentry France 51 I6
Commissioner's Salt Pan S. Africa 132 D7
Committee Bay Canada 165 K3
Commondale S. Africa 133 O4
Commonwealth Bay Antarctica 223 J2
Commonwealth Territory admin. div. Australia see Jervis Bay Territory
Como Italy 56 B3
Como, Lago di l. Italy see Como, Lake
Como, Lake Italy 56 B3
also known as Como, Lago di
Como Chamling l. China 89 E6
Comodoro Rivadavia Arg. 205 D7
Comoé r. Côte d'Ivoire see Komoé
Comonfort Mex. 185 E4
Comores country Africa see Comoros
Comorin, Cape India 94 C4
also known as Kanniya Kumari

▶Comoros country Africa 129 D7
known as Al Qumur in Arabic; also spelt Comores in French
africa [countries] ▶▶ 114–117

Comox Canada 166 E5
Compiègne France 51 I3
Compostela Mex. 184 D4
Compostela Phil. 74 C5
Comprida, Ilha i. Brazil 203 C8
Compton CA U.S.A. 182 F8
Compton IL U.S.A. 172 D9

Comrat Moldova 58 J2
formerly spelt Komrat
Con, Sông r. Vietnam 78 D4
Cona China 89 E7
also spelt Tsona

▶Conakry Guinea 124 B4
Capital of Guinea.

Conambo Ecuador 198 B5
Conambo r. Ecuador 198 B5
Cona Niyeo Arg. 205 D6
Conay Chile 204 C3
Concarán Arg. 204 D4
Concarneau France 50 C5
Conceição Amazonas Brazil 199 F5
Conceição Mato Grosso Brazil 201 F1
Conceição Paraíba Brazil 202 E3
Conceição Rondônia Brazil 201 E2
Conceição Roraima Brazil 199 F4
Conceição r. Brazil 207 H3
Conceição da Barra Brazil 203 E6
Conceição das Alagoas Brazil 206 E6
Conceição de Macabu Brazil 207 L9
Conceição do Araguaia Brazil 202 B4
Conceição do Coité Brazil 202 E4
Conceição do Mato Dentro Brazil 203 D6
Conceição do Maú Brazil 199 G4
Concepción Corrientes Arg. 204 F3
Concepción Tucumán Arg. 204 D2
Concepción Beni Bol. 200 D2
Concepción Santa Cruz Bol. 201 E4
Concepción Chile 204 B5
Concepción Mex. 185 E3
Concepción r. Mex. 184 B2
Concepción Panama 186 C5
Concepción Para. 201 F5
Concepción, Canal sea chan. Chile 205 B8
Concepción, Punta pt Mex. 184 C3
Concepción del Uruguay Arg. 204 F4
Conception, Point U.S.A. 182 D7
Conception Bay Namibia 130 B4
Concesio Italy 56 C3
Concession Zimbabwe 131 F3
Concha Mex. 184 D4
Conchas Brazil 206 E9
Conchas Lake U.S.A. 181 F6
Conches-en-Ouche France 50 G4
Conchi Chile 200 C5
Concho Mex. 184 D3
Concho U.S.A. 183 O7
Concho r. U.S.A. 179 C6
Conchos r. Chihuahua Mex. 184 D2
Conchos r. Nuevo León/Tamaulipas Mex. 185 F3
Concord CA U.S.A. 182 B4
Concord MI U.S.A. 173 I8
Concord NC U.S.A. 174 D5

▶Concord NH U.S.A. 177 N2
State capital of New Hampshire.

Concord PA U.S.A. 176 H5
Concord VA U.S.A. 176 G8
Concord VT U.S.A. 177 N1
Concordia Arg. 204 F3
Concórdia Amazonas Brazil 199 E6
Concórdia Santa Catarina Brazil 203 A8
Concordia Antioquia Col. 198 C3
Concordia Meta Col. 198 C4
Concordia Mex. 184 D4
Concordia Peru 198 C6
Concordia S. Africa 132 B6
Concordia U.S.A. 178 C4
Concord Peak Afgh. 101 H2
Con Cuông Vietnam 78 D4
Conda Angola 127 B7
Condamine Australia 149 F5
Condamine r. Australia 147 F1
Conde Brazil 202 E4
Condega Nicaragua 186 B4
Condeixa Brazil 202 B2
Condé-sur-Noireau France 50 F4
Condeúba Brazil 202 D5
Condobolin Australia 147 E3
Condoe Moz. 131 G3
Condom France 50 G9
Condon U.S.A. 180 B3
Condor, Cordillera del mts Ecuador/Peru 198 B6
Conecuh r. U.S.A. 175 C6
Conejos Mex. 184 E3
Conejos U.S.A. 181 F5
Conejos r. U.S.A. 181 F5
Conemaugh r. U.S.A. 176 F5
Conero, Monte hill Italy 56 F5
Conestogo Lake Canada 173 M7
Conesus Lake U.S.A. 176 H3
Conesville IA U.S.A. 172 B9
Conesville OH U.S.A. 176 D5
Coney Island Sing. see Serangoon, Pulau
Coney Island U.S.A. 177 L5
Conflict Group is P.N.G. 149 F1
Confluence U.S.A. 176 F6
Confoederatio Helvetica country Europe see Switzerland
Confolens France 50 G6
Confusion Range mts U.S.A. 183 K3
Confuso r. Para. 201 F6
Congdü China see Nyalam
Conghua China 87 E4
Congjiang China 87 D3
also known as Bingmei
Congleton U.K. 47 J10
▶Congo country Africa 126 B5
formerly known as Congo (Brazzaville) or French Congo or Middle Congo or Moyen Congo; long form Congo, Republic of
africa [countries] ▶▶ 114–117

▶Congo r. Congo/Dem. Rep. Congo 127 B6
2nd longest river in Africa and 8th in the world. Formerly known as Zaïre.
africa [landscapes] ▶▶ 112–113

Congo (Brazzaville) country Africa see Congo
Congo (Kinshasa) country Africa see Congo, Democratic Republic of

▶Congo, Democratic Republic of country Africa 126 D5
3rd largest and 4th most populous country in Africa. Formerly known as Zaire or Belgian Congo or Congo (Kinshasa) or Congo Free State.
africa [countries] ▶▶ 114–117

Congo, Republic of country Africa see Congo
Congo Basin Dem. Rep. Congo 126 D5
Congo Free State country Africa see Congo, Democratic Republic of
Congonhas Brazil 207 J7
Congonhinhas Brazil 206 C10
Congress U.S.A. 183 L7
Conguillo, Parque Nacional nat. park Chile 204 C5
Conhuas Mex. 185 H5
Cónico, Cerro mt. Arg. 205 C6
Conil de la Frontera Spain 54 E8
Coniston Canada 173 M4
Coniston U.K. 47 I9
Conjuboy Australia 149 E3
Conkal Mex. 185 H4
Conklin Canada 167 I4
Conkouati, Réserve de Faune nature res. Congo 126 A5
Conlara r. Arg. 204 D4
Conn r. Canada 168 E2
Conn, Lough l. Rep. of Ireland 47 C9
Connacht reg. Rep. of Ireland see Connaught
Connaught Canada 173 M2
Connaught reg. Rep. of Ireland 47 C10
also spelt Connacht
Conneaut U.S.A. 176 E4
Conneaut Lake U.S.A. 176 E4
Conneautville U.S.A. 176 E4
Connecticut r. U.S.A. 177 M4
Connecticut state U.S.A. 177 M4
Connel U.K. 46 G7
Connells Lagoon Conservation Reserve nature res. Australia 148 C3
Connemara Australia 149 D5
Connemara reg. Rep. of Ireland 47 C10
Connemara National Park Rep. of Ireland 47 C10
Conner, Mount hill Australia 148 A5
Connersville U.S.A. 174 C4
Connolly, Mount Canada 166 C2
Connors Range hills Australia 149 F4
Cononaco Ecuador 198 C5
Cononaco r. Ecuador 198 C5
Conover U.S.A. 172 D4
Conquista Bol. 200 D2
Conquista Brazil 206 F6
Conrad U.S.A. 180 E2
Conroe U.S.A. 179 D6
Conroe, Lake U.S.A. 179 D6
Consecon Canada 173 P6
Consejo Belize 186 A3
Conselheiro Lafaiete Brazil 203 D7
Conselheiro Pena Brazil 203 D6
Conselice Italy 56 D4
Consett U.K. 47 K9
Consolación del Sur Cuba 186 C2
Côn Sơn i. Vietnam 79 D6
Consort Canada 167 I4
Constance Germany see Konstanz
Constance, Lake Germany/Switz. 51 P5
also known as Bodensee
Constância dos Baetas Brazil 199 F6
Constanța Romania 58 J4
also spelt Küstence; historically known as Tomi
Constanța airport Romania see Kogălniceanu
Constantia tourist site Cyprus see Salamis
Constantia Germany see Konstanz
Constantina Spain 54 F7
Constantine Alg. 123 G1
also known as Qacentina; historically known as Cirta
Constantine U.S.A. 172 H9
Constantine, Cape U.S.A. 164 D4
Constantinople Turkey see İstanbul
Constitución de 1857, Parque Nacional nat. park Mex. 184 B1
Consuelo Australia 149 F5
Consuelo Brazil 201 E3
Consul Canada 167 I5
Consul r. Canada 167 K1
Contagem Brazil 207 I6
Contamana Peru 200 B1
Contarina Italy 56 E3
Contas r. Brazil 202 E5
Conthey Switz. 51 N6
Contoocook r. U.S.A. 177 N2
Contoy, Isla i. Mex. 186 B2
Contratacion Col. 198 C3
Contreras, Embalse de resr Spain 55 J5
Contreras, Isla i. Chile 205 B8
Contres France 50 H5
Contria Brazil 207 I5
Contwoyto Lake Canada 167 I1
Convención Col. 198 C2
Convent U.S.A. 175 B6
Convoy U.S.A. 176 A5
Conway S. Africa 133 J8
Conway AR U.S.A. 179 D5
Conway KY U.S.A. 176 A8
Conway NC U.S.A. 177 H9
Conway NH U.S.A. 177 N2
Conway SC U.S.A. 175 E5
Conway, Cape Australia 149 F4
Conway, Lake salt flat Australia 146 B2
Conway National Park Australia 149 F4
Conway Springs U.S.A. 178 C4
Coober Pedy Australia 146 B2
Cooch Behar India see Koch Bihar
Coogoon r. Australia 147 F1
Cook Australia 146 A2
Cook U.S.A. 172 A3
Cook, Bahía de b. Chile 205 C9
Cook, Cape Canada 166 E5
▶Cook, Mount Canada/U.S.A. 166 B2
oceania [landscapes] ▶▶ 136–137

▶Cook, Mount N.Z. 153 E11
Highest mountain in New Zealand. Also known as Aoraki or Aorangi.

Cook Atoll Kiribati see Tarawa
Cookes Peak U.S.A. 181 F6
Cookeville U.S.A. 174 C4
Cookhouse S. Africa 133 J9
Cook Ice Shelf Antarctica 223 K2
Cook Inlet sea chan. U.S.A. 164 D3

▶Cook Islands S. Pacific Ocean 221 H7
Self-governing New Zealand Territory.
oceania [countries] ▶▶ 138–139

Cooksburg U.S.A. 177 K3
Cooks Passage Australia 149 E2
Cookstown U.K. 47 F9
Cook Strait N.Z. 152 I8
Cooktown Australia 149 E2
Coolabah Australia 147 E2
Cooladdi Australia 149 E5
Coolah Australia 147 F2
Coolamon Australia 147 E3
Coolgardie Australia 151 C6
Coolibah Australia 148 A2
Coolimba Australia 151 A6
Cooloola National Park Australia 149 G5
Coolum Beach Australia 149 G5
Cooma Australia 147 F4
Coombah Australia 146 D3
Coonabarabran Australia 147 F2
Coonalpyn Australia 146 C3
Coonamble Australia 147 F2
Coonana Aboriginal Reserve Australia 151 C6
Coondambo Australia 146 B2
Coondapoor India see Kundapura
Coongan r. Australia 150 B4
Coongan Aboriginal Reserve Australia 150 B4
Coongoola Australia 147 E1
Coon Rapids U.S.A. 174 A2
Cooper r. Australia 148 B2
Cooper U.S.A. 179 D5
Cooper Creek watercourse Australia 146 C2
also known as Barcoo Creek
Cooperdale U.S.A. 176 C5
Coopernook Australia 147 G2
Coopersburg U.S.A. 177 J5
Coopers Mills U.S.A. 177 P1
Cooper's Town Bahamas 186 D1
Cooperstown ND U.S.A. 178 C2
Cooperstown NY U.S.A. 177 K3
Coopracambra National Park Australia 147 F4
Coor-de-Wandy hill Australia 151 B5
Coorong National Park Australia 146 C4
Cooroy Australia 149 G5
Coosa r. U.S.A. 175 C5
Coos Bay U.S.A. 180 A4
Coos Bay b. U.S.A. 180 A4
Cootamundra Australia 147 F3
Cooum r. India 94 D3
Copahue, Volcán vol. Chile 204 C5
Copainalá Mex. 185 G5
Copala Mex. 185 F5
Copal Urcu Peru 198 C5
Copán tourist site Hond. 186 A4
Cope, Cabo c. Spain 55 J7
Copemish U.S.A. 172 H6

▶Copenhagen Denmark 45 K5
Capital of Denmark. Also known as København.

Copere Bol. 201 E4
Copetonas Arg. 204 E5
Copeton Reservoir Australia 147 F2
Cô Pi, Phou mt. Laos/Vietnam 78 D4
Copiapó Chile 204 C2
Copiapo, Volcán vol. Chile 204 C2
Copley Australia 146 C2
Coporaque Peru 200 C3
Copparo Italy 56 D4
Coppename r. Suriname 199 G3
Copperbelt prov. Zambia 127 E8
formerly known as Western Province
Copperfield r. Australia 149 D3
Copper Harbor U.S.A. 172 F3
Coppermine Canada see Kugluktuk
Coppermine r. Canada 167 H1
Coppermine Point Canada 168 C4
Copperton S. Africa 132 G6
Copperton U.S.A. 183 L1
Copp Lake Canada 167 H2
Copșa Mică Romania 58 F2
Coqên China 89 D6
Coquilhatville Dem. Rep. Congo see Mbandaka
Coquille i. Micronesia see Pikelot
Coquille U.S.A. 180 A4
Coquimbo Chile 204 C3
Coquimbo admin. reg. Chile 204 C3
Coquitlam Canada 166 F5
Corabia Romania 58 F5
Coração de Jesus Brazil 202 C6
Coracesium Turkey see Alanya
Coracora Peru 200 B3
Coral Bay Australia 150 A4
Coral Harbour Canada 165 K3
Coral Sea S. Pacific Ocean 145 E3

▶Coral Sea Islands Territory terr. Australia 145 E3
Australian External Territory.
oceania [countries] ▶▶ 138–139

Coralville U.S.A. 172 B9
Corangamite, Lake Australia 147 D4
Corazuli Arg. 200 D5
Coraopolis U.S.A. 176 E5
Corato Italy 56 I7
Corbett National Park India 96 C3
Corbie France 51 I3
Corbin U.S.A. 176 A9
Corbones r. Spain 54 F7
Corbu Romania 58 J4
Corby U.K. 47 L11
Corcaigh Rep. of Ireland see Cork
Córcoles r. Spain 55 H5
Corcoran U.S.A. 182 E5
Corcovado Arg. 205 C6
Corcovado, Golfo de sea chan. Chile 205 B6
Corcovado, Parque Nacional nat. park Costa Rica 186 C5
Corcyra i. Greece see Corfu
Cordeiro Brazil 207 K9
Cordele U.S.A. 175 D6
Cordelia U.S.A. 182 B3
Cordell U.S.A. 179 C5
Cordillera de los Picachos, Parque Nacional nat. park Col. 198 C4
Cordillera Range mts Phil. 74 B4
Cordillo Downs Australia 149 D5
Cordisburgo Brazil 207 I6
Córdoba Córdoba Arg. 204 D3
Córdoba Río Negro Arg. 204 C6
Córdoba prov. Arg. 204 E4
Córdoba dept Col. 198 C2
Córdoba Durango Mex. 185 E3
Córdoba Veracruz Mex. 185 F5
Córdoba Spain 54 G7
historically known as Cordova or Corduba or Karmona
Córdoba, Sierras de mts Arg. 204 D4
Cordova Peru 200 B3
Cordova Spain see Córdoba
Cordova AK U.S.A. 164 E3
Cordova IL U.S.A. 172 C9
Cordova Bay U.S.A. 166 C4
Corduba Spain see Córdoba
Coreaú Brazil 202 D2
Corella r. Australia 149 D3
Corella Lake salt flat Australia 148 B3
Corfield Australia 149 D4
Corfu i. Greece 59 A9
also known as Kerkyra; also spelt Kérkira; historically known as Corcyra
Corguinho Brazil 203 A6
Coria Spain 54 E5
Coria del Río Spain 54 E7
Coribe Brazil 202 C5
Coricudgy mt. Australia 147 F3
Corigliano, Golfo di b. Italy 57 I9
Corigliano Calabro Italy 57 I9
Coringa Islands Australia 149 F3
Corinium U.K. see Cirencester
Corinne Canada 167 J5
Corinth Greece 59 D11
also spelt Korinthos; historically known as Corinthus
Corinth MS U.S.A. 174 B5
Corinth NY U.S.A. 177 L2
Corinth, Gulf of sea chan. Greece 59 D10
also known as Korinthiakos Kolpos
Corinthus Greece see Corinth
Corinto Brazil 203 C6
Corinto Nicaragua 186 B4
Corixa Grande r. Bol./Brazil 201 F4
Corixinha r. Brazil 201 F4
Cork Rep. of Ireland 47 D12
also spelt Corcaigh
Corlay France 50 C4
Corleone Sicilia Italy 57 F11
Çorlu Turkey 106 A2
Çorlu r. Turkey 58 I7
Cormeilles France 50 G3
Cormorant Canada 167 K4
Cormorant Lake Canada 167 K4
Cormorant Provincial Forest nature res. Canada 167 K4
Cornacchia, Monte mt. Italy 56 H7
Cornelia S. Africa 133 M4
Cornelia U.S.A. 179 G5
Cornélio Procópio Brazil 206 C10
Corneliskondre Suriname 199 G3
Cornell U.S.A. 172 B5
Cornellà de Llobregat Spain 55 N3
Corner Brook Canada 169 J3
Corneto Italy see Tarquinia
Cornetto mt. Italy 56 D3
Cornettsville U.S.A. 176 B8
Cornia r. Italy 56 C6
Corning AR U.S.A. 174 B4
Corning CA U.S.A. 182 B2
Corning IA U.S.A. 178 D3
Corning NY U.S.A. 177 H3
Corning OH U.S.A. 176 C6
Cornish watercourse Australia 149 E4
Cornish, Estrada b. Chile 205 B7
Corn Islands is Nicaragua see Maíz, Islas del
Corno, Monte mt. Italy 56 F6
Cornouaille reg. France 50 B4
Cornucopia U.S.A. 172 B4
Cornwall Ont. Canada 169 F4
Cornwall P.E.I. Canada 169 I4
Cornwall U.S.A. 177 I5
Cornwallis Island Canada 165 J2
Cornwall Island Canada 165 J2
Corny Point Australia 146 C3
Coro Venez. 198 D2
Coroaci Brazil 203 D6
Coroatá Brazil 202 C3
Corocoro Bol. 200 C4
Corocoro, Isla i. Venez. 199 F2
Coroglen N.Z. 152 J4
Coroico Bol. 200 D4
Corolla U.S.A. 177 J9
Coromandel Brazil 206 F5
Coromandel N.Z. 152 J4
Coromandel Coast India 94 D4
Coromandel Forest Park nature res. N.Z. 152 J5
Coromandel Peninsula N.Z. 152 J4
Coromandel Range hills N.Z. 152 J4
Coron Phil. 74 B3
Corona CA U.S.A. 182 G8
Corona NM U.S.A. 181 F6
Coronado U.S.A. 183 G9
Coronado, Bahiá de b. Costa Rica 186 C5
Coronation Canada 167 I4
Coronation Gulf Canada 165 H3
Coronation Island S. Atlantic Ocean 222 U2
Coronation Islands Australia 150 D2
Coron Bay Phil. 74 B4
Coronda Arg. 204 E3
Coronel Brandsen Arg. 204 F4
Coronel Dorrego Arg. 204 E5
Coronel Fabriciano Brazil 203 D6
Coronel Francisco Sosa Arg. 204 D6
Coronel Moldes Arg. 204 D2
Coronel Murta Brazil 207 K3
Coronel Oviedo Para. 201 F6
Coronel Portillo Peru 198 B5
Coronel Pringles Arg. 204 E5
Coronel Sapucaia Brazil 201 G5
Coronel Suárez Arg. 204 E5
Coronel Vidal Arg. 204 F5
Corovodë Albania 58 B8
Corowa Australia 147 E3
Corozal Belize 185 H5
Corozal Venez. 187 H5
Corozo Pando Venez. 199 E2
Corpen Aike Arg. 205 C8
Corpus Christi U.S.A. 179 C7
Corpus Christi, Lake U.S.A. 179 C6
Corque Bol. 200 D4
Corral Chile 204 B5
Corral de Almaguer Spain 55 H5
Corral de Cantos mt. Spain 54 G5
Corralilla Cuba 186 C2
Corralitos U.S.A. 182 C5
Corrandibby Range hills Australia 151 A5
Corrane Moz. 131 H2
Corrasi, Punta mt. Sardegna Italy 57 B8
Corraun Peninsula Rep. of Ireland 47 C10
Córrego do Ouro Brazil 206 C3
Córrego Novo Brazil 207 K6
Corrente Brazil 202 C4
Corrente r. Bahia Brazil 202 D5
Corrente r. Minas Gerais Brazil 206 C6
Corrente Grande r. Brazil 207 K6
Correntes Brazil 203 A6
Correntes r. Brazil 201 G4
Correnti, Isola delle i. Sicilia Italy 57 H12
Correntina Brazil 202 C5
Correntina r. Brazil see Éguas
Corrèze France 50 H7
Corrèze r. France 51 H7
Corrib, Lough l. Rep. of Ireland 47 C10
Corrientes Arg. 204 F2
Corrientes prov. Arg. 204 F3
Corrientes r. Arg. 204 F3
Corrientes r. Peru 198 C5
Corrientes, Cabo c. Arg. 204 F5
Corrientes, Cabo c. Col. 198 B3
Corrientes, Cabo c. Cuba 186 B2
Corrientes, Cabo c. Mex. 184 D4
Corrigan U.S.A. 179 D6
Corrigin Australia 151 B7
Corriverton Guyana 199 G3
Corrubedo, Cabo c. Spain 54 B2
Corry U.S.A. 176 F4
Corryong Australia 147 E4
Corsaglia r. Italy 51 N8
Corse admin. reg. France 56 B6
Corse i. France see Corsica
Corse, Cap c. Corse France 51 P9
▶Corsica i. France 51 O10
also known as Corse
europe [environments] ▶▶ 36–37
Corsicana U.S.A. 179 C5
Corsico, Baie de b. Gabon 126 A4
Cort Adelaer, Kap c. Greenland see Kangeq
Cortale Italy 57 I10
Corte Corse France 51 P10
Cortegana Spain 54 E7
Cortes Spain 55 J3
Cortés, Sea of g. Mex. see California, Gulf of
Cortes de la Frontera, Reserva Nacional de nature res. Spain 54 F8
Cortez U.S.A. 181 E5
Cortez Mountains U.S.A. 183 H1
Cortina d'Ampezzo Italy 56 E2
Cortland NY U.S.A. 177 I3
Cortland OH U.S.A. 176 E4
Cortona Italy 56 D5
Corubal r. Guinea-Bissau 124 B4
Coruche Port. 54 C6
Çoruh Turkey see Artvin
Çoruh r. Turkey 107 E2
Çorum Turkey 106 C2
Corumbá Brazil 201 F4
Corumbá r. Brazil 206 E5
Corumbá de Goiás Brazil 206 E2
Corumbaíba Brazil 206 E5
Corumbataí r. Brazil 206 B10
Corumbaú, Ponta pt Brazil 207 N3
Corund Romania 58 G2
Corunna Canada 173 K8
Corunna Spain see A Coruña
Corunna U.S.A. 173 I8
Coruripe Brazil 202 E4
Corvallis U.S.A. 180 B3
Corwen U.K. 47 I11
Corydon IA U.S.A. 174 A3
Corydon IN U.S.A. 174 C4
Coryville U.S.A. 176 G4
Cos i. Greece see Kos
Cosalá Mex. 184 D3
Cosamaloapan Mex. 185 G5
Coscaya Chile 200 C4
Cosentia Italy see Cosenza
Cosenza Italy 57 I9
historically known as Cosentia
Coșereni Romania 58 H4
Coshocton U.S.A. 176 D5
Cosmoledo Atoll Seychelles 129 E7
Cosmo Newbery Aboriginal Reserve Australia 151 C6
Cosmópolis Brazil 206 F9
Cosne-Cours-sur-Loire France 51 I5
Cosquín Arg. 204 D3
Cossato Italy 56 A3
Cossé-le-Vivien France 50 F5
Costa Brazil 202 D3
Costa Blanca coastal area Spain 55 K6
Costa Brava coastal area Spain 55 O3
Costa de la Luz coastal area Spain 54 D7
Costa del Azahar coastal area Spain 55 K5
Costa del Sol coastal area Spain 54 F8
Costa Dorada coastal area Spain 55 N3
Costa Marques Brazil 201 D3
Costa Rica Brazil 203 A6
▶Costa Rica country Central America 186 B5
northamerica [countries] ▶▶ 158–159
Costa Rica Mex. 184 D3
Costa Verde coastal area Spain 54 E1
Costermansville Dem. Rep. Congo see Bukavu
Costești Romania 58 F4
Costești Romania 58 I2
Costigan Lake Canada 167 J3
Coșustea r. Romania 58 E4
Cotabambas Peru 200 B3
Cotabato Phil. 74 C5
Cotacajes r. Bol. 200 D4
Cotagaita Bol. 200 D5
Cotahuasi Peru 200 B3
Cotaxé r. Brazil 203 D6
Cote, Mount U.S.A. 166 D3
Coteau des Prairies slope U.S.A. 178 C2
Coteau du Missouri slope ND U.S.A. 178 B1
Coteau du Missouri slope SD U.S.A. 178 B2
Coteaux Haiti 187 E3
Côte d'Azur coastal area France 51 N9
▶Côte d'Ivoire country Africa 124 D4
formerly known as Ivory Coast
africa [countries] ▶▶ 114–117
Côte Française de Somalis country Africa see Djibouti
Cotegipe Brazil 202 C4
Cotentin pen. France 50 E3
Côtes de Meuse ridge France 51 K3
Coti r. Brazil 200 D2
Cotiaeum Turkey see Kütahya
Cotiella mt. Spain 55 L2
Cotingo r. Brazil 199 F4
Cotmeana r. Romania 58 F4
Cotonou Benin 125 F5
Cotopaxi prov. Ecuador 198 B5
Cotopaxi, Volcán vol. Ecuador 198 B5
Cotovsc Moldova see Hîncești
Cotswold Hills U.K. 47 J12
Cottage Grove U.S.A. 180 B4
Cottbus Germany 49 L4
Cotteliar r. India 94 D3
Cottian Alps mts France/Italy 51 M8
also known as Cottiennes, Alpes or Cozie, Alpi
Cottica Suriname 199 H4
Cottiennes, Alpes mts France/Italy see Cottian Alps
Cotton U.S.A. 172 A3
Cottonbush Creek watercourse Australia 148 C4
Cottonwood AZ U.S.A. 183 L7
Cottonwood CA U.S.A. 182 B1
Cottonwood r. KS U.S.A. 178 C4
Cottonwood r. MN U.S.A. 178 D2
Cottonwood Creek watercourse U.S.A. 181 G7
Cottonwood Falls U.S.A. 178 C4
Cottonwood Wash watercourse U.S.A. 183 N7
Cotuí Dom. Rep. 187 F3
Cotulla U.S.A. 179 C6
Couchman Range hills Australia 150 D2
Coudersport U.S.A. 176 G4
Coudres, Île aux i. Canada 169 G4
Couëdic, Cape de Australia 146 C4
Couëron France 50 E5
Couesnon r. France 50 E4
Couiza France 51 I10
Coulee Dam U.S.A. 180 C3
Coulman Island Antarctica 223 L2
Coulogne France 51 H2
Couloir 1 well Alg. 123 H4
Coulommiers France 51 J4
Coulonge r. Canada 168 E4
Coulterville U.S.A. 182 D4
Council U.S.A. 180 C3
Council Bluffs U.S.A. 178 D3
Council Grove U.S.A. 178 C4
Councillor Island Australia 147 E4
Coupeville U.S.A. 180 B2
Courageous Lake Canada 167 I1
Courantyne r. Guyana 199 G3
Courland Lagoon b. Lith./Rus. Fed. 42 C6
also known as Kurshskiy Zaliv or Kurskiy Zaliv or Kuršių marios
Cournon-d'Auvergne France 51 J7
Coursan France 51 J9
Courtenay Canada 166 E5
Courthézon France 51 K8
Courtland U.S.A. 177 H9
Courtrai Belgium see Kortrijk
Coushatta U.S.A. 179 D5
Coutances France 50 E3
Coutinho Moz. see Ulongue
Couto de Magalhães de Minas Brazil 207 J5
Coutras France 50 F7
Coutts Canada 167 I5
Couvin Belgium 51 K2
Couzeix France 50 H7
Covaleda Spain 55 I3
Covasna Romania 58 H3
Cove Fort U.S.A. 183 L3
Cove Island Canada 173 L5
Covelo U.S.A. 182 A2
Cove Mountains hills U.S.A. 176 G6
Covendo Bol. 200 D3
Coventry U.K. 47 K11
Covesville U.S.A. 176 G8
Covilhã Port. 54 D4
Covington GA U.S.A. 175 D5
Covington IN U.S.A. 174 C3
Covington KY U.S.A. 176 A6
Covington LA U.S.A. 175 B6
Covington OH U.S.A. 176 A5
Covington TN U.S.A. 174 B5
Covington VA U.S.A. 176 E8
Cow r. Canada 173 J3
Cowal, Lake dry lake Australia 147 E3
Cowan U.S.A. 176 B7
Cowan, Lake salt flat Australia 151 C6
Cowcowing Lakes salt flat Australia 151 B6
Cowdenbeath U.K. 46 I7
Cowell Australia 146 C3
Cowen U.S.A. 176 E7
Cowes Australia 147 E4
Cowley Australia 149 E5
Cowlitz r. U.S.A. 180 B3
Cowpasture r. U.S.A. 176 F8
Cowra Australia 147 F3
Cox r. Australia 148 B2
Coxá r. Brazil 207 I1
Coxen Hole Hond. see Roatán
Coxilha de Santana hills Brazil/Uruguay 204 G3
Coxilha Grande hills Brazil 203 A9
Coxim Brazil 203 A6
Coxim r. Brazil 203 A6
Coxsackie U.S.A. 177 L3
Cox's Bazar Bangl. 97 F5
Coyah Guinea 124 B4
Coy Aike Arg. 205 C8
Coyame Mex. 181 F7
Coyanosa Creek watercourse U.S.A. 179 B6
Coyote r. Mex. 181 D7
Coyote, Punta pt Mex. 184 C3
Coyote Lake U.S.A. 183 H6
Coyote Peak hill U.S.A. 183 J9
Coyote Peak U.S.A. 182 F5
Coyotitán Mex. 184 D4
Coyuca de Benítez Mex. 185 E5
Coyuca de Catalán Mex. 185 E5
Cozad U.S.A. 178 C3
Cozia, Vârful mt. Romania 58 F3
Cozie, Alpi mts France/Italy see Cottian Alps
Cozumel Mex. 185 I4
Cozumel, Isla de i. Mex. 185 I4
Cozzo del Pellegrino mt. Italy 57 I9
Crab Island Australia 149 D1
Crab Orchard U.S.A. 176 A8
Cracovia Poland see Kraków
Cracow Australia 149 F5
Cracow Poland see Kraków
Cradle Mountain Lake St Clair National Park Australia 147 E5
Cradock Australia 146 C2
Cradock S. Africa 133 J9
Crafthole S. Africa 132 I3
Craig AK U.S.A. 166 C4
Craig CO U.S.A. 180 F4
Craigavon U.K. 47 F9
Craigieburn Australia 147 E4
Craigieburn N.Z. 153 F11
Craigieburn Forest Park nature res. N.Z. 153 F11
Craignure U.K. 46 G7
Craigsville VA U.S.A. 176 F7
Craigsville WV U.S.A. 176 E7
Crail U.K. 46 J7
Crailsheim Germany 48 H6
Craiova Romania 58 E4
Cramlington U.K. 47 K8
Cramond S. Africa 132 F4
Cranberry Junction Canada 166 D4
Cranberry Lake U.S.A. 177 K1
Cranberry Portage Canada 167 K4
Cranbourne Australia 147 E4
Cranbrook Canada 167 H5
Crandon U.S.A. 172 E5
Crane OR U.S.A. 180 C4
Crane TX U.S.A. 179 B6
Crane Lake l. Canada 167 I5
Crane Lake U.S.A. 172 A2
Cranston KY U.S.A. 176 B7
Cranston RI U.S.A. 177 N4
Cranz Rus. Fed. see Zelenogradsk
Craolândia Brazil 202 C3
Craon France 50 F5
Crary Ice Rise Antarctica 223 M1
Crary Mountains Antarctica 222 P1
Crasna Romania 58 I1
Crasna r. Romania 58 D1
Crater Lake National Park U.S.A. 180 B4
Crater Peak U.S.A. 182 C1
Craters of the Moon National Monument nat. park U.S.A. 180 D4
Crateús Brazil 202 D3
Crato Brazil 202 E3
Crato Port. 54 D5
Cravari r. Brazil 201 F3
Cravinhos Brazil 206 F8
Cravo Norte Col. 198 D3
Crawford U.S.A. 178 B3
Crawford Point Phil. 74 A4
Crawford Range hills Australia 148 B4
Crawfordsville U.S.A. 174 C3
Crawfordville U.S.A. 175 C6
Crawley U.K. 47 L12
Crazy Mountains U.S.A. 180 E3
Crean Lake Canada 167 J4
Crécy-en-Ponthieu France 51 H2
Crediton U.K. 47 I13
Cree r. Canada 167 J3
Creede U.S.A. 181 F5
Creedmoor U.S.A. 176 G9
Creel Mex. 184 D3
Cree Lake Canada 167 J3
Creighton Canada 167 K4
Creighton S. Africa 133 N7
Creil France 51 I3
Crema Italy 56 B3
Cremona Canada 167 H5
Cremona Italy 56 C3
Crepori r. Brazil 199 G6
Crépy-en-Valois France 51 I3
Cres Croatia 56 G4
Cres i. Croatia 56 G4
Crescent City U.S.A. 180 A4
Crescent Group is Paracel Is 72 D3
Crescent Head Australia 147 G2
Crescent Junction U.S.A. 183 O3
Crescent Lake National Wildlife Refuge nature res. U.S.A. 178 B3
Crescent Peak U.S.A. 183 I6
Crescent Valley U.S.A. 183 H1
Cresco U.S.A. 174 A3
Crespo Arg. 204 E4
Cresswell watercourse Australia 148 B3
Cresswell Downs Australia 148 B3
Crest France 51 L8
Crest Hill hill Hong Kong China 87 [inset]
also known as Tai Shek Mo
Crestline U.S.A. 176 C5
Creston Canada 167 G5
Creston IA U.S.A. 178 D3
Creston WY U.S.A. 180 F4
Crestview U.S.A. 175 C6
Creta i. Greece see Crete
Crêt de la Neige mt. France 51 L6
Crete i. Greece 59 F13
also spelt Kriti; historically known as Creta
Crete U.S.A. 178 C3
Crêt Monniot mt. France 51 M5
Creus, Cap de c. Spain 55 O2
Creuse r. France 51 G5
Crevalcore Italy 56 D4
Crevasse Valley Glacier Antarctica 222 O1
Crevillente Spain 55 K6
Crewe U.K. 47 J10
Crewe U.S.A. 176 G8
Crianlarich U.K. 46 H7
Criccieth U.K. 47 H11
Criciúma Brazil 203 B9
Cricova Moldova 58 J1
formerly spelt Krikovo
Cricovu Sărat r. Romania 58 H4
Cridersville U.S.A. 176 A5
Crieff U.K. 46 I7
Criffell hill U.K. 47 I9
Crikvenica Croatia 56 G3
Crillon, Mount U.S.A. 166 B3
Crimea pen. Ukr. 41 E7
also known as Kryms'kyy Pivostriv; short form Krym'
Crimmitschau Germany 49 J5
Cripple Creek U.S.A. 180 F5
Crișan Romania 58 K3
Crisfield U.S.A. 177 J8
Cristais, Serra dos mts Brazil 206 F4
Cristal, Monts de mts Equat. Guinea/Gabon 125 H6
Cristalândia Brazil 202 B4
Cristalina Brazil 206 F3
Cristalino r. Brazil 201 G2
Cristalino r. Brazil see Mariembero
Cristianópolis Brazil 206 E4
Cristina Brazil 207 H9
Cristino Castro Brazil 202 C4
Cristuru Secuiesc Romania 58 G2
Crișul Alb r. Romania 58 C2
Crișul Negru r. Romania 58 C2
Crișul Repede r. Romania 58 C1
Crișurilor, Câmpia plain Romania 58 C2
Criterion mt. Peru 200 B3
Criuleni Moldova 58 K1
formerly spelt Kriulyany
Crivitz Germany 48 I2
Crivitz U.S.A. 172 E5
Crixás Brazil 202 B5
Crixás Açu r. Brazil 202 B5
Crixás Mirim r. Brazil 202 B5
Crna r. Macedonia 58 C7
Crna Glava mt. Yugo. 58 A6
Crna Gora mts Macedonia/Yugo. 58 C6
Crna Gora aut. rep. Yugo. 58 A6
English form Montenegro
Crna Trava Srbija Yugo. 58 D6
Crni Drim r. Macedonia 58 B7
Crni Timok r. Yugo. 58 D5
Črni vrh mt. Slovenia 56 H2
Črnomelj Slovenia 56 H3

index

C

D

Crnook mt. Yugo. **58** D6
Croajingolong National Park Australia **147** F4
▶**Croatia** country Europe **56** H3
known as Hrvatska in Croatian
europe [countries] ▶ 32–35
Crocco, Monte mt. Italy **57** I10
Crocker, Banjaran mts Malaysia **77** F1
Crocker Range National Park Sabah Malaysia **77** G1
Crockett U.S.A. **179** D6
Croghan U.S.A. **177** J2
Croisette, Cap c. France **51** I4
Croisic, Pointe de pt France **50** D5
Croisilles France **51** I2
Croker, Cape Australia **148** B1
Croker, Cape Canada **173** M6
Croker Island Australia **148** B1
Cromarty U.K. **46** H6
Cromer U.K. **47** N11
Cromwell N.Z. **153** D13
Cromwell U.S.A. **172** A4
Cronadun N.Z. **153** F10
Crooked r. U.S.A. **180** B3
Crooked Creek U.S.A. **166** A1
Crooked Harbour b. Hong Kong China **87** [inset]
also known as Kat O Hoi
Crooked Island Bahamas **187** E2
Crooked Island Hong Kong China **87** [inset]
also known as Kat O Chau
Crooked Island Passage Bahamas **187** E2
Crooked Lake Canada/U.S.A. **172** B2
Crooked River Canada **167** K4
Crookston U.S.A. **178** C2
Crooksville U.S.A. **176** C6
Crookwell Australia **147** F3
Crosbie r. Australia **149** E5
Crosby U.K. **47** I10
Crosby MN U.S.A. **174** A2
Crosby ND U.S.A. **178** B1
Crosbyton U.S.A. **179** B5
Cross r. Nigeria **125** H5
Cross Bay Canada **167** M2
Cross City U.S.A. **175** D6
Crosse, Île-à-la- Canada **167** J4
Crossett U.S.A. **175** C5
Cross Fell hill U.K. **47** J9
Crossfield Canada **167** H5
Cross Harbour b. Bahamas **186** D1
Cross Lake Canada **167** L4
Cross Lake I. Canada **167** L4
Cross Lake I. U.S.A. **173** Q7
Crossman Peak U.S.A. **183** J8
Cross River state Nigeria **125** H5
Cross Sound sea chan. U.S.A. **166** B3
Croswell U.S.A. **173** K7
Crotch Lake Canada **173** Q6
Croton Italy see Crotone
Crotone Italy **57** J9
historically known as Croton
Crow r. Canada **166** E3
Crow Agency U.S.A. **180** F3
Crowal watercourse Australia **147** E2
Crow Creek r. U.S.A. **180** F4
Crow Creek Indian Reservation res. U.S.A. **178** C2
Crowdy Bay National Park Australia **147** G2
Crowell U.S.A. **179** C5
Crow Indian Reservation res. U.S.A. **180** F3
Crowl watercourse Australia **147** E3
Crowley U.S.A. **179** D6
Crowley, Lake U.S.A. **182** F4
Crown Point U.S.A. **181** E6
Crownpoint U.S.A. **181** I6
Crown Point NY U.S.A. **177** L2
Crown Prince Olav Coast Antarctica **223** C2
Crown Princess Martha Coast Antarctica **223** W1
Crows Nest Australia **147** G1
Crowsnest Pass Canada **167** H5
Crowsnest Pass pass Canada **167** H5
Crow Wing r. U.S.A. **178** D2
Croydon Australia **149** D3
Crozet U.S.A. **176** G7
Crozet, Îles is Indian Ocean **219** K9
English form Crozet Islands
Crozet Islands Indian Ocean see Crozet, Îles
Crozier Channel Canada **165** G2
Crozon France **50** B4
Crucea Romania **58** G3
Crucero Peru **200** C3
Cruces Cuba **186** C2
Cruces, Punta c. Col. **198** B3
Cruillas Mex. **185** F3
Crum U.S.A. **176** C8
Cruz mt. Spain **55** I5
Cruz Venez. **199** E3
Cruz, Cabo c. Cuba **186** D3
Cruz Alta Brazil **203** A9
Cruz del Eje Arg. **204** D3
Cruzeiro Brazil **203** C7
Cruzeiro do Sul Brazil **200** B1
Cruzen Island Antarctica **222** O2
Cruz Grande Mex. **185** F5
Crvenka Vojvodina, Srbija Yugo. **58** A3
Cry Lake Canada **166** D3
Crysdale, Mount Canada **166** F4
Crystal Brook Australia **146** C3
Crystal City Canada **167** L5

Crystal City MO U.S.A. **174** B4
Crystal City TX U.S.A. **179** C6
Crystal Falls U.S.A. **172** E4
Crystal Lake U.S.A. **172** E8
Crystal River U.S.A. **175** D6
Crystal Springs U.S.A. **175** B6
Csabrendek Hungary **49** O8
Csanádpalota Hungary **49** R9
Csépa Hungary **49** R9
Cserhát hills Hungary **49** Q8
Cserszegtomaj Hungary **49** O9
Csongrád Hungary **49** R9
Csorna Hungary **49** O8
Csorvás Hungary **49** R9
Csóványos hill Hungary **49** P8
Csurgó Hungary **49** O9
Ctesiphon tourist site Iraq **107** F4
also known as Tayspun
Cua r. Spain **54** E2
Cu'a Dinh An r. mouth Vietnam **79** D6
Cuadrada, Sierra hills Arg. **205** C7
Cuale Angola **127** C7
Cualedro Spain **54** D3
Cuamato Angola **127** B9
Cuamba Moz. **131** H1
formerly known as Nova Freixa
Cuando r. Angola/Zambia **127** D9
Cuando Cubango prov. Angola **127** C8
Cuangar Angola **127** C9
Cuango Lunda Norte Angola **127** C7
Cuango Uíge Angola **127** C6
Cuango r. Angola **127** C6
also spelt Kwango
Cuanza r. Angola **127** B7
also spelt Kwanza
Cuanza Norte prov. Angola **127** B7
Cuanza Sul prov. Angola **127** B7
Cuareim r. Uruguay **204** F3
Cuaró Uruguay **204** F3
Cuarto r. Arg. **204** E4
Cuatir r. Angola **127** C9
Cuatro Ciénegas Mex. **185** E3
Cuatro Ojos Bol. **201** E4
Cuauhtémoc Mex. **184** D2
Cuautla Mex. **185** F5
Cuba NY U.S.A. **176** G3
Cuba OH U.S.A. **176** B6

▶**Cuba** country West Indies **186** C2
5th largest island and 5th most populous country in North America.
northamerica [landscapes] ▶ 156–157
northamerica [countries] ▶ 158–159

Cubagua, Isla i. Venez. **199** E2
Cubal Angola **127** B8
Cubal r. Angola **127** B7
Cubango r. Angola/Namibia **127** D9
Cubara Col. **198** C3
Cubatão Brazil **206** G10
Cub Hills Canada **167** J4
Cubillas r. Spain **55** H7
Çubuk Turkey **106** C2
Çucao Chile **205** B6
Cucapa, Sierra mts Mex. **183** I9
Cuchi Angola **127** C8
Cuchilla Grande hills Uruguay **204** G4
Cuchilla Grande Inferior hills Uruguay **204** F4
Cuchillo-Có Arg. **204** D5
Cucu, Vârful mt. Romania **58** G2
Cucuí Brazil **199** F4
Cucumbi Angola **127** C7
Cucurrupí Col. **198** B3
Cúcuta Col. **198** C3
Cucutas hills Spain **55** K3
Cudalbi Romania **58** I3
Cuddalore India **94** C4
Cuddapah India **94** C3
Cuddapan, Lake salt flat Australia **149** D5
Cuddeback Lake U.S.A. **182** G6
Cudi watercourse Turkey **109** K1
Cudi Dağı mt. Turkey **109** J1
Cudillero Spain **54** E1
Cue Australia **151** B5
Cuebe r. Angola **127** C8
Cueio r. Angola **127** D8
Cuéllar Spain **54** G3
Cuemba Angola **127** C8
Cuenca Ecuador **198** B5
Cuenca Phil. **74** B3
Cuenca Spain **55** I4
Cuenca, Serranía de mts Spain **55** I4
Cuencamé Mex. **184** E3
Cuernavaca Mex. **185** F5
Cuero U.S.A. **179** C6
Cuers France **51** M9
Cuervos Mex. **183** J9
Cueto Cuba **186** E2
Cuevo Bol. **201** E5
Cugir Romania **58** E3
Cugir r. Romania **58** E3
Cugnaux France **50** H9
Cugo r. Angola **127** C6
Cuiabá Brazil **201** F3
Cuiabá r. Brazil **201** F4
Cuicatlan Mex. **185** F5
Cuihua China see Daguan
Cuijiang China see Ninghua
Cuilapa Guat. **185** H6
Cuilcagh hill Rep. of Ireland/U.K. **47** E9
Cuillin Hills U.K. **46** F6
Cuillin Sound sea chan. U.K. **46** F6
Cuilo r. Angola **127** C7
Cuilo-Futa Angola **127** B6
Cuiluan China **82** C3
Cuimba Angola **127** B6
Cuité r. Brazil **207** L6
Cuito r. Angola **127** C8
Cuito Cuanavale Angola **127** C8
Cuitzeo, Laguna de l. Mex. **185** E5
Cuiuni r. Brazil **199** F5
Cuivre r. U.S.A. **174** B4
Cujangan r. Phil. **74** B5
Cujmir Romania **58** D4
Cukai Malaysia **76** C1
also spelt Chukai
Çuke Albania **59** B9
Çukurca Turkey **107** E3
also known as Çal
Çukurova plat. Turkey **108** G1
Cula r. Moldova **58** J1
Culai Shan mt. China **85** H4
Cu Lao Cham i. Vietnam **78** E5
Cu Lao Re i. Vietnam **79** E5
Cu Lao Thu i. Vietnam **79** E6
Culasi Phil. **74** B4
Culberston U.S.A. **180** F2
Culcairn Australia **147** E3
Culebras Peru **200** A2
Culebras i. Angola **127** B7
also spelt Dzhul'fa
Culfa Azer. **107** G3
Culiacán Mex. **184** D3
Culion Phil. **74** A4
Culion i. Phil. **74** A4
Cúllar-Baza Spain **55** I7
Cullen U.S.A. **179** D5
Cullen Point Australia **149** D1
Cullera Spain **55** K5
Cullinan S. Africa **133** M4
Cullman U.S.A. **174** C5
Cul Mor hill U.K. **46** G5
Culpeper U.S.A. **176** H7
Culuene r. Brazil **202** A4
Culver, Point Australia **151** D7
Culverden N.Z. **153** G10
Cumã, Baía do inlet Brazil **202** C2

Cumaná Venez. **199** E2
Cumbal, Nevado de vol. Col. **198** B4
Cumberland KY U.S.A. **176** C9
Cumberland MD U.S.A. **176** G6
Cumberland OH U.S.A. **176** D6
Cumberland VA U.S.A. **176** G8
Cumberland WI U.S.A. **172** A5
Cumberland r. U.S.A. **176** B9
Cumberland Bay S. Georgia **205** [inset]
Cumberland Head U.S.A. **176** B4
Cumberland House Canada **167** K4
Cumberland Islands Australia **149** F4
Cumberland Mountain mts U.S.A. **176** B9
Cumberland Peninsula Canada **165** M3
Cumberland Plateau U.S.A. **174** C5
Cumberland Point U.S.A. **172** D3
Cumberland Sound sea chan. Canada **165** M3
Cumbernauld U.K. **46** I8
Cumbre Alta mt. Spain **54** G5
Cumbre Negro mt. Arg. **205** C7
Cumbres de Majalca, Parque Nacional nat. park Mex. **184** D2
Cumbum India **94** C3
Cuminá Brazil **199** G5
Cummins Australia **146** B3
Cummins Range hills Australia **150** D3
Cumnock U.K. **46** H8
Cumpas Mex. **184** C2
Çumra Turkey **106** C3
Cumuruxatiba Brazil **207** N4
Cunani Brazil **199** I4
Cuñaré Col. **198** C4
Cundeelee Aboriginal Reserve Australia **151** C6
Cunderdin Australia **151** B6
Cundinamarca dept Col. **198** C3
Cunene prov. Angola **127** B9
Cunene r. Angola **127** A9
also spelt Kunene
Cuneo Italy **51** N5
Cung Son Vietnam **79** E5
Çüngüş Turkey **107** D3
Cunha Brazil **207** I10
Cunhinga Angola **127** C8
formerly known as Vouga
Cunnamulla Australia **147** E2
Cunshamayo Peru **200** B1
Cununa r. Romania **58** C4
Čuokkaraš'ša mt. Norway **44** N1
Cuorgnè Italy **51** N7
Cupar U.K. **46** I7
Cupari r. Brazil **199** H5
Cupica Col. **198** B3
Cupra Marittima Italy **56** F5
Ćuprija Srbija Yugo. **58** C5
Cupula, Pico mt. Mex. **184** C3
Curaçá Brazil **199** K5
Curaçá r. Brazil **199** K5
Curaçá r. Brazil **198** D6
Curaçao i. Neth. Antilles **187** F4
Curacó r. Arg. **204** D5
Curaculo r. Angola **127** B7
Curahuara de Carangas Bol. **200** C4
Curanilahue Chile **204** B5
Curanja r. Peru **200** C2
Curaray r. Ecuador **198** C5
Curatabaca Venez. **199** F3
Curaya r. Arg. **204** E4
Curdlawidny Lagoon salt flat Australia **146** C2
Curé r. Col. **198** D5
Cure r. France **51** J5
Curia Switz. see Chur
Curiapo Venez. **199** F2
Curicó Chile **204** C4
Curicuriari, Serra hill Brazil **199** E5
Curieuriari r. Brazil **199** E5
Curimata Brazil **202** C4
Curiplaya Col. **198** C4
Curitiba Brazil **203** B8
Curitibanos Brazil **203** B8
Curiúva Brazil **206** C11
Curnamona Australia **146** C2
Curoca r. Angola **127** A8
Curral de Dentro Brazil **207** L2
Curralinho Brazil **202** B2
Curralulla watercourse Australia **148** B5
Curral Velho Cape Verde **124** [inset]
Currawilla Australia **149** D5
Currawinya National Park Australia **147** E2
Current Bahamas **186** D1
Current r. U.S.A. **174** B4
Currie Australia **147** D4
Currie U.S.A. **183** J1
Currituck U.S.A. **177** I9
Currituck Sound inlet U.S.A. **177** J9
Curtea de Argeş Romania **58** F3
Curtici Romania **58** C2
Curtis Channel Australia **149** G5
Curtis Group is Australia **147** E4
Curtis Island Australia **149** F4
Curtis Island N.Z. **145** I5
Curuá Brazil **199** H5
Curuá r. Brazil **199** H6
Curuaés r. Brazil **202** A3
Curuaí Brazil **199** H5
Curuapanema r. Brazil **199** H5
Curuá Una r. Brazil **199** H5
Curuçá Brazil **202** C2
Curumu Brazil **199** I5
Curupira Brazil **199** H5
Curupira, Serra mts Brazil/Venez. **199** E4
Cururu Bol. **201** E3
Cururu r. Brazil **201** F1
Cururupu Brazil **202** C2
Curuzú Cuatiá Arg. **204** F3
Curvelo, Cerro mt. Venez. **199** F3
Curvelo Brazil **203** D6
Curwood, Mount hill U.S.A. **172** E4
Cusco Peru **200** C3
also spelt Cuzco
Cusco dept Peru **200** B3
Cushendun U.K. **47** F8
Cushing U.S.A. **179** C4
Cusset France **51** J6
Cusseta U.S.A. **175** C5
Custer MT U.S.A. **180** F3
Custer SD U.S.A. **178** B3
Cutato Angola **127** C8
Cut Bank U.S.A. **180** D2
Cut Bank Creek r. U.S.A. **180** D2
Cuthbert U.S.A. **175** C6
Cuthbertson Falls Australia **148** B2
Cutler U.S.A. **182** E5
Cutler Ridge U.S.A. **175** D7
Cut Off U.S.A. **175** B6
Cutral-Co Arg. **204** C5
Cutro Italy **57** I9
Cuttaburra Creek r. Australia **147** D2
Cuttack India **95** E1
Cuvelai Angola **127** B8
Cuvette admin. reg. Congo **126** C5
Cuvette-Ouest admin. reg. Congo **126** B4
Cuvier, Cape Australia **151** A5
Cuvier Island N.Z. **152** J4
Cuvillier, Lac l. Canada **173** Q2
Cuxhaven Germany **48** F2
Cuya Chile **200** C4
Cuyahoga Valley National Recreation Area park U.S.A. **176** D4
Cuyama U.S.A. **182** E7
Cuyama r. U.S.A. **182** D7
Cuyapo Phil. **74** B3
Cuyo Phil. **74** B4
Cuyo East Passage Phil. **74** B4
Cuyo Islands Phil. **74** B4
Cuyo West Passage Phil. **74** B4
Cuyuni r. Guyana **199** G3

Cuyutingni Nicaragua see Kuyu Tingni
Cuzco Peru see Cusco
Cuzco Peru **200** A1
Cwmbran U.K. **47** I12
Cyangugu Rwanda **126** F5
Cybinka Poland **49** L3
Cyclades is Greece **59** F11
also spelt Kikládhes or Kyklades
Cygnet U.S.A. **176** B4
Cymru admin. div. U.K. see Wales
Cynthiana U.S.A. **176** A7
Cypress Hills Canada **167** I5
Cypress Hills Provincial Park Canada **167** I5
▶**Cyprus** country Asia **108** D3
spelt Kypros in Greek or Kibris in Turkish; historically known as Alashiya
asia [countries] ▶ 64–67
Cyrenaica reg. Libya **120** D1
Cyrene tourist site Libya **120** D1
also known as Cirene
Cythera i. Greece see Kythira
Czaplinek Poland **49** N2
Czar Canada **167** I4
Czarna r. Poland **49** Q4
Czarna r. Poland **49** S5
Czarna Białostocka Poland **49** U2
Czarna Nida r. Poland **49** R5
Czarna Struga r. Poland **49** O3
Czarne Poland **49** N2
Czarnków Poland **49** N3

▶**Czechoslovakia**
Divided in 1993 into the Czech Republic and Slovakia.

Czechowice-Dziedzice Poland **49** Q6
▶**Czech Republic** country Europe **49** K6
also known as Česká Republika
europe [countries] ▶ 32–35
Czempiń Poland **49** N3
Czerniejewo Poland **49** O3
Czernowitz Ukr. see Chernivtsi
Czersk Poland **49** O2
Czerwieńsk Poland **49** M3
Częstochowa Poland **49** Q5
formerly known as Chenstokhov
Człopa Poland **49** N2
Człuchów Poland **49** O2

⬇ **D**

Đa, Sông r. Vietnam see Black River
Da'an China **85** J2
formerly known as Dalai
Daanbantayan Phil. **74** B4
Dabab, Jabal el mt. Jordan **108** G6
Dabaga Tanz. **129** B7
Dabajuro Venez. **198** D2
Dabakala Côte d'Ivoire **124** D4
Daban China **85** H3
also known as Bairin Youqi
Dabao China **86** B3
Dabas Hungary **49** Q8
Daba Shan mts China **87** D1
Dabat Eth. **104** B3
Dabba China see Daocheng
Dabeiba Col. **198** B3
Dabein Myanmar **78** B4
Dabhoi India **96** B5
Dabhol India **94** B2
Dabi, Wādi al watercourse Jordan **109** H6
Dabie Shan mts China **87** E2
Dąbki Poland **49** N1
Dabl, Wādī watercourse Saudi Arabia **109** H8
Daiquiri Cuba **186** E3
Daireaux Arg. **204** E5
Dairen China see Dalian
Dairût Egypt **121** F3
Dairyland U.S.A. **172** A4
Dai-sen vol. Japan **91** C7
Daisen-Oki National Park Japan **91** C7
Daisetsu-zan National Park Japan **90** H3
Daishan China **87** G2
also known as Gaotingzhen
Daiyue China see Shanyin
Daiyun Shan mts China **87** F3
Dajarra Australia **148** C4
Dajie China see Jiangchuan
Dajin Chuan r. China **86** B2
Dajing China **87** G3
Da Juh China **84** B4

▶**Dakar** Senegal **124** A3
Capital of Senegal.

Dakar el Arak well Sudan **121** F5
Dakhal, Wādī el watercourse Egypt **108** D9
Dakhin Shahbazpur Island Bangl. **97** F5
Dakhla W. Sahara see Ad Dakhla
Dakhla Oasis Egypt **121** F3
Đâk Lak Vietnam **79** D5
Đâk Nghe r. Vietnam **79** D5
Dakoank India **95** G5
Dakol'ka r. Belarus **43** J9
Dakor India **96** B5
Dakoro Niger **125** G3
Dakota City IA U.S.A. **178** D3
Dakota City NE U.S.A. **178** C3
Đakovica Kosovo, Srbija Yugo. **58** B6
also spelt Đakovica
Dakovo Croatia **56** K3
Dala Angola **127** D7
Dalaba Guinea **124** B4
Dalad Qi China see Shulinzhao
Dalai China see Da'an
Dalai Hob China **84** D3
also known as Ejin Qi
Dalai Nur l. China **85** H3
Dalâkī Iran **100** B4
Dalälven r. Sweden **45** L3
Dalaman Turkey **106** B3
Dalaman r. Turkey **106** B3
Dalandzadgad Mongolia **84** D3
Dalanganem Islands Phil. **74** B4
Dalaoba China **88** C3
Dalap-Uliga-Darrit Marshall Is see Delap-Uliga-Djarrit
Dalarna county Sweden **45** K3
formerly known as Kopparberg
Dalarna reg. Sweden **45** K3
Dalat Sarawak Malaysia **77** E2
Đa Lat Vietnam **79** E6
Dalatando Angola see N'dalatando
Dalay Mongolia **84** D3
Dalbandin Pak. **101** E4
Dalbeg Australia **149** E4
Dalbosjön l. Sweden **45** K4
Dalby Australia **147** F1
Dalby Sweden **45** K5
Dalcahue Chile **205** B6
Dale Hordaland Norway **45** I3
Dale Sogn og Fjordane Norway **45** I3
Dale City U.S.A. **177** H7
Dale Hollow Lake U.S.A. **174** C4
Dalen Norway **45** J4
Dalet Myanmar **78** A4
Dalfors Sweden **45** K3
Dalgaranger, Mount hill Australia **151** B5
Dalgety r. Australia **151** A5
Dalhart U.S.A. **179** B4
Dalhousie Canada **169** H3
also known as Rongzhag or Zhangguo

Dalhousie, Cape Canada **164** G2
Dali Shaanxi China **87** D1
Dali Yunnan China **86** B3
also known as Xiaguan
Dali r. China **85** I4
Dalian China **85** I4
formerly known as Dairen or Dalny or Lüda
Daliang China see Shunde
Daliang Shan mts China **86** B3
Dalian Wan b. China **85** I4
Dalin China **85** I3
Daling r. China **85** I3
Dalinghe China see Linhai
Dalizi China **82** B4
Dalj Croatia **56** K3
Dalkola India **97** E4
Dallas OR U.S.A. **180** B3
Dallas TX U.S.A. **179** C5
Dallas City U.S.A. **172** B10
Dalles City U.S.A. see The Dalles
Dall Island U.S.A. **164** F4
Dallol Bosso watercourse Mali/Niger **125** F3
Dalmā i. U.A.E. **105** F2
▶**Dalmatia** reg. Croatia **56** H4
also spelt Dalmacija
europe [landscapes] ▶ 30–31
Dalmellington U.K. **46** H8
Dalmeny Canada **167** J4
Dal'negorsk Rus. Fed. **82** D3
formerly known as Tetyukhe
Dal'nerechensk Rus. Fed. **82** D3
formerly known as Iman
Dal'niye Zelentsy Rus. Fed. **40** F1
Dalny China see Dalian
Daloa Côte d'Ivoire **124** D5

▶**Dalol** Eth. **128** D1
Highest recorded annual mean temperature in the world.
world [climate and weather] ▶ 16–17

Dalou Shan mts China **86** C2
Dalqān well Saudi Arabia **105** D2
Dalrymple, Lake Australia **149** E4
Dalrymple, Mount Australia **149** F4
Dalsbruk Fin. **42** D1
Daltenganj India **97** E4
formerly spelt Daltonganj
Dalton Canada **168** C3
Dalton S. Africa **133** O6
Dalton GA U.S.A. **174** C5
Dalton MA U.S.A. **177** L3
Dalton OH U.S.A. **176** D5
Dalton PA U.S.A. **177** J4
Dalton Iceberg Tongue Antarctica **223** I2
Dalton Mills Canada **173** I2
Daludalu Indon. **76** C2
Daluo Shan mt. China **87** E4
Dalupiri i. Phil. **74** B2
Dalvík Iceland **44** [inset]
Dalwallinu Australia **151** B6
Dalwhinnie U.K. **46** H7
Daly r. Australia **148** A2
Daly City U.S.A. **182** B4
Daly River Australia **148** A2
Daly River/Port Keats Aboriginal Land res. Australia **148** A2
Daly Waters Australia **148** B3
Damagaram Takaya Niger **125** H3
Damalisques de Leshwe nature res. Dem. Rep. Congo **127** F8
Daman India **94** B1
formerly spelt Damão
Daman and Diu union terr. India **94** A1
Damanava Belarus **42** G9
Damâne well Mauritania **124** B2
Damaneh Iran **100** B3
Damanhur Egypt **121** F2
Damant Lake Canada **167** J2
Damão India see Daman
Damaq Iran **100** B3
Damaqun Shan mts China **85** G3
Damar Indon. **75** C2
Damar i. Moluccas Indon. **75** D3
Damar i. Moluccas Indon. **75** D4
Damara Cent. Afr. Rep. **126** C3
Damaraland reg. Namibia **130** C4
Damariscotta Lake U.S.A. **177** P1
Damar Laut, Pulau i. Sing. **76** [inset]
Damas Syria see Damascus

▶**Damascus** Syria **109** H4
Capital of Syria. Also known as Ash Sham or Damas; also spelt Dimashq.

Damascus MD U.S.A. **177** H6
Damascus VA U.S.A. **176** D9
Damaturu Nigeria **125** I4
Damāvand Iran **100** C3
Damāvand, Qolleh-ye mt. Iran **100** C3
English form Demavend
Damba Angola **127** C6
Dambai Ghana **125** F4
Dambatta Nigeria **125** H3
Damboa Nigeria **125** I4
Dâmboviţa r. Romania **58** G4
Damchara India **97** G4
Damdy Kazakh. **103** F2
formerly known as Zhalanash
Dame Marie Haiti **187** E3
Damghan Iran **100** C2
Damietta Egypt see Dumyât
Daming China **85** G4
Daming Shan mt. China **87** D4
Damjong China **97** G2
Damlasu Turkey **109** K1
Dammai i. Phil. **74** B5
Dammam Saudi Arabia **105** E2
also spelt Ad Dammām
Dammastock mt. Switz. **51** O6
Damme Germany **48** F3
Damoh India **96** C5
Damongo Ghana **125** E4
Damour Lebanon **108** G4
Dampelas, Tanjung pt Indon. **75** A2
Dampier Australia **150** B4
Dampier Archipelago is Australia **150** B4
Dampier Island P.N.G. see Karkar Island
Dampier Land reg. Australia **150** C3
Dampierre-sur-Salon France **51** L5
Dampier Strait P.N.G. **145** D2
Dampit Indon. **77** F5
Damqoq Zangbo r. China see Maquan He
Dam Qu r. China **84** B4
Dâmrei, Chuŏr Phnum mts Cambodia **79** D6
Damroh India **97** G3
Damxoi China see Comai
Damxung China **89** E6
also known as Gongtang
Dan r. U.S.A. **176** F9
Dana i. Indon. **75** D5
Dana Nepal **97** D3
Dana, Mount U.S.A. **182** E4
Danakil reg. Eritrea/Eth. see Denakil
Danané Côte d'Ivoire **124** C5
Đa Năng Vietnam **78** E4
formerly known as Tourane
Đa Năng, Vinh b. Vietnam **78** E4
Dananhu China **84** B3
Danao Phil. **74** B4
Danata Turkm. **102** C5
Danba China **86** B2
also known as Rongzhag or Zhangguo

Danbury CT U.S.A. 177 L4
Danbury NC U.S.A. 176 E9
Danbury NH U.S.A. 177 N2
Danbury WI U.S.A. 172 A4
Danby U.S.A. 177 M2
Danby Lake U.S.A. 183 I7
Dancheng China 87 E1
Dancheng China see Xiangshan
Dande r. Angola 127 B7
Dande Eth. 128 C3
Dandel'dhura Nepal 96 D3
Dandeli India 94 B3
Dando Angola 127 C7
Dandong China 83 B4
formerly known as Andong
Dandridge U.S.A. 174 D4
Danė r. Lith. 42 C6
Daneborg Greenland 165 Q2
Daneţi Romania 58 F5
Dänew Turkm. see Dyanev
Danfeng China 87 D1
also known as Longjuzhai
Danfeng China see Shizong
Dangan Liedao i. China 87 E4
Dangara Tajik. see Danghara
Dangbizhen Rus. Fed. 82 C3
Dangchang China 86 C1
Dangchengwan China see Subei
Dange Angola 127 B6
formerly known as Quitexe
Danger Islands atoll Cook Is see Pukapuka
Danger Point S. Africa 132 D11
Dangé-St-Romain France 50 G6
Danggali Conservation Park nature res. Australia 146 D3
Danghara Tajik. 101 G2
also spelt Dangara
Danghe Nanshan mts China 84 B4
Dangila Eth. 128 C2
Dangjin Shankou pass China 84 B4
Dangla Shan mts China see Tanggula Shan
Dan Gorayo Somalia 128 F2
Dangori India 97 G4
Dangqên China 89 E6
Dangriga Belize 185 H5
formerly known as Stann Creek
Dangshan China 87 F1
Dangtu China 87 F2
Dan-Gulbi Nigeria 125 G4
Dangur Eth. 128 B2
Dangur Mountains Eth. 128 B2
Dangyang China 87 D2
Daniel's Harbour Canada 169 J3
Daniëlskuil S. Africa 132 H5
Danielson U.S.A. 177 N4
Danielsrus S. Africa 133 M4
Danielsville U.S.A. 175 D5
Danilkovo Rus. Fed. 43 S2
Danilov Rus. Fed. 43 V3
Danilovgrad Crna Gora Yugo. 58 A6
Danilovka Kazakh. 103 G1
Danilovka Rus. Fed. 41 H6
Danilovskaya Vozvyshennost' hills Rus. Fed. 40 F4
Daning China 85 F4
Dänizkänarı Azer. 107 G2
Danjiang China see Leishan
Danjiangkou China 87 D1
formerly known as Junxian
Danjiangkou Shuiku resr China 87 D1
Danjo-guntō is Japan 91 A8
Dank Oman 105 G3
Dankalia prov. Eritrea 104 C5
Dankov Rus. Fed. 43 U8
Dankova, Pik mt. Kyrg. 103 I4
Danleng China 86 B2
Danlí Hond. 186 B4
Danmark Fjord inlet Greenland 165 Q1
English form Denmark Fjord
Dannebrog Ø i. Greenland see Qillak
Dannemora U.S.A. 177 L1
Dannenberg (Elbe) Germany 48 I2
Dannet well Niger 125 G2
Dannevirke N.Z. 152 K8
Dannhauser S. Africa 133 O5
Dan Sai Thai. 78 C4
Danshui Taiwan see Tanshui
Dansville U.S.A. 176 H3
Danta Gujarat India 96 B4
Danta Rajasthan India 89 A7
Dantewara India 94 D2
Dantu China 87 F1
also known as Zhenjiang

▶Danube r. Europe 58 J3
2nd longest river in Europe. Also spelt Donau (Austria/Germany) or Duna (Hungary) or Dunaj (Slovakia) or Dunărea (Romania) or Dunav (Bulgaria/Croatia/Yugoslavia) or Dunay (Ukraine).
europe [landscapes] ▶ 30–31

Danube Delta Romania 58 K3
also known as Dunării, Delta
Danubyu Myanmar 78 A4
Danumparai Indon. 77 F2
Danum Valley Conservation Area nature res. Sabah Malaysia 77 G1
Danville AR U.S.A. 179 D5
Danville IL U.S.A. 174 C3
Danville IN U.S.A. 174 C4
Danville KY U.S.A. 176 A8
Danville OH U.S.A. 176 C5
Danville VA U.S.A. 176 F9
Danville VT U.S.A. 177 M1
Danxian China see Danzhou
Danyang China 87 F2
Danzhai China 87 C3
also known as Longquan
Danzhou Guangxi China 87 D3
Danzhou Hainan China 87 D5
also known as Nada; formerly known as Danxian
Danzhou China see Yichuan
Danzig Poland see Gdańsk
Danzig, Gulf of Poland/Rus. Fed. see Gdańsk, Gulf of
Dao Phil. 74 B4
Dão r. Port. 54 C4
Daocheng China 86 B2
also known as Dabba or Jinzhu
Daojiang China see Daoxian
Daokou China see Huaxian
Daoshiping China 87 D2
Daotanghe China 84 D4
Dao Tay Sa is S. China Sea see Paracel Islands
Dao Timmi Niger 125 I1
Daoud Alg. see Aïn Beïda
Daoudi well Mauritania 124 D3
Daoukro Côte d'Ivoire 124 E5
Daoxian China 87 D3
also known as Daojiang
Daozhen China 87 C2
also known as Yuxi
Dapa Phil. 74 C4
Dapaong Togo 125 F4
Dapchi Nigeria 125 H3
Daphabum mt. India 97 H4
Daphnae tourist site Egypt 108 D7
also known as Kawm Dafanah
Daphne U.S.A. 175 C6
Dapiak, Mount Phil. 74 B4
Dapingdi China see Yanbian
Dapitan Phil. 74 B4
Daqahlīya governorate Egypt 108 C6
Da Qaidam Zhen China 84 B4
Daqiao China 86 B3
Daqing China 82 B3
also known as Anda; formerly known as Sartu
Daqing Shan mts China 85 F3
Daqin Tal China 85 I3
also known as Naiman Qi
Daqiu China 87 F3
Daqq-e Patargān salt flat Iran 101 E3
Daqq-e-Tundi, Dasht-e imp. l. Afgh. 101 E3
Daquan China 84 B3
Daquanwan China 84 B3
Dāqūq Iraq 107 F4
Daqu Shan i. China 87 G2
Dara Senegal 124 B3
formerly spelt Dahra
Dar'ā Syria 108 H5
Dar'ā governorate Syria 108 H5
Dâra, Gebel mt. Egypt 106 C6
Daraá r. Brazil 199 E5
Dārāb Iran 100 C4
Daraga Phil. 74 B3
Darahanava Belarus 43 J8
Daraim Afgh. 96 A1
Daraina Madag. 131 [inset] K2
Daraj Libya 120 A2
Daram i. Phil. 74 C4
Dārān Iran 100 B3
Đa Rāng, Sông r. Vietnam 79 E5
Darasun Rus. Fed. 85 G1
Daraut-Korgan Kyrg. see Daroot-Korgan
Đaravica mt. Yugo. 58 B6
Darazo Nigeria 125 H4
Darb Saudi Arabia 104 C4
Darband Iran 100 D4
Darband Uzbek. see Derbent
Darband, Kūh-e mt. Iran 100 D4
Darb-e Behesht Iran 100 D4
Darbėnai Lith. 42 C5
Dar Ben Karricha el Behri Morocco 54 F9
Darbhanga India 97 E4
Darcang China 86 A1
Dar Chabanne Tunisia 57 C12
Dar Chaoui Morocco 54 F9
D'Arcy Canada 166 F5
Darda Croatia 56 K3
Dardanelle AR U.S.A. 179 D5
Dardanelle CA U.S.A. 182 E3
Dardanelle, Lake U.S.A. 179 D5
Dardanelles strait Turkey 106 A2
also known as Çanakkale Boğazı; historically known as Hellespont
Dardo China see Kangding
Dar el Beida Morocco see Casablanca
Darende Turkey 107 D3

▶Dar es Salaam Tanz. 129 C6
Former capital of Tanzania.

Dārestān Iran 100 C4
Darfield N.Z. 153 G11
Darfo Boario Terme Italy 56 C3
Dargai Pak. 101 G3
Darganata Turkm. 103 E4
Dargaville N.Z. 152 H3
Dargin, Jezioro l. Poland 49 S1
Dargo Australia 147 E4
Darhan Mongolia 85 E1
Darhan Muminggan Lianheqi China see Bailingmiao
Darica Turkey 58 K8
Darıcı Turkey 59 J9
Darien CT U.S.A. 177 L4
Darien GA U.S.A. 175 D6
Darién, Golfo del g. Col. 198 B2
Darién, Parque Nacional de nat. park Panama 186 D6
Darién, Serranía del mts Panama 186 D5
Dar'inskiy Kazakh. 103 H2
also known as Dariya
Dar'inskoye Kazakh. 102 B2
Darío Nicaragua 186 B4
Dariya Kazakh. see Dar'inskiy
Dariz Oman 105 G3
Darjeeling India 97 F4
also spelt Darjiling
Darjiling India see Darjeeling
Dārkhovīn Iran 100 B4
Darlag China 86 A1
also known as Gyümai

▶Darling r. Australia 147 D3
2nd longest river in Oceania. Part of the longest (Murray-Darling).
oceania [landscapes] ▶ 136–137

Darling S. Africa 132 C10
Darling Downs hills Australia 147 F1
Darling Range hills Australia 151 A7
Darlington U.K. 47 K9
Darlington SC U.S.A. 175 E5
Darlington WI U.S.A. 172 C8
Darlington Dam resr S. Africa 133 J10
Darlington Point Australia 147 E3
Darlot, Lake salt flat Australia 151 C5
Darłowo Poland 49 N1
Dărmănești Romania 58 H2
Darma Pass China/India 89 C6
Darmaraopet India 94 C2
Darmstadt Germany 48 F6
Darna r. India 94 B1
Darnah Libya 120 D1
also spelt Derna
Darnall S. Africa 133 P6
Darnick Australia 147 D3
Darnley, Cape Antarctica 223 E2
Darnley Bay Canada 164 G3
Daroca Spain 55 J3
Daroot-Korgan Kyrg. 103 H5
also spelt Daraut-Kurgan
Darovskoy Rus. Fed. 40 H4
Dar Pahn Iran 100 D5
Darr watercourse Australia 149 D4
Darregueira Arg. 204 E5
Darreh Bid Iran 100 D3
Darreh Gaz Iran 101 D2
also known as Mohammadābād
Darreh Gozaru r. Iran see Gīzeh Rūd
Darreh-ye Bāhābād Iran 100 C4
Darreh-ye Shahr Iran 100 A3
Darreh-ye Shekārī r. Afgh. 101 G3
Darreh-ye Shekārī r. Afgh. 101 G3
Darro watercourse Eth. 128 D3
Darsa i. Yemen 105 F5
Darsi India 94 C3
Darß pen. Germany 49 J1
Darßer Ort c. Germany 49 J1
Darta Turkm. 102 C4
formerly known as Kianly; formerly spelt Tarta
Dar Ta'izzah Syria 109 H1
Dartang China see Baqên
Dartford U.K. 47 M12
Dartmoor Australia 146 D4
Dartmoor hills U.K. 47 H13
Dartmoor National Park U.K. 47 I13
Dartmouth Canada 169 I4
Dartmouth U.K. 47 I13
Dartmouth, Lake salt flat Australia 149 E5
Dartmouth Reservoir Australia 147 E4
Daru P.N.G. 73 J8
Daru waterhole Sudan 121 G5
Daruba Indon. 75 D2
Daruvar Croatia 56 J3
Darvaza Turkm. 102 D4
also spelt Derweze
Darvi Mongolia 84 B2
Darvi Mongolia see Bulgan
Darvinskiy Gosudarstvennyy Zapovednik nature res. Rus. Fed. 43 S3
Darvoz, Qatorkŭhi mts Tajik. 101 G2
Darwendale Zimbabwe 131 F3
Darwha India 94 C1

▶Darwin Australia 148 A2
Capital of the Northern Territory. Historically known as Palmerston.

Darwin Falkland Is 205 F8
Darwin, Canal sea chan. Chile 205 B7
Darwin, Monte mt. Chile 205 C9
Darya Khan Pak. 101 G4
Dar'yalyktakyr, Ravnina plain Kazakh. 103 F3
Daryānah Libya 120 D1
Dar"yoi Amu r. Asia see Amudar'ya
Dar"yoi Sir r. Asia see Syrdar'ya
Dārzīn Iran 100 D4
Dās i. U.A.E. 105 F2
Dasada India 96 A5
Dasha r. China 85 G4
Dashbalbar Mongolia 85 G1
Dashhowuz Turkm. see Dashkhovuz
Dashiqiao China 85 I3
formerly known as Yingkou
Dashitou China 88 E3
Dashizhai China 85 I2
Dashkawka Belarus 43 L8
Dashkesan Azer. see Daşkäsän
Dashkhovuz Turkm. 102 D4
also known as Dashoguz; also spelt Dashhowuz; formerly known as Tashauz
Dashkhovuz Oblast admin. div. Turkm. see Dashkhovuzskaya Oblast'
Dashkhovuzskaya Oblast' admin. div. Turkm. 102 D4
English form Dashkhovuz Oblast; formerly known as Tashauzskaya Oblast'
Dashköpri Turkm. see Tashkepri
Dashoguz Turkm. see Dashkhovuz
Dasht Iran 100 D2
Dasht r. Pak. 101 E5
Dashtak Qalehsi Iran 100 D2
formerly spelt Dashtak Qal'ehsi
Dashtak Qal'ehsi Iran see Dashtak Qalehsi
Dasht-e Bar Iran 100 D4
Dasht-e Palang r. Iran 100 C4
Dashtiari Iran 101 E5
Dashuikeng China 85 E4
Dashuiqiao China 84 C4
Dashuitou China 84 E4
Daska Pak. 101 H3
Daşkäsän Azer. 107 F2
also spelt Dashkesan
Daskop S. Africa 132 G10
Dasongshu China 86 C3
Daspar mt. Pak. 101 H2
Dassa Benin 125 F5
Dassalan i. Phil. 74 B5
Dassen Island S. Africa 132 C10
Dastakān, Ra's-e pt Iran 100 C5
Da Suifen He r. China 82 C4
Dasuya India 96 B3
Dasville S. Africa 133 M3
Datadian Indon. 77 F2
Datça Turkey 106 A3
Date Japan 90 G3
Date Creek watercourse U.S.A. 183 K7
Dateland U.S.A. 183 K9
Datha India 96 B5
Datia India 96 C4
Datian China 87 F3
also known as Junxi
Datian Ding mt. China 87 D4
Datong China see Tong'an
Datong Heilong. China 82 B3
Datong Qinghai China 84 D4
also known as Qiaotou
Datong Shanxi China 85 G3
Datong He r. China 84 D4
Datong Shan mts China 84 C4
Datta Rus. Fed. 82 F2
Datu i. Indon. 77 E2
Datu, Tanjung c. Indon./Malaysia 77 E2
Datuk, Tanjung pt Indon. 76 C3
Datu Piang Phil. 74 C5
also known as Dulawan
Daudkandi Bangl. 97 F5
Daud Khel Pak. 101 G3
Daudnagar India 97 E4
Daudzeva Latvia 42 G5
Daugai Lith. 42 F7
Daugailiai Lith. 42 G6
Daugava r. Latvia 42 F4
Daugavpils Latvia 42 H6
also known as Dvinsk; formerly known as Dünaburg
Daugyvenė r. Lith. 42 E5
Daulatabad Afgh. 101 F2
Daulatabad Iran see Malāyer
Daulatpur Bangl. 97 F5
Daule Ecuador 198 B5
Daun Germany 48 D5
Daund India 94 B2
Daung Kyun i. Myanmar 79 B5
also known as Ross Island
Daungyu r. Myanmar 78 A3
Dauphin Canada 167 K5
Dauphiné reg. France 51 L7
Dauphiné, Alpes du mts France 51 L8
Dauphin Island U.S.A. 175 B6
Dauphin Lake Canada 167 L5
Daura Nigeria 125 H3
Daurie Creek r. Australia 151 A5
Dauriya Rus. Fed. 85 H1
Daurskiy Khrebet mts Rus. Fed. 85 F1
Dausa India 96 C4
Dâu Tiêng, Hô resr Vietnam 79 D6
Däväçi Azer. 107 G2
also spelt Divichi
Davangere India 94 B3
Davao Phil. 74 C5
Davao Gulf Phil. 74 C5
Dāvarān Iran 100 D4
Dāvar Panāh Iran 101 E5
also known as Sarāvān
Davel S. Africa 133 N3
Davenport IA U.S.A. 174 B3
Davenport NY U.S.A. 177 K3
Davenport WA U.S.A. 180 C3
Davenport Downs Australia 149 D5
Davenport Range hills Australia 148 B4
Daveyton S. Africa 133 M3
David Panama 186 C5
David City U.S.A. 178 C3
Davidson Canada 167 J5
Davidson, Mount hill Australia 148 A4
Davidson Lake Canada 167 L4
Davies, Mount Australia 146 A1
Davinópolis Brazil 206 F5
Davis research station Antarctica 223 F2
Davis r. Australia 150 C4
Davis i. Myanmar see Than Kyun
Davis CA U.S.A. 182 C3
Davis WV U.S.A. 176 F6
Davis, Mount hill U.S.A. 176 F6
Davis Bay Antarctica 223 I2
Davis Dam U.S.A. 183 J6
Davis Dam dam U.S.A. 183 J6
Davis Inlet Canada 169 I2
Davison U.S.A. 173 J7
Davis Sea Antarctica 223 G2
Davis Strait Canada/Greenland 165 N3
Davlekanovo Rus. Fed. 40 J5
Davlia Greece 59 D10
also spelt Dhávlia
Davos Switz. 51 P6
Davutlar Turkey 59 I11
Davy U.S.A. 176 D8
Davyd-Haradok Belarus 42 I9
Davydkovo Rus. Fed. see Tolbukhino
Davydovo Rus. Fed. 43 T4
Davy Lake Canada 167 I3
Dawa China 85 I3
Dawa Co l. China 89 D6
Dawāsir reg. Saudi Arabia 104 D3
Dawāsir, Wādī ad watercourse Saudi Arabia 104 D3
Dawa Wenz r. Eth. 128 D3
Dawaxung China 89 D6
Dawê China 86 B2
Dawei Myanmar see Tavoy
Dawei b. Myanmar see Tavoy
Dawen r. China 85 H5
Dawera i. Indon. 75 D4
Dawhat Bilbul b. Saudi Arabia 105 E2
Dawhinava Belarus 42 I7
Dawna Range mts Myanmar/Thai. 78 B4
Dawqah Oman 105 F4
Dawqah Saudi Arabia 104 C4
Dawrān Yemen 104 D5
Dawson r. Australia 149 F4
Dawson Canada 166 B1
Dawson GA U.S.A. 175 C6
Dawson ND U.S.A. 180 H3
Dawson, Isla i. Chile 205 C9
Dawson, Mount Canada 167 G5
Dawson Bay Canada 167 K4
Dawson Creek Canada 166 F4
Dawson Inlet Canada 167 M2
Dawson Range mts Canada 166 A2
Dawsons Landing Canada 166 E5
Dawu Hubei China 87 E2
Dawu China see Maqên
Dawu Sichuan China 86 B2
also known as Xianshui
Dawu Taiwan see Tawu
Dawukou China see Shizuishan
Dawu Shan hill China 87 E2
Dawwah Oman 105 G3
Dax France 50 E9
Daxian China see Dazhou
Daxiang Ling mts China 86 B2
Daxihaizi Shuiku l. China 88 D3
Daxin China 87 C4
also known as Taocheng
Daxing China see Ninglang
Daxing China see Lüchun
Daxue China see Wencheng
Daxue Shan mts China 86 B2
Dayan China see Lijiang
Dayang r. China 85 I4
Dayangshu China 85 J1
Dayan Nuur l. Mongolia 84 A1
Dayao China 86 B3
also known as Jinbi
Dayao Shan mts China 87 D4
Dâyat en Nahârât well Mali 124 E2
Daye China 87 E2
Dayi China 86 B2
also known as Jinyuan
Daying Jiang r. China 86 A3
Dayishan China see Guanyun
Daylesford Australia 147 E4
Dayong China 87 D2
formerly known as Zhangjiajie
Dayr Abū Sa'īd Jordan 108 G5
Dayr az Zawr Syria 109 L2
also spelt Deir-ez-Zor
Dayr az Zawr governorate Syria 109 L2
Dayr Ḩāfir Syria 109 I1
Daysland Canada 167 H4
Dayton OH U.S.A. 176 A6
Dayton TN U.S.A. 174 C5
Dayton TX U.S.A. 179 D6
Dayton VA U.S.A. 176 G7
Dayton WA U.S.A. 180 C3
Daytona Beach U.S.A. 175 D6
Dayu China 87 E3
also known as Nan'ao
Dayu Indon. 77 F3
Dayu Ling mts China 87 E3
Da Yunhe canal China 87 F1
English form Grand Canal
Dayyina i. U.A.E. 105 F2
Dazaifu Japan 91 B8
Dazhe China see Pingyuan
Dazhongji China see Dafeng
Dazhou China 87 C2
formerly known as Daxian
Dazhou Dao i. China 87 D5
Dazhu China 87 C2
also known as Zhuyang
Dazu China 86 C2
also known as Longgang
De Aar S. Africa 132 I7
Dead r. U.S.A. 172 F4
Deadman's Cay Bahamas 187 E2
Dead Mountains U.S.A. 183 J7

▶Dead Sea salt l. Asia 98 B3
Lowest point in the world and in Asia. Also known as Bahrat Lut or HaMelah, Yam.

Deadwood U.S.A. 178 B2
Deakin Australia 151 E6
Deal U.K. 47 N12
Dealesville S. Africa 133 J5
Dean r. Canada 166 E4
De'an China 87 E2
also known as Puting
Dean Channel Canada 166 E4
Deán Funes Arg. 204 D3
Deanuvuotna inlet Norway see Tanafjorden
Dearborn U.S.A. 173 J8
Dease r. B.C. Canada 166 D3
Dease r. N.W.T. Canada 167 G1
Dease Arm b. Canada 166 F1
Dease Lake Canada 166 D3
Dease Lake l. Canada 166 D3
Dease Strait Canada 165 I3
Death Valley U.S.A. 183 H5

▶Death Valley depr. U.S.A. 183 G5
Lowest point in the Americas.
northamerica [landscapes] ▶ 156–157

Death Valley Junction U.S.A. 183 H5
Death Valley National Park U.S.A. 183 G5
Deaver U.S.A. 180 E3
Debagram India 97 F5
Debak Sarawak Malaysia 77 E2
Debao China 86 C4
Debar Macedonia 58 B7
Debark Eth. 128 C1
Debay well Yemen 105 E4
Debden Canada 167 J4
De Beers Pass S. Africa 133 N5
Debert Canada 169 I4
Debesy Rus. Fed. 40 J4
Dębica Poland 49 S5
De Biesbosch, Nationaal Park nat. park Neth. 48 B4
Debila Alg. 123 G2
Debin Rus. Fed. 39 P3
Dęblin Poland 49 S4
Dębno Poland 49 L3
Débo, Lac l. Mali 124 D3
Deborah East, Lake salt flat Australia 151 B6
Deborah West, Lake salt flat Australia 151 B6
Deboyne Islands P.N.G. 149 G1
Debre Birhan Eth. 128 C2
Debrecen Hungary 49 S8
Debre Markos Eth. 128 C2
Debre Sina Eth. 128 C2
Debre Tabor Eth. 128 C2
Debre Werk' Eth. 128 C2
Debre Zeyit Eth. 128 C2
Debrzno Poland 49 O2
Deçan Kosovo, Srbija Yugo. see Dečani
Dečani Kosovo, Srbija Yugo. 58 B6
also spelt Deçan
Decatur AL U.S.A. 174 C5
Decatur GA U.S.A. 175 C5
Decatur IL U.S.A. 174 B4
Decatur IN U.S.A. 176 A5
Decatur MI U.S.A. 172 H8
Decatur MS U.S.A. 175 B5
Decatur TN U.S.A. 174 C5
Decatur TX U.S.A. 179 C5
Decazeville France 51 I8

▶Deccan plat. India 94 C2
Plateau making up most of southern and central India.

Deception watercourse Botswana 130 E4
Deception Bay Australia 147 G1
Dechang China 86 B3
also known as Dezhou
Decheng China see Deqing
Děčín Czech Rep. 49 L5
Decize France 51 J6
Decorah U.S.A. 174 B3
Dedap i. Indon. see Penasi, Pulau
Dedaye Myanmar 78 A4
Dedebağı Turkey 59 K11
Dedegöl Dağları mts Turkey 106 B3
Deder Eth. 128 D2
Dedinovo Rus. Fed. 43 U6
Dedo de Deus mt. Brazil 206 F11
Dedop'listsqaro Georgia 107 F2
formerly known as Tsiteli Tskaro
Dédougou Burkina 124 E3
Dedovichi Rus. Fed. 43 K4
Dedu China 82 B2
also known as Qingshan
Dedurovka Rus. Fed. 102 C2
Dedza Malawi 129 B8
Dedza Mountain Malawi 131 G2
Dee r. England/Wales U.K. 47 I10
Dee r. Scotland U.K. 46 J6
Deeg India 96 C4
Deelfontein S. Africa 132 H7
Deep Bay Hong Kong China 87 [inset]
also known as Shenzhen Wan
Deep Bight inlet Australia 150 D2
Deep Creek Lake U.S.A. 176 F6
Deep Creek Range mts U.S.A. 183 K2
Deep Gap U.S.A. 176 D9
Deep River Canada 168 E4
Deep River U.S.A. 177 M4
Deer Creek r. U.S.A. 182 B2
Deer Creek Reservoir U.S.A. 183 M1
Deeri Somalia 128 E3
Deering, Mount Australia 151 E5
Deer Island Canada 169 H4
Deer Island AK U.S.A. 164 C4
Deer Island ME U.S.A. 177 Q1
Deer Isle U.S.A. 177 Q1
Deer Lake Nfld. Canada 169 J3
Deer Lake Ont. Canada 167 M4
Deer Lake l. Canada 167 M4
Deer Lodge U.S.A. 180 D3
Deer Park U.S.A. 180 C3
Deerpass Bay Canada 166 F1
Deesa India see Disa
Defeng China see Liping
Defensores del Chaco, Parque Nacional nat. park Para. 201 E5
Defiance U.S.A. 176 A4
Defiance Plateau U.S.A. 183 O6
Défirou well Niger 125 I1
De Funiak Springs U.S.A. 175 C6
Degana India 96 B4
Degano r. Italy 56 E2
Dêgê China 86 A2
also known as Gengqing
Degebe r. Port. 54 D6
Degeberga Sweden 45 K5
Degeh Bur Eth. 128 D2
Dégelis Canada 169 G4
formerly known as Ste-Rose-du-Dégelé
Degema Nigeria 125 G5
Degerfors Sweden 45 K4
Deggendorf Germany 49 J7
Degh r. Pak. 101 H4
Değirmencik r. Turkey 59 J9
Değirmenlik Cyprus see Kythrea
Degodia reg. Eth. 128 D3
De Grey Australia 150 B4
De Grey r. Australia 150 B4
Degtevo Rus. Fed. 41 G6
Degtyarevka Rus. Fed. 43 N8
Dehaj Iran 100 C4
Dehak Iran 101 E5
Dehalak Deset i. Eritrea 121 I6
Deh Bakrī Iran 100 D4
Deh Barez Iran see Fāryāb
Deh Bīd Iran 100 C4
Deh-Dasht Iran 100 B4
Dehdez Iran 100 B4
Dehej India 96 B5
Deh-e Khalīfeh Iran 100 B4
Deh-e Kohneh Iran 100 B4
Dehel Island Eritrea 104 B5
Dehgāh Iran 100 B2
Deh Golān Iran 100 A3
Dehi Afgh. 101 F3
Deh Khvājeh Iran 100 C4
Dehkūyeh Iran 100 C5
Dehloran Iran 100 A3
Deh Mollā Iran 100 C3
De Hoge Veluwe, Nationaal Park nat. park Neth. 48 C3
De Hoop Nature Reserve S. Africa 132 E11
De Hoop Vlei l. S. Africa 132 E11
Dehqonobod Uzbek. see Dekhkanabad
Dehra Dun India 96 C3
Dehri India 97 E4
Deh Shū Afgh. 101 E4
Dehua China 87 F3
also known as Longxun
Dehui China 82 B3
Deim Zubeir Sudan 126 E3
Deinze Belgium 51 J2
Deïr el Qamar Lebanon 108 G4
Deir-ez-Zor Syria see Dayr az Zawr
Dej Romania 58 E1
Dejë, Mal mt. Albania 58 B7
Dejen Eth. 128 C2
Deji China see Rinbung
Dejiang China 87 D2
also known as Jiangsi
Deka Drum Zimbabwe 131 E3
De Kalb IL U.S.A. 174 B3
De Kalb MS U.S.A. 175 B5
De Kalb TX U.S.A. 179 D5
De Kalb Junction U.S.A. 177 J1
De-Kastri Rus. Fed. 81 O2
Dekemhare Eritrea 121 H6
Dekese Dem. Rep. Congo 126 D5
Dekhkanabad Uzbek. 103 F5
also spelt Dehqonobod
Dékoa Cent. Afr. Rep. 126 C3
Delaki Indon. 75 C5
Delamar Lake U.S.A. 183 J4
Delami Sudan 128 A2
De Land U.S.A. 175 D6
Delano U.S.A. 182 E6
Delano Peak U.S.A. 183 L3

▶Delap-Uliga-Djarrit Marshall Is 220 F5
Capital of the Marshall Islands, on Majuro atoll. Also spelt Dalap-Uliga-Darrit or Djarrit-Uliga-Dalap.

Delārām Afgh. 101 E3
Delareyville S. Africa 133 J3
Delaronde Lake Canada 167 J4
Delavan U.S.A. 172 E8
Delaware U.S.A. 176 B5
Delaware r. KS U.S.A. 178 D4
Delaware r. NJ/PA U.S.A. 177 J6
Delaware state U.S.A. 177 J7
Delaware, East Branch r. U.S.A. 177 J4
Delaware, West Branch r. U.S.A. 177 J4
Delaware Bay U.S.A. 177 J6
Delaware City U.S.A. 177 J6
Delaware Water Gap National Recreational Area park U.S.A. 177 K4
Delay r. Canada 169 G1
Delbarton U.S.A. 176 C8
Delbeng Sudan 126 F3
Del Bonita Canada 167 H5
Delburne Canada 167 H4
Delčevo Macedonia 58 D7
Delegate Australia 147 F4
Delémont Switz. 51 N5
Delevan CA U.S.A. 182 B2
Delevan NY U.S.A. 176 G3
Delfinópolis Brazil 206 G7
Delft Neth. 48 B3
Delft Island Sri Lanka 94 C4
Delfzijl Neth. 48 D2
Delgado, Cabo c. Moz. 129 D7
Delgermörön Mongolia 84 C2
Delger Mörön r. Mongolia 84 D1
Delgo Sudan 121 F4
Delhi Canada 173 M8
Delhi China 84 C4
formerly known as Delingha

▶Delhi India 96 C3
world [cities] ▶ 24–25

Delhi admin. div. India 89 B6
Delhi CA U.S.A. 182 D4
Delhi LA U.S.A. 175 B5
Delhi NY U.S.A. 177 K3
Deli i. Indon. 77 D4
Deli r. Turkey 107 C3
Delice Turkey 106 C3
Delice r. Turkey 106 C2
Délices Fr. Guiana 199 H3
Delījān Iran 100 B3
Deliktaş Turkey 59 H10
Déline Canada 166 F1
formerly known as Fort Franklin
Delingha China see Delhi
Delisle Canada 167 J5
Delitua Indon. 76 B2
Delitzsch Germany 49 J4
Dell Rapids U.S.A. 178 C3
Dellys Alg. 123 F1
Del Mar U.S.A. 183 G9
Delmar DE U.S.A. 177 J7
Delmar IA U.S.A. 172 C8
Delmas S. Africa 133 M3
Delmenhorst Germany 48 F2
Delmont U.S.A. 176 F5
Delmore Downs Australia 148 B4
Delnice Croatia 56 G3
Del Norte U.S.A. 181 F5
Delong China 86 C4
De-Longa, Ostrova is Rus. Fed. 39 P2
English form De Long Islands
De Long Islands Rus. Fed. see De-Longa, Ostrova
De Long Mountains U.S.A. 164 C3
De Long Strait Rus. Fed. see Longa, Proliv
Deloraine Australia 147 E5
Deloraine Canada 167 K5
Delphi tourist site Greece 59 D10
Delphi U.S.A. 174 C3
Delphos U.S.A. 176 A5
Delportshoop S. Africa 133 I5
Delray Beach U.S.A. 175 D7
Del Rio Mex. 184 C2
Del Rio U.S.A. 179 B6
Delsbo Sweden 45 L3
Delta state Nigeria 125 G5
Delta CO U.S.A. 181 E5
Delta OH U.S.A. 176 A4
Delta UT U.S.A. 183 L2
Delta Amacuro state Venez. 199 F2
Delta du Saloum, Parc National du nat. park Senegal 124 A3
Delta Junction U.S.A. 164 E3
Delta National Wildlife Refuge nature res. U.S.A. 175 B6
Delta Reservoir U.S.A. 177 J2
Deltona U.S.A. 175 D6
Delungra Australia 147 F2
Delvada India 94 A1
Delvinë Albania 59 B9
Dema r. Rus. Fed. 102 C1
Demak Indon. 77 E4
Demavend mt. Iran see Damāvand, Qolleh-ye
Demba Dem. Rep. Congo 127 D6
Dembava Lith. 42 F6
Dembia Cent. Afr. Rep. 126 E3
Dembi Dolo Eth. 128 B2
Demerara Guyana see Georgetown
Demidov Rus. Fed. 43 M6
Deming U.S.A. 181 F6
Demini r. Brazil 199 F5
Demini, Serras do mts Brazil 199 F4
Demirci Turkey 106 B3
Demir Hisar Macedonia 58 C7
Demirköprü Barajı resr Turkey 106 B3
Demirköy Turkey 58 I7
Demirler r. Turkey 59 K10
Demistkraal S. Africa 133 I10
Demmin Germany 49 K2
Democracia Brazil 199 F6
Demopolis U.S.A. 175 C5
Dempo, Gunung vol. Indon. 76 C4
Dempster Highway Canada 166 B1
Dêmqog Jammu and Kashmir 96 C2
Demyakhi Rus. Fed. 43 N6
Dem'yanovo Rus. Fed. 40 H3
Demyansk Rus. Fed. 43 N4
De Naawte S. Africa 132 F7
Denair U.S.A. 182 D4
Denakil reg. Eritrea/Eth. 121 I6
also spelt Danakil
Denali National Park and Preserve U.S.A. 164 D3
formerly known as Mount McKinley National Park
Denan Eth. 128 D3
Denare Beach Canada 167 K4
Denau Uzbek. 103 F5
also spelt Denow
Denbigh Canada 168 E4
Denbigh U.K. 47 I10
also spelt Dinbych
Den Bosch Neth. see 's-Hertogenbosch
Den Burg Neth. 48 B2
Den Chai Thai. 78 C4
Dendang Indon. 77 D3
Dendâra Mauritania 124 D2
Dendermonde Belgium 51 K1
also known as Termonde
Đeneral Janković Kosovo, Srbija Yugo. 58 C6
also spelt Djeneral Jankovič
Denezhkin Kamen', Gora mt. Rus. Fed. 40 K3
Dengas Niger 125 H3
Denge Nigeria 125 G3
Dengfeng China 87 E1
Dênggar China 89 D6
Dengjiabu China see Yujiang
Dêngka China see Têwo
Dêngkagoin China see Têwo
Dengkou China 85 E3
also known as Bayan Gol
Dêngqên China 97 G3
also known as Gyamotang
Dengta China 87 E4
Denguiro Cent. Afr. Rep. 126 D3
Dengxian China see Dengzhou
Dengzhou China 87 E1
formerly known as Dengxian
Dengzhou China see Penglai
Den Haag Neth. see The Hague
Denham Australia 151 A5
Denham r. Australia 150 E2
Denham Range mts Australia 149 F4
Denham Sound sea chan. Australia 151 A5
Den Helder Neth. 48 B3
Denholm Canada 167 I4
Denia Spain 55 L6

Denial Bay Australia 146 B3
Deniliquin Australia 147 E3
Deniskovichi Rus. Fed. 43 M9
Denison *IA* U.S.A. 178 D3
Denison *TX* U.S.A. 179 C5
Denison, Cape Antarctica 223 J2
Denison Plains Australia 150 E3
Denisovka Kazakh. see Ordzhonikidze
Denizli Turkey 106 B3
historically known as Laodicea *or* Laodicea
ad Lycum
Denizli *prov.* Turkey 59 K11
Denman Australia 147 F3
Denman Glacier Antarctica 223 G2
Denmark Australia 151 B7
▶Denmark *country* Europe 45 J5
europe [countries] ▶▶ 32–35
Denmark U.S.A. 172 F6
Denmark Fjord *inlet* Greenland *see*
Danmark Fjord
Denmark Strait Greenland/Iceland 165 Q3
Dennilton S. Africa 133 N2
Dennis, Lake *salt flat* Australia 150 E4
Dennison U.S.A. 176 D5
Dennisville U.S.A. 177 K6
Denow Uzbek. see Denau
Denpasar Indon. 77 F5
Densongi Indon. 75 B3
Denton *MD* U.S.A. 177 J7
Denton *TX* U.S.A. 179 C5
D'Entrecasteaux, Point Australia 151 A7
D'Entrecasteaux, Récifs *reef*
New Caledonia 145 F3
D'Entrecasteaux Islands P.N.G. 145 E2
D'Entrecasteaux National Park Australia
151 A7
Dents du Midi *mt.* Switz. 51 M6
▶Denver U.S.A. 180 E5
State capital of Colorado.
Denys *r.* Canada 168 E2
Deo India 97 F4
Deoband India 96 C3
Deobhog India 95 D2
Deogarh *Orissa* India 97 E5
Deogarh *Rajasthan* India 96 B4
Deogarh *mt.* India 97 D5
Deoghar India 97 E4
also spelt Devghar
Deoli India 94 C4
Déols France 50 H6
Deori India 96 C5
Deoria India 97 D4
Deosai, Plains of Jammu and Kashmir
96 B2
Dep *r.* Rus. Fed. 82 B1
Depalpur India 96 B5
De Pas, Rivière *r.* Canada 169 H2
De Pere U.S.A. 172 E6
Depew U.S.A. 176 G3
Deposit U.S.A. 177 J3
Depot-Forbes Canada 173 Q3
Depot-Rowanton Canada 173 P4
Depsang Point *hill* Aksai Chin 89 B5
Depue U.S.A. 172 D9
Deputatskiy Rus. Fed. 39 N3
Dêqên *Xizang* China 89 E6
Dêqên *Xizang* China 89 E6
Dêqên China *see* Dagzê
Dêqên *Yunnan* China 86 A2
also spelt Deqin
Deqing *Guangdong* China 87 D4
also known as Dechang
Deqing *Zhejiang* China 87 G2
De Queen U.S.A. 179 D5
De Quincy U.S.A. 179 D6
Der, Lac du *l.* France 51 K4
Dera India 96 C4
Dera Bugti Pak. 101 G4
Dera Ghazi Khan Pak. 101 G4
Deraheib *reg.* Sudan 121 G4
Dera Ismail Khan Pak. 101 G4
Derajat *reg.* Pak. 101 G4
Deram, Mount Antarctica 223 C2
Derbent Rus. Fed. 102 B4
Derbent Uzbek. 103 F5
formerly spelt Darband
Derbisiye Turkey *see* Şenyurt
Derby Australia 150 C3
Derby S. Africa 133 L2
Derby U.K. 47 K11
Derby *CT* U.S.A. 177 L4
Derby *KS* U.S.A. 178 C4
formerly known as El Paso
Derby Line U.S.A. 177 M1
Dereeske Hungary 49 S8
Dereköy Turkey 108 D1
Dereköy Turkey 59 K11
Dereva Rus. Fed. 43 P5
Derg, Lough *l.* Rep. of Ireland 47 D11
Dergachi Rus. Fed. 102 B2
Dergachi Ukr. *see* Derhachi
Dergholm State Park *nature res.* Australia
146 D4
Derhachi Ukr. 41 F6
also spelt Dergachi
De Ridder U.S.A. 179 D6
Derik Turkey 107 E3
Derinkuyu Turkey 106 C3
Derkali *well* Kenya 128 D4
Derna Libya *see* Darnah
Dêrong China 86 A2
also known as Songmai
Derow Iran 102 B5
Derre Moz. 131 H3
Derry U.K. *see* Londonderry
Derry U.S.A. 177 N3
Derryveagh Mountains *hills* Rep. of Ireland
47 D9
Derstei China 84 D3
Dêrub China *see* Rutog
Derudeb Sudan 121 H5
De Rust S. Africa 132 G10

Deruta Italy 56 E6
Derventa Bos.-Herz. 56 J4
Derwent *r.* Australia 147 E5
Derwent *r. Derbyshire, England* U.K. 47 K11
Derwent *r. England* U.K. 47 L10
Derweze Turkm. see Darvaza
Deryugino Rus. Fed. 43 Q9
Derza *r.* Rus. Fed. 43 P5
Derzhavino Rus. Fed. 102 C1
Derzhavinsk Kazakh. 103 F2
formerly known as Derzhavinskiy
Derzhavinskiy Kazakh. *see* Derzhavinsk
Desa Romania 58 E5
Desaguadero *r.* Arg. 204 D4
Desaguadero *r.* Bol. 200 C4
Désappointement, Îles du *is* Fr. Polynesia
221 I6
English form Disappointment Islands
Des Arc U.S.A. 174 B5
Desatoya Mountains U.S.A. 182 G2
Desbarats Canada 173 J4
Descalvado Brazil 201 F4
Descalvado *São Paulo* Brazil 206 F8
Descartes France 50 G6
Deschambault Lake Canada 167 K4
Deschambault Lake *l.* Canada 167 K4
Deschutes *r.* U.S.A. 170 B2
Desē Eth. 128 C2
formerly spelt Dessye
Deseado Chile 200 C5
Deseado Arg. 205 D7
Deseado *r.* Arg. 205 D7
Desemboque Del Granma National Park
tourist site Cuba 186 D3
Desemboque Mex. 184 B2
Desengaño, Punta *pt* Arg. 205 D8
Deseret India 94 C2
Deseret Peak U.S.A. 183 L1
Deseronto Canada 173 P6
Désert, Lac *l.* Canada 173 Q5
Desertas *is* Madeira 122 A2
Desert Canal Pak. 101 G4
Desert Center U.S.A. 183 I8
Desert Hot Springs U.S.A. 183 H8
Desert Lake U.S.A. 183 I3
Desert National Wildlife Refuge
nature res. U.S.A. 183 I5
Desert View U.S.A. 183 M5
Deshler U.S.A. 176 B4
Deshnok India 96 B3
Desiderio Tello *Arg.* 204 D3
Desierto Central de Baja California,
Parque Natural del *nature res.* Mex.
184 B2
Desierto de Sechura *des.* Peru 198 A6
Deskati Greece 59 C9
also spelt Dheskáti
De Smet U.S.A. 178 C2
▶Des Moines *IA* U.S.A. 178 B4
State capital of Iowa.
Des Moines *NM* U.S.A. 178 B4
Des Moines *r.* U.S.A. 178 D2
Desna *r.* Rus. Fed./Ukr. 41 D6
Desnăţui *r.* Romania 58 E5
Desnogorsk Rus. Fed. 43 O7
Desnogorskoye Vodokhranilishche *resr*
Rus. Fed. 43 O7
Desnudo, Cerro *mt.* Arg. 205 C7
Desolación, Isla *i.* Chile 205 B9
Desolation Point Phil. 74 C4
DeSoto U.S.A. 172 B7
Despatch S. Africa 133 J10
Despen Rus. Fed. 84 B1
Des Plaines U.S.A. 172 F8
Despotovac Srbija Yugo. 58 C4
Dessau Germany 49 J4
Destor Canada 173 O2
D'Estrees Bay Australia 146 C3
Destruction Bay Canada 166 B2
Desvres France 51 H2
Deta Romania 58 C3
Detah Canada 167 H2
Detchino Rus. Fed. 43 R7
Dete Zimbabwe 131 E3
formerly spelt Dett
De Teut Natuurreservaat *nature res.*
Belgium 51 L2
Deti Jon *b.* Albania/Greece 59 A8
Đetinja *r.* Yugo. 58 B5
Detmold Germany 48 F4
Detour, Point U.S.A. 172 G5
De Tour Village U.S.A. 173 J5
Detrital Wash *watercourse* U.S.A. 183 J5
Detroit U.S.A. 173 J8
Detroit Lakes U.S.A. 178 D2
Dett Zimbabwe *see* Dete
Detva Slovakia 49 Q7
Deua National Park Australia 147 F3
Deurne Neth. 48 E4
Deutschland *country* Europe *see* Germany
Deutschlandsberg Austria 49 M9
Deutsch-Luxemburgischer Naturpark
nature res. Germany 48 E6
Deux-Rivières Canada 173 O4
Deva Romania 58 D3
Deva U.K. *see* Chester
Devadurga India 94 C2
Devakottai India 94 C4
Devana U.K. *see* Aberdeen
Devanhalli India 94 C3
Devarkonda India 94 C2
Deve Bair *pass* Macedonia *see*
Velbüzhdki Prokhod
Devecser Hungary 49 O8
Develi Turkey 106 C3
also known as Everek
Deveron *r.* U.K. 46 J8
Devesel Romania 58 D4
Devět Skal *hill* Czech Rep. 49 N6
Devgadh Bariya India 96 B5
Devghar India *see* Deoghar
Devikot India 96 A4
Devil River Peak N.Z. 152 G8
Devils *r.* U.S.A. 179 B6
Devil's Gate *pass* U.S.A. 182 E3
Devils Lake U.S.A. 178 C1
Devil's Lake *l.* U.S.A. 179 B6
Devil's Paw *mt.* U.S.A. 164 F4
Devil's Peak U.S.A. 182 E4
Devil's Point Bahamas 187 E1
Devil's Thumb *mt.* Canada/U.S.A. 166 C3
Devin Bulg. 58 F7
Devine U.S.A. 179 C6
Devizes U.K. 47 K12
Devli India 96 B4
Devnya Bulg. 58 I5
Devoll *r.* Albania 58 A8
Dévoluy *mts* France 51 L8
Devon *Alta* Canada 180 D1
Devon *Ont.* Canada 173 J3
Devon S. Africa 133 N4
Devon Island Canada 165 J2
Devonport Australia 147 E5
Devore U.S.A. 182 G7
Devrek Turkey 106 B2
Devrez *r.* Turkey 106 C2
Dévrukh India 94 B2
Dewa, Tanjung *pt* Indon. 76 A2
Dewakang Besar *i.* Indon. 77 G4
Dewanganj Bangl. 97 F4
Dewangiri Bhutan 97 F4
Dewas India 96 C5
De Weerribben, Nationaal Park *nat. park*
Neth. 48 E3
Dewele Eth. 128 D2
Dewetsdorp S. Africa 133 K6

De Witt *AR* U.S.A. 174 B5
De Witt *IA* U.S.A. 174 B3
Dexing China 87 F2
formerly known as Yincheng
Dexter *MI* U.S.A. 174 B4
Dexter *MO* U.S.A. 174 B4
Dexter *NM* U.S.A. 181 F6
Dexter *NY* U.S.A. 177 I1
Deyang China 86 C2
Dey-Dey Lake *salt flat* Australia 146 A2
Deyhuk Iran 100 D3
Deynau Turkm. see Dyanev
Deyong, Tanjung *pt* Indon. 73 I8
Dêyü Co *l.* China 89 D5
Deyyer Iran 100 B5
Dez *r.* Iran 100 B4
Dez, Sadd-e *resr* Iran 107 G4
formerly known as Mohammad Reza Shah
Pahlavi Dam
Dezadeash Canada 166 B2
Dezadeash Lake Canada 166 B2
Dezfūl Iran 100 B4
▶Dezhneva, Mys *c.* Rus. Fed. 39 T3
Most easterly point of Asia. English form
East Cape.
Dezhou China 85 H4
Dezhou China *see* Dechang
Dezh Shāhpūr Iran *see* Marivān
Dhading Nepal 97 E4
Dhahab, Wādī adh *r.* Syria 108 G5
Dhāhiriya West Bank 108 F6
Dhahlān, Jabal *hill* Saudi Arabia 104 D2
Dhahran Saudi Arabia 105 E2
also spelt Az Zahrān
▶Dhaka Bangl. 97 F5
Capital of Bangladesh and 5th most
populous city in Asia. Formerly spelt Dacca.
world [cities] ▶▶ 24–25
Dhaka *admin. div.* Bangl. 97 F5
Dhalbhum *reg.* India 97 E5
Dhaleswari *r.* Bangl. 97 F5
Dhaleswari *r.* India 97 G4
Dhalgaon India 94 B2
Dhamār Yemen 104 D5
Dhamār *governorate* Yemen 104 D5
Dhamnod India 96 B5
Dhampur India 96 C3
Dhamtari India 94 D1
Dhanbad India 97 E5
Dhandhuka India 96 B5
Dhanera India 96 B4
Dhangarhi Nepal 96 D3
Dhang Range *mts* Nepal 97 D3
Dhankuta Nepal 97 E4
Dhar India 96 B5
Dhar Adrar *hills* Mauritania 124 B2
Dharampur India 94 B1
Dharan Bazar Nepal 97 E4
Dharapuram India 94 C4
Dharhara India 97 E4
Dhari India 96 A5
Dharmanagar India 97 G4
Dharmapuri India 94 C3
Dharmavaram India 94 C3
Dharmjaygarh India 97 D5
also known as Rabkob
Dharmkot India 96 B3
Dharoor *watercourse* Somalia 128 F2
Dhar Oualâta *hills* Mauritania 124 D2
Dhar Tichît *hills* Mauritania 124 C2
Dharug National Park Australia 147 F3
Dharur India 94 C2
Dharwad India 94 B3
formerly known as Dharwar
Dharwar India *see* Dharwad
Dhasa India 96 A5
Dhasan *r.* India 96 C4

▶Dhaulagiri *mt.* Nepal 97 D3
7th highest mountain in the world and in
Asia. Also spelt Dhawlagiri.
world [physical features] ▶▶ 8–9
Dhaulpur India 96 C4
Dhaurahra India 96 D4
Dhávlia Greece *see* Davlia
Dhawlagiri *mt.* Nepal *see* Dhaulagiri
Dhebar Lake India 96 B4
Dhekelia Sovereign Base Area
military base Cyprus 108 E2
Dhekiajuli India 97 G4
Dhenkanal India 95 E1
Dheskáti Greece *see* Deskati
Dhiafánion Greece *see* Diafani
Dhibān Jordan 108 G6
Dhidhimótikhon Greece *see* Didymoteicho
Dhing India 97 G4
Dhirwāh, Wādī adh *watercourse* Jordan
109 H6
Dhodhekánisos *is* Greece *see* Dodecanese
Dhofar *admin. reg.* Oman *see* Ẓufār
Dhokós *i.* Greece *see* Dokos
Dhola India 96 A5
Dholka India 96 B5
Dhomokós Greece *see* Domokos
Dhone India 94 C3
Dhoomadheere Somalia 128 D4
Dhoraji India 96 A5
Dhori India 96 A5
Dhragónádha *i.* Greece *see* Dragonada
Dhragónisos *i.* Greece *see* Dragonisi
Dhrangadhra India 96 A5
Dhrol India 96 A5
Dhrosia Greece *see* Drosia
Dhubāb Yemen 104 C5
Dhuburi India 97 F4
also spelt Dhubri
Dhule India 94 B1
formerly known as Dhulia
Dhulia India *see* Dhule
Dhulian India 97 E4
Dhuma India 96 C5
Dhunche Nepal 97 E4
Dhūudo Somalia 128 F2
Dhuusa Marreeb Somalia 128 E3
Dhuwaybān *basin* Saudi Arabia 104 D2
Dhytiki Ellas *admin. reg.* Greece *see*
Dytiki Ellas
Dhytiki Makedhonia *admin. reg.* Greece *see*
Dytiki Makedonia
Dia *i.* Greece 59 G13
Diablo, Mount U.S.A. 182 C4
Diablo Range *mts* U.S.A. 182 C4
Diaca Moz. 129 C7
Diafani Greece 59 J13
also known as Dhiafánion
Diafarabé Mali 124 D3
Diaka *r.* Mali 124 D3
Dialakoto Senegal 124 B3
Diallassagou Mali 124 E3
Diamante Arg. 204 E4
Diamante *r.* Arg. 204 D4
Diamante Italy 57 H9
Diamantina *watercourse* Australia 149 C5
Diamantina *Amazonas* Brazil 199 F6
Diamantina *Minas Gerais* Brazil 203 D6
Diamantina, Chapada *plat.* Brazil 202 D5
Diamantina Gates National Park Australia
149 D4
Diamantina Lakes Australia 149 D4
Diamantino *Mato Grosso* Brazil 201 F3
Diamantino *Mato Grosso* Brazil 202 A6
Diamond Harbour India 97 F5
Diamond Islets Australia 149 F3
Diamond Peak U.S.A. 183 C4
Diamond Springs U.S.A. 182 D3

Diamondville U.S.A. 180 E4
Diamou Mali 124 C3
Diamounguél Senegal 124 B3
Dianbai China 87 D4
Dianbu China *see* Feidong
Diancang Shan *mt.* China 86 B3
Dian Chi *l.* China 86 B3
Diandioumé Mali 124 C3
Diane Bank *sea feature* Australia 149 F3
Diangounté Kamara Mali 124 C3
Diani *r.* Guinea 124 C5
Dianjiang China 87 D2
also known as Guixi
Diano Marina Italy 56 A5
Dianópolis Brazil 206 C2
Dianra Côte d'Ivoire 124 C4
Diaobingshan China *see* Tiefa
Diaokou China 85 H4
Diaoling China 82 C3
Diapaga Burkina 125 F3
Diapitos *r.* Greece 59 E11
Diariazos *r.* Cyprus 108 D2
Diatifèrè Guinea 124 C3
Diavolo, Mount *hill* India 95 G3
Diaz Point Namibia 130 B5
Dib, Rās *pt* Egypt 108 E9
Dibā al Ḩiṣn U.A.E. 105 G2
Dibab Oman 105 G3
Dibang *r.* India *see* Dingba Qu
Dibaya Dem. Rep. Congo 127 D6
Dibbis Sudan 120 E6
Dibek Dağı *mt.* Turkey 59 J10
Dibella *well* Niger 125 I2
Dibeng S. Africa 132 G4
Dibīlē Eth. 128 D2
Dibis Iraq 109 P2
Diboli *r.* India 94 C2
Dibrugarh India 97 G4
Dibulla Col. 198 C2
Dickens U.S.A. 179 B5
Dickeyville U.S.A. 172 C8
Dickinson U.S.A. 178 B2
Dickson U.S.A. 174 C4
Dicle *r.* Turkey 107 E3 *see* Tigris
Dida Galgalu *reg.* Kenya 128 C4
Didah *well* Saudi Arabia 104 A5
Didao China 82 C3
Didi, Jabal *ad hill* Syria 109 K2
Didicas *i.* Phil. 74 B2
Diéni Mali 124 D3
Didima Hills Sudan 128 B3
Dido *waterhole* Kenya 128 D5
Didwana India 96 B4
Didymoteicho Greece 58 H7
also known as Dhidhimótikhon
Didžiasalis Lith. 42 H6
Didžiulis *l.* Lith. 42 F7
Die France 51 L8
Die Berg *mt.* S. Africa 133 O2
Diébougou Burkina 124 E4
Dieburg Germany 48 F6
Diedenhofen France *see* Thionville
Diefenbaker, Lake Canada 167 J5
Diego de Almagro, Isla *i.* Chile 205 B8
Diego Garcia *i.* British Indian Ocean Terr.
159 L6
Diego Martin Trin. and Tob. 187 H5
Diégo Suarez Madag. *see* Antsiranana
Diégrãga *well* Mauritania 124 C2
Diéké Guinea 124 C5
Diekirch Lux. 51 M3
Diélette France 50 D4
Diemelsee *park* Germany 48 F4
Diên Châu Vietnam 78 D4
Dienvidsusēja *r.* Latvia 42 F5
Diepholz Germany 48 F3
Dieppe France 50 H3
Dierks U.S.A. 179 D5
Di'er Nonchang Qu *r.* China 85 E4
Di'er Songhua Jiang *r.* China 82 B3
Diest Belgium 51 L2
Dietikon Switz. 51 O5
Dieveniškes Lith. 42 G7
Diffa Niger 125 I3
Diffa *dept* Niger 125 I2
Difnein Island Eritrea 104 B4
Dig *well* Eth. 128 E3
Diga Diga *well* Niger 125 F3
Digapahandi India 95 E2
Digba Dem. Rep. Congo 126 F4
Digboi India 97 G4
Digby Canada 169 H4
Digerbergen *hill* Sweden 45 K3
Diggi India 96 B4
Dighton U.S.A. 178 B4
Diglur India 94 C2
Digne-les-Bains France 51 M8
Digoin France 51 J6
Digos Phil. 74 C5
Digras India 94 C1
Digri Pak. 101 G5
Digul *r.* Indon. 73 I8
Digya National Park Ghana 125 E5
Dihang *r.* India 97 G3 *see* Brahmaputra
Diib, Wadi *watercourse* Sudan 104 B3
Dijlah *r.* Iraq/Syria 107 F4 *see* Tigris
Dijlah - Ath Tharthār, Qanāt *canal* Iraq
109 O4
English form Tharthār Canal
Dijon France 51 L5
Dik Chad 126 C2
Dikanäs Sweden 44 L2
Diken India 96 B4
Dikhil Djibouti 128 D2
Dikho *r.* India 97 G4
Diksal India 94 B2
Diksmuide Belgium 51 I1
Dikson Rus. Fed. 39 I2
Dikwa Nigeria 125 I3
Dila Indon. 73 I8
Dīla *r.* Iraq/Syria 107 F4 *see* Tigris
Dilārām Iran 100 D4
Dir mii Geçidi *pass* Turkey 108 A1
Dirk Hartog Island Australia 151 A5
Dirxou Niger 125 I2
Dirranbandi Australia 147 F2
Dirri Dem. Rep. Congo 126 E4
▶Dili East Timor 75 C5
Capital of East Timor.
Dili Dem. Rep. Congo 126 E4
Dilia *watercourse* Niger 125 I3
Dilijan Armenia 107 F2
Dilijan Argelanots' *nature res.* Armenia
107 F2
Di Linh Vietnam 79 E6
Dilion Cone *mt.* N.Z. 153 H10
Dilizhan Armenia *see* Dilijan
Dillenburg Germany 48 F5
Dilley U.S.A. 179 C6
Dilli Mali 124 D3
Dilling Sudan 121 F6
Dillingen an der Donau Germany 48 H7
Dillingham U.S.A. 164 D4
Dillinya Aboriginal Land *res.* Australia
148 B2
Dillon Canada 167 I4
Dillon *r.* Canada 167 I4
Dillon *MT* U.S.A. 180 D3
Dillon *SC* U.S.A. 174 E5
Dillsburg U.S.A. 177 H5
Dillwyn U.S.A. 176 F8
Dilolo Dem. Rep. Congo 127 D7
Dilos *i.* Greece 59 G11
Diltāwa Iraq 107 F4
Dimako Cameroon 125 I5
Dimapur India 97 G4
Dimas Mex. 184 D4
Dimashq Syria *see* Damascus

Dimashq *governorate* Syria 109 I4
Dimbelenge Dem. Rep. Congo 127 D6
Dimbokro Côte d'Ivoire 124 D5
Dimbocla Australia 147 D4
Dimbulah Australia 149 E3
Dimitrovgrad Bulg. 58 G6
Dimitrovgrad Rus. Fed. 41 I5
formerly known as Melekess
Dimitrovgrad *Srbija* Yugo. 58 D5
formerly known as Tsaribrod
Dimitrovo Bulg. *see* Pernik
Dimmitt U.S.A. 179 B5
Dimona Israel 108 G6
Dinagat *i.* Phil. 74 C4
Dinagat Sound *sea chan.* Phil. 74 C4
Dinajpur Bangl. 97 F4
Dinan France 50 D4
Dinanagar India 96 B3
Dinangourou Mali 125 E3
Dinant Belgium 51 K2
Dinapur India 97 E4
Dinar Turkey 106 B3
historically known as Apamea
Dīnār, Kūh-e *mt.* Iran 100 B4
Dinara *mt.* Bos.-Herz. 56 I4
Dinara Planina *mts* Bos./Croatia *see*
Dinaric Alps
Dinard France 50 D4
Dinaric Alps *mts* Bos.-Herz./Croatia 56 I4
also known as Dinara Planina
Dinas *r.* Kenya 128 C4
Dinbych U.K. *see* Denbigh
Dinbych-y-Pysgod U.K. *see* Tenby
Dinder *r.* Sudan 121 G6
Dinder el Agaliyin *r.* Sudan 104 A5
Dinder National Park Sudan 121 G6
Dindi *r.* India 94 C2
Dindigul India 94 C4
Dindima Nigeria 125 H4
Dindori *Madhya Pradesh* India 96 D5
Dindori *Maharash'ra* India 94 B1
Dinek Turkey 106 C2
Dinga Dem. Rep. Congo 127 C6
Dinga Pak. 101 H3
Dingalan Bay Phil. 74 B3
Dingba Qu *r.* India 97 G4
also known as Dibang
Dingcan China *see* Dibang
Dingbujie China 87 E2
Dindiéni Mali 124 D3
Dingelstädt Germany 48 H4
Dingin, Bukit *mt.* Indon. 76 C3
Dingla Nepal 97 E4
Dingle Rep. of Ireland 47 B11
Dingle Bay Rep. of Ireland 47 B11
Dingnan China 87 E3
also known as Lishi
Dinge Australia 149 C5
Dingcheng China *see* Linshui
Dingxing China *see* Dingzhou
Dingxian China *see* Dingzhou
Dingxiang China 85 G4
Dingxin China 84 C3
Dingxing China 85 G4
Dingyuan China 87 F1
Dingzhou China 85 G4
formerly known as Dingxian
Dingzi Gang *b.* China 85 I4
Dingzixou China 84 B4
Dinhata India 97 F4
Diên Châu Vietnam 78 D4
Dinh Lâp Vietnam 78 D3
Dinkel *r.* Neth. 48 D3
Dinkelsbühl Germany 48 H6
Dinnebito Wash *watercourse* U.S.A. 183 M6
Dinngyê China 89 D6
also known as Gyangkar
Dinokwe Botswana 131 E4
Dinosaur U.S.A. 183 O1
Dinosaur National Monument *nat. park*
U.S.A. 183 O1
Dintifeladas Indon. 77 D4
Dinuba U.S.A. 182 E4
Dinwiddie U.S.A. 176 H8
Diofila Mali 124 D3
Dioïla Mali 124 D3
Dion *r.* Guinea 124 C4
Diorisio Brazil 207 K6
Diório Cerqueira Brazil 203 A8
Diorama Brazil 206 B3
Dioscurias Georgia *see* Sokhumi
Diosig Romania 58 D1
Diospolis Magna *tourist site* Egypt *see*
Thebes
Dioulaoulou Senegal 124 A3
Dioumara Mali 124 C3
Dioundiou Niger 125 F3
Dioura Mali 124 D3
Diourbel Senegal 124 A3
Dipalpur Pak. 101 H4
Dipayal Nepal 96 D3
Diphu India 97 G4
Dipkarpaz Cyprus *see* Rizokarpason
Diplo Pak. 101 G5
Diplolog Phil. 74 B4
Dipperu National Park Australia 149 F4
Dipton N.Z. 153 C13
Dipu China *see* Anji
Dir Pak. 101 G3
Dirah U.A.E. 105 F2
Dirang India 97 G4
Diré Mali 124 E2
Direction, Cape Australia 149 D2
Dirê Dawa Eth. 128 D2
Dirfys *mts* Greece 59 E10
Dirhami Eston.a 42 E2
Diriamba Nicaragua 186 B5
Dirico Angola 127 D9
Dir lo *r. Sicilia* Italy 57 H11
Dirranbandi Australia 147 F2
Dirs Saudi Arabia 104 C4
Dirty Devil *r.* U.S.A. 183 N4
formerly known as Deesa
Disang *r.* India 97 G4
Disappointment, Cape Antarctica 223 T2
Disappointment, Cape S. Georgia 205 [inset]
Disappointment, Lake *salt flat* Australia
150 C4
Disappointment Islands Fr. Polynesia *see*
Désappointement, Îles du
Disappointment Lake Canada 169 I2
Discovery Bay Australia 146 C4
Discovery Bay *Hong Kong* China 87 [inset]
also known as Tai Pak Wan
Discovery Bay Coastal Park *nature res.*
Australia 146 C4
Disentis Muster Switz. 51 O6
Disgrazia, Monte *mt.* Italy 56 B2
Dishna Egypt 121 G3
Disko *i.* Greenland *see* Qeqertarsuaq
Disko Bugt *b.* Greenland *see*
Qeqertarsuup Tunua
Dismal Lakes Canada 167 G1
Dismal Mountains Antarctica 223 H2
Dismal Swamp U.S.A. 177 I9
Disneyland Paris *tourist site* France 51 I4
Dispur India 97 F4
Disputanta U.S.A. 177 H8
Disraëli Canada 169 G4
Diss U.K. 47 N11

Dissän Island Saudi Arabia 104 C4
▶Distrito Federal *admin. dist.* Brazil 206 F2
English form Federal District
Distrito Federal *admin. dist.* Mex. 185 F5
Distrito Federal *admin. dist.* Venez. 199 E2
English form Federal District
Disūq Egypt 108 B6
Ditloung S. Africa 132 G5
Dittaino *r. Sicilia* Italy 57 H11
Diu India 94 A1
Diuata Mountains Phil. 74 C4
Diuata Point Phil. 74 C4
Divān Darreh Iran 100 A3
Divehi *country* Indian Ocean *see* Maldives
Divénié Congo 126 B5
Dives *r.* France 50 F3
Divichi Azer. *see* Däväçi
Divide Mountain U.S.A. 166 A3
Divilacan Bay Phil. 74 B2
Divinésia Brazil 207 J7
Divinópolis Brazil 203 C7
Divisões, Serra das *mts* Brazil 206 B4
also known as Santa Maria, Serra de
Divisor, Sierra de *mts* Peru *see*
Ultraoriental, Cordillera
Divjaka *nat. park* Albania 58 A8
Divnoye Rus. Fed. 41 G7
Divo Côte d'Ivoire 124 C5
Divo Rus. Fed. 43 U3
Divor *r.* Port. 54 C6
Divouinia *i.* Greece 59 H13
Diviği Turkey 107 E2
Divuma Dem. Rep. Congo 127 D7
Div'ya Rus. Fed. 40 K4
Dīwaniyah Iraq *see* Ad Dīwānīyah
Dixcove Ghana 125 E5
Dixfield U.S.A. 177 O1
Dix Milles, Lac des *l.* Canada 173 S3
Dixmont U.S.A. 177 P1
Dixon *CA* U.S.A. 182 C3
Dixon *IL* U.S.A. 174 C3
Dixon Entrance *sea chan.* Canada/U.S.A.
164 F4
Dixon's Bahamas 175 F7
Dixonville Canada 167 G3
Diyadin Turkey 107 E3
Diyālá *governorate* Iraq 107 F4
Diyarbakır Turkey 107 E3
historically known as Amida
Diyodar India 96 A4
Diz Pak. 101 E5
Dizak Iran *see* Dāvar Panāh
Dizangué Cameroon 125 H6
Diz Chah Iran 100 C3
Dize Turkey *see* Yüksekova
Dizney U.S.A. 176 B9
Dja *r.* Cameroon 126 C5
Dja, Réserve de *nature res.* Cameroon
125 I6
Djado Niger 125 I1
Djado, Plateau du Niger 125 I1
Djakarta Indon. *see* Jakarta
Djakovica *Kosovo, Srbija* Yugo. *see*
Đakovica
Djamâa Alg. 123 G2
Djamba Dem. Rep. Congo 127 D7
Djambala Congo 126 B5
Djampie Dem. Rep. Congo 126 C5
Djampiel Cameroon 125 I5
Djanet Alg. 123 H4
Djarrit-Uliga-Dalap Marshall Is *see*
Delap-Uliga-Djarrit
Djebr *mt.* Alg. 123 F4
Djébrène Chad 126 C2
Djédaa Chad 120 C6
Djedid *well* Alg. 123 E4
Djelfa Alg. 123 F2
Djéma Cent. Afr. Rep. 126 E3
Djèmber Chad 126 C2
Djeneral Janković *Kosovo, Srbija* Yugo. *see*
Đeneral Janković
Djenné Mali 124 D3
also spelt Jenne
Djerdap *nat. park* Yugo. 58 D4
Djermaya Chad 120 B6
Djia Dem. Rep. Congo 126 D5
Djibo Burkina 125 E3
Djibouti Côte d'Ivoire 124 C4
▶Djibouti *country* Africa 128 D3
spelt Jībūtī in Arabic; formerly known as
Côte Française de Somalis in French or
French Somaliland or French Territory of the
Afars and Issas
africa [countries] ▶▶ 114–117
▶Djibouti Djibouti 128 D2
Capital of Djibouti. Also spelt Jibuti.
Djidjelli Alg. *see* Jijel
Djiguéni Mauritania 124 C3
Djinet, Cap *c.* Alg. 55 O8
Djipologo Dem. Rep. Congo 126 D4
Djolu Dem. Rep. Congo 126 D4
Djombo Kibbit Chad 120 C6
Djoua *r.* Congo/Gabon 126 B4
Djoubissi Cent. Afr. Rep. 126 C3
Djougou Benin 125 F4
Djoum Cameroon 125 I6
Djugu Dem. Rep. Congo 126 F4
Djuma Dem. Rep. Congo 126 C5
Djúpivogur Iceland 44 [inset] D2
Djurås Sweden 45 K3
Djurdjura National Park Alg. 55 P8
spelt nationalpark in part Sweden 45 K4
Djäiri India 94 C4 ... Dairi India 94 C4
Dmitriya Lapteva, Proliv *sea chan.*
Rus. Fed. 39 O2
Dmitriyevka *Primorskiy Kray* Rus. Fed. 90 C3
Dmitriyevka *Samarskaya Oblast'* Rus. Fed.
102 B1
Dmitriyev-L'govskiy Rus. Fed. 43 Q9
Dmitriyevsk Ukr. *see* Makiyivka
Dmitriyevskoye Rus. Fed. 43 S7
Dmitrov Rus. Fed. 43 S5
Dmitrovo Rus. Fed. 43 O9
Dmitrovskiy Pogost Rus. Fed. 43 U6
Dmitrovsk-Orlovskiy Rus. Fed. 43 Q9
Dmytriyevs'k Ukr. *see* Makiyivka
Dnepr *r.* Rus. Fed. *see* Dnieper
Dneprodzerzhinsk Ukr. *see*
Dniprodzerzhyns'k
▶Dnieper *r.* Europe 41 D6
3rd longest river in Europe. Also spelt
Dnepr (Rus. Fed.) or Dnipro (Ukraine) or
Dnyapro (Belarus).
europe [landscapes] ▶▶ 30–31
Dniester *r.* Moldova 58 L2
also spelt Nistru
Dniester *r.* Ukr. 41 D6
also spelt Dnister (Ukraine) *or* Nistru
(Moldova)
Dnipro *r.* Ukr. 41 D6 *see* Dnieper
Dniprodzerzhyns'k Ukr. 41 E6
also spelt Dneprodzerzhinsk; *formerly*
known as Kamenskoye
Dnipropetrovs'k Ukr. 41 E6
also spelt Dnepropetrovsk; *formerly known*
as Yekaterinoslav
Dniprorudne Ukr. 41 E6
also spelt Dneprorudnoye
Dnister *r.* Ukr. 41 D6 *see* Dniester
Dnistrov'k'y Lyman *l.* Ukr. 58 L2
Dno Rus. Fed. 43 K4

Dnyapro r. Belarus 41 D5 see Dnieper
Dnyaprowska-Buhski, Kanal canal Belarus 42 F9
Doa Moz. 131 G3
Doabi Mekh-i-Zarin Afgh. 101 F3
Doaktown Canada 169 H4
Doangdoangan Besar i. Indon. 77 G4
Doangdoangan Kecil i. Indon. 77 G4
Doany Madag. 131 [inset] K2
Doba Chad 126 C2
Doba China see Toiba
Doabasna r. Belarus 43 L9
Dobbertiner Seenlandschaft park Germany 49 J2
Dobbs, Cape Canada 167 O1
Dobczyce Poland 49 R6
Dobele Latvia 42 E5
Döbeln Germany 49 K4
Doberai, Jazirah pen. Indon. 73 H7
English form Doberai Peninsula; formerly known as Vogelkop Peninsula
Doberai Peninsula Indon. see Doberai, Jazirah
Döbern Germany 49 L4
Dobiegniew Poland 49 M3
Doblas Arg. 204 D5
Dobo Indon. 73 H8
Doboj Bos.-Herz. 56 K4
Do Borji Iran 100 C4
Dobra Poland 49 P4
Dobre Miasto Poland 49 R2
Dobreşti Romania 58 D2
Dobrich Bulg. 58 I5
formerly known as Tolbukhin
Dobrinka r. Belarus 41 G5
Dobrești Romania 58 I2
Dobroval r. Russ. Fed. 42 D7
Dobroye Rus. Fed. 43 U9
Dobruchi Rus. Fed. 42 G4
Dobrudzhansko Plato plat. Bulg. 58 I5
Dobrun Romania 58 F4
Dobrush Belarus 43 M9
Dobryanka Rus. Fed. 40 K4
Dobryanka Ukr. 43 M9
Dobrynikha Rus. Fed. 43 S6
Dobskie, Jezioro l. Poland 49 S1
Dobson N.Z. 153 F11
Dobson r. N.Z. 153 D12
Dobzha China 89 E6
Doc Can reef Phil. 74 A5
Doce r. Espírito Santo Brazil 203 E6
Doce r. Goiás Brazil 206 B5
Do China Qala Afgh. 101 G4
Doctor Arroyo Mex. 185 E4
Doctor Belisario Domínguez Mex. 184 D2
Doctor Hicks Range hills Australia 150 F6
Doctor Petru Groza Romania see Ştei
Doda China 129 C6
Dod Ballapur India 94 C3
Dodecanese is Greece 59 I13
also spelt Dodekanisos or Dhodhekánisos
Dodekanisos is Greece see Dodecanese
Dodge Center U.S.A. 174 A2
Dodge City U.S.A. 178 B4
Dodgeville U.S.A. 172 C6
Dodman Point U.K. 47 H13
Dodola Eth. 128 C3
▶Dodoma Tanz. 129 B6
Capital of Tanzania.
Dodoma admin. reg. Tanz. 129 B6
Dodori National Reserve nature res. Kenya 128 D5
Dodsonville U.S.A. 176 B6
Doetinchem Neth. 48 D4
Dofa Indon. 75 C3
Doftana r. Romania 58 F2
Dog r. Canada 168 B3
Dogai Coring salt l. China 89 E5
Dogaicoring Qangco salt l. China 89 E5
Doğanbey Aydın Turkey 59 H11
Doğanbey İzmir Turkey 59 H10
Doğanşehir Turkey 107 D3
Dog Creek Canada 166 F5
Doghārūn Iran 101 E3
Dog Island Canada 169 I1
Dog Lake Man. Canada 167 L5
Dog Lake Ont. Canada 168 B3
Dog Lake Ont. Canada 168 C3
Dognecea Romania 58 C3
Dōgo i. Japan 91 C6
Dogole well Somalia 128 E2
Dogondoutchi Niger 125 G3
Dogoumbo Chad 126 C2
Dõgo-yama mt. Japan 91 C6
Dog Rocks is Bahamas 186 D1
Doğubeyazıt Turkey 107 F3
Dogxung Zangbo r. China 89 D6
also known as Raka Zangbo
▶Doha Qatar 105 E2
Capital of Qatar. Also spelt Ad Dawḩah.
Dohad India see Dahod
Dohazari Bangl. 78 A3
Dohrighat India 89 C7
Doi r. Fiji 145 H4
also spelt Ndoi
Doi Inthanon National Park Thai. 78 B4
Doi Luang National Park Thai. 78 B4
Doilungdêqên China 89 E6
also known as Namka
Doi Saket Thai. 78 B4
Doisanagar India 97 H5
Dois Córregos Brazil 206 E9
Dois Irmãos, Serra dos hills Brazil 202 D4
Dojran, Lake Greece/Macedonia 58 D7
also spelt Doïranis, Limni or Dojransko Ezero
Dojransko Ezero l. Greece/Macedonia see Dojran, Lake
Doka Sudan 121 G6
Dokali Iran 100 C3
Dokhara, Dunes de des. Alg. 123 G2
Dokos i. Greece 59 E11
also spelt Dhokós
Dokri Pak. 101 G5
Dokshukino Rus. Fed. see Nartkala
Dokshytsy Belarus 42 I7
Doksy Czech Rep. 49 L5
Dokuchayeva, Mys c. Rus. Fed. 90 J2
Dokuchayevsk Kazakh. 103 F2
Dokuchayevs'k Ukr. 41 F7
formerly known as Olenivs'ki Kar"yery or Yelenovskiye Kar'yery
Dolak, Pulau i. Indon. 73 I8
also known as Yos Sudarso
Dolan Springs U.S.A. 183 J6
Dolbeau Canada 169 F3
Dole France 51 L5
Dolgellau U.K. 47 I11
Dolgeville U.S.A. 177 K2
Dolgiy, Ostrov i. Rus. Fed. 40 K1
Dolgorukovo Rus. Fed. 43 T9
Dolgoye Lipetskaya Oblast' Rus. Fed. 43 U8
Dolgoye Orlovskaya Oblast' Rus. Fed. 43 S9
Dolgusha Rus. Fed. 43 R6
Dolhasca Romania 58 H1
Dolianova Sardegna Italy 57 B9
Dolinsk Rus. Fed. 82 F3
Dolisie Congo see Loubomo

Dolit Indon. 75 C3
Doljevac Srbija Yugo. 58 C5
also known as Tongcheng
Dolleman Island Antarctica 222 T2
Dolna Lipnitsa Bulg. 58 G5
Dolni Chiflik Bulg. 58 I5
formerly known as Georgi Traykov
Dolní Dubník Bulg. 58 F5
Dolno Kamartsi Bulg. 58 E6
Dolno Levski Bulg. 58 F5
Dolný Kubín Slovakia 49 Q6
Dolo Indon. 75 B3
Dolomites mts Italy 56 D3
also known as Dolomiti or Dolomitiche, Alpi
Dolomiti mts Italy see Dolomites
Dolomiti Bellunesi, Parco Nazionale delle nat. park Italy 56 D2
Dolomitiche, Alpi mts Italy see Dolomites
Dolon, Pereval pass Kyrg. see Dolon Ashuusu
Dolon Ashuusu pass Kyrg. 103 H4
also known as Dolon, Pereval
Dolonnur China see Duolun
Dolo Odo Eth. 128 D3
Doloon Mongolia 85 E2
Dolores Arg. 204 F5
Dolores Guat. 185 H5
Dolores Mex. 184 C3
Dolores Uruguay 204 F4
Dolores r. U.S.A. 183 O3
Dolores Hidalgo Mex. 185 E4
Dolovo Vojvodina, Srbija Yugo. 58 B4
Dolphin, Cape Falkland Is 205 F8
Dolphin and Union Strait Canada 164 H3
Dolphin Head Namibia 130 B5
Dolphin Island Nature Reserve Australia 150 B4
Đô Lương Vietnam 78 D4
Dolzhitsy Rus. Fed. 43 K3
Dom, Gunung mt. Indon. 73 I7
Domaniç Turkey 106 B3
also known as Hisarköy
Domar Bangl. 97 F4
Domartang China see Banbar
Domažlice Czech Rep. 49 J6
Domba China 97 G2
Dombarovskiy Rus. Fed. 102 D2
Dombe Moz. 131 G3
Dombe Grande Angola 127 B8
Dombegyház Hungary 49 S9
Dombóvár Hungary 49 P9
Dombra Angola 127 C8
Dombrau Poland see Dąbrowa Górnicza
Dombrovitsa Ukr. see Dubrovytsya
Dombrowa Poland see Dąbrowa Górnicza
Dom Cavati Brazil 207 K6
Domda China see Qingshuihe
Dome Argus ice feature Antarctica 223 F1
Dome Charlie ice feature Antarctica 223 H2
also known as Dome Circe
Dome Circe ice feature Antarctica see Dome Charlie
Dome Fuji research station Antarctica 223 C1
Domeikava Lith. 42 E7
Domel Island Myanmar see Letsok-aw Kyun
Dome Rock Mountains U.S.A. 183 J8
Domett, Cape Australia 150 E2
Domett, Mount N.Z. 152 G9
Domeyko Chile 204 C3
Dom Feliciano Brazil 203 A9
Domfront France 50 F4
Domfront Germany 50 I5
Domingos Martins Brazil 207 M7
▶Dominica country West Indies 187 H4
northamerica [countries] ▶▶▶ 158–159
Dominical Costa Rica 186 C5
Dominicana, República country West Indies see Dominican Republic
▶Dominican Republic country West Indies 187 F3
also known as Dominicana, República; historically known as Santo Domingo
northamerica [countries] ▶▶▶ 158–159
Dominica Passage Dominica/Guadeloupe 187 H4
Dominion, Cape Canada 165 L3
Dominique i. Fr. Polynesia see Hiva Oa
Domiongo Dem. Rep. Congo 126 D6
Dom Joaquim Brazil 207 J5
Domka Bhutan 97 F4
Domneşti Romania 58 F3
Domneşti Romania 58 G4
Domo Eth. 128 E3
Domodedovo Rus. Fed. 43 S6
Domodossola Italy 56 A2
Domokos Greece 59 D9
also spelt Dhomokós
Domoni Comoros 129 E8
Domozhirovo Rus. Fed. 43 O1
Dom Pedrito Brazil 203 A9
Dom Pedro Brazil 202 C3
Dompu Indon. 77 G5
Domula China 89 C5

Dong'e China 85 H4
also known as Tongcheng
Dongfang China 87 D5
Dongfanghong China 82 D3
Donggala Indon. 75 A3
Donggang China 83 B5
formerly known as Dadong or Donggou
Donggi Cona r. China see Donggar
Donggou China see Donggang
Donggu China 87 E3
Donghai China 87 F1
also known as Niushan
Dong Hai sea N. Pacific Ocean see East China Sea
Donghai Dao i. China 87 D4
Dong He r. China 86 C2
Dong He watercourse China 84 D3
Đông Hôi Vietnam 78 D4
Dong Jiang r. China 87 E4
Dongjingcheng China 82 C3
Dongkai, Tanjung pt Indon. 75 A3
Dongkou China 87 D3
Donglan China 87 C4
Dongle China 84 C4
Dongliao r. China 85 I3
Donglük China 88 F3
Dongmen China see Luocheng
Dongming China 85 G5
Dongnan China 82 C3
Dongo Angola 127 B8
Dongo Gongo 126 C4
Dongobesh Tanz. 129 B6
Dongola Sudan 121 F5
Dongotona Mountains Sudan 128 B3
Dongou Congo 126 C4
Dong Phraya Fai mts Thai. 78 C4
Dong Phraya Yen mts Thai. 79 C5
Dongping Guangdong China 87 E4
Dongping China see Anhua
Dongping Shandong China 85 H5
Dongpo China see Meishan
Dongqiao China 89 E6
Dongshan Fujian China 87 F4
also known as Xibu
Dongshan Jiangsu China 87 G2
Dongshan China see Shangyou
Dongshan China see Xuan'en
Dongsha Qundao is China 81 J3
English form Pratas Islands
Dongsheng China 85 F4
Dongshuan China see Tangdan
Dongtai China 87 G1
Dongtaijnar Hu l. China 84 B4
Dongting Hu l. China 87 E2
Dongtou China 87 G3
Dongxi China see Bei'ao
Donguena Angola 127 B9
Dongula Gabon 126 A4
Dong Ujimqin Qi China see Uliastai
Dongxiang China see Xuanhan
Dongxiangzu China see Xiaonan
Dongxing China 82 B3
Dongyang China 87 F2
Dongying China 85 H4
Dongzhen China 84 D4
Dongzhi China 87 F2
also known as Yaodu
Doniphan U.S.A. 174 B4
Donja Dubnica Kosovo, Srbija Yugo. 58 C5
Donjek r. Canada 166 B2
Donji Miholjac Croatia 56 K3
Donji Milanovac Srbija Yugo. 58 D4
Donji Vakuf Bos.-Herz. 56 J4
also known as Srbobran
Donji Zemunik Croatia 56 H4
Donkerpoort S. Africa 133 J4
Donmanick Islands Bangl. 97 F5
Donna r. Norway 44 K2
Donnacona Canada 169 G4
Donnelly Canada 167 G4
Donnellys Crossing N.Z. 152 H3
Donner Pass U.S.A. 182 D2
Donnersberg hill Germany 48 E6
Donnybrook Australia 151 A7
Donostia - San Sebastián Spain 55 J1
Donoussa Greece 59 G11
Donoussa i. Greece 59 G11
Donovan U.S.A. 172 F10
Donskoy Rus. Fed. 43 T7
Donskoye Lipetskaya Oblast' Rus. Fed. 43 T9
formerly known as Vodopyanovo
Donskoye Stavropol'skiy Kray Rus. Fed. 41 G7
Donsol Phil. 74 B3
Donthami r. Myanmar 78 B4
Donzenac France 50 H7
Doomadgee Australia 148 C3
Doomadgee Aboriginal Reserve Australia 148 C3
Doon, Loch l. U.K. 46 H9
Doon r. India 94 C2
Doon r. Mex. 184 C4
▶Don r. Rus. Fed. 43 U9
5th longest river in Europe.
europe [landscapes] ▶▶▶ 30–31
Don r. U.K. 46 J6
Don, Xé r. Laos 79 D5
Donadeu Arg. 204 E2
Donald Australia 147 D4
Donaldsonville U.S.A. 175 B6
Donalnes, Cerro mt. Chile 204 C2
Donalsonville U.S.A. 175 C6
Doñana, Parque Nacional de nat. park Spain 54 E8
Donau r. Austria/Germany 49 L7 see Danube
Donaueschingen Germany 48 F8
Donauwörth Germany 48 H7
Don Benito Spain 54 F6
Doncaster U.K. 47 K10
Dondo Moz. 131 G3
Dondo, Tanjung pt Indon. 75 B2
Dondo, Teluk b. Indon. 75 B2
Dondonay i. Phil. 74 B4
Dondra Head Sri Lanka 94 D5
Donegal Rep. of Ireland 47 D9
Donegal Bay Rep. of Ireland 47 D9
Dönenbay Kazakh. see Dunenbay
Donets'k Ukr. 41 F7
formerly known as Stalino or Yuzovka
Donets'kyy Kryazh hills Rus. Fed./Ukr. 41 F6
Denfoss Norway 45 J3
Donga r. Cameroon/Nigeria 125 H4
Donga Nigeria 125 H5
Dong'an China 87 D3
Dong'an China see Baiyashi
Dongara Australia 151 A6
Dongargaon India 94 C2
Dongargarh India 96 C5
Dongbatu China 84 C3
Dongbo China see Mêdog
Dongchuan China 86 B3
formerly known as Xincun
Dongchuan China see Yao'an
Dongco China 89 D5
Dongcun China see Haiyang
Dongcun China see Lanxian

Dorokhovo Rus. Fed. 43 R6
Dorokhsh Iran 101 D3
Dörööö Nuur salt l. Mongolia 84 B2
Dorostol Bulg. see Silistra
Dorotea Sweden 44 L2
Dorowa Zimbabwe 131 F3
Dorpat Estonia see Tartu
Dorre Island Australia 151 A5
Dorrigo Australia 147 G2
Dorris U.S.A. 180 B4
Dorsale Camerounaise slope Cameroon/Nigeria 125 I5
Dorset Canada 173 O5
Dorset U.K. 47 J13
Dorsoidong Co l. China 89 E5
Dortmund Germany 48 E4
Dorton U.S.A. 176 C8
Dortyol Turkey 107 D3
Doruma Dem. Rep. Congo 126 E3
Dorüneh Iran 100 D3
Dorylaeum Turkey see Eskişehir
Do Sãri Iran 100 D4
Dos Bahías, Cabo c. Arg. 205 D6
Dos Cabezas Mountains U.S.A. 183 O9
Dos de Mayo Peru 198 C6
Dos Hermanas Spain 54 F7
Dos Lagunos Guat. 185 H5
Doshakh, Koh-i- mt. Afgh. 101 E3
Dos Palos U.S.A. 182 D5
Dos Pozos Arg. 205 D6
Dosse r. Germany 49 J3
Dosso Niger 125 F3
also spelt Dossé
Dosso, Réserve Partielle de nature res. Niger 125 F3
Dossor Kazakh. 102 C3
Dostyk Kazakh. 88 C2
also spelt Dostyy; formerly known as Druzhba
Dostyy Kazakh. see Dostyk
Dothan U.S.A. 175 C6
Döttingen Germany 48 F3
Douai France 51 J2
Douako Guinea 124 C4
Douala Cameroon 125 H5
Douala-Edéa, Réserve nature res. Cameroon 125 H6
Douarnenez France 50 B4
Douarnenez, Baie de b. France 50 B4
Double Island Hong Kong China 87 [inset]
also known as Wong Wan Chau
Double Island Point Australia 149 G5
Double Mountain Fork r. U.S.A. 179 B5
Double Peak U.S.A. 182 F6
Double Point Australia 149 E3
Double Springs U.S.A. 174 C5
Doubs r. France/Switz. 51 L6
Doubtful Bay Australia 150 D3
Doubtful Island Bay Australia 151 B7
Doubtful Sound N.Z. 153 B13
Doué-la-Fontaine France 50 F5
Douentza Mali 124 E3
Dougga tourist site Tunisia 123 H1
▶Douglas Isle of Man 47 H9
Capital of the Isle of Man.
Douglas N.Z. 152 I7
Douglas S. Africa 132 H6
Douglas AZ U.S.A. 181 E7
Douglas GA U.S.A. 175 D6
Douglas WY U.S.A. 180 F4
Douglas Channel Canada 166 D4
Douglas City U.S.A. 182 B1
Douglas Creek watercourse Australia 146 C2
Douglas Creek r. U.S.A. 183 P1
Douglas Range mts Antarctica 222 T2
Douglas Reef i. Japan see Okino-Tori-shima
Douglasville U.S.A. 175 C5
Dougoulé well Niger 125 H3
Douhi Chad 125 H3
Douhudi China see Gong'an
Doukato, Akra c. Greece 59 B10
Doulaincourt-Saucourt France 51 L4
Douliu Taiwan see Touliu
Doullens France 51 I2
Doumé Benin 125 F4
Doumé Cameroon 125 I5
Doumé r. Cameroon 125 I5
Doumen China 87 E4
Douna Mali 125 E3
Dounkassa Benin 125 F4
Doupovské Hory mts Czech Rep. 49 K5
Dourada, Cachoeira waterfall Brazil 206 D5
Dourada, Serra hills Brazil 202 B5
Dourada, Serra mts Brazil 202 B5
Dourados Brazil 203 A7
Dourados r. Brazil 203 A7
Dourados, Serra dos hills Brazil 203 A7
Dourbali Chad 126 B2
Dourdan r. France 51 I3
Dourdoure Chad 126 C2
Douro r. Port. 54 C3
also known as Duero (Spain)
Doushi China see Gong'an
Doushui Shuiku resr China 87 E3
Doutor Camargo Brazil 206 A10
Douz Tunisia 123 H2
Douze r. France 50 F8
Douziat Chad 126 C6
Dove r. U.K. 47 K11
Dove Brook Canada 169 J2
Dove Bugt b. Greenland 165 Q2
Dove Creek U.S.A. 183 P4
Dover U.K. 47 N12
historically known as Dubris
▶Dover DE U.S.A. 177 J6
State capital of Delaware.
Dover NH U.S.A. 177 O2
Dover NJ U.S.A. 177 K5
Dover OH U.S.A. 176 D5
Dover TN U.S.A. 174 C4
Dover, Point Australia 151 D7
Dover, Strait of France/U.K. 50 H2
also known as Pas de Calais
Dover-Foxcroft U.S.A. 174 G2
Dover Plains U.S.A. 177 L4
Dovey r. U.K. see Dyfi
Doveyrich, Rūd-e r. Iran/Iraq 107 G5
Dovnsklint cliff Denmark 48 H1
Dovre Norway 44 J3
Dovrefjell Nasjonalpark nat. park Norway 44 J3
Dow, Lake Botswana see Xau, Lake
Dowa Malawi 129 B8
Dowagiac U.S.A. 172 G9
Dowgha'i Iran 100 D3
Dowi, Tanjung pt Indon. 76 B2
Dowlatābād Afgh. 101 F2
Dowlatābād Fārs Iran 100 C4
Dowlatābād Fārs Iran 100 D4
Dowlatābād Khorāsān Iran 100 D3
Dowlatābād Khorāsān Iran 101 D3
Dowlatābād Khorāsān Iran 101 D3
Dowl at Yār Afgh. 101 F3
Downey CA U.S.A. 182 F8
Downey ID U.S.A. 180 D4
Downham Market U.K. 47 M11
Downieville U.S.A. 182 D2

Downpatrick U.K. 47 G9
Downs U.S.A. 178 C4
Downsville NY U.S.A. 177 K3
Downsville WI U.S.A. 172 B6
Downton, Mount Canada 166 E4
Dow Rūd Iran 100 B3
Dow Sar Iran 100 A3
Dowshī Iran 101 G3
Dowzha Belarus 43 L6
Doyle U.S.A. 182 D1
Doyles Canada 169 J4
Doyrentsi Bulg. 58 F5
Dozdān r. Iran 100 D5
Dözen is Japan 91 C6
Dozois, Réservoir Canada 168 E4
Drâa, Oued watercourse Morocco 122 C3
Dracena Brazil 206 B8
Drachenwerth S. Africa 133 I4
Drachten Neth. 48 D2
Dragalina Romania 58 I4
Dragan l. Sweden 44 K2
Drăgăneşti-Olt Romania 58 F4
Drăgăneşti-Vlaşca Romania 58 F4
Drăgăşani Romania 58 F3
Draghoender S. Africa 132 G4
Dragoman Bulg. 58 C5
Dragonada i. Greece 59 H13
Dragonera, Isla i. Spain see Sa Dragonera
Dragones Arg. 201 E5
Dragonisi i. Greece 59 G11
also known as Dhragónisos
Dragon Rocks Nature Reserve Australia 151 B7
Dragon's Mouths strait Trin. and Tob./Venez. 187 H5
Dragoon U.S.A. 183 N9
Dragor Denmark 45 K5
Dragos Vodă Romania 58 I4
Dragsfjärd Fin. 45 M3
Draguignan France 51 M9
Drahichyn Belarus 42 G9
also spelt Drogichin
Drakensberg mts Lesotho/S. Africa 133 M6
Drakensberg mts S. Africa 131 F5
Drakensberg Garden S. Africa 133 N6
Draken's Rock mt. S. Africa 133 M7
Drakes Bay U.S.A. 182 A4
Drakulya r. Ukr. 58 I3
Drama Greece 58 F7
Drammen Norway 45 J4
Drang, Prêk r. Cambodia 79 D5
Drangajökull ice cap Iceland 44 [inset] B2
Drangedal Norway 45 J4
Drangme Chhu r. Bhutan 97 F4
Dranov, Lacul l. Romania 58 K4
Dranske Germany 43 K1
Draper U.S.A. 183 M1
Draper, Mount U.S.A. 166 B3
Drapsaca Afgh. see Kunduz
Dras Jammu and Kashmir 96 C2
Drau r. Austria 49 L8
also spelt Drava or Dráva
Drava r. Europe 49 N9
also spelt Drau or Dráva
Dráva r. Hungary 56 M3
also spelt Drau or Drava
Dravinja r. Slovenia 56 H2
Dravograd Slovenia 56 H2
Drawa r. Poland 49 M3
Drawieński Park Narodowy nat. park Poland 49 M2
Drawno Poland 49 M2
Drawsko, Jezioro l. Poland 49 N2
Drawsko Pomorskie Poland 49 N2
Drayton Valley Canada 167 H4
Drebber Germany 48 F3
Dreieich Germany 48 F6
Dreistelzberge hill Germany 48 G5
Drenovci Croatia 56 K3
Drenovets Bulg. 58 D5
Drepano, Akra pt Greece 59 G11
Dresden Canada 173 K8
Dresden Germany 49 K4
Dresden U.S.A. 174 C4
Dretun' Belarus 43 K5
Dreux France 50 H4
Drevsjø Norway 45 K3
Drewryville U.S.A. 177 H9
Drezdenko Poland 49 M3
Driceni Latvia 42 I5
Dridża r. Latvia 42 I6
Driftwood U.S.A. 176 G4
Driggs U.S.A. 180 E4
Drillham Australia 149 F5
Drin r. Albania 58 A6
Drin, Gjiri i b. Albania 58 A6
Drina r. Bos.-Herz./Yugo. 56 L4
Drincea r. Romania 58 D4
Drini i Zi r. Albania 58 B6
Drinit, Gjiri i b. Albania 58 A7
Drino r. Albania 59 B8
Driscoll Island Antarctica 222 O1
Drissa r. Belarus see Vyerkhnyadzvinsk
Drissa r. Belarus see Vyerkhnyadzvinsk
Drobeta - Turnu Severin Romania 58 D4
also known as Turnu Severin
Drochtersen Germany 48 G2
Drogheda Rep. of Ireland 47 F10
Drogichin Belarus see Drahichyn
Drogobych Ukr. see Drohobych
Drohiczyn Poland 49 T3
Drohobych Ukr. 53 C2
also spelt Drogobych
Droichead Átha Rep. of Ireland see Drogheda
Droitwich U.K. 47 J11
Dronne r. France 50 F7
Dronning Ingrid Land reg. Greenland 165 O3
Dronning Louise Land reg. Greenland 165 Q2
Dronning Maud Land reg. Antarctica see Queen Maud Land
Droogmakerij de Beemster tourist site Neth. 48 B3
Dropt r. France 50 F7
Drosh Pak. 101 G3
Drosia Greece 59 E10
Droskovo Rus. Fed. 43 S9
Drovyanaya Rus. Fed. 85 G1
Drowning r. Canada 168 C3
Druk-Yul country Asia see Bhutan
Drumheller Canada 167 H5
Drummond atoll Kiribati see Tabiteuea
Drummond, Lake U.S.A. 177 I9
Drummond Island U.S.A. see McKean
Drummond Island Kiribati see McKean
Drummond Range hills Australia 149 E5
Drummondville Canada 169 F4
Drummore U.K. 46 H9
Drumnadrochit U.K. 46 H6
Drury Lake Canada 166 C2
Druskieniki Lith. see Druskininkai
Druskininkai Lith. 42 F8
formerly known as Druskieniki
Drusti Latvia 42 I4
Druts' r. Belarus 43 L8
Druya Belarus 42 I6
Druzhba Kazakh. see Dostyk
Druzhina Rus. Fed. 39 O3
Druzhnaya Gorka Rus. Fed. 43 L2
Druzhnoye, Ozero l. Rus. Fed. 43 S1
Drweca r. Poland 49 P2

Dry r. Australia 148 B2
Dryanovo Bulg. 58 G5
Dryazhno Rus. Fed. 43 J3
Dry Bay U.S.A. 166 B3
Dryberry Lake Canada 168 A3
Drybin Belarus 43 M7
Dry Cimarron r. U.S.A. 178 B4
Dryden Canada 168 A3
Dryden NY U.S.A. 177 I3
Dryden TX U.S.A. 176 C9
Dry Fork r. U.S.A. 180 F5
Drygalski Fjord inlet S. Georgia 205 [inset]
Drygalski Ice Tongue Antarctica 223 L1
Drygalski Island Antarctica 223 I9
Drygarn Fawr hill U.K. 47 I11
Dry Harts r. S. Africa 133 I4
Dry Lake U.S.A. 183 J5
Dry Lake l. U.S.A. 182 G2
Dry Ridge U.S.A. 176 A7
Drysa r. Belarus 43 J5
Drysdale r. Australia 150 D2
Drysdale Island Australia 148 B1
Drysdale River National Park Australia 150 D2
Drysvaty, Vozyera l. Belarus/Lith. see Drūkšiu ežeras
Dry Tortugas is U.S.A. 175 D7
Drzewica Poland 49 R4
Dschang Cameroon 125 H5
Dua r. Dem. Rep. Congo 126 D4
Düāb r. Iran 100 B3
Du'an China 87 D4
also known as Anyang
Duancun China see Wuxiang
Duaringa Australia 149 F4
Duars reg. India 97 F4
Duarte, Pico mt. Dom. Rep. 187 F3
formerly known as Trujillo, Monte
Duba Saudi Arabia 104 A2
Dubai U.A.E. 105 F2
also spelt Dubayy
Dubakella Mountain U.S.A. 182 A1
Dubăsari Moldova 58 L1
formerly known as Dubăsar' or Dubossary
Dubăsari prov. Moldova 53 H2
Dubawnt r. Canada 167 L2
Dubawnt Lake Canada 167 K2
Dubayy U.A.E. see Dubai
Dubbagh, Jabal ad mt. Saudi Arabia 104 A2
Dubbo Australia 147 F3
Dube r. Liberia 124 C4
Dübendorf Switz. 51 O5
Dübener Heide park Germany 49 J4
Dubesar' Moldova see Dubăsari
Dubets U.S.A. 182 A1
Dubičiai Lith. 42 I7
Dubinës, Maja e mt. Albania 58 A6
Dubingiai Lith. 42 G6
Dublán Mex. 184 D2
Dublin Canada 172 F2
▶Dublin Rep. of Ireland 47 F10
Capital of the Republic of Ireland. Also known as Baile Átha Cliath.
Dublin GA U.S.A. 175 D5
Dublin VA U.S.A. 176 E8
Dubna r. Latvia 42 I5
Dubna Moskovskaya Oblast' Rus. Fed. 43 S5
Dubna Tul'skaya Oblast' Rus. Fed. 43 R7
Dubnica nad Váhom Slovakia 49 P7
Dubno Ukr. 41 C6
Dubois U.S.A. 180 D3
Du Bois U.S.A. 176 G4
Dubossary Moldova see Dubăsari
Dubovaya Roshcha Rus. Fed. 43 T8
Dubovka Rus. Fed. 41 H6
Dubovka Volgogradskaya Oblast' Rus. Fed. 41 H6
Duboovoye, Ozero l. Rus. Fed. 43 V6
Dubovskoye Rus. Fed. 41 G7
Dübrar Pass Azer. 107 G2
Dubréka Guinea 124 B4
Dubris U.K. see Dover
Dubrovichi Rus. Fed. 43 U7
Dubrovka Bryanskaya Oblast' Rus. Fed. 43 O8
Dubrovka Pskovskaya Oblast' Rus. Fed. 43 K4
Dubrovka Pskovskaya Oblast' Rus. Fed. 43 K4
Dubrovnik Croatia 56 L5
historically known as Ragusa
Dubrovytsya Ukr. 41 C6
formerly known as Dombrovitsa
Dubrowna Belarus 43 L7
Dubun Kazakh. 103 J4
Dubuque U.S.A. 174 B2
Dubysa r. Lith. 42 E6
Duc de Gloucester, Îles du is Fr. Polynesia 221 I7
English form Duke of Gloucester Islands
Ducey France 50 E4
Duchang China 87 F2
Duchateau Entrance sea chan. P.N.G. 149 G1
Ducherow Germany 49 K2
Duchesne U.S.A. 183 N1
Duchesne r. U.S.A. 183 O1
Duchess Australia 148 C4
Duchess Canada 167 I5
Ducie Island Pitcairn Is 221 J7
Duck r. U.S.A. 174 C5
Duck Bay Canada 167 K4
Duck Creek r. Australia 150 A4
Duck Lake Canada 167 J4
Duck Valley Indian Reservation res. U.S.A. 180 C4
Duckwater U.S.A. 183 I3
Duckwater Peak U.S.A. 183 I3
Đức Trọng Vietnam 79 E6
Duda r. Col. 198 C4
Duderstadt Germany 48 H4
Dudeşti Vechi Romania 58 B2
Dudhi India 97 D4
Dudinka Rus. Fed. 39 I3
Dudley U.K. 47 J11
Dudleyville U.S.A. 183 N9
Dudna r. India 94 C2
Duduza S. Africa 133 N4
Duékoué Côte d'Ivoire 124 D5
Duen, Bukit vol. Indon. 76 C3
Duero r. Spain 55 I3
also spelt Douro (Portugal)
Dufault, Lac l. Canada 173 O2
Dufferin, Cape Canada 168 E1
Duffer Peak U.S.A. 180 C4
Duffield U.S.A. 176 C9
Duff Islands Solomon Is 145 F2
Dufftown U.K. 46 I6
Dufourspitze mt. Italy/Switz. 56 A3
Dufrost Canada 167 L5
Dugal Uzbek. 103 F5
also spelt Dughoba
Dugald r. Australia 149 D3
Duga-Zapadnaya, Mys c. Rus. Fed. 39 Q4
Dughoba Uzbek. see Dugal
Dugi Otok i. Croatia 56 G4
Dugi Rat Croatia 56 I5
Dugna Rus. Fed. 43 R7
Dugopolje Croatia 56 I5
Dugo Selo Croatia 56 I3
Dugui Qarag China 85 F4
Dügüncübaşı Turkey 58 I7
Dugway U.S.A. 183 L1
Du He r. China 87 D1

251

Duhūn Tārsū *mts* Chad/Libya **120** C4
Duida-Marahuaca, Parque Nacional *nat. park* Venez. **199** E4
Duifken Point Australia **149** D2
Duisburg Germany **48** D4
Duitama Col. **198** C3
Dujiangyan China **86** B2
formerly known as Guanxian
Dūkān Dam Iraq **107** F3
Dukat Rus. Fed. **39** P3
Dukat *mt.* Yugo. **58** D6
Dukathole S. Africa **133** K7
Duke Island U.S.A. **166** D4
Duke of Clarence *atoll* Tokelau *see* Nukunonu
Duke of Gloucester Islands Fr. Polynesia *see* Duc de Gloucester, Îles du
Duke of York *atoll* Tokelau *see* Atafu
Duk Fadiat Sudan **128** A3
Duk Faiwil Sudan **128** A3
Dukhān Qatar **105** E2
Dukhnah Saudi Arabia **104** C2
Dukhovnitskoye Rus. Fed. **102** B1
Dukhovshchina Rus. Fed. **43** N6
Dukhovshehinskaya Vozvyshennost' *hills* Rus. Fed. **43** M6
Duki Rus. Fed. **82** D2
Duki *r.* Rus. Fed. **82** D2
Dukku Nigeria **125** H4
Dukla Poland **49** S6
Dukou China *see* Panzhihua
Dūkštas Lith. **42** I6
Dukwe Botswana **131** E4
Dulaanhaan Mongolia **85** E1
Dulac U.S.A. **175** B6
Dulan China **84** C4
also known as Qagan Us
Dulawan Phil. *see* Datu Piang
Dulce *r.* Arg. **204** E3
Dulce *r.* Spain **55** I4
Dulce U.S.A. **181** F5
Dulce, Golfo *b.* Costa Rica **186** C5
Dulce Nombre de Culmi Hond. **186** B4
Dulcinea Chile **204** C2
Dul'durga Rus. Fed. **85** G1
Dulgalakh *r.* Rus. Fed. **39** N3
Dülgopol Bulg. **58** I5
Dulhunty *r.* Australia **149** D1
Dulishi Hu *salt l.* China **89** C5
Dulit, Pegunungan *mts* Sarawak Malaysia **77** F2
Duliu Jiang *r.* China **87** C3
Duljugan Point Phil. **74** C4
Dullabchara India **97** G4
Dullstroom S. Africa **133** O2
Dülmen Germany **48** E4
Dulovka Rus. Fed. **43** J4
Dulovo Bulg. **58** I5
Duluth U.S.A. **174** A2
Dulyapino Rus. Fed. **43** V4
Dūmā Syria **109** H4
Dumaguete Phil. **74** B4
Dumai Indon. **76** C2
Dumanquilas Bay Phil. **74** B5
Dumaran *i.* Phil. **74** A4
Dumarchen *i.* Indon. **75** C1
Dumaresq *r.* Australia **147** F2
Dumas *AR* U.S.A. **174** B5
Dumas *TX* U.S.A. **179** B5
Dumayr Syria **107** D4
Dumayr, Jabal *mts* Syria **109** H4
Dumbarton U.K. **46** H8
Dumbe S. Africa **133** O4
Dumbéa New Caledonia **145** F4
Dümbier *mt.* Slovakia **49** Q7
Dumbleyung Australia **151** B7
Dumbleyung, Lake *salt flat* Australia **151** B7
Dumbo Cameroon **125** H5
Dumdum *i.* Indon. **77** D2
Dumfries U.K. **47** I8
Dumești Romania **58** I1
Duminichi *Kaluzhskaya Oblast'* Rus. Fed. **43** Q8
Duminichi *Kaluzhskaya Oblast'* Rus. Fed. **43** Q8
Dûmitra Romania **58** F1
Dumka India **97** E4
Dummaguden India **94** C4
Dümmer, *Naturpark nature res.* Germany **48** F3
Dummerstorf Germany **49** J1
Dumoga Indon. **75** C2
Dumoine *r.* Canada **168** E4
Dumoine, Lac *l.* Canada **173** P4
Dumont, Lac *l.* Canada **173** P4
Dumont d'Urville *research station* Antarctica **223** I2
Dumont d'Urville Sea Antarctica **223** I2
Dumraon India **97** E4
Dumsuk *i.* Saudi Arabia **104** C4
Dumyât Egypt **121** F7
English form Damietta
Dumyât, Masabb *est.* Egypt **108** C6
Dumyât *governorate* Egypt **108** C6
Duna *r.* Hungary **49** P9 *see* Danube
Dünaburg Latvia *see* Daugavpils
Dunaföldvár Hungary **49** P9

Dunaj *r.* Slovakia **49** O8 *see* Danube
Dunajec *r.* Poland **49** R5
Dunajská Streda Slovakia **49** O8
Dunajs'ki Plavni *nature res.* Ukr. **58** K3
Dunakeszi Hungary **49** Q8
Dunanbay Kazakh. *see* Dunenbay
Dunany Point Rep. of Ireland **47** F10
Dunapataj Hungary **49** P9
Dunārea *r.* Romania **58** J3 *see* Danube
Dunării, Delta Romania *see* Danube Delta
Dunaszekcsö Hungary **49** P9
Dunaújváros Hungary **49** P9
formerly known as Sztálinváros
Dunav *r.* Bulg./Croatia/Yugo. **58** H5 *see* Danube
Dunavtsi Bulg. **58** D5
Dunay Rus. Fed. **90** C3
Dunay *r.* Ukr. **58** J3 *see* Danube
Dunay, Ostrova *is* Rus. Fed. **39** M2
Dunayivtsi Ukr. **41** C6
Dunback N.Z. **153** E13
Dunbar Australia **149** D3
Dunbar *PA* U.S.A. **176** F6
Dunbar *WI* U.S.A. **172** E5
Dunbar *WV* U.S.A. **176** D7
Dunbeath U.K. **46** I5
Duncan Canada **166** F5
Duncan *AZ* U.S.A. **183** I9
Duncan *OK* U.S.A. **179** C5
Duncan, Cape Canada **168** D2
Duncan Lake *B.C.* Canada **167** G5
Duncan Lake *N.W.T.* Canada **167** H2
Duncannon U.S.A. **177** I5
Duncan Passage India **95** G4
Duncansby Head U.K. **46** I5
Duncan Town Bahamas **186** E2
Dundaga Latvia **42** D4
Dundalk Rep. of Ireland **47** F9
also known as Dún Dealgan
Dundalk U.S.A. **177** I6
Dundalk Bay Rep. of Ireland **47** F10
Dundas Canada **173** N7
Dundas Greenland **165** M2
also known as Uummannaq
Dundas, Lake *salt flat* Australia **151** C7
Dundas Island Canada **166** D4
Dundas Nature Reserve Australia **151** C7
Dundas Peninsula Canada **165** H2
Dundas Strait Australia **148** A1
Dundbürd Mongolia **85** F2
Dún Dealgan Rep. of Ireland *see* Dundalk
Dundee S. Africa **133** O5
Dundee U.K. **46** J7
Dundee U.S.A. **177** I3
Dundgovi *prov.* Mongolia **85** E2
Dundoo Australia **147** E5
Dundrum Bay U.K. **47** G9
Dundwa Range *mts* India/Nepal **97** D4
Dune, Lac *l.* Canada **169** F1
Dunedin N.Z. **153** E13
Dunedin U.S.A. **175** D6
Dunenbay Kazakh. **103** J2
also known as Dönenbay; *formerly spelt* Dunanbay
Dunfermline U.K. **46** I7
Dungannon U.K. **47** F9
Dún Garbhán Rep. of Ireland *see* Dungarvan
Dungargarh India **96** B3
Dungarpur India **96** B5
Dungarvan Rep. of Ireland **47** E11
also known as Dún Garbhán
Dung Co *l.* China **89** E6
Dungeness *hd* U.K. **47** M13
Dungeness, Punta *pt* Arg. **205** C9
Dungu Dem. Rep. Congo **126** F4
Dungun Malaysia **76** C1
formerly known as Kuala Dungun
Dungunab Sudan **104** B3
Dunhua China **82** C4
Dunhuang China **84** B3
Dunkeld Australia **149** T5
Dunkeld U.K. **46** I7
Dunkerque France *see* Dunkirk
Dunkirk France **51** I1
also spelt Dunkerque
Dunkirk U.S.A. **176** F3
Dunkwa Ghana **125** E5
Dún Laoghaire Rep. of Ireland **47** F10
Dunlap *IA* U.S.A. **178** D3
Dunlap *TN* U.S.A. **172** H9
Dunlap *TN* U.S.A. **174** C5
Dunluce *tourist site* U.K. **47** F8
Dunmanway Rep. of Ireland **47** C12
Dunmarra Australia **148** B3
Dunmore *PA* U.S.A. **177** J4
Dunmore *WV* U.S.A. **176** F7
Dunmore Town Bahamas **186** D1
Dunn U.S.A. **174** E5
Dunnet Head U.K. **46** I5
Dunnigan U.S.A. **182** C3
Dunning U.S.A. **178** C3
Dunn Rock Nature Reserve Australia **151** B7
Dunnville Canada **173** N8
Dunolly Australia **147** D4
Dunphy U.S.A. **183** H1
Duns U.K. **46** J8
Dunsandel N.Z. **153** G11
Dunsborough Australia **151** A7
Dunsmuir U.S.A. **180** B4
Dunstan Mountains N.Z. **153** D13
Duntroon N.Z. **153** F12
Dunvegan U.K. **46** F6
Dunvegan Lake Canada **167** J2
Dunyapur Pak. **101** G4
Duobukur *r.* China **85** J1
Duolun China **85** H3
also known as Dolonnur
Dupadu India **94** C3
Dupang Ling *mts* China **87** D3
Duparquet Canada **145** F4
Duparquet, Lac *l.* Canada **173** N2
Duperré Alg. *see* Aïn Defla
Dupnitsa Bulg. **58** E6
formerly known as Stanke Dimitrov
Dupree U.S.A. **178** B2
Dupuy, Cape Australia **150** A4
Duqaylah *i.* Saudi Arabia **104** C4
Duque de Bragança Angola *see* Calandula
Duque de Caxias Brazil **207** J8
Duque de York, Isla *i.* Chile **205** B8
Duquette U.S.A. **172** A4
Dura *r.* Eth. **128** C2
Dūrā West Bank **108** G6
Durack *r.* Australia **150** D3
Durack Range *hills* Australia **150** D3
Dura Europos Syria *see* Aş Şāliḥiyah
Durağan Turkey **106** C2
Durance *r.* France **51** K9
Durand *MI* U.S.A. **173** J8
Durand *WI* U.S.A. **172** B6
Durango Baja California Mex. **183** I9
Durango *Durango* Mex. **184** D3
Durango *state* Mex. **184** D3
Durango Spain **55** I2
Durango U.S.A. **181** F5
Durani *reg.* Afgh. **101** F4
Dúrankulak Bulg. **58** J5
Duranno, Monte *mt.* Italy **56** E2
Durant *IA* U.S.A. **172** B9
Durant *MS* U.S.A. **175** B5
Durant *OK* U.S.A. **179** C5
Duratón *r.* Spain **54** G3
Durazno Uruguay **204** F4
Durazno Uruguay **204** F4
Durazzo Albania *see* Durrës
Durban S. Africa **133** P6

Durban-Corbières France **51** I10
Durbanville S. Africa **132** C10
Durbin U.S.A. **176** F7
Durbuy Belgium **51** L2
Đurđevac Croatia **56** J2
Durdura, Raas *pt* Somalia **128** F2
Düre China **84** A2
Düren Germany **48** D5
Düren Iran **100** D3
Durg India **97** D5
Durgapur Bangl. **97** F4
Durgapur India **97** E5
Durham Canada **173** M6
Durham U.K. **47** K9
Durham *CA* U.S.A. **182** C2
Durham *NC* U.S.A. **174** E5
Durham *NH* U.S.A. **177** O2
Durham Downs Australia **146** D1
Durhi *well* Eth. **128** D3
Duri Indon. **76** C2
Durlas Rep. of Ireland *see* Thurles
Durleşti Moldova **58** J2
Durmitor *mt.* Yugo. **58** A5
also known as Bobotov Kuk
Durmitor *nat. park* Yugo. **58** A5
Durness U.K. **46** H5
Durocortorum France *see* Reims
Durostorum Bulg. *see* Silistra
Duroverum U.K. *see* Canterbury
Durrës Albania **58** A7
formerly called Durazzo; *historically known as* Dyrrhachium *or* Epidamnus
Dursey Island Rep. of Ireland **47** B12
Dursunbey Turkey **106** B3
Durtal France **50** F5
Duru China *see* Wuchuan
Duru *r.* Dem. Rep. Congo **126** F4
Duru *reg.* Oman **105** F5
Dürûn Iran **101** E3
Durukhsi Somalia **128** E2
Durusu Gölü *l.* Turkey **58** J7
Durūz, Jabal ad *mt.* Syria **109** H5
D'Urville, Tanjung *pt* Indon. **73** I7
D'Urville Island N.Z. **152** H8
Durzab Afgh. **101** F3
Dusetos Lith. **42** H5
Dushan China **87** C3

► **Dushanbe** Tajik. **101** G2
Capital of Tajikistan. Formerly known as Stalinabad.

Dushanzi China **88** D2
also known as Maytag
Dushore U.S.A. **177** I4
Dusia *l.* Lith. **42** E7
Dusky Sound *inlet* N.Z. **153** A13
Dussejour, Cape Australia **150** E2
Düsseldorf Germany **48** D4
Dusti Tajik. **101** G3
formerly known as Pyandzh
Dustlik Uzbek. **103** G4
Dusty U.S.A. **180** D3
Duszniki-Zdrój Poland **49** N5
Dutch East Indies *country* Asia *see* Indonesia
Dutch Guiana *country* S. America *see* Suriname
Dutch Mountain U.S.A. **183** K1
Dutch New Guinea *prov.* Indon. *see* Irian Jaya
Dutch West Indies *terr.* West Indies *see* Netherlands Antilles
Outsan-Wai Nigeria **125** H4
Dutse Nigeria **125** H4
Dutsin-Ma Nigeria **125** G3
Dutton *r.* Australia **149** D4
Dutton Canada **173** L8
Dutton, Lake *salt flat* Australia **146** C2
Dutton, Mount U.S.A. **183** L3
Duval Canada **167** J5
Duved Sweden **44** K3
Duvergé Dom. Rep. **187** F3
Duvert, Lac *l.* Canada **169** G3
Duvno Bos.-Herz. *see* Tomislavgrad
Duweihin *well* Saudi Arabia **100** B5
Duweihin, Khor *b.* Saudi Arabia/U.A.E. **105** E2
Duwin Iraq **107** F3
Duyinzeik Myanmar **78** B4
Duyun China **87** C3
Duzab Pak. **101** E5
Düzce Turkey **106** B2
Duzdab Iran *see* Zāhedān
Dvarets Belarus **42** H9
Dve Mogili Bulg. **58** G5
Dviete Latvia **42** H5
Dvinitsa *r.* Rus. Fed. **43** V2
Dvinsk Latvia *see* Daugavpils
Dvinskaya Guba *g.* Rus. Fed. **40** F2
Dvin'ye, Ozero *l.* Rus. Fed. **43** M5
Dvor Croatia **56** I3
Dvorichi Rus. Fed. **43** T5
Dvoryanka Rus. Fed. **90** B2
Dvoyni Rus. Fed. **43** U6
Dwangwa Malawi **129** B8
Dwarka India **96** A5
Dwarsberg S. Africa **133** K1
Dwellingup Australia **151** B7
Dwesa Nature Reserve S. Africa **133** M9
Dweshula S. Africa **133** O6
Dwight U.S.A. **172** E9
Dwingelderveld, Nationaal Park *nat. park* Neth. **48** D3
Dwyka S. Africa **132** F10
Dwyka *r.* S. Africa **132** F10
D'yakonovo Rus. Fed. **43** V3
Dyanev Turkm. **103** F5
also spelt Dänew; *formerly spelt* Deynau
Dyankovo Bulg. **58** H5
Dyat'kovo Rus. Fed. **43** P8
Dyce U.K. **46** J6
Dyer, Cape Canada **165** M3
Dyer Bay Canada **173** L5
Dyer Plateau Antarctica **222** T2
Dyersburg U.S.A. **174** B4
Dyersville U.S.A. **172** B8
Dyfi *r.* U.K. **47** I11
also spelt Dovey
Dyje *r.* Austria/Czech Rep. **49** N7

► **Dykh-Tau, Gora** *mt.* Rus. Fed. **41** G8
2nd highest mountain in Europe.
europe [landscapes] ▶▶▶ 30–31

Dylewska Góra *hill* Poland **49** Q2
Dymi U.S.A. **178** B4
Dynevor Downs Australia **147** E2
Dynów Poland **49** T6
Dyoki S. Africa **133** M8
Dyrrhachium Albania *see* Durrës
Dysart Australia **149** F4
Dysna *r.* Lith. **42** H6
Dysnų ežeras *l.* Lith. **42** H6
Dysselsdorp S. Africa **132** G10
Dytiki Ellas *admin. reg.* Greece **59** B10
also spelt Dhytiki Ellás
Dytiki Makedonia *admin. reg.* Greece **59** C8
also spelt Dhytiki Makedhonia
Dyulino Rus. Fed. **39** N3
Dyurtyuli Rus. Fed. **40** J5
Dyviziya Ukr. **58** L2
Dzaanhushuu Mongolia **84** D2
Dzadgay Mongolia **84** C3
Dzag Gol *r.* Mongolia **84** C2
Dzalaa Mongolia **84** D1
Dzamïn Üüd Mongolia **85** F3

► **Dzaoudzi** Mayotte **129** E8
Capital of Mayotte.

Dzaudzhikau Rus. Fed. *see* Vladikavkaz
Dzavhan *prov.* Mongolia **84** B1
Dzavhan Gol *r.* Mongolia **84** B1
Dżbán *mts* Czech Rep. **49** K5
Dzegstey Mongolia **84** D1
Dzelter Mongolia **85** E1
Dzeni Latvia **42** H4
Dzerzhinsk Belarus *see* Dzyarzhynsk
Dzerzhinsk Rus. Fed. **40** G4
Dzerzhinskoye Kazakh. *see* Kabanbay
Dzhagdy, Khrebet *mts* Rus. Fed. **82** C1
Dzhaki-Unakhta Yakbyyana, Khrebet *mts* Rus. Fed. **82** D2
Dzhaksy Kazakh. *see* Zhaksy
Dzhakul', Gora *mt.* Rus. Fed. **84** B1
Dzhalagash Kazakh. **103** G4
also spelt Zhalaghash
Dzhalalabad Azer. *see* Cälilabad
Dzhalal-Abad Kyrg. *see* Jalal-Abad
Dzhalal-Abadskaya Oblast' *admin. div.* Kyrg. *see* Jalal-Abad
Dzhalil' Rus. Fed. **40** J5
Dzhalinda Rus. Fed. **82** A1
Dzhaltyr Kazakh. *see* Zhaltyr
Dzhambeyty Kazakh. *see* Zhympity
Dzhambul Kazakh. *see* Taraz
Dzhambulskaya Oblast' *admin. div.* Kazakh. *see* Zhambylskaya Oblast'
Dzhanga Turkm. **102** C4
also known as Jangnga
Dzhangala Kazakh. **102** C2
formerly known as Kisykkamys
Dzhangel'dy Uzbek. **103** E4
also spelt Jangeldi; *formerly spelt* Dzhankel'dy *or* Dzhingil'dy
Dzhankel'dy Uzbek. *see* Dzhangel'dy
Dzhankoy Ukr. **41** E7
Dzhansugorov Kazakh. **103** I3
also spelt Zhansügirov
Dzhanybek Kazakh. **102** A2
also known as Zhänibek
Dzharkent Kazakh. *see* Zharkent
Dzharkurgan Uzbek. **103** F5
Dzhebariki-Khaya Rus. Fed. **39** N3
Dzhebel Bulg. **58** G7
Dzhebel Turkm. **102** C5
also spelt Jebel
Dzheltulak Rus. Fed. **82** B1
Dzhergalan Kyrg. *see* Jyrgalang
Dzhetygara Kazakh. *see* Zhitikara
Dzhetymtau, Gory *hills* Uzbek. **103** F4
Dzhetysay Kazakh. *see* Zhetysay
Dzheykhun Turkm. **103** E5
also spelt Jeyhun; *formerly known as* Farāb-Pristan'
Dzhezdy Kazakh. *see* Zhezdy
Dzhezkazgan Kazakh. *see* Zhezkazgan
Dzhida Rus. Fed. **84** D1
Dzhida *r.* Rus. Fed. **84** E1
Dzhidinskiy, Khrebet *mts* Mongolia/Rus. Fed. **84** D1
Dzhigirbent Turkm. **103** E4
also spelt Jigerbent
Dzhilandy Tajik. **101** H2
also spelt Dzhelondi *or* Jelondí
Dzhingil'dy Uzbek. *see* Dzhangel'dy
Dzhirgatal' Tajik. *see* Jirgatol
Dzhizak Uzbek. **103** F4
also spelt Jizzakh
Dzhizak Oblast *admin. div.* Uzbek. *see* Dzhizakskaya Oblast'
Dzhizakskaya Oblast' *admin. div.* Uzbek. **103** F5
English form Dzhizak Oblast; *also known as* Jizzakh Wiloyati
Dzhokhar Ghala Rus. Fed. *see* Groznyy
Dzhubga Rus. Fed. **41** F7
Dzhu-Dzhu-Klu Turkm. **102** E5
Dzhugdzhur, Khrebet *mts* Rus. Fed. **39** N4
Dzhul'fa Azer. *see* Culfa
Dzhuma Uzbek. **103** F5
also spelt Juma
Dzhungarskiy Alatau, Khrebet *mts* China/Kazakh. **88** B2
Dzhurun Kazakh. *see* Zhuryn
Dzhusaly Kazakh. **103** F3
also spelt Zhosaly
Dzialdowo Poland **49** R2
Dzibalchén Mex. **185** H5
Dzierzgoń Poland **49** Q2
Dzierzoniów Poland **49** N5
Dzilam de Bravo Mex. **185** H4
Dzioua Alg. **123** G2
Dzisna Belarus **43** J6
Dzitás Mex. **185** H4
Dzitva *r.* Belarus **42** G8
Dzodze Ghana **125** F5
Dzogsool Mongolia **84** E2
Dzöölön Mongolia **84** C1
Dziükija *nat. park* Lith. **42** F7
Dzungarian Basin China *see* Junggar Pendi
Dzungarian Gate *pass* China/Kazakh. **88** C2
also known as Alataw Shankou
Dzüünbayan Mongolia **85** F2
Dzüünharaa Mongolia **85** E1
Dzuunmod Mongolia **85** E2
Dzüyl Mongol a **84** B2
formerly known as Tonhil
Dzyaniskavichy Belarus **42** H9
Dzyarzhranja Belarus **43** M8
Dzyarzhynsk Belarus **42** I8
Dzyarzhynsk Belarus **43** J6
Dzyarzhynsk Belarus **42** I8
formerly spelt Dzerzhinsk; *formerly known as* Kaydanovo
Dzyatlava Belarus **42** G8
Dzyatlavichy Belarus **42** H9
Dzyerkawshchyna Belarus **42** I6

↓ **E**

Eabamet Lake Canada **168** C3
Eads U.S.A. **178** B4
Eagar U.S.A. **183** O7
Eagle *r.* Canada **169** J2
Eagle *AK* U.S.A. **166** D3
Eagle *CO* U.S.A. **180** E5
Eagle Cap *mt.* U.S.A. **180** C3
Eagle Crags *mt.* U.S.A. **183** G6
Eagle Creek *r.* Canada **167** J4
Eagle Lake *CA* U.S.A. **182** D1
Eagle Lake *ME* U.S.A. **174** G1
Eagle Lake *l.* U.S.A. **181** F7
Eagle Mountain *hill* U.S.A. **174** B2
Eagle Pass U.S.A. **179** B6
Eagle Passage Falkland Is **205** F9
Eaglesham Canada **167** G4
Eagle Tail Mountains U.S.A. **183** K8
Eagle Village U.S.A. **166** A1
Earaheedy Australia **151** C5
Ear Falls Canada **168** A3
Earlimart U.S.A. **182** E5
Earl Mountains N.Z. **153** B13
Earlton Canada **173** N3
Earn *r.* U.K. **46** I7
Earnscleugh N.Z. **153** D13

Earnslaw, Mount N.Z. **153** C12
also known as Pikirakatahi
Earth U.S.A. **179** B5
Easky U.S.A. **174** D5
East, Mount *hill* Australia **151** C6
East Alligator *r.* Australia **148** B2
East Antarctica *reg.* Antarctica **223** H1
East Aurat U.S.A. **177** J4
East Aurora U.S.A. **176** G3
East Baines *r.* Australia **148** A2
East Bay *r.* U.S.A. **175** B6
East Bay *inlet* U.S.A. **175** C6
East Bengal *country* Asia *see* Bangladesh
East Berlin U.S.A. **177** I6
Eastbourne N.Z. **152** I9
Eastbourne U.K. **47** M13
East Branch U.S.A. **176** F5
East Branch Clarion River Reservoir U.S.A. **176** G4
East Caicos *i.* Turks and Caicos Is **187** F2
East Cape N.Z. **152** M5
East Cape Rus. Fed. *see* Dezhneva, Mys
East Carbon City U.S.A. **183** N2
East Chicago U.S.A. **172** F9
East China Sea N. Pacific Ocean **81** L6
also known as Dong Hai
East Coast Bays N.Z. **152** I4
East Dereham U.K. **47** M11
East Dubuque U.S.A. **172** C8
Eastend Canada **167** I5
Easter Group *is* Australia **151** A6

► Easter Island S. Pacific Ocean **221** K7
Part of Chile. Also known as Pascua, Isla de.

Eastern *admin. reg.* Ghana **125** E5
Eastern *prov.* Kenya **128** E5
Eastern *prov.* Sierra Leone **124** C4
Eastern *prov.* Zambia **127** C4
Eastern Cape *prov.* S. Africa **133** K8
Eastern Creek *r.* Australia **149** D4
Eastern Desert Egypt **121** G3
also known as Şaḥra el Sharqīya
Eastern Equatoria *state* Sudan **128** B3
Eastern Ghats *mts* India **94** C3

► Eastern Island *HI* U.S.A. **220** G4
Mos: northerly point of Oceania.

Eastern Lesser Sunda Islands *prov.* Indon. *see* Nusa Tenggara Timur
Eastern Nara *canal* Pak. **101** G5
Eastern Samoa *terr.* S. Pacific Ocean *see* American Samoa
Eastern Sayan Mountains Rus. Fed. *see* Vostochnyy Sayan
Eastern Taurus *plat.* Turkey *see* Güneydoğu Toroslar
Eastern Transvaal *prov.* S. Africa *see* Mpumalanga
Easterville Canada **167** L4
East Falkland *i.* Falkland Is **205** F9
East Frisian Islands Germany **48** E2
also known as Ostfriesische Inseln
East Grand Forks U.S.A. **178** D2
East Grand Rapids U.S.A. **172** H8
Easthampton U.S.A. **177** M3
East Hampton U.S.A. **177** N4
East Hartford U.S.A. **177** M4
East Haydon Australia **149** D3
East Holden U.S.A. **177** Q1
East Island P.N.G. **149** G1
East Jamaica U.S.A. **173** M4
East Jordan U.S.A. **173** H5
East Kazakhstan Oblast *admin. div.* Kazakh. *see* Vostochnyy Kazakhstan
East Kilbride U.K. **46** H8
East Lamma Channel Hong Kong China **87** [inset]
also known as Tung Pok Liu Hoi Hap
Eastland U.S.A. **179** C5
East Lansing U.S.A. **173** I8
Eastleigh U.K. **47** K13
East Linton U.K. **46** J8
East Liverpool U.S.A. **176** E5
East London S. Africa **133** L10
also known as Oos-Londen
East Longmeadow U.S.A. **177** M3
Eastmain Canada **168** E2
Eastmain *r.* Canada **168** E2
Eastman U.S.A. **175** D5
East Middlebury U.S.A. **177** L2
East Millinocket U.S.A. **174** H2
East Naples U.S.A. **175** D7
Easton *CA* U.S.A. **182** E5
Easton *MD* U.S.A. **177** I7
Easton *PA* U.S.A. **177** K5
East Pakistan *country* Asia *see* Bangladesh
East Park Reservoir U.S.A. **182** B2
East Peoria U.S.A. **172** D10
East Point Canada **169** I4
Eastpoint *ME* U.S.A. **174** H2
Eastport *MI* U.S.A. **172** H5
East Range *mts* U.S.A. **182** G1
East Retford U.K. *see* Retford
East Ridge U.S.A. **174** C5
East St Louis U.S.A. **174** B4
East Sea N. Pacific Ocean *see* Japan, Sea of
East Shoal Lake Canada **167** L5
East Siberian Sea Rus. Fed. **39** Q2
also known as Vostochno-Sibirskoye More
East Side Canal *r.* U.S.A. **182** E6
East Tavaputs Plateau U.S.A. **183** O2
East Tawas U.S.A. **173** J6

► Eastern Timor *terr.* Asia **75** C5
Former Portuguese territory. Part of Indonesia 1976-1999, awaiting independence. Formerly known as Portuguese Timor *or* Timor Timur.
asia [countries] ▶▶▶ 64–67

East Tons *r.* India **97** E4
East Troy U.S.A. **172** E8
East Verde *r.* U.S.A. **183** M7
Eastview Canada *see* Vanier
East Walker *r.* U.S.A. **182** E3
East York Canada **173** N7

► **Edinburgh** U.K. **46** I8
Capital of Scotland.

Edincik Turkey **59** I8
Edinet Moldova **41** D7
Edinet *prov.* Moldova **53** H2
Edingeni Malawi **129** B8
Edirne Turkey **106** A2
Edirne *prov.* Turkey **58** H8
Edisto *r.* U.S.A. **175** D5
Edith, Mount U.S.A. **180** E3
Edithburgh Australia **146** C3
Edith Cavell, Mount Canada **166** G4
Edith Ronne Land *ice feature* Antarctica *see* Ronne Ice Shelf
Edith Withnell, Lake *salt flat* Australia **151** C2
Edjeleh Libya **120** A3
Edjérir *watercourse* Mali **125** F2
Edjudina Australia **151** C5
Edmond U.S.A. **179** C5
Edmonds U.S.A. **180** B3
Edmonton Australia **149** E3

► **Edmonton** Canada **167** H4
Provincial capital of Alberta.

Edmonton U.S.A. **174** C4
Edmore U.S.A. **173** H7
Edmund Lake Canada **167** M4
Edmundston Canada **169** G4
Edna U.S.A. **179** C6
Edo Japan *see* Tōkyō
Edo *state* Nigeria **125** G5
Edolo Italy **56** C2
Edom *reg.* Israel/Jordan **108** G7
Edremit Turkey **106** A3
historically known as Adramyttium
Edremit Körfezi *b.* Turkey **106** A3
historically known as Adramyttium, Gulf of
Edrengiyn Nuruu *mts* Mongolia **84** C2
Edsbro Sweden **45** L4

Ebamet Lake Canada **168** C3
Earp U.S.A. **183** J7
Ebla *tourist site* Syria **109** H2
Ebo Angola **127** B7
Ebola *r.* Dem. Rep. Congo **126** D4
Ebolowa Cameroon **125** H6
Ebony Namibia **130** B4
Ebonyi *state* Nigeria **125** H5
Ebre *r.* Spain *see* Ebro
Ebro *r.* Spain **55** I4
also spelt Ebre
Ebro, Embalse del *resr* Spain **54** H1
Eburacum U.K. *see* York
Ebusus *i.* Spain *see* Ibiza
Ecbatana Iran *see* Hamadän
Eccles U.S.A. **176** D8
Eceabat Turkey **59** H8
also spelt Maydos
Echague Phil. **74** B2
Echarri-Aranaz Spain **55** I2
also spelt Etxarri-Aranatz
Ech Chélif Alg. **123** F1
formerly known as El Asnam *or* Orléansville
Ech Cherita, Sebkhet *salt pan* Tunisia **57** C13
Echeng China *see* Ezhou
Echinades *i.* Greece **59** B10
Echinos Greece **58** F7
also spelt Ekhínos
Echizen-misaki *pt* Japan **91** D7
Echmiadzin Armenia *see* Ejmiatsin
Echo Bay *N.W.T.* Canada **167** G1
formerly known as Port Radium
Echo Bay *Ont.* Canada **168** C4
Echo Cliffs *esc.* U.S.A. **183** M5
Echoing *r.* Canada **167** M4
Échouani, Lac *l.* Canada **173** R3
Echternach Lux. **51** M4
Echuca Australia **147** E4
Écija Spain **54** F7
Ečka Vojvodina, Srbija Yugo. **58** B3
Eckerman U.S.A. **173** H4
Eckernförde Germany **48** G1
Eckerö Fin. **45** I3
Eckerö *i.* Fin. **42** A1
Eclipse Sound *sea chan.* Canada **165** K2
Ecoporanga Brazil **207** M5
Écrins, Parc National des *nat. park* France **51** M8

► **Ecuador** *country* S. America **198** B5
southamerica [countries] ▶▶▶ 192–193
southamerica [contrasts] ▶▶▶ 194–195

Écueillé France **50** H5
Ed Eritrea **121** I6
Ed Sweden **45** J4
Eday *i.* U.K. **46** J4
Ed Da'ein Sudan **126** E2
Ed Damazin Sudan **128** B2
Ed Damer Sudan **121** G5
also spelt Ad Damir
Ed Debba Sudan **121** F5
also spelt Ad Dabbah
Eddeki *well* Chad **120** C5
Eddies Cove Canada **169** J3
Ed Dueim Sudan **121** G6
also spelt Ad Duwaym
Eddystone Point Australia **147** F5
Eddyville U.S.A. **174** B4
Ede Neth. **48** C3
Edéa Cameroon **125** H6
Edehon Lake Canada **167** L2
Edéia Brazil **206** D4
Eden Australia **147** F4
Eden *r.* U.K. **47** I9
Eden *NC* U.S.A. **176** F9
formerly known as Leaksville
Eden *TX* U.S.A. **179** C5
Edenburg S. Africa **133** J6
Edendale N.Z. **153** C14
Edendale S. Africa **133** O6
Edenderry Rep. of Ireland **47** E10
Edenhope Australia **146** D4
Edenton U.S.A. **177** I9
Edenvale S. Africa **133** M3
Edenville S. Africa **133** L4
Eder *r.* Germany **48** G4
Eder-Stausee *resr* Germany **51** O1
Edessa Greece **58** D8
also spelt Edhessa
Edessa Turkey *see* Şanlıurfa
Edevik Sweden **44** K3
Edfu Egypt *see* Idfu
Edgar Ranges *hills* Australia **150** C3
Edgartown U.S.A. **177** O4
Edgecumbe N.Z. **152** K5
Edgecumbe Island Solomon Is *see* Utupua
Edgefield U.S.A. **175** D5
Edge Island Svalbard *see* Edgeøya
Edgeøya *i.* Svalbard **38** C2
English form Edge Island
Edgerton Canada **167** I4
Edgerton *OH* U.S.A. **176** A4
Edgerton *VA* U.S.A. **176** H9
Edgerton *WI* U.S.A. **172** D8
Edgewood U.S.A. **177** I6
Édhessa Greece *see* Edessa
Edievale N.Z. **153** D13
Edigan Rus. Fed. **88** D1
Édikel *well* Niger **125** G2
Edina U.S.A. **174** B3
Edinboro U.S.A. **176** E4
Edinburg *TX* U.S.A. **179** C7
Edinburg *VA* U.S.A. **176** G7

Edsbyn Sweden 45 K3
Edsele Sweden 44 L3
Edson Canada 167 G4
Eduardo Castex Arg. 204 D4
Eduni, Mount Canada 166 D1
Edward r. N.S.W. Australia 147 E3
Edward r. Qld Australia 149 D2
Edward, Lake Dem. Rep. Congo/Uganda 126 F5
also known as Rutanzige, Lake; formerly known as Idi Amin Dada, Lake
Edward, Mount Antarctica 222 T1
Edwardesabad Pak. see Bannu
Edward Island Australia 148 B2
Edward Island Canada 172 E2
Edward River Aboriginal Reserve Australia 149 D2
Edwards U.S.A. 177 J1
Edwards Plateau U.S.A. 179 B6
Edwardsville U.S.A. 174 B4
Edward VIII Bay Antarctica 223 D2
Edward VII Peninsula Antarctica 223 N1
Edwin B. Forsythe National Wildlife Refuge nature res. U.S.A. 177 K6
Edziza, Mount Canada 166 D3
Edzo Canada see Rae-Edzo
Eel r. U.S.A. 182 A1
Eel, South Fork r. U.S.A. 182 A1
Eendekuil S. Africa 132 C9
Eenzamheid Pan salt pan S. Africa 132 E4
Eesti country Europe see Estonia
Éfaté i. Vanuatu 145 F3
also spelt Vaté; formerly known as Sandwich Island
Efes tourist site Turkey see Ephesus
Effingham U.S.A. 174 B4
Eflâni Turkey 106 C2
Efsus Turkey see Afşin
Eftimie Murgu Romania 58 D4
Eg Mongolia 85 F1
Ega r. Spain 55 J2
Egadi, Isole is Sicilia Italy 57 D10
English form Egadi Islands
Egadi Islands is Sicilia Italy see Egadi, Isole
Egan Range mts U.S.A. 183 J3
Eganville Canada 173 P5
Egbe Nigeria 125 G4
Egedesminde Greenland see Aasiaat
Egentliga Finland reg. Fin. see Varsinais-Suomi
Eger r. Germany 49 J5
Eger Hungary 49 R8
Egersund Norway 45 I4
Egerton, Mount hill Australia 151 B5
Eggenfelden Germany 49 J7
Egg Harbor U.S.A. 172 F5
Egg Harbor City U.S.A. 177 K6
Egg Lake Canada 167 J4
Eggum Norway 44 K1
Egilsstaðir Iceland 44 [inset] D2
Eğin Turkey see Kemaliye
Eginbah Australia 150 B4
Egindibulaq Kazakh. see Yegindybulak
Egindy Kazakh. 103 H2
Eğirdir Turkey 106 B3
Eğirdir Gölü l. Turkey 106 B3
Egiyn Gol r. Mongolia 84 D1
Égletons France 51 I7
Eglinton Island Canada 165 H2
Eglisau Switz. 51 O5
Egmont, Cape N.Z. 152 H7
Egmont, Mount vol. N.Z. see Taranaki, Mount
Egmont National Park N.Z. 152 I7
Egmont Village N.Z. 152 I7
Egua Col. 199 E3
Éguas r. Brazil 202 C5
also known as Correntina
Egvekinot Rus. Fed. 39 S3

►Egypt country Africa 121 F3
2nd most populous country in Africa. Known as Misr or Mudraya in Arabic; formerly known as United Arab Republic; historically known as Aegyptus.
africa [countries] ►►► 114–117

Ehcel well Mali see Agous-n-Ehsel
Ehen Hudag China 84 D4
also known as Alxa Youqi
Ehime pref. Japan 91 C8
Ehingen (Donau) Germany 48 G7
Ehrenberg U.S.A. 183 J8
Ehrenberg Range hills Australia 148 A4
Eibar Spain 55 I1
Eibergen Neth. 48 D3
Eichstätt Germany 48 I7
Eide Norway 44 I3
Eider r. Germany 48 F1
Eidfjord Norway 45 I3
Eiði Faroe Is 46 E1
Eidsvåg Norway 44 J3
Eidsvold Australia 149 F5
Eidsvoll Norway 45 J3
Eifel hills Germany 48 D5
Eigg i. U.K. 46 F7
Eight Degree Channel India/Maldives 94 B5
Eights Coast Antarctica 222 R2
Eighty Mile Beach Australia 150 C3
Eilat Israel 108 F8
also spelt Elat
Eildon, Lake Australia 147 E4
Eildon State Park nature res. Australia 147 E4
Eileen Lake Canada 167 J2
Eilenburg Germany 49 J4
Eilerts de Haan, Natuurreservaat nature res. Suriname 199 G4
Eilerts de Haan Gebergte mts Suriname 199 G4
Eil Malk i. Palau 73 H5
also known as Mecherchar
Einasleigh Australia 149 E3
Einasleigh r. Australia 149 D3
Einbeck Germany 48 G4
Eindhoven Neth. 48 C4
Eindpaal Namibia 132 D2
Einme Myanmar 78 A4
Einsiedeln Switz. 51 O5
Éire country Europe see Ireland, Republic of
Eiriosgaigh i. U.K. see Eriskay
Eiru r. Brazil 198 D6
Eirunepé Brazil 198 D6
Eisberg hill Germany 48 G4
Eiseb watercourse Namibia 130 D3
Eisenach Germany 48 H5
Eisenerz Austria 49 L8
Eisenerzer Alpen mts Austria 49 L8
Eisenhower, Mount Canada see Castle Mountain
Eisenhüttenstadt Germany 49 L3
Eisenstadt Austria 49 N8
Eišiškės Lith. 42 F7
Eisleben Lutherstadt Germany 48 I4
Eistow N.Z. 152 J5
Eitape P.N.G. see Aitape
Eivinvik Norway 45 I3
Eivissa Spain see Ibiza
Eivissa i. Spain see Ibiza
Ejea de los Caballeros Spain 55 J2
Ejeda Madag. 131 [inset] J5
Ejin Horo Qi China see Altan Shiret
Ejin Qi China see Dalain Hob
Ej Jill, Sebkhet salt flat Mauritania 122 B5
Ejmiadzin Armenia see Ejmiatsin
Ejmiatsin Armenia 107 F2
formerly spelt Echmiadzin or Ejmiadzin
Ejura Ghana 125 E5
Ekalaka U.S.A. 180 F3
Ekang Nigeria 125 H5
Ekangala S. Africa 133 M2
Ékata Gabon 126 B4
Ekawasaki Japan 91 C8
Ekenäs Fin. 45 M4
also known as Tammisaari
Ekenäs Sweden 45 K4
Ekenäs skärgårds Nationalpark nat. park Fin. 45 M4
also known as Tammisaaren Saariston Kansallispuisto
Ekerem Turkm. see Okarem
Eket Nigeria 125 G5
Eketahuna N.Z. 152 J8
Ekhínos Greece see Echinos
Ekhmîm Egypt see Akhmîm
Ekibastuz Kazakh. 103 H2
Ekimchan Rus. Fed. 82 D1
Ekinyazı Turkey 109 K1
Ekiti state Nigeria 125 G5
Ekka Island Canada 166 F1
Ekoli Dem. Rep. Congo 126 E5
Ekonda Rus. Fed. 39 K3
Ekondo Titi Cameroon 125 H5
Ekostrovskaya Imandra, Ozero l. Rus. Fed. 44 P2
Ekouamou Congo 126 C4
Ekpoma Nigeria 125 G5
Eksere Turkey see Gündoğmuş
Ekshärad Sweden 45 K3
Eksjö Sweden 45 K4
Ekskavatornyy Rus. Fed. 82 A1
Eksteenfontein S. Africa 132 B5
Ekström Ice Shelf Antarctica 223 X2
Ekträsk Sweden 44 L2
Ekwan r. Canada 168 D2
Ekwan Point Canada 168 D2
Ela Myanmar 78 B4
El Aaiún W. Sahara see Laâyoune
El Abbasiya Sudan 121 F6
Elafonisos i. Greece 59 D12
Elafonisou, Steno sea chan. Greece 59 D12
El 'Agrûd well Egypt 108 F7
Elaia, Cape Cyprus 108 F2
also known as Zeytin Burnu; also spelt Elea, Cape
El Aiadia well Sudan 121 G5
El 'Aiyat Egypt 108 C8
El 'Alamein Egypt 121 F2
also spelt Al 'Alamayn
El Alamo Mex. 184 A2
El Alia Alg. 123 G2
El Alia Tunisia 57 B11
El Alto Peru 198 A6
El 'Amirîya Egypt 108 A6
El Amria Alg. 55 J9
Elands r. S. Africa 133 N1
Elands r. S. Africa 133 O2
Elandsberg mt. S. Africa 133 K9
Elandsdoorn S. Africa 133 N2
Elandsdrif S. Africa 133 J9
Elandskraal S. Africa 133 O5
Elandslaagte S. Africa 133 N5
Elandsputte S. Africa 133 K2
El Aouinet Alg. 57 A13
El Arahal Spain 54 F7
El Araïche Morocco see Larache
El Arco Mex. 184 B2
El Aricha Alg. 123 E2
El 'Arîsh Egypt 121 G2
Elasa i. Greece 59 H13
El Ashmûnein Egypt 121 F3
historically known as Hermopolis Magna
El Asnam Alg. see Ech Chélif
Elassona Greece 59 D9
El Astillero Spain 54 H1
Elat Israel see Eilat
El 'Aţf reg. W. Sahara 122 B5
Elati mt. Greece 59 B10
Elato atoll Micronesia 73 K5
Elazığ Turkey 107 D3
Elba U.S.A. 175 C6
Elba, Isola d' i. Italy 56 C6
historically known as Ilva
El Bahr El Ahmar governorate Egypt 108 C9
El'ban Rus. Fed. 82 E2
El Banco Col. 198 C2
El Bânoûn well Mauritania 124 D2
El Barco de Ávila Spain 54 F4
El Barco de Valdeorras Spain see O Barco
El Barreal salt l. Mex. 184 D2
El Barun Sudan 128 B2
Elbasan Albania 58 B7
Elbaşı Turkey 106 C3
El Bauga Sudan 121 G5
El Baúl Venez. 199 D2
El Bayadh Alg. 123 F2
formerly known as Géryville
Elbe r. Germany 48 G2
also known as Labe (Czech Republic)
'Elb el Fçâl des. Mauritania 124 C2
El Beqa'a valley Lebanon 109 H3
El Berié well Mauritania 124 C2
Elberta U.S.A. 183 M2
Elberton U.S.A. 175 D5
El Beru Hagia Somalia 128 D4
Elbeuf France 50 H3
Elbeyli Turkey 109 I1
El Beyyed well Mauritania 122 C5
El Beyyed well Mauritania 124 C2
El Billete, Cerro mt. Mex. 185 E5
Elbing Poland see Elbląg
Elbistan Turkey 107 D3
Elbląg Poland 49 Q1
historically known as Elbing
Elbląski, Kanał canal Poland 49 Q1
El Bluff Nicaragua 186 C4
El Bolsón Arg. 205 C6
El Bordj Alg. 55 L9
El Borma Tunisia 123 H3
El Boulaïda Alg. see Blida
Elbow Canada 167 J5
Elbow Lake U.S.A. 178 C2
El Bozal Mex. 185 E4

►Elbrus mt. Rus. Fed. 41 G8
Highest mountain in Europe.
europe [landscapes] ►►► 30–31

El Buheyrat state Sudan 126 F3
El Buitre mt. Spain 55 J6
El Burg Egypt 108 C6
El Burgo de Osma Spain 55 H3
El Burumbul Egypt 108 C8
Elburz Mountains Iran 100 B2
also known as Alborz, Reshteh-ye
El Cain Arg. 205 C6
El Cajon U.S.A. 183 H9
El Callao Venez. 199 F3
El Campo U.S.A. 179 C6
El Canton Venez. 198 D3
El Capulin r. Mex. 179 B7
El Carmelo Venez. 198 D2
El Carmen Arg. 200 D6
El Carmen Beni Bol. 201 E3
El Carmen Santa Cruz Bol. 201 F4
El Carmen Ecuador 198 B5
El Carmen Venez. 199 E4
El Caroche mt. Spain 55 K5
also spelt Caroch
El Casco Mex. 184 D3
El Cebú, Cerro mt. Mex. 185 G6
El Centro U.S.A. 183 I9
El Cerro Bol. 201 E4
El Chaparro Venez. 199 E2
Elche Spain 55 K6
historically known as Illici
El Chichónal vol. Mex. 185 G5
El Chilicote Mex. 184 D2
Elcho U.S.A. 172 D5
Elcho Island Australia 148 B1
El Coca Ecuador see Puerto Francisco de Orellana
El Cocuy, Parque Nacional nat. park Col. 198 C3
El Collado hill Spain 54 G6
El Contador, Puerto de pass Spain 55 I7
El Cotorro Cuba 186 C2
El Cuy Arg. 204 C5
El Cuyo Mex. 185 I4
Elda Spain 55 K6
El Dab'a Egypt 53 H5
El Dalgamûn Egypt 108 B7
Eldama Ravine Kenya 128 B4
Elde r. Germany 48 I2
El Debb well Eth. 128 D3
Eldee Canada 173 N4
El Deir Egypt 108 C7
Eldena U.S.A. 172 D9
Elderon U.S.A. 172 D6
El Desemboque Mex. 181 D7
Eldhraun lava field Iceland 44 [inset] C3
El Diamante Mex. 184 E2
El Difícil Col. 198 C2
El'dikan Rus. Fed. 39 N3
El Diviso Col. 198 B4
El Djezair Alg. see Algiers
El Doctor Mex. 184 B2
Eldon U.S.A. 178 D4
Eldorado Arg. 204 G2
Eldorado Brazil 203 B8
El Dorado Col. 198 D4
El Dorado Mex. 184 D3
El Dorado AR U.S.A. 179 D5
El Dorado KS U.S.A. 178 C4
Eldorado U.S.A. 179 B6
El Dorado Venez. 199 F3
Eldorado Mountains U.S.A. 183 J6
Eldoret Kenya 128 B4
Eldridge U.S.A. 172 C9
Eldridge, Mount U.S.A. 166 A1
Elea, Cape Cyprus see Elaia, Cape
Eleanor U.S.A. 176 D7
Electric Peak U.S.A. 180 E3
El Eglab plat. Alg. 122 D4
El 'Ein well Sudan 121 F5
Eleja Latvia 42 E5
El Ejido Spain 55 I8
Elek Hungary 49 S9
Elek r. Rus. Fed. see Ilek
Elekmonar Rus. Fed. 88 D1
Elektrėnai Lith. 42 F7
Elektrogorsk Rus. Fed. 43 T6
Elektrostal' Rus. Fed. 43 T6
Elektrougli Rus. Fed. 43 T6
Elele Nigeria 125 G5

►Elemi Triangle terr. Africa 128 B3
Disputed territory (Ethiopia/Kenya/Sudan) administered by Kenya.

Elena Bulg. 58 G6
El Encanto Col. 198 C5
El Encinal Mex. 183 H9
Elephanta Caves tourist site India 94 B2
Elephant Butte Reservoir U.S.A. 181 F6
Elephant Island Antarctica 222 U2
Éléphants de Kaniama, Réserve des nature res. Dem. Rep. Congo 127 E6
Éléphants de Sakania, Réserve Partielle aux nature res. Dem. Rep. Congo 127 F7
Eleshnitsa Bulg. 58 E7
Eleşkirt Turkey 107 E3
also known as Aleşkirt
El Espinar Spain 54 G4
El Estor Guat. 185 H6
Eleuthera i. Bahamas 186 D1
Eleva U.S.A. 172 B6
Eleven Point r. U.S.A. 178 E4
El Fahs Tunisia 57 B12
El Faiyûm Egypt 121 F2
also spelt Al Fayyūm
El Faiyûm governorate Egypt 108 B8
El Faouar Tunisia 123 H2
El Fasher Sudan 120 E6
El Fashn Egypt 106 B5
El Fendek Morocco 54 F9
El Ferrol Spain see Ferrol
El Ferrol del Caudillo Spain see Ferrol
El Fud Eth. 128 D3
El Fuerte Mex. 184 C3
El Fula Sudan 126 F2
Elgå Norway 45 J3
Elgal waterhole Kenya 128 C4
El Gamâlîya Egypt 108 C6
El Gçaib well Mali 122 D5
formerly known as El Ksaib Ounane
El Geili Sudan 121 G6
El Geneina Sudan 120 D6
El Geteina Sudan 121 G6
El Gezira state Sudan 121 G6
El Ghaba Sudan 121 F5
El Ghalla, Wadi watercourse Sudan 126 E2
El Ghallâouîya well Mauritania 122 C5
El Gheddiya Mauritania 124 C2
El Ghor plain Jordan/West Bank see Al Ghawr
Elgin U.K. 46 I6
Elgin IL U.S.A. 178 E3
Elgin NV U.S.A. 183 J4
Elgin OR U.S.A. 180 C3
Elgin TX U.S.A. 179 C6
Elgin Down Australia 149 E4
El'ginskiy Rus. Fed. 39 O3
El Gir well Sudan 121 E5
El Gîza Egypt see Giza
El Gîza governorate Egypt 108 A9
El Gogorrón, Parque Nacional nat. park Mex. 185 E4
El Goléa Alg. 123 F3
El Golfo de Santa Clara Mex. 184 B2
Elgon, Mount Uganda 128 B4
Elgoras, Gora hill Rus. Fed. 44 O1
El Guante Mex. 184 D2
El Guetar Tunisia 123 H2
El Guettâra well Mali 123 E5
El'gyay Rus. Fed. 39 L3
El Haddâdi Egypt 108 B6
El Hamma Tunisia 123 H2
El Hammâm Egypt 121 F2
El Ḥammâmi reg. Mauritania 122 C5
El Hâmûl Egypt 108 C6
El Hank reg. Alg. 122 D4
El Hank esc. Mali/Mauritania 122 C5
El Haouaria Tunisia 57 D11
El Harra Egypt 121 E3
El Hasira Sudan 104 A5
El Hato del Volcán Panama 186 C5
El Hawata Sudan 121 G6
El Heiz Egypt 106 B5
El Hierro i. Canary Is 122 A4
El Higo Mex. 185 F4
El Hilla Sudan 121 E6
El Homr Alg. 123 F3
El Homra Sudan 121 F6
El Houeïtat well Mauritania 124 C2
El Huecu Arg. 204 C5
El Huseinîya Egypt 108 C7
Eli well Niger 125 H3
Elias Garcia Angola 127 D7
Elías Piña Dom. Rep. 187 F3
Elichpur India see Achalpur
Elihu U.S.A. 176 A8
Elila Dem. Rep. Congo 126 E5
Elila r. Dem. Rep. Congo 126 E5
El 'Ilw el Ahmar el Qibli hill Egypt 108 B9
Elim S. Africa 132 D11
Elim U.S.A. 164 C3
Elimäki Fin. 42 H1
Elimberrum France see Auch
Elin Pelin Bulg. 58 E6
Eliot, Mount Canada 169 I1
Eliozondo Spain 55 J1
Elipa Dem. Rep. Congo 126 E5
Elisabetha Dem. Rep. Congo 126 D4
also known as Lokutu
Élisabethville Dem. Rep. Congo see Lubumbashi
Eliseu Martins Brazil 202 D4
El Iskandarîya Egypt see Alexandria
El Iskandarîya governorate Egypt 108 A6
Elista Rus. Fed. 41 H7
formerly known as Stepnoy
Elizabeth U.S.A. 177 K5
Elizabeth, Mount hill Australia 150 D3
Elizabeth City U.S.A. 177 I9
Elizabeth Creek r. Australia 148 C3
Elizabeth Island Pitcairn Is see Henderson Island
Elizabeth Islands U.S.A. 177 O4
Elizabeth Point Namibia 130 B5
Elizabeth Reef Australia 145 E4
Elizabethton U.S.A. 176 C9
Elizabethtown KY U.S.A. 174 C4
Elizabethtown NC U.S.A. 174 E5
Elizabethtown NY U.S.A. 177 L1
Elizabethville U.S.A. 177 I5
Elizavety, Mys c. Rus. Fed. 39 O4
El Jadida Morocco 122 C2
formerly known as Mazagan
El Jaralito Mex. 184 D3
El Jebelein Sudan 121 G6
El Jem Tunisia 123 H2
El Jicaro Nicaragua 186 B4
El Juile Mex. 185 G5
Elk r. Canada 167 H5
Ełk Poland 49 T2
historically known as Lyck
Ełk r. Poland 49 T2
Elk r. MD U.S.A. 177 J6
Elk r. TN U.S.A. 174 C5
El Kaa Lebanon see Qaa
El Kab Sudan 121 G5
Elkader U.S.A. 174 B3
El Kala Alg. 123 H1
formerly spelt La Calle
El Kamlin Sudan 121 G6
El Karabi Sudan 121 G5
Elkas kalns hill Latvia 42 G4
Elk City U.S.A. 179 C5
Elk Creek U.S.A. 182 B2
Elkedra Australia 148 B4
Elkedra watercourse Australia 148 C4
El Kelaâ des Srarhna Morocco 122 D2
El Kerē Eth. 128 D3
Elkford Canada 167 H5
Elk Grove U.S.A. 182 C3
El Khalil West Bank see Hebron
El Khandaq Sudan 121 F5
El Khârga Egypt 121 F3
also spelt Al Khārijah
Elkhart IN U.S.A. 174 C3
Elkhart KS U.S.A. 178 B4
El Khartûm Sudan see Khartoum
El Khatatba Egypt 108 B7
El Khenachich esc. Mali see El Khnâchîch
El Khnâchîch esc. Mali 122 D5
also spelt El Khenachich
Elkhorn U.S.A. 172 E8
Elkhorn r. U.S.A. 178 C3
Elkhorn City U.S.A. 176 C8
Elkhovo Bulg. 58 H6
Elki Turkey see Beytüşşebap
Elkin U.S.A. 176 E9
Elkins U.S.A. 176 F7
Elk Island National Park Canada 167 H4
Elk Lake Canada 168 D4
Elk Lake l. U.S.A. 172 H6
Elkland U.S.A. 177 H4
Elk Mountain U.S.A. 180 F4
Elko Canada 167 H5
Elko U.S.A. 183 I1
El K'oran Eth. 128 E3
Elk Park U.S.A. 176 D9
Elk Point Canada 167 I4
Elk Point U.S.A. 178 C3
Elk River U.S.A. 174 A2
El Ksaib Ounane well Mali see El Gçaib
El Ksour Tunisia 57 A13
Elk Springs U.S.A. 183 P1
Elkton KY U.S.A. 174 C4
Elkton MD U.S.A. 177 J6
Elkton VA U.S.A. 176 G7
Elkview U.S.A. 176 D7
El Lagowa Sudan 126 F2
Ellas country Europe see Greece
Ellavalla Australia 151 A5
Ellaville U.S.A. 175 C5
Ell Bay Canada 167 O1
Ellef Ringnes Island Canada 165 I2
El Lēh Eth. 128 C4
El Lein well Kenya 128 D5
Elleker Australia 151 B7
Elléloyé well Chad 120 C5
Ellen, Mount U.S.A. 183 N3
Ellenabad India 96 B3
Ellenboro U.S.A. 176 D6
Ellenburg Depot U.S.A. 177 L1
Ellendale DE U.S.A. 177 J7
Ellendale ND U.S.A. 178 C2
Ellensburg U.S.A. 180 B3
Ellenville U.S.A. 177 K4
El León, Cerro mt. Mex. 184 D3
Ellesmere N.Z. 153 G11
Ellesmere, Lake N.Z. 153 G11

►Ellesmere Island Canada 165 K2
4th largest island in North America and 10th in the world.
northamerica [landscapes] ►►► 156–157

Ellesmere Island National Park Reserve Canada 165 L1
Ellesmere Port U.K. 47 J10
Ellice r. Canada 167 K1
Ellice Island atoll Tuvalu see Funafuti
Ellice Islands country S. Pacific Ocean see Tuvalu
Ellicott City U.S.A. 177 I6
Ellicottville U.S.A. 176 G3
Ellijay U.S.A. 174 C5
El Limón Mex. 185 F4
Elliot Australia 148 B3
Elliot S. Africa 133 L8
Elliot, Mount Australia 149 E3
Elliotdale S. Africa 133 M8
also known as Xhora
Elliot Knob mt. U.S.A. 176 F7
Elliot Lake Canada 168 D4
Elliot Price Conservation Park nature res. Australia 146 C2
Ellis U.S.A. 178 C4
Ellisras S. Africa 131 E4
Elliston Australia 146 B3
Elliston U.S.A. 176 E8
Ellisville U.S.A. 175 B6
Ellon U.K. 46 J6
Ellora Caves tourist site India 94 B1
Ellsworth KS U.S.A. 178 C4
Ellsworth ME U.S.A. 177 Q1
Ellsworth WI U.S.A. 174 A2
Ellsworth Land reg. Antarctica 222 R1
Ellsworth Mountains Antarctica 222 S1
Ellwangen (Jagst) Germany 48 H7
El Macao Dom. Rep. 187 F3
El Mahalla el Kubra Egypt 108 C7
El Mahâriq Egypt 121 F3
El Maharraqa Egypt 108 C8
El Mahia reg. Mali 123 E5
El Maitén Arg. 205 C6
El Maks el Bahari Egypt 121 F3
Elmakuz Dağı mt. Turkey 108 E1
Elmalı Turkey 106 B3
El Mallâha marsh Egypt 108 E9
El Malpais National Monument nat. park U.S.A. 181 F6
El Ma'mûra Egypt 108 B6
El Managil Sudan 121 G6
El Mango Venez. 199 E4
El Mansûra Egypt 121 F2
also spelt Al Manşūrah
El Mansûrîya Egypt 108 C7
El Manteco Venez. 199 F3
El Manzla Morocco 54 F9
El Marsa Tunisia 57 C12
El Matarîya Egypt 108 D6
El Medo Eth. 128 D3
El Meghaïer Alg. 123 G2
El Melemm Sudan 126 F2
El Melhes well Mauritania 124 B2
El Mesellemiya Sudan 121 G6
El Messir well Chad 120 C6
El Mex Egypt 108 A6
El Miamo Venez. 199 F3
Elmina Ghana 125 E5
also known as São Jorge da Mina
El Mina Lebanon 108 G3
El Minya Egypt 108 C8
El Minya Egypt 121 F2
El Minya governorate Egypt 108 B9
Elmira Ont. Canada 173 M7
Elmira P.E.I. Canada 169 I4
Elmira MI U.S.A. 173 I5
Elmira NY U.S.A. 177 I3
El Mirage U.S.A. 183 L8
El Moïnane well Mauritania 124 C2
Elmore Australia 147 E4
El Morro mt. Arg. 204 D4
El Mraïfig well Mauritania 124 C3
El Mraïti well Mali 125 E2
El Mreyyé reg. Mauritania 124 D2
Elmshorn Germany 48 G2
El Muglad Sudan 126 E2
El Mugrón mt. Spain 55 J6
Elmwood U.S.A. 172 D10
El Mzereb well Mali 122 D4
Elne France 51 I10
Elnesvågen Norway 44 I3
El Nido Phil. 74 A4
El Oasis Mex. 183 I9
El Obeid Sudan 121 F6
El Ocote, Parque Natural nature res. Mex. 185 G5
El Odaiya Sudan 121 F6
El Oro prov. Ecuador 198 B5
El Oro Mex. 184 E3
Elos Greece 59 E13
El Oued Alg. 123 G2
Eloy U.S.A. 183 M9
El Palmar Venez. 199 F3
El Palmito Mex. 184 D3
El Pao Bolívar Venez. 199 F2
El Pao Cojedes Venez. 199 E2
Elpaputih, Teluk b. Indon. 75 D3
El Paraíso Hond. 186 B4
El Paso IL U.S.A. 174 B3
El Paso U.S.A. see Derby
El Paso TX U.S.A. 181 F7
El Peñón Arg. 204 D2
El Perelló Spain 55 L4
Elphinstone i. Myanmar see Thayawthadangyi Kyun
El Pilar Venez. 199 F2
El Pino, Sierra mts Mex. 185 E2
El Pintado Arg. 201 E6
El Pluma Arg. 205 C7
El Pocito Bol. 201 E3
El Portete b. Col. 198 C1
El Porvenir Col. 198 D3
El Porvenir Mex. 183 H9
El Porvenir Mex. 184 D2
El Porvenir Panama 186 D5
El Prat de Llobregat Spain 55 N3
also known as Prat de Llobregat
El Progreso Guat. 185 H6
also known as Guastatoya
El Puente Bol. 200 D5
El Puente Nicaragua 186 B4
El Puerto de Santa María Spain 54 E8
El Qâ' valley Egypt 108 E9
El Qâhira Egypt see Cairo
El Qâhira governorate Egypt 108 C8
El Qanâtir el Qahiriya Egypt 108 C7
El Qantara Egypt 106 C5
El Qantara el Sharqiya Egypt 108 D7
El Qasimiye r. Lebanon 108 G4
El Qasr Egypt 121 F3
El Quds Israel/West Bank see Jerusalem
El Quebrachal Arg. 204 D2
El Quss Abû Sa'îd plat. Egypt 121 E3
El Real Panama 186 D5
El Regocijo Mex. 184 D4
El Reno U.S.A. 179 C5
El Retorno Mex. 185 E4
El Rey, Parque Nacional nat. park Arg. 201 D6
El Ridisîya Bahari Egypt 121 G3
El Rio U.S.A. 182 E7
El Rôda Egypt 108 B8
El Rosario watercourse Mex. 181 D7
Elrose Canada 167 I5
Elroy U.S.A. 172 C7
El Rucio Mex. 185 E4
Elsa Canada 166 C2
Elsa r. Italy 56 C5
El Saff Egypt 121 F2
El Sahuaro Mex. 184 B2
El Salado Arg. 205 D6
El Salado Mex. 185 E3
El Sâlhîya Egypt 108 D7
El Salto Mex. 184 D4
►El Salvador country Central America 185 H6
also known as Salvador
northamerica [countries] ►►► 158–159
El Salvador Chile 204 C2
El Salvador Mex. 185 E3
El Salvador Phil. 74 C4
El Samán de Apure Venez. 198 D3
Elsas Canada 173 K2
El Sauz Mex. 184 D2
El Seibo Dom. Rep. 187 F3
Elsen Nur l. China 84 B5
El Serrat Andorra 55 M2
El Shab well Egypt 121 F4
El Shâyib hill Egypt 108 B8
El Shuhada Egypt 108 B7
Elsie U.S.A. 173 I7
Elsinore Denmark see Helsingør
Elsinore CA U.S.A. 183 G8
Elsinore UT U.S.A. 183 L3
Elsinore Lake U.S.A. 183 G8
Elsnes Norway 44 M1
El Sosneado Arg. 204 C4
Elsterniederung und Westliche Oberlausitzer Heide park Germany 49 K4
Elsterwerda Germany 49 K4
El Sueco Mex. 184 D2
El Suweis Egypt see Suez
El Suweis governorate Egypt 108 C8
El Tajin tourist site Mex. 185 F4
El Tama, Parque Nacional nat. park Venez. 198 C3
El Tarabîl hill Egypt 108 D8
El Tarf Alg. 123 H1
El Teleno mt. Spain 54 E2
El Temascal Mex. 185 F3
Eltham N.Z. 152 I7
El Thamad Egypt 121 G2
El Tigre Venez. 199 E2
El Tigre, Parque Nacional nat. park Guat. 185 H5
El Tocuyo Venez. 198 D2
El'ton Rus. Fed. 102 A2
El'ton, Ozero l. Rus. Fed. 102 A2
El Toro Chile 204 C3
El Totumo Venez. 198 C2
El Trébol Arg. 204 E4
El Tren Mex. 184 B2
El Triunfo Mex. 184 C4
El Tunal Arg. 204 D2
El Tuparro, Parque Nacional nat. park Col. 198 D3
El Tûr Egypt 121 G2
El Turbio Chile 205 B8
El Turbón mt. Spain 55 L2
El Uqsur Egypt see Luxor
Eluru India 94 D2
El 'Uteishan well Sudan 121 G5
Elva Estonia 42 H3
El Vallecillo Mex. 184 C2
Elvanlı Turkey see Tömük
Elvas Port. 54 D6
Elvebakken Norway 44 M1
Elven France 50 D5
El Vendrell Spain 55 M3
also spelt Vendrell
Elvenes Norway 44 O1
Elverum Norway 45 J3
El Viejo mt. Col. 198 C3
El Viejo Nicaragua 186 B4
El Vigía, Cerro mt. Mex. 184 D4
Elvira Brazil 198 C6
Elvire r. Australia 150 E3
Elvire Aboriginal Reserve Australia 150 D3
Elvo r. Italy 56 A3
El Wâdi El Jadid governorate Egypt 106 A6
El Wak Kenya 128 D4
El Wasta Egypt 108 C8
El Watya well Egypt 121 E2
Elwood IN U.S.A. 174 C3
Elwood NE U.S.A. 178 C3
Elwood NJ U.S.A. 177 K6
El Wuz Sudan 121 F6
Ely U.K. 47 M11
Ely MN U.S.A. 174 B2
Ely NV U.S.A. 183 J2
El Yagual Venez. 198 D3
El Yibo well Kenya 128 C3
Elyria U.S.A. 176 C4
Elysburg U.S.A. 177 I5
El Zacatón, Cerro mt. Mex. 185 F5
El Zape Mex. 184 D3
El Zawâmil Egypt 108 C7
Emajõgi r. Estonia 42 I3
Emām Qolī Iran 100 D2
Emāmrūd Iran 100 C2
formerly known as Shāhrūd
Emām Şaḩeb Afgh. 101 G2
Emām Taqī Iran 101 D2
formerly known as Shāh Taqī
Emangusi S. Africa 133 Q3
E. Martínez Mex. see Emiliano Martínez
Emas, Parque Nacional das nat. park Brazil 206 A5
Emazar Kazakh. 88 C2
Emba Kazakh. 102 D2
also known as Embi or Zhem
Emba r. Kazakh. 102 C3
Embalenhle S. Africa 133 N3
Embarcación Arg. 201 D5
Embarras Portage Canada 167 I3
Embarrass U.S.A. 172 A3
Embetsu Japan see Enbetsu
Embi Kazakh. see Emba
Embiah, Mount hill Sing. 76 [inset]
Embira r. Brazil see Envira
Émbonas Greece see Emponas
Emborcação, Represa de resr Brazil 206 F5
Emborion Greece see Emporeio
Embu Brazil 206 G10
Embu Kenya 128 C5
Embundo Angola 127 C9
Emden Germany 48 E2
Emecik Turkey 59 I12
Emei China see Emeishan
Emeishan China 86 B2
formerly known as Emei
Emei Shan mt. China 86 B2
Emel' r. Kazakh. 88 C2
Emerald Australia 149 F4
Emeril Canada 169 H2
Emerita Augusta Spain see Mérida
Emerson Canada 167 L5
Emerson U.S.A. 176 B7
Emery U.S.A. 183 M3
Emesa Syria see Homs
Emet Turkey 106 B3
Emigrant Gap U.S.A. 182 D2
Emigrant Pass U.S.A. 183 H1
Emigrant Valley U.S.A. 183 I4
eMijindini S. Africa 133 P2
Emi Koussi mt. Chad 120 C5
Emile r. Canada 167 G2
Emiliano Martínez Mex. 184 D3
short form E. Martínez
Emiliano Zapata Mex. 185 H5
Emilia-Romagna admin. reg. Italy 56 D4
Emin China 88 C2
also known as Dorbiljin
Emine, Nos pt Bulg. 58 I6
Eminence U.S.A. 174 B4
Emin He r. China 88 C2
Eminska Planina hills Bulg. 58 I6
Emirdağ Turkey 106 B3
Emir Dağı mt. Turkey 106 B3
Emlenton U.S.A. 176 F4
Emmaboda Sweden 45 K4
Emmahaven Indon. see Telukbayur
Emmaste Estonia 42 D3
Emmaus Rus. Fed. 43 R5
Emmaus U.S.A. 177 J5
Emmeloord Neth. 48 C3
Emmelshausen Germany 48 E5
Emmen Neth. 48 D3
Emmen Switz. 51 O5
Emmendingen Germany 48 E7
Emmerich Germany 48 D4
Emmet Australia 149 E5
Emmetsburg U.S.A. 178 D3
Emmett U.S.A. 180 C4
Emmiganuru India 94 C3
formerly spelt Yemmiganur
Emmitsburg U.S.A. 177 H6
Emo Canada 168 A3
Emőd Hungary 49 R8
Emona Slovenia see Ljubljana
Emory U.S.A. 179 D5
Emory Peak U.S.A. 179 B6
Empada Guinea-Bissau 124 B4
Empalme Mex. 184 C3
Empanadas mt. Spain 55 I7
Empangeni S. Africa 133 P5
Empedrado Arg. 204 F2
Empexa, Salar de salt flat Bol. 200 C5
Empire U.S.A. 172 G6
Empoli Italy 56 C5
Emponas Greece 59 I12
also spelt Émbonas
Emporeio Greece 59 G12
also known as Emborion
Emporia KS U.S.A. 178 C4
Emporia VA U.S.A. 176 H9
Emporium U.S.A. 176 G4
Empress Canada 167 I5
Empress Mine Zimbabwe 131 F3
Empty Quarter des. Saudi Arabia see Rub' al Khālī
'Emrānī Iran 100 D3
Ems r. Germany 48 E2
Emsdale Canada 173 N5
Emsdetten Germany 48 E3
Ems-Jade-Kanal canal Germany 48 E2
Emthonjeni S. Africa 133 O2
Emu Creek r. Australia 149 D3
Emumägi hill Estonia 42 I3
Emu Park Australia 149 F4
Emur Shan mts China 82 A1
Emzinoni S. Africa 133 N3
Ena Japan 91 E7
Enafors Sweden 44 K3
Enambú Col. 198 D4

Enamuna Brazil 199 F3
Enarotali Indon. 73 I7
Ena-san mt. Japan 91 E7
Enbetsu Japan 90 G2
  also spelt Embetsu
Encanadé mt. Japan 55 L4
Encantadas, Serra das hills Brazil 203 A9
Encanto, Cape Phil. 74 B3
Encarnación Mex. 185 E4
Encarnación Para. 201 G6
Enchi Ghana 124 E5
Encinas mt. Spain 54 H6
Encinitas U.S.A. 183 G8
Encino U.S.A. 181 F6
Encón Arg. 204 D4
Encontrados Venez. 198 C2
Encounter Bay Australia 146 C3
Encruzilhada Brazil 202 D5
Encruzilhada do Sul Brazil 203 A9
Encs Hungary 49 S7
Endako Canada 166 E4
Endau Malaysia 76 C2
Endau r. Malaysia 76 C2
Endeavour Strait Australia 149 D1
Endeh Indon. 75 B5
Enderbury i. Kiribati 145 H2
Enderby Canada 166 G5
Enderby Land reg. Antarctica 223 D2
Endicott Mountains U.S.A. 164 D3
Endimari r. Brazil 200 D2
Endla riiklik looduskaitseala nature res. Estonia 42 H3
Endom Cameroon 125 I6
Endwell U.S.A. 177 I3
Endzele Latvia 42 G4
Ene r. Peru 200 B2
Eneabba Australia 151 A6
Enemutu Brazil 199 I4
EnenKio terr. N. Pacific Ocean see Wake Atoll
Energeticheskiy Kazakh. 103 I4
Energetik Rus. Fed. 102 D2
Energía Arg. 204 F5
Enewetak atoll Marshall Is 220 E5
Enez Turkey 106 A2
  historically known as Aenus
Enfiâo, Ponta do pt Angola 127 A8
Enfidaville Tunisia 57 C12
Enfield Canada 169 I4
Enfield U.S.A. 174 E4
Engan Norway 44 J3
Engaño, Cabo c. Dom. Rep. 187 F3
Engaños, Rio de los r. Col. See Yari
Engaru Japan 90 H2
Engcobo S. Africa 133 L8
Engelhard U.S.A. 174 F5
Engel's Rus. Fed. 102 A2
  also known as Pokrovsk
Engelschmangat sea chan. Neth. 48 B2
Engenheiro Beltrão Brazil 206 A10
Engenheiro Navarro Brazil 207 J4
Engenina watercourse Australia 146 B2
Engerdal Norway 45 J3
Enghershatu mt. Eritrea 121 H5
  also known as Yagda
Engineer Canada 166 C3
Engkililli Sarawak Malaysia 77 E2
England admin. div. U.K. 47 K11
Englee Canada 169 K3
Englehart Canada 168 E4
Englewood FL U.S.A. 175 D7
Englewood OH U.S.A. 176 A6
English r. Canada 167 M5
English U.S.A. 174 C4
English Bazar India see Ingraj Bazar
English Channel Fr./U.K. 47 K14
  also known as La Manche
English Coast Antarctica 222 S2
Engozero Rus. Fed. 40 F2
Engstingen Germany 48 G7
Engure Latvia 42 E4
Engures ezers l. Latvia 42 E4
Enguri r. Georgia 107 E2
Enhlalakahle S. Africa 133 O6
Enid U.S.A. 179 C4
Enipefs r. Greece 59 D9
Eniwa Japan 90 G3
eNjesuthi mt. S. Africa 133 N6
Enkan, Mys pt Rus. Fed. 39 O4
Enkeldoorn Zimbabwe see Chivhu
Enkhuizen Neth. 48 D3
Enköping Sweden 45 L4
Enle China see Zhenyuan
Enna Sicilia Italy 57 G11
Ennadai Lake Canada 167 K2
En Nahud Sudan 121 F6
Ennadai Australia 147 E2
Ennis Rep. of Ireland 47 D11
  also spelt Inis
Ennis MT U.S.A. 180 E3
Ennis TX U.S.A. 179 C5
Enniscorthy Rep. of Ireland 47 F11
  also spelt Inis Córthaidh
Enniskerry Rep. of Ireland 47 F10
Enniskillen U.K. 47 E9

Ennistymon Rep. of Ireland 47 C11
Enn Nâqoûra Lebanon 108 G4
Enns Austria 49 L7
Enns r. Austria 49 L7
Eno Fin. 44 O3
Enonkoski Fin. 44 O3
Enontekiö Fin. 44 M1
Enoree r. U.S.A. 174 D5
Enosburg Falls U.S.A. 177 M1
Enping China 87 E4
Enrekang Indon. 75 A3
Enrile Phil. 74 B2
Enriquillo Dom. Rep. 187 F3
Enriquillo, Lago de l. Dom. Rep. 187 F3
Enschede Neth. 48 D3
Ensenada Baja California Norte Mex. 184 A2
Ensenada Baja California Sur Mex. 184 C4
Ensenada de Utria nat. park Col. 198 B3
Enshi China 87 D2
Ensley U.S.A. 175 C6
Entebbe Uganda 128 B4
Enterprise Canada 167 G2
Enterprise AL U.S.A. 175 C6
Enterprise OR U.S.A. 180 C3
Enterprise UT U.S.A. 183 K4
Enterprise Point Phil. 74 A4
Entrance Canada 167
Entrepeñas, Embalse de resr Spain 55 I4
Entre Ríos prov. Arg. 204 F3
Entre Rios Bol. 201 D5
Entre Rios Bahia Brazil 202 E4
Entre Rios Pará Brazil 199 I6
Entre Rios Moz. see Malema
Entre Rios de Minas Brazil 203 C7
Entroncamento Port. 54 C5
Entuba Zimbabwe 131 E3
Entumeni S. Africa 133 P5
Enugu Nigeria 125 G5
Enugu state Nigeria 125 G5
Enurmino Rus. Fed. 39 S3
Envigado Col. 104 B3
Envira Brazil 200 C1
Envira r. Brazil 200 C1
  also known as Embira
Enying Hungary 49 P9
Enys, Mount N.Z. 153 F11
Enzan Japan 91 F7
Eo r. Spain 54 D1
Eochaill Rep. of Ireland see Youghal
Eokuk Lake Canada 167 H1
Eooa i. Tonga see Eua
Epe Nigeria 125 F5
Epéna Congo 126 C4
Épernay France 51 J3
Ephesus tourist site Turkey 59 I11
  also known as Efes
Ephraim U.S.A. 183 M2
Ephrata PA U.S.A. 177 I5
Ephrata WA U.S.A. 180 C3
Epidamnus Albania see Durrës
Epidavros tourist site Greece 59 E11
Epidavrou Limiras, Kolpos b. Greece 59 E12
Épila Spain 55 J3
Épinac France 51 K6
Épinal France 51 M4
Epirus admin. reg. Greece see Ipeiros
Episkopi Cyprus 108 D3
Episkopi Bay Cyprus 108 D3
Episkopis, Kolpos b. Cyprus see Episkopi Bay
Epping U.K. 47 M12
Epping U.S.A. 177 N2
Epping Forest National Park Australia 149 E4
Eppynt, Mynydd hills U.K. 47 I11
Epsom U.K. 47 L12
Epte r. France 50 H3
Epu-pel Arg. 204 E5
Epuyén Arg. 205 C6
Équateur prov. Dem. Rep. Congo 126 D4
▶**Equatorial Guinea** country Africa 125 H6
  known as Guinea Ecuatorial in Spanish; formerly known as Spanish Guinea
  africa [countries] ➤➤ 114–117
Equeipa Venez. 199 F3
Équerdreville-Hainneville France 50 E3
Era r. Italy 56 C5
Erac Creek watercourse Australia 149 E5
Eraclea Italy 56 E3
Erakurri mt. Spain 55 J1
Eran Bay Phil. 74 A4
Erandol India 94 B1
Erawadi r. Myanmar see Irrawaddy
Erawan National Park Thai. 79 B5
Erba, Jebel mt. Sudan 121 H4
Erbaa Turkey 107 D2
Erbendorf Germany 48 J6
Erbeskopf hill Germany 48 E6
Ercan airport Cyprus 108 D2
Erçek Turkey 107 E3
Erçiş Turkey 107 E3
Erciyes Dağı mt. Turkey 106 C3
Ercsi Hungary 49 P8
Érd Hungary 49 P8
Erdalsfjellet hill Norway 44 N1
Erdaobaihe China see Baihe
Erdaogou China 84 A2
Erdek Turkey 106 A2
Erdemli Turkey 106 C3
Erdenet Hövsgöl Mongolia 84 C1
  also known as Yagda
Erdenet Orhon Mongolia 84 E1
Erdenetsogt Bayankhongor Mongolia 84 D2
Erdenetsogt Ömnögovĭ Mongolia 85 E3
Erding Germany 48 I7
Erdniyevskiy Rus. Fed. 102 A3
Erdre r. France 50 E5
Eré Peru 198 C4
Eré, Campos hills Brazil 206 A11
Erebato r. Venez. 199 F3
Erebus, Mount vol. Antarctica 223 L1
Erech tourist site Iraq 107 F5
  also spelt Uruk
Erechim Brazil 203 A8
Ereentsav Mongolia 85 G1
Ereğli Konya Turkey 106 C3
  historically known as Cabistra or Heraclea
Ereğli Zonguldak Turkey 106 B2
  historically known as Heraclea Pontica
Erego Moz. see Errego
Erei, Monti mts Sicilia Italy 57 G11
Ereikoussa i. Greece 59 A9
  also spelt Erikoussa
Erementau Mex. 185 E5
Erendira Mex. 185 E5
Erenhaberga Shan mts China 88 D3
Erenhot China 85 G3
Erenik r. Yugo. 58 B6
Erenköy Cyprus see Kokkina
Eresk Iran 100 D3
Eresma r. Spain 54 G3
Eresos Greece 59 G9
Eretria Greece 59 E10
Erevan Armenia see Yerevan
Erfenis Dam S. Africa 133 K5
Erfenis Dam Nature Reserve S. Africa 133 K5
Erfoud Morocco 122 D2
Erfurt Germany 48 I5
Ergani Turkey 107 D3
Erg Atouila des. Mali 122 D5
Erg Bourarhet des. Alg. 123 H4
'Erg Chech des. Alg./Mali 122 D5
Erg d'Amer des. Alg. 123 H4
Erg du Djourab des. Chad 120 C5
Erg du Ténéré des. Niger 125 H2
Ergel Mongolia 85 F3
Érgeme Latvia 42 G4

Ergene r. Turkey 106 A2
Erg Iabès des. Alg. 123 E4
Erg Iguidi des. Alg./Mauritania 122 D4
'Erg I-n-Sâkâne des. Mali 123 E5
Erg Issaouane des. Alg. 123 G4
Erg Kilian des. Alg. 123 H5
Erg Mehedjibat des. Alg. 123 F4
Erg Tassedjefit des. Alg. 123 F4
Erguig r. Chad 126 B2
Ergun China 85 I1
  formerly known as Ergun Youqi or Labudalin
Ergun Youqi China see Ergun
Ergun Youqi China see Argun'
Er Hai l. China 86 B3
Eria r. Spain 54 F2
Erice Sicilia Italy 57 E10
Ericht, Loch l. U.K. 46 H7
Erickson Man. Canada 167 L5
Erie KS U.S.A. 178 D4
Erie PA U.S.A. 176 F4
Erie, Lake Canada/U.S.A. 173 M8
'Erigât des. Mali 124 D2
Erik Eriksenstretet sea chan. Svalbard 38 C2
Erikoússi i. Greece see Ereikoussa
Eriksdale Canada 167 L5
Erillas hill Spain 54 F6
Erimo Japan 90 H3
Erimo-misaki c. Japan 90 H4
Erin Canada 173 M7
Erin U.S.A. 174 C4
Eriskay i. U.K. 46 E6
  also spelt Eiriosgaigh
Erithraí Greece see Erythres
Erithropótamos r. Greece see Erydropotamos
▶**Eritrea** country Africa 121 H6
  africa [countries] ➤➤ 114–117
Erkech-Tam Kyrg. 103 H5
  formerly spelt Irkeshtam
Erkner Germany 49 K3
Erkowit Sudan 104 D3
Erlangen Germany 48 I6
Erlangping China 87 D1
Erldunda Australia 148 B5
Erlong Shan mt. China 82 C4
Ermak Kazakh. see Aksu
Ermana, Khrebet mts Rus. Fed. 85 G1
Ermelo S. Africa 133 N3
Ermenek Turkey 106 C3
Ermenek r. Turkey 108 E1
Ermil Sudan 121 F6
Ermioni Greece 59 E11
Ermoupoli Greece 59 F11
Ernakulam India 94 C4
Erne r. Rep. of Ireland/U.K. 47 D9
Ernée France 50 F4
Ernest Giles Range hills Australia 151 C5
Ernest Sound sea chan. U.S.A. 166 C4
Erode India 94 C4
Eromanga Australia 149 D5
Erongo admin. reg. Namibia 130 B4
Erp Neth. 48 D3
Erqu China see Zhouzhi
Errabiddy Hills Australia 151 A5
Er Rachidia Morocco 122 D3
  formerly known as Ksar-es-Souk
Er Rahad Sudan 121 F6
Erramala Hills India 94 C3
Er Raoui des. Alg. 123 E3
Errego Moz. 131 H3
  formerly known as Erego
Er Renk Sudan 128 B2
Errigal hill Rep. of Ireland 47 D8
Errinundra National Park Australia 147 F4
Erris Head Rep. of Ireland 47 B9
Erro r. Spain 55 J1
Er Rogel Sudan 121 G5
Erromango i. Vanuatu 145 F3
Erronan i. Vanuatu see Futuna
Er Roseires Sudan 128 B2
Er Ru'at Sudan 121 G6
Ersekë Albania 59 B8
Erta Ale vol. Eth. 128 D1
Ertai China 84 A2
Ertil' Rus. Fed. 41 G6
Ertis Kazakh. see Irtyshsk
Ertis r. Kazakh./Rus. Fed. see Irtysh
Ertix He r. China/Kazakh. 88 D1
  also known as Chernyy Irtysh or Qara Ertis
Erufu Nigeria 125 G4
Erugu Nigeria 125 G5
Eru Iaht b. Estonia 42 G2
Eruwa Nigeria 125 F5
Erval Brazil 204 G4
Ervália Brazil 207 K7
Erve r. France 50 F5
Erwin U.S.A. 178 G4
Erwitte Germany 48 F4
Erydropotamos r. Greece 58 H7
  also spelt Erithropótamos
Erythres Greece 59 E10
  also known as Erithraí
Erzgan China 86 A3
  also known as Yuhu
Erzen r. Albania 58 A7
Erzerum Turkey see Erzurum
Erzgebirge mts Czech Rep./Germany 49 K5
  historically known as Ore Mountains
Erzhan China 82 B2
Erzin Rus. Fed. 84 B1
Erzin Turkey 106 D3
Erzincan Turkey 107 D3
Erzurum Turkey 107 E3
  formerly spelt Erzerum
Erzvikas Lith. 42 D6
Esa-ala P.N.G. 145 E2
Esan-misaki c. Japan 90 G4
Esashi Hokkaidō Japan 90 H2
Esashi Iwate Japan 90 G5
Esbjerg Denmark 45 J5
Esbo Fin. see Espoo
Escada Brazil 202 F3
Escalante Phil. 74 B4
Escalante r. U.S.A. 183 N4
Escalante Desert U.S.A. 183 K4
Escalón Mex. 184 D3
Escalón r. U.S.A. 182 D4
Escambia r. U.S.A. 175 C6
Escanaba U.S.A. 172 F5
Escandón, Puerto de pass Spain 55 K4
Escárcega Mex. 185 H5
Escarpada Point Phil. 74 B2
Escaut r. Belgium 51 J1
Eschede Germany 48 H3
Esch-sur-Alzette Lux. 51 L3
Eschwege Germany 48 H4
Eschweiler Germany 48 D5
Escocesa, Bahía b. Dom. Rep. 187 F3
Escoma Bol. 200 C3
Escondido r. Mex. 179 B6
Escondido r. Nicaragua 186 C4
Escondido U.S.A. 183 G8
Escudilla mt. U.S.A. 183 O8
Escuinapa Mex. 184 D4
Escuintla Guat. 185 H6
Escuintla Mex. 185 G6
Escuque Venez. 198 D2
Escurso r. Brazil 206 C4
Escusa mt. Spain 54 C4
Eséka Cameroon 125 H6
Ese-Khayya Rus. Fed. 39 N3
Eşen Turkey 106 B3
Eşen r. Turkey 59 K12
Esengully Turkm. 102 C5
  formerly spelt Gasan-Kuli or Hasan Guli
Esenköy Turkey 58 J8
Esenyurt Turkey 58 J7
Ésera r. Spain 55 L2
Eşfahān Iran 100 B3
  English form Isfahan; formerly spelt Ispahan

Esfandak Iran 101 E5
Esfarayen, Reshteh-ye Iran 100 D2
Esfideh Iran 101 D3
Esgueva r. Spain 54 G3
Eshan China 86 B3
  also known as Shuangjiang
Eshanguzar Kyrg. 103 I4
  formerly known as imeni Voroshilova or Kalinin
Eshimba Dem. Rep. Congo 127 E6
Eshkamesh Afgh. 101 G2
Eshowe S. Africa 133 P5
Esigodini Zimbabwe 131 F4
  formerly known as Essexvale
Esikhawini S. Africa 133 Q5
Esil Kazakh. see Yesil'
Esil r. Kazakh./Rus. Fed. see Ishim
Esino r. Italy 56 F5
Esk Australia 147 G1
Esk r. Australia 147 I9
Eskdale r. U.K. 47 I9
Esker Canada 169 I3
Eskifjörður Iceland 44 [inset] D2
Eski Gediz Turkey 106 B3
Eskilstuna Sweden 45 L4
Eskimo Lakes Canada 164 F3
Eskimo Point Canada see Arviat
Eski Mosul Iraq 107 E3
Eski-Nookat Kyrg. 103 H4
  formerly spelt Iski-Naukat
Eskipazar Turkey 106 C2
Eskişehir Turkey 106 B3
  historically known as Dorylaeum
Esla r. Spain 54 E3
Esla, Embalse de resr Spain see Ricobayo, Embalse de
Eslāmābād-e Gharb Iran 100 A3
  formerly known as Shāhābād
Esler Dağı mt. Turkey 59 K11
Eslöv Sweden 45 K5
Esma'īlī-ye Soflá Iran 100 C4
Eşme Turkey 106 B3
Esmeralda Cuba 186 D2
Esmeralda, Isla i. Chile 205 B8
Esmeraldas Brazil 207 I6
Esmeraldas Ecuador 198 B4
Esmeraldas prov. Ecuador 198 B4
Esmont r. Bol. 200 D3
Esmont U.S.A. 176 G8
Esnagi Lake Canada 173 I2
Espalha r. Brazil see São Francisco
Espalion France 51 I8
Espalmador, Isla i. Spain see S'Espalmador
Espana country Europe see Spain
Espanola Canada 168 D4
Espanola U.S.A. 181 F5
Esparreguera Spain 55 M3
Esparta Hond. 186 B4
Esparto U.S.A. 182 B3
Espe Kazakh. 103 H4
Espelette France 50 E9
Esperance Australia 151 C7
Esperance Bay Australia 151 C7
Esperantinópolis Brazil 202 C3
Esperanza research station Antarctica 222 U2
Esperanza Santa Cruz Arg. 205 C8
Esperanza Santa Fé Arg. 204 E3
Esperanza Mex. 184 C3
Esperanza Peru 200 C2
Esperanza Phil. 74 C4
Espichel, Cabo c. Port. 54 B6
Espiel Spain 54 G6
Espigão, Serra do mts Brazil 203 B8
Espinazo Mex. 185 E3
Espinheira Angola 127 B9
Espinhaço, Serra do mts Brazil 203 D6
Espinheira hill Port. 54 B6
Espinho Port. 54 C3
Espinilho, Serra do hills Brazil 203 A9
Espino Venez. 199 E2
Espinosa Brazil 202 D5
Espinosa de los Monteros Spain 55 H1
Espírito Santo Brazil see Vila Velha
Espírito Santo state Brazil 203 D6
Espíritu 74 B2
Espíritu Santo Bol. 200 D3
Espíritu Santo i. Vanuatu 145 F3
Espíritu Santo, Bahía del b. Mex. 185 I5
Espíritu Santo, Isla i. Mex. 184 C3
Espita Mex. 185 H4
Esplanada Brazil 202 E4
Espoo Fin. 45 N3
  also spelt Esbo
Espuña mt. Spain 55 J7
Espungabera Moz. 131 G4
Esqueda Mex. 184 C2
Esquel Arg. 205 B6
Esquimalt Canada 166 F5
Esquina Arg. 204 F3
Esquipulas Guat. 185 H6
Esrange Sweden 44 M2
Essaouira Morocco 122 C2
  formerly known as Mogador
Es Semara W. Sahara 122 C4
▶**Essen** Germany 48 E4
  4th most populous city in Europe.
  world [cities] ➤➤ 24–25
Essendon, Mount hill Australia 151 C5
Essex Canada 173 K8
Essex CA U.S.A. 183 I7
Essex MA U.S.A. 177 O3
Essex MD U.S.A. 177 I6
Essex NY U.S.A. 177 L1
Essex Junction U.S.A. 177 L1
Essexville U.S.A. 173 J7
Essexvale Zimbabwe see Esigodini
Esslingen am Neckar Germany 48 G7
Esso Rus. Fed. 39 P4
Essonne r. France 51 I4
Est prov. Cameroon 125 I6
Estaca de Bares, Punta da pt Spain 54 D1
Estación Coahuila Mex. 183 I9
Estado r. Brazil 206 C4
Estados, Isla de los i. Arg. 205 D9
Estagno Point Phil. 74 B2
Eştahbān Iran 100 C4
  also known as Savanat
Estaire Canada 173 M4
Estância Goiás Brazil 206 B4
Estância Sergipe Brazil 202 E4
Estancia U.S.A. 181 F6
Estancia Camerón Chile 205 C9
Estancia Carmen Arg. 205 C9
Estand, Küh-e mt. Iran 101 E4
Estarreja Port. 54 C4
Estats, Pic d' mt. France/Spain 55 M2
Estcourt S. Africa 133 M4
Este Italy 56 D3
Este, Parque Nacional del nat. park Dom. Rep. 187 F3
Esteban Mex. 184 B2
Esteban de Urizar Arg. 201 D5
Estela Brazil 203 B8
Esteli Nicaragua 186 B4
Estella Spain 55 I2
  also known as Lizarra
Estena r. Spain 54 G5
Estepa Spain 54 G7
Estepona Spain 54 G8
Esteras r. Spain 54 G5
Esterel reg. France 51 M9
Esterhazy Canada 167 K5
Estero Bay U.S.A. 182 C6
Esteros Para. 201 E5

Este Sudeste, Cayos del is Col. 198 A1
Estevan Canada 167 K5
Estevan Group is Canada 166 D4
Estherville U.S.A. 178 D3
Estill U.S.A. 175 D5
Estiva Brazil 207 G9
Estiva r. Brazil 202 C3
Eston Canada 167 I5
▶**Estonia** country Europe 42 F3
  known as Eesti in Estonian; formerly known as Estonskaya S.S.R.
  europe [countries] ➤➤ 32–35
Estonskaya S.S.R. country Europe see Estonia
Estreito Brazil 204 H3
Estrela, Serra da mts Port. 54 D4
Estrela do Indaiá Brazil 207 H6
Estrela do Sul Brazil 206 F5
Estrella mt. Spain 55 H6
Estrella, Punta pt Mex. 184 B2
Estrella, Sierra mts U.S.A. 183 L8
Estrema Brazil 200 D3
Estremadura reg. Port. 54 B5
Estremoz Port. 54 D6
Estrondo, Serra hills Brazil 202 B3
Estuaire prov. Gabon 126 A4
Estún Iran 101 D3
Esztergom Hungary 49 P8
  also known as G'ran
Étables-sur-Mer France 50 D4
Etadunna Australia 146 C4
Etah India 96 C4
Étain France 51 L3
Etamamiou Canada 169 J3
Étampes France 51 I4
Etamunbanie, Lake salt flat Australia 148 C5
Étaples France 50 H2

▶**Everest, Mount** China/Nepal 97 E4
  Highest mountain in the world and in Asia. Also known as Qomolangma Feng or Sagarmatha.
  world [physical features] ➤➤ 8–9

	mountain	height	location	page#
1 ▶	Mount Everest	8 848m / 29 028ft	China/Nepal Asia	➤➤ 97 E4
2 ▶	K2	8 611m / 28 251ft	China/Jammu and Kashmir Asia	➤➤ 96 C2
3 ▶	Kangchenjunga	8 586m / 28 169ft	India/Nepal Asia	➤➤ 97 E3
4 ▶	Lhotse	8 516m / 27 939ft	China/Nepal Asia	➤➤ 97 E3
5 ▶	Makalu	8 463m / 27 765ft	China/Nepal Asia	➤➤ 97 E3
6 ▶	Cho Oyu	8 201m / 26 906ft	China/Nepal Asia	➤➤ 97 E3
7 ▶	Dhaulagiri	8 167m / 26 794ft	Nepal Asia	➤➤ 97 D3
8 ▶	Manaslu	8 163m / 26 781ft	Nepal Asia	➤➤ 97 D3
9 ▶	Nanga Parbat	8 126m / 26 660ft	Jammu and Kashmir Asia	➤➤ 96 B2
10 ▶	Annapurna I	8 091m / 25 545ft	Nepal Asia	➤➤ 97 D3

highest mountains

Etawah Rajasthan India 96 C4
Etawah Uttar Pradesh India 96 C4
Etchojoa Mex. 184 C3
Etelä-Suomi prov. Fin. 45 N3
eThandakukhanya S. Africa 133 O3
Ethel watercourse Australia 151 B5
Ethelbert Canada 167 K5
Ethel Creek Australia 150 C4
E'Thembini S. Africa 132 G6
Etheridge r. Australia 149 D3
▶**Ethiopia** country Africa 128 C2
  3rd most populous country in Africa. Spelt Ityopia in Amharic; historically known as Abyssinia.
  africa [countries] ➤➤ 114–117
Ethiopian Highlands mts Eth. 128 C2
Etili Turkey 59 H9
  also known as Gölçük
Etimesgut Turkey 106 C3
Etna r. Norway 45 J3
Etna, Monte vol. Sicilia Italy 57 H11
  also known as Etna, Mount
Etna, Mount vol. Sicilia Italy see Etna, Monte
Etne Norway 45 I4
Etobicoke Canada 173 N7
Etolin Island U.S.A. 164 F4
Etorofu-tō i. Rus. Fed. see Iturup, Ostrov
Etosha National Park Namibia 130 B3
Etosha Pan salt pan Namibia 130 C3
Etoumbi Congo 126 B4
Etowah r. U.S.A. 175 C5
Étrek r. Iran/Turkm. see Atrek
Étrépagny France 50 H3
Étropole Bulg. 58 F6
Etsha Botswana 130 D3
Ettelbruck Lux. 51 M3
Etten-Leur Neth. 48 E4
Ettlingen Germany 48 F7
Ettrick r. U.K. 46 J8
Ettumanur India 94 C4
Etxarri-Aranatz Spain see Echarri-Aranaz
Etztalán Mex. 184 D4
Etzicom Coulee r. Canada 167 I5
Eua i. Tonga 145 H4
  formerly known as Eooa
Euabalong Australia 147 E3
Eubank U.S.A. 176 A9
Euboea i. Greece see Evvoia
Eucla Australia 151 E6
Euclid U.S.A. 176 D4
Euclides da Cunha Brazil 202 E4
Eucumbene, Lake Australia 147 F4
Eudora U.S.A. 175 B5
Eudunda Australia 146 C3
Eufaula AL U.S.A. 175 C6
Eufaula OK U.S.A. 179 D5
Eufaula Lake resr U.S.A. 179 D5
Eugene U.S.A. 180 B3
Eugenia r. Brazil 201 F2
Eugenia, Punta pt Mex. 184 B3
Euic Australia 147 E2
Eungella Australia 149 F4
Eungella National Park Australia 149 F4
Eunice LA U.S.A. 179 D6
Eunice NM U.S.A. 177 B5
Eupen Belgium 51 L2
▶**Euphrates** r. Asia 107 G7
  Longest river in western Asia. Also known as Al Furāt (Iraq/Syria) or Fırat (Turkey).
Eupora U.S.A. 175 B5
Eura Fin. 45 M3
Eure r. France 50 H3
Eure-et-Loir dept France 50 H4
Eureka CA U.S.A. 180 A4
Eureka IL U.S.A. 168 B5
Eureka KS U.S.A. 178 C4
Eureka MT U.S.A. 180 D2
Eureka NV U.S.A. 183 I2
Eureka OH U.S.A. 176 D7
Eureka SD U.S.A. 178 C2
Eureka UT U.S.A. 183 L2
Eureka Springs U.S.A. 179 D4
Eureka Sound sea chan. Canada 165 K2
Eureka Valley U.S.A. 182 G4
eudapolis Brazil 207 I3
Eurnilla watercourse Australia 146 L1
Eurombah Australia 149 F5
Eurombah Creek r. Australia 149 F5
Europa, Île i. Indian Ocean 218 J7
  English form Europa Island
Europa, Picos de mts Spain 54 F1
Europa, Punta de pt Gibraltar see Europa Point
Europa Island Indian Ocean see Europa, Île

Europa Point Gibraltar 54 F8
  also known as Europa, Punta de
Eustis U.S.A. 175 D6
Euston Australia 147 D3
Eutaw U.S.A. 175 C5
Eutin Germany 48 H1
Eutsuk Lake Canada 166 E4
Evale Angola 127 B9
Evans, Lac l. Canada 168 E3
Evans City U.S.A. 176 E5
Evans Ice Stream Antarctica 222 S1
Evans Strait Canada 165 K3
Evanston IL U.S.A. 172 F8
Evanston WY U.S.A. 180 E4
Evansville IN U.S.A. 174 C4
Evansville WI U.S.A. 172 D8
Evansville WY U.S.A. 180 F4
Eva Perón Arg. see La Plata
Eva Perón prov. Arg. see La Pampa
Evart U.S.A. 173 I3
Evaton S. Africa 133 L3
Evaz Iran 100 C5
Evcili Turkey 108 D1
Eveleth U.S.A. 172 A3
Evening Shade U.S.A. 174 B4
Evensk Rus. Fed. 39 P3
Evenskjær Norway 44 L1
Everard, Cape Australia 147 F4
Everard, Lake salt flat Australia 146 B2
Everard, Mount N.T. Australia 148 B4
Everard, Mount S.A. Australia 148 B4
Everard Range hills Australia 146 B1
Everek Turkey see Develi
▶**Everest, Mount** China/Nepal 97 E4
  Highest mountain in the world and in Asia. Also known as Qomolangma Feng or Sagarmatha.
  world [physical features] ➤➤ 8–9
Everett PA U.S.A. 176 G5
Everett WA U.S.A. 180 B3
Evergem Belgium 51 J1
▶**Everglades** swamp U.S.A. 175 D7
  world [land cover] ➤➤ 18–19
Everglades National Park U.S.A. 175 D7
Evergreen U.S.A. 175 C6
Everman, Volcán vol. Mex. 184 C5
Everson U.S.A. 180 B2
Evertsberg Sweden 45 K3
Evesham Australia 149 D4
Evesham U.K. 47 K11
Évian-les-Bains France 51 M6
Evijärvi Fin. 44 M3
Evinayong Equat. Guinea 125 H6
Evington U.S.A. 176 F8
Evinos r. Greece 59 C10
Evje Norway 45 I4
Évora admin. dist. Port. 54 C6
Évora Port. 54 D6
Evoron, Ozero l. Rus. Fed. 82 C2
Évosmo Greece 58 E8
Evowghli Iran 100 A2
Évreux France 50 H3
Evron France 50 F4
Evros r. Greece/Turkey 58 H8
  also spelt Hebros
Evrotas r. Greece 59 D12
Évry France 51 I4
Evrychou Cyprus 108 D2
  also spelt Evrykhou
Evrykhou Cyprus see Evrychou
Evvoia i. Greece 59 F10
  English form Euboea; also known as Negroponte
Ewa Beach U.S.A. 181 [inset] Z1
Ewan Australia 149 E3
Ewaso Ngiro r. Kenya 128 C5
Ewbank S. Africa 132 H3
Ewe, Loch b. U.K. 46 G6
Ewen U.S.A. 172 D4
Ewenkizu Zizhiqi China see Bayan Tohoi
Ewing Island Antarctica 222 T2
Ewirgol China 88 D3
Ewo Congo 126 B5
Exaltación Bol. 200 D3
Excelsior S. Africa 133 L5
Excelsior Mountain U.S.A. 182 E3
Excelsior Mountains U.S.A. 182 F3
Excelsior Springs U.S.A. 178 D4
Exe r. U.K. 47 I13
Executive Committee Range mts Antarctica 222 P1
Exeland U.S.A. 172 B4
Exeter Canada 173 L7
Exeter U.K. 47 I13
Exeter CA U.S.A. 182 E5
Exeter NH U.S.A. 177 O3
Exeter Lake Canada 167 I1
Exmoor hills U.K. 47 I12
Exmore U.S.A. 177 J8
Exmouth Australia 150 A4
Exmouth U.K. 47 I13
Exmouth, Mount Australia 147 F2
Exmouth Gulf Australia 150 A4
Exmouth Lake Canada 167 H1
Expedition National Park Australia 149 F5
Expedition Range mts Australia 149 F5
Exploits r. Canada 169 K3
Exton U.S.A. 177 J5
Extremadura aut. comm. Spain 54 H5
Extrême-Nord prov. Cameroon 125 I4
Exuma Cays Bahamas 186 D1
Exuma Sound sea chan. Bahamas 186 E1
Eya r. Rus. Fed. 41 F7
Eyangu Dem. Rep. Congo 126 C5
Eyasi, Lake salt l. Tanz. 129 B5
Eyawadi r. Myanmar see Irrawaddy
Eydehavn Norway 45 J4
Eyeberry Lake Canada 167 J2
Eyelenoborsk Rus. Fed. 40 L2
Eyemouth U.K. 46 J8
Eyjafjallajökull ice cap Iceland 44 [inset] C3
Eyjafjörður inlet Iceland 44 [inset] C2
Eyl Somalia 128 F3
Eylau Rus. Fed. see Bagrationovsk
Eymet France 50 G8
Eymir Turkey 59 J11
Eymoutiers France 50 H7
Eyre r. France 50 E8
Eyre (South), Lake salt flat Australia 146 C2
▶**Eyre, Lake** salt flat Australia 146 C2
  Largest lake in Oceania and lowest point in Oceania.
  oceania [landscapes] ➤➤ 136–137
  oceania [features] ➤➤ 142–143
Eyre Creek watercourse Australia 148 C5

Eyre Mountains N.Z. 153 C13
Eyre Peak N.Z. 153 C13
Eyre Peninsula Australia 146 B3
Eyrieux r. France 51 K8
Eystfuroy i. Faroe Is 46 F1
Eyumojok Cameroon 125 H5
Eyvänaki Iran 100 C3
Ezakheni S. Africa 133 O5
eZamokuhle S. Africa 133 N3
'Ezbet el Burg Egypt 108 C6
Ezbet el Gezira Egypt 108 C6
Ezbet Gamasa el Gharbiya Egypt 108 C6
Ezel U.S.A. 176 B8
Ezenzeleni S. Africa 133 M4
Ezequiel Ramos Mexia, Embalse resr Arg.
  204 C5
Ezernieki Latvia 42 I5
Ezhou China 87 E2
  formerly known as Echeng
Ezhva Rus. Fed. 40 I3
  formerly known as Sloboda
Ezine Turkey 106 A3
Ezinepazar Turkey 106 D2
Ezo i. Japan see Hokkaidō
Ezousa r. Cyprus 108 E3
Ezra's Tomb tourist site Iraq 107 F5

↓ F

Faadhippolhu Atoll Maldives 94 B5
Fabens U.S.A. 181 F7
Faber, Mount hill Sing. 76 [inset]
Faber Lake Canada 167 E2
Fåberg Norway 45 J3
Fåborg Denmark 45 J5
Fabriano Italy 56 E3
Facatativá Col. 198 C3
Fachi Niger 125 H2
Factoryville U.S.A. 177 J4
Facundo Arg. 205 C7
Fada Chad 120 D5
Fada-Ngourma Burkina 125 F3
Faḍilah well Saudi Arabia 105 E3
Faḍli reg. Yemen 105 D5
Fadnoun, Plateau du Alg. 123 H4
Faenza Italy 56 D4
Færingehavn Greenland see
  Kangerluarsoruseq
Færoerne terr. N. Atlantic Ocean see
  Faroe Islands
Faeroes terr. N. Atlantic Ocean see Faroe Islands
Fafa r. Cent. Afr. Rep. 126 C3
Fafanlap Indon. 73 H7
Fafe Port. 54 C3
Fafen Shet' watercourse Eth. 128 E3
Faga watercourse Burkina 125 F3
Fågåraş Romania 58 F3

▶ Fagatogo American Samoa 145 H3
  Capital of American Samoa.

Fagersta Sweden 45 K4
Fåget Romania 58 D3
Fagnano, Lago l. Arg./Chile 205 C9
Fagne reg. Belgium 51 I4
Fagochia well Niger 125 G2
Faguibine, Lac l. Mali 124 D2
Fagurhólsmýri Iceland 44 [inset] C3
Fagwir U.K. 46 J8
Fahlian, Rūdkhāneh-ye watercourse Iran
  100 B4
Fahraj Iran 100 D4
Fahūd, Jabal hill Oman 105 G3
Faillon, Lac l. Canada 173 O5
Fairbanks U.S.A. 164 E3
Fairborn U.S.A. 176 A6
Fairbury U.S.A. 178 C3
Fairchild U.S.A. 172 C6
Fairfax N.Z. 153 C14
Fairfax IA U.S.A. 172 B9
Fairfax VA U.S.A. 177 H7
Fairfax VT U.S.A. 177 L1
Fairfield CA U.S.A. 182 B3
Fairfield IA U.S.A. 174 B3
Fairfield ID U.S.A. 180 D4
Fairfield IL U.S.A. 174 B4
Fairfield OH U.S.A. 176 A6
Fairfield TX U.S.A. 179 C6
Fairfield VA U.S.A. 177 L1
Fairfield VA U.S.A. 176 F7
Fairgrove U.S.A. 173 J7
Fairhaven U.S.A. 177 O3
Fair Haven U.S.A. 177 L2
Fair Head U.K. 47 F8
Fair Isle i. U.K. 46 K4
Fairlee U.S.A. 177 M2
Fairlie N.Z. 153 E12
Fairmont MN U.S.A. 178 D3
Fairmont WV U.S.A. 176 E6
Fairmont Hot Springs Canada 167 H5
Fairplay U.S.A. 180 F5
Fairview Australia 149 D2
Fairview Canada 166 G3
Fairview IL U.S.A. 172 C10
Fairview KY U.S.A. 176 B7
Fairview MI U.S.A. 173 I6
Fairview OK U.S.A. 179 C4
Fairview PA U.S.A. 176 E4
Fairview UT U.S.A. 183 M2
Fairview WV U.S.A. 172 C2
Fairview Park Hong Kong China 87 [inset]
Fairweather, Cape U.S.A. 166 B3
Fairweather, Mount Canada/U.S.A. 164 F4
Fais i. Micronesia 73 J5
  formerly known as Lyallpur
Faisalabad Pak. 101 H4
Faizabad Afgh. see Feyzābād
Faizabad Afgh. 101 H2
Faizabad India 97 D4
Fäj aş Şulubi watercourse Saudi Arabia109 M7
Fajj, Wādī al watercourse Iraq 109 O5
Fajr, Wādī al watercourse Saudi Arabia 107 D5
Fakaofo atoll Tokelau 145 H2
  also spelt Fakaofu; formerly known as
  Bowditch
Fakaofu atoll Tokelau see Fakaofo
Fakel Rus. Fed. 40 J4
  formerly known as Sergiyevskiy
Fakenham U.K. 47 M11
Fåker Sweden 44 K3
Fakfak Indon. 73 H7
Fakhrabad Iran 100 C4
Fakiragram India 97 F4
Fakiyska Reka r. Bulg. 58 I6
Fakse Denmark 45 K5
Fakse Bugt b. Denmark 45 K5
Faku China 85 I3
Falaba Sierra Leone 124 C4
Falagountou Burkina 125 F3
Falaise France 50 F4
Falaise Lake Canada 167 G2
Falakata India 97 F4
Falam Myanmar 78 A3
Falavarjan Iran 100 B3
Falcarragh Rep. of Ireland 47 D8
Falces Spain 55 J2
Fălciu Romania 58 J2
Falcon, Cap c. Alg. 55 K9
Falcon state Venez. 198 D2
Falcon Island Tonga see Fonuafo'ou
Falcon Lake Canada 167 M5
Falcon Lake l. Mex./U.S.A. 185 E3
Falelima Samoa 145 H3

Falémé r. Mali/Senegal 124 B3
Falerii Italy see Civita Castellana
Falfurrias U.S.A. 179 C7
Falher Canada 167 G4
Falkatt Germany 49 K4
Falkenberg Germany 49 K4
Falkenberg Sweden 45 K4
Falkensee Germany 49 K3
Falkirk U.K. 46 I8

▶ Falkland Islands terr. S. Atlantic Ocean
  205 F8
  United Kingdom Overseas Territory. Also
  known as Malvinas, Islas.
  southamerica [countries] ▶▶ 192–193

Falkland Sound sea chan. Falkland Is
  205 E9
Falkner Arg. 204 D6
Falkonera i. Greece 59 E12
Falköping Sweden 45 K4
Fall r. U.S.A. 178 D4
Fall Branch U.S.A. 176 C9
Fallbrook U.S.A. 182 G8
Fall Creek U.S.A. 172 B6
Fallières Coast Antarctica 222 T2
Fallon U.S.A. 182 F2
Fall River U.S.A. 177 N4
Fall River Pass U.S.A. 180 F4
Falls City U.S.A. 178 D3
Falls Creek U.S.A. 176 F4
Falmouth Antigua and Barbuda 187 H3
Falmouth Jamaica 186 D3
Falmouth U.K. 47 G13
Falmouth KY U.S.A. 176 A7
Falmouth MA U.S.A. 177 O4
Falmouth ME U.S.A. 177 O2
Falmouth VA U.S.A. 176 H7
Falou Mali 124 D3
False r. Canada 169 G1
False Bay S. Africa 132 C11
False Bay Park S. Africa 133 Q4
False Point India 95 E1
Falso, Cabo c. Dom. Rep. 187 F3
Falso, Cabo c. Hond. 186 C4
Falso Cabo de Hornos c. Chile 205 C9
Falster i. Denmark 45 K5
Fălticeni Romania 58 H1
Falun Sweden 45 K3
Falzarego, Passo di pass Italy 56 E2
Famagusta Cyprus 108 E2
  also known as Ammochostos or Gazimağusa
  or Magosa
Famagusta Bay Cyprus see Ammochostos Bay
Famatina Arg. 204 D3
Famatina, Sierra de mts Arg. 204 C3
Famenin Iran 100 B3
Fame Range hills Australia 151 C5
Family Lake Canada 167 M5
Family Well Australia 150 D4
Fanad Head Rep. of Ireland 47 E8
Fanambana Madag. 131 [inset] K2
Fanandrana Madag. 131 [inset] K3
Fanari, Akra pt Greece 59 H11
Fanchang China 87 F2
Fandriana Madag. 131 [inset] J4
Fang Thai. 78 B4
Fangak Sudan 128 A2
Fangcheng China see Fangchenggang
Fangcheng China 87 E1
Fangchenggang China 87 D4
  formerly known as Fangcheng
Fangdou Shan mts China 87 D2
Fangliao Taiwan 87 G4
Fangshan Taiwan 87 G4
Fangxian China 87 D1
Fangzheng China 82 C3
Fani i Vogël r. Albania 58 A7
Fanipal' Belarus 42 I8
Fankuai China 87 D2
  formerly known as Fankuaidian
Fankuaidian China see Fankuai
Fanling Hong Kong China 87 [inset]
Fanrrem Norway 44 J3
Fannůj Iran 101 D5
Fano i. Denmark 45 J5
Fano Italy 56 F5
  historically known as Colonia Julia Fenestris
  or Fanum Fortunae
Fanoualie i. Tonga see Fonualei
Fanshan Anhui China 87 F2
Fanshan Zhejiang China 87 G3
Fanshi China 85 G4
Fan Si Pan mt. Vietnam 78 C3
Fanum Fortunae Italy see Fano
Fanxian China 85 G5
  also known as Yingtaoyuan
Farab Turkm. see Farap
Faraba Mali 124 C3
Farab-Pristan'i Turkm. see Dzheykhan
Faradje Dem. Rep. Congo 126 F4
Faradofay Madag. see Tôlañaro
Farafangana Madag. 131 [inset] J4
Farafenni Gambia 124 B3
Farafra Oasis Egypt 121 F3
Farāgheh Iran 100 C4
Farāh Afgh. 101 E3
  historically known as Alexandria Prophthasia
Farāh prov. Afgh. 101 E3
Farāhābād Iran see Khezerābād
Farah Rūd watercourse Afgh. 101 E3
Farakhulm Afgh. 101 G2
Farallon de Medinilla i. N. Mariana Is 73 K3
  also known as Bird Island
Farallon de Pajaros vol. N. Mariana Is 73 K3
  also known as Largeau
Farallon National Wildlife Refuge
  nature res. U.S.A. 182 A4
Faranah Guinea 124 C4
Faraoani Romania 58 H2
Far'aoun well Mauritania 124 B2
Farap Turkm. 103 E5
  formerly known as Farab
Fararah Oman 105 F4
Farasān Saudi Arabia 104 C3
Farasān, Jazā'ir is Saudi Arabia 104 C4
Faratsiho Madag. 131 [inset] J3
Faraulep atoll Micronesia 73 J5
  also known as Fattoilep; also spelt Foraulep;
  formerly known as Gardner
Fardes r. Spain 55 I7
Farewell, Cape Greenland 165 O3
  also known as Farvel, Kap or Nunap Isua or
  Uummannarsuaq
Farewell, Cape N.Z. see Farewell, Cape
Farewell Spit N.Z. 152 G8
Färgelanda Sweden 45 J4
Farghona Uzbek. see Fergana
Farg'ona Wiloyati admin. div. Uzbek. see
  Ferganskaya Oblast'
Fargo U.S.A. 178 C2
Faribault U.S.A. 174 A2
Faribault, Lac l. Canada 169 G1
Faridabad India 96 C3
  formerly known as Fort Gouraud
Faridpur Bangl. 97 F5
Faridpur India 96 C3
Fārig Iran 100 D4
Fārigh, Wādī al watercourse Libya 120 C2
Färila Sweden 45 K3
Farim Guinea-Bissau 124 B3
Farīmān Iran 101 D3
Farinha r. Brazil 202 C3
Farish Uzbek. 103 F4
  English form Farish
Fārisķūr Egypt 108 C6
Färjestaden Sweden 45 L4
Farkadhon Greece 59 D9
Farkhar Afgh. see Farkhato

Farkhato Afgh. 101 G2
  also spelt Farkhar
Farkhor Tajik. 101 G2
  also spelt Farkhar
Farley U.S.A. 172 B8
Farmahin Iran 100 B3
Farmakonisi i. Greece 59 I11
Farmer City U.S.A. 174 B3
Farmer Island Canada 168 D1
Farmerville U.S.A. 179 D5
Farmington Canada 166 F4
Farmington IA U.S.A. 172 B10
Farmington IL U.S.A. 172 C10
Farmington ME U.S.A. 177 O1
Farmington MO U.S.A. 174 B4
Farmington NH U.S.A. 177 N2
Farmington NM U.S.A. 181 F5
Farmington UT U.S.A. 180 E4
Farmington Hills U.S.A. 173 ,8
Far Mountain Canada 166 E4
Farmville U.S.A. 176 G8
Farne Islands U.K. 46 K8
Farnham U.S.A. 177 H8
Farnham, Lake salt flat Australia 151 D5
Farnham, Mount Canada 167 G5
Faro Brazil 199 G5
Faro r. Cameroon 125 I4
Faro Canada 166 C2
Faro Port. 54 C7
Faro admin. dist. Port. 54 C7
Fårö i. Sweden 45 L4
Faro, Réserve du nature res. Cameroon 125 I4
Faro, Serra do mts Spain 54 D2

▶ Faroe Islands terr. N. Atlantic Ocean 46 E2
  Self-governing Danish Territory. Also spelt
  Faeroes; also known as Færoerne or Føroyar.
  europe [countries] ▶▶ 32–35

Fårösund Sweden 45 L4
Farquhar Atoll Seychelles 129 F7
Farquhar Islands Seychelles 129 F7
Farquharson Tableland hills Australia 151 C5
Farrandsville U.S.A. 176 H4
Farrars Creek watercourse Australia 149 D5
Farrāsh, Jabal al mt. Saudi Arabia 104 C4
Farrāshband Iran 100 C4
Farr Bay Antarctica 223 G2
Farrellton Canada 173 R5
Farrokhī Iran 100 D3
Farrukhabad India see Fatehgarh
Fars prov. Iran 100 C4
Farsala Greece 59 D9
Farsaliotis r. Greece 59 D9
Fārsī, Jazireh-ye i. Iran 107 G2
Farson U.S.A. 180 E4
Farsund Norway 45 I4
Fartak, Jabal mts Yemen 105 E5
Fartak, Ra's c. Yemen 105 F5
Fârţăneşti Romania 58 I3
Fartura r. Brazil 206 C3
Fartura, Serra da mts Brazil 203 A8
Farvel, Kap c. Greenland see Farewell, Cape
Farwell MI U.S.A. 173 I7
Farwell TX U.S.A. 179 B5
Fāryāb prov. Afgh. 101 F2
Fāryāb Hormozgan Iran 100 D5
  also known as Deh Barez
Fāryāb Kermān Iran 100 D4
Farynava Belarus 43 J6
Fasā Iran 100 C4
Fasano Italy 56 J8
Făsikan Geçidi pass Turkey 108 D1
Fasil Ghebbi and Gonder Monuments
  tourist site Eth. 128 C1
Fāsteh, Ra's-e pt Iran 101 E5
Fastiv Ukr. 41 D6
  also spelt Fastov
Fastov Ukr. see Fastiv
Fatehabad India 96 B3
Fatehgarh Madhya Pradesh India 96 C4
Fatehgarh Uttar Pradesh India 96 C4
  formerly known as Farrukhabad
Fatehnagar India 96 B4
Fatehpur Rajasthan India 96 B4
Fatehpur Uttar Pradesh India 96 D4
Fatehpur Sikri India 96 C4
Fateyevka Rus. Fed. 43 Q9
Fatezh Rus. Fed. 43 Q9
Fatḥābād Iran 100 C4
Fathai Sudan 128 A2
Fati, Lac l. Mali 124 D2
Fatick Senegal 124 A3
Fattoilep atoll Micronesia see Faraulep
Fatuma Dem. Rep. Congo 127 F6
Faulkton U.S.A. 178 C2
Faulquemont France 51 M3
Fauquier Canada 166 G5
Fauresmith S. Africa 133 J6
Fauske Norway 44 K2
Faust Canada 167 H4
Favalto, Monte mt. Italy 56 E5
Favara Sicilia Italy 57 E11
Favignana, Isola i. Sicilia Italy 57 E11
Fawcett Canada 167 H4
Fawn r. Canada 168 B2
Fawnleas S. Africa 133 O6
Fawwārah Saudi Arabia 104 C2
Faxaflói b. Iceland 44 [inset] B2
Faxälven r. Sweden 44 L3
Faxian Hu l. China 86 B3
Faya Chad 120 C5
Fayaoué New Caledonia 145 F4
Faydat al Adyān waterhole Iraq 109 M6
Faydat al Habbārīyah waterhole Iraq 109 N5
Fayette AL U.S.A. 175 C5
Fayette MI U.S.A. 172 E8
Fayette MO U.S.A. 178 D4
Fayette MS U.S.A. 175 B6
Fayette OH U.S.A. 176 A4
Fayetteville AR U.S.A. 179 D4
Fayetteville GA U.S.A. 175 C5
Fayetteville NC U.S.A. 174 E5
Fayetteville NY U.S.A. 177 I2
Fayetteville TN U.S.A. 174 C5
Fayetteville WV U.S.A. 176 D7
Fayfā Saudi Arabia 104 C4
Fayḩālah, Wādī watercourse Saudi Arabia
  109 O8
Fāyid Egypt 108 D7
Faylakah i. Kuwait 107 G5
Fayl-la-Forêt France 51 L5
Fazair al Ghrazi watercourse Saudi Arabia
  109 H8
Fazao Malfakassa, Parc National de
  nat. park Togo 125 F4
Fazel well Niger 125 H2
Fazilka India 96 B3
Fazrān, Jabal hill Saudi Arabia 105 D2
Fdérik Mauritania 122 B5
  formerly known as Fort Gouraud
Fead Group is P.N.G. see Nuguria Islands
Feale r. Rep. of Ireland 47 C11
Fear, Cape U.S.A. 175 E5
Feather r. U.S.A. 182 C3
Feather, North Fork r. U.S.A. 182 C3
Featherston N.Z. 152 J8
Fécamp France 50 G3
Federación Arg. 204 F3
Federación Arg. 204 F3
Federación, Embalse resr Arg.
  204 C5
Federal Arg. 204 F3
Federal Capital Territory admin. div.
  Nigeria 125 G4

Federal District admin. dist. Brazil see
  Distrito Federal
Federal District admin. dist. Venez. see
  Distrito Federal
Federalsburg U.S.A. 177 J7
Federated Malay States country Asia see
  Malaysia
Federation of Bosnia and Herzegovina
  aut. div. Bos.-Herz. see
  Fédéracija Bosna i Hercegovina
Fedorov Kazakh. see Fedorovka
Fedorovka Kustanayskaya Oblast' Kazakh.
  103 F1
Fedorovka Pavlodarskaya Oblast' Kazakh.
  103 I1
Fedorovka Zapadnyy Kazakhstan Kazakh.
  102 B2
Fedorovskoye Rus. Fed. 43 U5
Fehérgyarmat Hungary 49 T8
Fehet Lake Canada 167 M1
Fehmarn i. Germany 48 I1
Fehmarn Belt strait Denmark/Germany 45 J5
  also known as Femer Bælt
Fehrbellin Germany 49 J3
Feia, Lagoa lag. Brazil 203 D7
Feicheng China see Feixian
Feidong China 87 F2
  also known as Dianbu
Feijó Brazil 200 C2
Feilai Fei tourist site Hong Kong China see
  Kowloon Peak
Feira Zambia see Luangwa
Feira de Santana Brazil 202 E5
Feira do Monte Spain 54 D1
Feirān Egypt 108 E9
Feirān, Wādī watercourse Egypt 108 E9
Feirān, Gebel mt. Egypt 108 F9
Feixi China 87 F2
  also known as Shangpai; formerly known as
  Shangpaihe
Feixian China 85 H5
Feixiang China 85 G4
Fejaj, Chott el salt l. Tunisia 123 H2
Feje i. Denmark 48 I1
Feke Turkey 106 C3
Felanitx Spain 55 O5
Felaou well Alg. 125 G2
Feldberg mt. Ger. 51 N5
Feldbach Austria 48 G3
Feldkirch Austria 48 G8
Feldkirchen in Kärnten Austria 49 L9
Feldru Romania 58 E1
Feliciano r. Arg. 204 F3
Felicity U.S.A. 176 A7
Felidhu Atoll Maldives 93 D10
Felipe C. Puerto Mex. 185 H5
Felix, Cape Canada 165 J3
Felixarco Brazil 203 C6
Felixlândia Brazil 203 C6
Felixstowe U.K. 47 N12
Felletin France 51 I7
Fellowsville U.S.A. 176 F6
Felsberg Germany 48 G4
Felsina Italy see Bologna
Feltre Italy 56 D2
Femeas r. Brazil 202 C5
Femer Bælt strait Denmark/Germany see
  Fehmarn Belt
Femi i. Denmark 48 I1
Femund l. Norway 44 K3
Femundsmarka Nasjonalpark nat. park
  Norway 44 K3
Fen r. China 85 F5
Fenambosy, Lohatanjona pt Madag.
  131 [inset] I5
Fenelon Falls Canada 173 O6
Fener Burnu hd Turkey 108 G1
  also known as Karatas Burnu
Fénérive Madag. see Fenoarivo Atsinanana
Fengari mt. Greece 59 G3
Fengcheng China see Lianjiang
Fengcheng China see Yongding
Fengcheng China see Anxi
Fengcheng China see Xin'eng
Fengcheng Jiangxi China 87 E2
Fengcheng Liaoning China 83 B5
Fengchuan China see Fengxin
Fengdu China 87 C2
  also known as Xiucaiwan; formerly known as
  Mingshan
Fenggang China see Shaxian
Fenggang China 87 C3
  also known as Longquan
Fenggang China see Yihuang
Fenggeling China 86 D1
Fenghua China 87 G2
Fenghuang China see Tuojiang
Fengjiaba China see Wangcang
Fengjie China 87 D2
  also known as Yong'an
Fengkai China 87 D3
  also known as Jiangkou
Fenglin Taiwan 87 G4
Fengming China see Qishan
Fengnan China 85 H4
Fengning China see Fengcheng
Fengqing China see Luotian
Fengqing China see Fengqing
Fengqiu Shuiku resr China 87 E3
Fengshui Shan mt. China 82 A1
Fengtai China 87 F1
Fengtongzai Giant Panda Reserve
  nature res. China 86 B2
Fengxian Jiangsu China 85 H5
Fengxian Shaanxi China 86 C1
  also known as Shuangshipu
Fengxian Shanghai China 87 G2
  also known as Nanqiao
Fengxiang China see Luobei
Fengxiang China see Lincang
Fengxin China 87 E2
  also known as Fengchuan
Fengyang China 87 F1
  also known as Fucheng
Fengyi China see Zheng'an
Fengyi China see Maoxian
Fengyi Taiwan 87 F3
Fengzhen China 85 G3
Fengzhou China China 85 F4
Feni Bangl. 97 F5
Feni Islands P.N.G. 145 E2
Fenny r. Bangl./India 97 F5
Feno, Capo di c. Corse France 56 A7
Fenoarivo Madag. see Fenerive
Fenoarivo Atsinanana Madag. 131 [inset] K3
  formerly known as Fénérive
Fenoarivo Be Madag. 131 [inset] J3
Fenton U.S.A. 173 J8
Fenua Ura atoll Fr. Polynesia see Manuae
Fenwick U.S.A. 176 E7
Fenwood Canada 167 K5
Fenyang China 85 F4
Fenyi China 87 E3
Feodosiya Ukr. 41 F7
  also known as Caffa or Kafa or Kefe;
  historically known as Theodosia
Fer, Cap de c. Alg. 123 G1
Férai Greece see Feres
Ferapontovo Rus. Fed. 43 V2
Ferdinandshof Germany 49 K2
Ferdows Iran 100 D3

Fère-Champenoise France 51 J4
Feres Greece 59 H8
  also known as Férei
Férfer Somalia 128 E3
Fergana Uzbek. 103 H4
  also spelt Farghona; formerly known as
  Novyy Margelan or Skobelev
Fergana Oblast admin. div. Uzbek. see
  Ferganskaya Oblast'
Fergana Range mts Kyrg. see
  Fergana Too Tizmegi
Fergana Too Tizmegi mts Kyrg. 103 H4
  English form Fergana Range; also known as
  Ferganskiy Khrebet
Ferganskaya Oblast' admin. div. Uzbek.103 G4
  English form Fergana Oblast; also known as
  Farghona Wiloyati
Ferganskiy Khrebet mts Kyrg. see
  Fergana Too Tizmegi
Fergus Canada 173 M7
Fergus Falls U.S.A. 178 C2
Ferguson Lake Canada 167 L2
Fergusson r. Australia 148 L2
Fergusson Island P.N.G. 145 E2
Fériana Tunisia 123 H2
Feridu India see Fatehgarh
Feriana Tunisia 123 H2
Ferjukot Iceland 44 [inset] B2
Ferkessédougou Côte d'Ivoire 124 D4
Ferlach Austria 49 L9
Ferlo, Vallée du watercourse Senegal 124 B3
Ferlo-Nord, Réserve de Faune du
  nature res. Senegal 124 B3
Ferlo-Sud, Réserve de Faune du
  nature res. Senegal 124 B3
Fermo Italy 56 F5
  historically known as Firmum or Firmum
  Picenum
Fermont Canada 169 H2
Fermoselle Spain 54 D3
Fermoy Rep. of Ireland 47 D11
Fernandina Beach U.S.A. 175 D6
Fernando de Magallanes, Parque
  Nacional nat. park Chile 205 B9
Fernando de Noronha i. Brazil 216 L6
Fernandópolis Brazil 206 C7
Fernando Poó i. Equat. Guinea see Bioco
Fernão Núñez Spain 54 G7
Fernão Dias Brazil 207 J3
Fernão Veloso Moz. 131 I2
Ferndale U.S.A. 180 B2
Ferndown U.K. 47 K13
Fernhill N.Z. 152 K7
Fernie Canada 167 H5
Fernley U.S.A. 182 E2
Fern ridge Germany 48 I4
Ferozepore India see Firozpur
Ferrara Italy 56 D4
Ferrato, Capo c. Sardegna Italy 57 C9
Ferreira Spain 54 D1
Ferreira do Alentejo Port. 54 C6
Ferreñafe Peru 198 B6
Ferreira r. Brazil 200 C2
Ferreira U.S.A. 175 B6
Ferro, Capo c. Sardegna Italy 56 C7
Ferro i. Canary Is see El Ferro; long form El Ferrol
  del Caudillo
Ferron U.S.A. 183 M2
Ferros Brazil 203 D6
Ferrum U.S.A. 176 E9
Ferryland Canada 169 K4
Ferryville Tunisia see Menzel Bourguiba
Fertő-tavi nat. park Hungary 49 N8
Ferzikovo Rus. Fed. 43 P7
Fès Morocco 122 D2
  also spelt Al Fas or Fez
Feshi Dem. Rep. Congo 127 C6
Fessenden U.S.A. 178 C2
Fet Dom, Tanjung pt Indon. 75 D3
Fété Bowé Senegal 124 B3
Ficalho hill Port. 54 D7
Fiche Eth. 128 C2
Fichtelgebirge hills Germany 48 J5
Fichtelgebirge park Germany 48 J5
Ficksburg S. Africa 133 L5
Fidă oasis Saudi Arabia 105 F4
Fidenza Italy 56 C4
Fidîmîn Egypt 108 B8
Fidjeland Norway 45 I4
Fieberbrunn Austria 49 J8
Field B.C. Canada 167 H5
Field Ont. Canada 173 M4
Field Island Australia 148 B2
Fiemanka r. Latvia 42 H5
Fieni Romania 58 G3
Fier Albania 58 A8
Fiery Creek r. Australia 149 C3
Fierzes, Liqeni i resr Albania 58 B6
Fife Lake U.S.A. 172 H6
Fife Ness pt U.K. 46 J7
Fifield U.S.A. 172 C5
Fifteenth of May City Egypt see
  Medinet 15 Mayo
Fifth Cataract rapids Sudan see 5th Cataract
Fifth Meridian Canada 167 H3
Figalo, Cap c. Alg. 55 J9
Figari, Cap c. Sardegna Italy 56 C7
Figeac France 51 I8
Figueira a. Foz Port. 54 C4
Figueira do Foz Port. 54 C4
Figueiró dos Vinhos Port. 54 C5
Figueras Spain see Figueres
Figueres Spain 55 N2
  also spelt Figueras
Figuig Morocco 123 E2
Figuil Cameroon 125 I4

▶ Fiji country S. Pacific Ocean 145 G3
  4th most populous and 5th largest country
  in Oceania.
  oceania [countries] ▶▶ 138–139

Fik' Eth. 128 D2
Filabusi Zimbabwe 131 F4
Filadelfia Italy 57 I10
Filadelfia Costa Rica 186 B5
Filadelfia Para. 201 E5
Fiľakovo Slovakia 49 Q7
Filamana Mali 124 D4
Filchner Ice Shelf Antarctica 222 V1
Filey U.K. 47 L9
Filiași Romania 58 E4
Filiates Greece 59 B9
Filiatra Greece 59 C11
Filibe Bulg. see Plovdiv
Filicudi, Isola i. Isole Lipari Italy 57 G10
Filingué Niger 125 F3
Filiouri r. Greece see Lissos
Filipinas country Asia see Philippines
Filippa, Mys hd Rus. Fed. 82 E1

Fère-Champenoise France 51 J4
Feres Greece 59 H8
Filippiada Greece 59 B9
Filippoi tourist site Greece 58 F7
Filipstad Sweden 45 K4
Fillan Norway 44 J3
Fillira Greece see Fillyra
Fillmore Canada CA U.S.A. 182 F7
Fillmore UT U.S.A. 183 L3
Fillyra Greece 58 G7
  also spelt Fillira
Filtu Eth. 128 D3
Fimbul Ice Shelf Antarctica 223 A2
Fina, Réserve de nature res. Mali 124 C3
Finale Ligure Italy 56 B4
Fincastle U.S.A. 176 F8
Finch'a'ā Hāyk' l. Eth. 128 C2
Findhorn r. U.K. 46 I6
Findık Turkey 107 E3
  also known as Parona
Findlay U.S.A. 176 B4
Fine U.S.A. 177 J1
Finger Lake Canada 167 M4
Finger Lakes U.S.A. 177 I3
Fingeshwar India 94 D1
Fingoè Moz. 131 F2
Finiels, Sommet de mt. France 51 J8
Finike Turkey 106 B3
Finike Körfezi b. Turkey 106 C3
Finisterre Spain see Fisterra
Finisterre, Cabo c. Spain 54 B2
  also known as Finisterre, Cabo or Fisterra, Cabo
Finke Australia 148 B5
Finke watercourse Australia 148 B5
Finke, Mount hill Australia 146 B3
Finke Aboriginal Land res. Australia 148 C5
Finke Bay Australia 148 B2
Finke Flood Flats lowland Australia 148 B5
Finke Gorge National Park Australia 148 B5

▶ Finland country Europe 44 M3
  known as Suomi in Finnish
  europe [countries] ▶▶ 32–35
  europe [environments] ▶▶ 36–37

Finland U.S.A. 172 B3
Finland, Gulf of Europe 42 C3
Finlay r. Canada 166 E3
Finlay, Mount Canada 166 E3
Finlay Forks Canada 166 F4
Finlayson U.S.A. 172 A4
Finlayson Australia 147 E3
Finley U.S.A. 178 C2
Finmark Canada 172 D3
Finn r. Rep. of Ireland 47 E9
Finne ridge Germany 48 I4
Finnigan, Mount Australia 149 E2
Finniss r. Australia 148 C2
Finniss, Cape Australia 146 B3
Finnis Springs Aboriginal Land res.
  Australia 146 C2
Finnmark county Norway 44 N1
Finnmarksvidda reg. Norway 44 M1
Finnsjøen Norway 45 K3
Finnsnes Norway 44 L1
Finschhafen P.N.G. 73 K8
Finspång Sweden 45 K4
Finsteraarhorn mt. Switz. 51 O6
Finsterwalde Germany 49 K4
Finström Fin. 42 A1
Fintona U.K. 47 E9
Finucane Range hills Australia 149 D4
Fiora r. Italy 56 D6
Fiordland National Park N.Z. 153 B13
Fiorenzuola d'Arda Italy 56 B4
Fir reg. Saudi Arabia 105 D1
Firat r. Turkey 107 E3 see Euphrates
Firavahana Madag. 131 [inset] J4
Firebaugh U.S.A. 182 D5
Firedrake Lake Canada 167 J2
Firenze Italy see Florence
Fire River Canada 173 J2
Fireside Canada 166 E3
Firesteel Creek r. U.S.A. 178 C3
Firiña Venez. 199 E3
Firk, Sha'ib watercourse Iraq 107 F5
Firkachi well Niger 125 I3
Firmat Arg. 204 E4
Firminy France 51 K7
Firmum Italy see Fermo
Firmum Picenum Italy see Fermo
Firovo Rus. Fed. 43 O3
Firozabad India 96 C4
Firozkoh reg. Afgh. 101 F3
Firozpur Haryana India 96 C3
Firozpur Punjab India 96 B3
  formerly spelt Ferozepore
First Cataract rapids Egypt see 1st Cataract
First Three Mile Opening sea chan.
  Australia 149 E2
Firuzabad Iran see Rāsk
Firūzābād Iran 100 C4
Firūzeh Iran 100 D2
Firūzkūh Iran 100 C3
Fischersbrunn Namibia 130 B5
Fish watercourse Namibia 130 C5
Fish r. S. Africa 132 F7
Fisher Bay Antarctica 223 J2
Fisher Glacier Antarctica 223 F1
Fisher River Canada 167 L5
Fisher Strait Canada 165 K3
Fishersville U.S.A. 176 G7
Fishguard U.K. 47 H11
  also known as Abergwaun
Fishing Creek U.S.A. 177 I7
Fishing Lake Canada 167 M4
Fish Lake MN U.S.A. 172 A4
Fish Lake UT U.S.A. 183 M3
Fish Point U.S.A. 173 J7
Fisk, Cape Antarctica 222 T1
Fiskebøl Norway 44 K1
Fiskenæsset Greenland see Qeqertarsuatsiaat
Fismes France 51 J3
Fisterra Spain 54 B2
  also spelt Finisterre
Fisterra, Cabo c. Spain see Finisterre, Cape
Fitampito Madag. 131 [inset] J4
Fitchburg MA U.S.A. 177 N3
Fitchburg WI U.S.A. 172 C8
Fitful Head U.S.A. 176 C14
Fitiaui Greece see Fyteies
Fitjar Norway 45 I4
Fitri, Lac l. Chad 120 C6
Fitzcarrald Peru 200 C3
Fitzgerald Canada 167 I3
Fitzgerald River National Park Australia 151 B7
Fitz Hugh Sound sea chan. Canada 166 D5
Fitzmaurice r. Australia 148 A2
Fitz Roy Arg. 205 D7
Fitz Roy, Cerro mt. Arg. 205 B8
Fitzroy r. Qld Australia 149 F4
Fitzroy r. W.A. Australia 150 C3
Fitzroy Aboriginal Land res. Australia 148 A2
Fitzroy Crossing Australia 150 D3
Fitzwilliam Island Canada 168 D4
Fiume Croatia see Rijeka
Fiumefreddo di Sicilia Sicilia Italy 57 H11
Five Fingers Peninsula N.Z. 153 A13
Five Forks U.S.A. 153 E13
Five Points U.S.A. 182 D5
Fivizzano Italy 56 C4
Fizi Dem. Rep. Congo 126 F5
Fizuli Azer. see Füzuli
Fjällbacka Sweden 44 L2
Fjellerup Denmark 44 L1
Fjerritslev Denmark 45 J4
Fkih Ben Salah Morocco 122 D2
Flå Norway 45 J3
Flaga Iceland 44 [inset] C3

Flagstaff S. Africa 133 N8
also known as Siphaqeni
Flagstaff U.S.A. 183 M6
Flagstaff Lake U.S.A. 174 G2
Flaherty Island Canada 168 E1
Flakaberg Sweden 44 M2
Flåm Norway 45 I3
Flambeau r. U.S.A. 172 B5
Flamborough Head U.K. 47 L9
Flamenco, Isla i. Arg. 204 E6
Fläming hills Germany 49 J3
Flaming Gorge Reservoir U.S.A. 180 E4
Flaminksvlei salt pan S. Africa 132 F7
Flanagan r. Canada 167 M4
Flandreau U.S.A. 178 C2
Flannagan Lake U.S.A. 176 C8
Flannan Isles U.K. 46 E5
Flåsjön l. Sweden 44 K2
Flat r. Canada 166 E2
Flat r. U.S.A. 172 H8
Flateyjardalsheiði reg. Iceland 44 [inset] C2
Flathead r. U.S.A. 180 D2
Flathead, Middle Fork r. U.S.A. 167 H5
Flathead Indian Reservation res. U.S.A. 180 D3
Flathead Lake U.S.A. 180 D3
Flatiron mt. U.S.A. 180 D3
Flat Island Mauritius 72 E4
Flat Lick U.S.A. 176 B9
Flat Point N.Z. 152 J9
Flattery, Cape Australia 149 E2
Flattery, Cape U.S.A. 180 A2
Flat Top mt. Canada 166 B2
Flatwillow Creek r. U.S.A. 180 F3
Flatwoods KY U.S.A. 176 C7
Flatwoods WV U.S.A. 176 E7
Flechtinger Höhenzug park Germany 48 I3
Fleetwood U.K. 47 I10
Fleetwood U.S.A. 177 J5
Flekkefjord Norway 45 I4
Flemingsburg U.S.A. 176 B7
Flemington U.S.A. 177 K5
Flen Sweden 45 L4
Flensborg Fjord inlet Denmark/Germany 45 J5
also known as Flensburger Förde
Flensburg Germany 48 G1
Flensburger Förde inlet Denmark/Germany
see Flensborg Fjord
Flers France 50 F4
Flesherton Canada 173 M6
Flesko, Tanjung pt Indon. 75 C2
Fletcher Lake Canada 167 I2
Fletcher Peninsula Antarctica 222 S2
Fletcher Pond l. U.S.A. 173 J6
Fleurance France 50 G9
Fleur de Lys Canada 169 J3
Fleur-de-May, Lac l. Canada 169 H3
Fleury-les-Aubrais France 51 H5
Flinders r. Australia 149 D3
Flinders Bay Australia 151 A7
Flinders Chase National Park Australia 146 C3
Flinders Group is Australia 149 E2
Flinders Group National Park Australia 149 E2
Flinders Island S.A. Australia 146 B3
Flinders Island Tas. Australia 147 F4
Flinders Passage Australia 149 F3
Flinders Ranges mts Australia 146 C3
Flinders Ranges National Park Australia 146 C2
Flinders Reefs Australia 149 F3
Flin Flon Canada 167 K4
Flint U.K. 47 I10
also known as Y Fflint
Flint U.S.A. 173 J7
Flint r. GA U.S.A. 175 C6
Flint r. MI U.S.A. 173 J7
Flint Island Kiribati 221 H6
Flintstone U.S.A. 176 G6
Flisa Norway 45 K3
Flisa r. Norway 45 K3

▶Flissingskiy, Mys c. Rus. Fed. 38 G2
Most easterly point of Europe.

Flix Spain 55 L3
Flöha Germany 49 K5
Flood Range mts Antarctica 222 P1
Flora r. Australia 148 A2
Flora U.S.A. 172 G10
Florac France 51 J8
Flora U.S.A. 175 C6
Flora Reef Australia 149 E3
Floraville Australia 148 C3
Flor de Punga Peru 198 C6
Florence Italy 56 D5
also known as Firenze; historically known as Florentia
Florence AL U.S.A. 174 C5
Florence AZ U.S.A. 183 M8
Florence CO U.S.A. 181 F5
Florence KY U.S.A. 176 A7
Florence OR U.S.A. 180 A4
Florence SC U.S.A. 175 E5
Florence Junction U.S.A. 183 M8
Florencia Arg. 204 F3
Florencia Col. 198 C4
Florentia Italy see Florence
Florentino Ameghino Arg. 205 D6
Florentino Ameghino, Embalse resr Arg. 205 D6
Flores Brazil 202 D3
Flores Guat. 185 H5
Flores i. Indon. 75 B5
Florescência Brazil 200 C2
Flores de Goiás Brazil 202 C5
Flores Island Canada 166 E5
Flores Sea Indon. 75 A4
Floresta Brazil 202 E4
Floresville U.S.A. 179 C6
Floriano Brazil 202 D3
Floriano Peixoto Brazil 200 D2
Florianópolis Brazil 203 B8
Florida Bol. 201 E4
Florida Chile 204 B5
Florida Cuba 186 D2
Florida Uruguay 204 F4
Florida state U.S.A. 175 D6
Florida, Straits of Bahamas/U.S.A. 186 C2
Florida Bay U.S.A. 175 D7
Florida Keys is U.S.A. 175 D7
Florida Negra Arg. 205 D8
Flórida Paulista Brazil 206 B8
Floridia Sicilia Italy 57 H11
Florii, Vârful hill Romania 58 E1
Florin U.S.A. 182 C3
Florina Greece 58 C8
Florínia Brazil 206 C9
Floriskraaldam l. S. Africa 132 F10
Florissant U.S.A. 174 B4
Florø Norway 45 I3
Flour Lake Canada 169 H2
Floyd U.S.A. 176 E9
Floyd, Mount U.S.A. 183 L6
Floydada U.S.A. 179 B5
Fluchthorn mt. Austria/Switz. 51 Q6
Fluk Indon. 75 C3
Flums Switz. 51 P5
Flushing Neth. see Vlissingen
Flushing OH U.S.A. 176 D5
Fluvià r. Spain 55 O2
Fly r. P.N.G. 73 J8
Flying Fish, Cape Antarctica 222 R2
Flying Fox Creek r. Australia 148 B2
Foam Lake Canada 167 K5
Foča Bos.-Herz. 56 K5
also known as Srbinje
Foça Turkey 106 A3
Focşani Romania 58 I3
Focuri Romania 58 I1
Fodé Cent. Afr. Rep. 126 D3
Foelsche r. Australia 148 C2
Fogang China 87 E4
also known as Shijiao
Fog Bay Australia 148 A2
Fogelsville U.S.A. 177 J5
Foggåret el Arab Alg. 123 F4
Foggia Italy 56 H7
Fogi Indon. 75 C3
Foglia r. Italy 56 E5
Föglö Fin. 45 M3
Fogo i. Cape Verde 124 [inset]
Fogo Island Canada 169 K3
Fogoleva Kazakh. 103 G4
Föhr i. Germany 48 F1
Foinaven hill U.K. 46 H5
Foix France 50 H10
Fokino Rus. Fed. 43 P8
formerly known as Tsementnyy
Fokku Nigeria 125 G4
Folarskarnuten mt. Norway 45 I3
Folda sea chan. Norway 44 K2
Foldereid Norway 44 K2
Foldfjorden sea chan. Norway 44 J2
Folegandros Greece 59 F12
Folegandros i. Greece 59 F12
Foley Botswana 131 E4
Foley AL U.S.A. 175 C6
Foley MN U.S.A. 174 A2
Foleyet Canada 168 D3
Foley Island Canada 165 L3
Folgares Angola see Capelongo
Folger, Cape Antarctica 223 H2
Foligno Italy 56 E6
Folkestone U.K. 47 N12
Folkston U.S.A. 175 D6
Folldal Norway 45 J3
Folletts U.S.A. 172 C9
Föllinge Sweden 44 K3
Follonica Italy 56 C6
Folsom U.S.A. 176 E6
Folsom Lake U.S.A. 182 C3
Fomboni Comoros 129 D8
Fómento Cuba 186 D2
Fomin Rus. Fed. 41 G7
Fominskoye Rus. Fed. 40 G4
Fonda U.S.A. 177 K3
Fond-du-Lac Canada 167 J3
Fond du Lac r. Canada 167 J3
Fond du Lac U.S.A. 172 E7
Fond du Lac Indian Reservation res. U.S.A. 174 A2
Fonde U.S.A. 176 B9
Fondevila Spain 54 C3
Fondi Italy 56 F7
historically known as Fundi
Fon Going ridge Guinea 124 C4
Fonni Sardegna Italy 57 B8
Fonsagrada Spain see A Fonsagrada
Fonseca Col. 198 C2
Fontainebleau France 51 I4
Fontanges Canada 169 G2
Fontas Canada 166 F3
Fontas r. Canada 166 F3
Fonte Boa Brazil 199 E5
Fonte do Pau-d'Agua Brazil 201 F3
Fontenay-le-Comte France 50 F6
Fonteneau, Lac l. Canada 169 I3
Fontur pt Iceland 44 [inset] D2
Fonuafo'ou i. Tonga 145 H4
also known as Falcon Island; also spelt Fonuafu'u
Fonuafu'u i. Tonga see Fonuafo'ou
Fonualei i. Tonga 145 H3
also spelt Fanoualie; formerly known as Amargura Island
Fonyód Hungary 49 O9
Foochow China see Fuzhou
Fool Creek Reservoir U.S.A. 183 L2
Foot's Bay Canada 173 N5
Foping China 87 D1
also known as Yuanjiazhuang
Foraker, Mount U.S.A. 164 D3
Forat Iran 100 C3
Foraulep atoll Micronesia see Faraulep
Forbes Australia 147 F3
Forbesganj India 97 E4
Forbes Reef Swaziland 133 P3
Forchheim Germany 48 I6
Ford r. Canada 169 H1
Ford r. U.S.A. 172 F5
Ford City CA U.S.A. 182 E6
Ford City PA U.S.A. 176 F5
Førde Hordaland Norway 45 I4
Førde Sogn og Fjordane Norway 45 I3
Forde Lake Canada 167 L2
Fordell N.Z. 152 J7
Fordingbridge U.K. 50 E2
Ford Range mts Antarctica 222 O1
Fords Bridge Australia 147 E2
Fordyce U.S.A. 179 D5
Forécariah Guinea 124 B4
Forel, Mont mt. Greenland 165 P3
Foreman U.S.A. 179 D5
Foremost Canada 167 I5
Foresight Mountain Canada 166 E4
Forest Canada 168 D5
Forest MS U.S.A. 175 B5
Forest OH U.S.A. 176 B5
Forest VA U.S.A. 176 F8
Forestburg Canada 167 H4
Forest City U.S.A. 177 J4
Forest Creek r. Australia 149 D3
Foresthill U.S.A. 182 D2
Forest Junction U.S.A. 172 E6
Forest Lake U.S.A. 172 A5
Forest Lakes U.S.A. 183 N7
Forest Park U.S.A. 175 C5
Forest Ranch U.S.A. 182 C2
Forestville Canada 169 G3
Forestville CA U.S.A. 182 B3
Forestville MI U.S.A. 173 K7
Forestville NY U.S.A. 176 F3
Forêt des Deux Balé nat. park Burkina 124 E4
Forêt de Togodo nature res. Togo 125 F5
Forfar U.K. 46 J7
Forges-les-Eaux France 50 H3
Forillon, Parc National de nat. park Canada 169 H3
Forish Uzbek. see Farish
Forked River U.S.A. 177 K6
Forks U.S.A. 180 A3
Forksville U.S.A. 177 I4
Fork Union U.S.A. 176 G8
Forlì Italy 56 E4
Forman U.S.A. 178 C2
Formby U.K. 47 I10
Formentera i. Spain 55 M6
Formentor, Cap de c. Spain 55 O5
Formerie France 50 H3
Former Yugoslav Republic of Macedonia country Europe see Macedonia
Formia Italy 56 F7
Formiga Brazil 203 C7
Formigine Italy 56 C4
Formosa Arg. 204 F2
Formosa prov. Arg. 204 F2
Formosa country Asia see Taiwan
Formosa Brazil 206 F2
Formosa, Serra hills Brazil 201 G3
Formosa do Rio Preto Brazil 202 C4
Formosa Strait China/Taiwan see Taiwan Strait
Formoso Brazil 202 B4
Formoso r. Bahia Brazil 202 C5
Formoso r. Goiás Brazil 206 A5
Formoso r. Tocantins Brazil 202 B4
also known as Javaés
Fornos Moz. 131 G4
Forolshogna mt. Norway 44 J3
Føroyar terr. N. Atlantic Ocean see Faroe Islands
Forres U.K. 46 I6
Forrest Australia 151 E6
Forrest r. Australia 150 E2
Forrest U.S.A. 174 B3
Forrestal Range mts Antarctica 222 U1
Forrest City U.S.A. 174 B5
Forrest Lakes salt flat Australia 151 E6
Forreston U.S.A. 172 D8
Forsand Norway 45 I4
Forsayth Australia 149 D3
Forsbakken Norway 44 L1
Forshaga Sweden 45 K4
Forssa Fin. 45 M3
Forst Germany 49 L4
Forster Australia 147 G3
Forsyth GA U.S.A. 175 D5
Forsyth MO U.S.A. 178 D4
Forsyth MT U.S.A. 180 F3
Forsythe Canada 173 Q2
Forsyth Islands Australia 148 C3
Forsyth Range hills Australia 149 D4
Fort Abbas Pak. 101 H4
Fort Albany Canada 168 D2
Fortaleza Pando Bol. 200 D2
Fortaleza Pando Bol. 200 D3
Fortaleza Brazil 202 E2
formerly known as Ceará
Fortaleza de Santa Teresa Uruguay 204 G4
Fort Apache Indian Reservation res. U.S.A. 183 N8
Fort Archambault Chad see Sarh
Fort Ashby U.S.A. 176 G6
Fort Assiniboine Canada 167 H4
Fort Atkinson U.S.A. 172 E8
Fort Augustus U.K. 46 H6
Fort Babine Canada 166 E4
Fort Beaufort S. Africa 133 K9
Fort Belknap Indian Reservation res. U.S.A. 180 E2
Fort Benton U.S.A. 180 E3
Fort Berthold Indian Reservation res. U.S.A. 178 B2
Fort Black Canada 167 J4
Fort Brabant Canada see Tuktoyaktuk
Fort Bragg U.S.A. 182 A2
Fort Carillon U.S.A. see Ticonderoga
Fort Carnot Madag. see Ikongo
Fort Charlet Alg. see Djanet
Fort Chimo Canada see Kuujjuaq
Fort Chipewyan Canada 167 I3
Fort Collins U.S.A. 180 F4
Fort Constantine Australia 149 D4
Fort-Coulonge Canada 168 E4
Fort Covington U.S.A. 177 K1
Fort Crampel Cent. Afr. Rep. see Kaga Bandoro
Fort-Dauphin Madag. see Tôlañaro
Fort Davis U.S.A. 179 B6

▶Fort-de-France Martinique 187 H4
Capital of Martinique.

Fort de Kock Indon. see Bukittinggi
Fort de Polignac Alg. see Illizi
Fort Deposit U.S.A. 175 C5
Fort Dodge U.S.A. 178 D3
Fort Donald S. Africa 133 N7
Fort Duchesne U.S.A. 183 O1
Forte, Monte hill Sardegna Italy 57 A8
Fort Edward U.S.A. 177 L2
Forte Nordeste Angola 127 D6
Fort Erie Canada 173 O8
Fortescue r. Australia 150 B4
Forte Veneza Brazil 199 H6
Fortezza, Monte della hill Italy 56 C6
Fort Flatters Alg. see Bordj Omer Driss
Fort Foureau Cameroon see Kousséri
Fort Franklin Canada see Déline
Fort Gaines U.S.A. 175 C6
Fort Gardel Alg. see Zaouatallaz
Fort Garland U.S.A. 181 F5
Fort Gay U.S.A. 176 C7
Fort Gibson Lake U.S.A. 179 D5
Fort Good Hope Canada 166 D1
Fort Gouraud Mauritania see Fdérik
Forth r. U.K. 46 I7
Forth, Firth of est. U.K. 46 I7
Fort Hall Kenya see Muranga
Fort Hall Indian Reservation res. U.S.A. 180 D4
Fort Hertz Myanmar see Putao
Fortification Range mts U.S.A. 183 J3
Fortín Aroma Para. 201 E5
Fortín Ávalos Sánchez Para. 201 E5
Fortín Boquerón Para. 201 F5
Fortín Capitán Demattei Para. 201 E5
Fortín Carlos Antonio López Para. 201 F5
Fortín Coronel Bogado Para. 201 E5
Fortín Coronel Eugenio Garay Para. 201 E5
Fortín Galpón Para. 201 F4
Fortín General Caballero Para. 201 F6
Fortín General Díaz Para. 201 E5
Fortín General Mendoza Para. 201 E5
Fortín Hernandarias Para. 201 E5
Fortín Infante Rivarola Para. 201 E5
Fortín Juan de Zalazar Para. 201 F5
Fortín Lagerenza Para. 201 E5
Fortín Lavalle Arg. 204 E2
Fortín Leonardo Britos Para. 201 E5
Fortín Leonida Escobar Para. 201 E5
Fortín Linares Para. 201 E5
Fortín Madrejón Para. 201 F5
Fortín May Alberto Gardel Para. 201 E5
Fortín Nueva Asunción Para. 201 E5
Fortín Pilcomayo Arg. 201 E5
Fortín Presidente Ayala Para. 201 F5
Fortín Ravelo Bol. 201 E4
Fortín Suárez Arana Bol. 201 E4
Fortín Teniente Juan Echauri López Para. 201 E5
Fortín Teniente Mountania Para. 201 F5
Fortín Teniente Primero hill Mendoza Para. 201 F4
Fortín Teniente Rojas Silva Para. 201 E6
Fort Jameson Zambia see Chipata
Fort Johnston Malawi see Mangochi
Fort Kent U.S.A. 174 G2
Fort Laperrine Alg. see Tamanrasset
Fort Lauderdale U.S.A. 175 D7
also known as Port Everglades
Fort Liard Canada 166 F2
Fort Liberté Haiti 187 F3
Fort Loudon U.S.A. 176 H6
Fort Mackay Canada 167 I3
Fort Macleod Canada 167 H5
formerly known as MacLeod
Fort Madison U.S.A. 174 B3
Fort Manning Malawi see Mchinji
Fort McCoy U.S.A. 172 C6
Fort McMurray Canada 167 I3
Fort McPherson Canada 164 F3
Fort Morgan U.S.A. 178 B3
Fort Mtombeni S. Africa 133 O6
Fort Myers U.S.A. 175 D7
Fort Nelson Canada 166 F3
Fort Nelson r. Canada 166 F3
Fort Norman Canada see Tulit'a
Fort Orange U.S.A. see Albany
Fortore r. Italy 56 H7
Fort Payne U.S.A. 174 C5
Fort Peck Indian Reservation res. U.S.A. 180 F2
Fort Peck Reservoir U.S.A. 180 F3
Fort Pierce U.S.A. 175 D7
Fort Pierre U.S.A. 178 B2
Fort Portal Uganda 128 A4
Fort Providence Canada 167 G2
Fort Qu'Appelle Canada 167 K5
Fort Randall U.S.A. see Cold Bay
Fort Recovery U.S.A. 176 A5
Fort Resolution Canada 167 H2
Fortrose N.Z. 153 C14
Fortrose U.K. 46 H6
Fort Rosebery Zambia see Mansa
Fort Rousset Congo see Owando
Fort Rupert Canada see Waskaganish
Fort St James Canada 166 E4
Fort St John Canada 166 F3
Fort Sandeman Pak. see Zhob
Fort Saskatchewan Canada 167 H4
Fort Scott U.S.A. 178 D4
Fort Severn Canada 168 C1
Fort-Shevchenko Kazakh. 102 B3
Fort Simpson Canada 166 F2
Fort Smith Canada 167 H2
Fort Smith U.S.A. 179 D5
Fort Stockton U.S.A. 179 B6
Fort Sumner U.S.A. 181 F6
Fort Totten (Devils Lake Sioux) Indian Reservation res. U.S.A. 178 C2
Fort Trinquet Mauritania see Bîr Mogreïn
Fortuna U.S.A. 180 A4
Fortune Bay Canada 169 K4
Fort Valley U.S.A. 175 D5
Fort Vermilion Canada 167 G3
Fort Victoria Zimbabwe see Masvingo
Fort Walton U.S.A. see Fort Walton Beach
Fort Walton Beach U.S.A. 175 C6
formerly known as Fort Walton
Fort Ware Canada see Ware
Fort Wayne U.S.A. 174 C3
Fort Wellington Guyana 199 G3
Fort White Myanmar 78 A3
Fort William U.K. 46 G7
Fort Worth U.S.A. 179 C5
Fort Yates U.S.A. 178 B2
Fortymile r. Canada/U.S.A. 166 A1
Forty Mile Scrub National Park Australia 149 E3
Forty-Second Hill S. Africa see 42nd Hill
Fort Yukon U.S.A. 164 E3
Forum Iulii France see Fréjus
Forūr, Jazīreh-ye i. Iran 100 C5
Forvik Norway 44 K2
Fos, Golfe de b. France 51 K9
Foshan China 87 E4
Fo Shek Chau i. Hong Kong China see Basalt Island
Foskvallen Sweden 45 K3
Fosna pen. Norway 44 J3
Foso Ghana 125 E5
Foss Iceland 44 [inset] C3
Fossano Italy 51 N8
Fosshóll Iceland 44 [inset] C2
Fossil U.S.A. 180 B3
Fossil Downs Australia 150 D3
Fossombrone Italy 56 E5
Fos-sur-Mer France 51 K9
Foster Australia 147 E4
Foster U.S.A. 176 A7
Foster, Mount Canada/U.S.A. 166 C3
Foster Bugt b. Greenland 165 Q2
Foster Lakes Canada 167 J3
Fostoria U.S.A. 176 B4
Fotadrevo Madag. 131 [inset] J5
Fotuna i. Vanuatu see Futuna
Fouesnant France 50 B5
Fougamou Gabon 126 A5
Fougères France 50 E4
Foula i. U.K. 46 J3
Foulamôri Guinea 124 B3
Foul Bay Egypt 121 G4
Foulenzem Gabon 126 A5
Foulness Point U.K. 47 M12
Foul Point Sri Lanka 94 D4
Foulpointe Madag. see Mahavelona
Foulwind, Cape N.Z. 153 F9
Foumban Cameroon 125 H5
Foumbot Cameroon 125 H5
Foum Zguid Morocco 122 D3
Foundation Ice Stream glacier Antarctica 222 T1
Founougo Benin 125 F4
Fount U.S.A. 176 B9
Fountain Green U.S.A. 183 M2
Fountains Abbey tourist site U.K. 47 K9
Four, Pointe de pt France 50 C6
Fourchambault France 51 J5
Fourches, Mont des hill France 51 L4
Four Corners U.S.A. 182 G7
Fouriesburg S. Africa 133 M5
Fournier, Lac l. Canada 169 H3
Fournoi Greece 59 H11
Fournoi i. Greece 59 H11
Fourteen Mile Point U.S.A. 172 D4
Fourth Cataract rapids Sudan see 4th Cataract
Fouta Djallon reg. Guinea 124 B4
Foveaux Strait N.Z. 153 B14
Fowl Cay i. Bahamas 175 E7
Fowler CA U.S.A. 182 E5
Fowler CO U.S.A. 181 F5
Fowler IN U.S.A. 174 C3
Fowler MI U.S.A. 173 I7
Fowler Ice Rise Antarctica 222 S1
Fowlers Bay Australia 146 B2
Fowlers Bay b. Australia 146 B3
Fowlerville U.S.A. 173 I8
Fox r. B.C. Canada 166 E3
Fox r. Man. Canada 167 M3
Fox r. IL U.S.A. 174 B3
Fox r. WI U.S.A. 172 D7
Foxas Spain 54 C1
Fox Creek Canada 167 G4
Foxe Basin g. Canada 165 L3
Foxe Channel Canada 165 K3
Foxen l. Sweden 45 J4
Foxe Peninsula Canada 165 L3
Fox Glacier N.Z. 153 E11
Fox Islands U.S.A. 164 C4
Fox Lake Canada 167 H3
Fox Mountain Canada 166 C2
Foxton N.Z. 152 J8
Foxton Beach N.Z. 152 J8
Fox Valley Canada 167 I5
Foyle r. Rep. of Ireland/U.K. 47 E9
Foyle, Lough b. Rep. of Ireland/U.K. 47 E8
Foz Spain 54 D1
Foz de Areia, Represa de resr Brazil 203 B8
Foz de Gregório Brazil 198 D6
Foz de Copeá Brazil 199 F5
Foz do Cunene Angola 127 A9
Foz do Iguaçu Brazil 203 A8
Foz do Jamari Brazil 201 E2
Foz do Jutaí Brazil 199 E5
Foz do Mamoriá Brazil 199 E5
Foz do Riosinho Brazil 200 C1
Frackville U.S.A. 177 I5
Fraga Arg. 204 D4
Fraga Spain 55 L3
Fraile Muerto Uruguay 204 G4
Frakes, Mount Antarctica 222 Q1
Framingham U.S.A. 177 N3
Framnes Mountains Antarctica 223 E2
Fram Peak Antarctica 223 D2
Franca Brazil 206 F7
Français, Récif des reef New Caledonia 145 F3
Francavilla al Mare Italy 56 G6
Francavilla Fontana Italy 57 J8

▶France country Europe 50 F5
3rd largest and 4th most populous country in Europe. Historically known as Gallia or Gaul.
europe [countries] ▶▶ 32–35

France, Île de i. Greenland 165 R2
Frances Australia 146 D4
Frances r. Canada 166 D2
Francés, Punta pt Cuba 186 C2
Frances Lake Canada 166 D2
Frances Lake l. Canada 166 D2
Francesville U.S.A. 172 G10
Franceville Gabon 126 B5
also known as Masuku
Franche-Comté admin. reg. France 51 M5
Francis Canada 167 K5
Francis atoll Kiribati see Beru
Francisco de Orellana Ecuador see Puerto Francisco de Orellana
Francisco de Orellana Peru 198 C5
Francisco I. Madero Coahuila Mex. 185 E3
Francisco I. Madero Durango Mex. 184 D3
Francisco Meeks Arg. 204 F5
Francisco Sá Brazil 202 D6
Francisco Zarco Mex. 184 A1
Francistown Botswana 131 E4
Franco da Rocha Brazil 206 G10
Francofonte Sicilia Italy 57 G11
François Lake Canada 166 E4
Francois Peron National Park Australia 151 A5
Francs Peak U.S.A. 180 E4
Frankenberg (Eder) Germany 48 F4
Frankenhöhe park Germany 48 H6
Frankenmuth U.S.A. 173 J7
Frankenthal (Pfalz) Germany 48 F6
Frankenwald mts Germany 48 I5
Frankenwald park Germany 48 I5
Frankford Canada 173 P6
Frankfort S. Africa 133 M4
Frankfort IN U.S.A. 174 C3

▶Frankfort KY U.S.A. 176 A7
State capital of Kentucky.

Frankfort MI U.S.A. 172 G6
Frankfort OH U.S.A. 176 B6
Frankfurt am Main Germany 48 F5
Frankfurt an der Oder Germany 49 L3
Frank Hann National Park Australia 151 C7
Franklin Lake U.S.A. 183 I1
Fränkische Alb hills Germany 48 H7
Fränkische Schweiz reg. Germany 48 I6
Fränkische Schweiz Veldensteiner Forst park Germany 48 I5
Frankland r. Australia 151 B7
Frankland, Cape Australia 147 E4
Franklin S. Africa 133 N7
Franklin AZ U.S.A. 183 O9
Franklin IN U.S.A. 174 C4
Franklin KY U.S.A. 174 C4
Franklin LA U.S.A. 175 B6
Franklin MA U.S.A. 177 N3
Franklin ME U.S.A. 177 Q1
Franklin NC U.S.A. 174 D5
Franklin NE U.S.A. 178 C3
Franklin NH U.S.A. 177 N2
Franklin NJ U.S.A. 177 K4
Franklin OH U.S.A. 176 A6
Franklin PA U.S.A. 176 F4
Franklin TN U.S.A. 174 C5
Franklin TX U.S.A. 179 C6
Franklin VA U.S.A. 177 I9
Franklin WI U.S.A. 172 E8
Franklin WV U.S.A. 176 F7
Franklin Bay Canada 164 G3
Franklin D. Roosevelt Lake U.S.A. 180 C2
Franklin Furnace U.S.A. 176 C7
Franklin-Gordon National Park Australia 147 E5
Franklin Grove U.S.A. 172 D9
Franklin Island Antarctica 223 L1
Franklin Lake Canada 167 M1
Franklin Mountains Canada 166 F2
Franklin Mountains N.Z. 153 B12
Franklin Sound sea chan. Australia 147 E5
Franklin Strait Canada 165 J2
Franklinton LA U.S.A. 175 B6
Franklinton NC U.S.A. 176 G9
Franklinville U.S.A. 176 G3
Frankrike Sweden 44 K3
Frankston Australia 147 E4
Fransenhof S. Africa 132 G6
Fransfontein Namibia 130 B4
Franske Øer is Greenland 165 R2
Fränsta Sweden 44 L3
Frantsa-Iosifa, Zemlya is Rus. Fed. 38 F2
English form Franz Josef Land
Franz Canada 168 C3
Franz Josef Glacier N.Z. 153 E11
Franz Josef Land is Rus. Fed. see Frantsa-Iosifa, Zemlya
Frasca, Capo della c. Sardegna Italy 57 A9
Frascati Italy 56 E7
Fraser r. Australia 150 C3
Fraser r. B.C. Canada 166 F5
Fraser r. Nfld. Canada 169 I1
Fraser, Mount hill Australia 151 B5
Fraserburg S. Africa 132 F8
Fraserburgh U.K. 46 J6
Fraserdale Canada 168 D3
Fraser Island Australia 149 G5
also known as Great Sandy Island
Fraser Island National Park Australia 149 G5
Fraser Lake Canada 166 E4
Fraser National Park Australia 147 E4
Fraser Plateau Canada 166 E4
Fraser Range Australia 151 C7
Fraser Range hills Australia 151 C7
Frasertown N.Z. 152 L6
Frater Canada 173 I3
Frătești Romania 58 G5
Frauenfeld Switz. 51 O5
Fray Bentos Uruguay 204 F4
Fray Marcos Uruguay 204 G4
Frazeysburg U.S.A. 176 C5
Frazier Downs Aboriginal Reserve Australia 150 C3
Frazier Park U.S.A. 182 F7
Frecăței Romania 58 J4
Frederic MI U.S.A. 173 I6
Frederic WI U.S.A. 172 A5
Frederica U.S.A. 177 J6
Fredericia Denmark 45 J5
Frederick r. Australia 150 B5
Frederick MD U.S.A. 176 H6
Frederick OK U.S.A. 179 C5
Frederick E. Hyde Fjord inlet Greenland 165 P1
Frederick Hills Australia 148 B2
Frederick Reef Australia 149 G4
Fredericksburg TX U.S.A. 179 C6
Fredericksburg VA U.S.A. 176 H7
Frederick Sound sea chan. U.S.A. 166 C3
Fredericktown MO U.S.A. 174 B4
Fredericktown OH U.S.A. 176 C5

▶Fredericton Canada 169 H4
Provincial capital of New Brunswick.

Fredericton airport Canada 174 H2
Frederikshåb Greenland see Paamiut
Frederikshavn Denmark 45 J4
Frederikssund Denmark 45 K5
Frederiksted Virgin Is (U.S.A.) 187 G3
Frederiksværk Denmark 45 K5
Fredonia AZ U.S.A. 183 L5
Fredonia KS U.S.A. 178 D4
Fredonia NY U.S.A. 176 F3
Fredonia PA U.S.A. 176 E4
Fredonia WI U.S.A. 172 F7
Fredrika Sweden 44 L2
Fredriksberg Sweden 45 K3
Fredrikshamn Fin. see Hamina
Fredrikstad Norway 45 J4
Freedonyer Peak U.S.A. 182 D1
Freehold U.S.A. 177 K5
Freeland U.S.A. 177 J4
Freeling Heights hill Australia 146 C2
Freel Peak U.S.A. 182 E3
Freels, Cape Canada 169 K3
Freeman U.S.A. 178 C3
Freeman, Lake U.S.A. 172 G10
Freeport IL U.S.A. 174 B3
Freeport ME U.S.A. 177 O2
Freeport PA U.S.A. 176 F5
Freeport TX U.S.A. 179 D6
Freeport City Bahamas 186 D1
Freer U.S.A. 179 C7
Freesoil U.S.A. 172 G6
Free State prov. S. Africa 133 K5
formerly known as Orange Free State

▶Freetown Sierra Leone 124 B4
Capital of Sierra Leone.

Freewood Acres U.S.A. 177 K5
Fregenal de la Sierra Spain 54 E6
Fregon Australia 146 B1
Fréhel, Cap c. France 50 D4
Freiberg Germany 49 K5
Freiburg Switz. see Fribourg
Freiburg im Breisgau Germany 48 E7
Frei Gonzaga Brazil 207 L4
Frei Inocêncio Brazil 207 L5
Freising Germany 48 I7
Freistadt Austria 49 L7
Freital Germany 49 K5
Freixo de Espada à Cinta Port. 54 E3
Fréjus France 51 M9
historically known as Forum Iulii
Frekhaug Norway 45 I3
Fremantle Australia 151 A7
Fremont CA U.S.A. 182 C4
Fremont IN U.S.A. 176 A4
Fremont MI U.S.A. 172 H7
Fremont NE U.S.A. 178 C3
Fremont OH U.S.A. 176 B4
Fremont WI U.S.A. 172 E6
Fremont r. U.S.A. 183 N3
Fremont Junction U.S.A. 183 M3
Frenchburg U.S.A. 176 B8
French Congo country Africa see Congo
French Creek r. U.S.A. 176 F4

▶French Guiana terr. S. America 199 H4
French Overseas Department. Known as Guyane Française in French.
southamerica [countries] ▶▶ 192–193

French Guinea country Africa see Guinea
French Island Australia 147 E4
Frenchman r. U.S.A. 180 F2
Frenchman Bay U.S.A. 177 Q1
Frenchman Creek r. U.S.A. 178 B3
Frenchman Lake CA U.S.A. 182 D2
Frenchman Lake NV U.S.A. 183 I5
French Pass N.Z. 152 H8

▶French Polynesia terr. S. Pacific Ocean 221 I7
French Overseas Territory. Known as Polynésie Française in French.
world [land images] ▶▶ 12–13
oceania [countries] ▶▶ 138–139
oceania [issues] ▶▶ 140–141

French Somaliland country Africa see Djibouti

▶French Southern and Antarctic Lands terr. Indian Ocean 218 L8
French Overseas Territory. Known as Terres Australes et Antarctiques Françaises in French.
asia [countries] ▶▶ 64–67

French Sudan country Africa see Mali
French Territory of the Afars and Issas country Africa see Djibouti
Frenchtown U.S.A. 177 J5
Frenda Alg. 123 F2
Frenštát pod Radhoštěm Czech Rep. 49 P6
Frere S. Africa 133 N5
Fresco r. Brazil 199 I6
Fresco Côte d'Ivoire 124 D5
Freshfield, Cape Antarctica 223 K2
Fresnillo Mex. 185 E4
Fresno U.S.A. 182 E5
Fresno r. U.S.A. 182 D5
Fressel, Lac l. Canada 169 F2
Fresvikbreen glacier Norway 45 I3
Freu, Cap des c. Spain 55 O5
Freudenstadt Germany 48 F7
Frew watercourse Australia 148 B4
Frewsburg U.S.A. 176 F3
Freycinet Estuary inlet Australia 151 A5
Freycinet Peninsula Australia 147 F5
Freyming-Merlebach France 51 M3
Freyre Arg. 204 E3
Freyung Germany 49 K7
Fria Guinea 124 B4
Fria, Cape Namibia 130 B3
Friant U.S.A. 182 E5
Friant-Kern Canal U.S.A. 182 E6
Frias Arg. 204 D3
Fribourg Switz. 51 N6
also known as Freiburg
Frick Switz. 51 O5
Friday Harbor U.S.A. 180 B2
Fridtjof Nansen, Mount Antarctica 223 M1
Friedberg Germany 48 H7
Friedens U.S.A. 176 G5
Friedland Germany 49 K2
Friedland Rus. Fed. see Pravdinsk
Friedrichshafen Germany 48 G8
Friend U.S.A. 178 C3
Friendly Islands country S. Pacific Ocean see Tonga
Friendship U.S.A. 176 G3
Friesach Austria 49 L9

Friesack Germany 49 J3
Friesoythe Germany 48 E2
Friggesund Sweden 45 L3
Frio r. TX U.S.A. 179 C6
Frio watercourse U.S.A. 179 B5
Friol Spain 54 D1
Frisco U.S.A. 180 F5
Frisco Mountain U.S.A. 183 K3
Frissell, Mount hill U.S.A. 177 L3
Friuli - Venezia Giulia admin. reg. Italy 56 F2
Friza, Proliv strait Rus. Fed. 81 P3
Froan nature res. Norway 44 J2
Frobisher Bay Canada see Iqaluit
Frobisher Bay b. Canada 165 M3
Frobisher Lake Canada 167 I3
Frohavet b. Norway 44 J3
Frohburg Germany 49 J4
Frohnleiten Austria 49 M8
Frolovo Rus. Fed. 41 G6
Frombork Poland 49 Q1
Frome watercourse Australia 146 C2
Frome U.K. 47 J12
Frome, Lake salt flat Australia 146 C2
Fromveur, Passage du strait France 50 A4
Fronteira Port. 54 D5
Fronteiras Brazil 202 D3
Frontera Coahuila Mex. 185 E3
Frontera Tabasco Mex. 185 G5
Frontera, Punta pt Mex. 185 G5
Fronteras Mex. 184 C2
Frontignan France 51 J9
Front Royal U.S.A. 176 G7
Frosinone Italy 56 F7
historically known as Frusino
Frosta Norway 44 J3
Frostburg U.S.A. 176 G6
Frost Glacier Antarctica 223 I2
Frøya i. Norway 44 J3
Fruges France 51 I2
Fruita U.S.A. 183 P2
Fruitland IA U.S.A. 172 B9
Fruitland MD U.S.A. 177 J7
Fruitland UT U.S.A. 183 N1
Fruitport U.S.A. 172 G7
Fruitvale U.S.A. 183 P2
Fruktovaya Rus. Fed. 43 U7
Frunze Kyrg. 103 G4
also known as Frunzenskoye
Frunze Kyrg. see Bishkek
Frunzenskoye Kyrg. see Frunze
Frunzivka Ukr. 58 K1
Frusino Italy see Frosinone
Fruska Gora nat. park Yugo. 58 A3
Frutigen Switz. 51 N6
Frutillar Chile 205 B6
Frutuoso Brazil 201 E3
Fryanovo Rus. Fed. 43 T5
Fryazino Rus. Fed. 43 T6
Frýdek-Místek Czech Rep. 49 P6
Fryeburg U.S.A. 177 O1
Fu'an China 87 F3
Fucheng China see Fengyang
Fucheng China see Fuxian
Fuchū Japan 91 C7
Fuchuan China 87 D3
also known as Fuyang
Fuchun Jiang r. China 87 G2
Fudai Japan 90 G4
Fude China 87 F3
Fuding China 87 G3
Fudua waterhole Kenya 128 C5
Fudul reg. Saudi Arabia 105 D3
Fuengirola Spain 54 G8
Fuenlabrada Spain 54 H4
Fuente-Álamo Spain 55 J6
Fuente Álamo Spain 55 J7
Fuente Albilla, Cerro de mt. Spain 55 J6
Fuente de Cantos Spain 54 E6
Fuente Obejuna Spain 54 F6
Fuentesaúco Spain 54 F3
Fuentes de Ebro Spain 55 K3
Fuerte Olimpo Para. 201 F5
Fuerteventura i. Canary Is 122 B3
Fuga i. Phil. 74 B2
Fugloy i. Faroe Is 46 F1
Fuglstad Norway 44 K2
Fugou China 87 E1
Fugu China 85 F4
Fuguo China see Zhanhua
Fuhai China 88 D2
also known as Burultokay
Fuḥaymī Iraq 109 N3
Fujairah U.A.E. 105 G2
also spelt Al Fujayrah or Fujeira
Fujeira U.A.E. see Fujairah
Fuji China see Luxian
Fuji Japan 91 F7
Fujian prov. China 87 F3
English form Fukien
Fu Jiang r. China 86 C2
Fujieda Japan 91 F7
Fuji-Hakone-Izu National Park Japan 91 F7
Fujiidera Japan 91 D7
Fujin China 82 C3
Fujinomiya Japan 91 F7
Fujioka Japan 91 F6
Fuji-san vol. Japan 91 F7
Fujiyoshida Japan 91 F7
Fūka Egypt 106 A5
Fukagawa Japan 90 H3
Fukang China 88 D2
Fukaura Japan 90 F4
Fukaya Japan 91 F6
Fukien prov. China see Fujian
Fukuchiyama Japan 91 D7
Fukue Japan 91 A8
Fukue-jima i. Japan 91 A8
Fukui Japan 91 E6
Fukui pref. Japan 91 E7
Fukuno Japan 91 E6
Fukuoka Japan 91 B8
Fukuoka pref. Japan 91 B8
Fukushima Fukushima Japan 90 G6
Fukushima Hokkaidō Japan 90 G4
Fukushima pref. Japan 90 G6
Fukuyama Japan 91 B9
Fûl, Gebel hill Egypt 108 D8
Fulacunda Guinea-Bissau 124 B4
Fūlād Maialleh Iran 100 C2
also known as Amirabad
Fulayj Oman 105 G3
Fulchhari Bangl. 97 F4
Fulda Germany 48 G5
Fulda r. Germany 48 G4
Fule China 86 C3
Fuli China see Jixian
Fuliji China 87 F1
Fulin China see Hanyuan
Fuling China 87 C2
Fulitun China see Jixian
Fullerton CA U.S.A. 182 G8
Fullerton NE U.S.A. 178 C3
Fullerton, Cape Canada 167 N2
Fulnek Czech Rep. 49 O6
Fulton KY U.S.A. 174 B4
Fulton MO U.S.A. 174 B4
Fulton MS U.S.A. 174 B5
Fulton NY U.S.A. 177 I2
Fulufjället naturreservat nature res. Sweden 45 K3
Fulunäs Sweden 45 K3
Fumay France 51 K3
Fumel France 50 G8
Fumin China 86 B3
also known as Yongding
Funabashi Japan 91 F7
Funafuti atoll Tuvalu 145 G2
formerly known as Ellice Island
Funan China 87 E1
Funan China see Fusui
Funäsdalen Sweden 44 K3
▶Funchal Madeira 122 A2
Capital of Madeira.
Fundación Col. 198 C2
Fundão Brazil 203 D6
Fundão Port. 54 D4
Fundi Italy see Fondi
Fundición Mex. 184 C3
Fundo das Figueiras Cape Verde 124 [inset]
Fundulea Romania 58 H4
Fundy, Bay of g. Canada 169 H4
Fünen i. Denmark see Fyn
Funeral Peak U.S.A. 183 H5
Fünfkirchen Hungary see Pécs
Fung Wong Shan hill Hong Kong China see Lantau Peak
Funhalouro Moz. 131 G4
Funing Jiangsu China 87 F1
Funing Yunnan China 86 C4
also known as Xinhua
Funiu Shan mts China 87 D1
Funnel Creek r. Australia 149 F4
Funsi Ghana 125 E4
Funtua Nigeria 125 G4
Funzie U.K. 46 L3
Fuping China 85 G4
Fuqing China 87 F3
Fuquan China 87 C3
also known as Chengxian
Furancungo Moz. 131 G2
Furano Japan 90 H3
Fürgun, Kūh-e mt. Iran 100 D5
Furmanov Rus. Fed. 40 G4
Furmanovka Kazakh. see Moyynkum
Furmanovo Kazakh. see Zhalpaktal
Furmanovo Rus. Fed. 90 D3
Furnas, Represa resr Brazil 207 G8
Furneaux Group is Australia 147 F5
Furnes Belgium see Veurne
Furong China see Wan'an
Fürstenau Germany 48 E3
Fürstenberg Germany 49 K2
Fürstenfeld Austria 49 N8
Fürstenfeldbruck Germany 48 I7
Fürstenwalde Germany 49 L3
Fürth Germany 48 H6
Furth im Wald Germany 49 J6
Furubira Japan 90 G3
Furudal Sweden 45 K3
Furukawa Japan 90 G5
Fury and Hecla Strait Canada 165 K3
Fusagasugá Col. 198 C3
Fusan S. Korea see Pusan
Fushan Shandong China 85 I4
Fushan Shanxi China 85 F5
Fushë-Krujë Albania 58 A7
Fushun Liaoning China 82 A4
Fushun Sichuan China 86 C2
Fusong China 82 B4
Fusui China 87 C4
also known as Xinning; formerly known as Funan
Futago-san vol. Japan 91 B8
Futaleufú Chile 205 C6
Fu Tau Pun Chau i. Hong Kong China 87 [inset]
Futog Vojvodina, Srbija Yugo. 58 A3
Futtsu Japan 91 F7
Futuna i. Vanuatu 145 G3
also spelt Fotuna; formerly known as Erronan
Futuna, Île i. Wallis and Futuna Is 145 H3
Futuna Islands Wallis and Futuna Is 145 H3
English form Hoorn Islands; also known as Hoorn, Îles de or Horne, Îles de.
Futun Xi r. China 87 F3
Fuwa Egypt 108 B6
Fuwayriṭ Qatar 105 E2
Fuxian China see Wafangdian
Fuxian China 85 F5
also known as Fucheng
Fuxin Liaoning China 85 I3
also known as Fuxinzhen
Fuxin Liaoning China 85 I3
Fuxing China see Wangmo
Fuxinzhen China see Fuxin
Fuya Japan 90 F5
Fuyang Anhui China 87 E1
Fuyang China see Fuchuan
Fuyang Zhejiang China 87 F2
Fuyang r. China 85 H4
Fuying Dao i. China 87 G3
Fuyu Heilong. China 85 J2
Fuyu China see Songyuan
Fuyu Jilin China 82 B3
formerly known as Sanchahe
Fuyuan Heilong. China 82 D2
Fuyuan Yunnan China 86 C3
also known as Zhong'an
Fuyun China 84 A2
also known as Koktokay
Füzesabony Hungary 49 R8
Füzesgyarmat Hungary 49 S8
Fuzhou China 87 F3
formerly spelt Foochow
Fuzhou China see Linchuan
Füzuli Azer. 107 F3
also spelt Fizuli; formerly known as Karyagino
Fwamba Dem. Rep. Congo 127 D6
Fyn county Denmark 45 J5
Fyn i. Denmark 38 B4
also known as Fünen
Fyne, Loch inlet U.K. 46 G8
Fyresvatn l. Norway 45 J4
F.Y.R.O.M. country Europe see Macedonia
Fyteies Greece 59 C10
also known as Fitíai

↓ G

Gaâfour Tunisia 57 B12
Gaalkacyo Somalia 128 E3
Ga'âr, Birket el salt l. Egypt 108 B7
Gaat r. Sarawak Malaysia 77 F2
Gab watercourse Namibia 132 B4
Gabakly Turkm. see Kabakly
Gabangab well Eth. 128 E3
Gabas r. France 50 F9
Gabasumdo China see Tongde
Gabbac, Raas pt Somalia 128 F2
Gabbs Valley Range mts U.S.A. 182 F3
Gabd Pak. 101 E5
Gabela Angola 127 B7
Gaberones Botswana see Gaborone
Gabès Tunisia 123 H2
Gabès, Golfe de g. Tunisia 123 H2
English form Gabès, Gulf of
Gabès, Gulf of Tunisia see Gabès, Golfe de
Gabgaba, Wadi watercourse Sudan 121 G4
Gable End Foreland hd N.Z. 152 M6
▶Gabon country Africa 126 A5
africa [countries] ▶▶ 114–117
Gabon, Estuaire du est. Gabon 126 A4

▶Gaborone Botswana 131 E5
Capital of Botswana. Formerly spelt Gaberones.

Gabou Senegal 124 B3
Gabriel Vera Bol. 200 D4
Gabriel y Galán, Embalse de resr Spain 54 E4
Gābrīk Iran 100 D5
Gābrīk watercourse Iran 100 D5
Gabrovnitsa Bulg. 58 E5
Gabrovo Bulg. 58 G6
Gabú Guinea-Bissau 124 B3
Gabuli vol. Eth. 128 D1
Gacé France 50 G4
Gacko Bos.-Herz. 56 K5
Gädäbäy Azer. 107 F2
Gadabedji, Réserve Totale de Faune de nature res. Niger 125 G3
Gadag India 94 B3
Gadaisu P.N.G. 149 F1
Gäddede Sweden 44 K2
Gadê China 86 A1
also known as Pagqên
Gadebusch Germany 48 I2
Gades Spain see Cádiz
Gadhada India 96 A5
Gadhra India 94 A1
Gadsden U.S.A. 175 C5
Gadwal India 94 C2
Gadyach Ukr. see Hadyach
Gadyn Turkm. 103 E5
Gadzi Cent. Afr. Rep. 126 C3
Gadžin Han Srbija Yugo. 58 D5
Gæi'dnuvuop'pi Norway 44 M1
Gael Hamke Bugt b. Greenland 165 Q2
Găeşti Romania 58 G4
Gaeta Italy 56 F7
Gaeta, Golfo di g. Italy 56 F7
Gafanha da Nazaré Port. 54 C4
Gaferut i. Micronesia 73 K5
Gaffney U.S.A. 174 D5
Gafra, Wâdi el watercourse Egypt 108 C7
Gafsa Tunisia 123 H2
historically known as Capsa
Gag i. Indon. 75 D3
Gagal Chad 126 B2
Gagaon India 96 B5
Gagarin Rus. Fed. 43 Q6
formerly known as Gzhatsk
Gagarin Uzbek. 103 G4
also known as Yerzhar
Gagere watercourse Nigeria 125 G3
Gagliano del Capo Italy 57 K9
Gagnoa Côte d'Ivoire 124 D5
Gagnon Canada 169 G3
Gago Coutinho Angola see Lumbala N'guimbo
Gagra Georgia 107 E2
Gaià r. Spain 55 M3
also spelt Gayá
Gaiab watercourse Namibia 130 C6
Gaibandha Bangl. 97 F4
Găiceana Romania 58 I2
Gaifi, Wâdi el watercourse Egypt 108 F7
Gail r. Austria 49 K9
Gail U.S.A. 179 B5
Gaillac France 50 H9
Gaillimh Rep. of Ireland see Galway
Gaillon France 50 H3
Gaindaingoinkor China see Lhünzhub
Gainesboro U.S.A. 178 F4
Gainesville FL U.S.A. 175 D6
Gainesville GA U.S.A. 174 D5
Gainesville MO U.S.A. 178 D4
Gainesville TX U.S.A. 179 C5
Gainsborough U.K. 47 L10
Gairdner r. Australia 151 B7
Gairdner, Lake salt flat Australia 146 B2
Gairloch U.K. 46 G6
Gairo Tanz. 129 C6
Gaixian China see Gaizhou
Gaizhou China 85 I3
also known as Gaixian
Gaiziņkalns hill Latvia 42 G5
Gaja r. Hungary 49 P8
Gajah Hutan, Bukit hill Malaysia 76 C1
Gajapatinagaram India 95 D2
Gajar r. Nigeria 125 H4
Gajiram Nigeria 125 I3
Gajol India 97 F4
Gajos well Kenya 128 C4
Gakarosa mt. S. Africa 132 H4
Gakem Nigeria 125 H5
Gakuch Jammu and Kashmir 96 B1
Gala China 89 E6
Galaasiya Uzbek. 103 F5
also spelt Galosiyo
Galâla el Baḥarîya, Gebel el plat. Egypt 108 C8
Galán, Cerro mt. Arg. 204 D2
Galana r. Kenya 128 D5
Galand Iran 100 C2
Galang Besar i. Indon. 76 D2
Galangue Angola 127 C8
Galanta Slovakia 49 O7
Galaosiyo Uzbek. see Galaasiya
Galápagos, Islas is Pacific Ocean see Galapagos Islands

▶Galapagos Islands is Pacific Ocean 221 M6
Part of Ecuador. Most westerly point of South America. Also known as Galápagos, Islas or Colón, Archipiélago de.
southamerica [contrasts] ▶▶ 194–195

Galashiels U.K. 46 J8
Galata Bulg. 58 I5
Galatea N.Z. 152 K6
Galați Romania 58 J3
Galatina Italy 57 K8
Galatini Greece 59 C8
Galatista Greece 59 E8
Galatone Italy 57 K8
Galax U.S.A. 176 E9
Galaymor Turkm. see Kala-I-Mor
Galdhøpiggen mt. Norway 45 J3
Galeana Chihuahua Mex. 184 D2
Galeana Nuevo León Mex. 185 E3
Galegu Sudan 121 G6
Galela Indon. 75 C2
Galena AK U.S.A. 164 D3
Galena IL U.S.A. 174 B3
Galena KS U.S.A. 178 D4
Galena MD U.S.A. 177 J6
Galena MO U.S.A. 178 D4
Galena Bay Canada 166 G5
Galera, Punta pt Chile 204 B6
Galera, Punta pt Ecuador 198 A4
Galera, Punta pt Mex. 185 F6
Galera Point Trin. and Tob. 187 H5
Galeras vol. Col. 198 B4
Galesburg IL U.S.A. 174 B3
Galesburg MI U.S.A. 172 H8
Galeshewe S. Africa 133 I5
Galesville U.S.A. 172 B6
Galeton U.S.A. 176 H4
Galga r. Hungary 49 Q8
Galguduud admin. reg. Somalia 128 E3
Gal Hareeri Somalia 128 E3
Gália Brazil 206 D9
Galicea Mare Romania 58 E4
Galich Rus. Fed. 40 G4
Galichskaya Vozvyshennost' hills Rus. Fed. 40 G4
Galicia aut. comm. Spain 54 D2
Galičica nat. park Macedonia 58 B7
Galilee, Sea of l. Israel 108 G5
also known as Tiberias, Lake or Kinneret, Yam
Galiléia Brazil 207 L6
Galissas Greece 59 F11
Galitsa Rus. Fed. 43 S8
Galiwinku Australia 148 B2
Gallabat Sudan 121 H6
Gallarate Italy 56 A3
Gallatin MO U.S.A. 178 D4
Gallatin TN U.S.A. 174 C4
Gallatin r. U.S.A. 180 E3
Galle Sri Lanka 94 D5
Gállego r. Spain 55 K3
Gallegos r. Arg. 205 C8
Gallegos, Cabo c. Chile 205 B7
Gallia country Europe see France

▶Gallinas, Punta pt Col. 198 D1
Most northerly point of South America.

Gallipoli Italy 57 K8
Gallipoli Turkey 106 A2
also spelt Gelibolu; historically known as Callipolis
Gallipolis U.S.A. 176 C7
Gällivare Sweden 44 M2
Gallneukirchen Austria 49 L7
Gallo r. Spain 55 I4
Gällö Sweden 44 K3
Gallo, Capo c. Sicilia Italy 57 F10
Gallup KY U.S.A. 176 C7
Gallup NM U.S.A. 181 E6
Gallur Spain 55 J3
Gallura reg. Sardegna Italy 56 A8
Gallyaaral Uzbek. 103 F4
also spelt Ghallaorol
Galma watercourse Nigeria 125 G4
Galoya Sri Lanka 94 D4
Gal Oya National Park Sri Lanka 94 D5
Gal Shiikh Somalia 128 E2
Galt U.S.A. 182 C3
Gal Tardo Somalia 128 E4
Galtat Zemmour W. Sahara 122 B4
Galtee Mountains hills Rep. of Ireland 47 D11
Galtymore hill Rep. of Ireland 47 D11
Galūgāh, Kūh-e mts Iran 100 C4
Galūgāh-e Āsīyeh Iran 101 D3
Galunggung, Gunung vol. Indon. 77 E4
Galva U.S.A. 172 C9
Galveias Port. 54 D5
Galveston IN U.S.A. 172 G10
Galveston TX U.S.A. 179 D6
Galveston Bay U.S.A. 179 D6
Gálvez Arg. 204 E4
Galwa Nepal 97 D3
Galway Rep. of Ireland 47 C10
also spelt Gaillimh
Galway Bay Rep. of Ireland 47 C10
Gâm r. Vietnam 78 D3
Gamá Brazil 206 E3
Gama, Isla i. Arg. 204 E6
Gamaches France 50 H3
Gamagōri Japan 91 E7
Gamalakhe S. Africa 133 O7
Gamalama vol. Indon. 75 C2
Gamarra Col. 198 C2
Gámas Fin. see Kaamanen
Gamawa Nigeria 125 H3
Gamay Bay Phil. 74 C3
Gamba China 89 E6
also known as Gongbalou
Gamba Gabon 126 A5
Gambēla Eth. 128 B2
Gambēla admin. reg. Eth. 128 B3
Gambēla National Park Eth. 128 B3
Gambell U.S.A. 164 B3
▶Gambia country Africa 124 A3
africa [countries] ▶▶ 114–117
Gambia r. Gambia 124 A3
Gambie r. Senegal 124 B3
Gambier, Îles is Fr. Polynesia 221 J7
English form Gambier Islands; also known as Mangareva Islands
Gambier Islands Australia 146 C3
Gambier Islands Fr. Polynesia see Gambier, Îles
Gambo Canada 169 K3
Gamboma Congo 126 B5
Gamboola Australia 149 D3
Gamboula Cent. Afr. Rep. 126 B3
Gamda China see Zamtang
Gamka r. S. Africa 132 F10
Gamkunoro, Gunung vol. Indon. 75 C2
Gamlakarleby Fin. see Kokkola
Gamleby Sweden 45 L4
Gammams well Sudan 121 G5
Gammelstaden Sweden 44 M2
Gammon Ranges National Park Australia 146 C2
Gamoep S. Africa 132 C6
Gamova, Mys pt Rus. Fed. 82 C4
Gampaha Sri Lanka 94 D5
Gampola Sri Lanka 94 D5
Gams Switz. 51 P5
Gamshadzai Kūh mts Iran 101 E4
Gamtog China 86 A2
Gamtoos r. S. Africa 133 J10
Gamud mt. Eth. 128 C3
Gamvik Norway 44 O1
Gan r. China 85 J1
Gana China see Gengda
Ganado U.S.A. 183 O6
Ganâg Egypt 108 B7
Gananoque Canada 168 E4
Ganāveh Iran 100 B4
Gäncä Azer. 107 F2
also spelt Gandzha; formerly known as Kirovabad; formerly spelt Gyandzha
Gand Belgium see Ghent
Ganda Angola 127 B8
formerly known as Mariano Machado
Gandadiwata, Bukit mt. Indon. 75 A3
Gandai India 96 D5
Gandajika Dem. Rep. Congo 127 D6
Gándara Spain 54 C1
Gandarbal Jammu and Kashmir 96 B2
Gandari Mountain Pak. 101 G4
Gandava Pak. 101 F4
Gander Canada 169 K3
Gander r. Nfld. Canada 169 K3
Ganderkesee Germany 48 F2
Gander Lake Canada 169 K3
Gandesa Spain 55 L3
Gandevi India 94 B1
Gandhidham India 96 A5
Gandhinagar India 96 B5
Gandhi Sagar resr India 96 B4
Gandi, Wadi watercourse Sudan 126 E2
Gandía Spain 55 K6
Gand-i-Zureh plain Afgh. 101 E4
Gandomān Iran 100 B4
Gandu Brazil 202 E5
Gandvik Norway 44 O1
Gandzha Azer. see Gäncä
Ganeb well Mauritania 124 C2
Ganga r. Bangl./India see Ganges
Ganga Nigeria 125 G4
Ganga r. Sri Lanka 94 D5
Gangakher India 94 C2
Gangán Arg. 205 C6
Gangán, Pampa de plain Arg. 205 C6
Ganganagar India 96 B3
Gangapur India 94 B2
Gangapur Maharashtra India 94 B2
Gangapur Rajasthan India 96 B4
Gangapur Rajasthan India 96 C4
Gangara Niger 125 H3
Gangavali r. India 94 B3
Gangaw Myanmar 78 A3
Gangawati India 94 C3
Gangaw Range mts Myanmar 78 B3
Gangca China 84 D4
also known as Shaliuhe
Gangdhar India 96 B5
Gangdisê Shan mts China 89 C6
English form Kailas Range
Ganges r. Bangl./India 96 F5
also known as Ganga or Padma (Bangl.)
Ganges France 51 J9
▶Ganges, Mouths of the Bangl./India 97 F5
asia [landscapes] ▶▶ 62–63
Gangi Sicilia Italy 57 G11
Ganglota Liberia 124 C5
Gangouyi China 84 E5
Gangra Turkey see Çankırı
Gangrar India 96 B4
Gangtok India 97 F4
Gangu China 86 C1
Gangziyao China 85 G4
Ganhezi China 88 E2
Gani Indon. 75 D3
Ganiakali Guinea 124 C4
Ganjam India 95 E2
Gan Jiang r. China 87 F2
Ganjig China 85 I3
also known as Horqin Zuoyi Houqi
Gankovo Rus. Fed. 43 O2
Ganluo China 86 B2
also known as Xinshiba
Gannan China 85 I2
Gannat France 51 J6
Gannett Peak U.S.A. 180 E4
Ganq China 84 B4
Ganquan China 85 F4
Gansbaai S. Africa 132 D11
Gänserndorf Austria 49 N7
Ganshui China 86 C2
Ganskuil S. Africa 133 K1
Gansu prov. China 84 C3
English form Kansu
Gantamaa Somalia 128 D4
Gantapara India 95 D1
Gantheaume Point Australia 150 C3
Gant'iadi Georgia 107 E2
formerly known as Pilenkovo
Ganting China see Huxian
Gantsevichi Belarus see Hantsavichy
Ganxian China 87 E3
also known as Meilin
Ganyal r. India 94 C1
Ganye Nigeria 125 I4
Ganyesa S. Africa 132 I3
Ganyu China 87 F1
also known as Qingkou
Ganyushkino Kazakh. 102 B3
Ganzhe China see Minhou
Ganzhou China 87 E3
Ganzi Sudan 128 A3
Ganzurino Rus. Fed. 85 E1
Gao Mali 125 E2
Gao admin. reg. Mali 125 F2
Gao'an China 87 E2
Gaocheng China 85 G4
Gaocheng China see Litang
Gaochun China 87 F2
also known as Chunxi
Gaocun China see Mayang
Gaohebu China 87 F2
Gaojian China 87 E3
Gaolan China 84 C4
formerly known as Shidongsi
Gaoleshan China see Xianfeng
Gaoliangjian China see Hongze
Gaoligong Shan mts China 86 A3
Gaoling China 87 D1
also known as Luyuan
Gaomi China 85 H4
Gaomutang China 87 D3
Gaoping China 85 G5
Gaoqing China 85 H4
also known as Tianzhen
Gaotai China 84 C4
Gaotang China 85 H4
Gaotangling China see Wangcheng
Gaotingzhen China see Daishan
Gaotouyao China 85 F4
Gaoua Burkina 124 E4
Gaoual Guinea 124 B4
Gaoxian China 86 C2
also known as Wenjiang
Gaoxiong Taiwan see Kaohsiung
Gaoyang China 85 G4
Gaoyi China 85 G4
Gaoyou China 87 F1
Gaoyou Hu l. China 87 F1
Gaozhou China 87 D4
Gap France 51 M8
Gapan Phil. 74 B3
Gapuwiyak Australia 148 B2
Gaqol China 89 C6
Gar China 99 K3
also known as Gargunsa or Shiquanhe
Gar Pak. 101 E5
Gar' r. Rus. Fed. 82 C1
Garaa Tebourt well Tunisia 123 H3
Garabekevyul Turkm. 103 F5
formerly spelt Karabekaul
Garabil Belentligi hills Turkm. see Karabil', Vozvyshennost'
Garabinzam Congo 126 B4
Garabogazköl Aylagy b. Turkm. see Kara-Bogaz-Gol, Zaliv
Garabogazköl Bogazy sea chan. Turkm. see Kara-Bogaz-Gol, Proliv
Garacad Somalia 128 F3
Garachiné Panama 186 D5
Garachiné, Punta pt Panama 186 D5
Garadag Somalia 128 E2
Gara Ekar hill Alg. 123 G6
Garagoa Col. 198 C3
Garagum des. Kazakh. see Karakum Desert
Garagum des. Turkm. see Karakum Desert
Garah Australia 147 F2
Garalo Mali 124 D4
Garamätnyýaz Turkm. see Karamet-Niyaz
Garamba r. Dem. Rep. Congo 126 F4
Garanhuns Brazil 202 E4
Ga-Rankuwa S. Africa 133 L2
Garapu Brazil 202 A5
Garapuava Brazil 206 G3
Garar, Plaine de plain Chad 126 D2
Garawa Aboriginal Land res. Australia 148 C3
Garba Cent. Afr. Rep. 126 D2
Garbahaarey Somalia 128 D4
Garba Tula Kenya 128 C4
Garberville U.S.A. 182 A1
Garbo China see Lhozhag
Garbosh, Kūh-e mt. Iran 100 B3
Gărbova, Vârful hill Romania 58 H3
Garbsen Germany 48 G3
Garça Brazil 206 D9
Garças, Rio das r. Brazil 206 A2
Gârceni Romania 58 I2
Garcias Brazil 206 A7
Garcia Sola, Embalse de resr Spain 54 F5
Gârcina Romania 58 H2
Gard r. France 51 K9
Garda Italy 56 C3
Garda, Lago di l. Italy see Garda, Lake
Garda, Lake Italy 56 C3
also known as Garda, Lago di
Gardabani Georgia 107 F2
Gârda de Sus Romania 58 D2
Garde Lake Canada 167 J2
Gardelegen Germany 48 I3
Garden City U.S.A. 178 B4
Garden Corners U.S.A. 172 G5
Garden Grove U.S.A. 182 G8
Garden Hill Canada 167 M4
Garden Island U.S.A. 172 H5
Garden Mountain U.S.A. 176 D8
Gardermoen airport Norway 45 J3
also known as Oslo
Gardez Afgh. 101 G3
Gardinas Belarus see Hrodna
Gardiner U.S.A. 177 P1
Gardiner, Mount Australia 148 B4
Gardiner Range hills Australia 148 A3
Gardiners Island U.S.A. 177 M4
Gardiner's Range mts Australia 148 B4
Gardner atoll Micronesia see Faraulep
Gardner IL U.S.A. 172 E9
Gardner MA U.S.A. 177 N3
Gardner Inlet Antarctica 222 T1
Gardner Island Kiribati see Nikumaroro
Gardner Pinnacles is U.S.A. 221 G4
formerly known as Man-of-War Rocks or Pollard Islands
Gardnerville U.S.A. 182 E3
Gardno, Jezioro lag. Poland 49 O1
Gárdony Hungary 49 P8
Gardsjönås Sweden 44 L2
Gårdslösa Sweden 45 L4
Gáregasnjárga Fin. see Karigasniemi
Gares Spain see Puente la Reina
Garešnica Croatia 56 I3
Garet El Djenoun mt. Alg. 123 G4
Gare Tigre Fr. Guiana 199 H3
Garfield U.S.A. 181 F5
Garforth U.K. 47 K10
Gargalianoi Greece 59 C11
Gargáligas r. Spain 54 F5
Gargano, Parco Nazionale del nat. park Italy 56 H7
Gargantua, Cape Canada 168 C4
Gargunsa China see Gar
Gargždai Lith. 42 C6
Garhakota India 96 C5
Garhbeta India 97 E5
Garhchiroli India 94 D1
Garhi India 96 B5
Garhi Khairo Pak. 101 F4
Garhi Malehra India 96 C4
Garhmuktesar India 96 C3
Garhshankar India 96 C3
Garibaldi Brazil 203 B9
Garibaldi Canada 166 F5
Garibaldi, Mount Canada 166 F5
Garibaldi Provincial Park Canada 166 F5
Gariep Dam resr S. Africa 133 J7
Gariep Dam Nature Reserve S. Africa 133 J7
Garies S. Africa 132 B7
Garissa Kenya 128 C5
Garkalne Latvia 42 F4
Garkung Caka l. China 89 D5
Garland U.S.A. 179 C5
Garliava Lith. 42 E7
Gârliciu Romania 58 J4
Garlin France 50 F9
Garm Tajik. see Gharm
Garmab Afgh. 101 F3
Garmdasht Iran 100 B4
Garmeh Iran 100 D2
Garmī Iran 100 B2
Garmisch-Partenkirchen Germany 48 I8
Garmo, Qullai mt. Tajik. 101 G2
also known as Kommunizma, Pik or Kommunizm, Qullai
Garmsar Iran 100 C3
Garmsel reg. Afgh. 101 E4
Garner IA U.S.A. 174 A3
Garner KY U.S.A. 176 C8
Garnett U.S.A. 178 D4
Garnpung Lake imp. l. Australia 147 D3
Garo Hills India 97 F4
Garonne r. France 50 F8
Garoowe Somalia 128 F2
Garoth India 96 B4
Garou, Lac l. Mali 124 E2
Garoua Cameroon 125 I4
Garoua Boulai Cameroon 125 I5
Garqêntang China see Sog
Garrett U.S.A. 173 H9
Garrison KY U.S.A. 176 B7
Garrison ND U.S.A. 178 B2
Garrucha Spain 55 J7
Garrygala Turkm. 102 D5
formerly spelt Kara-Kala
Garry Lake Canada 167 K1
Garryowen S. Africa 133 L8
Garsen Kenya 128 D5
Garshy Turkm. see Karshi
Garsila Sudan 120 D6
Gartar China see Qianning
Gartempe r. France 50 G6
Gartog China see Markam
Gartok China see Garyarsa
Garut Indon. 77 D4
Garvie Mountains N.Z. 153 C13
Garwa India 97 D4
Garwolin Poland 49 S4
Gar Xincun China 89 C5
Gary IN U.S.A. 174 C3
Gary WV U.S.A. 176 D8
Garyarsa China 89 C6
also known as Gartok
Garyi China 86 A2
Garyū-zan mt. Japan 91 C7
Garza Arg. 204 E3
Gar Zangbo r. China 89 B5
Garzê China 86 A2
Garzón Col. 198 C4
Gasan-Kuli Turkm. see Esenguly
Gasan-Kuliyskiy Zapovednik nature res. Turkm. 102 C5
Gascogne reg. France see Gascony
Gascogne, Golfe de g. France/Spain see Gascony, Gulf of
Gasconade r. U.S.A. 174 B4
Gascony reg. France 50 F9
also spelt Gascogne
Gascony, Gulf of France/Spain 50 D9
also known as Gascogne, Golfe de or Gascuña, Golfo de
Gascoyne r. Australia 151 A5
Gascoyne, Mount hill Australia 151 B5
Gascoyne Junction Australia 151 A5
Gascuña, Golfo de g. France/Spain see Gascony, Gulf of
Gash and Setit prov. Eritrea 104 B5
Gasherbrum mt. Jammu and Kashmir 96 C2
Gash Setit Wildlife Reserve nature res. Eritrea 121 H6
Gasht Iran 101 E5
Gas Hu salt l. China 88 E4
Gashua Nigeria 125 H3
Gaspar Cuba 186 D2
Gaspar, Selat sea chan. Indon. 77 D3
Gaspé Canada 169 H3
Gaspé, Baie de b. Canada 169 H3
Gaspé, Cap c. Canada 169 H3
Gaspé, Péninsule de pen. Canada 169 H3
Gassan Burkina 124 E3
Gassan vol. Japan 90 G5
Gassane Senegal 124 B3
Gassaway U.S.A. 176 E7
Gassol Nigeria 125 H4
Gass Peak U.S.A. 183 I5
Gasteiz Spain see Vitoria-Gasteiz
Gastello Rus. Fed. 82 F2
Gaston U.S.A. 176 H9
Gaston, Lake U.S.A. 176 H9
Gastonia U.S.A. 174 D5
Gastouni Greece 59 C11
Gastre Arg. 205 C6
Gata, Cabo de c. Spain 55 I8
Gata, Cape Cyprus 108 E3
also known as Gatas, Akra
Gata, Sierra de mts Spain 54 E4
Gataga r. Canada 166 E3
Gătaia Romania 58 C3
Gatas, Akra c. Cyprus see Gata, Cape
Gatchina Rus. Fed. 43 L2
Gateshead U.K. 47 K9
Gates of the Arctic National Park and Preserve U.S.A. 164 D3
Gatesville U.S.A. 179 C6
Gateway U.S.A. 183 P3
Gatico Chile 200 C5
Gatineau Canada 168 F4
Gatineau r. Canada 168 F4
Gatlinburg U.S.A. 179 G5
Gatong China see Jomda
Gatooma Zimbabwe see Kadoma
Gatton Australia 147 G1
Gatún Panama 186 D5
Gatún, Lago l. Panama 186 C5
Gatvand Iran 100 B3
Gatwick airport U.K. 47 L12
Gaúcha do Norte Brazil 202 A5
Gaud-i-Zirreh depr. Afgh. 101 E4
Gauer Lake Canada 167 L3
Gauhati India see Guwahati
Gauja r. Latvia 42 F4
Gaujas nacionālais parks nat. park Latvia 42 G4
Gaul country Europe see France
Gaula r. Norway 44 J3
Gauley Bridge U.S.A. 176 D7
Gaupne Norway 45 I3
Gaurdak Turkm. see Govurdak

Gaurella India 97 D5
Gauribidanur India 94 C3
Gaurnadi Bangl. 97 F5
Gauteng prov. S. Africa 133 M3
also spelt Gauteng
formerly known as Pretoria-Witwatersrand-Vereeniging
Gaya Spain 55 N3
Gavarr Armenia see Kamo
Gavâter Iran 101 E5
Gâvbandi Iran 100 C5
Gâvbûs, Kûh-e mts Iran 100 C5
Gavdopoula i. Greece 59 F14

▶Gavdos i. Greece 59 F14
Most southerly point of Europe.

Gave r. France 50 E9
Gâveh Rûd r. Iran 100 A3
Gavião r. Brazil 202 D5
Gavião Port. 54 D5
Gävle Sweden 45 L3
Gävleborg county Sweden 45 K3
Gävlebukten b. Sweden 45 L3
Gavrilovka Vtoraya Rus. Fed. 41 G5
Gavrilov-Yam Rus. Fed. 43 U4
Gavrio Greece 59 F11
Gawachab Namibia 130 C5
Gawai Myanmar 78 B2
Gawan India 97 E4
Gawat well Libya 120 B3
Gawilgarh Hills India 96 C5
Gawler Australia 146 B3
Gawler Ranges hills Australia 146 B3
Gâwûr watercourse Turkm. see Gyaur
Gaxun Nur salt l. China 84 D3
Gay Rus. Fed. 102 D2
Gay U.S.A. 172 E3
Gaya r. China 82 C4
Gaya India 97 E4
Gaya i. Sabah Malaysia 77 G1
Gaya Niger 125 F4
Gayá r. Spain see Gaià
Gaya, Pulau i. Sabah Malaysia 77 G1
Gayam Indon. 77 F4
G'Aydat al Jhoucha ridge W. Sahara 122 C4
Gayéri Burkina 125 F3
Gaylord MI U.S.A. 173 I5
Gayndah Australia 149 F5
Gaynovo Rus. Fed. 43 R4
Gayny Rus. Fed. 40 J3
Gaysin Ukr. see Haysyn
Gayutino Rus. Fed. 43 T3
Gaz Iran 100 D3

▶Gaza terr. Asia 108 F6
Semi-autonomous region.
asia [countries] ▶▶ 64–67

▶Gaza Gaza 108 F6
Capital of Gaza. Also spelt 'Azza.

Gaza prov. Moz. 131 G4
Gaz-Achak Turkm. 103 E4
also spelt Gazojak
Gazalkent Uzbek. 103 G4
also spelt Ghazalkent
Gazandzhyk Turkm. 102 C5
formerly known as Kazandzhik
Gazawa Cameroon 125 I4
Gaziantep Turkey 107 D3
also known as Aintab
Gazibenli Turkey see Yahyalı
Gazik Iran 101 E3
Gazimağusa Cyprus see Famagusta
Gazimuro-Ononskiy Khrebet mts Rus. Fed. 85 F1
Gazimurskiy Zavod Rus. Fed. 85 H1
Gazipaşa Turkey 106 C3
Gazivode Jezero l. Yugo. 58 B6
Gazli Uzbek. 103 F4
Gazojak Turkm. see Gaz-Achak

Gbaaka Liberia 124 C5
Gbangbatok Sierra Leone 124 B5
Gbarnga Liberia 124 C5
Gbatala Liberia 124 C5
Gbéroubouè Benin 125 F4
Gboko Nigeria 125 H5
Gbwado Dem. Rep. Congo 126 D4
Gdańsk Poland 49 P1
historically known as Danzig
Gdańsk, Gulf of Poland/Rus. Fed. 49 Q1
also known as Gdańska, Zatoka; formerly known as Danzig, Gulf of
Gdańska, Zatoka g. Poland/Rus. Fed. see Gdańsk, Gulf of
Gdingen Poland see Gdynia
Gdov Rus. Fed. 42 I3
Gdyel Alg. 55 K9
Gdynia Poland 49 P1
historically known as Gdingen or Gotenhafen

Gearhart Mountain U.S.A. 180 B4
Gebe i. Indon. 75 D2
Gebeit Sudan 121 H5
Gebeit Mine Sudan 121 H4
Gebel Iweibid Egypt 108 D7
Gebre Guracha Eth. 128 C2
Gebze Turkey 58 K8
Gech'a Eth. 128 B3
Gecheng China see Chengkou
Gedang, Gunung mt. Indon. 76 C3
Gedaniu kalns hill Latvia 42 E5
Gedaref Sudan 121 G6
Gedaref state Sudan 121 G6
Gedern Germany 48 G5
Gediz Turkey 59 K10
Gediz r. Turkey 106 A3
Gêdo Eth. 128 C2
Gedo admin. reg. Somalia 128 D4
Gedong, Tanjong pt Malaysia 76 [inset]
Gedser Denmark 45 J5

Gedungpakuan Indon. 76 D4
Geel Belgium 51 L1
Geelong Australia 147 E4
Geelvink Channel Australia 151 A6
Geel Vloer salt pan S. Africa 132 E6
Geesthacht Germany 48 H2
Gefersa Eth. 128 C2
Gégé r. Lith. 42 C6
Geguzinė Lith. 42 F7
Gê'gyai China 89 C5
Ge Hu l. China 87 F2
Geidam Nigeria 125 H3
Geiersberg hill Germany 48 G6
Geikie r. Canada 167 K3
Geikie Island Canada 168 B3
Geikie Range hills Australia 149 D2
Geilo Norway 45 J3
Geiselhöring Germany 49 J7
Geislingen an der Steige Germany 48 G7
Geisūm, Gezâ'ir is Egypt see Qeisûm, Gezâ'ir
Geita Tanz. 128 C5
Gejiu China 86 B4
Gekdepe Turkm. 102 D5
also spelt Gökdepe; formerly spelt Geok-Tepe
Gel r. Sudan 128 A3
Gel watercourse Sudan 126 F2
Gela Sicilia Italy 57 G11
Gela r. Sicilia Italy 57 G11
Gela, Golfo di g. Sicilia Italy 57 G11
Geladaindong mt. China 89 E5
Geladi Eth. 128 E3
Gelai vol. Tanz. 128 C5
Gelam i. Indon. 77 E3
Geldern Germany 48 D4
Gelembe Turkey 59 I9
Gelemso Eth. 128 C3
Gelephu Bhutan 97 F4
also known as Hatisar
Gelibolu Turkey see Gallipoli
Gelibolu Yarımadası pen. Turkey 59 H8
Gelibolu Yarımadası Tarihi Milli Parkı nat. park Turkey 59 H8
Gelidonya Burnu pt Turkey see Yardımcı Burnu
Gelincik Dağı mt. Turkey 106 B3
Gelinsoor Somalia 128 E3
Gelmord Iran 100 D3
Gelnica Slovakia 49 R7
Gelsenkirchen Germany 48 E4
Gemas Malaysia 76 C2
Gembu Nigeria 125 H5
Gemena Dem. Rep. Congo 126 C4
Gemenci park Hungary 49 P9
Gemerek Turkey 106 D3
Gemlik Turkey 106 B2
Gemlik Körfezi b. Turkey 58 J8
Gemlufall Iceland 44 [inset] B2
Gemona del Friuli Italy 56 E2
Gémozac France 50 F7
Gemsa Egypt 121 G3
Gemsbok National Park Botswana 130 D5
Gemsbokplein well S. Africa 132 E3
Gemsbokvlakte S. Africa 133 I2
Gen r. China 85 H1
Genal r. Spain 54 F8
Genalë Wenz r. Eth. 128 D3
Gençay France 50 G6
Gendoa r. Eth. 104 B5
General Acha Arg. 204 D5
General Alvear Buenos Aires Arg. 204 E5
also spelt Yerakaroú
General Alvear Mendoza Arg. 204 D4
General Artigas Para. 201 F6
General Belgrano Arg. 204 F4
General Belgrano II research station Antarctica see Belgrano II
General Bernardo O'Higgins research station Antarctica 222 U2
General Cabrera Arg. 204 D4
General Carneiro Brazil 206 A2

▶General Carrera, Lago l. Arg./Chile 205 B7
Deepest lake in South America.

General Conesa Arg. 204 D6
General Escobedo Mex. 185 E3
General Freire Angola see Muxaluando
Generalísimo, Embalse del resr Spain 55 J5
General José de San Martín Arg. 204 E2
General Juan Madariaga Arg. 204 F5
General Lagos Chile 200 C4
General La Madrid Arg. 204 E5
General Luna Phil. 74 C4
General MacArthur Phil. 74 C4
General Machado Angola see Camacupa
General Martín Miguel de Güemes Arg. 200 D6
General Paz Arg. 204 F3
General Pico Arg. 204 E4
General Pinto Arg. 204 E4
General Roca Arg. 204 D5
General Saavedra Bol. 201 E4
General Salgado Brazil 206 C7
General San Martín research station Antarctica see San Martín
General Santos Phil. 74 C5
General Simón Bolívar Mex. 185 E3
General Terán Mex. 185 E3
General Toshevo Bulg. 58 J5
General Trias Mex. 184 D2
General Villegas Arg. 204 E4
Genemuiden Neth. 48 D3
Genesee r. U.S.A. 176 H2
Geneseo IL U.S.A. 174 B3
Geneseo NY U.S.A. 176 H3
Genet Eth. 128 C2
Geneva Switz. 51 M6
also known as Genève or Genf
Geneva IL U.S.A. 172 E8
Geneva NE U.S.A. 178 C3
Geneva NY U.S.A. 177 H3
Geneva OH U.S.A. 176 E4
Geneva, Lake France/Switz. 51 M6
also known as Léman, Lac
Genève Switz. see Geneva
Genf Switz. see Geneva
Gengda China 86 B2
formerly known as Gana
Gengenbach Germany 48 F7
Genglou China 87 E4
Gengqing China see Dêgê
Geni r. Sudan 128 B3
Genil r. Spain 54 F7
Genisea Greece 58 F7
also spelt Yenísea
Genk Belgium 51 L1
Genkai-nada b. Japan 91 B8
Gennargentu, Monti del mts Sardegna Italy 57 B9
Gennes France 50 F5
Genoa Australia 147 F4
Genoa Italy 56 A4
also spelt Genova; historically known as Genua
Genoa U.S.A. 172 E8
Genoa, Gulf of Italy 56 A4
also known as Genova, Gulf of
Genova Italy see Genoa
Genova, Gulf of Italy see Genoa, Gulf of
Gent Belgium see Ghent
Genteng Indon. 77 E4
Genteng i. Indon. 76 C3
Gevân-e Tâleb Khâni Iran 101 D3
also known as Vastan
Genthin Germany 49 J3
Gentio do Ouro Brazil 202 D4
Genua Italy see Genoa
Genzano di Roma Italy 56 E7
Geoagiu r. Romania 58 D3
Geographe Bay Australia 151 A7
Geographe Channel Australia 151 A5

Geographical Society Ø i. Greenland 165 Q2
Geok-Tepe Turkm. see Gekdepe
Georga, Zemlya i. Rus. Fed. 38 E1
English form George Land
George r. Canada 169 H1
George S. Africa 132 G11
George, Lake N.S.W. Australia 147 F3
George, Lake S.A. Australia 146 C4
George, Lake salt flat Australia 150 C3
George, Lake Uganda 128 A4
George, Lake FL U.S.A. 175 D6
George, Lake NY U.S.A. 177 L2
George Gills Range mts Australia 148 A4
George Land i. Rus. Fed. see Georga, Zemlya
Georges Mills U.S.A. 177 M2
George Sound inlet N.Z. 153 B12
George Town Australia 147 E5
George Town Bahamas 186 E1
Georgetown Canada 173 N7

▶George Town Cayman Is 186 C1
Capital of the Cayman Islands.

Georgetown Gambia 124 B3

▶Georgetown Guyana 199 G3
Capital of Guyana. Formerly known as Demerara; historically known as Stabroek.

George Town Malaysia 76 C1
also known as Pinang
Georgetown DE U.S.A. 177 J7
Georgetown GA U.S.A. 175 C6
Georgetown KY U.S.A. 176 A7
Georgetown OH U.S.A. 176 B7
Georgetown SC U.S.A. 175 E5
Georgetown TX U.S.A. 179 C6
George VI Sound sea chan. Antarctica 222 T2
George V Land reg. Antarctica 223 K2
George West U.S.A. 179 C6

▶Georgia country Asia 107 C2
known as Sakartvelo in Georgian; formerly known as Gruzinskaya S.S.R.
asia [countries] ▶▶ 64–67

Georgia state U.S.A. 175 D5
Georgia, Strait of Canada 166 E5
Georgian Bay Canada 168 D4
Georgian Bay Islands National Park Canada 173 N6
Georgi Dimitrov, Yazovir resr Bulg. see Koprinka, Yazovir
Georgina watercourse Australia 148 C5
Georgi Traykov Bulg. see Dolni Chiflik
Georgiu-Dezh Rus. Fed. see Liski
Georgiyevka Aktyubinskaya Oblast' Kazakh. 102 D2
Georgiyevka Vostochnyy Kazakhstan Kazakh. 103 J2
Georgiyevka Kazakh. see Korday
Georgiyevsk Rus. Fed. 41 G7
Georgiyevskoye Kostromskaya Oblast' Rus. Fed. 40 H4
Georgiyevskoye Vologod. Obl. Rus. Fed. 43 R2
Georg von Neumayer research station Antarctica see Neumayer
Gera Germany 48 J5
Gerakarou Greece 58 E8
also spelt Yerakaroú
Geraki Greece 59 D11
also known as Yeráki
Geraki, Akra pt Greece 59 B11
also known as Yeráki, Ákra
Geral de Goiás, Serra hills Brazil 202 C4
Geraldine N.Z. 153 F12
Geral do Paraná, Serra hills Brazil 206 F2
Geraldton Australia 151 A6
Gerama i. Indon. 75 C1
Geraneia mts Greece 59 E11
Gerar watercourse Israel 108 F6
Gérardmer France 51 M4
Gerāsh Iran 100 C5
Gerber U.S.A. 182 B1
Gercüş Turkey 107 E3
Gerdau S. Africa 133 K3
Gerdauen Rus. Fed. see Zheleznodorozhnyy
Gerecsei park Hungary 49 P8
Gerede Turkey 106 C2
Gerede r. Turkey 106 C2
Gereshk Afgh. 101 F4
Geretsried Germany 48 I8
Gergovie tourist site France 51 J7
Gerik Malaysia 76 C1
formerly spelt Grik
Gerimenj Iran 100 D3
Gering U.S.A. 178 B3
Gerlach U.S.A. 182 E1
Gerlachovský štít mt. Slovakia 49 R6
Gerlospaß pass Austria 48 J8
Germaine, Lac l. Canada 169 H2
Germania country Europe see Germany
Germania Land reg. Greenland 165 R2
Germencik Turkey 59 I11
Germersheim Germany 48 F6
Germiston S. Africa 133 M3
Gernika-Lumo Spain 55 I1
Gerolstein Germany 48 D5
Gerolzhofen Germany 48 H6
Gerona Spain see Girona
Gerrit Denys is P.N.G. see Lihir Group
Gers r. France 50 G8
Gers dept France 50 F9
Gersfeld (Rhön) Germany 48 G5
Gersoppa India 94 B3
Gêrzê China 89 D5
also known as Luring
Gerze Turkey 106 C2
Geschriebenstein hill Austria 49 N8
Gesoriacum France see Boulogne-sur-Mer
Gessler Arg. 204 E3
Geta Fin. 45 L3
Getafe Spain 55 H4
Getcheh, Kûh-e hills Iran 100 C3
Gete r. Belgium 51 L1
Getic, Podişul plat. Romania 58 E4
Gettorf Germany 48 H1
Gettysburg PA U.S.A. 177 H6
Gettysburg SD U.S.A. 178 C2
Gettysburg National Military Park nat. park U.S.A. 177 H6
Getu He r. China 86 C3
Getulina Brazil 206 D8
Getúlio Vargas Brazil 203 A8
Geumapang r. Indon. 76 B1
Geureudong, Gunung vol. Indon. 76 B1
Gevaş Turkey 107 F3
Gevgelija Macedonia 58 D7
Gevrai India 94 B2
Gevrey-Chambertin France 51 K5
Gewanē Wildlife Reserve nature res. Eth. 128 D2

Gex France 51 M6
Gexianzhuang China see Qinghe
Gey Iran see Nīkshahr
Geydik Dağları mts Turkey 108 D1
Geyikli Turkey 59 I9
Geylang Sing. 76 [inset]
Geylang r. Sing. 76 [inset]
Geyserville U.S.A. 182 B3
Gezarina Brazil 206 D3
Ghaap Plateau S. Africa 132 H4
Ghabeish Sudan 121 E6
Ghadaf, Wādī al watercourse Iraq 107 E4
Ghadaf, Wādī al watercourse Jordan 109 H6
Ghadamés Libya see Ghadāmis
Ghadāmis Libya 120 A2
also known as Ghudamis; formerly spelt Ghadamés
Ghaddūwah Libya 120 B3
Ghadir al Khayl waterhole Iraq 109 N6
Ghadir al Mulūsī well Iraq 109 K4
Ghaem Shahr Iran 100 C2
Ghaggar, Dry Bed of watercourse Pak. 101 H4
Ghaghara r. India 97 E4
formerly spelt Gogra
Ghaghra India 97 E5
formerly spelt Gogra
Ghaidah watercourse Iraq 109 M5
Ghalib Iran 100 C5
Ghallaorol Uzbek. see Gallyaaral
Ghanādah, Rās pt U.A.E. 105 F2
Ghānah well Oman 105 F4
Ghanim well Saudi Arabia 105 F4
Ghantiala India 96 B5
Ghantwar India 94 A1
Ghanwā Saudi Arabia 105 E2
Ghanzi Botswana 130 D4
Ghanzi admin. dist. Botswana 130 D4
Ghap'an Armenia see Kapan
Gharāmil, Jabal al hill Saudi Arabia 104 C3
Gharandal Jordan 108 G7
Gharandal, Wādī watercourse Egypt 108 D8
Gharbīya governorate Egypt 108 C7
Gharāt Tāris hill Syria 109 M2
Ghardimaou Tunisia 57 A12
Ghar el Melh Tunisia 57 C11
Gharghoda India 97 D5
Ghārib, Gebel mt. Egypt 121 G2
Ghārib, Rās pt Egypt 108 D7
Gharm Tajik. 101 G2
also spelt Garm
Gharo Pak. 101 F5
Gharyān Libya 120 B1
Gharz, Wādī al watercourse Syria 109 I5
Ghāt Libya 120 A3
Ghatampur India 96 D4
Ghatgan India 97 E5
Ghatol India 96 B5
Ghatsila India 97 E5
Ghauspur Pak. 101 G4
Ghawdex i. Malta see Gozo
Ghawr, Wādī al watercourse Syria 109 L3
Ghaymān Yemen 104 D5
Ghazal, Bahr el watercourse Chad 120 C6
Ghazal, Bahr el r. Sudan 128 A2
Ghazalkent Uzbek. see Gazalkent
Ghazaouet Alg. 123 E2
also known as Nemours
Ghaziabad India 96 C3
Ghazialah, Wādī watercourse Iraq 109 O3
Ghazipur India 97 D4
Ghazira, Wādī al watercourse Oman 105 G2
English form Malcolm Inlet
Ghazna Afgh. see Ghaznī
Ghaznī Afgh. 101 G3
Ghaznī r. Afgh. 101 G3
Ghazzāleh Saudi Arabia 104 C2
Ghelari Romania 58 D3
Ghelinţa Romania 58 H3
Ghemeis, Ras pt U.A.E. 105 E2
Ghent Belgium 51 J1
also spelt Gent or Gand
Ghent U.S.A. 176 D7
Gheorghe Gheorghiu-Dej Romania see Oneşti
Gheorghe Lazăr Romania 58 I4
Gheorgheni Romania 58 G2
Gherdi India 94 B2
Gherla Romania 58 E1
formerly known as Armenopolis
Ghijduwan Uzbek. see Gizhduvan
Ghilzai reg. Afgh. 101 G3
Ghināh, Wādī al watercourse Saudi Arabia 107 D5
Ghioroiu Romania 58 E4
Ghisonaccia Corse France 52 D3
Ghizao Afgh. 101 F3
Ghizar Jammu and Kashmir 96 B1
Ghizri Creek inlet Pak. 101 F5
Ghod India 94 B2
Ghod r. India 94 B2
Gholvad India 94 B3
Ghoraghat Bangl. 97 F4
Ghorak Afgh. 101 F3
Ghorband r. Afgh. 101 G3
Ghost Lake Canada 167 H2
Ghotaru India 96 A4
Ghotki Pak. 101 G5
Ghowr prov. Afgh. 101 F3
Ghuari r. India 97 E4
Ghubbah Yemen 105 F5
Ghudamis Libya see Ghadāmis
Ghugus India 94 C2
Ghulam Mohammed Barrage Pak. 101 G5
Ghurayfah hill Saudi Arabia 109 N6
Ghūri Iran 100 C5
Ghurian Afgh. 101 E3
Ghurrab, Jabal hill Saudi Arabia 104 D2
Ghurūb, Jabal hill Saudi Arabia 104 C3
Ghuzayn Oman 105 G3
Ghuzayyil, Sabkhat salt marsh Libya 120 C2
Ghuzor Uzbek. see Guzar
Gia Dinh Vietnam 79 D6
Giaginskaya Rus. Fed. 41 G7
Gialias r. Cyprus 108 E2
Giang r. Vietnam 78 D4
Gia Nghia Vietnam 79 D5
Giannitsa Greece 58 D8
also known as Yenije-i-Vardar; also spelt Yiannitsá
Giannutri, Isola di i. Italy 56 D6
Giant's Causeway lava field U.K. 47 C3
Gianyar Indon. 77 F5
Gianysada i. Greece 59 H13
Giardini-Naxos Sicilia Italy 57 H11
Giarmata Romania 58 C3
Giarre Sicilia Italy 57 H11
Giaveno Italy 51 N7
Giba Cuba 186 D2
Gibarrayo hill Spain 54 F7
Gibb r. Australia 150 D3
Gibbon U.S.A. 178 C3
Gibb River Australia 150 D3
Gibb River Aboriginal Reserve Australia 150 D3
Gibeon Namibia 130 C5
Gibraleón Spain 54 E7

▶Gibraltar Europe 54 F8
United Kingdom Overseas Territory.
europe [countries] ▶▶ 32–35

▶Gibraltar, Strait of Morocco/Spain 54 E9
europe [countries] ▶▶ 32–35

Gibraltar Range National Park Australia 147 G2
Gibson Australia 151 C7
Gibson City U.S.A. 174 B3
▶Gibson Desert Australia 150 C5
oceania [landscapes] ▶▶ 136–137
Gibson Desert Nature Reserve Australia 151 C5
Gibsons Canada 166 F5
Gichgeniyn Nuruu mts Mongolia 84 B2
Gīdamī Eth. 128 B2
Gidda Eth. 128 B2
Gidcalur India 94 C3
Gīddī, Gebel el hill Egypt 121 G2
English form Giddi Pass
Giddings U.S.A. 179 C6
Gīddī Pass hill Egypt see Gīddī, Gebel el
Gidê Eth. 128 C2
Gidolē Eth. 128 C3
Gien France 51 I5
Giesecke Isfjord inlet Greenland see Kanger-ussuaq
Gießen Germany 48 F5
Gīfan Iran 100 D2
Gifatin Egypt see Gifatin Island
Gifatin Island Egypt 104 A2
Gifhorn Germany 48 H3
Gift Lake Canada 167 H4
Gifu Japan 91 E7
Gifu pref. Japan 91 E7
Gigant Rus. Fed. 41 G7
Gigante, Cerro mt. Mex. 184 C3
Gigante Col. 198 C4
Gigha i. U.K. 46 G3
Giglio, Isola del i. Italy 56 C6
Gijón Spain 54 F1
Gikongoro Rwanda 126 F5
Gila r. U.S.A. 183 J9
Gila Bend U.S.A. 183 L9
Gila Bend Mountains U.S.A. 183 K8
Gila Mountains U.S.A. 183 J9
Gīlān prov. Iran 100 A2
Gīlān-e Gharb Iran 100 A3
Gila River Indian Reservation res. U.S.A. 183 M8
Gīlāu Romania 58 E2
Gīlāzī Azer. 107 G2
also spelt Kilyazi
Gilbert r. Australia 149 D3
Gilbert AZ U.S.A. 183 M8
Gilbert MN U.S.A. 172 A3
Gilbert WV U.S.A. 176 D8
Gilbert Islands country Pacific Ocean see Kiribati
Gilbert Range mts Australia 149 D3
Gilbert River Australia 149 D3
Gilbués Brazil 202 C4
Gile Moz. 131 H3
Gilead r. Jordan see Jil'ād
Giles Creek r. Australia 148 A3
Giles Meteorological Station Australia 151 E5
Gilf Kebir Plateau Egypt 121 D4
also known as Jilf al Kabīr, Haḍabat al
Gilgandra Australia 147 F3
Gil Gil Creek r. Australia 147 F2
Gilgit Jammu and Kashmir 96 B2
Gilgit r. Jammu and Kashmir 96 B2
Gilgunnia Australia 147 E3
Gili Iyang i. Indon. 77 F4
Gilimanuk Indon. 77 E5
Gilindire Turkey see Aydıncık
Gil am Canada 167 M3
Gilien watercourse Australia 148 B4
Gillen, Lake salt flat Australia 151 D5
Gilles, Lake salt flat Australia 146 C3
Gillespies Point N.Z. 153 D11
Gillett PA U.S.A. 177 I4
Gillett WI U.S.A. 172 E6
Gillette U.S.A. 180 F3
Gillhov Sweden 44 K3
Gilliat Australia 149 D4
Gilliat r. Australia 149 D4
Gillingham U.K. 47 M12
Gilman IL U.S.A. 174 C3
Gilman WI U.S.A. 172 C5
Gilmer U.S.A. 179 D5
Gilort r. Romania 58 E4
Gilroy U.S.A. 182 C4
Giluwe, Mount P.N.G. 73 J8
Gimbī Eth. 128 B2
Gimli Canada 167 L5
Gimo Sweden 45 L3
Gimont France 50 G9
Ginda Eritrea 121 H6
Gindie Australia 149 F4
Ginebra, Laguna l. Bol. 200 D3
Gineina, Rās el m. Egypt 108 E8
Gingee India 94 C3
Gin Gin Australia 149 F5
Gingin Australia 151 A6
Gingindlovu S. Africa 133 P6
Gingoog Phil. 74 C4
Ginīr Eth. 128 D3
Ginkūnai Lith. 42 E6
Ginzo de Limia Spain see Xinzo de Limia
Gioia, Golfo di b. Italy 57 H10
Gioia del Colle Italy 57 I8
Gioia Tauro Italy 57 H10
Gioura i. Greece 59 F9
also spelt Yioúra
Gipouloux r. Canada 169 F2
Gippsland reg. Australia 147 E4
Girâ, Wādī watercourse Egypt 108 E8
Girab India 96 A4
Gīrān Rīg mt. Iran 101 E3
Girar India 94 C1
Girard KS U.S.A. 178 D4
Girard OH U.S.A. 176 E4
Girard PA U.S.A. 176 E3
Girardin, Lac l. Canada 169 H1
Girdar Dhor r. Pak. 101 F5
Girdi Iran 101 D5
Giresun Turkey 107 D2
Girga Egypt 121 F3
Girgenti Sicilia Italy see Agrigento
Giri r. Dem. Rep. Congo 126 C4
Giridih India 97 E4
Girilambone Australia 147 E2
Girna r. India 96 B5
Girne Cyprus see Kyrenia
Giromagny France 51 M5
Giron Sweden see Kiruna
Girona Spain 55 N3
also spelt Gerona
Gironde est. France 50 E7
Girou r. France 50 H9
Girua Brazil 203 A9
Girvan U.K. 47 H8
Girvas Rus. Fed. 40 E3
Gisborne N.Z. 152 M6
Gisborne admin. reg. N.Z. 152 M6
Giscome Canada 166 F4
Gisenyi Rwanda 126 F5
Gislaved Sweden 45 K4
Gisors France 50 I3
Gissar Tajik. see Hisor
Gissar Range mts Tajik./Uzbek. 101 F2
also known as Gissarskiy Khrebet or Hisor Tizmasi
Gissarskiy Khrebet mts Tajik./Uzbek. see Gissar Range

Gissarskiy Zapovednik nature res. Uzbek. 103 F5
Gitarama Rwanda 126 F5
Gitega Burundi 126 F5
Giuba r. Somalia see Jubba
Giubega Romania 58 E4
Giubiasco Switz. 51 P6
Giugliano in Campania Italy 56 G8
Giulianova Italy 56 F6
Giurgeului, Munţii mts Romania 58 G2
Giurgiu Romania 58 G5
Givar Iran 100 C2
Give Denmark 45 J5
Givors France 51 K7
Giyani S. Africa 131 F4
Giyon Eth. 128 C2
Giza Egypt 121 F2
also spelt El Giza or Al Jīzah
▶Giza Pyramids tourist site Egypt 121 F2
also known as Ahrāmāt el Jīzah
africa [locations] ▶▶ 118–119
Gizeh Rûd r. Iran 100 A3
also known as Darreh Gozaru
Gizhduvan Uzbek. 103 F4
also spelt Ghijduwan
Gizhiga Rus. Fed. 39 Q3
Gizo Solomon Is 145 E2
Gizycko Poland 49 S1
Gjalicë e Lumës, Mal mt. Albania 58 B6
Gjerde Norway 44 I3
Gjerstad Norway 45 J4
Gjirokastër Albania 59 B8
formerly known as Argyrokastron
Gjoa Haven Canada 165 J3
Gjögur Iceland 44 [inset] B2
Gjøra Norway 44 J3
Gjøvik Norway 45 J3
Gjuhëzës, Kepi i pt Albania 58 A8
Glace Bay Canada 169 J4
Glacier Bay U.S.A. 166 C3
Glacier Bay National Park and Preserve U.S.A. 164 E3
Glacier National Park Canada 167 G5
Glacier National Park U.S.A. 180 D2
Glacier Peak vol. U.S.A. 180 B2
Glacier Spring U.S.A. 176 D9
Gladbeck Germany 48 E4
Gladenbach Germany 48 F5
Gladewater U.S.A. 179 D5
Gladstone Qld Australia 149 F4
Gladstone S.A. Australia 146 C3
Gladstone Canada 167 L5
Gladstone MI U.S.A. 172 F5
Gladstone MO U.S.A. 178 D4
Gladstone VA U.S.A. 176 G8
Gladwin U.S.A. 173 I7
Gladys U.S.A. 176 F8
Gladys Lake Canada 166 C3
Glamis U.K. 46 I7
Glamis U.S.A. 183 I9
Glämoč Bos.-Herz. 56 I4
Glan r. Austria 49 L9
Glan r. Germany 48 E6
Glan Phil. 74 C5
Glan i. Sweden 45 K4
Glarner Alpen mts Switz. 51 O6
Glarus Switz. 51 P5
Glasfjorden l. Sweden 45 K4
Glasford U.S.A. 172 D10
Glasgow U.K. 46 H8
Glasgow KY U.S.A. 174 C4
Glasgow MT U.S.A. 180 F2
Glasgow VA U.S.A. 176 F8
Glaskogens naturreservat nature res. Norway 45 K4
Glaslyn Canada 167 I4
Glassboro U.S.A. 177 J6
Glass Mountain U.S.A. 182 F4
Glass Peninsula U.S.A. 166 C3
Glauchau Germany 49 J5
Glavacioc r. Romania 58 G4
Glavan Bulg. 58 I6
Glavinitsa Bulg. 58 I5
Glavnik Kosovo, Srbija Yugo. 58 C6
Glazoué Benin 125 F5
Glazov Rus. Fed. 40 J4
Glazunovka Rus. Fed. 43 R9
Glazunovo Rus. Fed. 43 L6
Gleason U.S.A. 172 D5
Gleichen Canada 167 H5
Gleisdorf Austria 49 M8
Gleiwitz Poland see Gliwice
Glen Sweden 44 K3
Glen U.S.A. 177 N1
Glen Afton Canada 173 M4
Glen Afton N.Z. 152 I5
Glen Allen U.S.A. 176 H8
Glénan, Îles de is France 50 C5
Glen Arbor U.S.A. 172 H6
Glenavy N.Z. 153 F12
Glenboro Canada 167 L5
Glen Burnie U.S.A. 177 I6
Glen Canyon gorge U.S.A. 183 M4
Glen Canyon Dam U.S.A. 183 M5
Glencoe S. Africa 133 O5
Glencoe KY U.S.A. 176 A7
Glencoe MN U.S.A. 178 D2
Glenconnor S. Africa 133 J10
Glen Cove U.S.A. 177 L5
Glendale Canada 173 I4
Glendale AZ U.S.A. 183 L8
Glendale CA U.S.A. 182 F7
Glendale UT U.S.A. 183 L4
Glendale Lake U.S.A. 176 G5
Glendale Springs U.S.A. 176 D9
Glendambo Australia 146 B2
Glendive U.S.A. 180 F3
Glendon Canada 167 I4
Glendo Reservoir U.S.A. 180 F4
Glenelg r. Australia 146 D4
Glenfield U.S.A. 177 J2
Glenfinnan U.K. 46 G7
Glengarry Range hills Australia 151 B5
Glengyle Australia 148 C5
Glen Hill Aboriginal Reserve Australia 150 E3
Glen Innes Australia 147 F2
Glenlyon Peak Canada 166 C2
Glen Massey N.Z. 152 I5
Glen More U.K. 46 H6
Glenmorgan Australia 147 F1
Glen Murray N.Z. 152 I5
Glenn U.S.A. 182 B2
Glennallen U.S.A. 164 E3
Glennie U.S.A. 173 J6
Glenns Ferry U.S.A. 180 D4
Glenora Canada 166 D3
Glenore Australia 149 D3
Glenormiston Australia 148 C4
Glenorn Aboriginal Reserve Australia 151 C6
Glen Rock U.S.A. 177 I6
Glen Rogers U.S.A. 176 D8
Glen Rose U.S.A. 179 C5
Glenrothes U.K. 46 I7
Glenroy Australia 150 D3
Glens Falls U.S.A. 177 L2
Glen Shee valley U.K. 46 I7
Glenties Rep. of Ireland 47 D3
Glentunnel N.Z. 153 F11
Glenveagh National Park Rep. of Ireland 47 E3
Glenville U.S.A. 176 E7
Glenwater Canada 172 D2
Glen Wilton U.S.A. 176 F8
Glenwood AR U.S.A. 179 D5
Glenwood IA U.S.A. 178 D3
Glenwood MN U.S.A. 178 D2
Glenwood UT U.S.A. 183 M3
Glenwood City U.S.A. 172 A5
Glenwood Springs U.S.A. 180 F5

Glevum U.K. see Gloucester
Glina r. Bos.-Herz./Croatia 56 I3
Glina Croatia 56 I3
Glinka Rus. Fed. 43 N7
Glittertinden mt. Norway 45 J3
Gliwice Poland 49 P5
historically known as Gleiwitz
Globe U.S.A. 183 N8
Glodeanu-Sărat Romania 58 H4
Glodeni Romania 58 F2
Glogau Poland see Głogów
Gloggnitz Austria 49 M8
Glogovac Kosovo, Srbija Yugo. 58 B6
Głogów Poland 49 N4
historically known as Glogau
Głogówek Poland 49 O5
Głogów Małopolski Poland 49 S5
Glomfjord Norway 44 K2
Glomma r. Norway 45 J4
Glommersträsk Sweden 44 L2
Glória Brazil 202 E4
Glorieuses, Îles is Indian Ocean 129 E7
English form Glorioso Islands
Glorioso Islands Indian Ocean see Glorieuses, Îles
Gloucester Australia 147 F2
Gloucester P.N.G. 145 D2
Gloucester U.K. 47 J12
historically known as Glevum
Gloucester MA U.S.A. 177 O3
Gloucester VA U.S.A. 177 I8
Gloucester Island Australia 149 F4
Gloucester Point U.S.A. 177 I8
Glover Reef Belize 185 I5
Gloversville U.S.A. 177 K2
Glovertown Canada 169 K3
Glöwen Germany 48 J3
Głowno Poland 49 Q4
Głubczyce Poland 49 O5
Glubinnoye Rus. Fed. 82 D3
Glubokiy Rus. Fed. 41 G6
Glubokoye Belarus see Hlybokaye
Glubokoye Kazakh. 88 C1
Glubokoye, Ozero l. Rus. Fed. 43 K1
Glücksburg (Ostsee) Germany 48 G1
Glückstadt Germany 48 G2
Gluggarnir hill Faroe Is 46 F2
Glukhov Ukr. see Hlukhiv
Gmelinka Rus. Fed. 102 A2
Gmünd Austria 49 L7
Gmunden Austria 49 K8
Gnadenhutten U.S.A. 176 D5
Gnarp Sweden 45 L3
Gnarrenburg Germany 48 G2
Gnesen Poland see Gniezno
Gniew Poland 49 P2
Gniewkowo Poland 49 P3
Gniezno Poland 49 O3
historically known as Gnesen
Gnisvärd Sweden 45 L4
Gnjilane Kosovo, Srbija Yugo. 58 C6
Gnoien Germany 49 J2
Gnowangerup Australia 151 B7
Gnows Nest Range hills Australia 151 B6
Goa state India 94 B3
Goageb Namibia 130 C5
Goalpara India 97 F4
Goang Indon. 75 A5
Goaso Ghana 124 E5
Goat Fell hill U.K. 46 G8
Goba Eth. 128 D3
Gobabis Namibia 130 C4
Gobannium U.K. see Abergavenny
Gobas Namibia 130 C5
Gobernador Crespo Arg. 204 E3
Gobernador Duval Arg. 204 D5
Gobernador Gregores Arg. 205 C8
Gobernador Mayer Arg. 205 C8
Gobernador Virasoro Arg. 204 F3
Gobi des. China/Mongolia 85 E2
English form Gobi Desert
Gobi Desert China/Mongolia see Gobi
Gobiki Rus. Fed. 43 O8
Göblberg hill Austria 49 K7
Gobō Japan 91 D8
Goch Germany 48 D4
Gochas Namibia 130 C5
Go Công Vietnam 79 D6
Godagari Bangl. 97 F4
Godavari r. India 94 D2
Godbout Canada 169 H3
Godbout r. Canada 169 H3
Godda India 97 E4
Goddard, Mount U.S.A. 182 F4
Godē Eth. 128 D3
Godeal hill Port. 54 C6
Godech Bulg. 58 E5
Goderich Canada 168 D5
Goderville France 50 G3
Godhavn Greenland see Qeqertarsuaq
Godhra India 96 B5
Godinlabe Somalia 128 E3
Godo, Gunung mt. Indon. 75 C3
Gödöllő Hungary 49 Q8
Gods r. Canada 167 M3
Gods Lake Canada 167 M4
God's Mercy, Bay of Canada 167 O2
Godthåb Greenland see Nuuk
Goduċohkka mt. Sweden 44 L1
also spelt Kåtotjåkka
Godwin-Austen, Mount China/Jammu and Kashmir see K2
Goedemoed S. Africa 133 K7
Goedgegun Swaziland see Nhlangano
Goéland, Lac au l. Canada 168 E3
Goélands, Lac aux l. Canada 169 I2
Goes Neth. 48 A4
Goetzville U.S.A. 173 I4
Goffstown U.S.A. 177 N2
Gogama Canada 168 D4
Gogebic, Lake U.S.A. 172 D4
Gogebic Range hills U.S.A. 172 D4
Gögeç Turkey 109 K1
Gogland, Ostrov i. Rus. Fed. 42 H1
Gogoi Moz. 131 G4
Gogolevka Rus. Fed. 43 M7
Gogoșu Romania 58 D4
Gogounou Benin 125 F4
Gogra India see Ghaghra
Gogra r. India see Ghaghara
Gogrial Sudan 126 F2
Gogunda India 96 B4
Gohad India 96 C4
Gohana India 96 C3
Goharganj India 96 C5
Goiana Brazil 202 F3
Goianésia Brazil 206 D2
Goiânia Brazil 206 D3
Goianinha Brazil 202 F3
Goianira Brazil 206 D3
Goiás Brazil 206 C2
Goiás state Brazil 206 C3
Goiatuba Brazil 206 D5
Goincang China 86 B1
Goio-Erê Brazil 203 A8
Goi-Pula Dem. Rep. Congo 127 E6
Goito Italy 56 C3
Gojeb Wenz r. Eth. 128 C3
Gojra Pak. 101 H4
Gokak India 94 B2
Gokarn India 94 B3
Gök Çay r. Turkey 108 D1
Gökçeada i. Turkey 106 A2
also known as İmroz
Gökçedağ Turkey 106 B3
Gökçen Turkey 59 I10
Gökçeören Turkey 59 J10
Gökdepe Turkm. see Gëkdepe
Gökdere r. Turkey 108 D1
Gökirmak r. Turkey 106 C2
Goklenkuy, Solonchak salt l. Turkm. 102 D4
Gökova Turkey see Ula
Gökova Körfezi b. Turkey 106 A3
Gokprosh Hills Pak. 101 E5
Göksun Turkey 107 D3
Göksu Nehri r. Turkey 106 C3
Goksu Parkı Turkey 108 E1
Göktepe Turkey 108 D1
Gokwe Zimbabwe 131 F3
Gol Norway 45 J3
Gola India 96 D3
Golaghat India 97 G4
Golakganj India 97 F4
Golan hills Syria 108 G4
also spelt Al Jawlān or HaGolan
Gołańcz Poland 49 O3
Golbāf Iran 100 D4
Golbahār Afgh. 101 G3
Gölbaşı Turkey 107 D3
Gokteik Myanmar 78 B3
Golconda India 94 C2
Golconda IL U.S.A. 174 B4
Golconda NV U.S.A. 183 G1
Gölcük Turkey 59 I9
Gölcük Turkey 106 B2
Gölcük Turkey see Etili
Gölcük r. Turkey 59 J9
Golczewo Poland 49 L2
Gold U.S.A. 176 H4
Gołdap Poland 49 T1
Gołdapa r. Poland 49 S1
Gold Beach U.S.A. 180 A4
Goldberg Germany 49 J2
Gold Coast country Africa see Ghana
Gold Coast Australia 147 G2
formerly known as South Coast Town
Gold Coast coastal area Ghana 125 E5
Golden Canada 167 G5
Golden Bay N.Z. 152 G8
Goldendale U.S.A. 180 B3
Golden Downs N.Z. 153 G9
Golden Ears Provincial Park Canada 166 F5
Golden Gate Highlands National Park S. Africa 133 M5
Golden Hinde mt. Canada 166 E5
Golden Lake Canada 168 E4
Golden Meadow U.S.A. 175 B6
Golden Valley S. Africa 133 J9
Golden Valley Zimbabwe 131 F3
Goldfield U.S.A. 183 G4
Gold River Canada 166 E5
Goldsand Lake Canada 167 K3
Goldsboro U.S.A. 174 E5
Goldstone Lake U.S.A. 183 H6
Goldsworthy Australia 150 B4
Goldthwaite U.S.A. 179 C6
Goldvein U.S.A. 176 H7
Göle Turkey 107 E2
also known as Merdenik
Goleniów Poland 49 L2
Golestān Afgh. 101 E3
Golestān prov. Iran 100 C2
Goleta U.S.A. 182 E7
Golfito Costa Rica 186 C5
Golfo de Tehuantepec g. Mex. see Tehuantepec, Gulf of
Golfo di Orosei Gennargentu e Asinara, Parco Nazionale del nat. park Sardegna Italy 57 B8
Gölgeli Dağları mts Turkey 106 B3
Gölhisar Turkey 59 K11
Goliad U.S.A. 179 C6
Golija nat. park Yugo. 58 B5
Golija Planina mts Yugo. 58 B5
Golingka China see Gongbo'gyamda
Golitsyno Rus. Fed. 43 S6
Gölköy Turkey 107 D2
also known as Kuşluyan
Gollel Swaziland see Lavumisa
Gölmarmara Turkey 59 I10
Golmberg hill Germany 49 K3
Golmud China 84 B4
Golmud He r. China 84 B4
Golo i. Phil. 74 B3
Golobino Rus. Fed. 43 V6
Golodnaya Step' plain Uzbek. 103 F4
Golondrina Arg. 204 E3
Gölova Turkey 108 G1
Golovnino Rus. Fed. 90 I3
Golpāyegān Iran 100 B3
Gölpazarı Turkey 106 B2
Golspie U.K. 46 I6
Golub-Dobrzyń Poland 49 Q2
Golubovka Kazakh. 103 H1
Golungo Alto Angola 127 B7
Goluzino Rus. Fed. 43 V2
Gol Vardeh Iran 101 E3
Golweyn Somalia 128 E4
Golyama Syutkya mt. Bulg. 58 F7
Golyama Zhelyazna Bulg. 58 F6
Golyam Perelik mt. Bulg. 58 F7
Golyam Persenk mt. Bulg. 58 F7
Golyashi Belarus see Sasnovy Bor
Gölyazı Turkey 59 J8
Golynki Rus. Fed. 43 M7
Golyshi Rus. Fed. see Vetluzhskiy
Goma Dem. Rep. Congo 126 F5
Goma Uganda 128 A5
Gomang Co salt l. China 89 E6
Gomati r. India 96 D4
Gombak, Bukit hill Sing. 76 [inset]
Gombari Dem. Rep. Congo 126 F4
Gombe Nigeria 125 H4
Gombe state Nigeria 125 H4
Gombe r. Tanz. 129 A6
Gombi Nigeria 125 I4
Gombroon Iran see Bandar-e 'Abbās
Gömeç Turkey 59 H9
also known as Armutova
Gomel' Belarus see Homyel'
Gomel Oblast admin. div. Belarus see Homyel'skaya Voblasts'
Gomel'skaya Oblast' admin. div. Belarus see Homyel'skaya Voblasts'
Gómez Palacio Mex. 184 E3
Gómez Rendón Ecuador 198 A5
Gömil, Rūbār-e r. Iraq 109 O1
Gomishān Iran 100 C2
Gomo China 89 D5
Gomo Co salt l. China 89 D5
Gomorovichi Rus. Fed. 43 P1
Gomumu i. Indon. 75 C3
Gonabad Iran see Jüymand
Gonaïves Haiti 187 E3
Gonarezhou National Park Zimbabwe 131 F4
Gonbad-e Kavus Iran 100 C2
Gonda India 97 D4
Gondal India 96 A5
Gonda Libah well Eth. 128 E2
Gondar Col. 198 C5
Gondar Eth. see Gonder
Gonder Eth. 128 C1
formerly spelt Gondar
Gondey Chad 126 C2
Gondia India 96 D5
Gondomar Spain 54 C2
Gönen Turkey 106 A2
Gönen r. Turkey 59 I8
Gonfreville-l'Orcher France 50 G3
Gong'an China 87 E2
also known as Douhudi; formerly known as Doushi
Gongbalou China see Gamba
Gongbo'gyamda China 89 F6
also known as Golingka
Gongcheng China 87 D3
Gonggar China 89 E6
also known as Gyixong
Gongga Shan mt. China 86 B2
also known as Minya Konka
Gonghe China 84 D4
also known as Qabqa
Gonghe China see Mouding
Gonghui China 85 G3
Gongjiang China see Yudu
Gongliu China 88 C3
also known as Tokkuztara
Gongola r. Nigeria 125 I4
Gongolgon Australia 147 E2
Gongoué Gabon 126 A5
Gongpoquan China 84 C3
Gongquan China see Gongxian
Gongshan China 86 A3
also known as Cikai
Gongtang China see Damxung
Gongwang Shan mts China 86 B3
Gongxian China see Gongyi
Gongxian China 86 C2
also known as Gongquan
Gongyi China 87 E1
formerly known as Gongxian or Xiaoyi
Gongzhuling China 82 B4
formerly known as Huaide
Goniądz Poland 49 T2
Goniri Nigeria 125 I4
Gonjo China 86 A2
also known as Kasha
Gonjog China 89 D6
Gonnesa Sardegna Italy 57 A9
Gonnoi Greece 59 D9
Gonnosfanadiga Sardegna Italy 57 A9
Gōnoura Japan 91 A8
Gonubie S. Africa 133 M9
Gonzáles Mex. 185 F4
Gonzales CA U.S.A. 182 C5
Gonzales TX U.S.A. 179 C6
González Moreno Arg. 204 E4
Gonzalo Vásquez Panama 186 D5
Goochland U.S.A. 176 H8
Goode U.S.A. 176 F8
Goodenough, Cape Antarctica 223 I2
Goodenough Island P.N.G. 145 E2
Gooderham Canada 173 O6
Good Harbor Bay U.S.A. 172 H5
Good Hart U.S.A. 173 H5
Good Hope Botswana 133 J2
Good Hope U.S.A. 172 C10
Good Hope, Cape of S. Africa 132 C11
Good Hope Mountain Canada 166 E5
Goodland U.S.A. 178 B4
Goodman U.S.A. 172 E5
Goodooga Australia 147 E2
Goodparla Australia 148 B2
Goodrich U.S.A. 172 C5
Goodspeed Nunataks Antarctica 223 E2
Goodwood r. Canada 169 G2
Goole U.K. 47 L10
Goolgowi Australia 147 E3
Goolwa Australia 146 C3
Goomadeer r. Australia 148 B1
Goomalling Australia 151 B6
Goombalie Australia 147 E2
Goomeri Australia 149 G5
Goonda Moz. 131 G3
Goondiwindi Australia 147 F2
Goongarrie, Lake salt flat Australia 151 C6
Goongarrie National Park Australia 151 C6
Goonyella Australia 149 E4
Goorly, Lake salt flat Australia 151 B6
Goose r. Canada 169 I2
Goose r. U.S.A. 178 C2
Goose Bay Canada see Happy Valley - Goose Bay
Goose Creek U.S.A. 175 D5
Goose Creek r. U.S.A. 180 D4
Goose Green Falkland Is 205 F8
Goose Lake U.S.A. 180 B4
Goose Lake Canal r. U.S.A. 182 E6
Gooty India 94 C3
Gop India 95 E2
Gopalganj Bangl. 97 F5
Gopalganj India 97 E4
Gopeshwar India 96 C3
formerly known as Chamoli
Gopichettipalayam India 94 C4
Gopiganj India 97 D4
Göppingen Germany 48 G7
Góra Poland 49 N4
Goradiz Azer. see Horadiz
Goragorskiy Rus. Fed. 41 H8
Góra Kalwaria Poland 49 S4
Gorakhpur India 97 D4
Goražde Bos.-Herz. 56 K5
Gorbachevo Rus. Fed. 43 S8
Gorchukha Rus. Fed. 40 G4
Gorczański Park Narodowy nat. park Poland 49 R6
Gorda, Banco sea feature Hond. 186 C4
Gorda, Punta pt Nicaragua 186 C4
Gorda, Punta pt U.S.A. 180 A4
Gorda, Sierra mts Spain 54 G7
Gördalen Sweden 45 K3
Gördes Turkey 106 B3
Gordeyevka Rus. Fed. 43 M9
Gordon r. Canada 167 O1
Gordon NE U.S.A. 178 B3
Gordon WI U.S.A. 172 B4
Gordon, Isla i. Chile 205 C9
Gordon, Lake Australia 147 E5
Gordon Bay Australia 148 A1
Gordon Downs Australia 150 E3
Gordon Lake Canada 167 H2
Gordonsville U.S.A. 176 G7
Gordonvale Australia 149 E3
Goré Chad 126 C3
Gorē Eth. 128 B2
Gore N.Z. 153 C14
Gore U.S.A. 176 G6
Gore Bay Canada 173 K5
Gorelki Rus. Fed. 43 S7
Goreloye Rus. Fed. 41 G5
Gore Point U.S.A. 164 D4
Goretovo Rus. Fed. 43 Q6
Gorey Rep. of Ireland 47 F11
Gorg Iran 101 D4
Gorgān Iran 100 C2
also spelt Gurgan; formerly known as Asterabad or Astrabad; historically known as Hyrcania or Varkana
Gorgan Bay Iran 100 C2
Gorge Range hills Australia 150 B4
Gorge Range mts Australia 149 E3
Gorge Road N.Z. 153 C14
Gorges Namibia 132 B4
Gorgol admin. reg. Mauritania 124 B2
Gorgona, Isola di i. Italy 56 B5
Gorgora Eth. 128 C1
Gorgoram Nigeria 125 H3
Gorgova, Lacul l. Romania 58 K3
Gorham U.S.A. 177 N1
Gori Georgia 107 F2
Gorinchem Neth. 48 B4
Goris Armenia 107 F3
Goritsa Bulg. 58 I6
Goritsy Rus. Fed. 43 R4
Gorizia Italy 56 F3
Gorka Rus. Fed. 43 T5
Gorkhā Nepal 97 E4
Gorki Belarus see Horki
Gor'kiy Rus. Fed. see Nizhniy Novgorod
Gor'kovskaya Oblast' admin. div. Rus. Fed. see Nizhegorodskaya Oblast'
Gor'kovskoye Vodokhranilishche resr Rus. Fed. 43 V4
Gor'koye, Ozero salt l. Rus. Fed. 103 J1
Gor'koye, Ozero salt l. Rus. Fed. 103 J2
Gorlice Poland 49 S6
Görlitz Germany 49 L4
Gorlovka Ukr. see Horlivka
Gorlovo Rus. Fed. 43 U8
Gormi India 96 C4
Gorna Dzhumaya Bulg. see Blagoevgrad
Gorna Oryakhovitsa Bulg. 58 G5
Gorni Dŭbnik Bulg. 58 F5
Gornja Radgona Slovenia 56 H2
Gornja Toponica Srbija Yugo. 58 C5
Gornji Matejevac Srbija Yugo. 58 C5
Gornji Milanovac Srbija Yugo. 58 B4
Gornji Vakuf Bos.-Herz. 56 J5
also known as Uskoplje
Gorno Ablanovo Bulg. 58 G5
Gorno-Altaysk Rus. Fed. 80 D2
Gorno-Altayskaya Avtonomnaya Oblast' aut. rep. Rus. Fed. see Altay, Respublika
Gorno-Badakhshan aut. rep. Tajik. see Kŭhistoni Badakhshon
Gornopravdinsk Rus. Fed. 38 G3
Gornotrakiyska Nizina lowland Bulg. 58 G6
Gornozavodsk Rus. Fed. 40 K4
formerly known as Novopashiyskiy
Gornozavodsk Rus. Fed. 82 F3
Gornyak Rus. Fed. 88 C1
Gornyak Rus. Fed. 43 U8
Gornye Klyuchi Rus. Fed. 82 D3
Gornyy Khabarovskiy Kray Rus. Fed. 82 E2
formerly known as Solnechnyy
Gornyy Primorskiy Kray Rus. Fed. 90 C2
Gornyy Saratovskaya Oblast' Rus. Fed. 102 B2
Gornyy Altay aut. rep. Rus. Fed. see Altay, Respublika
Gornyy Badakhshan aut. rep. Tajik. see Kŭhistoni Badakhshon
Gornyy Balykley Rus. Fed. 41 H6
Goro Eth. 128 D3
Goro i. Fiji see Koro
Goroch'an mt. Eth. 128 C2
Gorodenka Ukr. see Horodenka
Gorodets Rus. Fed. 40 G4
Gorodishche Penzenskaya Oblast' Rus. Fed. 41 H5
Gorodishche Volgogradskaya Oblast' Rus. Fed. 41 H6
Gorodok Belarus see Haradok
Gorodok Belarus see Haradok
Gorodok Rus. Fed. see Zakamensk
Gorodok Ukr. see Horodok
Gorodovikovsk Rus. Fed. 41 G7
formerly known as Bashanta
Goroka P.N.G. 73 K8
Goroke Australia 146 D4
Gorokhovets Rus. Fed. 40 G4
Gorom Gorom Burkina 125 E3
Gorong, Kepulauan is Indon. 73 H7
Gorongosa Moz. 131 G3
formerly known as Vila Paiva de Andrada
Gorongosa mt. Moz. 131 G3
Gorongosa, Parque Nacional de nat. park Moz. 131 G3
Gorontalo Indon. 75 E2
Goronyo Nigeria 125 G3
Goroubi watercourse Niger 125 F3
Gorouol r. Burkina/Niger 125 F3
Górowo Iławeckie Poland 49 R1
Gorshechnoye Rus. Fed. 41 F6
Gór Stołowych, Park Narodowy nat. park Poland 49 N5
Goru, Vârful mt. Romania 58 H3
Görükle Turkey 59 J8
Gorumna Island Rep. of Ireland 47 C10
Gorutuba r. Brazil 207 J2
Goryachiy Klyuch Rus. Fed. 41 F7
Górzno Poland 49 Q2
Gorzów Wielkopolski Poland 49 M3
historically known as Landsberg
Gosainthan mt. China see Xixabangma Feng
Goschen Strait P.N.G. 149 F1
Gosford Australia 147 F3
Goshen CA U.S.A. 182 E5
Goshen IN U.S.A. 174 C3
Goshen NH U.S.A. 177 M2
Goshen NY U.S.A. 177 K4
Goshen VA U.S.A. 176 F8
Goshoba Turkm. see Koshoba
Goshogawara Japan 90 G4
Goslar Germany 48 H4
Gospić Croatia 56 H4
Gossas Senegal 124 A3
Gosse watercourse Australia 148 B3
Gossi Mali 125 E3
Gossinga Sudan 126 E2
Gostivar Macedonia 58 B7
Gostyń Poland 49 O4
Gostynin Poland 49 Q3
Gosu China 86 A1
Gota Eth. 128 D2
Götaälven r. Sweden 45 J4
Göteborg Sweden see Gothenburg
Gotel Mountains Cameroon/Nigeria 125 H5
Gotemba Japan see Gotenba
Gotenba Japan 91 F7
also spelt Gotemba
Götene Sweden 45 K4
Gotenhafen Poland see Gdynia
Gotha Germany 48 H5
Gothem Sweden 45 L4
Gothenburg Sweden 45 J4
also spelt Göteborg
Gothenburg U.S.A. 178 B3
Gothèye Niger 125 F3
Gotland i. Sweden 45 L4
Gotō-rettō is Japan 91 A8
Gotse Delchev Bulg. 58 E7
Gotska Sandön Sweden 45 L4
Gotska Sandön i. Sweden 45 L4
Gōtsu Japan 91 C7
Gottero, Monte mt. Italy 56 B4
Göttingen Germany 48 G4
Gottne Sweden 44 L3
Gott Peak Canada 166 F5
Gottwaldov Czech Rep. see Zlín
Gotval'd Ukr. see Zmiyiv
Gouako Cent. Afr. Rep. 126 D3
Gouda Neth. 48 B3
Gouda S. Africa 132 D10
Goudiri Senegal 124 B3
Goudoumaria Niger 125 H3
Goudreau Canada 173 I2
Gouéké Guinea 124 C4
Goûgaram Niger 125 G2

▶Gough Island S. Atlantic Ocean 217 N8
Dependency of St Helena.

Gouin, Réservoir Canada 169 F3
Goukamma Nature Reserve S. Africa 132 G11
Goulais River Canada 173 I4
Goulburn Australia 147 F3
Goulburn r. Australia 147 E4
Goulburn Islands Australia 148 B1
Goulburn River National Park Australia 147 F3
Gould, Mount hill Australia 151 B5
Gould City U.S.A. 172 H4
Gould Coast Antarctica 223 O1
Goulféy Cameroon 125 I3
Goulia Côte d'Ivoire 124 D4
Goulou atoll Micronesia see Ngulu
Goumbou Mali 124 D3
Goumenissa Greece 58 D8
Gouna Cameroon 125 I4
Goundam Mali 124 E2
Goundi Chad 126 C2
Gounou-Gaya Chad 126 B2
Gouraya Alg. 55 M8
Gouraye Mauritania 124 B3
Gourcy Burkina 124 E3
Gourdon France 50 H8
Gouré Niger 125 H3
Gourin France 50 C4
Gouripur Bangl. 97 F4
Gourits r. S. Africa 132 F11
Gourlay Lake Canada 173 I2
Gourma-Rharous Mali 125 E2
Goûrmél well Mauritania 124 C2
Gourmeur well Chad 120 D5
Gournay-en-Bray France 50 H3
Gouro Chad 120 C5
Goûr Oulad Ahmed reg. Mali 122 D5
Gourouro well Chad 120 D5
Goussainville France 51 I3
Gouvêa Brazil 207 J5
Gouveia Port. 54 D4
Gouverneur U.S.A. 177 J1
Gove U.S.A. 178 B4
Gove, Barragem do resr Angola 127 B8
Govedartsi Bulg. 58 E6
Govena, Mys hd Rus. Fed. 39 Q4
Gove Peninsula Australia 148 C2
Governador Valadares Brazil 203 D6
Governor Generoso Phil. 74 C5
Governor's Harbour Bahamas 186 D1
Govi-Altay prov. Mongolia 84 B2
Govi Altayn Nuruu mts Mongolia 84 C2
Govind Ballash Pant Sagar resr India 97 D4
Govindgarh India 97 D4
Govind Sagar resr India 96 C3
Govurdak Turkm. 103 F5
also spelt Gowurdak; formerly spelt Gaurdak
Gowanbridge N.Z. 153 G9
Gowanda U.S.A. 176 G3
Gowan Range hills Australia 149 E5
Gowd-e Aḥmar Iran 100 C4
Gowdeh, Rūd-e watercourse Iran 100 C5
Gowd-e Hasht Tekkeh waterhole Iran 100 D3
Gowganda Canada 173 M3
Gowganda Lake Canada 173 M3
Gowmal Kalay Afgh. 101 G3
Gowurdak Turkm. see Govurdak
Goya Arg. 204 F3
Göyçay Azer. 107 F2
Goyder r. Australia 148 B2
Goyder watercourse Australia 148 B5
Goyder Lagoon salt flat Australia 146 C1
Goymatdag hills Turkm. see Koymatdag, Gory
Göynük Antalya Turkey 108 B1
Göynük Bingöl Turkey 107 E3
also known as Oğnut
Göynük Bolu Turkey 106 B2
Göynükbelen Turkey 59 K9
Goyō-san mt. Japan 90 G5
Göytäpä Azer. 107 G3
Gözareh Afgh. 101 E3
Goz-Beïda Chad 120 D6
Gözcüler Turkey 108 G1
Gözene Turkey 107 D3
Gozha Co salt l. China 89 C5
Gözne Turkey 108 F1
Gozo i. Malta 57 G12
also known as Ghawdex
Goz Regeb Sudan 121 G5
Graaf-Reinet S. Africa 133 I9
Graafwater S. Africa 132 C9
Grabia r. Poland 49 P4
Grabo Côte d'Ivoire 124 D5
Grabouw S. Africa 132 D11
Grabovica Srbija Yugo 58 D4
Grabovo Kazakh. 103 H1
Grabow Germany 48 I2
Grabowa r. Poland 49 N1
Grabów nad Prosną Poland 49 P4
Gračac Croatia 56 H4
Gračanica Bos.-Herz. 56 K4
Gračanica Jezero l. Yugo. 58 A6
Graçay France 50 H5
Grace, Lake salt flat Australia 151 B7
Gracefield Canada 168 E4
Gracemere Australia 149 F4
Grachevka Rus. Fed. 102 C1
Grachi Kazakh. 103 I2
Gracias Hond. 186 A4
Gradačac Bos.-Herz. 56 K4
Gradaús Brazil 202 B3
Gradaús, Serra dos hills Brazil 202 B4
Gradets Bulg. 58 H6
Gradignan France 50 F8
Gradishte hill Bulg. 58 F6
Gradiška Bos.-Herz. see Bosanska Gradiška
Gradište Croatia 56 K3
Grădiștea Romania 58 H4
Grado Italy 56 F3
Grado Spain 54 E1
Grady U.S.A. 179 B5
Gräfenhainichen Germany 49 J4
Gräftåvallen Sweden 44 K3
Grafton Australia 147 G2
Grafton ND U.S.A. 178 C1
Grafton WI U.S.A. 172 F7
Grafton WV U.S.A. 176 E6
Grafton, Cape Australia 149 E3
Grafton, Mount U.S.A. 183 J3
Grafton Passage Australia 149 E3
Graham NC U.S.A. 176 F9
Graham TX U.S.A. 179 C5
Graham, Mount U.S.A. 183 O9
Graham Bell Island Rus. Fed. see Greem-Bell, Ostrov
Graham Island B.C. Canada 166 C4
Graham Island Nunavut Canada 165 J2
Graham Lake U.S.A. 177 Q1
Graham Land reg. Antarctica 222 T2
Graham Moore, Cape Canada 165 L2
Grahamstown S. Africa 133 K10
Graiguenamanagh Rep. of Ireland 47 F11
Grajagan Indon. 77 F5
Grajaú Brazil 202 C3
Grajaú r. Brazil 202 C2
Grajewo Poland 49 T2
Gram Denmark 45 J5
Gramada mt. Yugo. 58 D6
Gramat France 50 H8
Gramatikovo Bulg. 58 I6
Grammichele Sicilia Italy 57 G11
Grámmos mt. Greece 59 B8
Grammos mt. Albania/Greece 59 B8
Grampian U.S.A. 176 G5
Grampian Mountains U.K. 46 H7
Grampians, The mts Australia 147 D4
Grampians National Park Australia 147 D4
Gramsh Albania 58 B8
Gran Hungary see Esztergom
Granaatboskolk S. Africa 132 D7
Granada Col. 198 C4
Granada Nicaragua 186 B5
Granada Spain 55 H7
Granado hill Spain 54 D7
Gran Altiplanicie Central plain Arg. 205 C8
Granard Rep. of Ireland 47 E10
Gran Bajo San Julián valley Arg. 205 C8
Gran Bajo depr. Arg. 205 D7
Gran Bajo Salitroso salt flat Arg. 204 D5
Granbury U.S.A. 179 C5
Granby Canada 169 F4
Granby U.S.A. 180 F4
Gran Canaria i. Canary Is 122 B4
English form Grand Canary
Gran Chaco reg. Arg./Para. 201 E6
Grand r. MO U.S.A. 178 D3
Grand r. SD U.S.A. 178 B2
Grand, North Fork r. U.S.A. 178 B2
Grand, South Fork r. U.S.A. 178 B2
Grandas Spain 54 E1
Grand Atlas mts Morocco see Haut Atlas
Grand Bahama i. Bahamas 186 D1
Grand Bank Canada 169 K4
Grand-Bassam Côte d'Ivoire 124 E5
Grand Bay Canada 169 H4
Grand Bay U.S.A. 175 B6
Grand Bend Canada 168 D5
Grand Bérard mt. France 51 M8
Grand Bourg Guadeloupe 187 H4
Grand Caicos i. Turks and Caicos Is 187 F2
Grand Canal China see Da Yunhe
Grand Canal Rep. of Ireland 47 E10
Grand Canary i. Canary Is see Gran Canaria
Grand Canyon U.S.A. 183 L5
▶Grand Canyon gorge U.S.A. 183 L5
world [land images] ▶▶▶ 12–13
northamerica [landscapes] ▶▶▶ 156–157
Grand Canyon National Park U.S.A. 183 L5
Grand Cayman i. Cayman Is 186 C3
Grand Centre Canada 167 I4
Grand Combin mt. Switz. 51 N7
Grand Detour U.S.A. 172 D9
Grande r. Arg. 204 C5
Grande r. Santa Cruz Bol. 201 E4
Grande r. Santa Cruz Bol. 201 E4
also known as Guapay
Grande r. Bahia Brazil 202 D4
Grande r. São Paulo Brazil 206 C7
Grande r. Peru 200 B3
Grande, Bahía b. Arg. 205 C8
Grande, Cayo i. Cuba 186 D2
Grande, Cerro mt. Mex. 185 F5
Grande, Ciénaga lag. Col. 198 C2
Grande, Ilha i. Brazil 203 C7
Grande, Serra hills Brazil 201 E2
Grande, Serra mt. Brazil 199 F4
also known as Carauná
Grande Cache Canada 166 G4
Grande Comore i. Comoros see Njazidja
Grande de Manacapuru, Lago l. Brazil 199 F5
Grande-Entree Canada 169 I4
Grande Leyre r. France 50 F8
Grande Prairie Canada 166 G4
Grand Erg de Bilma des. Niger 125 I2
Grand Erg Occidental des. Alg. 123 E3
English form Great Western Erg
Grand Erg Oriental des. Alg. 123 G3
English form Great Eastern Erg
Grande-Rivière Canada 169 H3
Grande Ronde r. U.S.A. 180 C3
Grandes, Salinas salt marsh Arg. 200 D5
Grandes, Salinas salt marsh Arg. 204 D3
Gran Desierto del Pinacate, Parque Natural del nature res. Mex. 184 B2
Grande-Terre i. Guadeloupe 187 H3
Grande Terre i. Mayotte 129 E8
Grande Tête de l'Obiou mt. France 51 L8
Grande-Vallée Canada 169 H3
Grand Falls N.B. Canada 169 H4
Grand Falls Nfld. Canada 169 K3
Grandfather Mountain U.S.A. 176 D9
Grand Forks Canada 166 G5
Grand Forks U.S.A. 178 C2
Grand-Fougeray France 50 E5
Grand Gorge U.S.A. 177 K3
Grand Gosier Haiti 187 E3
Grand Harbour Canada 169 H4
Grand Haven U.S.A. 172 G7
Grandin, Lac l. Canada 167 G1
Grand Island U.S.A. 178 C3
Grand Island i. U.S.A. 172 G4
Grand Isle U.S.A. 175 B6
Grand Junction CO U.S.A. 183 P2
Grand Junction MI U.S.A. 172 G8
Grand-Lahou Côte d'Ivoire 124 D5
Grand Lake N.B. Canada 169 H4
Grand Lake Nfld. Canada 169 I2
Grand Lake Nfld. Canada 169 J3
Grand Lake LA U.S.A. 179 D6
Grand Lake LA U.S.A. 179 E6
Grand Lake MI U.S.A. 173 J5
Grand Lake St Marys U.S.A. 176 A5
Grand Ledge U.S.A. 173 I8
Grand Manan Island Canada 169 H4
Grand Marais MI U.S.A. 172 H4
Grand Marais MN U.S.A. 174 B2
Grand Marsh U.S.A. 172 D7
Grand-Mère Canada 169 F4
Grândola Port. 54 C6
Grândola, Serra de mts Port. 54 C6
Grand Pacific Glacier Canada 166 B3
Grand Passage New Caledonia 145 F3
Grand Rapids Canada 167 L4
Grand Rapids MI U.S.A. 172 H8
Grand Rapids MN U.S.A. 174 A2
Grand Récif de Cook reef New Caledonia 145 F3
Grand Récif du Sud reef New Caledonia 145 F4
Grand St Bernard, Col du pass Italy/Switz. see Great St Bernard Pass
Grand Santi Fr. Guiana 199 H3
Grand Teton mt. U.S.A. 180 E4
Grand Teton National Park U.S.A. 180 E4
Grand Traverse Bay U.S.A. 172 H6

▶Grand Turk Turks and Caicos Is 187 F2
Capital of the Turks and Caicos Islands. Also known as Cockburn Town.

Grand Turk i. Turks and Caicos Is 187 F2
Grand Valley Swaziland 133 P3
Grand View U.S.A. 172 B4
Grandville U.S.A. 172 H8
Grandvilliers France 51 H3
Grand Wash watercourse U.S.A. 183 J5
Grand Wash Cliffs mts U.S.A. 183 J6
Grañén Spain 55 K3
Graneros Chile 204 C4
Granger U.S.A. 180 E4
Grängesberg Sweden 45 K3
Grangeville U.S.A. 180 C3
Granhult Sweden 44 M2
Granisle Canada 166 E4
Granite City U.S.A. 174 B4
Granite Falls U.S.A. 178 D2
Granite Mountain U.S.A. 182 G1
Granite Mountains CA U.S.A. 183 I7
Granite Mountains CA U.S.A. 183 I8
Granite Peak MT U.S.A. 180 E3
Granite Peak UT U.S.A. 183 K1
Granite Range mts U.S.A. 182 E1
Granitogorsk Kazakh. 103 H4
Granitola, Capo c. Sicilia Italy 57 E11
Granity N.Z. 153 F9
Granja Brazil 202 D2
Gran Laguna Salada l. Arg. 205 D7
Gran Morelos Mex. 181 F7
Granollers Spain 55 N3
Gran Pajonal plain Peru 200 B2
Gran Paradiso mt. Italy 51 N7
Gran Paradiso, Parco Nazionale del nat. park Italy 51 N7
Gran Pilastro mt. Austria/Italy 48 I9
also known as Hochfeiler
Gran San Bernardo, Colle del pass Italy/Switz. see Great St Bernard Pass
Gran Sasso d'Italia mts Italy 56 F6
Gran Sasso e Monti della Laga, Parco Nazionale del nat. park Italy 56 F6
Gransee Germany 49 K2
Grant U.S.A. 178 B3
Grant, Mount NV U.S.A. 182 F3
Grant, Mount NV U.S.A. 182 G2
Grant City U.S.A. 178 D3
Grantham U.K. 47 L11
Grant Island Antarctica 222 P2
Grant Lake Canada 167 G1
Granton U.S.A. 172 C6
Grantown-on-Spey U.K. 46 I6
Grant Park U.S.A. 172 F9
Grant Range mts U.S.A. 183 I3
Grants U.S.A. 181 F6
Grantsburg U.S.A. 172 A5
Grants Pass U.S.A. 180 B4
Grantsville U.S.A. 183 L1
Granville Canada 166 B2
Granville France 50 E4
Granville AZ U.S.A. 183 O8
Granville IL U.S.A. 172 D9
Granville NY U.S.A. 177 L2
Granville OH U.S.A. 176 C5
Granville Lake Canada 167 K3

Granvin Norway 45 I3
Grão Mogol Brazil 202 D6
Grapevine Mountains U.S.A. 183 G5
Gras, Lac de i. Canada 167 I1
Graskop S. Africa 133 O1
Gräsö i. Sweden 45 L3
Grasplatz Namibia 130 B5
Grass r. Canada 167 L3
Grass r. U.S.A. 177 K1
Grasse France 51 M9
Grassflat U.S.A. 176 G4
Grass Lake U.S.A. 173 I8
Grasslands National Park Canada 167 J5
Grass Patch Australia 151 C7
Grassrange U.S.A. 180 E3
Grassridgedam r. S. Africa 133 J8
Grass River Provincial Park Canada 167 K4
Grass Valley U.S.A. 182 C2
Grassy Australia 147 E5
Grassy Creek r. Bahamas 186 D2
Grästorp Sweden 45 H4
Gratiot U.S.A. 172 C8
Gratkorn Austria 49 M8
Graudenz Poland see Grudziądz
Graulhet France 51 H9
Graus Spain 55 L2
Gravata Brazil 202 F4
Gravataí Brazil 203 B9
Gravdal Norway 44 K1
Grave, Pointe de pt France 50 E7
Gravelbourg Canada 167 J5
Gravenhurst Canada 168 E4
Grave Peak U.S.A. 180 D3
Gräveri Latvia 42 I5
Gravesend Australia 147 F2
Gravette U.S.A. 179 D4
Gravina in Puglia Italy 57 I8
Gravina Island U.S.A. 166 D4
Gravois, Pointe-à- pt Haiti 187 E3
Grawn U.S.A. 172 H6
Gray France 51 L5
Gray GA U.S.A. 175 D5
Gray KY U.S.A. 176 A9
Gray ME U.S.A. 177 O2
Gray TN U.S.A. 176 C9
Grayback Mountain U.S.A. 180 B4
Gray Lake Canada 167 I2
Grayling r. Canada 166 E3
Grayling U.S.A. 173 I6
Grays Harbor inlet U.S.A. 180 A3
Grays Lake U.S.A. 180 E4
Grayville U.S.A. 174 B4
Graz Austria 49 M8
Grdelica Srbija Yugo. 58 D6
Greasy Lake Canada 166 F2
Great Abaco i. Bahamas 186 D1
Great Australian Bight g. Australia 146 A3
Great Bahama Bank sea feature Bahamas 186 D1
Great Barrier Island N.Z. 152 J4

▶ Great Barrier Reef Australia 146 E1
oceania [landscapes] ⇒ 136-137
oceania [features] ⇒ 142-143

Great Barrier Reef Marine Park (Cairns Section) Australia 149 E3
Great Barrier Reef Marine Park (Capricorn Section) Australia 149 F4
Great Barrier Reef Marine Park (Central Section) Australia 149 F3
Great Barrier Reef Marine Park (Far North Section) Australia 149 E2
Great Barrington U.S.A. 177 L3
Great Basalt Wall National Park Australia 149 E3
Great Basin U.S.A. 183 H2
Great Basin National Park U.S.A. 183 J3
Great Bear r. Canada 166 E1

▶ Great Bear Lake Canada 166 F1
4th largest lake in North America and 8th in the world.
northamerica [landscapes] ⇒ 156-157

Great Belt sea chan. Denmark 45 J5
also known as Store Bælt
Great Bend KS U.S.A. 178 C4
Great Bend PA U.S.A. 177 J4
Great Bitter Lake Egypt 121 G2
also known as Buheirat-Murrat-el-Kubra, Buheirat
Great Blasket Island Rep. of Ireland 47 B11

▶ Great Britain i. U.K. 47 J9
Largest island in Europe and 8th in the world.
europe [landscapes] ⇒ 30-31

Great Coco Island Cocos Is 79 A5
Great Dismal Swamp National Wildlife Refuge nature res. U.S.A. 177 I9
Great Dividing Range mts Australia 145 D5
Great Driffield U.K. 47 L9
Great Duck Island Canada 173 K5
Great Eastern Erg des. Alg. see Grand Erg Oriental
Great Egg Harbor Inlet U.S.A. 177 K6
Greater Accra admin. reg. Ghana 125 F5
Greater Antilles is Caribbean Sea 171 J7
Greater Khingan Mountains China see Da Hinggan Ling
Greater Tunb i. The Gulf 105 F2
also known as Tonb-e Bozorg, Jazireh-ye or Tunb al Kubra
Great Exhibition Bay N.Z. 152 H2
Great Exuma i. Bahamas 186 E2

Great Falls U.S.A. 180 E3
Great Fish r. S. Africa 133 L10
Greatford N.Z. 152 J8
Great Gandak r. India 97 E4
Great Ganges atoll Cook Is see Manihiki
Great Guana Cay i. Bahamas 186 D1
Great Harbour Cay i. Bahamas 186 D1
Great Inagua i. Bahamas 187 E2
Great Karoo plat. S. Africa 132 H9
also known as Karroo
Great Kei r. S. Africa 133 M9
Great Lake Australia 147 E5

▶ Great Lakes Canada/U.S.A. 172
Consist of Lakes Erie, Huron, Michigan, Ontario and Superior.

Great Mercury Island N.Z. 152 J4
Great Miami r. U.S.A. 176 A6
Great Namaqualand reg. Namibia 130 C5
Great Nicobar i. India 95 G5
Great North East Channel Australia/P.N.G. 144 D2
Great Ouse r. U.K. 47 M11
Great Oyster Bay Australia 147 F5
Great Palm Island Australia 149 E3
Great Peconic Bay U.S.A. 177 M5
Great Plain of the Koukdjuak Canada 165 L3
Great Plains U.S.A. 178 B3
Great Point U.S.A. 177 O4
Great Rift Valley Africa 128 C5
Great Ruaha r. Tanz. 129 C6
Great Sacandaga Lake U.S.A. 177 K2
Great St Bernard Pass Italy/Switz. 51 N7
also known as Grand St Bernard, Col du or Gran San Bernardo, Colle del
Great Salt Lake U.S.A. 183 L1
Great Salt Lake Desert U.S.A. 183 K1
Great Sand Hills Canada 167 I5
Great Sand Sea des. Egypt/Libya 120 E2
Great Sandy Desert Australia 150 C4
Great Sandy Island Australia see Fraser Island
Great Sandy Island Nature Reserve Australia 150 A4
Great Sea Reef Fiji 145 G3

▶ Great Slave Lake Canada 167 H2
Deepest and 5th largest lake in North America.
northamerica [landscapes] ⇒ 156-157

Great Smoky Mountains U.S.A. 174 C5
Great Smoky Mountains National Park U.S.A. 174 D5
Great Snow Mountain Canada 166 E3
Great South Bay U.S.A. 177 L5
Great Usutu r. Africa see Usutu
Great Victoria Desert Australia 151 E6
Great Victoria Desert Conservation Park nature res. Australia 146 A2
Great Victoria Desert Nature Reserve Australia 151 E6
Great Wall research station Antarctica 222 U2
also known as Chang Cheng
▶ Great Wall tourist site China 85 H3
also known as Wan-li-ch'ang-ch'eng or Grand Western Erg
Great Western Erg des. Alg. see Grand Erg Occidental
Great West Torres Islands Myanmar 79 B6
Great Winterhoek S. Africa 132 D10
Great Yarmouth U.K. 47 N11
short form Yarmouth
Great Zab r. Iraq see Zāb al Kabīr, Nahr az
Great Zimbabwe National Monument tourist site Zimbabwe 131 F4
short form Zimbabwe
Grebbestad Sweden 45 J4
Grebenkovskiy Ukr. see Hrebinka
Grebnevo Rus. Fed. 43 U7
Grebyonka Ukr. see Hrebinka
Greci, Vârful hill Romania 58 J3
Greco, Cape Cyprus see Greko, Cape
Greco, Monte mt. Italy 56 H7
Gredos, Sierra de mts Spain 54 F4
Greece Chile 205 C9
▶ Greece country Europe 59 C10
known as Ellas in Greek; historically known as Hellas
europe [countries] ⇒ 32-35
Greece U.S.A. 176 H2
Greeley U.S.A. 180 F4
Greely Center U.S.A. 178 C3
Greely Fiord inlet Canada 165 K1
Greem-Bell, Ostrov i. Rus. Fed. 39 G1
English form Graham Bell Island
Green r. Canada 171 M2
Green r. KY U.S.A. 174 B5
Green r. ND U.S.A. 178 B2
Green r. WY U.S.A. 183 O3
Green Bay U.S.A. 172 E6
Green Bay b. U.S.A. 172 F5
Greenbrier r. U.S.A. 176 E8
Greenbushes Australia 151 B7
Greencastle Bahamas 175 E7
Greencastle IN U.S.A. 174 C4
Greencastle PA U.S.A. 176 H6
Green Cove Springs U.S.A. 175 D6
Greendale IN U.S.A. 176 A6
Greendale KY U.S.A. 176 A7
Greene ME U.S.A. 177 O1
Greene NY U.S.A. 177 J3
Greeneville U.S.A. 176 C9
Greenfield CA U.S.A. 182 C5
Greenfield IA U.S.A. 178 D3
Greenfield IN U.S.A. 174 C4
Greenfield MA U.S.A. 177 M3
Greenfield MO U.S.A. 178 D4
Greenfield OH U.S.A. 176 B6
Greenfield WI U.S.A. 172 D8
Great Head Australia 151 A8
Greenhill Island Australia 148 B1
Greenhills N.Z. 153 C14
Greening Canada 173 S2
Green Island i. Taiwan see Lü Tao
Green Island U.S.A. 172 C8
Green Island Bay Phil. 74 A4
Green Islands P.N.G. 145 E2
Green Lake Canada 167 J4
Green Lake l. Canada 166 F3
Green Lake U.S.A. 172 E7
▶ Greenland terr. N. America 165 O2
Self-governing Danish Territory. Largest island in the world and in North America. 3rd largest political entity in North America. Known as Grønland in Danish or Kalaallit Nunaat in Greenlandic.
world [physical features] ⇒ 8-9
world [land images] ⇒ 12-13
oceania [countries] ⇒ 138-139
northamerica [environments] ⇒ 162-163

Greenland U.S.A. 172 D4
Greenly Island Australia 146 B3
Green Mountains U.S.A. 177 M1
Greenock U.K. 46 H8
Greenough r. Australia 151 A6
Greenough U.S.A. 177 M4
Greenport U.S.A. 177 M5
Green River WY U.S.A. 180 E4
Greensboro AL U.S.A. 175 C5
Greensboro MD U.S.A. 177 J7
Greensboro NC U.S.A. 176 F9
Greensburg IN U.S.A. 174 C4
Greensburg KS U.S.A. 178 C4
Greensburg KY U.S.A. 174 C5
Greensburg LA U.S.A. 175 B6
Greensburg PA U.S.A. 176 F5
Greens Peak U.S.A. 183 O7
Green Swamp U.S.A. 175 E5
Greenup IL U.S.A. 174 B4
Greenup KY U.S.A. 176 C7
Green Valley U.S.A. 181 E7
Greenville Canada 166 D4
Greenville Liberia 124 C5
Greenville AL U.S.A. 175 C6
Greenville CA U.S.A. 182 D1
Greenville IL U.S.A. 174 C4
Greenville KY U.S.A. 174 C5
Greenville ME U.S.A. 174 G2
Greenville MI U.S.A. 172 H7
Greenville MO U.S.A. 174 B4
Greenville MS U.S.A. 175 B5
Greenville NC U.S.A. 174 E5
Greenville NH U.S.A. 177 N3
Greenville OH U.S.A. 176 A5
Greenville PA U.S.A. 176 E4
Greenville SC U.S.A. 174 D5
Greenville TX U.S.A. 179 C5
Greenwater Lake Canada 172 C2
Greenwater Provincial Park Canada 167 K4
Greenwich atoll Micronesia see Kapingamarangi
Greenwich CT U.S.A. 177 L4
Greenwich NY U.S.A. 177 L2
Greenwich OH U.S.A. 176 C4
Greenwood AR U.S.A. 179 D5
Greenwood IN U.S.A. 174 C4
Greenwood MS U.S.A. 175 B5
Greenwood SC U.S.A. 175 D5
Greenwood WI U.S.A. 172 C6
Greer U.S.A. 174 D5
Greers Ferry Lake U.S.A. 179 D5
Gregório r. Brazil 198 D6
Gregory r. Australia 148 C3
Gregory MI U.S.A. 173 I8
Gregory SD U.S.A. 178 C3
Gregory, Lake salt flat S.A. Australia 146 C2
Gregory, Lake salt flat W.A. Australia 150 D4
Gregory, Lake salt flat W.A. Australia 150 C4
Gregory Downs Australia 148 C3
Gregory National Park Australia 148 A3
Gregory Range hills Qld Australia 149 D3
Gregory Range hills W.A. Australia 150 C4
Greifswald Germany 49 K1
Greifswalder Bodden b. Germany 49 K1
Greifswalder Oie i. Germany 49 K1
Greiz Germany 49 J5
Greko, Cape Cyprus 108 F3
also spelt Greco, Cape
Gremikha Rus. Fed. 40 F1
Gremyachev Rus. Fed. 43 T7
Gremyachinsk Rus. Fed. 40 L4
Gremyachinsk Rus. Fed. 81 H2
Grená Denmark 45 J4
Grenada i. U.S. 175 B5
▶ Grenada country West Indies 187 H4
northamerica [countries] ⇒ 158-159
Grenade France 50 H9
Grenade-sur-l'Adour France 50 F9
Grenchen Switz. 51 N5
Grenen spit Denmark 45 J4
English form The Skaw
Grenfell Australia 147 F3
Grenfell Canada 167 K5
Grenoble France 51 L7
Grense-Jakobselv Norway 44 O1
Grenville, Cape Australia 149 D1
Grenville Grenada 187 H4
Grenville Island Fiji see Rotuma
Greshak Pak. 101 F5
Gresham U.S.A. 180 B3
Gresik Indon. 77 F4
Gressåmoen Nasjonalpark nat. park Norway 44 K2
Gretna LA U.S.A. 175 B6
Gretna VA U.S.A. 176 F9
Grevelingen sea chan. Neth. 48 A4
Greven Germany 48 E3
Grevena Greece 58 C8
Grevenbroich Germany 48 D4
Grevenmacher Lux. 51 H4
Grevesmühlen Germany 48 I2
Grey r. Canada 169 J4
Grey r. N.Z. 153 F10
Grey, Cape Australia 148 C2
Greybull U.S.A. 180 E3
Greybull r. U.S.A. 180 E3
Grey Hunter Peak Canada 166 C2
Grey Islands Canada 169 K3
Greylock, Mount U.S.A. 177 L3
Grey's Plains Australia 151 A5
Grey Range hills Australia 147 D2
Greystone Zimbabwe 131 F4
Greytown S. Africa 133 O6
Greytown U.S.A. 173 I3
Grez-Doiceau Belgium 51 K2
Gria, Akra pt Greece 59 H11
Gribanovskiy Rus. Fed. 41 G6
Gribingui r. Cent. Afr. Rep. 126 C3
Gribingui-Bamingui, Réserve de Faune du nature res. Cent. Afr. Rep. 126 C3
Gridley CA U.S.A. 182 C2
Gridley IL U.S.A. 172 E10
Grieskirchen Austria 49 K7
Griffin U.S.A. 175 C5
Griffith Australia 147 E3
Griffith Canada 173 P5
Grígiškės Lith. 42 G7
Grignols France 50 F8
Grigoriopol Moldova 58 K1
Grik Malaysia see Gerik
Grim, Cape Australia 147 E5
Grimari Cent. Afr. Rep. 126 D3
Grimma Germany 49 J4

Grimmen Germany 49 K1
Grimsby Canada 173 N7
Grimsby U.K. 47 L10
Grímsey i. Iceland 44 [inset] C2
Grimshaw Canada 167 G3
Grimstad Norway 45 J4
Grindaheim Norway 45 J3
Grindavík Iceland 44 [inset] B3
Grindu Romania 58 H4
Grindu Romania 58 J4
Grindul Chituc spit Romania 58 J4
Grindușu, Vârful mt. Romania 58 H2
Grinevo Rus. Fed. 43 O9
Grinnell U.S.A. 174 A3
Grinnell Peninsula Canada 165 J2
Grintjes Romania 58 G3
Grintovec mt. Slovenia 56 G2
Griqualand East reg. S. Africa 133 N7
Griqualand West reg. S. Africa 132 H5
Griquatown S. Africa 132 H5
Grise Fiord Canada 165 K2
Grishino Ukr. see Krasnoarmiys'k
Grisik Indon. 76 C3
Gris Nez, Cap c. France 50 H1
Grisolles France 50 H9
Grisslehamn Sweden 45 L3
Gritley U.K. 46 J5
Grizim well Alg. 123 C4
Grizzly Bear Mountain hill Canada 166 F1
Grmeč mts Bos.-Herz. 56 I4
Groais Island Canada 169 K3
Grobbendonk Belgium 51 K1
Grobiņa Latvia 42 C5
Groblersdal S. Africa 133 N2
Groblershoop S. Africa 132 G5
Gröbming Austria 49 K8
Grocka Srbija Yugo. 58 B4
Grodekovo Rus. Fed. 82 C3
Grodków Poland 49 O5
Grodno Belarus see Hrodna
Grodnenskaya Oblast' admin. div. Belarus see Hrodzyenskaya Voblasts'
Grodno Oblast admin. div. Belarus see Hrodzyenskaya Voblasts'
Grodzisk Mazowiecki Poland 49 R3
Grodzisk Wielkopolski Poland 49 N3
Groen watercourse N. Cape S. Africa 132 C7
Groen watercourse W. Cape/W. Cape S. Africa 132 E7
Groesbeck U.S.A. 179 C6
Gróf Iceland 44 [inset] B2
Groganville Australia 149 E3
Groix, Île de i. France 50 C5
Grójec Poland 49 R4
Grombalia Tunisia 57 C12
Grömitz Germany 48 H1
Gronau (Westfalen) Germany 48 E3
Grong Norway 44 K2
Groningen Neth. 48 D2
Groningen Suriname 199 H3
Grønland terr. N. America see Greenland
Grønnedal Greenland see Kangilinnguit
Groom Lake U.S.A. 183 I4
Groot r. E. Cape S. Africa 132 I10
Groot r. W. Cape S. Africa 132 D9
Groot r. W. Cape S. Africa 132 F10
Groot-Aar Pan salt pan S. Africa 132 E4
Groot Berg r. S. Africa 132 C9
Groot Brak r. S. Africa 133 C8
Grootdraaidam dam S. Africa 133 N3
Grootdrink S. Africa 132 F5
Groote Eylandt i. Australia 148 C2
Groote Eylandt Aboriginal Land res. Australia 148 C2
Grootfontein Namibia 130 C3
Groot-Grannapan salt pan S. Africa 133 J5
Groot Karas Berg plat. Namibia 130 C5
Groot Letaba r. S. Africa 131 F4
Grootmis S. Africa 132 B6
Grootpan S. Africa 133 J3
Grootrivierhoogte mts S. Africa 132 H10
Groot Swartberge mts S. Africa 132 F10
Grootvaalgraspan salt pan Namibia 132 C3
Grootvloer salt pan S. Africa 132 E6
Groot Winterberg mt. S. Africa 133 K9
Groot-Winterhoekberge mts S. Africa 133 I10
Gropeni Romania 58 I4
Grosa, Isla i. Spain 55 K7
Gros Islet St Lucia 187 H4
Gros Morne National Park Canada 169 J3
Grosne r. France 51 K6
Gross Barmen Namibia 130 C4
Großenhain Germany 49 K4
Großenkneten Germany 48 F3
Großenlüder Germany 48 G5
Großer Arber mt. Germany 49 K6
Großer Beerberg hill Germany 48 H5
Grösser Bösenstein mt. Austria 49 L8
Grosser Priel mt. Austria 49 L8
Großer Rachel mt. Germany 49 K7
Grosser Speikkofel mt. Austria 49 K9
Grosser Speikkogel mt. Austria 49 L9
Grosseto Italy 56 D6
Groß-Gerau Germany 48 F6
Großglockner mt. Austria 49 J8
Groß-Hesepe Germany 48 E3
Großräschen Germany 49 K4
Großrischen Germany 49 K3
Groß Schönebeck Germany 49 K3
Groß Uns Namibia 130 C4
Großvenediger mt. Austria 49 J8
Grosuplje Slovenia 56 G3
Grosvenor Mountains Antarctica 223 L1
Gros Ventre Range mts U.S.A. 180 E4
Groswater Bay Canada 169 J2
Groton CT U.S.A. 177 M4
Groton NY U.S.A. 177 I3
Groton SD U.S.A. 178 C2
Grottoes U.S.A. 176 G7
Grouard Mission Canada 167 G3
Grouard Lake Canada 167 G1
Grouin, Pointe du pt France 50 E4
Groumania Côte d'Ivoire 124 E5
Groundhog r. Canada 168 D3
Grove U.S.A. 178 D4
Grove City OH U.S.A. 176 B6
Grove Hill U.S.A. 175 C6
Grövelsjön Sweden 45 K3
Grove Mountains Antarctica 223 F1
Grover Beach U.S.A. 182 D6
Groveton NH U.S.A. 177 N1
Groveton TX U.S.A. 179 D6
Grovfjord Norway 44 L1
Groza'dovo Bulg. 58 F5
Groznyy Rus. Fed. 41 H8
also known as Dzhokhar Ghala
Grubišno Polje Croatia 56 J3
Grudovo Bulg. see Sredets
Grudziądz Poland 49 P2
historically known as Graudenz
Grumăzești Romania 58 H1
Grums Sweden 45 K4
Grünau Namibia 130 C5
Grünau-Grünheider Wald und Seengebiet park Germany 49 K4
Grünberg Germany 48 F5
Grünberg Poland see Zielona Góra
Grundagssätern Sweden 45 L3
Grundarfjördur Iceland 44 [inset] B2
Grundforsen Sweden 45 K3
Grundsee nature res. Austria 49 K8
Grundy U.S.A. 176 C8
Gruñidora Mex. 185 E3
Gruver U.S.A. 179 B4
Gruzdžiai Lith. 42 E5

Gruzinskaya S.S.R. country Asia see Georgia
Gryazi Rus. Fed. 43 U8
Gryaznoye Rus. Fed. 43 U7
Gryazovets Rus. Fed. 43 V3
Grybów Poland 49 R6
Gryfice Poland 49 M2
Gryfino Poland 49 L2
Gryfów Śląski Poland 49 M4
Gryllefjord Norway 44 L1
Grytgöl Sweden 45 K4
Grytviken S. Georgia 205 [inset]
Gua India 97 E5
Guà r. Italy 56 D3
Guabito Panama 186 C5
Guacanayabo, Golfo de b. Cuba 186 D2
Guacara Venez. 187 G5
Guachara r. Col. 193 D3
Guaçu Brazil 203 A7
Guaçuí Brazil 207 L7
Guadahortuna Spain 55 H7
Guadaira r. Spain 54 E6
Guadajira r. Spain 54 E6
Guadajoz r. Spain 54 G7
Guadalajara Mex. 185 E4
Guadalajara Spain 55 H4
Guadalaviar r. Spain 55 J4
Guadalcacín, Embalse de resr Spain 54 F8
Guadalcanal i. Solomon Is 145 F2
Guadalcanal Spain 54 F6
Guadalén r. Spain 55 H6
Guadales Arg. 204 D4
Guadalhorce r. Spain 54 G8
Guadalhorce, Embalse de resr Spain 54 G8
Guadalmar r. Spain 55 H7
Guadalmez r. Spain 54 G6
Guadalope r. Spain 55 K3
Guadalquivir r. Spain 54 F7
Guadalupe i. Mex. 170 C4
Guadalupe watercourse Mex. 183 H9
Guadalupe Nuevo León Mex. 185 E3
Guadalupe Zacatecas Mex. 185 E4
Guadalupe Peru 200 A1
Guadalupe AZ U.S.A. 183 M8
Guadalupe CA U.S.A. 182 D6
Guadalupe TX U.S.A. 179 C6
Guadalupe, Sierra de mts Spain 54 F5
Guadalupe Aguilera Mex. 184 D3
Guadalupe Mountains National Park U.S.A. 181 F7
Guadalupe Victoria Baja California Norte Mex. 183 I9
Guadalupe Victoria Durango Mex. 184 D3
Guadamez r. Spain 54 F6
Guadarrama r. Spain 54 G5
Guadarrama, Puerto de pass Spain 54 G4
Guadarrama, Sierra de mts Spain 54 G4
Guadazaón r. Spain 55 J5
▶ Guadeloupe terr. West Indies 187 H3
French Overseas Department.
northamerica [countries] ⇒ 158-159
Guadeloupe Passage Caribbean Sea 137 H3
Guadiamar r. Spain 54 D7
Guadiana r. Port./Spain 54 D7
Guadiana, Bahía de b. Cuba 186 B2
Guadiana Menor r. Spain 55 H7
Guadiaro r. Spain 54 F8
Guadiato r. Spain 54 F7
Guadiela r. Spain 55 I4
Guadix Spain 55 H7
Guafo, Isla i. Chile 205 B6
Guagua Phil. 74 B3
Guaíba Brazil 203 C6
Guaiçuí Brazil 203 C6
Guaicuras Brazil 201 F5
Guaillabamba r. Ecuador 198 B4
Guáimaro Cuba 186 D2
Guaina Venez. 199 F3
Guainía r. Col. 198 D4
Guainía r. Col./Venez. 198 E4
Guaiquinima, Cerro mt. Venez. 199 F3
Guaíra Brazil 203 A8
Guaíra Brazil 206 E7
Guairaçá Brazil 206 B7
Guaitecas, Islas is Chile 205 B6
Guajará Brazil 202 B2
Guajará Brazil 200 D2
Guajaratuba Brazil 199 F6
Guajará-Mirim Brazil 200 D1
Guaje, Laguna de l. Mex. 185 E2
Guaje, Llano de plain Mex. 185 E2
Guajira dept Col. 198 C2
Gualaceo Ecuador 198 B5
Gualala U.S.A. 182 A3
Gualán Guat. 185 H6
Gualaquiza Ecuador 198 B5
Gualdo Tadino Italy 56 E5
Gualeguay Arg. 204 F4
Gualeguay r. Arg. 204 F4
Gualeguaychu Arg. 204 F4
Gualicho, Salina salt flat Arg. 204 D6
Gualjaina Arg. 205 C6
Guallatiri vol. Chile 200 C5
▶ Guam terr. N. Pacific Ocean 73 J4
United States Unincorporated Territory.
oceania [countries] ⇒ 138-139
Guamblin, Isla i. Chile 205 B7
Guamaré Arg. 204 E5
Guamo Cuba 186 D2
Guampí, Sierra de mts Venez. 199 E3
Guamúchil Mex. 184 C3
Gu'an China 87 E1
Guan r. China 87 I1
Guanabacoa Cuba 186 C2
Guanabara Brazil 200 C2
Guanabara, Baía de b. Brazil 207 J9
Guanacaste, Parque Nacional nat. park Costa Rica 186 B5
Guanacevi Mex. 184 D3
Guanaja Hond. 186 B3
Guanajay Cuba 186 C2
Guanajuato Mex. 185 E4
Guanajuato state Mex. 185 E4
Guanambi Brazil 202 D5
Guanare Venez. 198 D2
Guanare Viejo r. Venez. 198 D2
Guanarito Venez. 198 D2
Guanay Bol. 200 D3
Guandacol Arg. 204 C3
Guandaokou China 87 D1
Guandi Shan mt. China 85 F4
Guandu r. Brazil 207 L6
Guane Cuba 186 B2
Guang'an China 86 C2
Guangchang China 87 F3
also known as Nonghui
Guangde China 87 F2
Guangdong prov. China 87 E4
English form Kwangtung
Guangfeng China 87 F2
also known as Yongfeng
Guanghai China 87 E4
Guanghan China 86 C2
Guangling China 85 G4
also known as Laohekou
Guangmao Shan mt. China 86 B3
Guangming Ding mt. China 87 F2

Guangnan China 86 C3
also known as Liancheng
Guangning China 87 E4
also known as Nanjie
Guangping China see Beining
Guangrao China 85 H4
Guangshan China 87 E2
Guangshui China 87 E2
Guangxi aut. reg. China see Guangxi Zhuangzu Zizhiqu
Guangxi Zhuangzu Zizhiqu aut. reg. China 87 D4
short form Guangxi; English form Kwangsi or Kwangsi Chuang Autonomous Region
Guangyuan China 86 C1
Guangze China 87 F3
also known as Hangchuan
Guangzhou China 87 E4
English form Canton; formerly spelt Kwangchow
Guanhães Brazil 203 D6
Guanhães r. Brazil 207 K6
Guanhe Kou r. mouth China 87 F1
Guánica Puerto Rico 187 G3
Guanipa r. Venez. 199 F2
Guanling China 86 C3
Guanmian Shan mts China 87 D2
Guanpo China 87 D1
Guansuo China see Guanling
Guanta Venez. 199 F2
Guantánamo Cuba 187 E2
Guantao China 85 G4
Guanxian China see Dujiangyan
Guanyang China 87 D3
Guanyinqiao China 86 B2
formerly known as Chuosijia
Guanyun China 87 F1
also known as Yishan; formerly known as Dayishan
Guapay r. Bol. see Grande
Guapé Brazil 203 C7
Guapi Col. 198 B4
Guapiara Brazil 206 E11
Guápiles Costa Rica 186 C5
Guaporé r. Bol./Brazil 200 D3
Guaporé Brazil 203 B9
Guaporé state Brazil see Rondônia
Guaquí Brazil 200 C4
Guará r. Brazil 202 C5
Guará r. Brazil 207 L6
Guara, Sierra de mts Spain 55 K2
Guarabira Brazil 202 F3
Guaranda Ecuador 198 B5
Guarani Brazil 207 L6
Guarantã Brazil 206 D8
Guaraparí Brazil 203 D7
Guarapuava Brazil 203 B8
Guararapes Brazil 206 C8
Guaratinga Brazil 202 E5
Guaratinguetá Brazil 207 H9
Guaratuba Brazil 203 B8
Guaratuba, Baía de b. Brazil 203 B8
Guaratos Bol. 200 C3
Guarda Port. 54 D4
Guarda admin. dist. Port. 54 D4
Guardafui, Cape Somalia see Caseyr, Raas
Guardal r. Spain 55 I7
Guardamar del Segura Spain 55 K6
Guardatinajas Venez. 199 E2
Guardia Escolta Arg. 204 E3
Guardiagrele Italy 56 G6
Guardiana de la Patria Mex. 183 I9
Guardo Spain 54 G2
Guardunha, Serra de mts Port. 54 D5
Guareña Spain 54 F6
Guariba r. Brazil 201 E1
Guárico state Venez. 199 E2
Guárico, Punta c. Cuba 187 E2
Guarojo r. Col. 198 D4
Guarujá Brazil 207 G10
Guarulhos Brazil 206 G10
Guasare r. Venez. 187 F5
Guasave Mex. 184 C3
Guasdualito Venez. 198 D3
Guasipati Venez. 199 F3
Guastatoya Guat. see El Progreso
Guasuba r. India 97 F5
▶ Guatemala country Central America 185 H6
4th most populous country in North America.

Guatemala Guat. see Guatemala City

▶ Guatemala City Guat. 185 H6
Capital of Guatemala. Also known as Guatemala.
northamerica [countries] ⇒ 158-159

Guatimozin Arg. 204 E4
Guatrache Arg. 204 E5
Guatrochi Arg. 205 D6
Guaviare dept Col. 198 D4
Guaviare r. Col. 198 D3
Guaxupé Brazil 206 G8
Guayabal Cuba 186 D2
Guayabal Cuba 186 D2
Guayaguas, Sierra da mts Arg. 204 D3
Guayama Puerto Rico 187 G3
Guayapo, Serranía mts Venez. 199 E3
Guayaquil Ecuador 198 B5
Guayaquil, Golfo de g. Ecuador 198 A5
Guayaramerín Bol. 200 D2
Guayas prov. Ecuador 198 A5
Guayatayoc, Lago de imp. l. Arg. 200 D5
Guaymas Mex. 184 C3
Guayquiraró r. Arg. 204 F3
Guazacapán Guat. 185 H6
Guba Eth. 128 B2
Gúbadag Turkm. 102 D4
formerly known as Tel'mansk
Guba Dolgaya Rus. Fed. 40 K1
Gubakha Rus. Fed. 40 K4
▶ Gûbâl, Geziret i. Egypt 104 A2
English form Gûbâl Island
Gûbâl Island Egypt see Gûbâl, Geziret
Guban plain Somalia 128 C2
Gubat Phil. 74 C3
Gúbbi India 94 C3
Gubbio Italy 56 E5
historically known as Iguvium
Gubdor Rus. Fed. 40 K3
Gubed Binna b. Somalia 128 F2
Guben Germany 49 L4
formerly known as Wilhelm-Pieck-Stadt
Gübene Bulg. 58 G6
Gubin Poland 49 L4
Gubio Nigeria 125 I3
Gubkin Rus. Fed. 41 F6
Gucheng Hebei China 85 G4
also known as Zhengkou; formerly known as Zhengjiakou
Gucheng Hubei China 87 D1
Gudalur India 94 C4
Gudar, Sierra de mts Spain 55 K4
Gudari India 95 D2
Gudaut'a Georgia 107 E2
Gudbrandsdalen valley Norway 45 J3
Guddu Barrage Pak. 101 G4
Gudermes Rus. Fed. 102 A4
Gudi Nigeria 125 H4
Gudivada India 94 D2
Gudiyattam India 94 C3
Gudong r. China 87 D4
Gudri r. Pak. 101 E4
Gudür Turkey 106 C2
Gúdúl Turkey 106 C2
Gudur Andhra Pradesh India 94 C4
Gudur Andhra Pradesh India 94 C3
Gudvangen Norway 45 I3
Gudzhal r. Rus. Fed. 82 D2

largest islands

	island	area sq km	area sq miles	location	page#
1 ▶	Greenland	2 175 600	840 004	North America	⇒ 165 O2
2 ▶	New Guinea	808 510	312 167	Oceania	⇒ 73 J8
3 ▶	Borneo	745 561	287 863	Asia	⇒ 77 F2
4 ▶	Madagascar	587 040	266 657	Africa	⇒ 131 J4
5 ▶	Baffin Island	507 451	195 927	North America	⇒ 165 L2
6 ▶	Sumatra	473 606	182 860	Asia	⇒ 76 B2
7 ▶	Honshū	227 414	87 805	Asia	⇒ 91 F6
8 ▶	Great Britain	218 476	84 354	Europe	⇒ 47 J9
9 ▶	Victoria Island	217 291	83 897	North America	⇒ 165 H2
10 ▶	Ellesmere Island	196 236	75 767	North America	⇒ 165 K2

Gudžiūnai Lith. 42 E6
Guè, Rivière du r. Canada 169 G1
Guebwiller France 51 N5
Guéckédou Guinea 124 C4
Guéguen, Lac l. Canada 173 P2
Guelb er Rîchât hill Mauritania 122 C5
Guélengdeng Chad 126 B2
Guelma Alg. 123 G1
Guelmine Morocco 122 C3
Guelph Canada 168 D5
Guémez Mex. 185 F4
Guendour well Mauritania 122 C6
Guéné Benin 125 F4
Guènt Paté Senegal 124 B3
Guer France 50 D5
Guéra pref. Chad 126 C2
Guéra, Massif du mts Chad 126 C2
Guérande France 50 D5
Guerara Alg. 123 G2
Guérard, Lac l. Canada 169 H1
Guercif Morocco 123 E2
Guéré watercourse Chad 120 C5
Guéréda Chad 120 D6
Guerende Libya 120 D4
Guéret France 50 H6
Guerneville U.S.A. 182 B3
Guernica Spain see Gernika-Lumo

▶Guernsey terr. Channel Is 50 D3
United Kingdom Crown Dependency.
europe [countries] ➡ 32–35

Guernsey U.S.A. 180 F4
Guérou Mauritania 124 C2
Guerrero Coahuila Mex. 179 B6
Guerrero Tamaulipas Mex. 185 F3
Guerrero state Mex. 185 E5
Guerrero Negro Mex. 184 B3
Guers, Lac l. Canada 169 H1
Guerzim Alg. 123 E3
Guetâtira well Mali 122 D4
Gueugnon France 51 K6
Guéyo Côte d'Ivoire 124 D5
Gufeng China see Pingnan
Gufu China see Xingshan
Gugë mt. Eth. 128 C3
Gügerd, Küh-e mts Iran 100 C3
Guglieri Arg. 204 E3
Guguan i. N. Mariana Is 73 K3
Gugu Mountains Eth. 128 C2
Guhakolak, Tanjung pt Indon. 76 D4
Guhe China 87 F2
Güh Küh mt. Iran 100 D5
Guhuai China see Pingyu
Guia Brazil 201 F3
Guiana Highlands mts S. America 199 E3
Guichen France 50 E5
Guichi China 87 F2
Guichicovi Mex. 185 G5
Guichón Uruguay 204 F4
Guidan-Roumji Niger 125 G3
Guidari Chad 126 C2
Guide China 84 D5
also known as Heyin
Guidel France 50 C5
Guider Cameroon 125 I4
Guidiguir Niger 125 H3
Guidimaka admin. reg. Mauritania 124 B3
Guiding China 87 C3
Guidong China 87 E3
Guidonia-Montecelio Italy 56 E7
Guier, Lac de l. Senegal 124 B2
Guietsou Gabon 126 A5
Guigang China 87 D4
Guiglo Côte d'Ivoire 124 D5
Güigüe Venez. 187 G5
Guija Moz. 131 G5
formerly known as Caniçado or Vila Alferes Chamusca
Gui Jiang r. China 87 D4
Guiji Shan mts China 87 G2
Guijuelo Spain 54 F4
Guildford U.K. 47 L12
Guilford U.S.A. 174 G2
Guilherand France 51 K8
Guilherme Capelo Angola see Cacongo
Guilin China 87 D3
Guillaume-Delisle, Lac l. Canada 168 E1
Guillaumes France 51 M8
Guillestre France 51 M8
Guimarães Brazil 202 C2
Guimarães Port. 54 C3
Guimaras i. Phil. 74 B4
Guimaras Strait Phil. 74 B4
Guimeng Ding mt. China 85 H5
Guinagourou Benin 125 F4
Guinan China 84 D5
also known as Mangra
Guindulman Phil. 74 C4
▶Guinea country Africa 124 B4
also known as Guinea-Conakry; spelt Guinée in French; formerly known as French Guinea
africa [countries] ➡ 114–117
Guinea, Gulf of Africa 125 G6
▶Guinea-Bissau country Africa 124 B3
also spelt Guiné-Bissau; formerly known as Portuguese Guinea
africa [countries] ➡ 114–117
Guinea-Conakry country Africa see Guinea
Guinea Ecuatorial country Africa see Equatorial Guinea
Guiné-Bissau country Africa see Guinea-Bissau
Guinée country Africa see Guinea
Guinée-Forestière admin. reg. Guinea 124 C4
Guinée-Maritime admin. reg. Guinea 124 B4
Güines Cuba 186 C2
Guînes France 51 H2
Guingamp France 50 C4
Guinguinéo Senegal 124 B3
Guiones, Punta pt Costa Rica 186 B5
Guipavas France 50 B4
Guiping China 87 D4
Güira de Melena Cuba 186 C2
Guiratinga Brazil 202 A6
Güiria Venez. 199 F2
Guisanbourg Fr. Guiana 199 I3
Guisborough U.K. 47 K9
Guise France 51 J3
Guishan China see Xinping
Guissefa well Mali 125 F2
Guitiriz Spain 54 D1
Guitri Côte d'Ivoire 124 D5
Guiuan Phil. 74 C4
Guivi hill Fin. 44 N1
Guixi China see Dianjiang
Guiyang Guizhou China 86 C3
formerly spelt Kweiyang
Guiyang Hunan China 87 E3
Guiyang Hunan China 87 E3
Guizhou prov. China 86 C3
English form Kweichow
Guizi China 87 D4
Gujan-Mestras France 50 E8
Gujarat state India 96 B5
formerly spelt Gujerat
Gujar Khan Pak. 101 H3
Gujba Nigeria 125 H4
Gujerat state India see Gujarat
Gujranwala Pak. 101 H3
Gujrat Pak. 101 H3
Gukou China 87 F3
Gukovo Rus. Fed. 41 F6
Gulabgarh Jammu and Kashmir 96 C2
Gulabie Uzbek. 102 D4
formerly known as Takhiatash
Gulang China 84 D4
Gulân Islands Egypt see Qul'ân, Gezâ'ir
Gülbahçe Turkey 59 H10
Gul'bakhor Uzbek. 103 G4
Gulbarga India 94 C2
Gul Basin dock Sing. 76 [inset]
Gulbene Latvia 42 H4
Gul'cha Kyrg. see Gülchö
Gülchö Kyrg. 103 H4
also spelt Gul'cha
Gülek Turkey 106 C3
also known as Çamalan
Gülek Boğazı pass Turkey 106 C3
English form Cilician Gates
Gulf, The Asia 105 E1
also known as Persian Gulf or Arabian Gulf
Gulfport U.S.A. 175 B6
Gulf Shores U.S.A. 175 C6
Gulgong Australia 147 F3
Gulian China 82 A1
Gulin China 86 C3
Gulistan Pak. 101 F4
Gulistan Uzbek. 103 G4
also spelt Guliston; formerly known as Mirzachul
Guliston Uzbek. see Gulistan
Guliya Shan mt. China 85 I1
Gulja China see Yining
Gul Kach Pak. 101 G4
Gul'kevichi Rus. Fed. 41 G7
Gull r. Canada 168 B3
Gullbrå Norway 45 I3
Gullkrona fjärd b. Fin. 45 M4
Gull Lake Canada 167 I5
Gullrock Lake Canada 167 M5
Gullspång Sweden 45 K4
Gullträsk Sweden 44 M2
Güllübahçe Turkey 59 I11
Güllük Turkey 59 I11
Güllük Körfezi b. Turkey 106 A3
Gulmarg Jammu and Kashmir 96 B2
Gülnar Turkey 106 C3
also known as Anaypazari
Gülpınar Turkey 59 H9
Gulrip'shi Georgia 107 E2
Gülşehir Turkey 106 C3
also known as Arapsun
Gul'shad Kazakh. 103 H3
Gulü China see Xincai
Gulu Uganda 128 B4
Gŭlŭbovo Bulg. 58 G6
Gulumba Gana Nigeria 125 I4
Gulwe Tanz. 129 C6
Gulyantsi Bulg. 58 F5
Gulyayevskiye Koshki, Ostrova is Rus. Fed. 40 J1
Guma China see Pishan
Gumal r. Pak. 101 G4
Gumare Botswana 130 D3
Gumbinnen Rus. Fed. see Gusev
Gumbiri mt. Sudan 128 A3
Gumdag Turkm. 102 C5
formerly spelt Kum-Dag
Gumel Nigeria 125 H3
Gümgüm Turkey see Varto
Gumla India 97 E5
Gumma pref. Japan see Gunma
Gummersbach Germany 48 E4
Gumpang r. Indon. 76 B1
Gumsi Nigeria 125 H3
Gümüşhane Turkey 107 D2
Gümüşsuyu Turkey 59 I10
Gümüşyaka Turkey 58 J7
Guna India 96 C4
Gunan China see Qijiang
Guna Terara mt. Eth. 128 C2
Gund r. Tajik. 101 G2
also spelt Gunt
Gundagai Australia 147 F3
Gunderi India 94 C3
Gundji Dem. Rep. Congo 126 D4
Gundlakamma r. India 94 D3
Gundlupet India 94 C4
Gündoğmuş Turkey 106 C3
also known as Eksere
Güneşli Turkey 59 J9
Güney Denizli Turkey 59 K10
Güney Kütahya Turkey 59 J9
Güneydoğu Toroslar plat. Turkey 107 E3
English form Eastern Taurus
Güneyyurt Turkey 108 D1
Gungilap Myanmar 78 B2
Gungu Dem. Rep. Congo 127 C6
Gungue Angola 127 B8
Gunib Rus. Fed. 102 A4
Gunisao r. Canada 167 L4
Gunja Croatia 56 K4
Günlüce Turkey 59 K9
Gunma pref. Japan 91 F6
also spelt Gumma
Gunna, Gebel mts Egypt 108 F9
Gunnarn Sweden 44 L2
Gunnbjørn Fjeld nunatak Greenland 165 Q3
Gunnedah Australia 147 F2
Gunnison CO U.S.A. 181 F5
Gunnison UT U.S.A. 183 M2
Gunnison r. U.S.A. 183 P2
Gunn Point Australia 148 A2
Gunong Ayer Sarawak Malaysia see Gunung Ayer
Gunpowder Creek r. Australia 148 C3
Güns Hungary see Kőszeg
Gun Sangari India 94 C3
Gunt r. Tajik. see Gund
Guntakal India 94 C3
Guntersville U.S.A. 174 C5
Guntur India 94 D2
Gununa Australia 148 C3
Gunungapi i. Indon. 75 C4
Gunung Ayer Sarawak Malaysia 77 E2
formerly spelt Gunong Ayer
Gunung Gading National Park Sarawak Malaysia 77 E2
Gunung Leuser National Park Indon. 76 B2
Gunung Mulu National Park Sarawak Malaysia 77 F1
Gunung Niyut Reserve nature res. Indon. 77 E2
Gunung Palung National Park Indon. 77 E3
Gunung Rinjani National Park Indon. 77 G5
Gunungsitoli Indon. 76 B2
Gunungsugih Indon. 76 D4
Gunungtua Indon. 76 B2
Gunupur India 95 D2
Günyüzü Turkey 106 B3
also known as Kozağacı
Gunza Angola see Porto Amboim
Günzburg Germany 48 H7
Gunzenhausen Germany 48 H6
Guochengyi China 84 E4
Guo He r. China 87 E1
Guo He r. China 87 F1
Guoluezhen China see Lingbao
Guoyang China 87 F1
Guozhen China see Baoji
Gupis Jammu and Kashmir 96 B1
Gura Caliței Romania 58 H3
Gurais Jammu and Kashmir 96 B2
Gura Portiței sea chan. Romania 58 J4
Gurara r. Nigeria 125 G4
Gura Şuţii Romania 58 G4
Gura Teghii Romania 58 H3
Gurba r. Dem. Rep. Congo 126 E4
Gurban Obo China 85 G3
Gurbantünggüt Shamo des. China 88 D2
Gurdaspur India 96 B2
Gurdim Iran 101 E5
Gurdon U.S.A. 179 D5
Güre Turkey 59 H9
Güre Turkey 106 B3
Gürgän Azer. 100 B1
Gurgan Iran see Gorgān
Gurgaon India 96 C3
Gurgei, Jebel mt. Sudan 120 E6
Gurghiu r. Romania 58 F2
Gurghiului, Munții mts Romania 58 F2
Gurgueia r. Brazil 202 D3
Gurha India 96 A4
Guri, Embalse de resr Venez. 199 F3
Gurig National Park Australia 148 B1
Gurinhatã Brazil 206 D6
Gurktaler Alpen mts Austria 49 K9
Gurlan Uzbek. see Gurlen
Gurlen Uzbek. 102 E4
also spelt Gurlan
Gurmatkal India 94 C2
Gurnee U.S.A. 172 F8
Guro Moz. 131 G3
Gürpınar Turkey 107 E3
also known as Kasrik
Gurramkonda India 94 C3
Gürsu Turkey 59 K8
also known as Kestel
Gurué Moz. 131 H2
formerly known as Vila de Junqueiro
Gürün Turkey 107 D3
Gurupá Brazil 199 I5
Gurupá, Ilha Grande de i. Brazil 199 I5
Gurupi Brazil 202 B4
Gurupi r. Brazil 202 C2
Gurupi, Cabo c. Brazil 202 C2
Gurupi, Serra do hills Brazil 202 B3
Guru Sikhar mt. India 96 B4
Guruve Zimbabwe 131 F3
also spelt Guruwe; formerly known as Chipuriro or Sipolilo
Guruwe Zimbabwe see Guruve
Guruzala India 94 C2
Gurvan Sayan Uul mts Mongolia 84 D3
Gur'yev Kazakh. see Atyrau
Gur'yevsk Rus. Fed. 42 B7
historically known as Neuhausen
Gur'yevskaya Oblast' admin. div. Kazakh. see Atyrauskaya Oblast'
Gusau Nigeria 125 G3
Gusev Rus. Fed. 42 D7
historically known as Gumbinnen
Gushgy Turkm. 101 E3
formerly spelt Kushka
Gushgy r. Turkm. 101 E2
Gushi China 87 E1
Gushiegu Ghana 125 E4
Gusinje Crna Gora Yugo. 58 A6
Gusino Rus. Fed. 43 M7
Gusinoozersk Rus. Fed. 85 E1
Gusinoye, Ozero l. Rus. Fed. 85 E1
Guskara India 97 E5
Gus'-Khrustal'nyy Rus. Fed. 40 G5
Guspini Sardegna Italy 57 A9
Güssing Austria 49 N8
Gustav Holm, Kap c. Greenland see Tasiilap Karra
Gustavia West Indies 187 H3
Gustavo Sotelo Mex. 184 B2
Gustavus U.S.A. 166 C3
Gustine U.S.A. 182 D4
Güstrow Germany 49 J2
Gütersloh Germany 48 F4
Guthrie AZ U.S.A. 183 O9
Guthrie KY U.S.A. 174 C4
Guthrie OK U.S.A. 179 C5
Guthrie TX U.S.A. 179 B5
Guthrie Center U.S.A. 178 D3
Gutian Fujian China 87 F3
Gutian Fujian China 87 F3
also known as Xincheng
Gutian Shuiku resr China 87 F3
Gutiérrez Bol. 201 E4
Guting China see Yutai
Guttenberg U.S.A. 174 B3
Gutu Zimbabwe 131 F3
Guvertfjället mts Sweden 44 L2
Guwahati India 97 F4
also spelt Gauhati
Guwër Iraq 107 E3
Guwlumayak Turkm. see Kuuli-Mayak
Guxian China 87 E3
▶Guyana country S. America 199 G3
formerly known as British Guiana
southamerica [countries] ➡ 192–193
Guyane Française terr. S. America see French Guiana
Guyang China see Guzhang
Guyang China 85 F3
Guyenne reg. France 50 F8
Guy Fawkes River National Park Australia 147 G2
Guyi China see Sanjiang
Guymon U.S.A. 178 B4
Güyom Iran 100 C4
Guyong China see Jiangle
Guyot Glacier Canada/U.S.A. 166 A2
Guyra Australia 147 F2
Guysborough Canada 169 I4
Guyu Zimbabwe 131 F4
Guyuan Hebei China 85 G3
also known as Pingdingbu
Guyuan Ningxia China 85 E5
Guzar Uzbek. 103 F5
also spelt Ghuzor
Güzelbağ Turkey 108 C1
Güzelhisar Barajı resr Turkey 59 I10
Güzeloluk Turkey 108 F1
Güzelyurt Cyprus see Morfou
Guzhang China 87 D2
also known as Gulin
Guzhen China 87 F1
Guzhou China see Rongjiang
Guzmán Mex. 184 D2
Guzmán, Lago de l. Mex. 184 D2
Gvardeysk Rus. Fed. 42 C7
historically known as Tapiau
Gvasyugi Rus. Fed. 82 E3
Gwa Myanmar 78 A4
Gwada Nigeria 125 G4
Gwadabawa Nigeria 125 G3
Gwadar Pak. 101 E5
formerly spelt Gwador
Gwadar West Bay Pak. 101 E5
Gwador Pak. see Gwadar
Gwaii Haanas National Park Reserve Canada 166 D4
Gwalior India 96 C4
Gwanda Zimbabwe 131 F4
Gwarzo Nigeria 125 G4
Gwatar Bay Pak. 101 E5
Gwayi Zimbabwe 131 E3
Gwayi r. Zimbabwe 131 E3
Gwda r. Poland 49 N2
Gweebarra Bay Rep. of Ireland 47 D9
Gweedore Rep. of Ireland 47 D8
Gwelo Zimbabwe see Gweru
Gweru Zimbabwe 131 F3
formerly spelt Gwelo
Gweta Botswana 131 E4
Gwinn U.S.A. 172 F4
Gwoza Nigeria 125 I4
Gwydir r. Australia 147 F2
Gyablung China 89 F6
Gyaca China 89 F6
also known as Ngarrab
Gyagartang China 86 B1
Gya'gya China see Saga
Gyaijêpozhanggê China see Zhidoi
Gyai Qu r. China 89 F6
Gyairong China 86 A1
Gyaisi China see Jiulong
Gyali i. Greece 59 I12
also spelt Yiali
Gyamotang China see Dêngqên
Gyamug China 89 C5
Gyandzha Azer. see Gäncä
Gyangkar China see Dinngyê
Gyangnyi Caka salt l. China 89 D5
Gyangrang China 89 D6
Gyangtse China see Gyangzê
Gyangzê China 89 E6
also spelt Gyangtse
Gyaring China 84 C5
Gyaring Co l. China 89 E6
Gyaring Hu l. China 86 A1
Gyaros Greece 59 F11
Gyaros i. Greece 59 F11
Gyaur watercourse Turkm. 102 C5
also spelt Gäwür
Gyaurs Turkm. see Sakhra
Gydan, Khrebet mts Rus. Fed. see Kolymskiy, Khrebet
Gydan Peninsula Rus. Fed. 39 H2
Gydopas pass S. Africa 132 D10
Gyêgu China see Yushu
Gyêmdong China 89 F6
Gyêsar Co l. China 89 D6
Gyêwa China 89 D6
also known as Zabqung
Gyigang China see Zayü
Gyimda China 89 F6
Gyirong Xizang China 89 D6
Gyirong Xizang China 89 D6
also known as Zongga
Gyitang China 86 A2
Gyixong China see Gonggar
Gyiza China 97 G2
Gyldenløve Fjord inlet Greenland see Umiiviip Kangertiva
Gyljen Sweden 44 M2
Gympie Australia 149 G5
Gyobingauk Myanmar 78 A4
Gyomaendrőd Hungary 49 R9
Gyöngyös Hungary 49 Q8
Győr Hungary 49 O8
historically known as Raab
Győrszentmárton Hungary see Pannonhalma
Gypsum Point Canada 167 H2
Gypsumville Canada 167 L5
Gytheio Greece 59 D12
also known as Yithion
Gyula Hungary 49 S9
Gyulafehérvár Romania see Alba Iulia
Gyümai China see Darlag
Gyumri Armenia 107 E2
also known as Kumayri; formerly known as Aleksandropol or Leninakan
Gyurgen Bair hill Turkey 58 H7
Gyzylarbat Turkm. 102 D5
formerly spelt Kizyl-Arbat
Gyzyletrek Turkm. 102 C5
formerly spelt Kizyl-Atrek
Gyzylsuw Turkm. see Kizyl-Su
Gzhat' r. Rus. Fed. 43 P6
Gzhatsk Rus. Fed. see Gagarin

↓ H

Ha Bhutan 97 F4
Haabneeme Estonia 42 F2
Häädemeeste Estonia 42 F3
Haag Austria 49 L7
Haanhöhiy Uul mts Mongolia 84 B1
Haanja Estonia 42 I3
Ha'ano i. Tonga 145 H3
Ha'apai Group is Tonga 145 H3
also spelt Habai Group
Haapajärvi Fin. 40 C3
Haapavesi Fin. 44 N2
Haapsalu Estonia 42 E3
Ha 'Arava watercourse Israel/Jordan see 'Arabah, Wādī al
Haarlem Neth. 48 B3
Haarlem S. Africa 132 H10
Haarstrang ridge Germany 48 E4
Haast N.Z. 153 D11
Haast r. N.Z. 153 D11
Haasts Bluff Aboriginal Land res. Australia 148 A4
Haaway Somalia 128 D4
Hab r. Pak. 101 F5
Habahe China 88 D1
also known as Kaba
Habai Group is Tonga see Ha'apai Group
Habana Cuba see Havana
Habarôn well Saudi Arabia 105 E3
Ḥabarūt Oman 105 F4
Habaswein Kenya 128 C4
Ḥabawnāh, Wādī watercourse Saudi Arabia 104 D4
Habay Canada 166 G3
Ḥabbān Yemen 105 D5
Ḥabbānīyah, Hawr al l. Iraq 107 E4
Habhab ash Shaykh, Ḥarrāt lava field Saudi Arabia 104 C4
Habicht mt. Austria 48 I8
Habichtswald park Germany 48 G4
Habiganj Bangl. 97 F4
Habirag China 85 G3
Ḥābis, Wādī al r. Jordan 108 G6
Habo Sweden 45 K4
Habra India 97 F5
Ḥabshīyah, Jabal mts Yemen 105 E4
Hacha Col. 198 C5
Hachijō-jima i. Japan 91 F8
Hachiman Japan 91 E7
Hachimori Japan 90 F4
Hachinohe Japan 90 G4
Hachiōji Japan 91 F7
Hachiryū Japan 90 F5
Hacıbekir Turkey 59 K9
Hacıbektaş Turkey 106 C3
Hacıköy Turkey see Çekerek
Hacıpaşa Turkey 109 H1
Hacı Zeynalabdin Azer. 107 G2
formerly known as Nasosnyy
Hack, Mount Australia 146 C2
Hackberry U.S.A. 183 K6
Hacker Valley U.S.A. 176 E7
Hackettstown U.S.A. 177 K5
Ha Côi Vietnam 78 D3
Hacufera Moz. 131 G4
formerly known as Algueirao
Hadabat al Budū plain Saudi Arabia 105 E3
Hadagalli India 94 B3
Hada Mountains Afgh. 101 F4
Ḥadan, Harrat lava field Saudi Arabia 104 C3
Hadano Japan 91 F7
Ḥadārah i. Saudi Arabia 104 C4
Ḥadârba, Râs pt Sudan 121 H4
Ḥadd, Ra's al pt Oman 105 G3
Haddad, Ouadi watercourse Chad 120 C6
Haddington U.K. 46 J8
Hadejia Nigeria 125 H3
Hadejia watercourse Nigeria 125 I3
Hadera Israel 108 F5
Hadera r. Israel 108 F5
Haderslev Denmark 45 J5
Hadgaon India 94 C2
Ḥadhah Saudi Arabia 104 C3
Ḥadh Banī Zaynān des. Saudi Arabia 105 E3
Hadhdhunmathi Atoll Maldives 93 D10
Hadhramaut reg. Yemen see Ḥaḍramawt
Hādī, Jabal al mts Jordan 109 H7
Hadiboh Yemen 105 F5
Hadilik China 88 D4
Hadım Turkey 106 C3
Hadjer Momou mt. Chad 120 D5
Hadley Bay Canada 165 I2
Ha Đông Vietnam 86 C4
Ḥadraj, Wādī watercourse Saudi Arabia 107 D5
Ḥaḍramawt governorate Yemen 105 E4
Ḥaḍramawt reg. Yemen 105 D5
also spelt Hadhramaut
Ḥaḍramawt, Wādī watercourse Yemen 105 E4
Hadranum Sicilia Italy see Adrano
Hadrian's Wall tourist site U.K. 47 J8
Hadrumetum Tunisia see Sousse
Hadseløy i. Norway 44 K1
Hadsten Denmark 45 J4
Hadsund Denmark 45 J4
Hadūs, Baḥr canal Egypt 108 D6
Hadyach Ukr. 41 E6
also spelt Gadyach
Hadzilavichy Belarus 43 L8
Haedo, Cuchilla de hills Uruguay 204 F4
Haeju N. Korea 83 B5
Haeju-man b. N. Korea 83 B5
Haena U.S.A. 181 [inset] Y1
Haenam S. Korea 83 B6
Ḥafar al 'Atk well Saudi Arabia 105 D2
Ḥafar al Bāṭin Saudi Arabia 105 D1
Haffküste park Germany 49 L2
Hafford Canada 167 J4
Hafik Turkey 107 D3
Ḥafirah, Qā' al depr. Jordan 108 H6
Ḥafirah, Wādī al watercourse Jordan 108 G6
Hafirat al'Aydā Saudi Arabia 104 B2
Hafirat Nasah Saudi Arabia 105 D2
Ḥafit Oman 105 F3
Ḥafit, Jabal mt. U.A.E. 105 F2
Hafizabad Pak. 101 H3
Haflong India 97 G4
Hafnarfjörður Iceland 44 [inset] B2
Haft Gel Iran 100 B4
Haftvān Iran 100 C5
Hafursfjörður b. Iceland 44 [inset] B2
Haga Myanmar see Haka
Hag Abdullah Sudan 121 G6
Haga-Haga S. Africa 133 M9
Hagar Canada 173 M4
Hagari r. India 94 C3
Hagar Nish Plateau Eritrea 121 H5

▶Hagåtña Guam 73 J4
Capital of Guam. Also known as Agana.

Hagen Germany 48 E4
Hagen, Mount P.N.G. 73 J8
Hagenow Germany 48 I2
Hagensborg Canada 166 E4
Hägere Hiywet Eth. 128 C2
Hagerhill U.S.A. 176 C8
Hagerstown U.S.A. 176 H6
Hagetmau France 50 F9
Häggenås Sweden 44 K3
Haggin, Mount U.S.A. 180 D3
Hagi Japan 91 B7
Ha Giang Vietnam 78 D3
Ha Giao, Sông r. Vietnam 79 E5
Hagiwara Japan 91 E7
HaGolan hills Syria see Golan
Hag's Head Rep. of Ireland 47 C11
Hague U.S.A. 177 L2
Haguenau France 51 N4
Hahajima-rettō is Japan 73 J1
Hai r. China 85 H4
Hai Tanz. 128 C5
Ḥai, Gebel el hill Egypt 108 C8
Hai'an China 87 G1
Haian Shanmo mts Taiwan see T'aitung Shan
Haib watercourse Namibia 130 C6
Haicheng China see Haifeng
Haicheng China 85 I3
Haicheng China see Haiyuan
Haidargarh India 97 D4
Hai Duong Vietnam 78 D3
Haifa Israel 108 F5
also spelt Hefa or Khefa
Haifa, Bay of Israel 108 G5
also known as Hefa, Mifraz
Haifeng China 87 E4
also known as Haicheng
Haikakan country Asia see Armenia
Haikang China see Leizhou
Haiki Japan 91 A8
Haikou China 87 D4
Ḥā'il Saudi Arabia 104 C2
Ḥā'il prov. Saudi Arabia 104 C2
Hailakandi India 97 G4
Hailar China 85 H1
also known as Hulun
Hailar r. China 85 H1
Hailey U.S.A. 180 D4
Haileybury Canada 168 E4
Hailin China 82 C3
Hailong China see Meihekou
Hails China 85 H3
Hailun China 82 B3
Hailuoto Fin. 44 N2
Hailuoto i. Fin. 44 N2
Haimen China 87 G2
Hainan i. China 87 D5
Hainan prov. China 81 H9
Hai-nang Myanmar 78 B3
Hainan Strait China 87 D5
also known as Qiongzhou Haixia
Hainaut reg. France 51 J2
Hainburg an der Donau Austria 49 N7
Haindi Liberia 124 C5
Haines U.S.A. 164 F4
Haines City U.S.A. 175 D6
Haines Junction Canada 166 B2
Haines Road Canada/U.S.A. 166 B2
Hainich ridge Germany 48 H4
Hainleite ridge Germany 48 H4
Haiphong Vietnam see Hai Phong
Hai Phong Vietnam 78 D3
English form Haiphong
Haiqing China 82 D3
Hairhan Namag China 84 D3
Haitan Dao i. China 87 F3
formerly known as Pingtan Dao
▶Haiti country West Indies 187 E3
historically known as St-Domingue
northamerica [countries] ➡ 158–159
Haiwee Reservoir U.S.A. 182 G5
Haiya Sudan 121 H5
Haiyaf l. Sudan 126 E2
Haiyan Qinghai China 84 D4
also known as Sanjiaocheng
Haiyan Zhejiang China 87 G2
also known as Wuyuan
Haiyang China see Xiuning
Haiyang China 85 I4
also known as Dongcun
Haiyou China see Sanmen
Haiyuan China 85 E4
also known as Haicheng
Haizhou Wan b. China 87 F1
Hāj Ali Qoli, Kavīr-e salt l. Iran 100 C3
Hajar, Jibāl mts Saudi Arabia 104 B2
Ḥajār, Oued el well Mali 124 E2
Hajdúböszörmény Hungary 49 S8
Hajdúnánás Hungary 49 S8
Hajdúszoboszló Hungary 49 S8
Hajeb El Ayoun Tunisia 57 B13
Ḥajhir mt. Yemen 105 F5
Hajiki-zaki pt Japan 90 F5
Hajipur India 97 E4
Hajir reg. Saudi Arabia 105 E2
Ḥājir Yemen 104 C5
Ḥajiyah, Wādī watercourse Iraq 109 N4
Ḥajjah Yemen 104 C5
Ḥajjah governorate Yemen 104 C4
Ḥājjīābād Fārs Iran 100 C4
Ḥājjīābād Iran 100 C2
Ḥājjīābād Hormozgan Iran 100 C4
Hajnówka Poland 49 U3
Hajo India 97 F4
Ḥājr, Wādī watercourse Yemen 105 E5
Ḥajrah Saudi Arabia 104 C3
Hajuu-Us Mongolia 85 E2
Haka Myanmar 78 A3
also spelt Haga or Hakha
Hakase-yama mt. Japan 90 F6
Hakataramea N.Z. 153 E12
Hakatere N.Z. 153 F11
Hakatere r. N.Z. see Ashburton
Hakelhuincul, Altiplanicie de plat. Arg. 204 C6
Hakha Myanmar see Haka
Hakippa, Har hill Israel 108 G7
Hakkâri Turkey 107 E3
also known as Çölemerik
Hakkas Sweden 44 M2
Hakken-zan mt. Japan 91 D7
Hakköda-san mt. Japan 90 G4
Hako-dake mt. Japan 90 H2
Hakodate Japan 90 G4
Hakodate-wan b. Japan 90 G4
Hakos Mountains Namibia 130 C4
Hakseen Pan salt pan S. Africa 132 E3
Hakui Japan 91 E6
Haku-san vol. Japan 91 E6
Haku-san National Park Japan 91 E6
Hal Belgium see Halle
Hala Pak. 101 G5
Ḥalā', Jabal al mt. Jordan 108 G7
Ḥalab Syria see Aleppo
Ḥalab governorate Syria 109 I1
Ḥalabān Saudi Arabia 104 D3
Ḥalabja Iraq 107 F4
Halach Turkm. see Khalach
Halachó Mex. 185 H4
Halahai China 82 B3
Halaib Sudan 121 H4

▶Halaib Triangle terr. Egypt/Sudan 121 G4
Disputed territory (Egypt/Sudan) administered by Sudan.

Ḥalāl, Gebel hill Egypt 108 E7
Ḥalāniyāt, Juzur al is Oman 105 G4
English form Kuria Muria Islands
Ḥalāniyāt, Khalīj al b. Oman 105 F4
English form Kuria Muria Bay
Ḥālat 'Ammār Saudi Arabia 106 D5
Hălăucești Romania 58 H1
Halawa U.S.A. 181 [inset] Z1
Halbā', Wādī al watercourse Saudi Arabia 109 M8
Halban Mongolia 84 C1
formerly known as Tsetserleg
Halberstadt Germany 48 I4
Halcon, Mount Phil. 74 B3
Halcyon Drift S. Africa 133 M7
Haldane r. Canada 166 F1
Halden Norway 45 J4
Haldensleben Germany 48 I3
Haldi r. India 97 F5
Haldia India 97 F5
Haldibari India 97 F4
Haldwani India 96 C3
Hale watercourse Australia 148 B5
Hale China 85 F3
Hale U.S.A. 173 J6
Hale, Mount hill Australia 151 B5
Haleakala National Park U.S.A. 181 [inset] Z1
Ḥāleh Iran 100 C5
Haleiwa U.S.A. 181 [inset] Y1
Halénia well Chad 120 D5
Haleparki Deresi r. Syria/Turkey see Quwayq, Nahr
Half Assini Ghana 124 E5
Halfeti Turkey 107 D3
Halfmoon Bay N.Z. 153 C14
Half Moon Bay U.S.A. 182 B4
Half Moon Lake salt flat Australia 146 B2
Halfway r. Canada 166 F3
Halfway U.S.A. 176 H6
Halfweg S. Africa 132 E7
Halhgol Mongolia 85 H2
Ḥalī, Wādī watercourse Saudi Arabia 104 C4
Ḥalib, Quwayrat al hill Iraq 109 N6
Haliburton Canada 173 O5
Haliburton Highlands hills Canada 168 E4
Halicarnassus Turkey see Bodrum
Halichy Rus. Fed. 43 N8

▶Halifax Canada 169 I4
Provincial capital of Nova Scotia.

Halifax U.K. 47 K10
Halifax NC U.S.A. 176 H9
Halifax VA U.S.A. 176 G9
Halifax, Mount Australia 149 E3
Halifax Bay Australia 149 E3
Halikko Fin. 42 E1
Ḥalīleh, Ra's-e pt Iran 100 B4
Halilulik Indon. 75 C5
Ḥalimah mt. Lebanon/Syria 109 H3
Halimun National Park Indon. 77 D4
Halinor Lake salt flat Australia 146 A2
Haliut China see Urad Zhongqi
Haliyā well Yemen 105 E4
Haliyal India 94 B3
Hall atoll Kiribati see Maiana
Hall U.S.A. 176 A8
Hälla Sweden 44 L3
Halland county Sweden 45 K4
Halla-san mt. S. Korea 83 B6
Halla-san National Park S. Korea 83 B6
Hall Beach Canada 165 K3
Halle Belgium 51 K2
also spelt Hal
Halle (Saale) Germany 48 I4
Halleck U.S.A. 183 I1
Hällefors Sweden 45 K4
Hälleforsnäs Sweden 45 L4
Hallein Austria 49 K8
Hallen Sweden 44 K3
Hallett, Cape Antarctica 223 L2
Hallettsville U.S.A. 179 C6
Hällevikstrand Sweden 45 J4
Halley research station Antarctica 222 W1
Hallgreen, Mount Antarctica 223 X2
Halliday Lake Canada 167 I2
Halligen is Germany 48 F1
Hallingdal valley Norway 45 J3
Hallingdalselva r. Norway 45 J4
Hall in Tirol Austria 48 I8
Hall Islands Micronesia 220 E5
Halliste r. Estonia 42 G3
Hällnäs Sweden 44 L2
Hallock U.S.A. 178 C1
Hall Peninsula Canada 165 M3
Hallsberg Sweden 45 K4
Halls Creek Australia 150 D3
Halls Lake Canada 173 O5
Hallstavik Sweden 45 L3
Hallvik Sweden 44 L2
Hallviken Sweden 44 K3
Hallyeo Haesang National Park S. Korea 83 C6
Halmahera i. Indon. 75 D2
also known as Jailolo Gilolo
Halmahera Sea Indon. 75 D3
Halmstad Sweden 45 K4
Halol India 96 B5
Haloze reg. Slovenia 56 H2
Hals Denmark 45 J4
Hal Saflieni Hypogeum tourist site Malta 57 G13
Hälsingborg Sweden see Helsingborg
Halsua Fin. 44 N3
Haltang r. China 84 B4
Haltwhistle U.K. 47 J9
Ḥālūl i. Qatar 105 F2
Halvad India 96 A5
Halvmåneøya i. Svalbard 38 C2
Ḥalwān hill Saudi Arabia 109 K9
Ham France 51 J3
Ham watercourse Namibia 132 D5

Ham, Oued el r. Alg. **55** O9
Hamab Namibia **132** D5
Hamada Japan **91** C7
Hamâda Çafia des. Mali **122** D5
Hamada ed Douakel plat. Mali **122** D4
Hamaguir Alg. **123** E3
Hamāh Syria **109** I2
Hamakita Japan **91** E7
Hamamasu Japan **90** G3
Hamamatsu Japan **91** E7
Hamapega hill Spain **54** F6
Hamar Norway **45** J3
Hamar Nafūr r. Oman **105** G4
Hamarøy Norway **44** K1
Hamasaka Japan **91** D7
Hamasien prov. Eritrea **104** B5
Hamâta, Gebel mt. Egypt **121** G3
Hamatonbetsu Japan **90** H2
Hambantota Sri Lanka **94** D5
Hambidge Conservation Park nature res.
  Australia **146** B3
Hambleton U.S.A. **176** F6
Hamburg Germany **48** G2
Hamburg S. Africa **133** L10
Hamburg AR U.S.A. **175** B5
Hamburg IA U.S.A. **174** E3
Hamburg NJ U.S.A. **177** K4
Hamburg NY U.S.A. **176** F3
Hamburg PA U.S.A. **177** J5
Hamburgisches Wattenmeer,
  Nationalpark nat. park Germany **48** F2
Ḥamḍ, Wādī al watercourse Saudi Arabia
  104 B2
Hamdah Saudi Arabia **104** C4
Hamdallay Niger **125** F3
Hamdānah Saudi Arabia **104** C4
Hamden U.S.A. **177** M4
Hamdibey Turkey **59** I9
Hamdili Turkey **108** G1
Hämeenkangas moorland Fin. **45** M3
Hämeenkoski Fin. **42** E1
  formerly known as Koski
Hämeenkyrö Fin. **45** M3
Hämeenlinna Fin. **45** N3
  also known as Tavastehus
HaMelah, Yam salt l. Asia see Dead Sea
Hamelin Australia **151** A5
Hamelin Pool b. Australia **151** A5
Hameln Germany **48** G3
Hamero Hadad Eth. **128** D3
Hamersley Australia **150** B4
Hamersley Lakes salt flat Australia **151** B6
Hamersley Range mts Australia **150** B4
Hamgyŏng-sanmaek mts N. Korea **82** C4
Hamhŭng N. Korea **83** B5
Hami China **84** B3
  also known as Kumul
Hamid Iran **100** B4
Hamid Sudan **121** F4
Hamidiye Turkey **58** H7
Hamilton Qld Australia **149** D4
Hamilton S.A. Australia **148** B5
Hamilton Vic. Australia **147** D4
Hamilton watercourse Qld Australia **149** C3
Hamilton watercourse S.A. Australia **146** B1
▶Hamilton Bermuda **171** N5
  Capital of Bermuda.
Hamilton Canada **168** E5
Hamilton r. Canada see Churchill
Hamilton N.Z. **152** J5
Hamilton U.K. **46** H8
Hamilton AL U.S.A. **174** C5
Hamilton MT U.S.A. **180** D3
Hamilton NY U.S.A. **177** K3
Hamilton OH U.S.A. **176** A6
Hamilton TX U.S.A. **179** C6
Hamilton, Mount CA U.S.A. **182** C4
Hamilton, Mount NV U.S.A. **183** I2
Hamilton Burn N.Z. **153** C13
Hamilton City U.S.A. **182** B2
Hamilton Downs Australia **148** B4
Hamilton Mountain hill U.S.A. **177** K2
Hamilton Sound sea chan. Canada **169** K3
Hamim, Wādī al watercourse Libya **120** D2
Hamina Fin. **45** N3
  also known as Fredrikshamn
Ḥāmir, Wādī al watercourse Saudi Arabia
  107 C3
Hamirpur Himachal Pradesh India **96** C3
Hamirpur Uttar Pradesh India **96** D4
Hamitabat Turkey see Isparta
Hamlet U.S.A. **174** E5
Hamley Bridge Australia **146** C3
Hamlin TX U.S.A. **177** J4
Hamlin TX U.S.A. **179** B5
Hamlin Lake U.S.A. **172** G6
Ham Luông, Sông r. mouth Vietnam **79** D6
Hamm Germany **48** E4
Hammada du Drâa plat. Alg. **122** C3
Hammâdât Tingharat des. Libya **120** A2
Hammam, Golfe de g. Tunisia **123** H1
Hammamet, Golfe de g. Tunisia **57** C12
Hammam-Lif Tunisia **57** C12
Hammam-Sousse Alg. **55** J9
Hammam Tunisia **57** C12
Hammamet Tunisia **57** C12
Hammari, Hawr al imp. l. Iraq **107** F5
Hammarland Fin. **42** H1
Hammarsdale S. Africa **133** O6
Hammarstrand Sweden **44** L3
Hammelburg Germany **48** G5
Hammerdal Sweden **44** L3
Hammerfest Norway **44** M1
Hammond IN U.S.A. **174** C3

Hammond LA U.S.A. **175** B6
Hammond Bay U.S.A. **173** I5
Hammondsport U.S.A. **177** H3
Hammonton U.S.A. **177** K6
Hambukt Norway **44** N1
Ham Ninh Vietnam **79** D6
Hamorton U.S.A. **177** J6
Hampden N.Z. **153** E13
Hampden Highlands U.S.A. **177** Q1
Hampden Sydney U.S.A. **176** G8
Hampi India **94** C3
  also known as Vijayanagar
Håmpjåkk Sweden **44** M2
Hampstead U.S.A. **177** I6
Hampton Canada **169** H4
Hampton AR U.S.A. **175** B5
Hampton IA U.S.A. **174** A3
Hampton NH U.S.A. **177** O3
Hampton SC U.S.A. **175** D5
Hampton TN U.S.A. **176** C9
Hampton VA U.S.A. **177** I8
Hampton Bays U.S.A. **177** M5
Hampton Tableland reg. Australia **151** D7
Hamra, Dhahrat Syria/Turkey see
  Ḩimâr, Wādī al
hamrat esh Sheikh Sudan **121** E6
Hamrin, Jabal hills Iraq **107** F4
Hams Fork r. U.S.A. **180** E4
Ham Tân Vietnam **79** D6
Hamta Pass India **96** C2
Hāmūn-e-Chah Gheybi salt pan Iran
  101 E4
Hāmūn-e Jaz Mūriān salt marsh Iran
  100 D5
Hāmūn Helmand salt flat Afgh./Iran **101** E4
Hamun-i-Lora dry lake Pak. **101** F4
Hamun-i-Mashkel salt flat Pak. **101** E4
Hāmūn Pu marsh Afgh. **101** F4
Hamur Turkey **107** E3
Hamwic U.K. see Southampton
Hamza Uzbek. see Khamza
Haná r. Czech Rep. **49** N6
Hana U.S.A. **181** [inset] Z1
Hanábana r. Cuba **175** D8
Hanahai watercourse Botswana/Namibia
  130 D4
Hanakpınar Turkey see Çınar
Hanalc Saudi Arabia **104** B2
Hanamaki Japan **90** G5
Hanamanioa, Cape U.S.A. **181** [inset] Z1
Hanam Plateau Namibia **132** B2
Hanang mt. Tanz. **129** B6
Hananui hill N.Z. see Anglem, Mount
Hanapepe U.S.A. **181** [inset] Y1
Hanau Germany **48** F5
Hancheng China **85** F5
Hanchuan China **87** E2
Hancheng China **85** F5
Hancock MD U.S.A. **176** G6
Hancock MI U.S.A. **172** E3
Hancock NY U.S.A. **177** J4
Handa Japan **91** E7
Handan China **85** G4
Handeni Tanz. **129** C6
Handian China see Changzhi
Handlová Slovakia **49** P7
HaNegev reg. Israel see Negev
Haneqarot watercourse Israel **108** G7
Hanerau-Hademarschen Germany **48** G1
Hanfeng China see Kaixian
Hanford U.S.A. **182** D4
Hangal India **94** B3
Hangan Myanmar **79** B5
Han-gang r. S. Korea **83** B5
Hangayn Nuruu mts Mongolia **84** C1
Hangchow China see Hangzhou
Hangchuan China see Guangze
Hanggin Houqi China see Xamba
Hanggin Qi China see Xin
Hangö Fin. see Hanko
Hangö östra fjärd b. Fin. **42** E2
Hangö västra fjärd b. Fin. **42** D2
Hangu China **85** H4
Hangu Pak. **101** G3
Hangya China **84** C4
Hangzhou China **87** G2
  formerly spelt Hangchow
Hangzhou Wan b. China **87** G2
Hani Turkey **107** E3
Ḩanidh Saudi Arabia **105** E2
Hanife r. Turkey **59** J8
Hanish Kabir i. Yemen **104** C5
Hanjia China see Pengshui
Hanjiang China **87** F1
  also known as Yangzhou
Han Jiang r. China **87** E4
Hanjiaoshui China **85** E4
Hankasalmi Fin. **44** N3
Hankey S. Africa **133** I10
Hanko Fin. **45** M4
  also spelt Hangö
Hanksville U.S.A. **183** N3
Hanle Jammu and Kashmir **96** C2
Hanley Canada **167** J5
Hanmer Forest Park nature res. N.Z.
  153 G10
Hanmer Springs N.Z. **153** G10
Hann r. Qld Australia **149** E2
Hann r. W.A. Australia **150** D3
Hann, Mount hill Australia **150** D2
Hanna Canada **167** I5
Hannagan Meadow U.S.A. **183** O8
Hannah Bay Canada **168** D3
Hannibal MO U.S.A. **174** B4
Hannibal NY U.S.A. **177** I2
Hannibal OH U.S.A. **176** E6
Hannover Germany **48** G3
  English form Hanover
Hannoversch Münden Germany **48** G4
Hann Range mts Australia **148** B4
Hanöbukten b. Sweden **45** K5
▶Ha Nôi Vietnam **78** D3
  Capital of Vietnam. English form Hanoi.
Hanoi Vietnam see Ha Nôi
Hanover Canada **168** D4
Hanover Germany see Hannover
Hanover S. Africa **133** I8
Hanover NH U.S.A. **177** M2
Hanover OH U.S.A. **176** C5
Hanover PA U.S.A. **177** H5
Hanover VA U.S.A. **176** H8
Hanover, Isla i. Chile **205** B8
Hanover Road S. Africa **133** I7
Hansen Mountains Antarctica **223** D2
Hanshou China **87** D2
Han Shui r. China **87** D2
Han India **96** C3
Hansnes Norway **44** L1
Hanson watercourse Australia **148** B4
Hansonville U.S.A. **176** C8
Hanson, Lake salt flat Australia **146** C3
Han Sum China **85** H2
Hantengri Feng mt. Kazakh./Kyrg. see
  Khan-Tengri, Pik
Hantsavichy Belarus **42** H9
  also spelt Gantsevichi
Hanumana India **97** D4
Hanumangarh India **96** B3
  also known as Bhatnair
Hanumari well Oman **105** F4
Hanur Gol r. Mongolia **84** D1
Hanyang China see Caidian
Hanyin China **87** D1
Hanyuan China **86** B2
  also known as Fulin
Hanzhong China **86** C1

Hao atoll Fr. Polynesia **221** I7
Haomen China see Menyuan
Haora India **97** F5
  formerly spelt Howrah
Haoud el Hamra Alg. **123** G2
Haouza W. Sahara **122** C4
Haparanda Sweden **44** N2
Haparanda skärgård nationalpark
  nat. park Sweden **44** M2
Hapch'ŏn S. Korea **91** A7
Hapoli India **97** G4
Happy Jack U.S.A. **183** M7
Happy Valley - Goose Bay Canada **169** I2
  also known as Goose Bay
Hapsu N. Korea **83** C4
Hapur India **96** C3
Haql Saudi Arabia **106** C5
Haqshah well Saudi Arabia **105** E3
Hara Alol mt. Djibouti **128** D2
Ḩaraḍ well Saudi Arabia **105** E2
Ḩaraḍ Yemen **104** C4
Ḩaraḍ, Jabal al mt. Jordan **108** G8
Haradah Saudi Arabia **105** D3
Haradak Belarus **43** K6
  also spelt Gorodok
Haradok Belarus **43** K6
  also spelt Gorodok
Haradotskaye Wzvyshsha hills Belarus
  43 K6
Harads Sweden **44** M2
Haradzishcha Belarus **42** H8
Haradzishcha Belarus **43** K8
Haradzyeya Belarus **42** H8
Haramachi Japan **90** G5
Haramukh mt. Jammu and Kashmir **96** B2
Haran Turkey see Harran
Harany Belarus **43** K6
Harappa Road Pak. **101** H4
▶Harare Zimbabwe **131** F3
  Capital of Zimbabwe. Formerly known as
  Salisbury.
Ha Rasebi S. Africa **133** J6
Ḩarāsīs, Jiddat al des. Oman **105** F4
  also known as a-Jiddét
Harat i. Iran **100** C4
Harat Island Eritrea **121** H5
Haraym well Saudi Arabia **105** E2
Har-Ayrag Mongolia **85** F2
Haraz-Djombo Chad **120** D1
Haraze-Mangueigne Chad **126** D2
Harbacheva Belarus **43** K6
Harbel Liberia **124** C5
Harbin China **82** B3
Harbke-Allertal park Germany **48** I3
Harboi Hills Pak. **101** F4
Harbor Beach U.S.A. **173** K7
Harbor Springs U.S.A. **173** I5
Harbour Breton Canada **169** K4
Harbutt Range hills Australia **150** C4
Harcuvar Mountains U.S.A. **183** K8
Harda Khas India **96** C5
Hardangerfjorden sea chan. Norway **45** I4
Hardangervidda Nasjonalpark nat. park
  Norway **45** I3
Hardap reg. Namibia **130** C5
Hardap Dam Namibia **130** C5
Hardbakke Norway **45** I3
Harden, Bukit mt. Indon. **77** F1
Hardenberg Neth. **48** D3
Harderwijk Neth. **48** C3
Hardeveld mts S. Africa **132** C8
Hardey r. Australia **150** B4
Hardin IL U.S.A. **174** B4
Hardin MT U.S.A. **180** F3
Harding r. Australia **150** B4
Harding S. Africa **133** N7
Harding Range hills W.A. Australia **150** D3
Harding Range hills W.A. Australia **151** B5
Hardoi India **96** D4
Hardwar India see Haridwar
Hardwick GA U.S.A. **175** D5
Hardwick VT U.S.A. **177** M1
Hardwicke Bay Australia **146** C3
Hardy r. Australia **150** B4
Hardy, Mount N.Z. see Rangipoua
Hardy, Península pen. Chile **205** C9
Hare Bay Canada **169** K3
Hareid Norway **44** I3
Hareidin, Wādī watercourse Egypt **108** E7
Hare Indian r. Canada **166** D1
Haren (Ems) Germany **48** E3
Hareøen i. Greenland see Qeqertarsuatsiaq
Härer Eth. **128** D2
Härer Wildlife Sanctuary nature res. Eth.
  128 D2
Harf el Mreffi mt. Lebanon **108** G4
Hargant China **85** H1
Hargeisa Somalia see Hargeysa
Hargele Eth. **128** D3
Hargeysa Somalia **128** E2
  also spelt Hargeisa
Harghita, Munţii mts Romania **58** G2
Harghita-Mădăraş, Vârful mt. Romania
  58 G2
Hargigo Eritrea **104** B5
Harhal Dağları mts Turkey **107** E3
Harhatan China **85** E4
Har Hu l. China **84** C4
Harib Yemen **105** D5
Haribomo, Lac l. Mali **124** E2
Haridwar India **96** C3
  formerly spelt Hardwar
Harif, Har mt. Israel **108** F7
  also known as Kharuf, Ra's
Harihar India **94** B3
Hariharpur India **94** B3
Harij India **96** A5
Härim Syria **109** H1
Harima-nada b. Japan **91** D7
Harūz-e Bālā Iran **100** D4
Harvard U.S.A. **172** E8
Harvard, Mount U.S.A. **180** F5
Harvey Canada **169** I4
Harvey MI U.S.A. **172** F4
Harvey ND U.S.A. **178** B2
Harvey Mountain U.S.A. **182** C1
Harwich U.K. **47** N12
Harwich Port U.S.A. **177** O4
Haryana state India **96** C3
Harz hills Germany **48** H4
Harz nat. park Germany **48** H4
Har Zin Israel **108** G7
Ḩaşāh, Wādī al watercourse
  Jordan/Saudi Arabia **109** I7
Hasalbag China **88** B3
Hasana, Wādī watercourse Egypt **108** E7
Hasan Dağı mts Turkey **106** C3
Hasan Guli Turkm. see Esenguly
Hasankeyf Turkey **107** E3
Hasan Langi Iran **100** D5
Hasanparti India **94** C2
Hasanur India **94** C4
Hasbaya Lebanon **108** G4
Hasbani r. Lebanon **106** C4
Hasbek Turkey **106** C3
Hasdo r. India **97** D5
Hase r. Germany **48** E3
Haselünne Germany **48** E3
Hashaat Mongolia **84** D2
HaSharon plain Israel see Sharon, Plain of
Hashimoto Japan **91** D7
Hashish, Ghubbat b. Oman **105** G3
Hashtgerd Iran **100** B3

Har Nuur l. Mongolia **84** C1
Haro Spain **55** I2
Harochychy Belarus **43** K9
Harold U.S.A. **176** C8
Haroldswick U.K. **46** L3
Harper Liberia **124** D5
Harper U.S.A. **178** C4
Harper, Mount Canada **166** B1
Harper Creek r. Canada **167** H3
Harper Lake U.S.A. **183** H6
Harpers Ferry U.S.A. **176** H6
Harpstedt Germany **48** F3
Harqin Qi China see Jinshan
Harqin Zuoqi Mongolzu Zizhixian China
  see Dachengzi
Harquahala Mountains U.S.A. **183** K8
Ḩarrā well Saudi Arabia **104** C3
Harrai India **96** C5
Harran Turkey **109** I1
  also spelt Haran; historically known as
  Carrhae
Harras of Dhamar vol. Yemen **104** D5
Ḩarrāt Kishb lava field Saudi Arabia **104** C3
Harricanaw r. Canada **168** E3
Harrietta U.S.A. **173** H6
Harriman U.S.A. **174** C5
Harriman Reservoir r. U.S.A. **177** M3
Harrington Australia **147** G2
Harrington DE U.S.A. **177** J7
Harrington ME U.S.A. **177** R1
Harris r. U.K. **46** F6
Harris, Lake salt flat Australia **146** B2
Harris, Mount Australia **148** A5
Harris, Sound of sea chan. U.K. **46** E6
Harrisburg Australia **146** B2
Harrisburg IL U.S.A. **174** B4
Harrisburg NE U.S.A. **178** B3
Harrisburg OH U.S.A. **176** B6
▶Harrisburg PA U.S.A. **177** I5
  State capital of Pennsylvania.
Harrismith S. Africa **133** N5
Harris Mountains N.Z. **153** C12
Harrison AR U.S.A. **179** D4
Harrison NE U.S.A. **178** B3
Harrison OH U.S.A. **176** A6
Harrison, Cape Canada **169** J2
Harrison Bay U.S.A. **164** D2
Harrisonburg LA U.S.A. **175** B6
Harrisonburg VA U.S.A. **176** G7
Harrison Lake Canada **166** F5
Harriston Canada **173** M7
Harrisville NY U.S.A. **177** J1
Harrodsburg U.S.A. **176** A8
Harrodsville N.Z. see Otorohanga
Harrogate U.K. **47** K10
Harrowsmith Canada **173** Q6
Harry S. Truman Reservoir r. U.S.A. **178** D4
Harsa Sweden **45** K3
Har Sai Shan mt. China **84** C5
Hârşeşti Romania **58** F4
Harsin Iran **100** A3
Harşit r. Turkey **107** D2
Hârşova Romania **58** I4
  formerly spelt Hîrşova
Harstad Norway **44** L1
Harsud India **96** C5
Harsvik Norway **44** J2
Hart r. Canada **166** E1
Hart U.S.A. **172** G7
Hart, Lake salt flat Australia **146** C2
Hart, Mount hill Australia **150** D3
Hartao China **85** I3
Hartbees r. S. Africa **132** E5
Ha Tiên Vietnam **79** D6
Ha Tinh Vietnam **78** D4
Hatisar Bhutan see Gelephu
Hato Corozal Col. **198** D3
Hatohud East Timor **75** C5
  formerly known as Hotahudo; formerly spelt
  Hato Hud
Hato Hud East Timor see Hatohud
Hato la Vergareña Venez. **199** F3
Hato Mayor Dom. Rep. **187** F3
Hat Piplia India **96** C4
Hatra Iraq **107** E4
  also known as Al Ḩaḍr
Hatsukaichi Japan **91** C7
Hatta Madhya Pradesh India **96** C4
Hatta Madhya Pradesh India **96** C4
Hattah Australia **147** D3
Hatteras, Cape U.S.A. **174** F5
Hattfjelldal Norway **44** K2
Hatti r. India **95** D7
Hattiesburg U.S.A. **175** B6
Hattingen Germany **48** E4
Hatton, Gunung hill Sabah Malaysia **77** G1
Hatton Bay Canada **166** F2
Hattras Passage Myanmar **79** B5
Hattula Fin. **45** N3
Hatvan Hungary **49** Q8
Hat Yai Thai. **79** C7
Haud reg. Eth. **128** D3
Haugesund Norway **45** I4
Hau Giang, Sông r. Vietnam **79** D6
Hauho Fin. **45** N3
Hauhungaroa Range mts N.Z. **152** J6
Haukeligrend Norway **45** I4
Haukipudas Fin. **44** N2
Haukivesi l. Fin. **44** O3
Haukivuori Fin. **45** N3
Haultain r. Canada **167** J4
Haungpa Myanmar **78** B2
Haup's S. Africa **133** K3
Hauraki Gulf N.Z. **152** J4
Hauraki Gulf Maritime Park nature res.
  N.Z. **152** I4
Haurangi Forest Park nature res. N.Z.
  152 J9
Hauroko, Lake N.Z. **153** B14
Hausach Germany **48** F7
Hausjärvi Fin. **42** F1
Haut, Isle au i. U.S.A. **177** Q1
Hautajärvi Fin. **44** O2
Hautes Atlas Morocco **122** C3
  English form High Atlas; also known as
  Grand Atlas
Haut-Congo prov. Dem. Rep. Congo see
  Orientale
Hautefort France **50** G7
Haute-Guinée admin. reg. Guinea **124** C4
Haute-Kotto pref. Cent. Afr. Rep. **126** D3
Haute-Normandie admin. reg. France **50** H3
Hauterive Canada **169** G3
Hauteurs de la Gâtine reg. France **50** F6
Haute-Volta country Africa see Burkina
Haut-Folin hill France **51** K6
Haut-Jura, Parc Naturel Régional du
  nat. res. France **51** L6
Haut-Languedoc, Parc Naturel Régional
  du nature res. France **51** J9
Haut-Mbomou pref. Cent. Afr. Rep. **126** E3
Haut-Ogooué prov. Gabon **126** B5
Hauts Plateaux Alg. **123** E2
Haut-Zaïre prov. Dem. Rep. Congo see
  Orientale
Hauvo Fin. see Nagu
Hauwai N.Z. **153** I9
Hauzenberg Germany **49** K7
▶Havana Cuba **186** C2
  Capital of Cuba. Also spelt Habana or La
  Habana.
Havana U.S.A. **174** B3
Havant U.K. **47** L13
Havasu, Lake U.S.A. **183** J7
Havel r. Germany **48** J3
Havelberg Germany **49** J3
Haveli Pak. **101** H4

Hashtpar Iran **100** B2
  formerly known as Tālesh
Hashtrud Iran **100** A2
  formerly known as Azaran or Sar Eskandar
Ḩasic Bos.-Herz. see Srnice
Hāsik Oman **105** F4
Hasilpur Pak. **101** H4
Haskell U.S.A. **179** C5
Hasle Denmark **45** K5
Haslemere U.K. **47** L12
Haslev Denmark **45** J5
Hăşmaşul Mare mt. Romania **58** G2
Hasparren France **50** E9
Ḩaşş, Jabal al hills Syria **109** I1
Hassa Turkey **109** I1
Hassan India **94** C3
Hassayampa watercourse U.S.A. **183** L8
Haßberge park Germany **48** H5
Hasselt Belgium **51** L2
Hassi Aridal well W. Sahara **122** B4
Hassi Bahbah Alg. **55** O9
Hassi Bedjedjene well Alg. **123** H4
Hassi Bel Guebbour Alg. **123** G3
Hassi Bou Bernous well Alg. **123** F4
Hassi Bourahla well Alg. **123** H4
Hassi Chebbaba well Alg. **123** F3
Hassi Daoula Alg. **123** F2
Hassi Doumas well W. Sahara **122** B5
Hassi el Ahmar well Alg. **123** F3
Hassi el Krenig well Alg. **123** F3
Hassi Fahl well Alg. **123** F3
Hassi Habadra well Alg. **123** G4
Hassi Ifertas well Libya **120** A2
Hassi I-n-Akeouet well Alg. **123** G4
Hassi I-n-Belrem well Alg. **123** F4
Hassi Inifel Alg. **123** F3
Hassi Khanem well Alg. **123** F3
Hassi Mdakene well Alg. **123** F3
Hassi Messaoud Alg. **123** G3
Hassi Msegguem well Alg. **123** F3
Hassi Nebka well Alg. **123** G4
Hassi Ntsel well Alg. **123** G4
Hassi Sebbakh well Alg. **123** G4
Hassi Tabelbalet well Alg. **123** G4
Hassi Tiguentourine well Alg. **123** G4
Hassi Ti-n Fouchaye well Alg. **123** H3
Hässleholm Sweden **45** K4
Hastière-Lavaux Belgium **51** K2
Hastings Australia **147** E4
Hastings Canada **173** P6
Hastings N.Z. **152** K7
Hastings U.K. **47** M13
Hastings MI U.S.A. **172** H8
Hastings MN U.S.A. **174** A2
Hastings NE U.S.A. **178** C3
Hastings Islanc P.N.G. **149** F1
Hasvik Norway **44** M1
Ḩaşwayl Yemen **105** F5
Ḩasy Haghe well Libya **120** A3
Hat India **97** D4
Hasy Msegguem well Libya **120** A3
Hatansuudal Mongolia **84** D2
Hatay Turkey see Antakya
Hatay prov. Turkey **108** H1
Hatch U.S.A. **183** L4
Hatches Creek Australia **148** B4
Hatchie r. U.S.A. **174** B5
Hat Creek U.S.A. **182** C1
Ḩateg Romania **58** D3
Hatepe N.Z. **152** K6
Hatfield Australia **147** D3
Hatgal Mongolia **84** D1
Hat Head National Park Australia **147** G2
Hathras India **96** C4
Hatia Bangl. **97** F5
Hatia Nepal **97** E4
Ḩāţibah, Ra's pt Saudi Arabia **104** B3

Havelian Pak. **101** H3
Havelock Canada **173** P6
Havelock N.Z. **152** H9
Havelock Swaziland see Bulembu
Havelock U.S.A. **174** E5
Havelock Island India **95** G4
Havelock Falls Australia **148** B2
Havelock North N.Z. **152** K7
Haven U.S.A. **178** C4
Haverdal Sweden **45** K4
Haverfordwest U.K. **47** H12
  also known as Hwlffordd
Haverhill U.K. **47** M11
Haverhill U.S.A. **177** N3
Haveri India **94** B3
Haverö Sweden **44** K3
Haverstraw U.S.A. **177** L4
Havličkův Brod Czech Rep. **49** M6
Havøysund Norway **44** N1
Havran Turkey **59** I9
Havran r. Turkey **59** H9
Havre U.S.A. **180** E2
Havre Aubert Canada **169** I4
Havre Aubert, Île du i. Canada **169** I4
Havre de Grace U.S.A. **177** I6
Havre Rock i. N.Z. **145** H5
Havre-St-Pierre Canada **169** I3
Havsa Turkey **58** H7
Havutlu Turkey **108** G1
Havza Turkey **106** C2
▶Hawaii i. U.S.A. **181** [inset] Z1
Hawai'i. The Gulf see Huwär
Hawahiya, Wādī watercourse Egypt **108** D9
Hawea, Lake N.Z. **153** D12
Hawea Flat N.Z. **153** D12
Hawera N.Z. **152** I7
Hawes U.K. **47** J9
Hawesville U.S.A. **174** C4
Hawick U.K. **46** J8
Ḩawīzah, Hawr al imp. l. Iraq **107** F5
Hawkdun Range mts N.Z. **153** D12
Hawke Bay N.Z. **152** L7
Hawke Island Canada **169** K2
Hawker Australia **146** C2
Hawkers Gate Australia **146** D2
Hawke's Bay admin. reg. N.Z. **152** K7
Hawkins Peak U.S.A. **183** K4
Hawk Junction Canada **173** L2
Haw Knob mt. U.S.A. **174** C5
Hawkesbill Cay i. Bahamas **175** E7
Hawksnest Point Bahamas **186** E1
Hawkswood N.Z. **153** H10
Hawlêr Iraq see Arbil
Hawley U.S.A. **177** J4
Hawng Luk Myanmar **78** B3
Hawr' Yemen **105** E5
Hawşal hills Saudi Arabia **108** G9
Hawshah, Jibāl al hills Saudi Arabia
  104 D3
Hawthorne U.S.A. **182** F3
Hawya r. Belarus **42** G8
Hawzën Eth. **104** B5
Hay Australia **147** E3
Hay watercourse Australia **148** C5
Hay r. Canada **167** H2
Hay r. U.S.A. **172** B6
Haya China **84** D3
Haya Indon. **75** D3
Hayachine-san mt. Japan **90** G5
Hayakita Japan **90** G3
Hayang S. Korea **91** A7
Haydän, Wādī r. Jordan **108** G6
  also known as Heidan
Haydarābād Iran **100** A2
Haydarba Turkey **59** I9
Hayden CO U.S.A. **180** F4
Hayden ID U.S.A. **180** C3
Hayes r. Man. Canada **167** M3
Hayes r. Nunavut Canada **165** J3
Hayes Center U.S.A. **178** B3
Hayes Creek Australia **148** A2
Hayes Halvø pen. Greenland **165** M2
Hayesville U.S.A. **174** D5
Ḩayf' Yemen **105** F5
Hayfield Reservoir U.S.A. **183** I8
Hayfork U.S.A. **182** A1
Ḩayl Oman **105** G2
Hayl, Wādī watercourse Syria **109** I4
Ḩayl, Wādī al watercourse Syria **109** K3
Haylaastay Mongolia **85** G2
Haymā' Oman **105** G4
Haymana Turkey **106** C3
Haymarket U.S.A. **176** H7
Hayna r. Belarus **42** J7
Haynesville U.S.A. **175** B5
Hayneville U.S.A. **175** C5
Hayotboshi Toghi mt. Uzbek. see
  Khayatbashi, Gora
Hayrabolu Turkey **106** A2
Hay River Canada **167** H2
Hay River Reserve Canada **167** H2
Hays U.S.A. **178** C4
Hays Yemen **104** C5
Hayshah, Sabkhat al salt pan Libya **120** B2
Haysi U.S.A. **176** C8
Hays Mountains Antarctica **223** N1
Haysville U.S.A. **178** C4
Haysyn Ukr. **41** D6
Hay well Oman **105** G2
Hayti S. U.S.A. **178** D2
Hayward CA U.S.A. **182** B4
Hayward WI U.S.A. **172** B4
Haywards Heath U.K. **47** L13
Ḩazy well Oman **105** F4
Hazarajat reg. Afgh. **101** F3
Hazard U.S.A. **176** B8
Hazaribag India **97** E5
Hazaribagh Range mts India **97** D5
Hazār Masjed, Kūh-e mts Iran **101** D2
Hazebrouck France **51** I2
Hazel Green U.S.A. **172** C8
Hazel Street U.S.A. **172** D5
Hazelton Canada **166** E4
Hazen U.S.A. **178** D2
Hazen Strait Canada **165** H2
Hazhdanahr reg. Afgh. **101** F2
Hazlehurst GA U.S.A. **175** D6
Hazlehurst MS U.S.A. **175** B5
Hazleton U.S.A. **177** J4
Hazlet salt flat Australia **150** C4
Hazorasp Uzbek. see Khazarasp
Hazrat Sultan Afgh. **101** F2
Hazro Pak. **101** H3
Hazro Turkey **107** E3
H. Bouchard Arg. **204** E4
Headingly Australia **148** C4
Head of Bight b. Australia **146** A2
Heafford Junction U.S.A. **172** D5
Healdsburg U.S.A. **182** B3
Healdton U.S.A. **179** C5
Healesville Australia **147** E4
Healing Springs U.S.A. **176** F8
▶Heard and McDonald Islands terr.
  Indian Ocean **219** L9
  Australian External Territory.
  asia [countries] ▶▶ 64–67
Heard Island Indian Ocean **219** L9
Hearne U.S.A. **179** C6
Hearne Lake Canada **167** H2
Hearst Canada **168** D3

Hearst Island Antarctica **222** T2
Heart *r.* U.S.A. **178** B2
Heath *r.* Bol./Peru **200** C3
Heathcote Australia **147** E4
Heathfield U.K. **47** M13
Heathrow *airport* U.K. **47** L12
Heathsville U.S.A. **177** I8
Heavener U.S.A. **179** D5
Hebbronville U.S.A. **179** C7
Hebei *prov.* China **85** G4
English form Hopei
Hebel Australia **147** E2
Heber *AZ* U.S.A. **183** N7
Heber *CA* U.S.A. **183** I9
Heber City U.S.A. **183** M1
Heber Springs U.S.A. **179** D5
Hebgen Lake U.S.A. **180** E3
Hebi China **85** G5
Hebian China **85** G4
Hebron Canada **169** I1
Hebron *IN* U.S.A. **172** F9
Hebron *MD* U.S.A. **177** J7
Hebron *NE* U.S.A. **178** C3
Hebron West Bank **108** G6
also known as Al Khalīl *or* El Khalil; *also spelt* Hevron
Hebron Fiord *inlet* Canada **169** I1
Hebros *r.* Greece/Turkey *see* **Evros**
Heby Sweden **45** L4
Hecate Strait Canada **166** D4
Hecelchakán Mex. **185** H4
Hecheng China *see* **Zixi**
Hecheng China *see* **Qingtian**
Hechi China **87** D3
also known as Jinchengjiang
Hechingen Germany **48** F7
Hechuan China **86** C2
Hechuan China *see* **Yongxing**
Hecla Island Canada **167** L5
Hector U.S.A. **178** D2
Hector Mountain *mts* N.Z. **153** C13
Hedberg Sweden **44** L2
Hede China *see* **Sheyang**
Hédé France **50** E4
Hede Sweden **44** K3
Hedemora Sweden **45** K3
Hedenäset Sweden **44** M2
Hede Shuiku *resr* China **87** D4
Hedesunda Sweden **45** L3
He Devil Mountain U.S.A. **180** C3
Hedgehope N.Z. **153** C14
Hedmark *county* Norway **45** J3
Heerenveen Neth. **48** C3
Heerhugowaard Neth. **48** B3
Heerlen Neth. **48** C5
Hefa Israel *see* **Haifa**
Hefa, Mifraz *b.* Israel *see* **Haifa, Bay of**
Hefei China **87** F2
Hefeng China **87** D2
also known as Rongmei
Heflin U.S.A. **175** C5
Hegang China **82** C3
Heggadadevankote India **94** C3
Heggenes Norway **45** J3
Hegura-jima *i.* Japan **90** E6
Heguri-jima *i.* Japan **91** C8
Heho Myanmar **78** B3
Heiban Sudan **128** A2
Heidan *r.* Jordan *see* **Haydān, Wādī al**
Heide Germany **48** G1
Heidelberg Germany **48** F6
Heidelberg *Gauteng* S. Africa **133** M3
Heidelberg *W. Cape* S. Africa **132** E11
Heidenheim an der Brenz Germany **48** H7
Heihe China **82** B2
formerly known as Aihui
Heilbron S. Africa **133** L4
Heilbronn Germany **48** G6
Heiligenbeil Rus. Fed. *see* **Mamonovo**
Heiligenhafen Germany **48** H1
Hei Ling Chau *i. Hong Kong* China **87** [inset]
Heilongjiang *prov.* China **85** I2
English form Heilungkiang
Heilong Jiang *r.* China **82** D2
also known as Amur
Heilungkiang *prov.* China *see* **Heilongjiang**
Heimaey *i.* Iceland **44** [inset] B3
Heinävesi Fin. **44** O3
Heinola Fin. **45** N3
Heinrichswalde Rus. Fed. *see* **Slavsk**
Heinz Bay Myanmar **79** B5
Heinze Islands Myanmar **79** B5
Heishan China **85** I3
Heishantou China **85** H1
Heishi Beihu *l.* China **89** C5
Heishui China **86** B1
also known as Luhua
Heisker Islands U.K. *see* **Monach Islands**
Heitān, Gebel *hill* Egypt **108** E7
Heituo Shan *mt.* China **85** G4
Hejaz *reg.* Saudi Arabia *see* **Hijaz**
Hejian China **85** H4
Hejiang China **86** C2
He Jiang *r.* China **87** D4
Hejin China **85** F5
Hejing China **88** D3
Heka China **84** C5
Hekimhan Turkey **107** D3
Hekla *vol.* Iceland **44** [inset] C3
Hekou *Gansu* China **84** D4
Hekou *Hubei* China **87** E2
Hekou China *see* **Yanshan**
Hekou China *see* **Yajiang**
Hekou *Yunnan* China **86** B4
Hekpoort S. Africa **133** L2
Hel Poland **49** P1
Helagsfjället *mt.* Sweden **44** K3
Helan Shan *mts* China **85** E4
Helegiu Romania **58** H2
Helem India **97** G4
Helen *i.* Palau **73** H6
Helen, Mount U.S.A. **183** H4
Helena *AR* U.S.A. **174** B5

▶**Helena** *MT* U.S.A. **180** D3
State capital of Montana.

Helena *OH* U.S.A. **176** B4
Helen Reef Palau **73** H6
Helensburgh U.K. **46** H7
Helensville N.Z. **152** I4
Helenwood U.S.A. **176** A9
Helgoland *i.* Germany **48** E1
English form Heligoland
Helgoländer Bucht *b.* Germany **48** F1
English form Heligoland Bight
Helgum Sweden **44** L3
Heligoland *i.* Germany *see* **Helgoland**
Heligoland Bight *b.* Germany *see* **Helgoländer Bucht**
Helixi China *see* **Ningguo**
Hella Iceland **44** [inset] B3
Hellas *country* Europe *see* **Greece**
Helleh *r.* Iran **100** B4
Hellertown U.S.A. **177** J5
Hellespont *strait* Turkey *see* **Dardanelles**
Hellevoetsluis Neth. **48** B4
Hellhole Gorge National Park Australia **149** E5
Helligskogen Norway **44** M1
Hellín Spain **55** J6
Hells Canyon *gorge* U.S.A. **180** C3
Hell-Ville Madag. *see* **Andoany**
Helm U.S.A. **182** D5
Helmand *prov.* Afgh. **101** E4
Helmand *r.* Afgh. **101** E4
Helmantica Spain *see* **Salamanca**
Helmbrechts Germany **48** I5
Helme *r.* Germany **48** I4
Helmeringhausen Namibia **130** C5
Helmond Neth. **48** C4
Helmsdale U.K. **46** I5
Helmsdale *r.* U.K. **46** I5
Helmsley U.K. **47** K9
Helmsley Aboriginal Holding *res.* Australia **149** D2
Helmstedt Germany **48** I3
Helodrano Antongila *b.* Madag. **131** [inset] K2
Helong China **82** C4
Helper U.S.A. **183** N2
Helpmekaar S. Africa **133** O5
Helsingborg Sweden **45** K4
formerly spelt Hälsingborg
Helsingfors Fin. *see* **Helsinki**
Helsingør Denmark **45** K4
historically known as Elsinore

▶**Helsinki** Fin. **45** N3
Capital of Finland. Also known as Helsingfors.

Helston U.K. **47** G13
Heltermaa Estonia **42** E3
Helvacı Turkey **59** I10
Helvécia Brazil **203** E6
Helvetic Republic *country* Europe *see* **Switzerland**
Helvetinjärven kansallispuisto *nat. park* Fin. **45** M3
Helwân Egypt **121** F2
also spelt Ḥulwān
Hemel Hempstead U.K. **47** L12
Hemet U.S.A. **183** H8
Hemlo Canada **172** H2
Hemlock Lake U.S.A. **176** H3
Hemmoor Germany **48** G2
Hemnesberget Norway **44** K2
Hemphill U.S.A. **179** D6
Hempstead U.S.A. **179** C6
Hemse Sweden **45** L4
Hemsedal Norway **45** J3
Hemsedal *valley* Norway **45** J3
Henan China **86** B1
also known as Yêgainnyin
Henan *prov.* China **87** E1
English form Honan
Hen and Chickens Islands N.Z. **152** I3
Henares *r.* Spain **55** H4
Henashi-zaki *pt* Japan **90** F4
Henbury Australia **148** B5
Hendawashi Tanz. **129** B5
Henderson *KY* U.S.A. **174** C4
Henderson *LA* U.S.A. **179** E6
Henderson *NC* U.S.A. **176** G9
Henderson *NV* U.S.A. **183** J5
Henderson *NY* U.S.A. **177** I2
Henderson *TN* U.S.A. **174** B5
Henderson *TX* U.S.A. **179** D5
Henderson Island Antarctica **223** G2
Henderson Island Pitcairn Is **221** J7
historically known as Elizabeth Island
Hendersonville *NC* U.S.A. **174** D5
Hendersonville *TN* U.S.A. **174** C4
Henderville *atoll* Kiribati *see* **Aranuka**
Hendijān Iran **100** B4
Hendorābī *i.* Iran **100** C5
Hendriksdal S. Africa **133** O2
Hendrina S. Africa **133** N3
Hengām, Jazīreh-ye *i.* Iran **100** C5
Hengch'un Taiwan **87** G4
Hengdong China **87** E3
Hengduan Shan *mts* China **86** A2
Hengelo Neth. **48** D3
Hengnan China *see* **Hengyang**
Hengshan *Heilong.* China **82** C3
Hengshan *Hunan* China **87** E3
Hengshan *Shaanxi* China **85** F4
Heng Shan *mt.* China **87** E3
Heng Shan *mts* China **85** G4
Hengshui China **85** G4
Hengshui China *see* **Chongyi**
Hengxian China **87** D4
also known as Hengzhou
Hengyang *Hunan* China **87** E3
also known as Hengnan
Hengyang *Hunan* China **87** E3
also known as Xidu
Hengzhou China *see* **Hengxian**
Henlopen, Cape U.S.A. **177** J7
Hennebont France **50** C5
Hennef (Sieg) Germany **48** E5
Hennenman S. Africa **133** L4
Hennessey U.S.A. **179** C4
Hennigsdorf Berlin Germany **49** K3
Henniker U.S.A. **177** N2
Henrichemont France **51** I5
Henrietta U.S.A. **179** C5
Henrietta Maria, Cape Canada **168** D2
Henrique de Carvalho Angola *see* **Saurimo**
Henry *r.* Australia **150** A4
Henry U.S.A. **172** D9
Henry, Cape U.S.A. **177** I9
Henryetta U.S.A. **179** D5
Henry Ice Rise Antarctica **222** T1
Henryk Arctowski *research station* Antarctica *see* **Arctowski**
Henry Kater, Cape Canada **165** M3
Henry Mountains U.S.A. **183** N3
Henrys Fork *r.* U.S.A. **180** E4
Hensall Canada **173** L7
Henshaw, Lake U.S.A. **183** H8
Henstedt-Ulzburg Germany **48** G2
Hentiesbaai Namibia **130** B4
Hentiy *prov.* Mongolia **85** F2
Henzada Myanmar **78** A4
also spelt Hinthada
Heping China *see* **Huishui**
Heping China *see* **Yanhe**
Hepo China *see* **Jiexi**
Heppner U.S.A. **180** C3
Hepu China **87** D4
also known as Lianzhou
Heqiaoyi China **84** D4
Heqing *Guangdong* China **87** E4
Heqing *Yunnan* China **86** B3
also known as Yunhe
Hequ China **85** F4
Heraclea Turkey *see* **Ereğli**
Heraclea Pontica Turkey *see* **Ereğli**
Heraklion Greece *see* **Iraklion**
Herald Cays *atolls* Australia **149** F3
Herāt Afgh. **101** E3
historically known as Alexandria Areion
Herāt *prov.* Afgh. **101** E3
Hérault *r.* France **51** J9
Herbagat Sudan **104** B4
Herbert *r.* Australia **149** E3
Herbert *watercourse* Australia **148** C3
Herbert Canada **167** J5
Herbert N.Z. **153** E13
Herbert Downs Australia **148** C4
Herberton Australia **149** E3
Herbert River Falls National Park Australia **149** E3
Herbertsdale S. Africa **132** F11
Herbertville N.Z. **152** K8
Herbert Wash *salt flat* Australia **151** D5
Herbignac France **50** D5
Herbstein Germany **48** G5
Herceg-Novi *Crna Gora* Yugo. **56** K6
Herculândia Brazil **206** C8
Hercules Dome *ice feature* Antarctica **223** Q1
Heredia Costa Rica **186** B5
Hereford U.K. **47** J11
Hereford U.S.A. **179** B5
Herekino N.Z. **152** H3
Heretaniwha Point N.Z. **153** D11
Herford Germany **48** F3
Héricourt France **51** M5
Herington U.S.A. **178** C4
Heriot N.Z. **153** D13
Herisau Switz. **51** P5
Heritage Range *mts* Antarctica **222** S1
Herkimer U.S.A. **177** K2
Herlen Mongolia **85** F2
Herlen Gol *r.* China/Mongolia *see* **Kerulen**
Herlen He *r.* China/Mongolia *see* **Kerulen**
Herlong U.S.A. **182** D1
Hermagor Austria **49** K9
Herma Ness *hd* U.K. **46** L3
Hermann U.S.A. **174** B4
Hermannsburg Australia **148** B4
Hermanus S. Africa **132** D11
Hermel Lebanon **109** H3
Hermes, Cape S. Africa **133** N8
Hermidale Australia **147** E2
Hermitage *MO* U.S.A. **178** D4
Hermitage *PA* U.S.A. **176** E4
Hermitage Bay Canada **169** J4
Hermite, Islas *is* Chile **205** D9
Hermit Islands P.N.G. **73** K7
Hermon, Mount Lebanon/Syria **108** G4
also known as Sheikh, Jebel esh
Hermonthis Egypt *see* **Armant**
Hermopolis Magna Egypt *see* **El Ashmûnein**
Hermosa, Valle *valley* Arg. **205** C7
Hermosillo Mex. **184** C2
Hernád *r.* Hungary **49** R8
also spelt Hornád (Slovakia)
Hernandarias Para. **201** G6
Hernando U.S.A. **174** B5
Hernani Spain **55** J1
Herndon *CA* U.S.A. **182** E5
Herndon *WV* U.S.A. **176** D8
Herne Germany **48** E4
Herning Denmark **45** J4
Heroica Nogales Mex. *see* **Nogales**
Heron Bay Canada **172** G2
Herong China **87** E2
Hérouville-St-Clair France **50** F3
Herowābād Iran *see* **Khalkhāl**
Herradura Mex. **185** E4
Herrenberg Germany **48** F7
Herrera Arg. **204** E3
Herrera del Duque Spain **54** F5
Herrero, Punta *pt* Mex. **185** I5
Herrieden Germany **48** H6
Herrin U.S.A. **174** B4
Herrljunga Sweden **45** K4
Herrvik Sweden **45** L4
Hers *r.* France **50** H9
Herschel S. Africa **133** L7
Herschel Island Canada **164** F3
Hershey U.S.A. **177** I5
Hertel U.S.A. **172** A5
Hertford U.K. **47** L12
Hertford U.S.A. **177** I9
Hertzogville S. Africa **133** J5
Hervey Bay Australia **149** G5
Hervey Islands Cook Is **221** H7
Herzberg Germany **49** K4
Herzliyya Israel **108** F5
Herzogenaurach Germany **48** H6
Herzogenburg Austria **49** M7
Ḥesār Iran **100** B4
Ḥeṣar Iran **100** B3
Hesdin France **51** I2
Heshan China **87** D4
Heshengqiao China **87** E2
Heshui China **85** F5
also known as Xihuachi
Heshun China **85** G4
Hesperia *CA* U.S.A. **183** G7
Hesperia *MI* U.S.A. **172** G7
Hesquiat Canada **166** E5
Hess *r.* Canada **166** C2
Hesse *land* Germany *see* **Hessen**
Hessel U.S.A. **173** I4
Hesselberg *hill* Germany **48** H6
Hessen *land* Germany **48** G5
English form Hesse
Hessischer Spessart, Naturpark *nature res.* Germany **48** G5
Hessisch Lichtenau Germany **48** G4
Hess Mountains Canada **166** C2
Hester Malan Nature Reserve S. Africa **132** C6
Hestvika Norway **44** J3
Het *r.* Laos **78** D3
Hetch Hetchy Aqueduct *canal* U.S.A. **182** B4
Hettinger U.S.A. **178** B2
Hettstedt Germany **48** I4
Heung Kong Tsai *Hong Kong* China *see* **Aberdeen**
Heuningneskloof S. Africa **133** I6
Heuningspruit S. Africa **133** L4
Heuningvlei *salt pan* S. Africa **132** H3
Heuvelton U.S.A. **177** J1
Heves Hungary **49** R8
Hevron West Bank *see* **Hebron**
Hewlett U.S.A. **176** H8
Hexenkopf *mt.* Austria **48** H8
Hexham U.K. **47** J9
Hexian China **87** F2
Hexigten Qi China *see* **Jingpeng**
Hexipu China **84** D4
Hexrivierberg *mts* S. Africa **132** D10
Heyang China *see* **Nanhe**
Heyang China **85** F5
Heydebreck Poland *see* **Kędzierzyn-Koźle**
Heydon S. Africa **133** I8
Heygali *well* Eth. **128** E3
Heyin China *see* **Guide**
Heyshope Dam S. Africa **133** O3
Heyuan China **87** E4
Heywood Australia **146** D4
Heze China **85** G5
also known as Caozhou
Hezhang China **86** C3
Hezheng China **84** D5
Hezhou China **87** D3
also known as Babu
Hezuozhen China **84** D5
Hhohho *reg.* Swaziland **133** P3
Hialeah U.S.A. **175** D7
Hiawassee U.S.A. **174** D5
Hiawatha U.S.A. **178** D4
Hibata *reg.* Saudi Arabia **104** C4
Hibberdene S. Africa **133** O7
Hibbing U.S.A. **174** A2
Hibbs, Point Australia **147** E5
Hibernia Reef Australia **150** C2
Hibiki-nada *b.* Japan **91** B7
Hīchān Iran **101** E5
Hickman U.S.A. **174** B4
Hickory U.S.A. **174** D5
Hicks Bay N.Z. **152** M5
Hicks Cays *is* Belize **185** H5
Hicksville *NY* U.S.A. **177** L5
Hicksville *OH* U.S.A. **176** A4
Hico U.S.A. **179** C5
Hidaka Japan **90** H3
Hidaka-sanmyaku *mts* Japan **90** H3
Hidalgo *Coahuila* Mex. **185** F3
Hidalgo *Tamaulipas* Mex. **185** F3
Hidalgo *state* Mex. **185** F4
Hidalgo del Parral Mex. **184** D3
Hidalgo Yalalag Mex. **185** F5
Hidasnémeti Hungary **49** S7
Hiddensee *i.* Germany **49** K1
Hidișelu de Sus Romania **58** D2
Hidrolândia Brazil **206** D3
Hierosolyma Israel/West Bank *see* **Jerusalem**
Hietaniemi Fin. **44** O2
Higashi-Hiroshima Japan **91** C7
Higashi-matsuyama Japan **91** F6
Higashine Japan **90** G5
Higashi-ōsaka Japan **91** D7
Higashi-suidō *sea chan.* Japan **91** A8
Higgins Bay U.S.A. **177** K2
Higgins Lake U.S.A. **173** I6
Higg's Hope S. Africa **132** H6
High Atlas *mts* Morocco *see* **Haut Atlas**
High Desert U.S.A. **180** B4
High Falls Reservoir U.S.A. **172** E5
Highflats S. Africa **133** O7
High Island *i. Hong Kong* China **87** [inset]
also known as Leung Shuen Wan Chau
High Island U.S.A. **179** D6
High Island *i.* U.S.A. **172** H5
High Island Reservoir *Hong Kong* China **87** [inset]
Highland *CA* U.S.A. **183** G7
Highland *MN* U.S.A. **172** B3
Highland *NY* U.S.A. **177** L4
Highland *WI* U.S.A. **172** C7
Highland Beach U.S.A. **177** I7
Highland Peak *CA* U.S.A. **182** E3
Highland Peak *NV* U.S.A. **183** J4
Highlands U.S.A. **177** L5
Highland Springs U.S.A. **177** H8
High Level Canada **167** G3
High Level Canal India **95** E1
Highline Canal U.S.A. **183** I9
Highmore U.S.A. **178** C2
High Point U.S.A. **174** E5
High Point *hill* U.S.A. **177** K4
High Prairie Canada **167** G4
High River Canada **167** H5
High Rock Bahamas **186** D1
Highrock Lake Canada **167** K4
High Rocky Point Australia **147** E5
High Springs U.S.A. **175** D6
High Tatras *mts* Poland/Slovakia *see* **Tatra Mountains**
Hightstown U.S.A. **177** K5
High Wycombe U.K. **47** L12
Higlale *well* Eth. **128** E3
Higuera de Abuya Mex. **184** D3
Higuera de Zaragoza Mex. **184** C3
Higüey Dom. Rep. **187** F3
Hihifo Tonga **145** H3
Hihnavaara Fin. **44** O2
Hiidenportin kansallispuisto *nat. park* Fin. **44** O3
Hiidenvesi *l.* Fin. **42** F1
Hiiraan Somalia **128** E3
Hiiraan *admin. reg.* Somalia **128** E3
Hiiumaa *i.* Estonia **42** D3
also known as Dagö; *historically known as* Oesel *or* Ösel
Hijānah, Buḩayrat al *imp. l.* Syria **109** H4
Hijāna, Wādī *watercourse* Syria **109** K3
Hijau, Gunung *mt.* Indon. **76** C3
Hijaz *reg.* Saudi Arabia **104** B2
English form Hejaz
Hiji Japan **91** B8
Hijo Phil. **74** C5
Hikari Japan **91** B8
Hiketa Japan **91** D7
Hikone Japan **91** E7
Hikurangi *mt.* N.Z. **152** M5
Hila Indon. **75** C4
Hilahila Indon. **75** B4
Hilaricos Chile **200** C5
Hilary Coast Antarctica **223** K1
Hildale U.S.A. **183** K4
Hildburghausen Germany **48** H5
Hilders Germany **48** H5
Hildesheim Germany **48** G3
Ḥilf, Ra's *c.* Oman **105** G3
Hili Bangl. **97** F4
Hillah Iraq **107** F4
also spelt Al Ḩillah
Hillandale S. Africa **132** E10
Hillard U.S.A. **176** B5
Hill City U.S.A. **178** C4
Hill Creek *r.* U.S.A. **183** O2
Hillerød Denmark **45** K5
Hillersen Germany **48** H3
Hillerse Germany **48** H3
Hillerstorp Sweden **45** K4
Hillesheim Germany **48** D5
Hillgrove Australia **149** E3
Hill Island Lake Canada **167** I2
Hillman U.S.A. **173** J5
Hillman, Lake *salt flat* Australia **151** B6
Hillsboro *IL* U.S.A. **174** B4
Hillsboro *MO* U.S.A. **174** B4
Hillsboro *ND* U.S.A. **178** C2
Hillsboro *NH* U.S.A. **177** N2
Hillsboro *OH* U.S.A. **176** B6
Hillsboro *OR* U.S.A. **180** B3
Hillsboro *TX* U.S.A. **179** C5
Hillsboro *WI* U.S.A. **172** C7
Hillsboro Canal U.S.A. **175** D7
Hillsborough Grenada **187** H4
Hillsborough U.S.A. **176** F9
Hillsborough, Cape Australia **149** F4
Hillsdale *MI* U.S.A. **173** I9
Hillsdale *NY* U.S.A. **177** L3
Hillsgrove U.S.A. **177** I4
Hillside Australia **150** B4
Hillsport Canada **168** C3
Hillston Australia **147** E3
Hillsville U.S.A. **176** E9
Hillswick U.K. **46** K3
Hilo U.S.A. **181** [inset] Z2
Hilton Australia **148** C4
Hilton U.S.A. **176** H2
Hilton Beach Canada **173** J4
Hilton Head Island U.S.A. **175** D5
Hilvan Turkey **107** D3
also known as Karacurun
Hilversum Neth. **48** C3
Ḩimā *well* Saudi Arabia **104** D4
Himachal Pradesh *state* India **96** C3
Ḩimā Ḑarīyah, Jabal *mt.* Saudi Arabia **104** C2

▶**Himalaya** *mts* Asia **97** C2
world [physical features] ⟶ 8–9
asia [landscapes] ⟶ 62–63

Himalchuli *mt.* Nepal **97** E3
Himanka Fin. **44** M2
Ḩimār, Wādī al *watercourse* Syria/Turkey **109** K1
also known as Hamra, Vâdii
Himarë Albania **59** A8
Ḩimār Umm Khunşur *hill* Saudi Arabia **109** M7
Himatangi Beach N.Z. **152** J8
Himatnagar India **96** B5
Himbirti Eritrea **104** B5
Himeji Japan **91** D7
Himekami-dake *mt.* Japan **90** G5
Himeville S. Africa **133** N6
Hime-zaki *pt* Japan **90** F5
Himi Japan **91** E6
Himora Eth. **128** C1
Ḩimş Syria *see* **Homs**
Ḩimş *governorate* Syria **109** J2
Ḩimş, Baḩrat *resr* Syria *see* **Qaţţīnah, Buḩayrat**
Hinako *i.* Indon. **76** B2
Hinakura N.Z. **152** J9
Hinatuan Phil. **74** C4
Hinatuan Passage Phil. **74** C4
Hîncești Moldova **58** J2
formerly known as Cotovsc *or* Kotovsk; *formerly spelt* Hânceşti *or* Khynchest' *or* Khynchesty
Hinche Haiti **187** E3
Hinchinbrook Island Australia **149** E3
Hinckley U.K. **47** K11
Hinckley *IL* U.S.A. **172** E9
Hinckley *ME* U.S.A. **177** P1
Hinckley *MN* U.S.A. **174** A2
Hinckley *UT* U.S.A. **183** L2
Hinckley Reservoir U.S.A. **177** J2
Hind, Wādī al *watercourse* Saudi Arabia **108** G8
Hinda Congo **126** B6
Hindan *r.* India **89** B6
Hindaun India **96** C4
Hindelang Germany **48** H8
Hindenburg Poland *see* **Zabrze**
Hindman U.S.A. **176** C8
Hindmarsh, Lake *dry lake* Australia **146** D4
Hindola India **95** E1
Hindoli India **96** B4
Hindoria India **96** C5
Hindri *r.* India **94** C3
Hinds N.Z. **153** F12
Hindu Kush *mts* Afgh./Pak. **101** F3
Hindupur India **94** C3
Hines Creek Canada **166** G3
Hinesville U.S.A. **175** D6
Hinganghat India **94** C1
Hingol *r.* Pak. **101** F5
Hingol *r.* Pak. *see* **Girdar Dhor**
Hınıs Turkey **107** E3
Hinks Conservation Park *nature res.* Australia **146** C3
Hinnøya *i.* Norway **44** K1
Hino Japan **91** C7
Hinobaan Phil. **74** B4
Hinojedo *mt.* Spain **55** I3
Hinojosa del Duque Spain **54** F6
Hino-misaki *pt* Japan **91** C7
Hinsdale U.S.A. **177** M3
Hinterzarten Germany **48** F8
Hinthada Myanmar *see* **Henzada**
Hinton *KY* U.S.A. **176** A7
Hinton *OK* U.S.A. **179** C5
Hinton *WV* U.S.A. **176** E8
Hinuera N.Z. **152** J5
Hiort *i.* U.K. *see* **Hirta**
Hipólito Mex. **185** E3
Hipponium Italy *see* **Vibo Valentia**
Hippopotames, Réserve de *nature res.* Dem. Rep. Congo **126** F6
Hippopotames, Réserve de Faune des *nature res.* Dem. Rep. Congo **126** E5
Hippopotames de Sakania, Réserve de *nature res.* Dem. Rep. Congo **127** F8
Hippo Regius Alg. *see* **Annaba**
Hippo Zarytus Tunisia *see* **Bizerte**
Hirabit Dağ *mt.* Turkey **107** F3
Hirado Japan **91** A8
Hirado-shima *i.* Japan **91** A8
Hirafok Alg. **123** G5
Hirakud Reservoir India **97** D5
Hiraman *watercourse* Kenya **128** C5
Hirata Japan **91** C7
Hiré-Watta Côte d'Ivoire **124** D5
Hiriyur India **94** C3
Hîrlău Romania *see* **Hârlău**
Hiroo Japan **90** H3
Hirosaki Japan **90** G4
Hirose Japan **91** C7
Hiroshima Japan **91** C7
Hiroshima *airport* Japan **91** C7
Hiroshima *pref.* Japan **91** C7
Hirota-wan *b.* Japan **90** G5
Hirschaid Germany **48** I6
Hirschberg Germany **48** I5
Hirschberg Poland *see* **Jelenia Góra**
Hirsingue France **51** N5
Hirson France **51** K3
Hîrșova Romania *see* **Hârșova**
Hirta *i.* U.K. **46** D6
also known as Hiort
Hirtshals Denmark **45** J4
Hisai Japan **91** E7
Hisaka-jima *i.* Japan **91** A8
Hisar India **96** B3
also spelt Hissar
Hisar, Koh-i- *mts* Afgh. **101** F3
Hisarcık Turkey **59** K9
Hisarköy Turkey *see* **Domaniç**
Hisarönü Turkey **106** C2
Hisarönü Körfezi *b.* Turkey **59** I12
Ḩisb, Sha'īb *watercourse* Iraq **107** F5
Ḩisn al Fuḑūl Yemen **105** E4
Hisor Tajik. **101** G2
also spelt Gissar
Hisor Tizmasi *mts* Tajik./Uzbek. *see* **Gissar Range**
Hispalis Spain *see* **Seville**
Hispania *country* Europe *see* **Spain**

▶**Hispaniola** *i.* Caribbean Sea **171** L7
Consists of the Dominican Republic and Haiti.

Hispur Glacier Jammu and Kashmir **96** B1
Hissar India *see* **Hisar**
Hisua India **97** E4
Hīt Iraq **107** E4
Hita Japan **91** B8
Hitachi Japan **91** G6
Hitachinaka Japan **91** G6
Hitachi-ōta Japan **91** G6
Hitoyoshi Japan **91** B8
Hitra *i.* Norway **44** J3
Hiuchi-nada *b.* Japan **91** C7
Hiva Oa *i.* Fr. Polynesia **221** I6
formerly known as Dominique
Hiwasa Japan **91** D8
Hixon Canada **166** F4
Hixson Cay *reef* Australia **149** G4
Hixton U.S.A. **172** B6
Hiyon *watercourse* Israel **108** G7
Hizan Turkey **107** E3
also known as Karasu
Hjallerup Denmark **45** J4
Hjälmaren *l.* Sweden **45** K4
Hjelle Norway **45** I3
Hjellestad Norway **46** R3
Hjelmeland Norway **45** I4
Hjerkinn Norway **44** J3
Hjo Sweden **45** K4
Hjørring Denmark **45** J4
Hjuvik Sweden **45** J4
Hka, Nam *r.* Myanmar **78** B3
Hkakabo Razi *mt.* Myanmar **78** B1
Hkok *r.* Myanmar **78** B3
Hkring Bum *mt.* Myanmar **78** B2
Hlabisa S. Africa **133** P5
Hlaing *r.* Myanmar **78** B4
Hlako Kangri *mt.* China *see* **Lhagoi Kangri**
Hlane Game Sanctuary *nature res.* Swaziland **133** P3
Hlatikulu Swaziland **133** P3
Hlazove Ukr. **43** O9
Hlegu Myanmar **78** B4
Hlinsko Czech Rep. **49** M6
Hlohlowane S. Africa **133** L5
Hlohovec Slovakia **49** O7
Hlotse Lesotho **133** M5
Hlučín Czech Rep. **49** P6
Hluhluwe S. Africa **133** Q5
Hluhluwe Game Reserve *nature res.* S. Africa **133** Q5
Hlukhiv Ukr. **41** E6
also spelt Glukhov
Hlung-Tan Myanmar **78** B3
Hlusha Belarus **43** J8
Hlusk Belarus **43** J9
Hlybokaye Belarus **42** I6
also spelt Glubokoye
Hnilec *r.* Slovakia **49** R7
Hnúšťa Slovakia **49** Q7
Ho Ghana **125** F5
Hoa Binh Vietnam **78** D3
Hoachanas Namibia **130** C4
Hoang Liên Son *mts* Vietnam **78** C3
Hoang Sa *is* S. China Sea *see* **Paracel Islands**
Hoanib *watercourse* Namibia **130** B3
Hoarusib *watercourse* Namibia **130** B3

▶**Hobart** Australia **147** E5
State capital of Tasmania.

Hobart U.S.A. **179** C5
Hobbs U.S.A. **179** B5
Hobbs Coast Antarctica **222** P1
Hobe Sound U.S.A. **175** D7
Hobhouse S. Africa **133** L6
Hobo Col. **198** C4
Hoboksar China **88** D2
also known as Qahar Youyi Zhongqi
Hobor China **85** G3
also known as Qahar Youyi Zhongqi
Hobot Xar Qi China *see* **Xin Bulag**
Hobro Denmark **45** J4
Hoburg Sweden **45** L4
Hoburgen *pt* Sweden **45** L4
Hobyo Somalia **128** F3
formerly spelt Obbia
Hochfeiler *mt.* Austria/Italy *see* **Gran Pilastro**
Hochfeld Namibia **130** C4
Hochgall *mt.* Austria/Italy *see* **Collalto**
Hochgolling *mt.* Austria **49** K8
Hochharz *nat. park* Germany **48** H4
Hô Chi Minh Vietnam *see* **Ho Chi Minh City**
Ho Chi Minh City Vietnam **79** D6
also known as Hô Chi Minh; *formerly known as* Saigon
Hochobir *mt.* Austria **49** L9
Hochschwab *mt.* Austria **49** M8
Hochtaunus *nature res.* Germany **48** F5
Hochtor *mt.* Austria **49** L8
Hocking *r.* U.S.A. **176** D6
Hôd *reg.* Mauritania **124** C2
Hodal India **96** C4
Hodda *mt.* Somalia **128** F2
Hodeidah Yemen **104** C5
also spelt Al Ḩudaydah
Hodein, Wâdi *watercourse* Egypt **121** G4
Hodgesville U.S.A. **176** E6
Hodgson Downs Australia **148** B2
Hodgson Downs Aboriginal Land *res.* Australia **148** B2
Hodh Ech Chargui *admin. reg.* Mauritania **124** D2
Hodh El Gharbi *admin. reg.* Mauritania **124** C2
Hódmezővásárhely Hungary **49** R9
Hodmo *watercourse* Somalia **128** E2
Hodna, Chott el *salt l.* Alg. **123** G2
Hodonín Czech Rep. **49** O7
Hodoșa Romania **58** F2
Hŏdrŏgŏ Mongolia **84** C1
Hodsons Peak Lesotho **133** N6
Hoek van Holland Neth. *see* **Hook of Holland**
Hoeryŏng N. Korea **82** C4
Hoeyang N. Korea **83** B5
Hof Germany **48** I5
Hoffman Mountain U.S.A. **177** L2
Hoffman's Cay *i.* Bahamas **186** D1
Hofmeyr S. Africa **133** J8
Höfn Iceland **44** [inset] D2
Hofors Sweden **45** L3
Hofsjökull *ice cap* Iceland **44** [inset] C2
Hofsós Iceland **44** [inset] C2
Hōfu Japan **91** B7
Hofūf Saudi Arabia *see* **Al Hufūf**
Höganäs Sweden **45** K4
Hogan Group *is* Australia **147** E4
Hogansburg U.S.A. **177** K1
Hoganthulla Creek *r.* Australia **149** E5
Hogg, Mount Canada **166** C2

▶**Hoggar** *plat.* Alg. **123** G5
also spelt Ahaggar
world [land cover] ⟶ 18–19

Hog Island U.S.A. **177** J8
Högsby Sweden **45** L4
Høgste Breakulen *mt.* Norway **45** I3
Hogsty Reef Bahamas **187** E2
Högyész Hungary **49** P9
Hoh *r.* U.S.A. **180** A3
Hohenems Austria **48** G8
Hohenlohe Ebene *plain* Germany **48** G6
Hohe Nock *mt.* Austria **49** L8
Hohensalza Poland *see* **Inowrocław**
Hohenwald U.S.A. **174** C5
Hohenwartetalsperre *resr* Germany **51** R2
Hoher Dachstein *mt.* Austria **49** K8
Hoh Ereg China *see* **Wuchuan**
Hoher Göll *mt.* Austria/Germany **49** K8
Hohe Rhön *mts* Germany **48** G5
Hohe Tauern *mts* Austria **49** J8
Hohe Tauern, Nationalpark *nat. park* Austria **49** J8
Hohe Venn *moorland* Belgium **51** M2
Hohhot China **85** F3
also spelt Huhhot; *formerly spelt* Huhehot
Hohoe Ghana **125** F5
Ho Hok Shan *Hong Kong* China **87** [inset]
Hōhoku Japan **91** B7
Hoh Xil Hu *salt l.* China **89** E5
Hoh Xil Shan *mts* China **80** D5
Hôi An Vietnam **78** E5
Hoima Uganda **128** A4
Hoisdorf Germany **48** H2
Hoisington U.S.A. **178** C4
Hoit Taria China **84** C4
Hôi Xuân Vietnam **78** D3
Hojagala Turkm. *see* **Khodzha-Kala**
Hojai India **97** G4
Hojambaz Turkm. *see* **Khodzhambaz**
Hōjo Japan **91** C8
Hökensås *hills* Sweden **45** K4
Hokio Beach N.Z. **152** J8
Hokitika N.Z. **153** E10
Hokkaidō *i.* Japan **81** O4
historically known as Ezo *or* Yezo
Hokkaidō *pref.* Japan **90** H3
Hokksund Norway **45** J4
Hokmābād Iran **100** D2
Hokonui N.Z. **153** C14
Hokonui Hills N.Z. **153** C13
Hokota Japan **91** G6
Hoktemberyan Armenia **107** F2
formerly spelt Oktemberyan
Hol *Buskerud* Norway **45** J3
Hol *Nordland* Norway **44** L1
Hola Kenya **128** C5
Holalkere India **94** C3
Holanda Bol. **200** D3
Holbæk Denmark **45** J5
Holberg Canada **166** D5
Holbrook Australia **147** E3
Holbrook U.S.A. **183** N7
Holcombe U.S.A. **172** B5
Holcombe Flowage *resr* U.S.A. **172** B5
Holden Canada **167** H4
Holden U.S.A. **183** L2
Holdenville U.S.A. **179** C5
Holdich Arg. **205** C7
Holdrege U.S.A. **178** C3
Hole Narsipur India **94** C3
Holgat *watercourse* S. Africa **132** A5
Holgate U.S.A. **176** A4
Holguín Cuba **186** D2
Holič Slovakia **49** O7
Höljes Sweden **45** K3
Hollabrunn Austria **49** N7
Holland *country* Europe *see* **Netherlands**
Holland *MI* U.S.A. **172** G8
Holland *NY* U.S.A. **176** G3
Hollandale U.S.A. **175** B5
Hollandia Indon. *see* **Jayapura**
Hollands Diep *est.* Neth. **48** B4
Hollick-Kenyon Peninsula Antarctica **222** T2
Hollick-Kenyon Plateau Antarctica **222** Q1
Hollis U.S.A. **179** C5
Hollister U.S.A. **182** C5
Hollóháza Hungary **49** S7
Hollola Fin. **45** N3
Hollum Neth. **48** C2
Holly U.S.A. **173** J8
Holly Springs U.S.A. **174** B5

Hollywood U.S.A. 175 D7
Holm Norway 44 K2
Holman Canada 165 H2
also known as Uluqsaqtuuq
Holmdene S. Africa 133 N3
Holmes Reef Australia 149 E3
Holmestrand Norway 45 J4
Holm Ø i. Greenland see Kiatassuaq
Holmögadarna naturreservat nature res. Sweden 44 M3
Holmön i. Sweden 44 M3
Holmsund Sweden 44 M3
Holmudden pt Sweden 45 L4
Holod r. Romania 58 J2
Holon Israel 108 F5
also spelt Kholon
Holoog Namibia 130 C5
Holothuria Banks reef Australia 150 D2
Holovets'ko Ukr. 49 T6
Holroyd r. Australia 149 D2
Holroyd Bluff hills Australia 151 C5
Holspruit r. S. Africa 133 M4
Holstebro Denmark 45 J4
Holsted Denmark 45 J5
Holstein U.S.A. 178 D4
Holsteinsborg Greenland see Sisimiut
Holston r. U.S.A. 176 B9
Holston Lake U.S.A. 176 B9
Holt U.S.A. 173 I8
Holton KS U.S.A. 178 D4
Holton MI U.S.A. 172 G7
Holtville U.S.A. 183 I9
Holtwood U.S.A. 177 I6
Holy Cross, Mount of the U.S.A. 180 F5
Holyhead U.K. 47 H10
also known as Caergybi
Holy Island England U.K. 46 K8
also known as Lindisfarne
Holy Island Wales U.K. 47 H10
Holyoke CO U.S.A. 178 B3
Holyoke MA U.S.A. 177 M3
Holy See Europe see Vatican City
Holzkirchen Germany 48 I8
Holzminden Germany 48 G4
Hom watercourse Namibia 132 C5
Homa Bay Kenya 128 B5
Homalin Myanmar 78 A2
Homathko r. Canada 166 E5
Homäyünshahr Iran see Khomeynīshahr
Homberg (Efze) Germany 48 G4
Hombetsu Japan see Honbetsu
Hombori Mali 125 E3
Hombre Muerto, Salar del salt flat Arg. 204 C2
Homburg Germany 48 E6
Home Bay Canada 165 M3
Home Hill Australia 149 E3
Home Point N.Z. 152 I3
Homer AK U.S.A. 164 D4
Homer LA U.S.A. 179 D5
Homer MI U.S.A. 174 D5
Homer MI U.S.A. 173 I8
Homer City U.S.A. 176 F5
Homerville U.S.A. 175 D6
Homestead Australia 149 E4
Homestead U.S.A. 175 D7
Homewood N.Z. 152 J9
Homewood U.S.A. 175 C6
Hommelvik Norway 44 J3
Homnabad India 94 C2
Homocea Romania 58 I2
Homodji well Niger 125 I2
Homoine Moz. 131 G4
Homs Libya see Al Khums
Homs Syria 109 H3
also spelt Hims; historically known as Emesa
Homyel' Belarus 43 M9
also spelt Gomel'
Homyel Oblast admin. div. Belarus see Homyel'skaya Voblasts'
Homyel'skaya Voblasts' admin. div. Belarus 43 K9
English form Homyel Oblast or Gomel Oblast; also known as Gomel'skaya Oblast'
Honaker U.S.A. 176 C9
Honan prov. China see Henan
Honaz Turkey 59 K11
historically known as Colossae
Hon Bai Canh i. Vietnam 79 D6
Honbetsu Japan 90 H3
also known as Hombetsu
Hon Chông Vietnam 79 D6
Hon Chuôi i. Vietnam 79 D6
Honda Col. 198 C3
Honda India 96 B3
Honda, Bahía b. Col. 198 C1
Honda Bay Phil. 74 A4
Hondapa India 95 E1
Hondeklipbaai S. Africa 132 B7
Hondo r. Belize/Mex. 185 H5
Hondo Japan 91 B8
Hondo NM U.S.A. 181 F6
Hondo TX U.S.A. 181 F6
Honduras country Central America 186 B4
northamerica [countries] 158-159
Honduras, Gulf of Belize/Hond. 186 B3
Hønefoss Norway 45 J3
Honesdale U.S.A. 177 J4
Honey Brook U.S.A. 177 J5

Honey Lake U.S.A. 182 D1
Honfleur France 50 G3
Hông, Sông r. Vietnam see Red River
Hong'an China 87 E2
Hongch'ŏn S. Korea 83 B5
Hongde China 84 E2
Honggouzi China 88 E4
Honggu China 84 D4
formerly known as Yaojie
Honghai Wan b. China 87 E4
Honghe China 86 B4
also known as Yisa
Hong He r. China 87 E1
Honghu China 87 E2
formerly known as Xindi
Hong Hu l. China 87 E2
Hongjialou China see Licheng
Hongjiang China 87 D3
Hongjiang China see Wangcang
▶Hong Kong Hong Kong China 87 [inset]
also known as Hsiang Kang or Xianggang
world [cities] 24-25
Hong Kong special admin. reg. China 87 [inset]
long form Xianggang Tebie Xingzhengqu
Hong Kong Harbour sea chan. Hong Kong China 87 [inset]
also known as Victoria Harbour
Hong Kong Island Hong Kong China 87 [inset]
also known as Hsiang Chang
Hongliu r. China 85 F4
Hongliu Daquan well China 84 C3
Hongliuwan China see Aksay
Hongliuyuan Gansu China 84 B3
Hongliuyuan Gansu China 84 D4
Hông Ngur Vietnam 79 D6
Hongor Mongolia 85 G2
Hongqiao China see Qidong
Hongqizhen China see Tongshi
Hongshan China 86 A2
formerly known as Mabating
Hongshui He r. China 87 D4
Hongtong China 85 F4
Hongū Japan 91 D8
Honguedo, Détroit d' sea chan. Canada 169 H3
Hongwansi China see Sunan
Hongwŏn N. Korea 83 B4
Hongyuan China 86 B1
Hongze China 87 F1
also known as Gaoliangjian
Hongze Hu l. China 87 F1

▶Honiara Solomon Is 145 E2
Capital of the Solomon Islands.

Honiton U.K. 47 I13
Honjō Japan 90 G5
Honkajoki Fin. 45 M3
Hon Khoai i. Vietnam 79 D6
Hon Mê i. Vietnam 78 D4
Hon Minh Hoa i. Vietnam 79 D6
Honnali India 94 B3
Honningsvåg Norway 44 N1
Honokaa U.S.A. 181 [inset] Z1

Honolulu U.S.A. 181 [inset] Z1
State capital of Hawaii.

Honor U.S.A. 172 G6
Hon Rai i. Vietnam 79 D6

Honshū i. Japan 91 F6
3rd largest island in Asia and 7th in the world.
asia [landscapes] 62-63

Honwad India 94 B2
Hood r. Canada 167 I1
Hood, Mount vol. U.S.A. 180 B3
Hood Point Australia 151 B7
Hood River U.S.A. 180 B3
Hoogeveen Neth. 48 D3
Hoogezand-Sappemeer Neth. 48 D2
Hooghly r. mouth India see Hugli
Hooker U.S.A. 178 B4
Hooker Creek Aboriginal Land res. Australia 148 A3
Hook Head Rep. of Ireland 47 F11
Hook of Holland Neth. 48 B4
also known as Hoek van Holland
Hook Reef Australia 149 F3
Hoolt Mongolia 84 D2
Hoonah U.S.A. 164 F4
Hoopa Valley Indian Reservation res. U.S.A. 180 B4
Hooper Bay U.S.A. 164 C3
Hooper Island U.S.A. 177 I7
Hoopstad S. Africa 133 J4
Hoorn Neth. 48 C3
Hoorn, Îles de is Wallis and Futuna Is see Futuna Islands
Hoorn Islands Wallis and Futuna Is see Futuna Islands
Hoosick U.S.A. 177 L3
Hoover Dam U.S.A. 183 J5
Hoover Memorial Reservoir U.S.A. 176 C5
Höövör Mongolia 84 D2
Hóp lag. Iceland 44 [inset] B2
Hopa Turkey 107 E2
Hope Canada 166 F5
Hope N.Z. 152 H9
Hope r. N.Z. 153 G10
Hope U.S.A. 179 D5
Hope, Lake salt flat S.A. Australia 146 C2
Hope, Lake salt flat W.A. Australia 151 C7
Hope, Point U.S.A. 164 C3
Hopedale Canada 169 I2
Hopefield S. Africa 132 C10
Hopei prov. China see Hebei
Hopelchén Mex. 185 H5
Hope Mountains Canada 169 I2
Hopen i. Svalbard 38 C2
Hopes Advance, Baie b. Canada 169 I1
Hopes Advance, Cap c. Canada 165 M3
Hopes Advance Bay Canada see Aupaluk
Hopetoun Vic. Australia 147 D3
Hopetoun W.A. Australia 151 C7
Hopetown S. Africa 132 I6
Hope Vale Aboriginal Reserve Australia 149 E2
Hope Valley U.S.A. 177 N4
Hopewell U.S.A. 177 H8
Hopewell Islands Canada 168 E1
Hopi Indian Reservation res. U.S.A. 183 N6
Hopin Myanmar 78 B2
Hopkins r. Australia 147 D4
Hopkins, Lake salt flat Australia 150 E5
Hopkinsville U.S.A. 174 C4
Hopland U.S.A. 182 A3
Hopong Myanmar 78 B3
Hopseidet Norway 44 N1
Hoquiam U.S.A. 180 B3
Hor Qinghai China 84 D5
also spelt Huoer
Horadiz Azer. 107 F3
also spelt Goradiz
Horasan Turkey 107 E2
Horažďovice Czech Rep. 49 K6
Hörb am Neckar Germany 48 F7
Hörby Sweden 45 K5
Horcajo de Santiago Spain 55 I5
Horcasitas Mex. 184 C2
Horcón Peru see Huaca
Horcones r. Arg. 204 C2
Horda Norway 45 I4
Houxia China 88 D3
Houzhai China see Nan'ao
Horezu Romania 58 E3
Horgo Mongolia 84 C1

Horgoš Vojvodina, Srbija Yugo. 58 A2
Hörh Uul mts Mongolia 85 E3
Horia Romania 58 J3
Horicon U.S.A. 172 E7
Horinger China 85 F3
Horiult Mongolia 84 D2

▶Horizon Deep sea feature
S. Pacific Ocean 220 G7
2nd deepest point in the world (Tonga Trench).

Horki Belarus 43 L7
also spelt Gorki
Horlick Mountains Antarctica 223 Q1
Horlivka Ukr. 41 F6
also spelt Gorlovka
Hormak Iran 101 E4
Hormoz i. Iran 100 D5
Hormoz, Küh-e mt. Iran 100 C5
Hormozgan prov. Iran 100 D5
Hormüd-e Bāgh Iran 100 C5
Hormüd-e Mir Khünd Iran 100 C5
Hormuz, Strait of Iran/Oman 105 G2
Horn Austria 49 M7
Horn r. Canada 167 G2
Horn c. Iceland 44 [inset] B2
▶Horn, Cape Chile 205 D9
Most southerly point of South America. Also known as Hornos, Cabo de.

Hornád r. Slovakia 49 R7
also spelt Hernád (Hungary)
Hornavan l. Sweden 44 L2
Hornbrook U.S.A. 180 B4
Horndal Sweden 45 L3
Horne, Îles de is Wallis and Futuna Is see Futuna Islands
Hörnefors Sweden 44 L3
Hornell U.S.A. 176 H3
Hornepayne Canada 168 C3
Hornillos Mex. 184 C3
Hornindal Norway 45 I3
Horn Island U.S.A. 175 B6
Hornkranz Namibia 130 C4
Horn Mountains Canada 166 F2
Hornos, Cabo de c. Chile see Horn, Cape
Hornos, Parque Nacional de nat. park Chile 205 D9
Hornoy-le-Bourg France 51 H3
Horn Peak Canada 166 D2
Hornsby Australia 147 F3
Hornsea U.K. 47 L10
Hornslandet pen. Sweden 45 L3
Hornslet Denmark 45 J4
Hornstrandir reg. Iceland 44 [inset] B2
Horodenka Ukr. 41 C6
also spelt Gorodenka
Horodnya Ukr. 41 L6
Horodok Ukr. 41 C6
also spelt Gorodok
Horokanai Japan 90 H2
Horo Shan mts China 88 C3
Horoshiri-dake mt. Japan 90 H3
Horqin Shadi reg. China 85 I3
Horqin Youyi Qianqi China see Ulanhot
Horqin Zuoyi Houqi China see Ganjig
Horqin Zuoyi Zhongqi China see Baokang
Horqueta Para. 201 F5
Horru China 89 E6
Horse Creek r. U.S.A. 180 F4
Horsefly Canada 166 F4
Horseheads U.S.A. 177 I3
Horse Lake U.S.A. 182 D1
Horsens Denmark 45 J5
Horseshoe Bend Australia 148 B5
Horseshoe Reservoir U.S.A. 183 M7
Horsham Australia 147 D4
Horsham U.K. 47 L12
Horten Norway 45 J4
Hortobágyi nat. park Hungary 49 S8
Horton r. Canada 164 G3
Horwood Lake Canada 168 D3
Ho Sai Hu l. China 84 B5
Hosa'ina Eth. 128 C3
Hosdurga India 94 C3
Hose, Pegunungan mts Sarawak Malaysia 77 F2
Hosenofu well Libya 120 D4
Hoşeynābād Iran 100 B3
Hoşeynīyeh Iran 100 B4
Hoshab Pak. 101 E5
Hoshangabad India 96 C5
Hoshiarpur India 96 B3
Hōsh 'Īsā Egypt 108 B7
Höshööt Arhangay Mongolia 84 D1
Höshööt Bayan-Ölgiy Mongolia 84 A1
Hoskins P.N.G. 145 E2
Hoşköy Turkey 58 I8
Hospet India 94 C3
Hosséré Vokre mt. Cameroon 125 I4
Hosszúpályi Hungary 49 S8
Hoste, Isla i. Chile 205 C9
Hosur India 94 C3
Hotahudo East Timor see Hatohud
Hotan China 89 C4
formerly spelt Khotan
Hotan He watercourse China 88 C3
Hotazel S. Africa 132 G4
Hot Creek r. U.S.A. 183 H3
Hotham r. Australia 151 B7
Hotham, Cape Australia 148 A2
Hoting Sweden 44 L3
Hot Springs AR U.S.A. 179 D5
Hot Springs SD U.S.A. 178 B3
Truth or Consequences
Hot Springs SD U.S.A. 178 B3
Hot Sulphur Springs U.S.A. 180 F4
Hottah Lake Canada 167 G1
Hottentots-Holland Nature Reserve S. Africa 132 C10
Hottentots Point Namibia 130 B5
Houaïlou New Caledonia 145 F4
Houdan France 50 H4
Houffalize Belgium 51 L2
Houghang Sing. 76 [inset]
Houghton MI U.S.A. 172 E4
Houghton NY U.S.A. 176 G3
Houghton Lake U.S.A. 173 I6
Houghton Lake l. U.S.A. 173 I6
Houghton le Spring U.K. 47 K9
Houhora N.Z. 152 H3
Houlton U.S.A. 174 H1
Houma China 85 F5
Houma U.S.A. 175 B6
Houmen China 87 E4
Houmt Souk Tunisia 123 H2
Houndé Burkina 124 E4
Hourtin et de Carcans, Étang d' l. France 50 E7
Housatonic U.S.A. 177 L3
Housatonic r. U.S.A. 177 L4
House Range mts U.S.A. 183 K2
Housesteads tourist site U.K. 47 J8
historically known as Vercovicium
Houston Canada 166 E4
Houston MN U.S.A. 172 B7
Houston MO U.S.A. 178 E4
Houston MS U.S.A. 175 B5
Houston TX U.S.A. 179 D6
Hout Bay S. Africa 132 C11
Houtkraal S. Africa 132 H6
Houtman Abrolhos is Australia 151 A6
Houtskär Fin. 42 C1
Houwater S. Africa 132 H7
Hov Denmark 45 J5
Hov Norway 45 J3

Hova Sweden 45 K4
Hovd Hovd Mongolia 84 A2
also known as Jargalant
Hovd Övörhangay Mongolia 84 D2
Hovd prov. Mongolia 84 B2
Hovden park Norway 45 I4
Hovd Gol r. Mongolia 84 B1
Hoveyzeh Iran 107 G5
Hovland U.S.A. 172 C3
Hovmantorp Sweden 45 K4
Hövsgöl Mongolia 85 F3
Hövsgöl prov. Mongolia 84 D1
Hövsgöl Nuur l. Mongolia 84 D1
Hövüün Mongolia 84 D2
Howa, Ouadi watercourse Chad/Sudan 120 D6
Howakil Bay Eritrea 104 C1
Howakil Island Eritrea 104 C1
Howar, Wadi watercourse Sudan 120 E5
Howard Australia 149 G5
Howard KS U.S.A. 178 C4
Howard SD U.S.A. 178 C2
Howard WI U.S.A. 172 E6
Howard City U.S.A. 172 H7
Howard Island Australia 148 B2
Howard Springs Australia 148 A2
Howden U.K. 47 L10
Howe, Cape Australia 147 F4
Howe, Mount Antarctica 223 O1
Howell U.S.A. 173 J8
Howes U.S.A. 180 C3
Howick S. Africa 133 O6
Howitt, Lake salt flat Australia 146 C1
Howland U.S.A. 174 G2

▶Howland Island N. Pacific Ocean 145 H1
United States Unincorporated Territory.
oceania [countries] 138-139

Howlong Australia 147 E3
Howrah India see Haora
Howz well Iran 100 D3
Howz-e Panj Iran 100 D4
Howz-e Panj waterhole Iran 100 C3
Howz-i-Khan well Iran 100 C3
Howz i-Mian i-Tak Iran 100 C3
Hoxie U.S.A. 178 B4
Höxter Germany 48 G4
Hoxtolgay China 88 D2
Hoxud China 88 D3
Hoy i. U.K. 46 I5
Høyanger Norway 45 I3
Hoyerswerda Germany 49 L4
Hoylandet Norway 44 K2
Hoyle Canada 173 L2
Höytiäinen l. Fin. 44 O3
Hoyt Peak U.S.A. 183 M1
Hozha Turkey 42 I8
Hpa-an Myanmar see Pa-an
Hradec Králové Czech Rep. 49 M5
Hradiště hill Czech Rep. 49 K5
Hradzyanka Belarus 43 J8
Hrasnica Bos.-Herz. 56 K5
Hraun slope Iceland 44 [inset] D2
Hrawzhynski Belarus 42 G7
Hrazdan Armenia 107 F2
also spelt Razdan; formerly known as Akhta
Hrazeni' Oblast Czech Rep. 49 L5
Hrebinka Ukr. 41 E6
also spelt Grebyonka; formerly known as Grebenkovskiy
Hrem"yach Ukr. 43 O9
Hristós Greece see Christos
Hrodna Belarus 42 E8
also known as Gardinas; also spelt Grodno
Hrodna Oblast admin. div. Belarus see Hrodzyenskaya Voblasts'
Hrodzyenskaya Voblasts' admin. div. Belarus 42 G8
English form Hrodna Oblast or Grodno Oblast; also known as Grodnenskaya Oblast'
Hron r. Slovakia 49 P8
Hrvatska country Europe see Croatia
Hrvatska Kostajnica Croatia 56 I3
Hsenwi Myanmar 78 B3
Hsiang Chang i. Hong Kong China see Hong Kong Island
Hsiang Kang Hong Kong China see Hong Kong
Hsin-hseng Myanmar 78 B3
Hsin, Nam r. Myanmar 78 B3
Hsin-chia-p'o country Asia see Singapore
Hsin-chia-p'o Sing. see Singapore
Hsinchu Taiwan 87 G3
also spelt Xinzhu
Hsinking China see Changchun
Hsinying Taiwan 87 G4
also spelt Xinying
Hsipaw Myanmar 78 B3
Hsi-sha Ch'un-tao is S. China Sea see Paracel Islands
Hsüeh Shan mt. Taiwan 87 G3
Hua'an China 87 F3
Huab watercourse Namibia 130 B4
Huachi Bol. 201 E4
Huacho Peru 200 A2
Huachón Peru 200 A2
Huachuan China 82 C3
also known as Yuelai
Huacrachuco Peru 200 A2
Huaculani Peru 200 C4
Huade China 85 G3
Huadian China 82 B4
Huadu China 87 E4
formerly known as Huaxian or Xinhua
Huafeng China see Hua'an
Huaihua China 87 D3
Hua Hin Thai. 79 B5
Huai'an Hebei China 85 G3
Huai'an Jiangsu China 87 F1
also known as Chaigoubu
Huai'an Jiangsu China see Chuzhou
Huaibei China 87 F1
Huaibin China 87 E1
formerly known as Wulongji
Huaicheng China see Huaiji
Huaide China see Gongzhuling
Huaidian China see Shenqiu
Huai Had National Park Thai. 78 D4
Huai He r. China 87 E1
Huaihua China 87 D3
also known as Yushuwan
Huaiji China 87 D4
also known as Huaicheng
Huai-nan China see Huainan
Huai-ku-khaeng Wildlife Reserve nature res. Thai. 79 B5
Huailai China 85 G3
Huai Luang r. Thai. 78 C4
Huaining China 87 F2
also known as Shipai
Huairen China 85 G4
formerly known as Shanyin
Huairou China 85 G3
Huai Samran r. Thai. 79 D5
Huaiyang China 87 E1
also known as Wangying
Huaiyin Jiangsu China 87 F1
formerly known as Qingjiang
Huaiyuan Anhui China 87 F1

Huaiyuan Guangxi China 87 D3
Huajialing China 84 E5
Huajuápan de León Mex. 185 F5
Huaki Indon. 75 C4
Hualahuises Mex. 185 F3
Hualapai Indian Reservation res. U.S.A. 183 K6
Hualapai Peak U.S.A. 183 K6
Hualfín Arg. 204 D2
Hualien Taiwan 87 G3
Hualla Peru 200 B3
Huallaga r. Peru 198 C6
Huallanca Peru 200 A2
Hualong China 84 D4
also known as Bayan
Huamachuco Peru 200 A1
Huamani Peru 200 B3
Huambo Angola 127 B8
formerly known as Nova Lisboa
Huambo prov. Angola 127 B8
Huams watercourse Namibia 132 B2
Huanan China 82 C3
Huancabamba Peru 198 B5
Huancache, Sierra mts Arg. 205 C6
Huancapi Peru 200 B3
Huancavelica Peru 200 B3
Huancavelica dept Peru 200 B3
Huancayo Peru 200 B3
Huanchaca China see Huanxian
Huangbei China 87 E3
Huangcaoba China see Xingyi
Huangchuan China 87 E1
Huanggang China 87 E2
Huanggang Shan mt. China 87 F2
also known as Tunxi
Huang He r. China see Yellow River
Huanghe Kou r. mouth China 85 H4
Huanghua China 85 H4
Huangjiajian China 87 G1
Huangling China 85 F5
also known as Qiaoshan
Huangliu China 87 D5
Huanglong China 85 F4
also known as Shipu
Huanglongsi China see Kaifeng
Huangmao Jian mt. China 87 F3
Huangmei China 87 E2
Huangnihe China 82 B4
Huangpi China 87 E2
Huangping China 87 D3
also known as Xinzhou
Huangshan China 87 F2
Huangshan China 87 F2
Huangsheugguan China 86 B1
Huangshi China 87 E2
Huang Shui r. China 84 D4
Huangtu Gaoyuan plat. China 85 E4
Huangxian China 85 I4
Huangyan China 87 G2
Huangyangzhen China 84 D4
Huangyuan China 84 D4
Huangzhong China 84 D4
also known as Lushar
Huangzhou China see Huanggang
Huaning China 86 B3
also known as Ningzhou
Huanjiang China 87 D3
also known as Si'en
Huan Jiang r. China 85 E4
Huanren China 82 B4
Huanshan China see Yuhuan
Huanta Peru 200 B3
Huantai China 85 H4
also known as Suozhen
Huánuco Peru 200 A2
Huánuco dept Peru 200 A2
Huanuhuanu Peru 200 B3
Huanuni Bol. 200 D4
Huanxian China 85 E4
also known as Huancheng
Huaping China 86 B3
also known as Zhongxin
Huap'ing Yü i. Taiwan 87 G3
Huar Bol. 200 D4
Huaral Peru 200 A2
Huaráz Peru 200 A2
Huariaca Peru 200 A2
Huarmey Peru 200 A2
Huarochirí Peru 200 A3
Huaron Peru 200 A2
Huarong China 87 E2
Huasaga r. Peru 198 B5
Huascarán, Parque Nacional nat. park Peru 200 A2
Huasco Chile 204 C3
Hua Shan mt. China 87 D1
Huashaoying China 85 G3
Huashixia China 84 C5
also known as Zogainrawar
Huashuguou China see Jingtieshan
Huatabampo Mex. 184 C3
Huatusco Mex. 185 F5
Huauchinango Mex. 185 F4
Huaura Peru 200 A2
Huautla Mex. 185 F5
Huaxian China see Huadu
Huaxian Henan China 85 G5
also known as Daokou
Huaxian Shaanxi China 87 D1
Huayacocotla Mex. 185 F4
Huayang China see Jixi
Huaylas Peru 200 A2
Huayuan China see Xiaochang
Huayuan China see Tianzhu
Huazangsi China see Tianzhu
Huazhaizi China 84 C4
Huazhou China 87 D4
Huaziha China see Huiyang
Hubba-d, Mount Canada/U.S.A. 166 B2
Hubbard, Pointe pt Canada 169 I1
Hubbard Lake U.S.A. 173 J6
Hubbard Point Canada 167 M3
Hubei prov. China 87 D2
English form Hupeh
Hubli India 94 B3
Hucal Arg. 204 D5
Huch'ang N. Korea 82 B4
Hückelhoven Germany 48 D4
Hückeswagen Germany 48 E4
Huddersfield U.K. 47 K10
Huder China 85 I1
Hudiksvall Sweden 45 L3
Hudson MA U.S.A. 177 N3
Hudson MD U.S.A. 177 I7
Hudson MI U.S.A. 173 I9
Hudson NH U.S.A. 177 N3
Hudson NY U.S.A. 177 L3
Hudson r. U.S.A. 177 L4
Hudson, Baie d' sea Canada see Hudson Bay
Hudson, Cerro mt. Chile 205 B7
Hudson, Détroit d' strait Canada see Hudson Strait
Hudson Bay Canada 167 K4
Hudson Bay Canada 165 K4
also known as Hudson, Baie d'
Hudson Falls U.S.A. 177 L2
Hudson Island Tuvalu see Nanumanga
Hudson Land reg. Greenland 165 Q2
Hudson Strait Canada 165 L3
also known as Hudson, Détroit d'
Hudson's Hope Canada 166 F3

Huelma Spain 55 H7
Huelva Spain 54 E7
Huelva r. Spain 54 E7
Huentelauquén Chile 204 C3
Huépac Mex. 184 C2
Huércal-Overa Spain 55 J7
Huerfano r. U.S.A. 181 F5
Huertecillas Mex. 185 E3
Huerva r. Spain 55 K3
Huesca Spain 55 K2
Huéscar Spain 55 I7
Huétamo Mex. 185 E5
Huete Spain 55 I4
Hueytown U.S.A. 175 C5
Huftarøy i. Norway 46 H0
Hugeilig l. Sudan 126 E2
Hugh watercourse Australia 148 B5
Hughenden Australia 149 E4
Hughes Australia 146 A2
Hughes r. Canada 167 L2
Hughes Bay Antarctica 222 T2
Hughesville MD U.S.A. 177 I7
Hughesville PA U.S.A. 177 I4
Hughson U.S.A. 182 C4
Hugli r. mouth India 97 E5
also spelt Hooghly
Hugli-Chunchura India 97 F5
Hugo CO U.S.A. 178 B4
Hugo OK U.S.A. 179 D5
Hugoton U.S.A. 178 B4
Huhehot China see Hohhot
Huhhot China see Hohhot
Huhudi S. Africa 133 I5
Huhus Fin. 44 O3
Hui'an China 87 F3
also known as Luocheng
Hui'anpu China 85 E4
Huiarau Range mts N.Z. 152 K6
Huib-Hoch Plateau Namibia 130 C5
Huichang China 87 E3
also known as Xiangjiang
Huichapán Mex. 185 F4
Huicheng China see Shexian
Huicheng China see Huilai
Huich'ŏn N. Korea 83 B4
Huidong Guangdong China 87 E4
also known as Pingshan
Huidong Sichuan China 86 B3
Huifa r. China 82 B4
Huihe China 85 H1
Huiji r. China 87 E1
Huila prov. Angola 127 B8
Huila dept Col. 198 C4
Huila, Nevado de vol. Col. 198 C4
Huilai China 87 F4
Huila Plateau Angola 127 B8
Huili China 86 B3
Huilongzhen China see Qidong
Huimanguillo Mex. 185 G5
Huimin China 85 H4
Huinahuaca Arg. 200 D5
Huinaimarca, Lago de l. Bol./Peru 200 C4
Huinan China 82 B4
also known as Chaoyang
Huinan China see Nanhui
Huinca Renancó Arg. 204 D4
Huining China 84 E5
also known as Huishi
Huishi China see Huining
Huishui China 86 C3
also known as Heping
Huisne r. France 50 G4
Huite Nur l. China 89 E5
Huitong China 87 D3
also known as Lincheng
Huittinen Fin. 45 M3
Huixian Gansu China 84 E5
Huixian Henan China 85 G5
Huixtla Mex. 185 G6
Huiyang China see Huizhou
Huize China 86 B3
also known as Zhongping
Huizhou China 87 E4
also known as Huiyang
Hujirt Arhangay Mongolia 84 D1
Hujirt Övörhangay Mongolia 84 D2
Hujirt Töv Mongolia 84 D2
Hukanui N.Z. 152 J8
Hukawng Valley Myanmar 78 B2
Hukou China 87 F2
also known as Shuangzhong
Hukuntsi Botswana 130 D4
Hulan China 82 B3
Hulan r. China 82 B3
Hulan Ergi China 85 I2
Hulayfah Saudi Arabia 104 C2
Hulayhilah well Syria 109 J3
Hulbert Lake U.S.A. 173 H4
Hulbert Lake l. U.S.A. 173 H4
Hulen U.S.A. 176 B9
Huliao China see Dabu
Hulin China 82 D3
Hull Canada 168 F4
Hull U.K. see Kingston upon Hull
Hull Island Kiribati see Orona
Hullo Estonia 42 D3
Hultsfred Sweden 45 K4
Hulu r. China 85 F5
Huludao China 85 I3
Hulun China see Hailar
Hulun Nur l. China 85 H1
Hulwän Egypt see Helwân
Hulyaypole Ukr. 41 F7
Huma China 82 B2
Huma r. China 82 B2
Humacao Puerto Rico 187 G3
Humahuaca Arg. 200 D5
Humaitá Brazil 201 E5
Humaitá Para. 201 F6
Humansdorp S. Africa 133 I11
Humay Peru 200 B3
Humaym well U.A.E. 105 F3
Humayyän, Jabal hill Saudi Arabia 104 C2
Humbe Angola 127 B9
Humbe, Serra do mts Angola 127 B8
Humber, Mouth of the U.K. 47 M10
Humberside airport U.K. 47 L10
Humberstone Chile 200 C5
Humberto de Campos Brazil 202 D2
Humboldt Canada 167 J4
Humboldt AZ U.S.A. 183 L7
Humboldt NE U.S.A. 178 D3
Humboldt NV U.S.A. 182 F1
Humboldt TN U.S.A. 174 B5
Humboldt r. U.S.A. 182 F1
Humboldt, Mont mt. New Caledonia 145 F4
Humboldt Bay U.S.A. 180 A4
Humboldt Gletscher glacier Greenland see Sermersuaq
Humboldt Lake U.S.A. 182 F1
Humboldt Mountain mts N.Z. 153 C12
Humboldt Range mts U.S.A. 182 F1
Humbolt Salt Marsh U.S.A. 182 G2
Hume r. Canada 166 D1
Humeda plain Arg. 204 E5
Humenné Slovakia 49 S7
Hume Reservoir Australia 147 E3
Humina reg. Bos.-Herz. 56 J5
Humka, Gora hill Croatia 56 I3
Humos, Cabo c. Chile 204 B4
Humpata Angola 127 B8
Humphrey Island atoll Cook Is see Manihiki
Humphreys, Mount U.S.A. 182 F4
Humphreys Peak U.S.A. 183 M6
Humpolec Czech Rep. 49 M6
Humppila Fin. 45 M3
Humpty Doo Australia 148 A2

Hun r. China 85 I3
Hūn Libya 120 B2
Húnaflói b. Iceland 44 [inset] B2
Hunan prov. China 87 D3
Hunchun China 82 C4
Hunchun r. China 82 C4
Hundorp Norway 45 J3
Hundred U.S.A. 176 E6
Hunedoara Romania 58 D3
Hünfeld Germany 48 G5
▶Hungary country Europe 49 P8
known as Magyar Köztársaság in Hungarian
europe [countries] ▶ 32–35
Hungerford Australia 147 E2
Hungerford U.K. 47 K12
Hung Fa Leng hill Hong Kong China see Robin's Nest
Hüngiy Gol r. Mongolia 84 B1
Hŭngnam N. Korea 83 B5
Hungry Horse Reservoir U.S.A. 180 D2
Hung Shui Kiu Hong Kong China 87 [inset]
Hungund India 94 C2
Hunissout Pan salt pan S. Africa 132 D7
Hunjiang China see Baishan
Hun Jiang r. China 82 B4
Hunnebostrand Sweden 45 J4
Huns Mountains Namibia 132 B4
Hunstanton U.K. 47 M11
Hunsur India 94 C3
Hunta Canada 173 L1
Hunte r. Germany 48 F2
Hunter r. Australia 147 F3
Hunter N.Z. 153 F12
Hunter r. N.Z. 153 D12
Hunterganj India 97 E4
Hunter Island Australia 147 E5
Hunter Island Canada 166 D5
Hunter Island S. Pacific Ocean 145 G4
Hunter Islands Australia 147 E5
Hunter Mountains N.Z. 153 B13
Hunter's Bay Myanmar 78 A4
Huntingdon U.K. 47 L11
Huntingdon PA U.S.A. 176 H5
Huntingdon TN U.S.A. 174 B4
Huntington IN U.S.A. 174 C3
Huntington UT U.S.A. 183 N2
Huntington WV U.S.A. 176 C7
Huntington Beach U.S.A. 182 F8
Huntington Creek r. U.S.A. 183 I1
Huntly N.Z. 152 J5
Huntly U.K. 46 J6
Hunt Mountain U.S.A. 180 F3
Hunt Peninsula Australia 146 C2
Huntsville Canada 168 E4
Huntsville AL U.S.A. 174 C5
Huntsville AR U.S.A. 179 D4
Huntsville MO U.S.A. 178 D4
Huntsville TX U.S.A. 179 D6
Hunucmá Mex. 185 H4
Hunyani r. Moz./Zimbabwe see Manyame
Hunyuan China 85 G4
Hunza Jammu and Kashmir 96 B1
Hunza reg. Jammu and Kashmir 96 B1
Hunza r. Pak. 101 H3
Hunze r. Neth. 48 D2
Huocheng China 88 C2
also known as Shuiding
Huoer China see Hor
Huojia China 85 G5
Huolin r. China 85 J2
Huolongmen China 82 B2
Huolu China see Luquan
Huong Thuy Vietnam 78 D4
Huon Peninsula P.N.G. 73 K8
Huonville Australia 147 E5
Huoqiu China 87 F1
Huoshan China 87 F2
Huo Shan mt. China 87 F2
Huoshao Tao i. Taiwan see Lü Tao
Huotsaus waterhole Namibia 130 B4
Huoxian China see Huozhou
Huozhou China 85 F4
formerly known as Huoxian
Hupeh prov. China see Hubei
Hupnik r. Turkey 109 H1
Ḩūr Iran 100 D4
Hurault, Lac l. Canada 169 G2
Huraymilā Saudi Arabia 105 D2
Huraysān reg. Saudi Arabia 105 D3
Hurbanovo Slovakia 49 P8
Hurd, Cape Canada 168 D4
Hurd Island Kiribati see Arorae
Hurdiyo Somalia 128 F2
Hure China 85 I3
also known as Hure Qi
Hüremt Mongolia 84 D1
Hürent Mongolia 84 D2
Hure Qi China see Hure
Hurghada Egypt 121 G3
also known as Al Ghardaqah
Huri mt. Kenya 128 C4
Huriel France 51 I6
Hurkett Canada 172 E2
Hurley U.S.A. 177 K4
Hurlock U.S.A. 177 J7
Huron CA U.S.A. 182 D5
Huron SD U.S.A. 178 C2
▶Huron, Lake Canada/U.S.A. 173 J5
2nd largest lake in North America and 4th in the world.
northamerica [landscapes] ▶ 156–157
Huron Bay U.S.A. 172 E4
Huron Beach U.S.A. 173 I5
Huronian Canada 172 C2
Huron Mountains hills U.S.A. 172 F4
Hurricane U.S.A. 183 K4
Hurricane Flats sea feature Bahamas 175 E8
Hurtado Chile 204 C3
Hurung, Gunung mt. Indon. 77 F2
Hurunui r. N.Z. 153 H10
Hurup Denmark 45 J4
Husain Nika Pak. 101 G4
Húsavík Norðurland eystra Iceland 44 [inset] C2
Húsavík Vestfirðir Iceland 44 [inset] B2
Husayn reg. Yemen 105 D4
Huseyinabat Turkey see Alaca
Huseyinli Turkey see Kızılırmak
Hushan China see Wuyi
Hushan China see Cixi
Husheib Sudan 121 G6
Huşi Romania 58 J2
Huskvarna Sweden 45 K4
Husn Jordan see Al Ḩişn
Ḩuşn Āl 'Abr Yemen 105 D4
Husnes Norway 45 I4
Husøy i. Norway 46 Q2
Hussainabad India 97 E4
Hustopeče Czech Rep. 49 N7
Husum Germany 48 G1
Husum Sweden 44 L3
Husvik S. Georgia 205 [inset]
Hutag Mongolia 84 D1
Hūtak Iran 100 D4
Hutanopan Indon. 76 B2
Hutaym, Ḩarrat lava field Saudi Arabia 104 C2
Hutchinson S. Africa 132 H8
Hutchinson KS U.S.A. 178 C4
Hutchinson MN U.S.A. 178 D2
Hutch Mountain U.S.A. 183 M7
Ḩūth Yemen 104 C4
Hutou China 82 D3
Huttah Kulkyne National Park Australia 147 D3
Hutton, Mount hill Australia 149 F5
Hutton Range hills Australia 151 C5
Hutubi China 88 D2
Hutubi He r. China 88 D2
Hutuo r. China 85 H4
Hutup watercourse Namibia 132 B2
Huu Đô Vietnam 78 D3
Huvadhu Atoll Maldives 93 D10
Hūvār Iran 101 E5
Hüvek Turkey see Bozova
Hüvīān, Kūh-e mts Iran 101 D5
Huwār i. The Gulf 105 E2
also spelt Hawar
Ḩuwaymī, Sha'īb al watercourse Iraq 109 P7
Huwaytat reg. Saudi Arabia 107 D5
Huxi China 87 E3
Huxian China 87 D1
also known as Ganting
Huxley, Mount hill Australia 150 D3
Huxley, Mount N.Z. 153 D12
Huy Belgium 51 L2
Hüzgān Iran 100 B4
Huzhen China 87 G2
Huzhou China 87 G2
formerly known as Wuxing
Huzhu China 84 D4
also known as Weiyuan
Huzurnagar India 94 C2
Hvalnes Iceland 44 [inset] D2
Hvammsfjörður inlet Iceland 44 [inset] B2
Hvannadalshnúkur vol. Iceland 44 [inset] C2
Hvar Croatia 56 I5
Hvar i. Croatia 56 I5
Hvardiys'ke Ukr. 41 E7
Hvarski Kanal sea chan. Croatia 56 I5
Hveragerði Iceland 44 [inset] B2
Hvide Sande Denmark 45 J4
Hvíta r. Iceland 44 [inset] B3
Hvítárvatn l. Iceland 44 [inset] C2
Hwadae N. Korea 83 C4
Hwange Zimbabwe 131 E3
formerly spelt Wankie
Hwange National Park Zimbabwe 131 E3
Hwang Ho r. China see Yellow River
Hwangju N. Korea 83 B5
Hwayang S. Korea 91 A7
Hwedza Zimbabwe 131 F3
Hwlffordd U.K. see Haverfordwest
Hyannis MA U.S.A. 177 O4
Hyannis NE U.S.A. 178 B3
Hyargas Nuur salt l. Mongolia 84 B1
Hyco Lake U.S.A. 176 F9
Hyde N.Z. 153 E13
Hyden Australia 151 B7
Hyden U.S.A. 176 B8
Hyderabad India 94 C2
Hyderabad Pak. 101 G5
Hydra i. Greece see Ydra
Hyères France 51 M9
Hyères, Îles d' is France 51 M10
Hyermanavichy Belarus 42 I6
Hyesan N. Korea 82 C4
Hyland r. Canada 166 D3
Hyland, Mount Australia 147 G2
Hyland Bay Australia 148 A2
Hyland Post Canada 166 D3
Hyllekrog i. Denmark 48 I1
Hyllestad Norway 45 I3
Hyltebruk Sweden 45 K4
Hyndman U.S.A. 176 G6
Hyndman Peak U.S.A. 180 D4
Hyōgo pref. Japan 91 D7
Hyōno-sen mt. Japan 91 D7
Hyrcania Iran see Gorgān
Hyrra Banda Cent. Afr. Rep. see Ira Banda
Hyrynsalmi Fin. 44 O2
Hysham U.S.A. 180 F3
Hythe Canada 166 G4
Hyūga Japan 91 B8
Hyvinkää Fin. 45 N3

↓ I

Ia A Dun r. Vietnam 79 E5
Iacanga Brazil 206 D8
Iaciara Brazil 202 C5
Iaco r. Brazil 200 C2
Iacobeni Romania 58 F2
Iacobeni Romania 58 G1
Iacri Brazil 206 C8
Iaçu Brazil 202 D5
Iadera Croatia see Zadar
Iaeger U.S.A. 176 D8
Iakora Madag. 131 [inset] J4
Ialomiţa r. Romania 58 I4
Ialomiţei, Balta marsh Romania 58 I4
Ialoveni Moldova 58 J2
formerly known as Kutuzov; formerly spelt Yaloven'
Ialpug r. Moldova 58 J2
formerly spelt Yalpukh
Ianca Romania 58 I3
Ian Calder Lake Canada 167 L1
Iancu Jianu Romania 58 F4
Iapu Brazil 207 K6
Iara r. Romania 58 E2
Iarauarune, Serra mts Brazil 199 F4
Iargara Moldova 58 J2
formerly spelt Yargara
Iaşi Romania 58 I1
also known as Jassy; also spelt Yaş
Iasmos Greece 58 G7
Iba Phil. 74 A3
Ibadan Nigeria 125 F5
Ibagué Col. 198 C3
Ibaiti Brazil 206 C10
Ibanda Uganda 128 A5
Ibăneşti Romania 58 F2
Ibañeta, Puerto de pass Spain 55 J1
Ibanga Kasai Occidental Dem. Rep. Congo 127 D6
Ibanga Sud-Kivu Dem. Rep. Congo 126 E5
Ibapah U.S.A. 183 K1
Ibar r. Yugo. 58 B5
Ibara Japan 91 C7
Ibaraki pref. Japan 91 G6
Ibarra Ecuador 198 B4
Ibarreta Arg. 204 F2
Ibaté Brazil 206 F8
Ibb Yemen 104 D5
Ibb governorate Yemen 104 D5
Ibba watercourse Sudan 126 F3
Ibbenbüren Germany 48 E3
Ibdeqqene watercourse Mali 125 F2
Iberá, Esteros del marsh Arg. 204 F3
Iberá, Lago l. Arg. 204 F3
Iberia Loreto Peru 198 C6
Iberia Madre de Dios Peru 200 C2
▶Iberian Peninsula Europe 54
Consists of Portugal, Spain and Gibraltar.
Ibertioga Brazil 207 J8
Iberville, Lac d' l. Canada 169 F2
also known as Upper Seal Lake
Ibestad Norway 44 L1
Ibeto Nigeria 125 G4
Ibi Indon. 76 B1
Ibi Nigeria 125 H4
Ibi Spain 55 K6
Ibiá Brazil 206 G6
Ibiapaba, Serra da hills Brazil 202 D2
Ibias r. Spain 54 E1
Ibicaraí Brazil 202 E5
Ibicuí Bahia Brazil 207 N1
Ibicuí Rio Grande do Sul Brazil 204 F3
Ibicuí r. Brazil 203 A9
Ibigawa Japan 91 E7
Ibimirim Brazil 202 E4
Ibina r. Dem. Rep. Congo 126 F4
Ibiporã Brazil 206 B10
Ibirá Brazil 206 D8
Ibiraçu Brazil 207 M6
Ibiranhém Brazil 207 M4
Ibitiara Brazil 202 D5
Ibitinga Brazil 206 E8
Ibiúna Brazil 206 F10
Ibiza Spain 55 M6
also spelt Eivissa
Ibiza i. Spain 55 M5
also spelt Eivissa; formerly spelt Iviza; historically known as Ebusus
Iblei, Monti mts Sicilia Italy 57 G11
İblis Burnu pt Turkey 59 J12
Ibn Buşayyiş well Saudi Arabia 105 D2
Ibn Hādī Saudi Arabia 104 C4
Ibotirama Brazil 202 D5
Iboundji, Mont hill Gabon 126 A5
Ibrā' Oman 105 G3
Ibra, Wadi watercourse Sudan 126 E2
Ibrāt, Wādī watercourse Iraq 109 N2
Ibresi Rus. Fed. 40 H5
'Ibrī Oman 105 G3
Ibu Indon. 75 C2
Ibuhos i. Phil. 74 B1
Ibusuki Japan 91 B9
Içá r. Brazil 198 E5
Ica Peru 200 B3
Ica dept Peru 200 B3
Icabarú Venez. 199 F3
Icaiché Mex. 185 H5
Içana Brazil 199 E4
Içana r. Brazil 198 E4
Icaraí Brazil 202 E2
Icaria i. Greece see Ikaria
Icatu Brazil 202 C2
Iceberg Canyon gorge U.S.A. 183 J5
İçel Turkey 106 C3
also known as Mersin
İçel prov. Turkey 108 E1
▶Iceland country Europe 44 [inset] B2
2nd largest island in Europe. Known as Ísland in Icelandic.
europe [landscapes] ▶ 30–31
europe [countries] ▶ 32–35
europe [environments] ▶ 36–37
Icem Brazil 206 D7
Ichak India 97 E4
Ichalkaranji India 94 B2
Ichchapuram India 95 E2
Ichihara Japan 91 G7
Ichilo r. Bol. 201 D4
Ichinoseki Japan 90 G5
Ichinskiy, Vulkan vol. Rus. Fed. 39 P4
Ichkeria aut. rep. Rus. Fed. see Chechenskaya Respublika
Ichkeul National Park Tunisia 57 B11
Ichnya Ukr. 41 E6
Ich'ŏn N. Korea 83 B5
Ich'ŏn S. Korea 83 B5
Ichuña Peru 200 C4
İçikler Turkey 59 J10
İçmeler Turkey 59 J12
Icó Brazil 202 E3
Iconha Brazil 207 M7
Iconium Turkey see Konya
Icosium Alg. see Algiers
Iculisma France see Angoulême
Icy Bay U.S.A. 166 A3
Icy Strait U.S.A. 166 C3
Ida, Mount N.Z. 153 E12
Idabdaba well Niger 125 H2
Idabel U.S.A. 179 D5
Idaga Hamus Eth. 104 B5
Ida Grove U.S.A. 178 D3
Idah Nigeria 125 G5
Idaho state U.S.A. 180 D3
Idaho City U.S.A. 180 D4
Idaho Falls U.S.A. 180 D4
Idalia National Park Australia 149 E5
Idanha-a-Nova Port. 54 D5
Idar India 96 B5
Idar-Oberstein Germany 48 E6
Ida Valley N.Z. 153 D13
Iday well Niger 125 H3
Iddan Somalia 128 F3
Idd el Asoda well Sudan 121 F6
Idd el Chanam Sudan 126 E2
Idd esh Shurak well Sudan 121 F5
Idefjorden inlet Norway/Sweden 45 J4
Ider Mongolia 84 C1
Ideriyn Gol r. Mongolia 84 D1
Idfina Egypt 108 B6
Idfu Egypt 121 G3
also spelt Edfu; historically known as Apollinopolis Magna
Idhān Awbārī des. Libya 120 A3
Idhān Murzūq des. Libya 120 B3
Idhra i. Greece see Ydra
Ídhras, Kólpos sea chan. Greece see Ydras, Kolpos
Idi Amin Dada, Lake Dem. Rep. Congo/Uganda see Edward, Lake
Idice r. Italy 56 D4
Idiofa Dem. Rep. Congo 126 C6
Idku Egypt 121 F2
Idlib Syria 109 H2
Idlib governorate Syria 109 H2
Idra i. Greece see Ydra
Idracowra Australia 148 B5
Idre Sweden 45 K3
Idrija Slovenia 56 G2
Idrijca r. Slovenia 56 F2
Idritsa Rus. Fed. 43 J5
Idstein Germany 48 F5
Idugala Tanz. 129 B6
Idukki India 94 C4
Idutywa S. Africa 133 M9
Idyllwild U.S.A. 183 H8
Idzhevan Armenia see Ijevan
Iecava Latvia 42 F5
Iecava r. Latvia 42 E5
Iepê Brazil 206 B9
Ieper Belgium 51 I2
also spelt Ypres
Ier r. Romania 49 T8
Ierapetra Greece 59 G13
Ierissou, Kolpos b. Greece 59 E8
Ifakara Tanz. 129 C7
'Ifāl, Wādī watercourse Saudi Arabia 104 A1
also known as Afal
Ifalik atoll Micronesia 73 J5
also spelt Ifaluk; formerly known as Wilson
Ifaluk atoll Micronesia see Ifalik
Ifanadiana Madag. 131 [inset] J4
Ifanirea Madag. 131 [inset] J4
Ife Nigeria 125 G5
Ifenat Chad 120 C6
Iferouâne Niger 125 H2
Ifetesene mt. Alg. 123 G4
Iffley Australia 149 D3
Ifjord Norway 44 N1
Ifôghas, Adrar des hills Mali 125 F2
also known as Iforas, Adrar des; short form Adrar
Ifon Nigeria 125 G5
Iforas, Adrar des hills Mali see Ifôghas, Adrar des
Ifould Lake salt flat Australia 146 B2
Ifrane Morocco 122 D2
Ifumo Dem. Rep. Congo 126 D5
Ifunda Tanz. 129 B7
Igan Sarawak Malaysia 72 D6
Igan r. Sarawak Malaysia 77 E2
Iganga Uganda 128 B4
Igarapava Brazil 206 F7
Igarapé Açú Brazil 202 C2
Igarapé Grande Brazil 202 C3
Igarapé Miri Brazil 202 B2
Igaratá Brazil 207 G10
Igarité Brazil 202 D4
Igarka Rus. Fed. 39 I3
Igatpuri India 94 B2
Igbeti Nigeria 125 G4
Igboho Nigeria 125 F4
Iğdır Turkey 107 F3
Iggesund Sweden 45 L3
Ighiu Romania 58 E2
Iglesia Arg. 204 C3
Iglesias Sardegna Italy 57 A9
Igli Alg. 123 E3
Iglino Rus. Fed. 40 K5
Igloolik Canada 165 K3
Igluligaarjuk Canada see Chesterfield Inlet
'Igma, Gebel el plat. Egypt 108 E8
Ignace Canada 168 B3
Ignacio Zaragosa Mex. 184 D2
Ignacio Zaragoza Mex. 185 F4
Ignalina Lith. 42 H6
İğneada Turkey 106 A2
İğneada Burnu pt Turkey 106 B2
Igoma Tanz. 129 B6
Igombe r. Tanz. 129 A6
Igorevskaya Rus. Fed. 43 O6
Igoumenitsa Greece 59 B9
Igra Rus. Fed. 40 J4
Igrim Rus. Fed. 38 G3
Iguaçu r. Brazil 203 A8
Iguaçu, Parque Nacional do nat. park Brazil 203 A8
Iguaçu, Saltos do waterfall Arg./Brazil see Iguaçu Falls
Iguaçu Falls Arg./Brazil 204 G2
also known as Iguazú, Cataratas do or Iguaçu, Saltos do
Iguaí Brazil 202 D5
Iguaje, Mesa de hills Col. 198 C4
Iguala Mex. 185 F5
Igualada Spain 55 M3
Iguape Brazil 203 C8
Iguaraçu Brazil 206 B10
Iguarapé Brazil 207 I7
Iguatemi Brazil 203 A7
Iguatemi r. Brazil 203 A7
Iguatu Brazil 202 E3
Iguazú, Cataratas do waterfall Arg./Brazil see Iguaçu Falls
Iguazú, Parque Nacional del nat. park Arg. 204 G2
Iguéla Gabon 126 A5
Igueña Spain 54 E2
Iguetti, Sebkhet salt flat Mauritania 122 C4
Igunga Tanz. 129 B6
Iguobazuwa Nigeria 125 G5
Igusule Tanz. 129 B5
Iguvium Italy see Gubbio
Iharaña Madag. 131 [inset] K2
formerly known as Vohémar or Vohimarina
Ihavandhippolhu Atoll Maldives 94 B5
Ihbulag Mongolia 85 E3
Ihhayrhan Mongolia 85 E2
Ihiala Nigeria 125 G5
Ihirène, Oued watercourse Alg. 123 G5
Ihosy Madag. 131 [inset] J4
Ihsuuj Mongolia 85 E1
Ih Tal China 85 I3
Iida Japan 91 E7
Iide-san mt. Japan 90 F6
Iijoki r. Fin. 44 N2
Iisalmi Fin. 44 N3
Iitti Fin. 42 H1
Iiyama Japan 91 F6
Iizuka Japan 91 B8
Ijâfene des. Mauritania 122 C5
Ijara Kenya 128 D5
Ijebu-Ode Nigeria 125 F5
Ijevan Armenia 107 F2
also spelt Idzhevan
IJmuiden Neth. 48 B3
Ijnâouene well Mauritania 124 B2
Ijoubbâne des. Mali 122 D5
IJssel r. Neth. 48 C3
IJsselmeer l. Neth. 48 C3
formerly known as Zuider Zee
Ijuí Brazil 203 A9
Ijuí r. Brazil 203 A8
Ijzer r. Belgium 51 I2
also known as Yser (France)
Ikaahuk Canada see Sachs Harbour
Ikaalinen Fin. 45 M3
Ikageleng S. Africa 133 K2
Ikageng S. Africa 133 L3
Ikahavo hill Madag. 131 [inset] J3
Ikalamavony Madag. 131 [inset] J4
Ikamatua N.Z. 153 F10
Ikang Nigeria 125 H5
Ikare Nigeria 125 G5
Ikaria i. Greece 59 H11
English form Icaria
Ikast Denmark 45 J4
Ikawai N.Z. 153 E12
Ikawhenua Range mts N.Z. 152 K6
Ikeda Hokkaidō Japan 90 H3
Ikeda Tokushima Japan 91 C7
Ikeja Nigeria 125 F5
Ikela Dem. Rep. Congo 126 D5
Ikelemba r. Dem. Rep. Congo 126 C4
Ikelenge Zambia 127 E7
Ikengo Dem. Rep. Congo 126 C5
Ikéngue Gabon 126 A5
Ikere Nigeria 125 G5
also spelt Ikerre
Ikerre Nigeria see Ikere
Ikhtiman Bulg. 58 E6
Ikhutseng S. Africa 133 I5
Iki i. Japan 91 A8
Iki-Burul Rus. Fed. 41 H7
Ikimba, Lake Tanz. 128 A5
Ikire Nigeria 125 G5
Ikla Estonia 42 F4
Ikom Nigeria 125 H5
Ikoma Tanz. 128 B5
Ikongo Madag. 131 [inset] J4
formerly known as Fort Carnot
Ikopa r. Madag. 131 [inset] J3
Ikorodu Nigeria 125 F5
Ikosi Dem. Rep. Congo 126 E5
Ikot Ekpene Nigeria 125 G5
Ikouhaouene, Adrar mt. Alg. 123 H4
Iksan S. Korea 83 B6
formerly known as Iri
Ikungu Tanz. 129 B6
Ila Nigeria 125 G4
Ilaferh, Oued watercourse Alg. 123 F5
Ilagala Tanz. 129 A6
Ilagan Phil. 74 B2
Ilaisamis Kenya 128 C4
Ilaiyankudi India 94 C4
Ilaka Atsinanana Madag. 131 [inset] K3
Īlām Iran 100 A3
Īlām prov. Iran 100 A3
Ilam Nepal 97 E4
Ilan Taiwan 87 G3
also spelt Yilan
Ilanz Switz. 51 P6
Ilaro Nigeria 125 F5
Ilave Peru 200 C4
Iława Poland 49 Q2
Ilazārān, Kūh-e mt. Iran 100 D4
Il Bogd Uul mts Mongolia 84 C2
Ile r. China/Kazakh. 88 B3
Île-à-la-Crosse, Lac l. Canada 167 J4
Ilebo Dem. Rep. Congo 126 D6
formerly known as Port Francqui
Île-de-France admin. reg. France 51 I4
Ileje Tanz. 129 B7
Ilek Kazakh. 102 C2
Ilek r. Rus. Fed. 102 C2
also spelt Elek
Ilen r. Rep. of Ireland 47 C12
Ileret Kenya 128 C3
Ilesa Nigeria 125 G5
also spelt Ilesha
Ilesha Nigeria see Ilesa
Ilet' r. Rus. Fed. 40 I5
Ileza Rus. Fed. 40 G3
Ilford Canada 167 M3
Ilfracombe Australia 149 E4
Ilfracombe U.K. 47 H12
Ilgaz Turkey 106 C2
Ilgaz Dağları mts Turkey 106 C2
Ilgın Turkey 106 B3
Ilhabela Brazil 203 C7
Ilha Grande Brazil 199 E5
Ilha Grande, Baía da b. Brazil 207 I10
Ilha Grande, Represa resr Brazil 203 A7
Ilha Solteira, Represa resr Brazil 206 B7
Ílhavo Port. 54 C4
Ilhéus Brazil 202 E5
Ili Kazakh. see Kapchagay
Ilia Romania 58 D3
Iliamna Lake U.S.A. 164 D4
İliç Turkey 107 D3
Il'ich Kazakh. 103 G4
Il'ichevsk Azer. see Şärur
Ilici Spain see Elche
Ilig, Raas pt Somalia 128 F3
Iligan Phil. 74 C4
Iligan Bay Phil. 74 C4
Iligan Point Phil. 74 B2
Ilijaš Bos.-Herz. 56 K5
Ilimanangip Nunaa i. Greenland 165 Q2
also known as Milne Land
Ilimpeya r. Rus. Fed. 39 K3
Il'inka Kazakh. 102 D2
Il'inka Kaluzhskaya Oblast' Rus. Fed. 43 R7
Il'inka Respublika Altay Rus. Fed. 88 D1
Il'inka Respublika Buryatiya Rus. Fed. 85 E1
Il'inka Respublika Tyva Rus. Fed. 84 B1
Il'ino Rus. Fed. 43 M6
Il'inskiy Permskaya Oblast' Rus. Fed. 40 J4
Il'inskiy Respublika Kareliya Rus. Fed. 43 N1
Il'inskiy Sakhalin Rus. Fed. 82 F3
Il'insko-Podomskoye Rus. Fed. 40 H3
Il'inskoye Orlovskaya Oblast' Rus. Fed. 43 Q8
Il'inskoye Tverskaya Oblast' Rus. Fed. 43 S5
Il'inskoye Yaroslavskaya Oblast' Rus. Fed. 43 T4
Il'inskoye-Khovanskoye Rus. Fed. 43 U5
Ilin Strait Phil. 74 B3
Iliomar East Timor 75 C5
Ilion U.S.A. 177 J2
Ilirska Bistrica Slovenia 56 G3
Ilium tourist site Turkey see Troy
Iliya r. Belarus 42 I7
Iliysk Kazakh. see Kapchagay
Ilk Hungary 49 T7
Il'ka Rus. Fed. 85 F1
Ilkal India 94 C3
Ill r. France 51 N4
Illana Bay Phil. 74 B5
Illapel Chile 204 C3
Illapel r. Chile 204 C3
Illbillee, Mount hill Australia 146 B1
Ille r. France 50 E4
Illela Nigeria 125 G3
Iller r. Germany 48 G7
Illertissen Germany 48 H7
Illescas Spain 54 H4
Illescas Uruguay 204 G4
Illimani, Nevado de mt. Bol. 200 D4
Illinois r. U.S.A. 174 B4
Illinois state U.S.A. 174 B4
Illinois and Mississippi Canal U.S.A. 172 D9
Illizi Alg. 123 H4
formerly known as Fort de Polignac
Illogwa watercourse Australia 148 B5
Illueca Spain 55 J3
Ilm r. Germany 48 I4
Ilma, Lake salt flat Australia 151 D6
'Ilmān, Jabal al hill Saudi Arabia 104 D4
Il'men', Ozero l. Rus. Fed. 43 M3
Ilmenau Germany 48 H5
Ilmtal park Germany 48 I5
Ilo Peru 200 C4
Ilobu Nigeria 125 G5
Iloc i. Phil. 74 A4
Iloilo Phil. 74 B4
Iloilo Strait Phil. 74 B4
Ilomantsi Fin. 44 O3
Ilongero Tanz. 129 B6
Ilorin Nigeria 125 G4
Ilovat' r. Rus. Fed. 41 H6
Ilovatka Rus. Fed. 41 H6
Ilovik i. Croatia 56 G4
Ilovlya Rus. Fed. 41 G6
Ilovlya r. Rus. Fed. 41 G6
Iłowa Poland 49 M4
Il-Ponta ta' Benghajsa pt Malta see Benghisa Point
Il'pyrskiy Rus. Fed. 39 Q3
formerly known as Il'pyrskoye
Il'pyrskoye Rus. Fed. see Il'pyrskiy
Ilūkste Latvia 42 H6
Ilulissat Greenland 165 N3
also known as Jakobshavn
Ilunde Tanz. 129 B6
Ilungu Tanz. 129 B6
Ilva i. Italy see Elba, Isola d'
Il'ya Belarus 42 I7
Il'yaly Turkm. see Yylanly
Ilych r. Rus. Fed. 40 K3
Iłżanka r. Poland 49 S4
Imabari Japan 91 C7
Imabetsu Japan 90 G4
Imabú r. Brazil 199 G5
Imagane Japan 90 G3
Imaichi Japan 91 F6
Imala Moz. 131 H2
Imām al Ḩamzah Iraq 107 F5
Imam-baba Turkm. 103 E5
Imamoğlu Turkey 106 C3
Iman Rus. Fed. see Dal'nerechensk
Iman r. Rus. Fed. 82 D3
Imantau, Ozero l. Kazakh. 103 G1
Imari Japan 91 A8
Imasgo Burkina 125 E3
also spelt Imassogo
Imassogo Burkina see Imasgo
Imata Peru 200 C3
Imataca, Serranía de mts Venez. 199 F3
Imatra Fin. 45 O3
Imavere Estonia 42 G3
Imazu Japan 91 E7
Imbabura prov. Ecuador 198 B4
Imbaimadai Guyana 199 F3
Imbituba Brazil 203 B9
imeni 26 Bakinskikh Komissarov Azer. see 26 Bakı Komissarı
imeni 26 Bakinskikh Komissarov Turkm. 102 C5
imeni Babushkina Rus. Fed. 40 G4
imeni C. A. Niyazova Turkm. 103 E5
formerly known as imeni Chapayevka
imeni Chapayevka Turkm. see imeni C. A. Niyazova
imeni Gastello Rus. Fed. 39 O3
imeni Kalinina Tajik. 101 H2
imeni Kerbabayeva Turkm. 102 E5
formerly known as Karrychirla
imeni Khamzy Khakikmzade Uzbek. see Khamza
imeni Kirova Kazakh. see Kopbirlik
imeni Kuybysheva Turkm. 103 E5
also known as Kuybyshew Adyndaky
imeni Petra Stuchki Latvia see Aizkraukle
imeni Poliny Osipenko Rus. Fed. 82 E1
imeni Voroshilova Kyrg. see Eshanguzar
imeni Zhelyabova Rus. Fed. 43 R3
Imeri, Serra mts Brazil 199 E4
Imese Dem. Rep. Congo 126 C4
Īmī Eth. 128 D3
Imishli Azer. see İmişli
İmişli Azer. 107 G3
also spelt Imishli
Imit Jammu and Kashmir 96 B1
Imja-do i. S. Korea 83 B6
Imjin-gang r. N. Korea/S. Korea 83 B5
Imlay U.S.A. 182 F1
Imlay City U.S.A. 173 J7
Imlili W. Sahara 122 B5
Immokalee U.S.A. 175 D7
Imo state Nigeria 125 G5
Imola Italy 56 D4
Imotski Croatia 56 J5
Imperatriz Brazil 202 C3
Imperia Italy 56 A5
Imperial Peru 200 A3
Imperial CA U.S.A. 183 I9
Imperial NE U.S.A. 178 B3
Imperial Beach U.S.A. 183 G9
Imperial Dam U.S.A. 183 J9
Imperial Valley plain U.S.A. 183 I9
Imperieuse Reef Australia 150 B3
Impfondo Congo 126 C4
Imphal India 97 G4
formerly known as Manipur
İmralı Adası i. Turkey 58 J8
Imrān Yemen 104 D5
İmroz Turkey 106 A2
İmroz i. Turkey see Gökçeada
Imrun Turkey see Pütürge
Imsil S. Korea 83 B6
Imst Austria 48 H8
Imtān Syria 109 H5
Imuris Mex. 184 C2
Imuruan Bay Phil. 74 A4
Imzouren Morocco 54 H9
In r. Rus. Fed. 82 D2
Ina Japan 91 E7
Ina r. Poland 49 L2
I-n-Abanghari well Niger 125 G2
Inabu Japan 91 E7
In Afaleleh well Alg. 123 H5
Inaguan Phil. 74 A4
Inago Moz. 131 H2
Inahuaya Peru 200 B1
Inajá Brazil 202 E4
Inaja, Serra do hills Brazil 201 H2
I-n-Akhmed well Mali 125 E2
I-n-Alchi well Mali 125 E2
I-n-Aleï well Mali 124 E2
Inamba-jima i. Japan see Inanba-jima
Inambari Peru 200 C3
Inambari r. Peru 200 C3
I-n-Amedde well Mali 124 D2
In Aménas Alg. 123 H3
In Amguel Alg. 123 G5
Inanba-jima i. Japan 91 F8
also spelt Inamba-jima
Inanda S. Africa 133 O6
Inangahua Junction N.Z. 153 F9
Inanwatan Indon. 73 H7
Iñapari Peru 200 C2
Inari Fin. 44 N1
also known as Aanaar or Anár
Inarigda Rus. Fed. 39 K3
Inarijärvi l. Fin. 44 N1
Inarijoki r. Fin./Norway 44 N1
I-n-Arouinat well Niger 125 G2
I-n-Atankarer well Mali 125 F2
Inauini r. Brazil 200 D2
Inawashiro-ko l. Japan 90 G6
In Azaoua well Alg. 123 G4
In-Azaoua well Alg. 123 G5
I-n-Azaoua watercourse Niger 125 G1
In Azar well Libya 120 A2
In Azāwah well Libya 120 A3
I-n-Azerraf well Mali 125 F2
In Belbel Alg. 123 F4
Inca Spain 55 N5
Inca de Oro Chile 204 C2
İnce Burnu pt Turkey 58 I8
İnce Burun pt Turkey 106 C2
Inceler Turkey 59 K11
Inchbonnie N.Z. 153 F10
İncheh Iran 100 D2
Inch'ini Terara mt. Eth. 128 C3
Inchiri admin. reg. Mauritania 122 B5
Inch'ŏn S. Korea 83 B5
also known as Jinsen; formerly known as Chemulpo
Inchope Moz. 131 G3
I-n-Choumaguene well Mali 125 F2
Incirli Turkey see Karasu
Incirlik Turkey 108 G1
Incomati r. Moz. 131 G5
Incudine, Monte mt. France 56 B7
Inčukalns Latvia 42 F4
Indaiá r. Brazil 207 H5
Indaiá Grande r. Brazil 206 A6
Indaiatuba Brazil 206 F10
Indalsälven r. Sweden 44 L3
Indalstø Norway 45 I3
Indargarh Madhya Pradesh India 96 C4
Indargarh Rajasthan India 96 C4
Inda Silasē Eth. 128 C1
Indawgyi, Lake Myanmar 78 B2
Indé Mex. 184 D3
I-n-Délimane well Mali 125 F3
Independence CA U.S.A. 182 F5
Independence IA U.S.A. 174 B3
Independence KS U.S.A. 178 D4
Independence KY U.S.A. 176 A7
Independence MO U.S.A. 178 D4
Independence VA U.S.A. 176 D9
Independence WI U.S.A. 172 B6
Independence Fjord inlet Greenland 165 Q1
Independence Mountains U.S.A. 180 C4
Independencia Bol. 200 D4
Independenta Romania 58 I4
Independenta Romania 58 J5
Independenta Romania 58 I3
Inder China 85 I2
also known as Jalaid
Inder, Ozero salt l. Kazakh. 102 B2
Inderborskiy Kazakh. 102 B2
Indi India 94 C2
▶India country Asia 93 E6
2nd most populous country in the world and in Asia. 3rd largest country in Asia and 7th in the world. Known as Bharat in Hindi.
world [countries] ▶ 10–11
world [population] ▶ 22–23
asia [landscapes] ▶ 62–63
asia [countries] ▶ 64–67
Indian r. U.S.A. 172 G4
Indiana U.S.A. 176 F5
Indiana state U.S.A. 174 C3
▶Indianapolis U.S.A. 174 C4
State capital of Indiana.
Indian Cabins Canada 167 G3
Indian Desert India/Pak. see Thar Desert
Indian Fields U.S.A. 176 B8
Indian Harbour Canada 169 J2
Indian Head Canada 167 K5
Indian Lake U.S.A. 177 K2
Indian Lake l. MI U.S.A. 172 G5
Indian Lake l. NY U.S.A. 177 K2
Indian Lake l. OH U.S.A. 176 B5
Indian Lake l. PA U.S.A. 176 G5
▶Indian Ocean 218 M7
3rd largest ocean in the world.
oceans [features] ▶ 210–211
Indianola IA U.S.A. 174 A3
Indianola MS U.S.A. 175 B5
Indian Peak U.S.A. 183 K3
Indian Springs U.S.A. 183 I5

J

index

Indian Wells U.S.A. 183 N6
Indiara Brazil 206 C4
Indiaroba Brazil 202 E4
Indibir Eth. 128 C2
Indiga Rus. Fed. 40 I2
Indigirka r. Rus. Fed. 39 O2
Indigskaya Guba b. Rus. Fed. 40 I2
Indija Vojvodina, Srbija Yugo. 58 B3
Indin Myanmar 78 A3
Indin Lake Canada 167 H1
Indio r. Nicaragua 186 C5
Indio U.S.A. 183 H6
Indispensable Reefs Solomon Is 145 F3
Indo-China reg. Asia 24 C4
Indomanka r. Rus. Fed. 43 S1
▶Indonesia country Asia 72 D8
  4th most populous country in the world and Asia. 5th largest country in Asia. Formerly known as Dutch East Indies.
  world [population] ➤ 22–23
  asia [countries] ➤ 64–67
Indore India 96 B5
Indragiri r. Indon. 76 C3
Indramayu Indon. 77 E4
Indramayu, Tanjung pt Indon. 77 E4
Indrapura, Gunung vol. Indon. see Kerinci, Gunung
Indrapura, Tanjung pt Indon. 76 C3
Indravati r. India 95 D2
Indre r. France 51 J3
Indulkana Australia 146 B1
Indur India see Nizamabad
Indura Belarus 42 E8
Indurti India 94 C2
Indus r. China/Pakistan 89 C5
  also known as Shiquan He
Indus, Mouths of the Pak. 101 F5
Indwe S. Africa 133 L8
Indwe r. S. Africa 133 L9
Indzhe Voyvoda Bulg. 58 I6
Inebolu Turkey 106 C2
I-n-Echaï well Mali 123 E5
Inegöl Turkey 106 B2
In Ekker Alg. 123 G4
Inerie vol. Indon. 75 B5
Ineu Romania 58 C2
Inevi Turkey see Cihanbeyli
Inez U.S.A. 176 C8
In Ezzane well Alg. 123 H5
Infanta, Cape S. Africa 132 E11
Infantas Col. 187 E6
Infantes Spain see Villanueva de los Infantes
Infiernillo, Presa resr Mex. 185 E5
Infiesto Spain 54 F1
Ing, Mae Nam r. Thai. 78 C3
Inga Dem. Rep. Congo 127 B6
Ingabu Myanmar 78 A4
Ingal Niger 125 G3
Ingalls, Mount U.S.A. 182 D2
Inganda Dem. Rep. Congo 126 D5
Inglestad Sweden 45 K4
Ingende Dem. Rep. Congo 126 C5
Ingeniero Guillermo Nueva Juárez Arg. 201 E5
Ingeniero Jacobacci Arg. 204 C6
Ingenika r. Canada 166 E3
Ingenio r. Peru 200 B3
Ingersoll Canada 173 M7
Ingessana Hills Sudan 128 B2
Ingettolgoy Mongolia 84 D1
Ingezi Zimbabwe see Ngezi
Ingham Australia 149 E3
Ingichka Uzbek. 103 F5
  formerly known as Rudnik Ingichka
Inglefield Land reg. Greenland 165 L2
Inglewood Qld Australia 147 F2
Inglewood Vic. Australia 147 D4
Inglewood N.Z. 152 I7
Inglewood U.S.A. 182 F4
Ingoka Pum mt. Myanmar 78 B2
Ingolf Fjord inlet Greenland 165 R1
Ingolstadt Germany 48 I7
Ingomar Australia 146 B2
Ingonish Canada 169 I4
Ingraj Bazar India 97 F4
  formerly known as English Bazar
Ingram VA U.S.A. 176 F9
Ingram WI U.S.A. 172 C5
Ingray Lake Canada 167 G1
Ingrid Christensen Coast Antarctica 223 F2
I-n-Guezzam Alg. 123 G6
I-n-Guita well Mali 125 F3
Ingulets Ukr. see Inhulets'
Ingulvsrak Norway 44 K2
Ingur r. Georgia/Rus. Fed. see Inguri
Ingushetia, Respublika aut. rep. Rus. Fed. see Ingushetiya, Respublika
Ingushetiya, Respublika aut. rep. Rus. Fed. 41 H8
  English form Ingushetia or Ingush Republic
Ingush Republic aut. rep. Rus. Fed. see Ingushetiya, Respublika
Ingwavuma S. Africa 133 Q4
Ingwavuma r. Swaziland see Ngwavuma

Ingwe Zambia 127 E8
Inhaca Moz. 133 Q2
Inhaca, Península pen. Moz. 131 G5
Inhafenga Moz. 131 G4
Inhambane Moz. 131 G4
Inhambane prov. Moz. 131 G4
Inhambupe Brazil 202 E4
Inhamitanga Moz. 131 G3
Inhapim Brazil 203 D6
Inharrime Moz. 131 G5
Inhassoro Moz. 131 G4
Inhaúmas Brazil 202 C5
I-n-Hihaou, Adrar hills Alg. 123 F5
Inhobim Brazil 207 M2
Inhulets' Ukr. 41 E7
  also spelt Ingulets
Inhumas Brazil 206 D3
Inielika vol. Indon. 75 B5
Iniesta Spain 55 J5
Inimutaba Brazil 207 I5
Iniö Fin. 42 C1
Inírida r. Col. 198 E4
Inis Rep. of Ireland see Ennis
Inis Córthaidh Rep. of Ireland see Enniscorthy
Inishark i. Rep. of Ireland 47 B10
Inishbofin i. Rep. of Ireland 47 B10
Inishmore i. Rep. of Ireland 47 C10
Inishmurray i. Rep. of Ireland 47 D9
Inishowen pen. Rep. of Ireland 47 E8
Inishowen Head Rep. of Ireland 47 F8
Inishtrahull i. Rep. of Ireland 47 E8
Inishturk i. Rep. of Ireland 47 B10
Injgan Sum China 85 H2
Injibara Eth. 128 C2
Injune Australia 149 F5
Inkardar'ya Kazakh. 103 F3
Inkerman Australia 149 D3
Inklin Canada 166 C3
Inklin r. Canada 166 C3
Inkylap Turkm. 103 E5
Inland Kaikoura Range mts N.Z. 153 H10
Inland Sea Japan see Seto-naikai
Inlet U.S.A. 177 K2
I-n-Milach well Mali 125 E2
Inn r. Europe 48 H9
Innaanganeq c. Greenland 165 M2
  also known as York, Kap
Innai Japan 91 B8
Innamincka Australia 146 D1
Innamincka Regional Reserve nature res. Australia 146 D1
Inndyr Norway 44 K2
Inner Mongolia aut. reg. China see Nei Mongol Zizhiqu
Inner Sound sea chan. U.K. 46 G6
Innes National Park Australia 146 C3
Innisfail Australia 149 E3
Innisfail Canada 167 H4
Innoket'yevka Rus. Fed. 82 C2
Innoshima Japan 91 C7
Innsbruck Austria 48 I8
Innukanik r. Canada 168 E1
Inny r. Rep. of Ireland 47 E10
Ino Japan 91 C8
Inobonto Indon. 75 C2
Inocência Brazil 206 B6
Inongo Dem. Rep. Congo 126 C5
Inoni Congo 126 B5
Inonias Peru 198 C5
Inönü Turkey 106 B3
Inosu Col. 198 D1
Inoucdjouac Canada see Inukjuak
Inovec hill Slovakia 49 P7
Inowrocław Poland 49 P3
  historically known as Hohensalza
Inquisivi Bol. 200 D4
In Salah Alg. 123 F4
  also spelt Ain Salah
▶Inscription, Cape Australia 151 A5
  Most westerly point of Oceania.
Insein Myanmar 78 B4
Insel Usedom park Germany 49 L2
Iñsko Poland 49 M2
In Sokki, Oued watercourse Alg. 123 F3
Insterburg Rus. Fed. see Chernyakhovsk
Instruch r. Rus. Fed. 42 C7
İnsuraţei Romania 58 I4
Insuza r. Zimbabwe 131 E3
Inta Rus. Fed. 40 L2
I-n-Tadera well Niger 125 H1
I-n-Tadrof well Niger 125 H2
In Takoufi, Oued watercourse Alg. 123 G4
I-n-Tassit well Mali 125 F2
I-n-Tebezas well Mali 125 F2
I-n-Téguift well Mali 125 F2
I-n-Telli well Mali 125 F2
I-n-Témegui well Mali 125 F2
Intepe Turkey 59 H8
Interamna Italy see Teramo
Interlaken Switz. 51 N6
International Falls U.S.A. 174 A1
Interview Island India 95 H3
Intích'o Eth. 104 B5
I-n-Touft well Mali 125 E2
Intracoastal Waterway canal U.S.A. 179 D6
Intutu Peru 198 C5
Inubō-zaki pt Japan 91 G7
Inukai Japan 91 B8
Inukjuak Canada 168 E1
  formerly known as Port Harrison; formerly spelt Inoucdjouac
Inuvik Canada 164 F3
Inuya r. Peru 200 B2
In'va r. Rus. Fed. 40 K4
Inveraray U.K. 46 G7
Inverbervie U.K. 46 J7
Invercargill N.Z. 153 C14
Inverell Australia 147 F2
Inverleigh Australia 149 D3
Inverness Canada 169 I4
Inverness U.K. 46 H6
Inverness CA U.S.A. 182 B3
Inverness FL U.S.A. 175 D6
Inverurie U.K. 46 J6
Inverway Australia 148 A3
Investigator Channel Myanmar 79 B5
Investigator Group is Australia 146 B3
Investigator Strait Australia 146 C3
Inwood U.S.A. 176 C5
Inxu r. S. Africa 133 M8
Inya r. Rus. Fed. 88 D1
Inyanga Zimbabwe see Nyanga
Inyanga Mountains Zimbabwe 131 G3
Inyangani mt. Zimbabwe 131 G3
  also spelt Inyangani
Inyanga National Park Zimbabwe see Nyanga National Park
Inyanti Zimbabwe see Nyathi
Inyazura Zimbabwe see Nyazura
Inyokern U.S.A. 182 G6
Inyo Mountains U.S.A. 182 F4
Inyonga Tanz. 129 B6
Inza Rus. Fed. 41 H5
Inzer r. Rus. Fed. 40 K5
Inzhavino Rus. Fed. 41 G5
Ioannina Greece 59 B9
  also spelt Yannina
Ioanninon, Limni l. Greece 59 B9
Iôl di Montasio mt. Italy 56 F7
Iô-jima i. Kazan-rettō Japan 73 J2
  also known as Iô-tô; also spelt Iwo Jima
Iô-jima i. Japan 91 B9
  also spelt Iô-shima
Iokanga r. Rus. Fed. 40 F2
Iola KS U.S.A. 178 C4
Iola WI U.S.A. 172 D6
Iolgo, Khrebet mts Rus. Fed. 88 D1

Iolotan' Turkm. see Yeloten
Iona Moz. see Iona
Iona i. Canada 169 I4
Iona i. U.K. 46 F7
Iona, Parque Nacional do nat. park Angola 127 B9
Iona Abbey tourist site U.K. 46 F7
Ione U.S.A. 182 C3
Ioneşti Romania 58 F4
Ionia U.S.A. 173 H8
Ionian Islands admin. reg. Greece see Ionioi Nisoi
Ionian Islands reg. Greece 59 A9
  also known as Ionioi Nisoi
Ionian Sea Greece/Italy 59 A11
Ionioi Nisoi admin. reg. Greece 59 A10
  English form Ionian Islands
Ionioi Nisoi reg. Greece see Ionian Islands
Iony, Ostrov i. Rus. Fed. 39 O4
Iordan Uzbek. 101 G1
  also spelt Yordan; formerly spelt Yardan
Iori r. Georgia 107 F2
Ios Greece 59 G12
Ios i. Greece 59 G12
Iô-shima i. Japan see Iô-jima
Iô-tô i. Japan see Iô-jima
Iouîk Mauritania 124 A2
Iowa r. U.S.A. 174 B3
Iowa state U.S.A. 174 A3
Iowa City U.S.A. 174 B3
Iowa Falls U.S.A. 174 A3
Ipameri Brazil 206 E4
Ipanema Brazil 203 D6
Ipanema r. Brazil 202 E4
Iparia Peru 200 B2
Ipatinga Brazil 203 D6
Ipatovo Rus. Fed. 41 G7
Ipauçu Brazil 206 D10
Ipeiros admin. reg. Greece 59 B9
  English form Epirus; also spelt Ípiros
Ipel' r. Slovakia 49 P8
  English form Ipoly; also spelt Ípoly
Ipelegeng S. Africa 133 J4
Ipiaçu Brazil 206 D5
Ipiales Col. 198 B4
Ipiaú Brazil 202 E5
Ipirá Brazil 202 E5
Ipiranga Amazonas Brazil 198 D5
Ipiranga Amazonas Brazil 199 F6
Ípiros admin. reg. Greece see Ipeiros
Ipixuna Brazil 200 B1
Ipixuna r. Amazonas Brazil 199 F6
Ipixuna r. Amazonas Brazil 200 B1
Ipoh Malaysia 76 C1
Ipoly r. Hungary/Slovakia see Ipel'
Ipopeng S. Africa 133 J6
Iporá Brazil 206 C4
Iporanga Brazil 206 E7
Ippy Cent. Afr. Rep. 126 D3
Ipsala Turkey 58 H8
Ipswich Australia 147 G1
Ipswich U.K. 47 N11
Ipswich U.S.A. 178 C2
Ipu Brazil 202 D3
Ipuã Brazil 206 E7
Ipueiras Brazil 202 D3
Ipupiara Brazil 202 D4
Iput' r. Rus. Fed. 43 M9
Iqaluit Canada 165 M3
  Territorial capital of Nunavut. Formerly known as Frobisher Bay.
Iqe He r. China 84 C4
Iquê r. Brazil 201 F3
  also known as Languiaru
Iquique Chile 200 C5
Iquiri r. Brazil see Ituxi
Iquitos Peru 198 C5
Ira Banda Cent. Afr. Rep. 126 D3
  formerly known as Hyra Banda
Iracoubo Fr. Guiana 199 H3
Irafshan reg. Iran 101 F5
Irai Brazil 203 A8
Irai Island P.N.G. 149 F1
Irakleia i. Greece 58 E7
Irakleia i. Greece 59 G12
  also spelt Iráklia
Irakleio Greece see Iraklion
Irakleiou, Kolpos b. Greece 59 G13
Iráklia i. Greece see Irakleia
Iraklion Greece 59 G13
  also spelt Heraklion or Irakleio; historically known as Candia
Irala Para. 201 G6
Iramaia Brazil 202 D5
▶Iran country Asia 100 C4
  formerly known as Persia
  asia [countries] ➤ 64–67
Iran, Pegunungan mts Indon. 77 F2
Īrānshāh Iran 100 A2
Īrānshahr Iran 101 E5
Irapa Venez. 199 F2
Irapuato Mex. 185 E4
▶Iraq country Asia 107 E4
  asia [countries] ➤ 64–67
Irarrarene reg. Alg. 123 G4
Irasville U.S.A. 177 M1
Iratapuru r. Brazil 199 H5
Irati Brazil 203 B8
Irati r. Spain 55 J2
Irayel' Rus. Fed. 40 J2
Irazu, Volcán vol. Costa Rica 186 C5
Irbe r. Latvia 42 D4
Irbes šaurums sea chan. Estonia/Latvia see Irbe Strait
Irbe Strait Estonia/Latvia 42 D4
  also known as Irbe väin or Irbes šaurums or Kura kurk or Sõrve väin
Irbe väin sea chan. Estonia/Latvia see Irbe Strait
Irbid Jordan 108 G5
Irbil Iraq see Arbil
Irbit Rus. Fed. 38 G4
Irebu Dem. Rep. Congo 126 C5
Irecê Brazil 202 D4
Iregua r. Spain 55 I2
▶Ireland i. International Feature 47 C11
  4th largest island in Europe.
  europe [landscapes] ➤ 30–31
▶Ireland, Republic of country Europe 47 D10
  known as Éire in Irish; formerly known as Irish Free State
  europe [countries] ➤ 32–35
Iren' r. Rus. Fed. 40 K4
Irene Arg. 204 E5
Irene, Mount N.Z. 153 B13
Ireng r. Guyana/Venez. 199 G4
Iretama Brazil 206 A11
Irgiz Kazakh. 103 E2
Irgiz r. Kazakh. 103 E2
  also spelt Yrghyz
Irgiz r. Kazakh. see Yrgyz
Irharrhar, Oued watercourse Alg. 123 G3
Irharrhar, Oued watercourse Alg. 123 G5
Irherm Morocco 122 C3
Irhil M'Goun mt. Morocco 122 D3
Irhzer Ediessane watercourse Alg. 120 A3
Iri S. Korea see Iksan
Irian, Teluk b. Indon. see Cenderawasih, Teluk
Irian Barat prov. Indon. see Irian Jaya
Irian Jaya prov. Indon. 73 I7
  also known as West Papua; formerly known as Dutch New Guinea or Irian Barat or West Irian
Irian Jaya reg. Indon. 73 I7
Iriba Chad 120 D5
Iricoumé, Serra hills Brazil 199 G4
Iri Dāgh mt. Iran 100 A2
Iriga Phil. 74 B3
Iriklinskiy Rus. Fed. 102 D2

Iriklinskoye Vodokhranilishche resr Rus. Fed. 102 D2
Iringa Tanz. 129 B6
Iringa admin. reg. Tanz. 129 B7
Iriri r. Brazil 199 H5
Iriri Novo r. Brazil 202 A4
Irish Free State country Europe see Ireland, Republic of
Irish Sea Rep. of Ireland/U.K. 47 G10
Irituia Brazil 202 C2
Iriya r. Rus. Fed. 43 O6
Irkeshtam Kyrg. see Erkech-Tam
Irkut r. Rus. Fed. 84 D1
Irkutsk Rus. Fed. 80 G2
Irkutskaya Oblast' admin. div. Rus. Fed. 84 D1
  English form Irkutsk Oblast
Irkutsk Oblast admin. div. Rus. Fed. see Irkutskaya Oblast'
Irma U.S.A. 172 D5
Irmak Turkey 106 C3
Irminio r. Sicilia Italy 57 G12
Irmo U.S.A. 175 D5
Irnijärvi l. Fin. 44 O2
Iro, Lac l. Chad 126 C2
Iroise, Mer d' g. France 50 B4
Iron Baron Australia 146 C3
Iron Bridge Canada 173 J4
Irondequoit U.S.A. 176 H2
Iron Junction U.S.A. 172 A3
Iron Knob Australia 146 C3
Iron Mountain U.S.A. 172 E5
Iron Mountain mt. U.S.A. 183 K4
Iron Range National Park Australia 149 D2
Iron River MI U.S.A. 172 E4
Iron River WI U.S.A. 172 B4
Ironton MO U.S.A. 174 B4
Ironton OH U.S.A. 176 C7
Ironwood U.S.A. 172 C4
Iroquois Canada 177 J1
Iroquois r. U.S.A. 172 F9
Iroquois Falls Canada 168 D3
Irosin Phil. 74 C3
Irpen' Ukr. see Irpin'
Irpin' Ukr. 41 D6
  also spelt Irpen'
Irqah Yemen 105 D5
'Irq al Ḥarūri des. Saudi Arabia 105 D2
'Irq al Maẓhūr des. Saudi Arabia 104 C2
'Irq Banbān des. Saudi Arabia 105 D2
'Irq Jahām des. Saudi Arabia 105 D2
'Irq Subay des. Saudi Arabia 104 C3
Irramarne Aboriginal Land res. Australia 148 C4
Irrawaddy admin. div. Myanmar 78 A4
Irrawaddy r. Myanmar 78 A3
  also spelt Ayeyarwady or Erawadi or Eyawadi
Irrawaddy, Mouths of the Myanmar 79 A5
Irsarybaba, Gory hills Turkm. 102 C4
  also known as Arsarybaba Erezi
Irshad Pass Afgh./Pak. 101 H2
▶Irtysh r. Kazakh./Rus. Fed. 38 G3
  5th longest river in Asia and 10th in the world. Part of the 2nd longest river in Asia (Ob'-Irtysh). Also spelt Ertis.
  asia [landscapes] ➤ 62–63
Irtyshsk Kazakh. 103 H1
  also known as Ertis; formerly known as Irtyshskoye
Irtyshskoye Kazakh. see Irtyshsk
Iruma Japan 91 F7
Irumu Dem. Rep. Congo 126 F4
Irún Spain 55 J1
Iruña Spain see Pamplona
Irvine U.K. 46 H8
Irvine CA U.S.A. 182 G8
Irvine KY U.S.A. 176 B8
Irvine Glacier Antarctica 222 T2
Irving U.S.A. 179 C5
Irwin r. Australia 151 A6
Irwinton U.S.A. 175 D5
Isa Nigeria 125 G3
Isā, Ra's pt Yemen 104 C5
Isaac r. Australia 149 F4
Isaac Lake Canada 166 F4
Isabela Negros Phil. 74 B4
Isabela Phil. 74 B5
Isabela, Cabo c. Dom. Rep. 187 F3
Isabela, Cordillera mts Nicaragua 186 B4
Isabella Indian Reservation res. U.S.A. 173 I7
Isabella Lake U.S.A. 182 F5
Isabelle, Point U.S.A. 172 E3
Isabey Turkey 106 B3
Isaccea Romania 58 J3
Isachenko, Ostrov i. Rus. Fed. 39 J2
Isachsen, Cape Canada 165 I2
Isafjarðardjúp est. Iceland 44 [inset] B2
Isafjörður Iceland 44 [inset] B2
Isagarh India 96 C4
Isahaya Japan 91 B8
Isai Kalat Pak. 101 E5
Isà Khel Pak. 101 G3
Isakogorka Rus. Fed. 40 G2
Isakovo Rus. Fed. 43 P6
Işalniţa Romania 58 E4
Isana r. Col. 198 D4
Isanga Dem. Rep. Congo 126 D5
Isangano National Park Zambia 127 F7
Isaouane-N-Tifernine des. Alg. 123 G4
Isar r. Germany 48 J7
Isbister U.K. 46 K3
Íscar Spain 54 G3
Iscayachi Bol. 200 D5
Ischia Italy 57 F8
Ischia, Isola d' i. Italy 57 F8
Isdell r. Australia 150 D3
Ise Japan 91 E7
Ise-wan b. Japan 91 E7
Iseyin Nigeria 125 F5
Isengi Dem. Rep. Congo 126 E4
Iseo, Lago d' l. Italy 56 C3
Isère r. France 51 K8
Isère, Pointe c. Fr. Guiana 199 H3
Iserlohn Germany 48 E4
Isernhagen Germany 48 G3
Isernia Italy 56 G7
  historically known as Aesernia
Ise-shima National Park Japan 91 E7
Isten dombja hill Hungary 49 N9
Īstgäh-e Eznä Iran 100 B3
Isfahan Iran see Eşfahān
Isfana Kyrg. 103 G5
Isfandaqeh Iran see Sangū'īyeh
Isfara Tajik. 101 G1
Isherim, Gora mt. Rus. Fed. 40 K3
Isherton Guyana 199 G4
Isheyevka Rus. Fed. 41 I5
Ishikari Japan 90 G3
Ishikari-gawa r. Japan 90 G3
Ishikari-wan b. Japan 90 G3
Ishikawa pref. Japan 91 E6
Ishim r. Kazakh./Rus. Fed. 103 F1
  also known as Esil
Ishimbay Rus. Fed. 102 D1
Ishinomaki Japan 90 G5
Ishioka Japan 91 G6
Ishizuchi-san mt. Japan 91 C8
Ishkafi, Jabal hill Iraq 109 N1
Ishkoshim Tajik. 101 G2
Ishnya Rus. Fed. 43 U4
Ishpeming U.S.A. 172 F4

Ishtikhon Uzbek. see Ishtykhan
Ishtragh Afgh. 101 G2
Ishtykhan Uzbek. 103 F5
  also spelt shtikhon
Ishurdi Bangl. 97 F4
Isigny-sur-Mer France 50 E3
Işıklı Turkey 106 B3
Isil'kul' Rus. Fed. 38 H4
'Isil wadi Saudi Arabia 109 I3
Isımbıra Tanz. 129 B6
Isinlivi Ecuador 198 B5
Isiolo Kenya 128 C4
Isipingo S. Africa 133 O6
Isiro Dem. Rep. Congo 126 E4
  formerly known as Paulis
Isisford Australia 149 E5
Iskabad Canal Afgh. 101 F2
Iskateley Rus. Fed. 40 J2
Iskele Cyprus see Trikomon
İskenderun Turkey 106 C3
  historically known as Alexandretta
İskenderun Körfezi b. Turkey 106 C3
İskilip Turkey 106 C2
Iski-Naukat Kyrg. see Eski-Nookat
Iskine Kazakh. 102 C3
Iskür r. Bulg. 58 F5
Iskūr, Yazovir resr Bulg. 58 E6
Iskushuban Somalia 128 F2
Iskut r. Canada 166 D3
Isla r. U.K. 46 I7
Isla, Wādī watercourse Egypt 108 E9
Isla Cristina Spain 54 D7
Isla de Salamanca, Parque Nacional nat. park Col. 198 C2
Isla Gorge National Park Australia 149 F5
İslahiye Turkey 107 C3
Islamabad Jammu and Kashmir see Anantnag
▶Islamabad Pak. 101 H3
  Capital of Pakistan.
Isla Magdalena, Parque Nacional nat. park Chile 205 B7
Islamkot Pak. 101 G5
Islamorada U.S.A. 175 D7
Islampur India 97 E4
Island r. Canada 166 F2
Ísland country Europe see Iceland
Island Bay Phil. 74 A4
Island Lagoon salt flat Australia 146 C2
Island Lake Canada 167 M4
Island Lake l. Canada 167 M4
Island Magee pen. U.K. 47 G9
Island Pond U.S.A. 177 N1
Islands, Bay of N.Z. 152 I3
Islas Baleares aut. comm. Spain 55 N5
Islas de Bahá, Parque Nacional nat. park Hond. 186 B3
Isley i. U.K. 46 F8
Islaz Romania 58 F5
Isle r. France 50 F8
▶Isle of Man i. Irish Sea 47 H9
  United Kingdom Crown Dependency.
  europe [countries] ➤ 32–35
Isle of Wight U.S.A. 177 I9
Isle Royale National Park U.S.A. 172 E3
Isluga, Parque Nacional nat. park Chile 200 C4
Ismail Ukr. see Izmayil
Ismâ'ilîya Egypt 121 G2
  also spelt Al Ismā'īlīyah
Ismâ'ilîya governorate Egypt 108 D7
Ismâ'ilîya, Tir'at el canal Egypt 108 D7
Ismailly Azer. see Ismayıllı
Isna Egypt 121 G3
İsoanala Madag. 131 [inset] J4
Isojoki Fin. 45 M3
Isoka Zambia 129 B7
Isokylä Fin. 44 N2
Isokyrö Fin. 44 M3
Isola del Liri Italy 56 F7
Isola di Capo Rizzuto Italy 57 J10
Isonzo r. Italy 56 F3
  also known as Soča
Isopa Tanz. 129 A7
Isorana Madag. 131 [inset] J4
Iso-Syöte hill Fin. 44 N2
Ispahan Iran see Eşfahān
Isparta Turkey 106 B3
  also known as Hamitabat
Isperikh Bulg. 58 H5
Ispica Sicilia Italy 57 G12
Ispir Turkey 107 E2
Ispisar Tajik. see Khŭjand
▶Israel country Asia 108 A7
  spelt Yizra'el in Hebrew or Isra'il in Arabic
  asia [countries] ➤ 64–67
Israelândia Brazil 206 C3
Israelite Bay Australia 151 C7
Isra'il country Asia see Israel
Issa Croatia see Vis
Issa r. Rus. Fed. 43 J5
Issano Guyana 199 G3
Issia Côte d'Ivoire 124 D5
Issimu Indon. 75 B2
Issin tourist site Iraq 107 F5
Is-sur-Tille France 51 L5
Issyk-Kul' Kyrg. see Balykchy
Issyk-Kul', Ozero salt l. Kyrg. see Ysyk-Köl
Issyk-Kul' Oblast admin. div. Kyrg. see Ysyk-Köl
Issyk-Kul'skaya Oblast' admin. div. Kyrg. see Ysyk-Köl
Ista r. Rus. Fed. 43 R8
Iştabāt 'Antar Saudi Arabia 104 B2
Iştablāt tourist site Iraq 107 F4
İstanbul Turkey 106 B2
  historically known as Byzantium or Constantinople
İstanbul prov. Turkey 58 J7
İstanbul Boğazı str. Turkey see Bosporus
İstanbul Boğazı strait Turkey see Bosporus
Isthilart Arg. 204 F3
Istiaía Greece 59 E10
Istik r. Tajik. 101 H2
Istmina Col. 198 B3
Istok Kosovo, Srbija Yugo. 58 B6
Istokpoga, Lake U.S.A. 175 D7
Istra Rus. Fed. 43 R6
Istra pen. Croatia see Istria
Istra r. Rus. Fed. 43 R5
Istres France 51 K9
Istria pen. Croatia 56 F3
  also spelt Istra
Istrița, Dealul hill Romania 58 H3
Is'ty'a r. Rus. Fed. 43 V7
Isuela r. Spain 55 J3
Iswaripur Bangl. 97 F5
Iswepe S. Africa 133 O3
Isyangulovo Rus. Fed. 102 D1
Isyk Kazakh. 103 I4
Itabaiana Brazil 202 E4
Itabaianinha Brazil 202 E4
Itabapoana Brazil 207 M8
Itabapoana r. Brazil 207 M8

Itaberaba Brazil 202 D5
Itaberaí Brazil 206 D3
Itabira Brazil 203 D6
Itabirito Brazil 203 D7
Itaboca Brazil 199 F6
Itaboraí Brazil 207 K9
Itabuna Brazil 202 E5
Itacaiuna r. Brazil 202 B3
Itacajá Brazil 202 C3
Itacambira Brazil 207 J4
Itacarambi Brazil 202 C5
Itacaré Brazil 202 E5
Itacayuna, Serra hills Brazil 201 H1
Itacoatiara Brazil 199 G5
Itacuaí r. Brazil 198 D5
Itaeté Brazil 202 D5
Itagmatana Iran see Hamadān
Itagmirim Brazil 207 N3
Itaguaçu Brazil 203 D6
Itaguaí Brazil 207 J9
Itaguajé Brazil 206 B9
Itaguara Brazil 207 I7
Itahuania Peru 200 C3
Itaí Brazil 206 D10
Itaim r. Brazil 202 D3
Itaiópolis Brazil 203 B8
Itaipu, Represa de resr Brazil 203 A8
Itäisen Suomenlahden kansallispuisto nat. park Fin. 45 N3
Itaituba Brazil 199 G6
Itajá Brazil 206 D3
Itajaí Brazil 203 B8
Itajobi Brazil 206 D8
Itajubá Brazil 203 C7
Itaju de Colônia Brazil 207 N2
Itajuipe Brazil 202 E5
Itaki India 97 E5
Itala Nature Reserve S. Africa 133 P4
▶Italia country Europe see Italy
Italy country Europe 56 C4
  5th most populous country in Europe. Known as Italia in Italian.
  europe [countries] ➤ 32–35
Itamaracá, Ilha de i. Brazil 202 F3
Itamaraju Brazil 203 E6
Itamarandiba Brazil 203 D6
Itamataré Brazil 202 C2
Itambacuri Brazil 207 L5
Itambacuri r. Brazil 207 L5
Itambé Brazil 207 L3
Itambé, Pico de mt. Brazil 203 D6
Itami airport Japan 91 D7
Itamirim Brazil 207 K1
Itampolo Madag. 131 [inset] I5
Itanagar India 97 G4
Itanguari r. Brazil 207 H1
Itanhaém Brazil 206 G11
Itanhauã r. Brazil 199 F6
Itanhém Brazil 203 E6
Itanhém r. Brazil 203 E6
Itanhomi Brazil 207 L6
Itany r. Fr. Guiana/Suriname 199 H4
Itaobím Brazil 202 D6
Itaocara Brazil 207 K8
Itapaci Brazil 206 D1
Itapajipe Brazil 206 D5
Itaparaná r. Brazil 199 F6
Itaparica, Represa de resr Brazil 202 E4
Itapé Brazil 207 N1
Itapebi Brazil 202 E5
Itapebí Uruguay 204 F3
Itapecerica Brazil 207 H7
Itapemirim Brazil 203 D7
Itapetinga Brazil 202 D5
Itapetininga Brazil 206 E10
Itapeva Brazil 206 E10
Itapeva, Lago l. Brazil 203 B9
Itapi r. Brazil 199 G5
Itapicuru r. Brazil 202 D2
Itapicuru r. Brazil 202 E4
Itapicuru r. Brazil 202 E4
Itapicuru, Serra de hills Brazil 202 C3
Itapicuru Mirim r. Brazil 202 C2
Itapinima Brazil 199 F6
Itapipoca Brazil 202 E2
Itapira Brazil 206 D9
Itapiranga Brazil 199 G5
Itapiraúna Brazil 206 C2
Itapiúna Brazil 202 E3
Itápolis Brazil 206 E8
Itaporanga Paraíba Brazil 202 E3
Itaporanga São Paulo Brazil 206 D10
Itapuã Brazil 203 D6
Itapuã Brazil 206 D2
Itaquaquecetuba Brazil 207 G10
Itaqui Brazil 204 F3
Itarana Brazil 207 M6
Itarantim Brazil 207 L2
Itararé r. Brazil 206 D10
Itararé r. Brazil 206 D11
Itarsi India 96 C5
Itarumã Brazil 206 C5
Itä-Suomi prov. Fin. 44 O3
Itatiba Brazil 206 E10
Itatuba Brazil 199 F6
Itatupã Brazil 199 I5
Itaúçu Brazil 206 D2
Itaueira r. Brazil 202 D3
Itaúna Amazonas Brazil 199 E5
Itaúna Minas Gerais Brazil 203 D6
Itaúnas r. Brazil 207 N5
Itbayat i. Phil. 74 B1
Itchen Lake Canada 167 H1
Ite Peru 200 C4
Itea Greece 59 D10
Itebero Dem. Rep. Congo 126 F5
Itemgen, Ozero l. Kazakh. 103 I3
Itende Tanz. 129 B6
Itezhi-Tezhi Dam Zambia 127 E8
Ithaca Greece see Ithaki
Ithaca MI U.S.A. 173 I7
Ithaca NY U.S.A. 177 I3
Ithaki Greece 59 B10
  English form Ithaca; also known as Vathi
Ithaki i. Greece 59 B10
  English form Ithaca
Ithakis, Steno sea chan. Greece 59 B10
Ith Hils ridge Germany 48 G3
Ithil, Wadi watercourse Saudi Arabia 109 I4
Itigi Tanz. 129 B6
Itihusa-yama mt. Japan 91 B8
Itilleq Greenland 165 N3
Itimbiri r. Dem. Rep. Congo 126 D4
Itinga Brazil 207 L3
Itiquira Brazil 201 F4
Itiquira r. Brazil 206 F9
Itirapuã Brazil 207 F7
Itiruçu Brazil 202 E5
Itiúba Brazil 202 E4
Itiúba, Serra de hills Brazil 202 E4
Itiyura r. Arg. 201 E5
Itkhari India 97 E4
Itmurinkol', Ozero l. Kazakh. 102 C2
Itō Japan 91 F7
Itoculo Moz. 131 I2
Itoigawa Japan 90 E6
Itoko Dem. Rep. Congo 126 D5
Iton r. France 50 G2
Itongafeno mt. Madag. 131 [inset] J4
Itororó Brazil 207 M1
Itsa Egypt 108 B8
Itsuki Japan 91 B8
Itsukushima Shrine tourist site Japan 91 C7
Ittiri Sardegna Italy 57 A8
Ittoqqortoormiit Greenland 165 Q2
  also known as Scoresbysund

Itu Brazil **206** F10
Itu Nigeria **125** G5
Itu Abu Island S. China Sea **72** D4
Ituaçu Brazil **202** D5
Ituberá Brazil **202** E5
Itui *r.* Brazil **198** D6
Ituiutaba Brazil **206** D5
Itula Dem. Rep. Congo **126** E5
Itumba Tanz. **129** B6
Itumbiara Brazil **206** D5
Itumbiara, Barragem *resr* Brazil **206** D5
Itungi Port Malawi **129** B7
Ituni Guyana **199** G3
Itupiranga Brazil **202** B3
Iturama Brazil **206** C6
Iturbe Para. **201** F6
Iturbide *Campeche* Mex. **185** H5
Iturbide *Nuevo León* Mex. **185** F3
Ituri *r.* Dem. Rep. Congo **126** E4
Iturup, Ostrov *i.* Rus. Fed. **82** G3
also known as Etorofu-tō
Itutinga Brazil **207** I8
Ituverava Brazil **206** F7
Ituxi *r.* Brazil **200** D1
also known as Iquiri
Ituzaingo Arg. **204** F2
Ityopia *country* Africa *see* **Ethiopia**
Itzehoe Germany **48** G2
Iuaretê Brazil **198** D4
Iuka U.S.A. **174** B5
Iul'tin Rus. Fed. **39** S3
Iuluti Moz. **131** H2
Iúna Brazil **207** L7
Iutica Brazil **198** D4
Ivaí *r.* Brazil **206** A10
Ivaiporã Brazil **206** B11
Ivakoany *mt.* Madag. **131** [inset] J4
Ivalo Fin. **44** N1
also known as Avveel or Avvil
Ivalojoki *r.* Fin. **44** N1
Ivanava Belarus **42** G9
also spelt Ivanovo
Ivanec Croatia **56** I2
Ivangorod Rus. Fed. **43** J2
Ivangrad *Crna Gora* Yugo. *see* **Berane**
Ivanhoe *N.S.W.* Australia **147** E3
Ivanhoe *W.A.* Australia **150** E2
Ivanhoe *r.* Canada **168** D3
Ivanhoe *CA* U.S.A. **182** E5
Ivanhoe *MN* U.S.A. **178** C2
Ivanhoe *VA* U.S.A. **176** E9
Ivanhoe Lake *N.W.T.* Canada **167** J2
Ivanhoe Lake *Ont.* Canada **173** K2
Ivanić-Grad Croatia **56** I3
Ivanishchi Rus. Fed. **43** V6
Ivanivka Ukr. **58** L2
Ivanjica *Srbija* Yugo. **58** B5
Ivankiv Ukr. **41** D6
Ivankovo Croatia **56** K3
Ivan'kovo Rus. Fed. **43** S7
Ivan'kovskiy Rus. Fed. **43** V5
Ivan'kovskoye Vodokhranilishche *resr* Rus. Fed. **43** R5
Ivankovtsy Rus. Fed. **82** D2
Ivano-Frankivs'k Ukr. **41** C6
also spelt Ivano-Frankovsk; formerly known as Stanislav
Ivano-Frankovsk Ukr. *see* **Ivano-Frankivs'k**
Ivanovka Kazakh. *see* **Kokzhayyk**
Ivanovka *Amurskaya Oblast'* Rus. Fed. **82** B2
Ivanovka *Orenburgskaya Oblast'* Rus. Fed. **102** C1
Ivanovo Belarus *see* **Ivanava**
Ivanovo *tourist site* Bulg. **58** G5
Ivanovo *Ivanovskaya Oblast'* Rus. Fed. **40** G4
Ivanovo *Pskovskaya Oblast'* Rus. Fed. **43** L5
Ivanovo *Tverskaya Oblast'* Rus. Fed. **43** S3
Ivanovo Oblast *admin. div.* Rus. Fed. *see* **Ivanovskaya Oblast'**
Ivanovskaya Oblast' *admin. div.* Rus. Fed. **43** U4
English form Ivanovo Oblast
Ivanovskiy Khrebet *mts* Kazakh. **88** C1
Ivanovskoye *Orlovskaya Oblast'* Rus. Fed. **43** R8
Ivanovskoye *Yaroslavskaya Oblast'* Rus. Fed. **43** U5
Ivanpah Lake U.S.A. **183** I6
Ivanšćica *mts* Croatia **56** H2
Ivanski Bulg. **58** I5
Ivanteyevka Rus. Fed. **102** B1
Ivantsevichi Belarus *see* **Ivatsevichy**
Ivato Madag. **131** [inset] J3
Ivatsevichy Belarus **42** G9
also spelt Ivantsevichi
Ivaylovgrad Bulg. **58** H7
Ivaylovgrad, Yazovir *resr* Bulg. **58** G7
Ivdel' Rus. Fed. **38** G3
Iveşti Romania **58** I3
Iveşti Romania **58** I2
Ivi, Cap *c.* Alg. **55** L8
Ivindo *r.* Gabon **126** B5
Ivinheima Brazil **203** A7
Ivittuut Greenland **165** O3
Iviza *i.* Spain *see* **Ibiza**
Ivohibe Madag. **131** [inset] J4
Ivolândia Brazil **206** C3
Ivolginsk Rus. Fed. **85** E1
Ivón Bol. **200** D2
Ivor U.S.A. **177** I9
Ivory Coast *country* Africa *see* **Côte d'Ivoire**
Ivösjön *l.* Sweden **45** K4
Ivot Rus. Fed. **43** P8
Ivrea Italy **51** N7
İvrindi Turkey **59** I9
Ivris Ugheltekhili *pass* Georgia **107** F2
Ivugivik Canada *see* **Ivujivik**
Ivujivik Canada **165** L3
formerly spelt Ivugivik
Ivuna Tanz. **129** B7
Ivvavik National Park Canada **164** F3
Ivyanyets Belarus **42** H8
Ivydale U.S.A. **176** D7
Iwaizumi Japan **90** G5
Iwaki Japan **90** G6
Iwaki-san *vol.* Japan **90** G4
Iwakuni Japan **91** C7
Iwamatsu Japan **91** C8
Iwamizawa Japan **90** G3
Iwan *r.* Indon. **77** F2
Iwanai Japan **90** G3
Iwanda Tanz. **129** B7
Iwanuma Japan **90** G5
Iwata Japan **91** E7
Iwate Japan **90** G5
Iwate *pref.* Japan **90** G5
Iwate-san *vol.* Japan **90** G5
Iwo Nigeria **125** G5
Iwo Jima *i.* Japan *see* **Iō-jima**
Iwupataka Aboriginal Land *res.* Australia **148** B4
Iwye Belarus **42** G8
Ixcamilpa Mex. **185** F5
Ixiamas Bol. **200** C3
Ixmiquilpán Mex. **185** F4
Ixopo S. Africa **133** O7
Ixtacomitán Mex. **185** G5
Ixtlán *Nayarit* Mex. **184** D4
Ixtlán *Oaxaca* Mex. **185** F5
Iya *i.* Indon. **75** B5
Iya *r.* Rus. Fed. **80** G1
Iyayi Tanz. **129** B7
İyirmi Altı Bakı Komissarı Azer. *see* **26 Bakı Komissarı**
Iyo Japan **91** C8
Iyomishima Japan **91** C8
Iyo-nada *b.* Japan **91** C8
Izabal, Lago de *l.* Guat. **185** H6
Izamal Mex. **185** H4
Izapa *tourist site* Mex. **185** G6
Izari-dake *mt.* Japan **90** G3
Izazi Tanz. **129** B6
Izbăşeşti *hill* Romania **58** F3
Izberbash Rus. Fed. **102** A4
Izdeshkovo Rus. Fed. **43** O6
Izeh Iran **100** B4
Izgagane *well* Niger **125** H2
Izhevsk Rus. Fed. **40** J4
formerly known as Ustinov
Izhma Rus. Fed. **40** J2
Izhma Rus. Fed. *see* **Sosnogorsk**
Izhma *r.* Rus. Fed. **40** J2
Izkī Oman **105** G3
Izmail Ukr. *see* **Izmayil**
Izmalkovo Rus. Fed. **43** S9
Izmayil Ukr. **41** D7
also spelt Izmail; formerly spelt Ismail
Izmeny, Proliv *sea chan.* Japan/Rus. Fed. *see* **Notsuke-suidō**
İzmir Turkey **106** A3
historically known as Smyrna
İzmir *prov.* Turkey **59** I10
İzmir Körfezi *g.* Turkey **106** A3
İzmit Turkey *see* **Kocaeli**
İzmit Körfezi *b.* Turkey **106** B2
Izmorene Morocco **54** H9
Iznajar, Embalse de *resr* Spain **54** G7
Iznalloz Spain **55** H7
İznik Turkey **58** K8
historically known as Nicaea
İznik Gölü *l.* Turkey **106** B2
Iznoski Rus. Fed. **43** Q7
Izoard, Col d' *pass* France **51** M8
Izobil'noye Rus. Fed. *see* **Izobil'nyy**
Izobil'nyy Rus. Fed. **41** G7
formerly known as Izobil'noye
Izola Slovenia **56** F3
Izoplit Rus. Fed. **43** R5
Izozog Bajo Bol. **201** E4
Izra' Syria **108** H5
Iztochni Rodopi *mts* Bulg. **58** G7
Izúcar de Matamoros Mex. **185** F5
Izu-hantō *pen.* Japan **91** F7
Izuhara Japan **91** A7
Izumi Japan **91** B8
Izumisano Japan **91** D7
Izumo Japan **91** C7

▶**Izu-Ogasawara Trench** *sea feature* N. Pacific Ocean **220** D3
5th deepest trench in the world.

Izu-shotō *is* Japan **91** F7
Izu-tobu *vol.* Japan **91** F7
Izvestiy Tsentral'nogo Ispolnitel'nogo Komiteta, Ostrova Rus. Fed. **39** I2
Izvestkovyy Rus. Fed. **82** C2
Izvoarele Romania **58** G4
Izvoarele Romania **58** F4
Izvoarele Romania **58** H3
Izvoru Romania **58** G4
Izyaslav Ukr. **41** C6
Iz"yayu Rus. Fed. **40** K2
Izyndy Kazakh. **102** D3
Izyum Ukr. **41** F6

↓ J

Jaama Estonia **42** I2
Ja'ar Yemen **105** D5
Jaba *watercourse* Iran **100** D3
Jabal as Sirāj Afgh. **101** G3
Jabal Dab Saudi Arabia **105** E3
Jabalón *r.* Spain **54** G6
Jabalpur India **96** C5
formerly spelt Jubbulpore
Jabbārah Fara Islands Saudi Arabia **104** C4
Jabbūl, Sabkhat al *salt flat* Syria **109** I2
Jabiluka Aboriginal Land *res.* Australia **148** B2
Jabir *reg.* Oman **105** G3
Jabiru Australia **148** B2
Jablah Syria **108** G2
Jablanica Bos.-Herz. **56** J5
Jablanica *r.* Yugo. **58** C5
Jablonec nad Nisou Czech Rep. **49** M5
Jabłonowo Pomorskie Poland **49** Q2
Jablunkov Czech Rep. **49** P6
Jaboticabal Brazil **206** E8
Jaboticatubas Brazil **207** J6
Jabuka *i.* Croatia **56** H5
Jabuka *Vojvodina, Srbija* Yugo. **58** B4
Jabung, Tanjung *pt* Indon. **76** D3
Jaburu Brazil **199** E6
Jabuti Brazil **199** G6
Jaca Spain **55** K2
Jacala Mex. **185** F4
Jacaraci Brazil **207** K1
Jacaré *Mato Grosso* Brazil **202** A5
Jacaré *Rondônia* Brazil **201** D2
Jacaré *r.* Brazil **199** F6
Jacaré *r.* Brazil **202** D4
Jacareacanga Brazil **199** G6
Jacareí Brazil **207** G10
Jacaretinga Brazil **201** F2
Jacarézinho Brazil **206** D10
Jáchal *r.* Arg. **204** D3
Jaciara Brazil **202** A5
Jacinto Brazil **202** D6
Jaciparaná Brazil **201** D2
Jaciparaná *r.* Brazil **201** D2
Jack *r.* Australia **149** E2
Jackfish Canada **172** G2
Jackfish Lake Canada **167** I4
Jack Lee, Lake *resr* U.S.A. **179** D5
Jacksboro *TN* U.S.A. **176** A9
Jacksboro *TX* U.S.A. **179** C5
Jackson Australia **149** F5
Jackson *AL* U.S.A. **175** C6
Jackson *CA* U.S.A. **182** D3
Jackson *GA* U.S.A. **175** D5
Jackson *KY* U.S.A. **176** B8
Jackson *MI* U.S.A. **173** I8
Jackson *MN* U.S.A. **178** D3
Jackson *MO* U.S.A. **174** B4

▶**Jackson** *MS* U.S.A. **175** B5
State capital of Mississippi.

Jackson *NC* U.S.A. **176** H9
Jackson *OH* U.S.A. **176** C6
Jackson *TN* U.S.A. **174** B5
Jackson *WI* U.S.A. **172** E7
Jackson *WY* U.S.A. **180** E4
Jackson, Cape N.Z. **152** I8
Jackson, Mount Antarctica **222** T2
Jackson Bay N.Z. **153** C11
Jackson Bay *b.* N.Z. **153** C11
also known as Okahu
Jackson Head N.Z. **153** C11
Jackson Island Rus. Fed. *see* Dzheksona, Ostrov
Jackson Lake U.S.A. **180** E4
Jacksonport U.S.A. **172** F6
Jacksons N.Z. **153** F10
Jackson's Arm Canada **169** J3
Jacksonville *AL* U.S.A. **175** C5
Jacksonville *AR* U.S.A. **179** D5
Jacksonville *FL* U.S.A. **175** D6
Jacksonville *IL* U.S.A. **174** B4
Jacksonville *NC* U.S.A. **174** E5
Jacksonville *OH* U.S.A. **176** C6
Jacksonville *TX* U.S.A. **179** D6
Jacksonville Beach U.S.A. **175** D6
Jack Wade U.S.A. **166** A1
Jacmel Haiti **187** E3
Jaco *i.* East Timor *see* **Jako**
Jacobabad Pak. **101** G4
Jacobina Brazil **202** D4
Jacob Lake U.S.A. **183** L5
Jacobsdal S. Africa **133** I6
Jacques-Cartier, Détroit de *sea chan.* Canada **169** H3
also known as Jacques Cartier Passage
Jacques Cartier, Mont *mt.* Canada **169** H3
Jacques Cartier Passage Canada *see* Jacques-Cartier, Détroit de
Jacquet River Canada **169** H4
Jacuba *r.* Brazil **206** A5
Jacuí Brazil **206** G8
Jacuí *r.* Brazil **203** B9
Jacuípe *r.* Brazil **202** E5
Jacunda Brazil **202** B3
Jacundá *r.* Brazil **202** B2
Jacupemba Brazil **207** M6
Jacupiranga Brazil **203** C8
Jacura Venez. **198** D2
Jadar *r.* Bos.-Herz. **56** L4
Jadar *r.* Yugo. **58** A4
Jadcherla India **94** C2
Jaddangi India **95** D2
Jaddi, Ras *pt* Pak. **101** E5
Jadebusen *b.* Germany **48** F2
Jadhdhānah Saudi Arabia **104** C4
Jādib Yemen **105** F4
J. A. D. Jensen Nunatakker *nunataks* Greenland **165** O3
Jadotville Dem. Rep. Congo *see* **Likasi**
Jadova *r.* Croatia **56** H4
Jadovnik *mt.* Bos.-Herz. **56** I4
Jaén Peru **198** B6
Jaen Phil. **74** B3
Jaén Spain **54** H7
Jæren *reg.* Norway **45** I4
Ja'farābād *Ardabil* Iran **100** B2
Ja'farābād *Khorāsan* Iran **100** D2
Jaffa Israel *see* **Tel Aviv-Yafo**
Jaffa, Cape Australia **146** C4
Jaffna Sri Lanka **94** C4
Jaffrey U.S.A. **177** M3
Jafr, Qa' al *imp. l.* Jordan **109** H7
Jagadhri India **96** C3
Jägala *r.* Estonia **42** G2
Jagalur India **94** C3
Jagdalak Afgh. **101** G3
Jagdalpur India **94** D2
Jagdaqi China **85** J1
Jagdishpur India **89** C7
Jagdispur India **97** E4
Jagersfontein S. Africa **133** J6
Jaggang China **89** B5
Jaggayyapeta India **94** D2
Jaghin Iran **100** D5
Jaghjaghah, Nahr *r.* Syria/Turkey **109** M1
Jagin *watercourse* Iran **100** D5
Jagkolk Vloer *salt pan* S. Africa **132** E6
Jagodina *Srbija* Yugo. **58** C5
formerly known as Svetozarevo
Jagok Tso *salt l.* China *see* **Urru Co**
Jagsamka China *see* **Luding**
Jagst *r.* Germany **48** G6
Jagtial India **94** C2
Jaguapitã Brazil **206** B10
Jaguarão *r.* Brazil/Uruguay **204** G4
also known as Yaguarón
Jaguarão Uruguay **204** G4
Jaguarari Brazil **202** D4
Jaguaretama Brazil **202** E3
Jaguari Brazil **203** A9
Jaguariaíva Brazil **206** D11
Jaguaribe Brazil **202** E3
Jaguaribe *r.* Brazil **202** E3
Jaguaripe Brazil **202** E5
Jaguaruana Brazil **202** E3
Jagüé Arg. **204** C3
Jagüey Grande Cuba **186** C2
Jahanabad India **97** E4
formerly spelt Jehanabad
Jahān Dāgh *mt.* Iran **100** B2
Jahleel, Point Australia **148** A1
Jahmah *well* Iraq **107** F5
Jahrom Iran **100** C4
Jāhyad Iran **100** D5
Jaicós Brazil **202** D3
Jaigarh India **94** B2
Jailolo Indon. **75** C2
Jailolo, Selat *sea chan.* Indon. **75** D3
Jailolo Gilolo *i.* Indon. *see* **Halmahera**
Jaiña Chile **200** C4
Jainca China **84** D5
also known as Magitang
Jaintiapur Bangl. **97** G4
Jaipur India **96** B4
Jaipurhat Bangl. **97** F4
Jais India **97** D4
Jaisalmer India **96** A4
Jaisinghnagar India **97** D5
Jaitaran India **96** B4
Jaitgarh *hill* India **94** C1
Jaitpur India **96** C4
Jajarkot Nepal **97** D3
Jajce Bos.-Herz. **56** J4
Jajnagar *state* India *see* **Orissa**
Jakar Bhutan **97** F4
also known as Byakar

▶**Jakarta** Indon. **77** D4
Capital of Indonesia. Formerly spelt Djakarta; historically known as Batavia or Sunda Kalapa.
world [cities] ▶ 24–25

Jakhan India **101** G6
Jakharrah Libya **120** D2
Jakin *mt.* Afgh. **101** F4
Jakkalsberg Namibia **130** C3
Jakkalsberg *hills* Namibia **132** A5
Jakki Kowr Iran **101** E5
Jäkkvik Sweden **44** L2
Jakliat India **96** B3
Jako *i.* East Timor **75** C5
also known as Jaco
Jakobshavn Greenland *see* **Ilulissat**
Jakobstad Fin. **44** M3
also known as Pietersaari
Jakupica *mts* Macedonia **58** C7
Jal U.S.A. **179** B5
Jalaid China *see* **Inder**
Jalājil Saudi Arabia **105** D2
Jalālābād Afgh. **101** G3
Jalalabad *Punjab* India **96** B3
Jalalabad *Uttar Pradesh* India **96** C3
Jalalabad *Uttar Pradesh* India **96** C4
Jalal-Abad Kyrg. **103** H4
also spelt Dzhalal-Abad
Jalal-Abad *admin. div.* Kyrg. **103** H4
English form Jalal-Abad Oblast; also known as Dzhalal-Abadskaya Oblast'
Jalal-Abad Oblast *admin. div.* Kyrg. *see* **Jalal-Abad**
Jalalpur *Gujarat* India **94** B1
Jalalpur *Uttar Pradesh* India **97** D4
Jalāmid, Ḩazm al *ridge* Saudi Arabia **107** D5
Ja'lān, Jabal *mts* Oman **105** G3
Jalandhar India **96** B3
formerly spelt Jullundur
Jalan Kayu Sing. **76** [inset]
Jalapa Guat. **185** H6
Jalapa Mex. **185** G5
Jalapa Nicaragua **186** B4
Jalapa Enríquez Mex. **185** F5
also known as Xalapa
Jalapur Pak. **101** H3
Jalapur Pirwala Pak. **101** G4
Jalasjärvi Fin. **44** M3
Jalaun India **96** C4
Jalawlā' Iraq **107** F4
also spelt Jalūlā
Jalboi *r.* Australia **148** B2
Jaldak Afgh. **101** F4
Jaldhaka *r.* Bangl. **97** F4
Jaldrug India **94** C2
Jales Brazil **206** C7
Jalesar India **96** C4
Jaleshwar India **97** E5
Jaleshwar Nepal *see* **Jaleswar**
Jaleswar Nepal **97** E4
also spelt Jaleshwar
Jalgaon India **96** B5
Jalībah Iraq **107** F5
Jalingo Nigeria **125** H4
Jalisco *state* Mex. **184** D5
Jallābī Iran **100** D5
Jalna India **94** B2
Jālo Iran **101** E5
Jalón *r.* Spain **55** J3
Jalor India **96** B4
Jalostotitlán Mex. **185** E4
Jalovik *Srbija* Yugo. **58** A4
Jalpa Mex. **185** E4
Jalpaiguri India **97** F4
Jalpan Mex. **185** F4
Jalrez Afgh. **101** G3
Jālū Libya **120** D2
Jalūlā Iraq *see* **Jalawlā'**
Jālū Oasis Libya **120** D2
Jām *r.* Iran **101** E3
Jām *reg.* Iran **101** E3
Jamaica Cuba **187** E2

▶**Jamaica** *country* West Indies **186** D3
northamerica [countries] ▶ 158–159

Jamaica Channel Haiti/Jamaica **187** E3
Jämaja Estonia **42** D3
Jamalpur Bangl. **97** F4
Jamalpur India **97** E4
Jamanxim *r.* Brazil **199** G6
Jamari Brazil **201** E2
Jamba Angola **127** C8
Jambi Indon. **76** C3
also known as Telanaipura
Jambi *prov.* Indon. **76** C3
Jambin Australia **149** F5
Jambo India **96** B4
Jamboaye *r.* Indon. **76** B1
Jambongan *i.* Sabah Malaysia **77** G1
Jambuair, Tanjung *pt* Indon. **76** B1
Jambūr Iraq **109** P2
Jambusar India **96** B5
Jamekunte India **94** C2
James *watercourse* Australia **148** C4
James *r.* Canada **167** I1
James *r. MO* U.S.A. **178** D4
James *r. ND/SD* U.S.A. **178** C3
James *r. VA* U.S.A. **177** I8
James, Isla *i.* Chile **205** B7
Jamesabad Pak. **101** G5
James Bay Canada **168** D2
Jamesburg U.S.A. **177** K5
James Cistern Bahamas **186** D1
Jameson Land *reg.* Greenland **165** Q2
Jameson Range *hills* Australia **151** D5
James Peak N.Z. **153** C13
James Ranges *mts* Australia **148** B5
James Ross Island Antarctica **222** U2
James Ross Strait Canada **165** J3
Jamestown Australia **146** C3
Jamestown Canada *see* **Wawa**
Jamestown S. Africa **133** K8

▶**Jamestown** St Helena **216** N7
Capital of St Helena and Dependencies.

Jamestown *CA* U.S.A. **182** D4
Jamestown *KY* U.S.A. **174** C4
Jamestown *ND* U.S.A. **178** C2
Jamestown *NY* U.S.A. **176** F3
Jamestown *PA* U.S.A. **176** E4
Jamestown *TN* U.S.A. **176** A9
Jāmijärvi Fin. **45** M3
Jamiltepec Mex. **185** F5
Jamkhandi India **94** B2
Jamkhed India **94** B2
Jammalamadugu India **94** C3
Jammerbugten *b.* Denmark **45** J4
Jammu Jammu and Kashmir **96** B2

▶**Jammu and Kashmir** *terr.* Asia **96** C2
Disputed territory (India/Pakistan). Short form Kashmir.
asia [countries] ▶ 64–67

Jamnagar India **96** A5
formerly known as Navangar
Jamner India **94** B1
Jamni *r.* India **96** C4
Jamno, Jezioro *lag.* Poland **49** N1
Jampang Kulon Indon. **77** D4
Jampur Pak. **101** G4
Jämsä Fin. **45** N3
Jämsänkoski Fin. **45** N3
Jamshedpur India **97** E5
Jamtara India **97** E5
Jamtari Nigeria **125** H5
Jämtland *county* Sweden **44** K3
Jamui India **97** E4
Jamuk, Gunung *mt.* Indon. **77** G2
Jamu Mare Romania **58** C3
Jamuna *r.* Bangl. **97** F5
Jamuna *r.* India **97** G4
Janā *i.* Saudi Arabia **105** E2
Janāb, Wādī al *watercourse* Jordan **109** H6
Janakpur India **97** D5
Janakpur Nepal **97** E4
Janaúba Brazil **202** D5
Janaucu, Ilha *i.* Brazil **202** B1
Jand Pak. **101** H3
Jandaia Brazil **206** C4
Jandaia do Sul Brazil **206** B10
Jandaq Iran **100** C3
Jandiala India **96** B3
Jandiatuba *r.* Brazil **198** D5
Jandongi Dem. Rep. Congo **126** D4
Jandowae Australia **149** F5
Jándula *r.* Spain **54** G6
Jandulilla *r.* Spain **55** H7
Janeiro *r.* Brazil **202** C5
Janesville *CA* U.S.A. **182** D1
Janesville *WI* U.S.A. **172** D8
Jang, Tanjung *pt* Indon. **76** D3
Jangal Iran **101** D3
Jangamo Moz. **131** G5
Jangaon India **94** C2
Jangeldi Uzbek. *see* **Dzhangel'dy**
Jangipur India **97** F4
Jangngai Turkm. *see* **Dzhanga**
Jangngai Ri *mts* China **89** D5
Jangngai Zangbo *r.* China **89** D5
Jānī Beyglū Iran **100** A2
Janikowo Poland **49** P3
Janiópolis Brazil **206** A11
Janja Bos.-Herz. **56** L4
Janja *r.* Bos.-Herz. **56** L4
Janjevo *Kosovo, Srbija* Yugo. **58** C6
Jan Kempdorp S. Africa **133** I4
formerly known as Andalusia
Jankov Kamen *mt.* Yugo. **58** B5

▶**Jan Mayen** *i.* Arctic Ocean **224** X2
Part of Norway.

Jänmuiža Latvia **42** G4
Jannatābād Iran **100** B3
Jaňona *mt.* Spain **54** E4
Janos Mex. **184** C2
Jánoshalma Hungary **49** Q9
Jánossomorja Hungary **49** O8
Janów Lubelski Poland **49** T5
Jans Bay Canada **167** I4
Jansenville S. Africa **133** I9
Jānua Coeli Brazil **202** B2
Januária Brazil **202** C5
Janūbī, Al Fulayj al *watercourse* Saudi Arabia **105** D1
Janūb Sīnā' *governorate* Egypt **108** E8
English form South Sinai; also known as Sinai al Janūbīya
Janwada India **94** C2
Janzar *mt.* Pak. **101** E5
Janzé France **50** E5
Jaora India **96** B5

▶**Japan** *country* Asia **90** E5
9th most populous country in the world. Known as Nihon or Nippon in Japanese.
world [population] ▶ 22–23
asia [countries] ▶ 64–67

Japan, Sea of N. Pacific Ocean **83** D5
also known as East Sea or Nippon Hai
Japan Alps National Park Japan *see* **Chibu-Sangaku National Park**
Japón Hond. **186** B4
Japurá *r.* Brazil **198** E5
Japvo Mount India **97** G4
Jaqué Panama **186** D6
Jarabacoa Dom. Rep. **187** F3
Jarābulus Syria **109** J1
Jarad Saudi Arabia **104** C4
Jaraguá Brazil **206** D2
Jaraguá do Sul Brazil **203** B8
Jaraguari Brazil **203** A7
Jaraiz de la Vera Spain **54** F4
Jarama *r.* Spain **55** H4
Jarash Jordan **108** G5
Jarauçu *r.* Brazil **199** H5
Järbo Sweden **45** L3
Jarboesville U.S.A. *see* **Lexington Park**
Jar-bulak Kazakh. *see* **Kabanbay**
Jardim *Ceará* Brazil **202** E3
Jardim *Mato Grosso do Sul* Brazil **201** F5
Jardin *r.* Spain **55** I6
Jardine River National Park Australia **149** D1
Jardinópolis Brazil **206** F8
Jargalant *Arhangay* Mongolia **84** D2
Jargalant *Bayanhongor* Mongolia **84** C2
Jargalant *Bayan-Ölgiy* Mongolia **84** A2
Jargalant *Dornod* Mongolia **85** G2
Jargalant *Govi-Altay* Mongolia **84** C2
Jargalant Mongolia *see* **Hovd**
Jargalant *Töv* Mongolia **85** E1
Jargalant Hayrhan *mt.* Mongolia **84** B2
Jargalthaan Mongolia **85** F2
Jari *r.* Brazil **199** I5
Jaria Jhanjail Bang. **97** F4
Jarmen Germany **49** K2
Järna *Dalarna* Sweden **45** K3
Järna *Stockholm* Sweden **45** L4
Jarnac France **50** F7
Jarocin Poland **49** O4
Jaroměř Czech Rep. **49** M5
Jarosław Poland **49** T5
Järpen Sweden **44** K3
Jarqŭrghon Uzbek. *see* **Dzharkurgan**
Jarrāh, Wādī *watercourse* Syria **109** M1
Jarrāhi *watercourse* Iran **100** B4
Jarratt U.S.A. **176** H9
Jarrettsville U.S.A. **177** I6
Jartai China **85** E4
Jartai Yanchi *salt l.* China **84** E4
Jarú Brazil **201** E2
Jarūb Yemen **105** F4
Jarud China *see* **Lubei**
Jarut *mt.* Yugo. **58** B5
Järvakandi Estonia **42** F3
Järvenpää Fin. **45** N3

▶**Jarvis Island** *terr.* N. Pacific Ocean **221** H6
United States Unincorporated Territory.
oceania [countries] ▶ 138–139

Järvsand Sweden **44** K2
Järvsö Sweden **45** L3
Jarwa India **97** D4
Jasdan India **96** A5
Jashpurnagar India **97** E5
Jasień Poland **49** M4
Jasiołka *r.* Poland **49** S6
Jāsk Iran **100** D5
Jāsk-e Kohneh Iran **100** D5
Jasliq Uzbek. *see* **Zhaslyk**
Jasło Poland **49** S6
Jašlūnai Lith. **42** G7
Jasmund *pen.* Germany **49** K1
Jasmund, Nationalpark *nature res.* Germany **49** K1
Jason Peninsula Antarctica **222** T2
Jasper Canada **166** G4
Jasper *AL* U.S.A. **175** C5
Jasper *AR* U.S.A. **179** D4
Jasper *FL* U.S.A. **175** D6
Jasper *GA* U.S.A. **174** C5
Jasper *IN* U.S.A. **174** C4
Jasper *NY* U.S.A. **176** H3
Jasper *OH* U.S.A. **176** B6
Jasper *TN* U.S.A. **174** C5
Jasper *TX* U.S.A. **179** D6
Jasper National Park Canada **167** G4
Jaşşān Iraq **107** F4
Jassy Romania *see* **Iaşi**
Jastarnia Poland **49** P1
Jastrebarsko Croatia **56** H3
Jastrowie Poland **49** N2
Jastrzębie-Zdrój Poland **49** P6
historically known as Bad Königsdorff
Jászárokszállás Hungary **49** Q8
Jászberény Hungary **49** Q8
Jataí Brazil **206** B4
Jatapu *r.* Brazil **199** G5
Jatara India **96** C4
Jati Pak. **101** G5
also known as Mughalbhin
Jatibarang Indon. **77** E4
Jatibonico Cuba **186** D2
Játiva Spain *see* **Xàtiva**
Jatiwangi Indon. **77** E4
Jatobá Brazil **202** A5
Jatoi Pak. **101** G4
Jättendal Sweden **45** L3
Jatuarana Brazil **201** E1
Jaú Brazil **206** E9
Jaú *r.* Brazil **199** F5
Jaú, Parque Nacional do *nat. park* Brazil **199** F5
Jauaperi *r.* Brazil **199** F5
Jaua Sarisariñama, Parque Nacional *nat. park* Venez. **199** E3
Jauco Cuba **187** E2
Jauja Peru **200** B2
Jaumave Mex. **185** F4
Jaunā *r.* Brazil **199** F6
Jaunanna Latvia **42** I4
Jaunay-Clan France **50** G6
Jaunjelgava Latvia **42** G5
Jaunkalsnava Latvia **42** G5
Jaunlutriņi Latvia **42** D5
Jaunmārupe Latvia **42** E5
Jaunpiebalga Latvia **42** H4
Jaunpils Latvia **42** E5
Jaunpur India **97** D4
Jaupaci Brazil **206** C3
Jauru Brazil **203** A6
Jauru *r.* Brazil **201** F4

▶**Java** *i.* Indon. **77** D5
5th largest island in Asia. Also spelt Jawa.
asia [landscapes] ▶ 62–63

Javadi Hills India **94** C3
Javaés *r.* Brazil *see* **Formoso**
Javaés, Serra dos *hills* Brazil **202** B4
Javalambre *mt.* Spain **55** K4
Javalambre, Sierra de *mts* Spain **55** J4
Javand Afgh. **101** F3
Javari *r.* Brazil **198** D6
also spelt Yavari
Javarthushuu Mongolia **85** G1
Java Sea Indon. **77** E4

▶**Java Trench** *sea feature* Indian Ocean **218** N6
Deepest point in the Indian Ocean.
oceans [features] ▶ 210–211

Jávea Spain **55** L6
Javier, Isla *i.* Chile **205** B7
Javor *mts* Yugo. **58** B5
Javořice *hill* Czech Rep. **49** M6
Javorie *mt.* Slovakia **49** Q7
Javornik *mt.* Slovenia **56** H2
Javorníky *mts* Slovakia **49** P6
Jävre Sweden **44** M2
Jawa *i.* Indon. *see* **Java**
Jawa Barat *prov.* Indon. **77** D4
Jawad India **96** B4
Jawai *r.* India **96** A4
Jawala Mukhi India **96** C3
Jawar India **96** C5
Jawa Tengah *prov.* Indon. **77** E4
Jawa Timur *prov.* Indon. **77** F4
Jawbān Bayk Syria **109** I1
Jawf, Wādī al *watercourse* Yemen **104** D5
Jawhar India **94** B2
Jawhar Somalia **128** E4
Jawor Poland **49** N4
Jaworzno Poland **49** Q5
Jawoyn Aboriginal Land *res.* Australia **148** B2
Jay U.S.A. **179** D4

▶**Jaya, Puncak** *mt.* Indon. **73** I7
Highest mountain in Oceania. Formerly known as Carstensz-top or Puntjak Sukarno.
oceania [landscapes] ▶ 136–137

Jayanca Peru **198** B6
Jayanti India **97** F4
Jayapura Indon. **73** J7
formerly known as Hollandia or Sukarnapura
Jayb, Wādī al *watercourse* Israel/Jordan **108** G6
Jaynagar *Bihar* India **97** E4
Jaynagar *W. Bengal* India **97** F5
Jaypur India **95** D2
Jayrūd Syria **109** H4
Jayton U.S.A. **179** B5
Jazīrat al Ḩamrā U.A.E. **105** F2
Jazminal Mex. **185** E3
Jbail Lebanon **108** G3
historically known as Biblos
J. C. Murphey Lake U.S.A. **172** F9
Jean U.S.A. **183** I6
Jeanerette U.S.A. **175** B6
Jean Marie River Canada **166** F2
Jebāl Bārez, Kūh-e *mts* Iran **100** D4
Jebel Libya **120** D2
Jebel Romania **58** C3
Jebel Turkm. *see* **Dzhebel**
Jebel Abyad Plateau Sudan **121** F5
Jebel Ali U.A.E. *see* **Mina Jebel Ali**
Jebel, Bahr el *r.* Sudan/Uganda *see* **White Nile**
Jeberos Peru **198** B6
Jebha Morocco **54** G9
Jebus Indon. **77** D3
Jedburgh U.K. **46** J8
Jeddah Saudi Arabia **104** B3
also spelt Jiddah
Jeddore Lake Canada **169** K3
Jedeida Tunisia **57** B12
Jędrzejów Poland **49** R5
Jedwabne Poland **49** T2
Jeetze *r.* Germany **48** I2
Jefferson *IA* U.S.A. **178** D3
Jefferson *NC* U.S.A. **176** D9
Jefferson *OH* U.S.A. **176** E4
Jefferson *TX* U.S.A. **179** D5
Jefferson *WI* U.S.A. **172** E7
Jefferson *r.* U.S.A. **180** E3
Jefferson, Mount U.S.A. **183** H3
Jefferson, Mount *vol.* U.S.A. **180** B3

▶**Jefferson City** *MO* U.S.A. **178** D4
State capital of Missouri.

Jefferson City *TN* U.S.A. **176** B9
Jeffersonton U.S.A. **176** H7
Jeffersonville *IN* U.S.A. **174** C4
Jeffersonville *KY* U.S.A. **176** B8
Jeffersonville *OH* U.S.A. **176** B6
Jeffrey U.S.A. **176** D8
Jeffrey's Bay S. Africa **133** I11
Jega Nigeria **125** G3
Jehanabad India *see* **Jahanabad**
Jēkabpils Latvia **42** G5
Jelbart Ice Shelf Antarctica **223** X2
Jelcz-Laskowice Poland **49** O4
Jeldēsa Eth. **128** D2
Jelenia Góra Poland **49** M5
historically known as Hirschberg
Jelep La *pass* China/India **89** E7
Jelgava Latvia **42** E5
Jellico U.S.A. **176** A9
Jellicoe Canada **168** C3
Jelloway U.S.A. **176** C5
Jelondi Tajik. *see* **Dzhilandy**
Jelow Gīr Iran **100** A3
Jemaja *i.* Indon. **77** D2
Jember Indon. **77** F5
Jemez Pueblo U.S.A. **181** F6
Jeminay China **88** D2
also known as Topterek
Jeminay Kazakh. **88** D2
Jemma *Bauchi* Nigeria **125** H4
Jemma *Kaduna* Nigeria **125** H4
Jemmel Tunisia **57** C13
Jemnice Czech Rep. **49** M6
Jempang, Danau *l.* Indon. **77** G3
Jena Germany **48** I5
Jena U.S.A. **179** D6
Jenda Malawi **129** B8
Jendouba Tunisia **123** H1
Jengish Chokusu *mt.* China/Kyrg. *see* **Pobeda Peak**
Jenīn West Bank **108** G5
Jenipapo Brazil **199** F6
Jenkinjones U.S.A. **176** D8
Jenkins U.S.A. **176** C8
Jenkintown U.S.A. **177** J5
Jenne Mali *see* **Djenné**
Jenner Canada **167** I5
Jennersdorf Austria **49** N9
Jennings *r.* Canada **166** C3
Jennings U.S.A. **179** D6
Jenpeg Canada **167** L4
Jeparra Indon. **77** E4
Jeparit Australia **147** D4
Jeppo Fin. **44** M3
Jequié Brazil **202** D5
Jequitaí Brazil **203** C6
Jequitaí *r.* Brazil **207** I4
Jequitinhonha Brazil **202** D6
Jequitinhonha *r.* Brazil **207** O2
Jerba, Île de *i.* Tunisia **123** H2
Jerbar Sudan **128** A3
Jereh Iran **100** B4
Jérémie Haiti **187** E3
Jeremoabo Brazil **202** E4
Jerer Shet' *watercourse* Eth. **128** D3
Jereweh Indon. **77** G5
Jerez Mex. **185** E4
Jerez de la Frontera Spain **54** E8
Jerez de los Caballeros Spain **54** E6
Jerfojaur Sweden **44** L2
Jerggul Norway **44** N1
Jergucat Albania **59** B9
Jericho Australia **149** E4
Jericho West Bank **108** G6
also known as Arīhā; also spelt Yerîḩo; historically known as Tell es-Sultan

index

J

K

Jerid, Chott el salt l. Tunisia 123 H2
Jerijih, Tanjong pt Sarawak Malaysia 77 E2
Jerilderie Australia 147 E3
Jermyn U.S.A. 177 J4
Jerome AZ U.S.A. 183 L7
Jerome ID U.S.A. 180 D4
Jerramungup Australia 151 B7

▶**Jersey** terr. Channel Is 50 D3
United Kingdom Crown Dependency.
europe [countries] ▶▶ 32–35

Jersey City U.S.A. 177 K5
Jerseyville U.S.A. 174 B4
Jerte r. Spain 54 E5
Jerumenha Brazil 202 D2

▶**Jerusalem** Israel/West Bank 108 G6
Capital of Israel. Also known as El Quds;
also spelt Yerushalayim; historically known
as Aelia Capitolina or Hierosolyma.
asia [issues] ▶▶ 66–67

Jerusalem N.Z. 152 J7
Jervis Bay Australia 147 E3
Jervis Bay Territory admin. div. Australia
147 E3
also known as Commonwealth Territory
Jervois Range hills Australia 148 B4
Jesenice Slovenia 56 G2
Jeseník Czech Rep. 49 O5
Jesi Italy 56 F5
Jesmond Canada 166 F5
Jesolo Italy 56 E3
Jesselton Sabah Malaysia see
Kota Kinabalu
Jessen Germany 49 J4
Jessheim Norway 45 J3
Jessore Bangl. 97 F5
Jesu Maria Island P.N.G. see
Rambutyo Island
Jesup U.S.A. 175 D6
Jesús Carranza Mex. 185 G5
Jesús María Arg. 204 D3
Jesús María, Barra spit Mex. 185 F3
Jetalsar India 96 A5
Jethro tourist site Saudi Arabia 104 A1
also known as Maghā'ir Shu'ayb
Jetmore U.S.A. 178 C4
Jevnaker Norway 45 J3
Jewett City U.S.A. 177 N4
Jewish Autonomous Oblast admin. div.
Rus. Fed. see
Yevreyskaya Avtonomnaya Oblast'
Jeyhun Turkm. see Dzheykhun
Jeziorak, Jezioro l. Poland 49 Q2
Jeziorany Poland 49 R2
Jeziorka r. Poland 49 S3
Jeziorsko, Jezioro l. Poland 49 P4
Jezzine Lebanon 108 G4
Jhabua India 96 B5
Jha Jha India 97 E4
Jhajjar India 96 C3
Jhajju India 96 B4
Jhal Pak. 101 F4
Jhalakati Bangl. 97 F5
Jhalawar India 96 C4
Jhalida India 97 E5
Jhalrapatan India 96 C4
Jhang Pak. 101 H4
Jhanjharpur India 97 E4
Jhansi India 96 C4
Jhanzi r. India 97 H4
Jhapa Nepal 97 E4
Jhargram India 97 E5
Jharia India 97 E5
Jharkhand state India 97 E5
Jharsuguda India 97 E5
Jhatpat Pak. 101 G4
Jhawani Nepal 97 E4
Jhelum r. India/Pak. 96 B3
Jhelum Pak. 101 H3
Jhenaidaha Bangl. see Jhenida
Jhenida Bangl. 97 F5
also known as Jhenaidaha
Jhinjhuvada India 96 A5
Jhinkpani India 97 E5
Jhudo Pak. 101 G5
Jhumritilaiya India 97 E4
Jhunjhunun India 96 B3
Jhusi India 97 D4
Jiachuan China 86 C1
formerly known as Jiachuanzhen
Jiachuanzhen China see Jiachuan
Jiading Sichuan China see Xinfeng
Jiading China 87 G2
Jiahe China 87 E3
Jiajiang China 86 B2
Jialing Jiang r. China 86 C2
Jialu r. China 87 E1
Jiamusi China 82 C3
Ji'an Jiangxi China 87 E3
also known as Dunhou
Ji'an Jiangxi China 87 E3
also known as Jizhou
Ji'an Jilin China 88 B4
Jianchang China see Nancheng
Jianchang China 85 H4
Jianchuan China 86 A3
also known as Jinhua
Jiandaoyu China see Zigui
Jiande China 87 F2
Jiang'an China 86 C2

Jiangbei China see Yubei
Jiangcheng China 86 B4
Jiangchuan China 86 B3
also known as Dajie
Jiangcun China 87 D3
Jiangdu China 87 F1
formerly known as Xiannümiao
Jiange China 86 C2
also known as Pu'an
Jiangjiehe China 87 C3
Jiangjin China 86 C2
Jiangjunmiao China 88 E2
Jiangjunmu China 85 H4
Jiangjuntai China 84 C3
Jiangkou China see Fengkai
Jiangkou Guizhou China 87 D3
also known as Shuangjiang
Jiangkou Shaanxi China see Pingchang
Jiangle China 87 F3
also known as Guyong
Jiangling China see Jingzhou
Jiangluozhen China 86 C1
Jiangmen China 87 E4
Jiangna China see Yanshan
Jiangning China 87 F2
also known as Dongshan
Jiangshan China 87 F2
Jiangsi China see Dejiang
Jiangsu prov. China 87 F1
English form Kiangsu
Jiangtaibu China 85 E5
Jiangxi prov. China 87 E3
English form Kiangsi
Jiangxia China see Wuchang
Jiangxian China 85 F5
Jiangxigou China 84 D4
Jiangyan China 87 G1
formerly known as Taixian
Jiangyin China 87 G2
Jiangyong China 87 D3
Jiangyou China 86 C2
formerly known as Zhongba
Jiangyu China 85 H4
Jiangzhesongrong China 89 D6
Jianhu China 87 F1
Jian Jiang r. China 87 D4
Jianjun China see Yongshou
Jianli China 87 E2
also known as Rongcheng
Jianning China 87 F3
also known as Suicheng
Jian'ou China 87 F3
Jianping Liaoning China 85 H3
also known as Yebaishou
Jianping Liaoning China 85 H3
also known as Jing
Jianshe China 86 A1
Jianshe China see Baiyü
Jianshi China 87 D2
also known as Yezhou
Jianshui China 86 B4
also known as Lin'an
Jianxing China 87 F2
Jianyang Fujian China 87 F3
Jianyang Sichuan China 86 C2
Jiaochang China 86 B1
formerly known as Jiaochangba
Jiaochangba China see Jiaoling
Jiaocheng China see Jiaoling
Jiaocheng China 85 G4
Jiaohe China 85 H4
Jiaohe Jilin China 82 B4
Jiaojiang China see Taizhou
Jiaokou China 85 G4
Jiaokou China see Yiliang
Jiaolai r. China 85 H4
Jiaolai r. China 85 I3
Jiaoling China 87 F3
also known as Jiaocheng
Jiaonan China 85 H5
formerly known as Wanggezhuang
Jiaowei China 87 F3
Jiaozhou China 85 I4
Jiaozhuo Wan b. China 85 I4
Jiaozuo China 85 G5
Jiapigou China 82 B4
Jiasa China 86 B3
Jiashan China see Mingguang
Jiashi China 88 B4
also known as Payzawat
Jia Tsuo La pass China 89 D6
Jiaxian Henan China 87 E1
Jiaxian Shaanxi China 85 F4
also known as Jialu
Jiaxiang China 85 H5
Jiaxing China 87 G2
Jiayi Taiwan see Chiai
Jiayin China 82 C2
also known as Chaoyang
Jiayu China 87 E2
also known as Yuyue
Jiayuguan China 84 C4
Jiazi China 87 F4
Jibou Romania 58 E1
Jibsh, Ra's c. Oman 105 G3
Jibuti country Africa see Djibouti
Jibuti Djibouti see Djibouti
Jicarilla Apache Indian Reservation res.
U.S.A. 181 F5
Jičín Czech Rep. 49 M5
Jiddah Saudi Arabia see Jeddah
Jidong China 82 C3
Jiehkkevarri mt. Norway 44 L1
Jiehu China see Yinan
Jieshi China 87 F4
Jieshou China 87 E1
Jiesjavrre l. Lith. 42 E7
Jiešjávri l. Norway 44 N1
Jiexi China 87 F4
also known as Hepo
Jiexiu China 85 F4
Jieyang China 87 F4
Jieznas Lith. 42 F7
Jigalong Aboriginal Reserve Australia
Jigalong Australia 150 C4
Jigawa state Nigeria 125 H3
Jigerbent Turkm. see Dzhigirbent
Jiggalong Australia 150 C4
Jiggs U.S.A. 183 I1
Jiguani Cuba 186 D2
Jigzhi China 86 B1
also known as Chugqênsumdo
Jihar, Wadi al watercourse Syria 109 I3
Jihlava Czech Rep. 49 N6
Jihlava r. Czech Rep. 49 N7
Jijel Alg. 123 G1
formerly spelt Djidjelli
Jijia r. Romania 58 J2
Jijiga Eth. 128 D3
Jijona Spain 55 K6
Jiju China 86 B2
Jil'ad reg. Jordan 108 G5
English form Gilead
Jīlān ash Shuwayḥiṭiyah esc. Saudi Arabia
109 K7
Jilava Romania 58 H4
Jilbadji Nature Reserve Australia 151 B6
Jilf al Kabīr, Haḍabat al plat. Egypt see
Gilf Kebir Plateau
Jilga r. Afgh. 101 F3
Jīlh al 'Ishār plain Saudi Arabia 105 D2
Jilib Somalia 128 D4
Jili Hu l. China 88 D2
Jilin China 82 B4
Jilin prov. China 85 J3
English form Kirin
Jiling China 87 F2
Jilin Hada Ling mts China 82 B4
Jiloca r. Spain 55 J3

Jilong Taiwan see Chilung
Jima Eth. 128 C3
Jima Ali well Eth. 128 E3
Jimani Haiti 187 F3
Jimbo Tanz. 129 C6
Jimbolia Romania 58 B3
Jimda China see Zindo
Jimena de la Frontera Spain 54 F8
Jiménez Chihuahua Mex. 184 D3
Jiménez Coahuila Mex. 185 E2
Jiménez Tamaulipas Mex. 185 F3
Jimeta Nigeria 125 I4
Jimi r. P.N.G. 73 J7
Jim Jim Creek r. Australia 148 B2
Jimo China 85 I4
Jimsar China 88 E3
Jina Romania 58 D3
Jinan China 85 H4
formerly spelt Tsinan
Jinbi China see Dayao
Jinchang China 84 D4
formerly known as Jinchuan
Jincheng China 85 G5
Jincheng China see Leibo
Jincheng China see Yilong
Jincheng China see Wuding
Jinchengjiang China see Hechi
Jinchuan China see Jinchang
Jinchuan China see Xingan
Jinchuan China 86 B2
also known as Quqên
Jind India 96 C3
Jindřichův Hradec Czech Rep. 49 M6
Jin'e China see Longchang
Jinfosi China 84 C4
Jing r. China 87 D1
Jing'an China see Doumen
Jingbian China 85 F4
also known as Zhangjiapan
Jingchuan China 85 E5
Jingde China 87 F2
also known as Jingyang
Jingdezhen China 87 F2
Jingdong China 86 B3
also known as Jinping
Jinggangshan China 87 E3
formerly known as Ciping
Jinggang Shan hill China 87 E3
Jinggongqiao China 87 F2
Jinggu China 86 B4
also known as Weiyuan
Jinghai China 85 H4
Jinghe China 88 C2
also known as Jing
Jinghong China 86 B4
formerly known as Yunjinghong
Jingjiang China 87 G1
Jingle China 85 G4
Jingmen China 87 E2
Jingning China 85 E5
Jingpeng China 85 H3
also known as Hexigten Qi
Jingpo Hu resr China 82 C3
Jingpo China 87 E2
Jingtai China 84 D4
also known as Yitiaoshan
Jingtieshan China 84 C4
formerly known as Huashugou
Jingxi China 86 C4
also known as Xinjing
Jingxian China 87 F2
Jingxian China see Jingzhou
Jingxin China see Yongshan
Jingyan China 86 C2
also known as Jingde
Jingyu China 82 B4
Jingyuan China 84 E4
Jingzhou Hubei China 87 E2
formerly known as Jiangling
Jingzhou Hubei China 87 E2
formerly known as Shashi
Jingzhou Hunan China 87 D3
also known as Quyang; formerly known as
Jingxian
Jinhe China see Jinping
Jinhua China see Jianchuan
Jinhua China 87 F2
Jining Nei Mongol China 85 G3
also spelt Tsining
Jining Shandong China 85 H5
formerly known as Chining
Jinja Uganda 128 B4
Jinjiang Fujian China 87 F3
Jinjiang China see Chengmai
Jinjiang Yunnan China 86 B3
Jin Jiang r. China 87 D3
Jin Jiang r. China 87 E2
Jinka Eth. 128 C3
Jinkouhe China 86 B2
Jinmen Taiwan see Chinmen
Jinmu Jiao pt China 87 D5
Jinning China 86 B3
also known as Kunyang
Jinotega Nicaragua 186 B4
Jinotepe Nicaragua 186 B5
Jinping Guizhou China 87 D3
also known as Sanjiang
Jinping China see Jingdong
Jinping Yunnan China 86 B4
also known as Jinhe
Jinping China see Qiubei
Jinping Shan mts China 86 B2
Jinsen S. Korea see Inch'ŏn
Jinsha China 87 D3
Jinsha Jiang r. China 78 B1
Jinsha Jiang r. China see Yangtze
Jinshan Nei Mongol China 85 H3
Jinshan Shanghai China 87 G2
also known as Zhujing
Jinshan China see Lufeng
Jinshi China 87 D2
Jinshi China see Xinning
Jinta China 84 C3
Jintan China 87 F2
Jintang China 86 C2
also known as Zhao
Jintotolo Channel Phil. 74 B4
Jintur India 94 C2
Jinxi China 87 F3
Jinxi China see Lianshan
Jin Xi r. China 87 F3
Jinxian China 87 F2
also known as Minhe
Jinxian China see Linhai
Jinxiang Shandong China 85 H5
Jinxiang Zhejiang China 87 G3
Jinxiu China 87 D3
Jinyang China 86 B3
also known as Tiandiba
Jinyun China see Dayi
Jinyun China 87 G2
also known as Wuyun
Jinz, Qa' al salt flat Jordan 108 H7
Jinzhai China see Meishan
Jinzhai China 87 E2
Jinzhong China 85 G4
Jinzhou Liaoning China 85 I3
Jinzhou Liaoning China 85 I4
Jinzhou Wan b. China 85 I4
Jinzu China see Daocheng
Ji-Paraná Brazil 201 F2
Jipijapa Ecuador 198 A5
Jiquilisco El Salvador 185 H6
Jiquipilan de Juárez Mex. 185 E5
Jiquitaia Brazil 207 N4

Jirau Brazil 200 D2
Jirgatol Tajik. 101 G2
also spelt Dzhirgatal'
Jiri r. India 97 G4
Jirin Gol China 85 H2
Jiroft Iran 100 C5
formerly known as Sabzvārān
Jirriiban Somalia 128 E3
Jirwān Saudi Arabia 105 E3
Jirzah Egypt 108 D3
Jishan China 85 F5
Jishi China see Xunhua
Jishou China 87 D3
Jishui China see Yongfeng
Jisr ash Shughūr Syria 108 H2
Jitian China see Lianshan
Jitra Malaysia 76 C1
Jiu r. Romania 58 F4
Jiudengkou China 85 F4
Jiuding Shan mt. China 86 B2
Jiugong Shan mt. China 87 E2
Jiujiang Jiangxi China 87 E2
also known as Shahejie; formerly known as
Shahezhen
Jiujiang Jiangxi China 87 E2
Jiulian China see Mojiang
Jiuling Shan mts China 87 E2
Jiulong Hong Kong China see Kowloon
Jiulong China 86 B2
Jiulong China see Yuechi
Jiuquan China 84 C4
formerly known as Suzhou
Jiutai China 85 J3
Jiuxian China 85 F4
Jiuxu China 87 C3
Jiuzhen China 87 F3
Jiwani Pak. 101 E5
Jiwen China 85 I1
Jixi Anhui China 87 F2
also known as Huayang
Jixi Heilong. China 82 C3
Jixian China see Jizhou
Jixian Heilong. China 82 C3
also known as Fuli; formerly known as Fulitun
Jixian Shanxi China 85 F5
also known as Weihui
Jixian China see Weihui
Jiyuan China 85 G5
Jiz, Wādi al r. Yemen 105 F4
Jīzān Saudi Arabia 104 C4
Jīzān prov. Saudi Arabia 104 C4
Jizera r. Czech Rep. 49 L5
Jizerské Hory mts Czech Rep. 49 M5
Jizhou China 85 G4
formerly known as Jixian
Jizl watercourse Saudi Arabia 104 B2
Jizō-zaki pt Japan 91 C7
Jizzakh Uzbek. see Dzhizak
Jizzakh Wiloyati admin. div. Uzbek. see
Dzhizakskaya Oblast'
Joaçaba Brazil 203 B8
Joachimsthal Germany 49 K3
Joaima Brazil 202 D6
Joal-Fadiout Senegal 124 A3
Joana Peres Brazil 202 B2
João Belo Moz. see Xai-Xai
João de Almeida Angola see Chibia
João Monlevade Brazil 207 J6
João Pessoa Brazil 202 F3
João Pinheiro Brazil 203 C6
Joaquim Felício Brazil 207 I4
Joaquin V. González Arg. 204 D2
Jobabo Cuba 186 D2
Jobat India 96 B5
Job Peak U.S.A. 182 F2
Jockfall Sweden 44 M2
Jocoli Arg. 204 C4
Joda India 97 E5
Jódar Spain 55 H7
Jodhpur India 96 B4
Jodiya India 96 A5
Joe Batt's Arm Canada 169 K3
Joensuu Fin. 44 O3
Joes Junction U.S.A. 178 B4
Joetsu Japan 90 F6
Jofane Moz. 131 G4
Joffre, Mount Canada 167 H5
Jogbani India 97 E4
Jogbura Nepal 96 D3
Jõgeva Estonia 42 H3
Jogighopa India 97 F4
Jogindarnagar India 96 C3
Jogjakarta Indon. see Yogyakarta
Jõgua Estonia 42 I2
Johannesburg S. Africa 133 L3
Johan Peninsula Canada 165 L2
Jōhen Japan 91 C8
Johilla r. India 96 D5
John Day U.S.A. 180 C3
John Day r. U.S.A. 180 C3
John Day, Middle Fork r. U.S.A. 180 C3
John Day, North Fork r. U.S.A. 180 C3
John d'Or Prairie Canada 167 H3
John F. Kennedy airport U.S.A. 177 L5
John hill Kerr Reservoir U.S.A. 176 G9
John Jay, Mount Canada/U.S.A. 166 D3
Johnny Hoe r. Canada 166 F1
John o'Groats U.K. 46 I5
Johnson U.S.A. 177 M1
Johnsonburg U.S.A. 176 G4
Johnson City NY U.S.A. 177 J3
Johnson City TN U.S.A. 176 C9
Johnson City TX U.S.A. 179 C6
Johnsondale U.S.A. 182 F6
Johnson's Crossing U.S.A. 175 D5
Johnston, Lake salt flat Australia 151 C7
Johnston and Sand Islands atoll
N. Pacific Ocean see Johnston Atoll

▶**Johnston Atoll** N. Pacific Ocean 220 G4
United States Unincorporated Territory. Also
known as Johnston and Sand Islands.
oceania [countries] ▶▶ 138–139

Johnstone Lake Canada see
Old Wives Lake
Johnstone Strait Canada 166 E5
Johnston Range hills Australia 151 B6
Johnstown NY U.S.A. 177 K2
Johnstown OH U.S.A. 176 C5
Johnstown PA U.S.A. 176 G5
Johor state Malaysia 76 ...
Johor, Selat strait Malaysia/Sing. 76 [inset]
Johor, Sungai Malaysia 76 [inset]
Johor Bahru Malaysia 76 C2
Jõhvi Estonia 42 I2
Joigny France 51 J5
Joinville Brazil 203 B8
Joinville France 51 L4
Joinville Island Antarctica 222 U2
Jojutla Mex. 185 F5
Jokela Fin. 42 F1
Jokelbugten b. Greenland 165 Q2
Jokioinen Fin. 45 M3
Jokiperä Fin. 44 M3
Jokkmokk Sweden 44 L2
Jökulbunga hill Iceland 44 [inset] B2
Jökulfirðir inlet Iceland 44 [inset] B2
Jökulsá á Dál r. Iceland 44 [inset] D2
Jökulsá á Fjöllum r. Iceland 44 [inset] C2
Jolarpettai India 94 C3
Jolfa Iran 100 A2
Joliet U.S.A. 174 B3
Joliette Canada 169 F4
Jolo i. Phil. 74 B5
Jolo Phil. 74 B5
Jolly Lake Canada 167 H1
Jolo i. Phil. 74 B5
Jomala i. Phil. 74 A2
Jomalig i. Phil. 74 B3
Jomard Entrance sea chan. P.N.G. 149 F1

Jombang Indon. 77 F4
Jomda China 86 A2
a so known as Gatong
Jomna Nepal see Yamuna
Jomsom Nepal 97 D3
Jonah Iran 100 C5
Jonancy U.S.A. 176 C5
Jonathan Point Belize 185 H5
Jonava Lith. 42 F6
Jondal Norway 45 I3
Jonê China 86 B1
also known as Liulin
Jonesboro AR U.S.A. 174 B5
Jonesboro IL U.S.A. 174 B4
Jonesboro LA U.S.A. 179 D5
Jonesboro TN U.S.A. 176 C9
Jones Mills U.S.A. 176 F5
Jones Mountains Antarctica 222 R2
Jonesport U.S.A. 174 I2
Jones Sound sea chan. Canada 165 K2
Jonestown KY U.S.A. 176 A8
Jonestown PA U.S.A. 177 I5
Jonesville LA U.S.A. 175 B6
Jonesville NC U.S.A. 176 E8
Jonesville VA U.S.A. 176 B9
Jonglei Sudan 128 A3
Jonglei state Sudan 128 A3
Jonglei Canal Sudan 128 A3
Joniškėlis Lith. 42 F6
Joniškis Lith. 42 E5
Jönk r. India 97 D5
Jönköping Sweden 45 K4
Jönköping county Sweden 45 K4
Jonquière Canada 169 G3
Jonuta Mex. 185 G5
Jonzac France 50 F7
Joplin U.S.A. 178 D4
Joppa Israel see Tel Aviv-Yafo
Jora India 96 C4

▶**Jordan** country Asia 108 G7
known as Al 'Urdun in Arabic
asia [countries] ▶▶ 64–67

Jordan r. Asia 103 G3
Jordan MT U.S.A. 180 F3
Jordan NY U.S.A. 177 I2
Jordan r. OR U.S.A. 180 C4
Jordan r. UT U.S.A. 183 L1
Jordânia Brazil 207 M2
Jordet Norway 45 K3
Jorge Montt, Isla i. Chile 205 B8
Jorhat India 97 G4
Jorm Afgh. 101 G2
Jörn Sweden 44 K2
Jörn Sweden 44 M2
Jöroinen Fin. 44 N2
Jørpeland Norway 45 I4
Jos Nigeria 125 H4
Jose Abad Santos Phil. 74 C5
Jose Bonifacio Rondônia Brazil 201 E3
José Bonifácio São Paulo Brazil 206 D8
José Cardel Mex. 185 F5
José de Freitas Brazil 202 D3
José de San Martín Arg. 205 C7
José Enrique Rodó Uruguay 204 F4
Joselândia Brazil 201 F3
José Pañganiban Phil. 74 B3
José Pedro Varela Uruguay 204 G4
Joseph, Lac l. Canada 169 H2
Joseph Bonaparte Gulf Australia 150 E2
Joseph City U.S.A. 183 N7
Joshimath India 96 C3
Jōshinetsu-kōgen National Park Japan
91 F6
Joshua Tree U.S.A. 183 H7
Joshua Tree National Park U.S.A. 183 I8
Jos Plateau Nigeria 125 H4
Josselin France 50 D5
Jossund Norway 44 K2
Jostedalsbreen glacier Norway 45 I3
Jostedalsbreen Nasjonalpark nat. park
Norway 45 I3
Josvainai Lith. 42 E6
Jotunheimen mts Norway 45 J3
Jotunheimen Nasjonalpark nat. park
Norway 45 J3
Joubertina S. Africa 132 H10
Jouberton S. Africa 133 K3
Joué-lès-Tours France 50 G5
Joukokylä Fin. 44 O2
Joûnié Lebanon 108 G4
Jourdanton U.S.A. 179 C6
Joussard Canada 167 H4
Joutsa Fin. 45 N3
Joutseno Fin. 45 N3
Joutsijärvi Fin. 44 O2
Jovellanos Cuba 186 C2
Jowai India 97 G4
Jowzjān prov. Afgh. 101 F2
Joy, Mount Canada 166 C3
Joya de Cerén tourist site El Salvador
185 H6
Jozini S. Africa 133 Q4
Jrayfiya well W. Sahara 122 B4
Jreïda Mauritania 124 A2
Juan Aldama Mex. 185 E3
Juancheng China 85 G5
Juan de Fuca Strait Canada/U.S.A. 164 G5
Juan de Garay Arg. 204 D5
Juan de Nova i. Indian Ocean 129 D9
Juan E. Barra Arg. 204 E5
Juan Fernández, Archipiélago is
S. Pacific Ocean see
Juan Fernández Islands
Juan Fernández Islands S. Pacific Ocean
221 M8
also known as Juan Fernández, Archipiélago
Juangriego Venez. 199 F2
Juan Jorge Arg. 204 F3
Juanjuí Peru 200 A2
Juankoski Fin. 44 O3
Juan Mata Ortiz Mex. 184 C2
Juanshui China see Tongcheng
Juan Stuven, Isla i. Chile 205 B7
Juara Brazil 201 F2
Juárez Mex. 185 E3
Juáréz, Sierra de mts Mex. 184 A1
Juatinga, Ponta da pt Brazil 207 I10
Juàzeiro Brazil 202 D4
Juazeiro do Norte Brazil 202 E3
Juazohn Liberia 124 C5
Juba r. Somalia see Jubba
Juba Sudan 128 A3
Juban Yemen 104 D5
Jubany research station Antarctica 222 U2
long form Teniente Jubany
Jubba r. Somalia 128 D4
also spelt Juba; formerly spelt Giuba
Jubbada Dhexe admin. reg. Somalia 128 D4
Jubbada Hoose admin. reg. Somalia 128 D4
Jubbah Saudi Arabia 104 C1
Jubbulpore India see Jabalpur
Jubilee Lake salt flat Australia 151 D6
Jubing Nepal 97 E4
Juby, Cap c. Morocco 122 B4
Júcar r. Spain 55 K5
Jucara Brazil 206 C2
Jucás Brazil 202 E3
Juchatengo Mex. 185 F5
Juchitán Mex. 184 D4
Juchitlán Mex. 185 F5
Jucurucu Brazil 203 E6
Jucurucu r. Brazil 207 M4
Judaberg Norway 45 I4
Judaidat al Hamir Iraq 107 E5
Judaydah Syria 109 I2
Judaydah waterhole Iraq 109 M5
Judayyidat 'Ar'ar well Iraq 107 E5
Judenburg Austria 49 L8
Judian China 86 A3
Judith r. U.S.A. 180 D3

Judith Gap U.S.A. 180 E3
Juegang China see Rudong
Juego de Bolos mt. Spain 55 H6
Juelsminde Denmark 45 J5
Juerana Brazil 207 N4
Jufari r. Brazil 199 F5
Jugon-les-Lacs France 50 D4
Jugoslavija country Europe see Yugoslavia
Juh China 85 F4
Juhaynah reg. Saudi Arabia 104 B2
Juigalpa Nicaragua 186 B4
Juillac France 50 H7
Juillet, Lac l. Canada 169 I2
Juína Brazil 201 F2
Juína r. Brazil 201 F3
Juist i. Germany 48 E2
Juiz de Fora Brazil 203 D7
Jujuhan r. Indon. 76 C3
Jujuy prov. Arg. 200 D5
Jukkasjärvi Sweden 44 M2
also known as Čohkkiras
Julaca Bol. 200 D5
Julesburg U.S.A. 178 B3
Juli Peru 200 C4
Julia Brazil 199 E5
Juliaca Peru 200 C3
Julia Creek Australia 149 D4
Julian U.S.A. 183 H8
Julian, Lac l. Canada 168 E2
Julian Alps mts Slovenia see Julijske Alpe
Julianatop mt. Indon. see Mandala, Puncak
Juliana Top mt. Suriname 199 G4
Julianehåb Greenland see Qaqortoq
Julijske Alpe mts Slovenia 56 F2
English form Julian Alps
Julimes Mex. 184 D2
Júlio de Castilhos Brazil 203 A9
Juliomagus France see Angers
Júlio Mesquita Brazil 206 D9
Julius, Lake Australia 148 C4
Jullundur India see Jalandhar
Juma r. Brazil 199 E6
Juma China 85 G4
Juma Uzbek. see Dzhuma
Jumanggoin China 86 A1
Jumba Somalia 128 D5
Jumilla Spain 55 J6
Jumla Nepal 97 D3
Jumna r. India see Yamuna
Jumna r. U.S.A. 172 B5
Jumprava Latvia 42 F4
Junagadh India 96 A5
Junagarh India 95 D2
Junan China 85 H5
also known as Shizilu
Jun Bulen China 85 H2
Junction TX U.S.A. 179 C6
Junction UT U.S.A. 183 L3
Junction Bay Australia 148 B1
Junction City KS U.S.A. 178 C4
Junction City KY U.S.A. 176 A8
Junction City OR U.S.A. 180 B3
Jundah Australia 149 D5
Jundiaí Brazil 206 G10

▶**Juneau** U.S.A. 164 F4
State capital of Alaska.

Juneau Icefield Canada 166 C3
Junee Australia 147 E3
Jūn el Khudr b. Lebanon 108 G4
Jungar Qi China see Shagedu
Jungfrau mt. Switz. 51 O6
Junggar Pendi basin China 88 D2
English form Dzungarian Basin
Jungshahi Pak. 101 F5
Junguls Sudan 128 B2
Juniata r. U.S.A. 177 H5
Junik Kosovo, Srbija Yugo. 58 A3
Junín Arg. 204 E4
Junín Peru 200 A2
Junín dept Peru 200 B2
Junior U.S.A. 176 F7
Juniper Mountains U.S.A. 183 K6
Junipero Serro Peak U.S.A. 182 C5
Junkerdalen Balvatnet nature res. Norway
44 K2
Junlian China 86 C2
Junnar India 94 B2
Junosuando Sweden 44 M2
Junqueirópolis Brazil 206 B8
Junsele Sweden 44 L3
Junshan Hu l. China 87 F2
Juntura U.S.A. 180 C4
Junturantta Fin. 44 O2
Junxi China see Datian
Junxian China see Danjiangkou
Ju'nyung China 86 A1
formerly known as Ju'nyunggoin
Ju'nyunggoin China see Ju'nyung
Juodkrantė Lith. 42 C6
Juodšiliai Lith. 42 G7
Juodupė Lith. 42 G5
Juoksengi Sweden 44 M2
Juosta r. Lith. 42 F6
Juostininkai Lith. 42 F6
Juozapinės kalnas hill Lith. 42 G7
Jüpär Iran 100 D4
Juparanã, Lagoa l. Brazil 207 M6
Jupiá Brazil 206 B8
Jupiter U.S.A. 175 D7
Jupiá, Represa resr Brazil 206 B8
Jupiter r. Canada 169 I3
Juquiá Brazil 206 F11
Juquiá r. Brazil 206 F10
Juquitiba Brazil 206 F11
Jur r. Sudan 126 F2
Jura mts France/Switz. 51 L7
Jura r. Lith. 42 D6
Jura i. U.K. 46 G7
Jura, Sound of sea chan. U.K. 46 G8
Juradó Col. 198 B3
Juramento Brazil 207 J3
Juranda Brazil 206 A11
Jurbarkas Lith. 42 D6
Juremal Brazil 202 D4
Jurf ad Darāwīsh Jordan 108 G7
Jurgurra r. Australia 150 B3
Jurh China 85 I2
Jurhen Ul Shan mts China 97 F2
Jüri Estonia 42 F2
Jurien Australia 151 A6
Jurien Bay Australia 151 A6
Jurilovca Romania 58 J4
Juriti Velho Brazil 199 G5
Jūrmala Latvia 42 E4
Jurmu Fin. 44 N2
Jurong China 87 F2
Jurong Sing. 76 [inset]
Jurong, Sungai r. Sing. 76 [inset]
Jurong Island reg. Sing. 76 [inset]
Juruá Brazil 199 E5
Juruá r. Brazil 199 E5
Juruena Brazil 201 F3
Juruena r. Brazil 200 C1
Jurumirim, Represa de resr Brazil 206 E10
Jurupari r. Brazil 200 C1
Juruti Brazil 199 G5
Jurva Fin. 44 M3
Jūsan-ko l. Japan 90 G4
Jusepín Venez. 199 F2
Jussari r. Fin. 42 E2
Jussara r. Brazil 199 E5
Jussey France 51 L5
Justice U.S.A. 176 D8
Justo Daract Arg. 204 D4
Jutaí Brazil 198 D5
Jutaí r. Brazil 198 E5
Jüterbog Germany 49 K4
Juti Brazil 203 A7
Jutiapa Guat. 185 H6
Jutiapa Hond. 186 B4

Juticalpa Hond. 186 B4
Jutis Sweden 44 L2
Jutland pen. Denmark 45 J4
also spelt Jylland
Juuka Fin. 44 O3
Juupajoki Fin. 45 N3
Juurikorpi Fin. 42 H1
Juva Fin. 45 N3
Juwain Afgh. 101 E4
Juwana Indon. 77 E4
Juxian China 85 H5
also known as Chengyang
Juye China 85 H3
Južanoukrajinsk Ukr. see Yuzhnoukrayinsk
Jwaneng Botswana 131 E5
Jylland pen. Denmark see Jutland
Jyrgalang Kyrg. 103 I4
also spelt Dzhergalan
Jyväskylä Fin. 44 N3

↓ K

▶K2 mt. China/Jammu and Kashmir 96 C2
2nd highest mountain in the world and in
Asia. English form Godwin-Austen, Mount;
also known as Qogir Feng.
world [physical features] >> 8–9

Ka r. Nigeria 125 G4
Kaabong Uganda 128 B4
Kaakha Turkm. see Kaka
Kaalpan salt pan S. Africa 132 I6
Kaalrug S. Africa 133 P2
Kaamanen Fin. 44 N1
also known as Gámas
Kaambooni Kenya 128 D5
Kääpa Estonia 42 I4
Kaapmuiden S. Africa 133 P2
Kaapstad S. Africa see Cape Town
Kaarina Fin. 45 M3
Kaarta reg. Mali 124 C3
Kaavi Fin. 44 O3
Kaba China see Habahe
Kaba r. China/Kazakh. 88 D2
Kabaena i. Indon. 75 B4
Kabakly Turkm. 103 E5
also spelt Gabakly
Kabala Sierra Leone 124 C4
Kabale Uganda 128 A5
Kabalega Falls National Park Uganda see
Murchison Falls National Park
Kabalo Dem. Rep. Congo 126 E6
Kabambare Dem. Rep. Congo 127 C6
Kabanbay Kazakh. 88 C2
also spelt Qabanbay; formerly known as
Dzerzhinskoye or Jar-bulak or Zharbulak
Kabanga Dem. Rep. Congo 127 C6
Kabangu Dem. Rep. Congo 127 D7
Kabanjahe Indon. 76 B2
Kabara r. Fiji 145 H3
also spelt Kambara; formerly known as
Appalla
Kabardino-Balkarskaya A.S.S.R. aut. rep.
Rus. Fed. see
Kabardino-Balkarskaya Respublika
Kabardino-Balkarskaya Respublika
aut. rep. Rus. Fed. 41 G8
formerly known as Kabardino-Balkarskaya
A.S.S.R.
Kabardino-Balkarskiy Zapovednik
nature res. Rus. Fed. 107 E2
Kabare Dem. Rep. Congo 126 F5
Kabarega National Park Uganda see
Murchison Falls National Park
Kabasalan Phil. 74 B5
Kabaung r. Myanmar see Kaka
Kabaw Valley Myanmar 78 A3
Kabba Nigeria 125 G5
Kabbani r. India 94 C3
Kâbdalis Sweden 44 M2
Kabd aş Şārim r. Syria 109 N3
Kabd Warqah reg. Syria 109 K3
Kabélawa Niger 125 I3
Kabenung Lake Canada 173 I2
Kaberneeme Estonia 42 G2
Kabertene Alg. 123 F3
Kab-hegy hill Hungary 49 O8
Kabinakagami r. Canada 168 C3
Kabinakagami Lake Canada 168 C3
Kabinda Dem. Rep. Congo 127 E6
Kabir r. Syria 108 G2
Kabirküh mts Iran 100 A3
Kabirwala Pak. 101 G4
Kabli Estonia 42 F3
Kabneshwar India 96 C5
Kabo Cent. Afr. Rep. 126 C3
Kabompo Zambia 127 E8
Kabompo r. Zambia 127 E8
Kabondo-Dianda Dem. Rep. Congo 127 E6
Kabongo Dem. Rep. Congo 127 E6
Kabosa Island Myanmar 79 B5
Kabou Cent. Afr. Rep. 126 C3
Kabou Togo 125 F4
Kabozha Rus. Fed. 43 S3
Kabrousse Senegal 124 A3
Kabshah, Jabal hills Saudi Arabia 104 C2
Kâbud Iran 101 E3
Kâbûd Gonbad Iran 101 E2
also known as Kalât
Kābud Rāhang Iran 100 B3
Kabugao Phil. 74 B2
▶Kābul Afgh. 101 G3
Capital of Afghanistan. Historically known
as Ortospana.

Kābul prov. Afgh. 101 G3
Kabul r. Afgh. 101 H3
Kabunda Dem. Rep. Congo 127 F8
Kabunduk Indon. 75 A5
Kaburuang i. Indon. 75 C2
Kabushiya Sudan 121 G5
Kabûtar Khân Iran 100 D3
Kabwe Zambia 127 F8
formerly known as Broken Hill
Kabyrga r. Kazakh. 103 E2
also spelt Qabyrgha
Kačanik Kosovo/Srbija Yugo. 58 C6
Kacepi Indon. 75 C3
Kacha Kuh mts Iran/Pak. 101 E4
Kachalinskaya Rus. Fed. 41 H6
Kachchh, Great Rann of marsh India see
Kachchh, Rann of
Kachchh, Gulf of India 96 A5
Kachchh, Rann of marsh India 96 A4
also known as Kachchh, Great Rann of; also
spelt Kutch, Rann of
Kachh Pak. 101 F4
Kachhola India 96 B4
Kachhwa India 97 D4
Kachia Nigeria 125 G4
Kachin state Myanmar 78 B2
Kachiry Kazakh. 103 I1
Kachisi Eth. 128 C2
Kacholola Zambia 127 F8
Kachug Rus. Fed. 80 D2
Kaçkar Dağı mt. Turkey 107 E2
Kada r. Poland 49 N4
Kada Japan 91 D7
Kadaingti Myanmar 78 B4

Kadaiyanallur India 94 C4
Kadam mt. Uganda 128 B4
Kadana Chad 120 D6
Kadanai r. Afgh./Pak. 101 F4
Kadan Kyun i. Myanmar 79 B5
Kadapongan i. Indon. 77 F4
Kadaura India 96 C4
Kadavu i. Fiji 145 G3
also spelt Kantavu
Kadavu Passage Fiji 145 G3
also known as Kedairu Passage; also spelt
Kandavu Passage
Kadaya Rus. Fed. 85 H1
Kaddam r. India 94 C2
Kade Ghana 125 E5
Kadéï r. Cent. Afr. Rep. 125 J6
Kadgo, Lake salt flat Australia 151 D5
Kādhimain Iraq see Al Kāzimīyah
Kadi India 96 B5
Kadiana Mali 124 D4
Kadiapattanam India 94 C4
Kadijica mt. Bulg. see Kadiytsa
Kadıköy Turkey 58 H8
historically known as Chalcedon
Kadıköy Turkey 106 B2
Kadiyevka Ukr. see Stakhanov
Kadiytsa mt. Bulg. 58 D7
also known as Kadijica
Kadmat i. India 94 B4
Kadnikov Rus. Fed. 43 V2
Kado Nigeria 125 H5
Ka-do i. N. Korea 83 B5
Kadok Malaysia 76 C1
Kadoka U.S.A. 178 B3
Kadoma Zimbabwe 131 F3
formerly spelt Gatooma
Kadonkani Myanmar 78 A5
Kadrina Estonia 42 H2
Kadugli Sudan 126 F2
Kaduna Nigeria 125 G4
Kaduna r. Nigeria 125 G4
Kaduna state Nigeria 125 G4
Kadur India 94 C3
Kadusam mt. China/India 86 A2
Kaduy Rus. Fed. 43 T3
Kadyy Rus. Fed. 40 H4
Kadzherom Rus. Fed. 40 J2
Kadzhi-Say Kyrg. see Kajy-Say
Kaechon N. Korea 83 B5
Kaédi Mauritania 124 B2
Kaegudeck Lake Canada 169 K3
Kaélé Cameroon 125 I4
Kaena Point U.S.A. 181 [inset] Y1
Kaeng Krachan National Park Thai. 79 B5
Kaeo N.Z. 152 H3
Kaesŏng N. Korea 83 B5
Kafa Ukr. see Feodosiya
Kafakumba Dem. Rep. Congo 127 D7
Kafan Armenia see Kapan
Kafanchan Nigeria 125 H4
Kafferrivier S. Africa 133 K6
Kaffin-Hausa Nigeria 125 H3
Kaffir r. S. Africa 133 J6
Kaffrine Senegal 124 A3
Kafia Kingi Sudan 126 D2
Kafiau i. Indon. 75 D3
Kafireas, Akra pt Greece 59 F10
Kafireos, Steno sea chan. Greece 59 F11
Kafiristan reg. Pak. 101 G3
also known as Kofarnihon
Kafjordbotn Norway 44 M1
Kafolo Côte d'Ivoire 124 D4
Kafr el Battikh Egypt 108 C6
Kafr el Garayda Egypt 108 B6
Kafr el Sheikh Egypt 108 C6
Kafr el Sheikh governorate Egypt 108 B6
Kafr el Zaiyât Egypt 108 B7
Kafret Rihama Egypt 121 E2
Kafr Silim Egypt 108 C6
Kafu r. Uganda 128 B4
Kafue Zambia 127 F8
Kafue r. Zambia 127 F8
Kafue Flats marsh Zambia 127 E8
Kafue National Park Zambia 127 E8
Kaga Japan 91 E6
Kaga Bandoro Cent. Afr. Rep. 126 C3
formerly known as Fort Crampel
Kagan Uzbek. 103 F5
also spelt Kogon
Kagang China 84 D5
Kaganovich Rus. Fed. see Tovarkovskiy
Kaganovichabad Tajik. see Kolkhozobod
Kaganovichi Pervyye Ukr. see Polis'ke
Kagarlyk Ukr. see Kaharlyk
Kagawa pref. Japan 91 D7
Kagawong Canada 173 K5
Kåge Sweden 44 M2
Kagera admin. reg. Tanz. 128 A5
Kagera, Parc National de la nat. park
Rwanda see Akagera National Park
Kagiso S. Africa 133 L3
Kağızman Turkey 107 E2
Kagmar Sudan 121 F6
Kagologolo Indon. 76 B3
Kagoshima Japan 91 B9
Kagoshima airport Japan 91 B9
Kagoshima pref. Japan 91 B9
Kagoshima-wan b. Japan 91 B9
Kagul Moldova see Cahul
Kaharlyk Ukr. 41 E6
also spelt Kagarlyk
Kahatola i. Indon. 75 C2
Kahawero waterhole Namibia 130 B3
Kahayan r. Indon. 77 F3
Kahemba Dem. Rep. Congo 127 C6
Kahla Germany 48 I5
Kahnûj Iran 100 D4
also known as Kahnu
Kahnu Iran see Kahnûj
Kahnuj Iran 100 D5
also known as Kahnu
Kahoka U.S.A. 174 B3
Kahoolawe i. U.S.A. 181 [inset] Z1
also spelt Kahulaui; formerly known as
Tahaurawe
Kahperusvaarat mts Fin. 38 C3
Kahramanmaraş Turkey 107 D3
formerly known as Maraş; historically known
as Germanica
Kahror Pak. 101 G4
Kahta Turkey 107 D3
Kahugish well Iran 100 D3
Kahuku Point U.S.A. 181 [inset] Y1
Kahul, Ozero l. Ukr. 58 J3
Kahulaui i. U.S.A. see Kahoolawe
Kahului U.S.A. 181 [inset] Z1
Kahûrak Iran 101 D4
Kahurangi National Park N.Z. 152 G9
formerly known as North West Nelson
Forest Park
Kahuta Pak. 101 H3
Kahuzi-Biega, Parc National du nat. park
Dem. Rep. Congo 126 F5
Kai, Kepulauan is Indon. 73 H8
Kaia r. Sudan 128 A3
Kaiama Nigeria 125 F4

Kaiapit P.N.G. 73 K8
Kaiapoi N.Z. 153 G11
Kaibab U.S.A. 183 L5
Kaibamardang China 84 C4
Kaibara Japan 91 D7
Kai Besar i. Indon. 73 H8
Kaibito Plateau U.S.A. 183 M5
Kaidu He r. China 88 D3
Kaieda r. Indon. as Karanakar
Kaieteur Falls Guyana 199 G3
Kaifeng Henan China 87 E1
also known as Huanglongsi
Kaifeng Henan China 87 E1
Kaihu N.Z. 152 H3
Kaihua China see Wenshan
Kaihua China 87 F2
Kaijiang China 87 C2
Kaiingveld reg. S. Africa 132 F6
also spelt Galaynor
Kai Kecil i. Indon. 73 H8
Kai Keung Leng Hong Kong China
87 [inset]
Kaikohe N.Z. 152 H3
Kaikoura N.Z. 153 H10
Kaikoura Peninsula N.Z. 153 H10
Kailahun Sierra Leone 124 C4
Kailas mt. China see Kangrinboqê Feng
Kailas Range mts China see Gangdisê Shan
Kaili China 87 C3
Kailongong waterhole Kenya 128 B3
Kailu China 85 I3
Kailua U.S.A. 181 [inset] Z1
Kailua Kona U.S.A. 181 [inset] Z2
Kaimai-Mamaku Forest Park nature res.
N.Z. 152 J5
Kaimai Range hills N.Z. 152 J5
Kaimana Indon. 73 H7
Kaimanawa Forest Park nature res. N.Z.
152 K6
Kaimanawa Mountains N.Z. 152 J7
Kaimar China 97 G2
Kaimganj India 96 C4
Kaimon-dake vol. Japan 91 B9
Kaimur Range hills India 97 D4
Käina Estonia 42 D3
Kainan Tokushima Japan 91 D8
Kainan Wakayama Japan 91 D7
Kainda Kyrg. see Kayyngdy
Kaindy Kyrg. see Kayyngdy
Kaingaroa Forest N.Z. 152 K6
Kaingiwa Nigeria 125 F3
Kainji Lake National Park Nigeria 125 G4
Kainji Reservoir Nigeria 125 G4
Kaintaragarh India 95 E1
Kaipara Harbour N.Z. 152 I4
Kaiparowits Plateau U.S.A. 183 M4
Kaiping China 87 E4
Kaiping China see Dêqên
Kaipokok Bay Canada 169 J2
Kaira India see Kheda
Kairakau Beach N.Z. 152 K7
Kairana India 96 C3
Kairatu Indon. 75 D3
Kairouan Tunisia 123 H2
Kaisepakte Sweden 44 L1
Kaiserslautern Germany 48 E6
Kaiser Wilhelm II Land reg. Antarctica
223 F2
Kaishantun China 82 C4
Kaišiadorys Lith. 42 F7
Kait, Tanjung pt Indon. 77 D3
Kaitaia N.Z. 152 H3
Kaitangata N.Z. 153 D14
Kaitawa N.Z. 152 L6
Kaithal India 96 C3
Kaitha India 96 C3
Kaitong China see Tongyu
Kaitum r. Sweden 44 M2
Kaitumälven r. Sweden 44 M2
Kaiwatu Indon. 75 C5
Kaiwi Channel U.S.A. 181 [inset] Z1
Kaixian China 87 D2
also known as Hanfeng
Kaiyang China 86 C3
Kaiyuan Liaoning China 85 J3
Kaiyuan Yunnan China 86 B4
Kajaani Myanmar 78 A3
Kajabbi Australia 149 D4
Kajaki Afgh. 101 F3
Kajang Malaysia 76 C2
Kajdar Iran 101 E3
Kajiado Kenya 128 C5
Kajo Kaji Sudan 128 B3
Kaju Iran 100 A2
Kajuligah Nature Reserve Australia 147 E3
Kajy-Say Kyrg. 103 I4
also known as Kadzhi-Say
Kak, Ozero salt l. Kazakh. 103 F1
also known as Qaq Köli
Kaka Sudan 128 B2
Kaka Turkm. 102 D5
formerly spelt Kaakha
Kakaban i. Indon. 77 G2
Kakabeka Falls Canada 168 B3
Kakabia i. Indon. 75 B4
Kakadu Aboriginal Land res. Australia
148 B2
Kakadu National Park Australia 148 B2
Kakagi Lake Canada 168 A3
Kakal r. Phil. 74 C5
Kakamas S. Africa 132 E5
Kakamega Kenya 128 B4
Kakamigahara Japan 91 E7
Kakamoéka Congo 126 A6
Kakana India 95 G4
Kakanj Bos.-Herz. 56 K4
Kakanui Mountains N.Z. 153 E13
Kakarahil well Niger 125 H3
Kakaramea N.Z. 152 I7
Kakaramea vol. N.Z. 152 J6
Kakata Liberia 124 C5
Kakatahi N.Z. 152 I7
Kakching India 97 C4
Kake Japan 91 C7
Kakenge Dem. Rep. Congo 126 D6
Kakesio Tanz. 128 B5
Kakhi Azer. see Qax
Kakhovka Ukr. 41 E7
Kakhovs'ke Vodoskhovyshche resr Ukr.
41 E7
Kakhul Moldova see Cahul
Kāki Iran 100 B4
Kakinada India 95 D2
also spelt Cocanada
Kakinjes, Maja nt. Albania 58 A6
Kakisa r. Canada 167 G2
Kakisa Lake Canada 167 G2
Kakogawa Japan 91 D7
Kakonko N. Korea see Tongyu
Kakpin Côte d'Ivoire 124 E4
Kakrala India 96 C3
Kakrima r. Guinea 124 B4
Kakshaal-Too mts China/Kyrg. see
Kokshaal-Tau
Kakuda Japan 90 G5
Kakuma Kenya 128 B4
Kakus r. Sarawak Malaysia 77 F2
Kakwa r. Canada 166 G4
Kal hill Croatia 56 G3
Kala Tanz. 129 A7
Kalaâ Kebira Tunisia 123 H2
Kalaallit Nunaat terr. N. America see
Greenland
Kalabagh Pak. 101 G3
Kalabahi Indon. 75 C5
Kalabak mt. Bulg./Greece see Radomir
Kalabáka Greece see Kalampaka
Kalabakan Sabah Malaysia 77 G1
Kalabaydh Togdheer Somalia 128 E3
Kalabaydh Woqooyi Galbeed Somalia 128 D2

Kalabo Zambia 127 D8
Kalach Rus. Fed. 41 G6
Kalacha Dida Kenya 128 C4
Kalach-na-Donu Rus. Fed. 41 G6
Kaladan r. India/Myanmar 95 G1
Kaladar Canada 168 E4
Kaladgi India 94 B2
Kalaena r. Indon. 75 B3
Kalahan Myanmar 78 B3
▶Kalahari Desert Africa 130 D4
world [population] >> 22–23
Kalahari Gemsbok National Park S. Africa
132 E2
Kalaikhum Tajik. see Qal'aikhum
Kalai-Khumb Tajik. see Qal'aikhum
Kala-I-Mor Turkm. 101 E3
also known as Qal'aikhum
Kalam Pak. 101 H3
Kalamare Botswana 131 E4
Kalamaria Greece 58 D8
Kalamata Greece 59 D11
also known as Kalámai
Kalamazoo U.S.A. 172 H8
Kalamazoo r. U.S.A. 172 G8
Kalambari i. Indon. 77 F4
Kalamnuri India 94 C2
Kalamos i. Greece 59 B10
Kalamos, Akra pt Greece 59 G12
Kalampaka Greece 59 C9
also known as Kalabáka
Kalana Estonia 42 D3
Kalana Mali 124 D4
Kalanaur Haryana India 89 B6
Kalanaur Punjab India 96 B3
Kalanchak pt Ukr. 41 E7
Kalandula Angola see Calandula
Kalangala Uganda 128 B5
Kalangali Tanz. 129 B6
Kalannie Australia 151 B6
Kalanwali India 96 B3
Kalao i. Indon. 75 B4
Kalaong Phil. 74 C5
Kalaotoa i. Indon. 75 B4
Kala Oya r. Sri Lanka 94 C4
Kalapana U.S.A. 181 [inset] Z2
Kalar watercourse Iran 101 E5
Kalār Iraq 107 F3
Kalarash Moldova see Călăraşi
Kalashnikovo Rus. Fed. 43 Q4
Kalasin Thai. 78 C4
Kalāt Iran 101 D5
Kalat Balochistan Pak. 101 F4
Kalat Balochistan Pak. 101 F5
Kalat, Küh-e mt. Iran 100 D3
Kalaus r. Rus. Fed. 41 H7
Kalavad India 96 A5
Kalavryta Greece 59 D10
Kalb, Ra's al c. Yemen 105 G5
Kalba U.A.E. 105 G2
Kālbăcār Azer. 107 F2
Kalbarri Australia 151 A5
Kalbatänai r. Lith. 42 G7
Kaltanénai Lith. 42 D6
Kalbinskiy Khrebet mts Kazakh. 148 C2
Kalbū Iran 100 D3
Kaldirim Turkey 108 G1
Kale r. N.Z. see Qalbi Zho̧asy
Kale Turkey 106 B3
Kaledupa i. Indon. 75 B4
Kalegauk Island Myanmar 79 B5
Kaleindaung inlet Myanmar 78 A4
Kalema Dem. Rep. Congo 126 E6
Kalémié Dem. Rep. Congo 127 F6
formerly known as Albertville
Kalemyo Myanmar 78 A3
Kalemoye Kazakh. 102 A3
Kalesija Bos.-Herz. 56 K4
Kalevala Rus. Fed. 44 O2
formerly known as Ukhta
Kaleybar Iran 100 A2
Kalga Rus. Fed. 85 H1
Kalgan r. Australia 151 B7
Kalgan China see Zhangjiakou
Kalghatgi India 94 B3
Kalgoorlie Australia 151 C6
Kaliakra, Nos pt Bulg. 58 J5
Kali Croatia 56 H4
Kali r. India/Nepal 96 D3
Kalianda Indon. 77 D4
Kalibo Phil. 74 B4
Kaliet Indon. 76 B3
Kali Gandaki r. Nepal 97 E3
Kaligiri India 94 C3
Kalikino Rus. Fed. 43 U9
Kalima Dem. Rep. Congo 126 E5
Kalimantan reg. Indon. 77 E2
Kalimantan Barat prov. Indon. 77 E2
Kalimantan Selatan prov. Indon. 77 F3
Kalimantan Tengah prov. Indon. 77 F3
Kalimantan Timur prov. Indon. 77 F2
Kalimedence park Hungary 49 O9
Kálimnos i. Greece see Kalymnos
Kalimpang India 97 F4
Kalinadi r. India 94 B3
Kali Nadi r. India 96 C4
Kalinin Kyrg. see Eshanguzar
Kalinin Rus. Fed. see Tver'
Kalinin Turkm. see Boldumsaz
Kalininabad Tajik. see Kalininobod
Kaliningrad Rus. Fed. 42 B7
historically known as Königsberg
see Kaliningrad Oblast admin. div.
Kaliningradskaya Oblast' admin. div.
Rus. Fed. 42 C7
Kaliningradskiy Zaliv b. Rus. Fed. 42 A7
Kalinino Armenia see Tashir
Kalinino Kostromskaya Oblast' Rus. Fed.
40 G4
Kalinino Omskaya Oblast' Rus. Fed. 103 H1
Kalinino Permskaya Oblast' Rus. Fed. 40 K4
Kalininobod Tajik. 101 G2
English form Kalininabad
Kalininsk Rus. Fed. 41 H6
formerly known as Balanda
Kalininskaya Rus. Fed. 41 F7
formerly known as Popovichskaya
Kalininskaya Oblast' admin. div. Rus. Fed.
see Tverskaya Oblast'
Kalinjara India 96 B5
Kalinkavichy Belarus 43 K9
also known as Kalinkovichi
Kalinkovichi Belarus see Kalinkavichy
Kalinovka Kazakh. 103 F1
also spelt Qalino
Kalinovo Slovakia 49 Q7
Kalipucang Indon. 77 E4
Kali Sindh r. India 96 C4
Kalispell U.S.A. 180 D2
Kalisz Poland 49 P4
also spelt Kalish
Kalisz Pomorski Poland 49 M2
Kalitva r. Rus. Fed. 41 G6

Kaliua Tanz. 129 A6
Kaliwari mt. N. Korea see Kwanmo-bong
Kalix Sweden 44 M2
Kalixälven r. Sweden 44 M2
Kalka India 96 C3
Kalkan Turkey 106 C3
Kalkaringi Australia 148 A3
Kalkaska U.S.A. 173 H6
Kalkfeld Namibia 130 C4
Kalkfeldpan S. Africa 133 J6
Kalkfontein Dam Nature Reserve S. Africa
133 J6
Kalkwerf S. Africa 132 F5
Kallakkurichh India see Kallakurichi
Kallakoopah Creek watercourse Australia
146 C1
Kallakurichi India 94 C4
Kallam India 94 C2
Kallang Sing. 76 [inset]
Kallang r. Sing. 76 [inset]
Kallaste Estonia 42 I3
Kallavesi l. Fin. 44 N3
Kållberget Sweden 44 K3
Kallifoni Greece 59 C9
Kallini Greece 59 C11
Kallir India 94 C1
Kalloni Greece 59 G9
Kallonis, Kolpos b. Greece 59 H9
Kallsjön l. Sweden 44 J2
Kallur India 94 C2
Kalmakkyrgan watercourse Kazakh. 103 F3
Kalmar Sweden 45 L4
Kalmar county Sweden 45 L4
Kalmarsund sea chan. Sweden 45 L4
Kalmthoutse Heide Natuurreservaat
nature res. Belgium 51 L1
Kalmunai Sri Lanka 94 D5
Kalmykia aut. rep. Rus. Fed. see
Kalmykiya - Khalm'g-Tangch, Respublika
Kalmykiya - Khalm'g-Tangch, Respublika
aut. rep. Rus. Fed. 41 H7
English form Kalmykiya; formerly known as
Kalmytskaya Avtonomnaya Oblast'
Kalmykovo Kazakh. see Taypak
Kalmytskaya Avtonomnaya Oblast'
aut. rep. Rus. Fed. see
Kalmykiya - Khalm'g-Tangch, Respublika
Kalnai Indon. 97 D5
Kalnciems Latvia 42 E5
Kalni r. Bangl. 97 F4
Kalnik mts Croatia 56 I2
Kaloko Dem. Rep. Congo 127 E6
Kaloko r. Dem. Rep. Congo 127 C6
Kaloma i. Indon. 75 C2
Kaloma Tanz. 129 A6
Kalomo Zambia 127 E9
Kalona U.S.A. 172 B5
Kalone Peak Canada 166 E4
Kalopanagiotis Cyprus 108 D3
Kalozhnoye, Ozero l. Rus. Fed. 44 O2
Kalpa India see Chini
Kalpeni i. India 94 B4
Kalpetta India 94 C4
Kalpi India 96 C4
Kalpin China see Kalpin
Kalquduq Uzbek. see Kulkuduk
Kalt Iran 101 D5
Kaltag U.S.A. 164 D3
Kaltenkirchen Germany 48 G2
Kaltungo Nigeria 125 H4
Kaluga Rus. Fed. 43 S6
Kaluga Oblast admin. div. Rus. Fed. see
Kaluzhskaya Oblast'
Kalukalukuang i. Indon. 77 G4
Kaluku Indon. 75 A3
Kalulong, Bukit mt. Sarawak Malaysia 77 F2
Kalulushi Zambia 127 E7
Kalumburu Australia 150 C2
Kalumburu Aboriginal Reserve Australia
150 C3
Kalundborg Denmark 45 J5
Kalupis Falls Sabah Malaysia 77 G1
Kalur Kot Pak. 101 G3
Kalush Ukr. 41 C6
Kaluszyn Poland 49 S3
Kalutara Sri Lanka 94 C5
Kaluzhskaya Oblast' admin. div. Rus. Fed.
43 O7
English form Kaluga Oblas
Kalvág Norway 45 I3
Kalvan India 94 B1
Kalvarija Lith. 42 E7
Kälviä Fin. 42 G7
Kälviä Fin. 40 D3
Kalvitsa Fin. 45 N3
Kalvola Fin. 45 N3
Kalwakurti India 94 C2
Kalyan India 94 B2
Kalyandurg India 94 C3
Kalyani India 94 C3
Kalyansingapuram India 95 D2
Kalyazin Rus. Fed. 43 S4
Kalymnos i. Greece 59 H12
Kalymnos r. Greece 59 H11
also spelt Kálimnos
Kalyshki Belarus 43 L6
Kama Dem. Rep. Congo 126 F5
Kama Myanmar 78 A4
▶Kama r. Rus. Fed. 40 J4
4th longest river in Europe.
europe [landscapes] >> 30–31
Kamaishi Japan 90 G5
Kamakura Japan 91 F7
Kamakusa Guyana 199 F3
Kamakwie Sierra Leone 124 C4
Kamal Chad 120 C6
Kamalapuram India 94 C3
Kamalia Pak. 101 H4
Kamamaung Myanmar 78 B4
Kaman India 96 C4
Kaman Turkey 106 C3
Kamanassie r. S. Africa 132 G10
Kamanassieberg mts S. Africa 132 G10
Kamanassie Lake Canada 173 P5
Kamanjab Namibia 130 B3
Kamaran Yemen 104 C5
Kamarán i. Yemen 104 C5
English form Kamaran Island
Kamarang Guyana 199 F3
Kamaran Island Yemen see Kamarán
Kamard reg. Afgh. 101 F3
Kamareddi India 94 C2
Kamares Dytiki Ellas Greece 59 C10
Kamares Sifnos Greece 59 F12
Kamaria Falls Guyana 199 G3
Kamarlu Armenia see Artashat
Kamas U.S.A. 183 M1
Kamashi Uzbek. 103 F5
also spelt Qamashi
Kamativi Zimbabwe 131 E3
Kamba Nigeria 125 F4
Kamba Kota Cent. Afr. Rep. 126 C3
Kambalda Australia 151 C6
Kambam India 94 C4
Kambang Indon. 76 C3
Kambangan i. Indon. 77 E5
Kambara i. Fiji see Kabara
Kambarka Rus. Fed. 40 J4
Kambia Sierra Leone 124 B4

Kambing, Pulau i. East Timor see Atauro
Kambo-san mt. N. Korea see Kwanmo-bong
Kambove Dem. Rep. Congo 127 E7
Kamburovo Bulg. 58 H5
Kambût Libya 120 E2
Kamchatka r. Rus. Fed. 39 Q4
Kamchatka, Poluostrov pen. Rus. Fed. see
Kamchatka Peninsula
▶Kamchatka Peninsula Rus. Fed. 39 P4
also known as Kamchatka, Poluostrov
asia [threats] >> 70–71
Kamchatskiy Proliv strait Rus. Fed. 39 Q4
Kamchatskiy Zaliv b. Rus. Fed. 39 Q4
Kamchiya r. Bulg. 58 I5
Kamchiyska Planina hills Bulg. 58 I6
Kamdesh Afgh. 101 H3
Kameia, Parque Nacional de nat. park
Angola see Cameia, Parque Nacional da
Kamelik r. Rus. Fed. 102 B1
Kamen Bulg. 58 G5
Kamen', Gory mts Rus. Fed. 39 J3
Kamende Dem. Rep. Congo 127 E6
Kamenets-Podol'skiy Ukr. see
Kam"yanets-Podil's'kyy
Kamenitsa r. Bulg. 58 F5
Kamenjak, Rt pt Croatia 56 F4
Kamenka Arkhangel'skaya Oblast' Rus. Fed.
40 H2
Kamenka Kaluzhskaya Oblast' Rus. Fed.
43 Q7
Kamenka Leningradskaya Oblast' Rus. Fed.
43 K1
Kamenka Lipetskaya Oblast' Rus. Fed. 43 T9
Kamenka Penzenskaya Oblast' Rus. Fed.
41 H5
Kamenka Primorskiy Kray Rus. Fed. 82 E3
Kamenka Smolenskaya Oblast' Rus. Fed.
43 N6
Kamenka-Bugskaya Ukr. see
Kam"yanka-Buz'ka
Kamenka-Strumilovskaya Ukr. see
Kam"yanka-Buz'ka
Kamenki Rus. Fed. 43 S5
Kamen'-na-Obi Rus. Fed. 80 C2
Kamenniki Rus. Fed. 43 T3
Kamennogorsk Rus. Fed. 43 K1
Kamennomostskiy Rus. Fed. 41 G7
Kamennoye, Ozero l. Rus. Fed. 44 O2
Kameno Bulg. 58 I5
Kamenongue Angola see Camanongue
Kamen'-Rybolov Rus. Fed. 82 D3
Kamenskiy Rus. Fed. 41 H6
Kamenskoye Koryakskiy Avtonomnyy Okrug
Rus. Fed. 39 Q3
Kamenskoye Zaporiz'ka Oblast' Rus. Fed.
43 T9
Kamenskoye Ukr. see Dniprodzerzhyns'k
Kamensk-Shakhtinskiy Rus. Fed. 41 G6
Kamensk-Ural'skiy Rus. Fed. 38 G4
Kamenz Germany 49 L4
Kameoka Japan 91 E7
Kamëz Albania 58 A7
Kameyama Japan 91 E7
Kamiah U.S.A. 180 C3
Kamienna r. Poland 49 S4
Kamień Pomorski Poland 49 L2
historically known as Cammin
Kamiesberg S. Africa 132 C7
Kamiesberg mts S. Africa 132 C7
Kamieskroon S. Africa 132 C6
Kamifurano Japan 90 H3
Kamikawa Japan 90 H3
Kamileroi Australia 149 D4
Kamina Dem. Rep. Congo 127 E7
Kamina Base Dem. Rep. Congo 127 E7
Kaminak Lake Canada 167 M2
Kaminokuni Japan 90 G4
Kaminoyama Japan 90 G5
Kaminške in Savinjske Alpe mts Slovenia
56 G2
Kaminuriak Lake Canada see
Qamanirjuaq Lake
Kamioka Japan 91 E6
Kamiros Greece 59 I12
Kamishihoro Japan 90 H3
Kamitsushima Japan 91 A7
Kamituga Dem. Rep. Congo 126 F5
Kamkaly Kazakh. 103 G3
Kamla r. India 97 E4
Kamla r. India 97 F4
Kamloops Canada 166 F5
Kamloops Lake Canada 166 F5
Kammuri-yama mt. Japan 91 C7
Kamnik Slovenia 56 G2
Kamo Armenia 107 F2
formerly known as Gavarr or Nor-Bayazet
Kamo N.Z. 152 I3
Kamob Sanha Sudan 121 H5
Kamogawa Japan 90 G3
Kamogawa Japan 91 G7
Kamoke Pak. 101 H4
Kamola Dem. Rep. Congo 127 E6
Kamonanira Tanz. 129 A6
Kamp r. Austria 49 M7

269

Kamyshla Rus. Fed. 41 J5
Kamyshlybash Kazakh. 103 E3
also spelt Qamyslybas; formerly spelt Kamyslybas
Kamysh-Samarskiye Ozera l. Kazakh. 102 B2
Kamyshnoye Kazakh. 103 E2
Kamyslybas Kazakh. see Kamyshlybash
Kamyslybas, Ozero l. Kazakh. 103 E3
Kamzyzak Rus. Fed. 102 B3
Kamzar Oman 105 G2
Kan r. Rus. Fed. 80 F2
Kan Sudan 128 A2
Kana r. Zimbabwe 131 E3
Kana, Bukit mt. Sarawak Malaysia 77 F2
Kanaaupscow r. Canada 169 E2
Kanab U.S.A. 183 L4
Kanab Creek r. U.S.A. 183 L5
Kanagawa pref. Japan 90 F7
Kanagi Japan 90 G4
Kanaima Falls Guyana 199 F3
Kanairiktok r. Canada 169 J2
Kanakapura India 94 C3
Kanala Greece 59 F11
Kanallaki Greece 59 B9
Kanan Sweden 44 K3
Kanana S. Africa 133 K3
Kananga Dem. Rep. Congo 127 D6
formerly known as Luluabourg
Kanangra-Boyd National Park Australia 147 F3
Kanarak India see Konarka
Kanarraville U.S.A. 183 K4
Kanash Rus. Fed. 40 H5
Kanas watercourse Namibia 132 B4
Kanas Köl l. China 88 D1
Kanawha r. U.S.A. 176 C7
Kanazawa Japan 91 E6
Kanbalu Myanmar 78 A3
Kanchanaburi Thai. 79 B5
Kanchanjunga mt. India/Nepal see Kangchenjunga
Kanchipuram India 94 C3
Kańczuga Poland 49 T6
Kand mt. Pak. 101 F4
Kandahār Afgh. 101 F4
also spelt Qandahar; historically known as Alexandria Arachoton
Kandahar India see Gandhidham
Kandalaksha Rus. Fed. 44 P2
Kandalakshskiy Zaliv g. Rus. Fed. 40 E2
Kandalakshskiy Zapovednik nature res. Rus. Fed. 44 P2
Kandang Indon. 76 B2
Kandangan Indon. 77 F3
Kandava Latvia 42 D4
Kandavu Passage Fiji see Kadavu Passage
Kandé Togo 125 F4
Kandhkot Pak. 101 G4
Kandi Benin 125 F4
Kandi, Tanjung pt Indon. 75 B2
Kandiaro Pak. 101 G5
Kandila Dytiki Ellas Greece 59 C10
Kandila Peloponnisos Greece 59 D11
Kandil Bouzou well Niger 125 H3
Kandra Turkey 106 B2
Kandja Cent. Afr. Rep. 126 D3
Kandla India 96 A5
Kandos Australia 147 F3
Kandra India 95 E1
Kandreho Madag. 131 [inset] J3
Kandri India 97 D5
Kandrian P.N.G. 145 D2
Kandukur India 94 C3
Kandy Sri Lanka 94 D5
Kandyagash Kazakh. 102 D2
also spelt Qandyaghash; formerly known as Oktyabr' or Oktyabr'sk
Kane U.S.A. 176 H4
Kane Bassin b. Greenland see Kane Bassin
Kane Bassin b. Greenland 165 M2
English form Kane Basin
Kaneh watercourse Iran 100 C5
Kanem pref. Chad 120 B5
Kaneohe U.S.A. 181 [inset] Z1
Kanevskaya Rus. Fed. 41 F7
Kaneyama Japan 90 G5
Kang Botswana 130 D4
Kanga r. Bangl. 97 F5
Kangaamiut Greenland 165 N3
Kangaarsussuaq c. Greenland 165 L2
also known as Parry, Kap
Kangaatsiaq Greenland 165 N3
Kangaba Mali 124 C4
Kangal Turkey 107 D3
Kangalassy Rus. Fed. 39 M3
Kangān Büshehr Iran 100 C5
Kangān Hormozgan Iran 100 D5
Kangan Aboriginal Reserve Australia 150 B4
Kangandala, Parque Nacional de nat. park Angola see Cangandala, Parque Nacional de
Kangar Malaysia 76 C1
Kangare Mali 124 C4
Kangaroo Island Australia 146 C3
Kangaroo Point Australia 148 C3
Kangaruma Guyana 199 G3
Kangasala Fin. 45 N3
Kangaslampi Fin. 44 O3
Kangasniemi Fin. 45 N3
Kangavar Iran 100 A3
Kangayam India 94 C4
Kangbao China 85 G3

▶Kangchenjunga mt. India/Nepal 97 F4
3rd highest mountain in the world and in Asia. Also spelt Kanchanjanga.
world [physical features] ▶▶ 8–9

Kangding China 86 B2
also known as Dardo or Lucheng
Kangean, Kepulauan is Indon. 77 F4
Kangen r. Sudan 128 B3

Kangeq c. Greenland 165 O3
Kangerluarsoruseq Greenland 165 N3
also known as Færingehavn
Kangerlussuaq Greenland 165 N3
also known as Søndre Strømfjord
Kangerlussuaq inlet Greenland 165 N2
also known as Giesecke Isfjord
Kangerlussuaq Greenland 165 N3
also known as Søndre Strømfjord
Kangerlussuaq inlet Greenland 165 P3
also known as Gyldenløves Fjord
Kangerlussuatsiaq inlet Greenland 165 O3
Kangersuatsiaq Greenland 165 N2
also known as Prøven
Kangertittivaq sea chan. Greenland 165 Q2
also known as Scoresby Sund
Kangertittivatsiaq inlet Greenland 165 P3
Kangetet Kenya 128 C4
Kanggye N. Korea 83 B4
Kangikajik c. Greenland 165 Q2
also known as Brewster, Kap
Kangilinnguit Greenland 165 O3
Kangiqsualujjuaq Canada 169 H1
formerly known as Port-Nouveau-Québec
Kangiqsujuaq Canada 165 L3
formerly known as Maricourt or Wakeham
Kangirsuk Canada 165 L3
formerly known as Bellin or Payne
Kang Krung National Park Thai. 79 B6
Kangle China 84 D5
Kangle China see Wanzai
Kanglong China 86 A1
Kangmar China 89 E6
Kangmar China see Kangxian
Kangnŭng S. Korea 83 C5
Kango Gabon 126 A4
Kangping China 85 I3
Kangra India 96 C2
Kangri Karpo Pass China/India 86 A2
Kangrinboqê Feng mt. China 89 C5
also known as Kailas
Kangsangdobdê China see Xainza
Kang Tipayan Dakula i. Phil. 74 A5
Kangto mt. China/India 89 F7
Kangtog China 89 D5
Kangxian China 86 C1
also known as Zuitai; formerly known as Zuitaizi
Kangxiwar China 89 B4
Kangyidaung Myanmar 78 A4
Kanhan r. India 96 C5
Kanhar r. India 97 D4
Kani Côte d'Ivoire 124 D4
Kani Myanmar 78 A3
Kaniama Dem. Rep. Congo 127 E6
Kanibadam Tajik. 101 G1
also spelt Konibodom
Kanibongan Sabah Malaysia 77 G1
Kaniere N.Z. 153 F10
Kanifing Gambia 124 A3
Kanigiri India 94 C3
Kanimekh Uzbek. 103 F4
Kanin, Poluostrov pen. Rus. Fed. 40 H2
Kanin Nos Rus. Fed. 40 H2
Kanin Nos, Mys c. Rus. Fed. 40 G1
Kaninskiy Bereg coastal area Rus. Fed. 40 G2
Kanita Japan 90 G4
Kaniva Australia 146 D4
Kanjiroba mt. Nepal 97 D3
Kanjiža Vojvodina, Srbija Yugo. 58 B2
also known as Magyarkanizsa
Kankaanpää Fin. 45 M3
Kankakee U.S.A. 174 C3
Kankakee r. U.S.A. 174 B3
Kankan Guinea 124 C4
Kankesanturai Sri Lanka 94 D4
Kankiya Nigeria 125 G3
Kankossa Mauritania 124 C3
Kanmaw Kyun i. Myanmar 79 B6
also known as Kisseraing Island
Kanmuri-yama mt. Japan 91 C7
also known as Kammuri-yama
Kannad India 94 B1
Kannapolis U.S.A. 174 D5
Kannauj India 96 C4
also known as Kanyakubja
Kanniyakumari India 94 C4
Kanniya Kumari r. India see Comorin, Cape
Kannod India 96 C5
Kannonkoski Fin. 44 N3
Kannur r. India see Cannanore
Kannus Fin. 44 M3
Kannuskoski Fin. 42 I1
Kano Nigeria 125 H3
Kano r. Nigeria 125 H4
Kano state Nigeria 125 H4
Kanona Zambia 127 F8
Kanonerka Kazakh. 103 I2
Kanonpunt pt S. Africa 132 F11
Kanor India 96 B4
Kanosh U.S.A. 183 L3
Kanovlei Namibia 130 C3
Kanowit Sarawak Malaysia 77 F2
Kanoya Japan 91 B9
Kanpur India 96 D4
also known as Cawnpore
Kanpur Pak. 101 G4
Kanrach reg. Pak. 101 F5
Kansai airport Japan 91 D7
Kansanshi Zambia 127 E8
Kansas r. U.S.A. 178 D4
Kansas state U.S.A. 178 C4
Kansas City KS U.S.A. 178 D4
Kansas City MO U.S.A. 178 D4
Kansenia Dem. Rep. Congo 127 E7
Kansk Rus. Fed. 80 F1
Kansu China 80 H1
Kansu prov. China see Gansu
Kanta mt. Eth. 128 B3
Kantala Fin. 44 N3
Kantang Thai. 79 B7
Kantara hill Cyprus 108 E2
Kantaralak Thai. 79 D5
Kantavu i. Fiji see Kadavu
Kantchari Burkina 125 F3
Kantemirovka Rus. Fed. 41 F6
Kanth India 96 C3
Kanti India 97 E4
Kantishna r. U.S.A. 164 D3
Kanton i. Kiribati 145 H2
also known as Abariringa; formerly spelt Canton Island
Kan-Too, Pik mt. Kazakh./Kyrg. see Khan-Tengri, Pik
Kanto-sanchi mts Japan 91 F7
Kantserava Belarus 45 O5
Kanttaji Aboriginal Land res. Australia 148 B3
Kanturk Rep. of Ireland 47 D11
Kanturpa Aboriginal Land res. Australia 148 B3
Kanuku Mountains Guyana 199 G4
Kanuma Japan 91 F6
Kanur India 94 C3
Kanus Namibia 132 C4
Kanuwe r. P.N.G. 73 J8
Kanyakubja India see Kannauj
KaNyamazane S. Africa 133 P2
Kanye Botswana 131 E5
Kanyemba Zimbabwe 131 F2
Kanyutno Rus. Fed. 43 O6
Kao Indon. 75 C2

Kao Niger 125 G3
Kao i. Tonga 145 H3
Kao, Teluk b. Indon. 75 C2
Kaohsiung Taiwan 87 G4
also spelt Gaoxiong
Kaôh Tang i. Cambodia 79 C6
Kaokoveld plat. Namibia 130 B3
Kaolack Senegal 124 A3
Kaoma Zambia 127 E8
Kaouadja Cent. Afr. Rep. 126 D3
Kapaa U.S.A. 181 [inset] Y1
Kapal Kazakh. 103 I3
also spelt Qapal
Kapalabuaya Indon. 75 C3
Kapan Armenia 107 F3
formerly spelt Ghap'an or Kafan
Kapanga Dem. Rep. Congo 127 D7
Kapareli Greece 59 E10
Kapatkyevichy Belarus 43 J9
Kapatu Zambia 127 F7
Kapchagay Kazakh. 103 I4
also spelt Qapshagay; formerly known as Ili or Iliysk
Kapchagayskoye Vodokhranilishche resr Kazakh. 103 I4
also known as Qapshagay Bögeni
Kapchorwa Uganda 128 B4
Kapčiamiestis Lith. 42 E8
Kap Dan Greenland see Kulusuk
Kapellen Belgium 51 K1
Kapello, Akra pt Greece 59 E12
Kapelskär Sweden 45 L4
also spelt Kapelskär
Kapelskär Sweden see Kapelskär
Kapfenberg Austria 49 M8
Kapili r. India 97 F4
Kapingamarangi atoll Micronesia 145 E2
formerly known as Greenwich
Kapıorman Dağları mts Turkey 106 B2
Kapiri Mposhi Zambia 127 F8
Kapisa prov. Afgh. 101 G3
Kapisillit Greenland 165 N3
Kapiskau r. Canada 168 D2
Kapiskong Lake Canada 173 L3
Kapit Sarawak Malaysia 77 F2
Kapiti Island N.Z. 152 I8
Kapiting Brazil 199 H4
Kapka well Chad 120 D5
Kapka, Massif du mts Chad 120 D6
Kaplamada, Gunung mt. Indon. 75 C3
Kaplankyr, Chink hills Turkm./Uzbek. 102 C4
Kaplankyrskiy Gosudarstvennyy Zapovednik nature res. Turkm. 102 D4
Kaplice Czech Rep. 49 L7
Kapoe Thai. 79 B6
Kapoeta Sudan 128 B3
Kaponda, Tanjung pt Indon. 75 B5
Kaponga N.Z. 152 I7
Kapos r. Romania 49 P9
Kaposvár Hungary 49 O9
Kappar Pak. 101 E5
Kappeln Germany 48 G1
Kapren India 96 C4
Kapsabet Kenya 128 B4
Kap Salt Swamp Pak. 101 E5
Kapsan N. Korea 83 C4
Kapsha r. Rus. Fed. 43 O2
Kapsukas Lith. see Marijampolė
Kaptai Bangl. 97 G5
Kaptsegaytuu Rus. Fed. 85 H1
Kapuas r. Indon. 77 E3
Kapuas r. Indon. 77 F3
Kapuas Hulu, Pegunungan mts Indon./Malaysia 77 F2
also known as Boven Kapuas Mountains
Kapunda Australia 146 C3
Kapuriya India 96 B3
Kapurthala India 96 B3
Kapuskasing Canada 168 D3
Kapuskasing r. Canada 168 D3
Kapustin Yar Rus. Fed. 41 H6
Kaputa Zambia 127 F7
Kaputar mt. Australia 147 F2
Kaputir Kenya 128 B4
Kapuvár Hungary 49 N8
Kapydzhik, Gora mt. Armenia/Azer. see Qazangödaği
Kapyl' Belarus 42 I8
also known as Kopyl'
Kap'yŏng S. Korea 83 B5
Kapyrevshchina Rus. Fed. 43 N6
Ka Qu r. China 89 D6
Kaqung China 88 B4
Kara r. India 97 D4
Kara r. Rus. Fed. 40 M1
Kara Togo 125 F4
Kara r. Turkey 107 E3
Kara Ada i. Turkey 59 I10
Karaali Turkey 106 C4
Kara Art Pass China 88 A4
Kara-Balta Kyrg. 103 H4
also spelt Karabalta
Karabanovo Rus. Fed. 43 T5
Karabas Kazakh. 103 H2
also spelt Qarabas
Karabekaul Turkm. see Garabekevyul
Karabiga Turkey 106 A2
Karabil', Vozvyshennost' hills Turkm. 103 E5
also known as Garabil Belentligi
Kara-Bogaz-Gol Turkm. see Karabogazkel'
Kara-Bogaz-Gol, Proliv sea chan. Turkm. 102 C4
also known as Garabogazköl Bogazy
Kara-Bogaz-Gol, Zaliv b. Turkm. 102 C4
also known as Garabogazköl Aylagy
asia [changes] ▶▶ 68–69
Karabogazkel' Turkm. 102 C4
formerly known as Kara-Bogaz-Gol
Karabük Turkey 106 C2
Karabulak Almatinskaya Oblast' Kazakh. 103 I3
also spelt Qarabulaq
Karabulak Vostochnyy Kazakhstan Kazakh. 88 D2
Karabulaksaya Kazakh. 103 H2
Karabura China see Yumin
Karaburun Turkey 106 A3
Karabutak Kazakh. 102 E2
Karacabey Turkey 106 B2
Karacadağ mt. Turkey 106 C3
Karacakılavuz Turkey 58 I7
Karacaköy Turkey 106 B2
Karaçalı Dağ mt. Turkey 107 D3
Karaçal Tepe mt. Turkey 108 C1
Karacasu Turkey 59 J11
Karaca Yarımadası pen. Turkey 108 B1
Karachay-Cherkess Republic aut. rep. Rus. Fed. see Karachayevo-Cherkesskaya Respublika
Karachayevo-Cherkesskaya A.S.S.R. aut. rep. Rus. Fed. see Karachayevo-Cherkesskaya Respublika
Karachayevo-Cherkesskaya Respublika aut. rep. Rus. Fed. 41 G8
English form Karachay-Cherkess Republic; formerly known as Karachayevo-Cherkesskaya A.S.S.R.
Karachayevsk Rus. Fed. 41 G8
formerly known as Klukhori
▶Karachi Pak. 101 F5
world [cities] ▶▶ 24–25
Karaçoban Turkey 107 E3
also spelt Karaköprü
Karaçulha Turkey 59 K12

Kara-Say Kyrg. 103 I4
Karasburg Namibia 130 C6
Kara Sea Rus. Fed. 39 H2
also known as Karskoye More
Kara-Darya r. Kyrg. 103 H4
Kara-Dar'ya Uzbek. see Payshanba
Kara Deniz sea Asia/Europe see Black Sea
Karaga Ghana 125 E4
Karaganda Kazakh. 103 H2
also spelt Qaraghandy
Karaganda Oblast admin. div. Kazakh. see Karagandinskaya Oblast'
Karagandinskaya Oblast' admin. div. Kazakh. 103 H2
English form Karaganda Oblast; also known as Qaraghandy Oblysy
Karagay Rus. Fed. 40 J4
Karagayly Kazakh. 103 H2
also spelt Qaraghayly
Karagez Turkm. 102 C5
Karaginskiy, Ostrov i. Rus. Fed. 39 Q4
Karagiye, Vpadina depr. Kazakh. 102 B4
Karaguzhikha Kazakh. 88 C1
Karagwe Tanz. 128 A5
Karahallı Turkey 58 I7
Karahasanlı Turkey 59 K10
Karahasanlı Turkey 106 C3
Karahisar Turkey 59 J11
Karaidel' Rus. Fed. 40 K5
Karaikal India 94 C4
Karaikkudi India 94 C4
Karaj Iran 100 B3
Karak Jordan see Al Karak
Kara-Kala Turkm. see Garrygala
Karakalli Turkey see Özalp
Karakalpakistan, Respublika aut. rep. Uzbek. 102 D4
also known as Karakalpaksraya Respublika or Karakalpakstan or Qaraqalpaqstan Respublikasy or Qoraqalpoghiston Respublikasi
Karakalpakiya Uzbek. 102 D3
also known as Qoraqalpogʻiston
Karakalpakskaya Respublika aut. rep. Uzbek. see Karakalpakistan, Respublika
Karakalpakstan aut. rep. Uzbek. see Karakalpakistan, Respublika
Kara Kara State Park nature res. Australia 147 D4
Karakatinskaya, Vpadina depr. Uzbek. 103 F4
Karakax China see Moyu
Karakax He r. China 89 C4
Karakax Shan mts China 89 C5
Karakeçi Turkey 107 D3
also known as Mizar
Karakeçili Turkey 106 C3
Karakelong i. Indon. 75 C1
Kara-Khol' Rus. Fed. 88 E1
Karaki China 89 C4
Karakitang i. Indon. 75 C1
Karaklis Armenia see Vanadzor
Karakoçan Turkey 107 E3
also known as Tepeköy
Karakoin salt l. Kazakh. see Karakoyyn, Ozero
Karakol' Rus. Fed. 102 C2
also spelt Qaraköl
Kara-Köl r. Kyrg. 103 H4
Karakol' Ysyk-Köl Kyrg. 103 I4
also known as Karakolka
Karakol Ysyk-Köl Kyrg. 103 I4
formerly known as Przheval'sk
Karaköprü Turkey see Karaçoban
Karakoram mts Asia 99 J2
Karakoram Pass China/Jammu and Kashmir 89 B5
Kara K'orē Eth. 128 C2
Karakoro r. Mali/Mauritania 124 B3
Karaköse Turkey see Ağrı
Karakoyyn, Ozero salt l. Kazakh. 103 G3
also known as Karakoin or Qaraqoyyn Köli
Kara Kul' Kyrg. see Kara-Köl
Karakul' Bukharskaya Oblast' Uzbek. 103 E5
Karakul', Ozero l. Tajik. see Qarokŭl
Kara-Kul'dzha Kyrg. see Kara-Kulja
Karakulino Rus. Fed. 40 J4
Kara-Kulja Kyrg. 103 H4
also spelt Kara-Kul'dzha
Karakum Kazakh. 103 I2
Karakum Desert Kazakh. 102 C3
also known as Garagum or Peski Karakum or Qaraqum
Karakum Desert Turkm. 102 E5
also known as Garagum or Peski Karakumy or Qaraqum
Karakumskiy Kanal canal Turkm. 103 E5
Karakurt Turkey 107 E2
Karakurt Turkey 59 I9
Karala Estonia 42 C3
Karalı Turkey 108 H1
Karalundi Australia 151 B5
Karama r. Indon. 75 A3
Karaman Turkey 106 C3
historically known as Laranda
Karaman prov. Turkey 108 D1
Karamanbeyli Geçidi pass Turkey 108 D1
Karamanlı Turkey 106 B3
Karamay China 88 D2
Karambar Pass Afgh./Pak. 101 H2
Karamea N.Z. 152 G9
Karamea r. N.Z. 152 F9
Karamea Bight b. N.Z. 152 F9
Karamet-Niyaz Turkm. 103 F5
also known as Garamätnyyaz
Karamian i. Indon. 77 F4
Karamiran China 89 D4
Karamiran He r. China 89 D4
Karamiran Shankou pass China 89 D4
Karamken Rus. Fed. 39 P3
Karamürsel Turkey 58 K8
Karamyshevo Rus. Fed. 43 J4
Karan i. Saudi Arabia 105 E2
Karan r. Afgh. 101 G2
Karan state Myanmar see Kayin
Karan i. Saudi Arabia 105 E2
Karang Senegal 124 A3
Karang, Tanjung pt Indon. 75 A3
Karangan Indon. 77 F4
Karangarua N.Z. 153 D11
Karangan Indon. 77 F5
Karangtang vol. Indon. 75 C2
Karanja India 94 C1
Karanja r. Congo 126 B4
Karanjia India 95 E1
Karanpara India 96 B3
Karaoba Kazakh. 103 I1
Karaova Turkey 59 I11
Karaoy Almatinskaya Oblast' Kazakh. 103 H3
Karaoy Almatinskaya Oblast' Kazakh. 103 H3
Karapelit Bulg. 58 I5
Karapınar Turkey 106 C3
also known as Sultanoye
Karapürçek Turkey 106 C2
Karaqi China 88 D3
Karas mts Namibia 130 C5
Karasay Turkey 106 C3
Karasay China 89 C4

Karijini National Park Australia 150 B4
Karikari, Cape N.Z. 152 H2
Karimata i. Indon. 77 E3
Karimata, Pulau-pulau is Indon. 77 E3
Karimata, Selat strait Indon. 77 E3
Karimganj India 97 G4
Karimnagar India 94 C2
Karimun Besar i. Indon. 76 C2
Karimunjawa i. Indon. 77 M8
Karimunjawa, Pulau-pulau is Indon. 77 E4
Karin Somalia 128 E2
Karinainen Fin. 45 M3
Käringsjön Sweden 44 K3
Karioi hill N.Z. 133 C2
Karis Fin. 45 M3
also known as Karjaa
Karisimbi, Mont vol. Rwanda 126 F5
Káristos Greece see Karystos
Karit Iran 100 D3
Karitsa Greece 59 D8
Kariya Japan 91 E7
Kariyangwe Zimbabwe 131 E3
Karjaa Fin. see Karis
Karjalohja Fin. 42 E1
Karka India 96 B5
Karjat India 94 B2
Karkai r. India 97 E5
Karkal India 94 B3
Karkamb India 94 B2
Karkams S. Africa 132 B7
Karkaralinsk Kazakh. 103 H2
also spelt Qarqaraly
Karkaralong, Kepulauan is Indon. 75 C1
Karkar Island P.N.G. 73 K7
also known as Dampier Island
Karkas, Kūh-e mts Iran 100 B3
Karkh Pak. 101 F5
Karkheh, Rūdkhāneh-ye r. Iran 100 A4
Karkinits'ka Zatoka g. Ukr. 41 E7
Karkkila Fin. 45 N3
Kärkölä Fin. 45 N3
Karkonoski Park Narodowy nat. park Czech Rep./Poland see Krkonošský národní park
Karksi-Nuia Estonia 42 G3
Karkūma, Ra's hd Saudi Arabia 104 B2
Karlantijpa North Aboriginal Land res. Australia 148 B3
Karlantijpa South Aboriginal Land res. Australia 148 B3
Karlik Shan mt. China 84 B3
Karlino Poland 49 M1
Karlıova Turkey 107 E3
Karlivka Ukr. 41 E6
also spelt Karlovka
Karl Marks, Qullai mt. Tajik. 101 H2
also known as Qaratomar Bögeni
Karl-Marx-Stadt Germany see Chemnitz
Karlovac Croatia 56 I3
Karlovka Ukr. see Karlivka
Karlovo Bulg. 58 F6
formerly known as Levskigrad
Karlovy Vary Czech Rep. 49 J5
historically known as Carlsbad
Karlsberg Sweden 45 L4
Karlsborg Sweden 45 K4
Karlsburg Romania see Alba Iulia
Karlshamn Sweden 45 K4
Karlskoga Sweden 45 K4
Karlskrona Sweden 45 K4
Karlsruhe Germany 48 F6
Karlstad Sweden 45 K4
Karlstadt Germany 48 G5
Karlyuk Turkm. 103 F5
Karma Belarus 43 L8
Karma, Ouadi watercourse Chad 120 C6
Karmala India 94 B2
Karmanovka Kazakh. 102 B2
Karmanovo Rus. Fed. 43 P6
Karmas Sweden 44 L2
Karmona Spain see Córdoba
Karnabchul', Step' plain Uzbek. 103 F5
Karnafuli Reservoir Bangl. 97 G5
Karnal India 96 C3
Karnali r. Nepal see Ghaghara
Karnaprayag India 96 C3
Karnataka state India 94 B3
formerly known as Mysore
Karnes City U.S.A. 179 C6
Karnobat Bulg. 58 H6
formerly known as Polyanovgrad
Karnul India see Kurnool
Karoi Zimbabwe 131 F3
Karokpi Myanmar 78 B5
Karong India 97 G4
Karonga Malawi 129 B7
Karonie Australia 151 C6
Karoo National Park S. Africa 132 G9
Karoonda Australia 146 C3
Karor Pak. 101 G4
Karora Eritrea 121 H5
Karos i. Greece see Keros
Karossa Indon. 75 A3
Karossa, Tanjung pt Indon. 77 G5
Karotis Greece 58 H7
Karouassa well Mali 125 E2
Karpasia pen. Cyprus see Karpas Peninsula
Karpas Peninsula Cyprus 108 F2
also known as Karpas Peninsula; also spelt Kırpaşa
Karpathos Greece 59 I13
Karpathos i. Greece 59 I13
formerly known as Scarpanto
Karpathou, Steno sea chan. Greece 59 I12
also known as Europe see Carpathian Mountains
Karpenisi Greece 59 C10
Karpilovka Belarus see Aktsyabrski
Karpinsk Rus. Fed. 38 G4
Karpogory Rus. Fed. 40 H3
Karpovichi Ukr. 43 N9
Karpuz r. Turkey 108 C1
Karpuzlu Aydın Turkey 59 I11
Karpuzlu Edirne Turkey 58 H7
Karratha Australia 150 B4
Karrats Fjord inlet Greenland see Nuugaatsiaap Imaa
Karri Iran 100 D4
Karringmelkspruit S. Africa 133 L7
Karroo plat. S. Africa see Great Karoo
Karroun Hill Nature Reserve Australia 151 B6
Karrukh Afgh. 101 E3
Karrychirla Turkm. see imeni Kerbabayeva
Kars Turkey 107 E2
Karsakpay Kazakh. 103 F3
also spelt Qarsaqbay
Kärsämäki Fin. 44 N3
Kārsava Latvia 42 I5
Karshi Turkm. 102 C5
Karshi Uzbek. 103 F5
also spelt Qarshi; historically known as Nautaca
Karshinskaya Step' plain Uzbek. 103 F5
also known as Qarshi Chūli
Karşıyaka Balıkesir Turkey 58 J8
Karşıyaka İzmir Turkey 59 I10
Karsiyang India 97 F4
Karskiye Vorota, Proliv strait Rus. Fed. 40 K1
English form Kara Strait
Karskoye More sea Rus. Fed. see Kara Sea
Karstädt Germany 48 I2
Karsu Turkey 109 H1
Karsun Rus. Fed. 41 H5
Kartal Turkey 106 B2
Kartala vol. Comoros 129 D7
Kartaly Rus. Fed. 103 E1

Kartarpur India 96 B3
Kartena Lith. 42 C6
Karthaus U.S.A. 176 G4
Kartsevo Rus. Fed. 43 L5
Kartsino, Akra pt Greece 59 F10
Karttula Fin. 44 N3
Kartuni Guyana 199 G3
Kartuzy Poland 49 P1
Karubwe Zambia 127 F8
Kārūkh, Jabal mt. Iraq 109 P1
Karumai Japan 90 G4
Karumba Australia 149 D3
Karun, Kūh-e hill Iran 100 B4
Kārūn, Rūd-e r. Iran 100 B4
Karunagapalli India 94 C4
Karungi Sweden 44 M2
Karungu Kenya 128 B5
Karuni Indon. 75 A5
Karunjie Australia 150 D3
Karup Denmark 45 J4
Karur India 94 C4
Karuzi Burundi 126 F5
Karvetnagar India 94 C3
Karvia Fin. 45 M3
Karviná Czech Rep. 49 P6
Karwar India 94 B3
Karwendelgebirge nature res. Austria 48 I8
Karwi India 96 D4
Karya Greece 59 B10
Karyagino Azer. see Füzuli
Karyes Greece 59 F8
Karymskoye Rus. Fed. 85 G1
Karynzharyk, Peski des. Kazakh. 102 C4
Karystos Greece 59 F10
also spelt Káristos
Kaş Turkey 106 B3
Kasa India 94 B2
Kasaba Turkey see Turgutlu
Kasaba Lodge Zambia 127 F7
Kasabonika Canada 168 B2
Kasai r. Dem. Rep. Congo 127 C5
Kasai Japan 91 D7
Kasai, Plateau du Dem. Rep. Congo 127 D6
Kasai Occidental prov. Dem. Rep. Congo 127 D6
Kasai Oriental prov. Dem. Rep. Congo 126 E6
Kasaji Dem. Rep. Congo 127 D7
Kasama Japan 91 G6
Kasama Zambia 127 F7
Kasan Uzbek. 103 F5
also spelt Koson
Kasane Botswana 131 E3
Kasanga Tanz. 129 A7
Kasangulu Dem. Rep. Congo 126 B6
Kasanka National Park Zambia 127 F8
Kasansay Uzbek. 103 G4
also spelt Kosonsoy
Kasanza Dem. Rep. Congo 127 C6
Kasar, Ras pt Sudan 121 H5
Kasaragod India 94 B3
Kasari r. Estonia 42 E3
Kasatkino Rus. Fed. 82 C2
Kasba Lake Canada 167 K2
Kasba Tadla Morocco 122 D2
Kasbi Uzbek. 103 F5
Kaseda Japan 91 B9
Kasempa Zambia 127 E8
Kasenga Katanga Dem. Rep. Congo 127 D7
Kasenga Katanga Dem. Rep. Congo 127 F7
Kasenye Dem. Rep. Congo 126 F4
Kasese Dem. Rep. Congo 126 E5
Kasese Uganda 128 A4
Kasevo Rus. Fed. see Neftekamsk
Kasganj India 96 C4
Kasha China see Gonjo
Kasha waterhole Kenya 128 D5
Kashabowie Canada 168 B3
Kāshān Iran 100 B3
Kashary Rus. Fed. 41 G6
Kashechewan Canada 168 D2
Kashgar China see Kashi
Kashi China 88 B4
formerly known as Kashgar or Kaxgar
Kashihara Japan 91 D7
Kashima Japan 91 B8
Kashima-nada b. Japan 91 G6
Kashin Rus. Fed. 43 S4
Kashinka r. Rus. Fed. 43 S4
Kashiobwe Dem. Rep. Congo 127 F7
Kashipur India 96 C3
Kashira Rus. Fed. 43 T7
Kashirka r. Rus. Fed. 43 T7
Kashiwazaki Japan 90 F6
Kashkadar'inskaya Oblast' admin. div. Uzbek. 103 F5
English form Kashkadarya Oblast; also known as Qashqadaryo Wiloyati
Kashkadar'ya r. Uzbek. 101 F2
also known as Qashqadaryo
Kashkadarya Oblast admin. div. Uzbek. see Kashkadar'inskaya Oblast'
Kashkanteniz Kazakh. 103 H3
also spelt Kashken-Teniz or Qashqantengiz
Kashken-Teniz Kazakh. see Kashkanteniz
Kashkurino Rus. Fed. 43 M6
Kāshmar Iran 100 D3
Kashmir terr. Asia see Jammu and Kashmir
Kashmir, Vale of valley India 96 B2
Kashmor Pak. 101 G4
Kashmund reg. Afgh. 101 G3
Kashyukulu Dem. Rep. Congo 127 E6
Kasi India see Varanasi
Kasia India 97 D4
Kasilovo Rus. Fed. 43 O8
Kasimbar Indon. 75 A3
Kasimov Rus. Fed. 40 G5
Kasingi Dem. Rep. Congo 126 F4
Kasiruta i. Indon. 75 C3
Kaskaskia r. U.S.A. 174 B4
Kaskattama r. Canada 167 N3
Kaskelen Kazakh. 103 I4
also spelt Qaskelen
Kaskinen Fin. 44 M3
also known as Kaskö
Kas Klong i. Cambodia see Kŏng, Kaôh
Kaskö Fin. see Kaskinen
Kaslo Canada 167 G5
Kasmere Lake Canada 167 K3
Kasnya r. Rus. Fed. 43 P6
Kasomeno Dem. Rep. Congo 127 F7
Kasongan Indon. 77 F3
Kasongo Dem. Rep. Congo 126 E6
Kasongo-Lunda Dem. Rep. Congo 127 C6
Kasonguele Dem. Rep. Congo 127 E6
Kasos i. Greece 59 H13
Kasou, Steno sea chan. Greece 59 I13
Kaspi Georgia 107 F2
Kaspīy Mangy Oypaty lowland Kazakh./Rus. Fed. see Caspian Lowland
Kaspiysk Rus. Fed. 102 A4
Kaspiyskiy Rus. Fed. see Lagan'
Kaspiyskoye More sea Asia/Europe see Caspian Sea
Kasplya Rus. Fed. 43 M7
Kasplya r. Rus. Fed. 43 L6
Kasrawad India 96 B5
Kasrik Turkey see Gürpınar
Kassa Slovakia see Košice
Kassaare laht b. Estonia 42 D3
Kassala Sudan 121 H6
Kassala state Sudan 121 G6
Kassandra pen. Greece 59 E8
Kassandras, Akra pt Greece 59 E9
Kassandras, Kolpos b. Greece 59 E8
Kassandreia Greece 59 E8
Kassel Germany 48 G4
Kasserine Tunisia 123 H2
Kassinga Angola see Cassinga
Kassouloua well Niger 125 H3
Kastamonu Turkey 106 C2
also known as Çandar
Kastelli Kriti Greece 59 E13
also known as Kastéllion
Kastelli Kriti Greece 59 G13
Kastéllion Greece see Kastelli
Kastellorizon i. Greece see Megisti
Kastellou, Akra pt Greece 59 I13
Kastoria Greece 58 C8
Kastorias, Limni l. Greece 58 C8
Kastornoye Rus. Fed. 41 F6
Kastos i. Greece 59 B10
Kastrakiou, Techniti Limni resr Greece 59 C10
Kastre Estonia 42 I3
Kastrova Belarus 43 J5
Kastsyukovichy Belarus 43 N8
also spelt Kostyukovichi
Kastsyukowka Belarus 43 L9
Kasugai Japan 91 E7
Kasuku Dem. Rep. Congo 126 E5
Kasulu Tanz. 129 A6
Kasumiga-ura l. Japan 91 G6
Kasumkent Rus. Fed. 102 B4
Kasungu Malawi 129 B8
Kasungu National Park Malawi 129 B8
Kasur Pak. 101 H4
Kataba Zambia 127 E9
Katagum Nigeria 125 H3
Katahdin, Mount U.S.A. 174 G2
Kataklik Jammu and Kashmir 96 C2
Katako-Kombe Dem. Rep. Congo 126 E5
Katakolo, Akra pt Greece 59 C11
Katakwi Uganda 128 B4
Katanda Dem. Rep. Congo 127 D6
Katanga prov. Dem. Rep. Congo 127 E7
formerly known as Shaba
Katangi Madhya Pradesh India 96 C5
Katangi Madhya Pradesh India 96 C5
Katangli Rus. Fed. 82 F2
Katanning Australia 151 B7
Kata Pusht Iran 100 B2
Katashin Rus. Fed. 43 N9
Katastari Greece 59 B11
Katavi National Park Tanz. 129 A6
Katawaz Afgh. 101 G3
Katawaz reg. Afgh. 101 F3
Katchall i. India 95 G5
Katchamba Togo 125 F4
Katea Dem. Rep. Congo 127 E6
Katerini Greece 59 D8
Katesh Tanz. 129 B6
Kate's Needle mt. Canada/U.S.A. 164 F4
Katete Zambia 129 B8
Katghora India 97 D5
Katha Myanmar 78 B2
Katherîna, Gebel mt. Egypt 121 G2
Katherine Australia 148 B2
Katherine r. Australia 148 A2
Katherine Gorge National Park Australia see Nitmiluk National Park
Kathi India 96 B5
Kathiawar pen. India 96 A5
Kathīb, Ra's al pt Yemen 104 C5
Kathîb el Henu des. Egypt 121 G2
Kathîb el Henu hill Egypt 108 D7
Kathîb el Makhâzin des. Egypt 108 D7
Kathleen Falls Australia 148 A2
Kathlehong S. Africa 133 M3

▶Kathmandu Nepal 97 E4
Capital of Nepal. English form Katmandu.

Kathu S. Africa 132 H4
Kathua Jammu and Kashmir 96 B2
Kathua watercourse Kenya 128 C5
Kati Mali 124 C3
Katibas r. Sarawak Malaysia 77 F2
Kati-ér r. Hungary 49 S8
Katihar India 97 E4
Katikati N.Z. 152 J5
Kati-Kati S. Africa 133 L9
Katima Mulilo Namibia 131 E3
Katimik Lake Canada 167 L4
Katino Rus. Fed. 43 U8
Katiola Côte d'Ivoire 124 D4
Kā Tiritiri o te Moana mts N.Z. see Southern Alps
Katiti Aboriginal Land res. Australia 148 A5
Katkop Hills S. Africa 132 E7
Katlabukh, Ozero l. Ukr. 58 J3
Katma China 88 D4
Katmai National Park and Preserve U.S.A. 164 D4
Katmandu Nepal see Kathmandu
Kato Achaïa Greece 59 C10
Kat O Chau i. Hong Kong China see Crooked Island
Katochi Greece 59 C10
Kato Figaleia Greece 59 C11
Kat O Hoi b. Hong Kong China see Crooked Harbour
Katol India 96 C5
Kåtölandet i. Fin. 44 M3
Katombe Dem. Rep. Congo 127 D6
Katompi Dem. Rep. Congo 127 E6
Katondwe Zambia 127 F8
Kato Nevrokopi Greece 58 E7
Katong Sing. 76 [inset]
Katonga r. Uganda 128 A4
Katon-Karagay Kazakh. 88 D1
also spelt Katonqaraghay
Katonqaraghay Kazakh. see Katon-Karagay
Katoomba Australia 147 F3
Katoposa, Gunung mt. Indon. 75 B3
Katosan India 96 B5
Kato Tithorea Greece 59 D10
Kåtotjåkka mt. Sweden see Godučohkka
Katowice Poland 49 Q5
formerly known as Stalinogród; historically known as Kattowitz
Katoya India 97 F5
formerly spelt Katwa
Katpur India 96 B5
Katrineholm Sweden 45 L4
Katse Dam Lesotho 133 M6
Katsepy Madag. 131 [inset] J2
Katsikas Greece 59 B9
Katsina Nigeria 125 G3
Katsina state Nigeria 125 G4
Katsina-Ala Nigeria 125 H5
Katsumoto Japan 91 A8
Katsuura Japan 91 G7
Katsuyama Japan 91 E6
Kattakurgan Uzbek. 103 F5
also spelt Kattaqŭrghon
Kattamudda Well Australia 150 D4
Kattaqŭrghon Uzbek. see Kattakurgan
Kattasang Hills Afgh. 101 F3
Kattavia Greece 59 I13
Kattegat strait Denmark/Sweden 45 J4
Kattisavan Sweden 44 L2
Kattowitz Poland see Katowice
Kattuputtur India 94 C4
Katumba Dem. Rep. Congo 127 E6
Katumbi Malawi 129 B7
Katun' r. Rus. Fed. 88 D1
Katunino Rus. Fed. 40 H4
Katunskiy Khrebet mts Rus. Fed. 88 D1
Katwa India see Katoya
Katwijk aan Zee Neth. 48 B3
Katyk Ukr. see Shakhtars'k
Katyn' Rus. Fed. 43 M7
Kąty Wrocławskie Poland 49 N4
Kauai i. U.S.A. 181 [inset] Y1
Kauai Channel U.S.A. 181 [inset] Y1
Kaudom Game Park nature res. Namibia 130 D3
Kaufbeuren Germany 48 H8
Kaufman U.S.A. 179 C5
Kauhajoki Fin. 44 M3
Kauhanevan-Pohjankankaan kansallispuisto nat. park Fin. 45 M3
Kauhava Fin. 44 M3
Kaukauna U.S.A. 172 E6
Kaukkwè Hills Myanmar 78 B2
Kaukonen Fin. 44 N2
Kauksi Estonia 42 I2
Kaulinranta Fin. 44 M2
Kaumajet Mountains Canada 169 I1
Kaunakakai U.S.A. 181 [inset] Z1
Kaunas Lith. 42 E7
formerly known as Kovno
Kaunata Latvia 42 I5
Kaundy, Vpadina depr. Kazakh. 102 C4
Kaunia Bangl. 97 F4
Kauno marios l. Lith. 42 F7
Kaupiri N.Z. 153 F10
Kaura-Namoda Nigeria 125 G3
Kau Sai Chau i. Hong Kong China 87 [inset]
Kaushany Moldova see Căușeni
Kaustinen Fin. 44 M3
Kautokeino Norway 44 M1
Kau-ye Kyun i. Myanmar 79 B6
Kavacha Rus. Fed. 39 Q3
Kavadarci Macedonia 58 D7
Kavajë Albania 58 A7
Kavak Turkey 58 H8
Kavak Turkey 106 D2
Kavak Dağı hill Turkey 59 H9
Kavaklıdere Manisa Turkey 59 J10
Kavaklıdere Muğla Turkey 59 J11
Kavala Greece 58 F8
Kavalas, Kolpos b. Greece 58 F8
Kavalerovo Rus. Fed. 82 D3
Kavali India 94 D3
Kavalpatnam India 94 C4
Kavalyova Belarus 43 L6
Kavanayen Venez. 199 F3
Kavār Iran 100 C4
Kavaratti India 94 B4
Kavaratti i. India 94 B4
Kavarna Bulg. 58 J5
Kavarskas Lith. 42 F6
Kavendou, Mont mt. Guinea 124 B4
Kaveri r. India 94 C4
Kaveripatnam India 94 C3
Kavi India 96 B5
Kavieng P.N.G. 145 E2
Kavīr Iran 100 B3
Kavīr, Dasht-e des. Iran 100 C3
Kavīr-e Abarkuh des. Iran 100 C4
Kavīr-i-Namak salt flat Iran 100 D3
Kavīr Kūshk well Iran 100 D3
Kavirondo Gulf Kenya see Winam Gulf
Kavkazskiy Zapovednik nature res. Rus. Fed. 41 G8
Kaw Fr. Guiana 199 H3
Kawabe Japan 90 G5
Kawachi-nagano Japan 91 D7
Kawagama Lake Canada 168 E4
Kawagoe Japan 91 F7
Kawaguchi Japan 91 F7
Kawahara Japan 91 D7
Kawai Japan 90 G5
Kawaihae U.S.A. 181 [inset] Z1
Kawaihoa Point U.S.A. 181 [inset] Y1
Kawakawa N.Z. 152 I3
Kawamata Japan 90 G6
Kawambwa Zambia 127 F7
Kawaminami Japan 91 B8
Kawana Zambia 127 E8
Kawangkoan Indon. 75 C2
Kawanishi Japan 91 D7
Kawardha India 96 D5
Kawartha Lakes Canada 168 E4
Kawasa Dem. Rep. Congo 127 F7
Kawasaki Japan 91 F7
Kawashiri-misaki pt Japan 91 B7
Kawato Indon. 75 B3
Kawaura Japan 91 B8
Kawawachikamach Canada 169 H2
Kawe i. Indon. 75 D2
Kaweah, Lake U.S.A. 182 F5
Kaweka Forest Park nature res. N.Z. 152 K7
Kaweka Range mts N.Z. 152 K7
Kawene Canada 172 B2
Kawerau N.Z. 152 K6
Kawhia N.Z. 152 I6
Kawich Peak U.S.A. 183 H4
Kawich Range mts U.S.A. 183 H4
Kawinaw Lake Canada 167 L4
Kawio i. Indon. 75 C1
Kawkabān Yemen 104 C5
Kawkareik Myanmar 78 B4
Kaw Lake U.S.A. 178 C4
Kawlin Myanmar 78 A3
Kawludo Myanmar 78 B4
Kawmapyin Myanmar 79 B5
Kawm Dafanah tourist site Egypt see Daphnae
Kawngmeum Myanmar 78 B3
Kawthaung Myanmar 79 B6
Kawthoolei state Myanmar see Kayin
Kawthule state Myanmar see Kayin
Kaxgar China see Kashi
Kaxgar He r. China 88 B4
Kax He r. China 88 C3
Kaxtax Shan mts China 89 C4
Kaya Burkina 125 E3
Kaya S. Korea 91 A7
Kayacı Dağı hill Turkey 59 H9
Kayadibi Turkey 107 D3
Kayah state Myanmar 78 B4
Kayambi Zambia 129 A7
Kayan r. Indon. 77 E3
Kayan r. Indon. 77 G2
Kayan Myanmar 78 B4
Kayanaza Burundi 126 F5
Kayangel atoll Palau 73 H5
also known as Ngcheangel
Kayankulam India 94 C4
Kayar India 94 C2
Kayasa Indon. 75 C2
Kaya-san National Park S. Korea 91 A7
Kaybagar, Ozero l. Kazakh. see Koybagar, Ozero
Kaydanovo Belarus see Dzyarzhynsk
Kayenta U.S.A. 183 N5
Kayes Mali 124 C3
Kayes admin. reg. Mali 124 C3
Kayga Kazakh. 103 F2
also known as Qayghy; formerly known as Kaygy
Kaygy Kazakh. see Kayga
Kayin state Myanmar 78 B4
also known as Karan; formerly known as Karen or Kawthoolei or Kawthule
Kaymanachikha Kazakh. 103 H1
Kaymaz Turkey 106 B3
Kaynar Kazakh. 103 I2
also spelt Qaynar
Kaynar Turkey 107 D3
Kaynarlı r. Turkey 58 I7
Kayoa i. Indon. 75 C2
Kayrakkum Tajik. see Qayroqqum
Kayrakkumskoye Vodokhranilishche resr Tajik. see Obanbori Qayroqqum
Kayrakty Kazakh. 103 H2
also spelt Qayraqty
Kayseri Turkey 106 C3
historically known as Caesarea Cappadociae or Mazaca
Kaysersberg France 51 N4
Kayuadi i. Indon. 75 B4
Kayuagung Indon. 76 D3
Kayuyu Dem. Rep. Congo 126 E5
Kayyerkan Rus. Fed. 39 I3
Kayyngdy Kyrg. 103 H4
formerly spelt Kainda or Kaindy; formerly known as Molotovsk
Kazachka Rus. Fed. 43 T8
Kazach'ye Rus. Fed. 39 N2
Kazakh Azer. see Qazax
Kazakhdar'ya Uzbek. 102 D4
also spelt Qozoqdaryo
Kazakhskaya S.S.R. country Asia see Kazakhstan
Kazakhskiy Melkosopochnik plain Kazakh. 103 G2
Kazakhskiy Zaliv b. Kazakh. 102 C4
also known as Qazaq Shyghanaghy

▶Kazakhstan country Asia 102 C2
4th largest country in Asia and 9th in the world. Also spelt Kazakstan or Qazaqstan in Kazakh; formerly known as Kazakhskaya S.S.R.
world [countries] 10–11
asia [countries] 64–67

Kazakhstan Kazakh. see Aksay
Kazaki Rus. Fed. 43 T9
Kazakstan country Asia see Kazakhstan
Kazalinsk Kazakh. 103 E3
also known as Qazaly
Kazan r. Canada 167 M2
Kazan' Rus. Fed. 40 I5
Kazanchunkur Kazakh. 103 J2
Kazancı Turkey 106 C3
Kazandzhik Turkm. see Gazandzhyk
Kazanje, Mal mt. Albania 59 B9
Kazanka r. Rus. Fed. 40 I5
Kazanketken Uzbek. 102 D4
also spelt Qozonketkan
Kazanlı Turkey 108 F1
Kazanlŭk Bulg. 58 G6
Kazanovka Rus. Fed. 43 T8
Kazanovo Rus. Fed. 85 G1
Kazan-rettō is N. Pacific Ocean see Volcano Islands
Kazatin Ukr. see Kozyatyn
Kazatskiy Kazakh. 102 D2
Kaza Wenz r. Eth. 128 C1

▶Kazbek mt. Georgia/Rus. Fed. 107 F2
4th highest mountain in Europe. Also known as Mqinvartsveri.
europe [landscapes] 30–31

Kaz Dağı mts Turkey 106 A3
Kāzerūn Iran 100 B4
Kazgorodok Kazakh. 103 G1
Kazhim Rus. Fed. 40 I3
Kazhmak r. Pak. 101 E5
Kazıkbelı Geçidi pass Turkey 59 K11
Kazi Magomed Azer. see Qazımämmäd
Kazimierza Wielka Poland 49 R5
Kazimierz Dolne Poland 49 S4
Kazincbarcika Hungary 49 R7
Kazinka Lipetskaya Oblast' Rus. Fed. 43 U9
formerly known as Novaya Zhizn
Kazinka Ryazanskaya Oblast' Rus. Fed. 43 U8
Kaziranga National Park India 97 G4
Kazlowshchyna Belarus 42 G8
Kazlowshchyna Belarus 42 J6
Kazlų Rūda Lith. 42 E7
Kazo Japan 91 F6
Kaztalovka Kazakh. 102 B2
Kazuma Pan National Park Zimbabwe 131 E3
Kazumba Dem. Rep. Congo 127 D6
Kazungula Zambia 127 E9
Kazuno Japan 90 G4
Kazy Turkm. 102 D5
Kazyany Belarus 43 K6
Kazygurt Kazakh. 103 G4
also spelt Qazyqurt; formerly known as Lenīn or Leninskoye
Kazym r. Rus. Fed. 38 G3
Kazymskiy Mys Rus. Fed. 38 G3
Kçirë Albania 58 A6
Kea Greece 59 F11
Kea i. Greece 59 F11
English form Ceos
Keaau U.S.A. 181 [inset] Z2
Keahole Point U.S.A. 181 [inset] Z2
Kealakekua Bay U.S.A. 181 [inset] Z2
Kealia U.S.A. 181 [inset] Z2
Keams Canyon U.S.A. 183 N6
Kéamu i. Vanuatu see Anatom
Kearney U.S.A. 178 C3
Kearneysville U.S.A. 176 H6
Kearny U.S.A. 183 N8
Keas, Steno sea chan. Greece 59 F11
Keate's Drift S. Africa 133 O5
Keban Turkey 107 D3
Keban Barajı resr Turkey 107 D3
Kebatu i. Indon. 77 E3
Kebbi state Nigeria 125 F3
Kébémèr Senegal 124 A3
Kébi r. Cameroon 125 I4
Kébi Côte d'Ivoire 124 D4
Kebili Tunisia 123 H2
Kebīr, Nahr al r. Lebanon/Syria 108 G3
Kebkabiya Sudan 120 E6
Kebnekaise mt. Sweden 44 L2
K'ebrī Dehar Eth. 128 E3
Kebumen Indon. 77 E4
Kecel Hungary 49 Q9
Kech reg. Pak. 101 E5
K'ech'a Terara mt. Eth. 128 C3
Kéché Cent. Afr. Rep. 126 D2
Kechika r. Canada 166 E3
Keçiborlu Turkey 106 B3
Kecskemét Hungary 49 Q9
Kedah state Malaysia 76 C1
Kédainiai Lith. 42 E6
Kedairu Passage Fiji see Kadavu Passage
Kédédéssé Chad 126 C2
Kedgwick Canada 169 H4
Kedian China 87 E2
Kediri Indon. 77 F4
Kedong China 82 B3
Kédougou Senegal 124 B3
Kedva r. Rus. Fed. 40 J2
Kędzierzyn-Koźle Poland 49 P5
historically known as Heydebreck
Keele r. Canada 166 E1
Keele Peak Canada 166 D2
Keeley Lake Canada 167 I4
Keeling Islands terr. Indian Ocean see Cocos Islands
Keelung Taiwan see Chilung
Keenapusan i. Phil. 74 A5
Keene CA U.S.A. 182 F6
Keene NH U.S.A. 177 M3
Keene OH U.S.A. 176 D5
Keep r. Australia 148 A2
Keepit, Lake resr Australia 147 F2
Keep River National Park Australia 148 A2
Keeromsberg mt. Free State S. Africa 133 K5
Keeromsberg mt. W. Cape S. Africa 132 D10
Keer-weer, Cape Australia 149 D2
Keetmanshoop Namibia 130 C5
Keewatin Canada 167 M5
Keewatin U.S.A. 174 A2
Kefallinía i. Greece see Cephalonia
Kefallonia i. Greece see Cephalonia
Kefalos Greece 59 H12
Kefalos, Akra pt Greece 59 F11
Kefamenanu Indon. 75 C5
Kefe Ukr. see Feodosiya
Keffi Nigeria 125 G4
Keflavík Iceland 44 [inset] B2
Kegalla Sri Lanka 94 D5
Kegayli Uzbek. see Kegeyli
Kegen Kazakh. 103 I4
Kegeyli Uzbek. 102 D4
also spelt Kegayli
Keglo, Baie de b. Canada 169 H1
Keg River Canada 167 G3
Kegul'ta Rus. Fed. 41 H7
Ķegums Latvia 42 F5
Keheili Sudan 121 G5
Kehl Germany 48 E7
Kehoula well Mauritania 124 C2
Kehra Estonia 42 G2
Kehsi Mansam Myanmar 78 B3
Kehtna Estonia 42 F3
Keibab Plateau U.S.A. 183 L5
Keighley U.K. 47 K10
Keihoku Japan 91 D7
Keila Estonia 42 F2
Keila r. Estonia 42 F2
Keilak Sudan 126 F2
Keili Sudan 128 B2
Kei Ling Ha Hoi b. Hong Kong China see Three Fathoms Cove
Keimoes S. Africa 132 E5
Kei Mouth S. Africa 133 M9
Kei Road S. Africa 133 L9
Keiskama r. S. Africa 133 L10
Keiskammahoek S. Africa 133 L9
Keïta Niger 125 G3
Kéita, Bahr r. Chad 126 C2
Keitele Fin. 44 N3
Keitele l. Fin. 44 N3
Keith Australia 146 D4
Keith U.K. 46 J6
Keith, Cape Australia 148 A1
Keith Arm b. Canada 166 F1
Keithley Creek Canada 166 F4
Keithsburg U.S.A 172 C9
Kejimkujik National Park Canada 169 H4
Kekaha U.S.A. 181 [inset] Y1
Këk-Art Kyrg. see Alaykuu
Ķekava Latvia 42 F5
Këkaygyr Kyrg. see Kök-Aygyr
Kekerengu N.Z. 153 H10
Kékes mt. Hungary 49 R8
Kekova Adası i. Turkey 108 A1
Kekra Rus. Fed. 39 O4
Kekri India 96 B4
Këk-Tash Kyrg. see Kök-Tash
K'elafo Eth. 128 E3
Kelai atoll Maldives 94 B5
Kelan China 85 F4
Kelang i. Indon. 75 C3
Kelang Malaysia 76 C2
formerly spelt Klang
Kelantan r. Malaysia 76 C1
Kelantan state Malaysia 76 C1
Kelārdasht Iran 100 B2
Kelawar i. Indon. 77 E3
Kelbia, Sebkhet salt pan Tunisia 57 C13
Kele Uganda 128 B4
Kelekçi Turkey 59 K11
Keles Turkey 59 K9
Keles Uzbek. 103 G4
Kelheim Germany 48 I7
Kelibia Tunisia 123 H1
Kelif Turkm. 103 F5
Kelifskiy Uzboy marsh Turkm. 103 E5
Kelkit Turkey 107 D2
also known as Çiftlik
Kelkit r. Turkey 107 D2
Kellavere hill Estonia 42 H2
Kéllé Congo 126 B5
Kellerberrin Australia 151 B6
Keller Lake Canada 166 F2
Kellerovka Kazakh. 103 G1
Kellett, Cape Canada 164 G2
Kelliher Canada 167 K5
Kellogg U.S.A. 180 C3
Kelloselkä Fin. 44 O2
Kells Rep. of Ireland 47 F10
also known as Ceanannus Mór
Kelly Lake Canada 166 E1
Kelly Range hills Australia 151 C5
Kelmė Lith. 42 D6
Kelo Chad 126 B2
Kelowna Canada 166 G5
Kelp Head Canada 166 E5
Kelsey U.S.A. 172 A3
Kelseyville U.S.A. 182 B3
Kelso N.Z. 153 D13
Kelso U.K. 46 J8
Kelso CA U.S.A. 183 I6
Kelso WA U.S.A. 180 B3
Kelti, Jebel mt. Morocco 54 F9
Keluang Malaysia 76 C2
formerly spelt Kluang
Kelujärvi Fin. 44 N2
Kelvington Canada 167 K4
Kelvin Island Canada 168 B3
Kelwara India 101 H5
Kem' Rus. Fed. 40 E2
Kem' r. Rus. Fed. 40 E2
Kema r. Rus. Fed. 43 S1
Ke Macina Mali see Massina
Kemah Turkey 107 D3
Kemal Turkey 58 H7
Kemaliye Turkey 107 D3
also known as Eğin
Kemalpaşa Turkey 59 I10
Kemano Canada 166 E4
Kembé Cent. Afr. Rep. 126 D3
Kembolcha Eth. 128 C2
Kemeneshát hills Hungary 49 O8
Kemer Antalya Turkey 106 B3
Kemer Antalya Turkey 108 A1
Kemer Muğla Turkey 106 B3
Kemer Barajı resr Turkey 106 B3
Kemerovo Rus. Fed. 80 D1
Kemerovo Oblast admin. div. Rus. Fed. see Kemerovskaya Oblast'
Kemerovskaya Oblast' admin. div. Rus. Fed. 80 D2
English form Kemerovo Oblast
Kemi Fin. 44 N2
Kemihaara Fin. 44 O2
Kemijärvi Fin. 44 N2
Kemijärvi l. Fin. 44 N2
Kemijoki r. Fin. 44 N2
Kemin Kyrg. 103 H4
formerly known as Bystrovka
Keminmaa Fin. 44 N2
Kemiö Fin. see Kimito
Kemir Turkm. 102 C5
formerly spelt Keymir
Kemlya Rus. Fed. 40 H5
Kemmerer U.S.A. 180 E4
Kemmuna i. Malta 57 G12
also known as Comino
Kémo pref. Cent. Afr. Rep. 126 C3
Kemp, Lake U.S.A. 179 C5
Kempazh r. Rus. Fed. 40 L2
Kempele Fin. 44 N2
Kempen reg. Belgium 51 K1
Kempendyay Rus. Fed. 39 L3
Kempisch Kanaal canal Belgium 51 L1
Kemp Land reg. Antarctica 223 D2
Kemp Peninsula Antarctica 222 U2
Kemp's Bay Bahamas 186 D1
Kempsey Australia 147 G2
Kempt, Lac l. Canada 169 F4
Kempten (Allgäu) Germany 48 H8
Kempton Australia 147 E5
Kempton Park S. Africa 133 M3
Kemptville Canada 173 R5
Kemujan i. Indon. 77 E4
Ken r. India 96 D4
Kenabeek Canada 173 N3
Kenai U.S.A. 164 D3
Kenai Fiords National Park U.S.A. 164 D4
Kenai Mountains U.S.A. 164 D4
Kenamu r. Canada 169 J2
Kenamuke Swamp Sudan 128 B3
Kenansville U.S.A. 174 E5
Kenawang, Bukit mt. Sarawak Malaysia 77 F2
Kenâyis, Râs el pt Egypt 121 E2
Kenbridge U.S.A. 176 G9
Kendal Indon. 77 E4
Kendal U.K. 47 J9
Kendall r. Australia 149 D2
Kendall U.S.A. 175 D7
Kendall, Cape Canada 167 O2
Kendall, Mount N.Z. 152 G9
Kendallville U.S.A. 172 H9
Kendari Indon. 75 B3
Kendawangan Indon. 77 E3
Kendawangan r. Indon. 77 E3
Kendégué Chad 126 C2
Kendhrikí Makedhonía admin. reg. Greece see Kentriki Makedonia
Kendraparha India 95 E1
Kendrew S. Africa 133 I9
Kendrick Peak U.S.A. 183 M6
Kendua Bangl. 97 F4
Kendujhargarh India 97 E5
Kendyktas mts Kazakh. 103 H4
Kendyrli-Kayasanskoye, Plato plat. Kazakh. 102 C4
Kendyrlisor, Solonchak salt l. Kazakh. 102 C4
Kenedy U.S.A. 179 C6
Keneka r. S. Africa 133 N7
Kenema Sierra Leone 124 C5
Kenepai, Gunung mt. Indon. 77 E2
Keneurgench Turkm. 102 D4
also spelt Köneürgench; formerly spelt Kunya-Urgench
Kenga Bhutan 97 F4
Kenge Dem. Rep. Congo 126 C6
Kengere Dem. Rep. Congo 127 E7
Keng Hkam Myanmar 78 B3
Kengis Sweden 44 M2
Keng Lap Myanmar 78 C3
Keng Lon Myanmar 78 B3
Keng-Peli Uzbek. 102 D4
Keng Tawng Myanmar 78 B3
Kengtung Myanmar 78 B3
Kenhardt S. Africa 132 F6
Kéniéba Mali 124 C3
Kéniébaoulé, Réserve de nature res. Mali 124 C3
Kénitra Morocco 122 D2
formerly known as Port-Lyautrey
Kenli China 85 H4
Kenmare Rep. of Ireland 47 C12
Kenmare U.S.A. 178 B1
Kenmare River inlet Rep. of Ireland 47 B12
Kenmaur Zimbabwe 131 F3
Kenmore U.S.A. 176 G3
Kenn Germany 48 D6
Kennebec U.S.A. 178 C3
Kennebec r. U.S.A. 174 G2
Kennebunk U.S.A. 177 O2
Kennebunkport U.S.A. 177 O2
Kennedy Australia 149 E3
Kennedy r. Australia 149 E2
Kennedy, Cape U.S.A. see Canaveral, Cape
Kennedy Range hills Australia 151 A5
Kennedy Range National Park Australia 151 A5
Kennedy's Vale S. Africa 133 O1
Kennedy Town Hong Kong China 87 [inset]
Kennedyville U.S.A. 177 J6
Kenner U.S.A. 175 B6
Kennet r. U.K. 47 L12
Kenneth Range hills Australia 150 B4
Kennett U.S.A. 174 B4
Kennewick U.S.A. 180 C3
Kenogami r. Canada 168 C3
Kenogami Lake Canada 173 M2
Kenogamissi Lake Canada 173 L2
Keno Hill Canada 166 C2
Kenora Canada 167 M5
Kenosha U.S.A. 172 F8
Kenova U.S.A. 176 C7
Kenozero, Ozero l. Rus. Fed. 40 F3
Kensington Canada 169 I4
Kent OH U.S.A. 176 D4
Kent TX U.S.A. 181 F7
Kent VA U.S.A. 176 D9
Kent WA U.S.A. 180 B3
Kentani S. Africa 133 M9
also spelt Centane
Kentau Kazakh. 103 G4
Kent Group is Australia 147 E4
Kentland U.S.A. 174 C3
Kenton MI U.S.A. 172 E4
Kenton OH U.S.A. 176 B5
Kenton-on-Sea S. Africa 133 K10
Kent Peninsula Canada 165 I3
Kentriki Makedonia admin. reg. Greece 58 E8
also spelt Kendhrikí Makedhonía
Kentucky r. U.S.A. 176 B8
Kentucky state U.S.A. 176 A8
Kentucky Lake U.S.A. 174 B4
Kentwood LA U.S.A. 175 B6
Kentwood MI U.S.A. 172 H8
▶Kenya country Africa 128 C4
africa [countries] 114–117

▶Kenya, Mount Kenya 128 C5
2nd highest mountain in Africa. Also known as Kirinyaga.
africa [landscapes] 112–113

Kenyir, Tasik resr Malaysia 76 C1
Kenzingen Germany 48 E7
Keokuk U.S.A. 174 B3
Keoladeo National Park India 96 C4
Keosauqua U.S.A. 174 B3
Keowee, Lake resr U.S.A. 174 D5
Kepa Rus. Fed. 44 P2
Kepa r. Rus. Fed. 44 P2
Kepahiang Indon. 76 C3
Kępice Poland 49 N1
Kepina r. Rus. Fed. 40 G2
Kepler Mountains N.Z. 153 B13
Kępno Poland 49 O4
Keppel Bay Australia 149 F4
Keppel Harbour sea chan. Sing. 76 [inset]
Keppel Island Tonga see Tafahi
Kepsut Turkey 106 B3
Kerala state India 94 B4
historically known as Chera
Kerang Australia 147 D3
Kerava Fin. 45 N3
Kerba Alg. 55 M8
Kerbau, Tanjung pt Indon. 76 C3
Kerbela Iraq see Karbalā'
Kerben Kyrg. 103 G4
also spelt Karavan
Kerbi r. Rus. Fed. 82 E1
Kerch Ukr. 41 F7
historically known as Panticapaeum
Kerchem'ya Rus. Fed. 40 J3
Kerchevskiy Rus. Fed. 40 K4
Kere Eth. 128 C3
Kerema P.N.G. 73 K8
Keremeos Canada 166 G5
Kerempe Burun pt Turkey 106 C2
Keren Eritrea 121 H6
Kerend Iran 100 A3
Kerepehi N.Z. 152 J5
Kerest' r. Rus. Fed. 43 M2
Keret' Rus. Fed. 44 P2
Keret' r. Rus. Fed. 44 P2
Keret', Ozero l. Rus. Fed. 44 P2
Kerewan Gambia 124 A3
Kerey watercourse Kazakh. 103 G2
formerly spelt Kirey
Kerey, Ozero salt l. Kazakh. 103 G2
formerly spelt Kirey, Ozero
Kergeli Turkm. 102 D5
Kerguélen, Îles is Indian Ocean 219 L9
English form Kerguelen Islands
Kerguelen Islands Indian Ocean see Kerguélen, Îles
Kericho Kenya 128 B5
Kerihun mt. Indon. 77 F2
Kerikeri N.Z. 152 H3
Kerimäki Fin. 44 O3
Kerinci, Danau l. Indon. 76 C3

Kerinci, Gunung vol. Indon. 76 C3
formerly known as Gunung Indrapura or
Kerintji
Kerinci Seblat National Park Indon. 76 C3
Kerio watercourse Kenya 128 C4
Keriya China see Yutian
Keriya He watercourse China 88 C4
Keriya Shankou pass China 89 C5
Kerka r. Romania 49 N9
Kerkebet Eritrea 104 B4
Kerkenah, Îles i. Tunisia 123 H2
Kerki Turkm. 103 F5
Kerkichi Turkm. 103 F5
Kerkini Oros mts Bulg./Macedonia see
Belasica
Kerkinitis, Limni l. Greece 58 E7
Kérkira i. Greece see Corfu
Kérkira Greece 58 A9
Kerkyra admin. div. Greece see Corfu
Kerkyra i. Greece see Corfu
Kerma Sudan 128 B3
Kermadec Islands S. Pacific Ocean 145 H5

▶Kermadec Trench sea feature
S. Pacific Ocean 220 C8
4th deepest trench in the world.

Kermān Iran 100 D4
also spelt Kirman; historically known as
Carmana
Kermān prov. Iran 100 D4
Kerman U.S.A. 182 D5
Kermānshāh Iran 100 A3
formerly known as Bākhtarān or
Qahremānshahr
Kermānshāh prov. Iran 100 A3
formerly known as Bākhtarān or
Kermānshāhān
Kermānshāhān prov. Iran see Kermānshāh
Kermine Uzbek. see Navoi
Kermit U.S.A. 179 B6
Kern r. U.S.A. 182 E6
Kern, South Fork r. U.S.A. 182 F6
Kernersville U.S.A. 176 E9
Kernertut, Cap c. Canada 169 H1
Kernot Range hills Australia 148 B5
Kernville U.S.A. 182 F6
Keros i. Greece 59 G12
also spelt Káros
Kérouané Guinea 124 C4
Kerpen Germany 48 D5
Kerr, Cape Antarctica 223 K1
Kerrobert Canada 167 I5
Kerrville U.S.A. 179 C6
Kerry Head Rep. of Ireland 47 C11
Kersa Dek Eth. 128 C3
Kershaw U.S.A. 174 D5
Kert, Oued r. Morocco 55 H9
Kerteminde Denmark 45 J5
Kertosono Indon. 77 F4
Kerulen r. China/Mongolia 85 H1
also known as Herlen Gol or Herlen He
Kerumutan Reserve nature res. Indon.
76 C3
Kerur India 94 C3
Kerva Rus. Fed. 43 U6
Keryneia Cyprus see Kyrenia
Kerzaz Alg. 123 E3
Kerzhenets r. Rus. Fed. 40 H4
Kesagami r. Canada 168 D3
Kesagami Lake Canada 168 D3
Kesälahti Fin. 44 O3
Keşan Turkey 106 A2
Keşap Turkey 107 D2
Kesarevo Bulg. 58 A9
Kesariya India 97 E4
Kesennuma Japan 90 G5
Keshan China 82 B2
Keshem Afgh. 101 G2
Keshendeh-ye Bala Afgh. 101 F2
Keshod India 96 A5
Keshorai Patan India 96 C4
Keskin Turkey 106 C3
Keskozero Rus. Fed. 40 E3
Kes'ma Rus. Fed. 43 S4
Kesova Gora Rus. Fed. 43 S4
Kesra Tunisia 57 B13
Kestel Turkey see Gürsu
Kestel Turkey 59 K8
Kestell S. Africa 133 M5
Kesten'ga Rus. Fed. 44 P2
Kestilä Fin. 44 N2
Keswick U.K. 47 I9
Keswick Dam U.S.A. 182 B1
Keszthely Hungary 49 O9
Ket' r. Rus. Fed. 39 J4
Keta Ghana 125 F5
Ketahun Indon. 76 C3
Ketam, Pulau i. Sing. 76 [inset]
Ketapang Jawa Timur Indon. 77 F4
Ketapang Kalimantan Barat Indon. 77 E3
Ketchikan U.S.A. 166 D4
Ketchum U.S.A. 180 D4
Kete Krachi Ghana 125 E5
Ketmen', Khrebet mts China/Kazakh.
88 C3
Kétou Benin 125 F5
Ketoy, Ostrov i. Rus. Fed. 81 Q3
Kętrzyn Poland 49 S1
Kétté Cameroon 125 I5
Kettering U.K. 47 L11
Kettering U.S.A. 176 A6
formerly known as Van Buren
Kettle r. Canada 166 G5
Kettle r. U.S.A. 174 A2
Kettle Creek r. U.S.A. 176 H4
Kettle Falls U.S.A. 180 C2
Kettleman City U.S.A. 182 E5
Kettle River U.S.A. 172 A4
Kettle River Range mts U.S.A. 180 C2
Ketungau r. Indon. 77 E2
Keuka U.S.A. 177 H3
Keuka Lake U.S.A. 177 H3

Keumgang, Mount N. Korea see
Kumgang-san
Keumsang, Mount N. Korea see
Kumgang-san
Keur Massène Mauritania 124 A2
Keurusselkä l. Fin. 45 N3
Keuruu Fin. 44 N3
Kevelaer Germany 48 D4
Kevon luonnonpuisto nature res. Fin.
44 N1
Kew Turks and Caicos Is 187 E2
Kewanee U.S.A. 174 B3
Kewaskum U.S.A. 172 E7
Kewaunee U.S.A. 172 F6
Keweenaw Bay U.S.A. 172 E4
Keweenaw Bay b. U.S.A. 172 E4
Keweenaw Peninsula U.S.A. 172 E3
Keweenaw Point U.S.A. 172 F3
Keyala Sudan 128 B3
Keya Paha r. U.S.A. 178 C3
Key Harbour Canada 168 D4
Keyi China 88 C3
Keyihe China 85 I1
Key Largo U.S.A. 175 D7
Key Largo National Marine Sanctuary
nature res. U.S.A. 175 D7
Keyling Inlet Australia 148 A2
Keymir Turkm. see Kemir
Keyser U.S.A. 176 G6
Keysers Ridge U.S.A. 176 F6
Keystone Lake OK U.S.A. 178 D4
Keystone Lake PA U.S.A. 176 F5
Keysville U.S.A. 176 G8
Keytesville U.S.A. 178 D4
Keytü Iran 100 B3
Keyvy, Vozvyshennost' hills Rus. Fed.
40 I2
Key West FL U.S.A. 175 D7
Key West IA U.S.A. 172 C8
Kez Rus. Fed. 40 J4
Kezar Falls U.S.A. 177 O2
Kezi Zimbabwe 131 F4
Kežmarok Slovakia 49 R6
Kgakala S. Africa 133 K4
Kgalagadi admin. dist. Botswana 130 D5
Kgatleng admin. dist. Botswana 131 E5
Kgotsong S. Africa 133 K4
Khabari al Hajm salt pan Saudi Arabia
109 K6
Khabarikha Rus. Fed. 40 J2
Khabarovo Rus. Fed. 40 L1
Khabarovsk Rus. Fed. 82 D2
Khabarovskiy Kray admin. div. Rus. Fed.
82 D2
English form Khabarovsk Kray
Khabarovsk Kray admin. div. Rus. Fed. see
Khabarovskiy Kray
Khabis Iran see Shahdād
Khabody Pass Afgh. 101 E3
Khabrā al'Arn salt pan Saudi Arabia
104 C3
Khabrah Şāfiyah hill Saudi Arabia 109 K6
Khābūr, Nahr al r. Syria 109 L1
Khachmas Azer. see Xaçmaz
Khachrod India 96 B5
Khadar, Jabal mt. Oman 105 G3
Khaḍārah Saudi Arabia 104 C4
Khadari watercourse Sudan 126 E2
Khadun' Belarus 43 M8
Khadyzhensk Rus. Fed. 41 F7
Khadzhidimovo Bulg. 58 E7
Khadzhybey's'kyy Lyman l. Ukr. 58 L2
Khaga India 96 D4
Khagaul India 97 E4
Khagrachari Bangl. 97 F5
also spelt Khagrachhari
Khagrachhari Bangl. see Khagrachari
Khairagarh Chhattisgarh India 96 D5
Khairagarh Uttar Pradesh India 89 B7
Khaïrpur Pak. 101 H4
Khairpur Pak. 101 G5
Khairwara India 96 B5
Khaja du Koh hill Afgh. 103 F5
Khakasiya, Respublika aut. rep. Rus. Fed.
80 E2
English form Khakassia; formerly known as
Khakasskaya A.S.S.R.
Khakassia aut. rep. Rus. Fed. see
Khakasiya, Respublika
Khakasskaya A.S.S.R. aut. rep. Rus. Fed.
see Khakasiya, Respublika
Khak-e Jabbar Afgh. 101 G3
Khakhea Botswana 130 D5
Khakir Afgh. 101 F3
Khakriz Afgh. 101 F4
Khalach Turkm. 103 F5
also spelt Halach
Khalajestan reg. Iran 100 B3
Khalamyer"ye Belarus 43 K6
Khalatse Jammu and Kashmir 96 C2
Khalidabad Iran 100 C3
Khalilabad Iran 100 D3
Khalilovo Rus. Fed. 102 D2
Khalkabad Turkm. 103 E4
Khalkabad Uzbek. 102 D4
also spelt Khalqobod
Khalkhāl Iran 100 B2
formerly known as Herowābād
Khálki i. Greece see Chalki
Khalkís Greece see Chalkida
Khallikot India 95 E2
Khal'mer-Yu Rus. Fed. 40 M2
Khalopyenichy Belarus 43 J7
Khalqobod Uzbek. see Khalkabad
Khalte Nepal 97 E4
Khalturin Rus. Fed. see Orlov
Khamar-Daban, Khrebet mts Rus. Fed.
84 D1
Khamaria India 96 D5
Khambhaliya India 96 A5
Khambhat India 96 B5
formerly known as Cambay
Khambhat, Gulf of India 94 A2
also known as Cambay, Gulf of
Khamgaon India 94 C1
Khamir Iran 100 C4
Khamir Yemen 104 C4
Khami Ruins National Monument
tourist site Zimbabwe 131 F4
Khamis Mushayţ Saudi Arabia 104 C3
Khamma well Saudi Arabia 105 D2
Khammam India 94 D2
Khampa Rus. Fed. 39 M3
Khampat Myanmar 78 A3
Khamra Rus. Fed. 39 L3
Khamseh reg. Iran 100 B3
Khamza Uzbek. 103 G4
also spelt Hamza; formerly known as imeni
Khamzy Khakimzade
Khan r. Namibia 130 B4
Khan, Nam r. Laos 78 C4
Khānābād Afgh. 101 G2
Khanabad Uzbek. 103 H4
also spelt Khonobod; formerly known as
Sovetabad
Khān al Baghdādī Iraq 107 E4
Khān al Hammād Iraq 109 P5
Khān al Maḩāwīl Iraq 107 F4
Khanapur Karnataka India 94 B3
Khanapur Maharashtra India 94 B2
Khānaqāh Iran 100 A2
Khān ar Raḩbah Iraq 107 F5
also known as Khan Ruḩbah
Khanasur Pass Iran/Turkey 107 F3

Khanbalik China see Beijing
Khânch Iran 100 A2
Khandagayty Rus. Fed. 84 B1
Khandala India 94 B2
Khandud Afgh. 101 H2
Khandwa India 96 C5
Khandyga Rus. Fed. 39 N3
Khâneh Khowreh Iran 100 C4
Khanewal Pak. 101 G4
Khangarh Pak. 101 G4
Khanh Dương Vietnam 79 E5
Khan Hung Vietnam see Soc Trăng
Khani Rus. Fed. 39 M4
Khaniá Greece see Chania
Khaniadhana India 96 C4
Khanino Rus. Fed. 43 R7
Khāni Yek Iran 100 C4
Khanka Uzbek. 102 E4
also spelt Khonqa; formerly spelt Khanki
Khanka, Lake China/Rus. Fed. see
Khanka, Ozero
Khanka, Ozero l. China/Rus. Fed. see
Khanka, Lake
Khankendi Azer. see Xankändi
Khanki Uzbek. see Khanka
Khanna India 96 C3
Khannā, Qāʻ salt pan Jordan 109 H5
Khannfoussa hill Alg. 123 G4
Khanovey Rus. Fed. 40 L2
Khanpur Pak. 101 G4
Khān Ruḩābah Iraq see Khān ar Raḩbah
Khān Shaykhūn Syria 109 H2
Khansiir, Raas pt Somalia 128 E2
Khantau Kazakh. 103 H3
Khantayskoye, Ozero l. Rus. Fed. 39 J3
Khantayskoye Vodokhranilishche resr
Rus. Fed. 39 I3
Khan-Tengri, Pik mt. Kazakh./Kyrg. 88 C3
also known as Hantengri Feng or
Kan-Too,Pik
Khanty-Mansiysk Rus. Fed. 38 G3
Khanty-Mansiyskiy Avtonomnyy Okrug
admin. div. Rus. Fed. 40 L3
English form Khanty-Mansy Autonomous
Okrug
Khanty-Mansy Autonomous Okrug
admin. div. Rus. Fed. see
Khanty-Mansiyskiy Avtonomnyy Okrug
Khān Yūnis Gaza 108 A4
Khao-ang-runai Wildlife Reserve
nature res. Thai. 79 C5
Khao Banthat Wildlife Reserve nature res.
Thai. 79 B7
Khao Chum Thong Thai. 79 B6
Khaoen Si Nakarin National Park Thai.
79 B5
Khao Laem National Park Thai. 79 B5
Khao Laem Reservoir Thai. 79 B5
Khao Luang National Park Thai. 79 B6
Khao Pu-Khao Ya National Park Thai.
79 B7
Khao-soi-dao Wildlife Reserve nature res.
Thai. 79 C5
Khao Sok National Park Thai. 79 B6
Khao Yai National Park Thai. 79 C5
Khapa India 96 C5
Khapcheranga Rus. Fed. 85 G1
Khaptad National Park Nepal 96 C3
Kharabali Rus. Fed. 102 A3
Kharaghoda India 96 A5
Kharagpur Bihar India 97 E4
Kharagpur W. Bengal India 97 E5
Kharaki Iran 100 C2
Khārān r. Iran 100 D3
Kharan Pak. 101 F4
Kharari India see Abu Road
Khardi India 94 B2
Khardung La pass Jammu and Kashmir
96 C2
also known as Laowohi
Kharfiyah Iraq 107 F5
Kharga r. Rus. Fed. 82 D1
Kharga Oasis Egypt 121 F3
also known as The Great Oasis
Khargapur India 96 C4
Kharg Islands Iran 100 B4
Khargon India 96 B5
Khari r. India 96 B4
Kharian Pak. 101 H3
Khariar India 95 D1
Kharīm, Gebel hill Egypt 108 E7
Kharkhara r. India 96 D5
Kharkhauda India 96 C3
Kharkiv Ukr. 41 F6
also spelt Khar'kov
Khar'kov Ukr. see Kharkiv
Khār Kūh mt. Iran 100 C4
Kharlu Rus. Fed. 40 D3
Kharmah, Ghubbat b. Yemen 105 F5
Kharmanli Bulg. 58 G7
Kharora India 97 D5
Kharovsk Rus. Fed. 43 V3
Kharovskaya Gryada hills Rus. Fed. 43 V2
Kharsawan India 97 E5
Kharsia India 97 D5

▶Khartoum Sudan 121 G6
Capital of Sudan. Also spelt El Khartûm.

Khartoum state Sudan 121 G6
Khartoum North Sudan 121 G6
Kharuf, Ra's mt. Israel see Harif, Har
Kharwar reg. Afgh. 101 F3
Khasab, Khor b. Oman 105 F2
Khasardag, Gora mt. Turkm. 102 D5
Khasav'yurt Rus. Fed. 102 A4
Khash Afgh. 101 E4
Khāsh Iran 101 E4
also known as Vasht
Khash Desert Afgh. 101 E4
Khashgort Rus. Fed. 38 G3
Khashm el Girba Sudan 121 G6
Khashm el Girba Dam Sudan 121 G6
Khash Rūd r. Afgh. 101 E4
Khashuri Georgia 107 E2
Khasi Hills India 97 F4
Khaskovo Bulg. 58 G7
Khasm al Mu'ayqil hill Saudi Arabia 105 E2
Khatam, Jabal al hill Saudi Arabia 104 B2
Khatanga Rus. Fed. 39 K2
Khatanga r. Rus. Fed. 39 K2
Khatanga, Gulf of Rus. Fed. see
Khatangskiy Zaliv
Khatangskiy Zaliv b. Rus. Fed. 39 K2
English form Khatanga, Gulf of
Khategaon India 96 C5
Khatinza Pass Pak. 101 G2
Khatlon admin. div. Tajik. 101 G2
English form Khatlon Oblast
Khatlon Oblast admin. div. Tajik. see
Khatlon
Khatmat al Malāha Oman 105 G2
Khatmia Pass Egypt 108 D7
Khātūnābād Iran 100 B3
Khatyrka Rus. Fed. 39 R3
Khavast Uzbek. 103 G4
also known as Khovos; formerly known as
Ursat'yevskaya
Khavda India 96 A5
Khawak Pass Afgh. 101 G3
Khawlaf, Ra's pt Yemen 105 F5
Khawr Shiban well Saudi Arabia 104 C4
Khaybar Saudi Arabia 104 B2
Khayamnandi S. Africa 133 J8
Khayatbashi, Gora mt. Uzbek. 103 F4
also known as Hayotboshi Toghi
Khaybar Saudi Arabia 104 B2
also known as Ash Shuray'
Khaydarken Kyrg. 103 G5
Khayelitsha S. Africa 132 C11
Khaypudyrskaya Guba b. Rus. Fed. 40 K1

Khayrān, Ra's al pt Oman 105 G3
Khazarasp Uzbek. 103 E4
also known as Hazorasp
Khé Bo Vietnam see Con Cuông
Khed Maharashtra India 94 B2
Khed Maharashtra India 94 B2
Kheda India 96 B5
formerly known as Kaira
Khedbrahma India 96 B4
Khedri Iran 100 D3
Khefa Israel see Haifa
Khehuene, Ponta pt Moz. 131 G4
Khelari India 97 E5
Khelyulya Rus. Fed. 44 O3
Khemarak Phumint Cambodia see
Krŏng Kaôh Kŏng
Khemis Anjra Morocco 54 F9
Khemis Beni Arous Morocco 54 F9
Khemis Miliana Alg. 123 F1
formerly known as Affreville
Khemisset Morocco 122 D2
Khenchela Alg. 123 G2
Khenifra Morocco 122 D2
Khenjan Afgh. 101 G3
Kherämeh Iran 100 C4
Kherli India 96 C4
Kherrah Iran 100 C5
Khersan r. Iran 100 B4
Kherson Ukr. 41 E7
Khe Sanh Vietnam 78 D4
Khesht Iran 100 B4
Kheta r. Rus. Fed. 39 K2
Khetolambina Rus. Fed. 44 P2
Kheyrābād Iran 100 C4
Khezerābād Iran 100 C2
also known as Farahābād
Khiaw, Khao mt. Thai. 79 C5
Khidr, Wādī al watercourse Iraq 109 O6
Khisarya Bulg. 58 F6
Khislavichi Rus. Fed. 43 N7
Khitai Pass Aksai Chin 89 B5
Khiva Uzbek. 102 E4
also spelt Khiwa
Khiwa Uzbek. see Khiva
Khiyāv Iran 100 A2
Khiytola Rus. Fed. 45 O3
Khlepen' Rus. Fed. 43 P6
Khlong, Mae r. Thai. 79 C5
Khlong-saeng Wildlife Reserve nature res.
Thai. 79 B6
Khlung Thai. 79 C5
Khmelezero Rus. Fed. 43 P1
Khmelinets Rus. Fed. 43 T9
Khmelita Rus. Fed. 43 O6
Khmel'nik Ukr. see Khmil'nyk
Khmel'nits'kyy Ukr. see Khmel'nyts'kyy
Khmel'nyts'kyy Ukr. 41 C6
also spelt Khmel'nitskiy; formerly known as
Proskurov
Khmer Republic country Asia see
Cambodia
Khmes, Jebel mt. Morocco 54 F9
Khmil'nyk Ukr. 41 C6
also spelt Khmel'nik
Khobda Kazakh. 102 C2
formerly known as Novoalekseyevka
Khodā Āfarīd spring Iran 100 D3
Khodasy Belarus 43 M8
Khodzha Davlet Uzbek. 103 E5
Khodzha-Kala Turkm. 102 D5
also spelt Hojagala
Khodzhaolen Turkm. 102 D5
Khodzhapir'yakh, Gora mt. Uzbek. 92 C3
Khodzhavend Azer. see Xocavänd
Khodzhent Tajik. see Khŭjand
Khodzheyli Uzbek. 102 D4
also spelt Khŭjayli
Khodzhycer r. Ukr. 58 K3
Khogali Sudan 126 E3
Khojand Tajik. see Khŭjand
Khokhlovo Rus. Fed. 43 S2
Khokhol'skiy Rus. Fed. 41 F6
Kholapur India 94 C1
Kholbon Rus. Fed. 85 H1
Kholm Afgh. 101 F2
also known as Tāshqurghān
Kholm Poland see Chełm
Kholm Novgorodskaya Oblast' Rus. Fed. 40 D4
Kholm Smolenskaya Oblast' Rus. Fed. 43 M6
Kholmechi Rus. Fed. 43 P9
Kholmogory Rus. Fed. 40 G2
Kholmsk Rus. Fed. 82 F3
Kholm-Zhirkovskiy Rus. Fed. 43 O6
Kholon Israel see Holon
Kholova r. Rus. Fed. 43 N3
Kholzun, Khrebet mts Kazakh./Rus. Fed.
88 D1
Khoman Iran 100 B3
Khomas admin. reg. Namibia 130 C4
Khomas Highland hills Namibia 130 B4
Khomeyn Iran 100 B3
Khomeynīshahr Iran 100 B3
formerly known as Homāyūnshahr
Khomutovo Rus. Fed. 43 S9
Khong, Mae Nam r. Myanmar see Salween
Khonj Iran 100 C5
Khonj, Kūh-e Iran 100 C5
Khon Kaen Thai. 78 C4
Khonobod Uzbek. see Khanabad
Khonqa Uzbek. see Khanka
Khonsa India 97 G4
Khonuu Rus. Fed. 39 N3
Khoper r. Rus. Fed. 41 G6
Khor Rus. Fed. 82 D3
Khor r. Rus. Fed. 82 D3
Khóra Greece see Chora
Khorāsan prov. Iran see Khorāsān
Khorat Plateau Thai. 78 C4
Khorazm Wiloyati admin. div. Uzbek. see
Khorezmskaya Oblast'
Khordha India 95 E1
Khoreyver r. Rus. Fed. 40 K2
Khorezm Oblast admin. div. Uzbek. see
Khorezmskaya Oblast'
Khorezmskaya Oblast' admin. div. Uzbek.
102 E4
English form Khorezm Oblast; also known as
Khorazm Wiloyati
Khorinsk Rus. Fed. 81 H2
Khorixas Namibia 130 B4
formerly known as Welwitschia
Khorixas Namibia 130 B4
Khormūj, Kūh-e mt. Iran 100 B4
Khorog Tajik. see Khorugh
Khorol Rus. Fed. 82 D3
Khorol Ukr. 41 E6
Khorramābād Iran 100 B3
Khorram Darreh Iran 100 B2
Khorramshahr Iran 100 B4
formerly known as Khūninshahr or
Muhammarah

Khorugh Tajik. 101 G2
also spelt Khorog
Khosedayu r. Rus. Fed. 40 K2
Khosf Iran 100 D3
Khosheutovo Rus. Fed. 102 A3
Khosravī Iran 100 B4
Khosrovi Argelanots' nature res. Armenia
107 F2
Khosta Rus. Fed. 41 F8
Khotan China see Hotan
Khotang Nepal 97 E4
Khotetovo Rus. Fed. 43 R9
Khot"kovo Rus. Fed. 43 S5
Khotyn Ukr. 41 C6
Khotynets Belarus 43 O8
Khouribga Morocco 122 D2
Khovaling Tajik. 101 G2
Khovu-Aksy Rus. Fed. 84 B1
Khowai India 97 F5
Khowos Uzbek. see Khavast
Khowrjān Iran 100 C4
Khewrnag, Kūh-e mt. Iran 100 C3
Khowst Afgh. 101 G3
also known as Matun
Khowst reg. Afgh./Pak. 101 G3
Khozap'ini, Tba l. Georgia 107 E2
Khozor Anghar Djibouti 104 C5
Khram, Ko i. Thai. 79 C5
Khri r. India 97 F4
Khrisoúpolis Greece see Chrysoupoli
Khristoforovo Rus. Fed. 40 H3
Khroma r. Rus. Fed. 39 N2
Khromtau Kazakh. 102 C2
Khru r. India 97 G4
Khrushchev Ukr. see Svitlovods'k
Khrushchovo Rus. Fed. 43 U9
Khrustalnyy Rus. Fed. 82 D3
Khrysokhou Bay Cyprus see
Chrysochou Bay
Khubbāz, Wādī watercourse Iraq 109 N4
Khubelu r. Lesotho 133 M6
Khudan r. Rus. Fed. 85 F1
Khudat Azer. see Xudat
Khude Hills Pak. 101 H4
Khudian Pak. 101 H4
Khudumelapye Botswana 131 E5
Khufaysah, Khashm al hill Saudi Arabia
105 D3
Khuff Saudi Arabia 104 C3
Khugiana Afgh. see Pirzada
Khūh Lab, Ra's pt Iran 101 E5
Khuis Botswana 132 F3
Khujand Tajik. 101 G1
also spelt Khocznent or Khojand or
Khudzhand; formerly known as Ispisar or
Leninabad or Leninobod
Khŭjand admin. div. Tajik. see Khodzheyli
Khŭjayli Uzbek. see Khodzheyli
Khu Khan Thai 79 D5
Khulays Saudi Arabia 104 B3
Khuldabad Ind a 94 B1
also known as Rauza
Khulga r. Rus. Fed. 40 L2
Khulkhuta Rus. Fed. 102 A3
Khulm r. Afgh. 101 F2
Khulna Bangl. 97 F5
Khulna admin. div. Bangl. 97 F5
Khuma S. Africa 133 K3
Khunayzir, Jabal al mts Syria 109 I3
Khunayzir, Wādī watercourse Syria 109 M1
Khuneiqa watercourse Sudan 121 F6
Khunik Bālā Iran 101 D3
Khūninshahr Iran see Khorramshahr
Khunjerab Pass China/Jammu and Kashmir
89 A4
Khunsar Iran 100 B3
Khunti India 97 E5
Khur Iran 100 D3
Khūr Iran 100 D3
Khurai India 96 C4
Khūran sea chan. Iran 100 C5
Khurays Saudi Arabia 105 E2
Khurd, Koh-i- mt. Afgh. 101 F3
Khureit Sudan 121 E6
Khuria Tank resr India see Maniari Tank
Khurja India 96 C3
Khurmalik Afgh. 101 E3
Khurmuli Rus. Fed. 82 E2
Khuzdar Pak. 101 F5
Khŭzestan prov. Iran 100 B4
Khvāf reg. Iran 101 E3
Khvājeh Iran 100 A2
Khvalynsk Rus. Fed. 102 B1
Khvashchevka Rus. Fed. 43 P5
Khvastovichi Rus. Fed. 43 Q8
Khvor Iran 100 C3
Khvord Narvan Iran 100 C3
Khvormūj Iran 100 B4
Khvorostyanka Rus. Fed. 102 B1
Khvosh Maqām Iran 100 A2
Khvoshna Belarus 102 L6
Khvoy Iran 100 A2
Khvoynaya Rus. Fed. 43 P3
Khvoynyy Rus. Fed. 82 B1
Khwae Noi r. Thai. 79 B5
Khwahan Afgh. 101 G2
Khwaja Amran mt. Pak. 101 F4
Khwaja-i-Ghar Afgh. 101 G2
Khwaja Muhammad Range mts Afgh.
101 G2
Khyber Pass Afgh./Pak. 101 G3
Khynchest' Moldova see Hîncești
Khynchesty Moldova see Hîncești
Kia'i r. Fin. 44 M2
Kiantajärvi r. Fin. 44 O2
Kiasar Iran see Darta
Kiate Greece 59 D10
Kibaha Tanz. 129 C6
Kibala Angola 127 B6
Kibale National Park Uganda 128 A4
Kibali r. Dem. Rep. Congo 126 F4
Kibangou Congo 126 B5
Kibara Tanz. 128 B5
Kibara, Monts mts Dem. Rep. Congo
127 E7
Kibawe Phil. 74 C5
Kibaya Tanz. 129 C6
Kiberashi Tanz. 129 C6
Kiboga Uganda 128 A4
Kibombo Dem. Rep. Congo 126 E5
Kibondo Tanz. 128 A5

Kibray Uzbek. 103 G4
also spelt Qibray
Kibre Mengist Eth. 128 C3
Kibris country Asia see Cyprus
Kibrît, Jabal al hill Saudi Arabia 108 F9
Kibungo Rwanda 126 F5
Kibuye Rwanda 126 F5
Kibwesa Tanz. 129 A6
Kičevo Macedonia 58 B7
Kichi-Kichi well Chad 120 C5
Kichmengskiy Gorodok Rus. Fed. 40 H4
Kichwamba Uganda 128 A5
Kicking Horse Pass Canada 167 G5
Kid, Wādī watercourse Egypt 108 F9
Kidal Mali 125 F2
Kidal admin. reg. Mali 125 F2
Kidatu Tanz. 129 C6
Kidderminster U.K. 47 J11
Kidepo Valley National Park Uganda
128 B4
Kidete Tanz. 129 C6
Kidira Senegal 124 B3
Kidmang Jammu and Kashmir 96 C2
Kidnappers, Cape N.Z. 152 L7
Kiel Germany 48 H1
Kiel U.S.A. 172 E7
Kiel Canal Germany see Nord-Ostsee-Kanal
Kielce Poland 49 R5
Kielder Water resr U.K. 47 J8
Kieler Bucht b. Germany 48 H1
Kieler Förde g. Germany 48 H1
Kiembara Burkina 124 E3
Kienge Dem. Rep. Congo 127 E7
Kietrz Poland 49 P5
Kiev Kazakh. see Kiyevka

▶Kiev Ukr. 41 D6
Capital of Ukraine. Also spelt Kiyev or Kyiv
or Kyyev or Kyyiv; historically known as
Kõnugard or Sambat.

Kiffa Mauritania 124 C2
Kifisia Greece 59 E10
Kifisos r. Greece 59 E10
Kifri Iraq 107 F4
Kifwanzondo Dem. Rep. Congo 126 C6

▶Kigali Rwanda 126 F5
Capital of Rwanda.

Kiğı Turkey 107 E3
Kiglapait Mountains Canada 169 I1
Kigliakvik Lake Canada 167 H1
Kignan Mali 124 C3
Kigoma Tanz. 129 A6
Kigoma admin. reg. Tanz. 129 A6
Kigwe Tanz. 129 C6
Kihambatang Indon. 77 F3
Kihei U.S.A. 181 [inset] Z1
Kihikihi N.Z. 152 J6
Kihlanki Fin. 44 M2
Kihniö Fin. 45 M3
Kihnu i. Estonia 42 E3
Kiik Kazakh. 103 H3
Kiikala Fin. 42 E1
Kiiminki Fin. 44 N2
Kii-nagashima Japan 91 E7
Kii-sanchi mts Japan 91 D8
Kii-suidō sea chan. Japan 91 D8
Kiiu Well Tanz. 129 C6
Kikerino Rus. Fed. 43 K2
Kikerk Lake Canada 167 H1
Kikinda Vojvodina, Srbija Yugo. 58 B3
Kikki Pak. 101 E5
Kikládhes is Greece see Cyclades
Kiknur Rus. Fed. 40 H4
Kikonai Japan 90 G4
Kikondja Dem. Rep. Congo 127 E7
Kikongo Dem. Rep. Congo 126 C6
Kikori P.N.G. 73 J8
Kikori r. P.N.G. 73 J8
Kikuchi Japan 91 B8
Kikwit Dem. Rep. Congo 126 C6
Kil Sweden 45 L4
Kilafors Sweden 45 L3
Kilakkarai India 94 C4
Kilan Iran 100 C3
Kilauea U.S.A. 181 [inset] Y1
Kilauea Crater U.S.A. 181 [inset] Z2
world [volcanoes] ▶ 14–15
Kilboghamn Norway 44 K2
Kilbotn Norway 44 L1
Kilchu N. Korea 83 C4
Kilcoy Australia 149 G5
Kildare Rep. of Ireland 47 F10
Kil'dinstroy Rus. Fed. 44 P1
Kildonan Zimbabwe 131 F3
Kilekale Lake Canada 166 F1
Kilemary Rus. Fed. 40 H4
Kilembe Dem. Rep. Congo 127 C6
Kilgore U.S.A. 179 D5
Kilgour r. Australia 148 B3
Kilia Ukr. see Kiliya
Kiliba Dem. Rep. Congo 126 F5
Kilibo Benin 125 F4
Kilifi Kenya 128 C5
Kilik Pass China 89 A4
Kilimanjaro admin. reg. Tanz. 129 C5

▶Kilimanjaro vol. Tanz. 128 C5
Highest mountain in Africa.
africa [landscapes] ▶ 112–113

Kilimanjaro National Park Tanz. 128 C5
Kilimatinde Tanz. 129 B6
Kilinailau Islands P.N.G. 145 E2
formerly known as Carteret Group or Nine
Islands
Kilindoni Tanz. 129 C6
Kilingi-Nõmme Estonia 42 F3
Kılıs Turkey 107 D3
Kılıs prov. Turkey 109 I1
Kiliya Ukr. 58 K3
also known as Chilia-Nouă; also spelt Kilia
Kilkee Rep. of Ireland 47 C11
Kilkenny Rep. of Ireland 47 E11
also spelt Cill Chainnigh
Kilkis Greece 58 D8
Killala Rep. of Ireland 47 C9
Killala Bay Rep. of Ireland 47 C9
Killala Lake Canada 172 G1
Killaloe Rep. of Ireland 47 D11
Killaloe Station Canada 173 P5
Killam Canada 167 I4
Killarney Australia 147 G2
Killarney Canada 168 D4
Killarney Rep. of Ireland 47 C11
also spelt Cill Airne
Killarney National Park Rep. of Ireland
47 C12
Killarney Provincial Park Canada 173 L4
Killary Harbour b. Rep. of Ireland 47 C10
Killeen U.S.A. 179 C6
Killin U.K. 46 H7
Killinek Island Canada see Killiniq Island
Killini mt. Greece see Kyllini
Killiniq Canada 165 M3
Killiniq Island Canada 165 M3
also spelt Killinek Island
Killorglin Rep. of Ireland 47 C11
Killybegs Rep. of Ireland 47 D9
Kilmarnock U.K. 46 H8
Kilmarnock U.S.A. 177 I8
Kil'mez' Rus. Fed. 40 I4
Kil'mez' r. Rus. Fed. 40 I4
Kilmore Australia 147 E4
Kilosa Tanz. 129 C6
Kilpisjärvi Fin. 44 M1
Kilpua Fin. 44 N2

Kilrush Rep. of Ireland 47 C11
Kilttan i. India 94 B4
Kilwa Dem. Rep. Congo 127 F7
Kilwa Masoko Tanz. 129 C7
Kilyazi Azer. see Gilăzi
Kim Chad 126 B2
Kimambi Tanz. 129 C7
Kimanis, Teluk b. Sabah Malaysia 77 F1
Kimasozero Rus. Fed. 44 O2
Kimasozero, Ozero l. Rus. Fed. 44 O2
Kimba Australia 146 C3
Kimba Congo 126 B5
Kimball NE U.S.A. 178 B3
Kimbe P.N.G. 145 E2
Kimberley Canada 167 H5
Kimberley S. Africa 133 I5
Kimberley Downs Australia 150 D3
Kimberley Plateau Australia 150 D3
Kimberley Range hills Australia 151 B5
Kimbirila-Sud Côte d'Ivoire 124 D4
formerly known as Kinbirila
Kimch'aek N. Korea 83 C4
also known as Sŏngjin
Kimch'ŏn S. Korea 83 C5
Kimhae S. Korea 83 C6
Kími Greece see Kymi
Kimito Fin. 45 M3
also known as Kemiö
Kimje S. Korea 83 B6
Kimmirut Canada 165 M3
formerly known as Lake Harbour
Kimobetsu Japan 90 G3
Kimolos i. Greece 59 F12
Kimolou-Sifnou, Steno sea chan. Greece 59 F12
Kimongo Congo 126 B6
Kimovaara Rus. Fed. 44 O3
Kimovsk Rus. Fed. 43 T8
formerly known as Mikhaylovka
Kimpanga Dem. Rep. Congo 127 E6
Kimpangu Dem. Rep. Congo 127 B6
Kimparana Mali 124 D3
Kimper U.S.A. 176 C8
Kimpese Dem. Rep. Congo 127 B6
Kimpoko Dem. Rep. Congo 126 B6
Kimpoku-san mt. Japan see Kinpoku-san
Kimry Rus. Fed. 43 S5
Kimsquit Canada 166 E4
Kimvula Dem. Rep. Congo 127 B6
Kinabalu, Gunung mt. Sabah Malaysia 77 G1
Kinabalu National Park Sabah Malaysia 77 G1
Kinabatangan r. Sabah Malaysia 77 G1
Kınalıada i. Turkey 58 K8
Kinango Kenya 129 C6
Kinaros i. Greece 59 H12
Kinaskan Lake Canada 166 D3
Kinbasket Lake Canada 166 G4
also known as McNaughton Lake
Kinbirila Côte d'Ivoire see Kimbirila-Sud
Kinbrace U.K. 46 I5
Kincaid Canada 167 J5
Kincardine Canada 168 D4
Kinchang Myanmar 78 B2
Kinchega National Park Australia 147 D3
Kincolith Canada 166 D4
Kinda Dem. Rep. Congo 127 E7
Kindamba Congo 126 B5
Kindat Myanmar 78 A3
Kinde U.S.A. 173 K7
Kindembe Dem. Rep. Congo 127 C6
Kinder U.S.A. 179 D6
Kindersley Canada 167 I5
Kindia Guinea 124 B4
Kindongo-Mbe Dem. Rep. Congo 126 C5
Kindu Dem. Rep. Congo 126 E5
Kinel' Rus. Fed. 41 I5
Kinel'-Cherkasy Rus. Fed. 41 I5
Kineshma Rus. Fed. 40 G4
King r. N.T. Australia 148 B2
King r. W.A. Australia 150 E2
King U.S.A. 176 E9
King, Canal sea chan. Chile 205 B7
King, Lake salt flat Australia 151 C5
King and Queen Courthouse U.S.A. 177 I8
Kingaroy Australia 149 F5
King City U.S.A. 182 C5
Kingcome r. Canada 166 E5
King Creek watercourse Australia 148 C5
King Edward r. Australia 150 D2
Kingfisher U.S.A. 179 C5
King George Bay Falkland Is 205 E8
King George Island Antarctica 222 U2
King George Islands Canada 168 E1
King George Islands Fr. Polynesia see Roi Georges, Îles du
King George Sound b. Australia 151 B7
King George VI Falls Guyana 199 F3
Kingimbi Dem. Rep. Congo 126 B6
Kingisepp Rus. Fed. 43 J2
King Island Australia 147 D4
King Island Canada 166 E4
King Island Myanmar see Kadan Kyun
Kingisseppa Estonia see Kuressaare
King Kirkland Canada 173 N2
Kinglake National Park Australia 147 E4
King Leopold and Queen Astrid Coast Antarctica 223 F2
King Leopold Range National Park Australia 150 D3
King Leopold Ranges hills Australia 150 D3
Kingman AZ U.S.A. 183 J6
Kingman KS U.S.A. 178 C4

▶Kingman Reef N. Pacific Ocean 221 H5
United States Unincorporated Territory.
oceania [countries] ▶ 138–139

King Mountain Canada 166 D3
King Mountain hill U.S.A. 179 B6
Kingombe Mbali Dem. Rep. Congo 126 E5
Kingondji Dem. Rep. Congo 127 C6
Kingoonya Australia 146 B2
King Peak Antarctica 223 S1
King Peninsula Antarctica 222 R2
Kingri Pak. 101 G4
Kings r. CA U.S.A. 182 D5
Kings r. NV U.S.A. 180 C4
Kingsburg U.S.A. 182 E5
Kings Canyon Australia 148 A5
Kings Canyon National Park U.S.A. 182 F5
Kingscote Australia 146 C3
Kingscourt Rep. of Ireland 47 F10
Kingseat N.Z. 152 I5
King Sejong research station Antarctica 222 U2
Kingsford U.S.A. 172 E5
Kingsland GA U.S.A. 175 D6
Kingsland IN U.S.A. 173 H10
Kingsley S. Africa 133 O4
Kingsley U.S.A. 172 H6
King's Lynn U.K. 47 M11
short form Lynn
Kingsmill Group is Kiribati 145 G2
Kings Sound b. Australia 150 C3
Kings Peak U.S.A. 183 N1
Kingsport U.S.A. 176 C9
Kingston Australia 147 E5
Kingston Canada 168 E4

▶Kingston Jamaica 186 D3
Capital of Jamaica.

▶Kingston Norfolk I. 220 F7
Capital of Norfolk Island.

Kingston N.Z. 153 C13
Kingston MA U.S.A. 177 O4
Kingston MO U.S.A. 178 D4
Kingston NY U.S.A. 177 K4
Kingston OH U.S.A. 176 C6
Kingston PA U.S.A. 177 J4
Kingston TN U.S.A. 174 C5
Kingston Peak U.S.A. 183 I6
Kingston South East Australia 146 C4
Kingston upon Hull U.K. 47 L10
short form Hull

▶Kingstown St Vincent 187 H4
Capital of St Vincent.

Kingstree U.S.A. 175 E5
Kingsville U.S.A. 179 C7
Kingswood U.K. 47 J12
Kington U.K. 47 I11
Kingungi Dem. Rep. Congo 127 C6
Kingurutik r. Canada 169 I1
Kingussie U.K. 46 H6
King William Island Canada 165 J3
King William's Town S. Africa 133 L9
Kingwood TX U.S.A. 179 D6
Kingwood WV U.S.A. 176 F6
Kiniama Dem. Rep. Congo 127 F7
Kınık Antalya Turkey 59 K12
Kınık İzmir Turkey 59 I9
Kinkala Congo 126 B6
Kinka-san i. Japan 90 G5
Kinleith N.Z. 152 J6
Kinloch N.Z. 153 C12
Kinlochleven U.K. 46 H7
Kinmen Taiwan see Chinmen
Kinmount Canada 173 O6
Kinna Sweden 45 K4
Kinnarasani r. India 94 D2
Kinnarodden pt Norway 44 N1
Kinnegad Rep. of Ireland 47 E10
Kinneret, Yam l. Israel see Galilee, Sea of
Kinniyai Sri Lanka 94 D4
Kinnula Fin. 44 N3
Kinoje r. Canada 168 D2
Kino-kawa r. Japan 91 D7
Kinomoto Japan 91 E7
Kinoosao Canada 167 K3
Kinpoku-san mt. Japan 90 F5
also spelt Kimpoku-san
Kinross S. Africa 133 N3
Kinsale Rep. of Ireland 47 D12
Kinsale U.S.A. 177 I7
Kinsarvik Norway 45 I3
Kinsele Dem. Rep. Congo 126 C6

▶Kinshasa Dem. Rep. Congo 126 B6
Capital of the Democratic Republic of Congo and 3rd most populous city in Africa. Formerly known as Léopoldville.
world [cities] ▶ 24–25

Kinshasa municipality Dem. Rep. Congo 126 C6
Kinsley U.S.A. 178 C4
Kinston U.S.A. 174 E5
Kintai Lith. 42 C6
Kintampo Ghana 125 E4
Kintata Dem. Rep. Congo 127 B6
Kintinian Guinea 124 C4
Kintom Indon. 75 B3
Kintop Indon. 77 F3
Kintore Australia 148 A4
Kintore, Mount Australia 146 A1
Kintyre pen. U.K. 46 G8
Kinu Myanmar 78 A3
Kinushseo r. Canada 168 D2
Kinuso Canada 167 H4
Kinwat India 94 C2
Kinyangiri Tanz. 129 B6
Kinyeti mt. Sudan 128 B4
Kinzhaly Kazakh. 102 D2
Kiomboi Tanz. 129 B6
Kiosk Canada 173 O4
Kiowa CO U.S.A. 180 F5
Kiowa KS U.S.A. 178 C4
Kipahigan Lake Canada 167 K4
Kipahulu U.S.A. 181 [inset] Z1
Kiparissia Greece see Kyparissia
Kipawa, Lac l. Canada 168 E4
Kipchak Pass China 88 B3
Kipelovo Rus. Fed. 43 U2
Kipen' Rus. Fed. 43 K2
Kipengere Range mts Tanz. 129 B7
Kipili Tanz. 129 A6
Kipini Kenya 128 D5
Kipling Canada 167 K5
formerly known as Kipling Station
Kipling Station Canada see Kipling
Kiptopeke U.S.A. 177 J8
Kipungo Angola see Quipungo
Kipushi Dem. Rep. Congo 127 E7
Kipushia Dem. Rep. Congo 127 F8
Kirakat India 97 D4
Kirakira Solomon Is 145 F3
Kiran Dağları hills Turkey 59 H10
Kirandul India 94 D2
Kirané Mali 124 C3
Kirawsk Belarus 43 K8
Kiraz Turkey 59 J10
Kirbla Estonia 42 E3
Kirbyville U.S.A. 179 D6
Kirchdorf an der Krems Austria 49 L8
Kirdimi Chad 120 C5
Kirenga r. Rus. Fed. 81 H1
Kirensk Rus. Fed. 81 H1
Kirey watercourse Kazakh. see Kerey
Kirey, Ozero salt l. Kazakh. see Kerey, Ozero
Kireyevsk Rus. Fed. 43 S8
Kirghizia country Asia see Kyrgyzstan
Kirghiz Range mts Asia 88 A3
also known as Kirgizskiy Khrebet
Kirgiziya Kazakh. 103 I2
Kirgiz-Miyaki Rus. Fed. 102 C1
Kirgizskaya S.S.R. country Asia see Kyrgyzstan
Kirgizskiy Khrebet mts Asia see Kirghiz Range
Kirgizstan country Asia see Kyrgyzstan
Kiri Dem. Rep. Congo 126 C5
Kiria Greece see Kyria
Kiriákion Greece see Kyriaki
▶Kiribati country Pacific Ocean 145 G2
formerly known as Gilbert Islands
oceania [countries] ▶ 138–139
Kiridh Somalia 128 E2
Kırıkhan Turkey 106 D3
Kırıkkale Turkey 106 C3
Kirikkuduk China 84 A2
Kirikopuni N.Z. 152 I3
Kirillov Rus. Fed. 43 T2
Kirillovo Rus. Fed. 82 F3
Kirillovskoye Rus. Fed. 43 K1
Kirin China see Jilin
Kirin prov. China see Jilin
Kirinyaga mt. Kenya see Kenya, Mount
Kirishi Rus. Fed. 43 N2
Kirishima-Yaku National Park Japan 91 B9
Kirishima-yama vol. Japan 91 B9
Kiritimati i. Kiribati 221 H5
Kiriwina Islands P.N.G. see Trobriand Islands
Kırkağaç Turkey 59 I9
Kirk Bulāg Dāgh mt. Iran 100 A2
Kirkby U.K. 47 J10
Kirkby Stephen U.K. 47 J9
Kirkcaldy U.K. 46 I7
Kirkcudbright U.K. 47 H9
Kirkenær Norway 45 K3
Kirkenes Norway 44 O1
Kirkfield Canada 173 O6
Kirkkonummi Fin. 45 N3
Kirkland AZ U.S.A. 183 L7
Kirkland IL U.S.A. 172 E8
Kirkland Lake Canada 168 D3
Kırklareli Turkey 106 A2
Kırklareli prov. Turkey 59 I7
Kırklareli Barajı resr Turkey 58 I7
Kirkliston Range mts N.Z. 153 E12
Kirkonmaanselkä b. Fin. 42 I1
Kirkovo Bulg. 58 G7
Kirkpatrick, Mount Antarctica 223 L1
Kirksville U.S.A. 174 A3
Kirkuk Iraq see Kirkūk
Kirkūk Iraq 107 F4
English form Kirkuk
Kirkwall U.K. 46 J5
Kirkwood S. Africa 133 J10
Kirkwood U.S.A. 172 C10
Kirman Iran see Kermān
Kırmır r. Turkey 106 B2
Kırobası Turkey see Mağara
Kirov Kazakh. see Balpyk Bi
Kirov Kyrg. see Kyzyl-Adyr
Kirov Kaluzhskaya Oblast' Rus. Fed. 43 P7
Kirov Kirovskaya Oblast' Rus. Fed. 40 I4
also known as Vyatka
Kirova, Zaliv b. Azer. see Qızılağac Körfäzi
Kirovabad Azer. see Gäncä
Kirovabad Tajik. see Panj
Kirovakan Armenia see Vanadzor
Kirovo Kazakh. 102 C2
Kirovo Ukr. see Kirovohrad
Kirovo Uzbek. see Besharyk
Kirov Oblast admin. div. Rus. Fed. see Kirovskaya Oblast'
Kirovo-Chepetsk Rus. Fed. 40 I4
formerly spelt Kirovo-Chepetskiy
Kirovo-Chepetskiy Rus. Fed. see Kirovo-Chepetsk
Kirovograd Ukr. see Kirovohrad
Kirovohrad Ukr. 41 E6
also spelt Kirovograd; formerly known as Kirovo or Yelizavetgrad or Zinovyevsk
Kirovsk Leningradskaya Oblast' Rus. Fed. 43 L2
formerly known as Nevdubstroy
Kirovsk Murmanskaya Oblast' Rus. Fed. 44 P2
Kirovsk Turkm. see Babadaykhan
Kirovskaya Oblast' admin. div. Rus. Fed. 40 I4
English form Kirov Oblast
Kirovskiy Kazakh. see Balpyk Bi
Kirovskiy Rus. Fed. 82 D3
Kirovskoye Kyrg. see Kyzyl-Adyr
Kirpaşa pen. Cyprus see Karpasia
Kirpili Turkm. 102 D5
Kirriemuir U.K. 46 I7
Kirs Rus. Fed. 40 J4
Kirsanov Rus. Fed. 41 G5
Kirsanovo Kazakh. 102 C2
Kırşehir Turkey 106 C3
Kirtachi Niger 125 F3
Kirthar National Park Pak. 101 F5
Kirthar Range mts Pak. 101 F5
Kiruna Sweden 44 M2
also spelt Giron
Kirundu Burundi 126 F5
Kirundu Dem. Rep. Congo 126 E5
Kirwan Escarpment Antarctica 223 X2
Kirya Rus. Fed. 40 H5
Kiryū Japan 91 F6
Kirzhach Rus. Fed. 43 T5
Kisa Sweden 45 K4
Kisakata Japan 90 F5
Kisaki Tanz. 129 C6
Kisama, Parque Nacional de nat. park Angola see Quiçama, Parque Nacional do
Kisangani Dem. Rep. Congo 126 E4
formerly known as Stanleyville
Kisar i. Indon. 75 C5
Kisaran Indon. 76 B2
Kisarawe Tanz. 129 C6
Kisarazu Japan 91 F7
Kis-Balaton park Hungary 49 O9
Kisbér Hungary 49 P8
Kiselevsk Rus. Fed. 80 D2
Kiseljak Bos.-Herz. 56 K5
Kisel'nya Rus. Fed. 43 N1
Kisel'ovka Rus. Fed. 82 E2
Kishanganj India 97 E4
Kishangarh Rajasthan India 96 A4
Kishangarh Rajasthan India 96 B4
Kishen Ganga r. India/Pak. 96 B2
Kishi-Karoy, Ozero salt l. Kazakh. 103 G1
Kishika-zaki pt Japan 91 B9
Kishinev Moldova see Chişinău
Kishiözen r. Kazakh./Rus. Fed. see Malyy Uzen'
Kishiwada Japan 91 D7
Kishkenekol' Kazakh. 103 H1
formerly known as Kzyltu or Qyzyltū
Kishorganj Bangl. 97 F4
Kishtwar Jammu and Kashmir 96 B2
Kisi Nigeria 125 F4
Kisi Tanz. 129 A6
Kisigo r. Tanz. 129 B6
Kisii Kenya 128 B5
Kisiju Tanz. 129 C6
Kiskittogisu Lake Canada 167 L4
Kiskitto Lake Canada 167 L4
Kisko Fin. 45 M3
Kiskőrös Hungary 49 Q9
Kiskunfélegyháza Hungary 49 Q9
Kiskunhalas Hungary 49 Q9
Kiskunlacháza Hungary 49 Q8
Kiskunmajsa Hungary 49 Q9
Kiskunsági nat. park Hungary 49 Q8
Kislovodsk Rus. Fed. 41 G8
Kismaayo Somalia 128 D5
formerly spelt Chisimaio or Kismayu
Kismayu Somalia see Kismaayo
Kisofukushima Japan 91 E7
Kisoro Uganda 128 A5
Kiso-sanmyaku mts Japan 91 E7
Kispiox Canada 166 E4
Kispiox r. Canada 166 E4
Kissamou, Kolpos b. Greece 59 E13
Kisseraing Island Myanmar see Kanmaw Kyun
Kissidougou Guinea 124 C4
Kissimmee U.S.A. 175 D6
Kissimmee r. U.S.A. 175 D7
Kissimmee, Lake U.S.A. 175 D7
Kississing Lake Canada 167 K4
Kissu, Jebel mt. Sudan 120 E4
Kistanje Croatia 56 H5
Kistelek Hungary 49 Q9
Kistna r. India see Krishna
Kistrand Norway 44 N1
Kisújszállás Hungary 49 R8
Kisuki Japan 91 C7
Kisumu Kenya 128 B5
Kisvárda Hungary 49 T7
Kisykkamys Kazakh. see Dzhangala
Kit r. Sudan 128 A3
Kita Mali 124 C3
Kitab Uzbek. 103 F5
also spelt Kitob
Kita-Daitō-jima i. Japan 81 M7
Kitagawa Japan 91 B8
Kitahiyama Japan 90 F3
Kitaibaraki Japan 90 G6
Kita-Iō-jima vol. Japan 73 J1
Kitakami Japan 90 G5
Kitakami-gawa r. Japan 90 G5
Kitakata Japan 90 F6
Kita-Kyūshū Japan 91 B8
Kitale Kenya 128 B4
Kitami Japan 90 H3
Kitami-sanchi mts Japan 90 H2
Kitanda Dem. Rep. Congo 127 E6
Kitaura Japan 91 B8
Kitchener Canada 168 D5
Kitchigama r. Canada 168 E3
Kiteba Dem. Rep. Congo 127 E6
Kitee Fin. 44 O3
Kitendwe Dem. Rep. Congo 127 F6
Kitgum Uganda 128 B4
Kíthira i. Greece see Kythira
Kíthnos i. Greece see Kythnos
Kíthnou, Stenón sea chan. Greece see Kythnou, Steno
Kiti, Cape Cyprus see Kition, Cape
Kitimat Canada 166 D4
Kitinen r. Fin. 44 N2
Kition, Cape Cyprus 108 E3
also known as Kiti, Cape or Kitiou, Akra
Kitiou, Akra c. Cyprus see Kition, Cape
Kitkatla Canada 166 D4
Kitob Uzbek. see Kitab
Kitriani i. Greece 59 F12
Kitsa Rus. Fed. 44 P1
Kitsault Canada 166 D4
Kitscoty Canada 167 I4
Kitsuki Japan 91 B8
Kittanning U.S.A. 176 F5
Kittatinny Mountains hills U.S.A. 177 K5
Kittilä Fin. 44 N2
Kittur India 94 B3
Kitty Hawk U.S.A. 177 J9
Kitui Kenya 128 C5
Kitumbeine vol. Tanz. 128 C5
Kitumbini Tanz. 129 C7
Kitunda Tanz. 129 B6
Kitwanga Canada 166 D4
Kitwe Zambia 127 F8
Kitzbühel Austria 49 J8
Kitzbüheler Alpen mts Austria 49 J8
Kitzingen Germany 48 H6
Kiu Kenya 128 C5
Kiu Lom Dam Thai. 78 B4
Kiunga P.N.G. 73 J8
Kiunga Marine National Reserve nature res. Kenya 128 D5
Kiuruvesi Fin. 44 N3
Kivalo ridge Fin. 44 N2
Kiverichi Rus. Fed. 43 R4
Kivijärvi Fin. 44 N3
Kivijärvi l. Fin. 42 I1
Kivijärvi l. Fin. 44 N3
Kivilompolo Norway 44 M1
Kiviõli Estonia 42 H2
Kivivaara Fin. 44 O3
Kivi-Vigala Estonia 42 F3
Kivu, Lake Dem. Rep. Congo/Rwanda 126 F5
Kiwaba N'zogi Angola 127 C7
formerly known as Brito Godins
Kiwai Island P.N.G. 73 J8
Kiwawa Tanz. 129 C7
Kiwirrkurra Aboriginal Reserve Australia 150 D4
Kiyakty, Ozero salt l. Kazakh. 103 G2
Kiyāt Saudi Arabia 104 C4
Kiyev Ukr. see Kiev
Kiyevka Kazakh. 103 G2
also known as Kiev
Kiyevka Rus. Fed. 90 C3
Kiyevskiy Rus. Fed. 43 R6
Kiyevskoye Vodokhranilishche resr Ukr. see Kyyivs'ke Vodoskhovyshche
Kıyıköy Turkey 58 J7
also known as Midye
Kiyma Kazakh. 103 F2
also spelt Qima
Kizel Rus. Fed. 40 K4
Kizema Rus. Fed. 40 H3
Kizhi, Ostrov i. Rus. Fed. 40 E3
Kizhinga Rus. Fed. 85 F1
Kiziba-Baluba, Réserve de nature res. Dem. Rep. Congo 127 E7
Kizigo Game Reserve nature res. Tanz. 129 B6
Kizil China 88 C3
Kızılcadağ Turkey 106 B3
Kızılca Dağ mt. Turkey 106 B3
Kızılcahamam Turkey 106 C2
also known as Yabanabat
Kızıldağ mt. Turkey 108 E1
Kızıldağ mt. Turkey 108 G1
Kızıl Dağı mt. Turkey 107 D3
Kızılırmak Turkey 106 C2
also known as Huseyinli
Kızılırmak r. Turkey 107 C2
Kızılören Turkey 106 C3
Kizil'skoye Rus. Fed. 102 D1
Kızıltepe Turkey 107 E3
also known as Koçhisar
Kizil"yurt Rus. Fed. 102 A4
Kızkalesi Turkey 108 F1
Kizlyar Rus. Fed. 102 A4
Kizlyarskiy Zaliv b. Rus. Fed. 102 A3
Kizner Rus. Fed. 40 I4
Kizreka Rus. Fed. 44 O2
Kizyl-Arbat Turkm. see Gyzylarbat
Kizyl-Atrek Turkm. see Gyzyletrek
Kizylayak Turkm. 103 F5
Kizyl Jilga Aksai Chin 89 B5
Kizyl-Su Turkm. 102 C5
also known as Gyzylsuw
Kjøllefjord Norway 44 N1
Kjøpsvik Norway 44 L1
Klaarstroom S. Africa 132 G10
Kladanj Bos.-Herz. 56 K4
Kladno Czech Rep. 49 L5
Kladovo Srbija Yugo. 58 D4
Klagan Sabah Malaysia 77 G1
Klagenfurt Austria 49 L9
also known as Celovec
Klagetoh U.S.A. 183 O6
Klaipėda Lith. 42 C6
historically known as Memel
Klaksvig Faroe Is see Klaksvík
Klaksvík Faroe Is 46 F1
also spelt Klaksvig
Klamath r. U.S.A. 180 A4
Klamath Falls U.S.A. 180 B4
Klamath Mountains U.S.A. 180 B4
Klampo Indon. 77 G2
Klang Malaysia see Kelang
Klappan r. Canada 166 D3
Klášterec nad Ohří Czech Rep. 49 K5
Klaten Indon. 77 E4
Klatovy Czech Rep. 49 K6
Klawer S. Africa 132 C8
Klawock U.S.A. 164 F4
Klazienaveen Neth. 48 D3
Klecko Poland 49 O3
Kleczew Poland 49 P3
Kleides Islands Cyprus 108 F2
also known as Zafer Adaları; also spelt Klidhes Islands
Kleinbegin S. Africa 132 F5
Klein Doring r. S. Africa 132 D8
Kleinegga mt. Norway 44 J3
Klein Karas Namibia 132 C4
Kleinmachnow Germany 49 K3
Kleinmond S. Africa 132 D11
Klein Roggeveldberge mts S. Africa 132 E10
Kleinsee S. Africa 132 B6
Kleinseenplatte Neustrelitz park Germany 49 J2
Klein Swartberg mt. S. Africa 132 F10
Klein-Vet r. S. Africa 133 K5
Kleitoria Greece 59 D11
also spelt Klitória
Klekovača mt. Bos.-Herz. 56 I4
Klemtu Canada 166 D4
Kleppesto Norway 45 I3
Klerksdorp S. Africa 133 K3
Klerkskraal S. Africa 133 L3
Kleszczele Poland 49 U3
Kletnya Rus. Fed. 43 O8
Kletsk Belarus see Klyetsk
Kletskaya Rus. Fed. 41 G6
formerly known as Kletskiy
Kletskiy Rus. Fed. see Kletskaya
Kleve Germany 48 D4
historically known as Cleves
Klichaw Belarus 43 K8
Klichka Rus. Fed. 85 H1
Klidhes Islands Cyprus see Kleides Islands
Klienpoort S. Africa 133 I10
Klimatino Rus. Fed. 43 S4
Klimavichy Belarus 43 M8
also spelt Klimovichi
Klimawka Belarus 43 M9
Kliment Bulg. 58 I5
Klimovichi Belarus see Klimavichy
Klimovo Rus. Fed. 43 N9
Klimovsk Rus. Fed. 43 S6
Klimov Zavod Rus. Fed. 43 P7
Klimpfjäll Sweden 44 K2
Klin Rus. Fed. 43 R5
Klina Kosovo, Srbija Yugo. 58 B6
Klinaklini r. Canada 166 E5
Kling Phil. 74 C5
Klingkang, Banjaran mts Indon./Malaysia 77 E2
Klinsko-Dmitrovskaya Gryada ridge Rus. Fed. 43 R5
Klintehamn Sweden 45 L4
Klintsovka Rus. Fed. 102 B2
Klintsy Rus. Fed. 43 N9
Klip r. S. Africa 133 N4
Klipdale S. Africa 132 D11
Klipfontein S. Africa 133 J10
Klippan Sweden 45 K4
Klipplaat S. Africa 133 I10
Kliprand S. Africa 132 C7
Klipskool S. Africa 133 O2
Klipvoor Dam S. Africa 133 L2
Klis Croatia 56 I5
Klishino Moskovskaya Oblast' Rus. Fed. 43 T7
Klishino Novgorodskaya Oblast' Rus. Fed. 43 O2
Klitmøller Denmark 45 J4
Klitória Greece see Kleitoria
Ključ Bos.-Herz. 56 I4
Kłobuck Poland 49 P5
Kłodawa Poland 49 P3
Kłodzko Poland 49 N5
Klondike r. Canada 166 B1
Klondike Goldrush National Historical Park nat. park U.S.A. 166 C3
Klooga Estonia 42 F2
Klosterneuburg Austria 49 N7
Klosters Switz. 51 P6
Klötze (Altmark) Germany 48 I3
Kluane r. Canada 166 B2
Kluane Game Sanctuary nature res. Canada 166 A2
Kluane Lake Canada 166 B2
Kluane National Park Canada 166 B2
Kluang Malaysia see Keluang
Kluang, Tanjung pt Indon. 77 E3
Kluczbork Poland 49 P5
Klukhori Rus. Fed. see Karachayevsk
Klumpang, Teluk b. Indon. 77 G3
Klungkung Indon. 77 F5
Klupro Pak. 101 G5
Klyastsitsy Belarus 43 J6
Klyava r. Belarus 43 J8
Klyavlino Rus. Fed. 40 J5
Klyaz'ma r. Rus. Fed. 43 U5
Klyetsk Belarus 42 H8
also spelt Kletsk
▶Klyuchevskaya, Sopka vol. Rus. Fed. 39 Q4
asia [threats] ▶ 70–71
Klyuchi Rus. Fed. 103 I1
Klyuchi Rus. Fed. 39 Q4
Knapdaar S. Africa 133 K7
Knapp Mound hill U.S.A. 172 C6
Knaresborough U.K. 47 K9
Knee Lake Man. Canada 167 M4
Knee Lake Sask. Canada 167 J4
Knesebeck Germany 48 H3
Knetzgau Germany 48 H6
Kneževi Vinogradi Croatia 56 K3
Knezha Bulg. 58 F5
Knić Srbija Yugo. 58 B5
Knife r. U.S.A. 178 B2
Knife River U.S.A. 172 B4
Knight Inlet Canada 166 E5
Knighton U.K. 47 I11
Knights Landing U.S.A. 182 C3
Knin Croatia 56 I4
Knittelfeld Austria 49 L8
Knivsta Sweden 45 L4
Knizhovnik Bulg. 58 G7
Knjaževac Srbija Yugo. 58 D5
Knob Lake Canada see Schefferville
Knob Peak hill Australia 150 E2
Knockaboy hill Rep. of Ireland 47 C12
Knock Hill hill U.K. 46 J6
Knockmealdown Mountains hills Rep. of Ireland 47 D11
Knokke-Heist Belgium 51 J1
Knosos tourist site Greece see Knossos
Knossos tourist site Greece 59 G13
also spelt Knosos or Knossós; historically known as Cnossus
Knossós tourist site Greece see Knossos
Knowles, Cape Antarctica 222 T2
Knox IN U.S.A. 172 G9
Knox PA U.S.A. 176 F4
Knox, Cape Canada 166 C4
Knox Atoll Kiribati see Tarawa
Knox Coast Antarctica 223 G2
Knoxville GA U.S.A. 175 D5
Knoxville IA U.S.A. 174 A3
Knoxville IL U.S.A. 172 C10
Knoxville TN U.S.A. 174 D5
Knud Rasmussen Land reg. Greenland 165 M2
Knyahinin Belarus 42 I7
Knyazevo Rus. Fed. 43 J5
Knyazhikha Rus. Fed. 43 R4
Knyazhitsy Rus. Fed. 43 J3
Knyazhytsy Belarus 43 L7
Knysna S. Africa 132 H11
Knyszyn Poland 49 T2
Ko, Gora mt. Rus. Fed. 82 E3
Koani Tanz. 129 C6
Koartac Canada see Quaqtaq
Koa Valley watercourse S. Africa 132 D6
Koba Indon. 77 D3
Kobayashi Japan 91 B9
Kobbfoss Norway 44 O1
Kobe Indon. 75 C2
▶Kōbe Japan 91 D7
world [earthquakes] ▶ 14–15
København Denmark see Copenhagen
Kobenni Mauritania 124 C3
Kobi Indon. 75 D3
Koblenz Germany 48 E5
formerly spelt Coblenz
K'obo Eth. 128 C1
Koboldo Rus. Fed. 82 D1
Kobozha r. Rus. Fed. 43 R3
Kobrin Belarus see Kobryn
Kobroör i. Indon. 73 H8
Kobryn Belarus 42 F9
also spelt Kobrin
Kobuk Valley National Park U.S.A. 164 D3
K'obulet'i Georgia 107 E2
Kobyay Rus. Fed. 39 M3
Kocaafşar r. Turkey 59 J8
Koca Dag mt. Turkey 59 K10
Kocaeli Turkey 106 B2
also known as İzmit; historically known as Astacus or Nicomedia
Kocaeli prov. Turkey 58 K8
Kocaeli Yarımadası pen. Turkey 58 K7
Kočani Macedonia 58 D7
Koçarlı Turkey 59 I11
Kocasu r. Turkey 106 B2
Kocatepe Turkey 109 I1
Koceljevo Srbija Yugo. 58 A4
Kočevje Slovenia 56 G3
Koch'ang S. Korea 83 B6
Koch Bihar India 97 F4
formerly spelt Cooch Behar
Kocher r. Germany 48 G6
Kocherinovo Bulg. 58 E6
Kochevo Rus. Fed. 40 J4
Kochi India see Cochin
Kōchi Japan 91 C8
Kōchi pref. Japan 91 C8
Koçhisar Turkey see Kızıltepe
Kochkor Kyrg. 103 H4
also known as Kochkorka
Kochkorka Kyrg. see Kochkor
Kochkurovo Rus. Fed. 41 H5
Kochubey Rus. Fed. 102 A3
formerly known as Chernyy Rynok
Kochylas hill Greece 59 F10
Kock Poland 49 T4
Kocs Hungary 49 P8
Kod India 94 B3
Kodaikanal India 94 C4
Kodala India 95 E2
Kodari Nepal 97 E4
Kodarma India 97 E4
Kodavere Estonia 42 I3
Kodiak U.S.A. 164 D4
Kodiak Island U.S.A. 164 D4
Kodinar India 94 A1
Kodino Rus. Fed. 40 F3
Kodiyakkarai India 94 C4
Kodok Sudan 128 B2
Kodomari Japan 90 G4
Kodori r. Georgia 107 E2
Kodumuru India 94 C3
Kodyma Ukr. 41 D6
Kodzhaele mt. Bulg./Greece 58 G7
Koedoesberg mts S. Africa 132 E9
Koedoeskop S. Africa 133 L1
Koegrabie S. Africa 132 E6
Koekenaap S. Africa 132 C8
Koës Namibia 130 C5
Kofa Mountains U.S.A. 183 K8
Kofa National Wildlife Refuge nature res. U.S.A. 183 J8
Kofarnihon Tajik. 101 G2
also spelt Kafirnigan; formerly known as Ordzhonikidzeabad or Orjonikidzeobod
Kofarnihon r. Tajik. 101 G2
Kofçaz Turkey 58 I7
Koffiefontein S. Africa 133 J6
Kofinas, Oros mt. Greece 59 G14
Köflach Austria 49 M8
Koforidua Ghana 125 E5
Kōfu Tottori Japan 91 C7
Kōfu Yamanashi Japan 91 F7
Kogălniceanu airport Romania 58 J4
also known as Cogălniceanu or Constanța
Kogaluc r. Canada 168 E1
Kogaluc, Baie de b. Canada 168 E1
Kogaluk r. Canada 169 I1
Kögart Kyrg. see Alaykuu
Køge Denmark 45 K5
Kogel' r. Rus. Fed. 40 K3
Kogi state Nigeria 125 G4
Kogon Uzbek. see Kagan
Kogoni Mali 124 D3
Kōhaihai pt N.Z. see Gillespies Point
Kohat Pak. 101 G3
Kohila Estonia 42 F2
Kohima India 97 G4
Kohistan reg. Pak. 101 H3
Kohkīlūyeh va Būyer Aḥmadī prov. Iran 100 B4
Kohler Range mts Antarctica 222 Q2
Kohls Ranch U.S.A. 183 M7
Kohlu Pak. 101 G4
Kohouro well Chad 120 D5
Kohrener Land park Germany 49 J4
Kohsan Afgh. 101 E3
Kohtla-Järve Estonia 42 I2
Kohyl'nyk r. Ukr. 58 K3
Koide Japan 90 F6
Koidern Canada 166 A2
Koidern Mountain Canada 166 A2
Koidu Sierra Leone see Sefadu
Koigi Estonia 42 G3
Koihoa India 95 G4
Koiingnaas S. Africa 132 B7
Koilkonda India 94 C2
Koilkuntla India 94 C3
Koin r. Rus. Fed. 40 I3
Koi Sanjaq Iraq 107 F3
Koitere l. Fin. 44 O3
Koivu Fin. 44 N2
Kōje-do i. S. Korea 83 C6
Ko-jima i. Japan 90 F4
Ko-jima i. Japan 91 F8
Kojonup Australia 151 B7
Kok r. Thai. 78 C3
Kokalaat Kazakh. 103 F2
Kokand Uzbek. 103 G4
also spelt Qŭqon
Kokankishlak Uzbek. see Pakhtaabad
Kokar Fin. 45 M4
Kokar i. Fin. 42 B2
Kök-Art Kyrg. see Alaykuu
Kokatahi N.Z. 153 F10
Kök-Aygyr Kyrg. 103 H4
also spelt Kékaygyr
Kokcha r. Afgh. 101 G2
Kokchetav Kazakh. see Kokshetau
Kokemäki Fin. 45 M3
Kokerboom Namibia 130 C6
Kokhanava Belarus 43 K7
Koki Senegal 124 B3
Kök-Janggak Kyrg. 103 H4
also spelt Kok-Yangak
Kokkina Cyprus 108 D2
also known as Erenköy
Kokkola Fin. 44 M3
also known as Gamlakarleby
Kok Kuduk well China 88 D2
Koknese Latvia 42 G5
Koko Nigeria 125 G4
Kokofata Mali 124 C3
Kokolo-Pozo Côte d'Ivoire 124 D5
Kokomo U.S.A. 174 C3
Kokong Botswana 130 D5
Kokonoe Japan 91 B8
Kokora Estonia 42 I3
Kokorevka Rus. Fed. 43 P9
Kokorevo Rus. Fed. 43 K4
Kokoro Benin 125 F4
Kokoshkino Rus. Fed. 43 S6
Kokosi S. Africa 133 L3
Kokou mt. Guinea 124 B4
Kokpekti Kazakh. 88 C1
Koksan N. Korea 83 B5
Koksaray Kazakh. 103 G4
Kokshaal-Tau mts China/Kyrg. 88 B3
also known as Kakshaal-Too
Kokshetau Kazakh. 103 G1
formerly spelt Kokchetav
Koksoak r. Canada 169 G1
Kokstad S. Africa 133 N7
Koksu Almatinskaya Oblast' Kazakh. 103 I3
Koksu Yuzhnyy Kazakhstan Kazakh. 103 G4
Koktal Kazakh. 103 I3
Kök-Tash Kyrg. 103 H4
also spelt Kek-Tash
Kokterek Kazakh. 103 G4
Koktokay China 84 A2
Koktokay China see Fuyun
Koktuma Kazakh. 88 C2
Koku, Tanjung pt Indon. 75 B4
Kokubu Japan 91 B9
Kok-Yangak Kyrg. see Kök-Janggak
Kokyar China 88 B4

Kolymskiy, Khrebet *mts* Rus. Fed. **39** Q3
  English form Kolyma Range; also known as
  Gydan, Khrebet
Kolymskoye Vodokhranilische resr
  Rus. Fed. **39** O3
Kolyshley Rus. Fed. **41** H5
Kolyuchinskaya Guba *b.* Rus. Fed. **39** S3
Kolyvan' Rus. Fed. **88** C1
Kom *mt.* Bulg. **58** E5
Kom China **88** D1
Komadugu-gana *watercourse* Nigeria
  125 I3
Komaga-take *mt.* Japan **90** F6
Komaga-take *vol.* Japan **90** F4
Komaggas S. Africa **132** B6
Komaggas Mountains S. Africa **132** B6
Komagvær Norway **44** O1
Komaki Japan **91** E7
Komandnaya, Gora *mt.* Rus. Fed. **82** E2
Komandorskiye Ostrova *is* Rus. Fed. **39** U4
Komarichi Rus. Fed. **43** P9
Komárno Slovakia **49** P8
Komarovo *Novgorodskaya Oblast'* Rus. Fed.
  43 O3
Komary Rus. Fed. **43** O6
Komati *r.* Swaziland **133** P2
Komatipoort S. Africa **133** P2
Komatsu Japan **91** E6
Komatsushima Japan **91** D7
Komba Dem. Rep. Congo **126** E4
Komba *i.* Indon. **75** B4
Kombakomba Indon. **75** B3
Kombat Namibia **130** C3
Kombe Dem. Rep. Congo **126** E6
Kombe Tanz. **129** A7
Kombissiri Burkina **125** E3
Komering *r.* Indon. **76** C3
Komga S. Africa **133** L9
Kôm Hamâda Egypt **108** B7
Komi, Respublika *aut. rep.* Rus. Fed. **40** I3
  English form Komi Republic; formerly known
  as Komi A.S.S.R.
  see
  Komi, Respublika
Komi A.S.S.R. *aut. rep.* Rus. Fed. *see*
  Komi, Respublika
Komi-Permyak Autonomous Okrug
  admin. div. Rus. Fed. *see*
  Komi-Permyatskiy Avtonomnyy Okrug
Komi-Permyatskiy Avtonomnyy Okrug
  admin. div. Rus. Fed. **40** I3
  English form Komi-Permyak Autonomous
  Okrug
Komi Republic *aut. rep.* Rus. Fed. *see*
  Komi, Respublika
Komiža Croatia **56** I5
Komkans S. Africa **132** C8
Komló Hungary **49** P9
Kommandokraal S. Africa **132** G10
Kommetjie S. Africa **132** C11
Kommissiepoort S. Africa **133** L6
Kommuna *r.* Indon. *see* Babadaykhan
Kommunarsk Ukr. *see* Alchevs'k
Kommunar *Kostromskaya Oblast'* Rus. Fed.
  40 G4
Kommunar *Leningradskaya Oblast'* Rus. Fed.
  43 L2
Kommunizm, Qullai *mt.* Tajik. *see*
  Garmo, Qullai
Kommunizma, Pik *mt.* Tajik. *see*
  Garmo, Qullai
Komodo *i.* Indon. **75** A5
Komodo National Park Indon. **75** A5
Komodou Guinea **124** C4
Komoé *r.* Côte d'Ivoire **124** E5
  also spelt Comoé
Kôm Ombo Egypt **121** G3
Komono Congo **126** B5
Komoran *i.* Indon. **73** I8
Komoro Japan **91** F6
Komotini Greece **58** G7
Kompong Cham Cambodia *see*
  Kâmpóng Cham
Kompong Chhnang Cambodia *see*
  Kâmpóng Chhnâng
Kompong Kleang Cambodia *see*
  Kâmpóng Khleăng
Kompong Som Bay Cambodia *see*
  Sihanoukville, Chhâk
Kompong Speu Cambodia *see*
  Kâmpóng Spœ
Kompong Thom Cambodia *see*
  Kâmpóng Thum
Komrat Moldova *see* Comrat
Komsberg *mts* S. Africa **132** F9
Komsberg *mts* S. Africa **132** C9
Komsomol Kazakh. *see* Komsomol'skiy
Komsomol Kazakh. *see* Komsomolets
Komsomol Turkm. *see* Komsomol'sk
Komsomolets Kazakh. **103** E2
  also known as Komsomol
Komsomolets, Ostrov *i.* Rus. Fed. **39** J1
Komsomolets, Zaliv *b.* Kazakh. **102** C3
Komsomol'sk *Ivanovskaya Oblast'* Rus. Fed.
  43 V4
Komsomol'sk *Kaliningradskaya Oblast'*
  Rus. Fed. *see* Kolsomyya
Komsomol'sk Turkm. **103** E5
  also known as Komsomol
Komsomol's'k Ukr. **41** F7
Komsomol's'ke Ukr. **41** F7
  formerly known as Karakubbud
Komsomol'skiy Kazakh. **102** C3
Komsomol'skiy *Chukotskiy Avtonomnyy*
  Okrug Rus. Fed. **39** R3
Komsomol'skiy Rus. Fed. *see* Yugorsk
Komsomol'skiy *Respublika Kalmykiya -*
  Khalm'g-Tangch Rus. Fed. **41** H7
  formerly known as Krasnyy Kamyshanik
Komsomol'skiy *Respublika Mordoviya*
  Rus. Fed. **41** H5
Komsomol'sk Rus. Fed. *see* Zavodskoy
Komsomol'sk-na-Amure Rus. Fed. **82** E2
Komsomol'skyy Kazakh. **103** E2
Komuniga Bulg. **58** G7
Kömürlü Turkey **107** E2
Kon India **97** D4
Konacık Turkey **108** C1
Konada India **95** D2
Konakli Turkey **108** C1
Konakovo Rus. Fed. **43** R5
Konar *prov.* Afgh. **101** G3
Konarak India **95** E2
  also known as Black Pagoda; formerly
  known as Kanarak or Konarak
Konch India **96** C4
Konchanskoye-Suvorovskoye Rus. Fed.
  43 P3
Konchezero Rus. Fed. **40** E3
Konchytsy Belarus **42** G9
Konda Rus. Fed. **44** P2
Kondagaon India **94** D2
Kondapalle India **94** D2
Kondapuram Andhra Pradesh India **94** C3
  Australia **149** E3
Kondavid India **94** D2
Kondiaronk, Lac *l.* Canada **173** O4
Kondinin Australia **151** B7
Kondinskoye Rus. Fed. **38** G3
  formerly known as Nakhrachi
Kondoa Tanz. **129** B5
Kondol' Rus. Fed. **41** H5
Kondopoga Rus. Fed. **40** E3
Kondoros Hungary **49** R9
Kondrat'yevo Rus. Fed. **43** J1

Kondrovo Rus. Fed. **43** Q7
Kondūz Afgh. **101** G2
  also spelt Kunduz; historically known as
  Drapsaca
Kondūz *prov.* Afgh. **101** G2
Konečka Planina *mts* Macedonia **58** D7
Konetsbor Rus. Fed. **40** K2
Koneürgench Turkm. *see* Keneurgench
Konevits, Ostrov *i.* Rus. Fed. **43** L1
Kong Cameroon **125** I5
Kong Côte d'Ivoire **124** D4
Kông, Kaôh *i.* Cambodia **79** C6
  formerly known as Kas Klong
Kông, Tônlé *r.* Cambodia **79** D5
Kong, Xé *r.* Laos **79** D5
Kongassambougou, Réserve de
  nature res. Mali **124** C3
Kongbo Cent. Afr. Rep. **126** D3
Kong Christian IX Land *reg.* Greenland
  165 P3
Kong Christian X Land *reg.* Greenland
  165 Q2
Kong Frederik IX Land *reg.* Greenland
  165 N3
Kong Frederik VIII Land *reg.* Greenland
  165 Q2
Kong Frederik VI Kyst *coastal area*
  Greenland **165** O3
Kong Karls Land *is* Svalbard **38** C2
Kong Kat *hill* Indon. **77** G2
Kongkemul *mt.* Indon. **77** G2
Kongola Namibia **130** D3
Kong Oscars Fjord *inlet* Greenland **165** Q2
Kongoussi Burkina **125** E3
Kongsberg Norway **45** J4
Kongsfjord Norway **44** O1
Kongsvinger Norway **45** K3
Kongur Shan *mt.* China **88** A4
  also known as Kungur
Kongwa Tanz. **129** C6
Kong Wilhelm Land *reg.* Greenland **165** Q2
Konibodom Tajik. *see* Kanibadam
Koniecpol Poland **49** P5
Königsberg Rus. Fed. *see* Kaliningrad
Königsbrunn Germany **48** H7
Königswartha Germany **49** L4
Königswinter Germany **48** E5
Königs Wusterhausen Germany **49** K3
Konimekh Uzbek. *see* Kanimekh
Konin Poland **49** P3
Konin *r.* Rus. Fed. **43** P1
Konitsa Greece **59** B8
Kóniz Switz. **51** N6
Konj *mt.* Bos.-Herz. **56** I6
Konjic Bos.-Herz. **56** J5
Konjuh *mts* Bos.-Herz. **56** K4
Könkämäeno *r.* Fin./Sweden **44** M1
Konkiep *watercourse* Namibia **130** C6
Kon'-Kolodez' Rus. Fed. **43** U9
Konkwesso Nigeria **125** F3
Konna Mali **124** D3
Konnarock U.S.A. **176** D9
Konnevesi Fin. **44** N3
Konongo Ghana **125** E5
Konoplyane Ukr. **58** L1
Konosha Rus. Fed. **40** G3
Kōnosu Japan **91** F6
Konotop Ukr. **41** E6
Kon Plong Vietnam **79** D5
Konqi He *r.* China **88** E3
Końskie Poland **49** R4
Konso Eth. **128** C3
Konstantinograd Ukr. *see* Krasnohrad
Konstantinovka Rus. Fed. **82** B2
Konstantinovka Ukr. *see* Kostyantynivka
Konstantinovo Rus. Fed. **43** T5
Konstantinovskiy Rus. Fed. **43** U4
Konstanz Germany **48** G8
  English form Constance; historically known
  as Constantia
Kontagora Nigeria **125** G4
Kontcha Cameroon **125** I5
Kontiolahti Fin. **44** O3
Kontiomäki Fin. **44** O2
Kon Tum Vietnam **79** D5
Kontum, Plateau du Vietnam **79** E5
Kōnugard Ukr. *see* Kiev
Konushin, Mys *pt* Rus. Fed. **40** H2
Konya Turkey **106** C3
  historically known as Iconium
Konyrat Kazakh. **103** H3
  also spelt Qongyrat; formerly known as
  Kounradskiy
Konyrolen Kazakh. **103** I3
  also spelt Qongyröleng
Konystanu Kazakh. **102** C2
  also spelt Qonystanū
Konz Germany **48** D6
Konzhakovskiy Kamen', Gora *mt.*
  Rus. Fed. **40** K4
Koocanusa, Lake *resr* Canada/U.S.A.
  167 H5
Kookynie Australia **151** C6
Kooline Australia **150** B4
Koolivoo, Lake *salt flat* Australia **148** C5
Koolkootinnie, Lake *salt flat* Australia
  146 C2
Koolyanobbing Australia **151** B6
Koondrook Australia **147** E3
Koongie Park Aboriginal Reserve Australia
  150 D3
Kooniba Australia **146** B2
Koopan-Suid S. Africa **132** F4
Koorawatha Australia **147** F3
Koorda Australia **151** B6
Koordarrie Australia **150** A4
Koorküla Estonia **42** G4
Koosa Estonia **42** I3
Koosharem U.S.A. **183** M3
Kooskia U.S.A. **180** C3
Kootenay *r.* Canada **167** G5
Kootenay Bay Canada **167** G5
Kootenay Lake Canada **167** G5
Kootenay National Park Canada **167** G5
Kootingal Australia **147** F2
Kootjieskolk S. Africa **132** E8
Kopa Kazakh. **103** H4
Kopa Zambia **127** F7
Kopanovka Rus. Fed. **102** A3
Kopaonik *mts* Yugo. **58** B5
Kopaonik *nat. park* Yugo. **58** B5
Koparberg *county* Sweden *see* Dalarna
Kopasker Iceland **44** [inset] C1
Kopbirlik Kazakh. **103** I3
  formerly known as imeni Kirova
Koper Slovenia **56** F3
Kopet Dag *mts* Iran/Turkm. **100** D2
  also known as Kopet-Dag, Khrebet; also
  spelt Koppeh Dāgh
Kopet-Dag, Khrebet *mts* Iran/Turkm. *see*
  Kopet Dag
Köping Sweden **45** L4
Koplik Albania **58** A6
Köpmanholmen Sweden **44** L3
Koporika Rus. Fed. **43** P6
Koppa India **94** B3
Koppal India **94** C3
Koppang Norway **45** J3
Koppány *r.* Romania **49** P9
Kopparberg Sweden **45** K4
Kopparberg *county* Sweden *see* Dalarna
  Kopet Dag
Kóppel *r.* Rus. Fed. **82** F2
Koppies S. Africa **133** L4
Koppies Dam Nature Reserve S. Africa
  133 L4

Koppieskraal Pan *salt pan* S. Africa **132** E3
Koprinka, Yazovir *resr* Bulg. **58** G6
  formerly known as Georgi Dimitrov, Yazovir
Koprivnica Croatia **56** I2
Köprü *r.* Turkey **106** C3
Köprübaşı Turkey **59** J10
Köprülü Turkey **106** C3
Köprülü Kanyon Milli Parkı *nat. park*
  Turkey **106** B3
Kopsava Belarus **42** G9
Kopsaya Gora Rus. Fed. **43** S7
Koptsi Belarus **43** L6
Kopu Estonia **42** E3
Kōpu *r.* Estonia **42** G3
Kopu N.Z. **152** J5
Kopyl' Belarus *see* Kapyl'
Kora India **96** D4
Korab *mts* Albania/Macedonia **58** B7
Korablino Rus. Fed. **43** V8
Koraf Eth. **128** E3
K'orahē Eth. **128** E3
Koramlik China **89** D4
Korana *r.* Bos.-Herz./Croatia **56** H3
Korangal India **94** C2
Koraput India **95** D2
Korat Thai. *see* Nakhon Ratchasima
Koratla India **94** C2
Korba India **97** D5
Korba Tunisia **57** C12
Korbach Germany **48** F4
Korbenichi Rus. Fed. **43** P1
Korbous Tunisia **57** C12
Korbu, Gunung *mt.* Malaysia **76** C1
Korçë Albania **58** B8
  formerly known as Koritsa
Korchino Rus. Fed. **103** J1
Korčula Croatia **56** J6
Korčula *i.* Croatia **56** I6
Korčulanski Kanal *sea chan.* Croatia **56** I5
Korday Kazakh. **103** H4
  formerly known as Georgiyevka
Kordestān *prov.* Iran **100** A3
Kord Kūy Iran **100** C2
Kordon Rus. Fed. **40** K4
Kords *reg.* Iran **100** D5
Korea, North *country* Asia **83** B4
  asia [countries] 64–67
Korea, South *country* Asia **83** B5
  asia [countries] 64–67
Korea Bay *g.* China/N. Korea **83** B5
Korea Strait Japan/S. Korea **83** C6
  also known as Tsushima-kaikyō
Koregaon India **94** B2
Korem Eth. **128** C1
Korenovsk Rus. Fed. **41** F7
  formerly known as Korenovskaya
Korenovskaya Rus. Fed. *see* Korenovsk
Korets' Ukr. **41** C6
Korf Rus. Fed. **39** Q3
Korfez Turkey **106** B2
Körfez Turkey **106** B2
  also known as Yarımca
Korff Ice Rise Antarctica **222** T1
Korfovskiy Rus. Fed. **82** D2
Korgas China **88** C2
Korgen Norway **44** K2
Korhogo Côte d'Ivoire **124** D4
Koriabo Guyana **199** G3
Koribundu Sierra Leone **124** C5
Kori Creek *inlet* India **96** A5
Koringberg S. Africa **132** C10
Koringplaas S. Africa **132** E9
Koriniti N.Z. **152** J7
Korinthiakos Kolpos *sea chan.* Greece
  see Corinth, Gulf of
Korinthos Greece *see* Corinth
Kórinthos Greece **59** F11
Korissia Greece **59** F11
Koritsa Albania *see* Korçë
Kōriyama Japan **90** G6
Korkana Fin. **44** O2
Korki Iran **100** D2
Korkino Rus. Fed. **38** G4
Korkodon *r.* Rus. Fed. **39** P3
Korkuteli Turkey **106** B3
Körkvere Estonia **42** E3
Korla China **88** E3
  formerly known as Kaku City
Kormakitis, Cape Cyprus **108** C2
Korman *mt.* Yugo. **58** A5
Körmend Hungary **49** N8
Körmör Iraq **109** P2
Kornat *i.* Croatia **56** H5
Kornat *nat. park* Croatia **56** H5
Korneyevka *Karagandinskaya Oblast'*
  Kazakh. **103** H2
Korneyevka *Severnyy Kazakhstan* Kazakh.
  103 G1
Kornsjø Norway **45** J4
Koro *r.* Côte d'Ivoire **124** D4
Koro *i.* Fiji **145** G3
  also spelt Goro
Koro Mali **124** D3
Korobets Rus. Fed. **43** O7
Koroc *r.* Canada **169** H1
Koroğlu Dağları *mts* Turkey **106** C2
Koroğlu Tepesi *mt.* Turkey **106** C2
Korogo *well* Eth. **128** C3
Korogwe Tanz. **129** C6
Korom, Bahr *watercourse* Chad **126** D2
Koroni Greece **59** C12
Koronowo Poland **49** O2
Koropi Greece **59** E11

Kos *i.* Greece **59** I12
  Engl sh form Cos
Kosa Rus. Fed. **40** J4
Kosa *r.* Rus. Fed. **40** J3
Kosagal Kazakh. **103** E2
Kosaka Japan **90** G4
Kosan N. Korea **83** B5
  formerly known as Sin'gosan
Kosava Belarus **42** G9
Kosaya Gora Rus. Fed. **43** S7
Koschagyl Kazakh. **102** C3
  also spelt Qosshaghyl
Kościan Poland **49** N3
Kościerzyna Poland **49** O1
Kosciusko U.S.A. **175** B5
Kosciusko, Mount Australia *see*
  Kosciuszko, Mount
Kosciusko Island U.S.A. **166** C3
  also spelt Kosciuszko, Mount
Kosciuszko National Park Australia **147** F4
Kose Estonia **42** G2
Köseçobanlı Turkey **108** E1
Köse Dağı *mt.* Turkey **107** D2
Kösedere Turkey **59** H9
Kosgi India **94** C2
Kosh-Agach Rus. Fed. **84** A1
Koshanicol' Kazakh. **102** B2
Koshbakakskoye Vodokhranilische resr
  Turkm. **103** E4
Kosh-Döbö Kyrg. **103** H4
Koshiki-jima-rettō *is* Japan **91** A9
Koshikino Rus. Fed. **103** J1
Koshimizu Japan **90** I3
Koshk Afgh. **101** F3
Koshk-e Kohneh Afgh. **101** E3
Koshki Rus. Fed. **41** I5
Koshkonong, Lake U.S.A. **172** E8
Koshkupyr Uzbek. **102** E4
  also spelt Qŭshkŭpir
Koshoba Turkm. **102** C4
  also spelt Goshoba
Koshrabad Uzbek. **103** F4
  alsc spelt Qŭshrabot
Koshtëbë Kyrg. *see* Kosh-Döbö
Kosi *r.* India **96** C3
Kosi Bay S. Africa **133** Q3
Kosi Bay Nature Reserve S. Africa **133** Q4
Košice Slovakia **49** S7
  a so known as Kassa
Kos *g.* India **94** B2
Kosi Reservoir Nepal **97** E4
Kos-Istek Kazakh. **102** C2
Košk Turkey **59** J11
Koski Rus. Fed. **43** O7
Koskol' Kazakh. **103** F2
Kos'kovo Rus. Fed. **43** O1
Koskuduk Kazakh. **103** I4
Koskullskulle Sweden **44** M2
Kóslan Rus. Fed. **40** I3
Kosma *r.* Rus. Fed. **40** I2
Kosmynino Rus. Fed. **43** V4
Kešnica *r.* Croatia **56** K3
Keson Uzbek. *see* Kasan
Kosŏng N. Korea **83** C4
Kosŏng S. Korea **83** A7
Kosŏng S. Korea **91** A7
Kosonsoy Uzbek. *see* Kasansay
Kosorzha Rus. Fed. **43** V9
Kosova *prov.* Yugo. *see* Kosovo
Kosovo *prov.* Yugo. **58** B6
  also known as Amselfeld; also spelt Kosova;
  long form Kosovo-Metohija
  europe [issues] 34–35
Kosovo-Metohija *prov.* Yugo. *see* Kosovo
Kosovo Polje Kosovo, Srbija Yugo. **58** B6
Kosovo Polje *plain* Yugo. **58** B6
Kosovska Kamenica Kosovo, Srbija Yugo.
  58 C6
Kosovska Mitrovica Kosovo, Srbija Yugo.
  58 B6
  formerly known as Titova Mitrovica; short
  form Mitrovica
Kosrae *atoll* Micronesia **220** E5
  also known as Ualan; formerly known as Kusaie
Kossa *well* Mauritania **124** C3
Kossatori *well* Niger **125** I3
Kossinine *hill* Germany **48** I6
Kossol Reef Palau **73** H5
Kossou, Lac de *l.* Côte d'Ivoire **124** D4
Kostanay Kazakh. **103** E1
  also spelt Qostanay; formerly spelt Kustanay
Kosta-Khetagurovo Rus. Fed. *see* Nazran'
Kostenets Bulg. **58** E6
Koster S. Africa **133** K4
Kosterevo Rus. Fed. **43** U6
Kosti Sudan **121** G6
Kostino Rus. Fed. **39** I3
Kostobobr Ukr. **43** N9
Kostolac *Srbija* Yugo. **58** C4
Kostomuksha Rus. Fed. **44** O2
Kostomukshskiy Zapovednik nature res.
  Rus. Fed. **44** O2
Kostopil' Ukr. **41** C6
  also spelt Kostopol'
Kostopol' Ukr. *see* Kostopil'
Kostroma *r.* Rus. Fed. **43** V4
Kostroma Rus. Fed. **40** G4
Kostroma Oblast admin. div. Rus. Fed. *see*
  Kostromskaya Oblast'
Kostromskaya Oblast' admin. div. Rus. Fed.
  40 G4
  English form Kostroma Oblast
Kostrzyn Poland **49** L3
Kostrzyń *r.* Poland **49** T3
Kostyantynivka Ukr. **41** F6
  formerly known as Konstantinovka
Kostyri Rus. Fed. **43** O7
Kostyukovichi Belarus *see* Kastsyukovichy
Kostyzhitsy Rus. Fed. **43** K4
Kosubosu Nigeria **125** F4
Kos'yu *r.* Rus. Fed. **40** K2
Kos'yu Rus. Fed. **40** K2
Koszalin Poland **49** N1
  historically known as Köslin
Kőszeg Hungary **49** N8
  also known as Güns
Kota *Chhattisgarh* India **97** D5
Kota *Rajasthan* India **96** B4
Kotaagung Indon. **76** D4
Kota Baharu Malaysia *see* Kota Bharu
Kotabaru *Kalimantan Barat* Indon. **77** E3
Kotabaru *Kalimantan Selatan* Indon. **77** G3
Kota Belud *Sabah* Malaysia **77** G1
Kota Bharu Malaysia **76** C1
  a so spelt Kota Baharu
Kotabumi Indon. **76** D3
Kot Addu Pak. **101** G4
Kota Kinabalu *Sabah* Malaysia **77** G1
  formerly known as Jesselton
Kotala Fin. **44** O2
Kotamobagu Indon. **75** C2
Kotaneelee Range *mts* Canada **166** E2
Kotaneneri, Gora *mt.* Kazakh. **103** I3
Kotapinang Indon. **76** C2
Kotar India **96** B4
Kotari *r.* India **96** B3

Kotawaringin Indon. **77** E3
Kotchandpur Bangl. **97** F5
Kotcho *r.* Canada **166** F3
Kotcho Lake Canada **166** F3
Kot Diji Pak. **101** G5
Kotdwara India **96** C3
Koteasro India **94** B5
Kotel Bulg. **58** H6
Kotel'nich Rus. Fed. **40** I4
Kotel'nikovo Rus. Fed. **41** G7
Kotel'nyy, Ostrov *i.* Rus. Fed. **39** N2
Kotemaori N.Z. **152** L7
Kotgar India **95** D2
Kotgarh India **96** C3
Kothagudem India *see* Kottagudem
Köthen (Anhalt) Germany **48** I4
Kothi India **96** D4
Kotiari Naoude Senegal **124** B3
Kotido Uganda **128** B4
Kotka Fin. **45** N3
Kot Kapura India **96** B3
Kotkino Rus. Fed. **40** I2
Kotlas Rus. Fed. **40** H3
Kotli Pak. **101** H3
Kotlik U.S.A. **164** C3
Kotlina Sandomierska *basin* Poland **49** S5
Kotlovan Rus. Fed. **43** P3
Kōtlutangi *pt* Iceland **44** [inset] C3
Kotly Rus. Fed. **43** J2
Koton-Karifi Nigeria **125** G4
Kotooka Japan **90** G4
Kotor *Crna Gora* Yugo. **56** K6
Kotorkoshi Nigeria **125** G3
Kotorosl' *r.* Rus. Fed. **43** U4
Kotorsko Bos.-Herz. **56** J4
Kotor Varoš Bos.-Herz. **56** I4
Kotouba Côte d'Ivoire **124** E4
Kotovo Rus. Fed. **41** H6
Kotovsk Moldova *see* Hînceşti
Kotovsk Rus. Fed. **41** G5
Kotovs'k Ukr. **41** D7
Kot Putli India **96** C4
Kotra *r.* Belarus **42** F8
Kotri *r.* India **94** D2
Kotri Pak. **101** G5
Kotronas Greece **59** D12
Korttas Kazakh. **102** D2
Kot Sarae Pak. **101** F6
Kottagudem India **94** D2
  also known as Bhadrachalam Road Station;
  also spelt Kothagudem
Kottayam *Kerala* India **94** C4
Kottayam *Pondicherry* India **94** B4
Kotte Sri Lanka *see*
  Sri Jayewardenepura Kotte
Kotto *r.* Cent. Afr. Rep. **126** D3
Kotturu India **94** C3
Kotuy *r.* Rus. Fed. **39** K2
Kotwar Peak India **97** D5
Kotzebue U.S.A. **164** C3
Kotzebue Sound *sea chan.* U.S.A. **164** C3
Kotzehoop S. Africa **132** B5
Kotzersus S. Africa **132** B7
Kouango Cent. Afr. Rep. **126** D3
Kouba Olanga Chad **120** D3
Koubia Guinea **124** C4
Kouchibouguac National Park Canada
  169 H4
Koudougou Burkina **124** E3
Kouebokkeveld *mts* S. Africa **132** D9
Kouéré Burkina **124** E4
Koueveldberge *mts* S. Africa **132** H9
Koufalia Greece **58** D8
Koufonisi *i.* Kriti Greece **59** H14
Koufonisi *i.* Greece **59** G12
Koufos Greece **59** E9
Kouga *r.* S. Africa **132** H10
Koui Cent. Afr. Rep. **126** C3
Kouilou admin. reg. Congo **126** A6
Kouki Cent. Afr. Rep. **126** C3
Koukourou *r.* Cent. Afr. Rep. **126** C3
Koukourou-Bamingui, Réserve de Faune
  du nature res. Cent. Afr. Rep. **126** C3
Koulamoutou Gabon **126** B5
Koulba Chad **120** D6
Koulikoro Mali **124** D3
Koulikoro admin. reg. Mali **124** C3
Kouloudia Chad **120** D3
Koum Cameroon **125** I4
Kouma *r.* Cent. Afr. Rep. **126** C3
Koumac New Caledonia **145** F4
Koumameyong Gabon **126** B4
Koumbia Cent. Afr. Rep. **126** D2
Koumbia Burkina **124** E4
Koumbia Guinea **124** B3
Koumenzi China **84** B3
Koumogo Chad **126** C2
Koumra Chad **126** C2
Koundâra Guinea **124** B3
Koundian Mali **124** C3
Koundougou Burkina **124** D4
Koungheul Senegal **124** C3
Kounoupoi *i.* Greece **59** H12
Kounradskiy Kazakh. *see* Konyrat
Kounsitél Guinea **124** B4
Kountchi *well* Niger **125** H3
Kountze U.S.A. **179** D6
Koup S. Africa **132** F10
Koupéla Burkina **125** E3
Kouqian China *see* Yongji
Kouridinga *well* Niger **125** I3
Kournas Greece **59** F13
Kourou Fr. Guiana **199** H3
Kourou *r.* Greece **58** G7
  also spelt Kurú
Kouroudjel Mauritania **124** C3
Kouroussa Guinea **124** C4
Koussanar Senegal **124** B3
Koussané Mali **124** C3
Kousséri Cameroon **125** I3
  formerly known as Fort Foureau
Koussountou Togo **125** F4
Koutiala Mali **124** D3
Kouto Côte d'Ivoire **124** D4
Kouvola Fin. **45** N3
Kouyou *r.* Congo **126** C5
Kovačica *Vojvodina, Srbija* Yugo. **58** B3
Kovarzino Rus. Fed. **43** T1
Kovda Rus. Fed. **44** P2
Kovdor Rus. Fed. **44** P2
Kovdozero Rus. Fed. **44** O2
Kovdozero, Ozero *l.* Rus. Fed. **44** P2
Kovel' Ukr. **41** C6
Kovernino Rus. Fed. **40** G4
Kovilj *Vojvodina, Srbija* Yugo. **58** B3
Kovilpatti India **94** C4
Kovin *Vojvodina, Srbija* Yugo. **58** B3
Kovno Lith. *see* Kaunas
Kovriga, Gora *hill* Rus. Fed. **40** I2
Kovrov Rus. Fed. **40** G4
Kovylkino Rus. Fed. **41** G5
Kovylnoye *r.* Rus. Fed. **43** S1
Kovzhskoye, Ozero *l.* Rus. Fed. **43** S1
Kowanyama Australia **149** D2
Kowanyama Aboriginal Reserve Australia
  149 D2
Kowares *waterhole* Namibia **130** B3
Kowary Poland **49** M5
Kowchale Belarus **43** K8
Kowhitirangi N.Z. **153** F10
Kowli Kosh, Gardaneh-ye *pass* Iran
  100 C4
Kowloon *Hong Kong* China **87** [inset]
  also known as Chiu Lung or Jiulong
Kowloon Peak *hill* Hong Kong China **87** [inset]
  also known as Fei Ngo Shan
Kowloon Peninsula *Hong Kong* China
  87 [inset]

Kowr-e-Koja *watercourse* Iran **101** E5
Kox Kuduk *well* China **84** B3
Kōya Japan **91** D7
Kōyama-misaki *pt* Japan **91** B7
Koybagar, Ozero *l.* Kazakh. **103** F1
formerly known as Kaybagar, Ozero
Köyceğiz Turkey **106** B3
Köyceğiz Gölü *l.* Turkey **59** J12
Koygorodok Rus. Fed. **40** I3
Koymatdag, Gory *hills* Turkm. **102** C4
also known as Goymatdag
Koynare Bulg. **58** F5
Koyna Reservoir India **94** B2
Koyp, Gora *mt.* Rus. Fed. **40** K3
Koyukuk *r.* U.S.A. **164** D3
Koyulhisar Turkey **107** D2
Koza Rus. Fed. **43** U3
Kozağacı Turkey *see* **Günyüzü**
Kō-zaki *pt* Japan **91** A7
Kozan Turkey **106** C3
also known as Sis
Kozani Greece **59** C8
Kozar, Ras *pt* Eritrea **104** C5
Kozara *mts* Bos.-Herz. **56** I3
Kozara *nat. park* Bos.-Herz. **56** J3
Kozarska Dubica Bos.-Herz. *see* **Bosanska Dubica**
Kozel'sk Rus. Fed. **43** Q7
Kozen *well* Chad **120** C4
Kozhabakhy Kazakh. **103** E3
Kozhakol', Ozero *l.* Kazakh. **103** G2
also known as Qozhaköl
Kozhevnikovo Rus. Fed. **39** L2
Kozhikode India *see* **Calicut**
Kozhim-Iz, Gora *mt.* Rus. Fed. **40** K3
Kozhva Rus. Fed. **40** K2
Kozhva *r.* Rus. Fed. **40** K2
Kozhym *r.* Rus. Fed. **40** K2
Kozienice Poland **49** S4
Kozlikha Rus. Fed. **43** V1
Kozloduy Bulg. **58** E5
Kozlovka *Chuvashskaya Respublika* Rus. Fed. **40** I5
Kozlovka *Voronezhskaya Oblast'* Rus. Fed. **41** G6
Kozlovo Rus. Fed. **43** R5
Kozlu Turkey **106** B2
Kozluk Bos.-Herz. **56** L4
Koźmin Poland **49** O4
Koz'modem'yansk Rus. Fed. **40** H4
Kozmoldak Kazakh. **103** G4
Koznitsa *mt.* Bulg. **58** E6
Kożuchów Poland **49** M4
Kožuf *mts* Greece/Macedonia **58** D7
Kōzu-shima *i.* Japan **91** F7
Kozyatyn Ukr. **41** D6
also spelt Kazatin
Kozyörük Turkey **58** H7
Kpalimé Togo **125** F5
Kpandae Ghana **125** E4
Kpandu Ghana **125** F5
Kpungan Pass India/Myanmar **97** H4
Kra, Isthmus of Thai. **79** B6
Kraai *r.* S. Africa **133** K7
Kraankuil S. Africa **132** I6
Krabi Estonia **42** H4
Krabi Thai. **79** B6
Kra Buri Thai. **79** B6
Krâchéh Cambodia **79** D5
also spelt Kratie
Kräckelbäcken Sweden **45** K3
Kraftino, Ozero *l.* Rus. Fed. **43** P4
Kragan Indon. **77** E4
Kragerø Norway **45** J4
Kragujevac *Srbija* Yugo. **58** B4
Krajenka Poland **49** O2
Krakatau *i.* Indon. **77** D4
Krakatau Volcano National Park Indon. **76** D4
Krakau Poland *see* **Kraków**
Kråklivollen Norway **44** J3
Kraków Poland **49** Q5
historically known as Cracovia *or* Cracow *or* Krakau
Krakow U.S.A. **172** E6
Kralendijk Neth. Antilles **187** F4
Kraljevića Croatia **56** G3
Kraljevo *Srbija* Yugo. **58** B5
formerly known as Rankovićevo
Kráľova hoľa *mt.* Slovakia **49** R7
Kráľovský Chlmec Slovakia **49** S7
Kralupy nad Vltavou Czech Rep. **49** L5
Kramators'k Ukr. **41** F6
Kramfors Sweden **44** L3
Krammer *est.* Neth. **48** B4
Kranidi Greece **59** E11
Kranj Slovenia **56** G2
Kranji Reservoir Sing. **76** [inset]
Kransfontein S. Africa **133** M5
Kranskop S. Africa **133** O5
Kranskop *mt.* S. Africa **133** N4
Krapanj Croatia **56** H5
Krapina Croatia **56** H2
Krapinske Toplice Croatia **56** H2
Krapivna *Kaluzhskaya Oblast'* Rus. Fed. **43** Q8
Krapivna *Smolenskaya Oblast'* Rus. Fed. **43** O7
Krapkowice Poland **49** O5
Krasavino Rus. Fed. **40** H3
Krasilov Ukr. *see* **Krasyliv**
Krasino Rus. Fed. **40** J1
Kraskino Rus. Fed. **82** C4
Krāslava Latvia **42** I6
Kraslice Czech Rep. **49** J5
Krasnapollye Belarus **43** M8
Krasnasyel'ski Belarus **42** F8
Krasnaya Gora Rus. Fed. **43** M8
Krasnaya Gorbatka Rus. Fed. **40** G5
Krasnaya Polyana Kazakh. **103** H2
Krasnaya Polyana Rus. Fed. **41** G8
Krasnaya Slabada Belarus **42** I9
Krasnaya Zarya Rus. Fed. **43** S9
Kraśnik Poland **49** T5
Krasnoarmeysk Kazakh. *see* **Tayynsha**
Krasnoarmeysk *Moskovskaya Oblast'* Rus. Fed. **43** T5
Krasnoarmeysk *Saratovskaya Oblast'* Rus. Fed. **41** H6
Krasnoarmeysk Ukr. *see* **Krasnoarmiys'k**
Krasnoarmeyskaya Rus. Fed. *see* **Poltavskaya**
Krasnoarmeyskiy *Chukotskiy Avtonomnyy Okrug* Rus. Fed. **39** R3
Krasnoarmeyskiy *Rostovskaya Oblast'* Rus. Fed. **41** G7
formerly known as Kuberle
Krasnoarmiys'k Ukr. **41** F6
also spelt Krasnoarmeysk; *formerly known as* Chervonoarmiys'k *or* Grishino *or* Postysheve
Krasnobarskiy Rus. Fed. **43** Q2
Krasnoborsk Rus. Fed. **40** H3
Krasnodar Rus. Fed. **41** F7
formerly known as Yekaterinodar
Krasnodar Kray *admin. div.* Rus. Fed. *see* **Krasnodarskiy Kray**
Krasnodarskiy Kray *admin. div.* Rus. Fed. **41** F7
English form Krasnodar Kray
Krasnodon Ukr. **41** F6
Krasnofarfornyy Rus. Fed. **43** M2
Krasnogorka Kazakh. *see* **Ul'ken Sulutar**
Krasnogorodskoye Rus. Fed. **43** J5
Krasnogorsk Rus. Fed. **43** S6
Krasnogorsk Rus. Fed. **82** F2
Krasnogorskoye Rus. Fed. **40** J4
Krasnograd Ukr. *see* **Krasnohrad**
Krasnogvardeysk Uzbek. *see* **Bulungur**
Krasnogvardeyskiy Rus. Fed. **43** V5
Krasnogvardeyskoye Rus. Fed. **41** G7
formerly known as Yevdokimovskoye
Krasnohrad Ukr. **41** E6
also spelt Krasnograd; *formerly known as* Konstantinograd
Krasnohvardiys'ke Ukr. **41** E7
Krasnokamensk Rus. Fed. **85** H1
Krasnokamsk Rus. Fed. **40** J4
Krasnokholm Rus. Fed. **102** C2
Krasnokutsk Kazakh. *see* **Aktogay**
Krasnokutskoye Kazakh. *see* **Aktogay**
Krasnolesnyy Rus. Fed. **41** F6
Krasnoles'ye Rus. Fed. **42** D7
Krasnomayskiy Rus. Fed. **43** P4
Krasnoostrovskiy Rus. Fed. **43** J1
Krasnoperekops'k Ukr. **41** E7
Krasnopol'ye Rus. Fed. **82** F2
Krasnorechenskiy Rus. Fed. **82** D3
Krasnosel'kup Rus. Fed. **39** I3
Krasnosel'skoye Rus. Fed. **43** K1
Krasnoslobodsk Rus. Fed. **41** G5
Krasnotur'insk Rus. Fed. **38** G4
Krasnoufimsk Rus. Fed. **40** K4
Krasnousol'skiy Rus. Fed. **40** K5
Krasnovishersk Rus. Fed. **40** K3
Krasnovodsk Turkm. *see* **Turkmenbashi**
Krasnovodskaya Oblast' *admin. div.* Turkm. *see* **Balkanskaya Oblast'**
Krasnovodskiy Gosudarstvennyy Zapovednik *nature res.* Turkm. **102** C5
Krasnovodskiy Zaliv *b.* Turkm. **102** C5
Krasnovodskoye Plato *plat.* Turkm. **102** C4
Krasnoyar Kazakh. **102** C2
Krasnoyarovo Rus. Fed. **82** C2
Krasnoyarsk Rus. Fed. **80** E1
Krasnoyarskiy Rus. Fed. **102** D2
Krasnoyarskiy Kray *admin. div.* Rus. Fed. **80** E1
English form Krasnoyarsk Kray
Krasnoyarsk Kray *admin. div.* Rus. Fed. *see* **Krasnoyarskiy Kray**
Krasnoye *Belgorodskaya Oblast'* Rus. Fed. **41** F6
Krasnoye *Bryanskaya Oblast'* Rus. Fed. **43** O8
Krasnoye *Lipetskaya Oblast'* Rus. Fed. **43** T9
Krasnoye *Pskovskaya Oblast'* Rus. Fed. **43** K5
Krasnoye Rus. Fed. *see* **Ulan Erge**
Krasnoye *Smolenskaya Oblast'* Rus. Fed. **43** M7
Krasnoye, Ozero *l.* Rus. Fed. **39** R3
Krasnoye Plamya Rus. Fed. **43** T5
Krasnoye Znamya Rus. Fed. **43** Q4
Krasnozatonskiy Rus. Fed. **40** I3
Krasnozavodsk Rus. Fed. **43** T5
Krasnoznamensk Rus. Fed. **42** D7
Krasnoznamenskiy Kazakh. *see* **Krasnoznamenskoye**
Krasnoznamenskoye Kazakh. **103** G2
formerly known as Krasnoznamenskiy
Krasnystaw Poland **49** U5
Krasnyy Rus. Fed. **43** M7
Krasnyy Chikoy Rus. Fed. **85** F1
Krasnyye Baki Rus. Fed. **40** H4
Krasnyye Barrikady Rus. Fed. **102** A3
Krasnyye Tkachi Rus. Fed. **43** U4
Krasnyy Kamyshanik Rus. Fed. *see* **Komsomol'skiy**
Krasnyy Kholm Rus. Fed. **43** S3
Krasnyy Kut Rus. Fed. **102** A2
Krasnyy Luch Rus. Fed. **43** L4
Krasnyy Luch Ukr. **41** F6
Krasnyy Lyman Ukr. **41** F6
Krasnyy Oktyabr' Rus. Fed. **43** T5
Krasnyy Profintern Rus. Fed. **43** V4
Krasnyy Rog *Bryanskaya Oblast'* Rus. Fed. **43** O8
Krasnyy Rog *Bryanskaya Oblast'* Rus. Fed. **43** O9
Krasnyy Tekstil'shchik Rus. Fed. **41** H6
Krasnyy Yar Kazakh. **103** G1
Krasnyy Yar Rus. Fed. **102** B3
Krasyliv Ukr. **41** C6
also spelt Krasilov
Kratie Cambodia *see* **Krâchéh**
Kratovo Macedonia **58** D6
Krauja Latvia **42** H6
Kraul Mountains Antarctica **223** X2
Kraulshavn Greenland *see* **Nuussuaq**
Krâvanh, Chuŏr Phnum *mts* Cambodia *see* **Cardamom Range**
Kraynovka Rus. Fed. **102** A4
Krechevitsy Rus. Fed. **43** M3
Krefeld Germany **48** D4
Krekenava Lith. **42** F6
Kremaston, Techniti Limni *resr* Greece **59** C10
Kremen *mt.* Croatia **56** H4
Kremenchug Ukr. *see* **Kremenchuk**
Kremenchuk Ukr. **41** E6
also spelt Kremenchug
Kremenchuts'ka Vodoskhovyshche *resr* Ukr. **41** E6
Kremenki Rus. Fed. **43** S7
Kremenskoye Rus. Fed. **43** Q6
Kremges Ukr. *see* **Svitlovods'k**
Kreml' Rus. Fed. *see* **Solovetskiy**
Kremmidi, Akra *pt* Greece **59** E12
Kremmling U.S.A. **180** F4
Krems an der Donau Austria **49** M7
Kremsmünster Austria **49** L7
Krenitzin Islands U.S.A. **164** C4
Krepoljin *Srbija* Yugo. **58** C4
Kresna Bulg. **58** E7
Kresta, Zaliv *g.* Rus. Fed. **39** S3
Krestena Greece **59** C11
Krest-Khal'dzhayy Rus. Fed. **39** N3
Krestovka Rus. Fed. **40** J2
Krestsy Rus. Fed. **43** N3
Kresty *Moskovskaya Oblast'* Rus. Fed. **43** S6
Kresty *Pskovskaya Oblast'* Rus. Fed. **43** M6
Kresty *Tul'skaya Oblast'* Rus. Fed. **43** T8
Krestyakh Rus. Fed. **39** L3
Kretinga Lith. **42** C6
Kreuth Germany **48** I8
Kreuzau Germany **48** D5
Kreuzeck Gruppe *mts* Austria **49** K9
Kreuzlingen Switz. **51** P5
Kreuztal Germany **48** E5
Kreva Belarus **42** H7
Kribi Cameroon **125** H6
Krichev Belarus *see* **Krychaw**
Krichim Bulg. **58** F6
Krieglach Austria **49** M8
Kriel S. Africa **133** N3
Krievukalns *hill* Latvia **42** C5
Krieza Greece **59** F10
Krikellos Greece **59** C10
Krikelos, Akra *pt* Greece **59** H12
Krikovo Moldova *see* **Cricova**
Kril'on, Mys *c.* Rus. Fed. **82** F3
Krios, Akra *pt* Greece **59** E13
Krishna *r.* India **94** D2
formerly known as Kistna
Krishnagiri India **94** C3
Krishnai *r.* India **97** F4
Krishnanagar India **97** F5
Krishnaraja Sagara *l.* India **94** C3
Krishnarajpet India **94** C3
Kristdala Sweden **45** L4
Kristiania Norway *see* **Oslo**
Kristiansand Norway **45** I4
Kristianstad Sweden **45** K4
Kristiansund Norway **44** I3
Kristiinankaupunki Fin. *see* **Kristinestad**
Kristinehamn Sweden **45** K4
Kristinestad Fin. **45** M3
also known as Kristiinankaupunki
Kristinopol' Ukr. *see* **Chervonohrad**
Kriti *admin. reg.* Greece **59** F14
Kriti *i.* Greece *see* **Crete**
Kriūkai Lith. **42** E6
Kriulyany Moldova *see* **Criuleni**
Kriusha Rus. Fed. **43** U7
Krivača *mt.* Yugo. **58** B5
Krivaja *r.* Bos.-Herz. **56** K4
Krivandino Rus. Fed. **43** U6
Kriva Palanka Macedonia **58** D6
Kriva Reka *r.* Macedonia **58** C6
Křivoklátská Vrchovina *hills* Czech Rep. **49** K6
Krivoles Rus. Fed. **43** N8
Krivoy Porog Rus. Fed. **40** E2
Krivoy Rog Ukr. *see* **Kryvyy Rih**
Križevci Croatia **56** I2
Krk *mt.* Bos.-Herz. **56** L4
Krk Croatia **56** G3
Krk *i.* Croatia **56** G3
Krka *r.* Croatia **56** H5
Krka *r.* Slovenia **56** H3
Krkonošský narodni park *nat. park* Czech Rep./Poland **49** M5
also known as Karkonoski Park Narodowy
Krnjača *Srbija* Yugo. **58** B4
Krnov Czech Rep. **49** O5
Krobia Poland **49** N4
Krohnwodoke Liberia **124** D5
Kroknes Norway **44** O1
Krokom Sweden **44** K3
Krókšfjarðarnes Iceland **44** [inset] B2
Krokstadøra Norway **44** J3
Krolevets' Ukr. **41** E6
Kroma *r.* Rus. Fed. **43** Q9
Kromdraai S. Africa **133** N2
Kromy Rus. Fed. **43** Q9
Kronach Germany **48** I5
Kronfjell *hill* Norway **45** J4
Krŏng Kaôh Kŏng Cambodia **79** C6
Kronli India **97** G3
Kronoberg *county* Sweden **45** K4
Kronoby Fin. **44** M3
Kronotskiy Poluostrov *pen.* Rus. Fed. **39** Q4
Kronotskiy Zaliv *b.* Rus. Fed. **39** Q4
Kronotskoye Ozero *l.* Rus. Fed. **39** Q4
Kronprins Christian Land *reg.* Greenland **165** Q1
Kronprins Frederik Bjerge *nunataks* Greenland **165** P3
Kronshagen Germany **48** H1
Kronshtadt Rus. Fed. **43** K2
English form Kronstadt
Kronstadt Romania *see* **Braşov**
Kronstadt Rus. Fed. *see* **Kronshtadt**
Kroonstad S. Africa **133** L4
Kropotkin Rus. Fed. **41** G7
Kropp Germany **48** G1
Krosno Poland **49** S6
Krosno Odrzańskie Poland **49** M3
Krossen Norway **45** J4
Krotoszyn Poland **49** O4
Krotz Springs U.S.A. **175** B6
Krousonas Greece **59** F13
Kroya Indon. **77** E4
Krško Slovenia **56** H3
Krstača *mt.* Yugo. **58** B6
Krugerdrifdam *resr* S. Africa **133** K5
Kruger National Park S. Africa **133** P2
Krugersdorp S. Africa **133** L3
Krugerspos S. Africa **133** O1
Kruglyakov Rus. Fed. *see* **Oktyabr'skiy**
Kruhlaye Belarus **43** K7
Krui Indon. **76** C4
Kruidfontein S. Africa **132** F9
Kruisfontein S. Africa **133** I11
Krujë Albania **58** A7
Krumë Albania **58** B6
Krumovgrad Bulg. **58** G7
Krungkao Thai. *see* **Ayutthaya**
Krung Thep Thai. *see* **Bangkok**
Kruoja *r.* Lith. **42** E5
Krupa Bos.-Herz. *see* **Bosanska Krupa**
Krupa na Uni Bos.-Herz. *see* **Bosanska Krupa**
Krupanj *Srbija* Yugo. **58** A4
Krupina Slovakia **49** Q7
Krupki Belarus **43** K7
Kruševac *Srbija* Yugo. **58** C5
Kruševo Macedonia **58** C7
Krušné Hory *mts* Czech Rep. **49** J5
Krustkalnu rezervāts *nature res.* Latvia **42** H5
Kruszwica Poland **49** P3
Krutoye *Orlovskaya Oblast'* Rus. Fed. **43** S9
Krutoye *Smolenskaya Oblast'* Rus. Fed. **43** M6
Kruzof Island U.S.A. **166** C3
Krybinka *r.* Belarus **43** K6
Krychaw Belarus **43** M8
also spelt Krichev
Kryezi Albania **58** B6
Krym' *pen.* Ukr. *see* **Crimea**
Krymsk Rus. Fed. **41** F7
formerly known as Krymskaya
Krymskaya Rus. Fed. *see* **Krymsk**
Kryms'kyy Pivostriv *pen.* Ukr. *see* **Crimea**
Kryms'kyy Zapovidnyk *nature res.* Ukr. **106** C1
Krynica Poland **49** R6
Krynica Morska Poland **49** Q1
Krynki Belarus **43** L6
Krystynopol Ukr. *see* **Chervonohrad**
Krytiko Pelagos *sea* Greece **59** G12
Kryvichy Belarus **42** I7
Kryvyy Rih Ukr. **41** E7
also spelt Krivoy Rog
Krzepice Poland **49** P5
Krzna *r.* Poland **49** U3
Krzna Południowa *r.* Poland **49** T4
Krzyż Wielkopolski Poland **49** N3
Ksabi Alg. **123** E3
Ksar Chellala Alg. **55** N9
formerly known as Reïbell
Ksar el Boukhari Alg. **123** F2
formerly known as Boghari
Ksar el Hirane Alg. **123** F2
Ksar el Kebir Morocco **122** D2
formerly spelt Alcazarquivir
Ksar-es-Souk Morocco *see* **Er Rachidia**
Ksenofontova Rus. Fed. **40** J3
Kshen' *r.* Rus. Fed. **43** S9
Kskyrbulak Yuzhnyy, Gora *hill* Turkm. **102** C4
Ksour, Monts des *mts* Alg. **120** A1
Ksour, Monts des *mts* Tunisia **123** H2
Ksour Essaf Tunisia **123** H2
Kstovo Rus. Fed. **40** H4
Ktsyn' Rus. Fed. **43** Q8
Kū', Jabal al *hill* Saudi Arabia **105** D2
Ku, Wadi el *watercourse* Sudan **121** E6
Kuaidamao China *see* **Tonghua**
Kuala Belait Brunei **77** F1
Kuala Dungun Malaysia *see* **Dungun**
Kualajelai Indon. **77** E3
Kuala Kangsar Malaysia **76** C1
Kualakapuas Indon. **77** F3
Kuala Kerai Malaysia **76** C1
Kuala Kinabatangan *r. mouth Sabah* Malaysia **77** G1
Kualakuayan Indon. **77** F3
Kuala Kubu Baharu Malaysia **76** C2
Kualakurun Indon. **77** F3
Kuala Lipis Malaysia **76** C1

▶**Kuala Lumpur** Malaysia **76** C2
Capital of Malaysia.

Kualapembuang Indon. **77** F3
Kuala Penyu *Sabah* Malaysia **77** F1
Kuala Pilah Malaysia **76** C2
Kualapuu U.S.A. **181** [inset] Z1
Kualasampit Indon. **77** F3
Kualasimpang Indon. **76** B1
Kuala Terengganu Malaysia **76** C1
Kualatungal Indon. **76** C3
Kuamut *Sabah* Malaysia **77** G1
Kuamut *r. Sabah* Malaysia **77** G1
Kuancheng China **85** H3
Kuandian China **83** B4
Kuangyuan China *see* **Yiliang**
Kuanshan Taiwan **87** G4
Kuantan Malaysia **76** C2
Kuaotuou N.Z. **152** J4
Kuba Azer. *see* **Quba**
Kuban' *r.* Rus. Fed. **41** F7
Kubār *Dayr az Zawr* Syria **109** K2
Kubārah Oman **105** G3
Kübassaare poolsaar *pen.* Estonia **42** E3
Kubaysah Iraq **107** E4
Kubbum Sudan **126** D2
Kubena *r.* Rus. Fed. **43** U2
Kubenskoye Rus. Fed. **43** U2
Kubenskoye, Ozero *l.* Rus. Fed. **43** U2
Kuberle Rus. Fed. *see* **Krasnoarmeyskiy**
Kubinka Rus. Fed. **43** R6
Kubitzer Bodden *b.* Germany **49** K1
Kubnya *r.* Rus. Fed. **40** I5
Kubokawa Japan **91** C8
Kubor, Mount P.N.G. **73** J8
Kubrat Bulg. **58** H5
Kubrinsk Rus. Fed. **43** T5
Kubumesaäi Indon. **77** F2
Kučevo *Srbija* Yugo. **58** C4
Kuchaman India **96** B4
Kuchema Rus. Fed. **40** G2
Kuchera India **96** B4
Kuching *Sarawak* Malaysia **77** E2
also spelt Kucing
Kuchinotsu Japan **91** B8
Kuchukskoye, Ozero *salt l.* Rus. Fed. **103** I1
Kuchurhan *r.* Ukr. **58** K2
Kucing *Sarawak* Malaysia *see* **Kuching**
Kuçovë Albania **58** A8
formerly known as Qyteti Stalin
Küçükköy Turkey **59** H9
Küçükmenderes *r.* Turkey **59** H8
Küçükmenderes *r.* Turkey **59** I11
Kuda India **96** A5
Kudachi India **94** B2
Kudal India **94** B3
Kudamatsu Japan **91** B8
Kudap Indon. **76** C2
Kudara-Somon Rus. Fed. **85** E1
Kudev *r.* Rus. Fed. **42** J4
Kudever' Rus. Fed. **43** K5
Kudirkos Naumiestis Lith. **42** D7
Kudligi India **94** C3
Kudremukh *mt.* India **94** B3
Kudrinskaya Rus. Fed. **43** Q7
Kudu Nigeria **125** G4
Kudus Indon. **77** E4
Kudymkar Rus. Fed. **40** J4
Kueishan Tao *i.* Taiwan **87** G3
Kufstein Austria **48** J8
Kugaly Kazakh. **103** I3
also spelt Qoghaly
Kugesi Rus. Fed. **40** H4
Kugka Lhai China **89** E6
Kugluktuk Canada **165** H3
formerly known as Coppermine
Kugmallit Bay Canada **164** F3
Kūh, Ra's-al- *pt* Iran **100** D5
Kūhak Iran **101** E5
Kūhbonān Iran **100** D4
Kūhdasht Iran **100** A3
Kūhestak Iran **100** D5
Kūhīn Iran **100** B2
Kūhīrī Iran **101** E5
Kūhistoni Badakhshon *aut. rep.* Tajik. **101** H2
also known as Gorno-Badakhshan *or* Gornyy Badakhshan; *formerly known as* Badakhshoni Kūhī; *short form* Badakhshan
Kühlung *park* Germany **48** I1
Kuhmo Fin. **44** O2
Kuhmoinen Fin. **45** N3
Kūhpāyeh Iran **100** C3
Kūhpāyeh *mt.* Iran **100** D4
Kūhrān, Kūh-e *mt.* Iran **100** D5
Kūhrang *r.* Iran **100** B4
Kui Buri Thai. **79** B5
Kuimetsa Estonia **42** G2
Kuis Namibia **130** C5
Kuiseb *watercourse* Namibia **130** B4
Kuitan China **87** E4
Kuitin China *see* **Kuytun**
Kuito Angola **127** C8
formerly known as Bié
Kuiu Island U.S.A. **166** C3
Kuivaniemi Fin. **44** N2
Kuivastu Estonia **42** E3
Kuja *r.* Latvia **42** H5
Kujang India **95** E1
Kujang N. Korea **83** B5
Kuji Japan **90** G4
Kuji-wan *b.* Japan **90** G4
Kujū-san *vol.* Japan **91** B8
Kukālār, Kūh-e *hill* Iran **100** B4
Kukan Rus. Fed. **82** D2
Kukatush Canada **173** K2
Kukawa Nigeria **125** I3
Kukerin Australia **151** B7
Kukës Albania **58** B6
Kuki Japan **91** F6
Kukkola Fin. **44** N2
Kukmor Rus. Fed. **40** I4
Kukoboy Rus. Fed. **43** U3
Kukruse Estonia **42** I2
Kukshi India **96** B5
Kukunuru India **94** D2
Kukup Malaysia **76** C2
Kukurtli Turkm. **102** D5
formerly known as Sernyy Zavod
Kukusan, Gunung *hill* Indon. **77** F3
Kukushtan Rus. Fed. **40** K4
Kūl *r.* Iran **100** C5
Kula Bulg. **58** D5
Kula *r.* Moldova *see* **Cula**
Kula Nigeria **125** G5
Kula Turkey **106** B3
Kula *Vojvodina, Srbija* Yugo. **58** A3
Kula *mt.* Yugo. **58** A6
Kulabu, Gunung *mt.* Indon. **76** B2
Kulachi Pak. **101** G4
Kulagi Rus. Fed. **43** N9
Kulagino Kazakh. **102** B2
Kula Kangri *mt.* Bhutan **97** F3
Kulal, Mount Kenya **128** C4
Kulaly, Ostrov *i.* Kazakh. **102** B3
also known as Qulaly Araly
Kulandy Kazakh. **102** D3
also spelt Qulandy
Kulaneh *reg.* Pak. **101** E5
Kulanotpes *watercourse* Kazakh. **103** G2
also spelt Qulanötpes
Kulao *r.* Pak. **101** F4
Kular Rus. Fed. **39** N2
Kulassein *i.* Phil. **74** B5
Kulat, Gunung *mt.* Indon. **77** G2
Kulautuva Lith. **42** E7
Kulawi Indon. **75** A3
Kulb Sudan **121** F4
Kuldīga Latvia **42** C5
Kuldja China *see* **Yining**
Kul'dur Rus. Fed. **82** C2
Kul'dzhuktau, Gory *hills* Uzbek. **103** E4
also known as Quljuqtog' Toghi
Kule Botswana **130** D4
Kulebaki Rus. Fed. **40** G5
Kuleshi Rus. Fed. **43** N6
Kület el Qrein *hill* Egypt **108** C8
Kulgera Australia **148** B5
Kulgunino Rus. Fed. **102** D1
Kulii Lith. **42** C6
Kuligi Rus. Fed. **40** J4
Kulikovo *Arkhangel'skaya Oblast'* Rus. Fed. **40** H3
Kulikovo *Lipetskaya Oblast'* Rus. Fed. **43** U9
Kulim Malaysia **76** C1
Kulittalai India **94** C4
Kulkuduk Uzbek. **103** E4
also spelt Kalquduq
Kulkyne *watercourse* Australia **147** E2
Kullamaa Estonia **42** F3
Kullu India **96** C3
Kulmbach Germany **48** I5
Kŭlob Tajik. **101** G2
also spelt Kulyab
Kulotino Rus. Fed. **43** O3
Kuloy Rus. Fed. **40** G3
Kuloy *r.* Rus. Fed. **40** G2
Kulp Turkey **107** E3
also known as Fasur
Kul'sary Kazakh. **102** C3
also spelt Qulsary
Kulshabi Sudan **126** F2
Kultuk Rus. Fed. **84** D1
Kulu Turkey **106** C3
Kulübe Tepe *mt.* Turkey **106** B3
Kulunda Rus. Fed. **103** I1
Kulunda *r.* Rus. Fed. **103** I1
Kulundinskaya Step' *plain* Kazakh./Rus. Fed. **103** H1
Kulundinskoye, Ozero *salt l.* Rus. Fed. **103** I1
Kulusuk Greenland **165** P3
also known as Kap Dan
Külvand Iran **100** C4
Kulwin Australia **147** D3
Kulyab Tajik. *see* **Kŭlob**
Kuma *r.* Rus. Fed. **44** O2
Kuma *r.* Rus. Fed. **102** A3
Kumagaya Japan **91** F6
Kumai, Teluk *b.* Indon. **77** E3
Kumaishi Japan **90** F3
Kumak *r.* Rus. Fed. **102** D2
Kumaka Guyana **199** G4
Kumalar Dağı *mts* Turkey **106** B3
Kumamoto Japan **91** B8
Kumamoto *pref.* Japan **91** B8
Kumano Japan **91** E8
Kumanovo Macedonia **58** C6
Kumara N.Z. **153** F10
Kumara Junction N.Z. **153** F10
Kumarkhali Bangl. **97** F5
Kumasi Ghana **125** E5
Ku-Mayima S. Africa **133** M8
Kumayri Armenia *see* **Gyumri**
Kumba Cameroon **125** H5
Kumbağ Turkey **58** I8
Kumbakonam India **94** C4
Kümbet Turkey **106** B3
Kumbharli Ghat *mt.* India **94** B2
Kumbher Nepal **97** D3
Kumbla India **94** B3
Kumbo Cameroon **125** H5
Kumbri Latvia **42** D5
Kumchuru Botswana **130** D4
Kum-Dag Turkm. *see* **Gumdag**
Kumdah Saudi Arabia **105** D3
Kumel *well* Iran **100** C3
Kumertau Rus. Fed. **102** C1
Kŭm-gang *r.* S. Korea **83** B6
Kumgang-san *mt.* N. Korea **83** C5
English form Keumgang, Mount; *formerly known as* Keumsang, Mount
Kumguri India **97** F4
Kumharsain India **89** B6
Kumher India **96** C4
Kŭmho-gang *r.* S. Korea **83** C6
Kumi S. Korea **83** C5
Kumi Uganda **128** B4
Kumkale Turkey **59** H9
Kum Kuduk *well* China **88** E3
Kumla Sweden **45** K4
Kumlinge Fin. **45** M3
Kumlu Turkey **109** H1
Kumluca Turkey **108** B1
Kummerower See *l.* Germany **49** J2
Kumo Nigeria **125** H4
Kŭmŏ-do *i.* S. Korea **83** B6
Kumola *watercourse* Kazakh. **103** F3
also spelt Qumola
Kumon Range *mts* Myanmar **78** B2
Kumphawapi Thai. **78** C4
Kumputunturi *hill* Fin. **44** N2
Kumta India **94** B3
Kumu Dem. Rep. Congo **126** E4
Kumukahi, Cape U.S.A. **181** [inset] Z2
Kumul China *see* **Hami**
Kumund India **95** D1
Kümüx China **88** E3
Kumylzhenskaya Rus. Fed. *see* **Kumylzhenskiy**
Kumylzhenskiy Rus. Fed. **41** G6
formerly known as Kumylzhenskaya
Kumyshtag, Pik *mt.* Kyrg. *see* **Kyumyush-Tak, Pik**
Kun *r.* Myanmar **78** B4
Kunar *r.* Afgh. **101** G3
Kunashir, Ostrov *i.* Rus. Fed. **82** G3
Kunashirskiy Proliv *sea chan.* Japan/Rus. Fed. *see* **Nemuro-kaikyō**
Kunchaung Myanmar **78** B3
Kunda Dem. Rep. Congo **126** E5
Kunda Estonia **42** H2
Kunda *r.* Estonia **42** H2
Kunda India **97** D4
Kunda-dia-Baze Angola **127** C7
Kunda laht *b.* Estonia **42** H2
Kundapura India **94** B3
formerly spelt Coondapoor
Kundar *r.* Afgh./Pak. **101** G3
Kundat *Sabah* Malaysia **77** G1
Kundelungu, Parc National de *nat. park* Dem. Rep. Congo **127** E7
Kundelungu Ouest, Parc National de *nat. park* Dem. Rep. Congo **127** E7
Kundgol India **94** B3
Kundian Pak. **101** G3
Kundur *i.* Indon. **76** C2
Kunduz Afgh. *see* **Kondūz**
Kunene *admin. reg.* Namibia **130** B3
Kunene *r.* Namibia **127** A9
also spelt Cunene
Künes China *see* **Xinyuan**
Künes Chang China **88** C3
Künes He *r.* China **88** C3
Künes Linchang China **88** D3
Kungälv Sweden **45** J4
Kungei Alatau *mts* Kazakh./Kyrg. **103** I4
Kunggar China *see* **Maizhokunggar**
Kunghit Island Canada **166** D4
Küngöy Ala-Too *mts* Kazakh./Kyrg. *see* **Kungei Alatau**
Kungrad Uzbek. **102** D4
also spelt Qongrat *or* Qŭnghirot; *formerly known as* Zheleznodorozhnyy
Kungradkol' Uzbek. **102** E4
Kungsbacka Sweden **45** K4
Kungshamn Sweden **45** J4
Kungsör Sweden **45** L4
Kungu Dem. Rep. Congo **126** C4
Kungur *mt.* China *see* **Kongur Shan**
Kungur Rus. Fed. **40** K4
Kungyangon Myanmar **78** A4
Kunhegyes Hungary **49** R8
Kuni *r.* India **94** C2
Kunié *i.* New Caledonia *see* **Pins, Île des**
Kunigai India **94** C3
Kunimi-dake *mt.* Japan **91** B8
Kuningaküla Estonia **42** I2
Kuningan Indon. **77** E4
Kunisaki Japan **91** B8
Kunjabar India **95** E1
Kunlavav India **96** A5
Kunlong Myanmar **78** B3
Kunlui *r.* India/Nepal **97** F4
Kunlun Shan *mts* China **84** B5
Kunlun Shankou *pass* China **84** B5
Kunmadaras Hungary **49** R8
Kunming China **86** B3
Kunmunya Aboriginal Reserve Australia **150** D2
Kuno *r.* India **96** C4
Kunoy *i.* Faroe Is **46** F1
Kunsan S. Korea **83** B6
Kunshan China **87** G2
Kunszentmárton Hungary **49** R9
Kunszentmiklós Hungary **49** Q8
Kuntshankoie Dem. Rep. Congo **126** D5
Kununurra Australia **150** E2
Kunwak *r.* Canada **167** L2
Kunwari *r.* India **96** C4
Kun'ya Rus. Fed. **43** L5
Kun'ya *r.* Rus. Fed. **43** M4
Kunyang China *see* **Yexian**
Kunyang China *see* **Jinning**
Kunyang China *see* **Pingyang**
Kunya-Urgench Turkm. *see* **Keneurgench**
Kunyu Shan *mts* China **85** I4
Künzelsau Germany **48** G6
Kuocang Shan *mts* China **87** G2
Kuolayarvi Rus. Fed. **44** O2
Kuopio Fin. **44** N3
Kuosku Fin. **44** O2
Kupa *r.* Croatia/Slovenia **56** I3
Kupang Indon. **75** B5
Kupang, Teluk *b.* Indon. **75** B5
Kupanskoye Rus. Fed. **43** T5
Kupari India **97** E5
Kupiškis Lith. **42** F6
Kuprava Latvia **42** I4
Kupreanof Island U.S.A. **164** F4
Kupreanof Point U.S.A. **164** D4
Kupuy Rus. Fed. **43** L5
Kupwara Jammu and Kashmir **96** B2
Kup"yans'k Ukr. **41** F6
Kuqa China **88** C3
Kür *r.* Azer. **107** G3
Kür *r.* Georgia **107** F2
Kur *r.* Rus. Fed. **82** D2
Kura *r.* Azer./Georgia **107** F2
Kura *r.* Rus. Fed. **41** G8
Kurabuka *r.* Australia **150** B5
Kuragaty Kazakh. **103** H4
also spelt Qoraghaty
Kuragwi Nigeria **125** H4
Kurakh Rus. Fed. **102** A4
Kura kurk *sea chan.* Estonia/Latvia *see* **Irbe Strait**
Kuramā, Harrat *lava field* Saudi Arabia **104** C2
Kurashasayskiy Kazakh. **102** D2
Kurashiki Japan **91** C7
Kurasia India **97** D5
Kura Soak *well* Australia **150** D3
Kurayn *i.* Saudi Arabia **105** E2
Kurayoshi Japan **91** C7
Kurayskiy Khrebet *mts* Rus. Fed. **84** A1
Kurba Rus. Fed. **43** U4
Kurban Dağı *mt.* Turkey **58** K8
Kurbin *r.* China **82** C2
Kurca *r.* Romania **58** B2
Kurchatov Rus. Fed. **41** E6
Kurchum Kazakh. **88** C1
also spelt Kürshim; *formerly known as* Kumashkino
Kurchum *r.* Kazakh. **88** C1
Kürdämir Azer. **107** G2
also spelt Kyurdamir
Kurday Kazakh. **103** H4
also spelt Qorday
Kür Dili *pt* Azer. **107** G3
Kurduvadi India **94** B2
Kŭrdzhali Bulg. **58** G7
Kure Japan **91** C7
Küre Turkey **106** C2
Kure Atoll U.S.A. **220** G4
also known as Ocean Island
Kuressaare Estonia **42** D3
formerly known as Kingisseppa
Kureya *r.* Rus. Fed. **43** K3
Kureyskoye Vodokhranilische *resr* Rus. Fed. **39** I3
Kurgal'dzhino Kazakh. *see* **Kurgal'dzhinskiy**
Kurgal'dzhinskiy Kazakh. **103** G2
also known as Qorghalzhyn; *formerly known as* Kurgal'dzhino
Kurgan Rus. Fed. **38** G4
Kurganinsk Rus. Fed. **41** G7
formerly known as Kurgannaya
Kurgannaya Rus. Fed. *see* **Kurganinsk**
Kurgantyube Tajik. *see* **Qŭrghonteppa**
Kuri India **96** A4
Kuria *is* Kiribati **145** G1
Kuria Muria Bay Oman *see* **Ḩalānīyāt, Khalīj al**
Kuria Muria Islands Oman *see* **Ḩalānīyāt, Juzur al**
Kuridala Australia **149** D4
Kurigram Bangl. **97** F4
Kurikka Fin. **44** M3
Kurikoma-yama *vol.* Japan **90** G5
Kurile, Mal *mt.* Albania **58** A6
Kuril Islands Rus. Fed. **82** G3
also known as Kuril'skiye Ostrova *or* Chishima-retto
Kurilovka Rus. Fed. **102** B2
Kuril'sk Rus. Fed. **81** P3
Kuril'skiye Ostrova *is* Rus. Fed. *see* **Kuril Islands**
Kuriyama Japan **90** G3
Kurkino Rus. Fed. **43** T8
Kurkurabazhi, Gora *mt.* Rus. Fed. **84** A1
Kurlkuta Aboriginal Reserve Australia **150** D4
Kurlovskiy Rus. Fed. **40** G5
Kurmanayevka Rus. Fed. **102** B1
Kurmashkino Kazakh. *see* **Kurchum**
Kurmene Latvia **42** F5
Kurmuk Sudan **128** B2
Kurnool India **94** C3
Kurobe Japan **91** E6
Kuroishi Japan **90** G4
Kuroiso Japan **90** G6
Kuromatsunai Japan **90** G3
Kuror, Jebel *mt.* Sudan **121** F4
Kuro-shima *i.* Japan **91** A9
Kurovskiy Rus. Fed. **82** B1
Kurovskoy Rus. Fed. **43** R7
Kurovskoye Rus. Fed. **43** T6
Kurow N.Z. **153** E12
Kurram *r.* Afgh./Pak. **101** G3
Kurri Kurri Australia **147** F3
Kuršėnai Lith. **42** D5
Kursh, Jabal *hill* Saudi Arabia **104** C3
Kürshim Kazakh. *see* **Kurchum**
Kurshskiy Zaliv *b.* Lith./Rus. Fed. *see* **Courland Lagoon**
Kurshynavichy Belarus **42** H9
Kursīši Latvia **42** D5
Kuršių marios *b.* Lith./Rus. Fed. *see* **Courland Lagoon**
Kuršių neringos nacionalinis parkas *nat. park* Lith. **42** B6
Kursk Rus. Fed. **41** F6
Kurskaya Rus. Fed. **41** H7
Kurskaya Oblast' *admin. div.* Rus. Fed. **41** F6
English form Kursk Oblast
Kurskiy Zaliv *b.* Lith./Rus. Fed. *see* **Courland Lagoon**
Kursk Oblast *admin. div.* Rus. Fed. *see* **Kurskaya Oblast'**
Kuršumlija *Srbija* Yugo. **58** C5
Kurşunlu Turkey **106** C2
Kurtalan Turkey **107** E3
also known as Misraç
Kürti *r.* Kazakh. *see* **Kurtty**
Kurtoğlu Burnu *pt* Turkey **106** B3

Kurtpınar Turkey **108** G1
Kurttepe Turkey **108** G1
Kurttu r. Kazakh. **103** I3
also spelt Kürti or Kurty
Kurty r. Kazakh. *see* **Kurttu**
Kuru Fin. **45** M3
Kurú r. Greece *see* **Kourou**
Kuru India **97** E5
Kuru *watercourse* Sudan **126** E2
Kurucaşile Turkey **106** C2
Kurud India **94** D1
Kurukshetra India **96** C3
Kuruman S. Africa **132** H4
Kuruman *watercourse* S. Africa **132** E3
Kuruman Hills S. Africa **132** H4
Kurume Japan **91** B8
Kurumkan Rus. Fed. **81** I2
Kurun r. Sudan **128** B3
Kurundi *watercourse* Australia **148** B4
Kurundwad India **94** B2
Kurunegala Sri Lanka **94** D5
Kurunzulay Rus. Fed. **85** H1
Kurupam India **95** D2
Kurupukari Guyana **199** G3
Kurush, Jebel *hills* Sudan **121** F4
Kur'ya Rus. Fed. **103** J2
Kur'ya Rus. Fed. **41** K3
Kuryk Kazakh. **102** B4
formerly known as Yeraliyev
Kuryong r. S. Korea **91** K9
Kuşadası Turkey **106** A3
Kuşadası Körfezi b. Turkey **106** A3
Kusaie atoll Micronesia *see* **Kosrae**
Kusary Azer. *see* **Qusar**
Kusawa Lake Canada **166** B2
Kuşcenneti Milli Parkı nat. park Turkey
59 I8
Kuse Japan **91** C7
Kus Gölü l. Turkey **106** A2
formerly known as Manyas Gölü
Kushalgarh India **96** B5
Kushalino Rus. Fed. **43** R4
Kushank Iran **100** D3
Kusheriki Nigeria **125** G4
Kushida-gawa r. Japan **91** E7
Kushikino Japan **91** B9
Kushima Japan **91** B9
Kushimoto Japan **90** I3
Kushiro Japan **90** G3
Kushiro-Shitsugen National Park Japan
90 I3
Kushka Turkm. *see* **Gushgy**
Kushmurun Kazakh. **103** F1
also known as Qusmuryn
Kushmurun, Ozero salt l. Kazakh. **103** F1
also known as Qusmuryn Köli
Kushnarenkovo Rus. Fed. **40** J5
Kushtagi India **94** C3
Kushtia Bangl. **97** F5
also spelt Kustia
Kushtih Iran **101** D4
Kushtozero, Ozero l. Rus. Fed. **43** R1
Kushui r. China **85** E4
Kushum Kazakh. **102** B2
Kushum r. Kazakh. **102** B2
Kuskan Turkey **107** E1
Kuskokwim r. U.S.A. **164** C3
Kuskokwim Bay U.S.A. **164** C4
Kuskokwim Mountains U.S.A. **164** D3
Kuskovo Rus. Fed. **44** H4
Kuşluyan Turkey *see* **Gölköy**
Kusŏng N. Korea **83** B5
Kussharo-ko l. Japan **90** I3
Kustanay Kazakh. *see* **Kostanay**
Kustanay Oblast admin. div. Kazakh. *see*
Kustanayskaya Oblast'
Kustanayskaya Oblast' admin. div. Kazakh.
103 E1
English form Kostanay Oblast; also known
as Qostanay Oblysy
Kustavi Fin. **45** M3
Küstence Romania *see* **Constanţa**
Kustia Bangl. *see* **Kushtia**
Kusu Indon. **75** C2
Kut, Ko i. Thai. **79** C6
Küt 'Abdollah Iran **100** B4
Kutacane Indon. **76** B2
Kütahya Turkey **106** B3
historically known as Cotiaeum
Kütahya prov. Turkey **106** B3
Kutai National Park Indon. **77** G2
K'ut'aisi Georgia **107** E2
Kutan Rus. Fed. **102** A3
Kutaraja Indon. *see* **Banda Aceh**
Kutarere N.Z. **152** L6
Kutayfat Turayf vol. Saudi Arabia
109 J6
Kutch, Gulf of India *see* **Kachchh, Gulf of**
Kutch, Rann of marsh India *see*
Kachchh, Rann of
Kutchan Japan **90** G3
Küt-e Gapu tourist site Iran **100** B3
Kutina Croatia **56** I3
Kutjevo Croatia **107** E2
Kutkai Myanmar **78** B3
Kutloanong S. Africa **133** K4
Kutná Hora Czech Rep. **49** M6
Kutno Poland **49** Q3
Kuttainen Sweden **44** M1
Kutu Dem. Rep. Congo **126** C5
Kutubdia Island Bangl. **97** F5

Kutum Sudan **120** E6
Kutuzov Moldova *see* **Ialoveni**
Kutztown U.S.A. **177** J5
Kuujjua r. Canada **165** H2
Kuujjuaq Canada **169** G1
formerly known as Fort Chimo
Kuujjuarapik Canada **168** E2
also known as Poste-de-la-Baleine
Kuuli-Mayak Turkm. **102** C4
also spelt Guwlumayak
Kuusajoki Fin. **44** N2
Kuusamo Fin. **44** O2
Kuusankoski Fin. **45** N3
Kuusjoki Fin. **42** E1
Kuutse mägi hill Estonia **42** H3
Kuvandyk Rus. Fed. **102** D2
Kuvango Angola **127** C8
formerly known as Artur de Paiva or
Capelongo or Vila da Ponte
Kuvshinovo Rus. Fed. **43** P4
▶**Kuwait** country Asia **107** F5
spelt Al Kuwayt in Arabic
world [changes]▶ 20–21
asia [countries]▶ 64–67

▶**Kuwait** Kuwait **107** F5
Capital of Kuwait. Also spelt Al Kuwayt.

Kuwait Jun b. Kuwait **107** F5
Kuwajleen atoll Marshall Is *see* **Kwajalein**
Kuwana Japan **91** E7
Kuybyshev Kazakh. *see* **Kuybyshevskiy**
Kuybyshev Rus. Fed. **80** B1
Kuybyshev Rus. Fed. *see* **Bolgar**
Kuybyshev Rus. Fed. *see* **Samara**
Kuybysheve Ukr. **41** F7
Kuybyshevka-Vostochnaya Rus. Fed. *see*
Belogorsk
Kuybyshevo Kazakh. *see* **Zhyngyldy**
Kuybyshevskaya Oblast' admin. div.
Rus. Fed. *see* **Samarskaya Oblast'**
Kuybyshevskiy Kazakh. **103** F2
also known as Küybyshev; formerly known
as Trudovoy
Kuybyshevskoye Vodokhranilishche resr
Rus. Fed. **40** I5
Kuybyshev Adyndaky Turkm. *see*
imeni Kuybysheva
Kuye r. China **85** F4
Kuyeda Rus. Fed. **40** J4
Kuygan Kazakh. **103** H3
also spelt Quyghan
Küysu China **84** B3
also spelt Kuitin
Kuytun He r. China **88** C2
Kuyucak Turkey **59** J11
Kuyukkol', Ozero salt l. Kazakh. **103** F2
Kuyuluk Turkey **108** F1
Kuyus Rus. Fed. **88** E1
Kuyu Tingni Nicaragua **186** C4
also known as Cuyuntingni
Kuyuwini r. Guyana **199** G4
Kuyvozi Rus. Fed. **43** L1
Kuzhenkino Rus. Fed. **43** O4
Kužiai Lith. **42** E6
Kuzino Rus. Fed. **43** T2
Kuz'minichi Rus. Fed. **43** O7
Kuz'minskoye Rus. Fed. **43** U7
Kuz'molovskiy Rus. Fed. **43** L1
Kuznechnoye Rus. Fed. **43** L1
Kuznetsk Rus. Fed. **41** H5
Kuznetsovo Rus. Fed. **90** F1
Kuznetsovs'k Ukr. **41** C6
Kuzomen' Rus. Fed. **40** F2
Kuzovatovo Rus. Fed. **41** H5
Kuzovka Rus. Fed. **43** T8
Kuzumaki Japan **90** G4
Kvænangen sea chan. Norway **44** M1
Kvaløya i. Norway **44** L1
Kvaløya i. Norway **44** M1
Kvalsund Norway **44** M1
Kvareli Georgia *see* **Qvareli**
Kvarkeno Rus. Fed. **102** D1
Kvarnberg Sweden **45** K3
Kvarner g. Croatia **56** G3
Kvarnerić sea chan. Croatia **56** G4
Kvèdarna Lith. **42** C6
Kvenvær Norway **44** J3
Kvichak Bay U.S.A. **164** D4
Kvikkjokk Sweden **44** L2
Kvinesdal Norway **45** I4
Kvissleby Sweden **45** L3
Kvitanosi mt. Norway **45** I3
Kvitegga mt. Norway **45** I3
Kvitøya ice feature Svalbard **38** D2
Kvitsøy Norway **45** I4
Kwa r. Dem. Rep. Congo **126** C5
Kwabhaca S. Africa *see* **Mount Frere**
KwaChibukhulu S. Africa **133** O3
Kwadacha Wilderness Provincial Park
Canada **166** E3
KwaDela S. Africa **133** N3
Kwadelen atoll Marshall Is *see* **Kwajalein**
Kwaga Tanz. **129** A6
KwaGuga S. Africa **133** N2
Kwajalein atoll Marshall Is **220** F5
also spelt Kuwajleen or Kwadelen
Kwakoegron Suriname **199** H3
Kwakwani Guyana **199** G3
Kwakwatse S. Africa **133** L4
Kwale Kenya **129** C6
Kwale Nigeria **125** G5
KwaMashu S. Africa **133** O6
Kwa-Mbonambi S. Africa **133** Q5
Kwame Danso Ghana **125** E5
KwaMhlanga S. Africa **133** M2
Kwamouth Dem. Rep. Congo **126** C5
Kwa Mtoro Tanz. **129** B6
Kwandang Indon. **75** B2
Kwangchow China *see* **Guangzhou**
Kwangju S. Korea **83** B6
Kwango r. Dem. Rep. Congo **126** C5
also spelt Cuango
Kwangsi aut. reg. China *see*
Guangxi Zhuangzu Zizhiqu
Kwangsi Chuang Autonomous Region
aut. reg. China *see*
Guangxi Zhuangzu Zizhiqu
Kwangtung prov. China *see* **Guangdong**
Kwangwazi Tanz. **129** C6
Kwania, Lake Uganda **128** B4
Kwanmo-bong mt. N. Korea **82** C4
also known as Kambo-san
Kwanobuhle S. Africa **133** J10
Kwanojoli S. Africa **133** K8
Kwanonqaba S. Africa **133** I8
Kwariza r. Angola *see* **Cuanza**
Kwa-Pita S. Africa **133** J3
Kwara state Nigeria **125** F4
KwaThandeka S. Africa **133** O3
Kwatinidubu S. Africa **133** N2
Kwawr Ummi Wu'al depr. Saudi Arabia
109 K6
KwaZamokhule S. Africa **133** N3
KwaZamukucinga S. Africa **133** I9
KwaZamuxolo S. Africa **133** I8
KwaZanele S. Africa **133** N3
Kwazulu-Natal prov. S. Africa **133** O5
formerly known as Natal
Kweichow China *see* **Guizhou**
Kweiyang China *see* **Guiyang**
Kwekwe Zimbabwe **131** E4
formerly spelt Que Que
Kwena Dam S. Africa **133** O2
Kweneng admin. dist. Botswana **131** E4
Kwetabohlegan r. Canada **168** D2
Kwezi-Naledi S. Africa **133** L7

Kwidzyn Poland **49** P2
historically known as Marienwerder
Kwihä Eth. **104** B5
Kwikila P.N.G. **73** K8
Kwilu r. Angola/Dem. Rep. Congo **127** C5
Kwisa r. Poland **49** M4
Kwitaro r. Guyana **199** G4
Kwo Chau Kwan To is Hong Kong China
see **Ninepin Group**
Kwoka mt. Indon. **73** H7
Kwoungo, Mont mt. Cent. Afr. Rep.
126 E3
Kwun Tong Hong Kong China **87** [inset]
Kyabé Chad **126** C2
Kyabra Australia **149** D5
Kyabra watercourse Australia **149** D5
Kyabram Australia **147** E4
Kyadet Myanmar **78** A3
Kyaiklat Myanmar **78** A4
Kyaikto Myanmar **78** B4
Kya-in Seikkyi Myanmar **78** B4
Kyakhta Rus. Fed. **85** E1
Kyalite Australia **147** D3
Kyancutta Australia **146** B3
Kyangin Irrawaddy Myanmar **78** A4
Kyangin Mandalay Myanmar **78** A3
Kyaukhnyat Myanmar **78** B4
Kyaukkyi Myanmar **78** B4
Kyaukme Myanmar **78** B3
Kyaukmyaung Myanmar **78** A3
Kyaukpadaung Myanmar **78** A3
Kyaukpyu Myanmar **78** A4
Kyaukse Myanmar **78** B3
Kyauktan Myanmar **78** B4
Kyauktaw Myanmar **78** A3
Kyaunggon Myanmar **78** A4
Kybartai Lith. **42** D7
Kybeyan Range mts Australia **147** F4
Ky Cung, Sông r. Vietnam **78** D3
Kyeburn N.Z. **153** E13
Kyeintali Myanmar **78** A4
Kyela Tanz. **129** B7
Kyenjojo Uganda **128** A4
Kyeraa Ghana **125** E5
Kyeylbelen, Gora hill Kazakh. **103** H3
Kyidaunggan Myanmar **78** B4
Kyikug China **84** D4
Kyinderi Ghana **125** E4
Kyiv Ukr. *see* **Kiev**
Kyjov Czech Rep. **49** O6
Kyklades is Greece *see* **Cyclades**
Kyle Canada **167** I5
Kyle of Lochalsh U.K. **46** G6
Kyll r. Germany **48** D6
Kyllini mt. Greece **59** D11
also spelt Killini
Kyllinis, Akra pt Greece **59** C11
Kymi Greece **59** F10
also spelt Kimi
Kymijoki r. Fin. **42** H1
Kymis, Akra pt Greece **59** F10
Kynna r. Norway **45** K3
Kynuna Australia **149** D4
Kyoga, Lake Uganda **128** B4
Kyōga-misaki pt Japan **91** D7
Kyogle Australia **147** G2
Kyom watercourse Sudan **126** F2
Kyondo Myanmar **78** B4
Kyŏngju S. Korea **83** D6
Kyongju National Park S. Korea **83** C6
Kyonpyaw Myanmar **78** A4
Kyōto Japan **91** D7
Kyōto pref. Japan **91** D7
Kyōwa Japan **90** G5
Kyparissia Greece **59** C11
also spelt Kiparissía
Kyparissiakos Kolpos b. Greece **59** C11
Kypros country Asia *see* **Cyprus**
Kypshak, Ozero salt l. Kazakh. **103** G2
also known as Qypshaq Köli
Kyra Rus. Fed. **85** G1
Kyra Panagia i. Greece **59** F9
Kyren Rus. Fed. **84** D2
Kyrenia Cyprus **108** E2
also known as Girne; also spelt Keryneia
Kyrenia Mountains Cyprus *see*
Pentadaktylos Range
▶**Kyrgyzstan** country Asia **103** H4
also spelt Kirgizstan; formerly known as
Kirghizia or Kirgizskaya S.S.R.
asia [countries]▶ 64–67
Kyrhyzh-Kytay r. Ukr. **58** K3
Kyria Greece **58** F7
also spelt Kíria
Kyriaki Greece **59** D10
also known as Kiriákion
Kyritz Germany **49** J3
Kyritz-Ruppiner Heide park Germany **49** J2
Kyrnychky Ukr. **58** K3
Kyrta Rus. Fed. **40** K3
Kysucké Nové Mesto Slovakia **49** P6
Kytalyktakh Rus. Fed. **39** N3
Kytay, Ozero l. Ukr. **58** K3
Kythira Greece **59** D12
Kythira i. Greece **59** D12
English form Cerigo; also spelt Kíthira;
historically known as Cythera
Kythnos i. Greece **59** F11
also spelt Kíthnos
Kythnou, Steno sea chan. Greece **59** F11
also spelt Kíthnou; Stenón
Kythrea Cyprus **108** E2
also known as Değirmenlik
Kyumyush-Tak, Pik mt. Kyrg. **103** G4
also spelt Kumyshtag, Pik
Kyunglung China **89** C6
Kyungyaung Myanmar **79** B5
Kyunhla Myanmar **78** A3
Kyuquot Canada **166** E5
Kyurdamir Azer. *see* **Kürdämir**
Kyushe Kazakh. **102** C3
▶**Kyūshū** i. Japan **91** B9
Kyūshū-sanchi mts Japan **91** B8
Kyustendil Bulg. **58** D6
Kywebwe Myanmar **78** B4
Kywong Australia **147** E3
Kyyev Ukr. *see* **Kiev**
Kyyiv Ukr. *see* **Kiev**
Kyyivs'ke Vodoskhovyshche resr Ukr. **41** D6
also known as Kiyevskoye Vodokhranilishche
Kyyjärvi Fin. **44** N3
Kyyvesi l. Fin. **45** N3
Kyzan Kazakh. **102** C3
also spelt Qyzan
Kyzketken Uzbek. **102** D4
also spelt Qizqetken
Kyzyl Moldova *see* **Ştefan Vodă**
Kyzyl Rus. Fed. **80** D2
Kyzyl-Adyr Kyrg. **103** G3
also known as Kirov or Kirovskoye
Kyzylagash Kazakh. **103** I3
Kyzyl-Art, Pereval pass Kyrg./Tajik. *see*
Kyzylart Pass
Kyzylart Pass Kyrg./Tajik. **101** H2
also spelt as Kyzyl-Art, Pereval or Qizil-Art,
Aghbai
Kyzyl-Burun Azer. *see* **Siyäzän**
Kyzylkesek Kazakh. **103** I2
also spelt Qyzylkesek; formerly known as
Kyzylkesken
Kyzylkesken Kazakh. *see* **Kyzylkesek**
Kyzyl-Khaya Rus. Fed. **88** E1
Kyzyl-Khem r. Rus. Fed. **84** C1
Kyzyl-Kiya Kyrg. *see* **Kyzyl-Kyya**
Kyzylkoga Kazakh. **102** C2
Kyzylkol', Ozero l. Kazakh. **103** G2
also spelt Qyzylköl
Kyzylkum, Peski des. Kazakh./Uzbek. *see*
Kyzylkum Desert

Kyzylkum Desert Kazakh./Uzbek. **103** F4
also known as Kyzylkum, Peski
also spelt Kyzyl-Kiya
Kyzyl-Mazhalyk Rus. Fed. **84** A1
Kyzylorda Kazakh. **103** F3
also spelt Kyzyl-Orda or Qyzylorda; formerly
known as Ak-Mechet
Kyzyl-Orda Oblast admin. div. Kazakh. *see*
Kyzyl-Ordinskaya Oblast'
Kyzylrabot Tajik. *see* **Qizilrabot**
Kyzylsay Kazakh. **102** C4
formerly known as Ozen or Uzen'
Kyzyl-Suu Kyrg. **103** G5
formerly known as Pokrovka
Kyzyl-Suu r. Kyrg. **103** G5
Kyzyltau Kazakh. **103** H3
also spelt Qyzyltaū
Kyzylzhar Kazakh. **103** G2
also spelt Qyzylzhar; formerly spelt Kyzyl-Dzhar
Kzyl-Dzhar Kazakh. *see* **Kyzylzhar**
Kzyl-Orda Kazakh. *see* **Kyzylorda**
Kzyl-Ordinskaya Oblast' admin. div.
Kazakh. **103** F3
English form Kyzyl-Orda Oblast; also known
as Qyzylorda Oblysy
Kzyl-Ordinskoye Vodokhranilishche resr
Kazakh. **103** F3
Kzyltu Kazakh. *see* **Kishkenekol'**

⬇ L

Laage Germany **49** J2
Laagri Estonia **42** F2
La Almunia de Doña Godina Spain **55** J3
La Amistad, Parque Internacional
nat. park Costa Rica/Panama **186** D5
La Angostura, Presa de resr Mex. **185** G6
Läänimaa prov. Estonia **42** I3
Läänimaa Estonia **42** I3
Laanle well Somalia **128** E3
La Antigua, Salina salt pan Arg. **204** D3
La Araucania admin. reg. Chile **204** B5
La Ardilla, Cerro mt. Mex. **185** E4
Laas Aano Somalia **128** E3
Laascaanood Somalia **128** E2
formerly known as Las Anod
La Ascensión, Bahía de b. Mex. **185** I5
Laas Dawaco Somalia **128** F2
Laasgoray Somalia **128** F2
La Asunción Venez. **199** F2
Laau Point U.S.A. **181** [inset] Z1
Lab r. Yugo. **58** C6
Laba r. Rus. Fed. **41** G7
La Babia Mex. **185** E2
La Bahia, Islas de is Hond. **186** B3
English form Bay Islands
La Baie Canada **169** G3
formerly known as Port-Alfred
Labala Indon. **75** B5
La Baleine, Grande Rivière de r. Canada
168 E2
La Baleine, Petite Rivière de r. Canada
168 E2
La Baleine, Rivière à r. Canada **169** H1
also known as Whale
La Banda Arg. **204** D2
La Bañeza Spain **54** F2
Labang Sarawak Malaysia **77** F2
Labanoras Lith. **42** G6
Labao China *see* **Liujiang**
La Barthe-de-Neste France **50** G9
La Baule-Escoublac France **50** D5
Labaz, Ozero l. Rus. Fed. **39** J2
Labazhskoye Rus. Fed. **40** J2
Labe r. Czech Rep. **49** L5
also known as Elbe (Germany)
Labé Guinea **124** B4
Labelle Canada **169** F4
La Belle U.S.A. **175** D7
Labengke i. Indon. **75** B3
La Bérarde France **50** H8
La Biche, Lac l. Canada **167** H4
Labin Croatia **56** G3
Labinsk Rus. Fed. **41** G7
Labis Malaysia **76** C2
La Bisbal d'Empordà Spain **55** O3
La Biznaga Mex. **184** C2
Labo Phil. **74** B3
La Bobia, Sierra de mts Spain **54** E1
Laboc i. Indon. **75** B3
La Bodera mt. Spain **55** I3
La Bomu, Réserve de Faune de nature res.
Dem. Rep. Congo **126** D3
La Boquilla Mex. **184** D3
Labora Namibia **130** C4
La Brea Peru **198** A4
La Brea Trin. and Tob. **187** H5
La Brenne, Parc Naturel Régional de
nature res. France **50** H6
Labruguière France **51** I9
Labuan Malaysia **77** F1
formerly known as Victoria
Labuan i. Malaysia **77** F1
Labuanbajo Indon. **75** B3
La Bufa, Cerro mt. Mex. **185** E5
Labuhan Indon. **77** D4
Labuhanbajo Indon. **75** A5
Labuhanbilik Indon. **76** C2
Labuhanruku Indon. **76** B2
Labuk, Telukan b. Sabah Malaysia **77** G1
Labutta Myanmar **78** A4
Labyrinth, Lake salt flat Australia **146** B2
Labytnangi Rus. Fed. **38** H3
Laç Albania **58** A7
Lac pref. Chad **120** B6
La Cabrera, Sierra de mts Spain **54** E2
La Cadena Mex. **184** D3
La Calderina mt. Spain **54** H5
La Calera Chile **204** C4
La Calle Alg. *see* **El Kala**
La Campana Spain **54** G7
La Canau, Étang de l. France **50** E8
Lacandón, Parque Nacional nat. park Guat.
185 H5
Lacanau France **50** E7
La Capelle France **51** J3
Lacapelle-Marival France **50** H8
Laćarak Vojvodina, Srbija Yugo. **58** A3
La Carlota Phil. **74** B4
La Carlota Spain **54** G7
Laferte Canada **173** O2

La Carolina Spain **55** H6
Laccadive, Minicoy and Amindivi Islands
union terr. India *see* **Lakshadweep**
Laccadive Islands India **94** B3
also known as Lakshadweep
Lac du Bonnet Canada **167** L5
Lac du Flambeau Canada **172** D5
La Ceiba Hond. **186** B3
Lacepede Bay Australia **146** C4
Lacepede Islands Australia **150** C3
Lacha, Ozero l. Rus. Fed. **40** F3
La Charité-sur-Loire France **51** I6
La Chartre-sur-le-Loir France **50** G5
La Chartreuse, Massif de mts France **51** L7
La Châtaigneraie France **50** F6
La Châtre France **51** H6
La Chaux-de-Fonds Switz. **51** M5
Lachine U.S.A. **173** J5
▶**Lachlan** r. Australia **147** D3
5th longest river in Oceania.
oceania [landscapes]▶ 136–137
La Chorrera Col. **198** C5
La Chorrera Panama **186** D5
Lachung India **97** F4
Lachute Canada **169** F4
Läçi Azer. **107** F2
Laçın Azer. **107** F3
La Ciotat France **51** L9
La Ciudad Mex. **184** D4
Lackawanna U.S.A. **176** G3
La Cocha Arg. **204** D2
La Cogulla mt. Spain **55** L3
La Colorada Sonora Mex. **184** C2
La Colorada Zacatecas Mex. **185** E4
Lacombe Canada **167** H4
La Comoé, Parc National de nat. park
Côte d'Ivoire **124** E4
Lacon U.S.A. **174** B3
La Concordia Mex. **185** G5
Laconi Sardegna Italy **57** B9
Laconia U.S.A. **177** N2
La Corey Canada **167** I4
La Corne Canada **173** O2
La Corse, Parc Naturel Régional de
nature res. Corse France **56** A6
La Coruña Spain *see* **A Coruña**
La Coubre, Pointe de pt France **50** E7
La Crescent U.S.A. **172** B3
La Crete Canada **167** H3
La Croix, Lac l. Canada/U.S.A. **172** B2
La Crosse KS U.S.A. **178** C4
La Crosse VA U.S.A. **176** G9
La Crosse WI U.S.A. **172** B7
La Cruz Arg. **204** F3
La Cruz Col. **198** B4
La Cruz Costa Rica **186** B5
La Cruz Chihuahua Mex. **184** D3
La Cruz Sinaloa Mex. **184** D4
La Cruz Tamaulipas Mex. **185** F3
La Cruz Nicaragua **186** B4
La Cruz Uruguay **204** F4
La Cruz, Cerro mt. Mex. **185** E5
La Cuenca Alta del Manzanares, Parque
Regional de park Spain **54** H4
La Cuesta Mex. **185** E2
La Culebra, Sierra de mts Spain **54** E3
La Curva Mex. **181** F7
La Cygne U.S.A. **178** D4
Ladainha Brazil **207** L4
Ladakh reg. Jammu and Kashmir **96** C2
English form Little Tibet
Ladakh Range mts India **96** C2
L'Adamaoua, Massif de mts Cameroon
125 I5
Ladang i. Thai. **79** B7
Ladd U.S.A. **172** D5
Lądek-Zdrój Poland **49** N5
La Demajagua Cuba **186** C2
also known as Santa Bárbara
La Demanda, Sierra de mts Spain **55** H3
La Dérouté, Passage de strait
Channel Is/France **50** D3
La Désirade i. Guadeloupe **187** H3
Ladik Turkey **106** C2
Ladismith S. Africa **132** F10
Ladispoli Italy **56** E7
Lādīz Iran **101** E4
Ladnun India **96** B4
▶**Ladoga, Lake** Rus. Fed. **43** M1
2nd largest lake in Europe. Also known as
Ladozhskoye Ozero.
europe [landscapes]▶ 30–31
Ladon r. Greece **59** C11
Ladozhskoye Ozero l. Rus. Fed. *see*
Ladoga, Lake
Ladra r. Spain **54** D1
Ladrillero, Canal sea chan. Chile **205** A8
Ladrones terr. N. Pacific Ocean *see*
Northern Mariana Islands
Ladrones, Islas is Panama **186** C6
Ladu mt. India **97** G4
Ladue r. Canada/U.S.A. **166** A2
Ladushkin Rus. Fed. **42** B7
historically known as Ludwigsort
Ladva Rus. Fed. **40** E3
Ladva-Vetka Rus. Fed. **40** E3
Ladwa India **96** C3
Lady Ann Strait Canada **165** K2
Lady Barron Australia **147** F5
Ladybrand S. Africa **133** L6
Lady Evelyn Lake Canada **173** M3
Lady Frere S. Africa **133** L8
Lady Grey S. Africa **133** L7
Lady Newnes Bay Antarctica **223** L2
Ladysmith Canada **166** F5
Ladysmith S. Africa **133** N5
Ladysmith U.S.A. **172** B5
Ladyzhenka Kazakh. **103** G1
Ladzhanurges Georgia *see* **Lajanurpekhi**
Lae P.N.G. **73** K8
Lae Thai. **78** C4
Laem Ngop Thai. **79** C5
La Encrucijada Venez. **187** G5
La Escala Spain *see* **L'Escala**
La Esmeralda Arg. **204** D3
La Esmeralda Bol. **201** E5
La Esmeralda Venez. **199** E4
Læsø i. Denmark **45** J4
La Esperanza Arg. **204** D3
La Esperanza Beni Bol. **200** D3
La Esperanza Santa Cruz Bol. **201** E3
La Esperanza Hond. **186** A4
La Estrella Bol. **201** E3
Laeva Estonia **42** H3
La Falda Arg. **204** D3
La Farge U.S.A. **172** B6
La Fargeville U.S.A. **177** J1
Lafayette CA U.S.A. **182** B4
Lafayette CO U.S.A. **180** F4
Lafayette IN U.S.A. **174** C3
Lafayette LA U.S.A. **179** D6
Lafayette OH U.S.A. **176** A4
Lafayette TN U.S.A. **174** C4
Lafé Cuba **186** B2
Laferte Canada **173** O2

Laferte r. Canada **167** G2
La Ferté-Bernard France **50** G4
La Ferté-Gaucher France **51** J4
La Ferté-Macé France **50** F4
La Ferté-St-Aubin France **51** H5
La Ferté-sous-Jouarre France **51** J4
Lafia Nigeria **125** H4
Lafiagi Nigeria **125** G4
Laflamme r. Canada **173** P1
La Fleche Canada **167** J5
La Flèche France **50** F5
Lafnitz r. Austria **49** N9
La Follette U.S.A. **176** A9
La Fontaine U.S.A. **172** H10
Laforce Canada **173** O3
Laforest Canada **173** L3
La Forest, Lac l. Canada **169** G2
Laforge Canada **169** F2
Laforge r. Canada **169** F2
Lafourche, Bayou r. U.S.A. **175** B6
Lafrançaise France **50** H8
La Frégate, Lac de l. Canada **169** F2
▶**La Galite** i. Tunisia **123** H1
Most northerly point of Africa.
La Galite, Canal de sea chan. Tunisia
123 H1
La Gallareta Arg. **204** E3
Lagamar Brazil **206** G5
Lagan' Rus. Fed. **102** A3
Lagan r. Sweden **45** K4
Lagana, Kolpos b. Greece **59** B11
Laganè well Niger **125** I3
La Garamba, Parc National de nat. park
Dem. Rep. Congo **126** F3
Lagarto Brazil **202** E4
Lagarto, Serra do hills Brazil **206** A10
Lagbar Senegal **124** B3
Lagdo, Lac de l. Cameroon **125** I4
Lågen r. Norway **45** J3
Lågen r. Norway **45** J4
Lagh Bogal watercourse Kenya/Somalia
128 D4
Lagh Bor watercourse Kenya/Somalia
128 D4
Lagh Kutulo watercourse Kenya/Somalia
128 D4
Laghmän prov. Afgh. **101** G3
Laghouat Alg. **123** F2
La Gineta Spain **55** J5
Lagkadas Greece **58** E8
also spelt Langadhás
Lagkor Co salt l. China **89** D5
La Gloria Col. **198** C2
La Gloria Mex. **185** F3
Lago prov. Moz. *see* **Niassa**
Lagoa da Prata Brazil **207** H7
Lagoa Dourada Brazil **207** I7
Lagoa Formosa Brazil **206** G5
Lagoa Santa Brazil **207** J6
Lagoa Vermelha Brazil **203** B9
Lago Belgrano Arg. **205** B7
Lago Cardiel Arg. **205** C8
Lago da Pedra Brazil **202** C3
Lagodekhi Georgia **107** F2
Lagolândia Brazil **206** D2
La Gomera i. Canary Is **122** A3
La Gomera Guat. **185** H6
La Gonâve, Île de i. Haiti **187** E3
Lagong i. Indon. **77** D2
Lagonoy Gulf Phil. **74** B3
Lagoon Creek r. Australia **148** C3
Lago Posadas Arg. **205** C7
La Gran Sabana plat. Venez. **199** F3
▶**Lagos** Nigeria **125** F5
Former capital of Nigeria. Most populous
city in Africa and 6th in the world.
world [cities]▶ 24–25
Lagos state Nigeria **125** F5
Lagos Port. **54** C7
Lagosa Tanz. **129** A6
Lagos de Moreno Mex. **185** E4
Lago Verde Brazil **201** E2
La Grita Venez. **198** D3
La Guajira, Península de pen. Col. **198** C1
La Guardia Arg. **204** D3
La Guardia Chile **204** C2
La Guardia Spain *see* **A Guardia**
Laguna Brazil **203** B9
Laguna U.S.A. **181** F6
Laguna, Ilha da i. Brazil **202** B2
Laguna Beach U.S.A. **182** G8
Laguna Dam U.S.A. **183** J8
Laguna de Laja, Parque Nacional nat. park
Chile **204** C5
Laguna de Perlas Nicaragua **186** C4
Laguna de Temascal, Parque Natural
nature res. Mex. **185** F5
Laguna Grande Arg. **205** C8
Laguna Lachua, Parque Nacional nat. park
Guat. **185** H6
Laguna Mountains U.S.A. **183** H9
Lagunas Chile **200** C5
Lagunas Peru **198** C6
Laguna San Rafael, Parque Nacional
nat. park Chile **205** B7
Lagunas de Catemaco, Parque Natural
nature res. Mex. **185** G5
Lagunas de Chacahua, Parque Nacional
nat. park Mex. **185** F6
Lagunas de Montebello, Parque Nacional
nat. park Mex. **185** G5
Laguna Yema Arg. **201** E6
Lagunillas Bol. **201** E4
Lagunillas Venez. **198** D2
Laha China **85** I1
La Habana Cuba *see* **Havana**
La Habra U.S.A. **182** G8
Lahad Datu Sabah Malaysia **77** G1
Lahad Datu, Telukan b. Sabah Malaysia
77 G1
La Hague, Cap de c. France **50** E3
Lahar India **96** C4
La Harpe U.S.A. **172** C10
Laharpur India **96** D4
Lahat Indon. **76** C3
Lahemaa rahvuspark nat. park Estonia
42 G2
Lahepere laht b. Estonia **42** F2
La Hève, Cap de c. France **50** G3
Lahewa Indon. **76** B2
Lahij Yemen **104** D5
Lahij governorate Yemen **104** D5
Lahishyn Belarus **42** H1
Lahn r. Germany **48** E5
Lahnstein Germany **48** E5
Laholm Sweden **45** K4

Laholmsbukten b. Sweden 45 K4
Lahontan Reservoir U.S.A. 182 E2
Lahore Pak. 101 H4
La Horqueta Venez. 199 F3
La Hotte, Massif de Haiti 187 K5
Lahoysk Belarus 42 I7
Lahr (Schwarzwald) Germany 48 E7
Lahti Fin. 45 N3
La Huerta Mex. 184 D5
L'Ahzar, Vallée de watercourse Niger 125 F3
Laï Chad 126 C2
Lai'an China 87 F1
also known as Xin'an
Laibach Slovenia see Ljubljana
Laibin China 87 D4
Laie U.S.A. 181 [inset] Z1
Laifeng China 87 D3
also known as Xiangfeng
Laihia Fin. 44 M3
Lai-hka Myanmar 78 B3
Lai-Hsak Myanmar 78 B3
Laingsburg S. Africa 132 E10
Laingsburg U.S.A. 173 I8
Lainioälven r. Sweden 44 M2
Lainsitz r. Austria 49 M7
Lair U.S.A. 176 A7
L'Aïr, Massif de mts Niger 125 H2
also known as Azbine
L'Aïr et du Ténéré, Réserve Naturelle Nationale de nature res. Niger 125 H2
Lairg U.K. 46 H5
Lais Indon. 76 C3
Lais Phil. 74 C5
La Isabela Cuba 186 C2
Laisälven r. Sweden 44 L2
La Isla Col. 198 B3
Laitila Fin. 45 M3
La Jagua Col. 198 C2
Lajamanu Australia 148 A3
Lajanurpekhi Georgia 107 E2
also known as Ladzhanurges
Lajeado Brazil 203 A9
Lajedo Brazil 202 E4
Laje dos Santos i. Brazil 207 G11
Lajinha Brazil 207 L7
Lajes Brazil 203 B8
La Jolla Peak hill U.S.A. 182 F7
Lajosmizse Hungary 49 Q8
La Joya Mex. 184 D3
La Joya Peru 200 C4
La Joya de los Sachas Ecuador 198 B5
Lajta r. Austria/Hungary 49 O8
La Junta Bol. 201 E3
La Junta Mex. 184 D2
La Junta U.S.A. 178 B4
La Juventud, Isla de i. Cuba 186 C2
formerly known as Pines, Isle of or Pinos, Isla de
Lakadiya India 96 A5
L'Akagera, Parc National de nat. park Rwanda see Akagera National Park
Lakathah Saudi Arabia 104 C4
Lakatraäsk Sweden 44 M2
Lake KY U.S.A. 176 B8
Lake WY U.S.A. 180 E3
Lake Alice N.Z. 152 J8
Lake Andes U.S.A. 178 C3
Lake Arthur U.S.A. 179 D6
Lake Butler U.S.A. 175 D6
Lake Cargelligo Australia 147 E3
Lake Charles U.S.A. 179 D6
Lake City AR U.S.A. 174 B5
Lake City CO U.S.A. 181 F5
Lake City FL U.S.A. 175 D6
Lake City IA U.S.A. 178 D3
Lake City MN U.S.A. 168 A4
Lake City SC U.S.A. 175 E5
Lake City TN U.S.A. 176 A9
Lake Clark National Park and Preserve U.S.A. 164 C3
Lake Clear U.S.A. 177 K1
Lake Coleridge N.Z. 153 F11
Lake Cowichan Canada 166 E5
Lake District National Park U.K. 47 I9
Lakefield Australia 149 E2
Lakefield Canada 168 E4
Lakefield National Park Australia 149 E2
Lake Fork r. U.S.A. 183 O1
Lake Frome Regional Reserve nature res. Australia 146 C2
Lake Gairdner National Park Australia 146 B2
Lake Geneva U.S.A. 172 E4
Lake Gilles Conservation Park nature res. Australia 146 C3
Lake Grace Australia 151 B7
Lake Gregory Aboriginal Reserve Australia 150 D4
Lake Harbour Canada see Kimmirut
Lake Havasu City U.S.A. 183 J7
Lakehurst U.S.A. 177 K5
Lake Isabella U.S.A. 182 F6
Lake Jackson U.S.A. 179 D6
Lakeland Australia 149 E2
Lakeland FL U.S.A. 175 D7
Lakeland GA U.S.A. 175 D6
Lake Linden U.S.A. 172 E3
Lake Louise Canada 167 G5
Lake Mackay Aboriginal Land res. Australia 148 A4
Lake Magenta Nature Reserve Australia 151 B7
Lake Manyara National Park Tanz. 128 B5
Lake Mburo National Park Uganda 128 A5
Lake Mills U.S.A. 174 A3
Lake Nash Australia 148 C4
Lake Paringa N.Z. 153 D11
Lake Placid U.S.A. 177 L1
Lake Providence U.S.A. 175 B5
Lakeport MI U.S.A. 173 K7
La Kéran, Parc National de nat. park Togo 125 F4
Lake Range mts U.S.A. 182 E1
Lake River Canada 168 D2
Lake St Peter Canada 173 O5
Lakes Entrance Australia 147 F4
Lakeshore U.S.A. 182 E4
Lakeside AZ U.S.A. 183 O7
Lakeside CA U.S.A. 183 H9
Lakeside MI U.S.A. 173 K7

Lakeview OR U.S.A. 180 B4
Lake Village U.S.A. 175 B5
Lakeville U.S.A. 174 A2
Lake Wales U.S.A. 175 D7
Lakewood CO U.S.A. 180 F5
Lakewood OH U.S.A. 176 D4
Lakewood WI U.S.A. 172 E5
Lakhdaria Alg. 55 O8
Lakhdenpokh'ya Rus. Fed. 45 O3
Lakhimpur India 96 H4
Lakhipur India 97 G4
Lakhisarai India see Luckeesarai
Lakhish r. Israel 108 F6
Lakhnadon India 96 C5
Lakhpat India 96 A5
Lakhtar India 96 A5
Lakhva r. Belarus 43 L8
Lakin U.S.A. 178 B4
Lakinsk Rus. Fed. 43 U5
formerly known as Lakinskiy
Lakinskiy Rus. Fed. see Lakinsk
Lakitusaki r. Canada 168 D2
Lakki Pak. 101 G3
Lakkoma Greece 59 G8
Lakonikos Kolpos b. Greece 59 D12
Lakor i. Indon. 75 D5
Lakota Côte d'Ivoire 124 D5
Lakota U.S.A. 178 C1
Laksefjorden sea chan. Norway 44 N1
Lakselv Norway 44 N1
Laksfors Norway 44 K2
Lakshadweep union terr. India 94 B4
formerly known as Laccadive, Minicoy and Amindivi Islands
Laksham Bangl. 97 F5
Lakshettipet India 94 C2
Lakshmeshwar India 94 B3
Lakshmikantapur India 97 F5
La Motte Canada 173 O2
Laktyshy Vodaskhovishcha resr Belarus 42 H9
Lala Phil. 74 B5
Lalago Tanz. 128 B5
La Laguna Arg. 204 E4
La Laguna, Picacho de mt. Mex. 184 C4
La Laguna Ojo de Liebre, Parque Natural de nature res. Mex. 184 B3
Lala Musa Pak. 101 H3
Lalapanzi Zimbabwe 131 F3
Lalapaşa Turkey 58 H7
Lalara Gabon 126 A4
Lalaua Moz. 131 H2
L'Albufera i. Spain 55 K5
La Léfini, Réserve de Chasse de nature res. Congo 126 B5
Laleham Australia 149 F4
La Lékoli-Pandaka, Réserve de Faune de nature res. Congo 126 B4
Lalganj India 97 E4
Lalgudi India 94 C4
Lälī Iran 100 B3
Lalībela Eth. 128 C1
La Libertad Ecuador 198 A5
La Libertad El Salvador 185 H6
La Libertad Guat. 185 H5
La Libertad Nicaragua 186 B4
La Libertad dept Peru 200 A2
La Ligua Chile 204 C4
Laliki Indon. 75 C4
Lalimboee Indon. 75 B3
Lalin China 82 B3
Lalin r. China 82 B3
Lalín Spain 54 C2
La Linde France 50 G8
La Línea de la Concepción Spain 54 F8
Lalitpur India 96 C4
Lalitpur Nepal see Patan
Lal-lo Phil. 74 B2
Lalmanirhat Bangl. 89 F4
Lalmikor Uzbek. see Lyal'mikar
La Loche Canada 167 I3
La Loche, Lac l. Canada 167 I3
La Loma Bol. 200 D5
La Loma Negra, Planicie de plain Arg. 204 D5
La Loupe France 50 H4
La Louvière Belgium 51 K2
Lalpur India 96 A5
Lal'sk Rus. Fed. 40 H3
Lalsot India 96 C4
La Lufira, Lac de retenue de resr Dem. Rep. Congo 127 E7
Laluni r. Indon. 75 C3
Lalung La pass China 89 D6
Lama Bangl. 97 G5
La Macarena, Parque Nacional nat. park Col. 198 C4
La Maddalena Sardegna Italy 56 B7
La Madeleine, Îles de is Canada 169 I4
Lamag Sabah Malaysia 77 G1
La Maiko, Parc National de nat. park Dem. Rep. Congo 126 E5
Lamaing Myanmar 79 B5
La Malbaie Canada 169 G4
La Maligne, Parque Nacional nat. park Mex. 185 F5
La Mancha Mex. 185 F5
La Manche strait France/U.K. see English Channel
La Manga del Mar Menor Spain 55 K7
La Manika, Plateau de Dem. Rep. Congo 127 E7
La Máquina Mex. 184 D2
Lamar CO U.S.A. 178 B4
Lamar MO U.S.A. 178 D4
La Maraoué, Parc National de nat. park Côte d'Ivoire 124 D4
La Marche, Plateaux de France 50 H6
Lamard Iran 100 C5
La Margeride, Monts de mts France 51 J7
Lamarque Arg. 204 D5
La Marque U.S.A. 179 D6
La Martre, Lac l. Canada 167 G2
Lamas r. Turkey 108 A1
La Matanzilla, Pampa de plain Arg. 204 C5
La Mauricie, Parc National de nat. park Canada 169 F4
La Maya Cuba 186 E3
Lamballe France 50 D4
Lambaréné Gabon 126 A5
Lambayeque Peru 198 B5
Lambayeque dept Peru 198 B6
Lambay Island Rep. of Ireland 47 G10
Lambeng Indon. 77 F3
Lambert atoll Marshall Is see Ailinglapalap
Lambert, Cape Australia 150 B4

Lameroo Australia 146 D3
La Mesa U.S.A. 183 G9
Lamesa U.S.A. 179 B5
L'Ametlla de Mar Spain 55 L4
Lamezia Italy 57 H11
Lamhar Touil, Sabkhet imp. l. W. Sahara 122 A5
Lamia Greece 59 D10
Lamigan Point Phil. 74 C5
Lamington National Park Australia 147 G2
Lamir Iran 100 B2
La Mirada U.S.A. 182 F8
also known as Mirada Hills
La Misa Mex. 184 C2
La Misión Mex. 183 H9
Lamitan Phil. 74 B5
also known as Anci
Lamma Island Hong Kong China 87 [inset]
also known as Pok Liu Chau
Lammerkop S. Africa 133 N2
Lammerlaw Range mts N.Z. 153 D13
Lammermuir Hills U.K. 46 J8
Lammhult Sweden 45 K4
Lammi Fin. 45 N3
Lammijärv lake channel Estonia/Rus. Fed. 42 I3
La Molle U.S.A. 172 D9
Lamoille r. U.S.A. 177 L1
La Moine r. U.S.A. 174 B4
La Mojonera Spain 55 I8
Lamon Bay Phil. 74 B3
Lamone r. Italy 56 E4
Lamongan Indon. 77 F4
Lamoni U.S.A. 174 A3
Lamont U.S.A. 182 F6
La Montagne d'Ambre, Parc National de nat. park Madag. 131 [inset] K2
La Montagne de Reims, Parc Naturel Régional de nature res. France 51 J3
Lamongne France 51 J6
La Morita Chihuahua Mex. 184 D2
La Morita Coahuila Mex. 185 E2
Lamotrek atoll Micronesia 73 K5
La Motte France 51 L8
Lamotte-Beuvron France 51 I5
La Motte-Servolex France 51 L7
La Mougalaba, Réserve de nature res. Gabon 126 A5
La Moure U.S.A. 178 C2
Lampa Peru 200 C3
Lampang Thai. 78 B4
Lam Pao Reservoir Thai. 78 C4
Lampasas U.S.A. 179 C6
Lampasas r. U.S.A. 179 C6
Lampazos Mex. 185 E3
Lampedusa, Isola di i. Sicilia Italy 57 E13
Lampeland Norway 45 J4
Lampeter U.K. 47 H11
also known as Llanbedr
Lamphun Thai. 78 B4
Lam Plai Mat r. Thai. 79 C5
Lampopnhya Rus. Fed. 40 H2
Lampsacus Turkey see Lâpseki
Lampung prov. Indon. 76 C4
Lampung, Teluk b. Indon. 76 D4
Lam Si Bai r. Thai. 79 D5
Lamta India 96 D5
Lam Tin Hong Kong China 87 [inset]
Lamu Kenya 128 D5
Lamu Myanmar 78 A4
La Muela mt. Spain 55 J5
La Mure France 51 L8
Lana r. Sardegna Italy 56 C7
Lana Italy 56 D2
Lanai i. U.S.A. 181 [inset] Z1
Lanai City U.S.A. 181 [inset] Z1
also known as Ranai
La Nao, Cabo de c. Spain 55 L6
Lanao, Lake Phil. 74 C5
Lanark Canada 173 Q5
Lanark U.K. 46 I8
Lanark r. U.S.A. 172 D8
Lanas Sabah Malaysia 77 G1
Lanbi Kyun i. Myanmar 79 B6
Lanboyan Point Phil. 74 B4
Lancang China 86 A4
also known as Menglang
Lancang Jiang r. China see Mekong
Lancaster CA U.S.A. 182 F7
Lancaster KY U.S.A. 176 A8
Lancaster MO U.S.A. 174 A3
Lancaster NH U.S.A. 177 N1
Lancaster OH U.S.A. 176 C6
Lancaster PA U.S.A. 177 I5
Lancaster SC U.S.A. 174 D5
Lancaster VA U.S.A. 177 I7
Lancaster WI U.S.A. 172 B7
Lancaster Sound strait Canada 165 K2
Lancelin Australia 151 A6
Lanch'khut'i Georgia 107 E2
Lanchow China see Lanzhou
Lanciano Italy 56 G6
Lancing U.S.A. 176 A9
Lanco Chile 204 B5
Lancun China 85 I4
Lańcut Poland 49 T5
Lancy Switz. 51 M6
Landak r. Indon. 77 E3
Landana Angola see Cacongo
Landau an der Isar Germany 49 J7
Landau in der Pfalz Germany 48 F6
Landeck Austria 48 H8
Lander watercourse Australia 148 A4
Lander U.S.A. 180 E4
Landerneau France 50 A4
Landes reg. France 50 F8
Landes de Gascogne, Parc Naturel Régional des nature res. France 50 F8
Landes de Lanvaux reg. France 50 D4
Landfall Island India 95 G3
Landik, Gunung mt. Indon. 76 C3
Landis Canada 167 I4
Landivisiau France 50 B4
Landless Corner Zambia 127 F8
Land O' Lakes U.S.A. 172 D4
Landor Australia 151 B5
Landquart Switz. 51 P5
Landrienne Canada 173 P2
Landrum U.S.A. 174 D5
Landsberg Poland see Gorzów Wielkopolski
Landsberg am Lech Germany 48 H7
Landsborough r. U.K. 47 D13
Land's End pt U.K. 47 G13
Landshut Germany 48 J7
Landskrona Sweden 45 K5
La Nedei mt. Romania 58 E3
La Negra Chile 200 C5
Lane Pool Reserve nature res. Australia 151 B7

Langeberg mts S. Africa 132 D10
Langehorn S. Africa 133 I3
Langeland i. Denmark 45 J5
Langelands Bælt strait Denmark 45 J5
Langen Germany 48 F5
Langenburg Canada 167 K5
Langenlois Austria 49 M7
Langenthal Switz. 51 N5
Langeoog Germany 48 E2
Langeoog i. Germany 48 E2
Langepas Rus. Fed. 38 H3
Langesund Norway 45 J4
Langfang China 85 H4
also known as Anci
Långfjällets naturreservat nature res. Sweden 45 K3
Langgapayung Indon. 76 C2
Langgar China 89 F6
Langgöns Germany 48 F5
Langham Canada 167 J4
Langhko Myanmar 78 B3
Langholm India 94 C3
also known as Langkon
Langholm U.K. 47 J8
Langjökull ice cap Iceland 44 [inset] B2
Langka Indon. 76 B1
Langkawi i. Malaysia 76 B1
Langkesi, Kepulauan is Indon. 75 C4
Lang Kha Toek, Khao mt. Thai. 79 B6
Langkon Sabah Malaysia 77 G1
Langlade Canada 166 F5
Langley Canada 166 F5
Langley U.S.A. 176 C8
Langlo watercourse Australia 149 E5
Langmusi China see Dagcanglhamo
Langnau France 51 J8
Langon France 50 F8
Langong, Xé r. Laos 78 D4
Langøya i. Norway 44 K1
Langqi China 87 F3
Langres France 51 K5
Langres, Plateau de France 51 K5
Langsa Indon. 76 B1
Langsa, Teluk b. Indon. 76 B1
Långsele Sweden 44 M3
Langshan China 85 E3
Lang Shan mts China 85 E3
Langsleth Norway 44 M1
Lang Son Vietnam 78 D3
Langtang National Park Nepal 97 E3
Langtao Myanmar 78 B2
Långträsk Sweden 44 M2
Langtry TX U.S.A. 179 B6
Languan China see Lantian
Languedoc-Roussillon admin. reg. France 51 I10
Languiaru r. Brazil see Iquê
Languíneo Arg. 205 C6
Langundu, Tanjung pt Indon. 77 G5
Långvinds bruk Sweden 45 L3
Langwedel Germany 48 G2
Langya Shan mt. China 85 G4
Langzhong China 86 C2
Laniel Canada 173 N3
Lanin, Parque Nacional nat. park Arg. 204 C5
Lanin, Volcán vol. Arg./Chile 204 C5
Lanini r. Sarawak Malaysia 77 E2
Lanji India 96 D5
Lanka country Asia see Sri Lanka
Lankao China 87 E1
formerly known as Lanfeng
Länkäran Azer. 107 G3
also spelt Lenkoran'
Lan Kok Tsui pt Hong Kong China see Black Point
Lanlacuni Bajo Peru 200 C3
Lannemezan France 50 G9
Lannion France 50 C4
L'Annonciation Canada 169 F4
La Noria Bol. 201 E3
La Noria Mex. 184 D4
Lansdale U.S.A. 177 J5
L'Anse U.S.A. 172 E4
L'Anse-St-Jean Canada 169 G3
Lansford U.S.A. 177 J5
Lansing r. Canada 166 C2
Lansing IA U.S.A. 172 B7
▶ Lansing MI U.S.A. 173 I8
State capital of Michigan.
Länsi-Suomi prov. Fin. 44 M3
Lansjärv Sweden 44 M2
Lanta, Ko i. Thai. 79 B7
Lantau Island Hong Kong China 87 [inset]
also known as Tai Yue Shan
Lantau Peak hill Hong Kong China 87 [inset]
also known as Fung Wong Shan
Lanterne r. France 51 M5
Lantian China see Lianyuan
Lantian China 87 D1
also known as Dongcun
Lanuza Phil. 74 C4
Lanuza Bay Phil. 74 C4
Lanxi Heilong. China 82 B3
Lanxi Zhejiang China 87 F2
Lanxian China 85 F4
also known as Dongcun
Lanya Sudan 128 A3
Lanyi r. China 85 F4
Lanyu i. Taiwan 87 G4
Lanzarote i. Canary Is 122 B3
Lanzhou China 84 D4
also spelt Lanchow
Lanzijing China 85 I2
Lanzo Torinese Italy 51 N7
Lao r. Italy 57 H9
Lao, Mae r. Thai. 78 B4
Laoag Phil. 74 B2
Laoang Phil. 74 C3
Laobie Shan mts China 86 A4
Laobukou China 87 D3
Lao Cai Vietnam 78 C3
Laodicea Syria see Latakia
Laodicea Turkey see Denizli
Laodicea ad Lycum Turkey see Denizli
Laodicea ad Mare Syria see Latakia
Laofengkou China 88 C2
Laoha r. China 85 I3
Laoheishan China 82 C3
Laohekou China 87 D1
also known as Guanghua
Laohutun China 85 I4
Laojunmiao China see Yumen
Lao Ling mts China 82 B4
Laolong China see Longchuan
Laon France 51 J3
Laona U.S.A. 172 E4
La Oroya Peru 200 B2
Laos country Asia 78 C4
asia [countries] ▶ 64–67
Laoshan China 85 I4
also known as Licun
Laotieshan Shuidao sea chan. China see Bohai Haixia
Laotougou China 82 C4
Laotuding Shan hill China 82 B4
Laou, Oued r. Morocco 54 F9
La Ouandja-Vakaga, Réserve de Faune de nature res. Cent. Afr. Rep. 126 D3
Laoudi-Ba Côte d'Ivoire 124 E4

Laowohi pass Jammu and Kashmir see Khardung La
also spelt Aryanah
Laoximiao China 84 D3
Laoye Ling mts China 82 C4
Lapa Brazil 203 B8
Lapachito Arg. 204 E2
Lapai Nigeria 125 G4
Lapalisse France 51 J6
La Palma i. Canary Is 122 A3
La Palma Panama 186 D5
La Palma U.S.A. 183 M9
La Palma del Condado Spain 54 E7
La Paloma Uruguay 204 G4
La Pampa prov. Arg. 204 D5
formerly known as Eva Perón
La Panza Range mts U.S.A. 182 D6
La Paragua Venez. 199 F3
La Paramera, Puerto de pass Spain 54 G4
La Paramera, Sierra de mts Spain 54 F4
Laparan i. Phil. 74 A5
La Parata, Pointe de pt Corse France 56 A7
La Paya, Parque Nacional nat. park Col. 198 C4
La Paz Entre Ríos Arg. 204 F3
La Paz Mendoza Arg. 204 D4
▶ La Paz Bol. 200 C4
Official capital of Bolivia.
world [countries] ▶ 10–11
southamerica [contrasts] ▶ 194–195
La Paz dept Bol. 200 C3
La Paz Hond. 186 B4
La Paz Mex. 184 C3
La Paz Nicaragua 186 B4
Lapaz U.S.A. 172 G9
La Paz Venez. 198 C2
La Paz, Bahía b. Mex. 184 C3
La Pedrera Col. 198 D5
Lapeer U.S.A. 173 J7
La Pelada Arg. 204 E3
La Peña Panama 186 C5
La Pendjari, Parc National de nat. park Benin 125 F4
La Pera Mex. 184 D2
La Pérouse Strait Japan/Rus. Fed. 90 G2
also known as Sōya-kaikyō
La Pesca Mex. 185 F4
La Piedad Mex. 185 E4
La Pila, Sierra de mts Spain 55 J6
La Pine U.S.A. 180 B4
Lapinig Phil. 74 C4
Lapinlahti Fin. 44 N3
La Pintada Panama 186 C5
Laplace U.S.A. 175 E6
Lap Lae Thai. 78 C4
La Plaine Ouanga, Réserve de nature res. Gabon 126 A5
Laplandsky Zapovednik nature res. Rus. Fed. 44 P2
La Plata Arg. 204 F4
formerly known as Eva Perón
La Plata MD U.S.A. 177 I7
La Plata MO U.S.A. 178 D3
La Plata, Río de sea chan. Arg./Uruguay 204 F4
La Plaza Spain 54 E1
La Plonge, Lac l. Canada 167 J4
Lapmeżciems Latvia 42 D4
La Pobla de Segur Spain 55 L2
La Pola de Gordón Spain 54 F2
La Poma Arg. 204 D2
Lapominka Rus. Fed. 40 G2
La Porte U.S.A. 173 G9
Laporte, Mount Canada 166 C2
Laposo, Bukit mt. Indon. 75 A4
La Potherie, Lac l. Canada 169 F1
Lapovo Srbija Yugo. 58 C4
La Poyata Col. 198 C3
Lappajärvi l. Fin. 44 M3
Lappeenranta Fin. 45 O3
Lappi Fin. 45 N4
Lappi reg. Europe 44 L2
Lapphojln Fin. 42 E7
Lappträsk Sweden 44 M2
Laprida Arg. 204 E5
La Pryor U.S.A. 179 C6
Lâpseki Turkey 106 A2
historically known as Lampsacus
Laptev Sea Rus. Fed. 39 M2
also known as Laptevykh, More
Laptevykh, More sea Rus. Fed. see Laptev Sea
Lapua Fin. 44 M3
Lapuanjoki r. Fin. 44 M3
La Puebla Spain see Sa Pobla
La Puebla del Río Spain 54 E7
La Puebla de Montalbán Spain 54 G5
La Puerta Catamarca Arg. 204 D3
La Puerta Córdoba Arg. 204 D3
La Puerta Venez. 198 D2
La Pumilla, Cordillera de mts Chile 204 C3
Lapurdum France see Bayonne
Lăpuşniu Mare Romania 58 F3
Lapusnik Kosovo, Srbija Yugo. 58 B5
Łapy Poland 49 T3
Laqiya Arbain well Sudan 121 F4
La Quiaca Arg. 204 D2
La Quinta U.S.A. 183 H8
Lar Iran 100 C5
Lara Australia 147 E4
Lara state Venez. 198 D2
Laracha Spain 54 C1
Larache Morocco 122 D2
formerly spelt El Araïche; historically known as Lixus
Laragne-Montéglin France 51 L8
Lărak i. Iran 100 D5
Laramie U.S.A. 180 F4
Laramie r. U.S.A. 180 F4
Laramie Mountains U.S.A. 180 F4
Laranda Turkey see Karaman
Laranjal Brazil 199 G6
Laranjal Paulista Brazil 206 F10
Laranjeiras Brazil 202 E4
Laranjeiras do Sul Brazil 203 A3
Larantuka Indon. 75 B5
Larat Indon. 73 H8
La Raygat reg. W. Sahara 122 A5
Larba Alg. 55 O8
L'Arbresle France 51 K7
Lárbro Sweden 45 L4
Larder Lake Canada 173 N2
Larder Lake l. Canada 173 N2
Laredo Spain 55 H1
Laredo U.S.A. 179 C7
La Reforma Sonora Mex. 181 E7
La Reforma Veracruz Mex. 185 F4
La Reina Adelaida, Archipiélago de is Chile 205 B9
English form from Queen Adelaide Islands
La Reine Canada 173 N2
La Réole France 50 F8
Largeau Chad see Faya
L'Argentière-la-Bessée France 51 M8
Largo U.S.A. 175 D7
Largo, Cayo i. Cuba 186 C2
Largs U.K. 46 H8

L'Ariana Tunisia 123 H1
Lariang Indon. 75 A3
Lariang r. Indon. 75 A3
Larimore U.S.A. 178 C1
La Rinconada Spain 54 E7
Larino Italy 56 G7
La Rioja Arg. 204 D3
La Rioja prov. Arg. 204 D3
La Rioja aut. comm. Spain 55 I2
Larionovo Rus. Fed. 43 L1
Larisa Greece 59 D9
also known as Yenişehir; also spelt Larissa
Larissa Greece see Larisa
Laristan reg. Iran 100 D5
Larkana Pak. 101 G5
Lark Harbour Canada 169 J3
Lar Koh mt. Afgh. 101 E3
Lark Passage Australia 149 E2
L'Arli, Parc National de nat. park Burkina 125 F4
L'Arli, Réserve Partielle de nature res. Burkina 125 F4
Larnaca Cyprus 108 E3
also spelt Larnaka
Larnaka Cyprus see Larnaca
Larne U.K. 47 G9
Larned U.S.A. 178 C4
Laro Cameroon 125 I4
La Robe Noire, Lac de l. Canada 169 I3
La Robla Spain 54 F2
La Roche-en-Ardenne Belgium 51 L2
La Rochefoucauld France 50 G7
La Rochelle France 50 E6
La Roche-sur-Yon France 50 E6
La Roda Spain 55 I5
La Romana Dom. Rep. 187 F3
La Ronge Canada 167 J4
La Ronge, Lac l. Canada 167 J4
La Rosa Mex. 185 E3
La Rosa de Castilla Mex. 183 H9
La Rosita Mex. 185 E2
Larouco, Serra do mts Spain 54 D3
Larrey Point Australia 150 B3
Larrimah Australia 148 B2
Larrimah Aboriginal Land res. Australia 148 B2
Lars Christensen Coast Antarctica 223 E2
▶ Larsen Ice Shelf Antarctica 222 T2
antarctica [features] ▶ 212–213
Larsnes Norway 44 I3
La Rubia Arg. 204 E3
Larvik Norway 45 J4
Lar'yak Rus. Fed. 39 I3
Larzac, Causse du plat. France 51 J8
La Sabana Arg. 204 F2
La Sabana Col. 198 D4
Las Adjuntas, Presa de resr Mex. 185 F4
La Sal U.S.A. 183 O3
La Sal, Cerros de mts Peru 200 B3
La Salle Canada 173 O3
La Salle U.S.A. 174 B3
La Salonga Nord, Parc National de nat. park Dem. Rep. Congo 126 D5
La Salonga Sud, Parc National de nat. park Dem. Rep. Congo 126 D5
Las Ánimas U.S.A. 178 B4
Las Ánimas, Punta pt Mex. 184 B2
Las Anod Somalia see Laascaanood
La Sarre Canada 168 E3
La Sauvette hill France 51 M9
Las Avispas Arg. 204 E3
Las Avispas Mex. 184 C2
La Savonnière, Lac l. Canada 169 F2
Las Bonitas Venez. 199 E3
Las Breñas Arg. 204 E2
Las Chapas Arg. 205 D6
La Scie Canada 169 K3
Las Conchas Bol. 201 F4
Las Cruces Mex. 184 D3
Las Cruces CA U.S.A. 182 D7
Las Cruces NM U.S.A. 181 F6
La Selle mt. Haiti 187 F3
La Serena Chile 204 C3
La Serena, Embalse de resr Spain 54 F6
Las Esperanças Mex. 185 E3
Las Estancias, Sierra de mts Spain 55 I7
Las Flores Buenos Aires Arg. 204 F5
Las Flores Salta Arg. 201 E6
Lashburn Canada 167 I4
Las Heras Arg. 204 D4
Las Hermosas, Parque Nacional nat. park Col. 198 C4
Las Herreras Mex. 184 D3
Lashio Myanmar 78 B3
Lashkar Gäh Afgh. 101 F4
La Sila reg. Italy 57 I9
Łasin Poland 49 Q2
Las Juntas Chile 204 C3
Las Lajas Arg. 204 C5
Las Lajitas Venez. 199 E3
Las Lavaderos Mex. 185 F4
Las Lomas Peru 198 A5
Las Lomitas Arg. 201 E6
Las Marismas marsh Spain 54 E7
Las Martinetas Arg. 205 D7
Las Médulas tourist site Spain 54 E2
Las Mercedes Venez. 199 E3
Las Mesteñas Mex. 184 D2
Las Minas Venez. 199 E3
Las Minas, Sierra de mts Guat. 185 H6
Las Mulatas is Panama see San Blas, Archipiélago de
Las Nieves Mex. 184 D3
Las Nopaleras, Cerro mt. Mex. 185 E4
La Solana Spain 55 H6
Las Orquídeas, Parque Nacional nat. park Col. 198 C3
La Souterraine France 50 H6
Las Ovejas Arg. 204 C5
Las Palmas watercourse Mex. 183 G9
Las Palmas Panama 186 C5
▶ Las Palmas de Gran Canaria Canary Is 122 B3
Joint capital of the Canary Islands.
Las Perlas, Archipiélago de is Panama 186 D5
Las Petas Bol. 201 F4
La Spezia Italy 56 B4
Las Piedras Uruguay 204 F4
Las Piedras, Río de r. Peru 200 C3
Las Pipinas Arg. 204 F5
Las Planchas Hond. 186 B4
Las Plumas Arg. 205 D6
Laspur Pak. 101 H3
Las Rosas Arg. 204 E4
Las Rozas de Madrid Spain 54 H4
Las Salinas, Pampa de salt pan Arg. 204 D3
Lassance Brazil 207 I4
Lassay-les-Châteaux France 50 F4
Lassen Peak vol. U.S.A. 182 C1
Lassen Volcanic National Park U.S.A. 182 C1
Las Tablas Panama 186 C6
Las Tablas de Daimiel, Parque Nacional de nat. park Spain 55 H5
Lastarria, Parque Nacional nat. park Chile 205 B7
Last Chance U.S.A. 178 B4
Las Termas Arg. 204 D2
Last Mountain Lake Canada 167 J5
Las Torres de Cotillas Spain 55 J6
Las Tórtolas, Cerro mt. Chile 204 C3

L

Lastoursville Gabon **126** B5
Lastovo *i.* Croatia **56** I6
Lastovski Kanal *sea chan.* Croatia **56** I6
Las Tres Vírgenes, Volcán *vol.* Mex. **184** B3
Las Trincheras Venez. **199** E3
Las Tunas Cuba **186** D2
Lasva Estonia **42** I4
Las Varas Col. **199** D3
Las Varas *Chihuahua* Mex. **184** D2
Las Varas *Nayarit* Mex. **184** D4
Las Varas Venez. **198** D3
Las Varillas Arg. **204** E3
Las Vegas *NM* U.S.A. **181** F6
Las Vegas *NV* U.S.A. **183** I5
Las Villuercas *mt.* Spain **54** F5
Las Yaras Peru **200** C4
Lata Solomon Is **145** F3
La Tabatière Canada **169** J3
Latacunga Ecuador **198** B5
Latady Island Antarctica **222** S2
La Tagua Col. **198** C5
Latakia Syria **108** G2
also known as Lattaquié; also spelt Al Lādhiqīyah; historically known as Laodicea or Laodicea ad Mare
Latalata *i.* Indon. **75** C3
Latchford Canada **173** N3
Latehar India **97** E5
La Teignouse, Passage de *strait* France **50** C5
Late Island Tonga **145** H3
also known as Latte Island or Lette Island
Latemar *mt.* Italy **56** D2
La Teste France **50** E8
La Tetilla, Cerro *mt.* Mex. **184** D4
Latgale reg. Latvia **42** I5
Latgales Augstiene *reg.* Latvia **42** I5
Latham Australia **151** B6
Lathi India **96** A5
Lathrop U.S.A. **182** C3
Latidān Iran **100** C5
Latimojong Mountains Reserve *nature res.* Indon. **75** B3
Latina Italy **56** E7
Latisana Italy **56** F3
La Toma Arg. **204** D4
La Tortue, Île de *i.* Haiti **187** G3
La Tortuga, Isla *i.* Venez. **199** E2
Latorytsya *r.* Ukr. **49** T7
Latouche Treville, Cape Australia **150** C3
Latouma *well* Niger **123** I5
La Tour-du-Pin France **51** L7
La Tranquera, Embalse de *resr* Spain **55** J3
La Tremblade France **50** E7
La Trinidad Nicaragua **186** B4
La Trinidad Phil. **74** B2
La Trinitaria Mex. **185** G5
La Trinité France **51** N9
Latronico Italy **57** I8
La Troya *r.* Arg. **204** C3
La Truite, Lac à *l.* Canada **173** O3
Latskoye Rus. Fed. **43** T3
Lattaquié Syria *see* Latakia
Latte Island Tonga *see* Late Island
Lattes France **51** J9
Latulipe Canada **173** N3
La Tuque Canada **169** F4
Latur India **94** C2
▶Latvia *country* Europe **42** E5
spelt Latvija in Latvian; formerly known as Latviyskaya S.S.R.
europe [countries] ▶ 32–35
Latvija *country* Europe *see* Latvia
Latviyskaya S.S.R. *country* Europe *see* Latvia
Lau Nigeria **125** H4
Lau *r.* Sudan **128** A3
Laua *r.* India **97** C3
Lauban *waterhole* Namibia **130** C4
Lauca, Parque Nacional *nat. park* Chile **200** C4
Lauenburg (Elbe) Germany **48** H2
Lauf an der Pegnitz Germany **48** I6
Laufen Germany **49** J8
Laufen Switz. **51** N5
Laugarbakki Iceland **44** [inset] B2
Laughland Lake Canada **167** M1
Laughlin, Mount Australia **148** F4
Laughlin Peak U.S.A. **181** F5
Lauhanvuoren kansallispuisto *nat. park* Fin. **45** M3
Lauka Estonia **42** D3
Laukaa Fin. **44** N3
Laukuva Lith. **42** D6
Laun Thai. **79** B6
Launay Canada **173** N2
Launceston Australia **147** E5
Launceston U.K. **47** H13
Launglon Myanmar **79** B5
Launglon Bok Islands Myanmar **79** B5
La Unidad Mex. **185** G6
La Unión Bol. **201** E4
La Unión Chile **204** B6
La Unión Col. **198** B4
La Unión El Salvador **185** I6
La Unión *Huánuco* Peru **200** A2
La Unión *Piura* Peru **198** A6
La Unión Spain **55** K7
Laur Phil. **74** B3
Laura Australia **149** E2
La Urbana Venez. **199** E3
Laurel *DE* U.S.A. **177** J7
Laurel *MS* U.S.A. **175** B6
Laurel *MT* U.S.A. **180** E3
Laureldale U.S.A. **177** J5
Laurel Hill *hills* U.S.A. **176** F6
Laurencekirk U.K. **46** J7
Laurens *IA* U.S.A. **178** D3
Laurens *SC* U.S.A. **174** D5

Laurentides, Réserve Faunique des *nature res.* Canada **169** G4
Lauri India **96** D4
Lauria Italy **57** H8
Laurie Island S. Atlantic Ocean **222** V2
Laurinburg U.S.A. **174** E5
Lauriston N.Z. **153** F11
Larium U.S.A. **172** E3
Lauru *i.* Solomon Is *see* Choiseul
Lausanne Switz. **51** M6
Lausitzer Grenzwall *park* Germany **49** K4
Laut *i.* Indon. **77** E1
Laut *i.* Indon. **77** E3
Laut *i.* Indon. **77** G3
Laut, Selat *sea chan.* Indon. **77** F3
Lauta Germany **49** L4
Lautaro Chile **204** B5
Lautaro, Cerro *vol.* Chile **205** B8
Lautem East Timor **75** C5
Lauterbrunnen Switz. **51** N6
Lautersbach (Hessen) Germany **48** G5
Laut Kecil, Kepulauan *is* Indon. **77** F4
Lautoka Fiji **145** G3
Laut Taka Bonerate National Park Indon. **75** B4
Lauttawar, Danau *l.* Indon. **76** B1
Lauvsnes Norway **44** J2
Lauvuskylä Fin. **44** O3
Lauwersmeer *l.* Neth. **48** D2
Lava *r.* Rus. Fed. **49** S1
Lava Beds National Monument *nat. park* U.S.A. **180** B4
Lavaca *r.* U.S.A. **179** C6
Laval Canada **169** F4
Laval France **50** F4
Lavalette U.S.A. **176** C7
Lävän Iran **100** C5
La Vanoise, Massif *de mts* France **51** M7
La Vanoise, Parc National de *nat. park* France **51** M7
Lavant *r.* Austria/Slovenia **49** L9
Lavapié, Punta *pt* Chile **204** B5
Lävar Iran **100** B4
Lavara Greece **59** J11
La Venta Hond. **186** B4
La Ventana, Sierra de *mts* Arg. **204** E5
Laventie France **51** I2
La Venturosa Col. **198** D3
La Vérendrye, Réserve Faunique de *nature res.* Canada **168** E4
Laverne U.S.A. **178** C4
Laverton Australia **151** C6
Lavia Fin. **45** M3
La Víbora Mex. **185** E3
La Victoria Venez. **187** G5
Lavieille, Lake Canada **173** O5
Lavigne Canada **173** M4
La Viña Arg. **204** D2
La Viña Peru **198** B6
Lavina U.S.A. **180** E3
La Virgen, Sierra de *mts* Spain **55** J3
Lavit France **50** G8
La Võge reg. France **51** M6
Lavongai *i.* P.N.G. *see* New Hanover
Lavoriškės Lith. **42** G7
La Voulte-sur-Rhône France **51** K8
Lavras Brazil **203** C7
Lavrio Greece **59** H11
Lavrov *Orlovskaya Oblast'* Rus. Fed. **43** R9
Lavrov *Vologod. Obl.* Rus. Fed. **43** S2
Lavumisa Swaziland **133** P4
formerly known as Gollel
Lavushi-Manda National Park Zambia **127** F8
Lawa *r.* Liberia **124** C5
Lawa Myanmar **78** B2
Lawagamau *r.* Canada **168** E3
Lawan India **97** D5
Lawang *i.* Indon. **77** G5
Lawashi *r.* Canada **168** D2
Lawdar Yemen **105** D5
Law Dome *ice feature* Antarctica **223** H2
Lawele Indon. **75** B4
Lawik Reef P.N.G. **149** G1
Lawit, Gunung *mt.* Indon./Malaysia **77** F2
Lawit, Gunung *mt.* Malaysia **76** C1
Lawksawk Myanmar **78** B3
Lawn Hill Australia **148** C3
Lawn Hill Creek *r.* Australia **148** C3
Lawn Hill National Park Australia **148** C3
Lawqah Saudi Arabia **109** M8
Lawqah *waterhole* Saudi Arabia **121** I2
Lawra Ghana **124** E4
Lawrence N.Z. **153** D13
Lawrence *KS* U.S.A. **178** D4
Lawrence *MA* U.S.A. **177** N3
Lawrenceburg *KY* U.S.A. **176** A7
Lawrenceburg *TN* U.S.A. **174** C5
Lawrenceville *IL* U.S.A. **174** B4
Lawrenceville *NJ* U.S.A. **177** K5
Lawrenceville *PA* U.S.A. **176** H3
Lawrenceville *VA* U.S.A. **176** H3
Lawrence Wells, Mount *hill* Australia **151** C5
Lawton U.S.A. **179** C5
Lawu, Gunung *vol.* Indon. **77** E4
Lawz, Jabal al *mt.* Saudi Arabia **104** A1
Laxå Sweden **45** K4
Laxey U.K. **47** H10
Lax Kw'alaams Canada **166** C4
formerly known as Port Simpson
Lay *r.* France **50** E6
Laya *r.* Rus. Fed. **40** K2
Layar, Tanjung *pt* Indon. **77** G4
La Yarada Peru **200** C4
La Yata-Ngaya, Réserve de Faune de *nature res.* Cent. Afr. Rep. **126** D2
Laydennyy, Mys *c.* Rus. Fed. **40** H1
Layeni Indon. **75** D4
Layla Saudi Arabia **105** D3
Layla *salt pan* Saudi Arabia **109** J6
Laylän Iraq **109** P2
Layon *r.* France **50** F5
L'Ayrolle, Étang de *lag.* France **51** J9
Laysan Island U.S.A. **221** G4
Laytonville U.S.A. **182** A2
La Zacatosa, Picacho *mt.* Mex. **184** C4
Lazarev Rus. Fed. **82** F1
formerly known as Mys Lazareva
Lazarevac *Srbija* Yugo. **58** B4
Lazarevo Rus. Fed. **43** S6
Lazarevskoye Rus. Fed. **107** D2
Lázaro, Sierra de San *mts* Mex. **184** C4
Lázaro Cárdenas *Baja California Norte* Mex. **184** B2
Lázaro Cárdenas *Baja California Norte* Mex. **184** B2
Lázaro Cárdenas *Michoacán* Mex. **185** D5
Lazcano Uruguay **204** G4
Lazdijai Lith. **42** E7
Lazinki Rus. Fed. **43** P7
Lazise Italy **56** C3
Lazo Arg. **204** F1
Lazo Rus. Fed. **82** D4
Lazo Rus. Fed. **39** N3
La Zorra *watercourse* Mex. **179** B6

Leach Island Canada **173** I3
Leader Canada **167** I5
Leadville U.S.A. **180** F5
Leaf *r.* U.S.A. **175** B6
Leaf Bay Canada *see* Tasiujaq
Leaf Rapids Canada **167** K3
Leahy, Cape Antarctica **222** Q2
Leake, Mount *hill* Australia **150** D3
Leakesville U.S.A. **175** B6
Leakey U.S.A. **179** C6
Leaksville U.S.A. *see* Eden
Leal, Mount *hill* Australia **150** B4
Leales Arg. **204** D2
Leamington Canada **168** D5
Leamington Spa, Royal U.K. **47** K11
Le'an China *see* Aoxi
Leandra S. Africa **133** N3
Leandro N. Alem Arg. **204** G2
Leanja Madag. **131** [inset] J2
Leasburg U.S.A. **176** F9
L'Eau Claire, Lac à *l.* Canada **169** F1
Le Havre France **50** G3
Lehi U.S.A. **183** M1
Leighton U.S.A. **177** J5
Lehliu-Gară Romania **58** H4
Lehlohonolo S. Africa **133** M7
Lehmi U.S.A. **180** D3
Lehtimäki Fin. **44** M3
Lehututu Botswana **130** D4
Leiah Pak. **101** G4
Leibnitz Austria **49** M9
Leibo China **86** B2
Leicester U.K. **47** K11
historically known as Ratae
Leichhardt *r.* Australia **148** C3
Leichhardt Falls Australia **148** C3
Leichhardt Range *mts* Australia **149** E4
Leiden Neth. **48** B3
historically known as Leyden
Leie *r.* Belgium **51** J1
Leifur Estonia **42** E3
Leigh *watercourse* Australia **146** C2
Leigh N.Z. **152** I4
Leigh Creek Australia **146** C2
Leighlinbridge Rep. of Ireland **47** F11
Leikanger Norway **45** J3
Leiktho Myanmar **78** B4
Leine *r.* Germany **48** G3
Leinefelde Germany **48** H4
Leinster Australia **151** C6
Leinster *reg.* Rep. of Ireland **47** F10
Leinster, Mount *h.* Rep. of Ireland **47** F11
Leipalingis Lith. **42** E7
Leipojärvi Sweden **44** M2
Leipsic U.S.A. **176** B4
Leipsoi *i.* Greece **59** H11
also spelt Lipsoí
Leipzig Germany **49** J4
Leipzig-Halle *airport* Germany **49** J4
Leira *More og Romsdal* Norway **44** J3
Leira *Oppland* Norway **45** J3
Leiria Port. **54** C5
Leiria *admin. dist.* Port. **54** C5
Leirvik *S. Africa* **133** M3
Leirvik *Sogn og Fjordane* Norway **45** I4
Leisha China **87** D3
also known as Danjiang
Lei Shui *r.* China **87** E3
Leisi Estonia **42** D3
Leisler, Mount *hill* Australia **148** A4
Leisler Hills Australia **146** A2
Leitchfield U.S.A. **174** C4
Leith U.K. **46** I8
Leithfield N.Z. **153** G11
Leivonmäki Fin. **45** N3
Leiyang China **87** E3
Leizhou China **87** D4
formerly known as Haikang
Leizhou Bandao *pen.* China **87** D4
English form for Luichow Peninsula
Leizhou Wan *b.* China **87** D4
Lek *r.* Neth. **48** B4
Leka *i.* Norway **44** J2
Lékana Congo **126** B5
Le Kef Tunisia **123** H1
historically known as Sicca Veneria
Lékéti *r.* Congo **126** B5
Lekhainá Greece *see* Lechaina
Lekhcheb Mauritania **124** C2
Lekkersing S. Africa **132** B6
Lekoes Norway **44** K1
Lékoni Gabon **126** B5
Leksozero, Ozero *l.* Rus. Fed. **44** O3
Lek'suiri Georgia *see* Lentekhi
Leksura Georgia *see* Lentekhi
Leksvik Norway **44** J3
Lelai, Tanjung *pt* Indon. **75** D2
Le Lamentin Martinique **187** [inset]
Leland Norway **44** K2
Leland *IL* U.S.A. **172** E9
Leland *MS* U.S.A. **175** B5
Leläng *l.* Sweden **45** K4
Le Lavandou France **51** M9
Leleque Arg. **205** C6
Leli China *see* Tianlin
Lelija *mt.* Bos.-Herz. **56** K5
Lelystad Neth. **48** C3
Le Maire, Estrecho de *sea chan.* Arg. **205** D9
Le Mans France **50** G4
Le Mars U.S.A. **178** C3
LeMay Range *mts* Antarctica **222** T2
Lembeh *i.* Indon. **75** C2
Lemberg *mt.* Germany **48** F7
Lemberg Ukr. *see* L'viv
Lembu Indon. **77** G2
Lembu, Gunung *mt.* Indon. **76** B1
Lembubut Indon. **77** G3
Lemdiyya Alg. *see* Médéa
Leme Brazil **206** F9
Le Merlu Rocher *mt.* France **51** L8
Lemeshkina Rus. Fed. **43** M9
Lemesos Cyprus *see* Limassol
Lemförde Germany **48** F3
Lemhi *r.* U.S.A. **180** D3
Lemhi Range *mts* U.S.A. **180** D3
Lemland Fin. **45** M3
Lemmenjoen kansallispuisto *nat. park* Fin. **44** N1
Lemmon U.S.A. **178** B2
Lemmon, Mount U.S.A. **183** N9
Lemnos *i.* Greece *see* Limnos
Le Môle St Nicolas Haiti **187** G3
Lemoncove U.S.A. **182** E5
Le Mont-Dore New Caledonia **145** G4
Le Mont-St-Michel *tourist site* France **50** E4
also known as Mont St Michel
Lemoore U.S.A. **182** E5
Lempäälä Fin. **45** M3
Lemreway U.K. **46** E5
Lemro *r.* Myanmar **78** A3
Lemtybozh Rus. Fed. **40** K3
Lemukutan *i.* Indon. **77** E2
Le Murge *hills* Italy **57** J8
Lemvig Denmark **45** J4
Lemyethna Myanmar **78** A4
Lem'yu *r.* Rus. Fed. **40** K3

Lefroy, Lake *salt flat* Australia **151** C6
Łęg *r.* Poland **49** S5
Legarde *r.* Canada **168** C3
Legaspi Phil. **74** B3
Legde France **50** E6
Legges Tor *mt.* Australia **147** E5
Leggett U.S.A. **182** A2
Leghorn Italy *see* Livorno
Legionowo Poland **49** R3
Legnago Italy **56** D3
Legnano Italy **56** B3
Legnica Poland **49** N4
historically known as Liegnitz
Legnone, Monte *mt.* Italy **56** B2
Le Grand U.S.A. **182** D4
Le Grand, Cape Australia **151** C7
Le Grand Coyer *mt.* France **51** M8
Le Grau-du-Roi France **51** K9
Leguena Chile **200** C5
Legune Australia **148** A2
Legwe *r.* Dem. Rep. Congo **126** E4
Leh Jammu and Kashmir **96** C2
Lehbei China *see* Jircheng
▶Lebanon *country* Asia **108** G3
spelt Lubnān in Arabic or Liban in French
asia [countries] ▶ 64–67
Lebanon *IN* U.S.A. **174** C3
Lebanon *MO* U.S.A. **178** D4
Lebanon *NH* U.S.A. **177** M2
Lebanon *NJ* U.S.A. **177** K5
Lebanon *OH* U.S.A. **176** A6
Lebanon *OR* U.S.A. **180** B3
Lebanon *PA* U.S.A. **177** J5
Lebanon *TN* U.S.A. **174** C4
Lebanon *VA* U.S.A. **176** C9
Lebap Turkm. **103** E5
Lebap Oblast *admin. div.* Turkm. *see* Lebapskaya Oblast'
Lebapskaya Oblast' *admin. div.* Turkm. **103** E5
English form Lebap Oblast; formerly known as Chardzhouskaya Oblast'
Lebda *tourist site* Libya *see* Leptis Magna
Lebec U.S.A. **182** F7
Lebedin Ukr. *see* Lebedyn
Lebedyan' Rus. Fed. **43** U8
Lebedyn Ukr. **41** E6
also spelt Lebedin
Lebel-sur-Quévillon Canada **168** E3
Lebiolali *well* Eth. **128** E3
Le Blanc France **50** H6
Lebo Dem. Rep. Congo **126** D3
Lebombo *mts* Moz. *see* Lebombomberg
Lebombomberg *hills* Moz. **133** Q3
also known as Lebomboberge
Lebonang S. Africa **133** M3
Lebork Poland **49** N1
Lebowakgomo S. Africa **131** M7
Lebrija Spain **54** E8
Łebsko, Jezioro *lag.* Poland **49** O1
Lebu Chile **204** B5
Le Bugue France **50** G8
Lebyazh'ye Kazakh. *see* Akku
Lebyazh'ye *Kirovskaya Oblast'* Rus. Fed. **40** I4
Lebyazh'ye *Leningradskaya Oblast'* Rus. Fed. **43** K2
Le Caire Egypt *see* Cairo
Lecce Italy **57** K8
Lecco Italy **56** B3
Lech *r.* Austria/Germany **48** H8
Lechaina Greece **59** C11
also spelt Lekhainá
Lechang China **87** E3
Le Chasseron *mt.* Switz. **51** M6
Le Château-d'Oléron France **50** E7
Lechința Romania **58** F1
Lechința *r.* Romania **58** F2
Lechtaler Alpen *mts* Austria **48** H8
Leck Germany **48** F1
Lecompte U.S.A. **179** D6
L'Écorce, Lac de *l.* Canada **173** Q3
Le Coteau France **51** K6
Le Creusot France **51** K6
Lectoure France **50** G9
Lecumberri Spain **55** J1
Łęczna Poland **49** T4
Łęczyca Poland **49** Q3
Ledang, Gunung *mt.* Malaysia **76** C2
Ledava *r.* Slovenia **56** I2
Ledbury U.K. **47** J11
Ledeč nad Sázavou Czech Rep. **49** M6
Ledengskoye Rus. Fed. **40** H4
Ledesma Spain **54** F3
Lediba Dem. Rep. Congo **126** C5
Ledong Hainan China **87** D5
also known as Baoyou
Le Dorat France **50** H6
Ledu China **84** D4
also known as Nianbai
Leduc Canada **167** H4
Le Duffre *mt.* France **51** L8
Ledyanaya, Gora *mt.* Rus. Fed. **39** M4
Lee *r.* Rep. of Ireland **47** D12
Leech Lake *l.* U.S.A. **174** A2
Leech Lake Indian Reservation *res.* U.S.A. **174** A2
Leeds U.K. **47** K10
Leek U.K. **47** J10
Leenane Rep. of Ireland **47** C10
Leeper U.S.A. **176** F4
Leer (Ostfriesland) Germany **48** E2
Leesburg *FL* U.S.A. **175** D6
Leesburg *GA* U.S.A. **175** C6
Leesburg *KY* U.S.A. **176** A7
Leesburg *VA* U.S.A. **176** H6
Lees Summit U.S.A. **178** D4
Le Steere Range *hills* Australia **151** C5
Leeston N.Z. **153** G11
Leesville U.S.A. **179** D6
Leesville Lake U.S.A. **176** F8
Leeton Australia **147** E3
Leeudoringstad S. Africa **133** K4
Leeu-Gamka S. Africa **132** F9
Leeukop *mt.* S. Africa **133** J5
Leeupoort S. Africa **133** L1
Leeuw *r.* S. Africa **132** F9
Leeuwarden Neth. **48** C2
Leeuwin, Cape Australia **151** A7
Leeward Islands Caribbean Sea **187** G3
Leewin-Naturaliste National Park Australia **151** A7
Le Faouët France **50** C4
Lefedzha *r.* Bulg. **58** G5
Lefka Cyprus **108** D2
also spelt Lefke
Lefkada Greece **59** B10
also known as Lefkás; formerly known as Leukas; historically known as Leucas
Lefkada *i.* Greece **59** B10
also known as Levkás or Santa Maura
Lefkás Greece *see* Lefkada
Lefke Cyprus *see* Lefka
Lefkimmi Greece **59** B9
also spelt Levkímmi
Lefkoşa Cyprus *see* Nicosia
Lefkosia Cyprus *see* Nicosia

Lena *r.* Rus. Fed. **80** H[1]
Lena *l.* U.S.A. **172** D8
Lena, Mount U.S.A. **183** O1
Lénakel Vanuatu **145** F3
Lencloître France **50** G6
Lençóis Brazil **202** D5
Lençóis Maranhenses, Parque Nacional dos *nat. park* Brazil **202** D2
Lençóis Paulista Brazil **206** E9
Lenda *r.* Dem. Rep. Congo **126** F4
Lendava Slovenia **56** I2
historically known as Liegnitz
Lendeh Iran **100** B4
Lendery Rus. Fed. **44** O3
Lendinara Italy **56** D3
Le Neubourg France **50** G3
Lengbarüt Iran **101** D4
Lenger Kazakh. **103** G4
Lengerich Germany **48** E3
Lenggries Germany **48** I8
Lenghuzhen China **84** B4
Lenglong Ling *mts* China **84** D4
Lengoué *r.* Congo **126** B4
Lengshuijiang China **87** D3
Lengshuitan China **87** D3
Lengua de Vaca, Punta *pt* Chile **204** C3
Lengwe National Park Malawi **129** B9
Lenhovda Sweden **45** K4
Lenin Tajik. **101** G2
also known as Kazygurt
Lenin, Qullai *mt.* Kyrg./Tajik. *see* Lenin Peak
Lenina, Kanal *canal* Rus. Fed. **41** J6
Lenina, Pik *mt.* Kyrg./Tajik. *see* Lenin Peak
Leninabad Tajik. *see* Khŭjand
Leninabad Uzbek. **102** D4
also spelt Leninobod
Leninakan Armenia *see* Gyumri
Lenin Atyndagy Choku *mt.* Kyrg./Tajik. *see* Lenin Peak
Lenine Ukr. **41** E7
also spelt Leninc; formerly known as Sem Kolodezey
Leningori Georgia *see* Akhalgori
Leningrad Rus. Fed. *see* St Petersburg
Leningrad Tajik. **101** G2
also known as Leningradskiy or Mŭ'minobod; formerly known as Muminabad
Leningrad Oblast *admin. div.* Rus. Fed. *see* Leningradskaya Oblast'
Leningradskaya Rus. Fed. **41** F7
Leningradskaya Oblast' *admin. div.* Rus. Fed. **43** L3
English form Leningrad Oblast
Leningradskiy Tajik. *see* Leningrad
Lenino Rus. Fed. **90** D2
Lenino Ukr. *see* Lenine
Leninobod Tajik. *see* Khŭjand
Leninobod *admin. div.* Tajik. **101** G2
English form Leninabad Oblast; also known as Khŭjand
Leninobod Uzbek. *see* Leninabad
Leninogor Kazakh. *see* Leninogorsk
Leninogorsk Kazakh. **88** C1
also known as Leninogor or Ridder
Leninogorsk Rus. Fed. **40** J5
formerly known as Novaya Pismyanka
Lenin Peak Kyrg./Tajik. **103** H5
also known as Lenina, Pik or Lenin, Qullai or Lenin Atyndagy Choku
Leninpol' Kyrg. **103** G4
Leninsk Kazakh. *see* Baykonur
Leninsk Rus. Fed. **41** H6
Leninsk Turkm. *see* Akdepe
Leninsk Uzbek. *see* Asaka
Leninskiy Kazakh. **102** C3
Leninskiy Rus. Fed. **43** U7
Leninsk-Kuznetskiy Rus. Fed. **80** D2
Leninskoye Kazakh. **102** D2
also known as Kazygurt
Leninskoye Rus. Fed. **40** H4
Leninskoye Rus. Fed. **82** D2
Lenkoran' Azer. *see* Länkäran
Lennard *r.* Australia **150** D3
Lenne *r.* Germany **51** N1
Lennox, Isla *i.* Chile **205** D9
Lennox-King Glacier Antarctica **223** L1
Lenoir U.S.A. **174** D5
Lenoir City U.S.A. **174** C5
Lenore U.S.A. **176** C8
Lenore Lake Canada **167** J4
Lenox U.S.A. **177** L3
Lens France **52** C1
Lensk Rus. Fed. **39** L3
formerly known as Mukhtuya
Lenti Hungary **49** N9
Lentini *Sicilia* Italy **57** H11
Lentua *l.* Fin. **44** O2
Lentvaras Lith. *see* Lentvaris
Lentvaris Lith. **42** G7
also known as Lentvaravas
Lent'yevo Rus. Fed. **43** R3
Lenwood U.S.A. **183** G7
Lenya Myanmar **79** B6
Léo Burkina **125** E4
Leoben Austria **49** N8
Leodhas, Eilean *i.* U.K. *see* Lewis, Isle of
Léogâne Haiti **187** E3
Leok Indon. **75** B2
Leola U.S.A. **178** B2
Leominster U.K. **47** J11
Leominster U.S.A. **177** N3
León Mex. **185** E4
León Nicaragua **186** B4
León Spain **54** F2
Leon *r.* U.S.A. **174** A3
Leon *r.* U.S.A. **179** C5
León, Montes de *mts* Spain **54** E2
Leonard U.S.A. **179** C5
Leonardo da Vinci *airport* Italy **56** E7
Leonardtown U.S.A. **177** I7
Leonardville Namibia **130** C4
Leone Vicario Mex. **185** I4
Leonforte *Sicilia* Italy **57** G11
Leongatha Australia **147** E4
Leonídi Greece **59** D11
Leonora Australia **151** C6
Leonovo Rus. Fed. **82** F2
Leopard *r.* Australia **150** D3
Leopold *r.* Australia **150** D3
Leopold Downs Australia **150** D3
Leopold Downs Aboriginal Reserve Australia **150** D3
Léopold II, Lac *l.* Dem. Rep. Congo *see* Mai-Ndombe, Lac
Leopoldina Brazil **203** D7
Leopoldo de Bulhões Brazil **206** E3
Léopoldville Dem. Rep. Congo *see* Kinshasa
Leoti U.S.A. **178** B4
Leova Moldova **58** J2
formerly spelt Leovo
Leoville Canada **167** J4
Leovo Moldova *see* Leova
Lepar *i.* Indon. **77** D3
Le Péage-de-Roussillon France **51** K7
spelt Belarus see Lyepyel'
Lepenou Greece **59** C10
Lephepe Botswana **131** E4
Lephoi S. Africa **133** J7
Leping China **87** F2
Lap'lana *r.* Rus. Fed. **40** G1
Lapoglava Croatia **56** I2
Le Poiré-sur-Vie France **50** E6
Le Pont France **51** M6
Lepontine, Alpi *mts* Italy/Switz. **56** A2
Leposavić *Kosovo, Srbija* Yugo. **58** B5

Leppävirta Fin. **44** N3
Lepreau, Point Canada **169** H4
Lepsa Kazakh. *see* Lepsy
Lepsa *r.* Kazakh. *see* Lepsy
Lepsi Kazakh. *see* Lepsinsk
Lepsinsk Kazakh. **103** J3
also known as Lepsi
Lepsy Kazakh. **103** I3
also known as Lepsa
Lepsy *r.* Kazakh. **103** I3
formerly known as Lepsa
Leptis Magna *tourist site* Libya **120** B1
also known as Lebda
Leptokarya Greece **59** D8
Le-Puy-en-Velay France **51** J7
Leqceïba Mauritania **124** B2
Léraba r. Burkina/Côte d'Ivoire **124** D4
Lerala Botswana **131** E4
Leratswana S. Africa **133** L5
Lercara Friddi *Sicilia* Italy **57** F11
Lerderderg State Park *nature res.* Australia **147** C4
Léré Chad **126** B2
Léré Mali **124** D3
Lere Nigeria **125** H4
Lereh, Tanjung *pt* Indon. **77** G4
Le Relecq-Kerhuon France **50** B4
Léric U.S.A. **198** D5
Lérida Spain *see* Lleida
Lerik Azer. **107** G3
Lerma Mex. **185** H5
Lerma Spain **54** H2
Lermontov Rus. Fed. **107** E1
formerly known as Lermontovskiy
Lermontovka Rus. Fed. **82** D3
Lermontovskiy Rus. Fed. *see* Lermontov
Lerno, Monte *mt.* Sardegna Italy **57** B8
Le Robert Martinique **187** [inset]
Leros *i.* Greece **59** H11
Le Roy U.S.A. **176** H3
Lerum Sweden **45** K4
Lerwick U.K. **46** K1
Ler Zerai *well* Sudan **126** E2
Les Agudes *mt.* Spain **55** N3
Les Borges Blanques Spain **55** L3
also spelt Borjas Blancas
Lesbos *i.* Greece **59** G9
also known as Mytilene; also spelt Lesvos
L'Escala Spain **55** O2
also spelt La Escala
Les Cayes Haiti **187** E3
Le Sentier Switz. **51** M6
Les Escaldes Andorra **55** M2
Les Escoumins Canada **169** G3
Le Seu d'Urgell Spain **55** M2
also spelt Seo de Urgell
Leshan China **86** B2
Les Herbiers France **50** E6
Leshou China *see* Xianxian
Leshukonskoye Rus. Fed. **40** H2
Lesina, Lago di *lag.* Italy **56** H7
Lesja Norway **45** J3
Lesjöfors Sweden **45** K4
Leskhimstroy Ukr. *see* Syeverodonets'k
Lesko Poland **49** T6
Leskovac *Srbija* Yugo. **58** C6
Leskovík Albania **59** B8
Leskov Island Antarctica **223** F2
Leslie U.S.A. **173** I8
Les Méchins Canada **169** H3
Les Mées France **51** L8
Les Minquiers *is* Channel Is **50** D4
Lesna *r.* Poland **49** L4
Lesneven France **50** B4
Lesnoy *Kirovskaya Oblast'* Rus. Fed. **40** J4
Lesnoy Rus. Fed. *see* Umba
Lesnoy *Smolenskaya Oblast'* Rus. Fed. **43** M6
Lesnoy, Ostrov *i.* Rus. Fed. **43** J1
Lesnoye Rus. Fed. **43** Q3
Lesnoye Rus. Fed. **40** J4
Lesogorsk Rus. Fed. **82** F2
Lesogorskiy Rus. Fed. **43** J1
Lesopil'noye Rus. Fed. **82** D3
Lesosibirsk Rus. Fed. **39** J4
▶Lesotho *country* Africa **133** L6
formerly known as Basutoland
africa [countries] ▶ 114–117
Lesotho Highlands Water Scheme Lesotho **133** M6
Lesozavodsk Rus. Fed. **82** D3
Lesozavodskiy Rus. Fed. **44** P2
Lesparre-Médoc France **50** F7
L'Espérance Rock *i.* N.Z. **145** I5
Les Pieux France **50** E3
L'Espina *mt.* Spain **55** L4
Les Ponts-de-Cé France **50** F5
Les Sables-d'Olonne France **50** E6
Lesse *r.* Belgium **51** K2
Les Sept-Îles *is* France **50** C4
Lesser Antilles *is* Caribbean Sea **187** G4
also known as Malyy Kavkaz
Lesser Caucasus *mts* Asia **41** G8
also known as Malyy Kavkaz
Lesser Himalaya *mts* India/Nepal **96** C3
Lesser Khingan Mountains China *see* Xiao Hinggan Ling
Lesser Slave Lake Canada **167** H4
Lesser Slave Lake Provincial Park Canada **167** H4
Lesser Tunb *i.* The Gulf **105** C2
also known as Tonb-e Kūchek, Jazireh-ye or Ţunb aş Şughrá
Lessingskop *mt.* S. Africa **133** K6
L'Est, Île de *i.* Canada **169** I4
L'Est, Pointe de *pt* Canada **169** I3
Lester U.S.A. **176** D8
Lestijärvi *l.* Fin. **44** M2
Lestijoki *r.* Fin. **44** M2
Les Triagoz *i.* France **50** C4
Les Trois Rivieres Cent. Afr. Rep. **126** C3
Lesung, Bukit *mt.* Indon. **77** F2
Les Vans France **51** K8
Lesvos *i.* Greece *see* Lesbos
Leszno Poland **49** N4
historically known as Lissa
Le Teil France **51** K8
Le Télégraphe *hill* France **51** K5
Letenye Hungary **49** N9
Leteri India **96** C4
Lethabile S. Africa **133** L2
Letha Range *mts* Myanmar **78** A3
Lethbridge *Alta* Canada **167** H5
Lethbridge *Nfld.* Canada **169** K3
Lethem Guyana **199** G4
Le Thillot France **51** M5
Leti *i.* Indon. **75** C5
Leti, Kepulauan *is* Indon. **75** C5
Leticia Col. **198** D6
Leting China **85** H4
Letjiesbos S. Africa **132** G9
Letlhakane Botswana **131** E4
Letlhakeng Botswana **131** E4
Letnerechenskiy Rus. Fed. **40** F2
Letniy Navolok Rus. Fed. **40** G2
Le Touquet-Paris-Plage France **50** H2
Letpadan Myanmar **78** A4
Le Tréport France **50** H2
Letsbo Sweden **45** K3
Letsok-aw Kyun *i.* Myanmar **79** B6
also known as Domel Island
Letsopa S. Africa **133** J3
Lette Island Tonga *see* Late Island
Letterkenny Rep. of Ireland **47** E9
Letung Indon. **77** D2
Letwurung Indon. **75** D4
Lëtzebuerg *country* Europe *see* Luxembourg
Leu Romania **58** F3
Léua Angola **127** D7
Leucas Greece *see* Lefkada
Leucate, Étang de *l.* France **51** J10
also known as Salses, Étang de

Leukas Greece see Lefkada
Leung Shuen Wan Chau i. Hong Kong China see High Island
Leunovo Rus. Fed. 40 G2
Leupp U.S.A. 183 N6
Leura Australia 149 F4
Leuser, Gunung mt. Indon. 76 B2
Leutkirch im Allgäu Germany 48 H8
Leuven Belgium 51 K2 also spelt Louvain
Levadeia Greece 59 D10
Levan Albania 58 A8
Levanger Norway 44 J3
Levante, Riviera di coastal area Italy 56 A4
Levanto Italy 56 B4
Levanzo, Isola di i. Sicilia Italy 57 E10
Levashi Rus. Fed. 102 A4
Levelland U.S.A. 179 B5
Levels N.Z. 153 F12
Leven U.K. 46 J7
Levens France 51 N9
Lévêque, Cape Australia 150 C3
Leverburgh U.K. 46 E6 also known as An t-Ob
Levering U.S.A. 173 I5
Leverkusen Germany 48 D4
Leverville Dem. Rep. Congo see Lusanga
Lévézou mts France 51 I8
Levice Slovakia 49 P7
Levidi Greece 59 D11
Levin N.Z. 152 J8
Lévis Canada 169 G4
Levitha i. Greece 59 H12
Levittown U.S.A. 177 K5
Levka Bulg. 58 H7
Levkás i. Greece see Lefkada
Levkimmi Greece see Lefkimmi
Levoča Slovakia 49 R6
Levočské vrchy mts Slovakia 49 R6
Levroux France 50 H6
Levski Bulg. 58 G5
Levskigrad Bulg. see Karlovo
Lev Tolstoy Rus. Fed. 43 U8
Levuka Fiji 145 G3
Lévuo r. Lith. 42 F5
Lewa Indon. 75 A5
Lewe Myanmar 78 B4
Lewer watercourse Namibia 132 B2
Lewerberg mt. S. Africa 132 B6
Lewes U.K. 47 M13
Lewes U.S.A. 177 J7
Lewin Brzeski Poland 49 O5
Lewis U.S.A. 183 P4
Lewis r. U.S.A. 180 B3
Lewis, Isle of i. U.K. 46 F5 also known as Leodhais, Eilean
Lewis, Lake salt flat Australia 148 B4
Lewisburg OH U.S.A. 176 A6
Lewisburg PA U.S.A. 177 I5
Lewisburg TN U.S.A. 174 C5
Lewisburg WV U.S.A. 176 E8
Lewis Cass, Mount Canada/U.S.A. 166 D3
Lewis Hills hill Canada 169 J3
Lewis Inlet India 95 G3
Lewis Pass N.Z. 153 G10
Lewis Pass National Reserve nature res. N.Z. 153 G10
Lewisporte Canada 169 K3
Lewis Range hills Australia 150 E4
Lewis Range mts U.S.A. 180 D2
Lewis Smith, Lake U.S.A. 175 C5
Lewiston CA U.S.A. 182 B1
Lewiston ID U.S.A. 180 C3
Lewiston ME U.S.A. 177 O1
Lewiston MN U.S.A. 172 B7
Lewistown IL U.S.A. 174 B3
Lewistown MT U.S.A. 180 E3
Lewistown PA U.S.A. 176 H5
Lewisville U.S.A. 179 D5
Lewisville, Lake U.S.A. 179 C5
Lewitz park Germany 48 I2
Lewotobi, Gunung vol. Indon. 75 B5
Lexington GA U.S.A. 175 D5
Lexington IL U.S.A. 172 E10
Lexington KY U.S.A. 176 A7
Lexington MI U.S.A. 173 K7
Lexington MO U.S.A. 178 D4
Lexington MS U.S.A. 175 B5
Lexington NC U.S.A. 174 D5
Lexington NE U.S.A. 178 C3
Lexington OH U.S.A. 176 C5
Lexington SC U.S.A. 175 D5
Lexington TN U.S.A. 174 B5
Lexington VA U.S.A. 176 F8
Lexington Park U.S.A. 177 I7 formerly known as Jarboesville
Leyden Neth. see Leiden
Leye China 86 C3 also known as Tongle
Leyla Dāgh mt. Iran 100 A2
Leyte i. Phil. 74 C4
Leyte Gulf Phil. 74 C4
Leżajsk Poland 49 T5
Lèze r. France 50 H9
Lezha Rus. Fed. 43 V3
Lezha r. Rus. Fed. 43 V2
Lezhë Albania 58 A7 formerly known as Alessio
Lezhi China 86 C2 also known as Tianchi
Lézignan-Corbières France 51 I9
Lezuza Spain 55 I6
L'gov Rus. Fed. 41 E6
Lhagoi Kangri mt. China 89 D6 also known as Hlako Kangri
Lhari China 89 F6 also known as Sirdingka
Lharidon Bight b. Australia 151 A5
Lharigarbo China see Amdo
Lhasa China 89 E6
Lhasa He r. China 89 E6
Lhasoi China 89 F6
Lhatog China 86 A2
Lhazê Xizang China 89 D6 also known as Quxar
Lhazê Xizang China 97 G3
L'Herbaudière, Pointe de pt France 50 D5
Lhokseumawe Indon. 76 B1
Lhoksukon Indon. 76 B1
Lhorong China 97 G3 also known as Zito

▶Lhotse mt. China/Nepal 97 E3
4th highest mountain in the world and in Asia.
world [physical features] 8–9

Lhozhag China 89 E6 also known as Garbo
Lhuentse Bhutan 97 F4
Lhünzê China 89 F6 also known as Xingba
Lhünzhub China 89 E6 also known as Gaindainqoinkor
Liancheng China 87 F3 also known as Lianfeng
Liancheng China see Qinglong
Liancheng China see Guangnan
Liancourt Rocks i. N. Pacific Ocean 91 B6 also known as Take-shima or Tokdo or Tok-tō or Tokto-ri
Lianfeng China see Liancheng
Liang Indon. 75 B3
Lianga Phil. 74 C4
Lianga Bay Phil. 74 C4
Liangaz Hu l. China 87 E2
Liangcheng China 85 G3
Liangdang China 86 C1
Liangfeng China 87 D3
Lianghe China 86 A3 also known as Zhedao
Lianghekou Gansu China 86 C1
Lianghekou Sichuan China 86 B2
Liangjiayoufang China see Youyu
Liangping China 87 C2 also known as Liangshan
Liangpran, Bukit mt. Indon. 77 F2
Liangshan China see Liangping
Liang Shan mt. Myanmar 78 B2
Liangshi China see Shaodong
Liang Timur, Gunung mt. Malaysia 76 C2
Liangwang Shan mts China 86 B3
Liangzhen China 85 F4
Liangzhou China see Wuwei
Lianhe China see Qianjiang
Lianhua China 87 E3 also known as Qinting
Lianhua Shan mts China 87 E4
Lianjiang Fujian China 87 F3 also known as Fengcheng
Lianjiang Guangdong China 87 D4
Lianjiang China see Xingguo
Lianjiangkou China 87 E3
Lian Jiang r. China 78 D2
Liannan China 87 E3 also known as Sanjiang
Lianping China 87 E3 also known as Yuanshan
Lianran China see Anning
Lianshan Guangdong China 87 E3 also known as Jitian
Lianshan Liaoning China 85 I3 formerly known as Jinxi
Liant, Cape pt Thai. see Samae San, Laem
Liantang China see Nanchang
Liantuo China 87 D2
Lianxian China see Lianzhou
Lianyin China 82 A1
Lianyuan China 87 D3 formerly known as Lantian
Lianyungang China 87 F1
Lianzhou China 87 E3 formerly known as Lianxian
Lianzhou China see Hepu
Lianzhushan China 82 C3
Liao r. China 85 I3
Liaocheng China 85 G4
Liaodong Bandao pen. China 85 I3
Liaodong Wan b. China 85 I3
Liaodun China 84 B3
Liaodunzhan China 84 B3
Liaoning prov. China 85 I3
Liaoyang China 85 I3
Liaoyuan China 82 B4
Liaozhong China 85 I3
Liapades Greece 59 A9
Liaqatabad Pak. 101 G3
Liard r. Canada 166 F2
Liard Highway Canada 166 F2
Liard Plateau Canada 166 E2
Liard River Canada 166 E3
Liari Pak. 101 F5
Liat i. Indon. 77 D3
Liathach mt. U.K. 46 G6
Liban country Asia see Lebanon
Liban, Jebel mts Lebanon 108 H3
Libano Col. 198 C3
Libau Latvia see Liepāja
Libby U.S.A. 180 D2
Libenge Dem. Rep. Congo 126 C4
Liberal U.S.A. 178 B4
Liberdade Brazil 207 I9
Liberdade r. Amazonas Brazil 200 C1
Liberdade r. Mato Grosso Brazil 202 A4
Liberec Czech Rep. 49 M5
▶Liberia country Africa 124 C5
africa [countries] 114–117
Liberia Costa Rica 186 B5
Libertad Venez. 198 D2
Libertador General San Martín Arg. 201 D5
Liberty AK U.S.A. 166 A1
Liberty IN U.S.A. 176 A6
Liberty KY U.S.A. 176 A8
Liberty ME U.S.A. 177 P1
Liberty MO U.S.A. 178 D4
Liberty NY U.S.A. 177 K4
Liberty TX U.S.A. 179 D6
Libertyville U.S.A. 172 F8
Libmanan Phil. 74 B3
Libni, Gebel hill Egypt 108 E7
Libo China 87 C3 also known as Yuping
Libobo, Tanjung pt Indon. 75 D3
Libode S. Africa 133 N8
Libohovë Albania 59 B8
Liboi Kenya 128 D4
Libong, Ko i. Thai. 79 B7
Libourne France 50 F8
Libral Well Australia 150 D4
Librazhd Albania 58 B7
Libre, Sierra mts Mex. 184 C2

▶Libreville Gabon 126 A4
Capital of Gabon.

Libuganon r. Phil. 74 C5

▶Libya country Africa 120 B3
4th largest country in Africa. Spelt Al Lībiyah in Arabic.
africa [countries] 114–117

Libyan Desert Egypt/Libya 120 E3
Libyan Plateau Egypt 121 E2
Licantén Chile 204 B4
Licata Sicilia Italy 57 F11
Lice Turkey 107 E3
Lichas pen. Greece 59 D10 also spelt Likhás
Licheng China see Xianyou
Licheng China see Lipu
Licheng Shandong China 85 H4 also known as Hongjialou
Licheng Shanxi China 85 G4
Lichfield N.Z. 152 J6
Lichfield U.K. 47 K11
Lichinga Moz. 129 B8 formerly known as Vila Cabral
Lichte Germany 48 I5
Lichtenburg S. Africa 133 K3
Lichtenfels Germany 48 I5
Lichuan Hubei China 87 D2
Lichuan Jiangxi China 87 F3 also known as Rifeng
Licínio de Almeida Brazil 207 K1
Liciro Moz. 131 H3
Licking r. U.S.A. 176 A6
Ličko Osik Croatia 56 H4
Licun China see Laoshan
Lid' r. Rus. Fed. 43 Q2
Lida Belarus 42 G8
Lidjombo Cent. Afr. Rep. 126 C4
Lidköping Sweden 45 K4
Lidsjöberg Sweden 44 K2
Lidumnieki Latvia 42 I5
Lidzbark Poland 49 Q2
Lidzbark Warmiński Poland 49 R1
Liebenbergs Vlei r. S. Africa 133 M4
Liebenwalde Germany 49 K3
Liebig, Mount Australia 148 A4
Lieblīng Romania 58 C3
▶Liechtenstein country Europe 51 P5
europe [countries] 32–35
Liège Belgium 51 L2 also known as Luik
Liegnitz Poland see Legnica
Lieksa Fin. 44 O3
Lielais Ludzas l. Latvia 42 I5
Lielupe r. Latvia 42 F4
Lielvārde Latvia 42 F5
Lien Sweden 44 L3
Lienz Austria 49 J9
Liepāja Latvia 42 C5 also spelt Liepaya, formerly spelt Libau
Liepaya Latvia see Liepāja
Liepna Latvia 42 I4
Liesjärven kansallispuisto nat. park Fin. 42 E1
Liestal Switz. 51 N5
Lieto Fin. 42 D1
Liétor Spain 55 J6
Lietuva country Europe see Lithuania
Liévin France 51 I2
Lièvre r. Canada 168 F4
Liezen Austria 49 L8
Lifamatola i. Indon. 75 C3
Lifanga Dem. Rep. Congo 126 D4
Liffey r. Rep. of Ireland 47 F10
Lifford Rep. of Ireland 47 E9
Liffré France 50 E4
Lifi Mahuida mt. Arg. 205 C6
Lifou i. New Caledonia 145 F4 also spelt Lifu; formerly known as Chabrol
Lifu i. New Caledonia see Lifou
Lifudzin Rus. Fed. see Rudnyy
Ligao Phil. 74 B3
Ligatne Latvia 42 G4
Lighthouse Reef Belize 185 I5
Lightning Ridge Australia 147 E2
Ligny-en-Barrois France 51 L4
Ligonha r. Moz. 131 H3
Ligonier IN U.S.A. 172 H9
Ligonier PA U.S.A. 176 F5
Ligoúrion Greece see Lygourio
Ligui Mex. 184 C3
Ligure, Mar sea France/Italy see Ligurian Sea
Liguria admin. reg. Italy 56 A4
Ligurian Sea France/Italy 51 O9 also known as Ligure, Mar or Ligurienne, Mer
Ligurienne, Mer sea France/Italy see Ligurian Sea
Ligurta U.S.A. 183 J9
Lihir Group is P.N.G. 145 E2 formerly known as Gerrit Denys
Lihou Reef and Cays Australia 149 F3
Lihue U.S.A. 181 [inset] Y1
Lihula Estonia 42 E3
Liivi laht b. Estonia/Latvia see Riga, Gulf of
Lijiang China 86 B3 also known as Dayan
Lijiang China see Yuanjiang
Lijiazhai China 87 E2
Lik, Nam r. Laos 78 C4
Lika reg. Croatia 56 H4
Likak Iran 100 B4
Likala Dem. Rep. Congo 126 C4
Likasi Dem. Rep. Congo 127 E7 formerly known as Jadotville
Likati Dem. Rep. Congo 126 D4
Likati r. Dem. Rep. Congo 126 E4
Likely Canada 166 F4
Likhachevo Ukr. see Pervomays'kyy
Likhachyovo Ukr. see Pervomays'kyy
Likhás pen. Greece see Lichas
Likhoslavl' Rus. Fed. 43 Q4
Likimi Dem. Rep. Congo 126 D4
Likino-Dulevo Rus. Fed. 43 T6
Likisia East Timor 75 C5 also spelt Liquiçá or Liquissa
Likma India 94 D1
Likolia Dem. Rep. Congo 126 D5
Likouala admin. reg. Congo 126 C4
Likouala r. Congo 126 C5
Likouala aux Herbes r. Congo 126 C5
Liku Indon. 77 E2
Liku Sarawak Malaysia 77 F1
Likupang Indon. 75 C2
L'Île-d'Anticosti, Réserve Faunique de nature res. Canada 169 I3
L'Île-Rousse Corse France 51 O10
Lilienfeld Austria 49 M7
Lilienthal Germany 48 F2
Liling China 87 E3
Liljendal Fin. 42 H1
Lilla Pak. 101 H3
Lilla Edet Sweden 45 K4
Lilla Luleälven r. Sweden 44 M2
Lillbliaken hill Sweden 44 L2
Lille Belgium 51 K1
Lille France 51 J2
Lille Bælt sea chan. Denmark see Little Belt
Lillebonne France 50 G3
Lillehammer Norway 45 J3
Lillesand Norway 45 J4
Lillestrøm Norway 45 J4
Lilley U.S.A. 172 H7
Lillian, Point hill Australia 151 D5
Lillie Glacier Antarctica 223 L2
Lillington U.S.A. 174 E5
Lillooet Canada 166 F5
Lillooet r. Canada 166 F5
Lillooet Range mts Canada 166 F5
Lilo r. Dem. Rep. Congo 126 E5
Lilong India 97 G4

▶Lilongwe Malawi 129 B8
Capital of Malawi.

Lilo Viejo Arg. 204 E2
Liloy Phil. 74 B4
Lily U.S.A. 172 E5
Lim r. Yugo. 58 A5

▶Lima Peru 200 A3
Capital of Peru and 4th most populous city in South America.
world [cities] 24–25

Lima dept Peru 200 A2
Lima MT U.S.A. 180 D3
Lima NY U.S.A. 176 H3
Lima OH U.S.A. 176 A5
Limaão Brazil 199 F4
Lima Duarte Brazil 207 J8
Līmah Oman 105 G2
Lima Islands China see Wanshan Qundao
Liman Rus. Fed. 102 A3
Limanowa Poland 49 R6
Limar Indon. 75 C4
Limari r. Chile 204 C3
Limas Indon. 76 D2
Limassol Cyprus 108 E3 also known as Lemesos
Limavady U.K. 47 F8
Limay r. Arg. 204 C5
Limay Mahuida Arg. 204 D5
Limbach-Oberfrohna Germany 49 J5
Limbang r. Sarawak Malaysia 77 F1
Limbani Peru 200 C3
Limbaži Latvia 42 F4
Limbdi India 96 A5
Limbe Cameroon 125 H5 formerly known as Victoria
Limboto Indon. 75 B2
Limboto, Danau l. Indon. 75 B2
Limbuè Moz. 131 H3
Limbungan Indon. 77 F3
Limbunya Australia 148 A3
Limburg an der Lahn Germany 48 F5
Lim Chu Kang Sing. 76 [inset]
Lim Chu Kang hill Sing. 76 [inset]
Lime Acres S. Africa 132 H5
Limehills N.Z. 153 C14
Limeira Brazil 206 F9
Limenaria Greece 58 F8
Limerick Rep. of Ireland 47 D11 also spelt Luimneach
Limestone U.S.A. 176 C9
Limestone Point Canada 167 L4
Limfjorden sea chan. Denmark 45 J4
Limia r. Spain 54 C3
Limin Chersonisou Greece 59 G13
Limingen Norway 44 K2
Limingen l. Norway 44 K2
Liminka Fin. 44 N2
Limmen Bight b. Australia 148 C2
Limmen Bight River r. Australia 148 B2
Limni Greece 59 E10
Limnos i. Greece 59 G9 also spelt Lemnos
Limoeiro Brazil 202 F3
Limoges France 50 H7
Limón Costa Rica 186 C5
Limón Hond. 186 B4
Limon U.S.A. 178 B4
Limonum France see Poitiers
Limoquije Bol. 200 D3
Limousin admin. reg. France 50 H7
Limousin, Plateaux du France 50 H7
Limoux France 51 I9
Limpopo r. S. Africa/Zimbabwe 131 G5
Limu China 87 D3
Limulunga Zambia 127 D8
Linaälven r. Sweden 44 M2
Līnah Saudi Arabia 104 C1
Linakeng Lesotho 133 M6
Linakhamari Rus. Fed. 44 O1
Lin'an China see Jianshui
Lin'an China 87 F2
Linao Bay Phil. 74 C5
Linapacan i. Phil. 74 A4
Linapacan Strait Phil. 74 A4
Linares Chile 204 C4
Linares Mex. 185 F3
Linares Spain 55 H6
Linas, Monte mt. Sardegna Italy 57 A9
Linau Balui plat. Sarawak Malaysia 77 F2
Lincang China 86 B4 also known as Fengxiang
Lincheng China see Lingao
Lincheng China see Huitong
Linchuan China 87 F3 formerly known as Fuzhou
Linck Nunataks Antarctica 222 R1
Lincoln Arg. 204 E4
Lincoln U.K. 47 L10 historically known as Lindum
Lincoln CA U.S.A. 182 C3
Lincoln IL U.S.A. 174 B3
Lincoln KS U.S.A. 178 C4
Lincoln ME U.S.A. 174 G2
Lincoln MI U.S.A. 173 J6

▶Lincoln NE U.S.A. 178 C3
State capital of Nebraska.

Lincoln City U.S.A. 180 A3
Lincoln Island Paracel Is 72 D3
Lincoln National Park Australia 146 B3
Lincoln Sea Canada/Greenland 165 O1
Lincolnshire Wolds hills U.K. 47 L10
Linda, Serra hills Brazil 202 D5
Lindas Norway 46 R3
Lindau (Bodensee) Germany 48 G8
Lindeman Group is Australia 149 F4
Linden Canada 167 H5
Linden Guyana 199 G3 formerly known as Mackenzie
Linden AL U.S.A. 175 C5
Linden CA U.S.A. 182 C3
Linden NJ U.S.A. 177 K5
Linden TN U.S.A. 174 C5
Linden TX U.S.A. 179 D5
Lindenow Fjord inlet Greenland see Kangerlussuatsiaq
Lindesberg Sweden 45 K4
Líndhos Greece see Lindos
Lindi r. Dem. Rep. Congo 126 E4
Lindi Tanz. 129 C7
Lindi admin. reg. Tanz. 129 C7
Lindisfarne i. U.K. see Holy Island
Lindley S. Africa 133 L4
Lindóia Brazil 206 G9
Lindome Sweden 45 K4
Lindong China 85 H3 also known as Bairin Zuoqi
Lindos Greece 59 J12 also spelt Líndhos
Lindos, Akra pt Greece 59 J12
Lindsay Canada 168 E4
Lindsay CA U.S.A. 182 E5
Lindsborg U.S.A. 178 C4
Lindsdal Sweden 45 L4
Lindside U.S.A. 176 E8
Lindum U.K. see Lincoln
Line Islands S. Pacific Ocean 221 H5
Linets Rus. Fed. 43 Q9
Linfen China 85 F4
Lingampet India 94 D2
Linganamakki Reservoir India 94 B3
Lingao China 87 D5 also known as Lincheng
Lingayen Phil. 74 B2
Lingayen Gulf Phil. 74 B2
Lingbao China 87 D1 formerly known as Guoluezhen
Lingbi China 87 F1
Lingcheng China see Lingshan
Lingcheng China see Lingshui
Lingcheng China see Lingxian
Lingchuan Guangxi China 87 D3
Lingchuan Shanxi China 85 G5
Lingelethu S. Africa 133 K9
Lingelihle S. Africa 133 J9
Lingen (Ems) Germany 48 E3
Lingga i. Indon. 76 D3
Lingga, Kepulauan is Indon. 76 D3
Linggo Co l. China 89 E5
Lingig Phil. 74 C5
Lingle U.S.A. 180 F4
Lingomo Dem. Rep. Congo 126 D4
Lingqiu China 85 G4
Lingshan China 87 D4 also known as Lingcheng
Lingshan Wan b. China 85 I5
Lingshi Bhutan see Lingzhi
Lingshi China 85 F4
Lingshui China 87 D5 also known as Lingcheng
Lingsugur India 94 C2
Lingtai China 85 E5 also known as Zhongtai
Linguère Senegal 124 B3
Lingui China 87 D3
Lingxi China see Yongshun
Lingxian China see Yanling
Lingxian China 85 H4 also known as Lingcheng
Lingxiang China 87 E2
Lingyuan China 85 H3
Lingyun China 86 C3 also known as Sicheng
Lingzhi Bhutan 97 F4 also spelt Lingshi
Lingzi Thang Plains l. Aksai Chin 89 B5
Linhai Liaoning China 85 I3 also known as Dalinghe; formerly known as Jinxian
Linhai Zhejiang China 87 G2
Linhares Brazil 203 D6
Linh Cam Vietnam 78 D4
Linhe China 85 E3
Linhpa Myanmar 78 A2
Linjiang China see Shanghang
Linjiang China 82 B4
Linköping Sweden 45 K4
Linkou China 82 C3
Linksness U.K. 46 I5
Linkuva Lith. 42 E5
Linli China 87 D2
Linlü Shan mt. China 85 G4
Linmingguan China see Yongnian
Linn U.S.A. 174 B4
Linn, Mount U.S.A. 182 B1
Linnansaaren kansallispuisto nat. park Fin. 44 O3
Linnhe, Loch inlet U.K. 46 G7
Linosa, Isola di i. Sicilia Italy 57 E13
Linova Belarus 42 F9
Linqing China 85 G4
Linru China see Ruzhou
Lins Brazil 206 D8
Linsan Guinea 124 B4
Linshui China 86 C2 also known as Dingping
Linta r. Madag. 131 [inset] J5
Lintah, Selat sea chan. Indon. 75 A5
Lintan China 86 B1
Lintao China 84 D5 also known as Taoyang
Linth r. Switz. 51 P5
Linthal Switz. 51 P6
Linton U.S.A. 178 B2
Lintong China 87 D1 also known as Lishan
Linville U.S.A. 176 D9
Linxi China 85 H3
Linxia China 84 D5
Linxian China see Linzhou
Linxian China 85 F4
Linxiang China 87 E2
Linyanti r. Botswana/Namibia 131 E3
Linyanti Swamp Namibia 130 D3
Linyi Shandong China 85 H4
Linyi Shandong China 85 H5
Linyi Shanxi China 85 F5
Linying China 87 E1
Linz Austria 49 L7
Linze China 84 D4 formerly known as Shahepu or Shahezhen
Linzhou China 85 G4 also known as Linxian
Lioma Moz. 131 H2
Lion, Golfe du g. France 51 J10 English form Lions, Gulf of
Lions, Gulf of France see Lion, Golfe du
Lions Den Zimbabwe 131 F3
Lion's Head Canada 173 L6
Lioua Chad 120 B6
Liouesso Congo 126 B4
Lipa Phil. 74 B3
Lipari Isole Lipari Italy 57 G10
Lipari, Isola i. Isole Lipari Italy 57 G10
Lipari, Isole is Italy 57 G10
Lipatkain Indon. 76 C2
Lipawki Belarus 42 I6
Liperi Fin. 44 O3
Lipetsk Rus. Fed. 43 U9
Lipetskaya Oblast' admin. div. Rus. Fed. 43 T9 English form Lipetsk Oblast
Lipetsk Oblast admin. div. Rus. Fed. see Lipetskaya Oblast'
Lipez, Cordillera de mts Bol. 200 D5
Lipiany Poland 49 L2
Lipin Bor Rus. Fed. 43 S1
Liping China 87 D3 also known as Defeng
Lipitsy Rus. Fed. 43 S8
Lipki Rus. Fed. 43 S8
Lipljan Kosovo, Srbija Yugo. 58 C6
Lipnaya Gorka Rus. Fed. 43 O2
Lipník nad Bečvou Czech Rep. 49 O6
Lipno Poland 49 Q3
Lipno, Vodní nádrž resr Czech Rep. 49 L7
Lipova Romania 58 C2
Lipovtsy Rus. Fed. 90 B2
Lipovu Romania 58 E4
Lippe r. Germany 48 D4
Lippstadt Germany 48 F4
Lipscomb U.S.A. 179 B4
Lipsk Poland 49 U2
Lipsko Poland 49 S4
Lipsoi i. Greece see Leipsoi
Lipti Lekh pass Nepal 96 D3
Liptovská Mara, Vodná nádrž resr Slovakia 49 Q6
Liptovský Hrádok Slovakia 49 Q6
Liptovský Mikuláš Slovakia 49 Q6
Liptrap, Cape Australia 147 E4
Liptsy Rus. Fed. 43 P6
Lipu China 87 D3 also known as Licheng
Lipusz Poland 49 O1
Liquiçá East Timor see Likisia
Liquissa East Timor see Likisia
Lira Uganda 128 B4
Liran i. Indon. 75 C4
Liranga Congo 126 C5
Liri r. Italy 56 F7
Liri, Jebel el mt. Sudan 128 A2
Lirung Indon. 75 C2
Lis Albania 58 B7
Lisa Romania 58 F3
Lisakovsk Kazakh. 103 E1
Lisala Dem. Rep. Congo 126 D4
L'Isalo, Massif de mts Madag. 131 [inset] J4
L'Isalo, Parc National de nat. park Madag. 131 [inset] J4
Lisboa Port. see Lisbon
Lisboa admin. dist. Port. 54 B5

▶Lisbon Port. 54 B6
Capital of Portugal. Also spelt Lisboa; historically known as Olisipo.

Lisbon IL U.S.A. 172 E9
Lisbon ME U.S.A. 177 O1
Lisbon ND U.S.A. 178 C2
Lisbon NH U.S.A. 177 N1
Lisbon OH U.S.A. 176 E5
Lisbon Falls U.S.A. 177 O2
Lisburn U.K. 47 F9
Liscannor Bay Rep. of Ireland 47 C11
Liscomb Game Sanctuary nature res. Canada 169 I4
Lisdoonvarna Rep. of Ireland 47 C10
Lisec mt. Macedonia 58 D7
L'Iseran, Col de pass France 51 N7
Lishan China see Lintong
Lishan Taiwan 87 G3
Lishe Jiang r. China 86 B3
Lishi China see Dingnan
Lishi China 85 F4
Līshtar-e Bālā Iran 100 B4
Lishu China 82 B4
Lishui Jiangsu China 87 F2
Lishui Zhejiang China 87 F2
Li Shui r. China 87 D2
Lisichansk Ukr. see Lysychans'k
Lisieux France 50 G3
Lisiy Nos Rus. Fed. 43 L1
Liskeard U.K. 47 H13
Liski Rus. Fed. 41 F6 formerly known as Georgiu-Dezh
L'Isle-en-Dodon France 50 G9
L'Isle-Jourdain France 50 H9
L'Isle-sur-la-Sorgue France 51 L9
L'Isle-sur-le-Doubs France 51 M5
Lismore Australia 147 G2
Lismore N.Z. 153 F11
Lismore Rep. of Ireland 47 E11
Lisne Ukr. 58 K2
Liss mt. Saudi Arabia 109 J6
Lissa Croatia see Vis
Lissa Poland see Leszno
Lisseri, Oued watercourse Tunisia 123 H2
Listafjorden b. Norway 45 I4
Lister, Mount Antarctica 223 K1
Listore watercourse Australia 148 C5
Listowel Canada 168 D5
Listowel Rep. of Ireland 47 C11
Listowel Downs Australia 149 E5
Listvyaga, Khrebet mts Kazakh./Rus. Fed. 88 D1
Listvyanka Rus. Fed. 84 E1
Liswarta r. Poland 49 P4
Lit Sweden 44 K3
Litang Guangxi China 87 D4
Litang Sichuan China 86 B2 also known as Gaocheng
Litang Qu r. China 86 B2
Litani r. Fr. Guiana/Suriname 199 H4
Lītani r. Lebanon 108 G4
Litchfield CA U.S.A. 182 D1
Litchfield IL U.S.A. 174 B4
Litchfield MI U.S.A. 173 I8
Litchfield MN U.S.A. 178 D2
Litembe Tanz. 129 D7
Litene Latvia 42 I4
Lith, Wādī al watercourse Saudi Arabia 104 C3
Lithgow Australia 147 F3
Lithino, Akra pt Greece 59 F14
▶Lithuania country Europe 42 E6
known as Lietuva in Lithuanian; formerly known as Litovskaya S.S.R.
europe [countries] 32–35
Litija Slovenia 56 G2
Lititz U.S.A. 177 I5
Litke, Mys c. Rus. Fed. 39 S2
Litochoro Greece 59 D8
Litoměřice Czech Rep. 49 L5
Litomyšl Czech Rep. 49 N6
Litovel Czech Rep. 49 O6
Litovko Rus. Fed. 82 D2
Litovskaya S.S.R. country Europe see Lithuania
Little r. LA U.S.A. 179 D6
Little r. OK U.S.A. 179 D5
Little r. TX U.S.A. 179 C6
Little Abaco i. Bahamas 186 D1
Little Abitibi r. Canada 168 D3
Little Abitibi Lake Canada 168 D3
Little Aden Yemen see 'Adan as Sughra
Little Andaman i. India 95 G4
Little Bahama Bank sea feature Bahamas 186 D1
Little Barrier i. N.Z. 152 J4
Little Bay de Noc U.S.A. 172 F5
Little Belt sea chan. Denmark 45 J5 also known as Lille Bælt
Little Belt Mountains U.S.A. 180 E3
Little Bighorn r. U.S.A. 180 F3
Little Bitter Lake Egypt 108 D7 also known as Murrat el Sughra, Buheirat
Little Blue r. U.S.A. 178 C4
Little Bow r. Canada 167 H5
Little Buffalo r. Canada 167 H2
Little Cayman i. Cayman Is 186 C3
Little Churchill r. Canada 167 M3
Little Coco Island Cocos Is 79 A5
Little Colorado r. U.S.A. 183 M5
Little Creek Peak U.S.A. 183 L4
Little Current Canada 168 D4
Little Current r. Canada 168 C3
Little Desert National Park Australia 146 D4
Little Egg Harbor inlet U.S.A. 177 K6
Little Exuma i. Bahamas 186 E2
Little Falls MN U.S.A. 178 D2
Little Falls NY U.S.A. 177 K2
Littlefield AZ U.S.A. 183 K5
Littlefield TX U.S.A. 179 B5
Little Fish r. S. Africa 133 K10
Little Fork r. U.S.A. 174 A1
Little Fort Canada 166 F5
Little Grand Rapids Canada 167 M4
Little Grass Valley Reservoir U.S.A. 182 C2
Little Inagua Island Bahamas 187 E2
Little Kanawha r. U.S.A. 176 D6
Little Karas Berg plat. Namibia 132 C4
Little Karoo plat. S. Africa 132 E10
Little Lake U.S.A. 182 G6
Little Mecatina r. Canada 169 I3 also known as Petit Mécatina
Little Mecatina Island Canada see Petit Mécatina, Île du
Little Miami r. U.S.A. 176 A6
Little Minch sea chan. U.K. 46 E6
Little Missouri r. U.S.A. 178 B2
Little Muskingum r. U.S.A. 176 D6
Little Nicobar i. India 95 G5
Little Olifants r. S. Africa 133 N2
Little Pamir mts Afgh. 101 H2
Little Pic r. Canada 172 G2
Little Powder r. U.S.A. 180 F3
Little Rann marsh India 96 A5
Little Red r. U.S.A. 179 E5
Little Red River Canada 167 H3
Little River N.Z. 153 G11
Little River U.S.A. 175 E5

▶Little Rock U.S.A. 179 D5
State capital of Arkansas.

Littlerock U.S.A. 182 G7
Little Sable Point U.S.A. 172 G7
Little Sachigo Lake Canada 168 A2
Little Salmon Lake Canada 166 C2
Little Salt Lake U.S.A. 183 L4
Little Sandy Desert Australia 150 B4
Little San Salvador i. Bahamas 186 E1
Little Sioux r. U.S.A. 178 C3
Little Smoky Canada 167 G4
Little Smoky r. Canada 167 G4
Little Snake r. U.S.A. 180 E4
Littlestown U.S.A. 177 H6
Little Tibet reg. Jammu and Kashmir see Ladakh
Littleton NC U.S.A. 176 H9
Littleton NH U.S.A. 177 N1
Littleton WV U.S.A. 176 E6
Little Traverse Bay U.S.A. 173 H5
Little Tupper Lake U.S.A. 177 K1
Little Turtle Lake Canada 172 A2
Little Valley U.S.A. 176 G3
Little Wabash r. U.S.A. 174 B4
Little Wanganui N.Z. 152 G9
Little White r. U.S.A. 178 B3
Little Wichita r. U.S.A. 179 C5
Little Wind r. U.S.A. 180 E4
Little Wood r. U.S.A. 180 D4
Little Zab r. Iraq see Zāb aş Şaghīr, Nahr az
Littoral prov. Cameroon 125 H5
Litunde Moz. 129 B8
Lituya Bay U.S.A. 166 B3
Litvínov Czech Rep. 49 K5
Liu r. China 85 H3
Liu r. China 85 I3
Liu Estonia 42 F3
Liuba China 86 C1
Liuchiu Yü i. Taiwan 87 G4
Liuchong He r. China 86 C3
Liuchow China see Liuzhou
Liugong Dao i. China 85 I4
Liugu r. China 85 I3
Liuhe China 82 B4
Liuheng Dao i. China 87 G2
Liujiachang China 87 D2
Liujiang China 87 D3 also known as Labao
Liujiaxia China see Yongjing
Liujiaxia Shuiku resr China 84 D5
Liulin China see Jonê
Liulin China 85 F4
Liupai China see Tian'e
Liupan Shan mts China 85 E5
Liupanshui China see Lupanshui
Liupo Moz. 131 H2
Liure Hond. 186 B4
Liushuquan China 84 B3
Liuwa Plain Zambia 127 D8
Liuwa Plain National Park Zambia 127 D8
Liuyang China 87 E2
Liuyang He r. China 87 E2
Liuzhangzhen China see Yuanqu

Liuzhou China **87** D3
formerly known as Liuchow
Livada, Akra *pt* Greece **59** G11
Livadi *i.* Greece **59** H12
Livadiya Rus. Fed. **82** D4
Līvāni Latvia **42** I5
Livarot France **50** G3
Livberze Latvia **42** F5
Live Oak *CA* U.S.A. **182** C2
Live Oak *FL* U.S.A. **175** D6
Liveringa Australia **150** D3
Livermore U.S.A. **182** C4
Livermore, Mount U.S.A. **181** F7
Liverpool Australia **147** F3
Liverpool Canada **169** H4
Liverpool U.K. **47** J10
Liverpool U.S.A. **177** I2
Liverpool Bay Canada **164** F3
Liverpool Plains Australia **147** F2
Liverpool Range *mts* Australia **147** F2
Livingston *AL* U.S.A. **182** D4
Livingston *CA* U.S.A. **182** D4
Livingston *KY* U.S.A. **176** A8
Livingston *LA* U.S.A. **175** B6
Livingston *MT* U.S.A. **180** E3
Livingston *TX* U.S.A. **177** K6
Livingston *WI* U.S.A. **172** C8
Livingston, Lake U.S.A. **179** D6
Livingstone Zambia **127** E9
also known as Maramba
Livingstonia Malawi **129** B7
Livingston Island Antarctica **222** T2
Livingston Manor U.S.A. **177** K4
Livingston Mountains N.Z. **153** C12
Livno Bos.-Herz. **56** J5
Livny Rus. Fed. **43** S9
Livo *r.* Rus. Fed. **44** O2
Livonia *MI* U.S.A. **173** J8
Livonia *NY* U.S.A. **176** H3
Livorno Italy **56** C5
historically known as Leghorn
Livradois, Monts du *mts* France **51** J7
Livradois Forez, Parc Naturel Régional du *nature res.* France **51** J7
Livramento do Brumado Brazil **202** D5
Livron-sur-Drôme France **51** K8
Liwā Oman **105** G2
Liwa', Wādī al *watercourse* Syria **109** H5
Liwale Tanz. **129** C7
Liwiec *r.* Poland **49** S3
Liwonde Malawi **129** B8
Liwonde National Park Malawi **129** B8
Liwu China *see* Lixian
Lixian *Gansu* China **86** C1
Lixian *Hebei* China **85** G4
also known as Liwu
Lixian *Hunan* China **87** D2
Lixian *Sichuan* China **86** B2
also known as Zagunao
Lixin China **87** F1
Lixouri Greece **59** B10
Lixus Morocco *see* Larache
Liyang China **87** F2
Liyuan China *see* Sangzhi
Liz *r.* Port. **54** C5
Lizarda Brazil **202** C4
Lizard Island Australia **149** E2
Lizard Point U.K. **47** G14
Lizarra Spain *see* Estella
Lizemores U.S.A. **176** D7
Liziping China **86** B2
Lizonne *r.* France **50** G7
Ljig Srbija Yugo. **58** E4
Ljubija Bos.-Herz. **56** I4

▶ **Ljubljana** Slovenia **56** G2
Capital of Slovenia. Historically known as
Emona or Laibach.

Ljubuški Bos.-Herz. **56** J5
Ljugarn Sweden **45** L4
Ljunga Sweden **44** L3
Ljungan *r.* Sweden **44** L3
Ljungaverk Sweden **44** L3
Ljungby Sweden **45** K4
Ljungskile Sweden **45** J4
Ljusdal Sweden **44** L3
Ljusnan *r.* Sweden **45** L3
Ljusne Sweden **45** L3
Ljutomer Slovenia **56** H2
Llagostera Spain **55** N3
Llaima, Volcán *vol.* Chile **204** C5
Llanbedr U.K. *see* Lampeter
Llançà Spain **55** O2
also spelt Llansá
Llancanelo, Salina *salt flat* Arg. **204** C4
Llandello U.K. **47** I12
Llandovery U.K. **47** I12
also known as Llanymddyfri
Llandrindod Wells U.K. **47** I11
Llandudno U.K. **47** I10
Llanelli U.K. **47** H12
Llanes Spain **54** F1
Llangollen U.K. **47** I11
Llangurig U.K. **47** I11
Llano *r.* Mex. **184** C2
Llano U.S.A. **179** C6
Llano *r.* U.S.A. **179** C6
Llano Estacado *plain* U.S.A. **179** B5
Llanos *plain* Col./Venez. **198** D3

Llanquihue, Lago *l.* Chile **205** B6
Llansá Spain *see* Llançà
Llanymddyfri U.K. *see* Llandovery
Llata Peru **200** A2
Lleida Spain **55** L3
also spelt Lérida
Llentrisca, Cap *c.* Spain **55** M6
Llerena Spain **54** E6
Llica Bol. **200** C4
Llíria Spain **55** K5
Llobregat *r.* Spain **55** M3
Llodio Spain **55** I1
Lloret de Mar Spain **55** N3
Llorgara *nat. park* Albania **59** A8
Lloyd Bay Australia **149** E1
Lloyd George, Mount Canada **166** E3
Lloyd Lake Canada **167** I3
Lloydminster Canada **167** I4
Lluchmayor Spain *see* Llucmajor
Llucmajor Spain **55** N5
also spelt Lluchmayor
Lô *r.* China/Vietnam **86** C1
Loa *r.* Chile **200** C5
Loa U.S.A. **183** M3
Loagan Bunut National Park *Sarawak*
Malaysia **77** F2
Loakulu Indon. **77** G3
Loanda Brazil **203** A7
Loano Italy **56** A4
Loay Phil. **74** C4
Lob' *r.* Rus. Fed. **43** Q5
Loban' *r.* Rus. Fed. **40** I4
Lobanovo Rus. Fed. **43** T8
Lobata Indon. **75** B3
Lôbau Germany **49** K4
Lobaye *pref.* Cent. Afr. Rep. **126** C3
Lobaye *r.* Cent. Afr. Rep. **126** C3
Löbenberg *hill* Germany **49** J4
Loberia Arg. **204** F5
Łobez Poland **49** M2
Lobito Angola **127** B8
Lobitos Peru **198** A6
Lobnya Rus. Fed. **43** S5
Loboko Congo **126** C5
Lobón Spain **54** E6
Lobos Arg. **204** F4
Lobos, Cabo *c.* Mex. **184** B2
Lobos, Isla de *i.* Mex. **185** F4
Lobos de Afuera, Islas *is* Peru **198** A6
Lobos de Tierra, Isla *i.* Peru **198** A6
Loburg Germany **48** J3
Loburn N.Z. **153** G11
Łobżenica Poland **49** O2
Locarno Switz. **51** O6
Lochaline U.K. **46** G7
Lochalsh Canada **173** I2
Lo Chau *i.* Hong Kong China *see*
Beaufort Island
Loch Baghasdail U.K. *see* Lochboisdale
Lochboisdale U.K. **46** E6
also spelt Loch Baghasdail
Lochem National Park Australia **149** D5
Loches France **50** G5
Loch Garman Rep. of Ireland *see* Wexford
Lochgilphead U.K. **46** G7
Lochiel S. Africa **133** O3
Lochinvar National Park Zambia **127** E8
Lochinver U.K. **46** G5
Lochmaddy U.K. **46** E6
also known as Loch nam Madadh
Lochnagar *mt.* U.K. **46** I7
Loch nam Madadh U.K. *see* Lochmaddy
Lochow Poland **49** S3
Lochranza U.K. **46** G8
Lochsa *r.* U.S.A. **180** D3
Lochy, Loch *l.* U.K. **46** H7
Lock Australia **146** B3
Lockbourne U.S.A. **176** C6
Lockeford U.S.A. **182** C3
Lockerbie U.K. **47** I8
Lockhart Australia **147** E3
Lockhart U.S.A. **179** C6
Lockhart River Australia **149** D2
Lockhart River Aboriginal Reserve
Australia **149** D2
Lock Haven U.S.A. **176** H4
Löcknitz *r.* Germany **48** I2
Lockport U.S.A. **176** G3
Locminé France **50** D5
Lôc Ninh Vietnam **79** D6
Locorotondo Italy **57** J8
Locri Italy **57** I10
Locumba *r.* Peru **200** C4
Lod Israel **108** F6
also known as Lydda
Loddon *r.* Australia **147** D3
Lode Latvia **42** G4
Lodève France **51** J9
Lodeynoye Pole Rus. Fed. **43** O1
Lodge, Mount Canada/U.S.A. **166** B3
Lodge Creek *r.* Canada/U.S.A. **167** I5
Lodhikheda India **96** C5
Lodhran Pak. **101** G4
Lodi Italy **56** B3
Lodi *CA* U.S.A. **182** D7
Lodi *OH* U.S.A. **176** C4
Lodi *WI* U.S.A. **172** D7
Loding Norway **44** K2
Lodingen Norway **44** K1
Lodja Dem. Rep. Congo **126** D5
Lodomeria Rus. Fed. *see* Vladimir
Lodosa Spain **55** I2
Lodrani India **96** A5
Lodwar Kenya **128** B4
Łódź Poland **49** Q4
Lodz Poland *see* Łódź
English form Lodz
Loei Thai. **78** C4
Loeriesfontein S. Africa **132** D7
Lofoten *is* Norway **44** K1
Lofsdalen Sweden **45** K3
Lofter S. Africa **133** J7
Lofty Range *hills* Australia **150** B5
Log Rus. Fed. **41** G6
Loga Niger **125** F3
Logageng S. Africa **133** I2
Logan *IA* U.S.A. **178** D3
Logan *NM* U.S.A. **181** G6
Logan *OH* U.S.A. **176** C6
Logan *UT* U.S.A. **180** E4
Logan *WV* U.S.A. **176** D8

▶ **Logan, Mount** Canada **166** A2
2nd highest mountain in North America.
northamerica [landscapes] ▶▶ 156–157

Logan, Mount U.S.A. **180** D2
Logan Creek *r.* Australia **149** E4
Logan Creek *r.* U.S.A. **178** D3
Logandale U.S.A. **183** J3
Logan Lake Canada **166** F5
Logan Mountains Canada **166** D2
Logansport *IN* U.S.A. **174** C3
Logansport *LA* U.S.A. **179** D6
Logatec Slovenia **56** G3
Lôgdeälven *r.* Sweden **44** L2
Loge *r.* Angola **127** B6
Logone *r.* Africa **126** B2
Logone Birni Cameroon **125** I4
Logone Occidental *pref.* Chad **126** B2
Logone Oriental *pref.* Chad **126** C2
Logreşti Romania **58** E4
Logroño Spain **55** I2
Løgstør Denmark **45** J4
Løgstrup Denmark **45** J4
Logtak Lake India **97** G4
Lohardaga India **97** E5
Loharu India **96** B3
Lohatlha S. Africa **132** H5

Lohawat India **96** B4
Lohil *r.* China/India *see* Zayü Qu
Lohīni Fin. **44** N2
Lohiniva Fin. **44** N2
Lohja Fin. **45** N3
Lohjanjärvi *l.* Fin. **42** E1
Löhne Germany **48** F3
Löhne (Oldenburg) Germany **48** F3
Lohtaja Fin. **44** M2
Lohusuu Estonia **42** I3
Loi, Nam *r.* Myanmar **78** C3
Loikaw Myanmar **78** B4
Loi Lan *mt.* Myanmar/Thai. **78** B4
Loi-lem Myanmar **78** B3
Loimaa Fin. **45** M3
Loimaan kunta Fin. **42** D1
Loipyet Hills Myanmar **78** B2
Loir *r.* France **50** F5
Loir, Les Vaux du *valley* France **50** G5
Loire *r.* France **51** D5
Loisach *r.* Germany **48** I8
Loi Sang *mt.* Myanmar **78** B3
Loi Song *mt.* Myanmar **78** B3
Loita Plains Kenya **128** B5
Loja Ecuador **198** B6
Loja *prov.* Ecuador **198** B6
Loja Spain **54** G7
Lokan *r.* Sabah Malaysia **77** G1
Lokandu Dem. Rep. Congo **126** E5
Lokan tekojärvi *l.* Fin. **44** N2
Lokchim *r.* Rus. Fed. **40** I3
Loken Belgium **51** K1
Loki *r.* Iceland **44** [inset] C2
Lokichar Kenya **128** B4
Lokichokio Kenya **128** B3
Lokilalaki, Gunung *mt.* Indon. **75** B3
Lokka Fin. **44** N2
Løkken Denmark **45** J4
Løkken Norway **44** J3
Loknya Rus. Fed. **43** L5
Lokofe Dem. Rep. Congo **126** D5
Lokoja Nigeria **125** G5
Lokolama Dem. Rep. Congo **126** C5
Lokolo *r.* Dem. Rep. Congo **126** C5
Lokomo Cameroon **125** I6
Lokoro *r.* Dem. Rep. Congo **126** C5
Lokosafa Cent. Afr. Rep. **126** C4
Lokossa Benin **125** F5
Lokot' Rus. Fed. **43** P9
Loksa Estonia **42** G2
Loktak, Lake India *see* Loktak Lake
Lokutu Dem. Rep. Congo *see* Elisabetha
Lol Sudan **126** F3
Lol *watercourse* Sudan **126** F2
Lola Angola **127** B8
Lola Guinea **124** C5
Lola, Mount U.S.A. **182** D2
Lolland *i.* Denmark **45** J5
Lolle *watercourse* Sudan **128** A2
Lollondo Tanz. **128** B5
Lolo Dem. Rep. Congo **126** C4
Lolo U.S.A. **180** D3
Loloda Indon. **75** C2
Loloda Utara, Kepulauan *is* Indon. **75** C2
Lolodorf Cameroon **125** H6
Lolo Pass U.S.A. **180** D3
Lolowau Indon. **76** B2
Lolwane S. Africa **132** H3
Lom Bulg. **58** E5
Lom Norway **45** J3
Lom Rus. Fed. **43** U4
Loma U.S.A. **182** D2
Loma Alta Bol. **200** D2
Lomako *r.* Dem. Rep. Congo **126** D4
Lomaloma Fiji **145** H3
Lomami *r.* Dem. Rep. Congo **126** D4
Loma Mountains Sierra Leone **124** C4
Lomar Pass Afgh. **101** F3
Lomas Peru **200** B3
Lomas Coloradas *hills* Arg. **205** D6
Lomas de Zamora Arg. **204** F4
Lomati *r.* S. Africa *see* Mlumati
Lombarda, Serra *hills* Brazil **199** H4
Lombardia *admin. reg.* Italy **56** B3
Lombardia Australia **150** C3
Lomblen *i.* Indon. **75** B5
Lombok *i.* Indon. **77** F5
Lombok *i.* Indon. **77** G1
Lombok, Selat *sea chan.* Indon. **77** F5

▶ **Lomé** Togo **125** F5
Capital of Togo.

Lomela *r.* Dem. Rep. Congo **126** D5
Lomié Cameroon **125** I6
Lomira U.S.A. **172** E7
Lommel Belgium **51** L1
Lomond Canada **169** J3
Lomond, Loch *l.* U.K. **46** H7
Lomonosov Rus. Fed. **43** K2
Lomont *hills* France **51** M5
Lomovoye Rus. Fed. **40** G2
Lomphat Cambodia *see* Lumphăt
Lompobattang, Gunung *mt.* Indon. **75** A4
Lompoc U.S.A. **182** D7
Lom Sak Thai. **78** C4
Łomża Sweden **44** L2
Łomża Poland **49** T2
Lonar India **94** C2
Lonato Italy **56** C3
Lonavale India **94** B2
Loncopue Arg. **204** C5
Londa Bangl. **97** F5
Londa India **94** B3
Londinium U.K. *see* London
Londoko Rus. Fed. **82** D2
London Canada **168** D5

▶ **London** U.K. **47** L12
Capital of the United Kingdom and of
England. 3rd most populous city in Europe.
Historically known as Londinium.
world [cities] ▶▶ 24–25
europe [environments] ▶▶ 36–37

London *KY* U.S.A. **176** A8
London *OH* U.S.A. **176** B6
London City *airport* U.K. **47** M12
Londonderry U.K. **47** E9
also known as Derry *or* Doire
Londonderry U.S.A. **177** M2
Londonderry, Cape Australia **150** D2
Londonderry, Isla *i.* Chile **205** B9
Londres Arg. **204** D2
Lone Mountain U.S.A. **183** I4
Lone Pine U.S.A. **182** F5
Long Thai. **78** B4
Longa Angola **127** C8
Longa *r. Bengo/Cuanza Sul* Angola **127** B7
Longa *r. Cuando Cubango* Angola **127** C9
Longa, Proliv *sea chan.* Rus. Fed. **39** R2
English form De Long Strait
Longagung Indon. **77** F2
Long Akah *Sarawak Malaysia* **77** F2
Long'an China **87** C4
Long'an China *see* Pingwu
Longarone Italy **56** E2
Longavi, Nevado de *mt.* Chile **204** C5
Long Bay U.S.A. **175** E5
Long Beach *CA* U.S.A. **182** F8
Long Beach *WA* U.S.A. **180** A3
Longbia Indon. **77** G2
Longboh Indon. **77** F2
Long Branch U.S.A. **177** L5
Longburn N.Z. **152** J8

Long Cay *i.* Bahamas **187** E2
Longchang China **86** C2
also known as Jin'e
Longcheng China *see* Longmen
Longcheng China *see* Pengze
Longcheng China *see* Chenggong
Longchuan China **87** E3
also known as Laolong
Longchuan China *see* Nanhua
Longchuan Jiang *r.* China **86** C3
Long Creek *r.* Canada **167** K5
Long Eaton U.K. **47** K11
Longfellow, Mount N.Z. **153** G10
Longford Rep. of Ireland **47** E10
Longgang China *see* Dazu
Longgang China *see* Yuli
Longgi *r.* Dem. Rep. Congo **126** C4
Long Harbour *Hong Kong China* **87** [inset]
also known as Tai Tan Hoi Hap
Longhope U.K. **46** I5
Longhua China **85** H3
Longhui China **87** D3
also known as Taohong; *formerly known as*
Taohuaping
Longhurst, Mount Antarctica **223** K1
Longibau Indon. **77** G2
Longido Tanz. **128** C5
Longikis Indon. **77** G3
Longing, Cape Antarctica **222** U2
Longiram Indon. **77** F3
Long Island Bahamas **187** E2
Long Island *N.S.* Canada **169** H4
Long Island *Nunavut* Canada **168** E2
Long Island India **95** G3
Long Island P.N.G. **73** K8
Long Island U.S.A. **177** M5
Long Island Sound *sea chan.* U.S.A.
177 L4
Longjiang China **85** I2
Long Jiang *r.* China **87** D3
Longjin China *see* Qingliu
Longjin China *see* Anyi
Longjuzhai China *see* Danfeng
Longkou China **85** I4
Longkou Wan *b.* China **85** I4
Longlac Canada **168** C3
Long Lake *l.* Canada **168** C3
Long Lake *l.* U.S.A. **177** K2
Long Lake *l. MI* U.S.A. **172** H6
Long Lake *l. MI* U.S.A. **173** J5
Long Lake *l. NY* U.S.A. **177** K1
Longli China **86** C3
also known as Longshan
Longlin China **86** C3
also known as Xinzhou
Longmeadow U.S.A. **177** M3
Longmen China **87** E4
also known as Longcheng
Longming China **86** C4
Longmont U.S.A. **180** F4
Longnan China **87** E3
Longnawan Indon. **77** F2
Longobucco Italy **57** I9
Longojo Angola **127** B8
Longotoma Chile **204** C4
Longpahangai Indon. **77** F2
Long Phu Vietnam **79** D6
Longping China *see* Luodian
Long Point Canada **168** D5
Long Point *pt Man.* Canada **167** L4
Long Point *pt Ont.* Canada **168** D5
Long Point Bay Canada **173** M8
Long Prairie U.S.A. **178** D2
Longpujungan Indon. **77** F2
Longquan China *see* Danzhai
Longquan China *see* Fenggang
Longquan China **87** F2
Longquan Xi *r.* China **87** F3
Long Range Mountains *Nfld.* Canada
169 J3
Longreach Australia **149** E4
Long Reef Australia **150** D2
Long Reef P.N.G. **149** F1
Longriba China **86** B1
Long Ridge U.S.A. **176** A7
Longshan China *see* Longli
Longshan China **87** D2
Longsheng China **87** D3
Longshou Shan *mts* China **84** D4
Long Teru *Sarawak Malaysia* **77** F2
Longtian China **87** D2
Longtom Lake Canada **167** G1
Long Tompas *pass* S. Africa **133** O2
Longtown U.K. **47** J8
Longué-Jumelles France **50** F5
Longueil Canada **169** H3
Longueuil Canada **169** H3
Longuyon France **51** L3
Longvale U.S.A. **182** A2
Long Valley U.S.A. **183** M7
Longview *TX* U.S.A. **179** D5
Longview *WA* U.S.A. **180** B3
Longwangmiao China **90** C2
Longwei Co *l.* China **89** E5
Longxi China **86** C1
Longxian China *see* Wengyuan
Longxian China **86** C1
Longyi Shan *mt.* China **87** F3
Longxun China *see* Dehua
Long Xuyên Vietnam **79** D6
Longyan China **87** F3
Longyao China **85** G4

▶ **Longyearbyen** Svalbard **38** B2
Capital of Svalbard.

Longzhen China **82** B3
Longzhou China **86** C4
Longzhouping China *see* Changyang
Lonigo Italy **56** D3
Lonja *r.* Croatia **56** I3
Lonjsko Polje *plain* Croatia **56** I3
Lonkin Madag. **131** [inset] K3
Lonoke U.S.A. **174** B5
Lönsboda Sweden **45** K4
Lønsdalen *valley* Norway **44** K2
Lons-le-Saunier France **51** L6
Lontar *i.* Indon. **75** D4
Lontra Brazil **199** I6
Lontra *r. Mato Grosso do Sul* Brazil
203 A7
Lontra *r. Tocantins* Brazil **202** C3
Looc Phil. **74** B3
Loochoo Islands Japan *see* Ryukyu Islands
Looking Glass *r.* U.S.A. **173** I8
Lookout, Cape Canada **168** D2
Lookout, Cape U.S.A. **174** E5
Lookout, Point *Qld* Australia **149** E2
Lookout, Point U.S.A. **173** J6
Lookout Mountain U.S.A. **175** C5
Lookout Point *W.A.* Australia **151** B7
Loolmalasin *vol. crater* Tanz. **128** C5
Looma Australia **150** D3
Loon Canada **168** B3
Loon *r.* Canada **167** H3
Loop Head Rep. of Ireland **47** C11
Lootsberg Pass S. Africa **133** I8
Lop China **89** C4
Lopandino Rus. Fed. **43** P9
Lopary Madag. **131** [inset] K4
Lopasnya Rus. Fed. *see* Chekhov
Lopatina, Gora *mt.* Rus. Fed. **82** F2
Lopatino Rus. Fed. **41** H5

Lopatinskiy Rus. Fed. **43** T6
Lopatka, Cape Rus. Fed. *see* Lopatka, Mys
Lopatka, Mys *c. Kamchatskaya Oblast'*
Rus. Fed. **39** P4
Lopatka, Mys *c. Respublika Sakha (Yakutiya)*
Rus. Fed. **39** P2
English form Lopatka, Cape
Lopatovo Rus. Fed. **43** J4
Lopazna Rus. Fed. **43** N8
Lop Buri Thai. **79** C5
also known as Tha Hin
Lopé-Okanda, Réserve de *nature res.*
Gabon **126** A5
Lopez Phil. **74** B3
Lopez, Cap *c.* Gabon **126** A5
Lop Nur *salt l.* China **88** C3
Lopori *r.* Dem. Rep. Congo **126** C4
Lopphavet *b.* Norway **44** M1
Loppi Fin. **45** N3
Lora *r.* Afgh. **101** F4
Lora Norway **45** J3
Lora del Río Spain **54** F7
Lorain U.S.A. **176** C4
Loralai *r.* Pak. **101** G4
Loralai Pak. **101** G4
Lora Spain **55** J7
Lorca Spain **55** J7
Lord Howe Atoll Solomon Is *see*
Ontong Java Atoll
Lord Howe Island Australia **145** E5
Lordsburg U.S.A. **181** G6
Lore Lindu National Park Indon. **75** B3
Lorena Brazil **203** C7
Lorengau P.N.G. **73** K7
Lorentz *r.* Indon. **73** I8
Lorentz National Park Indon. **73** I7
Lorenzo del Real Mex. **185** F4
Lorenzo Geyres Uruguay **204** F4
Lorestān *prov.* Iran **100** A3
Loretc Brazil **202** D5
Lorete Mex. **184** C3
Lorete *prov.* Peru **198** C5
Loreto Italy **56** F5
Loreto Para. **201** F5
Loreto *dept* Peru **198** C5
Loretto U.S.A. **172** C5
Lorian Swamp Kenya **128** C4
Lorica Col. **198** C2
Lorient France **50** C5
Lorillard *r.* Canada **167** N1
Lorn Afgh. **101** F4
Lorne *Qld* Australia **149** E5
Lorne *Vic.* Australia **147** D4
Lorc *r.* China **89** F6
Loropéni Burkina **124** E4
Lörrach Germany **48** E8
Lorrain, Plateau France **51** M4
Lorraine Australia **148** C3
Lorraine *admin. reg.* France **51** M3
Lorraine, Parc Naturel Régional de *park*
France **51** L4
Lort *r.* Australia **151** C7
Lörudden Sweden **44** L3
Los, Îles de *is* Guinea **124** B4
Losai National Reserve *nature res.* Kenya
128 C4
Losal India **96** B4
Los Alamitos, Sierra de *mt.* Mex. **185** E3
Los Alamos *CA* U.S.A. **182** D7
Los Alamos *NM* U.S.A. **181** F6
Los Alerces, Parque Nacional *nat. park*
Arg. **205** C3
Los Amores Arg. **204** F3
Los Andes Chile **204** C4
Los Angeles Chile **204** B5

▶ **Los Angeles** U.S.A. **182** F7
3rd most populous city in North America
and 7th in the world.
world [cities] ▶▶ 24–25
northamerica [threats] ▶▶ 160–161

Los Angeles Aqueduct *canal* U.S.A. **182** F6
Los Antiguos Arg. **205** C7
Los Arabos Cuba **186** C2
Los Argallanes, Sierra de *hills* Spain **54** F5
Los Banos U.S.A. **182** C5
Los Barrios Spain **54** F8
Los Barrios Spain **54** F8
Los Blancos Arg. **201** E5
Los Caballos Mesteños, Llano de *plain*
Mex. **184** D2
Los Canarreos, Archipiélago de *is* Cuba
186 C2
Los Chiles Costa Rica **186** B5
Los Choros, Archipiélago de *is* Chile
205 B7
Los Choros, Islas de *is* Chile **204** C3
Los Cisnes, Lagunas de *lakes* Arg. **204** C4
Los Corales del Rosario, Parque Nacional
nat. park Col. **198** C2
Los Coronados, Golfo de Chile **205** B6
Los Coronados, Islas *is* Mex. **183** G9
Los Corrales de Buelna Spain **54** G1
Los Cusis Beni Bol. **200** D3
Los Cusis Beni Bol. **201** D3
Los Difuntos, Laguna *l.* Uruguay *see*
Negra, Lago
Los Desventurados, Islas de *is* S. Pacific
Ocean **221** M7
Los Estados, Isla de *i.* Arg. **205** D9
historically known as Staten Island
Losevo Rus. Fed. **41** G6
Loseye *well* Tanz. **129** C6
Los Gatos U.S.A. **182** C4
Los Glaciares, Parque Nacional *nat. park*
Arg. **205** B8
Los Haïtises *nat. park* Dom. Rep. **187** F3
Los Hoyos Mex. **184** C2
Los Huemules, Parque Nacional *nat. park*
Chile **205** B7
Los Huicholes, Sierra de *mts* Mex. **184** D4
Łosice Poland **49** T3
Los Idolos Mex. **185** F4
Losini *i.* Croatia **56** G4
Los Jardines de la Reina, Archipiélago de
is Cuba **186** D2
Los Juríes Arg. **204** E3
Loskop S. Africa **133** N5
Loskop Dam Nature Reserve S. Africa
133 N2
Los Lagos Chile **204** B5
Los Lagos *admin. reg.* Chile **204** B6
Los Leones Mex. **184** C2
Los Lunas U.S.A. **181** F6
Los Mármoles, Parque Nacional *nat. park*
Mex. **185** F4
Los Menucos Arg. **204** C6
Los Mexicanos, Lago de *l.* Mex. **184** D2
Los Mochis Mex. **184** C3
Los Molinos U.S.A. **182** B1
Los Mosquitos, Golfo de *b.* Panama
186 C5
Los Navalmorales Spain **54** G5
Los Nevados, Parque Nacional *nat. park*
Col. **198** C3
Los Nodales, Bahía de *b.* Arg. **205** D7
Los Organos, Sierra de *hills* Cuba **175** C9
Los Palacios Cuba **186** C2
Los Palacios y Villafranca Spain **54** F7
Lospatos East Timor **75** C5
Los Pedroches *plat.* Spain **54** F6
Los Picos de Europa, Parque Nacional de
nat. park Spain **54** G1
Los Reyes Mex. **185** E5
Los Riachos, Islas de *is* Arg. **204** E6
Los Ríos *prov.* Ecuador **198** B5

Los Roques, Islas *is* Venez. **199** E2
Los Sauces Chile **204** B5
Lossiemouth U.K. **46** I6
Los Taques Venez. **198** D2
Lost Creek U.S.A. **176** B8
Los Telares Arg. **204** E3
Los Teques Venez. **199** E2
Los Testigos *is* Venez. **199** F2
Lost Hills U.S.A. **182** E6
Lost Tigres Arg. **204** E2
Lost Trail Pass U.S.A. **180** D3
Losuia P.N.G. **145** E2
Losvida, Vozyera *l.* Belarus **43** L6
Los Vientos Chile **200** C6
Los Vilos Chile **204** C3
Los Yébenes Spain **54** H5
Lot *r.* France **51** G8
Lota Chile **204** B5
Lotagipi Swamp Kenya **128** B3
Lote Norway **45** I3
Løten Norway **45** J3
Lotfābād Turkm. **102** D5
Loth U.K. **46** J4
Lothagum Hills Sudan **128** B3
Lothair S. Africa **133** O3
L'Oti, Réserve de Faune de *nature res.*
Togo **125** F4
Lotikipi Plain Kenya **128** B3
Loto Dem. Rep. Congo **126** D5
Lotoi *r.* Dem. Rep. Congo **126** C5
Lotoshino Rus. Fed. **43** Q5
Lot's Wife *i.* Japan *see* Sōfu-gan
Lotta *r.* Fin./Rus. Fed. **44** O1
also spelt Lutto
Louang Namtha Laos **78** C3
also spelt Luang Nam Tha
Louangphrabang Laos **78** C4
also spelt Luang Prabang
Louang Phrabang Range *mts* Laos/Thai.
78 C4
Loubomo Congo **126** B6
also known as Dolisie
Loučná *hill* Czech Rep. **49** K5
Loudéac France **50** D4
Loudi China **87** D3
Loudima Congo **126** B6
Loudon U.S.A. **174** C5
Loudonville U.S.A. **176** C5
Loudun France **50** G5
Louésé *r.* Congo **126** B5
L'Ouest, Pointe de *pt* Canada **169** H3
Louga Senegal **124** A3
Loughborough U.K. **47** K11
Lougheed Island Canada **165** I2
Loughrea Rep. of Ireland **47** D10
Louhans France **51** L6
Louisa *KY* U.S.A. **176** C7
Louisa *VA* U.S.A. **176** H7
Louisa Downs Aboriginal Reserve
Australia **150** D3
Louisbourg Canada **169** J4
formerly spelt Louisburg
Louisburg Canada *see* Louisbourg
Louisburg U.S.A. **176** G9
Louise Falls Canada **167** G2
Louis-Gentil Morocco *see* Youssoufia
Louisiade Archipelago *is* P.N.G. **149** G3
Louisiana U.S.A. **174** B4
Louisiana *state* U.S.A. **175** B6
Louis Trichardt S. Africa **131** F4
Louisvale S. Africa **132** F5
Louisville *GA* U.S.A. **175** D5
Louisville *IL* U.S.A. **174** B4
Louisville *KY* U.S.A. **174** C4
Louisville *MS* U.S.A. **175** B5
Louisville *OH* U.S.A. **176** D5
Louis-XIV, Pointe *pt* Canada **168** E2
Loukhi Rus. Fed. **44** P2
Loukoléla Congo **126** C5
Loukouo Congo **126** C5
Loulé Port. **54** C7
Loulouni Mali **124** D4
Loum Cameroon **125** H5
Louny Czech Rep. **49** K5
Loup *r.* U.S.A. **178** C3
Loup City U.S.A. **178** C3
Loups-Marins, Lacs des *lakes* Canada
169 F1
Lourdes Canada **169** J3
Lourdes France **50** F9
Lourenço Brazil **199** I4
Lourenço Marques Moz. *see* Maputo
Lourinhã Port. **54** B5
Louterwater S. Africa **132** H10
Louth Australia **147** E2
Louth U.K. **47** L10
Loutra Greece **59** F11
Loutra Aidipsou Greece **59** E10
Loutraki Greece **59** D11
Louvain Belgium *see* Leuven
Louviers France **50** H3
Louwsburg S. Africa **133** P4
Lövånger Sweden **44** M2
Lovasberény Hungary **49** P8
Lovat' *r.* Rus. Fed. **43** M3
Lövberga Sweden **44** L3
Lovćen *mts* Yugo. **56** K6
Lovech Bulg. **58** F5
Loveland U.S.A. **180** F4
Lovell *ME* U.S.A. **177** O1
Lovell *WY* U.S.A. **180** E3
Lovelock U.S.A. **182** F1
Lovenia, Mount U.S.A. **183** N1
Lovere Italy **56** C3
Lovers' Leap *mt.* U.S.A. **176** E9
Loves Park U.S.A. **172** D8
Loviisa Fin. **45** N3
Lovington U.S.A. **179** B5
Lovozero Rus. Fed. **40** E1
Lovran Croatia **56** G3
Lovrin Romania **58** D3
Lövsätuken *b.* Sweden **45** L3
Lovtsy Rus. Fed. **43** U6
Lôvua Angola **127** D7
Lóvua Angola **127** D7
Low Canada **173** R5
Lowa Dem. Rep. Congo **126** E5
Lowa *r.* Dem. Rep. Congo **126** E5
Lowari Pass Pak. **101** G3
Lowell *IN* U.S.A. **172** F9
Lowell *MA* U.S.A. **177** N3
Lowell *MI* U.S.A. **172** H8
Lowell *OR* U.S.A. **180** B4
Lowell *VT* U.S.A. **177** M1
Lowelli Sudan **128** B3
Löwen *watercourse* Namibia **132** B4
Lower Arrow Lake Canada **166** G5
Lower Brule Indian Reservation *res.*
U.S.A. **178** C2
Lower California *pen.* Mex. *see*
Baja California
Lower Garry Lake Canada **167** L1
Lower Glenelg National Park Australia
146 C4
Lower Granite Gorge U.S.A. **183** K6
Lower Hutt N.Z. **152** I9
Lower Klamath National Wildlife Refuge
nature res. U.S.A. **180** B4
Lower Laberge Canada **166** C2
Lower Lake U.S.A. **182** B3
Lower Lotení S. Africa **133** N6
Lower Lough Erne *l.* U.K. **47** E9
Lower Peirce Reservoir Sing. **76** [inset]
Lower Pitseng S. Africa **133** M7
Lower Red Lake U.S.A. **178** D2
Lower Sabie S. Africa **133** P2
Lower Saxony *land* Germany *see*
Niedersachsen
Lower Tunguska *r.* Rus. Fed. *see*
Nizhnyaya Tunguska
Lower Zambezi National Park Zambia
127 F8

Lowestoft U.K. **47** N11
Lowgar *prov.* Afgh. **101** G3
Łowicz Poland **49** Q3
Low Island Kiribati *see* **Starbuck Island**
Lowmoor U.S.A. **176** F8
Lowsville U.S.A. **176** E6
Lowville U.S.A. **177** J2
Loxton Australia **146** D3
Loxton S. Africa **132** G8
Loyalsock Creek *r.* U.S.A. **177** I4
Loyalton U.S.A. **182** D2
Loyalty Islands New Caledonia *see* **Loyauté, Îles**
Loyang China *see* **Luoyang**
Loyauté, Îles *is* New Caledonia **145** F4
English form Loyalty Islands
Loyd U.S.A. **172** C7
Loyengo Swaziland **133** P3
Loyev Belarus *see* **Loyew**
Loyew Belarus **41** D6
also spelt Loyev
Loyno Rus. Fed. **40** J4
Loyola, Punta *pt* Arg. **205** C8
Løypskardtinden *mt.* Norway **44** K2
Lozère, Mont *mt.* France **51** J8
Loznica *Srbija* Yugo. **58** A4
Loznitsa Bulg. **58** H5
Lozova Ukr. **41** F6
also spelt Lozovaya
Lozovaya Kazakh. *see* **Lozovoye**
Lozovaya Ukr. *see* **Lozova**
Lozovik *Srbija* Yugo. **58** C4
Lozovoye Kazakh. **103** I1
formerly known as Lozovaya
Loz'va *r.* Rus. Fed. **40** L3
Ltyentye Apurte Aboriginal Land *res.* Australia **148** B5
also known as Santa Teresa Aboriginal Land
Lu *r.* China **85** F4
Luabo Moz. **131** H3
Luacano Angola **127** D7
Luachimo *r.* Angola/Dem. Rep. Congo **127** D6
Lua Dekere *r.* Dem. Rep. Congo **126** C4
Luakila Dem. Rep. Congo **126** E6
Luala *r.* Moz. **131** H3
Luambe National Park Zambia **129** B8
Luampa *r.* Zambia **127** E8
Lu'an China **87** F2
Luanchuan China **87** D1
Luanco Spain **54** F1

▶**Luanda** Angola **127** B7
Capital of Angola.

Luanda *prov.* Angola **127** B7
Luando Angola **127** C7
Luando *r.* Angola **127** C7
Luando, Reserva Natural Integral do *nature res.* Angola **127** C7
Luang, Khao *mt.* Thai. **79** B6
Luanginga *r.* Zambia **127** D8
Luang Nam Tha Laos *see* **Louang Namtha**
Luang Prabang Laos *see* **Louangphrabang**
Luanguinga *r.* Angola **127** D8
Luangwa Zambia **127** F8
formerly known as Feira
Luangwa *r.* Zambia **127** F8
Luanhaizi China **84** B5
Luan He *r.* China **85** H4
Luannan China **85** H4
also known as Bencheng
Lua Nova Brazil **199** G6
Luanping China **85** H3
Luanshya Zambia **127** F8
Luanxian China **85** H4
also known as Luanzhou
Luanza Dem. Rep. Congo **127** F7
Luanzhou China *see* **Luanxian**
Luao Angola *see* **Luau**
Luapula *prov.* Zambia **127** F7
Luar, Danau *l.* Indon. **77** F2
Luarca Spain **54** E1
Luashi Dem. Rep. Congo **127** D7
Luatamba Angola **127** D8
Luau Angola **127** D7
formerly known as Teixeira de Sousa *or* Vila Teixeira de Sousa; *formerly spelt* Luao
Luba Equat. Guinea **125** H6
formerly known as San Carlos
Lubaczów Poland **49** U5
Lubalo Angola **127** C7
Lubań Poland **49** M4
Lubāna Latvia **42** H5
Lubānas ezers *l.* Latvia **42** H5
Lubang Phil. **74** B3
Lubang *i.* Phil. **74** B3
Lubang Islands Phil. **74** A3
Lubango Angola **127** B8
formerly known as Sá da Bandeira
Lubao Dem. Rep. Congo **127** E6
Lubartów Poland **49** T4
Lubawa Poland **49** Q2
Lübbecke Germany **48** F3
Lübben Germany **49** K4
Lübbenau Germany **49** K4
Lubbeskolk *salt pan* S. Africa **132** D6
Lubbock U.S.A. **179** B5
Lübeck Germany **48** H2
Lubeck U.S.A. **176** D6
Lübecker Bucht *b.* Germany **48** H1
Lubefu Dem. Rep. Congo **126** E6
Lubei China **85** I2
also known as Jarud
Lubelska, Wyżyna *hills* Poland **49** T4
Lüben Poland *see* **Lubin**
Lubenka Kazakh. **102** C2
Lubero Dem. Rep. Congo **126** F5
Lubéron, Montagne du *ridge* France **51** L9
Lubéron, Parc Naturel Régional du *nature res.* France **51** L9
Lubersac France **50** H7
Lubie, Jezioro *l.* Poland **49** M2
Lubienka *r.* Poland **49** P3
Lubień Kujawski Poland **49** Q3
Lubin Poland **49** N4
historically known as Lüben
Lubisi Dam *resr* S. Africa **133** L8
Lublin Poland **49** T4
Lubliniec Poland **49** P5
Lubnān *country* Asia *see* **Lebanon**
Lubny Ukr. **41** E6
Lubok Antu *Sarawak* Malaysia **77** E2
Luboń Poland **49** N3
Lubosalma Rus. Fed. **44** O3
Lubraniec Poland **49** P3
Lubrin Spain **55** I7
Lübtheen Germany **48** I2
Lubuagan Phil. **74** B2
Lubudi Dem. Rep. Congo **127** E7
Lubudi *r.* Dem. Rep. Congo **127** E7
Lubuklinggau Indon. **76** C3
Lubukpakam Indon. **76** B2
Lubuksikaping Indon. **76** C2
Lubumbashi Dem. Rep. Congo **127** E7
formerly known as Élisabethville
Lubunda Dem. Rep. Congo **127** E6
Lubungu Zambia **127** E8
Lubuta Zambia **127** D9
Lubutu Dem. Rep. Congo **126** E5
Lubutu *r.* Dem. Rep. Congo **126** E5
Lubwe Zambia **127** F7
Lubyanki Rus. Fed. **43** Q9
Lucala Angola **127** B7
Lucan Canada **173** L7
Lucanas Peru **200** B3
Lučani *Srbija* Yugo. **58** B5
Lucania, Mount Canada **166** A2
Lücaoshan China **84** B4
Lucapa Angola **127** D7
formerly known as Lukapa
Lucas Brazil **201** G3
Lucasville U.S.A. **176** C7
Lucca Italy **56** C5
Lucé France **50** H4
Lucea Jamaica **186** D3
Luce Bay U.K. **47** H9
Lucedale U.S.A. **175** B6
Lucélia Brazil **206** B8
Lucena Phil. **74** B3
Lucena Spain **54** G7
Lučenec Slovakia **49** Q7
Lucera Italy **56** H7
Lucerna Peru **200** C3
Lucerne Switz. **51** O5
also spelt Luzern
Lucerne U.S.A. **182** B2
Lucerne Valley U.S.A. **183** H7
Lucero Mex. **184** D2
Lucha *r.* Rus. Fed. **82** C1
Luchay Belarus **42** I6
Luchegorsk Rus. Fed. **82** D3
Lucheng China *see* **Luchuan**
Lucheng China **85** G4
Lucheng China *see* **Kangding**
Lucheringo *r.* Moz. **129** C7
Luchki Rus. Fed. **43** U5
Luchosa *r.* Belarus **43** L7
Lüchow Germany **48** I3
Luchuan China **87** D4
also known as Lucheng
Lüchun China **86** B4
also known as Daxing
Lucinda Australia **149** E3
Lucipara, Kepulauan *is* Indon. **75** C4
Lucira Angola **127** B8
Luciu Romania **58** I4
Łuck Ukr. *see* **Luts'k**
Luck U.S.A. **172** A5
Luckau Germany **49** K4
Luckeesarai India **97** E4
also spelt Lakhisarai
Luckenwalde Germany **49** K3
Luckhoff S. Africa **133** I6
Lucknow Canada **173** L7
Lucknow India **96** D4
Luçon France **50** E6
Lücongpo China **87** D2
Lucunga Angola **127** B6
Lucusse Angola **127** D8
Lucy Creek Australia **148** C4
Lüda China *see* **Dalian**
Luda Kamchiya *r.* Bulg. **58** I5
Ludbreg Croatia **56** I2
Lüdenscheid Germany **48** E4
Lüderitz Namibia **130** B5
Ludewa Tanz. **129** B7
Ludhiana India **96** B3
Ludian China **86** B3
also known as Wenping
Luding China **86** B2
also known as Jagsamka *or* Luqiao
Ludington U.S.A. **172** G7
Ludlow U.K. **47** J11
Ludlow *CA* U.S.A. **183** H7
Ludlow *VT* U.S.A. **177** M2
Ludogorie *reg.* Bulg. **58** H5
Ludogorsko Plato *plat.* Bulg. **58** H5
Ludoni Rus. Fed. **43** K3
Ludowici U.S.A. **175** D6
Luduș Romania **58** F2
Ludvika Sweden **45** K3
Ludwigsburg Germany **48** G7
Ludwigsfelde Germany **49** K3
Ludwigshafen am Rhein Germany **48** F6
Ludwigslust Germany **48** I2
Ludwigsort Rus. Fed. *see* **Ladushkin**
Ludza Latvia **42** I5
Luebo Dem. Rep. Congo **127** D6
Lueki Dem. Rep. Congo **126** E5
Lueki *r.* Dem. Rep. Congo **126** E5
Luembe Zambia **127** F8
Luena Angola **127** C7
formerly known as Luso
Luena Dem. Rep. Congo **127** E7
Luena Zambia **127** F7
Luena *r.* Zambia **127** D8
Luena Flats *plain* Zambia **127** D8
Luengé, Coutada Pública do *nature res.* Angola **127** D9
Luengue *r.* Angola **127** D9
Luenha *r.* Moz./Zimbabwe **131** G3
Luepa Venez. **199** F3
Lüeyang China **86** C1
Lufeng *Guangdong* China **87** E4
Lufeng China *see* **Xupu**
Lufeng *Yunnan* China **86** B3
also known as Jinshan
Lufira *r.* Dem. Rep. Congo **127** E7
Lufkin U.S.A. **179** D6
Lufu China *see* **Shilin**
Lug *r.* Yugo. **58** C4
Luga Rus. Fed. **43** K3
Luga *r.* Rus. Fed. **43** J2
Lugano Switz. **51** O6
Lugansk Ukr. *see* **Luhans'k**
Luganville Vanuatu **145** F3
Lugdunum France *see* **Lyon**
Lugela Moz. **131** H3
Lugela *r.* Moz. **131** H3
Lugenda *r.* Moz. **131** H1
Lugg *r.* U.K. **47** J11
Luggate N.Z. **153** D12
Luggudontsen *mt.* China **89** E6
Lughaye Somalia **128** D2
Lugo Italy **56** D4
Lugo Spain **54** D1
Lugoj Romania **58** C3
Lugovaya Rus. Fed. **43** S5
Lugovaya Proleyka Rus. Fed. *see* **Primorsk**
Lugovoy Kazakh. **103** H4
Lugovoye Kazakh. **103** H4
Lugus *i.* Phil. **74** B5
Luhanka Fin. **45** N3
Luhans'k Ukr. **41** F6
also spelt Lugansk; *formerly known as* Voroshilovgrad
Luhawskiya Belarus **43** L6
Luhe China **87** F1
Luḥfī, Wādī *watercourse* Jordan **109** H5
Luhin Sum China **85** H2
Luhit *r.* China/India *see* **Zayü Qu**
Luhit *r.* India **97** G3
Luhombero Tanz. **129** C7
Luhua China *see* **Heishui**
Luhuo China **86** B2
also known as Xindu *or* Zhaggo
Luhyny Ukr. **41** D6
Luia Angola **127** D7
Luia *r.* Angola **127** D6
Luia *r.* Moz. **131** G3
Luiana Angola **127** D9
Luiana *r.* Angola **127** D9
Luiana, Coutada Pública do *nature res.* Angola **127** D9
Luica Romania **58** H4
Luichow Peninsula China *see* **Leizhou Bandao**
Luik Belgium *see* **Liège**
Luilaka *r.* Dem. Rep. Congo **126** D5
Luimneach Rep. of Ireland *see* **Limerick**
Luing *i.* U.K. **46** G7
Luino Italy **56** A3
Luio *r.* Angola **127** D8
Luiro *r.* Fin. **44** N2
Luís Correia Brazil **202** D2
Luis Echeverría Álvarez Mex. **183** H9
Luís Gomes Brazil **202** E3
Luishia Dem. Rep. Congo **127** E7
Luis L. León, Presa *resr* Mex. **184** D2
Luis Moya *Durango* Mex. **184** E3
Luis Moya *Zacatecas* Mex. **185** E4
Luitpold Coast Antarctica **222** V1
Luiza Dem. Rep. Congo **127** D6
Luizi Dem. Rep. Congo **127** E6
Luján Arg. **204** F4
Luján de Cuyo Arg. **204** C4
Lujiang China **87** F2
Lukackek Rus. Fed. **82** D1
Lukala Dem. Rep. Congo **127** B6
Lukanga Dem. Rep. Congo **126** C6
Lukanga Swamps Zambia **127** E8
Lukapa Angola *see* **Lucapa**
Lukavac Bos.-Herz. **56** K4
Luke, Mount *hill* Australia **151** B5
Lukenga, Lac *l.* Dem. Rep. Congo **127** E7
Lukenie *r.* Dem. Rep. Congo **126** C5
Lukh *r.* Rus. Fed. **40** G4
Lukhovitsy Rus. Fed. **43** U7
Lŭki Bulg. **58** F7
Lukinskaya Rus. Fed. **43** P1
Luk Keng *Hong Kong* China **87** [inset]
Lukolela *Équateur* Dem. Rep. Congo **126** C5
Lukolela *Kasai Oriental* Dem. Rep. Congo **127** E6
Lukomskaye, Vozyera *l.* Belarus **43** K7
Lukou China *see* **Zhuzhou**
Lukovac *r.* Bos.-Herz. **56** L4
Lukovë Albania **59** A9
Lukovit Bulg. **58** F5
Lukovnikovo Rus. Fed. **43** P5
Łuków Poland **49** T4
Lukoyanov Rus. Fed. **40** H5
Luksagu Indon. **75** B3
Lukšiai Lith. **42** E7
Lukuga *r.* Dem. Rep. Congo **127** E6
Lukula Dem. Rep. Congo **127** B6
Lukuledi Tanz. **129** C7
Lukulu Zambia **127** D8
Lukumburu Tanz. **129** B7
Lukuni Dem. Rep. Congo **127** C6
Lukusashi *r.* Zambia **127** F8
Lukusuzi National Park Zambia **129** B8
Lula *r.* Dem. Rep. Congo **126** D5
Luleå Sweden **44** M2
Luleälven *r.* Sweden **44** M2
Lüleburgaz Turkey **106** A2
Lules Arg. **204** D2
Luliang China **86** B3
also known as Zhongshu
Lüliang Shan *mts* China **85** F4
Lulimba Dem. Rep. Congo **126** F6
Luling U.S.A. **179** C6
Lulong China **85** H4
Lulonga Dem. Rep. Congo **126** C4
Lulonga *r.* Dem. Rep. Congo **126** C4
Lulu *r.* Dem. Rep. Congo **126** D4
Luluabourg Dem. Rep. Congo *see* **Kananga**
Lülung China **89** D6
Lulworth, Mount *hill* Australia **151** B5
Lumachomo China **89** D6
Lumai Angola **127** D8
Lumajang Indon. **77** F5
Lumajangdong Co *salt l.* China **89** C5
Lumana Estonia **42** D3
Lümär Iran **107** F4
Lumbala Angola *see* **Lumbala N'guimbo**
Lumbala Angola *see* **Lumbala Kaquengue**
Lumbala Kaquengue Angola **127** D8
formerly known as Lumbala
Lumbala N'guimbo Angola **127** D8
formerly known as Gago Coutinho *or* Lumbala
Lumber *r.* U.S.A. **174** E5
Lumberton U.S.A. **174** E5
Lumbis Indon. **77** G1
Lumbrales Spain **54** E4
Lumding India **97** G4
Lumecha Tanz. **129** B7
Lumezzane Italy **56** C3
Lumi P.N.G. **73** J7
Lumijoki Fin. **44** N2
Lumina Romania **58** J4
Luminárias Brazil **207** I8
Lum-nan-pai Wildlife Reserve *nature res.* Thai. **78** B4
Lumparland Fin. **45** M3
Lumphăt Cambodia **79** D5
also spelt Lomphat
Lumpkin U.S.A. **175** C5
Lumsden Canada **167** J5
Lumsden N.Z. **153** C13
Lumut, Gunung *mt.* Indon. **77** F3
Lumut, Tanjung *pt* Indon. **77** D3
Lumwana Zambia **127** E7
Lün Mongolia **85** E2
Luna Phil. **74** B2
Luna *hill* Spain **54** F8
Luna *r.* Spain **54** F2
Lunan China **86** B3
also known as Lufu
Lunan Lake Canada **167** M1
Lunan Shan *mts* China **86** B3
Luna Pier U.S.A. **173** J9
Lunavada India **96** B5
Lunayyir, Ḥarrāt *lava field* Saudi Arabia **104** B2
Lunca Romania **58** F5
Lunca Bradului Romania **58** G2
Lunca Ilvei Romania **58** F1
Luncavăț *r.* Romania **58** F4
Lund Sweden **45** K5
Lund *NV* U.S.A. **183** I3
Lund *UT* U.S.A. **183** K3
Lunda Norte *prov.* Angola **127** C7
Lundar Canada **167** L5
Lunda Sul *prov.* Angola **127** D7
Lundazi Zambia **129** B8
Lundbreck Canada **167** H5
Lundi *r.* Zimbabwe *see* **Runde**
Lunds U.S.A. **172** E6
Lundu Tanz. **129** B7
Lundy Island U.K. **47** H12
Lune *r.* U.K. **47** J9
Lüneburg Germany **48** H2
Lüneburger Heide *reg.* Germany **48** H2
Lüneburger Heide, Naturpark *nature res.* Germany **48** G2
Lunel France **51** K9
Lünen Germany **48** E4
Lunenburg U.S.A. **176** G9
Lunestedt Germany **48** F2
Lunéville France **51** M4
Lunga Moz. **131** I2
Lunga *r.* Zambia **127** E8
Lunggar China **89** C6
Lunggar Shan *mts* China **89** C6
Lung Kwu Chau *i. Hong Kong* China **87** [inset]
Lungleh India *see* **Lunglei**
Lunglei India **97** G5
formerly spelt Lungleh
Lungmari *mt.* China **89** D6
Lungmu Co *salt l.* China **89** C5
Lungnaquilla Mountain *hill* Rep. of Ireland **47** F11
Lungro Italy **57** I9
Lungué-Bungo *r.* Angola **127** D8
Lungwebungu *r.* Zambia **127** D8
Lunh Nepal **97** D3
Luni *r.* India **96** A4
Luni *r.* Pak. **101** G4
Luninets Belarus *see* **Luninyets**
Lunino Rus. Fed. **41** H5
Luninyets Belarus **42** H9
also spelt Luninets
L'Union France **50** H9
Lunkaransar India **96** B3
Lunkha India **96** B3
Lunkho *mt.* Afgh./Pak. **101** H2
Lunkkaus Fin. **44** N2
Lunna Belarus **42** F8
Lunn Island P.N.G. **149** F1
Lunsar Sierra Leone **124** B4
Lunsemfwa *r.* Zambia **127** F8
Lunsklip S. Africa **131** F5
Luntai China **88** D3
also known as Bügür
Lunxhërisë, Mali i *ridge* Albania **59** B8
Lunyuk Indon. **77** G5
Lunzua Zambia **127** F7
Luo *r.* *Henan* China **87** E1
Luo *r.* *Shaanxi* China **87** D1
Luobei China **82** C3
also known as Fengxiang
Luobuzhuang China **88** E4
Luocheng China *see* **Hui'an**
Luocheng *Gansu* China **84** C4
Luocheng *Guangxi* China **87** D3
also known as Dongmen
Luochuan China **85** F5
also known as Fengqi
Luodian China **86** C3
also known as Longping
Luoding China **87** D4
Luodonselkä *sea chan.* Fin. **44** N2
Luodou Sha *i.* China **87** D4
Luohe China **87** E1
Luoma Hu *l.* China **87** F1
Luonan China **87** D1
Luoning China **87** D1
Luonnonsuojelualue *nature res.* Fin. **44** M3
Luonteri *l.* Fin. **45** N3
Luoping China **86** C3
also known as Luoxiong
Luopioinen Fin. **45** N3
Luoshan China **87** E1
Luotian China **87** E2
also known as Fengshan
Luovtejok Norway **44** O1
Luoxiao Shan *mts* China **87** E3
Luoxiong China *see* **Luoping**
Luoyang China *see* **Boluo**
Luoyang China **87** E1
formerly known as Loyang
Luoyang China *see* **Taishun**
Luoyuan China **87** F3
also known as Fengshan
Luozi Dem. Rep. Congo **126** B6
Luozigou China **82** C4
Lupa Market Tanz. **129** B7
Lupane Zimbabwe **131** E3
Lupanshui China **86** C3
also known as Shuicheng *or* Xiayingpan *or* Zhongshan; *formerly spelt* Liupanshui
Lupar *r.* *Sarawak* Malaysia **77** E2
Łupawa *r.* Poland **49** O1
L'Upemba, Parc National de *nat. park* Dem. Rep. Congo **127** E7
Lupeni Romania **58** G2
Lupeni Romania **58** E3
Luperón Dom. Rep. **187** F3
Lupilichi Moz. **129** B7
formerly known as Olivença
Lupire Angola **127** C8
Lupiro Tanz. **129** C7
Lupon Phil. **74** C5
Luppa Germany **49** J4
Lupton U.S.A. **183** O6
Lup'ya *r.* Rus. Fed. **40** J3
Luqiao China *see* **Luding**
Luqu China **86** B1
also known as Ma'ngê
Lu Qu *r.* China *see* **Tao He**
Luquan *Hebei* China **85** G4
formerly known as Huolu
Luquan *Yunnan* China **86** B3
also known as Pingshan
Luquembo Angola **127** C7
Lūrā Shīrīn Iran **107** F3
Luray U.S.A. **176** G7
Lure France **51** M5
Lure, Sommet de *mt.* France **51** L8
Lureco *r.* Moz. **129** C8
Luremo Angola **127** C7
Lurgan U.K. **47** F9
Lūrg-e Shotorān *salt pan* Iran **101** D3
Luribay Bol. **200** D4
Lurin Peru **200** A3
Luring China *see* **Gêrzê**
Lúrio Moz. **131** I2
Lurio *r.* Moz. **131** I2
Lusaheia *park* Norway **45** I4
Lusahunga Tanz. **128** A5
Lusaka Dem. Rep. Congo **127** F6

▶**Lusaka** Zambia **127** F8
Capital of Zambia.

Lusaka *prov.* Zambia **127** F8
Lusambo Dem. Rep. Congo **126** D6
Lusancay Islands and Reefs P.N.G. **145** E2
Lusanga Dem. Rep. Congo **126** C6
formerly known as Leverville
Lusangi Dem. Rep. Congo **126** E6
Luseland Canada **167** I4
Lusenga Plain National Park Zambia **127** F7
Lusewa Tanz. **129** C7
Lush, Mount *hill* Australia **150** D3
Lushan China **86** B2
also known as Luyang
Lushar China *see* **Huangzhong**
Lushi China **87** D1
Lushnjë Albania **58** A8
Lushoto Tanz. **129** C6
Lushui China **86** A3
Lüshun China **85** I4
formerly known as Port Arthur *or* Ryojun
Lüsi China **87** G1
Lusi *r.* Indon. **77** E4
Lusignan France **50** G6
Lusikisiki S. Africa **133** N8
Lusiwasi Zambia **127** F8
Lusk U.S.A. **180** F4
Luso Angola *see* **Luena**
Lussac-les-Châteaux France **50** G6
Lussusso Angola **127** B7
Lusushwana *r.* Swaziland **133** P3
Lusutufu *r.* Africa *see* **Usutu**
Lut, Bahrat *salt l.* Asia *see* **Dead Sea**
Lut, Dasht-e *des.* Iran **100** D4
Lutai China *see* **Ninghe**
Lü Tao *i.* Taiwan **87** G4
English form Green Island; *also known as* Huoshao Tao
Lutécia Brazil **206** C9
Luterskie, Jezioro *l.* Poland **49** R2
Lutetia France *see* **Paris**
Lūt-e Zangī Aḥmad *des.* Iran **100** D4
Luther Lake Canada **173** M7
Luthersburg U.S.A. **176** G4
Lutherstadt Wittenberg Germany **49** J4
also known as Wittenberg
Lutiba Dem. Rep. Congo **126** F5
Lütjenburg Germany **48** H1
Luton U.K. **47** L12
Lutong *Sarawak* Malaysia **77** F1
Lutope *r.* Zimbabwe **131** F3
Łutselk'e Canada **167** I2
formerly known as Snowdrift
Lutshima Dem. Rep. Congo **126** E6
Luts'k Ukr. **41** C6
formerly spelt Łuck
Luttig S. Africa **132** G9
Lutto *r.* Fin./Rus. Fed. *see* **Lotta**
Lutuai Angola **127** D8
Lutynia *r.* Poland **49** O3
Lutz U.S.A. **175** D6
Lützow-Holm Bay Antarctica **223** C2
Lutzputs S. Africa **132** E5
Lutzville S. Africa **132** C8
Lumăki Fin. **45** N3
Luuq Somalia **128** D4
Luve Swaziland **133** P3
Luverne *AL* U.S.A. **175** C6
Luverne *MN* U.S.A. **178** C3
Luvia Fin. **45** M3
Luvo Angola **127** B6
Luvozero Rus. Fed. **44** O2
Luvua *r.* Dem. Rep. Congo **127** E6
Luvuei Angola **127** D8
Luvuvhu *r.* S. Africa **131** F4
Luwegu *r.* Tanz. **129** C7
Luwero Uganda **128** B4
Luwingu Zambia **127** F7
Luwo *i.* Indon. **75** D2
Luwuk Indon. **75** B3
▶**Luxembourg** *country* Europe **51** L3
Letzebuergesch form Lëtzebuerg; *also spelt* Luxemburg
europe [countries] ▶ 32–35

▶**Luxembourg** Lux. **51** M3
Capital of Luxembourg.

Luxemburg *country* Europe *see* **Luxembourg**
Luxemburg *IA* U.S.A. **172** B8
Luxemburg *WI* U.S.A. **172** F6
Luxeuil-les-Bains France **51** M5
Luxi *Hunan* China **87** D2
also known as Wuxi
Luxi *Yunnan* China **86** A3
also known as Mangshi
Luxi *Yunnan* China **86** B3
also known as Zhongshu
Luxian China **86** C2
also known as Fuji
Luxolweni S. Africa **133** J8
Luxor Egypt **121** G3
also spelt El Uqṣur *or* Al Uqṣur
Luyang China *see* **Lushan**
Luya Shan *mts* China **85** F4
Luy de France *r.* France **50** F9
Luyi China **87** E1
Luyuan China *see* **Gaoling**
Luz Brazil **207** H6
Luza Rus. Fed. **40** H3
Luza *r.* Rus. Fed. **40** H3
Luza *r.* Rus. Fed. **40** K2
Luzech France **50** H8
Luzern Switz. *see* **Lucerne**
Luzha *r.* Rus. Fed. **43** R7
Luzhai China **87** D3
Luzhi China **86** C3
also known as Xiayingpan
Luzhou China **86** C2
Luziânia Brazil **206** F3
Lužické Hory *mts* Czech Rep. **49** L5
Luzilândia Brazil **202** D2
Lūžņas Latvia **42** C4
Lužnice *r.* Czech Rep. **49** L6
Luzon *i.* Phil. **74** B3
Luzon Strait Phil. **74** B1
Luzy France **51** J6
Luzzi Italy **57** I9
L'viv Ukr. **41** C6
English form Lvov; *also spelt* L'vov; *formerly spelt* Lwów; *historically known as* Lemberg
L'vov Ukr. *see* **L'viv**
Lvov Ukr. *see* **L'viv**
L'vovskiy Rus. Fed. **43** S6
Lwów Ukr. *see* **L'viv**
Lwówek Poland **49** N3
Lyady Rus. Fed. **43** J3
Lyakhavichy Belarus **42** H8
also spelt Lyakhovichi
Lyakhovichi Belarus *see* **Lyakhavichy**
Lyakhovskiye Ostrova *is* Rus. Fed. **39** O2
Lyallpur Pak. *see* **Faisalabad**
Lyal'mikar Uzbek. **103** F5
also spelt Lalmikor
Lyamtsa Rus. Fed. **40** F2
Lyangar Uzbek. *see* **Langar**
Lyangar Uzbek. **103** F4
also spelt Langar
Lyapin *r.* Rus. Fed. **40** L3
Lyaskelya Rus. Fed. **44** O3
Lyaskovets Bulg. **58** G5
Lyasnaya Belarus **42** G9
Lyasnaya *r.* Belarus **42** E9
Lybster U.K. **46** I5
Lychkovo Rus. Fed. **43** N4
Lyck Poland *see* **Ełk**
Lycksele Sweden **44** L2
Lycopolis Egypt *see* **Asyūt**
Lydda Israel *see* **Lod**
Lyddan Island Antarctica **222** W2
Lydenburg S. Africa **133** O2
Lydia *reg.* Turkey **59** I10
Łydynia *r.* Poland **49** R3
Lyebyada *r.* Belarus **42** G8
Lyel'chytsy Belarus **41** D6
Lyell, Mount U.S.A. **182** E4
Lyell Island Canada **166** D4
Lyell Range *mts* N.Z. **153** G9
Lyenina Belarus **43** M9
Lyepyel' Belarus **43** J7
also spelt Lepel'
Lygourio Greece **59** E11
also known as Ligoúrion
Lygumai Lith. **42** E5
Lykens U.S.A. **177** I5
Lykoshino Rus. Fed. **43** O3
Lykso S. Africa **132** I4
Lyman Ukr. **58** K3
Lyman U.S.A. **180** E4
Lymans'ke Ukr. **58** K2
Lyme Bay U.K. **47** J13
Lymington U.K. **47** K13
Łyna *r.* Poland **49** S1
Lynch U.S.A. **176** C9
Lynchburg *TN* U.S.A. **174** C5
Lynchburg *VA* U.S.A. **176** F8
Lynches *r.* U.S.A. **175** E5
Lynch Station U.S.A. **176** F8
Lynchville U.S.A. **177** O1
Lynd *r.* Australia **149** D3
Lyndhurst *Qld* Australia **149** E3
Lyndhurst *S.A.* Australia **146** C2
Lyndon Australia **150** A4
Lyndon *r.* Australia **150** A4
Lyndon U.S.A. **178** D4
Lyndonville *NY* U.S.A. **176** G2
Lyndonville *VT* U.S.A. **177** M1
Lyngdal Norway **45** I4
Lyngen *sea chan.* Norway **44** M1
Lyngseidet Norway **44** M1
Lynher Reef Australia **150** C2
Lynn U.K. *see* **King's Lynn**
Lynn *IN* U.S.A. **176** A5
Lynn *MA* U.S.A. **177** O3
Lynn Canal *sea chan.* U.S.A. **166** C3
Lynndyl U.S.A. **183** L2
Lynn Haven U.S.A. **175** C6
Lynn Lake Canada **167** K3
Lynton U.K. **47** I12
Lyntupy Belarus **42** H6
Lynx Lake Canada **167** J2
Lynxville U.S.A. **172** B7
Lyon France **51** K7
English form Lyons; *historically known as* Lugdunum
Lyon Mountain U.S.A. **177** L1
Lyonnais, Monts du *hills* France **51** K7
Lyons Australia **146** B2
Lyons *r.* Australia **151** A5
Lyons France *see* **Lyon**
Lyons *GA* U.S.A. **175** D5
Lyons *KS* U.S.A. **178** C4
Lyons *NY* U.S.A. **177** I2
Lyons Falls U.S.A. **177** J2
Lyozna Belarus **43** L6
Lyra Reef P.N.G. **145** E2
Lysá Hora *mt.* Czech Rep. **49** P6
Lysekil Sweden **45** J4
Lyshchichi Rus. Fed. **43** N9
Łysica *hill* Poland **49** R5
Lyskovo Rus. Fed. **40** H4
Lys'va Rus. Fed. **40** K4
Lysychans'k Ukr. **41** F6
also spelt Lisichansk
Lysyye Gory Rus. Fed. **41** H6
Lytham St Anne's U.K. **47** I10
Lytkarino Rus. Fed. **43** S6
Lyttelton N.Z. **153** G11
Lytton Canada **166** F5
Lyuban' Belarus **42** J9
Lyuban' Rus. Fed. **43** M2
Lyubanskaye Vodaskhovishcha *resr* Belarus **42** J9
Lyubavichi Rus. Fed. **43** L7
Lyubazh Rus. Fed. **43** Q9
Lyubcha Belarus **42** H8
Lyubertsy Rus. Fed. **43** S6
Lyubeshiv Ukr. **41** C6
Lyubim Rus. Fed. **43** V3
Lyubimets Bulg. **58** H7
Lyubimovka Rus. Fed. **43** T8
Lyubishchytsy Belarus **42** G9
Lyubitovo Rus. Fed. **43** P3
Lyubokhna Rus. Fed. **43** P8
Lyubomirovo Rus. Fed. **43** T2
Lyubotin Ukr. *see* **Lyubotyn**
Lyubotyn Ukr. **53** J2
also spelt Lyubotin
Lyubyacha Belarus **42** I8
Lyubytino Rus. Fed. **43** O3
Lyudinovo Rus. Fed. **43** P8
Lyugovichi Rus. Fed. **43** O1
Lyulyakovo Bulg. **58** I6
Lyunda *r.* Rus. Fed. **40** H4
Lyusina Belarus **42** H9
Lyzha *r.* Rus. Fed. **40** K2
Lža *r.* Latvia **42** J4
Lzha *r.* Rus. Fed. **43** J4

↓ **M**

Ma *r.* Myanmar **78** B3
Ma, Nam *r.* Laos **78** C3
Ma, Sông *r.* Vietnam **78** D4
Maalhosmadulu Atoll Maldives **94** B5
Maamakundhoo *i.* Maldives *see* **Makunudhoo**
Maamba Zambia **127** E9
Ma'an Cameroon **125** H6
Ma'ān Jordan **108** G7
Maaninka Fin. **44** N3
Maaninkavaara Fin. **44** O2
Maanselkä Fin. **44** O3
Ma'anshan China **87** F2
Maanyt *Bulgan* Mongolia **84** D1
Maanyt *Töv* Mongolia **85** E2
Maardu Estonia **42** G2
Maarianhamina Fin. *see* **Mariehamn**
Ma'arrat an Nu'mān Syria **109** H2
Maartenshoop S. Africa **133** O1
Maas *r.* Neth. **48** B4
also spelt Meuse (Belgium/France)
Maaseik Belgium **51** L1
Maasin Phil. **74** C4
Maas-Schwalm-Nette *nat. park* Germany/Neth. **48** C4
Maastricht Neth. **48** C5
Maatsuyker Group *is* Australia **147** E5
Maba China **87** F1
Maba Indon. **75** D2
Maba, Ouadi *watercourse* Chad **120** D6
Mabalacat Phil. **74** B3
Mabalane Moz. **131** G4
Mabana Dem. Rep. Congo **126** F4
Mabanda Gabon **126** A5
Ma'bar Yemen **104** D5
Mabaruma Guyana **199** G2
Mabating China *see* **Hongshan**
Mabein Myanmar **78** B3
Mabel Creek Australia **146** B2
Mabel Downs Australia **150** D3
Mabella Canada **168** B3
Maberly Canada **173** Q6
Mabian China **86** B2
also known as Minjian
Mablethorpe U.K. **47** M10
Mably France **51** K6
Mabopane S. Africa **133** M2
Mabote Moz. **131** G4
Mabou Canada **169** I4
Mabrak, Jabal *mt.* Jordan **108** G7
Mabroûk *well* Mali **125** E2
Mabrous *well* Niger **125** I1
Mabuasehube Game Reserve *nature res.* Botswana **130** D5
Mabudis *i.* Phil. **74** B1
Mabula S. Africa **133** L1
Ma'būs Yūsuf *oasis* Libya **120** D3
Mabutsane Botswana **130** D5
Macá, Monte *mt.* Chile **205** B7
Macachín Arg. **204** E5
Macadam Plains Australia **151** B5
Macadam Range *hills* Australia **148** A2
Macaé Brazil **203** D7
Macael Spain **55** I7
Macaíba Brazil **202** F3
Macajalar Bay Phil. **74** C4
Macajuba Brazil **202** D5
Macaloge Moz. **129** B8
formerly known as Miranda *or* Vila Miranda
MacAlpine Lake Canada **167** K1
Macamic Canada **168** E3
Macan, Kepulauan *atolls* Indon. *see* **Taka'Bonerate, Kepulauan**
Macandze Moz. **131** G4
Macaneta, Ponta de *pt* Moz. **133** Q2
Macao China *see* **Macau**
Macapá *Amapá* Brazil **199** I4
Macapá *Amazonas* Brazil **200** D2
Macará Ecuador **198** B6
Macaracas Panama **186** C6
Macarani Brazil **202** D5
Macarena, Cordillera *mts* Col. **198** C4
Macareo, Caño *r.* Venez. **199** F2
Macas Ecuador **198** B5
Maçãs *r.* Port./Spain **54** E3
Macassar Indon. *see* **Ujung Pandang**
Macassar Strait Indon. *see* **Makassar Strait**
Macau Brazil **202** E3
Macau China **87** E4
also known as Aomen; *also spelt* Macao
Macaúã *r.* Brazil **200** C2
Macaúba Brazil **202** B4
Macaúbas Brazil **202** D5
Macauley Island N.Z. **145** H5
Macayari Col. **198** C4
Macbride Head Falkland Is **205** F8
Maccaretane Moz. **131** G5
Macclenny U.S.A. **175** D6
Macclesfield U.K. **47** J10
Macclesfield Bank *sea feature* S. China Sea **72** D3
also known as Zhongsha Qundao
Macdiarmid Canada **168** B3
Macdonald, Lake *salt flat* Australia **150** E4
MacDonnell Creek *watercourse* Australia **146** C2
Macdonnell Ranges *mts* Australia **148** A4
MacDowell Lake Canada **167** M4
Macedo de Cavaleiros Port. **54** E3
Macedon *country* Europe *see* **Macedonia**
▶**Macedonia** *country* Europe **58** C7
spelt Makedonija *in Macedonian; historically known as* Macedon; *long form* Former Yugoslav Republic of Macedonia; *short form* F.Y.R.O.M.
europe [countries] ▶ 32–35
Maceió Brazil **202** F4
Maceio, Ponta da *pt* Brazil **202** E3
Macenta Guinea **124** C4
Macerata Italy **56** F5
Macfarlane, Lake *salt flat* Australia **146** C3

index

M

Macgillycuddy's Reeks mts Rep. of Ireland 47 C12
Mach Pak. 101 F4
Macha Rus. Fed. 39 L3
Machacalis Brazil 207 H4
Machacamarca Bol. 200 D4
Machachi Ecuador 198 B5
Machadinho r. Brazil 201 E2
Machado Brazil 207 H8
Machadodorp S. Africa 133 O2
Machai Zambia 127 E8
Machaila Moz. 131 G4
Machakos Kenya 128 C5
Machala Ecuador 198 B5
Machali China see Madoi
Machanga Moz. 131 G4
Machareti Bol. 201 E5
Machar Marshes Sudan 128 B2
Machattie, Lake salt flat Australia 148 C5
Machatuine Moz. 133 Q2
Machaze Moz. see Chitobe
Machecoul France 50 E6
Macherla India 94 C2
Machesney Park U.S.A. 172 E8
Machhiwara India 96 C3
formerly spelt Machiwara
Machhlishahr India 97 E4
Machias ME U.S.A. 174 H2
Machias NY U.S.A. 176 H3
Machico Mauritius see Bioco
Machilipatnam India 94 D2
also known as Masulipatnam; formerly known as Bandar
Machina Malawi 129 B8
Machiques Venez. 198 C2
Machiwara India see Machhiwara
Māch Kowr Iran 101 E5
Macho, Arroyo del watercourse U.S.A. 181 F6
Machupicchu tourist site Peru 200 B3
Machupo r. Bol. 200 D3
Machynlleth U.K. 47 I11
Macia Moz. 131 G5
Macias Nguema i. Equat. Guinea see Bioco
Măcin Romania 58 J3
Macintyre r. Australia 147 F2
Macintyre Brook r. Australia 147 F2
Macizo de Tocate mts Peru 200 B3
Macka Turkey 107 D2
also known as Cevizlik
Mackay Australia 149 F4
MacKay r. Canada 167 I3
Mackay, Lake salt flat Australia 150 E4
MacKay Lake Canada 167 I2
Mackay Mountains Antarctica 222 O1
Mackenzie r. Australia 149 F4
Mackenzie B.C. Canada 166 F4
Mackenzie Ont. Canada 172 E2
►Mackenzie r. Canada 166 C2
northamerica [landscapes] ➤➤ 156–157
Mackenzie Guyana see Linden
Mackenzie atoll Micronesia see Ulithi
Mackenzie Bay Antarctica 223 F2
Mackenzie Bay Canada 164 F3
Mackenzie Bison Sanctuary nature res. Canada 167 G2
Mackenzie Highway Canada 167 G2
Mackenzie King Island Canada 165 H2
Mackenzie Mountains Canada 166 C1
►Mackenzie-Peace-Finlay r. Canada 166
2nd longest river in North America.
northamerica [landscapes] ➤➤ 156–157
Mackillop, Lake salt flat Australia see Yamma Yamma, Lake
Mackinac, Straits of lake channel U.S.A. 173 H5
Mackinac Island U.S.A. 173 I5
Mackinaw r. U.S.A. 174 B3
Macklin Canada 167 I4
Macksville Australia 147 G2
Mackunda Creek watercourse Australia 149 D4
Maclean Australia 147 G2
Macleantown S. Africa 133 L9
Maclear S. Africa 133 M8
Macleay r. Australia 147 G2
MacLeod Canada see Fort Macleod
MacLeod, Lake imp. l. Australia 150 A5
Macmillan r. Canada 166 C2
Macmillan Pass Canada 166 D2
Maçobere Moz. 131 G4
Macocola Angola 127 C6
Macomb U.S.A. 174 B3
Macomer Sardegna Italy 57 A8
Mâcon France 51 K6
Macon GA U.S.A. 175 D5
Macon MO U.S.A. 174 D4
Macon MS U.S.A. 175 B5
Macon OH U.S.A. 176 B7
Macon, Bayou r. U.S.A. 175 B6
Macondo Angola 127 D8
Macossa Moz. 131 G3
Macotera Spain 54 F4
Macoun Lake Canada 167 K3
Macovane Moz. 131 G4
Macpherson Robertson Land reg. Antarctica see Mac. Robertson Land
Macquarie r. N.S.W. Australia 147 E2
Macquarie r. Tas. Australia 147 E5
Macquarie Harbour Australia 147 E5
►Macquarie Island S. Pacific Ocean 220 E9
Part of Australia. Most southerly point of Oceania.
Macquarie Marshes Australia 147 E2
Macquarie Marshes Nature Reserve Australia 147 E2
Macquarie Mountain Australia 147 E3
Macraes Flat N.Z. 153 E13

MacRitchie Reservoir Sing. 76 [inset]
Mac. Robertson Land reg. Antarctica 223 E2
long form Macpherson Robertson Land
Macroom Rep. of Ireland 47 D12
Mactún Mex. 185 H5
Macú Brazil 198 D4
Macuira, Parque Nacional nat. park Col. 198 D1
Macuje Col. 198 C4
Macukull Albania 58 B7
Macumba Australia 146 B1
Macumba watercourse Australia 146 C1
Macururé Brazil 202 E4
Macusani Peru 200 C3
Macuspana Mex. 185 G5
Macuzari, Presa resr Mex. 184 C3
Macuze Moz. 131 H3
Madabá Jordan 108 G6
Madadeni S. Africa 133 O4

►Madagascar country Africa 131 [inset] J4
Largest island in Africa and 4th in the world.
africa [landscapes] ➤➤ 112–113
africa [countries] ➤➤ 114–117

Madagli Nigeria 125 I4
Madā'in Şāliḥ Saudi Arabia 104 B2
Madalena Brazil 202 E3
Madama Niger 123 I5
Madan Bulg. 58 F7
Madana Chad 126 C2
Madana well Chad 120 C5
Madanapalle India 94 C3
Madang P.N.G. 73 K8
Madaoara India 96 C4
Madaoua Niger 125 G3
Mādārāş Romania 58 C2
Madaripur Bangl. 97 F5
Madarounfa Niger 125 G3
Madau Turkm. 102 C5
also spelt Madaw; formerly known as Suidzhikurmsy
Madaw Turkm. see Madau
Madawaska India 93 P5
Madawaska r. Canada 168 E4
Madaya Myanmar 78 B3
Maddalena, Isola i. Sardegna Italy 56 B7
Maddaloni Italy 56 G7
Madded India 94 D2
Maddur India 94 C3
Madeir Sudan 126 F3

►Madeira r. Brazil 199 G5
4th longest river in South America.
southamerica [landscapes] ➤➤ 190–191

►Madeira terr. N. Atlantic Ocean 122 A2
Autonomous Region of Portugal. Long form Madeira, Arquipélago de.
africa [countries] ➤➤ 114–117

Madeira, Arquipélago da terr. N. Atlantic Ocean see Madeira
Madeirinha r. Brazil 201 E2
Madeley U.K. 47 J11
Madeline Island U.S.A. 172 C4
Madel Ouèï Chad 126 C2
Maden Turkey 107 D3
Madeniyet Kazakh. 103 I3
Madera Mex. 184 C2
Madera U.S.A. 182 D5
Madgaon India 94 B3
formerly known as Margao
Madgoul Djibouti 128 D1
Madhavpur India 96 A5
Madhepura India 97 E4
Madhoganj India 89 D7
Madhubani India 97 E4
Madhugiri India 94 C3
Madhya Pradesh state India 96 C5
formerly known as Central Provinces
Madi, Dataran Tinggi plat. Indon. 77 F2
Madibogo S. Africa 133 J3
Madikeri India 94 B3
Madill U.S.A. 179 C5
Madimba Angola 127 B6
Madimba Dem. Rep. Congo 126 B6
Madinani Côte d'Ivoire 124 D4
Madînat al 'Abîd Yemen 104 D5
Madînat ash Sha'b Yemen 104 D5
formerly known as Al Ittihad
Madinat ath Thawrah Syria 109 J2
also known as Tabaqah
Madingo-Kayes Congo 126 A6
Madinguou Congo 126 B6
Madingrin Cameroon 125 I4
Madini r. Bol. 200 D3
Madirovalo Madag. 131 [inset] J3
Madison AL U.S.A. 174 C5
Madison FL U.S.A. 175 D6
Madison GA U.S.A. 175 D5
Madison IN U.S.A. 174 C4
Madison ME U.S.A. 177 P1
Madison MN U.S.A. 178 C2
Madison NC U.S.A. 176 F9
Madison NE U.S.A. 178 C3
Madison OH U.S.A. 176 D4
Madison SD U.S.A. 178 C2
Madison VA U.S.A. 176 G7

►Madison WI U.S.A. 172 D7
State capital of Wisconsin.

Madison WV U.S.A. 176 D7
Madison r. U.S.A. 180 E3
Madison Heights U.S.A. 176 F8
Madisonville KY U.S.A. 174 C4
Madisonville TN U.S.A. 174 C5
Madisonville TX U.S.A. 179 D6
Madita Indon. 75 B5
Madiun Indon. 77 E4
Madjingo Gabon 126 B4
Madley, Mount hill Australia 150 C5
Madliena Latvia 42 G5
Mado Dem. Rep. Congo 126 F4
Madoc Canada 168 E4
Mado Gashi Kenya 128 C4
Madoi China 86 A1
also known as Machali
Madona Latvia 42 H5
Madongo Pan salt pan Botswana 130 D4
Madonie mts Sicilia Italy 57 F11
Madra Dağı mts Turkey 106 A3
Madrakah Saudi Arabia 104 A3
Madrakah, Ra's c. Oman 105 G4
Madras India see Chennai
Madras state India see Tamil Nadu
Madras U.S.A. 180 B3
Madre, Laguna lag. Mex. 185 F3
Madre, Laguna lag. U.S.A. 179 C7
Madre, Sierra mts Mex. 185 H6
also known as Madre de Chiapas, Sierra or Soconusco, Sierra de
Madre, Sierra mts Phil. 74 B2
Madre de Chiapas, Sierra mts Mex. see Madre, Sierra
Madre de Deus de Minas Brazil 207 I8
Madre de Dios dept Peru 200 C3
Madre de Dios, Isla i. Chile 205 B8
Madre del Sur, Sierra mts Mex. 185 F5
Madre Occidental, Sierra mts Mex. 184 C2
Madre Oriental, Sierra mts Mex. 185 F3
Madrès, Pic de mt. France 51 I10
Madrid India see Chennai

►Madrid Spain 54 H4
Capital of Spain.

Madrid aut. comm. Spain 54 H4
Madridejos Phil. 74 B4
Madridejos Spain 55 H5

Madrona, Sierra mts Spain 54 G6
Madruga Cuba 186 C2
Madrūsah Libya 120 B3
Maduda Dem. Rep. Congo 126 B6
Madugula India 95 D2
Madura r. Indon. 77 F4
Madura i. Indon. 77 F4
Madurai India 94 C4
Madurantakam India 94 C3
Madvār, Kūh-e mt. Iran 100 C4
Madwas India 97 D4
Madzhalis Rus. Fed. 102 A4
Madziwadzido Zimbabwe 131 F3
Madziwa Mine Zimbabwe 131 F3
Maebashi Japan 91 F6
Mae Hong Son Thai. 78 B4
Maelang Indon. 75 B2
Maella Spain 55 L3
Mae Ramat Thai. 78 B4
Māeriște Romania 58 D1
Mae Sariang Thai. 78 B4
Maeser U.S.A. 183 P1
Maes Howe tourist site U.K. 46 I4
Mae Sot Thai. 78 B4
Maestra, Sierra mts Cuba 186 D3
Mae Suai Thai. 78 B4
Mae Tuen Wildlife Reserve nature res. Thai. 78 B4
Maevatanana Madag. 131 [inset] J3
Maéwo i. Vanuatu 145 F3
also spelt Maiwo; formerly known as Aurora Island
Mae Wong National Park Thai. 78 B5
Mae Yom National Park Thai. 78 C4
Mafa Indon. 75 C2
Mafeking Canada 167 K4
Mafeking S. Africa see Mafikeng
Mafeteng Lesotho 133 L6
Mafia Channel Tanz. 129 C7
Mafia Island Tanz. 129 C6
Mafikeng S. Africa 133 J2
formerly spelt Mafeking
Mafinga Tanz. 129 B7
Mafra Brazil 201 H6
Mafra Port. 54 B6
Mafraq Jordan see Al Mafraq
Mafungabusi Plateau Zimbabwe 131 F3
Magabeni S. Africa 133 O7
Magaela hill Spain 54 F6
Magadan Rus. Fed. 39 P4
Magadi Kenya 128 C5
Magaliesburg S. Africa 133 L2
Magallanes Chile see Punta Arenas
Magallanes Phil. 74 B3
Magallanes, Estrecho de sea chan. Chile see Magellan, Strait of
Magallanes y Antártica Chilena admin. reg. Chile 205 D9
Magangue Col. 198 C2
Maganik mt. Yugo. 56 L6
Mağara Turkey 106 C3
also known as Kirobasi
Mağarali Turkey 109 J1
Magaramkent Rus. Fed. 102 B4
Magaria Niger 125 H3
Magas Iran see Zābolī
Magas Rus. Fed. 107 F2
Magat r. Phil. 74 B2
Magazine Mountain hill U.S.A. 179 D5
Magbakele Dem. Rep. Congo 126 D4
Magburaka Sierra Leone 124 C4
Magdagachi Rus. Fed. 82 B1
Magdalena Bol. 201 D3
Magdalena dept Col. 198 C2
Magdalena r. Col. 198 C2
Magdalena Mex. 184 C2
Magdalena, Bahía b. Col. 198 B3
Magdalena, Bahía b. Mex. 184 C3
Magdalena, Isla i. Chile 205 B7
Magdalena, Isla i. Mex. 184 B3
Magdalene, Gunung mt. Sabah Malaysia 77 G1
Magdeburg Germany 48 I3
Magdelaine Cays atoll Australia 149 F3
Magee U.S.A. 175 B6
Magelang Indon. 77 E4
Magellan, Strait of Chile 205 C9
also known as Magallanes, Estrecho de
Magenta Italy 56 B3
Magenta, Lake salt flat Australia 151 B7
Magereya i. Norway 44 N1
Mage-shima i. Japan 91 B9
Maggia r. Switz. 51 O6
Maggiorasca, Monte mt. Italy 56 C4
Maggiore, Lago l. Italy see Maggiore, Lake
Maggiore, Lake Italy 56 A3
also known as Maggiore, Lago
Maggiore, Monte hill Sardegna Italy 57 B8
Maghāgha Egypt 121 F2
Magh'ā'ir Shu'ayb tourist site Saudi Arabia see Jethro
Maghama Mauritania 124 B3
Maghāra, Gebel hill Egypt 108 E7
Maghera U.K. 47 F9
Maghnia Alg. 123 E2
Maghor Afgh. 101 E3
Mâgina, Sierra mts Spain 55 H7
Magingo Tanz. 129 B7
Magione Italy 56 E5
Magitang China see Jainca
Maglaj Bos.-Herz. 56 K4
Maglavit Romania 58 E4
Maglie Italy 57 K8
Magma U.S.A. 183 M8
Magna U.S.A. 183 L1
Magna Granite hill Italy 57 E12
Magnet Bay Antarctica 223 D2
Magnetic Island Australia 149 E3
Magnetic Passage Australia 149 E3
Magnitnyy Rus. Fed. 43 Q9
Magnitogorsk Rus. Fed. 102 D1
Magnolia AR U.S.A. 179 D5
Magnolia MS U.S.A. 175 B6
Magnor Norway 45 K4
Magny-en-Vexin France 50 H3
Mago Rus. Fed. 82 F1
Mágocs-er r. Hungary 49 R9
Mágoé Moz. 131 F2
Magole Tanz. 129 C6
Mago National Park Eth. 128 C3
Magosa Cyprus see Famagusta
Magoye Zambia 127 E8
Magozal Mex. 185 F4
Magpie Canada 169 H3
Magpie r. Canada 168 C4
Magpie r. Que. Canada 169 H3
Magpie, Lac l. Canada 169 H3
Magpie-Ouest r. Canada 169 H3
Magrath Canada 167 H5
Magre r. Spain 55 K5
Magruder Mountain U.S.A. 182 G4
Magrur, Wadi watercourse Sudan 121 D5
Magu Tanz. 128 B5
Maguan China 86 B4
Maguarinho, Cabo c. Brazil 202 C2
Magude Moz. 131 G3
Magudu S. Africa 133 P4
Magura Bangl. 97 F5
Māgura mt. Slovakia 49 P7
Magura, Vârful hill Romania 58 D1
Mägüri, Vârful mt. Romania 58 D3
Maguse Lake Canada 167 M2
Magwali S. Africa 133 L5
Magway Myanmar 78 A3
Magwe admin. div. Myanmar see Magwe

Magway admin. div. Myanmar see Magwe
Magwe Myanmar 78 A3
also spelt Magway
Magwe admin. div. Myanmar 78 A3
also spelt Magway
Magwegqana watercourse Botswana 130 D3
Magyarkanizsa Vojvodina, Srbija Yugo. see Kanjiža
Magyar Köztársaság country Europe see Hungary
Magyichaung Myanmar 78 A3
Mahābād Iran 100 A2
also known as Sāüjbolāgh
Mahabe Madag. 131 [inset] J4
Mahabharat Range mts Nepal 97 E4
Mahabo Toliara Madag. 131 [inset] J4
Mahabo Toliara Madag. 131 [inset] J4
Mahaboboka Madag. 131 [inset] J5
formerly known as Maneva
Mahad India 94 B2
Mahaddayweyne Somalia 128 E4
Mahadeo Hills India 96 C5
Mahadeopur India 94 D2
Mahaffey U.S.A. 176 G5
Mahagi Dem. Rep. Congo 126 F4
Mahagi Port Dem. Rep. Congo 126 F4
Mahaicony Guyana 199 G3
Mahajan India 96 A3
Mahajanga Madag. 131 [inset] J2
formerly spelt Majunga
Mahajanga prov. Madag. 131 [inset] J3
Mahakam r. Indon. 77 G3
Mahalapye Botswana 131 E4
Mahale Mountain National Park Tanz. 129 A6
also known as Makari Mountain National Park
Mahalevona Madag. 131 [inset] K2
Mahallāt Iran 100 B3
Maham India 96 C3
Māhān Iran 100 D4
Mahanadi r. India 95 E1
Mahanoro Madag. 131 [inset] K3
Maharajganj Bihar India 97 E4
Maharajganj Uttar Pradesh India 97 D4
Maharajpur India 96 C4
Maharashtra state India 94 B2
Mahārlū, Daryācheh-ye salt l. Iran 100 C4
Maha Sarakham Thai. 78 C4
Mahash, Wādi watercourse Egypt 108 E9
Mahasham, Wādi el watercourse Egypt 108 F7
Mahatalaky Madag. 131 [inset] J5
Maḥaţţat Dab'ah Jordan 108 H6
Mahavavy r. Madag. 131 [inset] J2
Mahavelona Madag. 131 [inset] K3
also known as Foulpointe
Mahaweli Ganga r. Sri Lanka 94 D5
Mahazoma Madag. 131 [inset] J3
Mahbub Sudan 121 F6
Mahbubabad India 94 D2
Mahbubnagar India 94 C2
Mahd adh Dhahab Saudi Arabia 104 C3
Mahdia Alg. 123 F2
Mahdia Guyana 199 G3
Mahdia Tunisia 123 H2
also spelt Mehdia
Mahe China 84 D5
Mahe India 94 B4
also known as Mayyazhi; formerly known as Mahé
Mahé i. Seychelles 218 K6
Mahendragarh India 96 C3
Mahendragiri mt. India 95 E2
Mahenge Tanz. 129 C7
Maheno N.Z. 153 E13
Mahesana India 96 B5
formerly spelt Mahsana
Maheshwar India 96 B5
Mahfirhin Yemen 105 F5
Māhfūr well Saudi Arabia 109 K7
Mahgawan India 96 C4
Mahi r. India 96 B5
Mahi watercourse Iran 101 D4
Mahia N.Z. 152 L7
Mahia Peninsula N.Z. 152 L7
Mahilyow Belarus 43 L8
also spelt Mogilev
Mahilyow Oblast admin. div. Belarus see Mahilyowskaya Voblasts'
Mahilyowskaya Voblasts' admin. div. Belarus 43 L8
English form Mahilyow Oblast or Mogilev Oblast; also known as Mogilevskaya Oblast'
Mahim India 96 B5
Mahina Mali 124 C3
Mahkene mt. Sweden 44 K3
Mahlabatini S. Africa 133 P5
Mahlaing Myanmar 78 A3
Mahlangasi S. Africa 133 P4
Mahlatswetsa S. Africa 133 L5
Mahmudabad India 96 D4
Mahmudabad Iran 100 C2
Maḥmūd-e 'Erāqī Afgh. 101 G3
Mahmudia Romania 58 K3
Mahmudiye Turkey 59 H9
Mahmutlar Turkey 108 D1
Mahmutşevketpaşa Turkey 58 K7
Mahnomen U.S.A. 178 C2
Mahoba India 96 C4
Mahoenui N.Z. 152 I6
Maholi India 96 C4
Mahón Spain 55 P5
also spelt Maó
Mahone Bay Canada 169 H4
Mahonga Game Park nature res. Namibia 130 D3
Mahony Lake Canada 166 E1
Mahou Mali 124 D3
Mahrāt, Jabal mt. Yemen 105 F4
Mahrāt, Wādi r. Yemen 105 E4
Mahrauni India 96 C4
Mähres Tunisia 123 H2
Māhrūd Iran 101 E3
Mahsana India see Mahesana
Mahuanggou China 84 B4
Mahur Assam India 97 G4
Mahur Maharashtra India 94 C2
Mahuta Tanz. 129 C7
Mahuva India 96 A5
Mahya Dağı mt. Turkey 58 I7
Mahyār Iran 100 B3
Mai i. Indon. 75 D4
Maia American Samoa 145 I3
Maia Moz. see Nacala
Maiaia atoll Kiribati 145 H2
formerly known as Hall
Maicao Col. 198 C1
Maicasagi r. Canada 168 E3
Maicasagi, Lac l. Canada 168 E3
Maiche France 51 M5
Maici r. Brazil 199 F6
Maicuru r. Brazil 199 H5
Maidens U.K. 46 H8
Maidi Indon. 75 C2
Maidstone Canada 167 I4
Maidstone U.K. 47 N12
Maiduguri Nigeria 125 I4
Maienga Rus. Fed. 102 A4
Maïeru Romania 58 F1
Maigh Nuad Rep. of Ireland see Maynooth
Mai Gudo mt. Eth. 128 C3
Maihar India 96 D4
Maihih N.Z. 152 J6
Maiji Shan mt. China 86 C1
Maijdi Bangl. 97 F5
Maiji Shan mt. China 86 C1
Maikal Range hills India 96 D5

Maiko r. Dem. Rep. Congo 126 E4
Mailani Hill mt. India 97 D5
Mailani India 96 D3
Mailao Chad 126 B2
Mailpy Pak. 101 H4
Ma'in tourist site Yemen 104 D4
Mainaguri India 97 F4
Main Brook Canada 169 K3
Main Channel lake channel Canada 173 L6
Maindargi India 94 C2
Mai-Ndombe, Lac l. Dem. Rep. Congo 126 C5
formerly known as Léopold II, Lac
Maine state U.S.A. 177 O1
Maine, Gulf of U.S.A. 177 P2
Mainé Hanari, Cerro hill Col. 198 C5
Maïné-Soroa Niger 125 H3
Maingkwan Myanmar 78 B2
Maingy Island Myanmar 79 B5
Mainhardt Germany 48 I7
Mainit Phil. 74 C4
Mainit, Lake Phil. 74 C4
Mainkung China 86 A2
Mainland i. Scotland U.K. 46 I4
Mainland i. Shetland, Scotland U.K. 46 K3
Mainling China 89 F6
also known as Tungdor
Mainoru Australia 148 B2
Mainoru r. Australia 148 B2
Mainpat reg. India 97 D5
Mainpuri India 96 C4
Main Range National Park Australia 147 G2
Maintenon France 50 H4
Maintirano Madag. 131 [inset] J3
Mainua Fin. 44 N2
Mainz Germany 48 F5
historically known as Mogontiacum
Maio i. Cape Verde 124 [inset]
Maipó, Volcán vol. Chile 204 F5
Maipú Buenos Aires Arg. 204 F5
Maipú Mendoza Arg. 204 C4
Maipures Col. 198 D4
Maipuri Landing Guyana 199 G4
Maiquetía Venez. 199 E2
Maiquinique Brazil 207 M2
Mairabari India 97 G4
Mairinque Brazil 206 G10
Mairipotaba Brazil 206 D4
Maisí Cuba 187 E2
Maïsiagala Lith. 42 G7
Maiskal Island Bangl. 97 F5
Maisons-Laffitte France 51 I4
Maitencillo Chile 204 C3
Maitengwe Botswana 131 E3
Maithon India 97 E5
Maitland N.S.W. Australia 147 F3
Maitland S.A. Australia 146 C3
Maitland r. Australia 148 B2
Maitland, Banjaran mts Sabah Malaysia 77 G1
Maitland, Lake salt flat Australia 151 C5
Maitri research station Antarctica 223 A2
Maiwo i. Vanuatu see Maéwo
Maiwok r. Australia 148 B2
Maiz, Islas del is Nicaragua 186 C4
also known as Corn Islands
Maizhokunggar China 89 E6
also known as Kunggar or Medu Konçar
Maizuru Japan 91 D7
Maja Jezercë mt. Albania 58 A6
Majagual Col. 198 C2
Majari r. Brazil 199 F4
Majdalah Yemen 105 F5
Majdanpek Srbija Yugo. 58 D4
Maje Brazil 207 J9
Majene Indon. 75 A3
Majevica mts Bos.-Herz. 56 K4
Majhgawan India 96 D4
Majholi India 96 C5
Majiang Guizhou China 87 D3
Majiang Guizhou China 87 C3
also known as Xingshan
Majol country N. Pacific Ocean see Marshall Islands
Major, Puig mt. Spain 55 N5
also spelt Mayor, Puig
Majorca i. Spain see Mallorca
also spelt Mallorca
Mâjro atoll Marshall Is see Majuro
Majuli Island India 97 G4
Majunga Madag. see Mahajanga
Majuriá Brazil 200 D1
Majuro atoll Marshall Is 220 F5
also spelt Mâjro; formerly spelt Meduro
Majwemasweu S. Africa 133 K5
Maka Senegal 124 B3
Makabana Congo 126 B5
Makahuena Point U.S.A. 181 [inset] Y1
Makak Cameroon 125 H6
Makale Indon. 75 A3
Makalehi i. Indon. 75 C2

►Makalu mt. China/Nepal 89 D7
5th highest mountain in the world and in Asia.
world [physical features] ➤➤ 8–9

Makalu Barun National Park Nepal 97 E4
Makamba Burundi 126 F6
Makanshy Kazakh. 88 C2
also spelt Maqanshy
Makanjila Malawi 129 B8
Makanya Tanz. 129 C6
Makanza Dem. Rep. Congo 126 C4
also spelt Mankanza; formerly known as Nouvelle Anvers
Makarakomb Madag. 131 [inset] J3
Makarewa N.Z. 153 C14
Makari Cameroon 125 I3
Makari Mountain National Park Tanz. see Mahale Mountain National Park
Makarov Rus. Fed. 82 F2
Makarska Croatia 56 I5
Makar'ye Rus. Fed. 40 I4
Makassar Indon. see Ujung Pandang
Makassar Strait Indon. 75 A3
also known as Macassar Strait
Makat Kazakh. 102 C3
also spelt Maqat
Makatini Flats lowland S. Africa 133 Q4
Makaw Myanmar 78 B2
Makay, Massif du mts Madag. 131 [inset] J4
Makedonija country Europe see Macedonia
Makelekete Sierra Leone 124 C4
Makeni Sierra Leone 124 C4
Makete Tanz. 129 B7
Makeyevka Ukr. see Makiyivka
Makgadikgadi salt pan Botswana 131 E4
Makgadikgadi Pans National Park Botswana 131 E4
Makhachkala Rus. Fed. 102 A4
Makhaleng r. Lesotho 133 L7
Makhambet Kazakh. 102 B3
formerly known as Yamankhalinka
Makhmar, Jabal al hill Saudi Arabia 104 C2
Makharadze Georgia see Ozurget'i
Makhmūr Iraq 107 F4
Makhfar al Ḩammām Syria 109 J2
Makhtal India 94 C2
Makhyah, Wādi r. Yemen 105 E4
Makin atoll Kiribati see Butaritari
Makindu Kenya 128 C5
Makinsk Kazakh. 103 G1

Makira i. Solomon Is see San Cristobal
Makiyivka Ukr. 41 F6
also spelt Makeyevka; formerly known as Dmitriyevsk or Dmytriyevs'k
Makkah Saudi Arabia see Mecca
Makkah prov. Saudi Arabia 104 C3
Makkaurhalveya Naturreservat nature res. Norway 44 O1
Makkovik Canada 169 J2
Makkovik, Cape Canada 169 J2
Maklaki Rus. Fed. 43 P7
Makljen pass Bos.-Herz. 56 J5
Makó Hungary 53 G2
Makoa, Serra hills Brazil 199 G4
Makokou Gabon 126 B4
Makokskraal S. Africa 133 K3
Makonde Plateau Tanz. 129 C7
Makongolosi Tanz. 129 B6
Makopong Botswana 130 D5
Makoro Dem. Rep. Congo 126 F4
Makotipoko Congo 126 C5
Makoua Congo 126 B5
Makovnik mt. Croatia 56 H3
Maków Mazowiecki Poland 49 S3
Makra i. Greece 59 G12
Makrakomi Greece 59 D10
Makran reg. Iran/Pak. 101 E5
Makrana India 96 B4
Makran Coast Range mts Pak. see Talar-i-Band
Makronisi i. Greece 59 F11
Makronisi i. Greece 59 H11
Maksatikha Rus. Fed. 43 Q4
Maksi India 96 C5
Maksimovka Rus. Fed. 82 E3
Maksotag Iran 101 E4
Maksudangarh India 96 C5
Makthar Tunisia 57 B13
Mākū Iran 100 A2
Makum India 97 G4
Makumbako Tanz. 129 B7
Makumbi Dem. Rep. Congo 127 D6
Makundu i. Maldives see Makunudhoo
Makunduchi Tanz. 129 C6
Makung Taiwan 87 F4
Makungwiro Tanz. 129 C7
Makunudhoo i. Maldives 94 B5
also known as Maamakundhoo; also spelt Makundu
Makurazaki Japan 91 B9
Makurdi Nigeria 125 H5
Makuri N.Z. 152 J8
Makuungo Somalia 128 D4
Makuyuni Tanz. 128 C5
Makwassie S. Africa 133 J4
Mal India 97 F4
Mala Peru 200 A3
Mala Rep. of Ireland see Mallow
Mala i. Solomon Is see Malaita
Malá Sweden 44 L2
Mala, Punta pt Panama 186 C6
Mala Aboriginal Land res. Australia 148 A4
Malabang Phil. 74 A4
Malabar Coast India 94 B3

►Malabo Equat. Guinea 125 H6
Capital of Equatorial Guinea. Formerly known as Santa Isabel.

Malabuñgan Phil. 74 A4
Malaca Spain see Málaga
Malacacheta Brazil 207 K4
Malacca Malaysia see Melaka
Malacca state Malaysia see Melaka
Malacca, Strait of Indon./Malaysia 76 B1
Malacky Slovakia 49 O7
Malad r. U.S.A. 180 D4
Malad City U.S.A. 180 D4
Maladzyechna Belarus 42 H7
also spelt Molodechno
Mala Fatra nat. park Slovakia 49 O6
Málaga Spain 54 G8
also spelt Malaca
Málaga NJ U.S.A. 177 J6
Malaga NM U.S.A. 181 F6
Malaga OH U.S.A. 176 D6
Malagarasi r. Burundi/Tanz. 129 A6
Malagarasi Tanz. 129 A6
Malagón Spain 54 H5
Malagón r. Spain 54 D7
Malahar Indon. 75 B5
Malaimbandy Madag. 131 [inset] J4
Mala Ina r. Poland 49 M2
Malaita i. Solomon Is 145 F2
also known as Mala; historically known as Carteret Island
Malaka mt. Indon. 77 G5
Malakal Sudan 128 A2
Malakanagiri India 94 D2
Mala Kapela mts Croatia 56 I3
Malakheti Nepal 96 D3
Malak Malak Aboriginal Land res. Australia 148 A2
Malakula i. Vanuatu 145 F3
Malakwal Pak. 101 H3
Malali Guyana 199 G3
Malamala Indon. 75 B3
Malamaui i. Phil. 74 B5
Malampaya Sound sea chan. Phil. 74 A4
Malan, Ras pt Pak. 101 F5
Malang Indon. 77 F4
Malanga Moz. 129 C8
Malangali Tanz. 129 B7
Malangana Nepal see Malangwa
Malange Angola see Malanje
Malangsedet Norway 44 L1
Malangwa Nepal 97 E4
also known as Malangana
Malanipa i. Phil. 74 B5
Malanje Angola 127 C7
formerly known as Malange
Malanje prov. Angola 127 C7
Malanut Bay Phil. 74 A4
Malanville Benin 125 F4
Malanzán Arg. 204 D3
Malanzán, Sierra de mts Arg. 204 D3
Malappuram India 94 C4
Malaren I. Sweden 45 L4
Malarpe Arg. 204 C4
Malaripó Brazil 199 H4
Malartic Canada 168 E3
Malartic, Lac l. Canada 173 O2
Malasoro, Teluk b. Indon. 75 A4
Malaspina Arg. 205 D7
Malaspina Glacier U.S.A. 166 A3
Malaspina Strait Canada 166 E5
Malatayur, Tanjung pt Indon. 77 F3
Malatya Turkey 107 D3
historically known as Melitene or Milid
Malaut India 96 B3
Malavalli India 94 C3
Malavate Fr. Guiana 199 H4
Malāvi Iran 100 A3
Malawali i. Sabah Malaysia 77 G1

►Malawi country Africa 129 B7
formerly known as Nyasaland
africa [countries] ➤➤ 114–117

Malawi, Lake Africa see Nyasa, Lake
Malawi National Park Zambia see Nyika National Park
Malawiya Sudan 121 H6
Malax Fin. 44 M3
Malaya pen. Malaysia see Peninsular Malaysia
Malaya Byerastavitsa Belarus 42 E8
Malaya Pera Rus. Fed. 40 J2
Malaya Vishera Rus. Fed. 43 N3
Malāyer Iran 100 B3
also known as Daulatabad
Malay Reef Australia 149 F3

Malay Sary Kazakh. 103 I3
▶Malaysia country Asia 76 C1
formerly known as Federated Malay States
asia [countries] 64–67
Malaysia, Semenanjung pen. Malaysia see Peninsular Malaysia
Malazgirt Turkey 107 E3
Malbaie r. Canada 169 G4
Malbaza Niger 125 G3
Malbon Australia 149 D4
Malbork Poland 49 Q1
historically known as Marienburg
Malbrán Arg. 204 E3
Malchin Germany 49 J2
Malcolm Australia 151 C6
Malcolm, Point Australia 151 C7
Malcolm Inlet Oman see Ghazira, Ghubbat al
Maldegem Belgium 51 J1
Malden U.S.A. 174 B4
Malden Island Kiribati 221 H6
▶Maldives country Indian Ocean 93 D10
also known as Divehi
asia [countries] 64–67
Maldon U.K. 47 M12
Maldonado Uruguay 204 G4
Maldonado, Punta pt Mex. 185 F5

▶Male Maldives 93 D10
Capital of the Maldives.
world [countries] 10–11

Male Myanmar 78 B3
Maléa Guinea 124 C4
Maleas, Akra pt Lesbos Greece 59 H9
Maleas, Akra pt Greece 59 E12
Male Atoll Maldives 93 D10
Malebogo S. Africa 133 J5
Malegaon Maharashtra India 94 B1
Malegaon Maharashtra India 94 C2
Malei Moz. 131 H3
Malé Karpaty hills Slovakia 49 O7
Malek Siāh, Kūh-e mt. Afgh. 101 E4
Malela Maniema Dem. Rep. Congo 126 E5
Malela Maniema Dem. Rep. Congo 126 E6
Malélé Congo 126 B6
Malele Dem. Rep. Congo 127 B6
Malema Moz. 131 H2
formerly known as Entre Rios
Malendo watercourse Nigeria 125 G4
Malente Germany 48 H1
Maleoskop S. Africa 133 N2
Målerås Sweden 45 K4
Maler Kotla India 96 B3
Maleševske Planine mts Bulg./Macedonia 58 D7
Malesherbes France 51 I4
Malesina Greece 59 E10
Mālestān Afgh. 101 F3
Malestroit France 50 D5
Maleta Rus. Fed. 85 F1
Malevka Rus. Fed. 43 T8
Malgas S. Africa 132 E11
Malgobek Rus. Fed. 41 H8
Malgomaj l. Sweden 44 L2
Malha Sudan 121 E6
Malhada Brazil 202 D5
Malham Saudi Arabia 105 D2
Malhargarh India 96 B4
Malheur r. U.S.A. 180 C3
Malheur Lake U.S.A. 180 C4
Malheur National Wildlife Refuge nature res. U.S.A. 180 C4
▶Mali country Africa 124 E2
formerly known as French Sudan
africa [countries] 114–117
Mali Dem. Rep. Congo 126 E5
Mali Guinea 124 B3
Malia Greece 59 G13
also spelt Mallia
Malian r. China 85 E5
Maliana East Timor 75 C5
Malianjing Gansu China 84 B3
Malianjing Gansu China 84 D4
Malibamatso r. Lesotho 133 M6
Malibu U.S.A. 182 F7
Maligay Bay Phil. 74 B5
Malihabad India 89 C7
Mali Hka r. Myanmar 78 B2
Malikdin Afgh. 101 G3
Malik Naro mt. Pak. 101 E4
Maliku Indon. 75 B3
Mali Kyun i. Myanmar 79 B5
also known as Tavoy Island
Malili Indon. 75 B3
Mali Lošinj Croatia 56 G4
Malimba, Monts mts Dem. Rep. Congo 127 F6
Malin Rep. of Ireland 47 E8
Malin Ukr. see Malyn
Malindi Kenya 128 D5
Malines Belgium see Mechelen
Malinga Gabon 126 B5
Malin Head Rep. of Ireland 46 E8
Malini Romania 58 H1
Malino Indon. 75 A4
Malino Rus. Fed. 43 T6
Malino, Gunung mt. Indon. 75 B2
Malinovka r. Rus. Fed. 82 D3
Malinovoye Ozero Rus. Fed. 103 I2
formerly known as Mikhaylovskiy
Malinyi Tanz. 129 C7
Malipo China 86 C4
Maliq Albania 58 B8
Mali Raginac mt. Croatia 56 H4
Malit, Qafa e pass Albania 58 B6
Malita Phil. 74 C5
Malitbog Phil. 74 C4
Maliwun Myanmar 79 B6
Maliya India 96 A5
Malka r. Rus. Fed. 41 H8
Malka Mary Kenya 128 D3
Malkapur Maharashtra India 94 B2
Malkapur Maharashtra India 94 C1
Malkara Turkey 106 A2
Mal'kavichy Belarus 42 H9
Malkhanskiy Khrebet mts Rus. Fed. 85 F1
Malko Tŭrnovo Bulg. 58 I7
Mallacoota Australia 147 F4
Mallacoota Inlet b. Australia 147 F4
Mallaig U.K. 46 G7
Mallanga well Chad 120 D5
Mallani reg. India 96 A4
Mallawi Egypt 121 F3
Mallee Cliffs National Park Australia 147 D3
Mållejus hill Norway 44 M1
Mallery Lake Canada 167 L1
Mallét Brazil 203 B8
Mallia Greece see Malia
Mallorca i. Spain see Majorca
Mallow Rep. of Ireland 47 D11
also spelt Mala
Mallowa Well Australia 150 D4
Malm Norway 44 J2
Malmberget Sweden 44 M2
Malmédy Belgium 51 M2
Malmesbury S. Africa 132 C10
Malmesbury U.K. 47 J12
Malmköping Sweden 45 L4
Malmö Sweden 45 K5
Malmö-Sturup airport Sweden 45 K5
Malmslätt Sweden 45 K4
Malmyzh Rus. Fed. 40 I4
Malo i. Indon. 75 C1
Maloarkhangel'sk Rus. Fed. 43 R9
Maloca Amazonas Brazil 199 F5
Maloca Pará Brazil 199 H4
Maloca Salamaim Brazil 201 E3
Malo Crniće Srbija Yugo. 58 C4
Malolos Phil. 74 B3
Malolotja Nature Reserve Swaziland 133 P3
Maloma Swaziland 133 P4
Malombe, Lake Malawi 129 B8
Malone U.S.A. 177 K1
Malong China 86 B3
also known as Tongquan
Malonga Dem. Rep. Congo 127 D7
Małopolska, Wyżyna hills Poland 49 R5
Maloshuyka Rus. Fed. 40 F3
Malovan pass Bos.-Herz. 56 J5
Malovăţ Romania 58 D4
Malowera Moz. 131 F2
formerly spelt Maluera
Måløy Norway 44 I3
Maloyaroslavets Rus. Fed. 43 R6
Maloye Borisovo Rus. Fed. 43 R2
Malozemel'skaya Tundra lowland Rus. Fed. 40 I2
Malpelo, Isla de i. N. Pacific Ocean 198 A4
Malpica Spain 54 C1
Mālpils Latvia 42 F4
Malprabha r. India 94 C2
Malpura India 96 B4
Malše r. Czech Rep. 49 L7
Malsiras India 94 B2
▶Malta country Europe 57 G13
europe [countries] 32–35
Malta Latvia 42 I5
Malta r. Latvia 42 I5
Malta i. Malta 57 G13
Malta U.S.A. 180 F2
Maltahöhe Namibia 130 C5
Maltam Cameroon 125 I3
Maltion luonnonpuisto nature res. Fin. 44 O2
Malton U.K. 47 L9
Maluera Moz. see Malowera
Malukken is Indon. see Moluccas
Maluku is Indon. see Moluccas
Maluku prov. Indon. 75 D3
Ma'lūlā, Jabal mts Syria 109 H4
Malului, Vârful hill Romania 58 D2
Malumfashi Nigeria 125 G4
Malundano Zambia 127 E9
Malung Sweden 45 K3
Maluti Mountains Lesotho 133 M6
Malu'u Solomon Is 145 F2
Malvan India 94 B2
Malvasia Greece see Monemvasia
Malvern AR U.S.A. 179 D5
Malvern OH U.S.A. 176 D5
Malvérnia Moz. see Chicualacuala
Malvinas, Islas terr. S. Atlantic Ocean see Falkland Islands
Malwa reg. India 96 C5
Malwal Sudan 128 A2
Malxe r. Germany 49 L4
Malý Dunaj r. Slovakia 49 P8
Malykay Rus. Fed. 39 L3
Malyn Ukr. 41 D6
also spelt Malin
Malyy, Ostrov i. Rus. Fed. 43 J1
Malyy Anyuy r. Rus. Fed. 39 Q3
Malyye Soli Rus. Fed. 43 V4
Malyy Irgiz r. Rus. Fed. 41 I5
Malyy Kavkaz mts Asia see Lesser Caucasus
Malyy Kunaley Rus. Fed. 85 E1
Malyy Lyakhovskiy, Ostrov i. Rus. Fed. 39 O2
Malyy Taymyr, Ostrov i. Rus. Fed. 39 K2
Malyy Uzen' r. Kazakh./Rus. Fed. 102 B2
also known as Kishiözen
Malyy Yenisey r. Rus. Fed. 84 B1
Malyy Zelenchuk r. Rus. Fed. 107 E1
Mama r. Rus. Fed. 39 O3
Mamadysh Rus. Fed. 40 I5
Mamafubedu S. Africa 133 M4
Mamahabane S. Africa 133 L5
Mamanuí N.Z. 152 H3
Mamasa Indon. 75 A3
Mambahenauhan i. Phil. 74 A5
Mambai Brazil 202 C5
Mambajao Phil. 74 C4
Mambal Cameroon 125 I5
Mambali Tanz. 129 B6
Mambasa Dem. Rep. Congo 126 F4
Mambéré r. Cent. Afr. Rep. 126 C4
Mambéré-Kadéï pref. Cent. Afr. Rep. 126 B3
Mambi Indon. 75 A3
Mambili r. Congo 126 C4
Mambolo Sierra Leone 124 B4
Mamboré Brazil 206 A11
Mambrui Kenya 128 D5
Mamburao Phil. 74 B3
Mamelodi S. Africa 133 M2
Mamers France 50 G4
Mamfé Cameroon 125 H5
Mamiá Brazil 199 F6
Mamili National Park Namibia 130 D3
Mamiña Chile 200 C5
Mamison Pass Georgia/Rus. Fed. 107 E2
Mammoth U.S.A. 183 N9
Mammoth Cave National Park U.S.A. 174 C4
Mammoth Lakes U.S.A. 182 F4
Mammoth Reservoir U.S.A. 182 E4
Mamonas Brazil 207 K2
Mamonovo Kaliningradskaya Oblast' Rus. Fed. 42 A7
historically known as Heiligenbeil
Mamonovo Ryazanskaya Oblast' Rus. Fed. 43 U8
Mamontovo Rus. Fed. 103 J1
Mamoré r. Bol./Brazil 200 D2
Mamori Brazil 199 E5
Mamori, Lago l. Brazil 199 F5
Mamoriá Brazil 200 D1
Mamou Guinea 124 B4
Mamoudzou Mayotte 129 E8
also spelt Mamoutsou or Mamutzu
Mamoutsou Mayotte see Mamoudzou
Mampikony Madag. 131 [inset] J3
Mampong Ghana 125 E5
Mamre S. Africa 132 C10
Mamry, Jezioro l. Poland 49 S1
Mamuju Indon. 75 A3
Ma'mūl Oman 105 F4
Mamuno Botswana 130 D4
Mamuras Albania 58 A7
Mamurogawa Japan 90 G5
Mamutzu Mayotte see Mamoudzou
Man Côte d'Ivoire 124 D5
Man r. India 94 B2
Man U.S.A. 176 D8

▶Man, Isle of i. Irish Sea 47 H9
United Kingdom Crown Dependency.
europe [countries] 32–35

Mana Fr. Guiana 199 H3
Mana U.S.A. 181 [inset] Y1
Mana Bárbara Venez. 198 C2
Manabí prov. Ecuador 198 B5
Manacacías r. Col. 198 C3
Manacapuru Brazil 199 F5
Manacor Spain 55 O5
Manado Indon. 75 C2

▶Managua Nicaragua 186 B4
Capital of Nicaragua.

Managua, Lago de l. Nicaragua 186 B4
Manah Oman 105 G3
Manaia N.Z. 152 I7
Manakara Madag. 131 [inset] J4
Manakau mt. N.Z. 153 H10
Manākhah Yemen 104 C5
Manali India 96 C2

▶Manama Bahrain 105 E2
Capital of Bahrain. Also spelt Al Manāmah.
world [countries] 10–11

Manamadurai India 94 C4
Manambaho r. Madag. 131 [inset] J3
Manambondro Madag. 131 [inset] J4
Manamelkudi India 94 C4
Manam Island P.N.G. 73 K7
also known as Vulcan Island
Manamo, Caño r. Venez. 199 F2
Manamoc i. Phil. 74 B4
Mananantañana r. Madag. 131 [inset] J4
Mananara r. Madag. 131 [inset] J4
Mananara, Parc National de nat. park Madag. 131 [inset] K3
Mananara Avaratra Madag. 131 [inset] K3
Manangoora Australia 148 C3
Mananjary Madag. 131 [inset] K4
Manankoliva Madag. 131 [inset] J5
Manankoro Mali 124 D4
Manantali, Lac de l. Mali 124 C3
Manantavadi India 94 C4
Manantenina Madag. 131 [inset] J5
Mana Pass China/India 89 B6
Mana Pools National Park Zimbabwe 131 F3
Manapouri N.Z. 153 B13

▶Manapouri, Lake N.Z. 153 B13
Deepest lake in Oceania.

Manapparai India 94 C4
Manarantsandry Madag. 131 [inset] J3
Manas China 88 D2
Manas r. India 97 F4
Manas, Gora mt. Uzbek. 103 G4
Manasa India 96 B4
Manas He r. China 88 D2
Manas Hu l. China 88 D2
Manāşir reg. U.A.E. 105 F3

▶Manaslu mt. Nepal 97 E3
8th highest mountain in the world and in Asia.
world [physical features] 8–9

Manasquan U.S.A. 177 K5
Manassas U.S.A. 176 H7
Manastir Macedonia see Bitola
Manas Wildlife Sanctuary nature res. Bhutan 97 F4
Manatang Indon. 75 C5
Manatuto East Timor 75 C5
Man-aung Kyun i. Myanmar see Cheduba Island
Manaus Brazil 199 F5
Manavgat Turkey 106 B3
Manavgat r. Turkey 108 C1
Manawa U.S.A. 172 E6
Manawar India 96 B5
Manawaru N.Z. 152 J5
Manawashei Sudan 120 E6
Manawatu r. N.Z. 152 J8
Manawatu-Wanganui admin. reg. N.Z. 152 J7
Manay Phil. 74 C5
Manayenki Rus. Fed. 43 R8
Manbazar India 97 E5
Manbij Syria 109 I1
Mancelona U.S.A. 173 H6
Manchar India 94 B2
Manchester U.K. 47 J10
Manchester CT U.S.A. 177 M4
Manchester IA U.S.A. 174 B3
Manchester KY U.S.A. 176 B8
Manchester MD U.S.A. 177 I6
Manchester MI U.S.A. 173 I8
Manchester NH U.S.A. 177 N3
Manchester OH U.S.A. 176 B7
Manchester TN U.S.A. 174 C5
Manchhar Lake Pak. 101 F5
Manciano Italy 56 D6
Mancılık Turkey 107 D3
Mancınık Dağı mts Turkey 59 I9
Mancos r. U.S.A. 183 P5
Mand Pak. 101 E5
Mand, Rūd-e r. Iran 100 B4
also known as Qara Āghach
Manda Bangl. 97 F4
Manda Malawi 129 B7
Manda Tanz. 129 B6
Manda, Jebel mt. Sudan 126 E2
Manda, Parc National de nat. park Chad 126 C2
Mandabe Madag. 131 [inset] J4
Mandaguaçu Brazil 206 A10
Mandaguari Brazil 206 B10
Mandai Sing. 76 [inset]
Mandal Afgh. 101 E3
Mandal Gujarat India 96 A5
Mandal Rajasthan India 96 B4
Mandal Bulgan Mongolia 84 D1
Mandal Töv Mongolia 85 E1
Mandal Norway 45 I4

▶Mandala, Puncak mt. Indon. 73 J7
3rd highest mountain in Oceania. Formerly known as Julianatop.
oceania [landscapes] 136–137

Mandalay Myanmar 78 B3
also spelt Mandale
Mandalay admin. div. Myanmar 78 A3
also spelt Mandale
Mandale Myanmar see Mandalay
Mandale admin. div. Myanmar see Mandalay
Mandalgarh India 96 B4
Mandalgovĭ Mongolia 85 E2
Mandalī Iraq 107 F4
Mandalt China 85 G3
also known as Sonid Zuoqi
Mandan U.S.A. 178 B2
Mandaon Phil. 74 B3
Mandapam India 94 C4
Mandar, Teluk b. Indon. 75 A3
Mandas Sardegna Italy 57 B9
Mandav Hills India 96 A5
Mandé, Mont de hill France 51 K6
Mandelieu-la-Napoule France 51 M9
Mandello del Lario Italy 56 B3
Mandera Kenya 128 D4
Manderfield U.S.A. 183 L3
Mandeville Jamaica 186 D3
Mandeville N.Z. 153 C13
Mandha India 96 A4
Mandheera Somalia 128 E2
Mandhoúdhion Greece see Mantoudi
Mandi India 96 C3
Mandiakui Mali 124 D3
Mandiana Guinea 124 C4
Mandi Burewala Pak. 101 H4
Mandidzuzure Zimbabwe see Chimanimani
Mandié Moz. 131 G3
Mandimba Moz. 131 G2
Manding, Monts mts Mali 124 C3
Mandioli i. Indon. 75 C3
Mandji Gabon 126 A5
Mandla India 96 D5
Mandor Indon. 77 E2
Mandorah Australia 148 A2
Mandoro Dem. Rep. Congo 126 F3
Mandoto Madag. 131 [inset] J3
Mandor Reserve nature res. Indon. 77 E2
Mandouri Togo 125 F4
Mandra Greece 59 E10
Mandraki Greece 59 I12
Mandrare r. Madag. 131 [inset] J5
Mandrenska r. Bulg. see Sredetska Reka
Mandritsara Madag. 131 [inset] K2
Mandsaur India 96 B4
Mandul i. Indon. 77 G2
Mandurah Australia 151 A7
Manduria Italy 57 J8
Mandvi Gujarat India 96 A5
Mandvi Gujarat India 96 B5
Mandya India 94 C3
Manekwara India 96 A5
Manendragarh India 97 D5
Maner India 97 E4
Maner r. India 94 C2
Manerbio Italy 56 C3
Maneromango Tanz. 129 C6
Manesht Kūh mt. Iran 100 A3
Mănești Romania 58 G4
Maneva Madag. see Mahaboboka
Manevychi Ukr. 41 C6
Manfalūt Egypt 121 F3
Manfredonia Italy 56 H7
Manfredonia, Golfo di g. Italy 56 I7
Manga Brazil 202 D5
Manga Burkina 125 E4
Mangabeiras, Serra das hills Brazil 202 C4
Manga Grande Angola 127 B6
Mangai Dem. Rep. Congo 126 C6
Mangai, Réserve de Faune des Hippopotames de nature res. Dem. Rep. Congo 126 C5
Mangaia i. Cook Is 221 H7
also spelt Mangea
Mangakino N.Z. 152 J6
Mangalagiri India 94 D2
Mangaldai India 97 G4
Mangalia Romania 58 J5
Mangalmé Chad 120 C6
Mangalore India 94 B3
Mangalvedha India 94 B2
Mangamaunu N.Z. 153 H10
Mangamuka N.Z. 152 H3
Mangania Dem. Rep. Congo 126 D4
Manganui r. N.Z. 152 H3
Mangaon India 94 B2
Mangapet India 94 D2
Mangarakau N.Z. 152 G8
Mangaratiba Brazil 207 I9
Mangareva Islands Fr. Polynesia see Gambier, Îles
Mangatainoka N.Z. 152 J8
Mangatawhiri N.Z. 152 J5
Mangaung S. Africa 133 K6
Mangawan India 97 D4
Mangaweka N.Z. 152 J7
Mangawhai N.Z. 152 I4
Mangde Chhu r. Bhutan see Trongsa Chhu
Ma'ngê China see Luqu
Mangea i. Cook Is see Mangaia
Mangembe Dem. Rep. Congo 126 E6
Manger Norway 45 I3
Manggar Indon. 77 E3
Mangghyshlaq Kazakh. see Mangistau
Mangghystaū Kazakh. see Mangistau
Mangghystaū Oblysy admin. div. Kazakh. see Mangistauskaya Oblast'
Mangghyt Uzbek. see Mangit
Manghit Uzbek. see Mangit
Mangistau Kazakh. 102 B4
also spelt Mangghystaū; formerly known as Mangghyshlaq or Mangyshlak
Mangistau, Gory hills Kazakh. 102 B3
Mangistauskaya Oblast' admin. div. Kazakh. 102 C4
also known as Mangghystaū Oblysy; formerly known as Mangyshlak Oblast or Mangyshlakskaya Oblast'
Mangit Uzbek. 102 E4
also spelt Mangghyt or Manghit
Mangkalihat, Tanjung pt Indon. 77 G2
Mangkutup r. Indon. 77 F3
Manglares, Punta pt Col. 198 B4
Mangnai China 88 E4
Mangnai Zhen China 88 E4
Mangoaka Madag. 131 [inset] K2
Mangochi Malawi 129 B8
formerly known as Fort Johnston
Mangodara Burkina 124 D4
Mangoky r. Toliara Madag. 131 [inset] I4
Mangoky r. Toliara Madag. 131 [inset] J4
Mangole i. Indon. 75 C3
Mangole, Selat sea chan. Indon. 75 C3
Mangoli India 94 B2
Mangombe Dem. Rep. Congo 126 E5
Mangonui N.Z. 152 H3
Mangoro r. Madag. 131 [inset] K3
Mangqystaū Shyghanaghy b. Kazakh. see Mangyshlakskiy Zaliv
Mangra China see Guinan
Mangral India 96 A5
Mangrol India 96 B4
Mangrul India 94 C1
Mangshi China see Luxi
Mangualde Port. 54 D4
Manguari Brazil 198 D5
Manguchar Pak. 101 F4
Mangueira, Lago l. Brazil 204 G4
Mangueirinha Brazil 203 A8
Manguéni, Plateau du Niger 123 H5
Mangui China 82 A2
Manguinha, Pontal do pt Brazil 202 E4
Mangula Zimbabwe see Mhangura
Mangum U.S.A. 179 C5
Mangunça, Ilha i. Brazil 202 C2
Mangut Rus. Fed. 85 G1
Mangyshlak Kazakh. see Mangistau
Mangyshlak, Poluostrov pen. Kazakh. 102 B3
also known as Tüpqaraghan Tübegi
Mangyshlak Oblast admin. div. Kazakh. see Mangistauskaya Oblast'
Mangyshlakskaya Oblast' admin. div. Kazakh. see Mangistauskaya Oblast'
Mangyshlakskiy Zaliv b. Kazakh. 102 B3
also known as Mangqystaū Shyghanaghy
Manhan Mongolia see Tögrög
Manhan Mongolia 84 C1
Manhattan U.S.A. 178 C4
Manhattan Beach U.S.A. 182 F8
Manhica Moz. 133 Q2
Manhoca Moz. 133 Q3
Manhuaçu Brazil 203 D7
Manhuaçu r. Brazil 207 L6
Manhumirim Brazil 207 L7
Mani Chad 120 B6
Mani well Chad 120 C5
Mani China 89 D5
Mani Col. 198 C3
Mani Nigeria 125 G3
Mānī', Wādī al watercourse Iraq 109 M3
Mania r. Madag. 131 [inset] J3
Maniago Italy 56 E2
Maniakoi Greece 58 C8
Maniari Tank resr India 97 D5
also known as Khuria Tank
Manica Moz. 131 G3
Manica prov. Moz. 131 G3
Manicaland prov. Zimbabwe 131 G3
Manicoré Brazil 199 F6
Manicoré r. Brazil 199 F6
Manicouagan Canada 169 G3
Manicouagan r. Canada 169 G3
Manicouagan, Réservoir Canada 169 G3
Manic Trois, Réservoir Canada 169 G3
Maniema prov. Dem. Rep. Congo 126 E5
Manīfah Saudi Arabia 105 E2
Manigango China 86 A2
Manigotagan Canada 167 L5
Manihari India 97 E4
Manihiki atoll Cook Is 221 H6
formerly known as Great Ganges or Humphrey Island
Maniitsoq Greenland 165 N3
also known as Sukkertoppen
Manji r. Pak. 101 F5
Manikchhari Bangl. 97 G5
Manikganj Bangl. 97 F5
Manikgarh India see Rajura
Manikpur India 96 D4

▶Manila Phil. 74 B3
Capital of the Philippines.
world [cities] 24–25

Manila U.S.A. 180 E4
Manila Bay Phil. 74 B3
Manilaid i. Estonia 42 F3
Manilla Australia 147 F2
Manily Rus. Fed. 39 Q3
Manimbaya, Tanjung pt Indon. 75 A3
Maningrida Australia 148 B2
Maninjau, Danau l. Indon. 76 C3
Manipa i. Indon. 75 C3
Manipa, Selat sea chan. Indon. 75 C3
Manipur India see Imphal
Manipur state India 97 G4
Manipur r. India/Myanmar 97 G5
Manisa Turkey 106 A3
Manisa prov. Turkey 59 J10
Manises Spain 55 K5
Manissauá Missu r. Brazil 202 A4
Manistee U.S.A. 172 G6
Manistee r. U.S.A. 172 G6
Manistique U.S.A. 172 G5
Manistique Lake U.S.A. 172 H4
Manitoba prov. Canada 167 L4
Manitoba, Lake Canada 167 L5
Manito Lake Canada 167 I4
Manitou Canada 167 L5
Manitou r. Canada 169 H3
Manitou, Lake Canada 168 D4
Manitou Beach U.S.A. 176 H2
Manitou Falls Canada 168 A3
Manitou Island U.S.A. 172 F3
Manitou Islands U.S.A. 172 G5
Manitoulin Island Canada 168 D4
Manitouwadge Canada 168 C3
Manitowaning Canada 173 L5
Manitowik Lake Canada 173 I2
Manitowish Waters U.S.A. 172 D4
Manitowoc U.S.A. 172 F6
Maniwaki Canada 168 F4
Manizales Col. 198 C3
Manja Madag. 131 [inset] J4
Manjacaze Moz. 131 G5
Manjak Madag. 131 [inset] J3
Manjam Umm Qurayyāt waterhole Egypt 104 A3
Manjarabad India 94 B3
Manjeri India 94 C4
Manjhand Pak. 101 G5
Man Jiang r. China 82 B4
Manjil Iran 100 B2
Manjimup Australia 151 B7
Manjo Cameroon 125 H5
Manjra r. India 94 C2
Man Kabat Myanmar 78 B2
Mankachar India 97 F4
Mankanza Dem. Rep. Congo see Makanza
Mankato KS U.S.A. 178 C4
Mankato MN U.S.A. 178 D2
Mankono Côte d'Ivoire 124 D4
Mankota Canada 167 J5
Manlleu Spain 55 N3
Manly U.S.A. 174 A3
Manmad India 94 B1
Mann r. Australia 148 B2
Mann, Mount Australia 148 A5
Manna Indon. 76 C4
Mannahill Australia 146 C3
Mannar Sri Lanka 94 C4
Mannar, Gulf of India/Sri Lanka 94 C4
Mannargudi India 94 C4
Manneru r. India 94 D3
Mannheim Germany 48 F6
Mannicolo Islands Solomon Is see Vanikoro Islands
Männikuste Estonia 42 F3
Manning Canada 167 G3
Manning ND U.S.A. 178 B2
Manning SC U.S.A. 175 D5
Manning Provincial Park Canada 166 F5
Mannington U.S.A. 176 E6
Männlifluh mt. Switz. 51 N6
Mann Ranges mts Australia 148 A5
Mannsville U.S.A. 177 I2
Mannu r. Sardegna Italy 57 A8
Mannu r. Sardegna Italy 57 A9
Mannu r. Sardegna Italy 57 B9
Mannu, Capo c. Sardegna Italy 57 A8
Mannville Canada 167 I4
Mano r. Liberia/Sierra Leone 124 C5
Manoa Bol. 200 D2
Man-of-War Rocks is U.S.A. see Gardner Pinnacles
Manoharpur India 89 B7
Manohar Thana India 96 C4
Manokotak U.S.A. 164 D4
Manokwari Indon. 73 H7
Manombo Atsimo Madag. 131 [inset] I4
Manompana Madag. 131 [inset] K3
Manono Dem. Rep. Congo 127 E6
Manora Head Pak. 101 F5
Mano River Liberia 124 C5
Manosque France 51 L9
Manouane, Lac l. Canada 169 G3
Mano-wan b. Japan 90 F5
Man Pan Myanmar 78 B3
Manp'o N. Korea 83 B4
Manpur India 96 B5
Manra i. Kiribati 145 H2
formerly known as Sydney Island
Manresa Spain 55 M3
Mansa Gujarat India 96 B5
Mansa Punjab India 96 B3
Mansa Zambia 127 F7
formerly known as Fort Rosebery
Mansabá Guinea-Bissau 124 B3
Mansa Konko Gambia 124 B3
Man Sam Myanmar 78 B3
Mansehra Pak. 101 H3
Mansel Island Canada 165 L3
Mansel'kya ridge Fin./Rus. Fed. 44 O2
Mansfield Australia 147 E4
Mansfield U.K. 47 K10
Mansfield AR U.S.A. 179 D5
Mansfield LA U.S.A. 179 D5
Mansfield MA U.S.A. 177 N3
Mansfield OH U.S.A. 176 C5
Mansfield PA U.S.A. 177 H4
Mansfield, Mount U.S.A. 177 M1
Man Si Myanmar 78 B2
Mansi Myanmar 78 A2
Mansidão Brazil 202 D4
Manso r. Brazil see Mortes, Rio das
Manso-Nkwanta Ghana 125 E5
Mansuela Indon. 75 D3
Mansurlu Turkey 106 C3
also known as Tapan
Manta Ecuador 198 A5
long form San Pablo de Manta
Mantalingajan, Mount Phil. 74 A4
Mantantale Dem. Rep. Congo 126 D5
Mantaro r. Peru 200 B3
Manteca U.S.A. 182 C4
Mantecal Venez. 198 D3
Mantehage i. Indon. 75 C2
Manteigas Port. 54 D4
Mantena Brazil 203 D6
Manteno U.S.A. 172 F9
Manteo U.S.A. 174 F5
Mantes-la-Jolie France 50 H4
Manthani India 94 C2
Manti U.S.A. 183 M2
Mantiqueira, Serra da mts Brazil 203 C7
Manto Hond. 186 B4
Manton U.S.A. 172 H6
Mantorville U.S.A. 168 A4
Mantos Blancos Chile 200 C5
Mantoudi Greece 59 E10
also known as Mandhoúdhion
Mantova Italy see Mantua
Mäntsälä Fin. 45 N3
Mänttä Fin. 45 N3
Mantua Cuba 186 B2
Mantua Italy 56 C3
also spelt Mantova
Mantua U.S.A. 176 D4
Mantuan Downs Australia 149 E5
Manturovo Rus. Fed. 40 H4
Mäntyharju Fin. 45 N3
Mäntyjärvi Fin. 44 N2
Manu r. Bol. see Mapiri
Manú r. Peru 200 C3
Manu, Parque Nacional nat. park Peru 200 B3
Manuae atoll Fr. Polynesia 221 H7
also known as Fenua Ura; formerly known as Scilly, Île
Manua Islands American Samoa 145 I3
Manubi S. Africa 133 M9
Manuel Alves r. Brazil 202 B4
Manuel J. Cobo Arg. 204 F4
Manuel Rodriguez, Isla i. Chile 205 B9
Manuel Urbano Brazil 200 C2
Manuel Vitorino Brazil 202 D5
Manuelzinho Brazil 202 A3
Manui i. Indon. 75 B3
Manūjān Iran 100 D5
Manukan Phil. 74 B4
Manukau N.Z. 152 I4
Manukau Harbour N.Z. 152 I5
Manuk Manka i. Phil. 74 A5
Manunda watercourse Australia 146 C3
Manupari r. Bol. 200 D2
Manurimi r. Bol. 200 D2
Manuripi r. Bol. 200 D2
Manusela National Park Indon. 75 D3
Manus Island P.N.G. 73 K7
Manutuke N.Z. 152 L6
Manvi India 94 C3
Manwat India 94 C2
Many U.S.A. 179 D6
Manyallaluk Aboriginal reserve res. Australia 148 B2
Manyame r. Moz./Zimbabwe 131 F2
formerly known as Hunyani
Manyara, Lake salt l. Tanz. 129 B5
Manyas Turkey 59 I8
Manyas Gölü l. Turkey see Kuş Gölü
Manyatseng S. Africa 133 L6
Manyberries Canada 167 I5
Manych-Gudilo, Ozero l. Rus. Fed. 41 G7
Many Farms U.S.A. 183 O5
Manyinga Zambia 127 E8
Many Island Lake Canada 167 I5
Manyoni Tanz. 129 B6
Many Peaks, Mount hill Australia 151 B7
Manzala, Bahra el lag. Egypt see Manzala, Lake
Manzala, Lake lag. Egypt 108 D6
also known as Manzala, Bahra el
Manzanal, Puerto del pass Spain 54 E2
Manzanares Spain 55 H5
Manzaneda, Cabeza de mt. Spain 54 D2
Manzanillo Cuba 186 D2
Manzanillo Mex. 184 D5
Manzanillo, Punta pt Panama 186 D5
Manzanza Dem. Rep. Congo 126 F6
Manzariyeh Iran 100 B3
Manzengele Dem. Rep. Congo 127 C6
Manzhouli China 85 H1
Manzini Swaziland 133 P3
formerly known as Bremersdorp
Manzini admin. dist. Swaziland 133 P3
Manzovka Rus. Fed. see Sibirtsevo
Mao Chad 120 B6
Mao Dom. Rep. 187 F3
formerly known as Valverde
Maó Spain see Mahón
Mao, Nam r. Myanmar see Shweli
Maoba Guizhou China 86 C3
Maoba Hubei China 87 D2
Maocifan China 87 E2
Mao'ergai China 86 B1
Maoke, Pegunungan mts Indon. 73 I7
Maokeng S. Africa 133 L4
Maokui Shan mt. China 83 A4
Maomao Shan mt. China 84 D4
Maoming China 87 D4
Ma On Shan hill Hong Kong China 87 [inset]
Maopi Cape Taiwan see Maopi T'ou
Maopi T'ou c. Taiwan 87 G4
English form Maopi Cape
Maopora i. Indon. 75 C4
Maotou Shan mt. China 86 B3
Maowen China see Maoxian
Maoxian China 86 B2
also known as Fengyi; formerly known as Maowen
Mapai Moz. 131 F4
Mapam Yumco l. China 89 C6
Mapane Indon. 75 B3
Mapanza Zambia 127 E9
Mapastepec Mex. 185 G6
Maphodi S. Africa 133 J7
Mapi r. Indon. 73 I8
Mapiche, Serranía mts Venez. 199 E3
Mapimí Mex. 184 E3
Mapimí, Bolsón de des. Mex. 184 D3
Mapin i. Phil. 74 A5
Mapinhane Moz. 131 G4
Mapire Venez. 199 E3
Mapireme Brazil 199 H4
Mapiri Bol. 200 C3
Mapiri r. Bol. 200 D2
also known as Manu
Mapirpán Col. 198 C4
Mapiu N.Z. 152 J6
Maple r. IA U.S.A. 178 D3
Maple r. MI U.S.A. 173 I8
Maple r. ND U.S.A. 178 C2
Maple r. ND U.S.A. 178 C2
Maple Creek Canada 167 I5
Maple Peak U.S.A. 183 O8
Mapleton IA U.S.A. 178 D3
Mapleton UT U.S.A. 183 M1
Maplewood U.S.A. 172 F6
Mapoon Australia 149 D1
Mapoon Aboriginal Reserve Australia 149 D2
Mapor i. Indon. 76 D2
Mapoteng Lesotho 133 L6
Maprik P.N.G. 73 J7
Mapuca India 94 B3
Mapuera r. Brazil 199 G5
Mapulanguene Moz. 131 G5
Mapunda Dem. Rep. Congo 127 E7

▶Maputo Moz. 131 G5
Capital of Mozambique. Formerly known as Lourenço Marques.

Maputo prov. Moz. 131 G5
Maputo r. Moz./S. Africa 133 Q3
Maputo, Baía de b. Moz. 133 Q3
Maputo Elephant Reserve nature res. Moz. 133 Q3
Maputsoe Lesotho 133 L5
Maqanshy Kazakh. see Makanchi
Maqar an Na'am well Iraq 107 E5
Maqat Kazakh. see Makat
Maqên China 86 B1
also known as Dawu
Maqên Gangri mt. China 86 A1
Maqla, Jabal al mts Saudi Arabia 108 G9

index

M

Maqnā Saudi Arabia **108** F9
Maqrat Yemen **105** E5
Maqteïr reg. Mauritania **122** C5
Maqu China **86** B1
   also known as Nyima
Ma Qu r. China see Yellow River
Maquan He r. China **89** D6
   also known as Damqoq Zangbo
Maquinchao Arg. **204** C6
Maquoketa U.S.A. **174** B3
Maquoketa r. U.S.A. **174** B3
Maquon U.S.A. **172** C10
Mar r. Pak. **101** F5
Mar, Serra do mts Rio de Janeiro/São Paulo Brazil **203** C7
Mar, Serra do mts Rio Grande do Sul/Santa Catarina Brazil **203** B9
Mar, Serra do mts Brazil **207** J9
Mara r. Canada **167** I1
Mara Guyana **199** G3
Mara India **97** C3
Mara admin. reg. Tanz. **128** B5
Maraã Brazil **199** E5
Maraba Brazil **202** B3
Marabahan Indon. **77** F3
Marabatua i. Indon. **77** F4
Marabitanas Brazil **199** E4
Maracá r. Brazil **199** I5
Maracaí Brazil **206** C9
Maracaibo Venez. **198** D2
Maracaibo, Lago de l. Venez. see Maracaibo, Lake
Maracaibo, Lake Venez. **198** D2
   also known as Maracaibo, Lago de
Maracaju Brazil **201** G5
Maracaju, Serra de hills Brazil **201** G5
Maracanã Brazil **202** C2
Maracanaquará, Planalto plat. Brazil **199** H5
Maracanda Uzbek. see Samarkand
Maracás Brazil **202** D5
Maracás, Chapada de hills Brazil **202** D5
Maracay Venez. **199** E2
Marachkova Belarus **43** J6
Maradi Libya **120** C2
Maradi dept Niger **125** G3
Maradi Niger **125** G3
Marāgheh Iran **100** A2
Maragogi Brazil **202** F4
Maragondon Phil. **74** B3
Marah Saudi Arabia **105** D2
Marahuaca, Cerro mt. Venez. **199** E4
Marais des Cygnes r. U.S.A. **178** D4
Marais du Cotentin et du Bessin, Parc Naturel Régional nature res. France **50** E3
Marais Poitevin, Val de Sèvre et Vendée, Parc Naturel Régional nature res. France **50** F6
Marajó, Baía de est. Brazil **202** B2
Marajó, Ilha de i. Brazil **202** B2
Marakei atoll Kiribati **145** G1
   also known as Maraki; formerly known as Matthew
Maraki atoll Kiribati see Marakei
Marakkanam India **94** C3
Maralal Kenya **128** C4
Maralbashi China see Bachu
Maraldy Kazakh. **103** I1
Maralinga Australia **146** A2
Maralinga-Tjarutja Aboriginal Lands res. Australia **146** A2
Maralwexi China see Bachu
Maramasike i. Solomon Is **145** F2
Marambio research station Antarctica **222** U2
   long form Vicecomodoro Marambio
Marampit i. Indon. **75** C1
Maran r. Pak. **101** E4
Marana U.S.A. **183** M9
Marand Iran **100** A2
Marandellas Zimbabwe see Marondera
Marang Myanmar **79** B6
Maranguape Brazil **202** E2
Maranhão r. Brazil **206** E1
Maranhão state Brazil **202** C3
Maranoa r. Australia **147** F1
Marañón r. Peru **198** C4
Marans France **50** F6
Marão Moz. **131** G3
   formerly known as Mau-é-ele
Marão mt. Port. **54** D3
Maraoué r. Côte d'Ivoire **124** C5
Marapanim Brazil **202** C2
Marape Brazil **201** F3
Marapi, Gunung vol. Indon. **76** C3
Marari Brazil **199** E5
Mararoa r. N.Z. **153** B13
Maraş Cyprus see Varosia
Maraş Turkey see Kahramanmaraş
Marasende i. Indon. **77** G4
Mărăşeşti Romania **58** I3
Măraşu Romania **58** I4
Maratea Italy **57** H9
Marathia, Akra pt Greece **59** B11
Marathokampos Greece **59** H11
Marathon Canada **168** C3
Marathon Greece see Marathonas
Marathón FL U.S.A. **175** D7
Marathon TX U.S.A. **179** B6
Marathon WI U.S.A. **172** D6
Marathonas Greece **59** E10
   also known as Marathón
Maratua i. Indon. **77** G2
Marauá Brazil **199** E5
Marauiá r. Brazil **199** E4
Maravatío Mex. **185** E5
Maravillas Creek watercourse U.S.A. **179** B6

Marāwah Libya **120** D1
Marawi Phil. **74** C4
Marayes Arg. **204** D3
Maray Lake Pak. **101** G4
Mar'ayt Yemen **105** E4
Märäzä Azer. **107** G2
Marbella Spain **54** G8
Marble Bar Australia **150** B4
Marble Canyon U.S.A. **183** M5
Marble Canyon gorge U.S.A. **183** M5
Marble Hall S. Africa **133** N1
Marble Hill U.S.A. **174** C4
Marble Island Canada **167** N2
Marbul Pass Jammu and Kashmir **96** B2
Marburg S. Africa **133** O7
Marburg Slovenia see Maribor
Marburg an der Lahn Germany **48** F5
Marca Peru **200** A2
Marca, Ponta da pt Angola **127** A9
Marcal r. Hungary **49** O8
Marcapata Peru **200** C3
Marcelino Brazil **199** E4
Marcellus MI U.S.A. **172** H8
Marcellus NY U.S.A. **177** I3
March r. Austria/Slovakia see Morava
March U.K. **47** M11
Marchant Hill hill Australia **146** C3
Marche reg. France **50** H6
Marche admin. reg. Italy **56** E5
Marche-en-Famenne Belgium **51** L2
Marchena Spain **54** F7
Mar Chiquita, Lago l. Arg. **204** E3
Marchtrenk Austria **49** L7
Mărciena Latvia **42** H5
Marcona Peru **200** B3
Marcos Juárez Arg. **204** E4
Marcy, Mount U.S.A. **177** L1
Mardan Pak. **101** H3
Mar de Ajó Arg. **204** F5
Mar del Plata Arg. **204** F5
Mardiän Afgh. **101** F2
Mardin Turkey **107** E3
Mårdudden Sweden **44** M2
Mardzad Mongolia **84** D2
Maré i. New Caledonia **145** F4
   formerly known as Britannia Island
Mare de Déu del Toro hill Spain **55** P5
Maree, Loch l. U.K. **46** G6
Mareeba Australia **149** E3
Maréna Mali **124** C3
Marendet Niger **125** G2
Marengo r. Australia **150** D3
Marengo IA U.S.A. **174** A3
Marengo IL U.S.A. **172** E8
Marengo WI U.S.A. **172** C4
Marenisco U.S.A. **172** D4
Marennes France **50** E7
Marerano Madag. **131** [inset] J4
Maret Islands Australia **150** D2
Marettimo, Isola i. Sicilia Italy **57** E11
Mareuil France **50** G7
Mareuil-sur-Lay-Dissais France **50** E6
Marevo Rus. Fed. **43** N4
Marfa U.S.A. **181** F7
Margam Ri mts China **89** D5
Marganets Kazakh. see Zhezdy
Marganets Ukr. see Marhanets'
Margao India see Madgaon
Margaret r. Australia **150** B3
Margaret watercourse Australia **146** C2
Margaret Lake Alta Canada **167** H3
Margaret Lake N.W.T. Canada **167** G2
Margaret River Australia **151** A7
Margaretville U.S.A. **177** K3
Margarita Arg. **204** E3
Margarita, Isla de i. Venez. **199** F2
Margaritovo Rus. Fed. **90** D3
Margate S. Africa **133** O7
Margate U.K. **47** N12
Margate City U.S.A. **177** K6
Märgau Romania **58** D2
Margherita India **97** G4
Margherita, Lake Eth. see Abaya, Lake

Margherita Peak Dem. Rep. Congo/Uganda **126** F4
   3rd highest mountain in Africa. Also known as Stanley, Mount or Marguerite, Pic.
   africa (landscapes) ▶ 112–113

Marghilon Uzbek. see Margilan
Marghita Romania **58** D1
Margilan Uzbek. **103** G4
   also spelt Marghilon
Margionys Lith. **42** F8
Margo, Dasht-i- des. Afgh. **101** E4
Margog Caka l. China **89** D5
Margos Peru **200** A2
Margosatubig Phil. **74** B5
Marguerite Canada **166** F4
Marguerite, Pic mt. Dem. Rep. Congo/Uganda see Margherita Peak
Marguerite Bay Antarctica **222** T2
Margyang China **89** E6
Marhaj Khalil Iraq **107** F4
Marhan Dägh hill Iraq **107** E3
Marhanets' Ukr. **41** E7
   also spelt Marganets; formerly known as Kominternn
Marhoum Alg. **123** E2
Mari r. Brazil **201** D1
Mari Myanmar **78** B2
Mari P.N.G. **73** J8
Maria r. Brazil **203** A7
Maria atoll Fr. Polynesia **221** H7
Maria Cleofas, Isla i. Mex. **184** D4
María Elena Chile **200** C5
Mariager Denmark **45** J4
María Ignacia Arg. **204** E5
Maria Island N.T. Australia **148** B2
Maria Island Tas. Australia **147** F5
Mariala National Park Australia **149** E5
María Madre, Isla i. Mex. **184** D4
   also known as Marqaköl
María Magdalena, Isla i. Mex. **184** D4
Marian Australia **149** F4
Mariana Brazil **207** J7
Mariano Loza Arg. **204** F3

▶ Mariana Trench sea feature
   N. Pacific Ocean **220** D5
   Deepest trench in the world.

Mariani India **97** G4
Mariánica, Cordillera mts Spain see Morena, Sierra
Marian Lake Canada **167** G2
Marianna AR U.S.A. **174** B5
Marianna FL U.S.A. **175** C6
Mariannelund Sweden **45** K4
Marínha r. Rus. Fed. **39** I3
Markham Canada **168** E5
Mariano Machado Angola see Ganda
Mariánské Lázně Czech Rep. **49** J6
   historically known as Marienbad
Mariapiri, Mesa de hills Col. **198** D4
Mariápolis Brazil **206** B9
Marias r. U.S.A. **180** E3
Marías, Islas is Mex. **184** D4

▶ Mariato, Punta pt Panama **186** C6
   Most southerly point of North America.

Maria van Diemen, Cape N.Z. **152** G2
Mariazell Austria **49** M8
Ma'rib Yemen **105** D5
Ma'rib governorate Yemen **105** D5
Maribel U.S.A. **172** F6

Maribo Denmark **48** I1
Maribor Slovenia **56** H2
   historically known as Marburg
Maricá Brazil **207** K9
Marica r. Bulg. see Maritsa
Marico r. S. Africa **133** K1
Marico Bosveld Nature Reserve S. Africa **133** K2
Maricopa AZ U.S.A. **183** L8
Maricopa CA U.S.A. **182** E6
Maricopa Mountains U.S.A. **183** L8
Maricourt Canada see Kangiqsujuaq
Maridi Sudan **126** F3
Maridi watercourse Sudan **126** F3
Marié r. Brazil **199** E5
Marie Byrd Land reg. Antarctica **222** P1
Marie-Galante i. Guadeloupe **187** H4
Mariehamn Fin. **45** L3
   also spelt Maarianhamina
Mari El aut. rep. Rus. Fed. see Mariy El, Respublika
Mariembero r. Brazil **202** B5
Marienbad Czech Rep. see Mariánské Lázně
Marienburg Poland see Malbork
Mariental Namibia **130** C5
Mariental U.S.A. **176** E5
Marienville U.S.A. **176** F4
Marienwerder Poland see Kwidzyn
Mariestad Sweden **45** K4
Mariet r. Canada **168** E1
Marietta GA U.S.A. **175** C5
Marietta OH U.S.A. **176** D6
Marietta OK U.S.A. **179** C5
Mariga r. Nigeria **125** G4
Marigliano Italy **56** D6
Marignane France **51** L9
Marigot Dominica **187** H4
Marigot r. Bulg. see Maritsa
Mariinsk Rus. Fed. **80** D1
Mariinskoye Rus. Fed. **103** E1
Marijampolė Lith. **42** E7
   formerly known as Kapsukas
Marília Brazil **206** D9
Marillana Australia **150** B4
Marimba Angola **127** C7
Marín Spain **54** C2
Marina di Gioiosa Ionica Italy **57** I10
Marolambo Madag. **131** [inset] K4
Maroldsweisach Germany **48** H5
Mar"ina Horka Belarus see Mar"ina Horka
Mar"ina Horka Belarus **42** J8
   also spelt Mar'ina Gorka
Marinduque i. Phil. **74** B3
Marine City U.S.A. **173** K8
Marinella, Golfo di b. Sardegna Italy **56** B7
Mariner Glacier Antarctica **223** L2
Marinette U.S.A. **172** F5
Maringá Brazil **206** B10
Maringa r. Dem. Rep. Congo **126** C4
Maringo U.S.A. **176** C5
Marinha Grande Port. **54** C5
Marinhas Iran **100** B3
Mar'insko Rus. Fed. **43** J3
Marion AL U.S.A. **175** C5
Marion AR U.S.A. **174** B5
Marion IA U.S.A. **172** B8
Marion IL U.S.A. **174** B4
Marion IN U.S.A. **174** C3
Marion KS U.S.A. **178** C4
Marion KY U.S.A. **174** B4
Marion NC U.S.A. **176** D5
Marion OH U.S.A. **176** B5
Marion SC U.S.A. **175** E5
Marion VA U.S.A. **176** D9
Marion WI U.S.A. **172** E6
Marion, Lake U.S.A. **175** D5
Marion Bay Australia **146** C3
Marion Lake U.S.A. **178** C4
Marion Reef Australia **149** G3
Mariou, Adrar mt. Alg. **123** H5
Maripa Venez. **199** E3
Maripasoula Fr. Guiana **199** H4
Maripipi i. Phil. **74** C4
Mariposa r. U.S.A. **182** E4
Mariposa r. U.S.A. **182** D4
Mariquita Col. **198** C3
Marir, Gezīret i. Egypt **104** A3
   English form Mirear Island
Marisa Indon. **75** B2
Mariscal Estigarribia Para. **201** E5
Mărişel Romania **58** E2
Mărişelu Romania **58** F1
Marite S. Africa **133** K1
Maritime Alps mts France/Italy **51** M8
   also known as Maritimes, Alpes or Maritime, Alpi
Maritime Kray admin. div. Rus. Fed. see Primorskiy Kray
Maritimes, Alpes mts France/Italy see Maritime Alps
Maritsa Bulg. see Simeonovgrad
Maritsa r. Bulg. **58** H7
   also spelt Marica
Maritime, Alpi mts France/Italy see Maritime Alps
Mari-Turek Rus. Fed. **40** I4
Mariupol' Ukr. **41** F7
   formerly known as Zhdanov
Mariusa nat. park Venez. **199** F2
Mariusa, Isla i. Venez. **199** F2
Marivän Iran **107** F4
   formerly known as Dezh Shähpur
Mariy El, Respublika aut. rep. Rus. Fed. **40** I4
   English form Mari El; formerly known as Mariyskaya A.S.S.R. or Mary A.S.S.R.
Mariyskaya A.S.S.R. aut. rep. Rus. Fed. see Mariy El, Respublika
Märjamaa Estonia **42** F3
Marjan Afgh. see Wazi Khwa
Marjayoûn Lebanon **108** G3
Markā i. Saudi Arabia **104** C4
Marka Somalia **128** E4
   formerly spelt Merca
Markaköl, Ozero l. Kazakh. **88** D1
   also known as Marqaköl
Markala Mali **124** D3
Markam China **86** A2
   formerly known as Gartog
Markapur India **94** C3
Markaryd Sweden **45** K4
Markawene well Eth. **128** E3
Markaz, Ra's c. Oman **105** G4
Markazi prov. Iran **100** B3
Markdale Canada **173** M6
Marken S. Africa **131** F4
Markermeer l. Neth. **48** C3
Market Harborough U.K. **47** L11
Market Rasen U.K. **47** L10
Market Weighton U.K. **47** L10
Markha r. Rus. Fed. **39** L3
Markham Canada **168** E5
Markham, Mount Antarctica **223** K1
Markhamet Uzbek. **103** H4
Markit China **88** B3
Markitta Sweden **44** M2
Markleeville U.S.A. **182** E3
Marklesburg U.S.A. **176** H5
Markounda Cent. Afr. Rep. **126** C2
Markovo Chükotskiy Avtonomnyy Okrug Rus. Fed. **39** Q3
Markovo Ivanovskaya Oblast' Rus. Fed. **43** V4

▶ Marshall Islands country
   N. Pacific Ocean **220** D5
   oceania (countries) ▶ 138–139

Marshalltown U.S.A. **174** A3
Marshfield MO U.S.A. **178** D4
Marshfield WI U.S.A. **172** C6
Marsh Harbour Bahamas **186** D1
Mars Hill U.S.A. **174** H2
Marsh Island U.S.A. **175** B6

Marktosis Canada **166** E5
Marktredwitz Germany **48** J5
Marlt Germany **48** E4
Marla Australia **146** B1
Marlboro U.S.A. **177** L4
Marlborough Australia **149** F4
Marlborough admin. reg. N.Z. **153** H9
Marlborough MA U.S.A. **177** N3
Marlborough NH U.S.A. **177** M3
Marle France **51** J3
Marlin U.S.A. **179** C6
Marlinton U.S.A. **176** E7
Marlo Australia **147** F4
Marloth Nature Reserve S. Africa **132** E11
Marmande France **50** G4
Marmara Turkey **58** I8
Marmara, Sea of g. Turkey **106** B2
   also known as Marmara Denizi
Marmara Adası i. Turkey **58** I8
Marmara Denizi g. Turkey see Marmara, Sea of
Marmaraereğlisi Turkey **58** I8
Marmara Gölü l. Turkey **59** J10
Marmarica reg. Libya **120** E2
Marmaris Turkey **106** B3
Marmaro Greece **59** I1
Marmelos r. Brazil **201** E1
Marmet U.S.A. **176** D7
Marmion, Lake salt l. Australia **151** C6
Marmion Lake Canada **168** B3
Marmolada mt. Italy **56** D2
Marmolejo Spain **54** G6
Marne r. France **51** I4
Marne Germany **48** G2
Marne, Source de la tourist site France **48** C8
Marne-la-Vallée France **51** I4
Marneuli Georgia **107** F2
   formerly known as Borchalo or Sarvani
Maro Chad **126** C2
Maroambihy Madag. **131** [inset] K3
Maroantsetra Madag. **131** [inset] K2
Maroba r. Brazil **206** B9
Marofandilia Madag. **131** [inset] J4
Marokopa N.Z. **152** I5
Marol Jammu and Kashmir **96** C2
Marolambo Madag. **131** [inset] K4
Maromandia Madag. **131** [inset] K3
Maromme France **50** H3
Maromokotro mt. Madag. **131** [inset] K2
Marondera Zimbabwe **131** F3
   formerly known as Marandellas
Maroni r. Fr. Guiana **199** H3
Maroochydore Australia **149** G5
Maroonah Australia **150** A4
Maroon Peak U.S.A. **180** F5
Maros Indon. **75** A4
Maros r. Romania **88** D2
Maroserana Madag. **131** [inset] K3
Maroûseh r. Madag. **131** [inset] K3
Marotandrano Madag. **131** [inset] K3
Marotolana Madag. **131** [inset] K2
Maroua Cameroon **125** I4
Marovato Antsirañana Madag. **131** [inset] K2
Marovato Toliara Madag. **131** [inset] J3
Marovoay Mahajanga Madag. **131** [inset] J3
Marovoay Atsimo Madag. **131** [inset] J4
Marowali Indon. **75** B3
Marowijne r. Suriname **199** H3
Marqab al Khubbāz hill Iraq **109** N4
Marqādah Syria **109** L2
Marqaköl l. Kazakh. see Markakol', Ozero
Mar Qu r. China **86** B1
Marquard S. Africa **133** L5
Marquesas Islands Fr. Polynesia **221** I6
   also known as Marquises, Îles
Marquesas Keys is U.S.A. **175** D7
Marquês de Valença Brazil **207** J9
Marquette U.S.A. **172** F4
Marquise France **51** H2
Marquises, Îles is Fr. Polynesia see Marquesas Islands
Marra r. Australia **147** E2
Marra, Jebel mt. Sudan **120** E6
Marra, Wādī watercourse Egypt **108** F9
Marra Aboriginal Land res. Australia **148** B2
Marradi Italy **56** D4
Marrakech Morocco **122** D3
   English form Marrakesh
Marrakesh Morocco see Marrakech
Marra Plateau Sudan **120** E6
Marrawah Australia **147** E5
Marree Australia **146** C2
Marrero U.S.A. **175** B6
Marresale Rus. Fed. **40** M1
Marromeu Moz. **131** G3
Marromeu, Reserva de nature res. Moz. **131** G3
Marrupa Moz. **129** C8
Marryat Australia **148** B5
Mars r. France **51** I7
Marsá 'Alam Egypt **121** G3
Marsá al Burayqah Libya **120** C2
Marsabit Kenya **128** C4
Marsabit National Reserve nature res. Kenya **128** C4
Marsa Darur Sudan **121** H5
Marsa Delwein Sudan **121** H4
Marsa 'Igli Egypt **104** A5
Marsala Sicilia Italy **57** E11
Marsa Mar'ob Sudan **104** B3
Marsa Matrûh Egypt **121** F2
   historically known as Paraetonium
Marsa Oseif Sudan **104** B3
Marsa Salak Sudan **104** B3
Marsa Shin'ab Sudan **104** B3
Marsa Tundaba Egypt **104** A2
Mars Bay Bahamas **186** D2
Marsberg Germany **48** G4
Marsciano Italy **56** E6
Marsden Australia **147** E3
Marsden Canada **167** I4
Marseille France **51** L9
   English form Marseilles; historically known as Massilia
Marseilles France see Marseille
Marseilles U.S.A. **172** E9
Marsella Bol. **200** D3
Marsh, Jabal mt. Saudi Arabia **108** F9
Marshall watercourse Australia **148** C4
Marshall AR U.S.A. **179** D5
Marshall IL U.S.A. **174** C4
Marshall MI U.S.A. **173** I8
Marshall MN U.S.A. **178** D2
Marshall MO U.S.A. **178** D4
Marshall TX U.S.A. **179** D5
Marshall VA U.S.A. **176** H7

Marsh Lake Canada **166** C2
Marsh Lake l. Canada **166** C2
Marshūn Iran **100** B2
Marsh Peak U.S.A. **133** O1
Märsta Sweden **45** L4
Marta Italy **56** D6
Marta r. Italy **56** D6
Martaban Myanmar **78** B4
   also known as Môktama
Martaban, Gulf of Myanmar **78** B4
Martani Besar i. Sabah Malaysia **77** G1
Martapura Kalimantan Selatan Indon. **77** F3
Martapura Sumatra Indon. **76** D4
Martel France **50** H8
Marten River Canada **168** E4
Marte R. Gómez, Presa resr Mex. **185** F3
Martés mt. Spain **55** K5
Martés, Serra mts Spain **55** J5
Martha's Vineyard i. U.S.A. **177** O4
Marti Cuba **186** D2
Martigny Switz. **51** N6
Martigues France **51** L9
Martin r. Canada **166** C2
Martin Slovakia **49** P6
Martin r. Spain **55** K4
Martin U.S.A. **178** B3
Martin, Lake U.S.A. **175** C5
Martina Franca Italy **57** J8
Martinborough N.Z. **152** J9
Martinet Spain **55** M2
Martinez Mex. **185** F4
Martinez CA U.S.A. **182** B3
Martinez GA U.S.A. **175** D5
Martinho Campos Brazil **203** C6

▶ Martinique terr. West Indies **187** H4
   French Overseas Department.
   oceania (countries) ▶ 138–139

Martinique Passage Dominica/Martinique **187** H4
Martino Greece **59** E10
Martinópolis Brazil **206** B9
Martin Peninsula Antarctica **222** Q2
Martins Bay N.Z. **153** B12
Martinsburg OH U.S.A. **176** C5
Martinsburg PA U.S.A. **176** G5
Martinsburg WV U.S.A. **176** H6
Martinsville IN U.S.A. **174** C4
Martinsville VA U.S.A. **176** F9

▶ Martin Vas, Ilhas is S. Atlantic Ocean **217** I7
   Most easterly point of South America.
   English form Martin Vaz Islands; also spelt Martim Vaz, Ilhas

Martin Vaz Islands S. Atlantic Ocean see Martin Vas, Ilhas
Martök Greece **59** E10
Marton N.Z. **152** J8
Martorell Spain **55** M3
Martos Spain **54** H7
Martuk Kazakh. **102** D2
   also spelt Martök
Martuni Armenia **107** F2
Maru Nigeria **125** G3
Maruchak Afgh. **101** E3
Marudi Sarawak Malaysia **77** F1
Marudu, Teluk b. Sabah Malaysia **77** G1
Marugame Japan **91** C7
Maruia r. N.Z. **153** G9
Maruim Brazil **202** F4
Marukhis Ughettekhili pass Georgia/Rus. Fed. **107** E2
Marum, Mount vol. Vanuatu **145** F3
Mārün r. Iran **100** B4
Marunga Angola **127** D9
Marusthali reg. India **96** A4
Maruwa Aboriginal Reserve Australia **150** D4
Maruwa Hills Sudan **128** B3
Marvast Iran **100** C4
Marv Dasht Iran **100** C4
Marvejols France **51** J8
Marvine, Mount U.S.A. **183** M3
Marwayne Canada **167** I4
Mary r. N.T. Australia **148** A2
Mary r. Qld Australia **149** G5
Mary r. W.A. Australia **150** D3
Mary Turkm. **103** E5
   historically known as Alexandria or Merv
Maryborough Qld Australia **149** G5
Maryborough Vic. Australia **147** D4
Marydale S. Africa **132** G6
Nar'yevka Rus. Fed. **102** I1
Mary Frances Lake Canada **167** J2
Maryland state U.S.A. **177** I7
Mary Oblast admin. div. Turkm. see Maryyskaya Oblast'
Mary's Harbour Canada **169** K3
Marystown Canada **169** K4
Marysvale U.S.A. **183** L3
Marysville CA U.S.A. **182** C2
Marysville KS U.S.A. **178** C4
Marysville MI U.S.A. **173** K8
Marysville OH U.S.A. **176** B5
Marysville WA U.S.A. **180** B2
Maryvale N.T. Australia **148** B5
Maryvale Qld Australia **149** F5
Maryville MO U.S.A. **178** D3
Maryville TN U.S.A. **174** D5
Maryyskaya Oblast' admin. div. Turkm. **103** E5
   English form Mary Oblast
Marzagão Brazil **206** E4
Marzo, Cabo c. Col. **198** B3
Masachapa Nicaragua **186** B5
Masada tourist site Israel **108** G6
   also spelt Metsada or Mezada
Masaff, Wādī watercourse Syria/Turkey **109** L1
Masagurc Tanz. **129** C7
Masāhün, Küh-e mt. Iran **100** C4
Masai Mara National Reserve nature res. Kenya **128** B5
Masai Steppe plain Tanz. **129** C6
Masaka Uganda **128** A5
Masakhane S. Africa **133** N8
Masalanyana Pan salt pan Botswana **130** D4
Masalembu Besar i. Indon. **77** F4
Masalembu Kecil i. Indon. **77** F4
Masalh Azer. **107** G3
Masamba Indon. **75** B3
Masamba mt. Indon. **75** B3
Masan S. Korea **83** C6
Masāqif i. Saudi Arabia **104** C4
Masasi Tanz. **129** C7
Masavi Bol. **201** E4
Masaya Nicaragua **186** B5
Masaya, Volcán de vol. Nicaragua **186** B5
Masbate Phil. **74** B3
Masbate i. Phil. **74** B4
Mascara Alg. **123** F2
   also spelt Mouaskar
Mascot U.S.A. **176** B9
Mascota Mex. **184** D4
Mascote Brazil **207** N2
Mascouche Canada **169** F4
Masein Myanmar **78** A3
Ma Sekatok b. Indon. **77** G3
Masela i. Indon. **75** D5
Masela i. Indon. **75** D5
Maseno Kenya **128** B4

Masères, Lac l. Canada **173** Q2

▶ Maseru Lesotho **133** L6
   Capital of Lesotho.

Masfjorden Norway **45** I3
Mashaba Zimbabwe see Mashava
Mashābih i. Saudi Arabia **104** B2
Mashai Lesotho **133** M6
Mashala Dem. Rep. Congo **126** D6
Mashan China **87** D4
   also known as Baishan
Mashava Zimbabwe **131** F4
   formerly spelt Mashaba
Masherbrum mt. Jammu and Kashmir **96** C2
Masheve Ukr. **43** N9
Mashhad Iran **101** D2
   English form Meshed
Mashi r. India **96** B4
Mashike Japan **90** G3
Mashket r. Pak. **101** E4
Mashki Chah Pak. **101** E4
Mäshkid r. Iran **101** E5
Mashonaland Central prov. Zimbabwe **131** F3
Mashonaland East prov. Zimbabwe **131** F3
Mashonaland West prov. Zimbabwe **131** F3
Mashtagi Azer. see Maştağa
Masiáca Mex. **184** C3
Masia-Mbia Dem. Rep. Congo **126** C5
Masibambane S. Africa **133** L8
Masif Baltim Egypt **108** A6
Masilah, Wādī al watercourse Yemen **105** E5
Masilo S. Africa **133** K5
Masi-Manimba Dem. Rep. Congo **126** C6
Masindi Uganda **128** A4
Masinloc Phil. **74** A3
Masinyusane S. Africa **132** H8
Masira, Gulf of Oman see Maşirah, Khalīj
Masira Channel Oman see Maşīrah, Tur'at
Maşīrah, Jazīrat i. Oman **105** G3
   English form Masira Island
Maşīrah, Khalīj b. Oman **105** G4
   English form Masira, Gulf of
Maşīrah, Tur'at sea chan. Oman **105** G3
   English form Masira Channel
Masira Island Oman see Maşīrah, Jazīrat
Masis Armenia **107** F2
Masisea Peru **200** B2
Masjaing S. Africa **133** L8
Masjed Soleymän Iran **100** B4
Mask, Lough l. Rep. of Ireland **47** C10
Maskanah Syria **109** J1
Maskütän Iran **101** D5
Maslti Pak. **101** E4
Masna'ah Yemen **105** E5
Masoala, Parc National nat. park Madag. **131** [inset] K3
Masoala, Tanjona c. Madag. **131** [inset] K3
Masohi Indon. **75** D3
Mason KY U.S.A. **176** A7
Mason MI U.S.A. **173** I8
Mason OH U.S.A. **176** A6
Mason TX U.S.A. **179** C6
Mason WV U.S.A. **172** B4
Mason WV U.S.A. **176** C6
Mason, Lake salt flat Australia **151** B5
Mason City U.S.A. **174** A3
Masoni i. Indon. **75** C3
Masontown PA U.S.A. **176** F6
Masontown WV U.S.A. **176** F6
Masqat Oman see Muscat
Masqat governorate Oman **105** G3
Masqat reg. Oman see Muscat
Massa Italy **56** C4
Massachusetts state U.S.A. **177** M3
Massachusetts Bay U.S.A. **177** O3
Massadona U.S.A. **183** P1
Massafra Italy **57** J8
Massa Marittimo Italy **56** C5
Massakory Chad **120** B6
Massalassef Chad **126** C2
Massa Marittima Italy **56** C5
Massambará Brazil **203** C7
Massana Gabon **126** A5
Massangena Moz. **131** G4
Massango Angola **127** C7
Massarosa Italy **56** C5
Massau Angola **127** C7
Massena U.S.A. **177** K1
Massenya Chad **120** C6
Masset Canada **166** C4
Masset Inlet Canada **166** C4
Masseube France **50** G5
Massey Canada **168** D4
Massiac France **51** J7
Massieville U.S.A. **176** C6
Massif Central mts France **51** J7
Massigui Mali **124** D4
Massilia France see Marseille
Massina Mali **124** D4
   formerly spelt Ke Macina
Massinga Moz. **131** G4
Massingir Moz. **131** G4
Massintonto r. Moz./S. Africa **133** Q2
Masson Canada **173** R5
Masson Island Antarctica **223** G2
Maştağa Azer. **107** G2
   also spelt Mashtagi
Mastchoh Tajik. **101** G2
   also known as Matcha
Masterton N.Z. **152** J9
Masticho, Akra pt Greece **59** H10
Mastic Point Bahamas **186** E1
Mastigouche, Réserve Faunique de nature res. Canada **169** F4
Mastrevik Norway **46** Q3
Mastuj Pak. **101** H2
Mastung Pak. **101** F4
Mastürah Saudi Arabia **104** B3
Masty Belarus **42** F8
   also spelt Mosty
Masuda Japan **91** B7
Masuku Dem. Rep. Congo **127** D6
Masuku Gabon see Franceville
Masuleh Iran **100** B2
Masulipatam India see Machilipatnam
Masuna i. American Samoa see Tutuila
Masurai, Bukit mt. Indon. **76** C3
Masvingo Zimbabwe **131** F4
   formerly known as Fort Victoria or Nyanda
Masvingo prov. Zimbabwe **131** F4
Maswe Tanz. **128** B5
Maswe Game Reserve nature res. Tanz. **128** B5
Maşyāf Syria **109** H2
Mat r. Albania **58** A7
Mata r. N.Z. **152** M5
Mata, Serranía de mts Venez. **199** E3
Mata Amarilla Arg. **205** C8
Mataba Zambia **127** E8
Matabaan Somalia **128** E3
Matabeleland North prov. Zimbabwe **131** E3
Matabhanga India **97** F4
Matachewan Canada **168** D4
Matachic Mex. **184** D2
Matadi Dem. Rep. Congo **127** B6
Matador U.S.A. **179** B5
Matagalpa Nicaragua **186** B5
Matagami Canada **168** E3
Matagami, Lac l. Canada **168** E3
Matagorda Brazil **202** D5
Matagrande Brazil **179** C6
Mata Grande Brazil **202** E3
Matahiwi N.Z. **152** J7

Mataigou China see Taole
Matak i. Indon. 77 D2
Matak Kazakh. 103 H2
Matakana Island N.Z. 152 K5
Matakaoa Point N.Z. 152 M5
Matakitaki N.Z. 153 C9
Matala Angola 127 B8
Mataleng S. Africa 133 I3
Matam Senegal 124 B3
Matamata N.Z. 152 J5
Mata-Mata S. Africa 132 E2
Matamau N.Z. 152 K8
Matameye Niger 125 H3
Matamoras U.S.A. 177 K4
Matamoros Campeche Mex. 185 H5
Matamoros Coahuila Mex. 185 E3
Matamoros Tamaulipas Mex. 185 F3
Ma'tan as Sārah well Libya 120 D4
Ma'tan Bishrah well Libya 120 D4
Matandu r. Tanz. 129 C7
Matane Canada 169 H3
Matane, Réserve Faunique de nature res.
Canada 169 H3
Mata Negra Venez. 199 F2
Matangi N.Z. 152 J5
Matanzas Cuba 186 C2
Matão Brazil 206 E8
Matão, Serra do hills Brazil 202 B4
Matapalo, Cabo c. Costa Rica 186 C1
Matapan, Cape pt Greece see Tainaro, Akra
Mata Panew r. Poland 49 R5
Matapédia, Lac r. Canada 169 H3
Mataporquera Spain 54 G2
Maţār well Saudi Arabia 105 D2
Matará Arg. 204 E3
Matara Sri Lanka 94 D5
also known as Matturai
Mataragka Greece 59 C10
also spelt Mataránga
Mataram Indon. 77 G5
Mataránga Greece see Mataragka
Mataranka Australia 148 B2
Matarinao Bay Phil. 74 C4
Matarka Morocco 123 E2
Matarma, Rās pt Egypt 108 D8
Mataroa N.Z. 152 J7
Matarombea r. Indon. 75 B3
Matarraña r. Spain 55 L3
Matasiri i. Indon. 77 F4
Matassi well Sudan 121 F5
Matassi Tanz. 129 C6
Matatiele S. Africa 133 M7
Matatila Dam India 96 C4
Matau N.Z. 152 I7
Mataura N.Z. 153 C14
Mataura r. N.Z. 153 C14

►Matā'utu Wallis and Futuna is 145 H3
Capital of Wallis and Futuna.

Matawai N.Z. 152 L6
Matawaia N.Z. 152 H3
Matawin r. Canada 169 F4
Matay Kazakh. 103 I3
Matbakh, Ra's al pt Qatar 105 E2
Matcha Tajik. see Mastchoh
Matchi-Manitou, Lac l. Canada 173 P2
Mategua Bol. 201 E3
Matehuala Mex. 185 E4
Matei Romania 58 F2
Mateke Hills Zimbabwe 131 F4
Matelica Italy 56 F5
Matelot Trin. and Tob. 187 H5
Matemanga Tanz. 129 C7
Matende Angola 127 C9
Matera Italy 57 I8
Matese, Monti del mts Italy 56 G7
Mátészalka Hungary 49 T8
Matetsi Zimbabwe 131 E3
Mateur Tunisia 57 B11
Mateus Leme Brazil 207 I6
Matewan U.S.A. 176 C8
Matha France 50 F7
Matheson Canada 168 D3
Mathews U.S.A. 177 I8
Mathias U.S.A. 176 G7
Mathrâki i. Greece 59 A9
Mathura India 96 C4
Mati Phil. 74 C5
Matiacoali Burkina 125 F3
Matianxu China 87 E3
Matiari Pak. 101 G5
Matias Barbosa Brazil 207 J8
Matias Cardoso Brazil 202 D5
Matías Romero Mex. 185 G5
Matibane Moz. 131 I2
Matimekosh Canada 169 H2
Matina Costa Rica 186 C5
Matinicus Island U.S.A. 177 Q2
Matizi China 86 B1
Matjiesfontein S. Africa 132 E10
Matla r. India 97 F5
Matli Pak. 101 G5
Matlock U.K. 47 K10
Matlwangtlwang S. Africa 133 L4
Matna Sudan 104 A5
Mato r. Venez. 199 E3
Mato, Cerro mt. Venez. 199 E3
Matoaka U.S.A. 176 D8
Matobo Hills Zimbabwe 131 F4
also spelt Matopo Hills
Matobo National Park Zimbabwe 131 F4
formerly known as Rhodes Matopos
National Park
Matogrossense, Pantanal marsh Brazil
201 G4
Mato Grosso Brazil 201 F3
►Mato Grosso state Brazil 206 A2
southamerica (contrasts) ▶▶ 194–195
Mato Grosso, Planalto do plat. Brazil
202 A5
Mato Grosso do Sul state Brazil 206 A6
Matola Moz. 131 G5
Matondo Moz. 131 G3
Matope Malawi 129 B8
Matopo Hills Zimbabwe see Matobo Hills
Matos r. Bol. 200 D3
Matosinhos Port. 54 C3
Matou China see Pingguo
Mato Verde Brazil 207 K2
Matozinhos Brazil 207 I6
Mátra mts Hungary 49 Q8
Maţraḩ Oman 105 E3
Matruh park Hungary 49 R8
Matrei in Osttirol Austria 49 J9
Matroosberg S. Africa 132 D10
Matroosberg mt. S. Africa 132 D10
Matrooster S. Africa 133 I3
Matrûh governorate Egypt 108 A8
Matsalu rüklik looduskaitseala nature res.
Estonia 42 E3
Matsap S. Africa 132 G5
Matse**... Matseŝta Rus. Fed. 107 D2
Matsudo Japan 91 F7
Matsue Japan 91 C7
Matsumae Japan 90 G4
Matsumoto Japan 91 E6
Matsusaka Japan 91 E7
Matsuura Japan 91 A8
Matsuyama Japan 91 C8
Matsuzaki Japan 91 F7

Mattagami r. Canada 168 D3
Mattamuskeet, Lake U.S.A. 174 E5
Mattawa Canada 168 E4
Matterhorn mt. Italy/Switz. 51 N7
Matterhorn mt. U.S.A. 180 D4
Mattersburg Austria 49 N8
Matthew atoll Kiribati see Marakei
Matthews U.S.A. 174 D5
Matthews Peak Kenya 128 C4
Matthews Ridge Guyana 199 F3
Matthew Town Bahamas 187 E2
Mattī, Sabkhat salt pan Saudi Arabia
105 F3
Mattituck U.S.A. 177 M5
Mattmar Sweden 44 K3
Mattô Japan 91 E6
Mattoon U.S.A. 174 B4
Måttsund Sweden 44 M2
Matturai Sri Lanka see Matara
Matu Sarawak Malaysia 77 E2
Matua, Ostrov i. Rus. Fed. 81 Q3
Matucana Peru 200 A2
Matugama Sri Lanka 94 D5
Matumbo Angola 127 C8
Matun Afgh. see Khowst
Maturín Venez. 199 F2
Maturuca Brazil 199 F3
Matusadona National Park Zimbabwe
131 F3
Matutuang i. Indon. 75 C1
Matveyev, Ostrov i. Rus. Fed. 40 K1
Matveyevka Rus. Fed. 102 C1
Matwabeng S. Africa 133 L4
Matxitxako, Cabo c. Spain 55 I1
Maty Island P.N.G. see Wuvulu Island
Matyrskiy Rus. Fed. 43 U9
Mau Madhya Pradesh India 96 C4
Mau Uttar Pradesh India 97 D4
Mau Uttar Pradesh India 97 D4
Mau Aimma India 97 D4
Maubermé, Pic de mt. France/Spain 55 L2
Maubin Myanmar 78 A4
Ma-ubin Myanmar 78 B2
Maubourguet France 50 G9
Mauchsberg S. Africa 133 O2
Maudaha India 96 C4
Maude Australia 147 E3
Maué-e-ele Moz. see Marão
Maués Brazil 199 G5
Maués r. Brazil 199 G5
Mauganj India 97 D4
Maug Islands N. Mariana Is 73 K2
Mauguio France 51 K9
Maui i. U.S.A. 181 [inset] Z1
Maukkadaw Myanmar 78 A3
Maulbronn Germany 48 F7
Maule admin. reg. Chile 204 B4
Maule r. Chile 204 B4
Mauléon France 50 F6
Mauléon-Licharre France 50 F9
Maullín Chile 205 B6
Maulvi Bazar Bangl. 97 F4
also spelt Moulvibazar
Maumaupaki hill N.Z. 152 J5
Maumee U.S.A. 176 B4
Maumee r. U.S.A. 176 B4
Maumee Bay U.S.A. 176 B4
Maumere Indon. 75 B5
Maun Botswana 130 D3
Mauna Kea vol. U.S.A. 181 [inset] Z2
Mauna Loa vol. U.S.A. 181 [inset] Z2
Maun Game Sanctuary nature res.
Botswana 130 D3
Maungatāniwha mt. N.Z. 152 K6
Maungatapere N.Z. 152 I3
Maungaturoto N.Z. 152 I4
Maungdaw Myanmar 78 A3
Maungmagan Islands Myanmar 79 B5
Maungmagon Myanmar 79 B5
Maupin U.S.A. 180 B3
Maurawan India 96 D4
Maurepas, Lake U.S.A. 175 B6
Maures, Massif des hills France 51 M9
Mauri r. Bol. 200 C4
Mauriac France 51 I7
Maurice country Indian Ocean see Mauritius
Maurice, Lake salt flat Australia 146 A2
Mauritania country Africa 122 B5
spelt Al Mūrītānīyah in Arabic or Mauritanie
in French
world [countries] ▶▶ 10–11
africa [countries] ▶▶ 114–117
Mauritanie country Africa see Mauritania
Mauritius country Indian Ocean 218 K7
also known as Maurice
africa [countries] ▶▶ 114–117
Mauro, Monte mt. Italy 56 G7
Mauron France 50 D4
Mauros mt. Greece 59 D8
Maurs France 51 I8
Mauston U.S.A. 172 J7
Mauvezin France 50 G9
Mauzé-sur-le-Mignon France 50 F6
Mava Dem. Rep. Congo 126 E4
Mavaca r. Venez. 199 E4
Mavago Moz. 129 C8
Mavasjaure l. Sweden 44 L2
Mavengue Angola 127 C9
Mavinga Angola 127 C9
Mavisdale U.S.A. 176 C8
Mavita Moz. 131 G3
Mavra r. Greece 59 H12
Mavrothalassa Greece 58 E8
Mavrovo nat. park Macedonia 58 B7
Mavume Moz. 131 G4
Mavuya S. Africa 133 L8
Mawa, Bukit mt. Indon. 77 F3
Ma Wan i. Hong Kong China 87 [inset]
Mâwān, Khashm hill Saudi Arabia 105 D3
Mawana India 96 C3
Mawanga Dem. Rep. Congo 127 C6
Mawasangka Indon. 75 B4
Mawdaung Pass Myanmar/Thai. 79 B6
Mawei China 87 F3
Mawhai Point N.Z. 152 M6
Mawheraiti N.Z. 153 F10
Mawheranui r. N.Z. see Grey
Māwiyah Yemen 104 D5
Mawjib, Wādī al r. Jordan 108 G6
also known as Arnon
Mawkhi Myanmar 78 B4
Mawkmai Myanmar 78 B3
Mawlaik Myanmar 78 A3
Mawlamyaing Myanmar see Moulmein
Mawlamyine Myanmar see Moulmein
Mawphlang India 97 F4
Mawqaq Saudi Arabia 104 C2
Mawshij Yemen 104 C5
Mawson research station Antarctica 223 E2
Mawson Coast Antarctica 223 E2
Mawson Escarpment Antarctica 223 E2
Mawson Peninsula Antarctica 223 K2
Maw Taung mt. Myanmar 79 B6
Mawza Yemen 104 C5
Maxaas Somalia 128 E4
Maxán Arg. 204 D3
Maxcanú Mex. 185 H4
Maxhamish Lake Canada 166 F3
Maxia, Punta mt. Sardegna Italy 57 A9
Maxinei Rcmania 58 I3
Maxixe Moz. 131 G4
Maxmo Fin. 44 M3
Maxwell U.S.A. 152 I7
Maxwelton Australia 149 D4
Maya i. Indon. 77 E3
Maya r. Rus. Fed. 39 N3

►Mbabane Swaziland 133 P3
Capital of Swaziland.

Mbacké Senegal 124 B3
Mbaéré r. Cent. Afr. Rep. 126 C4

index

M

Melhus Norway 44 J3
Meliadine Lake Canada 167 M2
Meliau, Gunung mt. Sabah Malaysia 77 G1
  also known as Melta, Mount
Melide Spain 54 D2
  also spelt Mellid
Meligalas Greece 59 C11

▶ Melilla N. Africa 55 I9
  Spanish Territory. Formerly known as Rusaddir.
  africa [countries] → 114–117
Melilli Sicilia Italy 57 H11
Melimoyu, Monte mt. Chile 205 B7
Melina, Mount N.Z. 153 D12
Melintang, Danau l. Indon. 77 G3
Melipilla Chile 204 C4
Melita Canada 167 K5
Melitene Turkey see Malatya
Melito di Porto Salvo Italy 57 H11
Melitopol' Ukr. 41 E7
Melk Austria 49 M7
Melka Guba Eth. 128 C3
Mellakoski Fin. 44 N2
Mellansel Sweden 44 L3
Mellansjö Sweden 45 K3
Mellanström Sweden 44 L2
Melle Germany 48 F3
Mellègue, Barrage dam Tunisia 57 A12
Mellerud Sweden 45 K4
Mellid Spain see Melide
Mellit Sudan 121 E6
Mellizo Sur, Cerro mt. Chile 205 B8
Mellor Glacier Antarctica 223 E2
Mellrichstadt Germany 48 H5
Mellum i. Germany 48 F1
Melmoth S. Africa 133 P5
Mel'nichoye Rus. Fed. 82 D3
Mělník Czech Rep. 49 L5
Mel'nikovo Rus. Fed. 43 K1
Melo Arg. 204 E4
Melo Uruguay 204 G4
Meloding S. Africa 133 K5
Melolo Indon. 75 B5
Mélong Cameroon 125 H5
Melovoye Ukr. see Milove
Melozitna r. U.S.A. 164 D3
Melrhir, Chott salt l. Alg. 123 G2
Melrose Australia 151 C5
Melrose U.K. 46 J8
Melrose U.S.A. 178 D2
Melsetter Zimbabwe see Chimanimani
Melsungen Germany 48 G4
Melta, Mount Sabah Malaysia see Meliau, Gunung
Meltaus Fin. 44 N2
Melton Australia 147 E4
Melton Mowbray U.K. 47 L11
Meluan Sarawak Malaysia 77 E2
Melun France 51 I4
Melur India 94 C4
Melut Sudan 128 D2
Melville Canada 167 K5
Melville, Cape Australia 149 E2
Melville, Lake Canada 169 J2
Melville Bay Australia 148 C1
Melville Bugt b. Greenland see Qimusseriarsuaq
Melville Island Australia 148 A1
Melville Island Canada 165 I2
Melville Peninsula Canada 165 K3
Melvin, Lough l. Rep. of Ireland/U.K. 47 D9
Mélykút Hungary 49 Q9
Memaliaj Albania 59 A8
Mêmar Co salt l. China 89 C5
Memba Moz. 131 I2
Memba, Baía de b. Moz. 131 I2
Memberamo r. Indon. 73 I7
Memboro Indon. 75 A5
Memel Lith. see Klaipėda
Memel S. Africa 133 N4
Mêmêle r. Latvia 42 F5
Memiakalnis hill Lith. 42 H6
Memmingen Germany 48 H8
Mempakul Sabah Malaysia 77 F1
Memphis tourist site Egypt 121 F2
Memphis MI U.S.A. 173 K8
Memphis MO U.S.A. 174 A3
Memphis TN U.S.A. 174 B5
Memphis TX U.S.A. 179 B5
Memuro-dake mt. Japan 90 H3
Mena Eth. 128 C3
Mena Indon. 75 C5
Mena Ukr. 41 E6
Mena U.S.A. 179 D5
Menabe mts Madag. 131 [inset] J4
Mènaka Mali 125 F3
Mènam Khong r. Asia 78 D4 see Mekong
Menanga Indon. 75 C3
Menarandra r. Madag. 131 [inset] J5
Menard U.S.A. 179 C6
Menasha U.S.A. 172 E6
Mencal mt. Spain 55 H7
Mencué arg. 204 C6
Mendanau i. Indon. 77 D3
Mendarda India 96 A5
Mendarik i. Indon. 77 D2
Mendawai Indon. 77 F3
Mendawai r. Indon. 77 F3
Mende France 51 J8
Mendebo Mountains Eth. 128 C3
Mendefera Eritrea 121 H6
  also known as Adi Ugri
Mendeleyevsk Rus. Fed. 40 J5
  formerly known as Bondyuzhskiy
Menden (Sauerland) Germany 48 E4
Mendenhall U.S.A. 175 B6
Mendenhall, Cape U.S.A. 164 C4
Mendenhall Glacier U.S.A. 166 C3
Menderes Turkey 59 I10
Méndez Mex. 185 F3
Mendez-Nuñez Phil. 74 B3

Mendi P.N.G. 73 J8
Mendip Hills U.K. 47 J12
Mendocino U.S.A. 182 A2
Mendocino, Cape U.S.A. 180 A4
Mendocino, Lake U.S.A. 182 A2
Mendota CA U.S.A. 182 D5
Mendota IL U.S.A. 174 B3
Mendota, Lake U.S.A. 172 D7
Mendoza Arg. 204 C4
Mendoza prov. Arg. 204 C4
Mendoza Bol. 200 D4
Mene de Mauroa Venez. 198 D2
Menemen Turkey 59 I10
Menez Bré hill France 50 C4
Menfi Sicilia Italy 57 E11
Menga, Puerto de pass Spain 54 F4
Mengalum i. Malaysia 77 F1
Mengban China 86 B4
Mengcheng China 87 F1
Mengding China 86 A3
Mengdingjie China see Mengding
Mengen Turkey 106 C2
Menggala Indon. 76 D4
Menghai China 86 B4
  also known as Xiangshan
Mengibar Spain 54 H6
Mengkiang r. Indon. 77 E2
Mengkoka, Gunung mt. Indon. 75 B3
Menglang China see Lancang
Menglie China see Jiangcheng
Mengmeng China see Shuangjiang
Mengong Cameroon 125 H6
Mengshan China 87 D3
Mengxian China see Mengzhou
Mengyang China see Mingshan
Mengyin China 85 H5
Mengzhou China 87 E1
  formerly known as Mengxian
Mengzi China 86 B4
  also known as Wenlan
Menihek Canada 169 H2
Menindee Australia 147 D3
Menindee Aboriginal Reserve Australia 147 D3
Menindee Lake Australia 147 D3
Meningie Australia 151 C6
Menkere Rus. Fed. 39 M3
Menna r. Eth. 104 B5
Mennecy France 51 I4
Mennonite Colony res. Para. 201 F3
Menominee U.S.A. 172 F5
Menominee r. U.S.A. 172 F5
Menominee Indian Reservation res. U.S.A. 172 E5
Menomonee Falls U.S.A. 172 E7
Menomonie U.S.A. 172 B6
Menongue Angola 127 C8
  formerly known as Serpa Pinto
Menor, Mar lag. Spain 55 K7
Menorca i. Spain see Minorca
Mensalong Indon. 77 G2
Men'shikova, Mys c. Rus. Fed. 40 K1
Mentakab Malaysia see Mentekab
Mentarang r. Indon. 77 G2
Mentawai, Kepulauan is Indon. 76 B3
Mentawai, Selat sea chan. Indon. 76 C3
Mentaya r. Indon. 77 F3
Mentekab Malaysia 76 C2
  formerly spelt Mentakab
Mentiras hill Port. 54 D6
Mentiras mt. Spain 55 I6
Mentok Indon. 76 D3
Menton France 51 N9
Mentone U.S.A. 179 B6
Mentor U.S.A. 176 D4
Mentuba r. Indon. 77 F3
Menufia governorate Egypt see Minūfiya
Menukung Indon. 77 F3
Menunu Indon. 75 B2
Menyapa, Gunung mt. Indon. 77 G2
Menyuan China 84 D4
  also known as Haomen
Menza r. Rus. Fed. 85 F1
Menzel Bourguiba Tunisia 123 H1
  formerly known as Ferryville
Menzelet Baraji resr Turkey 107 D3
Menzelinsk Rus. Fed. 40 J5
Menzel Temime Tunisia 57 D12
Menzies Australia 151 C6
Menzies, Mount Antarctica 223 E2
Meobbaai b. Namibia 130 B5
Meoqui Mex. 184 D2
Mepala Angola 127 B6
Meponda Moz. 131 G1
Meppel Neth. 48 D3
Meppen Germany 48 E3
Meqheleng S. Africa 133 L5
Mequéns r. Brazil 201 E3
Mequinenza, Embalse de resr Spain 55 L3
Mequon U.S.A. 172 F7
Mer France 50 H5
Merah Indon. 77 G2
Merak Indon. 77 D4
Meråker Norway 44 J3
Meramangye, Lake salt flat Australia 146 B2
Meramec r. U.S.A. 178 E4
Merano Italy 56 D2
Merapi, Gunung vol. Java Indon. 77 E4
Merapi, Gunung mt. Indon. 77 F5
Merari, Serra mt. Brazil 199 F3
Meratswe r. Botswana 131 E4
Meratus, Pegunungan mts Indon. 77 F3
Merauke Indon. 73 J8
Merawwah i. U.A.E. 105 F2
Merbau Indon. 76 C2
Merbein Australia 147 D3
Merca Somalia see Marka
Mercadal Spain 55 P5
Mercantour, Parc National du nat. park France 51 M8
Merced U.S.A. 182 D4
Merced r. U.S.A. 182 D4
Mercedario, Cerro mt. Arg. 204 C4
Mercedes Corrientes Arg. 204 F3
Mercedes San Luis Arg. 204 D4
Mercedes Uruguay 204 F4
Mercês Acre Brazil 200 C2
Mercês Minas Gerais Brazil 203 D7
Mercier Bol. 200 C2
Mercury U.S.A. 183 I5
Mercury Bay N.Z. 152 J4
Merdenik Turkey see Göle
Merdja Zerga, Réserve de nature res. Morocco 122 C2
Meredith U.S.A. 177 N2
Meredith, Cape Falkland Is 205 E9
Meredith, Lake U.S.A. 179 B5
Meredoua Alg. 123 F4
Mereeg Somalia 128 E4
Merefa Ukr. 41 F6
Meremäe Estonia 42 J4
Meremere N.Z. 152 I4
Merenkurkku strait Fin./Sweden 44 M3
Merepah Aboriginal Holding res. Australia 149 D2
Merezha Rus. Fed. 43 P2
Merga Oasis Sudan 121 E5
Mergenevo Kazakh. 102 B2
Mergui Myanmar 79 B6
  also known as Myeik
Mergui Archipelago is Myanmar 79 B6
Merhei, Lacul l. Romania 58 K3
Meribah Australia 146 D3
Meriç r. Greece/Turkey see Evros
Meriç r. Greece/Turkey 58 H8
Meriç Turkey 58 H7
Merichas Greece 59 F11

Mérida Mex. 185 H4
Mérida Spain 54 E6
  historically known as Emerita Augusta
Mérida Venez. 198 D2
Mérida state Venez. 198 D2
Mérida, Cordillera de mts Venez. 198 D3
Meriden U.S.A. 177 M4
Meridian MS U.S.A. 175 B5
Meridian TX U.S.A. 179 C6
Mérignac France 50 F8
Merijärvi Fin. 44 N2
Merikarvia Fin. 45 M3
Merimbula Australia 147 F4
Merin, Laguna l. Brazil/Uruguay see Mirim, Lagoa
Merinda Australia 149 F4
Meringur Australia 146 D3
Merir i. Palau 73 H6
  historically known as Warren Hastings Island
Merirumã Brazil 199 H4
Merivale r. Australia 149 E5
Merke Kazakh. 103 H4
Merkel U.S.A. 179 B5
Merkinė Lith. 42 F7
Merlimau, Pulau reg. Sing. 76 [inset]
Mermaid Reef Australia 150 B3
Merolia Australia 151 C5
Meron, Har mt. Israel 108 G5
Merošina Srbija Yugo. 58 C5
Merowe Sudan 121 F5
Meredin Australia 151 B6
Merrick hill U.K. 47 H8
Merrickville Canada 173 R6
Merrill MI U.S.A. 173 I7
Merrill WI U.S.A. 172 D5
Merrill, Mount Canada 166 E2
Merrillan U.S.A. 172 C6
Merrillville U.S.A. 172 F9
Merriman S. Africa 132 H6
Merriman U.S.A. 178 B3
Merritt Canada 166 F5
Merritt Island U.S.A. 175 D6
Merritt Island National Wildlife Refuge nature res. U.S.A. 175 D6
Merrygoen Australia 147 F2
Mersa Fatma Eritrea 121 I6
Mersa Gulbub Eritrea 121 H5
Mersa Teklay Eritrea 121 H5
Mersch Lux. 51 M3
Merse r. Italy 56 D5
Merseburg (Saale) Germany 48 I4
Mersin Turkey see İçel
Mersing Malaysia 76 C2
Mersing, Bukit mt. Sarawak Malaysia 77 F2
Mērsrags Latvia 42 E4
Mērsrags pt Latvia 42 E4
Merta India 96 B4
Merta Road India 96 B4
Merthyr Tydfil U.K. 47 I12
Merti Kenya 128 C4
Merti Plateau Kenya 128 C4
Mértola Port. 54 D7
Mertoutek Alg. 123 G4
Mertz Glacier Antarctica 223 J2
Mertz Glacier Tongue Antarctica 223 J2
Mertzon U.S.A. 179 B6
Méru France 51 I3
Meru Kenya 128 C4

▶ Meru vol. Tanz. 128 C5
  4th highest mountain in Africa.
  africa [landscapes] → 112–113
Meru Betiri National Park Indon. 77 F5
Merui Pak. 101 E4
Meru National Park Kenya 128 C4
Merv Turkm. see Mary
Merweville S. Africa 132 F9
Merzifon Turkey 106 C2
Merzig Germany 48 D6
Merz Peninsula Antarctica 222 T2
Mesa S. Africa 133 K3
Mesa r. Spain 55 J3
Mesa U.S.A. 183 M8
Mesabi Range hills U.S.A. 174 A2
Mesa Bolivar Venez. 198 D2
Mesagne Italy 57 J8
Mesara, Ormos b. Greece 59 F13
Mesa Verde National Park U.S.A. 181 E5
Mescalero Apache Indian Reservation res. U.S.A. 181 F6
Meschede Germany 48 F4
Meselefors Sweden 44 L2
Mesfinto Eth. 128 C1
Mesgouez, Lac Canada 169 F3
Mesha r. Rus. Fed. 40 I5
Meshchovsk Rus. Fed. 43 Q7
Meshed Iran see Mashhad
Meshekli Uzbek. 103 G4
Meshkān Iran 100 D2
Meshoppen U.S.A. 177 J4
Mesick U.S.A. 172 H6
Mesimeri Greece 59 E8
Meslay-du-Maine France 50 F5
Mesola Italy 56 E4
Mesolongi Greece 59 C10
  English form Missolonghi; also known as Mesolóngion
Mesolóngion Greece see Mesolongi
Mesopotamia Brazil 203 D6
Mesquite NV U.S.A. 183 I5
Mesquite TX U.S.A. 179 C5
Mesquite Lake U.S.A. 183 I6
Messaad Alg. 123 F2
Messak Mellet hills Libya 120 A3
Messalo r. Moz. 129 D7
Messana Sicilia Italy see Messina
Messaoud, Oued watercourse Alg. 123 E4
Messier, Canal sea chan. Chile 205 B8
Messina Sicilia Italy 57 H10
  historically known as Messana or Zancle
Messina S. Africa 131 F4
Messina, Strait of Italy 57 H10
  also known as Stretta di Messina
Messines Canada 173 Q4
Messini Greece 59 C11
Messiniakos Kolpos b. Greece 59 D12
Meßkirch Germany 48 G8
Messlingen Sweden 44 K3
Mesta r. Greece see Nestos
Mestghanem Alg. see Mostaganem
Meston, Akra pt Greece 59 G10
Mesudiye Turkey 107 D2
Mesuji r. Indon. 77 D4
Mesquil i. Indon. 77 G4
Meta dept Col. 198 C4
Meta r. Col./Venez. 198 D2
Métabetchouan Canada 169 G3
Metagama Canada 173 L3
Meta Incognita Peninsula Canada 165 M3
Metairie U.S.A. 175 B6
Metaliferi, Munţii mts Romania 58 D2
Metallifere, Colline mts Italy 56 C5
Metallostroy Rus. Fed. 43 L2
Metamora U.S.A. 172 D10
Metán Arg. 204 D2
Metanara Eth. 128 C2
Metangula Moz. 129 B8
  formerly known as Augusto Cardosa
Metapan El Salvador 185 H6
Meteghan Canada 169 H4
Metelys l. Lith. 42 E7
Metema Eth. 121 H6
Meteor Creek r. Australia 149 F5
Meteora tourist site Greece 59 C9
Metgethen Rus. Fed. see Midu
Methoni Greece 59 C12
Methuen U.S.A. 177 N3
Methven N.Z. 153 F11
Metiona Lake Canada 168 D3
Metković Croatia 56 I6
Metlakatla U.S.A. 166 D4

Metlaoui Tunisia 123 H2
Metlika Slovenia 56 H3
Metoro Moz. 131 H2
Metro Indon. 76 D4
Metropolis U.S.A. 174 B4
Metsada tourist site Israel see Masada
Metsäkylä Fin. 44 O2
Metsovo Greece 59 C9
Metter U.S.A. 175 D5
Mettler U.S.A. 182 F6
Mettuppalaiyam India 94 C4
Mettur India 94 C4
Metu Eth. 128 C3
Metundo, Ilha i. Moz. 129 D7
Metz France 51 M3
Metzingen Germany 48 G7
Meulaboh Indon. 76 B1
Meung-sur-Loire France 50 H5
Meurthe r. France 51 M4
Meuse r. Belgium/France 51 L1
  also spelt Maas (Netherlands)
Mêwa China 86 B1
Mexcala Mex. 185 F5
Mexia U.S.A. 179 C6
Mexiana, Ilha i. Brazil 202 B1
Mexicali Mex. 184 B1
Mexican Hat U.S.A. 183 O4
Mexican Water U.S.A. 183 O5

▶ Mexico country Central America 184 D4
  2nd most populous and 4th largest country in North America.
  northamerica [countries] → 158–159
México Mex. see Mexico City
México state Mex. 185 F5
Mexico ME U.S.A. 177 O1
Mexico MO U.S.A. 174 B4
Mexico NY U.S.A. 177 I2
Mexico, Gulf of Mex./U.S.A. 171 G7

▶ Mexico City Mex. 185 F5
  Capital of Mexico. Most populous city in North America and 2nd in the world. Also known as México.
  world [cities] → 24–25
Meybod Iran 100 C3
Meydani, Ra's-e pt Iran 100 D5
Meyenburg Germany 49 J2
Meyersdale U.S.A. 176 F6
Meyerton S. Africa 133 M3
Meylan France 51 L7
Meymac France 51 I7
Meymaneh Afgh. 101 F3
Meymeh Iran 100 B3
Meynypil'gyno Rus. Fed. 39 R3
Meyo Centre Cameroon 125 H6
Meyssac France 50 H7
Meza Myanmar 78 B2
Meza r. Rus. Fed. 43 V3
Mezada tourist site Israel see Masada
Mezas mt. Spain 54 E4
Mezcalapa r. Mex. 185 G5
Mezdra Bulg. 58 E5
Mèze France 51 J9
Mezen' Rus. Fed. 40 H2
Mezen' r. Rus. Fed. 40 H2
Mézenc, Mont mt. France 51 K8
Mezenskaya Guba b. Rus. Fed. 40 G2
Mezha r. Rus. Fed. 43 N4
Mezhdurechensk Rus. Fed. 40 I3
Mezhdurechensky Rus. Fed. 38 G4
Mezhdurechnyy Rus. Fed. see Shali
Mezhdusharskiy, Ostrov i. Rus. Fed. 40 J1
Mézidon-Canon France 50 F3
Mézin France 50 G8
Mezinovskiy Rus. Fed. 43 V6
Mezitli Turkey 108 F1
Mezőberény Hungary 49 S9
Mezőhegyes Hungary 49 R9
Mezőkövácsháza Hungary 49 R9
Mezőkövesd Hungary 49 R8
Mezőtúr Hungary 49 R9
Mezquital Mex. 184 D4
Mezquital r. Mex. 184 D4
Mezquitic Mex. 184 D4
Mežvidi Latvia 42 I5
Mezzolombardo Italy 56 D2
Mfouati Congo 126 B6
Mfuwe Zambia 127 F8
Mgachi Rus. Fed. 82 F2
Mgbidi Nigeria 125 G5
Mglin Rus. Fed. 43 N8
Mgwali r. S. Africa 133 M8
Mhail, Rubh' a' pt U.K. 46 F8
Mhangura Zimbabwe 131 F3
  formerly known as Mangula
Mhasvad India 94 B2
Mhlambanyatsi Swaziland 133 P3
Mhlume Swaziland 133 P3
Mhluzi S. Africa 133 N2
Mhow India 96 B5
Mi r. China 85 H4
Mi r. Myanmar 78 A3
Miahuatlán Mex. 185 F5
Miajadas Spain 54 F5
Miami Cent. Afr. Rep. 126 C2
Miami FL U.S.A. 175 D7
Miami OK U.S.A. 179 D4
Miami TX U.S.A. 179 B5
Miami Beach U.S.A. 175 D7
Miamisburg U.S.A. 176 A6
Miamitown U.S.A. 176 A6
Mi'ānābād Iran 100 D2
Mianaz Pak. 101 E5
Miancaowan China 84 C5
Mian Chanmun Pak. 101 H4
Mianchi China 87 D1
Miāndasht Iran 100 D2
Miandowāb Iran 100 A2
Miandrivazo Madag. 131 [inset] J3
Miāneh Iran 100 A2
Miangas i. Phil. 74 D5
Miani Hor b. Pak. 101 F5
Mianmian Shan mts China 86 B3
Mianning China 86 B2
  also known as Chengxiang
Mianwali Pak. 101 G3
Mianxian China 86 C1
Mianyang China see Xiantao
Mianyang China 86 C2
Miaodao Qundao is China 85 I4
Miao'ergou China 88 D2
  also known as Utu
Miaogao China see Suichang
Miaoli Taiwan 87 G3
Miao Ling mts China 87 B3
Miarinarivo Antananarivo Madag. 131 [inset] J3
Mifah Saudi Arabia 104 C4
Mifflin U.S.A. 176 C5
Mifflinburg U.S.A. 177 H5
Mifflintown U.S.A. 177 H5
Migang Shan mt. China 85 E5
Migdol S. Africa 133 J4
Migennes France 51 J5
Mignone r. Italy 56 D6
Micang Shan mts China 86 C1
Micaune Moz. 131 H3
Michalovce Slovakia 49 S7
Michel Canada 167 I4
Micheng China see Midu
Miches Dom. Rep. 187 F3
Michigan state U.S.A. 173 E4

▶ Michigan, Lake U.S.A. 172 F7
  3rd largest lake in North America and 5th in the world.
  northamerica [landscapes] → 156–157
Michigan City U.S.A. 174 C3
Michipicoten Bay Canada 168 C4
Michipicoten Island Canada 168 C4
Michipicoten River Canada 168 C4
Michoacán state Mex. 185 E5
Michurin Bulg. see Tsarevo
Michurinsk Rus. Fed. 41 G5
Micos Mex. 185 F4
Micoud St Lucia 187 H4
Micronesia i. Pacific Ocean 220 D5
Micronesia, Federated States of country N. Pacific Ocean 220 D5
  oceania [countries] → 138–139
Midai i. Indon. 77 D2
Midal well Niger 125 G2
Midale Canada 167 K5
Middelberg Pass S. Africa 132 D9
Middelburg Neth. 48 B4
Middelburg E. Cape S. Africa 133 J8
Middelburg Mpumalanga S. Africa 133 N2
Middelfart Denmark 45 J5
Middelharnis Neth. 48 B4
Middelpos S. Africa 132 E8
Middelwit S. Africa 133 L1
Middle Alkali Lake U.S.A. 180 B4
Middle Andaman i. India 95 G4
Middle Atlas mts Morocco see Moyen Atlas
Middle Bay Canada 169 J3
Middleboro U.S.A. 177 O4
Middleburg PA U.S.A. 177 H5
Middleburg VA U.S.A. 176 H7
Middleburgh U.S.A. 177 K3
Middlebury IN U.S.A. 172 H9
Middlebury VT U.S.A. 177 L1
Middle Concho r. U.S.A. 179 B6
Middle Congo country Africa see Congo
Middle Creek r. U.S.A. 149 C3
Middle Island U.S.A. 177 M5
Middle Loup r. U.S.A. 178 C3
Middlemount Australia 149 F4
Middleport OH U.S.A. 176 C6
Middle Raccoon r. U.S.A. 178 D3
Middle Ridge Wildlife Reserve nature res. Canada 169 K3
Middle River U.S.A. 176 H7
Middlesboro U.S.A. 176 B9
Middlesbrough U.K. 47 K9
Middlesex U.S.A. 177 H3
Middle Strait India see Andaman Strait
Middleton Australia 149 D4
Middleton Canada 169 H4
Middleton S. Africa 133 J9
Middleton U.S.A. 172 D7
Middletown CA U.S.A. 182 B3
Middletown CT U.S.A. 177 M4
Middletown DE U.S.A. 177 J6
Middletown MD U.S.A. 176 H6
Middletown NY U.S.A. 177 K4
Middletown OH U.S.A. 176 A6
Middletown PA U.S.A. 177 I5
Middleville MI U.S.A. 172 H8
Middleville NY U.S.A. 177 K2
Micelt Morocco 122 D2
Michishio well Somalia 128 E2
Midhurst U.K. 47 L13
Midi Yemen 104 C4
Midi, Canal du France 50 I9
Midi de Bigorre, Pic du mt. France 50 G10
Midi-Pyrénées admin. reg. France 50 I8
Midland Canada 168 D4
Midland CA U.S.A. 183 J8
Midland MI U.S.A. 173 I7
Midland TX U.S.A. 179 B5
Midland Junction Australia 151 A6
Midlands prov. Zimbabwe 131 F3
Midleton Rep. of Ireland 47 D12
Midlothian TX U.S.A. 179 C5
Midlothian UT U.S.A. 176 H8
Midmar Nature Reserve S. Africa 133 O6
Midnay Canada 173 L6
Midnapore India see Medinipur
Midongy Atsimo Madag. 131 [inset] J4
Midou r. France 50 F8
Midouze r. France 50 F9
Midsayap Phil. 74 C5
Midu China 86 B3
  also known as Micheng
Midvale U.S.A. 180 C3
Midway Oman see Thamarīt
Midway KY U.S.A. 176 A7
Midway UT U.S.A. 183 M1
▶ Midway Islands N. Pacific Ocean 220 G4
  United States Unincorporated Territory.
  oceania [countries] → 138–139
Midway Well Australia 150 C4
Midwest U.S.A. 180 F4
Midwest City U.S.A. 179 C5
Midyan reg. Saudi Arabia 104 A2
Midyat Turkey 107 E3
Midye Turkey see Kıyıköy
Midzhur mt. Bulg./Yugo. 58 D5
Mie Japan 91 E8
Mie pref. Japan 91 E7
Miechów Poland 49 R5
Miedwie, Jezioro l. Poland 49 L2
Międzychód Poland 49 N3
Międzylesie Poland 49 N5
Międzyrzec Podlaski Poland 49 T4
Międzyrzecz Poland 49 M3
Międzyzdroje Poland 49 L2
Miehikkälä Fin. 42 J1
Miekojärvi l. Fin. 44 N2
Mielec Poland 49 S5
Miembwe Tanz. 129 C7
Mień r. Poland 49 P3
Mienga Angola 127 C9
Miengwe Zambia 127 F8
Mienhua Yü i. Taiwan 87 G3
Mieraslompolo Fin. 44 N1
  also known as Mieraslouoppal
Mierasluoppal Fin. see Mieraslompolo
Miercurea-Ciuc Romania 58 G2
Mieres Spain 54 F1
Mieres del Camín Spain see Mieres
Mieres del Camino Spain see Mieres
Mieron Norway 44 N1
Mierzeja Helska pen. Poland 49 P1
Mierzeja Wiślana spit Poland 49 Q1
Miesbach Germany 48 I8
Mi'ēso Eth. 128 D2
Mieste Germany 48 I3
Mieszkowice Poland 49 L3
Mietoinen Fin. 45 M3

Mihaliçcık Turkey 106 B3
Mihara Japan 91 C7
Mihara-yama vol. Japan 91 F7
Mihidjan India see Chittaranjan
Mihijam India 97 E5
Mihumo Chini Tanz. 129 C7
Mijares r. Spain 55 K4
Mijas Spain 54 G8
Mijas mt. Spain 54 G8
Mikasa Japan 90 G3
Mikawa-wan b. Japan 91 E7
Mikhali Rus. Fed. 43 U6
Mikhalishki Belarus 42 H7
Mikhanavichy Belarus 42 I8
Mikha Tskhakaia Georgia see Senaki
Mikhaykovskiy Rus. Fed. see Prozorovo
Mikhaylov Rus. Fed. 43 U7
Mikhaylovgrad Bulg. see Montana
Mikhaylovka Amurskaya Oblast' Rus. Fed. 82 C2
Mikhaylovka Chitinskaya Oblast' Rus. Fed. 85 H1
Mikhaylovka Kurskaya Oblast' Rus. Fed. 43 Q9
Mikhaylovka Primorskiy Kray Rus. Fed. 82 D4
Mikhaylovka Rus. Fed. see Kimovsk
Mikhaylovka Volgogradskaya Oblast' Rus. Fed. 41 G6
Mikhaylovo Bulg. 58 E5
Mikhaylovskiy Rus. Fed. 103 I2
Mikhaylovskiy Rus. Fed. see Malinovoye Ozero
Mikhaylovskoye Rus. Fed. see Shpakovskoye
Mikhaylovskoye Rus. Fed. 43 V2
Mikhaytovo Island Antarctica 223 H1
Mikhnevo Rus. Fed. 43 S6
Miki Japan 91 D7
Mikines tourist site Greece see Mycenae
Mikir Hills India 97 G4
Mikkeli Fin. 45 N3
Mikkelin mlk Fin. 45 N3
Mikkwa r. Canada 167 H3
Mikonos i. Greece see Mykonos
Mikoyan Armenia see Yeghegnadzor
Mikropoli Greece 58 E7
Mikulkin, Mys c. Rus. Fed. 40 H2
Mikulov Czech Rep. 49 N7
Mikumi Tanz. 129 C6
Mikumi National Park Tanz. 129 C6
Mikun' Rus. Fed. 40 I3
Mikuni Japan 91 E6
Mikuni-sanmyaku mts Japan 91 F6
Mikura-jima i. Japan 91 F8
Mila Alg. 123 G1
Milaca U.S.A. 174 A2
Miladhunmadulu Atoll Maldives 94 B5
Milagres Brazil 202 E3
Milagro Arg. 204 D4
Milagro Ecuador 198 B5
Milan Italy 56 B3
  also spelt Milano; historically known as Mediolanum
Milan MI U.S.A. 173 I8
Milan MO U.S.A. 174 A3
Milan OH U.S.A. 176 C4
Milando, Reserva Especial do nature res. Angola 127 C7
Milange Australia 146 C3
Milange Moz. 131 H2
Milano Italy see Milan
Milano (Malpensa) airport Italy 51 O7
Milâs Romania 58 F2
Milas Turkey 106 A3
  historically known as Mylasa
Milavidy Belarus 42 G9
Milazzo Sicilia Italy 57 H10
  historically known as Mylae
Milazzo, Capo di c. Sicilia Italy 57 H10
Milbank U.S.A. 178 C2
Milde r. Germany 48 I3
Mildura Australia 147 D3
Mile China 86 B3
  also known as Miyang
Mîle Eth. 128 D2
Mileiz, Wâdi el watercourse Egypt 108 E7
Miles Australia 149 F5
Milesburg U.S.A. 176 H5
Miles City U.S.A. 180 F3
Mîle Serdo Reserve nature res. Eth. 128 D2
Miletin r. Romania 58 I1
Mileura Australia 151 B5
Milevsko Czech Rep. 49 L6
Mileyevo Rus. Fed. 43 Q8
Milford DE U.S.A. 177 J7
Milford IL U.S.A. 172 F10
Milford NE U.S.A. 178 C3
Milford NH U.S.A. 177 N3
Milford PA U.S.A. 177 K4
Milford UT U.S.A. 183 K3
Milford VA U.S.A. 176 H7
Milford Haven U.K. 47 G12
  also known as Aberdaugleddau
Milford Lake U.S.A. 178 C4
Milford Sound N.Z. 153 B12
Milford Sound inlet N.Z. 153 B12
  also known as Piopiotahi
Milgarra Australia 149 D3
Milgun Australia 151 B5
Milh, Bahr al l. Iraq see Razāzah, Buhayrat ar
Milh, Wādi al watercourse Iraq 109 P5
Milhat Ashqar salt l. Iraq 109 N2
Miliana Alg. 55 N8
Milicz Poland 49 O4
Milid Turkey see Malatya
Milikapiti Australia 148 A1
Miling Australia 151 B6
Milingimbi Australia 148 B2
Milip Vanuatu 145 F3
Milk r. U.S.A. 180 F2
Milk, Wadi el watercourse Sudan 121 F5
Milkovo Rus. Fed. 39 P4
Milk River Canada 167 H5
Millaa Millaa Australia 149 E3
Millárs r. Spain 55 K4
Millau France 51 J8
Millboro U.S.A. 176 F8
Millbrook Canada 173 O6
Millbrook U.S.A. 177 L4
Mill City U.S.A. 180 B3
Mill Creek r. U.S.A. 182 B1
Milledgeville GA U.S.A. 175 D5
Milledgeville IL U.S.A. 172 D9
Mille Lacs lakes U.S.A. 174 A2
Mille Lacs, Lac des l. Canada 168 B3
Millen U.S.A. 175 D5
Millenium Island Kiribati see Caroline Island
Miller S. Africa 132 H10
Miller U.S.A. 178 C2
Miller Dam Flowage resr U.S.A. 172 C5
Miller Lake Canada 173 L5
Millerovo Rus. Fed. 41 G6
Millersburg OH U.S.A. 173 I5
Millersburg PA U.S.A. 176 D5
Millers Creek U.S.A. 146 C2
Millers Falls U.S.A. 177 M3
Millers Flat N.Z. 153 D13
Millerton U.S.A. 177 L4
Millerton Lake U.S.A. 182 E4
Milleur Point U.K. 47 G8
Mill Glacier Antarctica 223 L1
Mill Hall U.S.A. 176 H4
Millicent Australia 146 D4

Millijiddie Aboriginal Reserve Australia 150 D3
Millington *MI* U.S.A. 173 J7
Millington *TN* U.S.A. 174 B5
Mill Inlet Antarctica 222 T2
Milliri, Cerro *mt.* Bol. 200 C5
Mill Island Antarctica 223 G2
Mill Island Canada 165 L3
Millmerran Australia 147 F1
Millom U.S.A. 47 I9
Millsboro U.S.A. 177 J7
Mills Creek *watercourse* Australia 149 D4
Mills Lake Canada 167 G2
Millston U.S.A. 172 C6
Millstone U.S.A. 176 D7
Millstream Australia 150 B4
Millstream-Chichester National Park Australia 150 B4
Milltown U.S.A. 172 A5
Millungera Australia 149 D3
Millvale S. Africa 133 K2
Mill Valley U.S.A. 182 B3
Millville *CA* U.S.A. 182 B1
Millville *NJ* U.S.A. 177 J6
Millwood Lake U.S.A. 179 D5
Milly-la-Forêt France 51 I4
Milly Milly Australia 151 B5
Milne Bay P.N.G. 149 F1
Milne Land *i.* Greenland *see* Ilimananngip Nunaa
Milo *r.* Guinea 124 C4
Milo U.S.A. 174 G2
Milogradovo Rus. Fed. 82 D4
Milolii U.S.A. 181 [inset] D2
Milos *i.* Greece 59 F12
Miloslavskoye Rus. Fed. 43 U8
Miłosław Poland 49 O3
Miloud *well* Alg. 122 D4
Milove Ukr. 41 G6
also spelt Melovoye
Milparinka Australia 146 D2
Milpitas U.S.A. 182 C4
Milroy U.S.A. 176 H5
Milton Canada 173 N7
Milton N.Z. 153 B14
Milton *DE* U.S.A. 177 J7
Milton *FL* U.S.A. 175 C6
Milton *VT* U.S.A. 177 L1
Milton *WV* U.S.A. 176 C7
Milton-Freewater U.S.A. 180 C3
Milton Keynes U.K. 47 L11
Miluo China 87 E2
Milverton Canada 173 M7
Milwaukee U.S.A. 172 F7
▶ **Milwaukee Deep** *sea feature* Caribbean Sea 216 J4
Deepest point in the Atlantic Ocean (Puerto Rico Trench).
oceans [features] ▶▶ 210–211
Mily Kazakh. 103 E2
Milybulabk Kazakh. 103 H2
formerly spelt Myylybulak
Milyushino Rus. Fed. 43 T3
Mimbelly Congo 126 C4
Mimbres *watercourse* U.S.A. 181 F6
Mimili Australia 146 B1
Mimisal India 94 C4
Mimizan France 50 E8
Mimoň Czech Rep. 49 L5
Mimongo Gabon 126 A5
Mimosa Rocks National Park Australia 147 F4
Mimoso Brazil 206 E2
Mimoso do Sul Brazil 207 L8
Mina Mex. 185 E3
Mina U.S.A. 182 F3
Mina, Nevado *mt.* Peru 200 C5
Mina, Oued *watercourse* Alg. 55 L9
Mināb Iran 100 D5
Mināb *r.* Iran 100 D5
Minabe Japan 91 D8
Mina Clavero Arg. 204 D3
Minaçu Brazil 202 C5
Minago *r.* Canada 167 L4
Minahasa, Semenanjung *pen.* Indon. 75 B2
English form Minahassa Peninsula
Minahassa Peninsula Indon. *see* Minahasa, Semenanjung
Mina Jebel Ali U.A.E. 105 F2
short form Jebel Ali
Minaker Canada *see* Prophet River
Minaki Canada 167 M5
Minamata Japan 91 B8
Minami Alps National Park Japan 91 F7
Minami-Daitō-jima *i.* Japan 81 M7
Minami-Iō-jima *vol.* Japan 73 J2
Min'an China *see* Longshan
Minaret Peaks N.Z. 153 D12
Minas Cuba 186 D2
Minas Indon. 76 C2
Minas Uruguay 204 G4
Mina' Sa'ud Kuwait 107 G5
Minas Basin *b.* Canada 169 H4
Minas Channel Canada 169 H4
Minas de Matahambre Cuba 186 C2
Minas Gerais *state* Brazil 207 J5
Minas Novas Brazil 207 K4
Minatitlán Mex. 185 G5
Minbu Myanmar 78 A3
Minbya Myanmar 78 A3
Minchinabad Pak. 101 H4
Minchinmávida *vol.* Chile 205 B6
Mincio *r.* Italy 56 D3
Mincivan Azer. 107 F3
also spelt Mindzhivan
Mindanao *i.* Phil. 74 C5
Mindanao *r.* Phil. 74 C5
Mindat Sakan Myanmar 78 A3
Mindelheim Germany 48 H7
Mindelo Cape Verde 124 [inset]
Minden Germany 48 F3
Minden *LA* U.S.A. 179 D5
Minden *NE* U.S.A. 178 C3
Minden *NV* U.S.A. 182 E3
Minden City U.S.A. 173 K7
Minderoo Australia 150 A4
Mindon Myanmar 78 A4
Mindona Lake *imp. l.* Australia 147 D2
Mindoro *i.* Phil. 74 B3
Mindoro Strait Phil. 74 A3
Mindouli Congo 126 B6
Mindszent Hungary 49 R9
Mindūrī Brazil 207 I8
Mindzhivan Azer. *see* Mincivan
Mine Japan 91 B7
Mine Centre Canada 172 A2
Minehead U.K. 47 I12
Mineiga, Gebel *mts* Chad/Sudan/Egypt/Sudan 104 A3
Mineola U.S.A. 179 D5
Mineral U.S.A. 176 H7
Mineral'nyye Vody Rus. Fed. 41 G7
Mineral Point U.S.A. 172 C8
Mineral Wells U.S.A. 179 C5
Minersville U.S.A. 176 H5
Minerva Reefs Fiji 145 H4
Minervino Murge Italy 56 I7
Minfeng China 89 C4
also known as Niya
Minga Dem. Rep. Congo 127 E7
Mingäçevir Azer. 107 F2
also spelt Mingechaur
Mingäçevir Su Anbarı *resr* Azer. 107 F2
English form Mingechaurskoye Vodokhranilishche
Mingala Cent. Afr. Rep. 126 D3

Mingan Canada 169 H3
Mingan, Îles de *is* Canada 169 I3
Mingbulak Uzbek. 103 E4
Mingechaur Azer. *see* Mingäçevir
Mingechaurskoye Vodokhranilishche *resr* Azer. *see* Mingäçevir Su Anbarı
Mingela Australia 149 E3
Mingenew Australia 151 A6
Mingera Creek *watercourse* Australia 148 C4
Mingfeng China *see* Yuan'an
Minggang China 87 E1
Mingguang China 87 F1
formerly known as Jiashan
Mingin Myanmar 78 A3
Mingin Range *mts* Myanmar 78 A3
Ming-Kush Kyrg. 103 H4
also spelt Min-Kush
Minglanilla Spain 55 J5
Mingo Junction U.S.A. 176 E5
Mingoyo Tanz. 129 C7
Mingshan China *see* Fengdu
Mingshan China 86 B2
also known as Mengyang
Mingshui *Gansu* China 84 C3
Mingshui *Heilong.* China 82 B3
Mingteke China 89 A4
Minguez, Puerto de *pass* Spain 55 J4
Mingulay *i.* U.K. 46 E7
also spelt Miughalaigh
Mingxi China 87 F3
also known as Xuefeng
Mingzhou China *see* Weixian
Mingzhou China *see* Suide
Minhe China *see* Jinxian
Minhe China 80 G5
also known as Shangchuankou
Minhla *Magwe* Myanmar 78 A4
Minhla *Pegu* Myanmar 78 A4
Minho *reg.* Port. 54 C2
Minhou China 87 F3
also known as Ganzhe
Minicoy *i.* India 94 B4
Minigwal, Lake *salt flat* Australia 151 C6
Minija *r.* Lith. 42 C6
Minilya Australia 150 A4
Minilya *r.* Australia 150 A4
Minímine Côte d'Ivoire 124 D4
Minipi Lake Canada 169 I2
Ministra, Sierra *mts* Spain 55 I3
Minitonas Canada 167 K4
Minitskaya Rus. Fed. 43 P1
Minjian China *see* Mabian
Min Jiang *r.* Sichuan China 86 C2
Min Jiang *r.* China 87 F3
Minjilang Australia 148 B1
Min-Kush Kyrg. *see* Ming-Kush
Minlaton Australia 146 C3
Minle China 84 D4
Minna Nigeria 125 G4
Minna Bluff *pt* Antarctica 223 L1
Minneapolis *KS* U.S.A. 178 C4
Minneapolis *MN* U.S.A. 174 A2
Minnedosa Canada 167 L5
Minnehaha Springs U.S.A. 176 F7
Minnesota *r.* U.S.A. 178 D2
Minnesota *state* U.S.A. 174 A2
Minnesota City U.S.A. 172 B6
Minnewaukan U.S.A. 178 C1
Min-ngaw Myanmar 78 B3
Minnie Creek Australia 150 A4
Minnipa Australia 146 B3
Minnitaki Lake Canada 168 B3
Miño *r.* Port./Spain 54 C3
Minokamo Japan 91 F7
Minonk U.S.A. 172 D10
Minorca *i.* Spain 55 O4
also spelt Menorca
Minot U.S.A. 178 B1
Minqār, Ghadir *imp. l.* Syria 109 I5
Minqār Khurayrit *hill* Egypt 108 B9
Minqin China 84 D4
Minqing China 87 F3
also known as Meicheng
Minquan China 87 E1
Min Shan *mts* China 86 B1
Minsin Myanmar 78 A2
▶ **Minsk** Belarus 42 I8
Capital of Belarus.
Minskaya Oblast' *admin. div.* Belarus *see* Minskaya Voblasts'
Minskaya Voblasts' *admin. div.* Belarus 42 I8
English form Minsk Oblast; also known as Minskaya Oblast'
Mińsk Mazowiecki Poland 49 S3
Minsk Oblast *admin. div.* Belarus *see* Minskaya Voblasts'
Minster U.S.A. 176 A5
Mintaka Pass China/Jammu and Kashmir 89 A4
Mintang China 86 B1
Mintlaw U.K. 46 K6
Minto *N.B.* Canada 169 H4
Minto *Y.T.* Canada 166 B2
Minto, Lac *l.* Canada 169 F1
Minto, Mount Antarctica 223 L2
Minto Inlet Canada 165 H2
Mintom Cameroon 125 I6
Minton Canada 167 J5
Minturn U.S.A. 180 F5
Minturnae Italy *see* Minturno
Minturno Italy 56 F7
historically known as Minturnae
Minudasht Iran 100 C2
Minūf Egypt 108 B7
Minūfīya *governorate* Egypt 108 B7
also spelt Menufia
Minusinsk Rus. Fed. 80 E2
Minutang India 86 A2
Minvoul Gabon 126 B4
Minxian China 84 D1
Minya Konka *mt.* China *see* Gongga Shan
Minyar Rus. Fed. 40 K5
Minywa Myanmar 78 A4
Minzong India 97 H4
Mio *well* Niger 125 H3
Mio U.S.A. 173 I6
Mionica *Srbija* Yugo. 58 B4
Mipia, Lake *salt flat* Australia 148 C3
Miquan China 88 D3
Miquelon Canada 168 E3
Miquelon *i.* St Pierre and Miquelon 169 J4
Mir Belarus 42 H8
Mi'r, Wādī al *watercourse* Egypt 108 D7
Mīra *r.* Col. 198 B4
Mira *r.* Port. 54 C7
Mira, Sierra de *mts* Spain 55 J5
Mirabela Brazil 202 C6
Miracema Brazil 207 K8
Miracema do Norte Brazil *see* Miracema do Tocantins
Miracema do Tocantins Brazil 202 B4
formerly known as Miracema do Norte
Mirada Hills U.S.A. *see* La Mirada
Mirador Brazil 206 A10
Mirador, Parque Nacional de *nat. park* Brazil 202 C2
Mirador-Dos Lagunos-Río Azul, Parque Nacional *nat. park* Guat. 185 H5
Miradouro Brazil 207 K7
Miraflores Boyacá Col. 198 D3
Miraflores Guaviare Col. 198 D4
Mirah, Wādī al *watercourse* Iraq/Saudi Arabia 107 E4
Mirai Brazil 207 K8
Miraj India 94 B2
Miralta Brazil 207 J3

Miramar Arg. 204 F5
Miramar, Canal *sea chan.* Chile 205 B8
Miramas France 51 L9
Miramichi Bay Canada 169 H4
Miram Shah Pak. 101 G3
Miran China 88 E4
Miraña Col. 198 D5
Miranda Brazil 201 F5
Miranda *r.* Brazil 201 F4
Miranda *U.S.A.* 182 A1
Miranda Moz. *see* Macaloge
Miranda *state* Venez. 199 E2
Miranda, Ilha *salt flat* Australia 151 C5
Miranda de Douro Port. 54 E3
Mirande France 50 F9
Mirandela Port. 54 D3
Mirandola Italy 56 D4
Mirante, Serra do *hills* Brazil 206 C9
Mirante do Paranapanema Brazil 206 B9
Mirapinima Brazil 199 F5
Miras Albania 58 B8
Mirassol Brazil 206 D7
Mir Bacheh Kowt Afgh. 101 G3
Mir-Bashir Azer. *see* Tärtär
Mirbāţ Oman 105 F4
Mirbāţ, Ra's *c.* Oman 105 F4
Mirear Island Egypt *see* Marīr, Gezīret
Mirebalais Haiti 187 E3
Mirebeau France 50 G6
Mirecourt France 51 M4
Miréménge Chad 120 B6
Mirepoix France 50 H9
Mirganj India 97 E4
Mirgorod Ukr. *see* Myrhorod
Miri *mt.* Pak. 101 E4
Miri India Niger 125 H3
Miri Sarawak Malaysia 77 F1
Miriaguda India 94 C2
formerly known as Miryalaguda
Miriam Vale Australia 149 F5
Miri Hills India 97 G4
Mirim, Lagoa *l.* Brazil/Uruguay 204 G4
also known as Merin, Laguna
Mirim, Lagoa do *l.* Brazil 203 B9
Mirimire Venez. 198 D2
Mirina Greece *see* Myrina
Mirjan India 94 B3
Mīrjāveh Iran 101 E4
Mirkovo Bulg. 58 F6
Mirna *r.* Croatia 56 F3
Mirny *research station* Antarctica 223 F2
Mirnyy *Arkhangel'skaya Oblast'* Rus. Fed. 40 H2
Mirnyy *Bryanskaya Oblast'* Rus. Fed. 43 M9
Mirnyy *Respublika Sakha (Yakutiya)* Rus. Fed. 39 L3
Miroč *hills* Yugo. 58 D4
Miromiro *mt.* N.Z. 153 G10
Mirond Lake Canada 167 K4
Mironovka *r.* N.Z. 152 J6
Mirosławiec Poland 49 N2
Mirow Germany 49 J2
Mirpur Pak. 101 H3
Mirpur Batoro Pak. 101 G5
Mirpur Khas Pak. 101 G5
Mirpur Sakro Pak. 101 F5
Mirsale Somalia 128 E3
Mirsali China 88 D3
Mirs Bay Hong Kong China 87 [inset]
also known as Tai Pang Wan
Mirtoan Sea Greece *see* Mirtoö Pelagos
Mirtoö Pelagos *sea* Greece 59 E12
English form Mirtoan Sea
Miruro Moz. 129 A8
Miryalaguda India *see* Mirialguda
Miryang S. Korea 83 C6
Mirzachirla Turkm. *see* Murzechirla
Mirzachul Uzbek. *see* Gulistan
Mirzapur India 97 D4
Misaki Japan 91 C7
Misakubo Japan 91 E7
Misan Iraq *see* Maysan
Misau Nigeria 125 H4
Misawa Japan 90 G4
Miscou Island Canada 169 H4
Misehkow *r.* Canada 168 B3
Misery, Mount St Kitts and Nevis 187 H3
Misgar Jammu and Kashmir 96 B1
Misha India 95 G5
Mishan China 82 D3
Mi'shaf, Rujm al *hill* Iraq 109 O6
Mishamattawa *r.* Canada 168 C2
Mishāsh al Ashāwī *well* Saudi Arabia 105 E2
Mishāsh al Ḩādī *well* Saudi Arabia 105 D3
Mishāsh aẓ Ẕuayyinī *well* Saudi Arabia 104 C2
Mishawaka U.S.A. 172 G9
Misheronskiy Rus. Fed. 43 U6
Mishibishu Lake Canada 172 H2
Mishima Japan 91 F7
Mi-shima *i.* Japan 91 B7
Mishlah, Khashm *hill* Saudi Arabia 105 D3
Mishmi Hills India 97 G3
Mishnutki Belarus 43 L5
Mislmeri *Sicilia* Italy 57 F10
Misima Island P.N.G. 149 F1
Misiones *prov.* Arg. 204 G2
Misis Dağ *hills* Turkey 108 G1
Miskah Saudi Arabia 104 C2
Miskitos, Cayos *is* Nicaragua 186 C4
Miskitos, Costa de *coastal area* Nicaragua *see* Mosquitos, Costa de
Miskolc Hungary 49 R7
Mislinja *r.* Slovenia 56 H2
Mismā, Jibāl al *mts* Saudi Arabia 104 C2
Mismā, Tall al ḥill *Jordan* 109 I5
Misoöl *i.* Indon. 75 D3
Misr *country* Africa *see* Egypt
Misraç Turkey *see* Kurtalan
Miṣrātah Libya 120 B1
also spelt Misuratah
Misrikh India 96 C4
Missanabie Canada 173 I2
Missão *r.* Canada 169 H3
Missinaibi *r.* Canada 168 D3
Missinaibi Lake Canada 168 D3
Mississippi Canada 167 J4
Mission *r.* Australia 149 D2
Mission *SD* U.S.A. 180 G4
Mission *TX* U.S.A. 179 C7
Mission Beach Australia 149 E3
Mission Viejo U.S.A. 182 G8
Missisa *r.* Canada 168 C2
Missisa Lake Canada 168 C2
Mississagi *r.* Canada 173 J3
Mississauga Canada 168 E5
Mississinewa Lake U.S.A. 172 H10
▶ **Mississippi** *r.* Canada 173 O4
world [changes] ▶▶ 20–21
▶ **Mississippi** *r.* U.S.A. 179 E6
4th longest river in North America. Part of the longest (Mississippi-Missouri).
northamerica [landscapes] ▶▶ 156–157
Mississippi *state* U.S.A. 175 B5
Mississippi Delta U.S.A. 175 B6
Mississippi Lake Canada 173 Q5
▶ **Mississippi-Missouri** *r.* U.S.A. 179 E6
Longest river in North America and 4th in world.
northamerica [landscapes] ▶▶ 156–157
Mississippi Sound *sea chan.* U.S.A. 175 B6
Missolonghi Greece *see* Mesolongi
Missoula U.S.A. 180 D3
Missour Morocco 122 E2

▶ **Missouri** *r.* U.S.A. 178 E4
3rd longest river in North America. Part of the longest (Mississippi-Missouri).
northamerica [landscapes] ▶▶ 156–157
Missouri *state* U.S.A. 174 A4
Missouri Valley U.S.A. 178 D3
Mistake Creek *r.* Australia 149 E3
Mistanipisipou *r.* Canada 169 I3
Mistassibi *r.* Canada 169 F3
Mistassini Canada 169 F3
Mistassini *r.* Canada 169 F3
Mistassini, Lac *l.* Canada 169 F3
Mistelbach Austria 49 N7
Misterbianco *Sicilia* Italy 57 H11
Mistissini Canada 169 F3
formerly known as Baie-du-Poste
Misty Fiords National Monument Wilderness *nat. park* U.S.A. 164 F5
Misuratah Libya *see* Miṣrātah
Misvær Norway 44 K3
Mita, Punta de *pt* Mex. 184 D4
Mitande Moz. 131 G2
Mītaraca *hill* Suriname 199 H4
Mitatib Sudan 121 H6
Mitchell Australia 147 E5
Mitchell *r.* N.S.W. Australia 147 G2
Mitchell *r.* Qld Australia 149 D2
Mitchell *r.* Vic. Australia 147 E4
Mitchell *OR* U.S.A. 180 B3
Mitchell *SD* U.S.A. 178 C3
Mitchell, Lake Australia 149 E3
Mitchell, Lake U.S.A. 173 H6
Mitchell, Mount U.S.A. 174 D5
Mitchell and Alice Rivers National Park Australia 149 D2
Mitchell Island Cook Is *see* Nassau
Mitchell Island Tuvalu *see* Nukulaelae
Mitchell Point Australia 148 B2
Mitchell Range *hills* Australia 148 B2
Mitchells Pass S. Africa 132 D10
Mitchelstown Rep. of Ireland 47 D11
Mitchinamécus, Lake Canada 173 R3
Mīt Ghamr Egypt 108 C7
Mithapur India 96 A5
Mitha Tiwana Pak. 101 H3
Mithi Pak. 101 G5
Mithimna Greece *see* Mithymna
Mithrani Can *canal* Pak. 101 G5
Mithymna Greece 59 H9
also spelt Mithimna
Mīt, Gebel *mts* Egypt 104 A2
Mitilini Greece *see* Mytilini
Mitishkino Rus. Fed. 43 O7
Mitkof Island U.S.A. 166 C3
Mito Japan 91 G6
Mitomoni Tanz. 129 B7
Mitre *mt.* N.Z. 152 J8
Mitre, Península *pen.* Arg. 205 D9
Mitre Island Solomon Is 145 G3
Mitrofanovka Rus. Fed. 41 F6
Mitrovica Kosovo, *Srbija* Yugo. *see* Kosovska Mitrovica
Mitsamiouli Comoros 129 D7
Mitsikeli *mt.* Greece 59 B9
Mitsinjo Madag. 131 [inset] J3
Mitsiwa Eritrea *see* Massawa
Mi-o-Chau Vietnam 78 D3
Mitsuke Japan 90 F6
Mittagong Australia 147 F3
Mittelbe *park* Germany 48 I3
Mittenwald Germany 48 I8
Mittersill Austria 49 J8
Mittersteig Germany 49 J6
Mittet Norway 44 I3
Mittimatalik Canada *see* Pond Inlet
Mittleres Saaletal *park* Germany 48 I5
Mītū Col. 198 D4
Mituas Col. 198 D4
Mitumba, Chaîne des *mts* Dem. Rep. Congo 127 E5
Mitumba, Monts *mts* Dem. Rep. Congo 126 F5
Mitwaba Dem. Rep. Congo 127 E7
Mīt Yazīd Egypt 108 C7
Mitzic Gabon 126 A4
Miuchalaigh *i.* U.K. *see* Mingulay
Miura Japan 91 F7
Mius *r.* Rus. Fed. 41 F7
Mixian China *see* Xinmi**
Miya-gawa *r.* Japan 91 E7
Miyagi *pref.* Japan 90 G5
Miyah, Wādī al *watercourse* Saudi Arabia 104 C2
Miyāh, Wādī al *watercourse* Syria 109 K3
Miyake-jima *i.* Japan 91 F7
Miyako Japan 90 G5
Miyakoji Japan 91 G6
Miyakonojō Japan 91 B9
Miyako-rettō *is* Japan 81 K8
Miyaluo China 86 B2
Miyaly Kazakh. 102 C2
Miyani India 94 A5
Miyanoura-dake *mt.* Japan 91 B9
Miyazaki Japan 91 B9
Miyazaki *pref.* Japan 91 B8
Miyazu Japan 91 D7
Miyi China 86 B3
Miyoshi Japan 91 C7
Miyun China 85 H3
Miyun Shuiku *resr* China 85 H3
Mizan Teferī Eth. 128 C3
Mizar Turkey *see* Karakeçi
Mizdah Libya 120 B1
Mizen Head Rep. of Ireland 47 C12
Mizhhir"ya Ukr. 53 C2
Mizhi China 85 F4
Mizil Romania 58 H3
Mizo Hills *state* India *see* Mizoram
Mizoram *state* India 97 G5
formerly known as Mizo Hills
Mizque Bol. 200 D4
Mizque *r.* Bol. 200 D4
Mizusawa Japan 90 G5

Mlaula *r.* Swaziland 133 Q3
Mlava *r.* Yugo. 53 C4
Mawa Poland 49 R2
Mlawula Nature Reserve Swaziland 133 Q3
Mlilwane Nature Reserve Swaziland 133 P3
Mljet *i.* Croatia 56 J6
Mljet *nat. park* Croatia 56 J6
Mljetski Kanal *sea chan.* Croatia 56 J6
Mlowoka Tanz. 129 C7
Mlumati *r.* S. Africa 133 P2
also known as Lomati
Mlungisi S. Africa 133 K8
Mmabatho S. Africa 133 J4
Mmadinare Botswana 131 E4
Mmashoro Botswana 131 E4
Mmathethe Botswana 133 E5
Mnjoli Dam Swaziland 133 P3
Mnogovershinnyy Rus. Fed. 82 E1
Mo Norway 45 I3
Moa *r.* Brazil 200 B5
Moa *i.* Indon. 75 D5
Moab U.S.A. 183 O3
Moabi Gabon 126 A5
Moaco *r.* Brazil 200 C1
Moa Island Australia 73 J9
Moala *i.* Fiji 145 G3
Moama N.Z. 153 F10
Moanda Gabon 126 B5
Moate Rep. of Ireland 47 E10
Moatize Moz. 131 G3
Moatize *r.* Moz. 131 G3
Moba Dem. Rep. Congo 127 F6
formerly known as Baudouinville
Mobara Japan 91 G7
Mobārakeh Iran 100 C4
Mobārakeh Iran 100 C4
Mobaye Cent. Afr. Rep. 126 D3
Mobayembongo Dem. Rep. Congo *see* Mobayi-Mbongo
Mobayi-Mbongo Dem. Rep. Congo 126 D3
also known as Mobayembongo; formerly known as Banzyville
Mobeka Dem. Rep. Congo 126 C4
Moberly U.S.A. 178 D4
Moberly Lake Canada 166 F4
Mobert Canada 172 F1
Mobile *AL* U.S.A. 175 B6
Mobile *AZ* U.S.A. 183 L8
Mobile Bay U.S.A. 175 B6
Mobile Point U.S.A. 174 B6
Moble *watercourse* Australia 147 E1
Mobo Phil. 74 B3
Mobridge U.S.A. 178 B2
Mobutu *r.* Dem. Rep. Congo/Uganda *see* Albert, Lake
Mobutu Sese Seko, Lake Dem. Rep. Congo/Uganda *see* Albert, Lake
Moca Gebçid *pass* Turkey 108 E1
Mocajuba Brazil 202 B2
Moçambicano, Planalto *plat.* Moz. 131 G4
Moçambique *country* Africa *see* Mozambique
Mocambo, Porto *b.* Moz. 131 I2
Moçambos Angola *see* Namibe
Moccasin U.S.A. 182 D4
Moccasin Gap U.S.A. 176 C9
Moc Hoa Vietnam 79 D6
Mocha *r.* Rus. Fed. 43 S6
Mocha Yemen 104 C5
also spelt Al Mukhā
Moji das Cruzes Brazil 207 G10
Moji-Guaçu *r.* Brazil 206 D7
Mojikob Japan 91 B9
Mojkovac Crna Gora Yugo. 58 A6
Mojo Bol. 200 D5
Mojo Eth. 128 C2
Mojokerto Indon. 77 F4
Mojones, Cerro *mt.* Arg. 204 C2
Mojos, Llanos de *plain* Bol. 200 D3
Mojo Shet' *r.* Eth. 128 C3
Mojotoro Bol. 200 D4
Moju Brazil 202 B2
Mōka Japan 91 G6
Mokai N.Z. 152 I7
Mokama India 97 E4
Mokambo Dem. Rep. Congo 127 F8
Mokaria Dem. Rep. Congo 126 C4
Mokau N.Z. 152 I6
Mokau *r.* N.Z. 152 I6
Mokéko Congo 126 B4
Mokelumne *r.* U.S.A. 182 C3
Mokelumne Aqueduct *canal* U.S.A. 182 C3
Mokohaobeng Pass Lesotho 133 M6
Mokhotlong Lesotho 133 N6
Mokhovoye Rus. Fed. 43 R9
Mokhsogollokh Rus. Fed. 39 M3
Mokimbo Dem. Rep. Congo 127 F6
Mokine Tunisia 57 C13
Mokohinau Islands N.Z. 152 I3
Mokokchung India 97 G4
Mokolo Cameroon 125 I4
Mokolo *r.* S. Africa 131 E4
Mokoreta N.Z. 153 D14
Mokotua N.Z. 153 C14
Mokp'o S. Korea 83 B6
Mokra Gora *mts* Yugo. 58 B6
Mokrin Vojvodina, *Srbija* Yugo. 58 B3
Mokrous Rus. Fed. 102 A2
Moksha *r.* Rus. Fed. 40 G5
Mokshan Rus. Fed. 41 H5
Môktama Myanmar *see* Martaban
Mokundurra India *see* Mukandwara
Mokwa Nigeria 125 G4
Mokwallo S. Africa 133 L4
Mola di Bari Italy 56 J7
Molai Greece 59 D12
Molalla U.S.A. 180 B3
Molango Mex. 185 F4
Molaoi Greece 59 D12
Molat *i.* Croatia 56 G4
Molatón *mt.* Spain 55 J6
Moldary Kazakh. 103 I2
Molde Norway 44 I3
Moldefjorden *inlet* Norway 44 I3
Moldjord Norway 44 K2
▶ **Moldova** *country* Europe 41 C6
formerly known as Moldavia or Moldavskaya S.S.R.
europe [countries] ▶▶ 32–35
Moldova *r.* Romania 58 H1
Moldova Nouă Romania 58 C4
Moldoveanu, Vârful *mt.* Romania 58 F3
Moldovei, Podișul *plat.* Romania 58 H1
Moldovei Centrale, Podișul *plat.* Moldova 58 I1
Moldovei de Sud, Cîmpia *plain* Moldova 58 J2
Molega Lake Canada 169 H4
Molegbwe Dem. Rep. Congo 126 D4
Molen *r.* S. Africa 133 N4
Mole National Park Ghana 125 E4
Molepolole Botswana 131 E5
Molētai Lith. 42 G6
Molfetta Italy 56 I7
Molfsee Germany 48 H1
Molina *r.* Arg. 204 C4
Molina de Aragón Spain 55 J4
Molina de Segura Spain 55 J6
Moline U.S.A. 174 B3
Molinella Italy 56 D4
Molinos *r.* Arg. 204 C2
Molins de Rei Spain 55 N3

Mogollon Plateau U.S.A. 183 M7
Mogontiacum Germany *see* Mainz
Mogor Eth. 128 D2
Mogoro *r.* Sardegna Italy 57 A9
Mogoșești Romania 58 H1
Mogroum Chad 126 B3
Moguer Spain 54 E7
Moguqi China 85 H2
Mogwase S. Africa 133 L2
Mogzon Rus. Fed. 85 G1
Mohács Hungary 49 P9
Mohaka *r.* N.Z. 152 L7
Mohala India 94 D1
Mohale's Hoek Lesotho 133 L7
Mohali India 96 C3
Mohammad Iran 100 D3
Mohammadabad Iran *see* Darreh Gaz
Mohammadia Alg. 123 F2
formerly known as Perrégaux
▶ **Mohammad Reza Shah Pahlavi Dam** *resr* Iran *see* Dez, Sadd-e
Mohan *r.* India/Nepal 96 D3
Mohana India 94 E2
Mohangarj Bangl. 97 F4
Mohave, Lake U.S.A. 183 J7
Mohawk U.S.A. 172 E3
Mohawk *r.* U.S.A. 177 L3
Mohawk Mountains U.S.A. 183 K9
Mohe China 82 A1
also known as Xilinji
Mohed Sweden 45 L3
Moheda Sweden 45 K4
Mohéli *i.* Comoros *see* Mwali
Mohembo Botswana 130 D3
Mohenjo Daro *tourist site* Pak. 101 G4
Mōhkō Fin. 44 O3
Möhne *r.* Germany 48 E4
Mohnyin Myanmar 78 B2
Moho Peru 200 C3
Mohol India 94 B2
Mohon Peak U.S.A. 183 K7
Mohoro Tanz. 129 C7
Mohyliv Podil's'kyy Ukr. 41 C6
also known as Mogilev Podol'skiy
Moi *Rogaland* Norway 45 I4
Moi *Vest-Agder* Norway 45 I4
Moijabana Botswana 131 E4
Moincêr China 89 C6
Moinda China 89 F6
also known as Zara
Moine Moz. 133 Q1
Moineşti Romania 58 H2
Moinkum Kazakh. *see* Moyyunkum, Peski
Mointy Kazakh. *see* Moyynty
Moirai Greece *see* Moires
Mo i Rana Norway 44 K2
Moirang India 97 G4
Moires Greece 59 F13
also known as Moirai
Moisakula Estonia 42 G3
Moisie Canada 169 H3
Moisie *r.* Canada 169 H3
Moissac France 50 H8
Moïssala Chad 126 C3
Moïtaco Venez. 199 E3
Mojácar Spain 55 J7
Mojados Spain 54 G3
Mojave U.S.A. 182 F6
Mojave *r.* U.S.A. 183 H7
Mojave Desert U.S.A. 183 G6
Mojerda *r.* Tunisia 57 C11
also known as Mejerda
Mojiang China 86 B4
also known as Jiulian

Mohile India 97 E4

Molise admin. reg. Italy 56 G7
Molkom Sweden 45 K4
Molledo Spain 54 G1
Mol Len mt. India 97 G4
Mollendo Peru 200 C4
Mollerin, Lake salt flat Australia 151 B6
Molleruosa Spain 55 L3
Mölln Germany 48 H2
Mölnlycke Sweden 45 K4
Molochnoye Rus. Fed. 43 U2
Molodechno Belarus see Maladzyechna
Molodezhnaya research station Antarctica 223 D2
Molod'kovo Rus. Fed. 43 N8
Molodoy Tud Rus. Fed. 43 O5
Molokai i. Rus. Fed. 43 S3
Molokovo Rus. Fed. 43 R3
Moloma r. Rus. Fed. 40 I4
Molong Australia 147 F3
Molopo watercourse Botswana/S. Africa 132 E5
Moloporivier Botswana 133 I2
Molos Greece 59 D10
Molotov Rus. Fed. see Perm'
Molotovsk Kyrg. see Kayyngdy
Molotovsk Rus. Fed. see Severodvinsk
Molotovsk Rus. Fed. see Nolinsk
Molotovskaya Oblast' admin. div. Rus. Fed. see Permskaya Oblast'
Moloundou Cameroon 125 I6
Molowaie Dem. Rep. Congo 127 D6
Molsheim France 51 N4
Molson Lake Canada 167 L4
Molteno S. Africa 133 K8
Moltenopass pass S. Africa 132 G9
Molu i. Indon. 73 H8
Moluccas is Indon. 75 C3
also known as Malukken or Maluku; historically known as Spice Islands
Molucca Sea Indon. 75 C3
Moluengo mt. Spain 55 J5
Molumbo Moz. 131 H2
Molvotitsy Rus. Fed. 43 N4
Molwe Dem. Rep. Congo 127 E7
Moma Moz. 131 H3
Momba Australia 147 D2
Mombaça Brazil 202 E3
Mombasa Kenya 129 C5
Mombenzélé Dem. Rep. Congo 126 C4
Mombetsu Japan see Monbetsu
Mombetsu Japan see Monbetsu
Momboyo r. Dem. Rep. Congo 126 C5
Mombuca, Serra da hills Brazil 206 A5
Momchilgrad Bulg. 58 G7
Momeik Myanmar see Möng Mit
Momence U.S.A. 172 F9
Momi, Ra's pt Yemen 105 F5
Momotombo, Volcán vol. Nicaragua 186 B4
Mompog Passage Phil. 74 B3
Mompono Dem. Rep. Congo 126 D4
Mompós Col. 198 C2
Momskiy Khrebet mts Rus. Fed. 39 O3
Mon i. Denmark 45 K5
Mon state Myanmar 78 B4
Mona U.S.A. 183 M2
Mona, Isla i. Puerto Rico 187 F3
Monaca U.S.A. 176 E6
Monach Islands U.K. 46 E6
also known as Heiskeir Islands
Monaco country Europe 51 N9
historically known as Portus Herculis Monoeci
europe [countries] 32–35
Monadhliath Mountains U.K. 46 H6
Monagas state Venez. 199 F2
Monaghan Rep. of Ireland 47 F9
also spelt Muineachán
Monahans U.S.A. 179 B6
Mona Passage Dom. Rep./Puerto Rico 187 F3
Monapo Moz. 131 J2
Mona Quimbundo Angola 127 C7
Monar, Loch l. U.K. 46 G6
Monarch Mountain Canada 166 E5
Monarch Pass U.S.A. 181 F5
Monashee Mountains Canada 166 G5
Monasterio del Suso tourist site Spain 55 I2
Monastery of St Catherine tourist site Egypt 108 E9
Monastery of St Anthony tourist site Egypt 108 D9
Monastery of St Paul tourist site Egypt 108 D9
Monastir Macedonia see Bitola
Monastir Tunisia 123 H2
Monastyrische Ukr. see Monastyryshche
Monastyrshchina Rus. Fed. 43 M7
Monastyryshche Ukr. 41 D6
also spelt Monastyrische
Monavale N.Z. 153 E12
Monbetsu Hokkaidō Japan 90 H2
also spelt Mombetsu
Monbetsu Hokkaidō Japan 90 H3
also spelt Mombetsu
Monboré Cameroon 125 I4
Moncalieri Italy 51 N7
Moncalvo mt. Spain 54 E2
Monchegorsk Rus. Fed. 44 P2
Mönchengladbach Germany 48 D4
formerly known as München-Gladbach
Monchique Port. 54 C7
Monchique, Serra de mts Port. 54 C7
Moncks Corner U.S.A. 175 D5
Monclova Mex. 185 E3
Moncton Canada 169 H4
Mondai Brazil 203 A8
Mondego r. Port. 54 C4
Mondego, Cabo c. Port. 54 C4
Mondimbi Dem. Rep. Congo 126 D4
Mondim de Basto Port. 54 D3
Mondjamboli Dem. Rep. Congo 126 D4
Mondlo S. Africa 133 O4

Mondo Chad 120 B6
Mondolfo Italy 56 F5
Mondoñedo Spain 54 D1
Mondovì Italy 51 N8
Mondovi U.S.A. 172 B6
Mondragón Spain see Arrasate
Mondragone Italy 56 F7
Mondsee l. Austria 49 K8
Mondúver hill Spain 55 K5
Monee U.S.A. 172 F9
Monemvasia Greece 59 E12
also known as Malvasia
Moneron, Ostrov i. Rus. Fed. 82 F3
also known as Maron
Monessen U.S.A. 176 F5
Monesterio Spain 54 E6
Monet Canada 173 R2
Moneta U.S.A. 176 F8
Monéteau France 51 J5
Monfalcone Italy 56 F3
Monflanquin France 50 G8
Monfort Col. 198 D4
Monforte Port. 54 D5
Monforte Spain 54 D2
Monfurado hill Port. 54 C6
Monga Katanga Dem. Rep. Congo 127 E7
Monga Orientale Dem. Rep. Congo 126 D3
Mongala r. Dem. Rep. Congo 126 C4
Mongar Bhutan 97 F4
Mongbwalu Dem. Rep. Congo 126 F4
Möng Cai Vietnam 78 D3
Mongemputu Dem. Rep. Congo 126 D5
Mongers Lake salt flat Australia 151 B6
Mong Hang Myanmar 78 B3
Monghidoro Italy 56 D4
Mong Hpayak Myanmar 78 B3
Mong Hsat Myanmar 78 B3
Mong Hsu Myanmar 78 B3
Monghyr India see Munger
Mong Kung Myanmar 78 B3
Mong Kyawt Myanmar 78 B3
Mong La Myanmar 78 C3
Mong Lin Myanmar 78 C3
Mong Loi Myanmar 78 C3
Mong Long Myanmar 78 B3
Möng Mit Myanmar 78 B3
also known as Momeik
Mong Nai Myanmar 78 B3
Mong Nawng Myanmar 78 B3
Mongo Chad 120 C6
Mongolia country Asia 84 C2
known as Mongol Uls in Mongolian; formerly known as Outer Mongolia
asia [countries] 64–67
Mongolküre China see Zhaosu
Mongol Uls country Asia see Mongolia
Mongomo Equat. Guinea 125 H6
Mongonu Nigeria 125 I3
Mongora Pak. 101 H3
Mongororo Chad 120 D6
Mongoumba Cent. Afr. Rep. 126 C4
Mong Pan Myanmar 78 B3
Mong Pat Myanmar 78 B3
Mong Ping Myanmar 78 B3
Mongu Zambia 127 D8
Mongua Angola 127 B9
Mong Un Myanmar 78 B3
Mong Yai Myanmar 78 B3
Mong Yang Myanmar 78 B3
Mong Yawng Myanmar 78 C3
Mong Yu Myanmar 78 B3
Mönhbulag Mongolia 84 D2
Monhegan Island U.S.A. 177 P2
Mönh Hayrhan Uul mt. Mongolia 84 A2
Monico U.S.A. 172 D5
Moniquirá Col. 198 C3
Monistrol-sur-Loire France 51 K7
Monitor Mountain U.S.A. 183 H3
Monitor Range mts U.S.A. 183 H3
Moñitos Col. 198 B2
Monjolos Brazil 207 I4
Monkey Bay Malawi 129 B8
Monkey Mia Australia 151 A5
Mońki Poland 49 T2
Monkira Australia 149 D5
Monkoto Dem. Rep. Congo 126 D5
Monkton Canada 173 L7
Monmouth U.K. 47 J12
also known as Trefynwy
Monmouth CA U.S.A. 182 E5
Monmouth IL U.S.A. 174 B3
Monmouth Mountain Canada 166 F5
Monnett U.S.A. 176 B5
Mono r. Togo 125 F5
Mono, Punta del pt Nicaragua 186 C5
Mono Lake U.S.A. 182 F3
Monolithos Greece 59 I12
Monon U.S.A. 172 G10
Monona U.S.A. 172 B7
Monopoli Italy 56 J8
Monor Hungary 49 Q8
Monorgahela r. U.S.A. 176 F5
Monou Chad 120 D5
Monóvar Spain 55 K6
Monowai, Lake N.Z. 153 B13
Monreal del Campo Spain 55 J4
Monreale Sicilia Italy 57 F10
Monroe GA U.S.A. 175 D5
Monroe LA U.S.A. 174 A3
Monroe MI U.S.A. 173 J9
Monroe MI U.S.A. 173 J9
Monroe NC U.S.A. 174 D5
Monroe NY U.S.A. 177 K4
Monroe UT U.S.A. 183 L3
Monroe VA U.S.A. 176 F8
Monroe WA U.S.A. 180 B3
Monroe WI U.S.A. 172 D8
Monroe Center U.S.A. 172 D6
Monroe City U.S.A. 174 B4
Monroe Lake U.S.A. 174 C4
Monroeton U.S.A. 177 I4
Monroeville AL U.S.A. 175 C6
Monroeville PA U.S.A. 176 A5
Monroeville OH U.S.A. 176 C4
Monrovia Liberia 124 C5
Capital of Liberia.
Mons Belgium 51 J2
Monsaráz, Ponta de pt Brazil 207 N6
Monselice Italy 56 D3
Mens Klint cliff Denmark 49 J1
Mönsterås Sweden 45 L4
Monstabaur Germany 48 E5
Montagu S. Africa 132 E10
Montague Canada 169 I4
Montague U.S.A. 179 C5
Montague Island U.S.A. 164 E3
Montague Range hills Australia 151 B5
Montague Sound b. Australia 150 D2
Montaigu France 50 E6
Montaigu-de-Quércy France 50 H8
Montalat r. Indon. 77 F3
Montalto mt. Italy 57 H10
Montalto di Castro Italy 56 D6
Montalto Uffugo Italy 57 H9
Montalvo Ecuador 198 B5
Montana Bulg. 58 E5
Montana state U.S.A. 180 E3
northamerica [environments] 162–163
Montaña de Comayagua, Parque Nacional nat. park Hond. 186 B4
Montaña de Cusuco, Parque Nacional nat. park Hond. 186 B4
Montaña de Yoro nat. park Hond. 186 B4
Montánchez, Sierra de mts Spain 54 E5
Montanha Brazil 207 N5
Montargis France 51 I5
Montauban France 50 H8
Montauk U.S.A. 177 N4
Montauk Point U.S.A. 177 N4
Mont-aux-Sources mt. Lesotho 133 M5
Montbard France 51 K5
Montbéliard France 51 M5
Mont Blanc mt. France/Italy 51 M7
5th highest mountain in Europe.
europe [landscapes] 30–31
Montblanc Spain 55 M3
also spelt Montblanch
Montblanch Spain see Montblanc
Montbrison France 51 K7
Montcalm U.S.A. 176 D8
Montceau-les-Mines France 51 K6
Montchanin France 51 K6
Montcuq France 50 H8
Mont-de-Marsan France 50 F9
Montdidier France 51 I3
Monte, Lago del l. Arg. 204 E5
Monteagudo Bol. 201 D4
Monte Alban tourist site Mex. 185 F5
Monte Alegre r. Brazil 206 C4
Monte Alegre Brazil 199 H5
Monte Alegre de Goiás Brazil 202 C5
Montealegre del Castillo Spain 55 J6
Monte Alegre de Minas Brazil 206 E5
Monte Apraziveí Brazil 206 D7
Monte Azul Paulista Brazil 206 E7
Montebello Canada 169 F4
Montebello Islands Australia 150 A4
Montebelluna Italy 56 E3
Monte Buey Arg. 204 E4
Monte-Carlo Monaco 51 N9
English form Monte Carlo
Monte Carlo Monaco see Monte-Carlo
Monte Carmelo Brazil 206 F5
Monte Caseros Arg. 204 F3
Montecatini Terme Italy 56 C5
Montecchio Maggiore Italy 56 D3
Montech France 50 H8
Monte Christo S. Africa 131 E4
Montecito U.S.A. 182 E7
Monte Cotugna, Lago di l. Italy 57 I8
Monte Cristi Dom. Rep. 187 F3
Montecristi Ecuador 198 A5
Monte Cristo Bol. 201 E3
Montecristo, Isola di i. Italy 56 C6
Monte da Rocha, Barragem do resr Port. 54 C7
Monte Dinero Arg. 205 C9
Monte Dourado Brazil 199 H5
Monte Escobedo Mex. 184 E4
Monte Falterona, Campigna e delle Foreste Casentinesi, Parco Nazionale del nat. park Italy 56 D5
Montefiascone Italy 56 D6
Montegiorgio Italy 56 F5
Montego Bay Jamaica 186 E5
Monte Hermoso Arg. 204 E5
Montehermoso Spain 54 E4
Monteiro Brazil 202 E3
Montejinnie Australia 148 A3
Montejunto, Serra do hill Port. 54 B5
Monte León Arg. 205 C8
Monte Libano Col. 198 C2
Montélimar France 51 K8
historically known as Acunum Acusio
Monte Lindo r. Para. 201 F5
Montello Italy 56 E3
Montemayor, Meseta de plat. Arg. 205 D7
Montemorelos Mex. 185 F3
Montemor-o-Novo Port. 54 C6
Montendre France 50 F7
Montenegro aut. rep. Yugo. see Crna Gora
Monte Patria Chile 204 C3
Montepuez Moz. 131 H1
Montepuez r. Moz. 129 D8
Monte Quemado Arg. 204 E2
Montereau-faut-Yonne France 51 I4
Monterey CA U.S.A. 182 C5
Monterey KY U.S.A. 176 A7
Monterey VA U.S.A. 176 F7
Monterey Bay U.S.A. 182 B5
Monterey Bay National Marine Sanctuary nature res. U.S.A. 182 B5
Montería Col. 198 C2
Monteriggioni Italy 56 D5
Montero Bol. 201 E4
Monteros Arg. 204 D2
Monterotondo Italy 56 E6
Monterrey Baja California Norte Mex. 183 I9
Monterrey Nuevo León Mex. 185 E3
also spelt Monterey
Montes Altos Brazil 202 C3
Montesano U.S.A. 180 B3
Montesano sulla Marcellana Italy 57 H8
Monte Sant'Angelo Italy 56 H7
Monte Santo Brazil 202 E4
Monte Santo de Minas Brazil 206 G8
Monte Santu, Capo di c. Sardegna Italy 57 B8
Montes Claros Brazil 202 D6
Montesilvano Italy 56 G6
Montesquieu-Volvestre France 50 H9
Montevideo Uruguay 204 F4
Capital of Uruguay.
Montevideo U.S.A. 178 D2
Monte Vista U.S.A. 181 F5
Montezinho, Parque Natural de nature res. Port. 54 E3
Montezuma U.S.A. 174 A3
Montezuma Creek U.S.A. 183 O4
Montezuma Creek r. U.S.A. 183 O4
Montezuma Peak U.S.A. 183 G4
Montfort-le-Gesnois France 50 G4
Montfragüe, Parque Natural de nature res. Spain 54 F5
Montgomery U.K. 47 I11
also known as Trefaldwyn
Montgomery AL U.S.A. 175 C5
State capital of Alabama.
Montgomery PA U.S.A. 177 I4
Montgomery WV U.S.A. 176 D7
Montgomery City U.S.A. 174 B4
Montgomery Islands Australia 150 C2
Montgri, hill Spain 55 M6
Monti Sardegna Italy 57 B8
Monticello AR U.S.A. 175 B5
Monticello FL U.S.A. 175 D6
Monticello IA U.S.A. 172 B8
Monticello IL U.S.A. 174 B3
Monticello IN U.S.A. 174 C3
Monticello KY U.S.A. 176 A8
Monticello MO U.S.A. 174 B3
Monticello NY U.S.A. 177 K4
Monticello UT U.S.A. 183 O4
Monticello WI U.S.A. 172 D8
Montichiari Italy 56 C3
Montiel, Cuchilla de hills Arg. 204 F3
Montier-en-Der France 51 K4
Montignac France 50 H7
Montigny, Lac l. Canada 173 P2
Montijo Spain 54 E6
Montilla Spain 54 G6
Montilla Spain 54 G7
Monti Sibillini, Parco Nazionale dei nat. park Italy 56 F5
Montivilliers France 50 G3
Mont-Joli Canada 169 G4
Mont-Laurier Canada 168 F4
Mont Louis Canada 169 H3
Montluçon France 51 I6

Montmagny Canada 169 G4
Montmarat Point Jamaica 186 D3
Montmédy France 51 L3
Montmirail France 51 J4
Montmoreau-St-Cybard France 50 G7
Montmorillon France 50 G6
Monto Australia 149 G5
Montoire-sur-le-Loir France 50 G5
Montoro Spain 54 G6
Montour Falls U.S.A. 177 I3
Montoursville U.S.A. 177 I4
Mont Peko, Parc National du nat. park Côte d'Ivoire 124 D5
Montpelier ID U.S.A. 180 E4
Montpelier IN U.S.A. 172 H10
Montpelier OH U.S.A. 176 A4
Montpelier VT U.S.A. 177 M1
State capital of Vermont.
Montpellier France 51 J9
Montpezat-de-Quercy France 50 H8
Montpon-Ménestérol France 50 G7
Montréal Canada 169 F4
English form Montreal; historically known as Ville-Marie
Montreal Canada see Montréal
Montreal r. Ont. Canada 168 C4
Montreal r. Ont. Canada 168 C4
Montreal Island Canada 173 I3
Montreal Lake Canada 167 J4
Montreal Lake l. Canada 167 J4
Montréal-Mirabel airport Canada 169 F4
Montreal River Canada 168 C4
Montreuil France 50 H2
Montreux Switz. 51 M6
Montrose well S. Africa 132 E3
Montrose U.K. 46 J7
Montrose CO U.S.A. 181 F5
Montrose MI U.S.A. 173 J7
Montrose PA U.S.A. 177 J4
Montrose WV U.S.A. 176 F6
Monts France 50 G5
Mont-St-Aignan France 50 H3
Mont-St-Michel, Baie du b. France 50 E4
Montsalvy France 51 J8
Mont Sangbé, Parc National du nat. park Côte d'Ivoire 124 D5
Montseny, Parque Natural del nature res. Spain 55 N3
Montserrat terr. West Indies 187 H3
United Kingdom Overseas Territory.
oceania [countries] 138–139
Mont St Michel tourist site France see Le Mont-St-Michel
Montuosa, Isla i. Panama 186 C6
Montvale U.S.A. 176 F8
Montviel, Lac l. Canada 169 G2
Monument Draw watercourse U.S.A. 179 B5
Monument Valley reg. U.S.A. 183 N5
Monveda Dem. Rep. Congo 126 D4
Monyakeng S. Africa 133 K4
Monywa Myanmar 78 A3
Monza Italy 56 B3
Monza r. Rus. Fed. 43 V3
Monze Zambia 127 F8
Monze, Cape pt Pak. see Muari, Ras
Monzhukly Turkm. 102 C5
Monzón Peru 200 A2
Monzón Spain 55 L3
Mooi r. Kwazulu-Natal S. Africa 133 O5
Mooi r. North West S. Africa 133 K3
Mooifontein Namibia 132 A3
Mooirivier S. Africa 133 O6
Mookane Botswana 131 E4
Moolawatana Australia 146 C2
Moomba Australia 146 D2
Moomin Creek r. Australia 147 F2
Moonbi Range mts Australia 147 F2
Moonda Lake salt flat Australia 149 D5
Moonie Australia 147 F1
Moonie r. Australia 147 F2
Moonta Australia 146 C3
Moora Australia 151 B6
Mooraberree Australia 149 D5
Moorcroft U.S.A. 180 F3
Moordenaarsnek pass S. Africa 133 M7
Moordoof (Südbrookmerland) Germany 48 E2
Moore r. Australia 151 A6
Moore U.S.A. 180 D5
Moore, Lake salt flat Australia 151 B6
Moore Embayment b. Antarctica 223 K1
Moorefield U.S.A. 176 G6
Moore Haven U.S.A. 175 D7
Moore Reef Australia 149 F3
Moore Reservoir U.S.A. 177 N1
Moore River National Park Australia 151 A6
Moorfoot Hills U.K. 46 I8
Moorhead U.S.A. 178 C2
Mooronnyah Lake imp. l. Australia 147 D3
Mooroopna Australia 147 E4
Moorpark U.S.A. 182 E7
Moorreesburg S. Africa 132 C10
Moorrinya National Park Australia 149 E4
Moosburg an der Isar Germany 48 I7
Moose r. Canada 168 D3
Moose r. Canada 168 D3
Moosehead Lake U.S.A. 174 A2
Moose Jaw Canada 167 J5
Moose Jaw r. Canada 167 J5
Moose Lake Canada 167 K4
Moose Mountain Creek r. Canada 167 K5
Moose River Canada 168 D3
Moosilauke, Mount U.S.A. 177 N1
Moosomin Canada 167 K5
Moosonee Canada 168 D3
Mootwingee National Park Australia 147 D2
Mopane S. Africa 131 F4
Mopeia Moz. 131 H3
Mopipi Botswana 131 E4
Mopti Mali 124 D3
Moqatta Sudan 104 A5
Moquegua Peru 200 C4
Moquegua dept Peru 200 C4
Mór Hungary 49 P8
Mora Cameroon 125 I4
Mora Port. 54 C6
Mora Spain 54 H5
Mora Sweden 45 K3
Mora MN U.S.A. 174 A2
Mora NM U.S.A. 181 F6
Mora r. U.S.A. 181 F6
Mora, Cerro mt. Arg./Chile 204 C4
Mora, r. Belarus 42 J9
Morada r. Belarus 42 J9
Moradabad India 96 C3
Morada Nova Ceará Brazil 200 C1
Morada Nova Ceará Brazil 202 E2
Morada Nova de Minas Brazil 207 H5
Morafenobe Madag. 131 [inset] J3
Morag Poland 49 Q2
Mórahalom Hungary 49 Q9
formerly known as Aslóközpont
Moraine Lake Canada 173 L6
Moral de Calatrava Spain 54 H6
Moraleda, Canal sea chan. Chile 205 B7
Moraleja Spain 54 E4
Moralcs Guat. 185 H6
Moramanga Madag. 131 [inset] K3
Moran Arg. 204 E5
Moran WY U.S.A. 180 E4
Moranbah Australia 149 F4
Morang Nepal see Biratnagar
Morangas Brazil 206 A9
Moranhat India 97 G4

Morant Cays is Jamaica 186 E3
Morant Point Jamaica 186 D3
Morapur India 94 C3
Morar, Loch l. U.K. 46 G7
Moratalla Spain 55 J6
Moratuwa Sri Lanka 94 C5
Morava reg. Czech Rep. see Moravia
Morava r. Europe 49 N7
also known as Marca
Moravia reg. Czech Rep. 49 O6
also known as Morava; formerly known as Mähren
Moravia U.S.A. 177 I3
Moravian Falls U.S.A. 176 D9
Moravice r. Yugo. 58 B5
Moravica r. Yugo. 58 B5
Moravice r. Czech Rep. 49 O6
Mcravská Třebová Czech Rep. 49 N6
Mcravské Budějovice Czech Rep. 49 M6
Mcravskoslezské Beskydy mts Czech Rep. 49 P6
Morawa Australia 151 A6
Morawhanna Guyana 199 G2
Meray Firth b. U.K. 46 H6
Meray Range hills Australia 148 A2
Morbach Germany 48 E6
Morbegno Italy 56 B2
Morbi India 96 A5
Morcenx France 50 F8
Morcillo Mex. 184 D3
Mordaga China 85 H1
Mordelles France 50 E4
Morden Canada 167 L5
Mordovia aut. rep. Rus. Fed. see Mordoviya, Respublika
Mordoviya, Respublika aut. rep. Rus. Fed. 41 H5
English form Mordovia or Mordvinia; formerly known as Mordovskaya A.S.S.R.
Mordovo Rus. Fed. 41 G6
Mordovskaya A.S.S.R. aut. rep. Rus. Fed. see Mordoviya, Respublika
Mordves Rus. Fed. 43 T7
Mordvinia aut. rep. Rus. Fed. see Mordoviya, Respublika
Moreč Poland 49 T3
Moreau r. U.S.A. 178 B2
Moreau, South Fork r. U.S.A. 178 B2
Morecambe U.K. 47 I9
Morecambe Bay U.K. 47 I9
Moree Australia 147 F1
Morehead P.N.G. 73 J8
Morehead U.S.A. 176 B7
Morehead City U.S.A. 174 E5
More.ra Brazil 199 F5
More-Iz, Gora hill Rus. Fed. 40 L1
Morel r. India 96 C4
Moreland U.S.A. 176 A8
Morelia Col. 198 C4
Morella Australia 149 E4
Morella Spain 55 K4
Morelos state Mex. 185 F5
Morena India 96 C4
Morena, Sierra mts Spain 54 E7
formerly known as Mariánica, Cordillera
Morenci U.S.A. 183 O8
Moreni Romania 58 G4
Moreno Mex. 184 C2
Moreno Valley U.S.A. 183 G8
Møre og Romsdal county Norway 44 I3
Morerú r. Brazil 201 F2
Mores Sardegna Italy 57 A8
Mcresby Island Canada 166 C4
Moreton Bay Australia 147 G1
Moreton Island Australia 147 G1
Moreuil France 51 I3
Morevo r. Rus. Fed. 40 K1
Morez France 51 M6
Morfou Cyprus 108 D2
also known as Güzelyurt; also spelt Morphou
Morfou Bay Cyprus 108 C2
Mor3au-Vijbus hill Fin. 44 N1
Morgan Australia 146 C3
Morgan r. U.S.A. 176 A7
Morgan, Mount U.S.A. 182 F4
Morgan City U.S.A. 175 B6
Morgan Hill U.S.A. 182 C4
Morgans Corner U.S.A. 177 I9
Morganton U.S.A. 174 D5
Morgantown KY U.S.A. 174 C4
Morgantown WV U.S.A. 176 F6
Morgenzon S. Africa 133 N3
Morges Switz. 51 M6
Mérgex Italy 51 N7
Merhar r. India 97 E4
Mori China 88 E3
Mori Japan 90 G3
Mori r. Indon. 75 B3
Mori, Cerro mt. Arg./Chile 204 C4
Moriah, Mount U.S.A. 183 J2
Moriarty U.S.A. 181 F6
Moriarty's Range hills Australia 147 E3
Moribaya Guinea 124 C4
Morice Lake Canada 166 E4
Moricetown Canada 166 E4
Morichal Col. 198 D4
Moricsala rezervāts nature res. Latvia 42 D4
Morija Lesotho 133 L6
Moriki Nigeria 125 G3
Morin Dawa China see Nirji
Morinville Canada 167 H4
Morioka Japan 90 G5
Morire Moz. 131 G3
Morisset Australia 147 F3
Moriyama Japan 91 E7
Moriyoshi Japan 90 G4
Moriyoshi-zan vol. Japan 90 G4
Mörjärv Sweden 44 M2
Morjen r. Pak. 101 E5
Morki Rus. Fed. 40 I4
Morkiny Gory Rus. Fed. 43 R4
Morlaix France 51 I3
Mörley Canada 167 H5
Mormal' Belarus 43 K9
Mormant France 51 I4
Mormon Lake U.S.A. 183 M7
Mormugao India see Marmagao
Morney watercourse Australia 149 D5
Mornington, Isla i. Chile 205 B8
Mornington Island Australia 148 C3
Mornos r. Greece 59 C10
Moro Pak. 101 F5
Moro r. Belarus 42 I9
Morobe P.N.G. 73 K8
Morocco country Africa 122 C3
africa [countries] 114–117
Morocco U.S.A. 172 F10
Moro Creek r. U.S.A. 179 D5
Morogoro Tanz. 129 C6
Morogoro admin. reg. Tanz. 129 C6
Moro Gulf Phil. 74 B5
Morojaneng S. Africa 133 L5
Morokweng S. Africa 132 H3
Moroleón Mex. 185 E4
Moromaho i. Indon. 75 C4
Morombe Madag. 131 [inset] I4
Moromore Bol. 201 D4
Morón Arg. 204 F4
Morón Cuba 186 D2
Mörön Mongolia 84 D1
Morona Ecuador 198 B5
Morona r. Peru 198 B5
Morona-Santiago prov. Ecuador 198 B5

Morondava Madag. 131 [inset] J4
Morón de la Frontera Spain 54 F7
Morondo Côte d'Ivoire 124 D4
Morongo Valley U.S.A. 183 H7
Moroni Comoros 129 D7
Capital of the Comoros.
Moroni U.S.A. 183 M2
Moron Us He r. China 84 B5
Moros r. Spain 54 G3
Morotai i. Indon. 75 D2
Morotai, Selat sea chan. Indon. 75 C2
Moroto Uganda 128 B4
Moroto, Mount Uganda 128 B4
Morotsuka Japan 91 B8
Morowai N.Z. 153 B13
Morowali Reserve nature res. Indon. 75 B3
Morozova Rus. Fed. 43 L2
Morozovo Rus. Fed. 43 V5
Morozovsk Rus. Fed. 41 G6
Morpara Brazil 202 D5
Morpeth Canada 173 L8
Morpeth U.K. 47 K8
Morphou Cyprus see Morfou
Morretes Brazil 203 B8
Morrill U.S.A. 176 A8
Morrilton U.S.A. 179 C5
Morrin Canada 167 H5
Morrinhos Brazil 206 D4
Morrinsville N.Z. 152 J5
Morris Canada 167 L5
Morris IL U.S.A. 174 B3
Morris MN U.S.A. 178 D2
Morris PA U.S.A. 177 H4
Morrisburg Canada 177 J1
Morris Jesup, Kap c. Greenland 165 P1
Most northerly point of North America.
Morrison U.S.A. 174 B3
Morrisons N.Z. 153 E13
Morristown AZ U.S.A. 183 L8
Morristown NJ U.S.A. 177 K5
Morristown NY U.S.A. 177 I6
Morristown TN U.S.A. 176 B9
Morrisville NY U.S.A. 177 J3
Morrisville VT U.S.A. 177 M1
Morr Morr Aboriginal Holding res. Australia 149 D3
Morro Brazil 207 I3
Morro, Punta c. Chile 204 C2
Morro Agudo Brazil 206 E7
Morro Bay U.S.A. 182 D6
Morro d'Anta Brazil 203 E6
Morro de Papanoa hd Mex. 185 E5
Morro de Petatlán hd Mex. 185 E5
Morro do Chapéu Brazil 202 D4
Morro do Coco Brazil 207 L8
Morro do Sinai hills Brazil 201 G2
Morros Brazil 202 C2
Morrosquillo, Golfo de b. Col. 198 C2
Morrumbala Moz. 131 G3
Morrumbene Moz. 131 G4
Mors reg. Denmark 45 J4
Morse Canada 167 J5
Morse U.S.A. 172 C4
Morse, Cape Antarctica 223 I2
Morshanka Rus. Fed. 41 G5
formerly known as Morshansk
Morshansk Rus. Fed. see Morshanka
Morsi India 96 C5
Mørsvik Norway 44 K2
Mort watercourse Australia 149 D4
Mortagne-au-Perche France 50 G4
Mortagne-sur-Sèvre France 50 F5
Mortain France 50 F4
Mortara Italy 56 A3
Morteau France 51 M5
Morteros Arg. 204 E3
Mortes, Rio das r. Minas Gerais Brazil 207 I3
Mortes, Rio das r. Tocantins Brazil 202 B4
also known as Manso
Mortimer's Bahamas 187 E2
Mortlach Canada 167 J5
Mortlake Australia 147 D4
Mortlock Islands Micronesia 220 E5
also known as Nomoi Islands
Mortlock Islands P.N.G. see Tauu Islands
Morton U.S.A. 174 B3
Morton TX U.S.A. 179 B5
Morton WA U.S.A. 180 B3
Morton National Park Australia 147 F3
Mortugaba Brazil 207 K1
Morundah Australia 147 E3
Mururoa atoll Fr. Polynesia see Mururoa
Moruya Australia 147 F3
Morvan, Parc Naturel Régional du nature res. France 51 K5
Morven Australia 149 E5
Morven N.Z. 153 F12
Morven hill U.K. 46 I5
Morvern reg. U.K. 46 G7
Morwell Australia 147 E4
Mor'ye Rus. Fed. 43 M1
Morzhovets, Ostrov i. Rus. Fed. 40 G2
Mosal'sk Rus. Fed. 43 P7
Mosbach Germany 48 F6
Mosby U.S.A. 180 F3
Moscarter, Punta des pt Spain 55 M5
Moscow Rus. Fed. 43 S6
Capital of the Russian Federation and 2nd most populous city in Europe. Also known as Moskva.
world [cities] 24–25
Moscow IA U.S.A. 172 B9
Moscow ID U.S.A. 180 C3
Moscow PA U.S.A. 177 J4
Moscow Oblast admin. div. Rus. Fed. see Moskovskaya Oblast'
Moscow University Ice Shelf Antarctica 223 I2
Mosel r. Germany 48 E5
Moselebe watercourse Botswana 130 D5
Moseley U.S.A. 176 H8
Moselle r. France 51 M3
Moses, Mount U.S.A. 183 G1
Moses Lake U.S.A. 180 C3
Mosgiel N.Z. 153 E13
Moshannon U.S.A. 176 G4
Moshaweng watercourse S. Africa 132 G3
Moshchnyy, Ostrov i. Rus. Fed. 42 I2
Moshenskoye Rus. Fed. 43 P3
Mosher Canada 173 I2
Moshi r. Nigeria 125 G4
Moshi Tanz. 128 C5
Mosina Poland 49 N3
Mosinee U.S.A. 172 D6
Mosi-oa-Tunya National Park Zimbabwe see Victoria Falls National Park
Mosita S. Africa 133 I3
Mosjøen Norway 44 K2
Moskal'vo Rus. Fed. 82 F1
Moskenesøy i. Norway 44 K2
Moskenstraumen sea chan. Norway 44 K2
Moskkugáisi mt. Norway 44 M1
Moskosel Sweden 44 L2
Moskovskaya Oblast' admin. div. Rus. Fed. 43 T6
English form Moscow Oblast
Moskovskiy Uzbek. see Shakhrikhan
Moskva Rus. Fed. see Moscow
Moskva r. Rus. Fed. 43 T6
Moskva Tajik. 101 G2
Moskvy, Kanal imeni canal Rus. Fed. 43 S5
Moşna Romania 49 N8
Mosonmagyaróvár Hungary 49 O8

Mosopo Botswana **133** J1
Mosor *mts* Croatia **56** I5
Mosquera Col. **198** B4
Mosquero U.S.A. **181** F6
Mosquitia *reg.* Hond. **186** C4
Mosquito Creek Lake U.S.A. **176** E4
Mosquito Lake Canada **167** K2
Mosquitos, Costa de *coastal area* Nicaragua **186** C4
also spelt Miskitos, Costa de
Moss Norway **45** J4
Mossaka Congo **126** C5
Mossâmedes Angola *see* Namibe
Mossâmedes Brazil **206** C3
Mossburn N.Z. **153** C13
Mosselbaai S. Africa *see* Mossel Bay
Mossel Bay S. Africa **132** G11
also spelt Mosselbaai
Mossel Bay b. S. Africa **132** G11
Mossendjo Congo **126** B5
Mossgiel Australia **147** E3
Mossman Australia **149** E3
Mossoró Brazil **202** E3
Moss Vale Australia **147** F3
Mossy r. Canada **167** K4
Most Bulg. **58** G7
Most Czech Rep. **49** K5
Mostaganem Alg. **123** F2
also spelt Mostaganem
Mostar Bos.-Herz. **56** I5
Mostardas Brazil **204** H3
Mostiştea r. Romania **58** H4
Móstoles Spain **54** H4
Mostoos Hills Canada **167** I4
Mostovskoy Rus. Fed. **41** G7
Mosty Belarus *see* Masty
Mosul Iraq **107** E3
also known as Al Mawşil
Mosvatn Austfjell *park* Norway **45** J4
Mosvatnet l. Norway **45** J4
Mosvik Norway **44** J3
Mot'a Eth. **128** C2
Motaba r. Congo **126** C4
Mota del Cuervo Spain **55** I5
Motagua r. Guat. **185** H6
Motal' Belarus **42** G3
Motala Sweden **45** K4
Mota Lava i. Vanuatu **145** F3
also known as Saddle Island or Valua
Motaze Moz. **131** G5
Motca Romania **58** H1
Motenge-Boma Dem. Rep. Congo **126** C4
Moteng Pass Lesotho **133** M5
Moth India **96** C4
Motherwell U.K. **46** I8
Mothibistat S. Africa **132** H5
Mothonaoi, Akra pt Greece **59** E12
Motihari India **97** E4
Motilla del Palancar Spain **55** J5
Motilla hill Spain **54** F4
Motiti Island N.Z. **152** K5
Motlan Ling hill China **83** A4
Motloutse r. Botswana **131** F4
Motokwe Botswana **130** E5
Motovskiy Zaliv sea chan. Rus. Fed. **44** P1
Motozintla Mex. **185** G6
Motril Spain **55** H8
Motru Romania **58** D4
Motru r. Romania **58** E4
Motshikiri S. Africa **133** L2
Mott U.S.A. **178** B2
Motueka N.Z. **152** H5
Motuhora Island N.Z. **152** K5
also known as Whale Island; *formerly known as* Moutohora Island
Motu Ihupuku i. N.Z. *see* Campbell Island
Motukarara N.Z. **153** G11
Motul Mex. **185** H4
Motupipi N.Z. **152** H5
Mouali Gbangba Congo **126** C4
Mouan, Nam r. Laos **78** D4
Mouaskar Alg. *see* Mascara
Moubray Bay Antarctica **223** L2
Mouchet, Mont r. France **51** J8
Mouchoir Bank sea feature Turks and Caicos Is **187** F2
Mouchoir Passage Turks and Caicos Is **187** F2
Mouding China **86** B3
also known as Gonghe
Moudjéria Mauritania **124** B2
Moudon Switz. **51** M6
Moudros Greece **59** G9
Mougri well Mauritania **124** B2
Mouhijärvi Fin. **45** M3
Mouhoun r. Africa **124** E4 see Black Volta
Mouila Gabon **126** A5
Moul well Niger **125** I3
Moulamein Australia **147** E3
Moulamein Creek r. Australia **147** D3
also known as Billabong Creek
Moulavibazar Bangl. *see* Maulvi Bazar
Moule Guadeloupe **187** H3
Moulèngui Binza Gabon **126** A5
Moulentär well Mali **124** D2
Moulhoulé Djibouti **128** D1
Moulins France **51** J6
Moulins-Engilbert France **51** J6
Moulie de Jaut, Pic du *mt.* France **50** F9
Moulmein Myanmar **78** A4
also known as Mawlamyaing or Mawlamyine
Moulmeingyun Myanmar **78** A4
Moulouya, Oued r. Morocco **122** E2
Moulton U.S.A. **174** C5
Moulton, Mount Antarctica **222** P1
Moultonborough U.S.A. **177** N2
Moultrie U.S.A. **175** D6
Moultrie, Lake U.S.A. **175** E5
Mounana Gabon **126** B5
Mound City IL U.S.A. **174** B4
Mound City KS U.S.A. **178** D4
Mound City MO U.S.A. **178** D3
Mound City SD U.S.A. **178** B2
Moundou Chad **126** C3
Moundsville U.S.A. **176** E7
Mounta, Akra pt Greece **59** B10
Mount Abu India **96** B4
Mountainair U.S.A. **181** F6
Mountain Brook U.S.A. **175** C5
Mountain City U.S.A. **176** D9
Mountain Grove U.S.A. **178** D4
Mountain Home AR U.S.A. **179** D4
Mountain Home ID U.S.A. **180** D4
Mountain Home UT U.S.A. **183** N1
Mountain Iron U.S.A. **172** A3
Mountain Lake Park U.S.A. **176** F6
Mountain Pass U.S.A. **183** I6
Mountain View AR U.S.A. **179** D5
Mountain View CA U.S.A. **182** B4
Mountain View HI U.S.A. **181** [inset] Z2
Mountain Village U.S.A. **164** C3
Mountain Zebra National Park S. Africa **133** J9
Mount Airy MD U.S.A. **177** H6
Mount Airy NC U.S.A. **176** E9
Mount Anderson Aboriginal Reserve Australia **150** B5
Mount Arapiles-Tooan State Park *nature res.* Australia **146** D4
Mount Aspiring National Park N.Z. **153** C12
Mount Assiniboine Provincial Park Canada **167** H5
Mount Augustus Australia **150** B5
Mount Ayliff S. Africa **133** N7
Mount Ayr U.S.A. **178** D3
Mount Baldy U.S.A. **182** G4
Mount Barker Australia **146** C3
Mount Barker W.A. Australia **151** B7
Mount Barnett Australia **150** D3

Mount Barnett Aboriginal Reserve Australia **150** D3
Mount Beauty Australia **147** E4
Mount Bellew Rep. of Ireland **47** D10
Mount Bruce N.Z. **152** J8
Mount Brydges Canada **173** L8
Mount Buffalo National Park Australia **147** E4
Mount Carmel IL U.S.A. **174** C4
Mount Carmel TN U.S.A. **176** C9
Mount Carmel Junction U.S.A. **183** L4
Mount Carroll U.S.A. **174** B3
Mount Clere Australia **151** B5
Mount Cook N.Z. *see* Aoraki
Mount Cook National Park N.Z. **153** E11
Mount Coolon Australia **149** E4
Mount Currie Nature Reserve S. Africa **133** N7
Mount Darwin Zimbabwe **131** F3
Mount Denison Australia **148** B4
Mount Desert Island U.S.A. **177** Q1
Mount Eba Australia **146** B2
Mount Eccles National Park Australia **146** D4
Mount Edziza Provincial Park Canada **166** D3
Mount Etna U.S.A. **172** H10
Mount Field National Park Australia **147** E5
Mount Fletcher S. Africa **133** M7
Mount Forest Canada **168** D4
Mount Frankland National Park Australia **151** B7
Mount Frere S. Africa **133** M7
also known as Kwabhaca
Mount Gambier Australia **146** D4
Mount Garnet Australia **149** E3
Mount Hagen P.N.G. **73** J8
Mount Holly U.S.A. **177** K6
Mount Holly Springs U.S.A. **177** H5
Mount Hope N.S.W. Australia **147** E3
Mount Hope S.A. Australia **146** B3
Mount Hope U.S.A. **176** D8
Mount Horeb U.S.A. **172** D7
Mount House Australia **150** D3
Mount Howitt Australia **149** D5
Mount Hutt N.Z. **153** F11
Mount Ida U.S.A. **179** D5
Mount Isa Australia **148** C4
Mount Jackson U.S.A. **176** G7
Mount James Aboriginal Reserve Australia **151** B5
Mount Jewett U.S.A. **176** G4
Mount Kaputar National Park Australia **147** F2
Mount Keith U.S.A. **151** C5
Mount Kenya National Park Kenya **128** C5
Mount Lebanon U.S.A. **176** E5
Mount Lofty Range mts Australia **146** C3
Mount MacDonald Canada **173** M3
Mount Magnet Australia **151** B6
Mount Manara Australia **147** D3
Mount Manning Nature Reserve Australia **151** B6
Mount Maunganui N.Z. **152** K5
Mount McKinley National Park U.S.A. *see* Denali National Park and Preserve
Mount Meadows Reservoir U.S.A. **182** D1
Mount Molloy Australia **149** E3
Mount Moorosi Lesotho **133** L7
Mount Morgan Australia **149** F4
Mount Morris IL U.S.A. **172** D8
Mount Morris MI U.S.A. **173** J7
Mount Morris NY U.S.A. **176** H3
Mount Olivet U.S.A. **176** A7
Mount Orab U.S.A. **176** B6
Mount Pearl Canada **169** K4
Mount Perry Australia **149** F5
Mount Pierre Aboriginal Reserve Australia **150** D3
Mount Pleasant Canada **169** H4
Mount Pleasant IA U.S.A. **174** B3
Mount Pleasant MI U.S.A. **173** I7
Mount Pleasant PA U.S.A. **176** F5
Mount Pleasant SC U.S.A. **175** E5
Mount Pleasant TX U.S.A. **179** D5
Mount Pleasant UT U.S.A. **183** M2
Mount Rainier National Park U.S.A. **180** B3
Mount Remarkable National Park Australia **146** C3
Mount Revelstoke National Park Canada **166** G5
Mount Richmond Forest Park nature res. N.Z. **152** H5
Mount Robson Provincial Park Canada **166** G4
Mount Rogers National Recreation Area park U.S.A. **176** D9
Mount Rupert S. Africa **133** I5
Mount St Helens National Volcanic Monument nat. park U.S.A. **180** B3
Mount's Bay U.K. **47** G13
Mount Shasta U.S.A. **180** B4
Mount Somers N.Z. **153** F11
Mount Sterling IL U.S.A. **174** B4
Mount Sterling KY U.S.A. **176** B7
Mount Sterling OH U.S.A. **176** B6
Mount Stewart S. Africa **133** I10
Mount Storm U.S.A. **176** F6
Mount Surprise Australia **149** E3
Mount Upton U.S.A. **177** J3
Mount Vernon Australia **150** B5
Mount Vernon GA U.S.A. **175** D5
Mount Vernon IA U.S.A. **172** B9
Mount Vernon IL U.S.A. **174** B4
Mount Vernon IN U.S.A. **174** C4
Mount Vernon KY U.S.A. **176** A8
Mount Vernon MO U.S.A. **178** D4
Mount Vernon OH U.S.A. **176** C5
Mount Vernon TX U.S.A. **179** D5
Mount Vernon WA U.S.A. **180** B2
Mount Wedge Australia **148** B4
Mount Welcome Aboriginal Reserve Australia **150** B4
Mount William National Park Australia **147** F5
Mount Willoughby Australia **146** B1
Moura Australia **149** F5
Moura Brazil **199** F5
Moura r. Brazil **200** B1
Mourão Port. **54** D6
Mouraya Chad **126** D2
Mourdi, Dépression du depr. Chad **120** D5
Mourdiah Mali **124** D3
Mourenx France **50** F9
Mourne Mountains hills U.K. **47** F9
Mourre de Chanier mt. France **51** M9
Mourtzeflos, Akra pt Greece **59** G9
Mousa i. U.K. **46** K3
Mouscron Belgium **51** J2
Mousgougou Chad **126** C2
Mousie U.S.A. **176** C8
Moussafoyo Chad **126** C2
Moussoro Chad **120** C6
Moutamba Congo **126** B5
Mouth of Wilson U.S.A. **176** D9
Moûtiers France **51** M7
Moutohora Island N.Z. *see* Motuhora Island
Moutong Indon. **75** B2
Mouydir, Monts du plat. Alg. **123** F4
Mouyondzi Congo **126** B5
Mouzaki Greece **59** C9
Mouzarak Chad **120** C5
Mouzon France **51** L3
Movas Mex. **184** C2
Mouzon France **51** L3
Movas Mex. **184** C2
Mouzon France **51** L3
Movila Miresii Romania **58** I3

Movileni Romania **58** F4
Mowanjum Aboriginal Reserve Australia **150** C3
Mowbullan, Mount Australia **149** F5
Mowhada U.S.A. **176** G6
Moxahala U.S.A. **176** C6
Moxey Town Bahamas **186** D1
Moxico prov. Angola **127** C8
Moy r. Rep. of Ireland **47** C9
Moyahua Mex. **185** E4
Moyale Eth. **128** C4
Moyamba Sierra Leone **124** B4
Moyen Atlas mts Morocco **122** D2
English form Middle Atlas
Moyen-Chari pref. Chad **126** C2
Moyen Congo country Africa *see* Congo
Moyeni Lesotho **133** L7
also known as Quthing
Moyenne-Guinée admin. reg. Guinea **124** B4
Moyen-Ogooué prov. Gabon **126** A5
Moynalyk Rus. Fed. **88** F1
Moyo i. Indon. **77** G5
Moyo Uganda **128** A4
Moyobamba Peru **198** B6
Moyowosi r. Tanz. **129** A6
Moysalen mt. Norway **44** M1
Moyto Chad **120** C6
Moytu China **89** B4
formerly known as Karakax
Moyum waterhole Kenya **128** C4
Moyynkum Kazakh. **103** H3
also known as Furmanovka
Moyynkum, Peski des. Kazakh. **103** F3
also known as Moinkum
Moyynty Kazakh. **103** H3
formerly spelt Mointy
► Mozambique country Africa **131** G4
spelt Moçambique in Portuguese; historically known as Portuguese East Africa
africa [countries] **114–117**
africa [features] **112–113**
Mozambique Channel Africa **131** I4
Mozambique Island Moz. *see* Moçambique
Mozdok Rus. Fed. **41** H8
Mozdūrān Iran **101** E2
Mozelle U.S.A. **176** B8
Mozhaysk Rus. Fed. **43** R6
Mozhga Rus. Fed. **40** J4
Mozhong China **86** A1
Mozo Myanmar **78** A3
Mozyr' Belarus *see* Mazyr
Mpal Senegal **124** A3
Mpanda Tanz. **129** A6
Mpandamatenga Botswana **131** E3
Mpande Zambia **127** F7
Mpé Congo **126** B5
Mpemvana S. Africa **133** O4
Mpessoba Mali **124** D3
Mpigi Uganda **128** A4
Mpika Zambia **127** F7
Mpoko r. Cent. Afr. Rep. **126** C3
Mpolweni S. Africa **133** O6
Mpongwe Zambia **127** F8
Mporokoso Zambia **127** F7
Mposa S. Africa **133** Q5
Mpouya Congo **126** C5
Mpui Tanz. **129** A7
Mpulungu Zambia **127** F7
Mpumalanga S. Africa **133** O6
Mpumalanga prov. S. Africa **133** N3
formerly known as Eastern Transvaal
Mpwapwa Tanz. **129** C6
Mqanduli S. Africa **133** M8
Mqinvartsveri mt. Georgia/Rus. Fed. *see* Kazbek
Mragowo Poland **49** S2
Mrewa Zimbabwe *see* Murehwa
Mrežnica r. Croatia **56** H3
Mrkonjić-Grad Bos.-Herz. **56** J4
Mrocza Poland **49** O2
Mroga r. Poland **49** Q4
M'Saken Tunisia **57** C13
Msambweni Kenya **129** C6
Msata Tanz. **129** C6
Mshinskaya Rus. Fed. **43** K2
M'Sila Alg. **123** G2
Msta Rus. Fed. **43** P4
Msta r. Rus. Fed. **43** O4
Mstinskiy Most Rus. Fed. **43** N3
Mstislavl' Belarus *see* Mstsislaw
Mstsislaw Belarus **43** M7
also spelt Mstislavl'
Msunduze r. S. Africa **133** Q4
Mszana Dolna Poland **49** R6
Mtama Tanz. **129** C7
Mtelo Kenya **128** B4
Mtera Reservoir Tanz. **129** B6
Mtoko Zimbabwe *see* Mutoko
Mtonjaneni S. Africa **133** P5
Mtorashanga Zimbabwe *see* Mutorashanga
Mtsensk Rus. Fed. **43** R8
Mts'khet'a Georgia **107** F2
Mtubatuba S. Africa **133** Q5
Mtunzini S. Africa **133** P5
Mtwara Tanz. **129** D7
Mtwara admin. reg. Tanz. **129** C7
Mu r. Myanmar **78** A3
Mu hu hl Port. *see* Mu'ao
Mu'āb, Jibāl reg. Jordan *see* Moab
Muaguide Moz. **129** C8
Mualama Moz. **131** H2
Muana Brazil **202** B2
Muanda Dem. Rep. Congo **127** B6
Muang Khammouan Laos **78** D4
Muang Khôngxédôn Laos **79** D5
Muang Luang r. Thai. **79** B6
Muang Pakbeng Laos **78** C4
Muang Pakxan Laos **78** C4
Muang Phin Laos **78** D4
Muang Phôn-Hông Laos **78** C4
Muang Sam Sip Thai. **79** D5
Muang Sing Laos **78** C3
Muang Thai country Asia *see* Thailand
Muang Vangviang Laos **78** C4
Muang Xaignabouri Laos **78** C4
Muanza Moz. **131** G3
Muar Malaysia **76** C2
Muar r. Malaysia **76** C2
Muara Brunei **77** F1
Muaraancalong Indon. **77** G2
Muarabeliti Indon. **76** C3
Muarabungo Indon. **76** C3
Muaradua Indon. **76** C4
Muaraenim Indon. **76** C3
Muarainu Indon. **77** G3
Muarakaman Indon. **77** G2
Muararupit Indon. **76** C3
Muarasoma Indon. **76** B2
Muaras Reef Indon. **76** F2
Muaratebo Indon. **76** C3
Muaratembesi Indon. **76** C3
Muarateweh Indon. **77** F3
Muara Tuang Sarawak Malaysia *see* Kota Samarahan
Muarawahau Indon. **77** G2
Muari, Ras pt Pak. **101** F5
Muarzug Libya *see* Murzuq
Muaymā, Wādī al watercourse Iraq **109** M5
Muazzam Shib Indon. **76** C3
Mubārak, Jabal mt. Jordan/Saudi Arabia **108** G8
Mubarraz well Saudi Arabia **107** E5

Mubarraz well Saudi Arabia **107** E5
Mubende Uganda **128** A4
Mubi Nigeria **125** I4
Mubrak Uzbek. *see* Mubarek
Mubur i. Indon. **77** D2
Mucajá Brazil **199** G5
Mucajaí r. Brazil **199** F4
Mucajaí, Serra do mts Brazil **199** F4
Mucalic r. Canada **169** H1
Mucari Bol. **201** E4
Mucheng China *see* Wuzhi
Muchinga Escarpment Zamb. a **127** F8
Muchiri Bol. **201** E4
Muchuan China **86** B2
also known as Muxi
Muck i. U.K. **46** F7
Muckadilla Australia **149** F5
Muckaty Aboriginal Land res. Australia **148** B3
Muco r. Col. **198** D3
Mucojo Moz. **129** D8
Muconda Angola **127** D7
formerly known as Nova Chaves
Mucope Angola **127** B9
Mucubela Moz. **131** H3
Mucum r. Brazil **199** E6
Mucumbura Moz. **131** F3
Mucunha Angola **127** C8
Mucupia Moz. **131** H3
Mucur Turkey **106** C3
Mucura Brazil **199** F5
Mucuri Brazil **207** N5
Mucuri r. Brazil **207** N5
Mucuripe Brazil **198** D5
Mucurune, Ponta de pt Brazil **202** E2
Mucusso, Coutada Pública do nature res. Angola **127** D9
Mucussueje Angola **127** D7
Muda r. Malaysia **76** C1
Mudabidri India **94** B3
Mudan Jiang r. China **82** C3
Mudanya Turkey **106** B2
Mudayrah Kuwait **107** F5
Mudaysisāt, Jabal hill Jordan **108** H6
Muddebihal India **94** C2
Muddy r. U.S.A. **183** J5
Muddy Boggy Creek r. U.S.A. **179** D5
Muddy Creek r. U.S.A. **183** J4
Muddy Gap Pass U.S.A. **180** F4
Muddy Peak U.S.A. **183** J5
Müd-e-Dahanāb Iran **101** D3
Muden S. Africa **133** O5
Mudgal India **94** C2
Mudhol India **94** B2
Mudgee Australia **147** F3
Mudhol India **94** C2
Mudigere India **94** B3
Mudjatik r. Canada **167** J3
Mudkhed India **94** C2
Mudki India **96** B3
Mud Lake U.S.A. **183** G4
Mudon Myanmar **78** B4
Mudraya country Africa *see* Egypt
Mudug admin. reg. Somalia **128** E3
Mudukani Tanz. **129** B5
Mudumu National Park Namibia **130** D3
Mudurnu Turkey **106** B2
Mud'yuga Rus. Fed. **40** F3
Muecaste Moz. **131** H2
Mueda Moz. **129** C8
Muela de Ares mt. Spain **55** K4
Mueller Range mts Australia **150** D3
formerly known as St Vila Caldas Xavier
Muerto, Mar lag. Mex. **185** G6
Muertos Cays is Bahamas **186** C1
Muftah well Sudan **121** G4
Muftyuga Rus. Fed. **40** H2
Mufulira Zambia **127** E8
Mufu Shan mts China **87** E2
Mufulu Dūzū lowland Azer. **107** G3
Muge r. Port. **54** C5
Mugeba Moz. **131** H3
Mughalbin Pak. *see* Jati
Mughal Sarai India **97** E4
Mūghār Iran **100** C3
Mughayrā' Saudi Arabia **107** D5
Mughayrā' Saudi Arabia **105** D3
Mughshin Oman **105** F4
Mughsu r. Tajik. **101** G2
also spelt Muksu
Mugia Spain *see* Muxía
Mugla Turkey **106** B3
Muğla prov. Turkey **59** J11
Mugodzharskaya Kazakh. **102** D2
Mugodzhary, Gory mts Kazakh. **102** D2
Mug Qu r. China **80** E6
Muguia Moz. **129** C8
Mugu Karnali r. Nepal **97** D3
Mugur-Aksy Rus. Fed. **84** A1
Muguxung China **89** E6
Mûḥ, Sabkhat imp. l. Syria **109** J3
Muhagiriya Sudan **126** E2
Muhala China *see* Yutian
Muhala Dem. Rep. Congo **127** F6
Muhammad, Rās pt Egypt **121** G3
Muhammadabad India **97** E3
Muhammad Qol Sudan **121** H4
Muhayriqah Saudi Arabia **105** D3
Muhaysh, Wādī al watercourse Jordan **108** H8
Muhaywir tourist site Iraq **109** H4
Muheza Tanz. **129** C6
► Mumbai India **94** B2
2nd most populous city in Asia and 3rd in the world. Formerly known as Bombay.
world [cities] **24–25**
Mühlacker Germany **48** F7
Mühldorf am Inn Germany **49** J7
Mühlhausen (Thüringen) Germany **48** H4
Mühlig-Hofmann Mountains Antarctica **223** A2

Mukachevo Ukr. *see* Mukacheve
Mukah Sarawak Malaysia **77** F2
Mukah r. Sarawak Malaysia **77** F2
Mukandarri India **96** B4
Mukandwara India **96** C4
also spelt Mokundura
Mukanga Dem. Rep. Congo **127** D6
Mukawa Japan **90** G3
Mu-kawa r. Japan **90** G3
Mukawwar, Gezirat i. Sudan **121** H4
Mukdahan Thai. **78** D4
Mukden China *see* Shenyang
Mukerian India **96** B3
Muketei r. Canada **168** C2
Mukhen Rus. Fed. **82** E2
Mukhino Rus. Fed. **82** B1
Mukhorshibir' Rus. Fed. **85** F1
Mukhtuya Rus. Fed. *see* Lensk
Mukinbudin Australia **151** B6
Mu Ko Chang National Park Thai. **79** C6
Mukomuko Indon. **76** C3
Mukono Uganda **128** B4
Mukoshi Zambia **127** F7
Mukry Turkm. **103** F5
Muksar India **96** A5
Muksu r. Tajik. *see* Mughsu
Muktinath Nepal **97** D3
Muktsar India **96** B3
Mukunsa Zambia **127** F6
Mukur Atyrauskaya Oblast' Kazakh. **102** C3
also known as Muqyr
Mukur Vostochnyy Kazakhstan Kazakh. **103** J2
Mukutawa r. Canada **167** L4
Mukwonago U.S.A. **172** E8
Mul India **94** C1
Mula r. India **94** B2
Mula Spain **55** J6
Mulainagiri hill India **94** B3
also known as Mulanay
Mulakatholhu Maldives **93** D10
formerly known as Mulaku
Mulaku atoll Maldives *see* Mulakatholhu
Mulaly Kazakh. **103** I3
also spelt Molaly
Mulan China **82** C3
Mulanay Phil. **74** B3
Mulanje Malawi **129** B9
Mulapula, Lake salt flat Australia **146** C2
Mulayh salt pan Saudi Arabia **109** J8
Mulayjah Saudi Arabia **105** E2
Mulbagal India **94** C3
Mulbekh Jammu and Kashmir **96** C2
Mulberry AR U.S.A. **179** D5
Mulberry NC U.S.A. **176** D9
Mulchatna r. U.S.A. **164** D3
Mulchén Chile **204** B5
Mulde r. Germany **49** J4
Muleba Tanz. **128** A5
Mule Creek U.S.A. **180** F4
Mulegé Mex. **184** C3
Mulekatembo Zambia **129** B7
Mules i. Indon. **75** B5
Muleshoe U.S.A. **179** B5
Mulevala Moz. **131** H3
Mulga Park Australia **148** A5
Mulgathing Australia **146** A2
Mulgrave r. Canada **167** J3
Mulhacén mt. Spain **55** H7
Mülhausen France *see* Mulhouse
Mülheim an der Ruhr Germany **48** D4
Mulhouse France **51** N5
also known as Mülhausen
Muli China **86** B3
Muli Rus. Fed. *see* Vysokogorniy
Mulilansolo Zambia **129** B7
Muling Heilong. China **82** C3
formerly known as Bamiantong
Muling Heilong. China **82** C3
Muling r. China **82** D3
Mull i. U.K. **46** G7
Mulla Ali Iran **100** A3
Mullaxoe Beyle Somalia **128** E2
Mullaittivu Sri Lanka **94** D4
Muller watercourse Australia **148** B4
Muller, Pegunungan mts Indon. **77** F2
Mullet Lake U.S.A. **173** I5
Mullewa Australia **151** A6
Müllheim Germany **48** E8
Mullica r. U.S.A. **177** K6
Mulligan watercourse Australia **148** C5
Mullingar Rep. of Ireland *see* An Muileann gCearr
Mullins U.S.A. **175** E5
Mull of Galloway c. U.K. **47** H9
Mull of Kintyre hd U.K. **47** G8
Mull of Oa hd U.K. **46** F8
Müllrose Germany **49** L3
Mullsjö Sweden **45** K4
Mullutu laht l. Estonia **42** D3
Mulobezi Zambia **127** E9
Mulondo Angola **127** B8
Mulonga Plain Zambia **127** D9
Mulongo Dem. Rep. Congo **127** E6
Mulsanne France **50** G5
Multai India **96** C5
Multan Pak. **101** G4
Multia Fin. **44** N3
Mulurulu Lake Australia **147** D3
Mulūşi, Wādī al watercourse Iraq **109** K4
Muma Dem. Rep. Congo **126** E4
Mūmān Iran **101** E5

Munda Solomon Is **145** E2
Mundel Lake Sri Lanka **94** C5
Mundiwindi Australia **150** C4
Mundo r. Spain **55** J6
Mundo Novo Brazil **202** D4
Mundra India **96** A5
Mundrabilla Australia **151** D6
Mundubbera Australia **149** F5
Mündwa India **96** B4
Muneru r. India **94** C2
Munfordville U.S.A. **174** C4
Mungallala Australia **149** E5
Mungallala Creek r. Australia **147** E2
Mungana Australia **149** E3
Mungaoli India **96** C4
Mungári Moz. **131** G3
Mungaroona Range Nature Reserve Australia **150** B4
Mungbere Dem. Rep. Congo **126** F4
Mungeli India **97** D5
Munger India **97** E4
formerly spelt Monghyr
Mungeranie Australia **146** C2
Mu Nggava i. Solomon Is *see* Rennell
Mungguresak, Tanjung pt Indon. **77** D2
Mungilli Aboriginal Reserve Australia **151** D5
Mungindi Australia **147** F2
Mungkarta Aboriginal Land res. Australia **148** B3
Mungla Bangl. **97** F5
Mungo Angola **127** C7
Mungo, Lake Australia **147** D3
Mungo National Park Australia **147** D3
Mungwi Zambia **127** F7
Mun'gyŏng S. Korea **83** B5
Munhango Angola **127** C7
Munhino Angola **127** B8
Munich Germany **48** I7
also known as München
Munising U.S.A. **172** G4
Muniz Freire Brazil **207** L7
Munkedal Sweden **45** J4
Munkflohögen Sweden **44** K3
Munku-Sardyk, Gora mt. Mongolia/Rus. Fed. **84** D1
Munro, Mount Australia **147** F5
Munse Indon. **75** B4
Munshiganj Bangl. **97** F5
Münsingen Switz. **51** N6
Münster Niedersachsen Germany **48** H3
Münster Nordrhein-Westfalen Germany **48** E4
Munster reg. Germany **48** E4
Münster reg. Rep. of Ireland **47** D11
Münsterland reg. Germany **48** E4
Münster-Osnabrück airport Germany **48** E3
Muntadgin Australia **151** B6
Munte Indon. **75** A2
Muntele Mare, Vârful mt. Romania **58** E2
Munteni Romania **58** I3
Mununga Zambia **127** F7
Munyal-Par sea feature India *see* Bassas de Pedro Padua Bank
Munyati r. Zimbabwe **131** F3
Munyu S. Africa **133** M8
Munzur Vadisi Milli Parkı nat. park Turkey **107** D3
Muodoslompolo Sweden **44** M2
Muojärvi l. Fin. **44** O2
Muonio Fin. **44** M2
Muonioälven r. Fin./Sweden **44** M2
also known as Muonionjoki
Muonionjoki r. Fin./Sweden *see* Muonioälven
Mupa Angola **127** B9
Mupa, Parque Nacional da nat. park Angola **127** B8
Mupfure r. Zimbabwe **131** F3
formerly known as Umfuli
Muping China **85** H3
Muqaddam watercourse Sudan **121** F5
Muqaybirah Yemen **105** D5
Muqaynimah well Saudi Arabia **105** E3
Muqdisho Somalia *see* Mogadishu
Muqnijat Oman **105** G3
Muqshin, Wādī r. Oman **105** F4
Muquém Brazil **202** B5
Muqur Afgh. *see* Mukur
Mur r. Austria **49** N9
also spelt Mura
Mura r. Croatia/Slovenia **49** N9
also spelt Mur
Muradiye Turkey **59** I10
Muradiye Turkey **107** F3
also known as Bargiri
Murai, Tanjong pt Sing. **76** [inset]
Murai Reservoir Sing. **76** [inset]
Murakami Japan **90** F5
Murallón, Cerro mt. Chile **205** B8
Muramvya Burundi **127** F5
Murán r. Slovakia **49** R7
formerly known as Fort Hall
Muras Spain **54** D1
Murashi Rus. Fed. **40** I4
Murat France **51** I7
Murat r. Turkey **107** E3
Muratli Turkey **106** A2
Murayama Japan **90** G5
Murayr, Jabal hill Saudi Arabia **104** C3
Muraysah, Ra's al pt Libya **120** D1
Murça Port. **54** D3
Murcheh Khvort Iran **100** B3
Murchison watercourse Australia **151** A5
Murchison, Mount Antarctica **223** L2
Murchison, Mount N.Z. **153** G9
Murchison watercourse Australia **151** A5
Murchison, Mount hill Australia **151** A5
Murchison Falls Uganda **128** A4
Murchison Falls National Park Uganda **128** A4
also known as Kabalega Falls National Park or Kabarega National Park
Murchison Island Canada **168** B3
Murchison Mountains N.Z. **153** B13
Murchison Range hills Australia **148** B4
Murcia Spain **55** J7
Murcia aut. comm. Spain **55** J7
Murciélagos Bay Phil. **74** B4
Mûr-de-Bretagne France **50** D4
Murdo U.S.A. **178** B3
Murdochville Canada **169** H3
Müretchie Turkey **106** A2
Muregi Nigeria **125** G4
Murehwa Zimbabwe **131** F3
formerly known as Mrewa or Murewa
Murewa Zimbabwe *see* Murehwa
Muret France **50** H9
Murfa Norway **44** K2
Murfreesboro AR U.S.A. **179** D5
Murfreesboro NC U.S.A. **177** I9
Murfreesboro TN U.S.A. **174** C5
Murgab Tajik. *see* Murghob
Murgab r. Afgh. *see* Murghab
Murgap Turkm. *see* Murgap
Murgap Tajik. *see* Murghob
Murgap r. Turkm. **103** E5
Murgap Turkm. *see* Murgap
Murgenella Australia **148** A1
Murgeni Romania **58** J2
Murgha Tarantina hills Italy **57** J8
Murghab r. Afgh. **101** F3
Murghab Tajik. *see* Murghob
Murgha Kibzai Pak. **101** G4

Murghob Tajik. 101 H2
Murgh Pass Afgh. 101 G3
Murgon Australia 149 F5
Murgoo Australia 151 B5
Muri Qinghai China 84 C4
Muri Qinghai China 84 D4
Muri India 97 E5
Müri Iran 100 C4
Muria, Gunung mt. Indon. 77 E4
Muriaé Brazil 203 D7
Muriege Angola 127 C7
Murii-dake mt. Japan 90 H3
Murillo Canada 172 D2
Müritz l. Germany 49 K2
Müritz, Nationalpark nat. park Germany 49 K2
Muriwai N.Z. 152 L6
Murjek Sweden 44 M2
Murkong Selek India 97 G4
Murmansk Rus. Fed. 44 P1
Murmanskaya Oblast' admin. div. Rus. Fed. 44 P1
English form Murmansk Oblast
Murmanskiy Bereg coastal area Rus. Fed. 40 E1
Murmansk Oblast admin. div. Rus. Fed. see Murmanskaya Oblast'
Murmashi Rus. Fed. 44 P1
Murmino Rus. Fed. 43 V7
Muro, Capo di c. Corse France 56 A7
Muro Lucano Italy 57 H8
Muron Canada 165 K2
Murongo Tanz. 128 A5
Muros Spain 54 B2
Muros e Noia, Ria de est. Spain 54 B2
Muroto Japan 91 D8
Muroto-zaki pt Japan 91 D8
Murowana-Goślina Poland 49 O3
Murphy ID U.S.A. 180 C4
Murphy NC U.S.A. 174 D5
Murphys U.S.A. 182 D3
Murrah reg. Saudi Arabia 105 E3
Murra Murra Australia 147 F2
Murranji Aboriginal Land res. Australia 148 B3
Murrat el Kubra, Buheirat l. Egypt see Great Bitter Lake
Murrat el Sughra, Buheirat l. Egypt see Little Bitter Lake
▶ Murray r. S.A. Australia 147 C3
3rd longest river in Oceania. Part of the longest (Murray-Darling).
oceania [landscapes] ▶ 136–137
Murray r. W.A. Australia 151 A7
Murray r. Canada 166 F3
Murray KY U.S.A. 174 B4
Murray UT U.S.A. 183 M1
Murray, Lake P.N.G. 73 J8
Murray, Lake U.S.A. 175 D5
Murray, Mount Canada 166 D2
Murray Bridge Australia 146 C3
Murray City U.S.A. 176 C6
▶ Murray-Darling r. Australia 144 D5
Longest river in Oceania.
oceania [landscapes] ▶ 136–137
Murray Downs Australia 148 B4
Murray Harbour Canada 169 I4
Murray Range hills Australia 151 E5
Murraysburg S. Africa 132 H8
Murray Sunset National Park Australia 146 D3
Murrayville Australia 146 D3
Murree Pak. 101 H3
Murrieta U.S.A. 183 G8
Murroa Moz. 131 H3
▶ Murrumbidgee r. Australia 147 D3
4th longest river in Oceania.
oceania [landscapes] ▶ 136–137
Murrupula Moz. 131 H2
Murrurundi Australia 147 F2
Murshidabad India 97 F4
Murska Sobota Slovenia 56 I2
Murtajapur India 94 C1
Murten Switz. 51 N6
Murter Croatia 56 H5
Murter i. Croatia 56 H5
Murtoa Australia 147 D4
Murtovaara Fin. 44 O2
Muru r. Brazil 200 C2
Murua i. P.N.G. see Woodlark Island
Murud India 94 B2
Murud, Gunung mt. Indon. 77 F2
Muruí r. Indon. 77 F3
Muruin Sum Shuiku resr China 85 H4
Murung r. Indon. 77 F3
Murung r. Indon. 77 F2
Muruntau Uzbek. 103 F4
Murupara N.Z. 152 K6
Mururoa atoll Fr. Polynesia 221 I7
also known as Moruroa; historically known as Osnaburg
Muruti, Ilha i. Brazil 199 I5
Murviedro Spain see Sagunto
Murwāni, Wādi watercourse Saudi Arabia 104 B3
Murwara India 96 D5
Murwillumbah Australia 147 G2
Murygino Kirovskaya Oblast' Rus. Fed. 40 I4
Murygino Smolenskaya Oblast' Rus. Fed. 43 N7
Mürz r. Austria 49 M8
Murzechirla Turkm. 102 E5
formerly spelt Mirzachirla
Murzūq Libya 120 B3
Mürzzuschlag Austria 49 M8
Muş Turkey 107 E3
Musa Dem. Rep. Congo 126 C4
Mūsa r. Latvia/Lith. 42 F5
Mūša r. Latvia/Lith. 42 F5
Mūsa, Gebel mt. Egypt see Sinai, Mount
Musa Ali Terara vol. Africa 128 D1
Musabani India 97 F5
Musabeyli Turkey 109 H1
Muşabih Saudi Arabia 104 C4
Musa Khel Bazar Pak. 101 G4
Musala mt. Bulg. 58 E6
Musala i. Indon. 76 B2
Musali Turkey 109 H1
Musan N. Korea 82 C4
Musandam admin. reg. Oman 105 G2
Musandam Peninsula Oman/U.A.E. 105 G2
Musa Qala, Rūd-i r. Afgh. 101 F3
Musay'id Qatar see Umm Sa'id
Musaymir Yemen 104 D5
Musbat well Sudan 120 E6
▶ Muscat Oman 105 G3
Capital of Oman. Also spelt Masqaṭ.

Muscat reg. Oman 105 G2
also spelt Masqaṭ
Muscat and Oman country Asia see Oman
Muscatine U.S.A. 174 B3
Muscoda U.S.A. 172 C2
Muscongus Bay U.S.A. 177 P2
Musé r. Lith. 42 F7
Musgrave Australia 149 D2
Musgrave, Mount N.Z. 153 E11
Musgrave Harbour Canada 169 K3
Musgrave Ranges mts Australia 148 A5
Mūshaki Afgh. 101 G3
Mushandike Sanctuary nature res. Zimbabwe 127 F10
Mushâsh al Kabid well Jordan 109 H8
Mushâsh Dabl well Saudi Arabia 109 H9
Mushâsh Muḑayyān well Saudi Arabia 109 J9
Mushayniqah well Yemen 105 D4
Mushayyish, Wādi al watercourse Jordan 108 H7
Mushenge Dem. Rep. Congo 126 D6
Mushie Dem. Rep. Congo 126 C5
Mushin Nigeria 125 F5
Musi r. India 94 C2
Musi r. Indon. 76 D3
Musica mt. Macedonia 58 C7
Music Mountain U.S.A. 183 K6
Musikot Nepal 97 D3
Musinia Peak U.S.A. 183 M2
Muskeg r. Canada 166 F2
Muskeget Channel U.S.A. 177 O4
Muskegon U.S.A. 172 G7
Muskegon r. U.S.A. 172 G7
Muskegon Heights U.S.A. 172 G7
Muskeg River Canada 166 G4
Muskingum r. U.S.A. 176 D6
Muskogee U.S.A. 179 C5
Muskoka Canada 173 N6
Muskoka, Lake Canada 168 E4
Muskrat Dam Lake Canada 168 B2
Muskwa r. Canada 166 F3
Muslimbagh Pak. 101 F4
Muslim-Croat Federation aut. div. Bos.-Herz. see
Federacija Bosna i Hercegovina
Musmar Sudan 121 G5
Musoma Tanz. 128 B5
Musombe Tanz. 129 B6
Musquanousse, Lac l. Canada 169 I3
Musquaro Canada 169 I3
Musquaro, Lac l. Canada 169 I3
Mussau Island P.N.G. 145 D2
Musselburgh U.K. 46 I8
Musselshell r. U.S.A. 180 F3
Mussende Angola 127 C7
Musserra Angola 127 B6
Mussidan France 50 G7
Mussolo Angola 127 C7
Mussoorie India 96 C3
Mussuma r. Angola 127 D8
Mussuma r. Angola 127 D8
Mustafabad India 97 E4
Mustafakemalpaşa Turkey 106 B2
Mustahil Eth. 128 E3
Mustamaa i. Fin. 42 I1
Mustang Draw watercourse U.S.A. 179 B6
Mustau, Gora mt. China 88 D2
Mustayevo Rus. Fed. 102 C2
Musters, Lago l. Arg. 205 C7
Mustique i. St Vincent 187 H4
Mustjala Estonia 42 E3
Mustjõgi r. Estonia 42 H4
Mustla Estonia 42 G3
Mustvee Estonia 42 H3
Musu-dan pt N. Korea 83 C4
Muswellbrook Australia 147 F3
Mut Egypt 121 F3
Mut Turkey 106 C3
Mutá, Ponta do pt Brazil 202 E5
Mutanda Zambia 127 E8
Mutare Zimbabwe 131 G3
formerly spelt Umtali
Mutarjim, Khashm hill Saudi Arabia 105 D3
Mutayr reg. Saudi Arabia 105 D2
Mutina Italy see Modena
Mutis, Col. 198 B3
Mutis, Gunung mt. Indon. 75 C5
Mutnyy Materik Rus. Fed. 40 J2
Mutoko Zimbabwe 131 G3
formerly spelt Mtoko
Mutombo Dem. Rep. Congo 127 D7
Mutooroo Australia 146 D3
Mutorashanga Zimbabwe 131 F3
formerly spelt Mtorashanga
Mutsamudu Comoros 129 E8
Mutshatsha Dem. Rep. Congo 127 E7
Mutsu Japan 90 G4
Mutsu-wan b. Japan 90 G4
Muttaburra Australia 149 E4
Muttonbird Islands N.Z. 153 B15
Muttukuru India 94 D3
Muttupet India 94 C4
Mutuali Moz. 131 H2
Mutum Brazil 207 L6
Mutum r. Brazil 198 D3
Mutum Biyu Nigeria 125 H4
Mutumparaná Brazil 200 D2
Mutungu-Tari Dem. Rep. Congo 127 C6
Mutur Sri Lanka 94 D4
Muuga Estonia 42 H2
Muurame Fin. 45 N3
Muurla Fin. 42 G1
Muurola Fin. 44 N2
Mu Us Shamo des. China 85 F4
Muxaluando Angola 127 B7
Muxi China see Muchuan
Muxía Spain 54 B1
also spelt Mugia
Muxima Angola 127 B7
Muyezerskiy Rus. Fed. 44 P3
Muynak Uzbek. 102 D4
also spelt Moynaq or Muynoq
Muynoq Uzbek. see Muynak

Muyombe Zambia 129 B7
Muyuka Cameroon 125 H5
Muyumba Dem. Rep. Congo 127 E6
Muyunkum, Peski des. Kazakh. 103 G3
Muyuping China 87 D2
Muzaffarabad Pak. 101 H3
Muzaffarnagar India 96 C3
Muzaffarpur India 97 E4
Muzamane Moz. 131 G4
Muzambinho Brazil 206 G8
Muzat He r. China 88 C3
Muze Moz. 131 F2
Muzillac France 50 D5
Müzin Iran 101 E5
Muzon, Cape U.S.A. 166 C4
Múzquiz Mex. 185 E3
Muztag mt. Xinjiang China 89 C5
Muztag mt. Xinjiang China 89 D4
Muztagata mt. China 88 A4
Muztor Kyrg. see Toktogul
Mvadi Gabon 126 B4
Mvangan Cameroon 125 H6
Mvolo Sudan 126 F3
Mvomero Tanz. 129 C6
Mvoung r. Gabon 126 B4
Mvouti Congo 126 B6
Mvuma Zimbabwe 131 F3
formerly spelt Umvuma
Mwali i. Comoros 129 D8
also spelt Mohéli
Mwanisenga Tanz. 129 B6
Mwanya Zambia 129 B8
Mwanza Malawi 129 B8
Mwanza Tanz. 128 B5
Mwanza admin. reg. Tanz. 128 B5
Mwape Angola 127 F8
Mweho Dem. Rep. Congo 126 E6
Mweka Dem. Rep. Congo 126 D6
Mwenda Zambia 127 F7
Mwene-Biji Dem. Rep. Congo 127 D7
Mwene-Ditu Dem. Rep. Congo 127 D6
Mwenezi Zimbabwe 131 F4
Mwenezi r. Zimbabwe 131 F4
formerly known as Nuanetsi
Mwenga Dem. Rep. Congo 126 F5
Mwereni Kenya 129 C6
Mweru, Lake Dem. Rep. Congo/Zambia 127 F7
formerly spelt Moero, Lake
Mweru Tanz. 129 C7
Mweru Wantipa, Lake Zambia 127 F7
Mweru Wantipa National Park Zambia 127 F7
Mwewa Zambia 129 A7
Mwimba Dem. Rep. Congo 127 D7
Mwingi Kenya 128 C5
Mwinilunga Zambia 127 E7
Mya, Oued watercourse Alg. 123 G3
Myadzyel Belarus 42 H7
Myadzyel, Vozyera l. Belarus 42 H7
Myaing Myanmar 78 A3
Myakishevo Rus. Fed. 43 J5
Myakit Rus. Fed. 39 P3
Myaksa Rus. Fed. 43 T3
Myall Lakes National Park Australia 147 G3
Myamoura-dake mt. Japan 91 B9
Myanaung Myanmar 78 A4
▶ Myanmar country Asia 78 A3
also known as Burma
asia [countries] ▶ 64–67
Myaretskiya Belarus 42 I6
Myatlevo Rus. Fed. 43 Q6
Myaundzha Rus. Fed. 39 O3
Myaungmya Myanmar 78 A4
Myawadi Thai. 78 B4
Mycenae tourist site Greece 59 D11
also known as Mikines or Mykines
Myeik Myanmar see Mergui
Myerkulavichy Belarus 43 L9
Myers U.S.A. 176 B7
Myingyan Myanmar 78 A3
Myinmoletkat mt. Myanmar 79 B5
Myinmu Myanmar 78 A3
Myittkyina Myanmar 78 B2
Myitson Myanmar 78 B3
Myitta Myanmar 79 B5
Myittha Myanmar 78 B3
Myittha r. Myanmar 95 G1
Myjava Slovakia 49 O7
Mykines i. Faroe Is 46 E1
Mykines tourist site Greece see Mycenae
Mykolayiv Ukr. 41 E7
Mykolayiv Chernihivs'ka Oblast' Ukr. 43 N9
Mykolayivka Odes'ka Oblast' Ukr. 58 K2
Mykolayivka-Novorosiys'ka Ukr. 58 K2
Mykonos Greece 59 G11
Mykonos i. Greece 59 G11
Mykonos tourist site Greece see Mikonos
Myla Rus. Fed. 40 I2
Myla r. Rus. Fed. 40 I2
Mylae Sicilia Italy see Milazzo
Mylasa Turkey see Milas
Mylipkoski Fin. 42 J1
Mymensing Bangl. see Mymensingh
Mymensingh Bangl. 97 F4
also spelt Mymensing; formerly known as Nasirabad
Mynäjoki r. Fin. 42 C1
Mynämäki Fin. 45 M3
also spelt Myngaral
Mynaral Kazakh. 103 H3
Mynfontein S. Africa 132 H7
Myngaral Kazakh. see Mynaral
Myohaung Myanmar 78 A3
Myŏnggan N. Korea 82 C4
Myory Belarus 42 I6
Myotha Myanmar 78 A3
Myozin-sho i. Japan see Myōjin-shō
Mýrdalsjökull ice cap Iceland 44 [inset] C3
Mýrdalssandur sand area Iceland 44 [inset] C3
Myre Norway 44 K1
Myrheden Sweden 44 M2
Myrhorod Ukr. 41 E6
also spelt Mirgorod
Myrina Greece 59 G9
also spelt Mirina
Myrlandshaugen Norway 44 L1
Myrnam Canada 167 I4
Myrnopillya Ukr. 58 K2
Myronivka Ukr. 41 D6
also spelt Mironovka
Myrskylä Fin. 45 N3
Myrtle Beach U.S.A. 175 E5
Myrtle Creek U.S.A. 180 B4
Myrtleford Australia 147 E4
Myrtle Point U.S.A. 180 A4
Myrzakent Kazakh. 103 G4
Mysen Norway 45 J4
Myshanka r. Belarus 42 G9
Myshkin Rus. Fed. 43 T4
Myshkino Rus. Fed. see Myshkin
Mys Lazareva Rus. Fed. see Lazarev
Myślenice Poland 49 Q6
Myślibórz Poland 49 L3
My Son tourist site Vietnam 78 E4
Mysore India 94 C3
Mysore state India see Karnataka
Mysovsk Rus. Fed. see Babushkin
Mys Shmidta Rus. Fed. 39 S3
Myszków Poland 49 Q5
Myszyniec Poland 49 S2
Myt Rus. Fed. 40 G4
My Tho Vietnam 79 D6
Mytilene i. Greece see Lesbos

Mytilini Greece 59 H9
also known as Mitilini
Mytilinioi Greece 59 H11
Mytilini Strait Greece/Turkey 59 H9
Mytishchi Rus. Fed. 43 S6
Myton U.S.A. 183 N1
Mývatn i. Iceland 44 [inset] C2
Mývatn-Laxá nature res. Iceland 44 [inset] C2
Mývatnsöræfi lava field Iceland 44 [inset] C2
Myylybulak Kazakh. see Milybulak
M'Zab Valley tourist site Alg. 123 F2
Mzamomhle S. Africa 133 K8
Mze r. Czech Rep. 49 J6
Mziha Tanz. 129 C6
Mzimba Malawi 129 B7
Mzingwani r. Zimbabwe 131 F4
also known as Umzingwani
Mzuzu Malawi 129 B7

↓ N

Na, Nam r. China/Vietnam 86 B4
Naab r. Germany 48 J6
Naalehu U.S.A. 181 [inset] Z2
Naam Sudan 126 F2
Naama Alg. 123 E2
Naantali Fin. 45 M3
also known as Nådendal
Naas Rep. of Ireland 47 F10
also spelt An Nás
Naba Estonia 42 I3
Naba Japan 81 L7
Nababeep S. Africa 132 B6
Nabadwip India see Navadwip
Nabāo r. Port. 54 C5
Nabarangapur India 95 D2
Nabas Phil. 74 B4
Nabatiyet et Tahta Lebanon 108 G4
Nabberu, Lake salt flat Australia 151 C5
Nabéré, Réserve Partielle de nature res. Burkina 124 E4
Naberera Tanz. 129 C6
Naberezhnyye Chelny Rus. Fed. 40 J5
formerly known as Brezhnev
Nabeul Tunisia 123 H1
Nabha India 96 C3
Nabileque r. Brazil 201 F5
Nabinagar India 97 E4
Nabire Indon. 73 I7
Nabi Younés, Ras en pt Lebanon 108 G4
English form Nablus; also known as Shekhem; also spelt Nâbulus
Nablus West Bank see Nāblus
Nabolo Ghana 125 E4
Naboomspruit S. Africa 131 F5
Nabra r. India 96 C2
Nabule Myanmar 79 B5
Nabulus West Bank see Nāblus
Nacajuca Mex. 185 G5
Nacala Moz. 131 I2
formerly known as Maiaia
Nacaome Hond. 186 B4
Nacaroa Moz. 131 H2
Nacebe Bol. 200 D2
Nacha Belarus 42 F7
Nacha r. Belarus 43 J7
Nachalovo Rus. Fed. 102 B3
Nachingwea Tanz. 129 C7
Nachna India 96 A4
Náchod Czech Rep. 49 N5
Nachuge India 95 G4
Nacimiento Chile 204 B5
Nacimiento Reservoir U.S.A. 182 D6
Nacogdoches U.S.A. 179 D6
Nacozari de García Mex. 184 C2
Nada China see Danzhou
Nadalevei r. Canada 166 C2
Nadbai India 96 C4
Nådendal Fin. see Naantali
Nadezhdinka Kazakh. 103 E1
formerly known as Nadezhdinskiy
Nadezhdinskiy Kazakh. see Nadezhdinka
Nadi Fiji 145 G3
Nadiad India 96 B5
Nădlac Romania 58 B2
Nador Morocco 123 E2
Nadporozh'ye Rus. Fed. 43 P1
Nădrag Romania 58 D3
Nadūshan Iran 100 C3
Nadvirna Ukr. 41 C6
also spelt Nadvornaya
Nadvornaya Ukr. see Nadvirna
Nadym Rus. Fed. 38 H3
Naenwa India 96 B4
Næstved Denmark 45 J5
Naf r. Bangl./Myanmar 97 G5
Nafas, Rās el m. Egypt 108 F5
Nafpaktos Greece 59 C10
also spelt Návpaktos
Nafplio Greece 59 D11
also known as Návplion
Naft r. Iraq see An Naft
Naftalan Azer. 107 F2
Naft-e Safid Iran 100 B4
Naft-e Shāh Iran see Naft Shahr
Naft Shahr Iran 107 F4
Nafūd ad Daḩl des. Saudi Arabia 105 D3
Nafūd al Ghuwayṭah des. Saudi Arabia 109 J8
Nafūd al Jur'ā des. Saudi Arabia 105 D2
Nafūd al 'Urayq des. Saudi Arabia 104 C2
Nafūd as Sirr des. Saudi Arabia 104 D2
Nafūd as Surrah des. Saudi Arabia 104 C3
Nafūd Qunayfidhah des. Saudi Arabia 105 D2
Nafūsah, Jabal hills Libya 120 A2
Nafy Saudi Arabia 104 C2
Nag, Co l. China 89 E5
Naga Phil. 74 B3
Nagagami r. Canada 168 C3
Nagahama Ehime Japan 91 C8
Nagahama Shiga Japan 91 E7
Naga Hills India 97 G4
Naga Hills state India see Nagaland
Nagai Japan 90 G5
Nagaland state India 97 G4
formerly known as Naga Hills
Nagambie Australia 147 E4
Nagano Japan 91 E6
Nagano pref. Japan 91 E6
Nagaoka Japan 90 F6
Nagaon India 97 G4
Nagap Namibia 132 D5
Nakop Namibia 132 D5
Nákotne Latvia 42 D5
Nagapalpatnam India see Nagapattinam
Nagappattinam India 94 C4
formerly spelt Nagapatam
Nagar r. Bangl./India 97 F4
Nagar Himachal Pradesh India 96 C2
Nagar Karnataka India 94 B3
Nagar Rajasthan India 96 C4
Nagaram India 94 D2
Nagarjuna Sagar Reservoir India 94 C2
Nagar Karnul India 94 C2
Nagarzê China 89 E6
Nagasaki Japan 91 A8
Nagasaki pref. Japan 91 A8
Naga-shima i. Japan 91 B8
Naga-shima i. Japan 91 B8
Nagato Japan 91 B7
Nagaur India 96 B4
Nagavali r. India 95 D2
Nagbhir India 94 C1
Nagda India 96 B5
Nagercoil India 94 C4
Nagha Kalat Pak. 101 F5

Nagina Incia 96 C3
Nagineh Iran 100 D3
Nagma Nepal 97 D3
Nagod India 96 D4
Nagold Germany 48 F7
Nagong Chu r. China see Parlung Zangbo
Nagorno-Karabakh aut. reg. Azer. see Dağlıq Qarabağ
Nagornyy Rus. Fed. 40 I4
Nagorsk Rus. Fed. 40 I4
Nagor'ye Rus. Fed. 43 T5
Nagpur India 96 C5
Nag Qu r. China 89 F6
Nagu Fin. 45 M3
also known as Hauvo
Nagua Dom. Rep. 187 F3
Nagurskoye Rus. Fed. 38 E1
Nagyatád Hungary 49 O9
Nagybecskerek Vojvodina, Srbija Yugo. see Zrenjanin
Nagycsed Hungary 49 T8
Nagyenyed Romania see Aiud
Nagyhalász Hungary 49 S7
Nagykálló Hungary 49 S8
Nagykanizsa Hungary 49 N9
Nagykáta Hungary 49 Q8
Nagykőrös Hungary 49 Q8
Nagykun-Sárrét reg. Hungary 49 R9
Nagyvárad Romania see Oradea
Naha Estonia 42 I3
Naha Japan 81 L7
Nahan India 96 C3
Nahang r. Iran/Pak. 101 E5
Nahanni Butte Canada 166 F2
also known as Tthenaagoo
Nahanni National Park Canada 166 E2
Nahanni Range mts Canada 166 F2
Nahari Japan 91 D8
Nahariyya Israel 108 G4
Nahāvand Iran 100 B3
N'Ahnet, Adrar mts Alg. 123 F4
Nahr, Jabal hill Saudi Arabia 104 D4
Nahr Ouassel, Oued watercourse Alg. 55 N9
Nahr 'Umr Iraq 100 A4
Nahue, Huapi Arg. 204 C6
Nahuel Huapí, Parque Nacional nat. park Arg. 204 C6
Nahuel Mapá Arg. 204 D4
Nahuel Niyeu Arg. 204 D6
Nahurta U.S.A. 175 D6
Naic Phil. 74 B3
Naica Mex. 184 D3
Naidor well Tanz. 129 C6
Naikliu Indon. 75 B5
Naik Murad Bangl. 97 F4
Nailung China 89 F6
Na'ima Sudan 121 G6
Naiman Qi China see Daqin Tal
Naim n Bulak well China 84 A2
Nain Canada 169 I1
Nā'īn Iran 100 C3
Naina India 97 D4
Nainour India 96 D5
Naioué Rus. Fed. 40 H3
Nairn U.K. 46 I6
Nairn Centre Canada 173 L4
▶ Nairobi Kenya 128 C5
Capital of Kenya.

Naissaar i. Estonia 42 F2
Naissus Srbija Yugo. see Niš
Naivasha Kenya 128 C5
Naizishan China 82 B4
Najafābād Iran 100 B3
Najasa r. Cuba 186 D2
Najd reg. Saudi Arabia 104 C2
English form Nejd
Nájera Spain 55 I2
Najibabad India 96 C3
Najin N. Korea 82 C4
Naji China see Naji
Naji China 85 I1
also known as Arun Qi; formerly known as Najitun
Najibabad India 96 C3
Najin N. Korea 82 C4
Najitun China see Naji
Najmah Saudi Arabia 105 D4
Najrān Saudi Arabia 104 C4
Najrān prov. Saudi Arabia 105 D4
Najrān, Wādi watercourse Saudi Arabia 104 D4
Nakadōri-shima i. Japan 91 A8
Naka-gawa r. Japan 91 D8
Nakalele Point U.S.A. 181 [inset] Z1
Nakama Japan 91 B8
Nakambé watercourse Burkina/Ghana 125 E4 see White Volta
Nakamura Japan 91 C8
Nakanbe watercourse Burkina/Ghana 125 E3 see White Volta
Nakano Japan 91 F6
Nakanojō Japan 91 F6
Nakano-shima i. Japan 83 C7
Nakapanya Tanz. 129 C7
Nakasatsunai Japan 90 H3
Nakashibetsu Japan 90 I3
Nakasongola Uganda 128 B4
Nakatonbetsu hill Japan 90 H2
Nakatsu Japan 91 B8
Nakatsugawa Japan 91 E7
Nakfa Eritrea 121 H5
Nakfa Wildlife Reserve nature res. Eritrea 121 H5
Nakhichevan' Azer. see Naxçıvan
Nakhl Egypt 121 F3
Nakhl-e Teqi Iran 100 C5
Nakhodka Rus. Fed. 82 D4
Nakhola India 97 G4
Nakhon Nayok Thai. 79 C5
Nakhon Pathom Thai. 79 C5
Nakhon Phanom Thai. 78 D4
Nakhon Ratchasima Thai. 79 C5
also known as Korat
Nakhon Sawan Thai. 79 B6
Nakhon Si Thammarat Thai. 79 B6
Nakhrachi Rus. Fed. see Kondinskoye
Nakhtarana India 96 A5
Nakina r. Canada 166 C3
Nakło nad Notecią Poland 49 O2
Naknek U.S.A. 164 D4
Nakodar India 96 B3
Nakonde Zambia 129 B7
Nakop Namibia 132 D5
Nākotne Latvia 42 D5
Naktong-gang r. S. Korea 83 C6
Nakuru Kenya 128 C5
Nakusp Canada 166 G5
Na-lang Myanmar 78 B3
Nalayh Mongolia 85 E2
Nalázi Moz. 131 G5
Nalbari India 97 F4
Nạldurg India 94 C2
Nalęczów Poland 49 T4
Nalgonda India 94 C2
Nalgonda India 94 C2
Nalhati India 97 F4
Nalitabari Bangl. 97 F4
Nalkhera India 96 C5
Nallamala Hills India 94 C3
Nallıhan Turkey 106 C2
Nalolo Zambia 127 D8

Nalón r. Spain 50 A9
Nālūt Libya 120 A2
Nama, Tanjung pt Indon. 75 D3
Namaacha Moz. 131 G5
Namacala Moz. 131 H2
Namacunde Angola 127 B9
Namacurra Moz. 131 H3
Namadgi National Park Australia 147 F3
Namahadi S. Africa 133 M4
Namacurra Moz. 131 H3
Namak, Daryācheh-ye salt flat Iran 100 B3
Namak-e Mīqhān, Kavīr-e salt flat Iran 100 B3
Nāmaki watercourse Iran 100 C4
Namakkal India 94 C4
Namakzar-e Shadad salt flat Iran 100 D4
Namanga Kenya 128 C5
Namangan Uzbek. 103 G4
Namangan Oblast admin. div. Uzbek. see Namanganskaya Oblast'
Namanganskaya Oblast' admin. div. Uzbek. 103 G4
English form Namangan Oblast; also known as Namangan Wiloyati
Namangan Wiloyati admin. div. Uzbek. see Namanganskaya Oblast'
Namanyere Tanz. 129 A6
Namapa Moz. 131 H2
Namaponda Moz. 131 H2
Namaqualand reg. S. Africa 132 A5
Namarrói Moz. 131 H2
Namasale Uganda 128 B4
Namatanai P.N.G. 145 E2
Namba Angola 127 B7
Nambol India 97 G4
Nambour Australia 149 G5
Nambucca Heads Australia 147 G2
Nambung National Park Australia 151 A6
Năm Căn Vietnam 79 D6
Namcha Barwa mt. China see Namjagbarwa Feng
Namche Bazar Nepal 97 E4
Namch'ŏn N. Korea 83 B5
Namco China 89 E6
Nam Co salt l. China 89 E6
Namdalen valley Norway 44 K3
Namdalseid Norway 44 J2
Nam Đinh Vietnam 78 D3
Namekagon r. U.S.A. 172 B5
Namen Belgium see Namur
Náměstovo Slovakia 49 Q6
Nametil Moz. 131 H2
Namew Lake Canada 167 K4
Nam-gang r. N. Korea 83 B5
Namhkam Myanmar 78 B3
Namhsan Myanmar 78 B3
Namialo Moz. 131 H2
▶ Namib Desert Namibia 130 B5
world [land images] ▶ 12–13
Namibe Angola 127 B8
formerly known as Moçâmedes or Mossâmedes
Namibe prov. Angola 127 B8
Namibe, Reserva de nature res. Angola 127 B8
▶ Namibia country Africa 130 B4
formerly known as South-West Africa; historically known as German South-West Africa
africa [countries] ▶ 114–117
Namib-Naukluft Game Park nature res. Namibia 130 B5
Namichiga Tanz. 129 C7
Namidobe Moz. 131 H3
Namie Japan 90 G6
Namies S. Africa 132 C5
Namín Iran 100 B2
Namina Moz. 131 H2
Namitete Malawi 129 B8
Namjagbarwa Feng mt. China 80 E7
also known as Namcha Barwa
Namji S. Korea 91 A7
Namka China see Doilungdêqên
Namkham Myanmar 78 B3
Namlang r. Myanmar 78 B3
Namlea Indon. 75 C3
Namling China 89 E6
also known as Nanmulingzha
Nam Nao National Park Thai. 78 C4
Nam Ngum Reservoir Laos 78 C4
Namoi r. Australia 147 F2
Nampa Canada 167 G3
Nampa mt. Nepal 96 D3
Nampala Mali 124 D3
Nampa N. Korea 83 B5
formerly known as Chinnamp'o
Nampula Moz. 131 H2
Nampula prov. Moz. 131 H2
Nam Pung Reservoir Thai. 78 C4
Namrole Indon. 75 C3
Namrup India 97 G4
Namsai Myanmar 78 B3
Namsang Myanmar 78 B3
Nam She Tsim hill Hong Kong China see Sharp Peak
Namsos Norway 44 J2
Namsskogan Norway 44 K3
Namtari Nigeria 125 I4
Namtok Myanmar 78 B5
Nam Tok Thai. 79 B5
Namtok Chattakan National Park Thai. 78 C4
Namtok Mae Surin National Park Thai. 78 B4
Namton Myanmar 78 B3
Namtsy Rus. Fed. 39 M3
Namtu Myanmar 78 B3
Namu Canada 166 E5
Namuli, Monte mt. Moz. 131 H2
Namuno Moz. 131 H2
Namur Belgium 51 K2
also known as Namen
Namutoni Namibia 130 C3
Namwala Zambia 127 E8
Namwera Malawi 129 B8
Namwŏn S. Korea 83 B6
Namya Ra Myanmar 78 B2
Namyit Island S. China Sea 72 D4
Namysłów Poland see Namysłow
Nan Thai. 78 C4
Nan, Mae Nam r. Thai. 78 C5
Nana r. Cent. Afr. Rep. 126 C3
Nana Bakassa Cent. Afr. Rep. 126 C3
Nana Barya r. Cent. Afr. Rep./Chad 126 C3
Nana-Grébizi pref. Cent. Afr. Rep. 126 C3
Nanaimo Canada 166 F5
Nana-Mambéré pref. Cent. Afr. Rep. 126 B3
Nan'an China 87 F3
Nanango Australia 149 G5
Nananib Plateau Namibia 130 C5
Nan'ao China 87 F4
also known as Houzhai
Nan'ao China see Dayu
Nanao Japan 91 E6
Nanatsu-shima i. Japan 90 E6
Nanay r. Peru 198 C5
Nanbai China see Zunyi
Nanbaxian China 84 B4
Nanbin China see Shizhu
Nanbu China 86 C2
Nancha China 82 C3
Nanchang Jiangxi China 87 E2
Nanchang Jiangxi China see Liantang
Nanchangshan China see Changdao
Nancheng China 87 F3
Nanchong China 86 C2
Nanchuan China 86 C2

Ñancorainza Bol. 201 E5
Nancowry i. India 95 G5
Nancut Canada 166 E4
Nancy France 51 M4
Nancy U.S.A. 176 A8
Nanda Devi mt. India 96 D3
Nanda Kot mt. India 96 D3
Nandan China 87 C3
Nanded India 94 C2
formerly known as Nander
Nander India see Nanded
Nandewar Range mts Australia 147 F2
Nandgaon India 94 B1
Nandi Zimbabwe 131 F4
Nandigama India 94 D2
Nandikotkur India 94 C3
Nanding He r. China 86 A4
Nandod India 96 B5
Nandu Jiang r. China 87 D4
Nandura India 94 C1
Nandurbar India 96 B5
Nandyal India 94 C3
Nănești Romania 58 I3
Nanfeng Guangdong China 87 D4
Nanfeng Jiangxi China 87 F3
also known as Qincheng
Nang China 89 F6
Nangade Moz. 129 C7
Nanga Eboko Cameroon 125 I5
Nangah Dedai Indon. 77 E3
Nangahembaloh Indon. 77 F2
Nangahkemangai Indon. 77 F3
Nangahmau Indon. 77 E3
Nangahpinoh Indon. 77 E3
Nangahsuruk Indon. 77 F2
Nangahtempuai Indon. 77 F2
Nangalala Australia 148 B2
Nanganga Tanz. 129 C7
Nangang Shan mts China 82 C4

Nanga Parbat mt. Jammu and Kashmir 96 B2
9th highest mountain in the world and in Asia.
world [physical features] ▶ 8–9

Nangarhār prov. Afgh. 101 G3
Nangatayap Indon. 77 E3
Nangbéto, Retenue de resr Togo 125 F5
Nangin Myanmar 79 B6
Nangis France 51 J4
Nangnim N. Korea 83 B4
Nangnim-sanmaek mts N. Korea 83 B4
Nangò Japan 90 F6
Nangong China 85 G4
Nangqên China 86 A1
also known as Xangda
Nangulangwa Tanz. 129 C7
Nanguneri India 94 C4
Nanhe China 85 G4
also known as Heyang
Nanhu China 84 B4
Nanhua Gansu China 84 C4
Nanhua Yunnan China 86 B3
also known as Longchuan
Nanhui China 87 G2
also known as Huinan
Nani Afgh. 101 G3
Nanisivik Canada 165 K2
Nanjangud India 94 C3
Nanjian China 86 B3
Nanjiang China 86 C1
Nanjie China see Guangning
Nanjing Fujian China 87 F3
also known as Shancheng
Nanjing Jiangsu China 87 F1
formerly spelt Nanking
Nanji Shan i. China 87 G3
Nanka Jiang r. China 86 A4
Nankang China 87 E3
formerly known as Rongjiang
Nankang China see Xingzi
Nanking China see Nanjing
Nankoku Japan 91 C8
Nankova Angola 127 C9
Nanlan He r. China 86 A4
Nanle China 85 G4
Nanling China 87 F2
Nan Ling mts China 87 D3
Nanliu Jiang r. China 87 D4
Nanlong China see Nanbu
Nanma China see Yiyuan
Nanmulingzue China see Namling
Nannine Australia 151 B5
Nanning China 87 D4
Nannup Australia 151 A7
Na Noi Thai. 78 C4
Nanortalik Greenland 165 O3
Nanouki atoll Kiribati see Nonouti
Nanouti atoll Kiribati see Nonouti
Nanpan Jiang r. China 86 C3
Nanpara India 97 D4
Nanpi China 85 H4
Nanpiao China 85 I3
Nanping Fujian China 87 F3
Nanping Sichuan China 86 C1
also known as Yongle
Nanpu China see Pucheng
Nanpu Xi r. China 87 F3
Nanqiao China see Fengxian
Nanri Dao i. China 87 F3
Nansa r. Spain 54 G1
Nansebo Eth. 128 C3
Nansei-shotō is Japan see Ryukyu Islands
Nansenga Zambia 127 E8
Nansen Land reg. Greenland 165 O1
Nansen Sound sea chan. Canada 165 J1
Nanshan Island S. China Sea 72 E4
Nanshankou China 84 B3
Nansha Qundao is S. China Sea see Spratly Islands
Nansio Tanz. 128 B5
Nantawarrina Aboriginal Land res. Australia 146 C2
Nantes France 50 E5
Nantes à Brest, Canal de France 50 D5
Nanthi Kadal lag. Sri Lanka 94 D4
Nantiat France 50 H6
Nanticoke Canada 168 D5
Nanticoke MD U.S.A. 177 J7
Nanticoke PA U.S.A. 177 I4
Nanticoke r. U.S.A. 177 J7
Nanton Canada 167 H5
Nantong Jiangsu China 87 G1
Nantong Jiangsu China 87 G2
Nantou China 87 [inset]
Nant'ou Taiwan 87 G4
Nantucket U.S.A. 177 O4
Nantucket Island U.S.A. 177 P4
Nantucket Sound g. U.S.A. 177 O4
Nantulo Moz. 129 C8
Nanty Glo U.S.A. 176 G5
Nanumaga i. Tuvalu see Nanumanga
Nanumanga i. Tuvalu 145 G2
also spelt Nanumaga; formerly known as Hudson Island
Nanumea i. Tuvalu 145 G2
Nanuque Brazil 203 D6
Nanusa, Kepulauan is Indon. 75 C1
Nanutarra Roadhouse Australia 150 A4
Nanxi China 86 C2
Nanxian China 87 E2
also known as Nanzhou
Nanxiong China 87 E3
formerly known as Xiongzhou
Nanyandang Shan mt. China 87 G3
Nanyang China 87 E1
Nanyō Japan 90 G5
Nanyuki Kenya 128 C5
Nanzamu China 82 B4
Nanzhang China 87 D2
Nanzhao China see Zhao'an
Nanzhao China 87 E1
Nanzheng China 86 C1
also known as Zhoujiaping
Nanzhou China see Nanxian
Naogaon Bangl. 97 F4
Naokot Pak. 101 G5
Naoli r. China 82 D3
Naomid, Dasht-e des. Afgh./Iran 101 E3
Naousa Greece 58 D8
Napa U.S.A. 182 B3
Napak mt. Uganda 128 B4
Napaktulik Lake Canada 167 H1
also known as Takijuq Lake
Napanee Canada 168 E4
Napasar India 96 B4
Napasoq Greenland 165 N3
Naperville U.S.A. 174 B3
Napier N.Z. 152 K7
Napier S. Africa 132 D11
Napier Broome Bay Australia 150 D2
Napier Mountains Antarctica 223 D2
Napier Peninsula Australia 148 B2
Napier Range hills Australia 150 D3
Naples Italy 57 G8
also known as Napoli; historically known as Neapolis
Naples FL U.S.A. 175 D7
Naples ME U.S.A. 177 O2
Naples NY U.S.A. 177 H3
Naples UT U.S.A. 183 O1
Napo China 86 C4
Napo prov. Ecuador 198 B5
Napo r. Ecuador 198 C5
Napoleon ND U.S.A. 178 C2
Napoleon OH U.S.A. 176 A4
Napoleonville U.S.A. 175 B6
Napoli Italy see Naples
Napoli, Golfo di b. Italy 57 G8
Naposta Arg. 204 E5
Nappanee U.S.A. 172 H9
Napperby Australia 148 B4
Naqadeh Iran 100 A2
Naqb Malha mt. Egypt 108 D8
Naqūb Yemen 105 D5
Nara Japan 91 D7
Nara pref. Japan 90 D7
Nara Mali 124 D3
Nara r. Rus. Fed. 43 S7
Narach Belarus 42 H7
Narach r. Belarus 42 H7
Narach, Vozyera l. Belarus 42 H7
Naracoorte Australia 146 D4
Naradhan Australia 147 E3
Narail Bangl. 97 F5
Naraina India 96 B4
Naranbulag Dornod Mongolia 85 G1
Naranbulag Uvs Mongolia 84 B1
Narang Afgh. 101 G3
Naranjal Ecuador 198 B5
Naranjal Peru 198 C6
Naranjos Mex. 185 F4
Naran Sebstein Bulag spring China 84 C3
Narao Japan 91 A8
Naraq Iran 100 B3
Narasannapeta India 95 E2
Narasapatnam, Point India 94 D2
Narasapur India 94 D2
Narasaraopet India 94 D2
Narasinghapur India 95 E1
Narasun Rus. Fed. 85 G1
Narat China 88 D3
Narathiwat Thai. 79 C7
Narat Shan mts China 88 C3
Nara Visa U.S.A. 179 B5
Narayanganj Bangl. 97 F5
Narayanganj India 96 D5
Narayangaon India 94 B2
Narayanpet India 94 C2
Naray Kelay Afgh. 101 G3
Narbada r. India see Narmada
Narbo France see Narbonne
Narbonne France 51 J9
historically known as Narbo
Narbuvoll Norway 44 J3
Narcea r. Spain 54 E1
Narcondam Island India 95 G3
Nardin Iran 100 C2
Nardò Italy 57 K8
Nare Arg. 204 E3
Narechi r. Pak. 101 G4
Naregal India 94 B3
Narembeen Australia 151 B7
Nares Strait Canada/Greenland 165 L2
Naretha Australia 151 D6
Narew r. Poland 49 R3
Narewka r. Poland 42 E9
Nari r. Pak. 101 F4
Naria Bangl. 97 F5
Narib Namibia 130 C5
Narie, Jezioro l. Poland 49 R2
Nariep S. Africa 132 B7
Narimanov Rus. Fed. 102 A3
formerly known as Nizhnevolzhsk
Narimskiy Khrebet mts Kazakh. 88 D1
Narin Afgh. 101 G2
Narin reg. Afgh. 101 G2
Narin China 85 F4
Narince Turkey 107 D3
Narin Gol watercourse China 84 B4
Nariño dept Col. 198 B4
Narita Japan 91 G7
Nariu-misaki pt Japan 91 D7
Nariwa Japan 91 C7
Narizon, Punta pt Mex. 184 C3
Narkaus Fin. 44 N2
Narken Sweden 44 M2
Narmada r. India 96 B5
also known as Narbada
Narnaul India 96 C3
Narni Italy 56 E6
historically known as Narnia
Narnia Italy see Narni
Narodnaya, Gora mt. Rus. Fed. 40 L2
Naro-Fominsk Rus. Fed. 43 R6
Narok Kenya 128 B5
Narooma Australia 147 F4
Narowlya Belarus 41 D6
Närpes Fin. 44 M3
Narrabri Australia 147 F2
Narragansett Bay U.S.A. 177 N4
Narran r. Australia 147 E2
Narrandera Australia 147 E3
Narran Lake Australia 147 E2
Narrogin Australia 151 B7
Narromine Australia 147 F3
Narrow Hills Provincial Park Canada 167 J4
Narrows U.S.A. 176 E8
Narrowsburg U.S.A. 177 J4
Narsalik Greenland 165 O3
Narsapur India 94 C2
Narsaq Greenland 165 O3
Narsarsuaq Greenland 165 O3
Narsimhapur India 96 C5
Narsingdi Bangl. 97 F5
Narsinghgarh India 96 C5
Narsipatnam India 95 D2
Nart China 85 G3
Nart Mongolia 85 E1
Nartë Albania 58 A8
Nartkala Rus. Fed. 107 E2
formerly known as Dokshukino
Naruko Japan 90 G5
Naruto Japan 91 D7
Narva Estonia 43 J2
Narva r. Estonia/Rus. Fed. 42 J2
Narva Bay Estonia/Rus. Fed. 42 I2
also known as Narva laht or Narvskiy Zaliv
Narvacan Phil. 74 B2
Narva-Jõesuu Estonia 43 J2
Narva laht b. Estonia/Rus. Fed. see Narva Bay
Narva Reservoir Estonia/Rus. Fed. see Narvskoye Vodokhranilishche
Narva veehoidla resr Estonia/Rus. Fed. see Narvskoye Vodokhranilishche
Narvik Norway 44 L1
Narvskiy Zaliv b. Estonia/Rus. Fed. see Narva Bay
Narvskoye Vodokhranilishche resr Estonia/Rus. Fed. 43 J2
English form Narva Reservoir; also known as Narva veehoidla
Narwana India 96 C3
Narwar India 96 C4
Narwinbi Aboriginal Land res. Australia 148 C3
Nar'yan-Mar Rus. Fed. 40 J2
Naryn Kyrg. 103 H4
Naryn admin. div. Kyrg. 103 H4
English form Naryn Oblast; also known as Narynskaya Oblast'; formerly known as Tien Shan Oblast or Tyanshanskaya Oblast'
Naryn r. Kyrg./Uzbek. 103 H4
Naryn Rus. Fed. 84 B1
Narynkol Kazakh. 88 C3
also spelt Naryngol
Naryn Oblast admin. div. Kyrg. see Naryn
Narynqol Kazakh. see Narynkol
Narynskaya Oblast' admin. div. Kyrg. see Naryn
Naryshkino Rus. Fed. 43 Q9
Năsăud Romania 58 F1
Näsby Sweden 45 K4
Naseby N.Z. 153 E13
Nashik India 94 B1
also spelt Nasik
Nashua U.S.A. 177 N3
Nashville AR U.S.A. 179 D5
Nashville GA U.S.A. 175 D6
Nashville IL U.S.A. 174 B4
Nashville NC U.S.A. 174 E5
Nashville OH U.S.A. 176 C5

Nashville TN U.S.A. 174 C4
State capital of Tennessee.

Našice Croatia 56 K3
Nasielsk Poland 49 R3
Näsijärvi l. Fin. 45 M3
Nasik India see Nashik
Nasir Sudan 128 B2
Nasirabad Bangl. see Mymensingh
Nasirabad India 96 B4
Nasirabad Pak. 101 G4
Naskaupi r. Canada 169 I2
Nasmganj India 97 E4
Nasondoye Dem. Rep. Congo 127 E7
Nasonville U.S.A. 172 C6
Nasosnyy Azer. see Hacı Zeynalabdin
Nasr Egypt 108 B7
Naṣrābād Eṣfahān Iran 100 B3
Naṣrābād Khorāsan Iran 101 D3
Naṣrānī, Jabal an mts Syria 109 I4
Nasratabad Iran see Zābol
Naṣrian-e-Pā'īn Iran 100 A3
Nass r. Canada 166 D4
Nassarawa Nigeria 125 G4
Nassarawa state Nigeria 125 H4
Nassau r. Australia 149 D2

Nassau Bahamas 186 D1
Capital of The Bahamas.

Nassau i. Cook Is 221 G6
formerly known as Mitchell Island
Nassau U.S.A. 177 L3
Nassau, Naturpark nature res. Germany 48 E5
Nassawadox U.S.A. 177 J8
Nasser, Lake resr Egypt 121 G4
Nassian Côte d'Ivoire 124 E4
Nässjö Sweden 45 K4
Nassuttooq inlet Greenland 165 N3
also known as Nordre Strømfjord
Nastapoca r. Canada 169 E1
Nastapoka Islands Canada 168 E1
Nastola Fin. 42 G1
Nasu-dake vol. Japan 90 F6
Nasugbu Phil. 74 B3
Nasva Rus. Fed. 43 L5
Nasva r. Rus. Fed. 43 L5
Nata Botswana 131 E4
Nata watercourse Botswana/Zimbabwe 131 E4
Natabu Indon. 75 C3
Natal Amazonas Brazil 201 E1
Natal Rio Grande do Norte Brazil 202 F3
Natal Indon. 76 B2
Natal prov. S. Africa see Kwazulu-Natal
Natal Drakensberg National Park S. Africa 133 N6
Naṭanz Iran 100 B3
Natashquan Canada 169 I3
Natashquan r. Canada 169 I3
Natchez U.S.A. 175 B6
Natchitoches U.S.A. 179 D6
Nathalia Australia 147 E4
Nathana India 96 B3
Nathdwara India 96 B4
Nati, Punta pt Spain 55 O4
Natiaboani Burkina 125 F4
National City U.S.A. 183 G9
National Park N.Z. 152 J7
National West Coast Tourist Recreation Area park Namibia 130 B4
Natitingou Benin 125 F4
Natividad, Isla i. Mex. 184 B3
Natividade Rio de Janeiro Brazil 207 L8
Natividade Tocantins Brazil 202 C4
Natla r. Canada 166 D2
Natmauk Myanmar 78 A3
Natogyi Myanmar 78 A3
Nator Bangl. 97 F4
Nátora Mex. 181 E7
Natori Japan 90 G5
Natron, Lake salt l. Tanz. 128 C5
Nattai National Park Australia 147 F3
Nattalin Myanmar 78 A4
Nattam India 94 C4
Nattaung mt. Myanmar 78 B4
Nattavaara Sweden 44 M2
Na'tū Iran 101 E3
Natuna, Kepulauan is Indon. 77 D1
also known as Bunguran, Kepulauan
Natuna Besar i. Indon. 77 E1
also known as Bunguran, Pulau
Natural Bridge U.S.A. 176 F8
Natural Bridges National Monument nat. park U.S.A. 183 N4
Naturaliste, Cape Australia 151 A7
Naturaliste Channel Australia 151 A5
Nature's Valley S. Africa 132 H10
Nau Tajik. see Nov
Naubinway U.S.A. 172 H4
Naucelle France 51 I8
Nauchas Namibia 130 C4
Nau Co l. China 89 C5
Naudesberg Pass S. Africa 133 I9
Nauen Germany 49 J3
Naugatuck U.S.A. 177 L4
Nau Hissar Pak. 101 F4
Naujan Phil. 74 B3
Naujoji Akmenė Lith. 42 D5
Naukh India 96 B4
Naulila Angola 127 B9
Naumburg (Saale) Germany 48 I4
Naungpale Myanmar 78 B4
Na'ūr Jordan 108 G6
Naurskaya Rus. Fed. 107 F2
Nauru i. Nauru 145 F2
Nauru country S. Pacific Ocean 145 F2
oceania [countries] ▶ 138–139
Naushahro Firoz Pak. 101 G5
Naushara Pak. 101 G5
Naushki Rus. Fed. 85 E1
Naustdal Norway 45 I3
Nauta Peru 198 C6
Nautaca Uzbek. see Karshi
Naute Dam Namibia 132 B3
Nautla Mex. 185 F4
Nautonwa India 97 D4
Nautsi Rus. Fed. 44 O1
Nauvoo U.S.A. 172 B10
Nava r. Dem. Rep. Congo 126 E4
Navabad Tajik. see Novobod
Navacerrada, Puerto de pass Spain 54 H4
Navachica mt. Spain 54 H8
Navadrutsk Belarus 42 I6
Navadwip India 97 F5
formerly spelt Nabadwip
Navahermosa Spain 54 G5
Navahrudak Belarus 42 G8
also spelt Novogrudok
Navahrudskaye Wzvyshsha hills Belarus 42 G8
Navajo r. U.S.A. 181 F5
Navajo Indian Reservation res. U.S.A. 183 O6
Navajo Lake U.S.A. 181 F5
Navajo Mountain U.S.A. 183 N4
Naval Phil. 74 C4
Navalmoral de la Mata Spain 54 F5
Navalvillar de Pela Spain 54 F5
Navan Rep. of Ireland 47 F10
also known as An Uaimh
Navangar India see Jamnagar
Navapolatsk Belarus 43 J6
also spelt Novopolotsk
Navarin, Mys c. Rus. Fed. 39 R3
Navarino, Isla i. Chile 205 D9
Navarra aut. comm. Spain 55 J2
English form Navarre
Navarre aut. comm. Spain see Navarra
Navarrenx France 50 F9
Navarro Peru 198 C6
Navarro r. U.S.A. 182 A2
Navashino Rus. Fed. 40 G5
Navasota U.S.A. 179 C6
Navasota r. U.S.A. 179 C6

Navassa Island terr. West Indies 187 E3
United States Unincorporated Territory.
oceania [countries] ▶ 138–139

Navasyolki Belarus 43 J9
Navayel'nya Belarus 42 G8
Naver r. U.K. 46 H5
Navesnoye Rus. Fed. 43 S9
Navesti r. Estonia 42 F3
Navia Spain 54 E1
Navia r. Spain 54 E1
Navidad Chile 204 C4
Navidad r. U.S.A. 179 C6
Naviraí Brazil 203 A7
Navlakhi India 96 A5
Navlya Rus. Fed. 43 P9
Navlya r. Rus. Fed. 43 P9
Năvodari Romania 58 J4
Navoi Uzbek. 103 F4
also spelt Nawoiy; formerly known as Kermine
Navoiyskaya Oblast' admin. div. Uzbek. 103 E4
English form Navoy Oblast; also known as Nawoiy Wiloyati
Navojoa Mex. 184 C3
Navolato Mex. 184 D3
Navoy Oblast admin. div. Uzbek. see Navoiyskaya Oblast'
Návpaktos Greece see Nafpaktos
Návplion Greece see Nafplio
Nävragöl Sweden 45 K4
Navrongo Ghana 125 E4
Navşar Turkey see Şemdinli
Navsari India 94 B1
Navua Fiji 145 G3
Nawa India 96 B4
Nawá Syria 108 H5
Nawabganj Bangl. 97 F4
Nawabganj India 97 D4
Nawabshah Pak. 101 G5
Nawada India 97 E4
Nāwah Afgh. 101 F3
Nawakot Nepal 97 E4
Nawalgarh India 96 B4
Nawar, Dasht-i imp. l. Afgh. 101 F3
Nawashahr India 89 B6
Nawāṣīf, Ḥarrāt lava field Saudi Arabia 104 C3
Nawnghkio Myanmar 78 B3
Nawngleng Myanmar 78 B3
Nawoiy Uzbek. see Navoi
Nawoiy Wiloyati admin. div. Uzbek. see Navoiyskaya Oblast'
Naws, Ra's c. Oman 105 F4
Naxçıvan Azer. 107 F3
also spelt Nakhichevan'
Naxi China 86 C2
Naxos Greece 59 G11
Naxos i. Greece 59 G11
Naya Col. 198 B4
Nayagarh India 95 E1
Nayak Afgh. 101 F3
Nayarit state Mex. 184 D4
Nāy Band, Kūh-e mt. Iran 100 D3
Nayfah oasis Saudi Arabia 105 E4
Nayong China 86 C3
also known as Yongxi
Nayoro Japan 90 H2
Nayt Yemen 105 F5
Nayuchi Malawi 129 B8
Nayudupeta India 94 C3
Nayyāl, Wādī watercourse Saudi Arabia 104 B1
Nazare Brazil 199 E4
Nazaré Brazil 199 H6
Nazareno Mex. 184 E3
Nazareth India 94 C4
Nazareth Israel 108 G5
Nazareth U.S.A. 177 J5
Nazário Brazil 206 D3
Nazas Mex. 184 D3
Nazas r. Mex. 184 D3
Nazca Peru 200 B3
Nāzīk Iran 100 A2
Nazilli Turkey 106 B3
Nazımiye Turkey 107 D3
Nazinon r. Burkina/Ghana 125 E4 see Red Volta
Nazira India 97 G4
Nazir Hat Bangl. 97 F5
Naziya Rus. Fed. 43 M2
Nazko Canada 166 F4
Nazko r. Canada 166 F4
Nazran' Rus. Fed. 41 H8
formerly known as Kosta-Khetagurovo
Nazrēt Eth. 128 C2
Nazwá Oman 105 G3
also spelt Nizwá
Nazyvayevsk Rus. Fed. 38 H4
formerly known as Novonazyvayevka
Nbâk Mauritania 124 B2
Ncanaha S. Africa 133 J10
Nchelenge Zambia 127 F7
Ncheu Malawi see Ntcheu
Ncora S. Africa 133 L8
Ncue Equat. Guinea 125 H6
Ndala Tanz. 129 B6
N'dalatando Angola 127 B7
formerly known as Salazar or Vila Salazar; formerly spelt Dalatando
Ndali Benin 125 F4
Ndanda Cent. Afr. Rep. 126 D3
Ndao i. Indon. 75 B5
Ndareda Tanz. 129 B6
Ndélé Cent. Afr. Rep. 126 D2
Ndélélé Cameroon 125 I5
Ndendé Gabon 126 A5
Ndende i. Solomon Is see Ndeni
Ndeni i. Solomon Is 145 F3
also spelt Ndende or Nitendi
Ndiael, Réserve de Faune du nature res. Senegal 124 A3
Ndikiniméki Cameroon 125 H5
Ndim Cent. Afr. Rep. 126 B3
N'Djamena Chad see Ndjamena

Ndjamena Chad 120 B6
Capital of Chad. Also spelt N'Djamena; formerly known as Fort Lamy.

Ndji r. Cent. Afr. Rep. 126 D3
Ndjim r. Cameroon 125 H5
Ndjolé Gabon 126 A5
Ndjouani i. Comoros see Nzwani
Ndjounou Gabon 126 B5
Ndofane Senegal 124 B3
Ndogo, Lagune lag. Gabon 126 A5
Ndoi i. Fiji see Doi
Ndok Cameroon 125 I5
Ndola Zambia 127 F8
Ndoto mt. Kenya 128 C4
Ndougou Gabon 126 A5
Nduke i. Solomon Is see Kolombangara
Ndumbwe Tanz. 129 C7
Ndumu S. Africa 133 Q3
Ndumu Game Reserve nature res. Moz. 133 Q3
Nduye Dem. Rep. Congo 126 F4
Ndwedwe S. Africa 133 O6
Nea Anchialos Greece 59 D9
Nea Apollonia Greece 58 E8
Nea Artaki Greece 59 E10
Neabul Creek r. Australia 147 E1
Neagh, Lough l. U.K. 47 F9
Neah Bay U.S.A. 180 A2
Neajlov r. Romania 58 G4
Nea Karvali Greece 58 F8
Neale, Lake salt flat Australia 148 A5
Neale Junction Nature Reserve Australia 151 D6
Neales watercourse Australia 146 C2
Nea Liosia Greece 59 E10
Nea Makri Greece 59 E10
Nea Moudania Greece 59 E8
Neamț r. Romania 58 H1
Nea Peramos Greece 58 F8
Neapoli Kriti Greece 59 G13
Neapoli Peloponnisos Greece 59 E12
Neapolis Italy see Naples
Nea Roda Greece 59 E8
Nea Santa Greece 58 D8
Neath U.K. 47 I12
also known as Castell-nedd
Nea Zichni Greece 58 E7
Nebbi Uganda 128 A4
Nebbou Burkina 125 E4
Nebesnaya, Gora mt. China 88 C3
Nebine Creek r. Australia 147 E2
Nebitdag Turkm. 102 C5
Nebo Australia 149 F4
Nebo, Mount U.S.A. 183 M2
Nebolchi Rus. Fed. 43 O2
Nebraska state U.S.A. 178 B3
Nebraska City U.S.A. 178 D3
Nebrodi, Monti mts Sicilia Italy 57 G11
Nebyloye Rus. Fed. 43 U5
Necedah U.S.A. 172 C6
Necedah National Wildlife Refuge nature res. U.S.A. 172 C6
Neches r. U.S.A. 179 D6
Nechí r. Col. 198 C2
Nechisar National Park Eth. 128 C3
Neckarsulm Germany 48 G6
Neckartal-Odenwald, Naturpark nature res. Germany 48 G6
Necker Island U.S.A. 221 H4
Necochea Arg. 204 F5
Necoclí Col. 198 B2
Nedelino Bulg. 58 G7
Nedelišće Croatia 56 I2
Nedel'noye Rus. Fed. 43 R7
Nederland country Europe see Netherlands
Nederlandse Antillen terr. West Indies see Netherlands Antilles
Neder Rijn r. Neth. 48 C4
Nedlouc, Lac l. Canada 169 F1
also known as Nedluk Lake
Nedluk Lake Canada see Nedlouc, Lac
Nědong China 89 E6
Nedre Soppero Sweden 44 M1
Nedstrand Norway 45 I4
Needham U.S.A. 177 N3
Needles U.S.A. 183 J7
Needmore U.S.A. 176 G6
Neemuch India see Nimach
Neenah U.S.A. 172 E6
Neepawa Canada 167 L5
Neergaard Lake Canada 165 K2
Nefta Tunisia 123 G2
Neftçala Azer. 107 G3
also spelt Neftechala
Neftechala Azer. see 26 Bakı Komissarı
Neftechala Azer. see Neftçala
Neftegorsk Sakhalin Rus. Fed. 82 F1
formerly known as Vostok
Neftegorsk Samarskaya Oblast' Rus. Fed. 102 B1
Neftekamsk Rus. Fed. 40 J4
formerly known as Kasevo
Neftekumsk Rus. Fed. 41 H7
Nefteyugansk Rus. Fed. 38 H3
formerly known as Ust'-Balyk
Neftezavodsk Turkm. see Seydi
Nefza Tunisia 57 B11
Negada Weyn well Eth. 128 E3
Negage Angola 127 B6
Négala Mali 124 C3
Negār Iran 100 D4
Negara Bali Indon. 77 F5
Negara Kalimantan Selatan Indon. 77 F3
Negara r. Indon. 77 F3
Negaunee U.S.A. 172 F4
Negēlē Oromia Eth. 128 C3
Negēlē Oromia Eth. 128 C3
Negeri Sembilan state Malaysia 76 C2
formerly spelt Negri Sembilan
Negev des. Israel 108 G7
also spelt HaNegev
Negomane Moz. 129 C7
Negombo Sri Lanka 94 C5
Negotin Srbija Yugo. 58 D4
Negotino Macedonia 58 D7
Negra, Cordillera mts Peru 200 A2
Negra, Lago l. Uruguay 204 G4
also known as Los Difuntos, Lago de
Negra, Punta pt Peru 198 A6
Negra, Serra mts Brazil 203 D6
Negra, Serranía de mts Bol. 201 E3
Negrais, Cape Myanmar 78 A5
Negratín, Embalse de resr Spain 55 I7
Negreira Spain 54 C2
Negreiros Chile 200 C4
Nègrepelisse France 50 H8
Negrești Romania 58 I2
Negri r. Australia 148 A3
Negri Romania 58 H2
Négrine Alg. 123 G2
Negri Sembilan state Malaysia see Negeri Sembilan
Negritos Peru 198 A6
Negro r. Arg. 204 E6
Negro r. Brazil 201 F4
Negro r. Para. 201 F6
Negro r. S. America 199 G5
Negro r. Uruguay 204 G4
Negro, Cabo c. Morocco 54 F9
Negroponte i. Greece see Evvoia
Negros i. Phil. 74 B4
Negru Vodă Romania 58 J5
Nehalem r. U.S.A. 180 B3
Nehavand Iran 100 B3
Nehbandān Iran 101 E4
Nehe China 85 J1
Nehoiu Romania 58 H3
Nehone Angola 127 C9
Neiafu Tonga 145 H3
Neiba Dom. Rep. 187 F3
Neijiang China 86 C2
Neilersdrif S. Africa 132 E5
Neill Island India 95 G4
Neillsville U.S.A. 172 C6
Nei Mongol Zizhiqu aut. reg. China 85 D3
English form Inner Mongolia
Neiqiu China 85 G4
Neiße r. Germany/Poland 49 L3
also known as Nysa Łużycka
Neiva Col. 198 C4
Neixiang China 87 D1
Nejanilini Lake Canada 167 L3
Nejapa Mex. 185 G5
Nejd reg. Saudi Arabia see Najd
Neka Iran 100 C2
Neka r. Iran 100 C2
Nek'emtē Eth. 128 C2
Nekhayevskaya Rus. Fed. 41 G6
formerly known as Nekhayevskiy
Nekhayevskiy Rus. Fed. see Nekhayevskaya
Neklyudovo Rus. Fed. 43 V6
Nekrasovskiy Rus. Fed. 43 S5
Nekrasovskoye Rus. Fed. 43 V4
Neksø Denmark 45 K5
Nela r. Spain 54 H2
Nelamangala India 94 C3
Nelas Port. 54 D4
Nelazskoye Rus. Fed. 43 S2
Nelia Australia 149 D4
Nelidovo Rus. Fed. 43 N5
Neligh U.S.A. 178 C3
Nel'kan Khabarovskiy Kray Rus. Fed. 39 N4
Nel'kan Respublika Sakha (Yakutiya) Rus. Fed. 39 O3
Nellie Lake Canada 173 M2
Nellim Fin. 44 O1
also spelt Njellim
Nellore India 94 C3
Nelluz watercourse Turkey 109 K1
Nelshoogte pass S. Africa 133 O2
Nelson Arg. 204 E3
Nelson Canada 166 G5
Nelson r. Canada 167 M3
Nelson N.Z. 152 H9
Nelson admin. reg. N.Z. 152 H9
Nelson AZ U.S.A. 183 K6
Nelson NE U.S.A. 178 C3
Nelson NV U.S.A. 183 J6
Nelson, Cape Australia 146 D4
Nelson, Estrecho strait Chile 205 B8
Nelson Bay Australia 147 G3
Nelson Creek N.Z. 153 F10
Nelson Forks Canada 166 F3
Nelson House Canada 167 L4
Nelson Lakes National Park N.Z. 153 G10
Nelspoort S. Africa 132 H9
Nelspruit S. Africa 133 O2
Nem r. Rus. Fed. 40 J3
Néma Mauritania 124 D2
Nema Rus. Fed. 40 I4
Nemadji r. U.S.A. 172 A4
Neman r. Belarus/Lith. see Nyoman
Neman Rus. Fed. 42 D6
Neman r. Rus. Fed. 42 D6
Ne'matābād Iran 100 D4
Nemausus France see Nîmes
Nembe Nigeria 125 G5
Nemda r. Rus. Fed. 40 G4
Nemea Greece 59 D11
Nemed Rus. Fed. 40 J3
Nemegos Canada 173 J3
Nemegosenda Lake Canada 173 J2
Nemenčine Lith. 42 G7
Nemetocenna France see Arras
Nemetskiy, Mys c. Rus. Fed. 44 O1
Nemirov Ukr. see Nemyriv
Némiscau r. Canada 168 E3
Nemor r. China 85 J1
Nemours Alg. see Ghazaouet
Nemours France 51 I4
Nemrut Dağı mt. Turkey 107 E3
Nemta r. Rus. Fed. 82 D2
Nemunas r. Lith. 42 C6
Nemunėlio Radviliškis Lith. 42 F5
Nemunelis r. Lith. 42 G5
Nemuro Japan 90 I3
Nemuro-hantō pen. Japan 90 I3
Nemuro-kaikyō sea chan. Japan/Rus. Fed. 90 I3
also known as Kunashirskiy Proliv
Nemuro-wan b. Japan 90 I3
Nemyriv Ukr. 41 D6
also spelt Nemirov
Nenagh Rep. of Ireland 47 D11
also known as An tAonach
Nenana U.S.A. 164 E3
Nenashevo Rus. Fed. 43 S7
Nene r. U.K. 47 M11
Nenets Autonomous Okrug admin. div. Rus. Fed. see Nenetskiy Avtonomnyy Okrug
Nenetskiy Avtonomnyy Okrug admin. div. Rus. Fed. 40 J2
English form Nenets Autonomous Okrug
Nenjiang China 85 J1
Nen Jiang r. China 85 J2
also known as Nonni
Neo Japan 91 E7
Neochori Greece 59 C9
also known as Neokhórion
Neo Karlovasi Greece 59 H11
also known as Néon Karlovásion
Neokhórion Greece see Neochori
Neola U.S.A. 183 N1
Neo Monastiri Greece 59 D9
Néon Karlovásion Greece see Neo Karlovasi
Neopit U.S.A. 172 E6
Neosho U.S.A. 178 D4
Neosho r. U.S.A. 178 D4
Neos Marmaras Greece 59 E8
Nepal country Asia 97 D3
asia [countries] ▶ 64–67
Nepalganj Nepal 97 D3
Nepanagar India 96 C5
Nepean Canada 168 F4
Nephi U.S.A. 183 M2
Nephin hill Rep. of Ireland 47 C9
Nephin Beg Range hills Rep. of Ireland 47 C9
Nepisiguit r. Canada 169 H4
Nepryadva r. Rus. Fed. 43 T8
Neptune U.S.A. 177 K5
Ner r. Poland 49 P3
Nera r. Italy 56 E6
Nérac France 50 G8
Neral India 94 B2
Nerang Australia 147 G1
Nera Tso l. Xizang China 89 F6
Neravai Lith. 42 F7
Nerchinsk Rus. Fed. 85 H1
Nerchinskiy Zavod Rus. Fed. 85 H1
Nereju Romania 58 H3
Nerekhta Rus. Fed. 43 V4
Nereta Latvia 42 G5
Neretva r. Bos.-Herz./Croatia 56 J5
Neretvanski Kanal sea chan. Croatia 56 J5
Neri India 94 C1
Nêri Pünco l. China 89 E6
Neriquinha Angola 127 D8
Neris r. Lith. 42 E7

Nerka, Lake U.S.A. 164 D4
Nerl' Ivanovskaya Oblast' Rus. Fed. 43 V5
Nerl' r. Rus. Fed. 43 S4
Nerl' Tverskaya Oblast' Rus. Fed. 43 T4
Nero, Ozero l. Rus. Fed. 43 U4
Nerópolis Brazil 206 D3
Neroyka, Gora mt. Rus. Fed. 40 K2
Ner Pinglai India 96 B4
Neruch' r. Rus. Fed. 43 R9
Nerussa r. Rus. Fed. 43 Q9
Neryungri Rus. Fed. 39 M4
Nes Norway 45 J3
Nes' Rus. Fed. 40 H2
Nes' r. Rus. Fed. 40 H2
Nesa' Iran 100 B2
Nesbyen Norway 45 J3
Nesebŭr Bulg. 58 I6
Neskaupstaður Iceland 44 [inset] D2
Nesna Norway 44 K2
Nesque r. France 51 K8
Nesri India 94 B2
Ness, Loch l. U.K. 46 H6
Ness City U.S.A. 178 C4
Nesse r. Germany 48 H9
Nesselrode, Mount Canada/U.S.A. 166 C3
Nesselwang Germany 48 H8
Neste r. France 50 G6
Nesterov Rus. Fed. 42 D7
Nesterovo Rus. Fed. 43 T3
Nestery Rus. Fed. 51 L4
Nestore r. Italy 56 E6
Nestor Falls Canada 168 A3
Nestoria U.S.A. 172 E4
Nestos r. Greece 58 F3
  also known as Mesta
Nesvizh Belarus see Nyasvizh
Netanya Israel 108 F5
Netarhat India 97 E5
Netcong U.S.A. 177 K5
▶Netherlands country Europe 48 B3
  also known as Holland; known as Nederland in Dutch
  europe [countries] ▶▶▶ 32–35
▶Netherlands Antilles terr. West Indies 187 F4
  Self-governing Netherlands Territory. Also known as Nederlandse Antillen; formerly known as Dutch West Indies.
  oceania [countries] ▶▶▶ 138–139
Neto r. Italy 57 J9
Netrakona Bangl. 97 F4
Netrang India 96 B5
Nettilling Lake Canada 165 L3
Nettuno Italy 56 E7
Neubari r. Sudan 128 B3
Neubrandenburg Germany 49 K2
Neubukow Germany 48 I8
Neuburg an der Donau Germany 48 I7
Neuchâtel Switz. 51 M6
Neuchâtel, Lac de l. Switz. 51 M6
Neuenhagen Berlin Germany 49 K3
Neuenkirchen Germany 48 J7
Neuenkirchen-Seelscheid Germany 48 E5
Neufchâteau Belgium 51 L4
Neufchâteau France 51 L4
Neufchâtel-en-Bray France 50 H3
Neuhausen Rus. Fed. see Gur'yevsk
Neuhof Germany 48 G5
Neuillé-Pont-Pierre France 50 G5
Neukirchen Rus. Fed. see Pionerskiy
Neumarkt in der Oberpfalz Germany 48 I6
Neumayer research station Antarctica 223 X2
  long form Georg von Neumayer
Neumünster Germany 48 G1
Neun, Nam r. Laos 78 C4
Neunkirchen Austria 49 N8
Neunkirchen Germany 48 E6
Neuquén Arg. 204 C5
Neuquén prov. Arg. 204 C5
Neuquén r. Arg. 204 C5
Neuruppin Germany 49 J3
Neu Sandez Poland see Nowy Sącz
Neuse r. U.S.A. 174 E5
Neusiedl am See Austria 49 N8
Neusiedler See l. Austria/Hungary 49 N8
Neusiedler See Seewinkel, Nationalpark nat. park Austria 49 N8
Neuss Germany 48 D4
Neustadt (Wied) Germany 48 E5
Neustadt an der Rübenberge Germany 48 G3
Neustadt an der Aisch Germany 48 H6
Neustadt an der Weinstraße Germany see Neustadt an der Weinstraße
Neustadt an der Weinstraße Germany 48 F6
  formerly known as Neustadt an der Hardt
Neustadt in Holstein Germany 48 H1
Neustadt in Sachsen Germany 49 L4
Neustift im Stubaital Austria 56 D1
Neustrelitz Germany 49 K2
Neuves-Maisons France 51 M4
Neuville-aux-Bois France 51 I4
Neuville-lès-Dieppe France 50 H3
Neuwerk i. Germany 48 F2
Neuwied Germany 48 E5
Nevada U.S.A. 174 C4
Nevada MO U.S.A. 178 D4
Nevada state U.S.A. 183 H1
Nevada, Sierra mt. Arg. 204 C2
Nevada, Sierra mts Spain 55 H7
Nevada, Sierra nature res. Spain 55 H7
Nevada, Sierra U.S.A. 182 C1
Nevada City U.S.A. 182 C2
Nevado, Cerro mt. Arg. 204 C4
Nevado, Sierra del mts Arg. 204 C5
Nevado de Colima, Parque Nacional nat. park Mex. 184 E5
Nevado de Toluca, Parque Nacional nat. park Mex. 185 F5
Nevasa India 94 B2
Nevdol'sk Rus. Fed. 43 P9
Neve, Serra da mts Angola 127 B8
Nevel' Rus. Fed. 43 K5

Nevel', Ozero l. Rus. Fed. 43 K6
Nevel'sk Rus. Fed. 82 F3
Neverkino Rus. Fed. 41 H5
Neveronys Lith. 42 F7
Nevers France 51 J5
Nevertire Australia 147 E2
Neves Brazil 207 J9
Nevesinje Bos.-Herz. 56 K5
Nevėžis r. Lith. 42 E7
Nevinnomyssk Rus. Fed. 41 G7
Nevis i. St Kitts and Nevis 187 H3
Nevşehir Turkey 106 C3
Nevskoye Rus. Fed. 00 C2
Nev r. CA U.S.A. 183 I8
Nev r. WV U.S.A. 176 D8
New Aiyansh Canada 166 D4
Newala Tanz. 129 C7
New Albany IN U.S.A. 174 C4
New Albany MS U.S.A. 174 B5
Newald U.S.A. 172 E5
New Amsterdam Guyana 199 G3
New Angledool Australia 147 E2
Newark CA U.S.A. 182 C4
Newark DE U.S.A. 177 J6
Newark NJ U.S.A. 177 K5
Newark NY U.S.A. 177 H2
Newark OH U.S.A. 176 C5
Newark airport U.S.A. 177 K5
Newark Lake U.S.A. 183 I2
Newark-on-Trent U.K. 47 L10
Newark Valley U.S.A. 177 I3
New Augusta U.S.A. 175 B6
Neway U.S.A. 172 H7
New Bedford U.S.A. 177 O4
Newberg U.S.A. 180 B3
New Berlin U.S.A. 174 E5
New Bern U.S.A. 174 E5
Newberry MI U.S.A. 172 H4
Newberry SC U.S.A. 175 D5
Newberry National Volcanic Monument nat. park U.S.A. 180 B4
Newberry Springs U.S.A. 183 H7
New Bethlehem U.S.A. 176 F4
New Bight Bahamas 187 E1
New Bloomfield U.S.A. 177 I5
Newboro Canada 168 E4
New Boston IL U.S.A. 172 C9
New Boston OH U.S.A. 176 C7
New Boston TX U.S.A. 179 D5
New Braunfels U.S.A. 179 C6
New Brighton U.S.A. 176 E5
New Britain i. P.N.G. 145 D2
New Brunswick prov. Canada 169 H4
New Brunswick U.S.A. 177 K5
New Buffalo U.S.A. 172 G9
Newburg U.S.A. 176 H5
Newburgh Canada 173 Q6
Newburgh U.K. 46 J6
Newburgh U.S.A. 177 K4
Newbury U.K. 47 K12
Newburyport U.S.A. 177 O3
New Caledonia i. S. Pacific Ocean see Nouvelle Calédonie
▶New Caledonia terr. S. Pacific Ocean 145 E3
  French Overseas Territory. Also known as Nouvelle Calédonie.
  oceania [countries] ▶▶▶ 138–139
  oceania [features] ▶▶▶ 142–143
New Carlisle Canada 169 I3
Newcastle Australia 147 F3
Newcastle N.B. Canada 169 H4
Newcastle Ont. Canada 168 E5
Newcastle S. Africa 133 N4
Newcastle U.K. 47 G9
Newcastle CA U.S.A. 182 C3
New Castle DE U.S.A. 177 J6
New Castle IN U.S.A. 174 C4
New Castle KY U.S.A. 176 A7
Newcastle ME U.S.A. 177 P1
New Castle PA U.S.A. 176 E4
Newcastle UT U.S.A. 183 K4
New Castle VA U.S.A. 176 E8
Newcastle WY U.S.A. 180 F4
Newcastle Creek r. Australia 148 B3
Newcastle Emlyn U.K. 47 H11
  also known as Castell Newydd Emlyn
Newcastle Range hills Australia 149 D3
Newcastle-under-Lyme U.K. 47 J10
Newcastle upon Tyne U.K. 47 K9
New Church U.S.A. 177 J8
Newchwang China see Yingkou
New City U.S.A. 177 L4
Newcomerstown U.S.A. 176 D5
New Concord U.S.A. 176 D6
Newdegate Australia 151 B7
▶New Delhi India 96 C3
  Capital of India.
New Don Pedro Reservoir U.S.A. 182 D4
Newell, Lake salt flat Australia 151 D5
Newell, Lake Canada 167 I5
New England Range mts Australia 147 F2
Newenham, Cape U.S.A. 164 C4
New Era U.S.A. 172 G7
Newfane U.S.A. 176 G2
Newfield U.S.A. 177 N2
Newfoundland i. Canada 169 J3
  historically known as Vinland
Newfoundland prov. Canada 165 N4
Newfoundland U.S.A. 177 J4
Newfoundland Evaporation Basin salt l. U.S.A. 183 K1
New Freedom U.S.A. 177 I6
New Galloway U.K. 47 H8
New Georgia i. Solomon Is 145 E2
New Georgia Islands Solomon Is 145 E2
New Georgia Sound sea chan. Solomon Is 145 E2
  also known as The Slot
New Glarus U.S.A. 172 D8
New Glasgow Canada 169 I4
Newgrange Tomb tourist site Rep. of Ireland 47 F10
▶New Guinea i. Indon./P.N.G. 73 J8
  Largest island in Oceania and 2nd in the world.
  oceania [landscapes] ▶▶▶ 136–137
New Halfa Sudan 121 G6
Newhall U.S.A. 182 F7
New Hampshire state U.S.A. 177 N1
New Hanover i. P.N.G. 145 E2
  also known as Lavongai
New Hanover S. Africa 133 O6
New Hartford U.S.A. 177 J2
New Haven CT U.S.A. 177 M4
New Haven IN U.S.A. 173 H9
New Haven WV U.S.A. 173 K8
New Hazelton Canada 166 E4
New Hebrides country S. Pacific Ocean see Vanuatu
New Hogan Reservoir U.S.A. 182 D3
New Holland country Oceania see Australia
New Holstein U.S.A. 172 E7
New Iberia U.S.A. 175 B6
Newington S. Africa 133 P1
New Ireland i. P.N.G. 145 E2
New Jersey state U.S.A. 177 K6
New Kandla India 96 A5
New Kensington U.S.A. 176 F5
New Kent U.S.A. 177 H8
Newkirk U.S.A. 178 C4
New Lanark tourist site U.K. 46 I8
Newland Range hills Australia 151 C6
New Lexington U.S.A. 176 C6
New Lisbon U.S.A. 172 C7
New Liskeard Canada 168 E4

New London CT U.S.A. 177 M4
New London IA U.S.A. 172 B10
New London OH U.S.A. 176 C4
New London WI U.S.A. 172 E6
New Madrid U.S.A. 174 B4
Newman Australia 150 B4
Newman U.S.A. 182 C4
Newman, Mount Australia 150 B4
Newman Island Antarctica 222 O1
Newmarket Canada 168 E4
Newmarket Rep. of Ireland 47 C11
Newmarket U.K. 47 M11
Newmarket U.S.A. 177 O2
New Market TN U.S.A. 176 B9
New Market VA U.S.A. 176 G7
Newmarket-on-Fergus Rep. of Ireland 47 D11
New Martinsville U.S.A. 176 E6
New Meadows U.S.A. 180 C3
New Mexico state U.S.A. 181 F6
New Miami U.S.A. 176 A6
New Milford CT U.S.A. 177 L4
New Milford PA U.S.A. 177 J3
Newnan U.S.A. 175 C5
New Norcia Australia 151 B6
New Norfolk Australia 147 E5
New Orleans U.S.A. 175 B6
New Oxford U.S.A. 177 H5
New Paltz U.S.A. 177 K4
New Paris IN U.S.A. 172 H9
New Paris OH U.S.A. 176 A6
New Philadelphia U.S.A. 176 D5
New Plymouth N.Z. 152 I7
Newport Isle of Wight, England U.K. 47 K13
Newport Newport, Wales U.K. 47 I12
  also known as Casnewydd
Newport AR U.S.A. 174 B5
Newport DE U.S.A. 177 J6
Newport IN U.S.A. 174 C4
Newport ME U.S.A. 177 P1
Newport NH U.S.A. 177 M2
Newport NJ U.S.A. 177 J6
Newport OR U.S.A. 180 A3
Newport PA U.S.A. 177 H5
Newport RI U.S.A. 177 N4
Newport TN U.S.A. 174 D5
Newport VT U.S.A. 177 M1
Newport Beach U.S.A. 182 G8
Newport News U.S.A. 177 I8
New Port Richey U.S.A. 175 D6
New Providence i. Bahamas 186 D1
Newquay U.K. 47 G13
New Richland U.S.A. 174 A3
New Richmond Canada 169 H3
New Richmond U.S.A. 172 A5
New River U.S.A. 183 L8
New Roads U.S.A. 175 B6
New Rockford U.S.A. 178 C2
New Ross Canada 169 H4
New Ross Rep. of Ireland 47 F11
Newry Australia 148 A3
Newry U.K. 47 F9
New Sharon U.S.A. 174 A3
New Siberia Islands Rus. Fed. 39 O2
  also known as Novosibirskiye Ostrova
New Smyrna Beach U.S.A. 175 D6
New South Wales state Australia 147 E3
New Stanton U.S.A. 176 F5
New Tazewell U.S.A. 176 B9
Newton GA U.S.A. 175 C6
Newton IA U.S.A. 174 A3
Newton IL U.S.A. 174 B4
Newton KS U.S.A. 178 C4
Newton MA U.S.A. 177 N3
Newton MS U.S.A. 175 B5
Newton NJ U.S.A. 177 K4
Newton TX U.S.A. 179 D6
Newton Abbot U.K. 47 I13
Newton Falls U.S.A. 177 K1
Newton Stewart U.K. 47 H9
Newtontoppen mt. Svalbard 38 B2
Newtown U.K. 47 I11
  also known as Y Drenewydd
New Town U.S.A. 178 B1
Newtown U.S.A. 177 K5
Newtownabbey U.K. 47 G9
Newtownards U.K. 47 G9
Newtownbutler U.K. 47 E9
Newtownmountkennedy Rep. of Ireland see Bunclody
Newtown St Boswells U.K. 46 J8
Newtownstewart U.K. 47 E9
New Ulm U.S.A. 178 D2
New Vienna U.S.A. 176 B6
Newville U.S.A. 176 H5
New Vineyard U.S.A. 177 O1
New Woodstock U.S.A. 177 J3

Ngarkat Conservation Park nature res. Australia 146 D3
Ngarrab China see Gyaca
Ngaruawahia N.Z. 152 J5
Ngaruroro r. N.Z. 152 K7
Ngatapa N.Z. 152 L6
Ngathainggyaung Myanmar 78 A4
Ngau Mei Hoi b. Hong Kong China see Port Shelter
Ngawa China see Aba
Ngawan Chaung r. Myanmar 79 B5
Ngawi Indon. 77 E4
Ngayok Bay Myanmar 78 A4
Ngcheangel atoll Palau see Kayangel
Ngeaur i. Palau 73 H6
Ngegera Tanz. 129 A6
Ngezi Zimbabwe 131 F4
  formerly known as Ingezi
Nggamea i. Fiji see Qelelevu
Nghabe r. Botswana 130 D4
Ngiap r. Laos 78 C4
Ngilmina Indon. 75 C5
Ngimbang Indon. 77 F4
Ngiva Angola see Ondjiva
Ngo Congo 125 I6
Ngoc Linh mt. Vietnam 79 D5
Ngofakiaha Indon. 75 C2
Ngoin, Co salt l. China 89 E6
Ngoko r. Cameroon/Congo 125 J6
Ngol Bembo Nigeria 125 H4
Ngoma Zambia 127 E8
Ngoma Bridge Botswana 131 E3
Ngoma Tsé-Tsé Congo 126 B5
Ngomba Tanz. 129 B7
Ngome S. Africa 133 P4
Ngong Cameroon 125 I4
Ngongola Angola 127 C8
Ngongotaha N.Z. 152 K6
Ngoqumalma China 89 D5
Ngoring China 86 A1
Ngoring Hu l. China 86 A1
▶Ngorongoro Conservation Area nature res. Tanz. 128 B5
  world [land cover] ▶▶▶ 18–19
Ngorongoro Crater Tanz. 128 B5
Ngoumou Cameroon 125 H5
Ngounié prov. Gabon 126 A5
Ngounié r. Gabon 126 A5
Ngouoni Gabon 126 B5
Ngoura Chad 120 C6
Ngouri Chad 120 C6
Ngourti Niger 125 I3
Ngoutchela weli Chad 120 C5
Ngozi Burundi 126 F5
Ngqeleni S. Africa 133 N8
Nguigmi Niger 125 I3
Nguiu Australia 148 A1
Ngukurr Australia 148 B2
Ngulu atoll Micronesia 73 I5
Ngum, Nam r. Laos 78 C4
Ngundu Zimbabwe 131 F4
Ngunguru Bay N.Z. 152 I3
Ngunju, Tanjung pt Indon. 75 B5
Ngunza Angola see Sumbe
Ngunza-Kabolu Angola see Sumbe
Nguru Nigeria 125 H3
Nguru Mountains Tanz. 129 C6
Nguyên Binh Vietnam 78 D3
Ngwaketse admin. dist. Botswana 131 E5
Ngwako Pan salt pan Botswana 130 D4
Ngwane country Africa see Swaziland
Ngwathe S. Africa 133 L4
Ngwavuma r. Swaziland 133 Q3
  also spelt Ingwavuma
Ngwelezana S. Africa 133 P5
Ngwempisi r. S. Africa 133 P3
Ngwezi r. Zambia 127 E9
Nhamatanda Moz. 131 G3
Nhamundá Brazil 199 G5
Nhamundá r. Brazil 199 G5
N'harea Angola 127 C7
Nha Trang Vietnam 79 E5
Nhecolândia Brazil 201 F4
Nhill Australia 146 D4
Nhlangano Swaziland 133 P4
  formerly known as Goedgegun
Nhlazatshe S. Africa 133 P5
Nhoma Namibia 130 D3
Nho Quan Vietnam 78 D3
Nhulunbuy Australia 148 C2
Nhu Pora Brazil 203 A9
Niabembe Dem. Rep. Congo 126 E5
Niablé Ghana 124 E5
Niacam Canada 167 J4
Niafounké Mali 124 E3
Niagara U.S.A. 172 F5
Niagara Falls Canada 168 E5
Niagara Falls U.S.A. 176 G2
Niagara Falls waterfall Canada/U.S.A. 176 G2
Niagara Falls U.S.A. 176 F2
Niagara-on-the-Lake Canada 173 N7
Niagassola Guinea 124 C4
Niagouelé, Mont du hill Guinea 124 C4
Niagu Aksai Chin 89 B5
Niah Sarawak Malaysia 77 F2
Niakaramandougou Côte d'Ivoire 124 D4
▶Niamey Niger 125 F3
  Capital of Niger.
Niamina Mali 124 D3
Nianbai China see Ledu
Niandan r. Guinea 124 C4
Niandankoro Guinea 124 C4
Niangandu Tanz. 129 C6
Niangara Dem. Rep. Congo 126 E4
Niangay, Lac l. Mali 124 E3
Niangoloko Burkina 124 D4
Niangua r. U.S.A. 178 D4
Niangxi China see Xinshao
Nia-Nia Dem. Rep. Congo 126 E4
Niankorodougou Burkina 124 D4
Niantic U.S.A. 177 M4
Nianzishan China 85 I3
Niari admin. reg. Congo 126 B5
Nias i. Indon. 76 B2
Niassa prov. Moz. 131 H2
Niassa, Lago l. Africa see Nyasa, Lake
Niassa, Reserva do nature res. Moz. 129 C8
Niaur i. Palau see Angaur
Nibil Well Australia 150 D4
Nica Latvia 42 C5
Nicaea Turkey see İznik
▶Nicaragua country Central America 186 B4
  5th largest country in North America.
  northamerica [countries] ▶▶▶ 158–159
Nicaragua, Lago de l. Nicaragua see Nicaragua, Lake
Nicaragua, Lake Nicaragua 186 B5
  also known as Nicaragua, Lago de
Nicaro Cuba 187 E2
Nicastro Italy 57 I10
Nice France 51 N9
  also known as Nizza
Nice U.S.A. 182 B2
Nicephorium Syria see Ar Raqqah
Niceville U.S.A. 175 C6
Nichicun, Lac l. Canada 169 G2
Nichihara Japan see Nichihara
Nichihara Japan 91 B7

Nichinan Japan 91 B9
Nichlaul India 97 D4
Nicholas Channel Bahamas/Cuba 186 C2
Nicholasville U.S.A. 176 B8
Nicholl's Town Bahamas 186 D1
Nichols IA U.S.A. 172 B9
Nichols NY U.S.A. 177 I3
Nicholson Australia 150 E3
Nicholson r. Australia 148 C3
Nicholson Canada 173 J3
Nicholson U.S.A. 177 J4
Nicholson Lake Canada 167 K2
Nicholson Range hills Australia 151 B5
Nicholville U.S.A. 177 K1
Nickol Bay Australia 150 B4
Nicobar Islands India 95 G4
Nicolae Bălcescu Romania 58 J4
Nicolás Bravo Mex. 185 H5
Nicolaus U.S.A. 182 C3
Nicomedia Turkey see Kocaeli
Nico Pérez Uruguay 204 G4
Nicopolis Bulg. see Nikopol
▶Nicosia Cyprus 108 E2
  Capital of Cyprus. Also known as Lefkosia or Lefkoşa.
Nicosia Sicilia Italy 57 G11
Nicotera Italy 57 H10
Nicoya Costa Rica 186 B5
Nicoya, Golfo de b. Costa Rica 186 B5
Nicoya, Península de pen. Costa Rica 186 B5
Nicuadala Moz. 131 H3
Niculiţel Romania 58 J3
Nida Lith. 42 B6
Nida r. Poland 49 R5
Nidadavole India 94 D2
Nidagunda India 94 C2
Nidym Rus. Fed. 39 J3
Nidže mt. Greece/Macedonia 58 C8
Nidzica Poland 49 R2

▶Nile r. Africa 121 F2
  Longest river in the world and in Africa. Also known as Nil, Bahr el.
  world [physical features] ▶▶▶ 8–9
  africa [issues] ▶▶▶ 116–117

longest rivers	river	length	location	page#
	1 ▶ Nile	6 695km / 4 160miles	Africa	121 F2
	2 ▶ Amazon	6 516km / 4 049miles	South America	202 B1
	3 ▶ Yangtze	6 380km / 3 964miles	Asia	87 G2
	4 ▶ Mississippi-Missouri	5 969km / 3 709miles	North America	179 E6
	5 ▶ Ob'-Irtysh	5 568km / 3 459miles	Asia	38 G3
	6 ▶ Yenisey-Angara-Selenga	5 550km / 3 448miles	Asia	39 I2
	7 ▶ Yellow	5 464km / 3 395miles	Asia	85 H4
	8 ▶ Congo	4 667km / 2 900miles	Africa	127 B4
	9 ▶ Rio de la Plata-Paraná	4 500km / 2 796miles	South America	204 F4
	10 ▶ Irtysh	4 440km / 2 759miles	Asia	38 G3

Nidzkie, Jezioro l. Poland 49 S2
Niebüll Germany 48 F1
Nied r. France 51 M3
Niederaula Germany 48 G5
Niederer Fläming park Germany 49 J3
Niedere Tauern mts Austria 49 K8
Niederlausitz reg. Germany 49 K4
Niedersachsen land Germany 48 G3
  English form Lower Saxony
Niedersächsisches Wattenmeer, Nationalpark nat. park Germany 48 D2
Niefang Equat. Guinea 125 H6
Niekerkshoop S. Africa 132 G6
Nielle Côte d'Ivoire 124 D4
Niem Cent. Afr. Rep. 126 B3
Niemba Dem. Rep. Congo 127 F6
Niemegk Germany 49 J3
Niemisel Sweden 44 M2
Niëna Mali 124 D4
Nienburg (Weser) Germany 48 G3
Niëri Ko watercourse Senegal 124 B3
Niers r. Germany 48 D4
Niesky Germany 49 L4
Nietverdiend S. Africa 133 K2
Nieuw Amsterdam Suriname 199 H3
Nieuwe Nickerie Suriname 199 G3
Nieuwoudtville S. Africa 132 D6
Nieuwpoort Belgium 51 I1
Nieves Spain see As Neves
Niğde Turkey 106 C3
Nigel S. Africa 133 M3
▶Niger country Africa 125 G4
  africa [countries] ▶▶▶ 114–117
▶Niger r. Africa 124 G5
  3rd longest river in Africa.
  africa [landscapes] ▶▶▶ 112–113
Niger state Nigeria 125 G4
Niger, Mouths of the Nigeria 125 G5
Niger, Source of the tourist site Guinea 124 C4
▶Nigeria country Africa 125 G4
  Most populous country in Africa and 10th in the world.
  world [population] ▶▶▶ 22–23
  africa [countries] ▶▶▶ 114–117
Nighasan India 96 D3
Nightcaps N.Z. 153 C13
Nighthawk Lake Canada 168 D3
Nigrande Latvia 42 C5
Nigrita Greece 58 E8
Nihing Pak. 101 F4
Nihommatsu Japan see Nihonmatsu
Nihon country Asia see Japan
Nihonmatsu Japan 90 G5
Niigata Japan 90 F6
Niigata pref. Japan 90 F6
Niigata-yake-yama vol. Japan 91 F6
Niihama Japan 91 C8
Niihau i. U.S.A. 181 [inset] Y1
Niikappu Japan 90 H3
Niimi Japan 91 C7
Niitsu Japan 90 F6
Nijar Spain 55 I8
Nijeveen Neth. 48 C3
Nijil, Wadi watercourse Jordan 108 G7
Nijmegen Neth. 48 C4
  also spelt Nimwegen
Nijverdal Neth. 48 D3
Nikaia Greece 59 D10
Nikel' Rus. Fed. 44 O1
Nikel'tau Kazakh. 102 D2
Nikiniki Indon. 75 C5
Nikitinca Kazakh. see Mykolayiv
Nikkaluokta Sweden 44 L2
Nikki Benin 125 F4
Nikko Japan 91 F6
Nikkō National Park Japan 90 F6
Nikola Rus. Fed. 40 H4
Nikolayevo Bulg. 58 G6
Nikolayev Ukr. see Mykolayiv
Nikolayevka Chelyabinskaya Oblast' Rus. Fed. 103 I1
Nikolayevka Khabarovskiy Kray Rus. Fed. 82 D2
Nikolayevka Ul'yanovskaya Oblast' Rus. Fed. 41 H5
Nikolayevo Rus. Fed. 43 K3
Nikolayevsk Rus. Fed. 41 H6
  formerly known as Nikolayevskiy
Nikolayevsk-na-Amure Rus. Fed. 82 F1
Nikol'sk Penzenskaya Oblast' Rus. Fed. 41 H5
  formerly known as Nikol'skaya Pestravka

Nikol'sk Vologod. Obl. Rus. Fed. 40 H4
Nikol'skaya Pestravka Rus. Fed. see Nikol'sk
Nikol'skiy Kazakh. see Satpayev
Nikol'skiy Rus. Fed. 43 P1
Nikol'skiy Torzhok Rus. Fed. 43 T2
Nikol'skoye Kamchatskaya Oblast' Rus. Fed. 39 Q4
Nikol'skoye Lipetskaya Oblast' Rus. Fed. 43 U9
Nikol'skoye Orenburgskaya Oblast' Rus. Fed. 102 C2
Nikol'skoye Vologod. Obl. Rus. Fed. 43 S2
Nikol'skoye Rus. Fed. see Sheksna
Nikopol Bulg. 58 F5
  historically known as Nicopolis
Nikopol' Ukr. 41 E7
Nik Pey Iran 100 B2
Niksar Turkey 107 D2
Nikshahr Iran 101 E5
  also known as Gey
Nikšić Crna Gora Yugo. 56 K6
Nikumaroro i. Kiribati 145 G2
  formerly known as Gardner Island
Nikunau i. Kiribati 145 G2
  also spelt Nukunau; formerly known as Byron Island
Nil, Bahr el r. Africa see Nile
Nila vol. Indon. 75 D4
Nilagiri India 97 E5
Nilakka l. Fin. 44 N3
Nilakkottai India 94 C4
Niland U.S.A. 183 I8
Nilandhoo Atoll Maldives 93 D10
Nilanga India 94 C2
Nilaveli Sri Lanka 94 D4
▶Nile r. Africa 121 F2
  Longest river in the world and in Africa. Also known as Nil, Bahr el.
  world [physical features] ▶▶▶ 8–9
  africa [issues] ▶▶▶ 116–117
Nile state Sudan 121 G5
▶Nile Delta Egypt 108 C6
  world [physical features] ▶▶▶ 8–9
  africa [issues] ▶▶▶ 116–117
Niles MI U.S.A. 172 G9
Niles OH U.S.A. 176 E4
Nileswaram India 94 B3
Nilgiri Hills India 94 C4
Nili r. Eth. 104 D3
Nilka China 88 C3
Nilópolis Brazil 207 J9
Nil Pass Afgh. 101 F3
Nilphamari Bangl. 97 F4
Nilsiä Fin. 44 O3
Niltepec Mex. 185 G5
Nilüfer r. Turkey 59 J8
Nimach India see Neemuch
Nimaj India 96 B4
Niman r. Rus. Fed. 82 D2
Nimba, Monts mts Africa see Nimba Mountains
Nimbahera India 96 B4
  also spelt Nimbhera
Nimbal India 94 B2
Nimba Mountains Africa 124 C5
  also known as Nimba, Monts
Nimberra Well Australia 150 C4
Nimbhera India see Nimbahera
Nimelen r. Rus. Fed. 82 E2
Nîmes France 51 K9
  historically known as Nemausus
Nimka Thana India 96 B4
Nimmitabel Australia 147 E4
Nimos i. Greece 59 I12
Nimpkish r. Canada 166 E5
Nimrod Glacier Antarctica 223 K1
Nimrūz prov. Afgh. 101 E4
Nimu Jammu and Kashmir 96 C2
Nimule Sudan 128 B4
Nimwegen Neth. see Nijmegen
Nina Estonia 42 I3
Ninawá governorate Iraq 107 E4
Ninawa tourist site Iraq see Nineveh
Ninda Angola 127 D8
Nindai Tanz. 129 B7
Nindigully Australia 147 F2
Nine Degree Channel India 94 B4
Nine Mile Lake salt flat Australia 147 D2
Ninemile Peak U.S.A. 183 H2
Ninepin Group is Hong Kong China 87 [inset]
  also known as Kwo Chau Kwan To
Ninety Mile Beach Australia 147 E4
Ninety Mile Beach N.Z. 152 G2
Nineveh tourist site Iraq 107 E4
  also spelt Ninawa
Ninfas, Punta pt Arg. 205 D6
Ningaloo Marine Park nature res. Australia 150 A4
Ning'an China 82 C3
Ningbo China 87 G2
  also known as Yinxian
Ningcheng China 85 H3
  also known as Tianyi
Ningde China 87 F3
Ningdu China 87 E3
  also known as Meijiang
Ning'er China see Pu'er
Ningguo China 87 F2
  also known as Helixi
Ninghai China 87 G2
Ninghe China 85 H4
  also known as Lutai
Ninghsia aut. reg. China see Ningxia Huizu Zizhiqu
Ningi Nigeria 125 H4
Ninging India 97 G3
Ningjin China see Songyuan
Ningjing Shan mts China 86 A2
Ninglang China see Daxing
Ningling China 87 E1
Ningming China 86 C4
  also known as Chengzhong
Ningnan China 86 B3
  also known as Pisha
Ningqiang China 87 D1
Ningshan China 87 D1
Ningsia aut. reg. China see Ningxia Huizu Zizhiqu
Ningxia aut. reg. China see Ningxia Huizu Zizhiqu
▶Ningxia Huizu Zizhiqu aut. reg. China 85 E4
  short form Ningxia; English form Ningsia or Ninghsia Hui Autonomous Region

Ningxian China 85 E5
also known as Xinning
Ningxiang China 87 E2
Ningyang China 85 H5
Ningyuan China 87 D3
Ningzhou China see Huaning
Ninh Binh Vietnam 78 D3
Ninh Hoa Vietnam 79 E5
Ninigo Group *i.* P.N.G. 73 J7
Ninnis Glacier Antarctica 223 J2
Ninnis Glacier Tongue Antarctica 223 K2
Ninohe Japan 90 G4
Ninualac, Canal *sea chan.* Chile 205 B7
Nioaque Brazil 201 E5
Niobrara *r.* U.S.A. 178 C3
Nioghalvfjerdsfjorden *inlet* Greenland 165 R2
Nioki Dem. Rep. Congo 126 C5
Niokolo Koba, Parc National du *nat. park* Senegal 124 B3
Niono Mali 124 C3
Nioro Mali 124 C3
Niort France 50 F6
Nioüt *well* Mauritania 124 D3
Nipa P.N.G. 73 J8
Nipani India 94 B2
Nipanipa, Tanjung *pt* Indon. 75 B3
Nipawin Canada 167 J4
Niphad India 94 B1
Nipigon Canada 168 B3
Nipigon, Lake Canada 168 B3
Nipigon Bay Canada 172 F2
Nipiodi Moz. 131 H3
Nipishish Lake Canada 169 I2
Nipissing Canada 173 N4
Nipissing, Lake Canada 168 E4
Nipomo U.S.A. 182 D6
Nippon *country* Asia see Japan
Nippon Hai *sea* N. Pacific Ocean see Japan, Sea of
Nippur *tourist site* Iraq 107 F4
Niquelândia Brazil 202 B5
Niquero Cuba 186 D2
Nir *Ardabil* Iran 100 A2
Nir *Yazd* Iran 100 C4
Nîr, Jabal an *hills* Saudi Arabia 104 C2
Nira *r.* India 94 B2
Nirasaki Japan 91 F7
Nirji China 85 J1
also known as Morin Dawa
Nirmal India 94 C2
Nirmali India 97 F4
Nirmal Range *hills* India 94 C2
Nirzas *l.* Latvia 42 I5
Niš Srbija Yugo. 58 C5
historically known as Naissus
Nisa Port. 54 D5
Nişab Yemen 105 D5
Nisah, Wādī *watercourse* Saudi Arabia 105 D2
Nišava *r.* Yugo. 58 C5
Niscemi *Sicilia* Italy 57 G11
Niseko Japan 90 G3
Nīshābūr Iran see Neyshābūr
Nishcha *r.* Belarus 43 J6
Nishibetsu-gawa *r.* Japan 90 I3
Nishikawa Japan 90 G5
Nishinomiya Japan 91 D7
Nishino-shima *i.* Japan 91 A8
Nishino-shima *vol.* Japan 81 O7
Nishi-Sonogi-hantō Japan 91 B9
Nishi-suidō *sea chan.* Japan/S. Korea 91 A7
also known as Chōsen-kaikyō
Nishiwaki Japan 91 D7
Nisia Floresta Brazil 202 F3
Nisibis Turkey see Nusaybin
Nisi-mera Japan 91 B8
Nisiros *i.* Greece see Nisyros
Niskanselkä *l.* Fin. 44 N3
Niskayuna U.S.A. 177 L3
Niskibi *r.* Canada 168 B1
Nisko Poland 49 T5
Nisling *r.* Canada 166 B2
Nisporeni Moldova 58 J1
Nissan *r.* Sweden 45 K4
Nisser *l.* Norway 45 I4
Nissum Bredning *b.* Denmark 45 J4
Nistru *r.* Moldova see Dniester
Nistrului Inferior, Cîmpia *lowland* Moldova 58 K1
Nisutlin *r.* Canada 166 C2
Nisyros *i.* Greece 59 I12
also spelt Nisiros
Nita Japan 91 C7
Nitchequon Canada 169 G2
Nitendi *i.* Solomon Is *see* Ndeni
Niterói Brazil 203 D7
Nith *r.* U.K. 47 I8
Niti Pass China 96 C3
Nitmiluk National Park Australia 148 B2
formerly known as Katherine Gorge National Park
Nitra Slovakia 49 P7
Nitra *r.* Slovakia 49 P8
Nitro U.S.A. 176 D7
Nittedal Norway 45 J3
Niuafo'ou *i.* Tonga 145 H3
also spelt Niuafu
Niuafu *i.* Tonga *see* Niuafo'ou
Niuatoputapu *i.* Tonga 145 H3
formerly known as Boscawen Island
Niubiziliang China 84 B4

▶ Niue *terr.* S. Pacific Ocean 145 I3
Self-governing New Zealand Overseas Territory.
oceania [countries] ▶ 138–139

Niujing China *see* Binchuan
Niulakita *i.* Tuvalu 145 G3
formerly known as Nurakita
Niulan Jiang *r.* China 86 B3
Niur, Pulau *i.* Indon. 76 C3
Niushan China *see* Donghai
Niutao *i.* Tuvalu 145 G2
Niuzhuang China 85 I3
Nivala Fin. 44 N3
Nivastroy Rus. Fed. 44 P2
Nive *watercourse* Australia 149 E5
Nive *r.* France 50 E9
Nive Downs Australia 149 E5
Nivelles Belgium 51 K2
Nivnoye Rus. Fed. 43 N8
Nivskiy Rus. Fed. 44 P2
Niwai India 96 B4
Niwari India 96 C4
Niwas India 96 D5
Nixia China *see* Sêrxu
Nixon U.S.A. 182 C4
Niya China *see* Minfeng
Niya He *r.* China 89 C4
Niyut, Gunung *mt.* Indon. 77 E2
Niz Rus. Fed. 43 Q2
Nizamabad India 94 C2
Nizampatnam India 94 D3
Nizam Sagar *l.* India 94 C2
Nizh Aydere Turkm. 102 D5
Nizhegorodskaya Oblast' *admin. div.* Rus. Fed. 40 H4
English form Nizhniy Novgorod Oblast; formerly known as Gor'kovskaya Oblast'
Nizhneangarsk Rus. Fed. 81 H1
Nizhnedevitsk Rus. Fed. 41 F6
Nizhnekamsk Rus. Fed. 40 J4
Nizhnekamskoye Vodokhranilishche *resr* Rus. Fed. 40 J5
Nizhnekolymsk Rus. Fed. 39 O3
Nizhne-Svirskiy Zapovednik *nature res.*

Nizhneudinsk Rus. Fed. 80 F2
Nizhnevartovsk Rus. Fed. 38 H3
Nizhnevolzhsk Rus. Fed. *see* Narimanov
Nizhneyansk Rus. Fed. 39 N2
Nizhniy Irginski Rus. Fed. 102 A2
Nizhniy Chir Rus. Fed. 41 G6
Nizhniye Kresty Rus. Fed. *see* Cherskiy
Nizhniye Ustriki Poland *see* Ustrzyki Dolne
Nizhniy Lomov Rus. Fed. 41 G5
Nizhniy Novgorod Rus. Fed. 40 G4
formerly known as Gor'kiy
Nizhniy Novgorod Oblast *admin. div.* Rus. Fed. *see* Nizhegorodskaya Oblast'
Nizhniy Odes Rus. Fed. 40 J3
Nizhniy Pyandzh Tajik. *see* Panji Poyon
Nizhniy Tagil Rus. Fed. 38 F4
Nizhniy Yenangsk Rus. Fed. 40 H4
Nizhnyaya Mola Rus. Fed. 40 H2
Nizhnyaya Omra Rus. Fed. 40 J3
Nizhnyaya Pesha Rus. Fed. 40 H2
Nizhnyaya Pirenga, Ozero *l.* Rus. Fed. 44 P2
Nizhnyaya Poyma Rus. Fed. 80 F1
Nizhnyaya Suyetka Rus. Fed. 103 I1
Nizhnyaya Tunguska *r.* Rus. Fed. 39 I3
English form Lower Tunguska
Nizhnyaya Tura Rus. Fed. 38 F4
Nizhnyaya Zolotitsa Rus. Fed. 40 G2
Nizhyn Ukr. 41 D6
also spelt Nezhin
Nizina Mazowiecka *reg.* Poland 49 R3
Nizip Turkey 107 D3
Nizkabor''ye Belarus 43 L6
Nízke Beskydy *hills* Slovakia 49 S6
Nízke Tatry *mts* Slovakia 49 Q7
Nízke Tatry *nat. park* Slovakia 49 Q7
Nizmennyy, Mys *pt* Rus. Fed. 90 D3
Nizwá Oman *see* Nazwá
Nizza France *see* Nice
Nizza Monferrato Italy 56 A4
Njallavárri *mt.* Sweden 44 L2
Njavve Sweden 44 L2
Njazidja *i.* Comoros 129 D7
also known as Grande Comore
Njegoš *mts* Yugo. 56 K6
Njellim Fin. 44 N1
Njinjo Tanz. 129 C7
Njombe Tanz. 129 B7
Njombe *r.* Tanz. 129 B6
Njutånger Sweden 45 L3
Nkai Zimbabwe *see* Nkayi
Nkambe Cameroon 125 H5
Nkandla S. Africa 133 P5
Nkasi Tanz. 129 A6
Nkawkaw Ghana 125 E5
Nkayi Zimbabwe 131 F3
formerly spelt Nkai
Nkhaïlé *well* Mauritania 124 D2
Nkhata Bay Malawi 129 B7
Nkhotakota Malawi 129 B8
Nkhotakota Game Reserve *nature res.* Malawi 129 B8
Nkomfap Nigeria 125 H5
Nkomi, Lagune *lag.* Gabon 126 A5
Nkondwe Tanz. 129 A6
Nkongsamba Cameroon 125 H5
Nkoranza Ghana 125 E5
Nkoteng Cameroon 125 I5
Nkululeko S. Africa 133 L7
Nkundi Tanz. 129 A6
Nkungwi Tanz. 129 A6
Nkurenkuru Namibia 130 C3
Nkwalini S. Africa 133 P5
Nkwanta Ghana 125 F4
Nkwenkwezi S. Africa 133 K10
Nmai Hka *r.* Myanmar 78 B2
Noa Dihing *r.* India 97 H4
Noakhali Bangl. 97 F5
Noamundi India 97 E5
Noatak *r.* U.S.A. 164 C3
Noatak National Preserve *nature res.* U.S.A. 164 D3
Nobeoka Japan 91 B8
Noblesville U.S.A. 174 C3
Nobokwe S. Africa 133 L8
Noboribetsu Japan 90 G3
Nobres Brazil 201 F3
Noccundra Australia 147 D1
Noce *r.* Italy 56 D2
Nocera Terinese Italy 57 I9
Nochistlán Mex. 185 E4
Nochixtlán Mex. 185 F5
Noco Italy 57 J8
Nockatunga Australia 147 D1
Nocoleche Nature Reserve Australia 147 E2
Nocona U.S.A. 179 C5
Noda Japan 91 F7
Nodaway *r.* U.S.A. 178 D4
Nodeland Norway 45 I4
Noel Kempff Mercado, Parque Nacional *nat. park* Bol. 201 E3
Noelville Canada 173 M4
Noenieput S. Africa 132 E4
also known as Heroica Nogales
Nogales U.S.A. 181 E7
Nogaro France 50 F9
Nogat *r.* Poland 49 Q1
Nogent-le-Rotrou France 50 G4
Nogent-sur-Oise France 51 I3
Nogent-sur-Seine France 51 J4
Noginsk *Evenkiyskiy Avtonomnyy Okrug* Rus. Fed. 39 J3
Noginsk *Moskovskaya Oblast'* Rus. Fed. 43 T6
Nogliki Rus. Fed. 82 F2
Nogo *r.* Australia 149 F5
Nogoa *r.* Australia 149 F4
Nōgōhaku-san *mt.* Japan 91 E7
Nogoyá Arg. 204 F4
Nohar India 96 B3
Noheji Japan 90 G4
Nohfelden Germany 48 E6
Nohili Point U.S.A. 181 [inset] Y1
Nohur Turkm. *see* Nokhur
Noia Spain 54 C2
also spelt Noya
Noidore *r.* Brazil 206 A1
Noire *r.* Canada 173 N4
Noire, Montagne *mts* France 51 I9
Noire, Pointe *pt* Morocco 55 H9
Noires, Montagnes *hills* France 51 D4
Noirmoutier, Île de *i.* France 50 D6
Noirmoutier-en-l'Île France 50 D5
Nojima-zaki *pt* Japan 91 F7
Nokaneng Botswana 130 D3
Nokesville U.S.A. 176 H7
Nokha India 96 B4
Nokhowch, Küh-e *mt.* Iran 101 E5
Nokhur Turkm. 102 D5
also spelt Nohur
Nokia Fin. 45 M3
Nõkis Uzbek. *see* Nukus
Nok Kundi Pak. 101 F4
Nokomis Canada 167 J5
Nokomis Lake Canada 167 K3
Nokou Chad 120 B6
Nokrek Peak India 97 F4
Nola Cent. Afr. Rep. 126 C4
Nolichucky *r.* U.S.A. 176 B9
Nolinsk Rus. Fed. 40 I4
formerly known as Molotovsk
Noll S. Africa 132 G10
Nólsoy *i.* Faroe Is 46 F1
Noma-misaki *pt* Japan 91 B9
Nomhon China 84 C4
Nomoi Islands Micronesia *see* Mortlock Islands
Nomonde S. Africa 133 K8
Nomo-zaki *pt* Japan 91 A8

Nomto Rus. Fed. 84 E1
Nomuka Tonga 145 H4
Nomzha Rus. Fed. 40 G4
Nonacho Lake Canada 167 I2
Nong'an China 82 B3
Nong Hong Thai. 79 C5
Nonghui China *see* Guang'an
Nong Khai Thai. 78 C4
Nongni *r.* China *see* Nen Jiang
Nongoma S. Africa 133 P4
Nongstoin India 97 F4
Nonni *r.* China *see* Nen Jiang
Nonoava Mex. 184 D3
Nonouti *atoll* Kiribati 145 G2
also known as Nanouki or Nanouti; formerly known as Sydenham
Nonsan S. Korea 83 B5
Nonthaburi Thai. 79 C5
Nontron France 50 G7
Nonwakazi S. Africa 132 I7
Nõo Estonia 42 I3
Nookawarra Australia 151 B5
Nookeyanna Lake *salt flat* Australia 146 C1
Noonamah Australia 148 A2
Noonkanbah Australia 150 D3
Noonkanbah Aboriginal Reserve Australia 150 D3
Noonthorangee Range *hills* Australia 147 D2
Noorama Creek *watercourse* Australia 147 F1
Noordbeveland *i.* Neth. 48 A4
Noordberhaaks *i.* Neth. 48 B3
Noordkaap S. Africa 133 P2
Noordkuil S. Africa 132 C9
Noordoewer Namibia 132 B6
Noordoost Polder Neth. 48 C3
Noordpunt *pt* Neth. Antilles 187 F4
Noormarkku Fin. 45 M3
Noorvik U.S.A. 164 C3
Nootka Island Canada 166 E5
Nóqui Angola 127 B6
Nora *r.* Rus. Fed. 82 C2
Norak Tajik. 101 G2
also spelt Nurek
Norala Phil. 74 C5
Noranda Canada 168 E3
Nor-Bayazet Armenia *see* Kamo
Norberg Sweden 45 L3
Nord *prov.* Cameroon 125 I4
Nord Greenland *see* Station Nord
Nord, Canal du France 48 A5
Nordaustlandet *i.* Svalbard 38 C2
Nordborg Denmark 48 G1
Nordbotn Norway 44 N1
Norddeg Canada 167 G4
Norden Germany 48 E2
Nordenshel'da, Arkhipelag *is* Rus. Fed. 39 J2
English form Nordenskjold Archipelago
Nordenskiold *r.* Canada 166 B2
Nordenskjold Archipelago *is* Rus. Fed. *see* Nordenshel'da, Arkhipelag
Norder Hever *sea chan.* Germany 48 F1
Norderney Germany 48 E2
Norderney *i.* Germany 48 E2
Norderstedt Germany 48 H2
Nordfjord Norway 44 O1
Nordfjord *inlet* Norway 44 I3
Nordfjordeid Norway 45 I3
Nordfold Norway 44 K2
Nordfriesische Inseln *is* Germany *see* North Frisian Islands
Nordhausen Germany 48 H4
Nordholz Germany 48 F1
Nordhorn Germany 48 E3
Nordhuglo Norway 45 I4
Nordingrå naturreservat *nature res.* Sweden 44 L3
Nordkapp *c.* Iceland *see* Horn
Nordkapp *c.* Norway *see* North Cape
Nord-Kivu *prov.* Dem. Rep. Congo 126 F5
Nord-Kvaløy *i.* Norway 44 L1
Nordkynhalvøya *i.* Norway 44 N1
Nordland *county* Norway 44 K2
Nordli Norway 44 K2
Nördliches Harzvorland *park* Germany 48 H4
Nördlingen Germany 48 H7
Nordmaling Sweden 44 L3
Nordmanvik Norway 44 M1
Nord- og Østgrønland, Nationalparken i *nat. park* Greenland 165 P2
Nordstrundingen *c.* Greenland *see* Northeast Foreland
Nord-Ostsee-Kanal *canal* Germany *see* Kiel Canal
Nord-Ouest *prov.* Cameroon 125 H5
Nord - Pas-de-Calais *admin. reg.* France 51 I2
Nord-Pas-de-Calais, Parc Naturel Régional du *nature res.* France 51 J2
Nordre Strømfjord *inlet* Greenland *see* Nassuttooq
Nordrhein-Westfalen *land* Germany 48 E4
English form North Rhine - Westphalia
Nordstrand *i.* Germany 48 F1
Nord-Trøndelag *county* Norway 44 K2
Norðurland eystra *constituency* Iceland 44 [inset] C2
Norðurland vestra *constituency* Iceland 44 [inset] B2
Nordvik *r.* Rus. Fed. 39 L2
Nordvika Norway 44 J3
Nore *r.* Rep. of Ireland 47 F11
Nore, Pic de *mt.* France 51 I9
Noreg *country* Europe *see* Norway
Noreikiškės Lith. 42 E7
Noresund Norway 45 J3
Norfolk *NE* U.S.A. 178 C3
Norfolk *NY* U.S.A. 177 K1
Norfolk *VA* U.S.A. 177 I8

▶ Norfolk Island *terr.* S. Pacific Ocean 145 G4
Australian External Territory.
oceania [countries] ▶ 138–139

Norfork Lake U.S.A. 179 D4
Norge *country* Europe *see* Norway
Norheimsund Norway 45 I3
Noria Chile 200 C5
Norikura-dake *vol.* Japan 91 E6
Noril'sk Rus. Fed. 39 I3
Norkyung China *see* Bainang
Norland Canada 173 O6
Norma *r.* Australia 149 D3
Normal U.S.A. 174 B3
Norman *r.* Australia 149 D3
Norman U.S.A. 179 C5
Norman, Lake *resr* U.S.A. 174 D5
Normanby *r.* Australia 149 E2
Normanby N.Z. 152 I7
Normanby Island P.N.G. 145 E2
Normandes, Îles *is* English Chan. *see* Channel Islands
Normandia Brazil 199 G4
Normandie *reg.* France *see* Normandy
Normandie, Collines de *hills* France 50 F4
Normandie-Maine, Parc Naturel Régional *nature res.* France 50 F4
Normandien S. Africa 133 N4
Normandy *reg.* France 50 F4
also spelt Normandie
Normanton Australia 149 D3
Norman Wells Canada 166 E1
Normétal Canada 173 N2
Noro Solomon Is 145 E2
Norogachic Mex. 184 D3
Norquay Canada 167 K5
Norquinco Arg. 205 C6

▶ North Island *c.* N.Z. 152 H6
3rd largest island in Oceania.
oceania [landscapes] ▶ 136–137

Norra Nebel Denmark 45 J5
Norrent-Fontes France 51 I2
Norrfjärden Sweden 44 M2
Norrhult-Klavreström Sweden 45 K4
Norris U.S.A. 180 E3
Norris Lake U.S.A. 176 B9
Norristown U.S.A. 177 J5
Norrköping Sweden 45 L4
Norrsundet Sweden 45 L3
Norrtälje Sweden 45 L4
Norseman Australia 151 C7
Norsewood N.Z. 152 K8
Norsjö Sweden 44 L2
Norsk Rus. Fed. 82 C1
Norske Øer *is* Greenland 165 R2
Norte, Punta *pt* Buenos Aires Arg. 204 F5
Norte, Punta *pt* Arg. 205 C8
Norte, Punta *pt* Arg. 205 E6
Norte, Serra do *hills* Brazil 201 F3
Norte de Santander *dept* Col. 198 C2
Nortelândia Brazil 201 F3
North, Cape Antarctica 223 I2
North, Cape Canada 169 I4
Northallerton U.K. 47 K9
Northam S. Africa 133 L1
Northam Australia 151 A6
Northampton MA U.S.A. 177 M3
Northampton U.K. 47 L11
Northampton PA U.S.A. 177 J5
Northampton Downs Australia 149 E5
North Andaman *i.* India 95 G3
North Anna *r.* U.S.A. 176 H8
North Anson U.S.A. 177 P1
North Arm *b.* Canada 167 H2
North Balabac Strait Phil. 74 A4
North Baltimore U.S.A. 176 B4
North Battleford Canada 167 I4
North Bay Canada 168 E4
North Bend U.S.A. 180 A4
North Bend PA U.S.A. 176 H4
North Bennington U.S.A. 177 L3
North Berwick U.K. 46 J7
North Berwick U.S.A. 177 O2
North Borneo *state* Malaysia *see* Sabah
North Bosque *r.* U.S.A. 179 C6
North Branch MI U.S.A. 173 J7
North Branch MN U.S.A. 172 A5
North Caicos *i.* Turks and Caicos Is 187 F2
North Canadian *r.* U.S.A. 179 C5
North Cape Canada 169 H4
North Cape Norway 44 N1
also known as Nordkapp
North Cape N.Z. 152 H2
North Caribou Lake Canada 168 B2
North Carolina *state* U.S.A. 176 F9
North Cascades National Park U.S.A. 180 B2
North Central Aboriginal Reserve Australia 150 D4
North Channel *lake channel* Canada 168 D4
North Channel *str.* Northern Ireland/Scotland U.K. 47 G9
North Charleston U.S.A. 175 E5
North Cheyenne Indian Reservation *res.* U.S.A. 180 F3
Northcliffe Australia 151 B7
Northcliffe Glacier Antarctica 223 G2
North Collins U.S.A. 176 G3
North Concho *r.* U.S.A. 179 B6
North Conway U.S.A. 177 N1
North Cowichan Canada 166 F5
North Creek U.S.A. 177 L2
North Dakota *state* U.S.A. 178 B2
North Downs *hills* U.K. 47 L12
North East *r.* Phil. 74 B5
North East U.S.A. 176 F3
North East Cay *reef* Australia 149 G4
North-Eastern *prov.* Kenya 128 D4

▶ Northeast Foreland *c.* Greenland 165 R1
Most easterly point of North America. Also known as Nordostrundingen.

North-East Frontier Agency *state* India *see* Arunachal Pradesh
Northeast Point Bahamas 175 F8
Northeast Providence Channel Bahamas 186 D1
North Edwards U.S.A. 182 G6
North End Point Bahamas 175 F7
Northeim Germany 48 G4
Northern *admin. reg.* Ghana 125 E4
Northern *prov.* S. Africa 133 M1
formerly known as Northern Transvaal
Northern *prov.* Sierra Leone 124 C4
Northern *state* Sudan 121 F4
Northern *prov.* Zambia 127 F7
Northern Aegean *admin. reg.* Greece *see* Voreio Aigaio
Northern Areas *admin. div.* Pak. 101 H2
Northern Bahr el Ghazal *state* Sudan 126 E2
Northern Cape *prov.* S. Africa 132 D6
Northern Darfur *state* Sudan 121 E6
Northern Donets *r.* Rus. Fed./Ukr. *see* Severskiy Donets
Northern Dvina *r.* Rus. Fed. *see* Severnaya Dvina
Northern Indian Lake Canada 167 L3
Northern Ireland *prov.* U.K. 47 F9
Northern Kordofan *state* Sudan 121 F6
Northern Light Lake Canada 168 B3

▶ Northern Mariana Islands *terr.* N. Pacific Ocean 73 J3
United States Commonwealth. Historically known as Ladrones.
oceania [countries] ▶ 138–139

Northern Rhodesia *country* Africa *see* Zambia
Northern Sporades *is* Greece *see* Voreioi Sporades
Northern Territory *admin. div.* Australia 148 B3
Northern Transvaal *prov.* S. Africa *see* Northern
North Fabius *r.* U.S.A. 174 B4
Northfield MA U.S.A. 177 M3
Northfield MN U.S.A. 174 A2
Northfield VT U.S.A. 177 M1
North Fiji Basin *sea feature* 156 H7
North Foreland *c.* U.K. 47 N12
North Fork U.S.A. 182 E4
North Fork Pass Canada 166 B1
North French *r.* Canada 168 D3
North Frisian Islands Germany 44 D1
also known as Nordfriesische Inseln
North Geomagnetic Pole Arctic Ocean 224 T1
North Haven U.S.A. 177 M4
North Head *r.* N.Z. 152 I4
North Henik Lake Canada 167 L2
North Highlands U.S.A. 182 C3
North Horr Kenya 128 C4
North Hudson U.S.A. 177 L2

▶ North Island *i.* N.Z. 152 H6
2nd largest island in Oceania.
oceania [landscapes] ▶ 136–137

North Island Phil. 74 B1
North Islet *reef* Phil. 74 B4
North Jadito Canyon *gorge* U.S.A. 183 N6
North Judson U.S.A. 172 G9
North Kazakhstan Oblast *admin. div.* Kazakh. *see* Severnyy Kazakhstan
North Kingsville U.S.A. 176 E4
North Knife *r.* Canada 167 M3
North Knife Lake Canada 167 M3
North Koel *r.* India 97 D4
North Komelik U.S.A. 183 M9

▶ North Korea *country* Asia 83 B4
asia [countries] ▶ 64–67

North Lakhimpur India 97 G4
Northland *admin. div.* N.Z. 152 I3
also known as Severnaya Zemlya
Northland Forest Park *nature res.* N.Z. 152 I3
North Las Vegas U.S.A. 183 I5
North Liberty U.S.A. 172 G9
North Little Rock U.S.A. 179 D5
North Loup *r.* U.S.A. 178 C3
North Luangwa National Park Zambia 129 B7
North Maalhosmadulu Atoll Maldives 94 B5
North Macmillan *r.* Canada 166 C2
North Magnetic Pole Canada 224 R1
North Mam Peak U.S.A. 180 F5
North Manchester U.S.A. 172 H10
North Moose Lake Canada 167 K4
North Muiron Island Australia 150 A4
North Nahanni *r.* Canada 166 F2
North Ossetia *aut. rep.* Rus. Fed. *see* Severnaya Osetiya-Alaniya, Respublika
North Palisade *mt.* U.S.A. 182 F4
North Platte U.S.A. 178 B3
North Platte *r.* U.S.A. 178 B3
North Point Australia 151 A6
North Point Hong Kong China 87 [inset] also known as Tsat Tsze Mui
North Pole Arctic Ocean 224 A1
Northport U.S.A. 175 C5
North Port U.S.A. 175 D7
North Reef Island India 95 G3
North Rhine - Westphalia *land* Germany *see* Nordrhein-Westfalen
North River Bridge Canada 169 I4
North Rona *i.* U.K. *see* Rona
North Ronaldsay *i.* U.K. 46 J4
North Saskatchewan *r.* Canada 167 J4
North Schell Peak U.S.A. 183 I2
North Sea Europe 46 N6
North Seal *r.* Canada 167 L3
North Sentinel Island India 95 G4
North Shoal Lake Canada 167 L5
North Shoshone Peak U.S.A. 183 G2
North Siberian Lowland Rus. Fed. 39 K2
also known as Severo-Sibirskaya Nizmennost'
North Simlipal National Park India 97 E5
North Sinai *governorate* Egypt *see* Shamāl Sīnā'
North Slope *plain* U.S.A. 164 E3
North Spirit Lake Canada 167 M4
North Stradbroke Island Australia 147 G1
North Stratford U.S.A. 177 N1
North Taranaki Bight *b.* N.Z. 152 I6
North Thompson *r.* Canada 166 G4
North Tonawanda U.S.A. 176 G3
North Trap *reef* N.Z. 153 B15
North Troy U.S.A. 177 M1
North Truro U.S.A. 177 O4
North Tuas Basin *dock* Sing. 76 [inset]
North Twin Island Canada 168 D2
North Twin Lake Canada 169 K3
North Ubian *i.* Phil. 74 B5
North Uist *i.* U.K. 46 E6
also known as Uibhist a' Tuath
Northumberland Isles Australia 149 F4
Northumberland National Park U.K. 46 J8
Northumberland Strait Canada 169 H4
North Umpqua *r.* U.S.A. 180 B4
North Vancouver Canada 166 F5
Northville U.S.A. 177 K2
North Wabasca Lake Canada 167 H3
North Walsham U.K. 47 N11
North Waterford U.S.A. 177 O1
North West *r.* S. Africa 133 J4
North West Cape Australia 150 A4
North-Western *prov.* Zambia 127 D8
North West Frontier *prov.* Pak. 101 G3
North West Nelson Forest Park *nat. park* N.Z. *see* Kahurangi National Park
Northwest Providence Channel Bahamas 186 D1
North West River Canada 169 J2
Northwest Territories *admin. div.* Canada 167 J2
North Wilkesboro U.S.A. 176 D9
North Windham U.S.A. 177 O2
Northwood IA U.S.A. 174 A3
Northwood ND U.S.A. 178 C2
Northwood NH U.S.A. 177 N2
Northwoods Beach U.S.A. 172 B5
North York Canada 173 N7
North York Moors *moorland* U.K. 47 L9
North York Moors National Park U.K. 47 L9
Norton Canada 169 H4
Norton KS U.S.A. 178 C4
Norton VT U.S.A. 174 D7
Norton de Matos Angola *see* Balombo
Norton Shores U.S.A. 172 G7
Norton Sound *sea chan.* U.S.A. 164 C3
Nortorf Germany 48 G1
Nort-sur-Erdre France 50 E5
Norvegia, Cape Antarctica 223 X2
Norwalk CT U.S.A. 177 L4
Norwalk WI U.S.A. 172 C7

▶ Norway *country* Europe 45 J3
known as Norge or Noreg in Norwegian
europe [countries] ▶ 32–35

Norway U.S.A. 177 O1
Norway Bay Canada 173 Q5
Norway House Canada 167 L4
Norwegian Bay Canada 165 J2
Norwegian Sea N. Atlantic Ocean 224 A2
Norwich Canada 173 M8
Norwich U.K. 47 N11
Norwich CT U.S.A. 177 M4
Norwich NY U.S.A. 177 H3
Norwood MA U.S.A. 177 N3
Norwood NY U.S.A. 177 K1
Norwood OH U.S.A. 176 A6
Norzagaray Phil. 74 B3
Nose Lake Canada 167 I1
Noshappu-misaki *hd* Japan 90 G2
Noshiro Japan 90 G4
Noshul' Rus. Fed. 40 I3
Nosivka Ukr. 41 D6
also known Nosovka
Nosop *watercourse* Africa *see* Nossob
Nosovaya Rus. Fed. 40 J1
Nosovka Ukr. *see* Nosivka
Noşratābād Iran 101 D4
Nossa Senhora da Glória Brazil 202 E4
Nossa Senhora do Livramento Brazil 201 F3
Nossen Germany 49 K4
Nossob *watercourse* Africa 132 E3
also known as Nossob
North Frisian Islands Germany 44 D1
also known as Nordfriesische Inseln
Nossob Camp S. Africa 132 E2
Nosy Varika Madag. 131 [inset] J4
Nota *r.* Fin./Rus. Fed. 44 O2
Notakwanon *r.* Canada 169 I2
Notch Peak U.S.A. 183 K2
Noteć *r.* Poland 49 M3
Notikewin *r.* Canada 166 G3

North Island Phil. 74 B1
North Islet *reef* Phil. 74 B4
Notio Aigaio *admin. reg.* Greece 59 H12
English form Southern Aegean; also spelt Nótion Aiyaíon
Nótion Aiyaíon *admin. reg.* Greece *see* Notio Aigaio
Notio Aigaio
Notios Evvoikos Kolpos *sea chan.* Greece 59 E10
Notio Steno Kerkyras *sea chan.* Greece 59 B9
Noto *Sicilia* Italy 57 H12
Noto Japan 90 E6
Noto, Golfo di *g. Sicilia* Italy 57 H12
Notodden Norway 45 J4
Noto-hantō *pen.* Japan 90 E6
Notre Dame, Monts *mts* Canada 169 G4
Notre Dame Bay Canada 169 K3
Notre-Dame-de-Koartac Canada *see* Quartaq
Notre-Dame-de-la-Salette Canada 173 R5
Notre-Dame-du-Laus Canada 173 R4
Notre-Dame-du-Nord Canada 173 N3
Notsé Togo 125 F5
Notsu Japan 91 C9
Notsuke-saki *pt* Japan 90 I3
Notsuke-suidō *sea chan.* Japan/Rus. Fed. 90 I3
Nottawasaga Bay Canada 173 M6
Nottaway *r.* Canada 168 E3
Nottingham U.K. 47 K11
Nottingham Island Canada 165 L3
Nottingham Road S. Africa 133 O6
Nottoway U.S.A. 176 G8
Nottoway *r.* U.S.A. 176 H9
Notukeu Creek *r.* Canada 167 J5
Nouâdhibou Mauritania 122 A5
formerly known as Port Étienne
Nouâdhibou, Râs *c.* Mauritania 122 A5
Nouakchott Mauritania 124 D2
Capital of Mauritania.

Noual *well* Mauritania 124 D2
Nouâmghâr Mauritania 124 A2
Nouei Vietnam 79 D5
Nouméa New Caledonia 145 G4
Capital of New Caledonia.

Noun *r.* Cameroon 125 H5
Nouna Burkina 124 E3
Noupoort S. Africa 133 I8
Nousu Fin. 44 O2
Nouveau-Comptoir Canada *see* Wemindji
Nouvelle Anvers Dem. Rep. Congo *see* Makanza
Nouvelle Calédonie *i.* S. Pacific Ocean 145 F4
also known as New Caledonia
Nouvelle Calédonie *terr.* S. Pacific Ocean *see* New Caledonia
Nouvelles Hébrides *country* S. Pacific Ocean *see* Vanuatu
Nov Tajik. 101 G1
also spelt Nau
Nõva Estonia 42 E2
Nova Almeida Brazil 207 M7
Nova América Brazil 206 D2
Nova Aurora Brazil 206 D2
Novabad Tajik. *see* Novobod
Novabad Tajik. *see* Novobod
Nova Baña Czech Rep. 49 P7
Nova Chaves Angola *see* Muconda
Novaci Romania 58 E3
Nova Crnja *Vojvodina, Srbija* Yugo. 58 B3
Nova Cruz Brazil 202 F3
Era Brazil 207 J6
Nova Esperança Angola *see* Buengas
Nova Esperança Brazil 206 A10
Nova Freixa Moz. *see* Cuamba
Nova Friburgo Brazil 203 D7
Nova Gaia Angola *see* Cambundi-Catembo
Nova Goa India *see* Panaji
Nova Gorica Slovenia 56 F3
Nova Gradiška Croatia 56 J3
Nova Granada Brazil 206 D7
Nova Iguaçu Brazil 203 D7
Nova Kakhovka Ukr. 41 E7
Nova Lima Brazil 203 D6
Nova Londrina Brazil 206 A9
Novalukoml' Belarus 43 K7
also spelt Novolukoml'
Nova Mambone Moz. 131 G4
Nova Nabúri Moz. 131 H3
Nova Odesa Ukr. 41 D7
also spelt Novaya Odessa
Nová Paka Czech Rep. 49 M5
Nova Paraiso Brazil 199 F4
Nova Pazova *Vojvodina, Srbija* Yugo. 58 B4
Nova Pilão Arcado Brazil 202 D4
Nova Ponte Brazil 206 E6
Nova Ponte, Represa *resr* Minas Gerais Brazil 207 H5
Nova Ponte, Represa *resr* Brazil 203 C6
Novara Italy 56 A3
Nova Remanso Brazil 202 D4
Nova Resende Brazil 206 G8
Nova Russas Brazil 202 D3
Nova Scotia *prov.* Canada 169 H4
historically known as Acadia
Nova Sento Sé Brazil 202 D4
Nova Serrana Brazil 207 I6
Nova Sintra Angola *see* Catabola
Nova Soure Brazil 202 E4
Nova Mezzola Italy 56 B2
Novato U.S.A. 182 B3
Nova Topola Bos.-Herz. 56 J3
Novator Rus. Fed. 40 I3
Nova Vanduzi Moz. 131 G3
Nova Varoš *Srbija* Yugo. 58 A5
Nova Venécia Brazil 207 M6
Nova Viçosa Brazil 207 N4
Nova Vida *Amazonas* Brazil 199 E5
Nova Vida *Rondônia* Brazil 201 E2
Nova Xavantino Brazil 206 A1
Novaya Kakhovka Ukr. *see* Nova Kakhovka
Novaya Kazanka Kazakh. 102 B2
also known as Zhanga Qazan
Novaya Ladoga Rus. Fed. 43 N1
Novaya Odessa Ukr. *see* Nova Odesa
Novaya Pismyanka Rus. Fed. *see* Leninogorsk
Novaya Sibir', Ostrov *i.* Rus. Fed. 39 O2

▶ Novaya Zemlya *is* Rus. Fed. 40 J1
3rd largest island in Europe.
europe [landscapes] ▶ 30–31
arctic [features] ▶ 214–215

Novaya Zhizn Rus. Fed. *see* Kazinka
Nova Zagora Bulg. 58 H6
Novelda Spain 55 K6
Novellara Italy 56 C4
Nové Město nad Metují Czech Rep. 49 N5
Nové Mlýny, Vodní nádrž *l.* Czech Rep. 49 N7
Nové Zámky Slovakia 49 P8
Novgorod Rus. Fed. *see* Velikiy Novgorod
Novgorodka Rus. Fed. 43 K4
Novgorod Oblast *admin. div.* Rus. Fed. *see* Novgorodskaya Oblast'
Novgorod-Severskiy Ukr. *see* Novhorod-Sivers'kyy
Novgorodskaya Oblast' *admin. div.* Rus. Fed. 43 N3
English form Novgorod Oblast
Novhorod-Sivers'kyy Ukr. 43 P9
also spelt Novgorod-Severskiy
Novhorodka Ukr. 41 D6
also spelt Novgorodka
Novhorod-Volyns'kyy Ukr. *see* Suvorovo

index N O

Novhorod-Sivers'kyy Ukr. 41 E6 *also spelt* Novgorod-Severskiy
Novi U.S.A. 173 J8
Novi Bečej *Vojvodina, Srbija* Yugo. 58 B3
Novichikha Rus. Fed. 103 J1
Novi Grad Bos.-Herz. *see* Bosanski Novi
Novi Iskŭr Bulg. 58 E6
Novikovo Rus. Fed. 82 F3
Novi Kozarci *Vojvodina, Srbija* Yugo. 58 B3
Novi Kritsim Bulg. *see* Stamboliyski
Novi Ligure Italy 56 A4
Novillero Mex. 184 D4
Novi Marof Croatia 56 I2
Novi Pazar Bulg. 58 I5
Novi Pazar *Srbija* Yugo. 58 B5
Novi Sad *Vojvodina, Srbija* Yugo. 58 A3 *also known as* Újvidék
Novi Travnik Bos.-Herz. 56 J4 *formerly known as* Pucarevo
Novi Vinodolski Croatia 56 G3
Novlenskoye Rus. Fed. 43 U2
Novoaleksandropov Rus. Fed. 82 F3
Novoaleksandrovsk Rus. Fed. 41 G7
Novoaleksandrovskiy Rus. Fed. 43 P7
Novoalekseyevka Kazakh. *see* Khobda
Novoaltaysk Rus. Fed. 80 C2 *formerly known as* Chesnokovka
Novoanninskiy Rus. Fed. 41 G6
Novo Aripuanã Brazil 199 F6
Novoazovs'k Ukr. 41 F7
Novo Beograd *Srbija* Yugo. 58 B4
Novobod Tajik. 101 G2 *also spelt* Novabad
Novobod Tajik. 101 G2 *also spelt* Navabad; *formerly known as* Shul'mak; *formerly spelt* Novabad
Novobogatīnsk Kazakh. *see* Novobogatinskoye
Novobogatinskoye Kazakh. 102 B3 *also known as* Novobogatīnsk
Novobureyskiy Rus. Fed. 82 C2 *formerly known as* Bureya-Pristan'
Novocheboksarsk Rus. Fed. 40 H4
Novocherkassk Rus. Fed. 41 G7
Novo Cruzeiro Brazil 203 D6
Novodolinka Kazakh. 103 H2
Novodugino Rus. Fed. 43 P6
Novodvinsk Rus. Fed. 40 G2 *formerly known as* Pervomayskiy
Novogeorgiyevka Rus. Fed. 82 B2
Novognezdilovo Rus. Fed. 43 Q9
Novogrudok Belarus *see* Navahrudak
Novogurovskiy Rus. Fed. 43 S7
Novo Hamburgo Brazil 203 B9
Novo Horizonte Brazil 206 D8
Novohrad-Volyns'kyy Ukr. 41 C6 *also spelt* Novgorod-Volynskiy
Novoil'insk Rus. Fed. 85 F1
Novokazalinsk Kazakh. *see* Ayteke Bi
Novokhopersk Rus. Fed. 41 G6
Novokhovansk Rus. Fed. 43 K6
Novokiyevskiy Uval Rus. Fed. 82 C2
Novokizhinginsk Rus. Fed. 85 F1
Novokubansk Rus. Fed. 107 E1 *formerly known as* Novokubanskiy
Novokubanskiy Rus. Fed. *see* Novokubansk
Novokuybyshevsk Rus. Fed. 102 B1
Novokuznetsk Rus. Fed. 80 D2 *formerly known as* Stalinsk
Novolazarevskaya *research station* Antarctica 223 A2
Novolukoml' Belarus *see* Novalukoml'
Novol'vovsk Rus. Fed. 43 T8
Novo Marapi Brazil 199 E5
Novomarkovka Kazakh. 103 H2
Novo Mesto Slovenia 56 H3
Novomichurinsk Rus. Fed. 43 U7
Novomikhaylovskiy Rus. Fed. 41 F7
Novo Miloševo *Vojvodina, Srbija* Yugo. 58 B3
Novomirgorod Ukr. *see* Novomyrhorod
Novomoskovsk Rus. Fed. 43 T7 *formerly known as* Bobriki *or* Stalinogorsk
Novomoskovs'k Ukr. 41 E6
Novomyrhorod Ukr. 41 D6 *also spelt* Novomirgorod
Novonazyvayevka Rus. Fed. *see* Nazyvayevsk
Novonikolayevka Kazakh. 103 G4
Novonikolayevsk Rus. Fed. *see* Novosibirsk
Novonikolayevskiy Rus. Fed. 41 G6
Novooleksiyivka Ukr. 41 E7
Novo Olinda do Norte Brazil 199 G5
Novo Oriente Brazil 202 D3
Novoorsk Rus. Fed. 102 D2
Novo Parnarama Brazil 202 D3
Novopashiyskiy Rus. Fed. *see* Gornozavodsk
Novopavlovka Rus. Fed. 85 F1
Novopokrovka *Kustanayskaya Oblast'* Kazakh. 103 F1
Novopokrovka *Severnyy Kazakhstan* Kazakh. 103 F1
Novopokrovka *Vostochnyy Kazakhstan* Kazakh. 103 J2
Novopokrovka Rus. Fed. 82 D3
Novopokrovskaya Rus. Fed. 41 G7
Novopolotsk Belarus *see* Navapolatsk
Novopolyan'ye Rus. Fed. 43 U8
Novopskov Ukr. 41 F6
Novo Redondo Angola *see* Sumbe
Novorepnoye Rus. Fed. 102 B2
Novorossiysk Rus. Fed. 41 F7
Novorossiyskiy Kazakh. *see* Novorossiyskoye
Novorossiyskoye Kazakh. 102 D2 *formerly known as* Novorossiyskiy
Novorybnaya Rus. Fed. 39 K2
Novorzhev Rus. Fed. 43 K4
Novoselki *Moskovskaya Oblast'* Rus. Fed. 43 T7
Novoselki *Tverskaya Oblast'* Rus. Fed. 43 M6
Novoselovo Rus. Fed. 43 U5
Novoselskoye Rus. Fed. *see* Achkhoy-Martan
Novosel'ye Rus. Fed. 43 J3
Novosergiyevka Rus. Fed. 102 C1
Novoshakhtinsk Rus. Fed. 41 F7
Novoshakhtinskiy Rus. Fed. 82 D3
Novosheshminsk Rus. Fed. 40 I5
Novosibirsk Rus. Fed. 80 C1 *formerly known as* Novonikolayevsk
Novosibirskaya Oblast' *admin. div.* Rus. Fed. 80 C1 *English form* Novosibirsk Oblast
Novosibirskiye Ostrova *is* Rus. Fed. *see* New Siberia Islands
Novosibirsk Oblast *admin. div.* Rus. Fed. *see* Novosibirskaya Oblast'
Novosil' Rus. Fed. 43 S9
Novosokol'niki Rus. Fed. 43 L5
Novospasskoye Rus. Fed. 41 H5
Novotroitsk Rus. Fed. 102 D2
Novotroitskoye Kazakh. *see* Tole Bi
Novotroitskoye Rus. Fed. 43 O8
Novotroyits'ke Ukr. 41 E7
Novoukrainka Ukr. *see* Novoukrayinka
Novoukrayinka Ukr. 41 D6 *also spelt* Novoukrainka
Novoural'sk Rus. Fed. 102 D2
Novouzensk Rus. Fed. 102 B2
Novovasylivka Ukr. 43 O9
Novovolyns'k Ukr. 41 C6
Novovoronezh Rus. Fed. 41 F6 *formerly known as* Novovoronezhskiy
Novovoronezhskiy Rus. Fed. *see* Novovoronezh
Novo-Voskresenovka Rus. Fed. 82 B1
Novovoznesenovka Kyrg. 103 I4
Novoyamskoye Rus. Fed. 43 P9
Novoye Dubovoye Rus. Fed. 43 U9
Novoyegor'yevskoye Rus. Fed. 103 J2
Novoye Leushino Rus. Fed. 43 V5
Novozavidovskiy Rus. Fed. 43 R5
Novozhilovskaya Rus. Fed. 40 I2
Novozybkov Rus. Fed. 43 M9
Novska Croatia 56 I3
Novy Boletsk Belarus 43 L6
Nový Bor Czech Rep. 49 L5
Novy Bykhaw Belarus 43 L8
Novy Dvor Belarus 42 F9
Nový Jičín Czech Rep. 49 O6
Novyya Kruki Belarus 42 I6
Novyya Zhuravichy Belarus 43 L8
Novyy Bor Rus. Fed. 40 J2
Novyye Burasy Rus. Fed. 102 A1
Novyye Ivaytenki Rus. Fed. 43 O9
Novyye Petushki Rus. Fed. *see* Petushki
Novyy Izborsk Rus. Fed. 42 I4
Novyy Kholmogory Rus. Fed. *see* Archangel
Novyy Margelan Uzbek. *see* Fergana
Novyy Nekouz Rus. Fed. 43 T4
Novyy Oskol Rus. Fed. 41 F6
Novyy Port Rus. Fed. 38 H3
Novyy Ropsk Rus. Fed. 43 N9
Novyy Sinets Rus. Fed. 43 R8
Novyy Urengoy Rus. Fed. 38 H3
Novyy Urgal Rus. Fed. 82 D2 *formerly known as* Raz"yezd 3km
Novyy Uzen' Kazakh. *see* Zhanaozen
Novyy Zay Rus. Fed. 40 J5
Now Iran 100 C4
Nowa Dęba Poland 49 S5
Nowa Ruda Poland 49 N5
Nowa Sarzyna Poland 49 T5
Nowa Sól Poland 49 M4
Nowata U.S.A. 178 D4
Now Dezh Iran 100 B3
Nowdī Iran 100 B2
Nowe Poland 49 P2
Nowe Miasteczko Poland 49 M4
Nowe Miasto Lubawskie Poland 49 Q2
Nowe Miasto nad Pilicą Poland 49 R4
Nowe Skalmierzyce Poland 49 O4
Now Gombad Iran 100 C3
Nowgong India *see* Nagaon
Nowgong India 96 C4
Now Kharegan Iran 100 C2
Nowleye Lake Canada 167 K2
Nowogard Poland 49 M2
Nowogród Poland 49 S2
Nowogród Bobrzański Poland 49 M4
Nowood *r.* U.S.A. 180 F3
Noworadomsk Poland *see* Radomsko
Nowra Australia 147 F3
Nowshahr Iran 100 B2
Now Shahr Iran 100 B2
Nowshera Pak. 101 H3
Nowsūd Iran 100 A3
Nowy Dwór Gdański Poland 49 Q1
Nowy Dwór Mazowiecki Poland 49 R3
Nowy Sącz Poland 49 R6 *historically known as* Neu Sandez
Nowy Staw Poland 49 Q1
Nowy Targ Poland 49 R6
Nowy Tomyśl Poland 49 N3
Noxen U.S.A. 177 I4
Noxubee National Wildlife Refuge *nature res.* U.S.A. 175 B5
Noy, Xé *r.* Laos 78 D4
Noy, Xé *r.* Laos 78 D4
Noya Spain *see* Noia
Noyabr'sk Rus. Fed. 38 H3
Noyant France 50 G5
Noyes Island U.S.A. 166 C4
Noyil *r.* India 94 C4
Noyon France 51 I3
Nozay France 50 E5
Nozizwe S. Africa 133 J7
Npitamaiong *mt.* Kenya 128 B4
Nqabeni S. Africa 133 O7
Nqamakwe S. Africa 133 L9
Nqutu S. Africa 133 O5
Nsalamu Zambia 127 F8
Nsambi Dem. Rep. Congo 126 C5
Nsanje Malawi 129 B9 *formerly known as* Port Herald
Nsawam Ghana 125 E5
Nseluka Zambia 127 F7
Nsoc Equat. Guinea 125 H6
Nsoko Swaziland 133 P4
Nsombo Zambia 127 F7
Nsukka Nigeria 125 G5
Nsumbu National Park Zambia *see* Sumbu National Park
Ntalfa *well* Mauritania 122 B5
Ntambu Zambia 127 E8
Ntandembele Dem. Rep. Congo 126 C5
Ntcheu Malawi 129 B8 *formerly spelt* Ncheu
Ntchisi Malawi 129 B8
Ntem *r.* Cameroon 125 H6 *formerly known as* Campo
Ntha S. Africa 133 L4
Ntibane S. Africa 133 M8
Ntiona Chad 120 B6
Ntomba, Lac *l.* Dem. Rep. Congo 126 C5
Ntoroko Uganda 128 A4
Ntoum Gabon 126 A4
Ntui Cameroon 125 H5
Ntungamo Uganda 128 A5
Ntwetwe Pan *salt pan* Botswana 131 E4
Ntywenka S. Africa 133 M8
Nuakata Island P.N.G. 149 F1
Nuanetsi *r.* Zimbabwe *see* Mwenezi
Nuangan Indon. 75 C2
Nu'aym *reg.* Oman 105 F3
Nuba, Lake *resr* Sudan 121 F4
Nuba Mountains Sudan 128 A2
Nubian Desert Sudan 121 G4
Nubivarri *hill* Norway 44 M1
Nucet Romania 58 D2
Nüden Mongolia 85 F3
Nudol' Rus. Fed. 43 R5
Nueces *r.* U.S.A. 179 C7
Nueltin Lake Canada 167 L2
Nueva, Isla *i.* Chile 205 D9
Nueva Alejandría Peru 198 C6
Nueva Arcadia Hond. 186 A4
Nueva Ciudad Guerrero Mex. 179 C7
Nueva Esparta *state* Venez. 199 E2
Nueva Florida Venez. 198 D2
Nueva Germania Para. 201 F5
Nueva Gerona Cuba 186 C2
Nueva Harberton Arg. 205 D9
Nueva Loja Ecuador 198 B4
Nueva Lubecka Arg. 205 C7
Nueva Ocotepeque Hond. 186 A4
Nueva Palmira Uruguay 204 F4
Nueva Rosita Mex. 185 E3
Nueva San Salvador El Salvador 185 H6
Nueva Villa de Padilla Mex. 185 F3
Nueve de Julio Arg. *see* 9 de Julio
Nuevitas Cuba 186 D2
Nuevo, Cayo *i.* Mex. 185 H4
Nuevo, Golfo *g.* Arg. 205 D6
Nuevo Casas Grandes Mex. 184 D2
Nuevo Ideal Mex. 184 D3
Nuevo Laredo Mex. 185 F3
Nuevo León Mex. 183 I9
Nuevo León *state* Mex. 185 F3
Nuevo Mamo Venez. 187 H5
Nufayyid Şabḩah *des.* Saudi Arabia 104 D3
Nuga Mongolia 84 B1
Nugaal *admin. reg.* Somalia 128 F2
Nugaal *watercourse* Somalia 128 F3
Nuga Nuga, Lake Australia 149 F5
Nugget Point N.Z. 153 D14
Nugr' *r.* Rus. Fed. 43 R8
Nugrus, Gebel *mt.* Egypt 121 G3
Nugu *r.* India 94 C3
Nuguria Islands P.N.G. 145 E2 *also known as* Fead Group
Nuh, Ras *pt* Pak. 101 E5
Nuhaka N.Z. 152 L7
Nui *i.* Tuvalu 145 G2
Nui Con Voi *r.* Vietnam *see* Red River
Nuijamaa Fin. 43 J1
Nui Ti On *mt.* Vietnam 79 D5
Nuits-St-Georges France 51 K5
Nu Jiang *r.* China 86 A3 *see* Salween
Nukey Bluff *hill* Australia 146 B3
Nukha Azer. *see* Şäki

▶Nuku'alofa Tonga 145 H4
Capital of Tonga.
world [countries] 10–11

Nukufetau *i.* Tuvalu 145 G2
Nukulaelae *i.* Tuvalu 145 G2 *also spelt* Nukulailai; *formerly known as* Mitchell Island
Nukulailai *i.* Tuvalu *see* Nukulaelae
Nukumanu Islands P.N.G. 145 E2
Nukunau *i.* Kiribati *see* Nikunau
Nukunono *atoll* Tokelau *see* Nukunonu
Nukunonu *atoll* Tokelau 145 H2 *also spelt* Nukunono; *formerly known as* Duke of Clarence
Nukus Uzbek. 102 D4 *also spelt* Nökis
Nulato U.S.A. 164 D3
Nules Spain 55 K5
Nullagine Australia 150 C4
Nullagine *r.* Australia 150 C4
Nullarbor Australia 146 A2
Nullarbor National Park Australia 146 A2
Nullarbor Plain Australia 146 A2
Nullarbor Regional Reserve *park* Australia 146 A2
Nuluarniavik, Lac *l.* Canada 168 E1
Nulu'erhu Shan *mts* China 85 H3
Num *i.* Indon. 73 I7
Num Nepal 97 E4
Numalla, Lake *salt flat* Australia 147 E2
Numan Nigeria 125 I4
Nu'mān *i.* Saudi Arabia 104 A2
Numata *Gumma* Japan 91 F6
Numata *Hokkaidō* Japan 90 G3
Numazu Japan 91 F7
Numbi Gate S. Africa 133 P2
Numbulwar Australia 148 B2
Numfoor *i.* Indon. 73 H7
Numin *r.* China 82 B3
Numkaub Namibia 130 C3
Nummi Fin. 45 M3
Numurkah Australia 147 E4
Nunaksaluk Island Canada 169 I2
Nunakuluut *i.* Greenland 165 O3 *also known as* Nunarsuit
Nunap Isua *c.* Greenland *see* Farewell, Cape
Nunarsuit *i.* Greenland *see* Nunakuluut
Nunavik *reg.* Canada 169 E1
Nunavut *admin. div.* Canada 167 L2
Nunda U.S.A. 176 H3
Nuneaton U.K. 47 K11
Nungatta National Park Australia 147 F4
Nungesser Lake Canada 167 M5
Nungnain Sum China 85 H2
Nungo Moz. 131 H2
Nunivak Island U.S.A. 164 C4
Nunkapasi India 95 E1
Nunkun *mt.* Jammu and Kashmir 96 C2
Nunligran Rus. Fed. 39 S3
Nuñoa Peru 200 C3
Nuñomoral Spain 54 E4
Nunukan *i.* Indon. 77 G2
Nuojiang China *see* Tongjiang
Nuomin *r.* China 85 J1
Nuoro *Sardegna* Italy 57 B8
Nupani *i.* Solomon Is 145 F3
Nuqayy, Jabal *mts* Libya 120 C4
Nuqrah Saudi Arabia 104 C2
Nuquí Col. 198 B3
Nur *r.* Iran 100 C2
Nura *r.* Kazakh. 103 G2
Nūrâbâd Iran 100 B4
Nurakita *i.* Tuvalu *see* Niulakita
Nurata Uzbek. 103 F4 *also spelt* Nurota
Nuratau, Khrebet *mts* Uzbek. 103 F4
Nur Dağları *mts* Turkey 107 C3
Nure *r.* Italy 56 B3
Nurek Tajik. *see* Norak
Nuremberg Germany 48 I6 *also spelt* Nürnberg
Nūr Gal Afgh. 101 G3
Nuri Mex. 184 C2
Nuri Sudan 121 G5
Nuri, Teluk *b.* Indon. 77 E3
Nuristan *reg.* Afgh. 101 G3
Nurla Jammu and Kashmir 96 C2
Nurlat Rus. Fed. 40 I5
Nurmes Fin. 44 O3
Nurmijärvi Fin. 45 N3
Nurmo Fin. 44 M3
Nürnberg Germany *see* Nuremberg
Nurota Uzbek. *see* Nurata
Nurpur Pak. 101 G4
Nurrai Lakes *salt flat* Australia 146 A2
Nurri, Mount *hill* Australia 147 E2
Nursfjellet *mt.* Norway 44 K2
Nurste Estonia 42 D3
Nürtingen Germany 48 G7
Nurzec *r.* Poland 49 T3
Nusa Tenggara Barat *prov.* Indon. 77 G5 *English form* Western Lesser Sunda Islands
Nusa Tenggara Timur *prov.* Indon. 75 B5 *English form* Eastern Lesser Sunda Islands
Nusaybin Turkey 107 E3 *historically known as* Nisibis
Nusela, Kepulauan *is* Indon. 75 D3
Nuşfalău Romania 58 D1
Nu Shan *mts* China 86 A3
Nushki Pak. 101 F4
Nutak Canada 169 I1
Nutarawit Lake Canada 167 L2
Nutrioso U.S.A. 183 O8
Nutwood Downs Australia 148 B2
Nuugaatsiaap Imaa *inlet* Greenland 165 N2 *also known as* Karrats Fjord
Nuugaatsiaq Greenland 165 N2

▶Nuuk Greenland 165 N3
Capital of Greenland. Also known as Godthåb.
world [countries] 10–11

Nuuksion kansallispuisto *nat. park* Fin. 42 F1
Nuupas Fin. 44 N2
Nuussuaq Greenland 165 N2 *also known as* Kraulshavn
Nuussuaq *pen.* Greenland 165 N2
Nuwakot Nepal 97 D3
Nuweiba el Muzeina Egypt 121 G2
Nuwekloof *pass* S. Africa 132 H10
Nuwerus S. Africa 132 C8
Nuweveldberge *mts* S. Africa 132 F9
Nuyts, Point Australia 151 B7
Nuyts Archipelago *is* Australia 146 B3
Nuyts Archipelago Conservation Park *nature res.* Australia 146 B3
Nuytsland Nature Reserve Australia 151 D7
Nuzvid India 94 D2
Nxai Pan National Park Botswana 131 E3
Nxaunxau Botswana 130 D3
Nyaän, Bukit *hill* Indon. 77 F2
Nyabessan Cameroon 125 H6
Nyabing Australia 151 B7
Nyack U.S.A. 177 L4
Nyagan' Rus. Fed. 38 G3 *formerly known as* Nyakh
Nyagquka China *see* Yajiang
Nyagrong China *see* Xinlong
Nyahua Tanz. 129 B6
Nyahururu Kenya 128 C4 *formerly known as* Thompson's Falls
Nyainqêntanglha Feng *mt.* China 89 E6
Nyainqêntanglha Shan *mts* China 89 E6 *English form* Nyenchen Tanglha Range
Nyainrong China 89 F5 *also known as* Sêrkang
Nyakahura *Kagera* Tanz. 128 A5
Nyakahura *Kagera* Tanz. 128 A5
Nyakaliro Tanz. 128 B5
Nyakallong S. Africa 133 K4
Nyakanazi Tanz. 128 A5
Nyåker Sweden 44 L3
Nyakh Rus. Fed. *see* Nyagan'
Nyakhachava Belarus 42 G9
Nyakrom Ghana 125 E5
Nyala Sudan 120 E6
Nyalam China 89 D6 *also known as* Congdü
Nyamandhiovu Zimbabwe 131 F3
Nyamapanda Zimbabwe 131 G3
Nyambiti Tanz. 128 B5
Nyamlell Sudan 126 E2
Nyamtumbo Tanz. 129 C7
Nyande Zimbabwe *see* Masvingo
Nyandoma Rus. Fed. 40 G3
Nyandomskiy Vozvyshennost' *hills* Rus. Fed. 40 F3
Nyanga Congo 126 A5
Nyanga Gabon 126 A5
Nyanga *prov.* Gabon 126 A5
Nyanga Zimbabwe 131 G3 *formerly spelt* Inyanga
Nyanga National Park Zimbabwe 131 G3 *formerly known as* Rhodes Inyanga National Park; *formerly spelt* Inyanga National Park
Nyang Qu *r.* China 89 E6
Nyang Qu *r.* China 89 F6
Nyankpala Ghana 125 E4
Nyanza *prov.* Kenya 128 B5
Nyapa, Gunung *mt.* Indon. 77 G2
Nyapongeth Sudan 128 B3
Nyar *r.* India 96 C3
Nyarling *r.* Canada 167 H2

▶Nyasa, Lake Africa 129 B7
3rd largest lake in Africa and 10th in the world. Also known as Malawi, Lake or Niassa, Lago.
africa [landscapes] 112–113

Nyasaland *country* Africa *see* Malawi
Nyashabozh Rus. Fed. 40 J2
Nyasvizh Belarus 42 H8 *also spelt* Nesvizh
Nyathi Zimbabwe 131 F3 *formerly spelt* Inyati
Nyaunglebin Myanmar 78 B4
Nyaungu Myanmar 78 A3
Nyays *r.* Rus. Fed. 40 L3
Nyazura Zimbabwe 131 G3 *formerly spelt* Inyazura
Nyborg Denmark 45 J5
Nyborg Norway 44 O1
Nyborg Sweden 44 M2
Nybro Sweden 45 K4
Nyeboe Land *reg.* Greenland 165 N1
Nyeharelaye Belarus 42 I8
Nyêmo China 89 E6 *also known as* Tarrong
Nyenchen Tanglha Range *mts* China *see* Nyainqêntanglha Shan
Nyeri Kenya 128 C5
Nyeshcharda, Vozyera *l.* Belarus 43 K6
Nyhammar Sweden 45 K3
Nyi, Co *l.* China 89 D5
Nyika National Park Zambia 129 B7 *also known as* Malawi National Park
Nyika Plateau Malawi 129 B7
Nyima China 89 D6
Nyimba Zambia 127 F8
Nyingchi China 89 F6 *also known as* Pula
Nyinma China *see* Maqu
Nyíradony Hungary 49 S8
Nyírbátor Hungary 49 T8
Nyírbéltek Hungary 49 T8
Nyíregyháza Hungary 49 S8
Nyiri Desert Kenya 128 C5
Nyiru, Mount Kenya 128 C4
Nykarleby Fin. 44 M3 *also known as* Uusikaarlepyy
Nykøbing Denmark 45 J5
Nykøbing Mors Denmark 45 J4
Nykøbing Sjælland Denmark 45 J5
Nyköping Sweden 45 L4
Nykvarn Sweden 45 L4
Nylstroom S. Africa 133 M1
Nylsvley *nature res.* S. Africa 133 M1
Nymagee Australia 147 E3
Nymboida National Park Australia 147 G2
Nymburk Czech Rep. 49 M5
Nynäshamn Sweden 45 L4
Nyngan Australia 147 E2
Nyogzê China 89 C6
Nyoman *r.* Belarus/Lith. 42 E8 *also spelt* Neman
Nyomanskaya Nizina *lowland* Belarus 42 G8
Nyon Switz. 51 M6
Nyong *r.* Cameroon 125 H6
Nyons France 51 L8
Nýřany Czech Rep. 49 K6
Nyrob Rus. Fed. 40 K3
Nyrud Norway 44 O1
Nysa Poland 49 O5
Nysa Kłodzka *r.* Poland 49 O5
Nysa Łużycka *r.* Germany/Poland *see* Neiße
Nysäter Sweden 45 K4
Nysätern Sweden 44 K3
Nysh Rus. Fed. 82 F2
Nyssa U.S.A. 180 C4
Nystad Fin. *see* Uusikaupunki
Nyūdō-zaki *pt* Japan 90 F5
Nyuk, Ozero *l.* Rus. Fed. 44 O2
Nyuksenitsa Rus. Fed. 40 H3
Nyunzu Dem. Rep. Congo 127 F6
Nyurba Rus. Fed. 39 L3
Nyuvchim Rus. Fed. 40 I3
Nyuya Rus. Fed. 39 L3
Nyuya *r.* Rus. Fed. 39 L3
Nyyskiy Zaliv *lag.* Rus. Fed. 82 F1
Nyzhn'ohirs'kyy Ukr. 41 E7
Nzambi Congo 126 A5
Nzara Sudan 126 F3
Nzébéla Guinea 124 C4
Nzega Tanz. 129 B6
Nzérékoré Guinea 124 C5
N'zeto Angola 127 B6 *formerly known as* Ambrizete
Nzi *r.* Côte d'Ivoire 124 D5
Nzilo, Lac *l.* Dem. Rep. Congo 127 E7
Nzingu Dem. Rep. Congo 126 E5
Nzo *r.* Côte d'Ivoire 124 D5
N'Zo, Réserve de Faune du *nature res.* Côte d'Ivoire 124 D5
Nzobe Dem. Rep. Congo 127 B6
Nzoia *r.* Kenya 128 B4
Nzoro *r.* Dem. Rep. Congo 126 F4
Nzwani *i.* Comoros 129 E8 *also known as* Arjouan; *also spelt* Ndjouani

↓ O

Oahe, Lake U.S.A. 178 B2
▶Oahu *i.* U.S.A. 181 [inset] Y1
northamerica [environments] 162–163
Oaitupu *i.* Tuvalu *see* Vaitupu
Oakbank Australia 146 D3
Oak Bluffs U.S.A. 177 O4
Oak City U.S.A. 183 L2
Oak Creek U.S.A. 172 F8
Oakdale *CA* U.S.A. 182 D4
Oakdale *LA* U.S.A. 179 D6
Oakes U.S.A. 178 C2
Oakey Australia 147 F1
Oakfield U.S.A. 176 G2
Oak Grove *LA* U.S.A. 175 B5
Oak Grove *MI* U.S.A. 173 I6
Oakham U.K. 47 L11
Oak Harbor *OH* U.S.A. 176 B4
Oak Harbor *WA* U.S.A. 180 B2
Oak Hill *OH* U.S.A. 176 C7
Oak Hill *WV* U.S.A. 176 D8
Oakhurst U.S.A. 182 E4
Oak Island U.S.A. 172 C4
Oak Knolls U.S.A. 182 D7
Oak Lake Canada 167 K5
Oakland *CA* U.S.A. 182 B4
Oakland *MD* U.S.A. 176 F6
Oakland *ME* U.S.A. 177 P1
Oakland *NE* U.S.A. 178 C3
Oakland *airport* U.S.A. 182 B4
Oakland City U.S.A. 174 C4
Oaklands Australia 147 E3
Oak Lawn U.S.A. 174 C3
Oakley *KS* U.S.A. 178 B4
Oakley *MI* U.S.A. 173 I7
Oakover *r.* Australia 150 C4
Oak Park U.S.A. 172 F9
Oakridge U.S.A. 180 B4
Oak Ridge U.S.A. 176 A9
Oakura N.Z. 152 H7
Oak View U.S.A. 182 E7
Oakville Canada 168 E5
Oamaru N.Z. 153 E13
Oaonui N.Z. 152 H7
Oaro N.Z. 153 H10
Oasis U.S.A. 182 G4
Oates Coast *reg.* Antarctica *see* Oates Land
Oates Land *reg.* Antarctica 223 K2 *also known as* Oates Coast
Oatlands Australia 147 E5
Oatlands S. Africa 133 I9
Oaxaca Mex. 185 F5
Oaxaca *state* Mex. 185 F5
Ob' *r.* Rus. Fed. 38 G3
Ob, Gulf of *sea chan.* Rus. Fed. *see* Obskaya Guba
Oba Canada 168 C3
Oba *i.* Vanuatu *see* Aoba
Obaghan *r.* Kazakh. *see* Ubagan
Obal' Belarus 43 K6
Obal' *canal* Belarus 43 K6
Obala Cameroon 125 H5
Oba Lake Canada 173 I2
Obama Japan 91 D7
Oban Nigeria 125 H5
Oban U.K. 46 G7
Obanazawa Japan 90 G5
Obanbori Qayroqqum *resr* Tajik. 101 G1 *also known as* Kayrakkumskoye Vodokhranilishche
Oban Hills *mt.* Nigeria 125 H5
O Barco Spain 54 E2 *also known as* El Barco de Valdeorras
Obbia Somalia *see* Hobyo
Obbola Sweden 44 M3
Obdorsk Rus. Fed. *see* Salekhard
Óbecse *Vojvodina, Srbija* Yugo. *see* Bečej
Obed Canada 167 G4
Obeliai Lith. 42 G6
Obelisk *mt.* N.Z. 153 D13
Oberá Arg. 204 G2
Oberau Germany 48 I8
Obere Donau *park* Germany 48 F7
Obere Saale *park* Germany 48 I5
Oberes Westerzgebirge *park* Germany 49 J5
Oberlausitzer Bergland *park* Germany 49 L4
Oberlin *KS* U.S.A. 178 B4
Oberlin *LA* U.S.A. 179 D6
Obernai France 51 N4
Oberndorf am Neckar Germany 48 F7
Oberon Australia 147 F3
Oberpfälzer Wald *mts* Germany 49 J6
Oberpullendorf Austria 49 N8
Oberstdorf Germany 48 H8
Oberviechtach Germany 49 J6
Oberwart Austria 49 N8
Obi *i.* Indon. 75 C3
Obi, Kepulauan *is* Indon. 75 C3
Obi, Selat *sea chan.* Indon. 75 C3
Óbidos Brazil 199 H5
Obigarm Tajik. 101 G2
Obihiro Japan 90 H3
Obilatu *i.* Indon. 75 C3
Obilić *Kosovo, Srbija* Yugo. 58 C6
Obil'noye Rus. Fed. 41 H7
Obion *r.* U.S.A. 174 B4
Obira Japan 90 G2

▶Ob'-Irtysh *r.* Asia 38 G3
2nd longest river in Asia and 5th in the world.
asia [landscapes] 62–63

Obispos Venez. 198 D2
Obluch'ye Rus. Fed. 82 C2
Obninsk Rus. Fed. 43 R6
Obnora *r.* Rus. Fed. 43 V3
Obo Cent. Afr. Rep. 126 E3
Obo China 84 D4
Obobogorap S. Africa 132 E4
Obock Djibouti 128 D2
Obokote Dem. Rep. Congo 126 E5
Obolo Nigeria 125 G5
Obong, Gunung *mt. Sarawak* Malaysia 77 F1
Oborniki Poland 49 N3
Obouya Congo 126 B5
Oboyan' Rus. Fed. 41 F6
Obozerskiy Rus. Fed. 40 G3
Obra India 97 D4
Obra *r.* Poland 49 M3
Obrage Arg. 204 F3
Obregón, Presa *resr* Mex. 184 C3
Obrenovac *Srbija* Yugo. 58 B4
O'Brien U.S.A. 180 B4
Obrochishte Bulg. 58 J5
Obruk Turkey 106 C3
Obrzycko Poland 49 N3
Observatory Hill *hill* Australia 146 B2
Observatory Inlet Canada 166 D4
Obsha *r.* Rus. Fed. 43 N6
Obshchiy Syrt *hills* Rus. Fed. 102 B2
Obskaya Guba *sea chan.* Rus. Fed. 38 H3 *English form* Ob, Gulf of
Obuasi Ghana 125 E5
Obubra Nigeria 125 H5
Obudovac Bos.-Herz. 56 K4
Obudu Nigeria 125 H5
Obukhovo Rus. Fed. 43 T6
Obva *r.* Rus. Fed. 40 J4
Ob"yachevo Rus. Fed. 40 I3
Ocala U.S.A. 175 D6
Ocampo Mex. 185 E3
Ocaña Col. 198 C2
Ocaña Peru 200 B3
Ocaña Spain 55 H5
Occidental, Cordillera *mts* Chile 200 C4
Occidental, Cordillera *mts* Col. 198 B4
Occidental, Cordillera *mts* Peru 200 C4
Oceana U.S.A. 176 D8
Ocean Beach U.S.A. 177 L5
Ocean Cape U.S.A. 166 B3
Ocean City *MD* U.S.A. 177 J7
Ocean City *NJ* U.S.A. 177 K6
Ocean Falls Canada 166 E4
Ocean Island Kiribati *see* Banaba
Ocean Island *atoll* U.S.A. *see* Kure Atoll
Oceano U.S.A. 182 D6
Oceans Cay *i.* Bahamas 186 D1
Oceanside U.S.A. 183 G8
Ocean Springs U.S.A. 175 B6
Ochakiv Ukr. 41 D7
Och'amch'ire Georgia 107 E2
Ocher Rus. Fed. 40 J4
Ochi *mt.* Greece 59 F10 *also known as* Ókhi Óros
Ōchi Japan 91 C7
Ochiishi-misaki *pt* Japan 90 I3
Ochil Hills U.K. 46 I7
Ochkyne Ukr. 43 O9
Ochlockonee *r.* U.S.A. 175 C6
Ochrida, Lake Albania/Macedonia *see* Ohrid, Lake
Ochsenfurt Germany 48 H6
Ochthonia Greece 59 F10 *also spelt* Okhthoniá
Ochthonia, Akra *pt* Greece 59 F10
Ocilla U.S.A. 175 D6
Ockelbo Sweden 45 L3
Ocland Romania 58 G2
Ocmulgee *r.* U.S.A. 175 D6
Ocna Mureş Romania 58 E2
Ocna Sibiului Romania 58 F3
Ocolaşul Mare, Vârful *mt.* Romania 58 G2
Ocoña Peru 200 B4
O'Connell Creek *r.* Australia 149 D4
Oconomowoc U.S.A. 172 E7
Oconto U.S.A. 172 F6
Oconto Falls U.S.A. 172 E6
O Corgo Spain 54 D2
Ocoruro Peru 200 C3
Ocos Guat. 185 G6
Ocosingo Mex. 185 G5
Ocotal Nicaragua 186 B4
Ocotlán Mex. 185 F5
Ocozocoautla Mex. 185 G5
October Revolution Island Rus. Fed. *see* Oktyabr'skoy Revolyutsii, Ostrov
Ocurí Bol. 200 D4
Ocussi East Timor *see* Pantemakassar
Ocussi *enclave* East Timor 75 C5
Oda Ghana 125 E5
Ōda Japan 91 C7
Oda, Jebel *mt.* Sudan 121 H4
Ódáðahraun *lava field* Iceland 44 [inset] C2
Ŏdaejin N. Korea 82 C4
Odae-san National Park S. Korea 83 C5
Ōdaigahara-zan *mt.* Japan 91 E7
Odanah U.S.A. 172 C4
Ōdate Japan 90 G4
Odawara Japan 91 F7
Odda Norway 45 I3
Odder Denmark 45 J5
Odei *r.* Canada 167 L3
Odell U.S.A. 172 E9
Odem U.S.A. 179 C7
Odemira Port. 54 C7
Ödemiş Turkey 106 A3
Ödenburg Hungary *see* Sopron
Odendaalsrus S. Africa 133 K4
Odensbacken Sweden 45 K4
Odense Denmark 45 J5
Oder *r.* Germany 48 G4 *also spelt* Odra (Poland)
Oderbucht *b.* Germany 49 L1
Oderhaff *b.* Germany 49 L2 *also known as* Stettiner Haff
Oderzo Italy 56 E3
Odesa Ukr. 41 D7 *also spelt* Odessa
Ödeshog Sweden 45 K4
Odes'ka Oblast' *admin. div.* Ukr. 58 K1 *English form* Odessa Oblast; *also spelt* Odesskaya Oblast'
Odessa Ukr. *see* Odesa
Odessa U.S.A. 179 B6
Odessa Oblast *admin. div.* Ukr. *see* Odes'ka Oblast'
Odesskaya Oblast' *admin. div.* Ukr. *see* Odes'ka Oblast'
Odessus Bulg. *see* Varna
Odi *watercourse* Sudan 121 H5
Odiel *r.* Spain 54 E7
Odienné Côte d'Ivoire 124 D4
Odintsovo Rus. Fed. 43 S6
Odobeşti Romania 58 I3
Odobeştilor, Măgura *hill* Romania 58 H3
Odolanów Poland 49 O4
Odom Inlet Antarctica 222 T2
Odorheiu Secuiesc Romania 58 G2
Odoyev Rus. Fed. 43 R8
Odra *r.* Poland 49 P6 *also spelt* Oder (Germany)
Odra *r.* Spain 54 G2
Odžaci *Vojvodina, Srbija* Yugo. 58 A3
Odzala, Parc National d' *nat. park* Congo 126 B4
Odzi Zimbabwe 131 G3
Odzi *r.* Zimbabwe 131 G3
Oea Libya *see* Tripoli
Oedong S. Korea 91 A7
Oeiras Brazil 202 D3
Oelde Germany 48 F4
Oelixdorf Germany 48 G2
Oelrichs U.S.A. 178 B3
Oelsnitz Germany 49 J5
Oelwein U.S.A. 174 B3
Oenpelli Australia 148 B2

Oesel *i.* Estonia *see* **Hiiumaa**
Oeufs, Lac des *l.* Canada **169** F2
Oeversee Germany **48** G1
Of Turkey **107** E2
O'Fallon *r.* U.S.A. **180** F3
Ofanto *r.* Italy **57** I7
Offa Nigeria **125** G4
Offenbach am Main Germany **48** F5
Offenburg Germany **48** E7
Offerdal Sweden **44** K3
Ofidoussa *i.* Greece **59** H12
Ofotfjorden *sea chan.* Norway **44** L1
Ōfunato Japan **90** G5
Oga *r.* Indon. **77** F2
Oga Japan **90** F5
Ogachi Japan **90** G5
Ogadēn *reg.* Eth. **128** E3
Oga-hantō *pen.* Japan **90** F5
Ōgaki Japan **91** E7
Ogallala U.S.A. **178** B3
Ogan *r.* Indon. **76** D3
Ogasawara-shotō *is* N. Pacific Ocean *see* **Bonin Islands**
Ogascanane, Lac *l.* Canada **173** O3
Ōgawa Japan **90** G6
Ogawara-ko *l.* Japan **90** G4
Ogbomosho Nigeria *see* **Ogbomoso**
Ogbomoso Nigeria **125** G4
also spelt Ogbomosho
Ogden *IA* U.S.A. **178** D3
Ogden *UT* U.S.A. **180** E4
Ogden, Mount Canada **166** C3
Ogdensburg U.S.A. **177** J1
Ogeechee *r.* U.S.A. **175** D6
Ogema U.S.A. **172** C5
Ogi Japan **90** F6
Ogidaki Canada **168** C4
Ogilvie *r.* Canada **164** F3
Ogilvie Mountains Canada **166** A1
'Oglât el Khnâchich *well* Mali **122** E5
Oglat Sbot *well* Alg. **122** D4
Oglio *r.* Italy **56** C3
Ogmore Australia **149** F4
Ognon *r.* France **51** L5
Oğnut Turkey *see* **Göynük**
Ogoamas, Gunung *mt.* Indon. **75** B2
Ogoja Nigeria **125** H5
Ogoki *r.* Canada **168** C3
Ogoki Lake Canada **168** C3
Ogoki Reservoir Canada **168** B3
Ogooué *r.* Gabon **126** A5
Ogooué-Ivindo *prov.* Gabon **126** B5
Ogooué-Lolo *prov.* Gabon **126** B5
Ogooué-Maritime *prov.* Gabon **126** A5
Ogoron Rus. Fed. **82** C1
Ogosta *r.* Bulg. **58** E5
Ogou *r.* Togo **125** F5
O'Grady, Lake *salt flat* Australia **151** B6
Ogražden *mts* Bulg./Macedonia **58** D7
also spelt Ograzhden
Ograzhden *mts* Bulg./Macedonia *see* **Ogražden**
Ogre Latvia **42** F5
Ogre *r.* Latvia **42** F5
Ogudnevo Rus. Fed. **43** T5
Ogulin Croatia **56** H3
Ogun *state* Nigeria **125** F5
Ogurchinskiy, Ostrov *i.* Turkm. **102** C5
also known as Ogurjaly Adasy *or* Turkmen Adasy
Ogurjaly Adasy *i.* Turkm. *see* **Ogurchinskiy, Ostrov**
Oğuz Azer. **107** F2
formerly known as Vartashen
Ohafia Nigeria **125** G5
Ohai N.Z. **153** B13
Ohakune N.Z. **152** J7
Ohanet Alg. **123** H3
Ohangwena *admin. reg.* Namibia **130** C3
Ōharu Japan **91** G7
O'Hare *airport* U.S.A. **172** F9
Ōhata Japan **90** G4
Ohau N.Z. **152** J8
Ohau, Lake N.Z. **153** D12
Ohcejohka Fin. *see* **Utsjoki**
O'Higgins Chile **200** C5
O'Higgins *admin. reg.* Chile **204** C4
O'Higgins, Lago *l.* Chile **205** B8
Ohio U.S.A. **172** D9
Ohio *r.* U.S.A. **178** E4
Ohio *state* U.S.A. **176** C5
Ohio Range *mts* Antarctica **223** Q1
Ohm *r.* Germany **51** O2
Ohne *r.* Estonia **42** H3
'Ohonua Tonga **145** H4
Ohope N.Z. **152** L5
Ohrdruf Germany **48** H5
Ohře *r.* Czech Rep. **49** L5
Ohre *r.* Germany **48** I3
Ohrid Macedonia **58** B7
Ohrid, Lake Albania/Macedonia **58** B7
also known as Ochrida, Lake *or* Ohridsko Ezero *or* Ohrit, Liqeni i
Ohridsko Ezero *l.* Albania/Macedonia *see* **Ohrid, Lake**
Ohrigstad S. Africa **133** O1
Ohrigstad Dam Nature Reserve S. Africa **133** O1
Öhringen Germany **48** G6
Ohrit, Liqeni i *l.* Albania/Macedonia *see* **Ohrid, Lake**
Ohura N.Z. **152** I6
Oiapoque Brazil **199** I4
Oiapoque *r.* Brazil/Fr. Guiana **199** I3
Oiba Col. **198** C3
Oich *r.* U.K. **46** H6
Oik Kazakh. *see* **Uyuk**
Oil City U.S.A. **176** F4
Oildale U.S.A. **182** E6
Oi Qu *r.* China **86** A2
Oirase-gawa *r.* Japan **90** G4
Oise *r.* France **51** I4
Oiseaux du Djoudj, Parc National des *nat. park* Senegal **124** A2
Ōita Japan **91** B8
Ōita *pref.* Japan **91** B8
Oiti *mt.* Greece **59** D10
Oiti *nat. park* Greece **59** D10
Oituz *r.* Romania **58** H2
Oiuru *well* Libya **120** C4
Oiwake Japan **90** G3
Ojai U.S.A. **182** E7
Ojailén *r.* Spain **54** H6
Ojalava *i.* Samoa *see* **Upolu**
Ojamaa *r.* Estonia **42** I2
Ojcowski Park Narodowy *nat. park* Poland **49** Q5
Öje Sweden **45** K3
Ojika-jima *i.* Japan **91** A8
Ojinaga Mex. **184** D2
Ojitlán Mex. **185** F5
Ojiya Japan **90** F6
Ojobo Nigeria **125** G5
Ojo de Laguna Mex. **184** D2
Ojo de Liebre, Lago *b.* Mex. **184** B3

▶**Ojos del Salado, Nevado** *mt.* Arg./Chile **204** C2
2nd highest mountain in South America.
southamerica [landscapes] 190–191

Ojuelos de Jalisco Mex. **185** E4
Ojung Sweden **45** K3
Oka Nigeria **125** G5
Oka *r.* Rus. Fed. **43** R9
Okahandja Namibia **130** C4
Okahu *b.* N.Z. *see* **Jackson Bay**
Okahukura N.Z. **152** J6
Okaihau N.Z. **152** H3
Okains Bay N.Z. **153** H11
Okains Bay *b.* N.Z. **153** H11
Okaka Nigeria **125** F4
Okakarara Namibia **130** C4
Okak Islands Canada **169** I1
Okanagan Falls Canada **166** G5
Okanagan Lake Canada **166** G5
Okanogan U.S.A. **180** C2
Okanogan *r.* U.S.A. **180** C2
Okanogan Range *mts* U.S.A. **180** B2
Okaputa Namibia **130** C4
Okara Pak. **101** H4
Okarem Turkm. **100** C2
also spelt Ekerem
Okarito Lagoon N.Z. **153** E11
Okaukuejo Namibia **130** B3
▶**Okavango** *r.* Botswana/Namibia **130** D3
world [land cover] 18–19
africa [issues] 116–117
Okavango *admin. reg.* Namibia **130** C3

▶**Okavango Delta** *swamp* Botswana **130** D3
Largest oasis in the world.

Ōkawa Japan **91** B8
Okaya Japan **91** F6
Okayama Japan **91** C7
Okayama *pref.* Japan **91** C7
Okazaki Japan **91** E7
Okeechobee U.S.A. **175** D7
Okeechobee, Lake U.S.A. **175** D7
Okeene U.S.A. **179** C4
Okefenokee National Wildlife Refuge and Wilderness *nature res.* U.S.A. **175** D6
Okefenokee Swamp U.S.A. **175** D6
Okemah U.S.A. **179** C5
Okene Nigeria **125** G5
Oker *r.* Germany **48** H3
Oketo Japan **90** H3
Okha India **96** A5
Okha Rus. Fed. **82** F1
Okhadunga Nepal *see* **Okhaldhunga**
Okhaldhunga Nepal **97** E4
also spelt Okhadunga
Okhansk Rus. Fed. **40** J4
Ókhi Óros *mt.* Greece *see* **Ochi**
Okhotino Rus. Fed. **43** T4
Okhotka *r.* Rus. Fed. **39** O4
Okhotsk Rus. Fed. **39** O4
Okhotsk, Sea of Japan/Rus. Fed. **90** I2
also known as Okhotskoye More
Okhotskoye More *sea* Japan/Rus. Fed. *see* **Okhotsk, Sea of**
Okhthoniá Greece *see* **Ochthonia**
Okhtyrka Ukr. **41** E6
also spelt Akhtyrka
Okhvat Rus. Fed. **43** N5
Okiep S. Africa **132** B6
Okinawa *i.* Japan **81** L7
Okinawa-guntō *is* Japan *see* **Okinawa-shotō**
Okinawa-shotō *is* Japan **81** L7
also known as Okinawa-guntō
Okino-Daitō-jima *i.* Japan **81** M8
Okino-shima *i.* Japan **91** B7
Okino-shima *i.* Japan **91** C8
Okino-Tori-shima *i.* Japan **81** N8
also known as Parece Vela; *formerly known as* Douglas Reef
Oki-shotō *is* Japan **91** C6
Okitipupa Nigeria **125** G5
Okkan Myanmar **78** A4
Oklahoma *state* U.S.A. **179** C5

▶**Oklahoma City** U.S.A. **179** C5
State capital of Oklahoma.

Oklawaha *r.* U.S.A. **175** D6
Okmulgee U.S.A. **179** C5
Oko, Wadi *watercourse* Sudan **121** H4
Okola Cameroon **125** H5
Okolona *MS* U.S.A. **174** B5
Okolona *OH* U.S.A. **176** A4
Okondja Gabon **126** B5
Okonek Poland **49** O2
Okor *r.* Hungary **56** J3
Okotoks Canada **167** H5
Okotusu *well* Namibia **130** A3
Okovskiy Les *for.* Rus. Fed. **43** N7
Okoyo Congo **126** B5
Okpety, Gora *mt.* Kazakh. **88** C2
Oksbøl Denmark **45** J5
Øksfjord Norway **44** M1
Oksovskiy Rus. Fed. **40** F3
Oksskolten *mt.* Norway **44** K2
Oksu *r.* Tajik. **101** H2
also spelt Aksu
Oktemberyan Armenia *see* **Hoktemberyan**
Oktumkum, Peski *des.* Turkm. **102** C4
Oktwin Myanmar **78** B4
Oktyabr' Kazakh. *see* **Kandyagash**
Oktyabr' Kazakh. **103** I4
Oktyabr' Rus. Fed. **43** S4
Oktyabr'sk Kazakh. *see* **Kandyagash**
Oktyabr'sk Rus. Fed. **41** I5
Oktyabr'skaya Belarus *see* **Aktsyabrskaya**
Oktyabr'skiy Belarus *see* **Aktsyabrski**
Oktyabr'skiy Belarus *see* **Aktsyabrski**
Oktyabr'skiy Kazakh. **103** E1
Oktyabr'skiy *Amurskaya Oblast'* Rus. Fed. **82** C1
Oktyabr'skiy *Arkhangel'skaya Oblast'* Rus. Fed. **40** G3
Oktyabr'skiy *Ivanovskaya Oblast'* Rus. Fed. **43** V4
Oktyabr'skiy *Kaluzhskaya Oblast'* Rus. Fed. **43** R7
Oktyabr'skiy *Kamchatskaya Oblast'* Rus. Fed. **39** P4
Oktyabr'skiy *Murmanskaya Oblast'* Rus. Fed. **44** P2
Oktyabr'skiy *Respublika Bashkortostan* Rus. Fed. **40** J5
Oktyabr'skiy *Ryazanskaya Oblast'* Rus. Fed. **43** T7
Oktyabr'skiy *Ryazanskaya Oblast'* Rus. Fed. **43** U8
Oktyabr'skiy *Sverdlovskaya Oblast'* Rus. Fed. **40** K4
Oktyabr'skiy *Volgogradskaya Oblast'* Rus. Fed. **41** G7
formerly known as Kruglyakov
Oktyabr'skoye Kazakh. **103** F1
Oktyabr'skoye Rus. Fed. **39** G3
formerly known as Kondinskoye
Oktyabr'skoye Rus. Fed. **102** C1
Oktyabr'skoy Revolyutsii, Ostrov *i.* Rus. Fed. **39** J2
English form October Revolution Island
Oktyah'sk Turkm. **102** D4
Okučani Croatia **56** J3
Ōkuchi Japan **91** B8
Okulovka Rus. Fed. **43** O3
Okuru N.Z. **153** C11
Okushiri-kaikyō *sea chan.* Japan **90** F3
Okushiri-tō *i.* Japan **90** F3
Okutango-hantō *pen.* Japan **91** D7
Okwa *watercourse* Botswana **130** E4
Ola Rus. Fed. **39** P4
Ola U.S.A. **179** D5
Ólafsvík Iceland **44** [inset] B2
Olaine Latvia **42** E5
Olan, Pic d' *mt.* France **51** M8
Olancha Peak U.S.A. **182** F5
Olanchito Hond. **186** B4
Öland *i.* Sweden **45** L4
Olanga Rus. Fed. **44** O2
Olary Australia **146** D3
Olary *watercourse* Australia **146** D3
Olathe U.S.A. **178** D4
Olavakod India **94** C4
Olavarría Arg. **204** E5
Oława Poland **49** O5
Olbernhau Germany **49** K5
Olbia *Sardegna* Italy **56** B8
Olbia, Golfo di *b. Sardegna* Italy **56** B8
Ol'chan Rus. Fed. **39** O3
Olcott U.S.A. **176** G2
Old Bahama Channel Bahamas/Cuba **186** D2
Old Bastar India **94** D2
Old Cherrabun Australia **150** D3
Old Cork Australia **149** D4
Old Crow Canada **164** F3
Oldeide Norway **45** I3
Oldenburg Germany **48** F2
Oldenburg in Holstein Germany **48** H1
Oldenzaal Neth. **48** D3
Olderdalen Norway **44** M1
Oldfield *r.* Australia **151** C7
Old Forge U.S.A. **177** K2
Old Gidgee Australia **151** B5
Oldham U.K. **47** J10
Old Head of Kinsale Rep. of Ireland **47** D12
Oldmeldrum U.K. **46** J6
Old Mkushi Zambia **127** F8
Old Morley S. Africa **133** N8
Old Orchard Beach U.S.A. **177** O2
Old Perlican Canada **169** K4
Old River U.S.A. **182** E6
Olds Canada **167** H5
Old Saybrook U.S.A. **177** M4
Old Speck Mountain U.S.A. **177** O1
Old Station U.S.A. **182** C1
Oldtown U.S.A. **176** C7
Old Town U.S.A. **174** G2
Olduvai Gorge *tourist site* Tanz. **128** B5
Old Washington U.S.A. **176** D5
Old Wives Lake Canada **167** J5
formerly known as Johnstone Lake
Old Woman Mountains U.S.A. **183** I7
Öldziyt *Arhangay* Mongolia **84** D1
Öldziyt *Dornogovĭ* Mongolia **85** F2
Olean U.S.A. **176** G3
Olecko Poland **49** T1
Oleggio Italy **56** A3
Olëkma *r.* Rus. Fed. **39** M3
Olekminsk Rus. Fed. **39** M3
Oleksandrivs'k Ukr. *see* **Zaporizhzhya**
Oleksandriya Ukr. **41** E6
also spelt Aleksandriya
Ølen Norway **45** I4
Olenegorsk Rus. Fed. **44** P1
formerly known as Olenya
Olenek Rus. Fed. **39** L3
Olenek *r.* Rus. Fed. **39** L2
Olenek Bay Rus. Fed. *see* **Oleneksky Zaliv**
Olenekskiy Zaliv *b.* Rus. Fed. **39** M2
English form Olenek Bay
Ölengti *r.* Kazakh. *see* **Olenti**
Olenino Rus. Fed. **43** O5
Olenitsa Rus. Fed. **40** E2
Olenivs'ki Kar"yery Ukr. *see* **Dokuchayevs'k**
Oleniy, Ostrov *i.* Rus. Fed. **39** H2
Olenti *r.* Kazakh. **102** C2
also spelt Ölengti
Olenti *r.* Kazakh. **103** H1
Olentuy Rus. Fed. **85** G1
Olenya Rus. Fed. *see* **Olenegorsk**
Oléron, Île d' *i.* France **50** E7
Oleshky Ukr. *see* **Tsyurupyns'k**
Oleśnica Poland **49** O4
Olesno Poland **49** P5
Olet Tongo *mt.* Indon. **77** G5
Olevs'k Ukr. **41** C6
Ølfjellet *mt.* Norway **44** K2
Ol'ga Rus. Fed. **82** D4
Olga, Lac *l.* Canada **168** E3
Olga, Mount Australia **148** A5
Ölgiy Mongolia **84** A1
Olhão Port. **54** D7
Olhava Fin. **44** N2
Olhos d'Agua Brazil **207** J4
Olia Chain *mts* Australia **148** A5
Oliana Spain **55** M2
Olib *i.* Croatia **56** G4
Oliena *Sardegna* Italy **57** B8
Olifants *watercourse* Namibia **130** C5
Olifants *r.* *W. Cape* S. Africa **132** C8
Olifants *r.* *W. Cape* S. Africa **132** F10
Olifants *r.* S. Africa **131** F4
Olifantshoek S. Africa **132** G4
Olifantsrivierberge *mts* S. Africa **132** C9
Olimarao *atoll* Micronesia **73** K5
Olimbos *hill* Cyprus *see* **Olympos**
Olimbos *mt.* Greece *see* **Olympus, Mount**
Olímpia Brazil **206** E7
Olimpos Beydağları Milli Parkı *nat. park* Turkey **106** B3
Olinalá Mex. **185** F5
Olinda Entrance *sea chan.* Australia **149** E1
Olinga Moz. **131** H3
Olio Australia **149** D4
Oliy Qoltyq Sory *dry lake* Kazakh. *see* **Sor Mertvyy Kultuk**
Olisipo Port. *see* **Lisbon**
Olite Spain **55** J2
Oliva Arg. **204** E4
Oliva Spain **55** K6
Oliva *hill* Spain **54** E6
Oliva, Cordillera de *mts* Arg./Chile **204** C3
Oliva de la Frontera Spain **54** E6
Olivares, Cerro de *mt.* Arg./Chile **204** C3
Olive Hill U.S.A. **176** B7
Olivehurst U.S.A. **182** C2
Oliveira Brazil **203** C7
Oliveira do Douro Port. **54** C3
Oliveira dos Brejinhos Brazil **202** D5
Olivença Moz. *see* **Lupilichi**
Olivença-a-Nova Angola *see* **Capunda Cavilongo**
Olivenza *r.* Port./Spain **54** D6
Olivenza Spain **54** D6
Oliver Canada **166** G5
Oliver Lake Canada **167** K3
Oliver Springs U.S.A. **176** A9
Olivet France **51** H5
Olivet U.S.A. **178** C3
Olivia U.S.A. **178** D2
Oljoro Wells Tanz. **129** C6
Ölkeyek *r.* Kazakh. *see* **Ul'kayak**
Ol'khovatka Rus. Fed. **41** F6
Ol'khovets Rus. Fed. **43** U8
Olkusz Poland **49** Q5
Ollachea Peru **200** C3
Ollagüe Chile **200** C5
Ollioules France **51** L9
Ollita, Cordillera de *mts* Arg./Chile **204** C3
Ollitas *mt.* Arg. **204** C3
Öllölä Fin. **44** O3
Ollombo Congo **126** B5
Olmaliq Uzbek. *see* **Almalyk**
Olmedo Spain **54** G3
Olmeto *Corse* France **56** A7
Olmos Peru **198** B6
Olmütz Czech Rep. *see* **Olomouc**
Olney *IL* U.S.A. **174** B4
Olney *MD* U.S.A. **177** H6
Olney *TX* U.S.A. **179** C5
Olochi Rus. Fed. **85** H1
Olofström Sweden **45** K4
Ol'oinka Kazakh. **103** F1
Olomane *r.* Canada **169** I3
Olomouc Czech Rep. **49** O6
also known as Olmütz
Olonets Rus. Fed. **43** N1
Olonetskaya Vozvyshennost' *hills* Rus. Fed. **43** O1
Olongapo Phil. **74** B3
Olongliko Indon. **77** F3
Olonne-sur-Mer France **50** E6
Oloron-Ste-Marie France **50** F9
Olosenga *i.* American Samoa *see* **Swains Island**
Olot Spain **55** N2
Olot Uzbek. *see* **Alat**
Olovo Bos.-Herz. **56** K4
Olovyannaya Rus. Fed. **85** G1
Oloy, Qatorkŭhi *mts* Asia *see* **Alai Range**
Olpad India **96** B5
Olpe Germany **48** E4
Ol'sa *r.* Belarus **43** K8
Olše *r.* Czech Rep. **49** P6
Ol'sha Rus. Fed. **43** M7
Olsztyn Poland **49** R2
historically known as Allenstein
Olsztynek Poland **49** R2
Olt *r.* Romania **58** F5
Olta Arg. **204** D3
Olte, Sierra de *mts* Arg. **205** C6
Olten Switz. **51** N5
Oltenița Romania **58** H4
Olteț *r.* Romania **58** F4
Oltina Romania **58** I4
Oltinkŭl Uzbek. *see* **Altynkul'**
Oltintopkan Tajik. **101** G1
also spelt Altyn-Topkan
Oltu Turkey **107** E2
Oluan Cape Taiwan *see* **Oluan Pi**
Oluan Pi *c.* Taiwan **87** G4
English form Oluan Cape
Olutanga *i.* Phil. **74** B5
Ölvega Spain **55** J3
Olvera Spain **54** F8
Ol'viopol' Ukr. *see* **Pervomays'k**
Olym *r.* Rus. Fed. **43** T9
Olymbos *hill* Cyprus *see* **Olympos**
Olympia *tourist site* Greece **59** C11

▶**Olympia** U.S.A. **180** B3
State capital of Washington.

Olympic National Park U.S.A. **180** B3
Olympos *hill* Cyprus **108** E2
also spelt Olimbos *or* Olymbos
Olympos *mt.* Greece *see* **Olympus, Mount**
Olympos *nat. park* Greece **59** D8
Olympus, Mount Greece **59** D8
also spelt Olimbos *or* Olympos
Olympus, Mount U.S.A. **180** B3
Olyutorskiy Rus. Fed. **39** Q3
Olyutorskiy, Mys *c.* Rus. Fed. **39** R4
Olyutorskiy Zaliv *b.* Rus. Fed. **39** Q4
Olzheras Rus. Fed. *see* **Mezhdurechensk**
Oma China **89** C5
Ōma Japan **90** G4
Oma *r.* Rus. Fed. **40** H2
Ōmachi Japan **91** E6
Omae-zaki *pt* Japan **91** F7
Ōmagari Japan **90** G5
Omagh U.K. **47** E9
Omaguas Peru **198** C6
Omaha U.S.A. **178** D3
Omaha Indian Reservation *res.* U.S.A. **178** C3
Omaheke *admin. reg.* Namibia **130** C4
Omakere N.Z. **152** K8
Omal'skiy Khrebet *mts* Rus. Fed. **82** E1
Omalur India **94** C4
▶**Oman** *country* Asia **105** F4
spelt 'Umān *in Arabic; formerly known as* Muscat and Oman
asia [countries] 64–67
Oman, Gulf of Asia **105** G2
Omangambo Namibia **130** B4
Omarama N.Z. **153** D12
Omarchevo Bulg. **58** H6
Omarska Bos.-Herz. **56** I4
Omaruru Namibia **130** B4
Omas Peru **200** A3
Omatako *watercourse* Namibia **130** D3
Omate Peru **200** C4
Omatjette Namibia **130** B4
Omaweneno Botswana **132** G2
Ōma-zaki *c.* Japan **90** G4
Omba *i.* Vanuatu *see* **Aoba**
Ombai, Selat *sea chan.* Indon. **75** C5
Ombalantu Namibia *see* **Uutapi**
Ombella-Mpoko *pref.* Cent. Afr. Rep. **126** C3
Ombika *waterhole* Namibia **130** B3
Omboué Gabon **126** A5
Ombrone *r.* Italy **56** D6
Ombu China **89** D6
Omdraaisvlei S. Africa **132** H7
Omdurman Sudan **121** G6
Ōme Japan **91** F7
Omedu Estonia **42** I3
Omegna Italy **56** A3
Omeo Australia **147** E4
Ömerler Turkey **59** K9
Ometepe, Isla de *i.* Nicaragua **186** B5
Ometepec Mex. **185** F5
Omgoy Wildlife Reserve *nature res.* Thai. **78** B4
Om Hajēr Eritrea **121** H6
Omīdīyeh Iran **100** B4
Ōmihachiman Japan **91** E7
Omihi N.Z. **153** G11
Omineca Mountains Canada **166** E3
Omiš Croatia **56** I5
Omitara Namibia **130** C4
Ōmiya Japan **91** F7
Ommaney, Cape U.S.A. **166** C3
Ommen Neth. **48** D3
Ömnögovĭ *prov.* Mongolia **84** E3
Omodeo, Lago *l. Sardegna* Italy **57** B8
Omoku Nigeria **125** G5
Omolon Rus. Fed. **39** Q3
Omolon *r.* Rus. Fed. **39** P3
Omo National Park Eth. **128** B3
Omono-gawa *r.* Japan **90** G5
Omo Wenz *r.* Eth. **128** C3
Omro U.S.A. **172** E6
Omsk Rus. Fed. **80** A1
Omskaya Oblast' *admin. div.* Rus. Fed. **80** A1
English form Omsk Oblast
Omsk Oblast *admin. div.* Rus. Fed. *see* **Omskaya Oblast'**
Omsukchan Rus. Fed. **39** P3
Ōmū Japan **90** H2
Omu, Vârful *mt.* Romania **58** G3
Omu-Aran Nigeria **125** G4
Omulew *r.* Poland **49** S2
Ōmura Japan **91** A8
Ōmura-wan *b.* Japan **91** A8
Omurtag Bulg. **58** H5
Omusati *admin. reg.* Namibia **130** B3
Omutninsk Rus. Fed. **40** J4
Onalaska U.S.A. **172** B7
Onaman Lake Canada **168** C3
Onancock U.S.A. **177** J8
Onang Indon. **75** A3
Onangué, Lac *l.* Gabon **126** A5
Onarga U.S.A. **172** E10
Onavas Mex. **184** C2
Onawa U.S.A. **178** C3
Onaway U.S.A. **173** I5
Onbingwin Myanmar **79** B5
Oncativo Arg. **204** E3
Oncócua Angola **127** B9
Öncül Turkey **109** K1
Onda Spain **55** K5
Ondal India *see* **Andal**
Ondangwa Namibia **130** B3
Ondarroa Spain **55** I1
Ondava *r.* Slovakia **49** S7
Onderstedorings S. Africa **132** E7
Ondjiva Angola **127** B9
also spelt Onjiva; *formerly known as* Pereira de Eça; *formerly spelt* N'giva
Ondo Nigeria **125** G5
Ondo *state* Nigeria **125** G5
Öndörhaan Mongolia **85** F2
Öndörshireet Mongolia **85** G1
Ondor Mod China **84** E3
Ondor Sum China **85** G3
One Botswana **130** D4
One and a Half Degree Channel Maldives **93** D10
One and a Half Mile Opening *sea chan.* Australia **149** E2
Onega Rus. Fed. **40** F3
Onega *r.* Rus. Fed. **40** F3

▶**Onega, Lake** Rus. Fed. **43** Q1
3rd largest lake in Europe. Also known as Onezhskoye Ozero.
europe [landscapes] 30–31

Onega Bay *g.* Rus. Fed. *see* **Onezhskaya Guba**
One Hundred and Fifty Mile House Canada *see* **150 Mile House**
One Hundred Mile House Canada *see* **100 Mile House**
Oneida *IL* U.S.A. **172** C9
Oneida *NY* U.S.A. **177** J2
Oneida *TN* U.S.A. **176** A9
Oneida Lake U.S.A. **177** J2
O'Neill U.S.A. **178** C3
Onekaka N.Z. **152** G8
Onekama U.S.A. **172** G6
Onekotan, Ostrov *i.* Rus. Fed. **39** P5
Oneonta *AL* U.S.A. **175** C5
Oneonta *NY* U.S.A. **177** J3
Oneroa N.Z. **152** J4
Onești Romania **58** H2
formerly known as Gheorghe Gheorghiu-Dej
Onet-le-Château France **51** I8
Onezhskaya Guba *g.* Rus. Fed. **40** E2
English form Onega Bay
Onezhskiy Kanal *canal* Rus. Fed. **43** O1
Onezhskoye Ozero *l.* Rus. Fed. *see* **Onega, Lake**
Ong *r.* India **95** D1
Onga Gabon **126** B5
Ongaonga N.Z. **152** K7
Ông Đôc, Sông *r.* Vietnam **79** D6
Ongeri Dem. Rep. Congo **126** E6
Ongers *watercourse* S. Africa **132** H6
Ongerup Australia **151** B7
Ongi *Dundgovĭ* Mongolia **84** D2
Ongi *Övörhangay* Mongolia **84** D2
Ongiyn Gol *r.* Mongolia **84** D2
Ongjin N. Korea **83** B5
Ongniud Qi China *see* **Wudan**
Ongole India **94** D3
Ongon Mongolia **84** D2
Ongtüstik Qazaqstan Oblysy *admin. div.* Kazakh. *see* **Yuzhnyy Kazakhstan**
Onguday Rus. Fed. **88** D1
Oni Georgia **107** E2
Onida U.S.A. **178** B2
Onilahy *r.* Madag. **131** [inset] I4
Onistagane, Lac *l.* Canada **169** G3
Onitsha Nigeria **125** G5
Onjati Mountain Namibia **130** C4
Onjiva Angola *see* **Ondjiva**
Onkamo Fin. **44** O3
Onkivesi *l.* Fin. **44** N3
Onnes Rus. Fed. **39** N3
Ōno *Fukui* Japan **91** E7
Ōno *Hokkaidō* Japan **90** G4
Onoda Japan **91** B8
Ono-i-Lau *i.* Fiji **145** H4
Ōnojō Japan **91** B8
Onomichi Japan **91** C7
Onon Mongolia **85** F1
Onon *r.* Rus. Fed. **85** G1
Onon Gol *r.* Mongolia **85** G1
Onor, Gora *mt.* Rus. Fed. **82** F2
Onotoa *atoll* Kiribati **145** G2
also spelt Onutu
Ons, Illa de *i.* Spain **54** C2
Onsan S. Korea **91** A7
Onseepkans S. Africa **132** D5
Onslow Australia **150** A4
Onslow Bay U.S.A. **174** E5
Onsŏng N. Korea **82** C4
Ontake-san *vol.* Japan **83** E6
Ontaratue *r.* Canada **166** D1
Ontario *prov.* Canada **167** N5
Ontario *CA* U.S.A. **182** G7
Ontario *OR* U.S.A. **180** C3
Ontario *WI* U.S.A. **172** C7
Ontario, Lake Canada/U.S.A. **173** P7
Onteniente Spain *see* **Ontinyent**
Ontinyent Spain **55** K6
also spelt Onteniente
Ontojärvi *l.* Fin. **44** O2
Ontong Java Atoll Solomon Is **145** E2
formerly known as Lord Howe Atoll
Ontur Spain **55** J6
Onutu *atoll* Kiribati *see* **Onotoa**
Onverwacht Suriname **199** H3
Onyx U.S.A. **182** F6
Oodnadatta Australia **146** B1
Oodweyne Somalia **128** E2
Ooldea Australia **146** A2
Ooldea Range *hills* Australia **146** A2
Oologah Lake *resr* U.S.A. **178** D4
Oombulgi Aboriginal Reserve Australia **150** D2
Ooratippra *r.* Australia **148** C4
Oorindi Australia **149** D4
Oos-Londen S. Africa *see* **East London**
Oostanaula *r.* U.S.A. **174** C5
Oostende Belgium *see* **Ostend**
Oosterhout Neth. **48** B4
Oosterschelde *est.* Neth. **48** A4
Oostvleteren Belgium **51** I2
Ootacamund India *see* **Udagamandalam**
Ootsa Lake Canada **166** E4
Ootsa Lake *l.* Canada **166** E4
Opalenica Poland **49** N3
Oparau N.Z. **152** I6
Opari N.Z. **152** J8
Opari Sudan **128** B4
Oparino Rus. Fed. **40** I4
Oparo *i.* Fr. Polynesia *see* **Rapa**
Opasatika *r.* Canada **168** D3
Opasatika Lake Canada **168** D3
Opasquia Canada **167** M4
Opasquia Provincial Park Canada **167** M4
Opataca, Lac *l.* Canada **169** F3
Opatija Croatia **56** G3
Opatów Poland **49** S5
Opava Czech Rep. **49** O6
Opava *r.* Czech Rep. **49** O5
Opechenskiy Posad Rus. Fed. **43** P3
Opelika U.S.A. **175** C5
Opelousas U.S.A. **179** D6
Opeongo Lake Canada **168** E4
Opheim U.S.A. **180** F2
Ophir Canada **173** J4
Ophir N.Z. **153** D13
Ophir, Gunung *vol.* Indon. **76** C2
Opihikao U.S.A. **181** [inset] Z2
Opinaca *r.* Canada **169** E2
Opinaca, Réservoir Canada **168** E2
Opinnagau *r.* Canada **168** D2
Opis *tourist site* Iraq **107** F4
Opiscotéo, Lac *l.* Canada **169** G2
Opobo Nigeria **125** G5
Opochka Rus. Fed. **43** J5
Opoco Bol. **200** D4
Opoczno Poland **49** R4
Opodepe Mex. **184** C2
Opole Poland **49** O5
historically known as Oppeln
Opole Lubelskie Poland **49** S4
Opononi N.Z. **152** H3
Opornyy Kazakh. **102** C3
Oporto Port. **54** C3
also known as Porto
Opotiki N.Z. **152** L6
Opovo *Vojvodina, Srbija* Yugo. **58** B3
Opp U.S.A. **175** C6
Oppdal Norway **44** J3
Oppedal Norway **45** I3
Oppeln Poland *see* **Opole**
Oppido Lucano Italy **57** H8
Oppland *county* Norway **45** J3
Opportunity U.S.A. **180** C3
Oprişor Romania **58** E4
Optaşi-Măgura Romania **58** F4
Opuatia N.Z. **152** I5
Opunake N.Z. **152** H7
Opuwo Namibia **130** B3
Opytnoye Kazakh. **102** B3
Oqqal"a Uzbek. *see* **Akkala**
Oqtosh Uzbek. *see* **Aktash**
Oquawka U.S.A. **174** B3
Or' *r.* Rus. Fed. **102** D2
Øra Norway **44** M1
Oracle U.S.A. **183** N9
Oradea Romania **58** C1
also known as Nagyvárad
Orahovac *Kosovo, Srbija* Yugo. **58** B6
Orahovica Croatia **56** J3
Orai India **96** C4
Oraibi U.S.A. **183** N6
Oraibi Wash *watercourse* U.S.A. **183** N6
Orain *r.* France **51** L6
Orajärvi Fin. **44** N2
Oral Kazakh. *see* **Ural'sk**
Oran Alg. **123** E2
also spelt Ouahran *or* Wahran
Orán Arg. **201** D5
Oran, Sebkha d' *salt pan* Alg. **55** K9
Ōrang N. Korea **82** C4
Orange Australia **147** F3
Orange France **51** K8
Orange *r.* Namibia/S. Africa **132** A5
also spelt Oranje
Orange *CA* U.S.A. **182** G8
Orange *TX* U.S.A. **179** D6
Orange *VA* U.S.A. **176** G7
Orange, Cabo *c.* Brazil **199** I3
Orangeburg U.S.A. **175** D5
Orange Cay *i.* Bahamas **186** D1
Orange City U.S.A. **178** C3
Orange Cove U.S.A. **182** E5
Orange Free State *prov.* S. Africa *see* **Free State**
Orange Park U.S.A. **175** D6
Orangerie Bay P.N.G. **149** F1
Orangevale U.S.A. **182** C3
Orangeville Canada **168** D5
Orangeville U.S.A. **183** M2
Orange Walk Belize **185** H5
Orani *Sardegna* Italy **57** B8
Orani Phil. **74** B3
Oranienburg Germany **49** K3
Oranje *r.* Namibia/S. Africa *see* **Orange**
Oranje Gebergte *hills* Suriname **199** H4
Oranjemund Namibia **130** C6
Oranjerivier S. Africa **133** I6

▶**Oranjestad** Aruba **187** F4
Capital of Aruba.

Oranjestad Neth. Antilles **187** H3
Oranjeville S. Africa **133** M3
Orantjugurr, Lake *salt flat* Australia **150** E4
Oranzherei Rus. Fed. **102** A3
Orapa Botswana **131** E4
Oras Phil. **74** C3
Orašac Bos.-Herz. **56** I4
Oras Bay Phil. **74** C3
Orăştie Romania **58** E3
Oraşul Stalin Romania *see* **Braşov**
Orava *r.* Slovakia **49** Q6
Orava, Vodná nádrž *resr* Slovakia **49** Q6
Oravais Fin. **44** M3
Oravița Romania **58** C3
Oravská Magura *mts* Slovakia **49** Q6
Orawia N.Z. **153** B14
Orba Co *l.* China **89** C5
Orbassano Italy **51** N7
Orbeasca Romania **58** G4
Orbec France **50** G3
Orbetello Italy **56** D6
Orbieu *r.* France **51** I9
Orbigo *r.* Spain **54** F3
Orbi Gorge Nature Reserve S. Africa **133** O7
Orbisonia U.S.A. **176** H5
Orbost Australia **147** F4
Orcadas *research station* S. Atlantic Ocean **222** V2
Orcera Spain **55** I6
Orchard Mesa U.S.A. **183** P2
Orchha India **96** C4
Orchila, Isla *i.* Venez. **199** E2
Orchomenos Greece **59** D10
also spelt Orkhomenós
Orchy *r.* U.K. **46** G7
Orcia *r.* Italy **56** D6
Orco *r.* Italy **51** N7
Orcotuna Peru **200** B2
Orcutt U.S.A. **182** D7
Ord *r.* Australia **150** E2
Ord U.S.A. **178** C3
Ord, Mount *hill* Australia **150** D3
Orda Rus. Fed. **40** K4
Órdenes Spain *see* **Ordes**
Ordes Spain **54** C1
also known as Órdenes
Ordesa - Monte Perdido, Parque Nacional de *nat. park* Spain **55** L2
Ord Mountain U.S.A. **183** H7
Ord River Dam Australia **150** E3
Ord River Nature Reserve Australia **150** E2
Ordu Turkey *see* **Yayladağı**
Ordu Turkey **107** D2
Ordubad Azer. **107** F3
Ordway U.S.A. **178** B4
Ordzhonikidze Kazakh. **103** E1
formerly known as Denisovka
Ordzhonikidze Rus. Fed. *see* **Vladikavkaz**
Ordzhonikidze Ukr. **41** E7
Ordzhonikidzeabad Tajik. *see* **Kofarnihon**
Ordzhonikidzevskaya Rus. Fed. *see* **Sleptsovskaya**
Ore Nigeria **125** G5
Öreälven *r.* Sweden **44** L3
Öreälven *r.* Sweden **45** K3
Oreana U.S.A. **182** F1
Örebro Sweden **45** K4
Örebro *county* Sweden **45** K4
Oredezh *r.* Rus. Fed. **43** K3
Oregon *IL* U.S.A. **174** B3
Oregon *OH* U.S.A. **176** B4
Oregon *WI* U.S.A. **172** D8
Oregon *state* U.S.A. **180** B4
Oregon City U.S.A. **180** B3
Öregrund Sweden **45** L3
Orekhi-Vydritsa Belarus *see* **Arekhawsk**
Orekhov Ukr. *see* **Orikhiv**
Orekhovo-Zuyevo Rus. Fed. **43** T6
Orekhovsk Belarus *see* **Arekhawsk**
Orel *Orlovskaya Oblast'* Rus. Fed. **43** R9
also spelt Oryol
Orel *Permskaya Oblast'* Rus. Fed. **40** K4
Orel, Gora *mt.* Rus. Fed. **82** E1
Orel', Ozero *l.* Rus. Fed. **82** E1
Orelek *mt.* Bulg. **58** E7
Orellana *prov.* Ecuador **198** B5
Orellana Peru **198** C6
Orellana, Embalse de *resr* Spain **54** F5
Orel Oblast *admin. div.* Rus. Fed. *see* **Orlovskaya Oblast'**
Orem U.S.A. **183** M1
Ore Mountains Czech Rep./Germany *see* **Erzgebirge**
Ören Turkey **59** K12
Ören Turkey **106** A3
Orenburg Rus. Fed. **102** C2
formerly known as Chkalov

Orenburg Oblast *admin. div.* Rus. Fed. *see* Orenburgskaya Oblast'
Orenburgskaya Oblast' *admin. div.* Rus. Fed. **102** B2
English form Orenburg Oblast; formerly known as Chkalovskaya Oblast'
Orense Arg. **204** F5
Orense Spain *see* Ourense
Oreón, Dhíavlos *sea chan.* Greece *see* Oreon, Diavlos
Oreon, Diavlos *sea chan.* Greece **59** D10
also spelt Oreón, Dhíavlos
Oreor Palau *see* Koror
Orepuki N.Z. **153** B14
Öreskilsälven *r.* Sweden **45** J4
Orestiada Greece **58** H7
also known as Orestiás
Orestiás Greece *see* Orestiada
Øresund *strait* Denmark/Sweden **45** K5
Oretana, Cordillera *mts* Spain *see* Toledo, Montes de
Oreti *r.* N.Z. **153** C14
Orewa N.Z. **152** I4
Orfane *well* Niger **125** G2
Orfanou, Kolpos *b.* Greece **58** E8
Orford Bay Australia **149** D1
Orford Ness *hd* U.K. **47** N11
Organabo Fr. Guiana **199** H3
Organ Pipe Cactus National Monument *nat. park* U.S.A. **183** L9
Orgeyev Moldova *see* Orhei
Orgil Mongolia **84** C1
Orgiva Spain **55** H8
Orgon Tal China **85** G3
Orgtrud Rus. Fed. **43** V5
Orgün Afgh. **101** G3
Orhaneli Turkey **106** B3
also known as Beyce
Orhangazi Turkey **59** K8
Orhei Moldova **58** J1
formerly spelt Orgeyev *or* Orkhey
Orhei *prov.* Moldova **58** J1
Orhon Gol *r.* Mongolia **84** E1
Orhontuul Mongolia **84** E1
Orhy, Pic d' *mt.* France/Spain **55** J2
Oria Spain **55** I7
Orichi Rus. Fed. **40** I4
Oriental, Cordillera *mts* Bol. **200** D4
Oriental, Cordillera *mts* Col. **198** C3
Oriental, Cordillera *mts* Peru **200** C3
Orientale *prov.* Dem. Rep. Congo **126** E4
formerly known as Haut-Congo *or* Haut-Zaïre
Oriente Brazil **201** D2
Orient Island U.S.A. **177** M4
Orihuela Spain **55** K6
Orikhiv Ukr. **41** E7
also known as Orekhov
Orikum Albania **59** A8
Orillia Canada **168** E4
Orimattila Fin. **45** N3
Orin U.S.A. **180** F4
▶**Orinoco** *r.* Col./Venez. **199** F2
world [land images] ▶▶▶ 12–13
Orinoco Delta Venez. **199** F2
Orion U.S.A. **172** C9
Oripää Fin. **45** M3
Oriskany U.S.A. **177** J2
Orissa *state* India **95** E1
formerly known as Jajnagar
Orissaare Estonia **42** E3
Oristano Sardegna Italy **57** A9
Oristano, Golfo di *b.* Sardegna Italy **57** A9
Orivesi Fin. **45** N3
Orivesi *l.* Fin. **44** O3
Oriximiná Brazil **199** H5
Orizaba Mex. **185** F5
▶**Orizaba, Pico de** *vol.* Mex. **185** F5
3rd highest mountain in North America.
Also known as Citlaltépetl.
northamerica [landscapes] ▶▶▶ 156–157
Orizona Brazil **206** D6
Orjonikidzeobod Tajik. *see* Kofarnihon
Örkelljunga Sweden **45** K4
Orkhey Moldova *see* Orhei
Orkhomenós Greece *see* Orchomenos
Orkney S. Africa **133** K3
Orkney *i.* U.K. **46** I5
Orla *r.* Poland **49** N4
Orla *r.* Poland **49** O2
Orland U.S.A. **182** B2
Orlândia Brazil **206** F7
Orlando U.S.A. **175** D6
Orleaes Brazil **203** B9
Orléans France **51** I5
Orleans *MA* U.S.A. **177** P4
Orleans *VT* U.S.A. **177** M1
Orléans, Île d' *i.* Canada **169** H4
Orléansville Alg. *see* Ech Chélif
Orlické Hory *mts* Czech Rep. **49** N5
Orlik Rus. Fed. **80** F2
Orlík, Vodní nádrž *resr* Czech Rep. **49** L6
Orljava *r.* Croatia **56** I3
Orlov Rus. Fed. **40** I4
formerly known as Khalturin
Orlov Gay Rus. Fed. **102** B2
Orlovo Rus. Fed. **43** P6
Orlovskaya Oblast' *admin. div.* Rus. Fed. **43** R9
English form Orel Oblast
Orlovskiy Rus. Fed. **41** G7

Orly *airport* France **51** I4
Ormankalns *hill* Latvia **42** G5
Ormara Pak. **101** F5
Ormara, Ras *hd* Pak. **101** F5
Ormilia Greece *see* Ormylia
Ormoc Phil. **74** C4
Ormond N.Z. **152** L6
Ormond Beach U.S.A. **175** D6
Ormskirk U.K. **47** J10
Ormylia Greece **59** E8
also spelt Ormilia
Ornans France **51** M5
Orne *r.* France **50** F3
Orne *r.* France **50** G4
Ørnes Norway **44** L2
Orneta Poland **49** R1
Ornö *i.* Sweden **45** L4
Örnsköldsvik Sweden **44** L3
Örö *i.* Fin. **42** I7
Oro N. Korea **83** B4
Oro, Lac *l.* Mali **124** E2
Orobayaya Bol. **201** E3
Orobie, Alpi *mts* Italy **56** B2
Orocó Brazil **202** E4
Orocué Col. **198** D3
Orodara Burkina **124** D4
Orofino U.S.A. **180** C3
Orog Nuur *salt l.* Mongolia **84** D2
Oro Grande U.S.A. **183** G7
Orol Dengizi *salt l.* Kazakh./Uzbek. *see* Aral Sea
Oromia *admin. reg.* Eth. **128** C2
Oromocto Canada **169** H4
Oromocto Lake Canada **169** H4
Oron Israel **108** G7
Oron Nigeria **125** H5
Orona *i.* Kiribati **145** H2
formerly known as Hull Island
Orono U.S.A. **174** G2
Oronoque Guyana **199** G4
Oronoque *r.* Guyana **199** G4
Orontes *r.* Lebanon/Syria **109** H3
also known as 'Āṣī *or* 'Aṣī, Nahr al
Orope Venez. **198** C2
Oropesa, Cabo de *c.* Spain **55** L4
Oroqen Zizhiqi China *see* Alihe
Oroquieta Phil. **74** B4
Ororbia Spain **55** J2
Orós Brazil **202** E3
Orós, Açude *resr* Brazil **202** E3
Orosei Sardegna Italy **57** B8
Orosei, Golfo di *b.* Sardegna Italy **57** B8
Orosháza Hungary **49** R9
Oroszlány Hungary **49** P8
Orotukan Rus. Fed. **39** P3
Oro Valley U.S.A. **183** N9
Oroville *CA* U.S.A. **182** C2
Oroville *WA* U.S.A. **180** C2
Oroville, Lake *resr* U.S.A. **182** C2
Orqohan China **85** I1
Orri, Monte *hill* Sardegna Italy **57** A9
Orrkjølen *hill* Norway **45** J3
Orroroo Australia **146** C3
Orsa Sweden **45** K3
Orsha Belarus **43** L7
Orsha Rus. Fed. **43** R5
Orshanka Rus. Fed. **40** H4
Orsjön *l.* Sweden **45** L3
Orsk Rus. Fed. **102** D2
Orșova Romania **58** D4
Ørsta Norway **44** I3
Örsundsbro Sweden **45** L4
Ortaca Turkey **59** J12
Orta Nova Italy **56** H7
Orta Toroslar *plat.* Turkey **108** E1
Orte Italy **56** E6
Ortegal, Cabo *c.* Spain **54** D1
Orteguaza *r.* Col. **198** C4
Orthez France **50** F9
Ortholmen Sweden **45** K3
Ortigueira Brazil **206** C11
Ortigueira Spain **54** D1
Orțișoara Romania **58** C3
Ortiz Mex. **184** C2
Ortiz Venez. **199** E2
Ortles *mt.* Italy **56** D2
Ortona Italy **56** G6
Ortonville U.S.A. **173** J8
Ortonville *MN* U.S.A. **178** C2
Ortospana Afgh. *see* Kābul
Orträsk Sweden **44** L2
Örtülü Turkey *see* Şenkaya
Oru Estonia **42** I2
Orulgan, Khrebet *mts* Rus. Fed. **39** M3
Orumbo Namibia **130** C4
Orumbo Boka *hill* Côte d'Ivoire **124** D5
Orūmīyeh Iran *see* Urmia
Orūmīyeh, Daryācheh-ye *salt l.* Iran *see* Urmia, Lake
Oruro Bol. **200** D4
Oruro *dept* Bol. **200** D4
Orüzgān *prov.* Afgh. **101** F3
Orvault France **50** F5
Orvieto Italy **56** E6
historically known as Urbs Vetus *or* Velsuna *or* Volsinii
Orville Coast Antarctica **222** T1
Orwell *OH* U.S.A. **176** E4
Orwell *VT* U.S.A. **177** L2
Orxon Gol *r.* China **85** H1
Oryakhovo Bulg. **58** E5
Oryol Rus. Fed. *see* Orel
Orzinuovi Italy **56** B3
Orzyc *r.* Poland **49** S3
Orzysz, Jezioro *l.* Poland **49** T2
Os Norway **44** J3
Oša *r.* Latvia **42** H5
Osa *r.* Poland **49** Q2
Osa, Península de *pen.* Costa Rica **186** C5
Osage *IA* U.S.A. **174** A3
Osage *WV* U.S.A. **176** E6
Osage *r.* U.S.A. **178** D4
Osage City U.S.A. **178** D4
▶**Ōsaka** Japan **91** D7
world [cities] ▶▶▶ 24–25
Ōsaka *pref.* Japan **91** D7
Ōsaka-wan *b.* Japan **91** D7
Osakarovka Kazakh. **103** H2
Osasco Brazil **206** G10
Osawatomie U.S.A. **178** D4
Osborn S. Africa **133** P5
Osborne U.S.A. **178** C4
Oscar Fr. Guiana **199** H4
Oscar Range *hills* Australia **150** D3
Osceola *AR* U.S.A. **174** B5
Osceola *IA* U.S.A. **174** A3
Osceola *MO* U.S.A. **178** D4
Osceola *NE* U.S.A. **178** C3
Osceola *WI* U.S.A. **172** A5
Oschatz Germany **49** K4
Oschersleben (Bode) Germany **48** I3
Oschiri Sardegna Italy **57** B8
Osečina Srbija Yugo. **58** A4
O Seixo Spain **54** C3
Ösel *i.* Estonia *see* Hiiumaa
Osensjøen *l.* Norway **45** J3
Osetr *r.* Rus. Fed. **43** T7
Ose-zaki *pt* Japan **91** A8
Osgode Canada **168** F4
Osgood Mountains U.S.A. **180** C4
Osh Kyrg. **103** H4
Osh *admin. div.* Kyrg. **103** H4
English form Osh Oblast; also known as Oshskaya Oblast'
Oshakati Namibia **130** B3
Oshamambe Japan *see* Oshamambe
Oshamambe Japan **90** G3
also spelt Oshamambe

Oshana *admin. reg.* Namibia **130** B3
Oshawa Canada **168** E4
Oshika Japan **90** G5
Oshika-hantō *pen.* Japan **90** G5
Oshikango Namibia **130** B3
Oshikoto *admin. reg.* Namibia **130** C3
Oshikuku Namibia **130** B3
Ō-shima *i.* Japan **90** F4
Ō-shima *i.* Japan **91** E8
Ō-shima *i.* Japan **91** F7
Oshima-hantō *pen.* Japan **90** F3
Oshin *r.* Nigeria **125** G4
Oshivelo Namibia **130** C3
Oshkosh *NE* U.S.A. **178** B3
Oshkosh *WI* U.S.A. **172** E6
Oshmyany Belarus *see* Ashmyany
Oshnovīyeh Iran **100** A2
Osh Oblast *admin. div.* Kyrg. *see* Osh
Oshogbo Nigeria **125** G5
also spelt Osogbo
Oshtorān Kūh *mt.* Iran **100** B3
Oshun *state* Nigeria *see* Osun
Oshwe Dem. Rep. Congo **126** C5
Osica de Sus Romania **58** F4
Osijek Croatia **56** K3
Osikovitsa Bulg. **58** F6
Osilinka *r.* B.C. Canada **166** E3
Osimo Italy **56** F5
Osipaonica Srbija Yugo. **58** C4
Osipenko Ukr. *see* Berdyans'k
Osipovichi Belarus *see* Asipovichy
Osire Namibia **130** C4
Osiyan India **96** B4
Osizweni S. Africa **133** O4
Osječenica *mts* Bos.-Herz. **56** I4
Oskaloosa *IA* U.S.A. **174** A3
Oskaloosa *KS* U.S.A. **178** D4
Oskarshamn Sweden **45** K4
Oskarström Sweden **45** K4
Oskélanéo Canada **173** P2
Öskemen Kazakh. *see* Ust'-Kamenogorsk
Oskil *r.* Ukr. *see* Oskol
Oskol *r.* Rus. Fed. **41** F6
also known as Oskil
Oskuya *r.* Rus. Fed. **43** M2
Oslava *r.* Czech Rep. **49** L6
Osława *r.* Poland **49** T6
▶**Oslo** Norway **45** J4
Capital of Norway. Historically known as Christiania or Kristiania.
Oslo *airport* Norway *see* Gardermoen
Oslob Phil. **74** B4
Oslofjorden *sea chan.* Norway **45** J4
Osmanabad India **94** C2
Osmancık Turkey **106** C2
Osmaneli Turkey **106** B2
Osmaniye Turkey **106** C3
Osmannagar India **94** C2
also known as Sultanabad
Os'mino Rus. Fed. **43** K2
Ōsmo Sweden **45** L4
Osmussaar *i.* Estonia **42** E2
Osnabrück Germany **48** F2
Osnaburg *atoll* Fr. Polynesia *see* Mururoa
Osno Lubuskie Poland **49** L3
Oso *r.* Dem. Rep. Congo **126** E5
Osogbo Nigeria *see* Oshogbo
Osogovske Planine *mts* Bulg./Macedonia **58** D6
Osor *hill* Croatia **56** G4
Osório Brazil **203** B9
Osorno Chile **204** B6
Osorno Spain **54** G2
Osoyoos Canada **166** G5
Osøyri Hordaland Norway **46** P3
Ospino Venez. **198** D2
Osprey Reef Australia **149** E2
Oss Neth. **48** C4
Ossa *hill* Port. **54** D6
Ossa, Mount Australia **147** E5
Osse *r.* Nigeria **125** G5
Osseo U.S.A. **172** C5
Ossian Sardegna Italy **57** A8
Ossineke U.S.A. **173** J6
Ossining U.S.A. **177** L4
Ossipee Lake U.S.A. **177** N2
Ossokmanuan Lake Canada **169** H2
Ossora Rus. Fed. **39** Q4
Ostashevo Rus. Fed. **43** Q5
Ostashkov Rus. Fed. **43** O4
Oste *r.* Germany **48** G2
Osten Germany **48** G2
Ostend Belgium **51** I1
also spelt Oostende *or* Ostende
Ostende Belgium *see* Ostend
Oster Rus. Fed. **43** N7
Oster *r.* Rus. Fed. **43** N8
Oster Ukr. **41** D6
Osterburg (Altmark) Germany **48** I3
Österbybruk Sweden **45** L3
Österbymo Sweden **45** K4
Österdalälven *r.* Sweden **45** K3
Österfärnebo Sweden **45** L3
Östergötland *county* Sweden **45** K4
Osterholz-Scharmbeck Germany **48** F2
Osterode am Harz Germany **48** H4
Österreich *country* Europe *see* Austria
Östersund Sweden **44** K3
Östervåla Sweden **45** L3
Osterzgebirge *park* Germany **49** K5
Østfold *county* Norway **45** J4
Ostfriesische Inseln *is* Germany *see* East Frisian Islands
Ostfriesland *reg.* Germany **48** E2
Ostgrönland *reg.* Germany **48** E2
Östhammar Sweden **45** L3
Ostra Kvarken *strait* Fin./Sweden **44** M3
Ostrava Czech Rep. **49** P6
Ostróda Poland **49** Q2
Ostrogozhsk Rus. Fed. **41** F6
Ostro Koplje *mt.* Yugo. **58** A4
Ostrołęka Poland **49** S3
▶**Ostrov** Czech Rep. **49** J5
Ostrov Romania **58** I4
Ostrov Rus. Fed. **43** J4
Ostrovets Poland *see* Ostrowiec Świętokrzyski
Ostrovskoye Rus. Fed. **40** G4
formerly known as Semyonovskoye
Ostrów Poland *see* Ostrów Wielkopolski
Ostrowiec Poland *see* Ostrowiec Świętokrzyski
Ostrowiec Świętokrzyski Poland **49** S5
formerly known as Ostrovets; *short form* Ostrowiec
Ostrów Lubelski Poland **49** T4
Ostrów Mazowiecka Poland **49** S3
Ostrowo Poland *see* Ostrów Wielkopolski
Ostrów Wielkopolski Poland **49** O4
formerly known as Ostrowo; *short form* Ostrów
Ostrzeszów Poland **49** O4
Ostseebad Binz Germany **48** K1
Ostseebad Kühlungsborn Germany **48** I1
Ostuni Italy **57** J8
Osuga *r.* Rus. Fed. **43** P4
Osuga *r.* Rus. Fed. **43** P4
O'Sullivan, Lac *l.* Canada **173** P2
Osum *r.* Albania **59** B8
Osŭm *r.* Bulg. **58** F5
Ōsumi-hantō *pen.* Japan **91** B9
Ōsumi-kaikyō *sea chan.* Japan **91** B9
Ōsumi-shotō *is* Japan **91** B9
Osun *state* Nigeria **125** G5
also spelt Oshun
Osuna Spain **54** F7

Osvaldo Cruz Brazil **206** C8
Oswego *IL* U.S.A. **172** E9
Oswego *KS* U.S.A. **178** D4
Oswego *NY* U.S.A. **177** I2
Oswego *r.* U.S.A. **177** I2
Oswestry U.K. **47** I11
Oświęcim Poland **49** Q5
historically known as Auschwitz
Osyno Rus. Fed. **43** J5
Ōta Japan **91** F6
Otago *admin. reg.* N.Z. **153** D13
Otago Peninsula N.Z. **153** E13
Otahiti *i.* Fr. Polynesia *see* Tahiti
Otairi N.Z. **152** J7
Otaki N.Z. **153** C13
Ōtaki Japan **91** J8
Otama N.Z. **153** C13
Otamauri N.Z. **152** K7
Otar Kazakh. **103** H4
Otaru Japan **90** G3
Otatara N.Z. **153** C14
Otautau N.Z. **153** B14
Otavalo Ecuador **198** B4
Otavi Namibia **130** C3
Ōtawara Japan **91** F6
Otchinjau Angola **127** B9
Otdia *atoll* Marshall Is *see* Wotje
Otekaieke N.Z. **153** E12
Otelnuc, Lac *l.* Canada **169** G1
Oțelu Roșu Romania **58** D3
Otematata N.Z. **153** E12
Otepää Estonia **42** H3
Otepää kõrgustik *hills* Estonia **42** H3
Oteren Norway **44** L1
Oteros *r.* Mex. **181** E8
Otgon Tenger Uul *mt.* Mongolia **84** C2
Othe, Forêt d' *for.* France **51** J4
Othello U.S.A. **180** C3
Othonoi *i.* Greece **59** A9
Oti *r.* Ghana/Togo **125** F4
Oti Indon. **75** A3
Otimati S. Africa **133** P6
Otinapa Mex. **184** D3
Otira N.Z. **153** F10
Otisco Lake U.S.A. **177** I3
Otish, Monts *hills* Canada **169** G3
Otjikondo Namibia **130** C4
Otjinene Namibia **130** C4
Otjitambi Namibia **130** B3
Otjiwarongo Namibia **130** B3
Otjovasandu *waterhole* Namibia **130** B3
Otjozondjupa *admin. reg.* Namibia **130** C4
Otobe Japan **90** G3
Otobe-dake *mt.* Japan **90** G3
Otofuke Japan **90** H3
Otog Qi China *see* Ulan
Otoineppu Japan **90** H2
Otok Croatia **56** K3
Otoka Bos.-Herz. **56** I4
Otoko N.Z. **152** L6
Otonga N.Z. **152** J6
Otoro, Jebel *mt.* Sudan **121** F7
Otorohanga N.Z. **152** J6
also known as Harrodsville
Otoskwin *r.* Canada **168** C3
Otoyo Japan **91** C8
Otpan, Gora *hill* Kazakh. **102** C3
Otpor Rus. Fed. *see* Zabaykal'sk
Otradinskiy Rus. Fed. **43** R8
Otradnoye Rus. Fed. **42** L2
Otradnoye, Ozero *l.* Rus. Fed. **43** M1
Otradnyy Rus. Fed. **41** I5
formerly known as Otradnoye
Otranto Italy **57** K8
Otranto, Strait of Albania/Italy **56** K7
Otrogovo Rus. Fed. *see* Stepnoye
Otrokovice Czech Rep. **49** O6
Otrozhnyy Rus. Fed. **39** R3
Ōtscher-Tormäuer *nature res.* Austria **49** M8
Otsego U.S.A. **172** H8
Otsego Lake U.S.A. **177** K3
▶**Ottawa** Canada **168** F4
Capital of Canada.
Ottawa *r.* Canada **168** F4
also known as Outaouais, Rivière des
Ottawa *IL* U.S.A. **174** D3
Ottawa *KS* U.S.A. **178** D4
Ottawa *OH* U.S.A. **176** A4
Ottawa Islands Canada **168** D1
Otter *r.* U.K. **47** I13
Otterburn U.K. **47** J8
Otter Creek U.S.A. **172** C8
Otterstad Sweden **45** K4
Ottignies Belgium **51** L2
Ottosdal S. Africa **133** J3
Ottoshoop S. Africa **133** J2
Ottumwa U.S.A. **174** A3
Otukpa Nigeria **125** H5
Otukpo Nigeria **125** H5
Otuyo Bol. **200** D4
Otway U.S.A. **176** B7
Otway, Bahía *b.* Chile **205** B9
Otway, Cape Australia **147** D4
Otway, Seno *b.* Chile **205** C9
Otway National Park Australia **147** D4
Otway Range *mts* Australia **147** D4
Otwock Poland **49** S3
Ötztaler Alpen *mts* Austria **48** H9
Ou *r.* Nam. *r.* Laos **78** C3
Ouacha Niger **125** H3
Ouachita U.S.A. **179** E6
Ouachita, Lake U.S.A. **179** D5
Ouachita Mountains U.S.A. **179** D5
Ouadâne *reg.* Mauritania **122** C3
Ouadda Cent. Afr. Rep. **126** D2
Ouaddaï *pref.* Chad **120** D6
Ouadjinkarem *well* Niger **125** G1
Ouâd Nâga Mauritania **124** B2
Ouadou *watercourse* Mauritania **124** C2
▶**Ouagadougou** Burkina **125** E3
Capital of Burkina.
Ouahigouya Burkina **124** E3
Ouahran Alg. *see* Oran
Ouaka *pref.* Cent. Afr. Rep. **126** D3
Ouaka *r.* Cent. Afr. Rep. **126** C3
Oualâta Mauritania **124** D2
Ouallé *r.* Mauritania **124** F4
Oualam Niger **125** F3
Ouallene *r.* Fr. Guiana **199** I3
Ouanazein *well* Chad **120** C5
Ouanda-Djalié Cent. Afr. Rep. **126** D2
Ouandja Haute-Kotto Cent. Afr. Rep. **126** D2
Ouandja Vakaga Cent. Afr. Rep. **126** D2
Ouando Cent. Afr. Rep. **126** D3
Ouango Cent. Afr. Rep. **126** D3
Ouangolodougou Côte d'Ivoire **124** D4
formerly known as Wangolodougou
Ouani Kalaoua *well* Niger **125** G3
Ouanne *r.* France **51** I5
Ouaqui Fr. Guiana **199** H4
Ouara *r.* Cent. Afr. Rep. **126** D3
Ouarâne *reg.* Mauritania **122** C3
Ouargaye Burkina **125** F3
also known as Ouaragou
Ouargla Alg. **123** G3
also spelt Wargla
Ouarissibitii *well* Mali **125** F2
Ouaritoufoulout *well* Mali **125** F2
Ouarkziz, Jbel *ridge* Alg./Morocco **122** C3
Ouarogou Burkina *see* Ouargaye

Ouarsenis, Massif de l' Alg. **55** M9
Ouarzazate Morocco **122** D3
Ouatagouna Mali **125** F3
Oubangui *r.* Cent. Afr. Rep./Dem. Rep. Congo *see* Ubangi
Oubergpas *pass* S. Africa **133** I9
Oudenaarde Belgium **51** J2
also spelt Audenarde
Oudon *r.* France **50** F5
Oudtshoorn S. Africa **132** G10
Oued Laou Morocco **54** F9
Oued Rhiou Alg. **55** L9
Oued Tlélat Alg. **55** K9
Oued Zem Morocco **122** D2
Ouéléssébougou Mali **124** D4
Ouémé *r.* Benin **125** F5
Ouessa Burkina **124** E4
Ouessant, Île d' France **50** A4
historically known as Ushant
Ouésso Congo **126** C4
Ouest *prov.* Cameroon **125** H5
Ouezzane Morocco **122** D2
Oughterard Rep. of Ireland **47** C10
Ougnat, Jbel *mt.* Morocco **122** D3
Ouham *pref.* Cent. Afr. Rep. **126** C3
Ouham *r.* Cent. Afr. Rep./Chad **126** C3
Ouham Pendé *pref.* Cent. Afr. Rep. **126** C3
Ouidah Benin **125** F5
historically known as Whydah
Ouinardane Mali **125** F3
Ouiriego Mex. **184** C3
Ouistreham France **50** F3
Oujáf *well* Mauritania **124** C2
Oujda Morocco **123** F2
Oujeft Mauritania **124** B2
Oulad Teïma Morocco **122** C3
Oulainen Fin. **44** N2
Oulangan kansallispuisto *nat. park* Fin. **44** O2
Ould Yenjé Mauritania **124** C3
Ouled Djellal Alg. **123** G2
Ouled Farès Alg. **55** M8
Ouled Naïl, Monts des *mts* Alg. **123** F2
Ouled Saïd *well* Alg. **123** F3
Ouli Cameroon **125** I5
Oullins France **51** K7
Oulu Fin. **44** N2
also known as Uleåborg
Oulu *prov.* Fin. **44** N2
Oulujärvi *l.* Fin. **44** N2
Oulujoki *r.* Fin. **44** N2
Oulx Italy **51** M7
Oum-Chalouba Chad **120** D6
Oume Côte d'Ivoire **124** D5
Oum el Bouaghi Alg. **123** H1
Oum-Hadjer Chad **120** C6
Oumm ed Droûs Guebli, Sebkhet *salt flat* Mauritania **122** C5
Oumm ed Droûs Telli, Sebkha *salt flat* Mauritania **122** C5
Oumm el A'sel *well* Mali **122** D5
Ounara Morocco **122** C3
Ounasjoki *r.* Fin. **44** N2
Oundle U.K. **47** M11
Ounga Canada **167** K5
Ounianga Kébir Chad **120** D5
Ounianga Sérir Chad **120** D5
Ounissoui *well* Niger **125** I2
Oupeye Belgium **51** L2
Our *r.* Lux. **51** N3
Oure-q *r.* France **51** J3
Ouré Kaba Guinea **124** C4
Ourém Brazil **202** C2
Ourense Spain **54** D2
a.so spelt Orense
Ouricuri Brazil **202** D3
Ourinhos Brazil **206** D9
Ourini Chad **120** D5
Ourique Port. **54** C7
Ouro Branco Brazil **207** J7
Ouro Fino Brazil **206** G9
Ouro Preto Brazil **203** D7
Oursi *r.* U.K. **47** L3
Ourthe *r.* Belgium **51** L2
Ouse *r.* U.K. **47** L10
Ouse *r.* France **50** D5
▶**Outamba Kilimi National Park** Sierra Leone **124** B4
Outaouais, Rivière des *r.* Canada *see* Ottawa
Outardes *r.* Canada **169** G3
Outardes Quatre, Réservoir Canada **169** G3
Outat Oulad el Haj Morocco **122** E2
Outeniekwaberge *mts* S. Africa **132** G10
Outer Hebrides *is* U.K. **46** E6
Outer Island U.S.A. **172** C3
Outer Mongolia *country* Asia *see* Mongolia
Outer Santa Barbara Channel U.S.A. **182** F8
Outjo Namibia **130** C4
Outlook Canada **167** J5
Outokumpu Fin. **40** D3
Outoul Alg. **123** G5
Outram N.Z. **153** E13
Out Skerries *is* U.K. **46** L3
Ouvéa *i.* New Caledonia **145** I4
also spelt Uéa *or* Uvéa
Ouyanghai Shuiku *resr* China **87** E3
Ouyen Australia **147** D3
Ova *r.* Turkey **108** C1
Ovace, Punta d' *mt.* Corse France **56** B7
Ovacık Turkey **107** D3
Ovada Italy **56** A4
Ovakışla Turkey **59** I11
Ovalle Chile **204** C3
Ovamboland *reg.* Namibia **130** B3
Ovan Gabon **126** B4
Ovar Port. **54** C4
Ovejas Col. **187** D3
Oveng Cameroon **125** I6
Ovens *r.* Australia **147** E4
Overberg *reg.* S. Africa **132** D11
Övergran Sweden **45** L4
Overhalla Norway **44** K2
Overkalix Sweden **44** M2
Overlander Roadhouse Australia **151** A5
Overland Park U.S.A. **178** D4
Övermark Fin. **44** M3
Overton *NV* U.S.A. **183** J5
Overton *TX* U.S.A. **179** D6
Övertorneå Sweden **44** M2
Överum Sweden **45** L4
Överuman *l.* Sweden **44** K2
Ovid *r.* Rus. Fed. **43** T7
Ovid *NY* U.S.A. **177** I3
Ovidiopol' Ukr. **58** L1
Ovidiu Romania **58** J4
Oviedo Spain **54** F1
Ovinishchenskaya Vozvyshennost' *hills* Rus. Fed. **43** R3
Ovišrags *hd* Latvia **42** C4
Oviston Nature Reserve S. Africa **133** J7
Övögdiy Mongolia **84** D1
Övoot Mongolia **85** G2
Övörhangay *prov.* Mongolia **84** D2
Övre Anarjokka Nasjonalpark *nat. park* Norway **44** N1
Øvre Ardal Norway **45** I3
Øvre Divdal Nasjonalpark *nat. park* Norway **44** L1
Øvre Pasvik Nasjonalpark *nat. park* Norway **44** O1
Øvre Rendal Norway **45** J3
Øvre Soppero Sweden **44** M1
Övt Mongolia **84** D2
Owahanga N.Z. **152** K8

Owakonze Canada **172** C2
Owando Congo **126** C5
formerly known as Fort Rousset
Owasco Lake U.S.A. **177** I3
Owase Japan **91** E7
Owasso U.S.A. **179** C4
Owatonna U.S.A. **174** A2
Owbeh Afgh. **101** E3
Owego U.S.A. **177** I3
Owendale S. Africa **132** H5
Owen Island Myanmar **79** B6
Owen Falls Dam Uganda **128** B4
Owen, Mount N.Z. **153** G9
Owen River N.Z. **153** G9
Owens *r.* U.S.A. **182** G5
Owensboro U.S.A. **174** C4
Owens Lake U.S.A. **182** G5
Owen Sound Canada **168** D4
Owen Sound *inlet* Canada **173** M6
Owen Stanley Range *mts* P.N.G. **145** D2
Owensville *MO* U.S.A. **174** B4
Owensville *OH* U.S.A. **176** A6
Owenton U.S.A. **176** A7
Owerri Nigeria **125** G5
Owhango N.Z. **152** J7
Owikeno Lake Canada **166** E5
Owings U.S.A. **177** I7
Owingsville U.S.A. **176** B7
Owl *r.* Canada **167** M3
Owl Creek *r.* U.S.A. **180** E4
Owminzatow Toghi *hills* Uzbek. *see* Auminzatau, Gory
Owo Nigeria **125** G5
Owosso U.S.A. **173** I8
Owyhee *r.* U.S.A. **180** C4
Owyhee Mountains U.S.A. **180** C4
Owyhee North Fork *r.* U.S.A. **180** C4
Owyhee South Fork *r.* U.S.A. **180** C4
Oxapampa Peru **200** B2
Öxarfjörður *b.* Iceland **44** [inset] C1
Oxbow Canada **167** K5
Ox Creek *r.* U.S.A. **180** E4
Oxelösund Sweden **45** L4
Oxford N.Z. **153** G11
Oxford U.K. **47** K12
Oxford *IA* U.S.A. **172** B9
Oxford *MA* U.S.A. **177** N3
Oxford *ME* U.S.A. **177** O1
Oxford *MI* U.S.A. **173** J8
Oxford *MS* U.S.A. **174** B5
Oxford *NC* U.S.A. **176** G6
Oxford *NY* U.S.A. **177** J3
Oxford *OH* U.S.A. **176** A6
Oxford *PA* U.S.A. **177** J6
Oxford *WI* U.S.A. **172** D7
Oxford House Canada **167** M4
Oxford Junction U.S.A. **172** C9
Oxford Lake Canada **167** M4
Oxkutzcab Mex. **185** H4
Oxley Australia **147** D3
Oxley Peak Australia **147** F2
Oxley Wild Rivers National Park Australia **147** G2
Ox Mountains *hills* Rep. of Ireland *see* Slieve Gamph
Oxnard U.S.A. **182** E7
Oxtongue Lake Canada **173** O5
Oxus *r.* Asia *see* Amudar'ya
Oxylithos Greece **59** F10
Oya *r.* Sarawak Malaysia **77** E2
Oyabe Japan **91** E6
Oyama Japan **91** F6
O-yama *mt.* Japan **91** F7
O-yama *vol.* Japan **83** E6
Oyapock *r.* Brazil/Fr. Guiana **199** I3
Oyapock, Baie d' *b.* Fr. Guiana **199** I3
Oyem Gabon **126** B4
Oyen Canada **167** I5
Øyeren *l.* Norway **45** J4
Oygon Mongolia **84** C1
Oykel *r.* U.K. **46** H6
Oymapınar Turkey **108** C1
Oymyakon Rus. Fed. **39** O3
Oyo Congo **126** B5
Oyo Nigeria **125** F5
Oyo *state* Nigeria **125** F4
Oyón Peru **200** A2
Oyonnax France **51** L6
Oyoqquduq Uzbek. *see* Ayakkuduk
Oyster Bay S. Africa **133** I11
Oytal Kazakh. **103** H4
Oy-Tal Kyrg. **103** H4
Oytograk China **89** C4
Oyukludağı *mt.* Turkey **108** D1
Oyyl Kazakh. *see* Uil
Oyyq Kazakh. *see* Uyuk
Ozalp Turkey **107** F3
formerly known as Karakalli
Ozamiz Phil. **74** B4
Ozark *AL* U.S.A. **175** C6
Ozark *AR* U.S.A. **179** D5
Ozark *MO* U.S.A. **178** D4
Ozark Plateau U.S.A. **178** D4
Ozarks, Lake of the U.S.A. **178** D4
Ożarów Poland **49** S5
Özbaşı Turkey **59** I11
Ozbekiston *country* Asia *see* Uzbekistan
Özd Hungary **49** R7
Özdere Turkey **59** I11
Özen Kazakh. *see* Kyzylsay
Özerevo Rus. Fed. **43** P7
Ozerishche Rus. Fed. **43** J7
Ozerne Ukr. **58** J3
Ozernovskiy Rus. Fed. **39** P4
Ozernoye Kazakh. **103** E1
formerly known as Ozernyy
Ozernoye Rus. Fed. **102** B2
Ozernyy Kazakh. *see* Shashubay
Ozernyy Kazakh. *see* Ozernoye
Ozernyy *Ivanovskaya Oblast'* Rus. Fed. **43** V4
Ozernyy *Orenburgskaya Oblast'* Rus. Fed. **103** E2
Ozernyy *Smolenskaya Oblast'* Rus. Fed. **43** N6
Ozerpakh Rus. Fed. **82** G5
Ozersk Rus. Fed. **42** C7
Ozerskiy Rus. Fed. **82** F3
Ozery Rus. Fed. **43** T7
Ozeryane Rus. Fed. **82** C2
Özgön Kyrg. **103** H4
also spelt Uzgen
Ozherel'ye Rus. Fed. **43** T7
Ozhogina *r.* Rus. Fed. **39** P3
Ozieri Sardegna Italy **57** B8
Ozimek Poland **49** P5
Ozinki Rus. Fed. **102** B2
Ozolnieki Latvia **42** E5
Ozona U.S.A. **179** B6
Ozorków Poland **49** P4
Özu Ehime Japan **91** C8
Özu Kumamoto Japan **91** B8
Ozuki Japan **91** B7
Ozuluama Mex. **185** F4
Ozurget'i Georgia **107** E2
formerly known as Makharadze

↓ P

Pâ Burkina **124** E4
Paakkola Fin. **44** N2
Paamiut Greenland **165** O3
also known as Frederikshåb
Pa-an Myanmar **78** B4
also spelt Hpa-an
Paanopa *i.* Kiribati *see* Banaba

Paarl S. Africa 132 C10
Paasvere Estonia 42 H2
Paatsjoki r. Europe see Patsoyoki
Paauilo U.S.A. 181 [inset] Z1
Pabaigh i. U.K. see Pabbay
Paballelo S. Africa 132 F5
P'abal-li N. Korea 83 C4
Pabbay i. Western Isles, Scotland U.K. 46 E6
Pabbay i. Western Isles, Scotland U.K. 46 E7
   also spelt Pabaigh
Pabianice Poland 49 Q4
   historically known as Pabianitz
Pabianitz Poland see Pabianice
Pabna Bangl. 97 F4
Pabradė Lith. 42 G7
Pab Range mts Pak. 101 F5
Pacaás, Serra dos hills Brazil 201 D2
Pacaás Novos, Parque Nacional nat. park
   Brazil 201 E2
Pacaembu Brazil 206 B8
Pacahuaras r. Bol. 200 D2
Pacajus Brazil 202 E3
Pacaraíma, Serra mts S. America see
   Pakaraima Mountains
Pacaraima Mountains S. America see
   Pakaraima Mountains
Pacarán Peru 200 B3
Pacasmayo Peru 200 A1
Pacatuba Brazil 202 E2
Pacaya r. Peru 198 C6
Pacaya, Volcán de vol. Guat. 185 H6
Pacaya Samiria, Reserva Nacional
   nature res. Peru 198 C5
Paceco Sicilia Italy 57 E11
Pacheco Chihuahua Mex. 184 C2
Pacheco Zacatecas Mex. 185 E3
Pachia i. Greece 59 G12
   also spelt Pakhiá
Pachino Sicilia Italy 57 H12
Pachitea r. Peru 200 B2
Pachiza Peru 200 A1
Pachor India 96 C5
Pachora India 94 B1
Pachpadra India 96 B4
Pachuca Mex. 185 F4
Pacifica U.S.A. 182 B4
Pacific Grove U.S.A. 182 C5

▶ Pacific Ocean 220
   Largest ocean in the world.
   oceans [features] ▶ 210–211

	ocean	area sq km	area sq miles	greatest depth	page#
1 ▶	Pacific	166 241 000	64 186 000	10 920m / 35 826ft	▶ 220–221
2 ▶	Atlantic	86 557 000	33 420 000	8 605m / 24 231ft	▶ 216–217
3 ▶	Indian	73 427 000	28 350 000	7 125m / 23 376ft	▶ 218–219
4 ▶	Arctic	9 485 000	3 662 000	5 450m / 17 880ft	▶ 224

Pacific Rim National Park Canada 166 E5
Pacijan i. Phil. 74 C4
Pacinan, Tanjung pt Indon. 77 F4
Pačir Vojvodina, Srbija Yugo. 58 A3
Pacitan Indon. 77 E5
Packsattel pass Austria 49 L6
Pacov Czech Rep. 49 M6
Pacoval Brazil 199 H5
Pacuí r. Brazil 207 I3
Paczków Poland 49 O5
Padada Phil. 74 C5
Padalere Indon. 75 B3
Padali Rus. Fed. see Amursk
Padamarang i. Indon. 75 B4
Padampur India 96 B3
Padang Kalimantan Barat Indon. 77 E3
Padang Sumatra Indon. 76 C3
Padang i. Indon. 76 C2
Padangpanjang Indon. 76 C3
Padangsidimpuan Indon. 76 B2
Padangtikar Indon. 77 E3
Padangtikar i. Indon. 77 E3
Padany Rus. Fed. 40 F3
Padarosk Belarus 42 F9
Padas r. Sabah Malaysia 77 F1
Padasjoki Fin. 45 N3
Padatha, Kūh-e mt. Iran 100 B4
Padauiri r. Brazil 199 F5
Padaung Myanmar 78 A4
Padcaya Bol. 201 D5
Paddington Australia 147 E3
Paderborn Germany 48 F4
Padeș, Vârful mt. Romania 58 D3
Padilla Bol. 201 D4
Padina Romania 58 I4
Padina Vojvodina, Srbija Yugo. 58 B3
Padinska Skela Srbija Yugo. 58 B4
Padjelanta nationalpark nat. park
   Sweden 44 L2
Padluzhzha Belarus 43 M8
Padma r. Bangl. see Ganges
Padmanabhapuram India 94 C4
Padmapur India 96 D5
Padova Italy see Padua
Padra India 96 B5
Padrão, Ponta pt Angola 127 B6
Padrauna India 97 E4
Padre Bernardo Brazil 206 E2
Padre Caro hill Spain 54 E7
Padre Island U.S.A. 179 C7
Padre Island National Seashore
   nature res. U.S.A. 179 C7
Padrón Spain 54 C2
Padrone, Cape S. Africa 133 K10
Padsvillye Belarus 42 I6
Padua India 95 C3
Padua Italy 56 D3
   also spelt Padova; historically known as
   Patavium
Paducah KY U.S.A. 174 B4
Paducah TX U.S.A. 179 B5
Padul Spain 55 H7
Padum Jammu and Kashmir 96 C2
Pădurea Craiului, Munții mts Romania
   58 D2
Paekakariki N.Z. 152 I8
Paekdu-san mt. China/N. Korea 82 C4
Paengnyŏng-do i. S. Korea 83 B5
Paerau N.Z. 153 D13
Paeroa N.Z. 152 J5
Paese Italy 56 E3
Paestum tourist site Italy 57 G8
   historically known as Poseidonia
Paete Phil. 74 B3
Pafos Cyprus see Paphos
Pafúri Moz. 131 F4
Pag Croatia 56 H4
Pag i. Croatia 56 G4
Paga r. Rus. Fed. 40 L2
Paga Conta Brazil 199 H6
Pagadenbaru Indon. 77 D4
Pagadian Phil. 74 B5
Pagai Selatan i. Indon. 76 C3
Pagai Utara i. Indon. 76 C3
Pagalu i. Equat. Guinea see Annobón
Pagan i. N. Mariana Is 73 K3
   also spelt Pagon
Pagaralam Indon. 76 C3
Pagasitikos Kolpos b. Greece 59 D9
Pagatan Kalimantan Selatan Indon. 77 F3
Pagatan Kalimantan Tengah Indon. 77 F3
Page U.S.A. 183 M5
Pagėgiai Lith. 42 C6
Pagerdewa Indon. 76 D3

Paget, Mount S. Georgia 205 [inset]
Paget Cay reef S. Georgia 149 G3
Paghman mt. Afgh. 101 G3
Pagirai Lith. 42 F6
Pagiriai Lith. 42 G7
Pagon i. N. Mariana Is see Pagan
Pagouda Togo 125 F4
Pagqên China see Gadê
Pagri China 89 E7
Pagwagh r. Canada 168 C3
Pagwi P.N.G. 73 J7
Pahala U.S.A. 181 [inset] Z2
Pahang r. Malaysia 76 C2
Pahang state Malaysia 76 C2
Paharpur tourist site Bangl. 97 F4
Paharpur Pak. 101 G3
Pahauman Indon. 76 C2
Pahia Point N.Z. 153 B14
Pahiatua N.Z. 152 J8
Pahlavi Dezh Iran see Āq Qal'eh
Pahlgam Jammu and Kashmir 96 C2
Pahokee U.S.A. 175 D7
Pahost Vodaskhovishcha resr Belarus
   42 H7
Pahra Kariz Afgh. 101 E3
Pahranagat Range mts U.S.A. 183 I4
Pahranichny Belarus 42 E8
   formerly known as Byerastavitsa
Pahrump U.S.A. 183 I5
Pahuj r. India 96 C4
Pahute Mesa plat. U.S.A. 183 H4
Paiaguás Brazil 201 F4
Paicines U.S.A. 182 C5
Paide Estonia 42 G3
Paignton U.K. 47 I13
Paihia N.Z. 152 I3
Paiján Peru 200 A1
Paikü Co l. China 89 D6
Paila r. Bol. 201 D4
Pailing China see Chun'an
Pailin Cambodia 79 C5
Paimio Fin. 45 M3
Paimpol France 50 C4
Painan Indon. 76 C3
Paine Chile 204 C4
Paine, Cerro mt. Chile 205 B8
Paineiras Brazil 207 H6
Painesdale U.S.A. 172 E4
Painesville U.S.A. 176 D4
Pains Brazil 207 H7

▶ Painted Desert U.S.A. 183 M5
Painted Rock Dam U.S.A. 183 K8
Paint Hills Canada see Wemindji
Paint Lake Canada 167 L4
Paint Lake Provincial Recreation Park
   Canada 167 L4
Paint Lick U.S.A. 176 A8
Paint Rock U.S.A. 179 C6
Paintsville U.S.A. 176 C8
Paipa Col. 198 C3
Pairi r. India 94 D1
Paisley Canada 173 L6
Paisley U.K. 46 H8
País Vasco aut. comm. Spain 55 I1
   English form Basque Country
Paita Peru 198 A6
Paitan, Teluk b. Sabah Malaysia 77 G1
Paithan India 94 B2
Paitou China 87 G2
Paiva r. Port. 54 C3
Paiva Couceiro Angola see Quipungo
Paixbán Mex. 185 H5
Pajala Sweden 44 M2
Pajan Ecuador 198 A5
Pajarito Col. 198 C3
Pájaros, Islotes Chile 204 C3
Pajęczno Poland 49 P4
Pakaia India 94 C4
Pakanbaru Indon. see Pekanbaru
Pakapki Lith. 42 E6
Pakaraima Mountains S. America 199 F4
   English form Pacaraima Mountains; also
   known as Pacaraimã, Serra or
   Paracaima, Sierra
Pakashkan Lake Canada 168 B3
Pakaur India 97 F4
Pakawau N.Z. 152 G8
Pakch'ŏn N. Korea 83 B5
Pakesley Canada 168 D4
Pakhachi Rus. Fed. 39 Q3
Pakhar' Kazakh. 103 C2
Pakhiá i. Greece see Pachia
Pakhoi China see Beihai
Pakhomovo Rus. Fed. 43 S7
Pakhtaabad Uzbek. 103 H4
   formerly known as Kokankishlak

▶ Pakistan country Asia 101 E4
   5th most populous country in Asia and 7th
   in the world.
   world [population] ▶ 22–23
   asia [countries] ▶ 64–67

Pak Ka Shan hill Hong Kong China see
   Parker, Mount
Pakkat Indon. 76 B2
Paklenica nat. park Croatia 56 H4
Paknampho Thai. see Nakhon Sawan
Pakokku Myanmar 78 A3
Pakoštane Croatia 56 H5
Pakpattan Pak. 101 H4
Pakowki Lake imp. l. Canada 167 I5
Pak Phanang Thai. 79 C6
Pak Phayun Thai. 79 C7
Pakra r. Croatia 56 I3
Pakrac Croatia 56 I3
Pakruojis Lith. 42 E6
Paks Hungary 49 P9
Pakse Laos see Pakxé
Pak Tam Chung Hong Kong China 87 [inset]
Pak Thong Chai Thai. 79 C5
Paktīā prov. Afgh. 101 G3
Paktīkā prov. Afgh. 101 G3
   also known as Mpal
Pakue Indon. 75 B3
Pakwash Lake Canada 167 M5
Pakxé Laos 79 D5
   also spelt Pakse
Pal Senegal see Mpal
Pala Chad 126 B2
Pala Myanmar 79 B5
Palabuhanratu Indon. 77 D4
Palabuhanratu, Teluk b. Indon. 77 D4
Palacios Bol. 200 D3
Palaestinia reg. Asia see Palestine
Palafrugell Spain 55 O3
Palagiano Italy 57 J8
Palagruža i. Croatia 56 I6
Palaia Fokaia Greece 59 E11
Palaikastro Greece 59 H13
   also spelt Palaiókastron
Palaiochora Greece 59 E13
Palaiókastron Greece see Palaikastro
Palairos Greece 59 B10

Palaiseau France 51 I4
Palakkat India see Palghat
Palamakoloi Botswana 130 D4
Palamás Greece 59 D9
Palam Pur India 96 C2
Palana India 96 B4
Palana Rus. Fed. 39 P4
Palanan Phil. 74 B2
Palanan Point Phil. 74 B2
Palancia r. Spain 55 K5
Palandur India 94 D1
Palanga Lith. 42 C6
Palangán, Kūh-e mts Iran 101 E3
Palani India 94 C4
Palanpur India 96 B4
Palanro Indon. 75 A4
Palantak Pak. 101 F5
Palapag Phil. 74 C3
Palapye Botswana 131 E4
Palar r. India 94 C3
Palas r. Belarus 43 J6
Palasa Indon. 75 B2
Palasbari India 97 F4
Palas de Rei Spain 54 D2
Palata r. Belarus 43 J5
Palatka Rus. Fed. 39 P3
Palatka U.S.A. 175 D6
Palau Sardegna Italy 56 B7

▶ Palau country N. Pacific Ocean 73 H5
   also spelt Belau
   asia [countries] ▶ 64–67

Palaui i. Phil. 74 B2
Palauig Phil. 74 A3
Palau Islands Palau 73 H5
Palauk Myanmar 79 B5
Palaw Myanmar 79 B5
Palawan i. Phil. 74 A4
   historically known as Paragua
Palawan Passage strait Phil. 74 A4
Palayan Phil. 74 B3
Palayankottai India 94 C4
Palazzo, Punta di Corse France 51 O10
Paldiski Estonia 42 F2
Pale Bos.-Herz. 56 K5
Palekh Rus. Fed. 43 V3
Paleleh Indon. 75 B2
Palembang Indon. 76 D3
Palena r. Aisén Chile 205 B6
Palena Los Lagos Chile 205 C6
Palencia Spain 54 G2
Palenque Mex. 185 G5
Palermo Arg. 201 D6
Palermo Sicilia Italy 57 F10
   historically known as Panormus
Palermo Punta Raísi airport Sicilia Italy
   57 F10
Palestine reg. Asia 108 G5
   historically known as Palaestinia
Palestine U.S.A. 179 D6
Paletwa Myanmar 78 A3
Palghar India 94 B2
Palghat India 94 C4
   also known as Palakkat
Palgrave, Mount hill Australia 150 A4
Palhoca Brazil 203 B8
Pali Madhya Pradesh India 96 D5
Pali Maharashtra India 94 B2
Pali Rajasthan India 96 B4
Palik Belarus 43 J7

▶ Palikir Micronesia 220 E5
   Capital of Micronesia.

Palimbang Phil. 74 C5
Palinuro, Capo c. Italy 57 H8
Paliouri Greece 59 E9
Paliouri, Akra pt Greece 59 E9
Palisade U.S.A. 180 E5
Palitana India 96 A5
Palivere Estonia 42 E3
Palja hill Sweden 44 M3
Paljakka hill Fin. 44 O2
Pálkāne Fin. 45 N3
Palk Bay Sri Lanka 94 C4
Palkino Rus. Fed. 42 I3
Palkonda India 95 D2
Palkonda Range mts India 94 C3
Palkot India 97 E5
Palk Strait India/Sri Lanka 94 C4
Palladani India see Palani
Pallapalla mt. Peru 200 B3
Pallas ja Ounastunturin kansallispuisto
   nat. park Fin. 44 M1
Pallasovka Rus. Fed. 102 A2
Pallavaram India 94 D3
Palleru r. India 94 D2
Pallinup r. Australia 151 B7
Pallisa Uganda 128 B4
Palliser, Cape N.Z. 152 J9
Palliser, Îles is Fr. Polynesia 221 I7
Palliser Bay N.Z. 152 J9
Pallu India 96 B3
Palma r. Brazil 202 C5
Palma Moz. 129 D7
Palma del Río Spain 54 F7
Palma de Mallorca Spain 55 N5
Palma di Montechiaro Sicilia Italy 57 F11
Palmanova Croatia 56 H3
Palmanova Italy 56 F3
Palmares Acre Brazil 200 D2
Palmares Pernambuco Brazil 202 F4
Palmares do Sul Brazil 203 B9
Palmarito Venez. 198 D3
Palmarola, Isola i. Italy 57 E8
Palmar Sur Costa Rica 186 C5
Palmas Paraná Brazil 203 B8
Palmas Tocantins Brazil 202 B4
Palmas, Cape Liberia 124 D5
Palmas, Golfo di b. Sardegna Italy 57 A10
Palma Soriano Cuba 186 E2
Palm Bay U.S.A. 175 D7
Palmdale U.S.A. 182 F7
Palm Desert U.S.A. 183 H8
Palmeira Brazil 203 B8
Palmeira das Missões Brazil 203 A3
Palmeira dos Índios Brazil 202 F4
Palmeirais Brazil 202 D3
Palmeiras r. Brazil 202 C5
Palmeiras de Goiás Brazil 206 D3
Palmeirinhas, Ponta das pt Angola
   127 B7

▶ Palmer research station Antarctica 222 T2
Palmer r. Australia 148 D3
Palmer watercourse Australia 148 B5
Palmer U.S.A. 164 E3
Palmer Land reg. Antarctica 222 T2
Palmerston Australia see Darwin
Palmerston Australia 148 A2
Palmerston atoll Cook Is 221 H7
Palmerston N.Z. 153 E13
Palmerston, Cape Australia 149 F4
Palmerston North N.Z. 152 J8
Palmerton U.S.A. 177 J5
Palmerville Australia 149 E2
Palmetto U.S.A. 175 D7
Palmi Italy 57 H10
Palmillas Mex. 185 F4
Palmira Col. 198 B4
Palmira Cuba 186 C2
Palmital Brazil 206 C9
Palmnicken Rus. Fed. see Yantarnyy
Palm Springs U.S.A. 183 H8
Palm Tree Creek r. Australia 149 F5
Palmyra Syria see Tadmur
Palmyra NY U.S.A. 177 H2
Palmyra PA U.S.A. 177 I5
Palmyra VA U.S.A. 176 G8

▶ Palmyra Atoll N. Pacific Ocean 221 H5
   United States Unincorporated Territory.
   oceania [countries] ▶ 138–139

Palmyras Point India 95 E1
Palni Hills India 94 C4
Palo Phil. 74 C4
Palo Alto U.S.A. 182 B4
Palo Blanco Arg. 204 C3
Palo Blanco Mex. 185 E3
Palo Chino watercourse Mex. 181 D7
Palo de las Letras Col. 198 B3
Paloh Sarawak Malaysia 77 E2
Paloich Sudan 128 B2
Palomani mt. Peru 200 C3
Palomares Mex. 185 G5
Palomar Mountain U.S.A. 183 H8
Palomas Arg. 200 D6
Palompon Phil. 74 C4
Palopo Indon. 75 B3
Palos, Cabo de c. Spain 55 K7
Palos, Santo Arg. 204 C2
Palouse r. U.S.A. 180 C3
Palo Verde U.S.A. 183 J8
Palo Verde, Parque Nacional nat. park
   Costa Rica 186 B5
Palovesi l. Fin. 45 M3
Palpa Ica Peru 200 B3
Palpa Lima Peru 200 A2
Palpetu, Tanjung pt Indon. 75 C3
Palsana India 96 B5
Paltamo Fin. 44 N2
Paltaselkä l. Fin. 44 N2
Pal'tso Rus. Fed. 43 P8
Palu Indon. 75 A3
Palu r. Indon. 75 A3
Palu Turkey 107 D3
Palwal India 96 C3
Palwancha India see Paloncha
Pal'yanovo Rus. Fed. 38 G3
Palyatskishki Belarus 42 G7
Palyavaam r. Rus. Fed. 39 R3
Palyeskaya Nizina marsh Belarus/Ukr. see
   Pripet Marshes
Palyessye Belarus 43 K9
Palyessye Belarus 43 M8
Pama r. Indon. 75 A3
Pama Burkina 125 F4
Pama, r. Cent. Afr. Rep. 126 C3
Pama, Réserve Partielle de nature res.
   Burkina 125 F4
Pamamaroo Lake Australia 147 D3

▶ Pamana i. Indon. 75 B5
   Most southerly point of Asia.

Pamanukan Indon. 77 D4
Pamar Col. 198 D5
Pamban Channel India 94 C4
Pambarra Moz. 131 G4
Pambula Australia 147 F4
Pamekasan Indon. 77 F4
Pameungpeuk Indon. 77 D4
Pamfila Greece 59 H9
Pamidi India 94 C3
Pamiers France 50 H9
Pamir r. Afgh./Tajik. 101 H2
Pamir mts Asia 99 I2
Pamirs Asia 99 I2
Pamlico r. U.S.A. 174 E5
Pamlico Sound sea chan. U.S.A. 174 E5
Pampa Chile 200 C5
Pampa U.S.A. 179 B5
Pampa Chica Arg. 205 C7
Pampachiri Peru 200 B3
Pampa de Infierno Arg. 204 E2
Pampa Grande Bol. 201 D4
Pampanua Indon. 75 B4
Pampas reg. Arg. 205 E5
   southamerica [landscapes] ▶ 190–191
Pampas Peru 200 B3
Pampas r. Peru 200 B3
Pampeluna Spain see Pamplona
Pampierstad S. Africa 133 I4
Pamplin U.S.A. 176 G8
Pamplona Col. 198 C3
Pamplona Phil. 74 B4
Pamplona Spain 55 J2
   also known as Iruña; historically known as
   Pampeluna
Pamukan, Teluk b. Indon. 77 G3
Pamukçu Turkey 59 I9
Pamukkale Turkey 59 K11
Pamukova Turkey 106 B2
Pamunkey r. U.S.A. 177 I8
Pamzal Jammu and Kashmir 96 C2
Pana Gabon 126 B5
Pana U.S.A. 174 B4
Panabá Mex. 185 H4
Panabo Phil. 74 C5
Panaca U.S.A. 183 J4
Panache, Lake Canada 168 D4
Panaci Romania 58 G1
Panaeati Island P.N.G. 149 G1
Panagar India 96 C5
Panagia i. Greece 58 F8
   also spelt Panayia
Panagtaran Point Phil. 74 A4
Panagyurishte Bulg. 58 F6
Panaitan i. Indon. 77 D4
Panaitolio Greece 59 C10
Panaji India 94 B3
   formerly known as Panjim; historically
   known as Nova Goa

▶ Panama country Central America 186 C5
   northamerica [countries] ▶ 158–159
Panamá Panama see Panama City
Panamá, Bahía de b. Panama 186 D5
Panamá, Golfo de g. Panama see
   Panama, Gulf of
Panama, Gulf of g. Panama 186 D6
   also known as Panamá, Golfo de
Panama Canal Panama 186 D5

▶ Panama City Panama 186 D5
   Capital of Panama. Also known as Panamá.

Panama City U.S.A. 175 C6
Panamint Range mts U.S.A. 183 G5
Panamint Valley U.S.A. 183 G5
Panao Peru 200 A2
Panaon i. Phil. 74 C4
Panapompom Island P.N.G. 149 G1
Panar r. India 97 F4
Panarea, Isola i. Isole Lipari Italy 57 H10
Panaro r. Italy 56 D4
Panarukan Indon. 77 F4
Panatinane Island P.N.G. 149 G1
Panay i. Phil. 74 B4
Panay Gulf Phil. 74 B4
Panayia i. Greece see Panagia
Panbult S. Africa 133 P3
Pancake Range mts U.S.A. 183 I3
Pancas Brazil 207 M6
Pančevo Vojvodina, Srbija Yugo. 58 B4
   also spelt Pancsova
Panchagarh Bangl. 97 F4
Panch'iao Taiwan 87 G3
Pancingapan, Bukit mt. Indon. 77 F2
Panciu Romania 58 I3
Pâncota Romania 58 C2
   formerly spelt Pîncota
Pancsova Vojvodina, Srbija Yugo. see
   Pancevo
Panda Moz. 131 G4
Pandan Panay Phil. 74 B4
Pandan Phil. 74 B3
Pandan, Selat strait Sing. 76 [inset]
Pandan Bay Phil. 74 B4
Pandan Reservoir Sing. 76 [inset]
Pandaria India 96 D5
Pandavapura India 94 C3
Paneas Syria see Bāniyās
Panelas Brazil 201 E3
Panevėžys Lith. 42 F6
Panfilov Kazakh. see Zharkent
Pang r. China 82 B1
Pang, Nam r. Myanmar 78 B3
Pangai Tonga 145 H3
Pangal Andhra Pradesh India 94 C2
Pangal Andhra Pradesh India 94 C2
Pangandaran Indon. 77 E4
Pangani Tanz. 129 C6
   also known as Ruvu
Pangani r. Tanz. 129 C6
Panganiban Phil. 74 C3
Pangar Djerem, Réserve du nature res.
   Cameroon 125 I5
Pangean Indon. 75 A3
Panghsang Myanmar 78 B3
Pangi Dem. Rep. Congo 126 E5
Pangi Range mts India 101 H3
Pangiabu China 85 I3
Pangkajene Indon. 75 A4
Pangkalanbuun Indon. 77 E3
Pangkalanlunang Indon. 77 E3
Pangkalansusu Indon. 76 B1
Pangkal Kalong Malaysia 76 C1
Pangkalpinang Indon. 76 D3
Pangkalsiang, Tanjung pt Indon. 75 B3
Panglang Myanmar 78 B3
Panglao i. Phil. 74 B4
Pangman Canada 137 J5
Pango Aluquém Angola 127 B7
Pangody Rus. Fed. 38 H3
Pangonda Cent. Afr. Rep. 126 D3
Pangong Tso salt l. China/Jammu and Kashmir
   see Bangong Co
Pangrango vol. Indon. 77 D4
Pang Sida National Park Thai. 79 C5
Pang Sua, Sungai r. Sing. 76 [inset]
Pangtara Myanmar 78 B3
Panguipulli Chile 204 B5
Panguitch U.S.A. 183 L4
Panguru N.Z. 152 H3
Panguruan Indon. 76 B2
Pangutaran Group i. Phil. 74 B5
Panhandle U.S.A. 179 B5
Pania-Mwanga Dem. Rep. Congo 127 E6
Pani Mines India 96 B5
Panino Tverskaya Oblast' Rus. Fed.
   43 P5
Panino Voronezhskaya Oblast' Rus. Fed.
   41 G6
Paninskaya Rus. Fed. 43 R1
Panipat India 96 C3
Panitan Phil. 74 A4
Panizowye Belarus 43 L7
Panj r. Afgh./Tajik. see Pyandzh
Panj Tajik. 101 G3
   also spelt Pyandzh; formerly known as
   Kirovabad
Panjāb Afgh. 101 F3
Panjakent Tajik. 101 F2
   also spelt Pendzhikent
Panjang Indon. 76 D4
Panjang i. Indon. 77 D3
Panjang, Bukit Sing. 76 [inset]
Panjang, Selat sea chan. Indon. 76 C2
Panjgur Pak. 101 F5
Panjhra r. India 96 B5
Panjim India see Panaji
Panjin China 85 I3
   also known as Panshan
Panji Poyon Tajik. 101 G3
Panjkora r. Pak. 101 G3
Panjnad r. Pak. 101 H4
Pankakoski Fin. 44 O3
Pankovka Rus. Fed. 43 M3
Panlian China see Miyi
Pan Ling mts China 82 C2
Panlong China see Queshan
Panna India 96 D4
Pannawonica Australia 150 B4
Pannonhalma Hungary 49 N8
   formerly known as Győrszentmárton
Pano Aqil Pak. 101 G5
Panopah Indon. 77 E3
Panoplis Egypt see Akhmim
Panorama Brazil 206 B8
Panormus Sicilia Italy see Palermo
Panruti India 94 C4
Panshan China see Panjin
Panshi China 82 B4
Panshui China see Pu'an
Pantaicermin, Gunung mt. Indon. 76 C3

▶ Pantanal marsh S. America 201 F3
   Largest area of wetlands in the world.

Pantanal de São Lourenço marsh Brazil
   201 F4
Pantanal do Taquari marsh Brazil
   201 F4
Pantanal Matogrossense, Parque
   Nacional do nat. park Brazil 201 F4
Pantar i. Indon. 75 C5
Pantelleria Sicilia Italy see Pantelleria
Pantelleria Sicilia Italy 57 C12
   historically known as Pantelaria
Pantelleria, Isola di i. Sicilia Italy 57 E12
Pantemakassar East Timor 75 C5
   formerly known as Ocussi
Pantha Myanmar 78 A3
Panticapaeum Ukr. see Kerch
Pantijan Aboriginal Reserve Australia
   150 D3
Pantokratoras hill Greece 59 A9
   also known as Pandokrátor
Panto watercourse Israel 108 G7
Pantukan Phil. 74 C5
Panu Dem. Rep. Congo 126 C5
Pánuco Mex. 185 F4
Pánuco r. Mex. 185 F4

Panvel India 94 B2
Panwari India 96 C4
Panxian China 86 C3
   also known as Shiqiao
Panzhihua China 86 B3
   also known as Dukou
Panzi Dem. Rep. Congo 127 C6
Panzos Guat. 185 H6
Pão de Açúcar Brazil 202 E3
Paola Italy 57 I9
Paola U.S.A. 178 D4
Paoli U.S.A. 174 C4
Paoni Indon. 75 D3
Paonia U.S.A. 180 F5
Paoua Cent. Afr. Rep. 126 C3
Paôy Pêt Cambodia 79 C5
Pap Uzbek. 103 G4
   also known as Pop
Pápa Hungary 49 O8
Papa, Monte del mt. Italy 57 H8
Papadianika Greece 59 D12
Papagaio r. Brazil 201 E2
Papagaios Minas Gerais Brazil 207 I6
Papagaios Rondônia Brazil 201 E2
Papagni r. India 94 C3
Papakura N.Z. 152 I5
Papallacta Ecuador 198 B5
Papamoa Beach N.Z. 152 K5
Papanasam Tamil Nadu India 94 C4
Papanasam Tamil Nadu India 94 C4
Papantla Mex. 185 F4
Paparhahandi India 95 D2
Paparoa N.Z. 152 I4
Paparoa National Park N.Z. 153 F10
Paparoa Range mts N.Z. 153 F10
Papas, Akra c. Greece 59 G11
Papa Stour i. U.K. 46 K3
Pápateszér Hungary 49 O8
Papatoetoe N.Z. 152 I5
Papatowai N.Z. 153 D14
Papa Westray i. U.K. 46 J4
   also known as Papay
Papay i. U.K. see Papa Westray

▶ Papeete Fr. Polynesia 221 I7
   Capital of French Polynesia.

Papenburg Germany 48 E2
Papendorp S. Africa 132 C8
Paphos Cyprus 108 D3
   also spelt Pafos; historically known as Paphus
Paphus Cyprus see Paphos
Papikio mt. Bulg./Greece 58 G7
Papilė Lith. 42 D5
Papillion U.S.A. 178 C3
Papineau-Labelle, Réserve Faunique de
   nature res. Canada 168 F2
Papiya hill Bulg. 58 I6
Papoose Lake U.S.A. 183 I4
Paposo Chile 204 C2

▶ Papua, Gulf of P.N.G. 73 J8

▶ Papua New Guinea country Oceania
   144 F2
   2nd largest and 2nd most populous country
   in Oceania.
   oceania [countries] ▶ 138–139

Papun Myanmar 78 B4
Papunya Australia 148 A4
Pará r. Brazil 203 C6
Pará state Brazil 199 I5
Para r. India 96 C4
Para r. Rus. Fed. 41 G5
Pará, Rio do r. Brazil 202 B2
Paraburdoo Australia 150 B4
Paracaima, Sierra mts S. America see
   Pakaraima Mountains
Paracale Phil. 74 B3
Paracambi Brazil 207 J9
Paracas Peru 200 A3
Paracas, Península pen. Peru 200 A3
Paracatu Brazil 206 F2
Paracatu r. Minas Gerais Brazil 206 H3
   also known as Pracu
Paracel Islands S. China Sea 72 D3
   also known as Dao Tay Sa or Hoang Sa or
   Hsi-sha Ch'ün-tao or Quan Dao Hoang Sa
   or Xisha Qundao
Parachilna Australia 146 C2
Parachinar Pak. 101 G3
Paracín Srbija Yugo. 58 C5
Parada, Punta c. Peru 200 A3
Pará de Minas Brazil 203 C6
Paradis Canada 168 E3
Paradise r. Canada 169 J2
Paradise Guyana 199 G3
Paradise CA U.S.A. 182 C2
Paradise MI U.S.A. 173 I4
Paradise NV U.S.A. 183 I5
Paradise Gardens Canada 167 H2
Paradise Hill Canada 167 I4
Paradise Peak U.S.A. 182 G3
Paradise River Canada 169 J2
Paradise Valley U.S.A. 183 M8
Parado Indon. 77 G5
Paradwip India 95 E1
Paraetonium Egypt see Marsa Matrûh
Paraf'yanava Belarus 42 I7
Paragominas Brazil 202 C2
Paragould U.S.A. 174 B4
Paragua r. Bol. 201 E3
Paragua r. Venez. 199 F3
Paraguaçu Brazil 207 F3
Paraguaçu r. Brazil 202 E5
Paraguaçu Paulista Brazil 206 C9
Paraguai r. Arg./Para. 201 F6

▶ Paraguay country S. America 201 F5
   southamerica [countries] ▶ 192–193

Paraíba r. Brazil 202 F3
Paraíba state Brazil 202 E3
Paraíba do Sul Brazil 207 J9
Paraíba do Sul r. Brazil 203 D7
Paraibuna Brazil 207 H10
Parainen Fin. see Pargas
Paraíso Brazil 206 A6
Paraíso Mex. 185 G5
Paraíso do Norte Brazil 202 B4
Paraisópolis Brazil 207 H9
Parakka Sweden 44 M2
Parakou Benin 125 F4
Parakylia Australia 146 C2
Paralakhemundi India 95 E2
   formerly spelt Parlakimedi
Paralia Greece 59 D10
Paramagudi India see Paramakudi
Paramakkudi India 94 C4
   formerly spelt Paramagudi

▶ Paramaribo Suriname 199 H3
   Capital of Suriname.

Paramillo mt. Col. 198 C3
Paramillo, Parque Nacional nat. park
   Col. 198 B3
Paramirim Brazil 202 D5
Paramirim r. Brazil 202 D4
Páramo hill Spain 54 C2
Páramo de Masa, Puerto del pass Spain
   54 H2
Paramonga Peru 200 A2
Paramushir, Ostrov i. Rus. Fed. 39 P4
Paran watercourse Israel 108 G7
Paraná Arg. 204 E3
Paraná Brazil 202 C5
Paraná r. Brazil 202 C5
Paraná state Brazil 206 B11

Paraná r. S. America 206 B7
Part of the Río de la Plata - Paraná, 2nd longest river in South America.
southamerica (landscapes) ▶ 190-191

Paranaguá Brazil 203 D8
Paranaíba Brazil 206 B6
Paranaíba r. Brazil 206 B7
Paraná Ibicuy r. Arg. 204 F4
Paranaiguara Brazil 206 B7
Paranaíta r. Brazil 201 F2
Paranapanema r. Brazil 206 B9
Paranapiacaba, Serra mts Brazil 203 B8
Paranapura Peru 198 B6
Paranari Brazil 199 E6
Paranavaí Brazil 206 A10
Parandak Iran 100 B3
Parang Phil. 74 B5
Parangi Aru r. Sri Lanka 94 D4
Parangipettai India 94 C4
  historically known as Porto Novo
Parang Pass India 96 C2
Parângul Mare, Vârful mt. Romania 58 E3
Parantij India 96 B5
Paraopeba Brazil 203 C6
Paraopeba r. Brazil 203 C6
Parapanda mt. Spain 54 H7
Parapara Indon. 75 C2
Pârâpâra Iraq 107 F4
Paraparaumu N.Z. 152 I8
Parapuã Brazil 206 C8
Paraque, Cerro mt. Venez. 199 E3
Paras Norway 44 N1
Paraspori, Akra pt Greece 59 I13
Parati Brazil 203 C7
Paratinga Brazil 202 D5
Paratoo Australia 146 C3
Paraú, Kûh-e mt. Iraq 107 T4
Parauapebas r. Brazil 202 B3
Parauaquara, Serra hill Brazil 199 H5
Parauari r. Brazil 199 E5
Paraúna Brazil 206 C4
Paray-le-Monial France 51 K6
Parbati r. India 96 C4
Parbatipur Bangl. 97 F4
Parchim Germany 48 I2
Parchment U.S.A. 172 H8
Parczew Poland 49 T4
Pardee Reservoir U.S.A. 182 D3
Pardeeville U.S.A. 172 D7
Pardina Romania 58 J3
Pardo Arg. 204 F5
Pardo r. Bahia Brazil 207 O2
Pardo r. Mato Grosso do Sul Brazil 206 A8
Pardo r. Minas Gerais Brazil 207 I2
Pardo r. São Paulo Brazil 206 E7
Pardoo Australia 150 B4
Pardubice Czech Rep. 49 M5
Pare Indon. 77 F4
Parece Vela i. Japan see Okino-Tori-shima
Parechcha Belarus 42 F8
Pare Chu r. China 89 B5
Parecis Brazil 201 F3
Parecis, Serra dos hills Brazil 201 E2
Paredes de Nava Spain 54 G2
Paredón Mex. 185 E3
Paremata N.Z. 152 I9
Parenda India 94 B2
Parent Canada 169 G4
Parentis-en-Born France 50 E8
Pareora N.Z. 153 F12
Parepare Indon. 75 A4
Parfino Rus. Fed. 43 M4
Parga Greece 59 B9
Pargas Fin. 45 M3
  also known as Parainen
Parghelia Italy 57 H10
Pargi India 94 C2
Pargolovo Rus. Fed. 43 L1
Paria Bol. 200 D4
Paria r. U.S.A. 183 M5
Paria, Gulf of Trin. and Tob./Venez. 187 H5
Paria, Península de pen. Venez. 199 F3
Pariaman Indon. 76 C3
Paria Plateau U.S.A. 183 L5
Paricatuba Brazil 199 F6
Parida, Isla i. Panama 186 C5
Parigi Indon. 75 B3
Parikkala Fin. 45 O3
Parikud Islands India 95 E2
Parima r. Brazil see Uatatás
Parima, Serra mts Brazil 199 E4
Parima-Tapirapecó, Parque Nacional nat. park Venez. 199 E4
Parinari Peru 198 C6
Pariñas, Punta pt Peru 198 A6
Parintins Brazil 199 G5
Paris Canada 173 M7

Paris France 51 I4
Capital of France and most populous city in Europe. Historically known as Lutetia.
world (cities) ▶ 24-25

Paris ID U.S.A. 180 D4
Paris IL U.S.A. 174 C4
Paris KY U.S.A. 176 A7
Paris ME U.S.A. 177 O1
Paris TN U.S.A. 174 B5
Paris TX U.S.A. 179 D5
Parish U.S.A. 177 I2
Parisienne, Île i. Canada 173 I4
Pariz Iran 100 C4
Parizh Rus. Fed. 103 E1
Park r. U.S.A. 178 C1
Parka Dem. Rep. Congo 126 C5
Parkajoki Sweden 44 M2
Parkal India 94 C2
Parkano Fin. 45 M3

Park City U.S.A. 183 M1
Parke Lake Canada 169 J2
Parkent Uzbek. 103 G4
Parker U.S.A. 183 J7
Parker, Mount hill Hong Kong China 87 [inset]
  also known as Pak Ka Shan
Parker Dam U.S.A. 183 J7
Parker Lake Canada 167 M2
Parker Range hills Australia 151 B7
Parkersburg U.S.A. 176 D6
Parkers Lake U.S.A. 176 A9
Parkes Australia 147 F3
Park Falls U.S.A. 172 C5
Park Forest U.S.A. 172 F9
Parkhar Tajik. see Farkhor
Parkhill Canada 173 L7
Parkinson Canada 173 J4
Parkman U.S.A. 176 D4
Park Rapids U.S.A. 178 D2
Parksley U.S.A. 177 J8
Parkston U.S.A. 178 C3
Parksville Canada 166 E5
Parkutta Jammu and Kashmir 96 C2
Parla Spain 54 H4
Parlakimedi India see Paralakhemundi
Parla Kimedi India 95 E2
Parli Vaijnath India 94 C2
Parlung Zangbo r. China 86 A2
  also known as Nagong Chu
Parma Italy 56 C4
Parma r. Italy 56 C4
Parma ID U.S.A. 180 C4
Parma MI U.S.A. 173 I8
Parma OH U.S.A. 176 D4
Parma Rus. Fed. 40 K2
Parmana Venez. 199 E3
Parnaguá Brazil 202 D4
Parnaíba Brazil 202 D2
Parnaíba r. Brazil 202 D2
Parnaibinha r. Brazil 202 C4
Parnarama Brazil 202 D3
Parnassos mt. Greece 59 D10
Parnassos nat. park Greece 59 D10
Parnassus N.Z. 153 H10
Parndana Australia 146 C3
Parner India 94 B2
Parnitha mt. nat. park Greece 59 E10
Parnon mts Greece 59 D11
Pärnu Estonia 42 F3
  formerly known as Pernov
Pärnu-Jaagupi Estonia 42 F3
Pärnu laht b. Estonia 42 F3
Paro Bhutan 97 F4
Paroa N.Z. 153 F10
Parona Turkey see Fındık
Paroo watercourse Australia 147 D2
Paroo Channel watercourse Australia 147 D2
Paropamisus mts Afgh. 101 E3
  also known as Safid Kûh
Paroreang, Bukit mt. Indon. 75 A3
Paros Greece 59 G11
Paros i. Greece 59 G11
Parow S. Africa 132 C10
Parowan U.S.A. 183 L4
Parral Chile 204 C5
Parral r. Mex. 181 D4
Parramatta Australia 147 F3
Parramore Island U.S.A. 177 J8
Parras Mex. 185 E3
Parrett r. U.S.A. 172 D5
Parrita Costa Rica 186 B5
Parrsboro Canada 169 H4
Parry, Kap c. Greenland see Kangaarsussuaq
Parry Bay Canada 165 K3
Parry Channel Canada 165 H2
Parry Islands Canada 165 H2
Parry Lagoons Nature Reserve Australia 150 F2
Parry Range hills Australia 150 A4
Parry Sound Canada 168 D4
Pars prov. Iran see Fārs
Parsa India 97 E4
Parsa prov. Iran see Fārs
Parsnip Peak U.S.A. 183 J3
Parsons KS U.S.A. 178 D4
Parsons WV U.S.A. 176 F6
Parsons Range hills Australia 148 B2
Partabgarh India 94 B2
Partabpur Chhattisgarh India 94 D2
Partabpur Chhattisgarh India 97 D5
Partakko Fin. 44 N1
Pártanna Sicilia Italy 57 E11
Pärte mt. Sweden 44 L2
Partenstein Germany 48 G5
Parthenay France 50 F6
Partida, Isla i. Mex. 184 C3
Partinico Sicilia Italy 57 F10
Partizansk Rus. Fed. 82 D4
  formerly known as Suchan
Partizánske Slovakia 49 P7
Partridge r. Canada 168 D3
Paru r. Brazil 199 G5
Parú, Serranía mts Venez. 199 E3
Parūd Iran 101 E5
Paru de Oeste r. Brazil 199 G5
Parvān prov. Afgh. 101 G3
Parvatipuram India 95 D2
Parvatsar India 96 B3
Paryang China 89 C5
Parychy Belarus 43 K9
Parygino Kazakh. 88 D1
Parys S. Africa 133 L3
Pas r. Spain 54 H1
Pasa Daği mt. Turkey 106 C3
Pasadena CA U.S.A. 182 F7
Pasadena TX U.S.A. 179 D6
Pasado, Cabo c. Ecuador 198 A5
Pasaje Ecuador 198 B5
Pa Sak, Mae Nam r. Thai. 79 C5
Pasan India 97 D5
Pasarwajo Indon. 75 B4
Pasawng Myanmar 78 B4
Pascagoula r. Canada 168 F3
Pascagoula U.S.A. 175 B6
Pascagoula r. U.S.A. 175 B6
Pascalis Canada 173 P2
Pașcani Romania 58 H1
Pasco dept Peru 200 C3
Pasco U.S.A. 180 C3
Pascoag U.S.A. 177 N4
Pascoal, Monte hill Brazil 203 E6
Pascoe r. Australia 149 E4
Pascua, Isla de i. S. Pacific Ocean see Easter Island
Pascual Phil. 74 B3
Pas de Calais strait France/U.K. see Dover, Strait of
Pasewalk Germany 49 L2
Pasfield Lake Canada 167 J3
Pasha Rus. Fed. 43 O1
Pasha r. Rus. Fed. 43 N1
Pashkovo Rus. Fed. 82 C2
Pashozero Rus. Fed. 43 O1
Pashtun Zarghun Afgh. 101 E3
Pasig Phil. 74 B3
Pasi Ga Myanmar 78 B2
Pasighat India 97 G3
Pasinler Turkey 107 E3
Pasir Gudang Malaysia 76 [inset]
Pasirian Indon. 77 F5
Pasir Laba, Tanjong pt Sing. 76 [inset]
Pasir Mas Malaysia 76 C1
Pasirpangarayan Indon. 76 C2
Pasir Panjang Sing. 76 [inset]

Pasir Panjang hill Sing. 76 [inset]
Pasir Putih Malaysia 76 C1
Pasitelu, Pulau-pulau is Indon. 75 B4
Paskevicha, Zaliv l. Kazakh. see Shevchenko, Zaliv
Paskūh Iran 101 E5
Pasłęk Poland 49 Q1
Pasłęka r. Poland 49 Q1
Paslīkaya Turkey 108 H1
Fašman i. Croatia 56 H5
Pasni Pak. 101 E5
Paso de Caballo Venez. 199 E2
Paso de Indios Arg. 205 C6
Paso del Limay Arg. 204 C6
Paso de los Libres Arg. 204 F3
Paso de los Toros Uruguay 204 F4
Paso del Sapo Arg. 205 C6
Paso de Patria Para. 201 F6
Paso de San Antonio Mex. 179 B6
Paso Real Hond. 186 B4
Paso Rio Mayo Arg. 205 C7
Paso Robles U.S.A. 182 D5
Pasquia Hills Canada 167 K4
Pasrur Pak. 101 H3
Passage Island U.S.A. 172 E2
Passagem Franca Brazil 202 D3
Passaic U.S.A. 177 K5
Passa Quatro Brazil 207 I9
Passa Tempo Brazil 207 I7
Passau Germany 49 K7
Passi Phil. 74 B4
Passo Fundo Brazil 203 A9
Passo Real, Barragem resr Brazil 203 A9
Passos Brazil 206 G7
Pastavy Belarus 42 H7
  also spelt Postavy
Pastaza prov. Ecuador 198 B5
Pastaza r. Peru 198 B6
Pasteur Arg. 204 E4
Pasto Col. 198 B4
Pasto Grande Brazil 201 E1
Pastora Peak U.S.A. 183 O5
Pastos Bons Brazil 202 D3
Pasu Jammu and Kashmir 96 B1
Pasuquin Phil. 74 B2
Pasur Turkey see Kulp
Pasuruan Indon. 77 F4
Pasvalys Lith. 42 F5
Pasvikelva r. Europe see Patsoyoki
Pasztó Hungary 49 Q8
Pata Bol. 200 C3
Pata i. Phil. 74 B5
Patagonia reg. Arg. 205 C8
  southamerica (contrasts) ▶ 194-195
Pataliputra India see Patna
Patan India 94 B2
Patan Gujarat India 96 B5
Patan Madhya Pradesh India 96 C5
Patan Maharashtra India 94 B2
Patan Nepal 97 E4
  also known as Lalitpur
Patancheru India 94 C2
Patandar, Koh-i- mt. Pak. 101 F5
Patani Indon. 75 D2
Patani Nigeria 125 G5
Patan Saongi India 96 C5
Pataudi India 96 C3
Patavium Italy see Padua
Patay Arg. 204 E2
Patchewollock Australia 147 D3
Patch Grove U.S.A. 172 C8
Patchogue U.S.A. 177 L5
Patea N.Z. 152 I7
Patea r. N.Z. 152 I7
Pate Island Kenya 128 D5
Patensie S. Africa 133 I10
Paternion Austria 49 K9
Paternò Sicilia Italy 57 G11
Paterson r. Australia 147 E2
Paterson S. Africa 133 J10
Paterson U.S.A. 177 K5
Paterson Inlet N.Z. 153 B14
  also known as Whaka a Te Wera
Paterson Range hills Australia 150 C4
Pathalgaon India 97 D5
Pathankot India 96 B3
Patharia India 96 C5
Pathein Myanmar see Bassein
Pathfinder Reservoir U.S.A. 180 F4
Pathiu Thai. 79 B6
Pathri India 94 C2
Pathum Thani Thai. 79 C5
Pati Indon. 77 E4
Patía r. Col. 198 B4
Patiala India 96 C3
Patini, Selat sea chan. Indon. 75 C3
Patitiri Greece 59 E9
Pativilca r. Peru 200 A2
Pātkai Bum mts India/Myanmar 78 A2
Patkaklik China 89 D4
Patlangıç Turkey 59 K12
Patmos Greece 59 H11
Patna India 97 E4
  historically known as Pataliputra
Patnagarh India 95 D1
Patnanongan i. Phil. 74 B3
Patnos Turkey 107 E3
Pato, Cerro mt. Chile 205 B7
Pato Branco Brazil 203 A8
Patoda India 94 B2
Patoka r. U.S.A. 174 C4
Patomskoye Nagor'ye mts Rus. Fed. 39 L4
Patoniva Fin. 44 N1
  also known as Buoddobohki
Patos Albania 58 A8
Patos Brazil 202 E3
Patos, Lagoa dos l. Brazil 203 B9
Patos, Rio dos r. Brazil 206 B5
Patos de Minas Brazil 206 G5
Patquía Arg. 204 D3
Patra Greece see Patras
Patrae Greece see Patras
Pátrai Greece see Patras
Patraïkos Kolpos b. Greece 59 C10
Patras Greece 59 C10
  also known as Patra or Pátrai; historically known as Patrae
Patrasaer India 97 E5
Patratu India 97 E5
Patreksfjörður Iceland 44 [inset] B2
Patri India 96 A5
Patricio Lynch, Isla i. Chile 205 B8
Patrick Creek watercourse Australia 149 E4
Patrick Springs U.S.A. 176 E9
Patrimônio Brazil 206 E6
Patrocínio Brazil 206 F5
Patsoyoki r. Europe 40 O1
  also known as Pasvikelva; also spelt Paatsjoki
Pattadakal tourist site India 94 B2
Pattanapuram India 94 C4
Pattani Thai. 79 C7
Pattani r. Thai. 79 C7
Pattaya Thai. 79 C5
Patten U.S.A. 174 G2
Patterson CA U.S.A. 182 C4
Patterson LA U.S.A. 175 B6
Patterson r. U.S.A. 176 G6
Patterson, Mount Canada 166 C1
Patterson Mountain U.S.A. 182 E5
Patterson, Point U.S.A. 172 H5
Patti India 97 D4
Patti Indon. 77 E4
Patti Sicilia Italy 57 G10
Pattijoki Fin. 44 N2
Pättikkä Fin. 44 M1
Pattikonda India 94 C3
Pattukkottai India 94 C4

Pattullo, Mount Canada 166 D3
Patu Brazil 202 E3
Patuakhali Bangl. 97 F5
Patuanak Canada 167 I4
Patuca, Parque Nacional nat. park Hond. 186 B4
Patuca, Punta pt Hond. 186 B4
Patur India 94 C1
Patutu mt. N.Z. 152 J7
Patuxent r. U.S.A. 177 I7
Patuxent Range mts Antarctica 223 S1
Patvinsuon kansallispuisto nat. park Fin. 44 O3
Pátzcuaro Mex. 185 E5
Pau France 50 F9
Pau-Brasil Brazil 207 N2
Paucartambo Peru 200 B2
Paucartambo r. Peru see Yavero
Pau d'Arco Brazil 202 B3
Pau d'Arco r. Brazil 201 H1
Pauhunri mt. China/India 89 E7
Pauillac France 50 F7
Pauini r. Brazil 199 D5
Pauini r. Brazil 200 D1
Pauk Myanmar 78 A3
Paukkaung Myanmar 78 A4
Paulatuk Canada 164 G3
Paulden U.S.A. 183 L7
Paulding Bay Antarctica 223 I2
Paulicéia Brazil 206 B8
Paulis Dem. Rep. Congo see Isiro
Paulista Brazil 202 F3
Paulistana Brazil 202 D4
Paulo Afonso Brazil 202 E4
Paulo de Faria Brazil 206 D7
Paulpietersburg S. Africa 133 O4
Pauls Valley U.S.A. 179 C5
Paulu, Îles is Fr. Polynesia see Tuamotu Islands
Păunești Romania 58 I2
Paung Myanmar 78 A4
Paungbyin Myanmar 78 A2
Paungde Myanmar 78 A4
Pauni India 94 C1
Pauri India 96 C3
Pausa Peru 200 B3
Pauto r. Col. 198 D3
Pauträsk Sweden 44 L2
Pauwela U.S.A. 181 [inset] Z1
Pavagada India 94 C3
Pavão Brazil 207 M5
Pavarandocito Col. 198 B3
Pāveh Iran 100 A3
Pavelets Rus. Fed. 43 U8
Pavia Italy 56 B3
  historically known as Ticinum
Pavilion U.S.A. 176 G3
Pavilosta Latvia 42 C5
Pavino Rus. Fed. 40 H4
Pavlikeni Bulg. 58 G5
Pavlinovo Rus. Fed. 43 O7
Pavlivka Ukr. 58 K1
Pavlodar Kazakh. 103 I1
Pavlodar Oblast admin. div. Kazakh. see Pavlodarskaya Oblast'
Pavlodar Oblysy admin. div. Kazakh. see Pavlodarskaya Oblast'
Pavlodarskaya Oblast' admin. div. Kazakh. 103 I1
  English form Pavlodar Oblast; also known as Pavlodar Oblysy
Pavlof Volcano U.S.A. 164 C4
Pavlograd Ukr. see Pavlohrad
Pavlohrad Ukr. 41 E6
  also spelt Pavlograd
Pavlovka Akmolinskaya Oblast' Kazakh. 103 H2
Pavlovka Kustanayskaya Oblast' Kazakh. 103 E1
Pavlovka Respublika Bashkortostan Rus. Fed. 40 K5
Pavlovka Ul'yanovskaya Oblast' Rus. Fed. 41 H5
Pavlovo Rus. Fed. 40 G5
Pavlovsk Leningradskaya Oblast' Rus. Fed. 43 L2
Pavlovsk Vorcnezhskaya Oblast' Rus. Fed. 41 G6
Pavlovskaya Rus. Fed. 41 F7
Pavlovskiy Kazakh. 103 E1
Pavlovskiy Posad Rus. Fed. 43 T6
Pavlovskoye Rus. Fed. 43 V1
Pavlovskoye Vodokhranilishche resr Rus. Fed. 40 K5
Pavullo nel Frignano Italy 56 C4
Pavy Rus. Fed. 43 K3
Pawai India 96 C4
Pawan r. Indon. 77 E3
Pawarenga N.Z. 152 H3
Pawayan India 96 D3
Pawhuska U.S.A. 178 C4
Pawling U.S.A. 177 L4
Pawn r. Myanmar 78 B4
Pawnee r. U.S.A. 178 C4
Pawnee City U.S.A. 178 C3
Paw Paw MI U.S.A. 172 H8
Paw Paw WV U.S.A. 176 G6
Pawu Aboriginal Land res. Australia 148 A3
Paxaro mt. Spain 54 C1
Paximadia i. Greece 59 H13
Paximadia i. Greece 59 F13
Paxoi i. Greece 59 B9
Paxson U.S.A. 164 E3
Paxton U.S.A. 174 B3
Payahe Incon. 75 C2
Payakumbuh Indon. 76 C3
Paya Lebar Sing. 76 [inset]
Payerne Switz. 51 M6
Payette U.S.A. 180 C3
Payette r. U.S.A. 180 C3
Pay-Khoy, Khrebet hills Rus. Fed. 40 L1
Payne Canada see Kangirsuk
Payne U.S.A. 176 A4
Payne, Lac l. Canada 169 F1
Paynes Creek U.S.A. 182 C1
Payne's Find Australia 151 B6
Paynesville Australia 147 E4
Paysandú Uruguay 204 F4
Pays de la Loire admin. reg. France 50 E5
Pays de Léon reg. France 50 B4
Payshanba Uzbek. see Kara-Dar'ya
Payson U.S.A. 183 M7
Payún, Cerro vol. Arg. 204 C5
Payyanur India 94 B3
Payzawat China see Jiashi
Paz, Río da r. Brazil 202 B4
Pazar Turkey 107 E2
Pazarcık Turkey 107 D3
Pazardzhik Bulg. 58 F6
Pazarköy Turkey 59 I9
Pazarlar Turkey 59 K10
Pazaryeri Turkey 59 K9
Paz de Ariporo Col. 198 D3
Paz de Rio Col. 198 C3
Pazin Croatia 56 F3
Pazña Bol. 200 D4
Pchevzha r. Rus. Fed. 43 M2
Pčinja r. Macedonia 58 C7
Pe Myanmar 79 B5
Pea r. U.S.A. 175 D7

Peace Point Canada 167 H3
Peace River Canada 167 G3
Peach Creek U.S.A. 176 D8
Peachland Canada 166 G5
Peach Springs U.S.A. 183 K6
Peacock Hills Canada 167 I1
Pea Island National Wildlife Refuge nature res. U.S.A. 174 F5
Peak Charles hill Australia 151 C7
Peak Charles National Park Australia 151 C7
Peak District National Park U.K. 47 K10
Peake watercourse Australia 146 C2
Peaked Mountain hill U.S.A. 174 G2
Peak Hill N.S.W. Australia 147 F3
Peak Hill W.A. Australia 151 B5
Peak Mountain U.S.A. 182 E7
Peak Range hills Australia 149 F4
Peaks Mill U.S.A. 176 A7
Peale, Mount U.S.A. 183 O3
Peanut U.S.A. 182 A1
Pearce Point Australia 148 A2
Pearisburg U.S.A. 176 E8
Pearl Canada 172 E2
Pearl r. U.S.A. 175 B5
Pearsall U.S.A. 179 C6
Pearson U.S.A. 175 D6
Pearson Islands Australia 146 B3
Pearston S. Africa 133 J9
Peary Channel Canada 165 J2
Peary Land reg. Greenland 165 P1
Pease r. U.S.A. 179 C5
Peawah r. Australia 150 B4
Peawanuck Canada 168 C2
Pebane Moz. 131 H3
Pebas Peru 198 D5
Pebble Island Falkland Is 205 F8
Pebendo Indon. 75 B3
Peć Kosovo, Srbija Yugo. 58 B6
  also known as Peje
Pecan Bayou r. U.S.A. 179 C6
Peçanha Brazil 207 K5
Pecatonica U.S.A. 172 D8
Pecha r. Rus. Fed. 44 O1
Pechenga Rus. Fed. 44 O1
  formerly known as Petsamo
Pechenga r. Rus. Fed. 43 P1
Pechora Rus. Fed. 40 K2
Pechora r. Rus. Fed. 40 K2
Pechora Sea Rus. Fed. see Pechorskoye More
Pechoro-Ilyichskiy Zapovednik nature res. Rus. Fed. 40 K3
Pechorskaya Guba b. Rus. Fed. 40 J1
Pechorskoye More sea Rus. Fed. 40 J1
  English form Pechora Sea
Pechory Rus. Fed. 42 I4
Pecica Romania 58 C2
Pecineaga Romania 58 J3
Peck U.S.A. 173 K7
Pecos U.S.A. 179 B6
Pecos r. U.S.A. 179 B6
Pécs Hungary 49 P9
  formerly known as Fünfkirchen
Pécsvárad Hungary 49 P9
Pedasí Panama 186 D6
Pedda Vagu r. India 94 C2
Pedder, Lake Australia 147 E5
Peddie S. Africa 133 L10
Pedernales Ecuador 198 A4
Pedernales Haiti 187 F3
Pedernales Mex. 181 F7
Pedernales r. U.S.A. 179 C6
Pedernales Venez. 199 F2
Pedernales, Salar de salt flat Chile 204 C2
Pederneiras Brazil 206 D9
Pedersöre Fin. 44 M3
Pediva Angola 127 B8
Pedra Azul Brazil 207 L3
Pedra Badejo Cape Verde 124 [inset]
Pedra Lume Cape Verde 124 [inset]
Pedra Preta, Serra da mts Brazil 202 B5
Pedras r. Brazil 202 C5
Pedras de Maria da Cruz Brazil 207 I2
Pedras Negras Brazil 201 E3
Pedregal Panama 186 C5
Pedregal Venez. 198 D2
Pedregulho Brazil 206 F7
Pedreiras Maranhão Brazil 202 C3
Pedreiras São Paulo Brazil 206 G9
Pedro, Point Sri Lanka 94 D4
Pedro Afonso Brazil 202 B4
Pedro Avelino Brazil 202 E3
Pedro Bank sea feature Jamaica 186 D3
Pedro Barros Brazil 206 F11
Pedro Cays is Jamaica 186 D3
Pedro Chico Col. 198 D4
Pedro Gomes Brazil 203 A6
Pedro Gómez Mex. 181 F7
Pedro II, Ilha reg. Brazil/Venez. 199 E4
Pedro Juan Caballero Para. 201 G5
Pedro Leopoldo Brazil 203 C6
Pedro Luro Arg. 204 E5
Pedro Muñoz Spain 55 I5
Pedro Osório Brazil 204 G3
Pedroso Port. 54 C3
Pedro Toledo Brazil 206 F11
Peebinga Australia 146 D3
Peebles U.K. 46 I8
Peebles U.S.A. 176 B7
Peedamulla Aboriginal Reserve Australia 150 A4
Pee Dee r. U.S.A. 175 E5
Peekskill U.S.A. 177 L4
Peel r. Canada 166 C1
Peel Isle of Man 47 H9
Peene r. Germany 49 K2
Peera Fin. 44 M1
Peera Peera Poolanna Lake salt flat Australia 148 C5
Peerless Lake Canada 167 H3
Peers Canada 167 G4
Peery Lake salt flat Australia 147 D2
Pegasus Bay N.Z. 153 G11
Pegnitz Germany 48 I6
Pego Spain 55 K6
Pegu Myanmar see Bago
Pegu admin. div. Myanmar 78 A4
  also spelt Bago
Pegu Yoma mts Myanmar 78 A4
Pehlivanköy Turkey 58 H7
Péhonko Benin 125 F4
Pehowa India 96 C3
Pehuajó Arg. 204 E4
Peikang Taiwan 87 G4
  also spelt Beigang
Peine Germany 48 H3
Peine, Cerro mt. Arg. 205 B8
Peint India 94 B1
Peipsi järv l. Estonia/Rus. Fed. see Peipus, Lake
Peipus, Lake Estonia/Rus. Fed. 42 I3
  also known as Chudskoye, Ozero or Peipsi järv
Peiraias Greece see Piraeus

Pei Shan mts China see Bei Shan
Peitz Germany 49 L4
Peixe Brazil 202 B5
Peixe r. Goiás Brazil 206 C1
Peixe r. Goiás Brazil 206 C1
Peixe r. São Paulo Brazil 206 B8
Peixe, Rio do r. Brazil 206 A3
Peixes r. Brazil 201 F2
Peixes r. Brazil 207 J9
Peixes, Rio dos r. Brazil 206 B1
Peixian China see Pizhou
Peixian China 87 F1
Peixoto, Represa resr Brazil 206 G7
Peixoto de Azevedo Brazil 202 A4
Peixoto de Azevedo r. Brazil 201 G2
Pejantan i. Indon. 77 D2
Peje Kosovo, Srbija Yugo. see Peć
Pek r. Yugo. 58 C4
Pekabata Indon. 75 A3
Pekalongan Indon. 77 E4
Pekan Malaysia 76 C2
Pekanbaru Indon. 76 C2
  also spelt Pakanbaru
Pékans, Rivière aux r. Canada 169 H2
Pekin U.S.A. 174 B3
Peking China see Beijing
Peklino Rus. Fed. 43 O8
Pelabuhan Kelang Malaysia 76 C2
  formerly known as Port Klang or Port Swettenham
Pelabuhan Sandakan inlet Sabah Malaysia 77 G1
Pelada, Pampa hills Arg. 205 C7
Pelado mt. Spain 55 J5
Pelagie, Isole is Sicilia Italy 57 E13
Pelagonija reg. Macedonia 58 C7
Pelagonisou, Diavlos sea chan. Greece 59 F9
Pelaihari Indon. 77 F3
Pelalawan Indon. 76 C3
Pelapis i. Indon. 77 E3
Pelasgia Greece 59 D10
  also spelt Pelasyia
Pelat, Mont mt. France 51 M8
Pelatsoeu mt. Lesotho 133 M5
Pelawanbesar Indon. 77 G2
Pełczyce Poland 49 M2
Peleaga, Vârful mt. Romania 58 D3
Pelechuco Bol. 200 C3
Peleči Latvia 42 H5
Pelée, Montagne vol. Martinique 187 H4
Pelee Island Canada 168 C5
Pelee Point Canada 168 D5
Peleliu i. Palau 73 H5
  also spelt Beliliou
Peleng i. Indon. 75 B3
Peleng, Selat sea chan. Indon. 75 B3
Peleng, Teluk b. Indon. 75 B3
Pelhřimov Czech Rep. 49 M6
Pelican Creek r. Australia 149 D3
Pelican Lake l. Canada 167 K4
Pelican Lake l. Canada 172 C1
Pelican Lake l. U.S.A. 178 D1
Pelican Narrows Canada 167 K4
Pelister mt. Macedonia 58 C8
Pelister nat. park Macedonia 58 C8
Pelješac pen. Croatia 56 J6
Pelkosenniemi Fin. 44 N2
Pellat Lake Canada 167 I1
Pellegrue France 50 G8
Pelleluhu Islands P.N.G. 73 J7
Pello Fin. 44 N2
Pellworm i. Germany 48 F1
Pelly r. Canada 166 B2
Pelly Bay Canada 165 K3
Pelly Crossing Canada 166 B2
Pelly Lake Canada 167 K1
Pelly Mountains Canada 166 C2
Pelokang is Indon. 77 G4
Peloponnese admin. reg. Greece see Peloponnisos
Peloponnese reg. Greece 59 C11
  also known as Peloponnisos; historically known as Peloponnesus
Peloponnisos admin. reg. Greece 59 D11
  English form Peloponnese; historically known as Peloponnesus
Peloponnisos reg. Greece see Peloponnese
Pelotas Brazil 204 G4
Pelotas, Rio das r. Brazil 203 B8
Pelovo Bulg. 58 F5
Pelplin Poland 49 P2
Pelsart Group is Australia 151 A6
Peltovuoma Fin. 44 N1
Pelusium tourist site Egypt 108 D6
Pelusium, Bay of Egypt see Tina, Khalîg el
Pelvoux, Massif du mts France 51 M8
Pemache r. Canada 173 J3
Pemadumcook Lake U.S.A. 174 G2
Pemalang Indon. 77 E4
Pemangkat Indon. 77 D2
Pemarung, Pulau i. Indon. 77 G3
Pematangsiantar Indon. 76 B2
Pemba Moz. 131 I2
  formerly known as Porto Amélia
Pemba Zambia 127 E9
Pemba, Baía de b. Moz. 129 D8
Pemba Channel Tanz. 129 C6
Pemba Island Tanz. 129 C6
Pemba North admin. reg. Tanz. 129 C6
Pemba South admin. reg. Tanz. 129 C6
Pemberton Australia 151 A7
Pemberton Canada 166 F5
Pemberton U.S.A. 177 K6
Pembina r. Canada 167 H4
Pembina r. U.S.A. 178 C1
Pembroke Canada 168 E4
Pembroke U.K. 47 H12
  also known as Penfro
Pembroke U.S.A. 175 D5
Pembroke, Cape Falkland Is 205 F8
Pembroke, Mount N.Z. 153 B12
Pembroke Pines U.S.A. 175 D7
Pembrokeshire Coast National Park U.K. 47 G12
Pembuanghulu Indon. 77 F3
Pemuco Chile 204 B5
Pen India 94 B2
Pen r. Myanmar 78 A3
Pena Barrosa Bol. 200 D5
Peña Cabollera mt. Spain 55 H3
Peña de Francia mt. Spain 54 E4
Peña de Izaga mt. Spain 55 J2
Peña de Oroel mt. Spain 55 K2
Peñafiel Port. 54 C3
Peñafiel Spain 54 H3
Peñagolosa mt. Spain 55 K4
Peñalara mt. Spain 54 H3
Peña de Santiago tourist site Spain 54 E2
Peñalsordo Spain 54 F5
Penamacor Port. 54 D4
Penambo Range mts Sarawak Malaysia see Tama Abu, Banjaran
Peña Mira mt. Spain 54 E3
Peña Nevada, Cerro mt. Mex. 185 F4
Penang state Malaysia see Pinang
Peñaranda de Bracamonte Spain 54 F4
Pen Argyl U.S.A. 177 J5
Penarie Australia 147 D3
Peñarroya mt. Spain 55 K4
Peñarroya-Pueblonuevo Spain 54 F6
Peñas, Cabo de c. Spain 54 F1
Penas, Golfo de g. Chile 205 B7
Peñas Blancas Nicaragua 186 B5
Peñasco watercourse U.S.A. 181 F6

Penasi, Pulau *i.* Indon. **76** A1
also known as Dedap
Peña Ubiña *mt.* Spain **54** F1
Peña Utrera *hill* Spain **54** E6
Pench *r.* India **96** C5
Pencheng China *see* **Ruichang**
Pench National Park India **96** C5
Penck, Cape Antarctica **223** F2
Pendé *r.* Cent. Afr. Rep. **126** C3
Pendembu Sierra Leone **124** B4
Pender U.S.A. **178** C3
Pender Bay Australia **150** C3
Pender Bay Aboriginal Reserve Australia **150** C3
Pendik Turkey **58** K8
Pendleton U.S.A. **180** C3
Pendleton Bay Canada **166** E4
Pendopo Indon. **76** C3
Pend Oreille *r.* U.S.A. **180** C2
Pend Oreille Lake U.S.A. **180** C2
Pendra India **97** D5
Penduv India **94** B2
Pendzhikent Tajik. *see* **Panjakent**
Penebangan *i.* Indon. **77** E3
Peneda Gerês, Parque Nacional da *nat. park* Port. **54** C3
Pene-Mende Dem. Rep. Congo **126** F6
Pénessoulou Benin **125** F4
Penetanguishene Canada **173** N6
Penfield U.S.A. **176** G4
Penfro U.K. *see* **Pembroke**
Peng'an China **86** C2
also known as Zhoukou
Penganga *r.* India **94** C2
Peng Chau *i. Hong Kong* China **87** [inset]
P'engchia Yü *i.* Taiwan **87** G3
Penge Dem. Rep. Congo **127** E6
P'enghu Ch'üntao *is* Taiwan **87** F4
English form Pescadores; *also known as* P'enghu Liehtao
P'enghu Liehtao *is* Taiwan *see* **P'enghu Ch'üntao**
P'enghu Tao *i.* Taiwan **87** F4
Pengiki *i.* Indon. **77** E2
Peng Kang *hill* Sing. **76** [inset]
Penglai China **85** I4
formerly known as Dengzhou
Pengshan China **86** B2
Pengshui China **87** D2
also known as Hanjia
Peng Siang, Sungai *r.* Sing. **76** [inset]
Pengwa Myanmar **78** A3
Pengxi China **86** C2
also known as Chicheng
Pengxian China *see* **Pengzhou**
Pengze China **87** F2
also known as Longcheng
Pengzhou China **86** B2
formerly known as Pengxian
Penhalonga Zimbabwe **131** G3
Penhoek Pass S. Africa **133** K8
Penhook U.S.A. **176** F9
Peniche Port. **54** B5
Penicuik U.K. **46** I8
Penida *i.* Indon. **77** F5
Peninga Rus. Fed. **40** E3
Peninsular Malaysia Malaysia **76** C2
also known as Malaya *or* Semenanjung Malaysia; *formerly known as* West Malaysia
Penitente, Serra do *hills* Brazil **202** C4
Pênjwin Iraq **107** F4
Penmarch France **50** B5
Penmarch, Pointe de *pt* France **50** B5
Penn U.S.A. *see* **Penn Hills**
Penna, Punta della *pt* Italy **56** G6
Penne Italy **56** F6
Pennell Coast Antarctica **223** L2
Penner *r.* India **94** D3
Penneshaw Australia **146** C3
Penn Hills U.S.A. **176** F5
formerly known as Penn
Pennine, Alpi *mts* Italy/Switz. **51** N7
English form Pennine Alps
Pennine Alps *mts* Italy/Switz. *see* **Pennine, Alpi**
Pennines *hills* U.K. **47** J9
Pennington S. Africa **133** O7
Pennington Gap U.S.A. **176** B9
Pennsboro U.S.A. **176** E6
Penns Grove U.S.A. **177** J6
Pennsville U.S.A. **177** J6
Pennsylvania *state* U.S.A. **176** G4
Penny Icecap Canada **165** M3
Penny Point Antarctica **223** K1
Peno Rus. Fed. **43** N5
Penobscot *r.* U.S.A. **177** Q1
Penobscot Bay U.S.A. **177** Q1
Penola Australia **146** D4
Peñón Blanco Mex. **184** D3
Penong Australia **146** B2
Penonomé Panama **186** C5
Penrhyn *atoll* Cook Is **221** H6
also known as Tongareva
Penrith Australia **147** F3
Penrith U.K. **47** J9
Pensacola U.S.A. **175** C6
Pensacola Bay *i.* U.S.A. **175** C6
Pensacola Mountains Antarctica **223** T1
Pensamiento Bol. **201** E3
Pensaukee U.S.A. **172** F6
Pentadaktylos Range *mts* Cyprus **108** E2
also known as Kyrenia Mountains *or* Beşparmak Dağları
Pentakota India **95** D2
Pentecost Island Vanuatu **145** F3
also known as Pentecôte, Île; *formerly known as* Whitsun Island
Pentecôte *r.* Canada **169** H3
Pentecôte, Île *i.* Vanuatu *see* **Pentecost Island**
Penteleu, Vârful *mt.* Romania **58** H3
Penticton Canada **166** G5
Pentire Point U.K. **47** G13
Pentland Australia **149** E4
Pentland Firth *sea chan.* U.K. **46** I5
Pentland Hills U.K. **46** I8
Pentwater U.S.A. **172** G7
Penukonda India **94** C3
Penunjok, Tanjong *pt* Malaysia **76** C1
Penwegon Myanmar **78** B4
Pen-y-Bont ar Ogwr U.K. *see* **Bridgend**
Penygadair *hill* U.K. **47** I11
Penylan Lake Canada **167** J2
Penyu, Kepulauan *is* Indon. **75** C4
Penza Rus. Fed. **41** H5
Penzance U.K. **47** G13
Penza Oblast *admin. div.* Rus. Fed. *see* **Penzenskaya Oblast'**
Penzenskaya Oblast' *admin. div.* Rus. Fed. **41** H5
English form Penza Oblast
Penzhinskaya Guba *b.* Rus. Fed. **39** Q3
Peoples Creek *r.* U.S.A. **180** E2
Peoria *AZ* U.S.A. **183** L8
Peoria *IL* U.S.A. **174** B3
Peoria Heights U.S.A. **172** D10
Pepeekeo U.S.A. **181** [inset] Z2
Pepel Sierra Leone **124** B4
Peper Sudan **128** B3
Pepworth S. Africa **133** N5
Pëqin Albania **58** A7
Pequi Brazil **207** I6
Pequop Mountains U.S.A. **183** J1
Pera Head Australia **149** D2
Peraitepuy Venez. **199** F3
Perak *i.* Malaysia **76** B1
Perak *r.* Malaysia **76** C1
Perak *state* Malaysia **76** C1
Perama Greece **59** F13
Perambalur India **94** C4
Perämeren kansallispuisto *nat. park* Fin. **44** N2
Perä-Posio Fin. **44** N2
Percé Canada **169** H3
Perche, Collines du *hills* France **50** G4
Percival Lakes *salt flat* Australia **150** D4
Percy France **50** E4
Percy U.S.A. **177** N1
Percy Isles Australia **149** F4
Percy Reach *l.* Canada **173** P6
Perdekop S. Africa **133** N4
Perdepoort *pass* S. Africa **132** H10
Perdida *r.* Brazil **202** C4
Perdido *r.* Brazil **201** F5
Perdido, Monte *mt.* Spain **55** L2
Perdiguère, Pic *mt.* France/Spain **55** L2
Perdika Greece **59** B9
Perdizes Brazil **206** F6
Perdões Brazil **207** H8
Perdu, Lac *l.* Canada **169** G3
Perechyn Ukr. **49** T7
Peregrebnoye Rus. Fed. **38** G3
Pereira Col. **198** C3
Pereira Barreto Brazil **206** B7
Pereira de Eça Angola *see* **Ondjiva**
Pereiro Brazil **202** E3
Perekhoda *r.* Rus. Fed. **43** M3
Perelub Rus. Fed. **102** B2
Pere Marquette *r.* U.S.A. **172** G7
Peremetnoye Kazakh. **102** B2
Peremul Par *reef* India **94** B4
Peremyshl' Rus. Fed. **43** R7
Peremyshlyany Ukr. **41** C6
Perené *r.* Peru **200** B2
Perenjori Australia **151** B6
Pereshnoye, Ozero *l.* Rus. Fed. **43** T1
Pereslavl'-Zalesskiy Rus. Fed. **43** T5
Pereslavskiy Natsional'nyy Park *nat. park* Rus. Fed. **43** T5
Peretu Romania **58** G4
Perevolotskiy Rus. Fed. **102** C2
Pereyaslavka Rus. Fed. **82** D3
Pereyaslav-Khmel'nitskiy Ukr. *see* **Pereyaslav-Khmel'nyts'kyy**
Pereyaslav-Khmel'nyts'kyy Ukr. **41** D6
also spelt Pereyaslav-Khmel'nitskiy
Pérez Chile **204** C2
Perg Austria **49** L7
Pergamino Arg. **204** E4
Perge *tourist site* Turkey **108** B1
Pergine Valsugana Italy **56** D2
Pergola Italy **56** E5
Perhentian Besar *i.* Malaysia **76** C1
Perho Fin. **44** N3
Periam Romania **58** B2
Péribonca *r.* Canada **169** F3
Perico Arg. **200** D6
Pericos Mex. **184** D3
Peridot U.S.A. **183** N8
Perieni Romania **58** I2
Périers France **50** E3
Perigoso, Canal *sea chan.* Brazil **202** B2
Périgueux France **50** G7
Perijá, Parque Nacional *nat. park* Venez. **198** C2
Perija, Sierra de *mts* Venez. **198** C2
Perim Island Yemen *see* **Barīm**
Peringat Malaysia **76** C1
Periprava Romania **58** K3
Perişoru Romania **58** I4
Peristera *i.* Greece **59** E9
Peristerio Greece **59** E10
Periteasca-Gura Portiţei *nature res.* Romania **58** K4
Perito Moreno Arg. **205** C7
Perito Moreno, Parque Nacional *nat. park* Arg. **205** B7
Perivar *r.* India **94** C4
Perlas, Laguna de *lag.* Nicaragua **186** C4
Perlas, Punta de *pt* Nicaragua **186** C4
Perleberg Germany **48** I2
Perlis *state* Malaysia **76** C1
Perm' Rus. Fed. **40** K4
formerly known as Molotov
Permas Rus. Fed. **40** H4
Përmet Albania **59** B8
Perm Oblast *admin. div.* Rus. Fed. *see* **Permskaya Oblast'**
Permskaya Oblast' *admin. div.* Rus. Fed. **40** K4
English form Perm Oblast; *formerly known as* Molotovskaya Oblast'
Permuda *i.* Croatia **56** G4
Pernā Fin. **42** H1
Pernambuco Brazil *see* **Recife**
Pernambuco *state* Brazil **202** E4
Pernatty Lagoon *salt flat* Australia **146** C2
Pernem India **94** B3
Pernik Bulg. **58** E6
formerly known as Dimitrovo
Perniö Fin. **45** M3
Pernov Estonia *see* **Pärnu**
Perolândia Brazil **206** A4
Peron, Cape Australia **151** A5
Peron Islands Australia **148** A2
Péronnas France **51** L6
Péronne France **51** I3
Peron Peninsula Australia **151** A5
Perote Mex. **185** F5
Perpignan France **51** I10
Perrégaux Alg. *see* **Mohammadia**
Perris U.S.A. **183** G8
Perros-Guirec France **50** C4
Perry Canada **173** I3
Perry *FL* U.S.A. **175** D6
Perry *GA* U.S.A. **175** D5
Perry *IA* U.S.A. **178** D3
Perry *MI* U.S.A. **173** I8
Perry *OK* U.S.A. **179** C4
Perry Hall U.S.A. **177** I6
Perrymennyy, Cape Antarctica **223** G2
Perrysburg U.S.A. **176** B4
Perryton U.S.A. **179** B4
Perryville *AR* U.S.A. **179** D5
Perryville *KY* U.S.A. **176** A8
Persepolis *tourist site* Iran **100** C4
Persia *country* Asia *see* **Iran**
Persian Gulf Asia *see* **The Gulf**
Persis *prov.* Iran *see* **Fārs**
Pertek Turkey **107** D3
Perth *Tas.* Australia **147** E5

▶**Perth** *W.A.* Australia **151** A6
State capital of Western Australia. 4th most populous city in Oceania.
world [cities] ⟫ 24–25

Perth Canada **168** E4
Perth U.K. **46** I7
Perth-Andover Canada **169** H4
Pertominsk Rus. Fed. **40** F2
Pertteli Fin. **42** E1
Pertuis France **51** L9
Pertuis Breton *sea chan.* France **50** E6
Pertuis d'Antioche *sea chan.* France **50** E6
Pertunmaa Fin. **45** N3
Pertusato, Capo *c. Corse* France **56** B7
Perú Bol. **200** D3
Peru *atoll* Kiribati *see* **Beru**

▶**Peru** *country* S. America **200** B2
3rd largest and 4th most populous country in South America.
southamerica [countries] ⟫ 192–193

Peru *IL* U.S.A. **172** D9
Peru *IN* U.S.A. **174** C3
Peru *NY* U.S.A. **177** L1
Perućko Jezero *l.* Croatia **56** I5
Perugia Italy **56** E5
historically known as Perusia
Perugorria Arg. **204** F3
Peruhumpenai Mountains Reserve *nature res.* Indon. **75** B3
Peruíbe Brazil **206** G11
Peruru India **94** C3
Perushtitsa Bulg. **58** F6
Perusia Italy *see* **Perugia**
Péruwelz Belgium **51** J2
Pervoavgustovskiy Rus. Fed. **43** Q9
Pervomaisc Moldova **58** K2
Pervomay Kyrg. **103** H4
also known as Pervomayskoye; *formerly known as* Pervomayskiy
Pervomaysk Rus. Fed. **40** G5
formerly known as Tashino
Pervomays'k Ukr. **41** D6
formerly known as Ol'viopol'
Pervomayskiy Kazakh. **103** J2
Pervomayskiy Kyrg. *see* **Pervomay**
Pervomayskiy Rus. Fed. *see* **Novodvinsk**
Pervomayskiy *Chitinskaya Oblast'* Rus. Fed. **85** G1
Pervomayskiy *Orenburgskaya Oblast'* Rus. Fed. **102** C2
Pervomayskiy *Smolenskaya Oblast'* Rus. Fed. **43** N7
Pervomayskiy *Tambovskaya Oblast'* Rus. Fed. **41** G5
formerly known as Bogoyavlenskoye
Pervomayskiy *Tul'skaya Oblast'* Rus. Fed. **43** S7
Pervomayskoye Kyrg. *see* **Pervomay**
Pervomayskoye Rus. Fed. **82** B1
Pervomayskoye Rus. Fed. **43** K1
Pervomays'kyy Ukr. **41** F6
formerly known as Likhachevo *or* Likhachyovo
Pervorechenskiy Rus. Fed. **39** Q3
Per'yevo Rus. Fed. **43** U2
Pes' Rus. Fed. **43** P3
Pes' *r.* Rus. Fed. **43** Q2
Pesa *r.* Italy **56** D5
Pesaguan *r.* Indon. **77** E3
Pesaro Italy **56** E5
historically known as Pisaurum
Pescadero U.S.A. **182** B4
Pescadores *is* Taiwan *see* **P'enghu Ch'üntao**
Pescadores, Punta *pt* Peru **200** B4
Pescara Italy **56** G6
Pescara *r.* Italy **56** G6
Pescari Romania **58** C4
Peschanokopskoye Rus. Fed. **41** G7
Peschanoye Rus. Fed. *see* **Yashkul'**
Peschanyy, Mys *pt* Kazakh. **102** B4
Peschici Italy **56** I7
Pescia Italy **56** C5
Pesebre, Punta *pt Canary Is* **122** B3
Pesha *r.* Rus. Fed. **40** H2
Peshanjan Afgh. **101** E3
Peshawar Pak. **101** G3
Peshkopi Albania **58** B7
Peshnyye, Ostrova *is* Kazakh. *see* **Bol'shiye Peshnyye, Ostrova**
Peshtera Bulg. **58** F6
Peshtigo U.S.A. **172** F5
Peshtigo *r.* U.S.A. **172** F6
Peski Kazakh. **103** F1
Peski *Moskovskaya Oblast'* Rus. Fed. **43** T6
Peski *Voronezhskaya Oblast'* Rus. Fed. **41** G6
Peski Turkm. **103** E5
Peski Karakum *des.* Kazakh. *see* **Karakum Desert**
Peski Karakumy *des.* Turkm. *see* **Karakum Desert**
Peskovka Rus. Fed. **40** J4
Pesnica Slovenia **56** H2
Pesochnoye Rus. Fed. **43** U3
Pesochnya Rus. Fed. **43** O8
Peso da Régua Port. **54** D3
Pespire Hond. **186** B4
Pesqueira Brazil **202** E4
Pesqueira Mex. **184** C2
Pessac France **50** F8
Pessinki naturreservat *nature res.* Sweden **40** B2
Pestovo Rus. Fed. **43** Q3
Pestravka Rus. Fed. **102** B1
Pestyaki Rus. Fed. **40** G4
Petah Tiqwa Israel **108** F5
Petaihari Martapura Reserve *nature res.* Indon. **77** F3
Petäjävesi Fin. **44** N3
Petalidi Greece **59** C12
Petalioi *i.* Greece **59** F10
Petaluma U.S.A. **182** B3
Pétange Lux. **51** L3
Petangis Indon. **77** F3
Petare Venez. **199** E2
Petas Greece **59** C9
Petatlán Mex. **185** E5
Petauke Zambia **127** F8
Petawaga, Lac *l.* Canada **173** R4
Petawawa Canada **173** P5
Petén Itzá, Lago *l.* Guat. **185** H5
Petenwell Lake U.S.A. **172** D6
Peterbell Canada **168** D3
Peterborough *S.A.* Australia **146** C3
Peterborough *Vic.* Australia **147** D4
Peterborough Canada **168** E4
Peterborough U.K. **47** L11
Peterborough U.S.A. **177** N3
Peterhead U.K. **46** K6
Peter I Island Antarctica **222** R2
also known as Peter I Øy
Peter I Øy *i.* Antarctica *see* **Peter I Island**
Peter Lougheed Provincial Park Canada **167** H5
Petermann Aboriginal Land *res.* Australia **148** A5
Petermann Bjerg *nunatak* Greenland **165** Q2
Petermann Ranges *mts* Australia **148** A5
Peter Pond Lake Canada **167** I4
Petersburg S. Africa **133** I9
Petersburg *AK* U.S.A. **164** F4
Petersburg *IL* U.S.A. **174** B4
Petersburg *IN* U.S.A. **174** C4
Petersburg *NY* U.S.A. **177** L3
Petersburg *OH* U.S.A. **176** E5
Petersburg *VA* U.S.A. **176** H8
Petersburg *WV* U.S.A. **176** F7
Petershagen Germany **48** F3
Peters Mine Guyana **199** G3
Peterstown U.S.A. **176** E8
Petersville U.S.A. **164** D3
Peter the Great Bay Rus. Fed. *see* **Petra Velikogo, Zaliv**
Pétervárad *Vojvodina, Srbija* Yugo. *see* **Petrovaradin**
Peterwardein *Vojvodina, Srbija* Yugo. *see* **Petrovaradin**
Peth India **94** B2
Petilia Policastro Italy **57** I9
Petit Atlas *mts* Morocco *see* **Anti Atlas**
Petitcodiac Canada **169** H4
Petite Creuse *r.* France **51** H6
Petit-Goâve Haiti **187** E3
Petitjean Morocco *see* **Sidi Kacem**
Petit Lac Manicouagan *l.* Canada **169** H2
Petit-Loango, Réserve de *nature res.* Gabon **126** A5
Petit Maine *r.* France **50** E5
Petit Mécatina *r.* Canada *see* **Little Mecatina**
Petit Mécatina *r.* Canada **169** J3
Petit Mécatina, Île du *i.* Canada **169** J3
also known as Little Mecatina Island
Petit Morin *r.* France **51** J4
Petitot *r.* Canada **166** F2
Petit St-Bernard, Col du *pass* France **51** M7
Petkino Rus. Fed. **43** U7
Petkula Fin. **44** N2
Petlad India **96** B5
Petlawad India **96** B5
Peto Mex. **185** H4
Petoskey U.S.A. **173** I5
Petra *tourist site* Jordan **108** G7
also spelt Batrā'
Petras, Mount Antarctica **222** P1
Petra tou Romiou *tourist site* Cyprus *see* **Aphrodite's Birthplace**
Petra Velikogo, Zaliv *b.* Rus. Fed. **82** C4
English form Peter the Great Bay
Petre, Point Canada **173** P7
Petrich Bulg. **58** E7
Petrified Forest National Park U.S.A. **183** O6
Petrijevci Croatia **56** K3
Petrikau Poland *see* **Piotrków Trybunalski**
Petrikov Belarus *see* **Pyetrykaw**
Petrila Romania **58** E3
Petrinja Croatia **56** I3
Petro, Cerro de *mt.* Chile **204** C3
Petroaleksandrovsk Uzbek. *see* **Turtkul'**
Petrodvorets Rus. Fed. **43** K2
Petrograd Rus. Fed. *see* **St Petersburg**
Petrokov Poland *see* **Piotrków Trybunalski**
Petrokrepost' Rus. Fed. *see* **Shlissel'burg**
Petrokrepost', Bukhta *b.* Rus. Fed. **43** M1
Petrolândia Brazil **202** E4
Petrolia Canada **173** K8
Petrolina *Amazonas* Brazil **199** E5
Petrolina *Pernambuco* Brazil **202** D4
Petrolina de Goiás Brazil **206** D3
Petron, Limni *l.* Greece **58** C8
Petropavl Kazakh. *see* **Petropavlovsk**
Petropavlovka Kazakh. **103** J3
Petropavlovka Rus. Fed. **85** E1
Petropavlovka Rus. Fed. **41** G5
Petropavlovsk Kazakh. **38** G4
also known as Petropavl
Petropavlovsk Rus. Fed. *see* **Petropavlovsk-Kamchatskiy**
Petropavlovsk-Kamchatskiy Rus. Fed. **39** P4
historically known as Petropavlovsk
Petrópolis Brazil **207** J9
Petroşani Romania **58** E3
Petrovac Bos.-Herz. *see* **Bosanski Petrovac**
Petrovac *Srbija* Yugo. **58** C4
Petrovaradin *Vojvodina, Srbija* Yugo. **58** A3
also known as Pétervárad; *historically known as* Peterwardein
Petrovichi Rus. Fed. **43** N8
Petrovsk Rus. Fed. **41** H5
Petrovskiy Rus. Fed. **43** V5
Petrovskoye *Moskovskaya Oblast'* Rus. Fed. **43** R5
Petrovskoye Rus. Fed. *see* **Svetlograd**
Petrovskoye *Yaroslavskaya Oblast'* Rus. Fed. **43** U4
Petrovsk-Zabaykal'skiy Rus. Fed. **85** F1
Petrov Val Rus. Fed. **41** H6
Petrozavodsk Rus. Fed. **40** E3
Petru Rareş Romania **58** F1
Petrusburg S. Africa **133** J6
Petrus Steyn S. Africa **133** M4
Petrusville S. Africa **133** I7
Petsamo Rus. Fed. *see* **Pechenga**
Petsana S. Africa **133** M4
Pettau Slovenia *see* **Ptuj**
Petukhovo Rus. Fed. **38** G4
Petushki Rus. Fed. **43** U6
formerly known as Novyye Petushki
Peuetsagu, Gunung *vol.* Indon. **76** B1
Peurasuvanto Fin. **44** N2
Peureula Indon. **76** B1
Pevek Rus. Fed. **39** R3
Pêxung China **89** F5
Peza *r.* Rus. Fed. **40** H2
Pézenas France **51** J9
Pezinok Slovakia **49** O7
Pfaffenhofen an der Ilm Germany **48** I7
Pfälzer Wald *hills* Germany **48** E6
Pfälzer Wald *park* Germany **48** E6
Pfarrkirchen Germany **49** J7
Pforzheim Germany **48** F7
Pfullendorf Germany **48** G8
Pfungstadt Germany **48** F6
Phagwara India **96** B3
Phahameng S. Africa **133** K5
Phalaborwa S. Africa **131** F4
Phalia Pak. **101** H3
Phalodi India **96** B4
Phalsbourg France **51** N4
Phalsund India **96** A4
Phaltan India **94** B2
Phalut Peak India/Nepal **97** F4
Phangan, Ko *i.* Thai. **79** C6
Phangnga Thai. **79** B6
Phan Rang Vietnam **79** E6
Phan Ri Vietnam **79** E6
Phan Thiêt Vietnam **79** E6
Phan Thiêt, Vinh *b.* Vietnam **79** E6
Phaphund India **96** C4
Phaplu Nepal **97** E4
Phat Diêm Vietnam **78** D3
Phatthalung Thai. **79** C7
Phayao Thai. **78** B4
Phek India **97** G4
Phelp *r.* Australia **148** B2
Phelps *NY* U.S.A. **177** H3
Phelps *WI* U.S.A. **172** D4
Phen Thai. **78** C4
Phenix U.S.A. **176** G8
Phenix City U.S.A. **175** C5
Phephane *watercourse* S. Africa **132** G2
Phet Buri Thai. **79** B5
Phetchabun Thai. **78** C4
Phichit Thai. **78** C4
Philadelphia Jordan *see* **'Ammān**
Philadelphia S. Africa **132** C10
Philadelphia Turkey *see* **Alaşehir**
Philadelphia *MS* U.S.A. **175** B5
Philadelphia *NY* U.S.A. **177** J1
Philadelphia *PA* U.S.A. **177** J6
Philae *tourist site* Egypt **121** G4
Philip U.S.A. **178** B2
Philip Atoll Micronesia *see* **Sorol**
Philippeville Alg. *see* **Skikda**
Philippeville Belgium **51** K2
Philippi U.S.A. **176** E6
Philippi, Lake *salt flat* Australia **148** C5
▶**Philippines** *country* Asia **74** A3
spelt Filipinas *or* Pilipinas *in* Filipino
asia [countries] ⟫ 64–67
Philippine Sea N. Pacific Ocean **74** B2

▶**Philippine Trench** *sea feature* N. Pacific Ocean **220** C5
3rd deepest trench in the world.

Philippolis S. Africa **133** J7
Philippolis Road S. Africa **133** J7
Philippopolis Bulg. *see* **Plovdiv**
Philipsburg Neth. Antilles **187** H3
Philipsburg U.S.A. **180** D3
Philip Smith Mountains U.S.A. **164** E3
Philipstown S. Africa **133** I7
Phillip Island Australia **147** E4
Phillips *r.* Australia **151** C7
Phillips *ME* U.S.A. **177** O1
Phillips *WI* U.S.A. **172** C5
Phillips Arm Canada **166** E5
Phillipsburg *KS* U.S.A. **178** C4
Phillipsburg *NJ* U.S.A. **177** J5
Phillips Inlet Canada **165** K1
Phillips Range *hills* Australia **150** D3
Phillipston U.S.A. **176** F5
Philmont U.S.A. **177** L3
Philomelium Turkey *see* **Akşehir**
Philpott Reservoir U.S.A. **176** E9
Phimun Mangsahan Thai. **79** D5
Phiritona S. Africa **133** L4
Phitsanulok Thai. **78** C4
Phlox U.S.A. **172** D5

▶**Phnom Penh** Cambodia **79** D6
Capital of Cambodia. Also spelt Phnum Pénh.

Phnum Pénh Cambodia *see* **Phnom Penh**
Pho, Laem *pt* Thai. **79** C7
Phoenicia U.S.A. **177** K3

▶**Phoenix** *AZ* U.S.A. **183** L8
State capital of Arizona.

Phoenix *NY* U.S.A. **177** I2
Phoenix Island Kiribati *see* **Rawaki**
Phoenix Islands Kiribati **145** H2
Phoenixville U.S.A. **177** J5
Phokwane S. Africa **133** N1
Phola S. Africa **133** N3
Phomolong S. Africa **133** L4
Phon Thai. **78** C5
Phong Nha Vietnam **78** D4
Phôngsali Laos **78** C3
also spelt Phong Saly
Phong Saly Laos *see* **Phôngsali**
Phong Thô Vietnam **78** C3
Phosphate Hill Australia **149** D4
Phrae Thai. **78** C4
Phra Nakhon Si Ayutthaya Thai. *see* **Ayutthaya**
Phrao Thai. **78** B4
Phra Saeng Thai. **79** B6
Phra Thong, Ko *i.* Thai. **79** B6
Phuchong-Nayoi National Park Thai. **79** D5
Phu Cuong Vietnam *see* **Thu Dâu Môt**
Phuduhudu Botswana **131** E4
Phuentsholing Bhutan **97** F4
also spelt Phuntsholing
Phuket Thai. **79** B7
Phuket, Ko *i.* Thai. **79** B7
Phu-khieo Wildlife Reserve *nature res.* Thai. **78** C4
Phulabani India **95** E1
Phulpur India **97** D4
Phu Luang Wildlife Reserve *nat. park* Thai. **78** C4
Phu Ly Vietnam **78** D3
Phumĭ Chhuk Cambodia **79** D6
also known as Chhuk
Phumĭ Kâmpóng Trâlach Cambodia **79** D5
Phumĭ Mlu Prey Cambodia **79** D5
Phumĭ Prâmaôy Cambodia **79** C5
Phumĭ Sâmraông Cambodia **79** C5
also known as Samrong
Phuntsholing Bhutan *see* **Phuentsholing**
Phu Phac Mo *mt.* Vietnam **78** D3
Phu Phan National Park Thai. **78** C4
Phu Quôc, Đao *i.* Vietnam **79** C6
formerly known as Quan Phu Quoc
Phuthaditjhaba S. Africa **133** M5
Phu Tho Vietnam **78** D3
Phu Vinh Vietnam *see* **Tra Vinh**
Pia Aboriginal Reserve Australia **151** B5
Piabung, Gunung *mt.* Indon. **77** F2
Piaca Brazil **202** C3
Piacá Brazil **206** C8
Piacenza Italy **56** B3
historically known as Placentia
Piacouadie, Lac *l.* Canada **169** G3
Piadena Italy **56** C3
Piagochioui *r.* Canada **168** E2
Pian *r.* Australia **147** F2
Piana di Catania *plain Sicilia* Italy **57** G11
Piangil Australia **147** D3
Pianguan China **85** F4
Pianoro Italy **56** D4
Pianosa, Isola *i.* Italy **56** C6
Piaseczno Poland **49** S3
Piaski Poland **49** T4
Piassabussu Brazil **202** E4
Piatã Brazil **202** D5
Piatra Romania **58** G5
Piatra Neamţ Romania **58** H2
Piatra Olt Romania **58** F4
Piatra Şoimului Romania **58** H2
Piauí *r.* Brazil **202** C3
Piauí *state* Brazil **202** D3
Piauí, Serra de *hills* Brazil **202** D4
Piave *r.* Italy **56** E3
Piazza Armerina *Sicilia* Italy **57** G11
Piazzi, Cima de' *mt.* Italy **56** C2
Piazzi, Isla *i.* Chile **205** B8
Pibor *r.* Sudan **128** B2
Pibor Post Sudan **128** B3
Pic *r.* Canada **168** C3
Pica Chile **200** C5
Picacho U.S.A. **183** M9
Picachos, Cerro dos *mt.* Mex. **184** B2
Picardie *admin. reg.* France **51** I3
Picardie *reg.* France *see* **Picardy**
Picardy *reg.* France **50** H3
also spelt Picardie
Picassent Spain **55** K5
Picayune U.S.A. **175** B6
Picháchic Mex. **184** D2
Pichanal Arg. **200** D5
Pichilemu Chile **204** B4
Pichilingue Mex. **184** C3
Pichi Mahuida Arg. **204** D5
Pichincha *prov.* Ecuador **198** B5
Pichor India **96** C4
Pichucalco Mex. **185** G5
Pic Island Canada **172** G2
Pickens U.S.A. **176** E7
Pickerel Lake Canada **172** B2
Pickering Canada **173** N7
Pickering U.K. **47** L9
Pickford U.S.A. **173** I4
Pickle Lake Canada **168** B3
Pico Bonito, Parque Nacional *nat. park* Hond. **186** B4
Pico da Neblina, Parque Nacional do *nat. park* Brazil **199** E4
Pico de Orizaba, Parque Nacional *nat. park* Mex. **185** F5
Pico de Tancítaro, Parque Nacional *nat. park* Mex. **185** E5
Picos Brazil **202** D3
Picos, Punta dos *pt* Spain **54** C3
Picota Peru **198** B6
Pico Truncado Arg. **205** D7
Pic River Canada **172** G2
Picton Australia **147** F3
Picton Canada **168** E5
Picton N.Z. **152** I9
Picton, Mount Australia **147** E5
Pictou Canada **169** I4
Picture Butte Canada **167** H5
Pictured Rocks National Lakeshore *nature res.* U.S.A. **172** G4
Picuí Brazil **202** E3
Picún Leufú Arg. **204** C5
Pidarak Pak. **101** E5
Pidurutalagala *mt.* Sri Lanka **94** D5
Piedade Brazil **206** F10
Pie de Palo, Sierra *mts* Arg. **204** C3
Piedimonte Matese Italy **56** G7
Piedmont *admin. reg.* Italy *see* **Piemonte**
Piedmont *MO* U.S.A. **174** B4
Piedmont *OH* U.S.A. **176** D5
Piedmont Lake U.S.A. **176** D5
Piedra *r.* Spain **55** J3
Piedrabuena Spain **54** G5
Piedra de Aguila Arg. **204** C6
Piedrafita Spain *see* **Pedrafita do Cebreiro**
Piedrahita Spain **54** F4
Piedralaves Spain **54** G4
Piedras, Punta *pt* Arg. **204** F4
Piedras Blancas Spain **54** F1
Piedras Blancas Point U.S.A. **182** C6
Piedras Negras Guat. **185** H5
Piedras Negras *Coahuila* Mex. **185** E2
Piedras Negras *Veracruz* Mex. **185** F5
Pie Island Canada **172** D2
Pieksämäki Fin. **44** N3
Pielavesi Fin. **44** N3
Pielavesi *l.* Fin. **44** N3
Pielinen *l.* Fin. **44** O3
Pieljekaise nationalpark *nat. park* Sweden **44** L2
Piemonte *admin. reg.* Italy **56** A4
English form Piedmont
Pienaarsrivier S. Africa **133** M2
Pieniężno Poland **49** R1
Pieniński Park Narodowy *nat. park* Poland **49** R6
Pieninský *nat. park* Slovakia **49** R6
Pieńsk Poland **49** M4
Pierce U.S.A. **178** C3
Pierce Lake Canada **167** M4
Pierceland Canada **167** I4
Pierceton U.S.A. **172** H9
Pieria *mts* Greece **59** D8

▶**Pierre** U.S.A. **178** B2
State capital of South Dakota.

Pierre, Bayou *r.* U.S.A. **175** B6
Pierre Bayou *r.* U.S.A. **179** D6
Pierrelatte France **51** K8
Pieskehaure *l.* Sweden **44** L2
Piešťany Slovakia **49** O7
Pietermaritzburg S. Africa **133** O6
Pietersaari Fin. *see* **Jakobstad**
Pietersburg S. Africa **131** F4
also known as Polokwane
Piet Plessis S. Africa **133** I3
Pietraperzia *Sicilia* Italy **57** G11
Pietrasanta Italy **56** C5
Pietra Spada, Passo di *pass* Italy **57** I10
Piet Retief S. Africa **133** O4
Pietrosu, Vârful *mt.* Romania **58** G1
Pieve di Cadore Italy **56** E2
Pievepelago Italy **56** C4
Pigeon *r.* Canada/U.S.A. **174** B1
Pigeon Bay Canada **173** K9
Pigeon Lake Canada **167** H4
Pigeon River U.S.A. **172** D2
Pigg *r.* U.S.A. **176** F8
Piggott U.S.A. **174** B4
Pigg's Peak Swaziland **133** P2
Pigon, Limni *l.* Greece **59** C9
Pigs, Bay of Cuba **186** C2
also known as Cochinos, Bahía de
Pigüé Arg. **204** E5
Piguicas *mt.* Mex. **185** F4
Piha N.Z. **152** I4
Pihama N.Z. **152** H7
Pihani India **96** D4
Pi He *r.* China **87** F1
Pihkva järv *l.* Estonia/Rus. Fed. *see* **Pskov, Lake**
Pihlajavesi *l.* Fin. **45** O3
Pihlava Fin. **45** M3
Pihtipudas Fin. **44** N3
Piikkiö Fin. **42** D1
Piippola Fin. **44** N2
Piirissaar *i.* Estonia **42** I3
Piirsalu Estonia **42** F2
Piispajärvi Fin. **44** O2
Pijiapan China *see* **Puge**
Pijijiapan Mex. **185** G6
Pikalevo Rus. Fed. **43** P2
Pike *NY* U.S.A. **176** G3
Pike *WV* U.S.A. **176** D6
Pikelot *i.* Micronesia **73** K5
formerly known as Coquille
Pikes Peak U.S.A. **180** F5
Piketberg S. Africa **132** C9
Pike Ton U.S.A. **176** B6
Pikeville *KY* U.S.A. **176** C8
Pikeville *TN* U.S.A. **174** C5
Pikihatiti *b.* N.Z. *see* **Port Pegasus**
Pikirakatahi *mt.* N.Z. *see* **Earnslaw, Mount**
Pikou China **85** I4
Pikounda Congo **126** C4
Pila Arg. **204** F5
Piła Poland **49** N2
historically known as Schneidemühl
Pila *mt.* Spain **55** J6
Pilagá *r.* Arg. **204** F2
Pilanesberg National Park S. Africa **133** L2
Pilani India **96** B3
Pilar *Buenos Aires* Arg. **204** F4
Pilar *Córdoba* Arg. **204** E3
Pilar Para. **201** F6
Pilar Phil. **74** C4
Pilar, Cabo *c.* Chile **205** B9
Pilar do Sul Brazil **206** F10
Pilas *i.* Phil. **74** B5
Pilas Spain **54** E7
Pilas Channel Phil. **74** B5
Pilat, Mont *mt.* France **51** K7
Pilat, Parc Naturel Régional du *nature res.* France **51** K7
Pilaya *r.* Bol. **201** D5
Pilcaniyeu Arg. **204** C6
Pilcomayo *r.* Bol./Para. **201** F6
Pilenkovo Georgia *see* **Gant'iadi**
Piler India **94** C3
Pili Greece *see* **Pyli**
Pili Phil. **74** B3
Pili, Cerro *mt.* Chile **200** D5
also known as Acamarachi
Pilikalnis *hill* Lith. **42** G6
Pilibangan India **96** B3
Pilibhit India **96** C3
Pilica *r.* Poland **49** S4
Piliga Nature Reserve Australia **147** F2
Pilipinas *country* Asia *see* **Philippines**
Pilisi *park* Hungary **49** P8
Pillau Rus. Fed. *see* **Baltiysk**
Pillcopata Peru **200** C3
Pilliga Australia **147** F2
Pillo, Isla del *i.* Arg. **204** E4
Pillsbury, Lake U.S.A. **182** B2
Pil'na Rus. Fed. **40** H5
Pil'nya, Ozero *l.* Rus. Fed. **40** K1
Pilões, Serra dos *mts* Brazil **206** F4
Pilón Cuba **186** D3
Pilón *r.* Mex. **179** C7
Pilos Greece *see* **Pylos**
Pilot Mountain *hill* U.S.A. **176** E9
Pilot Peak U.S.A. **182** G3
Pilot Point U.S.A. **164** D4
Pilot Rock U.S.A. **180** C3
Pilot Station U.S.A. **164** C3
Pilsen Czech Rep. *see* **Plzeň**
Pilsum U.S.A. **172** F6
Piltene Latvia **42** C4
Pilu, Nam *r.* Myanmar **78** B4
Pilvė *r.* Lith. **42** E7
Pilviškiai Lith. **42** E7
Pima U.S.A. **183** O9
Pimenta Bueno Brazil **201** E2
Pimpalner India **94** B1
Pimpri India **94** B1
Pimu Dem. Rep. Congo **126** D4
Pin *r.* Myanmar **78** A3
Pina *r.* Belarus **42** H9
Pinahat India **96** C4
Pinaleno Mountains U.S.A. **183** N9
Pinamalayan Phil. **74** B3
Pinamar Arg. **204** F5
Pinang Malaysia *see* **George Town**
Pinang *i.* Malaysia **76** C1
Pinang *state* Malaysia **76** C1
also known as Pulau Pinang; *formerly spelt* Penang
Pinar *mt.* Spain **54** F8
Pinar, Puerto del *pass* Spain **55** I6
Pinarbaşı Turkey **107** D3
also known as Aziziye
Pinar del Río Cuba **186** C2
Pinarhisar Turkey **106** A2

Piñas Ecuador 198 B5
Pinatubo, Mt vol. Phil. 74 F3
Pincher Creek Canada 167 H5
Pinckneyville U.S.A. 172 B4
Pinconning U.S.A. 173 J7
Pincota Romania *see* Pâncota
Pińczów Poland 49 R5
Pindaíba Brazil 206 A1
Pindamonhangaba Brazil 207 H9
Pindar Australia 151 A6
Pindar *r.* India 96 C3
Pindaré *r.* Brazil 202 C2
Pind Dadan Khay Pak. 101 H3
Pindi Gheb Pak. 101 H3
Pindobal Brazil 202 B2
Pindos *nat. park* Greece 59 C9
Pindus Mountains Greece 59 B9
  also known as Píndhos Óros;
  also spelt Pindos
Pindwara India 96 C4
Pine *watercourse* Australia 146 D3
Pine *r.* MI U.S.A. 172 H6
Pine *r.* MI U.S.A. 173 I7
Pine *r.* WI U.S.A. 172 C5
Pine *r.* WI U.S.A. 172 E5
Pine, Cape Canada 169 K4
Pine Bluff U.S.A. 174 A5
Pine City U.S.A. 178 D2
Pine Creek Australia 148 A2
Pine Creek *r.* U.S.A. 176 H4
Pine Creek *watercourse* U.S.A. 183 H1
Pinecrest U.S.A. 182 D3
Pinedale U.S.A. 180 E4
Pine Dock Canada 167 L5
Pine Falls Canada 167 L5
Pinega *r.* Rus. Fed. 40 G2
Pinegrove Australia 151 A5
Pine Grove KY U.S.A. 176 A7
Pine Grove PA U.S.A. 177 I5
Pine Hills CA U.S.A. 182 G7
Pine Hills FL U.S.A. 175 D6
Pinehouse Lake Canada 167 J4
Pineimuta *r.* Canada 168 C2
Pineios *r.* Greece 59 D9
  also spelt Piniós
Pineiou, Techniti Limni *resr* Greece 59 C11
Pine Island Bay Antarctica 222 R2
Pine Island Glacier Antarctica 222 R1
Pine Islands FL U.S.A. 175 D7
Pine Islands FL U.S.A. 175 D7
Pine Knot U.S.A. 176 A9
Pinellas Park U.S.A. 175 D7
Pine Mountain U.S.A. 182 C6
Pine Peak U.S.A. 183 K7
Pine Point Canada 167 H2
Pine Point *pt* Canada 167 H2
Pineridge U.S.A. 182 E4
Pine Ridge U.S.A. 178 B3
Pine Ridge Indian Reservation *res.* U.S.A. 178 B3
Pinerolo Italy 51 N8
Pines, Isle of *i.* Cuba *see*
  La Juventud, Isla de
Pines, Isle of *i.* New Caledonia *see*
  Pins, Île de
Pines, Lake o' the U.S.A. 179 D5
Pineto Italy 56 G6
Pinetop U.S.A. 183 O7
Pinetown S. Africa 133 O6
Pinetown *r.* Australia 151 A6
Pine Valley U.S.A. 177 I3
Pineville KY U.S.A. 176 B9
Pineville LA U.S.A. 179 D6
Pineville WV U.S.A. 176 D8
Ping, Mae Nam *r.* Thai. 78 C5
Pingal Jammu and Kashmir 96 B1
Ping'an China 84 D4
  formerly known as Ping'anyi
Ping'anyi China *see* Ping'an
Pingba China 86 C3
Pingbian China 86 B4
  also known as Yupin
Pingchang China 86 C2
Ping Dao *i.* China 85 H5
Pingding China 85 G4
Pingdingbu China *see* Guyuan
Pingdingshan China 87 E1
Pingdong Taiwan *see* P'ingtung
Pingdu China *see* Anfu
Pingdu China 85 H4
Pingguo China 86 C3
Pingguo China 87 C4
  also known as Matou
Pinghai China 87 F3
Pinghe China 87 F3
  also known as Xiaoxi
Pinghu China 87 G2
Pingjiang China 87 E2
Pingle China 87 D3
Pingli China 87 D1
Pingliang China 85 E5
Pinglu China 87 D1
  formerly known as Shengrenjian
Pingluo China 85 E4
Pingma China *see* Tiandong
Pingnan Fujian China 87 F3
Pingnan Guangxi China 87 D4
  also known as Gufeng
Pingquan China 85 H3
Pingshan China *see* Huidong
Pingshan Hebei China 85 G4
Pingshan Sichuan China 86 C2
  also known as Luquan
Pingtan China 87 F3
Pingtang China 86 C3
Pingtang China 87 F3
  also known as Tancheng

Pingtan Dao *i.* China *see* Haitan Dao
P'ingtung Taiwan 87 G4
  also spelt Pingdong
Pingwu China 86 C1
  also known as Long'an
Pingxi China *see* Yuping
Pingxiang China *see* Tongwei
Pingxiang Guangxi China 86 C4
Pingxiang Jiangxi China 87 E3
Pingyang Heilong. China 85 J1
Pingyang Zhejiang China 87 G3
  also known as Kunyang
Pingyao China 85 G4
Pingyi China 85 H5
Pingyin China 85 H4
Pingyu China 87 E1
  also known as Guhuai
Pingyuan Guangdong China 87 E3
  also known as Dazhe
Pingyuan Shandong China 85 H4
Pingyuanjie China 86 B4
Pingzhai China 87 D3
Pinhal Brazil 206 G9
Pinhal Novo Port. 54 C6
Pinheiro Brazil 202 C2
Pinheiro Machado Brazil 204 G3
Pinheiros Brazil 207 M5
Pinhel Port. 54 D4
Pinhuã *r.* Brazil 199 E6
Pini *i.* Indon. 76 B2
Pinilla *r.* Spain 55 I6
Piniós *r.* Greece *see* Pineios
Pinjarra Australia 151 A7
Pinjin Aboriginal Reserve Australia 151 C6
Pinkafeld Austria 49 N8
Pinkawilinie Conservation Park *nature res.* Australia 146 B3
Pinkerton Range *hills* Australia 148 A2
Pink Mountain Canada 166 F3
Pinlaung Myanmar 78 B3
Pinlebu Myanmar 78 A2
Pinnacle U.S.A. 176 E5
Pinnacle *hill* U.S.A. 176 G6
Pinnacles National Monument *nat. park* U.S.A. 182 C5
Pinnaroo Australia 146 D3
Pinneberg Germany 48 G2
Pinnes, Akra *pt* Greece 59 F8
Pinofranqueado Spain 54 E4
Pinoh *r.* Indon. 77 E3
Pinos, Isla de *i.* Cuba *see*
  La Juventud, Isla de
Pinos, Mount U.S.A. 182 E7
Pinoso Spain 55 J6
Pinoso *mt.* Spain 55 J6
Pinos-Puente Spain 54 H7
Pinotepa Nacional Mex. 185 F5
Pinrang Indon. 75 A3
Pins, Île des *i.* New Caledonia 145 F4
  English form Pines, Isle of;
  also known as Kunié
Pins, Pointe aux *pt* Canada 173 L8
Pinsk Belarus 42 H9
Pinta, Sierra *hill* U.S.A. 183 K9
Pintados Chile 200 C5
Pintasan Sabah Malaysia 77 G1
Pinto Spain 55 H4
Pintura U.S.A. 183 K4
Pinzolo Italy 56 C2
Pioche U.S.A. 183 J4
Pio IX Brazil 202 C2
Piombino Italy 56 C6
Pioneer OH U.S.A. 176 A4
Pioneer TN U.S.A. 176 A9
Pioneer, Ostrov *i.* Rus. Fed. 39 I2
Pionerskiy Kaliningradskaya Oblast'
  Rus. Fed. 42 B7
  historically known as Neukuhren
Pionerskiy Khanty-Mansiyskiy Avtonomnyy
  Okrug Rus. Fed. 38 G3
Pionki Poland 49 S4
Piopio N.Z. 152 J6
Piopiotahi *inlet* N.Z. *see* Milford Sound
Piorini *r.* Brazil 199 F5
Piorini, Lago *l.* Brazil 199 F5
Piotrków Trybunalski Poland 49 Q4
  formerly known as Petrokov; *historically
  known as* Petrikau
Piove di Sacco Italy 56 E3
Pip Iran 101 E5
Pipa Dingzi *mt.* China 82 C4
Pipanaco, Salar de *salt flat* Arg. 204 D3
Pipar India 96 B4
Pipar Road India 96 B4
Piperi *i.* Greece 59 F9
Piper Peak U.S.A. 182 G4
Pipestone Canada 167 K5
Pipestone *r.* Canada 168 B2
Pipestone U.S.A. 178 C3
Pipirig Romania 58 H1
Pipiriki N.Z. 152 J7
Pipli India 97 E5
Pipmuacan, Réservoir Canada 169 G3
Pippingarra Aboriginal Reserve
  Australia 150 B4
Pipriac France 50 E5
Piqan China *see* Shanshan
Piqanlik China 88 D5
Piqua U.S.A. 176 A5
Piqueras, Puerto de *pass* Spain 55 I2
Piquet Carneiro Brazil 202 E3
Piquete Brazil 207 H9
Piquiri *r.* Mato Grosso do Sul Brazil 201 G4
Piquiri *r.* Paraná Brazil 203 A8
Piracaia Brazil 206 G10
Piracanjuba *r.* Brazil 206 D4
Piracanjuba *r.* Brazil 206 D4
Piracicaba *r.* Minas Gerais Brazil 203 D6
Piracicaba *r.* São Paulo Brazil 206 E9
Piraçununga Brazil 206 F8
Piracuruca Brazil 202 D2
Piraeus Greece 59 E11
  also spelt Peiraias *or* Piraiévs
Piraí do Sul Brazil 203 B8
Piraiévs Greece *see* Piraeus
Piraju Brazil 206 D10
Pirajuba Brazil 206 E7
Pirajuí Brazil 206 D8
Pirallahı Adası Azer. 107 G2
Pirané Arg. 204 F2
Piranga Brazil 207 J7
Piranga *r.* Brazil 207 K7
Piranhas Alagoas Brazil 202 E4
Piranhas Amazonas Brazil 199 F6
Piranhas Goiás Brazil 206 B5
Piranhas *r.* Goiás Brazil 206 B3
Piranhas *r.* Rio Grande do Norte
  Brazil 202 E3
Pirapemas Brazil 202 C2
Pirapetinga Amazonas Brazil 201 E1
Pirapetinga Minas Gerais Brazil 207 K8
Pirapó *r.* Brazil 206 A9
Pirapora Brazil 203 C6
Pirapozinho Brazil 206 B9
Piraputangas Brazil 201 F4
Pirara Guyana 199 G4
Pirarajá Uruguay 204 G4
Piratini Brazil 204 G3
Piratininga Brazil 206 D8
Piratininga *r.* Brazil 207 G2
Pirawa India 96 C4
Pirdop Bulg. 58 F6
Pire Mahuida, Sierra *mts* Arg. 205 C6
Pirenópolis Brazil 206 C2
Pires do Rio Brazil 206 D4
Pirganj Bangl. 97 F4
Pirgos Greece *see* Pyrgos
Pirgovo Bulg. 58 G5
Piriaka N.Z. 152 J6

Pirápolis Uruguay 204 G4
P'irin *mts* Bulg. 58 E7
Pirineos *mts* Europe *see* Pyrenees
Piripá Brazil 207 L1
Piripiri Brazil 202 D3
Pírita *r.* Estonia 42 F2
Piritu *Falcón* Venez. 198 D2
Piritu *Portuguesa* Venez. 198 D2
Firmed India 94 C4
Pirna Germany 49 K5
Pirojpur Bangl. 97 F5
Pirón *r.* Spain 54 H3
Pirongia N.Z. 152 J5
Pirongia *vol.* N.Z. 152 J5
Pirongia Forest Park *nature res.*
  N.Z. 152 J5
Piros, Ozero *l.* Rus. Fed. 43 O3
Pirot *Srbija* Yugo. 58 D5
Pírpainti India 97 E4
Pirrasit Dağ *hill* Turkey 107 E3
Pirsagat Azer. 100 D2
Pirsaatçay *r.* Azer. 107 G2
Piru Indon. 75 D3
Piru, Teluk *b.* Indon. 75 D3
Pir'yakh, Gora *mt.* Tajik. 101 G2
  also known as Piryakh, Kŭhi
Piryakh, Kŭhi *mt.* Tajik. *see* Pir'yakh, Gora
Piryatin Ukr. *see* Pyryatyn
Piryetós Greece *see* Pyrgetos
Piryíon Greece *see* Pyrgi
Pirzada Afgh. 101 F4
  also known as Khugiana
Pisa Italy 56 C5
  historically known as Pisae
Pisa *r.* Poland 49 S2
Pisac Peru 200 C3
Pisae Italy *see* Pisa
Pisagua Chile 200 C4
Pisang *i.* Indon. 75 D3
Pisa Range *mts* N.Z. 153 D12
Pisau, Tanjong *pt* Malaysia 77 G1
Pisaurum Italy *see* Pesaro
Pisba, Parque Nacional *nat. park*
  Col. 198 C3
Pisco Peru 200 A3
Pisco *r.* Peru 200 A3
Piseco Lake U.S.A. 177 K2
Písek Czech Rep. 49 L6
Pishan China *see* Ningnan
Pishan China 88 B4
  also known as Guma
Pishin Iran 101 E5
Pishin Pak. 101 F4
Pishin Lora *r.* Pak. 101 F4
Pishkek Kyrg. *see* Bishkek
Pishtar Rus. Fed. 82 B4
Pisidia *reg.* Turkey 106 B3
Pising Indon. 75 B4
Pisinimo U.S.A. 183 L9
Piskent Uzbek. *see* Pskent
Piso Firme Bol. 201 E3
Pisogne Italy 56 C3
Pissa *r.* Rus. Fed. 42 C7

Piz Platta *mt.* Switz. 51 P6
Pizzo Italy 57 I10
Pizzo Carbonara *mt. Sicilia* Italy 57 G11
Pizzuto, Monte *mt.* Italy 56 E6
Placentia Canada 169 K4
Placentia Italy *see* Piacenza
Placentia Bay Canada 169 K4
Placer *Masbate* Phil. 74 B4
Placer *Mindanao* Phil. 74 C4
Placerville CA U.S.A. 182 D3
Placerville CO U.S.A. 181 E5
Placetas Cuba 186 D2
Plácido de Castro Brazil 200 D3
Plain Dealing U.S.A. 179 D5
Plainfield IN U.S.A. 174 C4
Plainfield NJ U.S.A. 177 K5
Plainfield VT U.S.A. 177 M1
Plainfield WI U.S.A. 172 D6
Plains U.S.A. 179 B5
Plainview NE U.S.A. 178 C3
Plainview NY U.S.A. 177 L5
Plainview TX U.S.A. 179 B5
Plainville U.S.A. 178 C4
Plainwell U.S.A. 172 H8
Plaisance France 50 G9
Plaisance Haiti 187 E3
Plaistow U.S.A. 177 N3
Plaju Indon. 76 D3
Plaka, Akra *pt* Greece 59 H13
Plakoti, Cape Cyprus 108 F2
  also known as Yassi Burnu
Plampang Indon. 77 G5
Plana Cays *is* Bahamas 187 E2
Planada U.S.A. 182 D4
Planaltina Brazil 206 D2
Planalto Brazil 207 M1
Plancoët France 50 D5
Plandište *Vojvodina, Srbija* Yugo. 58 C3
Plane *r.* Germany 49 J3
Plankinton U.S.A. 178 C3
Plano IL U.S.A. 172 E9
Plano TX U.S.A. 179 C5
Plant City U.S.A. 175 D7
Planura Brazil 206 E7
Plaquemine U.S.A. 175 B6
Plasencia Spain 54 E4
Plaški Croatia 56 H3
Plaster City U.S.A. 183 I9
Plaster Rock Canada 169 H4
Plaston S. Africa 133 P2
Plastun Rus. Fed. 82 E3
Platamon, Rt *pt* Yugo. 56 K6
Platamonas Greece 59 D9
Platanal Peru 200 C4
Platani *r. Sicilia* Italy 57 F11
Platanistos Greece 59 F10
Platanos Greece 59 C11
Platbakkies S. Africa 132 C7
Platberg *mt.* S. Africa 133 N5

Ploudalmézeau France 50 B4
Ploufragan France 50 D4
Plouguerneau France 50 B4
Plouha France 50 D4
Plouzané France 50 B4
Plouzévédé France 50 B4
Plovdiv Bulg. 58 F6
  also known as Filibe; *historically known as*
  Philippopolis
Plover U.S.A. 172 D6
Plover *r.* U.S.A. 172 D5
Plover Cove Reservoir Hong Kong China
  87 [inset]
Plozk Poland *see* Płock
Pluckemin U.S.A. 177 K5
Plum U.S.A. 176 F5
Plum Coulee Canada 167 L5
Plummer U.S.A. 180 C3
Plumridge Lakes *salt flat* Australia 151 D6
Plumridge Lakes Nature Reserve Australia
  151 D6
Plumtree Zimbabwe 131 E4
Plungė Lith. 42 C6
Plutarco Elías Calles, Presa *resr*
  Mex. 181 E7
Plutarco Elís Calles, Presa *resr*
  Mex. 184 C2
Pluto, Lac *l.* Canada 169 G2
Pluvigner France 50 C5
Plužine *Crna Gora* Yugo. 58 A5
Plyeshchanitsy Belarus 42 I7
  also spelt Pleshchenitsy
Ply Huey Wati, Khac *mt.* Myanmar/Thai.
  78 B4

▶ Plymouth Montserrat 187 H3
  Capital of Montserrat, largely abandoned in
  1997 owing to volcanic activity.

Plymouth Trin. and Tob. 187 H5
Plymouth U.K. 47 H13
Plymouth CA U.S.A. 182 D3
Plymouth IN U.S.A. 172 G9
Plymouth MA U.S.A. 177 N3
Plymouth NC U.S.A. 174 E5
Plymouth NH U.S.A. 177 N2
Plymouth WI U.S.A. 172 F7
Plymouth Bay U.S.A. 177 O4
Plynlimon *hill* U.K. 47 I11
Plyussa Rus. Fed. 43 K3
Plyussa *r.* Rus. Fed. 43 J3
Plzeň Czech Rep. 49 K6
  historically known as Pilsen
Po *r.* Burkina 125 E4
Po *r.* Italy 56 E3
Pê, Parc National de *nat. park* Burkina
  125 E4
Po, Tanjong *pt* Sarawak Malaysia 77 E2
Poás, Volcán *vol.* Costa Rica 186 B5
Poat *i.* Indon. 75 B3
Pobeda, Gora *mt.* Rus. Fed. 39 O3
Pobeda Peak China/Kyrg. 88 B3
  also known as Jergish Chokusu *or* Tomur
  Feng; *formerly known as* Pobedy, Pik *or*
  Shengli Feng
Pobedinskiy Rus. Fed. *see* Zarechnyy
Pobedy, Pik *mt.* China/Kyrg. *see*
  Pobeda Peak
Pobiedziska Poland 49 O3
Poca U.S.A. 176 D7
Pocahontas IA U.S.A. 178 D3
Pocatalico *r.* U.S.A. 176 D7
Pocatello U.S.A. 180 D4
Pochala Sudan 128 D3
Pocheny Ukr. 41 C5
Pochep Rus. Fed. 43 N8
Pochinki Rus. Fed. 40 H5
Pochinok Smolenskaya Oblast'
  Rus. Fed. 43 N7
Pochinok *Tverskaya Oblast'* Rus. Fed. 43 P4
Pochutla Mex. 185 F6
Pock, Gunung *hill Sabah* Malaysia 77 G1
Pocking Germany 49 J7
Poções Brazil 202 D5
Pocomoke City U.S.A. 177 J7
Pocomoke Sound *b.* U.S.A. 177 J8
Pocona Bol. 200 D4
Poconé Brazil 201 F4
Pocono Mountains *hills* U.S.A. 177 J4
Pocono Summit U.S.A. 177 J4
Poço Ranakah *vol.* Indon. 75 B5
Poços de Caldas Brazil 206 G8
Pocrane Brazil 207 L6
Podberez'ye Rus. Fed. 43 L4
Podborany Czech Rep. 49 K5
Podborov'ye Rus. Fed. 43 K5
Podcher'ye Rus. Fed. 40 K3
Poddębice Poland 49 P4
Poddor'ye Rus. Fed. 43 M4
Podensac France 50 F8
Podgorac *Srbija* Yugo. 58 C5
Podgorenskiy Rus. Fed. 41 F6
Podgorica *Crne Gora* Yugo. 58 A6
  formerly known as Titograd
Podgornoye Rus. Fed. 39 I4
Podile India 94 C3
Podişul Transilvaniei *plat.* Romania *see*
  Transylvanian Basin
Pockamennaya Tunguska Rus. Fed. 39 J3
Pockamennaya Tunguska *r.* Rus. Fed. 39 J3
Podkhozheye Rus. Fed. 43 T7
Podlesnoye Rus. Fed. 102 A2
Podocarpus, Parque Nacional *nat. park*
  Ecuador 198 B6
Podoleni Romania 58 H2
Podolsk Rus. Fed. 43 S6
Podor Senega 124 B2
Podosinki Rus. Fed. 43 R6
Podozerskiy Rus. Fed. 43 U4
Podporozh'ye Rus. Fed. 43 P1
Podsvil'ye Belarus 42 I7
Podujevo *Kosovo, Srbija* Yugo. 58 B5
Podyuga Rus. Fed. 40 G3
Podvot'ye Rus. Fed. 40 H3
Poel *i.* Germany 48 I1
Poeppel Corner *salt flat* Australia 148 C5
Poetovio Slovenia *see* Ptuj
Pcfadder S. Africa 132 C6
Pcgamasing Canada 173 L4
Pegan Rus. Fed. 102 B3
Poggibonsi Italy 56 D5
Poggio Ballone *hill* Italy 56 C6
Poggio di Montieri *mt.* Italy 56 D5
Poggio Rusco Italy 56 D3
Pogled mt. *see* Bo Hai
Pogoreloye-Gorodishche Rus. Fed. 43 P5
Pogrebishche Ukr. *see* Pohrebyshche
Po Hai *g.* China *see* Bo Hai
P'ohang S. Korea 83 C5
Pohja Fin. 45 M3
Pohnpei *atoll* Micronesia 220 E5
  formerly spelt Ponape; *historically known as*
  Ascension
Pohrebyshche Ukr. 41 D6
Pohri India 96 C4
Poiana Mare Romania 58 E5
Poiana Ruscă, Munţii *mts* Romania 58 D3
Poiana Stampei Romania 58 G1
Poienești Romania 58 I2
Poienița, Vârful *mt.* Romania 58 E2
Poindimié New Caledonia 145 F4
Poinsett, Cape Antarctica 223 H2
Point au Fer Island U.S.A. 175 B6
Point-Comfort Canada 173 R4
Pointe à la Hache U.S.A. 175 B6
Pointe-à-Pitre Guadeloupe 187 H3
Pointe au Baril Station Canada 173 M5

Pointe Aux Pins U.S.A. 173 I5
Pointe-Noire Congo 126 A6
Pointe Noire Guadeloupe 187 H3
Point Hope U.S.A. 164 C2
Point Kenny Australia 146 B3
Point Lake Canada 167 H1
Point Nepean National Park Australia
  147 E4
Point of Rocks MD U.S.A. 176 H6
Point of Rocks WY U.S.A. 180 E5
Point Pelee National Park Canada 173 K9
Point Pleasant U.S.A. 177 K5
Point Reyes National Seashore *nature res.*
  U.S.A. 182 A3
Point Salvation Aboriginal Reserve
  Australia 151 C6
Point Samson Australia 144 A4
Poisevo Rus. Fed. 40 J5
Poisson Blanc, Lac du *l.* Canada 173 R5
Poissonnier Point Australia 150 B3
Poitiers France 50 G6
  historically known as Limonum
Poitou, Plaines et Seuil du *plain* France
  50 G6
Poitou-Charentes *admin. reg.* France 50 F6
Poix-de-Picardie France 51 H3
Pojo Bol. 200 D4
Pojuca Brazil 202 E5
Pokaran India 96 A4
Pokataroo Australia 147 F2
Pokats' *r.* Belarus 43 L9
Pokcha Rus. Fed. 40 K3
Pokeno N.Z. 152 J5
Pokhara Nepal 97 D3
Pokhvistnevo Rus. Fed. 41 J5
Pokigron Suriname 199 H3
Pokka Fin. 44 N1
Pok Liu Chau *i. Hong Kong* China *see*
  Lamma Island
Poko Dem. Rep. Congo 126 E4
Pokров Smolenskaya Oblast' Rus. Fed. 43 Q6
Pokrov Vladimirskaya Oblast' Rus. Fed. 43 U6
Pokrovka Kazakh. 103 G4
Pokrovka Kyrg. 103 G4
Pokrovka Kyrg. *see* Kyzyl-Suu
Pokrovka Moskovskaya Oblast'
  Rus. Fed. 43 R5
Pokrovka Orenburgskaya Oblast'
  Rus. Fed. 102 C2
Pokrovka Primorskiy Kray Rus. Fed. 82 C4
Pokrovka Primorskiy Kray Rus. Fed. 90 C2
Pokrovsk Rus. Fed. 39 M3
Pokrovsk Rus. Fed. *see* Engel's
Pokrovskoye Lipetskaya Oblast'
  Rus. Fed. 43 S9
Pokrovskoye Orlovskaya Oblast'
  Rus. Fed. 43 R9
Pokrovskoye Rostovskaya Oblast'
  Rus. Fed. 41 F7
Pokrovsk-Ural'skiy Rus. Fed. 40 K3
Pokshen'ga *r.* Rus. Fed. 40 H3
Pol' *r.* Rus. Fed. 43 V6
Pola Croatia *see* Pula
Pola Phil. 74 B3
Pola Rus. Fed. 43 M4
Pola *r.* Rus. Fed. 43 M4
Polacca U.S.A. 183 N6
Polacca Wash *watercourse* U.S.A. 183 N6
Pola de Allande Spain 54 E1
Pola de Laviana Spain 54 F1
Pola de Lena Spain 54 F1
Pola de Siero Spain 54 F1
Pola de Somiedo Spain 54 E1
Polán Iran 101 E5
Polán Spain 54 H5
Polana *mt.* Slovakia 49 Q7
▶ Poland *country* Europe 49 N3
  known as Polska in Polish

  europe [countries] ▶ 32–35

Połaniec Poland 49 S5
Polanów Poland 49 N1
Polar Bear Provincial Park Canada 168 D2
Polar Plateau Antarctica 223 V1
Polar Times Glacier Antarctica 223 E2
Polatlı Turkey 106 C3
Polatsk Belarus 43 J6
  also spelt Polotsk
Polatskaya Nizina *lowland* Belarus 42 J6
Polavaram India 94 D2
Polazna Rus. Fed. 40 K4
Polcirkeln Sweden 44 N2
Połczyn Zdrój Poland 49 N2
Poldarsa Rus. Fed. 40 H3
Pol-e Fāsā Iran 100 C4
Pole-Khatum Iran 101 E2
Pol-e Khomrī Afgh. 101 G3
Pol-e Safīd Iran 100 C2
Polessk Rus. Fed. 42 C7
Poles'ye *marsh* Belarus/Ukr. *see*
  Pripet Marshes
Polewali Indon. 75 A3
Poli Cameroon 125 I4
Poli Cyprus *see* Polis
Poliaigos *i.* Greece *see* Polyaigos
Poliçan Albania 58 B8
Policastro, Golfo di *b.* Italy 57 H9
Police Poland 49 L2
Polichnitos Greece 59 H9
  also spelt Polikhnitos
Policoro Italy 57 I8
Polídhrosos Greece *see* Polydroso
Polignano a Mare Italy 56 J8
Poligny France 51 L6
Polikastron Greece *see* Polykastro
Polikhnitos Greece *see* Polichnitos
Polikrayshte Bulg. 58 G5
Polillo *i.* Phil. 74 B3
Polillo Islands Phil. 74 B3
Polillo Strait Phil. 74 B3
Polis Cyprus 108 D2
  also known as Poli
Polis'ke Ukr. 41 D6
  formerly known as Kaganovichi Pervyye
Polis'kyy Zapovidnyk *nature res.* Ukr. 41 D6
Polist' *r.* Rus. Fed. 43 M3
Polistena Italy 57 I10
Polisto, Ozero *l.* Rus. Fed. 43 L4
Politovo Rus. Fed. 40 I2
Políyiros Greece *see* Polygyros
Polk U.S.A. 176 F4
Polkorona Latvia 42 H5
Polkowice Poland 49 N4
Polla Italy 57 H8
Pollachi India 94 C4
Pollard Lakes U.S.A. *see*
  Gardner Pinnacles
Pöllauer Tal *nature res.* Austria 49 M8
Pollença Spain 55 O5
  also spelt Pollensa
Pollensa Spain *see* Pollença
Pollino, Parco Nazionale del *nat. park*
  Italy 57 I9
Poloc Harbour *b.* Phil. 74 B5
Pollock Pines U.S.A. 182 D3
Pollock Reef Australia 151 C7
Pollok N.Z. 152 I5
Polmak Norway 44 N1
Polnovat Rus. Fed. 38 G3
Polo Fin. 44 O2
Polo U.S.A. 172 D9
Pologi Ukr. *see* Polohy
Polohy Ukr. 41 F7
  also spelt Pologi; *formerly known as*
  Chubarovka
Polokwane S. Africa *see* Pietersburg
Polomet' *r.* Rus. Fed. 43 N4
Polomoloc Phil. 74 C5
Polonnaruwa Sri Lanka 94 D5
Polonne Ukr. 41 D6
  also spelt Polonnoye

Polonnoye Ukr. see **Polonne**
Polotnyanyy Zavod Rus. Fed. **43** Q7
Polotsk Belarus see **Polatsk**
Polovinka Rus. Fed. see **Ugleural'skiy**
Polovragi Romania **58** E3
Pöls r. Austria **49** L8
Polska country Europe see **Poland**
Polski Trŭmbesh Bulg. **58** G5
Polson U.S.A. **180** D3
Polta r. Rus. Fed. **40** G2
Poltár Slovakia **49** Q7
Poltava Ukr. **41** E6
Poltavka Rus. Fed. **82** C3
Poltavskaya Rus. Fed. **41** F7
formerly known as Krasnoarmeyskaya
Poltoratsk Turkm. see **Ashgabat**
Põltsamaa Estonia **42** G3
Põltsamaa r. Estonia **42** H3
Polur India **94** C3
Põlva Estonia **42** I3
Polvadera U.S.A. **181** F6
Polvijärvi Fin. **44** O3
Polya r. Rus. Fed. **43** U6
Polyaigos i. Greece **59** F12
also spelt Poliaigos
Polyanovgrad Bulg. see **Karnobat**
Polyany Rus. Fed. **43** K1
Polyarnoye Rus. Fed. see **Russkoye Ust'ye**
Polyarnyy Chukotskiy Avtonomnyy Okrug Rus. Fed. **39** R3
Polyarnyy Murmanskaya Oblast' Rus. Fed. **44** P1
Polyarnyye Zori Rus. Fed. **44** P2
Polyarnyy Krug Rus. Fed. **44** P2
Polyarnyy Ural mts Rus. Fed. **40** L2
Polydroso Greece **59** D10
also known as Polídhrosos
Polygyros Greece **59** E8
also spelt Políyiros
Polyiagou-Folegandrou, Steno sea chan. Greece **59** F12
Polykastro Greece **58** D8
also known as Políkastron
Polynesia is Oceania **220** G5
Polynésie Française terr. S. Pacific Ocean see **French Polynesia**
Pomabamba Peru **200** A2
Pomahaka r. N.Z. **153** D14
Pomarance Italy **56** C5
Pomarkku Fin. **45** M3
Pomba r. Brazil **203** D7
Pombal Pará Brazil **199** H5
Pombal Paraíba Brazil **202** E3
Pombal Port. **54** C5
Pombas r. Brazil **199** F6
Pombas Cape Verde **124** [inset]
Pombo r. Brazil **206** A7
Pomene Moz. **131** G4
Pomeroy S. Africa **133** O5
Pomeroy OH U.S.A. **176** C6
Pomeroy WA U.S.A. **180** C3
Pomezia Italy **56** E7
Pomfret S. Africa **132** H2
Pomio P.N.G. **145** E2
Pomokaira reg. Fin. **44** N2
Pomona Namibia **130** B5
Pomona U.S.A. **182** G7
Pomorie Bulg. **58** I6
Pomorska, Zatoka b. Poland **49** L1
Pomorskie, Pojezierze reg. Poland **49** O2
Pomorskiy Bereg coastal area Rus. Fed. **40** E2
Pomorskiy Proliv sea chan. Rus. Fed. **40** I1
Pomos Point Cyprus **108** D2
also known as Pomou, Akra
Pomo Tso l. China see **Puma Yumco**
Pomou, Akra pt Cyprus see **Pomos Point**
Pompei Italy **57** G8
historically known as Pompeii
Pompéia Brazil **206** C9
Pompeii Italy see **Pompei**
Pompéu Brazil **203** C6
Pompton Lakes U.S.A. **177** K4
Ponape atoll Micronesia see **Pohnpei**
Ponask Lake Canada **167** M4
Ponazyrevo Rus. Fed. **40** H4
Ponca U.S.A. **178** C3
Ponca City U.S.A. **178** C4
Ponce Puerto Rico **187** G3
Ponce de Leon Bay U.S.A. **175** D7
Poncha Springs U.S.A. **181** F5
Ponda India **94** B3
Pondicherry India **94** C4
also spelt Pondichéry or Puduchcheri
Pondicherry union terr. India **95** C4
Pondichéry India see **Pondicherry**
Pond Inlet Canada **165** L2
also known as Mittimatalik; formerly known as Ponds Bay
Pondoland reg. S. Africa **133** N8
Ponds, Island of Canada **169** K2
Ponds Bay Canada see **Pond Inlet**
Poneloya Nicaragua **186** B4
Ponente, Riviera di coastal area Italy **56** A5
Ponferrada Spain **54** E2
Pongakawa N.Z. **152** K5
Pongara, Pointe pt Gabon **126** A4
Pongaroa N.Z. **152** K8
Pongo watercourse Sudan **126** E3
Pongo de Manseriche gorge Peru **198** B6
Pongola S. Africa **133** P4
Pongola r. S. Africa **133** Q3
Pongolapoort Dam l. S. Africa **133** P4
Pongolapoort Public Resort Nature Reserve S. Africa **133** P4
Poniatowa Poland **49** T4
Poniki, Gunung mt. Indon. **75** B2
Ponindilisa, Tanjung pt Indon. **75** B3
Ponizov'ye Rus. Fed. **43** M6
Ponnaganur Myanmar **78** A3
Ponnaivar r. India **94** C4
Ponnampet India **94** B3
Ponnani India **94** B4
Ponnani r. India **94** B4
Ponneri India **94** D3
Ponnyadaung Range mts Myanmar **78** A3
Ponoka Canada **167** H4
Ponomarevka Rus. Fed. **102** C1
Ponorogo Indon. **77** E4
Ponoy r. Rus. Fed. **40** G2
Pons r. Canada **169** G1
Pons France **50** F7
Pons Spain see **Ponts**
Ponsacco Italy **56** C5
Ponsul r. Port. **54** D5
Pontacq France **50** F9

▶**Ponta Delgada** Azores **216** M3
Capital of the Azores.

Ponta de Pedras Brazil **202** B2
Ponta dos Índios Brazil **199** I3
Ponta do Sol Cape Verde **124** [inset]
Ponta Grossa Brazil **203** B8
Pontal do Ipiranga Brazil **207** N6
Pontalina Brazil **206** D4
Pont-à-Mousson France **51** M4
Pontant Arg. **204** E5
Pontão Brazil **202** B3
Ponta Porã Brazil **201** G5
Pontarlier France **51** M6
Pontassieve Italy **56** D5
Pont-Audemer France **50** G3
Pont-Aven France **50** C5
Pontax r. Canada **168** E3
Pontchartrain, Lake U.S.A. **175** B6
Pontchâteau France **50** D5
Pont-d'Ain France **51** L6
Pont-de-Roide France **51** M5
Pont de Suert Spain **55** L2
Ponte Alta do Norte Brazil **202** C4
Ponteareas Spain **54** C2
also spelt Puenteareas
Pontebba Italy **56** F2
Ponte Branca Brazil **206** A3
Ponte-Ceso Spain **54** C1
Pontecorvo Italy **56** F7
Ponte de Pedra Brazil **201** F3
Pontedera Italy **56** C5
Ponte de Sor Port. **54** C5
Ponte do Rio Verde Brazil **203** A6
Ponte Firme Brazil **206** G5
Ponteix Canada **167** J5
Ponteland U.K. **47** K8
Ponte Nova Brazil **203** D7
Pontes-e-Lacerda Brazil **201** F3
Pontevedra Spain **54** C2
Pontevedra, Ría de est. Spain **54** C2
Ponthierville Dem. Rep. Congo see **Ubundu**
Pontiac IL U.S.A. **174** B3
Pontiac MI U.S.A. **173** J8
Pontiae is Italy see **Ponziane, Isole**
Pontianak Indon. **77** E3
Pontine Islands is Italy see **Ponziane, Isole**
Pontivy France **50** D4
Pont-l'Abbé France **50** B5
Pontoetoe Suriname **199** H4
Pontoise France **51** I3
Ponton watercourse Australia **151** C6
Ponton Canada **167** L4
Pontotoc U.S.A. **174** B5
Pontremoli Italy **56** B4
Ponts Spain **55** M3
also spelt Pons
Pont-St-Esprit France **51** K8
Pont-sur-Yonne France **51** J4
Pontypool Canada **173** O6
Pontypool U.K. **47** I12
Pontypridd U.K. **47** I12
Ponui Island N.Z. **152** J4
Ponyatovka Rus. Fed. **43** N8
Ponyri Rus. Fed. **43** R9
Ponza Italy **57** E8
Ponza, Isola di i. Italy **56** E8
Ponziane, Isole is Italy **56** E8
English form Pontine Islands; historically known as Pontiae
Poochera Australia **146** B3
Pool admin. reg. Congo **126** B5
Poole U.K. **47** K13
Poolowanna Lake salt flat Australia **148** C5
Poona India see **Pune**
Pooncarie Australia **147** D3
Poopelloe Lake Australia **147** E2
Poopó Bol. **200** D4
Poopó, Lago de l. Bol. **200** D4
Poor Knights Islands N.Z. **152** I3
Pop Uzbek. see **Pap**
Popa Mountain Myanmar **78** A3
Popayán Col. **198** B4
Pope Latvia **42** C4
Popes Creek U.S.A. **177** I7
Popigay r. Rus. Fed. **39** K2
Popiltah Lake imp. l. Australia **146** D3
Popio Lake Australia **146** D3
Poplar r. Man. Canada **167** L4
Poplar r. N.W.T. Canada **166** G2
Poplar U.S.A. **172** B4
Poplar r. U.S.A. **180** F2
Poplar, West Fork r. U.S.A. **180** F2
Poplar Bluff U.S.A. **174** B4
Poplar Camp U.S.A. **176** E9
Poplar Plains U.S.A. **176** B7
Poplarville U.S.A. **175** B6
Poplevinskiy Rus. Fed. **43** U8

▶**Popocatépetl, Volcán** vol. Mex. **185** F5
5th highest mountain in North America.
northamerica [landscapes] ▶ 156–157
northamerica [threats] ▶ 160–161

Popoh Indon. **77** E5
Popokabaka Dem. Rep. Congo **127** C6
Popoli Italy **56** F6
Popondetta P.N.G. **145** D2
Popovača Croatia **56** I3
Popovichskaya Rus. Fed. see **Kalininskaya**
Popovka Vologod. Obl. Rus. Fed. **43** S2
Popovka Vologod. Obl. Rus. Fed. **43** U1
Popovo Bulg. **58** H5
Popovo Polje plain Bos.-Herz. **56** J6
Popovska Reka r. Bulg. **58** H6
Poppberg hill Germany **48** I6
Poppenberg hill Germany **48** H4
Poprad r. Poland **49** R6
Poprad Slovakia **49** R6
Poquis, Nevado de mt. Chile **200** D5
Poquoson U.S.A. **177** I8
Por r. Poland **49** U5
Porali r. Pak. **101** F5
Porangahau N.Z. **152** K8
Porangatu Brazil **202** B5
Porazava Belarus **42** F9
Porbandar India **96** A5
Porcher Island Canada **166** D4
Porciúncula Brazil **207** K7
Porco Bol. **200** D4
Porcsalma Hungary **49** T8
Porcuna Spain **54** G7
Porcupine r. Canada/U.S.A. **164** E3
Porcupine, Cape Canada **169** J2
Porcupine Creek r. U.S.A. **180** F2
Porcupine Gorge National Park Australia **149** E4
Porcupine Hills Canada **167** K4
Porcupine Mountains U.S.A. **172** D4
Porcupine Plain Canada **167** K4
Porcupine Provincial Forest nature res. Canada **167** K4
Pordenone Italy **56** E3
Pordim Bulg. **58** F5
Pore Col. **198** D3
Poreč Croatia **56** F3
Porecatu Brazil **206** B9
Porech'ye Moskovskaya Oblast' Rus. Fed. **43** Q6
Porech'ye Pskovskaya Oblast' Rus. Fed. **43** L5
Porech'ye Tverskaya Oblast' Rus. Fed. **43** R3
Porech'ye-Rybnoye Rus. Fed. **43** U4
Poretskoye Rus. Fed. **40** H5
Porga Benin **125** F4
Pori Fin. **45** M3
also known as Björneborg
Porirua N.Z. **152** I9
Porjus Sweden **44** L2
Porkhov Rus. Fed. **43** K4
Porkkalafjärden b. Fin. **42** F2
Porlamar Venez. **199** F2
Porma r. Spain **54** F2
Pormpuraaw Australia **149** D2
Pornainen Fin. **45** N3
Pornic France **50** D5
Poro i. Phil. **74** C4
Poro, Monte hill Italy **57** H10
Poronaysk Rus. Fed. **82** F2
Porong China see **Baingoin**
Pôrông, Stœng r. Cambodia **79** D5
Poros Greece **59** E11
Poros i. Greece **59** E11
Porosozero Rus. Fed. **40** E3
Porpoise Bay Antarctica **223** I2
Porquerolles, Île de i. France **51** M10
Porquis Junction Canada **173** M2
Porrentruy Switz. **51** N5
Porriño Spain **54** C2
Porsangen sea chan. Norway **44** N1
Porsangerhalvøya pen. Norway **44** N1
Porsgrunn Norway **45** J4
Porsuk r. Turkey **106** B3
Portadown U.K. **47** F9
Portaferry U.K. **47** G9
Portage IN U.S.A. **172** F9
Portage MI U.S.A. **172** H8
Portage PA U.S.A. **176** G5
Portage WI U.S.A. **172** D7
Portage Lakes U.S.A. **176** D5
Portage la Prairie Canada **167** L5
Portal U.S.A. **178** B1
Port Alberni Canada **166** E5
Port Albert Australia **147** E4
Portalegre Port. **54** D5
Portalegre admin. dist. Port. **54** D5
Portales U.S.A. **179** B5
Port-Alfred Canada see **La Baie**
Port Alfred S. Africa **133** K10
Port Alice Canada **166** E5
Port Allegany U.S.A. **176** G4
Port Alma Australia **149** F4
Port Angeles U.S.A. **180** B2
Port Antonio Jamaica **186** D3
Port-à-Piment Haiti **187** E3
Portarlington Rep. of Ireland **47** E10
Port Arthur Australia **147** E5
Port Arthur China see **Lüshun**
Port Arthur U.S.A. **179** D6
Port Askaig U.K. **46** F8
Port Augusta Australia **146** C3
Port-au-Port Bay Canada **169** J3

▶**Port-au-Prince** Haiti **187** E3
Capital of Haiti.

Port aux Choix Canada **169** J3
Port Beaufort S. Africa **132** E11
Port Blair India **95** G4
Port Bolster Canada **173** N6
Portbou Spain **55** O2
Port Bradshaw b. Australia **148** C2
Port Broughton Australia **146** C3
Port Burwell Canada **173** M8
Port Campbell Australia **147** D4
Port Campbell National Park Australia **147** D4
Port Canning India **97** F5
Port Carling Canada **173** N5
Port-Cartier Canada **169** H3
formerly known as Shelter Bay
Port Chalmers N.Z. **153** E13
Port Charles N.Z. **152** J4
Port Charlotte U.S.A. **175** D7
Port Clements Canada **166** C4
Port Clinton OH U.S.A. **176** C4
Port Clyde U.S.A. **177** P2
Port Colborne Canada **168** E5
Port Credit Canada **173** N7
Port Darwin b. Australia **148** A2
Port Davey b. Australia **147** E5
Port-de-Paix Haiti **187** E3
Port de Pollença Spain **55** O5
also spelt Puerto de Pollensa
Port Dickson Malaysia **76** C2
Port Douglas Australia **149** E3
Port Dover Canada **173** M8
Port Easington inlet Australia **148** A1
Porte des Morts lake channel U.S.A. **172** G5
Port Edward Canada **166** D4
Port Edward S. Africa **133** O8
Port Edwards U.S.A. **172** D6
Porteira Brazil **199** G5
Porteirinha Brazil **202** D5
Portel Brazil **202** B2
Portel Port. **54** D6
Portelândia Brazil **206** A4
Port Elgin N.B. Canada **169** H4
Port Elgin Ont. Canada **168** D4
Port Elizabeth S. Africa **133** J10
Port Ellen U.K. **46** F8
Port Erin Isle of Man **47** H9
Porter Lake N.W.T. Canada **167** J2
Porter Lake Sask. Canada **167** J3
Porter Landing Canada **166** D3
Porterville S. Africa **132** C10
Porterville U.S.A. **182** E5
Portes-lès-Valence France **51** K8
Port Étienne Mauritania see **Nouâdhibou**
Port Everglades U.S.A. see **Fort Lauderdale**
Port Fairy Australia **147** D4
Port Fitzroy N.Z. **152** J4
Port Francqui Dem. Rep. Congo see **Ilebo**
Port-Gentil Gabon **126** A5
Port Gibson U.S.A. **175** B6
Port Grosvenor S. Africa **133** N8
Port Harcourt Nigeria **125** G5
Port Hardy Canada **166** E5
Port Harrison Canada see **Inukjuak**
Port Hawkesbury Canada **169** I4
Porthcawl U.K. **47** I12
Port Hedland Australia **150** B4
Port Henry U.S.A. **177** L1
Port Herald Malawi see **Nsanje**
Porthmos Zakynthou sea chan. Greece **59** B11
Port Hope Canada **173** O7
Port Hope U.S.A. **173** K7
Port Hope Simpson Canada **169** K2
Port Hueneme U.S.A. **182** E7
Port Huron U.S.A. **173** K8
Port-Ilіç Azer. **107** G3
Portillo Cuba **186** D3
Portimão Port. **54** C7
Port Island Hong Kong China **87** [inset]
also known as Chek Chau
Port Jackson Australia see **Sydney**
Port Jackson inlet Australia **147** F3
Port Jefferson U.S.A. **177** L5
Port Kaituma Guyana **199** G3
Port Keats Australia see **Wadeye**
Port Kent U.S.A. **177** L1
Port Klang Malaysia see **Pelabuhan Kelang**
Port Láirge Rep. of Ireland see **Waterford**
Portland Australia **146** D4
Portland IN U.S.A. **176** A5
Portland ME U.S.A. **177** O2
Portland MI U.S.A. **173** I8
Portland OR U.S.A. **180** B3
Portland, Isle of pen. U.K. **47** J13
Portland Bay Australia **146** D4
Portland Bill hd U.K. see **Bill of Portland**
Portland Canal inlet Canada **166** D4
Portland Creek Pond l. Canada **169** J3
Portland Inlet Canada **166** D4
Portland Point Jamaica **186** D3
Portland Roads Australia **149** D2
Portlaoise Rep. of Ireland **47** E10
Port Lavaca U.S.A. **179** C6
Port Lincoln Australia **146** B3
Port Loko Sierra Leone **124** B4
Port Louis Guadeloupe **187** H3

▶**Port Louis** Mauritius **219** K7
Capital of Mauritius.

Port-Lyautrey Morocco see **Kénitra**
Port MacDonnell Australia **146** D4
Port Macquarie Australia **147** G2
Port Manvers inlet Canada **169** I1
Port McArthur b. Australia **148** C2
Port McNeill Canada **166** E5
Port-Menier Canada **169** H3
Port Moller b. U.S.A. **164** C4
Port Morant Jamaica **186** D3

▶**Port Moresby** P.N.G. **73** K8
Capital of Papua New Guinea.

Port Musgrave b. Australia **149** D1
Portnacroish U.K. **46** G7
Portnahaven U.K. **46** F8
Port Neches U.S.A. **179** D6
Port Neill Australia **146** C3
Port Nelson Bahamas **187** E2
Portneuf r. Canada **169** G3
Portneuf, Réserve Faunique de nature res. Canada **169** F4
Port Nis U.K. **46** F5
Port Nolloth S. Africa **132** A6
Port Norris U.S.A. **177** J6
Port-Nouveau-Québec Canada see **Kangiqsualujjuaq**
Porto Brazil **202** D2
Porto Port. see **Oporto**
Porto admin. dist. Port. **54** C3
Porto, Golfe de b. Corse France **51** O10
Porto Acre Brazil **200** D2
Porto Alegre Amazonas Brazil **200** D2
Porto Alegre Mato Grosso do Sul Brazil **203** A7
Porto Alegre Pará Brazil **199** H6
Porto Alegre Rio Grande do Sul Brazil **203** B9
Porto Alencastro Brazil **206** C6
Porto Alexandre Angola see **Tombua**
Porto Amarante Brazil **201** E3
Porto Amboim Angola **127** B7
also known as Gunza
Porto Amélia Moz. see **Pemba**
Porto Artur Brazil **201** G3
Porto Azzurro Italy **56** C6
Porto Belo Brazil **203** B8
Portobelo Panama **186** D5
Portobelo, Parque Nacional nat. park Panama **186** D5
Porto Camargo Brazil **203** A7
Porto Cavlo Brazil **202** F4
Porto da Fôlha Brazil **202** E4
Porto da Lontra Brazil **199** H6
Porto de Meinacos Brazil **202** A5
Porto de Moz Brazil **199** H5
Porto de Santa Cruz Brazil **207** L2
Porto do Barka Brazil **199** H6
Porto do Massacas Brazil **201** E3
Porto dos Gaúchos Óbidos Brazil **201** F2
Porto do Son Spain **54** B2
also spelt Puerto del Son
Porto Empedocle Sicilia Italy **57** F11
Porto Esperança Brazil **201** F4
Porto Esperidião Brazil **201** F3
Porto Estrêla Brazil **201** F3
Porto Feliz Brazil **206** F10
Portoferraio Italy **56** C6
Porto Ferreira Brazil **206** F8
Porto Firme Brazil **207** J7
Porto Franco Brazil **202** C3

▶**Port of Spain** Trin. and Tob. **187** H5
Capital of Trinidad and Tobago.

Porto Grande Brazil **199** I4
Portogruaro Italy **56** E3
Porto Inglês Cape Verde **124** [inset]
Porto Jofre Brazil **201** F4
Portola U.S.A. **182** D2
Porto Luceno Brazil **203** A8
Portomaggiore Italy **56** D4
Porto Mauá Brazil **203** A8
Porto Murtinho Brazil **201** F5
Porto Nacional Brazil **202** B4

▶**Porto-Novo** Benin **125** F5
Capital of Benin.

Porto Novo Cape Verde **124** [inset]
Porto Novo India see **Parangipettai**
Portopalo di Capo Passero Sicilia Italy **57** H12
Porto Primavera, Represa resr Brazil **206** A8
Port Orange U.S.A. **175** D6
Port Orchard U.S.A. **180** B3
Port Orford U.S.A. **180** A4
Porto Rincão Cape Verde **124** [inset]
Porto San Giorgio Italy **56** F5
Porto Santana Brazil **199** I5
Porto Sant'Elpidio Italy **56** F5
Porto Santo, Ilha de i. Madeira **122** A2
Portoscuso Sardegna Italy **57** A9
Porto Seguro Brazil **202** E6
Porto Tolle Italy **56** E4
Porto Torres Sardegna Italy **56** A8
historically known as Turris Libisonis
Porto Triunfo Brazil **201** E3
Porto União Brazil **203** B8
Porto-Vecchio Corse France **52** D3
Porto Velho Brazil **201** E2
Portoviejo Ecuador **198** A5
Porto Wálter Brazil **200** B2
Portpatrick U.K. **47** G9
Port Pegasus b. N.Z. **153** B15
also known as Pikihatiti
Port Perry Canada **173** O6
Port Phillip Bay Australia **147** E4
Port Pirie Australia **146** C3
Portree U.K. **46** F6
Port Renfrew Canada **166** E5
Port Rexton Canada **169** K3
Port Roper b. Australia **148** B2
Port Rowan Canada **173** M8
Port Royal U.S.A. **177** H7
Port Royal Sound inlet U.S.A. **175** D5
Port Said Egypt **121** G2
also known as Būr Sa'īd
Port St Joe U.S.A. **175** C6
Port St Johns S. Africa **133** N8
Port-St-Louis Madag. see **Antsohimbondrona**
Port-St-Louis-du-Rhône France **51** K9
Port Saint Lucie City U.S.A. **175** D7
Port Salvador Falkland Is **205** F8
Ports de Beseit mts Spain **55** L4
also spelt Puertos de Beceite
Port Severn Canada **173** N6
Port Shelter b. Hong Kong China **87** [inset]
also known as Ngau Mei Hoi
Port Shepstone S. Africa **133** O7
Port Simpson Canada see **Lax Kw'alaams**
Portsmouth Dominica **187** H4
Portsmouth U.K. **47** K13
Portsmouth NH U.S.A. **177** O2
Portsmouth OH U.S.A. **176** C7
Portsmouth VA U.S.A. **177** I9
Port Stanley Falkland Is see **Stanley**
Port Stephens Falkland Is **205** E9
Port Sudan Sudan **121** H5
also known as Būr Sudan
Port Sulphur U.S.A. **175** B6
Port-sur-Saône France **51** M5
Port Swettenham Malaysia see **Pelabuhan Kelang**
Port Talbot U.K. **47** I12
Port Tambang b. Phil. **74** B3
Porttipahdan tekojärvi l. Fin. **44** N1
Port Townsend U.S.A. **180** B2
▶**Portugal** country Europe **54** C7
europe [countries] ▶ 32–35
Portugalete Spain **55** H1
Portugália Angola see **Chitato**
Portuguesa state Venez. **198** D2
Portuguese East Africa country Africa see **Mozambique**
Portuguese Guinea country Africa see **Guinea-Bissau**
Portuguese Timor terr. Asia see **East Timor**
Portuguese West Africa country Africa see **Angola**
Portumna Rep. of Ireland **47** D10
Portus Herculis Monoeci country Europe see **Monaco**
Port-Vendres France **51** J10
Port Victoria Australia **146** C3

▶**Port Vila** Vanuatu **145** F3
Capital of Vanuatu. Also known as Vila.

Portville U.S.A. **176** G3
Port Vladimir Rus. Fed. **44** P1
Port Waikato N.Z. **152** I5
Port Wakefield Australia **146** C3
Port Warrender Australia **150** D2
Port Washington U.S.A. **172** F7
Port Wing U.S.A. **172** B4
Porumamilla India **94** C3
Porus'ya r. Rus. Fed. **43** M4
Porvenir Pando Bol. **200** C2
Porvenir Santa Cruz Bol. **201** E3
Porvenir Chile **205** C9
Porvoo Fin. **45** N3
also known as Borgå
Porvoonjoki r. Fin. **42** G1
Por'ya Guba Rus. Fed. **44** P2
Poryŏng S. Korea **83** B5
formerly known as Taech'ŏn
Porzuna Spain **54** G5
Posada Sardegna Italy **57** B8
Posada r. Sardegna Italy **57** B8
Posada Spain **54** F1
Posadas Arg. **204** G2
Posadas Spain **54** F7
Posadowsky Bay Antarctica **223** G2
Posavina reg. Bos.-Herz./Croatia **56** I3
Poschiavo Switz. **51** Q6
Poseidonia Greece **59** F11
Poseidonia tourist site Italy see **Paestum**
Posen Poland see **Poznań**
Posen U.S.A. **173** J5
Poshekhon'ye Rus. Fed. **43** U3
formerly known as Poshekhon'ye-Volodarsk
Poshekhon'ye-Volodarsk Rus. Fed. see **Poshekhon'ye**
Posht watercourse Iran **100** D4
Posht-e Badam Iran **100** C3
Poshteh-ye Chaqvir hill Iran **100** D4
Posht-e Kūh mts Iran **100** A3
Posht Kūh hill Iran **100** B2
Posio Fin. **44** O2
Poskam China see **Zepu**
Poso Indon. **75** B3
Poso r. Indon. **75** B3
Poso, Danau l. Indon. **75** B3
Poso, Teluk b. Indon. **75** B3
Posof Turkey **107** E2
Posorja Ecuador **198** A5
Pospelikha Rus. Fed. **103** J1
Posse Brazil **202** C5
Possession Islands Antarctica **223** L2
Pößneck Germany **48** I5
Post U.S.A. **179** B5
Poşta Câlnău Romania **58** H3
formerly spelt Poşta Cîlnău
Poşta Cîlnău Romania see **Poşta Câlnău**
Postavy Belarus see **Pastavy**
Poste-de-la-Baleine Canada see **Kuujjuarapik**
Postmasburg S. Africa **132** H5
Postojna Slovenia **56** G3
Poston U.S.A. **183** J7
Postville Canada **169** J2
Postville U.S.A. **174** B3
Post Weygand Alg. **123** F4
Postysheve Ukr. see **Krasnoarmiys'k**
Posušje Bos.-Herz. **56** J5
Pos'yet Rus. Fed. **82** C4
Pota Indon. **75** B5
Potamia Greece **58** F8
Potamos Greece **59** D12
Potanino Rus. Fed. **43** N1
Potchefstroom S. Africa **133** L3
Potcoava Romania **58** F4
Poté Brazil **203** D6
Poteau U.S.A. **179** D5
Potegaon India **94** D2
Potentia Italy see **Potenza**
Potenza Italy **57** H8
historically known as Potentia
Potenza r. Italy **56** F5
Poteriteri, Lake N.Z. **153** B14
Potfontein S. Africa **132** I7
Potgietersrus S. Africa **131** F5
Poti r. Brazil **202** D3
P'ot'i Georgia **107** E2
Potikal India **94** D2
Potiraguá Brazil **202** E5
Potiskum Nigeria **125** H4
Potnarvin Vanuatu **145** F3
Po Toi i. Hong Kong China **87** [inset]
also spelt Putoi
Potomac r. U.S.A. **177** I7
Potomac, South Branch r. U.S.A. **176** G6
Potomac, South Fork South Branch r. U.S.A. **176** F7
Potomana, Gunung mt. Indon. **75** C5
Potoru Sierra Leone **124** C5
Potosí Bol. **200** D4
Potosí dept Bol. **200** D5
Potosi U.S.A. **174** B4
Potosi Mountain U.S.A. **183** I6
Pototan Phil. **74** B4
Potrerillos Chile **204** C2
Potrero del Llano Mex. **184** D2
Potro r. Peru **198** B6
Potsdam Germany **49** K3
Potsdam U.S.A. **177** K1
Potsdamer Havelseengebiet park Germany **49** J3
Pottangi India **95** D2
Pottendorf Austria **49** N8
Potter U.S.A. **178** B3
Potter Valley U.S.A. **182** A2
Potterville U.S.A. **176** A3
Pottstown U.S.A. **177** J5
Pottsville U.S.A. **177** I5
Potwar reg. Pak. **101** H3
Pouancé France **50** E5
Pouce Coupe Canada **166** F4
Pouch Cove Canada **169** K4
Poughkeepsie U.S.A. **177** L4
Poultney U.S.A. **177** L2
Pouma Cameroon **125** H6
Pound U.S.A. **176** C8
Poupan S. Africa **132** I7
Pourerere N.Z. **152** K8
Pouso Alegre Brazil **207** H9
Pouso Alegre, Serra mts Brazil **206** D2
Pouso Alto Brazil **206** A3
Poutasi Samoa **145** H3
Poŭthĭsăt Cambodia **79** C5
also spelt Pursat
Pouto N.Z. **152** I4
Pouzauges France **50** F6
Povarovo Rus. Fed. **43** S5
Považská Bystrica Slovakia **49** P6
Poved' r. Rus. Fed. **43** P4
Povenets Rus. Fed. **40** E3
Povlen mt. Yugo. **58** A4
Povoação Brazil **207** N6
Póvoa de Varzim Port. **54** C3
Povorino Rus. Fed. **41** G6
Povorotnyy, Mys hd Rus. Fed. **82** D4
Poway U.S.A. **183** G9
Powder r. MT U.S.A. **180** F3
Powder r. OR U.S.A. **180** C3
Powder, South Fork r. U.S.A. **180** F4
Powder River U.S.A. **180** F4
Powell U.S.A. **180** E3
Powell r. U.S.A. **176** B9
Powell, Lake resr U.S.A. **183** N4
Powell Creek watercourse Australia **149** D5
Powell Mountain U.S.A. **182** F3
Powell River Canada **166** E5
Powellsville U.S.A. **177** I9
Powers U.S.A. **172** F5
Powhatan U.S.A. **176** H8
Powhatan Point U.S.A. **176** E6
Powidzkie, Jezioro l. Poland **49** O3
Powo China **86** A1
Poxoréu Brazil **202** A5
Poyan, Sungai r. Sing. **76** [inset]
Poyang China see **Boyang**
Poyang Hu l. China **87** F2
Poyan Reservoir Sing. **76** [inset]
Poyarkovo Rus. Fed. **82** C2
Poygan, Lake U.S.A. **172** E6
Poynette U.S.A. **172** D7
Poyo, Cerro mt. Spain **55** I7
Poysdorf Austria **49** N7
Pöytyä Fin. **45** M3
Pozantı Turkey **106** C3
Požarevac Srbija Yugo. **58** C4
Poza Rica Mex. **185** F4
Požega Croatia **56** J3
formerly known as Slavonska Požega
Požega Srbija Yugo. **58** B5
Pozharskoye Rus. Fed. **90** D1
Pozhnya Rus. Fed. **43** M5
Pozhva Rus. Fed. **40** K4
Poznań Poland **49** N3
historically known as Posen
Pozo Alcón Spain **55** I7
Pozo Betbeder Arg. **204** D2
Pozoblanco Spain **54** G6
Pozo Colorado Para. **201** F5
Pozo del Tigre Arg. **201** E6
Pozo Hondo Arg. **204** D2
Pozohondo Spain **55** J6
Pozo Nuevo Mex. **184** C2
Pozos, Punta pt Arg. **205** D7
Pozo San Martin Arg. **204** E2
Pozsony Slovakia see **Bratislava**
Pozuzo Peru **200** B2
Pozzallo Sicilia Italy **57** G12
Pozzuoli Italy **57** G8
historically known as Puteoli
Pra r. Ghana **125** E5
Prabumulih Indon. **76** D3
Prabuty Poland **49** Q2
Prachatice Czech Rep. **49** L6
Prachi r. India **95** E2
Prachin Buri Thai. **79** C5
Prachuap Khiri Khan Thai. **79** B6
Pradairo mt. Spain **54** D1
Praděd mt. Czech Rep. **49** O5
Pradera Col. **198** B4
Prades France **51** I10
Prado Brazil **203** E6
Pradópolis Brazil **206** E8

▶**Prague** Czech Rep. **49** L5
Capital of the Czech Republic. Also known as Praha.

Praha Czech Rep. see **Prague**
Prahova r. Romania **58** H4

▶**Praia** Cape Verde **124** [inset]
Capital of Cape Verde.

Praia a Mare Italy **57** H9
Praia do Bilene Moz. **131** G5
Praia Grande Brazil **206** G11
Praia Rica Brazil **201** G3
Prainha Amazonas Brazil **201** E1
Prainha Pará Brazil **199** H5
Prairie Australia **149** E4
Prairie r. U.S.A. **174** A2
Prairie City U.S.A. **180** C3
Prairie Dog Town Fork r. U.S.A. **179** B5
Prairie du Chien U.S.A. **172** B7
Prairie River Canada **167** K4
Prakhon Chai Thai. **79** C5
Pram r. Austria **49** K7
Pramanta Greece **59** C9
Pran r. Thai. **79** C5
Pran Buri Thai. **79** B5
Prangli i. Estonia **42** G2
Pranhita r. India **94** C2
Prapat Indon. **76** B2
Prasonisi, Akra pt Greece **59** I13
Praszka Poland **49** P4
Prat i. Chile **205** B8
Prata Brazil **206** E6
Prata r. Goiás Brazil **206** A5
Prata r. Minas Gerais Brazil **206** D5
Prata r. Minas Gerais Brazil **207** G4
Pratapgarh India **96** B4
Pratas Islands China see **Dongsha Qundao**
Prat de Llobregat Spain see **El Prat de Llobregat**
Prathes Thai country Asia see **Thailand**
Pratinha Brazil **206** G6
Prato Italy **56** D5
Pratt U.S.A. **178** C4
Prattville U.S.A. **175** C5
Pravara r. India **94** B2
Pravda Bulg. **58** I5
Pravdinsk Rus. Fed. **42** C7
historically known as Friedland
Pravia Spain **54** E1
Praya Indon. **77** G5
Prazaroki Belarus **45** O5
Preah, Prêk r. Cambodia **79** D5
Preăh Vihear Cambodia **79** D5
Prechistoye Smolenskaya Oblast' Rus. Fed. **43** N6
Prechistoye Yaroslavskaya Oblast' Rus. Fed. **43** V3
Precipice National Park Australia **149** F5
Predazzo Italy **56** D2
Predeal Romania **58** G3
Preeceville Canada **167** K5
Pré-en-Pail France **50** F4
Preetz Germany **48** H1
Pregolya r. Rus. Fed. **42** B7
Preiļi Latvia **42** I5
Preissac, Lac l. Canada **173** O2
Prekornica mts Yugo. **58** A6
Prelate Canada **167** I5
Prémery France **51** J5
Premnitz Germany **49** J3
Prenj mts Bos.-Herz. **56** J5
Prentiss U.S.A. **175** B6
Prenzlau Germany **49** K2
Preobrazheniye Rus. Fed. **82** D4
Preparis Island Cocos Is **79** A5
Preparis North Channel Cocos Is **79** A5
Preparis South Channel Cocos Is **79** A5
Přerov Czech Rep. **49** O6
Presa de la Amistad, Parque Natural nature res. Mex. **185** E2
Presanella, Cima mt. Italy **56** C2
Presa San Antonio Mex. **185** E3
Prescott Canada **168** F4
Prescott AR U.S.A. **179** D5
Prescott AZ U.S.A. **183** L7
Prescott Valley U.S.A. **183** L7
Preservation Inlet N.Z. **153** A14
Preševo Srbija Yugo. **58** C6
Presidencia Roca Arg. **204** F2
Presidencia Roque Sáenz Peña Arg. **204** E2
Presidente Bernardes Brazil **206** B9
Presidente de la Plaza Arg. **204** F2
Presidente Dutra Brazil **202** C3
Presidente Eduardo Frei research station Antarctica **222** U2
Presidente Epitácio Brazil **206** A8
Presidente Hermes Brazil **201** E2
Presidente Jânio Quadros Brazil **207** L1
Presidente Juan Perón prov. Arg. see **Chaco**
Presidente Juscelino Brazil **207** I5
Presidente Olegário Brazil **206** G5
Presidente Prudente Brazil **206** B9
Presidente Venceslau Brazil **206** B8
Presidio U.S.A. **181** F7
Preslav Bulg. see **Veliki Preslav**
Prešov Slovakia **49** S7
Prespa, Lake Europe **58** C8
also known as Prespansko Ezero or Prespës, Liqeni i
Prespansko Ezero l. Europe see **Prespa, Lake**

Prespes nat. park Greece 58 C8
Prespes, Liqeni i. Europe see Prespa, Lake
Presque Isle ME U.S.A. 174 G2
Presque Isle MI U.S.A. 173 J5
Presque Isle WI U.S.A. 172 F4
Presque Isle Point U.S.A. 172 F4
Pressbaum Austria 49 N7
Pressburg Slovakia see Bratislava
Prestea Ghana 125 E5
Presteigne U.K. 47 I11
Přeštice Czech Rep. 49 K6
Preston U.K. 47 J10
Preston GA U.S.A. 175 C5
Preston IA U.S.A. 172 C8
Preston ID U.S.A. 180 E4
Preston MD U.S.A. 177 J7
Preston MN U.S.A. 174 A3
Preston, Cape Australia 150 B4
Prestonsburg U.S.A. 176 C8
Prestwick U.K. 46 H8
Preto r. Amazonas Brazil 199 F5
Preto r. Bahia Brazil 202 D4
Preto r. Goiás Brazil 206 C5
Preto r. Minas Gerais Brazil 206 G3
Preto r. Rondônia Brazil 201 E2
Preto r. São Paulo Brazil 206 D7
▶ Pretoria S. Africa 133 M2
Official capital of South Africa.
world [countries] ▶▶▶ 10–11

Pretoria-Witwatersrand-Vereeniging prov.
S. Africa see Gauteng
Preussisch-Eylau Rus. Fed. see
Bagrationovsk
Preußisch Stargard Poland see
Starogard Gdański
Preveza Greece 59 B10
Prey Vêng Cambodia 79 D6
Priamurskiy Rus. Fed. 82 D2
formerly known as Pokrovka
Priaral'skiye Karakumy, Peski des.
Kazakh. 103 E3
Priargunsk Rus. Fed. 85 I11
also known as Tsurukhaytuy
Pribinić Bos.-Herz. 56 J4
Priboj Srbija Yugo. 58 A5
Příbram Czech Rep. 49 L6
Price r. Austral.a 148 A2
Price Canada 169 G3
Price NC U.S.A. 176 F9
Price UT U.S.A. 183 N2
Price r. U.S.A. 183 N2
Price Island Canada 166 D4
Prichaly Rus. Fed. 42 C6
Prichard AL U.S.A. 175 B6
Prichard WV U.S.A. 176 C7
Priego de Córdoba Spain 54 G7
Priekule Latvia 42 C5
Priekulė Lith. 42 C6
Priekuļi Latvia 42 G4
Prienai Lith. 42 E7
Prienai Lith. 42 G7
Prieska S. Africa 132 G6
Prieskapoort pass S. Africa 132 G6
Priest Lake U.S.A. 180 C2
Prievidza Slovakia 49 P7
Prigor'ye Rus. Fed. 43 O8
Prijedor Bos.-Herz. 56 I4
Prijepolje Srbija Yugo. 58 A5
Prikaspiyskaya Nizmennost' lowland
Kazakh./Rus. Fed. see Caspian Lowland
Prikro Côte d'Ivoire 124 E5
Prilep Macedonia 58 B4
Priluki Rus. Fed. 43 U2
Priluki Ukr. see Pryluky
Primavera Bol. 200 D2
Primavera do Leste Brazil 202 A5
Primeira Cruz Brazil 202 D2
Primero de Enero Cuba 186 D2
also known as Violeta
Primghar U.S.A. 178 D3
Primorsk Leningradskaya Oblast'
Rus. Fed. 43 J1
Primorsk Volgogradskaya Oblast'
Rus. Fed. 41 H6
formerly known as Lugovaya Proleyka
Primorskiy Rus. Fed. 82 C4
formerly known as Ust'-Mongunay
Primorskiy Khrebet mts Rus. Fed. 85 E1
Primorskiy Kray admin. div. Rus. Fed. 82 D3
English form Maritime Kray
Primorsko-Akhtarsk Rus. Fed. 41 F7
Primrose r. Canada 166 B2
Primrose Lake Canada 167 I4
Prince Albert Canada 167 J4
Prince Albert S. Africa 132 G10
Prince Albert Mountains Antarctica
223 K1
Prince Albert National Park Canada
167 J4
Prince Albert Peninsula Canada 165 H2
Prince Albert Road S. Africa 132 G10
Prince Albert Sound sea chan. Canada
165 H2
Prince Alfred, Cape Canada 164 G2
Prince Charles Island Canada 165 L3
Prince Charles Mountains Antarctica
223 E2
Prince Edward Island prov. Canada 169 I4

▶ Prince Edward Islands Indian Ocean
219 J9
Part of South Africa.

Prince Edward Point Canada 173 Q7
Prince Frederick U.S.A. 177 I7
Prince Frederick Harbour Australia 150 D2
Prince George Canada 166 F4
Prince Gustav Adolf Sea Canada 165 I1
Prince Harald Coast Antarctica 223 C2
also known as Prins Harald Kyst
Prince Karl Foreland i. Svalbard see
Prins Karls Forland
Prince of Wales, Cape U.S.A. 164 C3
Prince of Wales Island Australia 149 D1
Prince of Wales Island Canada 165 J2
Prince of Wales Island U.S.A. 164 F4
Prince of Wales Strait Canada 165 H2
Prince Patrick Island Canada 165 H2
Prince Regent r. Australia 150 D2
Prince Regent Inlet sea chan. Canada
165 J2
Prince Regent Nature Reserve Australia
150 D2
Prince Rupert Canada 166 D4
Princess Anne U.S.A. 177 J7
Princess Astrid Coast Antarctica 223 A2
Princess Charlotte Bay Australia 149 D2
Princess Elizabeth Land reg. Antarctica
223 F2
Princess Mary Lake Canada 167 L1
Princess May Range hills Australia 150 D2
Princess Mountains N.Z. 153 B13
Princess Ragnhild Coast Antarctica 223 B2
Princess Royal Island Canada 166 D4
Princeton Canada 166 F5
Princeton CA U.S.A. 182 B2
Princeton IL U.S.A. 174 B3
Princeton IN U.S.A. 174 C4
Princeton KY U.S.A. 174 C4
Princeton MO U.S.A. 174 A3
Princeton NJ U.S.A. 177 K5
Princeton WI U.S.A. 172 D6
Prince William Sound b. U.S.A. 164 E3
Príncipe i. São Tomé and Príncipe 125 G6
Prineville U.S.A. 180 B3
Prinos Greece 58 F8
Prins Harald Kyst coastal area Antarctica
see Prince Harald Coast
Prins Karls Forland i. Svalbard 38 B2
English form Prince Karl Foreland
Prinzapolca Nicaragua 186 C4
Priolo Gargallo Sicilia Italy 57 H11
Prior, Cabo c. Spain 54 C1
Priozernyy Kazakh. see Tugyl
Priozersk Rus. Fed. 43 L1
also spelt Priozyorsk
Priozyorsk Rus. Fed. see Priozersk
Pripet r. Belarus/Ukr. 41 C5
also spelt Pryp"yat' (Ukraine) or Prypyats'
(Belarus)
Pripet Marshes Belarus/Ukr. 41 C6
also known as Palyeskaya Nizina or Poles'ye
Pripolyarnyy Ural mts Rus. Fed. 40 K2
Priponeşti Romania 58 I2
Prirechnyy Rus. Fed. 44 O1
Prisăcani Romania 58 I1
Priseka hill Croatia 56 I3
Pristan' Przheval'sk Kyrg. see
Przheval'sk Pristany
Priština Kosovo, Srbija Yugo. 58 C6
Prithvipur India 96 C4
Pritzwalk Germany 49 J2
Privas France 51 K8
Privlaka Croatia 56 H4
Privokzal'nyy Rus. Fed. 43 Q6
Privolzhsk Rus. Fed. 40 G4
Privolzhskaya Vozvyshennost' hills
Rus. Fed. 41 H6
English form Volga Upland
Privolzh'ye Rus. Fed. 41 I5
Priyutnoye Rus. Fed. 41 G7
Prizren Kosovo, Srbija Yugo. 58 B6
Prizzi Sicilia Italy 57 F11
Prnjavor Bos.-Herz. 56 J4
Probištip Macedonia 58 C5
Probolinggo Indon. 77 F4
Prochowice Poland 49 N4
Proctor MN U.S.A. 172 A2
Proctor VT U.S.A. 177 L2
Proctorville U.S.A. 176 C7
Proddatur India 94 C3
Proença-a-Nova Port. 54 D5
Professor van Blommestein Meer resr
Suriname 199 H3
also known as Brokopondo Stuwmeer
Progreso Hond. 186 B4
Progreso Coahuila Mex. 185 E3
Progreso Hidalgo Mex. 185 F4
Progreso Yucatán Mex. 185 H4
Progress Rus. Fed. 82 C2
Progresso Brazil 200 C2
Project City U.S.A. 182 B1
Prokhladnyy Rus. Fed. 41 H8
Prokletije mts Albania/Yugo. 58 A6
Prokop'yevsk Rus. Fed. 80 D2
Prokuplje Srbija Yugo. 58 C5
also known as Nanpu
Proletariy Rus. Fed. 43 L4
Proletarsk Rus. Fed. 41 G7
formerly known as Proletarskaya
Proletarskaya Rus. Fed. see Proletarsk
Prome Myanmar see Pyè
Promissão Brazil 201 E2
Promissão, Represa resr Brazil 206 D8
Pronino Rus. Fed. 40 G4
Pronsk Rus. Fed. 43 U7
Pronya r. Belarus 43 M8
Prophet r. Canada 166 F3
Prophet River Canada 166 F3
formerly known as Minaker
Prophetstown U.S.A. 172 D5
Propriá Brazil 202 E4
Proserpine Australia 149 F4
Proshkava Belarus 42 J6
Proskurov Ukr. see Khmel'nyts'kyy
Prosna r. Poland 49 O3
Prosotsani Greece 58 E7
Prospect NJ U.S.A. 177 J2
Prospect OH U.S.A. 176 B5
Prospect OR U.S.A. 180 B4
Prospect PA U.S.A. 176 E5
Prosperidad Phil. 74 C4
Prosser U.S.A. 180 C3
Prostějov Czech Rep. 49 O6
Proston Australia 149 F5
Proszowice Poland 49 R5
Protem S. Africa 132 E11
Proti i. Greece 59 C11
Protva r. Rus. Fed. 43 R6
Protva r. Rus. Fed. 43 S7
Provadiya Bulg. 58 I5
Prøven Greenland see Kangersuatsiaq
Provence-Alpes-Côte-d'Azur admin. reg.
France 51 M9
Providence U.S.A. see Annapolis

▶ Providence U.S.A. 177 N4
State capital of Rhode Island.

Providence, Cape N.Z. 153 A14
Providence Atoll Seychelles 129 F7
Providence Bay Canada 173 K5
Providencia Ecuador 198 B5
Providencia, Isla de i. Caribbean Sea
186 C4
Providência, Serra de hills Brazil 201 E2
Providenciales Island Turks and Caicos Is
187 E2

Provideniya Rus. Fed. 39 S3
Providential Channel Australia 149 D2
Provincetown U.S.A. 177 O3
Provincia Col. 198 C3
Frovins France 51 J4
Frovo U.S.A. 183 M1
Provost Canada 167 I4
Prozor Bos.-Herz. 56 J5
Prozorovo Rus. Fed. 43 S3
formerly known as Mikhaykovskiy
Prrenjas Albania 58 B7
Pru r. Ghana 125 E4
Prudentópolis Brazil 203 B8
Prudhoe Bay U.S.A. 164 E2
Prudhoe Island Australia 149 F4
Prudki Rus. Fed. 43 T7
Prudnik Poland 49 O5
Prudzinki Belarus 43 J6
Prundeni Romania 58 F4
Prundu Romania 58 H4
Prundu Bârgăului Romania 58 F1
formerly spelt Prundu Bîrgăului
Prundu Bîrgăului Romania see
Prundu Bârgăului
Pruntytown U.S.A. 176 E6
Prusa Turkey see Bursa
Prushkov Poland see Pruszków
Pruszcz Gdański Poland 49 P1
Pruszków Poland 49 R3
historically known as Prushkov
Prut r. Europe 58 J3
Pruzhany Belarus 42 F9
Prvić i. Croatia 56 G4
Prydz Bay Antarctica 223 F2
Pryelbrussky Natsional'nyy Park nat. park
Rus. Fed. 41 G8
Pryluky Ukr. 41 E6
Prymors'k Ukr. 41 F7
also spelt Primorsk
Prymors'ke Ukr. see Sartana
Prymors'ke Ukr. 58 K1
Pryor U.S.A. 179 D4
Pryp"yat' r. Ukr. see Pripet
Prypyats' r. Belarus 41 C5 see Pripet
Przasnysz Poland 49 R2
Przedbórz Poland 49 Q4
Przemyśl Poland 49 T6
Przeworsk Poland 49 T5
Przheval'sk Kyrg. see Karakol
Przheval'skoye Rus. Fed. 43 M6
formerly known as Sloboda
Przheval'sk Pristany Kyrg. 103 I4
also known as Pristan' Przheval'sk
Przysucha Poland 49 R4
Psachna Greece 59 E10
also spelt Psakhná
Psakhná Greece see Psachna
Psalidis, Akra pt Greece 59 F12
Psara i. Greece 59 G10
Psará i. Greece 59 F9
Psebay Rus. Fed. 41 G7
Pserimos i. Greece 59 I12
Pskent Uzbek. 103 G4
also known as Piskent
P'skhus Nakrdzali nature res. Georgia
107 E2
Pskov Rus. Fed. 43 J4
Pskov, Lake Estonia/Rus. Fed. 42 I3
also known as Pihkva järv
or Pskovskoye Ozero
Pskova r. Rus. Fed. 43 J4
Pskov Oblast admin. div. Rus. Fed. see
Pskovskaya Oblast'
Pskovskaya Oblast' admin. div.
Rus. Fed. 43 K4
English form Pskov Oblast
Pskovskoye Ozero l. Estonia/Rus. Fed. see
Pskov, Lake
Psunj mts Croatia 56 J3
Ptan' r. Rus. Fed. 43 T8
Ptich' Belarus see Ptsich
Ptolemaïda Greece 58 C8
Ptolemais Israel see 'Akko
Ptsich Belarus 43 J9
also spelt Ptich'
Ptuj Slovenia 56 H2
also known as Pettau; historically
known as Poetovio
Pu r. China 85 H5
Pu'an China 86 C3
also known as Panshui
Pu'an China see Jiange
Puaka hill Sing. 76 [inset]
Pucacuro Peru 198 C5
Pucacuro r. Peru 198 C5
Pucalá Peru 198 B6
Pucallpa Peru 200 B2
Pucará Bol. 201 D4
Pucara Peru 200 C4
Pucarani Bol. 200 C4
Pucarevo Bos.-Herz. see Novi Travnik
Puca Urco Peru 198 D5
Pucheng Fujian China 87 F3
also known as Nanpu
Pucheng Shaanxi China 87 D1
Puchezh Rus. Fed. 40 H4
Puch'ŏn S. Korea 83 B5
Pucioasa Romania 58 G3
Pucio Point Phil. 74 B4
Pucka, Zatoka b. Poland 49 P1
Puckford, Mount hill Australia 151 B5
Pucol Spain 55 K5
also spelt Puzol
Pucón Chile 204 B5
Pudai watercourse Afgh. see Dor
Pūdanū Iran 100 C3
Pudasjärvi Fin. 44 N2
Pudimoe S. Africa 133 I4
Puding China 86 C3
Pudozh Rus. Fed. 40 F3
Puducherri India see Pondicherry
Pudukkottai India 94 C4
Puebla Baja California Norte Mex. 183 I9
Puebla Puebla Mex. 185 F5
long form Puebla de Zaragoza
Puebla state Mex. 185 F5
Puebla de Don Fadrique Spain 55 I7
Puebla de Obando Spain 54 D5
Puebla de Zaragoza Mex. see Puebla
Pueblo U.S.A. 181 F5
Pueblo Hundido Chile 204 C2
Pueblo Viejo Col. 199 E4
Pueblo Viejo, Laguna de lag. Mex. 185 F4
Pueblo Yaqui Mex. 184 C3
Puech de Rouet hill France 51 I8
Puelches Arg. 204 D5
Puelén Arg. 204 D5
Puente Alto Chile 204 C4
Puente de Ixtla Mex. 185 F5
Puente del Inca Arg. 204 C4
Puente-Genil Spain 54 G7
Puente la Reina Spain 55 J2
also known as Gares
Puentes de García Rodríguez Spain see
As Pontes de García Rodríguez
Puente Torres Venez. 198 D3
also known as Ning'er
Puerco watercourse NM U.S.A. 183 N7
Puerco watercourse NM U.S.A. 181 F6
Puerto Acosta Bol. 200 C3
Puerto Aisén Chile 205 B7
Puerto Alegre Bol. 201 E3
Puerto Alejandría Bol. 200 D3
Puerto Alfonso Col. 198 D5
Puerto América Peru 198 B6

Puerto Ángel Mex. 185 F6
Puerto Antequera Para. 201 F6
Puerto Arista Mex. 185 G6
Puerto Armuelles Panama 186 C5
Puerto Asís Col. 198 B4
Puerto Ayacucho Venez. 199 E3
Puerto Bajo Pisagua Chile 205 B7
Puerto Barrios Guat. 185 H6
Puerto Berrío Col. 198 C3
Puerto Boyacá Col. 198 C3
Puerto Cabello Venez. 199 D2
Puerto Cabezas Nicaragua 186 C4
Puerto Cabo Gracias á Dios Nicaragua
186 C4
Puerto Carreño Col. 199 E3
Puerto Casado Para. 201 F5
Puerto Cavinas Bol. 200 D3
Puerto Cerpera Peru 198 C5
Puerto Ceticayo Peru 200 C2
Puerto Cisnes Chile 205 B7
Puerto Córdoba Col. 198 D5
Puerto Coig Arg. 205 C8
Puerto Cortés Costa Rica 186 C5
Puerto Cortés Hond. 186 B4
Puerto Cortés Mex. 184 C3
Puerto Cuemani Col. 198 C4
Puerto Cumarebo Venez. 198 E2
Puerto de Cabras Canary Is see
Puerto del Rosario
Puerto de Cayo Ecuador 198 A5
Puerto Definitivo Peru 200 C3
Puerto de Hierro Venez. 187 H5
Puerto de Los Ángeles, Parque Natural
nature res. Mex. 184 C4
Puerto del Rosario Canary Is 122 B3
formerly known as Puerto de Cabras
Puerto del Son Spain see Porto do Son
Puerto de Morelos Mex. 185 I4
Puerto de Nutrias Venez. 198 D2
Puerto de Pollensa Spain see
Port de Pollença
Puerto Escondido Mex. 185 F6
Puerto Estrella Col. 198 D1
Puerto Flamenco Chile 204 C2
Puerto Francisco de Orellana
Ecuador 198 B5
also known as El Coca; short form
Francisco de Orellana
Puerto Génova Bol. 200 D3
Puerto Grether Bol. 201 D4
Puerto Guarani Para. 201 F5
Puerto Harberton Arg. 205 D9
Puerto Heath Bol. 200 C3
Puerto Huitoto Col. 198 C4
Puerto Inca Peru 200 B2
Puerto Ingeniero Ibáñez Chile 205 B7
Puerto Inírida Col. 199 E4
Puerto Irigoyen Arg. 201 E5
Puerto Isabel Bol. 201 F4
Puerto Jesús Costa Rica 186 B5
Puerto Juárez Mex. 185 I4
Puerto La Paz Arg. 201 E5
Puerto Leguizamo Col. 198 C5
Puerto Lempira Hond. 186 C4
Puerto Libertad Mex. 184 B2
Puertollano Spain 54 G6
Puerto Lobos Arg. 205 D6
Puerto López Col. 198 C3
Puerto López Col. 198 C3
Puerto López Ecuador 198 A5
Puerto Lumbreras Spain 55 J7
Puerto Madero Mex. 185 G6
Puerto Madryn Arg. 205 D6
Puerto Magdalena Mex. 184 B3
Puerto Maldonado Peru 200 C3
Puerto Mamoré Bol. 200 D3
Puerto Manatí Cuba 186 D2
Puerto Máncora Peru 198 A6
Puerto María Auxiliadora Para. 201 F5
Puerto Marquez Bol. 200 D3
Puerto Melinka Chile 205 B6
Puerto Mercedes Col. 198 C4
Puerto México Mex. see Coatzacoalcos
Puerto Mihanovich Para. 201 F5
Puerto Miranda Venez. 199 E3
Puerto Montt Chile 205 B6
Puerto Morazán Nicaragua 186 B4
Puerto Natales Chile 205 B8
Puerto Nuevo Col. 198 D3
Puerto Olaya Col. 198 C3
Puerto Ordaz Venez. 199 F2
Puerto Ospina Col. 198 C4
Puerto Padre Cuba 186 D2
Puerto Pardo Peru 198 B5
Puerto Pariamanu Peru 200 C3
Puerto Peñasco Mex. 184 B2
Puerto Pinasco Para. 201 F5
Puerto Pirámides Arg. 205 D6
Puerto Piritu Venez. 199 E2
Puerto Pizarro Col. 198 C5
Puerto Plata Dom. Rep. 187 F3
Puerto Portillo Peru 200 B2
Puerto Prado Peru 200 B2
Puerto Presidente Stroessner Para. see
Ciudad del Este
Puerto Princesa Phil. 74 A4
Puerto Quepos Costa Rica 186 B5
Puerto Quetzal Guat. 185 H6
Puerto Real Spain 54 E8
Puerto Rico Arg. 204 G2
Puerto Rico Bol. 200 D2
Puerto Rico Bol. 200 D3

▶ Puerto Rico terr. West Indies 187 G3
United States Commonwealth
oceania [countries] ▶▶▶ 138–139

▶ Puerto Rico Trench sea feature
Caribbean Sea 216 J4
Deepest trench in the Atlantic Ocean.

Puerto Saavedra Chile 204 B5
Puerto Salgar Col. 198 C3
Puerto Sama Cuba see Samá
Puerto San Agustín Peru 198 D5
Puerto San Carlos Chile 205 B7
Puerto Sandino Nicaragua 186 B4
formerly known as Puerto Somoza
Puerto San José Guat. 185 H6
Puerto Santa Cruz Arg. 205 C8
Puerto Sastre Para. 201 F5
Puerto Saucedo Bol. 201 E3
Puertos de Beceite mts Spain see
Ports de Beseit
Puerto Serrano Spain 54 F8
Puerto Siles Bol. 200 D3
Puerto Socorro Peru 198 C4
Puerto Somoza Nicaragua see
Puerto Sandino
Puerto Suárez Bol. 201 F4
Puerto Supe Peru 200 A2
Puerto Tahuantsuyo Peru 200 C3
Puerto Tejado Col. 198 B4
Puerto Tunigrama Peru 198 B5
Puerto Valdés Arg. 205 E6
Puerto Vallarta Mex. 184 D4
Puerto Varas Chile 205 B6
Puerto Victoria Peru 200 B2
Puerto Villazón Bol. 201 E3
Puerto Visser Arg. 205 D7
Puerto Wilches Col. 198 C3
Puerto Yartou Chile 205 C9
Puerto Arturo Peru 198 C5
Puga Brazil 201 F4
Pugachev Rus. Fed. 102 B1
Pugachevo Rus. Fed. 40 J4
Pugal India 96 B3

Puga Puga, Ilha i. Moz. 131 H2
Puge China 86 B3
also known as Pijie
Puger Indon. 77 F5
Puglia admin. reg. Italy 56 H7
Pugwash Canada 169 I4
Puhja Estonia 42 H3
Pui Romania 58 E3
Pui O Wan b. Hong Kong China 87 [inset]
Puiești Romania 58 I3
Puig de Cemanegra mt. Spain 55 N2
Puig des Galatzó mt. Spain 55 N5
Puigmal mt. France/Spain 55 N2
Pui O Wan b. Hong Kong China 87 [inset]
Puiseaux France 51 I4
Puits 29 well Chad 120 C6
Puits 30 well Chad 120 C6
Pujada Bay Phil. 74 C5
Pujehun Sierra Leone 124 C5
Puji China see Wugong
Pujiang China 87 F2
also known as Puyang
Pukaki, Lake N.Z. 153 E12
Puk'an-san National Park S. Korea 83 B5
Pukapuka atoll Cook Is 221 G6
also known as Danger Islands
Pukaskwa r. Canada 172 H2
Pukaskwa National Park Canada 168 C3
Pukatawagan Canada 167 K4
Pukchin N. Korea 83 B4
Pukch'ŏng N. Korea 83 C4
also known as Xinjin
Pukchong N. Korea see Pukch'ŏng
Pukearuhe N.Z. 152 I6
Pukehoi N.Z. 152 K7
Pukekohe N.Z. 152 I5
Pukenui N.Z. 152 H2
Pukeokahu N.Z. 152 J7
Pukeranga Bay N.Z. 152 I9
Puketeraki Range mts N.Z. 153 G11
Puketiri N.Z. 152 K7
Puketoi Range hills N.Z. 152 K8
Puketutu N.Z. 152 J6
Pukeuri Junction N.Z. 153 F13
Pukhnovo Rus. Fed. 43 M6
Pukkila Fin. 42 G1
Puksoozero Rus. Fed. 40 G3
Pukulu i. Palau 73 I8
Pula Croatia 56 F3
formerly spelt Pola
Pula Sardegna Italy 57 B9
Pulacayo Bol. 200 D5
Pulandian China 85 I4
formerly known as Xinjin
Pulandian Wan b. China 85 I4
Pulangi r. Phil. 74 C5
Pulangpisau Indon. 77 F3
Pular, Cerro mt. Chile 200 C6
Pulasi i. Indon. 75 A3
Pulaski NY U.S.A. 177 I2
Pulaski TN U.S.A. 174 C5
Pulaski VA U.S.A. 176 E8
Pulaski WI U.S.A. 172 E6
Pulau r. Indon. 73 I8
Pulau Pinang state Malaysia see Pinang
Puławy Poland 49 S4
Pulheim Germany 48 D4
Pulicat India 94 D3
Pulicat Lake inlet India 94 D3
Pulivendla India 94 C3
Pulkau r. Austria 49 N7
Pülküb Fin. 44 N2
Pullman U.S.A. 180 C3
Pulo Anna i. Palau 73 H6
Pulog, Mount Phil. 74 B2
Pulozero Rus. Fed. 40 E1
Púlpite, Punta c. Mex. 184 C3
Pulsano Italy 57 J8
Pultusk Poland 49 S3
Fulu China 89 A3
Pülümür Turkey 107 D3
Puluton Indon. 75 C1
Pulyatin Rus. Fed. 90 C3
Puma Tanz. 129 B6
Puma Yumco l. China 89 E6
also known as Pomo Tso
Pumiao China see Yongning
Pumpkin Creek r. U.S.A. 180 F3
Puná, Isla i. Ecuador 198 A5
Puna de Atacama plat. Arg. 204 D2
Punakaiki N.Z. 153 F10
Punakha Bhutan 97 F4
Punalur U.S.A. 181 [inset] Z2
Punata Bol. 200 D4
Punch Pak. 101 H3
Punchaw Canada 166 F4
Punda Maria S. Africa 131 F4
Pundri India 96 B3
Pune India 94 B2
formerly spelt Poona
Pungol Sing. 76 [inset]
Punggol, Sungai r. Sing. 76 [inset]
P'ungsan N. Korea 83 C4
Pünguè r. Moz. 131 F3
Punia Dem. Rep. Congo 126 E5
Puning China 87 F4
Punitaqui Chile 204 C3
Punjab prov. Pak. 101 G4
Punjab prov. Pak. 101 G4
Punkaharju Fin. 45 O3
Punmah Glacier China/Jammu and Kashmir
89 B5
Puno Peru 200 C3
short form Puno 200 C3
Punpun r. India 97 E4
Punta, Cerro de mt. Puerto Rico 187 G3
Punta Alta Arg. 204 E5
Punta Arenas Chile 205 C9
formerly known as Magallanes
Punta Balestrieri mt. Sardegna Italy 57 B8
Punta de Bombón Peru 200 C4
Punta de Diaz Chile 204 C2
Punta de Delgada Arg. 205 D6
Punta de los Llanos Arg. 204 D3
Punta Gorda Belize 185 H5
Punta Gorda Nicaragua 186 C5
Punta Gorda U.S.A. 175 D7
Punta Negra, Salar salt flat Chile 200 C6
Punta Norte Arg. 205 E6
Punta Prieta Mex. 184 B2
Puntarenas Costa Rica 186 B5
Puntas Negras, cerro mt. Chile 200 D5
Punta Umbría Spain 54 E7
Punta Fijo Venez. 198 D2
Punxsutawney U.S.A. 176 F5
Puokio Fin. 44 N2
Puolanka Fin. 44 O2
Puquio Peru 200 B3
Puquios Chile 200 C4
Pur r. Rus. Fed. 39 J3
Puracé, Parque Nacional nat. park Col.
198 B4
Puranpur India 96 D3
Purari r. P.N.G. 73 J8
Purbalingga Indon. 77 E4
Purcell U.S.A. 179 C5
Purcellville U.S.A. 176 H6
Purcell Mountains Canada 167 G5
Pureba Conservation Park nature res.
Australia 146 B2
Purekkari neem pt Estonia 42 G2
Puren Chile 204 B5
Pureora Forest Park nature res. N.Z.
152 J6

Puri India 95 E2
Purmerend Neth. 48 B3
Purna India 94 C2
Purna r. Maharashtra India 94 C2
Purna r. Maharashtra India 96 C5
Purnabhaba r. India 97 F4
Purnia India 97 F4
Purndu Saltpan salt flat Australia 146 A1
Purnea India see Purnia
Purnia India 97 F4
formerly spelt Purnea
Purnululu National Park Australia 150 E3
formerly known as Bungle Bungle
National Park
Purranque Chile 204 B6
Pursat Cambodia see Poŭthĭsăt
Purtuniq Canada 165 L3
formerly known as Asbestos Hill
Puruandíro Mex. 185 E4
Puruê r. Brazil 198 D5
Purukcahu Indon. 77 F3
Puruliya India 97 E5

▶ Purus r. Peru 199 F5
3rd longest river in South America.
southamerica [landscapes] ▶▶▶ 190–191

Puruvesi l. Fin. 45 O3
Purvis U.S.A. 175 B6
Pürvomay Bulg. 58 G6
Purwa India 96 C4
Purwakarta Indon. 77 D4
Purwareja Indon. 77 E4
Purwodadi Indon. 77 E4
Purwokerto Indon. 77 E4
Puryŏng N. Korea 82 C4
Pus r. India 94 C2
Puša Latvia 42 I5
Pusa r. Spain 54 G5
Pusad India 94 C2
Pusan S. Korea 83 C6
also known as Busan or Fusan
Pusan Point Phil. 74 C5
Pusatdamai Indon. 77 E2
Pusatdarul mt. Turkey 108 E1
Pushchino Rus. Fed. 43 S7
Pushemskiy Rus. Fed. 40 H3
Pushkar India 96 B4
Pushkin Rus. Fed. 43 L2
Pushkino Azer. see Bilăsuvar
Pushkino Rus. Fed. 102 A2
Pushkinskaya, Gora mt. Rus. Fed. 82 F3
Pushkinskiye Gory Rus. Fed. 43 J4
Pusht-i Āsmān spring Iran 100 D3
Pusht-i-Rud reg. Afgh. 101 E4
Püspökladány Hungary 49 S8
Püssi Estonia 42 I2
Pusti Lisac mt. Yugo. 56 K6
Pustoshka Rus. Fed. 43 K5
Pusula Fin. 42 F1
Pusur r. Bangl. 97 F5
Puszcza Augustowska for. Poland 49 U2
Puszcza Natecka for. Poland 49 M3
Pusztaszeri park Hungary 49 R9
Putahow Lake Canada 167 K3
Putao Myanmar 78 B2
formerly known as Fort Hertz
Putaruru N.Z. 152 J6
Putbus Germany 49 K1
Puteoli Italy see Pozzuoli
Puteran i. Indon. 77 F4
Putere N.Z. 152 L6
Puteyets Rus. Fed. 40 K2
Puthein Myanmar see Bassein
Putian China 87 F3
Putignano Italy 56 J8
Putilovo Rus. Fed. 40 H4
Putimets Rus. Fed. 43 R9
Putina Peru 200 C3
Puting China see De'an
Puting, Tanjung pt Indon. 77 E3
Putla Mex. 185 F5
Putlitz Germany 48 J2
Putna r. Romania 58 H3
Putnam U.S.A. 177 N4
Putney U.S.A. 177 M3
Putoi i. Hong Kong China see Po Toi
Putorana, Gory mts Rus. Fed. 39 J3
Putrajaya Malaysia 76 C2
Putre Chile 200 C3
Putsonderwater S. Africa 132 F6
Puttalam Sri Lanka 94 C4
Puttalam Lagoon Sri Lanka 94 C4
Puttgarden Germany 48 I1
Puttur India 94 B3
Putú Chile 204 B4
Putubumba Dem. Rep. Congo 126 E5
Putumayo dept Col. 198 C4
Putumayo r. Col. 198 D5
Pütürge Turkey 107 D3
also known as Imrun
Putusibau Indon. 77 F2
Putyvl' Ukr. 41 E6
Puula l. Fin. 45 N3
Puumala Fin. 45 O3
Puuwai U.S.A. 181 [inset] Y1
Puvurnituq Canada 165 L3
Puxian China 85 F4
Puyallup U.S.A. 180 B3
Puyang China see Pujiang
Puy de Dôme mt. France 51 I7
Puy de Montoncel mt. France 51 J7
Puy de Sancy mt. France 51 I7
Puyehue, Parque Nacional nat. park Chile
204 C6
Puyel Arg. 205 C6
Puy Gris mt. France 51 M7
Puymorens, France 51 I9
Puyo Ecuador 198 B5
Puysegur Point N.Z. 153 A14
Puzol Spain see Puçol
Pwani admin. reg. Tanz. 129 C6
formerly known as Coast
Pweto Dem. Rep. Congo 127 F7
Pwllheli U.K. 47 H11
Pyalitsa Rus. Fed. 40 F2
Pyal'ma Rus. Fed. 40 F3
Pyamalaw r. Myanmar 78 A5
Pyandzh r. Afgh./Tajik. 101 G2
also known as Ab-i-Panja; also spelt Panj
Pyandzh Tajik. see Panj
Pyaozero, Ozero l. Rus. Fed. 44 O2
Pyaozerskiy Rus. Fed. 44 O2
Pyapon Myanmar 78 A4
Pyasina r. Rus. Fed. 39 I2
Pyasinskiy Zaliv b. Rus. Fed. 39 I3
Pyasúchnik r. Bulg. 58 F6
Pyatigorsk Rus. Fed. 41 G7
Pyatikhatki Ukr. see P"yatykhatky
Pyatimar Kazakh. see Pyatimarskoye
Pyatimarskoye Kazakh. 102 B2
formerly known as Pyatimar
Pyatirech'ye Rus. Fed. 43 L1
Pyatovskiy Rus. Fed. 43 R7
P"yatykhatky Ukr. 41 E6
also spelt Pyatikhatki
Pyaunglaung r. Myanmar 78 B4
Pyawbwe Myanmar 78 B3
Pyazhelka Rus. Fed. 43 Q1
Pyazhozero, Ozero l. Rus. Fed. 43 Q1
Pyè Myanmar 78 A4
also known as Pyin; formerly
known as Prome
Pyershamayski Belarus 42 G8
Pyeski Belarus 42 F8
Pyes Pa N.Z. 152 K5
Pyetrykaw Belarus 43 J9
also spelt Petrikov
Pygmalion Point India 95 G5
Pyhäjärvi l. Fin. 42 E1

Pyhäjärvi *l.* Fin. **44** N3
Pyhäjärvi *l.* Fin. **44** N3
Pyhäjärvi *l.* Fin. **44** O3
Pyhäjärvi *l.* Fin. **45** M3
Pyhäjoki Fin. **44** N2
Pyhäjoki *r.* Fin. **44** N2
Pyhältö Fin. **42** I1
Pyhäntä Fin. **44** N2
Pyhäranta Fin. **45** M3
Pyhäsalmi Fin. **44** N3
Pyhäselkä Fin. **44** O3
Pyhäselkä *l.* Fin. **44** O3
Pyhätunturin kansallispuisto *nat. park* Fin. **44** N2
Pyhtää Fin. **45** N3
Pyin Myanmar *see* **Pyè**
Pyingaing Myanmar **78** A3
Pyinmana Myanmar **78** B4
Pyli Greece **59** I12
also spelt Pili
Pyl'karamo Rus. Fed. **39** I3
Pylos Greece **59** C12
also spelt Pílos
Pymatuning Reservoir U.S.A. **176** E4
Pyŏksŏng N. Korea **83** B5
Pyŏktong N. Korea **83** B4
P'yŏnggang N. Korea **83** B5
P'yŏngsong N. Korea **83** B5
P'yŏngt'aek S. Korea **83** B5

▶**P'yŏngyang** N. Korea **83** B5
Capital of North Korea.

Pyŏnsan Bando National Park S. Korea **83** B6
Pyramid Lake U.S.A. **182** E1
Pyramid Lake Indian Reservation *res.* U.S.A. **182** E1
Pyramid Range *mts* U.S.A. **182** E2
Pyrenees *mts* Europe **55** N2
also spelt Pyrénées *or* Pirineos
Pyrénées *mts* Europe *see* **Pyrenees**
Pyrénées Occidentales, Parc National des *nat. park* France/Spain **55** K2
Pyrgetos Greece **59** D9
also spelt Piryetós
Pyrgi Greece **59** G10
also known as Piryion
Pyrgos Greece **59** C11
also spelt Pírgos
Pyrton, Mount *hill* Australia **150** B4
Pyryatyn Ukr. **41** E6
also spelt Piryatin
Pyrzyce Poland **49** L2
Pyshchug Rus. Fed. **40** H4
Pyshna Belarus **43** J7
Pyszna *r.* Poland **49** M5
Pytalovo Rus. Fed. **42** I4
Pythonga, Lac *l.* Canada **173** Q4
Pyu Myanmar **78** B4
Pyxaria *mt.* Greece **59** E10
also spelt Pixariá

Q

Qā', Wādī al *watercourse* Saudi Arabia **104** B2
Qaa Lebanon **109** H3
formerly spelt El Kaa
Qaanaaq Greenland *see* **Thule**
Qabanbay Kazakh. *see* **Kabanbay**
Qabātiya West Bank **108** G5
Qābil Oman **105** F3
Qabka China *see* **Xaitongmoin**
Qabnag China **89** F6
Qabqa China *see* **Gonghe**
Qabr Bandar *tourist site* Iraq **107** E5
Qabr Hūd Oman **105** E4
Qabyrgha *r.* Kazakh. *see* **Kabyrga**
Qacentina Alg. *see* **Constantine**
Qacha's Nek Lesotho **133** M7
Qadā' Chāy *watercourse* Iraq **109** P3
Qadamgāli Iran **100** D2
Qādes Afgh. **101** E3
Qadīmah Saudi Arabia **104** B3
Qādir Karam Iraq **107** F4
Qādisīyah, Buḩayrat al *resr* Iraq **109** N3
Qādisīyah, Sadd *dam* Iraq **107** E4
English form Qadisiyah Dam
Qadisiyah Dam Iraq *see* **Qādisīyah, Sadd**
Qādub Yemen **105** F5
Qa'emabad Iran **101** E4
Qā'emīyeh Iran **100** B4
Qagan China **85** H1
Qagan Ders China **85** E3
Qagan Nur *Nei Mongol* China **85** F4
Qagan Nur *Nei Mongol* China **85** G3
also known as Xulun Hobot Qagan Qi *or* Zhengxiangbai Qi
Qagan Nur *Nei Mongol* China **85** G3
Qagan Nur *Qinghai* China **84** C4
Qagan Nur *l.* China **85** J2
Qagan Nur *resr* China **85** G3
Qagan Teg China **85** G3
Qagan Tohoi China **84** B5
Qagan Us China *see* **Dulan**
Qagan Us He *r.* China **84** C4
Qagca China **86** A1
formerly known as Cacagoin
Qagchêng China *see* **Xiangcheng**
Qahar Youyi Houqi China *see* **Bayan Qagan**
Qahar Youyi Qianqi China *see* **Togrog Ul**
Qahar Youyi Zhongqi China *see* **Hobor**
Qā' Ḩazawzā' *depr.* Saudi Arabia **107** D5
Qahd, Wādī *watercourse* Saudi Arabia **104** C2
Qahr, Jibāl al *hills* Saudi Arabia **104** D4
Qahremānshahr Iran *see* **Kermānshāh**
Qaḩṭān *reg.* Saudi Arabia **104** C3
Qaidam He *r.* China **84** B4
Qaidam Pendi *basin* China **84** B4
English form Tsaidam Basin
Qaidar China *see* **Cêtar**
Qainaqangma China **89** E5
Qaisar Afgh. **101** F3
Qaisar *r.* Afgh. **101** F2
Qaisar, Koh-i- *mt.* Afgh. **101** F3
Qalabotjha S. Africa **133** M4
Qalā Diza Iraq **107** F3
Qala'en Nahl Sudan **121** G6
Qala-i-Fateh Afgh. **101** E4
Qala-i-Kang Afgh. **101** E4
Qal'aikhum Tajik. **101** G2
also spelt Kalaikhum; *formerly spelt* Kalai-Khumb
Qalamat Abū Shafrah Saudi Arabia **105** F3
Qalamat Al Juḩaysh *oasis* Saudi Arabia **105** E3
Qalamat ar Rakabah *oasis* Saudi Arabia **105** F3
Qalamat Fāris *oasis* Saudi Arabia **105** E4
Qalamat Nadqān *well* Saudi Arabia **105** E3
Qalamat Shutfah *well* Saudi Arabia **105** F3
Qalansīyah Yemen **105** F5
Qala Shinia Takht Afgh. **101** F3
Qalāt Afgh. **101** F3
Qal'at al Azlam Saudi Arabia **104** A2
Qal'at al Ḩiṣn *tourist site* Syria **109** H3
Qal'at al Marqab *tourist site* Syria **108** G2
Qal'at al Mu'azzam Saudi Arabia **104** B2
Qal'at Bīshah Saudi Arabia **104** C3
Qal'at Muqaybirah, Jabal *mt.* Syria **109** J2
Qal'at Ṣāliḩ Iraq **107** F5
Qala Vali Afgh. **101** E3
Qalbī Zhotasy *mts* Kazakh. *see* **Kalbinskiy Khrebet**
Qal'eh Iran **100** C2
Qal'eh Dāgh *mt.* Iran **100** A2
Qal'eh Tirpul Afgh. **101** E3
Qal 'eh-ye Bost Afgh. **101** F4
Qal 'eh-ye Now Afgh. **101** E3
Qal'eh-ye Shūrak *well* Iran **100** D3
Qalhāt Oman **105** G3
Qalīb Bāqūr *well* Iraq **107** F5
Qalqīlya West Bank **108** F5
Qalqutan Kazakh. *see* **Koluton**
Qalti el Adusa *well* Sudan **121** E5
Qalyūb Egypt **121** F2
Qalyūbīya *governorate* Egypt **108** C7
Qamalung China **86** A1
Qamanirjuaq Lake Canada **167** M2
also known as Kaminuriak Lake
Qamanittuaq Canada *see* **Baker Lake**
Qamar, Ghubbat al *b.* Yemen **105** F4
English form Qamar Bay
Qamar, Jabal al *mts* Oman **105** F4
Qamar Bay Yemen *see* **Qamar, Ghubbat al**
Qamashi Uzbek. *see* **Kamashi**
Qamdo China **86** A2
also spelt Chamdo
Qam Hadīl Saudi Arabia **104** C4
Qamīnis Libya **120** C2
Qamruddin Karez Pak. **101** G4
Qamṣar Iran **100** B3
Qamystybas Kazakh. *see* **Kamyshlybash**
Qanawt Oman **105** F4
Qandahar Afgh. *see* **Kandahār**
Qandala Somalia **128** F2
Qandaranbashi *mt.* Iran **100** A2
Qandyaghash Kazakh. *see* **Kandyagash**
Qangzê China **89** B6
Qanṭara, Gebel *hill* Egypt **108** B7
Qapal Kazakh. *see* **Kapal**
Qapan Iran **100** C2
Qapqal China **88** C3
Qapshagay Kazakh. *see* **Kapchagay**
Qapshagay Bögeni *resr* Kazakh. *see* **Kapchagayskoye Vodokhranilishche**
Qaq Köli *salt l.* Kazakh. *see* **Kak, Ozero**
Qaqortoq Greenland **165** O3
also known as Julianehåb
Qara Egypt **106** A5
Qarā', Jabal al *mts* Oman **105** F4
Qara Āghach *r.* Iran *see* **Mand, Rūd-e**
Qara Anjīr Iraq **109** P2
Qaraaoun Lebanon **108** G4
Qarabas Kazakh. *see* **Karabas**
Qarabulaq Kazakh. *see* **Karabulak**
Qarabutaq Kazakh. *see* **Karabutak**
Qaraçala Azer. **100** B2
Qarachōq, Jabal *mts* Iraq **107** E4
Qara Ertis *r.* China/Kazakh. *see* **Ertix He**
Qaraghandy Kazakh. *see* **Karaganda**
Qaraghandy Oblysy *admin. div.* Kazakh. *see* **Karagandinskaya Oblast'**
Qaraghayly Kazakh. *see* **Karagayly**
Qārah Saudi Arabia **107** E5
Qārah, Jabal al *hill* Saudi Arabia **104** D4
Qarah Bāgh *Ghaznī* Afgh. **101** G3
Qarah Bāgh *Kābul* Afgh. **101** G3
Qarak China **88** B4
Qaraköl Kazakh. *see* **Karakol'**
Qaranqu *r.* Iran **100** A2
Qaraoy Kazakh. *see* **Karaoy**
Qara Özek Uzbek. *see* **Karauzyak**
Qaraqalpaqstan Respublikasy *aut. rep.* Uzbek. *see* **Karakalpakistan, Respublika**
Qara Qōsh Iraq **109** O1
Qaraqoyyn Köli *salt l.* Kazakh. *see* **Karakoyyn, Ozero**
Qaraqozha Kazakh. *see* **Karaguzhikha**
Qaraqum *des.* Kazakh. *see* **Karakum Desert**
Qaraqum *des.* Turkm. *see* **Karakum Desert**
Qarasū Kazakh. *see* **Karasu**
Qara Şū Chāy *r.* Syria/Turkey *see* **Karasu**
Qara Tarai *mt.* Afgh. **101** F3
Qarataū Kazakh. *see* **Karatau**
Qarataū Zhotasy *mts* Kazakh. *see* **Karatau, Khrebet**
Qaratöbe Kazakh. *see* **Karatobe**
Qaratoghay Kazakh. *see* **Karatogay**
Qaratomar Bögeni *resr* Kazakh. *see* **Karatomarskoye Vodokhranilishche**
Qaraton Kazakh. *see* **Karaton**
Qaraūyl Kazakh. *see* **Karaul**
Qarazhal Kazakh. *see* **Karazhal**
Qardho Somalia **128** F2
Qardud Sudan **126** F2
Qareh Chāy *r.* Iran **100** B3
Qareh Dāgh *mts* Iran **100** A2
Qareh Qāch, Kūh-e *mts* Iran **100** C3
Qareh Sū *r.* Iran **100** A2
Qāret Gahannam *hill* Egypt **108** B8
Qarhan China **84** B4
Qarkilik China *see* **Ruoqiang**
Qarnayṭ, Jabal *hill* Saudi Arabia **104** C3
Qarnein *i.* U.A.E. **105** F2
Qarn el Kabsh, Gebel *mt.* Egypt **121** G2
Qarokŭl *l.* Tajik. **101** H2
also known as Karakul', Ozero
Qarqan China *see* **Qiemo**
Qarqan He *r.* China **88** D4
Qarqaraly Kazakh. *see* **Karkaralinsk**
Qarqi *Xinjiang* China **88** C3
Qarqi *Xinjiang* China **88** D3
Qārqī Iran **102** C5
Qarqīn Afgh. **101** F2
Qarrit, Qafa e *pass* Albania **58** B8
Qarsaqbay Kazakh. *see* **Karsakpay**
Qarshi Uzbek. *see* **Karshi**
Qarshi Chŭli *plain* Uzbek. *see* **Karshinskaya Step'**
Qartaba Lebanon **108** G3
Qārūh, Jazīrat *i.* Kuwait **107** G5
Qārūn Egypt **108** B8
Qaryat al Ulyā Saudi Arabia **105** D2
Qaṣab, Wādī al *watercourse* Iraq **109** O2
Qasamī Iran **100** D3
Qasa Murg *mts* Afgh. **101** E3
Qasba India **97** E4
Qaṣbah, Ra's al *pt* Saudi Arabia **108** F9
Qāsemābād *Khorāsan* Iran **100** D3
Qāsemābād *Khorāsan* Iran **101** D2
Qashqadaryo *r.* Uzbek. *see* **Kashkadar'ya**
Qashqadaryo Wiloyati *admin. div.* Uzbek. *see* **Kashkadar'inskaya Oblast'**
Qash Qai *reg.* Iran **100** B4
Qashqantengiz Kazakh. *see* **Kashkanteniz**
Qasigianguit Greenland **165** N3
also known as Christianshåb
Qasim *reg.* Saudi Arabia **104** C2
Qaskeleñ Kazakh. *see* **Kaskelen**
Qasq China **85** F3
also known as Tumd Zuoqi
Qaşr ad Dayr, Jabal *mt.* Jordan **108** G7
Qaşr al Azraq Jordan **109** H6
Qaşr al Ḩayr *tourist site* Syria **109** I3
Qaşr al Khubbāz Iraq **107** E4
Qaşr 'Amīj Iraq **109** M4
Qaşr 'Amrah *tourist site* Jordan **109** H6
Qaşr aş Şabiyah Kuwait **107** G5
Qaşr Burqu' *tourist site* Jordan **109** I5
Qaşr-e-Qand Iran **101** E5
Qaşr-e Shīrīn Iran **107** F4
Qasr Farafra Egypt **121** E3
Qaşr Ḩimām Saudi Arabia **105** D3
Qaşr Larocu Libya **120** B3
Qaşr Shaqrah *tourist site* Iraq **107** F5
Qassimiut Greenland **165** O3
Qa'tabah Yemen **104** D5
Qatana Syria **108** H4
▶**Qatar** *country* Asia **105** E2
asia [countries] ▶▶ 64–67
Qatlish Iran **100** D2
Qaṭrâni, Gebel *esc.* Egypt **121** F2
Qaṭrūyeh Iran **100** C4
Qaṭṭāfī, Wādī al *watercourse* Jordan **109** I6
Qaṭṭâra, Râs *esc.* Egypt **121** E2
Qaṭṭâra Depression Egypt **121** E2
also known as Qaṭṭārah, Munkhafaḍ al
Qaṭṭārah, Munkhafaḍ al *depr.* Egypt *see* **Qaṭṭâra Depression**
Qaṭṭīnah, Buḩayrat *resr* Syria **109** H3
also known as Ḩimş, Baḩrat
Qavāmābād Iran **100** D4
Qax Azer. **107** F2
also spelt Kakhi
Qāyen Iran **100** D3
Qayghy Kazakh. *see* **Kayga**
Qaynar Kazakh. *see* **Kaynar**
Qayraqty Kazakh. *see* **Kayrakty**
Qayroqqum Tajik. **101** G1
formerly spelt Kayrakkum
Qaysīyah, Qa' al *imp. l.* Jordan **109** H6
Qayyārah Iraq **107** E4
Qazaly Kazakh. *see* **Kazalinsk**
Qazangödağ *mt.* Armenia/Azer. **107** F3
also known as Kapydzhik, Gora
Qazaq Shyghanaghy *b.* Kazakh. *see* **Kazakhskiy Zaliv**
Qazaqstan *country* Asia *see* **Kazakhstan**
Qazax Azer. **107** F2
also spelt Kazakh
Qazi Ahmad Pak. **101** G5
Qazımämmäd Azer. **107** G2
also spelt Kazi Magomed
Qazvīn Iran **100** B2
Qazvīn *prov.* Iran **100** B2
Qazyqurt Kazakh. *see* **Kazygurt**
Qedir China **88** D3
Qeh China **84** D3
Qeisûm, Gezâ'ir *is* Egypt **104** A2
English form Qeisûm Islands; *also spelt* Geisûm, Gezâ'ir
Qeisûm Islands Egypt *see* **Qeisûm, Gezâ'ir**
Qelelevu *i.* Fiji **145** H3
also spelt Nggelelevu
Qena Egypt **121** G3
also spelt Qinā
Qena *governorate* Egypt **104** A2
Qena, Wâdi *watercourse* Egypt **121** G3
Qeqertarsuaq Greenland **165** N3
also known as Godhavn
Qeqertarsuaq *i.* Greenland **165** N3
also known as Disko
Qeqertarsuatsiaat Greenland **165** N3
also known as Fiskenæsset
Qeqertarsuatsiaq *i.* Greenland **165** N2
also known as Hareøen
Qeqertarsuup Tunua *b.* Greenland **165** N3
also known as Disko Bugt
Qeshlāq Iran **100** A3
Qeshm Iran **100** D5
Qeshm *i.* Iran **100** D5
Qeydār Iran **100** B2
Qeys *i.* Iran **100** C5
Qezel Owzan, Rūdkhāneh-ye *r.* Iran **100** B2
Qezi'ot Israel **108** F7
Qi *r.* China **85** G5
Qian *r.* China **87** C1
Qian'an *Hebei* China **85** H4
Qian'an *Jilin* China **85** J2
Qiancheng China **87** D3
Qiang *r.* China **87** F1
Qian Gorlos China *see* **Qianguozhen**
Qianguozhen China **82** B3
also known as Qian Gorlos
Qianjiang *Chongqing* China **87** D2
also known as Lianhe
Qianjiang *Hubei* China **87** E2
Qianjin China **82** D3
formerly known as Weidongmen
Qianning China **86** B2
also known as Gartar
Qianqihao China **85** I2
Qianshan China **87** F2
also known as Meicheng
Qian Shan *mts* China **85** I3
Qianshanlaoba China **88** D2
Qianwei China **86** B2
also known as Yujin
Qianxi *Guizhou* China **86** C3
Qianxi *Hebei* China **85** H3
also known as Xingcheng
Qianxian China **87** D1
Qianyang *Hunan* China **87** D3
also known as Anjiang
Qianyang *Shaanxi* China **86** C1
Qianyang *Zhejiang* China **87** F2
Qianyou China *see* **Zhashui**
Qiaocun China **85** G4
Qiaojia China **86** B3
also known as Xinhua
Qiaoshan China *see* **Huangling**
Qiaotou China *see* **Datong**
Qiaotou China **86** B3
Qiaowa China *see* **Muli**
Qiaowan China **84** C3
Qiaozhuang China *see* **Qingchuan**
Qibā' Saudi Arabia **104** D2
Qibing S. Africa **133** L6
Qibray Uzbek. *see* **Kibray**
Qichun China **87** E2
also known as Caohe; *formerly known as* Caojiahe
Qidong *Hunan* China **87** E3
formerly known as Hongqiao
Qidong *Jiangsu* China **87** G2
also known as Huilongzhen
Qiemo China **88** D4
formerly known as Cherchen *or* Qarqan
Qihe China **85** H4
also known as Yancheng
Qijiang China **86** C2
also known as Gunan
Qijiaojing China **88** E3
Qikiqtarjuaq Canada **165** M3
formerly known as Broughton Island
Qiktim China **88** E3
Qila Ladgasht Pak. **101** E5
Qilaotu Shan *mts* China **85** H3
Qila Safed Pak. **101** E4
Qila Saifullah Pak. **101** G4
Qili China *see* **Shitai**
Qilian China **84** D4
also known as Babao
Qilian Shan *mt.* China **84** C4
Qilian Shan *mts* China **84** C4
Qillak *i.* Greenland **165** P3
also known as Dannebrog Ø
Qīma Kazakh. *see* **Kiyma**
Qiman el 'Arûs Egypt **108** C8
Qimantag *mts* China **89** E4
Qimen China **87** F2
also known as Qishan
Qimusseriarsuaq *b.* Greenland **165** M2
also known as Melville Bugt
Qin *r.* China **87** E1
Qinā Egypt *see* **Qena**
Qināb, Wādī *r.* Yemen **105** E4
Qin'an China **86** C1
also known as Xingguo
Qincheng China *see* **Nanfeng**
Qing *r.* China **82** A4
Qing'an China **82** B3
Qingcheng China *see* **Qingyang**
Qingchengzi China **83** A4
Qingchuan China **86** C1
also known as Qiaozhuang
Qingdao China **85** I4
formerly spelt Tsingtao
Qinggang China **82** B3
Qinggil China *see* **Qinghe**
Qingguandu China **87** D2
Qinghai *prov.* China **84** C4
English form Chinghai; *formerly known as* Chinghai
Qinghai Hu *salt l.* China **84** D4
Qinghai Nanshan *mts* China **84** C4
Qinghe *Hebei* China **85** G4
also known as Gexianzhuang
Qinghe *Xinjiang* China **84** A2
also known as Qinggil
Qinghua China *see* **Bo'ai**
Qingjian China **85** F4
also known as Xiuyan
Qingjiang China *see* **Huaiyin**
Qingjiang China *see* **Zhangshu**
Qing Jiang *r.* China **87** D2
Qingkou China *see* **Ganyu**
Qingliu China **87** F3
also known as Longjin
Qinglong *Guizhou* China **86** C3
also known as Liancheng
Qinglong *Hebei* China **85** H3
Qinglong *r.* China **85** H4
Qingpu China **87** G2
Qingquan China *see* **Xishui**
Qingshan China *see* **Dedu**
Qingshizui China **84** D4
Qingshui China *see* **Qingshuipu**
Qingshui China **86** C1
also known as Yongqing
Qingshuihe *Nei Mongol* China **85** F4
Qingshuihe *Qinghai* China **86** A1
also known as Domda
Qingshuihezi China **88** C2
Qingshuilang Shan *mts* China **86** A3
Qingshuipu China **84** C4
formerly known as Qingshui
Qingtian China **87** G2
also known as Hecheng
Qingtongxia China **85** E4
also known as Xiaoba
Qingxian China **85** H4
also known as Qingzhou
Qingxu China **85** G4
also known as Qingyuan
Qingyang *Anhui* China **87** F2
also known as Rongcheng
Qingyang *Gansu* China **85** E4
also known as Qingcheng
Qingyang China *see* **Sihong**
Qingyuan China *see* **Weiyuan**
Qingyuan *Guangdong* China **87** E4
Qingyuan China *see* **Yizhou**
Qingyuan *Liaoning* China **82** B4
Qingyuan China *see* **Qingxu**
Qingyuan *Zhejiang* China **87** F3
Qingyun China **85** H4
formerly known as Xiejiaji
Qingzang Gaoyuan *plat.* China *see* **Tibet, Plateau of**
Qingzhen China **86** C3
Qingzhou China *see* **Qingxian**
Qingzhou *Hubei* China **87** D2
Qingzhou *Shandong* China **85** H4
formerly known as Yidu
Qinhuangdao China **85** H4
Qinjiang China *see* **Shicheng**
Qin Ling *mts* China **87** C1
Qinshui China **85** G5
Qinting China *see* **Lianhua**
Qinxian China **85** G4
Qinyang China **85** G5
Qinyuan China **85** G4
Qinzhou China **87** D4
Qinzhou Wan *b.* China **87** D4
Qionghai China **87** D5
Qiongjiexue China *see* **Qonggyai**
Qionglai China **86** B2
Qionglai Shan *mts* China **86** B2
Qiongshan China **87** D5
Qiongxi China *see* **Hongyuan**
Qiongzhou Haixia *strait* China *see* **Hainan Strait**
Qiqihar China **85** I2
formerly spelt Tsitsihar
Qiquanhu China **88** E3
Qir Iran **100** C4
Qira China **89** C4
Qiraīya, Wādī *watercourse* Egypt **108** F7
Qiryat Gat Israel **108** F6
Qiryat Shemona Israel **108** G4
Qishan China *see* **Qimen**
Qishan China **87** C1
also known as Fengming
Qishn Yemen **105** E5
Qishon *r.* Israel **108** G5
Qishrān Island Saudi Arabia **104** C3
Qitab ash Shāmah *vol. crater* Saudi Arabia **107** D5
Qitai China **88** E3
Qitaihe China **82** C3
Qitbīt, Wādī *r.* Oman **105** F4
Qiubei China **86** C3
also known as Jinping
Qiujin China **87** E2
Qixia China **85** I4
Qixian *Henan* China **85** G5
formerly known as Zhaoge
Qixian *Henan* China **87** E1
Qixian *Shanxi* China **85** G4
Qixing *r.* China **82** D3
Qiyang China **87** D3
Qiying China **85** E4
Qizhou Liedao *i.* China **87** D5
Qızılağac Körfäzi *b.* Azer. **100** B2
formerly known as Kirova, Zaliv
Qizil-Art, Aghbai *pass* Kyrg./Tajik. *see* **Kyzylart Pass**
Qizilrabot Tajik. **101** H2
also spelt Kyzylrabot
Qizqetkan Uzbek. *see* **Kyzketken**
Qoboqobo S. Africa **133** M9
Qoghaly Kazakh. *see* **Kugaly**
Qogir Feng *mt.* China/Jammu and Kashmir *see* **K2**
Qog Qi China **85** E3
Qojūr Iran **100** A2
Qolora Mouth S. Africa **133** M9
Qoltag *mts* China **88** E3
Qom Iran **100** B3
Qom *prov.* Iran **100** B3
Qomdo China *see* **Qumdo**
Qomisheh Iran *see* **Shahrezā**
Qomolangma Feng *mt.* China/Nepal *see* **Everest, Mount**
Qonaqkänd Azer. **107** G2
Qonggyai China **89** E6
also known as Qiongjiexue; *also spelt* Chonggye
Qongj China **85** F3
Qongkol China **88** D3
Qongrat Uzbek. *see* **Kungrad**
Qongyrat Kazakh. *see* **Kounradskiy**
Qongyrat Kazakh. *see* **Konyrat**
Qongyröleng Kazakh. *see* **Konyrolen**
Qonj China **84** C4
Qonystanū Kazakh. *see* **Konystanu**
Qooriga Neegro *b.* Somalia **128** F3
Qoornoq Greenland **165** N3
Qoqek China *see* **Tacheng**
Qoqodala S. Africa **133** K8
Qoradaryo *r.* Kyrg. *see* **Kara-Darya**
Qoraghaty Kazakh. *see* **Kuragaty**
Qoraqalpoghiston Uzbek. *see* **Karakalpakiya**
Qoraqalpoghiston Respublikasi *aut. rep.* Uzbek. *see* **Karakalpakistan, Respublika**
Qoraūzak Uzbek. *see* **Karauzyak**
Qorday Kazakh. *see* **Kurday**
Qorghalzhyn Kazakh. *see* **Kurgal'dzhinskiy**
Qornet es Saouda *mt.* Lebanon **108** H3
Qorowulbozor Uzbek. *see* **Karaulbazar**
Qoroy, Gardaneh-ye *pass* Iran **100** B2
Qorveh Iran **100** A3
Qosh Tepe Iraq **107** E3
Qosshaghyl Kazakh. *see* **Koschagyl**
Qostanay Kazakh. *see* **Kostanay**
Qostanay Oblysy *admin. div.* Kazakh. *see* **Kustanayskaya Oblast'**
Qotbābād Iran **100** D5
Qotūr Iran **100** A2
Qozhaköl *l.* Kazakh. *see* **Kozhakol', Ozero**
Qozonketkan Uzbek. *see* **Kazanketken**
Qozoqdaryo Uzbek. *see* **Kazakhdar'ya**
Quabbin Reservoir U.S.A. **177** M3
Quadra Island Canada **166** E5
Quadros, Lago dos *l.* Brazil **203** B9
Quaggasfontein Poort *pass* S. Africa **132** E8
Quail Mountains U.S.A. **183** G6
Quairading Australia **151** B7
Quakenbrück Germany **48** E3
Quamby Australia **149** D4
Quanah U.S.A. **179** C5
Quanbao Shan *mt.* China **87** D1
Quân Đao Cô Tô *is* Vietnam **78** D3
Quan Dao Hoang Sa *is* S. China Sea *see* **Paracel Islands**
Quân Đao Nam Du *i.* Vietnam **79** D6
Quan Dao Truong Sa *is* S. China Sea *see* **Spratly Islands**
Quang Ngai Vietnam **79** E5
Quang Tri Vietnam **78** D4
Quang Yen Vietnam **78** D3
Quan He *r.* China **87** E1
Quanjiang China *see* **Suichuan**
Quan Long Vietnam *see* **Ca Mau**
Quannan China **87** E3
also known as Chengxiang
Quan Phu Quoc *i.* Vietnam *see* **Phu Quôc, Đao**
Quanshang China **87** F3
Quanwan *Hong Kong* China *see* **Tsuen Wan**
Quanzhou *Fujian* China **87** F3
Quanzhou *Guangxi* China **87** D3
Qu'Appelle *r.* Canada **167** K5
Quaqtaq Canada **165** M3
formerly known as Notre-Dame-de-Koartac; *formerly spelt* Koartac
Quarai Brazil **204** F3
Quarry Bay *Hong Kong* China **87** [inset]
Quarryville U.S.A. **177** I6
Quarteira Port. **54** C7
Quartu Sant'Elena *Sardegna* Italy **57** B9
Quartzite Mountain U.S.A. **183** H4
Quartzsite U.S.A. **183** J8
Quaryat al Faw *tourist site* Saudi Arabia **105** D4
Quba Azer. **107** G2
also spelt Kuba
Quchan Iran **100** D2
Qudaysah *well* Oman **105** G4
Qudeni S. Africa **133** O5
Queanbeyan Australia **147** F3

▶**Québec** Canada **169** G4
Provincial capital of Québec.

Québec *prov.* Canada **169** F2
Quebra Anzol *r.* Brazil **206** F6
Quedas Moz. **131** G3
Quedlinburg Germany **48** I4
Queen Adelaide Islands Chile *see* **La Reina Adelaida, Archipiélago de**
Queen Alia *airport* Jordan **108** G6
Queen Anne U.S.A. **177** J7
Queen Bess, Mount Canada **166** E5
Queen Charlotte Canada **166** C4
Queen Charlotte Bay Falkland Is **205** E8
Queen Charlotte Islands Canada **166** C4
Queen Charlotte Sound *sea chan.* Canada **166** D5
Queen Charlotte Strait Canada **166** E5
Queen Creek U.S.A. **183** M8
Queen Elizabeth Islands Canada **165** I2
Queen Elizabeth National Park Uganda **128** A5
formerly known as Ruwenzori National Park
Queen Elizabeth Range *mts* Antarctica **223** K1
Queen Fabiola Mountains Antarctica **223** C2
Queen Mary Land *reg.* Antarctica **223** G2
Queen Maud Bird Sanctuary *nature res.* Canada **167** K1
Queen Maud Gulf Canada **165** I3
Queen Maud Land *reg.* Antarctica **223** A2
also known as Dronning Maud Land
Queen Maud Mountains Antarctica **223** O1
Queensburgh S. Africa **133** O6
Queens Channel Australia **148** A2
Queenscliff Australia **147** E4
Queensland *state* Australia **149** E4
Queenstown Australia **147** E5
Queenstown N.Z. **153** C13
Queenstown Rep. of Ireland *see* **Cóbh**
Queenstown S. Africa **133** K8
Queenstown Sing. **76** [inset]
Queenstown U.S.A. **177** I7
Queen Victoria Spring Nature Reserve Australia **151** C6
Quehua Bol. **200** D4
Quehué Arg. **204** D5
Queiba *well* Chad **120** D5
Queimada Brazil **201** E2
Queimada, Ilha *i.* Brazil **202** B2
also known as Serraria, Ilha
Queimadas Brazil **202** E4
Queiroz Brazil **206** C8
Quela Angola **127** C7
Quelimane Moz. **131** H3
Quelite Mex. **184** D4
Quellón Chile **205** B6
Quelpart Island S. Korea *see* **Cheju-do**
Queluz Brazil **207** I9
Quemada Grande, Ilha *i.* Brazil **206** G11
Quemado U.S.A. **181** E6
Quembo *r.* Angola **127** D8
Quemchi Chile **205** E6
Quemoy *i.* Taiwan *see* **Chinmen Tao**
Quemú-Quemú Arg. **204** E5
Quepem India **94** B3
Que Que Zimbabwe *see* **Kwekwe**
Quequén Arg. **204** F5
Querência Brazil **202** A5
Querétaro Mex. **185** E4
Querétaro *state* Mex. **185** F4
Querfurt Germany **48** I4
Querobabi Mex. **184** C2
Querpon Peru **198** B6
Quesada Spain **55** H7
Quesat *watercourse* W. Sahara **122** C4
Queshan China **87** E1
also known as Panlong
Quesnel Canada **166** F4
Quesnel *r.* Canada **166** F4
Quesnel Lake Canada **166** F4
Questembert France **50** D5
Quetena de Lipez *r.* Bol. **200** D5
Quetico Provincial Park Canada **172** B2
Quetta Pak. **101** F4
Queuco Chile **204** C5
Queulat, Parque Nacional *nat. park* Chile **205** B7
Queupán Arg. **204** D6
Queyras, Parc Naturel Régional du *nature res.* France **51** M8
Quezaltenango Guat. **185** H6
Quezaltepeque El Salvador **185** H6
Quezon *Negros* Phil. **74** B4
Quezon *Palawan* Phil. **74** A4

▶**Quezon City** Phil. **74** B3
Former capital of the Philippines.

Qufu China **85** H5
Qugaryatang China **89** E6
Quibala Angola **127** B7
Quibaxe Angola **127** B7
Quibdó Col. **198** B3
Quiberon France **50** C5
Quiberon, Baie de *b.* France **50** C5
Quíbor Venez. **198** D2
Quicama, Parque Nacional do *nat. park* Angola **127** B7
also spelt Kisama, Parque Nacional de
Quiet Lake Canada **166** C2
Quihita Angola **127** B8
Quiindy Para. **201** F6
Quilá Mex. **184** D3
Quilalí Nicaragua **186** B4
Quilán, Cabo *c.* Chile **205** B6
Quilandi India **94** B4
Quilca Peru **200** B4
Quilenda Angola **127** B7
Quilengues Angola **127** B8
Quillacollo Bol. **200** D4
Quillan France **51** I10
Quill Lakes Canada **167** J5
Quillota Chile **204** C4
Quilmes Arg. **204** F4
Quilon India **94** C4
also known as Kollam
Quilpie Australia **149** E5
Quilpué Chile **204** C4
Quimbele Angola **127** C6
Quimili Arg. **204** E2
Quimome Bol. **201** E4
Quimper France **50** B5
Quimperlé France **50** C5
Quinault *r.* U.S.A. **180** A3
Quinault Indian Reservation *res.* U.S.A. **180** A3
Quince Mil Peru **200** C3
Quincinetto Italy **51** N7
Quincy *CA* U.S.A. **182** D2
Quincy *FL* U.S.A. **175** C6
Quincy *IL* U.S.A. **174** B4
Quincy *MI* U.S.A. **173** I9
Quincy *OH* U.S.A. **176** B5
Quindio *dept* Col. **198** C3
Quines Arg. **204** D4
Quinga Moz. **131** I2
Quinhagak U.S.A. **164** C4
Quinhámel Guinea-Bissau **124** B4
Qui Nhon Vietnam **79** E5
Quinigua, Cerro *mts* Venez. **199** E3
Quiniluban *i.* Phil. **74** B4
Quinkan Aboriginal Holding *res.* Australia **149** E2
Quinn *r.* U.S.A. **180** C4
Quinn Canyon Range *mts* U.S.A. **183** I4
Quinnimont U.S.A. **176** D8
Quiñones Bol. **200** D2
Quintana Brazil **206** C9
Quintana de la Serena Spain **54** F6
Quintanar de la Orden Spain **55** H5
Quintanar del Rey Spain **55** J5
Quintana Roo *state* Mex. **185** H5
Quintin France **50** D4
Quinto *r.* Arg. **204** D4
Quinto Spain **55** K3
Quinzau Angola **127** B6
Quinze, Lac des *l.* Canada **173** N3
Quionga Moz. **129** D7
Quiotepec Mex. **185** F5
Quipapá Brazil **202** F4
Quipungo Angola **127** B8
formerly known as Paiva Couceiro; *formerly spelt* Kipungo
Quiquive *r.* Bol. **200** D3
Quiriguá *tourist site* Guat. **185** H6
Quirihue Chile **204** B5
Quirima Angola **127** C7
Quirindi Australia **147** F2
Quirinópolis Brazil **206** C5
Quirke Lake Canada **173** K4
Quiroga Bol. **200** D4
Quiroga Spain **54** D2
Quisiro Venez. **198** D2
Quissac France **51** K9
Quissamã Brazil **207** L9
Quitapa Angola **127** C7
Quita Sueño Bank *sea feature* Caribbean Sea **186** C4
Quiterajo Moz. **129** D7
Quitéria *r.* Brazil **206** B7
Quitexe Angola *see* **Dange**
Quitilipi Arg. **204** E2
Quitman *GA* U.S.A. **175** D6
Quitman *MS* U.S.A. **175** B5

▶**Quito** Ecuador **198** B5
Capital of Ecuador.

Quitovac Mex. **184** B2
Quitralco, Parque Nacional *nat. park* Chile **205** B7
Quixadá Brazil **202** E3
Quixeramobim Brazil **202** E3
Qujiang China *see* **Quxian**
Qu Jiang *r.* China **86** C2
Qujing China **86** B3
Quko S. Africa **133** M9
Qulaly Araly *i.* Kazakh. *see* **Kulaly, Ostrov**
Qul'ân, Gezâ'ir *i.* Egypt **104** A2
English form Gulân Islands
Qulandy Kazakh. *see* **Kulandy**
Qulanötpes *watercourse* Kazakh. *see* **Kulanotpes**
Qulbān Layyah *well* Iraq **107** F5
Quljuqtow Toghi *hills* Uzbek. *see* **Kul'dzhuktau, Gory**
Qulsary Kazakh. *see* **Kul'sary**
Qulûsana Egypt **106** B5
Qulzum, Baḩr el *b.* Egypt *see* **Suez Bay**
Qumar He *r.* China **84** B5
Qumarheyan China **84** B5
Qumarlêb China **84** B5
also known as Yiggêtang
Qumbu S. Africa **133** M8
Qumdo China **97** G3
formerly spelt Qomdo
Qumola *watercourse* Kazakh. *see* **Kumola**
Qumrha S. Africa **133** L9
Qunayy *well* Saudi Arabia **105** D3
Qunayyin, Sabkhat al *salt marsh* Libya **120** D2
Qunfudh Yemen **105** E4
Qŭnghirot Uzbek. *see* **Kungrad**
Qu'nyido China **86** A2
Quoich *r.* Canada **167** M1
Quoin Island Australia **148** A2
Quoin Point S. Africa **132** D11
Quong Muztag *mt.* China **89** C5
Quorn Australia **146** C3
Quoxo *r.* Botswana **131** E4
Quqên China *see* **Jinchuan**
Qŭqon Uzbek. *see* **Kokand**
Qurayat Oman **105** G3
Qurayyah *tourist site* Saudi Arabia **108** H9
Qurayyat al Milḩ *l.* Jordan **109** I6
Qŭrghonteppa Tajik. **101** G2
also spelt Kurgantyube
Qus Egypt **121** G3
Qusar Azer. **107** G2
also spelt Kusary
Quşay'ir Saudi Arabia **105** E5
Quseir Egypt **121** G3
Qushan China *see* **Beichuan**
Qūshchī Iran **100** A2
Qūsheh Dāgh *mts* Iran **100** A2
Qŭshkŭpir Uzbek. *see* **Koshkupyr**
Qŭshrabot Uzbek. *see* **Koshrabad**
Qusmuryn Kazakh. *see* **Kushmurun**
Qusmuryn Köli *salt l.* Kazakh. *see* **Kushmurun, Ozero**
Qusum *Xizang* China **89** B5
Qusum *Xizang* China **89** F6
also known as Xiajiang
Quthing Lesotho *see* **Moyeni**
Quthing *r.* Lesotho **133** M7
Quṭn, Jabal *hill* Saudi Arabia **104** C2

Qutú' Island Saudi Arabia 104 C4
Quwayq, Nahr r. Syria/Turkey 109 I2
  also known as Haleparki Deresi
Qū' Wishām reg. Oman 105 F4
Quwu Shan mts China 85 E4
Quxar China see Lhazê
Quxian China 86 C2
  also known as Quijiang
Qüxü China 89 E6
  also known as Xoi
Quyang China see Jingzhou
Quyghan Kazakh. see Kuygan
Quyon Canada 173 Q5
Qüyün Eshek i. Iran 100 A3
Qüz Saudi Arabia 104 C4
Quzhou Hebei China 85 G4
Quzhou Zhejiang China 87 F2
Quzi China 85 E4
Qvareli Georgia 107 F2
  also spelt Kvareli
Qypshaq Köli salt l. Kazakh. see
  Kypshak, Ozero
Qyteti Stalin Albania see Kuçovë
Qyzan Kazakh. see Kyzan
Qyzylagash Kazakh. see Kyzylagash
Qyzylkesek Kazakh. see Kyzylkesek
Qyzylköl i. Kazakh. see Kyzylkol', Ozero
Qyzylorda Kazakh. see Kyzylorda
Qyzylorda Oblysy admin. div. Kazakh. see
  Kzyl-Ordinskaya Oblast'
Qyzyltaū Kazakh. see Kyzyltau
Qyzyltü Kazakh. see Kishkenekol'
Qyzylzhar Kazakh. see Kyzylzhar

↓ R

Raab r. Austria 49 N9
Raab Hungary see Györ
Raahe Fin. 44 N2
Rääkkylä Fin. 44 O3
Raalte Neth. 48 D3
Ra'an, Khashm ar hill Saudi Arabia 104 C2
Raanujärvi Fin. 44 N2
Raas i. Indon. 77 F4
Raasay i. U.K. 46 F6
Raasiku Estonia 42 H2
Rab i. Croatia 56 G4
Rába r. Hungary 49 O8
Raba Indon. 77 F5
Raba r. Poland 49 R5
Rabaale Somalia 128 E2
Rabang China 89 C5
Rabat Gozo Malta see Victoria
Rabat Malta 53 E4

▶ Rabat Morocco 122 D2
Capital of Morocco.

Rabatakbaytal Tajik. see Akbaytal
Rabât-e Kamah Iran 100 D3
Rabaul P.N.G. 145 E2
Rabaul vol. P.N.G. 145 E2
Rabbath Ammon Jordan see 'Amman
Rabbi r. Italy 56 E4
Rabbit r. Canada 166 E3
Rabbit Flat Australia 148 A4
Rabbitskin r. Canada 166 F2
Rábca r. Hungary 49 O8
Rabezha Rus. Fed. 43 U6
Rabidine well Niger 125 G3
Rābigh Saudi Arabia 104 B3
Rabka Poland 49 Q6
Rabkob India see Dharmjaygarh
Rabnabad Islands Bangl. 97 G5
Râbnița Moldova see Rîbnița
Rābor Iran 100 D4
Rabotoqbaytal Tajik. see Akbaytal
Rabt Sbayta res. W. Sahara 122 B5
Rabyânah oasis Libya 120 D3
Rača Srbija Yugo. 58 B4
Racalmuto Sicilia Italy 57 F11
Racconigi Italy 51 N8
Raccoon Cay i. Bahamas 186 E2
Raccoon Creek r. U.S.A. 176 C7
Raceland U.S.A. 175 B6
Race Point U.S.A. 177 O3
Rachaïya Lebanon 108 G4
Rachel U.S.A. 183 I4
Rachevo Rus. Fed. 43 S3
Rach Gia Vietnam 79 D6
Rach Gia, Vinh b. Vietnam 79 D6
Raciąż Poland 49 Q3
Racibórz Poland 49 P5
  historically known as Ratibor
Racine WI U.S.A. 172 F8
Racine WV U.S.A. 176 D7
Racine Lake Canada 173 J2
Racu Romania 58 F2
Racoş Romania 58 G2
Racovita Romania 58 I3
Radá' Yemen 104 D5
Radashkovichy Belarus 42 I7
  also spelt Radoshkovichi
Rădăuți Romania 41 I7
Radbuza r. Czech Rep. 49 K6
Radchenko Rus. Fed. 43 R5
Radcliff U.S.A. 174 C5
Radd, Wâdî ar watercourse Syria 109 M1

Radde Rus. Fed. 82 C2
Rade Norway 45 J4
Radebeul Germany 49 K4
Radenthein Austria 49 K9
Radew r. Poland 49 M1
Radford U.S.A. 176 E8
Radford Point Australia 148 A1
Radhanpur India 96 A5
Radishchevo Rus. Fed. 102 A1
Radisson Que. Canada 168 E2
Radisson Sask. Canada 167 J4
Raditsa-Krylovka Rus. Fed. 43 P8
Radium S. Africa 133 M2
Radium Hot Springs Canada 167 G5
Radlinski, Mount Antarctica 222 R1
Radnevo Bulg. 58 G6
Rado de Tumaco inlet Col. 198 B4
Radogoshcha Rus. Fed. 43 P2
Radolfzell am Bodensee Germany 48 F8
Radom Poland 49 S4
Radom Sudan 126 E2
Radomir Bulg. 58 D6
Radomir mt. Bulg./Greece 58 E7
  formerly known as Kalabak
Radomka r. Poland 49 S4
Radom National Park Sudan 126 D2
Radomsko Poland 49 P4
  formerly known as Noworadomsk
Radomyshl Ukr. 41 D6
Radoshkovichi Belarus see Radashkovichy
Radovets Bulg. 58 H7
Radoviš Macedonia 58 D7
Radovitskiy Rus. Fed. 43 U6
  formerly known as Tsentral'nyy
Radovljica Slovenia 56 G2
Radøy i. Norway 46 Q3
Radstock, Cape Australia 146 B3
Radun' Belarus 42 F7
Radunia r. Poland 49 P1
Radviliškis Lith. 42 E6
Radwá, Jabal mt. Saudi Arabia 104 B2
Radymno Poland 49 T6
Radziejów Poland 49 P3
Radzyń Podlaski Poland 49 T4
Rae Bareli India 96 D4
Raecreek r. Canada 166 B1
Rae-Edzo Canada 167 G2
  also known as Edzo
Raeford U.S.A. 174 E5
Raeside, Lake salt flat Australia 151 C6
Raetihi N.Z. 152 J7
Rãf hill Saudi Arabia 107 D5
Rafaela Arg. 204 E3
Rafaḥ Gaza see Rafaḥ
Rafaï Cent. Afr. Rep. 126 D3
Raffadali Sicilia Italy 57 F11
Rafḥā' Saudi Arabia 107 E5
Rafiaḥ Gaza 108 F5
  also spelt Rafaḥ
Rafina Greece 59 F10
Rafsanjan Iran 100 D4
  also known as Bahämabäd
Raft r. U.S.A. 180 D4
Raga Sudan 126 E3
Ragag Sudan 126 E2
Ragana Latvia 42 F4
Ragang, Mount vol. Phil. 74 C5
Ragay Gulf Phil. 74 B3
Ragged, Mount hill Australia 151 C7
Ragged Island Bahamas 186 E2
Ragged Island U.S.A. 177 Q2
Raghogarh India 96 C4
Raghwah waterhole Saudi Arabia 109 P9
Raghwan, Wâdî watercourse Yemen
  104 D5
Raglan N.Z. 152 I5
Rago Nasjonalpark nat. park Norway 44 L2
Ragueneau Canada 169 G3
Ragusa Croatia see Dubrovnik
Ragusa Sicilia Italy 57 G12
Raha Indon. 75 B4
Raha r. Indon. 75 B4
Rahachow Belarus 43 L8
  also spelt Rogachev
Rahad r. Sudan 121 G6
Rahad Canal Sudan 121 G6
Rahad el Berdi Sudan 126 D2
Rahad Wahal well Sudan 120 E6
Rahaeng Thai. see Tak
Rahat, Harrat lava field Saudi Arabia 104 C3
Rahatgaon India 96 C5
Rahimatpur India 94 B2
Rahimyar Khan Pak. 101 G4
Râhjerd Iran 100 B3
Rahotu N.Z. 152 H7
Rahouia Alg. 55 M9
Rahumäe Estonia 42 I3
Rahuri India 94 B2
Rahzanak Afgh. 101 E3
Raïa r. Fr. Polynesia 221 H7
  also known as Uliatea
Raibu i. Indon. see Air
Raichur India 94 C2
Raiganj India 97 F4
Raigarh Chhattisgarh India 97 D5
Raigarh Orissa India 94 D3
Raijua i. Indon. 75 B5
Raikot India 96 B3
Railroad Valley U.S.A. 183 I3
Raimangal r. Bangl. 97 F5
Raimbault, Lac l. Canada 169 G2
Rainbow Lake Canada 166 G3
Raine Entrance sea chan. Australia 149 E1
Raine Island Australia 149 E1
Rainelle U.S.A. 176 E8
Raini r. Pak. 101 G4
Rainier, Mount vol. U.S.A. 180 B3
Rainy r. U.S.A. 174 A1
Rainy Lake Canada 168 A3
Raippaluoto i. Fin. 44 M3
Raipur Bangl. 97 F5
Raipur Chhattisgarh India 97 D5
Raipur Rajasthan India 96 B4
Raipur Jammu and Kashmir 96 B2
Raipur W. Bengal India 97 E5
Rairangpur India 97 E5
Raisen India 96 C5
Raisinghnagar India 96 B3
Raisio Fin. 45 M3
Raistakka Fin. 44 O2
Raith Canada 172 D4
Rai Valley N.Z. 152 H9
Raivavae i. Fr. Polynesia 221 I7
  also known as Vavitao
Raiwind Pak. 101 H4
Raja Estonia 42 I3
Raja, Ujung pt Indon. 76 B2
Rajaampat, Kepulauan is Indon. 75 D3
Rajabasa, Gunung vol. Indon. 77 D4
Rajagangapur India 97 E5
Rajahmundry India 94 D2
Raja-Joosseppi Fin. 44 O1
  also known as Räjijovsset
Rajaldesar India 96 B3
Rajamäki Fin. 42 F1
Rajampet India 94 C3
Rajang r. Sarawak Malaysia 77 E2
Rajapalaiyam India 94 C4
Rajapur India 94 B2
Rajasthan state India 96 B4
  historically known as Rajputana Agency
Rajasthan Canal India 96 B3
Rajauli India 97 E4
Rajbari Bangl. 97 F5
Rajgarh Madhya Pradesh India 96 C4
Rajgarh Maharashtra India 94 B2
Rajgarh Rajasthan India 96 B3
Rajgarh Rajasthan India 96 C4
Rajgir India 97 F4

Rajgród Poland 49 T2
Räjijovsset Fin. see Raja-Joosseppi
Rajim India 94 D1
Rajince Srbija Yugo. 58 C6
Rajkot India 96 A5
Rajmahal India 86 A5
Rajmahal Hills India 97 E4
Raj Nandgaon India 96 D5
Rajpipla India 96 B5
Rajpur India 96 B5
Rajpura India 96 C3
Rajputana Agency state India see
  Rajasthan
Rajsamand India 96 B4
Rajshahi Bangl. 97 F4
  also known as Rampur Boalia
Rajshahi admin. div. Bangl. 97 F4
Râju Syria 109 H1
Rajula India 96 A5
Rajur India 94 C1
Rajura India 94 C2
Rajura India see Ahmadpur
Raka China 89 D6
Rakahuri r. N.Z. see Ashley
Rakai Uganda 128 A5
Rakaia N.Z. 153 G11
Rakaia r. N.Z. 153 G11
Rakan, Ra's pt Qatar 105 E2
Rakaposhi mt. Jammu and Kashmir 96 B1
Raka Zangbo r. China see Dogxung Zangbo
Rakeahua, Mount hill N.Z. 153 B14
Rakhaing state Myanmar see Arakan
Rakhine state Myanmar see Arakan
Rakhiv Ukr. 53 G2
Rakhshan r. Pak. 101 E5
Rakiraki Fiji 145 G3
Rakit i. Indon. 77 D4
Rakitnitsa r. Bulg. 58 G6
Rakitnoye Rus. Fed. 82 D3
Rakitnoye Rus. Fed. 41 E6
Rakitu Island N.Z. 152 J4
Rakiura i. N.Z. see Stewart Island
Rakke Estonia 42 I3
Rakkestad Norway 45 J4
Rakhnanovskie Klyuchi Kazakh. 88 D1
Rakni r. Pak. 101 F4
Rakoniewice Poland 49 N3
Rakops Botswana 131 E4
Rakovitsa Bulg. 58 D5
Rakovník Czech Rep. 49 K5
Rakovski Bulg. 58 F6
Rakushechnyy, Mys pt Kazakh. 102 B4
Rakvere Estonia 42 I2

▶ Raleigh NC U.S.A. 174 E5
State capital of North Carolina.

Raleighvallen Voltsberg, Natuurreservaat
nature res. Suriname 199 G3
Ralla Indon. 75 A4
Ralph U.S.A. 172 F4
Ralston Canada 167 I5
Ralston U.S.A. 177 I4
Ram r. Canada 166 F2
Rama Israel 108 G5
Rama Nicaragua 186 B4
Ramacca Sicilia Italy 57 G11
Ramādī, Saddat ar dam Iraq 109 O4
Ramah Canada 169 I1
Ramales de la Victoria Spain 55 H1
Ramalho, Serra do hills Brazil 202 C5
Ramallah West Bank 108 G6
Ramallo Arg. 204 E4
Ramanagaram India 94 C4
Ramanathapuram India see Ramnad
Ramanuj Ganj India 97 D5
Ramas, Cape India 94 B3
Ramasukha Rus. Fed. 43 L8
  also spelt Rogachev
Ramatlabama watercourse
  Botswana/S. Africa 133 J2
Ramatlabama S. Africa 133 J2
Ramayampet India 94 C2
Ramberg Norway 44 K1
Rambervilliers France 51 M4
Rambouillet France 50 H4
Rambutyo Island P.N.G. 73 K7
  historically known as Jesu Maria Island
Ramdurg India 94 B3
Ramechhap Nepal 97 E4
Rame Head S. Africa 133 N8
Rame Head U.K. 47 H13
Ramenskoye Rus. Fed. 43 T6
Rameshki Rus. Fed. 43 R4
Rameswaram India 94 C4
Ramezān Kalak Iran 101 E5
Ramgarh Bangl. 97 F5
Ramgarh Jharkhand India 97 E5
Ramgarh Rajasthan India 96 A4
Ramgarh Rajasthan India 96 C4
Ramgul r. Afgh. 101 G3
Rämhormoz Iran 100 B4
Ramingining Australia 148 B2
Ramit Tajik. see Romit
Ramitan Uzbek. see Romitan
Ramla Israel 108 F6
Ramlat al Ghafah des. Saudi Arabia 105 F3
Ramlat al Wahibah des. Oman 105 G4
Ramlat Amilhayt des. Oman 105 F4
Ramlat as Sab'atayn des. Yemen 105 D5
Ramlat Dahm des. Saudi Arabia/Yemen
  105 D4
Ramlat Rabyânah des. Libya see
  Rebiana Sand Sea
Ramm, Jabal mts Jordan 108 G8
  also spelt Rum, Jebel
Ramni Belarus 43 L6
Râmnicu Sărat r. Romania 58 I3
Râmnicu Sărat Romania 58 I3
  formerly spelt Rîmnicu Sărat
Râmnicu Vâlcea Romania 58 F3
  formerly spelt Rîmnicu Vîlcea
Ramo Eth. 128 D3
Ramokgwebane Botswana 131 E4
Ramón Spain 183 H8
Ramón Lista Arg. 205 D7
Ramonville-St-Agne France 50 H9
Ramore Canada 173 M2
Ramos Arizpe Mex. 185 E3
Ramos Botswana 131 F4
Rampart of Genghis Khan tourist site Asia
  85 G1
Ramparts r. Canada 166 D1
Rampur Himachal Pradesh India 89 B6
Rampur Uttar Pradesh India 96 C3
Rampur Uttar Pradesh India 96 C3
Rampura India 96 C4
Rampur Boalia Bangl. see Rajshahi
Rampur Hat India 97 F4
Ramree Myanmar 78 A4
Ramree Island Myanmar 78 A4
Ramsele Sweden 44 L3
Ramsey Canada 173 K3
Ramsey Isle of Man 47 H9
Ramsey U.S.A. 183 I6
Ramsey Lake Canada 168 D4
Ramsgate S. Africa 133 O7
Ramsgate U.K. 47 N12
Ramshai Hat India 97 F4
Ramsin Iran 100 D4
Ramsing India 97 G3

Ramsjö Sweden 45 K3
Ramtek India 96 C5
Ramu Bangl. 97 G5
Ramu r. P.N.G. 73 J7
Ramundberget Sweden 44 K3
Ramusio, Lac l. Canada 169 I2
Ramvik Sweden 44 L3
Ramygala Lith. 42 F6
Rana, Cerro hill Col. 199 D4
Rañadoiro, Puerto de pass Spain 54 E2
Rañadoiro, Sierra de mts Spain 54 E2
Ranaghat India 97 F5
Ranai i. U.S.A. see Lanai
Rana Pratap Sagar resr India 96 B4
Ranapur India 96 B5
Rânåsfoss Norway 45 J3
Ranau Sabah Malaysia 77 G1
Ranau, Danau l. Indon. 76 C4
Rancagua Chile 204 C4
Rance r. France 50 D4
Rancharia Brazil 206 C9
Rancheria r. Canada 166 D2
Rancheria r. Canada 166 D2
Ranchester U.S.A. 180 F3
Ranchi India 97 E5
Rancho Cordova U.S.A. 182 C3
Rancho de Caçados Tapiúnas Brazil
  201 F2
Ranchos de Taos U.S.A. 181 F5
Rancho Veloz Cuba 175 D8
Ranco, Lago l. Chile 204 B6
Randalstown U.K. 47 I9
Randangan Panua Reserve nature res.
  Indon. 75 B3
Randazzo Sicilia Italy 57 G11
Randburg S. Africa 133 L3
Randers Denmark 45 J4
Randfontein S. Africa 133 L3
Randijaure r. Sweden 44 L2
Randolph MA U.S.A. 177 N3
Randolph ME U.S.A. 177 P1
Randolph NY U.S.A. 176 G3
Randolph UT U.S.A. 180 E4
Randolph VT U.S.A. 177 M2
Randow r. Germany 49 L2
Randsburg U.S.A. 182 G6
Randsfjorden l. Norway 45 J3
Randsverk Norway 45 J3
Råneå Sweden 44 M2
Ranfurly N.Z. 153 E13
Ranga r. India 78 A2
Rangae Thai. 79 C7
Rangamati Bangl. 97 G5
Rangapara North India 97 G4
Rangas, Tanjung pt Indon. 75 A3
Rangasa, Tanjung pt Indon. 75 A3
Rangaunu Bay N.Z. 152 H2
Rangeley Lake U.S.A. 177 O1
Rangely U.S.A. 183 P1
Ranger Lake Canada 168 D4
Ranger Lake l. Canada 173 J4
Rangi India 94 D1
Rangia Patharughat India 97 F4
Rangiauria i. S. Pacific Ocean see
  Pitt Island
Rangiora N.Z. 153 G11
Rangipoua mt. N.Z. 152 L5
  also known as Hardy, Mount
Rangitaiki N.Z. 152 K6
Rangitata N.Z. 153 D11
Rangitata r. N.Z. 153 F12
Rangitikei r. N.Z. 152 J7
Rangitoto Islands N.Z. 152 H8
Rangiwaea Junction N.Z. 152 J7
Rangiwaia N.Z. 152 J7
Rangkasbitung Indon. 77 D4
Rangke China see Zamtang
Rangkül Tajik. 101 H2
Rangôn Myanmar see Rangoon
Rangôn admin. div. Myanmar see Yangôn

▶ Rangoon Myanmar 78 B4
Capital of Myanmar. Also known as Yangôn;
also spelt Rangôn; historically known as
Dagon.

Rangoon admin. div. Myanmar see Yangôn
Rangoon r. Myanmar 78 B4
Rangpur Bangl. 97 F4
Rangsang i. Indon. 76 C2
Rangse Myanmar 78 A2
Rani India 96 B4
Rania India 96 B3
Ranibennur India 94 B3
Raniganj India 97 E5
Ranijula Peak India 97 D5
Ranikhet India 96 C3
Ranipur India 96 C4
Raniwara India 96 B4
Ranken watercourse Australia 148 C4
Rankin U.S.A. 179 B6
Rankin Inlet Canada 167 M2
Rankin Inlet inlet Canada 167 M2
Rankin's Springs Australia 147 E3
Ranković Srbija Yugo. see Kraljevo
Ranna Estonia 42 I3
Rannes Australia 149 F5
Ranneye Rus. Fed. 102 C2
Rannu Estonia 42 I3
Rannoch, Loch l. U.K. 46 H7
Rano Nigeria 125 H4
Ranobe r. Madag. 131 [inset] J3
Ranohira Madag. 131 [inset] J4
Ranomafana Madag. 131 [inset] K3
Ranomatana Madag. 131 [inset] J5
Ranong Thai. 79 B6
Ranongga i. Solomon Is 145 E2
Ranopiso Madag. 131 [inset] J5
Ranot Thai. 79 C7
Ranotsara Avaratra Madag. 131 [inset] J4
Ranova r. Rus. Fed. 43 V7
Ranpur India 96 A5
Ransiki Indon. 73 I7
Ransom U.S.A. 172 E9
Ranta Fin. 44 N1
Rantabe Madag. 131 [inset] K2
Rantasalmi Fin. 44 O3
Rantau Indon. 77 F3
Rantau i. Indon. 76 C2
Rantaukampar Indon. 76 C2
Rantaupanjang Kalimantan Tengah Indon.
  77 F2
Rantaupanjang Kalimantan Timur Indon.
  77 G2
Rantauprapat Indon. 76 B2
Rantaupulut Indon. 77 F3
Rantemario, Gunung mt. Indon. 75 B3
Rantepao Indon. 75 A3
Rantoul U.S.A. 174 B3
Rantsevo Rus. Fed. 43 P5
Rantsila Fin. 44 N2
Ranua Fin. 44 N2
Ranxë Albania 58 A7
Rånya Iraq 107 F3
Ranyah, Wâdî watercourse Saudi Arabia
  104 C3
Rao Go mt. Laos/Vietnam 78 D4
Raohe China 82 D3
Raon-l'Étape France 51 M4
Raoul Island N.Z. 145 H4
Rapa i. Fr. Polynesia 221 I7
  also known as Oparo or Rapa-iti
Rapa-iti i. Fr. Polynesia see Rapa
Rapallo Italy 56 B4
Rapar India 96 A5
Rapch r. Iran 101 D5
Rapel r. Chile 204 C4
Raper, Cape Canada 165 M3
Rapidan r. U.S.A. 176 H7
Rapid Bay Australia 146 C3

Rapid City U.S.A. 178 B2
Rapide-Deux Canada 173 O3
Rapide-Sept Canada 173 O3
Rápina Estonia 42 I3
Rapla Estonia 42 G3
Rappahannock r. U.S.A. 177 I8
Rappang Indon. 78 A3
Rapti r. India 97 D4
Rapulo r. Eol. 200 D3
Rapur Andhra Pradesh India 94 C3
Rapur Gujarat India 96 A5
Rapurapu i. Phil. 74 C3
Raqqa Syria see Ar Raqqah
Raquette r. U.S.A. 177 K2
Raquette Lake U.S.A. 177 K2
Rara National Park Nepal 97 D3
Raritan Bay U.S.A. 177 K5
Raroia atoll Fr. Polynesia 221 I7
  historically known as Barclay de Tolly
Rarotonga i. Cook Is 221 H7
  historically known as Armstrong Island or
  Roxburgh Island
Ras India 96 B4
Raša r. Croatia 56 G3
Rasa i. Phil. 74 A4
Rasa, Punta pt Arg. 204 E6
Ra's ad Daqm Oman 105 G4
Ra's al 'Ayn Syria 109 L1
Ra's al Hadd Oman 105 G3
Ras al Khaimah U.A.E. 105 F2
  Ra's al Khaymah
Ra's al Khaymah U.A.E. 105 F2
  English form Ras al Khaimah
Ra's al Mish'āb Saudi Arabia 105 E1
Ra's an Naqb Jordan 108 G7
Ra's ash Shaykh Humayd Saudi Arabia
  104 A1

▶ Ras Dashen mt. Eth. 128 C1
5th highest mountain in Africa.
africa [landscapes] ▶ 112–113

Raseiniai Lith. 42 E6
Ras el Ma Alg. 123 E2
  formerly known as Bedeau
Ra's el Mâ Mali 124 D2
Râs Ghârib Egypt 121 F2
Rashaant Bayan-Ölgiy Mongolia 84 A2
Rashaant Dundgovi Mongolia 85 E2
Rashad Sudan 128 A2
Rashid Egypt 121 F2
  historically known as Rosetta
Rashid reg. Saudi Arabia 105 F3
Rashshah Yemen 105 D5
Rasht Iran 100 B2
Rasina r. Yugo. 58 C5
Rasine r. Yugo. 58 C5
Rậsjö Sweden 44 K3
Rãsk Iran 101 E5
Raskam mts China 89 B4
Ras Koh mt. Pak. 101 F4
Raskoh mts Pak. 101 F4
Râs Muhammad National Park Egypt
  104 A2
Rasmussen Basin sea feature Canada
  165 J3
Rasna Belarus 43 M7
Rasna Belarus 43 K7
Râşnov Romania 58 G3
  formerly spelt Rîşnov
Raso i. Cape Verde 124 [inset]
Raso da Catarina hills Brazil 202 E4
Rason Lake salt flat Australia 151 C5
Rasony Belarus 43 J6
  also spelt Rossony
Rasova Romania 58 I4
Rasovo Bulg. 58 E5
Rasra India 97 E4
Ra's Sāq, Jabal hill Saudi Arabia 104 B2
Ra's Sharwayn c. Yemen 105 E5
Rasshua, Ostrov i. Rus. Fed. 81 Q3
Ra's Şirāb Oman 105 G3
Rass Jebel Tunisia 57 C11
Rasskazovo Rus. Fed. 41 G5
Rast Romania 58 E5
Rasta r. Belarus 43 L8
Ras Tannûrah Saudi Arabia 105 E2
Rastatt Germany 48 F7
Rastede Germany 48 F2
Råstojaure l. Sweden 44 M1
Rastkogel mt. Austria see Vidnoye
Ratamka Belarus 42 I8
Ratak Chain is Marshall Is 220 F5
Ratangarh Madhya Pradesh India 96 B4
Ratangarh Rajasthan India 96 B3
Ratanpur Chhattisgarh India 97 D5
Ratanpur Gujarat India 96 B5
Rätansbyn Jämtland Sweden 44 K3
Rat Buri Thai. 79 B5
Ratchino Rus. Fed. 102 C1
Rate-fontein S. Africa 132 C8
Rath India 96 C4
Rathbun Lake U.S.A. 174 A3
Rathdowney Myanmar 78 A3
Rathenow Germany 49 J3
Rathenower Wald- und Seengebiet park
  Germany 49 J3
Rathlin Island U.K. 47 I8
Rathluirc Rep. of Ireland 47 D11
  also known as Charleville
Ratibor Poland see Racibórz
Ratisbon Germany see Regensburg
Ratitovec mt. Slovenia 56 G2
Ratiya India 96 B3
Ratjäh, Wâdî watercourse Jordan 108 H4
Rat Lake Canada 167 L3
Ratlam India 96 B5
Ratnagiri India 94 B2
Ratnapura Sri Lanka 94 C5
Ratne Ukr. 41 K4
  also spelt Ratno
Ratno Ukr. see Ratne
Ratn Dero Pak. 101 G5
Raton U.S.A. 181 F5
Ratnagh, Wâdî ar watercourse Iraq 109 L4
Rattray Head U.K. 46 K6
Rättvik Sweden 45 K3
Ratz, Mount Canada 166 C3
Ratzeburg Germany 48 H2
Rau i. Indon. 75 C2
Raub Malaysia 76 C2
Rauch Arg. 204 F5
Rauðamýri Iceland 44 [inset]
Raudanjoki r. Fin. 44 N2
Rãu de Mori Romania 58 D3
Raudhatain Kuwait 107 F5
Raudondvaris Lith. 42 E7
Raufarhöfn Iceland 44 [inset] D1
Raukumara r. N.Z. 152 L6
Raukumara Forest Park nature res. N.Z.
  152 L5
Raukumara Range mts N.Z. 152 L6
Raul r. India 95 D1
Raul Soares Brazil 207 K7
Rauma Fin. 45 M3
Rauna Latvia 42 G4
Raurimu N.Z. 152 J7
Raurkela India 97 E5
Rauschen Rus. Fed. see Svetlogorsk
Rausu Japan 90 I2
Rausu-dake mt. Japan 90 I2
Rautalampi Fin. 44 N3

Rautavaara Fin. 44 O3
Rautjärvi Fin. 45 O3
Rauza India see Khuldabad
Ravalli U.S.A. 180 D3
Ravānsar Iran 100 A3
Ravanusa Sicilia Italy 57 F11
Rávar Iran 100 D4
Ravat Kyrg. 101 G2
Ravena U.S.A. 177 L3
Ravenna Italy 56 E4
Ravenna NE U.S.A. 178 C3
Ravenna OH U.S.A. 176 D4
Ravensburg Germany 48 G8
Ravenshoe Australia 149 E3
Ravensthorpe Australia 151 C7
Ravenswood Australia 149 E4
Ravenswood U.S.A. 176 D7
Raver India 96 C5
Ravi r. Pak. 101 G4
Ravna Gora Croatia 56 G3
Ravna Gora hill Croatia 56 J3
Ravnina Turkm. see Ravnina
  also spelt Rawnina
Ravshan Uzbek. 103 E5
Rawa Aopa Watumohe National Park
  Indon. 75 B4
Rãwah Iraq 107 E4
Rawai well Sudan 104 A4
Rawaki i. Kiribati 145 H2
  formerly known as Phoenix Island
Rawala Kot Pak. 101 H3
Rawalpindi Pak. 101 H3
Rawalpindi Lake Canada 167 H1
Rawa Mazowiecka Poland 49 R4
Rawāndiz Iraq 107 F3
Rawāndiz, Rūbâr-i r. Iraq 109 P1
Rawas r. Indon. 76 C3
Rawatsar India 96 B3
Rawdah Yemen 104 D5
Rawdah, Sabkhat ar salt flat Syria 109 M2
Rawghah watercourse Saudi Arabia 109 I9
Rawhide Lake Canada 173 K4
Rawi i. Thai. 79 B7
Rawicz Poland 49 N4
Rawka r. Poland 49 R4
Rawlinna Australia 151 D6
Rawlins U.S.A. 180 F4
Rawlinson, Mount hill Australia 151 D5
Rawlinson Range hills Australia 151 E5
Rawnina Turkm. see Ravnina
Rawson Arg. 205 D6
Rawson Mountains Antarctica 223 N1
Raxaul China 86 A2
Ray, Cape Canada 169 J4
Raya, Bukit mt. Kalimantan Indon. 77 E3
Raya, Bukit mt. Kalimantan Indon. 77 F3
Rayachoti India 94 C3
Rayadurg India 94 C3
Rayagarha India 95 D2
Rayak Lebanon 108 H4
Raychikhinsk Rus. Fed. 82 C2
Rayda Rus. Fed. 43 R3
Raydah Yemen 104 D5
Raydâr Iraq 109 P2
Râyen Iran 100 D4
Rayes Peak U.S.A. 182 E7
Rayevskiy Rus. Fed. 40 J5
Raymān i. Saudi Arabia 108 G9
Raymond Canada 167 H5
Raymond NH U.S.A. 177 N2
Raymond WA U.S.A. 180 B3
Raymond Terrace Australia 147 F3
Raymondville U.S.A. 179 C7
Raymore Canada 167 J5
Rayón India 97 E5
Rayner Glacier Antarctica 223 D2
Rayón Mex. 185 F4
Rayones Mex. 185 E3
Rayong Thai. 79 C5
Raystown Lake U.S.A. 176 G5
Raysût Oman 105 F4
Rayth al Khayl watercourse Saudi Arabia
  109 I9
Rayton S. Africa 133 M3
Rayville U.S.A. 175 B5
Rayyis Saudi Arabia 104 B3
Raz, Pointe du pt France 50 A4
Razam India 95 D2
Razan Iran 100 B3
Ražanj Srbija Yugo. 58 C5
Razăzah, Buhayrat ar l. Iraq 107 E4
  formerly known as Milḥ, Baḥr al
Razdan Armenia see Hrazdan
Razdel'naya Ukr. see Rozdil'na
Razdol'noye Rus. Fed. 82 C4
Razeh Iran 100 B3
Razgrad Bulg. 58 H5
Razhene Zangbo r. China 89 E6
Razim, Lacul lag. Romania 58 J4
Razlog Bulg. 58 E7
Raz"yezd 3km Rus. Fed. see Novyy Urgal
R. D. Bailey Lake U.S.A. 176 D8
Ré, Île de i. France 50 D6
Reading U.K. 47 L12
Reading MI U.S.A. 173 I9
Reading OH U.S.A. 176 A6
Reading PA U.S.A. 177 J5
Readsboro U.S.A. 177 M3
Readstown U.S.A. 172 C7
Reagile S. Africa 133 K2
Real r. Brazil 202 E4
Real Spain 54 F4
Reales mt. Spain 54 F8
Realicó Arg. 204 D4
Réalmont France 51 I9
Reăng Kesei Cambodia 79 C5
Reata Mex. 185 E3
Reate Italy see Rieti
Rebaa Alg. 123 H3
Rebbenesøy i. Norway 44 L1
Rebecca, Lake salt flat Australia 151 C6
Rebiana Sand Sea des. Libya 120 D3
  also known as Ramlat Rabyânah
Rebollera mt. Spain 54 G6
Reboly Rus. Fed. 44 P3
Rebrebti Dhubo well Eth. 128 E3
Rebrikha Rus. Fed. 103 J1
Rebun-tô i. Japan 90 G2
Recanati Italy 56 F5
Recea Romania 58 I3
Recco Italy 56 B4
Rechane Rus. Fed. 43 M5
Recherche, Archipelago of the is Australia
  151 C7
Recherche Archipelago Nature Reserve
  Australia 151 C7
Rechitsa Belarus see Rechytsa
Rechna Doab lowland Pak. 101 H4
Rechytsa Belarus 43 L9
Recife Brazil 202 F4
  formerly known as Pernambuco
Recife, Cape S. Africa 133 J11
Recinto Chile 204 C5
Recklinghausen Germany 48 E4
Recknitz r. Germany 49 J2
Reconquista Arg. 204 F3
Recovery Glacier Antarctica 223 V1
Recreio Mato Grosso Brazil 201 F2
Recreio Minas Gerais Brazil 207 K8
Recreo Arg. 204 D3
Rectortville U.S.A. 176 D7
Recz Poland 49 M2
Red r. Australia 149 D3
Red r. Canada/U.S.A. 167 L5
Red, North Fork r. U.S.A. 179 C5
Redang i. Malaysia 76 C1

Red Bank NJ U.S.A. 177 K5
Red Bank TN U.S.A. 174 C5
Red Basin China see Sichuan Pendi
Red Bay Canada 169 J3
Redberry Lake Canada 167 J4
Red Bluff hill Australia 151 B5
Red Bluff U.S.A. 182 B1
Red Bluff Lake U.S.A. 179 B6
Red Butte mt. U.S.A. 183 L6
Redcar U.K. 47 K9
Redcliff Canada 167 I5
Red Cliff U.S.A. 172 C4
Redcliff Zimbabwe 131 F3
Redcliffe, Mount hill Australia 151 C6
Red Cliffs Australia 147 D3
Red Cloud U.S.A. 178 C3
Red Deer Canada 167 H4
Red Deer r. Alta/Sask. Canada 167 I5
Red Deer r. Man./Sask. Canada 167 K4
Red Deer Lake Canada 167 K4
Reddersburg S. Africa 133 K6
Redding U.S.A. 182 B1
Redditch U.K. 47 K11
Red Earth Creek Canada 167 H3
Redelinghuys S. Africa 132 C9
Redenção Pará Brazil 202 B3
Redenção Piauí Brazil 202 C4
Redeyef Tunisia 123 H2
Redfield U.S.A. 178 C2
Red Granite Mountain Canada 166 B2
Redhill Australia 146 C3
Red Hills U.S.A. 178 C4
Red Hook U.S.A. 177 L4
Red Idol Gorge China 89 E6
Red Indian Lake Canada 169 J3
Redkino Rus. Fed. 43 R5
Redknife r. Canada 166 G2
Red Lake Canada 167 M5
Red Lake l. Canada 167 M5
Red Lake U.S.A. 183 L6
Red Lake r. U.S.A. 178 C2
Red Lake Falls U.S.A. 178 C2
Red Lake Indian Reservation res. U.S.A. 178 D1
Red Lakes U.S.A. 178 D1
Redlands U.S.A. 183 G7
Red Lion NJ U.S.A. 177 K6
Red Lion PA U.S.A. 177 I6
Red Lodge U.S.A. 180 E3
Red Mercury Island N.Z. 152 J4
Redmond OR U.S.A. 180 B3
Redmond UT U.S.A. 183 M2
Red Oak U.S.A. 178 D3
Redojari waterhole Kenya 128 C5
Redon France 50 D5
Redonda i. Antigua and Barbuda 187 H3
Redondela Spain 54 C2
Redondo Port. 54 D6
Redondo Beach U.S.A. 182 F8
Red Peak U.S.A. 180 D3
Red River r. Vietnam 78 D3
also known as Hồng, Sông or Nui Con Voi
Red Rock Canada 168 B3
Red Rock AZ U.S.A. 183 M9
Red Rock PA U.S.A. 177 I4
Red Rock r. U.S.A. 180 D3
Red Sea Africa/Asia 104 A2
Red Sea state Sudan 121 G5
Redstone Canada 166 F4
Redstone r. N.W.T. Canada 166 E1
Redstone r. Ont. Canada 173 L2
Red Volta r. Burkina/Ghana 125 E4
also known as Nazinon (Burkina)
Redwater r. U.S.A. 180 F2
Redway U.S.A. 182 A1
Red Willow Creek r. U.S.A. 178 B3
Red Wine r. Canada 169 J2
Red Wing U.S.A. 174 A2
Redwood City U.S.A. 182 B4
Redwood Falls U.S.A. 178 D2
Redwood National Park U.S.A. 180 A4
Redwood Valley U.S.A. 182 A2
Ree, Lough l. Rep. of Ireland 47 E10
Reed City U.S.A. 172 H7
Reed Lake Canada 167 K4
Reedley U.S.A. 182 E5
Reedsburg U.S.A. 172 D7
Reedsport U.S.A. 180 A4
Reedsville OH U.S.A. 176 D6
Reedsville PA U.S.A. 176 H5
Reedville U.S.A. 177 I8
Reedy U.S.A. 176 D7
Reedy Creek watercourse Australia 149 E4
Reedy Glacier Antarctica 223 P1
Reefton N.Z. 153 F10
Reese U.S.A. 173 J7
Reese r. U.S.A. 183 H1
Refahiye Turkey 107 D3
Reform U.S.A. 175 B5
Reforma Mex. 185 G5
Refugio U.S.A. 179 C6
Rega r. Poland 49 M1
Regen Germany 49 K7
Regência Brazil 207 N6
Regensburg Germany 48 J6
historically known as Castra Regina or Ratisbon
Regenstauf Germany 51 S3
Regente Feijó Brazil 206 B9
Reggane Alg. 123 F4
Reggio Italy see Reggio di Calabria
Reggio Italy see Reggio nell'Emilia
Reggio di Calabria Italy 57 H10
historically known as Rhegium; short form Reggio
Reggio Emilia Italy see Reggio nell'Emilia
Reggio nell'Emilia Italy 56 C4
also known as Reggio Emilia; historically known as Regium Lepidum; short form Reggio
Reghin Romania 58 F2
Regi Afgh. 101 F3

▶Regina Canada 167 J5
Provincial capital of Saskatchewan.

Régina Fr. Guiana 199 H3
Registan reg. Afgh. 101 F4
Registro Brazil 206 F11
Registro do Araguaia Brazil 206 B2
Regium Lepidum Italy see Reggio nell'Emilia
Regozero Rus. Fed. 44 O2
Rehli India 96 C5
Rehoboth Namibia 130 C4
Rehoboth Bay U.S.A. 177 J7
Rehoboth Beach U.S.A. 177 J7
Rehovot Israel 108 F6
Reïbell Alg. see Ksar Chellala
Reichenbach Germany 49 J5
Reichshoffen France 51 N4
Reid Australia 151 E6
Reidsville GA U.S.A. 175 D5
Reidsville NC U.S.A. 176 F9
Reigate U.K. 47 L12
Reiley Peak U.S.A. 183 N9
Reims France 51 K3
English form Rheims; historically known as Durocortorum or Remi
Reinach Switz. 51 N5
Reinbek Germany 48 H2
Reindeer r. Canada 167 K4
Reindeer Island Canada 167 L4
Reindeer Lake Canada 167 K3
Reine Norway 44 K2
Reinersville U.S.A. 176 D6
Reineskarvet mt. Norway 45 J3
Reinga, Cape N.Z. 152 G2
Reinosa Spain 54 G2
Reinsfeld Germany 48 D6
Reipholsfjöll hill Iceland 44 [inset] B2
Reisa Nasjonalpark nat. park Norway 44 M1
Reisjärvi Fin. 44 N3
Reisterstown U.S.A. 177 I6
Reitz S. Africa 133 M4
Reitzburg S. Africa 133 L4
Reiu r. Estonia 42 F3
Reivilo S. Africa 132 I4
Rejowiec Fabryczny Poland 49 U4
Rekapalle India 94 D2
Rekohua i. S. Pacific Ocean see Chatham Island
Rekovac Srbija Yugo. 58 C5
Rėkyvos ežeras l. Lith. 42 E6
Reliance Canada 167 I2
Relizane Alg. 123 F2
Rellano Mex. 184 D3
Relli India 95 D2
Remada Tunisia 123 H2
Remarkable, Mount hill Australia 146 C3
Rembang Indon. 77 E4
Remedios Cuba 186 D2
Remedios, Punta pt El Salvador 185 H6
Remel el Abiod des. Tunisia 123 H3
Remennikovo Rus. Fed. 43 J5
Remeshk Iran 100 D5
Remeskylä Fin. 44 N3
Remi France see Reims
Remington U.S.A. 176 H7
Rémire Fr. Guiana 199 H3
Remiremont France 51 M4
Remmel Mountain U.S.A. 180 B2
Remo Glacier Jammu and Kashmir 96 C2
Remontnoye Rus. Fed. 41 G7
Rempang i. Indon. 76 D2
Remscheid Germany 48 E4
Remus U.S.A. 173 H7
Rena Norway 45 J3
Rena r. Norway 45 J3
Renabie Canada 173 J2
Renaix Belgium see Ronse
Renapur India 94 C2
Renard Islands P.N.G. 149 G1
Rende China see Xundian
Rende Italy 57 I9
Rend Lake U.S.A. 174 B4
Rendsburg Germany 48 G1
Renedo Spain 54 H1
René-Levasseur, Île i. Canada 169 G3
Renens Switz. 51 M6
Renews Canada 169 K4
Renfrew Canada 168 E4
Rengat Indon. 76 C3
Rengo Chile 204 C4
Ren He r. China 87 D1
Renheji China 87 E2
Renhou China see Tangxian
Renhua China 87 E3
Renhuai China 86 C3
Reni Ukr. 41 D7
Renick U.S.A. 176 E8
Renigunta India 94 C3
Renko Fin. 42 F1
Renland reg. Greenland see Tuttut Nunaat
Renmark Australia 146 D3
Rennell i. Solomon Is 145 F3
also known as Mu Nggava
Rennell, Islas is Chile 205 B8
Rennerod Germany 48 F5
Renner Springs Australia 148 B3
Rennes France 50 E4
Rennes, Bassin de basin France 50 E4
Rennick Glacier Antarctica 223 K2
Rennie Canada 167 M5
Reno r. Italy 56 E4
Reno MN U.S.A. 172 B7
Reno NV U.S.A. 182 E2
Renoster r. S. Africa 133 K3
Renoster watercourse S. Africa 132 E8
Renosterkop S. Africa 132 G9
Renovo U.S.A. 176 H4
Renqiu China 85 H4
Renshou China 86 C2
also known as Wenlin
Rensselaer IN U.S.A. 174 C3
Rensselaer NY U.S.A. 177 L3
Rentjärn Sweden 44 L2
Renton U.S.A. 180 B3
Renukut India 97 D4
Renwick N.Z. 152 H9
Renya r. Rus. Fed. 43 S3
Réo Burkina 124 E3
Reo Indon. 75 B5
Repartimento Brazil 199 G5
Repembe r. Moz. 131 G4
Repetek Turkm. 103 E5
Repetekskiy Zapovednik nature res. Turkm. 103 E5
Repino Rus. Fed. 43 N6
Repokaira reg. Fin. 44 N1
Repolka Rus. Fed. 43 K2
Reporoa N.Z. 152 K6
Reposaari Fin. 45 M3
Republic OH U.S.A. 176 B4
Republic WA U.S.A. 180 C2
Republican r. U.S.A. 178 C4
Republican, South Fork r. U.S.A. 178 B3
Republika Srpska aut. div. Bos.-Herz. 56 J4
Repulse Bay b. Australia 149 F4
Repulse Bay Canada 165 K3
Repvåg Norway 44 N1
Requena Peru 198 C6
Requena Spain 55 J5
Requista France 51 I8
Reriutaba Brazil 202 D3
Reşadiye Turkey 107 E3
also known as Sorp
Reşadiye Turkey 107 D2
Reşadiye Yarımadası pen. Turkey 59 I12
Resag, Gunung mt. Indon. 76 D4
Resava r. Yugo. 58 C4
Resavica Srbija Yugo. 58 C4
Resen Macedonia 58 C7
Resende Brazil 207 I9
Reserva Brazil 203 B8
Reserve U.S.A. 181 E6
Reshetnikovo Rus. Fed. 43 R5
Reshi China 87 D2
Resia, Passo di pass Austria/Italy 48 H9
Resistencia Arg. 204 F2
Reșita Romania 58 C3
Resko Poland 49 M2
Resolute Bay Canada 165 J2
Resolution Island Canada 165 M3
Resolution Island N.Z. 153 A13
Resplendor Brazil 207 L6
Ressa r. Rus. Fed. 43 Q7
Ressango Garcia S. Africa 133 P2
Resseta r. Rus. Fed. 43 Q8
Restefond, Col de pass France 51 M8
Restelica Kosovo, Srbija Yugo. 58 B7
Restinga de Marambaia coastal area Brazil 207 I10
Restinga Seca Brazil 203 A9
Restrepo Col. 198 C3
Resülayn Turkey see Ceylanpınar
Retalhuleu Guat. 185 H6
Retem, Oued er watercourse Alg. 123 G2
Retén Llico Chile 204 B4
Retezat, Parcul Național nat. park Romania 58 D3
Retford U.K. 47 L10
also known as East Retford
Rethel France 51 K3
Réthimnon Greece see Rethymno
Rethymno Greece 59 F13
also known as Réthimnon
Retiers France 50 E5
Retortillo tourist site Spain 54 G2
Rettikhovka Rus. Fed. 90 C2
Retuerta mt. Spain 55 J4

▶Réunion terr. Indian Ocean 218 K7
French Overseas Department. Historically known as Bourbon.
africa [countries] 114–117

Reus Spain 55 M3
Reusam, Pulau i. Indon. 76 B2
Reutlingen Germany 48 G7
Reutov Rus. Fed. 43 S6
Reval Estonia see Tallinn
Revda Rus. Fed. 44 P2
Reveille Peak U.S.A. 183 H4
Revel Estonia see Tallinn
Revel France 51 I9
Revelganj India 97 E4
Revelstoke Canada 166 G5
Reventazón Peru 198 A6
Revermont reg. France 51 L7
Reviga Romania 58 I4
Reviga r. Romania 58 I4
Revigny-sur-Ornain France 51 K4
Revillagigedo, Islas is Mex. 184 B5
Revillagigedo Island U.S.A. 164 F4
Revna r. Rus. Fed. 43 P9
Revolyutsii, Pik mt. Tajik. see Revolyutsiya, Qullai
Revolyutsiya, Qullai mt. Tajik. 101 H2
also known as Revolyutsii, Pik
Revsnes Norway 44 L1
Revúca Slovakia 49 R7
Revuè r. Moz. 131 G3
Revyakino Rus. Fed. 43 S7
Rewa India 97 D4
Rewari India 96 C3
Rex, Mount Antarctica 222 S2
Rexburg U.S.A. 180 E4
Rexton Canada 169 H4
Rey, Isla del i. Panama 186 D5
Reyes Bol. 200 D3
Reyes, Point U.S.A. 182 A3
Reyes, Punta pt Col. 198 B4
Reyhanlı Turkey 109 H1
Reykir Iceland 44 [inset] B2
Reykjanes constituency Iceland 44 [inset] B3
Reykjanestá pt Iceland 44 [inset] B3

▶Reykjavík Iceland 44 [inset] B2
Capital of Iceland. English form Reykjavik.

Reykjavik Iceland see Reykjavík
Reynolds Range mts Australia 148 B4
Reynosa Mex. 185 F3
Reyssouze r. France 51 K6
Rezā, Kūh-e hill Iran 100 B3
Rezā'īyeh Iran see Urmia
Rezā'īyeh, Daryācheh-ye salt l. Iran see Urmia, Lake
Rēzekne Latvia 42 I5
Rēzekne r. Latvia 42 I5
Rezinjski vrh mt. Slovenia 56 G3
Rezovska Reka r. Bulg./Turkey 58 J7
Rezvāndeh Iran see Rezvānshahr
Rezvānshahr Iran 100 B2
formerly known as Rezvāndeh
R. F. Magón Mex. see Ricardo Flores Magón
Rgotina Srbija Yugo. 58 D4
Rharbi, Oued el watercourse Alg. 123 F3
Rhegium Italy see Reggio di Calabria
Rheims France see Reims
Rhein r. Germany 48 D4 see Rhine
Rheine Germany 48 E3
Rheinland-Pfalz land Germany 48 E6
English form Rhineland-Palatinate
Rheinsberg Germany 49 J2
Rhein-Taunus, Naturpark nature res. Germany 48 F5
Rheinwaldhorn mt. Switz. 51 P6
Rhemilès well Alg. 122 D3
Rheris, Oued watercourse Morocco 122 D3
Rhin r. France 51 N4 see Rhine
Rhine r. Europe 48 D4
also spelt Rhein (Germany) or Rhin (France)
Rhinebeck U.S.A. 177 L4
Rhinelander U.S.A. 172 D5
Rhineland-Palatinate land Germany see Rheinland-Pfalz
Rhinluch marsh Germany 49 J3
Rhino Camp Uganda 128 A4
Rhinow Germany 49 J3
Rhir, Cap c. Morocco 122 C3
Rho Italy 56 B3
Rhode Island state U.S.A. 177 N4
Rhodes Greece 59 J12
also spelt Rodos
Rhodes i. Greece 59 J12
also spelt Rodos or Ródhos; formerly known as Rodi; historically known as Rhodus
Rhodesia country Africa see Zimbabwe
Rhodes Inyanga National Park Zimbabwe see Nyanga National Park
Rhodes Matopos National Park Zimbabwe see Matobo National Park
Rhodes Peak U.S.A. 180 D3
Rhodope Mountains mts Bulg. 58 E7
Rhodope Mountains Bulg./Greece 58 E7
also known as Rodopi Planina
Rhodus i. Greece see Rhodes
Rhône r. France/Switz. 51 K9
Rhône-Alpes admin. reg. France 51 L7
Rhube, Oasis of Syria see Ruhbah
Rhuthun U.K. see Ruthin
Rhyl U.K. 47 I10
Riaba Equat. Guinea 125 H6
Riachão Brazil 202 C3
Riachão das Neves Brazil 202 C4
Riacho de Santana Brazil 202 D5
Riacho dos Machados Brazil 207 J2
Ri'al Fuhah hill Saudi Arabia 108 H9
Rialma Brazil 206 D2
Rialp, Pantà de resr Spain 55 M3
Rialto U.S.A. 183 G7
Riangnom Sudan 126 F2
Riaño, Embalse de resr Spain 54 F2
Rianópolis Brazil 206 D2
Riansáres r. Spain 55 H5
Riasi Jammu and Kashmir 96 B2
Riau prov. Indon. 76 C2
Riau, Kepulauan is Indon. 76 D2
Riaza r. Spain 55 H3
Ribadavia Spain 54 C2
Ribadeo Spain 54 D1
Ribadesella Spain 54 F1
Ribas de Fresser Spain see Ribes de Freser
Ribas do Rio Pardo Brazil 203 A7
Ribat Afgh. 101 G2
Ribat-i-Shur waterhole Iran 100 D3
Ribáuè Moz. 131 H2
Ribble r. U.K. 47 J10
Ribe Denmark 45 J5
Ribeira Branco Brazil 206 E11
Ribeirão das Neves Brazil 207 I6
Ribeirão do Pinhal Brazil 206 C10
Ribeirão Preto Brazil 206 F8
Ribeiro Gonçalves Brazil 202 C4
Ribera Sicilia Italy 57 F11
Ribérac France 50 G7
Riberalta Bol. 200 D2
Ribes de Freser Spain 55 N2
also spelt Ribas de Fresser
Ribnica Slovenia 56 G3
Rîbnița Moldova 41 D7
formerly spelt Râbnita or Rybnitsa
Ribnitz-Damgarten Germany 49 J1
Ribnovo Bulg. 58 E7
Rica Aventura Chile 200 C5
Říčany Czech Rep. 49 L6
Ricardo Flores Magón Mex. 184 D2
short form R. Magón
Riccione Italy 56 E5
Rice CA U.S.A. 183 J7
Rice VA U.S.A. 176 G8
Rice Lake l. Ont. Canada 168 E4
Rice Lake l. Ont. Canada 173 K3
Rice Lake U.S.A. 172 B5
Riceville U.S.A. 176 C8
Richards Bay S. Africa 133 Q5
Richards Inlet Antarctica 223 L1
Richards Island Canada 164 F3
Richardson r. Canada 167 I3
Richardson Island Canada 167 G1
Richardson Lakes U.S.A. 177 O1
Richardson Mountains Canada 164 F3
Richardson Mountains N.Z. 153 C12
Richard Toll Senegal 124 B2
Richelieu France 50 G5
Richfield U.S.A. 183 L3
Richfield Springs U.S.A. 177 K3
Richford NY U.S.A. 177 I3
Richford VT U.S.A. 177 M1
Richgrove U.S.A. 182 E6
Richibucto Canada 169 H4
Rich Lake Canada 167 I4
Richland U.S.A. 180 C3
Richland Center U.S.A. 172 C7
Richlands U.S.A. 176 D8
Richmond N.S.W. Australia 147 F3
Richmond Qld Australia 149 D4
Richmond Ont. Canada 173 R5
Richmond Que. Canada 169 F4
Richmond N.Z. 152 H9
Richmond Kwazulu-Natal S. Africa 133 O6
Richmond N. Cape S. Africa 132 H8
Richmond U.K. 47 K9
Richmond CA U.S.A. 182 B4
Richmond IL U.S.A. 172 E8
Richmond IN U.S.A. 176 A6
Richmond KY U.S.A. 176 A8
Richmond ME U.S.A. 177 P1
Richmond MI U.S.A. 173 K8
Richmond TX U.S.A. 179 D6

▶Richmond VA U.S.A. 176 H8
State capital of Virginia.

Richmond VT U.S.A. 177 M1
Richmond, Mount N.Z. 152 H9
Richmond Dale U.S.A. 176 C6
Richmond Hill Canada 168 E5
Richmond Hill U.S.A. 175 D6
Richmond Range hills Australia 147 G2
Richmond Range mts N.Z. 152 H9
Richmondville U.S.A. 177 K3
Rich Square U.S.A. 177 H9
Richtersveld National Park S. Africa 132 B5
Richvale U.S.A. 182 C2
Richwood OH U.S.A. 176 B5
Richwood WV U.S.A. 176 E7
Ricklеån r. Sweden 44 M2
Ricobayo, Embalse de resr Spain 54 F3
also known as Esla, Embalse de
Ricomagus France see Riom
Riddell Nunataks Antarctica 223 E2
Ridder Kazakh. see Leninogorsk
Riddlesburg U.S.A. 176 G5
Rideau r. Canada 173 R5
Rideau Lakes Canada 168 E4
Ridge r. Canada 168 C3
Ridgecrest U.S.A. 182 G6
Ridgefield U.S.A. 177 L4
Ridgeland MS U.S.A. 175 B5
Ridgeland SC U.S.A. 175 D5
Ridgeland WI U.S.A. 172 B5
Ridgetown Canada 173 L8
Ridgeway U.S.A. 176 F9
Ridgway U.S.A. 176 G4
Riding Mountain National Park Canada 167 K5
Ridley r. Australia 150 B4
Riebeek-Kasteel S. Africa 132 C10
Riebeek-Oos S. Africa 133 K10
Riebeek Wes S. Africa 132 C10
Riecito Venez. 198 D2
Ried im Innkreis Austria 49 K7
Riedlingen Germany 48 G7
Riekertsdam S. Africa 133 K2
Rieppesgai'sa mt. Norway 44 M1
Riesa Germany 49 K4
Riesco, Isla i. Chile 205 B9
Riesi Sicilia Italy 57 G11
Riestedt Germany 48 I4
Riet r. S. Africa 133 H6
Riet watercourse S. Africa 132 E8
Rietavas Lith. 42 C6
Rietberg Germany 48 F4
Rietbron S. Africa 132 H9
Rietfontein S. Africa 132 E3
Riethuiskraal S. Africa 132 F11
Rieti Italy 56 E6
historically known as Reate
Rietpoort S. Africa 132 C7
Rietschen Germany 49 L4
Riet se Vloer salt pan S. Africa 132 E7
Rietvlei S. Africa 133 O6
Rieumes France 50 H9
Rifā'ī, Tall mt. Jordan/Syria 109 H5
Rifaina Brazil 206 F7
Rifeng China see Lichuan
Rifle U.S.A. 180 F5
Rift Valley prov. Kenya 128 B4
Rift Valley Lakes National Park Eth. see Abijatta-Shalla National Park

▶Rīga Latvia 42 F5
Capital of Latvia. English form Riga.

Riga Latvia see Rīga
Riga, Gulf of Estonia/Latvia 42 E4
also known as Liivi laht or Rīgas jūras līcis or Riia laht
Rigacikun Nigeria 125 G4
Rigaio Greece 59 D9
Rīgān Iran 100 D4
Rīgas jūras līcis b. Estonia/Latvia see Riga, Gulf of
Rigby U.S.A. 180 E4
Rig-Rig Chad 120 B6
Riguel r. Spain 55 J2
Riia laht b. Estonia/Latvia see Riga, Gulf of
Riihimäki Fin. 45 N3
Riiser-Larsen Ice Shelf Antarctica 223 W2
Riisipere Estonia 42 F2
Riisitunturin kansallispuisto nat. park Fin. 44 O2
Rijau Mex. 184 B1
Rijau Nigeria 125 G4
Riječki Zaliv b. Croatia 56 G3
Rijeka Croatia 56 G3
formerly known as Fiume
Rijm al Mudhari hill Iraq 109 K5
Rikā, Wādī ar watercourse Saudi Arabia 104 D3
Rikubetsu Japan 90 H3
Rikuchū-kaigan National Park Japan 90 H5
Rikuzen-takata Japan 90 G5
Rila Bulg. 58 E6
Rila mts Bulg. 58 E6
Rila China 89 D6
Riley U.S.A. 180 C4
Rileyville U.S.A. 176 G7
Rillieux-la-Pape France 51 K7
Rillito U.S.A. 183 M9
Rima watercourse Niger/Nigeria 125 G3
Rimah, Wādī al watercourse Saudi Arabia 104 C2
Rimau, Pulau i. Indon. 76 D3
Rimava r. Slovakia 49 R7
Rimavská Sobota Slovakia 49 R7
Rimbey Canada 167 H4
Rimbo Sweden 45 L4
Rimersburg U.S.A. 176 F4
Rimetea Romania 58 E2
Rimforsa Sweden 45 K4
Rimini Italy 56 E4
historically known as Ariminum
Râmnicu Sărat Romania see Râmnicu Sărat
Râmnicu Vâlcea Romania see Râmnicu Vâlcea
Rimouski Canada 169 G3
Rimouski, Réserve Faunique de nature res. Canada 169 G3
Rimutaka Forest Park nature res. N.Z. 152 J9
Rinbung China 89 E6
also known as Deji
Rinca i. Indon. 75 A5
Rincão Brazil 206 E8
Rincon Morocco see Mdiq
Rincón, Cerro del mt. Chile 200 D6
Rinconada Arg. 200 D5
Rincón del Bonete, Lago Artificial de resr Uruguay 204 F4
Rincón de los Sauces Arg. 204 C5
Rincón de Romos Mex. 185 E4
Rind r. India 96 D4
Rinda r. Latvia 42 C4
Rindal Norway 44 J3
Rineia i. Greece 59 G11
also spelt Rinía
Riner U.S.A. 176 E8
Ringarooma Bay Australia 147 E5
Ringas India 96 B4
Ringe Denmark 45 J5
Ringebu Norway 45 J3
Ringgold U.S.A. 176 C5
Ringim Nigeria 125 H3
Ringkøbing Denmark 45 J4
Ringkøbing Fjord lag. Denmark 45 J5
Ringsted Denmark 45 J5
Ringvassøy i. Norway 44 L1
Ringwood U.K. 47 K13
Ringwood U.S.A. 177 K4
Rinía i. Greece see Rineia
Rinópolis Brazil 206 C8
Rinteln Germany 48 G3
Rinya r. Romania 49 O9
Rio WI U.S.A. 172 D7
Rio Alegre Brazil 201 F4
Riobamba Ecuador 198 B5
Rio Bananal Brazil 207 M6
Rio Blanco U.S.A. 180 F5
Rio Bonito Brazil 207 K9
Rio Branco Brazil 200 D2
Rio Branco state Brazil see Roraima
Rio Branco, Parque Nacional do nat. park Brazil 199 F4
Río Bravo, Parque Internacional del nat. park Mex. 185 E2
Rio Brilhante Brazil 203 A7
Río Bueno Chile 204 B6
Río Caribe Venez. 199 F2
Rio Casca Brazil 203 D7
Río Chico Arg. 205 C8
Río Chico Venez. 199 E2
Rio Claro Rio de Janeiro Brazil 207 I9
Rio Claro São Paulo Brazil 206 F9
Rio Claro Trin. and Tob. 187 H5
Río Claro Venez. 187 F5
Río Colorado Arg. 204 D5
Río Corrientes Ecuador 198 B5
Río Cuarto Arg. 204 D4
Rio das Almas r. Brazil 201 H3
Rio das Pedras Moz. 131 G4

▶Rio de Janeiro Brazil 203 D7
3rd most populous city in South America. Former capital of Brazil.
world [cities] 24–25

Rio de Janeiro state Brazil 203 D7
Río de Jesús Panama 186 C6

▶Río de la Plata - Paraná r. S. America 204 F4
2nd longest river in South America and 9th in the world.
southamerica [landscapes] 190–191

Rio Dell U.S.A. 180 A4
Rio do Sul Brazil 203 B8
Rio Formoso Brazil 202 F4
Río Frío Costa Rica 186 C5
Río Gallegos Arg. 205 C8
Rio Grande Arg. 205 D9
Rio Grande Bol. 200 D5
Rio Grande Brazil 204 G4
Rio Grande Mex. 185 E4
Rio Grande r. Mex./U.S.A. 185 F3
also known as Bravo del Norte, Río
Río Grande, Salar de salt flat Arg. 204 C2
Rio Grande City U.S.A. 179 C7
Rio Grande do Norte state Brazil 202 E3
Rio Grande do Sul state Brazil 203 A9
Riohacha Col. 198 C2
Río Hato Panama 186 C5
Río Hondo, Embalse resr Arg. 204 D2
Rioja Peru 198 B6
Río Lagartos Mex. 185 H4
Rio Largo Brazil 202 F4
Riom France 51 J7
historically known as Ricomagus
Rio Maior Port. 54 C5
Riom-ès-Montagnes France 51 I7
Río Muerto Arg. 204 E2
Río Mulatos Bol. 200 D4
Río Muni reg. Equat. Guinea 125 H6
Río Negro prov. Arg. 204 D5
Rio Negro Brazil 203 B8
Río Negro Chile 204 B6
Rionero in Vulture Italy 56 H8
Rioni r. Georgia 107 E2
Rio Novo Brazil 207 J8
Rio Novo do Sul Brazil 207 M7
Rio Pardo de Minas Brazil 202 D5
Río Plátano, Reserva Biósfera del nature res. Hond. 186 B4
Rio Pomba Brazil 207 J8
Rio Preto Brazil 207 J9
Rio Preto, Serra do hills Brazil 206 G3
Rio Rancho U.S.A. 181 F6
Ríos Spain 54 D3
Riosucio Col. 198 B3
Río Tercero Arg. 204 D4
Río Tigre Ecuador 198 B5
Rio Tinto Brazil 202 F3
Río Tuba Phil. 74 A4
Riou, Oued watercourse Alg. 55 L9
Riou Lake Canada 167 J3
Rio Verde Brazil 206 C4
Río Verde Chile 205 C9
Rioverde Ecuador 198 B4
Río Verde Quintana Roo Mex. 185 H5
Río Verde San Luis Potosí Mex. 185 F4
Rio Verde de Mato Grosso Brazil 203 A6
Rio Vermelho Brazil 207 J5
Rio Vista U.S.A. 182 C3
Riozinho Brazil 200 D2
Riozinho r. Amazonas Brazil 199 E5
Riozinho r. Mato Grosso do Sul Brazil 201 F4
Ripanj Srbija Yugo. 58 B4
Ripats Sweden 44 M2
Ripky Ukr. 41 D6
Ripley MS U.S.A. 174 B5
Ripley NY U.S.A. 176 F3
Ripley OH U.S.A. 176 B7
Ripley TN U.S.A. 174 B5
Ripley WV U.S.A. 176 D7
Ripoll Spain 55 N2
Ripon U.K. 47 K9
Ripon CA U.S.A. 182 C4
Ripon WI U.S.A. 172 E7
Riposto Sicilia Italy 57 H11
Risalpur Pak. 101 H3
Risân 'Aneiza hill Egypt 108 E7
Risaralda dept Col. 198 C3
Risasi Dem. Rep. Congo 126 E5
Risbäck Sweden 44 K2
Riscle France 50 F9
Risco Plateado mt. Arg. 204 C4
Risha, Birket Umm salt l. Egypt 108 B7
Rishā', Wādī ar watercourse Saudi Arabia 104 D2
Rishikesh India 96 C3
Rishiri-Rebun-Sarobetsu National Park Japan 90 G2
Rishiri-tō i. Japan 90 G2
Rishiri-zan vol. Japan 82 F3
Rishon Le Ziyyon Israel 108 F6
Rising Sun IN U.S.A. 176 A7
Rising Sun MD U.S.A. 177 I6
Risle r. France 50 G3
Risnjak nat. park Croatia 56 G3
Rîşnov Romania see Râșnov
Rison U.S.A. 179 D5
Risør Norway 45 J4
Rissa Norway 44 J3
Rissington N.Z. 152 K7
Rissu, Gebel hill Egypt 108 B8
Ristiina Fin. 45 N3
Ristijärvi Fin. 44 O2
Ristikent Rus. Fed. 44 O1
Risum China 89 B5
Ritan r. Indon. 77 F2
Ritausma Latvia 42 F5
Ritchie S. Africa 133 I6
Ritchie's Archipelago is India 95 G3
Ritch Island Canada 167 G1
Ritscher Upland mts Antarctica 223 X2
Ritsem Sweden 44 L2
Ritsis Nakrdzali nature res. Georgia 107 E2
Ritter, Mount U.S.A. 182 E4
Rītupe r. Latvia 42 I5
Ritzville U.S.A. 180 C3
Riu, Mount hill P.N.G. 149 G1
Rīva r. Latvia 42 C5
Rivadavia Buenos Aires Arg. 204 E4
Rivadavia Mendoza Arg. 204 C4
Rivadavia Salta Arg. 201 E6
Rivadavia Chile 204 C3
Riva del Garda Italy 56 C3
Riva Palacio Mex. 181 F7
Rivarolo Canavese Italy 51 N7
Rivas Nicaragua 186 B5
Rivash Iran 100 D3
Rive-de-Gier France 51 K7
Rivera Arg. 204 E5
Rivera Uruguay 204 G3
River Cess Liberia 124 C5
Riverdale U.S.A. 182 E5
Riverhead U.S.A. 177 M5
Riverina Australia 151 C6
Riverina reg. Australia 147 E3
Rivero, Isla i. Chile 205 B7
Rivers state Nigeria 125 G5
Riversdale N.Z. 153 C13
Riversdale S. Africa 132 F11
Riversdale Beach N.Z. 152 K9
Riverside S. Africa 133 N7
Riverside CA U.S.A. 182 G8
Riverside IA U.S.A. 172 B9
Riversleigh Australia 148 C3
Riverton Canada 167 L5
Riverton N.Z. 153 C14
also known as Aparima
Riverton S. Africa 133 I5
Riverton UT U.S.A. 183 M1
Riverton VA U.S.A. 176 G7
Riverton WY U.S.A. 180 E4
Riverview Canada 169 H4
River View S. Africa 133 Q5
Rives France 51 L7
Rivesaltes France 51 I10
Rivesville U.S.A. 176 E6
Rivière-au-Renard Canada 169 H3
Rivière Bleue Canada 169 G4
Rivière-du-Loup Canada 169 G4
Rivière-Pentecote Canada 169 H3
Rivière-Pigou Canada 169 H3
Rivière-Pilote Martinique 187 H4
Riviersonderend S. Africa 132 D11
Riviersonderend Mountains S. Africa 132 D11
Rivne Ukr. 41 C6
also spelt Rovno; formerly spelt Równe
Rivoli Italy 51 N7
Rivulets S. Africa 133 O2
Rivungo Angola 127 D9
Riwaka N.Z. 152 G9
Riwoqê China 86 A2

▶Riyadh Saudi Arabia 105 D2
Capital of Saudi Arabia. Also spelt Ar Riyāḍ.

Riyan Yemen 105 E5
Riyue Shankou pass China 84 D4
Riza well Iran 100 C3
Rizal Phil. 74 B3
Rize Turkey 107 E2
Rizhao Shandong China 85 H5
formerly known as Shijiusuo
Rizhao Shandong China 85 H5
Rizokarpaso Cyprus see Rizokarpason
Rizokarpason Cyprus 108 F2
also known as Dipkarpaz or Rizokarpaso
Rīzū well Iran 100 D3
Rīzū'īyeh Iran 100 D4
Rjukan Norway 45 J4
Rkîz, Lac l. Mauritania 124 B2
Roa Norway 45 J3
Roa Spain 54 H3
Roach Lake U.S.A. 183 I6
Roads U.S.A. 176 C6

▶Road Town Virgin Is (U.K.) 187 G3
Capital of the British Virgin Islands.

Roan Norway 44 J2
Roan Cliffs ridge U.S.A. 183 O2
Roan Fell hill U.K. 47 J8
Roan Mountain U.S.A. 176 C9
Roanne France 51 K6
Roanoke AL U.S.A. 175 C5
Roanoke IL U.S.A. 172 D10
Roanoke VA U.S.A. 176 F8
Roanoke r. U.S.A. 176 I9
Roanoke Rapids U.S.A. 176 H9
Roan Plateau U.S.A. 183 O2
Roaringwater Bay Rep. of Ireland 47 C12
Roatán Hond. 186 B3
also known as Coxen Hole
Robat r. Afgh. 101 E4
Robāţ Iran 100 D4
Robāţ-e Khān Iran 100 D3
Robāţ-e Shahr-e Bābak Iran 100 C4
Robāţe Tork Iran 100 B3
Robāţ-e Ţoroq Iran 101 D2
Robāţ Karīm Iran 100 B3
Robāt-Sang Iran 101 D3
Robat Thana Pak. 101 E4
Robb Canada 167 G4
Robben Island S. Africa 132 C10
Robbins U.S.A. 176 A9
Robbins Island Australia 147 E5
Robbinsville U.S.A. 174 D5
Robe r. Australia 150 A4
Robe, Mount hill Australia 146 D2
Röbel Germany 49 J2
Robert Glacier Antarctica 223 D2
Robert Lee U.S.A. 179 B6
Roberts U.S.A. 180 D4
Roberts, Mount Australia 147 G2
Robertsburg U.S.A. 176 D7
Roberts Butte mt. Antarctica 223 K2
Roberts Creek Mountain U.S.A. 183 I2
Robertsfors Sweden 44 M2
Robertsganj India 97 D4

Rocky Harbour Canada **169** J3
Rocky Hill U.S.A. **176** C7
Rocky Lane Canada **167** G3
Rocky Mount NC U.S.A. **174** E5
Rocky Mount VA U.S.A. **176** F9
Rocky Mountain House Canada **167** H4
Rocky Mountain National Park U.S.A.
    180 F4
Rocky Mountains Canada **170** E3
Rocky Mountains Forest Reserve
    nature res. Canada **167** G4
Rocroi France **51** K3
Rødberg Norway **45** J3
Roddickton Canada **169** K3
Rode S. Africa **133** N7
Rödeby Sweden **45** K4
Rodeo Mex. **184** D3
Roderick r. Australia **151** B5
Rodez France **51** I8
Rodholivos Greece see Rodolivos
Rodhópolis Greece see Rodopoli
Ródhos i. Greece see Rhodes
Rodi i. Greece see Rhodes
Roding Germany **49** J6
Rodino Rus. Fed. **103** J1
Rødlia Norway **44** J4
Rodna Romania **58** F1
Rodney, Cape N.Z. **152** I4
Rodnichek Rus. Fed. see Rodnichok
Rodnichok Rus. Fed. **41** G6
    also spelt Rodnichek
Rodnya Belarus **43** N8
Rodnykovka Kazakh. **102** D2
Rodolfo Sanchez Toboada Mex. **184** A2
Rodolivos Greece **58** E8
    also spelt Rodholivos
Rodonit, Kepi i pt Albania **58** A7
Rodopi Planina mts Bulg./Greece see
    Rhodope Mountains
Rodopoli Greece **58** E7
    also known as Rodhópolis
Rodopos Greece **59** E13
Rodos Greece **58** I7
Rodos i. Greece see Rhodes
Rodosto Turkey see Tekirdağ
Rodovoye Rus. Fed. **42** I4
Rodøya i. Norway **44** K2
Rodrigues Peru **198** C6
Rodrigues i. Mauritius **218** L7
Rødsand Norway **44** O1
Roe r. Australia **150** B4
Roebourne Australia **150** B4
Roebuck Bay Australia **150** C3
Roedtan S. Africa **131** F5
Roe Plains Australia **151** D6
Roermond Neth. **48** C4
Roermond S. Africa see Roulers
    also known as Roulers
Roes Welcome Sound sea chan. Canada
    167 O2
Rogachev Belarus see Rahachow
Rogachevo Rus. Fed. **43** S5
Rogagua, Laguna l. Bol. **200** D3
Rogaland county Norway **45** I4
Rogaška Slatina Slovenia **49** M9
Rogatica Bos.-Herz. **56** L5
Roger, Lac l. Canada **173** O2
Rogers Canada **167** G5
Rogers U.S.A. **179** D4
Rogers City U.S.A. **173** J5
Rogers Lake U.S.A. **182** G4
Rogersville U.S.A. **176** B9
Roggan r. Canada **168** E2
Roggeveld plat. S. Africa **132** E9
Roggeveldberge esc. S. Africa **132** E9
Rogliano Italy **57** I9
Rognan Norway **44** K2
Rognedino Rus. Fed. **43** O8
Rögnitz r. Germany **48** H2
Rogoźno Poland **49** O3
Rogue r. U.S.A. **180** A4
Roha India **94** B2
Rohnert Park U.S.A. **182** B3
Rohrbach in Oberösterreich Austria
    49 K7
Rohri Pak. **101** G5
Rohtak India **96** C3
Rohuküla Estonia **42** E3
Roi Et Thai. **78** C4
Roi Georges, Îles du is Fr. Polynesia **221** I6
    English form King George Islands
Roine l. Fin. **45** N3
Roing India **97** G3
Rojas Arg. **204** E4
Rojdåfors Sweden **45** K3
Rojhan Pak. **101** G4
Rojo, Cabo c. Mex. **185** F4
Rojo, Cabo c. Puerto Rico **187** G3
Rojo Aguado, Laguna l. Bol. **200** D3
Rokan r. Indon. **76** C2
Rokeby Australia **149** D2
Rokeby National Park Australia **149** D2
Rokiškis Lith. **42** G6
Rokkasho Japan **90** G4
Rokkō-zaki pt Japan **90** E6
Rokland Norway **44** K2
Roknäs Sweden **44** M2
Rokycany Czech Rep. **49** K6
Rokytne Ukr. **41** C6
Rola Kangri mt. China **89** E5
Ropinsalmi Fin. **44** M1
Roquebrune-sur-Argens France **51** M9
Roquefort France **50** F8
Roquetas de Mar Spain **55** I8
Roraima state Brazil **199** F4
    formerly known as Rio Branco
Roraima, Mount Guyana **199** F3
Rorey Lake Canada **166** D1
Røros Norway **44** J3
Rorschach Switz. **51** P5
Rørvik Norway **44** J2
Ros' r. Belarus **42** H9
Roś, Jezioro l. Poland **49** S2
Rosa, Lake Bahamas **187** E2
Rosa, Punta pt Mex. **184** C3
Rosal de la Frontera Spain **54** D7
Rosales Mex. **184** D2
Rosalia U.S.A. **180** C3
Rosalind Bank sea feature Caribbean Sea
    186 C3
Rosamond U.S.A. **182** F7
Rosamond Lake U.S.A. **182** F7
Rosamorada Mex. **184** D4
Rosario Arg. **204** E4
Rosario Baja California Norte Mex. **184** B2
Rosario Coahuila Mex. **185** E3
Rosario Sinaloa Mex. **184** C3
Rosario Sonora Mex. **184** C3
Rosario Para. **202** A5
Rosario Luzon Phil. **74** B2
Rosario Luzon Phil. **74** B3
Rosário Venez. **198** C2
Rosario, Cayo del i. Cuba **186** C2
Rosario, Sierra del hills Cuba **175** D8
Rosario de la Frontera Arg. **204** D2
Rosario de Lerma Arg. **200** D5
Rosário do Sul Brazil **203** A9
Rosarito Baja California Norte Mex. **184** A1
Rosarito Baja California Norte Mex. **184** B2
Rosarito Baja California Sur Mex. **184** B3
Rosarno Italy **57** H10
Rosas Spain see Roses
Rosas, Golfo de b. Spain see
    Roses, Golf de
Rosa Zárate Ecuador **198** B4

►Rome Italy **56** E7
Capital of Italy. Also spelt Roma.

Rome GA U.S.A. **179** F5
Rome ME U.S.A. **177** P1
Rome NY U.S.A. **177** J2
Romeo U.S.A. **173** J8
Romford U.K. **47** M12
Romilly-sur-Seine France **51** J4
Romit Tajik. **101** G2
    also known as Ramit
Romitan Uzbek. **103** F5
    formerly spelt Ramitan
Romney U.K. see Ramit
Romny Ukr. **41** E6
Romo i. Denmark **45** J5
Romorantin-Lanthenay France **50** H5
Rompin r. Malaysia **76** C2
Romppala Fin. **44** O3
Romsey U.K. **47** K13
Romu mt. Indon. **77** G5
Romulus U.S.A. **173** J8
Ron India **94** B3
Rona i. U.K. **46** G4
    also known as North Rona
Ronas Hill hill U.K. **46** K3
Roncador, Serra do hills Brazil **202** A3
Roncador Cay i. Caribbean Sea **186** C4
Roncador Reef Solomon Is **145** E2
Roncevorte U.S.A. **176** E8
Ronchi Italy **56** E2
Ronciglione Italy **56** E6
Ronda Spain **54** F8
Ronda, Serranía de mts Spain **54** F8
Ronda, Serranía de nature res. Spain
    54 G8
Ronda das Salinas Brazil **201** E3
Rondane Nasjonalpark nat. park Norway
    45 J3
Ronde i. Grenada **187** H4
Rondon Brazil **206** A10
Rondón Col. **198** D3
Rondônia state Brazil **201** E2
    formerly known as Guaporé
Rondonópolis Brazil **202** A6
Rondout Reservoir U.S.A. **177** K4
Rong'an China **87** D3
    also known as Chang'an
Rongbaca China **86** A2
Rongchang China **86** C2
Rongcheng China see Qingyang
Rongcheng China see Rongxian
Rongcheng China see Jianli
Rongcheng China **85** I4
    formerly known as Yatou
Rongcheng Wan b. China **85** I4
Rong Chu r. China **89** E6
Rongelap atoll Marshall Is **220** F6
    also known as Kongelap; also spelt Rönlap
Rongjiang China **87** D3
    also known as Guzhou
Rongjiang China see Nankang
Rong Jiang r. China **87** D3
Rongjiawan China see Yueyang
Rongklang Range mts Myanmar **78** A3
Rongmei China see Hefeng
Rongshui China **87** D3
Rongwo China see Tongren
Rongxian Guangxi China **87** D4
    also known as Rongcheng
Rongxian Sichuan China **86** C2
    also known as Xuyang
Rongzhag China see Danba
Rönlap atoll Marshall Is see Rongelap
Ronne Denmark **45** K5
Ronne r. see Renaix
Ronuro r. Brazil **202** A5
Roodebank S. Africa **133** N3
Rooiberg mt. Free State S. Africa **133** M5
Rooiberg mt. W. Cape S. Africa **132** F10
Rooikloof pass S. Africa **132** E9
Rooikraal S. Africa **133** I2
Rooke Island P.N.G. see Umboi
Rookh Aboriginal Reserve Australia
    150 B4
Roorkee India **96** C3
Roosboom S. Africa **133** N5
Roosendaal Neth. **48** B4
Roosevelt AZ U.S.A. **183** M8
Roosevelt UT U.S.A. **183** O1
Roosevelt, Mount Canada **166** E3
Roosevelt Island Antarctica **223** N1
Roosenekal S. Africa **133** N2
Root r. Canada **166** F2
Root r. U.S.A. **174** B3
Ropa r. Poland **49** S6
Ropaži Latvia **42** F5
Ropczyce Poland **49** S5
Roper r. Australia **148** B2
Roper Bar Australia **148** B2
Roper Bar Aboriginal Land res. Australia
    148 B2
    also known as Yutpundji Djindiniwirrit
Roper Creek r. Australia **149** F4
Ropinsalmi Fin. **44** M1
Ropsha Rus. Fed. **43** L5
Ros'ha Afgh. **101** G2
Roslağ Fårs Iran **100** C5
Roştāq Hormozgan Iran **100** C5
Rosthern Canada **167** J4
Rostock Germany **48** J1
Rostonsölkä ridge Sweden **44** M1
Rostov Rus. Fed. **43** U4
Rostov-na-Donu Rus. Fed. **41** F7
    English form Rostov-on-Don
Rostov Oblast admin. div. Rus. Fed. see
    Rostovskaya Oblast'
Rostov-on-Don Rus. Fed. see
    Rostov-na-Donu
Rostovskaya Oblast' admin. div. Rus. Fed.
    41 G7
    English form Rostov Oblast
Rostrenen France **50** C4
Rostrevor U.K. **47** F9
Rosvik Norway **44** K2
Rosvik Sweden **44** M2
Roswell GA U.S.A. **175** C5
Roswell NM U.S.A. **181** F6
Rota i. N. Mariana Is **73** K4
    formerly known as Sarpan
Rotch Island Kiribati see Tamana
Rote i. Indon. **75** B5
    also spelt Roti
Rotenburg (Wümme) Germany **48** G2
Rote Wand mt. Austria **48** G8
Roth Germany **48** I6
Rothenburg ob der Tauber Germany **48** H6
Rotherham U.K. **47** K10
Rothes U.K. **46** I6
Rothesay U.K. **46** G8
Rothschild U.S.A. **172** D6
Rothschild Island Antarctica **222** T2
Roti i. Indon. see Rote
Roti i. Indon. **75** B5
Roto Australia **147** E3
Rotoaira, Lake N.Z. **152** J7
Rotomagus France see Rouen
Rotomanu N.Z. **153** F10
Rotondo, Monte mt. Corse France **56** B6
Rotorua N.Z. **152** K6
Rotorua, Lake N.Z. **152** K6
Rott r. Germany **49** K7
Rottenburg am Neckar Germany **48** F7

►Roseau Dominica **187** H4
Capital of Dominica.

Roseau r. U.S.A. **178** D1
Roseau U.S.A. **178** C1
Roseberth Australia **148** C4
Rosebery Australia **147** E5
Rose Blanche Canada **169** J4
Rosebud r. Canada **167** H5
Rosebud Creek r. U.S.A. **180** F3
Rosebud Indian Reservation res. U.S.A.
    178 B3
Roseburg U.S.A. **180** B4
Rose City U.S.A. **173** I6
Rosedale MS U.S.A. **174** B5
Rosedale TN U.S.A. **176** A9
Rosedene S. Africa **132** G9
Rosehall Guyana **199** G3
Roseires Reservoir Sudan **128** B2
Rosemary Island Australia **150** B4
Rosenberg U.S.A. **179** D6
Rosendal Norway **45** I4
Rosendal S. Africa **133** L5
Rosendale U.S.A. **172** E7
Rosengarten Germany **48** G2
Rosenheim Germany **48** J8
Rose Peak U.S.A. **183** C8
Rose Point Canada **166** D4
Roses Spain **55** O2
Roses, Golf de b. Spain **55** O2
    also known as Rosas, Golfo de
Roseto degli Abruzzi Italy **56** G6
Rosetown Canada **167** J5
Rosetta Egypt see Rashid
Rosetta Creek r. Australia **149** E4
Rose Valley Canada **167** K4
Roseville CA U.S.A. **182** C3
Roseville IL U.S.A. **174** B3
Roseville MI U.S.A. **173** K8
Roseville OH U.S.A. **176** C6
Roshal' Rus. Fed. **43** U6
Roshchino Rus. Fed. **43** K1
Roshchino Rus. Fed. **90** D2
Roshkhvār Iran **101** D3
Rosholt U.S.A. **172** D6
Rosh Pinah Namibia **130** C5
Rosignano Marittimo Italy **56** C5
Rosignol Guyana **199** G3
Rosiori Romania **58** I4
Roşiori de Vede Romania **58** G4
Rositsa Bulg. **58** I5
Rositsa r. Bulg. **58** G5
Roskilde Denmark **45** K5
Roskovec Albania **58** A8
Roskruge Mountains U.S.A. **183** M9
Roslavl' Rus. Fed. **43** N8
Roslyakovo Rus. Fed. **44** P1
Roslyatino Rus. Fed. **40** H4
Rosmead S. Africa **133** J8
Rosolina Italy **56** E3
Rosolini Sicilia Italy **57** G12
Rosporden France **50** C5
Ross r. Australia **147** E5
Ross r. Canada **166** C2
Ross N.Z. **153** E10
Ross, Mount hill N.Z. **152** J9
Rossan Point Rep. of Ireland **47** D9
Ross Barnett Reservoir U.S.A. **175** B5
Ross Bay Junction Canada **169** H2
Ross Dependency Antarctica **222** N2
Rosseau, Lake Canada **173** N5
Rossel Lagoon P.N.G. **149** G1
Ross Ice Shelf Antarctica **223** M1
Rossignol, Lac l. Canada **169** F2
Rössing Namibia **130** B4
Ross Island Antarctica **223** L1
Ross Island Myanmar see Daung Kyun
Rossiter Bay Australia **151** C7
Rossiyskaya Sovetskaya Federativnaya
    Sotsialisticheskaya Respublika country
    Asia/Europe see Russian Federation
Rossland Canada **166** G5
Rosslare Rep. of Ireland **47** F11
Rosslare Harbour Rep. of Ireland **47** F11
Rosso Mauritania **124** B2
Rossön Sweden **44** L3
Ross-on-Wye U.K. **47** J12
Rossony Belarus see Rasony
Rossosh' Rus. Fed. **41** F6
Rossouw S. Africa **133** L8
Rossport Canada **172** F2
Ross River Australia **148** B4
Ross River Canada **166** C2
Ross Sea Antarctica **223** L1
Ressvatnet l. Norway **44** K2
Rossville U.S.A. **172** B7
Rosswood Canada **166** D4
Rōst Iraq **107** F3
Røst i. Norway **44** K2
Rostaq Afgh. **101** G2

Rottenmann Austria **49** L8
Rotterdam Neth. **48** B4
Rotterdam U.S.A. **177** L3
Rottnest Island Australia **151** A7
Rottweil Germany **48** F7
Rotuma i. Fiji **145** G3
    formerly known as Grenville Island
Rotunda Romania **58** F5
Rötviken Sweden **44** K3
Rötz Germany **49** J6
Roubaix France **51** J2
Roudnice nad Labem Czech Rep. **49** L5
Rouen France **50** H3
    historically known as Rotomagus
Rôuge Estonia **42** H4
Rouge-Matawin, Réserve Faunique
    nature res. Canada **169** F4
Rougemont U.S.A. **176** E8
Rough Ridge N.Z. **153** D13
Rouhia Tunisia **57** B13
Roui, Oued er watercourse Niger **125** H1
Roulers Belgium see Roeselare
Roulette U.S.A. **176** G4
Roulpmaulpma Aboriginal Land res.
    Australia **148** B4
Roumania country Europe see Romania
Roundeyed Lake Canada **169** G2
Roundhead U.S.A. **176** B5
Round Hill Nature Reserve Australia
    147 E3
Round Lake Canada **168** E4
Round Mountain mt. Australia **147** G2
Round Mountain U.S.A. **183** G3
Round Rock AZ U.S.A. **183** O5
Round Rock TX U.S.A. **179** C6
Roundup U.S.A. **180** E3
Roura Fr. Guiana **199** H3
Rousay i. U.K **46** I4
Rouses Point U.S.A. **177** L1
Roussillon France **51** K7
Routh Bank sea feature Phil. see
    Seahorse Bank
Rouxville S. Africa **133** K7
Rouyn Canada **168** E3
Rouyuan China see Huachi
Rouyuanchengzi China see Huachi
Rovaniemi Fin. **44** N2
Rovato Italy **56** C3
Roven'ki Rus. Fed. **41** F6
Rovereto Italy **56** D3
Roverni Arg. **204** E2
Rovigo Italy **56** D3
Rovinari Romania **58** E4
Rovinj Croatia **56** F3
Rovkul'skoye, Ozero l. Rus. Fed. **44** O3
Rovno Ukr. see Rivne
Rovnoye Rus. Fed. **102** A2
Rowlesburg U.S.A. **176** F6
Rowley Island Canada **165** L3
Rowley Shoals sea feature Australia **150** B3
Rownaye Belarus **43** K6
Röwne Ukr. see Rivne
Rów Polski r. Poland **49** N4
Rowsburg U.S.A. **176** D5
Roxas Luzon Phil. **74** B2
Roxas Mindanao Phil. **74** B4
Roxas Mindoro Phil. **74** B3
Roxas Palawan Phil. **74** A4
Roxas Panay Phil. **74** B4
Roxboro U.S.A. **176** E8
Roxborough Downs Australia **148** C4
Roxburgh Island Cook Is see Rarotonga
Roxby Downs Australia **146** C2
Roxen l. Sweden **45** K4
Roxo r. Port. **54** C7
Roxo, Barragem do resr Port. **54** C7
Royal Canal Rep. of Ireland **47** E10
Royal Center U.S.A. **172** G10
Royal Chitwan National Park Nepal **97** E4
Royale, Île i. Canada see
    Cape Breton Island
Royale, Isle i. U.S.A. **172** E2
Royal National Natural Park S. Africa **133** N6
Royal Society Range mts Antarctica
    223 K1
Royalton U.S.A. **172** E6
Royan France **50** E7
Roye France **51** I3
Roy Hill Australia **150** B4
Royston U.K. **47** L11
Royston U.S.A. **175** D5
Rožaje Crna Gora Yugo. **58** B6
Rózan Poland **49** S3
Rozani hill Yugo. **58** A4
Rozdil'na Ukr. **41** D7
    also known as Razdel'naya
Rozdol'ne Ukr. **41** E7
Rozhdestvenka Kazakh. **103** G2
Rozhdestveno Tverskaya Oblast' Rus. Fed.
    43 P5
Rezhdestveno Yaroslavskaya Oblast'
    Rus. Fed. **43** S4
Rozhdestvenskoye Rus. Fed. **40** H4
Rozhdestvo Rus. Fed. **43** P9
Rozivka Ukr. **41** F7
Rožňava Slovakia **49** R7
Rozoy-sur-Serre France **51** K3
Roztoczański Park Narodowy nat. park
    Poland **49** U5
Rozveh Iran **100** B3
Rozzano Italy **56** B3
Rrëshen Albania **58** A7
Rrogozhinë Albania **58** A7
Rtishchevo Rus. Fed. **41** G5
Ruacana Namibia **130** B3
Ruahine National Park Tanz. **129** B6
Ruahine Forest Park nature res. N.Z.
    152 K7
Ruahine Range mts N.Z. **152** K8
Ruakaka N.Z. **152** I3
Ruanda country Africa see Rwanda
Ruapehu, Mount vol. N.Z. **152** J7
Ruapuke Island N.Z. **153** C14
Ruarwe Malawi **129** B7
Ruatangata N.Z. **152** I3
Ruatapu N.Z. **153** E10
Ruatoria N.Z. **152** M5
Ruba Belarus **43** L6
    formerly known as Vyarkhowye

Ruby Valley U.S.A. **183** I1
Rucăr Romania **58** G3
Ruchay Belarus **42** I6
    also known as Ruyuan
Rucheng China **87** E3
Ruciane-Nida Poland **49** S2
Ruckersville U.S.A. **176** G7
Rudall River National Park Australia **150** C4
Rudall watercourse Australia **150** C4
Rudarpur India **97** D4
Rudbar Afgh. **101** E4
Rüdbär Iran **100** B2
Rudauli India **97** D4
Rüd-e Kor watercourse Iran **100** C4
Rüdersdorf Berlin Germany **49** K3
Rudhumatal Hiri l. Iraq **109** N4
Rudina pass Iran **101** D3
Rüd-i-Shur watercourse Iran **100** D4
Rūdiškés Lith. **42** F7
Rudka r. Poland **49** U4
Rudkøbing Denmark **45** J5
Rudna Glava Srbija Yugo. **58** D4
Rudnaya Pristan' Primorskiy Kray Rus. Fed.
    82 D3
    formerly known as Tetyukhe-Pristan'
Rudnaya Pristan' Primorskiy Kray Rus. Fed.
    82 D4
Rudnichnyy Kazakh. **103** I3
Rudnichnyy Rus. Fed. **40** J4
Rudnik Poland **49** T5
Rudnik Ingichka Uzbek. see Ingichka
Rudnya Smolenskaya Oblast' Rus. Fed. **43** M7
Rudnya Tverskaya Oblast' Rus. Fed. **43** M5
Rudnya Volgogradskaya Oblast' Rus. Fed.
    41 H6
Rudnyy Kazakh. **103** E1
Rudnyy Rus. Fed. **82** D3
    formerly known as Lifudzin
Rudolf, Lake salt l. Eth./Kenya see
    Turkana, Lake

►Rudol'fa, Ostrov i. Rus. Fed. **38** F1
Most northerly point of Europe. English
form Rudolph Island.

Rudolph Island Rus. Fed. see
    Rudol'fa, Ostrov
Rudolstadt Germany **48** I5
Rudong China **87** G1
    also known as Juegang
Rudozem Bulg. **58** F7
Rüdsar Iran **100** B2
Rudzyensk Belarus **42** I8
Rue France **50** H2
Ruecas r. Spain **54** F5
Ruel Canada **173** M4
Ruen mt. Macedonia see Rujen
Ruenya r. Zimbabwe **131** G3
Rufa'a Sudan **121** G6
Rufe France **50** G6
Rufiji r. Tanz. **129** C7
Rufino Arg. **204** E4
Rufisque Senegal **124** A3
Rufunsa Zambia **127** F3
Rugåji Latvia **42** I4
Rugao China **87** G1
Rugby U.K. **47** K11
Rugby ND U.S.A. **178** B1
Rugby TN U.S.A. **176** B9
Rügen i. Germany **49** K1
Rügen, Naturpark park Germany **49** K1
Rugged Mountain Canada **166** E5
Rughiwa well Sudan **121** F5
Rugles France **50** G4
Ruhango Tanz. **129** C7
Ruhayyat al Hamr'ā' waterhole
    Saudi Arabia **105** C2
Ruhbah oasis Syria **109** I5
    English form Rhube, Oasis of
Ruhengeri Rwanda **126** F5
Ruhla Germany **48** H5
Ruhnu i. Estonia **42** E4
Rührupolding Germany **49** J8
Ruhr r. Germany **48** D4
Ruhudji r. Tanz. **129** B7
Ruhuna National Park Sri Lanka **94** D5
    also known as Yala National Park
Rui'an China **87** G3
Ruichang China **87** E2
    formerly known as Pencheng
Ruidoso U.S.A. **181** F6
Ruijin China **87** E3
Ruiz Mex. **184** D4
Ruiz, Nevado del vol. Col. **198** C3
Ruj mt. Bulg. **58** D6
Rūja r. Latvia **42** G4
Rujaylah, Harrat ar lava field Jordan **109** I5
Rujen mt. Macedonia **58** D6
    also spelt Ruen
Rūjiena Latvia **42** G4
Ruki r. Dem. Rep. Congo **126** C4
Rukumkot Nepal **97** D3
Rukungiri Uganda **128** A5
Rukwa admin. reg. Tanz. **129** A6
Rukwa Tanz. **129** A6
Rukwa, Lake Tanz. **129** B7
Rūl Dadnah U.A.E. **105** G2
Ruleville U.S.A. **175** B5
Rulin China see Chengbu
Rulong China see Xinlong
Rūm Iran **101** D3
Rum i. U.K. **46** F7
Rum r. U.S.A. **174** A2
Rum, Jebel mts Jordan see Ramm, Jabal
Ruma Nigeria **125** G3
Rumah Saudi Arabia **105** D2
Ruma National Park Kenya **128** B5
Rumania country Europe see Romania
Rumaylah waterhole Iraq **109** O4
Rumaylah, Wādī watercourse Syria **109** M1
Rumayn l. Saudi Arabia **104** C3
Rumbek Sudan **126** E3
Rumblar r. Spain **54** H6
Rumburk Czech Rep. **49** L5
Rum Cay i. Bahamas **187** E2
Rumford U.S.A. **177** O1
Rumia Poland **49** P1
Rumilly France **51** L7
Rummah, Jabal ar mts Saudi Arabia **104** C2
Rummānā hill Syria **109** H3
Runan China **87** E1
    also known as Runing
Runanga N.Z. **153** F10
Runaway, Cape N.Z. **152** L5
Runcorn U.K. **47** J10
Runcu Romania **58** E4
Runde r. Zimbabwe **131** G4
Rundu Namibia **130** D3
Rundvik Sweden **44** L3
Rüng, Kaôh i. Cambodia **79** C6
Rungu r. Indon. **77** F3
Rungu Dem. Rep. Congo **126** E4
Rungwa Rukwa Tanz. **129** A6
Rungwa Singida Tanz. **129** B6
Rungwa r. Tanz. **129** B6
Rungwa Game Reserve nature res. Tanz.
    129 B6
Runing China see Runan
Rūnn-e Bālā Iran **101** D4
Runn r. Sweden **45** K3
Running Springs U.S.A. **183** H7
Running Water watercourse U.S.A. **179** B5
Ruokolahti Fin. **45** O3
Ruoqiang China **88** E4
    formerly known as Charkhlik or Qarkilik

Robert S. Kerr Reservoir U.S.A. **179** D5
Robertson r. Australia **149** D3
Robertson S. Africa **132** D10
Robertson, Lac l. Canada **169** J3
Robertson Island Antarctica **223** L2
Robertson Island Antarctica **222** U2
Robertson Point N.Z. **152** I9
Robertson Range hills Australia **150** C4
Robertsport Liberia **124** C5
Roberval Canada **169** F3
Robhanais, Rubha hd U.K. see Butt of Lewis
Robin's Nest hill Hong Kong China **87** [inset]
    also known as Hung Fa Leng
Robinson r. N.T. Australia **148** C3
Robinson r. W.A. Australia **150** D3
Robinson Canada **166** C2
Robinson IL U.S.A. **174** C3
Robinson KY U.S.A. **176** A7
Robinson Creek r. Australia **149** F5
Robinvale Australia **147** D3
Robles La Paz Col. **198** C2
Roblin Canada **167** K5
Robore Bol. **201** F4
Robson, Mount Canada **166** G4
Robstown U.S.A. **179** C7
Roby U.S.A. **179** B5
Roçadas Angola see Xangongo
Roca Partida, i. Mex. **184** B5
Rocas, Atol das atoll Brazil **202** F2
Rocas Alijos is Mex. **184** A3
Rocca Busambra mt. Sicilia Italy **57** F11
Rocca Imperiale Italy **57** I8
Roccastrada Italy **56** D5
Roc de Montalet mt. France **51** I9
Roc d'Enfer mt. France **51** M6
Rocha Uruguay **204** G4
Rochdale U.K. **47** J10
Rochechouart France **50** G7
Roche de Vic hill France **50** H7
Rochedo Brazil **203** A6
Rochefort Belgium **51** L2
Rochefort France **50** F7
Rochefort, Lac l. Canada **169** F1
Rochegda Rus. Fed. **40** G3
Rochelle U.S.A. **172** D9
Rochester IN U.S.A. **174** C3
Rochester MN U.S.A. **174** A2
Rochester NH U.S.A. **177** O2
Rochester NY U.S.A. **176** H2
Roc'h Trévezel hill France **50** C4
Rocina r. Spain **54** E8
Rock r. Canada **166** E2
Rock r. U.S.A. **172** F4
Rock r. IL U.S.A. **174** B3
Rock r. IL U.S.A. **178** C3
Rock Bay Canada **166** E5
Rock Creek r. Canada **166** B1
Rock Creek r. U.S.A. **180** F2
Rockdale U.S.A. **179** C6
Rockefeller National Wildlife Refuge
    nature res. U.S.A. **179** D6
Rockefeller Plateau Antarctica **222** O1
Rockford AL U.S.A. **175** C5
Rockford IL U.S.A. **174** B2
Rockford NC U.S.A. **176** E9
Rockford OH U.S.A. **176** A5
Rockglen Canada **167** J5
Rock Hall U.S.A. **177** I6
Rockhampton Australia **149** F4
Rockhampton Downs Australia **148** B3
Rock Hill U.S.A. **174** D5
Rockingham Australia **151** A7
Rockingham U.S.A. **174** D5
Rockingham Bay Australia **149** E3
Rockinghorse Lake Canada **167** H1
Rock Island Australia **150** B4
Rockland MA U.S.A. **177** N3
Rockland ME U.S.A. **177** P1
Rocklands Reservoir Australia **147** D4
Rocklea Australia **150** B4
Rocklin U.S.A. **182** C3
Rocknest Lake Canada **167** H1
Rock Point U.S.A. **183** O5
Rockport IN U.S.A. **174** C4
Rockport MA U.S.A. **177** O3
Rockport TX U.S.A. **179** C7
Rockport WV U.S.A. **176** D6
Rock Rapids U.S.A. **178** C3
Rock River U.S.A. **180** F4
Rock Sound Bahamas **186** D1
Rock Springs MT U.S.A. **180** F3
Rocksprings U.S.A. **179** B6
Rock Springs WY U.S.A. **180** E4
Rockstone Guyana **199** G3
Rockton U.S.A. **172** D8
Rockville IN U.S.A. **174** C4
Rockville MD U.S.A. **177** H6
Rockwall U.S.A. **179** C5
Rockwell City U.S.A. **178** D3
Rockwood U.S.A. **173** J5
Rocky Boy's Indian Reservation res. U.S.A.
    180 F2
Rockyford Canada **167** H5
Rocky Ford U.S.A. **178** B4
Rocky Fork U.S.A. **176** C9
Rocky Fork Lake U.S.A. **176** B6

►Rome Italy **56** E7

Romania country Europe **58** E3
    also spelt Roumania or Rumania
    europe [countries] ▬▬▬ 32–35
Roman-Kosh mt. Ukr. **41** E7
Romano, Cayo i. Cuba **186** D2
Romanovka Moldova see Basarabeasca
Romanovka Rus. Fed. **81** I2
Romanovo Rus. Fed. **41** G6
Romans-sur-Isère France **51** L7
Romanzof, Cape U.S.A. **164** C3
Romão Brazil **199** F5
Rombas France **51** M3
Romblon Phil. **74** B3
Romblon i. Phil. **74** B3
Romblon Passage Phil. **74** B3
Rombo, Ilhéus is Cape Verde see
    Secos, Ilhéus

Ruoqiang He r. China 88 E4
Ruo Shui watercourse China 84 D3
Ruotsinpyhtää Fin. 42 H1
Ruovesi Fin. 45 N3
Rupa India 97 G4
Rupat i. Indon. 76 C2
Rupea Romania 58 G2
Rupert r. Canada 168 E3
Rupert ID U.S.A. 180 D4
Rupert WV U.S.A. 176 E8
Rupert Bay Canada 168 E3
Rupert Coast Antarctica 222 O1
Rupert Creek r. Australia 149 D4
Rupnagar India 96 B4
Rupshu reg. Jammu and Kashmir 96 C2
Ruqayṭah Saudi Arabia 104 C3
Ruqqād, Wādī ar watercourse Israel 108 G5
Rural Hall U.S.A. 176 E9
Rural Retreat U.S.A. 176 D9
Rurrenabaque Bol. 200 D3
Rus Romania 58 E1
Rusaddir N. Africa see **Melilla**
Rusape Zimbabwe 131 G3
Rusca Montană Romania 58 D3
Ruschuk Bulg. see **Ruse**
Ruse Bulg. 58 G5
historically known as Ruschuk
Rusenski Lom nat. park Bulg. 58 H5
Rusera India 97 E4
Ruşeţu Romania 58 I4
Rushan China 85 I4
formerly known as Xiacun
Rushan Tajik. see **Rushon**
Rushanskiy Khrebet mts Tajik. see **Rushon, Qatorkŭhi**
Rush Creek r. U.S.A. 178 B4
Rushford U.S.A. 174 B3
Rush Lake U.S.A. 172 E7
Rushmere U.S.A. 177 I8
Rushon Tajik. 101 G2
also spelt Rushan
Rushon, Qatorkŭhi mts Tajik. 101 G2
also known as Rushanskiy Khrebet
Rushui r. China 85 E5
Rushville IL U.S.A. 174 B3
Rushville IN U.S.A. 174 C4
Rushville NE U.S.A. 178 B3
Rushville OH U.S.A. 176 C6
Rushworth Australia 147 E4
Rusk U.S.A. 179 D6
Ruskele Sweden 44 L2
Ruskin U.S.A. 175 D7
Rusnė Lith. 42 C6
Rusokastro Bulg. 58 I6
Rušona Latvia 42 H5
Rušonu ezers l. Latvia 42 H5
Russarö i. Fin. 42 D2
Russas Brazil 202 E3
Russell Man. Canada 167 K5
Russell Ont. Canada 173 R5
Russell N.Z. 152 I3
Russell KS U.S.A. 178 C4
Russell PA U.S.A. 176 F4
Russell Bay Antarctica 222 P2
Russell Island Canada 165 J2
Russell Lake Man. Canada 167 K3
Russell Lake N.W.T. Canada 167 H2
Russellville AL U.S.A. 174 C5
Russellville AR U.S.A. 179 D5
Russellville KY U.S.A. 174 C4
Russellville OH U.S.A. 176 B7
Rüsselsheim Germany 48 F5
Russi Italy 56 E4
Russia country Asia/Europe see **Russian Federation**

▶**Russian Federation** country Asia/Europe 38 F3
Largest country in the world, Europe and Asia. Most populous country in Europe, 3rd in Asia and 6th in the world. Formerly known as Russian Soviet Federal Socialist Republic or Rossiyskaya Sovetskaya Federativnaya Sotsialisticheskaya Respublika; short form Russia.
world [countries] ▶ 10–11
world [population] ▶ 22–23
europe [countries] ▶ 32–35
asia [countries] ▶ 64–67

largest countries

	country	area sq km	area sq miles	location	page#
1 ▶	Russian Federation	17 075 400	6 592 849	Asia/Europe	38 F3
2 ▶	Canada	9 970 610	3 849 674	North America	164 G3
3 ▶	USA	9 809 378	3 787 422	North America	170 E3
4 ▶	China	9 584 492	3 700 593	Asia	80 D5
5 ▶	Brazil	8 547 379	3 300 161	South America	202 B4
6 ▶	Australia	7 682 395	2 966 189	Oceania	144 A4
7 ▶	India	3 065 027	1 183 414	Asia	93 E6
8 ▶	Argentina	2 766 889	1 068 302	South America	204 C4
9 ▶	Kazakhstan	2 717 300	1 049 155	Asia	102 C2
10 ▶	Sudan	2 505 813	967 500	Africa	121 E5

Russian Soviet Federal Socialist Republic country Asia/Europe see **Russian Federation**
Russkaya-Polyana Rus. Fed. 103 H1
Russkiy, Ostrov i. Rus. Fed. 90 B3
Russkiy Brod Rus. Fed. 43 S9
Russkiy Kameshkir Rus. Fed. 41 H5
Russkiy Zavorot, Poluostrov pen. Rus. Fed. 40 J1
Russkoye Rus. Fed. 43 N8
Russkoye Ust'ye Rus. Fed. 39 O2
formerly known as Polyarnoye
Rust'avi Georgia 107 F2
Rustburg U.S.A. 176 F8
Rust de Winter S. Africa 133 M2
Rust de Winter Nature Reserve S. Africa 133 M2
Rustenburg S. Africa 133 L2
Rustenburg Nature Reserve S. Africa 133 L2
Rustfontein Dam l. S. Africa 133 K6
Rustig S. Africa 133 L4
Ruston U.S.A. 179 D5
Rut' r. Rus. Fed. 43 R6
Ruta Indon. 75 C3
Rutana Burundi 126 F5
Rutanzige, Lake Dem. Rep. Congo/Uganda see **Edward, Lake**
Rute Spain 54 G7
Ruteng Indon. 75 B5
Rutenga Zimbabwe 131 F4
Rutherfordton U.S.A. 174 D5
Rutherglen Canada 173 N4
Ruther Glen U.S.A. 176 H8
Ruthin U.K. 47 I10
also spelt Rhuthun
Rutland U.S.A. 177 M2
Rutland Island India 95 G4
Rutland Plains Australia 149 D2
Rutledge U.S.A. 176 B9
Rutledge Lake Canada 167 I2
Rutog Xizang China 89 B5
also known as Dêrub
Rutog Xizang China 89 D6
Rutog Xizang China 89 F6
Rutshuru Dem. Rep. Congo 126 F5
Rutter Canada 173 M4
Rutul Rus. Fed. 102 A4
Ruukki Fin. 44 N2
Ruusa Estonia 42 I3
Ruvaslahti Fin. 44 O3
Ruvo di Puglia Italy 56 I7
Ruvozero Rus. Fed. 44 O2
Ruvozero, Ozero l. Rus. Fed. 44 O2
Ruvu Tanz. see **Pangani**
Ruvuma r. Moz./Tanz. 129 D7
Ruvuma admin. reg. Tanz. 129 C7
Ruwaydah Saudi Arabia 105 D2
Ruwayshid, Wādī watercourse Jordan 109 I5
Ruwayṭah, Wādī watercourse Jordan 108 H8
Ruweijil pt Saudi Arabia 108 F8
Ruweis U.A.E. 105 F2
Ruwenzori mts Dem. Rep. Congo/Uganda 126 F5
Ruwenzori National Park Uganda see **Queen Elizabeth National Park**
Ruya r. Zimbabwe 131 G3
Ruyigi Burundi 126 F5
Ruyuan China 87 E3
also known as Rucheng
Ruza Rus. Fed. 43 R6
Ruzayevka Kazakh. 103 F1
Ruzayevka Rus. Fed. 41 H5
Ruzbugino Rus. Fed. 43 V3
Ruzhany Belarus 42 F9
Ruzhou China 87 E1
formerly known as Linru
Ružomberok Slovakia 49 Q6
▶**Rwanda** country Africa 126 F5
formerly spelt Ruanda
africa [countries] ▶ 114–117
Ryābād Iran 100 C2
Ryabovo Rus. Fed. 43 J1
Ryal Bush N.Z. 153 C14
Ryall, Mount N.Z. 153 F10
Ryan, Loch b. U.K. 47 G8
Ryazan' Rus. Fed. 43 U7
Ryazan Oblast admin. div. Rus. Fed. see **Ryazanskaya Oblast'**
Ryazanovskiy Rus. Fed. 43 U6
Ryazanskaya Oblast' admin. div. Rus. Fed. 43 V7
English form Ryazan Oblast
Ryazantsevo Rus. Fed. 43 U5
Ryazhsk Rus. Fed. 41 G5
Rybache Kazakh. 88 C2
Rybachiy, Poluostrov pen. Rus. Fed. 44 P1
Rybachiy Poselok Uzbek. 102 D3
Rybach'ye Kyrg. see **Balykchy**
Rybinsk Rus. Fed. 43 T3
formerly known as Andropov or Shcherbakov
Rybinskoye Vodokhranilishche resr Rus. Fed. 43 T3
Rybnik Poland 49 P5
Rybnitsa Moldova see **Rîbniţa**
Rybnoye Rus. Fed. 43 U7
Rybreka Rus. Fed. 40 E3
Rychnov nad Kněžnou Czech Rep. 49 N5
Rycroft Canada 166 G4
Ryd Sweden 45 K4
Rydberg Peninsula Antarctica 222 S2
Ryde U.K. 47 K13
Rye Beach U.S.A. 177 O3
Ryegate U.S.A. 180 E3
Rye Patch Dam U.S.A. 182 F1
Rye Patch Reservoir U.S.A. 182 F1
Ryki Poland 49 S4
Rykovo Ukr. see **Yenakiyeve**
Ryl'sk Rus. Fed. 41 E6
Rymanów Poland 49 S6
Rýmařov Czech Rep. 49 O6
Rymättylä Fin. 45 M3
Ryn Poland 49 S2
Ryn-Peski des. Kazakh. 102 B3
Ryńskie, Jezioro l. Poland 49 S2
Ryojun China see **Lüshun**
Ryōtsu Japan 90 F5
Rypin Poland 49 Q2
Rysjedal Norway 45 I3
Rytterknægten hill Denmark 45 K5
Ryttylä Fin. 42 F1
Ryukhovo Rus. Fed. 43 N9
Ryukyu Islands Japan 81 K8
also known as Ryūkyū-rettō or Nansei-shotō; historically known as Loochoo Islands
Ryūkyū-rettō is Japan see **Ryukyu Islands**
Ryzhikovo Rus. Fed. 43 M7
Ryzhkawka Belarus 43 L8
Rządza r. Poland 49 S3
Rzav r. Bos.-Herz. 56 L5
Rzepin Poland 49 L3
Rzeszów Poland 49 T5
Rzhaksa Rus. Fed. 41 G5
Rzhanitsa Rus. Fed. 43 O8
Rzhawka r. Belarus 43 L9
Rzhev Rus. Fed. 43 P5

↓ S

Sa'ābād Iran 100 D3
Saacow Somalia 128 D4
Sa'ādah al Barṣā' pass Saudi Arabia 109 H8
Sa'ādatābād Fārs Iran 100 C4
Sa'ādatābād Hormozgan Iran 100 C4
Saaifontein S. Africa 132 F8
Saalach r. Germany 49 K8
Saale park Germany 48 I4
Saale r. Germany 48 I4
Saalfeld Germany 48 I5
Saalfelden am Steinernen Meer Austria 49 J8
Saanen Switz. 51 N6
Saanich Canada 166 F5
Saar land Germany see **Saarland**
Saar r. Germany 48 D6
Saarbrücken Germany 48 D6
Saare Estonia 42 H3
Sääre Estonia 42 D4
Saaremaa i. Estonia 42 D3
Saarenkylä Fin. 44 N2
Saar-Hunsrück, Naturpark nature res. Germany 48 D6
Saari Fin. 45 O3
Saarijärvi Fin. 44 N3
Saari-Kämä Fin. 44 N2
Saarikoski Fin. 44 M1
Saariselkä Fin. 44 N1
also known as Suoločielgi
Saaristomeren Kansallispuisto nat. park Fin. see **Skärgårdshavets Nationalpark**
Saarland land Germany 48 D6
English form Saar
Saarlouis Germany 48 D6
Saatlı Azer. 107 G3
also spelt Saatly
Saatly Azer. see **Saatlı**
Saatse Estonia 42 I4
Saba i. Neth. Antilles 187 H3
Saba, Wādī watercourse Saudi Arabia 104 B1
Sab' Ābār Syria 109 I4
Šabac Srbija Yugo. 58 A4
Sabadell Spain 55 N3
Sabae Japan 91 E7
Sabah state Malaysia 77 G1
formerly known as North Borneo
Sabak Malaysia 76 C2
Sabaki r. Kenya 128 D5
Sabalan, Kūhhā-ye mts Iran 100 A2
Sabalana i. Indon. 75 A4
Sabalana, Kepulauan is Indon. 75 A4
Sabalgarh India 96 C4
Sabamagrande Hond. 186 B4
Saban Venez. 199 E2
Sabana, Archipiélago de is Cuba 186 C2
Sabana de la Mar Dom. Rep. 187 F3
Sabanalarga Col. 198 C2
Sabaneta Dom. Rep. 187 F3
Sabang Sulawesi Selatan Indon. 75 B3
Sabang Sulawesi Tengah Indon. 75 A2
Sabang Indon. 76 A1
Sabano Col. 198 C5
Şabanözü Turkey 106 C2
Săbăoani Romania 58 H1
Sabará Brazil 203 D6
Sabari r. India 94 D2
also known as Kolab
Sabarmati r. India 96 B5
Sabaru i. Indon. 75 A4
Sabastiya West Bank 108 G5
Sabaudia Italy 56 F7
Sabaya Bol. 200 C4
Şabāyā Island Saudi Arabia 104 C4
Sabelo S. Africa 132 H8
Sabena Desert Kenya 128 C4
Sabhā Libya 120 B3
Şabḩā' Saudi Arabia 104 D3
Sabhrai India 96 A5
Sabi r. India 96 C3
Sabi r. Moz./Zimbabwe see **Save**
Sabie Moz. 131 G5
Sabie r. Moz./S. Africa 133 Q2
Sabie S. Africa 133 O2
Sabile Latvia 42 D4
Sabina U.S.A. 176 B6
Sabinal Mex. 184 D2
Sabinal, Cayo i. Cuba 186 D2
Sabiñánigo Spain 55 K2
Sabinar, Punta del mt. Spain 55 I8
Sabinas Mex. 185 E3
Sabinas r. Coahuila Mex. 179 B7
Sabinas r. Nuevo León Mex. 179 C7
Sabinas Hidalgo Mex. 185 E3
Sabine r. U.S.A. 179 D6
Sabine Lake U.S.A. 179 D6
Sabine National Wildlife Refuge nature res. U.S.A. 179 D6
Sabinópolis Brazil 207 J5
Sabinov Slovakia 49 S6
Sabirabad Azer. 107 G2
Sablayan Phil. 74 B3
Sable, Cape Canada 169 H5
Sable, Cape U.S.A. 175 D7
Sable, Lac du l. Canada 169 H2
Sable, Rivière du r. Canada 169 G2
Sable Island Canada 169 J5
Sables, River aux r. Canada 173 K4
Sablé-sur-Sarthe France 50 F5
Sablon, Pointe du pt France 51 K9
Saboeiro Brazil 202 E3
Sabon Kafi Niger 125 H3
Sabou Burkina 125 E3
Sabourin, Lac l. Canada 173 P3
Sabres France 50 F8
Sabrina Coast Antarctica 223 H2
Sabtang i. Phil. 74 B1
Sabugal Port. 54 D4
Sabula U.S.A. 172 C8
Sabulu Indon. 75 B3
Sabunten i. Indon. 77 F4
Şabyā Saudi Arabia 104 C4
Sabzawar Afgh. see **Shīndand**
Sabzevār Iran 100 D2
Sabzvārān Iran see **Jīroft**
Saca, Vârful mt. Romania 58 G2
Sacaba Bol. 200 D4
Sa Cabaneta Spain 55 N5
Sacaca Bol. 200 D4
Sacalinul Mare, Insula i. Romania 58 K4
Sacandaga r. U.S.A. 177 K2
Sacaton U.S.A. 183 M8
Saccarel, Mont mt. France/Italy 51 N8
Sac City U.S.A. 178 D3
Sacco r. Italy 56 F7
Săcele Romania 58 G3
Săcele Romania 58 J4
Săceni Romania 58 G4
Sachanga Angola 127 C8
Sachigo r. Canada 168 B2
Sachigo Lake Canada 167 M4
Sachin India 96 B5
Sach'on S. Korea 83 C6
formerly known as Samch'ŏnp'o
Sach'ŏn S. Korea 91 A7
Sach Pass India 96 C2
Sachsen land Germany 49 K4
English form Saxony
Sachsen-Anhalt land Germany 48 I3
English form Saxony-Anhalt
Sachs Harbour Canada 164 G2
also known as Ikaahuk
Sächsische Schweiz park Germany 49 L5
Sacirsuyu r. Syria/Turkey see **Sājūr, Nahr**
Sackpfeife hill Germany 48 F5
Sackville Canada 169 H4
Saco U.S.A. 177 O2
Sacol i. Phil. 74 B5
Sacramento Brazil 206 F6

▶**Sacramento** U.S.A. 182 C3
State capital of California.

Sacramento r. U.S.A. 182 C3
Sacramento, Pampa del plain Peru 200 A1
Sacramento Mountains U.S.A. 181 F6
Sacramento Valley U.S.A. 182 B1
Sacratif, Cabo c. Spain 55 H8
Săcueni Romania 58 D1
Sacuriuiná r. Brazil 201 F3
Sacxán Mex. 185 H5
Sada S. Africa 133 K9
Sádaba Spain 55 J2
Sa'dābād Iran 100 B4
Sá da Bandeira Angola see **Lubango**
Şadad Syria 109 H3
Şa'dah Yemen 104 C4
Şa'dah governorate Yemen 104 C4
Sada-misaki pt Japan 91 C8
Sadang r. Indon. 75 A3
Sadani Tanz. 129 C6
Sadao Thai. 79 C7
Şadārah Yemen 105 E5
Sadaseopet India 94 C2
Saddat al Hindīyah Iraq 107 F4
Saddleback pass S. Africa 133 P2
Saddleback Mesa mt. U.S.A. 179 B5
Saddle Hill hill Australia 149 E2
Saddle Island Vanuatu see **Mota Lava**
Saddle Peak hill India 95 G3
Sa Đec Vietnam 79 D6
Sadḩ Oman 105 F4
Sadhaura India 96 C3
Sadi Eth. 128 B2
Sadieville U.S.A. 176 A7
Sadīj watercourse Iran 100 D5
Sadiqabad Pak. 101 G4
Sadiya India 80 F7
Sa'diya Saudi Arabia 104 B3
Sa'dīyah, Hawr as imp. l. Iraq 107 F4
Sa'diyyat i. U.A.E. 105 F2
Sadjoavato Madag. 131 [inset] K2
Sad-Kharv Iran 100 D2
Sado r. Port. 54 C6
Sadoga-shima i. Japan 90 F6
Sadon Rus. Fed. 41 H8
Sadong r. Sarawak Malaysia 77 E2
Sadovoye Rus. Fed. 41 H7
Sa Dragonera i. Spain 55 N5
also known as Dragonera, Isla
Sadri India 96 B4
Sadulshahar India 96 B3
Sādūs Saudi Arabia 105 D2
Sæby Denmark 45 J4
Saegertown U.S.A. 176 E4
Saena Julia Italy see **Siena**
Safad Israel see **Ẕefat**
Safâga, Gezîret i. Egypt 104 A2
English form Safâga Island
Safâga Island Egypt see **Safâga, Gezîret**
Safané Burkina 124 E3
Šafárikovo Slovakia see **Tornaľa**
Safayal Maqūf well Iraq 107 F5
Safed Khirs mts Afgh. 101 G2
Safed Koh mts Afgh. 101 F3
Safed Koh mts Afgh./Pak. 101 G3
Säffle Sweden 45 K4
Safford U.S.A. 183 O9
Safi Jordan see **Aş Şāfī**
Safi Morocco 122 C2
Safiabad Iran 100 D2
Safīd r. Iran 100 B2
Safidabeh Iran 101 E4
Safīdār, Kūh-e mt. Iran 100 C4
Safid Dasht Iran 100 B3
Safīd Kūh mts Afgh. see **Paropamisus**
Safīd Sagak Iran 101 E3
Sāfir Yemen 105 D5
Safiras, Serra das mts Brazil 203 D6
Şāfītā Syria 108 H3
Safonovo Arkhangel'skaya Oblast' Rus. Fed. 40 I2
Safonovo Smolenskaya Oblast' Rus. Fed. 43 O6
Safotu Samoa 145 H3
Safrā' al Asyāḩ esc. Saudi Arabia 104 C2
Safrā' as Sark esc. Saudi Arabia 104 D2
Safranbolu Turkey 106 C2
Safwān Iraq 107 F5
Şag Romania 58 C3
Saga China 89 D6
also known as Gya'gya
Saga Japan 91 E8
Saga pref. Japan 91 B8
Saga Kazakh. 103 F2
Sagae Japan 90 G5
Sagaing Myanmar 78 A3
Sagaing admin. div. Myanmar 78 A3
Sagala Mali see **Séguéla**
Sagamihara Japan 91 F7
Sagami-nada g. Japan 91 F7
Sagami-wan b. Japan 91 F7
Sagamu Nigeria 125 F5
also spelt Shagamu
Saganash Lake Canada 173 K1
Saganoseki Japan 91 B8
Saganthit Kyun i. Myanmar 79 B5
also known as Sellore Island
Sagar Karnataka India 94 B3
Sagar Karnataka India 94 C2
Sagar Madhya Pradesh India 96 C5
Sagaredzho Georgia see **Sagarejo**
Sagarejo Georgia 107 F2
also spelt Sagaredzho
Sagaria Bangl. 97 F5
Sagar Island India 97 F5
Sagarmatha mt. China/Nepal see **Everest, Mount**
Sagarmatha National Park Nepal 97 E4
Sagastyr Rus. Fed. 39 M2
Sagauli India 97 E4
Sagavanirktok r. U.S.A. 164 E2
Sage U.S.A. 180 E4
Sage Creek r. U.S.A. 180 E2
Saggi, Har mt. Israel 108 F7
Saghand Iran 100 C3
Saghyz Kazakh. see **Sagiz**
Sagileru r. India 94 C3
Saginaw MI U.S.A. 173 J7
Saginaw MN U.S.A. 172 A4
Saginaw Bay U.S.A. 173 J7
Sağırlar Turkey 59 J9
Sagiz Atyrauskaya Oblast' Kazakh. 102 C2
also spelt Saghyz
Sagiz Atyrauskaya Oblast' Kazakh. 102 C3
Sagiz r. Kazakh. see **Sagyz**
Sağlamtaş Turkey 58 I8
Sagleipie Liberia 124 C5
Saglek Bay Canada 169 I1
Saglouc Canada see **Salluit**
Sagly Rus. Fed. 88 E1
Sagone, Golfe de b. Corse France 56 A6
Sagra mt. Spain 55 I7
Sagres Port. 54 C7
Sagres, Ponta de pt Port. 54 C8
Sagsay watercourse Mongolia 84 C2
Sagu Indon. 75 B5
Sagu Myanmar 78 A3
Saguache U.S.A. 181 F5
Saguache Creek r. U.S.A. 181 F5
Sagua de Tánamo Cuba 187 E2
Sagua la Grande Cuba 186 C2
Saguaro National Park U.S.A. 183 N9
Saguenay r. Canada 169 G3
Sagunt Spain see **Sagunto**
Sagunto Spain 55 K5
also spelt Sagunt; historically known as Murviedro or Saguntum
Saguntum Spain see **Sagunto**
Sagwara India 96 B5
Sagyndyk, Mys pt Kazakh. 102 B3
Sagyz r. Kazakh. 102 C3
formerly spelt Sagiz
Saḩāb Jordan 108 H6
Sahabab India 96 C3
Sahagún Spain 54 F2
Sahand, Kūh-e mt. Iran 100 A2
▶**Sahara** des. Africa 123 F4
africa [landscapes] ▶ 112–113
africa [locations] ▶ 118–119
Sahara, Gebel mt. Egypt 108 F9
Şaḩara el Gharbîya des. Egypt see **Western Desert**
Şaḩara el Sharqîya des. Egypt see **Eastern Desert**
Saharan Atlas mts Alg. see **Atlas Saharien**
Saharanpur India 96 C3
Sahara Well Australia 150 C4
Saharsa India 97 E4
Sahaswan India 96 C3
Sahat, Kūh-e hill Iran 100 C3
Sahatwar India 97 E4
Sahavato Madag. 131 [inset] K4
Sahbā', Wādī as watercourse Saudi Arabia 105 E3
Şahbuz Azer. 107 F3
also spelt Shakhbuz
Saheira, Wâdi el watercourse Egypt 108 E7
Sahel reg. Africa 124 C3
Sahel prov. Eritrea 104 B4
Sahel, Réserve Partielle du nature res. Burkina 125 E3
Sahibganj India 97 E4
Sahiwal Punjab Pak. 101 H4
Sahiwal Punjab Pak. 101 H4
Sahlābād Iran 101 D3
Sahl al Maṭrān Saudi Arabia 104 B2
Sahl Rakbah plain Saudi Arabia 104 C3
Şaḩm Oman 105 G2
Şaḩneh Iran 100 A3
Şaḩrā al Ḩijārah reg. Iraq 107 F5
Şaḩragt el-Kubra Egypt 108 C7
Sahu China see **Zadoi**
Sahuaripa Mex. 184 C2
Sahuayo Mex. 185 E4
Şāḩūq reg. Saudi Arabia 104 C2
Şāḩūq, Wādī watercourse Saudi Arabia 104 C2
Šahy Slovakia 49 P7
Sahyadri mts India see **Western Ghats**
Sahyadriparvat Range hills India 94 B1
also known as Ajanta Range
Şahyūn tourist site Syria 108 H2
Sai r. India 96 D4
Saibai Island Australia 73 J8
Sai Buri Thai. 79 C7
Sai Buri r. Thai. 79 C7
Saïda Alg. 123 F2
Saïda Lebanon see **Sidon**
Saïda, Monts de mts Alg. 55 L9
Sai Dao Tai, Khao mt. Thai. 79 C5
Sa'id Bin Sahrān Oman 105 G3
Saïdia Morocco 55 I9
Saidpur Bangl. 97 F4
Saidpur India 97 D4
Saidu Pak. 101 H3
Saigō Japan 91 C6
Saigon Vietnam see **Ho Chi Minh City**
Saiha India 97 G5
Saihan Tal China 85 G3
also known as Sonid Youqi
Saihan Toroi China 84 D3
Saija Fin. 44 O2
Saijō Japan 91 C8
Saikai National Park Japan 91 A8
Saikanosy Masoala pen. Madag. 131 [inset] K2
Saiki Japan 91 B8
Sai Kung Hong Kong China 87 [inset]
Sailana India 96 B5
Sailyugem Mountains Rus. Fed. 84 A1
Saimaa l. Fin. 45 O3
Saimaankanava r. Fin. 45 O3
Saimbeyli Turkey 106 D3
Sain Alto Mex. 185 E4
Saindak Pak. 101 E4
Sa'īndezh Iran 100 A2
also known as Sa'īn Qal'eh; formerly known as Shāhīn Dezh
Sa'īn Qal'eh Iran see **Sa'īndezh**
Saïnsoubou Senegal 124 C3
Saint r. U.S.A. 178 E4
St Abb's Head U.K. 46 J8
St-Affrique France 51 I9
St-Aignan France 50 H5
St Alban's Canada 169 K4
St Albans U.K. 47 L12
historically known as Verulamium
St Albans VT U.S.A. 177 L1
St Albans WV U.S.A. 176 D7
St Alban's Head U.K. 47 J13
also known as St Aldhelm's Head
St Albert Canada 167 H4
St Aldhelm's Head U.K. see **St Alban's Head**
St-Amand-les-Eaux France 51 J2
St-Amand-Montrond France 51 I6
St-Ambroise Canada 169 G3
St-Amour France 51 L6
St-André, Cap pt Madag. see **Vilanandro, Tanjona**
St-André-de-Cubzac France 50 F8
St Andrews N.Z. 153 F12
St Andrews U.K. 46 J7
St Andrew Sound inlet U.S.A. 175 D6
Saint Anne U.S.A. 172 F9
St Ann's Bay Jamaica 186 D3
St Anthony Canada 169 K3
Saint Anthony U.S.A. 180 E4
St Arnaud Australia 147 D4
St Arnaud N.Z. 153 G9
St-Arnoult-en-Yvelines France 51 H4
St Asaph Bay Australia 148 A1
St-Astier France 50 G7
St-Aubin-du-Cormier France 50 E4
St-Augustin Canada 169 J3
St Augustin r. Canada 169 J3
St Augustine U.S.A. 175 D6
historically known as San Agostín
St-Aulaye France 50 G7
St Austell U.K. 47 H13
St-Avé France 50 D5
St Barbe Canada 169 J3
St-Barthélémi Canada 169 F4
St-Barthélemy i. West Indies 187 H3
St-Barthélemy, Pic de mt. France 50 H10
St Bathans N.Z. 153 D12
St Bees Head U.K. 47 I9
St Bernard mt. N.Z. 153 H10
St-Blaise Switz. 51 M5
St-Brice-en-Coglès France 50 E4
St Bride's Bay U.K. 47 G12
St-Brieuc France 50 D4
St-Brieuc, Baie de b. France 50 D4
St-Calais France 50 G5
St Catharines Canada 168 E5
St Catherine's Canada 169 K4
St Catherine's Point U.K. 47 K13
St-Céré France 50 H8
St-Chamond France 51 K7
St Charles Canada 173 M4
St Charles MD U.S.A. 177 I7
Saint Charles U.S.A. 173 I7
St Charles MO U.S.A. 174 B4
St-Chély-d'Apcher France 51 J8
St-Christol-lès-Alès France 51 K8
St Christopher i. St Kitts and Nevis see **St Kitts**
St Christopher and Nevis country West Indies see **St Kitts and Nevis**
St-Ciers-sur-Gironde France 50 F7
St Clair r. Canada/U.S.A. 174 D3
St Clair U.S.A. 173 K8
St Clair, Lake Canada/U.S.A. 173 K8
St Clairsville U.S.A. 176 E5
St-Claude France 51 L6
Saint Cloud U.S.A. 175 D6
St Cloud U.S.A. 178 D2
St-Coeur-de-Marie Canada 169 G3
St Croix r. Canada/U.S.A. 165 M5
St Croix r. U.S.A. 172 A5
St Croix Falls U.S.A. 172 A5
St Croix Island Virgin Is (U.S.A.) 187 G3
St-Cyr-sur-Loire France 50 G5
St David's U.K. 47 G12
also known as Tyddewi
St David's Head U.K. 47 G12
St-Denis France 51 I4

▶**St-Denis** Réunion 219 K7
Capital of Réunion.

St-Denis-du-Sig Alg. see **Sig**
St-Dié France 51 M4
St-Dizier France 51 K4
St-Domingue country West Indies see **Haiti**
Sainte Anne Canada 167 L5
Sainte Anne, Lac l. Alta Canada 167 H4
Sainte Anne, Lac l. Que. Canada 169 H3
Ste-Anne-de-Beaupré Canada 169 G4
Ste-Anne-de-Portneuf Canada 169 G3
Ste-Anne-des-Monts Canada 169 H3
Ste-Anne-du-Lac Canada 173 R4
Ste-Émélie-de-l'Énergie Canada 169 F4
Ste-Foy-la-Grande France 50 G8
Sainte Genevieve U.S.A. 174 B4
St-Égrève France 51 L7
Ste-Hermine France 50 E6
St Elias, Cape U.S.A. 164 E4

▶**St Elias, Mount** U.S.A. 166 A2
4th highest mountain in North America.
northamerica [landscapes] ▶ 156–157

St Elias Mountains Canada 166 A2
St Élie Fr. Guiana 199 H3
St-Éloy-les-Mines France 51 I6
Sainte Marguerite r. Canada 169 H3
Ste-Marie Canada 169 G4
Ste-Marie Martinique 187 H4
Ste-Marie, Cap c. Madag. see **Vohimena, Tanjona**
Ste-Maure-de-Touraine France 50 G5
Ste-Maxime France 51 M9
Ste-Rose Guadeloupe 187 H3
Ste-Rose-du-Dégelé Canada see **Dégelis**
Sainte Rose du Lac Canada 167 L5
Saintes France 50 F7
Saintes, Îles des is Guadeloupe 187 H4
Sainte Thérèse, Lac l. Canada 166 F1
St-Étienne France 51 K7
St-Étienne-de-Tinée France 51 M8
St-Étienne-du-Rouvray France 50 H3
St Eustatius i. Neth. Antilles 187 H3
St-Fabien Canada 169 G3
St Faith's S. Africa 133 O7
St-Félicien Canada 169 F3
St-Félix-de-Dalquier Canada 173 O2
St-Florentin France 51 J4
St-Florent-sur-Cher France 51 I6
St Floris, Parc National nat. park Cent. Afr. Rep. 126 D2
St-Flour France 51 J7
St Francesville U.S.A. 175 B6
St Francis r. Canada/U.S.A. 174 G2
St Francis r. U.S.A. 174 B5
St Francis, Cape S. Africa 133 I11
St Francis Bay S. Africa 133 J11
St Francis Isles Australia 146 B3
St-François r. Canada 169 F4
St-François, Lac l. Canada 169 G4
St-Gaudens France 50 G9
St-Gaultier France 50 H6
St-Gély-du-Fesc France 51 J9
St-Geniez-d'Olt France 51 I8
St George Australia 147 F2
St George r. Australia 149 E3
St George Canada 169 H4
St George AK U.S.A. 164 C4
St George SC U.S.A. 175 D5
St George UT U.S.A. 183 K4
St George, Cape P.N.G. 145 E2
St George, Point U.S.A. 180 A4
St George Head Australia 147 F3
St George Island AK U.S.A. 164 C4
St George Island FL U.S.A. 175 C6
St George Range hills Australia 150 D3
St George's Canada 169 J3
St-Georges Canada 169 G4
St Georges Fr. Guiana 199 I4

▶**St George's** Grenada 187 H4
Capital of Grenada.

St George's Bay Nfld. Canada 169 J3
St George's Bay N.S. Canada 169 I4
St George's Cay i. Belize 185 I5
St George's Channel India 95 G5
St George's Channel P.N.G. 145 E2
St George's Channel Rep. of Ireland/U.K. 47 F12
St Germain U.S.A. 172 D5
St-Germain-du-Puy France 51 I5
St-Germain-les-Belles France 50 H7
St-Gildas, Pointe de pt France 50 D5
St-Gildas-des-Bois France 50 D5
St-Gilles France 51 K9
St-Gilles-Croix-de-Vie France 50 E6
St Govan's Head U.K. 47 H12
St Helen U.S.A. 173 I6

▶**St Helena** terr. S. Atlantic Ocean 216 N7
United Kingdom Overseas Territory.

St Helena U.S.A. 182 B3
St Helena Bay S. Africa 132 C9
St Helena Bay b. S. Africa 132 C9
St Helena Sound inlet U.S.A. 175 D5
St Helens Australia 147 F5
St Helens U.K. 47 J10
St Helens U.S.A. 180 B3
▶**St Helens, Mount** vol. U.S.A. 180 B3
northamerica [threats] ▶ 160–161
St Helens Point Australia 147 F5

▶**St Helier** Channel Is 50 D3
Capital of Jersey.

St-Hilaire-du-Harcouët France 50 E4
Sainthiya India 97 E5
St-Hubert Belgium 51 L2
St-Hyacinthe Canada 169 F4
St Ignace U.S.A. 173 I5
St Ignace Island Canada 168 C3
St Ignatius Guyana 199 G4
St Ives U.K. 47 G13
St Jacques, Cap Vietnam see **Vung Tau**
St-Jacques-de-Dupuy Canada 168 E3
St-Jacques-de-la-Lande France 50 E4
St-James France 50 E4
St James MI U.S.A. 172 H5
St James MN U.S.A. 178 D3
St James MO U.S.A. 174 B4
St James NY U.S.A. 177 L5
St James, Cape Canada 166 D5
St-Jean r. Que. Canada 169 H3
St-Jean r. Que. Canada 169 H3
St Jean Fr. Guiana 199 H3
St-Jean, Lac l. Canada 169 F3
St-Jean-d'Acre Israel see **'Akko**
St-Jean-d'Angély France 50 F7
St-Jean-de-la-Ruelle France 50 H5
St-Jean-de-Luz France 50 E9
St-Jean-de-Maurienne France 51 M7
St-Jean-de-Monts France 50 D6
St-Jean-de-Port-Joli Canada 169 G4
St-Jean-sur-Richelieu Canada 169 F4
St-Jérôme Canada 169 F4
St Joe r. U.S.A. 180 C3
Saint John Canada 169 H4
St John r. Liberia 124 C5
St John U.S.A. 178 C4
St John r. U.S.A. 174 H2
St John, Cape Canada 169 K3
St John Bay Canada 169 J3
St John Island Canada 169 J3
St John Island Virgin Is (U.S.A.) 187 G3

▶**St John's** Antigua and Barbuda 187 H3
Capital of Antigua and Barbuda.

▶**St John's** Canada 169 K4
Provincial capital of Newfoundland.

St Johns AZ U.S.A. 183 O7
St Johns MI U.S.A. 173 I7
St Johns OH U.S.A. 176 A5
St Johns r. U.S.A. 175 D6
St Johnsbury U.S.A. 177 M1
St Johnsville U.S.A. 177 K3
St Joseph LA U.S.A. 175 B6
St Joseph MI U.S.A. 172 G8
St Joseph MO U.S.A. 178 D4
St Joseph r. MI U.S.A. 172 G8
St Joseph r. MI U.S.A. 173 H9
St Joseph, Lake Canada 168 B3
St-Joseph-d'Alma Canada see **Alma**
St Joseph Island Canada 168 D4
St Joseph Island U.S.A. 179 C7
St Jovité Canada 169 F4
St-Juéry France 51 I9
St-Julien-de-Concelles France 50 E5
St-Julien-en-Genevois France 51 M6
St-Junien France 50 G7
St-Just-en-Chaussée France 51 I3

St-Just-St-Rambert France 51 K7
St Kilda i. U.K. 46 D6
St Kitts i. St Kitts and Nevis 187 H3
also known as St Christopher
▶St Kitts and Nevis country West Indies 187 H3
also known as St Christopher and Nevis
northamerica [countries] ▶ 158–159
St-Laurent, Golfe du g. Canada see St Lawrence, Gulf of
St-Laurent-du-Maroni Fr. Guiana 199 H3
St Lawrence Australia 149 F4
St Lawrence Canada 169 K4
St Lawrence inlet Canada 169 I3
St Lawrence, Cape Canada 169 I4
St Lawrence, Gulf of Canada 169 I3
also known as St-Laurent, Golfe du
St Lawrence Island U.S.A. 164 C3
St Lawrence Islands National Park Canada 173 R6
St Lawrence Seaway sea chan. Canada/U.S.A. 174 F2
St Lazare Canada 169 F4
St-Léonard N.B. Canada 169 H4
St-Léonard Que. Canada 169 F4
St Leonard U.S.A. 177 I7
St-Léonard-de-Noblat France 50 H7
St Lewis Canada 169 K2
St Lewis r. Canada 169 K2
St-Lô France 50 E3
St-Louis France 51 N5
St Louis MI U.S.A. 173 I7
St Louis r. U.S.A. 174 B4
St Louis U.S.A. 174 A2
St-Louis du Nord Haiti 187 J3
St-Loup-sur-Semouse France 51 M5
▶St Lucia country West Indies 187 H4
northamerica [countries] ▶ 158–159
St Lucia, Lake S. Africa 133 Q5
St Lucia Channel Martinique/St Lucia 187 H4
St Lucia Estuary S. Africa 133 Q5
St Lucia Game Reserve nature res. S. Africa 133 Q5
St Lucia Park nature res. S. Africa 133 Q5
St Luke's Island Myanmar see Zadetkale Kyun
St-Macaire-en-Mauges France 50 F5
St Magnus Bay U.K. 46 K3
St-Maixent-l'École France 50 F6
St-Malo France 50 D4
St-Malo, Golfe de g. France 50 D4
St-Mandrier-sur-Mer France 51 L9
St Marc Haiti 187 E3
St-Marc, Canal de sea chan. Haiti 187 E3
St-Marcellin France 51 L7
St Margaret's Hope U.K. 46 J5
Saint Maries U.S.A. 180 C3
St Marks S. Africa 133 L9
St Mark's S. Africa see Cofimvaba
St Marks National Wildlife Refuge nature res. U.S.A. 175 C6
▶St Martin i. West Indies 187 H3
Dependency of Guadeloupe (France). The southern part of the island is the Dutch territory of Sint Maarten.
St Martin, Lake Canada 167 L5
St-Martin-de-Crau France 51 K9
St-Martin-de-Ré France 50 E6
St-Martin-d'Hères France 51 L7
St Mary r. Canada 167 H5
St Mary, Mount N.Z. 153 D12
St Marys Australia 147 F5
St Marys r. U.K. 47 F14
Saint Marys U.S.A. 178 C4
St Marys OH U.S.A. 176 A5
St Marys PA U.S.A. 176 G4
St Marys WV U.S.A. 176 D6
St Marys r. U.S.A. 176 A5
St Mary's, Cape Canada 169 K4
St Mary's Bay Canada 169 K4
St Marys City U.S.A. 177 I7
St-Mathieu Canada 173 G7
St-Mathieu, Pointe de pt France 50 B4
St Matthew Island U.S.A. 164 B3
Saint Matthews U.S.A. 175 D5
St Matthew's Island Myanmar see Zadetkyi Kyun
St Matthias Group is P.N.G. 145 D2
St Maurice r. Canada 169 F4
St-Maurice, Réserve Faunique du nature res. Canada 169 F3
St-Maximin-la-Ste-Baume France 51 L9
St-Médard-en-Jalles France 50 F8
St Michaels U.S.A. 177 I7
St Michael's Bay Canada 169 K2
St Michael's Mount tourist site U.K. 47 G13
St-Michel-de-Maurienne France 51 M7
St-Michel-des-Saints Canada 169 F4
St Mihiel France 51 L4
St-Nazaire France 50 D5
St Nicolas Belgium see Sint-Niklaas
St-Nicolas-de-Port France 51 M4
St Niklaus Switz. 51 N6
St-Omer France 51 I2
Saintonge reg. France 50 F7
St-Pacôme Canada 169 G4
St-Palais France 50 E9
St Paris U.S.A. 176 B5
St Pascal Canada 169 G4
St-Patrice, Lac Canada 173 P4
St Paul Canada 167 I4
St Paul r. Canada 169 J3
St Paul r. Liberia 124 C4
St Paul IA U.S.A. 172 B10
▶St Paul MN U.S.A. 174 A2
State capital of Minnesota.
St Paul NE U.S.A. 178 C3

St Paul VA U.S.A. 176 C9
St Paul, Île i. Indian Ocean 219 M8
English form St Paul Island
St-Paul-de-Fenouillet France 51 I10
St Paul Island Canada 169 I4
St Paul Island Indian Ocean see St Paul, Île
St-Paul-lès-Dax France 50 E9
St Paul Subterranean River National Park Phil. 74 A4
St Peter U.S.A. 174 A2
St Peter and St Paul Rocks is N. Atlantic Ocean see São Pedro e São Paulo
▶St Peter Port Channel Is 50 D3
Capital of Guernsey.
St Peter's Canada 169 I4
St Peters Canada 169 I4
▶St Petersburg Rus. Fed. 43 L2
5th most populous city in Europe. Also known as Sankt-Peterburg; formerly known as Leningrad; historically known as Petrograd.
world [cities] ▶ 24–25
St Petersburg U.S.A. 175 D7
St Petrus i. Indon. 77 E2
St-Philbert-de-Grand-Lieu France 50 E5
St-Pierre mt. France 51 I9
St Pierre Mauritius 129 F7
▶St-Pierre St Pierre and Miquelon 169 K4
Capital of St Pierre and Miquelon.
St-Pierre, Lac l. Canada 169 F4
▶St Pierre and Miquelon terr. N. America 169 J4
French Territorial Collectivity.
oceania [countries] ▶ 138–139
St-Pierre-des-Corps France 50 G5
St-Pierre-d'Oléron France 50 E7
St-Pierre-le-Moûtier France 51 J5
St-Pol-sur-Ternoise France 51 I2
St-Pons-de-Thomières France 51 I9
St-Pourçain-sur-Sioule France 51 J6
St Quentin Canada 169 H4
St-Quentin France 51 J3
St-Raphaël France 51 M9
St Regis r. U.S.A. 177 K1
St Regis Falls U.S.A. 177 K1
St-Renan France 50 B4
St-Rigaud, Mont mt. France 51 K6
St-Sauveur-des-Monts Canada 169 F4
St-Savin France 50 F7
St-Savinien France 50 F7
St-Sébastien-sur-Loire France 50 E5
St-Siméon, Mont de mt. France 51 M6
St Stephen U.S.A. 175 E5
St-Symphorien France 50 F8
St Terese U.S.A. 166 C3
St Theresa Point Canada 167 M4
St Thomas Canada 168 D5
St Thomas Virgin Is (U.S.A.) 187 G3
St-Tite-des-Caps Canada 169 G4
St-Tropez France 51 M9
St-Tropez, Cap de c. France 51 M9
St-Valery-en-Caux France 50 G2
St-Valery-sur-Somme France 50 H2
St-Vallier Bourgogne France 51 K6
St-Vallier Rhône-Alpes France 51 K7
St-Vaury France 50 H6
St Vincent Italy 51 N7
St Vincent i. West Indies 199 F1
St-Vincent, Cap pt Madag. see Ankaboa, Tanjona
St Vincent, Cape Australia 147 E5
St Vincent, Cape Port. see São Vicente, Cabo de
St Vincent, Gulf Australia 146 C3
▶St Vincent and the Grenadines i. West Indies 187 H4
northamerica [countries] ▶ 158–159
St-Vincent-de-Tyrosse France 50 E9
St Vincent Island U.S.A. 175 C6
St Vincent Passage St Lucia/St Vincent 187 H4
St Walburg Canada 167 I4
St-Yrieix-la-Perche France 50 H7
Saipal mt. Nepal 97 D3
Saipan i. N. Mariana Is 73 K3
also spelt Seypan
Saison r. France 50 F9
Saitama pref. Japan 90 F7
Saiteli Turkey see Kadınhanı
Saito Japan 91 B8
Saittanulkki hill Fin. 40 O2
Saivomuotka Sweden 44 M1
Sai Yok National Park Thai. 79 B5
Sajama, Nevado mt. Bol. 200 C4
Sajid Saudi Arabia 104 C2
Sājir, Ra's c. Oman 105 F4
Sajó r. Hungary 49 R8
Sajóhídvég Hungary 49 R7
Sajûr, Nahr r. Syria/Turkey 109 J1
also known as Bağırsak Deresi or Sacırsuyu
Sajzi Iran 100 B3
Sak watercourse S. Africa 132 F6
Saka Eth. 128 C2
Sakai Japan 91 G7
Sakaide Japan 91 C7
Sakaiminato Japan 91 C7
Sakākah Saudi Arabia 107 E5
also known as Sikaka
Sakakawea, Lake U.S.A. 178 B2
Sakala i. Indon. 77 E4
Sakaile Tanz. 129 A7
Sakami Canada 168 F2
Sakami r. Canada 169 E2
Sakami Lake Canada 168 E2
Sakania Dem. Rep. Congo 127 F8
Sakar mts Bulg. 58 H7
Sakar Turkm. 103 E5
Sakaraha Madag. 131 [inset] J4
Sakar-Chaga Turkm. 103 E5
Sakartvelo country Asia see Georgia
Sakarya Turkey 106 B2
also known as Adapazarı; formerly known as Adabazar
Sakarya r. Turkey 106 B2
Sakassou Côte d'Ivoire 124 C5
Sakata Japan 90 F5
Sakawa Japan 91 C7
Sakchu N. Korea 83 B4
Saken Seyfullin Kazakh. 103 H2
formerly known as Zharyk
Sa Keo r. Thai. 79 C5
Sakété Benin 125 F5
Sakhalin i. Rus. Fed. 82 F2
Sakhalin Oblast admin. div. Rus. Fed. see Sakhalinskaya Oblast'
Sakhalinskaya Oblast' admin. div. Rus. Fed. 82 F2
English form Sakhalin Oblast
Sakhalinskiy Zaliv b. Rus. Fed. 82 F1
Sakhnina, Mys c. Rus. Fed. 40 J1
Sakharovo Rus. Fed. 43 R5
Sakhelwe S. Africa 133 N3
Sakhile S. Africa 133 N3
Sakhra Turkm. 102 D5
Sakht-Sar Iran 100 B2
Şäki Azer. 107 F2
also spelt Sheki; formerly known as Nukha
Saki Nigeria 125 F4
also spelt Shaki
Saki Ukr. see Saky
Šakiai Lith. 42 E7
Sakiet Sidi Youssef Tunisia 57 A12

Sakir mt. Pak. 101 F4
Sakishima-shotō is Japan 81 K8
Sakleshpur India 94 B3
Sakmara r. Rus. Fed. 102 C2
Sa-koi Myanmar 78 B4
Sakoli India 96 C5
Sakon Nakhon Thai. 78 D4
Sakra, Pulau reg. Sing. 76 [inset]
Sakrand Pak. 101 G5
Sakrivier S. Africa 132 E7
Saksaul'skiy Kazakh. 103 E3
also known as Sekseüil; formerly known as Saksaul'skoye
Saksaul'skoye Kazakh. see Saksaul'skiy
Sakshaug Norway 44 J3
Sakti India 97 D5
Saku Japan 91 F6
Sakura Japan 91 G7
Sakura-jima vol. Japan 91 B9
Saky Ukr. 41 E7
also known as Saki
Säkylä Fin. 45 M3
Sal i. Cape Verde 124 [inset]
Sal r. Rus. Fed. 53 K2
Sal, Punta pt Hond. 186 B4
Sala Latvia 42 H5
Šaľa Slovakia 49 O7
Sala Sweden 45 L4
Salabangka, Kepulauan is Indon. 75 B3
Salaberry-de-Valleyfield Canada 169 F4
Salaca r. Latvia 42 H4
Salacgriva Latvia 42 F4
Sala Consilina Italy 57 H8
Salada, Bahía b. Chile 204 C2
Saiada, Laguna salt l. Mex. 184 B1
Saladas Arg. 204 F3
Salādin, Wādī watercourse Jordan 108 G8
Saladillo r. Córdoba Arg. 204 E4
Saladillo r. Santiago del Estero Arg. 204 E3
Salado r. Buenos Aires Arg. 204 F4
Salado r. Formosa Arg. 204 F2
Salado r. La Rioja Arg. 204 C3
Salado r. Río Negro Arg. 204 D6
Salado r. Arg. 204 D5
Salado r. Cuba 186 D2
Salado Ecuador 198 B5
Salado r. Mex. 185 F3
Salado r. Spain 54 E8
Salado watercourse U.S.A. 181 F6
Saladou Guinea 124 C4
Salaga Ghana 125 E4
Şalāh Saudi Arabia 104 C3
Şalāh, Tall hill Jordan 109 J4
Şalāh ad Dīn governorate Iraq 107 E4
Salahuddin India 97 F3
Salajwe Botswana 131 E4
Salakh, Jabal mt. Oman 105 G3
Salal Chad 120 C6
Salalah Sudan 121 H4
Şalālah Oman 105 F4
Salalé well Niger 125 I3
Salamá Guat. 185 H6
Salamá Hond. 186 B4
Salamajärven kansallispuisto nat. park Fin. 44 N3
Salamanca Chile 204 C3
Salamanca Mex. 185 E4
Salamanca Spain 54 F4
historically known as Helmantica or Salamantica
Salamanca U.S.A. 176 G3
Salamanga Moz. 131 G5
Salamantica Spain see Salamanca
Salamat pref. Chad 126 D2
Salamat, Bahr r. Chad 126 C2
Salāmatābād Iran 100 A3
Salamina Col. see Salamina
Salamina Greece 59 E11
Salamina i. Greece 59 E11
also known as Salamís
Salamís tourist site Cyprus 108 E2
also known as Constantia
Salamis i. Greece see Salamina
Salamiyah Syria 109 I2
Salamonie r. U.S.A. 172 H10
Salamonie Lake U.S.A. 172 H10
Salandi r. India 95 E1
Salantai Lith. 42 C5
Salaqi China 85 F3
also known as Tumd Youqi
Sālard Romania 58 D1
Salar de Pocitos Arg. 200 D6
Salas Spain 54 E1
Salas de los Infantes Spain 55 H2
Salaspils Latvia 42 F5
Salat r. France 50 H9
Salatiga Indon. 77 E4
Sălăuţa r. Romania 58 F1
Salavat Rus. Fed. 102 C1
Salaverry Peru 200 A2
Salawati i. Indon. 75 N7
Salawin Wildlife Reserve nature res. Thai. 78 B4
Salay Phil. 74 C4
Salaya India 96 A5
Salayar i. Indon. 75 B4
Salayar, Selat sea chan. Indon. 75 B4
Sala y Gómez, Isla i. S. Pacific Ocean 221 K7
Salazar Angola see N'dalatando
Salazar Arg. 204 E5
Salbris France 51 I5
Salcantay, Cerro mt. Peru 200 B3
Salcedo Dom. Rep. 187 F3
Sălciile Romania 58 H4
Šalčininkai Lith. 42 G7
Sălcioara Romania 58 H4
Saldae Alg. see Bejaïa
Salda Gölü l. Turkey 59 K11
Saldana Spain 54 G2
Saldanha S. Africa 132 B10
Saldanha Bay S. Africa 132 B10
Saldus Latvia 42 D5
Sale Australia 147 E4
Sale Myanmar 78 A3
Salea Indon. 75 B3
Saleh, Teluk b. Indon. 77 G5
Şālehābād Hamadān Iran 100 B3
Şālehābād Khorāsān Iran 101 E2
Salekhard Rus. Fed. 38 G3
historically known as Obdorsk
Salem India 94 C4
Salem S. Africa 133 K10
Salem AR U.S.A. 174 B4
Salem IL U.S.A. 172 B10
Salem IL U.S.A. 174 B4
Salem MA U.S.A. 177 O3
Salem MO U.S.A. 174 B4
Salem NJ U.S.A. 177 J6
Salem NY U.S.A. 177 L2
▶Salem OR U.S.A. 180 B3
State capital of Oregon.
Salem SD U.S.A. 178 C3
Salem UT U.S.A. 183 M1
Salem VA U.S.A. 176 E8
Salem WV U.S.A. 176 E6
Salemi Sicilia Italy 57 E11
Sälen Sweden 45 K3
Salerno Italy 57 G8
historically known as Salernum
Salerno, Golfo di g. Italy 57 G8
Salernum Italy see Salerno
Sales Oliveira Brazil 206 F7

Salesópolis Brazil 207 H10
Salford U.K. 47 J10
Salgada Brazil 199 F5
Salgado Brazil 202 E4
Salgótarján Hungary 49 Q7
Salgueiro Brazil 202 E4
Sali Alg. 123 E4
Salian Afgh. 101 E4
Salibabu i. Indon. 75 C2
Salida U.S.A. 181 F5
Saliena Latvia 42 H5
Salignac-Eyvignes France 50 H8
Salihli Turkey 106 B3
Salihorsk Belarus 42 I9
also spelt Soligorsk
Salīkénié Senegal 124 B3
Salimi Dem. Rep. Congo 127 D7
Salimo Moz. 129 C8
Salina KS U.S.A. 178 C4
Salina UT U.S.A. 183 M3
Salina, Isola i. Isole Lipari Italy 57 G10
Salina Cruz Mex. 185 F5
Salinas Brazil 202 D6
Salinas Ecuador 198 A5
Salinas Mex. 185 E4
Salinas r. Mex. 179 C7
Salinas U.S.A. 182 C5
Salinas r. U.S.A. 182 C5
Salinas, Cabo de c. Spain see Ses Salines, Cap de
Salinas, Ponta das pt Angola 127 B8
Salinas, Punta pt Dom. Rep. 187 F3
Salinas de Garci Mendoza Bol. 200 D4
Saline U.S.A. 173 J8
Saline r. AR U.S.A. 179 D5
Saline r. KS U.S.A. 178 C4
Saline Valley depr. U.S.A. 182 G5
Salineville U.S.A. 176 E5
Salingyi Myanmar 78 A3
Salinópolis Brazil 202 C2
Salinosó Lachay, Punta pt Peru 200 A2
Salisbury U.K. 47 K12
Salisbury MD U.S.A. 177 J7
Salisbury NC U.S.A. 174 D5
Salisbury PA U.S.A. 176 F6
Salisbury Zimbabwe see Harare
Salisbury Island Canada 165 L3
Salisbury Plain U.K. 47 J12
Sălişte Romania 58 E3
Salitre r. Brazil 202 D4
Şalkhad Syria 109 H5
Salki r. India 95 E1
Salla Fin. 44 P2
Salliqueló Arg. 204 E5
Sallisaw U.S.A. 179 D5
Sallom Sudan 104 B4
Sallum Canada 165 L3
formerly known as Saglouc
Sallyana Nepal see Salyan
Salma Syria 109 H2
Salmás Iran 100 A2
also known as Shāhpūr
Salmi Rus. Fed. 40 D3
Salmivaara Fin. 44 O2
Salmo Canada 167 G5
Salmon U.S.A. 180 D3
Salmon r. U.S.A. 180 C3
Salmon, Middle Fork r. U.S.A. 180 D3
Salmon Arm Canada 166 G5
Salmon Falls Creek r. U.S.A. 180 D4
Salmon Gums Australia 151 C7
Salmon Reservoir U.S.A. 177 J2
Salmon River Mountains U.S.A. 180 D3
Salmonsdam Nature Reserve S. Africa 132 D11
Salmtal Germany 48 D6
Salo Cent. Afr. Rep. 126 C4
Salo Fin. 45 M3
Salò Italy 56 C3
Saloinen Fin. 44 N2
Salome U.S.A. 183 K8
Salon India 97 D4
Salon-de-Provence France 51 L9
Salonga r. Dem. Rep. Congo 126 D5
Salonica Greece see Thessaloniki
Salonika Greece see Thessaloniki
Salonta Romania 58 C2
Salor r. Spain 54 D5
Salou Spain 55 M3
Salou, Cap de c. Spain 55 M3
Saloum watercourse Senegal 124 A3
Salpausselkä reg. Fin. 45 N3
Salsacate Arg. 204 D3
Salsbruket Norway 44 J2
Salses, Étang de l. France see Leucate, Étang de
Salsk Rus. Fed. 41 G7
Salso r. Sicilia Italy 57 F11
Salso r. Sicilia Italy 57 G11
Salsomaggiore Terme Italy 56 B4
Salt Jordan see As Salt
Salt watercourse S. Africa 132 H10
Salt Spain 55 N3
Salt r. AZ U.S.A. 183 L8
Salt r. MO U.S.A. 178 E4
Salt r. WY U.S.A. 180 E4
Salta Arg. 200 D6
Salta prov. Arg. 204 D2
Saltanovka Rus. Fed. 43 P9
Saltcoats Canada 167 K5
Saltee Islands Rep. of Ireland 47 F11
Saltery Bay Canada 166 E5
Saltfjellet Svartisen Nasjonalpark nat. park Norway 44 K2
Salt Fork r. U.S.A. 178 C4
Salt Fork Arkansas r. U.S.A. 178 C4
Salt Fork Brazos r. U.S.A. 179 B5
Salt Fork Lake U.S.A. 176 D5
Salt Fork Red r. U.S.A. 179 C5
Saltillo Mex. 185 E3
Salt Lake salt l. India 89 A7
▶Salt Lake City U.S.A. 183 M1
State capital of Utah.
Salt Lick U.S.A. 176 B7
Salt Marsh Lake salt l. U.S.A. 183 K2
Salto Brazil 206 F10
Salto Uruguay 204 F3
Salto r. Italy 56 E6
Salto da Divisa Brazil 202 E6
Salto de Agua Mex. 185 G5
Salto del Guairá Para. 201 G5
Salto Grande Brazil 206 D9
Salto Grande, Embalse de resr Uruguay 204 F3
Salton City U.S.A. 183 H8
Salton Sea salt l. U.S.A. 183 I3
Saltpond Ghana 125 E5
Salt River Canada 167 H2
Saltrou Haiti see Belle-Anse
Saltville U.S.A. 176 C8
Saltyki Rus. Fed. 43 U8
Saluda SC U.S.A. 175 D5
Saluda VA U.S.A. 177 I8
Saluda r. U.S.A. 174 D5
Saluebesar r. Indon. 75 B3
Salue Timpaus, Selat sea chan. Indon. 75 B3
Salûm Egypt 106 A5
Salûm, Gulf of Egypt 121 E2
Salumbar India 96 B4
Saluq, Küh-e mt. Iran 100 D2

Salur India 95 D2
Saluzzo Italy 51 N8
Salvador Brazil 202 E5
formerly known as Bahia
Salvador country Central America see El Salvador
Salvador, Lake U.S.A. 175 B6
Salvador Mazza Arg. 201 E5
Salvaterra Brazil 202 C2
Salvatierra Mex. 185 E4
Salvation Creek r. U.S.A. 183 N3
Salwah Saud. Arabia 105 E2
Salwah, Dawhat b. Qatar/Saudi Arabia 105 E2
Salween r. China/Myanmar 78 B4
also known as Mae Nam Khong or Thanlwin (Myanmar) or Nu Jiang (China)
Salyan Azer. 107 G3
also spelt Sal'yany
Sal'yany Azer. see Salyan
Salyersville U.S.A. 176 B8
Salza r. Austria 49 L8
Salzach r. Austria/Germany 49 J7
Salzbrunn Namibia 130 C5
Salzburg Austria 49 K8
Salzgitter Germany 48 I4
formerly known as Watenstadt-Salzgitter
Salzkotten Germany 48 F4
Salzwedel Germany 48 I3
Salzwedel-Diesdorf park Germany 48 H3
Sam Gabon 126 A4
Sam India 96 A4
Sam, Nam r. Laos/Vietnam 78 D4
Samá Cuba 136 E2
Samac Bos.-Herz. see Bosanski Šamac
Samad Oman 105 G3
Samae San, Laem pt Thai. 79 C5
English form Liant, Cape
Samagaltay Rus. Fed. 84 B1
Samah well Saudi Arabia 105 D3
Samaida Iran see Someydeh
Samaipata Bol. 201 E4
Samak, Tanjung pt Indon. 77 D3
Samakoulou Mali 124 C3
Samal i. Phil. 74 C5
Samalayuca Mex. 184 D2
Samal Island Phil. 74 C5
Samalkot India 95 D2
Samālūt Egypt 121 F2
Samana Dom. Rep. 187 E2
Samana India 96 C3
Samaná, Cabo c. Dom. Rep. 187 F3
Samana Cay i. Bahamas 187 E2
Samanala mt. Sri Lanka see Adam's Peak
Samandağı Turkey 106 C3
also known as Alevişik; historically known as Selancia Pieria
Samangan prov. Afgh. 101 F2
Samangan Iran 101 E3
Samani Japan 90 H3
Samaniego Col. 198 B4
Samannûd Egypt 108 C7
also known as Sebennytos
Samanqua r. Canada 169 G2
Samar i. Phil. 74 C4
Samar Rus. Fed. 102 B1
formerly known as Kuybyshev
Samara r. Rus. Fed. 102 C1
Samarahan Sarawak Malaysia see Sri Aman
Samarai P.N.G. 149 F1
Samara Oblast admin. div. Rus. Fed. see Samarskaya Oblast'
Samarga Rus. Fed. 82 E3
Samaria nat. park Greece 59 E13
Samariapo Venez. 199 E3
Samarinda Indon. 77 G3
Samarka Rus. Fed. 82 D3
Samarkand Uzbek. 103 F5
also spelt Samarqand; historically known as Maracanda
Samarkand, Fik r. Tajik. 101 G2
Samarkand Oblast admin. div. Uzbek. see Samarkandskaya Oblast'
Samarkandskaya Oblast' admin. div. Uzbek. 103 F5
English form Samarkand Oblast; also known as Samarqand Wiloyati
Samarobriva France see Amiens
Samarqand Uzbek. see Samarkand
Samarqand, Qullai mt. Tajik. see Samarkand, Pik
Samarqand Wiloyati admin. div. Uzbek. see Samarkandskaya Oblast'
Sämarrä' Iraq 107 E4
Sāmarrā', Saddat dam Iraq 109 O3
Samar Sea g. Phil. 74 C4
Samarskaya Oblast' admin. div. Rus. Fed. 102 B1
English form Samara Oblast; formerly known as Kuybyshevskaya Oblast'
Samarskoye Kazakh. 88 C1
also known as Samar
Samasata Pak. 101 G4
Samastipur India 97 E4
Samaúma Brazil 199 F6
Samba Dem. Rep. Congo 126 D5
Samba r. Indon. 77 F3
Samba Jammu and Kashmir 96 B2
Samba Cajú Angola 127 B7
Sambaliung mts Indon. 77 G2
Sambalpur India 97 D5
Sambar, Tanjung pt Indon. 77 E3
Sambas Indon. 77 E2
Sambava Madag. 131 [inset] K2
Sambhal India 96 C3
Sambhar Ukr. see Sambir
Sambhar India 96 C3
Sambhar Lake India 96 B4
Sambir Ukr. 53 B2
also spelt Sambor
Sambit i. Indon. 77 G2
Sambo Angola 127 C8
Sambo Indon. 75 B4
Samboja Indon. 77 G3
Sambor Ukr. see Sambir
Sâmbor Dam Cambodia 79 D5
Samborombón, Bahía b. Arg. 204 F5
Samch'ŏk S. Korea 83 C5
Samch'ŏnp'o S. Korea see Sach'on
Sameikkon Myanmar 78 A3
Samer France 50 H2
Semet' Rus. Fed. 43 V4
Samet, Ko i. Thai. 79 C5
Samfya Zambia 127 F7
Samhah i. Yemen 105 F5
Samhān, Jabal mts Oman 105 F4
Samí Pak. 101 E5
Samirah Saudi Arabia 104 C2
Samiria r. Peru 198 C6
Samirum Iran see 'Izad-e Khvāst
Samka Myanmar 78 B3
Şamkir Azer. 107 F2
also known as Shamkhor
Samná oasis Saudi Arabia 104 B2
Samnan va Damghan Iran 100 C3
Sam Neua Laos see Xam Nua
Samnû Libya 120 B3
▶Samoa country S. Pacific Ocean 145 H3
formerly known as Western Samoa or Samoa i Sisifo
oceania [countries] ▶ 138–139
Samoa i Sisifo country S. Pacific Ocean see Samoa

Samobor Croatia 56 H3
Samoded Rus. Fed. 40 G3
Samokov Bulg. 58 E6
Šamorín Slovakia 49 O7
Samos Greece 59 H11
Samos i. Greece 59 H11
Samosir i. Indon. 76 B2
Samothrace i. Greece see Samothraki
Samothraki Greece 58 G8
Samothraki i. Greece 59 G8
English form Samothrace
Samovodene Bulg. 58 G5
Samoylovka Rus. Fed. 41 G6
Sampa Côte d'Ivoire 124 E5
Sampacho Arg. 204 D4
Sampaga Indon. 75 A3
Sampang Indon. 77 F4
Sampit Indon. 77 F3
Sampit r. Indon. 77 F3
Sampit, Teluk b. Indon. 77 F3
Sampolawa Indon. 75 B4
Sampur Rus. Fed. 41 G5
Sampwe Dem. Rep. Congo 127 F6
Sam Rayburn Reservoir U.S.A. 179 D6
Samrebee Ghana 124 E5
Samr el 'Abd, Gebel mt. Egypt 108 D9
Samro, Ozero l. Rus. Fed. 43 J3
Samrong Cambodia see Phumĭ Sâmraông
Samsang China 89 C6
Sam Sao, Phou mts Laos/Vietnam 78 C3
Samsø i. Denmark 45 J5
Samsø Bælt sea chan. Denmark 45 J5
Sâm Son Vietnam 78 D4
Samsun Turkey 107 D2
historically known as Amisus
Samsy Kazakh. 103 I4
Samtens Germany 49 K1
Samthar India 96 C4
Samtredia Georgia 107 E2
Samui, Ko i. Thai. 79 C6
Samulun, Pulau i. Sing. 76 [inset]
Samundri Pak. 101 H4
Samur r. Azer./Rus. Fed. 107 G2
Samutlu Turkey see Temelli
Samut Prakan Thai. 79 C5
Samut Sakhon Thai. 79 C5
Samut Songkhram Thai. 79 C5
San Mali 124 D3
San r. Poland 49 S5
San, Phou mt. Laos 78 C4
San, Tônlé r. Cambodia 79 D5
Sana r. Bos.-Herz. 56 I3
▶San'ā' Yemen 104 D5
Capital of Yemen.
San'ā' governorate Yemen 104 D5
Sanaag admin. reg. Somalia 128 E2
San Adrián, Cabo de c. Spain 54 C1
Sanae research station Antarctica 223 X2
Sanaga r. Cameroon 125 H6
San Agostín U.S.A. see St Augustine
San Agustín Col. 198 B4
San Agustín, Cape Phil. 74 C5
Sanak Island U.S.A. 164 C5
Sanām Saudi Arabia 104 D3
San Ambrosio i. S. Pacific Ocean 200 A6
Sanana Indon. 75 C3
Sanandaj Iran 100 A3
also known as Sinneh
Sanando Mali 124 D3
San Andreas U.S.A. 182 D3
San Andrés Bol. 201 D3
San Andrés Col. 198 C4
San Andres Phil. 74 C3
San Andrés, Isla de i. Caribbean Sea 186 C4
San Andrés del Rabanedo Spain 54 F2
San Andres Mountains U.S.A. 181 F6
San Andres Tuxtla Mex. 185 G5
San Ángelo U.S.A. 179 B6
Sanankoroba Mali 124 C3
San Antolín de Ibias Spain 54 E1
San Antonio Arg. 204 D2
San Antonio Belize 185 H5
San Antonio Bol. 201 D3
San Antonio Chile 204 C3
San Antonio Hond. 186 B4
San Antonio Peru 200 C3
San Antonio Phil. 74 B3
San Antonio NM U.S.A. 181 F6
San Antonio r. CA U.S.A. 182 C5
San Antonio r. TX U.S.A. 179 D6
San Antonio Venez. 187 H5
San Antonio, Cabo c. Arg. 204 F5
San Antonio, Cabo c. Cuba 186 B2
San Antonio, Mount U.S.A. 182 G7
San Antonio Abad Spain 55 M6
San Antonio Bay Phil. 74 A4
San Antonio de Caparo Venez. 198 D3
San Antonio del Mar Mex. 184 A2
San Antonio de los Cobres Arg. 200 D6
San Antonio de Palé Equat. Guinea 125 G7
San Antonio de Tamanaco Venez. 199 E2
San Antonio Este Arg. 204 D6
San Antonio Oeste Arg. 204 D6
San Antonio Reservoir U.S.A. 182 D6
San Agustín Arg. 204 D5
San Agustín de Valle Fértil Arg. 204 D3
San Augustine U.S.A. 179 D6
Sanaw Yemen 105 E4
Sanawad India 96 C5
San Bartolo Mex. 185 E4
San Bartolomeo in Galdo Italy 56 H7
San Benedetto del Tronto Italy 56 F6
San Benedicto, Isla i. Mex. 184 C5
San Benito Guat. 185 H5
San Benito U.S.A. 179 C7
San Benito r. U.S.A. 182 C5
San Benito Mountain U.S.A. 182 D5
San Bernardino U.S.A. 183 G7
San Bernardino, Passo di pass Switz. 51 P6
San Bernardino Mountains U.S.A. 183 G7
San Bernardino Strait Phil. 74 C3
San Bernardo Chile 204 C4
San Bernardo Mex. 184 D3
San Blas Arg. 204 D6
San Blas Nayarit Mex. 184 D4
San Blas Sinaloa Mex. 184 C3
San Blas, Archipiélago de is Panama 186 D5
formerly known as Las Mulatas
San Blas, Cape U.S.A. 175 C6
San Blas, Cordillera de mts Panama 186 D5
San Borja Bol. 200 D3
San Buenaventura Mex. 185 E3
Sança Moz. 131 G3
San Candido Italy 56 E2
historically known as Aguntum
San Caprasio hill Spain 55 K3
San Carlos Mendoza Arg. 204 C4
San Carlos Salta Arg. 204 D2
San Carlos Chile 204 C5
San Carlos Equat. Guinea see Luba
San Carlos Coahuila Mex. 185 E2
San Carlos Tamaulipas Mex. 185 F3
San Carlos Nicaragua 186 B5
San Carlos Para. 201 F5
San Carlos Luzon Phil. 74 B3
San Carlos Negros Phil. 74 B4
San Carlos Uruguay 204 G4
San Carlos U.S.A. 183 N8
San Carlos Amazonas Venez. 199 E4
San Carlos Cojedes Venez. 198 D2
San Carlos Apure Venez. 199 E3
San Carlos de Bariloche Arg. 204 C6
San Carlos de Bolívar Arg. 204 E5

San Carlos de la Rápita Spain *see* **Sant Carles de la Ràpita**
San Carlos del Zulia Venez. **198** D2
San Carlos Indian Reservation *res.* U.S.A. **183** N8
San Carlos Lake U.S.A. **183** N8
San Cataldo *Sicilia* Italy **57** F11
San Cayetano Arg. **204** F5
San Celoni Spain *see* **Sant Celoni**
Sancerre France **51** I5
Sancerrois, Collines du *hills* France **51** I5
San Cesario di Lecce Italy **57** K8
Sancha *Gansu* China **86** C1
Sancha *Shanxi* China **85** F4
Sanchahe China *see* **Fuyu**
Sancha He *r.* China **86** C3
Sanchakou China **88** B4
Sanchi India **96** C5
San Chien Pau *mt.* Laos **78** C3
Sanchor India **96** A4
Sanchuan *r.* China **85** F4
Sanchursk Rus. Fed. **40** H4
San Ciro de Acosta Mex. **185** F4
San Clemente Chile **204** C4
San Clemente Spain **55** I5
San Clemente U.S.A. **182** G8
San Clemente del Tuyú Arg. **204** F5
San Clemente Island U.S.A. **182** F9
Sancoins France **51** I6
Sanco Point Phil. **74** C4
San Cristóbal Arg. **204** E3
San Cristóbal *Potosí* Bol. **200** D5
San Cristóbal *Santa Cruz* Bol. **201** E3
San Cristóbal Col. **198** C5
San Cristóbal Dom. Rep. **187** F3
San Cristobal *i.* Solomon Is **145** F3
also known as Arossi, *or* Makira
San Cristóbal Venez. **198** C3
San Cristóbal, Volcán *vol.* Nicaragua **186** B4
San Cristóbal de las Casas Mex. **185** G5
San Cristobal Wash *watercourse* U.S.A. **183** K9
Sancti Spíritus Cuba **186** D2
Sand Norway **45** I4
Sand *r. Free State* S. Africa **133** K5
Sand *r. Northern* S. Africa **131** F4
Sanda Japan **91** D7
Sandagou Rus. Fed. **90** D3
Sandai Indon. **77** E3
Sandakan *Sabah* Malaysia **77** G1
Sandakphu Peak India **97** F4
Sandane Norway **45** I3
Sandanski Bulg. **58** E7
Sandaohezi China *see* **Shawan**
Sandaré Mali **124** C3
Sanday *i.* U.K. **46** J4
Sandberg S. Africa **132** C9
Sandbukt Norway **44** M1
Sand Cay *reef* India **94** B4
Sande *Sogn og Fjordane* Norway **45** I3
Sande *Vestfold* Norway **45** J4
Sandefjord Norway **45** J4
Sandefjord (Torp) *airport* Norway **45** J4
Sandercock Nunataks Antarctica **223** D2
Sanders U.S.A. **183** O6
Sanderson U.S.A. **179** B6
Sandersville U.S.A. **175** D5
Sandfire Roadhouse Australia **150** C3
Sandfloeggi *mt.* Norway **45** I4
Sand Hill *r.* U.S.A. **178** C2
Sand Hills U.S.A. **178** B3
Sandhornøy *i.* Norway **44** K2
Sandi India **96** D4
Sandia Peru **200** C3
San Diego Mex. **181** E7
San Diego *CA* U.S.A. **183** G9
San Diego *TX* U.S.A. **179** C7
San Diego, Cabo *c.* Arg. **205** D9
San Diego, Sierra *mts* Mex. **184** C2
San Diego de Cabrutica Venez. **199** E2
Sandıklı Turkey **106** B3
Sandila India **96** D4
Sanding *i.* Indon. **76** C3
Sand Island U.S.A. **172** C4
Sandivey *r.* Rus. Fed. **40** K2
Sand Lake Canada **168** C4
Sand Lake *l.* Canada **167** M5
Sandnes Norway **45** I4
Sandnessjøen Norway **44** K2
Sandø *i.* Faroe Is *see* **Sandoy**
Sandoa Dem. Rep. Congo **127** D7
Sandomierz Poland **49** S5
Sândominic Romania **58** G2
formerly spelt Sîndominic
San Domino, Isole *i.* Italy **56** H6
Sandoná Col. **198** B4
San Donà di Piave Italy **56** E3
Sandover *watercourse* Australia **148** C4
Sandovo Rus. Fed. **43** R3
Sandow, Mount Antarctica **223** G2
Sandoway Myanmar **78** A4
also known as Thandwè
Sandoy *i.* Faroe Is **46** F2
also spelt Sandø
Sandpoint U.S.A. **180** C2
Sandray *i.* U.K. **46** E7
also spelt Sanndraigh
Sandringham Australia **148** C5
Sand River Reservoir Swaziland **133** P3
Sandsele Sweden **44** L2
Sandspit Canada **166** D4
Sand Springs *IA* U.S.A. **172** B8
Sand Springs *OK* U.S.A. **179** C4
Sand Springs Salt Flat U.S.A. **182** F2
Sandspruit *r.* S. Africa **133** K4
Sandstone Australia **151** B5
Sandstone U.S.A. **174** A2
Sand Tank Mountains U.S.A. **183** L9
Sandton S. Africa **133** M3
Sandu *Guizhou* China **87** C3
also known as Sanhe
Sandu *Hunan* China **87** E3
Sandur India **94** C3
Sandusky *MI* U.S.A. **173** K7
Sandusky *OH* U.S.A. **176** C4
Sandusky Bay U.S.A. **176** C4
Sandveld *mts* S. Africa **132** C8
Sandveld Nature Reserve S. Africa **133** J4
Sandverhaar Namibia **132** B3
Sandvika *Akershus* Norway **45** J4
Sandvika *Nord-Trøndelag* Norway **44** K3
Sandviken Sweden **45** L3
Sandvlakte S. Africa **133** I10
Sandwich U.S.A. **177** O4
Sandwich Bay Canada **169** J2
Sandwich Island Vanuatu *see* **Éfaté**
Sandwip Bangl. **97** F5
Sandwip Channel Bangl. **97** F5
Sandy U.S.A. **183** M1
Sandy *r.* U.S.A. **177** P1
Sandy Bay Canada **167** K4
Sandy Bight *b.* Australia **151** C7
Sandy Cape *Qld* Australia **149** G5
Sandy Cape *Tas.* Australia **147** E5
Sandy Creek *r.* Australia **148** C3
Sandy Island Australia **150** C2
Sandykachi Turkm. **103** E5
Sandykly Gumy *des.* Turkm. *see* **Sundukli, Peski**
Sandy Lake *Alta* Canada **167** H4
Sandy Lake *Ont.* Canada **167** M4
Sandy Lake *l.* Canada **167** M4
Sandy Springs U.S.A. **175** C5
Sandyville U.S.A. **176** D7
Sân el Hagar Egypt **108** C7
San Estanislao Para. **201** F6
San Esteban Hond. **186** B4
San Esteban, Isla *i.* Mex. **184** B2
San Fabián de Alico Chile **204** C5
San Felipe Chile **204** C4
San Felipe *Baja California Norte* Mex. **184** B2
San Felipe *Chihuahua* Mex. **184** D3
San Felipe *Guanajuato* Mex. **185** E4
San Felipe *mt.* Spain **55** J4
San Felipe Venez. **198** D2
San Felipe, Cayos de *is* Cuba **186** C2
San Feliú de Guíxols Spain *see* **Sant Feliu de Guíxols**
San Félix, Isla *i.* S. Pacific Ocean **221** M7
San Fernando Arg. **204** F4
San Fernando Chile **204** C4
San Fernando *Baja California Norte* Mex. **184** B2
San Fernando *Tamaulipas* Mex. **185** F3
San Fernando *Luzon* Phil. **74** E2
San Fernando *Luzon* Phil. **74** B3
San Fernando Spain **54** E8
San Fernando Trin. and Tob. **187** H5
San Fernando U.S.A. **182** F7
San Fernando de Apure Venez. **199** E3
San Fernando de Atabapo Venez. **199** E3
San Filipe Creek *watercourse* U.S.A. **183** I8
Sånfjället nationalpark *nat. park* Sweden **45** K3
Sanford *r.* Australia **151** A5
Sanford *FL* U.S.A. **175** D6
Sanford *ME* U.S.A. **177** O2
Sanford *MI* U.S.A. **173** I7
Sanford *NC* U.S.A. **174** E5
San Francisco Arg. **204** E3
San Francisco Bol. **200** D3
San Francisco Mex. **184** B2
▶**San Francisco** U.S.A. **182** B4
world [cities] ▶▶ 24–25
world [communications] ▶▶ 26–27
San Francisco *r.* U.S.A. **181** E6
San Francisco, Paso de *pass* Arg. **204** C2
San Francisco, Sierra *mts* Mex. **184** B3
San Francisco Bay *inlet* U.S.A. **182** B4
San Francisco del Oro Mex. **184** D3
San Francisco de Macorís Dom. Rep. **187** F3
San Francisco de Paula, Cabo *c.* Arg. **205** D8
San Francisco Gotera El Salvador **185** H6
San Francisco Javier Spain **55** M6
Sanga Dem. Rep. Congo **127** F6
San Gabriel Ecuador **198** B4
San Gabriel, Punta *pt* Mex. **184** B2
San Gabriel Mountains U.S.A. **182** F7
Sangachaly Azer. *see* **Sanqaçal**
Sangai, Parque Nacional *nat. park* Ecuador **198** B5
Sangaigerong Indon. **76** D3
Sa'ngain China **86** A2
San Gallan, Isla *i.* Peru **200** A3
Sangam India **94** C3
Sangameshwar India **94** B2
Sangamner India **94** B2
Sangamon *r.* U.S.A. **174** B3
Sangān Iran **101** D3
Sangan, Koh-i- *mt.* Afgh. **101** F3
Sangar *r.* Pak. **101** G4
Sangar Rus. Fed. **39** M3
Sangaréa Guinea **124** B4
Sangareddi India **94** C2
Sangarédi Guinea **124** B4
Sangaria India **96** B3
Sangasanga Indon. **77** G3
Sanga Sanga *i.* Phil. **74** A5
Sangasso Mali *see* **Zangasso**
Sangaste Estonia **42** H4
San Gavino Monreale *Sardegna* Italy **57** A9
Sangay, Volcán *vol.* Ecuador **198** B5
Sang Bast Iran **101** D3
Sangbé Cameroon **125** I5
Sangboy Islands Phil. **74** B5
Sangbur Afgh. **101** E3
Sangeang *i.* Indon. **77** G5
Sangejing China **85** E3
Sângeorgiu de Pădure Romania **58** F2
formerly spelt Sîngeorgiu de Pădure
Sângeorz-Băi Romania **58** F1
formerly spelt Sîngeorz-Băi
Sangequanzi China **88** E3
Sânger Romania **58** F2
Sanger U.S.A. **182** E5
Sângera Moldova *see* **Sîngera**
Sangerfield U.S.A. **177** J3
Sangerhausen Germany **48** I4
San Germán Puerto Rico **187** G3
Sanggan *r.* China **85** G3
Sanggar, Teluk *b.* Indon. **77** G5
Sanggarmai China **86** B1
Sanggau Indon. **77** E2
Sanggou Wan *b.* China **85** I4
Sangha *admin. reg.* Congo **126** B4
Sangha *r.* Congo **126** C5
Sangha-Mbaéré *pref.* Cent. Afr. Rep. **126** C4
Sanghar Pak. **101** G5
San Gil Col. **198** C3
Sangilen, Nagor'ye *mts* Rus. Fed. **84** B1
San Giovanni in Fiore Italy **57** I9
San Giovanni Rotondo Italy **56** H7
San Giovanni Suegiu *Sardegna* Italy **57** A9
Sangir India **96** B5
Sangir *i.* Indon. **75** C2
Sangir, Kepulauan *is* Indon. **75** C2
Sangiran *tourist site* Indon. **77** E4
San Giuliano Terme Italy **56** C5
San Giustino Italy **56** E5
Sangiyn Dalay Mongolia **84** E2
Sangiyn Dalay Nuur *salt l.* Mongolia **84** C1
Sangju S. Korea **83** C5
Sangkapura Indon. **77** F4
Sangkarang, Kepulauan *is* Indon. **75** A4
Sângke, Stœng *r.* Cambodia **79** C5
Sangkulirang Indon. **77** G2
Sangkulirang, Teluk *b.* Indon. **77** G2
Sangla Pak. **101** H4
Sangli India **94** B2
San Glorio, Puerto de *pass* Spain **54** G1
Sangmélima Cameroon **125** H6
Sango Zimbabwe **131** F4
formerly known as Vila Salazar *or* Villasalazar
Sangod India **96** C4
Sangole India **94** B2
San Gorgonio Mountain U.S.A. **183** H7
Sangowo Indon. **75** D2
Sangpi China *see* **Xiangcheng**
Sang Qu *r.* China **86** A2
Sangre de Cristo Range *mts* U.S.A. **181** F5
San Gregorio de Polanco Uruguay **204** G4
Sangre Grande Trin. and Tob. **187** H5
Sangri China **89** F6
also known as Xueba
Sangro *r.* Italy **56** G6
Sangrur India **96** B3
Sangsang China **89** D6
Sangu *r.* Bangl. **97** F5
Sangue *r.* Brazil **201** F2
Sangüesa Spain **55** J2
San Guiliano Milanese Italy **56** B3
Sangū'iyeh Iran **100** D4
also known as Isfandaqeh
Sangyuan China *see* **Wuqiao**
Sangzhi China **87** D2
also known as Liyuan
Sanhe China *see* **Sandu**
Sanhe China **85** I1
Sanhezhen China **87** F2
San Hilario Mex. **184** C3
San Hipólito, Punta *pt* Mex. **184** B3
Sanhūr Egypt **121** F2
San Ignacio Belize **185** H5
San Ignacio *Beni* Bol. **200** D3
San Ignacio *Santa Cruz* Bol. **201** E4
San Ignacio *Santa Cruz* Bol. **201** E3
San Ignacio *Baja California Sur* Mex. **184** B3
San Ignacio *Sonora* Mex. **184** C2
San Ignacio Para. **201** F6
San Ignacio Peru **198** B6
San Ignacio, Laguna *l.* Mex. **184** B3
Sanikiluaq Canada **168** E1
San Ildefonso Peninsula Phil. **74** B2
Sanin-kaigan National Park Japan **91** D7
Sanipas *pass* S. Africa **133** N6
Sanislău Romania **49** T8
Sanitz Germany **49** J1
Sāniyat al Fawākhir *well* Libya **120** C3
San Jacinto Col. **198** C2
San Jacinto Phil. **74** B3
San Jacinto U.S.A. **183** H8
San Jacinto Peak U.S.A. **183** H8
Sanjai *r.* India **97** E5
San Jaime Arg. **204** F3
San Javier Arg. **204** F3
San Javier *Beni* Bol. **200** D3
San Javier *Santa Cruz* Bol. **201** E4
San Javier Spain **55** K7
San Javier de Loncomilla Chile **204** C4
Sanjawi Pak. **101** G4
Sanjbod Iran **100** B2
San Jerónimo Mex. **185** E5
San Jerónimo Peru **200** B1
Sanjiang China *see* **Liannan**
Sanjiang China **87** D3
also known as Guyi
Sanjiang China *see* **Jinping**
Sanjiangkou China *see* **Haiyan**
Sanjiaoping China **87** D2
Sanjie China **87** G2
Sanjō Japan **90** F6
San Joaquín Bol. **200** D3
San Joaquín Para. **201** F6
San Joaquin U.S.A. **182** D5
San Joaquin *r.* U.S.A. **182** C3
San Joaquin Valley U.S.A. **182** D4
San Jon U.S.A. **178** B5
San Jorge Arg. **204** E3
San Jorge, Golfo de *g.* Arg. **205** D7
San Jorge, Golfo de *g.* Spain *see* **Sant Jordi, Golf de**
San José Col. **199** D4
▶**San José** Costa Rica **186** B5
Capital of Costa Rica.
San José *watercourse* Mex. **181** D8
San Jose *Luzon* Phil. **74** B3
San Jose *Mindoro* Phil. **74** B3
San Jose *Mindoro* Phil. **74** B3
San Jose *CA* U.S.A. **182** C4
San Jose *NM* U.S.A. **181** F6
San Jose *watercourse* U.S.A. **181** F6
San José Venez. **199** E2
San José, Cabo *c.* Arg. **205** D7
San José, Cuchilla de *hills* Uruguay **204** F3
San José, Golfo *g.* Arg. **205** D6
San José, Isla *i.* Mex. **184** C3
San José, Volcán *vol.* Chile **204** C4
San José de Amacuro Venez. **199** F2
San José de Bavicora Mex. **184** D2
San José de Buenavista Phil. **74** B4
San José de Chiquitos Bol. **201** E4
San José de Comondú Mex. **184** C3
San José de Gracia *Baja California Sur* Mex. **184** B3
San José de Gracia *Sonora* Mex. **184** C2
San José de Guaribe Venez. **187** G5
San José de Jáchal Arg. **204** C3
San José de la Brecha Mex. **184** C3
San José de la Dormida Arg. **204** E3
San José de la Mariquina Chile **204** B5
San José del Boquerón Arg. **204** E2
San José del Cabo Mex. **184** C4
San José del Guaviare Col. **198** C4
San José de Mayo Uruguay **204** F4
San José de Ocuné Col. **198** D3
San José de Primas Mex. **181** E7
San José de Raíces Mex. **185** E3
San Juan Arg. **204** C3
San Juan *prov.* Arg. **204** C3
San Juan Bol. **201** E4
San Juan Col. **198** B2
San Juan *r.* Col. **198** B3
San Juan *r.* Costa Rica/Nicaragua **186** C5
San Juan *mt.* Cuba **186** C2
San Juan *Chihuahua* Mex. **184** D3
San Juan *Coahuila* Mex. **185** E3
San Juan Peru **200** B3
San Juan Phil. **74** C4
▶**San Juan** Puerto Rico **187** G3
Capital of Puerto Rico.
San Juan *r. CA* U.S.A. **182** D6
San Juan *r. UT* U.S.A. **183** N4
San Juan Venez. **199** E3
San Juan, Cabo *c.* Arg. **205** E9
San Juan, Cabo *c.* Equat. Guinea **125** H6
San Juan, Punta *pt* El Salvador **186** A4
San Juan Bautista Para. **201** F6
San Juan Bautista Spain **55** M5
San Juan Bautista U.S.A. **182** C5
San Juan Bautista Tuxtepec Mex. **185** F5
San Juan Capistrano U.S.A. **182** G8
San Juancito Hond. **186** B4
San Juan de César Col. **198** C2
San Juan de Guadalupe Mex. **185** E3
San Juan de la Costa Chile **204** B6
San Juan de la Peña, Sierra de *mts* Spain **55** K2
San Juan del Norte Nicaragua **186** C5
San Juan del Norte, Bahía de *b.* Nicaragua **186** C5
San Juan de los Cayos Venez. **198** D2
San Juan de los Morros Venez. **199** E2
San Juan del Río *Durango* Mex. **184** D3
San Juan del Río *Querétaro* Mex. **185** F4
San Juan del Sur Nicaragua **186** B5
San Juan de Salvamento Arg. **205** E9
San Juan Evangelista Mex. **185** G5
San Juan Islands U.S.A. **180** B2
San Juanito Mex. **184** D3
San Juanito, Isla *i.* Mex. **184** D4
San Juan Mountains U.S.A. **181** F5
San Juan y Martínez Cuba **186** C2
San Julián Arg. **205** D8
San Just *mt.* Spain **55** K4
San Justo Arg. **204** E3
Sankarani *r.* Côte d'Ivoire/Guinea **124** C4
Sankarankovil India **94** C4
Sankeshwar India **94** B2
Sankh *r.* India **97** E5
Sankosh *r.* Bhutan *see* **Sunkosh**
Sankra *Chhattisgarh* India **94** D1
Sankra *Rajasthan* India **96** A4
Sankt Andrä Austria **49** L9
Sankt Gallen Switz. **51** P5
Sankt Gotthard Hungary *see* **Szentgotthárd**
Sankt Johann im Pongau Austria **49** K8
Sankt Moritz Switz. **51** P6
Sankt-Peterburg Rus. Fed. *see* **St Petersburg**
Sankt Peter-Ording Germany **48** F1
Sankt Pölten Austria **49** M7
Sankt Veit an der Glan Austria **49** L9
Sankt Wendel Germany **48** E6
Sankuru *r.* Dem. Rep. Congo **126** D6
San Lázaro Para. **201** F5
San Lázaro, Cabo *c.* Mex. **184** B3
San Leandro U.S.A. **182** B4
San Leonardo in Passiria Italy **56** D2
Şanlıurfa Turkey **107** D3
formerly known as Urfa; *historically known as* Edessa
Şanlıurfa *prov.* Turkey **109** J1
San Lorenzo *Corrientes* Arg. **204** F3
San Lorenzo *Santa Fé* Arg. **204** E4
San Lorenzo *Beni* Bol. **200** D3
San Lorenzo *Pando* Bol. **200** D2
San Lorenzo *Tarija* Bol. **200** D5
San Lorenzo Ecuador **198** B4
San Lorenzo Hond. **186** B4
San Lorenzo Mex. **184** D2
San Lorenzo Peru **200** C2
San Lorenzo *mt.* Spain **55** I2
San Lorenzo, Cabo *c.* Ecuador **198** A5
San Lorenzo, Cerro *mt.* Arg./Chile **205** B7
San Lorenzo, Isla *i.* Mex. **184** B2
San Lorenzo, Isla *i.* Peru **200** A3
Sanlúcar de Barrameda Spain **54** E8
San Lucas Bol. **200** D5
San Lucas *Baja California Sur* Mex. **184** B3
San Lucas *Baja California Sur* Mex. **184** C4
San Lucas, Cabo *c.* Mex. **184** C4
San Lucas, Serranía de *mts* Col. **198** C3
San Luis Arg. **204** D4
San Luis *prov.* Arg. **204** D4
San Luis Brazil **200** D2
San Luis Cuba **186** E2
San Luis Guat. **185** H5
San Luis Mex. **185** E5
San Luis Peru **198** C5
San Luis *AZ* U.S.A. **183** J9
San Luis *AZ* U.S.A. **183** M9
San Luis *CO* U.S.A. **181** F5
San Luis Venez. **198** D2
San Luis, Isla *i.* Mex. **184** B2
San Luis, Sierra de *mts* Arg. **204** D4
San Luis de la Paz Mex. **185** E4
San Luis del Palmar Arg. **204** F2
San Luis Gonzaga Mex. **184** C3
San Luisito Mex. **184** B2
San Luis Obispo U.S.A. **182** D6
San Luis Obispo Bay U.S.A. **182** D6
San Luis Potosí Mex. **185** E4
San Luis Potosí *state* Mex. **185** E4
San Luis Reservoir U.S.A. **182** C4
San Luis Río Colorado Mex. **184** B1
Sanluri *Sardegna* Italy **57** A9
San Manuel U.S.A. **183** N9
San Marcello Pistoiese Italy **56** C4
San Marcial, Punta *pt* Mex. **184** C3
San Marco, Capo *c. Sardegna* Italy **57** A9
San Marco, Capo *c. Sicilia* Italy **57** F11
San Marcos Chile **204** C3
San Marcos Col. **198** C2
San Marcos Guat. **185** H6
San Marcos Hond. **186** B4
San Marcos Mex. **185** F5
San Marcos Peru **200** A1
San Marcos U.S.A. **179** C6
San Marcos *r.* U.S.A. **179** C6
San Marcos, Isla *i.* Mex. **184** B3
▶**San Marino** *country* Europe **56** E5
europe [countries] ▶▶ 32–35
▶**San Marino** San Marino **56** E5
Capital of San Marino.
San Martín *research station* Antarctica **222** T2
long form General San Martín
San Martín *Catamarca* Arg. **204** D3
San Martín *Mendoza* Arg. **204** C4
San Martín *r.* Bol. **201** E3
San Martín *dept* Peru **200** A1
San Martín, Lago *l.* Arg./Chile **205** B8
San Martín, Volcán *vol.* Mex. **185** G5
San Martín de los Andes Arg. **204** C6
San Martín de Valdeiglesias Spain **54** G4
San-Martino-di-Lota *Corse* France **51** P10
San Mateo Peru **198** D5
San Mateo U.S.A. **182** B4
San Mateo Venez. **199** E2
San Matías Bol. **201** F4
San Matías, Golfo *g.* Arg. **204** D6
San Mauricio Venez. **199** E2
Sanmen China **87** G2
also known as Haiyou
Sanmen Wan *b.* China **87** G2
Sanmenxia China **87** D1
San Miguel Arg. **204** F3
San Miguel Bol. **201** E4
San Miguel *r.* Bol. **201** E3
San Miguel *r.* Col. **198** C4
San Miguel El Salvador **185** H6
San Miguel Panama **186** D5
San Miguel Peru **200** B3
San Miguel U.S.A. **182** D6
San Miguel *r.* U.S.A. **181** E5
San Miguel Bay Phil. **74** B3
San Miguel de Allende Mex. **185** E4
San Miguel de Cruces Mex. **184** D3
San Miguel de Horcasitas *r.* Mex. **184** C2
San Miguel de Huachi Bol. **200** D3
San Miguel del Monte Arg. **204** F4
San Miguel de Tucumán Arg. **204** D2
short form Tucumán
San Miguel do Araguaia Brazil **202** E5
San Miguel el Alto Mex. **185** E4
San Miguel Island U.S.A. **182** D7
San Miguel Islands Phil. **74** A5
San Miguelito Panama **186** D5
San Miguel Sola de Vega Mex. **185** F5
Sanming China **87** F3
San Miniato Italy **56** C5
Sanna *r.* Poland **49** S5
San Narciso Phil. **74** B3
Sannaspos S. Africa **133** K6
Sanndatti India **94** B3
Sanndraigh *i.* U.K. *see* **Sandray**
Sannicandro Garganico Italy **56** H7
San Nicolás Mex. **185** F3
San Nicolas Phil. **74** B2
San Nicolás, Bahía *b.* Peru **200** B3
San Nicolás de los Arroyos Arg. **204** E4
San Nicolás del Presidio Mex. **184** D3
San Nicolas Island U.S.A. **182** E8
Sânnicolau Mare Romania **58** B2
formerly spelt Sînnicolau Mare
Sannieshof S. Africa **133** J3
Sanniquellie Liberia **124** C5
Sannohe Japan **90** G4
Sañogasta, Sierra de *mts* Arg. **204** D3
Sanok Poland **49** T6
San Onofre Col. **198** C2
San Pablo Arg. **205** D9
San Pablo *Potosí* Bol. **200** D5
San Pablo *Santa Cruz* Bol. **201** E3
San Pablo *r.* Bol. **201** E3
San Pablo Col. **198** D3
San Pablo Mex. **185** F4
San Pablo Phil. **74** B3
San Pablo U.S.A. **182** B4
San Pablo de Manta Ecuador *see* **Manta**
San Pedro *Buenos Aires* Arg. **204** F4
San Pedro *Catamarca* Arg. **204** D2
San Pedro *Jujuy* Arg. **200** D6
San Pedro *Misiones* Arg. **204** G2
San Pedro Belize **185** I5
San Pedro *Beni* Bol. **200** D3
San Pedro *Santa Cruz* Bol. **201** E4
San Pedro *r.* Bol. **200** D4
San-Pédro Côte d'Ivoire **124** D5
San Pedro *r.* Cuba **186** D2
San Pedro Mex. **184** C4
San Pedro *r.* Mex. **181** F7
San Pedro Peru **200** C2
San Pedro Phil. **74** B3
San Pedro *watercourse* U.S.A. **183** N9
San Pedro, Punta *pt* Costa Rica **186** C5
San Pedro, Sierra de *mts* Spain **54** D5
San Pedro Carchá Guat. **185** H6
San Pedro Channel U.S.A. **182** F8
San Pedro de Atacama Chile **200** C5
San Pedro de las Colonias Mex. **185** E3
San Pedro de Lloc Peru **200** A1
San Pedro del Pinatar Spain **55** K7
San Pedro de Macorís Dom. Rep. **187** F3
San Pedro de Ycuamandyyú Para. **201** F6
San Pedro el Saucito Mex. **184** C2
San Pedro Mártir, Parque Nacional *nat. park* Mex. **184** B2
San Pedro Sula Hond. **186** A4
San Pietro, Isola di *i. Sardegna* Italy **57** A9
San Pietro in Cariano Italy **56** C3
San Pitch *r.* U.S.A. **183** M2
Sanqaçal Azer. **107** G2
also spelt Sangachaly
Sanquhar U.K. **46** I8
Sanquianga, Parque Nacional *nat. park* Col. **198** B4
San Quintín, Cabo *c.* Mex. **184** A2
San Rafael Arg. **204** C4
San Rafael Bol. **201** E4
San Rafael U.S.A. **182** B4
San Rafael *r.* U.S.A. **183** N3
San Rafael Venez. **198** D2
also known as San Rafael del Moján
San Rafael del Moján Venez. *see* **San Rafael**
San Rafael del Norte Nicaragua **186** B4
San Rafael del Yuma Dom. Rep. **187** F3
San Rafael Knob *mt.* U.S.A. **183** N3
San Rafael Mountains U.S.A. **182** D7
San Ramón *Beni* Bol. **200** D3
San Ramón *Santa Cruz* Bol. **201** E4
San Remo Italy **51** N9
San Rodrigo *watercourse* Mex. **179** B6
San Román, Cabo *c.* Venez. **198** D1
San Roque *Andalucía* Spain **54** F8
San Roque *Galicia* Spain **54** C1
San Roque *Galicia* Spain **54** C2
San Roque, Punta *pt* Mex. **184** B3
San Saba U.S.A. **179** C6
San Saba *r.* U.S.A. **179** C6
Sansalé Guinea **124** B4
San Salvador Arg. **204** F3
San Salvador *i.* Bahamas **187** E1
formerly known as Watling Island
▶**San Salvador** El Salvador **185** H6
Capital of El Salvador.
San Salvador Peru **198** D5
San Salvador de Jujuy Arg. **200** D6
San Salvo Italy **56** G6
Sansané Haoussa Niger **125** F3
Sansanné-Mango Togo **125** F4
San Sebastián Arg. **205** C9
San Sebastián *hill* Spain **54** C2
San Sebastián, Bahía de *b.* Arg. **205** C9
San Sebastián de los Reyes Spain **55** H4
Sansepolcro Italy **56** E5
San Severino Marche Italy **56** F5
San Severo Italy **56** H7
Sansha China **87** G3
San Silvestre Bol. **200** C2
San Silvestre Venez. **198** D2
San Simon U.S.A. **183** O9
Sanski Most Bos.-Herz. **56** I4
Sanson N.Z. **152** J8
Sansoral Islands Palau *see* **Sonsorol Islands**
Sansui China **87** D3
also known as Bagong
Santa Peru **200** A2
Santa *r.* Peru **200** A2
Santa Adélia Brazil **206** E8
Santa Ana Arg. **204** D2
Santa Ana *La Paz* Bol. **200** D3
Santa Ana *Santa Cruz* Bol. **201** F4
Santa Ana El Salvador **185** H6
Santa Ana Mex. **184** C2
Santa Ana U.S.A. **182** G8
Santa Ana de Yacuma Bol. **200** D3
Santa Anita Mex. **184** C4
Santa Anna U.S.A. **179** C6
Santa Bárbara Brazil **201** F3
Santa Bárbara Cuba *see* **La Demajagua**
Santa Bárbara Hond. **186** A4
Santa Bárbara Mex. **184** D3
Santa Bárbara *mt.* Spain **55** I7
Santa Bárbara *mt.* Spain **55** J6
Santa Barbara U.S.A. **182** E7
Santa Bárbara *Amazonas* Venez. **199** E4
Santa Bárbara *Barinas* Venez. **198** D3
Santa Barbara, Ilha *i.* Brazil **207** O4
Santa Bárbara, Parque Nacional *nat. park* Hond. **186** A4
Santa Bárbara, Serra de *hills* Brazil **203** A7
Santa Barbara Channel U.S.A. **182** D7
Santa Bárbara d'Oeste Brazil **206** F9
Santa Barbara do Sul Brazil **203** A9
Santa Barbara Island U.S.A. **182** E8
Santa Catalina Chile **204** C2
Santa Catalina Panama **186** C5
Santa Catalina Venez. **199** F2
Santa Catalina, Gulf of U.S.A. **182** G8
Santa Catalina, Isla *i.* Mex. **184** C3
Santa Catalina de Armada Spain **54** C1
Santa Catalina Island U.S.A. **182** F8
Santa Catarina *state* Brazil **203** B8
Santa Catarina *Baja California Norte* Mex. **184** B2
Santa Catarina *Nuevo León* Mex. **185** E3
Santa Catarina Neth. Antilles **187** F4
also spelt Santa Catharina
Santa Catarina, Ilha de *i.* Brazil **203** B8
Santa Catharina Neth. Antilles *see* **Santa Catarina**
Santa Clara Col. **198** D5
Santa Clara Cuba **186** D2
Santa Clara *r.* Mex. **181** F7
Santa Clara *CA* U.S.A. **182** C4
Santa Clara *UT* U.S.A. **183** K4
Santa Clara *r.* U.S.A. **182** E7
Santa Clara, Barragem de *resr* Port. **54** C7
Santa Clarita U.S.A. **182** F7
Santa Clotilde Peru **198** C5
Santa Coloma de Farners Spain **55** N3
Santa Coloma de Gramanet Spain **55** N3
Santa Comba Angola *see* **Waku-Kungo**
Santa Comba Dão Port. **54** C4
Santa Croce Camerina *Sicilia* Italy **57** G12
Santa Cruz *prov.* Arg. **205** C8
Santa Cruz *r.* Arg. **205** C8
Santa Cruz Bol. **201** E4
Santa Cruz *dept* Bol. **201** E4
Santa Cruz *Espírito Santo* Brazil **207** M6
Santa Cruz *Pará* Brazil **199** H5
Santa Cruz *Pará* Brazil **202** B2
Santa Cruz Costa Rica **186** B5
Santa Cruz Mex. **184** C2
Santa Cruz Peru **198** C6
Santa Cruz *Luzon* Phil. **74** A3
Santa Cruz *Luzon* Phil. **74** B3
Santa Cruz *Luzon* Phil. **74** B3
Santa Cruz *mt.* Spain **55** J3
Santa Cruz U.S.A. **182** B5
Santa Cruz *watercourse* U.S.A. **183** L8
Santa Cruz, Isla *i.* Mex. **184** C3
Santa Cruz, Puerto *inlet* Arg. **205** C8
Santa Cruz Barillas Guat. **185** H6
Santa Cruz Cabrália Brazil **202** E6
Santa Cruz das Palmeiras Brazil **206** F8
Santa Cruz de Goiás Brazil **206** E4
Santa Cruz de la Palma Canary Is **122** A3
Santa Cruz del Quiché Guat. **185** H6
Santa Cruz del Sur Cuba **186** D2
Santa Cruz de Mudela Spain **55** H6
▶**Santa Cruz de Tenerife** Canary Is **122** A3
Joint capital of the Canary Islands.
Santa Cruz de Yojoa Hond. **186** B4
Santa Cruz do Rio Pardo Brazil **206** D9
Santa Cruz do Sul Brazil **203** A9
Santa Cruz Island U.S.A. **182** E7
Santa Cruz Islands Solomon Is **145** F3
Santa Efigênia de Minas Brazil **207** K5
Santa Elena *Buenos Aires* Arg. **204** E5
Santa Elena *Entre Ríos* Arg. **204** F3
Santa Elena Bol. **200** D5
Santa Elena Peru **198** C6
Santa Elena Venez. **199** F3
Santa Elena, Cabo *c.* Costa Rica **186** B5
Santa Elena, Punta *pt* Ecuador **198** A5
Santa Eufemia, Golfo di *g.* Italy **57** I10
Santa Eugenia Spain **54** C2
Santa Eulalia del Río Spain **55** M6
Santa Fé Arg. **204** E3
Santa Fé *prov.* Arg. **204** E3
Santa Fé Cuba **186** C2
Santa Fé Panama **186** C5
Santa Fe Phil. **74** B3
Santa Fe Spain **54** H7
▶**Santa Fe** U.S.A. **181** F6
State capital of New Mexico.
Santa Fé de Bogotá Col. *see* **Bogotá**
Santafé de Bogotá *municipality* Col. **198** C4
Santa Fé de Minas Brazil **202** C6
Santa Fé do Sul Brazil **206** C7
Santa Filomena Brazil **202** C4
Sant'Agata di Militello *Sicilia* Italy **57** G10
Santa Helena Brazil **202** C2
Santa Helena de Goiás Brazil **206** C4
Santai *Sichuan* China **86** C2
also known as Tongchuan
Santai *Xinjiang* China **88** C2
Santa Inês *Bahia* Brazil **202** E5
Santa Inês *Maranhão* Brazil **202** C2
Santa Inés, Isla *i.* Chile **205** B9
Santa Isabel Arg. **204** D5
Santa Isabel Bol. **200** D5
Santa Isabel Brazil **201** E3
Santa Isabel Equat. Guinea *see* **Malabo**
Santa Isabel *i.* Solomon Is **145** E2
formerly spelt Santa Ysabel
Santa Isabel, Ilha Grande de *i.* Brazil **202** D2
Santa Isabel, Sierra *mts* Mex. **184** B2
Santa Isabel de Sihuas Peru **200** B4
Santa Isabel do Araguaia Brazil **201** H1
Santa Juliana Brazil **206** F6
Santalpur India **96** A5
Santa Lucia Chile **200** C5
Santa Lucía Ecuador **198** B5
Santa Lucia Guat. **185** H6
Santa Lucía, Cerro de *mt.* Spain **54** G7
Santa Lucia Range *mts* U.S.A. **182** C5
Santa Luzia *Maranhão* Brazil **202** C3
Santa Luzia *Paraíba* Brazil **202** E3
Santa Luzia *i.* Cape Verde **124** [inset]
Santa Magdalena Arg. **204** E4
Santa Margarita Arg. **204** E3
Santa Margarita Spain **55** O5
Santa Margarita U.S.A. **182** D6
Santa Margarita, Isla *i.* Mex. **184** C3
Santa María Arg. **204** D2
Santa Maria Bol. **201** E3
Santa Maria *Amazonas* Brazil **199** F5
Santa Maria *Amazonas* Brazil **199** G5
Santa Maria *Pará* Brazil **199** H5
Santa Maria *Rio Grande do Sul* Brazil **203** A9
Santa Maria *r.* Brazil **203** A9
Santa Maria *r.* Brazil **206** G1
Santa Maria Cape Verde **124** [inset]
Santa María Mex. **185** H5
Santa María *r.* Mex. **184** D2
Santa Maria U.S.A. **182** D7
Santa Maria *r.* U.S.A. **183** K7
Santa María Venez. **199** E3
Santa Maria, Cabo de *c.* Moz. **131** G5
Santa Maria, Cabo de *c.* Port. **54** D8
Santa Maria, Cape Bahamas **175** F8
Santa María, Cayo *i.* Cuba **186** D2
Santa Maria, Chapadão de *hills* Brazil **202** C5
Santa María, Isla *i.* Chile **204** B5
Santa María, Punta *pt* Peru **200** B3
Santa Maria, Serra de *hills* Brazil **206** G1
Santa Maria Capua Vetere Italy **56** G7
Santa Maria da Boa Vista Brazil **202** E4
Santa Maria das Barreiras Brazil **202** B4
Santa Maria da Vitória Brazil **202** C5
Santa María de Ipire Venez. **199** E2
Santa María del Oro Mex. **184** D3
Santa María del Río Mex. **185** E4
Santa Maria di Leuca, Capo *c.* Italy **57** K9
Santa Maria do Salto Brazil **207** M3
Santa Maria do Suaçuí Brazil **203** D6
Santa Maria Island Vanuatu **145** F3
Santa Maria Mountains U.S.A. **183** L7
Santa Marina Salina *Isole Lipari* Italy **57** G10
Santa Marinella Italy **56** D6
Santa Marta Col. **198** C2
Santa Marta, Cabo de *c.* Angola **127** B8
Santa Marta, Serra de *mts* Brazil *see* **Divisões, Serra das**
Santa Marta Grande, Cabo de *c.* Brazil **203** B9
Santa Martha, Cerro *mt.* Mex. **185** G5
Santa Maura *i.* Greece *see* **Lefkada**
Santa Monica U.S.A. **182** F7
Santa Monica Bay U.S.A. **182** F8
Santan Indon. **77** G3
Santana *Amazonas* Brazil **199** E4
Santana *Bahia* Brazil **202** D5
Santana *r.* Brazil **206** B6
Sântana Romania **58** C2
Santana da Boa Vista Brazil **203** A9
Santana do Acaraú Brazil **202** D2
Santana do Araguaia Brazil **202** B4
Santana do Cariri Brazil **202** E3
Santana do Livramento Brazil **204** G3
Santander Col. **198** B4
Santander *dept* Col. **198** C3
Santander Spain **54** H1
Santa Nella U.S.A. **182** C4
Sant'Angelo in Lizzola Italy **56** E5
Sant'Angelo Lodigiano Italy **56** B3
Santanghu China **84** B2
Santanilla, Islas *is* Caribbean Sea *see* **Swan Islands**
Santan Mountain *hill* U.S.A. **183** M8
Sant'Anna, Ilha de *i.* Brazil **207** L9
Sant'Antioco *Sardegna* Italy **57** A9
historically known as Sulci *or* Sulcis
Sant'Antioco, Isola di *i. Sardegna* Italy **57** A9
Santañy Spain *see* **Santanyí**
Santanyí Spain **55** O5
also spelt Santañy
Santa Paula U.S.A. **182** E7
Santapilly India **95** D2
Santa Pola Spain **55** K6
Santa Pola, Cabo de *c.* Spain **55** K6
Santaquin U.S.A. **183** M2
Santa Quitéria Brazil **202** D3
Sant Arcangelo Italy **57** I8
Santarém Brazil **199** H5
Santarém Port. **54** C5
Santarém *admin. dist.* Port. **54** C5
Santa Rita *Mato Grosso* Brazil **201** F1
Santa Rita *Paraíba* Brazil **202** F3
Santa Rita Col. **198** C4
Santa Rita Mex. **185** E3
Santa Rita *Guárico* Venez. **199** E2
Santa Rita *Zulia* Venez. **198** D2
Santa Rita de Cassia Brazil **202** C4
Santa Rita do Araguaia Brazil **206** A3
Santa Rita do Pardo Brazil **206** A8
Santa Rita do Sapucaí Brazil **207** H9
Santa Rita do Weil Brazil **198** D5
Santa Rosa *Corrientes* Arg. **204** F3
Santa Rosa *La Pampa* Arg. **204** D5
Santa Rosa *Río Negro* Arg. **204** D6
Santa Rosa *Salta* Arg. **200** D6
Santa Rosa Bol. **200** D3
Santa Rosa *Acre* Brazil **200** C2
Santa Rosa *Rio Grande do Sul* Brazil **203** A8
Santa Rosa Col. **198** D4

Santa Rosa Ecuador 198 B5
Santa Rosa Mex. 185 H5
Santa Rosa Para. 201 F6
Santa Rosa Loreto Peru 198 C5
Santa Rosa Puno Peru 200 C3
Santa Rosa CA U.S.A. 182 B3
Santa Rosa NM U.S.A. 181 F6
Santa Rosa Venez. 199 E4
Santa Rosa de Copán Hond. 186 A4
Santa Rosa de la Roca Bol. 201 E4
Santa Rosa del Conlara Arg. 204 D4
Santa Rosa del Palmar Bol. 201 E4
Santa Rosa de Osos Col. 198 C2
Santa Rosa de Vigo Bol. 200 D3
Santa Rosa de Viterbo Brazil 206 F8
Santa Rosa Island U.S.A. 182 D8
Santa Rosalía Mex. 184 B3
Santa Rosa Mountains U.S.A. 183 H8
Santa Rosa Range mts U.S.A. 180 C5
Santa Rosa Wash watercourse U.S.A. 183 L8
Santa Sylvina Arg. 204 E2
Santa Teresa Australia 148 B5
Santa Teresa Brazil 207 M6
Santa Teresa r. Brazil 202 B3
Santa Teresa Mex. 185 F3
Santa Teresa, Embalse de resr Spain 54 F4
Santa Teresa Aboriginal Land res. Australia see Ltyentye Apurte Aboriginal Land
Santa Teresa di Gallura Sardegna Italy 56 B7
Santa Terezinha Brazil 202 B4
Santa Vitória Brazil 206 D5
Santa Vitória do Palmar Brazil 204 G4
Santa Vittoria, Monte mt. Sardegna Italy 57 B9
Santa Ynez r. U.S.A. 182 D7
Santa Ysabel i. Solomon Is see Santa Isabel
Sant Carles de la Ràpita Spain 55 L4
also spelt San Carlos de la Rápita
Sant Celoni Spain 55 N3
also spelt San Celoni
Santee U.S.A. 183 H9
Santee r. U.S.A. 175 E5
Santeramo in Colle Italy 57 I8
Santerno r. Italy 56 D4
Sant Feliu de Guíxols Spain 55 O3
also spelt San Feliú de Guíxols
Santiago Brazil 203 A9

▶Santiago Chile 204 C4
Capital of Chile.
southamerica [countries] ▶ 192–193

Santiago admin. reg. Chile 204 C4
Santiago Dom. Rep. 187 F3
long form Santiago de los Caballeros
Santiago Baja California Sur Mex. 184 C4
Santiago Nuevo León Mex. 185 E3
Santiago Panama 186 C5
Santiago Para. 201 F6
Santiago Peru 200 B3
Santiago r. Peru 198 B6
Santiago, Cabo c. Chile 205 B8
Santiago, Cerro mt. Panama 186 C5
Santiago, Río Grande de r. Mex. 184 D4
Santiago, Sierra de mts Bol. 201 F4
Santiago Astata Mex. 185 G5
Santiago de Cao Peru 200 A1
Santiago de Compostela Spain 54 C2
Santiago de Cuba Cuba 186 E2
Santiago de la Espada Spain 55 I6
Santiago del Estero Arg. 204 D2
Santiago del Estero prov. Arg. 204 D2
Santiago de los Caballeros Dom. Rep. see Santiago
Santiago de Mendez Ecuador 198 B5
Santiago de Pacaguaras Bol. 200 C3
Santiago do Cacém Port. 54 C6
Santiago Ixcuintla Mex. 184 D4
Santiago Peak U.S.A. 182 G8
Santiago Temple Arg. 204 E3
Santiago Vazquez Uruguay 204 F4
Santiaguillo, Laguna de l. Mex. 184 D3
Santillana Spain 54 G1
San Timoteo Venez. 198 D2
Santipur India see Shantipur
Santisteban del Puerto Spain 55 H6
Sant Jordi, Golf de g. Spain 55 L4
also spelt San Jorge, Golfo de
Sant Llorenç del Munt i la Serra de l'Obac, Parque Natural de nature res. Spain 55 M3
Santo Amaro Brazil 202 E5
Santo Amaro de Campos Brazil 207 L8
Santo Anastácio r. Brazil 206 A8
Santo André Brazil 207 I7
Santo André Port. 54 C6
Santo Ângelo Brazil 203 A9

▶Santo Antão i. Cape Verde 124 [inset]
Most westerly point of Africa.

Santo Antônio Amazonas Brazil 199 F5
Santo Antônio Maranhão Brazil 202 C2
Santo Antônio Rio Grande do Norte Brazil 202 F3
Santo Antônio r. Brazil 203 D6
Santo Antônio São Tomé and Principe 125 G6
Santo Antônio, Ponta pt Brazil 207 O3
Santo Antônio da Barra Brazil 202 D3
Santo Antônio da Cachoeira Brazil 199 H5
Santo Antônio da Platina Brazil 206 C10
Santo Antônio de Jesus Brazil 202 E5
Santo Antônio de Leverger Brazil 201 F3
Santo Antônio de Pádua Brazil 207 K8
Santo Antônio do Amparo Brazil 207 I7
Santo Antônio do Içá Brazil 199 E5
Santo Antônio do Jacinto Brazil 207 M3
Santo Antônio do Monte Brazil 207 H7
Santo Antônio do Rio Verde Brazil 206 F4
Santo Antônio dos Cavaleiros Port. 54 B6

Santo Antônio do Zaire Angola see Soyo
Santo Corazón Bol. 201 F4
Santo Domingo Cuba 186 C2

▶Santo Domingo Dom. Rep. 187 F3
Capital of the Dominican Republic. Formerly known as Ciudad Trujillo.

Santo Domingo Baja California Norte Mex. 184 B2
Santo Domingo San Luis Potosí Mex. 185 E4
Santo Domingo Nicaragua 186 B4
Santo Domingo Peru 200 D3
Santo Domingo country West Indies see Dominican Republic
Santo Domingo de la Calzada Spain 55 I2
Santo Domingo Pueblo U.S.A. 181 F6
Santo Domingo Tehuantepec Mex. 185 G5
Santo Eduardo Brazil 207 L8
Santo Hipólito Brazil 207 I5
Santo Inácio Brazil 206 B9
San Tomé Venez. 199 E2
Santoña Spain 55 H1
Santong r. China 82 B4
Santo Niño i. Phil. 74 C4
Santorini i. Greece see Thira
Santos Brazil 207 G10
Santos Dumont Brazil 207 J8
Santos Mercado Bol. 200 D2
Santo Stefano di Camastra Sicilia Italy 57 G10
Santo Tirso Port. 54 C3
Santo Tomás Chihuahua Mex. 181 F7
Santo Tomás Sonora Mex. 181 D7
Santo Tomás Nicaragua 186 B4
Santo Tomás Peru 200 B3
Santo Tomé Arg. 204 F3
Santrampur India 96 B5
Sanup Plateau U.S.A. 183 K5
San Valentin, Cerro mt. Chile 205 B7
San Vicente El Salvador 185 H6
San Vicente Mex. 184 A2
San Vicente Phil. 74 B2
San Vicente de Cañete Peru 200 A3
San Vicente de la Barquera Spain 54 G1
San Vicente del Caguán Col. 198 C4
San Vicente del Raspeig Spain 55 K6
San Vincenzo Italy 56 C5
San Vito, Capo c. Sicilia Italy 57 E10
San Vito al Tagliamento Italy 56 E3
San Vito dei Normanni Italy 57 J8
San Vito lo Capo Sicilia Italy 57 E10
Sanwer India 96 B5
Sanya China 87 D5
formerly known as Yaxian
San Yanaro Col. 198 D4
Sanyati r. Zimbabwe 131 F3
Sanyuan China 87 D1
Sanza Pombo Angola 127 C6
Sao, Phou mt. Laos 78 C4
São Bartolomeu r. Brazil 206 F3
São Benedito Brazil 202 D2
São Bento Amazonas Brazil 200 D1
São Bento Maranhão Brazil 202 C2
São Bento Roraima Brazil 199 F4
São Bento do Norte Brazil 202 F3
São Bernardo Brazil 202 D2
São Bernardo do Campo Brazil 206 G10
São Borja Brazil 204 F3
São Carlos Rondônia Brazil 201 D2
São Carlos Rondônia Brazil 201 E2
São Carlos São Paulo Brazil 206 F9
São Desidério Brazil 202 C5
São Domingos Brazil 202 C5
São Domingos r. Mato Grosso do Sul Brazil 203 A7
São Domingos r. Minas Gerais Brazil 206 C6
São Domingos r. Brazil 206 G2
São Domingos do Norte Brazil 207 M6
São Felipe, Serra de hills Brazil 202 C5
São Félix Bahia Brazil 202 D5
São Félix Mato Grosso Brazil 202 B4
São Félix Pará Brazil 199 I6
São Fidélis Brazil 203 D7
São Filipe Cape Verde 124 [inset]
São Francisco Acre Brazil 200 C2
São Francisco Amazonas Brazil 199 F6
São Francisco Minas Gerais Brazil 202 C5
São Francisco r. Brazil 200 D2
also known as Espalha

▶São Francisco r. Brazil 207 H4
5th longest river in South America.
southamerica [landscapes] ▶ 190–191

São Francisco, Ilha de i. Brazil 203 B8
São Francisco de Assis Brazil 203 A8
São Francisco de Goiás Brazil 206 D2
São Francisco de Paula Brazil 203 B9
São Francisco de Sales Brazil 206 D5
São Francisco do Sul Brazil 203 B8
São Gabriel Brazil 203 A9
São Gabriel da Palha Brazil 207 M6
São Gabriel de Goiás Brazil 206 F2
São Gonçalo Brazil 203 D7
São Gonçalo do Abaeté Brazil 203 C6
São Gotardo Brazil 207 H6
Sao Hill Tanz. 129 B7
São Jerônimo da Serra Brazil 206 C10
São João Brazil 199 I6
São João, Ilhas de is Brazil 202 C2
São João, Serra de hills Brazil 201 E2
São João da Aliança Brazil 206 E2
São João da Barra Brazil 203 D7
São João da Boa Vista Brazil 206 F8
São João da Ponte Brazil 207 I2
São João das Duas Pontas Brazil 206 C7
São João do Rei Brazil 203 C7
São João de Meriti Brazil 207 J9
São João do Araguaia Brazil 202 B2
São João do Caiuá Brazil 206 A8
São João do Cariri Brazil 202 E3
São João do Paraíso Brazil 202 D5
São João do Piauí Brazil 202 D3
São João dos Patos Brazil 202 D3
São João do Sul Angola 127 B8
São João Evangelista Brazil 207 K5
São Joaquim Amazonas Brazil 199 F4
São Joaquim Santa Catarina Brazil 203 B9
São Jorge da Mina Ghana see Elmina
São José Amazonas Brazil 199 E5
São José Santa Catarina Brazil 203 B8
São José do Anauá Brazil 199 F4
São José do Belmonte Brazil 202 E3
São José do Divino Brazil 207 L5
São José do Egito Brazil 202 E3
São José do Jacuri Brazil 207 K5
São José do Norte Brazil 204 G4
São José do Peixe Brazil 202 D3
São José do Rio Pardo Brazil 206 E8
São José do Rio Preto Brazil 206 D7
São José dos Campos Brazil 207 H10
São José dos Dourados r. Brazil 206 D7
São José dos Pinhais Brazil 203 B8
São Lourenço Brazil 207 H9
São Lourenço r. Brazil 201 F3
São Lourenço do Sul Brazil 204 H3
São Lucas Brazil 206 D2
São Luís Brazil 202 D2
São Luís de Montes Belos Brazil 206 D3
São Luís do Paraitinga Brazil 207 H10
São Luís do Quitunde Brazil 202 F4
São Luís Gonzaga Brazil 203 A9
São Manuel Brazil 206 E9
São Marceline Brazil 199 E4
São Marcos r. Brazil 206 E4
São Marcos, Baía de b. Brazil 202 C2
São Martinho Brazil 199 G6

São Mateus Brazil 203 E6
São Mateus r. Brazil 207 N5
São Mateus do Sul Brazil 203 B8
São Miguel i. Azores 216 M3
São Miguel r. Brazil 206 G3
São Miguel Arcanjo Brazil 206 F10
São Miguel do Tapuio Brazil 202 D3
São Miguel Jesuit Missions tourist site Brazil 203 A9
Saona, Isla i. Dom. Rep. 187 F3
Saône r. France 51 K7
São Nicolau Angola see Bentiaba
São Nicolau i. Cape Verde 124 [inset]

▶São Paulo Brazil 206 G10
Most populous city in South America and 4th in the world.
world [cities] ▶ 24–25

São Paulo state Brazil 206 E9
São Paulo de Olivença Brazil 198 D5
São Pedro Amazonas Brazil 199 G6
São Pedro Mato Grosso do Sul Brazil 206 B6
São Pedro Rondônia Brazil 201 E2
São Pedro São Paulo Brazil 206 F9
São Pedro da Aldeia Brazil 203 D7
São Pedro do Desterro Brazil 200 D2
São Pedro do Ivaí Brazil 206 B10
São Pedro do Sul Brazil 203 A9
São Pedro do Sul Port. 54 C4
São Pedro e São Paulo is N. Atlantic Ocean 216 M5
English form St Peter and St Paul Rocks
São Pires r. Brazil see Teles Pires
São Raimundo das Mangabeiras Brazil 202 C3
São Raimundo Nonato Brazil 202 D4
São Romão Amazonas Brazil 199 E6
São Romão Minas Gerais Brazil 202 C6
São Roque Brazil 206 F10
São Roque de Minas Brazil 206 G7
São Salvador Angola see M'banza Congo
São Salvador do Congo Angola see M'banza Congo
São Sebastião Amazonas Brazil 200 C1
São Sebastião Pará Brazil 199 H6
São Sebastião Rondônia Brazil 201 E2
São Sebastião São Paulo Brazil 203 C7
São Sebastião, Ilha de i. Brazil 203 C7
São Sebastião da Amoreira Brazil 206 C10
São Sebastião da Boa Vista Brazil 202 B2
São Sebastião do Paraíso Brazil 206 G7
São Simão Mato Grosso do Sul Brazil 201 F5
São Simão Minas Gerais Brazil 206 C6
São Simão, Barragem de resr Brazil 206 C6
São Simão, Represa de resr Brazil 206 D5
Sao-Siu Indon. 75 C2
São Tiago Brazil 207 I7
São Tiago i. Cape Verde 124 [inset]

▶São Tomé São Tomé and Principe 125 G6
Capital of São Tomé and Principe.

São Tomé i. São Tomé and Principe 125 G6
São Tomé, Cabo de c. Brazil 203 D7
São Tomé, Pico de mt. São Tomé and Principe 125 G6

▶São Tomé and Principe country Africa 125 G6
africa [countries] ▶ 114–117

Saoura, Oued watercourse Alg. 123 E3
São Vicente Brazil 206 G10
São Vicente i. Cape Verde 124 [inset]
São Vicente, Cabo de c. Port. 54 C7
English form St Vincent, Cape
São Vicente Ferrer Brazil 202 C2
Sápai Greece see Sapes
Sapallanga Peru 200 B3
Sapanca Turkey 106 B2
Sapão r. Brazil 202 C4
Saparua Indon. 75 D3
Saparua i. Indon. 75 D3
Sape, Selat sea chan. Indon. 75 A5
Sape, Teluk b. Indon. 77 G5
Sapele Nigeria 125 G5
Sapes Greece 58 G7
also known as Belören
Saphane Turkey 59 K9
Sapientza i. Greece 59 C12
Sapo, Serranía del mts Panama 186 D6
Sa Pobla Spain 55 O5
also spelt La Puebla
Sapo National Park Liberia 124 C5
Sapozerka Brazil 206 C10
Sapotskin Belarus 42 E8
Sapouy Burkina 125 E4
Sapozhok Rus. Fed. 41 G5
Sappa Creek r. U.S.A. 178 C3
Sapporo Japan 90 H3
Saptamukhi r. India 97 F5
Sapucaí r. Minas Gerais Brazil 207 H8
Sapucaí r. Brazil 206 E7
Sapucaia Brazil 199 G5
Sapudi i. Indon. 77 F4
Sapulpa U.S.A. 179 C4
Sapulut Sabah Malaysia 77 G1
Saq, Jabal hill Saudi Arabia 104 C2
Sāqī Iran 101 D3
Saqqaq Greenland 165 N2
Saqqez Iran 100 A2
Sara Bangl. 97 F4
Sarā Iran 100 A2
Sarāb Iran 100 A2
Sarabit el Khādim tourist site Egypt 108 E8
Sara Buri Thai. 79 C5
Saracá, Lago l. Brazil 199 G5
Saraf Doungous Chad 120 C6
Saragossa Spain see Zaragoza
Saraguro Ecuador 198 B5
Saraikela India 97 E5
Sarai Sidhu Pak. 101 H4
Sārāisniemi Fin. 44 N2
Sarakhs Turkm. 102 E5
Sarakiniko, Akra pt Greece 59 E10
Sarakino i. Greece 59 F10
Saraktash Rus. Fed. 102 D2
Saraland U.S.A. 175 B6
Saralzhin Kazakh. 102 C2
Saramati mt. India/Myanmar 97 G4
Saramériza Peru 198 B6
Saran France 51 H5
Saran' Kazakh. 103 H2
Saran, Gunung mt. Indon. 77 E3
Saranac r. U.S.A. 177 L1
Saranac Lake U.S.A. 177 L1
Sarandë Albania 59 B9
Sarandi Paraná Brazil 206 B10
Sarandi Rio Grande do Sul Brazil 203 A8
Sarandi del Yi Uruguay 204 F4
Sarangani i. Phil. 74 C5
Sarangani Bay Phil. 74 C5
Sarangani Islands Phil. 74 C5
Sarangani Strait Phil. 74 C5
Sarangarh India 97 D5
Saransk Rus. Fed. 41 H5
Sara Peak Nigeria 125 H4
Sarapul Rus. Fed. 40 J4
Sarasota U.S.A. 175 D7
Saraswati r. India 96 K5
Sǎrata r. Moldova 58 J2
Sǎrata r. Romania 58 H4
Sarata Ukr. 41 D7
Sarata r. Ukr. 58 K3

Saratoga CA U.S.A. 182 B4
Saratoga WY U.S.A. 180 F4
Saratoga Springs U.S.A. 177 L2
Saratok Sarawak Malaysia 77 E2
Saratov Rus. Fed. 102 B1
Saratov Oblast admin. div. Rus. Fed. see Saratovskaya Oblast'
Saratovskaya Oblast' admin. div. Rus. Fed. 102 A2
English form Saratov Oblast
Saratovskoye Vodokhranilishche resr Rus. Fed. 102 A1
Saravan Iran 101 E5
Saravan Laos 79 D5
Sarawa r. Myanmar 78 B5
Sarawak state Malaysia 77 E2
Saray Turkey 106 A2
Saraya Guinea 124 C4
Saraya Senegal 124 C3
Saraya, Pulau reg. Sing. 76 [inset]
Sarayçık Turkey 59 J12
Saraydüzü Turkey 106 B3
Saraylar Turkey 58 I8
Sarayönü Turkey 106 C3
Sarbāz r. Iran 101 E5
Sarbāz reg. Iran 101 E5
Sārbelah Bhutan 97 F4
Sarbisheh Iran 101 D3
Sárbogárd Hungary 49 P9
Sarca r. India/Nepal 99 K4
Sarda r. India/Nepal 99 K4
Sardarpur India 96 B5
Sardarshahr India 96 B3
Sardasht Iran 100 B4
Sardasht Khūzestān Iran 100 B4
Sardegna admin. reg. Italy 57 B8
Sardegna i. Italy see Sardinia
Sardica Bulg. see Sofia
Sardinata Col. 198 C2
Sardinia Costa Rica 186 B5
Sardinia i. Italy 57 C8
also spelt Sardegna
Sardis U.S.A. 174 B5
Sardis Lake resr U.S.A. 174 B5
Sardpol Port. 54 C5
Sareb, Rás-as- pt U.A.E. 105 E2
Sareks nationalpark nat. park Sweden 44 L2
Sarektjåkkå mt. Sweden 44 L2
Sarempaka, Gunung mt. Indon. 77 F3
Sar-e Pol Afgh. 101 F2
Sar-e Pol prov. Afgh. 101 F2
Sarezskoye Ozero l. Tajik. see Sarez, Küli
Sargasso Sea Europe 216 J4
Sargentu Loros Peru 198 C5
Sargodha Pak. 101 H3
Sarh Chad 126 C2
formerly known as Fort Archambault
Sarhad reg. Iran 101 E4
Sarhro, Jbel mt. Morocco 122 D3
Sārī Iran 100 C2
Saria i. Greece 59 I13
Sari-i-Bum Afgh. 101 F3
Sáric Mex. 184 C2
Sarichioi Romania 58 J4
Sarigan i. N. Mariana Is 73 K3
Sarıgöl Turkey 59 K11
Sarıkamış Turkey 107 E2
Sarikei Sarawak Malaysia 77 E2
Sarkemer Turkey 59 I11
Sarıköy Turkey 59 I8
Sarıkül, Qatorkühi mts China/Tajik. see Sarykol Range
Sarila India 96 C4
Sarimbun Reservoir Sing. 76 [inset]
Sarina Australia 149 F4
Sariñena Spain 55 K3
Sarıoğlan Turkey see Belören
Sari-Pül Afgh. see Sar-e Pol
Sārī Qamish Iran 100 C2
Sariqamish Kuli salt l. Turkm./Uzbek. see Sarykamyshskoye Ozero
Sarir Tibesti des. Libya 120 C4
Sarir Water Wells Field Libya 120 D3
Sarishabari Bangl. 97 F4
Sarita U.S.A. 179 C7
Sarnveliler Turkey 108 D1
Sariwŏn N. Korea 83 B5
Sarıyer Turkey 106 B2
Sarız Turkey 107 D3
Sark i. Channel Is 50 D3
Sarkad Hungary 49 S9
Sarkari Tala India 96 A4
Sarkikaraağaç Turkey 106 C3
Sārkisalo Fin. 42 D1
Şarkışla Turkey 107 D3
Sarkör watercourse Iran 101 E5
Şarköy Turkey 106 A2
Sarlath Range mts Afgh./Pak. 101 F4
Sarlat-la-Canéda France 50 H8
Sarmanovo Rus. Fed. 40 J5
Sarmento r. Italy 57 I8
Sarmi Indon. 73 I7
Sarmiento Arg. 205 C7
Särna Sweden 45 K3
Särnate Latvia 42 C4
Sarneh Iran 100 A3
Sarnen Switz. 51 O6
Sarni India see Amla
Sarnia Canada 168 D5
Sarny Ukr. 41 C6
Saroako Indon. 75 B3
Sarogozha r. Rus. Fed. 43 Q3
Sarolangun Indon. 76 C3
Saroma-ko l. Japan 90 H2
Saroma U.S.A. 172 B5
Saronikos Kolpos g. Greece 59 E11
Saros Körfezi b. Turkey 106 A2
Sarotra India 96 B5
Sarova Rus. Fed. 40 G5
Sarowbī Afgh. 101 G3
Sarpa, Ozero l. Rus. Fed. 41 H7
Sarpan i. N. Mariana Is see Rota
Šar Planina mts Macedonia/Yugo. 58 B7
Sarpsborg Norway 45 J4
Sarqant Kazakh. see Sarkand
Sarre r. France 51 N3
Sarrebourg France 51 N4
Sarreguemines France 51 N3
Sarre-Union France 51 N4
Sarria Spain 54 D2
Sarrión Spain 55 K4
Sarro Mali 124 D3
Sarròch Sardegna Italy 57 B9
Sars Rus. Fed. 40 K4
Sartana Ukr. 41 F7
formerly known as Prymors'ke
Sartène Corse France 56 A7
Sarthe r. France 50 F5
Sarti Greece 59 E8
Sartininkai Lith. 42 C6
Sartu China see Daqing
Sarud, Rūdkhāneh-ye r. Iran 100 B3
Saruhanlı Turkey 59 I10
Saruna r. Pak. 101 F5
Sarupsar India 96 B3

Şārūr Azer. 107 F3
also spelt Sharur; formerly known as Il'ichevsk
Saru Tara tourist site Afgh. 101 E4
Särvābād Iran 100 A3
Sarvani Georgia see Marneuli
Sárvár Hungary 49 N8
Sarvestān Iran 100 C4
Sárvíz r. Romania 49 P9
Sarya r. India 94 B2
Saryagach Kazakh. 103 G4
Sary-Bulak Kyrg. 103 H4
Sarydhaz r. Kyrg. see Sary-Jaz
Sarydzhas Kazakh. see Saryzhaz
Sarygamysh Köli salt l. Turkm./Uzbek. see Sarykamyshskoye Ozero
Sary-Ishikotrau, Peski des. Kazakh. see Saryyesik-Atyrau, Peski
Sary-Jaz r. Kyrg. 103 I4
also spelt Sarydhaz
Sarykamys Kazakh. 102 C3
also spelt Saryqamys
Sarykemer Kazakh. 103 G4
formerly known as Mikhaylovka
Sarykiyak Kazakh. 103 H2
Sarykol Range mts China/Tajik. 88 A4
also known as Sarikül, Qatorkühi
Sarymoyyn, Ozero salt l. Kazakh. 103 F2
formerly known as Zhaksy Sarysu
Saryozek Kazakh. 103 I3
Saryqamys Kazakh. see Sarykamys
Saryshagan Kazakh. 103 H3
Sarysu watercourse Kazakh. 103 F3
formerly known as Zhaksy Sarysu
Sary-Tash Kyrg. 103 H5
Saryter, Gora mt. Kyrg. 103 I4
Saryumir Kazakh. 102 D2
Sary Yazikskoye Vodokhranilishche resr Turkm. 103 E5
Saryyesik-Atyrau, Peski des. Kazakh. 103 H3
Saryzhal Kazakh. 103 I2
Saryzhaz Kazakh. 103 I4
also spelt Sarydzhas
Sarzhal Kazakh. 103 I2
also spelt Saryzhal
Sasak Indon. 76 B2
Sasar, Tanjung pt Indon. 75 A5
Sasaram India 97 E4
Sásd Hungary 49 P9
Sasebo Japan 91 A8
Saskatchewan prov. Canada 167 J4
Saskatchewan r. Canada 167 K4
Saskatoon Canada 167 J4
Saskylakh Rus. Fed. 39 L2
Saslaya mt. Nicaragua 186 B4
Saslaya, Parque Nacional nat. park Nicaragua 186 B4
Sasnovy Bor Belarus 43 K9
also spelt Sosnovyy Bor; formerly known as Golyashi
Sasolburg S. Africa 133 L3
Sasovo Rus. Fed. 41 G5
Sassandra Côte d'Ivoire 124 D5
Sassandra r. Côte d'Ivoire 124 D5
Sassari Sardegna Italy 57 A8
Sassnitz Germany 49 K1
Sassoferrato Italy 56 E5
historically known as Sentinum
Sasso Marconi Italy 56 D4
Sass Fiigais mt. Italy 56 D2
Sass Town Liberia 124 C5
Sassuolo Italy 56 C4
Sastobe Kazakh. 103 G4
also known as Saztöbe
Sastre Arg. 204 E3
Sasvad India 94 B2
Sasykkol', Ozero l. Kazakh. 103 J5
also known as Sasyqköl
Satadougou Mali 124 C3
Satahual i. Micronesia see Satawal
Sata-misaki c. Japan 91 B9
Satana India 94 B1
Satara India 94 B2
Satara S. Africa 131 F5
Satawal i. Micronesia 73 K5
also spelt Satahual
Sätbaev Kazakh. see Satpayev
Satchinez Romania 58 C3
Satéma Cent. Afr. Rep. 126 D3
Satengar i. Indon. 77 G4
Säter Sweden 45 K3
Setevó Mex. 184 D3
Saticoy U.S.A. 182 E7
Satihaure l. Sweden 44 L2
Satilla r. U.S.A. 175 D6
Satipo Peru 200 B2
Satiri Burkina 124 D4
Satirler Turkey see Yeşilova
Satka Rus. Fed. 38 F4
Satkania Bangl. 97 G5
Satkhira Bangl. 97 F5
Satluj r. India/Pak. see Sutlej
Satmala Range hills India 94 B1
Satmala Range hills Afgh./Pak. 101 F4
Satna India 96 D4
Sátoraljaújhely Hungary 49 S7
Satorina mt. Croatia 56 H4
Satpayev Kazakh. 103 F3
also spelt Sätbaev; formerly known as Nikol'skiy
Satpura Range mts India 96 B5
Šatrijos kalnis hill Lith. 42 D6
Satsuma-hantō pen. Japan 91 B9
Satsunai-gawa r. Japan 90 H3
Sattahip Thai. 79 C5
Sattanen Fin. 44 N2
Sattenapalle India 94 C2
Satthwa Myanmar 78 A4
Satti Jammu and Kashmir 96 C2
Satu Mare Romania 53 G2
Satun Thai. 79 C7
Satwas India 96 C5
Saubi i. Indon. 77 F4
Sauce Arg. 204 F3
Sãuceaua Mountains U.S.A. 183 L9
Sauce de Luna Arg. 204 F3
Saucillo Mex. 184 D2
Sauda Norway 45 I4
Saudakent Kazakh. 103 G4
also known as Baykadam or Bayqadam
Sauðárkrókur Iceland 44 [inset] C2

▶Saudi Arabia country Asia 104 C3
known as Al 'Arabīyah as Su'ūdīyah in Arabic
asia [landscapes] ▶ 62–63
asia [countries] ▶ 54–67

Saue Estonia 42 F3
Sauêruiná r. Brazil 201 F3
also known as Papagaio
Saug r. Phil. 74 C5
Saugeen r. Canada 168 D4
Saugerties U.S.A. 177 L3
Saugues France 51 J8
Saújbolāgh Iran see Mahābād
Saujil Arg. 204 D2
Saujon France 50 F7
Saukas ezers l. Latvia 42 G5
Sauk Center U.S.A. 178 D2
Sauk City U.S.A. 172 D7
Sauland Norway 45 J4
Sauldre r. France 51 H5
Saulgau Germany 48 G7
Saulieu France 51 K5

Saulkrasti Latvia 42 F4
Sault: Sainte Marie Canada 168 C4
Sault Ste Marie U.S.A. 173 I4
Saumalköl' Kazakh. 103 G1
formerly known as Volodarskoye
Saumarez Reef Australia 149 G4
Saumlakki Indon. 73 H8
Saumur France 50 F5
Saunavaara Fin. 44 N2
Saunders, Mount hill Australia 148 A2
Saunders Coast Antarctica 222 O1
Saunders Island Falkland Is 205 E8
Saunemin U.S.A. 172 E10
Sauquoit U.S.A. 177 J2
Saur, Khrebet mts China/Kazakh. 88 D2
Sauriesti Latvia 42 F5
Sáurimo Angola 127 D7
formerly known as Henrique de Carvalho
Sausalito U.S.A. 182 B4
Sausar India 96 C5
Sautar Angola 127 C7
Sava r. Europe 49 M9
Savá Hond. 186 B4
Sava Italy 57 J8
Savage U.S.A. 177 I6
Savage River Australia 147 E5
Savai'i i. Samoa 145 H3
historically known as Chatham Island
Savala r. Rus. Fed. 41 G6
Savalou Benin 125 F5
Savana r. Canada 169 G3
Savane r. Canada 169 G3
Savane Moz. 131 G3
Savanna U.S.A. 174 B3
Savannah GA U.S.A. 175 D5
Savannah MO U.S.A. 178 D4
Savannah OH U.S.A. 176 C5
Savannah TN U.S.A. 174 B5
Savannah r. U.S.A. 175 D5
Savannah Sound Bahamas 186 D1
Savannakhét Laos 78 D4
Savanna-la-Mar Jamaica 186 D3
Savanne Canada 172 C2
Savant Lake Canada 168 B3
Savantvadi India see Vadi
Savanur India 94 B3
Sävar Sweden 44 M3
Săvârșin Romania 58 D2
Sävast Sweden 44 M2
Savaştepe Turkey 106 A3
Savè Benin 125 F5
Save r. France 50 H9
Save r. Moz./Zimbabwe 131 G4
formerly spelt Sabi
Sāveh Iran 100 B3
Savelugu Ghana 125 E4
Savenay France 50 E5
Saveretik Guyana 199 G3
Saverne France 51 N4
Savigliano Italy 51 N3
Savino Rus. Fed. 40 G4
Savinskiy Rus. Fed. 40 G3
Savinskoye Rus. Fed. 43 U6
Savio r. Italy 56 E4
Savitaipale Fin. 45 N3
Savitri r. India 94 B2
Sävja Sweden 45 L4
Savna Cerra Gora Yugo. 58 A6
Savoie reg. France see Savoy
Savona Italy 56 A4
Savonlinna Fin. 45 O3
Savonranta Fin. 44 O3
Savoonga U.S.A. 164 B3
Savoy reg. France 51 M6
also spelt Savoie
Savozero, Ozero l. Rus. Fed. 43 O1
Şavşat Turkey 107 E2
Sävsjö Sweden 45 K4
Savu i. Indon. 75 B5
also spelt Sawu
Saudrija, Rt Croatia 56 F3
Savukoski Fin. 44 O2
Savur Turkey 107 E3
Savute r. Botswana 130 E3
Savuti Botswana 131 E3
Saw Myanmar 78 A3
Sawab, Wādī as watercourse Iraq 109 M3
Sawāb, Wādī as watercourse Syria 109 L3
Sawahlunto Indon. 76 C3
Sawai, Teluk b. Indon. 75 D3
Sawai Madhopur India 96 C4
Sawan Indon. 77 F3
Sawan Myanmar 78 B2
Sawankhalok Thai. 78 B4
also known as Wang Mai Khon
Sawar India 96 B4
Sawara Japan 91 G7
Sawasaki-bana pt Japan 90 F6
Sawata Japan 90 F6
Sawatch Range mts U.S.A. 180 F5
Sawdā', Jabal as hills Libya 120 B2
Sawi, Ao b. Thai. 79 B6
Sawl Egypt 108 E7
Sawla Ghana 124 E4
Sawmills Zimbabwe 131 F3
Sawpit Australia 147 G2
Şawqirah, Dawhat b. Oman 105 G4
English form Şawqirah Bay
Şawqirah, Ra's c. Oman 105 G4
Şawqirah Bay Oman see Şawqirah, Dawhat
Sawtell Australia 147 G2
Sawtooth Mountains hills U.S.A. 174 D2
Sawtooth Range ID U.S.A. 180 D3
Sawtooth Range WA U.S.A. 180 B2
Sawu Indon. 75 B5
Sawu i. Indon. see Savu
Sawu Sea Indon. 75 B5
Saxby r. Australia 149 D3
Saxnäs Sweden 44 K2
Saxony land Germany see Sachsen
Saxony-Anhalt land Germany see Sachsen-Anhalt
Saxton KY U.S.A. 176 A9
Saxton PA U.S.A. 176 G5
Say Mali 124 D3
Say Niger 125 F3
Sayabouri Laos see Muang Xaignabouri
Sayafi i. Indon. 75 D2
Sayak Kazakh. 103 I3
also spelt Sayaq
Sayalkudi India 94 C4
Sayam well Niger 125 I3
Sayán Peru 200 A2
Sayang i. Indon. 75 D2
Sayano-Shushenskoye Vodokhranilishche resr Rus. Fed. 80 C2
Sayaq Kazakh. see Sayak
Sayat Turkm. 103 E5
also spelt Sayot; formerly spelt Sayyod
Sayda Lebanon see Sidon
Sayen Iran 100 D2
Sayghān Afgh. 101 F3
Sayh al Ahmar reg. Oman 105 G3
Sayh al Uwayr reg. Oman 105 G3
Sayhūt Yemen 105 E5
Sayingpan China 86 B3
Saykhin Kazakh. 102 A2
also spelt Sayqyn
Şāylac Somalia 128 D2
Saylan country Asia see Sri Lanka
Saynshand Mongolia 85 F2
Sayn-Ust Mongolia 84 B2
Sayot Turkm. see Sayat
Sayo-Ōtesh Kazakh. see Say-Utes
Şayqal, Bahr imp. l. Syria 109 I4
Sayqyn Kazakh. see Saykhin
Sayram Hu salt l. China 88 C2

Sayramskiy, Pik mt. Uzbek. 103 G4
Sayre OK U.S.A. 179 C5
Sayre PA U.S.A. 177 I4
Sayreville U.S.A. 177 K5
Sayula Jalisco Mex. 184 E5
Sayula Veracruz Mex. 185 G5
Say'ūn Yemen 105 E4
Say-Utes Kazakh. 102 C3 also spelt Say-Ötesh
Sayward Canada 166 E5
Sayy well Oman 105 G4
Sayyod Turkm. see Sayat
Sazan i. Albania 58 A8
Sázava r. Czech Rep. 49 L6
Sazonovo Rus. Fed. 43 Q2
Saztöbe Kazakh. see Sastobe
Sbaa Alg. 123 E3
Sbeitla Tunisia 123 H2
Sbiba Tunisia 57 B13
Scaddan Australia 151 C7
Scaër France 50 C4
Scafell Pike hill U.K. 47 I9
Scalea Italy 57 H9
Scaletta Zanclea Sicilia Italy 57 H10
Scalloway U.K. 46 K3
Scalpaigh, Eilean i. U.K. see Scalpay
Scalpay i. U.K. 46 F6 also known as Scalpaigh, Eilean
Scandicci Italy 56 D5
Scansano Italy 56 D6
Scânteia Romania 58 I4
Scanzano Jonico Italy 57 I8
Scapa Flow inlet U.K. 46 I5
Scarba i. U.K. 46 G7
Scarborough Canada 168 E5
Scarborough Trin. and Tob. 187 H5
Scarborough U.K. 47 L9
Scarborough Shoal sea feature S. China Sea 73 E3
Scargill N.Z. 153 G10
Scarinish U.K. 46 F7
Scarp i. U.K. 46 E5
Scarpanto i. Greece see Karpathos
Scaterie Island Canada 169 J4
Scawfell Shoal sea feature S. China Sea 77 D1
Sceale Bay Australia 146 B3
Šćedro i. Croatia 56 I5
Schaale r. Germany 48 H2
Schaalsee l. Germany 48 H2
Schaalsee park Germany 48 H2
Schaffhausen Switz. 51 O5
Schagen Neth. 48 B3
Schakalskuppe Namibia 130 C5
Schao watercourse Afgh./Iran 101 E4
Scharbeutz Germany 48 H1
Schärding Austria 49 K7
Scharhörn sea feature Germany 48 F2
Schaumburg U.S.A. 172 E8
Scheeßel Germany 48 G2
Schefferville Canada 169 H2 formerly known as Knob Lake
Scheibbs Austria 49 M7
Schell Creek Range mts U.S.A. 183 J3
Schellsburg U.S.A. 176 G5
Schellville U.S.A. 182 B3
Schenectady U.S.A. 177 L3
Schenefeld Germany 48 G2
Schertz U.S.A. 179 C6
Schesaplana mt. Austria/Switz. 51 P5
Scheßlitz Germany 48 I6
Schierling Germany 48 J7
Schiermonnikoog i. Neth. 48 D2
Schiermonnikoog Nationaal Park nat. park Neth. 48 D2
Schiers Switz. 51 P6
Schimatari Greece 59 E10 also known as Skhimatárion
Schio Italy 56 D3
Schirmeck France 51 N4
Schitu Duca Romania 58 I1
Schiza i. Greece 59 C12 also spelt Skhíza
Schkeuditz Germany 49 J4
Schladen Germany 48 H3
Schladming Austria 49 K8
Schlei r. Germany 48 H1
Schleiz Germany 48 I5
Schleswig Germany 48 G1
Schleswig-Holstein land Germany 48 G1
Schleswig-Holsteinisches Wattenmeer, Nationalpark nat. park Germany 48 F1
Schlosshof tourist site Austria 49 N7
Schloß Holte-Stukenbrock Germany 48 F4
Schluchsee Germany 48 F8
Schlüchtern Germany 48 G5
Schlüsselburg Rus. Fed. see Shlissel'burg
Schmallenberg Germany 48 F4
Schmidt Island Rus. Fed. see Shmidta, Ostrov
Schmidt Peninsula Rus. Fed. see Shmidta, Poluostrov
Schmidtsdrif S. Africa 132 I5
Schneidemühl Poland see Piła
Schneverdingen Germany 48 G2
Schoemanskloof pass S. Africa 133 O2
Schoharie U.S.A. 177 K3
Schokland tourist site Neth. 48 C3
Schombee S. Africa 133 J8
Schönebeck (Elbe) Germany 48 I3
Schönefeld airport Germany 49 K3
Schöningen Germany 48 H3
Schoodic Point U.S.A. 177 R1
Schoolcraft U.S.A. 172 H8
Schoonhoven Neth. 48 B4
Schöpfl hill Austria 49 M7
Schorfheide reg. Germany 49 K3
Schouten Island Australia 147 F5
Schouten Islands P.N.G. 73 J7
Schrankogel mt. Austria 48 I8
Schreiber Canada 168 C3
Schrems Austria 49 M7
Schrobenhausen Germany 48 I7
Schroon Lake U.S.A. 177 L2
Schröttersburg Poland see Płock
Schulenburg U.S.A. 179 C6
Schull Rep. of Ireland 47 C12
Schultz Lake Canada 167 L1
Schuyler U.S.A. 178 C3
Schuyler Lake U.S.A. 177 J3
Schuylerville U.S.A. 177 L2
Schuylkill Haven U.S.A. 177 I5
Schwaan Germany 49 J2
Schwabach Germany 48 I6
Schwäbische Alb mts Germany 48 F8
Schwäbisch-Fränkischer Wald, Naturpark nature res. Germany 48 G7
Schwäbisch Hall Germany 48 G6
Schwabmünchen Germany 48 H7
Schwalm r. Germany 48 G4
Schwanden Switz. 51 P5
Schwandorf Germany 48 J6
Schwaner, Pegunungan mts Indon. 77 F3
Schwangau Germany 48 H8
Schwartz Range mts Antarctica 223 D2
Schwarzenbek Germany 48 H2
Schwarzenberg Germany 49 J5
Schwarzer Mann hill Germany 48 D5
Schwarzrand mts Namibia 130 C5
Schwarzwald mts Germany see Black Forest
Schwaz Austria 48 I8
Schwedeneck Germany 48 H1
Schwedt an der Oder Germany 49 L2
Schweinfurt Germany 48 H5
Schweiz country Europe see Switzerland
Schweizer-Reneke S. Africa 133 J4
Schwerin Germany 48 I2
Schweriner See l. Germany 48 I2
Schweriner Seenlandschaft park Germany 48 I2
Schwyz Switz. 51 O5
Sciacca Sicilia Italy 57 F11
Scicli Sicilia Italy 57 G12
Science Hill U.S.A. 176 A8
Scilla Italy 57 H10
Scilly, Île atoll Fr. Polynesia see Manuae
Scilly, Isles of U.K. 47 F14
Scio U.S.A. 176 D5
Scioto r. U.S.A. 176 C7
Scipio U.S.A. 183 L2
Scobey U.S.A. 180 F2
Scodra Albania see Shkodër
Scofield Reservoir U.S.A. 183 M2
Scone Australia 147 F3
Scordia Sicilia Italy 57 G11
Scoresby Land reg. Greenland 165 Q2
Scoresbysund Greenland see Ittoqqortoormiit
Scoresby Sund sea chan. Greenland see Kangertittivaq
Scorniceşti Romania 58 F4
Scorpion Bight b. Australia 151 D7
Scorzè Italy 56 E3
Scotia Sea S. Atlantic Ocean 217 K9
▶Scotland admin. div. U.K. 46 I6 historically known as Caledonia europe [environments] 36–37
Scotland U.S.A. 177 I7
Scotstown Canada 169 G4
Scott, Cape Australia 148 A2
Scott, Cape Canada 166 D5
Scott, Mount hill U.S.A. 179 C5
Scott Base research station Antarctica 223 L1
Scottburgh S. Africa 133 O7
Scott City U.S.A. 178 B4
Scott Coast Antarctica 223 K1
Scott Glacier Antarctica 223 G2
Scott Glacier Antarctica 223 N1
Scott Inlet Canada 165 L2
Scott Island Antarctica 223 L2
Scott Islands Canada 166 D5
Scott Mountains Antarctica 223 D2
Scott Reef Australia 150 C2
Scottsbluff U.S.A. 178 B3
Scottsboro U.S.A. 174 C5
Scottsburg U.S.A. 174 C4
Scottsdale Australia 147 E5
Scotts Head Dominica 187 H4
Scottsville KY U.S.A. 174 C4
Scottsville VA U.S.A. 176 G8
Scottville U.S.A. 172 G7
Scourie U.K. 46 G5
Scranton U.S.A. 177 J4
Scugog, Lake Canada 168 E4
Scunthorpe U.K. 47 L10
Scuol Switz. 51 Q6
Scupi Macedonia see Skopje
Scutari Albania see Shkodër
Scutari, Lake Albania/Yugo. 58 A6 also known as Shkodrës, Liqeni i or Skardarsko Jezero
Seaboard U.S.A. 176 H9
Seabrook, Lake salt flat Australia 151 E6
Seaca Romania 58 F4
Seaford U.K. 47 M13
Seaford U.S.A. 177 J7
Seaforth Canada 173 L7
Seahorse Bank sea feature Phil. 74 A4 also known as Routh Bank
Seal r. Canada 167 M3
Seal, Cape S. Africa 132 H11
Sea Lake Australia 147 D3
Seal Bay Antarctica 223 X2
Seal Cove Canada 169 J3
Seal Island U.S.A. 177 Q2
Seal Lake Canada 169 I2
Sealy U.S.A. 179 C6
Seaman U.S.A. 176 B7
Seaman Range mts U.S.A. 183 I4
Searcy U.S.A. 174 B5
Searles Lake U.S.A. 183 G6
Searsport U.S.A. 177 Q1
Seascale U.K. 47 I9
Seaside CA U.S.A. 182 C5
Seaside OR U.S.A. 180 B3
Seaside Park U.S.A. 177 K6
Seaton Glacier Antarctica 223 D2
Seattle U.S.A. 180 B3
Sea View S. Africa 133 J11
Seaview Range mts Australia 149 E3
Seaville U.S.A. 177 K6
Seaward Kaikoura Range mts N.Z. 153 H10
Seba Indon. 75 B5
Sebaco Nicaragua 186 B4
Sebago Lake U.S.A. 177 O2
Sebakwe Recreational Park Zimbabwe 127 F9
Sebangan, Teluk b. Indon. 77 F3
Sebangka i. Indon. 76 D2
Sebastea Turkey see Sivas
Sebastian U.S.A. 175 D7
Sebastián Vizcaíno, Bahía b. Mex. 184 B2
Sebasticook r. U.S.A. 177 P1
Sebastopol Ukr. see Sevastopol'
Sebastopol U.S.A. 182 B3
Sebatik i. Indon. 77 G1
Sebauh Sarawak Malaysia 77 F2
Sebayan, Bukit mt. Indon. 77 E3
Sebba Burkina 125 F3
Sebderat Eritrea 121 H6
Sebdou Alg. 123 E2
Sébékoro Mali 124 C3
Seben Turkey 106 B2
Sebenico Croatia see Šibenik
Sebennytos Egypt see Samannûd
Sebeş Romania 58 E3
Sebeş r. Romania 58 E2
Sebewaing U.S.A. 173 J7
Sebezh Rus. Fed. 43 J5
Şebinkarahisar Turkey 107 D2
Sebiş Romania 58 D2
Sebisseb, Oued r. Alg. 55 O9
Sebla r. Rus. Fed. 43 S3
Seblat, Gunung mt. Indon. 76 C3
Sebrell U.S.A. 177 H9
Sebring U.S.A. 175 D7
Sebuku i. Indon. 77 G3
Sebuku r. Indon. 77 G1
Sebuku, Teluk b. Indon. 77 G2
Sečanj Vojvodina, Srbija Yugo. 58 B3
Secaş r. Romania 58 E2
Secas, Islas is Panama 186 C6
Secchia r. Italy 56 D3
Seccia Mountains Eth. 128 C3
Sechelt Canada 166 F5
Sechenovo Rus. Fed. 40 H5
Sechura Peru 198 A6
Sechura, Bahía de b. Peru 198 A6
Second Cataract rapids Sudan see 2nd Cataract
Second Mesa U.S.A. 183 N6
Second Three Mile Opening sea chan. Australia 149 D2
Secos, Ilhéus is Cape Verde 124 [inset] also known as Rombo, Ilhéus do
Sečovce Slovakia 49 S7
Secretary Island N.Z. 153 A13
Secunda S. Africa 133 N3
Secunderabad India 94 C2
Sécure r. Bol. 200 D3
Seda Latvia 42 G4
Seda r. Latvia 42 G4
Seda Lith. 42 D5
Seda r. Port. 54 C6
Sedalia U.S.A. 178 D4
Sedan France 51 K3
Sedan U.S.A. 178 C4
Sedan Dip Australia 149 D3
Seddon N.Z. 153 I9
Seddonville N.Z. 153 F9
Sedeh Fārs Iran 100 C4
Sedeh Khorāsan Iran 101 D3
Sedgefield U.S.A. 176 F9
Sedgewick Canada 167 I4
Sedgwick U.S.A. 177 Q1
Sédhiou Senegal 124 B3
Sedico Italy 56 E2
Sedlčany Czech Rep. 49 L6
Sedlets Poland see Siedlce
Sedom Israel 108 G6
Sedona U.S.A. 183 M7
Sédrata Alg. 123 G1
Šeduva Lith. 42 E6
Sędziszów Poland 49 R5
Seebad Heringsdorf Germany 49 L2
Seeberg pass Austria/Slovenia 49 L9
Seehausen (Altmark) Germany 48 I3
Seeheim Namibia 130 C5
Seeheim-Jugenheim Germany 48 F6
Seekoegat S. Africa 132 G10
Seekoei r. S. Africa 133 I7
Seekoevlei Nature Reserve S. Africa 133 N4
Seela Pass Canada 166 B1
Seeley U.S.A. 183 I9
Seelig, Mount Antarctica 222 R1
Seelow Germany 49 L3
Seenu Atoll Maldives see Addu Atoll
Sées France 50 G4
Seesen Germany 48 H4
Seevetal Germany 48 H2
Sefadu Sierra Leone 124 C4 also known as Koidu
Seferihisar Turkey 59 H10
Sefid, Kūh-e mt. Iran 100 B3
Sefid, Kūh-e mts Iran 100 B4
Sefophe Botswana 131 E4
Ségala Mali 124 C3
Segalstad Norway 45 J3
Segama r. Sabah Malaysia 77 G1
Segamat Malaysia 76 C2
Segangane Morocco 55 H9
Şegarcea Romania 58 E4
Sêgbana Benin 125 F4
Segen Wenz watercourse Eth. 128 C3
Segera Tanz. 129 C6
Segezha Rus. Fed. 40 E3
Seggueur, Oued watercourse Alg. 123 F2
Seghnān Afgh. 101 G2
Seghouane Alg. 55 N8
Segiz, Ozero salt l. Kazakh. 103 F3
Segontia U.K. see Caernarfon
Segontium U.K. see Caernarfon
Segonzac France 50 F7
Segorbe Spain 55 K5
Ségou Mali 124 D3
Ségou admin. reg. Mali 124 D3
Segovia Col. 198 C3
Segovia r. Hond./Nicaragua see Coco
Segovia Spain 54 G4
Segozerskoye, Ozero resr Rus. Fed. 40 E3
Segré France 50 F5
Segre r. Spain 55 L3
Séguédine Niger 125 I1
Séguéla Côte d'Ivoire 124 D5
Séguéla Mali 124 D3 formerly spelt Sagala
Séguénéga Burkina 125 E3
Seguin U.S.A. 179 C6
Segura r. Spain 55 K6
Segura, Sierra de mts Spain 55 I7
Sehithwa Botswana 130 D4
Sehlabathebe Lesotho 133 N6
Sehlabathebe National Park Lesotho 133 N6
Seho i. Indon. 75 C3
Sehore India 96 C5
Sehwan Pak. 101 F5
Seiche r. France 50 E5
Seignelay r. Canada 169 G3
Seikpyu Myanmar 78 A3
Seiland i. Norway 44 M1
Seiling U.S.A. 179 C4
Seille r. France 51 K6
Seille r. France 51 M3
Šeimena r. Lith. 42 D7
Sein, Île de i. France 50 B4
Seinäjoki Fin. 44 M3
Seine r. Canada 168 B3
Seine r. France 51 G3
Seine, Baie de b. France 50 F3
Seine, Sources de la tourist site France 51 K5
Seine, Val de valley France 51 J4
Seipinang Indon. 77 F3
Seistan reg. Iran see Sīstān
Seitsemisen kansallispuisto nat. park Fin. 45 M3
Seival Brazil 204 G3
Sejny Poland 49 U1
Sekadau Indon. 77 E2
Sekanak, Teluk b. Indon. 76 D3
Sekatak Bengara Indon. 77 G2
Sekayu Indon. 76 C3
Sekčov r. Slovakia 49 S7
Seke China see Sêrtar
Seke-Banza Dem. Rep. Congo 127 B6
Sekhukhune S. Africa 133 O1
Seki Japan 91 E7
Seki Turkey 108 A1
Seki r. Turkey 108 A1
Sekicau, Gunung vol. Indon. 76 D4
Sekoma Botswana 131 D5
Sekondi Ghana 125 E5
Sek'ot'a Eth. 128 C1
Sekseuil Kazakh. see Saksaul'skiy
Seküheh Iran 101 E4
Sela Rus. Fed. see Shali
Selagan r. Indon. 76 C3
Selah U.S.A. 180 B3
Selangor state Malaysia 76 C2
Selargius Sardegna Italy 57 B9
Selaru i. Indon. 73 H8
Selatan, Tanjung pt Indon. 77 F4
Selatpanjang Indon. 76 C2
Selawik U.S.A. 164 C3
Selbjørnsfjorden sea chan. Norway 46 Q4
Selbu Norway 44 J3
Selby U.K. 47 K10
Selby U.S.A. 178 B2
Selbyville U.S.A. 177 J7
Selçuk Turkey 59 I11 also known as Akıncılar
Sele r. Italy 57 G8
Selebi-Phikwe Botswana 131 E4 formerly spelt Selebi-Pikwe
Selebi-Pikwe Botswana see Selebi-Phikwe
Selečka Planina mts Macedonia 58 C7
Selemdzha r. Rus. Fed. 82 C1
Selemdzhinskiy Khrebet mts Rus. Fed. 82 D1
Selendi Turkey 59 J10
Selenduma Rus. Fed. 85 E1

▶Selenga r. Rus. Fed. 85 E1
Part of the Yenisey-Angara-Selenga, 3rd longest river in Asia.
asia [landscapes] 62–63

Selenge Dem. Rep. Congo 126 C5
Selenge Mongolia 84 D1
Selenge prov. Mongolia 85 E1
Selenge Mörön r. Mongolia 85 E1
Selenginsk Rus. Fed. 85 E1
Selenicë Albania 58 A8
Sélestat France 51 N4
Seletar Sing. 76 [inset]
Seletar, Pulau i. Sing. 76 [inset]
Seletar Reservoir Sing. 76 [inset]
Seletinskoye Kazakh. 103 H1 also known as Sileti
Selety r. Kazakh. see Sileti
Seletyteniz, Ozero salt l. Kazakh. see Siletiteniz, Ozero
Seleucia Turkey see Silifke
Seleucia Pieria Turkey see Samandağı
Seleznevo Rus. Fed. 43 J1
Selezni Rus. Fed. 43 M6
Selfoss Iceland 44 [inset] B3
Sel'gon Stantsiya Rus. Fed. 82 D2
Selib Rus. Fed. 40 I3
Sélibabi Mauritania 124 B3
Seligenstadt Germany 48 F5
Seliger, Ozero l. Rus. Fed. 43 O4
Seligman U.S.A. 183 L6
Selikhino Rus. Fed. 82 E2
Selîma Oasis Sudan 121 F4
Selimiye Turkey 59 I11
Sélingué, Lac de l. Mali 124 C4
Selinnkegni Mali 124 C3
Selinous r. Greece 59 D10
Selinsgrove U.S.A. 177 I5
Selinunte tourist site Sicilia Italy 57 E11
Selishche Rus. Fed. 43 O5
Selishchi Rus. Fed. 41 G5
Selitrennoye Rus. Fed. 102 A3
Selii i. Indon. 77 D3
Selizharovo Rus. Fed. 43 O5
Selje Norway 44 I3
Seljord Norway 45 J4
Selkirk Canada 167 L5
Selkirk U.K. 46 J8
Selkirk Mountains Canada 167 G4
Selkopp Norway 44 N1
Sellia Marina Italy 57 I10
Sellore Island Myanmar see Saganthit Kyun
Selma AL U.S.A. 175 C5
Selma CA U.S.A. 182 E5
Selmer U.S.A. 174 B5
Selmet Wielki, Jezioro l. Poland 49 T2
Selong Indon. 77 G5
Selongey France 51 L5
Selonsrivier S. Africa 133 N2
Sélouma Guinea 124 C4
Selous, Mount Canada 166 C2
Selous Game Reserve nature res. Tanz. 129 C7
Selseleh-ye Pīr Shūrān mts Iran 101 E4
Selsey Bill hd U.K. 47 L13
Sel'tso Bryanskaya Oblast' Rus. Fed. 43 P8
Sel'tso Bryanskaya Oblast' Rus. Fed. 43 P8
Selty Rus. Fed. 40 J4
Seluan i. Indon. 77 D1
Selukwe Zimbabwe see Shurugwi
Selvagens, Ilhas is Madeira 122 B3
Selvānā Iran 100 A2
Selvas reg. Brazil 199 D6
Selviria Brazil 206 B7
Selway r. U.S.A. 180 D3
Selwyn Lake Canada 167 J2
Selwyn Mountains Canada 166 D1
Selwyn Range hills Australia 149 C4
Seman r. Albania 58 A8
Semangka, Teluk b. Indon. 76 D4
Semarang Indon. 77 E4
Sematan Sarawak Malaysia 77 E2
Semau i. Indon. 75 B5
Semayang, Danau l. Indon. 77 G3
Sembakung r. Indon. 77 G2
Sembawang Sing. 76 [inset]
Sembawang, Sungai r. Sing. 76 [inset]
Sembé Congo 126 B4
Şemdinli Turkey 107 F3 also known as Navşar
Semendire Srbija Yugo. see Smederevo
Semendua Dem. Rep. Congo 126 C5
Semendyayevo Rus. Fed. 43 T4
Semenic, Vârful mt. Romania 58 D3
Semenivka Ukr. 41 E5 also spelt Semenovka
Semenov Rus. Fed. 40 H4
Semenovka Ukr. see Semenivka
Semenovskoye Rus. Fed. 43 U3
Semeru, Gunung vol. Indon. 77 F5
Semey Kazakh. see Semipalatinsk
Semhar prov. Eritrea 104 B5
Semibratovo Rus. Fed. 43 U4
Semidi Islands U.S.A. 164 D4
Semigorodnyaya Rus. Fed. 43 V2
Semikarakorsk Rus. Fed. 41 G7
Semiluki Rus. Fed. 41 F6
Semily Czech Rep. 49 M5
Seminoe Reservoir U.S.A. 180 F4
Seminole U.S.A. 179 B5
Seminole, Lake U.S.A. 175 C6
Semiozernoye Kazakh. 103 F1
Semipalatinsk Kazakh. 103 J2 also known as Semey
Semirara i. Phil. 74 B3
Semirara Islands Phil. 74 B4
Semirom Iran 100 B4
Semitau Indon. 77 E2
Semiyarka Kazakh. 103 I2
Semizbuga Kazakh. 103 H2 also known as Semizbughy
Semizbughy Kazakh. see Semizbuga
Semkhoz Rus. Fed. 43 T5
Sem Kolodezey Ukr. see Lenine
Semlac Romania 58 B2
Semlevo Smolenskaya Oblast' Rus. Fed. 43 O6
Semlevo Smolenskaya Oblast' Rus. Fed. 43 O6
Semnān Iran 100 C3
Semnān prov. Iran 100 B3
Sêmnyi China 84 D4
Semois r. Belgium 51 K3
Semonkong Lesotho 133 M6
Sempach Switz. 51 O5
Semporna Sabah Malaysia 77 G1
Sempu i. Indon. 77 F5
Sem Tripa Brazil 199 H6
Semtsy Rus. Fed. 43 O9
Semyonovskoye Rus. Fed. see Bereznik
Semyonovskoye Rus. Fed. see Ostrovskoye
Sên, Stœng r. Cambodia 79 D5
Sena Bol. 200 D2
Senador Canedo Brazil 206 D3
Senador Pompeu Brazil 202 E3
Senafe Eritrea 104 B5
Senaki Georgia 107 E2 formerly known as Mikha Tskhakaia or Tskhakaia
Sena Madureira Brazil 200 C2
Senanayake Samudra l. Sri Lanka 94 D5
Senanga Zambia 127 D9
Sénas France 51 L9
Senatobia U.S.A. 174 B5
Sendai Kagoshima Japan 91 B9
Sendai Miyagi Japan 90 G5
Sendai-wan b. Japan 90 G5
Sendelingsfontein S. Africa 133 K3
Senden Germany 48 H7
Şendreni Romania 58 I3
Sene r. Ghana 125 E5
Senebui, Tanjung pt Indon. 76 C2
Seneca IL U.S.A. 172 E9
Seneca KS U.S.A. 178 C4
Seneca OR U.S.A. 180 C3
Seneca PA U.S.A. 176 F4
Seneca Lake U.S.A. 177 I3
Seneca Rocks U.S.A. 176 F7
Senecaville Lake U.S.A. 176 D6
▶Senegal country Africa 124 B3
world [countries] 10–11
africa [countries] 114–117
Sénégal r. Mauritania/Senegal 124 A2
Seneka, Mys hd Rus. Fed. 82 E1
Senekal S. Africa 133 L5
Seney National Wildlife Refuge nature res. U.S.A. 172 G4
Senftenberg Germany 49 L4
Senga Malawi 129 B8
Senga Hill Zambia 127 F7
Sengar r. India 96 C4
Sengata Indon. 77 G2
Sengerema Tanz. 128 B5
Sengés Brazil 206 D11
Sengeyskiy, Ostrov i. Rus. Fed. 40 I1
Sengiley Rus. Fed. 41 I5
Sengirli, Mys pt Kazakh. see Syngyrli, Mys
Sengirli, Mys pt Kazakh. 102 C4 also spelt Syngyrli, Mys
Sêngli Co l. China 89 D6
Senguerr r. Arg. 205 C7
Sengwa r. Zimbabwe 131 F3
Senhit prov. Eritrea 104 B5
Senhor do Bonfim Brazil 202 D4
Senica Slovakia 49 O7
Senigallia Italy 56 F5
Senj Croatia 56 G4
Senja i. Norway 44 L1
Senjehopen Norway 44 L1
Şenkaya Turkey 107 E2 also known as Örtülü
Senko Guinea 124 C4
Senkobo Zambia 127 E9
Sen'kove Ukr. 41 F6
Sen'kovo Rus. Fed. 43 L6
Şenköy Turkey 108 H1
Senku Jammu and Kashmir 96 C2
Senlac S. Africa 132 H2
Senlin Shan mt. China 82 C4
Senlis France 51 I3
Senmonorom Cambodia 79 D5
Sennar Sudan 121 G6
Sennar state Sudan 121 G6
Senneterre Canada 168 E3
Senno Belarus see Syanno
Senonches France 50 H4
Senorbì Sardegna Italy 57 B9
Senqu r. Lesotho 133 L7
Sens France 51 J4
Sensuntepeque El Salvador 185 H6
Senta Vojvodina, Srbija Yugo. 58 B3 also spelt Zenta
Sentinel Peak Canada 166 F4
Sentinel Range mts Antarctica 222 S1
Sentinum Italy see Sassoferrato
Sentosa i. Sing. 76 [inset] formerly known as Blakang Mati, Pulau
Şenyurt Turkey 107 E3 also known as Derbesiye
Seo de Urgell Spain see La Seu d'Urgell
Seonath r. India 97 D5
Seondha India 96 C4
Seoni India 96 C5
Seoni Chhapara India 96 C5
Seoni-Malwa India 96 C5

▶Seoul S. Korea 83 B5
Capital of South Korea. Also spelt Sŏul.
world [cities] 24–25

Séoune r. France 50 G8
Sepanjang i. Indon. 77 F4
Separation Point N.Z. 152 G8
Separation Well Australia 150 C4
Separ Shāhābād Iran 100 A3
Sepasu Indon. 77 G2
Sepatini r. Brazil 200 D1
Sepetiba, Baía de b. Brazil 207 I10
Sepik r. P.N.G. 73 J7
Sepinang Indon. 77 G2
Sepino Italy 56 G7
Sep'o N. Korea 83 B5
Sępólno Krajeńskie Poland 49 O2
Sepotuba r. Brazil 201 F3
Seppa India 97 G4
Şepreuş Romania 58 C2
Septèmes-les-Vallons France 51 L9
Sept-Îles Canada 169 H3 also known as Seven Islands
Sept-Îles-Port-Cartier, Réserve Faunique de nature res. Canada 169 H3
Sepupa Botswana 130 D3
Seputih r. Indon. 77 D4
Sequillo r. Spain 54 F3
Sequoia National Park U.S.A. 182 F5
Serae prov. Eritrea 104 B5
Serafimovich Rus. Fed. 41 G6
Seraitang China see Baima
Seram i. Indon. 75 D3 English form Ceram
Seram Sea Indon. 75 D3 English form Ceram Sea
Serang Indon. 77 D4
Serangoon, Pulau i. Sing. 76 [inset] also known as Coney Island
Serangoon, Sungai r. Sing. 76 [inset]
Serangoon Harbour b. Sing. 76 [inset]
Serapeum Egypt 108 D7
Serapong, Mount hill Sing. 76 [inset]
Serasan i. Indon. 77 E2
Serasan, Selat sea chan. Indon. 77 E2
Seraya i. Indon. 77 E2
Serbâl, Gebel mt. Egypt 108 E9
Serbia aut. rep. Yugo. see Srbija
Sêrbug Co l. China 89 E5
Sêrca China 97 G3
Serdica Bulg. see Sofia
Serdo Eth. 128 D2
Serdoba r. Rus. Fed. 41 H5
Serdobsk Rus. Fed. 41 H5
Serebryanka Rus. Fed. 40 J3
Serebryansk Kazakh. 88 C1
Serebryanyye Prudy Rus. Fed. 43 T7
Sered' Slovakia 49 O7
Sereda Moskovskaya Oblast' Rus. Fed. 43 Q6
Sereda Yaroslavskaya Oblast' Rus. Fed. 43 V4
Seredeyskiy Rus. Fed. 43 Q7
Seredka Rus. Fed. 43 J3
Serednikovo Rus. Fed. 43 U6
Seredniy Kuyal'nyk r. Ukr. 58 L2
Seredyna-Buda Rus. Fed. 43 P9
Seredyne Ukr. 49 T7
Şereflikoçhisar Turkey 106 C3
Serein r. France 51 J5
Seremban Malaysia 76 C2
Serengeti National Park Tanz. 128 B5
Serengeti Plain Tanz. 128 E5
Serenje Zambia 127 F8
Serere Uganda 128 B4
Serezha r. Rus. Fed. 40 G5
Serezha r. Rus. Fed. 43 L5
Sergach Rus. Fed. 40 H5
Sergeikha Rus. Fed. 43 V5
Sergelen Dornod Mongolia 85 G1
Sergelen Sühbaatar Mongolia 85 F2
Sergen Turkey 58 I7
Sergeyevka Rus. Fed. 90 C3
Sergeyevka Akmolinskaya Oblast' Kazakh. 103 G2
Sergeyevka Severnyy Kazakhstan Kazakh. 103 F1
Sergino Rus. Fed. 38 G3
Sergipe state Brazil 202 E4
Sergiyev Posad Rus. Fed. 43 T5 formerly known as Zagorsk
Sergiyevskiy Rus. Fed. see Fakel
Sergiyevskoye Rus. Fed. 43 S9
Sergo Ukr. see Stakhanov
Serhiyivka Ukr. 58 L2
Seria Brunei 77 F1
Serian Sarawak Malaysia 77 E2
Seribu, Kepulauan is Indon. 77 D4
Seribudolok Indon. 76 B2
Serifos Greece 59 F11
Serifos i. Greece 59 F11
Serifou, Steno sea chan. Greece 59 F11
Sérignan France 51 J9
Sérigny r. Canada 169 G2
Sérigny, Lac l. Canada 169 G2
Serik Turkey 106 B3
Serikbuya China 88 B4
Serikkembelo Indon. 75 C3
Sèrinama Madag. 131 [inset] J3
Seringa, Serra da hills Brazil 199 I6
Seringapatam Reef Australia 150 C2
Serinhisar Turkey 59 K11
Serio r. Italy 56 B3
Serio, Parco del park Italy 56 B3
Sêrkang China see Nyainrong
Sermata i. Indon. 75 D5
Sermata, Kepulauan is Indon. 75 D5
Sermersuaq glacier Greenland 165 M2 also known as Humboldt Gletscher
Sermersuaq glacier Greenland 165 N2 also known as Steenstrup Gletscher
Sērmūkši Latvia 42 G4
Sernovodsk Rus. Fed. 41 I5
Sernur Rus. Fed. 40 I4
Sernyy Zavod Turkm. see Kukurtli
Serón Spain 55 I7
Seronga Botswana 130 D3
Serouenout well Alg. 123 G4
Serov Rus. Fed. 38 G4
Serowe Botswana 131 E4
Serpa Port. 54 D7
Serpa Pinto Angola see Menongue
Serpent r. Canada 169 G3
Serpent, Vallée du watercourse Mali 124 C3
Serpentine r. Australia 151 A7
Serpentine Lakes salt flat Australia 146 A2
Serpent's Mouth sea chan. Trin. and Tob./Venez. 187 H5
Serpeysk Rus. Fed. 43 Q7
Serpis r. Spain 55 K6
Serpneve Ukr. 58 K2
Serpukhov Rus. Fed. 43 S7
Serra Brazil 203 D7
Serra Bonita Brazil 206 G2
Serra da Bocaina, Parque Nacional da nat. park Brazil 203 C7
Serra da Canastra, Parque Nacional da nat. park Brazil 206 G7
Serra da Capivara, Parque Nacional da nat. park Brazil 202 D4
Serra da Estrela, Parque Natural da nature res. Port. 54 D4
Serra da Mesa, Represa resr Brazil 202 B5
Serra das Araras Brazil 207 H2
Serra de Outes Spain 54 C2
Serradilla Spain 54 E5
Serra do Divisor, Parque Nacional da nat. park Brazil 200 B2
Serra do Navio Brazil 199 H4
Serra dos Aimorés Brazil 207 M4
Serra do Salitre Brazil 206 G6
Sérrai Greece see Serres
Serramanna Sardegna Italy 57 A9
Serrana Brazil 206 F8
Serrana Bank sea feature Caribbean Sea 186 C4
Serranía de la Neblina, Parque Nacional nat. park Venez. 199 E4
Serranilla Bank sea feature Caribbean Sea 186 D4
Serrano i. Chile 205 B8
Serranópolis Brazil 206 A5
Serraria, Ilha i. Brazil see Queimada, Ilha
Serra San Bruno Italy 57 I10
Serras de Aire e Candeeiros, Parque Natural das nature res. Port. 54 C5
Serra Talhada Brazil 202 E3
Serravalle Scrivia Italy 56 A4
Serre r. France 51 J3
Serres Greece 58 E7 also known as Sérrai
Serrezuela Arg. 204 D3
Serrinha Brazil 202 E4
Serrita Brazil 202 E3
Sêrro Brazil 203 D6
Serrota mt. Spain 54 F4
Sers Tunisia 57 A12
Sersou, Plateau du Alg. 55 M9
Sertã Port. 54 C5
Sertânia Brazil 202 E4
Sertanópolis Brazil 206 B10
Sertão de Camapuã reg. Brazil 206 A6
Sertãozinho Brazil 206 F8
Sêrtar China 86 B1 also known as Seke
Sertavul Geçidi pass Turkey 108 E1
Sertolovo Rus. Fed. 43 L1
Serua vol. Indon. 75 D4
Serui Indon. 73 I7
Serule Botswana 131 E4
Serutu i. Indon. 77 E3
Seruyan r. Indon. 77 F3
Servach r. Belarus 42 I7
Servia Greece 59 D8
Servol r. Spain 55 L4 also spelt Cerbol
Serwaru Indon. 75 C5
Sêrxu China 86 A1 also known as Nixia
Sesayap Indon. 77 G2
Sesayap r. Indon. 77 G2
Sese Dem. Rep. Congo 126 E4
Sesekinika Canada 173 M2
Sesel country Indian Ocean see Seychelles
Sesepe Indon. 75 C3
Sesfontein Namibia 130 B3
Seshachalam Hills India 94 C3
Seshcha Rus. Fed. 43 O8
Sesheke Zambia 127 E9
Sesia r. Italy 56 A3
Seskar Furö i. Sweden 44 M2
Sesklio i. Greece 59 I12
Sesostris Bank sea feature India 94 A3
S'Espalmador i. Spain 55 M6 also known as Espalmador, Isla
Sessa Angola 127 D8
Ses Salines, Cap de c. Spain 55 O5 also spelt Salinas, Cabo de
Sestra r. Rus. Fed. 43 S5
Sestri Levante Italy 56 B4
Sestroretsk Rus. Fed. 43 K1
Sestrunj i. Croatia 56 G4
Sestu Sardegna Italy 57 B9
Šešupė r. Lith./Rus. Fed. 42 D6
Sesvete Croatia 56 I3
Set r. Spain 55 L3
Set, Phou mt. Laos 79 D5
Sète France 51 J9
Sete Barras Brazil 206 F11
Šetekšna r. Lith. 42 G6
Sete Lagoas Brazil 203 C6
Setermoen Norway 44 L1
Setesdal valley Norway 45 I4
Seti r. Nepal 97 D3
Seti r. Nepal 97 E4
Setia Italy see Sezze
Sétif Alg. 123 G1 also spelt Stif
Setit r. Africa 121 H6
Seto Japan 91 E7
Seto-naikai sea Japan 91 C8 English form Inland Sea
Seto-naikai National Park Japan 91 C7
Setsan Myanmar 78 A4
Settat Morocco 122 D2
Setté Cama Gabon 126 A5
Settepani, Monte mt. Italy 56 A4
Settimo Torinese Italy 51 N7
Settle U.K. 47 J9
Settlement Creek r. Australia 148 C3
Settlers S. Africa 133 M1
Setúbal Port. 54 C6
Setúbal admin. dist. Port. 54 C6
Setúbal, Baía de b. Port. 54 B6
Setubinha Brazil 207 K4
Seugne r. France 50 F7
Seul, Lac l. Canada 168 A3
Seurre France 51 L5
Sev r. Rus. Fed. 43 P9

S

Sevan Armenia **107** F2
Sevan, Lake Armenia **107** F2
also known as Sevan, Ozero or Sevana Lich
Sevan, Ozero *l.* Armenia *see* Sevan, Lake
Sevana Lich *l.* Armenia *see* Sevan, Lake
Sevaruyo Bol. **200** D4
Sevastopol' Ukr. **41** E7
English form Sebastopol
Seven Islands Canada *see* Sept-Îles
Sevenoaks S. Africa **133** O6
Sevenoaks U.K. **47** M12
Seventeen Seventy Australia **149** F5
Seventy Mile House Canada *see*
70 Mile House
Sévérac-le-Château France **51** J8
Severino Ribeiro Brazil **204** G3
Severka *r.* Rus. Fed. **43** T6
Severn *r.* Australia **147** F2
Severn *r.* Canada **168** C2
Severn *mt.* N.Z. **153** H10
Severn S. Africa **132** G3
Severn *r.* U.K. **47** J12
Severn U.S.A. **177** H9
Severnaya Dvina *r.* Rus. Fed. **40** G2
English form Northern Dvina
Severnaya Mylva *r.* Rus. Fed. **40** K3
Severnaya Osetiya-Alaniya, Respublika
aut. rep. Rus. Fed. **41** H8
English form North Ossetia; formerly known
as Severo-Osetinskaya A.S.S.R.
Severnaya Sos'va *r.* Rus. Fed. **38** G3
Severnaya Zemlya *is* Rus. Fed. **39** K1
English form North Land
Severn Lake Canada **168** B2
Severnoye Rus. Fed. **43** J5
formerly known as Sol-Karmala
Severnyy Moskovskaya oblast' Rus. Fed.
43 S5
Severnyy Nenetskiy Avtonomnyy Okrug
Rus. Fed. **40** I1
Severnyy Respublika Komi Rus. Fed. **40** M2
Severnyy Anyuyskiy Khrebet *mts* Rus. Fed.
39 R3
Severnyy Berezovyy, Ostrov *i.* Rus. Fed.
43 J1
Severnyy Chink Ustyurta *esc.* Kazakh.
102 D3
Severnyy Kazakhstan *admin. div.* Kazakh.
103 G1
English form North Kazakhstan Oblast; also
known as Soltüstik Qazaqstan Oblysy; long
form Severo-Kazakhstanskaya Oblast'
Severnyy Kommunar Rus. Fed. **40** J4
Severnyy Suchan Rus. Fed. *see*
Uglekamensk
Severnyy Ural Rus. Fed. **40** K3
Severobaykal'sk Rus. Fed. **81** H1
Severo-Baykal'skoye Nagor'ye *mts*
Rus. Fed. **81** I1
Severodonetsk Ukr. *see* Syeverodonets'k
Severodvinsk Rus. Fed. **40** F2
formerly known as Molotovsk
Severo-Kazakhstanskaya Oblast'
admin. div. Kazakh. *see* Severnyy Kazakhstan
Severo-Kuril'sk Rus. Fed. **39** Q4
Severomorsk Rus. Fed. **44** P1
formerly known as Vayenga
Severoonezhsk Rus. Fed. **40** F3
Severo-Osetinskaya A.S.S.R. *aut. rep.*
Rus. Fed. *see*
Severnaya Osetiya-Alaniya, Respublika
Severo-Sibirskaya Nizmennost' *lowland*
Rus. Fed. *see* North Siberian Lowland
Severoural'sk Rus. Fed. **40** K3
Severo-Yeniseyskiy Rus. Fed. **39** J3
Severo-Zadonsk Rus. Fed. **43** T7
Severskaya Rus. Fed. **107** D1
Severskiy Donets *r.* Rus. Fed./Ukr. **41** G7
English form Northern Donets; also spelt
Sivers'ky Donets
Seveso Italy **51** N4
Sevettijärvi Fin. **44** O1
also spelt Čeʹvetjäuʹrr
Sevier *r.* U.S.A. **183** L1
Sevier Bridge Reservoir U.S.A. **183** M2
Sevier Desert U.S.A. **183** L2
Sevier Lake U.S.A. **183** K3
Sevierville U.S.A. **174** D5
Sevilla Col. **198** C3
Sevilla Spain *see* Seville
Seville Spain **54** F7
also spelt Sevilla; historically known as
Hispalis
Sevlievo Bulg. **58** G5
Sevnica Slovenia **56** H2
Sevojno Srbija Yugo. *see*
Sèvre Nantaise *r.* France **50** E5
Sevsk Rus. Fed. **43** P9
Sewand *r.* India **94** B2
Sewani India **96** B3
Seward AK U.S.A. **164** E3
Seward IL U.S.A. **172** D8
Seward NE U.S.A. **178** C4
Seward PA U.S.A. **176** F5
Seward Mountains Antarctica **222** T2
Seward Peninsula U.S.A. **164** C3
Sewell Chile **204** C4
Sewell Inlet Canada **166** C4
Sexi Spain *see* Almuñécar
Sexsmith Canada **166** G4
Sextin *r.* Mex. **184** D3
Sextín Mex. **184** D3
Seyah Band Koh *mts* Afgh. **101** E3
Seyakha Rus. Fed. **38** H2
Seybaplaya Mex. **185** H5
▶ Seychelles *country* Indian Ocean **218** K6
also spelt Sesel
africa [countries] ▶ 114–117
Seýdi Turkm. **103** E5
formerly known as Neftezavodsk
Seydişehir Turkey **106** C3
Seyðisfjörður Iceland **44** [inset] D2
Seyfe Gölü *salt flat* Turkey **106** C3
Seyhan Turkey *see* Adana

Seyhan *r.* Turkey **106** C3
Seyitgazi Turkey **106** B3
Seyitömer Turkey **59** K9
Seym *r.* Rus. Fed./Ukr. **41** E6
Seymchan Rus. Fed. **39** P3
Seymour Australia **147** E4
Seymour S. Africa **133** K9
Seymour IN U.S.A. **174** C4
Seymour TX U.S.A. **179** C5
Seymour Inlet Canada **166** E5
Seymour Range *mts* Australia **148** B5
Seynod France **51** M7
Seypan *i.* N. Mariana Is *see* Saipan
Seytan *i.* Turkey **58** I7
Seyyedābād Afgh. **101** G3
Sežana Slovenia **56** F3
Sézanne France **51** J4
Sezela S. Africa **133** O7
Sezha *r.* Rus. Fed. **43** P6
Sezze Italy **56** F7
historically known as Setia
Sfakia Greece **59** F13
Sfântu Gheorghe Romania **58** G3
formerly known as Sfîntu Gheorghe
Sfântu Gheorghe Romania **58** K4
Sfântu Gheorghe, Brațul *watercourse*
Romania **58** K3
Sfântu Gheorghe-Palade-Perișor
nature res. Romania **58** K4
Sfax Tunisia **123** H2
also spelt Aş Şafāqis
Sfendami Greece **59** D8
Sfîntu Gheorghe Romania *see*
Sfântu Gheorghe
Sfizef Alg. **55** K9
Sgiersch Poland *see* Zgierz
's-Gravenhage Neth. *see* The Hague
Sgurr Alasdair *hill* U.K. **46** F6
Sgurr Mòr *mt.* U.K. **46** G6
Sgurr na Cìche *mt.* U.K. **46** G6
Sha *r.* China **85** G4
Shaanxi *prov.* China **87** D1
English form Shensi
Shaartuz Tajik. *see* Shahrtuz
Shaba *prov.* Dem. Rep. Congo *see* Katanga
Shāba Egypt **108** B6
Shabani Zimbabwe *see* Zvishavane
Shabbaz Uzbek. *see* Beruni
Shabeellaha Dhexe *admin. reg.* Somalia
128 E4
Shabeellaha Hoose *admin. reg.* Somalia
128 D4
Shabestar Iran **100** A2
Shabla Bulg. **58** J5
Shabla, Nos *pt* Bulg. **58** J5
Shablykino Rus. Fed. **43** Q9
Shabogamo Lake Canada **169** H2
Shabunda Dem. Rep. Congo **126** E5
Shabwah Yemen **105** D5
Shabwah *governorate* Yemen **105** D5
Shacha *r.* Rus. Fed. **43** V3
Shache China **88** B4
formerly known as Yarkand or Yarkant
Shacheng China *see* Huailai
Shackleton Coast Antarctica **223** L1
Shackleton Glacier Antarctica **223** M1
Shackleton Ice Shelf Antarctica **223** G2
Shackleton Range *mts* Antarctica **223** V1
Shadād Saudi Arabia **104** C3
Shadadkot Pak. **101** F5
Shadaogou China **87** D2
Shade U.S.A. **176** C6
Shādegān Iran **100** B4
Shadīkām *watercourse* Iran **100** C4
Shadrinsk Rus. Fed. **38** G4
Shadwan Island Egypt *see* Shākir, Gezīret
Shadwell U.S.A. **176** G7
Shady Grove U.S.A. **180** B4
Shady Spring U.S.A. **176** E7
Sha'fat al Bashir *hill* Syria **109** K2
Shafer, Lake U.S.A. **172** G10
Shafi'abad Iran **100** C4
Shafirkan Uzbek. **103** F4
also spelt Shofirkon; formerly spelt Shafrikan
Shafranovo Rus. Fed. **40** L5
Shafrikan Uzbek. *see* Shafirkan
Shafter U.S.A. **182** E6
Shaftesbury U.K. **47** J12
Shag *r.* N.Z. **153** E13
Shagamu *r.* Canada **168** C2
Shagamu Nigeria *see* Sagamu
Shagan *watercourse* Kazakh. **102** D3
Shagan *watercourse* Kazakh. **103** I2
Shagedu China **85** F4
also known as Jungar Qi
Shaghab *oasis* Saudi Arabia **104** B2
Shaghan Kazakh. *see* Chagan
Shaghyray Üstirti *plat.* Kazakh. *see*
Shagyray, Plato
Shagonar *Respublika Tyva* Rus. Fed. **84** I1
Shagonar *Respublika Tyva* Rus. Fed. **84** B1
Shag Point N.Z. **153** E13
Shag Rocks *is* S. Georgia **217** L9
Shagyray, Plato *plat.* Kazakh. **102** D3
also known as Shaghyray Üstirti; formerly
known as Chagrayskoye Plato
Shagyrlyk Kazakh. **102** D4
Shahabad *Andhra Pradesh* India **94** C2
Shahabad *Haryana* India **96** C3
Shahabad *Karnataka* India **94** C2
Shahabad *Rajasthan* India **96** C4
Shahabad *Uttar Pradesh* India **96** D4
Shāhābād Iran *see* Eslāmābād-e Gharb
Shahada India **96** B5
Shah Alam Malaysia **76** C2
Shahana Pak. **101** E5
Shahapur *Karnataka* India **94** B3
Shahapur *Maharashtra* India **94** A2
Shahbā' Syria **109** H5
Shahbazpur *sea chan.* Bangl. **97** F5
Shahdād Iran **100** D4
also known as Khabis
Shahdadpur Pak. **101** F5
Shahdol India **97** D5
Shahe *Chongqing* China **87** D2
Shahe *Shandong* China **85** H4
Shahe *Shanxi* China **85** G4
Shahejie China *see* Jiujiang
Shahepu China *see* Linze
Shahezhen China *see* Linze
Shahezhen China *see* Jiujiang
Shah Fuladi *mt.* Afgh. **101** F3
Shahganj India **97** D4
Shahgarh *Madhya Pradesh* India **96** C4
Shahgarh *Rajasthan* India **96** A4
Shahhāt Libya **120** D1
Shāhīn Dezh Iran *see* Sa'īndezh
Shahjahanpur *Uttar Pradesh* India **96** C4
Shah Ismail Afgh. **101** E4
Shahjahanpur *Uttar Pradesh* India **96** C4
Shāh Jehān, Kūh-e *mts* Iran **100** D2
Shāh Jūy *mt.* Iran **101** F3
Shāh Kūh *mt.* Iran **101** D4
Shahpur *Karnataka* India **94** C2
Shahpur *Madhya Pradesh* India **96** C5
Shahpur *Madhya Pradesh* India **96** C5
Shāhpūr Iran *see* Salmās
Shahpur *Balochistān* Pak. **101** G4
Shahpur *Punjab* Pak. **101** G3
Shahpur *Sindh* Pak. **101** G5
Shahpura *Madhya Pradesh* India **96** C5
Shahpura *Madhya Pradesh* India **96** C5
Shahpura *Rajasthan* India **96** B4
Shahr oasis Saudi Arabia **105** E4
Shahrak Afgh. **101** F3
Shāhrakht Iran **101** E3
Shahram reg. Saudi Arabia **104** C4
Shahr-e Bābak Iran **100** C4
Shahr-e Kord Iran **100** B3
Shahr-e Now Iran **101** E3
Shahrezā Iran *see* Qomishēh

Shahrisabz Uzbek. *see* Shakhrisabz
Shahriston Tajik. *see* Shakhriston
also spelt Shakhristan
Shahr Rey Iran **100** B3
Shahr Sultan Pak. **101** G4
Shahrtuz *Tajik.* **101** G2
also spelt Shaartuz
Shāhrūd Iran *see* Emāmrūd
Shāhrūd, Rūdkhāneh-ye *r.* Iran **100** B2
Shahrud Bustam *reg.* Iran **100** C3
Shāh Savārān, Kūh-e *mts* Iran **100** D4
Shah Taqi Iran *see* Emām Taqī
Sha'ibān el Jiranīyat *watercourse*
Saudi Arabia **109** J6
Shaidara, Step' *plain* Kazakh. **103** F4
Shaikh Husain *mt.* Pak. **101** F4
Shā'ir, Jabal *mts* Syria **109** I3
Sha'īra, Gebel *mt.* Egypt **108** F8
Shaj'ah, Jabal *mt.* Saudi Arabia **105** E2
Shajapur India **96** C5
Shakar Bolāghī Iran **100** A2
Shakaskraal S. Africa **133** P6
Shakaville S. Africa **133** P6
Shakawe Botswana **130** D3
Shakespeare Island Canada **168** B3
Shakh Tajik. **101** G2
also known as Shoh
Shakhbuz Azer. *see* Şahbuz
Shakhovskaya Rus. Fed. **43** Q5
Shakhrikhan Uzbek. **103** H4
formerly known as Moskovskiy or Stalino
Shakhrisabz Uzbek. **103** F5
also spelt Shahrisabz
Shakhriston Tajik. *see* Shahriston
Shakhtars'k Ukr. **41** F6
also spelt Shakhtersk or Shakhtyorsk;
formerly known as Katyk
Shakhtersk Ukr. *see* Shakhtars'k
Shakhtinsk Kazakh. **103** H2
Shakhty Rus. Fed. **41** G7
Shakhun'ya Rus. Fed. **40** H4
Shaki Nigeria *see* Saki
Shākir, Gezīret *i.* Egypt **121** G3
English form Shadwan Island
Shakopee U.S.A. **178** D2
Shakotan-hantō *pen.* Japan **90** G3
Shakotan-misaki *c.* Japan **90** G3
Shakou China *see* Shalu
S'hala Häyk' *l.* Eth. **128** C3
Shalakusha Rus. Fed. **40** G3
Shālamzār Iran **100** B3
Shalday Kazakh. **103** I1
Shalginskiy Kazakh. **103** G3
also known as Shalqīya; formerly known as
Shalgiya
Shalgiya Kazakh. *see* Shalginskiy
Shali Rus. Fed. **41** H8
also known as Şela; formerly known as
Mezhdurechnye
Shalim Oman **105** F4
Shaliuhe China *see* Gangca
Shalkar, Ozero *salt l.* Kazakh. **102** B2
also known as Shalqar Köli; formerly spelt
Chalkar, Ozero
Shalkar Karashatau *salt l.* Kazakh. **103** E2
Shalkar-Yega-Kara, Ozero *l.* Rus. Fed.
103 E2
Shālma Egypt **108** B6
Shalqar Kazakh. *see* Chelkar
Shalqar Köli *salt l.* Kazakh. *see*
Shalkar, Ozero
Shalqīya Kazakh. *see* Shalginskiy
Shaluli Shan *mts* China **86** A2
Shaluni *mt.* India **97** H3
Shama *r.* Tanz. **129** B6
Shamāl Sīnā' *governorate* Egypt **108** D7
English form North Sinai; also known as
Sinai ash Shamālīya
Shamalzā'ī Afgh. **101** F4
Shamary Rus. Fed. **40** K4
Shāmat al Akbād *des.* Saudi Arabia **104** C1
Shamattawa Canada **167** M3
Shamattawa *r.* Canada **168** C2
Shamava Belarus **43** M7
Shambār Iran **100** A3
Shambe Sudan **128** A3
Shambu Eth. **128** C2
Shambuanda Dem. Rep. Congo **127** D6
Sham Chun *r.* China **87** [inset]
Shamgarh India **96** C4
Shamgong Bhutan *see* Zhemgang
Shamis U.A.E. **105** F3
Shamkhal Rus. Fed. **102** A4
Shamkhor Azer. *see* Şämkir
Shammar, Jabal *reg.* Saudi Arabia **104** C2
Shamoksha Rus. Fed. **43** O1
Shamrock U.S.A. **179** B5
Shamva Zimbabwe **131** F3
Shan *state* Myanmar **78** B3
Shancheng China *see* Nanjing
Shancheng China *see* Shanxian
Shand Afgh. **101** E4
Shandan China **84** D4
Shandian *r.* China **85** H3
Shandīz Iran **101** D2
Shandong *prov.* China **85** H4
English form Shantung
Shandong Bandao *pen.* China **85** I4
Shandrükh Iraq **107** F4
Shandur Pass Pak. **101** H2
Shangani *r.* Zimbabwe **131** E3
Shangcai China **87** E1
also known as Caidu
Shangcheng China **87** E2
Shang Chu *r.* China **89** E6
Shangchuan Dao *i.* China **87** E4
Shangchuankou China *see* Minhe
Shangdu China **85** G3
Shangganling China **82** C3
Shanggao China **87** E2
also known as Aoyang

▶ Shanghai China **87** G2
4th most populous city in Asia and 9th in
the world.
world [cities] ▶ 24–25

Shanghai *municipality* China **87** G2
Shanghang China **87** F3
also known as Linjiang
Shanghe China **85** H4
Shanghekou China **83** B4
Shangji China *see* Xichuan
Shangjie China *see* Yangbi
Shangjin China **87** D1
Shangkuli China **85** I1
Shangnan China **87** D1
Shangombo Zambia **127** D9
Shangpai China *see* Feixi
Shangqiu *Henan* China **87** E1
Shangqiu *Henan* China **87** E1
also known as Zhuji
Shangrao China **87** F2
Shangshui China **87** E1
Shangsi China **87** D4
also known as Siyang
Shangtang China *see* Yongjia
Shangyou China **87** E3
also known as Dongshan
Shangyou Shuiku *salt flat* China **88** C3
Shangyu China **87** G2
Shangzhi China **82** B3
Shangzhou China **87** D1
Shanhaiguan China **85** H3
Shanhe China *see* Zhengning
Shanhetun China **82** B3
Shani Nigeria **125** I4

Shankou China **84** B3
Shannon N.Z. **152** J8
Shannon *airport* Rep. of Ireland **47** D11
Shannon *est.* Rep. of Ireland **47** D11
Shannon *r.* Rep. of Ireland **47** D11
Shannon S. Africa **133** K6
Shannon *i.* Greenland **165** P2
Shannon, Mouth of the Rep. of Ireland
47 C11
Shannon National Park Australia **151** B7
Shannon Ø *i.* Greenland **165** P2
Shan Plateau Myanmar **78** B2
Shanshan China **88** E3
also known as Piqan
Shanshanzhan China **88** E3
Shansi *prov.* China *see* Shanxi
Shantarskiye Ostrova *is* Rus. Fed. **39** N4
Shan Tei Tong *hill* Hong Kong China *see*
Stenhouse, Mount
Shan Teng *hill* Hong Kong China *see*
Victoria Peak
Shantipur India **97** F5
Shantou China **87** F4
formerly known as Swatow
Shantung *prov.* China *see* Shandong
Shanwei China **87** F4
Shanxi *prov.* China **85** F4
English form Shansi
Shanxian China **87** F1
Shanya *r.* Rus. Fed. **43** Q7
Shanyang China **87** D1
Shanyin China **85** G4
Shaodong China **87** D3
also known as Liangshi
Shaoguan China **87** E3
Shaoshan China **87** E3
Shaowu China **87** F3
Shaoxing China **87** G2
Shaoyang China **87** D3
Shapa China **87** D4
Shapembe Dem. Rep. Congo **126** D6
Shaping China *see* Ebian
Shapinsay *i.* U.K. **46** J4
Shapki *r.* Rus. Fed. **43** M2
Shapkina *r.* Rus. Fed. **40** J2
Shapsha Rus. Fed. **43** P1
Shapyalyevichy Belarus **43** K7
Shaqlāwa Iraq **109** P1
Shaqq el Giefer, Wadi *watercourse* Sudan
121 E6
Shaqq el Khadir Sudan **121** E6
Shaqrā' Saudi Arabia **105** D2
Shar Kazakh. **103** J2
formerly known as Charsk
Shār, Jabal *mt.* Saudi Arabia **104** A2
Sharaf *well* Iraq **107** F4
Sharāh, Jibāl ash *mts* Jordan **108** G2
Sharalday Rus. Fed. **85** E1
Sharanga Rus. Fed. **40** H4
Sharan Jogizai Pak. **101** G4
Sharārīp, Rās *pt* Egypt **108** E9
Sharawrā, Jabal *hills* Saudi Arabia **109** H9
Sharawrā', Qa' *salt pan* Saudi Arabia
109 H9
Sharbaqty Kazakh. *see* Shcherbakty
Sharbithah, Ra's *c.* Oman **105** G4
Sharbulag Mongolia **84** D1
Sharchino Rus. Fed. **103** J1
Shardara Kazakh. **103** F4
formerly known as Chardara
Shardara Bögeni *resr* Kazakh./Uzbek. *see*
Chardarinskoye Vodokhranilishche
Shardi Pak. **101** H3
Sharga *Govĭ-Altay* Mongolia **84** B2
Sharga *Hövsgöl* Mongolia **84** C1
formerly known as Tsagaan-Uul
Shargun' Uzbek. **103** F5
Sharhorod Ukr. **41** D6
also known as Teïhe; formerly known as
Taïhezhen
Sharhulsan Mongolia **84** E2
Shari *r.* Cameroon/Chad *see* Chari
Shari Japan **90** I3
Shārī, Buhayrat *imp. l.* Iraq **107** F4
Shari-dake *vol.* Japan **90** I3
Sharīra Reg. Egypt **108** F9
Sharjah U.A.E. **105** F2
also known as Ash Shāriqah
Sharka-leb La *pass* China **89** E6
Sharkawshchyna Belarus **42** I6
Shark Bay Australia **151** A5
Shark Fin Bay Phil. **74** A4
Sharkhāt Yemen **105** E5
Shark Reef Australia **149** E2
Sharlawuk Turkm. *see* Sharlouk
Sharlouk Turkm. **102** C5
also spelt Sharlawuk
Sharlyk Rus. Fed. **102** C1
Sharmah Saudi Arabia **104** A1
Sharm el Sheikh Egypt **121** G3
Sharon PA U.S.A. **176** E4
Sharon WI U.S.A. **172** E8
Sharon, Plain of Israel **108** F5
also known as HaSharon
Sharon Springs U.S.A. **178** B4
Sharonville U.S.A. **176** A6
Sharpe, Lake *salt flat* Australia **151** C6
Sharpe, Lake Canada **167** M4
Sharp Peak *hill* Hong Kong China **87** [inset]
also known as Nam She Tsim
Sharpsburg U.S.A. **176** D6
Sharqat Iraq *see* Ash Sharqāt
Sharqī, Jabal ash *mts* Lebanon/Syria **108** G4
English form Anti Lebanon
Sharqīya *governorate* Egypt **108** C7
Sharqpur Pak. **101** H4
Sharur Azer. *see* Şärur
Shary *wall* Saudi Arabia **104** C2
Shar'ya *r.* Rus. Fed. **40** H4
Shar'ya *r.* Rus. Fed. **43** N2
Sharyn Kazakh. *see* Charyn
Shashe *r.* Botswana/Zimbabwe **131** F4
Shashemené Eth. **128** C3
Shashi China *see* Jingzhou
Shashubay Kazakh. **103** H3
formerly known as Ozernyy
Shasta, Mount *vol.* U.S.A. **180** B4
Shasta Dam U.S.A. **182** B1
Shasta Lake U.S.A. **182** B1
Shatalovo Rus. Fed. **43** N6
Shāṭi', Wādī ash *watercourse* Libya **120** B3
Shatilki Belarus *see* Svyetlahorsk
Sha Tin Hong Kong China **87** [inset]
Shatki Rus. Fed. **40** H5
Sha Tong Hau Shan *i.* Hong Kong China *see*
Bluff Island
Shatoy Rus. Fed. **41** H8
also known as Sovetskoye
Shatsk Rus. Fed. **41** G5
Shatsk Ukr. **42** E9
Shats'k *nat. park* Ukr. **41** B6
Shatt, Ra's osh *pt* Iran **100** B4
Shaṭṭ al 'Arab *r.* Iran/Iraq **107** G5
Shaṭṭ al Gharrāf *r.* Iraq **107** F4
Shattuck U.S.A. **179** C4
Shatura Rus. Fed. **43** U6
Shaturtorf Rus. Fed. **43** U6
Shaubak Jordan *see* Ash Shawbak
Shäüildir Kazakh. *see* Shaul'der
Shaul'der Kazakh. **103** G3
also spelt Shäüildir

Shaunavon Canada **167** I5
Shaverki Rus. Fed. **44** O3
Shaver Lake U.S.A. **182** E4
Shavers Fork *r.* U.S.A. **176** F7
Shaw *r.* Australia **150** B4
Shawan China **88** D2
also known as Sancaohezi
Shawano U.S.A. **172** E6
Shawano Lake U.S.A. **172** E6
Shawāq *well* Saudi Arabia **104** B2
Shawnee U.S.A. **179** C5
Shawsville U.S.A. **176** E8
Sha Xi *r.* China **87** F3
Shaxian China **87** F3
also known as Fenggang
Shayan Kazakh. **103** G3
formerly spelt Chayan
Shaybārā *i.* Saudi Arabia **104** B2
Shayboveyem *r.* Rus. Fed. **39** Q3
Shay Gap Australia **150** C4
Shaykh, Sha'ib ash *watercourse* Iraq
109 N5
Shaykh Jūwī Iraq **107** F4
Shaykh Sa'd Iraq **107** F4
Shaykovka Rus. Fed. **43** P7
Shāzand Iran **100** B3
Shazaoyuan China **84** B4
Shazāz, Jabal *mt.* Saudi Arabia **104** C2
Shāzī Hāmir, Wādī *watercourse*
Saudi Arabia **109** M6
Shazud Tajik. **101** H2
Shchara *r.* Belarus **42** F8
Shchekino Rus. Fed. **43** S7
Shchekino Rus. Fed. **43** S7
Shchelkanovo Rus. Fed. **43** Q7
Shchelkovo Rus. Fed. **43** T6
Shchel'yayur Rus. Fed. **40** J2
Shcherbakov Rus. Fed. *see* Rybinsk
Shcherbakty Kazakh. **103** I1
also spelt Sharbaqty
Shchetinskoye Rus. Fed. **43** T3
Shchigry Rus. Fed. **41** F6
Shchokino Rus. Fed. **43** S7
Shchors Ukr. **41** D6
formerly known as Snovsk
Shchuchin Belarus *see* Shchuchyn
Shchuchinsk Kazakh. **103** G1
Shchuchyn Belarus **42** F8
also spelt Shchuchin
Shchuger *r.* Rus. Fed. **40** K2
Shchytkavichy Belarus **42** J8
Shea Guyana **199** G4
Shebalino Rus. Fed. **88** D1
Shebandowan Lakes Canada **172** C2
Shebekino Rus. Fed. **41** F6
Sheberghän Afgh. **101** F2
Sheboygan U.S.A. **172** F7
Shebshi Mountains Nigeria **125** H4
Shebunino Rus. Fed. **82** F3
Shecheng China *see* Shexian
Shediac Canada **169** H4
Shedin Peak Canada **166** E4
Shedok Rus. Fed. **107** E1
Sheelin, Lough *l.* Rep. of Ireland **47** E10
Sheepmoor S. Africa **133** O3
Sheep Peak U.S.A. **183** I5
Sheerness U.K. **47** M12
Sheet Harbour Canada **169** I4
Shefar'am Israel **108** G5
Sheffield N.Z. **153** G11
Sheffield U.K. **47** K10
Sheffield AL U.S.A. **174** C5
Sheffie d IL U.S.A. **172** D9
Sheffield PA U.S.A. **176** F4
Sheffield TX U.S.A. **179** B6
Sheffield Lake Canada **169** J3
Shegaon India **94** C1
Sheguiandah Canada **173** L5
Shēh Husēn Eth. **128** D3
Shehong China **86** C2
Sheikh, Jebel esh *mt.* Lebanon/Syria *see*
Hermon, Mount
Sheikh, Wādī es *watercourse* Egypt **108** D9
Sheikh Othman Yemen *see*
Ash Shaykh 'Uthman
Shekak *r.* Canada **168** C3
Shekhawati *reg.* India **96** B4
Shekhupura Pak. **101** H4
Sheki Azer. *see* Şäki
Shekka Ch'ün-Tao *is* Hong Kong China *see*
Soko Islands
Shek Kwu Chau *i.* Hong Kong China **87** [inset]
Shekou China **87** [inset]
Shek Pik *resr* Hong Kong China *see*
Shek Pik Reservoir
Shek Pik Reservoir Hong Kong China
87 [inset]
also known as Shek Pik
Sheksna Rus. Fed. **43** T2
formerly known as Nikol'skoye
S'eksna *r.* Rus. Fed. **43** T2
Sheksninskoye Vodokhranilishche *resr*
Rus. Fed. **43** T2
Shek Uk Shan *mt.* Hong Kong China
87 [inset]
Shela China **89** F6
Shelag *watercourse* Afgh./Iran **101** E4
Shelagskiy, Mys *pt* Rus. Fed. **39** R2
Shelbiana U.S.A. **176** C8
Shelbina U.S.A. **178** D4
Shelburn U.S.A. **174** C4
Shelburne N.S. Canada **169** H5
Shelburne Ont. Canada **173** M6
Shelburne Bay Australia **149** D1
Shelburne Falls U.S.A. **177** M3
Shelby MS U.S.A. **174** B5
Shelby MT U.S.A. **180** E2
Shelby NC U.S.A. **174** D5
Shelby OH U.S.A. **176** C5
Shelbyville IL U.S.A. **174** B4
Shelbyville IN U.S.A. **174** C4
Shelbyville MO U.S.A. **178** D4
Shelbyville TN U.S.A. **174** C5
Shelbyville, Lake U.S.A. **174** B4
Sheldon S. Africa **133** J10
Sheldon IA U.S.A. **178** D3
Sheldon IL U.S.A. **172** F10
Sheldon WI U.S.A. **172** C5
Sheldon National Wildlife Refuge
nature res. U.S.A. **180** C4
Sheldon Springs U.S.A. **177** M1
Sheldrake Canada **169** H3
Shelek Kazakh. *see* Chilik
Shelekhov Rus. Fed. **81** F2
Shelikhova, Zaliv *g.* Rus. Fed. **39** P3
Shelikof Strait U.S.A. **164** D4
Shellbrook Canada **167** J4
Shelley U.S.A. **180** D4
Shell Lake U.S.A. **172** B5
Shell Lakes *salt flat* Australia **151** D6
Shell Mountain U.S.A. **182** A1
Shellsburg U.S.A. **172** B9
Shelon' *r.* Rus. Fed. **43** L3
Shelopugino Rus. Fed. **85** H1
Shelter Bay Canada *see* Port-Cartier
Shelter Island U.S.A. **177** M4
Shelter Point N.Z. **153** C15
Shelton U.S.A. **180** B3
Sheltozero Rus. Fed. **43** R1
Shemakha Azer. *see* Samaxı
Shemankar *r.* Nigeria **125** H4
Shemenichi Rus. Fed. **43** P1
Shemonaikha Kazakh. **103** J1
Shemordan Rus. Fed. **40** I4
Shemursha Rus. Fed. **40** H5

Shenandoah IA U.S.A. **178** D3
Shenandoah PA U.S.A. **177** I5
Shenandoah VA U.S.A. **176** G6
Shenandoah *r.* U.S.A. **176** H6
Shenandoah Mountains U.S.A. **176** F7
Shenandoah National Park U.S.A. **176** G7
Shenchi China **85** G4
Shendam Nigeria **125** H4
Shendi Sudan **121** G5
Shending Shan *hill* China **82** D3
Shenge Sierra Leone **124** B5
Shengel'dy Kazakh. **103** G4
Shengel'dy Kazakh. **103** G4
formerly spelt Chengel'dy
Shēngjin Albania **58** A7
Shengli China **87** E2
Shengli Daban *pass* China **88** D3
Shengli Feng *mt.* China/Kyrg. *see*
Pobeda Peak
Shengrenjian China *see* Pinglu
Shengsi China **87** H2
also known as Caiyuanzhen
Shengsi Liedao *is* China **87** G2
Shengxian China *see* Shengzhou
Shengzhou China **87** G2
formerly known as Shengxian
Shenkoll Albania **58** A7
Shenkursk Rus. Fed. **40** G3
Shenmu China **85** G4
Shennongjia China **87** D2
also known as Songbai
Shenqiu China **87** E1
also known as Huaidian
Shenshu China **82** C3
Shensi *prov.* China *see* Shaanxi
Shentala Rus. Fed. **40** I5
Shenton, Mount *hill* Australia **151** C6
Shenxian China **85** G4
Shenxian China **85** G4
Shenyang China **85** I3
formerly known as Mukden
▶ Shenzhen China **87** [inset]
also known as Bao'an
world [changes] ▶ 20–21
Shenzhen Wan *b.* Hong Kong China *see*
Deep Bay
Shenzhou China **85** G4
also known as Shenxian
Sheoganj India **96** A4
Sheopur India **96** C4
Shepard Island Antarctica **222** P2
Shepetivka Ukr. **41** C6
also spelt Shepetovka
Shepetovka Ukr. *see* Shepetivka
Shepherd Islands Vanuatu **145** F3
Shepparton Australia **147** E4
Sheptaky Ukr. **43** O9
Sheqi China **87** E1
Sherabad Uzbek. **103** F5
also known as Sherodod
Sherard, Cape Canada **165** K2
Sherborne S. Africa **133** I8
Sherborne U.K. **47** J13
Sherbro Island Sierra Leone **124** B5
Sherbrooke N.S. Canada **169** I4
Sherbrooke Que. Canada **169** G4
Sherburne U.S.A. **177** J3
Shercock Rep. of Ireland **47** F10
Sherda *well* Chad **120** C4
Sherdoyak Kazakh. **88** C1
Shereiq Sudan **121** G5
Shergarh India **96** A4
Sherghati India **97** E4
Sheridan AR U.S.A. **179** D5
Sheridan WY U.S.A. **180** F3
Sherkaly Rus. Fed. **38** G3
Sherlock *r.* Australia **150** B4
Sherlovaya Gora Rus. Fed. **85** H1
Sherman NY U.S.A. **176** F3
Sherman TX U.S.A. **179** C5
Sherman Mountain U.S.A. **183** I1
Sherobod Uzbek. *see* Sherabad
Sherovichi Rus. Fed. **43** M7
Sherpur *Dhaka* Bangl. **97** F4
Sherpur *Rajshahi* Bangl. **97** F4
Sherridon Canada **167** K4
Shertally India **94** C4
also known as Cherthala
's-Hertogenbosch Neth. **48** C4
also known as Den Bosch
Sherwood U.S.A. **176** A4
Sherwood Downs N.Z. **153** E11
Sherwood Lake Canada **167** K2
Sheryshevo Rus. Fed. **82** C2
Sheshegwaning Canada **173** K5
Sheshtamad Iran **100** D2
Sheslay Canada **166** D3
Sheslay *r.* Canada **166** C3
Shestikhino Rus. Fed. **43** T4
Shethanei Lake Canada **167** L3
Shetland *admin. div.* U.K. **46** L3
Shetpe Kazakh. **102** C3
Sheung Shui Hong Kong China **87** [inset]
Sheung Sze Mun *sea chan.* Hong Kong
China **87** [inset]
Sheung Yue Ho *r.* Hong Kong China
87 [inset]
Shevaroy Hills India **94** C4
Shevchenko Kazakh. *see* Aktau
Shevchenko, Zaliv *l.* Kazakh. **102** C3
formerly known as Paskevicha, Zaliv
Shevgaon India **94** B2
Shevli *r.* Rus. Fed. **82** D1
Shexian *Anhui* China **87** F2
also known as Huicheng
Shexian *Hebei* China **85** G4
also known as Shecheng
Sheya Rus. Fed. **39** L3
Sheyang China **87** G1
also known as Hede
Sheybukhta Rus. Fed. **43** V2
Sheyenne *r.* U.S.A. **178** C2
Sheykh Sho'eyb *i.* Iran **100** C5
Sheykino Rus. Fed. **43** M5
Shey Phoksundo National Park Nepal
97 D3
Shiant Islands U.K. **46** F6
Shiashkotan, Ostrov *i.* Rus. Fed. **81** Q3
Shiawassee *r.* U.S.A. **173** J7
Shibām Yemen **105** E5
Shibar Pass Afgh. **101** G3
Shibazhan China **82** B1
Shibetsu *Hokkaidō* Japan **90** H2
Shibetsu *Hokkaidō* Japan **90** I3
Shibīn el Kôm Egypt **121** F2
Shibing China **87** D3
Shibogama Lake Canada **168** B2
Shibotsu-jima *i.* Rus. Fed. *see*
Zelenyy, Ostrov
Shibukawa Japan **91** F6
Shibushi Japan **91** B9
Shibushi-wan *b.* Japan **91** B9
Shicheng China *see* Zhouning
Shicheng China **87** F3
Shicheng Dao *i.* China **85** I4
Shichinohe Japan **90** G4
Shickshinny U.S.A. **177** I4
Shicun China *see* Xiangfen
Shidād al Mismā' *hill* Saudi Arabia **109** J6
Shidao China **85** I4
Shiderti *r.* Kazakh. **103** H1
Shidongsi China *see* Gaolan
Shiel, Loch *l.* U.K. **46** F7
Shield, Cape Australia **148** C2
Shieli Kazakh. *see* Chiili
Shifa, Jabal ash *mts* Saudi Arabia **104** A1
Shifang China **86** C2
Shiga *pref.* Japan **91** D7
Shigatse China *see* Xigazê

Shiggaon India 94 B3
Shigong China 88 F3
Shigony Rus. Fed. 41 I5
Shiguai China 85 F3
formerly known as Shiguaigou
Shiguaigou China see Shiguai
Shihan Yemen 105 F4
Shiḥan, Wādī r. Oman 105 F4
Shihezi China 88 D2
Shihkiachwang China see Shijiazhuang
Shiikh Somalia 128 E2
Shijak Albania 58 A7
Shijiao China see Fogang
Shijiazhuang China 85 G4
formerly spelt Shihkiachwang
Shijiu Hu l. China 87 F2
Shijiusuo China see Rizhao
Shikabe Japan 90 G3
Shikag Lake Canada 168 B3
Shikar r. Pak. 101 E4
Shikarpur India 94 B3
Shikarpur Pak. 101 G5
Shikengkong mt. China 87 E3
Shikhany Rus. Fed. 102 A1
Shikohabad India 96 C4
Shikoku i. Japan 91 C8
Shikoku-sanchi mts Japan 91 C8
Shikotan, Ostrov i. Rus. Fed. 82 G4
also known as Shikotan-tō
Shikotan-tō i. Rus. Fed. see Shikotan, Ostrov
Shikotsu vol. Japan 90 G3
also known as Tarumae-san
Shikotsu-Tōya National Park Japan 90 G3
Shil'da Rus. Fed. 102 D2
Shilega Rus. Fed. 40 H2
Shiliguri India 97 F4
also spelt Siliguri
Shilipu China 87 E2
Shiliu China see Changjiang
Shilka Rus. Fed. 85 H1
Shilla mt. Jammu and Kashmir 96 C2
Shillelagh Rep. of Ireland 47 F11
Shillington Canada 173 M2
Shillo r. Israel 108 F5
Shillong India 97 F4
Shilou China 85 F4
Shilovo Ryazanskaya Oblast' Rus. Fed. 41 G5
Shilovo Tul'skaya Oblast' Rus. Fed. 43 T8
Shilüüstey Mongolia see Balgatay
Shimabara Japan 91 B8
Shimabara-wan b. Japan 91 B8
Shimada Japan 91 F7
Shimamaki Japan 90 G3
Shimane pref. Japan 91 C7
Shimane-hantō pen. Japan 91 C7
Shimanovsk Rus. Fed. 82 B1
Shimbiris mt. Somalia 128 E2
also known as Surud Ad
Shimbirre waterhole Kenya 128 D4
Shimen China 87 D2
Shimian China 86 B2
also known as Xinmian
Shimizu Hokkaidō Japan 90 H3
Shimizu Shizuoka Japan 91 F7
Shimla India 96 C3
formerly spelt Simla
Shimminato Japan see Shinminato
Shimoda Japan 91 F7
Shimodate Japan 91 F6
Shimoga India 94 B3
Shimokawa Japan 90 H2
Shimokita-hantō pen. Japan 90 G4
Shimoni Kenya 129 C6
Shimonoseki Japan 91 B8
formerly known as Akamagaseki
Shimotsuma Japan 91 F6
Shimsha r. India 94 C3
Shimshal Jammu and Kashmir 96 B1
Shimsk Rus. Fed. 43 L3
Shin, Loch l. U.K. 46 H5
Shināfīyah Iraq see Ash Shanāfīyah
Shinan China 87 D4
Shindand Afgh. 101 E3
also known as Sabzawar
Shingbwiyang Myanmar 78 B2
Shinghshal Pass Pak. 101 H2
Shinglehouse U.S.A. 176 G4
Shingleton U.S.A. 172 G4
Shingletown U.S.A. 182 C1
Shing Mun Reservoir Hong Kong China 87 [inset]
also known as Ngan Hei Shui Tong
Shingozha Kazakh. 103 J3
also spelt Shyngqozha
Shingū Japan 91 E8
Shingwedzi S. Africa 131 F4
Shining Tree Canada 173 L3
Shinjō Japan 90 G5
Shinkai Hills Afgh. 101 G3
Shinkāy Afgh. 101 F4
Shinminato Japan 91 E6
also spelt Shimminato
Shinnan-yō Japan 91 B7
Shinnston U.S.A. 176 E6
Shinshiro Japan 91 E7
Shintoku Japan 90 H3
Shinyanga Tanz. 128 B5
Shinyanga admin. reg. Tanz. 129 B5
Shiogama Japan 90 G5
Shiojiri Japan 91 E6
Shiono-misaki c. Japan 91 D8
Shioya-zaki pt Japan 90 G6
Shipai China see Huaining
Ship Chan Cay i. Bahamas 175 E7
Shipchenski Prokhod pass Bulg. 58 G6
Shipilovo Rus. Fed. 43 T4
Shiping China 86 B4
also known as Yilong
Shipki Pass China/India 89 B6
Shipman U.S.A. 176 G8
Shippegan Canada 169 H4
Shippegan Island Canada 169 H4
Shippensburg U.S.A. 176 H5
Shippenville U.S.A. 176 F4
Shiprock U.S.A. 183 P5
Shiprock Peak U.S.A. 183 P5
Shipu China see Huanglong
Shipu China 87 G2
Shipunskiy, Mys hd Rus. Fed. 39 Q4
Shiqian China 87 D3
Shiqiao China see Panyu
Shiqizhen China see Zhongshan
Shiqqat al Kharītah des. Saudi Arabia 105 D4
Shiquan China 87 D1
Shiquanhe China see Ali
Shiquanhe China see Gar
Shiquanh He r. China see Indus
Shi'r, Jabal hill Saudi Arabia 104 C2
Shirā'awh i. Qatar 105 F2
Shirābād Iran 100 B2
Shirakami-misaki pt Japan 90 G4
Shirakawa Fukushima Japan 90 G6
Shirakawa Gifu Japan 91 E6
Shirane-san mt. Japan 91 F7
Shirane-san vol. Japan 90 F6
Shiranuka Japan 90 I3
Shiraoi Japan 90 G3
Shirase Coast Antarctica 223 O1
Shirase Glacier Antarctica 223 C2
Shirataki Japan 90 H3
Shirati Tanz. 128 B5
Shīrāz Iran 100 C4
Shirbīn Egypt 108 C6
Shire r. Malawi 129 B9
Shireet Mongolia 85 G2
Shirega Rus. Fed. 40 I3
Shiretoko-hantō pen. Japan 90 I3
Shiretoko-misaki c. Japan 90 I2
Shiretoko National Park Japan 90 I2
Shirin Uzbek. 103 G4
Shirinab r. Pak. 101 F4
Shīrīn Tagāb Afgh. 101 F2
Shiriya-zaki c. Japan 90 G4
Shirkala reg. Kazakh. 102 D3
Shīr Kūh mt. Iran 100 C4
Shiroishi Japan 90 G6
Shirone Japan 90 F6
Shiroro Reservoir Nigeria 125 G4
Shirotori Japan 91 E7
Shirpur India 96 B5
Shirten Höloy Gobi des. China 84 C3
Shīrvān Iran 100 D2
Shisanjianfang China 88 E3
Shisanzhan China 82 B2
Shiselweni admin. dist. Swaziland 133 P4
Shishaldin Volcano U.S.A. 164 C4
Shisha Pangma mt. China see Xixabangma Feng
Shishou China 87 E2
Shishovka Rus. Fed. 43 T3
Shitai China 87 F2
also known as Qili
Shitan China 87 E3
Shitang China 87 G2
Shitanjing China 85 E4
Shithāthah Iraq 109 O5
Shiv India 96 A4
Shiveluch, Sopka vol. Rus. Fed. 39 Q4
Shivpuri India 96 C4
Shivta tourist site Israel 108 F7
also known as Subeita
Shivwits U.S.A. 183 K4
Shivwits Plateau U.S.A. 183 K5
Shiwan Dashan mts China 87 C4
Shiwa Ngandu Zambia 127 F7
Shixing China 87 E3
also known as Taiping
Shiyan China 87 D1
Shizhu China 87 D2
also known as Nanbin
Shizilu China see Junan
Shizipu China 87 F2
Shizong China 86 B3
also known as Danfeng
Shizugawa Japan 90 G5
Shizuishan China 85 E4
also known as Dawukou
Shizukuishi Japan 90 G5
Shizuoka Japan 91 F7
historically known as Sumpu
Shizuoka pref. Japan 91 F7
▶Shkhara mt. Georgia/Rus. Fed. 107 E2
3rd highest mountain in Europe.
europe [landscapes] 30–31
Shklov Belarus see Shklow
Shklow Belarus 43 L7
also spelt Shklov
Shkodër Albania 58 A6
formerly known as Scutari; historically known as Scodra
Shkodrës, Liqeni i l. Albania/Yugo. see Scutari, Lake
Shkotovo Rus. Fed. 90 C3
Shkumbin r. Albania 58 A7
Shlina r. Rus. Fed. 43 P4
Shlino, Ozero l. Rus. Fed. 43 O4
Shlissel'burg Rus. Fed. 43 M2
also spelt Schlüsselburg; formerly known as Petrokrepost'
Shmidta, Ostrov i. Rus. Fed. 39 J1
English form Schmidt Island
Shmidta, Poluostrov pen. Rus. Fed. 82 F1
English form Schmidt Peninsula
Shmoylovo Rus. Fed. 43 J4
Shoalhaven r. Australia 147 F3
Shoal Lake Man. Canada 167 K5
Shoal Lake Sask. Canada 167 K4
Shoals U.S.A. 174 C4
Shoalwater Bay Australia 149 F4
Shōbara Japan 91 C7
Shōdo-shima i. Japan 91 D7
Shoemakersville U.S.A. 177 J5
Shofirkon Uzbek. see Shafirkan
Shoghlābād Iran 100 D2
Shoh Tajik. see Shakh
Shohi Pass Pak. see Tal Pass
Shokanbetsu-dake mt. Japan 90 G3
Shokotsu-gawa r. Japan 90 H2
Shokpar Kazakh. see Chokpar
Shola r. Rus. Fed. 43 S1
Sholakskay Kazakh. 103 F2
also spelt Sholaqsay
Sholapur India see Solapur
Sholaqorghan Kazakh. see Shollakorgan
Sholaqsay Kazakh. see Sholaksay
Shollakorgan Kazakh. 103 G4
also spelt Sholaqorghan; formerly spelt Chulakkurgan
Shomba r. Rus. Fed. 40 E2
Shongar Bhutan 97 F4
Shonzha Kazakh. see Chundzha
Shopsha Rus. Fed. 43 U4
Shoptykol' Kazakh. 103 H2
Shoqpar Kazakh. see Chokpar
Shoranur India 94 C4
Shorap Pak. 101 F5
Shorapur India 94 C2
Shorawak reg. Afgh. 101 F4
Shor Barsa-Kel'mes salt marsh Uzbek. 102 D4
Shorghun Uzbek. see Shargun'
Shorkot Pak. 101 H4
Shorkozakhly, Solonchak depr. Turkm. 102 D4
Shornaq Kazakh. see Chernak
Shorobe Botswana 130 D3
Shortandy Kazakh. 103 G2
Shortsville U.S.A. 177 H3
Shosambetsu Japan see Shosanbetsu
Shosanbetsu Japan 90 G2
also spelt Shosambetsu
Shosha r. Rus. Fed. 43 R5
Shoshone CA U.S.A. 183 H6
Shoshone ID U.S.A. 180 D4
Shoshone r. U.S.A. 180 E3
Shoshone Mountains U.S.A. 183 G2
Shoshone Peak U.S.A. 183 H5
Shoshong Botswana 131 E4
Shoshoni U.S.A. 180 E4
Shostka Ukr. 41 E6
Shouguang China 85 H4
Shouxian China 87 F1
Shouyang China 85 G4
Shouyang Shan mt. China 87 D1
Showak Sudan 121 G6
Show Low U.S.A. 183 N7
Shoyna Rus. Fed. 40 H2
Shpakovskoye Rus. Fed. 41 G7
formerly known as Mikhaylovskoye
Shpola Ukr. 41 D6
Shqipërisë, Republika e country Europe see Albania
Shreve U.S.A. 176 C5
Shreveport U.S.A. 179 D5
Shrewsbury U.K. 47 J11
Shrigonda India 94 B2
Shri Lanka country Asia see Sri Lanka
Shri Mohangarh India 96 A4
Shrirampur India 97 F5
Shrirangapattana India 94 C3
Shtefan-Vode Moldova see Ştefan Vodă
Shtërmen Albania 58 B8
Shtiqën Albania 58 B6
Shu r. China 87 F1
Shu Kazakh. 103 H4
formerly spelt Chu
Shu'ab, Ghubbat b. Yemen 105 F5
Shu'ab, Ra's pt Yemen 105 F5
Shu'aiba Iraq 107 F5
Shuajingsi China 86 B1
Shuangbai China 86 B3
also known as Tuodian
Shuangcheng China see Zherong
Shuangcheng China 82 B3
Shuanghe China 87 E2
Shuanghechang China 87 C2
Shuanghedagang China 82 C2
Shuanghuyu China see Zizhou
Shuangjiang China see Jiangkou
Shuangjiang China see Tongdao
Shuangjiang China 86 A4
also known as Mengmeng
Shuangjiang China see Eshan
Shuangliao China 85 I3
formerly known as Zhengjiatun
Shuangpai China 87 D3
Shuangshipu China see Fengxian
Shuangyang China 82 B4
Shuangyashan China 82 C3
Shuangzhong China see Hukou
Shu'ayt, Wādī r. Yemen 105 E4
Shubarkuduk Kazakh. 102 D2
Shubarshi Kazakh. 102 D2
Shubayh well Saudi Arabia 109 J7
Shubrâ el Kheima Egypt 121 F2
Shubrāmīyah well Saudi Arabia 104 C3
Shucheng China 87 F2
Shucushuyacu Peru 198 C6
Shufu China 88 A4
Shuganu India 97 G4
Shughnon, Qatorkŭhi mts Tajik. 101 G2
also known as Shugnanskiy Khrebet
Shugnanskiy Khrebet mts Tajik. see Shughnon, Qatorkŭhi
Shugozero Rus. Fed. 43 P2
Shugur Rus. Fed. 38 G3
Shuicheng China see Lupanshui
Shuiding China see Huocheng
Shuidong China see Dianbai
Shuihu China see Changfeng
Shuiji China 87 F3
Shuiji China see Laixi
Shuijing China 86 C1
Shuikou Guangdong China 87 E4
Shuikou Hunan China 87 D3
also known as Tuojiang
Shuikouguan China 86 C4
Shuikoushan China 87 E3
Shuiluocheng China see Zhuanglang
Shuiquanzi China 84 D4
Shuituo He r. China 86 B3
Shuizhai China see Wuhua
Shujaabad Pak. 101 G4
Shulan China 82 B3
Shule China 88 B4
Shule He r. China 84 B3
Shule Nanshan mts China 84 C4
Shulinzhao China 85 F3
also known as Dalad Qi
Shul'mak Tajik. see Novobod
Shulu China see Xinji
Shum Rus. Fed. 43 M2
Shumagin Islands U.S.A. 164 C4
Shumanay Uzbek. 102 D4
Shumarinai-ko l. Japan 90 H2
Shumen Bulg. 58 H5
formerly known as Kolarovgrad
Shumensko Plato nat. park Bulg. 58 H5
Shumerlya Rus. Fed. 40 H5
Shumikha Rus. Fed. 38 G4
Shumilina Belarus 43 K6
Shumshu, Ostrov i. Rus. Fed. 39 P4
Shumyachi Rus. Fed. 43 N8
Shunak, Gora mt. Kazakh. 103 H3
Shūnat Nimrīn Jordan 108 G6
Shunde China 87 E4
also known as Daliang
Shunga Rus. Fed. 43 V4
Shunyi China 85 H3
Shuolong China 86 C4
Shuoxian China see Shuozhou
Shuozhou China 85 G4
formerly known as Shuoxian
Shupiyan Jammu and Kashmir 89 A5
Shuqqat Najrān depr. Saudi Arabia 105 D4
Shuqrah Yemen 105 D5
Shūr r. Iran 100 C4
Shūr r. Iran 100 D4
Shūr r. Iran 101 E3
Shūr r. Iran 101 E4
Shūr watercourse Iran 100 C4
Shūr watercourse Iran 100 C4
Shur watercourse Iran 100 C5
Shur watercourse Iran 100 D3
Shūrāb Chahār Maḥāll va Bakhtīārī Iran 100 B3
Shūr Āb Iran 100 B3
Shūrāb Khorāsan Iran 100 D3
Shūrāb Yazd Iran 100 C3
Shūr Āb watercourse Iran 100 C4
Shurab Tajik. see Shŭrob
Shurchi Uzbek. 103 F5
Shureghestan Iran 100 C3
Shūr Gaz Iran 101 D4
Shūrjestān Iran 100 C4
Shurma Rus. Fed. 40 I4
Shŭrob Tajik. 101 G1
also spelt Shurab
Shūrū Iran 101 E4
Shurugwi Zimbabwe 131 F3
formerly spelt Selukwe
Shuruppak tourist site Iraq 107 F5
Shusf Iran 101 E4
Shūsh Iran 100 B3
Shusha Azer. see Şuşa
Shushicë r. Albania 59 A8
Shushkodom Rus. Fed. 43 V3
Shushtar Iran 100 B3
Shuswap Lake Canada 166 G5
Shutar Khun Pass Afgh. 101 F3
Shuwaysh, Tall ash hill Jordan 109 I6
Shuya Ivanovskaya Oblast' Rus. Fed. 40 G4
Shuya Respublika Kareliya Rus. Fed. 40 E3
Shuyak Island U.S.A. 164 D4
Shuyang China 87 F1
Shuyskoye Rus. Fed. 43 V2
Shvartsevskiy Rus. Fed. 43 S7
Shwebandaw Myanmar 78 A4
Shwebo Myanmar 78 A3
Shwedaung Myanmar 78 A4
Shwedwin Myanmar 78 A2
Shwegun Myanmar 78 B4
Shwegyin Myanmar 78 B4
Shwelaung r. Myanmar 78 A4
Shweli r. Myanmar 78 B3
also known as Mao, Nam
Shwenyaung Myanmar 78 B3
Shweudaung mt. Myanmar 78 B3
Shyghanaq Kazakh. see Chiganak
Shyghys Qazaqstan Oblysy admin. div. Kazakh. see Vostochnyy Kazakhstan
Shyghys-Qongyrat Kazakh. see Shygys Konyrat
Shygys Konyrat Kazakh. 103 H3
also spelt Shyghys-Qongyrat; formerly known as Vostochno-Kounradskiy
Shymkent Kazakh. 103 G4
formerly spelt Chimkent
Shynggyrlaū Kazakh. see Chingirlau
Shyngqozha Kazakh. see Shingozha
Shyok r. India 96 B2
Shyok Jammu and Kashmir 96 C2
Shypuvate Ukr. 41 F6
Shyshchytsy Belarus 42 I8
Si, Laem pt Thai. 79 B6
Sia Indon. 73 H8
Siabu Indon. 76 B2
Siachen Glacier Jammu and Kashmir 96 C2
Siahan Range mts Pak. 101 E5
Sīah Chashmeh Iran 100 A2
Siahgird Afgh. 101 F2
Siah Koh mts Afgh. 101 F3
Sīāh Kūh mts Iran 100 C3
Siak r. Indon. 76 C2
Siak Sri Inderapura Indon. 76 C2
Sialkot Pak. 101 H3
Siam country Asia see Thailand
Sian China see Xi'an
Sianów Poland 49 N1
Siantan i. Indon. 77 D2
Siapa r. Venez. 199 E4
Siargao i. Phil. 74 C4
Siasconset U.S.A. 177 P4
Siasi Phil. 74 B5
Siasi i. Phil. 74 B5
Siatista Greece 59 C8
Siaton Phil. 74 B4
Siau i. Indon. 75 C2
Šiauliai Lith. 42 E6
Siavonga Zambia 127 F9
Siayan i. Phil. 74 B1
Siazan' Azer. see Siyäzän
Sib Iran 101 E5
Sīb Oman 105 G3
Sibanicú Cuba 186 D2
Sibati China see Xibet
Sibay i. Phil. 74 B4
Sibay Rus. Fed. 102 D1
Sibayi, Lake S. Africa 133 Q4
Sibbald, Cape Antarctica 223 L2
Sibbo Fin. 45 N3
Sibbofjärden b. Fin. 42 G1
Šibenik Croatia 56 H5
formerly spelt Sebenico
Siberia Rus. Fed. see Central Siberian Plateau
Siberut i. Indon. 76 B3
Siberut, Selat sea chan. Indon. 76 B3
Siberut National Park Indon. 76 B3
Sibi Pak. 101 F4
Sibidiri P.N.G. 73 J8
Sibigo Indon. 76 A2
Sibiloi National Park Kenya 128 C4
Sibirtsevo Rus. Fed. 82 D3
formerly known as Manzovka
Sibiryakova, Ostrov i. Rus. Fed. 39 H2
Sibiti Congo 126 B5
Sibiu Romania 58 F3
Sibley U.S.A. 178 D3
Siboa Indon. 75 B2
Sibolga Indon. 76 B2
Siborongborong Indon. 76 B2
Sibowe r. Swaziland 133 P3
Sibsagar India 97 G4
Sibu Sarawak Malaysia 77 E2
Sibuco Phil. 74 B5
Sibuco Bay Phil. 74 B5
Sibuguey r. Phil. 74 B5
Sibuguey Bay Phil. 74 B5
Sibut Cent. Afr. Rep. 126 C3
Sibutu i. Phil. 74 A5
Sibutu Passage Phil. 74 A5
Sibuyan i. Phil. 74 B3
Sibuyan Sea Phil. 74 B3
Sic Romania 58 E2
Sicamous Canada 166 G5
Sicapoo mt. Phil. 74 B2
Sicca Veneria Tunisia see Le Kef
Siccus watercourse Australia 146 C2
Sicheng China see Lingyun
Sichon Thai. 79 B6
Sichuan prov. China 86 B2
English form Szechwan
Sichuan Pendi basin China 86 C2
English form Red Basin
Sicié, Cap c. France 51 L9
Sicilia admin. reg. Italy 57 G11
Sicilia i. Italy see Sicily
Sicilian Channel Italy/Tunisia 57 E11
Sicily i. Italy 57 G10
also known as Sicilia
Sicuani Peru 200 C3
Šid Vojvodina, Srbija Yugo. 58 A3
Sidangoli Indon. 75 C2
Siddhapur India 96 B5
also spelt Sidhpur
Siddharthanagar Nepal see Bhairawa
Siddipet India 94 C2
Sideby Fin. 45 M3
also known as Siipyy
Sidéia Island P.N.G. 149 F1
Sid el Na'âm, Gebel hill Egypt 108 C8
Sidenreng, Danau l. Indon. 75 A3
Sidensjö Sweden 44 L3
Sidéradougou Burkina 124 D4
Sideros, Akra pt Greece 59 H13
Sidesaviwa S. Africa 132 G9
Sidhauli India 96 D4
Sidhi India 97 D4
Sidhirókastron Greece see Sidirokastro
Sidhpur India see Siddhapur
Sidi Aïssa Alg. 55 O9
Sidi Ali Alg. 55 L8
Sidi Ameur Alg. 55 O9
Sidi Barrani Egypt 121 E2
Sidi Bel Abbès Alg. 123 E2
Sidi Bennour Morocco 122 C2
Sidi Bou Sa'id Tunisia see Sidi Bouzid
Sidi Bouzid Tunisia 123 H2
also known as Sidi Bou Sa'id
Sidi El Hani, Sebkhet de salt pan Tunisia 123 H2
Sidi el Mokhtâr well Mali 124 E2
Sidi Ifni Morocco 122 C3
Sidi Kacem Morocco 122 D2
formerly known as Petitjean
Sidikalang Indon. 76 B2
Sidi Khaled Alg. 123 G2
Sidi Ladjel Alg. 55 N9
Sidi Mannsour well Alg. 123 E3
Sidi Mhamed well W. Sahara 122 B5
Sidi Okba Alg. 123 G2
Sidirokastro Greece 58 E7
also known as Sidhirókastron
Sidi Saâd, Barrage dam Tunisia 57 B13
Sidi Sâlim Egypt 108 B6
Sidi-Smaïl Morocco 122 C2
Sid Lake Canada 167 J2
Sidlaw Hills U.K. 46 I7
Sidley, Mount Antarctica 222 P1
Sidmouth U.K. 47 I13
Sidmouth, Cape Australia 149 D2
Sidnaw U.S.A. 172 E4
Sidney Canada 166 F5
Sidney IA U.S.A. 178 D3
Sidney MT U.S.A. 180 F3
Sidney NE U.S.A. 178 B3
Sidney NY U.S.A. 177 J3
Sidney OH U.S.A. 176 A5
Sidney Lanier, Lake U.S.A. 174 D5
Sido Mali 124 D4
Sidoan Indon. 75 B2
Sidoarjo Indon. 77 F4
Sidoktaya Myanmar 78 A3
Sidon Lebanon 108 G4
also spelt Saïda or Sayda
Sidorovo Rus. Fed. 43 V3
Sidra r. Poland 49 U2
Sidri, Wâdi watercourse Egypt 108 E9
Sidrolândia Brazil 203 A7
Sidvokodvo Swaziland 133 P3
Sidwadweni S. Africa 133 M8
Sidzhak Uzbek. 103 G4
also spelt Sijjak; formerly spelt Sydzhak
Siebe Norway 44 M1
Siedlce Poland 49 T3
historically known as Sedlets
Sieg r. Germany 48 E5
Siegen Germany 48 F5
Siemianówka, Jezioro l. Poland 49 T3
Siemiatycze Poland 49 T3
Siĕmréab Cambodia 79 C5
also spelt Siem Reap
Siem Reap Cambodia see Siĕmréab
Si'en China see Huanjiang
Siena Italy 56 D5
historically known as Saena Julia
Sieniawa Poland 49 T5
Sieppijärvi Fin. 44 M2
Sieradz Poland 49 P4
Sieraków Poland 49 N3
Sierpc Poland 49 Q3
Sierpienica r. Poland 49 Q3
Sierra Bahoruco nat. park Dom. Rep. 187 F3
Sierra Blanca U.S.A. 181 F7
Sierra Chica Arg. 204 E5
Sierra Colorada Arg. 204 D6
Sierra de Cazorla Segura y las Villas park Spain 55 I6
Sierra del Gistral mts Spain see Xistral, Serra do
Sierra Grande Arg. 205 D6
▶Sierra Leone country Africa 124 B4
africa [countries] 114–117
Sierra Madre Mountains U.S.A. 182 D6
Sierra Mojada Mex. 184 E3
Sierra Nevada, Parque Nacional nat. park Venez. 198 D2
Sierra Nevada de Santa Marta, Parque Nacional nat. park Col. 198 C2
Sierraville U.S.A. 182 D2
Sierra Vista U.S.A. 181 E7
Sierre Switz. 51 N6
Siesartis r. Lith. 42 D7
Siesartis r. Lith. 42 F6
Şieu Romania 58 F1
Şieu r. Romania 58 F1
Sieve r. Italy 56 D5
Sievi Fin. 44 N3
Sifang Ling mts China 87 C4
Sifeni Eth. 128 D1
Sifié Côte d'Ivoire 124 D5
Sifnos i. Greece 59 F11
Sifnou, Steno sea chan. Greece 59 F11
Sig Alg. 123 E2
formerly known as St-Denis-du-Sig
Sig, Ozero l. Rus. Fed. 43 O4
Sigani well Saudi Arabia 105 F4
Sigatoka Fiji 145 G3
also spelt Singatoka
Sigave Wallis and Futuna Is 145 H3
also known as Leava; also spelt Singave
Sigean France 51 I9
Sigep, Tanjung pt Indon. 76 B3
Sigguup Nunaa pen. Greenland 165 N2
also known as Svartenhuk Halvø
Sighişoara Romania 58 F2
Sigiriya Sri Lanka 94 D5
Siglap Sing. 76 [inset]
Sigli Indon. 76 A1
Siglufjörður Iceland 44 [inset] C2
Sigma Phil. 74 B4
Sigmaringen Germany 48 G7
Signal de Mailhebiau mt. France 51 J8
Signal de Randon mt. France 51 J8
Signal du Pic hill France 50 H7
Signal Peak U.S.A. 183 J8
Signy-l'Abbaye France 51 K3
Sigoga S. Africa 133 M7
Sigoisooinan Indon. 76 B3
Sigourney U.S.A. 174 A3
Sigri, Akra pt Greece 59 G9
Siguatepeque Hond. 186 B4
Sigüeiro Spain 54 C2
Sigüenza Spain 55 I3
Siguiri Guinea 124 C4
Sigulda Latvia 42 F4
Sigurd U.S.A. 183 M3
Sihanoukville Cambodia 79 C6
formerly known as Kâmpóng Saôm or Kompong Som
Sihanoukville, Chhâk b. Cambodia 79 C6
formerly known as Kompong Som Bay
Sihaung Myauk Myanmar 78 A3
Sihawa India 94 D1
Sihhoya Swaziland 133 P2
Sihong China 87 F1
also known as Qingyang
Sihora Madhya Pradesh India 96 D5
Sihora Maharashtra India 96 C5
Sihou China see Changdao
Sihuas Peru 200 A2
Sihui China 87 E4
Siikainen Fin. 45 M3
Siikajoki Fin. 44 N2
Siikajoki r. Fin. 44 N2
Siilinjärvi Fin. 44 N3
Siipyy Fin. see Sideby
Siirt Turkey 107 E3
historically known as Tigranocerta
Sijjak Uzbek. see Sidzhak
Sijunjung Indon. 76 C3
Sika India 96 A5
Sikaka Saudi Arabia see Sakākah
Sikakap Indon. 76 C3
Sikandra Rao India 96 C4
Sikanni Chief Canada 166 F3
Sikanni Chief r. Canada 166 F3
Sikar India 96 B4
Sikaram mt. Afgh. 101 G3
Sikasso Mali 124 D4
Sikasso admin. reg. Mali 124 D4
Sikaw Myanmar 78 B3
Sikea Greece 59 E8
Sikeli Indon. 75 B4
Sikeston U.S.A. 174 B4
Sikhote-Alin' mts Rus. Fed. 82 D4
Sikhote-Alinskiy Zapovednik nature res. Rus. Fed. 82 E3
Sikinos Greece 59 G12
Sikinos i. Greece 59 G12
Sikirevci Croatia 56 K3
Sikkim state India 97 F4
Siklós Hungary 56 K3
Sikongo Zambia 127 D8
Siksjö Sweden 44 L2
Sikta India 97 E4
Sikuaishi China see Changhai
Sikuati Sabah Malaysia 77 G1
Sila' i. Saudi Arabia 104 A2
Silago Phil. 74 C4
Šilalė Lith. 42 D6
Silandro Italy 56 C2
Si Lanna National Park Thai. 78 B4
Silao Mex. 185 E4
Sila Point Phil. 74 C3
Silawaih Agam vol. Indon. 76 A1
Silay Phil. 74 B4
Silba i. Croatia 56 G4
Silchar India 97 G4
Şile Turkey 58 K7
Šilene Latvia 42 H6
Siler City U.S.A. 174 E5
Sileru r. India 94 D2
Silesia reg. Czech Rep./Poland 49 N5
Silet Alg. 123 G5
Sileti Kazakh. see Seletinskoye
Sileti r. Kazakh. 103 H1
formerly spelt Selety
Siletiteniz, Ozero salt l. Kazakh. 103 H1
formerly spelt Seletyteniz, Ozero
Silgadi Nepal see Silgarhi
Silgarhi Nepal 96 D3
also spelt Silgadi
Silghat India 97 G4
Siliana Tunisia 123 H1
Silifke Turkey 106 C3
historically known as Seleucia
Siliguri India see Shiliguri
Sililo Zambia 127 E9
Siling Co salt l. China 89 E6
Silipur India 96 C4
Silisili, Mount Samoa 145 H3
Silistat Turkey see Bozkır
Siliştea Romania 58 G4
Siliştea Nouă Romania 58 F4
Silistra Bulg. 58 I4
historically known as Dorostol or Durostorum or Silistria
Silistria Bulg. see Silistra
Silivri Turkey 106 B2
Siljan Norway 45 J4
Siljan l. Sweden 45 K3
Silkaatskop S. Africa 133 K2
Silkeborg Denmark 45 J4
Silla Spain 55 K5
Sillamäe Estonia 42 I2
Sillaro r. Italy 56 D4
Sille Turkey 106 C3
Silleda Spain 54 C2
Silleiro, Cabo c. Spain 54 C2
Sillé-le-Guillaume France 50 F4
Silli India 97 E5
Sillod India 94 B1
Sillon de Talbert pen. France 50 C4
Siloam Springs U.S.A. 179 D4
Silobela S. Africa 133 O3
Silovayakha r. Rus. Fed. 40 L2
Silsbee U.S.A. 179 D6
Silsby Lake Canada 167 M4
Siltaharju Fin. 44 N2
Siltakylä Fin. 42 H1
Siltou well Chad 120 B5
Siluas Indon. 77 E2
Silūp r. Iran 101 E5
Šilutė Lith. 42 C6
Silutshana S. Africa 133 O5
Šiluva Lith. 42 E6
Silva Jardim Brazil 207 K9
Silvan Turkey 107 E3
Silvânia Brazil 206 E3
Silvassa India 94 B1
Silver Bank sea feature Turks and Caicos Is 187 F2
Silver Bank Passage Turks and Caicos Is 187 F2
Silver Bay U.S.A. 174 B2
Silver City Canada 166 B2
Silver City U.S.A. 181 E6
Silver Creek U.S.A. 176 F3
Silver Creek r. U.S.A. 183 N7
Silverdale N.Z. 152 I4
Silver Islet Canada 172 E2
Silver Lake U.S.A. 172 D6
Silver Lake l. CA U.S.A. 183 H6
Silver Lake l. MI U.S.A. 172 F4
Silvermine Mountains hills Rep. of Ireland 47 D11
Silver Peak Range mts U.S.A. 182 G4
Silver Spring U.S.A. 177 I7
Silver Springs U.S.A. 182 E2
Silverthrone Mountain Canada 166 E5
Silvertip Mountain Canada 180 B2
Silverton Australia 146 D2
Silverton Canada 166 G5
Silverton CO U.S.A. 181 F5
Silverton TX U.S.A. 179 B5
Silver Water Canada 173 K5
Silves Brazil 199 G5
Silves Port. 54 C7
Silvia Col. 198 B4
Silvies r. U.S.A. 180 C4
Silvituc Mex. 185 H5
Silvretta Gruppe mts Switz. 51 Q6
Sim r. Rus. Fed. 40 K5
Sima Comoros 129 E8
Sima Rus. Fed. 43 U5
Simao China 86 B4
Simão Dias Brazil 202 E4
Simaraña Venez. 199 F3
Simàrd, Lac l. Canada 173 O3
Simaria Jharkhand India 97 E4
Simaria Madhya Pradesh India 96 D4
Simatang i. Indon. 75 B2
Simav Turkey 106 B3
Simav Dağları mts Turkey 106 B3
Şimayr i. Saudi Arabia 104 C4
Simba Dem. Rep. Congo 126 D4
Simbirsk Rus. Fed. see Ul'yanovsk
Simbruini, Monti mts Italy 56 F7
Simbukhovo Rus. Fed. 43 R6
Simcoe Canada 168 D5
Simcoe, Lake Canada 168 E4
Simdega India 97 E5
Simeå Sweden 45 L3
Simēn Mountains National Park Eth. 128 C1
Simēn Mountains Eth. 128 C1
Simeonovgrad Bulg. 58 G6
formerly known as Maritsa
Simeria Romania 58 E3
Simeto r. Sicilia Italy 57 H11
Simeuluë i. Indon. 76 B2
Simferopol' Ukr. 41 E7
Simi i. Greece see Symi
Simikot Nepal 97 D3
Simindou Cent. Afr. Rep. 126 D3
Siminy mt. Slovakia 49 R6
Simitli Bulg. 58 E7
Simi Valley U.S.A. 182 F7
Simla India see Shimla
Şimleu Silvaniei Romania 58 D1
Simmern (Hunsrück) Germany 48 E6
Simmesport U.S.A. 175 B6
Simm's Bahamas 187 E2
Simnas Lith. 42 E7
Simo Fin. 44 N2
Simojärvi l. Fin. 44 N2
Simonette r. Canada 166 G4
Simonhouse Canada 167 K4
Šimonka mt. Slovakia 49 S7
Simons U.S.A. 176 E4
Simon's Town S. Africa 132 C11
Simontornya Hungary 49 P9
Simon Wash watercourse U.S.A. 183 O9
Simpang Indon. 76 D3
Simpang Mangayau, Tanjong pt Sabah Malaysia 77 G1
Simplício Mendes Brazil 202 D3
Simplon Pass Switz. 51 O6
Simpson Canada 167 J5
Simpson Desert Australia 148 C5
Simpson Desert Conservation Park nature res. Australia 148 C5
Simpson Desert National Park Australia 148 C5
Simpson Desert Regional Reserve nature res. Australia 146 C1
Simpson Hill hill Australia 151 D5
Simpson Island Canada 172 F2
Simpson Islands Canada 167 H2
Simpson Park Mountains U.S.A. 183 H2
Simpson Peninsula Canada 165 K3
Simpsonville U.S.A. 174 D5
Simra Nepal 97 E4
Simrishamn Sweden 45 K5
Simuk i. Indon. 76 B3
Simulubek Indon. 76 B3
Simunjan Sarawak Malaysia 77 E2
Simunul i. Phil. 74 A5
Simushir, Ostrov i. Rus. Fed. 81 Q3
Sina r. India 94 B2
Sīnā', Shibh Jazīrat pen. Egypt see Sinai
Sinabang Indon. 76 B2
Sinabung vol. Indon. 76 B2
Sina Dhaqa Somalia 128 E3
▶Sinai pen. Egypt 121 G2
also known as Sīnā', Shibh Jazīrat
world [physical features] 8–9
Sinai, Mont hill France 51 K3
Sinai, Mount Egypt 108 E9
also known as Mūsa, Gebel
Sinaia Romania 58 G3
Sinai al Janūbîya governorate Egypt see Janūb Sīnā'
Sinai ash Shamâlîya governorate Egypt see Shamāl Sīnā'
Si Nakarin Reservoir Thai. 79 B5

index

S

Sinaloa state Mex. **184** C3
Sinamaica Venez. **198** D2
Sinan China **87** D3
Sinancha Rus. Fed. see Cheremshany
Sinanju N. Korea **83** B5
Sinarades Greece **59** A9
Sinäwin Libya **120** A2
Sinazongwe Zambia **127** E9
Sinbaungwe Myanmar **78** A4
Sinbo Myanmar **78** B2
Sinbyugyun Myanmar **78** A3
Sincan Turkey **107** D3
Sincé Col. **198** C2
Sincelejo Col. **198** C2
Sinchu Taiwan see T'aoyüan
Sinclair, Lake U.S.A. **175** D5
Sinclair Mills Canada **166** F4
Sincora, Serra do hills Brazil **202** D5
Sind r. India **96** C4
Sind prov. Pak. see Sindh
Sinda Rus. Fed. **82** E2
Sinda Zambia **127** F8
Sindal Denmark **45** J4
Sindangan Phil. **74** B4
Sindangan Bay Phil. **74** B4
Sindangbarang Indon. **77** D4
Sindara Gabon **126** A5
Sindari India **96** A4
Sindeh, Teluk b. Indon. **75** B5
Sindelfingen Germany **48** F7
Sindgi India **94** C2
Sindh prov. Pak. **101** G5
  formerly spelt Sind
Sindhnur India **94** C3
Sindhuli Garhi Nepal **97** E4
  also known as Sindhulimadi
Sindhulimadi Nepal see Sindhuli Garhi
Sindi Estonia **42** F3
Sindi India **94** C1
Sindırgı Turkey **106** B3
Sindkhed India **94** C2
Sindkheda India **96** B5
Sindominic Romania see Sândominic
Sindor Rus. Fed. **40** I3
Sindou Burkina **124** D4
Sindphana r. India **94** C2
Sindri India **97** E5
Sind Sagar Doab lowland Pak. **101** G4
Sinegor'ye Rus. Fed. **40** I4
Sinekçi Turkey **59** I8
Sinel'nikovo Ukr. see Synel'nykove
Sinendé Benin **125** F4
Sines Port. **54** C7
Sines, Cabo de c. Port. **54** C7
Sinettä Fin. **44** N2
Sinezerki Rus. Fed. **43** P8
Sinfra Côte d'Ivoire **124** D5
Sing Myanmar **78** B3
Singa Sudan **121** G6
Singahi India **96** D3
Singaingmyo Myanmar **78** B3
▶**Singapore** country Asia **76** C2
  known as Hsin-chia-p'o in Chinese; spelt
  Singapura in Malay
  asia [countries] ▶ 64–67
▶**Singapore** Sing. **76** C2
  Capital of Singapore. Also known as Hsin-
  chia-p'o; also spelt Singapura; historically
  known as Tumasik.
Singapore, Strait of Indon./Sing. **76** C2
Singapura country Asia see Singapore
Singapura Sing. see Singapore
Singaraja Indon. **77** F5
Singareni India **94** D2
Singatoka Fiji see Sigatoka
Singave Wallis and Futuna Is see Sigave
Sing Buri Thai. **79** C5
Singen (Hohentwiel) Germany **48** F8
Singeorgiu de Pădure Romania see
  Sângeorgiu de Pădure
Singeorz-Bãi Romania see Sângeorz-Bãi
Singera Moldova **58** J2
  formerly spelt Sângera
Singgimtay China **88** B3
  formerly known as Singim
Singh India **89** A6
Singhampton Canada **173** M6
Singida Tanz. **129** B6
Singida admin. reg. Tanz. **129** B6
Singidunum Srbija Yugo. see Belgrade
Singim China see Singgimtay
Singkaling Hkamti Myanmar **78** A2
Singkang Indon. **75** B4
Singkawang Indon. **77** E2
Singkep i. Indon. **76** C3
Singkil Indon. **76** B2
Singkuang Indon. **76** B2
Singleton Canada **173** M6
Singleton, Mount hill N.T. Australia **148** A1
Singleton, Mount hill W.A. Australia **151** B6
Singoli India **96** B4
Singon Myanmar **78** B3
Singora Thai. see Songkhla
Sin'gosan N. Korea see Kosan
Singou, Réserve Totale du nature res.
  Burkina **125** F4
Singra India **97** F4
Singu Myanmar **78** A3
Singureni Romania **58** G4
Sin'gye N. Korea **83** B5
Sinhala country Asia see Sri Lanka
Sinharaja Forest Reserve nature res.
  Sri Lanka **94** D5
Sinhŭng N. Korea **83** B4
Siniloan Phil. **74** B3
Sining China see Xining
Siniscola Sardegna Italy **57** B8
Sini Vrŭkh mt. Bulg. **58** G7
Siniy-Shikhan Rus. Fed. **103** E2
Sinj Croatia **56** I5
Sinjai Indon. **75** B4

Sinjār Iraq **107** E3
Sinjār, Jabal mt. Iraq **107** E3
Sinkat Sudan **121** H5
Sinkiang aut. reg. China see
  Xinjiang Uygur Zizhiqu
Sinkiang Uighur Autonomous Region
  aut. reg. China see Xinjiang Uygur Zizhiqu
Sinking Spring U.S.A. **176** B6
Sinkyewichy Belarus **42** I9
Sinmi-do i. N. Korea **83** B5
Sinnamary Fr. Guiana **199** H3
Sinnar India **94** B2
Şinnar, Khashm hill Saudi Arabia **109** O8
Sinn Bishr, Gebel hill Egypt **108** D8
Sinneh Iran see Sanandaj
Sinn el Kaddâb esc. Egypt **121** F4
Sinnemahoning U.S.A. **176** G4
Sinni r. Italy **57** I8
Sînnicolau Mare Romania see
  Sânnicolau Mare
Sinnûris Egypt **108** B8
Sinoia Zimbabwe see Chinhoyi
Sinoie, Lacul lag. Romania **58** J4
Sinole Latvia **42** H4
Sinop Brazil **201** G2
Sinop Turkey **106** C2
  historically known as Sinope
Sinope Turkey see Sinop
Sinoquipe Mex. **184** C2
Sinp'a N. Korea **83** C4
Sinp'o N. Korea **83** C4
Sinp'yŏng N. Korea **83** B5
Sinsang N. Korea **83** B5
Sinsheim Germany **48** F6
Sintang Indon. **77** E2
Sint-Laureins Belgium **51** J1

▶**Sint Maarten** i. Neth. Antilles **187** H3
  Part of the Netherlands Antilles. The
  northern part of the island is the French
  territory of St Martin.

Sint Nicolaas Aruba **187** F4
Sint-Niklaas Belgium **51** K1
  also spelt St Nicolas
Sinton U.S.A. **179** C6
Sintsovo Rus. Fed. **43** R5
Sint-Vith Belgium **51** M2
Sinú r. Col. **198** C2
Sinŭiju N. Korea **83** B4
Sinujiif Somalia **128** F2
Sinyaya r. Rus. Fed. **43** J4
Siocon Phil. **74** B5
Siófok Hungary **49** P9
Sioma Zambia **127** D9
Sioma Ngwezi National Park Zambia
  127 D9
Sion Switz. **51** N6
Siorapaluk Greenland **165** L2
Sioule r. France **51** J6
Sioux Center U.S.A. **178** C3
Sioux City U.S.A. **178** C3
Sioux Falls U.S.A. **178** C3
Sioux Lookout Canada **168** B3
Sipacate Guat. **185** H6
Sipalay Phil. **74** B4
Šipan i. Croatia **56** I5
Sipang, Tanjong pt Sarawak Malaysia **77** E2
Siphaqeni S. Africa see Flagstaff
Siping China **82** B3
Sipiwesk Canada **167** L4
Sipiwesk Lake Canada **167** L4
Siple, Mount Antarctica **222** P2
Siple Coast Antarctica **223** N1
Siple Island Antarctica **222** P2
Sipolilo Zimbabwe see Guruve
Šipovo Bos.-Herz. **56** I4
Sipsey r. U.S.A. **175** B5
Sipura i. Indon. **76** B3
Sipura, Selat sea chan. Indon. **76** B3
Siq, Wādī el watercourse Egypt **108** D8
Siqirah Yemen **105** F5
Siqueira Campos Brazil **206** D10
Siquijor Phil. **74** B4
Siquijor i. Phil. **74** B4
Siquisique Venez. **198** D2
Sir r. Pak. **101** G6
Sira India **94** C3
Sira Norway **45** I4
Şīr Abū Nu'āyr i. U.A.E. **105** F2
Si Racha Thai. **79** C5
Siracusa Sicilia Italy see Syracuse
Siraha Nepal see Sirha
Sirajganj Bangl. **97** F4
Sir Alexander, Mount Canada **166** F4
Şiran Turkey **107** D2
Širathu India **97** D4
Sirba r. Burkina/Niger **125** F3
Şīr Banī Yās i. U.A.E. **105** F2
Sircilla India see Sirsilla
Sirdaryo r. Asia see Syrdar'ya
Sirdaryo Azer. see Syrdar'ya
Sirdaryo Wiloyati admin. div. Uzbek. see
  Syrdar'inskaya Oblast'
Sirdingka China see Lhari
Sire Tanz. **129** A6
Sir Edward Pellew Group is Australia
  148 C2
Siren U.S.A. **172** A5
Siret r. Romania **58** J3
Sir Graham Moore Islands Australia
  150 D2
Sirha Nepal **97** F4
  also spelt Sirha
Sirhān, Wādī as watercourse
  Jordan/Saudi Arabia **109** I6
Sirhind India **96** C3
Siri, Cape P.N.G. **149** G1
Širia Romania **58** C2
Širik Iran **100** D5
Sirik, Tanjong pt Sarawak Malaysia **77** E2
Sirikit Reservoir Thai. **78** C4
Sirina i. Greece see Syrna
Siritoi r. Pak. **101** G4
Sirjā Iran **101** E5
Sir James MacBrien, Mount Canada
  166 E2
Sīrjān Iran **100** C4
Sīrjān salt flat Iran **100** C4
Sir Joseph Banks Group Conservation
  Park nature res. Australia **146** C3
Sirkka Fin. **44** N2
Sirmaur India **96** C3
  formerly spelt Sirmur
Sirmium Vojvodina, Srbija Yugo. see
  Sremska Mitrovica
Sirmour India **97** D4
Sirmur India see Sirmaur
Şırnak Turkey **107** F3
Širniö Fin. **44** O2
Sirohi India **96** B4
Sironcha India **94** D2
Sironj India **96** C4
Siros i. Greece see Syros
Sirotsina Belarus **43** K6
Siroua, Jbel mt. Morocco **122** D3
Sirpur India **94** D2
Sirrayn Island Saudi Arabia **104** C4
Sirrei Eth. **128** D3
Sirretta Peak U.S.A. **182** F6
Sirri, Jazireh-ye i. Iran **100** C5
Sirsa India **96** B3
Sir Sandford, Mount Canada **166** G5
Sirs el Laiyâna Egypt **108** B7
Sirsi Karnataka India **94** B3
Sirsi Uttar Pradesh India **96** C3
Sirsilla India **94** C2
  formerly spelt Sircilla
Sirte Libya **120** C2
Sirte, Gulf of Libya **120** C2
  also known as Surt, Khalīj

Sir Thomas, Mount hill Australia **146** A1
Siruguppa India **94** C3
Sirupa r. Mex. **181** E7
Sirur Karnataka India **94** B2
Sirur Maharashtra India **94** B2
Širutiškis Lith. **42** E6
Sirvan Turkey **107** E3
Sirvel India **94** C3
Širvintos Lith. **42** F6
Şirwāh Yemen **104** D5
Sirwān r. Iraq **107** F4
Sir Wilfrid Laurier, Mount Canada **166** F4
Sir William Thompson Range hills Australia
  149 D2
Siryan Iran **100** D3
Sis Turkey see Kozan
Sisak Croatia **56** I3
  historically known as Siscia
Sisaket Thai. **79** D5
Sisal Mex. **185** H4
Sisante Spain **55** I5
Siscia Croatia see Sisak
Sishen S. Africa **132** H4
Sishilipu China **85** E5
Sisian Armenia **107** F3
Sisimiut Greenland **165** N3
  also known as Holsteinsborg
Sisipuk Lake Canada **167** K4
Siskiwit Bay U.S.A. **172** E3
Sisogu'ichic Mex. **184** D3
Sīsŏphŏn Cambodia **79** C5
Sisquoc r. U.S.A. **182** D7
Sissach Switz. **51** N5
Sissili r. Burkina **125** E4
Sissonville U.S.A. **176** D7
Sīstān reg. Iran **101** E4
  also spelt Seistan
Sīstān, Daryācheh-ye marsh Afgh. **101** E4
Sister Bay U.S.A. **172** F5
Sisteron France **51** L8
Sisters U.S.A. **180** B3
Sistersville U.S.A. **176** E6
Sisto r. Italy **56** F7
Sit' r. Rus. Fed. **43** S3
Sitalike Tanz. **129** A6
Sitamarhi India **97** E4
Sitamau India **96** B5
Sitampiky Madag. **131** [inset] J3
Sitapur India **96** D4
Siteia Greece **59** H13
  formerly spelt Stegi
Siteki Swaziland **133** P3
  formerly spelt Stegi
Sithonia pen. Greece **59** E9
Sitia Greece see Siteia
Sitian China **84** B3
Sitila Moz. **131** G4
Siting China **87** C3
Sitio da Abadia Brazil **202** C5
Sitio do Mato Brazil **202** D5
Sitka U.S.A. **164** F4
Sitnica r. Yugo. **58** B6
Sitno mt. Slovakia **49** P7
Sitnya r. Rus. Fed. **43** K4
Sitra oasis Egypt **121** E3
Sitsyenyets Belarus **43** K5
Sittang r. Myanmar **78** B4
  also spelt Sittaung or Sittoung
Sittard Neth. **48** C5
Sittaung Myanmar **78** A2
Sittaung r. Myanmar see Sittang
Sittoung r. Myanmar see Sittang
Sittwe Myanmar **78** A3
  formerly known as Akyab
Situbondo Indon. **77** F4
Siu A Chau i. Hong Kong China **87** [inset]
Siumpan, Rubha an t- hd U.K. see
  Tiumpan Head
Siumpu i. Indon. **75** B4
Siuna Nicaragua **186** B4
Siuntio Fin. **42** F1
Siuri India **97** E5
Siva Rus. Fed. **40** J4
Sivaganga India **94** C4
Sivakasi India **94** C4
Sivaki Rus. Fed. **82** B1
Sivand Iran **100** C4
Sivas Turkey **107** D3
  historically known as Sebasteia
Sivaslı Turkey **106** B3
Siverek Turkey **107** D3
Sivers i. Latvia **42** I5
Siverskiy Rus. Fed. **43** L2
Sivers'kyy Donets' r. Rus. Fed./Ukr. see
  Severskiy Donets
Sivomaskinskiy Rus. Fed. **40** L2
Sivrice Turkey **107** D3
Sivrihisar Turkey **106** B3
Sivukile S. Africa **133** N3
Siwa Egypt **121** E2
Siwa Indon. **75** B3
Siwalik Range mts India/Nepal **96** C3
Siwan India **97** E4
Siwana India **96** A4
Siwa Oasis Egypt **121** E2
Six Cross Roads Barbados **187** I4
Six-Fours-les-Plages France **51** L9
Sixian China **87** F1
Sixmile Canada **166** A1
Siyabuswa S. Africa **133** N2
Siyang China **87** F1
  also known as Zhongxing
Siyathemba S. Africa **133** M3
Siyathuthuka S. Africa **133** O2
Siyäzän Azer. **107** G2
  also known as Siazan'; formerly known as
  Kyzyl-Burun
Siyitang China **85** F3
Siyom r. India **78** A1
Siyuni Iran **100** C3
Siziwang Qi China see Ulan Hua
Sizyabsk Rus. Fed. **40** J2
Sjælland i. Denmark see Zealand
Sjaunja naturreservat nature res. Sweden
  44 L2
Sjenica Srbija Yugo. **58** B5
Sjoa Norway **45** J3
Sjøbo Sweden **45** K5
Sjøholt Norway **44** I3
Sjona sea chan. Norway **44** K2
Sjoutnäset Sweden **44** K2
Sjøvegan Norway **44** L1
Sjulsmark Sweden **44** M2
Sjuøyane is Svalbard **38** C1
Skäckerfjällen mts Sweden **44** K3
Skadarsko Jezero nat. park Yugo. **58** A4
Skadovs'k Ukr. **41** E7
Skælsør Denmark **45** J5
Skærbæk Denmark **45** I5
Skærfjorden inlet Greenland **165** R2
Skaftá r. mouth Iceland **44** [inset] C3
Skaftárós r. mouth Iceland **44** [inset] C3
Skagafjörður inlet Iceland **44** [inset] C2
Skagaheiði reg. Iceland **44** [inset] B2
Skagen Denmark **45** J4
Skagern l. Sweden **45** K4
Skagerrak strait Denmark/Norway **45** J4
Skagit r. U.S.A. **180** B2
Skagit Mountain Canada **166** F5
Skagway U.S.A. **164** F4
Skaidi Norway **44** N1
Skaidiškes Lith. **42** G7
Skala Notio Aigaio Greece **59** H11
Skala Peloponnisos Greece **59** D11
Skala Kallonis Greece **59** H9
Skaland Norway **44** L1
Skalino Rus. Fed. **43** V3

Skalleiv Norway **44** O1
Skalmodal Sweden **44** K2
Skanderborg Denmark **45** J4
Skåne county Sweden **45** K5
Skaneateles U.S.A. **177** I3
Skaneateles Lake U.S.A. **177** I3
Skånevik Norway **45** I4
Skansholm Sweden **44** L2
Skantzoura i. Greece **59** F9
Skara Sweden **45** K4
Skara Brae tourist site U.K. **46** I4
Skarberget Norway **44** L1
Skärbläcka Sweden **45** K4
Skardarsko Jezero l. Albania/Yugo. see
  Scutari, Lake
Skardu Jammu and Kashmir **96** B2
Skåre Norway **45** I4
Skärgårdshavets Nationalpark nat. park
  Fin. **45** M4
  also known as Saaristomeren Kansallispuisto
Skarnes Norway **45** J3
Skärplinge Sweden **45** L3
Skärsjövalen Sweden **45** K3
Skarstind mt. Norway **45** J3
Skarszewy Poland **49** P1
Skarvedalsseggen mt. Norway **45** J3
Skarvsjöby Sweden **44** L2
Skaryszew Poland **49** S4
Skarżysko-Kamienna Poland **49** R4
Skaudvilė Lith. **42** D6
Skaulo Sweden **44** M2
Skaupsjøen-Hardangerjøkulen park
  Norway **45** I3
Skawa r. Poland **49** Q6
Skawina Poland **49** Q6
Skaymat W. Sahara **122** B4
Skeena r. Canada **166** D4
Skeena Mountains Canada **166** D3
Skegness U.K. **47** M10
Skeiðarársandur sand area Iceland
  44 [inset] C3
Skeleton Coast Game Park nature res.
  Namibia **130** B3
Skellefteå Sweden **44** M2
Skellefteälven r. Sweden **44** M2
Skelleftebukten b. Sweden **44** M2
Skellefteham Sweden **44** M2
Skeppshamn Sweden **44** L3
Skerries Rep. of Ireland **47** F10
Skhimatárion Greece see Schimatari
Skhira Tunisia **123** H2
Skhiza i. Greece see Schiza
Ski Norway **45** J4
Skiathos Greece **59** E9
Skiathos i. Greece **59** E9
Skibbereen Rep. of Ireland **47** C12
Skibotn Norway **44** M1
Skidal' Belarus **42** F8
  also spelt Skidel'
Skiddaw hill U.K. **47** I9
Skidegate Mission Canada **166** D4
Skidel' Belarus see Skidal'
Skiemonys Lith. **42** G6
Skien Norway **45** J4
Skierniewice Poland **49** R4
Skikda Alg. **123** G1
  formerly known as Philippeville
Škilbéni Latvia **42** I4
Skinari, Akra pt Greece **59** B11
Skinnskatteberg Sweden **45** K4
Skio Jammu and Kashmir **96** C2
Skipskop S. Africa **132** E11
Skipton Australia **147** D4
Skipton U.K. **47** J10
Skiropoúla i. Greece see Skyropoula
Skíros i. Greece see Skyros
Skive Denmark **45** I4
Skjálfandafljót r. Iceland **44** [inset] C2
Skjálfandi b. Iceland **44** [inset] C2
Skjelatinden mt. Norway **44** K2
Skjellbreid Norway **44** K2
Skjellinhovde hill Norway **45** J3
Skjerkeknuten hill Norway **44** K2
Skjervøy Norway **44** M1
Skjolden Norway **45** I3
Sknyatino Rus. Fed. **43** S4
Skobelev Uzbek. see Fergana
Skobeleva, Pik mt. Kyrg. **103** H5
Skocjanske Jame tourist site Slovenia
  56 F3
Skoenmakerskop S. Africa **133** J11
Škofja Loka Slovenia **56** G2
Skog Sweden **45** L3
Skoganvarre Norway **44** N1
Skogfoss Norway **44** O1
Skoki Poland **49** N3
Skokie U.S.A. **172** F8
Skol' Kazakh. **103** F2
Sköllersta Sweden **45** K4
Skomvær i. Norway **44** J2
Skoonspruit r. S. Africa **133** K4
Skopelos Greece **59** E9
Skopelos i. Greece **59** E9
Skopia hill Greece **59** C9
Skopin Rus. Fed. **43** U8

▶**Skopje** Macedonia **58** C7
  Capital of Macedonia. Also spelt Skopje;
  historically known as Scupi.

Skopje Macedonia see Skopje
Skopunarfjørður sea chan. Faroe Is **46** F2
Skórcz Poland **49** P2
Skorodnoye Rus. Fed. **41** F6
Skorping Denmark **45** J4
Skotoussa Greece **59** E8
Skotterud Norway **45** K4
Skoutari Greece **58** E7
Skoutaros Greece **59** H9
Skövde Sweden **45** K4
Skovorodino Rus. Fed. **82** A1
Skowhegan U.S.A. **177** P1
Skriveri Latvia **42** G5
Skrlatica mt. Slovenia **56** F2
Skröven Sweden **44** M2
Skrunda Latvia **42** C5
Skrwa r. Poland **49** Q3
Skrydlyeva Belarus **43** L6
Skúgvoy i. Faroe Is **46** F2
Skukum, Mount Canada **166** C2
Skukuza S. Africa **133** O2
Skuleskogens nationalpark nat. park
  Sweden **44** L3
Skull Peak U.S.A. **183** H5
Skull Valley U.S.A. **183** L7
Skultuna Sweden **45** L4
Skunk r. U.S.A. **174** B3
Skuodas Lith. **42** C5
Skuratovskiy Rus. Fed. **43** S7
Skurup Sweden **45** K5
Skút r. Bulg. **58** E5
Skutskär Sweden **45** L3
Skvyra Ukr. **41** D6
Skwierzyna Poland **49** M3
Skye i. U.K. **46** F6
Skykula hill U.S.A. **183** H5
Skyring, Seno b. Chile **205** B9
Skyropoula i. Greece **59** F10
  also spelt Skiropoúla
Skyros i. Greece **59** F10
Skyros i. Greece **59** F10
Skytrain Ice Rise Antarctica **222** S1
Slabodka Belarus **42** I6
Slabozia Belarus **42** J8
Slade U.S.A. **176** B7
Slættaratindur hill Faroe Is **46** F1
Slagelse Denmark **45** J5
Slagnäs Sweden **44** L2
Slamet, Gunung vol. Indon. **77** E4
Slaná r. Slovakia **49** R7

Slaney r. Rep. of Ireland **47** F11
Slănic Romania **58** H3
Slănic r. Romania **58** H3
Slănic Moldova Romania **58** H2
Slănské Vrchy mts Slovakia **49** S7
Slantsy Rus. Fed. **43** J2
Slaný Czech Rep. **49** L5
Slapaberžė Lith. **42** E6
Slashers Reefs Australia **149** E3
Slate Islands Canada **168** C3
Slatina Croatia **56** J3
Slatina Romania **58** F4
Slatina r. Slovakia **49** Q7
Slatina-Timiş Romania **58** D3
Slaty Fork U.S.A. **176** E7
Slautnoye Rus. Fed. **39** Q3
Slave r. Canada **167** H2
Slave Coast Africa **125** F5
Slave Lake Canada **167** H4
Slave Point Canada **167** H2
Slavgorod Belarus see Slawharad
Slavgorod Rus. Fed. **80** D1
Slavkovichi Rus. Fed. **43** K4
Slavonia reg. Croatia **56** J3
  also spelt Slavonija
Slavonija reg. Croatia see Slavonia
Slavonska Požega Croatia see Požega
Slavonski Brod Croatia **56** K3
Slavsk Rus. Fed. **42** C7
  historically known as Heinrichswalde
Slavuta Ukr. **41** C6
Slavutych Ukr. **41** D6
Slavyanka Kazakh. see Myrzakent
Slavyanka Rus. Fed. **82** C4
Slavyanovo Bulg. **58** F5
Slavyansk Ukr. see Slov''yans'k
Slavyanskaya Rus. Fed. see
  Slavyansk-na-Kubani
Slavyansk-na-Kubani Rus. Fed. **41** F7
  formerly known as Slavyanskaya
Sława Poland **49** N4
Sławharad Belarus **43** M8
  also spelt Slavgorod
Sławno Poland **49** N1
Slayton U.S.A. **178** D3
Sleaford U.K. **47** L10
Sleaford Bay Australia **146** B3
Slea Head Rep. of Ireland **47** B11
Sleat, Sound of sea chan. U.K. **46** G6
Sled Lake Canada **167** J4
Sleeper Islands Canada **168** E1
Sleeping Bear Dunes National Lakeshore
  nature res. U.S.A. **172** G6
Sleeping Bear Point U.S.A. **172** G6
Sleep Island Hong Kong China **87** [inset]
Sleman Indon. **77** E4
Sleptsovskaya Rus. Fed. **41** H8
  also known as Ordzhonikidzevskaya
Slessor Glacier Antarctica **223** W1
Ślesza hill Poland **49** N5
Slick Rock U.S.A. **183** P3
Slidell U.S.A. **175** B5
Slide Mountain U.S.A. **177** K4
Slidre Norway **45** J3
Slieve Donard hill U.K. **47** G9
Slieve Car hill Rep. of Ireland **47** C9
Slieve Gamph hills Rep. of Ireland **47** C10
  also known as Ox Mountains
Slieve Mish Mountains hills Rep. of Ireland
  47 B11
Sligachan U.K. **46** F6
Sligeach Rep. of Ireland see Sligo
Sligo Rep. of Ireland **47** D9
  also spelt Sligeach
Sligo U.S.A. **176** F4
Sligo Bay Rep. of Ireland **47** D9
Slipper Island N.Z. **152** J5
Slippery Rock U.S.A. **176** E4
Sliterss rezervāts nature res. Latvia **42** C4
Sliven Bulg. **58** H6
Slivnitsa Bulg. **58** E6
Slivo Pole Bulg. **58** H5
Sljeme mt. Croatia **56** H3
Sloan r. Canada **167** G1
Sloan U.S.A. **183** I6
Sloat U.S.A. **182** D2
Sloboda Rus. Fed. see Ezhva
Sloboda Rus. Fed. **43** P7
Slobodchikovo Rus. Fed. **40** I3
Slobodka Rus. Fed. **43** N7
Slobodskoy Rus. Fed. **40** I4
Slobodzeya Moldova see Slobozia
Slobodzeya Moldova **58** J2
  formerly spelt Slobodzeya
Slobozia Romania **58** I4
Slobozia Bradului Romania **58** I3
Słomniki Poland **49** R5
Slonim Belarus **42** G8
Słonsk Poland **49** L3
Słough U.K. **47** L12
Slovakia country Europe **49** P7
  known as Slovensko in Slovakian
  europe [countries] ▶ 32–35
Slovenia country Europe **56** H2
  spelt Slovenija in Slovenian
  europe [countries] ▶ 32–35
Slovenj Gradec Slovenia **56** H2
Slovenska Bistrica Slovenia **56** H2
Slovenske Gorice hills Slovenia **56** H2
Slovenské Rudohorie mts Slovakia **49** Q7
Slovensko country Europe see Slovakia
Slovensky kras mts Slovakia **49** R7
Slovensky raj nat. park Slovakia **49** R7
Slov''yans'k Ukr. **41** F6
  formerly known as Slavyansk
Słubice Poland **49** L3
Sluch r. Belarus **42** I9
Sluch r. Ukr. **53** H1
Sludka Rus. Fed. **40** I4
Slunj Croatia **56** H3
Słupca Poland **49** O3
Słupia r. Poland **49** N1
Słupsk Poland **49** O1
  formerly known as Stolp
Slussfors Sweden **44** L2
Slutsk Belarus **42** I8
Slyna r. Lith. **42** D6
Slyne Head Rep. of Ireland **47** B10
Slyudyanka Rus. Fed. **84** D1
Smackover U.S.A. **179** D5
Smäland reg. Sweden **45** K4
Smålandsstenar Sweden **45** K4
Small Point U.S.A. **177** P2
Smallwood Reservoir Canada **169** H2
Smalowka Belarus **43** J6
Smalyavichy Belarus **42** J7
Smarhon' Belarus **42** H7
Smarthon' Belarus see Smorgon'
Smartt Syndicate Dam resr S. Africa
  132 H7
Smeaton Canada **167** J4
Smederevo Srbija Yugo. **58** B4
  historically known as Semendire
Smederevska Palanka Srbija Yugo. **58** B4
Smedjebacken Sweden **45** K3
Smela Ukr. see Smila
Smelror Norway **44** O1
Smethport U.S.A. **176** G4
Smigiel Poland **49** N3
Smila Ukr. **41** D6
  also known as Smela
Smilavichy Belarus **42** J8
Smiltene Latvia **42** G4
Smiltiņu kalns hill Latvia **42** I5
Smines Norway **44** K1
Smirnykh Rus. Fed. **82** F2
Smoča r. Italy see Isonzo

Smith Canada **167** H4
Smith r. MT U.S.A. **180** E3
Smith r. VA U.S.A. **176** F3
Smith Arm b. Canada **166** F1
Smith Bay U.S.A. **164** D2
Smith Center U.S.A. **178** C4
Smithers Canada **166** E4
Smithers Landing Canada **166** E4
Smithfield S. Africa **133** K7
Smithfield NC U.S.A. **174** E5
Smithfield UT U.S.A. **180** E4
Smithfield VA U.S.A. **177** I9
Smith Glacier Antarctica **222** Q1
Smith Island Antarctica **222** T2
Smith Island India **95** G3
Smith Island MD U.S.A. **177** I7
Smith Island VA U.S.A. **177** J8
Smithland U.S.A. **174** B4
Smith Mountain Lake U.S.A. **176** F8
Smith River Canada **166** E3
Smithsburg U.S.A. **176** H6
Smiths Falls Canada **168** E4
Smith Sound sea chan. Canada/Greenland
  165 L2
Smithton Australia **147** E5
Smithville TN U.S.A. **174** C5
Smithville WV U.S.A. **176** D6
Smitskraal S. Africa **133** I10
Smjörfjöll mts Iceland **44** [inset] D2
Smoke Creek Desert U.S.A. **182** E1
Smoky r. Canada **166** G3
Smoky Bay Australia **146** B3
Smoky Cape Australia **147** G2
Smoky Falls Canada **168** D3
Smoky Hill r. U.S.A. **178** B4
Smoky Hill, North Fork r. U.S.A. **178** B4
Smoky Hills KS U.S.A. **178** C4
Smoky Lake Canada **167** H4
Smoky Mountains U.S.A. **180** D4
Smela r. Norway **44** I3
Smolenka Rus. Fed. **102** B2
Smolensk Rus. Fed. **43** N7
Smolenskaya Oblast' admin. div. Rus. Fed.
  43 O7
  English form Smolensk Oblast
Smolensk Oblast admin. div. Rus. Fed. see
  Smolenskaya Oblast'
Smolensko-Moskovskaya Vozvyshennost'
  hills Rus. Fed. **43** N7
Smolevichi Belarus see Smalyavichy
Smolikas mt. Greece **59** B8
Smolyan Bulg. **58** F8
Smolyoninovo Rus. Fed. **82** D4
Smooth Rock Falls Canada **168** D3
Smoothrock Lake Canada **168** B3
Smoothstone Lake Canada **167** J4
Smørfjord Norway **44** N1
Smorgon' Belarus see Smarhon'
Smotrova Buda Rus. Fed. **43** N9
Smyadovo Bulg. **58** I5
Smyley Island Antarctica **222** S2
Smyrna Turkey see İzmir
Smyrna DE U.S.A. **177** J6
Smyrna GA U.S.A. **175** C5
Smyrna TN U.S.A. **174** C5
Smyth, Canal sea chan. Chile **205** B8
Snæfell mt. Iceland **44** [inset] D2
Snaefell hill Isle of Man **47** H9
Snæfellsjökull ice cap Iceland **44** [inset] B2
Snæfellsnes pen. Iceland **44** [inset] B2
Snake r. Canada **166** C1
Snake r. NE U.S.A. **178** B3
Snake r. U.S.A. **180** B3
Snake Range mts U.S.A. **183** J2
Snake River Canada **166** F3
Snake River Plain U.S.A. **180** D4
Snare r. Canada **167** G2
Snare Lake Canada **167** J3
Snare Lakes Canada see Wekweti
Snares Islands N.Z. **145** F6
  also known as Tini Heke
Snåsa Norway **44** K2
Snåsvatn l. Norway **44** K2
Sneedville U.S.A. **176** B9
Sneek Neth. **48** C2
Sneem Rep. of Ireland **47** C12
Sneeuberge mts S. Africa **132** H8
Snegamook Lake Canada **169** I2
Snegurovka Ukr. see Tetiyiv
Snelling U.S.A. **182** D4
Sněpele Latvia **42** C5
Snezhed' r. Rus. Fed. **43** R8
Snezhnogorsk Rus. Fed. **39** I3
Snežka mt. Czech Rep. **49** M5
  also spelt Sněžka
Snežnik mt. Slovenia **56** G3
Śniardwy, Jezioro l. Poland **49** S2
Sniečkus Lith. see Visaginas
Sněžka mt. Czech Rep. see Snězka
Śnieżnik mt. Poland **49** N5
Snihurivka Ukr. **41** E7
Snina Slovakia **49** T7
Snøhetta mt. Norway **44** J3
Snohomish U.S.A. **180** B3
Snønuten mt. Norway **45** I4
Snopot' r. Rus. Fed. **43** O8
Snov r. Ukr. **43** N9
Snova r. Rus. Fed. **43** R9
Snova r. Rus. Fed. **43** T9
Snovsk Ukr. see Shchors
Snow Belarus **42** H8
Snowbird Lake Canada **167** K2
Snowcrest Mountain Canada **167** G5
Snowdon mt. U.K. **47** H10
Snowdonia National Park U.K. **47** I11
Snowdrift r. Canada **167** I2
Snowdrift Canada see Łutselk'e
Snowflake U.S.A. **183** N7
Snow Hill MD U.S.A. **177** J7
Snow Hill NC U.S.A. **174** E5
Snow Lake Canada **167** K4
Snowtown Australia **146** C3
Snow Water Lake U.S.A. **183** J1
Snowy r. Australia **147** F4
Snowy Mountain U.S.A. **177** K2
Snowy Mountains Australia **147** E4
Snowy, Vozyera l. Belarus **42** I6
Snug Corner Bahamas **187** E2
Snug Harbour Nfld. Canada **169** K2
Snug Harbour Ont. Canada **173** M5
Snyder OK U.S.A. **179** C5
Snyder TX U.S.A. **179** B5
Snyderspoort pass S. Africa **132** E8
Snykhovo Rus. Fed. **43** R8
Soahany Madag. **131** [inset] J4
Soaigh i. U.K. see Soay
Soalala Madag. **131** [inset] J3
Soamanonga Madag. **131** [inset] J4
Soanierana-Ivongo Madag. **131** [inset] K3
Soan-kundo is S. Korea **83** B6
Soata Col. **198** C3
Soavinandriana Madag. **131** [inset] J3
Soay i. U.K. **46** E7
  also spelt Soaigh
Sobaek-sanmaek mts S. Korea **83** B6
Sobaek-san National Park S. Korea **83** C5
Sobat r. Sudan **128** A2
Soběslav Czech Rep. **49** L6
Sobger r. Indon. **73** J7
Sobinka Rus. Fed. **43** V6
Sobolevo Rus. Fed. **43** T6
Sobo-san mt. Japan **91** B8
Sobradinho Brazil **206** F2
Sobradinho, Barragem de resr Brazil
  202 D4
Sobrado Bahia Brazil **202** D4
Sobrado Pará Brazil **199** H6
Sobral Brazil **202** D2
Sobrance Slovakia **49** T7

Soča r. Slovenia 56 F3
Sochaczew Poland 49 R3
Sochi Rus. Fed. 41 F8
Sŏch'ŏn S. Korea 83 B5
Sochos Greece 58 E8 also spelt Sokhós
Société, Archipel de la is Fr. Polynesia see Society Islands
▶Society Islands Fr. Polynesia 221 H7 also known as Société, Archipel de la oceania [issues] 140–141
Socol Romania 58 C4
Socompa Chile 200 C6
Soconusco, Sierra de mts Mex. see Madre, Sierra
Socorro Brazil 206 G9
Socorro Col. 198 C3
Socorro U.S.A. 181 F6
Socorro, Isla i. Mex. 184 C5
Socota Peru 198 B6
Socotra i. Yemen 105 F5 also spelt Suquṭrā
Socovos Spain 55 J6
Soc Trăng Vietnam 79 D6 formerly known as Khan Hung
Socuéllamos Spain 55 I5
Soda Lake CA U.S.A. 182 E6
Soda Lake CA U.S.A. 183 H6
Sodankylä Fin. 44 N2
Soda Plains Aksai Chin 89 B5
Soda Springs U.S.A. 180 E4
Söderhamn Sweden 45 L3
Söderköping Sweden 45 L4
Södermanland county Sweden 45 L4
Södertälje Sweden 45 L4
Sodiri Sudan 121 F6
Sodium S. Africa 132 H7
Sodo Eth. 128 C3
Södra Kvarken strait Fin./Sweden 45 L3
Sodus U.S.A. 177 H2
Sodwana Bay National Park S. Africa 133 Q4
Soë Indon. 75 C5
Soekmekaar S. Africa 131 F4
Soela väin sea chan. Estonia 42 D3
Soerabaia Indon. see Surabaya
Soest Germany 48 F4
Soetdoring Nature Reserve S. Africa 133 K5
Soetendalsvlei l. S. Africa 132 D11
Sofades Greece 59 D9
Sofala Moz. 131 G4
Sofala prov. Moz. 131 G3 formerly known as Beira
Sofala, Baía de b. Moz. 131 G4
▶Sofia Bulg. 58 E6 Capital of Bulgaria. Also spelt Sofiya; historically known as Sardica or Serdica or Sredets.
Sofia r. Madag. 131 [inset] J2
Sofiko Greece 59 E11
Sofiya Bulg. see Sofia
Sofiyevka Ukr. see Vil'nyans'k
Sofiysk Khabarovskiy Kray Rus. Fed. 82 D1
Sofiysk Khabarovskiy Kray Rus. Fed. 82 E2
Sofporog Rus. Fed. 44 O2
Sofrino Rus. Fed. 43 S5
Sofra Kalesi tourist site Turkey 108 D1
Sōfu-gan i. Japan 81 O7 English form Lot's Wife
Sog China 89 F6 also known as Garqêntang
Sogamoso Col. 198 C3
Sogat China 88 D3 formerly spelt Süget
Sogda Rus. Fed. 82 D2
Sogma China 89 C5
Søgne Norway 45 I4
Sognefjorden inlet Norway 45 I3
Sogn og Fjordane county Norway 45 I3
Sogo Rus. Fed. 39 M2
Sogod Phil. 74 C4
Sogod Bay Phil. 74 C4
Sogo Hills Kenya 128 C4
Sogolle well Chad 120 B6
Sogo Nur l. China 84 D3
Sogozha r. Rus. Fed. 43 U3
Söğüt Turkey 106 B2
Söğüt Dağı mts Turkey 106 B3
Sŏgwip'o S. Korea 83 B6
Sohâg Egypt 121 F3 also spelt Sūhāj
Sohagpur India 96 C5
Sohalinskiy Kazakh. 103 G2
Sohan r. Pak. 101 G3
Sohano P.N.G. 145 E2
Sohar Oman see Şuḩār
Sohela India 97 D5
Sohna India 96 C3
Sohng Gwe, Khao hill Myanmar/Thai. 79 B5
Soignies Belgium 51 K2
Soila China 86 A2
Soini Fin. 44 N3
Soissons France 51 J3
Sōja Japan 91 C7
Sojat India 96 B4
Sojat Road India 96 B4
Sojoton Point Phil. 74 B4
Sok r. Rus. Fed. 41 I5
Sokch'o S. Korea 83 C5
Söke Turkey 106 A3
Sokele Dem. Rep. Congo 127 E7
Sokhondo, Gora mt. Rus. Fed. 85 F1
Sokhor, Gora mt. Rus. Fed. 85 E1
Sokhós Greece see Sochos
Sokhumi Georgia 107 E2 also known as Aq'a; also spelt Sukhumi; historically known as Dioscurias or Sukhum-Kale
Sokiryany Ukr. see Sokyryany
Sokkuram Grotto tourist site S. Korea 90 A7
Soknedal Norway 44 J3
Sokobanja Srbija Yugo. 58 C5
Sokodé Togo 125 F4
Soko Islands Hong Kong China 87 [inset] also known as Shekka Ch'ün-Tao
Sokol Rus. Fed. 82 F3
Sokol Rus. Fed. 43 V2
Sokolac Bos.-Herz. 56 K5
Sokółka Poland 49 U2
Sokol'niki Tul'skaya Oblast' Rus. Fed. 43 T7
Sokol'niki Tverskaya Oblast' Rus. Fed. 43 P5
Sokolo Mali 124 D3
Sokolov Czech Rep. 49 J5
Sokolovka Rus. Fed. 90 C3
Sokołów Małopolski Poland 49 T5
Sokołow Podlaski Poland 49 T3
Sokolozero, Ozero l. Rus. Fed. 44 O2
Sokone Senegal 124 A3
Sokosti hill Fin. 44 O1
Sokoto Nigeria 125 G3
Sokoto r. Nigeria 125 G4
Sokoto state Nigeria 125 G3
Sokourala Guinea 124 C4
Sokyryany Ukr. 41 C6 also spelt Sokiryany
Sola Cuba 186 D2
Sola r. Poland 49 Q6
Sola i. Tonga see Ata
Solan India 96 C3
Solana Beach U.S.A. 183 G9
Solander Island N.Z. 153 A14
Solanet Arg. 204 F5
Solano Phil. 74 B2
Solano Venez. 199 E4
Solapur India 94 B2 formerly spelt Sholapur
Soldado Bartra Peru 198 C5
Soldotna U.S.A. 164 D3
Solec Kujawski Poland 49 P2
Soledad Arg. 204 E3
Soledad U.S.A. 182 C5
Soledad Venez. 199 F2
Soledad de Doblado Mex. 185 F5
Soledade Brazil 198 D6
Solen mt. Norway 45 J3
Solenoye Rus. Fed. 41 G7
Solenzo Burkina 124 D3
Solfjellsjøen Norway 44 K2
Solginskiy Rus. Fed. 40 G3
Solhan Turkey 107 E3
Soligalich Rus. Fed. 40 G4
Soligorsk Belarus see Salihorsk
Solihull U.K. 47 K11
Solikamsk Rus. Fed. 40 K4
Sol'-Iletsk Rus. Fed. 102 C2
Soliman Tunisia 57 C12
Solimón, Punta pt Mex. 185 I5
Solingen Germany 48 E4
Solita Col. 198 C4
Solita Venez. 187 F5
Sol-Karmala Rus. Fed. see Severnoye
Sölktäler nature res. Austria 49 K8
Sollefteå Sweden 44 L3
Sollentuna Sweden 45 L4
Sóller Spain 55 N5
Sollerön Sweden 45 K3
Solling hills Germany 48 G4
Solnechnogorsk Rus. Fed. 43 R5
Solnechnyy Rus. Fed. 82 E2
Solnechnyy Rus. Fed. see Gornyy
Solo r. Java Indon. 77 E4
Solo r. Sulawesi Indon. 75 B3
Solofra Italy 57 G8
Solok Indon. 76 C3
Sololá Guat. 185 H6
Solomon U.S.A. 183 O9
Solomon r. U.S.A. 178 C4
Solomon, North Fork r. U.S.A. 178 C4
Solomon, South Fork r. U.S.A. 178 C4
▶Solomon Islands country S. Pacific Ocean 145 F2 4th largest and 5th most populous country in Oceania. Formerly known as British Solomon Islands. oceania [countries] 138–139
Solomon Sea P.N.G./Solomon Is 145 E2
Solon China 85 I2
Solon U.S.A. 172 B9
Solor i. Indon. 75 B5
Solor, Kepulauan is Indon. 75 B5
Solotcha Rus. Fed. 43 U7
Solothurn Switz. 51 N5
Solovetskiy Rus. Fed. 40 E2 formerly known as Kreml'
Solovetskiye Ostrova is Rus. Fed. 40 E2
Solovetskoye Rus. Fed. 40 H4
Solov'yevo Rus. Fed. 43 N7
Solov'yevsk Mongolia 85 G1
Solov'yevsk Rus. Fed. 82 B1
Solsona Spain 55 M3
Solt Hungary 49 Q9
Šolta i. Croatia 56 I5
Soltānābād Khorāsan Iran 100 D2
Soltānābād Iran 101 D3
Soltānābād Tehrān Iran 100 B3
Soltān-e Bakva Afgh. 101 E3
Soltānī, Khowr-e b. Iran 100 B4
Soltanqolī Iran 100 A3
Soltau Germany 48 G3
Sol'tsy Rus. Fed. 43 L3
Soltüstik Qazaqstan Oblysy admin. div. Kazakh. see Severnyy Kazakhstan
Soltvadkert Hungary 49 Q9
Solunska Glava mt. Macedonia 58 C7
Solvang U.S.A. 182 D7
Solvay U.S.A. 177 I2
Sölvesborg Sweden 45 K4
Sol'vychegodsk Rus. Fed. 40 H3
Solway Firth est. U.K. 47 I9
Solwezi Zambia 127 E8
Sōma Japan 90 G6
Soma Turkey 106 A3
Somabhula Zimbabwe 131 F3 formerly spelt Somabula
Somabula Zimbabwe see Somabhula
Somali admin. reg. Eth. 128 D3
▶Somalia country Africa 128 E4 spelt Soomaaliya in Somali; long form Somali Republic africa [countries] 114–117
Somali Republic country Africa see Somalia
Somanga Tanz. 129 C7
Somanya Ghana 125 E5
Sombang, Gunung mt. Indon. 77 G2
Sombo Angola 127 D7
Sombor Vojvodina, Srbija Yugo. 58 A3 also spelt Zombor
Sombrerete Mex. 184 E4
Sombrero i. Anguilla 187 H3
Sombrero Chile 205 C9
Sombrero Channel India 95 G5
Somdari India 96 B4
Somero Fin. 45 M3
Somerset KY U.S.A. 176 A8
Somerset MA U.S.A. 177 N4
Somerset MI U.S.A. 173 I8
Somerset OH U.S.A. 176 C6
Somerset PA U.S.A. 176 F6
Somerset East S. Africa 133 J9
Somerset Island Canada 165 J2
Somerset West S. Africa 132 C11
Somersworth U.S.A. 177 O2
Somerton U.S.A. 183 J9
Someru Estonia 42 H2
Somerville NJ U.S.A. 177 K5
Somerville TN U.S.A. 174 B5
Somerville Reservoir U.S.A. 179 C6
Someşan, Podişul plat. Romania 58 E2
Someş Cald r. Romania 58 E2
Someşul Mare r. Romania 58 E1
Someşu Mic r. Romania 58 E1
Somesville U.S.A. 177 Q1
Someydeh Iran 100 A3 also spelt Samaida
Somino Rus. Fed. 43 P2
Somkele S. Africa 133 Q5
Sommarøy Norway 44 L1
Somme r. France 50 H2
Sommen l. Sweden 45 K4
Sömmerda Germany 48 I4
Sommet, Lac du l. Canada 169 G2
Somnath India 94 A1 also known as Patan
Somogyszob Hungary 49 O9
Somosomo Fiji 145 H3
Somotillo Nicaragua 186 B4
Somoto Nicaragua 186 B4
Somovo Orlovskaya Oblast' Rus. Fed. 43 Q9
Somovo Tul'skaya Oblast' Rus. Fed. 43 R8
Sompeta India 95 E2
Sompolno Poland 49 P3
Somport, Col du pass France/Spain 55 K2
Šomrda hill Yugo. 58 C4
Somuncurá, Mesa Volcánica de plat. Arg. 204 D6
Somvarpet India 94 B3
Son r. India 96 E4
Soná Panama 186 C6
Sonag China see Zêkog
Sonai r. India 97 G4
Sonai r. India 97 G4
Sonakhan India 97 D5
Sonala India 94 C1
Sonaly Kazakh. 103 G2
Sonamukhi India 97 E5
Sonapur India 95 D1
Sonari India 97 G4
Sŏnch'ŏn N. Korea 83 B5
Sondalo Italy 56 C2
Sønderå r. Denmark 48 F1
Sønderborg Denmark 45 J5
Sondershausen Germany 48 H4
Sønderup Denmark 45 J4
Søndre Strømfjord Greenland see Kangerlussuaq
Søndre Strømfjord inlet Greenland see Kangerlussuaq
Søndre Upernavik Greenland see Upernavik Kujalleq
Sondrio Italy 56 B2
Sonepet India 94 C2
Song Nigeria 125 I4
Songa Indon. 75 C3
Songad India 96 A5
Songbai China see Shennongjia
Songbu China 87 E2
Sông Cau Vietnam 79 E5
Songcheng China see Xiapu
Sông Đa, Hô resr Vietnam 78 D3
Songea Tanz. 129 B7
Sŏnggan N. Korea 83 B4
Songhua Hu resr China 82 B4
Songhua Jiang r. China 82 D3 English form Sungari
Songjiachuan China see Wubu
Songjiang Jilin China 82 C4 formerly known as Antu
Songjiang Shanghai China 87 G2 formerly known as Sungkiang
Songjianghe China 82 B4
Sŏngjin N. Korea see Kimch'aek
Sŏngju S. Korea 91 A7
Songkan China 86 C2
Songkhla Thai. 79 C7 also known as Singora
Song Khram, Mae Nam r. Thai. 78 D4
Songköl l. Kyrg. 103 H4 also known as Sonkël', Ozero
Songling China 85 I2
Song Ling mts China 85 H3
Songmai China see Dêrong
Songming China 86 B3 also known as Songyang
Sŏngnam S. Korea 83 B5
Songnim N. Korea 83 B5
Songni-san National Park S. Korea 83 B5
Songo Angola 127 B6
Songo Moz. 131 G2
Songololo Dem. Rep. Congo 127 B6
Songololo Dem. Rep. Congo see Mbanza-Ngungu
Songpan China 86 B1 also known as Jin'an or Sungqu
Songsak India 97 F4
Sŏngsan S. Korea 83 B6
Songshan China see Ziyun
Song Shan mt. China 87 E1
Songtao China 87 D2
Songxi China 87 F3 also known as Songyuan
Songxian China 87 E1
Songyang China see Songming
Songyuan China see Songxi
Songyuan China 82 B3 also known as Ningjiang; formerly known as Fuyu
Songzi China 87 D2 formerly known as Xinjiangkou
Sonhat India 97 D5
Sonid Youqi China see Saihan Tal
Sonid Zuoqi China see Mandalt
Sonipat India 96 C3
Sonkach India 96 C5
Sonkajärvi Fin. 44 N3
Sonkël', Ozero l. Kyrg. see Songköl
Sonkovo Rus. Fed. 43 S4
Sơn La Vietnam 78 C3
Sonmiani Bay Pak. 101 F5
Sonneberg Germany 48 I5
Sonnenjoch mt. Austria 48 J8
Sono r. Minas Gerais Brazil 203 C6
Sono r. Tocantins Brazil 202 B4
Sonoita watercourse Mex. 181 D7
Sonoma U.S.A. 182 B3
Sonoma Peak U.S.A. 182 G1
Sonora r. Mex. 184 C2
Sonora state Mex. 184 C2
Sonora CA U.S.A. 182 D4
Sonora TX U.S.A. 179 B6
Sonora Peak U.S.A. 182 E3
Sonqor Iran 100 A3
Sonseca Spain 54 H5
Son Servera Spain 55 O5
Sonsón Col. 198 C3
Sonsonate El Salvador 185 H6
Sonsorol Islands Palau 73 H5 also spelt Sansoral Islands
Sonstraal S. Africa 132 G4
Son Tây Vietnam 78 D3
Sonthofen Germany 48 H8
Sonwabile S. Africa 133 M8
Soochow China see Suzhou
Soodla r. Estonia 42 G2
Soomaaliya country Africa see Somalia
Soperton U.S.A. 175 D5
Sopi, Tanjung pt Indon. 75 D2
Sopo watercourse Sudan 126 E2
Sopot Bulg. 58 F6
Sopot Poland 49 P1
Sopot Srbija Yugo. 58 B4
Sopron Hungary 49 N8 historically known as Ödenburg
Sopu-Korgon Kyrg. 88 A3 also known as Sufi-Kurgan
Sopur Jammu and Kashmir 96 B2
Soputan, Gunung vol. Indon. 75 C2
Sor r. France 51 I9
Sôr r. Port. 54 C6
Sor r. Spain 54 D1
Sora Italy 56 F7
Sorab India 94 B3
Söråker Sweden 44 L3
Sŏrak-san mt. S. Korea 83 C5
Sorak-san National Park S. Korea 83 C5
Sorata Bol. 200 C3
Sør-Audnedal Norway 45 I4
Sorbas Spain 55 I7
Sorbe r. Spain 55 H4
Sor Donyztau dry lake Kazakh. 102 D3
Sorel Canada 169 F4
Sorell Australia 147 E5
Soreq r. Israel 108 F6
Sørfjorden inlet Norway 45 I3
Sorgono Sardegna Italy 57 B8
Sorgues France 51 K8
Sorgues r. France 51 I9
Sorgun Yozgat Turkey 106 C3 also known as Yeşilova
Sorgun r. Turkey 108 F1
Soria Spain 55 I3
Sorikmarapi vol. Indon. 76 B2
Sørkappøya i. Svalbard 38 B2
Sor Kaydak dry lake Kazakh. 102 C3
Sorkh, Kūh-e mts Iran 100 C3
Sorkheh Iran 100 C3
Sørland Norway 44 K2
Sørli Norway 44 K2
Sor Mertvyy Kultuk dry lake Kazakh. 102 C3 also known as Öli Qoltyq Sory
Sörmjöle Sweden 44 M3
Sorø Denmark 45 J5
Soro India 97 E5
Soro, Monte mt. Sicilia Italy 57 G11
Soroca Moldova 41 D6 formerly spelt Soroki
Sorocaba Brazil 206 F10
Sorochinsk Rus. Fed. 102 C1
Soroki Moldova see Soroca
Sorokino Rus. Fed. 43 K4
Sorol atoll Micronesia 73 J5 formerly known as Philip Atoll
Sorong Indon. 73 H7
Sororó r. Brazil 202 B3
Sororoca Brazil 199 F4
Sorot' r. Rus. Fed. 43 J4
Soroti Uganda 128 B4
Sørøya i. Norway 44 M1
Sørøysundet sea chan. Norway 44 M1
Sorp Turkey see Reşadiye
Sorraia r. Port. 54 C5
Sørreisa Norway 44 L1
Sorrento Italy 57 G8
Sorsakoski Fin. 44 N3
Sorsatunturi hill Fin. 44 O2
Sorsele Sweden 44 L2
Sorso Sardegna Italy 57 A8
Sorsogon Phil. 74 C3
Sortavala Rus. Fed. 45 O3
Sortland Norway 44 K1
Sortot Sudan 121 F5
Sør-Trøndelag county Norway 44 J3
Sørvær Norway 44 M1
Sørvågen Norway 44 K2
Sõrve väin sea chan. Estonia/Latvia see Irbe Strait
Sŏsan S. Korea 83 B5
Sosedno Rus. Fed. 43 J3
Sosenskiy Rus. Fed. 43 Q7
Soshanguve S. Africa 133 M2
Soskovo Rus. Fed. 43 Q9
Sosna r. Rus. Fed. 43 T9
Sosnogorsk Rus. Fed. 40 J3 formerly known as Izhma
Sosnovka Kazakh. 103 I2
Sosnovka Arkhangel'skaya Oblast' Rus. Fed. 40 H3
Sosnovka Murmanskaya Oblast' Rus. Fed. 40 G2
Sosnovka Tambovskaya Oblast' Rus. Fed. 41 G5
Sosnovka Vologod. Obl. Rus. Fed. 43 S3
Sosnovka Vologod. Obl. Rus. Fed. 43 U2
Sosnovo Rus. Fed. 43 L1
Sosnovoborsk Rus. Fed. 41 H5
Sosnovo-Ozerskoye Rus. Fed. 81 I2
Sosnovyy Rus. Fed. 44 P2
Sosnovyy Bor Belarus see Sasnovy Bor
Sosnovyy Bor Rus. Fed. 43 K2
Sosnowiec Poland 49 Q5 historically known as Sosnowitz
Sosnowitz Poland see Sosnowiec
Sosny Belarus 42 I9
Sosso Cent. Afr. Rep. 126 B4
Sos'va Rus. Fed. 38 G4
Sot' r. Rus. Fed. 43 V4
Sota r. Benin 125 F4
Sotang China 97 G3
Sotério r. Brazil 201 D2
Sotillo r. Spain 54 F6
Sotkamo Fin. 44 O2
Soto Arg. 204 D3
Soto la Marina Mex. 185 F4
Sotouboua Togo 125 F4
Sotteville-lès-Rouen France 50 H3
Sottunga Fin. 45 M3
Sotuta Mex. 185 H4
Souanké Congo 126 B4
Soubré Côte d'Ivoire 124 D5
Soucis, Cape N.Z. 152 H9
Souda Greece 59 F13
Soudan Australia 148 C4
Soudas, Ormos b. Greece 59 F13
Soúdha Greece see Souda
Soufli Greece 58 H7
Soufrière vol. Guadeloupe 187 H3
Soufrière St Lucia 187 H4
Soufrière vol. St Vincent 199 F1
Soufrière Hills Montserrat 187 H3
Souguéta Guinea 124 B4
Sougueur Alg. 55 M9
Souillac France 50 H8
Souilly France 51 L3
Souk Ahras Alg. 123 G1
Souk el Arbaâ du Rharb Morocco 122 D2
Souk el Had el Rharbia Morocco 54 F9
Souk el Kella Morocco 54 F9
Souk Khemis du Sahel Morocco 54 E9
Soukoukoutane Niger 125 F3
Souk Tleta Taghramet Morocco 54 F9
Souk-Tnine-de-Sidi-el-Yamani Morocco 54 F9
Sŏul S. Korea see Seoul
Soulac-sur-Mer France 50 E7
Sounding Creek r. Canada 167 I4
Sounfat well Mali see Tessoûnfat
Sounio nat. park Greece 59 F11
Soûr Lebanon see Tyre
Sourdeval France 50 F4
Soure Brazil 202 B2
Sour el Ghozlane Alg. 55 O8
Souris Man. Canada 167 K5
Souris P.E.I. Canada 169 I4
Souris r. Canada 167 L5
Souriya country Asia see Syria
Souroumelli well Mauritania 124 C2
Sous, Oued watercourse Morocco 122 C3
Sousa Brazil 202 E3
Sousa Lara Angola see Bocoio
Sousel Port. 54 D6
Sousse Tunisia 123 H2 also spelt Susah; historically known as Hadrumetum
Soussellem, Oued watercourse Alg. 55 N9
Soustons France 50 E9
Sout r. S. Africa 132 C8
Sout watercourse S. Africa 132 E5
South Africa country Africa see South Africa, Republic of
▶South Africa, Republic of country Africa 130 D6 known as Suid-Afrika in Afrikaans; short form South Africa africa [countries] 114–117
South Alligator r. Australia 148 B2
Southampton Canada 168 D4
Southampton U.K. 47 K13 historically known as Hamwic
Southampton U.S.A. 177 M5
Southampton Island Canada 167 O1
South Andaman i. India 95 G4
South Anna r. U.S.A. 176 H8
South Aulatsivik Island Canada 169 I1
South Australia state Australia 146 B2
Southaven U.S.A. 174 B5
South Baldy mt. U.S.A. 181 F6
South Bay U.S.A. 175 D7
South Bend IN U.S.A. 174 C3
South Bend WA U.S.A. 180 B3
South Bluff pt Bahamas 187 E2
South Boston U.S.A. 176 G9
Southbridge N.Z. 153 G11
Southbridge U.S.A. 177 M3
South Brook Canada 169 J3
South Burlington U.S.A. 177 L1
Southburn N.Z. 153 F12
South Carolina state U.S.A. 175 D5
South Charleston OH U.S.A. 176 B6
South Charleston WV U.S.A. 176 D7
South China Sea N. Pacific Ocean 72 E4
South Coast Town Australia see Gold Coast
South Dakota state U.S.A. 178 B2
South Deerfield U.S.A. 177 M3
South Downs hills U.K. 47 L13
South East admin. dist. Botswana 133 J2
South East Cape Australia 147 E5
South East Isles Australia 151 C7
Southend Canada 167 K3
Southend-on-Sea U.K. 47 M12
Southern admin. reg. Eth. 128 C3
Southern admin. reg. Malawi 129 B8
Southern prov. Sierra Leone 124 B5
Southern prov. Zambia 127 E9
Southern Aegean admin. reg. Greece see Notio Aigaio
Southern Alps mts N.Z. 153 E11 also known as Kā Tiritiri o te Moana
Southern Central Aboriginal Reserve Australia 151 D5
Southern Cross Australia 151 B6
Southern Darfur state Sudan 126 E2
Southern Indian Lake Canada 167 L3
Southern Kordofan state Sudan 128 A2
Southern Lau Group is Fiji 145 H3
Southern National Park Sudan 126 F3
Southern Ocean 222 F3
Southern Pines U.S.A. 174 E5
Southern Rhodesia country Africa see Zimbabwe
Southern Uplands hills U.K. 46 H8
Southern Urals mts Rus. Fed. see Yuzhnyy Ural
Southern Ute Indian Reservation res. U.S.A. 181 F5
South Esk Tableland reg. Australia 150 D3
Southey Canada 167 J5
Southeyville S. Africa 133 L8
South Fabius r. U.S.A. 178 E4
Southfield U.S.A. 173 J8
Southfields U.S.A. 177 K4
South Fork CA U.S.A. 182 A1
South Fork CO U.S.A. 181 F5
South Fork PA U.S.A. 176 G5
South Fox Island U.S.A. 172 H5
Southgate r. Canada 166 E5
South Geomagnetic Pole (2000) Antarctica 223 H1
▶South Georgia and South Sandwich Islands terr. S. Atlantic Ocean 217 L9 United Kingdom Overseas Territory. southamerica [countries] 192–193
South Gillies Canada 172 D2
South Grand r. U.S.A. 178 D4
South Hatia Island Bangl. 97 F5
South Haven U.S.A. 172 G8
South Head N.Z. 152 I4
South Head N.Z. 152 I4
South Henik Lake Canada 167 L2
South Hero U.S.A. 177 L1
South Hill U.S.A. 176 G9
South Horr Kenya 128 C4
South Indian Lake Canada 167 L3
South Island India 94 B4
▶South Island N.Z. 153 G12 2nd largest island in Oceania. Also known as Te Waipounamu. oceania [landscapes] 136–137
South Islet reef Phil. 74 A4
South Junction Canada 167 M5
South Kazakhstan Oblast admin. div. Kazakh. see Yuzhnyy Kazakhstan
South Kitui National Reserve nature res. Kenya 128 C5
South Koel r. India 97 E5
▶South Korea country Asia 83 B5 asia [countries] 64–67
South Lake Tahoe U.S.A. 182 D3
Southland admin. reg. N.Z. 153 B13
South Loup r. U.S.A. 178 C3
South Luangwa National Park Zambia 127 F8
South Macmillan r. Canada 166 C2
South Magnetic Pole (2000) Antarctica 223 J2
South Manitou Island U.S.A. 173 G5
South Mills U.S.A. 177 I9
Southminster U.K. 47 M12
South Moose Lake Canada 167 K4
South Mountains hills U.S.A. 177 H6
South Muiron Island Australia 150 A4
South Nahanni r. Canada 166 D1
South Negril Point Jamaica 186 D3
South New Berlin U.S.A. 177 J3
South Orkney Islands S. Atlantic Ocean 222 V2
South Paris U.S.A. 177 O1
South Passage Australia 151 A5
South Patrick Shores U.S.A. 175 D6
South Platte r. U.S.A. 178 B3
South Point pt U.S.A. 181 [inset] Z2
South Pole Antarctica 223 T1
South Porcupine Canada 173 L2
Southport Australia 147 E5
Southport U.K. 47 I10
Southport NC U.S.A. 175 E5
Southport NY U.S.A. 177 I3
South Portland U.S.A. 177 O2
South River Canada 173 N5
South Ronaldsay i. U.K. 46 J5
South Royalton U.S.A. 177 M2
South Salt Lake U.S.A. 183 M1
South San Francisco U.S.A. 182 B4
South Saskatchewan r. Canada 167 J4
South Seal r. Canada 167 L3
South Shetland Islands Antarctica 222 U2
South Shields U.K. 47 K8
South Sinai governorate Egypt see Janūb Sīnā'
South Skunk r. U.S.A. 174 A3
South Taranaki Bight b. N.Z. 152 I7
South Tent mt. U.S.A. 183 M2
South Tons r. India 97 D4
South Tucson U.S.A. 183 N9
South Turkana Nature Reserve Kenya 128 B4
South Twin Island Canada 168 E2
South Twin Lake Canada 169 K3
South Uist i. U.K. 46 E6 also known as Uibhist a' Deas
South Umpqua r. U.S.A. 180 B4
South Wellesley Islands Australia 148 C3
South-West Africa country Africa see Namibia
South West Cape Australia 147 E5
South West Cape N.Z. 153 B15 also known as Puhiwaero
South West Cay reef Australia 149 G4
Southwest Conservation Area nature res. Australia 147 E5
South West Entrance sea chan. P.N.G. 149 F1
Southwest Harbor U.S.A. 177 Q1
South West Island Australia 149 F3
South West National Park Australia 147 E5
South West Rocks Australia 147 G2
South Whitley U.S.A. 172 H9
South Williamson U.S.A. 176 C8
South Williamsport U.S.A. 177 I4
South Windham U.S.A. 177 O2
Southwold U.K. 47 N11
Southwood National Park Australia 147 F1
South Zanesville U.S.A. 176 C6
Soutpansberg mts S. Africa 131 F4
Souttouf, Adrar mts W. Sahara 122 B5
Souvigny France 51 J6
Sovata Romania 58 G2
Soveja Romania 58 H2
Soverato Italy 57 I10
Sovet Tajik. 101 G2
Sovetabad Uzbek. see Khanabad
Sovetsk Kaliningradskaya Oblast' Rus. Fed. 42 C6 historically known as Tilsit
Sovetsk Kirovskaya Oblast' Rus. Fed. 40 I4
Sovetsk Tul'skaya Oblast' Rus. Fed. 43 S8
Sovetskaya Rus. Fed. 107 F1
Sovetskaya Gavan' Rus. Fed. 82 F2
Sovetskiy Khanty-Mansiyskiy Avtonomnyy Okrug Rus. Fed. 38 G3
Sovetskiy Leningradskaya Oblast' Rus. Fed. 43 J1
Sovetskiy Respublika Mariy El Rus. Fed. 40 I4
Sovetskiy Tajik. see Sovet
Sovetskoye Rus. Fed. see Shatoy
Sovetskoye Rus. Fed. 102 A2
Sovetskoye Rus. Fed. see Zelenokumsk
Soviči Bos.-Herz. 56 J5
Sowa Botswana 131 E4
Sowa China 86 A2 formerly known as Dagxoi
Sowa Pan salt pan Botswana 131 E4
Soweto S. Africa 133 L3
Sōya-kaikyō strait Japan/Rus. Fed. see La Pérouse Strait
Soyaló Mex. 185 G5
Sōya-misaki c. Japan 90 G2
Soyana r. Rus. Fed. 40 G2
Soyang-ho l. S. Korea 83 B5
Soyaux France 50 G7
Sōya-wan b. Japan 90 G2
Soylan Armenia see Vayk'
Soyma r. Rus. Fed. 40 I2
Soyo Angola 127 B6 formerly known as Santo António do Zaire
Sozaq Kazakh. see Suzak
Sozh r. Europe 43 L9
Sozimskiy Rus. Fed. 40 J4
Sozopol Bulg. 58 I6 historically known as Apollonia
Spaatz Island Antarctica 222 T2
Spadafora Sicilia Italy 57 H10
▶Spain country Europe 54 F4 4th largest country in Europe. Known as España in Spanish; historically known as Hispania. europe [countries] 32–35
Spalato Croatia see Split
Spalatum Croatia see Split
Spalding Australia 146 C3
Spalding U.K. 47 L11
Spaniard's Bay Canada 169 K4
Spanish Canada 168 D4
Spanish r. Canada 168 D4
Spanish Fork U.S.A. 183 M1
Spanish Guinea country Africa see Equatorial Guinea
Spanish Netherlands country Europe see Belgium
Spanish Point Rep. of Ireland 47 C11
Spanish Sahara terr. Africa see Western Sahara
Spanish Town Jamaica 186 D3
Spanish Wells Bahamas 175 E7
Sparagio, Monte mt. Sicilia Italy 57 E10
Sparks U.S.A. 182 E2
Sparta Greece see Sparti
Sparta GA U.S.A. 175 D5
Sparta MI U.S.A. 172 H7
Sparta NC U.S.A. 176 D9
Sparta TN U.S.A. 174 C5
Sparta WI U.S.A. 172 C7
Spartanburg U.S.A. 174 D5
Spartansburg U.S.A. 176 F4
Spartel, Cap c. Morocco 54 F9
Sparti Greece 59 D11 historically known as Lacedaemon or Sparta
Spartivento, Capo c. Sardegna Italy 57 A10
Spartivento, Capo c. Italy 57 I11
Sparwood Canada 167 H5
Spas-Demensk Rus. Fed. 43 P7
Spas-Klepiki Rus. Fed. 43 V6
Spassk Rus. Fed. 43 Q6
Spasskaya Polist' Rus. Fed. 43 M3
Spassk-Dal'niy Rus. Fed. 82 D3
Spasskoye Kazakh. 103 G1
Spasskoye-Lutovinovo Rus. Fed. 43 R8
Spas-Ugol Rus. Fed. 43 S5
Spatha, Akra pt Greece 59 E13
Spatsizi Plateau Wilderness Provincial Park Canada 166 D3
Spean Bridge U.K. 46 H7
Spearfish U.S.A. 178 B2
Spearman U.S.A. 179 B4
Speers Canada 167 J4
Speightstown Barbados 187 I4
Speikkogel mt. Austria 49 M8
Speke Gulf Tanz. 128 B5
Spence Bay Canada see Taloyoak
Spencer IA U.S.A. 178 D3
Spencer ID U.S.A. 180 D3
Spencer IN U.S.A. 174 C4
Spencer MA U.S.A. 177 N3
Spencer NY U.S.A. 177 I3
Spencer VA U.S.A. 176 E9
Spencer, Cape Australia 146 C3
Spencer, Cape U.S.A. 166 B3
Spencer, Point U.S.A. 39 T3
Spencer Gulf est. Australia 146 C3
Spencer Range hills N.T. Australia 148 A2
Spencer Range hills N.T. Australia 148 B2
Spences Bridge Canada 166 F5
Spenser Mountains N.Z. 153 G10
Spercheios r. Greece 59 D10 also spelt Sperkhiós
Sperkhiós r. Greece see Spercheios
Spermezeu Romania 58 F1
Sperrin Mountains hills U.K. 47 E9
Sperryville U.S.A. 176 G7
Spétsai i. Greece see Spetses
Spetses Greece 59 E11
Spetses i. Greece 59 E11 also known as Spétsai
Spey r. U.K. 46 I6
Speyer Germany 48 F6
Spezand Pak. 101 F4
Spice Islands Indon. see Moluccas
Spiekeroog i. Germany 48 E2
Spiez Switz. 51 N6
Spijkenisse Neth. 48 B4
Spil Dağı Milli Parkı nat. park Turkey 59 I10
Spilimbergo Italy 56 E2
Spin Búldak Afgh. 101 F4
Spioenkop Dam Nature Reserve S. Africa 133 N5
Spirit Lake U.S.A. 178 D3
Spiritwood Canada 167 J4
Spirovo Rus. Fed. 43 P4
Spišská Nová Ves Slovakia 49 R7
Spitak Armenia 107 F2
Spiti r. India 96 C3
Spit Point Australia 150 B4
▶Spitsbergen i. Svalbard 38 B2 5th largest island in Europe. Also spelt Spitzbergen. europe [landscapes] 30–31
Spitskop mt. S. Africa 132 G10
Spitskopvlei S. Africa 133 J8
Spitsyno Rus. Fed. 42 I3
Spittal an der Drau Austria 49 K9
Spitzbergen i. Svalbard see Spitsbergen
Split Croatia 56 I5 formerly known as Spalato; historically known as Spalatum
Split Lake Canada 167 L3
Split Lake l. Canada 167 L3
Spokane U.S.A. 180 C3
Spokane r. U.S.A. 180 C3
Spokane Indian Reservation res. U.S.A. 180 C3
Spoon r. U.S.A. 174 B3
Spooner U.S.A. 172 B5
Spot Bay Cayman Is 186 D3
Spotsylvania U.S.A. 176 H7
Spragge Canada 173 K4
Sprague r. U.S.A. 180 B4
Spranger, Mount Canada 166 F4
Spratly Islands S. China Sea 72 D5
Spratly Islands S. China Sea 72 D5 also known as Nansha Qundao or Dan Dao Truong Sa or Truong Sa

Spread Eagle U.S.A. **172** E5
Spreča r. Bos.-Herz. **56** K4
Spree r. Germany **49** K3
Spreewald park Germany **49** L4
Spremberg Germany **49** L4
Spring r. U.S.A. **178** D4
Spring Bay Canada **173** K5
Springbok S. Africa **132** C6
Spring City U.S.A. **183** M2
Spring Creek r. Australia **148** C3
Spring Creek U.S.A. **183** I1
Springdale Canada **169** K3
Springdale U.S.A. **179** D4
Springe Germany **48** J3
Springer U.S.A. **181** F5
Springerville U.S.A. **183** O7
Springfield N.Z. **153** F11
Springfield CO U.S.A. **178** B4
Springfield GA U.S.A. **175** D5
▶ Springfield IL U.S.A. **174** B4
  State capital of Illinois.
Springfield KY U.S.A. **174** C4
Springfield MA U.S.A. **177** M3
Springfield MN U.S.A. **178** D2
Springfield MO U.S.A. **178** D4
Springfield OH U.S.A. **176** B6
Springfield OR U.S.A. **180** B3
Springfield TN U.S.A. **174** C4
Springfield VT U.S.A. **177** M2
Springfield WV U.S.A. **176** G6
Springfontein S. Africa **133** J7
Spring Garden Guyana **199** G3
Spring Glen U.S.A. **183** N2
Spring Green U.S.A. **172** C7
Spring Grove MN U.S.A. **172** B7
Spring Grove VA U.S.A. **177** I8
Springhill Canada **169** H4
Springhill U.S.A. **175** D6
Springhouse Canada **166** F5
Spring Mountains U.S.A. **183** I5
Springport U.S.A. **173** I8
Springs S. Africa **133** M3
Springs Junction N.Z. **153** G10
Springsure Australia **149** F5
Spring Valley S. Africa **133** K9
Spring Valley U.S.A. **183** H9
Springview U.S.A. **178** C3
Springville CA U.S.A. **182** F5
Springville NY U.S.A. **176** G3
Springville PA U.S.A. **177** J4
Springville UT U.S.A. **183** M1
Springwater U.S.A. **176** H3
Spruce Grove Canada **167** H4
Spruce Knob mt. U.S.A. **176** F7
Spruce Mountain CO U.S.A. **183** P3
Spruce Mountain NV U.S.A. **183** I1
Spulico, Capo c. Italy **57** I9
Spurn Head U.K. **47** M10
Spurr, Mount vol. U.S.A. **164** D3
Spuzzum Canada **166** F5
Squamish Canada **166** F5
Squam Lake U.S.A. **177** N2
Square Lake U.S.A. **174** G2
Squillace Italy **57** I10
Squillace, Golfo di g. Italy **57** I10
Squinzano Italy **57** K8
Squire U.S.A. **182** F1
Squires, Mount hill Australia **151** D5
Sragen Indon. **77** E4
Srbica Kosovo, Srbija Yugo. **58** B6
Srbija aut. rep. Yugo. **58** B5
  English form Serbia
Srbinje Bos.-Herz. see Foča
Srbobran Bos.-Herz. see Donji Vakuf
Srbobran Vojvodina, Srbija Yugo. **58** A3
Srebarna tourist site Bulg. see
  Srebarna
Srebarna Bulg. **58** J6
  formerly known as Grudovo
Srebrenica Bos.-Herz. **56** L4
Sredets Bulg. **58** I6
  formerly known as Sofia
Sredetska Reka r. Bulg. **58** I6
  formerly known as Grudovo
Sredinnyy Khrebet mts Rus. Fed. **39** P4
Srediste Bulg. **58** I5
Sredna Gora mts Bulg. **58** E6
Srednebelaya Rus. Fed. **82** B2
Srednekolymsk Rus. Fed. **39** N3
Sredne-Russkaya Vozvyshennost' hills
  Rus. Fed. see Central Russian Upland
Sredne-Sibirskoye Ploskogor'ye plat.
  Rus. Fed. see Central Siberian Plateau
Sredneye Kuyto, Ozero l. Rus. Fed. **44** O2
Srednogorie Bulg. **58** E6
Srednyaya Akhtuba Rus. Fed. **41** H6
Šrem Poland **49** O3
Srem reg. Yugo. **58** A3
Sremska Mitrovica Vojvodina, Srbija Yugo.
  58 A4
  historically known as Sirmium
Srêpôk, Tônlé r. Cambodia **79** D5
Sretensk Rus. Fed. **81** J2
Sri Aman Sarawak Malaysia **77** E2
  formerly known as Samarahan
Sriharikota India **94** D3
Sringeri India **94** B3
Sri Pada mt. Sri Lanka see Adam's Peak
Srirangam India **94** C4
Srisailam India **94** C2
Srivaikuntam India **94** C4
Srivardhan India **94** B2
Srivilliputtur India **94** C4
Srnetica mts Bos.-Herz. **56** I4
Srnice Bos.-Herz. **56** K4
  also known as Hasič
Środa Śląska Poland **49** N4
Środa Wielkopolska Poland **49** O3
Srpska Crnja Vojvodina, Srbija Yugo. **58** B3
Srpska Kostajnica Bos.-Herz. see
  Bosanska Kostajnica
Srpski Brod Bos.-Herz. see Bosanski Brod
Srpski Itebej Vojvodina, Srbija Yugo. **58** B3
Srungavarapukota India **95** D2
Sselki Rus. Fed. **43** U9
Staansaam S. Africa **132** D4
Staaten r. Australia **149** D3
Staaten River National Park Australia
  149 D3
Stabbursdalen Nasjonalpark nat. park
  Norway **44** M1
Staberhuk c. Germany **48** I1
Stabroek Guyana see Georgetown
Stade Germany **48** J2
Städjan-Nipfjällets naturreservat
  nature res. Sweden **45** K3
Stadskanaal Neth. **48** D3
Stadtallendorf Germany **48** G5
Stadthagen Germany **48** G3
Staffa i. U.K. **46** F7
Staffelstein Germany **48** H5
Stafford U.K. **47** J11
Stafford Creek Bahamas **186** D1
Stafford's Post S. Africa **133** N7
Stafford Springs U.S.A. **177** M4
Stagen Indon. **77** G3
Stagg Lake Canada **167** H2
Stahlstown U.S.A. **176** F5
Stahle Latvia **42** I4
Stakhanov Ukr. **41** F6
  formerly known as Kadiyevka or Sergo
Stakhanovo Rus. Fed. see Zhukovskiy
Stalin Bulg. see Varna
Stalin, Mount Canada **166** E3
Stalinabad Tajik. see Dushanbe
Stalingrad Rus. Fed. see Volgograd
Stalingradskaya Oblast' admin. div.
  Rus. Fed. see Volgogradskaya Oblast'
Staliniri Georgia see Ts'khinvali
Stalino Ukr. see Donets'k
Stalino Uzbek. see Shakhrikhan
Stalinogorsk Rus. Fed. see Novomoskovsk
Stalinogród Poland see Katowice
Stalinsk Rus. Fed. see Novokuznetsk
Stalowa Wola Poland **49** T5
Stalwart Point S. Africa **133** L10
Stamboliyski Bulg. **58** F6
Stamford Australia **149** D4
Stamford U.K. **47** L11
Stamford CT U.S.A. **177** L4
Stamford NY U.S.A. **177** K3
Stamford TX U.S.A. **179** C5
Stampalia i. Greece see Astypalaia
Stampriet Namibia **130** C5
Stamsund Norway **44** J1
Stanardsville U.S.A. **176** G7
Stancomb-Wills Glacier Antarctica **223** W1
Standerton S. Africa **133** N3
Standing Rock Indian Reservation res.
  U.S.A. **178** B2
Standish U.S.A. **173** J7
Stăneşti Romania **58** F4
Stanfield U.S.A. **183** M9
Stanford S. Africa **132** D11
Stanford KY U.S.A. **176** A8
Stanford MT U.S.A. **180** E3
Stangenestind hill Norway **44** O1
Stanger S. Africa **133** P6
Stănileşti Romania **58** J1
Stanislav Ukr. see Ivano-Frankivs'k
Stânişoarei, Munţii mts Romania **58** G1
Stanke Dimitrov Bulg. see Dupnitsa
Stanley Australia **147** E5
Stanley Hong Kong China **87** [inset]
  also known as Chek Chue
▶ Stanley Falkland Is **205** F8
  Capital of the Falkland Islands. Long form
  Port Stanley.
Stanley ID U.S.A. **180** D3
Stanley ND U.S.A. **178** B1
Stanley VA U.S.A. **176** G7
Stanley WI U.S.A. **172** C6
Stanley, Chutes waterfall Dem. Rep. Congo
  see Boyoma Falls
Stanley, Mount hill N.T. Australia **148** A4
Stanley, Mount hill Tas. Australia **147** F5
Stanley, Mount Dem. Rep. Congo/Uganda
  see Margherita Peak
Stanley Reservoir India **94** C4
Stanleyville Dem. Rep. Congo see
  Kisangani
Stann Creek Belize see Dangriga
Stanos Greece **59** C10
Stanovaya Rus. Fed. **43** T9
Stanovoye Rus. Fed. **43** T9
  formerly known as Ploskoye
Stanovoy Khrebet mts Rus. Fed. **81** K1
Stanovoy Kolodez' Rus. Fed. **43** R9
Stans Switz. **51** O6
Stansmore Range hills Australia **150** E4
Stansted airport U.K. **47** M12
Stanthorpe Australia **147** F2
Stanton KY U.S.A. **176** B8
Stanton MI U.S.A. **173** H7
Stanton ND U.S.A. **178** B2
Stanton NE U.S.A. **178** C3
Stanton TX U.S.A. **179** B5
Stantsiya Babarykino Rus. Fed. **43** T9
Stantsiya Skuratovo Rus. Fed. **43** S8
Stantsiya-Yakkabag Uzbek. see Yakkabag
Staples U.S.A. **178** D2
Stapleton U.S.A. **178** C3
Stąporków Poland **49** R4
Star r. U.S.A. **178** A7
Starachowice Poland **49** S4
Stara Huta Ukr. **43** O9
Stará Ľubovňa Slovakia **49** R6
Stara Pazova Vojvodina, Srbija Yugo. **58** B3
Stara Planina mts Bulg./Yugo. see
  Balkan Mountains
Staraya Kulatka Rus. Fed. **102** A1
Staraya Poltavka Rus. Fed. **102** A2
Staraya Russa Rus. Fed. **43** M5
Staraya Toropa Rus. Fed. **43** M5
Stara Zagora Bulg. **58** G6
Starbuck Island Kiribati **221** H6
  formerly known as Barren Island or Low
  Island or Starve Island
Starchiojd Romania **58** H3
Star City AR U.S.A. **174** B5
Star City IN U.S.A. **172** G10
Stargard in Pommern Poland see
  Stargard Szczeciński
Stargard Szczeciński Poland **49** M2
  historically known as Stargard in Pommern
Stari Ras and Sopoćani tourist site Yugo.
  58 B5
Staritsa Rus. Fed. **43** P5
Starke U.S.A. **175** D6
Starkey U.S.A. **176** F8
Starkovo Rus. Fed. **43** V6
Starkville U.S.A. **175** B5
Star Lake U.S.A. **177** J1
Starling Inlet Hong Kong China **87** [inset]
  also known as Sha Tau Kok Hoi
Starnberg Germany **48** I8
Starnberger See l. Germany **48** I8
Staroaleyskoye Rus. Fed. **88** C1
Starobel'sk Ukr. see Starobil's'k
Starobil's'k Ukr. **41** F6
  also known as Starobel'sk
Starobyn Belarus **42** I9
Starodub Rus. Fed. **43** N9
Starogard Gdański Poland **49** P2
  historically known as Preußisch Stargard
Starokonstantinov Ukr. see
  Starokostyantyniv
Starokostyantyniv Ukr. **41** C6
  also spelt Starokonstantinov
Starokozache Ukr. **58** K2
Starokozvove Bulg. **58** I6
Staromaksimkino Rus. Fed. **40** J5
Staroshcherbinovskaya Rus. Fed. **41** F7
Starosubkhangulovo Rus. Fed. **102** D1
Staroye Rus. Fed. **43** V2
Staroye Istomino Rus. Fed. **43** O6
Staroye Melkovo Rus. Fed. **43** P5
Staroye Sandovo Rus. Fed. **43** R3
Staroye Syalo Belarus **43** K6
Starcyur'yevo Rus. Fed. **41** G5
Starozhilovo Rus. Fed. **43** U7
Star Peak U.S.A. **182** F1
Starve Island Kiribati see Starbuck Island
Starynki Belarus **42** I7
Staryya Darohi Belarus **43** J8
  also spelt Staryye Dorogi
Staryy Dvor Rus. Fed. **43** V5
Staryye Dorogi Belarus see Staryya Darohi
Staryye Yurkovichi Rus. Fed. **43** M9
Staryy Kayak Rus. Fed. **39** K2
Staryy Nadym Rus. Fed. **38** H3
Staryy Oskol Rus. Fed. **41** F6
Staryy Sambir Ukr. **49** T6
  also spelt Staryy Sambor
Staryy Sambor Ukr. see Staryy Sambir
Staßfurt Germany **48** I4
Staszów Poland **49** S5
State College U.S.A. **176** H5
State Road U.S.A. **176** H5
State Road U.S.A. **176** E9
Statesboro U.S.A. **175** D5
Statesville U.S.A. **174** D5
Stathelle Norway **45** J4
Station r. U.K. **45** J3
Station No. 6 Sudan **121** G4
Station No. 10 Sudan **121** G5
Station Nord Greenland **165** R1
  also known as Nord
Statzberg hill Austria **49** M7
Stăuceni Moldova **58** J1
Staunton U.S.A. **176** F7
Stavanger Norway **45** I4
Stavertsi Bulg. **58** F5
Stavropol' Rus. Fed. **41** G7
  formerly known as Voroshilovsk
Stavropolka Kazakh. **103** F1
Stavropol' Kray admin. div. Rus. Fed. see
  Stavropol'skiy Kray
Stavropol'-na-Volge Rus. Fed. see Tol'yatti
Stavropol'skaya Vozvyshennost' hills
  Rus. Fed. **41** G7
Stavropol'skiy Kray admin. div. Rus. Fed.
  41 G7
  English form Stavropol Kray
Stavros Greece **58** E8
Stavros, Akra pt Kriti Greece **59** F13
Stavros, Akra pt Naxos Greece **59** G11
Stawbun Belarus **43** M9
Stawell Australia **147** D4
Stawell r. Australia **149** D4
Stawiski Poland **49** T2
Stawiszyn Poland **49** P4
Stawki, Park Krajobrazowy Poland **49** Q5
Stayki Rus. Fed. **43** Q8
Stayner Canada **173** M6
Stayton U.S.A. **180** B3
Steamboat U.S.A. **182** E2
Steamboat Springs U.S.A. **180** F4
Stearns U.S.A. **176** A9
Stebbins U.S.A. **164** C3
Steekdorings S. Africa **133** I4
Steel r. Canada **168** C3
Steele Island Antarctica **222** T2
Steelpoort S. Africa **133** O1
Steelton U.S.A. **177** I5
Steelville U.S.A. **174** B4
Steen r. Canada **167** G3
Steenkampsberge mts S. Africa **133** O2
Steen River Canada **167** G3
Steens Mountain U.S.A. **180** C4
Steenstrup Gletscher glacier Greenland
  see Sermersuaq
Steenvoorde France **51** I2
Steenwijk Neth. **48** D3
Steep Point Australia **151** A5
Stefanovci Greece **59** C10
Stefansson Bay Antarctica **223** D2
Stefansson Island Canada **165** I2
Ştefan Vodă Moldova **58** K2
  formerly known as Biruinţa or Kyzyl or
  Suvorovo; formerly spelt Ştefan-Vode
Ştefan Voda Romania **58** I4
Stege Denmark **45** K5
Stegi Swaziland see Siteki
Stegi Romania **58** I2
  formerly known as Doctor Petru Groza
Steiermark land Germany **48** F6
Steigerwald mts Germany **48** H6
Steigerwald park Germany **48** H6
Steilrand S. Africa **133** P4
Steinar Iceland **44** [inset] C3
Steinbach Canada **167** L5
Steinfurt Germany **48** E3
Steingaden Germany **48** H8
Steinhausen Namibia **130** C4
Steinhuder Meer, Naturpark nature res.
  Germany **48** G3
Steinkjer Norway **44** J2
Steinkopf S. Africa **132** C6
Steinsland Norway **46** R3
Stekaar S. Africa **132** H8
Stella S. Africa **133** I3
Stella Maris Bahamas **187** E2
Stellenbosch S. Africa **132** C10
Stello, Monte mt. Corse France **51** P10
Stelvio, Parco Nazionale dello nat. park
  Italy **56** C2
Stelvio, Passo dello pass Italy **56** C2
Stenay France **51** L3
Stendal Germany **48** I3
Stende Latvia **42** D4
Stenhouse, Mount hill Hong Kong China
  87 [inset]
  also known as Shan Tei Tong
Stenudden Sweden **44** L2
Stenungsund Sweden **45** J4
Steornabhagh U.K. see Stornoway
Stepanakert Azer. see Xankändi
Stepantsevo Rus. Fed. **43** R5
Stepantsevo Rus. Fed. **43** R5
Stephens, Cape N.Z. **152** H8
Stephens City U.S.A. **176** G6
Stephens Lake Canada **167** N3
Stephenson, Mount Antarctica **222** T2
Stephenville Canada **169** J3
Stephenville U.S.A. **179** C5
Stepne Ukr. **43** O9
Stepnogorsk Kazakh. **103** H1
Stepnoy Rus. Fed. see Elista
Stepnoye Saratovskaya Oblast' Rus. Fed.
  102 A2
Stepnoye Stavropol'skiy Kray Rus. Fed.
  107 F1
Stepnyak Kazakh. **103** G1
Stepojevac Srbija Yugo. **58** B4
Stepurino Rus. Fed. **43** Q5
Sterea Ellas admin. reg. Greece **59** E10
Sterkfontein Dam resr S. Africa **133** N5
Sterkspruit S. Africa **133** L7
Sterkstroom S. Africa **133** K8
Sterlet Lake Canada **167** I1
Sterlibashevo Rus. Fed. **102** C1
Sterling S. Africa **132** F8
Sterling CO U.S.A. **178** B3
Sterling IL U.S.A. **174** B3
Sterling KS U.S.A. **178** C4
Sterling MI U.S.A. **173** I6
Sterling UT U.S.A. **183** M2
Sterling City U.S.A. **179** B6
Sterling Heights U.S.A. **173** J8
Sterlitamak Rus. Fed. **102** C1
Sternberg Germany **48** I2
Šternberk Czech Rep. **49** O6
Stes-Maries-de-la-Mer France **51** K9
Steszew Poland **49** N3
Stettin Poland see Szczecin
Stettiner Haff b. Germany see Oderhaff
Stettler Canada **180** D1
Steubenville KY U.S.A. **176** A9
Steubenville OH U.S.A. **176** E5
Stevenage U.K. **47** L12
Stevens, Mount N.Z. **152** G8
Stevenson U.S.A. **180** B3
Stevenson Lake Canada **167** L4
Stevens Point U.S.A. **172** D6
Stevensville MD U.S.A. **177** I7
Stevensville MI U.S.A. **172** G8
Stevensville PA U.S.A. **177** I4
Steventon Island Antarctica **222** O1
Stewart r. Australia **149** D2
Stewart Canada **166** E4
Stewart r. Canada **166** B2
Stewart, Cape Australia **148** B1
Stewart, Isla i. Chile **205** C9
Stewart Crossing Canada **166** B2
Stewart Island nature res. N.Z. **153** B15
  also known as Rakiura
Stewart Islands Solomon Is **145** F2
Stewarts Point U.S.A. **182** A3
Stewart Valley Canada **167** J5
Stewiacke Canada **169** I4
Steynrus S. Africa **133** L4
Steynsburg S. Africa **133** J8
Steyr Austria **49** I7
Steytlerville S. Africa **133** I10
▶ St Helena and Dependencies terr.
  S. Atlantic Ocean **216**
  Consists of St Helena, Ascension, Tristan da
  Cunha and Gough Island.
  africa [countries] ▶ 114–117
Stif Alg. see Sétif
Stigler U.S.A. **179** D5
Stigliano Italy **57** I8
Stigtomta Sweden **45** L4
Stikine r. Canada **166** D3
Stikine Plateau Canada **166** D3
Stilbaai S. Africa **132** F11
Stilfontein S. Africa **133** K3
Stilis Greece see Stylida
Stillwater MN U.S.A. **172** A5
Stillwater OK U.S.A. **179** C4
Stillwater r. U.K. **47** N12
Stillwater National Wildlife Refuge
  nature res. U.S.A. **182** F2
Stillwater Range mts U.S.A. **182** F2
Stilo r. Kent, England U.K. **47** K13
Stilo, Punta pt Italy **57** I10
Štitit mt. Bos.-Herz. **56** J5
Stilwell U.S.A. **179** D4
Štimlje Kosovo, Srbija Yugo. **58** C6
Stinear, Mount Antarctica **223** E2
Stinnett U.S.A. **179** B5
Štip Macedonia **58** D7
Stipanov Grič mt. Croatia **56** H4
Stirling Australia **148** A3
Stirling Canada **173** P6
Stirling U.K. **46** I7
Stirling Creek r. Australia **148** A3
Stirling Range mts Australia **151** B7
Stirling Range National Park Australia
  151 B7
Stirrat U.S.A. **176** C8
Stittsville Canada **173** R5
Stjernøya i. Norway **44** M1
Stjørdalshalsen Norway **44** J3
Stockach Germany **48** G8
Stockbridge U.S.A. **173** I8
Stockerau Austria **49** N7
▶ Stockholm Sweden **45** L4
  Capital of Sweden.
Stockholm county Sweden **45** L4
Stockinbingal Australia **147** E3
Stockport U.K. **47** J10
Stocksbridge U.K. **47** K10
Stockton CA U.S.A. **182** C4
Stockton IL U.S.A. **172** C8
Stockton KS U.S.A. **178** C4
Stockton UT U.S.A. **183** L1
Stockton Island U.S.A. **172** C4
Stockton Lake U.S.A. **178** D4
Stockton-on-Tees U.K. **47** K9
Stockton Plateau U.S.A. **179** B6
Stockton Springs U.S.A. **177** Q1
Stockville U.S.A. **178** B3
Stoczek Łukowski Poland **49** S4
Stöde Sweden **44** L3
Stodolishche Rus. Fed. **43** N7
Stoeng Trêng Cambodia **79** D5
  also spelt Stung Treng
Stogovo Planina mts Macedonia **58** B7
Stoke-on-Trent U.K. **47** J10
Stokes, Mount N.Z. **152** H9
Stokes Inlet U.S.A. **157** C7
Stokes Point Australia **147** D5
Stokes Range hills Australia **148** A3
Stokkseyri Iceland **44** [inset] B3
Stokkvågen Norway **44** K2
Stokmarknes Norway **44** K1
Stol mt. Yugo. **58** D4
Stolac Bos.-Herz. **56** J5
Stolberg (Rheinland) Germany **48** D5
Stolbovoy Rus. Fed. **38** F2
Stolbovoy, Ostrov i. Rus. Fed. **39** N2
Stolbtsy Belarus see Stowbtsy
Stolice hill Bos.-Herz. **56** K4
Stolin Belarus **41** C6
Stollberg Germany **49** J5
Stołp Poland see Słupsk
Stolsheimen park Norway **45** I3
Stolzenau Germany **48** G3
Stompneusbaai S. Africa **132** B9
Stone U.K. **47** J11
Stoneboro U.S.A. **176** E4
Stonecliffe Canada **168** E4
Stonecutters' Island pen. Hong Kong China
  87 [inset]
  also known as Ngong Shuen Chau
Stoneham U.S.A. **180** G4
Stone Harbor U.S.A. **177** K6
Stonehaven U.K. **46** J7
Stonehenge Australia **149** D5
Stonehenge tourist site U.K. **47** K12
Stoneville U.S.A. **176** F9
Stonewall Canada **167** L5
Stoney Creek Canada **173** N7
Stony Point Canada **173** K7
Stonington U.S.A. **177** Q1
Stony Creek U.S.A. **176** H9
Stony Gorge Reservoir U.S.A. **182** B2
Stony Lake Canada **167** L3
Stony Point U.S.A. **177** I2
Stony Rapids Canada **167** J3
Stooping r. Canada **168** D2
Stör r. Germany **48** G2
Stora Le l. Sweden **45** J4
Stora Lulevatten l. Sweden **44** L2
Stora Sjöfallets nationalpark nat. park
  Sweden **44** L2
Storavan l. Sweden **44** L2
Storbäcken Sweden **45** K3
Storbekkfjellet mt. Norway **45** J3
Storbo Sweden **45** K3
Stord i. Norway **45** I4
Stordai Norway **44** I3
Storjuktan l. Sweden **44** L2
Storen Norway **44** J3
Store Sotra i. Norway **45** I3
Storfjärden l. Sweden **45** L3
Storfjorden sea chan. Svalbard **38** D2
Storforshei Norway **44** K2
Storjola Sweden **44** K2
Storjord Norway **44** K2
Storkarho mt. Norway **44** J3
Storkerson Peninsula Canada **165** I2
Storm Bay Australia **147** E5
Stormberg S. Africa **133** K8
Stormberg mt. S. Africa **133** K7
Stormberg r. S. Africa **133** K7
Stormberge mts S. Africa **133** K8
Storm Lake U.S.A. **178** D3
Stormsrivier S. Africa **132** H10
Stornoway U.K. **46** F5
  also spelt Steornabhagh
Storøya i. Svalbard **38** G2
Storseleby Sweden **44** L2
Storsjøen l. Norway **45** J3
Storsjön l. Sweden **45** K3
Storsjön l. Sweden **44** J3
Storskog Norway **44** L2
Storslett Norway **44** M1
Storstremmen sea chan. Denmark **45** J5
Stortemelk sea chan. Neth. **48** C2
Storuman Sweden **44** L2
Storuman l. Sweden **44** L2
Storvigelen mt. Norway **44** K3
Storvik Sweden **45** L3
Storvorde Denmark **45** J4
Storvreta Sweden **45** L3
Stosch, Isla i. Chile **205** B8
Stoŭng, Stœng r. Cambodia **79** D5
Stour r. Dorset, England U.K. **47** K13
Stour r. Kent, England U.K. **47** N12
Stout Lake Canada **168** A2
Stovall U.S.A. **176** G9
Stowbtsy Belarus **42** H8
  also known as Stolbtsy
Stowmarket U.K. **47** M11
Stoyba Rus. Fed. **82** C1
Straatsdrif S. Africa **133** K2
Strabane U.K. **47** E9
Stradella Italy **56** I3
Strahan Australia **147** E5
Straight Cliffs ridge U.S.A. **183** M4
Strakonice Czech Rep. **49** K6
Straldzha Bulg. **58** H6
Stralsund Germany **49** K1
Strand S. Africa **132** C11
Stranda Norway **44** I3
Strangford Leugh inlet U.K. **47** G9
Strängnäs Sweden **45** L4
Strangways r. Australia **148** B3
Strangways Range mts Australia **148** B4
Stranraer U.K. **47** G9
Strasbourg France **51** N4
  historically known as Argentoratum, or
  Strassburg
Strasburg Germany **49** K2
Strasburg OH U.S.A. **176** D5
Strasburg PA U.S.A. **177** I6
Strasburg VA U.S.A. **176** G7
Strășeni Moldova see Strășeni
Strassburg France see Strasbourg
Straßwalchen Austria **49** K8
Stratford Canada **168** D4
Stratford N.Z. **152** I7
Stratford CA U.S.A. **182** E5
Stratford CT U.S.A. **177** L4
Stratford TX U.S.A. **179** B4
Stratford WI U.S.A. **172** C6
Stratford-upon-Avon U.K. **47** K11
Strathalbyn Australia **146** C3
Strathcona, Mount Antarctica **223** D2
Strathcona Provincial Park Canada **166** E5
Strathgordon Australia **147** E5
Strathmore Canada **167** I5
Strathmore r. U.K. **46** I4
Strathnaver Canada **166** F4
Strathroy Canada **173** L8
Strathspey valley U.K. **46** I6
Stratton Mountain U.S.A. **177** M2
Straubing Germany **48** J7
Straumen Norway **44** K1
Straumen Nordland Norway **44** K2
Straumen Nordland Norway **44** K2
Straumnes pt Iceland **44** [inset] B2
Strausberg Germany **49** K3
Strawberry Mountain U.S.A. **180** C3
Strawberry Point U.S.A. **172** B8
Strawberry Reservoir U.S.A. **183** M1
Strawn U.S.A. **179** C5
Straža mt. Macedonia **58** D6
Strazhitsa Bulg. **58** H5
Strážnice Czech Rep. **49** O6
Streaky Bay Australia **146** B3
Streaky Bay b. Australia **146** B3
Streator U.S.A. **174** B3
Strehaia Romania **58** E4
Strei r. Romania **58** D3
Střela r. Czech Rep. **49** K6
Strelcha Bulg. **58** F6
Strelka Rus. Fed. **39** P3
Strelkovo Rus. Fed. **43** P1
Strelley Australia **150** B4
Strelley r. Australia **150** B4
Strelley Aboriginal Reserve Australia **150** B4
Strel'na r. Rus. Fed. **40** F2
Strenči Latvia **42** G4
Stretta di Messina strait Italy see
  Messina, Strait of
Streymoy i. Faroe Is **46** E1
Strezhevoy Rus. Fed. **38** H3
Stříbro Czech Rep. **49** J6
Strickland r. P.N.G. **73** J8
Strimonas r. Greece **58** E8
Strizivojna Croatia **56** K3
Stroeder Arg. **204** E6
Stofades i. Greece **59** C11
Ströhen Germany **48** F3
Stromberg U.K. **46** I5
Stromboli, Isola i. Isole Lipari Italy **57** H10
Stromeferry U.K. **46** G6
Stromness S. Georgia **205** [inset]
Stromness U.K. **46** I5
Sromsburg U.S.A. **178** C3
Strömsmo Norway **44** L1
Strömstad Sweden **45** J4
Strömsund Sweden **44** K3
Strongoli Italy **57** J9
Strongsville U.S.A. **176** D4
Stronsay i. U.K. **46** J4
Stropkov Slovakia **49** S6
Stroud U.K. **47** J12
Strücklingen (Saterland) Germany **48** E2
Struer Denmark **45** J4
Struga Macedonia **58** B7
Strugi-Krasnyye Rus. Fed. **43** K3
Struis Bay S. Africa **132** E11
Struis Bay b. S. Africa **132** E11
Struma r. Bulg. **58** E7
Strumica Macedonia **58** D7
Strumica r. Macedonia **58** D7
Strumino Rus. Fed. **43** T5
Struthers U.S.A. **176** E4
Stryama r. Bulg. **58** F6
Strydenburg S. Africa **132** H6
Stryn Norway **45** I3
Stryy Ukr. **52** G2
Strzegomka r. Poland **49** N5
Strzelce Krajeńskie Poland **49** M3
Strzelce Opolskie Poland **49** P5
Strzelecki, Mount hill Australia **148** B4
Strzelecki Creek watercourse Australia
  146 C1
Strzelecki Regional Reserve nature res.
  Australia **146** C1
Strzelin Poland **49** O5
Strzelno Poland **49** P3
Strzyżów Poland **49** S6
Stuart r. Australia **149** F5
Stuart FL U.S.A. **175** D7
Stuart IA U.S.A. **178** D3
Stuart VA U.S.A. **176** E9
Stuart Bluff Range mts Australia **148** B4
Stuart Lake Canada **166** E4
Stuart Mountains N.Z. **153** B13
Stuart Range hills Australia **146** B2
Stuarts Draft U.S.A. **176** F7
Stubaier Alpen mts Austria **48** I8
Stubbenkammer hd Germany **49** K1
Stubica Srbija Yugo. **58** C5
Stubline Srbija Yugo. **58** B4
Stuchka Latvia see Aizkraukle
Stučka Latvia see Aizkraukle
Studenica tourist site Yugo. **58** B5
Studen Kladenets, Yazovir resr Bulg. **58** G7
Studenoye Rus. Fed. **43** S9
Studholme Junction N.Z. **153** F12
Studis S. Africa **132** I10
Stugun Sweden **44** K3
Stulpicani Romania **58** G1
Stung Treng Cambodia see Stœng Trêng
Stupart r. Canada **167** M4
Stupino Rus. Fed. **43** T7
Stura di Demonte r. Italy **51** N8
Sturge Island Antarctica **223** K2
Sturgeon r. Ont. Canada **168** D4
Sturgeon r. Sask. Canada **167** J4
Sturgeon U.S.A. **172** G5
Sturgeon, Lake Canada **172** B2
Sturgeon Bay b. Canada **167** L4
Sturgeon Bay U.S.A. **172** F6
Sturgeon Bay b. U.S.A. **173** I5
Sturgeon Bay Canal lake channel U.S.A.
  172 F6
Sturgeon Falls Canada **168** E4
Sturgeon Lake Canada **173** O6
Sturgis KY U.S.A. **174** C4
Sturgis MI U.S.A. **172** H9
Sturgis SD U.S.A. **178** B2
Šturlić Bos.-Herz. **56** H3
Sturt, Mount hill Australia **146** D2
Sturt Bay Australia **146** C3
Sturt Creek watercourse Australia **150** D3
Sturtevant U.S.A. **172** F8
Sturt National Park Australia **146** D2
Sturt Plain Australia **148** B3
Sturt Stony Desert Australia **146** D2
Stutterheim S. Africa **133** L9
Stuttgart Germany **48** G7
Stuttgart U.S.A. **174** B5
Stykkishólmur Iceland **44** [inset] B2
Stylida Greece **59** D10
  also known as Stilis
Styr r. Belarus/Ukr. **38** G4
Suaçuí Grande r. Brazil **203** D6
Suai East Timor **75** C5
Suaita Col. **198** C3
Suakin Sudan **121** H5
Suakin Archipelago is Sudan **121** H5
Suao Dem. Rep. Congo **127** D6
Suao Taiwan **87** G3
Suaqui Grande Mex. **184** C2
Suara, Mount Eritrea **121** H5
Suardi Arg. **204** E3
Suárez Col. **198** B4
Suata Venez. **199** E3
Suau P.N.G. **149** F1
Subačius Lith. **42** F6
Subang Indon. **77** D4
Subansiri r. India **78** A2
Subanarekha r. India **97** E5
Subashi Iran **100** B3
Subaşı Turkey **58** J7
Subate Latvia **42** G5
Subay reg. Saudi Arabia **105** C3
Şubayhah Saudi Arabia **109** J7
Şubayhī reg. Yemen **104** C5
Subcetate Romania **58** G2
Subei China **84** C4
  also known as Dangchengwan
Subi Besar i. Indon. **77** E2
Subi Kecil i. Indon. **77** E2
Sublette U.S.A. **178** B4
Subotica Vojvodina, Srbija Yugo. **58** A2
  also known as Szabadka
Subucle mt. Eritrea **121** I6
Success, Lake U.S.A. **182** F5
Suceava Romania **53** I9
  formerly spelt Sucsava
Sucha Beskidzka Poland **49** Q6
Suchan, Rus. Fed. **82** D4
Suchedniów Poland **49** R4
Suchitepéquez Mex. **185** F5
Suchan r. Rus. Fed. **82** D4
Suciu de Sus Romania **58** F2
Suck r. Rep. of Ireland **47** D10
Sucker Creek Landing Canada **173** M4
▶ Sucre Bol. **200** D4
  Legislative capital of Bolivia.
  world [countries] ▶ 10–11
Sucre dept Col. **198** C2

Sucre state Venez. 199 F2
Sucuaro Col. 198 D3
Sucumbíos prov. Ecuador 198 B5
Sucunduri r. Brazil 199 G6
Sucuriú r. Brazil 206 B7
Suczawa Romania see Suceava
Sud prov. Cameroon 125 H6
Sud, Rivière du r. Canada 177 L1
Suda Rus. Fed. 43 S2
Suda r. Rus. Fed. 43 S2
Sudak Ukr. 41 E7

▶Sudan country Africa 121 E5
Largest country in Africa and 10th largest in the world. Historically known as Anglo-Egyptian Sudan.
world [countries] 10–11
africa [countries] 114–117

Suday Rus. Fed. 40 G4
Sudayr reg. Saudi Arabia 105 D2
Sudayr, Sha'īb watercourse Iraq 107 F5
Sudbishchi Rus. Fed. 43 S9
Sud'bodarovka Rus. Fed. 102 C1
Sudbury Canada 168 D4
Sudbury U.K. 47 M11
Sudd swamp Sudan 126 F3
Suddie Guyana 199 G3
Sude r. Germany 48 H2
Sudest Island P.N.G. see Tagula Island
Sudetenland mts Czech Rep./Poland see Sudety
Sudety mts Czech Rep./Poland 49 M5
historically known as Sudetenland
Sudimir Rus. Fed. 43 P8
Sudislavl' Rus. Fed. 40 G4
Sud-Kivu prov. Dem. Rep. Congo 126 F5
Sudlersville U.S.A. 177 J6
Sudogda Rus. Fed. 40 G5
Sudomskiye Vysoty hills Rus. Fed. 43 K4
Sudost' r. Rus. Fed. 43 O9
Sud-Ouest prov. Cameroon 125 H5
Sudr Egypt 121 G2
Sudr, Râs el pt Egypt 108 D8
Suðurland constituency Iceland 44 [inset] B2
Suðuroy i. Faroe Is 46 F2
Suðuroyarfjørður sea chan. Faroe Is 46 F2
Sue watercourse Sudan 126 F3
Sueca Spain 55 K5
Sŭedinenie Bulg. 58 F6
Suez Egypt 121 G2
also spelt El Suweis or As Suways
Suez, Gulf of Egypt 121 G2
also known as Suweis, Khalîg el or Suways, Khalīj as
Suez Bay Egypt 108 D8
also known as Qulzum, Baḥr el
Suez Canal Egypt 121 G2
also known as Suweis, Qanâ el
Şufaynah Saudi Arabia 104 C3
Suffolk U.S.A. 177 I9
Sūfiān Iran 100 A2
Sufi-Kurgan Kyrg. see Sopu-Korgon
Sug-Aksy Rus. Fed. 88 E1
Sugar r. U.S.A. 172 D8
Sugarbush Hill hill U.S.A. 172 E5
Sugar Grove NC U.S.A. 176 D9
Sugar Grove OH U.S.A. 176 C6
Sugarloaf Mountain U.S.A. 174 G2
Sugarloaf Point Australia 147 G3
Sugar Notch U.S.A. 173 R9
Sugbuhan Point Phil. 74 C4
Süget China see Sogat
Sugi i. Indon. 76 C2
Sugun China 88 B4
Sugut r. Sabah Malaysia 77 G1
Sugut, Tanjong pt Sabah Malaysia 77 G1
Suhaia Romania 58 G5
Suhai Hu l. China 84 B4
Suhait China 84 E4
Sūhāj Egypt see Sohâg
Şuḩār Oman 105 G2
English form Sohar
Sühbaatar Mongolia 85 E1
Sühbaatar prov. Mongolia 85 G2
Suheli Par i. India 94 B4
Suhl Germany 48 H5
Suhopolje Croatia 56 J3
Suhul reg. Saudi Arabia 105 D3
Suhūl al Kidan plain Saudi Arabia 105 F3
Suhum Ghana 125 E5
Şuhut Turkey 106 B3
Suiá Missur r. Brazil 202 A4
Sui'an China see Zhangpu
Suibin China 82 C3
Suichang China 87 F2
also known as Miaogao
Suicheng China see Jianning
Suicheng China see Suixi
Suichuan China 87 E3
also known as Quanjiang
Suid-Afrika country Africa see South Africa, Republic of
Suide China 85 F4
also known as Mingzhou
Suidzhikurmsy Turkm. see Madau
Suifen r. China 82 C4
Suifenhe China 82 C3
Suigam India 96 A4
Suihua China 82 B3
Suijiang China 86 B2
also known as Zhongcheng
Suileng China 82 B3
Suining Hunan China 87 D3
also known as Changpu
Suining Jiangsu China 87 F1
Suining Sichuan China 86 C2
Suiping China 87 E1
also known as Zhuoyang
Suippes France 51 K3
Suir r. Rep. of Ireland 47 E11
Suisse country Europe see Switzerland
Suixi Anhui China 87 F1
Suixi Guangdong China 87 D4
also known as Suicheng
Suixian China 87 E1
Suixian China see Suizhou
Suiyang China 87 C3
also known as Yangchuan
Suizhai China see Xiancheng
Suizhong China 85 I3
Suizhou China 87 E2
formerly known as Suixian
Sujangarh India 96 B4
Sujawal Pak. 101 G5
Sukabumi Indon. 77 D4
Sukadana Kalimantan Barat Indon. 77 E3
Sukadana Sumatra Indon. 77 D4
Sukadana, Teluk b. Indon. 77 E3
Sukagawa Japan 90 G6
Sukaramai Indon. 77 E3
Sukarnapura Indon. see Jayapura
Sukarno, Puntjak mt. Indon. see Jaya, Puncak
Suket India 96 C4
Sukeva Fin. 44 N3
Sukhanovka Rus. Fed. 90 C1
Sukhary Belarus 43 L8
Sukhinichi Rus. Fed. 43 Q7
Sukhodol'skoye, Ozero l. Rus. Fed. 43 L1
Sukhodrev r. Rus. Fed. 43 Q7
Sukhona r. Rus. Fed. 43 V2
Sukhothai Thai. 78 B4
Sukhoverkovo Rus. Fed. 43 Q5
Sukhumi Georgia see Sokhumi
Sukhum-Kale Georgia see Sokhumi
Sukkertoppen Greenland see Maniitsoq
Sukkozero Rus. Fed. 40 E3
Sukkur Pak. 101 G5
Sukkur Barrage Pak. 101 G5
Sukma India 94 D2
Sukpay Rus. Fed. 82 E3
Sukpay r. Rus. Fed. 82 E3
Sukri r. India 96 B4
Sukromlya Rus. Fed. 43 P5
Sukromny Rus. Fed. 43 R4
Sukses Namibia 130 C4
Suktel r. India 95 D1
Sukumo Japan 91 C8
Sukun i. Indon. 75 B5
Sul, Canal do sea chan. Brazil 202 B2
Sul, Pico do mt. Brazil 207 J7
Sula i. Norway 46 Q2
Sula r. Rus. Fed. 40 I2
Sula, Kepulauan is Indon. 75 C3
Sula, Ozero l. Rus. Fed. 44 O3
Sulabesi i. Indon. 75 C3
Sulaiman Ranges mts Pak. 101 G4
Sulak Rus. Fed. 102 A4
Sulak r. Rus. Fed. 102 A4
Sūlār Iran 100 B4
Sula Sgeir i. U.K. 46 F4
Sulasih, Gunung vol. Indon. 76 C3
Sulat Phil. 74 C4
Sulawesi i. Indon. see Celebes
Sulawesi Selatan prov. Indon. 75 A3
Sulawesi Tengah prov. Indon. 75 B3
Sulawesi Tenggara prov. Indon. 75 B4
Sulawesi Utara prov. Indon. 75 C2
Sulaymān Beg Iraq 107 F4
Sulayyimah Saudi Arabia 105 D3
Sulci Sardegna Italy see Sant'Antioco
Sulcis Sardegna Italy see Sant'Antioco
Sulechów Poland 49 M3
Sulęcin Poland 49 M3
Suledeh Iran 100 B2
Sulejów Poland 49 Q4
Sulejowskie, Jezioro l. Poland 49 Q4
Suleman, Teluk b. Indon. 75 A2
Sule Skerry i. U.K. 46 H4
Sule Stack i. U.K. 46 H4
Süleymanlı Turkey 107 D3
Suliki Indon. 76 C3
Sulima Sierra Leone 124 C5
Sulina Romania 58 K3
Sulina, Braţul watercourse Romania 58 K3
Suliskongen mt. Norway 44 L2
Sulitjelma Norway 44 L2
Sulkava Fin. 45 O3
Sullana Peru 198 A6
Süller Turkey 59 K10
Sullivan IL U.S.A. 174 B4
Sullivan IN U.S.A. 174 C4
Sullivan Bay Canada 166 E5
Sullivan Island Myanmar see Lanbi Kyun
Sullivan Lake Canada 167 I5
Sully-sur-Loire France 51 I5
Sulmo Italy see Sulmona
Sulmona Italy 56 F6
historically known as Sulmo
Süloğlu Turkey 58 H7
Sulphur LA U.S.A. 179 D6
Sulphur OK U.S.A. 179 C5
Sulphur r. U.S.A. 179 D5
Sulphur Draw watercourse U.S.A. 179 E5
Sulphur Springs U.S.A. 179 D5
Sulphur Springs Draw watercourse U.S.A. 179 B5
Sultan Canada 168 D4
Sultan Libya 120 D2
Sultan, Koh-i- mts Pak. 101 E4
Sultanabad India see Osmannagar
Sultanabad Iran see Arāk
Sultanbeyli Turkey 58 K8
Sultanhanı Turkey 106 C3
Sultanhisar Turkey 59 J11
Sultaniça Turkey 58 H8
Sultanıye Turkey see Karapınar
Sultanpur India 97 D4
Sultansandzharskoye Vodokhranilische resr Turkm. 103 E4
Sulu Dem. Rep. Congo 126 E6
Suluan i. Phil. 74 C4
Sulu Archipelago is Phil. 74 B5
Sülüklü Turkey 106 C3
Sülüktü Kyrg. 103 G5
also spelt Sulyukta
Suluntah Libya 120 D1
Sulūq Libya 120 D2
Suluru India 94 D3
Sulu Sea N. Pacific Ocean 74 A4
Sulyukta Kyrg. see Sülüktü
Sulzbach-Rosenberg Germany 48 I6
Sulzberger Bay Antarctica 222 N1
Sumaco, Volcán vol. Ecuador 198 B5
Šumadija reg. Yugo. 58 B4
Sumāil Oman 105 G3
Sumalata Indon. 75 B2
Sumampa Arg. 204 E3
Sumangat, Tanjong pt Sabah Malaysia 74 A5
Sumapaz, Parque Nacional nat. park Col. 198 C4
Sumatera i. Indon. see Sumatra
Sumatera Barat prov. Indon. 76 C3
Sumatera Selatan prov. Indon. 76 C3
Sumatera Utara prov. Indon. 76 B2

▶Sumatra i. Indon. 76 B2
2nd largest island in Asia and 6th in the world. Also spelt Sumatera.
asia [landscapes] 62–63

Sumaúma Brazil 201 E1
Šumava mts Czech Rep. 49 K6
Šumava nat. park Czech Rep. 49 K6
Sumba i. Indon. 75 B5
Sumba, Île i. Dem. Rep. Congo 126 C4
Sumba, Selat sea chan. Indon. 75 A5
Sumbar r. Turkm. 102 C5
Sumbawa i. Indon. 77 G5
Sumbawabesar Indon. 77 G5
Sumbawanga Tanz. 129 A6
Sumbay Peru 200 C3
Sumbe Angola 127 B7
formerly known as Ngunza or Ngunza-Kabolu or Novo Redondo
Sumbing, Gunung vol. Indon. 76 C3
Sumbu Zambia 127 F7
Sumbu National Park Zambia 127 F7
also spelt Nsumbu National Park
Sumburgh U.K. 46 K4
Sumburgh Head U.K. 46 K4
Sumbuya Sierra Leone 124 C5
Sumdo Aksai Chin 89 B5
Sumdo China 86 B2
Sumdum, Mount U.S.A. 166 C3
Sumé Brazil 202 E3
Sumedang Indon. 77 D4
Sume'eh Sarā Iran 100 B2
Sümeg Hungary 49 O9
Sumeih Sudan 126 E2
Sumenep Indon. 77 F4
Sumerpur India 96 B4
Sumgait Azer. see Sumqayıt
Sumisu-jima i. Japan 91 G9
Sümiyn Bulag Mongolia 85 G1
Summēl Iraq 107 E3
Summer Beaver Canada 168 B2
Summerdown Namibia 130 C4
Summerford Canada 169 K3
Summer Island U.S.A. 172 G5
Summerland Canada 166 G5
Summerside Canada 169 I4
Summersville U.S.A. 176 E7
Summersville Lake U.S.A. 176 E7
Summerville GA U.S.A. 174 C5
Summerville SC U.S.A. 175 D5
Summit Lake B.C. Canada 166 E3
Summit Lake B.C. Canada 166 F4
Summit Mountain U.S.A. 183 H2
Summit Peak U.S.A. 181 F5
Sumnal Aksai Chin 89 B5
Sumner U.S.A. 174 B5
Sumner, Lake N.Z 153 G10
Sumner Strait U.S.A. 166 C3
Sumon-dake mt. Japan 90 F6
Sumoto Japan 91 D7
Sumpangbinangae Indon. 75 A4
Šumperk Czech Rep. 49 N6
Sumprabum Myanmar 78 B2
Sumpu Japan see Shizuoka
Sumqayıt Azer. 107 G2
also spelt Sumgait
Sumqayıt r. Azer. 107 G2
Sumsar Kyrg. 103 G4
Sumskiy Posad Rus. Fed. 40 E2
Sumter U.S.A. 175 D5
Sumur Jammu and Kashmir 96 C2
Sumy Ukr. 41 E6
Sun r. U.S.A. 180 E3
Suna Rus. Fed. 40 I4
Sunagawa Japan 90 G3
Sunam India 96 B3
Sunamganj Bangl. 97 F4
Sunan China 84 C4
also known as Hongwansi
Sunan N. Korea 83 B5
Şunaynah Oman 105 F3
Sunaysilah salt l. Iraq 109 M2
Sunbright U.S.A. 176 A9
Sunbula Kuh mts Iran 100 A3
Sunbury Australia 147 E4
Sunbury NC U.S.A. 177 I9
Sunbury OH U.S.A. 176 C5
Sunbury PA U.S.A. 177 I5
Sunchales Arg. 204 E3
Suncho Corral Arg. 204 E2
Sunch'ŏn N. Korea 83 B5
Sunch'ŏn S. Korea 83 B6
Sun City S. Africa 133 L2
Sun City U.S.A. 183 L8
Suncook U.S.A. 177 N2
Sund Fin. 42 B1
Sunda, Selat strait Indon. 77 D4
English form Sunda Strait
Sunda Kalapa Indon. see Jakarta
Sundance U.S.A. 180 F3
Sundarbans reg. Bangl./India 97 F5
Sundarbans National Park Bangl./India 97 F5
Sundargarh India 97 E5
Sundarnagar India 96 C3
Sunda Strait Indon. see Sunda, Selat
Sundays r. E. Cape S. Africa 133 J10
Sundays r. Kwazulu-Natal S. Africa 133 O5
Sunday Strait Australia 150 C3
Sunderland U.K. 47 K9
Sündiken Dağları mts Turkey 106 B3
Sundre Canada 167 H5
Sundridge Canada 168 E4
Sundsvall Sweden 45 L3
Sundukli, Peski des. Turkm. 103 E5
also known as Sandykly Gumy
Sundumbili S. Africa 133 P6
Sunel India 96 C4
Sunga Tanz. 129 C6
Sungaiapit Indon. 76 C2
Sungaiguntung Indon. 76 C2
Sungailiat Indon. 77 D3
Sungaipenuh Indon. 76 C3
Sungaipinyuh Indon. 77 E2
Sungai Tuas Basin dock Sing. 76 [inset]
Sungari r. China see Songhua Jiang
Sungei Petani Malaysia 76 C1
Sungei Seletar Reservoir Sing. 76 [inset]
Sungguminasa Indon. 75 A4
Sungikai Sudan 121 F6
Sungkiang China see Songjiang
Sung Kong i. Hong Kong China 87 [inset]
Sungo Moz. 131 G3
Sungqu China see Songpan
Sungurlare Bulg. 58 H6
Sungurlu Turkey 106 C2
Sunja Croatia 56 I3
Sunkar, Gora mt. Kazakh. 103 H3
Sunkosh r. Bhutan 97 F4
also spelt Sankosh
Sun Kosi r. Nepal 97 E4
Sunndal Norway 45 I3
Sunndalsøra Norway 44 J3
Sunne Sweden 45 K4
Sunnyside UT U.S.A. 183 N2
Sunnyside WA U.S.A. 180 C3
Sunnyvale U.S.A. 182 B4
Sun Prairie U.S.A. 172 D7
Sunsas, Sierra de hills Bol. 201 F4
Sunset House Canada 167 G4
Sunset Peak hill Hong Kong China 87 [inset]
also known as Tai Tung Shan
Sunshine Island Hong Kong China 87 [inset]
also known as Chau Kung To
Suntar Rus. Fed. 39 L3
Suntsar Pak. 101 E5
Suntu Eth. 128 C2
Sunwi-do i. N. Korea 83 B5
Sunwu China 82 B2
Sunyani Ghana 124 E5
Suojanperä Fin. 44 O1
Suolahti Fin. 44 N3
Suolijärvet l. Fin. 40 D2
Suoločielgi Fin. see Saariselkä
Suoluvuobmi Norway 44 M1
Suomenniemi Fin. 45 N3
Suomi Canada 172 D2
Suomi country Europe see Finland
Suomusjärvi Fin. 42 E1
Suomussalmi Fin. 44 O2
Suō-nada b. Japan 91 B8
Suonenjoki Fin. 44 N3
Suŏng Cambodia 79 D6
Suong r. Laos 78 C4
Suontee Fin. 44 N3
Suontienselkä l. Fin. 44 N3
Suoyarvi Rus. Fed. 40 E3
Suozhen China see Huantai
Supa India 94 B3
Supai U.S.A. 183 L5
Supaul India 97 E4
Superfosfatnyy Uzbek. 103 F5
Superior AZ U.S.A. 183 M8
Superior MT U.S.A. 180 D3
Superior NE U.S.A. 178 C3
Superior WI U.S.A. 172 A4
Superior, Laguna lag. Mex. 185 G5

▶Superior, Lake Canada/U.S.A. 172 F3
Largest lake in North America and 2nd in the world.
northamerica [landscapes] 156–157

Supetar Croatia 56 I5
Suphan Buri Thai. 79 C5
Süphan Dağı mt. Turkey 107 E3
Supiori i. Indon. 73 I7
Suponevo Rus. Fed. 43 P8
Support Force Glacier Antarctica 223 V1
Supraśl Poland 49 U2
Supraśl r. Poland 49 U2
Sup'sa r. Georgia 107 E2
Supung N. Korea 83 B4
Sūq al Inān Yemen 104 D4
Sūq ar Rubū' Saudi Arabia 104 C3
Sūq ash Shuyūkh Iraq 107 F5
Suqian China 87 F1
Sūq Suwayq Saudi Arabia 104 B2
Suquṭrā i. Yemen see Socotra
Sur r. Ghana 125 E4
Súr Hungary 49 P8
Şūr Oman 105 G3
Sur, Point U.S.A. 182 C5
Sur, Punta pt Arg. 204 F5
Sura Rus. Fed. 41 H5
Sura r. Rus. Fed. 41 H4
Şuraabad Azer. 107 G2
Surab Pak. 101 F4
Surabaya Indon. 77 F4
formerly spelt Soerabaia
Surajpur India 97 D5
Sūrak Iran 100 D5
Surakarta Indon. 77 E4
Suramana Indon. 75 A3
Şura Mare Romania 58 F3
Sūrān Iran 101 E5
Şūrān Syria 109 H2
Surára Brazil 199 F6
Surat Australia 147 F1
Surat India 96 B5
Suratgarh India 96 B3
Surat Thani Thai. 79 B6
also known as Ban Don
Suraż Poland 49 T3
Surazh Belarus 43 L6
Surazh Rus. Fed. 43 N8
Surbiton Australia 149 E4
Sūrdāsh Iraq 107 F4
Surdila-Greci Romania 58 I3
Surduc Romania 58 E1
Surdulica Srbija Yugo. 58 D6
Sûre r. Germany/Lux. 51 M3
Surendranagar India 96 A5
formerly known as Wadhwan
Suretka Costa Rica 186 C5
Surf U.S.A. 182 D7
Surgana India 94 B1
Surgères France 50 F6
Surgidero de Batabanó Cuba 186 C2
Surgut Rus. Fed. 38 H3
Suri India see Siuri
Suriapet India 94 C2
also spelt Suryapet
Surigao Phil. 74 C4
Surigao Strait Phil. 74 C4
Surimena Col. 198 C4
Surin Thai. 79 C5
Surinam country S. America see Suriname
▶Suriname country S. America 199 G3
also spelt Surinam; formerly known as Dutch Guiana
southamerica [countries] 192–193
Suriname r. Suriname 199 H3
Suripá Venez. 198 D3
Suriyān Iran 100 C4
Surkhābād Iran 100 C3
Surkhandar'inskaya Oblast' admin. div. Uzbek. 103 F5
English form Surkhandarya Oblast; also known as Surkhondaryo Wiloyati
Surkhandar'ya r. Uzbek. 103 F5
also spelt Surkhondaryo
Surkhandarya Oblast admin. div. Uzbek. see Surkhandar'inskaya Oblast'
Surkhet Nepal 97 D3
also known as Birendranagar
Surkhob r. Tajik. 101 G2
Surkhondaryo r. Uzbek. see Surkhandar'ya
Surkhondaryo Wiloyati admin. div. Uzbek. see Surkhandar'inskaya Oblast'
Surmāq Iran 100 C4
Sürmene Turkey 107 E2
Surnadalsøra Norway 44 J3
Sŭrnevo Bulg. 58 G6
Surovikino Rus. Fed. 41 G6
Surprise Canada 166 C3
Surprise Lake Canada 166 C3
Surrey Canada 166 F5
Surskoye Rus. Fed. 41 H5
Surt Libya see Sirte
Surt, Khalīj g. Libya see Sirte, Gulf of
Surtsey i. Iceland 44 [inset] B3
Sūrū Iran 100 D5
Suru, Vârful mt. Romania 58 F3
Surubiú r. Brazil 202 B2
Sürüç Turkey 107 D3
Surud, Raas pt Somalia 128 E2
Surud Ad mt. Somalia see Shimbiris
Suruga-wan b. Japan 91 F7
Surulangun Indon. 76 C3
Surumú r. Brazil 199 F4
Surup Phil. 74 C5
Suryapet India see Suriapet
Şuşa Azer. 107 F3
also spelt Shusha
Susa Italy 51 N7
Susa Japan 91 B7
Sušac i. Croatia 56 I6
Susah Tunisia see Sousse
Susak i. Croatia 56 G4
Susaki Japan 91 C8
Susami Japan 91 D8
Susan U.S.A. 177 I8
Sūsangerd Iran 100 B4
Susanville U.S.A. 182 D1
Suşehri Turkey 107 D2
Sushitsa Bulg. 58 G5
Sushui r. China 87 D1
Sušice Czech Rep. 49 K6
Šuškova Latvia 43 J5
Susner India 96 C5
Susong China 87 F2
Susquehanna U.S.A. 177 J4
Susquehanna r. U.S.A. 177 I6
Susquehanna, West Branch r. U.S.A. 176 I5
Susques Arg. 200 D5
Sussex Canada 169 H4
Sussex U.S.A. 177 K4
Susua Indon. 75 B3
Susuman Rus. Fed. 39 O3
Susupu Indon. 75 C2
Susurluk Turkey 106 B3
Šušvė r. Lith. 42 E6
Suswa, Mount Kenya 128 B5
Susz Poland 49 Q2
Sutak Jammu and Kashmir 96 C2
Sutaşı Turkey 108 G1
Sutay Uul mt. Mongolia 84 B2
Sutherland Australia 147 F3
Sutherland S. Africa 132 E9
Sutherland NE U.S.A. 178 B3
Sutherland VA U.S.A. 176 H8
Sutherland Range hills Australia 151 D5
Sutjeska nat. park Bos.-Herz. 56 K5
Sutlej r. India/Pak. 96 A3
also spelt Satluj
Sutlepa meri l. Estonia 42 E2
Sütlüce Turkey 108 E1
Sütlüce Turkey 58 I7
Sutter U.S.A. 182 C2
Sutter Creek U.S.A. 182 D3
Sutton r. Canada 168 D2
Sutton N.Z. 153 E13
Sutton NE U.S.A. 178 C3
Sutton WV U.S.A. 176 E7
Sutton Coldfield U.K. 47 K11
Sutton Lake Canada 168 C2
Sutton Lake U.S.A. 176 E7
Suttor r. Australia 149 E4
Suttsu Japan 90 G3
Sutwik Island U.S.A. 164 D4
Sutyr' r. Rus. Fed. 82 D2
Suugant Mongolia 85 E2
Suurberg mt. S. Africa 133 J8
Suurberg mts S. Africa 133 J10
Suurbraak S. Africa 132 E11
Suure-Jaani Estonia 42 G3
Suuremõisa Estonia 42 D3
Suur katel b. Estonia 42 D3
Suur-Pakri i. Estonia 42 E2
Suurpea Estonia 42 G2
Suur väin sea chan. Estonia 42 E3

▶Suva Fiji 145 G3
Capital of Fiji.

Suvalki Poland see Suwałki
Suva Reka Kosovo, Srbija Yugo. 58 B6
Suvorov atoll Cook Is see Suwarrow
Suvorov Rus. Fed. 43 R7
Suvorove Ukr. 58 J3
Suvorovo Bulg. 58 I5
formerly known as Novgradets
Suvorovo Moldova see Ştefan Vodă
Suwa Japan 91 F6
Suwakong Indon. 77 F3
Suwałki Poland 49 T1
formerly spelt Suvalki
Suwannaphum Thai. 79 C5
Suwannee r. U.S.A. 175 D6
Suwanose-jima i. Japan 83 C7
Suwaran, Gunung mt. Indon. 77 G2
Suwarrow atoll Cook Is 221 H6
also known as Anchorage Island; also spelt Suvorov
Suwaylih Jordan 108 G5
also spelt Suweilih
Suwayqīyah, Hawr as imp. l. Iraq 107 F4
Suwayr well Saudi Arabia 107 E5
Suways, Khalīj as g. Egypt see Suez, Gulf of
Suweilih Jordan see Suwaylih
Suweis, Khalîg el g. Egypt see Suez, Gulf of
Suweis, Qanâ el canal Egypt see Suez Canal
Suwŏn S. Korea 83 B5
Suxu China 87 D4
Suykbulak Kazakh. 103 J2
also spelt Sūyqbulaq
Suyo Peru 198 A6
Sūyqbulaq Kazakh. see Suykbulak
Suz, Mys pt Kazakh. 102 C4
Sūzā Iran 100 D5
Suzak Kazakh. 103 G3
also spelt Sozaq
Suzaka Japan 91 F6
Suzdal' Rus. Fed. 43 V5
Suzemka Rus. Fed. 43 P9
Suzhou Anhui China 87 F1
Suzhou China see Jiuquan
Suzhou Jiangsu China 87 G2
formerly spelt Soochow
Suzi r. China 82 B4
Suzu Japan 90 E6
Suzuka Japan 91 E7
Suzu-misaki pt Japan 83 E5
Suzzara Italy 56 C4
Sværholthalvøya pen. Norway 44 N1

▶Svalbard terr. Arctic Ocean 38 A2
Part of Norway.

Svalenik Bulg. 58 H5
Svanstein Sweden 44 M2
Svapa r. Rus. Fed. 43 Q9
Svappavaara Sweden 44 M2
also known as Veaikevárri
Svapushcha Rus. Fed. 43 N4
Svärdsjö Sweden 45 K3
Svarta r. Fin. 42 G1
Svartälven r. Sweden 45 K4
Svartbyn Sweden 44 M2
Svartenhuk Halvø pen. Greenland see Sigguup Nunaa
Svartlä Sweden 44 M2
Svatove Ukr. 41 F6
Svay Riěng Cambodia 79 D6
Svecha Rus. Fed. 40 H4
Švėdasai Lith. 42 G6
Sveg Sweden 45 K3
Svegsjön l. Sweden 45 K3
Sveio Norway 45 I4
Sveki Latvia 42 H4
Švėkšna Lith. 42 C6
Svelgen Norway 45 I3
Svellingen Norway 44 J3
Švenčionėliai Lith. 42 G6
Švenčionys Lith. 42 H6
Svendborg Denmark 45 J5
Svenljunga Sweden 45 K4
Svenstavik Sweden 44 K3
Šventoji r. Lith. 42 F6
Sverchkovo Rus. Fed. 43 Q6
Sverdlovsk Rus. Fed. see Yekaterinburg
Sverdlovs'k Ukr. 41 F6
Sverdlovsk Uzbek. 103 F5
Sverdlovskaya Oblast' admin. div. Rus. Fed. 40 L4
English form Sverdlovsk Oblast
Sverdlovsk Oblast admin. div. Rus. Fed. see Sverdlovskaya Oblast'
Sverdrup Channel Canada 165 J2
Sverdrup Islands Canada 165 J2
Sverige country Europe see Sweden
Sveta Andrija i. Croatia 56 H5
Švėtė r. Lith. 42 E5
Sveti Ivan Zelina Croatia see Zelina
Sveti Jure mt. Croatia 56 J5
Sveti Nikole Macedonia 58 C7
Svetlaya Rus. Fed. 82 E3
Svetlodarskoye Rus. Fed. 82 F2
Svetlogorsk Belarus see Svyetlahorsk
Svetlogorsk Kaliningradskaya Oblast' Rus. Fed. 42 B7
historically known as Rauschen
Svetlogorsk Krasnoyarskiy Kray Rus. Fed. 39 I3
Svetlograd Rus. Fed. 41 G7
formerly known as Petrovskoye
Svetlopolyansk Rus. Fed. 40 J4
Svetlovodsk Ukr. see Svitlovods'k
Svetlyy Rus. Fed. 42 B7
historically known as Zimmerbude
Svetlyy Rus. Fed. 103 E2
Svetlyy Yar Rus. Fed. 41 H6
Svetogorsk Rus. Fed. 43 J1
Svetozarevo Srbija Yugo. see Jagodina
Svētupe r. Latvia 42 F4
Svíahnúkar vol. Iceland 44 [inset] C2
Svidník Slovakia 49 S6
Sviibi Estonia 42 E3
Svilaja mts Croatia 56 I5
Svilajnac Srbija Yugo. 58 C4
Svilengrad Bulg. 58 H7
Svinecea Mare, Vârful mt. Romania 58 D4
Svinø i. Faroe Is see Svínoy
Svínoy i. Faroe Is 46 F1
also spelt Svinø
Svintsovyy Rudnik Turkm. 103 F5
Svir Belarus 42 H7
Svir' r. Rus. Fed. 43 P1
Svir, Vozyera l. Belarus 42 H7
Sviritsa Rus. Fed. 43 N1
Svirskaya Guba b. Rus. Fed. 43 N1
Svir'stroy Rus. Fed. 43 O1
Svishtov Bulg. 58 G5
Svislach Hrodzyenskaya Voblasts' Belarus 42 F8
Svislach Minskaya Voblasts' Belarus 42 I8
Svislach r. Belarus/Poland 42 F8
also spelt Svisloch or Świstocz
Svislach r. Belarus 42 J8
also spelt Svisloch
Svisloch r. Belarus see Svislach
Svisloch r. Belarus see Svislach
Svit Slovakia 49 R6
Svitava r. Czech Rep. 49 N7
Svitavy Czech Rep. 49 N6
Svitlovods'k Ukr. 41 E6
also spelt Svetlovodsk; formerly known as Khrushchev or Kremges
Svizzera country Europe see Switzerland
Svoboda Rus. Fed. 42 C7
Svobodnyy Rus. Fed. 82 C2
Svoge Bulg. 58 E6
Svol'nya r. Belarus 43 J6
Svolvær Norway 44 K1
Svratka r. Czech Rep. 49 N6
Svrljig Srbija Yugo. 58 D5
Svrljiške Planine mts Yugo. 58 D5
Svyantsyanskiya Hrady hills Belarus 42 H7
Svyatoy Nos, Mys c. Rus. Fed. 40 I2
Svyatsk Rus. Fed. 43 M9
Svyetlahorsk Belarus 43 K9
also spelt Svetlogorsk; formerly known as Shatilki
Svyha r. Ukr. 43 O9
Swabi Pak. 101 H3
Swaershoek S. Africa 133 J9
Swaershoekpas pass S. Africa 133 J9
Swain Reefs Australia 149 G4
Swainsboro U.S.A. 175 D5
Swains Island American Samoa 145 H3
also known as Olosenga
Swakop watercourse Namibia 130 B4
Swakopmund Namibia 130 B4
Swale r. U.K. 47 K9
Swallow Islands Solomon Is 145 F3
Swampy r. Canada 169 G1
Swan r. Australia 151 A6
Swan r. Man./Sask. Canada 167 K4
Swan r. Ont. Canada 168 D2
Swanage U.K. 47 K13
Swana-Mume Dem. Rep. Congo 127 E7
Swandale U.S.A. 176 E7
Swanepoelspoort mt. S. Africa 132 H10
Swan Hill Australia 147 D3
Swan Hills Canada 167 H4
Swan Islands is Caribbean Sea 186 C3
also known as Santanilla, Islas
Swan Lake B.C. Canada 166 D4
Swan Lake Man. Canada 167 K4
Swan Lake U.S.A. 178 D2
Swanlinbar Rep. of Ireland 47 E9
Swanquarter U.S.A. 174 E5
Swanquarter National Wildlife Refuge nature res. U.S.A. 174 E5
Swan Reach Australia 146 C3
Swan River Canada 167 K4
Swansea Australia 147 F5
Swansea U.K. 47 I12
also known as Abertawe
Swansea Bay U.K. 47 I12
Swans Island U.S.A. 177 Q1
Swanton CA U.S.A. 182 B4
Swanton VT U.S.A. 177 L1
Swartberg S. Africa 133 N7
Swartberg mt. S. Africa 132 D11
Swartbergpas pass S. Africa 132 F10
Swartdoorn r. S. Africa 132 B7
Swart Kei r. S. Africa 133 L9
Swartkolkvloer salt pan S. Africa 132 E7
Swartkops r. S. Africa 133 J10
Swart Nossob watercourse Namibia see Black Nossob
Swartplaas S. Africa 133 K3
Swartputs S. Africa 132 H5
Swartput se Pan salt pan Namibia 132 D3
Swartruggens S. Africa 133 K2
Swartruggens mts S. Africa 133 K2
Swartz Creek U.S.A. 173 J8
Swarzędz Poland 49 O3
Swasey Peak U.S.A. 183 K2
Swastika Canada 173 M2
Swat r. Pak. 101 G3
Swat Kohistan reg. Pak. 101 H3
Swatow China see Shantou
▶Swaziland country Africa 133 P3
known as Ngwane in Swazi
africa [countries] 114–117

▶Sweden country Europe 45 K4
5th largest country in Europe. Known as Sverige in Swedish.
europe [countries] 32–35

Swedesburg U.S.A. 172 B9
Sweet Briar U.S.A. 176 F8
Sweet Home U.S.A. 180 B3
Sweet Springs U.S.A. 176 E8
Sweetwater U.S.A. 179 B5
Sweetwater r. U.S.A. 180 F4
Swellendam S. Africa 132 E11
Swempoort S. Africa 133 L8
Świder r. Poland 49 S3
Świdnica Poland 49 N5
Świdnik Poland 49 T4
Świdwin Poland 49 M2
Świebodzice Poland 49 N5
Świebodzin Poland 49 M3
Świecie Poland 49 P2
Świętokrzyskie, Góry hills Poland 49 R5
Świętokrzyski Park Narodowy nat. park Poland 49 R5
Swift r. U.S.A. 177 O1
Swift Current Canada 167 J5
Swiftcurrent Creek r. Canada 167 J5
Swilly, Lough inlet Rep. of Ireland 47 E8
Swindon U.K. 47 K12
Swinkpan imp. l. S. Africa 133 J5
Świnoujście Poland 49 L2
Swiss Confederation country Europe see Switzerland
Swiss National Park Switz. 51 Q6
Świstocz r. Belarus see Svislach
▶Switzerland country Europe 51 N6
known as Schweiz in German or Suisse in French or Svizzera in Italian; also known as Swiss Confederation; long form Confoederatio Helvetica
europe [countries] 32–35
Swords Rep. of Ireland 47 F10
Swords Range hills Australia 149 D4
Syalyets Belarus 43 L8
Syalyets Vodaskhovishcha resr Belarus 42 F9
Syamozero, Ozero l. Rus. Fed. 40 E3
Syamzha Rus. Fed. 43 V2
Syang Nepal 97 D3
Syanno Belarus 43 K7
also spelt Senno
Syarednenemanskaya Nizina lowland Belarus/Lith. 42 F8
Syas' r. Rus. Fed. 43 N1
Syas'troy Rus. Fed. 43 N1
Sybrandskraal S. Africa 133 M2
Sycamore U.S.A. 172 E9
Sychevka Rus. Fed. 43 P6
Sychevo Rus. Fed. 43 R6
Syców Poland 49 O4
Sydenham atoll Kiribati see Nonouti

▶Sydney Australia 147 F3
State capital of New South Wales. Most populous city in Oceania. Historically known as Port Jackson.
world [cities] 24–25
oceania [features] 142–143

Sydney Canada 169 I4
Sydney Island Kiribati see Manra
Sydney Lake Canada 167 M5
Sydney Mines Canada 169 I4
Sydzhak Uzbek. see Sidzhak
Syedra tourist site Turkey 108 D1
Syeverodonets'k Ukr. 41 F6
also spelt Severodonetsk; formerly known as Leskhimstroy
Sykesville U.S.A. 176 G4
Sykkylven Norway 44 I3
Syktyvkar Rus. Fed. 40 I3
Sylacauga U.S.A. 175 C5
Sylhet Bangl. 97 F4
Sylhet admin. div. Bangl. 97 F4
Sylt i. Germany 48 F1
Sylva r. Rus. Fed. 40 K4
Sylva U.S.A. 174 D5
Sylvania GA U.S.A. 175 D5
Sylvania OH U.S.A. 176 B4
Sylvan Lake Canada 167 H4
Sylvester U.S.A. 175 D6
Sylvester, Lake salt flat Australia 148 B3
Sylvia, Mount Canada 166 E3

↓ T

→ 318

Symi Greece 59 I12
Symi i. Greece 59 I12
also spelt Sími
Syndicate Phil. 74 B3
Synel'nykove Ukr. 41 E6
also spelt Sinel'nikovo
Syngyrli, Mys pt Kazakh. 41 J8
also spelt Sengirli, Mys
Synnagyn, Khrebet mts Rus. Fed. 39 M4
Synnfjell mt. Norway 45 J3
Synnott Range hills Australia 150 D3
Synya r. Rus. Fed. 40 K2
Synya i. Rus. Fed. 40 K2
Syowa research station Antarctica 223 C2
Syracusae Sicilia Italy see Syracuse
Syracuse Sicilia Italy 57 H11
also spelt Siracusa; historically known as Syracusae
Syracuse KS U.S.A. 178 B4
Syracuse NY U.S.A. 177 I2
Syrdar'inskaya Oblast' admin. div. Uzbek. 103 G4
English form Syr Darya Oblast; also known as Sirdaryo Wiloyati
Syr Darya r. Asia see Syrdar'ya
Syrdar'ya r. Asia 99 H1
English form Syr Darya; also known as Dar'yoi Sir; also spelt Sirdaryo
Syrdar'ya Uzbek. 103 G4
also spelt Sirdaryo; formerly known as Syrdaryinskiy
Syrdarya Oblast admin. div. Uzbek. see Syrdar'inskaya Oblast'
Syrdaryinskiy Uzbek. see Syrdar'ya
▶ Syria country Asia 109 I2
spelt As Sūriyah or Souriya in Arabic
asia [countries] ▶ 64–67
Syriam Myanmar 78 B4
Syrian Desert Asia 107 D4
also known as Bādiyat ash Shām
Syrna i. Greece 59 H12
also spelt Sirina
Syrokvashino Rus. Fed. 43 L5
Syros i. Greece 59 F11
also spelt Síros
Syrskiy Rus. Fed. 43 U9
Sysmä Fin. 45 N3
Sysola r. Rus. Fed. 40 I3
Sysoevo Rus. Fed. 43 R2
Syumsi Rus. Fed. 40 I4
Syun r. Rus. Fed. 40 I5
Syurkum Rus. Fed. 82 F2
Syurkum, Mys pt Rus. Fed. 82 F2
Syzran' Rus. Fed. 41 I5
Szabadka Vojvodina, Srbija Yugo. see Subotica
Szabadszállás Hungary 49 Q9
Szadek Poland 49 P4
Szamocin Poland 49 O2
Szamos r. Hungary 49 T7
Szamotuły Poland 49 N3
Szany Hungary 49 O8
Szarvas Hungary 49 R9
Szatmár-Beregi park Hungary 49 T7
Szczebrzeszyn Poland 49 T5
Szczecin Poland 49 L2
historically known as Stettin
Szczecinek Poland 49 N2
Szczekociny Poland 49 Q5
Szczuczyn Poland 49 T2
Szczytno Poland 49 R2
Szechwan prov. China see Sichuan
Szeged Hungary 49 R9
Szeghalom Hungary 49 S8
Székesfehérvár Hungary 49 P8
Szekszárd Hungary 49 P9
Szentes Hungary 49 R9
Szentgotthárd Hungary 49 N9
historically known as Sankt Gotthard
Szentőrinc Hungary 49 O9
Szerencs Hungary 49 S7
Szeska Góra hill Poland 49 T1
Szigetszentmiklós Hungary 49 Q8
Szigetvár Hungary 49 O9
Szkwa r. Poland 49 S2
Szlichtyngowa Poland 49 N4
Szolnok Hungary 49 R8
Szombathely Hungary 49 N8
Szprotawa Poland 49 M4
Sztálinváros Hungary see Dunaújváros
Sztum Poland 49 Q2
Szubin Poland 49 O2
Szücsi Hungary 49 Q8
Szydłowiec Poland 49 R4
Szypliszki Poland 49 U1

↓ T

Taabo, Lac de l. Côte d'Ivoire 124 D5
Taagga Duudka reg. Somalia 128 E3
Taal, Lake Phil. 74 B3
Tab Hungary 49 P9
Tabaco Phil. 74 B3
Tăbah Saudi Arabia 104 C2
Tabajara Brazil 201 E2
Tabakat well Mali 123 E5
Tabanan Indon. 77 F5
Tabang r. Indon. 77 F2
Tabankulu S. Africa 133 N7
Tabaqah Syria 109 J2
Tabaqah Syria see Madīnat ath Thawrah
Tabar Islands P.N.G. 145 E2
Tabarka Tunisia 57 A12
Tabas Khorāsān Iran 100 D3
Tabas Khorāsān Iran 101 E3
Tabasalu Estonia 42 F2
Tabasco state Mex. 185 G5
Tabāsīn Iran 100 D4
Tābask, Kūh-e mt. Iran 100 B4
Tabatinga Brazil 198 D6
Tabatinga, Serra da hills Brazil 202 C4
Tabayoo, Mount Phil. 74 B2
Tabbita Australia 147 E3
Tabelbala Alg. 123 E3
Taber Canada 167 H5
Taberdga Alg. 123 G2
Tabernas Spain 55 I7
Tabernes de Valldigna Spain see Taverhes de la Valldigna
Tabet, Nam r. Myanmar 78 B2
Tabia Tsaka salt l. China 89 C5
Tabin Wildlife Reserve nature res. Sabah Malaysia 77 G1
Tabir r. Indon. 76 C3
Tabiteuea atoll Kiribati 145 G2
also spelt Taputeouea; formerly known as Drummond
Tabivere Estonia 42 H3
Tablas i. Phil. 74 B3
Tablas Strait Phil. 74 B3
Table Bay S. Africa 132 C10
Table Cape N.Z. 152 L7
Table Islands India 79 A5
Table Mountain hill S. Africa 132 C10
Table Point Phil. 74 A4
Table Rock Reservoir U.S.A. 178 D4
Tabligbo Togo 125 F5
Taboca Brazil 199 F5
Tabocal r. Brazil 199 F6
Tabocó r. Brazil 201 D4
Tabong Myanmar 78 B2
Tábor Czech Rep. 49 L6
Tabora Tanz. 129 B6
Tabora admin. reg. Tanz. 129 B6
Taboshar Tajik. 101 G3
Tabou Côte d'Ivoire 124 D5
Tabrichat well Mali 123 F3
Tabrīz Iran 100 A2
Tabuaeran i. Kiribati 221 H5
Tabūk Saudi Arabia 104 B1
Tabūk prov. Saudi Arabia 104 B1
Tabulam Indon. 75 B3
Tabuny Rus. Fed. 103 I1
Tabuyung Indon. 76 B2
Täby Sweden 45 L4
Tacaipu, Serra hills Brazil 199 H5
Tacalé Brazil 199 H4
Tacámbaro Mex. 185 E5
Tacaná, Volcán de vol. Mex. 185 G6
Tacarcuna, Cerro mt. Panama 186 D5
Tachdaït well Niger 125 G3
also known as Qoqek; formerly known as Chuguchak
Tachibana-wan b. Japan 91 A8
Tachie Canada 166 E4
Tachikawa Tōkyō Japan 91 F7
Tachikawa Yamagata Japan 90 F5
Táchira state Venez. 198 C2
Tachiumet well Libya 120 A3
Tachov Czech Rep. 49 J6
Tacina r. Italy 57 I10
Taciuă, Lago i. Brazil 199 F6
Tacloban Phil. 74 C4
Tacna Col. 198 D5
Tacna Peru 200 C4
Tacna dept Peru 200 C4
Tacoma U.S.A. 180 B3
Taconite Harbor U.S.A. 172 C3
Taco Pozo Arg. 204 E2
Tacuarembó Uruguay 204 G3
Tacupeto Mex. 184 C2
Tadami Japan 91 F6
Tadami-gawa r. Japan 91 F6
Tadélaka well Niger 125 G3
Tademaït, Plateau du Alg. 123 F3
English form Tademaït Plateau
Tademaït Plateau Alg. see Tademaït, Plateau du
Tadine New Caledonia 145 F4
Tadjentourt hill Alg. 123 H4
Tadjeraout, Oued watercourse Alg. 123 F5
also known as Chengliang
Tadjikistan country Asia see Tajikistan
Tadjoura Djibouti 128 D2
Tadjoura, Golfe de g. Djibouti 128 D2
Tadjrouna Alg. 123 F2
Tadmur Syria 109 J3
also known as Tamar; historically known as Palmyra
Tadó Col. 198 B3
Tadohae Haesang National Park S. Korea 83 B6
Tadoule Lake Canada 167 L3
Tadoussac Canada 169 G3
Tadpatri India 94 C3
Tadrart Acacus tourist site Libya 120 A3
Tadwale India 94 C2
Tadzhikabad Tajik. see Tojikobod
Tadzhikistan country Asia see Tajikistan
Tadzhikskaya S.S.R. country Asia see Tajikistan
T'aean Haean National Park S. Korea 83 B5
T'aebaek-sanmaek mts N. Korea/S. Korea 83 B5
Taebla Estonia 42 E3
Taech'ŏn S. Korea see Poryŏng
Taech'ŏng-do i. S. Korea 83 B5
Taedong-gang r. N. Korea 83 B5
formerly known as Daido
Taedong-man b. N. Korea 83 B5
Taegu S. Korea 83 C6
Taehŭksan-kundo is S. Korea 83 B6
Taejŏn S. Korea 83 B5
Taejŏng S. Korea 83 B6
T'aepaek S. Korea 83 C5
Taevaskoja Estonia 42 I3
Tafahi i. Tonga 145 I3
formerly known as Keppel Island
Tafalla Spain 55 J2
Tafassasset, Oued watercourse Alg./Niger 123 H5
Tafelberg S. Africa 133 J8
Tafelberg mt. S. Africa 132 F9
Tafelberg mt. Suriname 199 G4
Tafelberg, Natuurreservaat nature res. Suriname 199 G4
Tafila Jordan see At Tafilah
Tafiré Côte d'Ivoire 124 D4
Tafi Viejo Arg. 204 D2
Tafjord Norway 44 I3
Tafouralt Morocco 122 C3
Tafresh Iran 100 B3
Taft Iran 100 C4
Taft U.S.A. 182 E6
Taftān, Kūh-e mt. Iran 101 E4
Taftanāz Syria 109 I1
Tagab Sudan 121 F5
Tagajō Japan 90 G5
Tagânet Keyna well Mali 124 C2
Taganrog Rus. Fed. 41 F7
also known as Taganrogskiy Zaliv or Tahanroz'ka Zatoka
Taganrogskiy Zaliv b. Rus. Fed./Ukr. see Taganrog, Gulf of
Tagant admin. reg. Mauritania 124 C2
Tagarev, Gora mt. Iran/Turkm. 100 D2
Tagawa Japan 91 B8

Tabang r. Indon. 77 F2
Tabankulu S. Africa 133 N7
Tabaqah Syria 109 J2
Tabaqah Syria see Madīnat ath Thawrah
Tabar Islands P.N.G. 145 E2
Tabarka Tunisia 57 A12
Tabas Khorāsān Iran 100 D3
Tabas Khorāsān Iran 101 E3
Tabasalu Estonia 42 F2
Tabasco state Mex. 185 G5
Tabāsīn Iran 100 D4
Tābask, Kūh-e mt. Iran 100 B4
Tabatinga Brazil 198 D6
Tabatinga, Serra da hills Brazil 202 C4
Tabayoo, Mount Phil. 74 B2
Tabbita Australia 147 E3
Tabelbala Alg. 123 E3
Taber Canada 167 H5
Taberdga Alg. 123 G2
Tabernas Spain 55 I7
Tabernes de Valldigna Spain see Taverhes de la Valldigna
Tabet, Nam r. Myanmar 78 B2
Tabia Tsaka salt l. China 89 C5
Tabin Wildlife Reserve nature res. Sabah Malaysia 77 G1
Tabir r. Indon. 76 C3
Tabiteuea atoll Kiribati 145 G2
also spelt Taputeouea; formerly known as Drummond
Tabivere Estonia 42 H3
Tablas i. Phil. 74 B3
Tablas Strait Phil. 74 B3
Table Bay S. Africa 132 C10
Table Cape N.Z. 152 L7
Table Islands India 79 A5
Table Mountain hill S. Africa 132 C10
Table Point Phil. 74 A4
Table Rock Reservoir U.S.A. 178 D4
Tabligbo Togo 125 F5
Taboca Brazil 199 F5
Tabocal r. Brazil 199 F6
Tabocó r. Brazil 201 D4
Tabong Myanmar 78 B2
Tábor Czech Rep. 49 L6
Tabora Tanz. 129 B6
Tabora admin. reg. Tanz. 129 B6
Taboshar Tajik. 101 G3
Tabou Côte d'Ivoire 124 D5
Tabrichat well Mali 123 F3
Tabrīz Iran 100 A2
Tabuaeran i. Kiribati 221 H5
Tabūk Saudi Arabia 104 B1
Tabūk prov. Saudi Arabia 104 B1
Tabulam Indon. 75 B3
Tabuny Rus. Fed. 103 I1
Tabuyung Indon. 76 B2
Täby Sweden 45 L4

Tagaza well Niger 125 G2
also known as Luoyang
Tagbilaran Phil. 74 B4
Tagchagpu Ri mt. China 89 C5
Tagdempt Alg. see Tiaret
Taggia Italy 51 N9
Taghmanant well Mali 122 D4
also spelt Tarhmanant
Tagish Canada 166 C3
Tagish Lake Canada 166 C3
Tagliacozzo Italy 56 F6
Tagliamento r. Italy 56 F3
Tagnout Chaggueret well Mali see Tagnout Chaggueret
Tagoloan r. Phil. 74 C4
Tagomago i. Spain 55 M5
Tagouaret well Mauritania 124 D2
Tagta Turkm. 102 D4
Tagtabazar Turkm. 101 E3
formerly spelt Takhta-Bazar
Taguatinga Minas Gerais Brazil 206 E2
Taguatinga Tocantins Brazil 202 C5
Tagudin Phil. 74 B2
Taguenout Haggueret well Mali see Tagnout Chaggueret
Tagula P.N.G. 149 F1
Tagula Island P.N.G. 149 G1
also known as Sudest Island
Tagus r. Port./Spain 54 D5
also known as Tajo (Spain) or Tejo (Portugal)
Tah, Sabkhat salt pan Morocco 122 B4
Taha China 85 J2
Tahaetkun Mountain Canada 166 G5
Tahalra reg. Alg. 123 G5
Tahan, Gunung mt. Malaysia 76 C1
Tahanroz'ka Zatoka b. Rus. Fed./Ukr. see Taganrog, Gulf of
Tahat, Mont mt. Alg. 123 G5
Tahaurawe i. U.S.A. see Kahoolawe
Tahe China 82 B1
Taheke N.Z. 152 H3
Tāhemaa Estonia 42 I3
Tahifet Alg. 123 G5
Tahili Mongolia 84 C2
Tahiti i. Fr. Polynesia 221 I7
also spelt Otahiti
Tahkuna nina pt Estonia 42 D2
Tahlab r. Iran/Pak. 101 E4
Tahlab, Dasht-i plain Pak. 101 E4
Tahlequah U.S.A. 179 D5
Tahoe, Lake U.S.A. 182 D2
Tahoe City U.S.A. 182 D2
Tahoe Vista U.S.A. 182 D2
Tahoka U.S.A. 179 B5
Tahora N.Z. 152 J7
Tahorakuri N.Z. 152 K6
Tahoua Niger 125 G3
Tahoua dept Niger 125 G3
Tahrūd Iran 100 D4
Tahrūd r. Iran 100 D4
Taht, Oued El watercourse Alg. 55 L9
Tahta Egypt 121 F3
Tahtalı Dağ mt. Turkey 108 B1
Tahtsa Peak Canada 166 E4
Tahua Bol. 200 D4
Tahuamanú r. Bol. 200 D2
Tahuamanú Peru 200 C2
Tahulandang i. Indon. 75 C2
Tahuna Indon. 75 C2
Taï, Parc National de nat. park Côte d'Ivoire 124 D5
Tai A Chau i. Hong Kong China 87 [inset]
Tai'an Liaoning China 85 I3
Tai'an Shandong China 85 H4
Taibai China 87 C1
also known as Zuitou
Taibai Shan mt. China 87 C1
Taibei Taiwan see T'aipei
Taibet Alg. 123 G2
Taibilla r. Spain 55 I6
Taibilla, Sierra de mts Spain 55 I6
Taibus Qi China see Baochang
T'aichung Taiwan 87 G3
also spelt Taizhong
Taidong Taiwan see T'aitung
Taieri r. N.Z. 153 E14
Taigu China 85 G4
Taihang Shan mts China 85 G4
Taihang Shan mts China 85 G4
Taihape N.Z. 152 J7
Taihe Anhui China 87 E1
Taihe Jiangxi China 87 E3
also known as Chengjiang
Taihe China see Shehong
Taihezhen China see Shehong
Tai Ho Wan Hong Kong China 87 [inset]
Taihu China 87 E2
Tai Hu l. China 87 G2
Taikang Heilong. China 85 J2
formerly known as Dorbod
Taikang Henan China 87 E1
Taikkyi Myanmar 78 A4
Tailai China 85 I2
Tailako East Timor 75 C5
Taketa Japan 91 B8
Tai Lam Chung Reservoir Hong Kong China 87 [inset]
Taileleo Indon. 76 B3
Tailem Bend Australia 146 C3
Tai Long Wan b. Hong Kong China 87 [inset]
Tailuge Taiwan see T'ailuko
T'ailuko Taiwan 87 G3
also spelt Tailuge
Taim Brazil 204 G4
Taimani reg. Afgh. 101 E3
Tai Mo Shan hill Hong Kong China 87 [inset]
Tain r. Ghana 124 E4
Tain U.K. 46 H6
T'ainan Taiwan 87 G4
Tainaro, Akra pt Greece 59 D12
English form Matapan, Cape
Tai O Hong Kong China 87 [inset]
Taiobeiras Brazil 202 D5
Taipa Brazil 202 F3
Taipa N.Z. 152 H3
Tai Pak Wan b. Hong Kong China see Discovery Bay
Tai Pang Wan b. Hong Kong China see Mirs Bay
Taipei Taiwan see T'aipei
▶ T'aipei Taiwan 87 G3
Capital of Taiwan. English form Taipei; also spelt Taibei.

Taiping China see Shixing
Taiping Guangdong China 87 E4
Taiping China see Chongzuo
Taiping Guangxi China 87 C4
Taiping Malaysia 76 C1
Taiping Ling mt. China 85 I2
Tai Po Hong Kong China 87 [inset]
Tai Po Hoi b. Hong Kong China see Tolo Harbour
Tai Poutini National Park N.Z. see Westland National Park
Taipu Brazil 202 F3
Taipudia India 97 G4
Taiqian China 85 G5
Tairadate-kaikyō sea chan. Japan 90 G4
Tairbeart U.K. see Tarbert
Tai Rom Yen National Park Thai. 79 B6
Tairua N.Z. 152 J5
Taisei Nigeria 125 H5
Takundi Dem. Rep. Congo 126 C6
Tainaro Japan 91 B8
Tai Wan b. Hong Kong China see Joss House Bay
Tai To Yan mt. Hong Kong China 87 [inset]
T'aitung Taiwan 87 G4
also known as Taidong
Tai Tung Shan hill Hong Kong China see Sunset Peak
T'aitung Shan mts Taiwan 87 G4
also known as Haian Shanmc
Taivalkoski Fin. 44 O2
Taivaskero mt. Fin. 44 N1
Taivassalo Fin. 45 M3
▶ Taiwan country Asia 87 G4
also known as China, Republic of or Chung-hua Min-kuo; formerly known as Formosa
asia [countries] ▶ 64–67
Taiwan Haixia strait China/Taiwan see Taiwan Strait
Taiwan Shan mts Taiwan see Chungyang Shanmo
Taixing China 87 F1
Taiwan Strait China/Taiwan 87 F4
also known as Taiwan Haixia; formerly known as Formosa Strait
Taixian China see Jiangyan
Taixing China 87 G1
Taïyetos Óros mts Greece see Tavgetos
Taiyuan China 85 G4
Tai Yue Shan i. Hong Kong China see Lantau Island
Taiyue Shan mts China 85 F4
Taizhao China 89 C6
Taizhong Taiwan see T'aichung
Taizhou Jiangsu China 87 F1
Taizhou Zhejiang China 87 G2
also known as Jiaojiang
Taizhou Liedao i. China 87 G2
Taizhou Wan b. China 87 G2
Taizi r. China 83 B4
Ta'izz Yemen 104 C5
Ta'izz governorate Yemen 104 C5
Tajam, Tanjong pt Sing. 76 [inset]
Tajamulco, Volcán de vol. Guat. 185 H6
Tajarhī Libya 120 B3
Tajem, Gunung hill Indon. 77 D3
Tāj-e Maleki Iran 100 B4
Tajerouine Tunisia 123 H2
▶ Tajikistan country Asia 101 G2
spelt Tojikiston in Tajik; formerly known as Tadzhikskaya S.S.R.; formerly spelt Tadjikistan
asia [countries] ▶ 64–67
Tajima Japan 90 F6
Tajitos Mex. 184 B2
Taj Mahal tourist site India 96 C4
Tajo r. Spain 54 D5 see Tagus
Tajoom India 86 B2
Tajsara, Cordillera de mts Bol. 200 D5
Tajuña r. Spain 55 H4
Tak Thai. 78 B4
Takāb Iran 100 A2
Takabba Kenya 128 D4
Taka'Bonerate, Kepulauan atolls Indon. 75 B4
also known as Macan, Kepulauan
Taka Bol. Cent. Afr. Rep. 126 D2
Takahagi Japan 90 G6
Takahashi Japan 91 C7
Takahe, Mount Antarctica 222 Q1
Takaka N.Z. 152 G8
Takal India 96 C5
Takalaou Chad 126 C2
Takalous, Oued watercourse Alg. 123 G5
Takama Guyana 199 G3
Takamatsu Japan 91 D7
Takamori Japan 91 B8
Takanabe Japan 91 B8
Takanosu Japan 90 G4
Takaoka Japan 91 E6
Takapau N.Z. 152 K8
Takapuna N.Z. 152 I4
Takara-jima i. Japan 83 C7
Takasaki Japan 91 F6
Takatokwane Botswana 131 E5
Takatshwaane Botswana 130 D4
Takatsuki Japan 91 D7
Takatsuki-yama mt. Japan 91 C8
Takatu r. Brazil/Guyana 199 G3
Ta-Kaw Myanmar 78 B3
Takayama Japan 91 E6
Tak Bai Thai. 79 C7
Takefu Japan 91 E7
Takehara Japan 91 C7
Takengon Indon. 76 B1
Takeo Cambodia see Takêv
Takeo Japan 91 B8
Take-shima i. N. Pacific Ocean see Liancourt Rocks
Takêv Cambodia 79 D6
also spelt Takeo
Takfon Tajik. 101 G2
Takhādīd well Iraq 107 F5
Takhar prov. Afgh. 101 G2
Takhatpur India 97 D5
Takhemaret Alg. 55 L9
Takhiatash Uzbek. see Gulabie
Takhini r. Canada 166 C2
Takhini Hotspring Canada 166 C2
Ta Khli Thai. 79 C5
Takht Apān, Kūh-e mt. Iran 100 B3
Takhta-Bazar Turkm. see Tagtabazar
Takhtabrod Kazakh. 103 F1
Takhtakupyr Uzbek. 102 E4
Takht-i-Sulaiman mt. Pak. 101 G4
Takht-i-Suleiman mt. Iran 100 B2
Takiéta Niger 125 H3
Takijuq Lake Canada see Napaktulik Lake
Takikawa Japan 90 H3
Takinoue Japan 90 I2
Takisung Indon. 77 F3
Takitimu Mountains N.Z. 153 B13
Takla Lake Canada 166 E4
Takla Landing Canada 166 E4
▶ Taklimakan Desert China 88 C4
also known as Takla Makan or Taklimakan Shamo
world [land images] ▶ 12–13
Taklimakan Shamo des. China see Taklimakan Desert
Takob Tajik. 101 G2
Takoradi Ghana 125 E5
Takpa Shiri mt. China 89 F6
Takti r. Canada/U.S.A. 164 F4
Taku Canada 166 C3
Taku Japan 91 B8
Takua Pa Thai. 79 B6
Takua Thung Thai. 79 B6
Takum Nigeria 125 H5
Takundi Dem. Rep. Congo 126 C6
Tal India 96 B5
Tala Uruguay 204 G4
Talachyn Belarus 43 K7
Talagang Pak. 101 H3

Talaiassa, Serra hill Spain 55 M6
Talaja India 96 B5
Talakan Amurskaya Oblast' Rus. Fed. 82 C2
Talakan Khabarovskiy Kray Rus. Fed. 82 D2
Talala India 96 A5
Talandzha Rus. Fed. 82 C2
Talang, Gunung vol. Indon. 76 C3
Talangbetutu Indon. 76 D3
Talara Peru 198 A6
Talar-i-Band mts Pak. 101 E5
also known as Macran Coast Range
Talas r. Kazakh./Kyrg. 103 G3
Talas Kyrg. 103 H4
Talas admin. div. Kyrg. 103 G4
English form Talas Oblast; also known as Talasskaya Oblast'
Talas Ala-Too mts Kyrg. 103 G4
English form Talas Range; also known as Talasskiy Alatau, Khrebet
Talas Ala-Too mts Kyrg. see Talas Ala-Too
Talas Oblast admin. div. Kyrg. see Talas
Talas Range mts Kyrg. see Talas Ala-Too
Talasskaya Oblast' admin. div. Kyrg. see Talas
Talasskiy Alatau, Khrebet mts Kyrg. see Talas Ala-Too
Tal'at al Jamā'ah, Rujm mt. Jordan 108 G7
Talata-Mafara Nigeria 125 G3
Țal 'at Mūsá mt. Lebanon/Syria 109 H3
Talaud, Kepulauan is Indon. 75 C1
Talavera de la Reina Spain 54 G5
Talawanta Australia 149 C3
Talawgyi Myanmar 78 B2
Talayan Phil. 74 C5
Talayuela Spain 54 F5
Talayuelo mt. Spain 55 I5
Talbehat India 96 C4
Talbot, Mount hill Australia 151 D5
Talbot Inlet Canada 165 L2
Talbot Lake Canada 167 L4
Talbotton U.S.A. 175 C5
Talbragar r. Australia 147 F3
Talca Chile 204 C4
Talca, Punta pt Chile 204 C4
Talcahuano Chile 204 B5
Talcher India 95 E1
Taldan Rus. Fed. 82 B1
Taldom Rus. Fed. 43 S5
Taldyk r. Kazakh. 102 D4
Taldyk, Pereval pass Kyrg. 103 H5
Taldykorgan Kazakh. 103 I3
also known as Taldyqorghan; formerly spelt Taldy-Kurgan
Taldy-Kurgan Kazakh. see Taldykorgan
Taldyqorghan Kazakh. see Taldykorgan
Taldysu Kyrg. see Taldy-Suu
Taldy-Suu Kyrg. 103 I4
also spelt Taldysu
Talegaon Maharashtra India 94 B2
Talegaon Maharashtra India 94 C1
Talen India 96 C5
Taleni S. Africa 133 M9
Tâlesh Iran see Hashtpar
Talets, Ozero l. Rus. Fed. 43 R2
Talga r. Australia 150 B4
Talgar Kazakh. 103 I4
Talgar, Pik mt. Kazakh. 103 I4
Talḩah Saudi Arabia 104 C4
Taliabu i. Indon. 75 C3
Taliang Phil. 74 C5
Talikota India 94 C2
Talikud i. Phil. 74 C5
Talimardzhan Uzbek. 103 F5
also spelt Tallymerjen or Tollimarjon
Taliouine Morocco 122 D3
Talipaamba India 94 B3
also spelt Thaliparamba
Talisay Phil. 74 B4
Talisayan Indon. 77 G2
Talisayan Phil. 74 C4
Talış Dağları mts Azer./Iran 107 G3
also known as Talyshskiye Gory
Talisei i. Indon. 75 C3
Talitsa Kostromskaya Oblast' Rus. Fed. 40 H4
Talitsa Lipetskaya Oblast' Rus. Fed. 43 T9
Taliwang Indon. 77 G5
Tal'ka Belarus 43 J8
Tallacootra, Lake salt flat Australia 146 B2
Talladega U.S.A. 175 C5
▶ Tallahassee U.S.A. 175 C6
State capital of Florida.
Tallangatta Australia 147 E4
Tallapoosa r. U.S.A. 175 C5
Tallaringa Conservation Park nature res. Australia 146 B2
Tall 'Afar Iraq 107 E3
Tallard France 50 E6
Tall Baydar Syria 109 L1
▶ Tallinn Estonia 42 F2
Capital of Estonia. Historically known as Reval or Revel.
Tallina laht b. Estonia 42 F2
Tall Kalakh Syria 108 H3
Tall Kayf Iraq 107 E3
Tall Kūjik Syria 109 N1
Tall Tamir Syria 109 L1
Tallmadge U.S.A. 176 D4
Tallulah U.S.A. 175 B5
Tall 'Uwaynāt Iraq 107 E3
Tallymerjen Uzbek. see Talimardzhan
Tălmaciu Romania 58 F3
Talmisã Brazil 199 H4
Talmont-St-Hilaire France 50 E6
Tal'ne Ukr. 41 D6
also spelt Tal'noye
Tal'noye Ukr. see Tal'ne
Talod India 96 B5
Taloda India 96 B5
Talodi Sudan 128 A2
Taloga U.S.A. 179 C4
Taloi Range mts Pak. 101 F5
Talon, Lac l. Canada 169 H2
Taloqān Afgh. 101 G2
Talos Dome ice feature Antarctica 223 K2
Ta Loung San mt. Laos 78 C3
Taloyoak Canada 165 J3
formerly known as Spence Bay
Talpa Mex. 184 D4
Tal Pass Pak. 101 H3
also known as Shohi Pass
Talras well Niger 125 H3
Talsi Latvia 42 D5
Tal Siyāh Iran 101 D4
Taltal Chile 204 C2
Taltson r. Canada 167 H2
Talu China 89 F6
Taluk Indon. 76 C3
Taluti, Teluk b. Indon. 75 D3
Talvik Norway 44 M1
Talwood Australia 147 F2
Taly Rus. Fed. 41 G6
Talyawalka r. Australia 147 D3
Talyshskiye Gory mts Azer./Iran see Talış Dağları
Talyy Rus. Fed. 40 J2
Tama Abu, Banjaran mts Sarawak Malaysia 77 F2
also known as Penambo Range or Tamabo Range
Tamabo Range mts Sarawak Malaysia see Tama Abu, Banjaran
Tamadaw Myanmar 78 A3
Tamai, Nam r. Myanmar 78 B2

Tamaki Strait N.Z. 152 I4
Tamala Australia 151 A5
Tamala Rus. Fed. 41 G5
Tamalameque Col. 187 E5
Tamale Ghana 125 E4
Tamalet well Mali 125 F3
Tamalung Indon. 77 F3
Tamana Japan 91 B8
Tamana i. Kiribati 145 G2
formerly known as Rotch Island
Tamanar Morocco 122 C3
Tamanco Peru 198 C6
Tamanhint Libya 120 B3
Tamani Mali 124 D3
Taman Negara National Park Malaysia 76 C1
Tamano Japan 91 C7
Tamanrasset Alg. 123 G5
also known as Tamenghet; formerly known as Fort Laperrine
Tamanrasset, Oued watercourse Alg. 123 F5
Tamanthi Myanmar 78 A2
Tamaqua U.S.A. 177 J5
Tamar India 97 E5
Tamar r. Syria see Tadmur
Tamar r. U.K. 47 H13
Tamar India 94 B1
Tamaradant well Mali 125 F2
Tamarai Japan 91 B8
Tamarugal, Pampa de plain Chile 200 D4
Tamasane Botswana 131 E4
Tamási Hungary 49 P9
Tamaşi Romania 58 I2
Tamatave Madag. see Toamasina
Tamaulipas state Mex. 185 F4
Tamaulipas, Sierra de mts Mex. 185 F4
Tama Wildlife Reserve nature res. Eth. 128 C3
Tamayama Japan 90 G5
Tamazula Durango Mex. 184 D3
Tamazula Jalisco Mex. 185 E5
Tamazulápam Mex. 185 F5
Tamazunchale Mex. 185 F4
Tambach Kenya 128 B4
Tambacounda Senegal 124 B3
Tambangsawah Indon. 76 C3
Tambankulu Swaziland 133 P3
Tambaoura, Falaise de esc. Mali 124 C3
Tambaqui Brazil 199 F6
Tambara Moz. 131 G3
Tambau Brazil 206 F8
Tambawel Nigeria 125 G3
Tambelan, Kepulauan is Indon. 77 D2
Tambelan Besar i. Indon. 77 D2
Tambellup Australia 151 B7
Tamberu Indon. 77 F4
Tambisan Sabah Malaysia 77 G1
Tambo Australia 149 E5
Tambo r. Australia 147 E4
Tambo r. Peru 200 C4
Tambobamba Peru 200 B3
Tambo Grande Peru 198 A6
Tambohorano Madag. 131 [inset] I3
Tambopata r. Peru 200 C3
Tambor Angola 127 B9
Tambora, Gunung vol. Indon. 77 G5
Tamboril Brazil 202 D3
Tamboryacu r. Peru 198 C5
Tamboura Cent. Afr. Rep. 126 E3
Tambov Rus. Fed. 41 G5
Tambovka Rus. Fed. 82 C2
Tambov Oblast admin. div. Rus. Fed. see Tambovskaya Oblast'
Tambovskaya Oblast' admin. div. Rus. Fed. 41 G5
English form Tambov Oblast
Tambre r. Spain 54 C2
Tambu, Teluk b. Indon. 75 A2
Tambunan Sabah Malaysia 77 G1
formerly known as Tibabar
Tambunan, Bukit well Sabah Malaysia 77 G1
Tambura Sudan 126 E3
Tambuyukon, Gunung mt. Sabah Malaysia 77 G1
Tâmchekket Mauritania 124 C2
Tamdy Kazakh. 102 D4
Tamdybulak Uzbek. 103 F4
also spelt Tomdibuloq
Tamdytau, Gory hills Uzbek. 103 F4
also known as Tomditow Toghi
Tame Col. 198 D3
Tâmega r. Port. 54 C3
Tamel Aike Arg. 205 C8
Tamelos, Akra pt Greece 59 F11
Tamenghest Alg. see Tamanrasset
Tamenglong India 97 G4
Tamerlanovka Kazakh. see Temirlanovka
Tamesna reg. Niger 125 G2
Tamgak, Adrar mt. Niger 125 H2
Tamgout de Lalla Khedidja mt. Alg. 55 P8
Tamgué, Massif du mt. Guinea 124 B3
Tamia India 96 C5
Tamiahua Mex. 185 F4
Tamiahua, Laguna de lag. Mex. 185 F4
Tamiami Canal U.S.A. 175 D7
Tamiang r. Indon. 76 B1
Tamiang, Ujung pt Indon. 76 B1
Tamil Nadu state India 94 C4
formerly known as Madras
Tamin Gol r. Mongolia 84 C2
Tamiš r. Yugo. 58 B4
Tāmiya Egypt 121 F2
Tamiyah, Jabal hill Saudi Arabia 104 C2
Tamit well Niger 125 H1
Tamlelt, Plaine de plain Morocco 123 E2
Tamluk India 97 E5
Tammaro r. Italy 56 G7
Tammela Etelä-Suomi Fin. 42 E1
Tammela Oulu Fin. 44 O2
Tammerfors Fin. see Tampere
Tammio i. Fin. 42 I1
Tammisaaren Saariston Kansallispuisto nat. park Fin. 42 I1
Ekenäs skärgårds Nationalpark
Tammisaari Fin. see Ekenäs
Tammispää Estonia 42 I2
Tamnava r. Yugo. 58 B4
Tamou Niger 125 F3
Tamou, Réserve Totale de Faune de nature res. Niger 125 F3
Tampa U.S.A. 175 D7
Tampa Bay U.S.A. 175 D7
Tampang Indon. 76 D4
Tampere Fin. 45 M3
also known as Tammerfors
Tampico Mex. 185 F4
Tampines Sing. 76 [inset]
Tampines, Sungai r. Sing. 76 [inset]
Tampo Indon. 75 B4
Tamrah Saudi Arabia 105 D3
Tamsagbulag Mongolia 85 H2
Tamsalu Estonia 42 H2
Tamshiyacu Peru 198 C6
Tamsweg Austria 49 K8
Tamu Myanmar 78 A2
Tamuin Mex. 185 F4
Tamur r. Nepal 97 F4
Tamworth Australia 147 F2
Tamworth U.K. 47 K11
Tan Kazakh. 103 I2
Tana r. Fin./Norway see Tenojoki
Tana r. Kenya 128 D5
Tana Madag. see Antananarivo
Tana i. Vanuatu see Tanna
Tana, Lake Eth. 128 C2
also known as T'ana Hāyk'
Tanabe Japan 91 D8
Tanabi Brazil 206 D7
Tana Bru Norway 44 O1

Tanafjorden inlet Norway 44 O1
also known as Deanuvuotna
Tanagro r. Italy 57 H8
Tanah, Tanjung pt Indon. 77 E4
T'ana Hāyk' l. Eth. see Tana, Lake
Tanahbala i. Indon. 76 B3
Tanahgrogot Indon. 77 G3
Tanahjampea i. Indon. 75 B4
Tanahmasa i. Indon. 76 B3
Tanahmerah Indon. 77 G2
Tanahputih Indon. 76 C2
Tanakeke i. Indon. 75 A4
Tanakpur India 96 D3
Tanambung Indon. 75 A3
Tanami Australia 148 A3
Tanami Desert Australia 148 A3
Tanami Downs Aboriginal Land res. Australia 148 A4
Tân An Vietnam 79 D6
Tananarive Madag. see Antananarivo
Tanandava Madag. 131 [inset] I4
Tanāqib, Ra's pt Saudi Arabia 105 E2
Tanaro r. Italy 56 A3
Tanauan Phil. 74 C4
Tanbar Australia 149 D5
Tancheng China see Pingtan
Tancheng China 87 F1
Tanch'ŏn N. Korea 83 C4
Tanda Côte d'Ivoire 124 E5
Tanda Uttar Pradesh India 96 C3
Tanda Uttar Pradesh India 97 D4
Tandag Phil. 74 C4
Țăndărei Romania 58 I4
Tandaué Angola 127 C9
Tandek Sabah Malaysia 77 G1
formerly known as Taritipan
Tandi India 96 C2
Tandil Arg. 204 F5
Tandjilé pref. Chad 126 C2
Tando Adam Pak. 101 G5
Tando Alahyar Pak. 101 G5
Tando Bago Pak. 101 G5
Tando Muhammad Khan Pak. 101 G5
Tandou Lake imp. l. Australia 147 D3
Tandsjöborg Sweden 45 K3
Tandubatu i. Phil. 74 B5
Tandula r. India 96 D5
Tandur Andhra Pradesh India 94 C2
Tandur Andhra Pradesh India 94 C2
Taneatua N.Z. 152 K6
Tanega-shima i. Japan 91 B9
Taneichi Japan 90 G4
Tanen Taunggyi mts Thai. 78 B4
Taneti i. Indon. 75 C3
Tanew r. Poland 49 T5
Taneytown U.S.A. 177 H6
Tanezrouft reg. Alg./Mali 123 E5
Tanezrouft Tan-Ahenet reg. Alg. 123 E5
Ţanf, Jabal aţ hill Syria 109 J4
Tang, Ra's-e pt Iran 101 D5
Tanga Rus. Fed. 85 F1
Tanga Tanz. 129 C6
Tanga admin. reg. Tanz. 129 C6
Tangaehe N.Z. 152 I4
Tangail Bangl. 97 F4
Tanga Islands P.N.G. 145 E2
Tangalla Sri Lanka 94 D5
Tanganyika country Africa see Tanzania

▶Tanganyika, Lake Africa 127 F6
Deepest and 2nd largest lake in Africa and 7th largest in the world.
africa [landscapes] ▶▶▶ 112–113

Tangar Iran 100 C2
Tangasseri India 94 C4
Tangdan China 86 B3
formerly known as Dongshuan
Tangeli Iran 100 C2
Tange Promontory hd Antarctica 223 D2
Tanger Morocco see Tangier
Tangerang Indon. 77 D4
Tangermünde Germany 48 I3
Tang-e Sarkheh Iran 101 D5
Tanggor China 86 B1
Tanggu China 85 H4
Tanggulashan China see Tuotuoheyan
Tanggula Shan mt. China 89 E5
Tanggula Shan mts China 89 E5
also known as Dangla Shan
Tanggula Shankou pass China 89 E5
Tangguo China 89 D6
Tanghe China 87 E1
Tang He r. China 87 E1
Tangi Pak. 101 G3
Tangier Morocco 122 D2
also spelt Tanger or Tanjah; historically known as Tingis
Tangimoana N.Z. 152 J8
Tangkittebak, Gunung mt. Indon. 76 D4
Tang La pass China 89 E7
Tanglag China 86 A1
Tanglin Sing. 76 [inset]
Tangmai China 97 G3
Tango Japan 91 D7
Tangorin Australia 149 E4
Tangra Yumco salt l. China 89 D6
Tangse Indon. 76 A1
Tangshan China 85 H4
Tangsyq Kazakh. see Tansyk
Tangte mt. Myanmar 78 B3
Tangub Mindanao Phil. 74 B4
Tangub Negros Phil. 74 B4
Tanguieta Benin 125 F4
Tangwan China 87 D3
Tangwang r. China 82 C3
Tangwanghe China 82 C2
Tangxian China 85 G4
also known as Renhou
Tangxianzhen China 87 E2
Tang-yan Myanmar 78 B3
Tangyan He r. China 87 D2
Tangyin China 85 G5
Tangyuan China 82 C3
Tanhaçu Brazil 202 D5
Tanhua Fin. 44 N2
Taniantaweng Shan mts China 86 A2
Tanimbar, Kepulauan is Indon. 73 H8
Tanintharyi Myanmar see Tenasserim
Tanintharyi Myanmar see Tenasserim
Tanintharyi admin. div. Myanmar see Tenasserim
Taninthayi Myanmar see Tenasserim
Taniwel Indon. 75 D3
Tanjah Morocco see Tangier
Tanjay Phil. 74 B4
Tanjore India see Thanjavur
Tanjung Kalimantan Selatan Indon. 77 F3
Tanjung Sumatra Indon. 76 D3
Tanjungbalai Sumatra Indon. 76 B2
Tanjungbalai Sumatra Indon. 76 C2
Tanjungbaliha Indon. 75 C3
Tanjungbatu Kalimantan Timur Indon. 77 G2
Tanjungbatu Sumatra Indon. 76 C2
Tanjungbuayabuaya, Pulau i. Indon. 77 G2
Tanjunggaru Indon. 77 G3
Tanjungkarang-Telukbetung Indon. 76 D4
also known as Telukbetung; formerly known as Bandar Lampung
Tanjungpandan Indon. 77 D3
Tanjungpinang Indon. 76 D2
Tanjungpura Indon. 76 B2
Tanjung Puting National Park Indon. 77 F3
Tanjungraja Indon. 76 D3
Tanjungredeb Indon. 77 G2
Tanjungsaleh i. Indon. 77 E3
Tanjungsatai Indon. 77 E3
Tanjungselor Indon. 77 G2
Tank Pak. 101 G3
Tankara India 96 A5
Tankavaara Fin. 44 N1
Tankhala India 96 B5
Tankhoy Rus. Fed. 85 E1
Tankse Jammu and Kashmir 96 C2
Tankuhi India 97 E4
Tankwa r. S. Africa 132 D9
Tankwa-Karoo National Park S. Africa 132 D9
Tanlwe r. Myanmar 78 A4
Tanna i. Vanuatu 145 F3
also spelt Tana
Tännäs Sweden 44 K3
Tanner, Mount Canada 166 G5
Tannila Fin. 44 N2
Tannu-Ola, Khrebet mts Rus. Fed. 84 A1
Tannu Tuva aut. rep. Rus. Fed. see Tyva, Respublika
Tano Japan 91 B9
Tañon Strait Phil. 74 B4
Tanot India 96 A4
Tanout Niger 125 H3
Tanquian Mex. 185 F4
Tansen Nepal 97 D4
Tanshui Taiwan 87 G3
also spelt Danshui
Tansilla Burkina 124 D3
Tansyk Kazakh. 103 I3
also spelt Tangsyq
Tanta Egypt 121 F2
Tantabin Pegu Myanmar 78 B4
Tantabin Sagaing Myanmar 78 A3
Tan-Tan Morocco 122 C3
Tantoyuca Mex. 185 F4
Tantpur India 96 C4
Tantu China 85 I2
Tantura Israel 108 F5
Tanuku India 94 D2
Tanumshede Sweden 45 J4
Tanwakka, Sabkhat well W. Sahara 122 B5
▶Tanzania country Africa 129 B6
formerly known as Tanganyika
africa [countries] ▶▶▶ 114–117
Tanzilla r. Canada 166 D3
Tao, Ko i. Thai. 79 B6
Tao'an China see Taonan
Taocheng China see Yongchun
Taocheng China see Daxin
Taodeni Mali see Taoudenni
Tao'er r. China 85 I2
Tao He r. China 84 D5
also known as Lu Qu
Taohong China see Longhui
Taohuaping China see Longhui
Taojiang China 87 E2
Taolanaro Madag. see Tôlañaro
Taole China 85 E4
also known as Mataigou
Taonan China 85 I2
formerly known as Tao'an
Taongi atoll Marshall Is 220 F5
Taormina Sicilia Italy 57 H11
Taos U.S.A. 181 F5
Taouârdeï well Mali 125 F2
Taoudenni Mali 122 E5
also spelt Taodeni
Taounate Morocco 122 D2
Taounnant well Mali 123 E5
formerly known as Tin Tounnant
Taourirt Morocco 123 E2
Taoxi China 87 F3
Taoyang China see Lintao
Taoyuan China 87 D2
T'aoyüan Taiwan 87 G3
also known as Sinchu
Taozhou China see Guangde
Tapa Estonia 42 G2
Tapaan Passage Phil. 74 B5
Tapachula Mex. 185 G6
Tapajós r. Brazil 199 H5
Tapaktuan Indon. 76 B2
Tapalqué Arg. 204 E5
Tapan Indon. 76 C3
Tapan Turkey see Mansurlu
Tapanahoni r. Suriname 199 H3
Tapanatepec Mex. 185 G5
Tapanuli, Teluk b. Indon. 76 B2
Tapará, Ilha Grande do i. Brazil 199 H5
Tapara, Serra do hills Brazil 199 H5
Tapat i. Indon. 75 C3
Tapauá Brazil 199 E6
Tapauá r. Brazil 199 E6
Tapawera N.Z. 152 G9
Tapera Rio Grande do Sul Brazil 203 A9
Tapera Roraima Brazil 199 F5
Tapera Chile 205 C7
Taperoá Brazil 202 E5
Tapes Brazil 203 B9
Tapeta Liberia 124 C5
Tapi r. India 96 B5
Tapia, Sierra de hills Bol. 201 F4
Tapi Aike Arg. 205 C8
Tapiantana i. Phil. 74 B5
Tapiau Rus. Fed. see Gvardeysk
Tapiche r. Peru 198 C6
Tápió r. Hungary 49 R8
Tapiocanga, Chapada do hills Brazil 206 F3
Tápiószecső Hungary 49 Q8
Tapira Brazil 206 G6
Tapiracanga Brazil 202 C5
Tapirai Brazil 206 F10
Tapirapé r. Brazil 202 B4
Tapirapecó, Sierra mts Brazil/Venez. 199 E4
Tapirapuã Brazil 201 F3
Tapis mt. Malaysia 76 C1
Tapisuelas Mex. 184 C3
Taplejung Nepal 97 E4
Tap Mun Chau i. Hong Kong China 87 [inset]
Tapoa watercourse Burkina 125 F3
Tapol Chad 126 B2
Tapolca Hungary 49 O9
Ta-pom Myanmar 78 B3
Tappahannock U.S.A. 177 I8
Tappal India 96 C3
Tappeh, Kūh-e hill Iran 100 B3
Tappi-zaki pt Japan 90 G4
Taprobane country Asia see Sri Lanka
Tapuaenuku mt. N.Z. 153 H9
Tapul Phil. 74 B5
Tapul Group is Phil. 74 B5
Tapulonanjing mt. Indon. 76 B2
Tapung r. Indon. 76 C2
Tapurú Brazil 199 E5
Tapurucuara Brazil 199 E5
Taputeouea atoll Kiribati see Tabiteuea
Taqar mt. Yemen 104 D5
Taqtaq Iraq 107 F4
Taquara Brazil 203 B9
Taquaral, Serra do hills Brazil 206 A2
Taquari Brazil 203 A6
Taquari r. Brazil 201 F4
Taquaritinga Brazil 206 E8
Taquarituba Brazil 206 D10
Taquaruçu r. Brazil 206 A8
Tara Australia 147 F1
Tara r. Bos.-Herz./Yugo. 56 K5
Tara nat. park Yugo. 58 A5
Taraba r. Nigeria 125 H4
Taraba state Nigeria 125 H4
Tarabai Brazil 206 B9
Tarabuco Bol. 200 D4
Țarābulus Libya see Tripoli
Taraclia Moldova 58 J3
formerly spelt Tarakliya
Taraco Peru 200 C3
Taracua Brazil 198 D4
Taradale N.Z. 152 K7
Tarāghin Libya 120 B3
Tarai reg. India 97 F4
Taraira r. Brazil see Traira
Tarairí Bol. 201 E5
Tarakan Indon. 77 G2
Tarakan i. Indon. 77 G2
Tarakki reg. Afgh. 101 F3
Taraklı Turkey 106 B2
Tarakliya Moldova see Taraclia
Tarakua Fiji 145 H3
Taran, Mys pt Rus. Fed. 42 A7
Tarana India 96 C5
Taranagar India 96 B3
Taranaki admin. reg. N.Z. 152 H7
Taranaki, Mount vol. N.Z. 152 I7
also known as Egmont, Mount
Tarancón Spain 55 H4
Tarangambadi India 94 C4
Tarangara Chad 126 C2
Tarangire National Park Tanz. 129 C6
Tarangul l. Kazakh. see Taranköl', Ozero
Taranköl', Ozero l. Kazakh. 103 G1
formerly known as Tarangul
Taranovskoye Kazakh. 103 E1
formerly known as Viktorovka
Taranto Italy 57 J8
historically known as Tarentum
Taranto, Golfo di g. Italy 57 J8
Tarapacá admin. reg. Chile 200 C4
Tarapacá Col. 198 D5
Tarapoto Peru 198 B6
Țaraq an Na'ājah reg. Syria 109 K3
Tarare France 51 K7
Tararua Forest Park nature res. N.Z. 152 J8
Tararua Range mts N.Z. 152 J8
Tarascon-sur-Ariège France 50 H10
Tarashcha Ukr. 41 D6
Tarasht Iran 100 D3
Tarasovskiy Rus. Fed. 41 G6
Tarat Alg. 123 H4
Tarata Peru 200 C4
Tarauacá Brazil 200 C2
Tarauacá r. Brazil 198 D6
Taravo r. Corse France 56 A7
Tarawa atoll Kiribati 145 G1
formerly known as Cook Atoll or Knox Atoll
Tarawera N.Z. 152 K7
Tarawera, Lake N.Z. 152 K6
Tarawera, Mount N.Z. 152 K6
Taraz Kazakh. 103 G4
formerly known as Dzhambul or Zhambyl; historically known as Auliye Ata
Tarazona Spain 55 J3
Tarazona de la Mancha Spain 55 J5
Tarbagatay Kazakh. 103 J3
Tarbagatay Rus. Fed. 85 E1
Tarbagatay, Khrebet mts Kazakh. 88 C2
Tarbat Ness pt U.K. 46 I6
Tarbert Rep. of Ireland 47 C11
Tarbert Argyll and Bute, Scotland U.K. 46 G8
Tarbert Western Isles, Scotland U.K. 46 F6
also spelt Tairbeart
Tarbes France 50 G9
Tarbet U.K. 46 H7
Tarboro U.S.A. 174 E5
Tarcoola Australia 146 B2
Tarcoon Australia 147 E2
Tarcoonyinna watercourse Australia 146 B1
Țarcului, Munții mts Romania 58 D3
Tardes r. France 51 I6
Tardoire r. France 50 G7
Tardoki-Yani, Gora mt. Rus. Fed. 82 E2
Taree Australia 147 G2
Tareifing Sudan 128 B2
Tärendö Sweden 44 M2
Tarentum Italy see Taranto
Tareya Rus. Fed. 39 J2
Țarfā, Ra's aț pt Saudi Arabia 104 C4
Tarfaya Morocco 122 B4
formerly known as Cabo Yubi or Cape Juby or Villa Bens
Targa well Niger 125 G2
Targan Kazakh. see Targyn
Targhee Pass U.S.A. 180 E3
Târgoviște Romania 58 G4
formerly spelt Tîrgoviște
Târgu Bujor Romania 58 I3
formerly spelt Tîrgu Bujor
Târgu Cărbunești Romania 58 E4
formerly spelt Tîrgu Cărbunești
Târgu Frumos Romania 58 H1
formerly spelt Tîrgu Frumos
Targuist Morocco 122 D2
Târgu Jiu Romania 58 E3
formerly spelt Tîrgu Jiu
Târgu Lăpuș Romania 58 E1
formerly spelt Tîrgu Lăpuș
Târgu Mureș Romania 58 F2
also known as Marosvásárhely; formerly spelt Tîrgu Mureș
Târgu Neamț Romania 58 H1
formerly spelt Tîrgu Neamț
Târgu Ocna Romania 58 H2
formerly spelt Tîrgu Ocna
Târgu Secuiesc Romania 58 H2
formerly spelt Tîrgu Secuiesc
Targyailing China 89 D6
Targyn Kazakh. 88 C1
formerly spelt Targan
Tarhān Iran 100 A3
Tarhmanant well Mali see Taghmanant
Tarhūnah Libya 120 B1
Tari P.N.G. 73 J8
Tarian Gol China 85 F4
Tarib, Wādī watercourse Saudi Arabia 104 C4
Tarif U.A.E. 105 F2
Tarifa Spain 54 F8
Tarifa, Punta de pt Spain 54 F8
Tarigtig Point Phil. 74 B2
Tarija Bol. 201 D5
Tarija dept Bol. 201 D5
Tarikere India 94 B3
Tariku r. Indon. 73 I7
Tarīm Yemen 105 E4
Tarim Basin China 88 C4
also known as Tarim Pendi
Tarime Tanz. 128 B5
Tarim He r. China 88 D3
Tarim Liuchang China 88 D3
Tarim Pendi basin China see Tarim Basin
Taringuiti Bol. 201 E5
Tarin Kowt Afgh. 101 F3
Taritatu r. Indon. 73 I7
Taritipan Sabah Malaysia see Tandek
Tarjil Iraq 109 P2
Tarka r. S. Africa 133 J9
Tarka, Vallée de watercourse Niger 125 G3
Tarkastad S. Africa 133 K9
Tarkio U.S.A. 178 D3
Tarko-Sale Rus. Fed. 38 H3
Tarkwa Ghana 125 E5
Tarlac Phil. 74 B3
Tarlac r. Phil. 74 B2
Tarlo River National Park Australia 147 F3
Tarlton U.S.A. 176 C6
Tarma Junín Peru 200 B2
Tarma Loreto Peru 198 D5
Tarn r. France 51 H8
Tarna r. Hungary 49 Q8
Tärnaby Sweden 44 K2
Tarnak r. Afgh. 101 F4
Târnava Mare r. Romania 58 E2
Târnava Mică r. Romania 58 E2
Târnăveni Romania 58 F2
formerly spelt Tîrnăveni
Tarnica mt. Poland 49 T6
Tarnobrzeg Poland 49 S5
Tarnogród Poland 49 T5
Tarnogskiy Gorodok Rus. Fed. 40 G3
Tarnopol Ukr. see Ternopil'
Tarnos France 50 E9
Târnova Romania 58 C3
Tarnów Poland 49 R5
Tarnowitz Poland see Tarnowskie Góry
Tarnowskie Góry Poland 49 P5
historically known as Tarnowitz
Tårnvik Norway 44 K2
Taro r. Italy 56 C4
Tarō Japan 90 G5
Taro Co salt l. China 89 C6
Țārom Iran 100 C4
Taroom Australia 149 F5
Taroudannt Morocco 122 C3
Tarpasa Bangl. 97 F5
Tarpaulin Swamp Australia 148 C3
Tarpon Springs U.S.A. 175 D6
Tarpum Bay Bahamas 175 E7
Tarq Iran 100 B3
Tarquinia Italy 56 D6
historically known as Corneto or Tarquinii
Tarquinii Italy see Tarquinia
Tarrabool Lake salt flat Australia 148 B3
Tarracina Italy see Terracina
Tarraco Spain see Tarragona
Tarragona Spain 55 M3
historically known as Tarraco
Tårrajaur Sweden 44 L2
Tarraleah Australia 147 E5
Tarrant Point Australia 148 C3
Tarras N.Z. 153 D12
Tarrasa Spain see Terrassa
Tàrrega Spain 55 M3
Tarrong China see Nyêmo
Tarso Ahon mt. Chad 120 C4
Tarso Emissi mt. Chad 120 C4
Tarso Kobour mt. Chad 120 C4
Tarsus Turkey 106 C3
Tarta Turkm. see Darta
Tartagal Salta Arg. 201 E5
Tartagal Santa Fé Arg. 204 F3
Tärtär Azer. 107 F2
also spelt Terter; formerly known as Mir-Bashir
Tartas France 50 F9
Tartu Estonia 42 H3
formerly known as Yur'yev; historically known as Dorpat
Țarțūs Syria 108 G3
Țarțūs governorate Syria 108 H2
Tarumae-san vol. Japan see Shikotsu
Tarumirim Brazil 207 L6
Tarumizu Japan 91 B9
Tarumovka Rus. Fed. 102 A3
Tarung Hka r. Myanmar 78 B2
Tarusa Rus. Fed. 43 S7
Tarusa r. Rus. Fed. 43 S7
Tarūt Saudi Arabia 105 E2
Tarutung Indon. 76 B2
Tarutyne Ukr. 58 K2
Tarvisio Italy 56 F2
Tarvisium Italy see Treviso
Tarvo Bol. 201 E3
Tarz Iran 100 D4
Tasaral Kazakh. 88 A2
Tasbuget Kazakh. 103 F3
Taschereau Canada 173 O2
Taseko Mountain Canada 166 F5
Tasendjanet, Oued watercourse Alg. 123 F4
Tasgaon India 94 B2
Tashauz Turkm. see Dashkhovuz
Tashauzskaya Oblast' admin. div. Turkm. see Dashkhovuzskaya Oblast'
Tashbunar r. Ukr. 58 J3
Tashi China 84 B3
Tashi Chho Bhutan see Thimphu
Tashigang Bhutan see Trashigang
Tashino Rus. Fed. see Pervomaysk
Tashir Armenia 107 F2
formerly known as Kalinino
Tashk, Daryācheh-ye l. Iran 100 C4

▶Tashkent Uzbek. 103 G4
Capital of Uzbekistan. Also spelt Toshkent.

Tashkent Oblast admin. div. Uzbek. see Tashkentskaya Oblast'
Tashkentskaya Oblast' admin. div. Uzbek. 103 G4
English form Tashkent Oblast; also known as Toshkent Wiloyati
Tashkepri Turkm. 103 E5
also spelt Dashköpri
Tash-Kömür Kyrg. 103 H4
also spelt Tash-Kumyr
Tash-Kumyr Kyrg. see Tash-Kömür
Tashla Rus. Fed. 102 C2
Tashqurghan Afgh. see Kholm
Tasialujjuaq, Lac l. Canada 169 F1
Tasiat, Lac l. Canada 169 F1
Tasiilap Karra c. Greenland 165 P3
also known as Gustav Holm, Kap
Tasiilaq Greenland see Ammassalik
Tasikmalaya Indon. 77 E4
Tasiujaq Canada 169 G1
formerly known as Baie-aux-Feuilles or Leaf Bay
Tasiusaq Greenland 165 N2
Tåsjö Sweden 44 K2
Task well Niger 125 H3
Tasker Niger 125 H3
Taskesken Kazakh. 103 J3
Taşköprü Turkey 106 C2
Taşlıçay Turkey 107 E3
Tasman N.Z. 152 H9
Tasman admin. reg. N.Z. 152 G9
Tasman r. N.Z. 153 E12
Tasman, Mount N.Z. 153 E11
Tasman Bay N.Z. 152 H9

▶Tasmania state Australia 147 E5
4th largest island in Oceania. Historically known as Van Diemen's Land.
oceania [landscapes] ▶▶▶ 136–137

Tasman Mountains N.Z. 152 G9
Tasman Peninsula Australia 147 F5
Tasman Sea S. Pacific Ocean 145 G6
Tășnad Romania 58 D1
Taşova Turkey 107 D2
also known as Yemişenbükü
Tassara Niger 125 G2
Tasselot, Mont hill France 51 K5
Tassi Gabon 126 A5
Tassialouc, Lac l. Canada 169 F1
Tassili du Hoggar plat. Alg. 123 G5
Tassili n'Ajjer plat. Alg. 123 G4
Tassin-la-Demi-Lune France 51 K7
Tåstrup Denmark 45 K5
Tas-Tumus Rus. Fed. 39 M3
Tasty Kazakh. 103 G3
Tasty-Taldy Kazakh. 103 F2
Tasu Canada 166 C4
Taşucu Turkey 108 E1
Tas-Yuryakh Rus. Fed. 39 L3
Tata Hungary 49 P8
Tata Morocco 122 D3
Tataba Indon. 75 B3
Tatabánya Hungary 49 P8
Tatamagouche Canada 169 I4
Tata Mailau, Gunung mt. East Timor 75 C5
Tatanagar India 97 E5
Tataouine Tunisia 123 H2
Tatarbunary Ukr. 41 D7
Tatarka Belarus 43 J8
Tatarpur India 96 C4
Tatarsk Rus. Fed. 80 B1
Tatarsk Rus. Fed. 43 M7
Tatarskaya A.S.S.R. aut. rep. Rus. Fed. see Tatarstan, Respublika
Tatarskiy Proliv strait Rus. Fed. 82 F2
English form Tatar Strait
Tatarstan, Respublika aut. rep. Rus. Fed. 40 I5
formerly known as Tatarskaya A.S.S.R.
Tatar Strait Rus. Fed. see Tatarskiy Proliv
Tătăruși Romania 58 H1
Tatau Sarawak Malaysia 77 F2
Tatavi r. Iran 100 A2
Tate r. Australia 149 D3
Tatebayashi Japan 91 F6
Tateyama Japan 91 F7
Tate-yama vol. Japan 91 E6
Tathlina Lake Canada 167 G2
Tathlīth Saudi Arabia 104 C4
Tathlīth, Wādī watercourse Saudi Arabia 104 D3
Tathra Australia 147 F4
Tati Botswana 131 E4
Tâtîlt well Mauritania 124 B2
Tatishchevo Rus. Fed. 41 H6
Tatkon Myanmar 78 B3
Tatla Lake Canada 166 E5
Tatlatui Provincial Park Canada 166 E3
Tatlayoko Lake Canada 166 E5
Tatlikbulak China 88 D4
Tatnam, Cape Canada 167 N3
Tatra Mountains Poland/Slovakia 49 Q6
also known as High Tatras or Tatry
Tatrang China 88 D4
Tatranský nat. park Slovakia 49 R6
Tatry mts Poland/Slovakia see Tatra Mountains
Tatrzański Park Narodowy nat. park Poland 49 Q6
Tatshenshini r. Canada 166 B3
Tatshenshini-Alsek Provincial Wilderness Park Canada 166 B3
Tatsuno Japan 91 D7
Tatta Pak. 101 F5
Tatti Kazakh. 103 H4
formerly spelt Tatty
Tatty Kazakh. see Tatti
Tatui Brazil 206 F10
Tatuk Mountain Canada 166 E4
Tatula r. Lith. 42 F5
Tatum NM U.S.A. 178 B5
Tatum TX U.S.A. 179 D5
Tatvan Turkey 107 E3
Tau i. American Samoa 145 I3
Taua Brazil 202 D3
Tauapeçaçu Brazil 199 F5
Tauariã Brazil 199 F6
Taubaté Brazil 203 C7
Tauber r. Germany 48 G6
Tauberbischofsheim Germany 48 G6
Tauchik Kazakh. 102 B3
also spelt Taūshyq
Taufkirchen (Vils) Germany 48 J7
Tauhara mt. N.Z. 152 K6
Tauhoa N.Z. 152 I4
Tauini r. Brazil 199 G4
Taukum, Peski des. Kazakh. 103 H3
Taumarunui N.Z. 152 J6
Taumaturgo Brazil 200 B2
Taunay Brazil 201 G5
Taung S. Africa 133 I4
Taungbon Myanmar 79 B5
Taungdwingyi Myanmar 78 A3
Taunggyi Myanmar 78 B3
Taunglau Myanmar 78 B3
Taungnyo Range mts Myanmar 78 B4
Taungtha Myanmar 78 A3
Taungup Myanmar 78 A4
Taunsa Pak. 101 G4
Taunton U.K. 47 I12
Taunton U.S.A. 177 N4
Taunus hills Germany 48 E5
Taupiri N.Z. 152 J5
Taupo N.Z. 152 K6
Taupo, Lake N.Z. 152 J6
Tauragė Lith. 42 D6
Tauralaukis Lith. 42 C6
Tauramena Col. 198 C3
Tauranga N.Z. 152 K5
Taurasia Italy see Turin
Taureau, Réservoir Canada 169 F4
Taurianova Italy 57 I10
Taurikura N.Z. 152 I3
Taurion r. France 50 H7
Tauroa Point N.Z. 152 H3
Taurus Mountains Turkey 106 C3
also known as Toros Dağları
Taūshyq Kazakh. see Tauchik
Tauste Spain 55 J3
Tauu Islands P.N.G. 145 E2
formerly known as Mortlock Islands
Tauwharepare N.Z. 152 M6
Tauyskaya Guba g. Rus. Fed. 39 P4
Tauz Azer. see Tovuz
Tavagnacco Italy 56 F2
Tavankut Vojvodine, Srbija Yugo. 58 A2
Tavares U.S.A. 175 D6
Tavas Turkey 106 B3
also known as Yarangüme
Tavastehus Fin. see Hämeenlinna
Tavda Rus. Fed. 38 G4
Tavelsjö Sweden 44 M2
Tavernes de la Valldigna Spain 55 K5
also spelt Tabernes de Valldigna
Taveuni i. Fiji 145 H3
Tavgetos mts Greece 59 D11
also known as Taïyetos Óros
Taviano Italy 57 K9
Tavignano r. Corse France 56 B6
Tavil'dara Tajik. 101 G2
also spelt Tovil'-Dora
Tavira Port. 54 D7
Tavistock Canada 173 M7
Tavistock U.K. 47 H13
Tavolara, Isola i. Sardegna Italy 56 B8
Tavolzhan Kazakh. 103 I1
also spelt Tobylzhan
Távora r. Spain 54 D3
Tavoy Myanmar 79 B5
also known as Dawei; also spelt Tawè
Tavoy r. Myanmar 79 B5
also known as Dawei
Tavoy Island Myanmar see Mali Kyun
Tavoy Point Myanmar 79 B5
Tavrichanka Rus. Fed. 90 B3
Tavricheskoye Kazakh. 103 J2
also known as Tavrīl
Tavrīl Kazakh. see Tavricheskoye
Tavşanlı Turkey 106 B3
Tavua Fiji 145 G3
Taw r. U.K. 47 H12
Tawakoni, Lake U.S.A. 179 D5
Tawallah Range hills Australia 148 B2
Tawang India 97 F4
Tawas Bay U.S.A. 173 J6
Tawas City U.S.A. 173 J6
Tawau Sabah Malaysia 77 G1
Tawau, Telukan b. Sabah Malaysia 77 G1
Tawè Myanmar see Tavoy
Taweisha Sudan 121 E6
Tawi r. India 96 B2
Ţawī Ḩafīr well U.A.E. 105 F2
Tawila Sudan 120 E6
Tawila, Gezâ'ir is Egypt 104 A2
English form Tawila Islands
Tawila Islands Egypt see Tawila, Gezâ'ir
Ţawī Murra well U.A.E. 105 F2
Tawitawi i. Phil. 74 A5
Tawmaw Myanmar 78 B2
Tawu Taiwan 87 G4
also spelt Dawu
Taxco Mex. 185 F5
Taxkorgan China 88 A4
Tay r. Canada 166 C2
Tay r. U.K. 46 I7
Tay, Firth of est. U.K. 46 I7
Tay, Lake salt flat Australia 151 C7
Tay, Loch l. U.K. 46 H7
Tayabamba Peru 200 A2
Tayabas Bay Phil. 74 B3
Tayan Indon. 77 E2
Tayeeglow Somalia 128 E3
Tayga Rus. Fed. 80 D1
Taygan Mongolia 84 C2
Taykanskiy Khrebet mts Rus. Fed. 82 D1
Taylor Canada 166 F3
Taylor AZ U.S.A. 183 N7
Taylor NE U.S.A. 178 C3
Taylor TX U.S.A. 179 C6
Taylor, Mount N.Z. 153 F11
Taylor, Mount U.S.A. 181 F6
Taylorsville U.S.A. 174 C4
Taylorville U.S.A. 174 B4
Taymā' Saudi Arabia 104 B2
Taymura r. Rus. Fed. 39 J3
Taymyr, Ozero l. Rus. Fed. 39 K2
Taymyr, Poluostrov pen. Rus. Fed. see Taymyr Peninsula
Taymyr Peninsula Rus. Fed. 39 I2
also known as Taymyr, Poluostrov
Tây Ninh Vietnam 79 D6
Taypak Kazakh. 102 B2
also spelt Taypaq; formerly known as Kalmykovo
Taypaq Kazakh. see Taypak
Tayport U.K. 46 J7
Tayshet Rus. Fed. 80 F1
Taysoygan, Peski des. Kazakh. 102 C2
Tayspun tourist site Iraq see Ctesiphon
Taytan Turkey 59 J10
Taytay Luzon Phil. 74 B3
Taytay Palawan Phil. 74 A4
Taytay Bay Phil. 74 A4
Tayu Indon. 77 E4
Tayuan China 82 B2
Tayyebād Iran 101 E3
Tayynsha Kazakh. 103 G1
formerly known as Krasnoarmeysk
Taz r. Rus. Fed. 39 H3
Taza Morocco 122 E2
Taza-Bazar Uzbek. see Shumanay
Tāza Khurmātū Iraq 107 F4
Taze Myanmar 78 A3
Tazeh Kand Azer. 107 F3
Tazenakht Morocco 122 D3
Tazewell TN U.S.A. 176 B9
Tazewell VA U.S.A. 176 D8
Tazin r. Canada 167 I2
Tāzirbū Libya 120 D3
Tazirbu Water Wells Field Libya 120 D3
Tazizilet well Niger 125 H2
Tazlău Romania 58 H2
Tazlău r. Romania 58 H2
Tazmalt Alg. 55 P8
Tazoghrane Tunisia 57 C12
Tazouikert hill Mali 123 E5
Tazovskaya Guba sea chan. Rus. Fed. 39 H3
Tazovskiy Rus. Fed. 39 H3
Tazrouk Alg. 123 G5
Tazzarine Morocco 122 D3
Tazzouguert Morocco 122 E2
Tbessa Alg. see Tébessa

▶T'bilisi Georgia 107 F2
Capital of Georgia. English form Tbilisi; historically known as Tiflis.

Tbilisi Georgia see T'bilisi
Tchabal Mbabo mt. Cameroon 125 I5
Tchad country Africa see Chad
Tchamba Togo 125 F4
Tchaourou Benin 125 F4
Tchetti Benin 125 F5
Tchibanga Gabon 126 A5
Tchidoutene watercourse Niger 125 G2
Tchié well Chad 120 C5
Tchigaï, Plateau du Niger 123 I5
Tchikala-Tcholohanga Angola 127 C8
formerly known as Vila Nova
Tchin-Tabaradene Niger 125 G3
Tcholliré Cameroon 125 I4
Tczew Poland 49 P1
historically known as Dirschau
Te, Prêk r. Cambodia 79 D5
Tea r. Brazil 199 E5
Teacapán Mex. 184 D4
Teague, Lake salt flat Australia 151 C5
Te Anau N.Z. 153 B13
Te Anau, Lake N.Z. 153 B13
Te Anga N.Z. 152 I6
Teano Italy 56 G7
historically known as Teanum Sidicinum
Teano Range mts Australia 150 B5
Teanum Sidicinum Italy see Teano
Teapa Mex. 185 G5
Te Araroa N.Z. 152 M5
Te Aroha N.Z. 152 J5
Te Aroha, Mount hill N.Z. 152 J5
Teate Italy see Chieti
Te Awamutu N.Z. 152 J6
Tébarat Niger 125 F3
Tebedu Sarawak Malaysia 77 E2
Teberda Rus. Fed. 41 G8
Teberdinskiy Zapovednik nature res. Rus. Fed. 107 E2
Tebesjuak Lake Canada 167 L2
Tébessa Alg. 123 H2
also spelt Tbessa; historically known as Theveste
Tébessa, Monts de mts Alg. 123 H2
Tebicuary Para. 201 F6
Tebicuary r. Para. 201 F6
Tebingtinggi Sumatra Indon. 76 B2
Tebingtinggi Sumatra Indon. 76 C3
Tebo r. Indon. 76 C3
Téboursouk Tunisia 57 B12
Tebulos Mt'a Georgia/Rus. Fed. 41 H8
Tecalitlán Mex. 185 E5
Tecate Mex. 184 A1
Tece Turkey 108 F1
Tech r. France 51 I10
Techiman Ghana 125 E5
Techirghiol Romania 58 J4
Tecka Arg. 205 C6
Tecka r. Arg. 205 C6
Tecoh Mex. 185 H4
Tecolutla Mex. 185 F4
Tecomán Mex. 184 E5
Tecopa U.S.A. 183 H6
Tecoripa Mex. 184 C2
Técpan Mex. 185 E5
Tecuala Mex. 184 D4
Tecuci Romania 58 I3
Tecumseh MI U.S.A. 173 J9
Tecumseh NE U.S.A. 178 C3
Ted Somalia 128 D3
Tedzhen Turkm. 102 E5
also spelt Tejen
Tedzhen r. Turkm. 102 E5
Tedzhenstroy Turkm. 102 E5
Teec Nos Pos U.S.A. 183 O5
Teekloof Pass S. Africa 132 F9
Teel Mongolia 84 D1
Teeli Rus. Fed. 84 A1
Tees r. U.K. 47 K9
Teeswater Canada 173 L6
Tefé Brazil 199 E5
Tefé r. Brazil 199 E5
Tefé, Lago l. Brazil 199 E5
Tefedest mts Alg. 123 G4
Téfoûlet well Mali 125 F2
Tegal Indon. 77 E4
Tegel airport Germany 49 K3
Tegina Nigeria 125 G4

▶Tegucigalpa Hond. 186 B4
Capital of Honduras.

Teguidda-n-Tessoumt Niger 125 G2
Tehachapi U.S.A. 182 F6
Tehachapi Mountains U.S.A. 182 E7
Tehachapi Pass U.S.A. 182 F6
Te Hana N.Z. 152 I4
Te Hauke N.Z. 152 K7
Tehek Lake Canada 167 M1
Teheran Iran see Tehrān
Tehery Lake Canada 167 M1
Téhini Côte d'Ivoire 124 E4
Tehran Iran see Tehrān

► Tehrān Iran 100 B3
  Capital of Iran. Also spelt Teheran.

Tehrān prov. Iran 100 B3
Tehri India see Tikamgarh
Tehri India 96 C3
Tehuacán Mex. 185 F5
Tehuantepec, Gulf of Mex. 185 G6
  also known as Tehuantepec, Golfo de
Tehuantepec, Istmo de isthmus Mex.
  185 G5
Tehuitzingo Mex. 185 F5
Teiču rezervāts nature res. Latvia 42 H5
Teide, Pico del vol. Canary Is 122 A3
Teifi r. U.K. 47 H11
Teignmouth U.K. 47 I13
Teiskot well Mali 125 F2
Teita Hills Kenya 128 C5
Teiu Romania 58 G4
Teiuş Romania 58 E2
Teixeira Brazil 202 E3
Teixeira da Silva Angola see Bailundo
Teixeira de Freitas Brazil 207 N4
Teixeira de Sousa Angola see Luau
Teixeiras Brazil 207 K7
Tejakula Indon. 77 F5
Tejeda y Almijara, Sierra de nature res.
  Spain 54 H8
Tejen Turkm. see Tedzhen
Tejgaon Bangl. 97 F5
Tejira well Niger 125 H3
Tejo r. Port. 54 C5 see Tagus
Tejupan, Punta pt Mex. 184 E5
Te Kaha N.Z. 152 L5
Te Kao N.Z. 152 I2
Tekapo r. N.Z. 153 E12
Tekapo, Lake N.Z. 153 E11
Tekari India 97 E4
Te Kauwhata N.Z. 152 J5
Tekax Mex. 185 H4
Tekeli Kazakh. 103 G4
Teke r. Turkey 108 C1
Teke, Ozero salt l. Kazakh. 103 H1
Teke (Aktyubinskaya Oblast') Kazakh. 102 E2
Tekeli (Almatinskaya Oblast') Kazakh. 103 I3
Tekes China 88 C3
Tekes Kazakh. 103 J4
Tekes He r. China 88 C3
Tekezē Wenz r. Eritrea/Eth. 121 H6
Tekiliktag mt. China 89 C4
Tekin Rus. Fed. 82 C2
Tekirdağ Turkey 106 A2
  formerly known as Rodosto
Tekirdağ prov. Turkey 58 I7
Tekirova Turkey 108 B3
Tekkali India 95 E2
Tekman Turkey 107 E3
Teknaf Bangl. 97 G5
Tekoa, Mount N.Z. 153 G10
Tekong Kechil, Pulau i. Sing. 76 [inset]
Te Kopuru N.Z. 152 H4
Tekouiat, Oued watercourse Alg. 123 F5
Te Kowhai N.Z. 152 J5
Tökro well Chad 120 D5
Tektek Dağları hills Turkey 109 K1
Teku Indon. 75 B3
Te Kuiti N.Z. 152 J6
Tel r. India 95 D1
Tela Hond. 186 B4
Telanaipura Indon. see Jambi
Télataï Mali 125 F2
T'elavi Georgia 107 F2
Tel Aviv-Yafo Israel 108 F5
  English form Tel Aviv; also known as Yafa;
  historically known as Joppa
Telč Czech Rep. 49 M6
Telchac Puerto Mex. 185 H4
Tel'ch'ye Rus. Fed. 43 R8
Telciu Romania 58 E1
Tele r. Dem. Rep. Congo 126 D4
Télé, Lac l. Mali 124 E2
Teleajen r. Romania 58 F3
Telegapulang Indon. 77 F3
Telegraph Creek Canada 166 D3
Telekhany Belarus see Tsyelyakhany
Telêmaco Borba Brazil 203 B8
Telemark county Norway 45 J4
Telén Arg. 204 D5
Telen r. Indon. 77 G2
Teleorman r. Romania 58 F4
Telertheba, Djebel mt. Alg. 123 G4
Telescope Peak U.S.A. 183 G5
Teles Pires r. Brazil 201 T4
  also known as São Pires
Teletskoye, Ozero l. Rus. Fed. 88 D1
Telfer Mining Centre Australia 150 C4
Telford U.K. 47 J11
Telfs Austria 48 I8
Telig well Mali 120 C5
Télimélé Guinea 124 B4
Télissour well Chad 120 D5
Teljo, Jebel mt. Sudan 121 E6
Telkwa Canada 166 E4
Tellaro r. Sicilia Italy 57 H12
Tell Atlas mts Alg. see Atlas Tellien
Teller U.S.A. 164 C3
Tell es-Sultan West Bank see Jericho
Tellicherry India 94 B4
  also known as Thalassery
Telloar Ukr. 58 L2
Telloh Iraq 107 F5
Tell Rāk Egypt 108 D7
Telluride U.S.A. 181 F5
Tel'mansk Turkm. see Gubadag
Tel Megiddo tourist site Israel 108 G5
  historically known as Armageddon
Telmen Nuur salt l. Mongolia 84 C1
Telo Indon. 76 [inset]
Teloloapán Mex. 185 F5
Telo Martius France see Toulon
Tel'pos-Iz, Gora r. Rus. Fed. 40 K3
Telsen Arg. 205 D6
Telšiai Lith. 42 D6

Teluk Anson Malaysia 76 C1
  also known as Teluk Intan
Telukbajur Indon. see Telukbayur
Telukbatang Indon. 77 E3
Telukbayur Indon. 76 E3
  formerly known as Emmahaven; formerly
  spelt Telukbajur
Telukbetung Indon. see
  Tanjungkarang-Telukbetung
Telukdalam Indon. 76 B2
Teluk Intan Malaysia see Teluk Anson
Telukkuantan Indon. 76 C3
Teluknaga Indon. 77 D4
Telukpakedai Indon. 77 E3
Telyazh'ye Rus. Fed. 43 S9
Tema Ghana 125 F5
Temagami Canada 173 N3
Temagami Lake Canada 168 E4
Temaju r. Indon. 77 E2
Temanggung Indon. 77 E4
Temapache Mex. 185 F4
Te Mapou N.Z. 152 I7
Temax Mex. 185 H4
Temba S. Africa 133 M2
Tembagapura Indon. 73 I7
Tembe r. Moz. 133 Q3
Tembe Elephant Park nature res. S. Africa
  133 Q3
Tembenchi r. Rus. Fed. 39 J3
Tembesi r. Indon. 76 C3
Tembilahan Indon. 76 C3
Tembisa S. Africa 133 M3
Tembo Aluma Angola 127 C6
Tembué Moz. see Chifunde
Tembuland reg. S. Africa 133 M8
Tembwe Zambia 129 B7
Teme r. U.K. 47 J11
Temecula U.S.A. 183 G8
Temelli Turkey 106 C3
  also known as Samutlu
Temenchula, Gora mt. Rus. Fed. 84 C1
Temengor, Tasik resr Malaysia 76 C1
Temerin Vojvodina, Srbija Yugo. 58 A3
Temerloh Malaysia 76 C2
Teminabuan Indon. 73 H7
Temir Kazakh. 102 D2
Temir Kazakh. see Tumur
Temirlan Kazakh. see Temirlanovka
Temirlanovka Kazakh. 103 G4
  also known as Temirlan; also spelt
  Tamerlanovka
Temirtau Kazakh. 103 H2
Témiscamie r. Canada 169 F3
Témiscaming Canada 168 E4
Témiscamingue, Lac l. Canada 173 N3
  also known as Timiskaming, Lake
Témiscouata, Lac l. Canada 169 G4
Temiyang r. Indon. 76 D2
Temkino Rus. Fed. 43 P6
Temmes Fin. 44 N2
Temnikov Rus. Fed. 41 G5
Temo r. Sardegna Italy 57 A8
Temora Australia 147 E3
Temósachic Mex. 184 D2
Tempe U.S.A. 183 M8
Tempe, Danau l. Indon. 75 A4
Tempe Downs Australia 148 B5
Tempio Pausania Sardegna Italy 56 B8
Temple MI U.S.A. 173 H6
Temple TX U.S.A. 179 C6
Temple Bay Australia 149 D2
Templemore Rep. of Ireland 47 E11
Templer Bank sea feature Phil. 74 A4
Templeton watercourse Australia 148 C4
Templeton r. N.Z. 153 G11
Templeton U.S.A. 182 D6
Templin Germany 49 K2
Tempoal Mex. 185 F4
Tempoal Angola 127 C8
Tempy Rus. Fed. 43 S5
Temryuk Rus. Fed. 41 F7
Temryukskiy Zaliv b. Rus. Fed. 41 F7
Temuco Chile 204 B5
Temuka N.Z. 153 F12
Temul China see Butuo
Temyasovo Rus. Fed. 102 D1
Tena Ecuador 198 B5
Tenabo Mex. 185 H4
Tenabo, Mount U.S.A. 183 H1
Tenala Fin. 42 E1
Tenali India 94 D2
Tenango Mex. 185 F5
Tenasserim Myanmar 79 B5
  also known as Tanintharyi or Tanintharyi or
  Taninthayi
Tenasserim admin. div. Myanmar 79 B5
  also known as Tanintharyi
Tenasserim r. Myanmar 79 B5
Tenby U.K. 47 H12
  also known as Dinbych-y-Pysgod
Tenby Bay Canada 173 J4
Tence France 51 K7
Tendaho Eth. 128 D2
Tende France 51 N6
Tende, Col de pass France/Italy 51 N8
Ten Degree Channel India 95 G4
Tendelti Sudan 121 G7
Te-n-Dghamcha, Sebkhet salt marsh
  Mauritania 124 A2
Tendö Japan 90 G5
Tendrara Morocco 123 F2
Tendre, Mont mt. Switz. 51 M6
Tendukheda India 96 C5
Téné r. Guinea 124 C4
Tenedos i. Turkey see Bozcaada
Ténénkou Mali 124 D3
Tenenys r. Lith. 42 D6
Ténéré du Tafassâsset des. Niger 125 H1
Tenerife i. Canary Is 122 A3
Ténès Alg. 123 F1
Ténès, Cap c. Alg. 55 M8
Tenevo Bulg. 58 H6
Teng, Nam r. Myanmar 78 B4
Tengah, Kepulauan is Indon. 77 G4
Tengah, Sungai r. Sing. 76 [inset]
Tengcheng China see Tengxian
Tengchong China 86 A3
Tenge Kazakh. 102 C4
Tengeh Reservoir Sing. 76 [inset]
Tenggarong Indon. 77 G3
Tengger Shamo des. China 84 E4
Tengiz, Ozero salt l. Kazakh. 103 G2
Tengréla Côte d'Ivoire 124 D4
  formerly spelt Tingréla
Ten'gushevo Rus. Fed. 40 G5
Tengxian China see Tengcheng
Tengxian China 87 D4
  also known as Tengzhou
Tengzhou China 85 H5
  formerly known as Tengxian
Teniente Enciso, Parque Nacional
  nat. park Para. 201 E5
Teniente Jubany research station
  Antarctica see Jubany
Te-n-loubrar, Sebkhet salt marsh
  Mauritania 124 A2
Tenkasi India 94 C4
Tenke Dem. Rep. Congo 127 E7
Tenkeli Rus. Fed. 39 O2
Tenkodogo Burkina 125 F4
Ten Mile Lake salt flat Australia 151 C5
Ten Mile Lake Canada 169 J3
Tenna r. Italy 56 F5
Tennant Creek Australia 148 B3
Tennessee r. U.S.A. 174 B4
Tennessee state U.S.A. 174 C4
Tennessee Pass U.S.A. 180 F5
Tennevoll Norway 44 L1
Tennholmfjorden sea chan. Norway 44 K2

Tenniöjoki r. Fin./Rus. Fed. 44 O2
Tennyson U.S.A. 172 C8
Teno Chile 204 C4
Tenojoki r. Fin./Norway 44 O1
  also known as Tana
Tenom Sabah Malaysia 77 F1
Tenosique Mex. 185 H5
Tenryū Japan 91 E7
Tenryū-gawa r. Japan 91 E7
Tenteno Indon. 75 B3
Tenterfield Australia 147 G2
Ten Thousand Islands U.S.A. 175 D7
Tentolomatinan, Gunung mt. Indon. 75 B2
Tentudia mt. Spain 54 E6
Tenu r. France 50 E5
Teocaltiche Mex. 185 E4
Teocelo Mex. 185 F5
Teodoro Sampaio Brazil 206 A9
Teófilo Otôni Brazil 203 D6
Teomabal i. Phil. 74 B5
Teonthar India 97 D4
Teopisca Mex. 185 G5
Teotihuacán tourist site Mex. 185 F5
Tepa Ghana 125 E5
Tepa Indon. 75 D4
Tepache Mex. 184 C2
Te Paki N.Z. 152 G2
Tepasto Fin. 44 N2
Tepatitlán Mex. 185 E4
Tepecik Turkey 58 J7
Tepehuanes Mex. 184 D3
Tepeji Mex. 185 F5
Tepeköy Turkey see Karakoçan
Tepel'meme de Morelos Mex. 185 F5
Tepelenë Albania 59 B8
Tepic Mex. 184 D4
Tepla r. Czech Rep. 49 J5
Teplaya Gora Rus. Fed. 40 K4
Teplice Czech Rep. 49 K5
Teploye (Lipetskaya Oblast') Rus. Fed. 43 T8
Teploye (Tul'skaya Oblast') Rus. Fed. 43 S8
Tepopa, Punta c pt Mex. 184 B2
Te Puke N.Z. 152 K5
Te Puna N.Z. 152 K5
Tequila Mex. 184 E4
Tequisistlán Mex. 185 G5
Tecuisquiapán Mex. 185 F4
Ter r. Spain 55 O2
Téra Niger 125 F3
Tera r. Port. 54 C6
Tera r. Spain 54 F3
Terakeka Sudan 128 A3
Teram Kangri mt.
  China/Jammu and Kashmir 89 B5
Teramo Italy 56 F6
  historically known as Interamna
Terang Australia 147 D4
Teratani r. Pak. 101 G4
Terbuny Rus. Fed. 43 T9
Tärcan Turkey 107 E3
Tereben' Rus. Fed. 43 Q8
Terebovlya Ukr. 41 C6
Terebush Rus. Fed. 43 T7
Teregova Romania 58 D3
Terek Rus. Fed. 107 F2
Terek r. Rus. Fed. 41 H8
Tere-Khol' Rus. Fed. 84 F1
Tere-Khol', Ozero l. Rus. Fed. 84 C1
Terek-Say Kyrg. 103 G4
Terektinskiy Khrebet mts Rus. Fed. 88 D1
Terekty (Karagandinskaya Oblast') Kazakh. 103 G2
Terekty (Vostochnyy Kazakhstan Kazakh. 88 D1
  formerly known as Alekseyevka
Teren'ga Rus. Fed. 41 I5
Terengganu state Malaysia 76 C1
  formerly spelt Trengganu
Terengözek Kazakh. see Terenozek
Terenos Brazil 203 A7
Terenozek Kazakh. 103 F3
  also spelt Terengözek or Teren-Uzyak
Terensay Rus. Fed. 102 D2
Terentang, Pulau i. Indon. 77 G3
Teren-Uzyak Kazakh. see Terenozek
Tereshka r. Rus. Fed. 41 I6
Teresina Brazil 202 D3
Teresina de Goias Brazil 202 C5
Teresita Col. 198 D4
Teresópolis Brazil 207 K9
Terespol Poland 42 I9
Teressa Island India 95 G4
Terezinha Brazil 199 H4
Terges r. Port. 54 D7
Tergeste Italy see Trieste
Tergnier France 51 J3
Terhiyn Tsagaan Nuur l. Mongolia 84 C1
Teriberka Rus. Fed. 44 P1
Teriberka r. Rus. Fed. 44 P1
Teriberskiy, Mys pt Rus. Fed. 44 P1
Terisakkan r. Kazakh. 103 F2
  formerly spelt Tersakkan
Terjit well Mauritania 122 B5
Terka Reba Eth. 128 D3
Terkezi well Chad 120 D5
Terlingua Creek r. U.S.A. 179 B6
Terma, Ras pt Eritrea 104 C3
Termas de Socos Chile 200 C3
Terme Turkey 107 D2
Termessos Milli Parkı nat. park Turkey
  108 B3
Termez Uzbek. 103 F5
  also spelt Termiz
Termination Island Australia 151 C7
Termini Imerese Sicilia Italy 57 F11
Termini Imerese, Golfo di b. Sicilia Italy
  57 F10
Términos, Laguna de lag. Mex. 185 H5
Termit well Niger 120 D3
Termit, Massif de hill Niger 125 H2
Termit-Kaobol Niger 125 H3
Termiz Uzbek. see Termez
Termo U.S.A. 182 D1
Termoli Italy 56 G7
Termonde Belgium see Dendermonde
Tern r. U.K. 47 J11
Ternate Indon. 75 C2
Ternate i. Indon. 75 C2
Terneuzen Neth. 48 A4
Terney Rus. Fed. 82 E3
Terni Italy 56 E6
Ternitz Austria 49 N8
Ternopil' Ukr. 41 C6
  also known as Ternopol'; formerly spelt Tarnopol
Ternopol' Ukr. see Ternopil'
Terowie Australia 146 C3
Terpeniya, Mys c. Rus. Fed. 82 G2
Terpeniya, Zaliv g. Rus. Fed. 82 F2
Terra Alta U.S.A. 176 F6
Terra Bella U.S.A. 182 E6
Terra Boa Brazil 206 A10
Terrace Canada 166 D4
Terrace Bay Canada 168 C3
Terracina Italy 56 F7
  formerly spelt Tarracina; historically known
  as Anxur
Terra Firma S. Africa 132 H2
Terralba Sardegna Italy 57 B9
Terra Nova Bay Antarctica 223 K1
Terra Nova National Park Canada 169 K3
Terranuova Bracciolini Italy 56 D5
Terra Preta Brazil 198 D6
Terra Rica Brazil 206 A9
Terrasini Sicilia Italy 57 F10
Terrassa Spain 55 N3
  also spelt Tarrasa
Terrasson-la-Villedieu France 50 H7

Terrazas Mex. 184 D2
Terre Adélie reg. Antarctica see Adélie Land
Terrebonne Bay U.S.A. 175 B6
Terre Haute U.S.A. 174 C4
Terrell U.S.A. 179 C5
Terre Plaine plain France 51 K5
Terrero Mex. 184 D2
Terres Australes et Antarctiques
  Françaises terr. Indian Ocean see
  French Southern and Antarctic Lands
Terril mt. Spain 54 F8
Terry mt. U.S.A. 180 F3
Tersakkan r. Kazakh. see Terisakkan
Terschelling i. Neth. 48 C2
Terskey Alatau, Khrebet mts Kyrg. see
  Terskey Ala-Too
Terskey Ala-Too mts Kyrg. 103 I4
  also known as Terskey Alatau, Khrebet
Terskiy Bereg coastal area Rus. Fed.
  40 F2
Tertenia Sardegna Italy 57 B9
Terter Azer. see Tärtär
Terutao i. Thai. 79 B7
Terutao National Park Thai. 79 B7
Tervakoski Fin. 42 F1
Tervel Bulg. 58 I5
Tervo Fin. 44 N3
Tervola Fin. 44 N2
Teryayevo Rus. Fed. 43 R5
Teshani Bos.-Herz. 56 J4
Teseney Eritrea 121 H6
Tesha r. Rus. Fed. 40 G5
Teshekpuk Lake U.S.A. 164 D2
Teshikaga Japan 90 I3
Teshio Japan 90 H2
Teshio-dake mt. Japan 90 H3
Teshio-gawa r. Japan 90 H2
Teshio-sanchi mts Japan 90 G2
Tešlica Srbija Yugo. 58 B4
Tesiyn Gol r. Mongolia 84 B1
Teslić Bos.-Herz. 56 J4
Teslin Canada 166 C2
Teslin r. Canada 166 C2
Teslin Lake Canada 166 C2
Teslui r. Romania 58 F4
Teso Santo hill Spain 54 F3
Tesouras r. Brazil 206 C1
Tesouro Brazil 206 A2
Tesovo-Netyl'skiy Rus. Fed. 43 M3
Tesovskiy Rus. Fed. 43 L3
Tessala, Monts du mts Alg. 55 K9
Tessalit Mali 123 F4
Tessaoua Niger 125 G3
Tesséroukane well Niger 125 G2
Tessolo Moz. 131 G4
Tessoûnfat well Mali 123 F5
  formerly spelt Sounfat
Test r. U.K. 47 K13
Testour Tunisia 123 H1
Tetachuck Lake U.S.A. 166 E4
Tetagouche r. Canada 169 H4
Tetas, Punta pt Chile 200 C3
Tete Moz. 131 G3
Tete prov. Moz. 131 G2
Tetehosi Indon. 76 B2
Tête Jaune Cache Canada 166 G4
Te Teko N.Z. 152 K6
Teterino Rus. Fed. 43 V3
Teteriv r. Ukr. 41 D6
Teterow Germany 49 J2
Teteven Bulg. 58 F6
Tetiyiv Ukr. 41 D6
  also spelt Tetiyev; formerly known as
  Snegurovka
Teton r. U.S.A. 180 E3
Te Toro U.S.A. 180 E4
Tétouan Morocco 122 D2
  also known as Tetuán; historically known as
  Titawin
Tetovo Macedonia 58 B6
Tetuán Morocco see Tétouan
Tetulia sea chan. Bangl. 97 F5
Tetyukhe Rus. Fed. see Dal'negorsk
Tetyukhe-Pristan' Rus. Fed. see
  Rudnaya Pristan'
Tetyushi Rus. Fed. 40 I5
Teuchezhsk Rus. Fed. see Adygeysk
Teuchi Japan 91 A9
Teuco r. Arg. 204 E2
Teulada Sardegna Italy 57 A10
Teulada, Capo c. Sardegna Italy 57 A10
Teul de González Ortega Mex. 184 E4
Teun vol. Indon. 75 D4
Teunom Indon. 76 A1
Teunom r. Indon. 76 A1
Teupitz-Köriser Seengebiet park Germany
  49 K3
Teuri-tō i. Japan 90 G2
Teustepe Nicaragua 186 B4
Teutoburger Wald hills Germany 48 E3
Teuva Fin. 44 M3
Tevere r. Italy see Tiber
Teverya Israel see Tiberias
Teviot N.Z. 153 C13
Teviot r. U.K. 46 J8
Tevriz Rus. Fed. 38 I4
Te Waewae N.Z. 153 B14
Te Waewae Bay N.Z. 153 B14
Te Waipounamu i. N.Z. see South Island
Tewane Botswana 131 E5
Tewantin Australia 149 G5
Teweh r. Indon. 77 F3
Te Wera North I. N.Z. 152 I7
Te Wera North I. N.Z. 152 L6
Te Wharau N.Z. 152 J9
Tewkesbury U.K. 47 J12
Têwo China 86 B1
  also known as Dêngka; formerly known as
  Dengkagoin
Texarkana AR U.S.A. 179 D5
Texarkana TX U.S.A. 179 D5
Texas Australia 147 F2
Texas state U.S.A. 179 C6
Texas City U.S.A. 179 D6
Texcoco Mex. 185 F5
Texel i. Neth. 48 B2
Texoma, Lake U.S.A. 179 C5
Teyateyaneng Lesotho 133 L6
Teykovo Rus. Fed. 43 V5
Teyvareh Afgh. 101 F3
Tezu r. Rus. Fed. 40 G4
Teza S. Africa 133 Q5
Teziutlán Mex. 185 F5
Tezpur India 97 G4
Tezu India 97 H4
Tfaritity W. Sahara 122 C4
Tha, Nam r. Laos 78 C3
Tha-anne r. Canada 167 M2
Thabana-Ntlenyana mt. Lesotho 133 N6
Thaba Nchu S. Africa 133 K6
Thabankulu mt. S. Africa 133 O4
Thaba Putsoa mt. Lesotho 133 L7
Thaba Putsoa mts S. Africa 133 L5
Thabazimbi S. Africa 131 F4
Thabeikkyin Myanmar 78 B3
Thaba-Tseka Lesotho 133 M6
Thabong S. Africa 133 K4
Thabt, Gebel at mt. Egypt 108 F9
Thabyedaung Myanmar 78 B3
Thac Ba, Hô l. Vietnam 78 D3
Thade r. Myanmar 78 A4
Thādiq Saudi Arabia 105 D3
Thagyettaw Myanmar 79 B5
Tha Hin Thai. see Lop Buri

Thai Binh Vietnam 78 D3
► Thailand country Asia 78 C4
  known in Thai as Muang Thai or Prathes
  Thai; formerly known as Siam
  asia [countries] ▶▶ 64–67
Thailand, Gulf of Asia 79 C6
Thai Muang Thai. 79 B6
Thai Nguyên Vietnam 78 D3
Thaj Saudi Arabia 105 E2
Thakurgaon Bangl. 97 F4
Thakurtola India 96 D5
Thal Pak. 101 G3
Thala Tunisia 123 H2
Thalang Thai. 79 B3
Thalassery India see Tellicherry
Thal Desert Pak. 101 G4
Thale (Harz) Germany 48 I4
Thale Luang lag. Thai. 79 C7
Thalgau Austria 49 K8
Tha Li Thai. 78 C4
Thaliparamba India see Taliparamba
Thallon Australia 147 F2
Thamad Bū Hash'shah well Libya 120 C3
Thamaga Botswana 131 E5
Thamar, Jabal mt. Yemen 105 D5
Thamarit Oman 105 F4
  English form Micway
Thames r. Canada 173 K8
Thames N.Z. 152 J5
Thames est. U.K. 47 M12
Thames r. U.K. 47 M12
Thames, Firth of b. N.Z. 152 J4
Thamesford Canada 173 M7
Thamesville Canada 173 L8
Thamūd Yemen 105 E4
Thamugadi tourist site Alg. see Timgad
Thana India see Thane
Thana Bula Khan Pak. 101 F5
Thandla India 96 B5
Thandwe Myanmar see Sandoway
Thane India 94 B2
  formerly spelt Thana
Thangadh India 96 A5
Thangoo Australia 150 C3
Thanh Hoa Vietnam 78 D4
Thanjavur India 94 C4
  also known as Tanjore
Than Kyun i. Brazil 206 C1
Thanlwin r. Myanmar 79 B6
  also known as Davis
Thanlwin r. Myanmar see Salween
Thano Bula Khan Pak. 101 F5
Than Uyen Vietnam 86 B4
Thaoge r. Botswana 130 D3
Thaolintoa Lake Canada 167 L2
Thap Put Thai. 79 B6
Thap Sakae Thai. 79 B5
Thara India 96 A4
Tharad India 96 A4
Tharaka Kenya 128 C5
Thar Desert India/Pak. 96 A4
  also known as Indian Desert
Thargomindah Australia 147 D1
Tharrawaddy Myanmar 78 A4
Tharraway Myanmar 78 A5
Tharthār, Buhayrat ath l. Iraq 107 E4
Tharthār Canal Iraq see
  Dijlah - Ath Tharthār, Qanāt
Tharwāniyyah U.A.E. 105 F3
Thasos Greece 58 F8
Thasos i. Greece 58 F8
Thatcher U.S.A. 183 O9
Thaton Myanmar 78 B4
Thatta Pak. 101 F5
Thaungdut Myanmar 78 A2
Thaungyn r. Myanmar/Thai. 78 B4
Thaton Myanmar 78 B4
Thau, Bassin de lag. France 51 J9
Thaungyn r. Myanmar/Thai. 78 B4
Tha Uthen Thai. 78 D4
Thawr, Jabal mt. Jordan 108 G8
Thayawthadangyi Kyun i. Myanmar 79 B5
Thazi Myanmar 78 B3
The Aldermen Islands N.Z. 152 K4
Theba U.S.A. 183 L9
Thebae tourist site Egypt see Thebes
► The Bahamas country West Indies 186 D1
  northamerica [countries] ▶▶ 158–159
Thebes tourist site Egypt 121 G3
  also known as Diospolis Magna or
  Thebae
Thebes Greece see Thiva
The Bluff Bahamas 186 D1
The Broads nat. park U.K. 47 N11
The Brothers is Yemen see Al Ikhwān
The Brothers is Hong Kong China 87 [inset]
  also known as Tei Siu Mo To
The Calvados Chain is P.N.G. 149 G1
The Cheviot hill U.K. 46 J8
The Coorong inlet Australia 146 C3
The Dalles U.S.A. 180 B3
  also known as Dalles City
Thecford U.S.A. 178 B3
The English Company's Islands Australia
  148 C1
The Entrance Australia 147 F3
Theewaterskloof Dam resr S. Africa
  132 D11
The Fens reg. U.K. 47 L11
► The Gambia country Africa 124 A3
  africa [countries] ▶▶ 114–117
The Great Oasis Egypt see Kharga Oasis
The Grenadines is St Vincent 187 H4
The Gulf Asia 105 E1
  also known as Persian Gulf or Arabian Gulf
The Hague Neth. 48 B3
  Seat of government of the Netherlands.
  Also known as Den Haag or 's-Gravenhage.
  world [countries] ▶▶ 10–11
The Haven S. Africa 133 M9
The Horseshoe mt. S. Africa 132 H8
The Hunters Hills N.Z. 153 E12
Theinkun Myanmar 79 B6
Theinzeik Myanmar 78 B4
The Key N.Z. 153 B13
Thekulthiel Lake Canada 167 I2
The Lakes National Park Australia 147 E4
Thelon r. Canada 167 L1
Thelon Game Sanctuary nature res.
  Canada 167 K1
The Lynd Junction Australia 149 E3
Themar Germany 48 H5
Thembalesizwe S. Africa 132 I9
Thembalihle S. Africa 133 N4
The Minch sea chan. U.K. 46 E5
The Mullet b. Rep. of Ireland 47 B9
The Needles stack U.K. 47 K13
Theni India 96 C5
Thenia Alg. 55 O8
Théniet El Had Alg. 55 N9
Thenon France 50 H7
Theodore Australia 149 F5
Theodore U.S.A. 175 B6
Theodore Roosevelt r. Brazil 201 E1
Theodore Roosevelt Lake U.S.A. 183 M8
Theodore Roosevelt National Park U.S.A.
  178 B2
Theodosia Ukr. see Feodosiya
The Officer Creek watercourse Australia
  146 B1
The Pas hill Rep. of Ireland 47 C11
The Pas Canada 167 K4
Thera i. Greece see Thira
Thérain r. France 51 I3
The Remarkables mts N.Z. 153 C13
Theresa U.S.A. 177 J1
Theresa Creek r. Australia 149 F4
Therma Greece see Thermo

Thermaïkos Kolpos g. Greece 59 D8
Thermo Greece 59 C10
  also known as Thérmon
Thérmon Greece see Thermo
Thermopolis U.S.A. 180 E4
The Salt Lake salt flat Australia 147 D2
► The Settlement Christmas I. 220 B6
  Capital of Christmas Island.

Thesiger Bay Canada 164 G2
The Skaw spit Denmark see Grenen
The Slot sea chan. Solomon Is see
  New Georgia Sound
The Solent strait U.K. 47 K13
Thesprotiko Greece 59 B9
Thessalia admin. reg. Greece 59 C9
  English form Thessaly
Thessalon Canada 168 D4
Thessalonica Greece see Thessaloniki
Thessaloniki Greece 58 D8
  also known as Salonika or Thessalonica;
  formerly known as Salonica
Thessaly admin. reg. Greece see Thessalia
The Storr hill U.K. 46 F6
The Teeth mt. Phil. 74 A4
The Terraces hills Australia 151 C6
Thetford U.K. 47 M11
Thetford Mines Canada 169 G4
The Thumbs mt. N.Z. 153 E11
Thetkethaung r. Myanmar 78 A4
The Triangle mts Myanmar 78 B2
The Twins Australia 146 B2
Theun r. Laos 78 D4
Theunissen S. Africa 133 K5
Theva-i-Ra reef Fiji see Ceva-i-Ra
► The Valley Anguilla 187 H3
  Capital of Anguilla.

Thevenard Australia 146 B3
Thevenard Island Australia 150 A4
Thévenet, Lac l. Canada 169 G1
Theveste Alg. see Tébessa
The Wash b. U.K. 47 M11
The Weald reg. U.K. 47 M12
The Woodlands U.S.A. 179 D6
Thiamis r. Greece see Thyamis
Thibodaux U.S.A. 179 E6
Thief River Falls U.S.A. 178 C1
Thiel Neth. see Tiel
Thiel Mountains Antarctica 223 R1
Thielsen, Mount U.S.A. 180 B4
Thielt Belgium see Tielt
Thiers France 51 J7
Thiès Senegal 124 A3
Thika Kenya 128 C5
Thikombia i. Fiji see Cikobia
Thiladhunmathee Atoll Maldives 94 B5
Thilogne Senegal 124 B3
  also spelt Tilogne
Thimbu Bhutan see Thimphu
► Thimphu Bhutan 97 F4
  Capital of Bhutan. Also known as Tashi
  Chho; also spelt Thimbu.

Thingvallavatn (Pingvallavatn) l. Iceland
  44 [inset] B3
Thingvellir (Pingvellir) Iceland 44 [inset] B2
Thionville France 51 M3
  formerly known as Diedenhofen
Thira Greece 59 G12
Thira i. Greece 59 G12
  also known as Santorini; historically known
  as Thera
Thirasia i. Greece 59 G12
Third Cataract rapids Sudan see
  3rd Cataract
Thirsk U.K. 47 K9
Thirty Mile Lake Canada 167 L2
Thiruvananthapuram India see Trivandrum
Thiruvarur India 94 C4
Thiruvattiyur India see Tiruvottiyur
Thissavros, Techniti Limni resr Greece
  58 F7
Thisted Denmark 45 J4
Thistilfjörður (Pistilfjörður) b. Iceland
  44 [inset]
Thistle Creek Canada 166 B2
Thistle Island Australia 146 C3
Thistle Lake Canada 167 I1
Thityabin Myanmar 78 A3
Thiva Greece 59 E10
  also known as Thívai; historically known as
  Thebes
Thívai Greece see Thiva
Thiviers France 50 H7
Thjórsá (Pjórsá) r. Iceland 44 [inset] B3
Thlewiaza r. Canada 167 M2
Thoa r. Canada 167 I2
Thô Chu, Đao i. Vietnam 79 C6
Thoen Thai. 78 B4
Thoeng Thai. 78 C4
Thohoyandou S. Africa 131 F4
Tholen i. Neth. 48 B4
Thomas Australia 151 B5
Thomas, Lake salt flat Australia 148 C5
Thomas Hill Reservoir U.S.A. 178 D4
Thomas Hubbard, Cape Canada 165 J1
Thomas Mountain U.S.A. 183 H8
Thomaston CT U.S.A. 177 L4
Thomaston GA U.S.A. 175 C5
Thomaston ME U.S.A. 177 P1
Thomastown Rep. of Ireland 47 E11
Thomasville AL U.S.A. 175 C6
Thomasville NC U.S.A. 174 D5
Thomomde Haiti 187 F3
Thompson Canada 167 L4
Thompson r. Canada 166 F5
Thompson MI U.S.A. 172 G5
Thompson UT U.S.A. 183 O3
Thompson r. U.S.A. 174 A4
Thompson Falls U.S.A. 180 D3
Thompson Peak U.S.A. 181 F6
Thompson's Falls Kenya see Nyahururu
Thompson Sound Canada 166 E5
Thompson Sound inlet N.Z. 153 A13
Thompsonville U.S.A. 177 M4
Thomson watercourse Australia 149 D5
Thomson GA U.S.A. 175 D5
Thomson IL U.S.A. 172 C9
Thon Buri Thai. 79 C5
Thongwa Myanmar 78 B4
Thonon-les-Bains France 51 M6
Thoreau U.S.A. 181 E6
Thorhild Canada 167 H4
Thórisvatn (Pórisvatn) l. Iceland 44 [inset] C2
Thorn Poland see Toruń
Thornapple r. U.S.A. 173 H8
Thornbury U.S.A. 153 C14
Thorncliffe Canada 173 N4
Thorne U.K. 47 L10
Thorne U.S.A. 182 F3
Thornton r. Australia 148 C3
Thornton U.S.A. 172 E6
Thornhill U.K. 47 I8
Thorsby Canada 167 H4
Thorshavn Faroe Is see Tórshavn
Thorshavnfjella reg. Antarctica see
  Thorshavnheiane
Thorshavnheiane reg. Antarctica 223 E2
  also known as Thorshavnfjella
Thórshöfn (Pórshöfn) Iceland 44 [inset] D2
Thorvaldsfell (Porvaldsfell) vol. Iceland
  44 [inset]
Thota-ea-Moli Lesotho 133 L6
Thouars France 50 F6
Thoubal India 97 G4
Thouet r. France 50 F5

Thouin, Cape pt Australia 150 B4
Thourout Belgium see Torhout
Thousand Islands Canada/U.S.A. 173 Q6
Thousand Lake Mountain U.S.A. 183 M3
Thousand Oaks U.S.A. 182 F7
Thousand Palms U.S.A. 183 H8
Thousandsticks U.S.A. 176 B8
Thrace reg. Turkey 106 A2
also spelt Thraki or Trakiya or Trakya
Thraki reg. Turkey see Thrace
Thrakiko Pelagos sea Greece 58 F8
Thredbo Australia 147 F4
Three Fathoms Cove b. Hong Kong China 87 [inset]
also known as Kei Ling Ha Hoi
Three Forks U.S.A. 180 E3
▶Three Gorges Project resr China 87 D2
asia [changes] ▶▶ 68–69
Three Hummock Island Australia 147 E5
Three Kings Islands N.Z. 152 G2
Three Oaks U.S.A. 172 G9
Three Pagodas Pass Myanmar/Thai. 79 B5
Three Points U.S.A. 183 M9
Three Points, Cape Ghana 125 E5
Three Rivers CA U.S.A. 182 F5
Three Rivers MI U.S.A. 172 H9
Three Rivers TX U.S.A. 179 C6
Three Sisters S. Africa 132 H8
Three Sisters mt. U.S.A. 180 B3
Three Springs Australia 151 A6
Thrissur India see Trichur
Throckmorton U.S.A. 179 C5
Throssell, Lake salt flat Australia 151 D5
Throssel Range hills Australia 150 C4
Thrushton National Park Australia 147 E1
Thubun Lakes Canada 167 I2
Thu Dâu Môt Vietnam 79 D6
formerly known as Phu Cuong
Thuin Belgium 51 K2
Thul Sudan 128 B2
Thul watercourse Sudan 128 A2
Thulaythawāt Gharbī, Jabal hill Syria 109 K2
Thule Greenland 165 M2
also known as Qaanaaq
Thuli Zimbabwe 131 F4
Thuli r. Zimbabwe 131 F4
Thumayl, Wādī watercourse Iraq 109 O4
Thun Switz. 51 N6
Thunda Australia 149 D5
Thundelarra Australia 151 B6
Thunder Bay Canada 168 B3
Thunder Bay b. Canada 168 B3
Thunder Bay b. U.S.A. 173 J5
Thunder Creek r. Canada 167 J5
Thunder Knoll sea feature Caribbean Sea 186 C3
Thuner See l. Switz. 51 N6
Thung Salaeng Luang National Park Thai. 78 C4
Thung Song Thai. 79 B6
Thung Wa Thai. 79 B7
Thung-yai-naresuan Wildlife Reserve nature res. Thai. 79 B5
Thur r. Switz. 51 O5
Thüringen land Germany 48 H4
English form Thuringia
Thüringer Becken reg. Germany 48 I4
Thüringer Wald mts Germany 48 H5
English form Thuringian Forest
Thüringer Wald park Germany 48 H5
Thuringia land Germany see Thüringen
Thuringian Forest mts Germany see Thüringer Wald
Thurles Rep. of Ireland 47 E11
also spelt Durlas
Thurmont U.S.A. 176 H6
Thursby U.K. 47 I9
Thursday Island Australia 149 D1
Thurso U.K. 46 I5
Thurso r. U.K. 46 I5
Thurston Island Antarctica 222 R2
formerly known as Thurston Peninsula
Thurston Peninsula i. Antarctica see Thurston Island
Thusis Switz. 51 P6
Thwaites Glacier Tongue Antarctica 222 Q1
Thy reg. Denmark 45 J4
Thyamis r. Greece 59 B9
also spelt Thiamis
Thyatira Turkey see Akhisar
Thyborøn Denmark 45 J4
Thylungra Australia 149 D5
Thymaina i. Greece 59 H11
Thyolo Malawi 129 B9
Thyou Burkina 125 E4
Thyou Burkina see Tiou
Thysville Dem. Rep. Congo see Mbanza-Ngungu
Tiāb Iran 100 D5
Tiahuanaco Bol. 200 C4
Tiancang China 84 C3
Tianchang China 87 F1
Tiancheng China see Chongyang
Tianchi China see Lezhi
Tiandeng China 87 C4
Tiandiba China see Jinyang
Tiandong China 86 C4
Tian'e China 87 C3
also known as Liupai
Tianfanjie China 87 F2
Tiângol Louggueré watercourse Senegal 124 B3
Tianguá Brazil 202 D2
Tianjin China 85 H4
English form Tientsin
Tianjin municipality China 85 H4
English form Tientsin
Tianjun China 84 C4
also known as Xinyuan
Tiankoye Senegal 124 B3
Tianlin China 86 C3
also known as Leli
Tianmen China 87 E2
Tianmu Shan mts China 87 F2
Tianqiaoling China 82 C4
Tianquan China 86 B2
also known as Chengxiang
Tianshan China 85 I3
also known as Ar Horqin Qi
Tian Shan mts China/Kyrg. see Tien Shan
Tianshifu China 82 B4
Tianshui China 86 C1
Tianshuihai Aksai Chin 89 B5
Tianshuijing China 84 B3
Tiantai China 87 G2
Tiantaiyong China 85 H3
Tiantang China see Yuexi
Tianyang China 86 C4
also known as Tianzhou
Tianyi China see Ningcheng
Tianzhen China see Gaoqing
Tianzhen China 85 G3
Tianzhou China see Tianyang
Tianzhu Gansu China 84 D4
also known as Huazangsi
Tianzhu Guizhou China 87 D3
Tiaret Alg. 123 F2
also known as Tagdempt
Tiaret well Tunisia 123 H3
Tiassalé Côte d'Ivoire 124 D5
Tibabar Sabah Malaysia see Tambunan
Tibagi Brazil 203 B8
Tibagi r. Brazil 206 C10
also spelt Tibaji
Tibaji r. Brazil see Tibagi
Tibal, Wādī watercourse Iraq 107 E4
Tibaná Col. 198 C3
Tibati Cameroon 125 I5
Tibba Pak. 101 G4
Tibé, Pic de mt. Guinea 124 C4
Tiber r. Italy 56 E7
also spelt Tevere
Tiberghamine Alg. 123 F3
Tiberias Israel 108 G5
also spelt Teverya
Tiberias, Lake Israel see Galilee, Sea of
Tiber Reservoir U.S.A. 180 E2
Tibesti mts Chad 120 C4
Tibet aut. reg. China see Xizang Zizhiqu
Tibet, Plateau of China 89 D5
also known as Qingzang Gaoyuan or Xizang Gaoyuan
Tibet Autonomous Region aut. reg. China see Xizang Zizhiqu
Tibiri Niger 125 G3
Țibleș, Vârful mt. Romania 58 F2
Tiboku Falls Guyana 199 G3
Tibooburra Australia 147 D2
Tibrikot Nepal 97 D3
Tibuga, Ensenada b. Col. 198 B3
Tibur Italy see Tivoli
Tiburón, Isla i. Mex. 184 B2
Ticao i. Phil. 74 B3
Ticha r. Bulg. 58 H5
Tichak mt. Bulg. 58 D6
Tichau Poland see Tychy
Tichborne Canada 173 Q6
Tichégami r. Canada 169 F3
Tichet well Mali 125 F2
Tichit Mauritania 124 C2
Tichla W. Sahara 122 B5
Ticino r. Italy/Switz. 56 B3
Ticinum Italy see Pavia
Țicleni Romania 58 E4
Ticonderoga U.S.A. 177 L2
historically known as Fort Carillon
Ticul Mex. 185 H4
Ticumbia i. Fiji see Cikobia
Tiddim Myanmar 78 A3
Tideridjaounine, Adrar mts Alg. 123 F5
Tidikelt, Plaine du plain Alg. 123 F4
Tidioute U.S.A. 176 F4
Tidjerouene well Mali 125 F2
Tidjikja Mauritania 124 C2
Tidore i. Indon. 75 C2
Tiébissou Côte d'Ivoire 124 D5
Tiéboro Chad 120 C4
Tiefa China 85 I3
also known as Diaobingshan
Tiel Neth. 48 C4
formerly spelt Thiel
Tiel Senegal 124 B3
Tieli China 82 B3
Tieling China 82 A4
Tielongtan Aksai Chin 89 B5
Tielt Belgium 51 J2
also spelt Thielt
Tiémé Côte d'Ivoire 124 D4
Tiene Liberia 124 C5
Tienen Belgium 51 K2
also known as Tirlemont
Tien Shan mts China/Kyrg. 88 B3
also spelt Tian Shan or Tyan' Shan'
Tien Shan Oblast admin. div. Kyrg. see Naryn
Tientsin China see Tianjin
Tientsin municipality China see Tianjin
Tiên Yên Vietnam 78 D3
Tierfontein S. Africa 133 K5
Tierp Sweden 45 L3
Tierra Amarilla U.S.A. 181 F5
Tierra Blanca Mex. 185 F5
Tierra Blanca Peru 198 C6
Tierra Colorada Mex. 185 F5
Tierra del Fuego prov. Arg. 205 D9

▶Tierra del Fuego, Isla Grande de i. Arg./Chile 205 C9
Largest island in South America.
southamerica [landscapes] ▶▶ 190–191

Tierra del Fuego, Parque Nacional nat. park Arg. 205 D9
Tierra Llana de Huelva plain Spain 54 D7
Tierralta Col. 198 B2
Tiétar r. Spain 54 F5
Tiétar, Valle de valley Spain 54 F4
Tietê Brazil 206 F10
Tietê r. Brazil 206 B7
Tieyon Australia 148 B5
Tiffin U.S.A. 176 B4
Tiflis Georgia see T'bilisi
Tifore i. Indon. 75 C2
Tifton U.S.A. 175 D6
Tifu Indon. 75 C3
Tiga i. Sabah Malaysia 77 F1
Tigane S. Africa 133 K3
Tigănești Romania 58 G5
Tigapuluh, Pegunungan mts Indon. 76 C3
Tigen Kazakh. 102 B3
Tīgh Āb Iran 101 E5
Tigheciului, Dealurile hills Moldova 58 J3
Tighina Moldova 58 K2
formerly known as Bender or Bendery
Tigiretskiy Khrebet mts Kazakh./Rus. Fed. 88 C1
Tigiria India 95 E1
Tignère Cameroon 125 I5
Tignish Canada 169 H4
Tigoda r. Rus. Fed. 43 M2
Tigranocerta Turkey see Siirt
Tigray admin. reg. Eth. 128 C1
Tigre r. Ecuador/Peru 198 C6
Tigre, Cerro del mt. Mex. 185 F4
Tigris r. Asia 107 F4
also known as Dicle (Turkey) or Dijlah, Nahr (Iraq/Syria)
Tigrovaya Balka Zapovednik nature res. Tajik. 101 G2
Tiguent Mauritania 124 B2
Tiguesmat hills Mauritania 122 C4
Tiguidit, Falaise de esc. Niger 125 G2
Tiguir well Niger 125 H2
Tīh, Gebel el plat. Egypt 121 G2
Tihāmah reg. Saudi Arabia 104 C4
Tihuatlán Mex. 185 F4
Tijamuchi r. Bol. 200 D3
Tijara India 96 C4
Tiji Libya 120 A1
Tijirīt reg. Mauritania 122 B5
Tijuana Mex. 184 A1
Tijucas Brazil 203 B8
Tijucas, Bahía de b. Brazil 203 B8
Tijuco r. Brazil 206 C5
Tikal tourist site Guat. 185 H5
Tikal, Parque Nacional nat. park Guat. 185 H5
Tikamgarh India 96 C4
also known as Tehri
Tikanlik China 88 D3
Tikchik Lake U.S.A. 164 D4
Tikherón Greece see Tykhero
Tikhmenevo Rus. Fed. 43 T3
Tikhonova Pustyn' Rus. Fed. 43 R7
Tikhoretsk Rus. Fed. 41 G7
Tikhtozero Rus. Fed. 44 O2
Tikhvin Rus. Fed. 43 O2
Tikhvinka r. Rus. Fed. 43 O2
Tikhvinskaya Gryada ridge Rus. Fed. 43 O2
Tikiktene well Niger 125 G2
Tikitiki N.Z. 152 M5
Tikkakoski Fin. 44 N3
Tikkurila Fin. 42 G1
Tikokino N.Z. 152 K7
Tikrīt Iraq 107 E4
Tiksheozero, Ozero l. Rus. Fed. 44 P2
Tiksi Rus. Fed. 39 M2
Tikumbia i. Fiji see Cikobia
Tikveš Ezero l. Macedonia 58 C7
Tikwana S. Africa 133 J4
Tila r. Nepal 97 D3
Tilaiya Reservoir India 97 E4
Tilavar Iran 100 C2
Tilbeşar Ovasi plain Turkey 109 I1
Tilbooroo Australia 147 E1
Tilburg Neth. 48 C4
Tilbury Canada 173 K8
Tilbury U.K. 47 M12
Tilcara Arg. 200 D5
Tilcha Australia 146 D2
Tilden U.S.A. 179 C6
Tileagd Romania 58 D1
Tilemsès Niger 125 G3
Tilemsi, Vallée du watercourse Mali 125 F2
Tilghman U.S.A. 177 I7
Tilhar India 96 C4
Tilia, Oued watercourse Alg. 123 F4
Tilimsen Alg. see Tlemcen
Tilin Myanmar 78 A3
Tillabéri Niger 125 F3
Tillabéri dept Niger 125 F3
Tillamook U.S.A. 180 B3
Tillanchong Island India 95 G4
Tille r. France 51 L5
Tilley Canada 167 I5
Tillia Niger 125 G2
Tillsonburg Canada 168 D5
Tiloa Niger 125 F3
Tilogne Senegal see Thilogne
Tilomonte Chile 200 C5
Tilos i. Greece 59 I12
Tilpa Australia 147 E2
Tilsa r. Latvia 42 I5
Tilsit Rus. Fed. see Sovetsk
Tilton U.S.A. 177 N2
Tilža Latvia 42 I5
Tim Rus. Fed. 41 F6
Tim r. Rus. Fed. 43 S9
Tima Egypt 121 F3
Timakara i. India 94 B4
Timane r. Para. 201 F5
Timanskiy Kryazh ridge Rus. Fed. 40 I2
Timar Turkey 107 E3
Timaru N.Z. 153 F12
Timashevsk Rus. Fed. 41 F7
formerly known as Timashevskaya
Timashevskaya Rus. Fed. see Timashevsk
Timbákion Greece see Tympaki
Timbalier Bay U.S.A. 175 B6
Timbaúba Brazil 202 F3
Timbedgha Mauritania 124 C2
Timber Creek Australia 148 A2
Timber Lake U.S.A. 178 B2
Timber Mountain U.S.A. 183 H4
Timberville U.S.A. 176 G7
Timbiquí Col. 198 B4
Timbué, Ponta pt Moz. 131 H3
Timbuktu Mali 124 E2
also spelt Tombouctou
Timbun Mata i. Sabah Malaysia 77 G1
Timelkam Austria 49 K7
Timétrine Mali 125 E2
Timétrine reg. Mali 125 E2
Timgad tourist site Alg. 123 G2
also known as Thamugadi
Timia Niger 125 H2
Timïaouine Alg. 123 F5
Timimoun Alg. 123 F3
Timirist, Râs pt Mauritania 124 A2
Timiryazev Kazakh. 103 F1
Timiryazevo Kazakh. 103 F1
Timiș r. Romania 58 B3
Timiskaming, Lake Canada see Témiscamingue, Lac
Timișoara Romania 58 C3
Timișului, Câmpia plain Romania 58 B3
Timkovichi Belarus see Tsimkavichy
Ti-m-Meghsoi watercourse Niger 125 G2
Timmelsjoch pass Austria/Italy 48 I9
Timmins Canada 168 D3
Timms Hill hill U.S.A. 172 C5
Timok r. Yugo. 58 D4
Timokhino Rus. Fed. 43 R2
Timon Brazil 202 D3
Timor i. Indon. 75 C5
Timor Sea Australia/Indon. 144 B3
Timor Timur terr. Asia see East Timor
Timoshino Rus. Fed. 43 R1
Timóteo Brazil 207 K6
Timoudi Alg. 123 E3
Timperley Range hills Australia 151 C5
Timrå Sweden 44 L3
Timsâh, Bahra el l. Egypt 108 D7
Tims Ford Lake U.S.A. 174 C5
Timshor r. Rus. Fed. 40 J3
Timur Kazakh. see Tumur
Timurni Muafi India 96 C5
Tin, Jabal hill Saudi Arabia 104 C2
Tina r. S. Africa 133 N8
Tina, Khalîg el b. Egypt 108 D6
English form Pelusium, Bay of
Ti-n-Aguelhaj well Mali 125 E2
Tin Alkoum Libya 120 A3
Tin Amzi, Oued watercourse Alg. 123 G5
Ti-n-Azabo well Mali 125 F2
Ti-n-Bessaïs well Mauritania 122 C5
Tin Can Bay Australia 149 G5
Tinchebray France 50 F4
Ti-n-Didine well Mali 123 E5
Tindivanam India 94 C3
Tindouf Alg. 122 C4
Tiné Chad 120 D6
Ti-n-Echeri well Mali 125 E2
Tinée r. France 51 N9
Tineo Spain 54 E1
Tinerhir Morocco 122 D3
Ti-n-Etissane well Mali 125 E2
Tinfouchy Alg. 122 D3
Tinggi i. Malaysia 76 D2
Tingi Mountains Sierra Leone 124 C4
Tingis Morocco see Tangier
Ting Jiang r. China 87 F3
Tingkawk Sakan Myanmar 78 B2
Tinglev Denmark 45 J5
Tingo Maria Peru 200 B2
Tingrela Côte d'Ivoire see Tengréla
Tingri China 89 D6
Tingsryd Sweden 45 K4
Tingstäde Sweden 45 L4
Tingvatn Norway 45 I4
Tingvoll Norway 44 J3
Tingzhou China see Changting
Tinharé, Ilha de i. Brazil 202 E5
Tinian i. N. Mariana Is 73 K4
formerly known as Buena Vista
Tiniéré well Mauritania 124 B2
Tinigua, Parque Nacional nat. park Col. 198 C4
Tini Heke is N.Z. see Snares Islands
Tiniroto N.Z. 152 L6
Tinja r. Bos.-Herz. 56 K4
Tinjar r. Sarawak Malaysia 77 F1
Tinkisso r. Guinea 124 C4
Tinline, Mount N.Z. 153 H10
Tinn Norway 45 J4
Tinnelvelly India see Tirunelveli
Tinnsjø l. Norway 45 J4
Tinogasta Arg. 204 D3
Tinompo Indon. 75 B2
Tinos Greece 59 G11
Tinos i. Greece 59 G11
Tiñosa mt. Spain 54 G7
Ti-n-Rerhoh well Alg. 123 G5
Tinrhert, Plateau du Alg. 123 G3
Ti-n-Srir well Mali 125 F2
Tinsukia India 97 G4
Tintagel Canada 166 E4
Țînțâne Mauritania 124 C2
Ti-n-Tarabine well Alg. 123 G5
Ti-n-Tarabine, Oued watercourse Alg. 123 G5
Ti-n-Tehoun well Mali 124 E2
Tintejert, Adrar mt. Alg. 123 F4
Ti-n-Tersi well Mali 125 F2
Tintina Arg. 204 E2
Tintinara Australia 146 D3
Tinto r. Spain 54 E7
Tin Tounnant well Mali see Taounnant
Tinui N.Z. 152 K8
Ti-n-Zaouâtene Mali 125 F2
Tioga ND U.S.A. 178 B1
Tioga PA U.S.A. 177 H4
Tioga r. U.S.A. 177 H3
Tioman i. Malaysia 76 D2
Tionaga Canada 173 K2
Tioribougou Mali 124 C3
Tiou Burkina 124 E3
formerly spelt Thyou
Tioughnioga r. U.S.A. 177 J3
Tipasa Alg. 123 F1
Tipitapa Nicaragua 186 B4
Tipler U.S.A. 172 E5
Tippecanoe r. U.S.A. 174 C3
Tipperary Rep. of Ireland 47 D11
Tiptala Bhanjyang pass Nepal 97 E4
Tipton CA U.S.A. 182 E5
Tipton IA U.S.A. 174 B3
Tipton MO U.S.A. 178 D4
Tipton, Mount U.S.A. 183 J6
Tiptonville U.S.A. 174 B4
Tiptop U.S.A. 176 D8
Tip Top Hill hill Canada 168 C3
Tiptur India 94 C3
Tipuani Bol. 200 C3
Tiquié r. Brazil 198 D4
Tiquisate Guat. 185 H6
Tiracambu, Serra do hills Brazil 202 C3
Tirahart, Oued watercourse Alg. 123 F5
Tīrān Iran 100 B3
Tīrān i. Saudi Arabia 104 A2

▶Tirana Albania 58 A7
Capital of Albania. Also spelt Tiranë.

Tiranë Albania see Tirana
Tirano Italy 56 C2
Tiraouene well Niger 125 G2
Tirap India 97 G4
Tiraraouine well Mali 125 E2
Tirari Desert Australia 146 C1
Tiraspol Moldova 58 K2
Tirau N.Z. 152 J5
Tiraumea N.Z. 152 K8
Tiraz Mountains Namibia 130 C5
Tire Turkey 59 I10
Tiree i. U.K. 46 F7
Tirek well Alg. 123 F5
Tirest well Mali 123 F5
Tîrgoviște Romania see Târgoviște
Tîrgu Bujor Romania see Târgu Bujor
Tîrgu Cărbunești Romania see Târgu Cărbunești
Tîrgu Frumos Romania see Târgu Frumos
Tîrgu Jiu Romania see Târgu Jiu
Tîrgu Lăpuș Romania see Târgu Lăpuș
Tîrgu Mureș Romania see Târgu Mureș
Tîrgu Neamț Romania see Târgu Neamț
Tîrgu Ocna Romania see Târgu Ocna
Tîrgu Secuiesc Romania see Târgu Secuiesc
Tirich Mir mt. Pak. 101 G2
Tiririne, Oued watercourse Alg. 123 H5
Tiris Zemmour admin. reg. Mauritania 122 C5
Tirkšliai Lith. 42 D5
Tirlemont Belgium see Tienen
Tirna r. India 94 C2
Tîrnăveni Romania see Târnăveni
Tirnavos Greece see Tyrnavos
Tiro hill Spain 54 F6
Tirodi India 96 C5
Tiros Brazil 203 C6
Tiroungoulou Cent. Afr. Rep. 126 D2
Tirourda, Col de pass Alg. 55 P8
Tirreno, Mare sea France/Italy see Tyrrhenian Sea
Tirso r. Sardegna Italy 57 A9
Tirthahalli India 94 B3
Tiruchchendur India 94 C4
Tiruchchirappalli India 94 C4
formerly known as Trichinopoly
Tiruchengodu India 94 C4
Tirukkoyilur India 94 C3
Tirumangalam India 94 C4
Tirunelveli India 94 C4
formerly known as Tinnelvelly
Tiruntán Peru 200 B1
Tirupati India 94 C3
Tiruppattur Tamil Nadu India 94 C3
Tiruppattur Tamil Nadu India 94 C4
Tiruppur India 94 C4
Tiruttani India 94 C3
Tiruttaraippundi India 94 C4
Tiruvallur India 94 C3
Tiruvannamalai India 94 C3
Tiruvettipuram India 94 C3
Tiruvottiyur India 94 D3
also spelt Thiruvattiyur
Tiru Well Australia 150 D4
Tiryns tourist site Greece 59 D11
Tirza r. Latvia 42 H4
Tisa r. Yugo. 58 B3
also known as Tisza
Tisa r. Yugo. 58 C5
Tisaiyanvilai India 94 C4
Tisău Romania 58 H3
Tisdale Canada 167 J4
Tishomingo U.S.A. 179 C5
Tiska, Mont mt. Alg. 123 H5
Tissemsilt Alg. 123 F2
formerly known as Vialar
Tista r. India 97 F4
Tisza r. Hungary see Tisa
Tiszabezdéd Hungary 49 T7
Tiszaföldvár Hungary 49 R9
Tiszafüred Hungary 49 R8
Tiszakécske Hungary 49 R9
Tiszaújváros Hungary 49 S8
also known as Búdszentmihály
Tiszavasvári Hungary 49 S8
Tit Alg. 123 F4
Tit Alg. 123 G5
Titabar India 97 G4
Titan Dome ice feature Antarctica 223 K1
Titao Burkina 125 E3
Titarisios r. Greece 59 D9
Tit-Ary Rus. Fed. 39 M2
Titawin Morocco see Tétouan
Titel Vojvodina, Srbija Yugo. 58 B3
Tithwal Pak. 101 H3
Titicaca, Lago l. Bol./Peru see Titicaca, Lake

▶Titicaca, Lake Bol./Peru 200 C3
Largest lake in South America. Also known as Titicaca, Lago.
southamerica [landscapes] ▶▶ 190–191
southamerica [countries] ▶▶ 192–193

Titiroa mt. N.Z. see Aspiring, Mount
Titlagarh India 95 D1
Titlis mt. Switz. 51 O6
Titograd Crna Gora Yugo. see Podgorica
Titova Mitrovica Kosovo, Srbija Yugo. see Kosovska Mitrovica
Titov Drvar Bos.-Herz. 56 I4
Titovka r. Rus. Fed. 44 O1
Titovo Užice Srbija Yugo. see Užice
Titovo Velenje Slovenia see Velenje
Titov Veles Macedonia see Veles
Titov Vrbas Vojvodina, Srbija Yugo. see Vrbas
Ti Tree Australia 148 B4
Tittabawassee r. U.S.A. 173 J7
Titteri mts Alg. 55 O8
Tittmoning Germany 49 J7
Titu Romania 58 G4
Titule Dem. Rep. Congo 126 E4
Titusville FL U.S.A. 175 D6
Titusville PA U.S.A. 176 F4
Tiu Chung Chau i. Hong Kong China 87 [inset]
Tiumpan Head U.K. 46 F5
also known as Siumpain, Rubha an t-
Tiva watercourse Kenya 128 C5
Tivari India 96 B4
Tivat Crna Gora Yugo. 56 K6
Tiveden nationalpark nat. park Sweden 45 K4
Tiverton Canada 173 L6
Tiverton U.K. 47 I13
Tivoli Italy 56 E7
historically known as Tibur
Tiwal, Wadi watercourse Sudan 126 D2
Tiwāl al 'Abā reg. Syria 109 K1
Tiwi Oman 105 G3
Tiwi Aboriginal Land res. Australia 148 A1
Tiworo, Selat sea chan. Indon. 75 B4
Tixkokob Mex. 185 H4
Tixtla Mex. 185 F5
Tiya tourist site Eth. 128 C2
Tizi El Arba hill Alg. 55 O8
Tizi Mighert pass Morocco 122 C3
Tizimín Mex. 185 H4
Tizi-n-Test pass Morocco 122 C3
Tizi-n-Tichka pass Morocco 122 D3
Tizi Ouzou Alg. 123 G1
Tiznap He r. China 88 B4
Tiznit Morocco 122 C3
Tizoc Mex. 185 E3
Tjaktjajaure l. Sweden 44 L2
Tjåmotis Sweden 44 L2
Tjaneni Swaziland 133 P2
Tjappsåive Sweden 44 L2
Tjautas Sweden 44 M2
Tjeggelvas l. Sweden 44 L2
Tjirebon Indon. see Cirebon
Tjirrkarli Aboriginal Reserve Australia 151 D5
Tjolotjo Zimbabwe see Tsholotsho
Tjörn i. Sweden 45 J4
Tjörnes pen. Iceland 44 [inset] C2
Tjøtta Norway 44 K2
Tkibuli Georgia see Tqibuli
Tkvarcheli Georgia see Tqvarch'eli
Tlacolula Mex. 185 F5
Tlacotalpán Mex. 185 G5
Tlacotepec, Cerro mt. Mex. 185 E5
Tlalnepantla Mex. 185 F5
Tlancualpican Mex. 185 F5
Tlapa Mex. 185 F5
Tlapacoyan Mex. 185 F5
Tlaxcala Mex. 185 F5
Tlaxcala state Mex. 185 F5
Tlaxco Mex. 185 F5
Tlaxcoapán Mex. 185 F4
Tlaxiaco Mex. 185 F5
Tlell Canada 166 D4
Tlemcen Alg. 123 E2
formerly spelt Tilimsen
Tleta Rissana Morocco 54 F9
Tlhabologang S. Africa 133 K3
Tlhakalatlou S. Africa 132 H5
Tlhakgameng S. Africa 133 I3
Tlholong S. Africa 133 M5
Tlokweng Botswana 131 E5
Tluszcz Poland 49 S3
Tlyarata Rus. Fed. 107 F2
T'ma r. Rus. Fed. 43 Q5
Tmeïmîchât Mauritania 122 B5
Tnaôt, Prêk r. Cambodia 79 D6
To r. Myanmar 78 B4
also known as China Bakir
Toad r. Canada 166 E3
Toad River Canada 166 E3
Toamasina Madag. 131 [inset] K3
formerly known as Tamatave
Toamasina prov. Madag. 131 [inset] K3
Toana mts U.S.A. 183 J1
Toano U.S.A. 177 I8
Toa Payoh Sing. 76 [inset]
Toast U.S.A. 176 E9
Toatoa N.Z. 152 L6
To Awai well Sudan 121 G4
Toay Arg. 204 D5
Toba China 86 A2
Toba Japan 91 E7
Toba, Danau l. Indon. 76 B2
English form Toba, Lake
Toba, Lake Indon. see Toba, Danau
Toba and Kakar Ranges mts Pak. 101 F4
Tobago i. Trin. and Tob. 187 H5
Toba Inlet Canada 166 E5
Tobarra Spain 55 J6
Tobas Arg. 204 E3
Toba Tek Singh Pak. 101 H4
Tobelo Indon. 75 C2
Tobermorey Australia 148 C4
Tobermory Australia 147 D1
Tobermory Canada 168 D4
Tobermory U.K. 46 F7
Tōbetsu Japan 90 G3
Tobi i. Palau 73 H6
Tobias Barreto Brazil 202 E4
Tobin, Lake salt flat Australia 150 D4
Tobin, Mount U.S.A. 183 G1
Tobin Lake Canada 180 G1
Tobique r. Canada 169 H4
Tobi-shima i. Japan 90 F5
Toboali Indon. 77 D3
Tobol Kazakh. 103 E1
also spelt Tobyl
Tobol r. Kazakh./Rus. Fed. 103 E1
also spelt Tobyl
Tobol'sk Rus. Fed. 38 G4
Toboso Phil. 74 B4
Tobruk Libya see Tubruq
Tobyhanna U.S.A. 177 J4
Tobyl Kazakh. see Tobol
Tobyl r. Kazakh./Rus. Fed. see Tobol
Tobylzhan Kazakh. see Tavolzhan
Tobysh r. Rus. Fed. 40 I2
Tocache Nuevo Peru 200 A2
Tocantinópolis Brazil 202 C3
Tocantins r. Pará Brazil 199 G6
Tocantins r. Brazil 202 B2
Tocantins state Brazil 202 B4
Toccoa U.S.A. 174 D5
Toce r. Italy 56 A3
Tochi r. Pak. 101 G3
Tochigi Japan 91 F6

	city	population	location	page#
largest cities	1 ▶ Tōkyō	26 444 000	Japan Asia	91 F7
	2 ▶ Mexico City	18 131 000	Mexico North America	185 F5
	3 ▶ Mumbai (Bombay)	18 066 000	India Asia	94 B2
	4 ▶ São Paulo	17 755 000	Brazil South America	206 G10
	5 ▶ New York	16 640 000	USA North America	177 L5
	6 ▶ Lagos	13 427 000	Nigeria Africa	125 F5
	7 ▶ Los Angeles	13 140 000	USA North America	182 F7
	8 ▶ Kolkata (Calcutta)	12 918 000	India Asia	97 F5
	9 ▶ Shanghai	12 887 000	China Asia	87 G2
	10 ▶ Buenos Aires	12 560 000	Argentina South America	204 F4

Tochigi pref. Japan 91 F6
Tochio Japan 90 F6
Töcksfors Sweden 45 J4
Tocoa Hond. 186 B4
Tocopilla Chile 200 C5
Tocorpuri, Cerros de mts Bol./Chile 200 D5
Tocumwal Australia 147 E3
Tod, Mount Canada 166 G5
Toda Bhim India 96 C4
Toda Rai Singh India 96 B4
Todd watercourse Australia 148 B5
Todd Range hills Australia 151 D5
Todi Italy 56 E6
historically known as Tuder
Todi mt. Switz. 51 O6
Todog China 88 C2
formerly spelt Todok
Todohokke Japan 90 G4
Todok China see Todog
Todos os Santos r. Brazil 207 M4
Todos Santos Bol. 200 D4
Todos Santos Mex. 184 C4
Todtmoos Germany 48 E8
Toe Jaga, Khao hill Thai. 79 B5
Toekomstig Stuwmeer resr Suriname 199 G4
Toéni Burkina 124 E3
Tofield Canada 167 H4
Tofino Canada 166 E5
Toft U.K. 46 K3
Tofte U.S.A. 172 C3
Toftlund Denmark 45 J5
Tofua i. Tonga 145 H3
Toga U.S.A. 176 G8
Tōgane Japan 91 G7
Togdheer admin. reg. Somalia 128 E2
Togi Japan 91 E6
Togiak U.S.A. 164 C4
Togian i. Indon. 75 B3
Togian, Kepulauan is Indon. 75 B3
Togliatti Rus. Fed. see Tol'yatti
▶Togo country Africa 125 F4
africa [countries] ▶▶ 114–117
Tograsay He r. China 88 E4
Tögrög Mongolia 84 B2
formerly known as Manhan
Togrog Ul China 85 G3
also known as Qahar Youyi Qianqi
Togtoh China 85 F3
Toguchin Rus. Fed. 80 C1
Toguz Kazakh. 103 E3
Tog Wajaale Somalia 128 D2
Tohamiyam Sudan 121 H5
Tohana India 96 B3
Tohenbatu mt. Sarawak Malaysia 77 F2
Tohmajärvi Fin. 44 O3
Tohmajärvi l. Fin. 44 O3
Toholampi Fin. 44 N3
Tohom China 85 E3
Töhöm Mongolia 85 F2
Tohono O'Odham (Papago) Indian Reservation res. U.S.A. 183 L9
Tohoun Togo 125 F5
Toi Hokkaidō Japan 90 G4
Toi Shizuoka Japan 91 F7
Toiba China 89 E6
also spelt Doba
Toijala Fin. 45 M3
Toili Indon. 75 B3
Toi-misaki pt Japan 91 B9
Toineke Indon. 75 C5
Toiyabe Range mts U.S.A. 183 G2
Tojikiston country Asia see Tajikistan
Tojikobod Tajik. 101 G2
also spelt Tadzhikabad
Tōjō Japan 91 C7
Tok r. Rus. Fed. 102 C1
Tok U.S.A. 164 E3
Tokachi-gawa r. Japan 90 H3
Tōkai Japan 91 E7
Tokaj Hungary 49 S7
Tokala, Gunung mt. Indon. 75 B3
Tōkamachi Japan 90 F6
Tokanui N.Z. 153 C14
Tokar Sudan 121 H5
Tokarahi N.Z. 153 E12
Tokara-rettō is Japan 81 L7
Tokarevka Kazakh. 103 H2
Tokat Turkey 107 D2
Tokatoka N.Z. 152 H4
Tŏkch'ok-to i. S. Korea 83 B5
Tŏkch'ŏn N. Korea 83 B5
Tokdo i. N. Pacific Ocean see Liancourt Rocks

▶Tokelau terr. S. Pacific Ocean 221 G6
New Zealand Overseas Territory.
oceania [countries] ▶▶ 138–139

Tokhtamysh Tajik. see Tŭkhtamish
Toki Japan 91 E7
Tokkuztara China see Gongliu
Tokmak Kyrg. 103 H4
also spelt Tokmok; formerly known as Bol'shoy Tokmak
Tokmak Ukr. 41 E7
formerly known as Bol'shoy Tokmak or Velykyy Tokmak
Tokmok Kyrg. see Tokmak
Tokomaru Bay N.Z. 152 M6
Tokoroa N.Z. 152 J6
Tokoro-gawa r. Japan 90 I2
Tokounou Guinea 124 C4
Tokoza S. Africa 133 M3
Tokrau watercourse Kazakh. see Tokyrau
Toksu China see Xinhe
Toksun China 88 E3
Tok-tō i. N. Pacific Ocean see Liancourt Rocks
Toktogul Kyrg. 103 H4
formerly known as Muztor
Toktogul'skoye Vodokhranilishche resr Kyrg. see Toktogul Suu Saktagychy
Toktogul Suu Saktagychy resr Kyrg. 103 H4
also known as Toktogul'skoye Vodokhranilishche
Tokto-ri i. N. Pacific Ocean see Liancourt Rocks
Tokty Kazakh. 88 C2
Tokû i. Tonga 145 H3
Tokur Rus. Fed. 82 D1
Tokushima Japan 91 D7
Tokushima pref. Japan 91 D8
Tokuyama Japan 91 B7
Tokwe r. Zimbabwe see Tugwi
Tokyo Japan see Tōkyō

▶Tōkyō Japan 91 F7
Capital of Japan. Most populous city in the world and in Asia. English form Tokyo; historically known as Edo.
world [population] ▶▶ 22–23
world [cities] ▶▶ 24–25

Tōkyō municipality Japan 90 F7
Tōkyō-wan b. Japan 91 F7
Tokyrau watercourse Kazakh. 103 H3
also spelt Toqyraū; formerly spelt Tokrau
Tokyu-san National Park S. Korea 83 B6
Tokzār Afgh. 101 F3
Tolaga Bay N.Z. 152 M6

Tôlañaro Madag. 131 [inset] J5
also known as Faradofay; formerly known as Fort-Dauphin; formerly spelt Taolanaro
Tolar, Cerro mt. Arg. 204 D2
Tolbazy Rus. Fed. 40 I3
Tolbo Mongolia 84 A1
Tolbukhin Bulg. see Dobrich
Tolbukhino Rus. Fed. 43 V4
formerly known as Davydkovo
Tolchin, Mount Antarctica 223 T1
Tolé Panama 186 C5
Tole Bi Kazakh. 103 H4
formerly known as Novotroitskoye
Toledo Amazonas Brazil 198 C6
Toledo Paraná Brazil 203 A8
Toledo Ohio Brazil 204 C2
Toledo Spain 54 G4
historically known as Toletum
Toledo IA U.S.A. 174 A3
Toledo OH U.S.A. 176 B4
Toledo OR U.S.A. 180 B3
Toledo, Montes de mts Spain 54 G5
formerly known as Oretana, Cordillera
Toledo Bend Reservoir U.S.A. 179 D6
Tolentino Italy 56 F6
Toletum Spain see Toledo
Tolga Norway 44 J3
Toli China 88 C2
Toliara Madag. 131 [inset] I4
formerly spelt Tuléar
Toliara prov. Madag. 131 [inset] J4
Tolima dept Col. 198 C4
Toling China see Zanda
Tolitoli Indon. 75 B2
Tol'ka Rus. Fed. 39 I3
Tolkmicko Poland 49 Q1
Tollense r. Germany 49 K2
Tollensesee-Becken park Germany 49 K2
Tolleson U.S.A. 183 L8
Tollimarzhan Uzbek. see Talimardzhan
Tolmachevo Rus. Fed. 43 K3
Tolmezzo Italy 56 F2
Tolmin Slovenia 56 F2
Tolna Hungary 49 P9
Tolo, Dem. Rep. Congo 126 C5
Tolo Channel Hong Kong China 87 [inset]
also known as Chek Mun Hoi Hap
Tolochin Belarus see Talachyn
Tolo Harbour b. Hong Kong China 87 [inset]
also known as Tai Po Hoi
Tolonen Fin. 44 N1
Tolosa France see Toulouse
Tolosa Spain 55 I1
Tolsan-do i. S. Korea 83 B6
Tolsmaville Canada 173 J5
Tolstoy, Mys c. Rus. Fed. 39 Q4
Toltén Chile 204 B5
Tolú Col. 198 C2
Toluca Mex. 185 F5
Tolvand, Ozero l. Rus. Fed. 44 O2
Tol'yatti Rus. Fed. 41 I5
English form Togliatti; formerly known as Stavropol'-na-Volge
Tolybay Kazakh. 103 E2
Tom' r. Rus. Fed. 82 B2
Toma Burkina 124 E3
Tomah U.S.A. 172 C7
Tomahawk U.S.A. 172 D5
Tomakomai Japan 90 G3
Tomales U.S.A. 182 B3
Tomamae Japan 90 G2
Tomani Sabah Malaysia 77 F1
Tomar Brazil 199 F5
Tomari Rus. Fed. 82 F3
Tomaros mt. Greece 59 B9
Tomarza Turkey 106 C3
Tomatlán Mex. 184 D5
Tomave Bol. 200 D5
Tomazina Brazil 206 D10
Tombador, Serra do hills Bahia Brazil 202 D4
Tombador, Serra do hills Mato Grosso Brazil 201 F3
Tombigbee r. U.S.A. 175 C6
Tombo S. Africa 133 N8
Tomboco Angola 127 B6
Tombos Brazil 207 K7
Tombouctou Mali see Timbuktu
Tombouctou admin. reg. Mali 124 E2
Tombstone U.S.A. 181 E7
Tombua Angola 127 A8
formerly known as Porto Alexandre
Tom Burke S. Africa 131 E4
Tomdibuloq Uzbek. see Tamdybulak
Tomditow Toghi hills Uzbek. see Tamdytau, Gory
Tome Chile 204 B5
Tome Moz. 131 D4
Tomea i. Indon. 75 B4
Tomelilla Sweden 45 K5
Tomelloso Spain 55 H5
Tomenaryk Kazakh. 103 F4
formerly spelt Tyumen'-Aryk
Tomi Romania see Constanța
Tomiko Canada 173 N4
Tominé r. Guinea 124 B3
Tomingley Australia 147 F3
Tomini, Teluk g. Indon. 75 B3
Tominian Mali 124 D3
Tomioka Fukushima Japan 90 G6
Tomioka Gunma Japan 91 F6
Tomislavgrad Bos.-Herz. 56 J5
formerly known as Duvno
Tomkinson Ranges mts Australia 146 A1
Tømmerneset Norway 44 K2
Tommot Rus. Fed. 39 M4
Tomo Col. 199 E4
Tomo r. Col. 198 D4
Tomóchic Mex. 184 D2
Tomorit, Maja e mt. Albania 58 B8
Tomorlog China 88 E4

Tomortei China 85 G3
Tompa Hungary 49 Q9
Tompira Indon. 75 B3
Tompi Seleka S. Africa 133 N1
Tompo Indon. 75 A3
Tompo Rus. Fed. 39 N3
Tom Price Australia 150 B4
Tomra China 89 D7
Tomsk Rus. Fed. 80 D1
Toms River U.S.A. 177 K6
Tomtor Rus. Fed. 39 O3
Tömük Turkey 108 F1
also known as Elvanlı
Tomuraushi-yama mt. Japan 90 H3
Tomur Feng mt. China/Kyrg. see Pobeda Peak
Tomuzlovka r. Rus. Fed. 41 H7
Tom White, Mount U.S.A. 164 E3
Tonalá Chiapas Mex. 185 G5
Tonalá Veracruz Mex. 185 G5
Tonami Japan 91 E6
Tonantins Brazil 199 E5
Tonate Fr. Guiana 199 H3
Tonawanda U.S.A. 176 G2
Tonb-e Bozorg, Jazireh-ye i. The Gulf see Greater Tunb
Tonb-e Küchek, Jazireh-ye i. The Gulf see Lesser Tunb
Tonbridge U.K. 47 M12
Tondano Indon. 75 C2
Tondela Port. 54 C4
Tønder Denmark 45 J5
Tondi India 94 C4
Toney Mount Antarctica 222 Q1
Tonga Cameroon 125 H5
▶Tonga country S. Pacific Ocean 145 H3
historically known as Friendly Islands
oceania [countries] ➡ 138–139
Tonga Sudan 128 A2
Tongaat S. Africa 133 P6
Tonga Plateau Zambia 127 E9
Tongaporutu N.Z. 152 I6
Tongareva atoll Cook Is. see Penrhyn
Tongariro vol. N.Z. 152 J7
Tongariro National Park N.Z. 152 J7
Tongatapu i. Tonga 145 H4
Tongatapu Group is Tonga 145 H4
▶Tonga Trench sea feature S. Pacific Ocean 220 G7
2nd deepest trench in the world.
Tongbai China 87 E1
Tongbai Shan mts China 87 E1
Tongcheng Anhui China 87 F2
Tongcheng Hubei China 87 E2
also known as Juanshui
Tongcheng China see Dong'e
T'ongch'ŏn N. Korea 83 B5
Tongchuan China 85 F5
Tongchuan China see Santai
Tongdao China 87 D3
also known as Shuangjiang
Tongde China 84 D5
also known as Gabasumdo
Tongduch'ŏn S. Korea 83 B5
Tongeren Belgium 51 L2
also spelt Tongres
Tonggu China 87 E2
also known as Yongning
Tongguan China 87 D2
Tonggu Jiao pt China 87 D5
Tonghae S. Korea 83 C5
also known as Xiushan
Tonghe China 82 C3
Tonghua Jilin China 82 B4
also known as Kuaidamao
Tonghua Jilin China 82 B4
Tongi Bangl. see Tungi
Tongjiang Heilong. China 82 D3
Tongjiang Sichuan China 87 C2
also known as Nuojiang
Tongken r. China 82 B3
Tongking, Gulf of China/Vietnam 78 E3
also known as Tongkin
Tongliao China 85 I3
Tongliao China 85 I3
Tongling Anhui China 87 F2
Tongling Anhui China 87 F2
Tonglu China 87 F2
Tongnae S. Korea 91 A7
Tongo Australia 147 D2
Tongobory Madag. 131 [inset] J4
Tongquan China see Malong
Tongquil i. Phil. 74 B5
Tongren Guizhou China 87 D3
Tongren Qinghai China 84 D5
also known as Rongwo
Tongres Belgium see Tongeren
Tongsa Bhutan see Trongsa
Tongshan China 87 F1
also known as Xuzhou
Tongshi China 87 D5
formerly known as Hongqizhen
Tongta Myanmar 78 B3
Tongtian He r. China see Yangtze
Tongue U.K. 46 H5
Tongue r. U.S.A. 180 F3
Tongue of the Ocean sea chan. Bahamas 186 E2
Tongwei China 84 E5
also known as Pingxiang
Tongxian China see Tongzhou
Tongxiang China 87 G2
Tongxin China 85 E4
T'ongyŏng S. Korea 83 C6
Tongyu China 85 I3
also known as Kaitong
Tongzhou China 85 H4
formerly known as Tongxian
Tongzi China 86 C2
Tonhil Mongolia see Dzüyl
Tonica U.S.A. 172 D9
Tónichi Mex. 184 C2
Tonila Mex. 184 E5
Tonj Sudan 126 F3
Tonj watercourse Sudan 126 F3
Tonk India 96 B4
Tonkābon Iran 100 B2
Tonkawa U.S.A. 178 C4
Tonkin reg. Vietnam 78 E3
Tônlé Repou r. Laos 79 D5
Tônlé Sab l. Cambodia see Tonle Sap
▶Tonle Sap l. Cambodia 79 C5
Largest lake in Southeast Asia. Also spelt Tônlé Sab.
Tonnay-Charente France 50 F7
Tonneins France 50 G8
Tonnerre France 51 J5
Tönning Germany 48 F1
Tōno Japan 90 G5
Tonopah AZ U.S.A. 183 L8
Tonopah NV U.S.A. 183 G3
Tonosí Panama 186 C6
Tons r. India 89 B6
Tønsberg Norway 45 J4
Tonshalovo Rus. Fed. 43 S2
Tonstad Norway 45 I4
Tontelbos S. Africa 132 E7
Tonto Basin U.S.A. 183 M8
Tonto Creek watercourse U.S.A. 183 M8
Tonzang Myanmar 78 A3
Toobeah Australia 147 F2
Toobli Liberia 124 C4
Tooele U.S.A. 183 L1
Toolonga Nature Reserve Australia 151 A5

Toompine Australia 147 E1
Toorberg mt. S. Africa 132 I9
Toowoomba Australia 147 F1
Tooxin Somalia 128 F2
Top Afgh. 101 G2
Topalki Rus. Fed. 43 R3
Topana Romania 58 F4
Topaz Lake U.S.A. 182 E3
▶Topeka U.S.A. 178 D4
State capital of Kansas.
Topia Mex. 184 D3
Topkancvo Rus. Fed. 43 T7
Topki Rus. Fed. 80 D1
Topla reg. India 96 D5
Topla r. Slovakia 49 S7
Toplana, Gunung mt. Indon. 75 D3
Topley Canada 166 E4
Topley Landing Canada 166 E4
Toplica r. Yugo. 58 C5
Topliţa Romania 58 G2
Topocalma, Punta pt Chile 204 B4
Topock U.S.A. 183 J7
Topol'čany Slovakia 49 P7
Topolnitsa r. Bulg. 58 F6
Topolobampo Mex. 184 C3
Topoleg Romania 58 J4
Topolog r. Romania 58 F3
Topoloveni Romania 58 G4
Topolovgrad Bulg. 58 H6
Topozero, Ozero l. Rus. Fed. 44 P2
Toppenish U.S.A. 180 B3
Topraisar Romania 58 J4
Topterek China see Jeminay
Topuni N.Z. 152 I5
Tor Eth. 128 B3
Tora Dem. Rep. Congo 126 F4
Tor Baldak mt. Afgh. 101 F4
Torbali Turkey 106 A3
Torbat-e Heydariyeh Iran 101 D3
Torbat-e Jām Iran 101 E3
Torbay Bay Australia 151 B7
Torbeyevo Respublika Mordoviya Rus. Fed. 41 G5
Torbeyevo Smolenskaya Oblast' Rus. Fed. 43 P6
Torch r. Canada 167 K4
Torchino Rus. Fed. 43 V5
Tordesillas Spain 54 G3
Tordino r. Italy 56 F6
Töre Sweden 44 M2
Töreboda Sweden 45 K4
Torelló Spain 55 N2
Toreno Spain 54 E2
Toreo Indon. 75 B3
Torere N.Z. 152 L5
Torey Rus. Fed. 84 I1
Torgau Germany 49 J4
Torgelow Germany 49 L2
Torghay Kazakh. see Turgay
Torgun r. Rus. Fed. 102 A2
Torhamn Sweden 45 K4
Torhout Belgium 51 J1
also spelt Thourout
Tori Estonia 42 G3
Tori India 97 E5
Tori r. Sudan 128 A3
Torigni-sur-Vire France 50 F3
Torine pass Bos.-Herz. 56 K5
Torino Italy see Turin
Tori-shima i. Japan 91 G9
Torit Sudan 128 B3
Torixoreu Brazil 206 A3
Torkamān Iran 100 A2
Torkovichi Rus. Fed. 43 L3
Torma Estonia 42 H3
Törmänen Fin. 44 N1
Torment, Point Australia 150 C3
Tormes r. Spain 54 E3
Tornado Mountain Canada 167 H5
Tornalla Slovakia 49 R7
formerly known as Šafárikovo
Tornavacas, Puerto de pass Spain 54 F4
Torneå Fin. see Tornio
Torneälven r. Sweden 44 N2
Torneträsk Sweden 44 L1
Torneträsk l. Sweden 44 L1
Torngat, Monts mts Canada see Torngat Mountains
Torngat Mountains Canada 169 H1
also known as Torngat, Monts
Tornik mt. Yugo. 58 A5
Tornio Fin. 44 N2
also spelt Torneå
Tornquist Arg. 204 E5
Toro Nigeria 125 H4
Toro Spain 54 F3
Toro, Lago del l. Chile 205 B8
Toro, Pico del mt. Mex. 185 E3
Torodi Niger 125 F3
Törökszentmiklós Hungary 49 R8
▶Toronto Canada 168 E4
Provincial capital of Ontario and 5th most populous city in North America.
world [cities] ➡ 24–25
Toronto U.S.A. 176 E5
Toropatsa Rus. Fed. 43 M5
Toro Peak U.S.A. 183 H8
Toropets Rus. Fed. 43 M5
Tororo Uganda 128 B4
Toros Dağları mts Turkey see Taurus Mountains
Toroshino Rus. Fed. 43 J4
Torquato Severo Brazil 204 G4
Torquay Australia 147 E4
Torrance U.S.A. 182 F5
Torre r. Spain 54 D3
Torre de Annunziata Italy 57 G8
Torreblanca Spain 55 L4
Torre Blanco, Cerro mt. Mex. 184 B1
Torrecerredo mt. Spain 54 G1
Torrecilla mt. Spain 54 G8
Torre del Greco Italy 57 G8
Torre de Moncorvo Port. 54 D3
Torredonjimeno Spain 54 H7
Torrejón de Ardoz Spain 55 H4
Torrejón-Tajo, Embalse de resr Spain 54 F5
Torrelaguna Spain 55 H4
Torrelavega Spain 54 G1
Torremaggiore Italy 56 H7
Torremolinos Spain 54 G8
▶Torrens, Lake salt flat Australia 146 C2
2nd largest lake in Oceania.
oceania [landscapes] ➡ 136–137
Torrens Creek Australia 149 E4
Torrent Arg. 204 F3
Torrent Spain 55 K5
also spelt Torrente
Torrente Spain see Torrent
Torreón Mex. 185 E3
Torreorgaz hill Spain 54 D5
Torres Brazil 203 B9
Torres del Paine, Parque Nacional nat. park Chile 205 B8
Torres Islands Vanuatu 145 F3
Torres Novas Port. 54 C5
Torres Strait Australia 144 D1
Torres Vedras Port. 54 B5

Torrevieja Spain 55 K7
Torrey U.S.A. 183 M3
Torridge r. U.K. 47 H13
Torriglia Italy 56 B4
Torrijos Spain 54 G5
Torrington U.S.A. 180 F4
Torroella de Montgrí Spain 55 O2
Torrón i. Sweden 44 K3
Torsa Chhu r. Bhutan 97 F4
Torsby Sweden 45 K3
▶Tórshavn Faroe Is. 46 F1
Capital of the Faroe Islands. Also spelt Thorshavn.
Torsvåg Norway 44 L1
Tortilla Flat U.S.A. 183 M8
Tortkuduk Kazakh. 103 H2
Tortola i. Virgin Is (U.K.) 187 G3
Tortoli Sardegna Italy 57 B9
Tortomanu Romania 58 J4
Tortona Italy 56 A4
Tortorici Sicilia Italy 57 G10
Tortosa, Punta pt Mex. 184 C3
Tortuga, Laguna l. Mex. 185 F4
Tortuguero, Parque Nacional nat. park Costa Rica 186 C4
Tortum Turkey 107 E2
Torūd Iran 100 D2
Torugart, Pereval pass China/Kyrg. see Turugart Pass
Torul Turkey 107 E2
Toruń Poland 49 P2
historically known as Thorn
Torva Estonia 42 G3
Torvlieysa mt. Norway 44 I3
Tory Island Rep. of Ireland 47 D8
Torysa r. Slovakia 49 S7
Tory Sound sea chan. Rep. of Ireland 47 D8
Torzhkovskaya Gryada hills Rus. Fed. 43 P5
Torzhok Rus. Fed. 43 P4
Tosa Japan 91 C8
Tosashimizu Japan 91 C8
Tosa-wan b. Japan 91 C8
Tosa-yamada Japan 91 C8
Tosbotn Norway 44 K3
Toscana admin. reg. Italy 56 D5
English form Tuscany
Toscana reg. Italy see Tuscany
Toscana, Arcipelago is Italy 56 B5
Tosenfjorden inlet Norway 44 K3
To-shima i. Japan 91 F7
Tōshima-yama mt. Japan 90 G4
Toshkent Uzbek. see Tashkent
Toshkent Wiloyati admin. div. Uzbek. see Tashkentskaya Oblast'
Tosno Rus. Fed. 43 U2
Tosno Rus. Fed. 43 L2
Toson Hu l. China 84 C4
Tosontsengel Mongolia 84 C1
Tossa de Mar i. Spain 55 M3
Tossal de l'Orri mt. Spain 55 M3
Tostado Arg. 204 E3
Tõstamaa Estonia 42 E3
Tostedt Germany 48 G2
Tosu Japan 91 B8
Tosya Turkey 106 C2
Toszek Poland 49 P5
Totana Spain 55 J7
Totapola mt. Sri Lanka 94 D5
Totaranui N.Z. 152 G8
Toteng Botswana 130 D4
Tôtes France 50 H3
Tot'ma Rus. Fed. 40 G4
Totness Suriname 199 H3
Totolapan Mex. 185 F5
Totonicapán Guat. 185 H6
Totora Bol. 200 D4
Totoral Chile 204 C2
Totoralejos Arg. 204 D3
Totoya i. Fiji 145 H3
Totskoye Rus. Fed. 102 C1
Tottori Japan 91 D7
Tottori Japan 91 C7
Touâret well Niger 125 G1
Touba Côte d'Ivoire 124 C4
Touba Senegal 124 B3
Toubkal, Parc National nat. park Morocco 122 D3
Touboro Cameroon 125 I5
Touchet r. U.S.A. 180 C3
Toucy France 51 J5
Toudaohu China 85 E3
Toueirma well Mauritania 122 B5
Touérât well Mali 122 D4
Toufourine well Mali 122 D4
Tougan Burkina 124 E3
Tougourt Alg. 123 G2
Tougouri Burkina 125 E3
Touil Mauritania 124 C3
Toukoto Mali 124 C3
Toul France 51 M4
Toulépleu Côte d'Ivoire 124 C4
Toulfé Burkina 125 E3
Touliu Taiwan 87 G4
also known as Douliu
Toulnustouc r. Canada 169 G3
Toulon France 51 L9
historically known as Telo Martius
Toulouk well Niger 125 G2
Toulouse France 50 H9
historically known as Tolosa
Toumbélaga well Niger 125 G3
Toummo well Niger 123 I5
Toumodi Côte d'Ivoire 124 D5
Toungo Nigeria 125 I4
Toungoo Myanmar 78 B4
Toupai China 87 D3
Touques r. France 50 G3
Touraine reg. France 50 G5
Tourane Vietnam see Da Năng
Tourassine well Mauritania 122 C4
Tourba Chad 120 B6
Tourgis Lake Canada 167 J1
Tourinán, Cabo c. Spain 54 B1
Tourlaville France 50 E3
Tour Matagrin hill France 51 K7
Tournai Belgium 51 J2
Tournavista Peru 200 B2
Tourndo, Oued watercourse Alg./Niger 123 H5
Tournon-sur-Rhône France 51 K7
Tournus France 51 K6
Touros Brazil 202 F3
Tours France 50 G5
historically known as Caesarodunum or Turones
Tous, Embalse de resr Spain 55 K5
Toussiana Burkina 124 D4
Toussidé, Pic mt. Chad 120 C4
Toussoro, Mont mt. Cent. Afr. Rep. 126 D2
Toutai China 82 B3
Toutouwai i. S. Africa 132 C10
Touwsrivier S. Africa 132 E10
Tôv prov. Mongolia 85 E2
Tovar Venez. 198 D2
Tovarkovo Rus. Fed. as Kaganovich
Tovarnik Croatia 56 L3
Tovil'-Dora Tajik. see Tavil'dara
Tovu Fiji 145 H3

Tovuz Azer. 107 F2
also spelt Tauz
Towada Japan 90 G4
Towada-Hachimantai National Park Japan 90 G5
Towai N.Z. 152 I3
Towakaima Guyana 199 G3
Towak Mountain hill U.S.A. 164 C3
Towanda U.S.A. 177 I4
Towaoc U.S.A. 183 P4
Towari Indon. 75 B4
Tower U.S.A. 172 A3
Tower City U.S.A. 177 I5
Towerhill Creek watercourse Australia 149 E4
Towner U.S.A. 178 B1
Towns r. Australia 148 B2
Townsend MA U.S.A. 177 N2
Townsend MT U.S.A. 180 E3
Townshend Island Australia 149 F4
Townsville Australia 149 E3
Towori, Teluk b. Indon. 75 B3
Towot Sudan 128 B3
Towr Kham Afgh. 101 G3
Towson U.S.A. 177 I6
Towuti, Danau l. Indon. 75 B3
Toy U.S.A. 182 F1
Toyah U.S.A. 179 B6
Tōya-ko l. Japan 90 G3
Toyama Japan 91 E6
Toyama pref. Japan 91 E6
Toyama-wan b. Japan 90 E6
Tōyo Japan 91 C8
Toyohashi Japan 91 E7
Toyokawa Japan 91 E7
Toyonaka Japan 91 D6
Toyooka Japan 91 D7
Toyosaka Japan 90 F6
Toyota Japan 91 E7
Toyotomi Japan 90 G2
Tōyōshi Fiji 145 H3
Toytepa Uzbek. 103 G4
Tozal del Orri mt. Spain see Tossal de l'Orri
Tozanlı Turkey see Almus
Tozé Kangri mt. China 89 C5
Tozeur Tunisia 123 H2
Tqibuli Georgia 107 E2
also spelt Tkibuli
Tqvarch'eli Georgia 107 E2
also spelt Tkvarcheli
Trâblous Lebanon see Tripoli
Trabotivište Macedonia 58 D7
Trabzon Turkey 107 D2
English form Trebizond; historically known as Trapezus
Tracy CA U.S.A. 182 C4
Tracy MN U.S.A. 178 D2
Trade Lake U.S.A. 172 A5
Trading r. Canada 168 D3
Træna i. Norway 44 J2
Trænfjorden sea chan. Norway 44 K2
Traer U.S.A. 174 A3
Trafalgar, Cabo c. Spain 54 E8
Traffic Mountain Canada 166 D2
Traian Romania 58 J2
Traiguén Chile 204 B5
Trail Canada 166 G5
Traill Island Greenland see Traill Ø
Traill Ø i. Greenland 165 Q2
English form Traill Island
Traipu Brazil 202 E4
Traira r. Brazil 198 D5
also spelt Taraíra
Trairas r. Brazil 206 G4
Trairi Brazil 202 F3
Traisen r. Austria 49 M7
Trajano de Morais Brazil 207 K9
Trajectum Neth. see Utrecht
Traka r. S. Africa 132 H10
Trakai Lith. 42 F7
Trakai nat. park Lith. 42 F7
Trakiya reg. Turkey see Thrace
Trakt Rus. Fed. 40 I3
Trakya reg. Turkey see Thrace
Tralee Rep. of Ireland 47 C11
also known as Trá Li
Trá Li Rep. of Ireland see Tralee
Trá Mhór Rep. of Ireland see Tramore
Tramonti, Serra de mts Spain 55 N5
Tramore Rep. of Ireland 47 E11
also known as Trá Mhór
Tranäs Sweden 45 K4
Trancas Arg. 204 C2
Trancoso Port. 54 D3
Tranebjerg Denmark 45 J5
Tranemo Sweden 45 K4
Trang Thai. 79 B7
Trangan i. Indon. 73 H8
Trangie Australia 147 E3
Trani Italy 56 I7
Tranqueras Uruguay 204 G3
Transantarctic Mountains Antarctica 223 K2
Trans Canada Highway Canada 167 H5
Transcona Canada 167 L5
Transtrand Sweden 45 K3
Transylvanian Alps mts Romania 58 D3
also known as Carpații Meridionali
Transylvanian Basin plat. Romania 58 F2
Trapani Sicilia Italy 57 E10
Trapezus Turkey see Trabzon
Trapper Peak U.S.A. 180 D3
Trappes France 51 H4
Trapua r. Brazil 203 A9
Traralgon Australia 147 E4
Traras, Morts des mts Alg. 55 J9
Trarza admin. reg. Mauritania 124 B2
Trasacco Italy 56 F7
Trăscăului, Munții mts Romania 58 E2
Trashigang Bhutan 97 F4
also known as Tashigang
Trasimeno, Lago l. Italy 56 E5
Trás-os-Montes reg. Port. 54 D3
Trasvase, Canal de Spain 55 I5
Trasvase Tajo-Segura, Canal de Spain 55 I5
Traun Austria 49 L7
Traun r. Austria 49 L7
Traunreut Germany 49 J8
Traunsee l. Austria 49 L8
Traunstein Germany 49 J8
Traupis Lith. 42 F6
Trave r. Germany 48 H2
Travellers Lake imp. l. Australia 147 D3
Traverse City U.S.A. 172 H6
Travesía Puntana des. Arg. 204 D4
Travesía Tunuyán des. Arg. 204 D4
Travessão Brazil 207 L8
Travis, Lake U.S.A. 179 C6
Travnik Bos.-Herz. 56 J4
Travo r. Corse France 56 B7
Trbovlje Slovenia 56 H2
Trebević nat. park Bos.-Herz. 56 K5
Trebel r. Germany 49 K2
Trèbes France 51 I9
Trebić Czech Rep. 49 M6
Trebinje Bos.-Herz. 56 K6
Trebisacce Italy 57 I9
Trebišnjica r. Bos.-Herz. 56 K6
Trebišov Slovakia 49 S7
Trebizond Turkey see Trabzon
Trebnje Slovenia 56 H3
Trebon Czech Rep. 49 L6

Tree r. Canada 167 I1
Tree Island India 94 B4
Treene r. Germany 48 G1
Trefaldwyn U.K. see Montgomery
Tre'gosse Islets and Reefs Australia 149 F3
Treignac France 50 H7
Treinta y Tres Uruguay 204 G3
Trelew Arg. 205 D6
Trelleborg Sweden 45 K5
Trélon France 51 K2
Trem mt. Yugo. 58 D5
Tramblant, Mont hill Canada 169 F4
Trembleur Lake Canada 166 E4
Tremiti, Isole i. Italy 56 H6
Tremlya r. Belarus 43 K9
Tremont U.S.A. 177 I5
Tremonton U.S.A. 180 D4
Tremp Spain 55 L2
Trempealeau r. U.S.A. 172 B6
Trenche r. Canada 169 F4
Trenčín Slovakia 49 P7
'Trenggalek Indon. 77 E5
Trengganu state Malaysia see Terengganu
Trenque Lauquén Arg. 204 E4
Trent Italy see Trento
Trent r. U.K. 47 L10
Trentino - Alto Adige admin. reg. Italy 56 D2
Trento Italy 56 D2
English form Trent; historically known as Tridentum
Trenton Canada 168 E4
Trenton FL U.S.A. 175 D6
Trenton GA U.S.A. 174 C5
Trenton MO U.S.A. 174 A3
Trenton NC U.S.A. 174 E5
Trenton NE U.S.A. 178 B3
▶Trenton NJ U.S.A. 177 K5
State capital of New Jersey.
Trepang Bay Australia 148 A1
Trepassey Canada 169 K4
Tres Arboles Uruguay 204 F4
Tres Arroyos Arg. 204 E5
Tres Cerros Arg. 205 D8
Três Corações Brazil 203 C7
Tres Cruces Arg. 200 D5
Tres Cruces Chile 204 C3
Tres Esquinas Col. 198 C4
Três Irmãos, Represa resr Brazil 206 C7
Tres Isletas Arg. 204 E2
Treska r. Macedonia 58 C6
Treski Estonia 42 I4
Três Lagoas Brazil 206 B7
Tres Lagos Arg. 205 C8
Tres Lomas Arg. 204 E5
Três Marias, Represa resr Brazil 203 C6
Três Marias Brazil 207 H5
Tres Matas Venez. 199 F2
Tres Montes, Península pen. Chile 205 B7
Tres Picachos, Sierra mts Mex. 181 F7
Tres Picos mt. Arg. 205 C6
Tres Picos Mex. 185 G6
Tres Picos, Cerro mt. Arg. 204 E5
Tres Picos, Cerro mt. Mex. 185 G5
Tres Piedras U.S.A. 181 F5
Tres Pinos U.S.A. 182 C4
Três Pontas Brazil 203 C7
Tres Puentes Chile 204 C2
Tres Puntas, Cabo c. Arg. 205 D7
Três Ranchos Brazil 206 F5
Três Rios Brazil 203 D7
Třešť Czech Rep. 49 M6
Trestino Rus. Fed. 43 Q4
Tretna Rus. Fed. 43 Q4
Três Unidos Brazil 198 D6
Tres Zapotes tourist site Mex. 185 G5
Tretten Norway 45 J3
Treuchtlingen Germany 48 H7
Treuenbrietzen Germany 49 J3
Treungen Norway 45 J4
Trevelin Arg. 205 C6
Treves Germany see Trier
Trevi Italy 56 E6
Treviglio Italy 56 B3
Treviso Italy 56 E3
Trevose Head U.K. 47 G13
Trgoviste Srbija Yugo. 58 D6
Triabunna Australia 147 E5
Tri An, Hồ resr Vietnam 79 D6
Triánda Greece see Trianta
Triangle U.S.A. 177 H7
Triánta Greece 59 J12
also spelt Triánda
Tribal Areas admin. div. Pak. 101 G3
Tribeč mts Slovakia 49 P7
Tri Brata, Gora hill Rus. Fed. 82 F1
Tribune U.S.A. 178 B4
Tricarico Italy 57 I8
Tricase Italy 57 K9
Trichinopoly India see Tiruchchirappalli
Trichonida, Limni l. Greece 59 C10
Trichur India 94 C4
also known as Thrissur
Trida Australia 147 E3
Tridentum Italy see Trento
Trier Germany 48 D6
historically known as Augusta Treverorum or Treves
Trieste Italy 56 F3
historically known as Tergeste
Trieste, Golfo di g. Europe see Trieste, Gulf of
Trieste, Gulf of Europe 56 F3
also known as Trieste, Golfo di
Trie-sur-Baïse France 50 G9
Trieux r. France 50 C4
Triggiano Italy 56 I7
Triglavski Narodni Park nat. park Slovenia 56 F2
Trigno r. Italy 56 G6
Trikala Greece 59 C9
also spelt Trikkala
Trikkala Greece see Trikala
Trikomo Cyprus see Trikomon
Trikomon Cyprus 108 E2
also known as Trikomo or İskele
Trikora, Puncak mt. Indon. 73 I7
2nd highest mountain in Oceania.
oceania [landscapes] ➡ 136–137
Trikorfa mt. Greece 59 D10
Trilj Croatia 56 I5
Trim Rep. of Ireland 47 F10
Trincheras Mex. 184 C2
Trincomalee Sri Lanka 94 D4
Trindade Brazil 206 D3
Trindade, Ilha da i. S. Atlantic Ocean 217 L7
Tringia mt. Greece 59 C9
Trinidad Bol. 200 D3
Trinidad Cuba 186 C2
Trinidad Uruguay 204 F4
Trinidad U.S.A. 181 F5
Trinidad, Golfo b. Chile 205 B8
▶Trinidad and Tobago country West Indies 187 H5
northamerica [countries] ➡ 158–159
Trinitápoli Italy 56 I7
Trinity U.S.A. 179 D6
Trinity r. CA U.S.A. 182 A1
Trinity r. TX U.S.A. 179 D6
Trinity, West Fork r. U.S.A. 179 C5

Trinity Bay Australia **149** E3
Trinity Bay Canada **169** K4
Trinity Dam U.S.A. **182** B1
Trinity Islands U.S.A. **164** D4
Trinity Range *mts* U.S.A. **182** E1
Trinkat Island India **95** G4
Trinkitat Sudan **104** B4
Trino Italy **56** A3
Trinway U.S.A. **176** C5
Trionto, Capo *c.* Italy **57** I9
Tripa *r.* Indon. **76** B2
Tripoli Greece **59** D11
also known as Trípolis
Tripoli Lebanon **108** G3
also known as Trâblous; *historically known as* Tripolis

Tripoli Libya **120** B1
Capital of Libya. Also known as Ţarābulus; historically known as Oea.

Trípolis Greece *see* **Tripoli**
Tripolis Lebanon *see* **Tripoli**
Tripolitania *reg.* Libya **120** B2
Tripunittura India **94** C4
Tripura *state* India **97** F5
Trischen *i.* Germany **48** F1

Tristan da Cunha *i.* S. Atlantic Ocean **217** N8
Dependency of St Helena.

Tristao, Îles *is* Guinea **124** B4
Trisul *mt.* India **96** C3
Triton Canada **169** K3
Triton Island *atoll* Paracel Is **72** D3
Triunfo *Pernambuco* Brazil **202** E3
Triunfo *Rondônia* Brazil **200** D2
Triunfo Hond. **186** B4
Trivandrum India **94** C4
also spelt Thiruvananthapuram
Trivento Italy **56** G7
Trizina Greece **59** E11
Trnava Slovakia **49** O7
Trobriand Islands P.N.G. **145** E2
also known as Kiriwina Islands
Trofa Port. **54** C3
Trofaiach Austria **49** M8
Trofors Norway **44** K2
Trogir Croatia **56** I5
Troglav *mt.* Croatia **56** I5
Troina *Sicilia* Italy **57** G11
Troisdorf Germany **48** E5
Trois Fourches, Cap des *c.* Morocco **123** E2
also known as Tres Forcas, Cabo *or* Uarc, Ras
Trois-Pistoles Canada **169** G3
Trois-Rivières Canada **169** F4
Troitsa Rus. Fed. **38** G3
Troitsk *Chelyabinskaya Oblast'* Rus. Fed. **38** G4
Troitsk *Moskovskaya Oblast'* Rus. Fed. **43** S6
formerly known as Troitskiy
Troitskiy Rus. Fed. *see* **Troitsk**
Troitsko-Pechorsk Rus. Fed. **40** K3
Troitskoye *Khabarovskiy Kray* Rus. Fed. **82** E2
Troitskoye *Orenburgskaya Oblast'* Rus. Fed. **102** C1
Troitskoye *Respublika Bashkortostan* Rus. Fed. **102** D1
Troitskoye *Respublika Kalmykiya - Khalm'g-Tangch* Rus. Fed. **41** H7
Trolla *well* Chad **120** B6
Trollhättan Sweden **45** K4
Trollheimen *park* Norway **44** J3
Trombetas *r.* Brazil **199** G5
Tromelin, Île *i.* Indian Ocean **218** K7
English form Tromelin Island
Tromelin Island Indian Ocean *see* **Tromelin, Île**
Tromelin Island Micronesia *see* **Fais**
Tromen, Volcán *vol.* Arg. **204** C5
Trompsburg S. Africa **133** J7
Troms *county* Norway **44** L1
Tromsø Norway **44** L1
Trona U.S.A. **183** G6
Tronador, Monte *mt.* Arg. **204** C6
Tronçais, Forêt de *for.* France **51** I6
Trondheim Norway **44** J3
Trondheimsfjorden *sea chan.* Norway **44** J3
Trondheimsleia *sea chan.* Norway **44** J3
Trongsa Bhutan **97** F4
also spelt Tongsa
Trongsa Chhu *r.* Bhutan **97** F4
also known as Mangde Chhu
Tronto *r.* Italy **56** F6
Troödos, Mount Cyprus **108** D3
Troödos Mountains Cyprus **108** D3
Troon U.K. **46** H8
Tropaia Greece **59** C11
Troparevo Rus. Fed. **43** Q6
Tropas *r.* Brazil **199** G6
Tropea Italy **57** H10
Tropeiros, Serra dos *hills* Brazil **202** C5
Tropic U.S.A. **183** L4
Trosh Rus. Fed. **40** J2
Trosna Rus. Fed. **43** Q9
Trostan' Rus. Fed. **43** N9
Trostan *hill* U.K. **47** F8
Trostberg Germany **49** J7
Trotuş *r.* Romania **58** H2
Trout *r.* *B.C.* Canada **166** E3
Trout *r.* *N.W.T.* Canada **166** G2
Trout Creek Canada **173** N5
Trout Creek U.S.A. **172** D4
Trout Dale U.S.A. **176** D9
Trout Lake *Alta* Canada **167** H3
Trout Lake *N.W.T.* Canada **166** F2
Trout Lake *l.* *N.W.T.* Canada **166** F2
Trout Lake *l.* *Ont.* Canada **167** M5
Trout Lake *l.* U.S.A. **172** D4
Trout Run U.S.A. **177** H4
Troutville U.S.A. **176** F8
Trowbridge U.K. **47** J12
Trowutta Australia **147** E5
Troy *tourist site* Turkey **106** A3
also known as Truva; *historically known as* Ilium
Troy *AL* U.S.A. **175** C6
Troy *KS* U.S.A. **178** D4
Troy *MI* U.S.A. **173** J8
Troy *MO* U.S.A. **174** B4
Troy *NC* U.S.A. **174** E5
Troy *NH* U.S.A. **177** M3
Troy *NY* U.S.A. **177** L3
Troy *OH* U.S.A. **176** A5
Troy *PA* U.S.A. **177** I4
Troyan Bulg. **58** F6
Troyekurovo *Lipetskaya Oblast'* Rus. Fed. **43** T9
Troyekurovo *Lipetskaya Oblast'* Rus. Fed. **43** U8
Troyes France **51** K4
Troy Lake U.S.A. **183** H7
Troy Peak U.S.A. **183** I3
Trstenik *Srbija* Yugo. **58** C5
Trubchevsk Rus. Fed. **43** O9
Trubetchino Rus. Fed. **43** U9
Trubia *r.* Spain **54** F1
Truc Giang Vietnam *see* **Bên Tre**
Trucial Coast *country* Asia *see* **United Arab Emirates**
Trucial States *country* Asia *see* **United Arab Emirates**
Truckee U.S.A. **182** D2
Trud Rus. Fed. **43** O4
Trudovoy Kazakh. *see* **Kuybyshevskiy**
Trudovoy Rus. Fed. *see* **Yusta**
Trudovoye Rus. Fed. **82** D4
Trudy *r.* Rus. Fed. **43** S9
Truer Range *hills* Australia **148** A4
Trufanovo Rus. Fed. **40** H2
Trujillo Hond. **186** B4
Trujillo Peru **200** A2
Trujillo Spain **54** F5
Trujillo Venez. **198** D2
Trujillo *state* Venez. **198** D2
Trujillo, Monte *mt.* Dom. Rep. *see* **Duarte, Pico**
Trumann U.S.A. **174** B5
Trumansburg U.S.A. **177** I3
Trumbull U.S.A. **177** L4
Trumbull, Mount U.S.A. **183** K5
Trumon Indon. **76** B2
Trŭn Bulg. **58** D6
Trun France **50** G4
Trŭna *mt.* Bulg. **58** E6
Trung Khanh Vietnam **78** D3
Truong Sa *is* S. China Sea *see* **Spratly Islands**
Truro Canada **169** I4
Truro U.K. **47** G13
Trusan *Sarawak* Malaysia **77** F1
Trusan *r.* *Sarawak* Malaysia **77** F1
Truskmore *hill* Rep. of Ireland **47** D9
Trus Madi, Gunung *mt.* *Sabah* Malaysia **77** G1
Trŭstenik Bulg. **58** F5
Trutch Canada **166** F3
Trutch Creek *r.* Canada **166** F3
Truth or Consequences U.S.A. **181** F6
formerly known as Hot Springs
Trutnov Czech Rep. **49** M5
Truva *tourist site* Turkey *see* **Troy**
Truyère *r.* France **51** I8
Truzhenik Rus. Fed. **43** Q3
Tryavna Bulg. **58** G6
Tryon U.S.A. **178** B3
Trypiti, Akra *pt* *Kriti* Greece **59** F13
Trypiti, Akra *pt* Greece **59** F9
Trysil Norway **45** K3
Trysilelva *r.* Norway **45** K3
Trysilfjellet *mt.* Norway **45** K3
Tryškiai Lith. **42** D5
Tržac Bos.-Herz. **56** H4
Trzcianka Poland **49** N2
Trzebiatów Poland **49** M1
Trzebinia Poland **49** Q5
Trzebnica Poland **49** O4
Trzemeszno Poland **49** O3
Tržič Slovenia **56** G2
Trzrcińsko-Zdrój Poland **49** L3
Tsagaannuur *Bayan-Ölgiy* Mongolia **84** A1
Tsagaannuur *Dornod* Mongolia **85** H2
Tsagaan Nuur *salt l.* Mongolia **84** B2
Tsagaan-Olom Mongolia **84** C2
Tsagaan-Ovoo Mongolia **85** G1
Tsagaan-Ovoo Mongolia **84** D2
Tsagaan-Uul Mongolia *see* **Sharga**
Tsagan Aman Rus. Fed. **102** A3
formerly known as Burunniy
Tsagan Khurtey, Khrebet *mts* Rus. Fed. **85** F1
Tsagan-Nur Rus. Fed. **41** H7
Tsaidam Basin China *see* **Qaidam Pendi**
Tsåktso *mt.* Sweden **44** M1
Tsalenjikha Georgia **107** E2
Tsama I Congo **126** B5
Tsangatjåkkå *mt.* Sweden **44** K2
Tsao Botswana **130** D4
Tsaratanana, Massif du *mts* Madag. **131** [inset] K2
Tsarevo Bulg. **58** I6
formerly known as Michurin
Tsarevo-Zaymishche Rus. Fed. **43** P6
Tsaribrod *Srbija* Yugo. *see* **Dimitrovgrad**
Tsarimir Bulg. **58** F6
Tsaritsyn Rus. Fed. *see* **Volgograd**
Tsatsana *mt.* S. Africa **133** M7
Tsat Tsze Mui *pt* *Hong Kong* China *see* **North Point**
Tsaukaib Namibia **130** B5
Tsavo East National Park Kenya **128** C5
Tsavo West National Park Kenya **129** C5
Tsazo S. Africa **133** L8
Tsebanana Botswana **131** E3
Tseel Mongolia **84** B2
Tsefat Israel *see* **Ẕefat**
Tselina Rus. Fed. **41** G7
Tselinnyy Rus. Fed. **103** E2
Tselinograd Kazakh. *see* **Astana**
Tselinogradskaya Oblast' *admin. div.* Kazakh. *see* **Akmolinskaya Oblast'**
Tsementnyy Rus. Fed. *see* **Fokino**
Tsengel Mongolia **84** D1
Tsenogora Rus. Fed. **40** H2
Tsentralen Balkan *nat. park* Bulg. **58** F6
Tsentral'nyy *Kirovskaya Oblast'* Rus. Fed. **40** I4
Tsentral'nyy Rus. Fed. *see* **Radovitskiy**
Tsentral'nyy *Ryazanskaya Oblast'* Rus. Fed. **43** U8
Tserkovishche Rus. Fed. **43** L6
Tserovo Bulg. **58** E5
Tses Namibia **130** C5
Tsetsegnuur Mongolia **84** B2
Tsetseng Botswana **130** D4
Tsetserleg Mongolia **84** D2
Tsetserleg Mongolia *see* **Halban**
Tsévié Togo **125** F5
Tshabong Botswana **130** D5
Tshad *country* Africa *see* **Chad**
Tshchikskoye Vodokhranilishche *resr* Rus. Fed. **41** F7
Tshela Dem. Rep. Congo **126** B6
Tshene Dem. Rep. Congo **126** C6
Tshibala Dem. Rep. Congo **127** D6
Tshibuka Dem. Rep. Congo **127** D6
Tshibwika Dem. Rep. Congo **127** D7
Tshidilamolomo Botswana **133** I2
Tshikapa Dem. Rep. Congo **127** D6
Tshikapa *r.* Dem. Rep. Congo **127** D6
Tshilenge Dem. Rep. Congo **127** D6
Tshimbulu Dem. Rep. Congo **127** D6
Tshing S. Africa **133** K3
Tshipise S. Africa **131** F4
Tshiumbe *r.* Angola/Dem. Rep. Congo **127** D6
Tshofa Dem. Rep. Congo **127** E6
Tshokwane S. Africa **133** P1
Tsholotsho Zimbabwe **131** E3
formerly spelt Tjolotjo
Tshootsha Botswana **130** D4
Tshuapa *r.* Dem. Rep. Congo **126** D5
Tshumbiri Dem. Rep. Congo **126** C5
Tsiazonano *mt.* Madag. **131** [inset] J3
Tsibritsa *r.* Bulg. **58** E5
Tsiigehtchic Canada **164** F3
formerly known as Arctic Red River
Tsil'ma *r.* Rus. Fed. **40** I2
Tsimkavichy Belarus **42** H8
also spelt Timkovichi
Tsimlyansk Rus. Fed. **41** G7
Tsimlyanskoye Vodokhranilishche *resr* Rus. Fed. **41** G7
Tsinan China *see* **Jinan**
Tsineng S. Africa **132** H4
Tsinghai *prov.* China *see* **Qinghai**
Tsing Shan *hill* *Hong Kong* China *see* **Castle Peak**
Tsing Shan Wan *b.* *Hong Kong* China *see* **Castle Peak Bay**
Tsing Shui Wan *b.* *Hong Kong* China *see* **Clear Water Bay**
Tsingtao China *see* **Qingdao**
Tsingy de Bemaraha, Réserve *nature res.* Madag. **131** [inset] J3
Tsing Yi *i.* *Hong Kong* China **87** [inset]
Tsining China *see* **Jining**
Tsinjomay *mt.* Madag. **131** [inset] J3
Tsintsabis Namibia **130** C3
Tsiombe Madag. **131** [inset] J5
Tsiroanomandidy Madag. **131** [inset] J3
Tsiteli Tskaro Georgia *see* **Dedop'listsqaro**
Tsitondroina Madag. **131** [inset] J4
Tsitsihar China *see* **Qiqihar**
Tsitsikamma Forest and Coastal National Park S. Africa **132** H11
Tsitsutl Peak Canada **166** E4
Tsivil'sk Rus. Fed. **40** H5
Tskhakaia Georgia *see* **Senaki**
Tskhaltubo Georgia *see* **Tsqaltubo**
Ts'khinvali Georgia **107** E2
formerly known as Staliniri
Tsna *r.* Belarus **42** I9
Tsna *r.* Rus. Fed. **41** G5
Tsna *r.* Rus. Fed. **43** P4
Tsna *r.* Rus. Fed. **43** U6
Tsnori Georgia **107** F2
Tsodilo Hills Botswana **130** D3
Tsolo S. Africa **133** M8
Tsomo S. Africa **133** L9
Tsomo *r.* S. Africa **133** L9
Tso Morari Lake Jammu and Kashmir **96** C2
Tson *r.* Rus. Fed. **43** R9
Tsona China *see* **Cona**
Tsopan *hill* Greece **58** G8
Tsqaltubo Georgia **107** E2
also spelt Tskhaltubo
Tsu Japan **91** E7
Tsubame Japan **90** F6
Tsubata Japan **91** E6
Tsubetsu Japan **90** I3
Tsuchiura Japan **91** G6
Tsuen Wan *Hong Kong* China **87** [inset]
also known as Quanwan
Tsugarū-kaikyō *strait* Japan **90** G4
English form Tsugaru Strait
Tsugaru Strait Japan *see* **Tsugarū-kaikyō**
Tsukigata Japan **90** G3
Tsukuba Japan **91** G6
Tsukumi Japan **91** B8
Tsul-Ulaan Mongolia **84** E2
Tsumeb Namibia **130** C3
Tsumis Park Namibia **130** C4
Tsumkwe Namibia **130** D3
Tsuno-shima *i.* Japan **91** B7
Tsuru Japan **91** F7
Tsuruga Japan **91** E7
Tsurugi-san *mt.* Japan **91** D8
Tsurukhaytuy Rus. Fed. *see* **Priargunsk**
Tsuruoka Japan **90** F5
Tsushima Japan **91** E7
Tsushima *is* Japan **91** A7
Tsushima-kaikyō *strait* Japan/S. Korea *see* **Korea Strait**
Tsuyama Japan **91** D7
Tsvetino Bulg. **58** E7
Tswaane Botswana **130** D4
Tswaraganang S. Africa **133** J5
Tswelelang S. Africa **133** J4
Tsyelyakhany Belarus **42** G9
also spelt Telekhany
Tsyerakhowka Belarus **43** M9
Ts'yl-os Provincial Park Canada **166** E5
Tsyomny Lyes Belarus **43** M7
Tsyp-Navolok Rus. Fed. **44** P1
Tsyurupyns'k Ukr. **41** E7
formerly known as Aleshki *or* Oleshky
Tthenaagoo Canada *see* **Nahanni Butte**
Tua *r.* Port. **54** D3
Tua, Tanjung *pt* Indon. **77** D4
Tuakau N.Z. **152** I5
Tual Indon. **73** H8
Tuam Rep. of Ireland **47** D10
Tuamarina N.Z. **152** H9
Tuamotu, Archipel des *is* Fr. Polynesia *see* **Tuamotu Islands**
Tuamotu Archipelago *is* Fr. Polynesia *see* **Tuamotu Islands**
Tuamotu Islands Fr. Polynesia **221** I6
English form Tuamotu Archipelago; *also known as* Tuamotu, Archipel des; *formerly known as* Paumotu, Îles
Tuân Giao Vietnam **78** C3
Tuangku *i.* Indon. **76** B2
Tuapeka Mouth N.Z. **153** D14
Tuapse Rus. Fed. **41** F7
Tuaran *Sabah* Malaysia **77** G1
Tuas Sing. **76** [inset]
Tuatapere N.Z. **153** B14
Tuath, Loch a' *b.* U.K. *see* **Broad Bay**
Tuba City U.S.A. **183** M5
Tubalai *i.* Indon. **75** D3
Tuban Indon. **77** F4
Tubarão Brazil **203** B9
Tūbās West Bank **108** G5
Tubau *Sarawak* Malaysia **77** F2
Tubbataha Reefs Phil. **74** A4
Tubeya Dem. Rep. Congo **127** D6
Tubigan *i.* Phil. **74** B5
Tübingen Germany **48** G7
Tubinskiy Rus. Fed. **102** D1
Tubmanburg Liberia **124** C5
Tubo *r.* Nigeria **125** G4
Tubod Phil. **74** B4
Tubou Fiji **145** H3
also spelt Tumbou
Tubruq Libya **120** D1
English form Tobruk
Tubu *r.* Indon. **77** G2
Tubuai *i.* Fr. Polynesia **221** I7
Tubuai Islands Fr. Polynesia **221** H7
also known as Australes, Îles
Tubutama Mex. **184** C2
Tucandera Brazil **199** F5
Tucannon *r.* U.S.A. **180** C3
Tucano Brazil **202** E4
Tucavaca Bol. **201** F4
Tucavaca *r.* Bol. **201** F4
Tuchitua Canada **166** D2
Tuchkovo Rus. Fed. **43** R6
Tuchodi *r.* Canada **166** F3
Tuchola Poland **49** O2
Tuchów Poland **49** S6
Tuckanarra Australia **151** B5
Tucker Glacier Antarctica **223** L2
Tuckerton U.S.A. **177** K6
Tucson U.S.A. **183** N9
Tucson Mountains U.S.A. **183** M9
Tuctuc *r.* Canada **169** H1
Tucumán Arg. *see* **San Miguel de Tucumán**
Tucumán *prov.* Arg. **204** D2
Tucumcari U.S.A. **179** B5
Tucunuco Arg. **204** C3
Tucuparé Brazil **199** H6
Tucupita Venez. **199** F2
Tucuracas Col. **198** C2
Tucuruí Brazil **202** B2
Tucuruí, Represa *resr* Brazil **202** B3
Tuczno Poland **49** N2
Tudela Spain **55** J2
also spelt Tutera
Tudela de Duero Spain **54** G3
Tuder Italy *see* **Todi**
Tudor Vladimirescu Romania **58** I3
Tudovka *r.* Rus. Fed. **43** O5
Tudu Estonia **42** H2
Tudulinna Estonia **42** I2
Tuen Mun *Hong Kong* China **87** [inset]
Tuensang India **97** G4
Tueré *r.* Brazil **199** I5
Tuerto *r.* Spain **50** A10
Tufanovo Rus. Fed. **43** V3
Ţufayḩ Saudi Arabia **105** E2
Tufi P.N.G. **145** D2
Tugela *r.* S. Africa **133** P6
Tugela Ferry S. Africa **133** O5
Tūghyl Kazakh. *see* **Tugyl**
Tuglung China **89** F6
Tugnug Point Phil. **74** C4
Tuguancun China **86** B3
Tuguegarao Phil. **74** B2
Tugur Rus. Fed. **82** E1
Tugurskiy Zaliv *b.* Rus. Fed. **82** E1
Tugwi *r.* Zimbabwe **131** F4
formerly spelt Tokwe
Tugyl Kazakh. **88** C2
also spelt Tūghyl; *formerly known as* Priozernyy
Tuhai *r.* China **85** H4
Tuhemberua Indon. **76** B2
Tui Spain **54** C2
also spelt Túy
Tuichi *r.* Bol. **200** D3
Tuilianpui *r.* Bangl./India **97** G5
Tuinplaas S. Africa **133** M1
Tuins *watercourse* S. Africa **132** E6
Tūja Latvia **42** F4
Tujiabu China *see* **Yongxiu**
Tujuh, Kepulauan *is* Indon. **77** D3
Tukan Rus. Fed. **102** D1
Tukangbesi, Kepulauan *is* Indon. **75** B4
Tukangbesi Marine Reserve *nature res.* Indon. **75** B4
Tukarak Island Canada **168** E1
Tukayel Eth. **128** E2
Tūkh Egypt **108** C7
Tukhavichy Belarus **42** G9
Tŭkhtamish Tajik. **101** H2
also spelt Tokhtamysh
Tukituki *r.* N.Z. **152** K7
Tūkrah Libya **120** D1
Tuktoyaktuk Canada **164** F3
formerly known as Fort Brabant
Tuktut Nogait National Park Canada **164** G3
Tukums Latvia **42** E5
Tukung, Bukit *mt.* Indon. **77** E3
Tukuringra, Khrebet *mts* Rus. Fed. **82** B1
Tukuyu Tanz. **129** B7
Tula *watercourse* Kenya **128** C5
Tula Mex. **185** F4
Tula Rus. Fed. **43** S7
Tulach Mhór Rep. of Ireland *see* **Tullamore**
Tulagt Ar Gol *r.* China **89** F4
Tulai China **84** C4
Tulai Nanshan *mts* China **84** C4
Tulai Shan *mts* China **84** C4
Tulak Afgh. **101** E3
Tula Mountains Antarctica **223** D2
Tulancingo Mex. **185** F4
Tulangbawang *r.* Indon. **76** D4
Tula Oblast *admin. div.* Rus. Fed. *see* **Tul'skaya Oblast'**
Tulare U.S.A. **182** E5
Tulare Lake Bed U.S.A. **182** E6
Tularosa U.S.A. **181** F6
Tulasi *mt.* India **94** D2
Tulcán Ecuador **198** B4
Tulcea Romania **58** J3
Tul'chin Ukr. *see* **Tul'chyn**
Tul'chyn Ukr. **41** D6
also spelt Tul'chin
Tule *r.* U.S.A. **182** E5
Tulé Venez. **187** E5
Tuléar Madag. *see* **Toliara**
Tulehu Indon. **75** D3
Tulelake U.S.A. **180** B4
Tule Mod China **85** I2
Tulghes Romania **58** G2
Tulia U.S.A. **179** B5
Tulihe China **85** I1
Tuliszków Poland **49** P3
Tulít'a Canada **166** E1
formerly known as Fort Norman
Tuljapur India **94** C2
Tulkarm West Bank *see* **Ţūlkarm**
Ţūlkarm West Bank **108** G5
English form Tulkarm
Tullahoma U.S.A. **174** C5
Tullamore Australia **147** E3
Tullamore Rep. of Ireland **47** E10
also spelt Tulach Mhór
Tulle France **50** H7
Tullibigeal Australia **147** E3
Tulln Austria **49** N7
Tullow Rep. of Ireland **47** F11
Tully Australia **149** E3
Tully Falls Australia **149** E3
Tulnici Romania **58** H3
Tuloma *r.* Rus. Fed. **44** P1
Tulos Rus. Fed. **44** O3
Tulppio Fin. **44** O2
Tulsa U.S.A. **179** D4
Tulsequah Canada **166** C3
Tulsipur Nepal **97** D3
Tul'skaya Oblast' *admin. div.* Rus. Fed. **43** S8
English form Tula Oblast
Tul'skoye Kazakh. **103** H1
Tuluá Col. **198** B3
Tulucești Romania **58** J3
Tuluksak U.S.A. **164** C3
Tulūl al Ashāqif *hills* Jordan **109** I5
Tulūl al Bissah *hills* Saudi Arabia **109** K6
Tulum *tourist site* Mex. **185** I4
Tulun Rus. Fed. **80** G2
Tulungagung Indon. **77** E5
Tulu-Tuloi, Serra *hills* Brazil **199** F4
Tulu Welel *mt.* Eth. **128** B2
Tulva *r.* Rus. Fed. **40** J4
Tuma Rus. Fed. **40** G5
Tumaco Col. **198** B4
Tumahole S. Africa **133** L3
Tumain China **89** E5
Tumak Rus. Fed. **102** B3
Tuman Iran **101** E3
Tuman-gang *r.* Asia *see* **Tumen Jiang**
Tumannaya *r.* Asia *see* **Tumen Jiang**
Tumannyy Rus. Fed. **40** E1
Tumanovo Rus. Fed. **43** P6
Tumanskiy Rus. Fed. **39** R3
Tumasik Sing. *see* **Singapore**
Tumatumari Guyana **199** G3
Tumazy Rus. Fed. **43** P1
Tumba Sweden **45** L4
Tumbangmiri Indon. **77** F3
Tumbangsamba Indon. **77** F3
Tumbangtiti Indon. **77** E3
Tumbao Phil. **74** C5
Tumbarumba Australia **147** F3
Tumbes Peru **198** A5
Tumbes *dept* Peru **198** A5
Tumbiscatio Mex. **185** E5
Tumbler Ridge Canada **166** F4
Tumbou Fiji *see* **Tubou**
Tumby Bay Australia **146** C3
Tumcha *r.* Fin./Rus. Fed. **44** C2
Tumd Youqi China *see* **Salaqi**
Tumd Zuoqi China *see* **Qasq**
Tumen *Jilin* China **82** C4
Tumen *Shaanxi* China **87** D1
Tumen Jiang *r.* Asia **82** C4
also known as Tuman-gang *or* Tumannaya
Tumeremo Venez. **199** F3
Tumereng Guyana **199** F3
Tumindao *i.* Phil. **74** A5
Tumiritinga Brazil **203** D6
Tumkur India **94** C3
Tumlingtar Nepal **97** E4
Tummo, Mountains of Libya/Niger **120** B4
Tumnin *r.* Rus. Fed. **82** F2
Tump Pak. **101** E5
Tumpah Indon. **77** F3
Tumpôr, Phnum *mt.* Cambodia **79** C5
Tumpu, Gunung *mt.* Indon. **75** B3
Tumputiga, Gunung *mt.* Indon. **75** B3
Tumsar India **96** C5
Tumshuk Uzbek. **103** F5
Tumu Ghana **125** E4
Tumucumaque, Serra *hills* Brazil **199** G4
Tumudibandh India **95** D2
Tumupasa Bol. **200** D3
Tumur Kazakh. **103** G4
also spelt Temir; *formerly spelt* Timur
Tumusla Bol. **200** D5
Tumut Australia **147** F3
Tumutuk Rus. Fed. **40** J5
Tumxuk China **88** C3
Tuna Ghana **124** E4
Tunapuna Trin. and Tob. **187** H5
Tunas de Zaza Cuba **186** D2
Ţunb al Kubrá *i.* The Gulf *see* **Greater Tunb**
Ţunb aş Şughrá *i.* The Gulf *see* **Lesser Tunb**
Tunbridge Wells, Royal U.K. **47** M12
Tunçbilek Turkey **59** K9
Tunceli Turkey **107** D3
Tuncurry Australia **147** G3
Tundla India **89** B7
Tundubai *well* Sudan **121** F5
Tunduma Tanz. **129** B7
Tundun-Wada Nigeria **125** H4
Tunduru Tanz. **129** C7
Tundzha *r.* Bulg. **58** H7
Tunes Tunisia *see* **Tunis**
Tunga Nigeria **125** H4
Tungabhadra *r.* India **94** C3
Tungabhadra Reservoir India **94** C3
Tungawan Phil. **74** B5
Tungdor China *see* **Mainling**
Tungi Bangl. **97** F5
also spelt Tongi
Tungku *Sabah* Malaysia **77** G1
Tungla Nicaragua **186** B4
Tung Lung Chau *i.* *Hong Kong* China *see* **Tung Lung Island**
Tung Lung Island *Hong Kong* China **87** [inset]
also known as Tung Lung Chau
Tungnaá *r.* Iceland **44** [inset] C2
Tungor Rus. Fed. **82** F1
Tungozero Rus. Fed. **44** O2
Tung Pok Liu Hoi Hap *sea chan.* *Hong Kong* China *see* **East Lamma Channel**
Tungsten Canada **166** D2
Tungun, Bukit *mt.* Indon. **77** F2
Tungurahua *prov.* Ecuador **198** B5
Tung Wan *b.* *Hong Kong* China **87** [inset]
Tuni India **95** D2
Tunica U.S.A. **174** B5
Tunica Canada **173** M2

Tunis Tunisia **123** H1
Capital of Tunisia. Historically known as Tunes.

Tunis, Golfe de *g.* Tunisia **123** H1
Tunisia *country* Africa **123** H2
spelt At Tūnisīyah *in Arabic; historically known as* Africa Nova
africa [countries] 114–117
Tunja Col. **198** C3
Tunkhannock U.S.A. **177** J4
Tunki Nicaragua **186** B4
Tunkinskiye Gol'tsy *mts* Rus. Fed. **84** D1
Tunliu China **85** G4
Tunnel City U.S.A. **172** C6
Tunnelton U.S.A. **176** F6
Tunnsjøen *l.* Norway **44** K2
Tunoshna Rus. Fed. **43** V4
Tuntsa Fin. **44** O2
Tunulic *r.* Canada **169** H1
Tununak U.S.A. **164** C3
Tunungayualok Island Canada **169** I1
Tunuyán Arg. **204** C4
Tunuyán *r.* Arg. **204** D4
Tunxi China *see* **Huangshan**
Tuo He *r.* China **87** F1
Tuojiang China *see* **Fenghuang**
Tuojiang China *see* **Shuikou**
Tuo Jiang *r.* China **86** C2
Tuolumne U.S.A. **182** D4
Tuolumne *r.* U.S.A. **182** C4
Tuolumne Meadows U.S.A. **182** E4
Tuoniang Jiang *r.* China **86** C3
Tuotuo He *r.* China **97** G2
Tuotuoheyan China **84** B5
also known as Tanggulashan
Tüp Kyrg. **103** I4
also spelt Typ
Tupã Brazil **206** C8
Tupaciguara Brazil **206** E5
Tupanaóca Brazil **199** F5
Tupanciretã Brazil **203** A9
Tupelo U.S.A. **174** B5
Tupinambarama, Ilha *i.* Brazil **199** G5
Tupi Paulista Brazil **206** B8
Tupiza Bol. **200** D5
Tupper Canada **166** F4
Tupper Lake U.S.A. **177** K1
Tupper Lake *l.* U.S.A. **177** K1
Tüpqaraghan Tübegi *pen.* Kazakh. *see* **Mangyshlak, Poluostrov**
Tupungato Arg. **204** C4

Tupungato, Cerro *mt.* Arg./Chile **204** C4
5th highest mountain in South America.
southamerica [landscapes] 190–191

Tuqayyid *well* Iraq **107** F5
Tuquan China **85** I2
Túquerres Col. **198** B4
Tuqu Wan *b.* China **87** D5
Tura China **89** D4
Tura India **97** F4
Tura Rus. Fed. **39** K3
Turabah *Hā'il* Saudi Arabia **104** C1
Turabah *Makkah* Saudi Arabia **104** C3
Turabah, Wādī *watercourse* Saudi Arabia **104** C3
Turagua, Serranía *mt.* Venez. **199** E3
Turakina N.Z. **152** J8
Turakina *r.* N.Z. **152** J8
Turana, Khrebet *mts* Rus. Fed. **82** C2
Turangi N.Z. **152** J6
Turan Lowland Asia **101** D2
also known as Turanskaya Nizmennost'
Turanskaya Nizmennost' *lowland* Asia *see* **Turan Lowland**
Ţuraq al 'Ilab *hills* Syria **109** J4
Tura-Ryskulova Kazakh. **103** G4
formerly known as Vannovka
Turaw Belarus **42** I9
Turayf Saudi Arabia **107** D5
Turayf *well* Saudi Arabia **105** E2
Ţurayf, Wādī *watercourse* Iraq **109** N4
Turba Estonia **42** F2
Turbaco Col. **198** C2
Turbacz *mt.* Poland **49** R6
Turbat Pak. **101** E5
Turbo Col. **198** B2
Turčianske Teplice Slovakia **49** P7
Turco Bol. **200** C4
Turda Romania **58** E2
Tūreh Iran **100** B3
Turek Poland **49** P3
Turfan China *see* **Turpan**
Turfan Depression China *see* **Turpan Pendi**
Turgay *Akmolinskaya Oblast'* Kazakh. **103** H2
Turgay *Kustanayskaya Oblast'* Kazakh. **103** E2
also spelt Torghay
Turgay *r.* Kazakh. **103** E3
Turgayskaya Dolina *valley* Kazakh. **103** E2
Turgayskaya Stolovaya Strana *reg.* Kazakh. **103** E2
Türgen Uul *mt.* Mongolia **84** A1
Türgen Uul *mts* Mongolia **84** A1
Turgeon *r.* Canada **168** E3
Tŭrgovishte Bulg. **58** H5
Turgut Turkey **106** B3
Turgut Turkey **59** J11
Turgutalp Turkey **59** I9
Turgutlu Turkey **106** A3
also known as Kasaba
Turgutreis Turkey **59** I12
Turhal Turkey **106** D2
Türi Estonia **42** G3
Turi Italy **56** J8
Turia *r.* Spain **55** K5
Turiaçu Brazil **202** C2
Turiaçu *r.* Brazil **202** C2
Turiaçu, Baía de *b.* Brazil **202** C2
Turiamo Venez. **199** E2
Turiec *r.* Slovakia **49** P6
Turin Canada **167** H5
Turin Italy **51** N7
also spelt Torino; *historically known as* Augusta Taurinorum *or* Taurasia
Turinsk Rus. Fed. **38** G4
Turiy Rog Rus. Fed. **82** C3
Türje Hungary **49** O9
Turka Rus. Fed. **81** H2
Turkana, Lake *salt l.* Eth./Kenya **128** B4
formerly known as Rudolf, Lake
Türkeli Turkey **58** I8
Türkeli Adası *i.* Turkey **58** I8
Turkestan Kazakh. **103** G4
also spelt Türkistan
Turkestan Range *mts* Asia **99** H2
Türkeve Hungary **49** R8
Turkey *country* Asia **106** B3
asia [countries] 64–67
Turkey U.S.A. **176** B8
Turkey *r.* U.S.A. **174** B3
Turki Rus. Fed. **41** G6
Türkistan Kazakh. *see* **Turkestan**
Turkmenabat Turkm. *see* **Chardzhev**
Turkmen Adasy *i.* Turkm. *see* **Ogurchinskiy, Ostrov**
Türkmen Aylagy *b.* Turkm. *see* **Turkmenskiy Zaliv**
Turkmenbashi Turkm. **102** C4
formerly known as Krasnovodsk
Türkmen Dağı *mt.* Turkey **106** B3
Turkmengala Turkm. **103** E5
also spelt Turkmen-Kala
Turkmenistan *country* Asia **102** D5
spelt Türkmenostan *in* Turkmen; *formerly known as* Turkmeniya *or* Turkmenskaya S.S.R.
asia [countries] 64–67
Turkmeniya *country* Asia *see* **Turkmenistan**
Turkmen-Kala Turkm. *see* **Turkmengala**
Turkmenkarakul' Turkm. **101** E3
Türkmenostan *country* Asia *see* **Turkmenistan**
Turkmenskaya S.S.R. *country* Asia *see* **Turkmenistan**
Turkmenskiy Zaliv *b.* Turkm. **102** C5
also known as Türkmen Aylagy
Türkoğlu Turkey **107** D3
Turkova Belarus **42** J6

Turks and Caicos Islands *terr.* West Indies **187** F2
United Kingdom Overseas Territory.
oceania [countries] 138–139

Turks Island Passage Turks and Caicos Is **187** F2
Turks Islands Turks and Caicos Is **187** F2
Turku Fin. **45** M3
also known as Åbo
Turkwel *watercourse* Kenya **128** C4
Turlock U.S.A. **182** D4
Turlock Lake U.S.A. **182** D4
Turmalina Brazil **203** D6
Turmus, Wādī at *watercourse* Saudi Arabia **104** C2
Turnagain *r.* Canada **166** E3
Turnagain, Cape N.Z. **152** K8
Turnbull, Mount U.S.A. **183** N8
Turneffe Islands Belize **185** I5
Turner *r.* Australia **150** B4
Turner *watercourse* Australia **151** B5
Turner U.S.A. **173** J6
Turner River Australia **150** E3
Turner's Peninsula Sierra Leone **124** B5
Turner Valley Canada **167** H5
Turnhout Belgium **51** K1
Turnor Lake Canada **167** I3
Turnor Lake *l.* Canada **167** I3
Turnov Czech Rep. **49** M5
Tŭrnovo Bulg. *see* **Veliko Tŭrnovo**
Turnu Măgurele Romania **58** F5
Turnu Severin Romania *see* **Drobeta - Turnu Severin**
Turon *r.* Australia **147** F3
Turones France *see* **Tours**
Turopolje *plain* Croatia **56** H3
Turovets Rus. Fed. **40** G4
Turovo Rus. Fed. **43** S7
Turpan China **88** E3
also spelt Turfan

Turpan Pendi *depr.* China **88** E3
Lowest point in northern Asia. English form Turfan Depression.

Turpan Zhan China **88** E3
also known as Daheyan
Turrialba Costa Rica **186** C5
Turriff U.K. **46** J6
Turris Libisonis *Sardegna* Italy *see* **Porto Torres**
Turşāq Iraq **107** F4
Turtkul' Uzbek. **103** E4
also spelt Törtköl; *formerly known as* Petroaleksandrovsk
Turtle Flambeau Flowage *resr* U.S.A. **172** C4
Turtleford Canada **167** I4
Turtle Island Australia **149** F3
Turtle Island Fiji *see* **Vatoa**
Turtle Islands Phil. **74** A5
Turtle Lake *l.* Canada **167** I4
Turtle Lake U.S.A. **172** A5
Turugart Pass China/Kyrg. **88** A3
also known as Torugart, Pereval *or* Turugart Shankou
Turugart Shankou *pass* China/Kyrg. *see* **Turugart Pass**
Turukhansk Rus. Fed. **39** I3
Turuna *r.* Brazil **199** G4
Turunçova Turkey **108** B1
Turush Kazakh. **102** D3
Turuvanur India **94** C3
Turvelândia Brazil **206** C4
Turvo Brazil **203** B9
Turvo *r.* *Goiás* Brazil **206** C4
Turvo *r.* *São Paulo* Brazil **206** D6
Turvo *r.* *São Paulo* Brazil **206** D9
Ţus Iran **101** D2
Tusayan U.S.A. **183** L6
Tuscaloosa U.S.A. **175** C5
Tuscania Italy **56** D6
Tuscany *admin. reg.* Italy *see* **Toscana**
Tuscany *reg.* Italy **56** C5
also known as Toscana
Tuscarawas *r.* U.S.A. **176** D5
Tuscarora Mountains *hills* U.S.A. **176** H5
Tuscola U.S.A. **174** B4
Tuscumbia *AL* U.S.A. **174** C5
Tuscumbia *MO* U.S.A. **178** D4
Tuskegee U.S.A. **175** C5
Tussey Mountains *hills* U.S.A. **176** G5
Tustin U.S.A. **172** H6
Tuszyn Poland **49** Q4
Tutak Turkey **107** E3
Tutaul Rus. Fed. **82** B1
Tutayev Rus. Fed. **43** U4
Tutera Spain *see* **Tudela**
Tuticorin India **94** C4
Tutoh *r.* *Sarawak* Malaysia **77** F2
Tutong Brunei **77** F1
Tutova *r.* Romania **58** I2
Tutrakan Bulg. **58** H4
Tuttle Creek Reservoir U.S.A. **178** C4
Tuttlingen Germany **48** F8

index T U V

Tuttut Nunaat *reg.* Greenland **165** Q2
also known as Renland
Tutuala East Timor **75** C5
Tutubu Tanz. **129** B6
Tutuila *i.* American Samoa **145** H3
formerly known as Masuna
Tutukaka N.Z. **152** I3
Tutume Botswana **131** E4
Tutûn Egypt **108** B8
Tutunendo Col. **198** B3
Tutupaca, Volcán *vol.* Peru **200** C4
Tuturumuri N.Z. **152** J9
Tututepec Mex. **185** F5
Tuul Gol *r.* Mongolia **85** E1
Tuun-bong *mt.* N. Korea **83** B4
Tuupovaara Fin. **44** O3
Tuusniemi Fin. **44** O3
Tuusula Fin. **45** N3
Tuva *aut. rep.* Rus. Fed. *see* **Tyva, Respublika**
▶**Tuvalu** *country* S. Pacific Ocean **145** G2
formerly known as Ellice Islands
oceania [countries] ▶▶▶ 138–139
Tuvana-i-Colo *i.* Fiji **145** H4
also spelt Tuvana-i-Tholo
Tuvana-i-Tholo *i.* Fiji *see* **Tuvana-i-Colo**
Tuve Sweden **45** J4
Tuve, Mount Antarctica **222** S2
Tuvinskaya A.S.S.R. *aut. rep.* Rus. Fed. *see* **Tyva, Respublika**
Tuvuk Kazakh. **103** I4
Tuwau *r.* Indon. **77** G2
Tuwayq, Jabal *hills* Saudi Arabia **105** D2
Tuwayq, Jabal *mts* Saudi Arabia **105** D3
Ṭuwayyil al Ḥājj *mt.* Jordan **108** G8
Ṭuwayyil ash Shihāq *mt.* Jordan **108** H7
Tuwwal Saudi Arabia **104** B3
Tuxer Gebirge *mts* Austria **48** I8
Tuxpan *Jalisco* Mex. **185** E5
Tuxpan *Nayarit* Mex. **184** D4
Tuxpan *Veracruz* Mex. **185** F4
Tuxtla Gutiérrez Mex. **185** G5
Túy Spain *see* **Tui**
Tuya Lake Canada **166** D3
Tuy Duc Vietnam **79** D5
Tuyên Quang Vietnam **78** D3
Tuy Hoa Vietnam **79** E5
Tuymazy Rus. Fed. **40** J5
Tūysarkān Iran **100** B3
Tüytepa Uzbek. *see* **Toytepa**
Tuz, Lake *salt l.* Turkey **106** C3
also known as Tuz Gölü
Tuz Gölü *salt l.* Turkey *see* **Tuz, Lake**
Tŭzha Bulg. **58** G6
Tuzha Rus. Fed. **40** H4
Tuz Khurmātū Iraq **107** F4
Tuzla Bos.-Herz. **56** K4
Tuzla Romania **58** J4
Tuzla Turkey **106** C3
Tuzla *r.* Turkey **107** E3
Tuzlov *r.* Rus. Fed. **41** G7
Tuzu *r.* Myanmar **78** A2
Tuzugu *well* Libya **120** C4
Tvååker Sweden **45** K4
Tvärålund Sweden **44** L2
Tvedestrand Norway **45** J4
Tver' Rus. Fed. **43** Q5
formerly known as Kalinin
Tver Oblast *admin. div.* Rus. Fed. *see* **Tverskaya Oblast'**
Tverskaya Oblast' *admin. div.* Rus. Fed. **43** Q4
English form Tver Oblast; formerly known as Kalininskaya Oblast'
Tvertsa *r.* Rus. Fed. **43** Q5
Tvøroyri Faroe Is **46** F2
Tvorozhkovo Rus. Fed. **43** J3
Tvŭrditsa Bulg. **58** G6
Twain Harte U.S.A. **182** D3
Twardogóra Poland **49** O4
Tweed Canada **173** P6
Tweed *r.* U.K. **46** J8
Tweed Heads Australia **147** G2
Tweedie Canada **167** I4
Tweedsmuir Provincial Park Canada **166** E4
Tweefontein S. Africa **132** D9
Tweeling S. Africa **133** M4
Twee Rivier Namibia **130** C5
Twee Rivieren Botswana **132** E3
Tweespruit S. Africa **133** L6
Twentynine Palms U.S.A. **183** H7
Twillingate Canada **169** K3
Twin Bridges U.S.A. **182** D3
Twin Buttes Reservoir U.S.A. **179** B6
Twin Falls Canada **169** H2
Twin Falls U.S.A. **180** D4
Twingi Zambia **127** F7
Twin Heads *hill* Australia **150** D4
Twin Mountain U.S.A. **177** N1
Twin Peak U.S.A. **182** D2
Twin Peaks *hill* Australia **151** B7
Twinsburg U.S.A. **176** D4
Twins Creek *watercourse* Australia **146** C2
Twisp U.S.A. **180** B2
Twitchen Reservoir U.S.A. **182** D6
Twitya *r.* Canada **166** D1
Twizel N.Z. **153** E12
Two Butte Creek *r.* U.S.A. **178** B4
Two Harbors U.S.A. **174** B2
Two Hills Canada **167** I4
Two Rivers U.S.A. **172** F6
Tyan' Shan' *mts* China/Kyrg. *see* **Tien Shan**
Tyanshanskaya Oblast' *admin. div.* Kyrg. *see* **Naryn**
Tyao *r.* India/Myanmar **97** G5
Tyatya, Vulkan *vol.* Rus. Fed. **82** G3
Tychy Poland **49** P5
historically known as Tichau
Tyczyn Poland **49** T6
Tydal Norway **44** J3
Tyddewi U.K. *see* **St David's**
Tygart Valley U.S.A. **176** F7
Tygda Rus. Fed. **82** B1
Tygda *r.* Rus. Fed. **82** B1
Tyinkrysset Norway **45** J3
Tykhero Greece **58** H7
also known as Tikherón
Tykocin Poland **49** T2
Tyler U.S.A. **179** D5
Tylertown U.S.A. **175** B6
Tylihul *r.* Ukr. **58** L1
Tyl'skiy Khrebet *mts* Rus. Fed. **82** D1
Tym' *r.* Rus. Fed. **82** F2
Tymonovychi Ukr. **43** N9
Tymovskoye Rus. Fed. **82** F2
Tympaki Greece **59** F13
also known as Timbákion
Tynda Rus. Fed. **81** K1
formerly known as Tyndinskiy
Tyndall U.S.A. **178** C3
Tyndinskiy Rus. Fed. *see* **Tynda**
Tyndrum U.K. **46** H7
Tyne *r.* U.K. **47** J7
Tyngsboro U.S.A. **177** N3
Tyngsjö Sweden **45** K3
Týn nad Vltavou Czech Rep. **49** L6
Tynset Norway **45** J3
Tyr Lebanon *see* **Tyre**
Tyras Ukr. *see* **Bilhorod-Dnistrovs'kyy**
Tyre Lebanon **108** G4
also known as Soûr; also spelt Tyr; historically known as Tyrus
Tyree, Mount Antarctica **222** S1
Tyrifjorden *l.* Norway **45** J3
Tyrma Rus. Fed. **82** D2
Tyrma *r.* Rus. Fed. **82** C2
Tyrnävä Fin. **44** N2
Tyrnavos Greece **59** D9
also spelt Tírnavos
Tyrnyauz Rus. Fed. **107** E2
Tyrone U.S.A. **176** G5
Tyrrell *r.* Australia **147** D3
Tyrrell, Lake *dry lake* Australia **147** D3
Tyrrell Lake Canada **167** J2
Tyrrhenian Sea France/Italy **57** C8
also known as Tirreno, Mare
Tyrus Lebanon *see* **Tyre**
Tysnesøy *i.* Norway **45** I4
Tyson Wash *watercourse* U.S.A. **183** J8
Tysse Norway **45** I3
Tytuvėnai Lith. **42** E6
Tyubelyakh Rus. Fed. **39** O3
Tyub-Karagan, Mys *pt* Kazakh. **102** B3
Tyukalinsk Rus. Fed. **38** H4
Tyulen'i, Ostrova *is* Kazakh. **102** B3
Tyul'gan Rus. Fed. **102** D1
Tyul'kino Rus. Fed. **40** K4
Tyumen' Rus. Fed. **38** G4
also spelt Tjumen'
Tyumen'-Aryk Kazakh. *see* **Tomenaryk**
Tyung *r.* Rus. Fed. **39** M3
Tyup Kyrg. *see* **Tüp**
Tyuratam Kazakh. *see* **Baykonur**
Tyuva-Guba Rus. Fed. **44** P1
Tyuyamuyunskoye Vodokhranilische *resr* Turkm./Uzbek. **103** E4
Tyva, Respublika *aut. rep.* Rus. Fed. **84** C1
formerly known as Tuva or Tuvinskaya A.S.S.R.; historically known as Tannu Tuva
Tywi *r.* U.K. **47** H12
Tzaneen S. Africa **131** F4
Tzucacab Mex. **185** H4

↓ U

Uacauyén Venez. **199** F3
Uaco Congo Angola *see* **Waku-Kungo**
Uainambi Brazil **198** D4
Ualan *atoll* Micronesia *see* **Kosrae**
Uälikhanov Kazakh. *see* **Valikhanovo**
Uamanda Angola **127** D9
Uape Moz. **131** H3
Uara Brazil **199** E5
Uarc, Ras *c.* Morocco *see* **Trois Fourches, Cap des**
Uari Brazil **199** G6
Uarini Brazil **199** E5
Uaroo Australia **150** A4
Uaruma Brazil **198** D4
Uasadi-jidi, Sierra *mts* Venez. **199** E3
Uatatás *r.* Brazil **199** F4
also known as Parima
Uatumã *r.* Brazil **199** G5
Uauá Brazil **202** E4
Uaupés Brazil **199** E5
Uaupés *r.* Brazil **198** E4
Uaxactún Guat. **185** H5
U'ayfirah *well* Saudi Arabia **104** D3
U'aylī, Wādī al *watercourse* Saudi Arabia **109** J7
U'aywij *well* Saudi Arabia **104** D1
U'aywij, Sha'īb al *watercourse* Saudi Arabia **109** P8
U'aywij, Wādī al *watercourse* Saudi Arabia **107** E5
Ub *Srbija* Yugo. **58** B4
Ubá Brazil **203** D7
Uba *r.* Kazakh. **103** J2
Ubagan *r.* Kazakh. **103** F1
also spelt Obaghan
Ubaí Brazil **202** C6
Ubaid *well* Sudan **121** E6
Ubaitaba Brazil **202** E5
'Ubāl Yemen **104** C5
Ubal Karabaur *hills* Uzbek. **102** C4
Ubal Muzbel' *hills* Kazakh. **102** C4
Ubangi *r.* Cent. Afr. Rep./Dem. Rep. Congo **126** C5
also spelt Oubangui
Ubangi-Shari *country* Africa *see* **Central African Republic**
Ubaporanga Brazil **207** K6
Ubate Col. **198** C3
Ubatuba Brazil **207** H10
Ubauro Pak. **101** G4
'Ubaydāt, Sha'īb al *watercourse* Iraq **109** N6
Ubayyid, Wādī al *watercourse* Iraq/Saudi Arabia **107** E4
Ube Japan **91** B8
Úbeda Spain **55** H6
Ubenazomozi Tanz. **129** C6
Uberaba Brazil **206** F6
Uberaba *r.* Brazil **206** E7
Uberlândia Brazil **206** E5
Überlingen Germany **48** G8
Ubin, Pulau *i.* Sing. **76** [inset]
Ubinskoye, Ozero *l.* Rus. Fed. **80** C1
Ubly U.S.A. **173** K7
Ubolratna Reservoir Thai. **78** C4
Ubombo S. Africa **133** Q4
Ubon Ratchathani Thai. **79** D5
Ubori Sudan **126** F3
Ubrique Spain **54** F8
Ubundu Dem. Rep. Congo **126** E5
formerly known as Ponthierville
Ucar Azer. **107** F2
also spelt Udzhary
Ucayali *dept* Peru **200** B2
Ucayali *r.* Peru **198** C6
Ucero *r.* Spain **55** H3
Uch Pak. **101** G4
Uch-Adzhi Turkm. **103** E5
also spelt Üçhajy
Üçhajy Turkm. *see* **Uch-Adzhi**
Üchān Iran **100** B2
Ucharal Kazakh. **103** J3
also spelt Üsharal
Uchinoura Japan **91** B9
Uchiura Japan **90** E6
Uchiura-wan *b.* Japan **90** G3
English form Volcano Bay
Uchiza Peru **200** A2
Uchkuduk Uzbek. **103** E4
also spelt Uchquduq
Uchkyay Uzbek. **103** F5
Uchquduq Uzbek. *see* **Uchkuduk**
Uchsay Uzbek. **102** D4
also spelt Uchsoy
Uchsoy Uzbek. *see* **Uchsay**
Uchte *r.* Germany **48** I3
Uchto *r.* Pak. **101** F5
Uchur *r.* Rus. Fed. **39** N4
Uckermark *reg.* Germany **49** K2
Uckfield U.K. **47** M13
Ucluelet Canada **166** E5
Uda *r.* Rus. Fed. **82** D1
Uda *r.* Rus. Fed. **85** E1
Udachnoye Rus. Fed. **102** A3
Udachnyy Rus. Fed. **39** L3
Udagamandalam India **94** C4
also spelt Udhagamandalam; formerly known as Ootacamund
Udaipur *Rajasthan* India **96** B4
Udaipur *Tripura* India **97** F5
Udaipura India **96** C5
Udayapur Garhi Nepal **97** E4
Udalguri India **97** G4
Udanti *r.* India/Myanmar **95** D1
Uda Walawe Reservoir Sri Lanka **94** D5
Udayagiri India **94** C3
'Udaynān *well* Saudi Arabia **105** E3
Uddeholm Sweden **45** K3
Uddevalla Sweden **45** J4
Uddjaure *l.* Sweden **44** L2
'Udeid, Khōr al *inlet* Qatar **105** E2
Uden Neth. **48** C4
Udgir India **94** C2
Udhagamandalam India *see* **Udagamandalam**
Udhampur Jammu and Kashmir **96** B2
Udimskiy Rus. Fed. **40** H3
Udine Italy **56** F2
Udjuktok Bay Canada **169** I2
Udmalaippettai India *see* **Udumalaippettai**
Udmurtia *aut. rep.* Rus. Fed. *see* **Udmurtskaya Respublika**
Udmurtskaya A.S.S.R. *aut. rep.* Rus. Fed. *see* **Udmurtskaya Respublika**
Udmurtskaya Respublika *aut. rep.* Rus. Fed. **40** J4
English form Udmurtia; formerly known as Udmurtskaya A.S.S.R.
Udokan, Khrebet *mts* Rus. Fed. **81** J1
Udomlya Rus. Fed. **43** Q4
Udon Thani Thai. **78** C4
Udskoye Rus. Fed. **82** D1
Udumalaippettai India **94** C4
also known as Udmalaippettai
Udupi India **94** B3
Udyl', Ozero *l.* Rus. Fed. **82** E1
Udzhary Azer. *see* **Ucar**
Uéa *i.* New Caledonia *see* **Ouvéa**
Uebonti Indon. **75** B3
Uecker *r.* Germany **49** L2
Ueckermünde Germany **49** L2
Ueda Japan **91** F6
Uekuli Indon. **75** B3
Uele *r.* Dem. Rep. Congo **126** D3
Uelen Rus. Fed. **39** T3
Uel'kal' Rus. Fed. **39** S3
Uelzen Germany **48** H3
Ueno Japan **91** E7
Uere *r.* Dem. Rep. Congo **126** E4
Ufa Rus. Fed. **40** J5
Ufa *r.* Rus. Fed. **40** K5
Uffing am Staffelsee Germany **48** I8
Uftyuga *r.* Rus. Fed. **40** H3
Uftyuga *r.* Rus. Fed. **43** U2
Ugab *watercourse* Namibia **130** B4
Ugāle Latvia **42** D4
Ugalla *r.* Tanz. **129** A6
Ugalla River Game Reserve *nature res.* Tanz. **129** A6
▶**Uganda** *country* Africa **128** A4
africa [countries] ▶▶▶ 114–117
Ugar *r.* Bos.-Herz. **56** J4
Ugento Italy **57** K9
Uggdal Norway **45** I3
Ughelli Nigeria **125** G5
Ugie S. Africa **133** M8
Ūgīnak Iran **101** E5
Ugine France **51** M7
Uglegorsk Rus. Fed. **82** F2
Uglekamensk Rus. Fed. **82** D4
formerly known as Severnyy Suchan
Ugleural'skiy Rus. Fed. **40** K4
formerly known as Polovinka
Uglich Rus. Fed. **43** T4
Ugljan *i.* Croatia **56** H4
Uglovka Rus. Fed. **43** O3
Uglovoye *Amurskaya Oblast'* Rus. Fed. **82** C2
Uglovoye *Primorskiy Kray* Rus. Fed. **82** D4
Uglovskoye Rus. Fed. **88** C1
Ugodskiy Zavod Rus. Fed. *see* **Zhukovo**
Ugol'noye Rus. Fed. **39** O3
Ugolnyy Rus. Fed. *see* **Beringovskiy**
Ugol'nyye Kopi Rus. Fed. **39** R3
Ugra Rus. Fed. **43** P7
Ugra *r.* Rus. Fed. **43** R7
Ugŭrchin Bulg. **58** F5
Ugut Rus. Fed. **38** H3
Uher Hudag China **85** F3
Uherské Hradiště Czech Rep. **49** O6
Úhlava *r.* Czech Rep. **49** K6
Uibaí Brazil **202** D4
Uibhist a' Deas *i.* U.K. *see* **South Uist**
Uibhist a' Tuath *i.* U.K. *see* **North Uist**
Uig U.K. **46** F6
Uíge Angola **127** B6
formerly known as Carmona or Vila Marechal Carmona
Uíge *prov.* Angola **127** B6
Ŭijŏngbu S. Korea **83** B5
Ŭiju N. Korea **83** B4
Uil Kazakh. **102** C2
also spelt Oyyl
Uil *r.* Kazakh. **102** C2
Uimaharju Fin. **44** O3
Uinkaret Plateau U.S.A. **183** K5
Uinskoye Rus. Fed. **40** K4
Uinta *r.* U.S.A. **183** O1
Uintah and Ouray Indian Reservation *res.* U.S.A. **183** O1
Uinta Mountains U.S.A. **183** N1
Ŭiryŏng S. Korea **91** A7
Uis Mine Namibia **130** B4
Uitenhage S. Africa **133** J10
Uithuizen Neth. **48** D2
Uitkyk S. Africa **132** C6
Uitsakpan *salt pan* S. Africa **132** E4
Uitspankraal S. Africa **132** D9
Újfehértó Hungary **49** S8
Ujhani India **96** C4
Uji Japan **91** D7
Uji-guntō *is* Japan **91** A9
Ujiyamada Japan *see* **Ise**
Ujjain India **96** B5
Újkígyós Hungary **49** S9
Ujohbilang Indon. **77** F2
Ujście Poland **49** N2
Ujung Kulon National Park Indon. **76** D4
Ujung Pandang Indon. **75** A4
formerly known as Macassar or Makassar
Újvidék *Vojvodina, Srbija* Yugo. *see* **Novi Sad**
Ukal Sagar *l.* India **96** B5
Ukata Nigeria **125** G4
'Ukayrishah *well* Saudi Arabia **104** D2
Ukerewe Island Tanz. **128** B5
Ukhaydir *tourist site* Iraq **107** E4
Ukhdūd *tourist site* Saudi Arabia **104** D4
Ukholovo Rus. Fed. **41** G5
Ukhra *r.* Rus. Fed. **43** U3
Ukhrul India **97** G4
Ukhta Rus. Fed. *see* **Kalevala**
Ukhta Rus. Fed. **40** J3
Ukhta *r.* Rus. Fed. **40** J3
Ukhtoma *r.* Rus. Fed. **43** U3
Ukhvala Belarus **43** K7
Ukiah U.S.A. **182** A2
Ukimbo Tanz. **129** B6
Ukkusissat Greenland **165** N2
Ukmergė Lith. **42** F6

▶**Ukraine** *country* Europe **41** D6
2nd largest country in Europe. Spelt Ukrayina in Ukrainian; formerly known as Ukrainskaya S.S.R.
europe [countries] ▶▶▶ 32–35

Ukrainka Kazakh. **88** C1
Ukrainskaya S.S.R. *country* Europe *see* **Ukraine**
Ukrayina *country* Europe *see* **Ukraine**
Ukrina *r.* Bos.-Herz. **56** J4
Uku Angola **127** B7
formerly known as Vila Nova do Seles
Uku-jima *i.* Japan **91** A8
Ukunna Angola **127** B8
Ukwi Botswana **130** D4
Ul *r.* India **89** B6
Ula Belarus **43** K6
Ula *r.* Belarus **43** K6
Ula Turkey **59** J11
also known as Gökova
Ulaanbaatar Mongolia *see* **Ulan Bator**
Ulaanbaatar *municipality* Mongolia **85** E2
Ulaan-Ereg Mongolia **85** F2
Ulaangom Mongolia **84** B1
Ulaanhudag Mongolia **84** E2
Ulaan Nuur *salt l.* Mongolia **84** D2
Ulaan-Uul *Bayanhongor* Mongolia **84** D2
Ulaan-Uul *Dornogovi* Mongolia **85** F2
Ulan *Nei Mongol* China **85** F4
also known as Otog Qi
Ulan *Qinghai* China **84** C4
also known as Xiligou

▶**Ulan Bator** Mongolia **85** E2
Capital of Mongolia. Also spelt Ulaanbaatar; historically known as Urga.

Ulanbel' Kazakh. **103** G3
Ulan Buh Shamo *des.* China **85** E3
Ulan Erge Rus. Fed. **41** H7
formerly known as Krasnoye
Ulanhad China *see* **Chifeng**
Ulanhot China **85** I2
also known as Horqin Youyi Qianqi
Ulan Hua China **85** F3
also known as Dorbod Qi or Siziwang Qi
Ulan-Khol Rus. Fed. **102** A3
Ulansuhai Nur *l.* China **85** F3
Ulan Tohoi China **84** D3
Ulan-Ude Rus. Fed. **85** E1
Ulan Ul Hu *l.* China **89** E5
Ulapes Arg. **204** D3
Ulaş Turkey **107** D3
Ulaş Turkey **58** I7
Ulastai China **88** D3
Ulaya Tanz. **129** C6
'Ulayyah, Ḥazma' hill Saudi Arabia **109** L9
Ulayyah *reg.* Saudi Arabia **105** D3
Ul'ba Kazakh. **88** C1
also spelt Ülbi
Ul'banskiy Zaliv *b.* Rus. Fed. **82** E1
UL Bend National Wildlife Refuge *nature res.* U.S.A. **180** F3
Ülbi Kazakh. *see* **Ul'ba**
Ulbroka Latvia **42** F5
Ulchin S. Korea **83** C5
Ulcinj *Crna Gora* Yugo. **58** A7
Ulco S. Africa **133** I5
Uldz Mongolia **85** F1
Uldz *r.* Mongolia **85** G1
Uleåborg Fin. *see* **Oulu**
Ulefoss Norway **45** J4
Ulei Vanuatu **145** F3
Ülenurme Estonia **42** H3
Ulety Rus. Fed. **85** G1
Ulfborg Denmark **45** J4
Ulgain Gol *r.* China **85** H2
Ul'gili Kazakh. **103** F1
Ulhasnagar India **94** B2
Uliastai China **85** H2
also known as Dong Ujimqin Qi
Uliastay Mongolia **84** C2
Uliatea *i.* Fr. Polynesia *see* **Raiatea**
Ulie *atoll* Micronesia *see* **Woleai**
Ulindi *r.* Dem. Rep. Congo **126** E5
Ulithi *atoll* Micronesia **73** I4
formerly known as Mackenzie
Ul'kayak *r.* Kazakh. **103** E2
also spelt Ölkeyek
Ul'ken-Karoy, Ozero *salt l.* Kazakh. **103** G1
Ülkenözen *r.* Kazakh./Rus. Fed. *see* **Bol'shoy Uzen'**
Ul'ken Sulutar Kazakh. **103** H4
formerly known as Krasnogorka
Ülken Vladimīrovka Kazakh. *see* **Bol'shaya Vladimirovka**
Ulla *r.* Spain **54** C2
Ulladulla Australia **147** F3
Ullapool U.K. **46** G6
Ullatti Sweden **44** M2
Ullawarra Aboriginal Reserve Australia **150** B4
Ulldecona Spain **55** L4
Ullmer, Mount Antarctica **222** S1
Ulloma Bol. **200** C4
Ullsfjorden *sea chan.* Norway **44** L1
Ullŭng-do *i.* S. Korea **83** C5
Ulm Germany **48** G7
Ul'ma *r.* Rus. Fed. **82** C2
Ulmeni Romania **58** H4
Ulmeni Romania **58** E1
Ulongue Moz. **131** G2
formerly known as Coutinho or Vila Coutinho
Uloowaranie, Lake *salt flat* Australia **148** C5
Ulricehamn Sweden **45** K4
Ulsan S. Korea **83** C6
Ulsberg Norway **44** J3
Ulsta U.K. **46** K3
Ulsteinvik Norway **44** I3
Ulster *reg.* Rep. of Ireland/U.K. **47** E9
Ulster U.S.A. **177** I4
Ultima Australia **147** D3
Ultraoriental, Cordillera *mts* Peru **200** B1
also known as Divisor, Sierra de
Ulu Indon. **75** C2
Ulu Sudan **128** B2
Ulua *r.* Hond. **185** I6
Ulubat Gölü *l.* Turkey **106** B2
Ulubey Turkey **106** B3
Uluborlu Turkey **106** B3
Uluçay *r.* Turkey **107** E3
Uludağ *mt.* Turkey **106** B2
Uludağ Milli Parkı *nat. park* Turkey **59** K8
Ulugqat China *see* **Wuqia**
Ulu Kali, Gunung *mt.* Malaysia **76** C2
Ulukışla Turkey **106** C3
Ulundi S. Africa **133** P5
Ulungur He *r.* China **84** A2
Ulungur Hu *l.* China **88** D2
Ulupalakua U.S.A. **181** [inset] Z1
Ulu Pandan Sing. **76** [inset]
Uluqsaqtuuq Canada *see* **Holman**
▶**Uluru** *hill* Australia **148** A5
also known as Ayers Rock
world [land cover] ▶▶▶ 18–19
oceania [features] ▶▶▶ 142–143
Uluru National Park Australia **148** A5
Ulus Dağı *mt.* Turkey **59** J9
Ulutau Kazakh. *see* **Ulytau**
Ulutau, Gory *mts* Kazakh. **103** F3
Ulverston U.K. **47** I9
Ulverstone Australia **147** E5
Ulvsjön Sweden **45** L3
Ul'yanikha Rus. Fed. **43** S3
Ul'yanino Rus. Fed. **43** T6
Ül'yanov Kazakh. *see* **Ul'yanovskiy**
Ul'yanovka Rus. Fed. **43** L2
Ul'yanovo *Kaliningradskaya Oblast'* Rus. Fed. **42** D7
Ul'yanovo *Kaluzhskaya Oblast'* Rus. Fed. **43** Q8
Ul'yanovo Uzbek. **103** G4
Ul'yanovsk Rus. Fed. **41** I5
also known as Simbirsk; also spelt Uljanovsk
Ul'yanovskaya Oblast' *admin. div.* Rus. Fed. **41** H5
English form Ulyanovsk Oblast
Ul'yanovskiy Kazakh. **103** H2
also known as Ül'yanov; formerly known as Ul'yanovskoye
Ulyanovsk Oblast *admin. div.* Rus. Fed. *see* **Ul'yanovskaya Oblast'**
Ul'yanovskoye Kazakh. *see* **Ul'yanovskiy**
Ul'yatuy Rus. Fed. **85** H1
Ulysses *KS* U.S.A. **178** B4
Ulysses *KY* U.S.A. **176** C8
Ulytau Kazakh. **103** F2
formerly spelt Ulutau
Uly-Zhylanshyk *r.* Kazakh. **103** E2
Umag Croatia **56** F3
Umala Bol. **200** D4
'Umān *country* Asia *see* **Oman**
Umán Mex. **185** H4
Uman' Ukr. **41** D6
Umango, Cerro *mt.* Arg. **204** C3
'Umarī, Qā' al *salt pan* Jordan **109** H6
Umaria India **96** D5
Umarkhed India **94** C2
Umarkot India **95** D2
Umarkot Pak. **101** G5
Umaroona, Lake *salt flat* Australia **146** C1
Umarpada India **96** B5
Umatilla U.S.A. **180** C3
Umayan *r.* Phil. **74** C4
'Umayrī, Wādī *watercourse* Oman **105** G3
Umba Rus. Fed. **40** E2
formerly known as Lesnoy
Umba *r.* Rus. Fed. **44** P2
Umbagog Lake U.S.A. **177** N1
Umbakumba Australia **148** C2
Umbeara Australia **148** B5
Umbelasha *watercourse* Sudan **126** E2
Umbertide Italy **56** E5
Umboi *i.* P.N.G. **73** K8
formerly known as Rooke Island
Umbozero Rus. Fed. **44** P2
Umbrella Mountains N.Z. **153** D13
Umbria *admin. reg.* Italy **56** E6
Umeå Sweden **44** M3
Umeälven *r.* Sweden **44** M3
Umet Rus. Fed. **41** G5
Umfolozi *r.* S. Africa **133** Q5
Umfolozi Game Reserve *nature res.* S. Africa **133** P5
Umfreville Lake Canada **167** M5
Umfuli *r.* Zimbabwe *see* **Mupfure**
Umgeni *r.* S. Africa **133** P6
Umhlanga S. Africa **133** P6
Umhlatuzi Lagoon S. Africa **133** Q5
Umiiviip Kangertiva *inlet* Greenland **165** O3
also known as Gyldenløve Fjord
Umingmaktok Canada **165** I3
Umirzak Kazakh. **102** B4
Umiujaq Canada **168** E1
Umkomaas S. Africa **133** O7
Umkomaas *r.* S. Africa **133** O7
Umlazi S. Africa **133** O6
Umma *tourist site* Iraq **107** F5
Umm ad Daraj, Jabal *mt.* Jordan **108** G5
Umm al Birak Saudi Arabia **104** B3
Umm al Ghār, Khabrat *waterhole* Iraq **109** N5
Umm al Hashīm, Jabal *mt.* Jordan **108** G8
Umm al Jamājim *well* Saudi Arabia **105** D2
Umm al Qaiwain U.A.E. *see* **Umm al Qaywayn**
Umm al Qaywayn U.A.E. **105** F2
English form Umm al Qaiwain
Umm ar Raghībah *waterhole* Iraq **109** N3
Umm ar Raqabah, Khabrat *imp. l.* Saudi Arabia **109** I8
Umm as Samīm *salt flat* Oman **105** F3
Umm at Qalbān Saudi Arabia **104** C2
Umm az Zumūl *well* Oman **105** F3
Umm Bāb Qatar **105** E2
Umm Badr Sudan **121** E6
Umm Dam Sudan **121** F6
Umm Ḥarb Saudi Arabia **104** B2
Umm Jumayyih *waterhole* Saudi Arabia **109** N9
Umm Keddada Sudan **121** E6
Umm Lajj Saudi Arabia **104** B2
Umm Mafrūd, Gebel *mt.* Egypt **108** F8
Umm Mukhbār, Jabal *hill* Saudi Arabia **104** B3
Umm Nukhaylah *hill* Saudi Arabia **109** J8
Umm Nukhaylah *well* Saudi Arabia **108** G9
Umm Qaṣr Iraq **107** F5
Umm Qurein *well* Sudan **121** F5
Umm Quṣur *i.* Saudi Arabia **104** A2
Umm Raqm, Gebel *hill* Egypt **108** C7
Umm Rumeila *well* Sudan **121** G5
Umm Ruwaba Sudan **121** F6
Umm Sa'ad Libya **120** E2
Umm Sa'id Qatar **105** E2
also known as Musay'īd
Umm Saiyala Sudan **121** F6
Umm Ṣalāl 'Alī Qatar **105** E2
Umm Samā Saudi Arabia **104** B3
Umm Saysabān, Jabal *mt.* Jordan **108** G8
Umm Shaitiya *well* Jordan **108** H8
Umm Shomar, Gebel *mt.* Egypt **108** E9
Umm Shugeira Sudan **121** F6
Umm Silsh, Sha'īb *watercourse* Iraq **109** O5
Umm Tināṣṣib, Gebel *mt.* Egypt **108** D9
Umm Urūmah *i.* Saudi Arabia **104** B2
Umm Wa'āl *hill* Saudi Arabia **109** J6
Umm Wazir *well* Saudi Arabia **105** D3
Umm Zanatir *mt.* Egypt **108** D9
Umnak Island U.S.A. **164** C4
Umphang Wildlife Reserve *nature res.* Thai. **78** B5
Umpilua Moz. **131** H2
Umpqua *r.* U.S.A. **180** A4
Umred India **94** C1
Umreth India **94** B1
Umtali Zimbabwe *see* **Mutare**
Umtamvuna *r.* S. Africa **133** O8
Umtata S. Africa **133** M8
Umtata *r.* S. Africa **133** N8
Umtata Dam *resr* S. Africa **133** M8
Umtentweni S. Africa **133** O7
Umuahia Nigeria **125** G5
Umuarama Brazil **203** A7
Umurbey Turkey **59** H8
Umurlar Turkey **59** J9
Umutoi N.Z. **152** J8
Umvoti *r.* S. Africa **133** P6
Umvuma Zimbabwe *see* **Mvuma**
Umzimkhlava *r.* S. Africa **133** N8
Umzimkulu S. Africa **133** N7
Umzimkulu *r.* S. Africa **133** O7
Umzimvubu *r.* S. Africa **133** N8
Umzingwani *r.* Zimbabwe *see* **Mzingwani**
Umzinto S. Africa **133** O7
Una Belarus **43** L6
Una *r.* Bos.-Herz./Croatia **56** I3
Una Brazil **202** E5
Una *r.* Brazil **202** F4
Una India **96** C3
Una, Mount N.Z. **153** G10
'Unāb, Jabal al *hill* Jordan **109** H8
English form Black Rock
'Unāb, Wādī al *watercourse* Jordan **109** H7
Unac *r.* Bos.-Herz. **56** I4
Unadilla U.S.A. **177** J3
Unadilla *r.* U.S.A. **177** J3
Unaí Brazil **206** G3
Unai Pass Afgh. **101** G3
Unalaska U.S.A. **164** C4
Unalaska Island U.S.A. **164** C4
Unango Moz. **129** B8
Unari Fin. **44** N2
Unauna *i.* Indon. **75** B3
'Unayzah Saudi Arabia **104** C2
'Unayzah, Jabal *hill* Iraq **107** D4
also spelt 'Aneiza, Jabal
Unchahra India **96** D4
Uncompahgre Plateau U.S.A. **183** P3
Unda *r.* Rus. Fed. **85** H1
Undara National Park Australia **149** E3
Unden *l.* Sweden **45** K4
Underberg S. Africa **133** N6
Underbool Australia **146** D3
Undersåker Sweden **44** K3
Undva Estonia **42** C3
Unecha Rus. Fed. **43** N9
Unecha *r.* Rus. Fed. **43** M9
Uneiuxi *r.* Brazil **199** E5
Unga Island U.S.A. **164** C4
Ungarie Australia **147** E3
Ungava, Baie d' *b.* Canada *see* **Ungava Bay**
Ungava, Péninsule d' *pen.* Canada **165** L3
also known as Ungava Peninsula
Ungava Bay Canada **169** H1
also known as Ungava, Baie d'
Ungava Peninsula Canada *see* **Ungava, Péninsule d'**
Ungeny Moldova *see* **Ungheni**
Unggi N. Korea **82** C4
Ungheni Moldova **58** I1
formerly spelt Ungeny
Ungheni Romania **58** F2
Unguana Moz. **131** G4
Unguja North *admin. reg.* Tanz. *see* **Zanzibar North**
Unguja South *admin. reg.* Tanz. *see* **Zanzibar South**
Unguja West *admin. reg.* Tanz. *see* **Zanzibar West**
Ungurași Romania **58** F1
Unguz, Solonchakovyye Vpadiny *salt flat* Turkm. **102** D5
Üngüz Angyrsyndaky Garagum *des.* Turkm. *see* **Zaunguzskiye Karakumy**
Ungvár Ukr. *see* **Uzhhorod**
Ungwana Bay Kenya **128** D5
Uni Rus. Fed. **40** I4
União *Acre* Brazil **200** C2
União *Minas Gerais* Brazil **206** C6
União da Vitória Brazil **203** B8
União do Marará Brazil **199** F5
União dos Palmares Brazil **202** F4
Uniara India **96** C4
Unicoi U.S.A. **176** C9
Uniejów Poland **49** P4
Unije *i.* Croatia **56** G4
Unimak Island U.S.A. **164** C4
Unini *r.* Brazil **199** F5
Unini Peru **200** B2
Unión Arg. **204** D4
Unión Para. **201** F6
Union *ME* U.S.A. **177** P1
Union *MO* U.S.A. **174** B4
Union *OR* U.S.A. **180** C3
Union *WV* U.S.A. **176** E8
Unión, Bahía *b.* Arg. **204** E5
Union, Mount U.S.A. **183** L7
Union City *OH* U.S.A. **176** A5
Union City *PA* U.S.A. **176** F4
Union City *TN* U.S.A. **174** B4
Uniondale S. Africa **132** H10
Unión de Reyes Cuba **186** C2

▶**Union of Soviet Socialist Republics**
Divided in 1991 into 15 independent nations: Armenia, Azerbaijan, Belarus, Estonia, Georgia, Kazakhstan, Kyrgyzstan, Latvia, Lithuania, Moldova, the Russian Federation, Tajikistan, Turkmenistan, Ukraine and Uzbekistan.

Union Springs *AL* U.S.A. **175** C5
Union Springs *NY* U.S.A. **177** I3
Uniontown U.S.A. **176** F6
Union Valley Reservoir U.S.A. **182** D3
Unionville *MI* U.S.A. **173** J7
Unionville *MO* U.S.A. **174** A3
Unionville *NV* U.S.A. **182** F1
Unionville *VA* U.S.A. **176** H7
▶**United Arab Emirates** *country* Asia **105** F3
known as Al Imārāt al 'Arabīyah al Muttaḥidah, in Arabic; formerly known as Trucial Coast or Trucial States
asia [countries] ▶▶▶ 64–67
United Arab Republic *country* Africa *see* **Egypt**

▶**United Kingdom** *country* Europe **47** L8
3rd most populous country in Europe.
europe [countries] ▶▶▶ 32–35

United Provinces *state* India *see* **Uttar Pradesh**

▶**United States of America** *country* N. America **170** E3
Most populous country in North America and 3rd in the world. 2nd largest country in North America and 3rd in the world.
world [countries] ▶▶▶ 10–11
world [changes] ▶▶▶ 20–21
world [population] ▶▶▶ 22–23
northamerica [countries] ▶▶▶ 158–159

United States Range *mts* Canada **165** M1
Unity Canada **167** I4
Unjab *watercourse* Namibia **130** B4
Unjha India **96** B5
Unnao India **96** D4
Ŭnp'a N. Korea **83** B5
Unsan N. Korea **83** B4
Ŭnsan N. Korea **83** B5
Unst *i.* U.K. **46** L3
Unstrut *r.* Germany **48** I4
Unstrut-Trias-Land *park* Germany **48** I4
Untari India **97** D4
Untere Havel *park* Germany **48** J3
Unteres Odertal *nat. park* Germany **49** L3
Unterschleißheim Germany **48** I7
Uniturán, Sierra de *mts* Venez. **199** E4
Unuk *r.* Canada/U.S.A. **166** D3
Unuli Horog China **97** F2

Un'ya r. Rus. Fed. 40 K3
Unzen-Amakusa National Park Japan 91 B8
Unzen-dake vol. Japan 91 B8
Unzha Rus. Fed. 40 H4
Uozu Japan 91 E6
Úpa r. Czech Rep. 49 M5
Upa r. Rus. Fed. 43 R7
Upalco U.S.A. 183 N1
Upar Ghat reg. India 97 E5
Upata Venez. 199 F2
Upemba, Lac l. Dem. Rep. Congo 127 E7
Upernavik Greenland 165 N2
Upernavik Kujalleq Greenland 165 N2
also known as Søndre Upernavik
Upi Phil. 74 C5
Upía r. Col. 198 C3
Upington S. Africa 132 F5
Upinniemi Fin. 45 N3
Upland U.S.A. 182 G7
Upleta India 96 A5
Upokongaro N.Z. 152 J7
Upoloksha Rus. Fed. 44 O2
Upolu i. Samoa 145 H3
formerly known as Ojalava
Upolu Point U.S.A. 181 [inset] Z1
Upper Alkali Lake U.S.A. 180 B4
Upper Arlington U.S.A. 176 B5
Upper Arrow Lake Canada 166 G5
Upper Chindwin Myanmar see Mawlaik
Upper East admin. reg. Ghana 125 E4
Upper Fraser Canada 166 F4
Upper Garry Lake Canada 167 K1
Upper Hutt N.Z. 152 J9
Upper Iowa r. U.S.A. 174 B3
Upper Klamath Lake U.S.A. 180 B4
Upper Liard Canada 166 D2
Upper Lough Erne l. U.K. 47 E9
Upper Marlboro U.S.A. 177 I7
Upper Mazinaw Lake Canada 173 P6
Upper Nile state Sudan 128 B2
Upper Peirce Reservoir Sing. 76 [inset]
Upper Preoria Lake U.S.A. 172 D10
Upper Red Lake U.S.A. 178 D1
Upper Sandusky U.S.A. 176 B5
Upper Saranac Lake U.S.A. 177 K1
Upper Seal Lake Canada see Iberville, Lac d'
Upper Takaka N.Z. 152 G9
Upper Tunguska r. Rus. Fed. see Angara
Upper Volta country Africa see Burkina
Upper West admin. reg. Ghana 125 E4
Uppinangadi India 94 B3
Upplands-Väsby Sweden 45 L4
Uppsala Sweden 45 L4
Uppsala county Sweden 45 L3
Upsala Canada 168 B3
Upshi Jammu and Kashmir 96 C2
Upson U.S.A. 172 C4
Upstart, Cape Australia 149 E3
Upstart Bay Australia 149 E3
Upton U.S.A. 177 N3
'Uqayqah, Wādī watercourse Jordan 108 G7
'Uqayribāt Syria 109 I2
Uqlat al 'Udhaybah well Iraq 107 F5
'Uqlat aş Şuqūr Saudi Arabia 104 C2
Uqturpan China see Wushi
Urabá, Golfo de b. Col. 198 B2
Urad Qianqi China see Xishanzui
Urad Zhongqi China 85 F3
also known as Haliut
Ūrāf Iran 100 D4
Uraga-suidō sea chan. Japan 91 F7
Uragawara Japan 90 F6
Ura-Guba Rus. Fed. 44 P1
Urahoro Japan 90 H3
Urakam India 94 C4
Urakawa Japan 90 H3
Ural hill Australia 147 E3
Ural r. Kazakh./Rus. Fed. 102 B3
also known as Zhayyq
Uralla Australia 147 F2
Ural Mountains Rus. Fed. 40 K2
also known as Ural'skiye Gory or Ural'skiy Khrebet
Uralovka Rus. Fed. 82 C1
Ural'sk Kazakh. 102 B2
also known as Oral
Ural'skaya Oblast' admin. div. Kazakh. see Zapadnyy Kazakhstan
Ural'skiye Gory mts Rus. Fed. see Ural Mountains
Ural'skiy Khrebet mts Rus. Fed. see Ural Mountains
Urambo Tanz. 129 B6
Uran India 94 B2
Urana Australia 147 E3
Urana, Lake Australia 147 E3
Urandangi Australia 148 C4
Urandi Brazil 202 D5
Uranium City Canada 167 I3
Urapunga Australia 148 B2
Urapuntja Australia 148 B4
Uraricoera Brazil 199 F4
Uraricoera r. Brazil 199 F4
Urartu country Asia see Armenia
Uras Sardegna Italy 57 A9
Ura-Tyube Tajik. see Ŭroteppa
Uravakonda India 94 C3
Uravan U.S.A. 183 P3
Urawa Japan 91 F7
Uray Rus. Fed. 38 G3
Uray'irah Saudi Arabia 105 E2
'Urayq ad Duḩūl des. Saudi Arabia 105 D2
'Urayq Sāqān des. Saudi Arabia 105 D2
Urazovka Rus. Fed. 40 H5
Urazovo Rus. Fed. 41 F6
Urbana IA U.S.A. 172 B8
Urbana IL U.S.A. 174 B3
Urbana IN U.S.A. 172 H10
Urbana OH U.S.A. 176 B5
Urbania Italy 56 E5
Urbano Santos Brazil 202 D2
Urbel r. Spain 54 H2
Urbino Italy 56 E5
historically known as Urbinum
Urbinum Italy see Urbino
Urbión mt. Spain 55 I2
Urbs Vetus Italy see Orvieto
Urcos Peru 200 C3
Urda Spain 54 H5
Ur'devarri hill Fin./Norway see Urtivaara
Urdoma Rus. Fed. 40 I3
Urd Tamir Gol r. Mongolia 84 D2
Urdyuzhskoye, Ozero l. Rus. Fed. 40 I2
Urdzhar Kazakh. 88 C2
also spelt Ürzhar
Ure r. U.K. 47 K9
Urechcha Belarus 42 I9
Urecheşti Romania 58 I2
Urein Egypt 108 B7
Uren' Rus. Fed. 40 H4
Urengoy Rus. Fed. 39 H3
Urenosi mt. Norway 45 I4
Urenui N.Z. 152 I6
Uréparapara i. Vanuatu 145 F3
Urewera National Park N.Z. 152 L6
Urfa Turkey see Şanlıurfa
Urga Mongolia see Ulan Bator
Urgal r. Rus. Fed. 82 D2
Urganch Uzbek. see Urgench
Urganlı Turkey 59 I10
Urgench Uzbek. 102 E4
also spelt Urganch
Ürgüp Turkey 106 C3
Urgut Uzbek. 103 F5
Urho China 88 D2
Urho Kekkosen kansallispuisto nat. park Fin. 44 N1
Uri Jammu and Kashmir 96 B2
Uribia Col. 198 C2
Uripitijuata, Cerro mt. Mex. 185 E5
Urique r. Mex. 181 F8
Urisino Australia 147 D2
Uritskiy Kazakh. 103 F1
Uritskoye Rus. Fed. 43 T9
Urī Wenz r. Eth. 104 B5
Urjala Fin. 45 M3
Urk Neth. 48 C3
Urkan Rus. Fed. 82 B1
Urkan r. Rus. Fed. 82 B1
Urkut Somalia 128 D4
Urla Turkey 106 A3
Urlaţi Romania 58 H4
Urlui r. Romania 58 G5
Urluk Rus. Fed. 85 E1
Urmai China 89 D6
Urmary Rus. Fed. 40 H5
Urmetan Tajik. 101 G2
Urmi r. Rus. Fed. 82 D2
Urmia Iran 100 A2
also spelt Orūmīyeh; formerly known as Reẕā'īyeh
Urmia, Lake salt l. Iran 100 A2
also known as Orūmīyeh, Daryācheh-ye; formerly known as Reẕā'īyeh, Daryācheh-ye
Urmston Road sea chan. Hong Kong China 87 [inset]
Uromi Nigeria 125 G5
Uroševac Kosovo, Srbija Yugo. 58 C6
Urosozero Rus. Fed. 40 E3
Ŭroteppa Tajik. 101 G2
also spelt Ura-Tyube
Urru Co salt l. China 89 D6
also known as Jagok Tso
Ursat'yevskaya Uzbek. see Khavast
Urshel'skiy Rus. Fed. 43 V6
Urt Mongolia 84 D3
Urtivaara hill Fin./Norway 44 M1
also spelt Ur'devarri
Urt Moron China 84 B4
Uru r. Brazil 206 D2
Uruáchic Mex. 184 C3
Uruaçu Brazil 202 B5
Uruana Brazil 206 D2
Uruapan Baja California Norte Mex. 184 A2
Uruapan Michoacán Mex. 185 E5
Urubamba Peru 200 B3
Urubaxi r. Brazil 199 E5
Urubu r. Brazil 199 G5
Urubupungá, Salto do waterfall Brazil 206 B7
Urucara Brazil 199 G5
Uruch'ye Rus. Fed. 43 O9
Urucu r. Brazil 199 F6
Uruçuí Brazil 202 C3
Uruçuí, Serra do hills Brazil 202 C4
Urucuia Brazil 202 C6
Urucuia r. Brazil 202 C6
Uruçui Preto r. Brazil 202 C3
Urucum Brazil 201 F4
Urucurituba Brazil 199 G5
Uruguai r. Brazil 203 A8
also spelt Uruguay
Uruguaiana Brazil 204 F3
Uruguay r. Arg./Uruguay 204 F4
also spelt Uruguai
▶Uruguay country S. America 204 F4
southamerica [countries] ▶ 192–193
Uruk tourist site Iraq see Erech
Urukthapel i. Palau 73 H5
Urumchi China see Ürümqi
Ürümqi China 88 D3
English form Urumchi
Urundi country Africa see Burundi
Urunga Australia 147 G2
Urup r. Rus. Fed. 41 G7
Urup, Ostrov i. Rus. Fed. 81 Q3
Urup, Proliv strait Rus. Fed. 81 Q3
Urupá r. Brazil 201 E2
Uru Pass China/Kyrg. 88 B3
'Urūq al Awārik des. Saudi Arabia 105 D4
'Urūq ash Shaybah des. Saudi Arabia 105 F3
Urusha Rus. Fed. 82 A1
Urusha r. Rus. Fed. 82 A1
Urussu Rus. Fed. 40 J5
Uruti N.Z. 152 I6
Uruwira Tanz. 129 A6
Uryl' Kazakh. 88 D1
Uryū Japan 90 G3
Uryupinsk Rus. Fed. 41 G6
Ürzhar Kazakh. see Urdzhar
Urzhum Rus. Fed. 40 I4
Urziceni Romania 58 H4
Usa r. Belarus 43 J8
Usa Japan 91 B8
Usa r. Rus. Fed. 40 K2
Usada i. Phil. 74 B5
Uşak Turkey 106 B3
Uşak prov. Turkey 59 K10
Usakos Namibia 130 B4
Usambara Mountains Tanz. 129 C6
Usangu Flats plain Tanz. 129 B7
Usarp Mountains Antarctica 223 K2
'Usaylān Yemen 105 D5
Usborne, Mount hill Falkland Is 205 F8
Usedom Germany 49 K2
Usedom i. Germany 49 L2
Useless Loop Australia 151 A5
Usengi Kenya 128 B5
Usfān Saudi Arabia 104 B3
Usha r. Belarus 42 G8
Usha r. Belarus 43 J8
Ushachi Belarus see Ushachy
Ushachy Belarus 43 J6
also spelt Ushachi
Ushakova, Ostrov i. Rus. Fed. 39 H1
Ushanovo Kazakh. 88 C1
Ushant i. France see Ouessant, Île d'
Üsharal Kazakh. see Ucharal
Usharal Kazakh. 103 G4
Ushayqir Saudi Arabia 105 D2
'Ushayrah Saudi Arabia 104 C3
Ushcha r. Rus. Fed. 43 K6
Ushcherp'ye Rus. Fed. 43 M9
Ushibuka Japan 91 B8
Ushirombo Tanz. 128 A5
Ushtobe Kazakh. 103 I3
formerly spelt Ush-Tyube
Ush-Tyube Kazakh. see Ushtobe
Ushuaia Arg. 205 C9
Uši Latvia 42 D4
Usina Brazil 202 A3
Usinsk Rus. Fed. 40 K2
Usk r. U.K. 47 J12
Uska India 97 D4
Uskhodni Belarus 42 I8
Uskoplje Bos.-Herz. see Gornji Vakuf
Üsküdar Turkey 106 B2
Üsküp Turkey 58 I7
Usma Latvia 42 D4
Usman' Rus. Fed. 41 F5
Usmas ezers l. Latvia 42 D4
Usmat Uzbek. 103 F5
formerly spelt Usmet
Usmet Uzbek. see Usmat
Usmyn' Rus. Fed. 43 M6
Uso r. Spain 54 F5
Usogorsk Rus. Fed. 40 I3
Usoke Tanz. 129 B6
Usol'ye Rus. Fed. 40 K4
Usol'ye-Sibirskoye Rus. Fed. 80 G2
Usora r. Bos.-Herz. 56 K4
Usozha r. Rus. Fed. 43 P9
Usozha r. Rus. Fed. 43 Q9
Uspallata Arg. 204 C4
Uspenka Kazakh. 103 I1
Uspenskiy Kazakh. 103 H2
Uspenskoye Rus. Fed. 43 L5
Uspen'ye Rus. Fed. 40 G4
Ussel France 51 I7
Ussuri r. Rus. Fed. 82 D2
also known as Wusuli Jiang
Ussuriysk Rus. Fed. 82 C4
formerly known as Voroshilov
Ust'-Abakanskoye Rus. Fed. see Abakan
Ust'-Alekseyevo Rus. Fed. 40 H3
Usta Muhammad Pak. 101 G4
Ust'-Balyk Rus. Fed. see Nefteyugansk
Ust'-Barguzin Rus. Fed. 81 H2
Ust'-Dolyssy Rus. Fed. 43 K5
Ust'-Donetskiy Rus. Fed. 41 G7
Ust'-Dzheguta Rus. Fed. 41 G7
formerly known as Ust'-Dzhegutinskaya
Ust'-Dzhegutinskaya Rus. Fed. see Ust'-Dzheguta
Uster Switz. 51 O5
Ustica, Isola di i. Sicilia Italy 57 F10
Ust'-Ilimsk Rus. Fed. 39 K4
Ust'-Ilimskiy Vodokhrinilishche resr Rus. Fed. 80 G1
Ust'-Ilya Rus. Fed. 85 G1
Ust'-Ilych Rus. Fed. 40 K3
Ústí nad Labem Czech Rep. 49 L5
Ústí nad Orlicí Czech Rep. 49 N6
Ustinov Rus. Fed. see Izhevsk
Ustirt plat. Kazakh./Uzbek. see Ustyurt Plateau
Ustka Poland 49 N1
Ust'-Kamchatsk Rus. Fed. 39 Q4
Ust'-Kamenogorsk Kazakh. 88 C1
also known as Öskemen
Ust'-Kan Rus. Fed. 88 D1
Ust'-Kara Rus. Fed. 40 M1
Ust'-Koksa Rus. Fed. 88 D1
Ust'-Kulom Rus. Fed. 40 J3
Ust'-Kut Rus. Fed. 80 H1
Ust'-Kuyga Rus. Fed. 39 N2
Ust'-Labinsk Rus. Fed. 41 F7
formerly known as Ust'-Labinskaya
Ust'-Labinskaya Rus. Fed. see Ust'-Labinsk
Ust'-Luga Rus. Fed. 43 J2
Ust'-Lyzha Rus. Fed. 40 K2
Ust'-Maya Rus. Fed. 39 N3
Ust'-Mongunay Rus. Fed. see Primorskiy
Ust'-Munduyka Rus. Fed. 39 I3
Ust'-Nem Rus. Fed. 40 J3
Ust'-Nera Rus. Fed. 39 O3
Ust'-Olenek Rus. Fed. 39 L2
Ust'-Omchug Rus. Fed. 39 O3
Ust-Orda Buryat Autonomous Okrug admin. div. Rus. Fed. see Ust'-Ordynskiy Buryatskiy Avtonomnyy Okrug
Ust'-Ordynskiy Rus. Fed. 80 G2
Ust'-Ordynskiy Buryatskiy Avtonomnyy Okrug admin. div. Rus. Fed. 80 G2
English form Ust-Orda Buryat Autonomous Okrug
Ust'-Port Rus. Fed. 39 I3
Ustrem Bulg. 58 H6
Ustrzyki Dolne Poland 49 T6
formerly known as Nizhniye Ustriki
Ust'-Sara Rus. Fed. 43 O1
Ust'-Shonosha Rus. Fed. 40 G3
Ust'-Tsil'ma Rus. Fed. 40 J2
Ust'-Ulagan Rus. Fed. 88 D1
Ust'-Umalta Rus. Fed. 82 D2
Ust'-Ura Rus. Fed. 40 H3
Ust'-Usa Rus. Fed. 40 K2
Ust'-Vayen'ga Rus. Fed. 40 G3
Ust'-Voya Rus. Fed. 40 K2
Ust'ya r. Rus. Fed. 40 G3
Ust'-Yansk Rus. Fed. 39 N2
Ust'ye Tverskaya Oblast' Rus. Fed. 43 M5
Ust'ye Vologod. Obl. Rus. Fed. 40 G4
Ust'ye Vologod. Obl. Rus. Fed. 43 U2
Ust'ye Yaroslavskaya Oblast Rus. Fed. 43 U4
Ust'ye r. Rus. Fed. 43 U4
Ust'ye-Kirovskoye Rus. Fed. 43 Q3
Ustyurt, Plato plat. Kazakh./Uzbek. see Ustyurt Plateau
Ustyurt Plateau Kazakh./Uzbek. 102 D4
also known as Ustirt or Ustyurt, Plato or Ustyurt Platosi
Ustyurt Platosi plat. Kazakh./Uzbek. see Ustyurt Plateau
Ustyutskoye Rus. Fed. 43 Q3
Ustyuzhna Rus. Fed. 43 R3
Usu China 88 D2
Usuki Japan 91 B8
Usulután El Salvador 185 H6
Usumacinta r. Guat./Mex. 185 G5
Usumbura Burundi see Bujumbura
Usun Apau, Dataran Tinggi plat. Sarawak Malaysia 77 F2
Usutu r. Africa 133 Q3
also known as Great Usutu or Lusutufu
Usvyaty Rus. Fed. 43 L6
Usvyeyka r. Belarus 43 K7
Uta Indon. 73 I7
Utah state U.S.A. 183 M2
Utah Lake U.S.A. 183 M1
Utajärvi Fin. 44 N2
Utan Indon. 77 G5
Utashinai Rus. Fed. see Yuzhno-Kuril'sk
'Utaybah reg. Saudi Arabia 104 C3
'Utaybah, Buḩayrat al imp. l. Syria 109 H4
Utayyiq Saudi Arabia 105 E2
Utbjoa Norway 45 I4
Utebo Spain 55 K3
Ute Creek r. U.S.A. 179 B5
Utembo r. Angola 127 D9
Ute Mountain Indian Reservation res. U.S.A. 183 P4
Utena Lith. 42 G6
Utete Tanz. 129 C7
Uthai Thani Thai. 79 C5
Uthal Pak. 101 F5
Utiariti Brazil 201 F3
Utica NY U.S.A. 177 J2
Utica OH U.S.A. 176 C5
Utiel Spain 55 J5
Utikuma Lake Canada 167 H4
Utila Hond. 186 B3
Utinga r. Brazil 202 D5
Utladalen park Norway 45 I3
Utlwanang S. Africa 133 J4
Uto Japan 91 B8
Utrata r. Poland 49 R3
Utraula India 97 D4
Utrecht Neth. 48 C3
historically known as Trajectum
Utrecht S. Africa 133 O4
Utrera Spain 54 F7
Utroya r. Rus. Fed. 42 J4
Utsira Norway 46 Q4
Utsjoki Fin. 44 N1
also spelt Ohcejohka
Utsunomiya Japan 91 F6
Utta Rus. Fed. 102 A3
Uttaradit Thai. 78 C4
Uttaranchal state India 96 C3
Uttarkashi India 96 C3
Uttar Pradesh state India 96 C4
formerly known as United Provinces
Utu China see Miao'ergou
Utubulak China 88 D2
Utupua i. Solomon Is 145 F3
formerly known as Edgecumbe Island
Utva r. Kazakh. 102 C2
Uulu Estonia 42 F3
Uummannaq Greenland see Dundas
Uummannaq Greenland 165 N2
Uummannaq Fjord inlet Greenland 165 N2
Uummannarsuaq c. Greenland see Farewell, Cape
Uurainen Fin. 44 N3
Üüreg Nuur salt l. Mongolia 84 A1
Üür Gol r. Mongolia 84 D1
Uusikaarlepyy Fin. see Nykarleby
Uusikaupunki Fin. 45 M3
also known as Nystad
Uutapi Namibia 130 B3
also known as Ombalantu
Uva r. Col. 198 D4
Uva Rus. Fed. 40 J4
Uvac r. Bos.-Herz./Yugo. 58 A5
Uvalde U.S.A. 179 C6
Uvaravichy Belarus 43 L9
Uvarovka Rus. Fed. 43 Q6
Uvarovo Rus. Fed. 41 G6
Uvéa i. New Caledonia see Ouvéa
Uver' r. Rus. Fed. 43 P3
Uvinza Tanz. 129 A6
Uvira Dem. Rep. Congo 126 F5
Uvod' r. Rus. Fed. 43 V4
Uvongo S. Africa 133 O7
Uvs prov. Mongolia 84 B1
Uvs Nuur salt l. Mongolia 84 B1
Uwa Japan 91 C8
Uwainid, Wādī al watercourse Saudi Arabia 109 H9
Uwajima Japan 91 C8
Uwa-kai b. Japan 91 C8
'Uwayfī Oman 105 G3
'Uwayja well Saudi Arabia 104 C2
'Uwaynāt Wannīn Libya 120 B2
'Uwayriḑ, Ḩarrat al lava field Saudi Arabia 104 B2
Uwaysiţ well Saudi Arabia 109 J7
Uweinat, Jebel mt. Sudan 120 E4
Uwemba Tanz. 129 B7
Uwi i. Indon. 77 D2
Uxin Ju China 85 F4
Uxin Qi China see Dabqig
Uxmal tourist site Mex. 185 H4
Uxxaktal China 88 D3
Uyaly Kazakh. 103 E3
Uyaly, Ozero l. Kazakh. see Koshkarkol', Ozero
Uyar Rus. Fed. 80 E1
Üydzin Mongolia 85 E2
Uyo Nigeria 125 G5
Üyönch Mongolia 84 B2
Üyönch Gol r. China 84 A2
Uyu Chaung r. Myanmar 78 A2
Uyuk Kazakh. 103 G4
also spelt Oyyq; formerly spelt Oik
Uyun Saudi Arabia 105 E2
Uyuni Bol. 200 D5
Uyuni, Salar de salt flat Bol. 200 D5
Uza r. Rus. Fed. 41 H5
'Uzaym, Nahr al r. Iraq 107 F4
▶Uzbekistan country Asia 102 D4
spelt O'zbekiston or Ŭzbekiston in Uzbek; formerly known as Uzbekskaya S.S.R. or Uzbek S.S.R.
asia [countries] ▶ 64–67
Ŭzbekiston country Asia see Uzbekistan
Uzbekskaya S.S.R. country Asia see Uzbekistan
Uzbek S.S.R. country Asia see Uzbekistan
Uzda Belarus 42 I8
Uzen' Kazakh. see Kyzylsay
Uzengyu-Kuush, Gora mt. China/Kyrg. 88 B3
Uzerche France 50 H7
Uzès France 51 K8
Uzgen Kyrg. see Özgön
Uzh r. Ukr. 49 T7
Uzha r. Rus. Fed. 43 O7
Uzhgorod Ukr. see Uzhhorod
Uzhhorod Ukr. 49 T7
also spelt Uzhgorod; formerly spelt Užhorod; historically known as Ungvár
Uzhok Ukr. 49 T7
Užhorod Ukr. see Uzhhorod
Užice Srbija Yugo. 58 A5
formerly known as Titovo Užice
Uzlovaya Rus. Fed. 43 T8
Uzola r. Rus. Fed. 40 G4
Üzümlü Turkey 59 K12
Uzun Uzbek. 103 G5
Uzun Ada i. Turkey 59 H10
Uzunagach Almatinskaya Oblast' Kazakh. 103 I4
also spelt Uzynaghash
Uzunagach Almatinskaya Oblast' Kazakh. 103 I4
Uzunbulak China 88 D2
Uzuncaburç Turkey 108 E1
Uzunköprü Turkey 106 A2
Užventis Lith. 42 D6
Uzvoz Rus. Fed. 43 M6
Uzyn Ukr. 41 D6
Uzynaghash Kazakh. see Uzunagach
Uzynkair Kazakh. 103 E3

↓ V

Vaajakoski Fin. 44 N3
Vaal r. S. Africa 132 H6
Vaala Fin. 44 N2
Vaalbos National Park S. Africa 133 I5
Vaal Dam S. Africa 133 M4
Vaal Dam Nature Reserve S. Africa 133 M3
Vaalplass S. Africa 133 M2
Vaalwater S. Africa 131 F5
Vaartsi Estonia 42 I4
Vaasa Fin. 44 M3
also spelt Vasa
Vabalninkas Lith. 42 F6
Vabich r. Belarus 43 K8
Vabkent Uzbek. 103 F4
also spelt Wobkent
Vablya r. Rus. Fed. 43 O9
Vác Hungary 49 Q8
Vacaré r. Brazil 207 H8
Vacaria Brazil 203 B9
Vacaria r. Mato Grosso do Sul Brazil 203 A7
Vacaria r. Minas Gerais Brazil 202 D6
Vacaria, Campo da plain Brazil 203 B9
Vacaria, Serra hills Brazil 203 A7
Vacaville U.S.A. 182 C3
Vache, Île-à- i. Haiti 187 E3
Väckelsång Sweden 45 K4
Vad Rus. Fed. 40 H5
Vad r. Rus. Fed. 41 G5
Vada India 94 B2
Vadakste r. Latvia/Lith. 42 D5
Vădăstriţa Romania 58 F5
Vadehavet nature res. Denmark 45 J5
Văđeni Romania 58 I3
Vadi India 94 B3
also known as Savantvadi
Vadodara India 96 B5
formerly known as Baroda
Vadsø Norway 44 O1
Vadstena Sweden 45 K4
Vadu Crişului Romania 58 D2

▶Vaduz Liechtenstein 48 G8
Capital of Liechtenstein.

Værøy i. Norway 44 K2
Vaga r. Rus. Fed. 43 V1
Vågåmo Norway 45 J3
Vaganski Vrh mt. Croatia 56 H4
Vágar i. Faroe Is 46 E1
Vagavaram India 94 D2
Vagnhärad Sweden 45 L4
Vagos Port. 54 C4
Vägsele Sweden 44 L2
Vågsfjorden sea chan. Norway 44 L1
Váh r. Slovakia 49 P8
Vahhābī Iran 100 D4
Vahsel, Cape S. Georgia 205 [inset]
Vahto Fin. 45 M3

▶Vaiaku Tuvalu 145 G2
Capital of Tuvalu, on Funafuti atoll.
world [countries] ▶ 10–11

Vaida Estonia 42 F2
Vaiden U.S.A. 175 B5
Vaigai r. India 94 C4
Vaijapur India 94 B2
Vaikam India 94 C4
Väike Emajõgi r. Estonia 42 H3
Väike-Maarja Estonia 42 H2
Väike-Pakri i. Estonia 42 E2
Vaikijaur Sweden 44 L2
Väimela Estonia 42 I4
Vaiņode Latvia 42 C5
Vaippar r. India 94 C4
Vair r. France 51 L4
Vairowal India 96 B3
Vaison-la-Romaine France 51 L8
Vaitupu i. Tuvalu 145 G2
also spelt Oaitupu
Vajrakarur India see Kanur
Vajszló Hungary 56 J3
Vakaga pref. Cent. Afr. Rep. 126 D2
Vakaga r. Cent. Afr. Rep. 126 D2
Vakhan Tajik. 96 B1
Vakhsh Tajik. 101 G2
formerly known as Vakhstroy
Vakhsh r. Tajik. 101 G2
Vakhstroy Tajik. see Vakhsh
Vakīlābād Iran 100 D4
Vaksdal Norway 45 I3
Vålådalen naturreservat nature res. Sweden 44 K3
Valamaz Rus. Fed. 40 J4
Valandovo Macedonia 58 D7
Valašské Klobouky Czech Rep. 49 P6
Valašské Meziříčí Czech Rep. 49 O6
Valaxa i. Greece 59 F10
Val-Barrette Canada 173 R4
Vâlcăneşti Romania 58 G3
Vâlcanului, Munţii mts Romania 58 D3
Valcheta Arg. 204 D6
Valdai Hills Rus. Fed. see Valdayskaya Vozvyshennost'
Valday Rus. Fed. 43 O4
Valdayskaya Vozvyshennost' hills Rus. Fed. 43 N5
English form Valdai Hills
Valdayskoye, Ozero l. Rus. Fed. 43 O3
Valdecañas, Embalse de resr Spain 54 F5
Val del Ticino, Parco della park Italy 56 A3
Valdemārpils Latvia 42 D4
Valdemarsvik Sweden 45 L4
Val-de-Meuse France 51 L4
Valdemoro Spain 54 H4
Valdepeñas Spain 55 H6
Valderaduey r. Spain 54 F3
Valderas Spain 54 F2
Val-de-Reuil France 50 H3
Valders U.S.A. 172 F6

▶Valdés, Península pen. Arg. 205 E6
Lowest point in South America.
southamerica [landscapes] ▶ 190–191

Val-des-Bois Canada 173 R5
Valdez U.S.A. 164 E3
Valdivia Chile 204 B5
Valdivia Col. 198 C3
Valdobbiadene Italy 56 D3
Val-d'Or Canada 168 E3
Valdosa mt. Spain 55 H3
Valdosta U.S.A. 175 D6
Valdres valley Norway 45 J3
Vale Georgia 107 E2
Vale U.S.A. 180 C3
Valea lui Mihai Romania 49 T8
Valea Lungă Romania 58 F2
Valea Lungă Romania 58 G3
Valemount Canada 166 G4
Valença Brazil 202 E5
Valença do Piauí Brazil 202 D3
Valençay France 50 H5
Valence Midi-Pyrénées France 50 G8
Valence Rhône-Alpes France 51 K8
Valencia Spain 55 K5
historically known as Valentia
Valencia aut. comm. Spain 55 K5
also known as Valenciana, Comunidad
Valencia Venez. 199 E2
Valencia, Golfo de g. Spain 55 L5
Valencia de Alcántara Spain 54 D5
Valencia de Don Juan Spain 54 F2
Valencia Island Rep. of Ireland 47 B12
Valenciana, Comunidad aut. comm. Spain see Valencia
Valenciennes France 51 J2
Vălenii de Munte Romania 58 H3
Valensole, Plateau de France 51 M9
Valentia Spain see Valencia
Valentin Rus. Fed. 82 D4
Valentine U.S.A. 178 B3
Valentine National Wildlife Refuge nature res. U.S.A. 178 B3
Valenza Italy 56 A3
Valenzuela Phil. 74 B3
Våler Norway 45 J3
Valera Venez. 198 D2
Vale Verde Brazil 207 N3
Valga Estonia 42 H4
Valgejõgi r. Estonia 42 G2
Valhalla Provincial Park Canada 166 G5
Valikhanovo Kazakh. 103 G1
also known as Ūālīkhanov
Valinco, Golfe de b. Corse France 56 A7
Valinhos Brazil 206 G9
Valjevo Srbija Yugo. 58 A4
Valka Latvia 42 H4
Valkeakoski Fin. 45 N3
Valkenswaard Neth. 48 C4
Valkla Estonia 42 G2
Valko Fin. 42 H1
also spelt Valkoni
Valkoni Fin. see Valko
Valky Ukr. 41 E6
Valkyrie Dome ice feature Antarctica 223 C1
Vallabhipur India 96 A5
Valladolid Mex. 185 H4
Valladolid Spain 54 G3
Vallard, Lac l. Canada 169 G2
Valldal Norway 44 I3
Vall de Uxó Spain 55 K5
Valle dept Col. 198 B4
Valle Norway 45 I4
Vallecito Arg. 204 D3
Valle d'Aosta admin. reg. Italy 51 N7
Valle de la Pascua Venez. 199 E2
Valle de Rosario Mex. 181 F8
Valle de Santiago Mex. 185 E4
Valle de Zaragoza Mex. 184 D3
Valledupar Col. 198 C2
Vallée-Jonction Canada 169 G4
Valle Fértil, Sierra de mts Arg. 204 C3
Valle Grande Bol. 201 D4
Valle Hermoso Mex. 185 F3
Vallejo U.S.A. 182 B3
Vallelunga Pratameno Sicilia Italy 57 F11
Valle Nacional Mex. 185 F5
Vallenar Chile 204 C3
Vallentuna Sweden 45 L4

▶Valletta Malta 57 G13
Capital of Malta.

Valley r. Canada 167 L5
Valley Center U.S.A. 183 G8
Valley City U.S.A. 178 C2
Valley Falls U.S.A. 180 B4
Valley Head Phil. 74 B2
Valley Head U.S.A. 176 E7
Valley of The Kings tourist site Egypt 121 G3
Valley Springs U.S.A. 182 D3
Valley Station U.S.A. 174 C4
Valley Stream U.S.A. 177 L5
Valleyview Canada 167 G4
Valley View U.S.A. 176 A8
Vallo della Lucania Italy 57 H8
Valls Spain 55 M3
Vallsta Sweden 45 L3
Val Marie Canada 167 J5
Valmaseda Spain see Balmaseda
Valmiera Latvia 42 G4
Valmy U.S.A. 183 G1
Valnera mt. Spain 55 H1
Valognes France 50 E3
Valona Albania see Vlorë
Valozhyn Belarus 42 H7
also spelt Volozhin
Valpaços Port. 54 D3
Val-Paradis Canada 168 E3
Valparai India 94 C4
Valparaíso Brazil 206 C8
Valparaíso Chile 204 C4
Valparaíso admin. reg. Chile 204 C4
Valparaíso Mex. 184 E4
Valparaiso FL U.S.A. 185 I2
Valparaiso IN U.S.A. 174 C3
Valpelline valley Italy 51 N7
Valpoi India 94 B3
Valpovo Croatia 56 K3
Valronquillo hill Spain 54 G5
Vals r. S. Africa 133 K4
Vals, Tanjung c. Indon. 73 I8
Valsad India 94 B1
Valshui Wash watercourse U.S.A. 181 D7
Valspan S. Africa 131 E5
Valsrivier S. Africa 133 M5
Valtimo Fin. 44 O3
Valtou mts Greece 59 C9
Valua i. Vanuatu see Mota Lava
Valuyets Rus. Fed. 43 O9
Valuyevka Rus. Fed. 41 G7
Valuyki Rus. Fed. 41 F6
Valverde Dom. Rep. see Mao
Valverde del Camino Spain 54 E7
Valverde del Fresno Spain 54 E4
Vam Co Dông r. Vietnam 79 D6
Vam Co Tay r. Vietnam 79 D6
Vamizi, Ilha i. Moz. 129 D7
Vammala Fin. 45 M3
Vampula Fin. 45 M3
Vamsadhara r. India 95 E2
Vamvakas, Akra pt Greece 59 H10
Van Turkey 107 E3
Van, Lake salt l. Turkey 107 E3
also known as Van Gölü
Vanadzor Armenia 107 F2
formerly known as Karaklis or Kirovakan
Vanajavesi l. Fin. 45 N3
Vana-Koiola Estonia 42 I4
Vanån r. Sweden 45 K3
Vânători Romania 58 J3
Vânători Romania 58 F2
Vanavara Rus. Fed. 39 K3
Van Buren AR U.S.A. 179 D5
Van Buren IN U.S.A. 172 H10
Van Buren MO U.S.A. 174 B4
Van Buren U.S.A. see Kettering
Vanceburg U.S.A. 176 B7
Vanch Tajik. see Vanj
Vanchskiy Khrebet mts Tajik. see Vanj, Qatorkŭhi
Vancleve U.S.A. 176 B8
Vancouver Canada 166 F5
Vancouver U.S.A. 180 B3
Vancouver, Mount Canada/U.S.A. 166 B2
Vancouver Island Canada 166 E5
Vanda Fin. see Vantaa
Vandalia IL U.S.A. 174 B4
Vandalia OH U.S.A. 176 A6
Vandavasi India 94 C3
formerly spelt Wandiwash
Vandekerckhove Lake Canada 167 K3
Vandellós Spain 55 L3
Vanderbijlpark S. Africa 133 L3
Vanderbilt U.S.A. 173 I5
Vandergrift U.S.A. 176 F5
Vanderhoof Canada 166 E4
Vanderkloof Dam resr S. Africa 133 I7
Vanderlin Island Australia 148 C2
Van Diemen, Cape N.T. Australia 148 A1
Van Diemen, Cape Qld Australia 148 C3
Van Diemen Gulf Australia 148 B1
Van Diemen's Land state Australia see Tasmania
Vändra Estonia 42 G3
Vandyksdrif S. Africa 133 N3
Vandžiogala Lith. 42 E6
Vāne Latvia 42 D5
Väner, Lake Sweden see Vänern

▶Vänern l. Sweden 45 K4
4th largest lake in Europe. English form Väner, Lake.
europe [landscapes] ▶ 30–31

Vänersborg Sweden 45 K4
Vaneteze r. Moz. 133 Q2
Vang, Mount Antarctica 222 T2
Vanga Kenya 129 C6
Vangaindrano Madag. 131 [inset] J4
Vangaži Latvia 42 F4
Van Gölü salt l. Turkey see Van, Lake
Vangsvik Norway 44 L1
Vanguard Canada 167 J5
Van Horn U.S.A. 181 F7
Vanier Canada 168 F4
formerly known as Eastview
Vanikoro Islands Solomon Is 145 F3
also known as Mannicolo Islands; formerly known as Pitt Islands
Vanil Noir mt. Switz. 51 N6
Vanimo P.N.G. 73 J7
Vanino Rus. Fed. 82 F2
Vanivilasa Sagara resr India 94 C3
Vaniyambadi India 94 C3
Vanj Tajik. 101 G2
also spelt Vanch
Vanj, Qatorkŭhi mts Tajik. 101 G2
also known as Vanchskiy Khrebet
Vänjaurträsk Sweden 44 L2
Vânju Mare Romania 58 D4
formerly spelt Vînju Mare
Vankarem Rus. Fed. 39 S3
Vankavesi l. Fin. 45 M3
Vanna i. Norway 44 L1
Vännäs Sweden 44 L3
Vanne r. France 51 J4
Vannes France 50 D5
Vannes, Lac l. Canada 169 H2
Vannovka Kazakh. see Tura-Ryskulova
Vanntindan mt. Norway 44 L1
Van Reenen S. Africa 133 N5
Van Rees, Pegunungan mts Indon. 73 I7
Vanrhynsdorp S. Africa 132 C8
Van Riebeeck Nature Reserve S. Africa 133 M2
Vanrook Australia 149 D3
Vanrook Creek r. Australia 149 D3
Vansada India 94 B1
Vansant U.S.A. 176 C8
Vansbro Sweden 45 K3
Vanse Norway 45 I4
Vansittart Bay Australia 150 D2
Vansittart Island Canada 165 K3
Vanstadensrus S. Africa 133 L6
Vantaa Fin. 45 N3
also spelt Vanda
Vantaa r. Fin. 42 F1
Van Truer Tableland reg. Australia 151 C5
Vant's Drift S. Africa 133 O5
Vanua Balavu i. Fiji 145 H3
also spelt Vanua Mbalavu or Vanua Valavo
Vanua Lava i. Vanuatu 145 F3
Vanua Levu i. Fiji 145 G3
Vanua Mbalavu i. Fiji see Vanua Balavu

Vanuatu country S. Pacific Ocean 145 F3
formerly known as New Hebrides or Nouvelles Hébrides
oceania [countries] 138–139
oceania [features] 142–143
Vanua Valavo i. Fiji see Vanua Balavu
Van Wert U.S.A. 176 A5
Van Wyksdorp S. Africa 132 F10
Vanwyksvlei S. Africa 132 F7
Vanwyksvlei l. S. Africa 132 F7
Van Zylsrus S. Africa 132 G3
Vao, Embalse de resr Spain 54 D2
also spelt Bao, Embalse del
Var r. France 51 N9
Vara Estonia 42 H3
Vara Sweden 45 K4
Varada r. India 94 C3
Varadero Cuba 186 C2
Varahi India 96 A5
Varaita r. Italy 51 N8
Varakļāni Latvia 42 H5
Varalé Côte d'Ivoire 124 E4
Varallo Italy 56 A3
Varāmīn Iran 100 B3
Varanasi India 97 D4
formerly known as Benares; historically known as Kasi
Varandey Rus. Fed. 40 K1
Varangerfjorden sea chan. Norway 44 O1
Varangerhalvøya pen. Norway 44 O1
also known as Várnjárg
Varano, Lago di lag. Italy 56 H7
Varapayeva Belarus 42 I6
Varaždin Croatia 56 I2
Varazze Italy 56 A4
Varberg Sweden 45 K4
Varbla Estonia 42 E3
Varda Greece 59 C10
Vardak prov. Afgh. 101 G3
Vardannapet India 94 C2
Vardar r. Macedonia 58 D7
Varde Denmark 45 J5
Vardenis Armenia 107 F2
formerly known as Basargechar
Vårdö Fin. 42 B1
Vardø Norway 44 O1
Varduva r. Lith. 42 D5
Varegovo Rus. Fed. 43 U4
Varel Germany 48 F2
Varela Arg. 204 D4
Varėna Lith. 42 F7
Vareš Bos.-Herz. 56 K4
Varese Italy 56 A3
Varfolomeyevka Rus. Fed. 82 D3
Vårgårda Sweden 45 K4
Vargas Arg. 204 C4
Vargem r. Brazil 202 E4
Vargem Alta Brazil 207 L7
Vargem Grande Brazil 202 D2
Vargem Grande do Sul Brazil 206 G8
Varginha Brazil 203 C7
Varhaug Norway 45 I4
Varkana Iran see Gorgān
Varkaus Fin. 44 N3
Varkhi Belarus 43 K6
Varmahlíð Iceland 44 [inset] C2
Varmeln l. Sweden 45 K4
Värmland county Sweden 45 K4
Värmlandsnäs i. Sweden 45 K4
Varna Bulg. 58 I5
formerly known as Stalin; historically known as Odessus
Varna r. India 94 B2
Varna Rus. Fed. 103 E1
Värnamo Sweden 45 K4
Värnäs Sweden 45 K3
Varnavino Rus. Fed. 40 H4
Varnek Rus. Fed. 40 L1
Varniai Lith. 42 D6
Varnja Estonia 42 I3
Várnjárg pen. Norway see Varangerhalvøya
Varnyany Belarus 42 H7
Varosha Cyprus see Varosia
Varosia Cyprus 108 E2
also known as Maraş; also spelt Varosha
Varoška Rijeka Bos.-Herz. 56 I3
Varpaisjärvi Fin. 44 N3
Várpalota Hungary 49 P8
Värriön luonnonpuisto nature res. Fin. 44 O2
Vărșag Romania 58 G2
Varsaj Afgh. 101 G2
Vărșand Romania 58 C2
Varsh, Ozero l. Rus. Fed. 40 H2
Varsinais-Suomi reg. Fin. 45 M3
also known as Egentliga Finland
Värska Estonia 42 I4
Vartashen Azer. see Oğuz
Vartdalsfjorden inlet Norway 44 I3
Vartholomio Greece 59 C11
Varto Turkey 107 E3
also known as Gümgüm
Vârtop Romania 58 E4
Vârtop, Pasul pass Romania 58 D2
Värtsilä Fin. 44 O3
Var'yegan Rus. Fed. 38 H3
Varzaneh Iran 100 C3
Várzea Alegre Brazil 202 E3
Várzea da Palma Brazil 203 C6
Várzea Grande Brazil 202 D3
Varzelândia Brazil 207 I2
Varzo Italy 56 A2
Varzob Tajik. 101 G2
Varzuga Rus. Fed. 40 F2
Vasa Fin. see Vaasa
Vasa Barris r. Brazil 202 E4
Vasai India 94 B2
Vasalemma Estonia 42 F2
Vasalemma r. Estonia 42 F2
Vásárosnamény Hungary 49 T7
Vascão r. Port. 54 D7
Vașcău Romania 58 D2
Vashka r. Rus. Fed. 40 H2
Vasht Iran see Khāsh
Vasilika Greece 58 E8
Vasilkov Ukr. see Vasyl'kiv
Vasilyevichy Belarus 43 K9
Vasil'yevo Rus. Fed. 42 I4
Vasil'yevskiy Mokh Rus. Fed. 43 Q4
Vas'kavichy Belarus 43 L8
Vaskivesi Fin. 45 M3
Vasknarva Estonia 42 I2
Vaslui Romania 58 I2
Vassar U.S.A. 173 J7
Vassenden Norway 45 I3
Vassfaret og Vidalen park Norway 45 J3
Vas-Soproni-síkság hills Hungary 49 N8
Vassouras Brazil 207 J9
Vastan Turkey see Gevaş
Västana Sweden 44 L3
Västanfjärd Fin. 42 D1
Västansjö Sweden 44 L2
Vastemõisa Estonia 42 G3
Vastenjaure l. Sweden 44 L2
Västerås Sweden 45 L4
Västerbotten county Sweden 44 K2
Västerdalälven r. Sweden 45 K3
Västerhaninge Sweden 45 L4
Västernorrland county Sweden 44 L3
Västervik Sweden 45 L4
Västmanland county Sweden 45 K4
Vasto Italy 56 G6
Västra Götaland county Sweden 45 K4
Västra Ormsjö Sweden 44 L2
Vastse-Kuuste Estonia 42 H3
Vasvár Hungary 49 N8
Vasyl'kiv Ukr. 41 D6
also spelt Vasilkov
Vatan France 50 H5
Väte Sweden 45 L4
Vaté i. Vanuatu see Éfaté
Vatersay i. U.K. 46 E7
Vathi Greece see Ithaki
Vathí Greece see Vathy
Vathia Greece 59 D12
Vathy Notio Aigaio Greece 59 H12
Vathy Voreio Aigaio Greece 59 H11
also spelt Vathí
Vatican City Europe 56 E7
Independent papal state, the smallest country in the world. English form Holy See; known as Città del Vaticano in Italian
world [countries] 10–11
europe [countries] 32–35
Vaticano, Capo c. Italy 57 H10
Vaticano, Città del Europe see Vatican City
Vatio Greece 59 I12
Vatnajökull ice cap Iceland 44 [inset] C2
Vatne Norway 44 I3
Vatoa i. Fiji 145 H3
also known as Turtle Island
Vatomandry Madag. 131 [inset] K3
Vatoussa Greece 59 H9
Vatra Dornei Romania 58 G1
Vätter, Lake Sweden see Vättern
Vättern l. Sweden 45 K4
English form Vätter, Lake
Vattrång Sweden 45 L3
Vatulele i. Fiji 145 G3
Vaucluse, Monts de mts France 51 L9
Vaucouleurs France 51 L4
Vaughan Springs Australia 148 A4
Vaughn U.S.A. 181 F6
Vaulx-en-Velin France 51 K7
Vaupés dept Col. 198 D4
Vaupés r. Col. 198 D4
Vauquelin r. Canada 168 E2
Vauvert France 51 K9
Vauxhall Canada 167 H5
Vav India 96 A4
Vavatenina Madag. 131 [inset] K3
Vava'u i. Tonga 145 H3
Vava'u Group is Tonga 145 H3
Vavitao i. Fr. Polynesia see Raivavae
Vavoua Côte d'Ivoire 124 D5
Vavozh Rus. Fed. 40 I4
Vavuniya Sri Lanka 94 D4
Vawkalata Belarus 42 I7
Vawkavichy Belarus 43 L8
also known as Volkovichi
Vawkavysk Belarus 42 F8
also known as Volkovysk
Vawkavyskaye Wzvyshsha hills Belarus 42 F8
also known as Volkovyskiye Vysoty
Växjö Sweden 45 K4
Vây, Đao i. Vietnam 79 C6
Vayalpad India 94 C3
Vayenga Rus. Fed. see Severomorsk
Vaygach, Ostrov i. Rus. Fed. 40 K1
Vayittiri India 94 C4
Vayk' Armenia 107 F3
formerly known as Azizbekov or Soylan
Vazante Brazil 206 G4
Vazáš Sweden see Vittangi
Vazobe mt. Madag. 131 [inset] J3
Vazuza r. Rus. Fed. 43 P6
Vazuzskoye Vodokhranilishche resr Rus. Fed. 43 P6
Veaikevárri Sweden see Svappavaara
Vecht r. Neth. 48 D3
also known as Vechte (Germany)
Vechta Germany 48 F3
Vechte r. Germany 48 D3
also known as Vecht (Neth.)
Vecmiķeļi Latvia 42 E5
Vecumnieki Latvia 42 F5
Vedana Rus. Fed. see Vedeno
Vedaranniyam India 94 C4
Vedasandur India 94 C4
Veddige Sweden 45 K4
Vedea Romania 58 F4
Vedea Romania 58 G5
Vedea r. Romania 58 G5
Vedeno Rus. Fed. 107 F2
also known as Vedana
Vedi Armenia 107 F3
Vedia Arg. 204 E4
Vedlozero Rus. Fed. 40 E3
Vedrych r. Belarus 43 L9
Veendam Neth. 48 D2
Veenendaal Neth. 48 C3
Vega i. Norway 44 J2
Vega U.S.A. 179 B5
Vegadeo Spain 54 D1
Vegarshei Norway 45 J4
Vegoritis, Limni l. Greece 58 C8
Vegreville Canada 167 H4
Végueta Peru 200 A2
Vehkalahti Fin. 42 I1
Vehmaa Fin. 45 M3
Vehoa r. Pak. 101 G4
Veidnes Norway 44 N1
Veinticinco de Mayo Arg. see 25 de Mayo
Veinticinco de Mayo Arg. see 25 de Mayo
Veinticinco de Mayo Arg. see 25 de Mayo
Veiros Brazil 199 H5
Veisiejis Lith. 42 E7
Veitsiluoto Fin. 44 N2
Vejer de la Frontera Spain 54 F8
Vejle Denmark 45 J5
Velachha India 96 B5
Vela Luka Croatia 56 I6
Velardena Mex. 184 E3
Vèlas, Cabo c. Costa Rica 186 B5
Velasco, Sierra de mts Arg. 204 D3
Vela Vrata, Kanal sea chan. Croatia 56 G3
Velázquez Uruguay 204 G4
Velbŭzhdki Prokhod pass Macedonia 58 D6
also known as Deve Bair
Velddrif S. Africa 132 C9
Velden am Wörther See Austria 49 L9
Veldhoven Neth. 48 C4
Veldurti India 94 C3
Velebit mts Croatia 56 G4
Velebitski Kanal sea chan. Croatia 56 G3
Veleka r. Bulg. 58 I6
Velen Germany 48 D4
Velenje Slovenia 56 H2
formerly known as Titovo Velenje
Veles Macedonia 58 C7
formerly known as Titov Veles
Velës, Mali i mt. Albania 58 A7
Velež mts Bos.-Herz. 56 J5
Vélez Col. 198 C3
Vélez-Málaga Spain 54 G8
Vélez-Rubio Spain 55 I7
Velhas r. Minas Gerais Brazil 203 C6
Velhas r. Minas Gerais Brazil 206 F6
Velia tourist site Italy 57 H8
Velibaba Turkey see Aras
Velichayevskoye Rus. Fed. 41 H7
Velika Drenova Srbija Yugo. 58 C5
Velika Gorica Croatia 56 I3
Velika Kapela mts Croatia 56 G3
Velika Kladuša Bos.-Herz. 56 H3
Velika Mlaka Croatia 56 I3
Velika Morava canal Yugo. 58 C4
Velika Plana Srbija Yugo. 58 C4
Velikaya Rus. Fed. 40 I4
Velikaya r. Rus. Fed. 39 R3
Velikaya r. Rus. Fed. 40 I4
Velikaya r. Rus. Fed. 43 J4
Velikaya Guba Rus. Fed. 40 E3
Velikaya Kema Rus. Fed. 82 E3
Veliki Drvenik i. Croatia 56 I5
Veliki Jastrebac mts Yugo. 58 C5
Veliki Preslav Bulg. 58 H5
formerly known as Preslav
Veliki Risnjak mt. Croatia 56 G3
Veliki Šiljegovac Srbija Yugo. 58 C5
Veliki Šturac mt. Yugo. 58 B4
Velikiye Luki Rus. Fed. 43 L5
Velikiy Novgorod Rus. Fed. 43 M3
formerly known as Novgorod; historically known as Holmgard
Velikiy Ustyug Rus. Fed. 40 H3
Velikonda Range hills India 94 C3
Velikooktyabr'skiy Rus. Fed. 43 O4
Veliko Tŭrnovo Bulg. 58 G5
formerly known as Tŭrnovo
Velikoye Vologod. Obl. Rus. Fed. 43 R2
Velikoye Yaroslavskaya Oblast' Rus. Fed. 43 U4
Velikoye, Ozero l. Rus. Fed. 43 R4
Velikoye, Ozero l. Rus. Fed. 43 V6
Vélingara Senegal 124 B3
Vélingara Senegal 124 B3
Velingrad Bulg. 58 F6
Velino r. Italy 56 E6
Velino, Monte mt. Italy 56 F6
Veliuona Lith. 42 E6
Velizh Rus. Fed. 43 M6
Velká Bíteš Czech Rep. 49 N6
Veľká Domaša, Vodná nádrž resr Slovakia 49 S6
Veľká Fatra mts Slovakia 49 P7
Velká Javořina hill Czech Rep./Slovakia 49 O7
Veľké Kapušany Slovakia 49 T7
Velké Meziříčí Czech Rep. 49 N6
Velkua Fin. 42 C1
Veľký Krtíš Slovakia 49 Q7
Veľký Meder Slovakia 49 O8
formerly known as Čalovo
Vella Lavella i. Solomon Is 145 E2
Vellar r. India 94 C4
Velletri Italy 56 E7
Vellinge Sweden 45 K5
Vellore India 94 C3
Vel'mo r. Rus. Fed. 39 J3
Velopoula i. Greece 59 E12
Vel'sk Rus. Fed. 40 G3
Velsuna Italy see Orvieto
Vel't Rus. Fed. 40 I1
Velten Germany 49 K3
Veluwezoom, Nationaal Park nat. park Neth. 48 C3
Velvendos Greece 59 D8
Vel'ye, Ozero l. Rus. Fed. 43 N4
Velyka Mykhaylivka Ukr. 58 K1
Velykodolyns'ke Ukr. 58 L2
Velykyy Tokmak Ukr. see Tokmak
Vel'yu r. Rus. Fed. 40 J3
Vemalwada India 94 C2
Vembanad Lake India 94 C4
Vemor'ye Rus. Fed. 82 F3
Vempalle India 94 C3
Venado Tuerto Arg. 204 E4
Venafro Italy 56 G7
Venamo r. Guyana/Venez. 199 F3
Venamo, Cerro mt. Venez. 199 F3
Venarey-les-Laumes France 51 K5
Venaria Italy 51 N7
Vencedor Brazil 199 F6
Venceslau Bráz Brazil 206 D10
Venciūnai Lith. 42 F7
Venda Nova Brazil 207 L7
Vendenheim France 51 N4
Vendeuvre-sur-Barse France 51 K4
Vendinga Rus. Fed. 40 H3
Vendôme France 50 H5
Vendrell Spain see El Vendrell
Venecia Col. 198 C4
Venegas Mex. 185 E4
Veneta, Laguna lag. Italy 56 E3
Venetia Italy see Venice
Veneto admin. reg. Italy 56 D3
Venev Rus. Fed. 43 T7
Venezia Italy see Venice
Venezia, Golfo di g. Europe see Venice, Gulf of
Venezuela country S. America 199 E3
5th most populous country in South America.
southamerica [countries] 192–193
Venezuela, Golfo de g. Venez. 198 D2
Vengurla India 94 B3
Veniaminof Volcano U.S.A. 164 D4
Venice Italy 56 E3
also known as Venezia; historically known as Venetia
Venice FL U.S.A. 175 D7
Venice LA U.S.A. 179 E6
Venice, Gulf of Europe 56 E3
also known as Venezia, Golfo di
Vénissieux France 51 K7
Venjan Sweden 45 K3
Venkatagiri India 94 C3
Venkatapuram India 94 D2
Venlo Neth. 48 D4
Vennesla Norway 45 I4
Venosa Italy 56 H8
historically known as Venusia
Venosta, Val valley Italy 56 C2
Venray Neth. 48 C4
Venta r. Latvia/Lith. 42 D5
Venta Lith. 42 D5
Venta de Baños Spain 54 G3
Ventania Brazil 206 C11
Ventersburg S. Africa 133 L5
Ventersdorp S. Africa 133 K3
Venterstad S. Africa 133 J7
Ventimiglia Italy 51 N9
Ventisquero mt. Arg. 205 C6
Ventnor U.K. 47 K13
Ventotene, Isola i. Italy 57 F8
Ventoux, Mont mt. France 51 L8
Ventspils Latvia 42 C4
historically known as Windau
Ventuari r. Venez. 199 E3
Ventura U.S.A. 182 E7
Venus Bay Australia 147 E4
Venusia Italy see Venosa
Venustiano Carranza, Presa resr Mex. 185 E3
Venzone Italy 56 F2
Vepsovskaya Vozvyshennost' hills Rus. Fed. 43 P1
Vera Arg. 204 E3
Vera Spain 55 J7
Verá, Lago l. Para. 201 F6
Vera Cruz Amazonas Brazil 200 D2
Vera Cruz São Paulo Brazil 206 D9
Vera Cruz Mex. see Veracruz
Veracruz Mex. 185 F5
also spelt Vera Cruz
Veracruz state Mex. 185 F4
Vera de Bidasoa Spain 55 J1
Veranópolis Brazil 203 B9
Veraval India 94 A1
Verbania Italy 56 A3
Verbilki Rus. Fed. 43 S5
Verbovskiy Rus. Fed. 40 G5
Vercelli Italy 56 A3
Vercors reg. France 51 L8
Vercors, Parc Naturel Régional du nature res. France 51 L8
Vercovicium tourist site U.K. see Housesteads
Verda r. Rus. Fed. 43 V8
Verdalsøra Norway 44 J3
Verde r. Arg. 205 D6
Verde r. Bahia Brazil 202 D4
Verde r. Goiás Brazil 206 C5
Verde r. Goiás/Minas Gerais Brazil 206 F5
Verde r. Mato Grosso Brazil 201 G2
Verde r. Mato Grosso do Sul Brazil 206 B8
Verde r. Minas Gerais Brazil 206 C6
Verde r. Minas Gerais Brazil 206 D6
Verde r. Minas Gerais Brazil 207 H8
Verde r. Brazil 206 E2
Verde r. Mex. 184 D3
Verde r. Para. 201 F5
Verde r. U.S.A. 183 M8
Verde, Cabo c. Senegal see Vert, Cap
Verde, Península pen. Arg. 204 E5
Verde Grande r. Brazil 202 D5
Verde Island Passage Phil. 74 B3
Verden (Aller) Germany 48 G3
Verde Pequeno r. Brazil 202 D5
Verdi U.S.A. 182 E2
Verdigris r. U.S.A. 178 D5
Verdikoussa Greece 59 C9
Verdinho r. Brazil 206 C4
Verdinho, Serra do mts Brazil 206 B5
Verdon r. France 51 L9
Verdun France 51 L3
Verdun-sur-Garonne France 50 H9
Vereeniging S. Africa 133 L3
Verena S. Africa 133 N2
Vereshchagino Rus. Fed. 40 J4
Verestovo, Ozero l. Rus. Fed. 43 R4
Vereya Rus. Fed. 43 R6
Verfeil France 50 H9
Verga, Cap c. Guinea 124 B4
Vergara Uruguay 204 G4
Vergeleë S. Africa 133 I2
Vergennes U.S.A. 177 L1
Vergina Greece 58 D8
also spelt Veryína
Véria Greece see Veroia
Verigino Rus. Fed. 43 T5
Verín Spain 54 D3
Veriora Estonia 42 I3
Veríssimo Brazil 206 E6
Veríssimo Sarmento Angola see Camissombo
Verkeerdevlei S. Africa 133 K5
Verkhne-Avzyan Rus. Fed. 102 D1
Verkhne-berezovskiy Kazakh. 88 C1
Verkhnedneprovsk Ukr. see Verkhn'odniprovs'k
Verkhnedneprovskiy Rus. Fed. 43 O7
Verkhneimbatsk Rus. Fed. 39 I3
Verkhnekolvinsk Rus. Fed. 40 K2
Verkhneruzskoye Vodokhranilishche resr Rus. Fed. 43 Q6
Verkhnespasskoye Rus. Fed. 40 H4
Verkhnetulomskiy Rus. Fed. 44 O1
Verkhnetulomskoye Vodokhranilishche resr Rus. Fed. 44 O1
Verkhneural'sk Rus. Fed. 102 D1
Verkhnevilyuysk Rus. Fed. 39 M3
Verkhnevolzhskoye Vodokhranilishche resr Rus. Fed. 43 N4
Verkhneyarkeyevo Rus. Fed. 40 J5
Verkhneye Kuyto, Ozero l. Rus. Fed. 44 O2
Verkhnezeysk Rus. Fed. 82 C1
Verkhniy At-Uryakh Rus. Fed. 39 P3
Verkhniy Baskunchak Rus. Fed. 102 A2
Verkhniye Koshevichi Rus. Fed. 43 M6
Verkhniye Mokhovichi Rus. Fed. 43 M6
Verkhniy Lomovets Rus. Fed. 43 T9
Verkhniy Mamon Rus. Fed. 41 G6
Verkhniy Shergol'dzhin Rus. Fed. 85 F1
Verkhniy Tatyshly Rus. Fed. 40 J4
Verkhniy Vyalozerskiy Rus. Fed. 40 E2
Verkhn'odniprovs'k Ukr. 41 E6
also spelt Verkhnedneprovsk
Verkhnyaya Inta Rus. Fed. 40 L2
Verkhnyaya Pakhachi Rus. Fed. 39 Q3
Verkhnyaya Taymyra r. Rus. Fed. 39 J2
Verkhnyaya Toyma Rus. Fed. 40 H3
Verkhnyaya Troitsa Rus. Fed. 43 S4
Verkhnyaya Tunguska r. Rus. Fed. see Angara
Verkhnyaya Yelovka Kazakh. 88 D1
Verkhoshizhem'ye Rus. Fed. 40 I4
Verkhovazh'ye Rus. Fed. 40 G3
Verkhov'ye Rus. Fed. 43 S9
Verkhoyanskiy Khrebet mts Rus. Fed. 39 M2
Verkhuba Kazakh. 88 C1
Verknė r. Lith. 42 F7
Verkola Rus. Fed. 40 H3
Verkykerskop S. Africa 133 N4
Verlatekloof pass S. Africa 132 E9
Verma Norway 44 J3
Vermaaklikheid S. Africa 132 F11
Vermelha, Serra hills Brazil 206 C10
Vermelho r. Mato Grosso Brazil 206 B1
Vermelho r. Pará Brazil 202 B3
Vermelho r. Tocantins Brazil 202 C3
Vermenton France 51 J5
Vermeş Romania 58 C3
Vermilion Canada 167 I4
Vermilion r. U.S.A. 174 B3
Vermilion Bay U.S.A. 179 E6
Vermilion Cliffs esc. AZ U.S.A. 183 L5
Vermilion Cliffs esc. UT U.S.A. 183 L4
Vermilion Lake U.S.A. 174 A2
Vermilion Range hills U.S.A. 172 A3
Vermillion U.S.A. 178 C3
Vermillion r. U.S.A. 178 C3
Vermillion Bay Canada 168 A3
Vermillon r. Canada 174 F2
Vermont state U.S.A. 177 M1
Vernadsky research station Antarctica 222 T2
long form Academician Vernadskiy
Vernal U.S.A. 183 O1
Verner Canada 168 D4
Verneuil-sur-Avre France 50 G4
Verneuk Pan salt pan S. Africa 132 F6
Vernier Switz. 51 M6
Vernio Italy 56 D4
Vernon Canada 166 G5
Vernon France 50 H3
Vernon AL U.S.A. 175 B5
Vernon TX U.S.A. 179 C5
Vernon, Mount hill Australia 150 B5
Vernon Islands Australia 148 A2
Vernoye Rus. Fed. 82 C2
Vernyy Kazakh. see Almaty
Vero Beach U.S.A. 175 D7
Veroia Greece 58 D8
also spelt Véria; historically known as Beroea
Verona Italy 56 C3
Verona VA U.S.A. 176 F7
Verona WI U.S.A. 172 D8
Verres Italy 51 N7
Versailles France 51 I4
Versailles IN U.S.A. 174 C4
Versailles KY U.S.A. 176 A7
Versailles MO U.S.A. 178 D4
Versailles OH U.S.A. 176 A5
Versalles Bol. 201 E3
Versec Vojvodina, Srbija Yugo. see Vršac
Verseka r. Lith. 42 F7
Versmold Germany 48 F3
Versoix Switz. 51 M6
Vert, Cap c. Senegal 124 A3
also known as Verde, Cabo
Vert, Île i. Canada 169 G3
Vertentes r. Brazil 202 B4
Vertesi park Hungary 49 P8
Vertientes Cuba 186 D2
Vertou France 50 E5
Vertus France 51 K4
Verulam S. Africa 133 P6
Verulamium U.K. see St Albans
Verviers Belgium 51 L2
Vervins France 51 J3
Verwoerdburg S. Africa see Centurion
Verwood Canada 167 J5
Veryína Greece see Vergina
Vesanto Fin. 44 N3
Vescovato Corse France 51 P10
Vesele Ukr. 41 E7
Veselevo Rus. Fed. 43 R6
Veselina r. Bulg. 58 G5
Veselí nad Lužnicí Czech Rep. 49 L6
Veselí nad Moravou Czech Rep. 49 O7
Veselovskoye Vodokhranilishche resr Rus. Fed. 41 G7
Veseloyarsk Rus. Fed. 88 C1
Veselyy Rus. Fed. 41 G7
Veselyy Podol Kazakh. 103 F1
Veshenskaya Rus. Fed. 41 G6
Vesijärvi l. Fin. 45 N3
Vesle r. France 51 J3
Veslyana r. Rus. Fed. 40 J3
Vesontio France see Besançon
Vesoul France 51 M5
Vesselyy Yar Rus. Fed. 90 D3
Vest-Agder county Norway 45 I4
Vesterålen is Norway 44 K1
Vesterålsfjorden sea chan. Norway 44 K1
Vestfirðir constituency Iceland 44 [inset] B2
Vestfjorddalen valley Norway 45 J4
Vestfjorden sea chan. Norway 44 K2
Vestfold county Norway 45 J4
Vestfold Hills Antarctica 223 F2
Vestmanna Faroe Is 46 E1
Vestmannaeyjar is Iceland 44 [inset] B3
English form Westman Islands
Vestnes Norway 44 I3
Vestre Jakobselv Norway 44 O1
Veststraumen Glacier Antarctica 223 X2
Vesturland constituency Iceland 44 [inset] B2
Vestvågøy i. Norway 44 K1
Vesuvio vol. Italy see Vesuvius
Vesuvio, Parco Nazionale del nat. park Italy 57 G8
Vesuvius vol. Italy 57 G8
also spelt Vesuvio
Ves'yegonsk Rus. Fed. 43 S3
Veszprém Hungary 49 O8
Vésztő Hungary 49 S9
Vet r. S. Africa 133 J4
Vetauua i. Fiji 145 H3
Veteli Fin. 44 M3
Veteran Canada 167 I4
Veternik Vojvodina, Srbija Yugo. 58 A3
Vetlanda Sweden 45 K4
Vetlefjorden Norway 45 I3
Vetluga Rus. Fed. 40 H4
Vetluga r. Rus. Fed. 40 H4
Vetluzhskiy Kostromskaya Oblast' Rus. Fed. 38 E4
formerly known as Golyshi
Vetluzhskiy Nizhegorodskaya Oblast' Rus. Fed. 40 H4
Vet'ma r. Rus. Fed. 43 O8
Vetovo Bulg. 58 H5
Vetralla Italy 56 E6
Vetren Bulg. 58 I6
formerly known as Zhitarovo
Vetrișoaia Romania 58 J2
Vetsikko Fin. 44 N1
Vettasjärvi Sweden 44 M2
Vettore, Monte mt. Italy 56 F6
Veurne Belgium 51 I1
also known as Furnes
Vevay U.S.A. 174 C4
Veveno r. Sudan 128 B3
Vevey Switz. 51 M6
Veydelevka Rus. Fed. 41 F6
Veyle r. France 51 K6
Veynes France 51 L8
Veyo U.S.A. 183 K4
Veys Iran 100 B4
Vėžaičiai Lith. 42 C6
Vézère r. France 50 G8
Vezhen mt. Bulg. 58 F6
Vezirköprü Turkey 106 C2
Via r. Liberia 124 C5
Viacha Bol. 200 C4
Viadana Italy 56 C4
Vialar Alg. see Tissemsilt
Viamao Brazil 203 B9
Viamonte Arg. 205 D9
Viana Angola 127 B7
Viana Espírito Santo Brazil 207 M7
Viana Maranhão Brazil 202 C2
Viana del Bollo Spain see Viana do Bolo
Viana do Alentejo Port. 54 D6
Viana do Bolo Spain 54 D2
also spelt Viana del Bollo
Viana do Castelo Port. 54 C3
Viana do Castelo admin. dist. Port. 54 C3
Vianden Lux. 51 M3
Viangchan Laos see Vientiane
Viangphoukha Laos 78 C3
Viaño Pequeno Spain 54 C1
Vianópolis Brazil 206 E3
Viar r. Spain 54 F7
Viareggio Italy 56 C5
Viaur r. France 51 H8
Viborg Denmark 45 J4
Viborg Rus. Fed. see Vyborg
Vibo Valentia Italy 57 I10
historically known as Hipponium
Vic Spain 55 N3
also spelt Vich
Vicam Mex. 184 C3
Vicdessos r. France 50 H10
Vicecomodoro Marambio research station Antarctica see Marambio
Vic-en-Bigorre France 50 G9
Vicente, Point U.S.A. 182 F8
Vicente Guerrero Mex. 184 A2
Vicenza Italy 56 D3
Vic-Fezensac France 50 G9
Vich Spain see Vic
Vichada dept Col. 198 D3
Vichada r. Col. 198 E3
Vichadero Uruguay 204 G3
Vichuga Rus. Fed. 40 G4
Vichy France 51 J6
Vicksburg AZ U.S.A. 183 K8
Vicksburg MI U.S.A. 172 H8
Vicksburg MS U.S.A. 175 B5
Vic-le-Comte France 51 J7
Vico, Lago di l. Italy 56 E6
Viçosa Alagoas Brazil 202 E4
Viçosa Minas Gerais Brazil 203 D7
Vic-sur-Cère France 51 I8
Victor, Mount Antarctica 223 C2
Victor Harbor Australia 146 C3
Victoria Arg. 204 E4
Victoria r. Australia 148 A2
Victoria state Australia 147 E4
Victoria Cameroon see Limbe
Victoria Canada 166 F5
Provincial capital of British Columbia.
Victoria La Araucania Chile 204 B5
Victoria Magallanes Chile 205 C9
Victoria Hond. 186 B4
Victoria Malaysia see Labuan
Victoria Malta 57 G12
also known as Rabat
Victoria Phil. 74 B3
Victoria Romania 58 I4
Victoria Romania 58 F3
Victoria Seychelles 218 K6
Capital of the Seychelles.
Victoria TX U.S.A. 179 C6
Victoria VA U.S.A. 176 G9
Victoria, Isla i. Chile 205 B7
Victoria, Lake Africa 128 B5
Largest lake in Africa and 3rd in the world.
africa [landscapes] 112–113
Victoria, Lake Australia 146 D3
Victoria, Mount Myanmar 78 A3
Victoria, Mount N.Z. 153 G10
Victoria, Mount P.N.G. 73 K8
Victoria and Albert Mountains Canada 165 L2
Victoria Falls waterfall Zambia/Zimbabwe 127 E9
africa [locations] 118–119
Victoria Falls Zimbabwe 131 E3
Victoria Falls National Park Zimbabwe 131 E3
also known as Mosi-oa-Tunya National Park
Victoria Fjord inlet Greenland 165 O1
Victoria Forest Park nature res. N.Z. 153 G9
Victoria Harbour sea chan. Hong Kong China see Hong Kong Harbour
Victoria Island Canada 165 H2
3rd largest island in North America and 9th in the world.
northamerica [landscapes] 156–157
Victoria Lake Canada 169 J3
Victoria Land coastal area Antarctica 223 K2
Victoria Peak hill Hong Kong China 87 [inset]
also known as Shan Teng
Victoria Range mts N.Z. 153 G10
Victoria River Australia 148 A2
Victoria River Downs Australia 148 A3
Victoria Valley N.Z. 152 H3
Victoriaville Canada 169 G4
Victoria West S. Africa 132 H8
Victorica Arg. 204 D5
Victorino Venez. 199 E4
Víctor Rosales Mex. 185 E4
Victorville U.S.A. 183 G7
Victory U.S.A. 177 I2
Victory Downs Australia 148 B5
Vicuña Chile 204 C3
Vicuña Mackenna Arg. 204 D4
Vidal, Isla i. Chile 205 B8
Vidalia U.S.A. 175 B6
Vidal Junction U.S.A. 183 J7
Vidamlya Belarus 42 E9
Videle Romania 58 G4
Viden mt. Bulg. 58 D6
Vidigueira Port. 54 D6
Vidima r. Bulg. 58 G6
Vidin Bulg. 58 D5
Vidisha India 96 C5
Vidlitsa Rus. Fed. 40 E3
Vidnoye Rus. Fed. 43 S6
formerly known as Rastorguyevo
Vidourle r. France 51 K9
Vidova Gora hill Croatia 56 I5
Vidsel Sweden 44 M2
Viduklė Lith. 42 D6
Viduša mts Bos.-Herz. 56 K6
Vidzemes Centrālā Augstiene hills Latvia 42 G5
Vidzy Belarus 42 H6
Viechtach Germany 49 J6
Viedgesville S. Africa 133 M8
Viedma Arg. 204 E6
Viedma, Lago l. Arg. 205 B8
southamerica [landscapes] 190–191
Viehberg mt. Austria 49 L7
Viejo, Cerro mt. Mex. 184 B2
Viekšniai Lith. 42 D5
Vielha Spain 55 L2
also spelt Viella
Viella Spain see Vielha
Vielsalm Belgium 51 L2
Vienenburg Germany 48 H4
Vienna Austria 49 N7
Capital of Austria. Also known as Wien; historically known as Vindobona.
Vienna GA U.S.A. 175 D5
Vienna IL U.S.A. 174 B4
Vienna MD U.S.A. 177 J7
Vienna MO U.S.A. 174 B4
Vienna WV U.S.A. 176 D6
Vienne France 51 K7
Vienne r. France 50 G5
Vientiane Laos 78 C4
Capital of Laos. Also spelt Viangchan.
Vieques i. Puerto Rico 187 G3
Vieremä Fin. 44 N3
Viersen Germany 48 D4
Vierwaldstätter See l. Switz. 51 O5
Vierzon France 51 I5
Viesca Mex. 185 E3
Viesīte Latvia 42 G5
Vieste Italy 56 I7
Viešvilės rezervatas nature res. Lith. 42 D6
Vietas Sweden 44 L2
Vietnam country Asia 78 D4
also spelt Viet Nam
asia [countries] 64–67
Viet Nam country Asia see Vietnam
Việt Tri Vietnam 78 D3
Vieux Comptoir, Lac du l. Canada 168 E2
Vieux-Fort Canada 169 J3
Vieux Fort St Lucia 187 H4
Vieux Poste, Pointe du pt Canada 169 I3
Vievis Lith. 42 F7
Vigala r. Estonia 42 F3
Vigan Phil. 74 B2
Vigeois France 50 H7
Vigevano Italy 56 A3
Vigia Brazil 202 B2
Vigia hill Port. 54 C7
Vigía Chico Mex. 185 I5
Viglio, Monte mt. Italy 56 F7
Vignemale mt. France 50 F10
Vignola Italy 56 D4
Vigny France 51 H3
Vigo Spain 54 C2
Vigo, Ría de est. Spain 54 C2
Vigors, Mount Australia 150 B4
Vihanti Fin. 44 N2
Vihari Pak. 101 H4
Vihiers France 50 F5
Vihorlat mt. Slovakia 49 T7
Vihterpalu r. Estonia 42 E2
Vihti Fin. 45 N3
Viiala Fin. 45 M3
Viipuri Rus. Fed. see Vyborg

Viirinkylä Fin. 44 N2
Viitasaari Fin. 44 N3
Viitka Estonia 42 I4
Vijainagar India 96 B3
Vijapur India 96 B5
Vijayadurg India 94 B2
Vijayanagar India see Hampi
Vijayapati India 94 C4
Vijayawada India 94 D2
also known as Bezwada
Vík Iceland 44 [inset] C3
Vik Norway 44 K2
Vikajärvi Fin. 44 N2
Vikarabad India 94 C2
Vikedal Norway 45 I4
Vikeke East Timor 75 C5
also known as Viqueque
Vikersund Norway 45 J4
Vikhra r. Rus. Fed. 43 M7
Vikhren mt. Bulg. 58 E7
Viking Canada 167 I4
Vikna i. Norway 44 J2
Vikos-Aoos nat. park Greece 59 B9
Vikøyri Norway 45 I3
Vikran Norway 44 L1
Viktorovka Kazakh. see Taranovskoye
Vila Spain 54 C3
Vila Vanuatu see Port Vila
Vila Alferes Chamusca Moz. see Guija
Vila Arriaga Angola see Bibala
Vila Bittencourt Brazil 198 D5
Vila Braga Brazil 199 G6
Vila Bugaço Angola see Camanongue
Vila Cabral Moz. see Lichinga
Vila Caldas Xavier Moz. see Muende
Vilacaya Bol. 200 D4
Vila Coutinho Moz. see Ulongue
Vila da Ponte Angola see Kuvango
Vila da Ribeira Brava Cape Verde 124 [inset]
Vila de Aljustrel Angola see Cangamba
Vila de Almoster Angola see Chiange
Vila de João Belo Moz. see Xai-Xai
Vila de Junqueiro Moz. see Gurué
Vila de Sal Rei Cape Verde 124 [inset]
Vila de Sena Moz. 131 G3
Vila de Trego Morais Moz. see Chókwè
Vila do Conde Port. 54 C3
Vila do Tarrafal Cape Verde 124 [inset]
Vila Flor Port. 54 D3
Vila Fontes Moz. see Caia
Vilafranca del Penedès Spain 55 M3
also spelt Villafranca del Penedès
Vila Franca de Xira Port. 54 C6
Vilagarcía de Arousa Spain 54 C2
also spelt Villagarcía de Arosa
Vila Gomes da Costa Moz. 131 G5
Vila Gouveia Moz. see Catandica
Vilaine r. France 50 D5
Viļaka Latvia 42 I4
Vilalba Spain 54 D1
Vila Luísa Moz. see Marracuene
Vila Marechal Carmona Angola see Uíge
Vila Miranda Moz. see Macaloge
Vila Murtinho Brazil 200 D2
Vilanandro, Tanjona pt Madag. 131 [inset] J3
formerly known as St-André, Cap
Vilanculos Moz. 131 G4
Viļāni Latvia 42 H5
Vila Nova Angola see Tchikala-Tcholohanga
Vila Nova da Fronteira Moz. 131 G3
Vilanova de Arousa Spain 54 C2
also spelt Villanueva de Arosa
Vila Nova de Foz Coa Port. 54 D3
Vila Nova de Gaia Port. 54 C3
Vila Nova de Ourém Port. 54 C5
Vila Nova de Paiva Port. 54 D4
Vila Nova do Seles Angola see Uku
Vilanova i la Geltrú Spain 55 M3
also spelt Villanueva-y-Geltrú
Vila Nova Sintra Cape Verde 124 [inset]
Vila Paiva de Andrada Moz. see Gorongosa
Vila Pery Moz. see Chimoio
Vila Pouca de Aguiar Port. 54 D3
Vila Real Port. 54 D3
Vila Real admin. dist. Port. 54 D3
Vila-real de los Infantes Spain 55 K5
also spelt Villarreal de los Infantes; formerly known as Villareal
Vilar Formoso Port. 54 E4
Vila Salazar Angola see N'dalatando
Vila Salazar Zimbabwe see Sango
Vila Teixeira de Sousa Angola see Luau
Vilavankod India 94 C4
Vila Velha Amapá Brazil 199 I4
Vila Velha Espírito Santo Brazil 203 D7
formerly known as Espírito Santo
Vila Velha de Ródão Port. 54 D5
Vila Verde Port. 54 C3
Vilcabamba, Cordillera mts Peru 200 B3
Vilcanota, Cordillera de mts Peru 200 C3
Vil'cheka, Zemlya i. Rus. Fed. 38 G1
English form Wilczek Land
Viled' r. Rus. Fed. 40 H3
Vileyka Belarus see Vilyeyka
Vil'gort Permskaya Oblast' Rus. Fed. 40 K3
Vil'gort Respublika Komi Rus. Fed. 40 I3
Vilhelmina Sweden 44 L2
Vilhena Brazil 201 E3
Viliya r. Belarus/Lith. 42 G7
Viljandi Estonia 42 G3
Viljoenskroon S. Africa 133 K4
Vilkaviškis Lith. 42 E7
Vilkija Lith. 42 E6
Vil'kitskogo, Ostrov i. Rus. Fed. 39 H2
Vil'kitskogo, Proliv strait Rus. Fed. 39 J2
Villa Abecia Bol. 200 D5
Villa Adriana tourist site Italy 56 E7
Villa Ahumada Mex. 184 D2
Villa Alba Arg. 204 E5
Villa Altagracia Dom. Rep. 187 F3
Villa Ana Arg. 204 F3
Villa Angela Arg. 204 E2
Villa Bella Bol. 200 D2
Villa Bens Morocco see Tarfaya
Villablino Spain 54 E2
Villacañas Spain 55 H5
Villacarrillo Spain 55 H6
Villach Austria 49 K9
also known as Beljak
Villacidro Sardegna Italy 57 A9
Villa Cisneros W. Sahara see Ad Dakhla
Villa Constitución Arg. 204 E4
Villa Constitución Mex. see Ciudad Constitución
Villa de Álvarez Mex. 184 E5
Villa de Cos Mex. 185 E4
Villa de Cura Venez. 199 E2
Villa de Guadalupe Mex. 185 H5
Villa del Rosario Arg. 204 E3
Villa del Totoral Arg. 204 D3
Villa Diego Arg. 204 E4
Villadiego Spain 54 G2
Villa Dolores Arg. 204 D3
Villadossola Italy 56 A2
Villa Flores Mex. 185 G5
Villafranca Spain 55 J2
Villafranca del Bierzo Spain 54 E2
Villafranca del Cid Spain 55 K4
Villafranca de los Barros Spain 54 E6
Villafranca del Penedès Spain see Vilafranca del Penedès
Villafranca di Verona Italy 56 C3
Villagarcía de Arosa Spain see Vilagarcía de Arousa
Villa Gesell Arg. 204 F5
Villagrán Mex. 185 F3
Villaguay Arg. 204 F3
Villa Guillermina Arg. 204 F3
Villa Hayes Para. 201 F6
Villahermosa Mex. 185 G5
Villa Hidalgo Mex. 181 E7
Villa Huidobro Arg. 204 D4
Villaines-la-Juhel France 50 F4
Villa Insurgentes Mex. 184 C3
Villa Iris Arg. 204 E5
Villajoyosa Spain 55 K6
Villa Juárez Mex. 181 E8
Villaldama Mex. 185 E3
Villálonga Arg. 204 E5
Villa María Arg. 204 E4
Villa María Grande Arg. 204 F3
Villa Martín Bol. 200 D5
Villamartín Spain 54 F8
Villa Matoque Arg. 204 E2
Villa Montes Bol. 201 E5
Villanova Monteleone Sardegna Italy 57 A8
Villa Nueva Arg. 204 E4
Villanueva Col. 198 C2
Villanueva Mex. 185 E4
Villanueva de Arosa Spain see Vilanova de Arousa
Villanueva de Córdoba Spain 54 G6
Villanueva de la Serena Spain 54 F6
Villanueva de los Castillejos Spain 54 D7
Villanueva de los Infantes Spain 55 I6
formerly known as Infantes
Villanueva-y-Geltrú Spain see Vilanova i la Geltrú
Villa Ocampo Arg. 204 F3
Villa Ocampo Mex. 184 D3
Villa O'Higgins Chile 205 B8
Villa Ojo de Agua Arg. 204 E3
Villa O. Pereyra Mex. see Villa Orestes Pereyra
Villa Orestes Pereyra Mex. 184 D3
short form Villa O. Pereyra
Villa Oropeza Bol. 200 D4
Villa Pesqueira Mex. 181 E7
Villaputzu Sardegna Italy 57 B9
Villar del Rey Spain 54 E5
Villareal Spain see Vila-real de los Infantes
Villarreal de los Infantes Spain see Vila-real de los Infantes
Villa Regina Arg. 204 D5
Villarrica Chile 204 B5
Villarrica Para. 201 F6
Villarrica, Lago l. Chile 204 B5
Villarrica, Parque Nacional nat. park Chile 204 C5
Villarrobledo Spain 55 I5
Villarrubia de los Ojos Spain 55 H5
Villas U.S.A. 177 K6
Villasalazar Zimbabwe see Sango
Villasana de Mena Spain 55 H1
Villa San Giovanni Italy 57 H10
Villa Sanjurjo Morocco see Al Hoceima
Villa San Martín Arg. 204 D3
Villasboas Uruguay 204 F4
Villa Serrano Bol. 201 D4
Villasimius Sardegna Italy 57 B9
Villa Unión Arg. 204 C3
Villa Unión Coahuila Mex. 185 E2
Villa Unión Durango Mex. 184 D4
Villa Unión Sinaloa Mex. 184 D4
Villa Valeria Arg. 204 D4
Villa Vasquez Dom. Rep. 187 F3
Villavicencio Col. 198 C3
Villaviciosa Spain 54 F1
Villaviciosa de Córdoba Spain 54 F6
Villa Viscarra Bol. 200 D4
Villazon Bol. 200 D5
Villedieu-les-Poêles France 50 E4
Villefranche-de-Lauragais France 50 H9
Villefranche-de-Rouergue France 51 I8
Villefranche-sur-Saône France 51 K7
Ville-Marie Canada see Montréal
Ville-Marie Canada 173 N3
Villemontel Canada 173 O2
Villemur-sur-Tarn France 50 H9
Villena Spain 55 K6
Villenauxe-la-Grande France 51 J4
Villeneuve-de-Marsan France 50 F9
Villeneuve-sur-Lot France 50 G8
Villeneuve-sur-Yonne France 51 J4
Ville Platte U.S.A. 179 D6
Villers-Bocage France 50 F3
Villers-Cotterêts France 51 J3
Villeta Para. 201 F6
Villeurbanne France 51 K7
Villicun, Sierra mts Arg. 204 C3
Villiers S. Africa 133 M4
Villingen Germany 48 F7
Villupuram India see Viluppuram
Vilna Canada 167 I4
Vilna Lith. see Vilnius
Vilnius Lith. 42 G7
Capital of Lithuania. Formerly known as Wilno; historically known as Vilna.
Vil'nyans'k Ukr. 41 E7
also spelt Vol'nyansk; formerly known as Chervonoarmeyskoye or Sofiyevka
Vilppula Fin. 45 N3
Vils r. Germany 48 I6
Vils r. Germany 49 K7
Vilsandi i. Estonia 42 C3
Vilsandi nature res. Estonia 42 C3
Vilsbiburg Germany 49 J7
Vilshofen Germany 49 K7
Viluppuram India 94 C4
also spelt Villupuram
Vilvoorde Belgium 51 K2
Vilyeyka Belarus 42 H7
also spelt Vileyka
Vilyeyskaye, Vozyera l. Belarus 42 I7
Vilyuy r. Rus. Fed. 39 M3
Vilyuyskoye Vodokhranilishche resr Rus. Fed. 39 L3
Vimbe mt. Zambia 127 F8
Vimercate Italy 56 B3
Vimianzo Spain 54 B1
Vimioso Port. 54 E3
Vimmerby Sweden 45 K4
Vimoutiers France 50 G4
Vimpeli Fin. 44 M3
Vimperk Czech Rep. 49 K6
Vina r. Cameroon 125 I5
also spelt Wina
Vina U.S.A. 182 B2
Viña del Mar Chile 204 C4
Vinalhaven U.S.A. 177 Q1
Vinalopó r. Spain 55 K6
Vinanivao Madag. 131 [inset] K2
Vinaròs Spain 55 L4
also spelt Vinaroz
Vinaroz Spain see Vinaròs
Vincelotte, Lac l. Canada 169 F2
Vincennes U.S.A. 174 C4
Vincennes Bay Antarctica 223 H2
Vinces r. Ecuador 198 B5
Vinchina Arg. 204 C3
Vinchos Peru 200 B3
Vindelälven r. Sweden 44 L3
Vindelfjällens naturreservat nature res. Sweden 44 K2
Vindeln Sweden 44 L2
Vindhya Range hills India 96 B5
Vindobona Austria see Vienna
Vineland U.S.A. 177 J6
Vinga Romania 58 C2
Vingăi, Câmpia plain Romania 58 C2
Vingåker Sweden 45 K4
Vinh Vietnam 78 D4
Vinhais Port. 54 E3
Vinh Long Vietnam 79 D6
Vinh Thuc, Đao i. Vietnam 78 D3
Vinh Yên Vietnam 78 D3
Vinica Macedonia 58 D7
Vinita U.S.A. 178 D4
Vinjhan India 96 A5
Vinju Mare Romania see Vânju Mare
Vinkovci Croatia 56 K3
Vinland i. Canada see Newfoundland
Vinni Estonia 42 H2
Vinnitsa Ukr. see Vinnytsya
Vinnitsy Rus. Fed. 43 P1
Vinnytsya Ukr. 41 D6
also spelt Vinnitsa
Vinogradov Rus. Fed. 43 T6
Vinson Massif mt. Antarctica 222 S1
Highest mountain in Antarctica.
antarctica [features] 212–213
Vinstra Norway 45 J3
Vintar Phil. 74 B2
Vinton U.S.A. 174 A3
Vinukonda India 94 C2
Vinza Congo 126 B5
Viola CA U.S.A. 182 C1
Viola IL U.S.A. 172 C9
Violeta Cuba see Primero de Enero
Violet Valley Aboriginal Reserve Australia 150 D3
Vioolsdrif S. Africa 132 B5
Viphya Mountains Malawi 129 B8
Vipiteno Italy 56 D2
Viqueque East Timor see Vikeke
Vir i. Croatia 56 H4
Virac Phil. 74 C3
Virac Point Phil. 74 C3
Viramgam India 96 B5
Viranşehir Turkey 107 D3
Virarajendrapet India 94 B3
Virawah Pak. 101 G5
Virawlya Belarus 43 K6
Vircava r. Latvia/Lith. 42 E5
Virchow, Mount hill Australia 150 B4
Virdáánjarga Fin. see Virtaniemi
Virden Canada 167 K5
Vire France 50 F4
Virei Angola 127 B8
Virful Highiş hill Romania 58 C2
Virgenes, Cabo c. Arg. 205 C9
Virgilina U.S.A. 176 G9
Virgin r. U.S.A. 183 J5
Virginatown Canada 173 N2
Virgin Gorda i. Virgin Is (U.K.) 187 G3
Virginia S. Africa 133 K5
Virginia U.S.A. 174 A2
Virginia state U.S.A. 176 G8
Virginia Beach U.S.A. 177 J9
Virginia City MT U.S.A. 180 E3
Virginia City NV U.S.A. 182 E2
Virginia Falls Canada 166 E2
Virgin Islands (U.K.) terr. West Indies 187 G3
United Kingdom Overseas Territory.
oceania [countries] 138–139
Virgin Islands (U.S.A.) terr. West Indies 187 G3
United States Unincorporated Territory.
oceania [countries] 138–139
Virgin Mountains U.S.A. 183 J5
Virginópolis Brazil 203 D6
Virje Croatia 56 J2
Virkkala Fin. 45 N3
Virmasvesi l. Fin. 44 N3
Virôchey Cambodia 79 D5
Virolahti Fin. 45 N3
Viroqua U.S.A. 172 C7
Virovitica Croatia 56 J3
Virpe Latvia 42 D4
Virrat Fin. 44 M3
Virserum Sweden 45 K4
Virtaniemi Fin. 44 O1
also known as Virdáánjarga
Virton Belgium 51 L3
Virtsu Estonia 42 E3
Virú Peru 200 A2
Virudunagar India 94 C4
Virunga, Parc National des nat. park Dem. Rep. Congo 126 F5
formerly known as Albert, Parc National
Virvytė r. Lith. 42 D5
Vis Croatia 56 I5
also known as Issa or Lissa
Vis i. Croatia 56 I5
Visaginas Lith. 42 H6
formerly known as Sniečkus
Visakhapatnam India see Vishakhapatnam
Visalia U.S.A. 182 E5
Visani Romania 58 I3
Visapur India 94 B2
Visavadar India 96 A5
Visayan Sea Phil. 74 B4
Visby Sweden 45 L4
Visconde do Rio Branco Brazil 207 K8
Viscount Melville Sound sea chan. Canada 165 H2
Vise, Ostrov i. Rus. Fed. 39 H2
Višegrad Bos.-Herz. 56 L5
Viseu Brazil 202 C2
Viseu Port. 54 D4
Viseu admin. dist. Port. 54 D4
Vishakhapatnam India 95 D2
also spelt Visakhapatnam; formerly spelt Vizagapatam
Vishegrad hill Bulg. 58 H7
Vishera r. Rus. Fed. 40 J3
Vishera r. Rus. Fed. 40 K3
Vishera r. Rus. Fed. 43 M3
Vishnevka Kazakh. 103 H2
Vishnyeva Belarus 42 H7
Visikums Latvia 42 I4
Visina Romania 58 G4
Viški Latvia 42 I5
Viški Kanal sea chan. Croatia 56 I5
Visnagar India 96 B5
Viso, Monte mt. Italy 51 N8
Viso del Marqués Spain 55 H6
Visoko Bos.-Herz. 56 K5
Visp Switz. 51 N6
Visrivier S. Africa 133 J8
Vissannapeta India 94 D2
Vista U.S.A. 183 G8
Vista Alegre Amazonas Brazil 199 D4
Vista Alegre Amazonas Brazil 199 D6
Vista Alegre Amazonas Brazil 199 F6
Vista Alegre Mato Grosso do Sul Brazil 201 F4
Vista Alegre Roraima Brazil 199 F4
Vista Lake U.S.A. 182 E6
Vistonida, Limni lag. Greece 58 G7
Vistula r. Poland 49 P1
also spelt Wisła
Vištytis Lith. 42 D7
Vit r. Bulg. 58 F5
Vita r. Col. 198 E3
Vitao mt. Yugo. 56 K5
Vitebsk Belarus see Vitsyebsk
Vitebskaya Oblast' admin. div. Belarus see Vitsyebskaya Voblasts'
Vitebsk Oblast admin. div. Belarus see Vitsyebskaya Voblasts'
Viterbo Italy 56 E6
Vitez Bos.-Herz. 56 J4
Vitez pass Bos.-Herz. 56 K5
Vitigudino Spain 54 E3
Viti Levu i. Fiji 145 G3
Vitim r. Rus. Fed. 81 I1
Vitimskoye Ploskogor'ye plat. Rus. Fed. 81 I2
Vitina Kosovo, Srbija Yugo. 58 C6
Vitomirica Kosovo, Srbija Yugo. 58 B6
Vitor Peru 200 C4
Vitor r. Peru 200 B4
Vitória Espírito Santo Brazil 203 D7
Vitória Pará Brazil 199 H5
Vitoria Spain see Vitoria-Gasteiz
Vitória da Conquista Brazil 202 D5
Vitoria-Gasteiz Spain 55 I2
also known as Gasteiz or Vitoria
Vitosha nat. park Bulg. 58 E6
Vitré France 50 E4
Vitrolles France 51 L9
Vitry-en-Artois France 51 I2
Vitry-le-François France 51 K4
Vitsyebsk Belarus 43 L6
English form Vitebsk
Vitsyebskaya Voblasts' admin. div. Belarus 43 J6
English form Vitebsk Oblast; also known as Vitebskaya Oblast'
Vittangi Sweden 44 M2
also known as Vazáš
Vitteaux France 51 K5
Vittel France 51 L4
Vittoria Sicilia Italy 57 G12
Vittorio Veneto Italy 56 E3
Vivarais, Monts du mts France 51 K8
Viveiro Spain 54 D1
also spelt Vivero
Vivero Spain see Viveiro
Vivian U.S.A. 179 D5
Vivo S. Africa 131 F4
Vivonne France 50 G6
Vivoratá Arg. 204 F5
Vivorillo, Cayos is Hond. 186 C4
Vizagapatam India see Vishakhapatnam
Vizcaíno Mex. 181 D8
Vizcaíno, Desierto de des. Mex. 184 B3
Vizcaíno, Sierra mts Mex. 184 B3
Vize Turkey 106 A2
Vizhas r. Rus. Fed. 40 H2
Vizianagaram India 95 D2
Vizinga Rus. Fed. 40 I3
Viziru Romania 58 I3
Vizzini Sicilia Italy 57 G11
V. J. José Perez Bol. 200 C3
Vjosë r. Albania 59 A8
Vlaardingen Neth. 48 B4
Vlădeasa, Vârful mt. Romania 58 D2
Vladičin Han Srbija Yugo. 58 D6
Vladikavkaz Rus. Fed. 41 H8
also known as Dzaudzhikau; formerly known as Ordzhonikidze
Vladimir Rus. Fed. 90 D3
Vladimir Rus. Fed. 43 V5
historically known as Lodomeria
Vladimiro-Aleksandrovskoye Rus. Fed. 82 D4
Vladimir Oblast admin. div. Rus. Fed. see Vladimirskaya Oblast'
Vladimirovka Kazakh. 103 F1
formerly known as Vladimirovskiy
Vladimirovo Bulg. 58 E5
Vladimirovskiy Kazakh. see Vladimirovka
Vladimirskaya Oblast' admin. div. Rus. Fed. 43 V6
English form Vladimir Oblast
Vladimirskiy Tupik Rus. Fed. 43 O6
Vladimir-Volynskiy Ukr. see Volodymyr-Volyns'kyy
Vladivostok Rus. Fed. 82 C4
Vladychnoye Rus. Fed. 43 U3
Vlăhita Romania 58 G2
Vlajna mt. Yugo. 58 C6
Vlasenica Bos.-Herz. 56 K4
Vlašić Planina mts Yugo. 58 A4
Vlašim Czech Rep. 49 L6
Vlasotince Srbija Yugo. 58 D6
Vlasovo Rus. Fed. 43 U6
Vlas'yevo Rus. Fed. 82 F1
Vlazovichi Rus. Fed. 43 N8
Vleesbaai b. S. Africa 132 F11
Vlieland i. Neth. 48 B2
Vlissingen Neth. 48 A4
historically known as Flushing
Vlorë Albania 58 A8
also known as Aulon or Valona; historically known as Avlona
Vlorës, Gjiri i b. Albania 58 A8
Vlotslavsk Poland see Włocławek
Vltava r. Czech Rep. 49 L5
Vnina r. Rus. Fed. 43 R2
Vöcklabruck Austria 49 K7
Vodice Croatia 56 H5
Vodlozero, Ozero l. Rus. Fed. 40 F3
Vodňany Czech Rep. 49 L6
Vodnjan Croatia 56 F4
Vodopyanovo Rus. Fed. see Donskoye
Voël r. S. Africa 133 J9
Vogan Togo 125 F5
Vogelkop Peninsula Indon. see Doberai, Jazirah
Vogelsberg hills Germany 48 F5
Voghera Italy 56 B4
Vognill Norway 44 J3
Vogošća Bos.-Herz. 56 K5
Vohburg an der Donau Germany 48 I7
Vohémar Madag. see Iharaña
Vohibinany Madag. see Ampasimanolotra
Vohilava Fianarantsoa Madag. 131 [inset] J4
Vohilava Fianarantsoa Madag. 131 [inset] K4
Vohimarina Madag. see Iharaña
Vohimena, Tanjona c. Madag. 131 [inset] J5
formerly known as Ste-Marie, Cap
Vohipeno Madag. 131 [inset] J4
Võhma Estonia 42 G3
Voi Kenya 128 C5
Voikoski Fin. 45 N3
Voineasa Romania 58 E3
Voineşti Romania 58 I1
Voinjama Liberia 124 C4
Voin Pervyy Rus. Fed. 43 R8
Voiron France 51 L7
Voitsberg Austria 49 M8
Vojvodina prov. Yugo. 58 A3
Voka Estonia 42 I2
Vokhma Rus. Fed. 40 H4
Vokhtoga Rus. Fed. 43 V3
Voknavolok Rus. Fed. 44 O2
Voko Cameroon 125 I4
Vol' r. Rus. Fed. 40 J3
Volaterrae Italy see Volterra
Volcán Arg. 200 D5
Volcán, Cerro vol. Bol. 200 D5
Volcán Barú, Parque Nacional nat. park Panama 186 C5
Volcano Bay Japan see Uchiura-wan
Volcano Islands N. Pacific Ocean 220 D4
Part of Japan. Also known as Kazan-rettō.
Volcans d'Auvergne, Parc Naturel Régional des nature res. France 51 I7
Volchas r. Belarus 43 M8
Volchikha Rus. Fed. 103 J1
Volchina r. Rus. Fed. 43 Q4
Volchiy Nos, Mys pt Rus. Fed. 43 N1
Volda Norway 44 I3
Vol'dino Rus. Fed. 40 J3
Volens U.S.A. 176 F9
Volga Rus. Fed. 43 T4
Volga r. Rus. Fed. 43 Q5
Longest river in Europe.
europe [landscapes] 30–31
Volga r. U.S.A. 172 B8
Volga Upland hills Rus. Fed. see Privolzhskaya Vozvyshennost'
Volgodonsk Rus. Fed. 41 G7
Volgograd Rus. Fed. 41 H6
formerly known as Stalingrad; historically known as Tsaritsyn
Volgograd Oblast admin. div. Rus. Fed. see Volgogradskaya Oblast'
Volgogradskaya Oblast' admin. div. Rus. Fed. 41 H6
English form Volgograd Oblast; formerly known as Stalingradskaya Oblast
Volgogradskoye Vodokhranilishche resr Rus. Fed. 41 H6
Volissos Greece 59 G10
Völkermarkt Austria 49 L9
Volkhov Rus. Fed. 43 N2
Volkhov r. Rus. Fed. 43 N1
Volkhovskaya Guba b. Rus. Fed. 43 N1
Volkhovskiy Rus. Fed. 43 M3
Völklingen Germany 48 D6
Volkovichi Belarus see Vawkavichy
Volkovo Rus. Fed. 43 L7
Volkovysk Belarus see Vawkavysk
Volkovyskiye Vysoty hills Belarus see Vawkavyskaye Wzvyshsha
Volksrust S. Africa 133 N4
Vol'no-Nadezhdinskoye Rus. Fed. 82 C4
Volnovakha Ukr. 41 F7
Vol'nyansk Ukr. see Vil'nyans'k
Volochanka Rus. Fed. 39 J2
Volochayevka-Vtoraya Rus. Fed. 82 D2
Volochisk Ukr. see Volochys'k
Volochys'k Ukr. 41 C6
also spelt Volochisk
Volodars'ke Ukr. 41 F7
Volodarskiy Rus. Fed. 102 B3
Volodarskoye Kazakh. see Saumalkol'
Volodymyr-Volyns'kyy Ukr. 41 C6
also spelt Vladimir-Volynskiy
Vologda Rus. Fed. 43 U2
Vologda r. Rus. Fed. 43 V2
Vologda Oblast admin. div. Rus. Fed. see Vologodskaya Oblast'
Vologodskaya Oblast' admin. div. Rus. Fed. 43 T1
English form Vologda Oblast
Volokolamsk Rus. Fed. 43 Q5
Volokonovka Rus. Fed. 41 F6
Volokoslavinskoye Rus. Fed. 43 T2
Volop S. Africa 132 G5
Volos Greece 59 D9
Voloshka Rus. Fed. 40 G3
Volosovo Rus. Fed. 43 K2
Volot Rus. Fed. 43 L4
Volovo Lipetskaya Oblast' Rus. Fed. 43 S9
Volovo Tul'skaya Oblast' Rus. Fed. 43 T8
Voloye Rus. Fed. 43 P7
Volozhin Belarus see Valozhyn
Volsini, Monti mts Italy 56 D6
Volsinii Italy see Orvieto
Vol'sk Rus. Fed. 102 A1
Volstruisleegte S. Africa 132 H10
Volstruispoort pass S. Africa 132 G7
Volta admin. reg. Ghana 125 F5
Volta r. Ghana 125 F5
Volta Blanche watercourse Burkina/Ghana see White Volta
Volta, Lake resr Ghana 125 F5
5th largest lake in Africa.
africa [landscapes] 112–113
Voltaire, Cape Australia 150 D2
Volta Noire r. Africa see Black Volta
Volta Redonda Brazil 203 C7
Volterra Italy 56 C5
historically known as Volaterrae
Voltoya r. Spain 54 G3
Volturino, Monte mt. Italy 57 H8
Volturno r. Italy 56 F7
Volubilis tourist site Morocco 122 D2
Voluntari Romania 58 H4
Volunteer Point Falkland Is 205 F8
Volvi, Limni l. Greece 58 E8
Vol'ya r. Rus. Fed. 40 L3
Volzhsk Rus. Fed. 40 I5
Volzhskiy Samarskaya Oblast' Rus. Fed. 41 I5
formerly known as Bol'shaya Tsarevshchina
Volzhskiy Volgogradskaya Oblast' Rus. Fed. 41 H6
Vomano r. Italy 56 G6
Vondanka Rus. Fed. 40 H4
Vondrozo Madag. 131 [inset] J4
Vonga Rus. Fed. 40 G2
Vonitsa Greece 59 B10
Võnnu Estonia 42 I3
Vonozero Rus. Fed. 43 P1
Vontimitta India 94 C3
Voorheesville U.S.A. 177 L3
Voosi kurk sea chan. Estonia 42 E2
Vop' r. Rus. Fed. 43 N7
Vopnafjörður Iceland 44 [inset] D2
Vopnafjörður b. Iceland 44 [inset] D2
Vörå Fin. 44 M3
also spelt Vöyri
Voran' Belarus 43 J6
Voranava Belarus 42 G7
Vordingborg Denmark 45 J5
Vordorf Germany 48 H3
Vorë Albania 58 A7
Voreio Aigaio admin. reg. Greece 59 G9
English form Northern Aegean
Voreioi Sporades is Greece 59 E9
English form Northern Sporades; also spelt Vorioi Sporádhes
Voreios Evvoïkos Kolpos sea chan. Greece 59 E10
Vorga Rus. Fed. 43 N8
Vorgashor Rus. Fed. 40 L2
Voriai Sporádhes is Greece see Voreioi Sporades
Vorijing mt. India 97 G3
Vorkuta Rus. Fed. 40 M2
Vormedalsheia park Norway 45 I4
Vormsi i. Estonia 42 E2
Vorob'yevka Lipetskaya Oblast' Rus. Fed. 43 U9
Vorob'yevka Voronezhskaya Oblast' Rus. Fed. 41 G6
Vorob"yivka Ukr. 43 O9
Vorogovo Rus. Fed. 39 I3
Vorona r. Rus. Fed. 41 G5
Voronezh Rus. Fed. 41 F6
Voronezh r. Rus. Fed. 43 U9
Voronezh Oblast admin. div. Rus. Fed. see Voronezhskaya Oblast'
Voronezhskaya Oblast' admin. div. Rus. Fed. 41 G6
English form Voronezh Oblast
Voronov, Mys pt Rus. Fed. 40 G2
Voronov, Mys pt Rus. Fed. 43 N1
Voronovo Rus. Fed. 43 S6
Vorontsovka Kazakh. 103 J2
Vorontsovo Rus. Fed. 43 J4
Vorontsovo-Aleksandrovskoye Rus. Fed. see Zelenokumsk
Voron'ye Rus. Fed. 40 G4
Voroshilov Rus. Fed. see Ussuriysk
Voroshilovgrad Ukr. see Luhans'k
Voroshilovsk Rus. Fed. see Stavropol'
Voroshilovsk Ukr. see Alchevs'k
Vorot'kovo Rus. Fed. 43 O6
Vorotynets Rus. Fed. 40 H4
Vorotynsk Rus. Fed. 43 R7
Vorozhba Ukr. 41 E6
Vorpommersche Boddenlandschaft, Nationalpark nat. park Germany 49 J1
Vorposten Peak Antarctica 223 B2
Vorskla r. Rus. Fed. 41 E6
Vorstershoop S. Africa 132 H2
Vorterkaka Nunatak mt. Antarctica 223 B2
Võrtsjärv l. Estonia 42 G3
Võru Estonia 42 I4
Vorukh Tajik. 101 G2
Vorya r. Rus. Fed. 43 P7
Vosburg S. Africa 132 G7
Vose Tajik. 101 G2
formerly known as Aral
Vosges mts France 51 M5
Vosges du Nord, Parc Naturel Régional des nature res. France 51 N4
Voshchazhnikovo Rus. Fed. 43 U4
Voskresensk Rus. Fed. 43 T6
Voskresenskoye Lipetskaya Oblast' Rus. Fed. 43 T8
Voskresenskoye Respublika Bashkortostan Rus. Fed. 102 D1
Voskresenskoye Tul'skaya Oblast' Rus. Fed. 43 S7
Voskresenskoye Vologod. Obl. Rus. Fed. 43 S2
Voskresenskoye Yaroslavskaya Oblast' Rus. Fed. 43 S4
Voss Norway 45 I3
Vostochnaya Litsa Rus. Fed. 40 F1
Vostochno-Kazakhstanskaya Oblast' admin. div. Kazakh. see Vostochnyy Kazakhstan
Vostochno-Kounradskiy Kazakh. see Shygys Konyrat
Vostochno-Sakhalinskiy Gory mts Rus. Fed. 82 F2
Vostochno-Sibirskoye More sea Rus. Fed. see East Siberian Sea
Vostochnyy Rus. Fed. 40 J4
Vostochnyy Chink Ustyurta esc. Uzbek. 102 D4
Vostochnyy Kazakhstan admin. div. Kazakh. 103 I2
English form East Kazakhstan Oblast; also known as Shyghys Qazaqstan Oblysy; long form Vostochno-Kazakhstanskaya Oblast'
Vostochnyy Sayan mts Rus. Fed. 80 E2
English form Eastern Sayan Mountains
Vostok research station Antarctica
Lowest recorded screen temperature in the world.
world [climate and weather] 16–17
Vostok Rus. Fed. 82 D3
Vostok Rus. Fed. see Neftegorsk
Vostok Island Kiribati 221 H6
Vostretsovo Rus. Fed. 82 D3
Vostroye Rus. Fed. 40 H3
Võsu Estonia 42 G2
Votkinsk Rus. Fed. 40 J4
Votkinskoye Vodokhranilishche resr Rus. Fed. 40 J4
Votorantim Brazil 206 F10
Votrya r. Rus. Fed. 43 N6
Votuporanga Brazil 206 D7
Voudi, Akra pt Greece 59 J12
Vouga Angola see Cunhinga
Vouga r. Port. 54 C4
Vouillé France 50 G6
Voula Greece 59 E11
Vourinos mt. Greece 59 C8
Vouziers France 51 K3
Voves France 50 H4
Vovodo r. Cent. Afr. Rep. 126 E3
Voxna Sweden 45 K3
Voxnan r. Sweden 45 L3
Voya r. Rus. Fed. 40 I4
Voyageurs National Park U.S.A. 174 A1
Voykar r. Rus. Fed. 40 M2
Voynitsa Rus. Fed. 44 O2
Vöyri Fin. see Vörå
Voyvozh Respublika Komi Rus. Fed. 40 J2
Voyvozh Respublika Komi Rus. Fed. 40 J3
Vozdvizhenskoye Moskovskaya Oblast' Rus. Fed. 43 R5
Vozdvizhenskoye Moskovskaya Oblast' Rus. Fed. 43 T5
Vozha r. Rus. Fed. 43 U7
Vozhayel' Rus. Fed. 40 I3
Vozhd' Proletariata Rus. Fed. 43 U6
Vozhe, Ozero l. Rus. Fed. 43 T1
Vozhega Rus. Fed. 43 V1
Vozhega r. Rus. Fed. 43 U1
Vozhgora Rus. Fed. 40 I2
Voznesenka Kazakh. 103 G1
Voznesens'k Ukr. 41 D7
Voznesen'ye Rus. Fed. 43 Q1
Vozrovdenye Uzbek. 102 D3
Vozrozhdeniya, Ostrov i. Uzbek. 102 D3
also known as Wozrojdeniye Oroli
Vozzhayevka Rus. Fed. 82 C2
Vrå Denmark 45 J4
Vrabevo Bulg. 58 F6
Vrachionas hill Greece 59 B11
also known as Vrakhiónas Óros
Vrachnaiika Greece 59 C10
also spelt Vrakhnaiika
Vrådal Norway 45 J4
Vrakhiónas Óros hill Greece see Vrachionas
Vrakhnaiika Greece see Vrachnaiika
Vran mt. Bos.-Herz. 56 J5
Vrana r. Bulg. 58 H5
Vrangel' Rus. Fed. 82 D4
Vrangelya, Mys pt Rus. Fed. 82 E1
Vrangelya, Ostrov i. Rus. Fed. see Wrangel Island
Vranjak Bos.-Herz. 56 K4
Vranje Srbija Yugo. 58 C6
Vranjska Banja Srbija Yugo. 58 D6
Vranov, Vodní nádrž resr Czech Rep. 49 M7
Vranov nad Topľou Slovakia 49 S7
Vrapčište Macedonia 58 B7
Vrasidas, Akra pt Greece 58 F8
Vratnik pass Bulg. 58 H6
Vratsa Bulg. 58 E5
Vrbanja r. Bos.-Herz. 56 J4
Vrbas r. Bos.-Herz. 56 J3
Vrbas Vojvodina, Srbija Yugo. 58 A3
formerly known as Titov Vrbas
Vrbno pod Pradědem Czech Rep. 49 O5
Vrbovec Croatia 56 I3
Vrbovsko Croatia 56 H3
Vrchlabí Czech Rep. 49 M5
Vrede S. Africa 133 N4
Vredefort S. Africa 133 L3
Vredenburg S. Africa 132 B9
Vredendal S. Africa 132 C8
Vredeshoop Namibia 132 D4
Vreed-en-Hoop Guyana 199 G3
Vrela Kosovo, Srbija Yugo. 58 B6
Vrhnika Slovenia 56 G3
Vriddhachalam India 94 C4
Vrigstad Sweden 45 K4
Vrindavan India 89 B7
Vrnjačka Banja Srbija Yugo. 58 B5
Vrolijkheid Nature Reserve S. Africa 132 D10
Vrrin Albania 58 A7
Vršac Vojvodina, Srbija Yugo. 58 C3
also known as Versec
Vryburg S. Africa 133 I3
Vryheid S. Africa 133 O4
Vsetín Czech Rep. 49 O6
Vsevolozhsk Rus. Fed. 43 L1
Vskhody Rus. Fed. 43 P7
Vtáčnik mt. Slovakia 49 P7
Vtáčnik mts Slovakia 49 P7
Vŭcha r. Bulg. 58 F7
Vučica r. Croatia 56 K3
Vučitrn Kosovo, Srbija Yugo. 58 B6
Vučje Srbija Yugo. 58 C6
Vuka r. Croatia 56 K3
Vukovar Croatia 56 L3
Vuktyl' Rus. Fed. 40 K3
Vukuzakhe S. Africa 133 N4
Vulcan Canada 167 H5
Vulcan Romania 58 E3
Vulcăneşti Moldova 58 J3
formerly spelt Vulkaneshty
Vulcan Island P.N.G. see Manam Island
Vulcano, Isola i. Isole Lipari Italy 57 G10
Vŭlchedrŭm Bulg. 58 E5
Vŭlchidol Bulg. 58 I5
Vulkaneshty Moldova see Vulcăneşti
Vulture Mountains U.S.A. 183 K8
Vung Dung Quat b. Vietnam 79 E5

Vung Tau Vietnam 79 D6
 formerly known as St Jacques, Cap
Vuohijärvi Fin. 42 H1
Vuohijärvi l. Fin. 45 N3
Vuokatti Fin. 44 O2
Vuoksa r. Rus. Fed. 43 L1
Vuoksa, Ozero l. Rus. Fed. 43 K1
Vuolijoki Fin. 44 N2
Vuollerim Sweden 44 M2
Vuolvojaure l. Sweden 44 L2
Vuotso Fin. 44 N1
Vürbitsa Bulg. 58 F1
Vurpär Romania 58 I3
Vürshets Bulg. 58 E5
Vustsye Belarus 42 I6
Vuyyuru India 94 D2
Vuzlove Ukr. 49 I7
Vuzlyanka l. Belarus 42 H7
Vvedenka Kazakh. 103 E1
Vwaza Game Reserve nature res. Malawi
 129 D7
Vyalikiya Bortniki Belarus 43 K8
Vyal'ye, Ozero l. Rus. Fed. 43 L2
Vyara India 96 B5
Vyarechcha Belarus 43 L6
Vyarkhovichy Belarus 42 E9
Vyarkhowye Belarus see Ruba
Vyatchyn Belarus 42 J9
Vyatka r. Rus. Fed. see Kirov
Vyatka r. Rus. Fed. 40 I4
Vyatskiye Polyany Rus. Fed. 40 I4
Vyatskoye Rus. Fed. 43 V4
Vyaz Rus. Fed. 43 K5
Vyazemskiy Rus. Fed. 82 D3
Vyaz'ma Rus. Fed. 43 P6
Vyaz'ma r. Rus. Fed. 43 O6
Vyazniki Rus. Fed. 40 G4
Vyazovka Rus. Fed. 102 A1
Vyazovka Rus. Fed. 41 G6
Vyazovo Rus. Fed. 43 U5
Vyborg Rus. Fed. 43 J1
 formerly known as Viipuri; formerly spelt
 Viborg
Vyborgskiy Zaliv b. Rus. Fed. 43 J1
Vychegda r. Rus. Fed. 40 H3
Vychegodskiy Rus. Fed. 40 H3
Vydrino Rus. Fed. 85 E1
Vyeramyeyki Belarus 43 M8
Vyerkhnyadzvinsk Belarus 42 I6
 formerly known as Drissa
Vyetka Belarus 43 M9
Vyetryna Belarus 42 J6
Vygonichi Rus. Fed. 43 P8
Vygozero, Ozero l. Rus. Fed. 40 E3
Vyksa Rus. Fed. 40 G5
Vylkove Ukr. 41 D7
Vym' r. Rus. Fed. 40 H3
Vypolzovo Rus. Fed. 43 Q4
Vyritsa Rus. Fed. 43 L2
Vyselki Rus. Fed. 41 F7
Vyshgorod Rus. Fed. 43 V7
Vyshhorod Ukr. 41 D6
Vyshkov Rus. Fed. 43 M9
Vyshkovo Rus. Fed. 49 J1
Vyshnevolotskaya Gryada ridge Rus. Fed.
 43 P5
Vyshnevolotskoye Vodokhranilishche resr
 Rus. Fed. 43 P4
Vyshney-Ol'shanoye Rus. Fed. 43 S9
Vyshniy-Volochek Rus. Fed. 43 P4
Vyskod' Rus. Fed. 43 L4
Vyškov Czech Rep. 49 O6
Vysoká Myto Czech Rep. 49 N6
Vysokinichi Rus. Fed. 43 R7
Vysokogorniy Rus. Fed. 82 E2
 formerly known as Muli
Vysokovsk Rus. Fed. 43 T4
Vysokovsk Rus. Fed. 43 R5
Vysokoye Belarus see Vysokaye
Vysokoye Rus. Fed. 43 P5
Vysotsk Rus. Fed. 43 J1
Vystupovychi Ukr. 41 D6
Vytebet' r. Rus. Fed. 43 Q8
Vytegra Rus. Fed. 40 F3
Vyvenka Rus. Fed. 39 Q3
Vyya r. Rus. Fed. 40 H3
Vyžuona r. Lith. 42 G6

↓ W

Wa Ghana 124 E4
Waajid Somalia 128 E3
Waal r. Neth. 48 B4
Waalwijk Neth. 48 C4
Waanyi/Garawa Aboriginal Land res.
 Australia 148 C2
Waat Sudan 128 B2
Wabag P.N.G. 73 J8
Wabakimi Lake Canada 168 B3
Wabal well Oman 105 G3
Wabamun Lake Canada 167 H4
Wabasca r. Canada 167 H3
Wabasca-Desmarais Canada 167 H4

Wabash IN U.S.A. 174 C3
Wabash OH U.S.A. 173 I10
Wabash r. U.S.A. 174 B4
Wabasha U.S.A. 174 A2
Wabassi r. Canada 168 C2
Wabatongushi Lake Canada 173 I2
Wabē Gestro r. Eth. 128 D3
Wabē Mena r. Eth. 128 D3
Wabeno U.S.A. 172 E5
Wabrah well Saudi Arabia 105 D2
Wabu China 87 F1
Wabuk Point Canada 168 C2
Wabush Canada 169 H2
Wabush Lake Canada 169 H2
Waccamaw r. U.S.A. 175 E5
Waccamaw, Lake U.S.A. 175 E5
Waccasassa Bay U.S.A. 175 D6
Wachapreague U.S.A. 177 J8
Wächtersbach Germany 48 I4
Wachusett Reservoir U.S.A. 177 N3
Waco Canada 169 H3
Waco U.S.A. 179 D6
Waconda Lake U.S.A. 178 C4
Wad Pak. 101 F5
Wada'a Sudan 121 E6
Wada Wadalla Aboriginal Land res.
 Australia 148 C2
Wadayama Japan 91 D7
Wad Banda Sudan 121 E6
Wadbilliga National Park Australia 147 F4
Waddān Libya 120 C2
Waddān, Jabal hills Libya 120 B2
Waddell Dam U.S.A. 183 L8
Waddeneilanden is Neth. see
 West Frisian Islands
Wadden Islands Neth. see
 West Frisian Islands
Waddenzee sea chan. Neth. 48 B3
Waddikee Australia 146 C3
Waddington, Mount Canada 166 E5
Waddinxveen Neth. 48 B3
Wadena Canada 167 K5
Wadena r. U.S.A. 178 D2
Wad en Nail Sudan 121 G6
Wadesboro U.S.A. 174 D5
Wadeye Australia 148 A2
 formerly known as Port Keats
Wadgaon Maharashtra India 94 B2
Wadgaon Maharashtra India 94 C1
Wad Hamid Sudan 121 G5
Wadhwan India 96 A5
Wadhwan India see Surendranagar
Wadi India 94 C2
Wadi r. India 94 B1
Wādī as Sir Jordan 108 G6
Wadian China 87 E1
Wādī Gimāl, Geziret i. Egypt 104 A2
 English form Wadi Gimal Island
Wādī Gimāl Island Egypt see
 Wādī Gimāl, Geziret
Wādī Halfa Sudan 121 F4
Wādī Hammah Saudi Arabia 104 C3
Wādī Mūsā Jordan 108 G7
Wad Medani Sudan 121 G6
Wadsworth NV U.S.A. 182 E2
Wadsworth OH U.S.A. 176 D4
Waegwan S. Korea 91 B6
Waenhuiskrans S. Africa 132 E11
Waesche, Mount Antarctica 222 P1
Wafangdian China 85 I4
 formerly known as Fuxian
Wafra Kuwait see Al Wafrah
Wagah India 96 C3
Wagait Aboriginal Land res. Australia
 148 A2
Wageningen Neth. 48 C4
Wageningen Suriname 199 G3
Wager Bay Canada 167 N1
Wagga Wagga Australia 147 E3
Wagin Australia 151 B7
Waglisla Canada 166 D4
Wagner Brazil 202 D5
Wagner U.S.A. 178 C3
Wagoner U.S.A. 179 D4
Wagon Mound U.S.A. 181 F5
Wagrowiec Poland 49 O3
Wah Pak. 101 H3
Wahai Indon. 75 D3
Wahda state Sudan 126 F2
Wahemen, Lac l. Canada 169 G2
Wahiawa U.S.A. 181 [inset] Y1
Wahoo U.S.A. 178 D3
Wahpeton U.S.A. 178 C2
Wahran Alg. see Oran
Wah Wah Mountains U.S.A. 183 K3
Wai India 94 B2
Waiapu r. N.Z. 152 M5
Waiau N.Z. 153 H10
Waiau r. North l. N.Z. 152 L6
Waiau r. South l. N.Z. 153 B13
Waiau r. South l. N.Z. 153 H10
Waidhofen an der Thaya Austria 49 M7
Waidhofen an der Ybbs Austria 49 L8
Waigama Indon. 75 D3
Waigeo i. Indon. 73 H7
Waihao Downs N.Z. 153 E12
Waiharara N.Z. 152 H2
Waiharoa N.Z. 152 J5
Waiheke Island N.Z. 152 J4
Waihi N.Z. 152 J5
Waihi Beach N.Z. 152 J5
Waihou r. N.Z. 152 J5
Waihua N.Z. 152 L7
Waikabubak Indon. 75 A5
Waikaia N.Z. 153 C13
Waikaia r. N.Z. 153 C13
Waikanae N.Z. 152 J8
Waikare, Lake N.Z. 152 J5
Waikaremoana, Lake N.Z. 152 K6
Waikaretu N.Z. 152 I5
Waikari N.Z. 153 G10
Waikato admin. reg. N.Z. 152 I5
Waikato r. N.Z. 152 I5
Waikawa N.Z. 153 D14
Waikeria N.Z. 152 J6
Waikerie Australia 146 C3
Waikii U.S.A. 181 [inset] Z2
Waikirikiri N.Z. 152 K6
Waikiloa Indon. 75 B5
Waikoikoi N.Z. 153 C13
Waikokopa N.Z. 152 L7
Waikouaiti N.Z. 153 E13
Wailuku U.S.A. 181 [inset] Z1
Waimahake N.Z. 153 C14
Waimakariri r. N.Z. 153 G11
Waimangaroa N.Z. 153 F9
Waimarama N.Z. 152 K7
Waimarie N.Z. 153 F12
Waimate N.Z. 153 F12
Waimatenui N.Z. 152 H3
Waimauku N.Z. 152 I4
Waimea U.S.A. 181 [inset] Z1
Wainganga r. India 94 C2
Waingapu Indon. 75 B5
Waini Point Guyana 199 G2
Wainwright Canada 167 I4
Wainwright U.S.A. 164 D2
Waiotira N.Z. 152 I3
Waiouru N.Z. 152 J7
Waipa r. N.Z. 152 I5
Waipahi N.Z. 153 C14
Waipapa N.Z. 152 I3
Waipapa Point N.Z. 153 C14
Waipara N.Z. 153 G11

Waipawa N.Z. 152 K7
Waipipi N.Z. 152 I5
Waipu N.Z. 152 I3
Waipukurau N.Z. 152 K7
Wairakei N.Z. 152 K6
Wairarapa, Lake N.Z. 152 J8
Wairau r. N.Z. 153 I9
Wairau Valley N.Z. 152 H9
Wairoa N.Z. 152 L7
Wairoa r. North l. N.Z. 152 I4
Wairoa r. North l. N.Z. 152 L7
Waishe China 87 F2
Waitahanui N.Z. 152 K6
Waitahuna N.Z. 153 D13
Waitakaruru N.Z. 152 J5
Waitaki N.Z. 153 F12
Waitaki r. N.Z. 153 F12
Waitangi S. Pacific Ocean 145 H6
Waitangitaona r. N.Z. 153 E11
Waitara N.Z. 152 I6
Waitati N.Z. 153 E13
Waite River Australia 148 B4
Waitomo Caves N.Z. 152 J6
Waitotara r. N.Z. 152 I7
Waitsburg U.S.A. 180 C3
Waiuku N.Z. 152 I5
Waiwera South N.Z. 153 D14
Waiyang China 87 F3
Waiyevu Fiji 145 H3
Wajid, Jabal al hills Saudi Arabia 104 D4
Wajiki Japan 91 D8
Wajima Japan 90 E6
Wajir Kenya 128 D4
Waka Dem. Rep. Congo 126 D5
Waka, Tanjung pt Indon. 75 C3
Wakami Lake Canada 173 K3
Wakasa Japan 91 D7
Wakasa-wan b. Japan 91 D7
Wakatipu, Lake N.Z. 153 C13
Wakatoma Lake Canada 173 J4
Wakaw Canada 167 J4
Wakaya Aboriginal Land res. Australia
 143 C3
Wakayama Japan 91 D7
Wakayama pref. Japan 91 D8
► Wake Atoll terr. N. Pacific Ocean 220 F4
 United States Unincorporated Territory. Also
 known as Āneen-Kio or EnenKio; formerly
 known as Wake Island.
 oceania [countries] ▶▶ 138–139
WaKeeney U.S.A. 178 C4
Wakefield Canada 173 R5
Wakefield N.Z. 152 H9
Wakefield U.K. 47 K10
Wakefield MI U.S.A. 172 D4
Wakefield RI U.S.A. 177 I9
Wakefield OH U.S.A. 176 B7
Wakefield VA U.S.A. 177 I9
Wakeham Canada see Kangiqsujuaq
Wake Island terr. N. Pacific Ocean see
 Wake Atoll
Wakema Myanmar 78 A4
Wakhan reg. Afgh. 101 H2
Waki Japan 91 D7
Wakinosawa Japan 90 G4
Wakkanai Japan 90 G3
Wakkerstroom S. Africa 133 O4
Wakool Australia 147 E3
Wakool r. Australia 147 D3
Wakuach, Lac l. Canada 169 H2
Waku-Kungo Angola 127 B7
 formerly known as Santa Comba; formerly
 spelt Uaco Congo
Wakuya Japan 90 G5
Wakwayowkastic r. Canada 168 D3
Walagunya Aboriginal Reserve Australia
 150 C4
Walajapet India 94 C3
Wałbrzych Poland 49 N5
 historically known as Waldenburg
Walcha Australia 147 F2
Walcott U.S.A. 180 F4
Walcz Poland 49 N3
Waldaist r. Austria 49 L7
Waldburg Range mts Australia 151 B5
Walden U.S.A. 177 K4
Waldenburg Poland see Wałbrzych
Waldkraiburg Germany 49 K7
Waldo U.S.A. 172 F7
Waldorf U.S.A. 177 I7
Waldport U.S.A. 180 A3
Waldron U.S.A. 179 D5
Waldron, Cape Antarctica 223 H2
Waldshut Germany 48 F8
Walea, Selat sea chan. Indon. 75 B3
Waleabahi i. Indon. 75 B3
Walēg China 86 B2
 formerly known as Warli
Walej, Sha'īb al watercourse Iraq 109 K5
Wales admin. div. U.K. 47 I11
 also known as Cymru; historically known as
 Cambria
Walewale Ghana 125 E4
Walford U.S.A. 172 B9
Walgett Australia 147 F2
Walgreen Coast Antarctica 222 Q1
Walhalla MI U.S.A. 172 G7
Walhalla ND U.S.A. 178 C1
Walhalla SC U.S.A. 174 D5
Walikale Dem. Rep. Congo 126 F5
Walker r. watercourse Australia 148 B5
Walker r. watercourse Australia 148 B2
Walker IA U.S.A. 172 B8
Walker MI U.S.A. 172 H7
Walker MN U.S.A. 178 D2
Walker r. U.S.A. 182 F3
Walker Bay S. Africa 132 D11
Walker Cay i. Bahamas 186 D1
Walker Creek r. Australia 149 D3
Walker Lake l. Canada 167 L4
Walker Lake l. U.S.A. 182 F3
Walker Lake l. U.S.A. 182 F3
Walker Mountains Antarctica 222 R2
Walker River Indian Reservation res.
 U.S.A. 182 F3
Walkersville U.S.A. 177 H6
Walkerville WV U.S.A. 176 E7
Walkerton U.S.A. 172 G9
Wall, Mount hill Australia 150 B4
Wallabi Group is Australia 151 A6
Wallaby Island Australia 149 D2
Wallace ID U.S.A. 180 C3
Wallace NC U.S.A. 174 E5
Wallace VA U.S.A. 176 C9
Wallaceburg Canada 168 D5
Wallal Downs Australia 150 C3
Wallambin, Lake salt flat Australia
 151 B6
Wallangarra Australia 147 F2
Wallaroo Australia 146 C3
Walla Walla U.S.A. 180 C3
Walldorn Germany 48 I6
Wallekraal S. Africa 132 B7
Wallenpaupack, Lake U.S.A. 177 J4
Wallingford CT U.S.A. 177 M4
Wallingford U.S.A. 177 M2
Wallis, Îles is Wallis and Futuna Is see
 Wallis Islands
► Wallis and Futuna Islands terr.
 S. Pacific Ocean 145 H3
 French Overseas Territory. Also known as
 Wallis et Futuna, Îs.
 oceania [countries] ▶▶ 138–139
Wallis et Futuna, Îles terr. S. Pacific Ocean
 see Wallis and Futuna Islands

Wallis Islands Wallis and Futuna Is 145 H3
 also known as Wallis, Îles
Wallis Lake inlet Australia 147 G3
Wallops Island U.S.A. 177 J8
Wallowa Mountains U.S.A. 180 C3
Walls U.K. 46 K3
Walls of Jerusalem National Park Australia
 147 E5
Wallumbilla Australia 149 F5
Walmsley Lake Canada 167 J2
Walney, Isle of i. U.K. 47 I9
Walnut Bottom U.S.A. 176 H5
Walnut Cove U.S.A. 176 E9
Walnut Creek r. U.S.A. 178 C4
Walnut Creek U.S.A. 182 B4
Walnut Grove U.S.A. 182 C3
Walnut Ridge U.S.A. 174 B4
Walong India 97 H3
Walpole U.S.A. 177 M2
Walpole, Île i. New Caledonia 145 F4
Walsall U.K. 47 K11
Walsenburg U.S.A. 181 F5
Walsh r. Australia 149 D3
Walsh U.S.A. 178 B4
Walsrode Germany 48 I3
Waltair India 95 D2
Walterboro U.S.A. 175 D5
Walter F. George Reservoir U.S.A. 175 C6
Walters U.S.A. 179 C5
Walter's Range hills Australia 147 E2
Walthall U.S.A. 175 B5
Waltham Canada 173 Q5
Waltham MA U.S.A. 177 N3
Waltham ME U.S.A. 177 Q1
Walton IN U.S.A. 172 G10
Walton KY U.S.A. 176 A7
Walton NY U.S.A. 177 J3
Walton WV U.S.A. 176 E7
Walton-on-the-Naze U.K. 47 N12
Walvisbaai Namibia see Walvis Bay
Walvis Bay Namibia 130 B4
Walvis Bay b. Namibia 130 B4
 also spelt Walvisbaai
Wamala, Lake Uganda 128 A4
Wamba Dem. Rep. Congo 126 E4
Wamba r. Dem. Rep. Congo 126 C6
Wamba Nigeria 125 H4
Wambardi Aboriginal Land res. Australia
 148 B3
Wamena Indon. 73 I7
Wami r. Tanz. 129 C6
Wamlana Indon. 75 C3
Wampaya Aboriginal Land res. Australia
 148 B3
Wampsville U.S.A. 173 R7
Wampusirpi Hond. 186 B4
Wanaaring Australia 147 E2
Wanaka N.Z. 153 D12
Wanaka, Lake N.Z. 153 D12
Wan'an China 87 E3
 also known as Furong
Wanapitei Lake Canada 173 M4
Wanaque Reservoir U.S.A. 177 K4
Wanasabari Indon. 75 B4
Wanbi Australia 146 C3
Wanci Indon. 75 B4
Wanda Arg. 204 G2
Wandana Nature Reserve Australia 151 A6
Wanda Shan mts China 82 D3
Wandering River Canada 167 H4
Wanding China 86 A3
 formerly known as Wandingzhen
Wandingzhen China see Wanding
Wandiwash India see Vandavasi
Wandle Downs N.Z. 153 H10
Wanditz Germany 49 K3
Wandoan Australia 149 F5
Wang, Mae Nam r. Thai. 78 B4
Wanganui N.Z. 152 I7
Wanganui r. North l. N.Z. 152 I7
Wanganui r. South l. N.Z. 153 E11
Wangaratta Australia 147 E4
Wangary Australia 146 B3
Wangcang China 87 C1
 also known as Hongjiang; formerly known as
 Fengjiaba
Wangcheng China 87 E2
 formerly known as Gaotangling
Wangda China see Zogang
Wangdu China 85 G4
Wangdue Phodrang Bhutan 97 F4
Wangerooge i. Germany 48 E2
Wanggamet, Gunung mt. Indon. 75 B5
Wang Gaxun China 84 C4
Wanggezhuang China see Jiaonan
Wangiwangi i. Indon. 75 B4
Wangjiang China 87 F2
Wangkui China 82 B3
Wang Mai Khon Thai. see Sawankhalok
Wangmao China 87 D4
Wangmo China 86 C3
 also known as Fuxing
Wangolodougou Côte d'Ivoire see
 Ouangolodougou
Wangqing China 82 C4
Wangying China see Huaiyin
Wangziguan China 85 G4
Wanie-Rukula Dem. Rep. Congo 126 E4
Wanimiyn Aboriginal Land res. Australia
 148 A2
Wankaner India 96 A5
Wankie Zimbabwe see Hwange
Wanlaweyn Somalia 128 E4
Wanna Lakes salt flat Australia 151 E6
Wannian China 87 F2
 also known as Chenying
Wanning China 87 D5
Wanrong China 85 F5
Wanshan China 87 F3
Wanshan Qundao is China 87 E4
 English form Lima Islands
Wanstead N.Z. 152 K8
Wantage U.K. 47 K12
Wanup Canada 173 M4
Wanxian China 87 K11
Wanxian China 87 C1
Wanyuan China 87 C1
Wanzai China 87 E2
 also known as Kangle
Wanzhi China see Wuhu
Wapakoneta U.S.A. 176 A5
Wapawekka Lake Canada 167 J4
Wapekka Lake Canada 168 B2
Wapello U.S.A. 172 B9
Wapikopa Lake Canada 168 C2
Wapiti r. Canada 166 G4
Wapotih Indon. 75 D3
Wappingers Falls U.S.A. 177 L4
Wapsipinicon r. U.S.A. 178 D3
Waqēn China 86 B1
Waqf aş Şawwān, Jibāl hills Jordan 109 H6
Waqisah well Iraq 107 E5
Waqr well Saudi Arabia 105 E3
Waqr Maryamah well Yemen 105 D4
War U.S.A. 176 D8
Wa'r, Wādī al watercourse Syria 109 L3
Warab Sudan 126 F2
Warab state Sudan 126 F2
Waradi waterhole Kenya 128 D4
Warah Pak. 101 F5
Warakurna-Wingellina-Irruntyu
 Aboriginal Reserve Australia 151 E5
Warandab Eth. 128 E3
Warangal India 94 C2
Waraseoni India 94 D5
Waratah Australia 147 E5
Warbreccan Australia 149 D5
Warburg Germany 48 H4
Warburton Vic. Australia 147 E4

Warburton W.A. Australia 151 D5
Warburton watercourse Australia 146 C1
Warburton S. Africa 133 O3
Warburton Aboriginal Reserve Australia
 151 D5
Warburton Bay Canada 167 J2
Warburton Range hills Australia 151 D5
Warche r. Belgium 51 L2
Ward watercourse Australia 149 E5
Ward N.Z. 153 I9
Ward, Mount Antarctica 222 P1
Ward, Mount South l. N.Z. 153 B13
Ward, Mount South l. N.Z. 153 D11
Wardang Island Australia 146 C3
Wardeglo waterhole Kenya 128 D4
Warden S. Africa 133 M4
Wardha India 94 C1
Wardha r. India 94 C2
Ware Canada 166 E3
Ware U.S.A. 177 M3
 also known as Fort Ware
Wareham U.K. 47 J13
Waremme Belgium 51 L2
Waren Germany 49 K2
Warendorf Germany 48 E4
Warginburra Peninsula Australia 149 F4
Wargla Alg. see Ouargla
War Gunbi waterhole Somalia 128 E2
Warialda Australia 147 F2
Wari Island P.N.G. 149 F1
Warin Chamrap Thai. 79 D5
Warka Poland 49 S4
Warkworth N.Z. 152 I4
Warman Canada 167 J4
Warmandi Indon. 73 H7
Warmba Namibia 130 C6
Warmbad S. Africa 133 M1
Warmbad Namibia 132 D4
Warmia reg. Poland 49 R1
Warm Springs NV U.S.A. 183 H3
Warm Springs VA U.S.A. 176 F7
Warm Springs Indian Reservation res.
 U.S.A. 180 B3
Warmwaterberg S. Africa 132 E10
Warmwaterberg mts S. Africa 132 E10
Warner Canada 167 I5
Warner Lakes U.S.A. 180 C4
Warner Mountains U.S.A. 180 B4
Warner Robins U.S.A. 175 D5
Warner Springs U.S.A. 183 H8
Warnes Bol. 201 E4
Warnow r. Germany 49 J1
Waronda India 94 C2
Waroona Australia 151 A7
Warora India 94 C1
Warra Australia 149 F5
Warrabri Aboriginal Land res. Australia
 148 B3
Warracknabeal Australia 147 D4
Warragamba Reservoir Australia 147 F3
Warragul Australia 147 E4
Warralakalna, Lake salt flat Australia
 146 C2
Warrambool hill Australia 151 B6
Warrambool r. Australia 147 E2
Warrandirrina, Lake salt flat Australia
 146 C1
Warrā el-'Arab Egypt 108 C7
Warrawagine r. Australia 150 C4
Warrego r. Australia 147 E2
Warrego Range hills Australia 149 E5
Warren Canada 173 M4
Warren IL U.S.A. 172 D8
Warren IN U.S.A. 172 H10
Warren MI U.S.A. 173 J8
Warren OH U.S.A. 176 E4
Warren PA U.S.A. 176 F4
Warren Hastings Island Palau see Merir
Warren Island U.S.A. 166 C4
Warrenpoint U.K. 47 F9
Warrens U.S.A. 172 C6
Warrensburg MO U.S.A. 178 D4
Warrensburg NY U.S.A. 177 L2
Warrenton S. Africa 133 I5
Warrenton GA U.S.A. 175 D5
Warrenton MO U.S.A. 178 E4
Warrenton NC U.S.A. 176 G9
Warrenton VA U.S.A. 176 H7
Warri Nigeria 125 G5
Warriedar hill Australia 151 B6
Warriners Creek watercourse Australia
 146 C2
Warrington N.Z. 153 E13
Warrington U.K. 47 J10
Warrington U.S.A. 175 C6
Warrnambool Australia 147 D4
Warroad U.S.A. 178 D1
Warrumbungle National Park Australia
 147 F2
Warrumbungle Range mts Australia 147 F2
Warruwi Australia 148 B1
Warry Warry watercourse Australia 146 D2
► Warsaw Poland 49 S3
 Capital of Poland. Also spelt Warszawa.
Warsaw IN U.S.A. 174 C3
Warsaw KY U.S.A. 176 A7
Warsaw MO U.S.A. 178 D4
Warsaw NY U.S.A. 176 G3
Warsaw VA U.S.A. 177 I8
Warsingsfehn Germany 48 E2
Warszawa Poland see Warsaw
Warta Poland 49 P4
Warta r. Poland 49 L3
 also known as Chenying
Wartburg U.S.A. 176 A9
Wartburg, Schloß tourist site Germany
 48 H4
Waru Indon. 77 G3
Warud India 96 C5
Warrumungu Aboriginal Land res. Australia
 148 B3
Warwick Australia 147 G2
Warwick U.K. 47 K11
Warwick NY U.S.A. 177 K4
Warwick RI U.S.A. 177 N4
Warwick Channel Australia 148 C2
Warzhong China 86 B2
Wasa Canada 167 H5
Wasaga Nigeria 125 G4
Wasaga Beach Canada 173 M6
Wasatch Range mts U.S.A. 183 M2
Wasbank S. Africa 133 O5
Wascana Creek r. Canada 167 J5
Wasco U.S.A. 182 E6
Wascott U.S.A. 172 A4
Waseca U.S.A. 174 A2
Wasekamio Lake Canada 167 I3
Washado Suriname 199 G3
Washap Pak. 101 E5
Washburn IL U.S.A. 172 D9
Washburn ND U.S.A. 178 B2
Washburn TN U.S.A. 176 B9
Washburn WI U.S.A. 172 C4
Washim India 96 C5
Washineska r. Canada 169 F3
► Washington DC U.S.A. 177 H7
 Capital of the United States of America.
 world [countries] ▶▶ 10–11
Washington IA U.S.A. 172 B9
Washington GA U.S.A. 175 D5
Washington IL U.S.A. 172 D10
Washington IN U.S.A. 174 C4
Washington KS U.S.A. 178 C4

Washington KY U.S.A. 176 B7
Washington NC U.S.A. 174 E5
Washington NH U.S.A. 177 M2
Washington NJ U.S.A. 177 K5
Washington UT U.S.A. 183 K4
► Washington state U.S.A. 180 B3
 world [changes] ▶▶ 20–21
Washington, Cape Antarctica 223 L2
Washington, Mount U.S.A. 177 N1
Washington Court House U.S.A. 176 B6
Washington Island U.S.A. 172 G5
Washington Land reg. Greenland 165 M2
Washir Afgh. 101 E3
Washita r. U.S.A. 179 C5
Washpool National Park Australia 147 G2
Washtucna U.S.A. 180 C3
Wasi' Saudi Arabia 104 D3
Wasi' well Saudi Arabia 105 D2
Wasiłków Poland 49 U2
Wesilla U.S.A. 164 D3
Wasit governorate Iraq 107 F4
Wasit tourist site Iraq 107 F4
Wāsiţah Saudi Arabia 104 D3
Waskaganish Canada 168 E3
 also known as Fort Rupert
Waskaiowaka Lake Canada 167 L3
Waskatenau Canada 167 H4
Wąsosz Poland 49 N4
Waspán Nicaragua 186 B4
Wassadou Senegal 124 B3
Wassamu Japan 90 H2
Wassenaar Neth. 48 B3
Wasser Namibia 130 C5
Wasserkuppe hill Germany 48 G5
Wassou Guinea 124 B4
Wassuk Range mts U.S.A. 182 F3
Wasswanipi, Lac l. Canada 168 E3
Watabeag Lake Canada 173 M2
Watambayoli Indon. 75 B3
Watampone Indon. 75 B4
Watapi Lake Canada 167 I4
Watarrka National Park Australia 148 A5
Watauga r. U.S.A. 176 C9
Watauga Lake U.S.A. 176 C9
Watenstadt-Salzgitter Germany see
 Salzgitter
Waterberg Namibia 130 C4
Waterberg Plateau Game Park nature res.
 Namibia 130 C4
Waterbury CT U.S.A. 177 L3
Waterbury VT U.S.A. 177 M1
Water Cays i. Bahamas 186 D2
Waterdown Canada 173 L7
Watereee r. U.S.A. 175 D5
Waterford Rep. of Ireland 47 E11
 also known as Port Láirge
Waterford S. Africa 133 J10
Waterford CA U.S.A. 182 D4
Waterford PA U.S.A. 176 F4
Waterford Harbour Rep. of Ireland 47 F11
Waterhen r. Canada 167 J4
Waterhen Lake Canada 167 L4
Waterhouse r. Australia 148 B2
Waterhouse Range mts Australia 148 B5
Waterloo Canada 168 D4
Waterloo Sierra Leone 124 B4
Waterloo IL U.S.A. 174 A3
Waterloo IL U.S.A. 174 B4
Waterloo NY U.S.A. 177 I3
Waterloo WI U.S.A. 172 E7
Waterlooville U.K. 47 K13
Waterman U.S.A. 172 E9
Waterpoort S. Africa 131 F4
Waterton Lakes National Park Canada
 167 H5
Waterton Park Canada 167 H5
Watertown NY U.S.A. 177 J2
Watertown SD U.S.A. 178 C2
Watertown WI U.S.A. 172 E7
Waterval r. S. Africa 133 M3
Waterval-Boven S. Africa 133 O2
Water Valley U.S.A. 174 B5
Waterville Rep. of Ireland 47 B12
Waterville ME U.S.A. 177 P1
Waterville WA U.S.A. 180 B3
Watervliet U.S.A. 177 L3
Wates Indon. 77 E4
Watford Canada 173 L8
Watford U.K. 47 L12
Watford City U.S.A. 178 B2
Wathaman r. Canada 167 K3
Wathaman Lake Canada 167 K3
Watheroo Australia 151 B6
Watheroo National Park Australia 151 A6
Watino Canada 167 G4
Watir, Wādī watercourse Egypt 108 F8
Watkins Glen U.S.A. 177 I3
Watkinsville U.S.A. 175 D5
Watling Island Bahamas see San Salvador
Watonga U.S.A. 179 C5
Watowato, Bukit mt. Indon. 75 D2
Watrous Canada 167 J5
Watrous U.S.A. 181 F6
Watsa Dem. Rep. Congo 126 F4
Watseka U.S.A. 174 C3
Watson r. Australia 149 D2
Watson Canada 167 J5
Watson Escarpment Antarctica 223 L1
Watson Lake Canada 166 D2
Watsonville U.S.A. 182 C4
Watt, Mount hill Australia 151 D5
Watterson Lake Canada 167 L2
Wattiwarriganna watercourse Australia
 146 C2
Watts Bar Lake resr U.S.A. 174 C5
Wattsburg U.S.A. 176 F3
Watubela, Kepulauan is Indon. 73 H7
Wau P.N.G. 73 K8
Wau Sudan 126 F2
Wau watercourse Sudan 126 E3
Waubay U.S.A. 178 C2
Wauchope N.S.W. Australia 147 G2
Wauchope N.T. Australia 148 B4
Wauchula U.S.A. 175 D7
Waukara, Gunung mt. Indon. 75 A3
Waukarlycarly, Lake salt flat Australia
 150 C4
Waukau U.S.A. 172 E7
Waukegan U.S.A. 174 C3
Waukesha U.S.A. 172 E7
Waukon U.S.A. 174 B3
Waunakee U.S.A. 172 D7
Waupaca U.S.A. 172 E7
Waupun U.S.A. 172 E7
Waurika U.S.A. 179 C5
Wausau U.S.A. 172 D6
Wauseon U.S.A. 174 D6
Wautoma U.S.A. 172 D6
Wave Hill Australia 148 A3
Waverley N.Z. 152 I7
Waverly IA U.S.A. 174 A3
Waverly NY U.S.A. 177 I3
Waverly OH U.S.A. 176 C6
Waverly TN U.S.A. 174 C4
Waverly VA U.S.A. 177 H8
Wavre Belgium 51 K2
Waw Myanmar 78 B4
Wawa Canada 168 C4
 formerly known as Jamestown
Wawa Nigeria 125 F4
Wawagosic r. Canada 168 E3
Wawalalindu Indon. 75 B3
Wāw al Kabīr Libya 120 C3
Wāw an Nāmūs waterhole Libya 120 C3
Wawasee, Lake U.S.A. 172 H9
Wawo Indon. 75 B3
Wawoi r. P.N.G. 73 J8
Wawotebi Indon. 75 B3
Waxahachie U.S.A. 179 C5

Waxü China 86 B1
Waxxari China 88 D4
Way, Lake salt flat Australia 151 C5
Wayabula Indon. 75 D2
Wayag i. Indon. 75 D2
Wayamli Indon. 75 D2
Wayaobu China see Zichang
Waycross U.S.A. 175 D6
Way Kambas National Park Indon. 77 D4
Waykilo Indon. 75 C3
Wayland KY U.S.A. 176 C8
Wayland MI U.S.A. 172 H8
Wayland NY U.S.A. 176 H3
Wayne MI U.S.A. 173 J8
Wayne NE U.S.A. 178 C3
Wayne WV U.S.A. 176 C7
Waynesboro GA U.S.A. 175 D5
Waynesboro MS U.S.A. 175 B6
Waynesboro PA U.S.A. 176 H6
Waynesboro TN U.S.A. 174 C5
Waynesboro VA U.S.A. 176 G7
Waynesburg U.S.A. 176 E6
Waynesville MO U.S.A. 178 D4
Waynesville NC U.S.A. 174 D5
Waza Myanmar 78 B2
Waza, Parc National de nat. park Cameroon 125 I4
Wazi Khwa Afgh. 101 G3
also known as Marjan
Wazirabad Pak. 101 H3
Wda r. Poland 49 P2
W du Niger, Parcs Nationaux du nat. park Niger 125 F4
We New Caledonia 145 F4
We, Pulau i. Indon. 76 A1
Weagamow Lake Canada 168 B2
Wear r. U.K. 47 K9
Weare U.S.A. 177 N2
Wearyan r. Australia 148 C3
Weatherford OK U.S.A. 179 C5
Weatherford TX U.S.A. 179 C5
Weatherly U.S.A. 177 J5
Weaver Lake Canada 167 L4
Weaverville U.S.A. 182 B1
Webequie Canada 168 C2
Weber N.Z. 152 K8
Weber r. U.S.A. 183 M1
Weber, Mount Canada 166 D4
Weber Basin sea feature Indon. 218 P6
Weber Inlet Antarctica 222 T2

▶Webi Shabeelle r. Somalia 128 D4
5th longest river in Africa.
africa [landscapes] 112–113

Webster MA U.S.A. 177 N3
Webster SD U.S.A. 178 C2
Webster WI U.S.A. 172 A5
Webster City U.S.A. 174 A3
Webster Springs U.S.A. 176 E7
Webuye Kenya 128 B4
formerly known as Broderick Falls
Wecho r. Canada 167 H2
Wecho Lake Canada 167 H2
Weda Indon. 75 C2
Weda, Teluk b. Indon. 75 D2
Weddell Island Falkland Is 205 E8
Weddell Sea Antarctica 222 V2
Wedderburn N.Z. 153 E13
Wedge Mountain Canada 166 F5
Weed U.S.A. 180 B4
Weedville U.S.A. 176 G4
Weenen S. Africa 133 O5
Weenen Nature Reserve S. Africa 133 O5
Weener Germany 48 E2
Weert Neth. 48 C4
Wee Waa Australia 147 F2
Wegberg Germany 48 D4
Węgliniec Poland 49 M4
Węgorzewo Poland 49 S1
Węgorzyno Poland 49 M2
Węgrów Poland 49 T3
Wehni Eth. 104 B5
Wei r. Henan China 85 G4
Wei r. Shaanxi China 86 D1
Wei r. Shandong China 85 H4
Weichang China 85 H3
Weiden in der Oberpfalz Germany 48 J6
Weidongmen China see Qianjin
Weifang China 85 H4
Weihai China 85 I4
Weihui China 85 G5
formerly known as Jixian
Weihu Ling mts China 82 B4
Weilburg Germany 51 O2
Weilheim in Oberbayern Germany 48 I8
Weimar Germany 48 I5
Weinan China 87 D1
Weingarten Germany 48 G8
Weinheim Germany 48 F6
Weining China 86 C3
Weipa Australia 149 D2
Weipa Aboriginal Reserve Australia 149 D2
Weipa South Aboriginal Reserve Australia 149 D2
Weiqu China see Chang'an
Weir r. Australia 147 F2
Weiragoo Range hills Australia 151 B5
Weir River Canada 167 M3
Weiser U.S.A. 180 C3
Weiser r. U.S.A. 180 C3
Weishan Shandong China 87 F1
also known as Xiazhen
Weishan Yunnan China 86 B3
also known as Wenhua
Weishan Hu l. China 87 F1
Weishi China 87 E1
Weiße Elster r. Germany 51 R1
Weißenburg in Bayern Germany 48 H6
Weißenfels Germany 48 I4
Weisshorn mt. Switz. 51 N6
Weiss Lake U.S.A. 179 F5
Weissmies mt. Switz. 51 O6
Weissrand Mountains Namibia 130 C5
Weißwasser Germany 49 L4
Weixian China 85 G4
also known as Mingzhou
Weixin China 86 C3
also known as Zhaxi
Weiya China 84 B3
Weiyuan China 84 E5
also known as Qingyuan
Weiyuan China see Huzhu
Weiyuan China see Jinggu
Weiyuan Jiang r. China 86 B4
Weiz Austria 49 M8
Weizhou China see Wenchuan
Weizhou Dao i. China 87 D4
Weizi China 85 I3
Wejherowo Poland 49 P1
Wekusko Canada 167 L4
Wekusko Lake Canada 167 L4
Wekweti Canada 167 H1
formerly known as Snare Lakes
Wel r. Poland 49 Q2
Welatam Myanmar 78 B2
Welbedacht Dam S. Africa 133 K6
Welbourn Hill Australia 146 B1
Welch U.S.A. 176 D8
Weld U.S.A. 177 O1
Weld, Mount hill Australia 151 C6
Weldiya Eth. 128 C2
Weldon U.S.A. 176 H9
Weld Range hills Australia 151 B5
Welford National Park Australia 149 D5
formerly known as Barcoo National Park
Welk'īt'ē Eth. 128 C2
Welkom S. Africa 133 K4
Welland Canada 173 N8
Welland r. U.K. 47 L11
Welland Canal Canada 173 N7
Wellesley Canada 173 M7
Wellesley Islands Australia 148 C3
Wellesley Islands Aboriginal Reserve Australia 148 C3
Wellesley Lake Canada 166 B2
Wellfleet U.S.A. 177 O4
Wellingborough U.K. 47 L11
Wellington Australia 147 F3
Wellington Canada 173 P7

▶Wellington N.Z. 152 I9
Capital of New Zealand.
world [countries] 10–11

Wellington admin. reg. N.Z. 152 J9
Wellington S. Africa 132 C10
Wellington CO U.S.A. 180 F4
Wellington KS U.S.A. 178 C4
Wellington NV U.S.A. 182 E3
Wellington OH U.S.A. 176 C4
Wellington TX U.S.A. 179 B5
Wellington UT U.S.A. 183 N2
Wellington, Isla i. Chile 205 B8
Wellington Range hills N.T. Australia 148 B2
Wellington Range hills W.A. Australia 151 C5
Wells Canada 166 F4
Wells U.S.A. 180 D4
Wells, Lake salt flat Australia 151 C5
Wellsboro U.S.A. 177 H4
Wellsford N.Z. 152 I4
Wells Gray Provincial Park Canada 166 F4
Wells-next-the-Sea U.K. 47 M11
Wellston U.S.A. 172 H6
Wellsville NY U.S.A. 176 H3
Wellsville OH U.S.A. 176 E5
Wellton U.S.A. 183 J9
Welna r. Poland 49 N3
Weloka U.S.A. 181 [inset] Z2
Wels Austria 49 L7
Welshpool U.K. 47 I11
also known as Y Trallwng
Welton U.S.A. 172 C9
Welwel Eth. 128 E3
Welwitschia Namibia see Khorixas
Wema Dem. Rep. Congo 126 D5
Wembere r. Tanz. 129 B6
Wembesi S. Africa 133 N6
Wembley Canada 166 G4
Wemindji Canada 168 E2
formerly known as Nouveau-Comptoir or Paint Hills
Wemyss Bight Bahamas 186 D1
Wen r. China 85 H5
Wenamu r. Guyana/Venez. 199 F3
Wenatchee U.S.A. 180 B3
Wenatchee Mountains U.S.A. 180 B3
Wenchang China 87 D5
Wenchang China see Zitong
Wencheng China 87 G3
also known as Daxue
Wenchi Ghana 125 E5
Wench'it Shet' r. Eth. 128 C2
Wenchow China see Wenzhou
Wenchuan China 86 B2
also known as Weizhou
Wendelstein mt. Germany 48 J8
Wenden Latvia see Cēsis
Wenden U.S.A. 183 K8
Wendeng China 85 I4
Wendo Eth. 128 C3
Wéndou Mbôrou Guinea 124 B4
Wendover U.S.A. 183 J1
Wenebegon Lake Canada 173 J3
Wenfeng China see Yongfeng
Wengshui China 86 A2
Wengyuan China 87 E3
also known as Longxian
Wenhua China see Weishan
Wenjiang China see Gaoxian
Wenjiashi China 87 E3
Wenlan China see Mengzi
Wenlin China see Renshou
Wenling China 87 G2
Wenlock r. Australia 149 D2
Wenona IL U.S.A. 172 D9
Wenona MD U.S.A. 177 J7
Wenping China see Ludian
Wenquan Chongqing China 87 D2
Wenquan Guizhou China 87 C2
Wenquan China see Yingshan
Wenquan Qinghai China 84 C5

▶Wenquan Qinghai China 89 E5
Highest settlement in the world.

Wenquan Xinjiang China 88 C2
also known as Arixang
Wenquanzhen China 87 E2
Wenshan China 86 C4
also known as Kaihua
Wenshui China 86 C2
Wensu China 88 C3
Wensum r. U.K. 47 N11
Wentworth Australia 146 D3
Wentworth NC U.S.A. 176 F9
Wentworth NH U.S.A. 177 N2
Wenxi China 85 F5
Wenxian China 86 C1
Wenyu r. China 85 F4
Wenzhou China 87 G3
formerly spelt Wenchow
Wer India 96 C4
Werda Botswana 130 D5
Werdau Germany 49 J5
Werder Eth. 128 E3
Werder Germany 49 J3
Wêreldend S. Africa 132 E1
Werinama Indon. 75 D3
Werl Germany 48 E4
Wermsdorfer Forst park Germany 49 J4
Wernberg-Köblitz Germany 49 J6
Wernecke Mountains Canada 166 B1
Wernigerode Germany 48 H4
Werota Eth. 128 C2
Werra r. Germany 48 G4
Werrimull Australia 146 D3
Werris Creek Australia 147 F2
Wertheim Germany 48 G6
Werwaru Indon. 75 D5
Wesel Germany 48 D4
Wesendorf Germany 48 H3
Weser r. Germany 48 F2
Weser sea chan. Germany 48 F2
Wesergebirge hills Germany 48 F3
Weska Weka Eth. 128 B3
Weslemkoon Lake Canada 173 P5
Wesley S. Africa 133 L10
Wesleyville Canada 169 K3
Wessel, Cape Australia 148 C1
Wessel Islands Australia 148 C1
Wesselsbron S. Africa 133 K4
Wesselsvlei S. Africa 132 H4
Wesselton S. Africa 133 N3
Wessington Springs U.S.A. 178 C2
West Alligator r. Australia 148 B2
West Allis U.S.A. 172 E7
West Antarctica reg. Antarctica 222 P1
West Baines r. Australia 148 A2
West Banas r. India 96 A5

▶West Bank terr. Asia 108 G6
Territory occupied by Israel.
asia [countries] 64–67

West Bay Canada 169 J2
West Bay Cayman Is 186 C3
West Bay b. U.S.A. 175 B6
West Bend U.S.A. 172 E7
West Bengal state India 97 E5
West Branch U.S.A. 173 I6
Westbrook U.S.A. 177 O2
West Burke U.S.A. 177 N1
Westby U.S.A. 172 C7
West Caicos i. Turks and Caicos Is 187 E2
West Cape N.Z. 153 A13
West Cape Howe Australia 151 B7
West Chester U.S.A. 177 J6
Westcliffe U.S.A. 181 F5
West Coast admin. reg. N.Z. 153 E10
West Coast National Park S. Africa 132 C10
West Dome mt. N.Z. 153 C13
West End Bahamas 175 E7
West End U.S.A. 177 J3
Westerburg Germany 48 E5
Westerholt Germany 48 E2
Westerland Germany 48 F1
Western watercourse Australia 149 D4
Western r. Canada 167 J1
Western admin. reg. Ghana 124 E5
Western prov. Kenya 128 B4
Western prov. Zambia 127 D8
Western Area admin. div. Sierra Leone 124 B4
Western Australia state Australia 146 A2
Western Bahr el Ghazal state Sudan 126 E3
Western Cape prov. S. Africa 132 E10
Western Darfur state Sudan 120 D6
Western Desert Egypt 121 F3
also known as Sahara el Gharbîya
Western Desert Aboriginal Land res. Australia 148 A3
Western Dvina r. Europe see Zapadnaya Dvina
Western Equatoria state Sudan 126 F3
Western Ghats mts India 94 B3
also known as Sahyadri
Western Kordofan state Sudan 126 F2
Western Lesser Sunda Islands prov. Indon. see Nusa Tenggara Barat
Western Port b. Australia 147 E4
Western Province prov. Zambia see Copperbelt

▶Western Sahara terr. Africa 122 B4
Disputed territory (Morocco). Formerly known as Spanish Sahara.
africa [countries] 114–117

Western Samoa country S. Pacific Ocean see Samoa
Western Sayan Mountains reg. Rus. Fed. see Zapadnyy Sayan
Westerschelde est. Neth. 48 A4
Westerstede Germany 48 E2
Westerville U.S.A. 176 C5
Westerwald hills Germany 48 E5
West Falkland i. Falkland Is 205 E8
West Fargo U.S.A. 178 C2
West Fayu atoll Micronesia 73 K5
Westfield MA U.S.A. 177 M3
Westfield NY U.S.A. 176 F3
Westfield PA U.S.A. 176 H4
Westfield WI U.S.A. 172 D7
West Frisian Islands Neth. 48 B2
also known as Wadden Islands or Waddeneilanden
Westgate Australia 149 E5
West Grand Lake U.S.A. 169 H4
West Hamlin U.S.A. 176 C7
West Hartford U.S.A. 177 M4
West Haven U.S.A. 177 M4
West Ice Shelf Antarctica 223 F2
West Indies N. America 171 L7
West Irian prov. Indon. see Irian Jaya
West Island India 95 G3
West Jordan U.S.A. 183 M1
West Kazakhstan Oblast admin. div. Kazakh. see Zapadnyy Kazakhstan
West Lafayette U.S.A. 174 C3
West Lamma Channel Hong Kong China 87 [inset]
Westland Australia 149 D4
Westland National Park N.Z. 153 E11
also known as Tai Poutini National Park
West Liberty IA U.S.A. 172 B9
West Liberty KY U.S.A. 176 B8
West Liberty OH U.S.A. 176 B5
Westlock Canada 167 H4
West Lorne Canada 168 D5
West Lunga r. Zambia 127 E8
West Lunga National Park Zambia 127 E8
West MacDonnell National Park Australia 148 B4
West Malaysia pen. Malaysia see Peninsular Malaysia
Westmalle Belgium 51 K1
Westman Islands Iceland see Vestmannaeyjar
Westmar Australia 147 F1
West Memphis U.S.A. 174 B5
West Milton U.S.A. 176 A6
Westminster U.S.A. 177 I6
West Monroe U.S.A. 179 D5
Westmoreland Australia 148 C3
Westmoreland U.S.A. 178 C4
Westmorland U.S.A. 183 I8
West Nicholson Zimbabwe 131 F4
West Nueces r. U.S.A. 179 C6
Westoe Dam S. Africa 133 O3
Weston OH U.S.A. 176 B4
Weston WV U.S.A. 176 E6
Westonaria S. Africa 133 L3
Weston-super-Mare U.K. 47 J12
Westover U.S.A. 177 J7
West Palm Beach U.S.A. 175 D7
West Papua prov. Indon. see Irian Jaya
West Plains U.S.A. 178 E4
West Point pt Australia 147 E5
West Point CA U.S.A. 182 D3
West Point IA U.S.A. 172 B10
West Point MS U.S.A. 175 B5
West Point NE U.S.A. 178 C3
West Point NY U.S.A. 177 L4
West Point OH U.S.A. 176 E5
West Point VA U.S.A. 177 I8
West Point Lake resr U.S.A. 175 C5
Westport Canada 173 Q6
Westport N.Z. 153 F9
Westport Rep. of Ireland 47 C10
Westport CA U.S.A. 182 A2
Westport NY U.S.A. 177 L1
Westray Canada 167 K4
Westray i. U.K. 46 I4
Westray Firth sea chan. U.K. 46 I4
Westree Canada 168 D4
West Road r. Canada 166 F4
West Rutland U.S.A. 177 L2
West Sacramento U.S.A. 182 C3
West Salem U.S.A. 176 C5
West Seneca U.S.A. 176 G3
West Siberian Plain Rus. Fed. 38 I3
also known as Zapadno-Sibirskaya Nizmennost' or Zapadno-Sibirskaya Ravnina
West Stewartstown U.S.A. 177 N1
West Topsham U.S.A. 177 M1
West Union IA U.S.A. 174 B3
West Union OH U.S.A. 176 B7
West Union WV U.S.A. 176 E6
West Valley City U.S.A. 183 M1
Westville IN U.S.A. 172 G9
Westville OK U.S.A. 179 D5
West Virginia state U.S.A. 176 E7
West Walker r. U.S.A. 182 E3
Westwood Australia 149 F4
Westwood U.S.A. 182 D1
West Wyalong Australia 147 E3
West York U.S.A. 177 I6
Wetan i. Indon. 75 D4
Wetar i. Indon. 75 C4
Wetar, Selat sea chan. Indon. 75 C5
Wetaskiwin Canada 167 H4
Wete Dem. Rep. Congo 126 E6
Wete Tanz. 129 C6
Wethersfield U.S.A. 177 M4
Wetmore U.S.A. 172 G4
Wetmore Glacier Antarctica 222 T2
Wetumpka U.S.A. 175 C5
Wetzlar Germany 48 F5
Wever U.S.A. 172 B10
Wewahitchka U.S.A. 175 C6
Wewak P.N.G. 73 J7
Wewoka U.S.A. 179 C5
Wexford Rep. of Ireland 47 F11
also known as Loch Garman
Wexford Harbour b. Rep. of Ireland 47 F11
Weyakwin Canada 167 J4
Weyauwega U.S.A. 172 E6
Weyburn Canada 167 K5
Weyer Markt Austria 49 L8
Weyhausen Germany 48 H3
Weyhe Germany 48 F3
Weymouth Canada 169 H4
Weymouth U.K. 47 J13
Weymouth U.S.A. 177 O3
Weymouth, Cape Australia 149 D2
Whakaari i. N.Z. 152 L5
also known as White Island
Whaka a Te Wera inlet N.Z. see Paterson Inlet
Whakaki N.Z. 152 L7
Whakamaru N.Z. 152 J6
Whakapunake hill N.Z. 152 L6
Whakarewarewa Forest Park nature res. N.Z. 152 K6
Whakatane N.Z. 152 K5
Whalan Creek r. Australia 147 F2
Whale r. Canada see La Baleine, Rivière à
Whale Bay U.S.A. 166 C3
Whale Cay i. Bahamas 186 D1
Whale Cove Canada 167 M2
Whale Island N.Z. see Motuhora Island
Whaleyville U.S.A. 177 I9
Whalsay i. U.K. 46 L3
Whampoa, Sungai r. Sing. 76 [inset]
Whangaehu r. N.Z. 152 J8
Whangamata N.Z. 152 J5
Whangamoa N.Z. 152 H9
Whangamomona N.Z. 152 I7
Whanganui Inlet N.Z. 152 G8
Whanganui National Park N.Z. 152 I7
Whangaparaoa N.Z. 152 I4
Whangara N.Z. 152 M6
Whangarei N.Z. 152 I3
Whangaroa Bay N.Z. 152 H3
Whapmagoostui Canada 168 E2
Wharanui N.Z. 153 I9
Whareama N.Z. 152 K8
Wharfe r. U.K. 47 K10
Wharncliffe Canada 173 J4
Wharncliffe U.S.A. 176 D8
Wharton U.S.A. 179 C6
Wharton Lake Canada 167 L1
Whataroa N.Z. 153 E11
Wha Ti Canada 167 G2
formerly known as Lac la Martre
Wheatland CA U.S.A. 182 C2
Wheatland IA U.S.A. 172 C9
Wheatland WY U.S.A. 180 F4
Wheatley Canada 173 K8
Wheatley U.S.A. 176 A7
Wheaton IL U.S.A. 174 B3
Wheaton MN U.S.A. 178 C2
Wheaton-Glenmont U.S.A. 177 H6
Wheeler TX U.S.A. 179 B5
Wheeler WI U.S.A. 172 B5
Wheeler Lake Canada 167 H2
Wheeler Lake resr U.S.A. 174 C5
Wheeler Peak NM U.S.A. 181 F5
Wheeler Peak NV U.S.A. 183 J3
Wheelersburg U.S.A. 176 C7
Wheeler Springs U.S.A. 182 E7
Wheeling U.S.A. 176 E5
Wheelwright Arg. 204 E4
Whernside hill U.K. 47 J9
Whim Creek Australia 150 B4
Whinham, Mount Australia 148 A5
Whirinaki Forest Park nature res. N.Z. 152 K6
Whiskey Jack Lake Canada 167 K3
Whiskeytown Lake U.S.A. 182 B1
Whispering Pines U.S.A. 182 B3
Whistler Canada 166 F5
Whitbourne Canada 169 K4
Whitby Canada 173 O7
Whitby U.K. 47 L9
Whitchurch U.K. 47 J11
Whitchurch-Stouffville Canada 173 N7
Whitcombe, Mount N.Z. 153 E11
White r. Canada 168 C3
White r. Canada/U.S.A. 166 B2
White r. AR U.S.A. 174 B5
White r. CO U.S.A. 183 O1
White r. IN U.S.A. 174 C4
White r. MI U.S.A. 172 G7
White r. NV U.S.A. 183 J5
White r. SD U.S.A. 178 C3
White r. VT U.S.A. 177 M2
White r. WI U.S.A. 172 C4
White watercourse AZ U.S.A. 183 N8
White watercourse TX U.S.A. 179 B5
White, East Fork r. U.S.A. 174 C4
White, Lake salt flat Australia 148 A4
White, North Fork r. U.S.A. 178 D4
White Bay Canada 169 J3
White Butte mt. U.S.A. 178 B2
White Canyon U.S.A. 183 N4
White Cliffs Australia 147 D2
White Cloud U.S.A. 172 H7
Whitecourt Canada 167 H4
White Earth Indian Reservation res. U.S.A. 178 D2
Whiteface Lake U.S.A. 172 A3
Whiteface Mountain U.S.A. 177 L1
Whitefield U.S.A. 177 N1
Whitefish Canada 173 L4
Whitefish r. Canada 166 E1
Whitefish U.S.A. 180 D2
Whitefish r. U.S.A. 172 G5
Whitefish Bay U.S.A. 172 F6
Whitefish Lake N.W.T. Canada 167 J2
Whitefish Lake Ont. Canada 172 D2
Whitefish Point U.S.A. 173 I4
White Hall U.S.A. 174 B4
Whitehall MI U.S.A. 172 G7
Whitehall MT U.S.A. 180 D3
Whitehall NY U.S.A. 177 L2
Whitehall OH U.S.A. 176 C6
Whitehall WI U.S.A. 172 B6
Whitehaven U.K. 47 I9
White Haven U.S.A. 177 J4
White Hill hill Canada 169 I4

▶Whitehorse Canada 166 C2
Territorial capital of Yukon.

White Horse, Vale of valley U.K. 47 K12
White Island Antarctica 223 D2
White Island N.Z. see Whakaari
White Kei r. S. Africa 133 L9
White Lake salt flat Australia 151 C5
White Lake Ont. Canada 168 C3
White Lake Ont. Canada 168 E4
White Lake LA U.S.A. 179 D6
White Lake MI U.S.A. 172 G7
Whitemark Australia 147 F5
White Mountain Peak U.S.A. 182 F4
White Mountains U.S.A. 177 N1
White Mountains National Park Australia 149 E4
Whitemouth r. Canada 171 G1
Whitemouth Lake Canada 167 M5
White Nile r. Sudan/Uganda 126 G1
also known as Abiad, Bahr el or Jebel, Bahr el
White Nile Dam Sudan 121 G6
White Nossob watercourse Namibia 130 C4
White Oak U.S.A. 176 B8
White Otter Lake Canada 168 B3
White Pass Canada/U.S.A. 166 C3
White Pine MI U.S.A. 172 D4
White Pine TN U.S.A. 176 B9
White Pine Range mts U.S.A. 183 I3
White River Canada 168 C3
Whiteriver U.S.A. 183 O8
White River U.S.A. 178 B3
White River Junction U.S.A. 177 M2
White River National Wildlife Refuge nature res. U.S.A. 174 B5
White River Valley U.S.A. 183 I3
White Rock Peak U.S.A. 183 J3
White Russia country Europe see Belarus
Whitesail Lake Canada 166 E4
White Salmon U.S.A. 180 B3
Whitesand r. Alta/N.W.T. Canada 167 H2
Whitesand r. Sask. Canada 167 K5
White Sands National Monument nat. park U.S.A. 181 F6
Whitesboro U.S.A. 177 J2
Whitesburg U.S.A. 176 C8
White Sea Rus. Fed. 40 F2
also known as Beloe More or Beloye More
White Stone U.S.A. 177 I8
White Sulphur Springs MT U.S.A. 180 E3
White Sulphur Springs WV U.S.A. 176 E8
Whitesville U.S.A. 176 D8
White Umfolozi r. S. Africa 133 P5
Whiteville U.S.A. 174 E5
White Volta watercourse Burkina/Ghana 125 E3
also known as Nakambé or Nakanbe or Volta Blanche
White Water U.S.A. 183 H8
Whitewater CO U.S.A. 183 P3
Whitewater WI U.S.A. 172 E8
Whitewater Baldy mt. U.S.A. 181 E6
White Well Australia 146 A2
White Woman Creek r. U.S.A. 178 B4
Whitewood Australia 149 D4
Whitewood Canada 167 K5
Whithorn U.K. 47 H9
Whitianga N.Z. 152 J4
Whitley City U.S.A. 176 A9
Whitmire U.S.A. 174 D5
Whitmore S. Africa 133 M8
Whitmore Mountains Antarctica 222 Q1
Whitney Canada 173 O5
Whitney, Lake U.S.A. 179 C5
Whitney, Mount U.S.A. 182 F5
Whitstable U.K. 47 N12
Whitsunday Group is Australia 149 F4
Whitsunday Island Australia 149 F4
Whitsunday Island National Park Australia 149 F4
Whitsunday Passage Australia 149 F4
Whitsun Island Vanuatu see Pentecost Island
Whittemore U.S.A. 173 J6
Whittier U.S.A. 182 F8
Whittington Range hills Australia 148 B3
Whittlesea S. Africa 133 K9
Whittlesey U.K. 47 L11
Whittlesey U.S.A. 172 C5
Whittlesey, Mount hill U.S.A. 172 C4
Whitton Australia 147 E3
Whitula watercourse Australia 149 D5
Wholdaia Lake Canada 167 J2
Why U.S.A. 183 L9
Whyalla Australia 146 C3
Whydah Benin see Ouidah
Wiang Kosai National Park Thai. 78 B4
Wiang Pa Pao Thai. 78 B4
Wiang Phran Thai. 78 B3
Wiang Sa Thai. 78 C4
Wiarton Canada 168 D4
Wiasi Ghana 125 E4
Wibaux U.S.A. 180 F3
Wichelen Belgium 48 A4
Wichita U.S.A. 178 C4
Wichita r. U.S.A. 179 C5
Wichita Falls U.S.A. 179 C5
Wichita Mountains U.S.A. 179 C5
Wichita Mountains National Wildlife Refuge nature res. U.S.A. 179 C5
Wick U.K. 46 I5
Wickenburg U.S.A. 183 L8
Wickepin Australia 151 B7
Wickham Australia 150 B4
Wickham r. Australia 148 A3
Wickham, Cape Australia 147 D4
Wicklow Rep. of Ireland 47 F11
also known as Cill Mhantáin
Wicklow Head Rep. of Ireland 47 G11
Wicklow Mountains Rep. of Ireland 47 F11
Wicklow Mountains National Park Rep. of Ireland 47 F10
Wicko, Jezioro lag. Poland 49 N1
Widawa r. Poland 49 O4
Widawka r. Poland 49 P4
Wide Bay Australia 149 G5
Wideroe, Mount Antarctica 223 B2
Widgeegoara watercourse Australia 147 E1
Widgiemooltha Australia 151 C6
Widi, Kepulauan is Indon. 75 D3
Wi-do i. S. Korea 83 B6
Więcbork Poland 49 O2
Wied r. Germany 48 E5
Wiehengebirge hills Germany 48 F3
Wiehl Germany 48 E5
Wieleń Poland 49 N3
Wielka Sowa mt. Poland 49 N5
Wielkopolskie, Pojezierze reg. Poland 49 O3
Wielkopolski Park Narodowy nat. park Poland 49 N3
Wieluń Poland 49 P4
Wien Austria see Vienna
Wiener Neustadt Austria 49 N8
Wiensberg mt. Austria 49 M7
Wieprz r. Poland 49 S4
Wieprza r. Poland 49 N1
Wieprz-Krzna, Kanał canal Poland 49 U4
Wieringerwerf Neth. 48 C3
Wieruszów Poland 49 P4
Wierzyca r. Poland 49 P2
Wiesbaden Germany 48 F5
Wiesloch Germany 48 F6
Wiesmoor Germany 48 E2
Wieżyca hill Poland 49 P1
Wigan U.K. 47 J10
Wiggins U.S.A. 175 B6
Wight, Isle of i. U.K. 47 K13
Wigierski Park Narodowy nat. park Poland 49 U1
Wignes Lake Canada 167 J2
Wigry, Jezioro l. Poland 49 U1
Wigtown U.K. 47 H9
Wigtown Bay U.K. 47 H9
Wijchen Neth. 48 C4
Wikieup U.S.A. 183 K7
Wik'ro Eth. 128 C1
Wikwemikong Canada 173 L5
Wil Switz. 51 P5
Wilber U.S.A. 178 C3
Wilberforce r. N.Z. 153 F11
Wilberforce, Cape Australia 148 C1
Wilbur U.S.A. 180 C3
Wilburton U.S.A. 179 D5
Wilcannia Australia 147 D2
Wilcox U.S.A. 176 G4
Wilczek Land i. Rus. Fed. see Vil'cheka, Zemlya
Wildalpener Salzatal nature res. Austria 49 M8
Wildcat Hill Wilderness Area nature res. Canada 167 K4
Wildcat Peak U.S.A. 183 H3
Wild Coast S. Africa 133 N8
Wilderness S. Africa 132 G10
Wilderness U.S.A. 176 H7
Wilderness National Park S. Africa 132 G11
Wildeshausen Germany 48 F3
Wild Goose Canada 172 D2
Wildhay r. Canada 167 G4
Wildhorn mt. Switz. 51 N6
Wild Horse Draw r. U.S.A. 181 F7
Wild Horse Hill mt. U.S.A. 178 B3
Wildon Austria 49 M9
Wild Rice r. MN U.S.A. 178 C2
Wild Rice r. ND U.S.A. 178 C2
Wild Rice Lake U.S.A. 172 A4
Wildwood Canada 167 H4
Wildwood FL U.S.A. 175 D6
Wildwood NJ U.S.A. 177 K7
Wiley Ford U.S.A. 176 G6
Wilga r. Poland 49 S4
Wilge r. Free State S. Africa 133 M4
Wilge r. Gauteng/Mpumalanga S. Africa 133 N2
Wilgena Australia 146 B2

▶Wilhelm, Mount P.N.G. 73 J8
5th highest mountain in Oceania.
oceania [landscapes] 136–137

Wilhelmina Gebergte mts Suriname 199 G4
Wilhelm-Pieck-Stadt Germany see Guben
Wilhelmsburg Austria 49 M7
Wilhelmshaven Germany 48 F2
Wilhelmstal Namibia 130 C4
Wilkes-Barre U.S.A. 177 J4
Wilkesboro U.S.A. 176 D9
Wilkes Coast Antarctica 223 I2
Wilkes Land reg. Antarctica 223 I2
Wilkie Canada 167 I4
Wilkinsburg U.S.A. 176 F5
Wilkins Coast Antarctica 222 T2
Wilkins Ice Shelf Antarctica 222 T2
Wilkinson Lakes salt flat Australia 146 B2
Will, Mount Canada 166 D3
Willamette r. U.S.A. 180 B3
Willandra Billabong watercourse Australia 147 E3
Willandra National Park Australia 147 E3
Willapa Bay U.S.A. 180 A3
Willard Mex. 184 C2
Willard NM U.S.A. 181 F6
Willard OH U.S.A. 176 C4
Willards U.S.A. 177 J7
Willcox U.S.A. 183 O9
Willcox Playa salt flat U.S.A. 183 O9
Willebroek Belgium 51 K1
Willem Pretorius Game Reserve nature res. S. Africa 133 L5

▶Willemstad Neth. Antilles 187 F4
Capital of the Netherlands Antilles.

Willeroo Australia 148 A2
William r. Canada 167 I3
William, Mount Australia 147 D4
William Creek Australia 146 C2
William Lake Canada 167 L4
Williams Australia 151 B7
Williams r. Qld Australia 149 D4
Williams r. W.A. Australia 151 B7
Williams AZ U.S.A. 183 L6
Williams CA U.S.A. 182 B2
Williamsburg IA U.S.A. 174 A3
Williamsburg KY U.S.A. 176 A9
Williamsburg MI U.S.A. 172 H6
Williamsburg OH U.S.A. 176 A6
Williamsburg PA U.S.A. 176 G5
Williamsburg VA U.S.A. 177 I8
Williams Lake Canada 166 F4
Williamson NY U.S.A. 177 H2
Williamson WV U.S.A. 176 C8
Williamsport IN U.S.A. 174 C3
Williamsport OH U.S.A. 176 B6
Williamsport PA U.S.A. 177 H4
Williamston MI U.S.A. 173 I8
Williamston NC U.S.A. 174 E5
Williamstown KY U.S.A. 176 A7
Williamstown MA U.S.A. 177 L3
Williamstown NY U.S.A. 177 J2
Willimantic U.S.A. 177 M4
Willis Group atolls Australia 149 F3
Willis Islands S. Georgia 205 [inset]
Williston S. Africa 132 E8
Williston FL U.S.A. 175 D6
Williston ND U.S.A. 178 B1
Williston SC U.S.A. 175 D5
Williston Lake Canada 166 F4
Willits U.S.A. 182 A2
Willmar U.S.A. 178 D2
Willmore Wilderness Provincial Park Canada 166 G4
Willochra watercourse Australia 146 C2
Willoughby U.S.A. 176 D4
Willow r. Canada 166 F4
Willow Beach U.S.A. 183 J6
Willow Bunch Canada 167 J5
Willow Creek r. Canada 167 H5
Willow Creek U.S.A. 180 B4
Willow Creek r. OR U.S.A. 180 B3
Willow Creek r. UT U.S.A. 183 O1
Willow Hill U.S.A. 176 H5
Willow Lake Canada 167 G2
Willowlake r. Canada 166 F2
Willowmore S. Africa 132 H10
Willowra Australia 148 B4
Willowra Aboriginal Land Trust res. Australia see Wirliyajarrayi Aboriginal Land Trust
Willow Reservoir U.S.A. 172 D5
Willows U.S.A. 182 B2
Willow Springs U.S.A. 178 E4
Willowvale S. Africa 133 M9
Wills, Lake salt flat Australia 150 E4
Wills Creek watercourse Australia 148 D4
Willunga Australia 146 C3
Wilmington Australia 146 C3
Wilmington DE U.S.A. 177 J6
Wilmington NC U.S.A. 175 E5
Wilmington OH U.S.A. 176 B6
Wilmington VT U.S.A. 177 M3
Wilmington Island U.S.A. 175 D5
Wilmore U.S.A. 176 A8
Wilno Lith. see Vilnius
Wilnsdorf Germany 48 F5
Wilpattu National Park Sri Lanka 94 D4
Wilpena watercourse Australia 146 C2
Wilson r. Australia 150 E3
Wilson watercourse Australia 147 D1
Wilson atoll Micronesia see Ifalik
Wilson MN U.S.A. 172 B7
Wilson NC U.S.A. 174 E5
Wilson NY U.S.A. 176 G2
Wilson, Mount CO U.S.A. 181 F5
Wilson, Mount NV U.S.A. 183 J3
Wilson, Mount OR U.S.A. 180 B3
Wilson Hills Antarctica 223 K2
Wilsonia U.S.A. 182 F5
Wilson Lake resr U.S.A. 174 C5
Wilsons U.S.A. 176 H8
Wilson's Promontory pen. Australia 147 E4
Wilson's Promontory National Park Australia 147 E4
Wilton r. Australia 148 B2
Wilton ME U.S.A. 177 O1
Wilton NH U.S.A. 177 N3
Wiltz Lux. 51 L3
Wiluna Australia 151 C5
Wimbledon N.Z. 152 K8
Wimereux France 50 H2
Wimmera r. Australia 147 D4
Wina r. Cameroon see Vina
Winamac U.S.A. 174 C3
Winam Gulf Kenya 128 B5
formerly known as Kavirondo Gulf
Winbin watercourse Australia 149 E5

Winburg S. Africa **133** L5
Wincanton S. Africa **132** G4
Wincanton U.K. **47** J12
Winchendon U.S.A. **177** M3
Winchester N.Z. **153** F12
Winchester U.K. **47** K12
Winchester IL U.S.A. **176** B4
Winchester IN U.S.A. **176** A5
Winchester KY U.S.A. **176** A8
Winchester NH U.S.A. **177** M3
Winchester TN U.S.A. **176** C8
Winchester VA U.S.A. **176** G6
Wind r. Canada **166** C1
Wind i. U.S.A. **180** E4
Windabout, Lake salt lake Australia **146** C2
Windau Latvia see Ventspils
Windber U.S.A. **176** G5
Wind Cave National Park U.S.A. **178** B3
Winder U.S.A. **175** D5
Windermere U.K. **47** J9
Windham U.S.A. **176** D4

▶ Windhoek Namibia **130** C4
Capital of Namibia.

Windidda Aboriginal Reserve Australia **151** C5
Windigo r. Canada **168** A2
Windigo Lake Canada **168** B2
Windischgarsten Austria **49** L8
Wind Mountain U.S.A. **181** F6
Windom U.S.A. **178** D3
Windorah Australia **149** D5
Window Rock U.S.A. **183** O6
Wind Point U.S.A. **172** F8
Wind Ridge U.S.A. **176** E6
Wind River Indian Reservation res. U.S.A. **180** E4
Wind River Range mts U.S.A. **180** E4
Winds, Bay of Antarctica **223** D22
Windsor Australia **147** F3
Windsor Nfld. Canada **169** K3
Windsor N.S. Canada **169** H4
Windsor Ont. Canada **168** D5
Windsor Que. Canada **169** F4
Windsor U.K. **47** L12
Windsor NC U.S.A. **174** E4
Windsor NY U.S.A. **177** J3
Windsor VA U.S.A. **177** I9
Windsor VT U.S.A. **177** M2
Windsor Dam U.S.A. **177** L4
Windsor Locks U.S.A. **177** M4
Windsorton S. Africa **133** I5
Windula watercourse Australia **149** D5
Windward Islands Caribbean Sea **187** H4
Windward Passage Cuba/Haiti **187** E3
Windy Harbour Australia **151** A7
Winefred Lake Canada **167** I4
Winfield AL U.S.A. **175** C5
Winfield IA U.S.A. **172** B9
Winfield KS U.S.A. **178** C4
Winfield WV U.S.A. **176** D7
Wingate Mountains hills Australia **148** A2
Wingene Belgium **51** J1
Wingham Canada **168** D5
Wini East Timor **75** C5
Winifred, Lake salt flat Australia **150** C4
Winifreda Arg. **204** D5
Winisk Canada **168** C2
Winisk r. Canada **168** C2
Winisk Lake Canada **168** C2
Winisk River Provincial Park Canada **168** C2
Winkana Myanmar **79** B5
Winkelhaaks r. S. Africa **132** D9
Winkelman U.S.A. **183** N9
Winkfelton S. Africa **133** K4
Winkler Canada **167** L5
Winlock U.S.A. **180** B3
Winnalls Ridge Australia **148** A5
Winneba Ghana **125** E5
Winnebago U.S.A. **178** D3
Winnebago, Lake U.S.A. **172** E6
Winnebago Indian Reservation res. U.S.A. **178** C3
Winneconne U.S.A. **172** E6
Winnemucca U.S.A. **182** G1
Winnemucca Lake U.S.A. **182** E1
Winner U.S.A. **178** B3
Winnett U.S.A. **180** F3
Winnfield U.S.A. **179** D6
Winnibigoshish, Lake U.S.A. **178** D2
Winning Australia **150** A4

▶ Winnipeg Canada **167** L5
Provincial capital of Manitoba.

Winnipeg r. Canada **167** L5
Winnipeg, Lake Canada **167** L5

Winnipegosis Canada **167** L5
Winnipegosis, Lake Canada **167** K4
Winnipesaukee, Lake U.S.A. **177** N2
Winnsboro SC U.S.A. **174** D5
Winnsboro TX U.S.A. **179** D5
Winona AZ U.S.A. **183** M6
Winona MI U.S.A. **172** E4
Winona MN U.S.A. **174** B2
Winona MO U.S.A. **174** B4
Winona MS U.S.A. **175** B5
Winooski U.S.A. **177** L1
Winooski r. U.S.A. **177** L1
Winschoten Neth. **48** D3
Winsen (Aller) Germany **48** G3
Winsen (Luhe) Germany **48** H2
Winslow AZ U.S.A. **183** N6
Winslow ME U.S.A. **177** P1
Winsted U.S.A. **177** L4
Winston-Salem U.S.A. **176** E9
Winter U.S.A. **172** B5
Winterberg Germany **48** F4
Winterberg mts S. Africa **133** K9
Winter Harbor U.S.A. **177** Q1
Winter Haven U.S.A. **175** D6
Winter Park U.S.A. **175** D6
Winterport U.S.A. **177** Q1
Winters CA U.S.A. **182** C3
Winters TX U.S.A. **179** C6
Winterset U.S.A. **178** D3
Winterswijk Neth. **48** D4
Winterthur Switz. **51** O5
Winterton S. Africa **133** N5
Winterveld S. Africa **133** M2
Winthrop U.S.A. **177** P1
Winton Australia **149** D4
Winton N.Z. **153** C14
Winton U.S.A. **177** I9
Wirliyajarrayi Aboriginal Land Trust res. Australia **148** B4
formerly known as Willowra Aboriginal Land Trust
Wirrabara Australia **146** C3
Wirraminna Australia **146** C2
Wirrida, Lake salt flat Australia **146** B2
Wirrulla Australia **146** B3
Wisbech U.K. **47** M11
Wiscasset U.S.A. **177** P1
Wisconsin r. U.S.A. **172** B7
Wisconsin state U.S.A. **174** B2
Wisconsin, Lake U.S.A. **172** D7
Wisconsin Dells U.S.A. **172** D7
Wisconsin Rapids U.S.A. **172** D6
Wise U.S.A. **176** C9
Wisil Dabarow Somalia **128** E3
Wisła r. Poland see Vistula
Wisłok r. Poland **49** T5
Wisłoka r. Poland **49** S5
Wismar Germany **48** I2
Wisner U.S.A. **178** C3
Wissota Lake U.S.A. **172** B6
Wistaria Canada **166** E4
Witbank S. Africa **133** N2
Witbooisvlei Namibia **130** C5
Witdraai S. Africa **132** E3
Witham r. U.K. **47** M11
Witherbee U.S.A. **177** L1
Withernsea U.K. **47** M10
Withlacoochee r. FL U.S.A. **175** D6
Withlacoochee r. FL U.S.A. **175** D6
Witjira National Park Australia **146** B1
Witkoppies mt. S. Africa **133** N4
Witkowo Poland **49** O3
Witkransnek pass S. Africa **133** J8
Witmos S. Africa **133** J9
Witnek S. Africa **133** M2
Witney U.K. **47** K12
Witnica Poland **49** L3
Witput S. Africa **133** P2
Witrivier S. Africa **133** N3
Witteberg mt. E. Cape S. Africa **132** G10
Witteberg mt. Free State S. Africa **133** M5
Witteberg mts S. Africa **133** L7
Witteberge mts S. Africa **132** E10
Wittenberg Germany see Lutherstadt Wittenberg
Wittenberg U.S.A. **172** D6
Wittenberge Germany **48** I3
Wittenburg Germany **48** I2
Wittenheim France **51** N5
Wittenoom Australia **150** B4
also known as Wittenoom Gorge
Wittenoom Gorge Australia see Wittenoom
Witti, Banjaran mts Sabah Malaysia **77** G1
Wittingen Germany **48** H3
Wittlich Germany **48** D6
Wittmund Germany **48** E2
Wittow pen. Germany **49** K1
Wittstock Germany **49** J2
Witu Kenya **128** D5
Witu Islands P.N.G. **145** D2
Witvlei Namibia **130** C4
Witwatersberg mts S. Africa **133** L3
Witwatersrand mts S. Africa **133** K3
Witzenhausen Germany **48** G4
Wivenhoe, Lake Australia **147** G1
Wkra r. Poland **49** R3
Władysławowo Poland **49** P1
Włocławek Poland **49** Q3
historically known as Vlotslavsk
Włoszczowa Poland **49** Q5
Wobkent Uzbek. see Vabkent
Wodonga Australia **147** E3
Wodzisław Śląski Poland **49** P5
historically known as Loslau
Wohko watercourse Sudan **126** F3
Wohlthat Mountains Antarctica **223** A2
Wōjja atoll Marshall Is see Wotje
Wokam i. Indon. **73** H8
Wokam r. China **82** C3
Wokha India **97** G4
Woking U.K. **47** L12
Wokingham watercourse Australia **149** D4
Woko National Park Australia **147** F2
Wolcott IN U.S.A. **172** F10
Wolcott NY U.S.A. **177** I2
Wolcott VT U.S.A. **177** M1
Wolcottville U.S.A. **172** H9
Wolczyn Poland **49** P4
Woldegk Germany **49** K2
Wolea atoll Micronesia see Woleai
Woleai atoll Micronesia **73** J5
also known as Ulie; Wolea
Woleu-Ntem prov. Gabon **126** A4
Wolf r. Canada **166** C2
Wolf r. U.S.A. **172** E6
Wolf Creek MT U.S.A. **180** D3
Wolf Creek OR U.S.A. **180** B4
Wolf Creek r. U.S.A. **179** C4
Wolf Creek Pass U.S.A. **181** F5
Wolfeboro U.S.A. **177** N2
Wolfen Germany **49** J4
Wolfenbüttel Germany **48** H3
Wolfhagen Germany **48** G4
Wolf Lake Canada **166** D2
Wolf Point U.S.A. **180** F2
Wolfsberg Austria **49** L9
Wolfsburg Germany **48** H3
Wolfstein Germany **48** E6
Wolfville Canada **169** H4
Wolgast Germany **49** K1
Wolhusen Switz. **51** O5
Wolin Poland **49** L2
Wolin i. Poland **49** L2
Woliński Park Narodowy nat. perk Poland **49** L2
Wolkersdorf Austria **49** N7
Wollaston, Islas is Chile **205** D9
Wollaston Lake Canada **167** K3
Wollaston Lake l. Canada **167** K3
Wollaston Peninsula Canada **165** H3
Wollemi National Park Australia **147** F3
Wollerau Switz. **51** O5

Wollongong Australia **147** F3
Wolmaransstad S. Africa **133** J4
Wolmirstedt Germany **48** I3
Wołomin Poland **49** S3
Wolong Reserve nature res. China **86** B2
Wolow Poland **49** N4
Wolowaru Indon. **75** B5
Wolseley S. Africa **132** D10
Wolsey U.S.A. **178** C2
Wolsztyn Poland **49** N3
Wolvega Neth. **48** D3
Wolverhampton U.K. **47** J11
Wolverine U.S.A. **172** H5
Wolwefontein S. Africa **133** I10
Wolwespruit S. Africa **133** J5
Wolya r. Indon. **76** A1
Wonarah Australia **148** C3
Wondai Australia **149** F5
Wonderfontein S. Africa **133** N2
Wonderkop mt. S. Africa **133** L5
Wondermere S. Africa **133** K2
Wongalarroo Lake salt l. Australia **147** E2
Wonga Wongué, Réserve de nature res. Gabon **126** A5
Wong Chhu r. Bhutan **97** F4
Wong Chuk Hang Hong Kong China **87** [inset]
Wong Leng hill Hong Kong China **87** [inset]
Wong Wan Chau i. Hong Kong China see Double Island
Wŏnju S. Korea **83** B5
Wonogiri Indon. **77** E4
Wonosari Indon. **77** E4
Wonosobo Indon. **77** E4
Wonowon Canada **166** F3
Wŏnsan N. Korea **83** B5
Wontaggi Australia **147** E4
Wonyulgunna, Mount hill Australia **151** B5
Woocalla Australia **146** C2
Wood, Mount Canada **166** A2
Woodbine U.S.A. **177** K6
Woodboro U.S.A. **172** D5
Woodbourne U.S.A. **177** K4
Woodbridge NJ U.S.A. **177** K5
Woodbridge U.K. **47** M11
Wood Buffalo National Park Canada **167** H3
Woodburn U.S.A. **176** A4
Woodburn OR U.S.A. **180** B3
Woodbury CT U.S.A. **177** L4
Woodbury MI U.S.A. **173** H8
Woodbury NJ U.S.A. **177** J6
Woodend Australia **147** E4
Woodfords U.S.A. **182** E3
Woodhall Spa U.K. **47** L10
Woodhull U.S.A. **172** C9
Wood Lake Canada **167** K4
Woodlake U.S.A. **182** E5
Woodland CA U.S.A. **182** C3
Woodland NC U.S.A. **177** H9
Woodland WA U.S.A. **180** B3
Woodland Park U.S.A. **180** F5
Woodlands Sing. **76** [inset]
Woodlark Island P.N.G. **145** E2
also known as Murua
Woodmurra Creek watercourse Australia **146** C1
Woodridge Canada **167** L5
Woodroffe watercourse Australia **148** C4
Woodroffe, Mount Australia **146** A1
Woodruff U.S.A. **172** D5
Woods, Lake salt flat Australia **148** B3
Woods, Lake of the Canada/U.S.A. **165** J5
Woodsfield U.S.A. **176** E6
Woods Hole U.S.A. **177** O4
Woodstock Australia **149** D4
Woodstock N.B. Canada **169** H4
Woodstock Ont. Canada **168** D5
Woodstock IL U.S.A. **172** E8
Woodstock VA U.S.A. **176** G7
Woodstock VT U.S.A. **177** M2
Woodstock Dam resr S. Africa **133** N5
Woodstown U.S.A. **177** J6
Woodsville U.S.A. **177** M1
Woodville N.Z. **152** J8
Woodville MS U.S.A. **175** B6
Woodville OH U.S.A. **176** B4
Woodville TX U.S.A. **179** D6
Woodward U.S.A. **179** C4
Woody U.S.A. **182** F6
Woöi Indon. **73** I7
Wooler U.K. **46** J8
Woolgar r. Australia **149** D4
Woolgoolga Australia **147** G2
Woolla Downs Australia **148** B4
Woollard, Mount Antarctica **222** R1
Wooltana Australia **146** C2
Woolwine U.S.A. **176** E9
Woomera Australia **146** C2
Woomera Prohibited Area Australia **146** B2
Woonsocket U.S.A. **178** C2
Woorabinda Australia **149** F5
Wooramel r. Australia **151** A5
Wooster U.S.A. **176** D5
Woqooyi Galbeed admin. reg. Somalia **128** D2
Worak-san National Park S. Korea **83** C5
Worb Switz. **51** N6
Worbody Point Australia **149** D2
Worcester S. Africa **132** D10
Worcester U.K. **47** J11
Worcester MA U.S.A. **177** N3
Worcester NY U.S.A. **177** K3
Wörgl Austria **48** J8
Workai i. Indon. **73** H8
Workington U.K. **47** I9
Worland U.S.A. **180** F3
Worms Germany **48** F6
Worms Head U.K. **47** H12
Worofla Côte d'Ivoire **124** D4
Wörth am Rhein Germany **48** F6
Worthing U.K. **47** L13
Worthington MN U.S.A. **178** D3
Worthington OH U.S.A. **176** B5
Wosi Indon. **75** C3
Wotjalum Aboriginal Reserve Australia **150** C3
Wotje atoll Marshall Is **220** H5
also spelt Wōjja; formerly known as Otdia
Wotu Indon. **75** B3
Wour Chad **120** B4
Wouri r. Cameroon **125** H5
Wowoni i. Indon. **75** B4
Wowoni, Selat sea chan. Indon. **75** B3
Wozrojdeniya Oroli i. Uzbek. see Vozrozhdeniya, Ostrov
Wrangel Island Rus. Fed. **39** S2
also known as Vrangelya, Ostrov
Wrangell U.S.A. **166** C3
Wrangell Island U.S.A. **166** C3
Wrangell Mountains U.S.A. **164** D3
Wrangell-St Elias National Park and Preserve U.S.A. **164** E3
Wrath, Cape U.K. **46** G5
Wray U.S.A. **178** B3
Wreck Reef Australia **149** G4
Wrecsam U.K. see Wrexham
Wrens U.S.A. **175** D5
Wrexham U.K. **47** J10
Wright Phil. **74** C4
Wrightmyo India **95** G4
Wrightson, Mount U.S.A. **181** E7
Wrightstown U.S.A. **172** E6
Wrightsville U.S.A. **175** D5
Wrightwood U.S.A. **182** G7
Wrigley Canada **166** F2
Wrigley U.S.A. **176** B7

Wrigley Gulf Antarctica **222** P2
Wrocław Poland **49** O4
historically known as Breslau
Wronki Poland **49** N3
Wrzesnia r. Poland **49** O3
Wrześnica r. Poland **49** O3
Wschowa Poland **49** N4
Wu'an China see Changtai
Wu'an China **85** G4
Wubalawun res. Australia see Larrimah Aboriginal Land
Wubin Australia **151** B6
Wubu China **85** F4
also known as Songjiachuan
Wuchagou China **85** I2
Wuchang Heilong. China **82** B3
Wuchang Hubei China **87** E2
formerly known as Jiangxia
Wucheng China **87** E2
Wuchow China see Wuzhou
Wuchuan Guangdong China **87** D4
also known as Meilu
Wuchuan Guizhou China **87** C2
also known as Duru
Wuchuan Nei Mongol China **85** F3
Wuda China **85** E4
Wudan China **85** H3
also known as Ongniud Qi
Wudang Shan mts China **87** D1
Wudao China **85** I4
Wuda'yah well Saudi Arabia **105** D4
Wudi China **85** H4
Wudil Nigeria **125** H4
Wuding China **86** B3
also known as Jincheng
Wuding r. China **85** F4
Wufeng China **86** C1
Wufeng China see Zhenxiong
Wugang China **87** D3
Wugong China **87** D1
also known as Puji
Wuhai China **85** E4
Wuhan China **87** E2
Wuhe China **87** F1
Wuhu Anhui China **87** F2
Wuhu Anhui China see Wanzhi
Wuhu China **87** F2
also known as Shuizhai
Wüjiang China **89** B5
Wujiang China **87** G2
Wu Jiang r. China **87** C2
Wujin China see Changzhou
Wujin China see Xinjin
Wukari Nigeria **125** H5
Wuleidao Wan l. China **85** I4
Wulian Feng mts China **86** B2
Wuliang Shan mts China **86** B3
Wuliaru i. Indon. **73** H8
Wuling China **87** C2
also known as Xingkou
Wulong r. China see Huaibin
Wulur Indon. **75** D4
Wum Cameroon **125** H5
Wumeng Shan mts China **86** B3
Wuming China **87** D4
Wümme r. Germany **48** F2
Wungda China **86** B2
Wuning China **87** E2
also known as Xinning
Wunnummin Lake Canada **168** B3
Wun Rog Sudan **126** E3
Wun Shwai Sudan **126** F2
Wunsiedel Germany **48** J5
Wunstorf Germany **48** G3
Wuntau Sudan **128** B2
Wuntho Myanmar **78** A3
Wupatki National Monument nat. park U.S.A. **183** M6
Wuping China **87** F3
Wuppertal Germany **48** E4
formerly known as Barmen-Elberfeld
Wuppertal S. Africa **132** D9
Wuqi China **85** F4
Wuqia Xinjiang China **88** A4
also known as Ukuqqat
Wuqia Xinjiang China **88** A4
Wuqiang China **85** G4
also known as Xiaofan
Wuqiao China **85** H4
also known as Sangyuan
Wuqing China **85** H4
also known as Yangcun
Wuquan China China see Buyang
Wuqub, Wādī watercourse Saudi Arabia **108** F9
Wuranga Australia **151** B6
Würm r. Germany **48** I7
Wurno Nigeria **125** G3
Wurralibi Aboriginal Land res. Australia **148** C2
Wurzbach Germany **48** I5
Würzburg Germany **48** G6
Wurzen Germany **49** J4
Wushan Chongqing China **87** D2
also known as Wuxia
Wushan China **86** C1
Wu Shan mts China **87** D2
Wusheng Sichuan China **86** B3
also known as Yankou
Wushi Zhejiang China **87** F2
also known as Uqturpan
Wusuli Jiang r. Rus. Fed. see Ussuri
Wutai China **85** G4
Wutai Shan mts China **85** G4
Wutong r. China **87** C2
Wutonggou China **88** D3
Wutongwozi Quan well China **84** B3
also known as Wuxia
Wuwei Anhui China **87** F2
Wuwei Gansu China **84** D4
formerly known as Liangzhou
Wuxi Chongqing China **87** D2
Wuxi China see Luxi
Wuxi China see Helong
Wuxia China see Wushan
Wuxiang China **85** G4
also known as Duancun
Wuxing China see Huzhou
Wuxuan China **87** D4
Wuxun China **87** D4
Wuxue China **87** E2
Wuyang China see Zhenyuan
Wuyang China **87** E1
also known as Wuquan
Wuyi China **87** F2
Wuyiling China **82** C2
also known as Gaoleshan
Wuyishan China **87** F3
formerly known as Chong'an
Wuyi Shan mts China **87** F3
Wuyi Shan tourist site China **87** F3
Wuyuan China **87** F2
also known as Ziyang
Wuyuan Nei Mongol China **85** F3
Wuyuan China see Haiyan
Wuyun China see Jinyun
Wuzhai China **85** G4
Wuzhi China **87** D4
Wuzhi Shan mts China **87** D5
Wuzhong China **85** E4

Wuzhou China **87** D4
formerly known as Wuchow
Wyaaba Creek r. Australia **149** C3
Wyalkatchem Australia **151** B6
Wyalong PA U.S.A. **177** I4
Wyalusing WI U.S.A. **172** B8
Wyandra Australia **147** E1
Wyanet U.S.A. **172** D9
Wyangala Reservoir Australia **147** F3
Wyara, Lake salt flat Australia **147** E2
Wye r. U.K. **47** J12
Wye Mills U.S.A. **177** I7
Wyemandoo hill Australia **151** B6
Wyk auf Föhr Germany **48** F1
Wyliesburg U.S.A. **176** G9
Wyloo Australia **150** B4
Wymondham U.K. **47** N11
Wymore U.S.A. **178** C3
Wynbring Australia **146** A2
Wyndham Australia **150** E2
Wyndham N.Z. **153** C14
Wyndham-Werribee Australia **147** E4
Wynne U.S.A. **174** B5
Wynniatt Bay Canada **165** H2
Wynyard Australia **147** E5
Wynyard Canada **167** J5
Wyocena U.S.A. **172** D7
Wyola Lake salt flat Australia **146** A2
Wyoming DE U.S.A. **177** J6
Wyoming IA U.S.A. **172** B8
Wyoming IL U.S.A. **172** D9
Wyoming MI U.S.A. **172** H8

▶ Wyoming state U.S.A. **180** F4
northamerica [environments] ▶▶ 162–163

Wyoming Peak U.S.A. **180** E4
Wyoming Range mts U.S.A. **180** E4
Wyong Australia **147** F3
Wyperfeld National Park Australia **146** D4
Wysoka Poland **49** O2
Wysokie Mazowieckie Poland **49** S3
Wysox U.S.A. **177** I4
Wyszków Poland **49** S3
Wyszogród Poland **49** Q3
Wyżnica r. Poland **49** S4

[↓] [X]

▶ Xaafun, Raas pt Somalia **128** F2
Most easterly point of Africa.

Xaafuun Somalia **128** F2
Xaçmaz Azer. **107** G2
also spelt Khachmas
Xade Botswana **130** D4
Xago China **89** C5
Xagquka China **89** F6
Xaidulla China **89** B4
Xainza China **89** E6
also known as Kangsangdobdê
Xaitongmoin China **89** E6
also known as Qabka
Xai-Xai Moz. **131** G5
formerly known as João Belo or Vila de João Belo
Xal, Cerro de hill Mex. **185** H4
Xalapa Mex. see Jalapa Enríquez
Xalin Somalia **128** E2
Xaltianguis Mex. **185** F5
Xamavera Angola **127** D9
Xamba China **85** E3
also known as Hanggin Houqi
Xambioá Brazil **202** B3
Xam Hua Laos **78** C3
formerly known as Sam Neua
Xá-Muteba Angola **127** C7
formerly known as Cinco de Outubro
Xan r. Laos **78** C4
Xan, Xé r. Vietnam **79** D5
Xangda China see Nangqên
Xangdin Hural China **85** H3
Xangdcring China see Xungba
Xangongo Angola **127** B9
formerly known as Roçadas
Xankändi Azer. **107** F3
also known as Stepanakert; also spelt Khankendi
Xanlar Azer. **107** F2
Xanthi Greece **58** F7
Xanxerê Brazil **203** A8
Xapuri Brazil **200** C2
Xarardheere Somalia **128** E3
Xar Burd China see Bayan Nuru
Xar Moron r. China **85** F3
Xar Moron r. China **85** I3
Xarrama r. Port. **54** C6
Xarrë Albania **59** B9
Xarsingma China see Yadong
Xassengue Angola **127** C7
Xátiva Spain **55** K6
also spelt Játiva
Xau, Lake Botswana **131** E4
also known as Dow, Lake
Xaudum watercourse Botswana/Namibia **130** D3
Xavantes, Represa de resr Brazil **206** D10
Xavantes, Serra dos hills Brazil **202** B5
Xa Vo Đat Vietnam **79** D6
Xayar China **88** C3
Xcalak Mex. **185** I5
X-Can Mex. **185** I4
Xekar China **88** B4
Xenia U.S.A. **176** B6
Xeriuini r. Brazil **199** F5
Xero Potamos r. Cyprus see Xeros
Xeros r. Cyprus **108** D3
also known as Xero Potamos
Xhora S. Africa see Elliotdale
Xhorodomo Pan salt pan Botswana **131** E4
Xi r. China **85** I3
Xiabancheng China **85** H3
Xiabole Shan mt. China **82** B2
Xiachengzi China **82** C3
Xiachuan Dao i. China **87** D4
Xiacun China see Rushan
Xiadong China **84** B3
Xiaguan China see Dali
Xiahe China **84** D5
also known as Labrang
Xiajiang China **87** E3
also known as Baqiu
Xiajiang China see Qusum
Xiajin China **85** G4
Xiamen China **87** F3
also known as Amoy
Xi'an China **87** D1
formerly spelt Sian
Xiancheng China **87** E1
Xiancheng China see Suizhai
Xianfeng China **87** D2
also known as Gaoleshan
Xiangcheng Henan China **87** E1
Xiangcheng Sichuan China **86** A2
also known as Qagchêng or Sangpi
Xiangcheng China see Xiangyang
Xiangtan China **87** E1
also known as Xiangxiang
Xiangfen China **85** F4
also known as Shicun
Xiangfeng China see Laifeng
Xianggang Hong Kong China see Hong Kong
Xianggang Tebie Xingzhengqu special admin. reg. China see Hong Kong
Xianghuang Qi China see Xin Bulag
Xiang Jiang r. China **87** E3
Xiangliang China see Huichang

Xiang Jiang r. China **87** E2
Xiangkhoang Laos **78** C4
Xiangkhoang Plateau Laos **78** C4
Xiangkou China see Wulong
Xiangning China **85** F5
Xiangquan He r. China **89** B6
Xiangride China **84** C5
Xiangshan China see Menghai
Xiangshan China **87** G2
Xiangshan Gang b. China **87** G2
Xiangshui China **87** F1
Xiangshuiba China **87** D3
Xiangtan China **87** E3
Xiangxiang China **87** E3
Xiangyang Hu l. China **89** E5
Xiangyin China **87** E2
Xiangyun China **87** E3
also known as Xiangcheng
Xianju China **87** G2
Xianning China **87** E2
Xianshui China see Jiangdu
Xianshui China see Dawu
Xianshui He r. China **86** B2
Xiantao China **87** E2
formerly known as Mianyang
Xianxia Ling mts China **87** F3
Xianxian China **85** H4
Xianyang China see Leshan
Xianyang China **87** D1
Xianyou China **87** F3
also known as Licheng
Xiaoba China see Qingtongxia
Xiaochang China **87** E2
also known as Huayuan
Xiaodong China **87** D4
Xiao'ergou China **85** I1
Xiaofan China see Wuqiang
Xiaogan China **87** E2
Xiaoguai China **88** D2
Xiao Hinggan Ling mts China **82** B2
English form Lesser Khingan Mountains
Xiaojin China **86** B2
also known as Meixing or Zainlha
Xiaomei China **87** F3
Xiaonan China **84** D5
also known as Dongxiangzu
Xiaonanchuan China **84** B5
Xiao Qaidam China **84** B4
Xiaoqing r. China **85** H4
Xiaosanjiang China **87** E3
Xiaoshan China **87** G2
Xiao Surmang China **86** A1
Xiaotao China **87** F3
Xiaowutai Shan mt. China **85** G4
Xiaoxi China see Pinghe
Xiaoxian China **87** F1
Xiaoxiang Ling mts China **86** B2
Xiaoyi China see Gongyi
Xiaoyi China **85** F4
Xiapu China **87** G3
also known as Songcheng
Xiaqiong China see Batang
Xiatil Mex. **185** H5
Xiaxian China **85** F4
Xiayanjing China see Yanjing
Xiayingpan China see Luzhi
Xiayingpan China see Lupanshui
Xiazhen China see Weishan
Xibdé China **86** A2
Xibing China **87** F3
Xibu China see Dongshan
Xichang China **86** B3
Xicheng China see Yangyuan
Xichou China **86** C4
also known as Xisa
Xichuan China **87** D1
formerly known as Shangji
Xide China **86** B2
also known as Guangming
Xidu China see Hengyang
Xié r. Brazil **199** E5
Xiejiaji China see Qingyun
Xiemahe' China **87** D2
Xieng Khouang Laos see Xiangkhoang
Xieyang Dao i. China **87** D4
Xifei He r. China **87** F1
Xifeng Gansu China **85** E5
formerly known as Xifengzhen
Xifeng Guizhou China **86** C3
also known as Yongjing
Xifeng Liaoning China **82** B4
also known as Yongjing
Xifengzhen China see Xifeng
Xigazê China **89** E6
formerly spelt Shigatse
Xihan Shui r. China **86** C1
Xihe China **86** C1
also known as Hanyuan
Xi He r. China **85** H3
Xihu China **84** B3
Xihua China **87** E1
Xihuachi China see Heshui
Xiji China **84** D5
Xi Jiang r. China **87** E4
Xijian Quan well China **84** C3
Xigir Ulan Hu salt l. China **97** D3
Xil China **85** G3
Xilaganí Greece see Xylagani
Xilaotou Shan mt. China **85** I2
Xiliao r. China **85** I3
Xiligou China see Ulan
Xilin China **86** C3
also known as Bada
Xilinhot China **85** H3
formerly known as Abagnar Qi
Xilinji China see Mohe
Xilókastron Greece see Xylokastro
Xilopolis Greece see Xylopoli
Ximiao China **84** D3
Xin China **85** F4
also known as Hanggin Qi
Xin'an China see Lai'an
Xin'an China see Anxin
Xin'an China **87** E1
Xin'anjiang Shuiku resr China **87** F2
Xinavane Moz. **133** Q2
Xin Barag Youqi China see Altan Emel
Xin Barag Zuoqi China see Amgalang
Xinbin China **82** B4
Xin Bulag China **85** G3
also known as Hobot Xar Qi or Xianghuang Qi
Xincai China **87** E1
also known as Gulü
Xinchang China **87** G2
Xinchang China see Yifeng
Xincheng China see Gutian
Xincheng Guangxi China **87** D3
also known as Dawu
Xincheng China see Yuancu
Xincheng China see Zhaojue
Xinchengbu China **85** F4
Xincun China China see Dongchuan
Xindi China **87** D4
Xindi China see Honghu
Xindu Guangxi China **87** D4
also known as Luhuo
Xindu Sichuan China **86** B2
Xinduqiao China **86** B2
Xinfeng Guangdong China **87** E3
also known as Fengcheng
Xinfeng Jiangxi China **87** E3
also known as Jiading
Xinfengjiang Shuiku resr China **87** E4
Xing'an China **87** D3

Xingan China 87 E3
also known as Jinchuan
Xingba China see Lhünzê
Xingcheng China see Qianxi
Xingcheng China 85 I3
Xingdi China 88 D3
Xinge Angola 127 C7
Xingguo China see Qin'an
Xingguo China 87 E3
also known as Lianjiang
Xinghai China 84 C5
also known as Ziketan
Xinghua China 87 F1
Xinghua Wan b. China 87 F3
Xingkai China 82 D3
Xingkai Hu l. China/Rus.Fed. see Khanka, Lake
Xinglong Hebei China 85 H3
Xinglong Heilong. China 82 B2
Xinglongzhen China 82 B3
Xingning China 87 E3
Xingou China 87 E2
Xingping China 87 D1
Xingren China 86 C3
Xingrenbu China 84 E4
Xingsagoinba China 86 B1
Xingshan China see Majiang
Xingshan China 87 D2
also known as Gufu
Xingtai China 85 G4
Xingtang China 85 G4
Xingu r. Brazil 199 H5
Xingu, Parque Indígena do res. Brazil 202 A4
Xinguara Brazil 202 B3
Xingxian China 85 F4
Xingxingxia China 84 B3
Xingyang China 87 E1
Xingyi China 86 C3
also known as Huangcaoba
Xingzi China 87 F2
also known as Nankang
Xinhe Hebei China 85 G4
Xinhe Xinjiang China 88 C3
also known as Toksu
Xin Hot China 85 G3
also known as Abag Qi
Xinhua China see Huadu
Xinhua China 87 D3
Xinhua China see Qiaojia
Xinhua China see Funing
Xinhuacun China 84 D4
Xinhuang China 87 D3
Xinhui China 85 H3
also known as Aohan Qi
Xining China 84 D4
formerly spelt Sining
Xinji China 85 G4
formerly known as Shulu
Xinji China see Xinxian
Xinjian China 87 E2
also known as Changleng
Xinjiang China 85 F5
Xinjiang aut. reg. China see Xinjiang Uygur Zizhiqu
Xin Jiang r. China 87 F2
Xinjiangkou China see Songzi
Xinjiang Uygur Autonomous Region aut. reg. China see Xinjiang Uygur Zizhiqu
Xinjiang Uygur Zizhiqu aut. reg. China 84 B3
English form Sinkiang Uighur Autonomous Region or Xinjiang Uygur Autonomous Region; short form Sinkiang or Xinjiang; formerly known as Chinese Turkestan
Xinjie China 85 F4
Xinjie China see Yuanyang
Xinjin China see Pulandian
Xinjin China 86 B2
also known as Wujin
Xinjing China see Jingxi
Xinkai r. China 85 I3
Xinling China see Badong
Xinlong China 86 B2
also known as Nyagrong or Rulong
Xinmi China 87 E1
formerly known as Mixian
Xinmian China see Shimian
Xinmin China 85 I3
Xinning China see Ningxian
Xinning China see Fusui
Xinning China 87 D3
also known as Jinshi
Xinning China see Wuning
Xinning China see Kaijiang
Xinping China 86 B3
also known as Guishan
Xinqing China 82 C2
Xinquan China 87 F3
Xinshan China see Anyuan
Xinshao China 87 D3
also known as Niangxi
Xinshi China see Jingshan
Xinshiba China see Ganluo
Xintai China 85 H5
Xintanpu China 87 E2
Xintian China 87 E3
Xinxian China 87 E2
also known as Xinji
Xinxiang China 85 G5
Xinxing China 87 E4
also known as Xincheng
Xinyang China 87 E1
Xinyang Gang r. China 87 G1
Xinye China 87 E1
Xinye r. China 87 F1
Xinyi Guangdong China 87 D4
Xinyi Jiangsu China 87 F1
Xinying China 87 D5
Xinying Taiwan see Hsinying
Xinyu China 87 E3
Xinyuan China see Tianjun
Xinyuan China 88 C3
also known as Künes
Xinzhangfang China 85 I1
Xinzheng China 87 E1
Xinzhou China see Longlin
Xinzhou China see Huangping
Xinzhou Hubei China 87 E2
Xinzhou Shanxi China 85 G4
Xinzhu Taiwan see Hsinchu
Xinzo de Limia Spain 54 D2
also spelt Ginzo de Limia
Xiongshan China see Zhenghe
Xiongzhou China see Nanxiong
Xipamanu r. Bol./Brazil 200 D2
Xiping Henan China 87 D1
also known as Baicheng
Xiping Henan China 87 E1
Xiqing Shan mts China 86 B1
Xique Xique Brazil 202 D4
Xiro hill Greece 59 E10
Xirokampo Greece 59 H11
Xiruá r. Brazil 198 E6
Xisa China see Xichou
Xishanzui China 85 F3
also known as Urad Qianqi
Xisha Qundao is S. China Sea see Paracel Islands
Xishuangbanna reg. China 86 B4
Xishui Guizhou China 86 C2
Xishui Hubei China 87 E2
also known as Qingquan
Xistral, Serra do mts Spain 54 D1
also spelt Sierra del Gistral
Xi Taijnar Hu l. China 84 B4
Xitole Guinea-Bissau 124 B4
Xiucaiwan China see Fengdu
Xiugu China see Jinxi
Xi Ujimqin Qi China see Bayan Ul Hot
Xiuning China 87 F2
also known as Haiyang
Xiushan China 87 D2
also known as Zhonghe
Xiushan China see Tonghai
Xiushui China 87 E2
also known as Yining
Xiu Shui r. China 87 E2
Xiuwen China 86 C3
Xiuwu China 85 G5
Xiuyan China 85 I3
Xiuyan China see Qingjian
Xiuying China 87 D4
Xiwanzi China see Chongli
Xiwu China 86 A1
Xixabangma Feng mt. China 89 D6
also known as Shisha Pangma; formerly known as Gosainthan
Xixia China 87 D1
Xixian Henan China 87 E1
Xixian Shanxi China 85 F4
Xixiang China 87 C1
Xixón Spain see Gijón
Xiyang China 85 G4
Xiyang Dao i. China 87 G3
Xiyang Jiang r. China 86 C3
Xizang aut. reg. China see Xizang Zizhiqu
Xizang Gaoyuan plat. China see Tibet, Plateau of
Xizang Zizhiqu aut. reg. China 86 A2
English form Tibet or Tibet Autonomous Region; short form Xizang
Xizhong Dao i. China 85 I4
Xocavänd Azer. 107 F3
also spelt Khodzhavend
Xodoto, Akra pt Greece 59 H12
Xoi China see Qüxü
Xolobe S. Africa 133 L9
Xom An Lôc Vietnam 79 D6
Xom Duc Hanh Vietnam 79 D6
Xonxa Dam S. Africa 133 L8
Xorkol China 88 E4
Xuancheng China see Xuanzhou
Xuan'en China 87 D2
also known as Zhushan
Xuanhan China 87 C2
also known as Dongxiang
Xuanhua China 85 G3
Xuân Lôc Vietnam 79 D6
Xuanwei China 86 C3
Xuanzhou China 87 F2
formerly known as Xuancheng
Xuchang Henan China 87 E1
Xucheng China see Xuwen
Xudat Azer. 107 G2
also spelt Khudat
Xuddur Somalia 128 D3
Xudun Somalia 128 E2
Xueba China see Sangri
Xuefeng China see Mingxi
Xuefeng Shan mts China 87 D3
Xuehua Shan hill China 87 D1
Xue Shan mts China 86 A3
Xugou China 87 F1
Xugui China 84 B5
Xuguit Qi China see Yakeshi
Xujiang China see Guangchang
Xulun Hobot Qagan Qi China see Qagan Nur
Xulun Hoh Qi China see Dund Hot
Xümatang China 86 A1
Xun r. China 82 C2
Xundian China 86 B3
also known as Rende
Xungba China 89 C5
also known as Xangdoring
Xungmai China 89 E6
Xung Qu r. China 89 F6
Xungru China 89 D6
Xunhe China 82 B2
Xun He r. China 87 D1
Xunhua China 84 D5
also known as Jishi
Xun Jiang r. China 87 D4
Xunke China 82 C2
Xunwu China 87 E3
also known as Changning
Xunxian China 85 G5
Xunyang China 87 D1
Xunyi China 85 F5
Xupu China 87 D3
also known as Lufeng
Xuru Co salt l. China 89 D6
Xushui China 85 G4
also known as Ansu
Xuwen China 87 D4
also known as Xucheng
Xuyang China see Rongxian
Xuyi China 87 F1
Xuyong China 86 C2
also known as Yongning
Xuzhou China see Tongshan
Xylagani Greece 58 G8
also spelt Xilagani
Xylokastro Greece 59 D10
also known as Xilókastron
Xylopoli Greece 58 E8
also known as Xilópolis

↓ Y

Ya'an China 86 B2
Yaapeet Australia 147 D3
Yabanabat Turkey see Kızılcahamam
Yabassi Cameroon 125 H5
Yabêlo Eth. 128 C3
Yabêlo Wildlife Sanctuary nature res. Eth. 128 C3
Yablanitsa Bulg. 58 F5
Yablanovo Bulg. 58 H6
Yablonovyy Khrebet mts Rus. Fed. 85 F1
Yabo Nigeria 125 G3
Yabrai Shan mts China 84 D4
Yabrai Yanchang China 84 D4
Yabrīn reg. Saudi Arabia 105 E3
Yabrūd Syria 109 H4
Yabuli China 82 C3
Yabuyanos Peru 198 C5
Yacha China see Baisha
Yacheng China 87 D5
Yachi He r. China 86 C3
Yacitetá, Isla i. Para. 201 F6
Yacyretá Apipé, Embalse resr Para. 201 F6
Yacuiba Bol. 201 E5
Yacurai Venez. 199 E3
Yadé, Massif du mts Cent. Afr. Rep. 126 B3
Yadgir India 94 C2
Yadiki India 94 C3
Yadkin r. U.S.A. 174 D5
Yadkinville U.S.A. 176 E9
Yadong China 89 E7
also known as Xarsingma; formerly known as Chomo
Yadrin Rus. Fed. 40 H5
Yaeyama-rettō is Japan 81 K8
Yafa Israel see Tel Aviv-Yafo
Yafran Libya 120 B1
Yagaba Ghana 125 E4
Yagaing state Myanmar see Arakan
Yağcılı Turkey 59 I9
Yağda Turkey see Erdemli
Yagman Turkm. 102 C5
Yagmo China 89 D6
Yagnitsa Rus. Fed. 43 S3
Yago Mex. 184 D4
Yagoda Bulg. 58 G6
Yagodnaya Polyana Rus. Fed. 41 H6
Yagodnoye Kaluzhskaya Oblast' Rus. Fed. 43 Q8
Yagodnoye Magadanskaya Oblast' Rus. Fed. 39 O3
Yagodnyy Rus. Fed. 82 E2
Yagoua Cameroon 125 I4
Yagra China 89 C6
Yagradagzê Shan mt. China 84 B5
Yaguajay Cuba 186 D2
Yaguarón r. Brazil/Uruguay see Jaguarão
Yaguas r. Peru 198 D5
Yaha Thai. 79 C7
Yahk Canada 167 G5
Yahualica Mex. 185 E4
Yahyalı Turkey 98 B2
also known as Gazibenli
Yahya Wana Afgh. 96 A3
Yai, Khao hill Thai. 79 B5
Yaita Japan 90 F6
Yaizu Japan 91 F7
Yajiang China 86 B2
also known as Hekou or Nyagquka
Yakacık Turkey 108 H1
Yakapınar Turkey 108 G1
Yakeshi China 85 I1
formerly known as Xuguit Qi
Yakhab waterhole Iran 100 D3
Yakhehal Afgh. 101 F4
Yakhroma Rus. Fed. 43 S5
Yakima U.S.A. 180 B3
Yakima r. U.S.A. 180 C3
Yakima Indian Reservation res. U.S.A. 180 B3
Yakinish Iran 100 C3
Yakkabag Uzbek. 103 F5
formerly known as Stantsiya-Yakkabag
Yakmach Pak. 101 E4
Yako Burkina 125 E3
Yakobi Island U.S.A. 166 B3
Yakoma Dem. Rep. Congo 126 D3
Yakoruda Bulg. 58 E6
Yakovlevka Rus. Fed. 82 D3
Yakumo Japan 90 G3
Yaku-shima i. Japan 91 B9
Yakutat U.S.A. 166 B3
Yakutat Bay U.S.A. 164 E4
Yakutsk Rus. Fed. 39 M3
Yakymivka Ukr. 41 E7
Yala Ghana 125 E4
Yala Thai. 79 C7
Yalai China 89 D6
Yalakdere Turkey 58 K8
Yala National Park Sri Lanka see Ruhuna National Park
Yalan Dünya Mağarası tourist site Turkey 108 D1
Yalata Aboriginal Lands res. Australia 146 A2
Yale Canada 166 F5
Yale U.S.A. 173 K7
Yalgoo Australia 151 B6
Yalıkavak Turkey 59 I11
Yalıköy Turkey 58 J7
Yalinga Cent. Afr. Rep. 126 D3
Yalizava Belarus 43 K8
Yalkubul, Punta pt Mex. 185 H4
Yalleroi Australia 149 E5
Yallo Burkina 124 E3
Yallourn Australia 147 E4
Yaloké Cent. Afr. Rep. 126 C3
Yalong Jiang r. China 86 B3
Yalova Turkey 106 B2
Yalova prov. Turkey 58 K8
Yaloven' Moldova see Ialoveni
Yalpirakinu Aboriginal Land res. Australia 148 B4
Yalpuh, Ozero l. Ukr. 58 J3
Yalpukh r. Moldova see Ialpug
Yalta Ukr. 41 E7
Yaltins'kyy Zapovidnyk nature res. Ukr. 106 C1
Yalu Jiang r. China 85 I2
Yalu Jiang r. China/N. Korea 83 B4
also known as Amnok-kang
Yalutorovsk Rus. Fed. 38 G4
Yalvaç Turkey 106 B3
Yām reg. Saudi Arabia 105 D4
Yamada Japan 90 G5
Yamaga Japan 91 B8
Yamagata Iwate Japan 90 G4
Yamagata Yamagata Japan 90 G5
Yamagata pref. Japan 90 F5
Yamaguchi Japan 91 B7
Yamaguchi pref. Japan 91 B7
Yamal, Poluostrov pen. Rus. Fed. see Yamal Peninsula
Yam Alin', Khrebet mts Rus. Fed. 82 D1
Yamal Peninsula Rus. Fed. 38 G2
also known as Yamal, Poluostrov
Yamanashi pref. Japan 90 F7
Yamanie Falls National Park Australia 149 E3
Yamankhalinka Kazakh. see Makhambet
Yamarovka Rus. Fed. 85 F1
Yamasaki Japan 91 D7
Yamatsuri Japan 90 G6
Yamba Australia 147 G2
Yambacoona Australia 147 D4
Yambarran Range hills Australia 148 A2
Yambéring Guinea 124 B4
Yambi, Mesa de hills Col. 198 D4
Yambio Sudan 126 F3
Yambol Bulg. 58 H6
Yambrasbamba Peru 198 B6
Yamdena i. Indon. 73 H8
Yame Japan 91 B8
Yamethin Myanmar 78 B3
Y'ami i. Phil. 74 B1

▶Yamin, Puncak mt. Indon. 73 I7
4th highest mountain in Oceania.
oceania [landscapes] ⟹ 136–137

Yamizo-san mt. Japan 90 G6
Yamkanmardi India 94 B2
Yamkhad Syria see Aleppo
Yamkino Rus. Fed. 43 K4
Yamm Rus. Fed. 43 J3
Yamma Yamma, Lake salt flat Australia 149 D5
also known as Mackillop, Lake

▶Yamoussoukro Côte d'Ivoire 124 D5
Capital of Côte d'Ivoire.

Yampil' Ukr. 41 D6
also spelt Yampol'
Yampol' Ukr. see Yampil'
Yamuna r. India 96 D4
English form Jumna
Yamunanagar India 96 C3
Yamzho Yumco l. China 89 E6
Yan r. China 85 F4
Yana r. Rus. Fed. 39 N2
Yanac Australia 146 D4
Yanachaga-Chemillen, Parque Nacional nat. park Peru 200 B2
Yanadani Japan 91 C8
Yanai Japan 91 C8
Yanam India 95 D2
formerly known as Yanaon
Yan'an China 85 F4
Yanaoca Peru 200 C3
Yanaon India see Yanam
Yanaul Rus. Fed. 40 J4
Yanavichy Belarus 43 L6
Yanayacu Peru 198 C5
Yanbian China 86 B3
also known as Dapingdi
Yanbu' al Bahr Saudi Arabia 104 B2
Yanbu' an Nakhl reg. Saudi Arabia 104 B2
Yanceyville U.S.A. 176 F9
Yanchang China 85 F4
Yancheng China 87 G1
Yancheng China see Qihe
Yancheng China see Jingyan
Yanchep Australia 151 A6
Yanchi Ningxia China 85 E4
Yanchi Xinjiang China 84 B3
Yanchuan China 85 F4
Yanco Creek r. Australia 147 E3
Yanco Glen Australia 146 D2
Yanda watercourse Australia 147 E2
Yandama Creek watercourse Australia 146 D2
Yandang Shan mts China 87 G3
Yandao China see Yingjing
Yandaxkak China 88 E4
Yandeyarra Aboriginal Reserve Australia 150 B4
Yandil Australia 151 B5
Yandina Solomon Is 145 E2
Yandja Dem. Rep. Congo 126 C5
Yandoon Myanmar 78 A4
Yandun China 84 B3
Yanega Rus. Fed. 43 O1
Yanfolila Mali 124 C4
Yang r. China 85 G3
Yangalia Cent. Afr. Rep. 126 D3
Yangambi Dem. Rep. Congo 126 E4
Ya'ngamdo Xizang China 89 F6
Ya'ngamdo Xizang China 89 F6
Yangasso Mali 124 D3
Yangbajain China 89 E6
Yangbi China 86 A3
also known as Shangjie
Yangcheng China see Yangshan
Yangcheng China 85 G5
Yangchuan China see Suiyang
Yangchun China 87 D4
Yangcun China 87 E4
Yangcun China see Wuqing
Yangdok N. Korea 83 B5
Yanggao China 85 G3
Yanggu China 85 G4
Yanghe China see Yongning
Yang Hu l. China 89 D5
Yangiaryk Uzbek. 102 E4
Yangi Davan pass Aksai Chin/China 89 B5
Yangi-Nishan Uzbek. 103 F5
Yangi Qal'eh Afgh. 101 G2
Yangirabad Uzbek. 103 F4
Yangiyul' Uzbek. 103 G4
Yangjialing China 85 F4
Yangjiang China 87 D4
Yangjiaqiao China 85 H4
Yangôn Myanmar see Rangoon
Yangôn admin. div. Myanmar 78 B4
English form Rangoon; also spelt Rangôn
Yangping China 87 D2
Yangquan China 85 G4
Yangshan China 87 E3
also known as Yangcheng
Yangshuo China 87 D3
Yang Talat Thai. 78 C4
Yangtouyan China 86 B3

▶Yangtze r. China 87 G2
Longest river in Asia and 3rd in the world. Also known as Yangtze Kiang or Chang Jiang or Jinsha Jiang or Tongtian He or Zhi Qu.
asia [landscapes] ⟹ 62–63

Yangtze Kiang r. China 87 F2
also known as Yangtze
Yangtze, Mouth of the China 87 G2
also known as Changjiang Kou
Yangudi Rassa National Park Eth. 128 D2
Yangweigang China 87 F1
Yangxian China 87 C1
Yangyang S. Korea 83 C5
Yangyuan China 85 G3
also known as Xicheng
Yangzhou China see Hanjiang
Yanhe China 87 D2
also known as Heping
Yanhu China 88 E3
Yaninee, Lake salt flat Australia 146 B3
Yanishpole Rus. Fed. 40 E3
Yanis"yarvi, Ozero l. Rus. Fed. 44 O3
Yanji China 82 C4
Yanjin Henan China 85 G5
Yanjin Yunnan China 86 C2
also known as Yanjing
Yanjing China see Yanyuan
Yanjing China 86 A2
also known as Xiayanjing; formerly known as Caka'lho
Yanjing China see Yanjin
Yankara National Park Nigeria 125 H4
Yankavichy Belarus 43 J6
Yankou China see Wusheng
Yankton U.S.A. 178 C3
Yankton Indian Reservation res. U.S.A. 178 C3
Yanling Henan China 87 E1
also known as Anling
Yanling Hunan China 87 E3
formerly known as Lingxian
Yannina Greece see Ioannina
Yano-Indigirskaya Nizmennost' lowland Rus. Fed. 39 O2
Yanovo Rus. Fed. 43 N7
Yanov-Stan Rus. Fed. 39 I3
Yan Oya r. Sri Lanka 94 D4
Yanqi China 88 D3
Yanqing China 85 G3
Yanqul Oman 105 G3
Yanrey r. Australia 150 A4
Yanshan Hebei China 85 H4
Yanshan Jiangxi China 87 F2
also known as Hekou
Yanshan Yunnan China 86 C4
also known as Jiangna
Yan Shan mts China 85 H3
Yanshi China 87 E1
Yanshiping China 97 G2
Yanshou China 82 C3
Yanskiy Zaliv g. Rus. Fed. 39 N2
Yantabulla Australia 147 E2
Yantai China 85 I4
formerly known as Chefoo
Yántales, Cerro mt. Chile 205 B6
Yantarnyy Rus. Fed. 42 A7
historically known as Palmnicken
Yanting China 86 C2
also known as Yunxi
Yantongshan China 82 B4
Yantou China 87 G2
Yantra r. Bulg. 58 G5
Yanūfi, Jabal al hill Saudi Arabia 104 C3
Yany-Kurgan Kazakh. see Zhanakorgan
Yanyuan China 86 B3
also known as Yanjing
Yanzhou China 85 H5
Yao'an China 86 B3
also known as Dongchuan
Yaodu China see Dongzhi
Yaojie China see Honggu
Yaoli China 87 F2

▶Yaoundé Cameroon 125 H6
Capital of Cameroon.

Yaoxian China 87 D1
Yao Yai, Ko i. Thai. 79 B6
Yaozhen China 85 F4
Yap i. Micronesia 73 I5
formerly spelt Eap
Yapacana, Parque Nacional nat. park Venez. 199 E4
Yapacani r. Bol. 201 D3
Yapen i. Indon. 73 I7
Yapen, Selat sea chan. Indon. 73 I7
Yappar r. Australia 149 D3
Yapukarri Guyana 199 G4
Yapuparra Aboriginal Reserve Australia 151 D5
Yaqui r. Mex. 184 C3
Yar Rus. Fed. 40 J4
Yara Cuba 186 D2
Yaracal Venez. 198 D2
Yaracuy state Venez. 198 D2
Yaradzha Turkm. see Yaradzhi
Yaradzhi Turkm. 102 D5
formerly spelt Yaradzha
Yaraka Australia 149 E5
Yarangüme Turkey see Tavas
Yaransk Rus. Fed. 40 H4
Yardan Uzbek. see Iordan
Yardea Australia 146 B3
Yardımcı Burnu pt Turkey 106 B3
also known as Gelidonya Burnu
Yardımlı Azer. 107 G3
also spelt Yardymly
Yardley U.S.A. 177 K5
Yardoi China 89 E6
Yardymly Azer. see Yardımlı
Yare r. U.K. 47 N11
Yarega Rus. Fed. 40 J3

▶Yaren Nauru 145 F2
Capital of Nauru.
world [countries] ⟹ 10–11

Yarenga r. Rus. Fed. 40 I3
Yarensk Rus. Fed. 40 I3
Yargara Moldova see Iargara
Yari r. Col. 198 C5
also known as Engaños, Río de los
Yariga-take mt. Japan 91 E6
Yarim Yemen 104 D5
Yarımca Turkey see Körfez
Yaringa watercourse Australia 148 C4
Yaripo Brazil 199 H4
Yaris well Niger 125 G3
Yaritagua Venez. 187 F5
Yarkand China see Shache
Yarkant China see Shache
Yarkant He r. China 88 B4
Yarker Canada 173 Q6
Yarkhun r. Pak. 101 H2
Yarlovo Bulg. 58 E6
Yarlung Zangbo r. China 89 D6 see Brahmaputra
Yarmouth Canada 169 H5
Yarmouth U.K. see Great Yarmouth
Yarmouth U.S.A. 177 O2
Yarmūk r. Asia 108 G5
Yarnell U.S.A. 183 L7
Yaroslavichi Rus. Fed. 43 P1
Yaroslavl' Rus. Fed. 43 U4
Yaroslavl Oblast admin. div. Rus. Fed. see Yaroslavskaya Oblast'
Yaroslavskaya Oblast' admin. div. Rus. Fed. 43 U4
English form Yaroslavl Oblast
Yaroslavskiy Rus. Fed. 82 D3
Yarqon r. Israel 108 F5
Yarrabah Aboriginal Reserve Australia 149 E3
Yarra Junction Australia 147 E4
Yarralin Aboriginal Land res. Australia 148 A3
Yarram Australia 147 E4
Yarraman Australia 149 F5
Yarrawonga Australia 147 E4
Yarra Yarra Lakes salt flat Australia 151 A6
Yarrie Australia 150 C4
Yarronvale Australia 149 E5
Yarrowmere Australia 149 E4
Yartsevo Krasnoyarskiy Kray Rus. Fed. 39 I3
Yartsevo Smolenskaya Oblast' Rus. Fed. 43 N6
Yaru r. China 89 D6
Yarumal Col. 198 C3
Yarwa China 86 A2
Yary Rus. Fed. 40 M1
Yarzhong China 86 A2
Yaş Romania see Iaşi
Yasa Dem. Rep. Congo 126 D5
Yasai r. India 95 E1
Yasawa Group is Fiji 145 G3
Yasenkovo Bulg. 58 H5
Yashi Nigeria 125 G3
Yashikera Nigeria 125 F4
Yashilkŭl l. Tajik. 101 H2
Yashkino Rus. Fed. 43 J5
Yashkul' Rus. Fed. 41 H7
formerly known as Peschanoye
Yasin Jammu and Kashmir 96 B1
Yaskavichy Belarus 42 I9
Yasna Polyana Bulg. 58 I6
Yasnogorsk Rus. Fed. 43 S7
formerly known as Laptevo
Yasnyy Amurskaya Oblast' Rus. Fed. 82 C1
Yasnyy Orenburgskaya Oblast' Rus. Fed. 102 D2
Yasothon Thai. 78 D5
Yass Australia 147 F3
Yass r. Australia 147 F3
Yassı Burnu c. Cyprus see Plakoti, Cape
Yasski Rus. Fed. 43 L4
Yasugi Japan 91 C7
Yāsūj Iran 100 B4
Yasuni nat. park Ecuador 198 C5
Yasur vol. Vanuatu 145 F3
Yat well Niger 125 I1
Yata r. Bol. 200 D2
Yata r. Cent. Afr. Rep. 126 D2
Yatağan Turkey 106 B3
Yatakala Niger 125 F3
Yata Plateau Kenya 128 C5
Yaté New Caledonia 145 F4
Yates r. Canada 167 H2
Yates Center U.S.A. 178 D4
Yathkyed Lake Canada 167 L2
Yathong Nature Reserve Australia 147 E3
Yatolema Dem. Rep. Congo 126 E4
Yatou China see Rongcheng
Yatsuga-take vol. Japan 91 F7
Yatsushiro Japan 91 B8
Yatsushiro-kai b. Japan 91 B8
Yaṭṭa West Bank 108 G6
also spelt Yuta
Yauca Peru 200 B3
Yauca r. Peru 200 B3
Yauco Puerto Rico 187 G3
Yauli Peru 200 A2
Yauna Maloca Col. 198 D5
Yauri Peru 200 C3
Yauricocha Peru 200 B3
Yau Tong b. Hong Kong China 87 [inset]
Yauyos Peru 200 B3
Yavan Tajik. see Yovon
Yavari r. Peru 198 D6
also spelt Javari
Yávaros Mex. 184 C3
Yavatmal India 94 C1
formerly spelt Yeotmal
Yavero r. Peru 200 B3
also known as Paucartambo
Yavi, Cerro mt. Venez. 199 E3
Yavr r. Fin./Rus. Fed. 44 O1
Yavuzlu Turkey 109 I1
Yawatahama Japan 91 C8
Yawatongguz He r. China 89 C4
Yawatongguzlangar China 89 C4
Yaw Chaung r. Myanmar 78 A3
Yawng-hwe Shan Myanmar 78 B3
Yaxchilan tourist site Guat. 185 H5
Yaxian China see Sanya
Yayladağı Turkey 108 H2
also known as Ordu
Yayva Rus. Fed. 40 K4
Yazagyo Myanmar 78 A3
Yazd Iran 100 C4
Yazd prov. Iran 100 C4
Yazdān Iran 101 E3
Yazd-e Khväst Iran 100 C4
also known as Samirum
Yazgulemskiy Khrebet mts Tajik. see Yazgulom, Qatorkŭhi
Yazgulom, Qatorkŭhi mts Tajik. 101 G2
also known as Yazgulemskiy Khrebet
Yazhelbitsy Rus. Fed. 43 N3
Yazıhan Turkey 107 D3
also known as Fethiye
Yazıkent Turkey 59 J11
Yazoo r. U.S.A. 175 B5
Yazoo City U.S.A. 175 B5
Yaz'va r. Rus. Fed. 40 K3
Ybakoura well Chad 120 B4
Y Bala U.K. see Bala
Ybbs r. Austria 49 M7
Ybbs an der Donau Austria 49 M7
Ybycuí Para. 201 F6
Yding Skovhøj hill Denmark 45 J5
Ydra Greece 59 E11
Ydra i. Greece 59 E11
English form Hydra; also spelt Idhra or Idra
Ydras, Kolpos sea chan. Greece 59 E11
also spelt Ídhras, Kólpos
Y Drenewydd U.K. see Newtown
Ye Myanmar 79 B5
Ye r. Myanmar 79 B5
Yebaishou China see Jianping
Yebawmi Myanmar 78 A2
Yebbi-Bou Chad 120 C4
Yebekshi Kazakh. 103 G4
Yecheng China 88 B4
formerly known as Karghalik or Kargilik
Yecla Spain 55 J6
Yécora Mex. 184 C2
Yedashe Myanmar 78 B4
Yedatore India 94 C3
Yedi Burun Başı pt Turkey 59 K12
Yedoma Rus. Fed. 40 H3
Yedri well Chad 120 C4
Yedrovo Rus. Fed. 43 O4
Yedy Belarus 42 I6
Yeed Eth. 128 D3
Yeeda River Australia 150 C3
Yeelanna Australia 146 B3
Yefimovskiy Rus. Fed. 43 P2
Yefremov Rus. Fed. 43 T8
Yêgainnyin China see Henan
Yeggueba well Niger 125 I2
Yeghegnadzor Armenia 107 F3
formerly known as Mikoyan; formerly spelt Yekhegnadzor
Yegindybulak Kazakh. 103 I2
also spelt Egindibulaq
Yegorlyk r. Rus. Fed. 41 G7
Yegorlykskaya Rus. Fed. 41 G7
Yegorova, Mys pt Rus. Fed. 82 E3
Yegor'ye Rus. Fed. 43 O6
Yegor'yevsk Rus. Fed. 43 U6
Yégué Togo 125 F4
Yei Sudan 128 A3
Yei r. Sudan 128 A3
Yeina Island P.N.G. 149 G1
Yeji China 87 E2
formerly known as Yejiaji
Yeji Ghana 125 E4
Yejiaji China see Yeji
Yekaterinburg Rus. Fed. 38 G4
formerly known as Sverdlovsk
Yekaterinodar Rus. Fed. see Krasnodar
Yekaterinoslav Ukr. see Dnipropetrovs'k
Yekaterinoslavka Rus. Fed. 82 C2
Yekaterinovka Lipetskaya Oblast' Rus. Fed. 43 T9
Yekaterinovka Saratovskaya Oblast' Rus. Fed. 41 H5
Yekhegnadzor Armenia see Yeghegnadzor
Yekimovichi Rus. Fed. 43 O7
Yekokora r. Dem. Rep. Congo 126 D4
Yelabuga Rus. Fed. 82 D2
Yelabuga Rus. Fed. 40 I5
Yelan' Rus. Fed. 41 G6
Yelbarsli Turkm. 103 E5
Yeleğen Turkey 59 J10
Yelenovskiye Kar'yery Ukr. see Dokuchayevs'k
Yelenskiy Rus. Fed. 43 Q8
Yelets Rus. Fed. 43 T9
Yeletskiy Rus. Fed. 40 M2
Yeligovo Rus. Fed. 43 O3
Yélimané Mali 124 C3
Yelino Rus. Fed. 43 U7
Yelizavetgrad Ukr. see Kirovohrad
Yelizovo Rus. Fed. 39 P4
Yelkhovka Rus. Fed. 41 I5
Yell i. U.K. 46 K3
Yellabina Regional Reserve nature res. Australia 146 B2
Yellandu India 94 D2
Yellapur India 94 B3
Yellareddi India 94 C2

▶Yellow r. China 85 H4
4th longest river in Asia and 7th in the world. Also known as Huang He or Ma Qu; formerly spelt Hwang Ho.
asia [landscapes] ⟹ 62–63

Yellow r. U.S.A. 172 C7
Yellow Bluff hd Canada 167 O1
Yellowdine Australia 151 B6
Yellowhead Pass Canada 166 G4

▶Yellowknife Canada 167 H2
Capital of Northwest Territories.

Yellowknife r. Canada 167 H2
Yellow Mountain hill Australia 147 E3
Yellow Sea N. Pacific Ocean 83 B6
Yellow Springs U.S.A. 176 B6
Yellowstone r. U.S.A. 178 B2
Yellowstone Lake U.S.A. 180 E3
▶Yellowstone National Park U.S.A. 180 E3
northamerica [environments] ⟹ 162–163
Yell Sound strait U.K. 46 K3
Yellville U.S.A. 179 D4
Yelm U.S.A. 180 B3
Yel'nya Rus. Fed. 43 O7
Yeloten Turkm. 103 E5
also spelt Yolöten; formerly spelt Iolotan'
Yelovo Rus. Fed. 40 J4
Yel'sk Belarus 41 D6
Yel'tsy Rus. Fed. 43 O5
Yelva r. Rus. Fed. 40 I3
Yelverton Bay Canada 165 K1
Yelwa Nigeria 125 H4
Yema Nanshan mts China 84 B4
Yema Shan mts China 84 B4
Yematan China 84 C4
Yembo Eth. 128 C2
▶Yemen country Asia 104 D5
asia [countries] ⟹ 64–67
Yemetsk Rus. Fed. 40 G3
Yemişenbükü Turkey see Taşova
Yemmiganur India see Emmiganuru
Yemtsa Rus. Fed. 40 G3
Yemva Rus. Fed. 40 I3
formerly known as Zheleznodorozhnyy
Yena Rus. Fed. 44 O2
Yenagoa Nigeria 125 G5
Yenakiyeve Ukr. 41 F6
also spelt Yenakiyevo; formerly known as Rykovo
Yenakiyevo Ukr. see Yenakiyeve
Yenangyat Myanmar 78 A3
Yenangyaung Myanmar 78 A3
Yenanma Myanmar 78 A4
Yên Bai Vietnam 78 D3
Yendi Ghana 125 E4
Yêndum China see Zhag'yab
Yénéganou Congo 126 B5
Yenge r. Dem. Rep. Congo 126 D5
Yengejeh Iran 100 A2
Yengema Sierra Leone 124 C4

Yexian China 87 E1
also known as Kunyang
Yexian China see Laizhou
Yeygen'yevka Kazakh. 103 I4
Yeyik China 89 C4
Yeysk Rus. Fed. 41 F7
Yeyungou China 88 D3
Yezerishche, Ozero l. Belarus/Rus. Fed.
43 L6
Yezhou China see Jianshi
Yezhua r. Rus. Fed. 40 H2
Yezo i. Japan see Hokkaidō
Yezyarysheha Belarus 43 K6
Y Fenni U.K. see Abergavenny
Y Fflint U.K. see Flint
Yi r. Henan China 87 E1
Yi r. Shandong China 87 F1
Yi r. Uruguay 204 F4
Yiali i. Greece see Gyali
Yi'allaq, Gebel mt. Egypt 108 E7
Yialousa Cyprus see Aigialousa
Yi'an China 82 B3
Yianisádha i. Greece see Giannitsa
Yiannitsá Greece see Giannitsa
Yibā, Wādī watercourse Saudi Arabia
104 C4
Yibin Sichuan China 86 C2
also known as Baixi
Yibin Sichuan China 86 C2
Yibug Caka salt l. China 89 D5
Yichang China 87 D2
Yicheng Hubei China 87 E2
Yicheng Shanxi China 85 F5
Yichuan Henan China 87 E1
Yichuan Shaanxi China 85 F5
also known as Danzhou
Yichun Heilong. China 82 C3
Yichun Jiangxi China 87 E3
Yidu China see Qingzhou
Yidun China 86 A2
also known as Dagxoi
Yifeng China 87 E2
also known as Xinchang
Yiggêtang China see Qumarlêb
Yihuang China 87 F3
also known as Fenggang
Yijiang China see Yiyang
Yijun China 85 F5
Yilaha China 85 J1
Yilan China 82 C3
Yilan Taiwan see Ilan
Yıldız Dağları mts Turkey 106 A2
Yıldızeli Turkey 107 D3
also known as Yenihan
Yilehuli Shan mts China 85 I1
Yiliang Yunnan China 86 B3
also known as Kuangyuan
Yiliang Yunnan China 86 C3
also known as Jiaokui
Yiliping China 84 B4
Yilliminning Australia 151 B7
Yilong Heilong. China 82 B3
Yilong Sichuan China 86 C2
also known as Jincheng
Yilong China see Shiping
Yilong Hu l. China 86 B4
Yimatu r. China 85 H3
Yimianpo China 82 C3
Yimin r. China 85 H1
Yiman China 85 H5
also known as Jiehu
Yincheng China see Dexing
Yinchuan China 85 E4
Yindarlgooda, Lake salt flat Australia
151 C6
Yingawunarri Aboriginal Land res.
Australia 148 A3
Yingcheng China 87 E2
Yingde China 87 E3
Ying He r. China 87 F1
Yingjing China 86 B2
also known as Yandao
Yingkou China 85 I3
historically known as Newchwang
Yingkou China see Dashiqiao
Yingpanshui China 84 E4
Yingshan Hubei China 87 E2
also known as Wenquan
Yingshan Sichuan China 86 C2
also known as Chengshou
Yingshang China 87 F1
Yingtan China 87 F2
Yingtaoyuan China see Fanxian
Yingxian China 85 G4
Yining China China see Xiushui
Yining China 88 C3
also known as Gulja; formerly known as
Kuldja
Yiningarra Aboriginal Land res. Australia
148 A4
Yinjiang China 87 D3
Yinkeng China 87 E3
Yinma r. China 82 B3
Yinmabin Myanmar 78 A3
Yinnyein Myanmar 78 B4
Yin Shan mts China 85 F3
Yinxian China see Ningbo
Yi'ong Zangbo r. China 89 F6
Yioúra i. Greece see Gioura
Yipinglang China 86 B3
Yiquan China see Meitan
Yira Chapeu, Monte mt. Brazil 207 I9
Yirol Sudan 128 A3
Yirrkala Australia 148 C2
Yirshi China see Yirxie
Yirxie China 85 H2
formerly known as Yirshi
Yisa China see Honghe
Yishan China see Yizhou
Yishan China see Guanyun
Yi Shan mt. China 85 H4
Yi Shan mts China 85 H4
Yishui China 85 H5
Yishun Sing. 76 [inset]
Yi Tchouma well Niger 125 I1
Yithion Greece see Gytheio
Yitiaoshan China see Jingtai
Yitong China 82 B4
Yitong r. China 82 B3
Yi Tu, Nam r. Myanmar 78 B3
Yitulihe China 85 I1
Yiwanquan China 84 B3
Yiwu China 84 B3
also known as Aratürük
Yiwulü Shan mts China 85 I3
Yixian Anhui China 87 F2
also known as Biyang
Yixian Hebei China 85 G4
also known as Yizhou
Yixian Liaoning China 85 I3
also known as Yizhou
Yixing China 87 F2
Yiyang Hunan China 87 E2
Yiyang Jiangxi China 87 F2
also known as Yijiang
Yiyuan China 85 H4
also known as Nanma
Yizhang China 87 E3
Yizheng China 87 F1
Yizhou China 87 D3
formerly known as Qingyuan or Yishan
Yizhou China see Yixian
Yizhou China see Yixian
Yizra'el country Asia see Israel
Ylä-Keitele l. Fin. 44 N3
Ylämaa Fin. 45 O3
Yläne Fin. 45 M3
Ylihärmä Fin. 44 M3
Yli-Ii Fin. 44 N2
Yli-Kärppä Fin. 44 N2

Ylikiiminki Fin. 44 N2
Yli-Kitka l. Fin. 44 O2
Ylistaro Fin. 44 M3
Ylitornio r n. 44 M2
Ylivieska Fin. 44 N2
Ylläs hill Fin. 44 N2
Ylöjärvi Fin. 45 M3
Ymer Nunatak Greenland 165 Q2
Ymer Ø i. Greenland 165 Q2
Ynykchanskiy Rus. Fed. 39 N3
Ynys Môn i. U.K. see Anglesey
Yoakum U.S.A. 179 C6
Yobe state Nigeria 125 H4
Yobetsu-dake vol. Japan 90 G3
Yoboki Djibouti 128 D2
Yogan, Cerro mt. Chile 205 C9
Yogoum well Chad 120 C3
Yogyakarta Indon. 77 E4
formerly spelt Jogjakarta
Yogyakarta admin. dist. Indon. 77 E5
Yoho National Park Canada 167 G5
Yoichi Japan 90 G3
Yoichi-dake mt. Japan 90 G3
Yojoa, Lago de l. Hond. 186 B4
Yōju S. Korea 83 B5
Yōka Japan 91 D7
Yokadouma Cameroon 125 I6
Yōkaichi Japan 91 E7
Yōkaichiba Japan 91 G7
Yokkaichi Japan 91 E7
Yoko Cameroon 125 I5
Yokohama Aomori Japan 90 G4
Yokohama Kanagawa Japan 91 F7
Yokosuka Japan 91 F7
Yokota Japan 90 G5
Yokotsu-dake mt. Japan 90 G4
Yola Nigeria 125 I4
Yolo U.S.A. 182 C3
Yolombo Dem. Rep. Congo 126 D5
Yolöten Turkm. see Yeloten
Yoluk Mex. 185 I4
Yom, Mae Nam r. Thai. 78 C5
Yomou Guinea 124 C5
Yonago Japan 91 D7
Yōnan N. Korea 83 B5
Yoneshiro-gawa r. Japan 90 G4
Yonezawa Japan 90 G6
Yŏng-am S. Korea 83 B6
Yong'an China see Fengjie
Yong'an China see Fengshou
Yongchang China 84 D4
Yongcheng China 87 F1
Yŏngch'ŏn S. Korea 83 C6
Yongchuan China 86 C2
Yongcheng China 87 E3
also known as Taocheng
Yongdeng China 84 D4
Yongding China 87 F3
also known as Fengcheng
Yongding China see Yongren
Yongding China see Fumin
Yongding r. China 85 H4
Yongfeng China 87 E3
also known as Wenfeng; formerly known as
Jishui
Yongfeng China see Guangfeng
Yongfengqu China 88 D3
Yongfu China 87 D3
Yŏnggwang S. Korea 83 B6
Yŏnghŭng N. Korea 83 B5
Yŏnghŭng-man b. N. Korea 83 B5
Yongji China 82 B4
Yongji China see Kouqian
Yongjia China 87 G2
also known as Shangtang
Yongjing China 84 D5
also known as Liujiaxia
Yongjing China see Xifeng
Yongjing China see Xifeng
Yongju S. Korea 83 C5
Yongkang China 87 G2
Yongle China see Zhen'an
Yongle China see Nanping
Yongling China 82 B4
Yongnian China 85 G4
also known as Linmingguan
Yongning Guangxi China 87 D4
also known as Pumiao
Yongning China see Tonggu
Yongning Ningxia China 85 E4
also known as Xuyong
Yongning China see Qingshui
Yongren China 86 B3
also known as Yongding
Yŏngsan-gang r. S. Korea 83 B6
Yongshan China 86 A3
also known as Jingxin
Yongsheng China 86 B3
also known as Yongbei
Yongshou China 85 E4
also known as Jianjun
Yongshun China 87 D2
also known as Lingxi
Yongtai China 87 F3
also known as Zhangcheng
Yŏngwŏl S. Korea 83 C5
Yongxi China see Nayong
Yongxing Hunan China 87 E3
Yongxing Jiangxi China 87 E3
also known as Hechuan
Yongxiu China 87 E2
Yongzhou China 87 D3
Yonkers U.S.A. 177 L5
Yonne r. France 51 I4
Yoo Baba well Niger 125 I2
Yopal Col. 198 C3
Yopurga China 88 B4
Yordon Uzbek. see Iordan
Yordu Jammu and Kashmir 96 B2
York Australia 151 B6
York r. Canada 167 M4
York U.K. 47 K10
historically known as Eburacum
York AL U.S.A. 175 B5
York NE U.S.A. 178 C3
York PA U.S.A. 177 I6
York, Cape Australia 149 C1
York, Kap c. Greenland see Innaanganeq
York Downs Australia 149 D2
Yorke Peninsula Australia 146 C3
Yorkshire Dales National Park U.K. 47 J9
Yorkshire Wolds hills U.K. 47 L10
York Springs U.S.A. 177 H5
Yorkton Canada 167 K5
Yorktown U.S.A. 177 I8
Yoro Hond. 186 B4
Yoronga i. Indon. 75 C3
Yörööö Gol r. Mongolia 85 E1
Yosemite U.S.A. 176 A8
Yosemite National Park U.S.A. 182 E4
Yosemite Village U.S.A. 182 E4
Yoshino-gawa r. Japan 91 C7
Yoshino-Kumano National Park Japan
91 E8
Yoshkar-Ola Rus. Fed. 40 H4
Yos Sudarso i. Indon. see Dolak, Pulau
Yōsu S. Korea 83 B6
Yotau Bol. 201 E4
Yōtei-zan mt. Japan 90 G3
Yotvata Israel 108 G8
Youbou Canada 166 E5
Youdunzi China 88 E4
Youghal Rep. of Ireland 47 E12
also known as Eochaill
You Jiang r. China 87 D4
Youlin China 85 H5
Young Australia 147 F3
Young r. Australia 151 C7

Young Uruguay 204 F4
Young U.S.A. 183 N7
Younghusband, Lake salt flat Australia
146 C3
Younghusband Peninsula Australia
146 C3
Young Island Antarctica 223 K2
Young Nicks Head N.Z. 152 L6
Young Range mts N.Z. 153 D12
Youngstown Canada 167 I5
Youngstown U.S.A. 176 E4
Youngsville NC U.S.A. 176 G9
Youngsville PA U.S.A. 176 F4
Yountville U.S.A. 182 B3
You Shui r. China 87 D2
Youssoufia Morocco 122 C2
formerly known as Louis-Gentil
Youvarou Mali 124 D3
Youxi China 87 F3
Youxian China 87 E3
Youyang China 87 D2
also known as Zhongduo
Youyi China 82 C3
Youyi Feng mt. China/Rus. Fed. 88 D1
Youyu China 85 F4
also known as Liangjiayoufang
Yovon Tajik. 101 G2
also spelt Yavan
Yowah watercourse Australia 147 E2
Yowereena Hill hill Australia 151 B5
Yozgat Turkey 106 C3
Ypé-Jhú Para. 201 G5
Yppäri Fin. 44 N2
Ypres Belgium see Ieper
Ypsilanti U.S.A. 173 J8
Yreka U.S.A. 180 B4
Yrghyz Kazakh. see Irgiz
Yr Wyddfa mt. U.K. see Snowdon
Yser r. France 51 K7
also known as IJzer (Belgium)
Yssingeaux France 51 K7
Ystad Sweden 45 K5
Ysyk-Köl Kyrg. see Balykchy
Ysyk-Köl admin. div. Kyrg. 103 I4
English form Issyk-Kul Oblast; also known as
Issyk-Kul'skaya Oblast'
Ysyk-Köl salt l. Kyrg. 103 I4
5th largest lake in Asia. Also known as
Issyk-Kul', Ozero.
asia [landscapes] 62–63
Y Trallwng U.K. see Welshpool
Ytre Vinje Norway see Åmot
Ytyk-Kyuyel' Rus. Fed. 39 N3
Yu r. Indon. 75 D3
Yu i. China. 75 D3
Yuan'an China 87 D2
Yuanbao Shan mt. China 87 D3
Yuanjiang Hunan China 87 E2
Yuanjiang Yunnan China 86 B4
also known as Lijiang
Yuan Jiang r. Hunan China 87 D2
Yuan Jiang r. Yunnan China 86 B4
Yuanjiazhuang China see Foping
Yuanli Taiwan 87 G3
Yuanlin China 85 H1
Yuanling China 87 D2
Yuanma China see Yuanmou
Yuanmou China 86 B3
also known as Yuanma
Yuanping China 85 G4
Yuanqu China 85 F5
also known as Xincheng; formerly known as
Liuzhangzhen
Yuanquan China see Anxi
Yuanshan China see Lianping
Yuanshanzi China 84 C4
Yuanyang China 86 B4
also known as Xinjie
Yuba City U.S.A. 182 C2
Yūbari Japan 90 G3
Yūbari-dake mt. Japan 90 H3
Yūbari-sanchi mts Japan 90 H3
Yubei China 86 C2
formerly known as Jiangbei
Yūbetsu Japan 90 H2
Yūbetsu-gawa r. Japan 90 H2
Yubu Sudan 126 E3
Yucaipa U.S.A. 183 G7
Yucatán pen. Mex. 185 H5
Yucatán state Mex. 185 H4
Yucatan Channel Cuba/Mex. 171 I7
Yucca U.S.A. 183 J7
Yucca Lake U.S.A. 183 H5
Yucca Valley U.S.A. 183 H7
Yucheng China see Yunan
Yucheng Henan China 87 E1
Yucheng Shandong China 85 H4
Yudino Moskovskaya Oblast' Rus. Fed. 43 S5
Yudino Yaroslavskaya Oblast' Rus. Fed.
43 U3
Yudoma r. Rus. Fed. 39 N4
Yudu China 87 E3
also known as Gongjiang
Yuecheng China see Yuexi
Yuechi China 86 C2
Yuelai China see Jiulong
Yueliang Pao l. China 85 I2
Yuendumu Australia 148 A4
Yuendumu Aboriginal Land res. Australia
148 A4
Yuen Long Hong Kong China 87 [inset]
Yueqing China 87 G2
Yuexi Anhui China 87 F2
also known as Tiantang
Yuexi Sichuan China 86 B2
also known as Yuecheng
Yueyang Hunan China 87 E2
also known as Rongjiawan
Yueyang China see Anyue
Yug Rus. Fed. 40 H4
Yug r. Rus. Fed. 40 H4
Yugan China 87 F2
Yugo-Kamskiy Rus. Fed. 40 J4
Yugorsk Rus. Fed. 38 G3
formerly known as Komsomol'skiy
Yugorskiy Poluostrov pen. Rus. Fed. 40 L1
Yugorskiy Shar Rus. Fed. 40 L1
Yugoslavia country Europe 58 B3
spelt Jugoslavija in Serbian
europe [countries] 32–35
Yugoslavia
Up to 1993 included Bosnia-Herzegovina,
Croatia, Macedonia and Slovenia.
Yuhang China 87 G2
Yuhu China see Eryuan
Yuhuan China 87 G2
also known as Huanshan
Yuhuang Ding mt. China 85 H4
Yuin Australia 151 B5
Yujiang China 87 F2
also known as Dengjiabu
Yu Jiang r. China 87 D4
Yujin China see Qianwei
Yukagirskoye Ploskogor'ye plat. Rus. Fed.
39 P3
Yukamenskoye Rus. Fed. 40 J4
Yukarı Sakarya Ovalanı plain Turkey 106 B3
Yukarısarıkaya Turkey 106 C3
Yukhavichy Belarus 43 J5
Yukhmachi Rus. Fed. 41 J5
Yukhnov Rus. Fed. 43 Q7
Yukhovo Rus. Fed. 43 L5

Yuki Dem. Rep. Congo 126 C5
Yuki Japan 91 C7
Yukon r. Canada/U.S.A. 164 C3
5th longest river in North America.
northamerica [landscapes] 156–157
Yukon-Charley Rivers National Preserve
nature res. U.S.A. 164 D3
Yukon Crossing Canada 166 B2
Yukon Territory admin. div. Canada
166 C2
Yüksekova Turkey 107 F3
also known as Dize
Yukuhashi Japan 91 B8
Yulara Australia 143 A5
Yuldybayevo Rus. Fed. 102 D1
Yule r. Australia 150 B4
Yuleba Australia 149 F5
Yuli China 88 D3
also known as Lopnur
Yuli Taiwan 87 G4
Yulin Guangxi China 87 D4
Yulin Shaanxi China 85 F4
Yulongxue Shan mt. China 86 B3
Yuma AZ U.S.A. 183 J9
Yuma CO U.S.A. 178 B3
Yuma Desert U.S.A. 183 J9
Yumaguzino Rus. Fed. 102 D1
Yumbarra Conservation Park nature res.
Australia 146 B2
Yumbi Bandundu Dem. Rep. Congo 126 C5
Yumbi Maniema Dem. Rep. Congo 126 E5
Yumbo Col. 198 B4
Yumen China 84 C4
also known as Laojunmiao
Yumendongzhan China 84 C4
Yumenguan China 84 B3
Yumenzhen China 84 C4
Yumin China 88 C2
also known as Karabura
Yumt Uul mt. Mongolia 84 C2
Yumurtalık Turkey 108 G1
Yuna Australia 151 A6
Yuna r. Dom. Rep. 187 F3
Yunak Turkey 106 B3
Yunan China 87 D4
also known as Yucheng
Yunchara Bol. 200 D5
Yuncheng Shandong China 85 G5
Yuncheng Shanxi China 87 D1
Yundamindera Australia 151 C6
Yunfu China 87 D4
Yungas reg. Bol. 200 D4
Yungay Chile 200 C6
Yungayo Peru 200 C3
Yun Gui Gaoyuan plat. China 86 B3
Yunhe China see Pizhou
Yunhe China see Heqing
Yunhe China 87 F2
Yunjinghong China see Jinghong
Yunkai Dashan mts China 87 D4
Yunnan prov. China 86 B3
Yun Shui r. China 87 E2
Yunta Australia 146 C3
Yunt Dağı mt. Turkey 108 D1
Yuntut National Park Canada 164 F3
Yunusler Turkey 59 K9
Yunwu Shan mts China 87 D4
Yunxi China 87 D1
Yunxi China see Yanting
Yunxian Hubei China 87 D1
Yunxian Yunnan China 86 B3
also known as Aihua
Yunxiao China 87 F4
also known as Yunling
Yun'yakha r. Rus. Fed. 40 L2
Yunyang Chongqing China 87 D2
Yunyang Henan China 87 E1
Yupin China see Pingbian
Yuping China see Libo
Yuping China 87 D3
also known as Pingxi
Yuqing China 87 D3
also known as Baini
Yura Bol. 200 D5
Yura r. Bol. 200 D5
Yuracpanin Peru 198 B6
Yura-çawa r. Japan 91 D7
Yūrappu-dake mt. Japan 90 G3
Yuratsishki Belarus 42 H7
Yuraygir National Park Australia 147 G2
Yurba Co l. China 89 D5
Yurga Rus. Fed. 80 C1
Yurimaguas Peru 198 B6
Yurino Rus. Fed. 40 H4
Yurla Rus. Fed. 40 J4
Yurungkax He r. China 89 C4
Yur'ya Rus. Fed. 40 I4
Yur'yakha r. Rus. Fed. 40 J2
Yuryev Estonia see Tartu
Yur'yevets Ivanovskaya Oblast' Rus. Fed.
40 G4
Yur'yevets Vladimirskaya Oblast' Rus. Fed.
43 V5
Yur'yev-Pol'skiy Rus. Fed. 43 U5
Yuscarán Hond. 186 B4
Yushan Fujian China 87 F2
a so known as Bingxi
Yü Shan mt. Taiwan 87 G4
Yushan Liedao is China 87 G2
Yushe China 85 G4
Yushino Rus. Fed. 40 I1
Yushkozero Rus. Fed. 40 F2
Yushu Jilin China 82 B3
Yushu Qinghai China 86 A1
Yushugou China 88 D3
Yusta r. Rus. Fed. 41 H7
Yushuwan China see Huaihua
Yusta Rus. Fed. 102 A3
Yusufeli Turkey 107 E2
Yusuhara Japan 91 C8
Yus'va Rus. Fed. 40 J4
Yuta West Bank see Yatta
Yutai China 87 F1
also known as Guting
Yutian Hebei China 85 H4
Yutian Xinjiang China 89 C4
also known as Keriya or Muhala
Yutpundji Djindiwirritj res. Australia see
Roper Bar Aboriginal Land
Yuty Para. 201 F6
Yuva Turkey 108 A1
Yuwang China 85 E4
Yuxi Hubei China 87 D2
Yuxi Yunnan China 86 B3
also known as Huanshan
Yuxiakou China 87 D2
Yuxian Shanxi China see Yuzhou
Yuxian Shanxi China 85 G4
Yuyao China 87 G2
Yuyue China see Jiayu
Yuza Japan 90 G5
Yuzawa Japan 90 G5
Yuzha Rus. Fed. 40 G4
Yuzhno-Alichurskiy, Khrebet mts Tajik. see
Alichuri Janubí, Qatorkŭhi
Yuzhno-Kamyshovyy ridge
Rus. Fed. 82 G3

Yuzhno-Kazakhstanskaya Oblast'
admin. div. Kazakh. see
Yuzhnyy Kazakhstan
Yuzhno-Kuril'sk Rus. Fed. 82 G3
also known as Utashinai
Yuzhno-Muyskiy Khrebet mts Rus. Fed.
81 I1
Yuzhno-Sakhalinsk Rus. Fed. 82 F3
Yuzhno-Sukhokumsk Rus. Fed. 41 H7
Yuzhnoukrayinsk Ukr. 41 D7
also spelt Yuzhnoukrajinsk
Yuzhnyy Rus. Fed. see Adyk
Yuzhnyy Rus. Fed. 41 G7
Yuzhnyy, Mys hd Rus. Fed. 39 P4
Yuzhnyy Altay, Khrebet mts Kazakh. 88 D1
Yuzhnyy Kazakhstan admin. div. Kazakh.
103 G4
English form South Kazakhstan Oblast'; also
known as Ongtüstik Qazaqstan Oblysy;
formerly known as Chimkentskaya Oblast';
long form Yuzhno-Kazakhstanskaya Oblast'
Yuzhnyy Ural mts Rus. Fed. 102 D1
English form Southern Urals
Yuzhong China 84 E5
also known as Yuxian
Yuzhou China see Yuxian
Yuzhou China 87 E1
Yuzkuduk Uzbek. 103 G4
also spelt Yuzquduq
Yuzovka Ukr. see Donets'k
Yuzquduq Uzbek. see Yuzkuduk
Yverdon Switz. 51 M6
Yvetot France 50 G3
Yweni Myanmar 78 A3
Ywathit Myanmar 78 B4
Yylanly Turkm. 102 D4
formerly spelt Il'yaly
Yzerfonteinpunt pt S. Africa 132 C10
Yzeure France 51 J6

↓ Z

Za, Oued r. Morocco 123 E2
Zaaimansdal S. Africa 132 H10
Zaamin Uzbek. 103 G5
also spelt Zomin
Zaandam Neth. 48 B3
Žabala r. Romania 58 H3
Žabalj Vojvodina, Srbija Yugo. 58 B3
Zāb al Kabīr, Nahr az r. Iraq 107 E3
English form Great Zab
Zabalova Latvia 42 I4
Zāb aş Şaghīr, Nahr az r. Iraq 107 E4
English form Little Zab
Zabaykal'sk Rus. Fed. 85 H1
formerly known as Otpor
Zab-e Kuchek r. Iran 100 A3
Zabia Dem. Rep. Congo 126 E4
Zabid Yemen 104 C5
Zabid, Wādī watercourse Yemen 104 C5
Ząbkowice Śląskie Poland 49 N5
Żabłudów Poland 49 U2
Żabno Poland 49 R5
Zabok Croatia 56 H3
Zábol prov. Afgh. 101 F3
Zābol Iran 101 E4
Zābol prov. Afgh. 101 E3
also known as Nasratabad
Zāboli Iran 101 E5
also known as Magas
Zabor'ye Rus. Fed. 43 Q2
Zabqung China see Gyêwa
Zăbrani Romania 58 C2
Zabré Burkina 125 E4
Zabrze Poland 49 P5
historically known to Hindenburg
Zaburun'ye Kazakh. 102 B3
Zacapa Guat. 185 H6
Zacapoaxtla Mex. 185 F5
Zacapu Mex. 185 E5
Zacatecas Mex. 185 E4
Zacatecas state Mex. 185 E4
Zacatecoluca El Salvador 185 H6
Zacatepec Morelos Mex. 185 F5
Zacatepec Oaxaca Mex. 185 F5
Zacatlán Mex. 185 F5
Zachagansk Kazakh. 102 B2
Zacharo Greece 59 C11
also spelt Zakháron
Zacoalco Mex. 184 E4
Zacualtipán Mex. 185 F4
Zacynthus i. Greece see Zakynthos
Zad, Col du pass Morocco 122 D2
Zadar Croatia 56 H4
formerly known as Zara; historically known
as ladera
Zadarski Kanal sea chan. Croatia 56 H4
Zadetkale Kyun i. Myanmar 79 B6
also known as St Luke's Island
Zadetkyi Kyun i. Myanmar 79 B6
also known as St Matthew's Island
Zadi Myanmar 79 B5
Zadoi China 97 G2
also known as Sahu
Zadonsk Rus. Fed. 43 T9
Zadran reg. Afgh. 101 G3
Za'farāna Egypt 108 D8
Za'farāna, Rās pt Egypt 108 D8
Zafarwal Pak. 101 H3
Zafer Adaları is Cyprus see Kleides Islands
Zafer Burnu c. Cyprus see
Apostolos Andreas, Cape
Zafora i. Greece 59 H12
Zafra Spain 54 E6
Zag Morocco 122 C3
Zagań Poland 49 M4
Żagarė Lith. 42 E5
Zagazig Egypt 121 F2
also spelt Az Zaqāzīq
Zaghdeh well Iran 100 D3
Zāgheh Iran 100 A3
Zāgheh-ye Bālā Iran 100 A3
Zaghouan Tunisia 123 H1
Zagon Romania 58 H3
Zagora Greece 59 E9
Zagora Morocco 122 D3
Zagorje ob Savi Slovenia 56 H3
Zagorsk Rus. Fed. see Sergiyev Posad
Zagórz Poland 49 T6
Zagrazhden Bulg. 58 F7

Zagreb Croatia 56 H3
Capital of Croatia. Historically known as
Agram.

Zagros, Kūhhā-ye mts Iran see
Zagros Mountains
Zagros Mountains Iran 100 A3
also known as Zagros, Kūhhā-ye
Žagubica Srbija Yugo. 58 C4
Zagunao China see Lixian
Za'gya Zangbo r. China 89 E5
Zahamena, Réserve de nature res. Madag.
131 [inset] K3
Zaḩawn, Wādī r. Yemen 105 E4
Zāhedān Balūchestān va Sīstān Iran 101 E4
also known as Duzdab
Zāhedān Fārs Iran 100 C4
Zāhedān Fārs Iran see Zakhmet
Zāḥlé Lebanon 108 G4
Zahmet Turkm. see Zakhmet
Zahrān Saudi Arabia 104 C4
Zahrat al Baṭn des. Iraq 109 N6
Zahrez Chergui salt pan Alg. 55 O9
Zaiceva Latvia 42 I4
Žaiginys Lith. 42 E6
Zaigrayevo Rus. Fed. 85 F1
Za'in, Jabal hill Saudi Arabia 104 C3
Zaindeh r. Iran 100 C3
Zainlha China see Xiaojin
Zair Uzbek. 102 D4
also spelt Zayyr or Zoir

Zaire country Africa see Congo, Democratic Republic of
Zaire prov. Angola 127 B6
Zaïre r. Congo/Dem. Rep. Congo see Congo
Zaječar Srbija Yugo. 58 D5
Zaka Zimbabwe 131 F4
Zakamensk Rus. Fed. 84 D1
formerly known as Gorodok
Zakataly Azer. see Zaqatala
Zakháro Greece see Zacharo
Zakharovka Kazakh. 103 G2
Zakharovo Rus. Fed. 43 U7
Zakhmet Turkm. 103 E5
also spelt Zähmet
Zākhō Iraq 107 E3
Zakhodnyaya Dzvina r. Europe see Zapadnaya Dvina
Zakhrebetnoye Rus. Fed. 40 F1
Zákinthos i. Greece see Zakynthos
Zakopane Poland 49 Q6
Zakouma Chad 126 C2
Zakouma, Parc National de nat. park Chad 126 C2
Zakros Greece 59 H13
Zakwaski, Mount Canada 166 F5
Zakynthos Greece 59 B11
Zakynthos i. Greece 59 B11
also spelt Zákinthos; historically known as Zacynthus
Zala Angola 127 B6
Zala r. Romania 49 O9
Zalābiyah tourist site Syria 109 K2
Zalaegerszeg Hungary 49 N9
Zalai-domsag hills Hungary 49 N9
Zalakomár Hungary 49 O9
Zalamea de la Serena Spain 54 F6
Zalanga Nigeria 125 H4
Zalantun China 85 I2
also known as Butha Qi
Zalaszentgrót Hungary 49 O9
Zalău Romania 58 E1
Zalavas Lith. 42 H7
Žalec Slovenia 56 H2
Zalegoshch' Rus. Fed. 43 R9
Zaleski U.S.A. 176 C6
Zales'ye Rus. Fed. 43 R3
Zalewo Poland 49 Q2
Zalew Szczeciński b. Poland 49 L2
Zalew Wiślany b. Poland 49 Q1
Zalim Saudi Arabia 104 C3
Zalingei Sudan 120 D6
Zalmā, Jabal az mt. Saudi Arabia 104 B2
Zaltan, Jabal hills Libya 120 C2
Zaluch'ye Rus. Fed. 43 M4
Zama Japan 91 F7
Zama Niger 125 F3
Zama City Canada 166 G3
Zamakh Saudi Arabia 105 D4
Zamani S. Africa 133 N4
Zamanti r. Turkey 106 C3
Zambales Mountains Phil. 74 B3
Zambeze r. Africa 131 G2 see Zambezi

▶Zambezi r. Africa 131 G2
4th longest river in Africa. Also spelt Zambeze.
africa [landscapes] ▶ 112–113

Zambezi Zambia 127 D8
Zambézia prov. Moz. 131 H3
Zambezi Escarpment Zambia/Zimbabwe 127 E9
Zambezi National Park Zimbabwe 131 E3
▶Zambia country Africa 127 E8
formerly known as Northern Rhodesia
africa [countries] ▶ 114–117
Zamboanga Phil. 74 B5
Zamboanga Peninsula Phil. 74 B5
Zamboanguita Phil. 74 B4
Zambrów Poland 49 T3
Zambue Moz. 131 F2
Zamfara state Nigeria 125 G3
Zamfara watercourse Nigeria 125 G3
Zamlat Amagraj hills W. Sahara 122 B4
Zamogil'ye Rus. Fed. 42 I3
Zamora Ecuador 198 B6
Zamora r. Ecuador 198 B5
Zamora Spain 54 F3
Zamora-Chinchipe prov. Ecuador 198 B5
Zamora de Hidalgo Mex. 185 E5
Zamość Poland 53 G1
formerly known as Zamost'ye
Zamost'ye Poland see Zamość
Zamtang China 86 B1
also known as Rangke; formerly known as Gamda
Zamuro, Punta pt Venez. 187 F5
Zamuro, Sierra del mts Venez. 199 F3
Zamzam, Wādī watercourse Libya 120 B2
Zanaga Congo 126 B5
Zanatepec Mex. 185 G5
Záncara r. Spain 55 I5
Zancle Sicilia Italy see Messina
Zanda China 89 B6
also known as Toling
Zandamela Moz. 131 G5
Zanderij Suriname 199 H3
Zandvliet Belgium 51 K1
Zanesville U.S.A. 176 C6
Zangasso Mali 124 D3
formerly spelt Sangasso
Zangelan Azer. see Zängilan
Zängilan Azer. 107 F3
also spelt Zangelan; formerly known as Pirchevan
Zangla Jammu and Kashmir 96 C2
Zangsêr Kangri mt. China 89 D5
Zanhuang China 85 G4
Zanjān Iran 100 B2
Zanjān prov. Iran 100 B2
Zanjān Rūd r. Iran 107 F3
Zannah, Jabal az hill U.A.E. 105 F2
Zanskar reg. Jammu and Kashmir see Zaskar
Zanthus Australia 151 C6
Zantiébougou Mali 124 D4
Zanzibar Tanz. 129 C6
Zanzibar Channel Tanz. 129 C6
Zanzibar Island Tanz. 129 C6
Zanzibar North admin. reg. Tanz. 129 C6
also known as Unguja North
Zanzibar South admin. reg. Tanz. 129 C6
also known as Unguja South
Zanzibar West admin. reg. Tanz. 129 C6
also known as Unguja West
Zaokskiy Rus. Fed. 43 S7
Zaonia Mornag Tunisia 57 C12
Zaoro-Songou Cent. Afr. Rep. 126 C3
Zaoshi Hubei China 87 E2
Zaoshi Hunan China 87 E3
Zaouatallaz Alg. 123 H4
formerly known as Fort Gardel
Zaouet el Kahla Alg. see Bordj Omer Driss
Zaouiet Kounta Alg. 123 E4
Zaoyang China 87 E1
Zaoyangzhan China 87 E1
Zaō-zan vol. Japan 90 G5
Zaozernyy Kazakh. 103 G1
formerly known as Aysarinskoye or Aysary
Zaozernyy Rus. Fed. 80 E1
Zaozer'ye Rus. Fed. 43 T4
Zaozhuang China 87 F1
Zap r. Turkey 107 E3
Zapadna Morava r. Yugo. 58 C5
Zapadnaya Dvina r. Europe 43 L6
English form Western Dvina; also spelt Zakhodnyaya Dzvina
Zapadnaya Dvina Rus. Fed. 43 N5
Zapadno-Kazakhstanskaya Oblast' admin. div. Kazakh. see Zapadnyy Kazakhstan
Zapadno-Sakhalinskiy Khrebet mts Rus. Fed. 82 F2
Zapadno-Sibirskaya Nizmennost' plain Rus. Fed. see West Siberian Plain
Zapadno-Sibirskaya Ravnina plain Rus. Fed. see West Siberian Plain
Zapadnyy Alamedin, Pik mt. Kyrg. 103 H4
Zapadnyy Berezovyy, Ostrov i. Rus. Fed. 43 J1
Zapadnyy Chink Ustyurta esc. Kazakh. 102 C4
Zapadnyy Kazakhstan admin. div. Kazakh. 102 B2
English form West Kazakhstan Oblast; also known as Batys Qazaqstan Oblysy; formerly known as Ural'skaya Oblast'; long form Zapadno-Kazakhstanskaya Oblast'
Zapadnyy Sayan reg. Rus. Fed. 80 D2
English form Western Sayan Mountains
Zapala Arg. 204 C5
Zapardiel r. Spain 54 F3
Zapata U.S.A. 179 C7
Zapata, Peninsula de pen. Cuba 186 C2
Zapatoca Col. 198 C3
Zapatón r. Spain 54 E6
Zapatoza, Ciénaga de l. Col. 198 C2
Zapiga Chile 200 C4
Zaplyus'ye Rus. Fed. 43 K3
Zăpodeni Romania 58 I2
Zapolyarnyy Murmanskaya Oblast' Rus. Fed. 44 O1
Zapolyarnyy Respublika Komi Rus. Fed. 40 L2
Zapol'ye Pskovskaya Oblast' Rus. Fed. 43 K3
Zapol'ye Vologod. Obl. Rus. Fed. 43 R2
Zaporizhzhya Ukr. 41 E7
also spelt Zaporozh'ye; formerly known as Aleksandrovsk or Oleksandrivs'k
Zaporozhskoye Rus. Fed. 43 L1
Zaporozh'ye Ukr. see Zaporizhzhya
Zapponeta Italy 56 H7
Zaprešić Croatia 56 H3
Zaprudnya Rus. Fed. 43 S5
Zaprudy Belarus 42 F9
Zapug China 89 C5
Zaqatala Azer. 107 F2
also spelt Zakataly
Zaqên China 97 G2
Zaqqui Libya 120 C2
Za Qu r. China 86 A2
Zaqungngomar mt. China 89 E5
Zara China see Moinda
Zara Croatia see Zadar
Zara Turkey 107 D3
Zarafshan Uzbek. 103 F4
also spelt Zarafshon
Zarafshon Tajik. 101 G2
also spelt Zeravshan
Zarafshon r. Tajik. 101 G2
also spelt Zeravshan
Zarafshon Uzbek. see Zarafshan
Zarafshon r. Uzbek. see Zeravshan
Zarafshon, Qatorkŭhi mts Tajik. 101 F2
also known as Zeravshanskiy Khrebet
Zaragoza Col. 198 C3
Zaragoza Mex. 185 E2
Zaragoza Spain 55 K3
English form Saragossa; historically known as Caesaraugusta
Zarand Kermān Iran 100 D4
Zarand Markazī Iran 100 B3
Zarandului, Munții hills Romania 58 D2
Zarang China 89 B6
Zaranj Afgh. 101 E4
Zarasai Lith. 42 H6
Zárate Arg. 204 F4
Zarautz Spain 55 I1
Zaraysk Rus. Fed. 43 T7
Zaraza Venez. 199 E2
Zarbdar Uzbek. 103 G4
Zārdab Azer. 107 F2
Zardak Iran 100 D3
Zard Kuh mts Iran 100 B3
Zarechensk Rus. Fed. 40 D2
Zarechka Belarus 42 G9
Zarechnyy Rus. Fed. 85 E1
Zarechnyy Rus. Fed. 43 U8
formerly known as Pobedinskiy
Zāreh Iran 100 B3
Zarembo Island U.S.A. 166 C3
Zarėnai Lith. 42 D6
Zarghat Saudi Arabia 104 C2
Zarghūn Shahr Afgh. 101 G3
Zargun mt. Pak. 101 F4
Zari Afgh. 101 F3
Zaria Nigeria 125 G4
Zariaspa Afgh. see Balkh
Zarichne Ukr. 41 C6
Zarīneh Rūd r. Iran 100 A2
Zaring China 89 E6
Zarmardan Afgh. 101 E3
Zărnești Romania 58 G3
Żarnowieckie, Jezioro l. Poland 49 P1
Zarqā' Jordan see Az Zarqā'
Zarqā', Nahr az r. Jordan 108 G5
Zarqān Iran 100 C4
Zarubino Rus. Fed. 43 O8
Zarubino Rus. Fed. 82 C4
Żary Poland 49 M4
Zarzaïtine Alg. 123 H3
Zarzal Col. 198 B3
Zarzis Tunisia 123 H2
Zasa Latvia 42 G5
Zashchita Kazakh. 88 C1
Zasheyek Rus. Fed. 44 O2
Zaskar r. India 96 C2
Zaskar reg. Jammu and Kashmir 96 C2
also spelt Zanskar
Zaskarki Belarus 43 J6
▶Zaskar Mountains India 96 C2
world [land images] ▶ 12–13
Zaslawkaye Vodaskhovishcha resr Belarus 42 I8
Zaslawye Belarus 42 I7
Zastron S. Africa 133 L7
Za'tarī, Wādī az watercourse Jordan 109 H5
Žatec Czech Rep. 49 K5
Zaterechnyy Rus. Fed. 107 F1
Zatobol'sk Kazakh. 103 E1
Zatoka Ukr. 58 L2
formerly known as Bugaz
Zatyshshya Ukr. 58 K1
Zaunguzskiye Karakumy des. Turkm. 102 D4
also known as Üngüz Angyrsyndaky Garagum
Zautla Mex. 185 F5
Zavadovskiy Island Antarctica 223 F2
Zavareh Iran 100 C3
Zavety Il'icha Rus. Fed. 82 F2
Zavidovići Bos.-Herz. 56 K4
Zavidovskiy Zapovednik nature res. Rus. Fed. 43 R5
Zavitaya Rus. Fed. see Zavitinsk
Zavitinsk Rus. Fed. 82 C2
formerly known as Zavitaya
Zavodskoy Rus. Fed. see Komsomol'skiy
Zavolzhsk Rus. Fed. 40 G4
formerly known as Zavolzh'ye
Zavolzh'ye Rus. Fed. see Zavolzhsk
Závora, Ponta pt Moz. 131 G5
Zavutstsye Belarus 42 J6
Zavyachellye Belarus 43 J6
Zav'yalova, Ostrov i. Rus. Fed. 39 P4
Zav'yalovo Rus. Fed. 103 J1
Zawa Qinghai China 84 D4
Zawa Xinjiang China 96 C1
Zawadzkie Poland 49 P5
Zawgyi r. Myanmar 78 B3
Zawiercie Poland 49 Q5
Zawilah Libya 120 B3
Zāwiyah, Jabal az hills Syria 109 H2
Zāwiyat Masūs Libya 120 D2
Zawlīyah, Jiddat az plain Oman 105 F3
Zawr, Ra's az pt Saudi Arabia 105 E2
Zâwyet Shammâs pt Egypt 106 A5
Zâwyet Sîdi Ghâzi Egypt 108 B6
Zay r. Rus. Fed. 40 I5
Zaydī, Wādī az watercourse Syria 109 H5
Zaysan Kazakh. 88 D2
Zaysan, Lake Kazakh. 88 C1
also known as Zaysan, Ozero
Zaysan, Ozero l. Kazakh. see Zaysan, Lake
Zaytsevo Rus. Fed. 43 J4
Zayü Xizang China 86 A2
Zayü Xizang China 86 A2
also known as Gyigang
Zayü Qu r. China/India 86 A2
also known as Lohil or Luhit
Zayyr Uzbek. see Zair
Zazafotsy Madag. 131 [inset] J4
Zazir, Oued watercourse Alg. 123 G6
Zbąszynek Poland 49 M3
Zborište mt. Yugo. 58 A5
Žďár nad Sázavou Czech Rep. 49 M6
Žďárské Vrchy hills Czech Rep. 49 M6
Zdolbuniv Ukr. 41 C6
also spelt Zdolbunov
Zdolbunov Ukr. see Zdolbuniv
Zduńska Wola Poland 49 P4
Zealand i. Denmark 45 J5
also spelt Sjælland
Zēbāk Afgh. 101 G2
Zeballos mt. Arg. 205 C7
Zeballos Canada 166 E5
Zēbār Iraq 107 F3
Zebargad, Gezîret i. Egypt 104 B3
English form Zebirget Island
Zebirget Island Egypt see Zebargad, Gezîret
Žebrák Czech Rep. 49 K6
Zebulon GA U.S.A. 175 C5
Zebulon KY U.S.A. 176 C8
Zebulon NC U.S.A. 174 E5
Zeebrugge Belgium 51 J1
Zeehan Australia 147 E5
Zeeland U.S.A. 172 G8
Zeerust S. Africa 133 K2
Ze'elim Israel 108 G5
also known as Safad; also spelt Tsefat
Zegrzyńskie, Jezioro l. Poland 49 S3
Zehdenick Germany 49 K3
Zeil, Mount Australia 148 B4
formerly spelt Ziel, Mount
Žeimelis Lith. 42 F5
Zeitz Germany 48 J4
Zêkog China 86 B1
also known as Sonag
Zela Turkey see Zile
Żelechów Poland 49 S4
Zelena Gora mt. Bos.-Herz. 56 J5
Zelenaya Roshcha Kazakh. 103 H1
Zelengora mts Bos.-Herz. 56 K5
Zelennik Rus. Fed. 40 H3
Zelenoborskiy Rus. Fed. 44 P2
Zelenodol'sk Rus. Fed. 40 I5
Zelenogorsk Rus. Fed. 43 K1
Zelenograd Rus. Fed. 43 S5
Zelenogradsk Rus. Fed. 42 B7
historically known as Cranz
Zelenokumsk Rus. Fed. 41 G7
formerly known as Sovetskoye or Vorontsovo-Aleksandrovskoye
Zelentsovo Rus. Fed. 40 H4
Zelenyy, Ostrov i. Rus. Fed. 82 G4
also known as Shibotsu-jima
Zelenyy Gay Kazakh. 103 G2
Železné Hory hills Czech Rep. 49 M6
Zelienople U.S.A. 176 E5
Želiezovce Slovakia 49 P7
Zelina Croatia 56 I3
formerly known as Sveti Ivan Zelina
Zelinggou China 84 C4
Želivka, Vodní nádrž resr Czech Rep. 49 L6
Željin mt. Yugo. 58 B5
Zell am See Austria 49 J8
Zellerrain pass Austria 49 M8
Zelów Poland 49 Q4
Zeltiņi Latvia 42 H4
Zel'va Belarus 42 F8
Žemaičių Naumiestis Lith. 42 C6
Žemaitijos nacionalinis parkas nat. park Lith. 42 C5
Zêmdasam China 86 B1
Zemen Bulg. 58 D6
Zemes Romania 58 H2
Zemetchino Rus. Fed. 41 G5
Zémio Cent. Afr. Rep. 126 E3
Zemmora Alg. 55 L9
Zémongo, Réserve de Faune de nature res. Cent. Afr. Rep. 126 E3
Zempleni park Hungary 49 S7
Zemplínska šírava l. Slovakia 49 T7
Zempoaltépetl, Nudo de mt. Mex. 185 G5
Zemtsy Rus. Fed. 43 N5
Zemun Srbija Yugo. 58 B4
Zênda China 86 A1
Zengcheng China 87 E4
Zengfeng Shan mt. China 82 C4
Zenica Bos.-Herz. 56 J4
Zenifim watercourse Israel 108 F7
Zenta Vojvodina, Srbija Yugo. see Senta
Zentsūji Japan 91 C7
Zenyeh Afgh. 101 G3
Zenzach Alg. 55 O9
Žepče Bos.-Herz. 56 K4
Zephyr Cove U.S.A. 182 E2
Zepu China 88 B4
formerly known as Poskam
Zeraf, Bahr el r. Sudan 128 A2
Zeravshan Tajik. see Zarafshon
Zeravshan r. Tajik. see Zarafshon
Zeravshan r. Uzbek. 103 E5
also spelt Zarafshon
Zeravshanskiy Khrebet mts Tajik. see Zarafshon, Qatorkŭhi
Zerenda Kazakh. 103 G1
Zeribet el Oued Alg. 123 G2
Zerków Poland 49 O3
Zermatt Switz. 51 N6
Zernograd Rus. Fed. 41 G7
formerly known as Zernovoy
Zernovoy Rus. Fed. see Zernograd
Zestafoni Georgia see Zestap'oni
Zestap'oni Georgia 107 E2
also spelt Zestafoni
Zeta r. Yugo. 58 A6
Zêtang China 89 E6
Zetea Romania 58 G2
Zeulenroda Germany 48 I5
Zeven Germany 48 G2
Zevenaar Neth. 48 D4
Zevgolatio Greece 59 D11
Zeya Rus. Fed. 82 B1
Zeya r. Rus. Fed. 82 B1
Zeydābād Iran 100 C4
Zēydar Iran 100 B2
Zeynalābād Iran 100 D4
Zeyskiy Zapovednik nature res. Rus. Fed. 82 B1
Zeysko-Bureinskaya Vpadina depr. Rus. Fed. 82 C2
Zeyskoye Vodokhranilishche resr Rus. Fed. 82 B1
Zeytin Burnu c. Cyprus see Elaia, Cape
Zeytindağ Turkey 59 I10
Zêzere r. Port. 54 C5
Zgharta Lebanon 108 G3
Zgierz Poland 49 Q4
historically known as Sgiersch
Zhabdün China 89 D6
Zhabinka Belarus 42 F9
Zhadove Ukr. 43 N9
Zhaggo China see Luhuo
Zhaglag China 86 A1
Zhag'yab China 86 A2
also known as Yêndum
Zhailma Kazakh. 103 E2
also spelt Zhayylma
Zhaksy Kazakh. 103 F2
also spelt Zhaqsy; formerly spelt Dzhaksy
Zhaksy-Kon watercourse Kazakh. 103 G2
Zhaksykylysh, Ozero salt l. Kazakh. 103 E3
Zhaksy Sarysu watercourse Kazakh. see Sarysu
Zhalaghash Kazakh. see Dzhalagash
Zhalanash Kazakh. 103 I4
Zhalanash Kazakh. see Damdy
Zhalgyztöbe Kazakh. see Zhangiztobe
Zhalpaktal Kazakh. 102 B2
also spelt Zhalpaqtal; formerly known as Furmanovo
Zhalpaqtal Kazakh. see Zhalpaktal
Zhaltyr Kazakh. 103 G2
formerly spelt Dzhaltyr
Zhaltyr, Ozero l. Kazakh. 102 B3
Zhaludok Belarus 42 F8
Zhamanakkol', Ozero salt l. Kazakh. 103 E2
Zhamansor Kazakh. 102 C3
Zhambyl Kazakh. 103 G3
Zhambyl Kazakh. see Taraz
Zhambyl Oblast admin. div. Kazakh. see Zhambylskaya Oblast'
Zhambylskaya Oblast' admin. div. Kazakh. 103 H3
English form Zhambyl Oblast; formerly known as Dzhambulskaya Oblast'
Zhameuka Kazakh. 103 J3
Zhamo China see Bomi
Zhan r. China 82 C2
Zhanakorgan Kazakh. 103 F4
also spelt Zhangaqorghan; formerly known as Yany-Kurgan
Zhanakurylys Kazakh. 103 E3
Zhanang China 89 E6
also known as Chatang
Zhanaortalyk Kazakh. 103 H3
Zhanaozen Kazakh. 102 C4
also spelt Zhangaözen; formerly known as Novyy Uzen'
Zhanatala Kazakh. 103 I4
Zhanatas Kazakh. 103 G4
also spelt Zhangatas
Zhanbay Kazakh. 102 B3
Zhanbei China 82 B2
formerly known as Zhanhe
Zhang r. China 85 G4
Zhangaözen Kazakh. see Zhanaozen
Zhangaqazaly Kazakh. see Ayteke Bi
Zhanga Qazan Kazakh. see Novaya Kazanka
Zhangaqorghan Kazakh. see Zhanakorgan
Zhangatas Kazakh. see Zhanatas
Zhangbei China 85 G3
Zhangcheng China see Yongtai
Zhangcunpu China 87 F1
Zhangde China see Anyang
Zhangdian China see Zibo
Zhanggu China see Danba
Zhangguangcai Ling mts China 82 C3
Zhanghua Taiwan see Changhua
Zhangiztobe Kazakh. 103 J2
also known as Zhalgyztöbe
Zhangjiajie China see Dayong
Zhangjiakou China 85 G3
also known as Kalgan
Zhangjiapan China see Jingbian
Zhangla China 86 B1
Zhanglou China 87 F1
Zhangping China 87 F3
Zhangpu China 87 F3
also known as Sui'an
Zhangqiu China 85 H4
Zhangshu China 87 E2
formerly known as Qingjiang
Zhangwei Xinhe r. China 85 H4
Zhangwu China 85 I3
Zhangxian China 86 C1
Zhangye China 84 D4
Zhangzhou China 87 F3
formerly spelt Changchow
Zhangzi China 85 G4
Zhanhe China see Zhanbei
Zhanhua China 85 H4
also known as Fuguo
Zhänibek Kazakh. see Dzhanybek
Zhanjiang China 87 D4
formerly spelt Changkiang
Zhansügirov Kazakh. see Dzhansugurov
Zhanterek Kazakh. 102 C3
Zhanyi China 86 B3
Zhao'an China 87 F4
also known as Nanzhao
Zhaodong China 82 B3
Zhaoge China see Qixian
Zhaojue China 86 B2
also known as Xincheng
Zhaoliqiao China 87 E2
Zhaoping China 87 D3
Zhaoqing China 87 E4
Zhaoren China see Changwu
Zhaosu China 88 C3
also known as Mongolküre
Zhaosutai r. China 85 I3
Zhaotong China 86 B3
Zhaoxian China 85 G4
also known as Zhaozhou
Zhaoyuan Heilong. China 82 B3
Zhaoyuan Shandong China 85 I4
Zhaozhen China see Jintang
Zhaozhou China see Zhaoxian
Zhaozhou China 82 B3
Zhapo China 87 D4
Zhaqsy Kazakh. see Zhaksy
Zharbulak Kazakh. see Kabanbay
Zharbulak Kazakh. 88 C2
Zhardzyazhzha Belarus 42 I7
Zhari Namco salt l. China 89 D6
Zharkamys Kazakh. 102 D3
Zharkent Kazakh. 103 J3
formerly known as Panfilov; formerly spelt Dzharkent
Zharkovskiy Rus. Fed. 43 N6
Zharma Kazakh. 103 J2
Zharmysh Kazakh. 102 C4
Zharsuat Kazakh. 103 J3
Zharyk Kazakh. see Saken Seyfullin
Zhashkiv Ukr. 41 D6
also spelt Zhashkov
Zhashkov Ukr. see Zhashkiv
Zhashui China 87 D1
also known as Qianyou
Zhaslyk Uzbek. 102 D4
also spelt Jasliq
Zhastkovo Rus. Fed. 43 N8
Zhaxi China see Weixin
Zhaxi Co salt l. China 89 D5
Zhaxigang China 89 B5
Zhaxizê China 86 A2
Zhayrem Kazakh. 103 G2
Zhayü China 86 A2
Zhayylma Kazakh. see Zhailma
Zhayyq r. Kazakh./Rus. Fed. see Ural
Zhdanov Ukr. see Mariupol'
Zhdanovo Kazakh. 103 G4
Zhdanovo Rus. Fed. 43 O4
Zhdanovsk Azer. see Beyläqan
Zhecheng China 87 E1
Zhedao China see Lianghe
Zhêhor China 86 B2
Zhejiang prov. China 87 G2
English form Chekiang
Zhelang China 87 E4
Zhelaniya, Mys c. Rus. Fed. 39 G2
Zhelcha r. Rus. Fed. 42 I3
Zhelezinka Kazakh. 103 H1
Zheleznodorozhnyy Rus. Fed. 42 C7
historically known as Gerdauen
Zheleznodorozhnyy Rus. Fed. see Yemva
Zheleznodorozhnyy Uzbek. see Kungrad
Zheleznogorsk Rus. Fed. 43 Q9
Zheleznya Rus. Fed. 43 S7
Zhelou China see Ceheng
Zheltorangy Kazakh. 103 H3
Zheltyye Vody Ukr. see Zhovti Vody
Zhelyu Voyvoda Bulg. 58 H6
Zhem Kazakh. see Emba
Zhemgang Bhutan 97 F4
Zhen'an China 87 D1
also known as Yongle
Zhenba China 87 C1
Zheng'an China 87 C2
also known as Fengyi
Zhengding China 85 G4
Zhenghe China 87 F3
also known as Xiongshan
Zhengjiakou China see Gucheng
Zhengjiatun China see Shuangliao
Zhengkou China see Gucheng
Zhenglan Qi China see Dund Hot
Zhengning China 85 F5
also known as Shanhe
Zhengxiangbai Qi China see Qagan Nur
Zhengyang China 87 E1
also known as Zhenyang
Zhengzhou China 87 E1
formerly spelt Chengchow
Zhenhai China 87 G2
Zhenjiang China see Dantu
Zhenjiangguan China 86 B1
Zhenlai China 85 I2
Zhenning China 86 C3
Zhenping China 87 D2
Zhenwudong China see Ansai
Zhenxi China 85 I2
Zhenxiong China 86 C3
also known as Wufeng
Zhenyang China see Zhengyang
Zhenyuan Gansu China 85 E5
Zhenyuan Guizhou China 87 D3
also known as Wuyang
Zhenyuan Yunnan China 86 B4
also known as Enle
Zhenziling China 87 D2
Zherdevka Rus. Fed. 41 G6
formerly known as Chibizovka
Zherdevo Rus. Fed. 43 R8
Zherong China 87 F3
also known as Shuangcheng
Zheshart Rus. Fed. 40 I3
Zhestylevo Rus. Fed. 43 S5
Zhetibay Kazakh. see Zhetybay
Zhetikara Kazakh. see Zhitikara
Zhetisay Kazakh. see Zhetysay
Zhetybay Kazakh. 102 C4
also spelt Zhetibay
Zhety-Kol', Ozero l. Rus. Fed. 103 E2
Zhetysay Kazakh. 103 G4
also spelt Zhetisay; formerly spelt Dzhetysay
Zhêxam China 89 D6
Zhexi Shuiku resr China 87 D2
Zhezdy Kazakh. 103 F2
formerly known as Marganets; formerly spelt Dzhezdy
Zhezkazgan Kazakh. 103 F3
also spelt Zhezqazghan; formerly spelt Dzhezkazgan
Zhezqazghan Kazakh. see Zhezkazgan
Zhicheng China see Changxing
Zhichitsy Rus. Fed. 43 M6
Zhidan China 85 F4
also known as Bao'an
Zhidoi China 97 G2
also known as Gyaijêpozhanggê
Zhigansk Rus. Fed. 39 M3
Zhigung China 89 E6
Zhijiang China 87 D3
Zhijin China 86 C3
Zhilevo Rus. Fed. 43 T7
Zhilino Rus. Fed. 43 R8
Zhilyanka Kazakh. see Kargalinskoye
Zhi Qu r. China see Yangtze
Zhirnovsk Rus. Fed. 41 H6
formerly known as Zhirnovskiy or Zhirnoye
Zhirnovskiy Rus. Fed. see Zhirnovsk
Zhirnoye Rus. Fed. see Zhirnovsk
Zhiryatino Rus. Fed. 43 O8
Zhitarovo Bulg. see Vetren
Zhitikara Kazakh. 103 E1
also spelt Zhetikara; formerly known as Dzhetygara
Zhitkovichi Belarus see Zhytkavichy
Zhitkovo Rus. Fed. 43 K1
Zhitkur Rus. Fed. 102 A2
Zhitomir Ukr. see Zhytomyr
Zhizdra Rus. Fed. 43 P8
Zhizdra r. Rus. Fed. 43 R7
Zhizhitsa Rus. Fed. 43 M5
Zhizhitskoye, Ozero l. Rus. Fed. 43 M5
Zhlobin Belarus 43 L9
Zhmerinka Ukr. see Zhmerynka
Zhmerynka Ukr. 41 D6
also spelt Zhmerinka
Zhob Pak. 101 G4
formerly known as Fort Sandeman
Zhob r. Pak. 101 G3
Zhodzina Belarus 43 J7
Zhokhova, Ostrov i. Rus. Fed. 39 P2
Zholnuskay Kazakh. 88 C1
Zholymbet Kazakh. 103 G2
Zhong'an China see Fuyuan
Zhongba China 87 E4
Zhongba China see Jiangyou
Zhongcheng China see Suijiang
Zhongdian China 86 A3
also known as Zhongxin
Zhongduo China see Youyang
Zhongguo country Asia see China
Zhongguo Renmin Gongheguo country Asia see China
Zhonghe China see Xiushan
Zhongmou China 87 E1
Zhongning China 85 E4
Zhongping China see Huize
Zhongshan research station Antarctica 223 F2
Zhongshan Guangdong China 87 E4
formerly known as Shiqizhen
Zhongshan Guangxi China 87 D3
Zhongshan China see Lupanshui
Zhongsha Qundao sea feature S. China Sea see Macclesfield Bank
Zhongshu China see Luxi
Zhongshu China see Luliang
Zhongtai China see Lingtai
Zhongtiao Shan mts China 87 D1
Zhongwei China 85 E4
Zhongxian China 87 D2
also known as Zhongzhou
Zhongxin China 87 E3
Zhongxin China see Zhongdian
Zhongxin China see Huaping
Zhongxing China see Siyang
Zhongxingji China 87 F2
Zhongyang China 85 F4
Zhongyicun China 86 B3
Zhongze China 87 E3
Zhongzhai China 86 C1
Zhongzhou China see Zhongxian
Zhosaly Kazakh. see Dzhusaly
Zhosaly Kazakh. 103 I2
Zhoujiajing China 84 D4
Zhoujiaping China see Nanzheng
Zhoukou China 87 E1
Zhoukou China see Peng'an
Zhouning China 87 F3
also known as Shicheng
Zhoushan China 87 G2
Zhoushan Dao i. China 87 G2
Zhoushan Qundao is China 87 G2
Zhouzhi China 87 D1
also known as Erqu
Zhovten' Ukr. 58 L1
Zhovti Vody Ukr. 41 E6
formerly known as Zheltyye Vody
Zhualy Kazakh. 103 E2
Zhuanghe China 85 I4
Zhuanglang China 85 E5
also known as Shuiluocheng
Zhuantobe Kazakh. 103 G3
Zhubgyügoin China 86 A1
Zhucheng China 85 H5
Zhudong Taiwan see Chutung
Zhugqu China 86 C1
Zhuhai China 87 E4
formerly known as Chuhai
Zhuji China see Shangqiu
Zhuji China 87 G2
Zhujia Chuan r. China 85 F4
Zhujing China see Jinshan
Zhukeng China 87 E4
Zhukopa r. Rus. Fed. 43 N5
Zhukovka Rus. Fed. 43 O8
Zhukovo Rus. Fed. 43 R6
formerly known as Ugodskiy Zavod
Zhukovskiy Rus. Fed. 43 T6
formerly known as Stakhanovo
Zhulong r. China 85 G4
Zhumadian China 87 E1
Zhumysker Kazakh. 102 B3
Zhuolu China 85 G3
Zhuoyang China see Suiping
Zhuozang r. China 85 G4
Zhuozhou China 85 H4
Zhuozi China 85 G3
also known as Zhuozishan
Zhuozishan China see Zhuozi
Zhuravlevka Kazakh. 103 G2
Zhurki Belarus 42 I6
Zhuryn Kazakh. 102 D2
formerly spelt Dzhurun
Zhusandala, Step' plain Kazakh. 103 H3
Zhushan China 87 D1
Zhushan China see Xuan'en
Zhuxi China 87 D1
Zhuyang China see Dazhu
Zhuzhou Hunan China 87 E3
also known as Lukou
Zhuzhou Hunan China 87 E3
Zhydachiv Ukr. 41 C6
Zhympity Kazakh. 102 C2
formerly known as Dzhambeyty
Zhyngyldy Kazakh. 102 B3
formerly known as Kuybyshevo
Zhytkavichy Belarus 42 I9
also spelt Zhitkovichi
Zhytomyr Ukr. 41 D6
also spelt Zhitomir
Zi r. China 85 H4
Ziama mt. Guinea 124 C4
Ziarat Iran 100 D2
Žiar nad Hronom Slovakia 49 P7
Zibā salt pan Saudi Arabia 109 J7
Zībār Iraq 107 E3
Zibo China 85 H4
formerly known as Zhangdian
Zichang China 85 F4
also known as Wayaobu
Zicheng China see Zijin
Zichtauer Berge und Klötzer Forst park Germany 48 I3
Ziddi Tajik. 101 G2
Zidi Pak. 101 F5
Ziębice Poland 49 O5
Ziel, Mount Australia see Zeil, Mount
Zielona Góra Poland 49 M4
historically known as Grünberg
Ziemelkursas Augstiene hills Latvia 42 D4
Ziemeris Latvia 42 I4
Ziemupe Latvia 42 C5
Ziesar Germany 49 J3
Zifta Egypt 121 F2
Zigaing Myanmar 78 A3
Zigê Tangco l. China 89 E5
Ziggurat of Ur tourist site Iraq 107 F5
Zighan Libya 120 D3
Zigon Myanmar 78 A4
Zigong China 86 C2
Ziguey Chad 120 B6
Zigui China 87 D2
also known as Jiandaoyu
Ziguinchor Senegal 124 A3
Žīguri Latvia 42 I4
Zihuatanejo Mex. 185 E5
Zijin China 87 E4
also known as Zicheng
Ziketan China see Xinghai
Zikeyevo Rus. Fed. 43 P8
Zikhron Ya'aqov Israel 108 F5
Zilair Rus. Fed. 102 D1
Zilaiskalns Latvia 42 G4
Zile Turkey 106 C2
historically known as Zela
Zilim r. Rus. Fed. 40 K5
Žilina Slovakia 49 P6
Zillah Libya 120 C2
Zillertaler Alpen mts Austria 48 I8
Zilupe Latvia 42 J5
Zima Rus. Fed. 80 G2
Zimapán Mex. 185 F4
Zimatlán Mex. 185 F5
Zimba Zambia 127 E9
▶Zimbabwe country Africa 131 F3
formerly known as Rhodesia or Southern Rhodesia
africa [countries] ▶ 114–117
Zimbabwe tourist site Zimbabwe see Great Zimbabwe National Monument
Zīmkān, Rūdkhāneh-ye r. Iran 100 A3
Zimmerbude Rus. Fed. see Svetlyy
Zimmi Sierra Leone 124 C5
Zimnicea Romania 58 G5
Zimniy Bereg coastal area Rus. Fed. 40 F2
Zimovniki Rus. Fed. 41 G7
Zin watercourse Israel 108 G6
Zinave, Parque Nacional de nat. park Moz. 131 G4
Zinder Niger 125 H3
Zinder dept Niger 125 H3
Zindo China 86 B2
formerly known as Jimda
Zing Nigeria 125 H4
Zinga Mulike Tanz. 129 C7
Ziniaré Burkina 125 E3
Zinihu China 85 E4
Zinjibār Yemen 105 D5
Zinkwazi Beach S. Africa 133 P6
Zinovo Rus. Fed. 43 V5
Zinoyevsk Ukr. see Kirovohrad
Zinzana Mali 124 D3
Zion U.S.A. 172 F8
Zion National Park U.S.A. 183 K4
Ziqudukou China 97 G2
Zīrab Iran 100 C2
Zirbitzkogel mt. Austria 49 L8
Zirc Hungary 49 O8
Žirje i. Croatia 56 H5
Zirkel, Mount U.S.A. 180 F4
Zīrkūh i. U.A.E. 105 F2
Ziro India 97 G4
Zi Shui r. China 87 E2
Zistersdorf Austria 49 N7
Zitácuaro Mex. 185 E5
Zitava r. Slovakia 49 P8
Žitište Vojvodina, Srbija Yugo. 58 B3
Zitiua r. Brazil 202 C2
Zito China see Lhorong
Zitong China 86 C2
also known as Wenchang

Žitorsđa Srbija Yugo. 58 C5
Zittau Germany 49 L5
Živinice Bos.-Herz. 56 K4
Ziway Hāyk' l. Eth. 128 C2
Zixi China 87 F3
  also known as Hecheng
Zixing China 87 E3
Ziya r. China 85 H4
Ziyanchurino Rus. Fed. 102 D2

Ziyang China see Wuyuan
Ziyang Shaanxi China 87 D1
Ziyang Sichuan China 86 C2
Ziyaret Dağı hill Turkey 108 F1
Ziyuan China 87 D3
  also known as Dahe
Ziyun China 86 C3
Ziz, Oued watercourse Morocco 122 D3
Zizhong China 86 C2
  also known as Chonglong
Zizhou China 85 F4
  also known as Shuanghuyu
Zlatar mts Yugo. 58 A5
Zlaté Moravce Slovakia 49 P7
Zlaten Rog Bulg. 58 D4
Zlatibor mts Yugo. 58 A5
Zlatica r. Yugo. 58 B3
Zlatna Romania 58 E2
Zlatni Pyasŭtsi nat. park Bulg. 58 J5
Zlatograd Bulg. 58 G7
Zlatoust Rus. Fed. 38 F4
Zlatoustovsk Rus. Fed. 82 D1
Zlatý Stôl mt. Slovakia 49 R7
Zlín Czech Rep. 49 O6
  formerly known as Gottwaldow
Zliţan Libya 120 B1
Złocieniec Poland 49 N2
Złoczew Poland 49 P4
Złotoryja Poland 49 M4
Złotów Poland 49 O2
Zlynka Rus. Fed. 43 M9
Zmeinogorsk Rus. Fed. 88 C1
Żmigród Poland 49 N4
Zmiyev Ukr. see Zmiyiv
Zmiyevka Rus. Fed. 43 R9
Zmiyiv Ukr. 41 F6
  also spelt Zmiyev; formerly known as Gotval'd
Znamenka Kazakh. 103 I2
Znamenka Altayskiy Kray Rus. Fed. 103 I1
Znamenka Orlovskaya Oblast' Rus. Fed. 43 O9
Znamenka Smolenskaya Oblast' Rus. Fed. 43 P7

Znamenka Ukr. see Znam"yanka
Znamenskoye Lipetskaya Oblast' Rus. Fed. 43 U8
Znamenskoye Orlovskaya Oblast' Rus. Fed. 43 Q8
Znam"yanka Ukr. 41 E6
  also spelt Znamenka
Žnin Poland 49 O3
Znobivka r. Ukr. 43 O9
Znob Novhorods'ke Ukr. 43 O9
Znojmo Czech Rep. 49 N7
Zoar S. Africa 132 F10
Zóbuè Mozc. 131 G2
Zogainrawar China see Huashixia
Zogang China 86 A2
  also known as Wangda
Zogqên China 86 A1
Zografos Greece 59 E11
Zohreh r. Iran 100 B4
Zoigê China 86 B1
Zoir Uzbek. see Zair
Zoissa Tanz. 129 C6
Zoji La pass Jammu and Kashmir 96 B3
Zola S. Africa 133 K9
Zolochev Ukr. see Zolochiv
Zolochev Ukr. see Zolochiv
Zolochiv Kharkivs'ka Oblast' Ukr. 41 E6
  also spelt Zolochev
Zolochiv L'vivs'ka Oblast' Ukr. 41 C6
  also spelt Zolochev
Zolotaya Gora Rus. Fed. 82 B1
Zolotinka Rus. Fed. 81 K1
Zolotonosha Ukr. 41 E6
Zolotukhino Rus. Fed. 43 R9
Zomandao r. Madag. 131 [inset] J4

▶ Zomba Malawi 129 B8
Former capital of Malawi.

Zombor Vojvodina, Srbija Yugo. see Sombor
Zomin Uzbek. see Zaamin
Zongga China see Gyirong
Zongo Dem. Rep. Congo 126 C3
Zonguldak Turkey 106 B2
Zongyang China 87 F2

Zonūz Iran 100 A2
Zoo Baba well Niger 125 I2
Zoppo, Portella dello pass Sicilia Italy 57 G11
Zorgho Burkina 125 E3
  also spelt Zorgo
Zorgo Burkina see Zorgho
Zorita Spain 54 F5
Zorleni Romania 58 I2
Zorlenţu Mare Romania 58 C3
Zorn r. France 51 O4
Zornitsa Bulg. 58 H6
Zorritos Peru 198 A5
Zorzor Liberia 124 C5
Zossen Germany 49 K3
Zouan-Hounien Côte d'Ivoire 124 C5
Zouar Chad 120 C4
Zoucheng China 85 H5
  formerly known as Zouxian
Zouérat Mauritania 122 B5
Zouina well Mauritania 124 D2
Zoulang Nanshan mts China 84 C4
Zouping China 85 H4
Zourvas, Akra pt Greece 59 E11
Zoushi China 87 D2
Zouxian China see Zoucheng
Zovka Rus. Fed. 43 J3
Zrenjanin Vojvodina, Srbija Yugo. 58 B3
  also known as Nagybecskerek
Zrmanja r. Croatia 56 H4
Zu Afgh. 101 G2
Zuata r. Venez. 199 E3
Zubālah, Wādi watercourse Saudi Arabia 109 O8
Zubayr, Jazā'ir i. Yemen 104 C5
Zubia Spain 55 H7
Zubkovo Rus. Fed. 43 R8
Zubova Polyana Rus. Fed. 41 G5
Zubovo Rus. Fed. 43 R1
Zubtsov Rus. Fed. 43 P5
Zuckerhütl mt. Austria 48 I9
Zuénoula Côte d'Ivoire 124 D5
Zuera Spain 55 K3
Żufār admin. reg. Oman 105 F4
  also spelt Dhofar

Zug Switz. 51 O5
Zugdidi Georgia 107 E2
Zuger See l. Switz. 51 O5
Zughaytūn r. Iraq 109 P3
Zugm, Birket el salt l. Egypt 108 B7
Zugu Nigeria 125 G4
Zuider Zee l. Neth. see IJsselmeer
Zuid-Willemsvaart canal Neth. 51 L1
Zuitaizi China see Kangxian
Zuitai China see Kangxian
Zuitou China see Taibai
Zújar r. Spain 54 F5
Żukowo Poland 49 P1
Zulia state Venez. 198 D2
Zülpich Germany 48 D5
Zumarraga Spain 55 I1
Zumba Ecuador 198 B6
Zumbo Moz. 131 F2
Zumbro r. U.S.A. 174 A2
Zumbrota U.S.A. 174 A2
Zummār Iraq 109 N1
Zumpango Mex. 185 F5
Zumpango del Rio Mex. 185 F5
Zungeru Nigeria 125 G4
Zunhua China 85 H3
Zuni U.S.A. 181 E5
Zuni watercourse U.S.A. 183 O7
Zuni Mountains U.S.A. 181 E6
Zun-Torey, Ozero l. Rus. Fed 85 G1
Zunyi Guizhou China 86 C3
  also known as Nanbai
Zunyi Guizhou China 86 C3
Zuo Jiang r. China/Vietnam 87 D4
Zuoquan China 85 G4
Zuoyun China 85 G4
Żupanja Croatia 56 K3
Žuromin Poland 49 Q2
Zuru Nigeria 125 G4
Zurzuna Turkey see Çıldır

Zusha r. Rus. Fed. 43 R8
Zusmarshausen Germany 48 H7
Zutphen Neth. 48 D3
Zuurberg National Park S. Africa 133 J10
Žuvinto rezervatas nature res. Lith. 42 E7
Zuwārah Libya 120 B1
Zuyevka Rus. Fed. 40 I4
Zuytdorp Nature Reserve Australia 151 A5
Zvečan Kosovo, Srbija Yugo. 58 B6
Zvejniekciems Latvia 42 F4
Zvenigorod Rus. Fed. 43 R6
Zvenigorodka Ukr. see Zvenyhorodka
Zvenyhorodka Ukr. 41 D6
  also spelt Zvenigorodka
Zverino Bulg. 58 E5
Zvezdë Albania 58 B8
Zvijezda mts Bos.-Herz. 56 K4
Zvishavane Zimbabwe 131 F4
  formerly spelt Shabani
Zvolen Slovakia 49 Q7
Zvornik Bos.-Herz. 56 L4
Zwarkop S. Africa 132 F7
Zwedru Liberia 124 C5
Zweibrücken Germany 48 E6
Zweletemba S. Africa 132 D10
Zwelitsha S. Africa 133 L9
Zwettl Austria 49 M7
Zwickau Germany 49 J5
Zwierzyniec Poland 49 T5
Zwiesel Germany 49 K6
Zwingli S. Africa 133 K1
Zwoleń Poland 49 S4
Zwolle Neth. 48 D3
Zyal'ki Belarus 43 J6
Zychlin Poland 49 Q3
Zyembin Belarus 43 J7
Żyrardów Poland 49 R3
Zyryan Kazakh. see Zyryanovsk
Zyryanka Rus. Fed. 39 P3
Zyryanovo Rus. Fed. 39 I3
Zyryanovsk Kazakh. 88 D1
  also known as Zyryan
Żywiec Poland 49 Q6

acknowledgements

MAPS AND DATA

General

Maps designed and created by HarperCollins Cartographic, Glasgow, UK

Design: One O'Clock Gun Design Consultants Ltd, Edinburgh, UK

Continental perspective views (pp30–31, 62–63, 112–113, 136–137, 156–157, 190–191) and globes (pp 14–15, 26–27, 214): Alan Collinson Design, Llandudno, UK

The publishers would like to thank all national survey departments, road, rail and national park authorities, statistical offices and national place name committees throughout the world for their valuable assistance, and in particular the following:

British Antarctic Survey, Cambridge, UK

Bureau of Rural Sciences, Barton, ACT, Australia, a scientific agency of the Department of Agriculture, Fisheries and Forestry, Australia

Tony Champion, Professor of Population Geography, University of Newcastle upon Tyne, UK

Mr P J M Geelan, London, UK

International Boundary Research Unit, University of Durham, UK

The Meteorological Office, Bracknell, Berkshire, UK

Permanent Committee on Geographical Names, London, UK

Data

Antarctica (pp222–223): Antarctic Digital Database (versions 1 and 2), © Scientific Committee on Antarctic Research (SCAR), Cambridge, UK (1993, 1998)

Bathymetric data: The GEBCO Digital Atlas published by the British Oceanographic Data Centre on behalf of IOC and IHO, 1994

Earthquakes data (pp14–15, 71): United States Geological Survey (USGS) National Earthquakes Information Center, Denver, USA

Coral reefs data (p141): UNEP World Conservation Monitoring Centre (UNEP-WCMC), Cambridge, UK. 'Reefs at Risk', 1998 Washington, DC, USA from World Resources Institute (WRI), the International Center for Living Aquatic Resources Management (ICLARM) and UNEP-WCMC

PHOTOGRAPHS AND IMAGES

page	image number	credit
3		NASA/Science Photo Library
6		NASA/Science Photo Library
7		NASA
8–9	1	NASA
	2	NASA/Science Photo Library
10–11	1	CNES, 1996 Distribution Spot Image/Science Photo Library
	2	US Geological Survey/Science Photo Library
	3	CNES, 1991 Distribution Spot Image/Science Photo Library
	4	CNES, 1986 Distribution Spot Image/Science Photo Library
12–13	1	NASA
	2	NASA/Science Photo Library
	3	NASA
	4	ImageState
	5	Bernhard Edmater/Science Photo Library
	6	Earth Science Corporation/Science Photo Library
	7	CNES, 1996 Distribution Spot Image/Science Photo Library
	8	Digital image © 1996 CORBIS; Original image courtesy of NASA/CORBIS
14–15	1	Axiom Photographic Agency Ltd
	2	David Parker/Science Photo Library
	3	Chris Johns/NGS Image Collection
16–17	Fig. 1	Courtesy of NASA/JPL/Caltech
	Fig. 2	Courtesy of NASA/JPL/Caltech
	Fig. 3	Courtesy of NASA/JPL/Caltech
	Fig. 4	NRSC Ltd/Science Photo Library
	Fig. 9	NASA/Goddard Space Flight Center
	Fig. 10	Reproduced by permission of The Met Office, Bracknell, Berkshire
	Fig. 11	Reproduced by permission of The Met Office, Bracknell, Berkshire
18–19	1	Francois Suchel/Still Pictures
	2	Earth Satellite Corporation/Science Photo Library
	3	NRSC/Still Pictures
	4	M & C Denis-Huot/Still Pictures
	5	Pictor International - London
	6	Dick Ross/Still Pictures
	7	ImageState
	8	Klaus Andrews/Still Pictures
20–21	1	NASA/Science Photo Library
	2	Earth Satellite Corporation/Science Photo Library
	3	Daniel Dancer/Still Pictures
	4 left	NASA - Goddard Space Flight Center Scientific Visualization Studio
	4 right	NASA - Goddard Space Flight Center Scientific Visualization Studio
	5 left	NPA Group www.satmaps.com
	5 right	NPA Group www.satmaps.com
22–23	1	David Reed/Panos pictures
	2	Cities Revealed ® aerial photography © The GeoInformation ® Group, 1998
24–25	1	Earth Satellite Corporation/Science Photo Library
	2	Spaceimaging.com
	3	NRSC/Still Pictures
	4	NASA
26–27	1	NRSC/Still Pictures
	Fig. 1	TeleGeography, Inc, Washington D.C., USA www.telegeography.com
	Fig. 2	TeleGeography, Inc, Washington D.C., USA www.telegeography.com
28		© Marc Garanger/CORBIS
29		NASA
30–31	1	Digital image © 1996 CORBIS; Original image courtesy of NASA/CORBIS
	2	NASA
	3	NASA
32–33	1	P. Tatlow/Panos Pictures
	2	CNES, 1993 Distribution Spot Image/Science Photo Library
	3	CNES, 1991 Distribution Spot Image/Science Photo Library
34–35	1	Wim Van Cappellen/Still Pictures
	2	NASA
	3	Andrew Tatlow/Panos Pictures

page	image number	credit
36–37	1	Geoslides Photography
	2	Pictor International - London
	3	CNES, 1992 Distribution Spot Image/Science Photo Library
	4	ESA, Eurimage/Science Photo Library
	5	Dick Ross/Still Pictures
	6	NRSC/Science Photo Library
	7	Cities Revealed ® aerial photography © The GeoInformation ® Group, 1999
60		Pictures Colour Library Ltd
61		NASA
62–63	1	ImageState
	2	CNES, 1992 Distribution Spot Image/Science Photo Library
	3	CNES, 1987 Distribution Spot Image/Science Photo Library
64–65	1	Digital image © 1996 CORBIS; Original image courtesy of NASA/CORBIS
	2	Marc Schlossman/Panos pictures
	3	Georg Gerster/NGS Image Collection
66–67	1	NASA
	2	© Hanan Isachar/CORBIS
	3	Pictor International - London
68–69	1 top	© Wolfgang Kaehler/CORBIS
	1 middle	© Keren Su/CORBIS
	1 bottom	DERA/Still Pictures
	2 top	NASA
	2 bottom	NASA
	3 top	Science Photo Library
	3 bottom	CNES, 1987 Distribution Spot Image/Science Photo Library
70–71	1	NOAA
	2	NASA
	3	Shehzad Nooran/Still Pictures
	4	Digital image © 1996 CORBIS; Original image courtesy of NASA/CORBIS
	5	NASA
110		Pictures Colour Library Ltd
111		NASA
112–113	1	CNES, 1988 Distribution Spot Image/Science Photo Library
	2	© CORBIS
	3	NASA/JPL/Caltech
114–115	1	Peter Hering
	2	Libe Taylor/Panos pictures
116–117	1	NASA
	2	NASA
	3	Christian Aid/Glynn Griffiths/Still Pictures
	4	Mark Edwards/Still Pictures
	5 left	CNES, 1998 Distribution Spot Image/Science Photo Library
	5 right	CNES, 2001 Distribution Spot Image/Science Photo Library
118–119	1	Paul Springett/Still Pictures
	2	CNES, 1994 Distribution Spot Image/Science Photo Library
	3	Alan Collinson Design
	4	Pierre Gleizes/Still Pictures
	5	Voltchev-Unep/Still Pictures
	6	Spaceimaging.com
134		Pictures Colour Library Ltd
135		NASA
136–137	1	Pictor International - London
	2	CNES, 1986 Distribution Spot Image/Science Photo Library
	3	Mike Schroder/Still Pictures
138–139	1	The aerial photograph on page 138 is Copyright © Commonwealth of Australia, AUSLIG, Australia's national mapping Agency. All rights reserved. Reproduced by permission of the General Manager, Autralian Surveying and Land Information Group, Department of Industry, Science and Resources, Canberra, ACT.
	2	eMAP Ltd
	3	eMAP Ltd
140–141	1 left	Pictor International - London
	1 right	NASA/Science Photo Library
	2	Bill van Aken © CSIRO Land and Water
	3 left	CNES, Distribution Spot Image/Science Photo Library
	3 right	Gerard & Margi Moss/Still Pictures
	Fig. 1	Bureau of Rural Sciences, Australia

page	image number	credit
142–143	1	NASA
	2	NASA
	3	ImageState
	4	Institute of Geological & Nuclear Sciences, New Zealand
	5	Spaceimaging.com
	6	NASA
	7	Image provided by ORBIMAGE © Orbital Imaging Corporation and processing by NASA Goddard Space Flight Center.
154		Pictures Colour Library Ltd
155		NASA
156–157	1	© Owen Franken/CORBIS
	2	© Lowell Georgia/CORBIS
	3	NASA
158–159	1	Gregor Turk
	2	NASA/Marshall Space Flight Center
	3	NASA
160–161	1	Infoterra Ltd
	2	© Roger Ressmeyer/CORBIS
	3	CNES, 1996 Distribution Spot Image/Science Photo Library
	4	NASA/Goddard Space Flight Center/Science Photo Library
	4 inset	NASA
162–163	1	NRSC/Still Pictures
	2	NASA
	3	Alex S. Maclean/Still Pictures
	4	NASA
	5	© David Muench/CORBIS
	6	Bernhard Edmaier/Science Photo Library
188		Pictures Colour Library Ltd
189		NASA
190–191	1	NASA
	2	© Yann Arthus-Bertrand/CORBIS
	3	NASA
192–193	1	Earth Satellite Corporation/Science Photo Library
	2	CNES, 1995 Distribution Spot Image/Science Photo Library
	3	NASA
194–195	1	Ron Giling/Still Pictures
	2	Jeremy Horner/Panos pictures
	3	NASA
	4	CNES, 1988 Distribution Spot Image/Science Photo Library
	5	Alan Collinson Design
	6	CNES, 1986 Distribution Spot Image/Science Photo Library
	7	Jacques Jangoux/Science Photo Library
	8	Digital image © 1996 CORBIS; Original image courtesy of NASA/CORBIS
	9	NASA
196–197	1	NASA/Science Photo Library
	2	Mark Edwards/Still Pictures
	3 top right	NASA/Goddard Space Flight Center/Science Photo Library
	3 left	Michael Nichols/NGS Image Collection
	3 bottom right	NASA/Goddard Space Flight Center/Science Photo Library
208		Pictures Colour Library Ltd
209		NASA
210–211	1	Alan Collinson Design
	2	WHF Smith, US National Oceanic and Atmospheric Administration (NOAA), USA
	Fig. 2	NASA/JPL
212–213	1	NASA
	2	Data provided by the EOS Distributed Active Archive Center (DAAC) processed at the National Snow and Ice Data Center, University of Colorado, Boulder, CO.
	3	NASA
	4	Courtesy of the David Vaughan/BEDMAP Consortium
	5	RADARSAT data Canadian Space Agency/Agence Spatiale Canadienne 1997. Received from the Canada Centre for Remote Sensing. Processed and distributed by RADARSAT International.
214–215	1	B&C Alexander
	2	Data provided by the EOS Distributed Active Archive Center (DAAC) processed at the National Snow and Ice Data Center, University of Colorado, Boulder, CO.
	3	Alan Collinson Design
	4 and 5	B&C Alexander
	6	NASA